New Standard Encyclopedia
Dictionary

Webster Illustrated
Contemporary
Dictionary
New Standard Encyclopedia Edition

Standard Educational Corporation
CHICAGO

Pro·crus·tes (prō·krus′tēz) *Gk. Myth.* A giant who tied travelers to an iron bed and amputated or stretched their limbs until they fitted it.

proc·tol·o·gy (prok·tol′ə·jē) *n.* The branch of medicine which deals with diseases of the lower colon, rectum, and anus. [< Gk. *proktos* anus + -LOGY] —**proc·to·log·i·cal** (prok′tə·loj′i·kəl) *adj.* —**proc·tol′o·gist** *n.*

proc·tor (prok′tər) *n.* 1 An agent acting for another; proxy. 2 A university or college official charged with maintaining order, supervising examinations, etc. —*v.t. & v.i.* To supervise (an examination). [< PROCURATOR] —**proc·to·ri·al** (prok·tôr′ē·əl, -tō′rē-) *adj.*

proc·to·scope (prok′tə·skōp) *n.* A surgical instrument for examining the interior of the rectum. —**proc·tos·co·py** (prok·tos′kə·pē) *n.*

pro·cum·bent (prō·kum′bənt) *adj.* 1 *Bot.* Lying on the ground; trailing. 2 Lying face down; prone. [< L *pro-* forward + *cubare* lie down]

proc·u·ra·tor (prok′yə·rā′tər) *n.* 1 A person authorized to manage the affairs of another. 2 In ancient Rome, one in charge of imperial revenues, esp. in a province. —**proc′u·ra·to′ri·al** (-rə·tôr′ē·əl, -tō′rē-) *adj.*

pro·cure (prō·kyŏŏr′) *v.* **·cured, ·cur·ing** *v.t.* 1 To obtain by some effort or means; acquire. 2 To bring about; cause. 3 To obtain for the sexual gratification of others. —*v.i.* 4 To obtain women for prostitution. [< L *procurare* look after] —**pro·cur′a·ble** *adj.* —**pro·cure′ment, pro·cur′er** *n.*

Pro·cy·on (prō′sē·on) *n.* The most conspicuous star in the constellation Canis Minor. [< Gk. *pro-* before + *kyōn* dog]

prod (prod) *v.t.* **prod·ded, prod·ding** 1 To punch or poke with or as with a pointed instrument. 2 To arouse mentally; urge; goad. —*n.* 1 Any pointed instrument used for prodding. 2 Something that incites one to action. [?] —**prod′der** *n.*

prod. produce; produced; product.

prod·i·gal (prod′ə·gəl) *adj.* 1 Wastefully extravagant, as of money, time, etc. 2 Yielding in profusion; bountiful. 3 Lavish; profuse. —*n.* One who is wastefully extravagant; a spendthrift. [< L *prodigus* wasteful] —**prod′i·gal′i·ty** (-gal′ə·tē) *n.* —**prod′i·gal·ly** *adv.*

pro·dig·ious (prə·dij′əs, prō-) *adj.* 1 Enormous or extraordinary in size, quantity, or degree. 2 Marvelous; amazing. —**pro·dig′ious·ly** *adv.* —**pro·dig′ious·ness** *n.*

prod·i·gy (prod′ə·jē) *n. pl.* **·gies** 1 Something extraordinary or awe-inspiring. 2 An exceptionally gifted child. 3 A monstrosity of nature. [< L *prodigium*]

pro·duce (prə·dyōōs′) *v.* **·duced, ·duc·ing** *v.t.* 1 To bring forth or bear; yield. 2 To bring forth by mental effort; compose, write, etc. 3 To cause to happen or be: His words *produced* a violent reaction. 4 To bring to view; exhibit; show: to *produce*. evidence. 5 To manufacture; make. 6 To bring to performance before the public, as a play. 7 To extend or lengthen, as a line. 8 *Econ.* To create (anything with exchangeable value). —*v.i.* 9 To yield or generate an appropriate product or result. —*n.* (prod′yōōs, prō′dyōōs) That which is produced, esp. farm products collectively. [< L *pro-* forward + *ducere* to lead] —**pro·duc′i·ble** *adj.*

pro·duc·er (prə·dyōō′sər) *n.* 1 One who or that which produces. 2 One who makes things for sale and use. 3 One in charge of the production of a public presentation, as of a play, motion picture, etc.

prod·uct (prod′əkt, -ukt) *n.* 1 Anything produced or obtained as a result of some operation or work. 2 *Math.* The result obtained by multiplication. 3 *Chem.* Any substance resulting from chemical change.

pro·duc·tion (prə·duk′shən) *n.* 1 The act or process of producing. 2 The amount produced. 3 Something produced, esp. an artistic work, as a play, motion picture, etc. 4 In political economy, a producing of goods or services.

pro·duc·tive (prə·duk′tiv) *adj.* 1 Producing easily or abundantly. 2 Characterized by fruitful work and accomplishment: a *productive* meeting. 3 Causing; resulting in: with *of*. —**pro·duc′tive·ly** *adv.* —**pro·duc·tiv·i·ty** (prō′duk·tiv′ə·tē), **pro·duc′tive·ness** *n.*

pro·em (prō′əm) *n.* A preface; prelude. [< Gk. *pro-* before + *oimē* song] —**pro·e·mi·al** (prō·ē′mē·əl) *adj.*

prof (prof) *n. Informal* PROFESSOR.

Prof. Professor. • See PROFESSOR.

prof·a·na·tion (prof′ə·nā′shən, prō·fə-) *n.* The act of profaning or the condition of being profaned.

pro·fane (prō·fān′, prə-) *v.t.* **·faned, ·fan·ing** 1 To treat (something sacred) with irreverence or abuse; desecrate. 2 To put to an unworthy or degrading use; debase. —*adj.* 1 Manifesting irreverence or disrespect toward sacred things. 2 Not sacred or religious in theme, content, use, etc.; secular. 3 Not esoteric; ordinary. 4 Vulgar. [< L *pro-* before + *fanum* temple] —**pro·fan′a·to·ry** (prō·fan′ə·tôr′ē, -tō′rē, prə-) *adj.* —**pro·fane′ly** *adv.* —**pro·fan′er** *n.*

pro·fan·i·ty (prō·fan′ə·tē, prə-) *n. pl.* **·ties** 1 The state of being profane. 2 Profane speech or action. Also **pro·fane′·ness** (-fān′nis).

pro·fess (prə·fes′, prō-) *v.t.* 1 To declare openly; avow; affirm. 2 To assert, usu. insincerely; make a pretense of: to *profess* remorse. 3 To declare or affirm faith in. 4 To have as one's profession: to *profess* the law. 5 To receive into a religious order. —*v.i.* 6 To make open declaration; avow; offer public affirmation. 7 To take the vows of a religious order. [< L *professus*, pp. of *profiteri* avow, confess] —**pro·fessed′** *adj.* —**pro·fess′ed·ly** (-fes′id·lē) *adv.*

pro·fes·sion (prə·fesh′ən) *n.* 1 An occupation that involves a higher education or its equivalent, and mental rather than manual labor, as law, medicine, teaching, etc. 2 The collective body of those following such an occupation. 3 Any calling or occupation requiring special skills, talents, etc.: the acting *profession*. 4 Any occupation. 5 The act of professing or declaring: *professions* of good will. 6 That which is avowed or professed.

pro·fes·sion·al (prə·fesh′ən·əl) *adj.* 1 Connected with, preparing for, engaged in, appropriate, or conforming to a profession: *professional* courtesy; *professional* skill. 2 Performing or doing for pay an activity often engaged in only for pleasure or recreation: a *professional* golfer. 3 Engaged in by performers, players, etc., who are paid: *professional* hockey. 4 Single-minded and zealous, often excessively so: a *professional* do-gooder. —*n.* 1 One who practices any profession or engages in any activity for pay. 2 One who is exceptionally skilled in some activity. —**pro·fes′sion·al·ism′** *n.* —**pro·fes′sion·al·ly** *adv.*

pro·fes·sion·al·ize (prə·fesh′ən·əl·īz′) *v.t.* **·ized, ·iz·ing** To make professional in character or quality: to *professionalize* tourism. —**pro·fes′sion·al·i·za′tion** *n.*

pro·fes·sor (prə·fes′ər) *n.* 1 A teacher of the highest grade in a university or college. 2 One who professes skill and offers instruction in some sport or art: a *professor* of gymnastics. 3 One who makes open declaration of his opinions, religious faith, etc. —**pro·fes·so·ri·al** (prō′fə·sôr′ē·əl, -sō′rē-, prof′ə-) *adj.* —**pro·fes·so′ri·al·ly** *adv.* —**pro·fes·so′ri·ate** (-it), **pro·fes′sor·ship** *n.* • In writing to a college or university professor, one may use either *Professor* or *Prof.* if the name is written in full or if the initials are used with the last name: *Professor Alfred Kern; Prof. C. E. Young.* If only the last name is used, *Professor* is spelled out.

prof·fer (prof′ər) *v.t.* To offer for acceptance. —*n.* The act of proffering, or that which is proffered. [< L *pro-* in behalf of + *offerre* to offer] —**prof′fer·er** *n.*

pro·fi·cien·cy (prə·fish′ən·sē) *n. pl.* **·cies** The fact or quality of being proficient; skill; competence; expertness.

pro·fi·cient (prə·fish′ənt) *adj.* Thoroughly competent; skilled; expert. —*n.* An expert. [< L *proficere* make progress, go forward] —**pro·fi′cient·ly** *adv.*

pro·file (prō′fīl, *esp. Brit.* prō′fēl) *n.* 1 A human head or face, as viewed from the side; also, a drawing of such a side view. 2 A drawing or view of something in outline or contour. 3 A somewhat brief biographical sketch. 4 Degree of exposure to public attention; public image: The army generals who seized control maintained a very low *profile*. 5 A vertical section of stratified soil or rock. —*v.t.* **·filed, ·fil·ing** 1 To draw a profile of; outline. 2 To write a profile of. [< Ital. *proffilare* draw in outline]

Profile *def. 1*

prof·it (prof′it) n. 1 Any benefit, advantage, or return. 2 *Often pl.* Excess of returns over outlay or expenditure. 3 *Often pl.* The gain obtained from invested capital; also, the ratio of gain to the amount of capital invested. 4 Income gained from property, stocks, etc. —v.i. 1 To be of advantage or benefit. 2 To derive gain or benefit. —v.t. 3 To be of profit or advantage to. [< L *profectus*, p.p. of *proficere* go forward] —**prof′it·less** adj.

prof·it·a·ble (prof′it·ə·bəl) adj. Bringing profit or gain. —**prof·it·a·bil·i·ty** (prof′ə·tə·bil′ə·tē), **prof′it·a·ble·ness** n. —**prof′it·a·bly** adv. —Syn. advantageous, beneficial, desirable, expedient, gainful, lucrative, productive, useful, worthwhile.

prof·i·teer (prof′ə·tir′) v.i. To seek or obtain excessive profits. —n. One who makes excessive profits, esp. to the detriment of others. —**prof′i·teer′ing** n.

profit sharing A system by which employees are given a percentage of the net profits of a business.

prof·li·ga·cy (prof′lə·gə·sē) n. The condition or quality of being profligate.

prof·li·gate (prof′lə·git, -gāt) adj. 1 Extremely immoral or dissipated; dissolute. 2 Recklessly extravagant. —n. A profligate person. [< L *profligare* strike to the ground, destroy] —**prof′li·gate·ly** adv.

pro·found (prə·found′, prō-) adj. 1 Intellectually deep or exhaustive: *profound* learning. 2 Reaching to, arising from, or affecting the depth of one's being: a *profound* look; *profound* respect. 3 Reaching far below the surface; deep: a *profound* chasm. 4 Complete; total: a *profound* revision of the book. [< L *pro-* very + *fundus* deep] —**pro·found′ly** adv. —**pro·found′ness** n.

pro·fun·di·ty (prə·fun′də·tē, prō-) n. pl. **·ties** 1 The state or quality of being profound. 2 A deep place. 3 A profound statement, theory, etc.

pro·fuse (prə·fyōōs′, prō-) adj. 1 Giving or given forth lavishly; extravagantly generous. 2 Copious; abundant: *profuse* vegetation. [< L *profusus*, pp. of *profundere* pour forth] —**pro·fuse′ly** adv. —**pro·fuse′ness** n.

pro·fu·sion (prə·fyōō′zhən, prō-) n. 1 A lavish supply or condition: a *profusion* of ornaments. 2 The act of pouring forth or supplying in great abundance; prodigality.

prog. progress; progressive.

pro·gen·i·tor (prō·jen′ə·tər) n. 1 A forefather or parent. 2 The originator or source of something. [< L *progignere* beget] —**pro·gen′i·tor·ship′** n.

prog·e·ny (proj′ə·nē) n. pl. **·nies** Offspring; descendants. [< L *progignere* beget]

pro·ges·ter·one (prō·jes′tə·rōn) n. An ovarian hormone active in preparing the uterus for reception of the fertilized ovum. Also **pro·ges·tin** (-tin). [< PRO-¹ + GE(STATION) + STER(OL) + -ONE]

prog·na·thous (prog′nə·thəs, prog·nā′-) adj. Having projecting jaws. Also **prog·nath·ic** (prog·nath′ik). [< PRO-² + Gk. *gnathos* jaw] —**prog·na·thism** (prog′nə·thiz′əm) n.

prog·no·sis (prog·nō′sis) n. pl. **·ses** (-sēz) A prediction or forecast, esp. as to the future course of a disease. [< Gk. *pro-* before + *gignōskein* know]

prog·nos·tic (prog·nos′tik) adj. 1 Predictive. 2 Of or useful in a prognosis. —n. 1 A sign of some future occurrence. 2 A basis for a prognosis.

prog·nos·ti·cate (prog·nos′tə·kāt) v.t. **·cat·ed, ·cat·ing** 1 To foretell by present indcations. 2 To indicate beforehand; foreshadow. —**prog·nos′ti·ca′tion, prog·nos′ti·ca′tor** n. —**prog·nos′ti·ca′tive** (-kā′tiv) adj.

pro·gram (prō′gram, -grəm) n. 1 A printed list giving in order the items, selections, etc., making up an entertainment; also, the selections, etc., collectively. 2 A printed list of the cast of characters, the performers, the acts or scenes, etc., in a play, opera, or the like. 3 A radio or television show. 4 Any prearranged plan or course of proceedings. 5 A sequence of instructions to be executed by a computer in solving a problem, usu. with means for automatically modifying the sequence depending on conditions that arise. *Brit. sp.* **·gramme.** —v.t. **·gramed** or **·grammed, ·gram·ing** or **·gram·ming** 1 To arrange a program of or for: to *program* one's day. 2 To schedule (an act, performer, etc.) for a program. 3 To furnish a program for (a computer). 4 To feed (information, instructions, etc.) into a computer. [< LL *programma* public announcement]

—pro·gram·mat·ic (prō′grə·mat′ik) adj. —**pro′gram·er, pro′·gram·mer** n.

programed instruction Instruction in which the learner responds to a prearranged series of questions, items, or statements, using various printed texts, audiovisual means, or a teaching machine. Also **programmed instruction.**

program music Music intended to suggest moods, scenes, or incidents.

prog·ress (prog′res, *esp. Brit.* prō′gres) n. 1 A moving forward in space, as toward a destination. 2 Advancement toward something better; improvement. —v.i. (prə·gres′) 1 To move forward or onward. 2 To advance toward completion or improvement. [< L *progressus*, pp. of *progredi* go forward]

pro·gres·sion (prə·gresh′ən) n. 1 The act of progressing. 2 A successive series of events, happenings, etc. 3 *Math.* A sequence of numbers or elements each of which is derived from the preceding by rule. 4 *Music* a An advance from one tone or chord to another. b A sequence or succession of tones or chords. 5 Course or lapse of time; passage. —**pro·gres′sion·al** adj. —**pro·gres′sion·ism** n.

pro·gres·sive (prə·gres′iv) adj. 1 Moving forward in space; advancing. 2 Increasing by successive stages: a *progressive* deterioration. 3 Aiming at or characterized by progress toward something better: a *progressive* country. 4 Favoring or characterized by reform, new techniques, etc.: a *progressive* party, jazz, etc. 5 Increasing in severity: said of a disease. 6 *Gram.* Designating an aspect of the verb which expresses continuing action: formed with any tense of the auxiliary *be* and the present participle; as, He *is speaking;* he *had been speaking.* —n. One who favors or promotes reforms or changes, as in politics. —**pro·gres′·sive·ly** adv. —**pro·gres′sive·ness** n.

pro·hib·it (prō·hib′it, prə-) v.t. 1 To forbid, esp. by authority or law; interdict. 2 To prevent or hinder. [< L *prohibere*] —**pro·hib′it·er** n. —Syn. 1 disallow, ban, deny, bar, debar. 2 impede, restrict, constrain, check, block, obstruct.

pro·hi·bi·tion (prō′ə·bish′ən) n. 1 A prohibiting or being prohibited. 2 A decree or order forbidding anything. 3 *Often cap.* The forbidding of the manufacture, transportation, and sale of alcoholic liquors as beverages. —**pro′hi·bi′tion·ist** n.

pro·hib·i·tive (prō·hib′ə·tiv, prə-) adj. Prohibiting or tending to prohibit. Also **pro·hib′i·to·ry** (-tôr′ē, -tō′rē). —**pro·hib′i·tive·ly** adv.

proj·ect (proj′ekt) n. 1 A course of action; a plan. 2 An organized, usu. rather extensive undertaking: a research *project.* 3 A group of single dwellings or of apartment houses forming a residential complex. —v.t. (prə·jekt′) 1 To cause to extend forward or out. 2 To throw forth or forward, as missiles. 3 To cause (an image, shadow, etc.) to fall on a surface. 4 To plan or estimate something in the future: to *project* living expenses. 5 To create or invent in the mind: to *project* an image of one's destiny. 6 To cause (one's voice) to be heard at a distance. 7 To have the ability to communicate (a dramatic role, one's personality, ideas, etc.) effectively, as to an audience. 8 *Psychol.* To ascribe or impute (one's own ideas, feelings, etc.) to another person, group, or object. 9 To make a projection (def. 4) of. —v.i. 10 To extend out; protrude. 11 To cause one's voice to be heard at a distance. 12 To communicate effectively, as to an audience. 13 *Psychol.* To impute one's own ideas, feelings, etc., to another person, group, or object. [< L *pro-* before + *jacere* throw]

pro·jec·tile (prə·jek′təl, -tīl) adj. 1 Projecting, or impelling forward. 2 Capable of being or intended to be projected or shot forth. —n. 1 A body projected or thrown forth by force. 2 A missile for discharge from a gun, cannon, etc.

pro·jec·tion (prə·jek′shən) n. 1 The act of projecting. 2 That which projects. 3 A prediction or estimation of something in the future based on current information, data, etc. 4 A system of lines drawn on a given fixed plane, as on a map, which represents, point for point, a given terrestrial or celestial surface. 5 *Psychol.* The process or an instance of projecting. 6 The exhibiting of pictures upon a screen. —**pro·jec′tive** adj. —**pro·jec′tive·ly** adv.

pro·jec·tion·ist (prə·jek′shən·ist) n. The operator of a motion-picture or slide projector.

pro·jec·tor (prə·jek′tər) n. One who or that which projects, esp. an apparatus for throwing images on a screen: a motion-picture *projector*.

pro·lapse (prō·laps′) v.i. **·lapsed, ·laps·ing** Med. To fall out of place, as an organ or part. —n. Med. (also prō′laps) Displacement of a part, esp. toward a natural orifice. [< L *pro-* forward + *labi* glide, fall]

pro·late (prō′lāt) adj. 1 Extended lengthwise. 2 Lengthened toward the poles. [< L *prolatus*]

prole (prōl) n. & adj. Informal PROLETARIAN.

pro·le·tar·i·an (prō′lə·târ′ē·ən) adj. Of the proletariat. —n. A member of the proletariat. [< L *proletarius* a Roman citizen of a class that, lacking property, served the state only by having children < *proles* offspring] —**pro′le·tar′i·an·ism** n.

pro·le·tar·i·at (prō′lə·târ′ē·ət) n. 1 Formerly, the lower classes. 2 The laboring class, esp. industrial wage earners.

pro·lif·er·ate (prō·lif′ə·rāt, prə-) v.t. & v.i. **·at·ed, ·at·ing** To create or reproduce in rapid succession. [< L *proles* offspring + *ferre* bear] —**pro·lif′er·a′tion** n. —**pro·lif′er·a′tive, pro·lif′er·ous** adj.

pro·lif·ic (prō·lif′ik, prə-) adj. 1 Producing abundantly, as offspring or fruit. 2 Producing creative or intellectual products abundantly: a *prolific* writer. [< L *proles* offspring + *facere* make] —**pro·lif′i·ca·cy** (-i·kə·sē), **pro·lif′ic·ness** n. —**pro·lif′i·cal·ly** adv.

pro·lix (prō′liks, prō·liks′) adj. 1 Unduly long and wordy. 2 Indulging in long and wordy discourse. [< L *prolixus* extended] —**pro·lix·i·ty** (prō·lik′sə·tē), **pro′lix·ness** n. —**pro′·lix·ly** adv.

pro·logue (prō′lôg, -log) n. 1 A preface, esp. an introduction, often in verse, spoken or sung by an actor before a play or opera. 2 Any anticipatory act or event. —v.t. To introduce with a prologue or preface. Also **pro′log.** [< Gk. *pro-* before + *logos* discourse]

pro·long (prə·lông′, -long′) v.t. To extend in time or space; continue; lengthen. Also **pro·lon′gate** (-lông′gāt, -long′-). [< L *pro-* forth + *longus* long] —**pro′lon·ga′tion, pro·long′ment, pro·long′er** n.

prom (prom) n. Informal A formal college or school dance or ball. [Short for PROMENADE]

prom. promenade; promontory.

prom·e·nade (prom′ə·nād′, -näd′) n. 1 A leisurely walk taken for pleasure. 2 A place for promenading. 3 A concert or ball opened with a formal march. —v. **·nad·ed, ·nad·ing** v.i. 1 To take a promenade. —v.t. 2 To take a promenade through or along. 3 To take or exhibit on or as on a promenade; parade. [< L *prominare* drive forward] —**prom′e·nad′er** n.

Pro·me·theus (prə·mē′thē·əs) Gk. Myth. A Titan who stole fire from heaven for mankind and as a punishment was chained to a rock, where an eagle daily devoured his liver. —**Pro·me′the·an** adj.

pro·me·thi·um (prə·mē′thē·əm) n. A radioactive element (symbol Pm) produced by uranium fission and belonging to the lanthanide series. [< PROMETHEUS]

prom·i·nence (prom′ə·nəns) n. 1 The state of being prominent; conspicuous. 2 Something that extends forth or protrudes. 3 Astron. One of the great luminous clouds arising from the sun's surface, seen during total eclipses: also **solar prominence.** Also **prom′i·nen·cy.**

prom·i·nent (prom′ə·nənt) adj. 1 Jutting out; projecting; protuberant. 2 Conspicuous. 3 Very well known; eminent: a *prominent* lawyer. [< L *prominere* to project] —**prom′i·nent·ly** adv. —**Syn.** 3 famous, noted, renowned, celebrated, popular, honored, outstanding.

prom·is·cu·i·ty (prom′is·kyōo′ə·tē, prō′mis-) n. pl. **·ties** The state, quality, or an instance of being promiscuous, esp. in sexual relations.

pro·mis·cu·ous (prə·mis′kyōo·əs) adj. 1 Composed of persons or things confusedly mingled. 2 Indiscriminate; esp., having sexual relations indiscriminately or casually with various persons. 3 Casual; irregular. [< L *promiscuus* mixed] —**pro·mis′cu·ous·ly** adv. —**pro·mis′cu·ous·ness** n.

prom·ise (prom′is) n. 1 An assurance given that a specified action will or will not be taken. 2 Reasonable ground for hope or expectation of future excellence, satisfaction, etc. 3 Something promised. —v. **·ised, ·is·ing** v.t. 1 To engage or pledge by a promise: He *promised* to do it. 2 To make a promise of (something) to someone. 3 To give reason for expecting. 4 Informal To assure (someone). —v.i. 5 To make a promise. 6 To give reason for expectation: often with *well* or *fair*. [< L *promissum,* pp. of *promittere* send forward] —**prom′is·er** n.

Promised Land 1 Canaan, promised to Abraham by God. Gen. 15:18. 2 Any longed-for place of happiness or improvement.

prom·is·ing (prom′is·ing) adj. Giving promise of good results or development. —**prom′is·ing·ly** adv.

prom·is·so·ry (prom′ə·sôr′ē, -sō′rē) adj. Containing or of the nature of a promise.

promissory note A written promise by one person to pay another unconditionally a certain sum of money at a specified time.

pro·mo (prō′mō) Slang n. PROMOTION (def. 3). —adj. Of, for, or relating to promotion (def. 3); promotional.

prom·on·to·ry (prom′ən·tôr′ē, -tō′rē) n. pl. **·ries** A high point of land extending into a body of water; headland. [< L *promunturium*]

pro·mote (prə·mōt′) v.t. **·mot·ed, ·mot·ing** 1 To contribute to the progress, development, or growth of; further; encourage. 2 To advance to a higher position, grade, or rank. 3 To advocate actively. 4 To publicize (a person, product, event, etc.), as by advertising, public appearances, etc. [< L *pro-* forward + *movere* to move] —**pro·mot′a·ble** adj.

pro·mot·er (prə·mō′tər) n. One who or that which promotes, esp. one who assists, by securing capital, etc., in promoting some enterprise, as a sports event, commercial venture, etc.

pro·mo·tion (prə·mō′shən) n. 1 Advancement in dignity, rank, grade, etc. 2 Furtherance or development, as of a cause. 3 Anything, as advertising, public appearances, etc., done to publicize a person, product, event, etc. —**pro·mo′tion·al** adj.

pro·mo·tive (prə·mō′tiv) adj. Tending to promote.

prompt (prompt) v.t. 1 To incite to action; instigate. 2 To suggest or inspire (an act, thought, etc.). 3 To remind of what has been forgotten or of what comes next; give a cue to. —v.i. 4 To give help or suggestions. —adj. 1 Quick to act, respond, etc.; ready. 2 Taking place at the appointed time; punctual. [< L *promptus* brought forth, hence, at hand] —**promp′ti·tude, prompt′ness** n. —**prompt′ly** adv.

prompt·er (promp′tər) 1 In a theater, one who follows the lines and prompts the actors. 2 One who or that which prompts.

prom·ul·gate (prom′əl·gāt, prō·mul′gāt) v.t. **·gat·ed, ·gat·ing** 1 To make known or announce officially, as a law, dogma, etc. 2 To make known or effective over a wide area or extent. [< L *promulgare* make known] —**prom·ul·ga′tion** (prom′əl·gā′shən, prō′mul-), **prom′ul·gat·or** n.

pron. pronoun; pronounced; pronunciation.

prone (prōn) adj. 1 Lying flat, esp. with the face, front, or palm downward; prostrate. 2 Leaning forward or downward. 3 Mentally inclined or predisposed: with *to.* [< L *pronus*] —**prone′ly** adv. —**prone′ness** n.

prong (prông, prong) n. 1 A pointed end of a fork. 2 Any pointed and projecting part, as the end of an antler, etc. —v.t. To prick or stab with a prong. [ME *pronge*] —**pronged** adj.

prong·horn (prông′hôrn′, prong′-) n. pl. **·horns** or **·horn** A small, deerlike mammal of w North America.

pro·nom·i·nal (prō·nom′ə·nəl) adj. Of, pertaining to, like, or having the nature of a pronoun. —**pro·nom′i·nal·ly** adv.

pro·noun (prō′noun) n. A word used as a substitute for a noun, as *he, she, that.* [< L *pro-* in place of + *nomen* name, noun]

pro·nounce (prə·nouns′) v.

Pronghorn

·nounced, ·nounc·ing v.t. **1** To utter or deliver officially or solemnly; proclaim. **2** To assert; declare, esp. as one's judgment: The judge *pronounced* her guilty. **3** To give utterance to; articulate (words, etc.). **4** To articulate in a prescribed manner: hard to *pronounce* his name. **5** To indicate the sound of (a word) by phonetic symbols. —v.i. **6** To make a pronouncement or assertion. **7** To articulate words; speak. [< L *pronuntiare* proclaim < *pro-* forth + *nuntiare* announce] —**pro·nounce'a·ble** adj. —**pro·nounc'er** n.

pro·nounced (prə·nounst') adj. Clearly noticeable; decided. —**pro·nounc·ed·ly** (prə·noun'sid·lē) adv.

pro·nounce·ment (prə·nouns'mənt) n. **1** The act of pronouncing. **2** A formal declaration or announcement.

pron·to (pron'tō) adv. Slang Quickly; promptly; instantly. [< L *promptus*]

pro·nun·ci·a·men·to (prə·nun'sē·ə·men'tō) n. pl. ·tos A public announcement; proclamation; manifesto. [< L *pronuntiare* pronounce]

pro·nun·ci·a·tion (prə·nun'sē·ā'shən) n. The act or manner of pronouncing words.

proof (proōf) n. **1** The act or process of proving; esp., the establishment of a fact by evidence or a truth by other truths. **2** A trial of strength, truth, fact, or excellence, etc.; a test. **3** Evidence and argument sufficient to induce belief. **4** *Law* Anything that serves to convince the mind of the truth or falsity of a fact or proposition. **5** The state or quality of having successfully undergone a proof or test. **6** The standard of strength of alcoholic liquors: see PROOF SPIRIT. **7** *Printing* A printed trial sheet showing the contents or condition of matter in type. **8** In engraving and etching, a trial impression taken from an engraved plate, stone, or block. **9** *Phot.* A trial print from a negative. **10** *Math.* A procedure that shows that a proposition is true. **11** Anything proved true; experience. **12** In philately, an experimental printing of a stamp. —adj. **1** Employed in or connected with proving or correcting. **2** Capable of resisting successfully; firm: with *against*: *proof* against bribes. **3** Of standard alcoholic strength, as liquors. —v.t. **1** To make a test or proof of. **2** To protect or make impervious: to *proof* a garment against stains. **3** PROOFREAD. [< L *probare* PROVE]

-proof combining form **1** Impervious to; not damaged by: *waterproof.* **2** Protected against: *mothproof.* **3** As strong as: *armorproof.* **4** Resisting; showing no effects of: *panicproof.*

proof·read (proōf'rēd') v.t. & v.i. **·read** (-red'), **·read·ing** (-rē'ding) To read and correct (printers' proofs). —**proof'·read'er** n.

prop[1] (prop) v.t. **propped, prop·ping 1** To support or keep from falling by or as by means of a prop. **2** To lean or place: usu. with *against.* **3** To support; sustain. —n. A support. [< MDu. *proppe* a vine prop]

prop[2] (prop) n. PROPERTY (def. 5).

prop[3] (prop) n. Informal PROPELLER.

prop. proper; properly; property; proposition; proprietor.

prop·a·gan·da (prop'ə·gan'də) n. **1** Any widespread scheme or effort to spread or promote an idea, opinion, or course of action in order to help or do damage to a cause, person, etc. **2** The ideas, opinions, etc., so spread or promoted: now often used disparagingly because of the deceitful or distorted character of much propaganda. [< NL *(congregatio de) propaganda (fide)* (the congregation for) propagating (the faith)]

prop·a·gan·dism (prop'ə·gan'diz·əm) n. The art, practice, or system of using propaganda. —**prop'a·gan'dist** adj., n. —**prop'a·gan·dis'tic** adj. —**prop'a·gan·dis'ti·cal·ly** adv.

prop·a·gan·dize (prop'ə·gan'dīz) v. **·dized, ·diz·ing** v.t. **1** To subject to propaganda. **2** To spread by means of propaganda. —v.i. **3** To carry on or spread propaganda.

prop·a·gate (prop'ə·gāt) v. **·gat·ed, ·gat·ing** v.t. **1** To cause (animals, plants, etc.) to multiply by natural reproduction; breed. **2** To reproduce (itself). **3** To spread abroad or from person to person; disseminate. **4** *Physics* To transmit (a form of energy) through space. —v.i. **5** To multiply by natural reproduction; breed. **6** *Physics* To pass or spread through space, as waves, heat, etc. [< L *propago* a slip for transplanting] —**prop'a·ga'tion, prop'a·ga'tor** n. —**prop'a·ga'tive** adj.

pro·pane (prō'pān) n. A gaseous hydrocarbon of the paraffin series. [< PROP(YL) + (METH)ANE]

pro·pel (prə·pel') v.t. **·pelled, ·pel·ling** To cause to move forward or ahead; drive or urge forward. [< L *pro-* forward + *pellere* drive]

pro·pel·lant (prə·pel'ənt) n. That which propels, esp. an explosive or fuel that propels a projectile, rocket, etc.

pro·pel·lent (prə·pel'ənt) adj. Propelling; able to propel.

pro·pel·ler (prə·pel'ər) n. **1** One who or that which propels. **2** Any device for propelling a craft through water or air; esp., a set of rotating vanes operating like a screw. Also **pro·pel'lor.**

Propeller

pro·pen·si·ty (prə·pen'sə·tē) n. pl. **·ties** Natural disposition to or for; tendency. [< L *pro-* forward + *pendere* hang]

PROOFREADER'S MARKS

Symbols in the column headed Margin are used only in the outer margins of the proof; the symbols used within the body of the text are given in the Text column.

Margin		Text
l.c.	Set in lower-case type	circled or /
cap.	Set in capitals	underscored
s.c.	Set in small capitals	underscored
c.+s.c.	Set in caps and small caps	
l.f.	Set in lightface type	circled
b.f.	Set in boldface type	underscored
Rom.	Set in roman type	circled
Ital.	Set in italic type	underscored
⊙	Insert period	∧
⩗ ⩘	Insert colon; semicolon	∧ ∧
⩘	Insert comma	∧
⩗	Insert apostrophe	∧
/?/	Insert question mark	∧
/!/	Insert exclamation mark	∧
/=/	Insert hyphen	∧
⩗	Insert quotation marks	∧
⩗	Insert superior figure or letter	∧
⩗	Insert inferior figure or letter	∧
1/m	Insert one em-dash	∧
℈	Take out (delete matter marked)	/
w.f.	Wrong font	circled or /

Margin		Text
✗	Broken letter: examine	circled
tr.	Transpose matter marked	
eq.#	Equalize spacing	
⌈	Move to left to point marked	⌈
⌉	Move to right to point marked	⌉
⌐	Raise to point marked	
⌐⌐	Lower to point marked	
∪	Push down space	/
⌒	Close up	⌒
⊄	Begin new paragraph	
no¶	Run on, not a paragraph	
⸗	Align type	
stet	Retain words crossed out	
⌇	Take out and close up	
‖	Line up matter	‖
Out	Omission here; see copy	∧
⌈	Move this to left	
⌉	Move this to right	
Qu.?	Query: is this right?	∧
Sp.	Spell out	circled
#	Insert space	∧

proof spirit An alcoholic liquor of a standard strength, in the U.S., containing ethyl alcohol in the amount of 50 percent of its volume, equal to 100 proof.

prop·er (prop'ər) adj. **1** Having special fitness; specially suited; appropriate. **2** Conforming to a standard; correct: the *proper* pronunciation. **3** Seemly; right; fitting: the

proper outfit. **4** Genteel and respectable, often excessively so. **5** Understood in the most correct or strict sense: usu. following the noun modified: Boston *proper*. **6** Naturally belonging to a person or thing: with *to:* Snow is *proper* to winter. —*n. Often cap.* That portion of the breviary or missal containing the prayers and collects suitable to special occasions. [< L *proprius* one's own] —**prop′er·ly** *adv.* —**prop′er·ness** *n.*

proper fraction A fraction in which the denominator exceeds the numerator.

proper noun A noun designating a specific person, place, or thing, always capitalized in English, as *John, Mount Everest, Apollo II.*

proper subset Any subset not identical with the entire set.

prop·er·tied (prop′ər·tēd) *adj.* Owning property.

prop·er·ty (prop′ər·tē) *n. pl.* **·ties 1** Any object that a person may lawfully acquire and own; any possession, esp. land or real estate. **2** A specific piece of land or real estate. **3** The legal right to the possession, use, and disposal of a thing. **4** An inherent quality or characteristic. **5** In the theater, movies, television, ballet, etc., any portable article, except scenery and costumes, used by the performers while performing. [< L *proprius* one's own]

proph·e·cy (prof′ə·sē) *n. pl.* **·cies 1** A prediction made under divine influence. **2** Any prediction. [< Gk. *pro-* before + *phanai* speak]

proph·e·sy (prof′ə·sī) *v.* **·sied, ·sy·ing** *v.t.* **1** To utter or foretell with or as with divine inspiration. **2** To predict (a future event). **3** To point out beforehand. —*v.i.* **4** To speak by divine influence. **5** To foretell the future. [< PROPHECY] —**proph′e·si′er** *n.*

proph·et (prof′it) *n.* **1** One who delivers divine messages or interprets the divine will. **2** One who foretells the future. **3** A religious leader. **4** An interpreter or spokesman for any cause. —**the Prophet** According to Islam, Mohammed. —**the Prophets** The Old Testament books written by the prophets. [< Gk. *pro-* before + *phanai* speak] —**proph′et·ess** *n. Fem.* —**proph′et·hood** (-hŏŏd) *n.*

pro·phet·ic (prə·fet′ik) *adj.* **1** Of or pertaining to a prophet or prophecy. **2** Predicting or foreshadowing a future event. Also **pro·phet′i·cal.** —**pro·phet′i·cal·ly** *adv.*

pro·phy·lac·tic (prō′fə·lak′tik, prof′ə-) *adj.* Pertaining to prophylaxis. —*n.* **1** A prophylactic medicine or appliance. **2** A condom.

pro·phy·lax·is (prō′fə·lak′sis, prof′ə-) *n.* Preventive treatment for disease. [< Gk. *pro-* before + *phylaxis* a guarding]

pro·pin·qui·ty (prō·ping′kwə·tē) *n.* **1** Nearness in place or time. **2** Kinship. [< L *propinquus* near]

pro·pi·ti·ate (prō·pish′ē·āt) *v.t.* **·at·ed, ·at·ing** To cause to be favorably disposed; appease; conciliate. [< L *propitiare* render favorable, appease] —**pro·pi·ti·a·ble** (prō·pish′ē·ə·bəl), **pro·pi′ti·a·tive, pro·pi′ti·a·to′ry** *adj.* —**pro·pi·ti·a·tion** (prō·pish′ē·ā′shən), **pro·pi′ti·a′tor** *n.* —**Syn.** pacify, placate, mollify, reconcile.

pro·pi·tious (prō·pish′əs) *adj.* **1** Kindly disposed; gracious. **2** Attended by favorable circumstances; auspicious. [< L *propitius* favorable] —**pro·pi′tious·ly** *adv.* —**pro·pi′·tious·ness** *n.* —**Syn.** **2** timely, fortunate, lucky, providential, happy, felicitous.

pro·po·nent (prə·pō′nənt) *n.* **1** One who makes a proposal or puts forward a proposition. **2** *Law* One who presents a will for probate. **3** One who advocates or supports a cause or doctrine. [< L *pro-* forth + *ponere* put]

pro·por·tion (prə·pôr′shən, -pōr′-) *n.* **1** Relative magnitude, number, or degree, as existing between parts, a part and a whole, or different things. **2** Balance and harmony; symmetry. **3** A proportionate or proper share. **4** *pl.* Size; dimensions. **5** An equality or identity between ratios. **6** *Math.* An identity or equation involving a pair of fractions, in the general form $4/2 = 8/4$. —*v.t.* **1** To adjust properly as to relative magnitude, amount, or degree. **2** To form with a harmonious relation of parts. [< L *pro-* before + *portio* a share] —**pro·por′tion·a·ble** *adj.* —**pro·por′tion·a·bly** *adv.* —**pro·por′tion·er** *n.*

pro·por·tion·al (prə·pôr′shən·əl, -pōr′-) *adj.* **1** Of, pertaining to, or being in proportion. **2** *Math.* Being the product of a given function or variable and a constant: The area of a circle is *proportional* to the square of the radius. —**pro·por′tion·al·ly** *adv.* —**pro·por′tion·al′i·ty** (-al′ə·tē) *n.*

pro·por·tion·ate (prə·pôr′shən·it, -pōr′-) *adj.* Being in due proportion; proportional. —*v.t.* (-āt) **·at·ed, ·at·ing** To make proportionate. —**pro·por′tion·ate·ly** *adv.* —**pro·por′·tion·ate·ness** *n.*

pro·po·sal (prə·pō′zəl) *n.* **1** An offer proposing something to be accepted or adopted. **2** An offer of marriage. **3** Something proposed.

pro·pose (prə·pōz′) *v.* **·posed, ·pos·ing** *v.t.* **1** To put forward for acceptance or consideration. **2** To nominate, as for admission or appointment. **3** To intend; purpose. **4** To suggest the drinking of (a toast or health). —*v.i.* **5** To form or announce a plan or design. **6** To make an offer, as of marriage. [< OF *pro-* forth + *poser* put] —**pro·pos′er** *n.*

prop·o·si·tion (prop′ə·zish′ən) *n.* **1** A scheme or proposal offered for consideration or acceptance. **2** *Informal* Any matter or person to be dealt with: a tough *proposition.* **3** *Informal* A proposal for illicit sexual intercourse. **4** A subject or statement presented for discussion. **5** *Logic* A statement in which the subject is affirmed or denied by the predicate. **6** *Math.* A statement whose truth is assumed or demonstrated. —*v.t.* *Informal* To make a proposal to (someone) to have illicit sexual intercourse. —**prop′o·si′·tion·al** *adj.* —**prop′o·si′tion·al·ly** *adv.*

pro·pound (prə·pound′) *v.t.* To put forward for consideration, solution, etc. [< L *proponere* set forth] —**pro·pound′·er** *n.*

pro·pri·e·tar·y (prə·prī′ə·ter′ē) *adj.* **1** Pertaining to a proprietor. **2** Protected as to name, composition, or process of manufacture by copyright, patent, etc. —*n. pl.* **·tar·ies 1** A proprietor or proprietors collectively. **2** Proprietorship. [< LL *proprietas* property]

pro·pri·e·tor (prə·prī′ə·tər) *n.* A person having the exclusive title to anything; owner. —**pro·pri′e·tor·ship′** *n.* —**pro·pri′e·tress** *n. Fem.*

pro·pri·e·ty (prə·prī′ə·tē) *n. pl.* **·ties** The character or quality of being proper; esp., accordance with recognized usage, custom, or principles. —**the proprieties** The standards of good social behavior. [< L *proprius* one's own]

pro·pul·sion (prə·pul′shən) *n.* **1** A propelling or being propelled. **2** Something that propels. [< L *propulsus*, pp. of *propellere* propel] —**pro·pul′sive** (-siv) *adj.*

pro·pyl (prō′pil) *n.* The univalent radical derived from propane.

pro ra·ta (prō rā′tə, rat′ə, rä′tə) Proportionate or proportionately: The loss was shared *pro rata.* [< L *pro rata (parte)* according to the calculated (share)]

pro·rate (prō·rāt′, prō′rāt′) *v.t. & v.i.* **·rat·ed, ·rat·ing** To distribute or divide proportionately. [< PRO RATA] —**pro·rat′a·ble** *adj.* —**pro·ra′tion** *n.*

pro·rogue (prō·rōg′) *v.t.* **·rogued, ·ro·guing** To discontinue a session of (an assembly, esp. the British Parliament). [< L *pro-* forth + *rogare* ask] —**pro·ro·ga·tion** (prō′rō·gā′shən) *n.*

pro·sa·ic (prō·zā′ik) *adj.* **1** Unimaginative; commonplace; dull. **2** Of or like prose. [< L *prosa* prose] —**pro·sa′i·cal·ly** *adv.* —**pro·sa′ic·ness** *n.*

pro·sce·ni·um (prō·sē′nē·əm) *n. pl.* **·ni·ums** or **·ni·a** (-nē·ə) **1** In a modern theater, that part of the stage between the curtain and the orchestra, sometimes including the curtain and its arch (**proscenium arch**). **2** In the ancient Greek or Roman theater, the stage. [< Gk. *proskēnion* < *pro-* before + *skēnē* a stage, orig. a tent]

pro·sciut·to (prō·shōō′tō) *n. pl.* **·ti** (-tē) or **·tos** A spicy, dry-cured ham, usu. sliced very thin. [Ital.]

pro·scribe (prō·skrīb′) *v.t.* **·scribed, ·scrib·ing 1** To denounce or condemn; prohibit; interdict. **2** To outlaw or banish. **3** In ancient Rome, to publish the name of (one condemned or exiled). [< L *pro-* before + *scribere* write] —**pro·scrib′er, pro·scrip′tion** (-skrip′shən) *n.* —**pro·scrip′tive** *adj.* —**pro·scrip′tive·ly** *adv.*

prose (prōz) *n.* **1** Speech or writing as found in ordinary conversation, letters, newspapers, etc. **2** Writing, esp. in literature, distinguished from poetry by the lack of conscious rhyme and usu. by rhythms suggesting ordinary speech or by a presentation in the form of a series of sentences with the initial letters capitalized. **3** Commonplace or tedious talk, style, quality, etc. —*adj.* **1** Of or in prose. **2** Tedious. —*v.t.* & *v.i.* **prosed, pros·ing** To write or speak in prose. [< L *prosa (oratio)* straight-forward (discourse)]

pros·e·cute (pros′ə·kyoot) *v.* **·cut·ed, ·cut·ing** *v.t.* **1** To go on with so as to complete; pursue to the end: to *prosecute* an inquiry. **2** To carry on or engage in, as a trade. **3** *Law* **a** To bring suit against for redress of wrong or punishment of crime. **b** To seek to enforce or obtain, as a claim or right, by legal process. —*v.i.* **4** To begin and carry on a legal proceeding. [< L *prosequi* pursue]

prosecuting attorney The attorney empowered to act in behalf of the government, whether state, county, or national, in prosecuting for penal offenses.

pros·e·cu·tion (pros′ə·kyoo′shən) *n.* **1** The act or process of prosecuting. **2** *Law* **a** The instituting and carrying forward of a judicial or criminal proceeding. **b** The party instituting and conducting it.

pros·e·cu·tor (pros′ə·kyoo′tər) *n.* **1** One who prosecutes. **2** *Law* **a** One who institutes and carries on a suit, esp. a criminal suit. **b** PROSECUTING ATTORNEY.

pros·e·lyte (pros′ə·līt) *n.* One who has been converted to any opinion, belief, sect, or party. —*v.t.* & *v.i.* **·lyt·ed, ·lyt·ing** PROSELYTIZE. [< Gk. *prosēlytos* a convert to Judaism] —**pros′e·lyt·ism** (-līt′iz·əm, -lə·tiz′əm), **pros′e·lyt·ist** *n.*

pros·e·lyt·ize (pros′ə·lə·tīz′) *v.t.* & *v.i.* **·ized, ·iz·ing** To convert or try to convert (a person) to one's religion, opinions, party, etc. —**pros′e·ly·tiz′er** *n.*

pro·sit (prō′sit) *interj.* A toast used in drinking health. [L, lit., may it benefit (you)]

pros·o·dy (pros′ə·dē, proz′-) *n.* The study of poetical forms, including meter, rhyme schemes, structural analysis, etc. [< Gk. *prosōidia* a song sung to music] —**pro·sod·ic** (prə·sod′ik, -zod′-) or **·i·cal** *adj.* —**pros′o·dist** *n.*

pros·pect (pros′pekt) *n.* **1** A future probability or something anticipated. **2** *Usu. pl.* Chances, as for success. **3** A scene; an extended view. **4** The direction in which anything faces; an exposure; outlook. **5** A potential buyer, candidate, etc. **6** The act of observing or examining; survey. **7** *Mining* **a** A place having signs of the presence of mineral ore. **b** The sample of mineral obtained by washing a small portion of ore or dirt. —*v.t.* & *v.i.* To explore (a region) for gold, oil, etc. [< L *pro-* forward + *specere* look]

pro·spec·tive (prə·spek′tiv) *adj.* **1** Anticipated; expected. **2** Looking toward the future; anticipatory. —**pro·spec′tive·ly** *adv.*

pros·pec·tor (pros′pek·tər) *n.* One who prospects for mineral deposits, oil, etc.

pro·spec·tus (prə·spek′təs) *n.* **1** A paper containing information of a proposed literary or business undertaking. **2** A summary; outline. [L, a look-out, prospect]

pros·per (pros′pər) *v.i.* **1** To thrive; flourish. —*v.t.* **2** To render prosperous. [< OF < L favorable]

pros·per·i·ty (pros·per′ə·tē) *n.* The state of being prosperous; esp., wealth or success.

pros·per·ous (pros′pər·əs) *adj.* **1** Successful; flourishing. **2** Wealthy; well-to-do. **3** Promising; favorable. [< L *prosper* favorable] —**pros′per·ous·ly** *adv.* —**pros′per·ous·ness** *n.*

pros·tate (pros′tāt) *adj.* Of the prostate gland. —*n.* PROSTATE GLAND. [< Gk. *prostatēs* one who stands before] —**pro·stat·ic** (prō·stat′ik) *adj.*

prostate gland A partly muscular gland at the base of the bladder around the urethra in male mammals.

pros·the·sis (pros·thē′sis, pros′thə-) *n. pl.* **·the·ses** (-thē′sēz) **1** Replacement of a missing part of the body with an artificial substitute. **2** A device used in prosthesis, as an artificial leg, eye, etc. [< Gk. *pros-* toward, besides + *tithenai* place, put] —**pros·thet·ic** (pros·thet′ik) *adj.*

pros·ti·tute (pros′tə·t(y)oot) *n.* **1** A woman who engages in sexual intercourse for money. **2** A person who engages in sexual acts for money: a male *prostitute*. **3** A person who uses his talents or gifts for unworthy or corrupt purposes. —*v.t.* **·tut·ed, ·tut·ing** **1** To put to base or unworthy purposes. **2** To offer (oneself or another) for lewd purposes, esp. for hire. [< L *prostituere* expose publicly, prostitute] —**pros′ti·tu′tion, pros′ti·tu′tor** *n.*

pros·trate (pros′trāt) *adj.* **1** Lying prone, or with the face to the ground. **2** Brought low in mind or body, as from grief, exhaustion, etc. **3** Lying at the mercy of another; defenseless. **4** *Bot.* Trailing along the ground. —*v.t.* **·trat·ed, ·trat·ing** **1** To bow or cast (oneself) down, as in adoration or pleading. **2** To throw flat; lay on the ground. **3** To overthrow or overcome; reduce to helplessness. [< L *prostratus,* pp. of *prosternere* lay flat] —**pros·tra′tion, pros′tra·tor** *n.*

pros·y (prō′zē) *adj.* **pros·i·er, pros·i·est** **1** Like prose. **2** Dull; commonplace. —**pros′i·ly** *adv.* —**pros′i·ness** *n.*

Prot. Protestant.

pro·tac·tin·i·um (prō′tak·tin′ē·əm) *n.* A radioactive element (symbol Pa) occurring in small amounts in uranium ores. [< PROT(O)- + ACTINIUM]

pro·tag·o·nist (prō·tag′ə·nist) *n.* **1** The actor who played the chief part in a Greek drama. **2** A leader in any enterprise or contest. [< Gk. *prōtos* first + *agōnistēs* a contestant, an actor]

pro·te·an (prō′tē·ən, prō·tē′ən) *adj.* Readily assuming different forms or aspects; changeable. [< PROTEUS]

pro·tect (prə·tekt′) *v.t.* **1** To shield or defend from attack, harm, or injury; guard; defend. **2** *Econ.* To assist (domestic industry) by protective tariffs. **3** In commerce, to provide funds to guarantee payment of (a draft, etc.). [< L *pro-* before + *tegere* to cover] —**pro·tec′tive** *adj.* —**pro·tec′tive·ly** *adv.* —**pro·tec′tive·ness, pro·tec′tor** *n.*

pro·tec·tion (prə·tek′shən) *n.* **1** The act of protecting or the state of being protected. **2** That which protects: Our dog is a great *protection*. **3** A system aiming to protect the industries of a country, as by imposing duties. **4** A safeconduct pass. **5** *Slang* Security purchased under threat of violence from racketeers; also, the money so paid.

pro·tec·tion·ism (prə·tek′shən·iz′əm) *n.* The economic doctrine or system of protection. —**pro·tec′tion·ist** *adj., n.* —**pro·tec′tion·is′tic** *adj.*

protective coloration Any natural coloration of a plant or animal that tends to disguise or conceal it from its enemies.

protective tariff A tariff that is intended to insure protection of domestic industries against foreign competition.

pro·tec·tor·ate (prə·tek′tər·it) *n.* **1** A relation of protection and partial control by a strong nation over a weaker power. **2** A country or region so protected.

pro·té·gé (prō′tə·zhā, prō·tə·zhā′) *n.* One aided, esp. in promoting a career, by another who is older or more powerful. [F, pp. of *protéger* protect] —**pro′té·gée** *n. Fem.*

pro·tein (prō′tēn, -tē·in) *n.* Any of a class of complex nitrogenous compounds found in all living matter and forming an essential part of the diet of animals. —*adj.* Composed of protein.

pro tem·po·re (prō tem′pə·rē) For the time being; temporary: usu. shortened to **pro tem.** [L]

Prot·er·o·zo·ic (prot′ər·ə·zō′ik, prō′tər-) *adj., n.* • See GEOLOGY. [< Gk. *proteros* former + *zōion* animal]

pro·test (prō′test) *n.* **1** An objection, complaint, or declaration of disapproval. **2** A public expression of dissent, esp. if organized. **3** A formal certificate attesting the fact that a note or bill of exchange has not been paid. —*adj.* Of or relating to public protest: *protest* demonstrations. —*v.* (prə·test′) *v.t.* **1** To assert earnestly or positively; state formally, esp. against opposition or doubt. **2** To make a protest against; object to. **3** To declare formally that payment of (a promissory note, etc.) has been duly submitted and refused. —*v.i.* **4** To make solemn affirmation. **5** To make a protest; object. [< L *pro-* forth + *testari* affirm] —**pro·test′er, pro·test′or** *n.*

Prot·es·tant (prot′is·tənt) *n.* Any Christian who is not a member of the Roman Catholic or Eastern Orthodox Churches. —*adj.* Pertaining to Protestants or Protestantism. —**Prot′es·tant·ism** *n.*

Protestant Episcopal Church A religious body in the U.S. which is descended from the Church of England.

prot·es·ta·tion (prot′is·tā′shən, prō′tes-) *n.* **1** The act of

protesting. **2** That which is protested. **3** Any protest or objection.

Pro·te·us (prō′tē·əs, -tyōōs) *Gk. Myth.* A sea god who had the power of assuming different forms. —**Pro′te·an** *adj.*

proto- *combining form* **1** First in rank or time; chief; typical: *protozoan.* **2** Primitive; original: *prototype.* Also **prot-.** [< Gk. *prōtos* first]

pro·to·col (prō′tə·kol) *n.* **1** The preliminary draft of an official document, as a treaty. **2** The preliminary draft or report of the negotiations and conclusions arrived at by a diplomatic conference, having the force of a treaty when ratified. **3** The rules of diplomatic and state etiquette and ceremony. —*v.i.* To write or form protocols. [< LGk. *prōtokollon* the first glued sheet of a papyrus roll]

pro·ton (prō′ton) *n.* A stable, positively charged subatomic particle found typically in atomic nuclei, having a charge equal in magnitude to that of an electron and a mass of about 1.672×10^{-24} gram. [< Gk. *prōtos* first]

pro·to·plasm (prō′tə·plaz′əm) *n.* The basic living substance of plant and animal cells. [< Gk. *prōtos* first + PLASMA] —**pro′to·plas′mic** *adj.*

pro·to·type (prō′tə·tīp) *n.* A first or original model; an archetype. —**pro′to·typ′al** (-tī′pəl), **pro′to·typ′ic** (-tip′ik), **pro′to·typ′i·cal** *adj.*

pro·to·zo·an (prō′tə·zō′ən) *n. pl.* **·zo·a** (-zō′ə) Any of a phylum of single-celled animals, including free-living, aquatic forms and pathogenic parasites. Also **pro′to·zo′on.** —*adj.* Pertaining or belonging to the phylum of protozoans: also **pro′to·zo′·ic.** [< PROTO- + Gk. *zōion* animal]

pro·tract (prō·trakt′, prə-) *v.t.* **1** To extend in time; prolong. **2** In surveying, to draw or map by means of a scale and protractor; plot. **3** *Zool.* To protrude or extend. [< L *protractus,* pp. of *protrahere* extend] —**pro·trac′tion** *n.* —**pro·tract′i·ble, pro·trac′tive** *adj.*

pro·tract·ed (prō·trak′tid, prə-) *adj.* Unduly or unusually extended or prolonged. —**pro·tract′ed·ly** *adv.* —**pro·tract′ed·ness** *n.*

pro·trac·tile (prō·trak′til) *adj.* Capable of being protracted or protruded; protrusile.

pro·trac·tor (prō·trak′tər) *n.* **1** An instrument for measuring and laying off angles. **2** One who or that which protracts.

pro·trude (prō·trōōd′, prə-) *v.t. & v.i.* **·trud·ed, ·trud·ing** To push or thrust out; project outward. [< L *pro-* forward + *trudere* thrust] —**pro·tru′dent** *adj.* —**pro·tru′sion** (-trōō′zhən) *n.*

pro·tru·sile (prō·trōō′sil) *adj.* Adapted to being thrust out, as a tentacle, etc. Also **pro·tru′si·ble.**

pro·tru·sive (prō·trōō′siv) *adj.* **1** Tending to protrude. **2** Pushing or driving forward. —**pro·tru′sive·ly** *adv.* —**pro·tru′sive·ness** *n.*

pro·tu·ber·ance (prō·tyōō′bər·əns) *n.* **1** Something that protrudes; a knob; prominence. **2** The state of being protuberant. Also **pro·tu′ber·an·cy.** [< LL *protuberare* bulge out] —**pro·tu′ber·ant** *adj.* —**pro·tu′ber·ant·ly** *adv.*

proud (proud) *adj.* **1** Moved by, having, or exhibiting a due sense of pride; self-respecting. **2** Characterized by excessive or immoderate pride. **3** Being a cause of honorable pride: a *proud* occasion. **4** Appreciative of an honor; glad: *proud* of his heritage. **5** High-mettled, as a horse; spirited. [< OE *prūd*] —**proud′ly** *adv.* —**Syn. 2** arrogant, haughty, supercilious, disdainful.

proud flesh An excessive growth of tissue at a healing wound or ulcer.

Prov, Prov. Proverbs.

prov. province; provincial; provisional; provost.

prove (prōōv) *v.* **proved, proved** or **prov·en** (prōō′vən), **prov·ing** *v.t.* **1** To show to be true or genuine, as by evidence or argument. **2** To determine the quality or genuineness of; test. **3** To establish the authenticity or validity of, as a will. **4** *Math.* To verify the accuracy of by an independent process. **5** *Printing* To take a proof of or from. **6** *Archaic* To learn by experience. —*v.i.* **7** To turn out to be: His hopes *proved* vain. [< L *probare* to test, try] —**prov′a·ble** *adj.* —**prov′er** *n.*

prov·e·nance (prov′ə·nəns) *n.* Origin or source, as of an archeological find or an object of art. [F< *provenant,* pr.p. of *provenir* come forth]

Pro·ven·çal (prō′vən·säl′, *Fr.* prō·vän·sál′) *n.* **1** The Romance language of Provence, France. **2** A native or resident of Provence. —*adj.* Of or pertaining to Provence, its inhabitants, or their language.

prov·en·der (prov′ən·dər) *n.* **1** Dry food for cattle, as hay. **2** Provisions. [< OF *provende* an allowance of food]

pro·ve·ni·ence (prō·vē′nē·əns, -vēn′yəns) *n.* PROVENANCE.

prov·erb (prov′ərb) *n.* **1** A terse expression of a popularly accepted piece of wisdom. **2** Something proverbial; a typical example; byword. [< L *pro-* before + *verbum* a word] —**Syn. 1** adage, aphorism, maxim, motto, saying, truism.

pro·ver·bi·al (prə·vûr′bē·əl) *adj.* **1** Of the nature of or pertaining to a proverb. **2** Generally known or remarked. —**pro·ver′bi·al·ly** *adv.*

Prov·erbs (prov′ərbz) *n.pl. (construed as sing.)* A book of the Old Testament consisting of moral sayings.

pro·vide (prə·vīd′) *v.* **·vid·ed, ·vid·ing** *v.t.* **1** To acquire for or supply; furnish. **2** To afford; yield: to *provide* pleasure. **3** To set down as a condition; stipulate. —*v.i.* **4** To take measures in advance: with *for* or *against.* **5** To furnish means of subsistence: usu. with *for.* **6** To make a stipulation. [< L *providere* foresee] —**pro·vid′er** *n.*

pro·vid·ed (prə·vī′did) *conj.* On condition that.

prov·i·dence (prov′ə·dəns) *n.* **1** *Often cap.* The care exercised by nature or God's will over the universe. **2** Care exercised for the future; foresight. [< L *providentia* < *providens,* pr.p. of *providere* foresee]

Prov·i·dence (prov′ə·dəns) *n.* God; the Deity.

prov·i·dent (prov′ə·dənt) *adj.* **1** Anticipating and preparing for future wants or emergencies; exercising foresight. **2** Economical; thrifty. —**prov′i·dent·ly** *adv.*

prov·i·den·tial (prov′ə·den′shəl) *adj.* **1** Resulting from or revealing the action of God's providence. **2** As if caused by divine intervention; wonderful. —**prov′i·den′tial·ly** *adv.*

pro·vid·ing (prə·vī′ding) *conj.* Provided; in case that.

prov·ince (prov′ins) *n.* **1** An administrative division within a country: the *provinces* of Canada. **2** A region or country ruled by the Roman Empire. **3** *pl.* Those regions that lie at a distance from the capital or major cities. **4** A sphere of knowledge or activity: the *province* of chemistry. **5** Proper concern or compass, as of responsibilities or duties: The *province* of the judge is to apply the laws. [< L *provincia* an official duty or charge, a province]

pro·vin·cial (prə·vin′shəl) *adj.* **1** Of or characteristic of a province. **2** Confined to a province; rustic. **3** Narrow; unsophisticated; uninformed. —*n.* **1** A native or inhabitant of a province. **2** One who is provincial. —**pro·vin′ci·al′i·ty** (-shē·al′ə·tē) *n.* —**pro·vin′cial·ly** *adv.*

pro·vin·cial·ism (prə·vin′shəl·iz′əm) *n.* **1** The quality of being provincial. **2** Provincial peculiarity, esp. of speech.

pro·vi·sion (prə·vizh′ən) *n.* **1** A measure taken in advance, as against future need. **2** *pl.* Food or a supply of food; victuals. **3** Something provided or prepared in anticipation of need. **4** A stipulation or requirement. —*v.t.* To provide with food or provisions. [< L *provisus,* p.p. of *providere* foresee] —**pro·vi′sion·er** *n.*

pro·vi·sion·al (prə·vizh′ən·əl) *adj.* Provided for a present service or temporary necessity: a *provisional* army. Also **pro·vi′sion·ar′y** (-er′ē). —**pro·vi′sion·al·ly** *adv.*

pro·vi·so (prə·vī′zō) *n. pl.* **·sos** or **·soes** **1** A conditional stipulation. **2** A clause, as in a contract or statute, limiting, modifying, or rendering conditional its operation. [< Med. L *proviso (quod)* it being provided (that)]

pro·vi·so·ry (prə·vī′zər·ē) *adj.* **1** Conditional. **2** Provisional. —**pro·vi′so·ri·ly** *adv.*

pro·vo (prō′vō) *n. pl.* **·vos** A youthful member of any of various groups committed to violent political action. [Du. < F *provocateur*]

prov·o·ca·tion (prov′ə·kā′shən) *n.* **1** The act of provoking. **2** Something that provokes or incites; esp., something that provokes anger or annoyance.

pro·voc·a·tive (prə·vok′ə·tiv) *adj.* Serving to provoke or excite; stimulating: a *provocative* theory. —*n.* That which

provokes or tends to provoke. —**pro·voc′a·tive·ly** adv. —**pro·voc′a·tive·ness** n.

pro·voke (prə·vōk′) v.t. **-voked, -vok·ing** 1 To stir to anger or resentment; irritate; vex. 2 To arouse or stimulate to some action. 3 To stir up or bring about: to *provoke* a quarrel. [< L *pro-* forth + *vocare* to call]

prov·ost (prō′vōst, prō′vəst, prov′əst) n. 1 A person having charge or authority over others. 2 The chief magistrate of a Scottish burgh. 3 An administrative official in some English and American colleges. 4 *Eccl.* The head of a collegiate chapter or a cathedral; a dean. [< L *praepositus* a prefect] —**prov′ost·ship** n.

pro·vost marshal (prō′vō) A military officer commanding a company of military police (**provost guard**).

prow (prou) n. 1 The forward part of a ship; the bow. 2 Any pointed projection, as of an airplane. [< Gk. *prōira*]

prow·ess (prou′is) n. 1 Strength, skill, and courage, esp. in battle. 2 Formidable skill; expertise. [< OF *prou* brave]

prowl (proul) v.t. & v.i. To roam about stealthily, as in search of prey or plunder. —n. The act of prowling. [ME *prollen*] —**prowl′er** n.

Prow of a ship

prowl car SQUAD CAR.

prox·i·mal (prok′sə·məl) adj. 1 Relatively nearer the center of the body or point of origin. 2 PROXIMATE. [< L *proximus* nearest] —**prox′i·mal·ly** adv.

prox·i·mate (prok′sə·mit) adj. Being in immediate relation with something else; next; near. [< L *proximus* nearest, superl. of *prope* near] —**prox′i·mate·ly** adv.

prox·im·i·ty (prok·sim′ə·tē) n. The state or fact of being near; nearness. [< L *proximus* nearest]

prox·i·mo (prok′sə·mō) adv. In or of the next or coming month. [< L *proximo (mense)* in the next (month)]

prox·y (prok′sē) n. pl. **prox·ies** 1 A person empowered by another to act for him. 2 The means or agency of one so empowered: to vote by *proxy*. 3 The office or right to act for another. 4 A document conferring the authority to act for another. [< L *procurare* procure]

pr.p. present participle.

prude (prōōd) n. One who displays an exaggerated devotion to modesty and propriety, esp. in sexual matters. [F < *prudefemme* an excellent woman] —**prud′ish** adj. —**prud′ish·ly** adv. —**prud′ish·ness** n.

pru·dence (prōōd′ns) n. 1 The exercise of thoughtful care, sound judgment, or discretion; cautious wisdom. 2 Economy; thrift. —**pru·den·tial** (prōō·den′shəl) adj.

pru·dent (prōōd′nt) adj. 1 Habitually careful to avoid errors and to follow the most reasonable or practical course; politic. 2 Exercising sound judgment; wise; judicious. 3 Characterized by discretion; cautious in manner. 4 Frugal; provident. [< L *prudens* knowing, skilled] —**pru′dent·ly** adv. —**Syn.** 1 shrewd. 2 sensible, sagacious, thoughtful. 3 circumspect.

prud·er·y (prōō′dər·ē) n. pl. **·er·ies** 1 Exaggerated devotion to modesty and propriety, esp. in sexual matters. 2 An action characteristic of a prude.

prune[1] (prōōn) n. 1 The dried fruit of any of several varieties of plum. 2 *Slang* A stupid or disagreeable person. [< Gk. *prounon* a plum]

prune[2] (prōōn) v.t. & v.i. **pruned, prun·ing** 1 To trim or cut superfluous branches or parts (from). 2 To cut off (superfluous branches or parts). [< OF *proignier*] —**prun′er** n.

pru·ri·ent (prŏŏr′ē·ənt) adj. 1 Tending to excite lustful thoughts or desires; lewd. 2 Characterized by or having lustful thoughts or desires: *prurient* interest. [< L *prurire* itch, long for] —**pru′ri·ence, pru′ri·en·cy** n. —**pru′ri·ent·ly** adv.

Prussian blue 1 A dark blue pigment or dye composed of various cyanogen compounds of iron. 2 A strong, blue color.

prussic acid HYDROCYANIC ACID.

pry[1] (prī) v.i. **pried, pry·ing** To look or peer carefully, curiously, or slyly; snoop. [ME *prien*]

pry[2] (prī) v.t. **pried, pry·ing** 1 To raise, move, or open by means of a lever. 2 To obtain by effort. —n. 1 A lever, as a bar, stick, or beam. 2 Leverage. [< PRIZE[2]]

pry·er (prī′ər) n. PRIER.

P.S. public school.

P.S., p.s. postscript.

Ps, Ps., Psa. Psalms.

psalm (säm) n. A sacred song or lyric, esp. one contained in the Old Testament Book of Psalms; a hymn. [< Gk. *psalmos* a song sung to the harp]

psalm·ist (sä′mist) n. A composer of psalms. —**the Psalmist** King David, the traditional author of many of the Scriptural psalms.

psalm·o·dy (sä′mə·dē, sal′-) n. pl. **·dies** 1 The singing of psalms in divine worship. 2 A collection of psalms. [< Gk. *psalmos* a psalm + *ōidē* a song] —**psalm′o·dist** n.

Psalms (sämz) n.pl. (construed as sing.) A lyrical book of the Old Testament, containing 150 hymns. Also **Book of Psalms.**

psal·ter (sôl′tər) n. A version of the Book of Psalms used in religious services. [< L *psalterium* a psaltery]

Psal·ter (sôl′tər) n. The Book of Psalms. Also **Psal′ter·y.**

psal·ter·y (sôl′tər·ē) n. pl. **·ter·ies** An ancient stringed musical instrument played by plucking. [< Gk. *psaltērion* < *psallein* to twitch, twang]

pseud. pseudonym.

pseu·do (sōō′dō) adj. Pretended; sham; false.

Psaltery

pseudo- combining form 1 False; pretended: *pseudonym*. 2 Closely resembling; serving or functioning as: *pseudopodium*. Also **pseud-.** [< Gk. *pseudēs* false]

pseu·do·nym (sōō′də·nim) n. A fictitious name; pen name. [< Gk. *pseudēs* false + *onyma* a name] —**pseu·don′y·mous** (sōō·don′ə·məs) adj. —**pseu·don′y·mous·ness, pseu·do·nym·i·ty** (sōō′də·nim′ə·tē) n.

pseu·do·po·di·um (sōō′də·pō′dē·əm) n. pl. **·di·a** (-dē·ə) A temporary extension of the protoplasm of a cell or unicellular organism, serving for taking in food, locomotion, etc. Also **pseu′do·pod** (-pod). [< PSEUDO- + Gk. *podion* little foot] —**pseu′do·po′di·al, pseu·do·po·o·dal** (sōō·dop′ə·dəl) adj.

psf, p.s.f. pounds per square foot.

pshaw (shô) interj. & n. An exclamation of annoyance, disgust, or impatience.

psi (sī, psī, psē) n. The twenty-third letter of the Greek alphabet (Ψ, ψ).

psi, p.s.i. pounds per square inch.

psi·lo·cy·bin (sī′lə·sī′bin) n. A hallucinogenic drug derived from a Mexican mushroom. [< *Psilocybe*, generic name of the mushroom + -IN]

psit·ta·co·sis (sit′ə·kō′sis) n. A viral infection affecting parrots, pigeons, etc., and sometimes humans, in whom it causes pneumonia, fever, etc. [< Gk. *psittakos* a parrot + -OSIS]

pso·ri·a·sis (sə·rī′ə·sis) n. A chronic skin condition characterized by reddish patches and white scales. [< Gk. *psōra* an itch] —**pso·ri·at·ic** (sôr′ē·at′ik, sō′rē-) adj.

PST, P.S.T., P.s.t. Pacific standard time.

psych (sīk) v.t. **psyched, psych·ing** Slang 1 To make mentally ready, as by inducing alertness or tension; key up: often with up. 2 To cause to lose self-assurance, esp. in order to place at a competitive disadvantage; demoralize: often with out: to psych rivals. 3 To manipulate by the use of psychology; esp., to outwit: often with out: psyched him into giving me a loan. 4 To understand: with out: couldn't psych it out. Also psych up. —**Syn.** 2 intimidate, distress, put off, disconcert, discountenance.

psych., psychol. psychologist; psychology.

psy·che (sī′kē) n. 1 The human soul. 2 The mind. [< Gk. *psyche* the soul < *psychein* breathe, blow]

Psy·che (sī′kē) Gk. & Rom. Myth. A maiden beloved by Cupid and regarded as a personification of the soul.

psy·che·de·li·a (sī′kə·dē′lē·ə, -dēl′yə) n. Psychedelic drugs and accessories, or things associated with them.

psy·che·del·ic (sī′kə·del′ik) adj. Causing or having to do with abnormal alterations of consciousness or perception: *psychedelic* drugs. [< Gk. *psychē* soul + *del(os)* manifest + -IC] —**psy′che·del′i·cal·ly** adv.

psy·chi·a·trist (sī·kī′ə·trist) *n.* A medical doctor specializing in the practice of psychiatry.

psy·chi·a·try (sī·kī′ə·trē) *n.* The branch of medicine concerned with mental and emotional disorders. [< PSYCH(O)- + Gk. *iatros* healer] —**psy·chi·at·ric** (sī′kē·at′rik) or ·**ri·cal** *adj.* —**psy′chi·at′ri·cal·ly** *adv.*

psy·chic (sī′kik) *adj.* **1** Of or pertaining to the psyche or mind. **2** Inexplicable with reference to present knowledge or scientific theory: *psychic* phenomena. **3** Sensitive or responsive to phenomena apparently independent of normal sensory stimuli: a *psychic* person. Also **psy′chi·cal.** — *n.* **1** A psychic person. **2** A spiritualistic medium. [< Gk. *psychē* soul] —**psy′chi·cal·ly** *adv.*

psy·cho (sī′kō) *n. pl.* ·**chos** *Slang* A mentally disturbed person; a neurotic or psychopath. —*adj.* **1** Psychologically disturbed. **2** Psychological or psychiatric. [< PSYCHO(NEUROTIC)]

psycho- *combining form* Mind; soul; spirit: *psychosomatic.* Also **psych-.** [< Gk. *psychē* spirit, soul]

psy·cho·ac·tive (sī′kō·ak′tiv) *adj.* Having an effect on the mind or on behavior.

psy·cho·a·nal·y·sis (sī′kō·ə·nal′ə·sis) *n.* **1** A method of psychotherapeutic treatment developed by Sigmund Freud and others, which seeks to alleviate certain mental and emotional disorders. **2** The theory or practice of such treatment. —**psy′cho·an′a·lyt′ic** (-an′ə·lit′ik) or ·**i·cal** *adj.* —**psy′cho·an′a·lyt′i·cal·ly** *adv.*

psy·cho·an·a·lyst (sī′kō·an′ə·list) *n.* One who practices psychoanalysis.

psy·cho·an·a·lyze (sī′kō·an′ə·līz) *v.t.* ·**lyzed, ·lyz·ing** To treat by psychoanalysis. *Brit. sp.* ·**lyse.**

psy·cho·dra·ma (sī′kō·drä′mə, -dram′ə) *n.* A form of psychotherapy in which the patient acts out, occasionally before an audience, situations involving his problems. — **psy′cho·dra·mat′ic** *adj.*

psy·cho·gen·ic (sī′kō·jen′ik) *adj.* Originating in the mind; caused by a mental or emotional condition. —**psy′·cho·gen′i·cal·ly** *adv.*

psy·cho·log·i·cal (sī′kō·loj′i·kəl) *adj.* **1** Of or pertaining to psychology. **2** Of or in the mind. **3** Suitable for affecting the mind: the *psychological* moment. Also **psy′cho·log′ic.** —**psy′cho·log′i·cal·ly** *adv.*

psy·chol·o·gist (sī·kol′ə·jist) *n.* A specialist in psychology.

psy·chol·o·gize (sī·kol′ə·jīz) *v.* ·**gized, ·giz·ing** *v.i.* **1** To theorize psychologically. —*v.t.* **2** To interpret psychologically.

psy·chol·o·gy (sī·kol′ə·jē) *n.* **1** The science of the mind in any of its aspects. **2** The systematic investigation of human or animal learning, behavior, etc. **3** The pattern of mental processes characteristic of an individual or type.

psy·cho·neu·ro·sis (sī′kō·nʸoo·rō′sis) *n. pl.* ·**ses** (-sēz) NEUROSIS. —**psy′cho·neu·rot′ic** (-rot′ik) *adj., n.*

psy·cho·path (sī′kō·path) *n.* One exhibiting severely deranged behavior. —**psy′cho·path′ic** *adj.*

psy·cho·pa·thol·o·gy (sī′kō·pə·thol′ə·jē) *n.* The pathology of the mind. —**psy′cho·path′o·log′i·cal** (-path′ə·loj′i·kəl) *adj.* —**psy′cho·pa·thol′o·gist** *n.*

psy·chop·a·thy (sī·kop′ə·thē) *n.* Mental disorder.

psy·cho·sis (sī·kō′sis) *n. pl.* ·**ses** (-sēz) A severe mental disorder marked by disorganization of the personality. [< Gk. *psychōsis* a giving of life]

psy·cho·so·mat·ic (sī′kō·sō·mat′ik) *adj.* **1** Of or pertaining to the interrelationships of mind and body, esp. with reference to disease. **2** Designating a physical ailment caused or influenced by emotional stress. [< PSYCHO- + SOMATIC]

psy·cho·sur·ger·y (sī′kō·sûr′jər·ē) *n.* Brain surgery performed to treat a mental disorder or alter behavior. — **psy′cho·sur′geon** (-sûr′jən) *n.* —**psy′cho·sur′gi·cal** *adj.*

psy·cho·ther·a·py (sī′kō·ther′ə·pē) *n.* The treatment of certain nervous and mental disorders by psychological techniques such as counseling, psychoanalysis, etc. Also **psy′cho·ther′a·peu′tics** (-ther′ə·pyoo′tiks). —**psy′cho·ther′·a·peu′tic** *adj.* —**psy′cho·ther′a·pist** *n.*

psy·chot·ic (sī·kot′ik) *n.* One suffering from a psychosis. —*adj.* Of psychosis or a psychotic. —**psy·chot′i·cal·ly** *adv.*

Pt platinum.

pt. (*pl.* **pts.**) part; payment; pint; point; port; preterit.

p.t. past tense; for the time being (L *pro tempore*).

PTA, P.T.A. Parent-Teacher Association.

ptar·mi·gan (tär′mə·gən) *n. pl.* ·**gans** or ·**gan** Any of various species of grouse of northern regions, usu. having white winter plumage. [< Scot. Gaelic *tarmachan*]

PT boat (pē′tē′) A high-speed, easily maneuverable motorboat equipped with torpedoes and, usu. machine guns and depth charges. [< *p(atrol) t(orpedo)*]

pter·i·do·phyte (ter′i·dō·fīt′) *n.* Any of a division of flowerless plants comprising the ferns, horsetails, and related plants with vascular stems, roots, and leaves. [< Gk. *pteris, pteridos* a fern + *phyton* a plant] —**pter′i·do·phyt′ic** (-fit′ik), **pter′i·doph′y·tous** (-dof′ə·təs) *adj.*

ptero- *combining form* Wing; feather; plume; resembling wings: *pterodactyl.* Also **pter-.** [< Gk. *pteron* wing]

pter·o·dac·tyl (ter′ə·dak′til) *n.* PTEROSAUR. [< Gk. *pteron* a wing + *daktylos* a finger]

pter·o·saur (ter′ə·sôr′) *n.* Any of various fossil reptiles having batlike wings. [< Gk. *pteros* wing + *sauros* lizard] —**pter′o·saur′i·an** *adj.*

-pterous *combining form* Having a specified number or kind of wings: *dipterous.* [< Gk. *pteron* wing]

ptg. printing.

Ptol·e·ma·ic (tol′ə·mā′ik) *adj.* Of or pertaining to Ptolemy, the astronomer who lived in the second century A.D., or to the Ptolemies who ruled Egypt.

Ptolemaic system The astronomical system of Ptolemy, which assumed that the earth was the central body around which the sun, planets, stars, etc., moved.

pto·maine (tō′mān, tō·mān′) *n.* Any of a class of usu. nontoxic compounds derived from decomposing protein. Also **pto′main.** [< Gk. *ptōma* a corpse]

ptomaine poisoning FOOD POISONING. •The term is based upon the erroneous idea that ptomaines usually cause food poisoning.

pty. proprietary.

pty·a·lin (tī′ə·lin) *n.* A digestive enzyme converting starch into dextrin and maltose.[< Gk. *ptyalon* saliva + -IN]

Pu plutonium.

pub (pub) *n. Brit.* A tavern or bar. [< PUB(LIC) (HOUSE)]

pub. public; publication; published; publisher.

pu·ber·ty (pyoo′bər·tē) *n.* **1** The state in an individual's development when he or she is physically capable of sexual reproduction. **2** The age at which puberty begins, usu. fixed legally at 14 years in boys and 12 in girls. [< L *pubes, puberis* an adult]

pu·bes (pyoo′bēz) *n.* **1** The hair that appears on the body at puberty. **2** The genital area that is covered with hair in the adult. [L, pubic hair]

pu·bes·cent (pyoo·bes′ənt) *adj.* **1** Arriving or having arrived at puberty. **2** *Biol.* Covered with fine hair or down, as leaves, etc. [< L *pubescere* attain puberty] —**pu·bes′·cence** *n.*

pu·bic (pyoo′bik) *adj.* Of or pertaining to the region in the lower part of the abdomen.

pu·bis (pyoo′bis) *n. pl.* ·**bes** (-bēz) Either of the two bones which join to form the front arch of the pelvis. [< L *(os) pubis* pubic (bone)]

publ. publication; published; publisher.

pub·lic (pub′lik) *adj.* **1** Of, pertaining to, or affecting the people at large. **2** Of or relating to the community as distinguished from private or personal matters. **3** For the use of or open to all; maintained by or for the community: *public* parks. **4** Well-known; open: a *public* scandal. **5** Occupying an official position. **6** Acting before or for the community: a *public* speaker. —*n.* **1** The people collectively. **2** A group of people sharing some attribute or purpose: the church-going *public.* [< L *publicus*] —**pub′lic·ly** *adv.* —**pub′lic·ness** *n.*

pub·li·can (pub′lə·kən) *n.* **1** In England, the keeper of a public house. **2** In ancient Rome, one who collected the public revenues. [< L *publicanus* a tax gatherer]

---

add, āce, câre, pälm; end, ēven; it, īce; odd, ōpen, ôrder; took, pool; up, bûrn; ə = a in *above*, u in *focus*; yoo = u in *fuse*; oil; pout; check; go; ring; thin; this; zh, *vision.* < derived from; ? origin uncertain or unknown.

pub·li·ca·tion (pub′lə·kā′shən) *n.* **1** The act of publishing. **2** That which is published; any printed work placed on sale or otherwise distributed.

public domain **1** Lands owned by a government. **2** The condition of being freely available for unrestricted use and not protected by copyright or patent.

public house **1** An inn, tavern, or hotel. **2** *Brit.* A saloon or bar.

pub·li·cist (pub′lə·sist) *n.* **1** One who publicizes, as an activity, a person, etc. **2** A writer on international law.

pub·lic·i·ty (pub·lis′ə·tē) *n.* **1** The state of being public. **2** Information, news, or promotional material intended to elicit public interest in some person, product, cause, etc.; also the work or business of preparing and releasing such material. **3** The attention or interest of the public.

pub·li·cize (pub′lə·sīz) *v.t.* **·cized, ·ciz·ing** To give publicity to; promote. *Brit. sp.* **pub′li·cise.**

public opinion The prevailing ideas, beliefs, or attitudes of a community.

public relations The business of representing and promoting the interests or reputation of a person or an organization in its relations with the public.

public school **1** A school maintained by public funds for the free education of the children of the community, usu. covering elementary and secondary grades. **2** In England, a private, endowed boarding school preparing students for the universities.

public servant A government official.

pub·lic-spir·it·ed (pub′lik·spir′it·id) *adj.* Showing an enlightened interest in the welfare of the community.

public utility A business organization which performs some public service, as the supplying of water or electric power, and is subject to governmental regulations.

public works Works built with public money, as post offices, roads, etc.

pub·lish (pub′lish) *v.t.* **1** To print and issue (a book, magazine, etc.) to the public. **2** To make known or announce publicly. **3** To print and issue the work of. —*v.i.* **4** To engage in the business of publishing books, magazines, newspapers, etc. **5** To have one's work printed and issued. [< L *publicare* make public] —**pub′lish·a·ble** *adj.* —**Syn. 2** promulgate, proclaim, declare, advertise.

pub·lish·er (pub′lish·ər) *n.* One who makes a business of publishing books, periodicals, etc.

puce (pyōōs) *n.* Dark purplish brown. —*adj.* Of this color. [F, lit., flea < L *pulex*]

puck[1] (puk) *n.* A mischievous sprite or hobgoblin. [< OE *pūca* a goblin] —**puck′ish** *adj.* —**puck′ish·ly** *adv.* —**puck′ish·ness** *n.*

puck[2] (puk) *n.* A hard rubber disk used in playing hockey. [? var. of POKE[1]]

puck·a (puk′ə) *adj.* PUKKA.

puck·er (puk′ər) *v.t. & v.i.* To gather or draw up into small folds or wrinkles. —*n.* A wrinkle. [?< POKE[2]]

pud·ding (pŏŏd′ing) *n.* **1** A sweetened and flavored dessert of soft food. **2** A sausage stuffed with seasoned, minced meat, blood, etc. [ME *poding*]

pud·dle (pud′l) *n.* **1** A small pool of water or other liquid. **2** A pasty mixture of clay and water. —*v.t.* **·dled, ·dling** **1** To convert (molten pig iron) into wrought iron by melting and stirring in the presence of oxidizing agents. **2** To mix (clay, etc.) with water to obtain a watertight paste. **3** To line, as canal banks, with such a mixture. **4** To make muddy; stir up. [ME < OE *pudd* a ditch] —**pud′dler** *n.*

pud·dling (pud′ling) *n.* The operation of making wrought iron from pig iron by agitation in a molten state with oxidizing agents present.

pu·den·dum (pyōō·den′dəm) *n. pl.* **·da** (-də) **1** The vulva. **2** *pl.* The external genitals of either sex. [L, neut. of *pudendus* (something) to be ashamed of] —**pu·den′·dal** *adj.*

pudg·y (puj′ē) *adj.* **pudg·i·er, pudg·i·est** Short and thick; fat. [< Scot. *pud* belly] —**pudg′i·ly** *adv.* —**pudg′i·ness** *n.*

pueb·lo (pweb′lō *for*

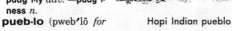

Hopi Indian pueblo

def. 1, pwä′blō *for def. 2) n. pl.* **·los** **1** A communal adobe or stone building or group of buildings of the Indians of the sw U.S. **2** A town or village of Indians or Spanish Americans, as in Mexico. [Sp., a town, people < L *populus*]

Pueb·lo (pweb′lō) *n.* A member of one of the Indian tribes of Mexico and the sw U.S.

pu·er·ile (pyōō′ər·il, pwer′il, -īl) *adj.* Childish; immature; silly. [< L *puer* boy] —**pu′er·ile·ly** *adv.* —**pu′er·il′i·ty, pu′er·ile·ness** *n.*

pu·er·per·al (pyōō·ûr′pər·əl) *adj.* Pertaining to or resulting from childbirth. [< L *puer* boy + *parere* bring forth]

Puerto Ri·co (pwer·tə rē′kō, pôr-) An island commonwealth of the West Indies, a part of the U.S., 3,423 sq. mi., cap. San Juan. •See map at DOMINICAN REPUBLIC. —**Puer′to Ri′can** *adj., n.*

puff (puf) *n.* **1** A short, mild explosive force or emission, as a gust of air or expelled breath. **2** The sound of such a force. **3** The air, breath, etc., so felt or emitted: a small *puff* of smoke. **4** The act of sucking in and exhaling in the course of smoking a cigarette, etc. **5** A light, air-filled piece of pastry. **6** A pad for dusting powder on the skin. **7** A small protuberance or swelling. **8** A loose roll of hair. **9** A quilted bed coverlet. **10** A part of a fabric gathered at the edges. **11** A public expression of fulsome praise. —*v.i.* **1** To blow in puffs, as the wind. **2** To breathe hard, as after violent exertion. **3** To emit smoke, steam, etc., in puffs. **4** To smoke a cigarette, etc., with puffs. **5** To move, act, or exert oneself while emitting puffs: with *away, up,* etc. **6** To swell, as with air or pride; dilate: often with *up.* —*v.t.* **7** To send forth or emit with short puffs or breaths. **8** To move, impel, or stir up with or in puffs. **9** To smoke, as a cigarette or pipe, with puffs. **10** To swell or distend. **11** To praise fulsomely. **12** To arrange (the hair) in a puff. [< OE *pyffan*] —**puff′i·ly** *adv.* —**puff′i·ness** *n.* —**puff′y** *adj.* (**·i·er, ·i·est**)

puff adder **1** A large African viper that puffs and hisses when disturbed. **2** HOGNOSE.

puff·ball (puf′bôl′) *n.* A globular fungus that puffs out dustlike spores if broken open when ripe.

puff·er (puf′ər) *n.* **1** One who puffs. **2** Any of various fishes that can inflate themselves with air or water.

puff·er·y (puf′ər·ē) *n.* Excessive praise, esp. to obtain publicity.

puf·fin (puf′in) *n.* Any of various northern sea birds with a chunky body and a large, triangular bill. [ME *poffin*]

Puffin

pug[1] (pug) *v.t.* **pugged, pug·ging** **1** To work (clay) with water in molding pottery or making bricks. **2** To fill in or cover with mortar, clay, felt, etc., to deaden sound. —*n.* A mixture of clay worked with water for brick-making, etc. [< dial. E]

pug[2] (pug) *n.* **1** A short-haired dog with a square body, upturned nose and curled tail. **2** PUG NOSE. [?]

pug[3] (pug) *n. Slang* A professional prizefighter. [Short for PUGILIST]

pu·gi·lism (pyōō′jə·liz′əm) *n.* BOXING. [< L *pugil* a boxer] —**pu′gi·list** *n.* —**pu′gi·lis′tic** *adj.* —**pu′gi·lis′ti·cal·ly** *adv.*

pug·na·cious (pug·nā′shəs) *adj.* Disposed or inclined to fight; quarrelsome. [< L *pugnus* fist] —**pug·na′cious·ly** *adv.* —**pug·nac·i·ty** (-nas′ə·tē), **pug·na′cious·ness** *n.*

pug nose A thick, short, upturned nose. [< PUG[2] + NOSE] —**pug′-nosed′** *adj.*

pu·is·sant (pyōō′ə·sənt, pyōō·is′ənt, pwis′ənt) *adj.* Powerful; mighty. [< L *posse* be able] —**pu′is·sance** *n.* —**pu′is·sant·ly** *adv.*

puke (pyōōk) *v.t. & v.i.* **puked, puk·ing,** *n. Informal* VOMIT. [?]

puk·ka (puk′ə) *adj.* Genuine; sound. [< Hind. *pakkā* cooked, ripe]

pul·chri·tude (pul′krə·t(y)ōōd) *n.* Beauty; grace. [< L *pulcher* beautiful] —**pul·chri·tu·di·nous** (-t(y)ōō′də·nəs) *adj.*

pule (pyōōl) *v.i.* **puled, pul·ing** To cry plaintively, as a child; whimper; whine. [< MF *pioler* chirp] —**pul′er** *n.*

Pul·it·zer Prize (po͞ol'it·sər, pyo͞o'lit-) Any of several annual awards for outstanding work in American journalism, literature, drama, and music, established by Joseph Pulitzer, 1847–1911, U.S. journalist.

pull (po͞ol) *v.t.* 1 To apply force to so as to cause motion toward or after the person or thing exerting force; drag; tug. 2 To draw or remove from a natural or fixed place: to *pull* a tooth or plug. 3 To give a pull or tug to. 4 To pluck, as a fowl. 5 To draw asunder; tear; rend: with *to pieces, apart,* etc. 6 To strain so as to cause injury: to *pull* a ligament. 7 In sports, to strike (the ball) so as to cause it to curve obliquely from the direction in which the striker faces. 8 *Informal* To put into effect; carry out: to *pull* off a robbery. 9 *Informal* To make a raid on; arrest. 10 *Informal* To draw out so as to use: to *pull* a knife. 11 To make or obtain by impression from type: to *pull* a proof. 12 In boxing, to deliver (a punch, etc.) with less than full strength. 13 In horse-racing, to restrain (a horse) so as to prevent its winning. 14 To operate (an oar) by drawing toward one. —*v.i.* 15 To use force in hauling, dragging, moving, etc. 16 To move: with *out, in, away, ahead,* etc. 17 To drink or inhale deeply. 18 *Informal* To attract attention or customers: an ad that *pulls.* 19 To row. —**pull for** 1 To strive in behalf of. 2 *Informal* To declare one's allegiance to. —**pull oneself together** To regain one's composure. —**pull through** To survive in spite of illness, etc. —**pull up** To come to a halt. —*n.* 1 The act or process of pulling. 2 Something that is pulled, as a handle. 3 A long swallow or a deep puff. 4 The drawing of an oar in rowing. 5 A steady, continuous effort, as in climbing: a long *pull* to the top. 6 *Informal* Influence, esp. with those in power: political *pull.* 7 An attractive force: the *pull* of gravity. [< OE *pullian* pluck] —**pull'er** *n.*

pull·back (po͞ol'bak') *n.* A withdrawal, as of troops.

pul·let (po͞ol'it) *n.* A young hen, usu. less than a year old. [< L *pullus* chicken]

pul·ley (po͞ol'ē) *n.* 1 A wheel or wheels grooved to receive a rope, usu. mounted in a block, used singly to reverse the direction of force applied, as in lifting a weight, and in various combinations to increase force at the expense of distance. 2 A flat or flanged wheel driving, carrying, or being driven by a flat belt, used to transmit power. [< Gk. *polos* a pivot, axis]

Pull·man (po͞ol'mən) *n.* A railroad car with compartments for sleeping or other special accommodations. Also **Pullman car.** [< George M. *Pullman,* 1831–97, U.S. inventor]

pull·out (po͞ol'out') *n.* 1 A withdrawal or removal, as of troops. 2 Something to be pulled out, as an oversize leaf folded into a magazine.

pull·o·ver (po͞ol'ō'vər) *adj.* Put on by being drawn over the head. —*n.* A garment put on in such a way, as a sweater.

pul·mo·nar·y (po͞ol'mə·ner'ē, pul'-) *adj.* 1 Pertaining to or affecting the lungs. 2 Having lunglike organs. 3 Designating the blood vessels carrying blood between the lungs and heart. Also **pul·mon·ic** (po͞ol·mon'ik, pul-). [< L *pulmo, pulmonis* lung] • See HEART.

Pul·mo·tor (po͞ol'mō'tər, pul'-) *n.* A machine for applying artificial respiration: a trade name.

pulp (pulp) *n.* 1 A moist, soft, slightly cohering mass, as the soft, succulent part of fruit. 2 A mixture of wood fibers or rags, made semifluid and forming the basis from which paper is made. 3 *pl.* Magazines printed on rough, unglazed, wood-pulp paper, and usu. having contents of a sensational nature. 4 Powdered ore mixed with water. 5 The soft tissue of vessels and nerves that fills the central part of a tooth. • See TOOTH. —*v.t.* 1 To reduce to pulp. 2 To remove the pulp from. —*v.i.* 3 To be or become pulp. [< L *pulpa* flesh, pulp] —**pulp'i·ness** *n.* —**pulp'y** *adj.*

pul·pit (po͞ol'pit, pul'-) *n.* 1 An elevated stand or desk for preaching in a church. 2 The office or work of preaching. 3 The clergy. [< L *pulpitum* platform]

pulp·wood (pulp'wo͞od') *n.* Soft wood used in the manufacture of paper.

pul·que (pul'kē, po͞ol'-; *Sp.* po͞ol'kä) *n.* A fermented Mexican drink made from agave. [Sp.]

pul·sar (pul'sär) *n.* An astronomical object that emits radio waves in pulses whose repetition rate is extremely stable. [< *puls(ating)* + (*st*)*ar*]

pul·sate (pul'sāt) *v.i.* **·sat·ed, ·sat·ing** 1 To move or throb with rhythmical impulses, as the pulse or heart. 2 To vibrate; quiver. [< L *pulsare,* freq. of *pellere* beat] —**pul·sa'tion, pul'sa·tor** *n.* —**pul'sa·tive** (-sə-tiv), **pul'sa·to·ry** *adj.*

pulse[1] (puls) *n.* 1 The rhythmic pressure in the arteries due to the beating of the heart. 2 Any short, regular throbbing; pulsation. 3 A brief surge of energy, esp. electrical or electromagnetic energy. 4 Feelings and attitudes sensitively perceived as belonging to a group or community; also, an indication of such feelings. —*v.i.* **pulsed, puls·ing** To manifest a pulse; pulsate; throb. [< L *pulsus* p.p. of *pellere* beat]

pulse[2] (puls) *n.* Leguminous plants collectively, as peas, beans, etc., or their edible seeds. [< L *puls* pottage]

pulse·jet (puls'jet') *n.* A jet engine that operates intermittently and produces power in rapid bursts.

pul·ver·ize (pul'və·rīz) *v.* **·ized, ·iz·ing** *v.t.* 1 To reduce to powder or dust, as by grinding or crushing. 2 To demolish; annihilate. —*v.i.* 3 To become reduced to powder or dust. *Brit. sp.* **·ise.** [< L *pulvis, pulveris* a powder, dust] —**pul'ver·iz'a·ble, pul'ver·a·ble** (pul'və·rə·bəl) *adj.* —**pul'ver·i·za'tion, pul'ver·iz'er** *n.*

pu·ma (pyo͞o'mə) *n.* MOUNTAIN LION. [< Quechua]

pum·ice (pum'is) *n.* Porous volcanic lava, used as an abrasive and polisher, esp. when powdered. Also **pumice stone.** —*v.t.* **·iced, ·ic·ing** To smooth, polish, or clean with pumice. [< L *pumex*] —**pu·mi·ceous** (pyo͞o·mish'əs) *adj.*

pum·mel (pum'əl) *v.t.* **·meled** or **·melled, ·mel·ing** or **·mel·ling** POMMEL.

pump[1] (pump) *n.* A device using suction or pressure to raise, circulate, exhaust, or compress a liquid or gas. —*v.t.* 1 To raise (a liquid) with a pump. 2 To remove the water, etc., from. 3 To inflate with air by means of a pump. 4 To propel, discharge, force, etc., from or as if from a pump. 5 To cause to operate in the manner of a pump. 6 To question persistently or subtly. 7 To obtain (information) in such a manner. —*v.i.* 8 To work a pump. 9 To raise water or other liquid with a pump. 10 To move up and down like a pump or pump handle. [< MDu. *pompe*] —**pump'er** *n.*

pump[2] (pump) *n.* A low-cut shoe without a fastening, worn esp. by women. [?]

pum·per·nick·el (pum'pər·nik'əl) *n.* A coarse, dark bread made with rye flour. [G]

pump·kin (pump'kin, pum'-, pung'-) *n.* 1 A coarse trailing vine with gourdlike fruit. 2 Its large, edible, orange-yellow fruit. [< Gk. *pepōn* a melon]

pun (pun) *n.* The humorous use of two words having the same or similar sounds but different meanings, or of a word having two more or less incongruous meanings. —*v.i.* **punned, pun·ning** To make a pun or puns. [? < Ital. *puntiglio* a fine point]

punch[1] (punch) *n.* 1 A tool for perforating or indenting, or for driving an object into a hole. 2 A machine for impressing a design or stamping a die. —*v.t.* To perforate, shape, indent, etc., with a punch. [ME *punchon puncheon*]

punch[2] (punch) *v.t.* 1 To strike sharply, esp. with the fist. 2 To poke with a stick; prod. 3 To drive (cattle). —*n.* 1 A swift blow with the fist. 2 A thrust or nudge. 3 *Informal* Vitality; effectiveness; force. — **punch in** (or **out**) To activate a time clock and record the hour at the start (or completion) of a period of work. [ME *punchen*] —**punch'er** *n.* —**Syn.** 1 hit, pound, pommel, box.

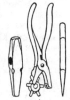

Punches
a. square.
b. revolving.
c. stamping.

punch[3] (punch) *n.* A hot or cold beverage made with fruit

---

add, āce, câre, pălm; end, ēven; it, īce; odd, ōpen, ôrder; to͞ok, po͞ol; up, bûrn; ə = a in *above, u* in *focus;* yo͞o = u in *fuse;* oil; pout; check; go; ring; thin; this; zh, *vision.* < derived from; ? origin uncertain or unknown.

juices, spices, and other ingredients, as tea or soda water, and often mixed with alcoholic spirits. [< Skt. *pañchan* five; from the five original ingredients]

Punch (punch) *n.* The quarrelsome, grotesque hero of a comic puppet show, **Punch and Judy.** —**pleased as Punch** Extremely pleased; highly gratified. [Short for PUNCHINELLO]

punch card In data processing, a card having an arrangement of positions into which holes may be punched for the storage of information. Also **punched card.**

pun·cheon (pun′chən) *n.* **1** An upright supporting timber. **2** A punch or perforating tool. **3** A broad, heavy piece of roughly dressed timber, having one flat, hewed side. **4** A liquor cask of variable capacity, from 72 to 120 gallons. **5** The amount held by such a cask. [< OF *poinçon, poinchon* a punch]

pun·chi·nel·lo (pun′chə·nel′ō) *n. pl.* ·los or ·loes **1** *Usu. cap.* A character in an Italian puppet show, the original of the English Punch. **2** A grotesque character; buffoon. [< dial. Ital. *Polcenella*]

punching bag An inflated or stuffed ball, usu. suspended, that is punched for exercise.

punch press A machine equipped with dies for cutting or forming metal.

punch·y (pun′chē) *adj.* **punch·i·er, punch·i·est** *Informal* **1** Dazed or confused, as from having been struck on the head: also **punch-drunk** (punch′drungk′). **2** Lively; snappy. —**punch′i·ly** *adv.* —**punch′i·ness** *n.*

punc·til·i·o (pungk·til′ē·ō) *n. pl.* ·til·i·os **1** A fine point of etiquette. **2** Preciseness in the observance of etiquette. [< L *punctum* a point]

punc·til·i·ous (pungk·til′ē·əs) *adj.* Very exacting in observing rules or conventions. [< Ital. *puntiglio* small point] —**punc·til′i·ous·ly** *adv.* —**punc·til′i·ous·ness** *n.*

punc·tu·al (pungk′chōō·əl) *adj.* **1** Arriving on time; prompt. **2** Habitually exact as to appointed time. **3** Consisting of or confined to a point. [< L *punctus* a point] —**punc′tu·al′i·ty** *n.* —**punc′tu·al·ly** *adv.*

punc·tu·ate (pungk′chōō·āt) *v.* ·at·ed, ·at·ing *v.t.* **1** To divide or mark with punctuation. **2** To interrupt at intervals. **3** To emphasize. —*v.i.* **4** To use punctuation. [< L *punctus* a point] —**punc′tu·a′tor** *n.*

punc·tu·a·tion (pungk′chōō·ā′shən) *n.* **1** The use of points or marks in written or printed matter to aid in the better comprehension of the meaning and grammatical relation of the words. **2** The marks so used.

punctuation mark Any of the marks used in punctuating, as the period or comma.

punc·ture (pungk′chər) *v.* ·tured, ·tur·ing *v.t.* **1** To pierce with a sharp point. **2** To make by pricking, as a hole. **3** To cause to collapse: to *puncture* a cherished illusion. —*v.i.* **4** To be pierced or punctured. —*n.* **1** A small hole, as one made by piercing. **2** The act of puncturing. [< L *punctus,* p.p. of *pungere* prick]

pun·dit (pun′dit) *n.* **1** One who is or assumes the part of an expert in making pronouncements, criticisms, predictions, etc. **2** In India, a Brahmin versed in Sanskrit lore, Hindu religion, etc. [< Skt. *paṇḍita* learned] —**pun′dit·ry** (-rē) *n.*

pun·gent (pun′jənt) *adj.* **1** Causing a sharp pricking, stinging, piercing, or acrid sensation. **2** Affecting the mind or feelings so as to cause pain; piercing; sharp. **3** Caustic; keen; cutting: *pungent* sarcasm. **4** Telling; pointed. [< L *pungere* prick] —**pun′gen·cy** *n.* —**pun′gent·ly** *adv.*

Pu·nic (pyōō′nik) *adj.* Of or pertaining to ancient Carthage or the Carthaginians.

pun·ish (pun′ish) *v.t.* **1** To subject (a person) to pain, confinement, or other penalty for a crime or fault. **2** To subject the perpetrator of (an offense) to a penalty. **3** To treat roughly; injure; hurt. [< L *punire*] —**pun′ish·a·ble** *adj.* —**pun′ish·a·bil′i·ty, pun′ish·er** *n.*

pun·ish·ing (pun′ish·ing) *adj.* Requiring exhausting effort; taxing; demanding: a *punishing* schedule.

pun·ish·ment (pun′ish·mənt) *n.* **1** Penalty imposed, as for a violation of law. **2** Any pain or loss inflicted in response to wrongdoing. **3** The act of punishing. **4** Physical damage or abuse.

pu·ni·tive (pyōō′nə·tiv) *adj.* Pertaining to or inflicting punishment. —**pu′ni·tive·ly** *adv.* —**pu′ni·tive·ness** *n.*

punk[1] (pungk) *n.* **1** Decayed wood, used as tinder. **2** Any substance that smolders when ignited. [< Algon.]

punk[2] (pungk) *Slang n.* **1** Rubbish; nonsense; anything worthless. **2** A petty hoodlum. **3** An inexperienced youth, esp. a young man: usu. contemptuous. —*adj.* Worthless; useless. [?]

pun·ky (pung′kē) *n. pl.* ·kies Any of various tiny, bloodsucking insects. Also **pun′key, pun′kie.** [< PUNK[1]]

pun·ster (pun′stər) *n.* One who enjoys making puns. Also **pun′ner.**

punt[1] (punt) *n.* A flat-bottomed, square-ended boat for use in shallow waters, and propelled with a pole. —*v.t.* **1** To propel (a boat) by pushing with a pole against the bottom of a shallow stream, lake, etc. **2** To convey in a punt. —*v.i.* **3** To go or hunt in a punt. [< L *ponto*] —**punt′er** *n.*

Punt

punt[2] (punt) *v.i.* To gamble or bet in certain card games, esp. against the banker. [< L *punctum* a point]

punt[3] (punt) *n.* In football, a kick made by dropping the ball from the hands and kicking it before it strikes the ground. —*v.t.* **1** To propel (a football) with a punt. —*v.i.* **2** In football, to make a punt. [?] —**punt′er** *n.*

pu·ny (pyōō′nē) *adj.* ·ni·er, ·ni·est Small or inferior, as in power, significance, etc. [< OF *puisne* born afterward] —**pu′ni·ly** *adv.* —**pu′ni·ness** *n.* —**Syn.** slight, minor, unimportant, frail.

pup (pup) *n.* The young of certain animals, as a dog, wolf, fox, seal, whale, etc. —*v.i.* **pupped, pup·ping** To bring forth pups. [Short for PUPPY]

pu·pa (pyōō′pə) *n. pl.* ·pae (-pē) or ·pas A quiescent stage between larva and adult in the metamorphosis of certain insects. [L, a girl, puppet] —**pu′pal** *adj.*

pu·pate (pyōō′pāt) *v.i.* ·pat·ed, ·pat·ing To enter upon or undergo the pupal condition. —**pu·pa′tion** *n.*

pu·pil[1] (pyōō′pəl) *n.* A person under the care of a teacher, as in a school. [< L *pupillus* and *pupilla,* dim. of *pupus* boy and *pupa* girl] —**pu′pil·age, pu′pil·lage** *n.* —**Syn.** student, disciple, scholar, learner.

pu·pil[2] (pyōō′pəl) *n.* The circular opening in the iris of the eye, through which light reaches the retina. [< L *pupilla* pupil of the eye] • See EYE.

Pupa of a butterfly

pup·pet (pup′it) *n.* **1** A small figure, as of a person or animal, manipulated usu. by the hands, or by pulling strings or wires attached to its jointed parts. **2** A person controlled by the will or whim of another. **3** A doll. —*adj.* **1** Of puppets. **2** Performing the will of an unseen power; not autonomous: a *puppet* state or government. [< L *pupa* a girl, doll, puppet] —**pup′pet·ry** (-rē) *n.*

pup·pet·eer (pup′i·tir′) *n.* One who manipulates puppets.

pup·py (pup′ē) *n. pl.* ·pies A young dog. [< L *pupa* a girl, doll]

puppy love Temporary affection or love that a boy and girl feel for each other.

pup tent A small tent providing shelter for one or two people.

pur (pûr) *n. & v.* PURR.

pur·blind (pûr′blind′) *adj.* **1** Partly blind. **2** Having little or no insight. **3** *Obs.* Totally blind. [< ME *pur* totally + *blind* blind] —**pur′blind′ly** *adv.* —**pur′blind′ness** *n.*

pur·chase (pûr′chəs) *v.t.* ·chased, ·chas·ing **1** To acquire by paying money or its equivalent; buy. **2** To obtain by exertion, sacrifice, flattery, etc. **3** To move, hoist, or hold by a mechanical purchase. —*n.* **1** The act of purchasing. **2** That which is purchased. **3** A mechanical hold or grip. **4** A device that gives a mechanical advantage, as a tackle or lever. [OF *porchacier* seek for] —**pur′chas·er** *n.* —**Syn. 1, 2** get, obtain, procure, secure.

pur·dah (pûr′də) *n.* **1** A curtain or screen used to seclude Muslim and Hindu women, esp. in India. **2** The state of seclusion so secured. [< Pers. *pardah* a veil]

pure (pyōōr) *adj.* **pur·er, pur·est 1** Free from mixture or contact with that which weakens, impairs, or pollutes. **2** Free from adulteration; clear; clean: *pure* water. **3** Fault-

less; righteous: *pure* motives. **4** Chaste; innocent. **5** Concerned with fundamental research, as distinguished from practical application: *pure* science. **6** Bred from stock having no admixture for many generations. **7** Nothing but; sheer: *pure* luck. [< L *purus* clean, pure] —**pure′ness** *n.*

pu·rée (pyŏŏ·rā′, pyŏŏr′ā) *n.* **1** A thick pulp, usu. of vegetables, boiled and strained. **2** A thick soup so prepared. — *v.t.* **·reed**, **·ree·ing** To put (cooked or soft food) through a sieve, blender, etc. Also **pu·ree′**. [F< OF *purer* strain< L *purus* pure]

pure·ly (pyŏŏr′lē) *adv.* **1** So as to be free from admixture, taint, or any harmful substance. **2** Chastely; innocently. **3** Merely; only: *purely* as a hobby. **4** Completely: *purely* up to him.

pur·ga·tive (pûr′gə·tiv) *adj.* Purging; cathartic. —*n.* A medication used in purging; cathartic.

pur·ga·to·ry (pûr′gə·tôr′ē, -tō′rē) *n. pl.* **·ries** **1** In Roman Catholic theology, a state or place where the souls of those who have died penitent are made fit for paradise by expiating venial sins. **2** Any place or state of temporary banishment, suffering, or punishment. [< AF < L *purgare* cleanse] —**pur′ga·to′ri·al** *adj.*

purge (pûrj) *v.* **purged**, **purg·ing** *v.t.* **1** To cleanse of what is impure or extraneous; purify. **2** To remove (impurities, etc.) in cleansing: with *away*, *off*, or *out*. **3** To rid (a group, nation, etc.) of individuals regarded as undesirable. **4** To remove or kill such individuals. **5** To cleanse or rid of sin, fault, or defilement. **6** *Med.* **a** To cause evacuation of (the bowels, etc.). **b** To induce evacuation of the bowels of. —*v.i.* **7** To become clean or pure. **8** *Med.* To have or induce evacuation of the bowels. —*n.* **1** The action of an organization, esp. a government, in removing from office or positions of power individuals regarded as undesirable. **2** The act of purging. **3** That which purges; a cathartic. [< L *purgare* cleanse] —**pur·ga·tion** (pûr·gā′shən), **purg′er** *n.*

pu·ri·fy (pyŏŏr′ə·fī) *v.* **·fied**, **·fy·ing** *v.t.* **1** To make pure or clean; rid of extraneous or noxious matter. **2** To free from sin or defilement. **3** To free of debasing elements. —*v.i.* **4** To become pure or clean. [< L *purus* pure + *facere* make] —**pu·rif·i·ca·to·ry** (pyŏŏ·rif′ə·kə·tôr′ē, -tō′rē) *adj.* —**pu·ri·fi·ca·tion** (pyŏŏr′ə·fə·kā′shən), **pu′ri·fi′er** *n.*

Pu·rim (pyŏŏr′im; *Hebrew* pōō·rēm′) *n.* A Jewish festival commemorating the defeat of Haman's plot to massacre the Jews. *Esth.* 9:26.

pur·ism (pyŏŏr′iz·əm) *n.* **1** Strong endorsement of a strict compliance with standards, rules, or conventions considered correct or pure, as in language. **2** Strict compliance with rules of correctness. **3** An instance of such compliance. —**pur′ist** *n.* —**pu·ris′tic**, **pu·ris′ti·cal** *adj.* —**pu·ris′ti·cal·ly** *adv.*

pu·ri·tan (pyŏŏr′ə·tən) *n.* One who is unusually or excessively strict regarding adherence to morality or religious practice. —*adj.* Of or characteristic of puritans. [< LL *puritas* purity] —**pu′ri·tan′ic** or **·i·cal** *adj.* —**pu′ri·tan′i·cal·ly** *adv.* —**pu′ri·tan′i·cal·ness**, **pu′ri·tan·ism** *n.*

Pu·ri·tan (pyŏŏr′ə·tən) *n.* One of a group of English Protestants of the 16th and 17th centuries, many of whom emigrated to the American colonies, who advocated simpler forms of creed and ritual in the Church of England. —*adj.* Of or relating to the Puritans. —**Pu′ri·tan′ic** or **·i·cal** *adj.* —**Pu′ri·tan·ism** *n.*

pu·ri·ty (pyŏŏr′ə·tē) *n.* **1** The character or state of being pure. **2** Absence of admixture or adulteration. **3** Innocence; blamelessness. **4** Degree of absence of white; saturation: said of a color.

purl¹ (pûrl) *v.i.* **1** To whirl; turn. **2** To flow with a bubbling sound. **3** To move in eddies. —*n.* **1** A circling movement of water; an eddy. **2** A gentle murmur, as of a rippling stream. [< Norw. *purla*]

purl² (pûrl) *v.t.* **1** To decorate, as with a border. **2** In knitting, to make (a stitch) backward. **3** To edge with lace, embroidery, etc. —*v.i.* **4** To do edging with lace, etc. —*n.* **1** An edge of lace, embroidery, etc. **2** In lacework, a spiral of gold or silver wire. **3** In knitting, the inversion of the knit stitch. [Earlier *pyrle*]

pur·lieu (pûr′lŏŏ) *n.* **1** *pl.* Outlying districts; outskirts. **2**

A place habitually visited; a haunt. **3** *pl.* Bounds. [< OF *puraler* go through]

pur·lin (pûr′lin) *n.* One of several horizontal timbers supporting rafters. Also **pur′line** (-lin). [ME *purlyn*]

pur·loin (pûr·loin′) *v.t. & v.i.* To steal; filch. [< AF *purloignier* remove, put far off] —**pur·loin′er** *n.*

pur·ple (pûr′pəl) *n.* **1** A color of mingled red and blue, between crimson and violet. **2** Cloth or a garment of this color, an emblem of royalty. **3** Royal power or dignity. **4** Preeminence in rank. —*adj.* **1** Of the color of purple. **2** Imperial; regal. **3** Conspicuously fanciful or ornate: *purple* prose. —*v.t. & v.i.* **·pled**, **·pling** To make or become purple. [< Gk. *porphyra* purple dye] —**pur′plish** *adj.*

Purple Heart A U.S. military decoration of honor awarded to members of the armed forces wounded in action.

pur·port (pər·pôrt′, -pōrt′, pûr′pôrt, -pōrt) *v.t.* **1** To have or bear as its meaning; signify; imply. **2** To claim or profess (to be), esp. falsely. —*n.* (pûr′pôrt, -pōrt) **1** That which is conveyed or suggested as the meaning. **2** The substance of a statement, etc., given in other than the exact words. [< L < *pro-* forth + *portare* carry] —**Syn.** *n.* **1** import, significance. **2** gist, meaning. —**pur·port′ed·ly** *adv.*

pur·pose (pûr′pəs) *n.* **1** An end of effort or action; something to be attained; plan; design; aim. **2** Settled resolution; determination. —**on purpose** Intentionally. —*v.t. & v.i.* **·posed**, **·pos·ing** To intend to do or accomplish; aim. [< OF *porposer*] —**pur′pose·less** *adj.* —**pur′pose·less·ly** *adv.* —**pur′pose·less·ness** *n.*

pur·pose·ful (pûr′pəs·fəl) *adj.* Having, or marked by, purpose; intentional. —**pur′pose·ful·ly** *adv.* —**pur′pose·ful·ness** *n.*

pur·pose·ly (pûr′pəs·lē) *adv.* Intentionally; deliberately; on purpose.

purr (pûr) *n.* An intermittent murmuring sound, such as a cat makes when pleased. —*v.i.* **1** To make such a sound. —*v.t.* **2** To express by purring. [Imit.]

purse (pûrs) *n.* **1** A small bag or pouch for money. **2** A receptacle carried usu. by women for holding personal articles, as a wallet, cosmetics, etc.; pocketbook. **3** Resources or means; a treasury. **4** A sum of money offered as a prize or gift. —*v.t.* **pursed**, **purs·ing** To contract into wrinkles or folds; pucker. [< Gk. *byrsa* a skin]

purs·er (pûr′sər) *n.* A ship's officer having charge of the accounts, records, payroll, etc.

purs·lane (pûrs′lin, -lān) *n.* Any of various prostrate, weedy plants with fleshy leaves and reddish stems. [< L *porcilaca*, var. of *portulaca*]

pur·su·ance (pər·sŏŏ′əns) *n.* The act of pursuing; a following after or following through: in *pursuance* of the truth.

pur·su·ant (pər·sŏŏ′ənt) *adj.* Pursuing. —**pursuant to** In accordance with; by reason of.

pur·sue (pər·sŏŏ′) *v.* **·sued**, **·su·ing** *v.t.* **1** To follow in an attempt to overtake or capture; chase. **2** To seek to attain or gain: to *pursue* fame. **3** To advance along the course of, as a path or plan. **4** To apply one's energies to or have as one's profession. **5** To follow persistently; harass; worry. —*v.i.* **6** To follow. **7** To continue. [< L *pro-* forth + *sequi* follow] —**pur·su′er** *n.*

pur·suit (pər·sŏŏt′) *n.* **1** The act of pursuing. **2** A continued employment, vocation, or preoccupation.

pur·sui·vant (pûr′swi·vənt) *n.* **1** An attendant upon a herald. **2** A follower; esp., a military attendant. [< OF *porsievre* pursue]

purs·y (pûr′sē) *adj.* **purs·i·er**, **purs·i·est** **1** Short-breathed. **2** Fat. [< OF *polser* pant, gasp] —**purs′i·ness** *n.*

pu·ru·lent (pyŏŏr′ə·lənt, -yə·lənt) *adj.* Consisting of or secreting pus; suppurating. [< L *pus*, *puris* pus] —**pu′ru·lence** or **·len·cy** *n.* —**pu′ru·lent·ly** *adv.*

pur·vey (pər·vā′) *v.t. & v.i.* To furnish or provide, as provisions. [< L *providere* foresee] —**pur·vey′or** *n.*

pur·vey·ance (pər·vā′əns) *n.* **1** The act of purveying. **2** Provisions.

pur·view (pûr′vyŏŏ) *n.* **1** Extent or scope of anything, as of official authority. **2** Range of view, experience, or under-

standing; outlook. **3** *Law* The body or the scope or limit of a statute. [< OF *porveier* purvey]

pus (pus) *n.* A viscid, usu. yellowish fluid consisting of bacteria, leukocytes, serum, and dead cells from inflamed tissue.

push (poŏsh) *v.t.* **1** To exert force upon or against (an object) for the purpose of moving. **2** To force (one's way), as through a crowd. **3** To develop, advocate, or promote vigorously and persistently: to *push* a new product. **4** To bear hard upon; press: to be *pushed* for time. **5** *Informal* To approach or come close to: He's *pushing* fifty. **6** *Slang* To sell (narcotic or other drugs) illegally. —*v.i.* **7** To exert pressure against something so as to move it. **8** To move or advance vigorously or persistently. **9** To exert great effort. —*n.* **1** The act of pushing; a propelling or thrusting pressure. **2** Anything pushed to cause action. **3** Determined activity; energy; drive. **4** A vigorous and persistent advance or effort. **5** An emergency; exigency. [< L *pulsare* to push, beat] —**Syn.** *v.* **1** shove, thrust, press, propel, drive.

push button A button or knob which, on being pushed, opens or closes an electric switch. —**push′·but′ton** *adj.*

push·cart (poŏsh′kärt′) *n.* A wheeled cart pushed by hand.

push·er (poŏsh′ər) *n.* **1** One who or that which pushes; esp., an active, energetic person. **2** *Slang* One who sells narcotic or other drugs illegally.

push·ing (poŏsh′ing) *adj.* **1** Enterprising; energetic. **2** Too aggressive; impertinent. —**push′ing·ly** *adv.*

push·o·ver (poŏsh′ō′vər) *n. Slang* **1** Anything that can be done with little or no effort. **2** Someone easily defeated, overcome, outwitted, etc.; one who represents no challenge to one's aims.

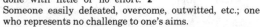
Supermarket pushcart

push·y (poŏsh′ē) *adj.* **·i·er**, **·i·est** Unpleasantly aggressive and persistent. —**push′i·ly** *adv.* —**push′i·ness** *n.*

pu·sil·lan·i·mous (pyoō′sə·lan′ə·məs) *adj.* Weak or cowardly in spirit; lacking strength of mind or courage. [< L *pusillus* very little + *animus* mind] —**pu′sil·la·nim′i·ty** (-lə·nim′ə·tē), **pu·sil·lan′i·mous·ness** *n.* —**pu·sil·lan′i·mous·ly** *adv.*

puss[1] (poŏs) *n.* **1** A cat. **2** A young girl: a term of affection. [?] •

puss[2] (poŏs) *n. Slang* The mouth; face. [< Ir. *pus* mouth, lips]

pus·sy[1] (poŏs′ē) *n. pl.* **·sies 1** PUSS[1]. **2** A fuzzy catkin, as of a willow.

pus·sy[2] (pus′ē) *adj.* **pus·si·er**, **pus·si·est** Full of or like pus. —**pus′si·ness** *n.*

pus·sy·foot (poŏs′ē·foŏt′) *v.i.* **1** To move softly and stealthily, as a cat does. **2** To act or proceed warily or tentatively, so as to be able to withdraw or change course before one's intentions are apparent. —**pus′sy·foot′er** *n.*

pus·sy willow (poŏs′ē) A small North American willow bearing velvety catkins in early spring.

pus·tu·late (pus′choō·lāt) *v.t. & v.i.* **·lat·ed**, **·lat·ing** To form into or become pustules. —*adj.* (-lāt, -lit) Covered with pustules. —**pus′tu·la′tion** *n.*

pus·tule (pus′choōl) *n.* **1** A small, circumscribed elevation of the skin with an inflamed base containing pus. **2** Any elevation resembling a pimple or a blister. [< L *pustula*] —**pus′tu·lar**, **pus′tu·lous** *adj.*

put (poŏt) *v.* **put**, **put·ting** *v.t.* **1** To bring into or set in a specified or implied place or position; lay: *Put* the dishes in the sink. **2** To bring into a specified state, condition, or relation: to *put* someone to work; to *put* merchandise on sale. **3** To order or bring about the establishment or placement of: to *put* a new store in Dallas; to *put* a man on the moon. **4** To send or direct, as by projecting or thrusting: to *put* a dart in the bull's-eye. **5** To throw with a pushing motion: to *put* the shot. **6** To bring to bear; apply: They *put* pressure on her. **7** To impose: to *put* a tax on air travel. **8** To effect; carry out: I'll *put* a stop to that. **9** To express; state:

Pussy willow

to *put* it simply. **10** To subject: to *put* his loyalty to the test. **11** To incite; prompt: Who *put* him up to it? **12** To ascribe or attribute: to *put* the wrong interpretation on a remark. **13** To propose for debate, consideration, etc.: to *put* the question. **14** To estimate: to *put* the time at five o'clock. **15** To establish; fix, as a price. **16** To risk; bet: to *put* money on a horse. —*v.i.* **17** To go; proceed: to *put* to sea. —**put about 1** *Naut.* To change to the opposite tack. **2** To change direction. —**put across 1** To carry out successfully. **2** To manage to be understood. **3** To bring about through deceit. —**put aside** (or **by**) **1** To place in reserve; save. **2** To thrust aside; discard. —**put away 1** PUT ASIDE. **2** *Informal* To eat or drink. **3** *Informal* To kill, as an injured or sick animal. —**put down 1** To repress; crush. **2** To degrade; demote. **3** To write. **4** *Slang* To humble or deflate. **5** To preserve or can. —**put forth 1** To grow, as shoots or buds. **2** To set out; leave port. **3** To proffer; suggest. **4** To publish. **5** To exert. —**put forward** To advance; advocate, as a proposal. —**put in 1** To submit or advance, as a claim or application. **2** To interject; interpolate. **3** *Naut.* To enter a harbor. **4** *Informal* To devote; expend, as time. —**put off 1** To delay; postpone. **2** To discard. **3** To make uneasy or uncomfortable; disconcert. —**put on 1** To clothe oneself in; don. **2** To bring into operation; effectuate: to *put on* a light. **3** To add: to *put on* weight. **4** To stage, as a play. **5** To simulate; pretend: to *put on* a sad face. **8** *Slang* To fool or deceive mischievously. —**put out 1** To extinguish, as a flame. **2** To expel; eject. **3** To disconcert; embarrass. **4** To inconvenience. **5** PUT FORTH. **6** In baseball, to retire (a batter or base runner). **7** To publish or manufacture, as a book or magazine. **8** *Slang* To use extra effort; exert oneself. —**put over 1** To delay; postpone. **2** To carry out successfully. **3** To bring about through deceit. —**put through 1** To bring to successful completion. **2** To cause to perform. **3** To establish a telephone connection for. —**put up 1** To erect; build. **2** To provide (money, capital, etc.). **3** To preserve or can. **4** To sheathe, as a weapon. **5** To nominate as a candidate. **6** To provide accommodations for. **7** *Informal* To incite. —**put up with** To endure; tolerate. —*n.* The act of putting or casting, esp. the shot. —*adj. Informal* Settled in place; fixed: My hat won't stay *put*. [< OE *putian* place] —**put′ter** *n.*

pu·ta·tive (pyoō′tə·tiv) *adj.* Supposed; reported; reputed. [< L *putare* think] —**pu′ta·tive·ly** *adv.*

put-down (poŏt′doun′) *n. Slang* Something that humbles or deflates, as a cutting remark.

put-on (poŏt′on′) *n. Slang* A hoax; deception.

put-out (poŏt′out′) *n.* In baseball, the act of causing an out, as of a batter or base runner.

pu·tre·fac·tion (pyoō′trə·fak′shən) *n.* **1** The process of rotting or decomposing, as by bacterial action. **2** The state of being putrefied. —**pu′tre·fac′tive** *adj.*

pu·tre·fy (pyoō′trə·fī) *v.t. & v.i.* **·fied**, **·fy·ing** To decay or cause to decay; rot. [< L *puter* rotten + *facere* make] —**pu′tre·fi′er** *n.*

pu·tres·cent (pyoō·tres′ənt) *adj.* **1** Becoming putrid. **2** Pertaining to putrefaction. [< L *putrescere* grow rotten] —**pu·tres′cence** *n.*

pu·trid (pyoō′trid) *adj.* **1** Being in a state of putrefaction; rotten. **2** Indicating or produced by putrefaction: a *putrid* smell. **3** Corrupt. [< L *putridus*] —**pu·trid·i·ty** (pyoō·trid′ə·tē), **pu′trid·ness** *n.*

putsch (poŏch) *n. Often cap.* An outbreak or rebellion; an attempted coup d'état. [G]

putt (put) *n.* In golf, a light stroke made on a putting green to place the ball in or near the hole. —*v.t. & v.i.* To strike (the ball) with such a stroke. [Var. of PUT]

put·tee (put′ē, pu·tē′) *n.* A strip of cloth or leather gaiter fastened about the leg from knee to ankle. [< Skt. *paṭṭa* a strip of cloth]

put·ter[1] (put′ər) *n.* **1** One who putts. **2** A golf club used in putting. • See GOLF.

put·ter[2] (put′ər) *v.i.* **1** To act, work, or proceed in a dawdling or ineffective manner. —*v.t.* **2** To waste or spend (time, etc.) in dawdling or puttering. [< OE *potion* push, kick]

put·ting green (put′ing) In golf, a smooth area of closely mown grass in which the hole is situated.

put·ty (put′ē) *n.* **1** A doughy mixture of clay and linseed

oil, used to cement panes in windows, fill cracks, etc. **2** Any substance similar in properties or uses. —*v.t.* **·tied, ·ty·ing** To fill, stop, fasten, etc., with putty. [< OF *potee* calcined tin, lit., a potful] —**put′ti·er** *n.*

put-up (pŏot′up′) *adj. Informal* Prearranged or contrived; staged: a *put-up* job.

put-up·on (pŏot′ə·pon′) *adj.* Beset or harassed, as by impositions; abused.

puz·zle (puz′əl) *v.* **·zled, ·zling** *v.t.* **1** To confuse or perplex; mystify. **2** To solve by investigation and study, as something perplexing: with *out.* —*v.i.* **3** To be perplexed or confused. —**puzzle over** To attempt to understand or solve. —*n.* **1** Something difficult to understand or explain; an enigma or problem. **2** A device, as a toy, or a problem designed for recreation and requiring ingenuity to solve. **3** The state of being puzzled; perplexity. [?] —**puz′zle·ment, puz′zler** *n.*

Pvt. Private.

PW prisoner of war.

pwt. pennyweight.

PX post exchange.

py·e·mi·a (pī·ē′mē·ə) *n.* Septicemia caused by pus-producing microorganisms. Also **py·ae′mi·a.** [< Gk. *pyon* pus + *haima* blood] —**py·e′mic** *adj.*

pyg·my (pig′mē) *adj.* Diminutive; dwarfish. —*n. pl.* **·mies 1** Someone of no importance. **2** A dwarfish person or animal.

Pyg·my (pig′mē) *n. pl.* **·mies** A member of a Negroid people of equatorial Africa, ranging in height from four to five feet. [< Gk. *pygmalos* a dwarf]

py·ja·mas (pə·jä′məz, -jam′əz) *n.pl. Brit.* PAJAMAS.

py·lon (pī′lon) *n.* **1** *Archit.* A monumental gateway, as to an Egyptian temple or other large edifice. **2** A tall, mastlike structure, as for supporting high-tension wires or for marking a course for aircraft. [< Gk. *pylōn* a gateway]

py·lo·rus (pī·lôr′əs, -lō′rəs, pi-) *n. pl.* **·ri** (-rī) The muscularly controlled opening between the stomach and the duodenum. [< Gk. *pylōros* a gatekeeper] —**py·lor′ic** (-lôr′ik, -lor′ik) *adj.*

py·or·rhe·a (pī′ə·rē′ə) *n.* A discharge of pus; esp., inflammation and pus discharge affecting the gums and tooth sockets. Also **py′or·rhoe′a.** [< Gk. *pys, pyos* pus + *rheein* flow] —**py′or·rhe′al** *adj.*

pyr·a·mid (pir′ə·mid) *n.* **1** A solid structure of masonry with a square base and triangular sides meeting in an apex, such as those constructed by the ancient Egyptians as royal tombs. **2** Something having the form of a pyramid. **3** *Geom.* A solid having a polygonal base and triangular sides that meet in a common vertex. —*v.i.* **1** To increase in a series of steps; escalate. **2** To buy or sell stock with paper profits used as margin to finance succeeding transactions. —*v.t.* **3** To increase by steps. **4** To buy and sell (stock) with paper profits used as margin to

Egyptian pyramids

finance succeeding transactions. [< Gk. *pyramis*] —**py·ram·i·dal** (pi·ram′ə·dəl, pir′ə·mid′əl), **pyr′a·mid′ic** or **·i·cal** *adj.* —**pyr′a·mid′i·cal·ly** *adv.*

pyre (pīr) *n.* A heap of combustibles arranged for burning a dead body as a funeral rite. [< Gk. *pyr* a fire]

py·reth·rum (pī·reth′rəm, -rē′thrəm) *n.* **1** A species of chrysanthemum. **2** An insecticide prepared from the powdered flowers of certain chrysanthemums. [L, feverfew]

Py·rex (pī′reks) *n.* A type of heat-resistant glass: a trade name.

pyr·i·dox·ine (pir′ə·dok′sēn, -sin) *n.* A constituent of the vitamin B complex. [< Gk. *pyr* fire + -ID(E) + OX(Y)- + -INE]

py·rite (pī′rīt) *n.* A lustrous, pale yellow, mineral sulfide of iron. [< Gk. *pyritēs* flint]

py·ri·tes (pī·rī′tēz, pī′rīts) *n. pl.* **py·ri·tes** (pī·rī′tēz) Any of various mineral sulfides with a metallic sheen, including pyrite: copper *pyrites.* —**py·rit′ic** (-rit′ik) or **·i·cal** *adj.*

pyro- *combining form* Fire; heat: *pyromania.* Also **pyr-.** [< Gk. *pyr* fire]

py·ro·ma·ni·a (pī′rə·mā′nē·ə, -mān′yə) *n.* A compulsion to commit arson. —**py′ro·ma′ni·ac** (-ak) *adj., n.* —**py·ro·ma·ni·a·cal** (pī′rō·mə·nī′ə·kəl) *adj.*

py·rom·e·ter (pī·rom′ə·tər) *n.* A thermometer designed to measure high temperatures. —**py·ro·met·ric** (pī′rə·met′rik) or **·ri·cal** *adj.* —**py·rom′e·try** *n.*

py·ro·tech·nics (pī′rə·tek′niks) *n. pl. (construed as sing. in def. 1)* **1** The art of making or using fireworks. **2** A display of fireworks. **3** An ostentatious display, as of oratory; virtuosity. [< PYRO- + Gk. *technē* an art] —**py′ro·tech′nic** or **·ni·cal** *adj.*

py·rox·y·lin (pī·rok′sə·lin) *n.* A nitrocellulose that is more stable than guncotton, used in making quick-drying lacquers, etc. Also **py·rox′y·line** (-lēn, -lin). [< Gk. *pyr, pyros* fire + *xylon* wood + -INE]

Pyr·rhic victory (pir′ik) A victory gained at a ruinous cost, such as that of Pyrrhus over the Romans in 279 B.C.

Py·thag·o·re·an theorem (pi·thag′ə·rē′ən) *Math.* The theorem that the sum of the squares of the two sides of a right triangle is equal to the square of the hypotenuse. [< *Pythagoras*, c. 500 B.C., Greek philosopher]

Python

Pyth·i·as (pith′ē·əs) See DAMON AND PYTHIAS.

py·thon (pī′thon, -thən) *n.* A large, nonvenomous snake that crushes its prey. [< Gk. *Pythōn* a serpent slain by Apollo]

py·tho·ness (pī′thə·nis, pith′ə-) *n.* **1** The priestess of the Delphic oracle. **2** Any woman supposed to be possessed of the spirit of prophecy; a witch. [< Gk. *Pytho* a familiar spirit, orig. Delphi]

pyx (piks) *n.* A container for keeping the consecrated wafer of the Eucharist or for carrying it to the sick. [< L *pyxis* a box]

pyx·is (pik′sis) *n. pl.* **pyx·i·des** (pik′sə·dēz) *Bot.* A dehiscent seed vessel with the upper portion separating as a lid. Also **pyx·id·i·um** (pik·sid′ē·əm). [< L, a box]

Q

Q, q (kyōō) *n. pl.* **Q's, q's** or **Qs, qs** (kyōōz) **1** The 17th letter of the English alphabet. **2** Any spoken sound representing the letter *Q* or *q*. **3** Something shaped like a Q. —*adj.* Shaped like a Q.

Q queen (chess).

Q. Quebec.

q. quart; quarter; quarterly; quarto; quasi; queen; query; question

Qa·tar (kä′tär) *n.* A British protected sheikdom on the w coast of the Persian Gulf, 8,500 sq. mi., cap. Doha. • See map at SAUDI ARABIA.

qb., q.b. quarterback.

Q.C. Quartermaster Corps; Queen's Counsel.

q.e. which is (L *quod est*).

Q.E.D. which was to be demonstrated (L *quod erat demonstrandum*).

Q.E.F. which was to be done (L *quod erat faciendum*).

QM, Q.M. Quartermaster.

QMC, Q.M.C. Quartermaster Corps.

QMG, Q.M.G., Q.M.Gen. Quartermaster General.

Qq. quartos.

qq.v. which see (L *quos vide*).

qr. quarter; quarterly; quire.

q.s. as much as suffices (L *quantum sufficit*).

qt. quart; quantity.

q.t. *Slang* quiet, esp. **on the q.t.** in secret.

qto. quarto.

qts, qts. quarts.

qu. quart; quarter; queen; query; question.

quack¹ (kwak) *v.i.* To utter a harsh, croaking cry, as a duck. —*n.* The sound made by a duck, or a similar croaking noise [Imit.]

quack² (kwak) *n.* **1** A pretender to medical knowledge or skill. **2** A charlatan. —*adj.* Of or pertaining to quacks or quackery. —*v.i.* To play the quack. [Short for QUACKSALVER] —**quack′ish** *adj.* —**quack′ish·ly** *adv.*

quack·er·y (kwak′ər·ē) *n. pl.* **·er·ies** The deceitful practices of a quack.

quack·sal·ver (kwak′sal′vər) *n.* QUACK². [< MDu. *quacsalven* use home remedies]

quad¹ (kwod) *n. Informal.* A quadrangle, as of a college or prison.

quad² (kwod) *n. Printing* A piece of type metal lower than the letters, used for spacing. [ME *quadrat,* a square instrument]

quad³ (kwod) *adj.* QUADRAPHONIC.

quad. quadrangle; quadrant; quadrat; quadruple.

Quad·ra·ges·i·ma (kwod′rə·jes′ə·mə) *n.* The first Sunday in Lent. Also **Quadragesima Sunday.** [L, fortieth]

quad·ran·gle (kwod′rang·gəl) *n.* **1** *Geom.* A plane figure having four sides and four angles. **2** An area shaped like a quadrangle, esp. when it is enclosed by buildings. **3** The buildings that enclose such an area. [< L *quattuor* four + *angulus* angle] —**quad·ran′gu·lar** *adj.*

quad·rant (kwod′rənt) *n.* **1** A quarter part of a circle; also, its circumference, having an arc of 90°. **2** An instrument having a graduated arc of 90°, with a movable radius for measuring angles on it. [< L *quattuor* four] — **quad·ran·tal** (kwod·ran′təl) *adj.*

Quadrant

quad·ra·phon·ic (kwod′rə·fon′ik) *adj.* Of, pertaining to, or employing a system of sound reproduction that uses four transmission channels and loudspeakers. [< QUADR(I)- + PHONIC]

quad·rat (kwod′rət) *n.* QUAD².

quad·rate (kwod′rāt, -rit) *adj.* Square; four-sided. —*v.* (-rāt) **·rat·ed, ·rat·ing** *v.i.* **1** To correspond or agree: with *with.* —*v.t.* **2** To cause to conform; bring in accordance with. [< L *quadrare* to square < *quattuor* four]

quad·rat·ic (kwod·rat′ik) *adj.* **1** Pertaining to or resembling a square. **2** Of or designating a quadratic equation. —*n. Math.* A quadratic equation.

quadratic equation An equation of the general form $ax^2 + bx + c = 0$, where *a, b, c* are constants.

quad·ra·ture (kwod′rə·chər) *n.* **1** The act or process of squaring. **2** The determining of the area of any surface.

quad·ren·ni·al (kwod·ren′ē·əl) *adj.* **1** Occurring once in four years. **2** Comprising four years. —*n.* A quadrennial period or event. [< QUADR(I)- + L *annus* year]

quadri- *combining form* Four: *quadrilateral.* Also **quadr-.** [< L *quattuor* four]

quad·ri·lat·er·al (kwod′rə·lat′ər·əl) *adj.* Formed or bounded by four lines; four-sided. —*n.* **1** *Geom.* A polygon of four sides. **2** A space or area defended by four enclosing fortresses. [< QUADRI- + L *latus, lateris* side]

qua·drille (kwə·dril′) *n.* **1** A square dance for four couples. **2** Music for such a dance. [< L *quattuor* four]

quad·ril·lion (kwod·ril′yən) *n. & adj.* See NUMBER. [< F *quatre* four + *(m)illion* million]

quad·ri·ple·gi·a (kwod′rə·plē′jē·ə) *n.* Paralysis of the arms and legs.

quad·ri·va·lent (kwod′rə·vā′lənt) *adj. Chem.* Having a valence of four. [< QUADRI- + L *valere* be worth]

quad·roon (kwod·rōōn′) *n.* A person having one Negro and three white grandparents. [< Sp. *cuarto* fourth]

quad·ru·ped (kwod′rōō·ped) *n.* A four-footed animal, esp. a mammal. —*adj.* Having four feet. [< L *quattuor* four + *pes* foot] —**quad·ru·pe·dal** (kwod·rōō′pə·dəl, kwod′·rōō·ped′l) *adj.*

quad·ru·ple (kwod·rōō′pəl, -rū′-, kwod′rōō·pəl) *adj.* **1** Four times as great or as many. **2** Having four parts or members. **3** Marked by four beats to the measure. —*n.* A number or sum four times as great as another. —*v.t. & v.i.* **·pled, ·pling** To multiply by four. —*adv.* Fourfold. [< L *quadruplus*]

quad·ru·plet (kwod·rōō′plit, -rū′-, kwod′rōō-) *n.* A combination of four objects. **2** One of four offspring born of the same mother at one birth.

quad·ru·pli·cate (kwod·rōō′plə·kit, -kāt) *adj.* **1** FOURFOLD. **2** Raised to the fourth power. —*v.t.* (-kāt) **·cat·ed, ·cat·ing** To multiply by four; quadruple. —*n.* The fourth of four like things: to file a *quadruplicate.* —**in quadruplicate** In four identical copies. —**quad·ru′pli·ca′tion** *n.*

quaes·tor (kwes′tər, kwēs′-) *n.* Any of a number of public officials in ancient Rome. Also **ques′tor.** [L < *quaerere* seek, inqure] —**quaes′to′ri·al** *adj.* —**quaes′tor·ship** *n.*

quaff (kwaf, kwof, kwôf) *v.t. & v.i.* To drink, esp. copiously or with relish. —*n.* The act of quaffing; also, that which is quaffed. [?] —**quaff′er** *n.*

quag·gy (kwag′ē, kwog′ē) *adj.* **·gi·er, ·gi·est** **1** Yielding to or quaking under the foot, as soft, wet earth; boggy. **2** Soft; yielding; flabby. [< QUAGMIRE]

quag·mire (kwag′mīr′, kwog′-) *n.* **1** Marshy ground that gives way under the foot; bog. **2** A difficult situation. [? < earlier *quab-* wetness + MIRE] —**quag′mired′** *adj.*

qua·haug (kwô′hôg, -hog, kwə·hôg′, -hog′) *n.* An edible, thick-shelled clam of the Atlantic coast of North America. Also **qua′hog.** [< Algon.]

quail¹ (kwāl) *n.* **1** Any of various small game birds related to the partridge. **2** BOBWHITE. [< OF *quaille*]

quail² (kwāl) *v.i.* To shrink with fear; lose heart or courage. [ME *quailen*]

quaint (kwānt) *adj.* **1** Pleasingly different, fanciful, or old-fashioned. **2** Unusual; odd; curious. [< L *cognitus* known] —**quaint′ly** *adv.* —**quaint′ness** *n.*

quake (kwāk) *v.i.* **quaked, quaking** **1** To shake, as with violent

Quail

emotion or cold; shudder; shiver. **2** To shake or tremble, as earth during an earthquake. —*n.* **1** A shaking or shuddering. **2** EARTHQUAKE. [< OE *cwacian* shake]

Quak·er (kwā′kər) *n.* A member of the Society of Friends: originally a term of derision, and still not used within the society. See SOCIETY OF FRIENDS. [< QUAKE, *v.;* with ref. to their founder's admonition to them to tremble at the word of the Lord] —**Quak′er·ish** *adj.* —**Quak′er·ism′** *n.*

quak·y (kwā′kē) *adj.* **quak·i·er, quak·i·est** Shaky; tremulous. —**quak′i·ly** *adv.* —**quak′i·ness** *n.*

qual·i·fi·ca·tion (kwol′ə·fə·kā′shən) *n.* **1** The act of qualifying, or the state of being qualified. **2** That which fits a person or thing for something. **3** A restriction; modification.

qual·i·fied (kwol′ə·fīd) *adj.* **1** Competent or eligible, as for public office. **2** Restricted or modified in some way. —**qual′i·fied′ly** *adv.*

qual·i·fy (kwol′ə·fī) *v.* **·fied, ·fy·ing** *v.t.* **1** To make fit or capable, as for an office, occupation, or privilege. **2** To make legally capable, as by the administration of an oath. **3** To limit, restrict, or lessen somewhat: He *qualified* his enthusiasm with a few criticisms. **4** To attribute a quality to; describe; characterize or name. **5** To make less strong or extreme; soften; moderate. **6** To change the strength or flavor of. **7** *Gram.* To modify. —*v.i.* **8** To be or become qualified. [< L *qualis* of such a kind + *facere* make] —**qual′i·fi′a·ble** *adj.* —**qual′i·fi′er** *n.*

qual·i·ta·tive (kwol′ə·tā′tiv) *adj.* Of or pertaining to quality. —**qual′i·ta′tive·ly** *adv.*

qualitative analysis The chemical identification of the elements or components in a compound or mixture.

qual·i·ty (kwol′ə·tē) *n. pl.* **·ties 1** That which makes a being or thing such as it is: a distinguishing element or characteristic; a *quality* of gases. **2** The basic nature or character of something: the *quality* of a summer's day. **3** Excellence: striving for *quality.* **4** Degree of excellence; relative goodness; grade: high *quality* of fabric. **5** A personal attribute, trait or characteristic: a woman with good and bad *qualities.* **6** *Archaic* Social rank; also, persons of rank, collectively. **7** *Music* That which distinguishes one tone from another, aside from pitch or loudness; timbre. —*adj.* Characterized by or having to do with quality: a *quality* product. [< L *qualis* of such a kind]

qualm (kwäm, kwôm) *n.* **1** A twinge of conscience; moral scruple. **2** A sensation of fear or misgiving. **3** A feeling of sickness. [? < OE *cwealm* death] —**qualm′ish, qualm′y** *adj.* —**qualm′ish·ly** *adv.* —**qualm′ish·ness** *n.*

quan·da·ry (kwon′dər·ē, -drē) *n. pl.* **·da·ries** A state of hesitation or perplexity; predicament. [?]

quan·ti·ta·tive (kwon′tə·tā′tiv) *adj.* **1** Of or pertaining to quantity. **2** Capable of being measured. —**quan′ti·ta′tive·ly** *adv.* —**quan′ti·ta′tive·ness** *n.*

quantitative analysis The precise determination of the relative amount of each chemical component in a compound or mixture.

quan·ti·ty (kwon′tə·tē) *n. pl.* **·ties 1** A definite or indefinite amount or number. **2** *pl.* Large amounts or numbers: *quantities* of food and drink. **3** That property of a thing which admits of exact measurement and numerical statement. **4** In prosody and phonetics, the relative period of time required to produce a given sound. [< L *quantus* how much, how large]

quan·tum (kwon′təm) *n. pl.* **·ta** (-tə) *Physics* A fundamental unit of energy or action as described in the quantum theory. [< L *quantus* how much]

quantum theory *Physics* A physical theory including as one of its essential features the postulate that energy is not continuous but divided into discrete packets, or quanta.

quar·an·tine (kwôr′ən·tēn, kwor′-) *n.* **1** A period of time fixed for the isolation and observation of persons, animals, or plants suspected of harboring an infectious disease. **2** A place for such isolation. **3** The isolation of subjects exposed to or infected with a communicable disease. —*v.t.* **·tined, ·tin·ing** To retain in quarantine. [< L *quadraginta* forty; a ref. to the original 40-day quarantine]

quark (kwärk) *n. Physics* Any of a group of three types of hypothetical fundamental particles proposed as the entities of which all other strongly interacting particles are composed. [Coined by M. Gell-Mann, born 1929, U.S. physicist]

quar·rel[1] (kwôr′əl, kwor′-) *n.* **1** An unfriendly, angry, or violent dispute. **2** A falling out or contention; breach of friendly relations: a lover's *quarrel.* **3** The cause for dispute. —*v.i.* **·reled** or **·relled, ·rel·ing** or **·rel·ling 1** To engage in a quarrel; dispute; contend; fight: to *quarrel* about money. **2** To break off a mutual friendship; fall out; disagree. **3** To find fault; cavil. [< L *querela* complaint] —**quar′rel·er** or **quar′rel·ler** *n.* —**Syn.** *n.* **1** altercation, bickering, brawl, controversy, feud, fracas, fray. **2** disagreement, fuss, misunderstanding, scene.

quar·rel[2] (kwôr′əl, kwor′-) *n.* **1** A dart or arrow with a four-edged head, formerly used with a crossbow. **2** A stonemason's chisel, glazier's diamond, or other tool having a several-edged point. [< L *quattuor* four]

quar·rel·some (kwôr′əl·səm, kwor′-) *adj.* Inclined to quarrel. —**quar′rel·some·ly** *adv.* —**quar′rel·some·ness** *n.*

quar·ri·er (kwôr′ē·ər, kwor′-) *n.* A workman in a stone quarry.

quar·ry[1] (kwôr′ē, kwor′ē) *n. pl.* **·ries 1** An animal being hunted down; game; prey. **2** Anything hunted, slaughtered, or eagerly pursued. [< L *corium* hide]

Quarrels
def. 1

quar·ry[2] (kwôr′ē, kwor′ē) *n. pl.* **·ries** An excavation from which stone is taken by cutting, blasting, or the like. —*v.t.* **·ried, ·ry·ing 1** To cut, dig, or take from or as from a quarry. **2** To establish a quarry in. [< LL *quadraria* place for squaring stone]

quart (kwôrt) *n.* **1 a** A U.S. measure of dry capacity equal to 2 pints or 1.10 liters. **b** A U.S. measure of fluid capacity equal to 2 pints or 0.946 liter. **2** A vessel of such capacity. [< L *quartus* fourth]

quar·ter (kwôr′tər) *n.* **1** One of four equal parts of something; a fourth. **2** Fifteen minutes or the fourth of an hour, or the moment with which it begins or ends. **3** A fourth of a year or three months. **4** A limb of a quadruped with the adjacent parts. **5** In the U.S. and Canada, a coin of the value of 25 cents. **6** *Astron.* **a** The time it takes the moon to make one fourth of its revolution around the earth. **b** Either of the phases of the moon between new moon and full moon. **7** *Nav.* One of the four principal points of the compass or divisions of the horizon; also, a point or direction of the compass. **8** A person, persons, or place, esp. as a source or origin of something: gossip coming from all *quarters.* **9** A particular division or district, as of a city. **10** *Usu. pl.* Proper or assigned station, position, or place, as of officers and crew on a warship. **11** *pl.* A place of lodging or residence. **12** *Naut.* The part of a vessel's after side, between the aftermost mast and the stern. **13** *Her.* Any of four equal divisions into which a shield is divided, or a figure or device occupying such a division. **14** Mercy shown to a vanquished foe by sparing his life; clemency. **15** One of the four periods into which a game, as football, is divided. —**at close quarters** Close by; at close range. —*adj.* **1** Consisting of a quarter. **2** Equal to a quarter. —*v.t.* **1** To divide into four equal parts. **2** To divide into a number of parts or pieces. **3** To cut the body of (an executed person) into four parts: He was hanged, drawn, and *quartered.* **4** To range from one side to the other of (a field, etc.) while advancing: The dogs *quartered* the field. **5** To furnish with quarters or shelter; lodge, station, or billet. **6** *Her.* **a** To divide (a shield) into quarters by vertical and horizontal lines. **b** To bear or arrange (different coats of arms) upon the quarters of a shield or escutcheon. —*v.i.* **7** To be stationed or lodged. **8** To range from side to side of an area, as dogs in hunting. **9** *Naut.* To blow on a ship's quarter: said of the wind. [< L *quartus* fourth]

quar·ter·back (kwôr′tər·bak′) *n.* In football, one of the backfield, who calls the signals and directs the offensive play of his team.

quarter day A day that begins a new quarter of the year, when quarterly payments, as of rent, etc., are due.

quar·ter·deck (kwôr′tər·dek′) *n. Naut.* The rear part of a ship's upper deck, reserved for officers.

quar·tered (kwôr′tərd) *adj.* 1 Divided into quarters. 2 Having quarters or lodgings. 3 Quartersawed.

quar·ter·ly (kwôr′tər·lē) *adj.* 1 Containing or being a quarter. 2 Occurring at intervals of three months. —*n. pl.* **·lies** A publication issued once every three months. —*adv.* 1 Once in a quarter of a year. 2 In or by quarters.

quar·ter·mas·ter (kwôr′tər·mas′tər, -mäs′-) *n.* 1 The officer on an army post who is responsible for the supply of food, clothing, etc. 2 On shipboard, a petty officer who assists the master or navigator.

quar·tern (kwôr′tərn) *n. Chiefly Brit.* A fourth part, as of certain measures or weights. [< L *quartus* fourth]

quarter note *Music* A note with one fourth the time value of a whole note. • See NOTE.

quar·ter·saw (kwôr′tər·sô′) *v.t.* **·sawed**, **·sawed** or **·sawn**, **·saw·ing** To saw (a log) lengthwise into quarters and then into planks or boards, in order to show the wood grain advantageously.

quar·ter·sec·tion (kwôr′tər·sek′shən) *n.* A tract of land half a mile square, containing one fourth of a square mile; 160 acres.

quar·ter·ses·sions (kwôr′tər·sesh′ənz) *n.* 1 In the U.S., any of various courts with criminal jurisdiction and, sometimes, administrative functions. 2 In England, a local court held quarterly that has limited criminal and civil jurisdiction and, often, administrative functions.

quar·ter·staff (kwôr′tər·staf′, -stäf′) *n. pl.* **·staves** (-stāvz′) A stout, iron-tipped staff about 6½ feet long, formerly used in England as a weapon.

quar·tet (kwôr·tet′) *n.* 1 A composition for four voices or instruments. 2 The four persons who render such a composition. 3 Any group of four persons or things. Also **quar·tette′**. [< Ital. *quarto* fourth]

quar·to (kwôr′tō) *adj.* Having four leaves or eight pages to the sheet: a *quarto* book. —*n. pl.* **·tos** 1 The size of a piece of paper obtained by folding a sheet into four leaves. 2 Paper of this size; also, a page of this size. 3 A book made of pages of this size. [< L *(in) quarto* (in) fourth]

quartz (kwôrts) *n.* A hard mineral form of silicon dioxide occurring in many varieties, some of which are valued as gems. [< G *Quarz*]

qua·sar (kwā′zär, -sär) *n. Astron.* QUASI-STELLAR OBJECT. [< QUAS(I) - (STELL)AR RADIO SOURCE]

quash[1] (kwosh) *v.t. Law* To make void or set aside, as an indictment; annul. [< LL *cassare* to empty]

quash[2] (kwosh) *v.t.* To put down or suppress forcibly or summarily. [< L *quassare*, freq. of *quatere* shake]

qua·si (kwā′zī, -sī; kwä′zē, -sē) *adj.* More in resemblance than in fact: a *quasi* scholar. [L, as if]

quasi- *combining form* Resembling but not quite; in some ways or to some extent: *quasi-legal, quasi-official.* [< L *quasi* as if]

qua·si·stel·lar object (kwā′zī·stel′ər, -sī-, kwä′zē-, -sē-) Any of various starlike objects emitting vast amounts of radiation over a broad spectrum and having large red shifts. Also **quasi-stellar radio source**.

quas·si·a (kwosh′ē·ə, kwosh′ə) *n.* 1 Any of several tropical trees having bitter wood and bark. 2 A bitter extract obtained from a quassia tree, used to allay fever. 3 An insecticide obtained from the wood of a certain quassia tree. [< Graman *Quassi*, a Surinam Negro who discovered its use in 1730]

qua·ter·na·ry (kwot′ər·ner′ē, kwə·tûr′nə·rē) *adj.* Consisting of four. [< L *quaterni* by fours]

Qua·ter·na·ry (kwot′ər·ner′ē, kwə·tûr′nə·rē) *adj. & n.* See GEOLOGY.

quat·rain (kwot′rān, kwot·rān′) *n.* A stanza of four lines. [< F *quatre* four]

quat·re·foil (kat′ər·foil′, kat′·rə-) *n.* 1 *Bot.* A leaf or flower with four leaflets or petals. 2 *Archit.* An ornament with four foils or lobes. [< OF *quatre* four + *foil* leaf]

Quatrefoil window

quat·tro·cen·to (kwät′trō·chen′tō) *n.* The 15th century, esp. in connection with Italian art and literature. —*adj.* Of or pertaining to the quattrocento. [< Ital., four hundred < *quattro* four + *cento* hundred]

qua·ver (kwā′vər) *v.i.* 1 To tremble or shake: said usu. of the voice. 2 To produce trills or quavers in singing or in playing a musical instrument. —*v.t.* 3 To utter or sing in a tremulous voice. —*n.* 1 A trembling or shaking, as in the voice. 2 A shake or trill, as in singing. 3 An eighth note. [< ME *cwafian* tremble] —**qua′ver·y** *adj.*

quay (kē) *n.* A wharf or artificial landing place where vessels load and unload. [F]

Que. Quebec.

quean (kwēn) *n.* A brazen woman; harlot; prostitute. [< OE *cwene* woman]

quea·sy (kwē′zē) *adj.* **·si·er**, **·si·est** 1 Feeling or causing nausea. 2 Easily nauseated; squeamish. 3 Causing or feeling uneasiness or discomfort. [ME *coysy*] —**quea′si·ly** *adv.* —**quea′si·ness** *n.*

Quech·ua (kech′wä) *n.* 1 One of a tribe of South American Indians which dominated the Inca empire prior to the Spanish conquest. 2 The language of the Quechuas. —**Quech′uan** *adj., n.*

queen (kwēn) *n.* 1 The wife of a king. 2 A female sovereign or monarch. 3 A woman preeminent in a given activity, accomplishment, etc. 4 A place or thing of great beauty, excellence, etc. 5 The most powerful piece in chess, capable of moving any number of squares in a straight or diagonal line. 6 A playing card bearing a conventional picture of a queen in her robes. 7 An egg-producing female in a colony of social insects, as bees, ants, etc. —*v.t.* 1 To make a queen of. —*v.i.* 2 To reign as or play the part of a queen: often with *it*. [< OE *cwēn* woman, queen] —**queen′ly** *adj., adv.* —**queen′li·ness** *n.*

Queen Anne's lace The wild carrot, having filmy white flowers resembling lace.

queen consort The wife of a reigning king.

queen dowager The widow of a king.

queen mother A queen dowager who is mother of a reigning sovereign.

queer (kwir) *adj.* 1 Different from the usual; strange; odd. 2 Of questionable character; open to suspicion; mysterious. 3 *Slang* Counterfeit. 4 Mentally unbalanced or eccentric. 5 Queasy or giddy. 6 *Slang* Homosexual: a contemptuous term. —*n. Slang* 1 Counterfeit money. 2 A homosexual, esp. a male homosexual: a contemptuous term. —*v.t. Slang* 1 To jeopardize or spoil. 2 To put into an unfavorable or embarrassing position. [< G *quer* oblique] —**queer′ly** *adv.* —**queer′ness** *n.* —**Syn.** *adj.* 1 bizarre, curious, droll, fantastic, grotesque, peculiar, singular. 2 suspect, suspicious. 4 peculiar, odd, deranged.

quell (kwel) *v.t.* 1 To put down or suppress by force; extinguish. 2 To quiet; allay, as pain. [< OE *cwellan* kill] —**quell′er** *n.*

quench (kwench) *v.t.* 1 To put out or extinguish, as a fire. 2 To slake or satisfy (thirst). 3 To suppress or repress, as emotions. 4 To cool, as heated iron or steel, by thrusting into water or other liquid. [ME *cwenken*] —**quench′a·ble** *adj.* —**quench′er** *n.*

quench·less (kwench′lis) *adj.* Incapable of being quenched; insatiable; irrepressible. —**quench′less·ly** *adv.* —**quench′less·ness** *n.*

quer·u·lous (kwer′ə·ləs, -yə·ləs) *adj.* 1 Disposed to complain or be fretful; faultfinding. 2 Indicating or expressing a complaint. [< L *queri* complain] —**quer′u·lous·ly** *adv.* —**quer′u·lous·ness** *n.* —**Syn.** 1 carping, captious, disparaging, critical, censorious.

que·ry (kwir′ē) *v.t.* **·ried**, **·ry·ing** 1 To inquire into; ask about. 2 To ask questions of; interrogate. 3 To express doubt concerning the correctness or truth of, esp., as in printing, by marking with a question mark. —*n. pl.* **·ries** 1 An inquiry; question. 2 A doubt. 3 A question mark. [< L *quaerere* ask]

ques. question.

quest (kwest) *n.* 1 The act of seeking; a looking for something. 2 A search, as an adventure or expedition in medieval romance; also, the person or persons making the search. —*v.i.* To go on a quest. [< L *quaerere* ask, seek] —**quest′er** *n.*

ques·tion (kwes′chən) *n.* 1 An inquiry, esp. to obtain information, test knowledge, etc. 2 A written or vocal expression of such an inquiry; an interrogative sentence, clause, or expression. 3 A subject of debate or dispute. 4 An issue or problem: It's not a *question* of time. 5 A doubt or uncertainty: There is no *question* of his skill. **—out of the question** Not to be considered as a possibility. *—v.t.* 1 To put a question or questions to; interrogate. 2 To be uncertain of; doubt. 3 To make objection to; challenge; dispute. *—v.i.* 4 To ask a question or questions. [< L *quaerere* ask] **—ques′tion·er** *n.*

ques·tion·a·ble (kwes′chən·ə·bəl) *adj.* 1 Open to question; debatable. 2 Dubious or suspect, as regards morality, integrity, respectability, etc.: *questionable* motives. **—ques′tion·a·bil′i·ty, ques′tion·a·ble·ness** *n.* **—ques′tion·a·bly** *adv.*

question mark A punctuation mark (?) indicating that the sentence it closes is a direct question. A question mark is also used to denote that a fact, statement, etc., is uncertain or doubtful.

ques·tion·naire (kwes′chə·nâr′) *n.* A written or printed form comprising a series of questions submitted to one or more persons in order to obtain data, as for a survey or report. [F]

quet·zal (ket·säl′) *n. pl.* **·zals** or **·zal·es** (-sä′läs) A crested bird of Central America having long, upper tail feathers in the male. 2 The monetary unit of Guatemala. Also **que·zal** (kä·säl′). [< Nahuatl]

queue (kyōō) *n.* 1 A braid of hair hanging from the back of the head; a pigtail. 2 A line of persons or vehicles waiting in the order of their arrival. *—v.i.* **queued, queu·ing** To form such a line: usu. with *up*. [< L *cauda* a tail]

quib·ble (kwib′əl) *n.* 1 An evasion of a point or question; an equivocation. 2 A minor objection; cavil. *—v.i.* **·bled, ·bling** To use quibbles. [< L *quibus*, ablative pl. of *qui* who, which] **—quib′bler** *n.*

quiche (kēsh) *n.* Any of various non-dessert, custardlike pies, having meat, cheese, vegetables, etc., as principal ingredients. [F]

quick (kwik) *adj.* 1 Done or occurring in a short time; expeditious; brisk; prompt; speedy: a *quick* answer. 2 Characterized by rapidity or readiness of movement or action; nimble; rapid; swift: a *quick* pace. 3 Alert; sensitive; perceptive: a *quick* ear; *quick* wit. 4 Responding readily; excitable; hasty: *quick-tempered*. 5 Lasting only a short time: a *quick* lunch. *—n.* 1 That which has life; those who are alive: chiefly in the phrase **the quick and the dead.** 2 The living flesh; esp., the tender flesh under a nail. 3 The most sensitive feelings: hurt to the *quick*. *—adv.* Quickly; rapidly. [< OE *cwic* alive]

quick bread Any bread, biscuits, etc., whose leavening agent makes immediate baking possible.

quick·en (kwik′ən) *v.t.* 1 To cause to move more rapidly; hasten or accelerate. 2 To make alive or quick; give or restore life to. 3 To excite or arouse; stimulate: to *quicken* the appetite. *—v.i.* 4 To move or act more quickly. 5 To come or return to life; revive. **—quick′en·er** *n.*

quick-freeze (kwik′frēz′) *v.t.* **-froze, -fro·zen, -freez·ing** To preserve by freezing rapidly and storing at a low temperature. **—quick′-fro′zen** *adj.*

quick·ie (kwik′ē) *n. Slang* Anything done hastily, as by short cuts or makeshift methods.

quick·lime (kwik′līm′) *n.* Unslaked lime.

quick·ly (kwik′lē) *adv.* In a quick manner; rapidly; soon.

quick·sand (kwik′sand′) *n.* A deep, wet bed of sand subjected to pressure by water below it and usu. incapable of supporting the weight of a person or animal.

quick·set (kwik′set′) *n.* 1 A slip, as of hawthorn, ready for planting. 2 A hedge made of such slips. *—adj.* Composed of quickset.

quick·sil·ver (kwik′sil′vər) *n.* Elemental mercury.

quick·step (kwik′step′) *n.* 1 A lively tune, esp. one in the rhythm of quick time. 2 A lively dance step, or a combination of such steps.

quick-tem·pered (kwik′tem′pərd) *adj.* Easily angered.

quick time A marching step of 120 paces a minute, each pace of 30 inches.

quick-wit·ted (kwik′wit′id) *adj.* Having a ready wit or quick discernment; keen; alert. **—quick′-wit′ted·ly** *adv.* **—quick′-wit′ted·ness** *n.*

quid[1] (kwid) *n.* A small portion, as of tobacco, to be chewed but not swallowed. [Var. of CUD]

quid[2] (kwid) *n. Brit. Slang* In England, a pound sterling, or a sovereign. [?]

quid·di·ty (kwid′ə·tē) *n. pl.* **·ties** 1 The essence of a thing. 2 A quibble; cavil. [< L *quid* which, what]

quid·nunc (kwid′nungk′) *n.* A gossip; busybody. [< L *quid nunc* what now]

quid pro quo (kwid′ prō kwō′) A thing given or received for another thing. [L, lit., something for something]

qui·es·cent (kwī·es′ənt, kwē-) *adj.* Being in a state of repose or inaction; quiet; still. [< L *quiescere* be quiet] **—qui·es′cence** *n.* **—qui·es′cent·ly** *adv.*

qui·et (kwī′ət) *adj.* 1 Being in a state of repose; still; calm; motionless. 2 Free from turmoil, strife, or busyness; tranquil; peaceful. 3 Having or making little or no noise; silent. 4 Gentle or mild, as of disposition. 5 Undisturbed by din or bustle; secluded. 6 Not showy or obtrusive, as dress. *—n.* The condition or quality of being free from motion, disturbance, noise, etc.; peace; calm. *—v.t. & v.i.* To make or become quiet: often with *down*. *—adv.* In a quiet or peaceful manner. [< L *quies* rest, repose] **—qui′et·ly** *adv.* **—qui′et·ness** *n.*

qui·et·en (kwī′ə·tən) *v.t. & v.i. Brit. or Regional* To make or become quiet: often with *down*.

qui·e·tude (kwī′ə·tyōōd) *n.* A state or condition of calm or tranquillity; repose; rest.

qui·e·tus (kwī·ē′təs) *n.* 1 A final discharge or settlement, as of a debt. 2 A release from or extinction of activity or life; death. 3 Something that silences or suppresses. 4 Something that kills. [< L *quietus (est)* (he is) quiet]

quill (kwil) *n.* 1 A large, strong, wing or tail feather. 2 The hollow, horny stem of a feather. 3 Something made from this, as a pen or a plectrum. 4 A spine of a porcupine or hedgehog. [ME *quil*]

quilt (kwilt) *n.* 1 A bedcover made by stitching together two layers of cloth with a soft padding between them. 2 Any bedcover, esp. if thick. 3 A quilted skirt or other quilted article. *—v.t.* 1 To stitch together (two pieces of material) with a soft substance between. 2 To stitch in ornamental patterns or crossing lines. *—v.i.* 3 To make a quilt or quilted work. [< L *culcita* mattress] **—quilt′work′** *n.*

Quill

quilt·ing (kwil′ting) *n.* 1 The act or process of making a quilt, or of stitching as in making a quilt. 2 Material for quiltwork. 3 A quilting bee or party.

quilting bee A social gathering of the women of a community for working on a quilt or quilts. Also **quilting party.**

quince (kwins) *n.* 1 A hard, acid, yellowish fruit, used for preserves. 2 The small tree, related to the apple, which bears quinces. [ME < Gk. *Kydōnia,* a town in Crete]

qui·nine (kwī′nīn, *esp. Brit.* kwi·nēn′) *n.* 1 A bitter alkaloid obtained from cinchona. 2 A medicinal compound of quinine, used to relieve the symptoms of malaria. [< Sp. *quina* cinchona bark + -INE]

Quin·qua·ges·i·ma (kwin′kwə·jes′ə·mə) *n.* The Sunday before Lent. Also **Quinquagesima Sunday.** [< L *quinquagesimus* fiftieth]

quin·sy (kwin′zē) *n.* An acute infection of the throat, esp. when suppurative. [< Gk. *kyōn* dog + *anchein* to choke]

quint (kwint) *n. Informal* A quintuplet. [< L *quinque* five]

quin·tal (kwin′təl) *n.* 1 A hundredweight. 2 In the metric system, 100 kilograms. [< Ar. *qintar*]

Quetzal

---

add, āce, câre, pälm; end, ēven; it, īce; odd, ōpen, ôrder; tŏŏk, pōōl; up, bûrn; ə = a in *above,* u in *focus;* yōō = u in *fuse;* oil; pout; check; go; ring; thin; this; zh, *vision.* < derived from; ? origin uncertain or unknown.

quin·tes·sence (kwin·tes′əns) n. 1 The essence of anything, esp. in its most pure, concentrated form. 2 The perfect manifestation or embodiment of anything. [< L *quinta essentia* fifth essence] —**quin·tes·sen·tial** (kwin′tə·sen′shəl) adj.

quin·tet (kwin·tet′) n. 1 A musical composition for five voices or instruments. 2 The five performers of such a composition. 3 Any group of five persons or things. Also **quin·tette′**. [< Ital. *quinto* fifth]

quin·til·lion (kwin·til′yən) n. & adj. See NUMBER. [< L *quintus* fifth + MILLION] —**quin·til′lionth** (-yənth) adj., n.

quin·tu·ple (kwin·t⁽ʸ⁾ōō′pəl, -tup′əl, kwin′t⁽ʸ⁾ōō·pəl) v.t. & v.i. ·pled, ·pling To multiply by five; make or become five times as large. —adj. 1 Consisting of five. 2 Being five times as much or as many. —n. A number or an amount five times as great as another. [< L *quintus* fifth + *-plex* -fold]

quin·tu·plet (kwin·tup′lit, -t⁽ʸ⁾ōō′plit, -t⁽ʸ⁾ōō′-, kwint′əp·lit) n. 1 Five things of a kind considered together. 2 One of five offspring born of the same mother at one birth.

quip (kwip) n. 1 A witty or sarcastic remark or retort; gibe. 2 A quibble. 3 An odd, fantastic action or object. —v.i. **quipped, quip·ping** To make a quip or quips. [< L *quippe* indeed] —**quip′pish** adj. —**quip′ster** n.

quire (kwīr) n. A set of 24 (or 25) sheets of paper of the same size and quality. [< L *quaterni* by fours]

Quir·i·nal (kwir′ə·nal) n. One of the seven hills on which Rome stands, containing the **Quirinal palace,** formerly a papal residence, after 1870 the royal residence, now the residence of the president of Italy. —adj. Pertaining to or situated on the Quirinal.

quirk (kwûrk) n. 1 A peculiar mannerism or trait; idiosyncracy. 2 An evasion; quibble. 3 A witticism; quip. 4 An abrupt curve or twist, as a flourish in writing. [?]

quirk·y (kwûrk′ē) adj. **quirk·i·er, quirk·i·est** Peculiar, unpredictable, and idiosyncratic: a *quirky* individual. —**quirk′i·ly** adv. —**quirk′i·ness** n.

quirt (kwûrt) n. A short-handled riding whip with a braided rawhide lash. —v.t. To strike with a quirt. [?]

quis·ling (kwiz′ling) n. One who betrays his country to the enemy and is then given political power by the conquerors. [< Vidkun *Quisling,* 1887–1945, Norwegian politician] —**quis′ling·ism** n.

quit (kwit) v. **quit** or **quit·ted, quit·ting** v.t. 1 To cease or desist from; discontinue. 2 To give up; renounce; relinquish: to *quit* a job. 3 To go away from; leave. 4 To let go of (something held). 5 To free; release. 6 To discharge; pay back. —v.i. 7 To resign from a position, etc. 8 To stop; cease; discontinue. 9 To leave; depart. —adj. Released, relieved, or absolved from something, as a duty, obligation, encumbrance, or debt; clear; free; rid. —n. The act of quitting. [< L *quies* rest, repose]

quit·claim (kwit′klām′) n. *Law* 1 The giving up of a claim, right, title, or interest. 2 An instrument by which one person gives up to another a claim or title to an estate. —v.t. To relinquish or give up claim or title to; release from a claim. [< QUIT + CLAIM]

quite (kwīt) adv. 1 Completely; fully; totally: not *quite* finished. 2 To a great or considerable extent; very: *quite* ill. 3 Positively; really: *quite* certain. [ME, rid of]

quit·tance (kwit′ns) n. 1 Discharge or release, as from a debt or obligation. 2 A document in evidence of this; receipt. 3 Something given or tendered by way of repayment. [< F *quiter* quit]

quit·ter (kwit′ər) n. One who quits needlessly; a shirker; slacker; coward.

quiv·er¹ (kwiv′ər) v.i. To shake with a slight, tremulous motion; vibrate; tremble. —n. The act or fact of quivering; a trembling or shaking. [?< QUAVER]

quiv·er² (kwiv′ər) n. A portable case or sheath for arrows; also, its contents. [< AF *quiveir*]

Quiver
of arrows

qui vive? (kē vēv′) "Who goes there?": used by French sentinels. —**be on the qui vive** To be on the look-out; be wide-awake. [F, who lives?]

quix·ot·ic (kwik·sot′ik) adj. 1 Pertaining to or like Don Quixote, the hero of a Spanish romance ridiculing knight-errantry. 2 Ridiculously chivalrous or romantic; having high but impractical sentiments, aims, etc. —**quix·ot′i·cal·ly** adv. —**quix·ot·ism** (kwik′sə·tiz′əm) n.

quiz (kwiz) n. pl. **quiz·zes** 1 The act of questioning; specifically, a brief oral or written examination. 2 A person given to ridicule or practical jokes. 3 A hoax; practical joke. —v.t. **quizzed, quiz·zing** 1 To examine by asking questions; question. 2 To make fun of; ridicule. [?] —**quiz′zer** n.

quiz program A television or radio program in which selected contestants or a panel of experts compete in answering questions.

quiz·zi·cal (kwiz′i·kəl) adj. 1 Mocking; teasing. 2 Perplexed; puzzled. 3 Queer; odd. —**quiz′zi·cal·ly** adv.

quod (kwod) n. *Brit. Slang* A prison. [?]

quoin (koin, kwoin) n. 1 An external angle of a building. 2 A large square stone forming such an angle. 3 A wedge-shaped stone, etc., as the keystone of an arch. [Var. of COIN]

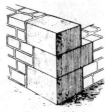

Quoins *def. 2*

quoit (kwoit, *esp. Brit.* koit) n. 1 A ring of iron or other material to be thrown over a stake, used in the game of quoits. 2 *pl.* A game played by throwing these disks at a short stake.

quon·dam (kwon′dəm) adj. Having been formerly; former. [L]

Quon·set hut (kwon′sit) A prefabricated metal structure in the form of half a cylinder resting lengthwise on its flat surface: a trade name.

Quonset hut

quo·rum (kwôr′əm, kwō′rəm) n. The number of members of any deliberative or corporate body that is necessary for the legal transaction of business, usu., a majority. [L, of whom]

quot. quotation.

quo·ta (kwō′tə) n. A proportional part or share given to or required from a person, group, etc. [< L *quotus* how great]

quo·ta·tion (kwō·tā′shən) n. 1 The act of quoting. 2 The words quoted. 3 A price quoted or current, as of securities, etc. —**quo·ta′tion·al** adj. —**quo·ta′tion·al·ly** adv.

quotation mark One of a pair of marks (" " or ' ') placed at the beginning and end of a quoted word or passage, the single marks usu. being used to set off a quotation within a quotation.

quote (kwōt) v. **quot·ed, quot·ing** v.t. 1 To repeat or reproduce the words of. 2 To repeat or cite (a rule, author, etc.), as for authority or illustration. 3 In commerce: **a** To state (a price). **b** To give the current or market price of. —v.i. 4 To make a quotation, as from a book. —n. 1 QUOTATION. 2 QUOTATION MARK. [< Med. L *quotare* distinguish by number < L *quot* how many] —**quot′a·bil′i·ty, quot′er** n. —**quot′a·ble** adj.

quoth (kwōth) v.t. *Archaic* Said or spoke; uttered: used only in the first and third persons, the subject always following the verb, as *quoth* he. [< OE *cwethan* say]

quo·tid·i·an (kwō·tid′ē·ən) adj. Recurring or occurring every day. —n. Something that returns every day, as a fever. [< L *quotidianus* daily]

quo·tient (kwō′shənt) n. *Math.* The result obtained by division; a factor by which a given number must be multiplied to produce a given product. [< L *quotiens* how often]

q.v. which see (L *quod vide*).

qy. query.

R

R, r (är) *n. pl.* **R's, r's, Rs, rs** (ärz) **1** The 18th letter of the English alphabet. **2** Any spoken sound representing the letter *R* or *r*. **3** Something shaped like an R. —**the three R's** Reading, writing, and arithmetic (regarded humorously as spelled *reading, 'riting,* and *'rithmetic*); the essential elements of a primary education. —*adj.* Shaped like an R.

R radical; ratio; Republican; rook (chess); registered (trademark).

R., r. rabbi; railroad; river; road; ruble; rupee.

r roentgen(s); radius.

r. range; rare; received; residence; retired; radius.

Ra (rä) The supreme Egyptian deity, the sun-god.

Ra radium.

rab·bet (rab′it) *n.* **1** A recess or groove in or near the edge of one piece of wood or other material to receive the edge of another piece. **2** A joint so made. —*v.t.* **1** To cut a rectangular groove in. **2** To unite in a rabbet. —*v.i.* **3** To be jointed by a rabbet. [< OF *rabattre* beat down]

rab·bi (rab′ī) *n. pl.* **·bis 1** A Jew authorized to teach or expound Jewish law. **2** The official head of a Jewish congregation. [< Heb. *rabbī* my master]

Ra

rab·bin·i·cal (rə·bin′i·kəl) *adj.* Of or pertaining to the rabbis or to their opinions, languages, writings, etc. Also **rab·bin·ic.** —**rab·bin′i·cal·ly** *adv.*

rab·bit (rab′it) *n.* **1** Any of numerous small, herbivorous mammals having soft fur, long legs and ears, and a short tail. **2** HARE. **3** The pelt of a rabbit or hare. —*v.i.* To hunt rabbits. [ME *rabette*] —**rab′bit·er** *n.*

rabbit fever TULAREMIA.

rabbit foot The left hind foot of a rabbit carried as a good-luck charm. Also **rabbit's foot.**

rab·ble (rab′əl) *n.* A disorderly crowd; mob. —**the rabble** The common people: a contemptuous term. [?]

rab·ble-rous·er (rab′əl·rou′zər) *n.* One who tries to incite mobs by arousing prejudices and passions. —**Syn.** demagogue, instigator, agitator.

Rab·e·lai·si·an (rab′ə·lā′zē·ən, -zhən) *adj.* **1** Of, pertaining to, or like Rabelais or his works. **2** Humorously coarse and boisterous; bawdy. —**Rab′e·lai′si·an·ism** *n.*

rab·id (rab′id) *adj.* **1** Affected with, arising from, or pertaining to rabies; mad. **2** Unreasonably zealous; fanatical. **3** Furious; raging. [< L *rabere* be mad] —**ra·bid·i·ty** (rə·bid′ə·tē), **rab′id·ness** *n.* —**rab′id·ly** *adv.*

ra·bies (rā′bēz) *n. pl.* **·bies** An acute viral disease affecting the central nervous system of dogs, bats, and other warm-blooded animals and transmissible to man by the bite of an infected animal. [< L *rabere* rave]

rac·coon (ra·kōōn′) *n.* **1** A North American nocturnal, tree-climbing mammal with a black face mask, long gray-brown fur, and a bushy, black-ringed tail. **2** The fur of this animal. Also **ra·coon′.** [< Algon.]

Raccoon

race¹ (rās) *n.* **1** A subdivision of mankind having a relatively constant set of physical traits, such as color of skin and eyes, stature, texture of hair, etc. **2** Any grouping of peoples according to geography, nation, etc. **3** A genealogical or family stock; clan: the *race* of MacGregor. **4** Any class of people having similar activities, interests, etc.: the *race* of lawyers. **5** *Biol.* A group of plants or animals within a species with distinct, inheritable characteristics; a variety. [< Ital. *razza*]

race² (rās) *n.* **1** A contest to determine the relative speed of the persons or animals which are in competition. **2** *pl.* A series of such contests, as for horses. **3** Any contest. **4** Duration of life; course; career. **5** A swift current of water or its channel. **6** A swift current or heavy sea. **7** A sluice or channel by which to conduct water to or from a water-wheel or around a dam. **8** Any guide or channel along which some part of a machine moves. **9** SLIPSTREAM. —*v.* **raced, rac·ing** *v.i.* **1** To take part in a race. **2** To move at great or top speed. **3** To move at an accelerated or too great speed, as an engine. —*v.t.* **4** To contend against in a race. **5** To cause to race. [< ON *rās*]

race·course (rās′kôrs′, -kōrs′) *n.* A course or track for racing.

ra·ceme (rā·sēm′, rə-) *n. Bot.* A flower cluster having flowers on short stalks arranged at intervals along a central stalk. [< L *racemus* cluster] —**rac·e·mose** (ras′ə·mōs) *adj.* —**rac′e·mose·ly** *adv.*

rac·er (rā′sər) *n.* **1** One who races. **2** Anything having unusually rapid speed, as a car, yacht, etc. **3** Any of a genus of large, agile snakes of North America.

race riot A riot caused by racial hostility, as between two groups of different races.

race·track (rās′trak′) *n.* A course or track for racing, esp. one for horse or dog racing.

Ra·chel (rā′chəl) In the Bible, the wife of Jacob and mother of Joseph.

ra·chi·tis (rə·kī′tis) *n.* RICKETS. [< Gk. *rhachitis* spinal inflammation] —**ra·chit′ic** (-kit′ik) *adj.*

ra·cial (rā′shəl) *adj.* **1** Of, pertaining to, or characteristic of a race. **2** Existing between races: *racial* brotherhood. —**ra′cial·ly** *adv.*

ra·cial·ism (rā′shəl·iz′əm) *n.* **1** The belief in or practice of racial superiority. **2** RACISM.

ra·cism (rā′siz·əm) *n.* **1** An excessive and irrational belief in the superiority of one's own racial group. **2** A doctrine, program, or practice based on such belief. —**ra′cist** *adj., n.*

rack¹ (rak) *n.* **1** Something on which various articles can be hung, stored, or canned. **2** A triangular frame for arranging the balls on a billiard table. **3** *Mech.* A bar having teeth that engage those of a gearwheel or pinion. **4** A machine for stretching or making tense; esp., an instrument of torture which stretches the limbs of victims. **5** Intense mental or physical suffering or its cause. **6** A wrenching or straining, as from a storm. —**on the rack** In great physical or mental pain. —*v.t.* **1** To place or arrange in or on a rack. **2** To torture on the rack. **3** To torment. **4** To strain, as with the effort of thinking: to *rack* one's brains. **5** To raise (rents) excessively. —**rack up** *Informal* To gain or achieve: to *rack up* a good score. [Prob. < MDu. *recken* to stretch] —**rack′er** *n.*

Rack *def. 3* and pinion

rack² (rak) *n.* SINGLE FOOT. —*v.i.* To proceed or move with this gait. [? Var. of ROCK²]

rack³ (rak) *n.* Thin, flying, or broken clouds. [< Scand.]

rack⁴ (rak) *n.* Destruction: obsolete except in the phrase **go to rack and ruin.** [Var. of WRACK]

rack·et¹ (rak′it) *n.* **1** A bat consisting of an oval, wooden or metal hoop strung with catgut, nylon, etc., and having a handle, used in playing tennis, etc. **2** *pl. (construed as sing.)* A game resembling court tennis, played in a court with four walls: also **rac·quets** (rak′its). [< Ar. *rāha* palm of the hand]

rack·et² (rak′it) *n.* **1** A loud, clattering or confused noise. **2** *Informal* A scheme for getting money or other benefits by fraud, intimidation, or other illegitimate means. **3**

Slang Any business or occupation. —*v.i.* To make a loud, clattering noise. [?] —**rack'et·y** *adj.*

rack·et·eer (rak'ə·tir') *n.* One who gets money or other benefits by fraud, intimidation, or other illegitimate means. —**rack'et·eer'ing** *n.*

rac·on·teur (rak'on·tûr', *Fr.* rá·kôn'tœr') *n.* A skilled storyteller. [F]

rac·y (rā'sē) *adj.* **rac·i·er, rac·i·est** 1 Full of spirit and vigor: a *racy* style. 2 Slightly immodest or risqué. 3 Spicy; piquant. [< RACE[1]] —**rac'i·ly** *adv.* —**rac'i·ness** *n.*

rad (rad) *n.* A unit of absorbed radiation equivalent to 100 ergs of absorbed energy per gram of absorbing material. [< R(ADIATION) + A(BSORBED) + D(OSE)]

rad radian.

ra·dar (rā'där) *n.* *Electronics* A device which detects, locates, and indicates the speed and approximate nature of aircraft, ships, objects, etc., by means of reflected microwaves. [< RA(DIO) D(ETECTING) A(ND) R(ANGING)]

ra·di·al (rā'dē·əl) *adj.* 1 Pertaining to, consisting of, or resembling a ray or radius. 2 Extending from a center like rays. 3 *Anat.* Of, pertaining to, or near the radius or forearm. 4 Developing uniformly on all sides. —*n.* 1 A radiating part. 2 RADIAL TIRE. —**ra'di·al·ly** *adv.*

radial tire A pneumatic tire with plies of fabric laid at right angles to the direction of the tread. Also **ra·di·al·ply tire** (rā'dē·əl·plī').

ra·di·an (rā'dē·ən) *n.* The angle subtended by an arc equal in length to the radius of the circle of which it is a part: a unit of measure. [< RADIUS]

ra·di·ance (rā'dē·əns) *n.* The quality or state of being radiant. Also **ra'di·an·cy, ra'di·ant·ness.**

ra·di·ant (rā'dē·ənt) *adj.* 1 Emitting rays of light or heat. 2 Beaming with brightness: a *radiant* smile. 3 Resembling rays. 4 Consisting of or transmitted by radiation: *radiant* heat. [< L *radiare* emit rays] —**ra'di·ant·ly** *adv.*

radiant energy *Physics* Energy transmitted by radiation, as electromagnetic waves.

ra·di·ate (rā'dē·āt) *v.* **·at·ed, ·at·ing** *v.i.* 1 To emit rays or radiation; be radiant. 2 To issue forth in rays. 3 To spread out from a center, as the spokes of a wheel. —*v.t.* 4 To send out or emit in rays. 5 To spread or show (joy, love, etc.) as if from a center. —*adj.* (-dē·it) Divided or separated into rays; having rays; radiating. [< L *radiare* emit rays] —**ra'di·a'tive** *adj.*

ra·di·a·tion (rā'dē·ā'shən) *n.* 1 The act or process of radiating or the state of being radiated. 2 That which is radiated, as energy in the form of particles or waves.

radiation sickness Sickness resulting from exposure to X-rays, nuclear explosions, etc.

ra·di·a·tor (rā'dē·ā'tər) *n.* 1 That which radiates. 2 A device for distributing heat, partly by radiation, as in heating or cooling systems.

rad·i·cal (rad'i·kəl) *adj.* 1 Thoroughgoing; extreme: *radical* measures. 2 Of, pertaining to, or professing policies and practices of extreme change, as in government. 3 Of or pertaining to the root or foundation; essential; basic. —*n.* 1 One who holds radical or extreme convictions. 2 In politics, one who advocates extreme governmental changes. 3 The primitive or underived part of a word; root. 4 *Math.* An indicated root of a number, expression, etc. 5 *Chem.* A group of atoms that act as a unit in a compound and remain together during a chemical reaction. [< L *radix, radicis* root] —**rad'i·cal·ly** *adv.* —**rad'i·cal·ness** *n.*

rad·i·cal·ism (rad'i·kəl·iz'əm) *n.* 1 The state of being radical. 2 Advocacy of radical or extreme measures.

rad·i·cal·ize (rad'i·kə·līz') *v.t.* **·ized, ·iz·ing** To make radical, as in politics. —**rad·i·cal·i·za·tion** (rad'i·kə·lə·zā'shən) *n.*

radical sign *Math.* The symbol $\sqrt{}$ placed around a number or expression to indicate that its root is to be taken. A number above it, not written when equal to 2, shows what root is to be taken; thus $\sqrt[n]{a}$ stands for the *n*th root of *a*.

rad·i·cle (rad'i·kəl) *n.* *Bot.* The embryonic root of a sprouting seed. [< L *radix, radicis* root]

ra·di·o (rā'dē·ō) *n. pl.* **·os** 1 The technology and process of communicating by means of radio waves. 2 A transmitter or receiver used in such communication. 3 The process, business, or industry of producing programs to be communicated in this way. —*adj.* Of, pertaining to, designat-

ing, employing, or produced by radiant energy, esp. electromagnetic waves: a *radio* beam. —*v.t. & v.i.* **·di·oed, ·di·o·ing** 1 To transmit (a message, etc.) by radio. 2 To communicate with (someone) by radio. [< RADIO(TELEGRAPHY)]

radio- *combining form* Radiation: *radioscopy.* [< L *radius* a ray]

ra·di·o·ac·tive (rā'dē·ō·ak'tiv) *adj.* Of, pertaining to, exhibiting, caused by, or characteristic of radioactivity.

ra·di·o·ac·tiv·i·ty (rā'dē·ō·ak·tiv'ə·tē) *n.* *Physics* The spontaneous disintegration of nuclei of certain elements and isotopes, with the emission of particles or rays.

radio astronomy The branch of astronomy which studies celestial phenomena by means of radio waves received from stars and other objects in space.

radio beacon A stationary radio transmitter which sends out signals for the guidance of ships and aircraft.

radio beam 1 A steady flow of radio signals concentrated along a given course or direction. 2 The narrow zone marked out for the guidance of aircraft by radio beacons.

ra·di·o·broad·cast (rā'dē·ō·brôd'kast', -käst') *v.t. & v.i.* **·cast** or **·cast·ed, ·cast·ing** To broadcast by radio. —*n.* BROADCAST. —**ra'di·o·broad'cast'er** *n.* —**ra'di·o·broad'cast'ing** *n.*

ra·di·o·car·bon (rā'dē·ō·kär'bən) *n.* CARBON 14.

radio frequency Any wave frequency from about 10 kilohertz to about 30,000 megahertz.

ra·di·o·gram (rā'dē·ō·gram') *n.* 1 A message sent by wireless telegraphy. 2 RADIOGRAPH.

ra·di·o·graph (rā'dē·ō·graf', -gräf') *n.* An image made by means of X-rays or the products of radioactivity. —*v.t.* To make a radiograph of. —**ra'di·og'ra·pher** (-og'rə·fər), **ra'di·og'ra·phy** *n.* —**ra'di·o·graph'ic** or **·i·cal** *adj.*

ra·di·o·i·so·tope (rā'dē·ō·ī'sə·tōp) *n.* A radioactive isotope, usu. one of an element having also a stable isotope.

ra·di·ol·o·gy (rā'dē·ol'ə·jē) *n.* That branch of science concerned with radioactivity, X-rays, etc., esp. in diagnostic and therapeutic applications. —**ra·di·o·log·i·cal** (rā'dē·ə·loj'i·kəl) or **ra'di·o·log'ic** *adj.* —**ra'di·ol'o·gist** *n.*

ra·di·om·e·ter (rā'dē·om'ə·tər) *n.* An instrument for detecting and measuring radiant energy by noting the speed of rotation of blackened disks suspended in a partially evacuated chamber.

ra·di·o·phone (rā'dē·ō·fōn') *n.* RADIOTELEPHONE.

ra·di·o·pho·to (rā'dē·ō·fō'tō) *n.* A photograph or image transmitted by radio. Also **ra'di·o·pho'to·graph.**

ra·di·o·scope (rā'dē·ō·skōp') *n.* An apparatus for detecting radioactivity or X-rays.

Radiometer

ra·di·os·co·py (rā'dē·os'kə·pē) *n.* Examination of bodies opaque to light by X-rays or other penetrating radiation. —**ra'di·o·scop'ic** (-skop'ik) or **·i·cal** *adj.*

ra·di·o·sonde (rā'dē·ō·sond') *n.* *Meteorol.* A device, usu. attached to a small balloon and sent aloft, which measures the pressure, temperature, and humidity of the upper air and radios the data to the ground. [< RADIO + F *sonde* sounding]

radio star A star that emits a sizable part of its energy as radio waves.

ra·di·o·tel·e·gram (rā'dē·ō·tel'ə·gram) *n.* A message sent by radiotelegraphy.

ra·di·o·te·leg·ra·phy (rā'dē·ō·tə·leg'rə·fē) *n.* Telegraphic communication by means of radio waves. Also **ra'di·o·tel'e·graph** (-tel'ə·graf, -gräf). —**ra'di·o·tel'e·graph'ic** *adj.*

ra·di·o·tel·e·phone (rā'dē·ō·tel'ə·fōn) *n.* A telephone set that uses radio waves to carry messages. —**ra'di·o·te·leph'o·ny** (-tə·lef'ə·nē) *n.*

radio telescope A sensitive radio receiver designed to receive radio waves from space.

Radiosonde

ra·di·o·ther·a·py (rā'dē·ō·ther'ə·pē) *n.* The use of X-rays and radioactivity in the treatment of disease.

radio wave Any electromagnetic wave of radio frequency.

rad·ish (rad′ish) n. 1 A tall, branching herb of the mustard family. 2 Its pungent, edible root, commonly eaten raw. [< L *radix, radicis* root]

ra·di·um (rā′dē·əm) n. A radioactive metallic element (symbol Ra) found in pitchblende as a disintegration product of uranium. [< L *radius* ray]

radium therapy The treatment of disease, esp. cancer, by means of radium.

ra·di·us (rā′dē·əs) n. pl. **·di·i** (-dē·ī) or **·di·us·es** 1 A straight line segment joining the surface of a sphere or circumference of a circle with its center. 2 *Anat.* The shorter of the two bones of the forearm. 3 *Zool.* A corresponding bone in the forelimb of other vertebrates. 4 *Bot.* A ray floret of a composite flower. 5 A raylike part, as a wheel spoke. 6 A circular area or boundary measured by its radius. 7 Sphere, scope, or limit, as of activity. 8 A fixed or circumscribed area or distance of travel. [L, spoke of a wheel, ray]

radius vector pl. **radius vectors** or **ra·di·i vec·to·res** (rā′dē·ī vek·tôr′ēz, -tō′rēz) *Math.* The distance in an indicated direction from a fixed origin to any point.

Radius def. 2

ra·dix (rā′diks) n. pl. **rad·i·ces** (rad′ə·sēz, rā′də-) or **ra·dix·es** *Math.* A number or symbol used as the base of a system of numeration. [L, root]

ra·dome (rā′dōm) n. A housing, transparent to microwaves, for a radar assembly. [< RA(DAR) + DOME]

ra·don (rā′don) n. A gaseous, radioactive element (symbol Rn) resulting from the decay of radium and having a half-life of about four days. [< RAD(IUM) + (NE)ON]

RAF, R.A.F. Royal Air Force.

raf·fi·a (raf′ē·ə) n. 1 A cultivated palm of Madagascar. 2 Fiber made from the leaves of this palm, used for weaving baskets, etc. [< Malagasy *rafia*]

raff·ish (raf′ish) adj. 1 Tawdry; gaudy; vulgar. 2 Disreputable. [< ME *raf* rubbish + -ISH]

raf·fle (raf′əl) n. A form of lottery in which a number of people buy chances on an object. —v. **·fled, ·fling** v.t. 1 To dispose of by a raffle: often with *off.* —v.i. 2 To take part in a raffle. [< OF *rafle* a game of dice] —**raf′fler** n.

raft[1] (raft, räft) n. 1 A float of logs, planks, etc., fastened together for transportation by water. 2 A flat, often inflatable object, as of rubber, that floats on water. —v.t. 1 To transport on a raft. 2 To form into a raft. —v.i. To travel by or work on a raft. [< ON *raptr* log] —**rafts′man** n.

raft[2] (raft, räft) n. *Informal* A large number or an indiscriminate collection of any kind. [< ME *raf* rubbish]

raft·er (raf′tər, räf′-) n. A timber or beam giving form, slope, and support to a roof. [< OE *ræfter*]

rag[1] (rag) v.t. **ragged, rag·ging** *Slang* 1 To tease or irritate. 2 To scold. —n. *Brit.* A prank. [?]

rag[2] (rag) n. 1 A waste, usu. torn piece of cloth. 2 A fragment of anything. 3 pl. Tattered or shabby clothing. 4 pl. Any clothing: a jocular use. 5 *Slang* A newspaper. —**chew the rag** *Slang* To talk or argue at length. —**glad rags** *Slang* One's best clothes. [< ON *rögg* tuft or strip of fur]

rag[3] (rag) n. RAGTIME. —v.t. **ragged, rag·ging** To compose or play in ragtime.

ra·ga (rä′gə) n. One of a large number of traditional melodic patterns, used by Hindu musicians as the basis for improvisation. [< Skt. *rāga* (musical) color]

rag·a·muf·fin (rag′ə·muf′in) n. Anyone, esp. a child, wearing very ragged clothes. [< *Ragamoffyn,* demon in *Piers Plowman* (1393), a long allegorical poem]

rag-bag (rag′bag′) n. 1 A bag in which rags or scraps of cloth are kept. 2 A miscellaneous collection; potpourri.

rage (rāj) n. 1 Violent anger; wrath; fury. 2 Any great violence or intensity, as of a fever or a storm. 3 Extreme eagerness or emotion. 4 Something that arouses great enthusiasm; craze; vogue. —v.i. **raged, rag·ing** 1 To feel or show violent anger. 2 To act or proceed with great vio-

lence. 3 To spread or prevail uncontrolled, as an epidemic. [< L *rabies* madness]

rag·ged (rag′id) adj. 1 Torn or worn into rags; frayed. 2 Wearing worn, frayed, or shabby garments. 3 Of rough or uneven character or aspect: a *ragged* performance. 4 Naturally of a rough or shabby appearance. —**rag′ged·ly** adv. —**rag′ged·ness** n.

rag·ged·y (rag′id·ē) adj. Ragged in appearance.

rag·lan (rag′lən) n. An overcoat or topcoat, the sleeves of which extend in one piece up to the collar. —adj. Of or designating such a sleeve or a garment with such sleeves. [< Lord Fitzroy *Raglan,* 1788–1855, Eng. field marshal]

rag·man (rag′man′, -mən) n. pl. **·men** (-men′, -mən) One who buys and sells old rags and other waste; a ragpicker.

ra·gout (ra·gōo′) n. A highly seasoned dish of stewed meat and vegetables. —v.t. **ra·gouted** (-gōod′), **ra·gout·ing** (-gōo′ing) To make into a ragout. [< F *ragoûter* revive the appetite]

rag·pick·er (rag′pik′ər) n. One who picks up and sells rags and other junk for a livelihood.

rag·time (rag′tīm′) n. 1 A kind of American dance music, popular 1890 to 1920, highly syncopated and in quick tempo. 2 The rhythm of this dance. [< *ragged time*]

rag·weed (rag′wēd′) n. Any of a genus of coarse, composite plants having pollen that often induces hay fever.

rag·wort (rag′wûrt′) n. GROUNDSEL (def. 1).

rah (rä) interj. Hurrah!: a cheer used esp. in school yells.

raid (rād) n. 1 A hostile or predatory attack, as by a rapidly moving body of troops. 2 AIR RAID. 3 Any sudden breaking into, invasion, or capture, as by the police. 4 A manipulative attempt to make stock prices fall by concerted selling. —v.t. 1 To make a raid on. —v.i. 2 To participate in a raid. [< OE *rād* a ride] —**raid′er** n.

rail[1] (rāl) n. 1 A bar, usu. of wood or metal, resting on supports, as in a fence, at the side of a stairway or roadway, or capping the bulwarks of a ship; a railing. 2 One of a series of parallel bars, of iron or steel, resting upon cross-ties, forming a support and guide for wheels, as of a railway. 3 A railroad: to ship by *rail.* —v.t. To furnish or shut in with rails; fence. [< L *regula* ruler]

rail[2] (rāl) n. Any of various small marsh and shore birds having short wings and tail. [< OF *raale, ralle*]

rail[3] (rāl) v.i. To use scornful, insolent, or abusive language: with *at* or *against.* [< MF *railler* to mock]

rail·ing (rā′ling) n. 1 A series of rails; a balustrade. 2 Rails or material from which rails are made.

rail·ler·y (rā′lər·ē) n. pl. **·ler·ies** Merry jesting or teasing. [< F *raillerie* jesting]

Rail

rail·road (rāl′rōd′) n. 1 A graded road, having metal rails supported by ties, for the passage of trains or other rolling stock drawn by locomotives. 2 The system of tracks, stations, etc., used in transportation by rail. 3 The corporation or persons owning or operating such a system. —v.t. 1 To transport by railroad. 2 *Informal* To rush or force with great speed or without deliberation: to *railroad* a bill through Congress. 3 *Slang* To cause to be imprisoned on false charges or without fair trial. —v.i. 4 To work on a railroad. —**rail′road′er** n.

railroad flat An apartment having rooms arranged one after another in a straight line without hallways.

rail·split·ter (rāl′split′ər) n. One who splits logs into fence rails.

rail·way (rāl′wā′) n. 1 A railroad, esp. one using comparatively light vehicles. 2 *Brit.* RAILROAD. 3 Any track having rails for wheeled equipment.

rai·ment (rā′mənt) n. Wearing apparel; clothing; garb. [< ARRAY + -MENT]

rain (rān) n. 1 The condensed water vapor of the atmosphere falling in drops. 2 The fall of such drops. 3 A fall or shower of anything in the manner of rain. 4 A rainstorm; shower. 5 pl. The rainy season in a tropical country. —v.i. 1 To fall from the clouds in drops of water. 2 To fall like

rain. **3** To send or pour down rain. —*v.t.* **4** To send down like rain; shower. [<OE *regn*]

rain·bow (rān′bō′) *n.* **1** An arch of light formed in the sky opposite the sun and exhibiting the colors of the spectrum. It is caused by refraction, reflection, and dispersion of sunlight in raindrops or mist. **2** Any brilliant display of color. **3** Any unfounded hope.

rain check 1 The stub of a ticket to an outdoor event entitling the holder to future admission if for any reason the event is called off. **2** Any postponed invitation.

rain·coat (rān′kōt′) *n.* A water-resistant coat giving protection against rain.

rain·drop (rān′drop′) *n.* A drop of rain.

rain·fall (rān′fôl′) *n.* **1** A fall of rain. **2** *Meteorol.* The amount of water precipitated in a given region over a stated time.

rain gauge An instrument for measuring rainfall.

rain·proof (rān′proof′) *adj.* Shedding rain. —*v.t.* To make rainproof.

rain·storm (rān′stôrm′) *n.* A storm accompanied by heavy rain.

rain·wa·ter (rān′wô′tər, -wot′ər) *n.* Water that falls or has fallen as rain.

rain·y (rā′nē) *adj.* **rain·i·er**, **rain·i·est** Of, abounding in, or bringing rain. —**rain′i·ly** *adv.* —**rain′i·ness** *n.*

rainy day A time of need; hard times.

raise (rāz) *v.* **raised**, **rais·ing** *v.t.* **1** To cause to move upward or to a higher level; lift; elevate. **2** To place erect; set up. **3** To construct or build; erect. **4** To make greater in amount, size, or value: to *raise* the price of corn. **5** To advance or elevate in rank, estimation, etc. **6** To increase the strength, intensity, or degree of. **7** To breed; grow: to *raise* chickens or tomatoes. **8** To rear (children, a family, etc.). **9** To cause to be heard: to *raise* a hue and cry. **10** To cause; occasion, as a smile or laugh. **11** To stir to action or emotion; arouse. **12** To waken; animate or reanimate: to *raise* the dead. **13** To obtain or collect, as an army, capital, etc. **14** To bring up for consideration, as a question. **15** To cause to swell or become lighter; leaven. **16** To put an end to, as a siege. **17** In card games, to bid or bet more than. **18** *Naut.* To cause to appear above the horizon, as land or a ship, by approaching nearer. —*v.i.* **19** *Regional* To rise or arise. **20** In card games, to increase a bid or bet. —**raise Cain** (or **the devil, the dickens, a rumpus,** etc.) *Informal* to make a great disturbance; stir up confusion. —*n.* **1** The act of raising. **2** An increase, as of wages or a bet. [<ON *reisa* lift, set up]

raised (rāzd) *adj.* **1** Elevated in low relief. **2** Made with yeast or leaven.

rai·sin (rā′zən) *n.* A grape of a special sort dried in the sun or in an oven. [<L *racemus* bunch of grapes]

rai·son d'ê·tre (re·zôn′ de′tr′) *French* A reason or excuse for existing.

raj (räj) *n.* In India, sovereignty; rule [<Hind. *rāj*]

ra·ja (rä′jə) *n.* **1** A prince or chief of India. **2** A Malay or Javanese ruler. Also **ra′jah.** [<Skt. *rājan* king]

rake[1] (rāk) *n.* A long-handled, toothed implement for drawing together loose material, making a surface smooth, etc. — *v.* **raked**, **rak·ing** *v.t.* **1** To gather together with or as with a rake. **2** To smooth, clean, or prepare with a rake. **3** To gather by diligent effort. **4** To search or examine carefully. **5** To direct heavy gunfire along the length of. —*v.i.* **6** To use a rake. **7** To scrape or pass roughly or violently: with *across, over,* etc. **8** To make a search. —**rake in** *Informal* To earn or acquire (money, etc.) in large quantities. —**rake up** *Informal* To make public or bring to light: to *rake up* old gossip. [<OE *raca*]

Rakes
a. garden. b. broom.

rake[2] (rāk) *v.* **raked**, **rak·ing** *v.i.* **1** To lean from the perpendicular, as a ship's masts. —*v.t.* **2** To cause to lean; incline. —*n.* Inclination from the perpendicular or horizontal, as the edge of a cutting tool. [?] —**raked** *adj.*

rake[3] (rāk) *n.* A dissolute, lewd man. [Orig. *rakehell* < ME *rakel* rash, wild] —**Syn.** roué, libertine, lecher, profligate.

rake-off (rāk′ôf′, -of′) *n.* *Slang* A percentage, as of profits; commission or rebate, usu. illegitimate.

rak·ish[1] (rā′kish) *adj.* **1** Dashing; jaunty. **2** *Naut.* Having the masts unusually inclined, usu. connoting speed. [<RAKE[2]] —**rak′ish·ly** *adv.* —**rak′ish·ness** *n.*

rak·ish[2] (rā′kish) *adj.* Like a rake; dissolute. —**rak′ish·ly** *adv.* —**rak′ish·ness** *n.*

ral·len·tan·do (ral′ən·tan′dō, *Ital.* räl′len·tän′dō) *adj.* & *adv. Music* Gradually slower. [Ital., pr.p. of *rallentare* slow down]

ral·ly[1] (ral′ē) *v.* **·lied**, **·ly·ing** *v.t.* **1** To bring together and restore to effective discipline: to *rally* fleeing troops. **2** To summon up or revive: to *rally* one's spirits. **3** To bring together for common action. —*v.i.* **4** To return to effective discipline or action: The enemy *rallied.* **5** To unite for common action. **6** To make a partial or complete return to a normal condition. **7** In tennis, badminton, etc. to engage in a rally. —*n. pl.* **·lies 1** An assembly of people, esp. to arouse enthusiasm. **2** A quick recovery or improvement, as of health, spirits, vigor, etc. **3** A reassembling, as of scattered troops. **4** In tennis, badminton, etc., an exchange of several strokes before one side wins the point. **5** A competition for automobiles that emphasizes driving and navigational skills rather than speed. [<F *re-* again + *allier* join]

ral·ly[2] (ral′ē) *v.t.* & *v.i.* To tease or ridicule; banter. [<F *railler* banter]

ram (ram) *n.* **1** A male sheep. **2** BATTERING-RAM. **3** Any device for forcing or thrusting, as by heavy blows. **4** A device for raising water by pressure of its own flow; a hydraulic ram. —*v.t.* **rammed**, **ram·ming 1** To strike with or as with a ram; dash against. **2** To drive or force down or into something. **3** To cram; stuff. [<OE]

Ram (ram) *n.* ARIES.

RAM Random access memory, a kind of computer memory in which information may be stored and/or erased repeatedly.

ram·ble (ram′bəl) *v.i.* **·bled**, **·bling 1** To walk about freely and aimlessly; roam. **2** To write or talk aimlessly or without sequence of ideas. **3** To proceed with turns and twists; meander. —*n.* **1** The act of rambling. **2** A meandering path; maze. [?]

ram·bler (ram′blər) *n.* **1** One who or that which rambles. **2** Any of several varieties of climbing roses.

ram·bunc·tious (ram·bungk′shəs) *adj. Informal* Difficult to control or manage; unruly. [?]

ram·e·kin (ram′ə·kin) *n.* **1** Any of various food mixtures, usu. containing cheese, baked and served in individual dishes. **2** Any small or individual baking dish. Also **ram′e·quin.** [<F *ramequin*]

ram·i·fi·ca·tion (ram′ə·fə·kā′shən) *n.* **1** The act or process of ramifying. **2** An offshoot or branch. **3** A result or consequence; ougrowth, as of an action.

ram·i·fy (ram′ə·fī) *v.t.* & *v.i.* **·fied**, **·fy·ing** To divide or spread out into or as into branches. [<L *ramus* branch + *facere* make]

ram·jet (ram′jet′) *n.* A type of jet engine consisting of a duct whose forward motion provides compressed air which mixes with fuel that burns and provides an exhaust velocity high enough to create thrust.

ra·mose (rā′mōs, rə·mōs′) *adj.* **1** Branching. **2** Consisting of or having branches. [<L *ramus* branch]

ramp[1] (ramp) *n.* **1** An inclined passageway or roadway that connects different levels. **2** A movable stairway or passageway for entering or leaving an airplane. **3** *Archit.* A concave part at the top or cap of a railing, wall, or coping. [<F *ramper* to climb]

ramp[2] (ramp) *v.i.* **1** To rear up on the hind legs and stretch out the forepaws. **2** To act in a violent or threatening manner. —*n.* The act of ramping. [<OF *ramper* to climb]

ram·page (ram′pāj) *n.* An outbreak of boisterous or angry agitation or violence. —*v.i.* (ram·pāj′) **·paged**, **·pag·ing** To rush or act violently; storm; rage [Orig. Scot.,? < RAMP[2]]

ram·pant (ram′pənt) *adj.* **1** Exceeding all bounds; unrestrained; wild. **2** Widespread; unchecked, as an erroneous belief. **3** Standing on the hind legs; rearing: said of a quadruped. **4** *Her.* Standing on the hind legs, with both forelegs elevated. [<OF *ramper* to climb] —**ram′pan·cy** *n.* —**ram′pant·ly** *adv.*

Rampant lion

ram·part (ram′pärt, -pərt) *n.* **1** The embankment surrounding a fort, on which the parapet is raised. **2** A bulwark or defense. —*v.t.* To supply with or as with ramparts; fortify. [< OF *re-* again + *emparer* prepare]

ram·pike (ram′pīk′) *n. Can.* A bare, dead tree, esp. one destroyed by fire. [?]

ram·rod (ram′rod′) *n.* **1** A rod used to compact the charge of a muzzleloading firearm. **2** A similar rod used for cleaning the barrel of a rifle, etc.

ram·shack·le (ram′shak′əl) *adj.* About to go to pieces from age and neglect. [?] —**Syn.** dilapidated, unsteady, shaky, battered.

ran (ran) *p.t.* of RUN.

ranch (ranch) *n.* **1** An establishment for rearing or grazing cattle, sheep, horses, etc., in large herds. **2** The buildings, personnel, and lands connected with it. **3** A large farm. —*v.i.* To manage or work on a ranch. [< Sp. *rancho* group eating together, mess] —**ranch′er, ranch′man** *n.*

ranch house 1 A long, one-story residence having a low-pitched roof. **2** The main house on a ranch.

ran·cid (ran′sid) *adj.* Having the bad taste or smell of spoiled fats. [< L *rancere* be rancid] —**ran·cid·i·ty** (ran·sid′-ə·tē), **ran′cid·ness** *n.*

ran·cor (rang′kər) *n.* Bitter and vindictive enmity. *Brit. sp.* **ran·cour.** [< L *rancere* be rank] —**ran′cor·ous** *adj.* —**ran′cor·ous·ly** *adv.* —**ran′cor·ous·ness** *n.* —**Syn.** malice, spite, hatred, hostility.

ran·dom (ran′dəm) *n.* Lack of definite purpose or intention: now chiefly in the phrase **at random,** without careful thought, planning, intent, etc.; haphazardly. —*adj.* **1** Done or chosen without deliberation or plan; chance; casual. **2** Chosen, determined, or varying without pattern, rule, or bias. [< OF *randonner, rander* move rapidly, gallop] —**ran′dom·ly** *adv.* —**ran′dom·ness** *n.*

ra·nee (rä′nē) *n.* RANI.

rang (rang) *p.t.* of RING².

range (rānj) *n.* **1** The area over which anything moves, operates, or is distributed. **2** An extensive tract of land over which cattle, sheep, etc., roam and graze. **3** Extent or scope: the whole *range* of political influence. **4** The extent of variation of anything: the temperature *range*. **5** A line, row, or series, as of mountains. **6** The horizontal distance between a gun and its target. **7** The horizontal distance covered by a projectile. **8** The maximum distance for which an airplane, ship, vehicle, etc., can be fueled. **9** The maximum effective distance, as of a weapon. **10** *Math.* The entire set of possible values of a dependent variable. **11** A place for shooting at a mark: a rifle *range*. **12** A large cooking stove. —*adj.* Of or pertaining to a range. —*v.* **ranged, rang·ing** *v.t.* **1** To place or arrange in definite order, as in rows. **2** To assign to a class, division, or category; classify. **3** To move about or over (a region, etc.), as in exploration. **4** To put (cattle) to graze on a range. **5** To adjust or train, as a telescope or gun. —*v.i.* **6** To move over an area in a thorough, systematic manner. **7** To rove; roam. **8** To occur; extend; be found: forests *ranging* to the east. **9** To vary within specified limits. **10** To lie in the same direction, line, etc. **11** To have a specified range. [< OF *ranger* arrange < *renc* row]

rang·er (rān′jər) *n.* **1** One who or that which ranges. **2** One of a group of mounted troops that protect large tracts of country. **3** One of a herd of cattle that feeds on a range. **4** A warden employed in patrolling forest tracts. **5** *Brit.* A government official in charge of a royal forest or park. **6** One of a group of soldiers trained esp. for raiding and close combat.

rang·y (rān′jē) *adj.* **rang·i·er, rang·i·est 1** Disposed to roam, or adapted for roving, as cattle. **2** Having long, slender limbs. **3** Roomy; spacious.

ra·ni (rä′nē) *n.* **1** The wife of a raja or prince. **2** A reigning Hindu queen or princess.

rank¹ (rangk) *n.* **1** A series of objects ranged in a line or row. **2** A degree of official standing: the *rank* of colonel. **3** A line of soldiers side by side in close order. **4** *pl.* An army; also, the common body of soldiers: to rise from the *ranks*. **5** Relative position in a scale; degree; grade: a writer of

low *rank*. **6** A social class or stratum: from all *ranks* of life. **7** High degree or position: a lady of *rank*. —*v.t.* **1** To place or arrange in a rank or ranks. **2** To assign to a position or classification. **3** To outrank: Sergeants *rank* corporals. —*v.i.* **4** To hold a specified place or rank. **5** To have the highest rank or grade. [< OF *ranc, renc*]

rank² (rangk) *adj.* **1** Flourishing and luxuriant in growth: *rank* weeds. **2** Strong and disagreeable to the taste or smell. **3** Utter; total: *rank* injustice. **4** Indecent; gross; vulgar. [< OE *ranc* strong] —**rank′ly** *adv.* —**rank′ness** *n.*

rank and file 1 The common soldiers of an army. **2** Those who form the main body of any organization, as distinguished from its leaders.

rank·ing (rangk′ing) *adj.* Taking precedence (over others): a *ranking* senator, officer, etc. —**Syn.** superior, senior.

ran·kle (rang′kəl) *v.* **·kled, ·kling** *v.i.* **1** To cause continued resentment, sense of injury, etc. **2** To become irritated or inflamed. —*v.t.* **3** To irritate; embitter. [< OF *rancler*]

ran·sack (ran′sak) *v.t.* **1** To search through every part of. **2** To search for plunder; pillage. [< ON *rann* house + *sækja* seek] —**ran′sack·er** *n.*

ran·som (ran′səm) *v.t.* **1** To secure the release of (a person, property, etc.) for a required price, as from captivity or detention. **2** To set free on payment of ransom. —*n.* **1** The price paid to ransom a person or property. **2** Release purchased, as from captivity. [< L *redimere* redeem] —**ran′som·er** *n.*

rant (rant) *v.i.* **1** To speak in loud, violent, or extravagant language. —*v.t.* **2** To exclaim or utter in a ranting manner. —*n.* Declamatory and bombastic talk. [< MDu. *ranten*] —**rant′er** *n.* —**rant′ing·ly** *adv.*

rap¹ (rap) *v.* **rapped, rap·ping** *v.t.* **1** To strike sharply and quickly; hit. **2** To utter in a sharp manner: with *out.* **3** *Slang* To criticize severely. —*v.i.* **4** To strike sharp, quick blows. **5** *Slang* To have a frank discussion; talk. —*n.* **1** A sharp blow. **2** A sound caused by or as by knocking. **3** *Slang* A severe criticism. **4** *Slang* Blame or punishment, as for wrongdoing: to take the *rap.* **5** *Slang* A prison sentence. **6** *Slang* A talk; discussion. —*adj. Slang* Marked by frank discussion: a *rap* session. [Imit.] —**rap′per** *n.*

rap² (rap) *n. Informal* The least bit: I don't care a *rap.* [?]

ra·pa·cious (rə·pā′shəs) *adj.* **1** Given to plunder or rapine. **2** Greedy; grasping. **3** Subsisting on prey seized alive, as hawks, etc. [< L *rapere* seize] —**ra·pa′cious·ly** *adv.* —**ra·pac·i·ty** (rə·pas′ə·tē), **ra·pa′cious·ness** *n.*

rape¹ (rāp) *v.* **raped, rap·ing** *v.t.* **1** To commit rape on. **2** To plunder or sack (a city, etc.). —*v.i.* **3** To commit rape. —*n.* **1** The act of a man who has sexual intercourse with a woman against her will or (called **statutory rape**) with a girl below the age of consent. **2** Any unlawful sexual intercourse or sexual connection by force or threat: homosexual *rape* in prison. **3** The plundering or sacking of a city, etc. **4** Any gross violation, assault, or abuse: the *rape* of natural forests. [< L *rapere* seize] —**rap′ist** *n.*

rape² (rāp) *n.* A plant related to mustard, grown for forage. [< L *rapum* turnip]

rape oil An oil obtained from seeds of the rape, used as a lubricant, etc. Also **rape·seed oil** (rāp′sēd′).

rap·id (rap′id) *adj.* **1** Having or done with great speed; swift; fast. **2** Marked or characterized by rapidity. —*n. Usu. pl.* A swift-flowing descent in a river. [< L *rapidus* < *rapere* seize, rush] —**ra·pid·i·ty** (rə·pid′ə·tē), **rap′id·ness** *n.* —**rap′id·ly** *adv.*

rap·id-fire (rap′id·fīr′) *adj.* **1** Firing or designed to fire shots rapidly. **2** Characterized by speed: *rapid-fire* repartee. Also **rap′id-fir′ing.**

rapid transit An urban passenger railway system.

ra·pi·er (rā′pē·ər, rāp′yər) *n.* **1** A long, pointed, two-edged sword with a large cup hilt, used in dueling, chiefly for thrusting. **2** A shorter straight sword without cutting edge and therefore used for thrusting only. [< F *rapière*]

Rapier

rap·ine (rap′in) n. The taking of property by force, as in war. [< L *rapere* seize] —**Syn.** plunder, pillage, looting, spoiling.

rap·port (ra·pôr′, -pōr′, *Fr.* rà·pôr′) n. Harmonious, sympathetic relationship; accord. —**en rapport** (äṅ rà·pôr′) *French* In close accord. [< F *rapporter* refer, bring back]

rap·proche·ment (rà·prôsh·mäṅ′) n. A state of harmony or reconciliation; restoration of cordial relations. [F]

rap·scal·lion (rap·skal′yən) n. A scamp; rascal. [Earlier *rascallion* < RASCAL]

rapt (rapt) adj. 1 Carried away with lofty emotion; enraptured; transported. 2 Deeply engrossed or intent. [< L *raptus*, pp. of *rapere* seize]

rap·to·ri·al (rap·tôr′ē·əl, -tō′rē-) adj. 1 Seizing and devouring living prey; predatory. 2 Having talons adapted for seizing prey: said esp. of hawks, vultures, eagle, owls, etc. [< L *raptus*, pp. of *rapere* seize]

rap·ture (rap′chər) n. 1 The state of being rapt or transported; ecstatic joy; ecstasy. 2 An expression of excessive delight. —*v.t.* **·tured, ·tur·ing** To enrapture; transport with ecstasy. —**rap′tur·ous** adj. —**rap′tur·ous·ly** adv.

rare[1] (râr) adj. **rar·er, rar·est** 1 Occurring infrequently; not common, usual, or ordinary. 2 Excellent in quality, merit, etc. 3 Rarefied: now said chiefly of the atmosphere. [< L *rarus*] —**Syn.** 2 extraordinary, distinctive, fine, choice.

rare[2] (râr) adj. **rar·er, rar·est** Not thoroughly cooked, as roasted or broiled meat retaining its redness and juices. [< OE *hrēre* lightly boiled]

rare·bit (râr′bit) n. WELSH RABBIT. [Alter. of (WELSH) RABBIT]

rare earth Any of the oxides of the rare-earth elements. —**rare-earth** (râr′ûrth′) adj.

rare-earth elements The series of metallic elements comprising atomic numbers 57 through 71. See PERIODIC TABLE OF ELEMENTS. Also **rare-earth metals.**

rar·e·fy (râr′ə·fī) *v.t. & v.i.* **·fied, ·fy·ing** 1 To make or become rare, thin, or less dense. 2 To make or become more refined, pure, subtle, etc. [< L *rarus* rare + *facere* make] —**rar′e·fac′tion** (-fak′shən) n. —**rar′e·fac′tive** adj.

rare·ly (râr′lē) adv. 1 Not often; infrequently. 2 With unusual excellence or effect; finely. 3 Exceptionally; extremely.

rar·ing (râr′ing) adj. *Informal* Full of enthusiasm; intensely desirous; eager: used with an infinitive: *raring* to go. [< dial. E, var. of REAR[2], to raise]

rar·i·ty (râr′ə·tē) n. pl. **·ties** 1 The quality or state of being rare, uncommon, or infrequent. 2 That which is exceptionally valued because scarce. 3 Thinness; tenuousness.

ras·cal (ras′kəl) n. 1 An unscrupulous person; scoundrel. 2 A mischievous person; tease; scamp. [< OF *rasque* filth, shavings] —**ras·cal′i·ty** (-kal′ə·tē) n. —**ras′cal·ly** adj. & adv.

rase (rāz) *v.* **rased, ras·ing** RAZE.

rash[1] (rash) adj. 1 Acting without due caution or regard of consequences; reckless. 2 Exhibiting recklessness or precipitancy. [ME *rasch*] —**rash′ly** adv. —**rash′ness** n.

rash[2] (rash) n. A patch of redness, itchiness, or other usu. temporary skin lesion.

rash·er (rash′ər) n. 1 A thin slice of meat, esp. of bacon. 2 A serving of several such slices. [?]

rasp (rasp, räsp) n. 1 A filelike tool having coarse, pointed projections. 2 The act or sound of rasping. —*v.t.* 1 To scrape with or as with a rasp. 2 To affect unpleasantly; irritate. 3 To utter in a rough voice. —*v.i.* 4 To grate; scrape. 5 To make a harsh, grating sound. [< OF *rasper* to scrape] —**rasp′er** n. —**rasp′y** adj. (**·i·er, ·i·est**)

rasp·ber·ry (raz′ber′ē, -bər·ē, räz′-) n. pl. **·ries** 1 A sweet, edible fruit, composed of drupelets clustered around a fleshy receptacle. 2 Any of a genus of brambles yielding this fruit. 3 *Slang* BRONX CHEER. [Earlier *rasp, raspis* raspberry + BERRY]

rat (rat) n. 1 Any of a genus of long-tailed rodents of worldwide distribution, larger and more aggressive than the mouse. 2 Any of various similar animals. 3 *Slang* A contemptible person, esp. one who deserts or betrays his associates. 4 A pad over which a woman's hair is combed to give more fullness. —*v.i.* **rat·ted, rat·ting** 1 To hunt rats. 2 *Slang* To desert one's party, companions, etc. 3 *Slang* To betray or inform: with *on*. [< OE *ræt*]

rat·a·ble (rā′tə·bəl) adj. That may be rated or valued. Also **rate′a·ble.** —**rat′a·bil′i·ty** n. —**rat′a·bly** adv.

ra·tan (ra·tan′) n. RATTAN.

ratch·et (rach′it) n. 1 A mechanism consisting of a notched wheel, the teeth of which engage with a pawl, permitting relative motion in one direction only. 2 The pawl or the wheel thus used. Also **ratchet wheel.** [< Ital. *rochetto* bobbin]

a. ratchet.
b. pawl.

rate[1] (rāt) n. 1 The quantity, quality, degree, etc., of a thing in relation to units of something else: a typing *rate* of 50 words per minute. 2 A price or value, esp. the unit cost of a commodity or service: the *rate* for electricity. 3 Rank or class: to be of the first *rate*. 4 A fixed ratio: the *rate* of exchange. 5 *Brit.* A local tax on property. —**at any rate** In any case; anyhow. —*v.* **rat·ed, rat·ing** *v.t.* 1 To estimate the value or worth of; appraise. 2 To place in a certain rank or grade. 3 To consider; regard: He is *rated* as a great statesman. 4 To fix the rate for the transportation of (goods), as by rail, water, or air. —*v.i.* 5 To have rank, rating, or value. [< L *ratus*, pp. of *reri* reckon] —**rat′er** n.

rate[2] (rāt) *v.t. & v.i.* **rat·ed, rat·ing** To reprove with vehemence; scold. [?]

rath·er (rath′ər, rä′thər) adv. 1 More willingly; preferably. 2 With more reason, justice, wisdom, etc.: We, *rather* than they, should leave first. 3 More accurately or precisely: my teacher, or *rather* my friend. 4 Somewhat; to a certain extent: *rather* tired. 5 On the contrary. —*interj.* *Chiefly Brit.* (ra′thûr′, rä′-) Most assuredly; absolutely. [< OE *hrathor* sooner]

raths·kel·ler (rath′skel·ər, räts′kel·ər) n. A beer hall or restaurant, often located below the street level. [< G *Rat* town hall + *Keller* cellar]

rat·i·fy (rat′ə·fī) *v.t.* **·fied, ·fy·ing** To give sanction to, esp. official sanction. [< L *ratus* fixed, reckoned + *facere* make] —**rat′i·fi·ca′tion, rat′i·fi′er** n. —**Syn.** confirm, approve, endorse, validate.

rat·ing (rā′ting) n. 1 A classification or evaluation based on a standard; grade; rank. 2 An evaluation of the financial standing of a business firm or an individual. 3 A classification of men in the armed services based on their specialties. 4 In radio and television, the popularity of a program as determined by polling public opinion. 5 Any of several classifications given a motion picture regarding the content or treatment of its subject matter.

ra·tio (rā′shō, -shē·ō) n. pl. **·tios** 1 Relation of degree, number, etc., between two similar things; proportion; rate. 2 A fraction or indicated quotient, esp. one used to compare the magnitudes of numbers. [L, computation < *reri* think]

ra·ti·oc·i·nate (rash′ē·ōs′ə·nāt, -os′-, rat′ē-) *v.i.* **·nat·ed, ·nat·ing** To make a deduction from premises; reason. [< L *ratiocinari* calculate, deliberate] —**ra′ti·oc′i·na′tion, ra′ti·oc′i·na′tor** n. —**ra′ti·oc′i·na′tive** adj.

ra·tion (rash′ən, rā′shən) n. 1 A portion; share. 2 A fixed allowance or portion of food or provisions, as alloted daily to a soldier, etc. 3 pl. Food or provisions, as for an army, expedition, etc. —*v.t.* 1 To issue rations to, as an army. 2 To give out or allot in rations. [< L *ratio* computation]

ra·tion·al (rash′ən·əl) adj. 1 Of, pertaining to, or attained by reasoning. 2 Able to reason; mentally sound; sane. 3 Sensible; judicious. 4 *Math.* a Of or being a rational number. b Denoting an algebraic expression, as $\sqrt{x^2 - y^2}$, containing a radical that can be solved. [< L *ratio* reckoning] —**ra′tion·al′i·ty** (-al′ə·tē), **ra′tion·al·ness** n. —**ra′tion·al·ly** adv.

ra·tion·ale (rash′ən·al′) n. 1 A logical basis or reason for something. 2 A rational exposition of principles.

ra·tion·al·ism (rash′ən·əl·iz′əm) n. 1 The formation of opinions by relying upon reason alone. 2 *Philos.* The theory that truth and knowledge are attainable through reason alone rather than through experience or sense perception. —**ra′tion·al·ist** adj., n. —**ra′tion·al·is′tic** adj. —**ra′tion·al·is′ti·cal·ly** adv.

ra·tion·al·ize (rash′ən·əl·īz′) *v.* **·ized, ·iz·ing** *v.t.* 1 To explain (one's behavior) plausibly without recognizing the actual motives. 2 To explain or treat from a rationalistic point of view. 3 To make rational or reasonable. 4 *Math.*

To solve the radicals of (an expression or equation containing variables). —*v.i.* **5** To think in a rational or rationalistic manner. **6** To rationalize one's behavior. —**ra′tion·al·i·za′tion** (-ə·zā′shən, -ī·zā′shən) *n.*

rational number A number expressible as a quotient of two integers; a fraction.

rat·ite (rat′īt) *adj.* Designating any of various large, flightless birds, as ostriches, kiwis, emus, etc. [< L *ratis* raft, in ref. to lack of a keel on the sternum]

rat·line (rat′lin) *n. Naut.* One of the small ropes fastened across the shrouds of a ship, used as a ladder for going aloft or descending. Also **rat′lin** (-lin), **rat′ling** (-ling). [?]

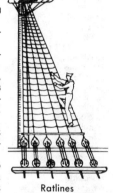

Ratlines

rat race *Slang* Frantic, usu. competitive activity or strife.

rats·bane (rats′bān′) *n.* Rat poison.

rat·tan (ra·tan′) *n.* **1** The long, tough, flexible stem of various climbing palms, used in wickerwork, etc. **2** Any of these palms. [< Malay *rotan*]

rat·ter (rat′ər) *n.* **1** A dog or cat that catches rats. **2** *Slang* A deserter or traitor.

rat·tle (rat′l) *v.* **·tled**, **·tling** *v.i.* **1** To make a series of sharp noises in rapid succession. **2** To move or act with such noises. **3** To talk rapidly and foolishly; chatter. —*v.t.* **4** To cause to rattle. **5** To utter or perform rapidly or noisily. **6** *Informal* To confuse; disconcert. —*n.* **1** A series of short, sharp sounds in rapid succession. **2** A plaything, implement, etc., adapted to produce a rattling noise. **3** The series of jointed horny rings in the tail of a rattlesnake, or one of these. **4** Rapid and noisy talk; chatter. **5** A sound caused by the passage of air through mucus in the throat. [< ME *ratelen*]

rat·tle·brain (rat′l·brān′) *n.* A talkative, flighty person; foolish chatterer. Also **rat′tle·head′** (-hed′), **rat′tle·pate′** (-pāt′). —**rat′tle·brained′** *adj.*

rat·tler (rat′lər) *n.* **1** RATTLESNAKE. **2** One who or that which rattles.

rat·tle·snake (rat′l·snāk′) *n.* Any of various venomous American snakes with a tail ending in a series of horny rings that rattle when the tail is vibrated.

rat·tle·trap (rat′l·trap′) *n.* Any rickety, clattering, or worn-out vehicle or article.

rat·ty (rat′ē) *adj.* **·ti·er**, **·ti·est** **1** Ratlike, or abounding in rats. **2** *Slang* Disreputable; treacherous. **3** *Slang* Rundown; shabby. —**rat′ti·ness** *n.*

rau·cous (rô′kəs) *adj.* **1** Rough in sound; hoarse; harsh. **2** Noisy and rowdy. [< L *raucus*] —**rau′cous·ly** *adv.* —**rau′cous·ness** *n.*

raunch·y (rôn′chē, rän′-) *adj. Slang* **raunch·i·er**, **raunch·i·est** **1** Sloppy; slovenly. **2** Sexually vulgar; lewd. **3** Lustful. [?] —**raunch′i·ly** *adv.* —**raunch′i·ness** *n.*

rav·age (rav′ij) *v.* **·aged**, **·ag·ing** *v.t.* **1** To lay waste, as by pillaging or burning; despoil; ruin. —*v.i.* **2** To wreak havoc; be destructive. —*n.* Violent and destructive action, or its result; ruin. [< F *ravir* ravish] —**rav′ag·er** *n.*

rave (rāv) *v.* **raved**, **rav·ing** *v.i.* **1** To speak wildly or incoherently. **2** To speak with extravagant enthusiasm. **3** To make a wild, roaring sound; rage. —*v.t.* **4** To utter wildly or incoherently. —*n.* **1** The act or state of raving. **2** *Informal* A highly favorable review. —*adj. Informal* Extravagantly enthusiastic: *rave* reviews. [< L *rabere* to rage] —**Syn. 1** babble, rant, gibber.

rav·el (rav′əl) *v.* **·eled** or **·elled**, **·el·ing** or **·el·ling** *v.t.* **1** To separate the threads or fibers of; unravel. **2** To make clear or plain; explain: often with *out*. —*v.i.* **3** To become separated, as threads or fibers; unravel; fray. —*n.* A raveled part or thread; a raveling. [? < MDu. *ravelen* to tangle] —**rav′el·er** or **rav′el·ler** *n.*

rav·el·ing (rav′əl·ing) *n.* A thread or threads raveled from a fabric. Also **rav′el·ling**.

ra·ven (rā′vən) *n.* A large, crowlike bird. —*adj.* Black and shining. [< OE *hræfn*]

rav·en·ing (rav′ən·ing) *adj.* **1** Seeking eagerly for prey; rapacious. **2** Mad. [< OF *raviner* ravage]

Raven

rav·en·ous (rav′ən·əs) *adj.* **1** Violently hungry; voracious. **2** Extremely eager; greedy; grasping: *ravenous* for praise. [< OF *ravine* rapine] —**rav′en·ous·ly** *adv.* —**rav′en·ous·ness** *n.*

ra·vine (rə·vēn′) *n.* A deep gorge or gully, esp. one worn by a flow of water. [F, small gully or torrent]

rav·ing (rā′ving) *adj.* **1** Furious; delirious; frenzied. **2** *Informal* Extraordinary; remarkable: a *raving* beauty. —*n.* Frenzied or irrational speech.

ra·vi·o·li (rä·vyō′lē, rä′vē·ō′lē, rav′ē-) *n.pl. (usu. construed as sing.)* Little envelopes of dough encasing meat, cheese, etc., which are boiled in broth and sauced. [Ital.]

rav·ish (rav′ish) *v.t.* **1** To fill with strong emotion, esp. delight; enrapture. **2** To rape. **3** To carry off by force. [< L *rapere* seize] —**rav′ish·er**, **rav′ish·ment** *n.*

rav·ish·ing (rav′ish·ing) *adj.* Very attractive, pleasing, etc. —**rav′ish·ing·ly** *adv.*

raw (rô) *adj.* **1** Not changed or prepared by cooking; uncooked. **2** In its original state or condition; not refined, processed, etc.: *raw* wool; *raw* sugar. **3** Having the skin torn or abraded: a *raw* wound. **4** Bleak; chilling: a *raw* wind. **5** Newly done; fresh: *raw* paint; *raw* work. **6** Inexperienced; undisciplined: a *raw* recruit. **7** Vulgar; off-color: a *raw* joke. **8** *Informal* Brutally harsh or unfair: a *raw* deal. —*n.* A sore or abraded spot. —**in the raw 1** In a raw, unspoiled, or unrefined state. **2** *Informal* Nude. [< OE *hrēaw*] —**raw′ly** *adv.* —**raw′ness** *n.*

raw-boned (rô′bōnd′) *adj.* Bony; gaunt.

raw·hide (rô′hīd′) *n.* **1** An untanned cattle hide. **2** A whip made of such hide.

ray¹ (rā) *n.* **1** A narrow beam of light. **2** Any of several lines radiating from an object. **3** *Geom.* A straight line emerging from a point and extending in one direction only. **4** A slight amount or indication: a *ray* of hope. **5** *Zool.* **a** A supporting spine of a fish's fin. **b** Any of numerous parts radiating from a common center, as the arms of a starfish. **6** *Bot.* **a** RAY FLOWER. **b** One of the flower stalks of an umbel. **7** *Physics* A stream of particles or waves. —*v.i.* **1** To emit rays; shine. **2** To radiate. —*v.t.* **3** To send forth as rays. **4** To mark with rays or radiating lines. [< L *radius*]

ray² (rā) *n.* Any of an order of marine fishes having a cartilaginous skeleton and a horizontally flattened body, dorsally placed eyes, and a thin, usu. long tail. [< L *raia*]

ray flower *Bot.* Any of the straplike flowers encircling certain composite flower heads, as in the daisy or sunflower. Also **ray floret.**

Ray

ray·on (rā′on) *n.* **1** A synthetic fiber made from a cellulose solution that is forced through spinnerets to produce solidified filaments. **2** A fabric made from these fibers. [F, ray, in ref. to its sheen]

raze (rāz) *v.t.* **razed**, **raz·ing** **1** To tear down; demolish. **2** To scrape or shave off. [< L *rasum*, pp. of *radere* scrape]

ra·zor (rā′zər) *n.* A sharp cutting implement used for shaving off the beard or hair. [< OF *raser* to scrape]

ra·zor·back (rā′zər·bak′) *n.* **1** FINBACK WHALE. **2** A lean half-wild hog of SE U.S. **3** A sharp ridge. —**ra′zor-backed′** *adj.*

razz (raz) *n. Slang* BRONX CHEER. —*v.t.* To heckle; deride. [< RASPBERRY]

raz·zle-daz·zle (raz′əl·daz′əl) *n. Slang* Any bewildering, exciting, or dazzling activity or performance. [Varied reduplication of DAZZLE]

Rb rubidium.

RBI, rbi, r.b.i. run(s) batted in.

R.C. Red Cross; Roman Catholic.

RCAF, R.C.A.F. Royal Canadian Air Force.
RCMP, R.C.M.P. Royal Canadian Mounted Police.
RCN, R.C.N. Royal Canadian Navy.
RCP, R.C.P. Royal College of Physicians.
RCS, R.C.S. Royal College of Surgeons
R.D. Rural Delivery.
R & D, R. & D., R and D research and development.
re[1] (rā) *n. Music* In solmization, the second tone of a diatonic scale. [< L *re(sonare)* resound. See GAMUT.]
re[2] (rē, rā) *prep.* Concerning; about; in the matter of: used in business letters, etc. [L, ablative of *res* thing]
re- *prefix* 1 Back: *remit* (to send back). 2 Again; anew; again and again: *regenerate.* [< L *re-, red-* back, again] • In the list of words below, *re-* is used solely to mean *again, anew, again and again.* These words are for the most part written solid. A hyphen, however, is sometimes used: **a** To prevent confusion with a similarly spelled word having a different meaning, as in *retreat* (to go back) and *re-treat* (to treat again). **b** In the formation of nonce words, as "We *reread* the contract and then *re-reread* it." Formerly, a hyphen was the rule before words beginning with *e,* as *re-edit,* but such words are now often written solid.

reabsorb	recharter	redraw
reabsorption	recheck	redrive
reaccess	rechoose	reecho
reaccommodate	rechristen	reedit
reaccredit	reclose	reelect
reaccuse	reclothe	reelection
readapt	recoin	reelevate
readdict	recoinage	reembark
readdress	recolonize	reembarkation
readjourn	recolor	reemerge
readjournment	recombination	reemergence
readjust	recombine	reemit
readjustment	recommence	reemphasize
readopt	recommission	reenact
readorn	recompose	reenaction
readvance	recompute	reenactment
readvertise	reconcentrate	reencourage
reaffirm	recondensation	reencouragement
realign	recondense	reendow
realignment	reconfirm	reengage
reanoint	reconjoin	reengagement
reappear	reconquer	reengrave
reappearance	reconquest	reenjoy
reapply	reconsecrate	reenjoyment
reappoint	reconsecration	reenlist
reappointment	reconsign	reenlistment
reapportion	reconsolidate	reenslave
reapportionment	reconsolidation	reenslavement
reargue	reconvene	reenter
reargument	reconvey	reenthrone
rearrest	recopy	reenthronement
reascend	recross	reentrance
reascension	recrystallization	reequip
reascent	recrystallize	reestablish
reassemblage	recultivate	reestablishment
reassemble	recultivation	reevaluate
reassert	redecorate	reevaluation
reassertion	rededicate	reexamination
reassign	rededication	reexamine
reassignment	redefine	reexchange
reassimilate	redeliberate	reexhibit
reassimilation	redeliver	reexpel
reassociate	redemand	reexperience
reattach	redemonstrate	reexport
reattachment	redeposit	reexportation
reattempt	redescend	reexpulsion
reavow	redescent	reface
reawake	redesign	refashion
reawakening	redesignate	refasten
rebaptism	redetermine	refertilize
rebaptize	redial	refind
rebid	redigest	reflavor
rebill	redirect	reflight
rebind	rediscover	reflorescence
rebloom	rediscovery	reflourish
reblossom	redispose	reflow
reboil	redissolve	reflower
reborn	redistill	refluctuation
rebottle	redistribute	refold
rebuild	redistribution	reformulate
recalibrate	redivide	refortification
recapitalize	redo	refortify
recharge	redraft	refreeze

refuel	reload	resegregate
refurbish	reloan	reseize
refurnish	relocate	reseizure
regalvanize	relocation	resell
regather	reman	resensitize
regerminate	remarriage	reseparate
regermination	remarry	re-serve
regild	remast	reset
regrade	remaster	resettle
regraft	remeasure	resettlement
regrant	remelt	reshape
regroup	remigrate	resharpen
rehandle	remigration	reshoot
rehang	remilitarize	reshuffle
rehearing	remix	re-sign
reheat	remold	resite
reheel	rename	resolder
rehire	renationalize	resole
rehybridize	renavigate	re-solve
rehydrate	renegotiate	re-sound
reimplant	renominate	resow
reimport	renomination	respeak
reimportation	renumber	respell
reimpose	renumerate	restart
reimposition	reobtain	restock
reimpress	reoccupation	restoke
reimprison	reoccupy	re-store
reinaugurate	reopen	restrengthen
reincorporate	reoppose	restress
reincur	reordain	restrike
reinduce	reorder	resubject
reinfect	reordination	resubjection
reinfection	reorient	resubjugate
reinflame	reorientation	resubmit
reinform	reossify	resummon
reinfuse	repacify	resummons
reingratiate	repack	resupply
reinhabit	repackage	resurprise
reinjure	repaint	resurvey
reinoculate	repartition	retake
reinoculation	repass	retarget
reinscribe	repassage	retell
reinsert	repeople	retool
reinsertion	rephrase	retrace
reinspect	replant	retrain
reinspection	replantation	re-treat
reinspire	replaster	retrial
reinstall	repledge	retrim
reinstruct	replunge	retry
reinsure	repolish	retune
reintegrate	repoll	re-turn
reintegration	repopulate	reunification
reinter	repopulation	reunify
reinterment	repossess	reurge
reintroduce	repour	reuse
reintroduction	re-press	reutilize
reinvest	reprocess	reutter
reinvestigate	reprogram	revaccinate
reinvestment	repropose	revaccination
reinvigorate	re-prove	revaluation
reinvigoration	republish	revalue
reinvitation	repurchase	revarnish
reinvite	repurify	revest
reinvolve	reread	re-view
reinvolvement	re-record	revindication
reissue	re-refer	revisit
rekindle	re-release	reweave
reknit	resail	reweigh
reland	resale	rewin
relaunch	resalute	rewind
relet	re-search	rewire
reliquidate	reseat	reword
reliquidation	reschool	rework

Re rhenium.
reach (rēch) *v.t.* 1 To stretch out or forth, as the hand. 2 To present or deliver; hand over. 3 To touch, grasp, or extend as far as: Can you *reach* the top shelf? 4 To arrive at or come to by motion or progress. 5 To achieve communication with; gain access to. 6 To amount to; total. 7 To have an influence on; affect. —*v.i.* 8 To stretch the hand, foot, etc., out or forth. 9 To attempt to touch or obtain something: He *reached* for his wallet. 10 To have extent in space, time, amount, influence, etc.: The ladder *reached* to the ceiling. 11 *Naut.* To sail on a tack with the wind on or forward of the beam. —*n.* 1 The act or power of reaching. 2 The distance one is able to reach, as with

the hand, an instrument, or missile. **3** An extent or result attained by thought, influence, etc.; scope; range. **4** An unbroken stretch, as of a stream; a vista or expanse. **5** *Naut.* The sailing, or the distance sailed, by a vessel on one tack. [< OE *ræcan*] —**reach′er** *n.*

re·act (rē·akt′) *v.i.* **1** To act in response, as to a stimulus. **2** To act in a manner contrary to some preceding act. **3** To be affected by a circumstance, influence, act, etc. **4** *Chem.* To undergo chemical change.

re·act (rē′akt′) *v.t.* To act again.

re·ac·tance (rē·ak′təns) *n.* *Electr.* The component of impedance that results from the presence of capacitance or inductance.

re·ac·tion (rē·ak′shən) *n.* **1** Any response, as to a stimulus, event, influence, etc. **2** A trend or tendency toward a former state of things; esp., a trend toward an earlier, usu. outmoded social, political, or economic policy or condition. **3** Any change in an organism effected by an agent, as a drug, food, allergen, etc., or an environmental condition, as heat, cold, etc. **4** *Physics* The force exerted on an agent by the body acted upon. **5** Any process involving a change in the composition or structure of an atomic nucleus, as fission, fusion, or radioactive decay. **6** *Chem.* A molecular change undergone by two or more substances in contact. —**re·ac′tion·al** *adj.* —**re·ac′tion·al·ly** *adv.*

re·ac·tion·ar·y (rē·ak′shən·er′ē) *adj.* Of, relating to, favoring, or characterized by reaction (def. 2). —*n.* *pl.* ·**ar·ies** One who generally opposes change or liberalism in political or social matters. Also **re·ac′tion·ist.**

re·ac·ti·vate (rē·ak′tə·vāt) *v.t.* ·**vat·ed,** ·**vat·ing** To make active or effective again. —**re·ac′ti·va′tion** *n.*

re·ac·tive (rē·ak′tiv) *adj.* **1** Tending to react, or resulting from reaction. **2** Responsive to a stimulus. —**re·ac′tive·ly** *adv.* —**re·ac′tiv′i·ty, re·ac′tive·ness** *n.*

re·ac·tor (rē·ak′tər) *n.* **1** One who or that which reacts. **2** An assembly of fissionable material, moderator, coolant, shielding, and other accessories, designed to control and utilize the energy released by atomic fission.

read (rēd) *v.* **read** (red), **read·ing** (rē′ding) *v.t.* **1** To apprehend the meaning of (a book, writing, etc.) by perceiving the form and relation of the printed or written characters. **2** To utter aloud (something printed or written). **3** To understand the significance of as if by reading: to *read* the sky. **4** To apprehend the meaning of something printed or written in (a foreign language). **5** To make a study of: to *read* law. **6** To discover the nature or significance of (a person, character, etc.) by observation or scrutiny. **7** To interpret (something read) in a specified manner. **8** To take as the meaning of something read. **9** To have or exhibit as the wording: The passage *reads* "principal," not "principle." **10** To indicate or register: The meter *reads* zero. **11** To extract (data) from storage: said of a computer or other information-retrieval system. **12** To bring into a specified condition by reading: I *read* her to sleep.′ —*v.i.* **13** To apprehend the characters of a book, musical score, etc. **14** To utter aloud the words or contents of a book, etc. **15** To gain information by reading: with *of* or *about.* **16** To learn by means of books; study. **17** To have a specified wording: The contract *reads* as follows. **18** To admit of being read in a specified manner. **19** To give a public reading or recital. —**read between the lines** To perceive or infer what is not expressed or obvious. —**read into** To discern (implicit meanings or implications) in a statement or position. —**read out** To expel from a religious body, political party, etc., by proclamation or concerted action. —**read up** (or **up on**) To learn by reading. —*adj.* (red) Informed by or acquainted with books or literature: *well-read.* [< OE *rædan* advise, read]

read·a·ble (rē′də·bəl) *adj.* **1** That can be read; legible. **2** Easy and pleasant to read. **3** MACHINE-READABLE. —**read′a·bil′i·ty, read′a·ble·ness** *n.* —**read′a·bly** *adv.*

read·er (rē′dər) *n.* **1** One who reads. **2** Any of various devices that provide readable images, as by projection on a screen, of material or microfilm, microcards, etc. **3** One who reads and criticizes manuscripts offered to publishers. **4** PROOFREADER. **5** A layman authorized to read the lesson in church services. **6** A professional reciter. **7** A textbook containing matter for exercises in reading.

read·ing (rē′ding) *n.* **1** The act or practice of one who reads. **2** The public recital of literary works. **3** Matter that is read or is designed to be read. **4** The datum indicated by an instrument, as a thermometer. **5** The form in which any passage or word appears in any copy of a work. **6** An interpretation, as of a musical composition. —*adj.* **1** Pertaining to or suitable for reading. **2** Inclined to read.

read·out (rēd′out′) *n.* **1** A display in intelligible form of specific items of information derived from data that have been recorded automatically or processed by computer. **2** The information so displayed.

read·y (red′ē) *adj.* **read·i·er, read·i·est** **1** Prepared for use or action. **2** Prepared in mind; willing. **3** Likely or liable: with *to*: *ready* to sink. **4** Quick to act, follow, occur, or appear; prompt. **5** Immediately available; convenient; handy. **6** Designating the standard position in which a rifle is held just before aiming. **7** Quick to understand; alert; quick; facile: a *ready* wit. —*n.* The position in which a rifle is held before aiming. —*v.t.* **read·ied, read·y·ing** To make ready; prepare. [< OE *ræde, geræde*] —**read′i·ly** *adv.* —**read′i·ness** *n.*

read·y-made (red′ē·mād′) *adj.* **1** Not made to order: *ready-made* clothing. **2** Not impromptu or original: *ready-made* opinions.

re·a·gent (rē·ā′jənt) *n.* Any substance used to induce a chemical reaction. [< RE- + AGENT]

re·al¹ (rē′əl, rēl) *adj.* **1** Having existence or actuality as a thing or state; not imaginary: a *real* event. **2** Not artificial or counterfeit; genuine. **3** Representing the true or actual, as opposed to the apparent or ostensible: the *real* reason. **4** Unaffected; unpretentious: a *real* person. **5** *Philos.* Having actual existence, and not merely possible, apparent, or imaginary. **6** *Law* Of or pertaining to things permanent and immovable: *real* property. **7** *Math.* Of or being a real number. —*n.* That which is real. —*adv.* *Informal* Very; extremely: to be *real* glad. [< Med. L *realis* < L *res* thing] —**re′al·ness** *n.*

re·al² (rē′əl, *Sp.* rä·äl′) *n.* *pl.* **re·als** or **re·a·les** (rä·ä′läs) **1** A former small silver coin of Spain. **2** *pl.* **reis** (rās) A former Portuguese and Brazilian coin; one thousandth of a milreis. [Sp., lit., royal]

real estate Land, including whatever is made part of or attached to it by man or nature, as trees, houses, etc. —**re′al·es·tate′** *adj.*

re·al·ism (rē′əl·iz′əm) *n.* **1** A disposition to deal solely with facts and reality and to reject the impractical or visionary. **2** In literature and art, the principle of depicting persons and scenes as they actually exist, without any idealization. **3** *Philos.* **a** The doctrine that universals or abstract concepts have actual, objective existence. **b** The doctrine that things have reality apart from the conscious perception of them. —**re′al·ist** *adj., n.* —**re′al·is′tic** *adj.* —**re′al·is′ti·cal·ly** *adv.*

re·al·i·ty (rē·al′ə·tē) *n.* *pl.* ·**ties** **1** The fact, state, or quality of being real, genuine, or true to life. **2** That which is real; an actual thing, situation, or event. **3** *Philos.* The absolute or the ultimate.

re·al·ize (rē′əl·īz) *v.* ·**ized,** ·**iz·ing** *v.t.* **1** To understand or appreciate fully. **2** To make real or concrete. **3** To cause to appear real. **4** To obtain as a profit or return. **5** To obtain money in return for: He *realized* his holdings for a profit. —*v.i.* **6** To sell property for cash. —**re′al·iz′a·ble** *adj.* —**re′al·i·za′tion, re′al·iz′er** *n.*

re·al·ly (rē′ə·lē, rē′lē) *adv.* **1** In reality; actually. **2** Truly; genuinely: a *really* fine play. —*interj.* Oh: used to express surprise, doubt, etc.

realm (relm) *n.* **1** A kingdom. **2** Domain; sphere: the *realm* of imagination. [< L *regalis* royal]

real number A number whose square is greater than or equal to zero.

re·al·tor (rē′əl·tər, -tôr) *n.* **1** A person engaged in the real-estate business. **2** *Usu. cap.* A member of the National Association of Real Estate Boards: a trade name.

re·al·ty (rē′əl·tē) *n.* *pl.* ·**ties** REAL ESTATE.

ream[1] (rēm) *n.* **1** A quantity of paper equal to 20 quires and consisting of 480, 500, or 516 sheets. **2** *pl. Informal* A prodigious amount. [< Ar. *rizmah* packet]

ream[2] (rēm) *v.t.* **1** To increase the size of (a hole), as with a rotating cutter or reamer. **2** To get rid of (a defect) by reaming. [< OE *rēman* enlarge, make room]

ream·er (rē′mər) *n.* **1** One who or that which reams. **2** A rotary tool with cutting edges for reaming. **3** A device with a ridged cone for extracting juice from citrus fruits.

Reamers

re·an·i·mate (rē-an′ə-māt) *v.t.* **·mat·ed, ·mat·ing 1** To bring back to life; resuscitate. **2** To revive; encourage. **—re′an·i·ma′tion** *n.*

reap (rēp) *v.t.* **1** To cut and gather (grain) with a scythe, reaper, etc. **2** To harvest a crop from: to *reap* a field. **3** To obtain as the result of action or effort. **—v.i. 4** To harvest grain, etc. **5** To receive a return or result. [< OE *repan*] — **reap′a·ble** *adj.* **—reap′ing** *n.*

reap·er (rē′pər) *n.* **1** One who reaps. **2** A machine for reaping grain.

rear[1] (rir) *n.* **1** The back or hind part. **2** A place or position at the back of or behind anything. **3** That division of a military force which is farthest from the front. **—adj.** Being in the rear. [< ARREAR]

rear[2] (rir) *v.t.* **1** To place upright; raise. **2** To build; erect. **3** To care for and bring to maturity. **4** To breed or grow. **—v.i. 5** To rise upon its hind legs, as a horse. **6** To rise high; tower, as a mountain. [< OE *ræran* set upright] **—rear′er** *n.*

rear admiral See GRADE.

rear guard A body of troops to protect the rear of an army.

re·arm (rē-ärm′) *v.t. & v.i.* **1** To arm again. **2** To arm with more modern weapons. **—re·ar′ma·ment** *n.*

rear·most (rir′mōst′) *adj.* Coming or stationed last.

re·ar·range (rē′ə-ranj′) *v.t. & v.i.* **·ranged, ·rang·ing** To arrange again or in some new way. **—re′ar·range′ment** *n.* — **Syn.** reorder, redispose, reorganize, readjust.

rear·ward (rir′wərd) *adj.* Coming last or toward the rear; hindward. **—adv.** Toward or at the rear; backward: also **rear′wards. —n.** The rear; end.

rea·son (rē′zən) *n.* **1** A motive or basis for an action, opinion, etc. **2** A statement which explains or accounts for an action, belief, etc. **3** The ability to think logically and rationally. **4** Sound thinking or judgment; common sense. **5** Sanity. **—by reason of** Because of. **—in (or within) reason** Within reasonable limits or bounds. **—it stands to reason** It is logical. **—with reason** Justifiably. **—v.i. 1** To think logically; obtain inferences or conclusions from known or presumed facts. **2** To talk or argue logically. **—v.t. 3** To think out carefully and logically; analyze: with *out.* **4** To influence or persuade by means of reason. **5** To argue; debate. [< L *ratio* computation] **—rea′son·er** *n.*

rea·son·a·ble (rē′zən-ə-bəl, rēz′nə-) *adj.* **1** Conformable to reason. **2** Having the faculty of reason; rational. **3** Governed by reason. **4** Not extreme or excessive; moderate. — **rea′son·a·bil′i·ty, rea′son·a·ble·ness** *n.* **—rea′son·a·bly** *adv.*

rea·son·ing (rē′zən·ing) *n.* **1** The act or process of using one's rational faculties to draw conclusions from known or assumed facts. **2** The reasons or proofs resulting from this process.

re·as·sure (rē′ə-shŏŏr′) *v.t.* **·sured, ·sur·ing 1** To restore to courage or confidence. **2** To assure again. **3** To reinsure. **—re′as·sur′ance** *n.* **—re′as·sur′ing·ly** *adv.*

re·bate (rē′bāt, ri·bāt′) *v.t.* **·bat·ed, ·bat·ing 1** To allow as a deduction. **2** To make a deduction from. **—n.** A deduction from a gross amount; discount: also **re·bate′·ment.** [< OF *rabattre* beat down] **—re′bat·er** *n.*

re·bec (rē′bek) *n.* A medieval bowed instrument, somewhat like a violin. Also **re′beck.** [< Ar. *rabāb*]

Rebec

Re·bec·ca (ri·bek′ə) In the Bible, wife of Isaac and mother of Esau and Jacob.

re·bel (ri·bel′) *v.i.* **·belled, ·bel·ling 1** To resist or fight against any authority, established custom, etc. **2** To react with violent aversion: usu. with *at.* **—n.** (reb′əl) One who rebels. **—adj.** (reb′əl) **1** Rebellious; refractory. **2** Of rebels. [< L *re-* again + *bellare* make war]

re·bel·lion (ri·bel′yən) *n.* **1** The act of rebelling. **2** Organized resistance to a government or to any lawful authority.

re·bel·lious (ri·bel′yəs) *adj.* **1** Being in a state of rebellion; insubordinate. **2** Of or pertaining to a rebel or rebellion. **3** Resisting control; refractory: a *rebellious* temper. **—re·bel′lious·ly** *adv.* **—re·bel′lious·ness** *n.*

re·birth (rē·bûrth′, rē′bûrth′) *n.* **1** A new birth. **2** A revival or renaissance.

re·bound (ri·bound′) *v.i.* **1** To bounce or spring back after or as after hitting something. **2** To recover, as from a difficulty. **3** To reecho. **—v.t. 4** To cause to rebound. **—n.** (rē′bound′, ri·bound′) **1** A bounding back; recoil. **2** Something that rebounds, as a basketball from a backboard. **3** Reaction after a disappointment: to fall in love on the *rebound.* [< F *re-* back + *bondir* bound]

re·broad·cast (rē·brôd′kast′, -käst′) *v.t.* **·cast** or **·cast·ed, ·cast·ing** To broadcast (the same program) again. **—n.** A program so transmitted.

re·buff (ri·buf′) *v.t.* **1** To reject or refuse abruptly or rudely. **2** To drive or beat back; repel. **—n. 1** A sudden repulse; curt denial. **2** A sudden check; defeat. **3** A beating back. [< Ital. *ribuffare*]

re·buke (ri·byōōk′) *v.t.* **·buked, ·buk·ing** To reprove sharply; reprimand. **—n.** A strong expression of disapproval. [< OF *re-* back + *bucher* beat] **—re·buk′er** *n.*

re·bus (rē′bəs) *n.* A representation of a word, phrase, or sentence by letters, numerals, pictures, etc., whose names suggest the same sounds as the words or phrases they represent. [L, ablative pl. of *res* thing]

Rebus meaning
I can see.

re·but (ri·but′) *v.t.* **·but·ted, ·but·ting** To dispute or show the falsity of, as by argument or by contrary evidence. [< OF *re-* back + *bouter* push, strike] **—re·but′ter** *n.* **—Syn.** disprove, refute, contradict.

re·but·tal (ri·but′l) *n.* The act of rebutting; refutation.

rec. receipt; recipe; record; recording.

re·cal·ci·trant (ri·kal′sə·trənt) *adj.* Not complying; obstinate; rebellious; refractory. **—n.** One who is recalcitrant. [< L *re-* back + *calcitrare* to kick] **—re·cal′ci·trance, re·cal′·ci·tran·cy** *n.*

re·call (ri·kôl′) *v.t.* **1** To call back; order or summon to return. **2** To summon back in awareness or attention. **3** To recollect; remember. **4** To take back; revoke; countermand. **—n.** (ri·kôl′, rē′kôl′) **1** A calling back. **2** An ability to remember. **3** Revocation, as of an order. **4** A system whereby public officials may be removed from office by popular vote.

re·cant (ri·kant′) *v.t.* **1** To withdraw formally one's belief in (something previously believed or maintained). **—v.i. 2** To disavow an opinion or belief previously held. [< L *re-* again + *cantare* sing] **—re·can·ta·tion** (rē′kan·tā′shən), **re·cant′er** *n.*

re·cap[1] (rē′kap′, rē·kap′) *v.t.* **·capped, ·cap·ping 1** To provide (a worn pneumatic tire) with a tread of new rubber. **2** To replace a cap on. **—n.** (rē′kap′) A tire which has been so treated. [< RE- + CAP]

re·cap[2] (rē′kap′) *v.t. & v.i.* **·capped, ·cap·ping** RECAPITULATE. **—n.** RECAPITULATION (def. 2).

re·ca·pit·u·late (rē′kə·pich′ŏŏ·lāt) *v.t. & v.i.* **·lat·ed, ·lat·ing** To restate or review briefly; sum up. [< LL *re-* again + *capitulare* draw up in chapters]

re·ca·pit·u·la·tion (rē′kə·pich′ŏŏ·lā′shən) *n.* **1** The act of recapitulating. **2** A brief summary. **—re′ca·pit′u·la′tive, re′·ca·pit′u·la·to·ry** (-lə·tôr′ē, -tō′rē) *adj.*

re·cap·ture (rē·kap′chər) *v.t.* **·tured, ·tur·ing 1** To capture again. **2** To recall; remember. **—n.** The act of recapturing or the state of being recaptured.

re·cast (rē·kast′, -käst′) *v.t.* **·cast, ·cast·ing 1** To form anew; cast again. **2** To fashion anew by changing style, arrangement, etc., as a sentence. **3** To calculate anew. **—n.** (rē′kast′, -käst′) Something which has been recast.

recd. received.

re·cede (ri·sēd′) v.i. ·ced·ed, ·ced·ing 1 To move back; withdraw, as flood waters. 2 To withdraw, as from an assertion, position, agreement, etc. 3 To slope backward: a *receding* forehead. 4 To become more distant or smaller. [< L *re-* back + *cedere* go]

re·cede (rē′sēd′) v.t. ·ced·ed, ·ced·ing To cede back; grant or yield to a former owner.

re·ceipt (ri·sēt′) n. 1 The act or state of receiving anything: to be in *receipt* of good news. 2 *Usu. pl.* That which is received: cash *receipts.* 3 A written acknowledgment of the payment of money, of the delivery of goods, etc. 4 RECIPE. —v.t. 1 To give a receipt for the payment of. 2 To write acknowledgment of payment on, as a bill. —v.i. 3 To give a receipt, as for money paid. [< L *receptus,* pp. of *recipere* take back, receive]

re·ceiv·a·ble (ri·sē′və·bəl) adj. 1 Capable of being received; fit to be received, as legal tender. 2 Due to be paid. —n. pl. Outstanding accounts listed as business assets.

re·ceive (ri·sēv′) v. ·ceived, ·ceiv·ing v.t. 1 To take into one's hand or possession (something given, offered, delivered, etc.). 2 To gain knowledge or information of. 3 To take from another by hearing or listening. 4 To bear; support. 5 To experience; meet with: to *receive* abuse. 6 To undergo; suffer: He *received* a wound in his arm. 7 To contain; hold. 8 To allow entrance to; admit; greet. 9 To perceive mentally: to *receive* a bad impression. 10 To regard in a specified way: The play was well *received.* —v.i. 11 To be a recipient. 12 To welcome visitors or callers. 13 *Telecom.* To convert incoming signals, as radio waves, into intelligible sounds or shapes, as in a radio or television set. [< L *re-* back + *capere* take]

re·ceived (ri·sēvd′) adj. *Chiefly Brit.* Accepted by established opinion or authority; standard.

re·ceiv·er (ri·sē′vər) n. 1 One who receives; a recipient. 2 An official assigned to receive money due. 3 *Law* A person appointed by a court to take into his custody the property or funds of another pending litigation. 4 One who knowingly buys or receives stolen goods. 5 Something which receives; a receptacle. 6 *Telecom.* An instrument designed to receive electric or electromagnetic signals and process them or transmit them to another stage.

re·ceiv·er·ship (ri·sē′vər·ship) n. 1 The office and functions pertaining to a receiver. 2 *Law* The state of being in the hands of a receiver.

re·cent (rē′sənt) adj. 1 Of or pertaining to a time not long past. 2 Occurring, formed, or characterized by association with a time not long past; modern; fresh; new. [< L *recens*] —re′cent·ly adv. —re′cen·cy, re′cent·ness n.

Re·cent (rē′sənt) adj. & n. See GEOLOGY.

re·cep·ta·cle (ri·sep′tə·kəl) n. 1 Anything that serves to contain or hold other things. 2 *Bot.* The base on which the parts of a flower grow. 3 An electric outlet. [< L *receptare,* freq. of *recipere* receive]

re·cep·tion (ri·sep′shən) n. 1 The act of receiving, or the state of being received. 2 A formal social entertainment of guests: a wedding *reception.* 3 The manner of receiving a person or persons: a warm *reception.* 4 *Telecom.* The act or process of receiving or, esp., the quality of reproduction achieved: poor radio *reception.*

re·cep·tion·ist (ri·sep′shən·ist) n. A person employed to receive callers, etc., as in a place of business.

re·cep·tive (ri·sep′tiv) adj. 1 Able or inclined to receive favorably: *receptive* to new ideas. 2 Able to contain or hold. —re·cep′tive·ly adv. —re·cep·tiv·i·ty (rē′sep·tiv′ə·tē), re·cep′tive·ness n.

re·cep·tor (ri·sep′tər) n. A sensory nerve ending adapted to receiving stimuli. [L, receiver]

re·cess (rē′ses, ri·ses′) n. 1 A depression or indentation in any otherwise continuous line or surface, esp. in a wall; niche. 2 A time of cessation from employment or occupation. 3 *Usu. pl.* A quiet and secluded spot; withdrawn or inner place: the *recesses* of the mind. —v. (usu. ri·ses′) v.t. 1 To place in or as in a recess. 2 To make a recess in. 3 To interrupt for a recess. —v.i. 4 To take a recess. [< L *recessus,* pp. of *recedere* go back]

re·ces·sion (ri·sesh′ən) n. 1 The act of receding; a withdrawal. 2 The procession of the clergy, choir, etc., as they leave the chancel after a church service. 3 A temporary economic setback occurring during a period of generally rising prosperity.

re·ces·sion (rē′sesh′ən) n. The act of ceding back, as to a former owner.

re·ces·sion·al (ri·sesh′ən·əl) adj. Of or pertaining to recession. —n. A hymn sung as the choir or clergy leave the chancel.

re·ces·sive (ri·ses′iv) adj. 1 Having a tendency to recede or go back. 2 *Genetics* Designating a hereditary factor that remains latent unless it is present in both members of a pair of chromosomes. —n. *Genetics* 1 A recessive factor or trait. 2 An organism having such factors or traits. —re·ces′sive·ly adv. —re·ces′sive·ness n.

re·cher·ché (rə·sher·shā′) adj. 1 Much sought after; choice; rare. 2 Elegant or refined, usu. to an excessive degree. [F]

re·cid·i·vism (rə·sid′ə·viz′əm) n. A tendency to relapse into a former state or condition, esp. into crime. [< L *recidivus* falling back] —re·cid′i·vist adj., n. —re·cid′i·vis′tic, re·cid′i·vous adj.

rec·i·pe (res′ə·pē) n. 1 A list of ingredients and directions for combining them, as in cooking, pharmacy, etc. 2 The means prescribed for attaining an end. [< L, imperative of *recipere* take]

re·cip·i·ent (ri·sip′ē·ənt) adj. Receiving or ready to receive; receptive. —n. One who or that which receives. —re·cip′i·ence, re·cip′i·en·cy n.

re·cip·ro·cal (ri·sip′rə·kəl) adj. 1 Done or given by each of two to the other; mutual. 2 Mutually interchangeable. 3 Related or corresponding, but in an inverse manner; opposite. 4 *Gram.* Expressive of mutual relationship or action: *One another* is a *reciprocal* phrase. 5 *Math.* Having a product of 1, as a pair of numbers. —n. 1 That which is reciprocal. 2 *Math.* Either of a pair of numbers having 1 as their product. [< L *reciprocus*] —re·cip′ro·cal·ly adv.

re·cip·ro·cate (ri·sip′rə·kāt) v. ·cat·ed, ·cat·ing v.t. 1 To cause to move backward and forward alternately. 2 To give and receive mutually; interchange. 3 To give, feel, do, etc., in return. —v.i. 4 To move backward and forward. 5 To make a return in kind. 6 To give and receive favors, gifts, etc., mutually. [< L *reciprocare* move to and fro] —re·cip′ro·ca′tion, re·cip′ro·ca′tor n. —re·cip′ro·ca′tive, re·cip′ro·ca·to′ry (-kə·tôr′ē, -kə·tō′rē) adj.

rec·i·proc·i·ty (res′ə·pros′ə·tē) n. 1 Reciprocal obligation, action, or relation. 2 A trade relation between two countries by which each makes concessions favoring the importation of the products of the other.

re·cit·al (ri·sīt′l) n. 1 A retelling in detail of an event, etc.; a narration; also, that which is retold. 2 A public delivery of something memorized. 3 A musical or dance program by a single performer or by a small group.

rec·i·ta·tion (res′ə·tā′shən) n. 1 The act of publicly reciting something that has been memorized. 2 That which is recited. 3 The reciting of a lesson in school or the time during a class when this takes place.

rec·i·ta·tive (res′ə·tə·tēv′, rə·sit′ə·tiv) n. *Music* 1 A style of singing that approaches ordinary speech in its rhythms and lack of melodic variation, used in opera and oratorio. 2 A passage so sung. Also *Italian* re·ci·ta·ti·vo (rä′chē·tä·tē′vō) —adj. Having the character of a recitative. [< Ital. *recitativo*]

re·cite (ri·sīt′) v. ·cit·ed, ·cit·ing v.t. 1 To declaim or say from memory, esp. formally, as in public or in a class. 2 To tell in particular detail; relate. 3 To enumerate. —v.i. 4 To declaim or speak something from memory. 5 To repeat or be examined in a lesson or part of a lesson in class. [< L *re-* again + *citare* cite] —re·cit′er n.

reck (rek) v.t. & v.i. *Archaic* 1 To heed; mind. 2 To be of concern or interest (to). [< OE *rēccan*]

reck·less (rek′lis) adj. 1 Foolishly heedless of danger; rash. 2 Careless; irresponsible. [< OE *reccelēas*] —reck′less·ly adv. —reck′less·ness n.

reck·on (rek′ən) v.t. 1 To count; compute; calculate. 2 To

look upon as being; regard. **3** *Regional* To suppose or guess; expect. —*v.i.* **4** To make computation; count up. **5** To rely or depend: with *on* or *upon*. —**reckon with 1** To settle accounts with. **2** To take into consideration; consider. [< OE *recenian* explain] —**reck′on·er** *n.*

reck·on·ing (rek′ən·ing) *n.* **1** The act of counting; computation. **2** A settlement of accounts. **3** Account; bill, as at a hotel. **4** An appraisal or estimate. **5** *Naut.* The calculation of a ship's position.

re·claim (ri·klām′) *v.t.* **1** To bring (a swamp, desert, etc.) into a condition to support cultivation or life, as by draining or irrigating. **2** To obtain (a substance) from used or waste products. **3** To cause to reform. —*n.* The act of reclaiming or state of being reclaimed. [< L *re-* against + *clamare* cry out] —**re·claim′a·ble** *adj.* —**re·claim′er, re·claim′ant** *n.*

re-claim (rē′klām′) *v.t.* To claim again.

rec·la·ma·tion (rek′lə·mā′shən) *n.* **1** The act of reclaiming. **2** Restoration, as to ownership, usefulness, etc.

re·cline (ri·klīn′) *v.t. & v.i.* **·clined, ·clin·ing** To assume or cause to assume a recumbent position; lie or lay down or back. [< L *re-* back + *clinare* lean] —**rec·li·na·tion** (rek′lə·nā′shən), **re·clin′er** *n.*

rec·luse (rek′lōōs, ri·klōōs′) *n.* One who lives in solitude and seclusion; hermit. —*adj.* Secluded or retired from the world. [< L *recludere* shut off] —**re·clu′sion** *n.* —**re·clu′sive** *adj.*

rec·og·ni·tion (rek′əg·nish′ən) *n.* **1** The act of recognizing or the condition of being recognized. **2** Special notice or acknowledgment; attention: His work has received much *recognition*. **3** Acknowledgment and acceptance on the part of one government of the independence and validity of another. —**re·cog·ni·to·ry** (ri·kog′nə·tôr′ē, -tō′rē), **re·cog′ni·tive** *adj.*

re·cog·ni·zance (ri·kog′nə·zəns, -kon′ə-) *n. Law* **1** An acknowledgment or obligation of record, with condition to do some particular act, as to appear and answer. **2** A sum of money deposited as surety for fulfillment of such act or obligation, and forfeited by its nonperformance. [< L *recognoscere* call to mind] —**re·cog′ni·zant** *adj.*

rec·og·nize (rek′əg·nīz) *v.t.* **·nized, ·niz·ing 1** To perceive as identical with someone or something previously known. **2** To identify or know, as by previous experience or knowledge: I *recognize* the symptoms. **3** To perceive as true; realize: I *recognize* my error. **4** To acknowledge the independence and validity of, as a newly constituted government. **5** To indicate appreciation or approval of. **6** To regard as valid or genuine: to *recognize* a claim. **7** To give (someone) permission to speak, as in a legislative body. **8** To admit the acquaintance of; greet. [Back formation < RECOGNIZANCE] —**rec·og·niz·a·ble** (rek′əg·nīz′ə·bəl) *adj.* —**rec′og·niz′a·bly** *adv.* —**rec′og·niz′er** *n.* —**Syn. 3** acknowledge, admit, allow.

re·coil (ri·koil′) *v.i.* **1** To start back, as in fear or loathing; shrink. **2** To spring back, as from force of discharge or impact. **3** To return to the source; react: with *on* or *upon*. **4** To move; retreat. —*n.* (rē′koil′) **1** A backward movement or impulse, as of a gun at the moment of firing. **2** A shrinking. [< OF *reculer*] —**re·coil′er** *n.*

re-coil (rē′koil′) *v.t. & v.i.* To coil again.

rec·ol·lect (rek′ə·lekt′) *v.t.* **1** To call back to the mind; remember. —*v.i.* **2** To have a recollection of something. [< L *recollectus*, pp. of *recolligere* gather together again]

re-col·lect (rē′kə·lekt′) *v.t.* **1** To collect again, as things scattered. **2** To collect or recover (one's thoughts, strength, etc.). **3** To compose (oneself). Also, for defs. 2 & 3, **rec·ol·lect** (rek′ə·lekt′). —**re′-col·lec′tion** *n.*

rec·ol·lec·tion (rek′ə·lek′shən) *n.* **1** The act or power of recollecting. **2** Something remembered. —**rec′ol·lec′tive** *adj.* —**rec′ol·lec′tive·ly** *adv.* —**rec′ol·lec′tive·ness** *n.*

rec·om·mend (rek′ə·mend′) *v.t.* **1** To commend or praise as desirable, worthy, etc. **2** To make attractive or acceptable. **3** To advise; urge. **4** To give in charge; commend. —**rec·om·mend′a·ble, rec·om·men·da·to·ry** (-də·tôr′ē, -tōr′ē) *adj.* —**rec′om·mend′er** *n.*

rec·om·men·da·tion (rek′ə·mən·dā′shən, -men-) *n.* **1** The act of recommending. **2** Something that recommends, as a letter or statement.

re·com·mit (rē′kə·mit′) *v.t.* **·mit·ted, ·mit·ting 1** To commit

again. **2** To refer back to a committee, as a bill. —**re′com·mit′ment, re′com·mit′tal** *n.*

rec·om·pense (rek′əm·pens) *v.t.* **·pensed, ·pens·ing 1** To give compensation to; pay or repay; reward. **2** To give compensation for, as a loss. —*n.* An equivalent for anything given, done, or suffered; payment; compensation; reward. [< L *re-* again + *compensare* compensate]

rec·on·cil·a·ble (rek′ən·sī′lə·bəl, rek′ən·sī′-) *adj.* Capable of being reconciled, adjusted, or harmonized. —**rec′on·cil′a·bil′i·ty, rec′on·cil′a·ble·ness** *n.* —**rec′on·cil′a·bly** *adv.*

rec·on·cile (rek′ən·sīl) *v.t.* **·ciled, ·cil·ing 1** To bring back to friendship after estrangement. **2** To settle or adjust, as a quarrel. **3** To bring to acquiescence, content, or submission. **4** To make or show to be consistent or congruous; harmonize. [< L *re-* again + *conciliare* unite] —**rec′on·cile′ment, rec·on·cil·i·a·tion** (rek′ən·sil′ē·a′shən) *n.* —**rec′on·cil′i·a·to·ry** (-sil′ē·ə·tôr′ē, -tō′rē) *adj.*

rec·on·dite (rek′ən·dīt, ri·kon′dīt) *adj.* **1** Beyond ordinary or easy understanding or perception; abstruse. **2** Dealing in difficult matters. **3** Hidden; obscure. [< L *recondere* put away, hide] —**rec′on·dite′ly** *adv.* —**rec′on·dite′ness** *n.*

re·con·di·tion (rē·kən·dish′ən) *v.t.* To put back into good or working condition, as by making repairs.

re·con·nais·sance (ri·kon′ə·səns, -säns) *n.* **1** An exploratory examination or survey, as of territory. **2** *Mil.* The act of obtaining information regarding the position, strength, and movement of enemy forces. [F]

re·con·noi·ter (rē′kə·noi′tər, rek′ə-) *v.t.* **1** To examine or survey, as for military, engineering, or geological purposes. —*v.i.* **2** To make a reconnaissance. *Brit. sp.* **·noi′tre.** [< OF *reconoistre*] —**re′con·noi′ter·er, re′con·noi′trer** *n.*

re·con·sid·er (rē′kən·sid′ər) *v.t. & v.i.* To consider again, esp. with a view to a reversal of a previous action. —**re′con·sid′er·a′tion** *n.*

re·con·sti·tute (rē·kon′stə·t^yōōt′) *v.t.* **·tut·ed, ·tut·ing** To constitute again, esp. to add water to a dehydrated or condensed substance. —**re·con′sti·tu′tion** *n.*

re·con·struct (rē′kən·strukt′) *v.t.* To construct again. —**Syn.** rebuild, refashion, reestablish, remodel.

re·con·struc·tion (rē′kən·struk′shən) *n.* **1** The act of reconstructing. **2** Something reconstructed. **3** *Usu. cap.* **a** The restoration of the seceded s States as members of the Union after the American Civil War. **b** The period of this restoration, from 1867–1877. —**re′con·struc′tive** *adj.*

re·con·vert (rē′kən·vûrt′) *v.t.* To change back, as to a former condition, form, religion, etc. —**re′con·ver′sion** (-vûr′zhən) *n.*

rec·ord (rek′ərd) *n.* **1** An account in written or other permanent form serving as evidence of a fact or event. **2** Something on which such an account is made, as a monument. **3** Information preserved and handed down: the heaviest rainfall on *record*. **4** The known career or performance of a person, animal, organization, etc. **5** The best listed achievement, as in a competitive sport. **6** *Law* **a** A written account of an act, statement, or transaction made by an officer acting under authority of law. **b** An official written account of a judicial or legislative proceeding. **7** A disk or cylinder, grooved so as to reproduce sounds that have been registered on its surface. —**go on record** To state publically or officially. —**off the record** Not for quotation or publication. —*adj.* Surpassing any previously recorded achievement or performance of its kind. —**re·cord** (ri·kôrd′) *v.t.* **1** To write down or otherwise inscribe, as for preservation, evidence, etc. **2** To indicate; register. **3** To offer evidence of. **4** To register and make permanently reproducible, as on tape, a phonograph record, etc. —*v.i.* **5** To record something. [< L *recordari* call to mind]

re·cord·er (ri·kôr′dər) *n.* **1** One who records. **2** A magistrate having criminal jurisdiction in a city or borough. **3** A type of flute blown at one end. **4** A device that records, as a tape recorder.

Recorder
def. 3

re·cord·ing (ri·kôr′ding) *n.* **1** The act or process of making a representation from which sound, video, data, etc., can be reproduced. **2** The material so represented.

record player A machine for reproducing sound from a record (def. 7).

re·count[1] (ri·kount′) v.t. **1** To relate the particulars of; narrate in detail. **2** To enumerate; recite. [< OF *reconter* relate] —**re·count′er** n.

re·count[2] (rē′kount′) v.t. To count again. —n. (rē′kount′) An additional count, esp. a second count of votes cast.

re·count·al (ri·koun′tǝl) n. A detailed narrative.

re·coup (ri·koop′) v.t. **1** To recover or make up for, as a loss. **2** To regain, as health. **3** To repay or reimburse. —n. The act of recouping. [< F *re-* again + *couper* to cut] —**re·coup′a·ble** adj. —**re·coup′ment** n.

re·course (rē′kôrs, -kōrs, ri·kôrs′, -kōrs′) n. **1** Resort to or application for help or security in trouble. **2** The person or thing resorted to. [< L *recursus* a running back]

re·cov·er (ri·kuv′ǝr) v.t. **1** To obtain again, as after losing; regain. **2** To make up for; retrieve, as a loss. **3** To restore (oneself) to natural balance, health, etc. **4** To reclaim, as land. **5** *Law* To gain or regain in judicial proceedings. —v.i. **6** To regain health, composure, etc. **7** *Law* To succeed in a lawsuit. [< L *recuperare*] —**re·cov′er·a·ble** adj.

re·cov·er (rē′kuv′ǝr) v.t. To cover again.

re·cov·er·y (ri·kuv′ǝr·ē) n. pl. **·er·ies 1** The act, process, or an instance of recovering. **2** The duration of recovering. **3** Restoration from sickness or from any undesirable or abnormal condition. **4** The extraction of usable substances and materials from byproducts, waste, etc. **5** The retrieval of a flying object, as a balloon, space vehicle, meteorite, etc., after it has fallen to earth.

rec·re·ant (rek′rē·ǝnt) adj. **1** Unfaithful to a cause or pledge; false. **2** Craven; cowardly. —n. A cowardly or faithless person; also, a deserter. [< L *re-* back + *credere* believe] —**rec′re·ance, rec′re·an·cy** n. —**rec′re·ant·ly** adv.

rec·re·ate[1] (rek′rē·āt) v. **·at·ed, ·at·ing** v.t. **1** To impart fresh vigor to; refresh, esp. after toil. —v.i. **2** To take recreation. [< L *recreare* create anew] —**rec′re·a′tive** adj.

re·cre·ate[2] (rē′krē·āt′) v.t. **·at·ed, ·at·ing** To create anew. —**re′cre·a′tion** n.

rec·re·a·tion (rek′rē·ā′shǝn) n. **1** Refreshment of body or mind, esp. after work; diversion; amusement. **2** Any pleasurable exercise or occupation. —**rec′re·a′tion·al** adj.

re·crim·i·nate (ri·krim′ǝ·nāt) v. **·nat·ed, ·nat·ing** v.t. **1** To accuse in return. —v.i. **2** To repel one accusation by making another in return. [< L *re-* again + *criminare* accuse] —**re·crim′i·na′tor** n. —**re·crim′i·na′tive, re·crim·i·na·to·ry** (ri·krim′ǝ·nǝ·tôr′ē, -tō′rē) adj.

re·crim·in·a·tion (ri·krim′ǝ·nā′shǝn) n. **1** The act of recriminating. **2** An accusation made in response to another.

re·cru·desce (rē′kroō·des′) v.i. **·desced, ·desc·ing** To reappear after lying dormant. [< L *re-* again + *crudescere* become harsh, break out] —**re′cru·des′cence** n. —**re′cru·des′cent** adj.

re·cruit (ri·kroōt′) v.t. **1** To enlist (men or women) for service, as in a military organization or a police force. **2** To muster; raise, as an army, by enlistment. **3** To enlist the aid, services, or support of: to *recruit* new members for a political party. **4** To replenish. —v.i. **5** To enlist new personnel for service, as in an army or other organization. **6** To gain or raise new supplies of anything lost or needed. —n. **1** A newly enlisted person, as a soldier or sailor. **2** Any new adherent of a cause, organization, or the like. [< F *recrute*] —**re·cruit′er, re·cruit′ment** n.

rec. sec. recording secretary.

rect. receipt; rectangle; rector; rectory.

rec·tal (rek′tǝl) adj. Pertaining to, for, or in the region of the rectum.

rec·tan·gle (rek′tang′gǝl) n. A parallelogram with all angles right angles. [< L *rectus* straight + *angulus* angle] • See PARALLELOGRAM.

rec·tan·gu·lar (rek·tang′gyǝ·lǝr) adj. **1** Having right angles. **2** Resembling a rectangle. —**rec·tan′gu·lar′i·ty** (-lar′ǝ·tē) n. —**rec·tan′gu·lar·ly** adv.

recti- *combining form* Straight: *rectilinear*. [< L *rectus* straight]

rec·ti·fi·er (rek′tǝ·fī′ǝr) n. **1** One who or that which recti-

fies. **2** *Electr.* A device that conducts in only one direction.

rec·ti·fy (rek′tǝ·fī) v.t. **·fied, ·fy·ing 1** To make right; correct; amend. **2** *Chem.* To refine or purify, as a liquid, by distillation. **3** *Electr.* To change (an alternating current) into a direct current. **4** To allow for errors or inaccuracies in, as a compass reading. [< L *rectus* right + *facere* make] —**rec′ti·fi′a·ble** adj. —**rec′ti·fi·ca′tion** (-tǝ·fǝ·kā′shǝn) n.

rec·ti·lin·e·ar (rek′tǝ·lin′ē·ǝr) adj. Pertaining to, consisting of, moving in, or bounded by a straight line or lines; straight. Also **rec′ti·lin′e·al.** —**rec′ti·lin′e·ar·ly** adv.

rec·ti·tude (rek′tǝ·tyōod) n. **1** Uprightness in principles and conduct. **2** Correctness of judgment, method, etc. [< L *rectus* right]

rec·tor (rek′tǝr) n. **1** In the Church of England, a priest who has full charge of a parish. **2** In the Protestant Episcopal Church, a priest in charge of a parish. **3** In the Roman Catholic Church: **a** A priest in charge of a congregation or church. **b** The head of a seminary or university. **4** In certain universities, colleges, and schools, the headmaster or principal. [< L *rectus,* pp. of *regere* rule] —**rec′tor·ate** (-it) n. —**rec·to·ri·al** (rek·tôr′ē·ǝl, -tō′rē-) adj.

rec·to·ry (rek′tǝr·ē) n. pl. **·ries 1** A rector's dwelling. **2** In England, a parish domain with its buildings, revenue, etc.

rec·tum (rek′tǝm) n. pl. **·tums** or **·ta** (-tǝ) The terminal part of the large intestine ending at the anus. [< NL *rectum (intestinum)* straight (intestine)]

re·cum·bent (ri·kum′bǝnt) adj. **1** Lying down, wholly or partly. **2** Resting; inactive. [< L *re-* back + *cumbere* lie] —**re·cum′bence, re·cum′ben·cy** n. —**re·cum′bent·ly** adv.

re·cu·per·ate (ri·kyōō′pǝ·rāt) v. **·at·ed, ·at·ing** v.i. **1** To regain health or strength. **2** To recover from loss, as of money. —v.t. **3** To obtain again after loss; recover. **4** To restore to vigor and health. [< L *recuperare*] —**re·cu′per·a′tion, re·cu′per·a′tor** n. —**re·cu′per·a·tive** adj.

re·cur (ri·kûr′) v.i. **·curred, ·cur·ring 1** To happen again or repeatedly. **2** To come back or return, as to the memory, in conversation, etc. [< L *re-* back + *currere* run]

re·cur·rent (ri·kûr′ǝnt) adj. **1** Happening or appearing again or repeatedly; recurring. **2** Turning back toward the source, as certain arteries and nerves. —**re·cur′rence, re·cur′ren·cy** n. —**re·cur′rent·ly** adv.

re·curve (ri·kûrv′) v.t. & v.i. **·curved, ·curv·ing** To curve or bend backward. [< L *re-* back + *curvus* curved] —**re·cur′·vate** (-kûr′vit, -vāt) adj.

re·cy·cle (rē·sī′kǝl) v.t. **·cy·cled, ·cy·cling** To reclaim (waste materials, as used newsprint, glass bottles, etc.) by using in the manufacture of new products. —**re·cy′cla·ble** adj.

red (red) adj. **red·der, red·dest 1** Having or being of a bright color resembling blood. **2** Of a hue approximating red: *red* hair. **3** Ultraradical in politics, esp. communistic. —n. **1** One of the primary colors, occurring at the opposite end of the spectrum from violet; the color of fresh human blood. **2** A hue or tint that approximates primary red. **3** Any pigment or dye having or giving this color. **4** A red animal or object. **5** *Often cap.* An ultraradical or revolutionary in politics, esp. a communist: from the red banner of revolution. —**in the red** *Informal* Operating at a loss; owing money. —**see red** To be very angry. [< OE *rēad*] —**red′dish** adj. —**red′ly** adv. —**red′ness** n.

red. reduce; reduction.

re·dact (ri·dakt′) v.t. **1** To prepare, as for publication; edit; revise. **2** To draw up or frame, as a message or edict. [< L *redactus,* pp. of *redigere* lead back, restore] —**re·dac′·tion, re·dac′tor** n.

red algae A class of marine algae having predominantly red pigment and usu. mosslike growth.

red·bait (red′bāt′) v.t. To denounce as being communist. —**red′bait′er** n.

red·bird (red′bûrd′) n. Any of various birds with red plumage in the male, as cardinals, certain tanagers, etc.

red·blood·ed (red′blud′id) adj. Having vitality and vigor. —**red′·blood′ed·ness** n.

red·breast (red′brest′) n. A robin.

red·cap (red′kap′) n. A porter, as in a railroad or airline terminal.

---

add, āce, câre, pälm; end, ēven; it, īce; odd, ōpen, ôrder; toŏk, poōl; up, bûrn; ǝ = a in above, u in focus; yōō = u in fuse; oil; pout; check; go; ring; thin; this; zh, vision. < derived from; ? origin uncertain or unknown.

red carpet A long red carpet traditionally used for important guests to walk on. **—red′-car′pet** *adj.*

Red China *Informal* The People's Republic of China.

red·coat (red′kōt′) *n.* **1** A British soldier during the American Revolution and the War of 1812. **2** *Can.* MOUNTIE.

red corpuscle ERYTHROCYTE.

Red Cross 1 An international society for bringing aid to victims of a war or disaster. **2** Any national branch of this society. **3** Their emblem, a red Greek cross on a white ground, symbol of neutrality.

red deer 1 A common deer of Europe and Asia. **2** The white-tailed deer in its summer coat.

red·den (red′n) *v.t.* **1** To make red. **—***v.i.* **2** To grow red, esp. to blush.

re·deem (ri·dēm′) *v.t.* **1** To regain possession of by paying a price. **2** To pay off, as a promissory note. **3** To convert into cash or a premium: to *redeem* stocks or trading stamps. **4** To set free; ransom. **5** *Theol.* To rescue from sin and its penalties. **6** To fulfill, as an oath or promise. **7** To make worthwhile. [< L *re-* back + *emere* buy] **—re·deem′a·ble, re·demp′ti·ble** (-demp′tə·bəl) *adj.*

re·deem·er (ri·dē′mər) *n.* One who redeems. **—the Redeemer** Jesus Christ.

re·demp·tion (ri·demp′shən) *n.* **1** The act of redeeming, or the state of being redeemed. **2** The recovery of what is mortgaged or pawned. **3** The payment of a debt or obligation, esp. the paying of the value of its notes, warrants, etc., by a government. **4** Deliverance or rescue, as by paying a ransom. **—re·demp′tive, re·demp′to·ry** *adj.*

re·de·ploy (rē′di·ploi′) *v.t.* To transfer (troops) from one zone of combat to another. **—re′de·ploy′ment** *n.*

re·de·vel·op (rē′di·vel′əp) *v.t.* **1** To develop again. **2** To rebuild, as a slum area. **3** *Phot.* To intensify with chemicals and put through a second developing process. **—***v.i.* **4** To develop again. **—re′de·vel′op·er, re′de·vel′op·ment** *n.*

red·eye (red′ī′) *n. Slang* Inferior whiskey.

red-hand·ed (red′han′did) *adj.* **1** Having just committed any crime. **2** Caught in the act of doing some particular thing. **—red′-hand′ed·ly** *adv.* **—red′-hand′ed·ness** *n.*

red·head (red′hed′) *n.* **1** A person with red hair. **2** A North American duck, the male of which has a red head. **—red′head′ed** *adj.*

redheaded woodpecker A North American woodpecker having a red head and neck.

red herring 1 Smoked herring. **2** An irrelevant topic introduced in order to divert attention from the main point under discussion.

red-hot (red′hot′) *adj.* **1** Heated to redness. **2** New; fresh. **3** Marked by excitement, agitation, or enthusiasm.

red·in·gote (red′ing·gōt′) *n.* An outer coat with long full skirts. [F< E *riding coat*]

re·dis·trict (rē′dis′trikt) *v.t.* To redraw the district boundaries of.

red lead (led) An oxide of lead, used as a red pigment.

red-let·ter (red′let′ər) *adj.* Happy or memorable: from the use on calendars of red letters to indicate holidays.

red light A traffic signal light meaning stop.

red-light district (red′līt′) That part of a city or town in which brothels are numerous: from the former use of red lights to mark brothels.

red man An American Indian.

red·neck (red′nek′) *n.* A white, usu. uneducated laborer of the South: a disparaging term. Also **red′-neck′**.

red·o·lent (red′ə·lənt) *adj.* **1** Fragrant; odorous. **2** Smelling: with *of*: a swamp *redolent* of decay. **3** Evocative: with *of*: *redolent* of the past. [< L *redolere* emit a smell] **—red′o·lence, red′o·len·cy** *n.* **—red′o·lent·ly** *adv.*

re·dou·ble (rē·dub′əl) *v.t. & v.i.* **1** To make or become double. **2** To increase greatly. **3** To echo or re-echo. **4** To fold or double back again. **5** In bridge, to double (an opponent's double).

re·doubt (ri·dout′) *n.* **1** A temporary fortification, as to defend a pass, a hilltop, etc. **2** Any place providing protection; stronghold. [< Med. L *reductus*, lit., a refuge]

re·doubt·a·ble (ri·dou′tə·bəl) *adj.* **1** Inspiring fear; formidable. **2** Deserving respect or deference. Also **re·doubt′· ed.** [< L *re-* thoroughly + *dubitare* doubt] **—re·doubt′a·ble·ness** *n.* **—re·doubt′a·bly** *adv.*

re·dound (ri·dound′) *v.i.* **1** To have an effect or result. **2** To return; reflect. **—***n.* A return by way of consequence; result. [< L *redundare* to overflow]

red pepper 1 Any of various capsicums having fruit that is red when ripe. **2** Such a fruit, or a condiment made from it, as cayenne, pimiento, etc.

red·poll (red′pōl′) *n.* A small finch of northern regions, having a reddish crown.

re·dress (ri·dres′) *v.t.* **1** To set right or make reparation for, as a wrong, by compensation or by punishment. **2** To make reparation to; compensate. **3** To remedy; correct. **—***n.* (rē′dres, ri·dres′) **1** Satisfaction for wrong done; reparation; amends. **2** A restoration; correction. [< F *redresser* straighten] **—re·dress′er** or **re·dres′sor** *n.*

red shift *Astron.* Displacement toward the red or low-frequency end of the spectrum of light or radio waves from a celestial body that is receding at high velocity.

red snapper Any of various reddish, marine fish highly esteemed as food.

red·start (red′stärt′) *n.* Any of various small warblers having red markings. [< RED + obs. *start* tail]

Red snapper

red tape Rigid official regulations, forms, or procedure involving delay or inaction: from the former practice of tying public documents with red tape.

red·top (red′top′) *n.* Any of certain grasses used for lawns and pasturage.

re·duce (ri·dy͞oos′) *v.* **·duced, ·duc·ing** *v.t.* **1** To make less in size, amount, number, intensity, etc.; diminish. **2** To bring into a certain system or order; classify. **3** To bring to a lower condition; degrade. **4** To bring to submission; subdue; conquer. **5** To bring to a specified condition or state: with *to*: to *reduce* rock to powder; *reduced* to tears. **6** To thin (paint, etc.) with oil or turpentine. **7** *Math.* To change (an expression) to a more elementary form. **8** *Chem.* **a** To remove oxygen from (a compound). **b** To add electrons to (an atom). **c** To decrease the positive valence of (an atom). **9** *Phot.* To diminish the density of (a photographic negative). **—***v.i.* **10** To become less in any way. **11** To decrease one's weight, as by dieting. [< L *re-* back + *ducere* lead] **—re·duc′er, re·duc′i·bil′i·ty** *n.* **—re·duc′i·ble** *adj.* **—re·duc′i·bly** *adv.*

reducing agent *Chem.* Any substance that reduces another substance and is thereby oxidized in a chemical reaction.

re·duc·ti·o ad ab·sur·dum (ri·duk′tē·ō ad ab·sûr′dəm, -shē·ō) Disproof of a proposition by showing that it is self-contradictory. [L, lit., reduction to absurdity]

re·duc·tion (ri·duk′shən) *n.* **1** The act or process of reducing. **2** Something that results from reducing. **3** The amount by which something is reduced. **—re·duc′tion·al, re·duc′tive** *adj.*

re·dun·dan·cy (ri·dun′dən·sē) *n. pl.* **·cies 1** The condition or quality of being redundant. **2** Something redundant, esp. unnecessary repetition. **3** Excess; surplus. **4** In information theory, repeated information in a message, used to lessen the probability of error. Also **re·dun′dance.**

re·dun·dant (ri·dun′dənt) *adj.* **1** Being more than is required; constituting an excess. **2** Unnecessarily repetitive or verbose. [< L *redundare* to overflow] **—re·dun′dant·ly** *adv.* **—Syn. 1** superfluous, excessive, inordinate, undue. **2** repetitious, iterative, reiterative, wordy.

re·du·pli·cate (ri·dy͞oo′plə·kāt) *v.* **·cat·ed, ·cat·ing** *v.t.* **1** To repeat again and again; copy; iterate. **2** *Ling.* To affix a reduplication to. **—***v.i.* **3** To undergo reduplication. **—***adj.* (-kit) Repeated again and again; duplicated. **—re·du′pli· ca′tive** *adj.*

re·du·pli·ca·tion (ri·dy͞oo′plə·kā′shən) *n.* **1** The act of reduplicating, or the state of being reduplicated; a redoubling. **2** *Ling.* **a** The repetition of an initial element or elements in a word. **b** The doubling of all or part of a word, often with vowel or consonant change, as in *fiddle-faddle.*

red·wing (red′wing′) *n.* **1** A North American blackbird with red and yellow wing patches in the male: also **red-winged blackbird.** **2** An Old World thrush with reddish orange on its wings.

red·wood (red′wo͞od′) *n.* **1** SEQUOIA. **2** Its wood.

reed (rēd) n. 1 The slender, frequently jointed stem of certain tall grasses growing in wet places; also, the grasses themselves. 2 *Music* a A thin, elastic plate of reed, wood, or metal nearly closing an opening, as in a pipe, used in reed organs, reed pipes of pipe organs, and some woodwind instruments, to produce a musical tone when vibrated by air. b An instrument having such a reed or reeds. 3 A crude musical pipe made of the hollow stem of a plant. 4 *Archit.* REEDING. 5 A comblike device on a loom that keeps the warp yarns evenly separated. —v.t. 1 To fashion into or decorate with reeds. 2 To thatch with reeds. —adj. *Music* Equipped with a reed or reeds. [< OE *hrēod*]

reed·ing (rē′ding) n. *Archit.* 1 Small, convex molding. 2 Parallel ornamentation using such molding.

reed organ A keyboard musical instrument sounding by means of reeds that vibrate freely in response to air currents.

re·ed·u·cate (rē·ej′o͞o·kāt) v.t. ·cat·ed, ·cat·ing 1 To educate again. 2 To rehabilitate, as a criminal, by education. —re′ed·u·ca′tion n.

reed·y (rē′dē) adj. reed·i·er, reed·i·est 1 Full of reeds. 2 Like a reed. 3 Having a tone like that of a reed instrument. —reed′i·ness n.

reef[1] (rēf) n. 1 A ridge of sand or rocks, or esp. of coral, at or near the surface of the water. 2 A lode, vein, or ledge. [< ON *rif* rib, reef] —reef′y adj. • See ATOLL.

reef[2] (rēf) *Naut.* n. 1 The part of a sail that is folded and secured or untied and let out in regulating its size on the mast. 2 The tuck taken in a sail when reefed. —v.t. 1 To reduce (a sail) by folding a part and tying it to a yard or boom. 2 To shorten or lower, as a topmast, by taking part of it in. [Prob. < ON *rif* rib]

reef·er[1] (rē′fər) n. 1 One who reefs. 2 A short, double-breasted coat or jacket.

reef·er[2] (rē′fər) n. *Slang* A marihuana cigarette. [?]

reef knot SQUARE KNOT.

reek (rēk) v.i. 1 To give off smoke, vapor, etc. 2 To give off a strong, offensive smell. 3 To be pervaded with anything offensive. —v.t. 4 To expose to smoke or its action. 5 To give off; emit. [< OE *rēocan*] —reek′er n. —reek′y adj. (·i·er, ·i·est)

reel[1] (rēl) n. 1 A rotatory device or frame for winding rope, cord, photographic film, or other flexible substance. 2 Such a device attached to a fishing rod. 3 The length of wire, film, thread, etc., wound on one reel. —v.t. 1 To wind on a reel or bobbin, as a line. 2 To draw in by reeling a line: with *in*: to *reel* a fish in. 3 To say, do, etc., easily and fluently: with *off*. [< OE *hrēol*] —reel′a·ble adj. —reel′er n.

Fishing reel

reel[2] (rēl) v.i. 1 To stagger, sway, or lurch, as when giddy or drunk. 2 To whirl round and round. 3 To have a sensation of giddiness or whirling: My head *reels*. 4 To waver or fall back, as attacking troops. —v.t. 5 To cause to reel. —n. A staggering motion; giddiness. [< REEL[1]] —reel′er n.

reel[3] (rēl) n. 1 A lively Scottish dance. 2 The music for such a dance. [?< REEL[1]]

re·en·force (rē′in·fôrs′, -en-, -fôrs′) v. ·forced, ·forc·ing REINFORCE.

re·en·try (rē·en′trē) n. 1 The act of entering again. 2 In whist and bridge, a card by which a player can regain the lead. 3 The return into the atmosphere of an object launched into space from the earth.

reeve[1] (rēv) v.t. reeved or rove (*for p.p. also* rov·en), reev·ing *Naut.* 1 To pass, as a rope or rod, through a hole, block, or aperture. 2 To fasten in such manner. 3 To pass a rope, etc., through (a block or pulley). [?< Du. *reven* reef a sail]

reeve[2] (rēv) n. In Canada, an elected official who presides over the council in certain villages and townships. [< OE *gerēfa* steward]

ref. referee; reference; referred; refining; reformed.

re·fec·tion (ri·fek′shən) n. 1 Refreshment by food and drink. 2 A light meal. [< L *refectus*, pp. of *reficere* remake, refresh]

re·fec·to·ry (ri·fek′tər·ē) n. pl. ·ries A room for eating, esp. in a monastery, convent, or college. [< Med. L *refectorium*]

re·fer (ri·fûr′) v. ·ferred, ·fer·ring v.t. 1 To direct or send for information or other purpose. 2 To hand over for consideration, settlement, etc. 3 To assign or attribute to a source, cause, group, class, etc. —v.i. 4 To make reference; allude. 5 To turn, as for information, help, or authority. [< L *re-* back + *ferre* bear, carry] —ref·er·a·ble (ref′ər·ə·bəl, ri·fûr′-), re·fer′ra·ble or re·fer′ri·ble adj. —re·fer′rer n.

ref·er·ee (ref′ə·rē′) n. 1 A person to whom a thing is referred for judgment or decision. 2 An official who sees that the rules of certain sports events are observed. —v.t. & v.i. To judge as a referee.

ref·er·ence (ref′ər·əns, ref′rəns) n. 1 The act of referring. 2 An incidental allusion or direction of the attention. 3 A note or other indication in a book, referring to some other book or passage. 4 One who or that which is or may be referred to. 5 A book or other source intended to be referred to for information, as a dictionary. 6 Relation: in *reference* to your inquiry. 7 A person to whom an employer may refer for information about a potential employee. 8 A written statement or testimonial referring to character or dependability. —ref′er·en′tial (-ən·shəl) adj. —ref′er·en′tial·ly adv.

ref·er·en·dum (ref′ə·ren′dəm) n. pl. ·dums or ·da (-də) 1 The submission of a proposed public measure or law, which has been passed upon by a legislature or convention, to a vote of the people for ratification or rejection. 2 The vote itself. [L, gerund of *referre* refer]

ref·er·ent (ref′ər·ənt) n. Something referred to, esp. the thing to which reference is made in any verbal statement.

re·fer·ral (ri·fûr′əl) n. 1 The act of referring or the condition of being referred. 2 One who has been referred.

re·fill (rē·fil′) v.t. & v.i. To fill or become filled again. —n. (rē′fil′) Any commodity packaged to fit and fill a container originally containing that commodity. —re·fill′a·ble adj.

re·fine (ri·fīn′) v. ·fined, ·fin·ing v.t. 1 To make fine or pure. 2 To make more elegant, polished, etc. 3 To improve or perfect. —v.i. 4 To become fine or pure. 5 To become more polished or cultured. 6 To make fine distinctions; use subtlety in thought or speech. [< RE- + FINE[1], v.] —re·fin′er n.

re·fined (ri·fīnd′) adj. 1 Characterized by refinement or polish. 2 Free from impurity. 3 Exceedingly precise or exact; subtle.

re·fine·ment (ri·fīn′mənt) n. 1 The act or process of refining. 2 The result of refining, esp. an improvement. 3 Fineness of thought, taste, language, etc.; freedom from coarseness or vulgarity. 4 A nice distinction; subtlety.

re·fin·er·y (ri·fī′nər·ē) n. pl. ·er·ies A plant for extracting useful products from raw material, as metal from ore, etc.

re·fit (rē·fit′) v.t. & v.i. ·fit·ted, ·fit·ting To make or be made fit or ready again, as by making or obtaining repairs, replacing equipment, etc. —n. The repair of damages or wear, esp. of a ship.

refl. reflection; reflex; reflexive.

re·flect (ri·flekt′) v.t. 1 To turn or throw back, as rays of light, heat, or sound. 2 To produce a symmetrically reversed image of, as a mirror. 3 To cause or bring as a result: with *on*: He *reflects* credit on his teacher. 4 To show or manifest: His writings *reflect* great imagination. —v.i. 5 To send back rays, as of light or heat. 6 To return in rays. 7 To give back an image; also, to be mirrored. 8 To think carefully; ponder. 9 To bring blame, discredit, etc.: with *on* or *upon*. [< L *re-* back + *flectere* bend]

re·flec·tion (ri·flek′shən) n. 1 The act of reflecting, or the state of being reflected. 2 *Physics* The throwing off or back (from a surface) of impinging light, heat, sound, or any form of radiant energy. 3 Reflected rays or an image thrown by reflection. 4 Careful, serious thought or consideration. 5 The result of such thought. 6 Censure; discredit; also, a remark or action tending to discredit. —re·flec′tion·al adj.

re·flec·tive (re·flek′tiv) adj. 1 Given to reflection or

thought; meditative. **2** Of or caused by reflection. **3** That reflects. —**re·flec'tive·ly** *adv.* —**re·flec'tive·ness, re'flec·tiv'i·ty** *n.*

re·flec·tor (ri·flek'tər) *n.* One who or that which reflects, esp. a device for reflecting light, heat, sound, etc.

re·flex (rē'fleks) *adj.* **1** Turned, bent, directed, or thrown backward. **2** *Physiol.* Of, pertaining to, or produced by an involuntary action or response. —*n.* **1** Reflection, as of light, or an image produced by reflection. **2** *Physiol.* An involuntary response to a stimulus: also **reflex action. 3** A habitual or automatic reaction. [< L *reflexus* reflected, pp. of *reflectere* bend back]

re·flex·ive (ri·flek'siv) *adj.* **1** REFLEX. **2** *Gram.* **a** Designating a verb whose object is identical with its subject, as "dresses" in "He dresses himself." **b** Designating a pronoun which is the direct object of a reflexive verb. —*n.* A reflexive verb or pronoun. —**re·flex'ive·ly** *adv.* —**re·flex'ive·ness, re·flex·iv'i·ty** (rē'flek·siv'ə·tē) *n.*

ref·lu·ent (ref'lōō·ənt) *adj.* Flowing back; ebbing, as the tide. [< L *re-* back + *fluere* flow] —**ref'lu·ence, ref'lu·en·cy** *n.*

re·flux (rē'fluks') *n.* A flowing back; ebb; return. [< L *refluxus,* pp. of *refluere* flow back]

re·for·est (rē·fôr'ist, -for'-) *v.t. & v.i.* To replant (an area) with trees. —**re'for·es·ta'tion** *n.*

re·form (ri·fôrm') *v.t.* **1** To make better by removing abuses, malpractice, etc. **2** To make better morally; persuade or educate from a sinful to a moral life. **3** To put an end to; stop (an abuse, malpractice, etc.). —*v.i.* **4** To give up sin or error; become better. —*n.* A correction or improvement of social or personal evils or errors. [< L *re-* again + *formare* to form] —**re·form'a·tive** *adj.* —**re·form'er** *n.* —**re·form'ist** *adj., n.*

re-form (rē'fôrm') *v.t. & v.i.* To form again. —**re'-for·ma'tion** *n.*

ref·or·ma·tion (ref'ər·mā'shən) *n.* **1** The act of reforming. **2** The state of being reformed.

Ref·or·ma·tion (ref'ər·mā'shən) *n.* The religious revolution of the 16th century that began by trying to reform Catholicism and ended with the establishment of Protestantism.

re·form·a·to·ry (ri·fôr'mə·tôr'ē, -tō'rē) *adj.* Tending or aiming to reform. —*n. pl.* **·ries** An institution for the reformation and instruction of juvenile offenders: also **reform school.**

re·fract (ri·frakt') *v.t.* **1** To deflect (a ray) by refraction. **2** *Optics* To determine the degree of refraction of (an eye or lens). [< L *refractus,* pp. of *refringere* turn aside]

re·frac·tion (ri·frak'shən) *n.* *Physics* The change of direction of a ray, as of light or heat, in oblique passage between media of different densities. —**re·frac'tive** *adj.* —**re·frac'·tive·ness, re·frac·tiv·i·ty** (rē'frak·tiv'ə·tē), re·frac'tor *n.*

re·frac·to·ry (ri·frak'tər·ē) *adj.* **1** Hard to control; stubborn; obstinate. **2** Resisting heat. **3** Resisting treatment, as a disease. —*n. pl.* **·ries 1** A refractory or obstinate person or thing. **2** Any of various highly heat-resistant materials. [< L *refractarius*] —**re·frac'to·ri·ly** *adv.* —**re·frac'to·ri·ness** *n.*

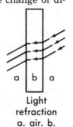

Light refraction
a. air. b. glass prism.

re·frain[1] (ri·frān') *v.i.* To hold oneself back. [< L *refrenare* curb] —**re·frain'er** *n.* —**Syn.** abstain, forbear, forgo, renounce.

re·frain[2] (ri·frān') *n.* **1** A phrase or verse repeated at intervals in a poem or a song. **2** The music for a refrain. [< OF *refraindre* to check, repeat]

re·fran·gi·ble (ri·fran'jə·bəl) *adj.* Capable of being refracted, as light. [< RE- + L *frangere* to break] —**re·fran'gi·bil'i·ty, re·fran'gi·ble·ness** *n.*

re·fresh (ri·fresh') *v.t.* **1** To revive (a person), as with food or rest. **2** To make fresh, clean, cool, etc. **3** To stimulate, as the memory. **4** To renew or replenish with or as with new supplies. —*v.i.* **5** To become fresh again; revive. **6** To take refreshment. —**re·fresh'er** *n.*

refresher course A course for reviewing and learning of recent developments in a profession or field of study.

re·fresh·ing (ri·fresh'ing) *adj.* **1** Serving to refresh. **2** Pleasing because new or unusual. —**re·fresh'ing·ly** *adv.*

re·fresh·ment (ri·fresh'mənt) *n.* **1** The act of refreshing, or the state of being refreshed. **2** That which refreshes. **3** *pl.* Food, or food and drink, served as a light meal.

re·frig·er·ant (ri·frij'ər·ənt) *adj.* **1** Cooling or freezing. **2** Allaying heat or fever. —*n.* **1** Any medicine or material that reduces fever. **2** A substance used to produce refrigeration.

re·frig·er·ate (ri·frij'ə·rāt) *v.t.* **·at·ed, ·at·ing 1** To keep or cause to become cold; cool. **2** To freeze or chill for preservative purposes, as foodstuffs. [< L *re-* thoroughly + *frigerare* to cool] —**re·frig'er·a'tion** *n.* —**re·frig'er·a'tive** *adj., n.* —**re·frig'er·a·to'ry** *adj.*

re·frig·er·a·tor (ri·frij'ə·rā'tər) *n.* A box, cabinet, room, railroad car, etc., equipped with a cooling apparatus for preserving the freshness of perishable foods, etc.

ref·uge (ref'yōōj) *n.* **1** Shelter or protection, as from danger or distress. **2** A safe place; asylum. **3** Something that brings relief, lessens difficulties, etc. [< L *refugere* to retreat]

ref·u·gee (ref'yōō·jē', ref'yōō·jē') *n.* One who flees to find refuge in another land or place, as from persecution or political danger.

re·ful·gent (ri·ful'jənt) *adj.* Shining; radiant; resplendent. [< L *refulgere* reflect light] —**re·ful'gence, re·ful'gen·cy** *n.* —**re·ful'gent·ly** *adv.*

re·fund[1] (ri·fund') *v.t.* **1** To give or pay back (money, etc.). **2** To repay (a person). —*v.i.* **3** To make repayment. —*n.* (rē'fund) A repayment; refunding; also, the amount repaid. [< L *refundere* pour back] —**re·fund'er, re·fund'ment** *n.*

re·fund[2] (rē'fund') *v.t.* To fund anew.

re·fus·al (ri·fyōō'zəl) *n.* **1** The act of refusing. **2** The privilege or opportunity of accepting or rejecting before others.

re·fuse[1] (ri·fyōōz') *v.* **·fused, ·fus·ing** *v.t.* **1** To decline to do, permit, take, or yield. **2** To decline to fulfill the request or desire of (a person). **3** To balk at jumping over (a ditch, hedge, etc.): said of a horse. —*v.i.* **4** To decline to do, permit, take, or yield something. [< L *refusus,* pp. of *refundere* pour back] —**re·fus'er** *n.*

ref·use[2] (ref'yōōs) *n.* Anything worthless; rubbish. [< OF *refus* refused]

re·fute (ri·fyōōt') *v.t.* **·fut·ed, ·fut·ing 1** To prove the incorrectness or falsity of (a statement). **2** To prove (a person) to be in error; confute. [< L *refutare*] —**re·fut'a·ble** *adj.* —**re·fut'a·bly** *adv.* —**ref·u·ta·tion** (ref'yə·tā'shən), **re·fu'tal, re·fut'er** *n.*

reg. regiment; region; register; registered; regular; regulation.

re·gain (ri·gān') *v.t.* **1** To get possession of again. **2** To reach again; get back to. —**re·gain'er** *n.*

re·gal (rē'gəl) *adj.* Belonging to or fit for a king; royal, stately, magnificent, etc. [< L *rex, regis* king] —**re·gal·i·ty** (ri·gal'ə·tē) *n.* —**re'gal·ly** *adv.*

re·gale (ri·gāl') *v.* **·galed, ·gal·ing** *v.t.* **1** To give unusual pleasure to; delight. **2** To entertain royally or sumptuously; feast. —*v.i.* **3** To feast. [< F *régaler*] —**re·gale'ment** *n.*

re·ga·li·a (ri·gā'lē·ə, -gāl'yə) *n. pl.* **1** The insignia and emblems of royalty, as the crown, scepter, etc. **2** The distinctive symbols, insignia, etc., of any society, order, or rank. **3** Fine clothes; fancy trappings.

re·gard (ri·gärd') *v.t.* **1** To look at or observe attentively. **2** To look on or think of in a certain way. **3** To take into account; consider. **4** To have relevance to. —*v.i.* **5** To pay attention. **6** To gaze or look. —*n.* **1** A look; gaze. **2** Careful attention; consideration. **3** Respect; esteem. **4** *Usu. pl.* Greetings; good wishes. **5** Reference; relation: with *regard to your letter.* [< OF *regarder* look at]

re·gard·ful (ri·gärd'fəl) *adj.* **1** Having or showing regard; heedful. **2** Respectful. —**re·gard'ful·ly** *adv.* —**re·gard'ful·ness** *n.*

re·gard·ing (ri·gär'ding) *prep.* In reference to; with regard to.

re·gard·less (ri·gärd'lis) *adj.* Having no regard or consideration; heedless; negligent. —*adv. Informal* In spite of everything. —**re·gard'less·ly** *adv.*

re·gat·ta (ri·gat'ə, -gä'tə) *n.* A boat race, or a series of such races. [Ital.]

re·gen·cy (rē'jən·sē) *n. pl.* **·cies 1** The government or office of a regent or body of regents. **2** The period during

which a regent or body of regents governs. **3** A body of regents. **4** The district under the rule of a regent. Also **re′gent·ship.**

re·gen·er·ate (ri·jen′ə·rāt) v. **·at·ed, ·at·ing** v.t. **1** To cause moral and spiritual reformation in. **2** To produce or form anew; reestablish; recreate. **3** Biol. To replace (a lost organ or tissue) with new growth. —v.i. **4** To form anew; be reproduced. **5** To become spiritually regenerate. **6** To effect regeneration. —adj. (ri·jen′ər·it) **1** Having new life; restored. **2** Spiritually renewed; regenerated. —**re·gen′er·a·cy** (-ər·ə·sē), **re·gen′er·a′tion, re·gen′er·a′tor** n. —**re·gen·er·a·tive** (ri·jen′ər·ə·tiv, -ə·rā′-) adj.

re·gent (rē′jənt) n. **1** One who rules in the name and place of a sovereign. **2** One of various officers having charge of education, as of a university or state. [< L regens, pr.p. of regere rule]

reg·i·cide (rej′ə·sīd) n. **1** The killing of a king. **2** The killer of a king. [< L rex, regis king + -CIDE] —**reg′i·ci′dal** adj.

re·gime (ri·zhēm′) n. **1** System of government or administration. **2** A particular government or its duration of rule. **3** A social system. **4** REGIMEN. Also **ré·gime** (rā·zhēm′). [< F < L regimen]

reg·i·men (rej′ə·mən) n. A system of diet, exercise, etc., used for therapeutic purposes. [< L regimen < regere to rule]

reg·i·ment (rej′ə·mənt) n. A military unit larger than a battalion and smaller than a division. —v.t. **1** To form into a regiment or regiments; organize. **2** To assign to a regiment. **3** To form into well-defined or specific units or groups; systematize. **4** To make uniform. [< LL regimentum < L regere to rule] —**reg′i·men′tal** adj. —**reg′i·men·ta′·tion** n.

reg·i·men·tals (rej′ə·men′təlz) n. pl. **1** Military uniform. **2** The uniform worn by the men and officers of a regiment.

re·gion (rē′jən) n. **1** An indefinite, usu. large portion of territory or space. **2** A specific area or place. **3** A specified area of activity, interest, etc.: the region of art. **4** A portion of the body. [< L regio < regere to rule]

re·gion·al (rē′jən·əl) adj. **1** Of or pertaining to a particular region; sectional; local: regional planning. **2** Of or pertaining to an entire region or section. —**re′gion·al·ly** adv.
• In this dictionary the label Regional is applied to terms used chiefly or exclusively within a particular region of the U.S., and constituting a part of that region's distinctive variety of speech or dialect. A user of regional speech should be aware that terms so labeled may be misunderstood or considered odd or illiterate in other parts of the country.

reg·is·ter (rej′is·tər) n. **1** An official record, as of names, events, transactions, etc. **2** The book containing such a record. **3** An item in such a record. **4** Any of various devices for adding or recording: a cash register. **5** REGISTRAR. **6** A device for regulating the admission of heated air to a room. **7** Music **a** The range or compass of a voice or instrument. **b** A series of tones of a particular quality or belonging to a particular portion of the compass of a voice or instrument. **8** Printing **a** Exact correspondence of the lines and margins on the opposite sides of a printed sheet. **b** Correct imposition of the colors in color printing. —v.t. **1** To enter in or as in a register; enroll or record officially. **2** To indicate on a scale. **3** To express or indicate: His face registered disapproval. **4** Printing To effect exact correspondence or imposition of. **5** To cause (mail) to be recorded, on payment of a fee, so as to insure delivery. —v.i. **6** To enter one's name in a register, poll, etc. **7** To have effect; make an impression. **8** Printing To be in register. [< L regestus, pp. of regerere record] —**reg·is·tra·ble** (rej′is·trə·bəl) adj. —**reg′is·trant** (-trənt) n.

reg·is·tered (rej′is·tərd) adj. **1** Recorded, as a birth, a voter, an animal's pedigree, etc. **2** Officially or formally qualified.

reg·is·trar (rej′is·trär) n. An authorized keeper of a register or of records, esp. of a college or court.

reg·is·tra·tion (rej′is·trā′shən) n. **1** The act of registering, as of voters, students, etc. **2** The number of persons registered. **3** An entry in a register.

reg·is·try (rej′is·trē) n. pl. **·tries 1** REGISTRATION. **2** A register, or the place where it is kept. **3** The nationality of a ship as entered in a register.

reg·nant (reg′nənt) adj. **1** Reigning in one's own right. **2** Predominant. **3** Widespread. [< L regnum reign]

re·gorge (ri·gôrj′) v.t. **·gorged, ·gorg·ing** To vomit up; disgorge. [< F re- again + gorge throat]

re·gress (ri·gres′) v.i. To go back; move backward; return. —n. (rē′gres) **1** A going back; return. **2** A return to a less perfect or lower state; retrogression. [< L regressus, pp. of regredi go back] —**re·gres′sive** adj. —**re·gres′sive·ly** adv. —**re·gres′sor** n.

re·gres·sion (ri·gresh′ən) n. **1** The act of regressing. **2** A return to a less perfect or lower state; retrogression. **3** Psychoanal. A retreat to earlier or infantile behavior.

re·gret (ri·gret′) v.t. **·gret·ted, ·gret·ting 1** To look back upon with a feeling of distress or loss. **2** To feel sorrow or grief concerning. —n. **1** Distress of mind in recalling some past event, act, loss, etc. **2** Remorseful sorrow; compunction. **3** pl. A polite refusal in response to an invitation. [< OF regreter] —**re·gret′ter** n.

re·gret·ful (ri·gret′fəl) adj. Feeling, expressive of, or full of regret. —**re·gret′ful·ly** adv. —**re·gret′ful·ness** n. —Syn. sorry, remorseful, contrite, apologetic.

re·gret·ta·ble (ri·gret′ə·bəl) adj. Deserving regret; unfortunate. —**re·gret′ta·bly** adv.

regt. regiment.

reg·u·lar (reg′yə·lər) adj. **1** Made, formed, or arranged according to a rule, standard, or type; symmetrical; normal. **2** Methodical; orderly: regular habits. **3** Conforming to a fixed or proper procedure or principle. **4** Customary; habitual: his regular breakfast. **5** Officially authorized. **6** Without variation or abnormality: His pulse is regular. **7** Thorough; unmitigated: a regular bore. **8** Informal Pleasant, good, honest, etc.: a regular guy. **9** Gram. Undergoing the inflection that is normal or most common. **10** Bot. Having all similar parts or organs of the same shape and size: said mainly of flowers. **11** Eccl. Belonging to a religious order: the regular clergy. **12** Mil. Pertaining or belonging to the permanent army. **13** In politics, designating, nominated by, or loyal to the official party organization or platform. **14** Geom. Having equal sides and angles. **15** Math. Controlled or formed by one law or operation throughout. —n. **1** A soldier belonging to a permanent or standing army. **2** In sports, a starting member of a team. **3** An habitual customer, patron, etc. **4** A clothing size for those of average height and weight. **5** Eccl. A member of a religious order. **6** A person loyal to a certain political party. [< L regula rule] —**reg′u·lar′i·ty** n. —**reg′u·lar·ly** adv.

reg·u·lar·ize (reg′yə·lə·rīz′) v.t. **·ized, ·iz·ing** To make regular. —**reg′u·lar·i·za′tion** n.

reg·u·late (reg′yə·lāt) v.t. **·lat·ed, ·lat·ing 1** To direct, manage, or control according to certain rules, principles, etc. **2** To adjust according to a standard, degree, etc.: to regulate currency. **3** To adjust to accurate operation. **4** To put in order; set right. [< L regula a rule < regere rule, lead straight] —**reg′u·la′tive, reg′u·la·to′ry** (-lə·tôr′ē, -tō′rē) adj.

reg·u·la·tion (reg′yə·lā′shən) n. **1** The act of regulating, or the state of being regulated. **2** A prescribed rule of conduct or procedure. —adj. **1** Required by rule or regulation. **2** Normal; customary.

reg·u·la·tor (reg′yə·lā′tər) n. **1** One who or that which regulates. **2** A device for regulating the speed of a watch. **3** A contrivance for controlling motion, flow, voltage, etc.

re·gur·gi·tate (rē·gûr′jə·tāt) v. **·tat·ed, ·tat·ing** v.i. **1** To flow backward. —v.t. **2** To cause to surge back, as partially digested food to the mouth from the stomach. [< LL reback + gurgitare flood, engulf] —**re·gur′gi·tant** adj. —**re·gur′gi·ta′tion** n.

re·ha·bil·i·tate (rē′hə·bil′ə·tāt, rē′ə-) v.t. **·tat·ed, ·tat·ing 1** To restore to a former state, capacity, privilege, rank, etc.; reinstate. **2** To restore to health or normal activity. [< Med. L rehabilitare] —**re′ha·bil′i·ta′tion** n.

re·hash (rē·hash′) v.t. To work into a new form; go over again. —n. (rē′hash′) The act or result of rehashing.

re·hears·al (ri·hûr′səl) n. 1 The act of rehearsing, as for a play. 2 The act of reciting or telling over again.

re·hearse (ri·hûrs′) v. ·hearsed, ·hears·ing v.t. 1 To practice privately in preparation for public performance, as a play or song. 2 To instruct or direct (a person) by way of preparation. 3 To say over again; repeat aloud; recite. 4 To give an account of; relate. —v.i. 5 To rehearse a play, song, dance, etc. [< OF *reherser* harrow over, repeat] —re·hears′er n.

Reich (rīkh, Ger. rīkh) n. Formerly, Germany, the German government, or its territory. —**Third Reich** The Nazi state under Adolf Hitler, 1933–45. [G]

reichs·mark (rīks′märk′, Ger. rīkhs′-) n. pl. ·marks or ·mark A monetary unit of Germany from 1924–48.

Reichs·tag (rīks′täg′, Ger. rīkhs′täkh′) n. The former legislative assembly of Germany.

reign (rān) n. 1 Sovereign power or rule; sovereignty. 2 The time or duration of a sovereign's rule. 3 Domination; sway: the *reign* of rationalism. —v.i. 1 To hold and exercise sovereign power. 2 To hold sway; prevail: Winter *reigns.* [< L *regnum* rule]

Reign of Terror The period of the French Revolution from May, 1793, to August, 1794, during which Louis XVI, Marie Antoinette, and thousands of others were guillotined.

re·im·burse (rē′im·bûrs′) v.t. ·bursed, ·burs·ing 1 To pay back (a person) an equivalent for what has been spent or lost; recompense. 2 To pay back; refund. [< RE- + < L *in*-in + *bursa* purse] —re′im·burs′a·ble adj. —re′im·burse′ment n.

rein (rān) n. 1 Usu. pl. A strap attached to each end of a bit to control a horse or other draft animal. 2 Any means of restraint or control. —v.t. 1 To guide, check, or halt with or as with reins. —v.i. 1 To check or halt a horse by means of reins: with *in* or *up.* [< OF *resne*]

re·in·car·nate (rē′in·kär′nāt) v.t. ·nat·ed, ·nat·ing To cause to undergo reincarnation.

re·in·car·na·tion (rē′in·kär·nā′shən) n. 1 The rebirth of a soul in a new body. 2 The Hindu doctrine that the soul, upon the death of the body, returns to earth in another body or a new form.

rein·deer (rān′dir′) n. pl. ·deer A European form of caribou, often domesticated. [< ON *hreinn* reindeer + *dyr* deer]

re·in·force (rē′in·fôrs′, -fōrs′) v.t. ·forced, ·forc·ing 1 To give new force or strength to. 2 *Mil.* To strengthen with more troops or ships. 3 To add some strengthening part or material to. 4 To increase the number of. [< RE- + *inforce,* var. of ENFORCE]

reinforced concrete Concrete containing metal bars, rods, or netting to increase its strength and durability.

re·in·force·ment (rē′in·fôrs′mənt, -fōrs′-) n. 1 The act of reinforcing. 2 Something that reinforces. 3 *Often pl. Mil.* A fresh body of troops or additional vessels.

re·in·state (rē′in·stāt′) v.t. ·stat·ed, ·stat·ing To restore to a former state, position, etc. —re′in·state′ment n.

reis (rās) n.pl. of REAL² (def. 2).

re·it·er·ate (rē·it′ə·rāt) v.t. ·at·ed, ·at·ing To say or do again and again. [< L *re*- again + *iterare* say] —re·it′er·a′tion n. —re·it′er·a′tive adj. —re·it′er·a′tive·ly adv. —Syn. iterate, repeat, retell, recapitulate.

re·ject (ri·jekt′) v.t. 1 To refuse to accept, recognize, believe, etc. 2 To refuse to grant; deny, as a petition. 3 To refuse (a person) recognition, acceptance, etc. 4 To expel; react against physiologically. 5 To cast away as worthless; discard. —n. (rē′jekt) A person or thing that has been rejected. [< L *re*- back + *jacere* to throw] —re·ject′er or re·jec′tor, re·jec′tion n.

re·joice (ri·jois′) v. ·joiced, ·joic·ing v.i. 1 To feel joyful; be glad. —v.t. 2 To fill with joy; gladden. [< L *re*- again + *ex*- thoroughly + *gaudere* be joyous] —re·joic′er, re·joic′ing n. —re·joic′ing·ly adv.

re·join¹ (ri·join′) v.t. 1 To say in reply; answer. —v.i. 2 To answer. [< F *rejoindre*]

re·join² (rē′join′) v.t. 1 To come again into company with. 2 To join together again; reunite. —v.i. 3 To come together again.

re·join·der (ri·join′dər) n. 1 An answer to a reply. 2 Any reply or retort. [< F *rejoindre* to answer, reply]

re·ju·ve·nate (ri·jōō′və·nāt) v.t. ·nat·ed, ·nat·ing To make young; give new vigor or youthfulness to. [< RE- again + L *juvenis* young + -ATE] —re·ju′ve·na′tion n.

rel. relating; relative; released; religion; religious.

re·lapse (ri·laps′) v.i. ·lapsed, ·laps·ing 1 To lapse back, as into disease after partial recovery. 2 To return to bad habits or sin; backslide. —n. (also rē′laps) 1 The act or an instance of relapsing. 2 The return of an illness after apparent recovery. [< L *relapsus,* pp. of *relabi* slide back] —re·laps′er n.

re·late (ri·lāt′) v. ·lat·ed, ·lat·ing v.t. 1 To tell the events or the particulars of; narrate. 2 To bring into connection or relation. —v.i. 3 To have relation: with *to.* 4 To have reference: with *to.* [< L *relatus,* pp. of *referre* to carry back] —re·lat′er n.

re·lat·ed (ri·lā′tid) adj. 1 Standing in relation; connected. 2 Of common ancestry; connected by blood or marriage; akin. 3 Narrated. —re·lat′ed·ly adv. —re·lat′ed·ness n.

re·la·tion (ri·lā′shən) n. 1 The fact or condition of being related or connected: the *relation* between poverty and disease. 2 Connection by blood or marriage; kinship. 3 A person connected by blood or marriage; a relative. 4 Reference; regard; allusion: in *relation* to your request. 5 *pl.* The contacts or dealings between or among individuals, groups, nations, etc.: race *relations;* political *relations.* 6 The act of relating or narrating; also, that which is related or told. —re·la′tion·al adj.

re·la·tion·ship (ri·lā′shən·ship) n. 1 The state or quality of being related; connection. 2 Kinship. 3 The kind or quality of association between people: a healthy *relationship.*

rel·a·tive (rel′ə·tiv) adj. 1 Having connection; pertinent: an inquiry *relative* to one's health. 2 Resulting from or depending upon a relation to or comparison with something else; comparative: a *relative* truth. 3 Intelligible only in relation to something else; not absolute. 4 *Gram.* Referring to or qualifying an antecedent: a *relative* pronoun. —n. 1 One who is related; a kinsman. 2 A relative word or term. —rel′a·tive·ly adv. —rel′a·tive·ness n.

relative clause *Gram.* A dependent clause introduced by a relative pronoun.

relative humidity At any given temperature, the percentage of the maximum possible water vapor content actually present in the air.

relative pronoun *Gram.* A pronoun that refers to an antecedent and introduces a dependent clause, as *who* in *We who knew him admired him.*

rel·a·tiv·i·ty (rel′ə·tiv′ə·tē) n. 1 The quality or condition of being relative; relativeness. 2 *Philos.* Existence viewed only as an object of, or in relation to, a thinking mind. 3 A condition of dependence or of close relation of one thing on or to another. 4 *Physics* The principle of the interdependence of matter, energy, space, and time, as mathematically formulated by Albert Einstein. The **special theory of relativity** states that the speed of light is the same in all frames of reference and that the same laws of physics hold in all frames of reference that are not accelerated. The **general theory of relativity** extends these principles to accelerated frames of reference and gravitational phenomena.

re·lax (ri·laks′) v.t. 1 To make lax or loose; make less tight or firm. 2 To make less stringent or severe, as discipline. 3 To abate; slacken, as efforts. 4 To relieve from strain or effort. —v.i. 5 To become lax or loose; loosen. 6 To become less stringent or severe. 7 To rest. 8 To unbend; become less formal. [< L *re*- again + *laxare* loosen] —re·lax′a·ble adj. —re·lax·a′tion, re·lax′er n.

re·lax·ant (ri·laks′ənt) adj. Pertaining to or causing relaxation. —n. A drug or other agent that reduces tension, esp. of muscles.

re·lay¹ (rē′lā) n. 1 A fresh set, as of men, horses, or dogs, to replace or relieve a tired set. 2 A supply of anything kept in store for anticipated use or need. 3 A relay race, or one of its laps or legs. 4 *Electr.* An electronically controlled switch. —v.t. (also ri·lā′) ·layed, ·lay·ing 1 To send onward by or as by relays. 2 To provide with relays. 3 *Telecom.* To retransmit (a message or signal). [< Ital. *rilasciare* leave behind]

re·lay² (rē′lā′) v.t. ·laid, ·lay·ing To lay again.

re·lay race (rē′lā) A race between teams, each runner of which runs only a set part of the course and is relieved by a teammate.

re·lease (ri·lēs′) v.t. **·leased, ·leas·ing** 1 To set free; liberate. 2 To deliver from worry, pain, obligation, etc. 3 To free from something that holds, binds, etc. 4 To permit the circulation, sale, performance, etc., of, as a motion picture, phonograph record, or news item. —n. 1 The act of releasing or setting free, or the state of being released. 2 A discharge from responsibility or penalty; also, a document authorizing this. 3 Law An instrument of conveyance by which one person surrenders and relinquishes all claims or rights to another person. 4 The releasing of something to the public; also, that which is released, as a news item, motion picture, etc. 5 Mech. Any catch or device to hold and release something. [< L relaxare relax] —re·leas′er n.

re·lease (rē′lēs′) v.t. **·leased, ·leas·ing** To lease again.

rel·e·gate (rel′ə·gāt) v.t. **·gat·ed, ·gat·ing** 1 To send off or consign, as to an obscure position or place. 2 To assign, as to a particular class or sphere. 3 To refer (a matter) to someone for decision, action, etc. 4 To banish; exile. [< L re- away, back + legare send] —rel′e·ga′tion n.

re·lent (ri·lent′) v.i. To soften in temper; become more gentle or compassionate. [< L relentescere grow soft]

re·lent·less (ri·lent′lis) adj. 1 Unremitting; continuous. 2 Not relenting; pitiless. —re·lent′less·ly adv. —re·lent′less·ness n.

rel·e·vant (rel′ə·vənt) adj. Fitting; pertinent; applicable. [< Med. L relevare bear upon] —rel′e·vance, rel′e·van·cy n. —rel′e·vant·ly adv.

re·li·a·ble (ri·lī′ə·bəl) adj. That may be relied upon; worthy of confidence. —re·li′a·bil′i·ty, re·li′a·ble·ness n. —re·li′a·bly adv. —Syn. trustworthy, dependable, loyal, constant.

re·li·ance (ri·lī′əns) n. 1 The act of relying. 2 Confidence; trust; dependence. 3 That upon which one relies.

re·li·ant (ri·lī′ənt) adj. 1 Having or manifesting reliance. 2 Dependent: with on. —re·li′ant·ly adv.

rel·ic (rel′ik) n. 1 Some remaining portion or fragment of that which has vanished or is destroyed. 2 A custom, habit, etc., from the past. 3 A keepsake or memento. 4 The body or part of the body of a saint, or any sacred memento. 5 pl. A corpse; remains. [< L reliquiae remains < relinquere leave]

re·lief (ri·lēf′) n. 1 The act of relieving, or the state of being relieved. 2 That which relieves. 3 Charitable aid, as money or food. 4 Release, as from a post or duty; also, the person or persons who take over for those released. 5 In architecture and sculpture, the projection of a figure, ornament, etc., from a surface; also, any such figure. 6 In painting, the apparent projection of forms and masses. 7 Geog. a The unevenness of land surface, as caused by mountains, hills, etc. b The parts of a map which portray such unevenness.

Relief def. 5

re·lieve (ri·lēv′) v.t. **·lieved, ·liev·ing** 1 To free wholly or partly from pain, stress, pressure, etc. 2 To lessen or alleviate, as pain or pressure. 3 To give aid or assistance to. 4 To free from obligation, injustice, etc. 5 To release from duty by providing a substitute. 6 To make less monotonous, harsh, or unpleasant; vary. 7 To bring into prominence; display by contrast. [< L relevare lift up] —re·liev′· a·ble adj. —re·liev′er n.

re·li·gion (ri·lij′ən) n. 1 A belief in a divine or superhuman power or principle, usu. thought of as the creator of all things. 2 The manifestation of such a belief in worship, ritual, conduct, etc. 3 Any system of religious faith or practice: the Jewish religion. 4 The religious or monastic life: to enter religion. 5 Anything that elicits devotion, zeal, dedication, etc.: Politics is his religion. [< L religio]

re·li·gi·os·i·ty (ri·lij′ē·os′ə·tē) n. The state or quality of being religious, esp. excessively or affectedly so.

re·li·gious (ri·lij′əs) adj. 1 Feeling and manifesting religion; devout; pious. 2 Of or pertaining to religion: a religious teacher. 3 Faithful and strict in performance; conscientious: a religious loyalty. 4 Belonging to the monastic life. —n. pl. **·ious** A monk or nun. —re·lig′ious·ly adv. —re·lig′ious·ness n.

re·lin·quish (ri·ling′kwish) v.t. 1 To give up; abandon. 2 To renounce: to relinquish a claim. 3 To let go (a hold or something held). [< L re- back, from + linquere leave] — re·lin′quish·er, re·lin′quish·ment n.

rel·i·quar·y (rel′ə·kwer′ē) n. pl. **·quar·ies** A casket, shrine, or other repository for relics. [< L reliquiae remains]

rel·ish (rel′ish) n. 1 Appetite; appreciation; liking. 2 The flavor, esp. when agreeable, in food and drink. 3 The quality in anything that lends spice or zest: Danger gives relish to adventure. 4 A savory food or condiment served with other food to lend it flavor or zest. 5 A hint, trace, or suggestion of some quality or characteristic. —v.t. 1 To like; enjoy: to relish a dinner or a joke. —v.i. 2 To have an agreeable flavor; afford gratification. [< OF relaisser leave behind] —rel′ish·a·ble adj.

re·live (rē·liv′) v.t. **·lived, ·liv·ing** To experience again, as in one's memory.

re·luc·tance (ri·luk′təns) n. 1 The state of being reluctant; unwillingness. 2 Electr. Capacity for opposing magnetic induction. Also **re·luc′tan·cy.**

re·luc·tant (ri·luk′tənt) adj. 1 Disinclined; unwilling. 2 Marked by unwillingness. [< L reluctari fight back] —re·luc′tant·ly adv.

re·ly (ri·lī′) v.i. **·lied, ·ly·ing** To place trust or confidence: with on or upon. [< L re- again + ligare to bind] —Syn. lean, depend, count, bank (all with on or upon).

re·main (ri·mān′) v.i. 1 To stay or be left behind after the removal, departure, or destruction of other persons or things. 2 To continue in one place, condition, or character. 3 To be left as something to be done, dealt with, etc. 4 To endure or last; abide. [< L re- back + manere stay, remain]

re·main·der (ri·mān′dər) n. 1 That which remains; something left over. 2 Math. a The result of subtraction; difference. b The difference of the product of the quotient and divisor subtracted from the dividend in division. 3 Law An estate in expectancy, but not in actual possession and enjoyment. 4 A copy or copies of a book remaining with a publisher after sales have fallen off or ceased. —adj. Left over; remaining. —v.t. To sell as a remainder (def. 4).

re·mains (ri·mānz′) n. pl. 1 That which is left after a part has been removed or destroyed; remnants. 2 A corpse. 3 Unpublished writings at the time of an author's death. 4 Survivals of the past, as fossils, monuments, etc.

re·make (rē·māk′) v.t. **·made, ·mak·ing** To make again or in a different form: to remake a silent film. —n. (rē′māk) Something that is remade, esp. a motion picture.

re·mand (ri·mand′, -mänd′) v.t. 1 To order or send back. 2 Law a To recommit to custody, as an accused person after a preliminary examination. b To send (a case) back to a lower court. —n. The act of remanding or the state of being remanded. [< L re- back + mandare to order] — re·mand′ment n.

re·mark (ri·märk′) n. 1 A comment or saying; casual observation. 2 The act of noticing, observing, or perceiving. —v.t. 1 To say or write by way of comment. 2 To take particular notice of. —v.i. 3 To make remarks: with on or upon. [< F re- again + marquer to mark] —re·mark′er n.

re·mark·a·ble (ri·mär′kə·bəl) adj. 1 Worthy of special notice. 2 Extraordinary; unusual. —re·mark′a·ble·ness n. —re·mark′a·bly adv.

re·me·di·a·ble (ri·mē′dē·ə·bəl) adj. Capable of being cured or remedied. —re·me′di·a·bly adv.

re·me·di·al (ri·mē′dē·əl) adj. Of the nature of or adapted to be used as a remedy: remedial measures. —re·me′di·al·ly adv.

rem·e·dy (rem′ə·dē) v.t. **·died, ·dy·ing** 1 To cure or heal, as by medicinal treatment. 2 To make right; repair; correct. 3 To overcome or remove (an evil or defect). —n. pl. **·dies** 1 A medicine or remedial treatment. 2 A means of correcting an evil, fault, etc. 3 Law A legal mode for enforcing

a right or redressing or preventing a wrong. [< L *re-* thoroughly + *mederi* heal, restore]

re·mem·ber (ri·mem′bər) *v.t.* **1** To bring back or present again to the mind or memory; recall. **2** To keep in mind carefully, as for a purpose. **3** To bear in mind with affection, respect, awe, etc. **4** To reward (someone) with a gift, legacy, tip, etc. —*v.i.* **5** To bring something back to or keep something in the mind. **6** To have or use one's memory. —**remember (one) to** To inform a person of the regard of: *Remember* me *to* your wife. [< L *re-* again + *memorare* bring to mind] —**re·mem′ber·er** *n.*

re·mem·brance (ri·mem′brəns) *n.* **1** The act or power of remembering or the state of being remembered. **2** The period within which one can remember. **3** That which is remembered. **4** A gift, memento, or keepsake. **5** An observance in commemoration.

re·mind (ri·mīnd′) *v.t.* To bring to (someone's) mind; cause to remember. —**re·mind′er** *n.* —**re·mind′ful** *adj.*

rem·i·nisce (rem′ə·nis′) *v.i.* ·**nisced**, ·**nisc·ing** To recall incidents or events of the past; indulge in reminiscences. [Back formation < REMINISCENCE]

rem·i·nis·cence (rem′ə·nis′əns) *n.* **1** The recalling to mind of past incidents and events. **2** A written or oral account of past experiences. **3** Anything that serves as a reminder of something else. [< L *reminisci* recollect] —**rem′i·nis′cent** *adj.* —**rem′i·nis′cent·ly** *adv.*

re·miss (ri·mis′) *adj.* Lax or careless in matters requiring attention; negligent. [< L *remittere* send back, slacken] —**re·miss′ness** *n.*

re·mis·si·ble (ri·mis′ə·bəl) *adj.* Capable of being remitted or pardoned, as sins. —**re·mis′si·bil′i·ty** *n.*

re·mis·sion (ri·mish′ən) *n.* **1** The act of remitting, or the state of being remitted. **2** Pardon, as of sins or a crime. **3** Release from a debt, penalty, or obligation. **4** Temporary abatement, as of pain, symptoms, etc.

re·mit (ri·mit′) *v.* ·**mit·ted**, ·**mit·ting** *v.t.* **1** To send, as money in payment for goods; transmit. **2** To refrain from exacting or inflicting, as a penalty. **3** To pardon; forgive. **4** To slacken; relax, as vigilance. **5** To restore; replace. **6** To put off; postpone. **7** *Law* To refer (a legal proceeding) to a lower court for further consideration. —*v.i.* **8** To send money, as in payment. **9** To diminish; abate. [< L *re-* back + *mittere* send] —**re·mit′ter** or **re·mit′tor** *n.*

re·mit·tal (ri·mit′l) *n.* REMISSION.

re·mit·tance (ri·mit′ns) *n.* **1** The act of remitting money or credit. **2** That which is remitted, as money.

re·mit·tent (ri·mit′nt) *adj.* Having temporary abatements: a *remittent* fever. —*n.* A remittent fever. [< L *remittere* remit] —**re·mit′tent·ly** *adv.*

rem·nant (rem′nənt) *n.* **1** That which remains of anything. **2** A piece of cloth, etc., left over after the last cutting. **3** A remaining trace or survival of anything: a *remnant* of faith. **4** A small remaining number or quantity, as of people. —*adj.* Remaining. [< OF *remaindre* remain]

re·mod·el (rē·mod′l) *v.t.* ·**eled** or ·**elled**, ·**el·ing** or ·**el·ling** **1** To model again. **2** To make over or anew.

re·mon·e·tize (rē·mon′ə·tīz) *v.t.* ·**tized**, ·**tiz·ing** To reinstate, esp. silver, as lawful money. [< RE- + L *moneta* money + -IZE] —**re·mon′e·ti·za′tion** *n.*

re·mon·strance (ri·mon′strəns) *n.* The act or an instance of remonstrating; protest.

re·mon·strant (ri·mon′strənt) *adj.* Protesting or opposing; expostulatory. —*n.* One who remonstrates.

re·mon·strate (ri·mon′strāt) *v.* ·**strat·ed**, ·**strat·ing** *v.t.* **1** To say or plead in protest or opposition. —*v.i.* **2** To protest; object. [< L *re-* again + *monstrare* show] —**re·mon·stra·tion** (rē′mon·strā′shən, rem′ən-), **re·mon′stra′tor** *n.* —**re·mon′·stra·tive** (-strə·tiv) *adj.*

re·morse (ri·môrs′) *n.* The keen or hopeless anguish caused by a sense of guilt; distressing self-reproach. [< LL *remorsus* a biting back] —**re·morse′ful** *adj.* —**re·morse′ful·ly** *adv.* —**re·morse′ful·ness** *n.*

re·morse·less (ri·môrs′lis) *adj.* Having no remorse or compassion. —**re·morse′less·ly** *adv.* —**re·morse′less·ness** *n.* —**Syn.** pitiless, cruel, merciless, ruthless.

re·mote (ri·mōt′) *adj.* **1** Located far from a specified place. **2** Removed far from present time. **3** Having slight bearing on or connection with: a problem *remote* from our discussion. **4** Distant in relation: a *remote* cousin. **5** Not

obvious; faint; slight: a *remote* likeness. **6** Cold; aloof: a *remote* manner. [< L *remotus,* p.p. of *removere* remove] —**re·mote′ly** *adv.* —**re·mote′ness** *n.*

remote control Control from a distance, as of a machine, apparatus, aircraft, etc.

re·mount (rē·mount′) *v.t.* & *v.i.* To mount again or anew. —*n.* (rē′mount′) **1** A new setting or framing. **2** A fresh riding horse.

re·mov·a·ble (ri·mōō′və·bəl) *adj.* Capable of being removed. —**re·mov′a·bil′i·ty, re·mov′a·ble·ness** *n.*

re·mov·al (ri·mōō′vəl) *n.* **1** The act of removing or the state of being removed. **2** Dismissal, as from office. **3** Changing of place, esp. of habitation.

re·move (ri·mōōv′) *v.* ·**moved**, ·**mov·ing** *v.t.* **1** To take or move away or from one place to another. **2** To take off. **3** To get rid of; do away with: to *remove* abuses. **4** To kill. **5** To displace or dismiss, as from office. **6** To take out; extract: with *from.* —*v.i.* **7** To change one's place of residence or business. **8** To go away; depart. —*n.* **1** The act of removing. **2** The distance or degree of difference between things: He is only one *remove* from a fool. [< L *re-* again + *movere* move] —**re·mov′er** *n.*

re·moved (ri·mōōvd′) *adj.* Separated, as by intervening space, time, or relationship, or by difference in kind: a cousin twice *removed.* —**re·mov·ed·ness** (ri·mōō′vid·nis) *n.*

re·mu·ner·ate (ri·myōō′nə·rāt) *v.t.* ·**at·ed**, ·**at·ing** **1** To pay (a person) for something, as for services, losses, etc. **2** To compensate or reward for (work, diligence, etc.). [< L *remunerari*] —**re·mu′ner·a′tion, re·mu′ner·a′tor** *n.* —**re·mu′·ner·a·tive** (-nər·ə·tiv, -nə·rā′tiv) *adj.* —**re·mu′ner·a·tive·ly** *adv.*

Re·mus (rē′məs) *Rom. Myth.* The twin brother of Romulus, by whom he was killed.

ren·ais·sance (ren′ə·säns′, -zäns′, ri·nā′səns) *n.* A new birth; resurrection; renascence. [F < *renaître* be reborn]

Ren·ais·sance (ren′ə·säns′, -zäns′, ri·nā′səns) *n.* **1** The revival of letters and art in Europe, marking the transition from the medieval to the modern world. **2** The period of this revival, from the 14th to the 16th century. **3** The style of art, literature, etc., marked by a classical influence, that was developed in and characteristic of this period. —*adj.* **1** Of, pertaining to, or characteristic of the Renaissance. **2** Pertaining to a style of architecture originating in Italy in the 15th century and based on the classical Roman style.

re·nal (rē′nəl) *adj.* Of or situated near the kidneys. [< L *renes* kidneys]

re·nas·cence (ri·nās′əns, -nas′-) *n.* A rebirth; revival. [< L *re-* again + *nasci* be born] —**re·nas′cent** *adj.*

Re·nas·cence (ri·nās′əns, -nas′-) *n.* RENAISSANCE.

rend (rend) *v.* **rent** or **rend·ed**, **rend·ing** *v.t.* **1** To tear apart forcibly. **2** To pull or remove forcibly: with *away, from, off,* etc. **3** To pass through (the air) violently and noisily. **4** To distress (the heart, etc.), as with grief or despair. —*v.i.* **5** To split; part. [< OE *rendan* tear, cut down] —**rend′er** *n.*

ren·der (ren′dər) *v.t.* **1** To give, present, or submit for action, approval, payment, etc. **2** To provide or furnish; give: to *render* aid. **3** To give as due: to *render* obedience. **4** To perform; do: to *render* great service. **5** To give or state formally. **6** To give by way of requital or retribution: to *render* good for evil. **7** To represent or depict, as in music or painting. **8** To cause to be: to *render* someone helpless. **9** To express in another language; translate. **10** To melt and clarify, as fat. **11** To give back; return: often with *back.* **12** To surrender; give up. [< L *reddere* give back] —**ren′der·a·ble** *adj.* —**ren′der·er** *n.*

ren·dez·vous (rän′dā·vōō, -də-) *n. pl.* ·**vous** (-vōōz) **1** An appointed place of meeting. **2** A meeting or an appointment to meet. —*v.t.* & *v.i.* ·**voused** (-vōōd), ·**vous·ing** (-vōō′ing) To assemble or cause to assemble at a certain place or time. [< F *rendez-vous,* lit., betake yourself]

ren·di·tion (ren·dish′ən) *n.* **1** A version or interpretation of a text. **2** A performance or interpretation, as of a musical composition, role, etc. **3** The act of rendering. [< OF *rendre* render]

ren·e·gade (ren′ə·gād) *n.* **1** One who abandons a previous loyalty, as to a religion, political party, etc. **2** One who gives up conventional or lawful behavior. —*adj.* Traitorous. [< Sp. *renegar* deny]

re·nege (ri·nig′, -neg′, -nēg′) v.i. **-neged, -neg·ing 1** In card games, to fail to follow suit when able or required by rule to do so. **2** To fail to fulfill a promise. [< L re- again + negare deny] —**re·neg′er** n.

re·new (ri·nyōo′) v.t. **1** To make new or as if new again. **2** To begin again; resume. **3** To repeat: to renew an oath. **4** To regain (vigor, strength, etc.). **5** To cause to continue in effect; extend: to renew a subscription. **6** To revive; reestablish. **7** To replenish or replace, as provisions. —v.i. **8** To become new again. **9** To begin or commence again. [< RE- + NEW] —**re·new′a·ble** adj. —**re·new′al, re·new′er** n. —**re·new′ed·ly** adv.

ren·i·form (ren′ə·fôrm, rē′nə-) adj. Kidney-shaped. [< L renes kidneys + -FORM]

ren·net (ren′it) n. **1** The mucous membrane lining the fourth stomach of a suckling calf or lamb. **2** An extract of this, used to curdle milk in making cheese, etc. **3** RENNIN. [< OE rinnan run together, coagulate]

ren·nin (ren′in) n. **1** A milk-curdling enzyme present in gastric juice. **2** This enzyme in partially purified form obtained from rennet.

re·nounce (ri·nouns′) v.t. **-nounced, -nounc·ing 1** To give up, esp. by formal statement. **2** To disown; repudiate. [< L renuntiare protest against] —**re·nounce′ment, re·nounc′· er** n. —**Syn. 1** abjure, disavow, disclaim, forswear.

ren·o·vate (ren′ə·vāt) v.t. **-vat·ed, -vat·ing 1** To make as good as new, as by repairing, cleaning, etc. **2** To renew; refresh; reinvigorate. [< L re- again + novare make new] —**ren′o·va′tion, ren′o·va′tor** n.

re·nown (ri·noun′) n. The state of being widely known for great achievements; fame. [< L re- again + nominare to name] —**re·nowned′** adj.

rent[1] (rent) n. Compensation, esp. payment in money, made by a tenant to a landlord or owner for the use of property, as land, a house, etc., usu. due at specified intervals. —**for rent** Available in return for a rent. —v.t. **1** To obtain the temporary possession and use of in return for paying rent. **2** To grant the temporary use of for a rent. —v.i. **3** To be let for rent. [< L reddita what is given back or paid] —**rent′a·ble** adj. —**rent′er** n.

rent[2] (rent) A p.t. & p.p. of REND. —n. **1** A hole or slit made by rending or tearing. **2** A violent separation; schism.

rent·al (ren′təl) n. **1** An amount paid or due to be paid as rent. **2** The revenue derived from rented property. **3** The act of renting. —adj. **1** Of or pertaining to rent. **2** Engaged in the business of renting or supervising rents.

re·nun·ci·a·tion (ri·nun′sē·ā′shən, -shē-) n. **1** The act of renouncing; repudiation. **2** A declaration in which something is renounced. —**re·nun′ci·a′tive** (-sē·ā′tiv), **re·nun′ci· a·to′ry** adj.

re·o·pen (rē·ō′pən) v.t. & v.i. **1** To open again. **2** To begin again; resume.

re·or·gan·i·za·tion (rē′ôr·gən·ə·zā′shən, -ī·zā′-) n. **1** The act of reorganizing. **2** The legal reconstruction of a corporation, usu. to avert a failure.

re·or·gan·ize (rē·ôr′gən·īz) v.t. & v.i. **-ized, -iz·ing** To organize anew. —**re·or′gan·iz′er** n.

rep[1] (rep) n. A silk, cotton, rayon, or wool fabric having a crosswise rib. [< F reps]

rep[2] (rep) n. Slang **1** REPERTORY. **2** REPRESENTATIVE. **3** REPUTATION.

Rep. Representative; Republic; Republican.

re·pair[1] (ri·pâr′) v.t. **1** To restore to sound or good condition after damage, injury, decay, etc. **2** To make up, as a loss; compensate for. —n. **1** The act or instance of repairing. **2** Condition after use or after repairing: in good repair. [< L re- again + parare prepare] —**re·pair′er** n.

re·pair[2] (ri·pâr′) v.i. To betake oneself; go: to repair to the garden. [< LL repatriare repatriate]

re·pair·man (ri·pâr′man′, -mən) n. pl. **-men** (-men′, -mən) A man whose work is to make repairs.

rep·a·ra·ble (rep′ər·ə·bəl) adj. Capable of being repaired. —**rep′a·ra·bly** adv.

rep·a·ra·tion (rep′ə·rā′shən) n. **1** The act of making amends; atonement. **2** That which is done or paid by way of making amends. **3** pl. Indemnities paid by defeated

countries for acts of war. **4** The act of repairing, or the state of being repaired. —**re·par·a·tive** (ri·par′ə·tiv) adj.

rep·ar·tee (rep′är·tē′, -ər-, -tā′) n. **1** Conversation marked by quick and witty replies. **2** Skill in such conversation. **3** A witty reply. [< F re- again + partir depart]

re·past (ri·past′, -päst′, rē′past) n. Food taken at a meal; a meal. [< LL repascere feed again]

re·pa·tri·ate (rē·pā′trē·āt) v.t. & v.i. **-at·ed, -at·ing** To send back to the country of birth, citizenship, or allegiance, as prisoners of war. —n. (rē·pā′trē·it) A person who has been repatriated. [< L re- again + patria native land] —**re·pa′· tri·a′tion** n.

re·pay (ri·pā′) v. **-paid, -pay·ing** v.t. **1** To pay back; refund. **2** To pay back or refund something to. **3** To make compensation or retaliation for. —v.i. **4** To make repayment or requital. —**re·pay′ment** n.

re·peal (ri·pēl′) v.t. To withdraw the authority to effect; rescind; revoke. —n. The act of repealing; revocation. [< OF rapeler recall] —**re·peal′a·ble** adj. —**re·peal′er** n.

re·peat (ri·pēt′) v.t. **1** To say again; reiterate. **2** To recite

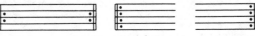

Repeats def. 2a

from memory. **3** To say (what another has just said). **4** To tell, as a secret, to another. **5** To do, make, or experience again. —v.i. **6** To say or do something again. **7** To vote more than once at the same election. —n. **1** The act of repeating. **2** Music **a** A sign indicating that a passage is to be repeated. **b** A passage meant to be repeated. [< L repetere do or say again] —**re·peat′a·ble** adj.

re·peat·ed (ri·pē′tid) adj. Occurring or spoken again and again. —**re·peat′ed·ly** adv.

re·peat·er (ri·pē′tər) n. **1** One who or that which repeats. **2** A firearm that can discharge several shots without being reloaded. **3** One who illegally votes more than once at the same election. **4** One who has been repeatedly imprisoned for criminal offenses.

re·pel (ri·pel′) v. **-pelled, -pel·ling** v.t. **1** To force or drive back; repulse. **2** To reject; refuse, as a suggestion. **3** To cause to feel distaste or aversion. **4** To fail to mix with or adhere to. —v.i. **5** To act so as to drive something back or away. **6** To cause distaste or aversion. [< L re- back + pellere drive] —**re·pel′ler** n.

re·pel·lent (ri·pel′ənt) adj. **1** Serving, tending, or having power to repel. **2** Exciting disgust; repugnant; repulsive. —n. Something that repels, as a substance that repels water, insects, etc. —**re·pel′len·cy, re·pel′lence** n.

re·pent (ri·pent′) v.i. **1** To feel remorse or regret, as for something done or undone; be contrite. **2** To change one's mind concerning past action: with of. —v.t. **3** To feel remorse or regret for (an action, sin, etc.). [< L re- again + poenitere cause to repent] —**re·pent′er** n.

re·pen·tance (ri·pen′təns) n. The act of repenting; sorrow for having done wrong. —**re·pen′tant** adj. —**re·pen′tant· ly** adv.

re·per·cus·sion (rē′pər·kush′ən) n. **1** Usu. pl. A long-range or unpredictable result, as of an event; aftereffect. **2** A reverberation; echo. [< L repercussus, p.p. of repercutere rebound] —**re′per·cus′sive** adj.

rep·er·toire (rep′ər·twär′) n. **1** A list of works, as of music or drama, that a company or person is prepared to perform. **2** Such works collectively. **3** The aggregate of devices, methods, etc., used in a particular line of activity: the teacher's repertoire of visual aids. [< LL repertorium inventory]

rep·er·to·ry (rep′ər·tôr′ē, -tō′rē) n. pl. **-ries 1** A theatrical group having a repertoire of productions: also **repertory company, repertory theater. 2** REPERTOIRE. **3** A place where things are gathered in readiness for use. [< L repertus, p.p. of reperire find, discover]

rep·e·ti·tion (rep′ə·tish′ən) n. **1** The doing, making, or saying of something again. **2** That which is repeated; a copy. —**re·pet·i·tive** (ri·pet′ə·tiv) adj. —**re·pet′i·tive·ly** adv.

rep·e·ti·tious (rep′ə·tish′əs) adj. Characterized by or

containing repetition, esp. useless or tedious repetition. —**rep′e·ti′tious·ly** *adv.* —**rep′e·ti′tious·ness** *n.*

re·pine (ri·pīn′) *v.i.* **·pined, ·pin·ing** To be discontented or fretful. [< RE- + PINE²] —**re·pin′er** *n.*

re·place (ri·plās′) *v.t.* **·placed, ·plac·ing 1** To put back in place. **2** To take or fill the place of; supersede. **3** To refund; repay. —**re·place′a·ble** *adj.* —**re·plac′er** *n.*

re·place·ment (ri·plās′mənt) *n.* **1** The act of replacing, or the state of being replaced. **2** Something used to replace, as a substitute.

re·play (rē·plā′) *v.t.* **1** To play again. **2** To show a replay of. —*n.* (rē′plā′) **1** The act of playing again. **2** The playing of a television tape, often in slow motion and usu. immediately following the live occurrence of the action shown. **3** The action shown in such a replay.

re·plen·ish (ri·plen′ish) *v.t.* **1** To fill again. **2** To bring back to fullness or completeness, as diminished supplies. [< L *re-* again + *plenus* full] —**re·plen′ish·er, re·plen′ish·ment** *n.*

re·plete (ri·plēt′) *adj.* **1** Full to the uttermost. **2** Gorged with food or drink; sated. **3** Abundantly supplied or stocked. [< L *repletus,* p.p. of *replere* fill again] —**re·ple′·tion, re·plete′ness** *n.*

rep·li·ca (rep′lə·kə) *n.* **1** A duplicate, as of a picture, executed by the original artist. **2** Any close copy or reproduction. [< L *replicare* to reply]

rep·li·cate (rep′lə·kāt) *v.t.* **·cat·ed, ·cat·ing 1** To make an indeterminate number of copies of; duplicate. **2** To fold over. —**rep′li·ca′tion** *n.*

re·ply (ri·plī′) *v.* **·plied, ·ply·ing** *v.i.* **1** To give an answer. **2** To respond by some act, gesture, etc. **3** To echo. **4** *Law* To file a pleading in answer to the statement of the defense. —*v.t.* **5** To say in answer: She *replied* that she would do it. —*n. pl.* **·plies** Something said, written, or done by way of answer. [< L *replicare* fold back, make a reply] —**re·pli′er** *n.*

re·port (ri·pôrt′, -pōrt′) *v.t.* **1** To make or give an account of; relate, as information obtained by investigation. **2** To bear back or repeat to another, as an answer. **3** To complain about, esp. to the authorities. **4** To state the result of consideration concerning: The committee *reported* the bill. —*v.i.* **5** To make a report. **6** To act as a reporter. **7** To present oneself, as for duty. —*n.* **1** That which is reported. **2** A formal statement of the result of an investigation. **3** Common talk; rumor. **4** Fame, reputation, or character. **5** A record of the transactions of a deliberative body. **6** An account prepared for publication in the press. **7** An explosive sound: the *report* of a gun. [< L *re-* back + *portare* carry] —**re·port′a·ble** *adj.* —**Syn** *v.* **1** describe, record, transcribe. *n.* **1, 2, 5, 6** account, statement, announcement. **3** gossip, hearsay.

re·port·age (ri·pôr′tij, -pōr′-, rep′ôr·täzh′) *n.* **1** The act or art of reporting, as for publication. **2** Reports that deal with events in a journalistic style. [F]

report card A periodic statement of a pupil's scholastic record.

re·port·ed·ly (ri·pôr′tid·lē, -pōr′-) *adv.* According to report.

re·port·er (ri·pôr′tər, -pōr′-) *n.* **1** One who reports. **2** One employed to gather and report news for publication or broadcasting. —**rep·or·to·ri·al** (rep′ər·tôr′ē·əl, -tō′rē-) *adj.*

re·pose¹ (ri·pōz′) *n.* **1** The state of being at rest. **2** Sleep. **3** Freedom from excitement or anxiety; composure. **4** Dignified calmness; serenity; peacefulness. —*v.* **·posed, ·pos·ing** *v.t.* **1** To lay or place in a position of rest. —*v.i.* **2** To lie at rest. **3** To lie in death. **4** To rely; depend: with *on, upon,* or *in.* [< LL *re-* again + *pausare* to pause] —**re·pose′ful** *adj.* —**re·pose′ful·ly** *adv.*

re·pose² (ri·pōz′) *v.t.* **·posed, ·pos·ing** To place, as confidence or hope: with *in.* [< L *repositus,* p.p. of *reponere* put back]

re·pos·i·to·ry (ri·poz′ə·tôr′ē, -tō′rē) *n. pl.* **·ries 1** A place in which goods may be stored; a depository. **2** Anything considered as a place of storage or assembly: a *repository* of Indian lore. **3** A person to whom a secret is entrusted. [< L *repositorium*]

re·pos·sess (rē′pə·zes′) *v.t.* To regain possession of, esp. as a result of the default of payments due. —**re′pos·ses′·sion** *n.*

rep·re·hend (rep′ri·hend′) *v.t.* To criticize sharply; find fault with. [< L *re-* back + *prehendere* hold] —**rep′re·hen′·sion** *n.* —**rep′re·hen′sive** *adj.* —**rep′re·hen′sive·ly** *adv.*

rep·re·hen·si·ble (rep′ri·hen′sə·bəl) *adj.* Deserving blame or censure. —**rep′re·hen′si·bil′i·ty, rep′re·hen′si·ble·ness** *n.* —**rep′re·hen′si·bly** *adv.*

rep·re·sent (rep′ri·zent′) *v.t.* **1** To serve as the symbol, expression, or designation of; symbolize: The dove *represents* peace. **2** To serve as an example, specimen, type, etc., of; typify: They *represent* the best in America. **3** To set forth a likeness or image of; depict; portray. **4** To serve as or be the delegate, agent, etc., of, as by legal authority or by election. **5** To act the part of; impersonate. **6** To bring before the mind; present clearly: Goya etchings that *represent* the horrors of war. **7** To set forth in words, esp. in a forceful and persuasive manner. **8** To describe as being of a specified character or condition: to *represent* a signature as authentic. [< L *re-* again + *praesentare* to present]

rep·re·sen·ta·tion (rep′ri·zen·tā′shən) *n.* **1** The act of representing, or the state of being represented. **2** A likeness or model. **3** A statement usu. purporting to be descriptive that represents a point of view and is intended to influence judgment. **4** A dramatic performance. **5** Representatives collectively.

rep·re·sen·ta·tive (rep′ri·zen′tə·tiv) *adj.* **1** Typifying a group or class. **2** Acting or having the power to act as an agent. **3** Made up of representatives. **4** Based on the political principle of representation. **5** Presenting, portraying, or representing. —*n.* **1** One who or that which is typical of a group or class. **2** One who is authorized as an agent or delegate. **3** *Often cap.* A member of a legislative body, esp., in the U.S., a member of the lower house of Congress or of a state legislature. —**rep′re·sen′ta·tive·ly** *adv.* —**rep′re·sen′ta·tive·ness** *n.*

re·press (ri·pres′) *v.t.* **1** To keep under restraint or control. **2** To block the expression of: to *repress* a groan. **3** To put down; quell, as a rebellion. [< L *repressus,* p.p. of *reprimere* press back] —**re·press′er, re·pres′sive·ness** *n.* —**re·press′i·ble, re·pres′sive** *adj.* —**re·pres′sive·ly** *adv.* —**Syn. 1** curb, rein. **2** suppress, hold in.

re·pres·sion (ri·presh′ən) *n.* **1** The act of repressing, or the condition of being repressed. **2** *Psychoanal.* The exclusion from consciousness of painful desires, memories, etc., and consequent manifestation through the unconscious.

re·prieve (ri·prēv′) *v.t.* **·prieved, ·priev·ing 1** To suspend temporarily the execution of a sentence upon. **2** To relieve for a time from suffering or trouble. —*n.* **1** The temporary suspension of a sentence. **2** Temporary relief or cessation of pain; respite. [< F *reprendre* take back]

rep·ri·mand (rep′rə·mand) *v.t.* To reprove sharply or formally. —*n.* Severe reproof or formal censure. [< L *reprimendus* to be repressed]

re·print (rē′print′) *n.* A printing that is an exact copy of a work already printed. —*v.t.* (rē·print′) To print again, esp. without alteration. —**re·print′er** *n.*

re·pri·sal (ri·prī′zəl) *n.* Any action done in retaliation for harm or injuries received, esp. an action involving the use of force and sanctioned by a government or political group. [< OF *reprendre* take back]

re·proach (ri·prōch′) *v.t.* To charge with or blame for something wrong; rebuke. —*n.* **1** The act of or an expression of reproaching; censure; reproof. **2** A cause of blame or disgrace. **3** Disgrace; discredit. [< OF *reprochier*] —**re·proach′ful** *adj.* —**re·proach′ful·ly** *adv.* —**re·proach′ful·ness** *n.*

rep·ro·bate (rep′rə·bāt) *adj.* **1** Utterly depraved; profligate; corrupt. **2** *Theol.* Abandoned in sin; condemned. —*n.* One who is reprobate. —*v.t.* **·bat·ed, ·bat·ing 1** To disapprove of heartily; condemn. **2** *Theol.* To abandon to damnation. [< LL *reprobare* reprove] —**rep′ro·ba′tion** *n.* —**rep′·ro·ba′tive** *adj.*

re·pro·duce (rē′prə·d^yōos′) *v.* **·duced, ·duc·ing** *v.t.* **1** To make a copy or image of. **2** To bring (offspring) into existence by sexual or asexual generation. **3** To replace (a lost part or organ) by regeneration. **4** To cause the reproduction of (plant life, etc.). **5** To produce again. **6** To recall to the mind; recreate mentally. —*v.i.* **7** To produce offspring. **8** To undergo copying, reproduction, etc. —**re′pro·duc′er** *n.* —**re′pro·duc′i·ble** *adj.*

re·pro·duc·tion (rē′prə·duk′shən) n. 1 The act or process of reproducing. 2 Any process by which animals or plants give rise to new organisms. 3 Something reproduced, as a photocopy. —**re′pro·duc′tive** adj. —**re′pro·duc′· tive·ly** adv. —**re′pro·duc′tive·ness** n.

re·prog·ra·phy (rē·prog′rə·fē) n. The reproduction of graphic material, esp. by electronic devices.

re·proof (ri·proof′) n. The act or an expression of reproving; censure.

re·prove (ri·proov′) v.t. **·proved, ·prov·ing** 1 To censure, as for a fault; rebuke. 2 To express disapproval of (an act). [< L re- again + probare to test]—**re·prov′er** n.—**re·prov′ing· ly** adv. —**Syn.** 1 admonish, chasten, chide, reproach, scold.

rep·tile (rep′tīl, -til) n. 1 Any of a class of cold-blooded, air-breathing verte- brates having a scaly skin, as crocodiles, liz- ards, snakes, turtles, etc. 2 A groveling, ab- ject person. —adj. 1 Of, like, or character- istic of a reptile. 2 Groveling, sly, base, etc. [< L reptus, p.p. of repere creep]—**rep·til·i·an** (rep·til′ē·ən) adj., n.

Reptile (crocodile)

re·pub·lic (ri·pub′lik) n. 1 A state in which the sover- eignty resides in the people entitled to vote for officers who represent them in governing. 2 This form of govern- ment. [< L res thing + publicus public]

re·pub·li·can (ri·pub′li·kən) adj. Pertaining to, of the na- ture of, or suitable for a republic. —n. An advocate of a republican form of government. —**re·pub′li·can·ism** n.

Re·pub·li·can (ri·pub′li·kən) n. A member of the Repub- lican Party in the U.S. —**Re·pub′li·can·ism** n.

Republican Party One of the two major political par- ties in the U.S.

re·pu·di·ate (re·pyoo′dē·āt) v.t. **·at·ed, ·at·ing** 1 To refuse to accept as valid, true, or authorized; reject. 2 To refuse to acknowledge or pay. 3 To cast off; disown, as a son. [< L repudium divorce]—**re·pu′di·a′tion, re·pu′di·a′tor** n.

re·pug·nance (ri·pug′nəns) n. 1 A feeling of strong dis- taste or aversion. 2 Contradiction; inconsistency.

re·pug·nant (ri·pug′nənt) adj. 1 Offensive to taste or feel- ing; exciting aversion. 2 Contradictory; inconsistent. [< L re back + pugnare to fight]—**re·pug′nant·ly** adv.

re·pulse (ri·puls′) v.t. **·pulsed, ·puls·ing** 1 To drive back; repel, as an attacking force. 2 To repel by coldness, dis- courtesy, etc.; rebuff. 3 To excite disgust in. —n. 1 The act of repulsing, or the state of being repulsed. 2 Rejection; refusal. [< L repulsus, p.p. of repellere repel]—**re·puls′er** n.

re·pul·sion (ri·pul′shən) n. 1 The act of repelling, or the state of being repelled. 2 Aversion; repugnance. 3 Physics The mutual action of two bodies that tends to drive them apart.

re·pul·sive (ri·pul′siv) adj. 1 Exciting strong feelings of dislike or disgust; offensive. 2 Such as to discourage ap- proach; forbidding. 3 Acting to repulse. —**re·pul′sive·ly** adv. —**re·pul′sive·ness** n.

rep·u·ta·ble (rep′yə·tə·bəl) adj. 1 Having a good reputa- tion; estimable; honorable. 2 Complying with the usage of the best writers. —**rep′u·ta·bil′i·ty** n.—**rep′u·ta·bly** adv.

rep·u·ta·tion (rep′yə·tā′shən) n. 1 The general estima- tion in which a person or thing is held by others, either good or bad. 2 High regard or esteem. 3 A particular credit ascribed to a person or thing: a reputation for honesty. [< L reputare be reputed.]

re·pute (ri·pyoot′) v.t. **·put·ed, ·put·ing** To regard or con- sider: usu. in the passive: reputed to be clever. —n. REPU- TATION (defs. 1 & 2). [< L re- again + putare think, count]

re·put·ed (ri·pyoo′tid) adj. Generally thought or sup- posed. —**re·put′ed·ly** adv.

re·quest (ri·kwest′) v.t. 1 To express a desire for, esp. politely. 2 To ask a favor of. —n. 1 The act of requesting; entreaty; petition. 2 That which is requested, as a favor. 3 The state of being requested: in request. [< L requisitus, p.p. of requirere seek again]

re·qui·em (rek′wē·əm, rē′kwē-) n. 1 Often cap. Any musi- cal composition or service for the dead. 2 Often cap. A musical setting for such a service. [< L Requiem rest, the first word of a Roman Catholic mass for the dead]

req·ui·es·cat (rek′wē·es′kat) n. A prayer for the repose of the dead. [L, may he (or she) rest]

re·quire (ri·kwīr′) v. **·quired, ·quir·ing** v.t. 1 To have need of; find necessary. 2 To call for, demand: Hunting requires patience. 3 To insist upon: to require absolute silence. 4 To command; order. —v.i. 5 To make a demand or request. [< L re- again + quaerere ask, seek]—**re·quir′er** n.

re·quire·ment (ri·kwīr′mənt) n. 1 That which is re- quired, as to satisfy a condition; a requisite. 2 A need or necessity.

req·ui·site (rek′wə·zit) adj. Required by the nature of things or by circumstances; indispensable. —n. That which cannot be dispensed with. —**req′ui·site·ly** adv. — **req′ui·site·ness** n.

req·ui·si·tion (rek′wə·zish′ən) n. 1 A formal request, as for supplies or equipment. 2 The act of requiring or de- manding, as that something be supplied. 3 The state of being required. —v.t. To make a requisition for or to.

re·qui·tal (ri·kwīt′l) n. 1 The act of requiting. 2 Adequate return for good or ill; reward, compensation, or retalia- tion.

re·quite (ri·kwīt′) v.t. **·quit·ed, ·quit·ing** 1 To make equiva- lent return for, as kindness, service, or injury. 2 To com- pensate or repay in kind. [< RE- + quite, obs. var. of QUIT] —**re·quit′er** n.

rere·dos (rir′ə dos, rer′ə-, rir′dos) n. An ornamental screen behind an altar. [< OF arere at the back + dos back]

re·run (rē′run′) n. A running over again, esp. a showing of a film of videotape after the initial showing. —v.t. (rē· run′) **·ran, ·run·ning** To run again.

res. research; reserve; residence; resolution.

re·scind (ri·sind′) v.t. To cancel or make void, as an order or an act. [< L re- back + scindere to cut]—**re·scind′ment, re·scind′er** n.

re·scis·sion (ri·sizh′ən) n. The act of rescinding. —**re· scis′si·ble, re·scis′so·ry** adj.

res·cue (res′kyoo) v.t. **·cued, ·cu·ing** 1 To save or free from danger, captivity, evil, etc. 2 Law To take or remove forci- bly from the custody of the law. —n. The act of rescuing. [< L re- again + excutere shake off]—**res′cu·er** n.

re·search (ri·sûrch′, rē′sûrch) n. Studious, systematic investigation or inquiry to ascertain, uncover, or assem- ble facts, used as a basis for conclusions or the formula- tion of theory. —v.t. 1 To do research on or for: to research an article. —v.i. 2 To do research; investigate. [< F recher- che]—**re·search′er** n.

re·sect (ri·sekt′) v.t. To perform a resection on. [< L re- back + secare cut, amputate]

re·sec·tion (ri·sek′shən) n. The surgical removal of a part of a bone, organ, etc.

re·sem·blance (ri·zem′bləns) n. 1 The quality of similarlity in nature, appearance, etc.; likeness. 2 A point or degree of similarity. 3 That which resembles a person or thing; semblance.

re·sem·ble (ri·zem′bəl) v.t. **·bled, ·bling** To be similar to in appearance, quality, or character. [< OF re- again + sem- bler seem]

re·sent (ri·zent′) v.t. To be indignant at, as an injury or insult. [< L re- again + sentire feel] —**re·sent′ful** adj. —**re· sent′ful·ly** adv. —**re·sent′ful·ness** n.

re·sent·ment (ri·zent′mənt) n. Anger and ill will caused by a feeling of injury or mistreatment.

res·er·va·tion (rez′ər·vā′shən) n. 1 A feeling of doubt or skepticism, expressed or unexpressed. 2 A qualification; condition; limitation. 3 An agreement to hold something back, as a hotel room, restaurant table, etc., for use at a particular time; also, a record of such an agreement. 4 The act of reserving. 5 A tract of public land set aside for some special purpose, as for the use of Indians or for the preser- vation of wildlife.

re·serve (ri·zûrv′) v.t. **·served, ·serv·ing,** 1 To hold back or set aside for special or future use. 2 To arrange for ahead

of time; have set aside for one's use. **3** To hold back or delay the determination or disclosure of: to *reserve* judgment. **4** To keep as one's own; retain: to *reserve* the right to quit. —*n.* **1** Something stored up for future use or set aside for a particular purpose. **2** A restrained quality of character or manner; reluctance to divulge one's feelings, thoughts, etc. **3** *Usu. pl.* **a** A military force held back from active duty to meet possible emergencies. **b** Members or units of such a force. **4** A substitute player on an athletic team. **5** Funds held back from investment, as in a bank, to meet regular demands. **6** The act of reserving; stint; qualification: without *reserve.* —**in reserve** Subject to or held for future use when needed. —*adj.* Constituting a reserve: a *reserve* supply. [< L *re-* back + *servare* keep] — **re·serv′er** *n.* —**Syn.** *n.* **2** reticence, diffidence, aloofness, modesty, restraint.

reserve clause In professional sports, the stipulation in a contract that commits a player to work for a particular team until released or traded by the employer or until retirement.

re·served (ri·zûrvd′) *adj.* **1** Showing or characterized by reserve of manner; undemonstrative. **2** Kept in reserve; held ready for use. —**re·serv·ed·ly** (ri·zûr′vid·lē) *adv.* —**re·serv′ed·ness** *n.*

re·serv·ist (ri·zûr′vist) *n.* A member of a military reserve.

res·er·voir (rez′ər·vwär, -vwôr -vôr) *n.* **1** A place where some material is stored for use, esp. a lake, usu. artificial, for collecting and storing water. **2** A receptacle for a fluid. **3** An extra supply; store.

re·shape (rē·shāp′) *v.t.* **·shaped, ·shap·ing** To give new form to; reorder the elements or structure of.

re·side (ri·zīd′) *v.i.* **·sid·ed, ·sid·ing** **1** To dwell for a considerable time; live. **2** To exist as an attribute or quality: with *in.* **3** To be vested: with *in.* [< L *residere* sit back]

res·i·dence (rez′ə·dəns) *n.* **1** The place or the house where one resides. **2** The act of residing. **3** The length of time one resides in a place. **4** The act or fact of residing. **5** The condition of residing in a particular place to perform certain duties or to pursue studies, often for a specified length of time.

res·i·den·cy (rez′ə·dən·sē) *n. pl.* **·cies 1** RESIDENCE. **2** A period of advanced training in a hospital, usu. in a medical specialty.

res·i·dent (rez′ə·dənt) *n.* **1** One who resides or dwells in a place. **2** A physician engaged in residency. **3** A diplomatic representative residing at a foreign seat of government. —*adj.* **1** Having a residence; residing. **2** Living in a place in connection with one's official work. **3** Not migratory: said of certain birds.

res·i·den·tial (rez′ə·den′shəl) *adj.* **1** Of, characteristic of, or suitable for residences. **2** Used by residents.

re·sid·u·al (ri·zij′o͞o·əl) *adj.* **1** Pertaining to or having the nature of a residue or remainder. **2** Left over as a residue. —*n.* **1** That which is left over from a total, as after subtraction. **2** *Often pl.* A payment made to a performer for each rerun of taped or filmed TV material in which he or she has appeared. —**re·sid′u·al·ly** *adv.*

re·sid·u·ar·y (ri·zij′o͞o·er′ē) *adj.* Entitled to receive the residue of an estate.

res·i·due (rez′ə·d yo͞o) *n.* **1** A remainder after a part has been separated or removed. **2** *Chem.* Matter left unaffected after combustion, distillation, evaporation, etc. **3** *Law* That portion of an estate which remains after all charges, debts, and particular bequests have been satisfied. [< L *residuus* remaining]

re·sid·u·um (ri·zij′o͞o·əm) *n. pl.* **·sid·u·a** (-zij′o͞o·ə) **1** RESIDUAL (def. 1). **2** RESIDUE (def. 3). [L]

re·sign (ri·zīn′) *v.t.* **1** To give up, as a position, office, or trust. **2** To relinquish (a privilege, claim, etc.). **3** To give over (oneself, one's mind, etc.), as to fate or domination. —*v.i.* **4** To resign a position, etc. [< OF< L *re-* back + *signare* to sign] —**re·sign′er** *n.*

res·ig·na·tion (rez′ig·nā′shən) *n.* **1** The act of resigning. **2** A formal notice of resigning. **3** The quality of being submissive; unresisting acquiescence.

re·signed (ri·zīnd′) *adj.* Characterized by resignation; submissive. —**re·sign·ed·ly** (ri·zī′nid·lē) *adv.* —**re·sign′ed·ness** *n.*

re·sil·ience (ri·zil′yəns) *n.* **1** The quality of being resilient; elasticity. **2** Cheerful buoyancy. Also **re·sil′ien·cy.**

re·sil·ient (ri·zil′yənt) *adj.* **1** Springing back to a former shape or position after being bent, compressed, etc. **2** Able to recover quickly; buoyant. [< L *resilire* to rebound] — **re·sil′ient·ly** *adv.*

res·in (rez′in) *n.* **1** A solid or semisolid, usu. translucent substance exuded from certain plants, used in varnishes, plastics, etc. **2** Any of various substances resembling this made by chemical synthesis. **3** ROSIN. —*v.t.* To apply resin to. [< Gk. *rhētinē*] —**res·i·na·ceous** (rez′ə·nā′shəs), **res·in·ous** *adj.*

re·sist (ri·zist′) *v.t.* **1** To stay the effect of; withstand; hold off: Steel *resists* corrosion. **2** To fight or struggle against; seek to foil or frustrate: to *resist* arrest; to *resist* temptation. —*v.i.* To offer opposition. [< L *re-* back + *sistere,* causative of *stare* stand] —**re·sist′er, re·sist′i·bil′i·ty** *n.* —**re·sist′i·ble, re·sis′tive** *adj.* —**re·sist′i·bly** *adv.*

re·sis·tance (ri·zis′təns) *n.* **1** The act of resisting. **2** Any force tending to hinder motion. **3** The capacity of an organism to ward off the effects of potentially harmful substances, as toxins. **4** *Electr.* The opposition of a body to the passage through it of an electric current. **5** The underground and guerrilla movement in a conquered country opposing the occupying power. —**re·sis′tant** *adj.*

re·sis·tor (ri·zis′tər) *n. Electr.* A device whose principal property is resistance.

res·o·lute (rez′ə·lo͞ot) *adj.* Having a fixed purpose; determined. [< L *resolutus,* p.p. of *resolvere* to resolve] —**res′o·lute·ly** *adv.* —**res′o·lute·ness** *n.* —**Syn.** steady, constant, firm, decisive.

res·o·lu·tion (rez′ə·lo͞o′shən) *n.* **1** The act of resolving or of reducing to a simpler form. **2** The making of a resolve. **3** The purpose or course resolved upon. **4** Firmness of purpose. **5** An outcome or result that serves to settle a problem, uncertainty, or conflict. **6** A statement expressing the intention or judgment of an assembly or group. **7** *Music* **a** The conventional replacement of a dissonant tone, chord, etc., by one that is consonant. **b** The tone or chord replacing the dissonant one. **8** The capacity of a telescope, microscope, etc., to give separate images of objects close together.

re·solve (ri·zolv′) *v.* **·solved, ·solv·ing** *v.t.* **1** To decide; determine (to do something). **2** To cause to decide or determine. **3** To separate or break down into constituent parts; analyze. **4** To clear away or settle, as a problem, uncertainty, or conflict; explain or solve. **5** To state or decide by vote. **6** *Music* To cause (a dissonant tone, chord, etc.) to undergo resolution. **7** To make distinguishable, as with a telescope or microscope. —*v.i.* **8** To make up one's mind: with *on* or *upon.* **9** To become separated into constituent parts. **10** *Music* To undergo resolution. —*n.* **1** Fixity of purpose; determination. **2** Something resolved upon; a decision. **3** A formal expression of the intention or judgment of an assembly or group. [< L *resolvere* loosen again] —**re·solv′a·ble** *adj.* —**re·solv′er** *n.*

res·o·nance (rez′ə·nəns) *n.* **1** The state or quality of being resonant; resonant sound. **2** Prolongation and amplification of a sound or tone by reverberation. **3** *Physics* A property of oscillatory systems whereby excitation at certain frequencies produces response of greater amplitude than at other frequencies.

res·o·nant (rez′ə·nənt) *adj.* **1** Having the quality of prolonging and amplifying sound by reverberation; producing resonance. **2** Resounding; displaying resonance. **3** Full of or characterized by resonance: a *resonant* voice. [< L *resonare* resound, echo] —**res′o·nant·ly** *adv.*

res·o·nate (rez′ə·nāt) *v.i.* **·nat·ed, ·nat·ing** To exhibit or produce resonance.

res·o·na·tor (rez′ə·nā′tər) *n.* Any device used to produce resonance or to increase sound by resonance.

re·sor·cin·ol (ri·zôr′sin·ōl, -ol) *n.* A derivative of phenol, used as an antiseptic and in making dyes, plastics, etc. Also **re·sor′cin.** [< RES(IN) + *orcinol* a phenol]

re·sort (ri·zôrt′) *v.i.* **1** To go frequently or habitually; repair. **2** To have recourse: with *to.* —*n.* **1** A hotel or other place that provides recreational facilities and sometimes entertainment, esp. for those on vacation. **2** The use of something as a means; a recourse; refuge. **3** A person

looked to for help. **4** A place frequented regularly. [< OF
re- again + *sortir* go out] —**re·sort′er** *n.*
re·sound (ri·zound′) *v.i.* **1** To be filled with sound; echo;
reverberate. **2** To make a loud, prolonged, or echoing
sound. **3** To ring; echo. **4** To be famed or extolled. —*v.t.* **5**
To give back (a sound, etc.); re-echo. **6** To celebrate; extol.
[< L *resonare*]
re·source (rē·sôrs, -sōrs, -zôrs, -zōrs, ri·sôrs′, -sōrs′,
-zôrs′, -zōrs′) *n.* **1** *Usu. pl.* That which can be drawn upon
as a means of help or support. **2** *Usu. pl.* Natural advantages, esp. of a country, as forests, oil deposits, etc. **3** *pl.*
Available wealth or property. **4** Skill or ingenuity in meeting any situation. **5** Any way or method of coping with a
difficult situation. [< L *re-* back + *surgere* to rise, surge]
re·source·ful (ri·sôrs′fəl, -sōrs′-, -zôrs′, -zōrs′) *adj.* Having the ability to meet the demands of any situation; ingenious. —**re·source′ful·ly** *adv.* —**re·source′ful·ness** *n.*
re·spect (ri·spekt′) *v.t.* **1** To have deferential regard for;
esteem. **2** To treat with propriety or consideration. **3** To
avoid intruding upon; regard as inviolable. **4** To have reference to; concern. —*n.* **1** A high regard for and appreciation of worth; esteem. **2** Due regard or consideration: *respect* for the law. **3** *pl.* Expressions of consideration;
compliments: to pay one's *respects*. **4** The condition of being honored or respected. **5** A specific aspect or detail: In
some *respects* the plan is impractical. **6** Reference or relation: usu. with *to*: with *respect* to profits. [< L *respectus,*
p.p. of *respicere* look back, consider] —**re·spect′er** *n.*
re·spect·a·ble (ri·spek′tə·bəl) *adj.* **1** Deserving of respect. **2** Conventionally correct; socially acceptable. **3**
Having a good appearance; presentable. **4** Moderate in
quality, size, or amount; fair: a *respectable* talent. —**re·
spect′a·bil′i·ty, re·spect′a·ble·ness** *n.* —**re·spect′a·bly** *adv.*
re·spect·ful (ri·spekt′fəl) *adj.* Characterized by or showing respect. —**re·spect′ful·ly** *adv.* —**re·spect′ful·ness** *n.*
re·spect·ing (ri·spek′ting) *prep.* In relation to.
re·spec·tive (ri·spek′tiv) *adj.* Relating separately to
each of those under consideration; several.
re·spec·tive·ly (ri·spek′tiv·lē) *adv.* Singly in the order
designated: to describe the duties of the judge and jury
respectively.
res·pi·ra·tion (res′pə·rā′shən) *n.* **1** The act of inhaling
air and expelling it; breathing. **2** The process by which an
organism takes in and uses oxygen and gives off carbon
dioxide and other waste products. —**re·spir·a·to·ry** (res′pər·
ə·tôr′ē, ri·spīr′ə·tôr′ē) *adj.*
res·pi·ra·tor (res′pə·rā′tər) *n.* **1** A screen, as of fine
gauze, worn over the mouth or nose, as a protection
against dust, etc. **2** An apparatus for artificial respiration.
re·spire (ri·spīr′) *v.* **·spired, ·spir·ing** *v.i.* **1** To inhale and
exhale air; breathe. —*v.t.* **2** To breathe. [< L *re-* again +
spirare breathe]
res·pite (res′pit) *n.* **1** Postponement; delay. **2** Temporary
relief from labor or effort; an interval of rest. [< Med. L
respectus delay]
re·splen·dent (ri·splen′dənt) *adj.* Shining with brilliant
luster; splendid; gorgeous. [< L *re-* again + *splendere* to
shine] —**re·splen′dence, re·splen′den·cy** *n.* —**re·splen′dent·ly**
adv.
re·spond (ri·spond′) *v.i.* **1** To give an answer; reply. **2** To
act in reply or return. **3** To react favorably: to *respond* to
treatment. —*v.t.* **4** To say in answer; reply. [< L *re-* back
+ *spondere* to pledge] —**re·spond′er** *n.*
re·spon·dent (ri·spon′dənt) *n.* **1** One who responds or
answers. **2** *Law* The party called upon to answer an appeal or petition; a defendant. —**re·spon′dence, re·spon′den·
cy** *n.*
re·sponse (ri·spons′) *n.* **1** Words or acts called forth as
a reaction; an answer or reply. **2** *Eccl.* A portion of a
church service said or sung by the congregation in reply
to the officiating priest. **3** *Biol.* Any reaction resulting
from a stimulus. **4** The action of a physical system when
energized or disturbed.
re·spon·si·bil·i·ty (ri·spon′sə·bil′ə·tē) *n. pl.* **·ties 1** The
state of being responsible or accountable. **2** That for which
one is responsible; a duty or trust. Also **re·spon′si·ble·ness.**

re·spon·si·ble (ri·spon′sə·bəl) *adj.* **1** Subject to being
called upon to account or answer for something; accountable. **2** Able to discriminate between right and wrong. **3**
Able to account or answer for something; able to meet
one's obligations. **4** Being the cause: Rain was *responsible*
for the delay. —**re·spon′si·bly** *adv.*
re·spon·sive (ri·spon′siv) *adj.* **1** Constituting a response.
2 Inclined to react with sympathy or understanding. **3**
Containing responses. —**re·spon′sive·ly** *adv.* —**re·spon′sive·
ness** *n.*
rest[1] (rest) *v.i.* **1** To cease working or exerting oneself for

Rests *def. 8b*
a. whole. b. half. c. quarter. d. eighth. e. sixteenth.
f. thirty-second. g. sixty-fourth.

a time; cease activity. **2** To obtain ease or refreshment by
lying down, sleeping, etc. **3** To sleep. **4** To be still or quiet;
cease all motion. **5** To be dead. **6** To be or lie in a specified
place: The blame *rests* with me. **7** To be supported; stand,
lean, lie, or sit: The rifle *rested* on the mantel. **8** To be
founded or based: That *rests* on the assumption of his
innocence. **9** To be directed, as the eyes. —*v.t.* **10** To give
rest to; refresh by rest. **11** To put, lay, lean, etc., as for
support or rest. **12** To found; base. **13** To direct (the gaze,
eyes, etc.). **14** *Law* To cease presenting evidence in (a case).
—*n.* **1** The act or state of resting. **2** A period of resting. **3**
Freedom from disturbance or disquiet; peace; tranquil-
lity. **4** Sleep. **5** Death. **6** That on which anything rests; a
support; basis. **7** A place for stopping or resting. **8** *Music*
a A measured interval of silence. **b** A character representing this. —**at rest** In a state of rest; motionless, peaceful,
asleep, or dead. [< OE *restan*] —**rest′er** *n.* —**Syn.** *n.* **1**
repose, quiet, inactivity, relaxation. **2** respite. **3** serenity,
peacefulness, calmness. **6** base, foundation.
rest[2] (rest) *n.* That which remains or is left over. —**the
rest** That or those which remain; the remainder; the others. —*v.i.* To be and remain: *Rest* content. [< L *restare*
stop, stand]
re·state (rē·stāt′) *v.t.* **·stat·ed, ·stat·ing** To state again or in
a new way. —**re·state′ment** *n.*
res·tau·rant (res′tə·ränt, -tränt, -tər·ənt) *n.* A place
where meals are prepared for sale and served on the
premises. [F, lit., restoring]
res·tau·ra·teur (res′tər·ə·tûr′) *n.* The proprietor of a restaurant. [F]
rest·ful (rest′fəl) *adj.* **1** Full of or giving rest. **2** Being at
rest; quiet. —**rest′ful·ly** *adv.* —**rest′ful·ness** *n.*
res·ti·tu·tion (res′tə·t^yōō′shən) *n.* **1** The act of restoring
something that has been taken away or lost. **2** Restoration
or return to a rightful owner. **3** The act of making good for
injury or loss. [< L *restituere* restore]
res·tive (res′tiv) *adj.* **1** Restless; fidgety: The audience
grew *restive.* **2** Unwilling to submit to control; unruly;
balky. [< F *rester* remain, balk] —**res′tive·ly** *adv.* —**res′·
tive·ness** *n.*
rest·less (rest′lis) *adj.* **1** Affording no rest or little rest;
disturbed: a *restless* sleep. **2** Uneasy; impatient; unquiet:
to feel *restless.* **3** Never resting; unending: the *restless*
waves. **4** Constantly seeking change or activity; unable or
unwilling to rest. —**rest′less·ly** *adv.* —**rest′less·ness** *n.*
res·to·ra·tion (res′tə·rā′shən) *n.* **1** The act of restoring,
or the state of being restored. **2** The bringing back to an
original or earlier condition, as a work of art or a building;
also, the object so restored. —**the Restoration 1** The return of Charles II to the English throne in 1660. **2** The
period following his return up to the revolution in 1688.
re·stor·a·tive (ri·stôr′ə·tiv, -stō′rə-) *adj.* Tending or able
to restore consciousness, strength, health, etc. —*n.* A re-
storative substance. —**re·sto′ra·tive·ly** *adv.* —**re·sto′ra·tive·
ness** *n.*
re·store (ri·stôr′, -stōr′) *v.t.* **·stored, ·stor·ing 1** To bring

into existence or effect again: to *restore* peace. **2** To bring back to a former or original condition, as a work of art or a building. **3** To put back in a former place or position; reinstate. **4** To bring back to health and vigor. **5** To give back (something lost or taken away); return. [< L *restaurare*] —**re·stor′er** *n.*

re·strain (ri·strān′) *v.t.* **1** To hold back from acting, proceeding, or advancing. **2** To restrict or limit. **3** To deprive of liberty, as by placing in a prison. [< L *re*- back + *stringere* draw tight] —**re·strain′ed·ly** (-strān′id·lē) *adv.* —**re·strain′er** *n.*

re·straint (ri·strānt′) *n.* **1** The act of restraining, or the state of being restrained. **2** Something that restrains, as a harness or similar device. **3** A restriction on conduct; stricture. **4** Control over the display of one's emotions, opinions, etc.; self-control.

re·strict (ri·strikt′) *v.t.* To hold or keep within limits or bounds; confine. [< L *re*- back + *stringere* draw tight]

re·strict·ed (ri·strik′tid) *adj.* **1** Limited or confined. **2** Available for use by certain persons or groups; also, excluding certain persons or groups.

re·stric·tion (ri·strik′shən) *n.* **1** The act of restricting, or the state of being restricted. **2** That which restricts; a limitation or restraint.

re·stric·tive (ri·strik′tiv) *adj.* **1** Serving, tending, or operating to restrict. **2** *Gram.* Limiting: a *restrictive* clause. —**re·stric′tive·ly** *adv.* • In *Will the man who spoke just now please stand up, who spoke just now* is a restrictive clause because it limits the application of *man,* which it modifies. It is not set off by commas, and is to be distinguished from a nonrestrictive clause, as in *The president, who will be 60 years old tomorrow, held a press conference today.*

rest room In a public building, a room or rooms provided with toilet facilities.

re·struc·ture (rē·struk′chər) *v.t.* **·tured, ·tur·ing** To reorganize on a different basis or into a new pattern.

re·sult (ri·zult′) *n.* **1** The outcome of an action, course, or process. **2** A quantity or value derived by calculation. —*v.i.* **1** To be a result or outcome; follow: with *from.* **2** To have as a consequence; end: with *in.* [< L *resultare* spring back]

re·sul·tant (ri·zul′tənt) *adj.* Arising or following as a result. —*n.* **1** That which results; a consequence. **2** *Physics* A vector representing the sum of two or more other vectors.

re·sume (ri·zōōm′) *v.* **·sumed, ·sum·ing** *v.t.* **1** To begin again after an interruption. **2** To take or occupy again: *Resume* your places. —*v.i.* **3** To continue after an interruption. [< L *resumere* take up again] —**re·sum′er** *n.*

rés·u·mé (rez′ōō·mā, rez′ōō·mā′) *n.* A summary, as of one's employment record, education, etc., used in applying for a new position. Also **res·u·mé′, res·u·me′.** [F]

re·sump·tion (ri·zump′shən) *n.* The act of resuming; a beginning again.

re·sur·face (rē·sûr′fis) *v.t.* **·faced, ·fac·ing 1** To provide with a new surface. —*v.i.* **2** To come into view again; become evident.

re·sur·gence (ri·sûr′jəns) *n.* A rising again, as from death, obscurity, or defeat; a surging back. Also **re·sur′gen·cy.** —**re·sur′gent** *adj.*

res·ur·rect (rez′ə·rekt′) *v.t.* **1** To bring back to life. **2** To bring back into use or to notice.

res·ur·rec·tion (rez′ə·rek′shən) *n.* **1** Any revival or renewal, as of a practice or custom. **2** *Theol.* **a** A rising from the dead. **b** The state of those who have risen from the dead. —**the Resurrection 1** The rising of Christ from the dead. **2** The rising again of all the dead at the day of final judgment. [< L *resurrectus,* p.p. of *resurgere*< *re*- again + *surgere* rise] —**res′ur·rec′tion·al** *adj.*

re·sus·ci·tate (ri·sus′ə·tāt) *v.t. & v.i.* **·tat·ed, ·tat·ing** To revive from unconsciousness or apparent death. [< L *re*- again + *suscitare* revive] —**re·sus′ci·ta′tion, re·sus′ci·ta′tor** *n.* —**re·sus′ci·ta′tive** *adj.*

ret (ret) *v.t.* **ret·ted, ret·ting** To steep or soak, as flax, to separate the fibers. [ME *reten*]

ret. retired.

re·tail (rē′tāl) *n.* The selling of goods in small quantities directly to the consumer. —**at retail 1** In small quantities to the consumer. **2** At retail prices. —*adj.* Of, pertaining

to, or engaged in the sale of goods at retail. —*adv.* AT RETAIL. —*v.t.* **1** To sell in small quantities directly to the consumer. **2** (ri·tāl′) To repeat, as gossip. —*v.i.* **3** To be sold at retail. [< OF *retailler* cut up] —**re′tail·er** *n.*

re·tain (ri·tān′) *v.t.* **1** To keep in one's possession; hold. **2** To maintain in use, practice, etc.: to *retain* one's standards. **3** To keep in a fixed condition or place. **4** To keep in mind; remember. **5** To hire or engage, as an attorney. [< L *re*- back + *tenere* to hold]

re·tain·er[1] (ri·tā′nər) *n.* **1** One employed in the service of a person of rank; servant. **2** One who or that which retains.

re·tain·er[2] (ri·tā′nər) *n.* **1** The fee paid to retain the services of an attorney or other adviser. **2** The act of retaining the services of an attorney, etc. [< OF *retenir* hold back]

retaining wall A wall to prevent a side of an embankment or cut from sliding.

re·tal·i·ate (ri·tal′ē·āt) *v.* **·at·ed, ·at·ing** *v.i.* **1** To return like for like; esp., to repay evil with evil. —*v.t.* **2** To repay (an injury, wrong, etc.) in kind; revenge. [< L *re*- back + *talio* punishment in kind] —**re·tal′i·a′tion** *n.* —**re·tal′i·a·tive, re·tal′i·a·to·ry** *adj.*

re·tard (ri·tärd′) *v.t.* **1** To hinder the advance or course of; impede; delay. —*v.i.* **2** To be delayed. —*n.* Delay; retardation. [< L *re*- back + *tardus* slow] —**re′tar·da′tion, re·tard′er** *n.* —**re·tard′a·tive** *adj.*

re·tard·ant (ri·tär′dənt) *n.* Something that retards: a fire *retardant.* —*adj.* Tending to retard.

re·tar·date (ri·tär′dāt) *n.* A mentally retarded person.

re·tard·ed (ri·tärd′id) *adj.* Abnormally slow in development, esp. mental development.

retch (rech) *v.i.* To make an effort to vomit; strain; heave. [< OE *hræcan* bring up (blood or phlegm)]

retd. retained; returned; retired.

re·ten·tion (ri·ten′shən) *n.* **1** The act of retaining, or the state of being retained. **2** The ability to retain data, images, etc., in the mind subject to later recall. **3** *Med.* A retaining within the body of materials normally excreted.

re·ten·tive (ri·ten′tiv) *adj.* Having the power or tendency to retain, esp. to retain in the mind: a *retentive* memory. —**re·ten′tive·ly** *adv.* —**re·ten′tive·ness, re·ten·tiv′i·ty** *n.*

re·think (rē·thingk′) *v.t.* **·thought** (-thôt), **·think·ing** To think about again, esp. in order to reassess; reconsider.

ret·i·cent (ret′ə·sənt) *adj.* **1** Reluctant to speak or speak freely; habitually silent; reserved. **2** Subdued or restrained; shunning bold statement: *reticent* prose. [< L *re*- again + *tacere* be silent] —**ret′i·cence, ret′i·cen·cy** *n.* —**ret′i·cent·ly** *adv.*

re·tic·u·lar (ri·tik′yə·lər) *adj.* **1** Like a net. **2** Intricate. **3** Of or pertaining to a reticulum. [< L *reticulum* network]

re·tic·u·late (ri·tik′yə·lāt) *v.* **·lat·ed, ·lat·ing** *v.t.* **1** To make a network of. **2** To cover with or as with lines of network. —*v.i.* **3** To form a network. —*adj.* (-lit, -lāt) Having the form or appearance of a network: also **re·tic′u·lat′ed.** —**re·tic′u·late·ly** *adv.* —**re·tic′u·la′tion** *n.*

ret·i·cule (ret′ə·kyōōl) *n.* A small handbag closed with a drawstring, formerly used by women. [< L *reticulum* network]

re·tic·u·lum (ri·tik′yə·ləm) *n. pl.* **·lums** or **·la** (-lə) The second stomach of a ruminant. [L, dim. of *rete* net]

ret·i·na (ret′ə·nə, ret′nə) *n. pl.* **·nas** or **·nae** (-nē) The light-sensitive membrane lining the back of the eyeball at the distal end of the optic nerve. [< L *rete* net] —**ret′i·nal** *adj.*

ret·i·nue (ret′ə·nyōō) *n.* The group of retainers attending a person of rank. [< F *retenir* retain]

re·tire (ri·tīr′) *v.* **·tired, ·tir·ing** *v.i.* **1** To withdraw oneself from business, public life, or active service. **2** To go away or withdraw, as for privacy, shelter, or rest. **3** To go to bed. **4** To fall back; retreat. **5** To move back; recede. —*v.t.* **6** To remove from active service. **7** To pay off and withdraw from circulation: to *retire* bonds. **8** To withdraw (troops, etc.) from action. **9** In baseball, to put out, as a batter. [< F *re*- back + *tirer* draw]

a. retina. b. lens. c. pupil. d. cornea. e. iris. f. optic nerve.

re·tired (ri·tīrd′) *adj.* **1** Withdrawn from business, public life, or active service; esp., no longer actively engaged in one's occupation or profession because of having reached a certain age. **2** Of or for those in retirement. **3** Withdrawn from public view; secluded.

re·tir·ee (ri·tīr′ē′) *n.* A person who is retired.

re·tire·ment (ri·tīr′mənt) *n.* **1** The act of retiring, or the state of being retired. **2** A withdrawal from active engagement in one's occupation or profession, esp. because of age. **3** An age or date at which retirement is planned. **4** A secluded place.

re·tir·ing (ri·tīr′ing) *adj.* Shy; modest; reserved. —**re·tir′· ing·ly** *adv.*

re·tort[1] (ri·tôrt′) *v.t.* **1** To direct (a word or deed) back upon the originator. **2** To reply to, as an accusation or argument, by a similar one. **3** To say in reply. —*v.i.* **4** To answer, esp. sharply. **5** To respond to an accusation, etc., in kind. —*n.* A sharp or witty reply that turns back a previously expressed accusation, insult, etc., upon its originator. [< L *retorquere* twist back] —**re·tort′er** *n.* —**Syn.** *n.* rejoinder, riposte, comeback.

re·tort[2] (ri·tôrt′) *n.* A stoppered vessel with a side tube, for heating or distilling substances. [< L *retortus* bent back]

re·touch (rē·tuch′) *v.t.* **1** To modify by changing details; touch up, as a painting. **2** To change or improve, as a photographic print, by a hand process. —*n.* (*also* rē′· tuch′) A retouching, as of a picture. —**re·touch′er** *n.*

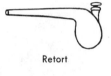

Retort

re·tract (ri·trakt′) *v.t.* & *v.i.* **1** To take back (an assertion, accusation, admission, etc.); disavow. **2** To draw back or in, as the claws of a cat. [< F < L *retractare* draw back] —**re· tract′a·ble, re·trac′tive** *adj.* —**re·trac′tion, re·trac′tor** *n.*

re·trac·tile (ri·trak′til) *adj. Zool.* Capable of being drawn back or in. —**re·trac·til·i·ty** (rē′trak·til′ə·tē) *n.*

re·tread (rē′tred′) *n.* A tire furnished with a new tread to replace a worn one. —*v.t.* (rē·tred′) To fit or furnish (a tire) with a new tread.

re·treat (ri·trēt′) *v.i.* **1** To go back or backward; withdraw. **2** To curve or slope backward. —*n.* **1** The act of retreating or drawing back, as from danger or conflict. **2** The retirement of an armed force from a position of danger. **3** In the armed forces, a signal, as by bugle, for the lowering of the flag at sunset. **4** A place of retirement or security; a refuge. **5** A period of religious contemplation and prayer by a group withdrawn from regular society. [< L *re-* again + *trahere* draw]

re·trench (ri·trench′) *v.t.* **1** To cut down or curtail (expenditures). **2** To cut off or away. —*v.i.* **3** To economize. [< MF *re-* back + *trencher* to cut] —**re·trench′er, re·trench′ment** *n.*

ret·ri·bu·tion (ret′rə·byōō′shən) *n.* **1** The impartial infliction of punishment, as for evil done. **2** That which is done or given in requital, as a reward or, esp., a punishment. [< L *re-* back + *tribuere* to pay] —**re·trib·u·tive** (ri·trib′yə· tiv), **re·trib′u·to′ry** *adj.* —**re·trib′u·tive·ly** *adv.*

re·triev·al (ri·trē′vəl) *n.* **1** The act or process of retrieving. **2** The power to restore or retrieve.

re·trieve (ri·trēv′) *v.* **·trieved, ·triev·ing** *v.t.* **1** To get back; regain. **2** To restore; revive, as flagging spirits. **3** To make up for; remedy the consequences of. **4** To call to mind; remember. **5** To locate and provide access to (data) in computer storage. **6** In tennis, etc., to return (a ball, etc.) after a run. **7** To find and bring in (wounded or dead game): said of dogs. —*v.i.* **8** To retrieve game. —*n.* The act of retrieving; recovery. [< OF *re-* again + *trouver* find] —**re·triev′a·bil′i·ty** *n.* —**re·triev′a·ble** *adj.*

re·triev·er (ri·trē′vər) *n.* **1** Any of various breeds of dog usu. trained to retrieve game. **2** A person who retrieves.

retro- *prefix* Back; backward: *retrograde*. [< L *retro* backward]

ret·ro·ac·tive (ret′rō·ak′tiv, rē′trō-) *adj.* Effective or applicable to a period prior to the time of enactment: a *retroactive* ruling granting wage increases as of last May. —**ret′ro·ac′tive·ly** *adv.* —**ret′ro·ac·tiv′i·ty** *n.*

ret·ro·grade (ret′rə·grād) *adj.* **1** Going, moving, or tend-

ing backward. **2** Declining toward a worse state or character. **3** Inverted in order. —*v.* **·grad·ed, ·grad·ing** *v.i.* **1** To move or appear to move backward. **2** To grow worse; decline; degenerate. [< L *retrogradus* a step backward] —**ret′ro·gra·da′tion** (-grā·dā′shən) *n.*

ret·ro·gress (ret′rə·gres) *v.i.* To go back to a more primitive or worse condition. [< L *retro-* backward + *gradi* walk] —**ret′ro·gres′sion** *n.* —**ret′ro·gres′sive** *adj.* —**ret′ro· gres′sive·ly** *adv.*

ret·ro·rock·et (ret′rō·rok′it) *n.* An auxiliary rocket that provides a backward thrust, as for reducing speed.

ret·ro·spect (ret′rə·spekt) *n.* A looking back on things past. —**in retrospect** In recalling or reviewing the past. [< L < *retro-* back + *specere* look] —**ret′ro·spec′tion** *n.*

ret·ro·spec·tive (ret′rə·spek′tiv) *adj.* **1** Looking back on the past. **2** RETROACTIVE. —*n.* An exhibition of works representing the entire period of an artist's productivity. —**ret′ro·spec′tive·ly** *adv.*

re·turn (ri·tûrn′) *v.i.* **1** To come or go back, as to or toward a former place or condition. **2** To come back or revert in thought or speech. **3** To revert to a former owner. **4** To answer; respond. —*v.t.* **5** To bring, carry, send, or put back; restore; replace. **6** To give in return, esp. with an equivalent: to *return* a favor. **7** To yield or produce, as a profit. **8** To send back; reflect, as light or sound. **9** To render (a verdict, etc.). **10** In sports, to throw, hit, or carry back (a ball). **11** In card games, to lead (a suit previously led by one's partner). —*n.* **1** The act of bringing back or restoring something to a former place or condition; restoration or replacement. **2** An appearing again; recurrence. **3** Something given or sent back, esp. in kind or as an equivalent; repayment. **4** Something, as an article of merchandise, returned for exchange or reimbursement. **5** *Often pl.* Profit or revenue; yield. **6** A response; answer; retort. **7** A formal or official report: a tax *return*. **8** *pl.* A report of the tabulated votes of an election. **9** In sports, the act of returning a ball. —**in return** In repayment; as an equivalent —*adj.* **1** Of or for a return: a *return* ticket. **2** Constituting a return or recurrence: a *return* engagement. **3** Returning. **4** Used for return: a *return* address. [< OF] —**re·turn′er** *n.*

re·un·ion (rē·yōōn′yən) *n.* **1** The act of reuniting. **2** A social gathering of persons who have been separated.

re·u·nite (rē′yōō·nīt′) *v.t.* & *v.i.* **·nit·ed, ·nit·ing** To bring or come together after separation. —**re′u·nit′er** *n.*

rev (rev) *Informal n.* A revolution, as of a motor. —*v.t.* **revved, rev·ving 1** To increase the speed of (an engine, motor, etc.): often with *up*. **2** To increase in tempo or intensity, with *up*. **3** To stimulate or excite: with *up*. —*v.i.* **4** To increase the speed of an engine, etc.: often with *up*. **5** To become stimulated or excited: with *up*.

Rev, Rev. Revelation; Reverend.

rev. revenue; reverse; review; revised; revision; revolution.

re·vamp (rē·vamp′) *v.t.* To make over or renovate.

re·vanch·ism (ri·vänsh′iz′əm) *n.* The revengeful desire to reacquire the land and power lost by a nation through war. [< F *revanche* revenge + -ISM] —**re·vanch′ist** *adj., n.*

re·veal (ri·vēl′) *v.t.* **1** To make known; disclose; divulge. **2** To make visible; expose to view. [< L *revelare* unveil] —**re·veal′er, re·veal′ment** *n.*

rev·eil·le (rev′i·lē) *n.* A morning signal by drum or bugle, notifying soldiers or sailors to rise. [< F *reveillez-vous*, imperative of *se reveiller* wake up]

rev·el (rev′əl) *v.i.* **·eled** or **·elled, ·el·ing** or **·el·ling 1** To take delight: with *in*: He *revels* in his freedom. **2** To make merry; engage in boisterous festivities. —*n.* **1** A boisterous festivity; celebration. **2** Merrymaking. [< OF < L *rebellare* to rebel] —**rev′el·er** or **rev′el·ler** *n.*

rev·e·la·tion (rev′ə·lā′shən) *n.* **1** The act of revealing. **2** That which is revealed, esp. news of a surprising nature. **3** *Theol.* **a** The act of revealing divine truth. **b** That which is so revealed.

Rev·e·la·tion (rev′ə·lā′shən) *n.* The Book of Revelation, the last book of the New Testament; the Apocalypse. Also **Rev′e·la′tions.**

---

add, āce, câre, pälm; end, ēven; it, īce; odd, ōpen, ôrder; tŏŏk, pōōl; up, bûrn; ə = *a* in *above*, *u* in *focus*; yōō = *u* in *fuse*; oil; pout; check; go; ring; thin; <u>th</u>is; zh, *vision*. < derived from; ? origin uncertain or unknown.

rev·el·ry (rev′əl·rē) *n. pl.* **·ries** Noisy or boisterous merriment.

re·venge (ri·venj′) *n.* **1** The act of returning injury for injury to obtain satisfaction. **2** A means of avenging oneself or others. **3** The desire for vengeance. **4** An opportunity to obtain satisfaction, esp. to make up for a prior defeat, humiliation, etc. —*v.t.* **·venged, ·veng·ing 1** To inflict punishment, injury, or loss in return for. **2** To take or seek vengeance in behalf of. [MF < L *re-* again + *vindicare* vindicate] —**re·venge′ful** *adj.* —**re·venge′ful·ly** *adv.* —**re·veng′er** *n.*

rev·e·nue (rev′ə·nyōō) *n.* **1** Total current income of a government. **2** Income from any property or investment. **3** A source or an item of income. [< F *revenir* to return]

re·ver·ber·ate (ri·vûr′bə·rāt) *v.* **·at·ed, ·at·ing** *v.i.* **1** To resound or reecho. **2** To be reflected or repelled. **3** To rebound or recoil. —*v.t.* **4** To echo back (a sound); reecho. **5** To reflect. [< L *reverberare* strike back, cause to rebound < *re-* back + *verberare* to beat] —**re·ver′ber·ant** *adj.* —**re·ver′ber·a′tor** *n.*

re·ver·ber·a·tion (ri·vûr′bə·rā′shən) *n.* **1** The act of reverberating, or the state of being reverberated. **2** The rebound or reflection of light, heat, or sound waves. —**re·ver′ber·a′tive, re·ver′ber·a·to′ry** *adj.*

re·vere (ri·vir′) *v.t.* **·vered, ·ver·ing** To regard with profound respect and awe; venerate. [< L *re-* again and again + *vereri* to fear] —**re·ver′er** *n.*

rev·er·ence (rev′ər·əns) *n.* **1** A feeling of profound respect often mingled with awe and affection. **2** An act of respect; an obeisance, as a bow or curtsy. **3** The state of being revered. **4** A reverend person: used as a title. —*v.t.* **·enced, ·enc·ing** To regard with reverence. —**Syn.** *n.* **1** adoration, awe, homage, honor, veneration.

rev·er·end (rev′ər·ənd) *adj.* **1** Worthy of reverence. **2** *Usu. cap.* Being a clergyman: used as a title. **3** Of or pertaining to the clergy. —*n.* A clergyman. • In informal usage, *Reverend* follows *the* and precedes the clergyman's full name or title of address and last name: *the Reverend Donald Smith; the Rev. Mr.* (or *Dr.*) *Smith.* Less formally, *Reverend* is used as a title of address: *Reverend Smith.* The use of *reverend* as a noun should be avoided, esp. in writing: *The reverend's sermon was much admired.*

rev·er·ent (rev′ər·ənt) *adj.* Feeling or expressing reverence. —**rev′er·ent·ly** *adv.*

rev·er·en·tial (rev′ə·ren′shəl) *adj.* Proceeding from or expressing reverence. —**rev′er·en′tial·ly** *adv.*

rev·er·ie (rev′ər·ē) *n. pl.* **·er·ies 1** Abstracted musing; daydreaming. **2** DAYDREAM. Also **rev′er·y.** [< F *rêver* dream]

re·vers (rə·vir′, -vâr′) *n. pl.* **·vers** (-virz′, -vârz′) A part of a garment folded over to show the inside, as the lapel of a coat. [< OF]

re·ver·sal (ri·vûr′səl) *n.* **1** The act of reversing. **2** A change to an opposite direction or course.

re·verse (ri·vûrs′) *adj.* **1** Turned backward; contrary or opposite in direction, order, etc. **2** Having the other side or back in view. **3** Causing backward motion. —*n.* **1** That which is directly opposite or contrary. **2** The back, rear, or secondary side or surface. **3** A change to an opposite position, direction, or state; reversal. **4** A change for the worse; a misfortune. **5** *Mech.* A gear that causes reverse motion. —*v.* **·versed, ·vers·ing** *v.t.* **1** To turn upside down or inside out. **2** To turn in an opposite direction. **3** To transpose; exchange. **4** To change completely or into something opposite: to *reverse* one's stand. **5** To set aside; annul: The higher court *reversed* the decision. **6** To apply (the charges for a telephone call) to the party receiving the call. **7** *Mech.* To cause to have an opposite motion or effect. —*v.i.* **8** To move or turn in the opposite direction. **9** To reverse its action: said of engines, etc. [< L *reversus,* p.p. of *revertere* turn around] —**re·verse′ly** *adv.* —**re·vers′er** *n.*

re·vers·i·ble (ri·vûr′sə·bəl) *adj.* **1** Capable of being worn or used with either side open to view, as a fabric, coat, rug, etc. **2** Capable of being reversed, as a chemical reaction. —*n.* A reversible coat, fabric, etc. —**re·vers′i·bil′i·ty** *n.* —**re·vers′i·bly** *adv.*

re·ver·sion (ri·vûr′zhən, -shən) *n.* **1** A return to some former condition or practice. **2** The act of reversing, or the state of being reversed. **3** *Biol.* The recurrence of ancestral characteristics; atavism. **4** *Law* The return of an es-

tate to the grantor or his heirs after the expiration of the grant. —**re·ver′sion·ar′y, re·ver′sion·al** *adj.*

re·vert (ri·vûrt′) *v.i.* **1** To go or turn back to a former place, condition, attitude, topic, etc. **2** *Biol.* To return to or show characteristics of an earlier, primitive type. [< L *re-* back + *vertere* to turn]

re·vet·ment (ri·vet′mənt) *n.* A facing or retaining wall, as of masonry, for protecting earthworks, river banks, etc. [< F *revêtement*]

re·view (ri·vyōō′) *v.t.* **1** To go over or examine again: to *review* a lesson. **2** To look back upon, as in memory. **3** To study carefully; survey or evaluate: to *review* test scores. **4** To write or make a critical evaluation of, as a new book or film. **5** *Law* To examine (something done or adjudged by a lower court) so as to determine its legality or correctness. —*v.i.* **6** To go over material again. **7** To review books, films, etc. —*n.* **1** An examination or study of something; a retrospective survey. **2** A lesson studied again. **3** A careful study or survey. **4** A critical evaluation, as of a new book or film. **5** A periodical featuring critical reviews. **6** A formal inspection, as of troops. **7** *Law* The process by which the proceedings of a lower court are reexamined by a higher court. [< MF < L *re-* again + *videre* see] —**re·view′a·ble** *adj.* —**re·view′er** *n.*

re·vile (ri·vīl′) *v.* **·viled, ·vil·ing** *v.t.* **1** To assail with abusive language; attack verbally. —*v.i.* **2** To use abusive language. [< OF *reviler* treat as vile] —**re·vile′ment, re·vil′er** *n.* —**Syn.** abuse, vilify, malign, slander, defame.

re·vise (ri·vīz′) *v.t.* **·vised, ·vis·ing 1** To read over so as to correct errors, make changes, etc. **2** To change; alter: to *revise* one's opinion. —*n.* **1** An instance of revising. **2** A corrected proof after having been revised. [< L *revisere* look back, see again] —**re·vis′er** or **re·vi′sor** *n.*

re·vi·sion (ri·vizh′ən) *n.* **1** The act or process of revising. **2** A revised version or edition. —**re·vi′sion·ar′y, re·vi′sion·al** *adj.*

re·vi·sion·ist (ri·vizh′ən·ist) *n.* **1** One who proposes a course of action regarded as a deviation from accepted ideas or established policy, as of a Communist state. **2** One who advocates revision. —*adj.* Of or characteristic of a revisionist. —**re·vi′sion·ism** *n.* —**re·vi′sion·is′tic** *adj.*

re·vi·tal·ize (rē·vī′təl·īz) *v.t.* **·ized, ·iz·ing** To restore vitality to; revive. —**re·vi′tal·i·za′tion** *n.*

re·viv·al (ri·vī′vəl) *n.* **1** The act of reviving, or the state of being revived. **2** A restoration or renewal after neglect or obscurity: the *revival* of radio drama. **3** An awakening of interest in religion. **4** A series of often emotional evangelical meetings.

re·viv·al·ist (ri·vī′vəl·ist) *n.* A preacher or leader of religious revivals. —**re·vi′val·ism** *n.* —**re·vi′val·is′tic** *adj.*

re·vive (ri·vīv′) *v.* **·vived, ·viv·ing** *v.t.* **1** To bring to life or consciousness again. **2** To give new vigor, health, etc., to. **3** To bring back into use or currency, as after a period of neglect or obscurity: to *revive* an old play. **4** To renew in the mind or memory. —*v.i.* **5** To return to consciousness or life. **6** To assume new vigor, health, etc. **7** To come back into use or currency. [< F < L *revivere* < *re-* again + *vivere* live] —**re·viv′er** *n.*

re·viv·i·fy (ri·viv′ə·fī) *v.t.* **·fied, ·fy·ing** To give new life or spirit to. [< L *re-* again + *vivificare* vivify] —**re·viv′i·fi·ca′tion, re·viv′i·fi·er** *n.*

rev·o·ca·ble (rev′ə·kə·bəl) *adj.* Capable of being revoked. —**rev′o·ca·bil′i·ty** *n.* —**rev′o·ca·bly** *adv.*

rev·o·ca·tion (rev′ə·kā′shən) *n.* The act of revoking, or the state of being revoked; repeal.

re·voke (ri·vōk′) *v.* **·voked, ·vok·ing** *v.t.* **1** To annul or make void; rescind. —*v.i.* **2** In card games, to fail to follow suit when possible and required by the rules. —*n.* In card games, neglect to follow suit. [< L *re-* back + *vocare* call] —**re·vok′er** *n.*

re·volt (ri·vōlt′) *n.* **1** An uprising against authority, esp. a government; a rebellion or insurrection. **2** An act of protest or refusal. —*v.i.* **1** To rise in rebellion against constituted authority. **2** To turn away in disgust or abhorrence. —*v.t.* **3** To cause to feel disgust or revulsion; repel. [< L *revolutus,* p.p. of *revolvere* revolve] —**re·volt′er** *n.*

re·volt·ing (ri·vōl′ting) *adj.* Abhorrent; loathsome; nauseating. —**re·volt′ing·ly** *adv.*

rev·o·lu·tion (rev′ə·lōō′shən) *n.* **1** The act or state of re-

volving. 2 A motion in a closed curve around a center, or a complete or apparent circuit made by a body in such a course. 3 Any turning, winding, or rotation about an axis. 4 A round or cycle of successive events or changes. 5 The period of space or time occupied by a cycle. 6 The overthrow and replacement of a government or political system by those governed. 7 Any extensive or drastic change.

rev·o·lu·tion·ar·y (rev′ə·lōō′shən·er′ē) adj. 1 Pertaining to or of the nature of revolution. 2 Causing or tending to produce a revolution. —n. pl. ·ar·ies One who advocates or takes part in a revolution: also rev′o·lu′tion·ist.

Revolutionary War AMERICAN REVOLUTION.

rev·o·lu·tion·ize (rev′ə·lōō′shən·īz) v.t. ·ized, ·iz·ing To bring about a radical or complete change in.

re·volve (ri·volv′) v. ·volved, ·volv·ing v.i. 1 To move in a circle or closed path about a center. 2 To rotate. 3 To recur periodically. —v.t. 4 To cause to move in a circle or closed path. 5 To cause to rotate. 6 To turn over mentally. [< L re- back + volvere roll, turn]

re·volv·er (ri·vol′vər) n. A handgun with a cylinder that revolves to make possible successive discharges without reloading.

revolving door A door rotating like a turnstile and consisting of three or four adjustable panels.

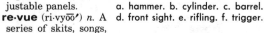

Revolver
a. hammer. b. cylinder. c. barrel.
d. front sight. e. rifling. f. trigger.

re·vue (ri·vyōō′) n. A series of skits, songs, dances, etc., often comical or satirical in nature. [F, review]

re·vul·sion (ri·vul′shən) n. 1 A sudden change of feeling; a strong reaction. 2 Complete disgust or aversion; loathing. [< L revulsus, p.p. of revellere pluck away] —re·vul′·sive adj.

re·ward (ri·wôrd′) n. 1 Something given or done in return, esp. to acknowledge and encourage merit, service, or achievement. 2 Money offered, as for the return of lost goods. —v.t. To give a reward to or for; recompense. [< AF rewarder look at] —re·ward′er n.

re·ward·ing (ri·wôrd′ing) adj. Yielding intangible rewards; satisfying: a rewarding career.

re·write (rē·rīt′) v.t. ·wrote, ·writ·ten, ·writ·ing 1 To write over again. 2 To revise or put into publishable form, as for a newspaper. —n. (rē′rīt′) A news item rewritten for publication.

RF, R.F., r.f. radio frequency.

RFD, R.F.D. Rural Free Delivery.

RH, R.H., r.h. right hand.

R.H. Royal Highness.

Rh rhodium.

r.h. relative humidity.

rhap·so·dize (rap′sə·dīz) v.t. & v.i. ·dized, ·diz·ing To express or recite with exaggerated sentiment and enthusiasm. —rhap′so·dist n.

rhap·so·dy (rap′sə·dē) n. pl. ·dies 1 Any rapturous or highly enthusiastic utterance or writing. 2 Music An instrumental composition of free form. [< Gk. rhaptein stitch together + ōidē song] —rhap·sod′ic (rap·sod′ik) or ·i·cal adj. —rhap·sod′i·cal·ly adv.

rhe·a (rē′ə) n. A ratite bird of South America, resembling but smaller than an ostrich, and having three toes. [NL]

rhe·ni·um (rē′nē·əm) n. A rare metallic element (symbol Re). [< L Rhenus Rhine]

rhe·o·stat (rē′ə·stat) n. Electr. A variable resistor used to control or limit current. [< Gk. rheos current + statos standing]

rhe·sus (rē′səs) n. A small macaque of India, widely used in research. Also rhesus monkey. [NL]

Rhe·sus factor (rē′səs) RH FACTOR.

rhet·o·ric (ret′ə·rik) n. 1 Skill in the use

Rhesus

of language, as in writing or speech. 2 The pretentious use of language. [< Gk. rhētorikē (technē) rhetorical (art)]

rhe·tor·i·cal (ri·tôr′i·kəl, -tor′-) adj. 1 Of the nature of rhetoric. 2 Designed for showy oratorical effect. —rhe·tor′·i·cal·ly adv. —rhe·tor′i·cal·ness n.

rhetorical question A question put only for effect, the answer being implied in the question.

rhet·o·ri·cian (ret′ə·rish′ən) n. A master or teacher of rhetoric.

rheum (rōōm) n. 1 A watery discharge from the nose or eyes. 2 A cold in the head. [< Gk. rheuma a flow] —rheum′y adj. (·i·er, ·i·est)

rheu·mat·ic (rōō·mat′ik) adj. Of, causing, or affected with rheumatism. —n. One affected with rheumatism.

rheumatic fever A disease chiefly affecting young persons following streptococcal infection, characterized by swollen joints and fever.

rheu·ma·tism (rōō′mə·tiz′əm) n. Any of various painful disorders of the joints. [< Gk. rheuma rheum] —rheu′ma·toid (-toid) adj.

rheumatoid arthritis A chronic, crippling disease of the joints.

Rh factor (är′ach′) A genetically transmitted substance in the blood of most individuals (**Rh positive**) and which may cause hemolytic reactions under certain conditions, as during pregnancy, or following transfusions with blood lacking this factor (**Rh negative**). [< RH(ESUS) monkey, the laboratory animal used in discovering this substance]

rhine·stone (rīn′stōn′) n. A highly refractive, colorless glass or paste, used as an imitation gemstone.

Rhine wine (rīn) A light, dry, white wine produced in the region of the Rhine River in W. CEN. Europe.

rhi·ni·tis (rī·nī′tis) n. Inflammation of the mucous membrane of the nose. [< Gk. rhis, rhinos nose + -ITIS]

rhi·no (rī′nō) n. pl. ·nos Informal A rhinoceros.

rhi·noc·e·ros (rī·nos′ər·əs) n. pl. ·ros·es or ·ros Any of various large, herbivorous, three-toed mammals of Africa and Asia, with one or two horns on the snout and a thick hide. [< Gk. rhis, rhinos nose + keras horn]

rhi·zome (rī′zōm) n. A specialized trailing or underground stem, producing roots from its lower surface and leaves or shoots from its upper surface or upturned tip. [< Gk. rhizōma mass of roots] —rhi·zom·a·tous (rī·zom′ə·təs, -zō′mə-) adj.

Indian rhinoceros

rho (rō) n. The 17th letter in the Greek alphabet (P, ρ).

Rhode Island Red (rōd) An American breed of chicken having reddish brown feathers.

Rho·de·sia (rō·dē′zhə, -zhē·ə) n. A British colony in CEN. Africa; unilaterally declared independence in 1965; 150,333 sq. mi., cap. Salisbury. —Rho·de′sian adj., n. • See map at AFRICA.

rho·di·um (rō′dē·əm) n. A hard, silvery metallic element (symbol Rh). [< Gk. rhodon rose; from the color of its salts]

Rhizome of bearded iris

rho·do·den·dron (rō′də·den′drən) n. Any of a genus of usu. evergreen shrubs or small trees with profuse clusters of flowers. [< Gk. rhodon rose + dendron tree]

rhom·boid (rom′boid) n. Geom. A parallelogram, esp. one with oblique angles, having unequal adjacent sides. —adj. Having the shape of a rhomboid or rhombus: also rhom·boi′dal. • See PARALLELOGRAM.

rhom·bus (rom′bəs) n. pl. ·bus·es or ·bi (-bī) Geom. An equilateral parallelogram, esp. one with oblique angles. [< Gk. rhombos spinning top, rhombus] —rhom′bic adj. • See PARALLELOGRAM.

rhu·barb (rōō′bärb) n. 1 Any of a genus of large-leaved perennial herbs. 2 The fleshy stalks of a species of rhubarb used in cooking. 3 Slang A heated argument or quarrel. [< Gk. rha rhubarb + barbaron foreign]

rhum·ba (rum′bə) *n. & v.* RUMBA.

rhyme (rīm) *n.* **1** A similarity of sounds of two or more words, esp. at the ends of lines of poetry. **2** A word wholly or partly similar in sound to another word. **3** A poem or verse employing such words, esp. at the ends of lines. **4** Poetry or verse in general. —*v.* **rhymed, rhy·ming** *v.i.* **1** To make rhymes or verses. **2** To be a rhyme. **3** To end in rhymes: said of verses. —*v.t.* **4** To write in rhyme. **5** To use as a rhyme. **6** To cause to be a rhyme or rhymes. [< Gk. *rhythmos* rhythm] —**rhym′er** *n.*

rhyme·ster (rīm′stər) *n.* A writer of light or inferior verse.

rhythm (rith′əm) *n.* **1** Movement or process characterized by the regular or harmonious recurrence of a beat, sound, action, development, etc.: the *rhythm* of the pulse; the *rhythm* of the seasons; the *rhythms* of speech. **2 a** The property of music that arises from comparison of the relative duration and accents of sounds. **b** A particular arrangement of durations and accents: a dance *rhythm.* **3** In literature, drama, etc., a forward-moving or compelling development toward a particular end, effect, etc.: The *rhythm* of the play was all off. **4** In art, the regular or harmonious recurrence of colors, forms, etc. **5** In prosody: **a** The cadenced flow of sound as determined by the succession of accented and unaccented syllables. **b** A particular arrangement of such syllables: iambic *rhythm.* [< Gk. *rhythmos* < *rheein* flow] —**rhyth′mic** or **·mi·cal** *adj.* — **rhyth′mi·cal·ly** *adv.* —**rhyth′mist** *n.*

rhythm method A method of birth control that consists of sexual abstinence during the woman's monthly period of ovulation.

RI Rhode Island (P.O. abbr.).

R.I. King and Emperor (L *Rex et Imperator*); Queen and Empress (L *Regina et Imperatrix*); Rhode Island.

ri·al (rī′al) *n.* A silver coin, the basic monetary unit of Iran. [< OF *rial, real* royal]

ri·al·to (rē·al′tō) *n. pl.* **·tos** A market or place of exchange. [< *Rialto,* an island of Venice]

rib (rib) *n.* **1** *Anat.* One of the series of curved bones attached to the spine of most vertebrates, and enclosing the chest cavity. **2** Something, as a structural element, likened to a rib: the *rib* of an umbrella. **3** The curved piece of an arch; also, one of the intersecting arches in vaulting. **4** A curved side timber bending away from the keel in a boat or ship. **5** A raised wale or stripe in cloth or knit goods. **6** A vein or nerve of a leaf or insect's wing. **7** A cut of meat including one or more ribs. **8** A wife: in jocular allusion to the creation of Eve from Adam's rib. *Gen.* 2:22. **9** *Slang* A practical joke. —*v.t.* **ribbed, rib·bing 1** To make with ridges: to *rib* a piece of knitting. **2** To strengthen by or enclose within ribs. **3** *Slang* To make fun of; tease. [< OE *ribb*]

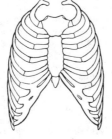

Human ribs

rib·ald (rib′əld) *adj.* Of or indulging in coarse, vulgar language or jokes. —*n.* A ribald person. [< OF *ribauld*] —**Syn.** *adj.* improper, unseemly, gross, obscene, impure.

rib·ald·ry (rib′əl·drē) *n. pl.* **·ries** Ribald language or jokes.

rib·bing (rib′ing) *n.* An arrangement of ribs, as in ribbed cloth, etc.

rib·bon (rib′ən) *n.* **1** A narrow strip of fabric made in a variety of weaves, used as trimming, for tying, etc. **2** Something shaped like or suggesting a ribbon. **3** *pl.* A narrow strip; a shred: torn to *ribbons.* **4** An ink-bearing strip of cloth in a typewriter. **5** A colored strip of cloth worn to signify the award of a prize, etc. **6** *Mil.* A strip of cloth worn to indicate campaigns served in, medals won, etc. —*v.t.* **1** To ornament with ribbons. **2** To tear into ribbons. [< OF *riban*]

ri·bo·fla·vin (rī′bō·flā′vin) *n.* A vitamin of the B complex found in many foods and required for normal growth.

ri·bo·nu·cle·ic acid (rī′bō·nyōō·klē′ik, -klā′ik) A substance that controls various processes within living cells, esp. the synthesis of proteins.

rice (rīs) *n.* **1** A cereal grass widely cultivated on wet land in warm climates. **2** The edible, starchy seeds of this plant. —*v.t.* **riced, ric·ing** To reduce (a food) to ricelike grains. [< Gk. *oryza*]

rice paper 1 A thin paper made from rice straw. **2** A similar paper made from the pith of a Chinese shrub, the **rice-paper plant.**

ric·er (rī′sər) *n.* A utensil consisting of a perforated container through which cooked potatoes, etc., are pressed.

rich (rich) *adj.* **1** Having large possessions, as of money, goods, or lands; wealthy. **2** Abundantly supplied: with *in* or *with.* **3** Yielding abundant returns; plentiful: a *rich* source of oil. **4** Of precious materials, fine workmanship, etc.: *rich* fabrics. **5** Luxuriant; sumptuous. **6** Having many choice ingredients, as butter, cream, etc.: a *rich* dessert. **7** Pleasingly full and resonant: a *rich* tone. **8** Deep; intense: a *rich* color. **9** Very fragrant; pungent: a *rich* perfume. **10** Containing a high percentage of fuel to air: said of fuel mixtures. **11** Abounding in desirable qualities: *rich* soil. **12** *Informal* Very funny: a *rich* joke. [< OE *rīce*] — **rich′ly** *adv.* —**rich′ness** *n.*

rich·es (rich′iz) *n. pl.* **1** Abundant possessions; wealth. **2** Abundance of whatever is precious.

Rich·ter scale (rik′tər) A logarithmic measure of the estimated energy released by earthquakes according to which 1 represents an imperceptible tremor and 10 a theoretical maximum about one thousand times greater than any recorded earthquake. [< Charles R. *Richter,* born 1900, U.S. seismologist]

rick (rik) *n.* A stack, as of hay, having the top rounded and thatched to protect the interior from rain. —*v.t.* To pile in ricks. [< OE *hrēac*]

rick·ets (rik′its) *n. pl. (construed as sing.)* A children's disease in which the bones do not harden normally, usu. due to vitamin D deficiency. [?]

rick·ett·si·a (rik·et′sē·ə) *n. pl.* **·si·ae** (-si·ē) Any of a genus of pathogenic bacterialike organisms parasitic in certain ticks and lice and transmissible to other animals and man. [< H. T. *Ricketts,* 1871–1910, U.S. pathologist] — **rick·ett′si·al** *adj.*

rick·et·y (rik′it·ē) *adj.* **1** Ready to fall; tottering. **2** Affected with rickets. **3** Feeble; infirm. —**rick′et·i·ly** *adv.* — **rick′et·i·ness** *n.*

rick·ey (rik′ē) *n. pl.* **rick·eys** A drink consisting of liquor, usu. gin, sweetened lime juice, and carbonated water. [?]

rick·rack (rik′rak′) *n.* Flat braid in zigzag form, used as trimming. [Reduplication of RACK¹]

rick·shaw (rik′shô) *n.* JINRIKSHA. Also **rick′sha.**

ric·o·chet (rik′ə·shā′, *esp. Brit.* -shet′) *v.i.* **·cheted** (-shād′) or **·chet·ted** (-shet′id), **·chet·ing** (-shā′ing) or **·chet·ting** (-shet′ing) To glance or rebound obliquely from a surface. —*n.* **1** A richocheting. **2** Something that ricochets. [< OF]

ri·cot·ta (ri·kot′ə; *Ital.* rē·kôt′tä) *n.* An unripened cheese, Italian in origin and similar to cottage cheese but smoother. [< L *recoquere* to cook again]

rid (rid) *v.t.* **rid** or **rid·ded, rid·ding** To free, as from a burden or annoyance: usu. with *of.* —*adj.* Free; clear; quit: with *of:* We are well *rid* of him. [< ON *rythja* clear (land) of trees]

rid·dance (rid′ns) *n.* **1** A removal of something undesirable. **2** The state of being rid.

rid·den (rid′n) *p.p.* of RIDE.

rid·dle¹ (rid′l) *v.t.* **·dled, ·dling 1** To perforate in numerous places, as with shot. **2** To sift through a coarse sieve. **3** To damage, injure, refute, etc., as if by perforating: to *riddle* a theory. —*n.* A coarse sieve. [< OE *hriddel* sieve] —**rid′· dler** *n.*

rid·dle² (rid′l) *n.* **1** A puzzling question or conundrum. **2** Any mysterious object or person. —*v.* **·dled, ·dling** *v.t.* **1** To solve; explain. —*v.i.* **2** To utter or solve riddles; speak in riddles. [< OE *rædels*]

ride (rīd) *v.* **rode** (*Regional* rid), **rid·den** (*Regional* rid), **rid·ing** *v.i.* **1** To sit on and be borne along by a horse or other animal. **2** To be borne along as if on horseback. **3** To travel or be carried on or in a vehicle or other conveyance. **4** To be supported in moving: The wheel *rides* on a shaft. **5** To float; be borne: The ship *rides* on the waves. **6** To carry a rider, etc., in a specified manner: This car *rides* well. **7** To seem to float in space, as a star. **8** To lie at anchor, as a ship. **9** To overlap or overlie, as broken bones. **10** To de-

pend: with *on:* Everything *rides* on him. **11** To be a bet: with *on:* They let their money *ride* on the filly. **12** *Informal* To continue unchanged: Let it *ride.* —*v.t.* **13** To sit on and control the motion of (a horse, bicycle, etc.). **14** To be borne or supported upon. **15** To overlap or overlie. **16** To travel or traverse (an area, certain distance, etc.) on a horse, in an automobile, etc. **17** To harass or bother oppressively: usu. in the past participle: *ridden* with shame. **18** To accomplish by riding: to *ride* a race. **19** To convey. **20** *Informal* To tease or torment by ridicule, criticisms, etc. **21** To keep somewhat engaged, usu. unnecessarily: to *ride* the brake. —**ride for a fall** To be headed for trouble, failure, etc. —**ride herd on** To control or supervise closely. —**ride out** To survive; endure successfully. —**ride up** To move upward out of place, as clothing. —*n.* **1** An excursion by any means of conveyance. **2** A means of transportation: to ask for a *ride.* **3** A manner of riding: a smooth *ride.* **4** A mechanical contrivance for riding, as at an amusement park. —**take for a ride** *Slang* **1** To remove (a person) to a place with the intent to murder. **2** To cheat; swindle. [< OE *rīdan*] —**rid′a·ble** *adj.*

rid·er (rī′dər) *n.* **1** One who or that which rides. **2** A piece of writing added to a document, contract, etc. **3** An addition to a legislative bill.

rid·er·less (rī′dər·lis) *adj.* Without a rider.

ridge (rij) *n.* **1** A raised mass of land long in proportion to its width and height. **2** A long, raised or top part of something, as the backbone of an animal, crest of a wave or mountain, ribbed part of a fabric, etc. **3** That part of a roof where the rafters meet the ridgepole. —*v.* **ridged, ridg·ing** *v.t.* **1** To mark with ridges. **2** To form into ridges. —*v.i.* **3** To form ridges. [< OE *hrycg* spine, ridge]

ridge·pole (rij′pōl′) *n.* A horizontal timber at the ridge of a roof. Also **ridge′beam′, ridge′-piece′, ridge′plate′.**

rid·i·cule (rid′ə·kyōōl) *n.* Language or actions expressing amused contempt or scorn; derision; mockery. —*v.t.* **·culed, ·cul·ing** To make fun of; hold up as a laughingstock; deride. [< L *ridiculum* a jest] —**rid′i·cul′er** *n.*

Ridgepole

Syn. *v.* banter, chaff, jeer, mock, taunt, satirize, scoff.

ri·dic·u·lous (ri·dik′yə·ləs) *adj.* **1** Absurdly comical: a *ridiculous* costume. **2** Unworthy of consideration; preposterous. —**ri·dic′u·lous·ly** *adv.* —**ri·dic′u·lous·ness** *n.* —**Syn. 1** droll, funny, grotesque, laughable. **2** absurd, nonsensical, foolish, stupid, asinine, senseless.

rid·ing[1] (rī′ding) *n.* The act of one who rides. —*adj.* **1** Suitable for riding: a *riding* horse. **2** To be used while riding: *riding* boots.

rid·ing[2] (rī′ding) *n.* **1** One of the three administrative divisions of Yorkshire, England. **2** Any similar administrative or electoral division, as in Canada, New Zealand, etc. [< OE *thrithing* the third part (of a county)]

rife (rīf) *adj.* **1** Prevalent; widespread. **2** Plentiful; abundant. **3** Containing in abundance: with *with.* [< OE *rīfe*]

riff (rif) *n.* In jazz music, a melodic phrase or motif played repeatedly as background or used as the main theme. —*v.i.* To perform a riff. [? Alter. of REFRAIN]

rif·fle (rif′əl) *n.* **1** A shoal or rocky obstruction lying beneath the surface of a stream and causing a stretch of choppy water. **2** Such a stretch of water. **3** A way of shuffling cards. —*v.t.* & *v.i.* **·fled, ·fling** **1** To cause or form a riffle. **2** To shuffle (cards) by bending up adjacent corners of two halves of the pack, and permitting the cards to slip together as they are released. **3** To thumb through (the pages of a book). [?]

riff·raff (rif′raf′) *n.* **1** Low, disreputable persons; rabble. **2** Miscellaneous rubbish. [< OF *rif et raf* every bit]

ri·fle[1] (rī′fəl) *n.* **1** A firearm having spiral grooves on the surface of the bore for imparting rotation to the projectile. **2** Such a weapon fired from the shoulder. **3** *pl.* A

Automatic rifle (M-14)

body of soldiers equipped with rifles. —*v.t.* **·fled, ·fling** To cut a spirally grooved bore in (a firearm, etc.). [< OF *rifler* to scratch]

ri·fle[2] (rī′fəl) *v.t.* **·fled, ·fling** **1** To search through and rob, as a safe. **2** To search and rob (a person). **3** To take away by force. [< OF *rifler* to scratch, plunder] —**ri′fler** *n.*

ri·fle·man (rī′fəl·mən) *n. pl.* **·men** (-mən) One armed or skilled with the rifle.

ri·fling (rī′fling) *n.* **1** The operation of forming the grooves in a rifle. **2** Such grooves collectively. ● See REVOLVER.

rift (rift) *n.* **1** An opening made by splitting; a cleft; fissure. **2** A break in friendly relations. —*v.t.* & *v.i.* To rive; burst open; split. [< Scand.]

rig[1] (rig) *v.t.* **rigged, rig·ging** **1** To fit out; equip. **2** *Naut.* **a** To fit, as a ship, with rigging. **b** To fit (sails, stays, etc.) to masts, yards, etc. **3** *Informal* To dress; clothe, esp. in finery: usu. with *out.* **4** To construct hurriedly or by makeshifts: often with *up.* **5** To prepare or arrange for special operation: controls *rigged* for the left hand only. —*n.* **1** The arrangement of sails, spars, etc., on a vessel. **2** *Informal* Dress or costume. **3** Gear, machinery, or equipment: an oil-well *rig.* **4** A carriage and its horse or horses. [< Scand.]

rig[2] (rig) *v.t.* **rigged, rig·ging** To control fraudulently: manipulate: to *rig* an election. [?]

rig·ger (rig′ər) *n.* One who rigs, esp. one who fits the rigging of ships, assembles lifting or hoisting gear, etc.

rig·ging (rig′ing) *n.* **1** *Naut.* The entire cordage system of a vessel. **2** Equipment or gear used in lifting, hauling, etc.

right (rīt) *adj.* **1** In accordance with some moral, just, or equitable law or standard; virtuous; upright. **2** Conformable to truth or fact; correct; accurate. **3** Proper; fitting; suitable. **4** Most desirable or preferable: to go to the *right* parties. **5** In an orderly or satisfactory state or condition: to put things *right.* **6** Sound; healthy; normal, as in mind or body. **7 a** Designating, being, or closest to that side of the body which is toward the south when one faces the sunrise. **b** Designating a corresponding side of anything. **8** Designating that surface or part of something designed to be worn outward or, when used, to be seen. **9** Politically conservative or reactionary. **10.** *Geom.* Formed by lines, segments, or planes perpendicular to a base. —*adv.* **1** According to some moral, just, or equitable law or standard. **2** Correctly; accurately. **3** In a straight line; directly: Go *right* home. **4** Precisely: He stood *right* in the doorway. **5** Suitably; properly: I can't fix it *right.* **6** Completely: burned *right* to the ground. **7** Thoroughly: He felt *right* at home. **8** Immediately: *right* after the storm. **9** Very: used regionally or in certain titles: a *right* nice day; the *Right* Reverend. **10** On or toward the right: to go *right.* —*n.* **1** That which is right, good, just, true, proper, etc. **2** *Often pl.* Any power or privilege to which a person has a moral, legal, or just claim: the *right* to vote. **3** *pl.* A claim or title to, or interest in, anything that is enforceable by law or custom: *rights* to property; fishing *rights.* **4** Something a person feels belongs justly or properly to him: a *right* to leave. **5** The correct or factual report or interpretation of something. **6** The right hand or side of a person or thing. **7** A direction to or a location on the right. **8** Something adapted for right-hand use or position. **9** In boxing: **a** A blow delivered with the right hand. **b** The right hand. **10** *Often cap.* In politics, a conservative or reactionary position, or a party or group advocating such a position, so designated because of the views of the party occupying seats on the right side of the presiding officer in certain European legislative bodies. —**by right** (or **rights**) Justly; properly. —**to rights** *Informal* Into a proper or orderly condition. —*v.t.* **1** To restore to an upright or normal position. **2** To put in order; set right. **3** To make correct or in accord with facts. **4** To make reparation for; redress or avenge: to *right* a wrong. **5** To make reparation to (a person); do justice to. —*v.i.* **6** To regain an upright or normal position. —*interj.* I agree! I understand! —**right on** *Informal* An interjectory phrase expressing enthusiastic agreement or encouragement: also used adjectivally: He was *right on* in that speech. [< OE *riht*]

right·a·bout (rīt′ə·bout′) *n.* A turning in or to the opposite direction, physically or mentally: also **right′a·bout′-face′** (-fās′).

right angle An angle with a measure of 90°. **—right′-an′-gled** *adj.* • See ANGLE.

right·eous (rī′chəs) *adj.* 1 Morally right and just. 2 Virtuous; blameless: a *righteous* man. 3 Justifiable; defensible: *righteous* anger. [< OE *riht* right + *wīs* wise] **—right′-eous·ly** *adv.* **—right′eous·ness** *n.*

right·ful (rīt′fəl) *adj.* 1 Owned or held by just or legal claim: *rightful* heritage. 2 Having a just or legal claim: the *rightful* heir. 3 Fair; upright; just. 4 Proper; suitable. **—right′ful·ly** *adv.* **—right′ful·ness** *n.*

right-hand (rīt′hand′) *adj.* 1 Of, pertaining to, or situated on the right side. 2 Of or for the right hand. 3 Most dependable or helpful: He was my *right-hand* man.

right-hand·ed (rīt′han′did) *adj.* 1 Using the right hand habitually or more easily than the left. 2 Done with the right hand. 3 Turning or moving from left to right, as the hands of a clock. 4 Adapted for use by the right hand, as a tool. **—right′-hand′ed·ness** *n.*

right·ism (rī′tiz·əm) *n.* Politically conservative or reactionary policies or principles. **—right′ist** *adj., n.*

right·ly (rīt′lē) *adv.* 1 Correctly. 2 Honestly; uprightly. 3 Properly; aptly.

right-mind·ed (rīt′mīn′did) *adj.* Having feelings or opinions that are right or sound.

right·ness (rīt′nis) *n.* The quality or condition of being right.

right of search 1 In international law, the right of a belligerent vessel in time of war to verify the nationality of a vessel and to ascertain, if neutral, whether it carries contraband goods. 2 A similar right in time of peace exercised to prevent piracy or to enforce revenue laws.

right of way 1 *Law* a The right, general or special, of a person to pass over the land of another. b The land over which such passage is made. 2 The strip of land over which a railroad, public highway, or high-tension power line is built. 3 The legal or customary precedence which allows one vehicle to cross in front of another. 4 Any right of precedence. Also **right′-of-way′**.

right triangle A triangle containing one right angle. • See TRIANGLE.

right whale Any of various large-headed, toothless whales that feed by straining water through whalebone plates in the mouth.

right wing 1 A political party or group advocating conservative or reactionary policies. 2 That part of any group advocating such policies. Also **Right Wing. —right′-wing′** *adj.* **—right′-wing′er** *n.*

rig·id (rij′id) *adj.* 1 Resisting change of form; stiff. 2 Rigorous; inflexible; severe; strict. 3 Precise; exact, as reasoning. [< L *rigere* be stiff] **—rig′id·ly** *adv.* **—ri·gid′i·ty, rig′id·ness** *n.*

rig·ma·role (rig′mə·rōl, rig′ə·mə-) *n.* Incoherent or uselessly complicated talk, writing, procedures, etc. [Alter. of *ragman roll* catalog, long list]

rig·or (rig′ər) *n.* 1 Harshness; strictness; severity, as of opinions, methods, temperament, etc. 2 Severe hardship, discomfort, etc. 3 Inclemency, as of the weather. 4 Exactitude; precision. 5 The condition of being stiff or rigid. *Brit. sp.* **rig′our.** [< L *rigere* be stiff] **—rig′or·is′tic** *adj.*

rig·or mor·tis (rig′ər môr′tis, rī′gər) The muscular stiffening that ensues within a few hours after death. [L, stiffness of death]

rig·or·ous (rig′ər·əs) *adj.* 1 Marked by or acting with rigor; severe. 2 Rigidly accurate; exact; strict. 3 Extremely difficult, arduous, or demanding. 4 Extremely variable, as weather; inclement. **—rig′or·ous·ly** *adv.* **—rig′or·ous·ness** *n.*

rile (rīl) *v.t. Informal* 1 To vex; irritate. 2 To roil; make muddy. [Var. of ROIL]

rill (ril) *n.* A small stream; rivulet. [< Du. *ril* or G *rille*]

rim (rim) *n.* 1 The edge or border of an object, usu. of a circular object. 2 The circumference of a wheel, esp., on an automobile wheel, the detachable, metal band over which the tire is fitted. **—v.t. rimmed, rim·ming** 1 To provide with or serve as a rim; border. 2 In sports, to roll around the edge of (the basket, cup, etc.) without falling in. [< OE *rima*]

rime[1] (rīm) *n., v.* **rimed, rim·ing** RHYME.

rime[2] (rīm) *n.* HOARFROST. **—v.t. & v.i. rimed, rim·ing** To cover with rime. [< OE *hrīm* frost] **—rim′y** *adj.*

rind (rīnd) *n.* The skin or outer coat that may be peeled or taken off, as of fruit, cheese, bacon, plants, etc. [< OE *rind* bark, crust]

ring[1] (ring) *n.* 1 Any object, line, or figure having the form of a circle or similar closed curve. 2 A rim or border of something circular. 3 A circular band of precious metal, worn on a finger. 4 Any metal or wooden band used for holding or carrying something: a napkin *ring.* 5 A group of persons or things in a circle. 6 A group of persons engaged in some common, often corrupt activity, business, etc.: a dope *ring.* 7 A place where the bark has been cut away around a branch or tree trunk. 8 A concentric layer of wood formed during a single year's growth in most trees and shrubs: also **annual ring.** 9 An area or arena, usu. circular, for exhibitions, etc.: a circus *ring.* 10 a A square area, usu. bordered with ropes, for boxing or wrestling matches. b The sport of prizefighting: with *the.* 11 Any field of competition or rivalry: He tossed his hat into the *ring.* **—v. ringed, ring·ing** *v.t.* 1 To surround with a ring; encircle. 2 To form into a ring or rings. 3 To provide or decorate with a ring or rings. 4 To cut a ring of bark from (a branch or tree); girdle. 5 To put a ring in the nose of (a pig, bull, etc.). 6 To hem in (cattle, etc.) by riding in a circle around them. 7 In certain games, to cast a ring over (a peg or pin). **—v.i.** 8 To form a ring or rings. 9 To move or fly in rings or spirals; circle. [< OE *hring*]

ring[2] (ring) *v.* **rang, rung, ring·ing** *v.i.* 1 To give forth a resonant sound, as a bell when struck. 2 To sound loudly or be filled with sound or resonance; reverberate; resound. 3 To cause a bell or bells to sound, as in summoning a servant. 4 To have or suggest, as by sounding, a specified quality: His story *rings* true. 5 To have a continued sensation of ringing or buzzing: My ears *ring.* **—v.t.** 6 To cause to ring, as a bell. 7 To produce, as a sound, by or as by ringing. 8 To announce or proclaim by ringing: to *ring* the hour. 9 To summon, escort, usher, etc., by or as by ringing: with *in* or *out*: to *ring* out the old year. 10 To strike (coins, etc.) on something so as to test their quality. 11 To call on the telephone: often with *up.* **—n.** 1 The sound produced by a bell. 2 A sound suggesting this: the *ring* of laughter. 3 Any loud, reverberating sound. 4 A telephone call. 5 A sound that is characteristic or indicative: with *of*: His words have the *ring* of truth. [< OE *hringan*] **—Syn.** *v.* 1 clang, resound, peal, toll, chime.

ring bolt A bolt having a ring through an eye in its head.

ringed (ringd) *adj.* 1 Wearing a ring or rings. 2 Encircled or marked by a ring or rings. 3 Composed of rings.

ring·er[1] (ring′ər) *n.* 1 One who or that which rings a bell, chime, etc. 2 *Slang* An athlete, horse, etc., illegally entered in a sports competition. 3 *Slang* A person who bears a marked resemblance to another.

ring·er[2] (ring′ər) *n.* 1 One who or that which rings or encircles. 2 A quoit or horseshoe that falls around one of the posts.

ring·lead·er (ring′lē′dər) *n.* A leader of any undertaking, esp. of an unlawful one.

ring·let (ring′lit) *n.* A long, spiral lock of hair; a curl.

ring·mas·ter (ring′mas′tər, -mäs′-) *n.* One who has charge of a circus ring and of the performances in it.

ring·side (ring′sīd′) *n.* 1 The space or seats immediately surrounding a ring, as at a prize fight. 2 Any area for close viewing.

ring·worm (ring′wûrm′) *n.* A contagious skin disease caused by certain fungi and marked by itchy lesions that spread ringlike from the site of infection.

rink (ringk) *n.* 1 A smooth surface of ice, used for sports, as ice-skating, hockey, curling, etc. 2 A smooth floor, used for roller-skating. 3 A building containing a surface for ice-skating or roller-skating. [< OF *renc* row, rank]

rinse (rins) *v.t.* **rinsed, rins·ing** 1 To remove soap, dirt, impurities, etc., from by immersing in or flooding with clear water. 2 To remove (soap, dirt, etc.) in this manner. 3 To wash lightly: often with *out.* 4 To use a rinse on (the hair). **—n.** 1 The act of rinsing. 2 A solution used for coloring hair. [? < L *recens* recent, fresh] **—rins′er** *n.*

rins·ing (rin′sing) *n.* 1 A rinse. 2 *Usu. pl.* a The liquid in

which anything is rinsed. **b** That which is removed by rinsing; dregs.

ri·ot (rī′ət) *n.* **1** A violent or tumultuous public disturbance by a large number of persons; uproar; tumult. **2** Any boisterous outburst: a *riot* of laughter. **3** A vivid show or display: a *riot* of color. **4** *Informal* An uproariously amusing person, thing, or performance. —**run riot 1** To act or move wildly and without restraint. **2** To grow profusely, as vines. —*v.i.* **1** To take part in a riot. **2** To live a life of unrestrained revelry. —*v.t.* **3** To spend (time, money, etc.) in riot or revelry. [< OF *riote*] —**ri′ot·er** *n.*

riot act Any forceful or vigorous warning or reprimand. —**read the riot act to** To reprimand bluntly and severely.

ri·ot·ous (rī′ət·əs) *adj.* **1** Of, pertaining to, like, or engaged in a riot. **2** Loud; boisterous. **3** Profligate: *riotous* spending. —**ri′ot·ous·ly** *adv.* —**ri′ot·ous·ness** *n.*

rip[1] (rip) *v.* **ripped, rip·ping** *v.t.* **1** To tear or cut apart, often roughly or violently. **2** To tear or cut from something else, often in a rough or violent manner: with *off, away, out,* etc. **3** To saw or split (wood) in the direction of the grain. —*v.i.* **4** To be torn or cut apart; split. **5** *Informal* To rush headlong. —**rip into** *Informal* To attack violently, as with blows or words. —**rip off** *Slang* **1** To steal or steal from. **2** To cheat, swindle, or dupe. —**rip out** *Informal* To utter with vehemence. —*n.* **1** A tear or split. **2** The act of ripping. [ME *rippen*] —**rip′per** *n.*

rip[2] (rip) *n.* **1** A ripple; a rapid in a river. **2** A riptide.

R.I.P. may he (she, or they) rest in peace (L *requiescat in pace*).

ri·par·i·an (ri·pâr′ē·ən, rī-) *adj.* Pertaining to, growing, or located on the banks of a river or other watercourse. [< L *ripa* bank of a river]

rip·cord (rip′kôrd′) *n.* The cord by which the canopy of a parachute is released from its pack.

ripe (rīp) *adj.* **rip·er, rip·est 1** Grown to maturity and fit for food, as fruit or grain. **2** Brought to a condition for use: *ripe* cheese. **3** Fully developed; matured; also, advanced, as in years. **4** In full readiness to do or try; prepared; ready: *ripe* for mutiny. **5** Resembling ripe fruit; rosy; luscious. **6** Ready for surgical treatment, as an abscess. [< OE *rīpe* ready for reaping] —**ripe′ly** *adv.* —**ripe′ness** *n.*

rip·en (rī′pən) *v.t. & v.i.* To make or become ripe; mature. —**rip′en·er** *n.*

rip·off (rip′of′, -ôf′) *n. Slang* **1** The act of ripping off; an act of stealing or cheating. **2** Anything dishonest, illegal, or exploitative.

ri·poste (ri·pōst′) *n.* **1** A return thrust, as in fencing. **2** A quick, clever reply or retort. Also **ri·post′.** [< L *respondere* to answer]

rip·ping (rip′ing) *adj. Brit. Slang* Splendid; excellent.

rip·ple (rip′əl) *v.* **·pled, ·pling** *v.i.* **1** To become slightly agitated on the surface, as water. **2** To flow with small waves or undulations. **3** To make a sound like water flowing in small waves. —*v.t.* **4** To cause to form ripples. —*n.* **1** A small wave or undulation on the surface of water. **2** Anything suggesting this in appearance. **3** Any sound like that made by rippling. [?] —**rip′pler** *n.* —**rip′pling** *adj.* —**rip′pling·ly** *adv.*

rip-roar·ing (rip′rôr′ing, -rōr′-) *adj. Slang* Excellent; exciting; boisterous.

rip·saw (rip′sô′) *n.* A saw designed for cutting wood in the direction of the grain.

rip·tide (rip′tīd′) *n.* Water violently agitated by conflicting tides or currents.

Ripsaw

rise (rīz) *v.* **rose, ris·en, ris·ing** *v.i.* **1** To move upward; go from a lower to a higher position. **2** To slope gradually upward: The ground *rises* here. **3** To have height or elevation; extend upward: The city *rises* above the plain. **4** To gain elevation in rank, status, fortune, or reputation. **5** To swell up: Dough *rises*. **6** To become greater in force, intensity, height, etc. **7** To become greater in amount, value, etc. **8** To become elated or more optimistic: Their spirits *rose*. **9** To become erect after lying down, sitting, etc.; stand up. **10** To get out of bed. **11** To return to life. **12** To revolt; rebel: The people *rose* against the tyrant. **13** To adjourn: The House passed the bill before *rising*. **14** To appear above the horizon: The sun *rose*. **15** To come to the surface, as a fish after a lure. **16** To have origin; begin. **17** To become perceptible to the mind or senses: The scene *rose* in his mind. **18** To occur; happen. **19** To be able to cope with an emergency, danger, etc.: Will he *rise* to the occasion? —*v.t.* **20** To cause to rise. —**rise above** To prove superior to; show oneself indifferent to. —*n.* **1** A moving or sloping upward; ascent. **2** An elevated place, as a small hill. **3** Appearance above the horizon. **4** The height of a stair step or of a flight of stairs. **5** Advance, as in rank, status, prosperity, etc. **6** Increase, as in price, volume, intensity, etc. **7** An origin, source, or beginning. **8** *Informal* An emotional reaction; a response or retort, esp. in the phrase **get a rise out of** (someone). **9** *Brit.* An increase in salary. [< OE *rīsan*]

ris·er (rī′zər) *n.* **1** One who rises or gets up, as from bed: an early *riser.* **2** The vertical part of a step or stair.

ris·i·bil·i·ty (riz′ə·bil′ə·tē) *n. pl.* **·ties 1** A tendency to laughter. **2** *Usu. pl.* Appreciation of what seems laughable or ridiculous.

ris·i·ble (riz′ə·bəl) *adj.* **1** Having the power of laughing. **2** Of a nature to excite laughter. **3** Pertaining to laughter. [< L *risus*, p.p. of *ridere* to laugh] —**ris′i·bly** *adv.*

ris·ing (rī′zing) *adj.* **1** Increasing in wealth, rank, fame, etc. **2** Ascending: the *rising* moon. **3** Sloping upward: a *rising* hill. **4** Advancing to adult years; maturing: the *rising* generation. —*n.* **1** The act of one who or that which rises. **2** That which rises. **3** An uprising or revolt.

risk (risk) *n.* **1** A chance of encountering harm or loss; hazard; danger. **2** In insurance: **a** Chance of loss. **b** Degree of exposure to loss or injury. **c** An applicant for an insurance policy considered with regard to the hazard of insuring him. —*v.t.* **1** To expose to a chance of injury or loss; hazard. **2** To incur the risk of. [< Ital. *risicare* to dare] —**risk′er** *n.*

risk·y (ris′kē) *adj.* **risk·i·er, risk·i·est** Attended with risk; hazardous; dangerous. —**Syn.** perilous, ticklish, unsafe, uncertain, critical.

ris·qué (ris·kā′) *adj.* Bordering on or suggesting impropriety; somewhat daring or improper. [F] —**Syn.** indelicate, lewd, smutty, dirty, unseemly, unbecoming.

ri·tar·dan·do (rē′tär·dän′dō) *adj. & adv. Music* In a gradually slower tempo. [< Ital. *ritardare* to delay]

rite (rīt) *n.* **1** A solemn ceremony performed in a prescribed manner. **2** The words or acts accompanying such a ceremony. **3** Any formal practice or custom. [< L *ritus*]

rit·u·al (rich′ōō·əl) *n.* **1** A prescribed form or method for the performance of a rite. **2** The use or performing of such rites. **3** A book setting forth such a system of rites or observances. **4** Any act, observance, or custom performed somewhat regularly or formally. —*adj.* Of, pertaining to, or consisting of a rite or rites. —**rit′u·al·ly** *adv.*

rit·u·al·ism (rich′ōō·əl·iz′əm) *n.* **1** The use or performance of ritual. **2** Slavish devotion to ritual. —**rit′u·al·ist** *n.* —**rit′u·al·is′tic** *adj.* —**rit′u·al·is′ti·cal·ly** *adv.*

ritz·y (rit′sē) *adj.* **ritz·i·er, ritz·i·est** *Slang* Smart; elegant; luxurious. [< C. *Ritz*, 1850–1918, Swiss hotelier] —**Syn.** classy, posh, swank, chic.

ri·val (rī′vəl) *n.* **1** One who strives to equal or excel another; a competitor. **2** A person or thing equaling or nearly equaling another, in any respect. —*v.t.* **·valed** or **·valled, ·val·ing** or **·val·ling 1** To strive to equal or excel; compete with. **2** To be the equal of or a match for. —*adj.* Being a rival or rivals; competing. [< L *rivalis*]

ri·val·ry (rī′vəl·rē) *n. pl.* **·ries 1** The act of rivaling. **2** The state of being a rival or rivals; competition.

rive (rīv) *v.* **rived, rived** or **riv·en, riv·ing** *v.t.* **1** To split asunder by force; cleave. **2** To break (the heart, etc.). —*v.i.* **3** To become split. [< ON *rifa* tear, rend] —**riv·er** (rī′vər) *n.*

riv·er (riv′ər) *n.* **1** A large, natural stream of water, usu. fed by converging tributaries along its course and discharging into a larger body of water. **2** A large stream of any kind; copious flow. —**sell down the river** To betray;

deceive. **—send up the river** *Slang* To send to a penitentiary. [< L *riparius*]

river basin An area of land drained by a river and its branches.

riv·er·head (riv′ər·hed′) *n.* The source of a river.

riv·er·side (riv′ər·sīd′) *n.* The land adjacent to a river.

riv·et (riv′it) *n.* A metal bolt, having a head on one end, used to join objects, as metal plates, by passing the shank through holes and forming a head by flattening out the plain end. **—***v.t.* **1** To fasten with or as with a rivet. **2** To fasten firmly. **3** To engross or attract (the eyes, attention, etc.). [< OF *river* to clench] **—riv′et·er** *n.*

riv·u·let (riv′yə·lit) *n.* A small stream or brook. [< L *rivus* brook]

RM, R.M., RM., r.m. Reichsmark(s).

rm. ream; room.

rms, r.m.s. root mean square.

rms. reams; rooms.

R.N. registered nurse; Royal Navy.

Rn radon.

RNA ribonucleic acid.

R.N.R. Royal Naval Reserve.

R.N.W.M.P. Royal Northwest Mounted Police.

roach[1] (rōch) *n.* **1** A European freshwater fish of the carp family. **2** One of other related fishes, as the American freshwater sunfish. [< OF *roche*]

roach[2] (rōch) *n.* **1** COCKROACH. **2** *Slang* The butt of a marihuana cigarette.

road (rōd) *n.* **1** An open way for public passage; a highway. **2** Any course followed in a journey or a project. **3** A railroad. **—on the road 1** On tour: said of circuses, theatrical companies, athletic teams, etc. **2** Traveling, as a canvasser or salesman. [< OE *rād* a ride, a riding]

road·bed (rōd′bed′) *n.* The foundation of a railroad track or of a road.

road·block (rōd′blok′) *n.* **1** An obstruction, as of men or materials, for blocking passage, as along a road. **2** Any obstacle to progress or advancement.

road·house (rōd′hous′) *n.* A restaurant, bar, etc., located at the side of a suburban or rural road.

road metal Broken stone or the like, used for making or repairing roads.

road·run·ner (rōd′run′ər) *n.* A long-tailed, very agile, crested ground cuckoo of sw North America.

road·stead (rōd′sted) *n. Naut.* A place of anchorage offshore, less sheltered than a harbor.

road·ster (rōd′stər) *n.* A light, open automobile having seats for two persons.

road·way (rōd′wā′) *n.* A road, esp. that part over which vehicles pass.

Roadrunner

roam (rōm) *v.i.* **1** To move about purposelessly from place to place; wander; rove. **—***v.t.* **2** To wander over; range: to *roam* the fields. **—***n.* The act of roaming. [ME *romen*] **—roam′er** *n.*

roan (rōn) *adj.* Of a color consisting of brown, reddish brown, black, or gray thickly interspersed with white hairs, as a horse. **—***n.* **1** A roan color. **2** An animal of a roan color. [< Sp. *roano*]

roar (rôr, rōr) *v.i.* **1** To utter a deep, prolonged cry, as of rage or distress. **2** To make a loud noise or din, as a cannon. **3** To laugh loudly. **4** To move, proceed, or act noisily. **—***v.t.* **5** To utter or express by roaring: The crowd *roared* its disapproval. **—***n.* **1** A full, deep, resonant cry. **2** Any loud, prolonged sound, as of wind or waves. **3** Loud, boisterous laughter. [< OE *rārian*] **—roar′er** *n.*

roast (rōst) *v.t.* **1** To cook by subjecting to the action of heat, as in an oven or by placing in hot ashes, embers, etc. **2** To heat to an extreme degree. **3** To dry and parch: to *roast* coffee. **4** *Informal* To criticize or ridicule severely. **—***v.i.* **5** To roast food in an oven, etc. **6** To be cooked or prepared by this method. **7** To be uncomfortably hot. **—***n.* **1** Something prepared for roasting, or that is roasted. **2** A social gathering where food is roasted: a corn *roast.* **3** *Informal* Severe criticism or ridicule. **—***adj.* Roasted. [< OHG *rōsten*]

roast·er (rōs′tər) *n.* **1** A person who roasts. **2** A pan for roasting. **3** Something suitable for roasting, as a chicken.

rob (rob) *v.* **robbed, rob·bing** *v.t.* **1** To seize and carry off the property of by unlawful violence or threat of violence. **2** To deprive (a person) of something belonging, necessary, due, etc.: *robbed* him of his honor. **3** To take something unlawfully from: to *rob* a store. **4** To steal: to *rob* gold. **—***v.i.* **5** To commit robbery. [< OHG *roubon*] **—rob′ber** *n.*

rob·ber·y (rob′ər·ē) *n. pl.* **·ber·ies** The act of robbing, esp. the taking away of the property of another unlawfully by using force or intimidation.

robe (rōb) *n.* **1** A long, loose, flowing, outer garment. **2** *pl.* Such a garment worn as a badge of office or rank. **3** A bathrobe or dressing gown. **4** A blanket or covering: lap *robe.* **—***v.* **robed, rob·ing** *v.t.* **1** To put a robe upon; clothe; dress. **—***v.i.* **2** To put on robes. [< OHG *roub* robbery]

rob·in (rob′in) *n.* **1** A large North American thrush with reddish brown breast and underparts. **2** A small European songbird with cheeks and breast yellowish red. [Dim. of *Robert*]

Robin Hood A legendary, English outlaw of great skill in archery, who robbed the rich to relieve the poor.

rob·in's-egg blue (rob′inz·eg′) A pale greenish blue.

Rob·in·son Cru·soe (rob′in·sən krōō′sō) The hero of Daniel

American robin

Defoe's *Robinson Crusoe* (1719), a sailor shipwrecked on a tropical island.

ro·bot (rō′bət, -bot) *n.* **1** A machine designed to resemble a person and perform human tasks. **2** Any mechanical device that performs complex, often humanlike actions automatically or by remote control. **3** A person who lives or works mechanically, without spontaneity, etc. [< Czech *robota* work, compulsory service]

robot bomb An early form of jet-powered guided missile having an explosive charge.

ro·bust (rō·bust′, rō′bust) *adj.* **1** Possessing or characterized by great strength or endurance. **2** Requiring strength. **3** Boisterous; rude: *robust* humor. **4** Rich, as in flavor: a *robust* soup. [< L *robur, roboris,* a hard variety of oak, strength] **—ro·bust′ly** *adv.* **—ro·bust′ness** *n.*

roc (rok) *n.* In Arabian and Persian legend, an enormous and powerful bird of prey.

Ro·chelle salt (rō·shel′) A potassium and sodium salt of tartaric acid, used as a cathartic, etc. [< La *Rochelle,* France]

rock[1] (rok) *n.* **1** A large mass of stone or stony matter, often forming a peak or cliff. **2** A piece of stone of any size. **3** *Geol.* Solid mineral matter, such as that forming an essential part of the earth's crust. **4** Any strong, solid person or thing, often acting as a support, refuge, defense, etc. **5** *Slang* A precious gem, esp. a diamond. **—on the rocks** *Informal* **1** In a ruined or disastrous condition. **2** Bankrupt; destitute. **3** Served with ice cubes: said of an alcoholic beverage. **—***adj.* Made or composed of rock; hard; stony. [< OF *roque*]

rock[2] (rok) *v.i.* **1** To move backward and forward or from side to side; sway. **2** To sway, reel, or stagger, as from a blow. **—***v.t.* **3** To move backward and forward or from side to side, esp. so as to soothe or put to sleep. **4** To cause to sway or reel. **—***n.* **1** The act of rocking or a rocking motion. **2** A type of popular music whose origins lie in jazz, country music, and blues, characterized by a strong, persistent rhythm, simple, often repeated melodies, and usu. performed by small, electronically amplified instrumental-singing groups: also **rock and roll, rock-and-roll, rock 'n' roll.** [< OE *roccian*]

rock·a·by (rok′ə·bī) *interj.* Go to sleep: used to lull a child to slumber. Also **rock′a·bye, rock′-a·bye.**

rock bottom 1 The very bottom; the lowest possible level. **2** The basis of any issue. **—rock′-bot′tom** *adj.*

rock-bound (rok′bound′) *adj.* Encircled by or bordered with rocks.

rock candy Sugar candied in hard, clear crystals.

rock crystal Colorless transparent quartz.

rock·er (rok′ər) *n.* **1** One who or that which rocks. **2** One

of the curved pieces on which a rocking chair or a cradle rocks. **3** ROCKING CHAIR.

rock·et (rok′it) *n.* **1 a** A usu. cylindrical firework, projectile, missile, or other device propelled by the reaction of ejected matter. **b** An engine that develops thrust by ejecting matter. **2** A vehicle propelled by rockets and designed for space travel. —*v.i. & v.t.* **1** To move or cause to move rapidly, as a rocket. **2** To rise or cause to rise rapidly: *Her career rocketed.* [< Ital. *rocchetta* spool]

rock·et·ry (rok′it·rē) *n.* The science and technology of rocket flight, design, and construction.

rock garden A garden with flowers and plants growing in rocky ground or among rocks arranged to imitate this.

rocking chair A chair having the legs set on rockers.

rocking horse A toy horse mounted on rockers.

rock ’n’ roll (rok′ən·rōl′) ROCK[2] *n.* (def. 2).

rock-ribbed (rok′ribd′) *adj.* **1** Surrounded or edged by rocks. **2** Inflexible; unchangeable.

rock salt Salt found in large, rocklike masses; halite.

rock·y[1] (rok′ē) *adj.* **rock·i·er, rock·i·est 1** Consisting of, abounding in, or resembling rocks. **2** Marked by difficulties, obstacles, etc. **3** Tough; unfeeling; hard. —**rock′i·ness** *n.*

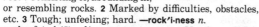

Rocking horse

rock·y[2] (rok′ē) *adj.* **rock·i·er, rock·i·est 1** Not firm; shaky; wobbly. **2** *Informal* Unsteady; dizzy. —**rock′i·ness** *n.*

Rocky Mountain goat MOUNTAIN GOAT.

ro·co·co (rə·kō′kō, rō′kə·kō′) *n.* **1** A style of decoration and architecture distinguished by profuse, elaborate, and delicately executed ornament, esp. prevalent during the 18th century. **2** Anything sometimes considered overly elaborate or delicate, as in literature, music, etc. —*adj.* **1** Having, or built in, the style of rococo. **2** Overelaborate; florid. [< F *rocaille* shellwork]

rod (rod) *n.* **1** A straight, usu. slim piece of wood, metal, etc. **2** A stick used to inflict punishment; also, the punishment itself. **3** A staff, wand, or scepter used as a badge of office, rank, rule, etc. **4** Dominion; rule; power, esp. if harsh. **5** FISHING ROD. **6** LIGHTNING ROD. **7** A measure of length, equal to 5.5 yards or 16.5 feet, or 5.03 meters. **8** A measuring rule. **9** One of the rodlike bodies of the retina sensitive to faint light. **10** *Slang* A pistol. [< OE *rod.*]

rode (rōd) *p.t.* of RIDE.

ro·dent (rōd′nt) *n.* Any of an order of gnawing mammals having incisors that grow continually, as a squirrel, beaver, or rat. —*adj.* **1** Gnawing. **2** Pertaining to the rodents. [< L *rodere* gnaw]

ro·de·o (rō′dē·ō, rō·dā′ō) *n. pl.* **·de·os 1** A roundup of cattle. **2** A public performance in which the riding of broncos or bulls, roping of calves, lariat-throwing, etc., are presented. [< Sp. *rodear* go around]

rod·o·mon·tade (rod′ə·mon·tād′, rō′də-, -täd′) *n.* Vain boasting; bluster. —*adj.* Bragging. [< Ital. *rodomontata*]

roe[1] (rō) *n.* A mass of eggs of fish or of certain crustaceans, as lobsters. [< MDu. *roge*]

roe[2] (rō) *n.* A small, graceful deer of Europe and w Asia. Also **roe deer.** [< OE *rā*]

roe·buck (rō′buk′) *n.* The male of the roe deer.

Roent·gen ray (rent′gən, runt′-, ren′chən) X-RAY. [< W. K. *Roentgen*, 1845–1923, German physicist]

Ro·ga·tion days (rō·gā′shən) *Eccl.* The three days immediately preceding Ascension Day, observed by litanies, processions, etc. [< L *rogare* ask]

rog·er (roj′ər) *interj.* **1** *Often cap.* Message received: a code signal used in radiotelephone communication. **2** *Informal* All right; O.K. [< *Roger*, code word for *r* used in telecommunication]

rogue (rōg) *n.* **1** A dishonest and unprincipled person; scoundrel. **2** One who is innocently mischievous or playful. **3** A dangerous animal separated from the herd: also used adjectively: a *rogue* elephant. —*v.* **rogued, ro·guing** *v.t.* **1** To practice roguery upon; defraud. —*v.i.* **2** To live or act like a rogue. [?] —*Syn.* ne′er-do-well, dastard, good-for-nothing, scamp, knave, rascal.

ro·guer·y (rō′gər·ē) *n. pl.* **·guer·ies 1** Knavery, cheating, or dishonesty. **2** Playful mischievousness.

rogues′ gallery A collection of photographs of criminals taken to aid the police in their future identification.

ro·guish (rō′gish) *adj.* **1** Playfully mischievous. **2** Knavish; dishonest. —**ro′guish·ly** *adv.* —**ro′guish·ness** *n.*

roil (roil) *v.t.* **1** To make muddy, as a liquid, by stirring up sediment. **2** To irritate or anger. [? < F *rouiller* rust, make muddy] —**roil′y** *adj.*

roist·er (rois′tər) *v.i.* **1** To act in a blustery manner; swagger. **2** To engage in revelry. [< L *rusticus* rustic] —**roist′er·er** *n.* —**roist′er·ing** *adj.*

ROK Republic of (South) Korea.

role (rōl) *n.* **1** A part or character taken by an actor. **2** Any assumed office or function. **3** A specific or acceptable pattern of behavior expected from those in a certain social status, profession, etc. Also **rôle.** [< F < Med. L *rotulus* roll of parchment]

roll (rōl) *v.i.* **1** To move upon a surface by turning round and round, as a wheel. **2** To move, be moved, travel about, etc., on or as on wheels. **3** To rotate wholly or partially: *Her eyes rolled.* **4** To assume the shape of a ball or cylinder by turning over and over upon itself. **5** To move or appear to move in undulations or swells, as waves or plains. **6** To sway or move from side to side, as a ship. **7** To rotate on a front-to-rear axis, as a projectile. **8** To walk with a swaying motion. **9** To make a sound as of heavy, rolling wheels; rumble: *Thunder rolled across the sky.* **10** To become spread or flat because of pressure applied by a roller, etc. **11** To perform a periodic revolution, as the sun. **12** To move ahead; progress. —*v.t.* **13** To cause to move by turning round and round or turning on an axis: to *roll* a ball; to *roll* a log. **14** To move, push forward, etc., on wheels or rollers. **15** To impel or cause to move onward with a steady, surging motion. **16** To begin to operate: *Roll* the presses. **17** To rotate, as the eyes. **18** To impart a swaying motion to. **19** To spread or make flat by means of a roller. **20** To wrap round and round upon itself. **21** To cause to assume the shape of a ball or cylinder by means of rotation and pressure: to *roll* a cigarette. **22** To wrap or envelop in or as in a covering. **23** To utter with a trilling sound: to *roll* one's r's. **24** To emit in a full and swelling manner, as musical sounds. **25** To beat a roll upon, as a drum. **26** To cast (dice) in the game of craps. **27** *Slang* To rob (a drunk or unconscious person). —**roll back** To cause (prices, wages, etc.) to return to a previous, lower level, as by government order. —**roll in 1** To arrive, usu. in large amounts: *Money rolled in.* **2** *Informal* To have large amounts of: *rolling in* money. —**roll out 1** To get out of (bed, etc.). **3** To flatten by means of rollers. —**roll up 1** To assume or cause to assume the shape of a ball or cylinder by turning over and over upon itself. **2** To accumulate; amass: to *roll up* large profits. **3** To arrive, as in an automobile. —*n.* **1** The act or an instance of rolling. **2** Anything rolled up. **3** A list of names, a register of items, etc.: an honor *roll.* **4** A long strip of something rolled upon itself: a *roll* of carpet. **5** Any food rolled up in preparation for eating or cooking, esp. small, variously shaped pieces of baked bread dough. **6** A roller. **7** A rolling gait or movement. **8** A rotation on an axis from front to rear, as of an aircraft. **9** A reverberation, as of thunder. **10** A trill. **11** A rapid beating of a drum. **12** An undulation or swell, as of waves or land. **13** *Slang* A wad of paper money; also, money in general. [< L *rota* wheel]

roll·a·way (rōl′ə·wā′) *adj.* Mounted on rollers for easy movement into storage.

roll·back (rōl′bak′) *n.* A return, esp. by government order, to a lower level, as of prices, wages, or rents.

roll call 1 The act of calling out a list of names to ascertain who is present. **2** The time of or signal for this.

roll·er (rō′lər) *n.* **1** One who or that which rolls anything. **2** Any cylindrical device that rolls, as for smoothing, crushing, imprinting, etc. **3** The wheel of a caster or roller skate. **4** A rod on which something is rolled up, as a curtain, map, hair, etc. **5** One of a series of long, swelling waves which break on a coast.

roller bearing A bearing employing rollers to lessen friction between parts.

roller coaster A railway having many steep inclines and sharp curves over which open cars run, as at an amusement park.

roller derby A race between two teams on roller skates, in which points are scored when a player overtakes opponents after skating around a track within a given time.

roll·er·skate (rō′lər·skāt′) v.i. **-skat·ed, -skat·ing** To go on roller skates. **—roller skater**

roller skate A metal frame on wheels, designed to be clamped to a shoe, or a shoe with wheels attached, for skating over a sidewalk, a wood floor, etc.

rol·lick·ing (rol′ik·ing) adj. Carelessly gay and frolicsome. Also **rol′lick·some** -(səm). [<earlier *rollick*, blend of ROMP and FROLIC]

Roller skate

rolling mill A machine or factory in which metal is rolled into sheets, bars, etc.

rolling pin A cylindrical roller of wood, glass, etc., for rolling out dough, etc.

rolling stock The wheeled transport equipment of a railroad.

roll·top (rōl′top′) adj. Having a flexible cover which slides back: a *rolltop* desk.

ro·ly·po·ly (rō′lē·pō′lē) adj. Short and fat; pudgy; dumpy. —n. **1** Brit. A pudding made of a sheet of pastry dough spread with fruit, preserves, etc., rolled up and cooked. **2** A pudgy person.

ROM Read-only memory, a kind of computer memory from which information may only be read, not altered or erased.

Ro·ma·ic (rō·mā′ik) adj. Pertaining to the language or people of modern Greece. —n. Modern Greek. [<Gk. *Rhōmaikos* Roman]

ro·maine (rō·mān′) n. A variety of lettuce having long leaves clustered in a head. [F, fem. of *romain* Roman]

ro·man (rō′mən) adj. *Printing* Designating a much-used style of type having serifs, and upright strokes thicker than horizontal strokes. —n. Roman type.

Ro·man (rō′mən) adj. **1** Of, pertaining to, or characteristic of Rome or its people. **2** Of the Roman Catholic Church. **3** LATIN. **4** Having a prominent, aquiline bridge: a *Roman* nose. —n. **1** A native, resident, or citizen of modern Rome or a citizen of ancient Rome. **2** A Roman Catholic.

ro·man à clef (rō·mäN′ ä·klā′) n. pl. **romans à clef** (-manz-) *French* A novel in which real persons or events appear under disguise; literally, novel with a key.

Roman calendar A calendar used by the ancient Romans. The day of the new moon (the calends), the full moon (the ides), and the ninth day before the ides (the nones) provided the bases for reckoning the day of the month.

Roman candle A tubular firework which discharges colored balls and sparks of fire.

Roman Catholic 1 A member of the Roman Catholic Church. **2** Of the Roman Catholic Church.

Roman Catholic Church The Christian church which recognizes the Pope as its supreme head on earth.

ro·mance (rō·mans′, rō′mans) n. **1** Adventurous, fascinating, or picturesque nature or appeal: the *romance* of faraway places. **2** A disposition to delight in the mysterious, adventurous, sentimental, etc.: a child of *romance*. **3** A love affair. **4** A long narrative from medieval legend, usu. involving heroes in strange adventures and affairs of love. **5** Any fictitious narrative embodying adventure, love affairs, etc. **6** The class of literature consisting of romances (defs. 4 and 5). **7** An extravagant falsehood. —v. (rō·mans′) **·manced, ·manc·ing** v.i. **1** To tell romances. **2** To think or act in a romantic manner. **3** *Informal* To make love. —v.t. **4** *Informal* To make love to; woo. [<OF *romans* a story written in French] **—ro·manc′er** n.

Ro·mance languages (rō·mans′) The languages developed from the vulgar Latin speech, including French, Italian, Spanish, Portuguese, and Rumanian.

Roman Empire The empire of ancient Rome, established in 27 B.C. and continuing until A.D. 395.

Ro·man·esque (rō′mən·esk′) adj. Of, pertaining to, or designating the style of architecture prevalent from the 5th to 12th centuries and characterized by the use of rounded arches and general massiveness. —n. Romanesque architecture.

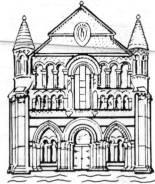

Romanesque façade

Roman holiday Enjoyment or profit derived from the sufferings of others. [< gladiatorial contests of ancient Rome]

Ro·ma·nia (rō·mā′nē·ə, -mān′yə) n. RUMANIA. **—Ro·man′ian** adj. n.

Ro·man·ic (rō·man′ik) adj. **1** Roman. **2** Of or pertaining to the Romance languages.

Ro·man·ism (rō′mən·iz′əm) n. The dogmas, forms, etc., of the Roman Catholic Church: a term used chiefly in disparagement. **—Ro′man·ist** adj., n.

Ro·man·ize (rō′mən·īz) v.t. & v.i. **·ized, ·iz·ing 1** To make or become Roman or Roman Catholic. **2** To write or speak in a Latinized style. **—Ro′man·i·za′tion** n.

Roman numerals The letters used until the tenth century as symbols in arithmetical notation. The basic letters are I (1), V (5), X (10), L (50), C (100), D (500), and M (1000). Intermediate and higher numbers are formed according to the following rules: Any symbol following another of equal or greater value adds to its value, as II = 2, XI = 11; any symbol preceding one of greater value subtracts from its value, as IV = 4, IX = 9, XC = 90; when a symbol stands between two of greater value, it is subtracted from the second and the remainder added to the first, as XIV = 14, LIX = 59.

ro·man·tic (rō·man′tik) adj. **1** Of, like, characterized or influenced by romance. **2** Given to feelings or thoughts of romance, adventure, idealism, etc. **3** Characterized by or conducive to love or amorousness. **4** Visionary; fantastic; impractical: a *romantic* scheme. **5** Strangely wild or picturesque: *romantic* scenery. **6** Of, pertaining to, or characteristic of romanticism (def. 1). —n. **1** An adherent of romanticism; a romanticist. **2** A romantic person. [<F *romance* romance, novel] **—ro·man′ti·cal·ly** adv.

ro·man·ti·cism (rō·man′tə·siz′əm) n. **1** *Often cap.* In the late 18th and early 19th centuries, a social and esthetic movement, beginning as a reaction to neo-classicism, and characterized, in art, literature, music, etc., by freedom of form, spontaneity of feeling, flights of lyricism and imagination, and a fascination with the remote past, nature, the strange and picturesque, etc. **2** The quality or characteristic of being romantic. **—ro·man′ti·cist** n.

ro·man·ti·cize (rō·man′tə·sīz) v.t. **·cized, ·ciz·ing** To regard or interpret in a romantic manner.

Romantic Movement ROMANTICISM (def. 1).

Rom·a·ny (rom′ə·nē) n. pl. **·nies 1** GYPSY. **2** The Indic language of the Gypsies. [<Romany *romani* < *rom* man]

Ro·me·o (rō′mē·ō) n. **1** In Shakespeare's tragedy *Romeo and Juliet,* the hero of the play. **2** Any ardent male lover.

romp (romp) v.i. **1** To play boisterously. **2** To win easily. —n. **1** One, esp. a girl, who romps. **2** Noisy, exciting frolic or play. **3** An easy victory. [Var. of RAMP[2]]

romp·er (rom′pər) n. **1** One who romps. **2** pl. A combination of waist and bloomers, as worn by young children.

Rom·u·lus (rom′yə·ləs) *Rom. Myth.* The founder of Rome, who, with his twin brother Remus, was reared by a she-wolf.

ron·do (ron′dō, ron·dō′) n. pl. **·dos** *Music* A composition or movement having a main theme that is repeated after each of several subordinate themes. [Ital., round]

rood (rōōd) n. **1** A cross or crucifix. **2** A square land measure, equivalent to one fourth of an acre, or 40 square rods. [<OE *rōd* rod]

roof (rōōf, rŏŏf) n. **1** The exterior upper covering of a building. **2** Any top covering, as of the mouth, a car, etc. **3** A

house; home. **4** The most elevated part of anything; top; summit. —*v.t.* To cover with or as with a roof. [< OE *hrōf*] —**roof′er** *n.*

roof garden 1 A garden on the roof of a building. **2** A gardenlike space on a roof used for a nightclub, restaurant, etc.

roof·ing (roo̅′fing, roof′ing) *n.* **1** Roofs collectively. **2** Material for roofs. **3** The act of covering with a roof.

rook[1] (rook) *n.* **1** An Old World bird similar to a crow. **2** A sharper; cheat; trickster. —*v.t. & v.i.* To cheat; defraud. [< OE *hrōc*]

rook[2] (rook) *n.* One of a pair of castle-shaped chessmen; a castle. [< Pers. *rukh*]

rook·er·y (rook′ər·ē) *n. pl.* **·er·ies 1** A place where rooks flock together and breed. **2** A breeding place of sea birds, seals, etc.

rook·ie (rook′ē) *n. Slang* **1** A raw recruit in the army, police, or any other service. **2** A first-year player in a major professional sport. [Prob. alter. of RECRUIT]

room (room, room) *n.* **1 a** A space for occupancy or use enclosed on all sides, as in a building. **b** The people in a room. **2** Space available or sufficient for some specified purpose: *room* to park. **3** Suitable or warrantable occasion; opportunity: room for doubt. **4** *pl.* Lodgings. —*v.i.* To occupy a room; lodge. [< OE *rūm* space]

room·er (roo̅′mər, room′ər) *n.* A lodger.

room·ette (roo̅·met′, room·et′) *n.* A compartment with a single bed in some railroad sleeping-cars.

room·ful (room′fool′, room′-) *n.* **1** As many or as much as a room will hold. **2** The number of persons in a room.

rooming house A house for roomers.

room·mate (room′māt′, room′-) *n.* One who occupies a room with another or others.

room·y (roo̅′mē, room′ē) *adj.* **room·i·er, room·i·est** Having abundant room; spacious. —**room′i·ly** *adv.* —**room′i·ness** *n.*

roor·back (roor′bak) *n. U.S.* A fictitious report circulated for political purposes. [< *Roorback,* purported author of a (nonexistent) book of travel]

roost (roost) *n.* **1 a** A perch upon which fowls rest at night. **b** Any place where birds resort to spend the night. **2** Any temporary resting place. —*v.i.* **1** To sit or perch upon a roost. **2** To come to rest; settle. [< OE *hrōst*]

roost·er (roo̅s′tər) *n.* The male of the chicken; cock. [< ROOST + -ER[1]]

root[1] (root, root) *n.* **1** The descending axis of a plant, usu. growing underground, providing support and absorbing moisture from the soil. **2** Any underground growth, as a tuber or bulb. **3** Some rootlike part of an organ or structure: the *root* of a tooth, hair, nerve, etc. • See TOOTH. **4** That from which something derives its origin, growth, life, etc.: Money is the *root* of all evil. **5.** *pl.* A mental or emotional attachment to some place or people, as through birth, childhood, etc. **6** The essence or basic part: the *root* of the problem. **7** *Ling.* A word or word part serving as the basic constituent element of a related group of words, as *know* in *unknown, knowledge, knowable,* and *knowingly.* **8** *Math.* A number or element that, taken a specified number of times as a factor, will produce a given number or element. **9** *Music* The principal tone of a chord. —*v.i.* **1** To put forth roots and begin to grow. **2** To be or become firmly fixed or established. —*v.t.* **3** To fix or implant by or as by roots. **4** To pull, dig, or tear up by or as by the roots; extirpate; eradicate: with *up* or *out.* [< OE *rōt*] —**root′y** *adj.*

root[2] (root, root) *v.t.* **1** To turn up or dig with the snout or nose, as swine. —*v.i.* **2** To turn up the earth with the snout. **3** To search for something; rummage. **4** To work hard; toil. [< OE *wrōtan* root up] —**root′er** *n.*

root[3] (root, root) *v.i. Informal* To give one's moral support to a contestant, team, cause, etc.: with *for.* [? < ROOT[2]] —**root′er** *n.*

Rooster

root beer A carbonated beverage flavored with the extracts of several roots.

root hair Any of numerous minute outgrowths on plant roots, having an absorbent function.

root·less (root′lis, root′-) *adj.* **1** Without roots. **2** Having no permanent or secure emotional attachment to a place, community, or culture. —**root′less·ness** *n.*

root·let (root′lit, root′-) *n.* A small root.

root·stock (root′stok′, root′-) *n.* RHIZOME.

rope (rōp) *n.* **1** An assembly of intertwined strands of fiber, wire, plastic, etc., forming a thick cord. **2** A collection of things plaited or united in a line. **3** A sticky or glutinous filament or thread of something, as of beaten egg yolks. **4 a** A cord or halter used in hanging. **b** Death by hanging. **5** LASSO. —*v.t.* **roped, rop·ing 1** To tie or fasten with or as with rope. **2** To enclose, border, or divide with a rope: usu. with *off:* He *roped* off the arena. **3** To catch with a lasso. **4** *Informal* To deceive: with *in.* [< OE *rāp*]

rop·y (rō′pē) *adj.* **rop·i·er, rop·i·est 1** That may be drawn into threads, as a glutinous substance; stringy. **2** Resembling ropes or cordage. —**rop′i·ly** *adv.* —**rop′i·ness** *n.*

Roque·fort cheese (rōk′fərt, *Fr.* rôk·fôr′) A strong cheese with a blue mold, made from ewe's and goat's milk. [< *Roquefort,* France, where first made]

ror·qual (rôr′kwəl) *n.* Any of various whales having a dorsal fin and marked lengthwise creases at the throat. [< Norw. *röyrkval*]

Rorqual

Ror·schach test (rôr′shäk, -shäkh, rôr′-) A psychological test based on the subject's interpretation of inkblot patterns. [< H. *Rorschach,* 1884–1922, Swiss psychiatrist]

ro·sa·ceous (rō·zā′shəs) *adj.* **1** Of, pertaining to, or designating the rose and related plants, as apple, hawthorn, etc. **2** Resembling a rose; rosy.

ro·sa·ry (rō′zə·rē) *n. pl.* **·ries** *Eccl.* **1** A string of beads for keeping count of a series of prayers, used esp. in Roman Catholicism. **2** The prayers. [< LL *rosarium* a rose garden]

rose[1] (rōz) *n.* **1** Any of a genus of hardy, erect or climbing shrubs with prickly stems and flowers of pink, red, white, yellow, etc. **2** The flower. **3** Any of various other plants or flowers having a likeness to the true rose. **4** A pinkish or purplish red color. **5** An ornamental knot, as of ribbon or lace; a rosette. **6** A form in which gems, esp. diamonds, are often cut. —*adj.* **1** Of, containing, or used for roses. **2** Of the color rose. **3** Rose-scented. [< L *rosa* < Gk. *rhodon*]

rose[2] (rōz) *p.t.* of RISE.

ro·se·ate (rō′zē·it, -āt) *adj.* **1** Of a rose color. **2** Optimistic; rosy. —**ro′se·ate·ly** *adv.*

rose·bud (rōz′bud′) *n.* The bud of a rose.

rose·bush (rōz′boosh′) *n.* A rose-bearing shrub.

rose chafer A hairy, fawn-colored beetle that feeds on the blossoms of roses and related plants. Also **rose beetle.**

rose fever A kind of hay fever that occurs in early summer when roses are in bloom. Also **rose cold.**

rose·mar·y (rōz′mâr′ē) *n. pl.* **·mar·ies 1** An evergreen, fragrant shrub related to mint. **2** Its leaves, used for their taste and aroma in cooking, perfumery, etc. [< L *ros* dew + *marinus* marine; infl. by *rose, Mary*]

rose of Sharon 1 In the Bible, an unidentified flower. **2** A species of hibiscus; althea. **3** A species of St. Johnswort.

ro·se·o·la (rō·zē·ō′lə, -zē′ə·lə) *n.* **1** A pink rash occurring as a symptom of various diseases. **2** A mild disease of infants, marked by fever and a pink rash. [< L *roseus* rosy]

Ro·set·ta stone (rō·zet′ə) A tablet containing an inscription in Egyptian hieroglyphics and in Greek, found near Rosetta, Egypt, in 1799. It supplied the key to the ancient inscriptions of Egypt.

ro·sette (rō·zet′) *n.* **1** A painted or sculptured architectural ornament with parts circularly arranged. **2** A ribbon badge shaped like a rose and worn to indicate possession of a certain military decoration. **3** Any flowerlike cluster as of leaves, markings, etc. [F, little rose]

rose water An aqueous extract of rose petals, used in perfumery and cooking. —**rose′·wa′ter** *adj.*

rose window A circular window filled with tracery that radiates from the center.

rose·wood (rōz′wŏŏd′) *n.* **1** The hard, dense, dark-colored wood of various tropical leguminous trees, valued for cabinet work. **2** Any tree yielding such a wood.

Rosh Ha·sha·na (rosh hə·shä′· nə, rōsh) The Jewish New Year, celebrated in September or early October. Also **Rosh Ha·sho′nah** (-shō′-). [< Hebrew *rōsh* head of + *hash-shānāh* the year]

Rose window

ros·in (roz′in) *n.* A hard, usu. amber-colored resin obtained from turpentine. —*v.t.* To apply rosin to. [Var. of RESIN] —**ros′in·y** *adj.*

ros·ter (ros′tər) *n.* **1** A list of officers and men enrolled for duty. **2** Any list of names. [< Du. *rooster* list]

ros·trum (ros′trəm) *n. pl.* **·trums** or **·tra** (-trə) **1** A stage or platform for public speaking. **2** Those speaking publically on a rostrum. **3** *pl.* **ros·tra** The orators' platform in the Roman forum. **4** A beak or snout. **5** One of various beaklike parts, as the prow of an ancient war galley. [< L *rostrum* beak]

ros·y (rō′zē) *adj.* **ros·i·er, ros·i·est** **1** Like a rose in color. **2** Blushing. **3** Fresh and blooming. **4** Favorable; optimistic. —**ros′i·ly** *adv.* —**ros′i·ness** *n.*

rot (rot) *v.* **rot·ted, rot·ting** *v.i.* **1** To undergo decomposition. **2** To fall or pass by decaying: with *away, off*, etc. **3** To become morally rotten. —*v.t.* **4** To cause to decompose; decay. —*n.* **1** The process of rotting or the state of being rotten. **2** Any of various plant and animal diseases characterized by destruction of tissue. **3** *Informal* Nonsense; bosh. —*interj.* Nonsense. [< OE *rotian*]

rot. rotating; rotation.

ro·ta·ry (rō′tər·ē) *adj.* **1** Turning on an axis, as a wheel. **2** Having some part that so turns: a *rotary* press. [< L *rota* wheel]

rotary engine An engine, as a turbine, in which rotary motion is directly produced without reciprocating parts.

ro·tate (rō′tāt, rō·tāt′) *v.t. & v.i.* **·tat·ed, ·tat·ing** **1** To turn or cause to turn on or as on its axis. **2** To alternate in a definite order or succession. [< L *rota* wheel] —**ro·tat′a·ble, ro′ta·tive** (-tə·tiv) *adj.* —**ro′ta·tor** *n.*

ro·ta·tion (rō·tā′shən) *n.* **1** The act or state of rotating. **2** Alternation or succession in some fixed order. **3** *Agric.* The practice of planting a field with a series of various crops to preserve the fertility of the field: also **crop rotation.** —**ro·ta′tion·al** *adj.*

ro·ta·to·ry (rō′tə·tôr′ē, -tō′rē) *adj.* **1** Of, pertaining to, or producing rotation. **2** Alternating or recurring.

ROTC, R.O.T.C. Reserve Officers' Training Corps.

rote (rōt) *n.* A routine, mechanical way of doing something. —**by rote** Mechanically; without intelligent attention: to learn *by rote.* [ME]

ro·ti·fer (rō′tə·fər) *n.* Any of numerous many-celled, aquatic microorganisms having rows of cilia at one end, which in motion resemble revolving wheels. [< L *rota* wheel + *ferre* to bear] —**ro·tif′er·al** (rō·tif′ər·əl), **ro·tif′er·ous** *adj.*

ro·tis·se·rie (rō·tis′ə·rē) *n.* **1** An establishment where meat is roasted and sold. **2** A device for roasting meat by rotating it on a spit before or over a source of heat. [< F *rôtir* to roast]

Rotifer

ro·to·gra·vure (rō′tə·grə·vyŏŏr′) *n.* **1** A printing process in which an impression is produced by rotating cylinders which have been etched from photographic plates. **2** Something printed by this process. [< L *rota* wheel + GRAVURE]

ro·tor (rō′tər) *n.* **1** A rotary part of a machine. **2** *Aeron.* The horizontally rotating airfoil assembly of a helicopter. [Contraction of ROTATOR]

rot·ten (rot′n) *adj.* **1** Decomposed; spoiled. **2** Smelling of decomposition or decay; putrid. **3** Untrustworthy; dishonest. **4** Weak or unsound, as if decayed. **5** *Informal* Disagreeable or very bad: a *rotten* disposition; a *rotten* movie. [< ON *rotinn*] —**rot′ten·ly** *adv.* —**rot′ten·ness** *n.*

rot·ter (rot′ər) *n. Chiefly Brit. Slang* A worthless or objectionable person.

ro·tund (rō·tund′) *adj.* **1** Rounded out, spherical, or plump. **2** Full-toned, as a voice or utterance. [< L *rota* wheel] —**ro·tun′di·ty, ro·tund′ness** *n.* —**ro·tund′ly** *adv.*

ro·tun·da (rō·tun′də) *n.* A circular building, room, hall, etc., esp. one with a dome. [< L *rotundus* round]

rou·ble (rŏŏ′bəl) *n.* RUBLE.

rouche (rŏŏsh) *n.* RUCHE.

rou·é (rŏŏ·ā′) *n.* A dissolute man; sensualist. [< F *rouer* break on the wheel]

Rotunda

rouge[1] (rŏŏzh) *n.* **1** Any cosmetic used for coloring the cheeks or lips. **2** A red powder, mainly ferric oxide, used in polishing. —*v.* **rouged, roug·ing** *v.t. & v.i.* To color with or apply rouge. [< L *rubeus* ruby]

rouge[2] (rŏŏzh) *n. Can.* A member of the Liberal party in Quebec. —*adj.* Of or pertaining to the Liberal party in Quebec.

rough (ruf) *adj.* **1** Having an uneven surface: a *rough* pavement. **2** Coarse in texture; shaggy: a *rough* tweed. **3** Disordered or ragged: a *rough* shock of hair. **4** Characterized by rude or violent action: *rough* sports. **5** Agitated; stormy: a *rough* passage. **6** Rude; coarse: a *rough* manner. **7** Lacking finish and polish; crude: a *rough* gem. **8** Done or made hastily and without attention to details: a *rough* sketch. **9** *Phonet.* Uttered with an aspiration, or *h* sound. **10** Harsh to the senses: *rough* sounds. **11** Without comforts or conveniences: the *rough* life of the poor. **12** Requiring physical strength: *rough* work. **13** *Informal* Difficult; trying: It's been a *rough* day. —**in the rough** In an unpolished or crude condition. —*n.* **1** Any rough ground. **2** A crude, incomplete, or unpolished object, material, or condition. **3** Any part of a golf course on which tall grass, bushes, etc., grow. **4** *Chiefly Brit.* A rude or violent person; ruffian. —*v.t.* **1** To make rough; roughen. **2** To treat roughly: often with *up.* **3** To make, cut, or sketch roughly: to *rough* in the details of a plan. —*v.i.* **4** To become rough. **5** To behave roughly. —**rough it** To live under or endure conditions that are hard, rustic, inconvenient, etc. —*adv.* In a rude manner. [< OE *rūh*] —**rough′ly** *adv.* —**rough′ness** *n.* —*Syn. adj.* **3** unkempt. **6** boorish, uncultivated.

rough·age (ruf′ij) *n.* Food containing bulky, indigestible constituents that stimulate peristalsis.

rough-and-read·y (ruf′ən·red′ē) *adj.* Crude or rough in quality but effective for a particular purpose.

rough-and-tum·ble (ruf′ən·tum′bəl) *adj.* Disregarding all rules of fighting; disorderly and violent. —*n.* A fight in which anything goes; a brawl.

rough-cast (ruf′kast′, -käst′) *v.t.* **-cast, -cast·ing** **1** To shape or prepare in a preliminary or incomplete form. **2** To coat, as a wall, with coarse plaster. —*n.* **1** Very coarse plaster for the outside of buildings. **2** A rude model of a thing in its first rough shape. —**rough′cast′er** *n.*

rough-dry (ruf′drī′) *v.t.* **-dried, -dry·ing** To dry (laundry) without ironing it afterward. —*adj.* Washed and dried but unironed.

rough·en (ruf′ən) *v.t. & v.i.* To make or become rough.

rough-hew (ruf′hyŏŏ′) *v.t.* **-hewed, -hewed** or **-hewn, -hew·ing** **1** To hew or shape roughly without smoothing. **2** To make crudely.

rough·house (ruf′hous′) *Slang n.* A noisy, boisterous disturbance; rough play. —*v.* (ruf′hous′, -houz′) **·housed, ·hous·ing** *v.i.* **1** To engage in roughhouse. —*v.t.* **2** To handle or treat roughly, usu. without hostile intent.

rough·neck (ruf′nek′) *n. Slang* A rowdy.

rough·rid·er (ruf′rī′dər) *n.* One skilled in breaking horses for riding, or accustomed to hard, rough riding.

Rough Riders The 1st U.S. Volunteer Cavalry in the Spanish-American War of 1898, commanded by Theodore Roosevelt.

rough-shod (ruf′shod′) *adj.* Shod with rough shoes to prevent slipping, as a horse. —**ride rough-shod (over)** To treat harshly and without consideration.

rou·lette (rōō·let′) *n.* **1** A gambling game in which participants place bets on which compartment of a rotating shallow bowl a small ball will fall into. **2** A toothed wheel for making marks or holes, as the tiny slits in a sheet of postage stamps. —*v.t.* ·**let·ted**, ·**let·ting** To use a roulette upon. [< L *rota* wheel]

Rou·ma·ni·a (rōō·mā′nē·ə, -mān′yə) *n.* RUMANIA. —**Rou·ma′ni·an** *adj., n.*

round (round) *adj.* **1** Having a shape like a ball, ring, or cylinder; spherical, circular, or cylindrical. **2** Semicircular: a *round* arch. **3** Plump. **4** Formed or moving in rotation or a circle: a *round* dance. **5** Approximate to the nearest ten, hundred, thousand, etc., as a number. **6** Pronounced with the lips forming a circle, as the vowel *o*. **7** Full; complete: a *round* dozen. **8** Large; ample; liberal: a good *round* fee. **9** Full in tone or resonance. **10** Free and easy; brisk: a *round* pace. —*n.* **1** Something round, as a globe, ring, or cylinder. **2** *Often pl.* A circular course or range; circuit; beat: to make one's *rounds*. **3** Motion in a circular path. **4** A series of recurrent actions; a routine: the daily *round* of life. **5** An outburst, as of applause. **6** In some sports and games, a division based on action or time. **7** A short canon for several voices. **8** A single shot fired by a weapon or by each of a number of weapons. **9** The ammunition used for such a shot. **10** ROUND DANCE (def. 1). **11** The state of being carved out on all sides: opposed to *relief.* **12** The state or condition of being circular; roundness. **13** A portion of a hind leg of beef, between the rump and lower leg. **14** A rung of a chair or ladder. —**go the rounds** To pass from person to person, as gossip, a rumor, etc. —*v.t.* **1** To make round or plump. **2** *Phonet.* To utter (a vowel) with the lips in a rounded position. **3** To travel or go around; make a circuit of. —*v.i.* **4** To become round or plump. **5** To make a circuit; travel a circular course. **6** To turn around. —**round off** (or **out**) **1** To make or become round. **2** To bring to perfection or completion. —**round up 1** To collect (cattle, etc.) in a herd, as for driving to market. **2** *Informal* To gather together; assemble. —*adv.* **1** On all sides; in such a manner as to encircle: A crowd gathered *round.* **2** In a circular path, or with a circular motion: The plane circled *round;* The wheel turns *round.* **3** To each of a number, one after the other: provisions enough to go *round.* **4** In circumference: a log three feet *round.* **5** From one position to another; here and there. **6** In the vicinity: to loiter *round.* **7** So as to complete a period of time: Will spring ever come *round* again? **8** In a circuitous or indirect way: Come *round* by way of the shopping center. **9** In the opposite direction: to turn *round.* —*prep.* **1** Enclosing; encircling: a belt *round* his waist. **2** On every side of; surrounding. **3** Toward every side of; about: He peered *round* him. **4** In the vicinity of: farms *round* the town. **5** To all or many parts of: driving friends *round* the city. **6** Here and there in: to look *round* a room. **7** So as to get to the other side of: walking *round* the corner. **8** In a group or mass surrounding: a rich socialite with hangers-on *round* him. [< L *rotundus*] —**round′ness** *n.*

round·a·bout (round′ə·bout′) *adj.* **1** Circuitous; indirect. **2** Encircling. —*n.* **1** A short, tight-fitting jacket for men and boys. **2** *Brit.* A merry-go-round.

round dance 1 A country dance in which the dancers form or move in a circle. **2** A dance with revolving or circular movements, as a waltz or polka, performed by two persons.

roun·de·lay (roun′də·lā) *n.* A simple song with a recurrent refrain. [< OF *rond* round]

round·er (roun′dər) *n.* **1** *Informal* A dissolute person; wastrel. **2** A tool for rounding a surface or edge.

Round·head (round′hed′) *n.* A member of the Parliamentary party in England in the civil war of 1642–49.

round·house (round′hous′) *n.* **1** A cabin on the after part of the quarter-deck of a vessel. **2** A round building with a turntable in the center, used for housing and repairing locomotives.

round·ly (round′lē) *adv.* **1** In a round manner or form. **2** Severely; vigorously; bluntly. **3** Thoroughly; completely.

round robin 1 A petition, protest, etc., on which signatures are written in a circle to avoid revealing the order of signing. **2** A tournament, as in tennis or chess, in which each player is matched with every other player.

round-shoul·dered (round′shōl′dərd) *adj.* Having the back rounded or the shoulders stooping.

round table 1 A group of persons meeting for a discussion. **2** Such a discussion. —**round′-ta′ble** *adj.*

Round Table 1 The table of King Arthur, made exactly circular so as to avoid any question of precedence among his knights. **2** King Arthur and his body of knights.

round trip A trip to a place and back again. —**round′-trip′** *adj.*

round·up (round′up′) *n.* **1** The bringing together of cattle scattered over a range for inspection, branding, etc. **2** The cowboys, horses, etc., employed in this work. **3** A bringing together, as of persons or things: a *roundup* of hobos.

round·worm (round′wûrm′) *n.* Any of a large phylum of worms with thin, cylindrical, unsegmented bodies; nematode worm.

rouse (rouz) *v.* **roused, rous·ing** *v.t.* **1** To cause to awaken from slumber, repose, unconsciousness, etc. **2** To excite to vigorous thought or action; stir up. **3** To startle or drive (game) from cover. —*v.i.* **4** To awaken from sleep or unconsciousness. **5** To become active. **6** To start from cover: said of game. —*n.* The act of rousing. [?] —**rous′er** *n.* —**Syn.** *v.* **2** animate, incite, arouse, stimulate.

rous·ing (rou′zing) *adj.* **1** Able to rouse or excite: a *rousing* speech. **2** Lively; vigorous: a *rousing* trade. **3** Exceptional; remarkable: a *rousing* success. —**rous′ing·ly** *adv.*

roust·a·bout (roust′ə·bout′) *n.* **1** A deck hand or dock worker. **2** An unskilled, semiskilled, or transient worker, as on an oil field or ranch. **3** A worker at a circus who helps to set up and dismantle tents, etc. [< *roust,* blend of ROUSE and ROUT]

rout[1] (rout) *n.* **1** A disorderly retreat or flight. **2** A boisterous and disorderly crowd; rabble. **3** An overwhelming defeat; debacle. —*v.t.* **1** To defeat disastrously. **2** To put to flight. [< L *ruptus,* p.p. of *rumpere* to break]

rout[2] (rout) *v.i.* **1** To turn up the earth with the snout, as swine. **2** To search; rummage. —*v.t.* **3** To dig or turn up with the snout. **4** To disclose to view; turn up as if with the snout: with *out.* **5** To hollow, gouge, or scrape, as with a scoop. **6** To drive or force out. [Var. of ROOT[2]]

route (rōōt, rout) *n.* **1** A course or way taken in passing from one point to another. **2** A road; highway. **3** The established passage which is regularly traveled by a person who delivers mail, milk, etc. **4** A way or means of approach: the *route* to success. —*v.t.* **rout·ed, rout·ing 1** To send by a certain way, as passengers, goods, etc. **2** To arrange an itinerary for. [< L *rupta (via)* broken (road)] —**rout′er** *n.*

rou·tine (rōō·tēn′) *n.* **1** A detailed method of procedure, prescribed or regularly followed. **2** Anything that has become customary or habitual. —*adj.* **1** Customary; habitual. **2** Uninspired; dull: a *routine* performance. [< F *route* way, road] —**rou·tine′ly** *adv.*

rove[1] (rōv) *v.* **roved, rov·ing** *v.i.* **1** To go from place to place without any definite destination. —*v.t.* **2** To roam over, through, or about. —*n.* The act of roving or roaming. [? < Du. *rooven* rob] —**Syn.** ramble, roam, wander.

rove[2] (rōv) A *p.t.* & *p.p.* of REEVE[1].

row[1] (rō) *n.* An arrangement or series of persons or things in a continued line, as a street lined with buildings on both sides, or a line of seats in a theater. —**a long row to hoe** A hard task or undertaking. —*v.t.* To arrange in a row: with *up.* [< OE *rāw* line]

row[2] (rō) *v.i.* **1** To use oars, sweeps, etc., in propelling a boat. **2** To be propelled by or as if by oars. —*v.t.* **3** To propel across the surface of the water with oars, as a boat. **4** To transport by rowing. **5** To be propelled by (a specific number of oars): said of boats. **6** To take part in (a rowing race). **7** To row against in a race. —*n.* **1** A trip in a rowboat; also, the distance covered. **2** The act of rowing, or an instance of it. [< OE *rōwan*]

row[3] (rou) *n.* A noisy disturbance or quarrel; dispute; brawl; clamor. —*v.t.* & *v.i.* To engage in a row. [?]

row·an (rō′ən, rou′-) *n.* **1** Any of various related trees having compound pinnate leaves, white flowers and red berries, as the European or American mountain ash. **2** The fruit of these trees: also **row′an·ber′ry**. [< Scand.]

row·boat (rō′bōt′) *n.* A boat propelled by oars.

row·dy (rou′dē) *n. pl.* **·dies** One inclined to create disturbances or engage in rows; a rough, quarrelsome person. — *adj.* **·di·er, ·di·est** Rough and loud; disorderly. [?] —**row′di·ly** *adv.* —**row′di·ness, row′dy·ism** *n.* —**row′dy·ish** *adj.*

row·el (rou′əl) *n.* A spiked or toothed wheel, as on a spur. —*v.t.* **·eled** or **·elled, ·el·ing** or **·el·ling** To prick with a rowel; spur. [< L *rota* wheel]

row·lock (rō′lok′) *n. Brit.* OARLOCK.

roy. royal.

roy·al (roi′əl) *adj.* **1** Of, pertaining to, or being a king, queen, or other sovereign. **2** Of, pertaining to, or under the patronage or authority of a sovereign. **3** Like or suitable for a sovereign. **4** Of superior quality or size: *royal* octavo. —*n.* A small sail or mast next above the topgallant. [< L *regalis* kingly] —**roy′al·ly** *adv.* —**Syn.** *adj.* **3** imperial, kingly, noble, regal, stately.

royal blue A vivid purplish or reddish blue.

roy·al·ist (roi′əl·ist) *n.* A supporter of a king, queen, or other sovereign. —**roy′al·ism** *n.*

roy·al·ty (roi′əl·tē) *n. pl.* **·ties** **1** The rank, status, or authority of a sovereign. **2** A royal personage; also, royal persons collectively. **3** Royal nature or quality. **4** A share of proceeds paid to a proprietor, author, inventor, etc.

rpm, r.p.m. revolutions per minute.

rps, r.p.s. revolutions per second.

rpt. report.

R.R. railroad; Right Reverend.

R.S. Recording Secretary; Reformed Spelling; Revised Statutes.

R.S.F.S.R. Russian Soviet Federated Socialist Republic.

RSV Revised Standard Version (of the Bible).

R.S.V.P., r.s.v.p. please reply (F *répondez s'il vous plaît*).

Rt. Hon. Right Honorable.

Rt. Rev. Right Reverend.

Rts. rights.

Ru ruthenium.

rub (rub) *v.* **rubbed, rub·bing** *v.t.* **1** To move or pass over the surface of with pressure and friction. **2** To cause (something) to move or pass with friction. **3** To cause to become frayed, worn, or sore from friction: This collar *rubs* my neck. **4** To clean, shine, dry, etc., by means of pressure and friction, or by means of a substance applied thus. **5** To apply or spread with pressure and friction: to *rub* polish on a table. **6** To force by rubbing: with *in* or *into*: to *rub* oil into wood. **7** To remove or erase by friction: with *off* or *out.* —*v.i.* **8** To move along a surface with friction; scrape. **9** To exert pressure and friction. **10** To become frayed, worn, or sore from friction; chafe. **11** To undergo rubbing or removal by rubbing: with *off, out,* etc. —**rub down** To massage. —**rub it in** *Slang* To harp on someone's errors, faults, etc. —**rub out** *Slang* To kill. —**rub the wrong way** To irritate; annoy. —*n.* **1** A subjection to frictional pressure; rubbing: Give it a *rub.* **2** A hindrance or doubt: There's the *rub.* **3** Something that injures the feelings; a sarcasm. [ME *rubben*]

ru·ba·to (rōō·bä′tō) *Music adj. & adv.* With certain notes lengthened or shortened at the performer's discretion. — *n. pl.* **·tos** A rubato passage or manner of playing [Ital.]

rub·ber[1] (rub′ər) *n.* **1** A tough, resilient, elastic material made from the latex of certain tropical plants, or synthesized from coal, petroleum, etc. **2** An article made of this material, as: **a** A rubber overshoe. **b** A condom. **3** One who or that which rubs. —*adj.* Made of rubber. [< RUB] — **rub′ber·y** *adj.*

rub·ber[2] (rub′ər) *n.* **1** In bridge, whist, and other card games, a series of games (3, 5, or 7) played by the same partners against the same adversaries, terminated when one side has won a majority (2 out of 3, etc.). **2** The odd game which breaks a tie between the players. [?]

rubber band A continuous elastic band of rubber, stretched to encircle and bind articles, etc.

rub·ber·ize (rub′ər·īz′) *v.t.* **·ized, ·iz·ing** To coat, impregnate, or cover with rubber or a rubber solution.

rub·ber·neck (rub′ər·nek′) *n. Slang* One who is extremely curious or inquisitive, as a tourist. —*v.i.* To look or listen with great curiosity.

rubber plant 1 Any of several plants yielding latex. **2** An Asian tree related to the fig, with oblong, leathery leaves, often kept as a house plant.

rub·ber-stamp (rub′ər·stamp′) *v.t.* **1** To endorse, initial, or approve with the mark made by a rubber stamping device. **2** *Informal* To pass or approve as a matter of course or routine.

rubber stamp 1 A stamp made of rubber which, when coated with ink, is used to print names, dates, etc. **2** A person or group of persons that approves something, as a policy or program, with little or no discussion, debate, etc. **3** Any routine approval.

rub·bish (rub′ish) *n.* **1** Waste refuse; garbage; trash. **2** Silly or worthless ideas, talk, etc.; nonsense. [?] —**rub′bish·y** *adj.* —**Syn.** **1** debris, litter. **2** absurdness, foolishness.

rub·ble (rub′əl) *n.* **1** Rough, irregular pieces of broken stone, brick, etc. **2** The debris to which buildings of brick, stone, etc., have been reduced by destruction or decay. **3** Masonry composed of irregular or broken stone: also **rub′ble·work′**.

rub·down (rub′doun′) *n.* A massage.

rube (rōōb) *n. Slang* An unsophisticated country person; rustic. [Abbr. of *Reuben*]

ru·bel·la (rōō·bel′ə) *n.* A contagious viral disease benign in children but linked to birth defects of children born of women infected in early pregnancy; German measles. [< L *rubellus* reddish, dim. of *ruber* red]

ru·be·o·la (rōō·bē·ō′lə, rōō·bē′ə·lə) *n.* A contagious viral disease usu. affecting children, marked by catarrh, fever, and a rash that persists for about a week; measles. [< L *rubeus* red] —**ru·be′o·lar** *adj.*

Ru·bi·con (rōō′bi·kon) *n.* A river in N CEN. Italy that formed the boundary separating Julius Caesar's province of Gaul from Italy; by crossing it under arms he committed himself to a civil war. —**cross the Rubicon** To commit oneself irrevocably to some course of action.

ru·bi·cund (rōō′bə·kənd) *adj.* Red, or inclined to redness; ruddy. [< L *rubicundus*] —**ru′bi·cun′di·ty** *n.*

ru·bid·i·um (rōō·bid′ē·əm) *n.* A soft, rare, metallic element (symbol Rb) resembling potassium. [< L *rubidus* red]

ru·ble (rōō′bəl) *n.* The basic monetary unit of the Soviet Union.

ru·bric (rōō′brik) *n.* **1** In early manuscripts and books, the heading of a chapter, an initial letter, etc., that appears in red, or in some distinctive type. **2** Any heading or title, as that of a statute. **3** A direction or rule as in a prayer book, missal, or breviary. [< L *ruber* red] —**ru′bri·cal** *adj.* —**ru′bri·cal·ly** *adv.*

ru·by (rōō′bē) *n. pl.* **·bies** **1** A translucent gemstone of a deep red color, a variety of corundum. **2** A rich red color like that of a ruby. —*adj.* Deep red. [< L *rubeus* red]

ruche (rōōsh) *n.* A pleated or gathered strip of fine fabric, worn about the neck or wrists of a woman's costume. [F< Med. L *rusca* tree bark]

ruch·ing (rōō′shing) *n.* **1** Material for ruches. **2** Ruches collectively.

ruck·sack (ruk′sak′, rōōk′-) *n.* KNAPSACK. [G, lit., back sack]

ruck·us (ruk′əs) *n. Slang* An uproar; commotion. [? blend of RUMPUS and *ruction,* alter. of INSURRECTION]

rud·der (rud′ər) *n.* **1** *Naut.* A broad, flat device hinged vertically at the stern of a vessel to direct its course. **2** Anything that guides or directs a course. **3** *Aeron.* A hinged or pivoted surface, used to turn an aircraft about its vertical axis. [< OE *rōthor* oar; scull] —**rud′der·less** *adj.*

rud·dy (rud′ē) *adj.* **·di·er, ·di·est** **1** Red or tinged with red. **2** Having a healthy glow; rosy: a *ruddy* complexion. [< OE *rudig*] —**rud′di·ly** *adv.* —**rud′di·ness** *n.*

rude (rōōd) *adj.* **rud·er, rud·est** **1** Offensively blunt or uncivil; impolite. **2** Characterized by lack of polish or refinement; uncouth. **3** Unskilfully made or done; crude. **4** Characterized by robust vigor; strong: *rude* health. **5** Barbarous; savage. **6**

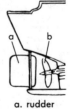

Rowel of spur

a. rudder
def. 1.
b. screw.

Jarring to the ear; harsh; discordant. **7** Lacking skill, training, accuracy, etc. [< L *rudis* rough] —**rude′ly** *adv.* —**rude′ness** *n.* —**Syn. 1** discourteous, impertinent. **2** boorish, uncivilized. **5** uncivilized.

ru·di·ment (rōō′də·mənt) *n.* **1** A first step, stage, or condition. **2** That which is undeveloped or partially developed. [< L *rudis* rough]

ru·di·men·ta·ry (rōō′də·men′tər·ē) *adj.* **1** Introductory; elementary: *rudimentary* knowledge. **2** Being in an imperfectly developed state; undeveloped. **3** Vestigial. Also **ru′di·men′tal.** —**ru′di·men′ta·ri·ly** *adv.* —**ru′di·men′ta·ri·ness** *n.*

rue[1] (rōō) *v.* **rued, ru·ing** *v.t.* **1** To feel sorrow or remorse for; regret extremely. —*v.i.* **2** To feel sorrow or remorse. —*n. Archaic* Sorrowful remembrance; regret. [< OE *hrēowan* be sorry] —**ru′er** *n.*

rue[2] (rōō) *n.* **1** A small, pungent shrub with bitter, evergreen leaves. **2** An infusion of rue leaves. [< Gk. *rhytē*]

rue·ful (rōō′fəl) *adj.* **1** Feeling or expressing sorrow, regret, or pity. **2** Causing sympathy or pity; pitiable. —**rue′ful·ly** *adv.* —**rue′ful·ness** *n.*

ruff[1] (ruf) *n.* **1** A pleated, round, heavily starched collar popular in the 16th century. **2** A natural collar of projecting feathers or hair around the neck of a bird or mammal. **3** The male of a European species of sandpiper, which has a large ruff in the breeding season. [Short for RUFFLE[1]] —**ruffed** *adj.*

ruff[2] (ruf) *n.* In a card game, the act of trumping. —*v.t. & v.i.* To trump. [< OF *roffle*]

Ruff

ruffed grouse (ruft) A North American grouse having in the male a fan-shaped tail and a black ruff.

ruf·fi·an (ruf′ē·ən, ruf′yən) *n.* A lawless, brutal person. —*adj.* Lawlessly or recklessly brutal or cruel. [< MF *rufian*] —**ruf′fi·an·ism** *n.* —**ruf′fi·an·ly** *adj.*

ruf·fle[1] (ruf′əl) *n.* **1** A pleated strip; frill, as for trim or ornament. **2** Anything resembling this, as a bird's ruff. **3** A disturbance; discomposure. **4** A ripple. —*v.* **·fled, ·fling** *v.t.* **1** To disturb or destroy the smoothness or regularity of: The wind *ruffles* the lake. **2** To draw into folds or ruffles; gather. **3** To furnish with ruffles. **4** To erect (the feathers) in a ruff, as a bird when frightened. **5** To disturb or irritate; upset. **6 a** To riffle (the pages of a book). **b** To shuffle (cards). —*v.i.* **7** To be or become rumpled or disordered. **8** To become disturbed or irritated. [ME *ruffelen* to ruffle]

ruf·fle[2] (ruf′əl) *n.* A low, continuous beat of a drum, not as loud as a roll. —*v.t.* **·fled, ·fling** To beat a ruffle upon, as a drum. [?]

rug (rug) *n.* **1** A covering for all or part of a floor, made of some heavy, durable fabric, strips of rag, animal skins, etc. **2** A warm covering, as of cloth, fur, etc., for the lap and feet.

rug·by (rug′bē) *n. Often cap.* A form of football. [< *Rugby* School, Rugby, England, where first played]

rug·ged (rug′id) *adj.* **1** Having a surface that is rough or uneven. **2** Rough; harsh: a *rugged* life. **3** Furrowed and irregular: *rugged* features. **4** Lacking polish and refinement. **5** Tempestuous; stormy: *rugged* weather. **6** Robust; sturdy: *rugged* health. [< Scand.] —**rug′ged·ly** *adv.* —**rug′ged·ness** *n.*

ru·in (rōō′in) *n.* **1** Destruction, downfall, or decay. **2** A person or thing that has decayed, fallen, or been destroyed. **3** *Usu. pl.* That which remains of something that has decayed or been destroyed: the *ruins* of Dresden. **4** That which causes destruction, downfall, or decay: Gambling was his *ruin.* **5** The state of being destroyed, fallen, decayed, etc: to fall into *ruin.* —*v.t.* **1** To bring to ruin; destroy. **2** To bring to disgrace or bankruptcy. **3** To deprive of chastity; seduce. —*v.i.* **4** To fall into ruin. [< L *ruere* to fall] —**ru′in·er** *n.* —**Syn.** *n.* **1** collapse, devastation, dilapidation. *v.* **1** demolish, ravage, raze.

ru·in·a·tion (rōō′in·ā′shən) *n.* **1** The act of ruining. **2** The state of being ruined. **3** Something that ruins.

ru·in·ous (rōō′in·əs) *adj.* **1** Causing or tending to ruin. **2** Falling to ruin. —**ru′in·ous·ly** *adv.* —**ru′in·ous·ness** *n.*

rule (rōōl) *n.* **1** Controlling power, or its possession and exercise; government; reign; also, the period of time during which a ruler or government is in power. **2** A method or principle of action; regular course of procedure: I make early rising my *rule.* **3** An authoritative direction or regulation about something to do or the way of doing it. **4** The body of directions laid down by or for a religious order: the *rule* of St. Francis. **5** A procedure or formula for solving a given class of mathematical problems. **6** An established usage fixing the form of words: a *rule* for forming the plural. **7** Something in the ordinary course of events or condition of things: In some communities illiteracy is the *rule.* **8** *Law* A judicial decision on some specific question or point of law. **9** A straight-edged instrument for use in measuring, or as a guide in drawing lines; a ruler. **10** *Printing* A strip of type-high metal for printing a rule or line. —**as a rule** Ordinarily; usually. —*v.* **ruled, rul·ing** *v.t.* **1** To have authority or control over; govern. **2** To influence greatly; dominate. **3** To decide judicially or authoritatively. **4** To restrain; keep in check. **5** To mark lines on, as with a ruler. —*v.i.* **6** To have authority or control. **7** To form and express a decision: The judge *ruled* on that point. —**rule out 1** To eliminate or exclude. **2** To preclude; prevent. [< L *regula* ruler, rule]

rule of thumb 1 A rule based on experience or common sense instead of scientific knowledge. **2** A method of procedure that is practical but not precise.

rul·er (rōō′lər) *n.* **1** One who rules or governs, as a sovereign. **2** A straight-edged strip of wood, metal, etc., used in drawing lines and in measuring.

rul·ing (rōō′ling) *adj.* **1** Exercising control. **2** Prevalent; predominant. —*n.* A decision, as of a judge or chairman.

rum[1] (rum) *n.* **1** An alcoholic liquor distilled from fermented molasses. **2** Any alcoholic liquor. [?]

rum[2] (rum) *adj. Brit. Slang* Queer; strange. [?]

Rum. Rumania; Rumanian.

Ru·ma·ni·a (rōō·mā′nē·ə, -mān′yə) *n.* A republic of SE Europe, 91,671 sq. mi., cap. Bucharest. • See map at BALKAN STATES.

Ru·ma·ni·an (rōō·mā′nē·ən, -mān′yən) *adj.* Of or pertaining to Rumania, its people, or their language. —*n.* **1** A native or citizen of Rumania. **2** The Romance language of the Rumanians.

rum·ba (rum′bə, *Sp.* rōōm′bä) *n.* **1** A dance originated by Cuban Negroes. **2** A ballroom dance based on this. **3** Music for such a dance. —*v.i.* To dance the rumba. [Sp.]

rum·ble (rum′bəl) *v.* **·bled, ·bling** *v.i.* **1** To make a low, heavy, rolling sound, as thunder. **2** To move or proceed with such a sound. —*v.t.* **3** To cause to make a low, heavy, rolling sound. **4** To utter with such a sound. —*n.* **1** A continuous low, heavy, rolling sound; a muffled roar. **2** A seat or baggage compartment in the rear of an automobile or carriage: also **rumble seat. 3** *Slang* A street fight involving a group, usu. deliberately provoked. [< MDu. *rommelen*]

ru·men (rōō′men) *n. pl.* **ru·mi·na** (rōō′mə·nə) or **ru·mens** The first chamber of the stomach of a ruminant. [L, throat]

ru·mi·nant (rōō′mə·nənt) *n.* Any of a division of even-toed ungulates, as a deer, sheep, cow, etc., that graze and chew the cud, which is temporarily stored in the first of the four chambers of the stomach. —*adj.* **1** Chewing the cud. **2** Of or pertaining to ruminants. **3** Meditative or thoughtful. [< L *ruminare* chew the cud, think over]

ru·mi·nate (rōō′mə·nāt) *v.t. & v.i.* **·nat·ed, ·nat·ing** **1** To chew (food previously swallowed and regurgitated) over again; chew (the cud). **2** To meditate or reflect (upon). —**ru′mi·nat′ing·ly, ru′mi·na′tive·ly** *adv.* —**ru′mi·na′tion, ru′mi·na′tor** *n.* —**Syn. 2** brood, consider, contemplate, muse.

rum·mage (rum′ij) *v.* **·maged, ·mag·ing** *v.t.* **1** To search through (a place, box, etc.) by turning over and disarranging the contents; ransack. **2** To find or bring out by searching: with *out* or *up.* —*v.i.* **3** To make a thorough search. —*n.* **1** Any act of rummaging. esp., disarranging things by searching thoroughly. **2** Odds and ends. [< MF *arrumer* pack or arrange cargo] —**rum′mag·er** *n.*

---

add, āce, câre, pälm; end, ēven; it, īce; odd, ōpen, ôrder; tŏŏk, pōōl; up, bûrn; ə = a in *above*, u in *focus*; yōō = u in *fuse;* oil; pout; check; go; ring; thin; ᵺis; zh, *vision.* < derived from; ? origin uncertain or unknown.

rummage sale A sale of donated miscellaneous objects to raise money, as for some charity.

rum·my[1] (rum′ē) *n.* Any of several card games the object of which is to match cards into sets of three or four of the same denomination or into sequences in the same suit. [?]

rum·my[2] (rum′ē) *n. pl.* **·mies** *Slang* A drunkard. —*adj.* Of, pertaining to, or affected by rum.

ru·mor (rōō′mər) *n.* **1** A story or report circulating without known foundation or authority. **2** Common gossip; hearsay. —*v.t.* To tell or spread as a rumor; report abroad. *Brit. sp.* **ru′mour.** [L, noise]

rump (rump) *n.* **1** The upper part of the hindquarters of an animal. **2** A cut of beef from this part. **3** The buttocks. **4** A last, often unimportant or undesirable part.

rum·ple (rum′pəl) *v.t. & v.i.* **·pled, ·pling** To form into creases or folds; wrinkle. —*n.* An irregular fold or crease; wrinkle. [< MDu. *rumpelen*]

rum·pus (rum′pəs) *n. Informal* A usu. noisy disturbance or commotion. [?]

rumpus room A room used for recreation, games, etc.

rum-run·ner (rum′run′ər) *n.* A person or ship involved in smuggling alcoholic liquor ashore or across a border.

run (run) *v.* **ran, run, run·ning** *v.i.* **1** To move by rapid steps, faster than walking. **2** To move rapidly; go swiftly. **3** To flee; take flight. **4** To make a brief or rapid journey: We *ran* over to Staten Island last night. **5** To make regular trips: This steamer *runs* between New York and Liverpool. **6 a** To take part in a race. **b** To be a candidate or contestant: to *run* for dogcatcher. **7** To finish a race in a specified position: I *ran* a poor last. **8** To move or pass easily: The rope *runs* through the pulley. **9** To pass or flow rapidly: watching the tide *run* out. **10** To proceed in direction or extent: This road *runs* north. **11** To flow: His nose *runs.* **12** To become liquid and flow, as wax; also, to spread or mingle confusedly, as colors when wet. **13** To move or roam about freely and easily: to *run* around town with friends. **14** To pass into a specified condition: to *run* to seed. **15** To unravel, as a fabric. **16** To give forth a discharge or flow. **17** To leak. **18** To continue or proceed without restraint: The conversation *ran* on and on. **19** To be operative; work: Will the engine *run?* **20** To continue or extend, as in time or space: Our property *runs* down to the sea. **21** To be reported or expressed: The story *runs* as follows. **22** To migrate, as salmon from the sea to spawn. **23** To occur or return to the mind: An idea *ran* through his head. **24** To occur with specified variation of size, quality, etc.: The corn is *running* small this year. **25** To be performed or repeated in continuous succession: The play *ran* for forty nights. **26** To pass or spread, as from mouth to mouth or point to point: rumors *running* wild. **27** To creep or climb, as a vine. —*v.t.* **28** To run or proceed along, as a route or path. **29** To make one's way over, through, or past: to *run* rapids. **30** To perform or accomplish by or as by running: to *run* a race or an errand. **31** To compete against in or as in a race. **32** To become subject to; incur: to *run* the risk of failure. **33** To present and support as a candidate. **34** To hunt or chase, as game. **35** To bring to a specified condition by or as by running: to *run* oneself out of breath. **36** To drive or force: with *out of, off, into, through,* etc. **37** To cause to move, as in some manner or direction: They *ran* the ship into port. **38** To move (the eye, hand, etc.) quickly or lightly: He *ran* his hand over the table. **39** To cause to move, slide, etc., as into a specified position: to *run* up a flag. **40** To transport or convey in a vessel or vehicle. **41** To smuggle. **42** To cause to flow: to *run* water into a pot. **43** To trace back: trying to *run* a bit of gossip to its source. **44** To mold, as from melted metal; found. **45** To sew (cloth) in a continuous line, usu. by taking a number of stitches with the needle at a time. **46** To control the motion or operation of; operate: to *run* an engine. **47** To direct or control; manage. **48** To allow to continue or mount up, as a bill. **49** In games, to make (a number of points, strokes, etc.) successively. **50** To publish in a magazine or newspaper: to *run* an ad. **51** To mark, set down, or trace, as a boundary line. **52** To suffer from (a fever, etc.). —**run across** To meet by chance. —**run down 1** To pursue and overtake, as a fugitive. **2** To strike down while moving. **3** To exhaust or damage, as by abuse or overwork. **4** To speak of disparagingly. —**run for it** To run to avoid some-

thing, to escape, seek safety, etc. —**run in 1** To insert; include. **2** *Slang* To arrest and place in confinement. —**run into 1** To meet by chance. **2** To collide with. —**run off 1** To produce on a typewriter, printing press, etc. **2** To decide (a tied race, game, etc.) by the outcome of another, subsequent race, game, etc. —**run out** To be exhausted, as supplies. —**run out of** To exhaust one's supply of. —**run over 1** To ride or drive over; run down. **2** To overflow. **3** To go over, examine, or rehearse. —**run through 1** To squander. **2** To stab or pierce. **3** To rehearse quickly. —**run up** To make hurriedly, as on a sewing machine. —*n.* **1** The act, or an act, of running or going rapidly. **2** A running pace: to break into a *run.* **3** Flow; movement; sweep: the *run* of the tide. **4** A distance covered by running. **5** A journey or passage, esp. between two points, made by a vessel, train, etc. **6** A rapid journey or excursion: take a *run* into town. **7** A swift stream or brook. **8** A migration of fish, esp. to up-river spawning grounds; also, the fish that so migrate. **9** A grazing or feeding ground for animals: a sheep *run.* **10** The regular trail or path of certain animals: an elephant *run.* **11** The privilege of free use or access: to have the *run* of the place. **12** A runway. **13** *Music* A rapid succession of tones. **14** A series, sequence, or succession. **15** A trend or tendency: the general *run* of the market. **16** A continuous spell (of some condition): a *run* of luck. **17** A surge of demands, as those made upon a bank or treasury to meet its obligations. **18** A period of continuous performance, occurrence, popularity, etc.: a play with a long *run.* **19** Class or type; also, the usual or general class or type. **20** A period of operation of a machine or device: an experimental *run.* **21** The output during such a period. **22** A period during which a liquid is allowed to run. **23** The amount of liquid allowed to flow at one time. **24** A narrow, lengthwise ravel, as in a sheer stocking. **25** An approach to a target made by a bombing plane. **26** In baseball, a score made by a player who completes a circuit of the bases from home plate before three outs are made. **27** An unbroken series of successful shots, strokes, etc., as in billiards. —**in the long run** As the ultimate outcome of any train of circumstances. —**on the run 1** Hastily: to eat *on the run.* **2** Running, running away, or retreating. —*adj.* **1** Made liquid; melted. **2** That has been melted or cast: *run* metal. [< OE *rinnan* to flow]

run·a·bout (run′ə·bout′) *n.* **1** A light, open automobile. **2** A light, open wagon. **3** A small motorboat. **4** A person who wanders or runs about from place to place; gadabout.

run·a·round (run′ə·round′) *n. Informal* Evasive or deceptive action or treatment: to get the *runaround* from someone.

run·a·way (run′ə·wā′) *adj.* **1** Escaping or escaped from restraint or control. **2** Brought about by running away: a *runaway* marriage. **3** Easily won, as a horse race. —*n.* **1** One who or that which runs away or flees, as a fugitive or deserter, or a horse of which the driver has lost control. **2** An act of running away.

run·down (run′doun′) *n.* **1** A summary; resumé. **2** In baseball, a play attempting to put out a base runner who is trapped between two bases.

run-down (run′doun′) *adj.* **1** Debilitated; tired out. **2** Dilapidated; shabby. **3** Stopped because not wound, as a watch. —*Syn.* **1** exhausted, weary. **2** decayed, ruined.

rune (rōōn) *n.* **1** A character of an ancient Germanic alphabet. **2** A Finnish or Old Norse poem; also, one of the sections of such a poem. **3** An obscure or mystic mark, song, poem, verse, or saying. [< ON *rūn* mystery, rune] —**ru′nic** *adj.*

Runes from an 11th-century tomb

rung[1] (rung) *n.* **1** A round crosspiece of a ladder or chair. **2** A spoke of a wheel. [< OE *hrung* crossbar]

rung[2] (rung) *p.p.* of RING[2].

run-in (run′in′) *n.* **1** A quarrel; bicker. **2** *Printing* Inserted or added matter. —*adj.* (run′in′) *Printing* That is inserted or added.

run·nel (run′əl) *n.* A little stream; a brook. Also **run′let** (-lit). [< OE *rinnan* to run]

run·ner (run′ər) *n.* **1** One who or that which runs. **2** One who operates or manages anything. **3** One who runs er-

rands or goes about on any kind of business, as a messenger. **4** That part on which an object runs or slides: the *runner* of a skate. **5** *Bot.* A slender horizontal stem that takes root at the nodes to produce new plants, as in the strawberry. **6** A smuggler. **7** A long, narrow rug or carpeting, used in hallways, etc. **8** A narrow strip of cloth, usu. of fine quality, used on tables, dressers, etc.

run·ner-up (run′ər·up′) *n. pl.* **·ners-up** or **·ner-ups** A contestant or team finishing second in a contest.

run·ning (run′ing) *adj.* **1** Inclined or trained to a running gait, as certain horses. **2** Done in or started with a run: a *running* jump. **3** Following one another without intermission; successive: He talked for three hours *running*. **4** Continuous: a *running* battle. **5** Characterized by easy flowing curves; cursive: a *running* hand. **6** Discharging, as pus from a sore. **7** Fluid or flowing. **8** In operation, as an engine. **9** Measured in a straight line: the cost per *running* foot. —*n.* **1** The act or movement of one who or that which runs. **2** That which runs or flows. —**in the running** Having a chance to win. —**out of the running** Having no chance to win.

running board A footboard, as on the side of a locomotive, certain automobiles, etc.

running head A heading or title at the top of each page or of every other page of a book, etc.: also **running title.**

running knot A knot made so as to slip along a noose and tighten when pulled upon.

running mate A candidate running with another but for a lesser position, as one seeking to be vice-president.

run·ny (run′ē) *adj.* **·ni·er, ·ni·est** Having a tendency to discharge: a *runny* nose. —**run′ni·ness** *n.*

run·off (run′ôf′ -of′) *n.* **1** Rainfall that drains from a particular area rather than soaking into the soil. **2** A final, deciding contest, game, etc.

run-of-the-mill (run′əv·thə·mil′) *adj.* Average; ordinary.

run-on (run′on′, -ôn′) *Printing n.* Appended or added matter. —*adj.* That is appended or added.

runt (runt) *n.* **1** A stunted animal, esp. the smallest of a litter. **2** A small or stunted person. [?] —**runt′i·ness** *n.* —**runt′y** *adj.* **(·i·er, ·i·est)**

run-through (run′throo′) *n.* A rapid reading through or rehearsal, as of a musical composition or a dramatic work.

run·way (run′wā′) *n.* **1** A way on, in, along, or over which something runs. **2** The path over which animals pass to and from their places of feeding or watering. **3** An enclosed place, as for chickens. **4** A strip of surfaced ground used for the takeoff and landing of airplanes. **5** A long, narrow platform extending from a stage into an auditorium.

ru·pee (roō·pē′, roō′pe) *n.* The basic monetary unit of India, Pakistan, and Sri Lanka. [< Skt. *rūpya* silver]

ru·pi·ah (roō·pē′ä) *n.* The basic monetary unit of Indonesia.

rup·ture (rup′chər) *n.* **1** The act of breaking apart or the state of being broken apart. **2** HERNIA. **3** Breach of peace and agreement between individuals or nations. —*v.t. & v.i.* **·tured, ·tur·ing 1** To break apart. **2** To affect with or suffer a rupture. [< L *ruptus*, p.p. of *rumpere* to break]

ru·ral (roor′əl) *adj.* Of or pertaining to the country, country people, country life, or agriculture. [< L *rus, ruris* country] —**ru′ral·ism, ru′ral·ist, ru′ral·ness** *n.* —**ru′ral·ly** *adv.*

rural free delivery Free mail delivery by carrier in rural districts.

ru·ral·ize (roor′əl·īz) *v.* **·ized, ·iz·ing** *v.t.* To make rural. — *v.i.* To go into or live in the country; rusticate. —**ru′ral·i·za′tion** *n.*

Rus., Russ. Russia; Russian.

ruse (roōs, roōz) *n.* An action intended to mislead or deceive; a stratagem; trick. [< F *ruser* dodge, detour]

rush[1] (rush) *v.i.* **1** To move or go swiftly, impetuously, forcefully, or violently. **2** To make an attack; charge: with *on* or *upon*. **3** To proceed recklessly or rashly; plunge: with *in* or *into.* **4** To come, go, pass, act, etc. with suddenness or haste: Ideas kept *rushing* to her mind. **5** To advance a football in a running play. —*v.t.* **6** To move, push, drive,

etc. with haste, impetuosity, or violence. **7** To do, perform, deliver, etc. hastily or hurriedly: to *rush* one's work. **8** To make a sudden assault upon. **9** *Slang* To seek the favor of with assiduous attentions. **10** To advance (a football) in a running play. —*n.* **1** The act of rushing; a sudden turbulent movement, drive, surge, etc. **2** Frantic activity; haste: the *rush* of city life. **3** A sudden pressing demand; a run: a *rush* on foreign bonds. **4** A sudden exigency; urgent pressure: a *rush* of business. **5** A sudden flocking of people, as to some new location. **6** A general contest or scrimmage between students from different classes. **7** In football, an attempt to take the ball through the opposing linemen and toward the goal. **8** *Usu. pl.* In motion pictures, the first film prints of a scene or series of scenes, before editing or selection. —**with a rush** Suddenly and hastily. — *adj.* Requiring urgency or haste: a *rush* order. [< AF *russher* to push] —**rush′er** *n.* —**Syn.** *v.* **1** dash, hasten, hurry.

rush[2] (rush) *n.* **1** Any of various grasslike plants common in marshy ground. **2** The pliant stem of certain rush plants, used for mats, basketry, etc. [< OE *rysc*] —**rush′y** *adj.* **(·i·er, ·i·est)**

rush hour A time when large numbers of people are traveling, as to or from work. —**rush′-hour′** *adj.*

rush·light (rush′līt′) *n.* A candle made by dipping a rush in tallow: also **rush light, rush candle.**

rusk (rusk) *n.* **1** Plain or sweet bread that is sliced after baking and then toasted or baked a second time until it is brown and crisp. **2** A light, soft, sweet biscuit. [< Sp. *rosca*, twisted loaf of bread]

rus·set (rus′it) *n.* **1** Reddish brown or yellowish brown. **2** A coarse homespun cloth, russet in color, formerly used by country people. **3** A winter apple of russet color. —*adj.* **1** Reddish brown or yellowish brown. **2** Made of russet. [< L *russus* reddish] —**rus′set·y** *adj.*

Rus·sia (rush′ə) *n.* **1** Loosely, the Union of Soviet Socialist Republics. **2** The Russian Soviet Federated Socialist Republic.

Rus·sian (rush′ən) *n.* **1** Loosely, a citizen or native of the Union of Soviet Socialist Republics. **2** A citizen or native of Russia. **3** The language of Russia and the official language of the Union of Soviet Socialist Republics. —*adj.* **1** Loosely, of or pertaining to the Union of Soviet Socialist Republics. **2** Of or pertaining to Russia or its people. **3** Of or pertaining to Russian, the language.

Russian dressing Mayonnaise combined with chili sauce, chopped pickles, etc.

Rus·sian·ize (rush′ən·īz) *v.t.* **·ized, ·iz·ing** To make Russian. —**Rus′sian·i·za′tion** *n.*

Russian leather A smooth, well-tanned, high-grade leather, often dark red, of calfskin or light cattle hide, dressed with birch oil and having a characteristic odor.

Russian Orthodox Church An autonomous branch of the Eastern Orthodox Church.

Russian Revolution The uprising of 1917 that resulted in the overthrow of the czarist regime. The revolution had two phases: first, the establishment of a moderate, provisional government under Kerensky (the **February Revolution**), and, second, the seizure of power by the Bolsheviks (Communists) under Lenin (the **October Revolution**).

Russian thistle A large tumbleweed common on the central plains of North America.

Russian wolfhound BORZOI.

Russo- *combining form* **1** Russia. **2** Russian and: *Russo*-Egyptian.

rust (rust) *n.* **1** A reddish or yellow coating on iron or iron alloys due to spontaneous oxidation. **2** A corroded spot or film of oxide on any metal. **3** Any of various parasitic fungi living on higher plants. **4** A plant disease caused by such fungi, which form spots on stems and leaves. **5** Any spot or film resembling rust on metal. **6** Any of several shades of reddish brown. —*v.t. & v.i.* **1** To become coated with rust. **2** To contract or cause to contract the plant disease rust. **3** To become or cause to become weakened because of disuse. [< OE *rūst*]

rus·tic (rus′tik) *adj.* **1** Of or pertaining to the country;

rural. **2** Uncultured; rude; awkward. **3** Unsophisticated; artless. **4** Made of the rough limbs of trees with the bark on them: *rustic* furniture. —*n.* **1** One who lives in the country. **2** An unsophisticated, coarse, or ignorant person, esp. one from a rural area. [< L *rus* country] —**rus′ti·cal·ly** *adv.*

rus·ti·cate (rus′tə·kāt) *v.* **·cat·ed, ·cat·ing** *v.i.* **1** To go to or live in the country. —*v.t.* **2** To send or banish to the country. **3** *Brit.* To suspend (a student) temporarily from a college for punishment. —**rus′ti·ca′tion, rus′ti·ca′tor** *n.*

rus·tic·i·ty (rus·tis′ə·tē) *n. pl.* **·ties 1** The condition or quality of being rustic. **2** A rustic trait or peculiarity.

rus·tle[1] (rus′əl) *v.t. & v.i.* **·tled, ·tling** To move or cause to move with a quick succession of small, light, rubbing sounds, as dry leaves or sheets of paper. —*n.* A rustling sound. [ME *rustelen*] —**rus′tler** *n.* —**rus′tling·ly** *adv.*

rus·tle[2] (rus′əl) *v.t. & v.i.* **·tled, ·tling 1** *Informal* To act with or obtain by energetic or vigorous action. **2** *Informal* To steal (cattle, etc.). [? Blend of RUSH and HUSTLE]

rus·tler (rus′lər) *n.* **1** *Slang* A person who is active and bustling. **2** *Informal* A cattle thief.

rust·y (rus′tē) *adj.* **rust·i·er, rust·i·est 1** Covered or affected with rust. **2** Consisting of or produced by rust. **3** Having the color or appearance of rust; discolored; faded, etc. **4** Not working well or freely; lacking nimbleness; stiff. **5** Impaired or deficient by neglect or want of practice: *rusty* in math. —**rust′i·ly** *adv.* —**rust′i·ness** *n.*

rut[1] (rut) *n.* **1** A sunken track worn by a wheel, as in a road. **2** A groove, furrow, etc., in which something runs. **3** A settled and tedious routine. —*v.t.* **rut·ted, rut·ting** To wear or make a rut or ruts in. [? Var. of ROUTE] —**rut′ti·ness** *n.* —**rut′ty** *adj.* (**·i·er, ·i·est**)

rut[2] (rut) *n.* The sexual excitement of various animals, esp. the male deer; also, the period during which it lasts. —*v.i.* **rut·ted, rut·ting** To be in rut. [< L *rugire* to roar]

ru·ta·ba·ga (rōō′tə·bā′gə) *n.* A variety of turnip having a large, yellowish root. [< dial. Sw. *rotabagge*]

ruth (rōōth) *n.* **1** Compassion; pity, mercy. **2** Grief; sorrow; remorse. [< OE *hrēow* sad]

Ruth (rōōth) In the Bible, a widow from Moab who left her people to live with her mother-in-law, Naomi. —*n.* The Old Testament book that tells her story.

ru·the·ni·um (rōō·thē′nē·əm) *n.* A rare metallic element (symbol Ru). [< *Ruthenia*, a region in the Ukraine]

ruth·less (rōōth′lis) *adj.* Having no compassion; merciless. —**ruth′less·ly** *adv.* —**ruth′less·ness** *n.*

R.V. Revised Version (of the Bible).

R.W. Right Worshipful; Right Worthy.

Rwan·da (rwän′də) *n.* A republic of CEN. Africa, 10,169 sq. mi., cap. Kigali. • See map at AFRICA.

Rx *symbol Med.* Take: the conventional heading for a prescription or formula. [Abbr. of L *recipe* take]

-ry Var. of -ERY.

Ry., ry. railway.

rye (rī) *n.* **1** A hardy, cultivated cereal grass. **2** The seeds of this grass. **3** Flour made from these seeds. **4** Whiskey consisting of a blend of bourbon and neutral spirits: also **rye whiskey.** [< OE *ryge*]

rye·grass (rī′gras′, -gräs′) *n.* A weedy grass sometimes cultivated for forage.

S

S, s (es) *n. pl.* **S's, s's, Ss, ss** (es′iz) **1** The 19th letter of the English alphabet. **2** Any spoken sound representing the letter *S* or *s*. **3** Something shaped like an S. —*adj.* Shaped like an S.

S Seaman; sulfur.

S. Sabbath; Saturday; Saxon; Senate; September; Signor; Sunday.

S., s. saint; school; senate; south; southern.

s. second; section; shilling; semi; series; shilling; son; southern; steamer; substantive; sun; surplus.

SA Seaman Apprentice.

S.A. Salvation Army; South Africa; South America.

Sab. Sabbath.

Sab·bath (sab′əth) *n.* **1** The seventh day of the week, a day of rest observed in Judaism and some Christian sects; Saturday. **2** The first day of the week as observed as a day of rest by Christians; Sunday. [< Heb. *shābath* to rest]

sab·bat·i·cal (sə·bat′i·kəl) *adj. Often cap.* Of the nature of or suitable for the Sabbath: also **sab·bat′ic.** —*n.* SABBATICAL YEAR (def. 2).

sabbatical year 1 In the ancient Jewish economy, every seventh year, in which the people were required to refrain from tillage. **2** In the U.S., a year of leave, or a shorter period, to be used for study and travel with full or partial salary, awarded to college faculty members, usu. every seven years: also **sabbatical leave.**

sa·ber (sā′bər) *n.* A heavy one-edged cavalry sword, often curved. —*v.t.* **·bered** or **·bred, ·ber·ing** or **·bring** To strike, wound, kill, or arm with a saber. Also, and *Brit. sp.*, **sa′bre.** [< MHG *sabel*]

Sa·bine (sā′bīn) *n.* A member of an ancient people of CEN. Italy, conquered and absorbed by Rome in 290 B.C. —*adj.* Of or pertaining to the Sabines.

sa·ble (sā′bəl) *n.* **1** A N Eurasian species of marten bearing costly fur. **2** The dressed fur of a sable. **3** *pl.* Garments made wholly or partly of this fur. **4** The color black. —*adj.* **1** Black; dark. **2** Made of sable fur. [< Med. L *sabelum*]

Saber

sa·bot (sab′ō, *Fr.* sȧ·bō′) *n.* **1** A wooden shoe, as of a French peasant. **2** A shoe having a wooden sole but flexible shank. [F]

sab·o·tage (sab′ə·täzh) *n.* **1** A wasting of materials or damage to machinery, tools, etc., by workmen to make management comply with their demands. **2** The destruction of bridges, railroads, supply depots, etc., either by enemy agents or by underground resisters. **3** Any deliberate effort to obstruct plans or aims. —*v.t. & v.i.* **·taged, ·tag·ing** To engage in, damage, or destroy by sabotage. [F < *saboter* work badly, damage]

sab·o·teur (sab′ə·tûr′, *Fr.* sȧ·bô·tœr′) *n.* One who engages in sabotage. [F]

sa·bra (sä′brə) *n. Often cap.* An Israeli born in Israel. [< Heb.]

sac (sak) *n.* A membranous pouch or cavity, often fluid-filled, in a plant or animal. [< L *saccus*]

SAC (sak) Strategic Air Command.

sac·cha·rin (sak′ər·in) *n.* A sweet compound derived from coal tar, used as a substitute for sugar. [< Gk. *sakcharon* sugar]

sac·cha·rine (sak′ər·in, -ə·rīn′, -ə·rēn′) *adj.* **1** Very sweet. **2** Cloyingly sweet: a *saccharine* voice. —*n.* SACCHARIN. —**sac′cha·rine·ly** *adv.* —**sac′cha·rin′i·ty** *n.*

sac·er·do·tal (sas′ər·dōt′l, sak′-) *adj.* Pertaining to a priest or priesthood; priestly. [< L *sacerdos* priest] —**sac′er·do′tal·ism** (-iz·əm) *n.* —**sac′er·do′tal·ly** *adv.*

sa·chem (sā′chəm) *n.* A North American Indian hereditary chief. [< Algon.]

sa·chet (sa·shā′) *n.* **1** A small bag for perfumed powder, used to scent closets, dresser drawers, etc. **2** The perfumed powder so used. [< L *saccus* a sack]

sack[1] (sak) *n.* **1** A large bag for holding heavy articles. **2** Such a bag and its contents: a *sack* of potatoes. **3** A measure or weight of varying amount. **4** A loosely hanging dress without a waistline, often worn without a belt: also **sack dress. 5** A short, loosely fitting coatlike garment worn by women and children. **6** *Slang* Dismissal, esp. in the phrases **get the sack, give (someone) the sack. 7** In baseball slang, a base. **8** *Slang* A bed; mattress. —**hit the sack** *Slang* To go to bed; retire for the night. —*v.t.* **1** To

put into a sack or sacks. **2** *Slang* To dismiss, as an employee. [< Gk. *sakkos* < Heb. *saq* sackcloth]

sack² (sak) *v.t.* To plunder or pillage (a town or city) after capturing. —*n.* The pillaging of a captured town or city. [< L *saccus* a sack (for carrying off plunder) —**sack′er** *n.*

sack³ (sak) *n.* Any of several strong, light-colored, dry Spanish wines, esp. sherry. [< L *siccus* dry]

sack·but (sak′but) *n.* **1** An early instrument resembling the trombone. **2** In the Bible, a stringed instrument. [< OF *saquer* to pull + *bouter* to push]

sack·cloth (sak′klôth′, -kloth′) *n.* **1** A coarse cloth used for making sacks. **2** Coarse cloth or haircloth worn in penance or mourning.

sack coat A man's short, loose-fitting coat with no waist seam, for informal wear.

sack·ful (sak′fool′) *n. pl.* **·fuls** Enough to fill a sack.

sack·ing (sak′ing) *n.* A coarse cloth made of hemp or flax and used for sacks.

sacque (sak) *n.* A jacket for a baby.

sac·ra·ment (sak′rə·mənt) *n.* **1** A rite ordained by Christ or by the church as an outward sign of grace, as baptism, confirmation, marriage, etc. **2** *Often cap.* **a** The Eucharist. **b** The consecrated bread and wine of the Eucharist: often with *the*. **3** Any solemn covenant or pledge. **4** Anything considered to have sacred significance. [< L *sacramentum* oath, pledge] —**sac′ra·men′tal** *adj.* —**sac′ra·men′tal·ly** *adv.*

sa·cred (sā′krid) *adj.* **1** Dedicated to religious use; hallowed. **2** Pertaining or related to religion: *sacred* books. **3** Consecrated by love or reverence: *sacred* to the memory of his father. **4** Dedicated to a person or purpose: a memorial *sacred* to those killed in battle. **5** Not to be profaned; inviolable: a *sacred* promise. [< L *sacer* holy] —**sa′cred·ly** *adv.* —**sa′cred·ness** *n.*

Sacred College COLLEGE OF CARDINALS.

sac·ri·fice (sak′rə·fīs) *n.* **1** The act of making an offering to a deity. **2** That which is sacrificed; a victim. **3** A giving up of something cherished or desired. **4** Loss incurred or suffered without return. **5** A reduction of price that leaves little profit or involves loss. **6** In baseball, a hit by which the batter is put out, but the base runner is advanced: also **sacrifice hit.** —*v.* **·ficed, ·fic·ing** *v.t.* **1** To give up (something valued) for the sake of something else: to *sacrifice* one's principles for expediency. **2** To sell or part with at a loss. **3** To make an offering, as to a god. **4** In baseball, to advance (one or more runners) by means of a sacrifice. —*v.i.* **5** To make a sacrifice. [< L *sacer* holy + *facere* to make] —**sac′ri·fic′er** *n.* —**sac′ri·fic′ing·ly** *adv.*

sac·ri·fi·cial (sak′rə·fish′əl) *adj.* Pertaining to, performing, or of the nature of a sacrifice. —**sac′ri·fi′cial·ly** *adv.*

sac·ri·lege (sak′rə·lij) *n.* The act of violating or profaning anything sacred. [< L *sacer* holy + *legere* to plunder]

sac·ri·le·gious (sak′rə·lij′əs, -lē′jəs) *adj.* Disrespectful or injurious to sacred persons or things. —**sac′ri·le′gious·ly** *adv.* —**sac′ri·le′gious·ness** *n.* —**Syn.** blasphemous, godless, impious, irreligious, profane.

sac·ris·tan (sak′ris·tən) *n.* A church official having charge of a sacristy and its contents. Also **sa′crist** (sā′-krist). [< L *sacer* sacred]

sac·ris·ty (sak′ris·tē) *n. pl.* **·ties** A room in a church for the sacred vessels and vestments; a vestry. [< Med. L *sacrista* sacristan]

sac·ro·il·i·ac (sak′rō·il′ē·ak) *adj.* Pertaining to the sacrum and the ilium and the joint between them.

sac·ro·sanct (sak′rō·sangkt) *adj.* Exceedingly sacred; inviolable: sometimes used ironically. [< L *sacer* holy + *sanctus* made holy] —**sac′ro·sanc′ti·ty** *n.*

sa·crum (sā′krəm, sak′rəm) *n. pl.* **·cra** (-krə) A triangular bone formed of fused vertebrae at the lower end of the spinal column and articulating with the hip bone. [< L *(os) sacrum* sacred (bone); from its being offered in sacrifices] • See PELVIS.

sad (sad) *adj.* **sad·der, sad·dest** **1** Sorrowful or depressed in spirits; mournful. **2** Causing sorrow or pity; distressing. **3** *Informal* Very bad; awful: a *sad* situation. **4** Dark-hued; somber. [< OE *sæd* sated] —**sad′ly** *adv.* —**sad′ness** *n.* —**Syn. 1** dejected, despondent, disconsolate, miserable, unhappy, depressed. **2** deplorable, grievous, lamentable, pitiful.

sad·den (sad′n) *v.t. & v.i.* To make or become sad.

sad·dle (sad′l) *n.* **1** A seat or pad for a rider, as on the back of a horse, bicycle, motorcycle, etc. **2** A padded cushion for a horse's back, as part of a harness or to support a pack, etc. **3.** The two hindquarters and part of the backbone of a carcass, as of mutton, venison, etc. **4** Some part or object like or likened to a saddle, as in form or position. —**in the saddle** In a position of control. —*v.t.* **·dled, ·dling** **1** To put a saddle on. **2** To load, as with a burden. **3** To place (a burden or responsibility) on a person. [< OE *sadol*]

American stock saddle
a. pommel or saddle
horn. b. cinches.
c. stirrup.

sad·dle·bag (sad′l·bag′) *n.* A large pouch, usu. one of a pair connected by a strap or band and slung over an animal's back behind the saddle.

saddle block A form of anesthesia used esp. during childbirth, in which the patient is injected in the lower spinal cord.

sad·dle·bow (sad′l·bō′) *n.* The arched front upper part of a saddle.

sad·dle·cloth (sad′l·klôth′, -kloth′) *n.* A thick cloth laid on an animal's back under a saddle.

saddle horse A horse used or trained for riding.

sad·dler (sad′lər) *n.* A maker of saddles, harness, etc.

sad·dler·y (sad′lər·ē) *n. pl.* **·dler·ies** **1** Saddles, harness, and fittings, collectively. **2** A shop or the work of a saddler.

saddle shoe A white sport shoe with a dark band of leather across the instep.

saddle soap A softening and preserving soap for leather, containing neat's-foot oil.

Sad·du·cee (saj′oo·sē, sad′yoo·sē) *n.* A member of an ancient Jewish sect, which during the time of Jesus rejected doctrines of the oral tradition, as resurrection, and adhered strictly to the Mosaic law. —**Sad′du·ce′an, Sad′du·cae′an** *adj.* —**Sad′du·cee′ism** *n.*

sad-i·ron (sad′ī′ərn) *n.* A heavy flatiron pointed at each end. [< SAD, in obs. sense "heavy" + IRON]

sad·ism (sā′diz·əm, sad′iz·əm) *n.* **1** The obtaining of sexual gratification by inflicting pain. **2** A morbid delight in cruelty. [< Comte Donatien de *Sade*, 1740–1814, French writer] —**sad·ist** (sā′dist, sad′ist) *n., adj.* —**sa·dis·tic** (sə·dis′tik, sā-) *adj.* —**sa·dis′ti·cal·ly** *adv.*

sad·o·mas·o·chism (sā′dō·mas′ə·kiz′m, sad′ō-, -maz′-) *n.* A tendency in one individual to be both a sadist and a masochist. [< SAD (ISM) + -O- + MASOCHISM] —**sad′o·mas′o·chist** *n.* —**sad′o·mas′o·chis′tic** *adj.*

sad sack *Slang* A well-meaning but bungling person, esp. a soldier.

sa·fa·ri (sə·fä′rē) *n. pl.* **·ris** A hunting expedition or journey, esp. in E Africa. [< Ar. *safara* travel]

safe (sāf) *adj.* **saf·er, saf·est** **1** Free or freed from danger. **2** Having escaped injury or damage. **3** Not involving risk or loss: a *safe* investment. **4** Not likely to disappoint: It is *safe* to promise. **5** Not likely to cause or do harm or injury: Is this ladder *safe?* **6** No longer in a position to do harm: a burglar *safe* in jail. **7** In baseball, having reached base without being retired. —*n.* **1** A strong iron-and-steel receptacle, usu. fireproof, for protecting valuables. **2** Any place of safe storage. [< L *salvus* whole, healthy] —**safe′ly** *adv.* —**safe′ness** *n.* —**Syn. 1** secure. **2** unharmed, unscathed. **3** dependable, reliable.

safe-con·duct (sāf′kon′dukt) *n.* **1** Permission to travel in foreign or enemy territories without risking arrest or injury. **2** An official document assuring such protection.

safe-crack·er (sāf′krak′ər) *n.* One who breaks into safes to rob them. —**safe′crack′ing** *n.*

safe-de·pos·it box (sāf′di·poz′it) A box, safe, or drawer, usu. fireproof, for valuable jewelry, papers, etc., generally located in a bank. Also **safe′ty-de·pos′it box.**

---

add, āce, câre, pälm; end, ēven; it, īce; odd, ōpen, ôrder; tŏŏk, pōōl; up, bûrn; ə = a in *above*, u in *focus*; yōō = u in *fuse*; oil; pout; check; go; ring; thin; this; zh, *vision*. < derived from; ? origin uncertain or unknown.

safe·guard (sāf′gärd′) n. 1 One who or that which guards or keeps in safety. 2 A mechanical device designed to prevent accident or injury. —v.t. To defend; guard.

safe·keep·ing (sāf′kē′ping) n. The act or state of keeping or being kept in safety; protection.

safe·ty (sāf′tē) n. pl. ·ties 1 Freedom from danger or risk. 2 Freedom from injury. 3 A device or catch designed as a safeguard. 4 In football, the touching of the ball to the ground behind the player's own goal line when the ball was propelled over the goal line by a member of his own team, scoring two points for the opposing team. 5 In baseball, a fair hit by which the batter reaches first base: also **base hit.** —adj. Providing protection.

safety belt 1 A strap that gives a workman needed freedom of movement and protection against falling. 2 SEAT BELT.

safety glass Glass strengthened by any of various methods to reduce the likelihood of its shattering upon impact.

safety match A match that ignites only if struck on a chemically prepared surface.

safety pin 1 A pin whose point springs into place within a protecting sheath. • See PIN. 2 A pin which prevents the premature detonation of a hand grenade.

safety razor A razor in which the blade is fixed and provided with a guard to reduce the risk of cuts.

safety valve 1 Mech. A valve for automatically relieving excessive pressure. 2 Any outlet for pent-up energy or emotion.

saf·flow·er (saf′lou′ər) n. A thistlelike herb with composite orange-red flowers and seeds that yield edible **safflower oil.** [< Ital. saffiore saffron]

saf·fron (saf′rən) n. 1 A species of crocus with orange stigmas. 2 The dried stigmas, used in cookery. 3 A deep yellow orange: also **saffron yellow.** —adj. Of the color or flavor of saffron. [< Ar. za′farān]

S. Afr. South Africa; South African.

sag (sag) v. sagged, sag·ging v.i. 1 To droop from weight or pressure, esp. in the middle. 2 To hang unevenly. 3 To lose firmness; weaken, as from exhaustion, age, etc. 4 To decline, as in price or value. —v.t. 5 To cause to sag. —n. 1 A sagging. 2 A depressed or sagging place: a sag in a roof. [ME saggen] —sag′ging·ly adv.

sa·ga (sä′gə) n. 1 A medieval Scandinavian narrative dealing with legendary and heroic exploits. 2 A story having the saga form or manner. [ON, history, narrative]

sa·ga·cious (sə·gā′shəs) adj. 1 Ready and apt to apprehend and to decide on a course; intelligent. 2 Shrewd and practical. [< L sagax wise] —sa·ga′cious·ly adv. —sa·ga′cious·ness n. —Syn. 1 acute, discerning, clear-sighted, keen, perspicacious.

sa·gac·i·ty (sə·gas′ə·tē) n. pl. ·ties The quality or an instance of being sagacious; discernment or shrewdness.

sag·a·more (sag′ə·môr, -mōr) n. A lesser chief among the Algonquian Indians of North America. [< Algon.]

sage¹ (sāj) n. A venerable man of profound wisdom, experience, and foresight. —adj. 1 Characterized by or proceeding from calm, far-seeing wisdom and prudence: a sage observation. 2 Profound; learned; wise. [< L sapere be wise] —sage′ly adv. —sage′ness n.

sage² (sāj) n. 1 A plant of the mint family with aromatic, gray-green leaves that are used for flavoring meats, etc. 2 Any of various related plants. 3 SAGEBRUSH. [< L salvia]

sage·brush (sāj′brush′) n. Any of various small, aromatic shrubs with composite flowers, native to the w U.S.

sage grouse A large grouse of the plains of the w U.S.

sage hen The sage grouse, esp. the female.

Sag·it·ta·ri·us (saj′ə·târ′ē·əs) n. A constellation and the ninth sign of the zodiac; the Archer. • See ZODIAC.

sag·it·tate (saj′ə·tāt) adj. Shaped like an arrowhead, as certain leaves. [< L sagitta an arrow] • See LEAF.

sa·go (sā′gō) n. pl. ·gos 1 Any of several varieties of East Indian palm. 2 The powdered pith of this palm, used as a thickening agent in puddings, etc. [< Malay sāgū]

sa·gua·ro (sə·gwä′rō, -wä′-) n. pl. ·ros A giant cactus of the sw U.S.: also **sa·hua·ro** (-wä′-). [< Sp.]

sa·hib (sä′ib) n. Master; lord; Mr.; sir: formerly used in India by natives in speaking of or addressing Europeans. Also **sa′heb.** [< Ar. sāhib a friend]

said (sed) p.t. & p.p. of SAY. —adj. Law Previously mentioned.

sail (sāl) n. 1 Naut. A piece of canvas, etc., attached to a mast, spread to catch the wind, and thus to propel a craft through the water. 2 Sails collectively. 3 pl. **sail** A sailing vessel or craft. 4 A trip in any watercraft. 5 Anything resembling a sail in form or use, as a windmill arm. —**set sail** To begin a voyage. —**take in sail** To lower the sails of a craft. —**under sail** With sails spread and driven by the wind. —v.i. 1 To move across the surface of water by the action of wind or steam. 2 To travel over water in a ship or boat. 3 To begin a voyage. 4 To manage a sailing craft: Can you sail? 5 To move, glide, or float in the air; soar. 6 To move along in a stately or dignified manner: She sailed by haughtily. 7 Informal To pass rapidly. 8 Informal To proceed boldly into action: with in. —v.t. 9 To move or travel across the surface of (a body of water) in a ship or boat. 10 To navigate. —**sail into** 1 To begin with energy. 2 To attack violently. [< OE segl]

sail·boat (sāl′bōt′) n. A small boat propelled by a sail or sails.

sail·cloth (sāl′klôth′, -kloth′) n. A very strong, firmly woven, cotton canvas suitable for sails.

sail·fish (sāl′fish′) n. pl. ·fish or ·fish·es Any of a genus of marine fishes allied to the swordfish, having a large dorsal fin likened to a sail.

Sailfish

sail·or (sā′lər) n. 1 An enlisted man in any navy. 2 One whose work is sailing. 3 One who works on a ship. 4 One skilled in sailing. 5 A passenger on a ship or boat, esp. in reference to seasickness: a good sailor. 6 A low-crowned, flat-topped hat with a brim. —sail′or·ly adj.

sail·plane (sāl′plān′) n. A light maneuverable glider used for soaring. —v.i. ·planed, ·plan·ing To fly a sailplane.

saint (sānt) n. 1 A holy or sanctified person. 2 Such a person who has died and been canonized by certain churches, as the Roman Catholic. 3 Often cap. A member of any of certain religious sects calling themselves saints. 4 A very patient, unselfish person. —v.t. To canonize; venerate as a saint. —adj. Holy; canonized. [< L sanctus holy, consecrated] —saint′hood n.

Saint Ber·nard (bər·närd′) A working dog of great size and strength, originally bred in Switzerland to rescue travelers in the Swiss Alps.

saint·ed (sān′tid) adj. 1 Canonized. 2 Of holy character; saintly.

saint·ly (sānt′lē) adj. ·li·er, ·li·est 1 Like a saint; godly; holy. 2 Unusually good, kind, etc. —saint′li·ness n. —Syn. 1 pious, sacred, blessed. 2 benevolent, charitable, kindly, righteous.

saith (seth, sā′ith) Archaic Present indicative third person singular of SAY.

sake¹ (sāk) n. 1 Purpose; motive; end: for the sake of peace and quiet. 2 Interest, regard, or consideration: for the sake of your children. [< OE saccu a (legal) case]

sa·ke² (sä′kē) n. A Japanese fermented alcoholic liquor made from rice: also **sa′ki.**

sal (sal) n. Salt: used esp. as a pharmaceutical term. [L]

sa·laam (sə·läm′) n. 1 An Oriental salutation resembling a low bow, the palm of the right hand being held to the forehead. 2 A respectful or ceremonious greeting. —v.t. & v.i. To make a salaam. [< Ar. salām peace]

sal·a·ble (sā′lə·bəl) adj. Such as can be sold; marketable. —sal′a·bil′i·ty, sal′a·ble·ness n. —sal′a·bly adv.

sa·la·cious (sə·lā′shəs) adj. Lascivious; lustful; lecherous. [< L salire to leap] —sa·la′cious·ly adv. —sa·la′cious·ness, sa·lac′i·ty (-las′ə·te) n.

sal·ad (sal′əd) n. 1 A dish of vegetables such as lettuce, cucumbers, tomatoes, etc., usu. uncooked and served with a dressing, sometimes mixed with chopped cold meat, fish, hard-boiled eggs, etc. 2 Any green vegetable that can be eaten raw. [< L salare to salt]

salad days Days of youth and inexperience.

salad dressing A sauce used on salads, as mayonnaise, oil and vinegar, etc.

sal·a·man·der (sal′ə·man′dər) *n.* **1** Any of an order of tailed amphibians having a smooth, moist skin. **2** A fabled reptile purportedly able to live in fire. [< L *salamandra*] —**sal′a·man′drine** (-drin) *adj.*

Salamander

sa·la·mi (sə·lä′mē) *n. pl.* **·mis** A salted, spiced sausage, originally Italian. [< L *sal* salt]

sal ammoniac AMMONIUM CHLORIDE. [L]

sal·a·ried (sal′ər·ēd) *adj.* **1** In receipt of a salary. **2** Yielding a salary.

sal·a·ry (sal′ər·ē) *n. pl.* **·ries** A periodic payment as compensation for official or professional services. —*v.t.* **·ried, ·ry·ing** To pay or allot a salary to. [< L *salarium* money paid Roman soldiers for their salt]

sale (sāl) *n.* **1** The exchange or transfer of property for money or its equivalent. **2** A selling of merchandise at prices lower than usual. **3** An auction. **4** Opportunity of selling; market: Stocks find no *sale*. **5** *Usu. pl.* The amount sold: last year's *sales.* —**for sale** Offered or ready for sale. —**on sale** For sale at bargain rates. [< OE *sala*]

sale·a·ble (sā′lə·bəl) *adj.* SALABLE.

sal·e·ra·tus (sal′ə·rā′təs) *n.* BAKING SODA. [< NL *sal aëratus* aerated salt]

sales·girl (sālz′gûrl′) *n.* A woman or girl hired to sell merchandise, esp. in a store.

sales·la·dy (sālz′lā′dē) *n. pl.* **·dies** *Informal* A woman or girl hired to sell merchandise, esp. in a store.

sales·man (sālz′mən) *n. pl.* **·men** (-mən) A man hired to sell goods, stock, etc., in a store or by canvassing.

sales·man·ship (sālz′mən·ship) *n.* **1** The work of a salesman. **2** Skill in selling.

sales·peo·ple (sālz′pē′pəl) *n.pl.* Salespersons.

sales·per·son (sālz′pûr′sən) *n.* A person hired to sell merchandise, esp. in a store: also **sales′clerk′** (-klûrk′).

sales resistance A resistance on the part of a potential customer to buying certain goods.

sales·room (sālz′rōōm′, -rōōm′) *n.* A room where merchandise is displayed for sale.

sales tax A tax on money received from sales of goods, usu. passed on to the buyer.

sales·wom·an (sālz′wōōm′ən) *n. pl.* **·wom·en** (-wim′in) A woman or girl hired to sell merchandise, esp. in a store.

Sal·ic (sal′ik) *adj.* Characterizing a law (the **Salic Law**) derived from Germanic sources in the fifth century, and providing that males only could inherit lands: later applied to the succession to the French and Spanish thrones.

sa·lic·y·late (sə·lis′ə·lāt, sal′ə·sil′āt) *n.* A salt or ester of salicylic acid.

sal·i·cyl·ic acid (sal′ə·sil′ik) A crystalline organic compound used in making aspirin and various analgesics. [< L *salix* willow]

sa·li·ent (sā′lē·ənt) *adj.* **1** Standing out prominently: a *salient* feature. **2** Extending outward; projecting: a *salient* angle. **3** Leaping; springing. —*n.* An extension, as of a fortification or a military line protruding toward the enemy. [< L *salire* to leap] —**sa′li·ence, sa′li·en·cy** *n.* —**sa′·li·ent·ly** *adv.* —**Syn. 1** conspicuous, noticeable, significant. **2** jutting.

sa·line (sā′lēn, sā′līn) *adj.* Constituting, consisting of, or characteristic of salt; salty. —*n.* **1** A metallic salt, esp. a salt of one of the alkalis or of magnesium. **2** A solution of sodium chloride or other salt. **3** A natural deposit of salt. [< L *sal* salt] —**sa·lin·i·ty** (sə·lin′ə·tē) *n.*

Salis·bur·y steak (sôlz′ber·ē, -brē) Ground beef mixed with bread crumbs, onion, seasoning, etc., cooked as patties and usu. served with gravy. [< J. H. *Salisbury*, 19th-century English physician]

Sa·lish (sā′lish) *n.* **1** A family of Indian languages of the NW U.S. and SW Canada. **2** A member of a tribe speaking any of these languages. —*adj.* Of or pertaining to the Salish languages or the people speaking them. Also **Sa′·lish·an** (-ən).

sa·li·va (sə·lī′və) *n.* A mixture of mucus and fluid secreted by glands in the cheeks and lower jaw. [L] —**sal·i·var·y** (sal′ə·ver′ē) *adj.*

sal·i·vate (sal′ə·vāt) *v.* **·vat·ed, ·vat·ing** *v.i.* **1** To secrete saliva. —*v.t.* **2** To cause to secrete saliva, esp. excessively. —**sal′i·va′tion** *n.*

sal·low (sal′ō) *adj.* Of an unhealthy yellowish color or complexion. —*v.t.* To make sallow. [< OE *salo*] —**sal′low·ness** *n.*

sal·ly (sal′ē) *v.i.* **·lied, ·ly·ing** **1** To rush out suddenly. **2** To set out energetically. **3** To go out, as from a room or building. —*n. pl.* **·lies** **1** A rushing forth, as of besieged troops against besiegers; sortie. **2** A going forth, as on a walk. **3** A witticism or bantering remark. [< L *salire* to leap]

sal·ma·gun·di (sal′mə·gun′dē) *n.* **1** A dish of chopped meat, anchovies, eggs, onions, etc., mixed and seasoned. **2** Any medley or miscellany. [? < Ital. *salami conditi* pickled meats]

salm·on (sam′ən) *n.* **1** Any of various anadromous food and game fishes inhabiting cool ocean waters and certain land-locked lakes. **2** The pinkish orange color of the flesh of certain salmon: also **salm′on·pink′**. —*adj.* Having the color salmon: also **salm′on·pink′**. [< L *salmo*]

Salmon

sal·mo·nel·la (sal′mō·nel′ə) *n. pl.* **·lae** (lē) or **·las** Any of a genus of aerobic bacteria that cause food poisoning and some diseases, including typhoid fever. [< D. E. *Salmon*, U.S. pathologist, 1850–1914]

salmon trout Any of various salmonlike fish, as the European sea trout, the namaycush, etc.

Sa·lo·me (sə·lō′mē, sal·ə·mā′) The daughter of Herodias, who asked from Herod the head of John the Baptist in return for her dancing.

sa·lon (sə·lon′, sal′on, *Fr.* sá·lôṅ′) *n.* **1** A room in which guests are received; a drawing-room. **2** The periodic gathering of noted persons, under the auspices of some distinguished personage. **3** A hall or gallery used for exhibiting works of art. **4** An establishment devoted to some specific purpose: a beauty *salon*. [< Ital. *sala* a room, hall]

sa·loon (sə·lōōn′) *n.* **1** A place where alcoholic drinks are sold; a bar. **2** A large room for public use, as on a passenger ship: a dining *saloon*. [< F *salon* salon] • In the U.S., *saloon* (def. 1) is now used mainly in historical contexts dealing with the American western frontier or as a rough equivalent of *dive* in describing a squalid bar.

sa·loon-keep·er (sə·lōōn′kē′pər) *n.* One who keeps a saloon (def. 1).

sal·si·fy (sal′sə·fē, ·fī) *n.* A plant with purple, composite flowers and a white, edible root of an oysterlike flavor. [< F *salsifis*]

sal soda Sodium carbonate; washing soda.

salt (sôlt) *n.* **1** A white, soluble, crystalline compound of sodium and chlorine, widely distributed in nature and found in all living organisms: also **table salt, common salt. 2** *Chem.* Any compound derived from an acid by replacement of all or part of the hydrogen by an electropositive radical or a metal. **3** *pl.* Any of various mineral compounds in common use, as Epsom salts, smelling salts, etc. **4** Piquant humor; dry wit. **5** That which preserves, corrects, or purifies: the *salt* of criticism. **6** A sailor. **7** A saltcellar. —**salt of the earth** A person or persons regarded as being fine, honest, kindly, etc. —**take with a grain of salt** To allow for exaggeration; have doubts about. —**worth one's salt** Worth one's pay or keep; hardworking. —*adj.* **1** Seasoned with salt; salty. **2** Cured or preserved with salt. **3** Containing, or growing or living in or near, salt water. —*v.t.* **1** To season with salt. **2** To preserve or cure with salt. **3** To furnish with salt: to *salt* cattle. **4** To add zest or piquancy to. **5** To add something to so as fraudulently to increase the value: to *salt* a mine with gold. —**salt away 1** To pack in salt for preserving. **2** *Informal* To store up; save. [< OE *sealt*] —**salt′er** *n.*

SALT, S.A.L.T. (sôlt) Strategic Arms Limitation Talks.

salt·cel·lar (sôlt′sel′ər) *n.* A small receptacle for table salt. [< ME *salt saler* < *salt* salt + *saler* saltcellar < OF *saliere;* form infl. by CELLAR]

salt chuck *Can. Regional* The sea.

salt·ed (sôl′tid) *adj.* 1 Treated or preserved with salt. 2 *Informal* Experienced or expert.

salting out The injection of a saline solution into the amniotic fluid to terminate a pregnancy.

salt lick A place to which animals go to lick salt from superficial natural deposits.

salt marsh Low coastal land frequently overflowed by the tide, usu. covered with coarse grass: also **salt meadow**.

salt·pe·ter (sôlt′pē′tər) *n.* 1 POTASSIUM NITRATE. 2 CHILE SALTPETER. Also **salt′pe′tre**. [< L *sal* salt + *petra* rock]

salt·shak·er (sôlt′shā′kər) *n.* A container with small apertures for sprinkling table salt.

salt·wa·ter (sôlt′wô′tər, -wot′ər) *adj.* Of, composed of, or living in salt water.

salt·works (sôlt′wûrks′) *n. pl.* **·works** An establishment where salt is made commercially.

salt·wort (sôlt′wûrt′) *n.* Any of a genus of weedy plants adapted to saline soils.

salt·y (sôl′tē) *adj.* **salt·i·er, salt·i·est** 1 Tasting of or containing salt. 2 Piquant; sharp, as speech, etc. —**salt′i·ly** *adv.* — **salt′i·ness** *n.*

sa·lu·bri·ous (sə·lōō′brē·əs) *adj.* Conducive to health; healthful; wholesome. [< L *salus* health] —**sa·lu′bri·ous·ly** *adv.* —**sa·lu′bri·ous·ness** *n.*

sal·u·tar·y (sal′yə·ter′ē) *adj.* 1 Beneficial. 2 Wholesome; healthful. [< L *salus* health] —**sal′u·tar′i·ly** *adv.* —**sal′u·tar′i·ness** *n.*

sal·u·ta·tion (sal′yə·tā′shən) *n.* 1 The act of saluting. 2 Any form of greeting. 3 The opening words of a letter, as *Dear Sir* or *Dear Madam*.

sa·lu·ta·to·ri·an (sə·lōō′tə·tôr′ē·ən, -tō′rē-) *n.* In colleges and schools, the graduating student who delivers the salutatory at commencement.

sa·lu·ta·to·ry (sə·lōō′tə·tôr′ē, -tō′rē) *n. pl.* **·ries** An opening oration, as at a college commencement. —*adj.* Of or relating to a salutatory address. [< L *salutare* SALUTE]

sa·lute (sə·lōōt′) *v.* **·lut·ed, ·lut·ing** *v.t.* 1 To greet with an expression or sign of welcome, respect, etc.; welcome. 2 To honor in some prescribed way, as by raising the hand to the cap, presenting arms, firing cannon, etc. —*v.i.* 3 To make a salute. —*n.* 1 An act of saluting; a greeting, show of respect, etc. 2 The attitude assumed in giving a military hand salute. [< L *salutare* < *salus* health] —**sa·lut′er** *n.*

Sal·va·dor (sal′və·dôr′, *Sp.* säl′vä·thôr′) *n.* EL SALVADOR.

Sal·va·do·ri·an (sal′və·dôr′ē·ən, -dō′rē-) *n.* A citizen or native of El Salvador. —*adj.* Of or pertaining to El Salvador or its people: also **Sal′va·do′ran**.

sal·vage (sal′vij) *v.t.* **·vaged, ·vag·ing** 1 To save, as a ship or its cargo, from wreck, capture, etc. 2 To save (material) from something damaged or discarded for reuse: to *salvage* aluminum. —*n.* 1 The saving of a ship, cargo, etc., from loss. 2 Any act of saving property. 3 The compensation allowed to persons by whose exertions a vessel, its cargo, or the lives of those sailing on it are saved from loss. 4 That which is saved from a wrecked or abandoned vessel or from after a fire. 5 Anything saved from destruction. [< OF *salver* to save] —**sal′vag·er** *n.*

sal·va·tion (sal·vā′shən) *n.* 1 The process or state of being saved. 2 A person or thing that delivers from evil, danger, or ruin. 3 *Theol.* Deliverance from sin and penalty; redemption. [< LL *salvare* to save]

Salvation Army A religious and charitable organization founded on semimilitary lines by William Booth in England in 1865. —**Sal·va′tion·ist** *n.*

salve[1] (sav, säv) *n.* 1 An emollient preparation for burns, cuts, etc. 2 Anything that heals, soothes, or mollifies. — *v.t.* **salved, salv·ing** 1 To dress with salve or ointment. 2 To soothe; appease, as conscience, pride, etc. [< OE *sealf*]

salve[2] (salv) *v.t.* **salved, salv·ing** To save from loss; salvage. [Back formation < SALVAGE]

sal·ver (sal′vər) *n.* A tray, as of silver. [< Sp. *salva*, orig. the foretasting of food, as for a king]

sal·vi·a (sal′vē·ə) *n.* 1 An ornamental species of sage with red flowers. 2 Any plant of the sage genus. [L]

sal·vo (sal′vō) *n. pl.* **·vos** or **·voes** 1 A simultaneous discharge of artillery, or of two or more bombs from an aircraft. 2 A sudden discharge or burst: a *salvo* of hail. 3 Tribute; praise. [< Ital. *salva* a salute]

sal vo·lat·i·le (sal vō·lat′ə·lē) Ammonium carbonate; smelling salts. [NL, volatile salt]

SAM (sam) surface-to-air missile.

S. Am., S. Amer. South America; South American.

sam·a·ra (sam′ər·ə, sə·mâr′ə) *n.* An indehiscent winged fruit, as of the elm or maple. [L, elm seed]

sa·mar·i·um (sə·mâr′ē·əm) *n.* A metallic element (symbol Sm) of the lanthanide series. [NL < Col. *Samarski*, 19th-century Russian mining official]

sam·ba (sam′bə, säm′bä) *n.* A dance of Brazilian origin in two-four time. —*v.i.* To dance the samba. [< a native African name]

Sam Browne belt (sam′ broun′) A military belt, with one or two light shoulder straps running diagonally across the chest from right to left. [< Sir Samuel J. Browne, 1824–1901, British army general]

same (sām) *adj.* 1 Identical; equal: They both are the *same* price. 2 Exactly alike; not different: The two children have the *same* first name. 3 Aforementioned; just spoken of. 4 Equal in degree of preference; indifferent. 5 Unchanged: The old place looks the *same*. —**all the same** 1 Nevertheless. 2 Equally acceptable or unacceptable. — **just the same** 1 Nevertheless. 2 Exactly identical or corresponding; unchanged. —*pron.* The identical person, thing, event, etc. —*adv.* In like manner; equally: with *the*. [< ON *samr, sami*] —**same′ness** *n.*

sam·i·sen (sam′i·sen) *n.* A three-stringed Japanese musical instrument played with a plectrum.

sa·mite (sā′mīt, sam′īt) *n.* A rich medieval fabric of silk, often interwoven with gold or silver. [< Gk. *hexamitos* woven with six threads]

Sa·mo·an (sə·mō′ən) *adj.* Of or pertaining to Samoa, its people, their language, culture, etc. —*n.* 1 A native or citizen of Samoa. 2 The language of the Samoans.

sam·o·var (sam′ə·vär) *n.* A metal urn containing a tube for charcoal for heating water, as for making tea. [Russ. < *samo-* self + *varit* boil]

Sam·o·yed (sam′ə·yed′) *n.* 1 One of a Mongoloid people inhabiting the Arctic coasts of Siberia. 2 A large Siberian dog with a thick white coat. —*adj.* Of or pertaining to the Samoyed people. Also **Sam′·o·yede′** (-yed′). —**Sam′o·yed′ic** *adj.*

Samovar

samp (samp) *n.* Coarsely ground Indian corn; also, a porridge made of it. [< Algon.]

sam·pan (sam′pan) *n.* Any of various small flat-bottomed boats used along rivers and coasts of China and Japan. [< Chin. *san* three + *pan* board]

sam·ple (sam′pəl) *n.* 1 A portion, part, or piece taken or shown as a representative of the whole. 2 An instance: This is a *sample* of his kindness. —*v.t.* **·pled, ·pling** To test or examine by means of a portion or sample. —*adj.* Serving as a sample: a *sample* dress. [< OF *essample* example]

Sampan

sam·pler (sam′plər) *n.* 1 One who tests by samples. 2 A device for removing a portion of a substance for testing. 3 A piece of needlework, designed to show a beginner's skill. [< L *exemplum* example]

Sam·son (sam′sən) In the Bible, a Hebrew judge of great physical strength, betrayed to the Philistines by Delilah.

sam·u·rai (sam′oo·rī) *n. pl.* **·rai** Under the Japanese feudal system, a member of the soldier class of the lower nobility; also, the class itself. [Jap.]

san·a·tive (san′ə·tiv) *adj.* Healing; health-giving. [< L *sanare* heal]

san·a·to·ri·um (san′ə·tôr′ē·əm, -tō′rē-) *n. pl.* **·to·ri·ums** or **·to·ri·a** (-tôr′ē·ə, -tō′rē·ə) An institution for the treatment of chronic disorders, as mental illness, alcoholism, etc. [< LL *sanatorius* healthy]

sanc·ti·fy (sangk′tə·fī) *v.t.* **·fied, ·fy·ing** 1 To set apart as holy; consecrate. 2 To free of sin; purify. 3 To render sacred or inviolable, as a vow. [< L *sanctus* holy + *facere* to make] —**sanc′ti·fi·ca′tion, sanc′ti·fi′er** *n.*

sanc·ti·mo·ni·ous (sangk′tə·mō′nē·əs) *adj.* Making an

ostentatious display or a hypocritical pretense of sanctity. —**sanc·ti·mo·ni·ous·ly** *adv.* —**sanc·ti·mo·ni·ous·ness** *n.*

sanc·ti·mo·ny (sangk′tə·mō′nē) *n.* Assumed or outward sanctity; a show of devoutness. [< L *sanctimonia* holiness]

sanc·tion (sangk′shən) *v.t.* **1** To approve authoritatively; confirm; ratify. **2** To countenance; allow. —*n.* **1** Final and authoritative confirmation; justification or ratification. **2** A formal decree. **3** A provision for securing conformity to law, as by the enactment of rewards or penalties or both. **4** *pl.* In international law, a coercive measure adopted by several nations to force a nation to obey international law, by limiting trade relations, by military force and blockade, etc. [< L *sanctus,* p.p. of *sancire* make sacred]

sanc·ti·ty (sangk′tə·tē) *n. pl.* **·ties 1** The state of being sacred or holy. **2** Saintliness; holiness. **3** Something sacred or holy.

sanc·tu·ar·y (sangk′chōō·er′ē) *n. pl.* **·ar·ies 1** A holy or sacred place, esp. one devoted to the worship of a deity. **2** The most sacred part of a place in a sacred structure; esp. the part of a church where the principal altar is situated. **3** A place of refuge: a wildlife *sanctuary.* **4** Immunity from the law or punishment. [< L *sanctus* holy] —**Syn. 1** church, shrine, temple. **3** preserve, shelter.

sanc·tum (sangk′təm) *n. pl.* **·tums** or **·ta** (-tə) **1** A sacred place. **2** A private room where one is not to be disturbed. [L < *sanctus* holy]

sanc·tum sanc·to·rum (sangk′təm sangk·tôr′əm, -tō′rəm) **1** HOLY OF HOLIES. **2** A place of great privacy: often used humorously. [LL, holy of holies]

sand (sand) *n.* **1** A hard, granular rock material finer than gravel and coarser than dust. **2** *pl.* Stretches of sandy desert or beach. **3** *pl.* Sandy grains, as those of the hourglass. **4** *Slang* Endurance; grit. —*v.t.* **1** To sprinkle or cover with sand. **2** To smooth or abrade with sand or sandpaper. [< OE]

san·dal (san′dəl) *n.* **1** A foot covering, consisting usu. of a sole only, held to the foot by thongs or straps. **2** A light, openwork slipper. [< Gk. *sandalion*] —**san′daled** *adj.*

san·dal·wood (san′dəl·wŏŏd′) *n.* **1** The fine-grained, dense, fragrant wood of any of several East Indian trees. **2** The similar wood of other trees. **3** Any tree yielding this wood. [< Med. L *sandalum* sandalwood + WOOD]

Sandal

sand·bag (sand′bag′) *n.* **1** A bag filled with sand, used for building fortifications, for ballast, etc. **2** A small bag filled with sand and used as a club. —*v.t.* **·bagged, ·bag·ging 1** To fill or surround with sandbags. **2** To strike or attack with a sandbag. —**sand′bag′ger** *n.*

sand·bank (sand′bangk′) *n.* A mound or ridge of sand.

sand·bar (sand′bär′) *n.* A ridge of silt or sand in rivers, along beaches, etc., formed by the action of currents or tides.

sand·blast (sand′blast′, -bläst′) *n.* **1** An apparatus for propelling a jet of sand, as for etching glass or cleaning stone. **2** The jet of sand. —*v.t.* To clean or engrave by means of a sandblast. —**sand′blast′er** *n.*

sand·box (sand′boks′) *n.* A box of sand for children to play in.

sand·er (san′dər) *n.* A device, esp. a machine powered by electricity, that smooths and polishes surfaces by means of a disk or belt coated with an abrasive: also **sanding machine.**

sand flea 1 CHIGOE. **2** Any of various tiny crustaceans that jump like fleas.

sand·hog (sand′hôg′, -hog′) *n.* One who works under air pressure, as in sinking caissons, building tunnels, etc.: also **sand hog.**

sand·lot (sand′lot′) *n.* A vacant lot in or near an urban area. —*adj.* Of or played in such a lot: *sandlot* baseball.

sand·man (sand′man′) *n.* In nursery lore, a mythical person supposed to make children sleepy by casting sand in their eyes.

sand·pa·per (sand′pā′pər) *n.* Strong paper coated with abrasive for smoothing or polishing. —*v.t.* To rub or polish with sandpaper.

sand·pi·per (sand′pī′pər) *n.* Any of certain small wading birds having long, thin bills and frequenting shores and marsh lands.

Sandpiper

sand·stone (sand′stōn′) *n.* A rock consisting chiefly of quartz sand cemented with other materials.

sand·storm (sand′stôrm′) *n.* A high wind by which clouds of sand or dust are carried along.

sand·wich (sand′wich, san′-) *n.* **1** Two or more slices of bread, having between them meat, cheese, etc. **2** Any combination of alternating dissimilar things pressed together. —*v.t.* To place between other persons or things. [< John Montagu, fourth Earl of *Sandwich,* 1718–92]

sandwich man *Informal* A man carrying boards, called **sandwich boards,** one in front and one behind, for the purpose of advertising or picketing.

sand·y (san′dē) *adj.* **sand·i·er, sand·i·est 1** Consisting of or characterized by sand; containing, covered with, or full of sand. **2** Yellowish red: a *sandy* beard. —**sand′i·ness** *n.*

sane (sān) *adj.* **san·er, san·est 1** Mentally sound; not deranged. **2** Proceeding from a sound mind. **3** Sensible; wise. [< L *sanus* whole, healthy] —**sane′ly** *adv.* —**sane′ness** *n.*

San·for·ize (san′fə·rīz) *v.t.* **·ized, ·iz·ing** To treat (cloth) by a special process so as to prevent more than slight shrinkage. [Back formation < *Sanforized,* a trade name]

sang (sang) *p.t.* of SING.

sang-froid (säng′frwä′, *Fr.* säṅ·frwä′) *n.* Calmness amid trying circumstances; composure. [F, lit., cold blood]

san·gui·nar·y (sang′gwə·ner′ē) *adj.* **1** Attended with bloodshed. **2** Prone to shed blood; bloodthirsty. [< L *sanguis* blood] —**san′gui·nar′i·ly** *adv.* —**san′gui·nar′i·ness** *n.*

san·guine (sang′gwin) *adj.* **1** Of buoyant disposition; hopeful. **2** Having the color of blood; ruddy: a *sanguine* complexion. **3** *Obs.* Bloodthirsty; sanguinary. Also **san·guin·e·ous** (sang·gwin′ē·əs). [< L *sanguis* blood] —**san′guine·ly** *adv.* —**san′guine·ness** *n.* —**Syn. 1** ardent, confident, enthusiastic, optimistic. **2** rubicund.

San·he·drin (san·hed′rən, -hēd′-, san′hi·drin, san′i-) *n.* In ancient times, the supreme council and highest court of the Jewish nation. Also **Great Sanhedrin.** [< Heb.]

san·i·tar·i·an (san′ə·târ′ē·ən) *n.* A person skilled in matters relating to sanitation and public health.

san·i·tar·i·um (san′ə·târ′ē·əm) *n. pl.* **·i·ums** or **·i·a** (-ē·ə) **1** A health resort. **2** SANATORIUM. [< L *sanitas* health]

san·i·tar·y (san′ə·ter′ē) *adj.* **1** Relating to the preservation of health and prevention of disease: *sanitary* measures. **2** Free from filth; clean; hygienic. —*n. pl.* **·tar·ies** A public toilet. [< L *sanitas* health] —**san′i·tar′i·ly** *adv.*

sanitary napkin An absorbent pad used by women during menstruation.

san·i·ta·tion (san′ə·tā′shən) *n.* **1** The science or process of establishing sanitary conditions, esp. as regards public health. **2** The removal of sewage, garbage, etc.

san·i·ta·tion·man (san′i·tā′shən·man′) *n. pl.* **·men** (-mən) A person, esp. a municipal employee, whose work is the collection of refuse and trash.

san·i·tize (san′ə·tīz) *v.t.* **·tized, ·tiz·ing 1** To make sanitary, as by scrubbing, washing, or sterilizing. **2** To make acceptable or unobjectionable, as by deleting offensive parts: a *sanitized* fairy tale. —**san′i·ti·zer** *n.*

san·i·ty (san′ə·tē) *n.* **1** The state of being sane or sound; mental health. **2** Sane moderation or reasonableness. [< L *sanus* healthy] —**Syn. 1** rationality, saneness. **2** common sense, level-headedness, sensibleness.

sank (sangk) *p.t.* of SINK.

San Ma·ri·no (mä·rē′nō) *n.* A republic located in an enclave of NE Italy, 23 sq. mi., cap. San Marino.

sans (sanz, *Fr.* säṅ) *prep.* Without. [< OF *sens, sanz*]

sans·cu·lotte (sanz′kyōō·lot′, *Fr.* säṅ·kü·lôt′) *n.* **1** A revolutionary: used by the aristocrats as a term of contempt for the poorly clad republicans who started the French Revolution of 1789. **2** Any revolutionary repub-

lican or radical. [F, lit., without knee breeches] —**sans'cu·lot'tic** adj. —**sans'cu·lot'tism** n.

san·se·vi·e·ri·a (san'sə·vir'ē·ə, -vi·ē'rē·ə) n. Any of a genus of succulent plants of the lily family with a cluster of tall, lance-shaped leaves. [< the Prince of Sanseviero, 1710–71, Italian scholar]

San·skrit (san'skrit) n. The ancient and classical language of the Hindus of India, belonging to the Indic branch of the Indo-Iranian subfamily of Indo-European languages: also **San'scrit**. [< Skt. samskrita well-formed]

sans ser·if (sanz ser'if) Printing A style of type without serifs.

San·ta Claus (san'tə klôz') In folklore, a friend of children who brings presents at Christmas time: usu. represented as a fat, jolly old man in a red suit; St. Nicholas. [< dial. Du. Sante Klaus Saint Nicholas]

Santa Fe Trail The trade route, important from 1821 to 1880, between Independence, Missouri and Santa Fe, New Mexico.

sap[1] (sap) n. 1 The juices of plants, which contain and transport the materials necessary to growth. 2 Any vital fluid; vitality. 3 Sapwood. 4 Slang A foolish, stupid, or ineffectual person. [< OE sæp]

sap[2] (sap) v. sapped, sap·ping v.t. 1 To weaken or destroy gradually and insidiously. 2 To approach or undermine (an enemy fortification) by digging trenches. —v.i. 3 To dig a sap or saps. —n. A deep, narrow trench dug so as to approach or undermine a fortification. [< MF sappe a spade] —Syn. v. 1 debilitate, disable, enervate, enfeeble.

sap·head (sap'hed') n. Slang A stupid person; simpleton. —**sap'head'ed** adj.

sa·pi·ent (sā'pē·ənt, sap'ē-) adj. Wise; sagacious: often ironical. [< L sapere know, taste] —**sa'pi·ence, sa'pi·en·cy** n. —**sa'pi·ent·ly** adv.

sap·ling (sap'ling) n. 1 A young tree. 2 A young person. [Dim. of SAP[1]]

sap·o·dil·la (sap'ə·dil'ə) n. 1 A large tropical American evergreen tree which yields chicle and an edible fruit. 2 Its apple-shaped fruit: also **sapodilla plum**. [< Nahuatl zapotl]

sap·o·na·ceous (sap'ə·nā'shəs) adj. Soapy. [< L sapo soap] —**sap'o·na'ceous·ness** n.

sa·pon·i·fy (sə·pon'ə·fī) v.t. ·fied, ·fy·ing To convert (a fat or oil) into soap by the action of an alkali. [< L sapo soap + facere to make] —**sa·pon'i·fi·ca'tion, sa·pon'i·fi'er** n.

sap·per (sap'ər) n. A soldier employed in making trenches, tunnels, and underground fortifications. [< SAP[2]]

sap·phire (saf'īr) n. 1 Any one of the hard, transparent, colored varieties of corundum, esp. a blue variety valued as a gem. 2 Deep blue. —**star sapphire** A sapphire cut without facets, showing six rays on the dome. —adj. Deep blue. [< Gk. sappheiros a gemstone]

sap·py (sap'ē) adj. ·pi·er, ·pi·est 1 Full of sap; juicy. 2 Slang Immature; silly. 3 Vital; pithy. —**sap'pi·ness** n.

sap·ro·phyte (sap'rə·fīt) n. An organism that lives on dead or decaying organic matter, as certain bacteria, fungi, etc. [< Gk. sapros rotten + -PHYTE] —**sap'ro·phyt'ic** (-fit'ik) adj.

sap·suck·er (sap'suk'ər) n. A small woodpecker that taps trees and drinks sap.

sap·wood (sap'wŏŏd') n. The new wood beneath the bark of a tree.

S.A.R. Sons of the American Revolution.

sar·a·band (sar'ə·band) n. 1 A stately Spanish dance in triple time, of the 17th and 18th centuries. 2 Music for this dance. Also **sar'a·bande**. [< Sp. zarabanda]

Sar·a·cen (sar'ə·sən) n. 1 Formerly, a Muslim enemy of the Crusaders. 2 An Arab. —adj. Of or pertaining to the Saracens. —**Sar'a·cen'ic** (-sen'ik) or ·i·cal adj.

Sar·ah (sâr'ə) In the Bible, the wife of Abraham and the mother of Isaac.

Sa·ran (sə·ran') n. A synthetic plastic material used as a textile fiber and as a transparent, moistureproof wrapping: a trade name.

sar·casm (sär'kaz·əm) n. 1 The use of keenly ironic or scornful remarks. 2 Such a remark. [< Gk. sarkazein tear flesh, speak bitterly] —**Syn.** 2 gibe, sneer, taunt.

Yellow-bellied sapsucker

sar·cas·tic (sär·kas'tik) adj. 1 Characterized by or of the nature of sarcasm. 2 Taunting. Also **sar·cas'ti·cal**. —**sar·cas'ti·cal·ly** adv.

sarce·net (särs'net) n. A fine, thin silk, used for linings. [< OF drap sarrasinois, lit. Saracen cloth]

sar·co·carp (sär'kō·kärp) n. The fleshy, usu. edible part of a drupe. [< Gk. sarx flesh + karpos a fruit]

sar·co·ma (sär·kō'mə) n. pl. ·mas or ·ma·ta (-mə·tə) A malignant tumor originating in connective tissue. [< Gk. sarkaein become fleshy] —**sar·co'ma·tous** (-kō'mə·təs) adj.

sar·coph·a·gus (sär·kof'ə·gəs) n. pl. ·gi (-jī) or ·gus·es 1 A stone coffin or tomb. 2 A large ornamental coffin of marble or other stone placed in a crypt or exposed to view. [< Gk. sarx flesh + phagein eat]

sard (särd) n. A deep brownish red variety of chalcedony, used as a gem. [< L sarda]

sar·dine (sär·dēn') n. 1 A small fish preserved in oil as a delicacy. 2 The young of the herring or some like fish similarly prepared. [< Gk. sarda a kind of fish]

sar·don·ic (sär·don'ik) adj. Scornful or derisive; sneering; mocking; cynical. [< Gk. sardanios bitter, scornful] —**sar·don'i·cal·ly** adv. —**sar·don'i·cism** n.

sar·do·nyx (sär·don'iks, sär'də·niks) n. A variety of onyx, containing layers of light-colored chalcedony and sard. [< Gk. sardios sard + onyx onyx]

sar·gas·so (sär·gas'ō) n. Any of a genus of large, floating brown seaweed: also **sargasso weed, sar·gas'sum**. [< Pg. sarga, a kind of grape]

sa·ri (sä'rē) n. pl. ·ris A length of cloth, constituting the principal garment of Hindu women, one end falling to the feet, and the other crossed over the bosom, shoulder, and sometimes over the head: also **sa'ree**. [< Skt. śāṭī]

Sari

sa·rong (sə·rong') n. A rectangular piece of colored cloth worn as a skirt by both sexes in the Malay Archipelago. [< Malay sārung]

sar·sa·pa·ril·la (sas'pə·ril'ə, sär'sə·pə·ril'ə) n. 1 A tropical American vine with fragrant roots. 2 An extract of these roots, used as flavoring. 3 Any of various plants resembling sarsaparilla. [< Sp. zarza a bramble + parilla little vine]

sar·to·ri·al (sär·tôr'ē·əl, -tō'rē-) adj. 1 Pertaining to a tailor or his work. 2 Pertaining to men's clothes. [< L sartor tailor] —**sar·to'ri·al·ly** adv.

sash[1] (sash) n. An ornamental band or scarf, worn around the waist or over the shoulder. [< Ar. shāsh muslin, turban]

sash[2] (sash) n. A frame, as of a window, in which glass is set. —v.t. To furnish with a sash. [Alter. of CHASSIS, taken as a pl.]

sa·shay (sa·shā') v.i. Informal To move or glide about, esp. ostentatiously. [< Fr. chassé a dance movement]

Sask. Saskatchewan.

sass (sas) Informal n. Impudence; back talk. —v.t. To talk to impudently. [Dial. alter. of SAUCE]

sas·sa·fras (sas'ə·fras) n. 1 A small North American tree related to laurel. 2 A flavoring agent made from the bark of its roots. [< Sp. sasafrás]

sas·sy (sas'ē) adj. ·si·er, ·si·est Informal Saucy; impertinent. —**sas'si·ly** adv. —**sas'si·ness** n.

sat (sat) p.t. of SIT.

SAT Scholastic Aptitude Test.

Sat. Saturday; Saturn.

Sa·tan (sā'tən) In the Bible, the great adversary of God and tempter of mankind; the Devil. [< Heb. sātān an enemy] —**sa·tan·ic** (sā·tan'ik, sə-), **sa·tan'i·cal** adj. —**sa·tan'i·cal·ly** adv.

satch·el (sach'əl) n. A small bag for carrying books, clothing, etc. [< L sacellus little sack]

sate[1] (sāt) v.t. sat·ed, sat·ing 1 To satisfy the appetite of. 2 To indulge with too much so as to weary or sicken; satiate. [< OE sadian] —**Syn** 1 gratify. 2 cloy, glut, stuff, surfeit.

sate[2] (sāt) Archaic p.t. of SIT.

sa·teen (sa·tēn') n. A smooth, shiny cotton fabric resembling satin. [Alter. of SATIN]

sat·el·lite (sat′ə·līt) n. 1 A body held in orbit about a more massive one; a moon. 2 An artificial body propelled into orbit, esp. around the earth. 3 One who attends upon a person in power. 4 Any obsequious attendant. 5 A small nation dependent on a great power. [< L satelles an attendant]

sa·ti·a·ble (sā′shē·ə·bəl, -shə·bəl) adj. Capable of being satiated. —**sa′ti·a·bil′i·ty, sa′ti·a·ble·ness** n. —**sa′ti·a·bly** adv.

sa·ti·ate (sā′shē·āt) v.t. ·at·ed, ·at·ing 1 To satisfy the appetite or desire of; gratify. 2 To fill or gratify excessively; glut. —adj. Filled to satiety; satiated. [< L satis enough] —**sa′ti·a′tion** n.

sa·ti·e·ty (sə·tī′ə·tē, sā′shē·ə·tē) n. pl. ·ties The state of being satiated; surfeit. [< L satis enough]

sat·in (sat′ən) n. A fabric of silk, rayon, etc., with glossy face and dull back. —adj. Of or similar to satin; glossy; smooth. [< OF] —**sat′in·y** adj.

sat·in·wood (sat′ən·wood′) n. 1 The smooth, hard wood of various trees, used in cabinetwork. 2 Any tree yielding such wood.

sat·ire (sat′īr) n. 1 The use of sarcasm, irony, or wit in ridiculing and denouncing abuses, follies, customs, etc. 2 A literary work that ridicules in this manner. [< L satira]

sa·tir·i·cal (sə·tir′i·kəl) adj. 1 Given to or characterized by satire: a satirical writer. 2 Sarcastic; caustic; biting. Also **sa·tir′ic.** —**sa·tir′i·cal·ly** adv. —**sa·tir′i·cal·ness** n.

sat·i·rist (sat′ə·rist) n. 1 A writer of satire. 2 A person fond of satirizing or ridiculing.

sat·i·rize (sat′ə·rīz) v.t. ·rized, ·riz·ing To subject to or criticize in satire. —**sat′i·riz′er** n.

sat·is·fac·tion (sat′is·fak′shən) n. 1 The act of satisfying, or the state of being satisfied. 2 The making of amends, reparation, or payment. 3 That which satisfies; compensation.

sat·is·fac·to·ry (sat′is·fak′tər·ē) adj. Giving satisfaction; answering expectations or requirements. —**sat′is·fac′to·ri·ly** adv. —**sat′is·fac′to·ri·ness** n. —Syn. adequate, gratifying, pleasing, sufficient.

sat·is·fy (sat′is·fī) v. ·fied, ·fy·ing v.t. 1 To supply fully with what is desired, expected, or needed. 2 To please; gratify. 3 To free from doubt or anxiety; convince. 4 To give what is due to. 5 To pay or discharge (a debt, obligation, etc.). 6 To answer sufficiently or convincingly, as a question or objection. 7 To make reparation for; expiate. —v.i. 8 To give satisfaction. [< L satis enough + facere do] —**sat′is·fi′er** n. —**sat′is·fy′ing·ly** adv.

sa·to·ri (sä·tō′rē) n. The sudden change of consciousness which is the goal of Zen Buddhism. [Jap.]

sa·trap (sā′trap, sat′rap) n. 1 A governor of a province in ancient Persia. 2 Any petty ruler under a despot. 3 A subordinate ruler or governor. [< O Pers. shathraparan, lit., a protector of a province]

sa·trap·y (sā′trə·pē, sat′rə·pē) n. pl. ·trap·ies The territory or the jurisdiction of a satrap. Also **sa·trap·ate** (sā′trə·pit, sat′rə-).

sat·u·rate (sach′ə·rāt) v.t. ·rat·ed, ·rat·ing To soak or imbue thoroughly to the utmost capacity for absorbing or retaining. —adj. Saturated. [< L satur full] —**sat′u·ra′tor** or **sat′u·rat′er** n.

sat·u·rat·ed (sach′ə·rā′tid) adj. 1 Replete; incapable of holding more of a substance: a saturated solution. 2 Chem. Designating an organic compound having no free or multiple valence bonds available for direct union with additional atoms. 3 Tending to increase the cholesterol content of the blood: said of some edible fats.

sat·u·ra·tion (sach′ə·rā′shən) n. 1 A saturating or being saturated. 2 A massive concentration, in any given area, as of advertising, military force, etc., for a specific purpose: often used attributively: saturation bombing.

saturation point 1 The maximum possible degree of impregnation of one substance with another. 2 A condition in which a person has reached the limit of patience, toleration, etc.

Sat·ur·day (sat′ər·dē, -dā) n. The seventh or last day of the week; the day of the Jewish Sabbath. [< OE Sæternesdæg Saturn's day]

Sat·urn (sat′ərn) Rom. Myth. The god of agriculture. —n. The planet of the solar system sixth in distance from the sun. •See PLANET. —**Sa·tur·ni·an** (sə·tûr′nē·ən) adj. [< L Saturnus]

sat·ur·na·li·a (sat′ər·nā′lē·ə) n.pl. (usu. construed as sing.) Any season or period of general license or revelry. —**sat′ur·na′li·an** adj.

Sat·ur·na·li·a (sat′ər·nā′lē·ə) n.pl. The feast of Saturn held in ancient Rome in mid-December, and marked by wild reveling and abandon. —**Sat′ur·na′li·an** adj.

sat·ur·nine (sat′ər·nīn) adj. 1 Having a grave, gloomy, or morose disposition or character. 2 In astrology, born under the supposed dominance of Saturn. [< L Saturnus Saturn] —**sat′ur·nine·ly** adv. —**sat′ur·nine′ness** n.

sat·yr (sā′tər, sat′ər) Gk. Myth. A wanton woodland deity with a man's body and goatlike legs. —n. A lascivious man. [< Gk. satyros] —**sa·tyr·ic** (sə·tir′ik) or ·**i·cal** adj.

sat·y·ri·a·sis (sat′ə·rī′ə·sis) n. An abnormally strong, insatiable sexual drive in males. [< Gk. satyros a satyr]

sauce (sôs) n. 1 An appetizing, usu. liquid relish for food to improve its taste. 2 A dish of fruit pulp stewed and sweetened: cranberry sauce. 3 Informal Pert or impudent language. 4 Slang Alcoholic liquor. —v.t. sauced, sauc·ing 1 To flavor or dress with sauce. 2 Informal To be saucy to. [< L salsus salted]

sauce·pan (sôs′pan′) n. A pan, usu. of metal or enamel, with projecting handle, for cooking food.

sau·cer (sô′sər) n. 1 A small dish for holding a cup. 2 Any round, shallow thing of similar shape. [< OF sauce sauce]

sau·cy (sô′sē) adj. ·ci·er, ·ci·est 1 Disrespectful to superiors; impudent. 2 Piquant; sprightly; amusing. —**sau′ci·ly** adv. —**sau′ci·ness** n.

Sau·di A·ra·bi·a (sou′dē ə·rä′bē·ə, sä·oo′dē) A kingdom

of N CEN. Arabia, 927,000 sq. mi., cap. Riyadh. —**Sau′di A·ra′bi·an** adj., n.

sauer·kraut (sour′krout′) n. Shredded and salted cabbage fermented in its own juice. [< G sauer sour + kraut cabbage]

Saul (sôl) In the Bible, the first king of Israel.

sau·na (sou′nə, sô′-) n. 1 A Finnish steam bath in which the steam is produced by running water over heated stones. 2 A bath in which the bather is exposed to very hot, dry air. 3 A room or enclosure for a sauna. [Finnish]

saun·ter (sôn′tər) v.i. To walk in a leisurely or lounging way; stroll. —n. 1 A slow, aimless manner of walking. 2 An idle stroll. [< ME santren muse] —**saun′ter·er** n. —**saun′ter·ing·ly** adv.

sau·ri·an (sôr′ē·ən) n. Any of the suborder of reptiles comprising the lizards. —adj. Pertaining to or having the characteristics of lizards. [< Gk. sauros a lizard]

-saurus *combining form* Zool. Lizard: *brontosaurus*. [< Gk. *sauros* a lizard]

sau·sage (sô′sij) *n.* Finely chopped and highly seasoned meat, commonly stuffed into a prepared animal intestine or other casing. [< L *salsus* salted]

sau·té (sô·tā′, sō-) *v.t.* **·téed, ·té·ing** To fry quickly in a little fat. —*n.* A sautéed dish. [F, p.p. of *sauter* to leap]

sau·terne (sô·tûrn′, sō-; *Fr.* sō·tern′) *n.* A sweet, white wine. [< *Sauternes*, district in sw France]

sav·age (sav′ij) *adj.* **1** Of a wild and untamed nature; not domesticated. **2** Fierce; ferocious. **3** Living in or belonging to the most primitive condition of human society; uncivilized. **4** Remote and wild: *savage* mountain country. —*n.* **1** A primitive or uncivilized human being. **2** A brutal and cruel person. —*v.t.* **sav·aged, sav·a·ging** To beat or maul cruelly. [< L *silva* a wood] —**sav′age·ly** *adv.* —**Syn.** *adj.* **1** undomesticated, feral. **2** brutal, bloodthirsty, barbarous. **3** uncultivated.

sav·age·ry (sav′ij·rē) *n. pl.* **·ries 1** The state of being savage. **2** Cruelty in disposition or action. **3** A savage act.

sa·van·na (sə·van′ə) *n.* A tract of level land covered with low vegetation; a treeless plain, esp. in or near the tropics: also **sa·van′nah**. [< Cariban]

sa·vant (sə·vänt′, sav′ənt; *Fr.* så·väṅ′) *n.* A person of exceptional learning. [F < L *sapere* be wise]

save[1] (sāv) *v.* **saved, sav·ing** *v.t.* **1** To preserve or rescue from danger, harm, etc. **2** To keep from being spent, expended, or lost. **3** To set aside for future use; accumulate: often with *up*. **4** To treat carefully so as to avoid fatigue, harm, etc.: to *save* one's eyesight. **5** To prevent by timely action: A stitch in time *saves* nine. **6** *Theol.* To deliver from the consequences of sin; redeem. —*v.i.* **7** To be economical. **8** To preserve something from harm, etc. **9** To accumulate money. [< L *salvus* safe] —**sav′er** *n.*

save[2] (sāv) *prep.* Except; but. —*conj.* **1** Except; but. **2** *Archaic* Unless. [< OF *sauf* being excepted, orig. safe]

sav·ing (sā′ving) *adj.* **1** That saves or rescues: *lifesaving* equipment. **2** Economical; frugal. **3** Holding in reserve; qualifying: a *saving* clause. —*n.* **1** Preservation from loss or danger. **2** Avoidance of waste; economy. **3** Any reduction in cost, time, etc.: a *saving* of 16 percent. **4** *pl.* Sums of money saved, esp. those deposited in a bank. —*prep.* **1** With the exception of; save. **2** With due respect for: *saving* your presence. —*conj.* With the exception of. —**sav′ing·ly** *adv.* —**sav′ing·ness** *n.*

savings account An account drawing interest at a savings bank.

savings bank An institution for receiving and investing savings and paying interest on deposits.

sav·ior (sāv′yər) *n.* One who saves. —**the Savior** Jesus Christ. *Brit. sp.* **sav′iour**.

sa·voir faire (så·vwår fâr′) Ability to see and to do the right thing; esp., sophisticated social poise. [F, lit., to know how to act]

sa·vor (sā′vər) *n.* **1** Taste and smell: a *savor* of garlic. **2** Specific or characteristic quality. **3** Relish; zest: The conversation had *savor*. —*v.i.* **1** To have savor; taste or smell: with *of*. **2** To have a specified savor or character: with *of*. —*v.t.* **3** To give flavor to; season. **4** To taste or enjoy with pleasure; relish. **5** To have the savor or character of. *Brit. sp.* **sa′vour**. [< L *sapere* taste, know] —**sa′vor·er** *n.* —**sa′vor·ous** *adj.*

sa·vor·less (sā′vər·lis) *adj.* Tasteless; insipid.

sa·vor·y[1] (sā′vər·ē) *adj.* **1** Of an agreeable taste and odor; appetizing. **2** In good repute. —*n. pl.* **·vor·ies** *Brit.* A small, hot serving of tasty food, usu. eaten at the end of a dinner. *Brit. sp.* **sa′vour·y**. [< OF *savourer* to taste] —**sa′vor·i·ly** *adv.* —**sa′vor·i·ness** *n.* —**Syn.** *adj.* **1** flavorful, palatable, piquant, tasty, toothsome. **2** respectable.

sa·vor·y[2] (sā′vər·ē) *n.* A hardy, annual herb of the mint family used for seasoning. Also **summer savory**. [< OF *savoreie*]

sa·voy (sə·voi′) *n.* A variety of cabbage with wrinkled leaves and a compact head. [< F *(chou de) Savoie* (cabbage of) Savoy]

Sa·voy·ard (sə·voi′ərd, sav′oi·ärd′) *n.* An actor or actress in or an admirer or producer of the Gilbert and Sullivan operas. [< the *Savoy*, London theater]

sav·vy (sav′ē) *Slang v.i.* **·vied, ·vy·ing** To understand; comprehend. —*n.* Understanding; know-how. —*adj.* Having good sense or know-how. [Alter. of Sp. ¿ *Sabe (usted)?* Do (you) know?]

saw[1] (sô) *n.* **1** A cutting tool with pointed teeth arranged continuously along the edge of a blade or disk. **2** A tool or machine having such teeth: a power *saw*. —*v.* **sawed, sawed** or **sawn, saw·ing** *v.t.* **1** To cut or divide with or as with a saw. **2** To shape or fashion with a saw. **3** To make a motion as if sawing: The speaker *saws* the air. —*v.i.* **4** To use a saw. **5** To cut: said of a saw. **6** To be cut with a saw: This wood *saws* easily. [< OE *sagu*] —**saw′er** *n.*

saw[2] (sô) *n.* A proverbial or familiar saying; old maxim. [< OE *sagu*]

saw[3] (sô) *p.t.* of SEE[1].

saw·bones (sô′bōnz′) *n. Slang* A surgeon.

saw·buck (sô′buk′) *n.* **1** A frame consisting of two X-shaped ends joined by connecting bars, for holding sticks of wood for sawing. **2** *Slang* A ten-dollar bill: from the resemblance of X, Roman numeral ten, to the ends of a sawbuck.

saw·dust (sô′dust′) *n.* Tiny particles of wood cut or torn out by sawing.

Sawbuck def. 1

saw·fish (sô′fish′) *n. pl.* **·fish** or **·fish·es** Any of a genus of large tropical fishes related to rays and having an elongated snout with teeth on each edge.

saw·fly (sô′flī′) *n. pl.* **·flies** A hymenopterous insect having in the female a pair of sawlike organs for piercing plants, wood, etc., in which to lay eggs.

saw·horse (sô′hôrs′) *n.* A frame consisting of a long wooden bar or plank supported by four extended legs.

saw·mill (sô′mil′) *n.* **1** An establishment for sawing logs with power-driven machinery. **2** A large sawing machine.

sawn (sôn) A *p.p.* of SAW[1].

Sawhorse

saw-toothed (sô′tōōtht′) *adj.* Having teeth or toothlike processes similar to those of a saw; serrate. Also **saw′tooth′** (-tōōth′).

saw·yer (sô′yər) *n.* One who saws logs, esp. a lumberman who fells trees by sawing, or one who works in a sawmill.

sax (saks) *n. Informal* A saxophone.

sax·i·frage (sak′sə·frij) *n.* Any of numerous perennial plants usu. having a basal rosette of leaves and growing in rocky places. [< L *(herba) saxifraga*, lit., stone-breaking (herb)]

Sax·on (sak′sən) *n.* **1** A member of a Germanic tribal group living in NW Germany in the early centuries of the Christian era. With the Angles and Jutes, the Saxons conquered England in the fifth and sixth centuries. **2** The language of the early Saxons. **3** An inhabitant of modern Saxony in Germany. —*adj.* Of or pertaining to the early Saxons, or to their language.

sax·o·phone (sak′sə·fōn) *n.* Any of a group of reed instruments having a straight metal body equipped with finger keys and terminating in a curved, conical bore. [< A. J. *Sax*, 1814–94, Belgian instrument maker] —**sax′o·phon′ist** *n.*

say (sā) *v.* **said, say·ing** *v.t.* **1** To speak. **2** To express in words; tell. **3** To state positively: *Say* which you prefer. **4** To recite; repeat: to *say* one's prayers. **5** To allege: They *say* that he lied. **6** To assume: He is worth, *say*, a million. —*v.i.* **7** To make a statement; speak. —**say nothing of** Without mentioning. —**that is to say** In other words. —*n.* **1** What one has said or has to say: Let him have his say. **2** *Informal* Right or turn to speak or choose: Now it is my *say*. —**the say** *Informal* Authority: Who has *the say* in this office? —*interj.* A hail or exclamation to command attention: also *Brit.* **I say!** [< OE *secgan*] —**say′er** *n.* —**Syn.** *v.* **1** articulate, pronounce, utter. **2** declare, affirm. **5** assert.

Saxophone

say·ing (sā'ing) *n.* **1** An utterance. **2** A maxim or saw. — **go without saying** To be so evident as to require no explanation.

say-so (sā'sō') *n. Informal* **1** An unsupported assertion or decision. **2** Right or power to make decisions: He has the *say-so.*

Sb antimony (L *stibium*).

SBA Small Business Administration.

SbE south by east.

SbW south by west.

SC Security Council (of the United Nations); South Carolina (P.O. abbr.).

S.C. Signal Corps; South Carolina; Supreme Court.

Sc scandium; stratocumulus.

sc. he (or she) carved or engraved it (L *sculpsit*); namely (L *scilicet*); scale; scene; science; screw; scruple (weight).

s.c. small capitals (printing).

scab (skab) *n.* **1** A crust on a wound or sore. **2** A contagious disease of sheep. **3** Any of certain plant diseases marked by a roughened or warty exterior. **4** A worker who will not join a labor union. **5** A worker who does the job of a person on strike. —*v.i.* **scabbed, scab·bing 1** To form or become covered with a scab. **2** To act or work as a scab. [< Scand.] —**scab'bi·ly** *adv.* —**scab'bi·ness** *n.* —**scab'by** *adj.* (**·i·er, ·i·est**)

scab·bard (skab'ərd) *n.* A sheath for a weapon, as for a bayonet or a sword. —*v.t.* To sheathe in a scabbard. [< OHG *scar* a sword + *bergan* hide, protect]

sca·bies (skā'bēz) *n.* A skin disease affecting man and various animals, caused by infestation by certain mites; the itch. [< L *scabere* to scratch, scrape] —**sca·bi·et·ic** (skā'bē·et'ik), **sca'bi·ous** (-əs) *adj.*

sca·bi·o·sa (skā'bē·ō'sə) *n.* Any of various plants related to the teasel, with showy, usu. prickly flowers. Also **sca'bi·ous** (-əs). [< Med. L *(herba) scabiosa* herb for scabies]

sca·brous (skā'brəs) *adj.* **1** Roughened with minute points. **2** Difficult to handle tactfully. **3** Suggestive; salacious. [< L *scabere* to scratch] —**sca'brous·ly** *adv.* —**sca'· brous·ness** *n.*

scads (skadz) *n.pl. Informal* A large amount or quantity. [?]

scaf·fold (skaf'əld, -ōld) *n.* **1** A temporary elevated structure for the support of workmen, materials, etc., as in constructing, painting, or repairing a building. **2** A platform for the execution of criminals. **3** Any raised platform. —*v.t.* To furnish or support with a scaffold. [< OF *escadafaut*]

scaf·fold·ing (skaf'əl·ding) *n.* **1** A scaffold, or system of scaffolds. **2** The materials for constructing scaffolds.

scag (skag) *n. Slang* Heroin.

sca·lar (skā'lər) *adj.* Defined by a single number, as a quantity having only magnitude. —*n.* A scalar quantity. [< L *scala* a ladder]

scal·a·wag (skal'ə·wag) *n.* **1** *Informal* A worthless person; rascal. **2** A Southern white who became a Republican during the Reconstruction period: a contemptuous term. Also **scal'la·wag, scal'ly·wag.** [?]

scald[1] (skôld) *v.t.* **1** To burn with hot liquid or steam. **2** To cleanse or treat with boiling water. **3** To heat (a liquid) to a point just short of boiling. **4** To cook in a liquid which is just short of the boiling point. —*v.i.* **5** To be or become scalded. —*n.* **1** A burn due to a hot fluid or steam. **2** Surface injury of plant tissue due to various causes, as exposure to sun, fungi, etc. [< L *ex-* very + *calidus* hot]

scald[2] (skôld, skäld) *n.* SKALD. —**scal·dic** (skôl'dik, skäl'-) *adj.*

scale[1] (skāl) *n.* **1** One of the thin, horny, usu. overlapping, protective plates covering most fishes, reptiles, etc. **2** SCALE INSECT. **3** A specialized leaf, as of a pine cone. **4** A flaky coating on metal, as from corrosion, etc. **5** Any thin, scalelike piece, as of skin. —*v.* **scaled, scal·ing** *v.t.* **1** To strip or clear of scale or scales. **2** To form scales on; cover with scales. **3** To take off in layers or scales; pare off. —*v.i.* **4** To come off in layers or scales; peel. **5** To shed scales. **6** To become incrusted with scales. [< OF *escale* a husk] — **scal'er** *n.*

scale[2] (skāl) *n.* **1** An object bearing accurately spaced

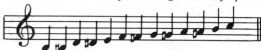

Ascending chromatic scale *def. 6*

marks for use in measurement, or the series of marks so used. **2** Any system of units of measurement. **3** A proportion used in representing distances, as on a map or blueprint. **4** *Math.* A system of numeration in which the successive places determine the value of digits, as the decimal system. **5** Any progressive or graded series; a graduation: the social *scale.* **6** *Music* A series of tones arranged in a sequence of ascending or descending pitches according to any of various systems of intervals. **7** *Phot.* The range of light values which may be reproduced by a photographic paper. **8** A succession of steps or degrees: a salary *scale.* **9** A relative degree or extent: to live on a modest *scale.* —*v.* **scaled, scal·ing** *v.t.* **1** To climb to the top of. **2** To make according to a scale. **3** To regulate or adjust according to a scale or ratio: with *up, down,* etc. — *v.i.* **4** To climb; ascend. **5** To rise, as in steps or stages: mountains *scaling* to the skies. [< L *scala* a ladder] — **scal'er** *n.*

scale[3] (skāl) *n.* **1** The bowl, scoop, or platform of a weighing instrument or balance. **2** *Usu. pl.* The balance itself. —**the Scales** LIBRA. —**turn the scales** To determine; decide. —*v.* **scaled, scal·ing** *v.t.* **1** To weigh in scales. **2** To amount to in weight. —*v.i.* **3** To be weighed. [< ON *skál* a bowl]

scale insect Any of numerous plant-feeding insects of which the adult female is sedentary under a scalelike, waxy shield.

sca·lene (skā'lēn, skā·lēn') *adj. Geom.* Having no two sides equal: said of a triangle. [< Gk. *skalēnos* uneven] • See TRIANGLE.

scal·lion (skal'yən) *n.* **1** A young, tender onion with a small white bulb. **2** A shallot or leek. [< L *(caepa) Ascalonia* (onion) of Ashkelon, a Palestinian seaport]

scal·lop (skal'əp, skol'-) *n.* **1** Any of various mollusks having a hinged shell with radiating ribs and wavy edge. **2** The edible abductor muscle of certain scallops. **3** A scallop shell. **4** One of a series of semicircular curves along an edge, as for ornament. —*v.t.* **1** To shape the edge of with scallops for ornamentation. **2** To bake (food) in a casserole with a sauce, usu. topped with bread crumbs. [< MF *escalope* shell] — **scal'lop·er** *n.*

Scallop shell

scalp (skalp) *n.* **1** The skin of the top and back of the skull, usu. covered with hair. **2** A portion of this, cut or torn away as a trophy among certain North American Indians. —*v.t.* **1** To cut or tear the scalp from. **2** *Informal* To buy (tickets) and sell again at prices exceeding the established rate. **3** *Informal* To buy and sell again quickly to make a small profit. —*v.i.* **4** *Informal* To scalp bonds, tickets, etc. [< Scand.] —**scalp'er** *n.*

scal·pel (skal'pəl) *n.* A small, sharp, surgical knife. [< L *scalpere* to cut]

scal·y (skā'lē) *adj.* **scal·i·er, scal·i·est 1** Having a covering of scales or flakes. **2** Of the nature of a scale. **3** Incrusted with a flaking deposit. —**scal'i·ness** *n.*

scamp[1] (skamp) *n.* A confirmed rogue; rascal. [< obs. *scamp* to roam] —**scamp'ish** *adj.* —**scamp'ish·ness** *n.*

scamp[2] (skamp) *v.t.* To perform (work) carelessly or dishonestly. [?] —**scamp'er** *n.*

scam·per (skam'pər) *v.i.* To run quickly or hastily. —*n.* A hurried flight. [< L *ex* out + *campus* a plain, battlefield] —**scam'per·er** *n.*

scam·pi (skam'pē) *n.pl.* Large shrimp, usu. served in a garlic sauce. [Ital.]

scan (skan) v. **scanned, scan·ning** v.t. **1** To examine in detail; scrutinize closely. **2** To pass the eyes over quickly; glance at. **3** To separate (verse) into metrical feet. **4** *Electronics* To cause a beam, as of light, electrons, microwaves, etc., to pass systematically over a surface or through a region. —v.i. **5** To scan verse. **6** To conform to metrical rules: said of verse. [< LL *scandere* scan verses] —**scan′ner** n.

Scan., Scand. Scandinavia; Scandinavian.

scan·dal (skan′dəl) n. **1** A discreditable action or circumstance offensive to public morals or feelings. **2** Injury to reputation. **3** General criticism that injures reputation; malicious gossip. **4** A person whose conduct arouses public censure. [< Gk. *skandalon* a snare] —**Syn. 2** discredit, disgrace, disrepute. **3** calumny, defamation, slander.

scan·dal·ize (skan′dəl·īz) v.t. **·ized, ·iz·ing** To shock the moral feelings of; outrage. —**scan′dal·i·za′tion, scan′dal·iz′er** n.

scan·dal·ous (skan′dəl·əs) adj. **1** Causing or being a scandal; disgraceful. **2** Consisting of evil or malicious reports. —**scan′dal·ous·ly** adv. —**scan′dal·ous·ness** n.

Scan·di·na·vi·a (skan′də·nā′vē·ə) n. The region of NW Europe occupied by Sweden, Norway, and Denmark; 315,-156 sq. mi; Finland, Iceland, and the Faroe Islands are often included: total area, 485,539 sq. mi. —**Scan′di·na′vi·an** adj., n.

scan·di·um (skan′dē·əm) n. A rare metallic element of low density. [< L *Scandia* Scandinavia]

scan·sion (skan′shən) n. The act or art of scanning verse to show its metrical parts.

scant (skant) adj. **1** Meager in measure or quantity. **2** Being just short of the measure specified: a *scant* half-hour; a *scant* five yards. —**scant of** Insufficiently supplied with: to be *scant of* breath from running. —v.t. **1** To restrict or limit in supply; stint. **2** To treat briefly or inadequately. —adv. *Regional* Scarcely; barely. [< ON *skammr* short] —**scant′ly** adv. —**scant′ness** n.

scant·ling (skant′ling) n. **1** A small beam or timber, esp. an upright timber in a structure. **2** Such timbers collectively. [< OF *eschantillon* specimen]

scant·y (skan′tē) adj. **scant·i·er, scant·i·est 1** Too little; not enough: a *scanty* meal. **2** Scarcely enough for what is needed; insufficient. [< SCANT] —**scant′i·ly** adv. —**scant′i·ness** n. —**Syn. 1** deficient, poor, sparse. **2** limited, restricted.

scape·goat (skāp′gōt′) n. **1** In the Bible, the goat upon whose head Aaron symbolically laid the sins of the people on the day of atonement, after which it was led away into the wilderness. *Lev.* 16. **2** Any person bearing blame for the misdeeds of others. —v.t. *Informal* To make a scapegoat of. [< ESCAPE + GOAT]

scape·grace (skāp′grās′) n. A mischievous or incorrigible person.

s. caps. small capitals (printing).

scap·u·la (skap′yə·lə) n. pl. **·las** or **·lae** (-lē) Either of the two large, flat bones of the upper back; shoulder blade. [< L *scapulae* shoulder blades]

scap·u·lar (skap′yə·lər) n. **1** A garment of certain religious orders consisting of two strips of cloth hanging down front and back. **2** Two small rectangular pieces of cloth connected by strings, worn as a badge of membership by certain religious orders. Also **scap′u·lar′y** (-ler′ē). [< L *scapula* shoulder]

Scapula

scar (skär) n. **1** The mark left after the healing of a lesion. **2** Any lingering sign, as from hardship, misfortune, etc.: the *scars* of poverty. —v.t. & v.i. **scarred, scar·ring** To mark or become marked with a scar. [< LL *eschara* a scab]

scar·ab (skar′əb) n. **1** Any of various beetles, esp. a large, black beetle held sacred by the ancient Egyptians. **2** A gemstone or other ornament in the form of this beetle. Also **scar·a·bee** (skar′ə·bē). [< L *scarabaeus*] —**scar′a·boid** (-boid) adj.

scar·a·bae·us (skar′ə·bē′əs) n. pl. **·bae·us·es** or **·bae·i** (-bē′ī) SCARAB. Also **scar′a·be′us** —**scar·a·bae′id** adj., n.

scar·a·mouch (skar′ə·mouch, -mōōsh) n. **1** A boastful, cowardly person. **2** *Usu. cap.* A similar character in old Italian comedy. Also **scar′a·mouche.** [< Ital. *Scaramuccia*, lit., a skirmish]

scarce (skârs) adj. **scarc·er, scarc·est 1** Rare and unusual: *scarce* antiques. **2** Scant; insufficient. —**make oneself scarce** *Informal* To go or stay away. [< OF *eschars* scanty, insufficient] —**scarce′ness** n.

scarce·ly (skârs′lē) adv. **1** Only just; barely: so weary he could *scarcely* walk. **2** Rarely: He *scarcely* goes out now. **3** Certainly not; probably not: That's *scarcely* possible.

scar·ci·ty (skâr′sə·tē) n. pl. **·ties 1** Scantiness; insufficiency: a *scarcity* of truffles. **2** Rarity: the *scarcity* of genius.

scare (skâr) v. **scared, scar·ing** v.t. **1** To strike with sudden fear; frighten. **2** To drive or force by frightening: with *off* or *away*. —v.i. **3** To take fright; become scared. —**scare up** *Informal* To get together hurriedly; produce: to *scare up* a meal from leftovers. —n. A sudden fright; alarm. —adj. *Informal* Intended to provoke alarm or concern: *scare* tactics. [< ON *skiarr* shy] —**scar′er** n. —**scar′ing·ly** adv. —**Syn.** v. **1** alarm, startle, terrify. n. fright, panic.

scare·crow (skâr′krō′) n. **1** Any effigy set up to scare crows and other birds from growing crops. **2** A cause of false alarm. **3** A person who is ragged and tattered or thin and gangling.

scare·head (skâr′hed′) n. *Informal* A newspaper headline in large type for sensational news.

scarf¹ (skärf) n. pl. **scarfs 1** In carpentry, a lapped joint made as by notching two timbers at the ends, and bolting them together to form a single piece: also **scarf joint. 2** The notched end of either of the timbers so cut. —v.t. **1** To unite with a scarf joint. **2** To cut a scarf in. [ME]

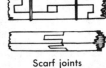

Scarf joints

scarf² (skärf) n. pl. **scarfs** or **scarves** (skärvz) **1** A long and wide band, worn about the head, neck, shoulders, or waist. **2** A necktie or cravat with dangling ends. **3** A runner for a bureau or table. —v.t. To cover or decorate with a scarf. [< OF *escharpe*]

scar·i·fy (skar′ə·fī) v.t. **·fied, ·fy·ing 1** To make shallow scratches in, as the skin. **2** To criticize severely. **3** To stir the surface of, as soil. [< Gk. *skariphasthai* scratch an outline] —**scar′i·fi′er, scar′i·fi·ca′tion** n.

scar·la·ti·na (skär′lə·tē′nə) n. A mild form of scarlet fever.

scar·let (skär′lit) n. **1** A brilliant red, inclining to orange. **2** Cloth or clothing of a scarlet color. —adj. Brilliant red. [< Pers. *saqalāt* a rich, scarlet cloth]

scarlet fever An acute streptococcal infection marked by fever, sore throat, and a red rash.

scarlet letter A scarlet "A" which adulterous women were once condemned to wear.

scarlet runner A climbing bean with vivid red flowers and long seed pods. Also **scarlet runner bean.**

scarp (skärp) n. **1** Any steep slope. **2** A steep artificial slope, esp. the inner slope, about a fortification. —v.t. To cut to a steep slope. [< Ital. *scarpa*]

scarves (skärvz) A pl. of SCARF².

scar·y (skâr′ē) adj. **scar·i·er, scar·i·est** *Informal* **1** Easily scared. **2** Giving cause for alarm. —**scar′i·ness** n.

scat¹ (skat) v.i. **scat·ted, scat·ting** *Informal* To go away quickly: usu. in the imperative. [?]

scat² (skat) n. Jazz singing that employs improvised nonsense syllables. —v.i. **scat·ted, scat·ting** To sing scat. [?]

scathe (skāth) v.t. **scathed, scath·ing 1** To criticize severely. **2** *Archaic* To injure severely. [< ON *skatha*]

scathe·less (skāth′lis) adj. Without harm or injury.

scath·ing (skā′thing) adj. Blasting; withering: a *scathing* rebuke. —**scath′ing·ly** adv.

sca·tol·o·gy (ska·tol′ə·jē, skə-) n. **1** The scientific study of excrement. **2** Preoccupation with obscenity or with excrement, as in literature. [< Gk. *skōr, skatos* dung + -LOGY] —**scat·o·log·i·cal** (skat′ə·loj′i·kəl) adj. —**sca·tol′o·gist** n.

scat·ter (skat′ər) v.t. **1** To throw about in various places; strew. **2** To disperse; rout. **3** *Physics* To reflect (radiation) in more than one direction. —v.i. **4** To separate and go in different directions. —n. The act of scattering or the con-

dition of being scattered. [ME *scateren*] —**scat′ter·er** *n.* —
Syn. *v.* **1** disseminate, sow, spread, sprinkle. **2** drive away.

scat·ter·brain (skat′ər-brān′) *n.* A heedless, flighty person. —**scat′ter-brained′** *adj.*

scat·ter·site (skat′ər-sīt) *adj.* Of or describing housing sponsored by government, esp. for low-income groups, located in various communities to avoid ghettoization.

scaup (skôp) *n.* A North American wild duck related to the canvasback, having the head and neck black in the male: also **scaup duck.** [Obs. var. of SCALP + DUCK]

scav·enge (skav′inj) *v.* **·enged, ·eng·ing** *v.t.* **1** To remove filth, rubbish, and refuse from, as streets. —*v.i.* **2** To act as a scavenger. **3** To search for food. [Back formation < SCAVENGER]

scav·en·ger (skav′in·jər) *n.* **1** Any organism that feeds on refuse, carrion, etc. **2** A person who removes refuse or unwanted things, as a garbage collector or a junkman. [< AF *scawage* inspection]

sce·nar·i·o (si-nâr′ē-ō, -nä′rē-ō) *n. pl.* **·nar·i·os 1** The plot or outline of a dramatic work. **2** The written plot and arrangement of incidents of a motion picture. **3** An outline or plan of a projected series of actions or events. [< LL *scenarius* of stage scenes] —**sce·nar′ist** *n.*

scene (sēn) *n.* **1** A locality and all connected with it, as presented to view; a landscape. **2** The setting for a dramatic action. **3** The place and surroundings of any event, as in literature or art. **4** A division of an act of a play. **5** A specific incident or episode in a play, novel, motion picture, etc.: the ghost *scene* in *Hamlet*. **6** The painted canvas, hangings, etc., for the background for a play. **7** An unseemly display of anger or excited feeling, esp. in public. **8** *Slang* A place or realm of a currently popular activity: the country music *scene*. —**behind the scenes 1** Out of sight of a theater audience; backstage. **2** Privately; in secret. [< Gk. *skēnē* a tent, a stage]

scen·er·y (sē′nər·ē) *n. pl.* **·er·ies 1** The features of a landscape; view. **2** The painted backdrops, etc., used in the theater to represent a setting in a play.

sce·nic (sē′nik, sen′ik) *adj.* **1** Of or relating to beautiful natural scenery: a *scenic* spot. **2** In art, representing a situation, action, etc. **3** Relating to stage scenery. —**sce′ni·cal·ly** *adv.*

scent (sent) *n.* **1** An odor. **2** The effluvium by which an animal can be tracked. **3** A clue aiding investigation. **4** A fragrant, fluid essence; perfume. **5** The sense of smell. —*v.t.* **1** To perceive by the sense of smell. **2** To form a suspicion of. **3** To cause to be fragrant; perfume. —*v.i.* **4** To hunt by the sense of smell. [< L *sentire* to sense]

scep·ter (sep′tər) *n.* **1** A staff or wand carried as the badge of command or sovereignty. **2** Kingly office or power. —*v.t.* To confer the scepter on; invest with royal power. Also, *esp. Brit.,* **scep′tre** (-tər). [< Gk. *skēptron* a staff]

scep·tic (skep′tik) *n.* SKEPTIC.

sched·ule (skej′ool, *Brit.* shed′yool) *n.* **1** A list specifying the details of some matter. **2** A timetable. **3** A detailed and timed plan for the steps in a procedure. —*v.t.* **·uled, ·ul·ing 1** To place in or on a schedule. **2** To appoint or plan for a specified time or date: He *scheduled* his appearance for five o′clock. [< LL *scedula*]

sche·ma (skē′mə) *n. pl.* **sche·ma·ta** (skē′mə·tə) A synopsis, summary, diagram, etc. [< Gk. *schēma*]

sche·mat·ic (skē-mat′ik) *adj.* Of or relating to a scheme, diagram, or plan. —*n.* A schematic diagram or drawing.

scheme (skēm) *n.* **1** A plan of something to be done; program. **2** An underhand plot: a *scheme* to defraud consumers. **3** A systematic arrangement: a color *scheme*. **4** An outline drawing; diagram. —*v.* **schemed, schem·ing** *v.t.* **1** To make a scheme for; plan. **2** To plan or plot in an underhand manner. —*v.i.* **3** To make schemes; plan. **4** To plot underhandedly. [< Gk. *schēma* a form, plan] —**schem′er** *n.*

Head of scepter

scher·zo (sker′tsō) *n. pl.* **·zos** or **·zi** (-tsē) *Music* A playful or light movement, as in a symphony. [Ital., a jest]

Schick test (shik) A test that indicates susceptibility to diphtheria if reddening of the skin occurs at the site of an injection of toxin. [< B. *Schick*, 1877–1967, Austrian physician]

schil·ling (shil′ing) *n.* The basic monetary unit of Austria.

schism (siz′əm, skiz′əm) *n.* **1** A division of a church into factions because of differences in doctrine. **2** A splitting into antagonistic groups. [< Gk. *schizein* to split]

schis·mat·ic (siz-mat′ik, skiz′-) *adj.* **1** Of or being a schism. **2** Promoting or guilty of schism. Also **schis·mat′i·cal.** —*n.* One who makes or participates in a schism. —**schis·mat′i·cal·ly** *adv.* —**schis·mat′i·cal·ness** *n.*

schist (shist) *n.* Any crystalline rock that readily splits or cleaves. [< Gk. *schizein* to split] —**schist′ous, schist·ose** (shis′tōs) *adj.*

schizo- *combining form* Split; divided: *schizophrenia*. [< Gk. *schizein* to split]

schiz·oid (skit′soid) *adj.* Pertaining to or resembling schizophrenia. —*n.* One having schizoid characteristics.

schiz·o·phre·ni·a (skit′sō-frē′nē-ə) *n.* Mental illness characterized in varying degrees by irrational thinking, disturbed emotions, bizarre behavior, etc. [< SCHIZO- + Gk. *phrēn* mind] —**schiz′o·phren′ic** (-fren′ik) *adj., n.*

schle·miel (shlə-mēl′) *n. Slang* An inept, easily duped person. Also **schle·mihl′.** [Yiddish, an unlucky person]

schlep (shlep) *Slang v.* **schlepped, schlep·ping** *v.t.* **1** To drag awkwardly; lug. —*v.i.* **2** To drag something awkwardly. **3** To proceed wearily or heavily: to *schlep* uptown. —*n.* **1** A difficult journey. **2** A stupid, awkward person. Also **schlepp.** [Yiddish *shleppen* to drag] —**schlep′per** *n.*

schlock (shlok) *Slang n.* Shoddy, inferior merchandise. —*adj.* Of inferior quality; tawdry. [Yiddish] —**schlock′y** *adj.* (**·i·er, ·i·est**)

schmaltz (shmälts) *n. Slang* **1** Anything which is overly sentimental, as in music or literature. **2** Extreme sentimentalism. [< G *Schmalz*, lit., melted fat] —**schmaltz′y** *adj.* (**·i·er, ·i·est**)

schnapps (shnäps, shnaps) *n.* **1** A strong gin. **2** Any strong alcoholic liquor. Also **schnaps.** [G, a dram, a nip]

schnau·zer (shnou′zər) *n.* A breed of terrier having a wiry coat. [< G *Schnauze* snout]

schnor·kel (shnôr′kəl) *n.* SNORKEL.

schnoz·zle (shnoz′əl) *n. Slang* Nose. [< G *Schnauze*]

Schnauzer

schol·ar (skol′ər) *n.* **1** A person eminent for learning. **2** An authority or specialist in an academic disicipline. **3** The holder of a scholarship. **4** One who learns under a teacher; a pupil. [< L *schola* school]

schol·ar·ly (skol′ər·lē) *adj.* **1** Of or characteristic of a scholar: a *scholarly* mind. **2** Exhibiting great learning. **3** Devoted to learning. —*adv.* After the manner of a scholar. —**schol′ar·li·ness** *n.* —**Syn.** *adj.* **2** erudite, intellectual, learned, lettered. **3** bookish, studious.

schol·ar·ship (skol′ər·ship) *n.* **1** Learning; erudition. **2** A stipend or other aid given to a student to enable him to continue his studies.

scho·las·tic (skō·las′tik, skə-) *adj.* **1** Pertaining to or characteristic of scholars, education, or schools. **2** Pertaining to or characteristic of the medieval schoolmen. Also **scho·las′ti·cal.** —*n. Often cap.* **1** A schoolman of the Middle ages. **2** An advocate of scholasticism. [< Gk. *scholazein* devote leisure to study] —**scho·las′ti·cal·ly** *adv.*

scho·las·ti·cism (skō·las′tə·siz′əm, skə-) *n.* **1** *Often cap.* The systematized logic, philosophy, and theology of medieval scholars. **2** Any system of teaching which insists on traditional doctrines and forms.

school[1] (skool) *n.* **1** An educational institution. **2** The building or group of buildings in which formal instruction is given. **3** A period or session of an educational institu-

tion: *School* begins tomorrow. **4** The pupils and teachers in an educational institution. **5** A subdivision of a university devoted to a special branch of higher education: a medical *school.* **6** The training of any branch of the armed services: gunnery *school.* **7** A body of disciples of a teacher or a group of persons whose work shows a common style or influence: a painting of the Flemish *school.* **8** Any sphere or means of instruction: the *school* of hard knocks. **9** A group of people having similar opinions, patterns of behavior, interests, etc.: He belongs to the old *school.* — *v.t.* **1** To instruct in a school; train. **2** To subject to rule or discipline. [< Gk. *scholē* leisure, school]

school[2] (skool) *n.* A congregation of fish, whales, etc., that feed or swim together. —*v.i.* To come together in a school. [< MDu. *schōle*]

school board A legal board or committee in charge of public schools

school·book (skool′book′) *n.* A book for use in school; textbook.

school·boy (skool′boi′) *n.* A boy attending school. —*adj.* Like or characteristic of a schoolboy.

school·fel·low (skool′fel′ō) *n.* A fellow pupil.

school·girl (skool′gûrl′) *n.* A girl attending school. — *adj.* Like or characteristic of a schoolgirl.

school·house (skool′hous′) *n.* A building in which a school is conducted.

school·ing (skoo′ling) *n.* **1** Instruction given at school. **2** The cost of educating and maintaining a student at a school. **3** The training of horses and riders.

school·man (skool′mən) *n.* *pl.* **·men** (-mən) One of the theologians of the Middle Ages.

school·marm (skool′märm′) *n.* *Informal* A woman schoolteacher, esp. one considered to be prudish.

school·mas·ter (skool′mas′tər, -mäs′-) *n.* A man who teaches in or is principal of a school.

school·mate (skool′māt′) *n.* A fellow pupil.

school·mis·tress (skool′mis′tris) *n.* A woman who teaches in or is principal of a school.

school·room (skool′room′, -room′) *n.* A room in which instruction is given.

school·teach·er (skool′tē′chər) *n.* One who teaches in a school below the college level.

schoon·er (skoo′nər) *n.* **1** A fore-and-aft rigged vessel having originally two masts, but later often three or more. **2** A large beer glass, holding about a pint. [< dial. *scoon* skim on water.]

schtick (shtik) *n.* SHTICK.

schuss (shoos) *v.i.* To ski down a steep slope at high speed. —*n.* **1** A straight, steep ski course. **2** The act of skiing down such a course. [G, lit., a shot] — **schuss′er** *n.*

Schooner

schwa (shwä, shvä) *n.* **1** A weak or obscure central vowel sound occurring in most of the unstressed syllables in English speech, as that of the *a* in *alone* or the *u* in *circus.* **2** The symbol (ə) for this sound. [< Heb. *shewa*]

sci. science; scientific.

sci·at·ic (sī·at′ik) *adj.* Pertaining to, in the area of, or affecting the hip. —*n.* A large leg nerve originating at the hip: also **sciatic nerve.** [< Gk. *ischion* hip, hip joint]

sci·at·i·ca (sī·at′i·kə) *n.* **1** Severe pain affecting the sciatic nerve. **2** Any painful affection of the hip and leg.

sci·ence (sī′əns) *n.* **1** Knowledge as of facts, phenomena, laws, and proximate causes, gained and verified by exact observation, organized experiment, and analysis. **2** Any of the various branches of such knowledge, as biology, chemistry, physics (**natural sciences**); economics, history, sociology (**social sciences**); agriculture, engineering (**applied sciences**). **3** Any department of knowledge in which the results of investigation have been systematized in the form of hypotheses and general laws subject to verification. **4** Expertness; skill: the *science* of statesmanship. **5** Originally, knowledge. [< L *scire* know]

Sci·ence (sī′əns) *n.* CHRISTIAN SCIENCE.

science fiction Novels and short stories dealing with actual or imaginary scientific developments and their effect on society or individuals. —**sci′ence-fic′tion** *adj.*

sci·en·tif·ic (sī′ən·tif′ik) *adj.* **1** Of, pertaining to, discovered by, derived from, or used in science. **2** Agreeing with the rules, principles, or methods of science; systematic. **3** Versed in science or a science. —**sci′en·tif′i·cal·ly** *adv.*

sci·en·tist (sī′ən·tist) *n.* One trained or learned in science or devoted to scientific study or investigation.

Sci·en·tist (sī′ən·tist) *n.* A Christian Scientist.

sci·en·tol·o·gy (sī′ən·tol′ə·jē) *n.* *Often cap.* A religious and psychotherapeutic cult purporting to solve personal problems, cure mental and physical disorders, and increase intelligence. [< L *scientia* science + -LOGY] —**sci′en·tol′o·gist** *n.*

sci-fi (sī′fī′) *Informal n.* Science fiction. —*adj.* Science-fiction.

scil·i·cet (sil′ə·set) *adv.* Namely; that is to say. [< L *scire licet* it is permitted to know]

scim·i·tar (sim′ə·tər) *n.* A curved sword or saber used by Turks. Also **scim′i·ter.** [MF < Pers. *shamshīr*]

scin·til·la (sin·til′ə) *n.* **1** A spark. **2** A trace; iota: a *scintilla* of truth. [L]

scin·til·late (sin′tə·lāt) *v.* **·lat·ed, ·lat·ing** *v.i.* **1** To give off sparks. **2** To be witty and brilliant in conversation. **3** To twinkle, as a star. —*v.t.* **4** To give off as a spark or sparks. [< L *scintilla* a spark] —**scin′til·la′ting·ly** *adv.* —**scin′til·la′tion** *n.* —**Syn. 1, 2** glitter, glow, shine, sparkle.

Scimitar

sci·o·lism (sī′ə·liz′əm) *n.* Pretentious, superficial knowledge. [< LL *sciolus* a smatterer] —**sci′o·list** *n.* —**sci′o·lis′tic** *adj.*

sci·on (sī′ən) *n.* **1** A child or descendant. **2** A bud or shoot from a plant or tree, used in grafting. [< OF *cion*]

scis·sion (sizh′ən, sish′-) *n.* **1** The act of cutting or splitting, or the state of being cut. **2** Any division. [< L *scissus,* p.p. of *scindere* to cut]

scis·sor (siz′ər) *v.t. & v.i.* To cut with scissors.

scis·sors (siz′ərz) *n.pl.* **1** A cutting implement with handles and a pair of blades pivoted face to face: sometimes a **pair of scissors. 2** *(construed as sing.)* In wrestling, a hold secured by clasping the legs about the body or head of the opponent. [< L *cisorium* a cutting instrument]

scissors kick In swimming, a kick in which both legs, bent at the knee, are thrust apart, then straightened and brought sharply together.

scis·sor·tail (siz′ər·tāl′) *n.* A flycatcher of the sw U.S. and Mexico having a forked tail.

scle·ra (skler′ə, sklir′ə) *n.* The firm, fibrous, white outer coat of the eyeball, continuous with the cornea: also **scle·rot·i·ca** (sklə·rot′i·kə). [< Gk. *sklēros* hard]

scle·ren·chy·ma (sklə·reng′kə·mə) *n.* *Bot.* Tissue composed of cells with hard, thick walls. [< Gk. *sklēros* hard + *enchyma* an infusion] —**scle·ren·chym·a·tous** (skler′en·kim′ə·təs, sklir′-, -kī′mə-) *adj.*

scle·ro·sis (sklə·rō′sis) *n.* Abnormal thickening and hardening of tissue. [< Gk. *sklēros* hard] —**scle·ro′sal** *adj.*

scle·rot·ic (sklə·rot′ik) *adj.* **1** Dense; firm, as the white of the eye. **2** Pertaining to or affected with sclerosis: also **scle·rosed** (-rōst′) [< Gk. *sklērotēs* hardness]

scoff (skôf, skof) *v.i.* **1** To speak with contempt or derision: often with *at.* —*v.t.* **2** To deride; mock. —*n.* **1** Words or actions of contempt. **2** A person or thing held in contempt. [ME *scof*] —**scoff′er** *n.* —**scoff′ing·ly** *adv.* —**Syn.** *v.* **1, 2** gibe, jeer, scorn, sneer, taunt.

scoff·law (skôf′lô, skof′-) *n.* A habitual or deliberate violator of traffic, safety, or public-health regulations.

scold (skōld) *v.t.* **1** To find fault with harshly. —*v.i.* **2** To find fault harshly or continuously. —*n.* One who scolds constantly: also **scold′er.** [< ON *skāld* a poet, satirist] —**scold′ing·ly** *adv.*

scol·lop (skol′əp) *n. & v.* SCALLOP.

sconce (skons) *n.* An ornamental wall bracket for holding a candle or other light. [< L *abscondere* to hide]

Wall sconce

scone (skōn, skon) *n.* **1** A thin oatmeal cake, baked on a griddle. **2** A teacake or soda biscuit. [?< MDu. *schoonbrot* fine bread]

scoop (skōōp) *n.* **1** The part of a dredge or steam shovel that lifts earth, sand, coal, etc. **2** A small shovellike implement for flour, sugar, ice cream, etc. **3** An implement for bailing, as water from a boat. **4** A spoon-shaped instrument for using in a cavity: a surgeon's *scoop*. **5** An act of scooping. **6** A scooping motion. **7** The amount scooped at once: a *scoop* of ice cream. **8** *Informal* A news story obtained and published ahead of rival papers. —*v.t.* **1** To take or dip out with a scoop. **2** To hollow out, as with a scoop; excavate. **3** *Informal* To heap up or gather in as if in scoopfuls; amass. **4** *Informal* To obtain and publish a news story before (a rival). [< MDu. *schōpe* a vessel for bailing out water] —**scoop'er** *n.*

scoop·ful (skōōp'fŏŏl') *n. pl.* **·fuls** As much as a scoop will hold.

scoot (skōōt) *v.i. Informal* To go quickly; dart off. —*n.* The act of scooting. [? < Scand.]

scoot·er (skōō'tər) *n.* **1** A child's vehicle consisting of a board mounted on two wheels and steered by a handle attached to the front axle, the rider standing with one foot on the board, using the other to push. **2** A similar vehicle powered by an internal-combustion engine and having a driver's seat: also **motor scooter.**

scope (skōp) *n.* **1** A range of view or action. **2** Capacity for achievement. **3** End in view; aim. **4** *Informal* A telescope, microscope, oscilloscope, etc. [< Gk. *skopos* a watcher]

-scope *combining form* An instrument for viewing, observing, or indicating: *microscope*. [< Gk. *skopos* a watcher]

sco·pol·a·mine (skō·pol'ə·mēn, -min, skō'pə·lam'ēn, -in) *n.* A depressant drug related to belladonna which blocks the formation of memories and various other functions of the brain. [< G. A. *Scopoli*, 1723–88, Italian naturalist]

-scopy *combining form* Observation; viewing: *microscopy*. [< Gk. *skopein* to watch]

scor·bu·tic (skôr·byōō'tik) *adj.* Of, like, or affected with scurvy. Also **scor·bu'ti·cal.** [< Med. L *scorbutus* scurvy] —**scor·bu'ti·cal·ly** *adv.*

scorch (skôrch) *v.t.* **1** To change the color, taste, etc., of, by slight burning. **2** To wither or shrivel by heat. **3** To criticize severely. —*v.i.* **4** To become scorched. **5** *Informal* To go at high speed. —*n.* **1** A superficial burn. **2** A mark caused by a slight burn. [ME *scorchen*] —**scorch'ing·ly** *adv.*

scorched-earth policy (skôrcht'ûrth') The policy of destroying all crops, industrial equipment, dwellings, etc., before the arrival of an advancing enemy.

scorch·er (skôr'chər) *n.* **1** A person or thing that scorches. **2** *Informal* A very hot day. **3** *Informal* One who moves at great speed.

score (skôr, skōr) *n.* **1** The record of the winning points, counts, runs, etc., in competitive games. **2** A record of indebtedness; bill. **3** *Music* A printed or written copy of a musical composition in which all vocal and instrumental parts are shown on two or more connected staves one above another. **4** A group of 20. **5** *pl.* An indefinite large number. **6** A value assigned to an individual or group response to a test or series of tests, as of intelligence or performance. **7** *Slang* A success, esp. in making a purchase of narcotics. —**to pay off** (or **settle**) **old scores** To get even with someone for past wrongs, injuries, etc. —*v.* **scored, scor·ing** *v.t.* **1** To mark with notches, cuts, or lines. **2** To mark with cuts or lines for the purpose of keeping a tally. **3** To delete by means of a line drawn through: with *out*. **4** To make or gain, as points, runs, etc. **5** To count for a score of, as in games: A touchdown *scores* six points. **6** To rate or grade, as an examination paper. **7** *Music* **a** To orchestrate. **b** To arrange or adapt for an instrument. **8** *Informal* To criticize severely; scourge. **9** In cooking, to make superficial cuts in (meat, etc.). —*v.i.* **10** To make points, runs, etc., as in a game. **11** To keep score. **12** To make notches, cuts, etc. **13** To achieve a success. **14** *Slang* To purchase marihuana or narcotics. **15** *Slang* To succeed in having sexual intercourse with someone. [< ON *skor* a notch] —**scor'er** *n.*

sco·ri·a (skôr'ē·ə, skō're·ə) *n. pl.* **·ri·ae** (-i·ē) **1** The refuse of melted metal or reduced ore. **2** Lava that is loose and cinderlike. [< Gk. *skōr* dung] —**sco'ri·a'ceous** (-ā'shəs) *adj.*

scorn (skôrn) *n.* **1** A feeling of contempt. **2** An object of supreme contempt. —*v.t.* **1** To hold in or treat with contempt; despise. **2** To reject with scorn; spurn. [< OF *escarn*] —**scorn'er, scorn'ful·ness** *n.* —**scorn'ful** *adj.* —**scorn'ful·ly** *adv.* —**Syn.** *n.* **1** disdain, scoffing. *v.* **1** contemn, detest.

Scor·pi·o (skôr'pē·ō) *n.* A constellation and the eighth sign of the zodiac; the Scorpion. Also **Scor·pi·us** (-əs). [< Gk. *skorpios*] • See ZODIAC.

scor·pi·on (skôr'pē·ən) *n.* **1** Any of an order of arachnids with long segmented tails bearing a poisonous sting. **2** In the Bible, a whip or scourge. [< Gk. *skorpios*]

Indian scorpion

Scorpion *n.* SCORPIO.

scot (skot) *n.* An assessment or tax. [< ON *skot*]

Scot (skot) *n.* A native of Scotland. • See SCOTCH.

Scot. Scotland; Scots; Scottish.

scotch (skoch) *v.t.* **1** To cut; scratch. **2** To wound so as to maim or cripple. **3** To quash or suppress: to *scotch* a rumor. —*n.* **1** A superficial cut; a notch. **2** A line traced on the ground, as for hopscotch. [?]

Scotch (skoch) *n.* **1** The people of Scotland collectively. **2** One or all of the dialects spoken by the people of Scotland. **3** Scotch whisky. —*adj.* Of or pertaining to Scotland, its inhabitants, or their dialects. • **Scotch, Scots, Scottish; Scot, Scotchman, Scotsman** Of the three proper adjectives, the form *Scotch* is accepted in Scotland only as applying to *Scotch plaid, Scotch terriers, Scotch whisky,* etc. In Scotland and northern England, the forms *Scots* and *Scottish* are preferred as applying to the people, language, culture, and institutions of Scotland: *Scots* or *Scottish English, the Scottish church.* In referring to an inhabitant of Scotland, *Scot* and *Scotsman* are preferred over the chiefly U.S. term *Scotchman.*

Scotch·man (skoch'mən) *n. pl.* **·men** (-mən) A Scot; Scotsman. • See SCOTCH.

Scotch tape A rolled strip of transparent adhesive tape: a trade name.

Scotch terrier A small terrier with compact body, short legs, and a grizzled coat.

Scotch whisky Whiskey made in Scotland from malted barley and having a rather smoky flavor. • Scotch whisky is traditionally spelled without the "e."

Scotch terrier

sco·ter (skō'tər) *n.* Any of several large ducks of northern regions, having black or dark brown plumage. [?< dial. E *scote*, var. of SCOOT]

scot-free (skot'frē') *adj.* **1** Free from any penalty, blame, or punishment. **2** Free from scot.

Scotland Yard **1** The headquarters of the London police: in full, **New Scotland Yard. 2** The London police force, esp. the detective bureau.

Scots (skots) *adj.* SCOTTISH. —*n.* The Scottish dialect of English. • See SCOTCH.

Scots·man (skots'mən) *n. pl.* **·men** (-mən) A Scot. • See SCOTCH.

Scot·ti·cism (skot'ə·siz'əm) *n.* A verbal usage or idiom peculiar to the Scottish people.

Scot·tish (skot'ish) *adj.* Pertaining to or characteristic of Scotland, its inhabitants, or their language. —*n.* **1** The dialect of English spoken in Scotland. **2** The people of Scotland collectively: with *the.* • See SCOTCH.

Scottish Gaelic The language of the Scottish Highlands.

Scottish terrier SCOTCH TERRIER. Also *Informal* **scot·tie** (skot'ē), **scot'ty.**

scoun·drel (skoun'drəl) *n.* An unscrupulous, dishonest person; villain. —*adj.* Villainous; base. [?] —**scoun'drel·ly** *adj.*

scour¹ (skour) *v.t.* **1** To clean or brighten by thorough

washing and rubbing. 2 To remove dirt, grease, etc., from; clean. 3 To clear by means of a strong current of water; flush. —*v.i.* 4 To rub something vigorously so as to clean or brighten it. 5 To become bright or clean by rubbing. —*n.* 1 The act of scouring. 2 A cleanser used in scouring. 3 *Usu. pl.* A dysentery affecting cattle. [<OF *escurer*] —**scour'er** *n.* —**Syn.** *v.* 1 polish, scrub. 2 cleanse.

scour[2] (skour) *v.t.* 1 To range over or through, as in making a search. 2 To move or run swiftly over or along. —*v.i.* 3 To range swiftly about, as in making a search. [ME *scoure*]

scourge (skûrj) *n.* 1 A whip for inflicting suffering or punishment. 2 Any severe punishment. 3 Any means for causing suffering or death: the *scourge* of cholera. —*v.t.* **scourged, scourg·ing** 1 To whip severely; flog. 2 To punish severely; afflict. [<LL *excoriare* flay] —**scourg'er** *n.*

scout[1] (skout) *n.* 1 A person, plane, etc., sent out to observe and get information, as of the position or strength of an enemy in war. 2 The act of scouting. 3 A person in search of promising performers in athletics, entertainment, etc.: a talent *scout*. 4 A member of the Girl Scouts or the Boy Scouts. 5 A fellow; guy: usu. in the phrase **a good scout**. —*v.t.* 1 To observe or spy upon for the purpose of gaining information. —*v.i.* 2 To go or act as a scout. — **scout around** To go in search. [<L *auscultare* to listen] —**scout'er** *n.*

scout[2] (skout) *v.t. & v.i.* To reject with disdain. [<Scand.]

scout·mas·ter (skout'mas'tər, -mäs'-) *n.* The adult leader of a troop of Boy Scouts.

scow (skou) *n.* A large boat with a flat bottom and square ends, chiefly used to carry freight, garbage, etc. [<Du. *schouw*]

scowl (skoul) *n.* 1 A lowering of the brows, as in anger. 2 Gloomy aspect. —*v.i.* 1 To contract the brows in anger, sullenness, or disapproval. 2 To look threatening; lower. —*v.t.* 3 To affect or express by scowling. [?<Scand.]

scr. scrip; script; scruple (weight).

scrab·ble (skrab'əl) *v.* **·bled, ·bling** *v.i.* 1 To scratch, scrape, or paw. 2 To scribble. 3 To struggle or strive. —*v.t.* 4 To scrible on. 5 To scrape together. —*n.* 1 The act of scrabbling; a moving on hands and feet or knees. 2 A scrambling effort. [<Du. *schrabbelen*] —**scrab'bler** *n.*

scrag (skrag) *v.t.* **scragged, scrag·ging** *Informal* To wring the neck of; garrote. —*n.* 1 *Slang* The neck. 2 A lean, bony person or animal. [?<Scand.]

scrag·gly (skrag'lē) *adj.* **·gli·er, ·gli·est** Uneven; irregular; jagged: a *scraggly* beard.

scrag·gy (skrag'ē) *adj.* **·gi·er, ·gi·est** 1 SCRAGGLY. 2 Lean; scrawny. —**scrag'gi·ly** *adv.* —**scrag'gi·ness** *n.*

scram (skram) *v.i.* **scrammed, scram·ming** *Slang* To go away; leave quickly. [Short for SCRAMBLE]

scram·ble (skram'bəl) *v.* **·bled, ·bling** *v.i.* 1 To move by clambering or crawling. 2 To struggle in a disorderly manner; scuffle. 3 To strive for something in such a manner. —*v.t.* 4 To mix together haphazardly or confusedly. 5 To gather or collect hurriedly or confusedly. 6 To cook (eggs) with the yolks and whites stirred together. 7 *Telecom.* To encode (a message) so that a special decoder is needed to make it intelligible. —*n.* 1 A difficult climb, as over rough terrain. 2 A struggle for possession: a *scramble* for power. [?] —**scram'bler** *n.*

scrap[1] (skrap) *n.* 1 A small piece; fragment. 2 A small part of something written. 3 *pl.* Bits of unused food. 4 Old or refuse metal. —*v.t.* **scrapped, scrap·ping** 1 To break up into scrap. 2 To discard. —*adj.* Having the form of scraps: *scrap* metal. [<ON *skrap* scraps] —**Syn.** 1 bit, chip, segment, shard. 3 leftovers.

scrap[2] (skrap) *Informal v.i.* **scrapped, scrap·ping** To fight; quarrel. —*n.* A fight; quarrel; squabble. [?<SCRAPE, *n.* (def. 2)] —**scrap'per** *n.*

scrap·book (skrap'bŏok') *n.* 1 A blank book in which to paste pictures, cuttings from periodicals, etc. 2 A personal notebook.

scrape (skrāp) *v.* **scraped, scrap·ing** *v.t.* 1 To rub, as with something rough or sharp, so as to abrade. 2 To remove an outer layer thus: with *off, away*, etc. 3 To rub (a rough or sharp object) across a surface. 4 To rub roughly across or against (a surface). 5 To dig or form by scratching or scraping. 6 To gather or accumulate with effort or difficulty. —*v.i.* 7 To scrape something. 8 To rub with a grating noise. 9 To make a grating noise. 10 To draw the foot backward along the ground in bowing. 11 To manage or get along with difficulty. 12 To be very or overly economical. —*n.* 1 The act or effect of scraping; also, the noise made by scraping. 2 A difficult situation. 3 A quarrel or fight. 4 A scraping or drawing back of the foot in bowing. [<ON *skrapa*] —**scrap'er** *n.*

scrap·ing (skrā'ping) *n.* 1 The act of one who or that which scrapes. 2 The sound so produced. 3 *Usu. pl.* Something scraped off or together.

scrap·ple (skrap'əl) *n.* Cornmeal cooked with scraps of pork and spices and molded into a firm loaf to be sliced for frying.

scrap·py[1] (skrap'ē) *adj.* **·pi·er, ·pi·est** Composed of scraps; fragmentary. —**scrap'pi·ly** *adv.* —**scrap'pi·ness** *n.*

scrap·py[2] (skrap'ē) *adj.* **·pi·er, ·pi·est** *Informal* 1 Ready and willing to fight. 2 Strongly competitive; gritty; tough. — **scrap'pi·ly** *adv.* —**scrap'pi·ness** *n.*

scratch (skrach) *v.t.* 1 To tear or mark the surface of with something sharp or rough. 2 To scrape or dig with something sharp or rough. 3 To scrape lightly with the nails, etc., as to relieve itching. 4 To rub with a grating sound; scrape. 5 To write or draw awkwardly or hurriedly. 6 To erase or cancel by scratches or marks. 7 To withdraw (an entry) from a competition, race, etc. —*v.i.* 8 To use the nails or claws, as in fighting or digging. 9 To scrape the skin, etc., lightly, as to relieve itching. 10 To make a grating noise. 11 To manage or get along with difficulty. 12 To withdraw from a game, race, etc. —*n.* 1 A mark or incision made on a surface by scratching. 2 A slight flesh wound or cut. 3 The sound of scratching. 4 The line from which contestants start, as in racing. 5 *Slang* Money. —**from scratch** From the beginning; from nothing. —**up to scratch** *Informal* Meeting the standard or requirement. —*adj.* 1 Done by chance; haphazard. 2 Made for hurried notes, figuring, etc.: a *scratch* pad. 3 Chosen hastily and at random: a *scratch* team. [<MDu. *cratsen*] —**scratch'er** *n.*

scratch·y (skrach'ē) *adj.* **scratch·i·er, scratch·i·est** 1 Consisting of scratches: *scratchy* handwriting. 2 Making a scratching noise. 3 Causing itching: a *scratchy* sweater. —**scratch'i·ly** *adv.* —**scratch'i·ness** *n.*

scrawl (skrôl) *v.t. & v.i.* To write hastily or illegibly. —*n.* Irregular or careless writing. [?] —**scrawl'er** *n.*

scraw·ny (skrô'nē) *adj.* **·ni·er, ·ni·est** Lean and bony. [?] —**scraw'ni·ness** *n.*

scream (skrēm) *v.i.* 1 To utter a prolonged, piercing cry, as of pain, terror, or surprise. 2 To make a piercing sound: the wind *screamed* in the trees. 3 To laugh loudly or immoderately. 4 To use heated, hysterical language. —*v.t.* 5 To utter with a scream. —*n.* 1 A loud, shrill, prolonged cry or sound. 2 *Informal* A hugely entertaining person or thing. [<ON *skraema* to scare] —**scream'ing·ly** *adv.*

scream·er (skrē'mər) *n.* 1 One who or that which screams. 2 A South American wading bird, related to the ducks. 3 *Slang* A sensational headline in a newspaper.

screech (skrēch) *n.* A shrill, harsh cry; shriek. —*v.t.* 1 To utter with a screech. —*v.i.* 2 To shriek. [<ON *skrækja*] — **screech'er** *n.* —**screech'y** *adj.* (**·i·er, ·i·est**)

screech owl 1 Any of various small owls emitting a high-pitched wail. 2 The barn owl.

screed (skrēd) *n.* A prolonged spoken or written tirade; harangue. [<OE *scréade*]

screen (skrēn) *n.* 1 Something that separates or shelters, as a light partition. 2 A coarse or fine metal mesh used for sifting, or as protection: a window *screen*. 3 Something that serves to conceal or protect: a smoke *screen*. 4 A surface, as a canvas or curtain, on which motion pictures and slides may be shown. 5 The surface of a cathode-ray tube, on which television pictures, computer information or graphics, etc., may be viewed. —**the screen** Motion pictures. —*v.t.* 1 To shield or conceal with or as with a screen. 2 To pass through a screen or sieve; sift. 3 To classify or scan for suitability, qualifications, etc.: to *screen* applicants for a job. 4 To project on a motion-picture screen. 5 To photograph (a motion picture); shoot. 6 To adapt (a play, novel, story, etc.) for motion pictures. —*v.i.* 7 To be suitable for representation as a motion picture. [<OF *escren*]

screen·ing (skrēn'ing) *n.* **1** A meshlike material, as for a window screen. **2** A showing of a motion picture. **3** *pl.* The parts of anything passed through or retained by a sieve; siftings.

screw (skrōō) *n.* **1** A device resembling a nail but having a slotted head and a tapering or cylindrical spiral for driving into wood, metal, plaster, etc., or for insertion into a corresponding threaded part. **2** A cylindrical socket with a spiral groove or thread **3** Anything having the form of a screw. **4** SCREW PRO-peller • See RUDDER. **5** A turn of or as of a screw. **6** Pressure; force. **7** *Slang* A prison guard. **8** *Brit. Slang* An old, worn-out, or bad-tempered horse. —**have a screw loose** *Slang* To be mentally deranged, eccentric, etc. —**put the screws on** (or to) *Slang* To exert pressure or force upon. —*v.t.* **1** To tighten, fasten, attach, etc., by a screw or screws. **2** To turn or twist. **3** To force; urge: to *screw* one's courage to the sticking point. **4** To contort, as one's features. **5** To practice oppression or extortion on; defraud. **6** To obtain by extortion. **7** *Slang* To act maliciously toward; harm. —*v.i.* **8** To turn as a screw. **9** To become attached or detached by means of twisting: with *on, off,* etc. **10** To twist or wind. **11** To practice oppression or extortion. —**screw up** *Slang* To botch; make a mess of: He *screwed up* his career. [< OF *escroue* nut] —**screw'er** *n.*

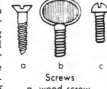

Screws
a. wood screw.
b. thumbscrew.
c. round-headed screw.

screw·ball (skrōō'bôl') *n.* **1** In baseball, a pitch thrown with a wrist motion opposite to that used for the outcurve. **2** *Slang* An unconventional or erratic person.

screw cap A cap or lid designed to screw onto the threaded top of a bottle, jar, or the like.

screw·driv·er (skrōō'drī'vər) *n.* A tool for turning screws.

screwed-up (skrōōd'up') *adj. Slang* **1** Disorganized or disorderly. **2** Mentally ill or emotionally distressed.

screw propeller An array of radial blades set at an angle on a rotary shaft to produce a spiral action in a fluid, used to propel ships, etc. • See RUDDER.

screw thread The spiral ridge of a screw or nut.

screw·y (skrōō'ē) *adj.* **screw·i·er, screw·i·est** *Slang* Irrational; eccentric. —**screw'i·ly** *adv.* —**screw'i·ness** *n.*

scrib·ble (skrib'əl) *v.* **·bled, ·bling** *v.t.* **1** To write hastily and carelessly. **2** To cover with careless or illegible writing. —*v.i.* **3** To write carelessly or hastily. **4** To make illegible or meaningless marks; scrawl. —*n.* **1** Hasty, careless writing. **2** Meaningless lines and marks; scrawl. [< L *scribere* write] —**scrib'bler** *n.* —**scrib'bly** *adj.*

scribe (skrīb) *n.* **1** One who copied manuscripts and books before printing was invented. **2** A clerk, public writer, or amanuensis. **3** An author: used humorously. **4** An ancient Jewish teacher of the Mosaic law. [< L *scribere* write] —**scrib'al** *adj.*

scrim (skrim) *n.* A lightweight, open-mesh, usu. cotton fabric, used for curtains, etc. [?]

scrim·mage (skrim'ij) *n.* **1** A rough-and-tumble contest; fracas. **2** In American football, a mass play from the line of scrimmage after the ball has been placed on the ground and snapped back, the play ending when the ball is dead. —**line of scrimmage** In football, the hypothetic line, parallel to the goal lines, on which the ball rests and along which the opposing linemen take position at the start of play. —*v.t.* & *v.i.* **·maged, ·mag·ing** To engage in a scrimmage. [Var. of SKIRMISH]

scrimp (skrimp) *v.i.* **1** To be very economical or stingy. —*v.t.* **2** To be overly sparing toward; skimp. **3** To cut too small, narrow, etc. [?] —**scrimp'er** *n.*

scrim·py (skrim'pē) *adj.* **·i·er, ·i·est** Skimpy or meager. —**scrimp'i·ly** *adv.* —**scrimp'i·ness** *n.*

scrim·shaw (skrim'shô) *n.* **1** The carving and engraving of usu. whalebone or whale ivory, as by American sailors. **2** An article so made. —*v.t.* **1** To make into scrimshaw by carving or engraving. —*v.i.* **2** To create scrimshaw. [?]

scrip (skrip) *n.* **1** Writing. **2** Any of various certificates showing that a person is entitled to receive something, as a fractional share of stock, a share of jointly owned property, etc. **3** A piece of paper money less than a dollar, formerly issued during emergencies in the U.S. [<SCRIPT] **Scrip.** Scriptural; Scripture(s).

script (skript) *n.* **1** Handwriting; also, a particular style of

This line is in script.

handwriting. **2** Printed matter in imitation of handwriting. **3** A manuscript or text. **4** The written text of a play, TV show, etc. [<L *scribere* write]

scrip·ture (skrip'chər) *n.* **1** The sacred writings of any people. **2** Any authoritative book or writing. [<L *scribere* write] —**scrip'tur·al** *adj.* —**scrip'tur·al·ly** *adv.*

Scripture (skrip'chər) *n.* **1** *Usu. pl.* The books of the Old and New Testaments; the Bible; also **(the) Holy Scripture. 2** A passage from the Bible.

scriv·en·er (skriv'ən·ər, skriv'nər) *n.* **1** A clerk or scribe. **2** A notary. [<L *scribere* write]

scrod (skrod) *n.* A young codfish, esp. when split and prepared for broiling. [<MDu. *schrode*]

scrof·u·la (skrof'yə·lə) *n.* Tuberculosis of the lymph glands. [<LL *scrofa* a breeding sow] —**scrof'u·lous** *adj.* —**scrof'u·lous·ly** *adv.* —**scrof'u·lous·ness** *n.*

scroll (skrōl) *n.* **1** A roll of parchment, paper, etc., esp. one containing or intended for writing. **2** The writing on such a roll. **3** Anything resembling a parchment roll, as a convoluted ornament or part. —*v.i.* To move one or more lines of copy off the top of a computer screen, so that additional lines may be displayed at the bottom, or vice versa. [<AF *escrowe*]

scroll saw A narrow-bladed saw for cutting thin sheets of wood into curved or convoluted shapes.

scrooge (skrōoj) *n.* A miserly, misanthropic person. [<Ebenezer *Scrooge,* a miserly character in Dickens' *A Christmas Carol*]

scro·tum (skrō'təm) *n. pl.* **·ta** (tə) or **·tums** The pouch that contains the testes. [L] —**scro'tal** *adj.*

scrounge (skrounj) *v.t.* & *v.i.* **scrounged, scroung·ing** *Slang* **1** To hunt about and take (something); pilfer. **2** To mooch; sponge. [?] —**scroung'er** *n.*

scrub[1] (skrub) *v.* **scrubbed, scrub·bing** *v.t.* **1** To rub vigorously in washing. **2** To remove (dirt, etc.) by such action. —*v.i.* **3** To rub something vigorously in washing. —*n.* The act of scrubbing. [<MDu. *schrobben*] —**scrub'ber** *n.*

scrub[2] (skrub) *n.* **1** A stunted tree. **2** A tract of stunted trees or shrubs. **3** A domestic animal of inferior breed. **4** A poor, insignificant person. **5** In sports, a player not on the varsity or regular team. **6** A game of baseball contrived hastily by a few players. —*adj.* **1** Undersized or inferior. **2** Consisting of or participated in by untrained players or scrubs: *scrub* team. [Var. of SHRUB]

scrub·by (skrub'ē) *adj.* **·bi·er, ·bi·est 1** Of stunted growth. **2** Covered with or consisting of scrub or underbrush. —**scrub'bi·ly** *adv.* —**scrub'bi·ness** *n.*

scrub oak Any of various dwarf oaks.

scruff (skruf) *n.* The nape or outer back part of the neck. [Earlier *scuff* < ON *skopt* hair]

scruf·fy (skruf'ē) *adj.* **·i·er, ·i·est 1** Shabby; seedy. **2** Worthless. [<OE *scruf* scurf] —**scruf'fi·ly** *adv.* —**scruf'fi·ness** *n.*

scrump·tious (skrump'shəs) *adj. Slang* Elegant or stylish; splendid. [? Var. of SUMPTUOUS] —**scrump'tious·ly** *adv.*

scru·ple (skrōō'pəl) *n.* **1** Doubt or uncertainty about what one should do. **2** Reluctance arising from conscientious disapproval. **3** An apothecaries' weight of 20 grains. **4** A minute quantity. —*v.t.* & *v.i.* **·pled, ·pling** To hesitate (doing) from considerations of right or wrong. [<L *scrupus* a sharp stone]

scru·pu·lous (skrōō'pyə·əs) *adj.* **1** Cautious in action for fear of doing wrong; conscientious. **2** Resulting from the exercise of scruples; careful. —**scru'pu·lous·ly** *adv.* —**scru'·pu·los'i·ty** (-los'ə·tē), **scru'pu·lous·ness** *n.* —**Syn.** 1 ethical, honest, upright. 2 exact, precise.

scru·ti·neer (skrōō'tə·nir') *n.* **1** One who scrutinizes. **2**

Brit. & Can. One who oversees a polling place, checking voters against the registry, etc.

scru·ti·nize (skrōō'tə·nīz) *v.t.* **·nized, ·niz·ing** To observe carefully; examine in detail. **—scru'ti·niz'er** *n.* **—scru'ti·niz'ing·ly** *adv.*

scru·ti·ny (skrōō'tə·nē) *n. pl.* **·nies** Close investigation; careful inspection. [< L *scrutari* examine]

scu·ba (skyōō'bə) *n.* A device worn by a free-swimming diver to provide a supply of air for breathing. [< *s(elf-) c(ontained) u(nderwater) b(reathing) a(pparatus)*]

scuba diving Swimming under water with the aid of a scuba. **—scuba diver**

scud (skud) *v.i.* **scud·ded, scud·ding** To move, run, or fly swiftly. **—n. 1** The act of scudding. **2** Light clouds driven rapidly before the wind. [?]

scuff (skuf) *v.i.* **1** To drag the feet in walking; shuffle. **— v.t. 2** To scrape (the floor, ground, etc.) with the feet. **3** To roughen the surface by rubbing or scraping: to *scuff* one's shoes. **—n.** The act of scuffing; also, the noise so made. [? < ON *skūfa* shove]

scuf·fle (skuf'əl) *v.i.* **·fled, ·fling 1** To struggle roughly or confusedly. **2** To drag one's feet; shuffle. **—n.** A disorderly struggle; fracas. [? < Scand.] **—scuf'fler** *n.*

scull (skul) *n.* **1** A long oar worked from side to side over the stern of a boat. **2** A light oar, used in pairs by one person. **3** A small boat for sculling. **—v.t. & v.i.** To propel (a boat) by a scull or sculls. [ME *sculle*] **—scull'er** *n.*

scul·ler·y (skul'ər·ē) *n. pl.* **·ler·ies** A room where kitchen utensils are kept and cleaned. [< L *scutella* a tray]

scul·lion (skul'yən) *n. Archaic* A servant who scours dishes, pots, and kettles. [< OF *escouillon* a mop]

scul·pin (skul'pin) *n.* Any of a family of spiny fishes having a large head and fanlike pectoral fins. [< L *scorpaena*, a scorpionlike fish]

sculpt (skulpt) *v.t. & v.i. Informal* SCULPTURE.

sculp·tor (skulp'tər) *n.* A person who sculptures. **— sculp'tress** (-tris) *n. Fem.*

sculp·ture (skulp'chər) *n.* **1** The art of fashioning three-dimensional figures, busts, abstract pieces, etc., of stone, wood, clay, bronze, or other material. **2** A piece or group produced by sculpture. **—v.t. ·tured, ·tur·ing 1** To fashion (stone, wood, metal, etc.) into sculpture. **2** To represent or portray by sculpture. **3** To embellish with sculpture. **4** To change (features on the surface of the earth) by erosion. **—v.i. 5** To work as a sculptor. [< L *sculpere* carve in stone] **—sculp'tur·al** *adj.* **—sculp'tur·al·ly** *adv.*

scum (skum) *n.* **1** A layer of impure or extraneous matter on the surface of a liquid. **2** Low, contemptible people. **— v. scummed, scum·ming** *v.t.* **1** To take scum from; skim. **— v.i. 2** To become covered with or form scum. [< MDu. *schuum*] **—scum'mi·ness** *n.* **—scum'my** *adj.* **(·mi·er, ·mi·est)**

scup (skup) *n.* A small porgy of the E coast of the U.S. [< Algon.]

scup·per (skup'ər) *n.* A hole or gutter bordering a ship's deck, to let water run off. [? < OF *escope* a bailing scoop]

scup·per·nong (skup'ər·nong) *n.* **1** A light-colored grape of the S U.S. **2** A sweet wine made from this grape. [< the *Scuppernong* River in N.C.]

scurf (skûrf) *n.* **1** Loose scales thrown off by the skin, as dandruff. **2** Any scaly matter adhering to a surface. [< OE] **—scurf'i·ness** *n.* **—scurf'y** *adj.* **(·i·er, ·i·est)**

scur·ri·lous (skûr'ə·ləs) *adj.* Grossly offensive or indecent; coarse and abusive: a *scurrilous* attack. [< L *scurra* a buffoon] **—scur·ril'i·ty** (skə·ril'ə·tē) *(pl.* **·ties), scur'ri·lous·ness** *n.* **—scur'ri·lous·ly** *adv.*

scur·ry (skûr'ē) *v.i.* **·ried, ·ry·ing** To move or go hurriedly; scamper. **—n. pl.** **·ries** The act or sound of scurrying. [?] — **Syn.** *v.* dart, dash, scoot, scuttle.

scur·vy (skûr'vē) A disease due to lack of vitamin C, marked by weakness, spotted skin, and bleeding gums. **— adj.** **·vi·er, ·vi·est** Low or contemptible. [< SCURF] **—scur'vi·ly** *adv.* **—scur'vi·ness** *n.*

scut (skut) *n.* A short tail, as of a rabbit or deer. [ME, a tail, a hare]

scutch·eon (skuch'ən) *n.* ESCUTCHEON.

scu·tel·late (skyōō·tel'it, skyōō'tə·lāt) *adj. Zool.* Covered with small plates or scales: also **scu'tel·lat'ed** (-lā'tid). [< L *scutum* a shield]

scu·tel·lum (skyōō·tel'əm) *n. pl.* **·la** (-ə) A small protective plate or scale, as on the tarsus of a bird. [< L *scutum* a shield] **—scu·tel'lar** *adj.*

scut·tle[1] (skut'l) *n.* **1** A small opening or hatchway with movable lid or cover, esp. in the roof or wall of a house, or in the deck or side of a ship. **2** The lid closing such an opening. **—v.t. ·tled, ·tling 1** To sink (a ship) by making holes below the water line. **2** To wreck or destroy. [< MF *escoutille* a hatchway]

scut·tle[2] (skut'l) *n.* A metal vessel or hod for coal. [< OE *scutel* a dish, platter]

scut·tle[3] (skut'l) *v.i.* **·tled, ·tling** To run in haste; scurry. **— n.** A hurried run or departure. [?] **—scut'tler** *n.*

scut·tle·butt (skut'l·but) *n.* **1** A drinking fountain aboard ship. **2** *Slang* Rumor; gossip. [Orig. *scuttled butt*, a lidded cask for drinking water]

scu·tum (skyōō'təm) *n. pl.* **·ta** (-tə) **1** A large shield carried by Roman foot soldiers. **2** *Zool.* A large, horny protective plate or scale: also **scute**. [L] **—scu·tate** (skyōō'tāt) *adj.*

Scyl·la (sil'ə) *Gk. Myth.* A sea monster who dwelt in a cave on the Italian coast opposite the whirlpool Charybdis. **—between Scylla and Charybdis** Between two equally menacing situations, one of which must be dealt with.

scythe (sīth) *n.* A tool composed of a long curved blade fixed at an angle to a long handle, used for mowing, reaping, etc. **—v.t. scythed, scyth·ing** To cut with a scythe. [< OE *sīthe*]

Scyth·i·a (sith'ē·ə) *n.* An ancient region of SE Europe, lying N of the Black Sea. **—Scyth'i·an** *adj., n.*

SD South Dakota (P.O. abbr.).

S.D., S. Dak. South Dakota.

SDR, S.D.R., SDRs, S.D.R.s Special Drawing Rights.

SE, S.E., se, s.e. southeast; southeastern.

Se selenium.

sea (sē) *n.* **1** The great body of salt water covering most of the earth's surface; the ocean. **2** A large body of salt water partly or wholly enclosed by land: the Adriatic *Sea*. **3** An inland body of water, esp. if salty: the *Sea* of Galilee. **4** The state of the ocean with regard to the course, flow, swell, or turbulence of the waves. **5** A heavy wave or swell. **6** Anything vast or boundless that resembles or suggests the sea. **—at sea 1** On the ocean. **2** Bewildered. **—follow the sea** To follow the occupation of a sailor. **—put to sea** To sail away from the land [< OE *sæ*]

sea anemone Any of various soft-bodied, sessile marine polyps with tentacles resembling the petals of a flower.

sea bass Any of various carnivorous food fishes of U.S. coastal waters.

Sea·bee (sē'bē') *n.* A member of one of the construction battalions of the U.S. Navy. [< *c(onstruction) b(attalion)*]

sea·board (sē'bôrd', -bōrd') *adj.* Bordering on the sea. **—n.** The seashore or seacoast and the adjoining region. [< SEA + *board* a border < OE *bord*]

Sea anemone
a. tentacles contracted. b. extended.

sea bread HARDTACK.

sea breeze A breeze blowing from the sea toward land.

sea calf A spotted seal of the E U.S. coast.

sea·coast (sē'kōst') *n.* The land on or close to the sea.

sea cow 1 Any of various large aquatic mammals, as the manatee or the dugong. **2** WALRUS.

sea cucumber Any of various cylindrical echinoderms having a rosette of tentacles at the mouth.

sea dog 1 SEAL[2]. **2** DOGFISH. **3** A sailor with long experience at sea.

sea eagle Any of various fish-eating birds related to the bald eagle.

sea·far·er (sē'fâr'ər) *n.* A sailor; mariner.

sea·far·ing (sē'fâr'ing) *n.* **1** The occupation of a sailor. **2** Traveling over the sea. **—adj.** Of, pertaining to, given to, or engaged in seafaring.

sea·food (sē'fōōd') *n.* Edible saltwater fish or shellfish.

sea·girt (sē'gûrt') *adj.* Surrounded by the sea.

sea·go·ing (sē'gō'ing) *adj.* **1** Designed or adapted for use on the ocean. **2** SEAFARING.

sea green Bluish green.

sea gull A gull, esp. one of a widely distributed gregarious species.

sea horse 1 Any of various small fishes found in warm seas, having a long curled tail and a head resembling that of a horse. 2 A walrus. 3 A mythical creature, half horse and half fish.

sea king A viking pirate chief of the Middle Ages.

seal[1] (sēl) *n.* 1 An impression made on a letter, document, etc., to prove its authenticity. 2 A wax wafer, piece of paper, etc., bearing such an authenticating impression. 3 A device with a raised or cut initial, word, or design, used to make such an impression. 4 A stamp, ring, etc., bearing such a device. 5 Something used to close or secure a letter, door, lid, wrapper, joint, passage, etc., firmly. 6 Anything that confirms, ratifies, or guarantees; pledge. 7 A sign or indication; token. 8 An ornamental stamp for packages, etc. —*v.t.* 1 To affix a seal to, as to prove authenticity or prevent tampering. 2 To stamp or otherwise impress a seal upon in order to attest to weight, quality, etc. 3 To fasten or close with a seal: to *seal* a glass jar. 4 To confirm the genuineness or truth of, as a bargain. 5 To establish or settle finally. 6 To secure, set, or fill up, as with plaster. [< L *sigillum* a small picture, seal] —**seal′a·ble** *adj.* —**seal′er** *n.*

Sea horse

seal[2] (sēl) *n.* 1 Any of various species of sea mammals with a short tail and four webbed flippers, with which it swims and waddles ashore. 2 The commercially valued fur of the **fur seal.** 3 Leather made from the hide of a seal. —*v.i.* To hunt seals. [< OE *seolh*] —**seal′er** *n.*

sea legs The ability to walk aboard a ship in motion without losing one's balance or suffering from seasickness.

Seal

sea level The average level of the surface of the ocean.

sea lily CRINOID.

sealing wax A pigmented mixture of shellac and resin with turpentine that is fluid when heated but becomes solid as it cools: used to seal papers, etc.

sea lion One of various large, eared seals, esp. the California sea lion.

seal ring SIGNET RING.

seal·skin (sēl′skin′) *n.* 1 The pelt or fur of the fur seal, often dyed dark brown or black. 2 An article made of this fur. —*adj.* Made of sealskin.

Sea·ly·ham terrier (sē′lē·ham, -əm) One of a breed of terriers with short legs, a wide skull, square jaws, and a wiry white coat. [Orig. bred in *Sealyham,* Wales]

seam (sēm) *n.* 1 A visible line of junction between parts, as the edges of two pieces of cloth sewn together. • See PINK[2]. 2 A line, ridge, or groove marking joined edges, as of boards. 3 Any similar line, ridge, etc., as that formed by a scar, wrinkle, etc. 4 A thin layer or stratum, as of rock or ore. —*v.t.* 1 To unite by means of a seam. 2 To mark with a cut, furrow, wrinkle, etc. —*v.i.* 3 To crack open; become fissured. [< OE *sēam*] —**seam′er** *n.*

sea·man (sē′mən) *n. pl.* **·men** (-mən) 1 An enlisted man in the navy or in the coast guard, graded according to his rank. 2 A mariner; sailor. —**sea′man·like′** (-līk′) *adj.* — **sea′man·ly** *adj., adv.*

sea·man·ship (sē′mən·ship) *n.* The skill of a seaman in handling sea craft.

sea mew A gull, esp. the European mew.

sea·mount (sē′mount′) *n.* A submarine mountain.

seam·stress (sēm′stris) *n.* A woman whose occupation is sewing. [< OE *sēam* seam + -ST(E)R + -ESS]

seam·y (sē′mē) *adj.* **seam·i·er, seam·i·est** 1 Like, formed by, or characterized by seams. 2 Showing an unworthy, unpleasant, or unpresentable aspect. —**seam′i·ness** *n.* — Syn. 2 sordid, degraded, squalid, disagreeable.

sé·ance (sā′äns) *n.* 1 A session or sitting. 2 A meeting of persons seeking to receive communications from spirits of the dead. [F < OF *seoir* sit]

sea·plane (sē′plān′) *n.* An airplane that can take off from and land on the water.

sea·port (sē′pôrt′, -pōrt′) *n.* 1 A harbor or port accessible to seagoing ships. 2 A town or city located at such a place.

sea purse The leathery egg case of certain sharks, rays, etc.

sear (sir) *v.t.* 1 To wither; dry up. 2 To burn the surface of; scorch. 3 To burn or cauterize; brand. 4 To make callous; harden. —*v.i.* 5 To become withered; dry up. —*adj.* Dried or blasted; withered. —*n.* A scar or brand. [< OE *sēar* dry]

search (sûrch) *v.t.* 1 To look through or explore thoroughly in order to find something. 2 To subject (a person) to a search. 3 To examine with close attention; probe. 4 To penetrate or pierce: The wind *searches* my clothes. 5 To learn by examination or investigation: with *out.* —*v.i.* 6 To make a search. —*n.* 1 The act of searching. 2 An act of boarding and inspecting a ship in pursuance of the right to search. [< LL *circare* go round, explore] — **search′a·ble** *adj.* —**search′er** *n.*

search·ing (sûr′ching) *adj.* 1 Investigating thoroughly. 2 Keenly penetrating. —**search′ing·ly** *adv.* —**search′ing·ness** *n.*

search·light (sûrch′līt′) *n.* 1 An apparatus consisting of a powerful light equipped with a reflector and mounted so that it can be projected in various directions. 2 The light so projected.

search warrant A warrant authorizing a police officer to search a house or other specified place, as for stolen goods.

sea·scape (sē′skāp′) *n.* 1 A view of the sea. 2 A picture presenting such a view.

sea·shell (sē′shel′) *n.* The shell of a marine mollusk.

sea·shore (sē′shôr′, -shōr′) *n.* Land bordering on the sea.

sea·sick (sē′sik′) *adj.* Suffering from seasickness.

sea·sick·ness (sē′sik′nis) *n.* Nausea, dizziness, etc., caused by the motion of a ship at sea.

sea·side (sē′sīd′) *n.* SEASHORE.

sea·son (sē′zən) *n.* 1 A division of the year as determined by the earth's position with respect to the sun: spring, summer, autumn, and winter. 2 A period of time. 3 A period of special activity or when a specified place is frequented: usu. with *the:* the opera *season;* the Palm Beach *season.* 4 A fit or suitable time. 5 The time of and surrounding a major holiday. —**in season** 1 At a time of availability and fitness, as for eating: Clams are *in season* during the summer. 2 In or at the right time. 3 Able to be killed or taken by permission of the law. 4 Ready to mate or breed: said of animals. —*v.t.* 1 To increase the flavor or zest of (food), as by adding spices, etc. 2 To add zest or piquancy to. 3 To render more suitable for use. 4 To make fit, as by discipline; harden. 5 To mitigate or soften; moderate. —*v.i.* 6 To become seasoned. [< LL *satio* sowing time] —**sea′son·er** *n.*

sea·son·a·ble (sē′zən·ə·bəl) *adj.* 1 Being in keeping with the season or circumstances. 2 Done or occurring at the proper or best time. —**sea′son·a·ble·ness** *n.* —**sea′son·a·bly** *adv.* —Syn. 1 timely, well-timed. 2 opportune, favorable, propitious, advantageous.

sea·son·al (sē′zən·əl) *adj.* Of, pertaining to, characteristic of, or happening during a season or the seasons. — **sea′son·al·ly** *adv.*

sea·son·ing (sē′zən·ing) *n.* 1 The process by which something is rendered fit for use. 2 Something added to give relish; esp., a condiment. 3 Something added to increase enjoyment, give zest, etc.

Great Seal of the United States

---

add, āce, câre, pälm; end, ēven; it, īce; odd, ōpen, ôrder; tòòk, pōōl; up, bûrn; ə = *a* in *above, u* in *focus;* yōō = *u* in *fuse;* oil; pout; check; go; ring; thin; this; zh, *vision.* < derived from; ? origin uncertain or unknown.

season ticket A ticket entitling the holder to something specified, as train trips, admission to entertainments, etc., during a certain period of time.

seat (sēt) *n.* 1 The thing on which one sits; a chair, bench, stool, etc. 2 That part of a thing upon which one rests in sitting, or upon which an object or another part rests. 3 That part of the person which sustains the weight of the body in sitting; buttocks. 4 That part of a garment which covers the buttocks. 5 The place where anything is situated or established: the *seat* of pain, the *seat* of a government. 6 A place of abode, esp. a large estate. 7 The privilege or right of membership in a legislative body, stock exchange, or the like. 8 The manner of sitting, as on horseback. 9 A surface or part upon which the base of anything rests. —*v.t.* 1 To place on a seat or seats; cause to sit down. 2 To have seats for; furnish with seats: The theater *seats* only 299 people. 3 To put a seat on or in; renew or repair the seat of. 4 To locate, settle, or center: usu. in the passive: The French government is *seated* in Paris. 5 To fix, set firmly, or establish in a certain position, place, etc. [< ON *sæti*]

seat belt A strap or harness that holds a passenger firmly in the seat, as while riding in a car or airplane.

seat·ing (sē′ting) *n.* 1 The act of providing with seats; also, the arrangement of such seats. 2 Fabric for upholstering seats. 3 A fitted support or base; a seat.

SEATO (sē′tō) Southeast Asia Treaty Organization.

sea urchin Any of various echinoderms shielded within a spine-covered, rounded case.

sea wall A wall for preventing erosion of the shore by the sea or for breaking the force of waves. —**sea-walled** (sē′wôld′) *adj.*

sea·ward (sē′wərd) *adj.* 1 Going or situated toward the sea. 2 Blowing, as wind, from the sea. —*adv.* In the direction of the sea: also **sea′wards.** —*n.* A direction or position toward the sea, away from land.

sea·way (sē′wā′) *n.* 1 A way or route over the sea. 2 An inland waterway that receives ocean shipping. 3 The headway made by a ship. 4 A rough sea.

sea·weed (sē′wēd′) *n.* Any marine plant or vegetation, esp. any multicellular alga.

sea·wor·thy (sē′wûr′thē) *adj.* In fit condition for a sea voyage. —**sea′wor′thi·ness** *n.*

se·ba·ceous (si·bā′shəs) *adj.* 1 Of, pertaining to, or resembling fat. 2 Secreting sebum. [< L *sebum* tallow]

se·bum (sē′bəm) *n.* An oily substance secreted by special glands in the skin. [L, tallow]

sec (sek) *adj. French* Dry: said of wines. Also *Italian* **sec·co** (sek′kō).

SEC, S.E.C. Securities and Exchange Commission.

sec. second(s); secondary; secretary; section(s); sector.

se·cant (sē′kant, -kənt) *adj.* Cutting, esp. into two parts; intersecting. —*n.* 1 *Geom.* A straight line intersecting a given curve. 2 *Trig.* A function equal to the reciprocal of the cosine. [< L *secare* to cut]

se·cede (si·sēd′) *v.i.* **·ced·ed, ·ced·ing** To withdraw formally from a union, fellowship, etc., esp. from a political or religious organization. [< L *se-* apart + *cedere* go] —**se·ced′er** *n.*

Ratio of AB to AD is the secant of angle BAD. AB is secant of arc CD.

se·ces·sion (si·sesh′ən) *n.* 1 The act of seceding. 2 *Usu. cap. U.S.* The withdrawal of the Southern States from the Union in 1860–61. —**se·ces′sion·al** *adj.* —**se·ces′sion·ism, se·ces′sion·ist** *n.*

Seck·el (sek′əl, sik′əl) *n.* A variety of small, sweet pear. Also **Seckel pear.** [< the Pennsylvania farmer who introduced it]

se·clude (si·klōōd′) *v.t.* **·clud·ed, ·clud·ing** 1 To remove and keep apart from the society of others; isolate. 2 To screen or shut off, as from view. [< L *se-* apart + *claudere* to shut]

se·clud·ed (si·klōō′did) *adj.* 1 Separated; living apart from others. 2 Protected or screened. —**se·clud′ed·ly** *adv.* —**se·clud′ed·ness** *n.*

se·clu·sion (si·klōō′zhən) *n.* 1 The act of secluding, or the state or condition of being secluded; solitude; retirement. 2 A secluded place. —**se·clu′sive** *adj.* —**se·clu′sive·ly** *adv.* —**se·clu′sive·ness** *n.*

sec·ond[1] (sek′ənd) *n.* 1 A unit of time, 1/60 of a minute. 2 A unit of angular measure, 1/60 of a minute. 3 An instant; moment: Wait a *second.* [< Med. L *seconda (minuta)*, lit., second (minute), i.e., the result of the second sexagesimal division]

sec·ond[2] (sek′ənd) *adj.* 1 Next in order, authority, responsibility, etc., after the first. 2 Ranking next below the first or best. 3 Of lesser quality or value; inferior; subordinate. 4 Identical with another or preceding one; other. 5 *Music* Lower in pitch, or rendering a secondary part. —*n.* 1 The one next after the first, as in order, rank, importance, etc. 2 The element of an ordered set that corresponds to the number two. 3 An attendant who supports or aids another, as in a duel. 4 *Often pl.* An article of merchandise of inferior quality. 5 *Music* a The interval between any one tone and another a whole step or half step away from or below it. b A subordinate part, instrument, or voice. 6 In parliamentary law, the act or declaration by which a motion is seconded: Do I hear a *second?* 7 *pl. Informal* A second portion of food. —*v.t.* 1 To act as a supporter or assistant of; promote; stimulate; encourage. 2 To support formally, as a motion, resolution, etc. —*adv.* In the second order, place, rank, etc. [< L *secundus* following]

sec·on·dar·y (sek′ən·der′ē) *adj.* 1 Of second rank, grade, or influence; subordinate. 2 Depending on, resulting from, or following what is primary. 3 Second in order of occurrence or development. 4 *Electr.* Of or pertaining to the output of a transformer. —*n. pl.* **·dar·ies** 1 One who or that which is secondary or subordinate. 2 *Electr.* A secondary circuit or coil. —**sec′on·dar′i·ly** *adv.*

secondary accent See ACCENT.

secondary education Education beyond the elementary or primary, and below the college, level.

secondary school A school providing secondary education.

second best One who or that which is next after the best. —**sec′ond-best′** *adj.*

second childhood A time or condition of dotage; senility.

sec·ond-class (sek′ənd·klas′, -kläs′) *adj.* 1 Ranking next below the first or best; inferior, inadequate, etc. 2 Of, pertaining to, or belonging to a class next below the first: *second-class* mail, *second-class* ticket, etc. —*adv.* By using second-class travel accommodations or second-class mail.

sec·ond-guess (sek′ənd·ges′) *v.t.* 1 To use hindsight in criticizing (an action, decision, etc., or the person responsible for it). 2 OUTGUESS. —**sec′ond-guess′er** *n.*

sec·ond-hand (sek′ənd·hand′) *adj.* 1 Previously owned, worn, or used by another; not new. 2 Received from another; not direct from the original source: *secondhand* information. 3 Of, pertaining to, or dealing in merchandise that is not new. —*adv.* Indirectly.

second hand The hand that marks the seconds on a clock or a watch.

second lieutenant See GRADE.

sec·ond·ly (sek′ənd·lē) *adv.* In the second place; second.

second nature An acquired trait or habit so ingrained as to seem innate.

sec·ond-rate (sek′ənd·rāt′) *adj.* Second or inferior in quality, size, rank, importance, etc.; second-class. —**sec′ond-rat′er** *n.*

second sight The supposed capacity to see objects not actually present, to see into the future, etc. —**sec′ond-sight′ed** *adj.*

sec·ond-sto·ry man (sek′ənd·stôr′ē, -stō′rē) *Informal* A burglar who enters a building through an upstairs window. Also **sec′ond-sto′ry-man.**

sec·ond-string (sek′ənd·string′) *adj. Informal* 1 In sports, being a substitute rather than a regular or starting player. 2 SECOND-RATE.

second thought A reevaluation or reconsideration of something following one's initial response or decision.

second wind 1 The return of easy breathing after a period of exertion or exercise. 2 A renewed capacity for the continuation of any effort.

se·cre·cy (sē′krə·sē) *n. pl.* **·cies** 1 The condition or quality of being secret; concealment. 2 The character of being secretive.

se·cret (sē′krit) adj. **1** Kept separate or hidden from view or knowledge, or from all persons except the individuals concerned; unseen. **2** Affording privacy; secluded. **3** Good at keeping secrets; close-mouthed. **4** Unrevealed or unavowed: a secret partner. **5** Not revealed to everyone; mysterious; esoteric. —n. **1** Something known only by a few people. **2** Something that is not explained or is kept hidden; mystery. **3** An underlying reason; key. —**in secret** In privacy; in a hidden place. [< L se- apart + cernere to separate] —**se′cret·ly** adv.

sec·re·tar·i·at (sek′rə·târ′ē·it, -at) n. **1** A secretary's position. **2** The place where a secretary transacts business and keeps records. **3** The entire staff of secretaries in an office; esp., a department headed by a secretary-general.

sec·re·tar·y (sek′rə·ter′ē) n. pl. **·tar·ies 1** An employee who deals with correspondence, records, and clerical business for a person, business, committee, etc. **2** An official in a business, club, etc., who has overall responsibility for somewhat similar work. **3** An executive officer presiding over and managing a department of government. **4** A writing desk with a bookcase on top. [< L secretum a secret] —**sec′re·tar′i·al** (-târ′ē·əl) adj.

secretary bird A large, predatory African bird having a crest resembling quill pens stuck behind the ear.

secretary general pl. **secretaries general** A chief administrative officer, esp. the head of a secretariat.

sec·re·tar·y·ship (sek′rə·ter′ē·ship) n. The work or position of a secretary.

se·crete (si·krēt′) v.t. **·cret·ed, ·cret·ing 1** To remove or keep from observation; conceal; hide. **2** Biol. To form and release (an enzyme, hormone, etc.). [Alter. of obs. secret, to conceal] —**se·cre′tor** n.

se·cre·tion (si·krē′shən) n. **1** Biol. The cellular process by which materials are separated from blood or sap and converted into new substances: the secretion of milk, urine, etc. **2** The substance secreted. **3** The act of concealing or hiding.

se·cre·tive (sē′krə·tiv, si·krē′tiv) adj. **1** Having or showing a disposition to secrecy. **2** (si·krē′tiv) SECRETORY. —**se′·cre·tive·ly** adv. —**se′cre·tive·ness** n.

se·cre·to·ry (si·krē′tər·ē) adj. Of, pertaining to, causing, or produced by secretion (def. 1).

secret service A department of the government concerned with work of a secret nature.

Secret Service A division of the U.S. Treasury Department concerned with the suppression of counterfeiting, the protection of the President, etc.

sect (sekt) n. **1** A religious denomination, esp. a body of dissenters from an established or older form of faith. **2** Adherents of a particular philosophical system or teacher, esp. a faction of a larger group. [< L sequi follow]

sect. section; sectional.

sec·tar·i·an (sek·târ′ē·ən) adj. **1** Of, pertaining to, or characteristic of a sect. **2** Having devotion to or prejudice in favor of a sect. **3** Narrow-minded; limited; parochial. —n. **1** A member of a sect. **2** A person who is blindly devoted to a sect or factional viewpoint. —**sec·tar′i·an·ism′** n.

sec·ta·ry (sek′tər·ē) n. pl. **·ries** A member of a sect.

sec·tion (sek′shən) n. **1** The act of cutting; a separating by cutting. **2** A slice or portion separated by or as if by cutting. **3** A separate part or division, as of a book or chapter. **4** A distinct part of a country, community, etc. **5** U.S. An area of land one square mile in extent and constituting ⅟₃₆ of a township. **6** A portion of a railroad's right of way under the care of a particular crew of men. **7** In a sleeping-car, a space containing two berths. **8** A representation of an object, as if cut by an intersecting plane. —v.t. **1** To divide into sections. **2** To shade (a drawing) so as to designate a section or sections. [< L sectus, p.p. of secare to cut]

sec·tion·al (sek′shən·əl) adj. **1** Of, pertaining to, or characteristic of a section. **2** Made up of sections. —**sec′tion·al·ly** adv.

sec·tion·al·ism (sek′shən·əl·iz′əm) n. Exaggerated concern for a particular section of a country rather than the whole. —**sec′tion·al·ist** n.

sec·tor (sek′tər) n. **1** Geom. A part of a circle bounded by two radii and the arc subtended by them. **2** Mil. **a** A part of a front in contact with the enemy. **b** Any of the subdivisions of a defensive position. **3** A distinct part, as of a society. —v.t. To divide into sectors. [< L sectus, p.p. of secare to cut] —**sec·to·ri·al** (-tôr′ē·əl, -tō′rē-) adj.

ACB is a sector of the circle.

sec·u·lar (sek′yə·lər) adj. **1** Of or pertaining to this world; temporal; worldly. **2** Not controlled by the church; civil; not ecclesiastical. **3** Not concerned with religion; not sacred: secular art. **4** Not bound by monastic vows, and not living in a religious community. **5** Of or describing a trend or process continuing for a long, indefinite period of time. —n. **1** A member of the clergy who is not bound by monastic vows and who does not live in a religious community. **2** A layman as distinguished from a member of the clergy. [< L saeculum generation, age]

sec·u·lar·ism (sek′yə·lə·riz′əm) n. **1** Regard for worldly as opposed to spiritual matters. **2** The belief that religion should not be introduced into public education or public affairs. —**sec′u·lar·ist** n. —**sec′u·lar·is′tic** adj.

sec·u·lar·ize (sek′yə·lə·rīz′) v.t. **·ized, ·iz·ing 1** To make secular; convert from sacred to secular possession or uses. **2** To make worldly. **3** To change (a regular clergyman) to a secular. —**sec′u·lar·i·za′tion** n.

se·cure (si·kyoŏr′) adj. **·cur·er, ·cur·est 1** Free from or not likely to be exposed to danger, theft, etc.; safe. **2** Free from fear, apprehension, etc. **3** Confident; certain. **4** In a state or condition that will not break, come unfastened, etc.: Is the door secure? **5** Reliable; steady; dependable: a secure job. —v. **·cured, ·cur·ing** v.t. **1** To make secure; protect. **2** To make firm, tight, or fast; fasten. **3** To make sure or certain; insure; guarantee. **4** To obtain possession of; get. —v.i. **5** To stop working: said of a ship's crew. **6** To berth; moor: said of a ship. [< L se- without + cura care] —**se·cur′a·ble** adj. —**se·cure′ly** adv. —**se·cure′ness, se·cur′er** n.

se·cur·i·ty (si·kyoŏr′ə·tē) n. pl. **·ties 1** The state of being secure; freedom from danger, risk, care, poverty, doubt, etc. **2** One who or that which secures or guarantees; surety. **3** pl. Written promises or something deposited or pledged for payment of money, as stocks, bonds, etc. **4** Defense or protection against espionage, attack, escape, etc. **5** Measures calculated to provide such defense or protection. **6** An organization or division of one charged with providing for safety and protection.

Security Council A permanent organ of the United Nations charged with the maintenance of international peace and security.

secy., sec′y. secretary.

se·dan (si·dan′) n. **1** A closed automobile having one compartment, front and rear seats, and two or four doors. **2** A closed chair, for one passenger, carried by two men by means of poles at the sides: also **sedan chair.** [?]

se·date (si·dāt′) adj. Not disturbed by excitement, passion, etc. [< L sedare make calm, settle] —**se·date′·ly** adv. —**se·date′ness** n. —Syn. calm, composed, staid.

Sedan def. 2

se·da·tion (si·dā′shən) n. The reduction of sensitivity to pain, stress, etc., by administering a sedative.

sed·a·tive (sed′ə·tiv) adj. Tending to calm or soothe; esp., acting to allay nervousness or emotional agitation. —n. A sedative medicine.

sed·en·tar·y (sed′ən·ter′ē) adj. **1** Accustomed to sit much or to work in a sitting posture. **2** Characterized by sitting. **3** Remaining in one place; not migratory. **4** Attached or fixed to an object. [< L sedere sit] —**sed′en·tar′·i·ly** adv. —**sed′en·tar′i·ness** n.

Se·der (sā'dər) *n. pl.* **Se·da·rim** (sə·där'im) or **Se·ders** In Judaism, a ceremonial dinner commemorating the Exodus, held on the eve of the first day of Passover, and traditionally on the eve of the second day by Jews outside of Israel. [< Heb. *sēdher* order]

sedge (sej) *n.* Any of a large family of grasslike plants growing in wet ground and usu. having triangular, solid stems and tiny flowers in spikes. [< OE *secg*] —**sedged, sedg'y** *adj.*

sed·i·ment (sed'ə·mənt) *n.* **1** Matter that settles to the bottom of a liquid; dregs; lees. **2** *Geol.* Fragmentary material deposited by water, ice, or air. [< L *sedere* sit, settle] **sed'i·men·ta'tion** *n.*

sed·i·men·ta·ry (sed'ə·men'tər·ē) *adj.* **1** Of, pertaining to, or having the character of sediment. **2** *Geol.* Designating rocks composed of compacted sediment. Also **sed'i·men'tal.**

se·di·tion (si·dish'ən) *n.* The incitement and act of resistance to or revolt against lawful authority. [< L *sed-* aside + *itio* a going]

se·di·tious (si·dish'əs) *adj.* **1** Of, pertaining to, or having the character of sedition. **2** Inclined to, taking part in, or guilty of sedition. —**se·di'tious·ly** *adv.* —**se·di'tious·ness** *n.*

se·duce (si·dyōōs') *v.t.* **·duced, ·duc·ing 1** To lead astray, as from a proper or right course: *seduced* by quick profits. **2** To entice into wrong, disloyalty, etc.; tempt. **3** To induce to have sexual intercourse. [< L *se-* apart + *ducere* lead] —**se·duc'er** *n.* —**se·duc'i·ble** or **se·duce'a·ble** *adj.*

se·duc·tion (si·duk'shən) *n.* **1** The act of seducing or the condition of being seduced. **2** Something which seduces; an enticement. Also **se·duce'ment.**

se·duc·tive (si·duk'tiv) *adj.* Tending to seduce. —**se·duc'tive·ly** *adv.* —**se·duc'tive·ness** *n.*

sed·u·lous (sej'ōō·ləs) *adj.* **1** Constant in application or attention; assiduous. **2** Diligent; industrious. [< L *se dolo* without guile] —**sed'u·lous·ly** *adv.* —**sed'u·lous·ness** *n.*

se·dum (sē'dəm) *n.* Any of a large genus of chiefly creeping or mat-forming plants with fleshy leaves, adapted to rocky terrain. [L, house leek]

see¹ (sē) *v.* **saw, seen, see·ing** *v.t.* **1** To perceive with the eyes; gain knowledge or awareness of by means of one's vision. **2** To perceive with the mind; comprehend. **3** To find out or ascertain; inquire about: *See* who is at the door. **4** To have experience or knowledge of; undergo: We have *seen* more peaceful times. **5** To encounter; chance to meet: I *saw* your husband today. **6** To have a meeting or interview with; visit or receive as a guest, visitor, etc.: The doctor will *see* you now. **7** To attend as a spectator; view. **8** To accompany; escort. **9** To take care; be sure: *See* that you do it! **10** In poker, to accept (a bet) or equal the bet of (a player) by betting an equal sum. —*v.i.* **11** To have or exercise the power of sight. **12** To find out; inquire. **13** To understand; comprehend. **14** To think; consider. **15** To take care; be attentive: *See* to your work. **16** To gain certain knowledge, as by awaiting an outcome: We will *see* if you are right. —**see about 1** To inquire into the facts, causes, etc., of. **2** To take care of; attend to. —**see through 1** To perceive the real meaning or nature of. **2** To aid or protect, as throughout a period of danger. **3** To finish. [< OE *sēon*]

see² (sē) *n.* **1** The official seat from which a bishop exercises jurisdiction. **2** The authority or jurisdiction of a bishop. [< L *sedes* a seat]

seed (sēd) *n.* **1** The ovule containing an embryo from which a plant may be reproduced. **2** That from which anything springs; source. **3** Offspring; children. **4** The male fertilizing element; semen; sperm. **5** Any small granular fruit, singly or collectively. —*v.t.* **1** To sow with seed. **2** To sow (seed). **3** To remove the seeds from: to *seed* raisins. **4** To strew (moisture-bearing clouds) with crystals, as of dry ice, silver iodide, etc., in order to initiate precipitation. **5** In sports: **a** To arrange (the drawing for positions in a tournament, etc.) so that the more skilled competitors meet only in the later events. **b** To rank (a skilled competitor) thus. —*v.i.* **6** To sow seed. **7** To grow to maturity and produce or shed seed. —**go to seed 1** To develop and shed seed. **2** To become shabby, useless, etc.; deteriorate. [< OE *sæd*] —**seed'er** *n.* —**seed'less** *adj.*

seed·bed (sēd'bed') *n.* **1** A protected bed of earth planted with seeds for later transplanting. **2** A place of early growth or nurture.

seed·case (sēd'kās') *n.* SEED VESSEL.

seed coat The integument of a seed. • See EMBRYO.

seed leaf COTYLEDON.

seed·ling (sēd'ling) *n.* **1** Any plant grown from seed. **2** A very small or young tree or plant.

seed oyster A young oyster, esp. one transplanted from one bed to another.

seed pearl A small pearl, esp. one used for ornamenting bags, etc., or in embroidery.

seed plant A plant which bears seeds.

seed vessel A pericarp, esp. one that is dry, as a pod.

seed·y (sē'dē) *adj.* **seed·i·er, seed·i·est 1** Abounding with seeds. **2** Gone to seed. **3** Poor and ragged; shabby. **4** Feeling or looking wretched. —**seed'i·ly** *adv.* —**seed'i·ness** *n.*

see·ing (sē'ing) *conj.* Since; in view of the fact; considering.

Seeing Eye dog The name used for a dog trained to lead the blind, esp. one trained by an organization (**Seeing Eye**) in New Jersey: a trade name.

seek (sēk) *v.* **sought, seek·ing** *v.t.* **1** To go in search of; look for. **2** To strive for; try to get. **3** To endeavor or try: He *seeks* to mislead me. **4** To ask or inquire for; request: to *seek* information. **5** To go to; betake oneself to: to *seek* a warmer climate. —*v.i.* **6** To make a search or inquiry. [< OE *sēcan*] —**seek'er** *n.*

seem (sēm) *v.i.* **1** To give the impression of being; appear. **2** To appear to oneself: I *seem* to remember her face. **3** To appear to exist: There *seems* no reason for hesitating. **4** To be evident or apparent: It *seems* to be raining. [< ON *sæma* honor, conform to]

seem·ing (sē'ming) *adj.* Having the appearance of reality but often not so: Her *seeming* nonchalance was solely due to three martinis. —*n.* Appearance; semblance; esp., false show. —**seem'ing·ly** *adv.* —**seem'ing·ness** *n.*

seem·ly (sēm'lē) *adj.* **·li·er, ·li·est 1** Befitting the proprieties; becoming; proper; decorous. **2** Handsome; attractive. —*adv.* Becomingly; appropriately. [< ON *sæmr* fitting] —**seem'li·ness** *n.*

seen (sēn) *p.p.* of SEE.

seep (sēp) *v.i.* To soak through pores or small openings; ooze. [< OE *sipian* soak] —**seep'y** *adj.*

seep·age (sē'pij) *n.* **1** The act or process of seeping; oozing; leakage. **2** The fluid that seeps.

seer (sē'ər for def. 1; sir for def. 2) *n.* **1** One who sees. **2** One who foretells events; a prophet. [< SEE¹ + -ER]

seer·suck·er (sir'suk'ər) *n.* A thin fabric, often striped, with crinkled surface. [< Pers. *shīr o shakkar,* lit., milk and sugar]

see·saw (sē'sô') *n.* **1** A game or contest in which persons sit or stand on opposite ends of a board balanced at the middle and make it move up and down. **2** A board balanced for this sport. **3** Any up-and-down or to-and-fro movement, tendency, change, etc. —*v.t. & v.i.* To move on or as if on a seesaw. —*adj.* Moving up and down or to and fro. [Reduplication of SAW¹]

seethe (sēth) *v.* **seethed, seeth·ing** *v.i.* **1** To boil. **2** To foam or bubble as if boiling. **3** To be agitated, as by rage. —*v.t.* **4** To soak in liquid; steep. **5** *Archaic* To boil. —*n.* The act or condition of seething. [< OE *sēothan*]

seg·ment (seg'mənt) *n.* **1** A part cut off or distinct from the other parts of anything: a section. **2** *Geom.* A part of a line or curve lying between two of its points. —*v.t. & v.i.* To divide into segments. [< L *secare* to cut] —**seg·men·tal** (seg·men'təl) *adj.* —**seg·men'tal·ly** *adv.* —**seg·men·tar·y** (seg'mən·ter'ē) *adj.*

seg·men·ta·tion (seg'mən·tā'shən) *n.* **1** Division into segments. **2** The process of repeated cleavage whereby a complex organism develops from a single cell.

se·go (sē'gō) *n. pl.* **·gos 1** A perennial plant of the lily family, having bell-shaped flowers. **2** Its edible bulb. Also **sego lily.** [< Ute]

seg·re·gate (seg'rə·gāt) *v.* **·gat·ed, ·gat·ing** *v.t.* **1** To place apart from others or the rest; isolate. **2** To cause the separation of (a race, social class, etc.) from the general mass of society or from a larger group. —*v.i.* **3** To separate from a mass and gather about nuclei, as in crystallization. —*adj.* (-git) Separated or set apart from others; segregated.

[< L *se-* apart + *grex* a flock] —**seg′re·ga′tive** *adj.* —**seg′re·ga′tor** *n.*

seg·re·ga·tion (seg′rə·gā′shən) *n.* **1** A segregating or being segregated or process of segregating. **2** The act or policy of separating a race, social class, etc., from the general mass of society or from a larger group.

Seid·litz powders (sed′lits) An effervescent mixture of salts, used as a laxative. Also **Seidlitz powder.** [< similarity to spring water in *Seidlitz,* Czechoslovakia]

sei·gnior (sān·yôr′, sān′yər) *n.* A man of rank, esp. a feudal lord. Also **sei·gneur** (sān′yər). [< L *senior* older] —**sei·gnio′ri·al** *adj.*

seign·ior·y (sān′yər·ē) *n. pl.* **·ior·ies** The territory, rights, or jurisdiction of a seignior.

seine (sān) *n.* Any long fishing net, having floats at the top edge and weights at the bottom. —*v.t. & v.i.* **seined, sein·ing** To fish or catch with a seine. [< Gk. *sagēnē* a fishing net]

seis·mic (sīz′mik, sīs′-) *adj.* Of, pertaining to, subject to, or produced by an earthquake or earthquakes. Also **seis′mal, seis′mi·cal.** [< Gk. *seismos* earthquake.]

seismo- *combining form* Earthquake: *seismograph.* [< Gk. *seismos* an earthquake]

seis·mo·gram (sīz′mə·gram, sīs′-) *n.* The record made by a seismograph.

seis·mo·graph (sīz′mə·graf, -gräf, sīs′-) *n.* An instrument for automatically recording the movements of the earth's crust. —**seis′mo·graph′ic** *adj.* —**seis·mog·ra·pher** (sīz·mog′rə·fər, sīs-), **seis·mog′ra·phy** *n.*

seis·mol·o·gy (sīz·mol′ə·jē, sīs-) *n.* The science dealing with earthquakes and related phenomena. —**seis·mo·log·ic**(sīz′mə·loj′ik, sīs′-) or **·i·cal** *adj.* —**seis′mo·log′i·cal·ly** *adv.* —**seis·mol′o·gist** *n.*

seize (sēz) *v.* **seized, seiz·ing** *v.t.* **1** To take hold of suddenly and forcibly; clutch; grasp. **2** To grasp mentally; understand. **3** To take possession of by authority or right. **4** To take possession of by or as by force. **5** To take prisoner; capture. **6** To act upon with sudden and powerful effect; attack; strike. **7** To take advantage of immediately, as an opportunity. **8** *Naut.* To fasten or bind by turns of cord, line, or small rope; lash. —*v.i.* **9** To take hold or make use: usu. with *on* or *upon.* [< OF *saisir, seisir*] —**seiz′a·ble** *adj.* —**seiz′er** *n.*

sei·zure (sē′zhər) *n.* **1** The act of seizing or the state of being seized. **2** A sudden incapacitation, as by disease.

se·lah (sē′lə) *n.* A Hebrew word of unknown meaning in the Psalms, usu. considered as a direction to readers or musicians.

sel·dom (sel′dəm) *adv.* At widely separated intervals, as of time or space; infrequently; rarely. —*adj.* Infrequent; rare. [< OE *seldan*]

se·lect (si·lekt′) *v.t.* **1** To take in preference to another or others; pick out; choose. —*v.i.* **2** To choose. —*adj.* **1** Chosen in preference to others. **2** Excellent; superior; choice. **3** Exclusive. **4** Very particular in selecting. [< L *se-* apart + *legere* choose] —**se·lect′ness, se·lec′tor** *n.*

se·lec·tee (si·lek′tē′) *n.* One called up for military service under selective service.

se·lec·tion (si·lek′shən) *n.* **1** A selecting or being selected. **2** Anything selected. **3** *Biol.* Any process, natural or artificial, which determines the survival of specific characteristics.

se·lec·tive (si·lek′tiv) *adj.* **1** Of, pertaining to, or characterized by selection. **2** Having the power or tendency to select. **3** Having or characterized by good selectivity, as a radio receiver. —**se·lec·tive·ly** *adv.* —**se·lec′tive·ness** *n.*

selective service Compulsory military service according to specified conditions of age, fitness, etc. —**se·lec′tive-ser′vice** *adj.*

se·lec·tiv·i·ty (si·lek′tiv′ə·tē) *n.* **1** The state or condition

of being selective. **2** *Telecom.* That characteristic of a radio receiver or filter by which frequencies can be sharply discriminated.

se·lect·man (si·lekt′mən) *n. pl.* **·men** (-mən) One of a board of town officers, elected annually in New England, except in Rhode Island, to manage local affairs.

sel·e·nite (sel′ə·nīt) *n.* A crystalline form of gypsum. [< Gk. *selēnītēs (lithos),* lit., moon(stone); so called because it was thought to wax and wane with the moon]

se·le·ni·um (si·lē′nē·əm) *n.* A nonmetallic element (symbol Se) of variable electrical resistance under the influence of light and having several allotropic forms. [< Gk. *selēnē* the moon]

self (self) *n. pl.* **selves 1** One's own person known or considered as the subject of his own consciousness. **2** The distinct and characteristic individuality or identity of any person or thing. **3** Personal interest or advantage. —*adj.* **1** Being uniform or of the same quality throughout. **2** Of the same kind (as in material, color, etc.,) as something else: a coat with a *self* belt. —*pron.* Myself, yourself, himself, or herself. [< OE]

self- *combining form* **1** Of oneself or itself: *self-analysis.* **2** By oneself or itself: *self-employed.* **3** In oneself or itself: *self-absorbed.* **4** To, with, for, or toward oneself: *self-satisfied.* **5** In or of oneself or itself inherently: *self-evident.*

self-ab·ne·ga·tion (self′ab′ni·gā′shən) *n.* The complete putting aside of self-interest. —**Syn.** self-sacrifice, self-denial, self-control, self-restraint.

self-a·buse (self′ə·byoos′) *n.* **1** The disparagement of one's own person or powers. **2** MASTURBATION.

self-ad·dressed (self′ə·drest′) *adj.* Addressed to oneself.

self-as·sured (self′ə·shoord′) *adj.* Confident in one's own abilities. —**self′-as·sur′ance** *n.*

self-cen·tered (self′sen′tərd) *adj.* Concerned exclusively with oneself and one's own needs and desires.

self-com·mand (self′kə·mand′, -mänd′) *n.* SELF-CONTROL.

self-con·fi·dence (self′kon′fə·dəns) *n.* Confidence in oneself or in one's own unaided powers, judgment, etc. —**self′-con′fi·dent** *adj.* —**self′-con′fi·dent·ly** *adv.*

self-con·scious (self′kon′shəs) *adj.* **1** Uncomfortably conscious that one is observed by others; ill at ease. **2** Displaying such consciousness: a *self-conscious* giggle. **3** Conscious of one's existence. —**self′-con′scious·ly** *adv.* —**self′-con′scious·ness** *n.*

self-con·tained (self′kən·tānd′) *adj.* **1** Keeping one's thoughts and feelings to oneself; impassive. **2** Exercising self-control. **3** Having within oneself or itself all that is necessary for independent existence or operation.

self-con·tra·dic·tion (self′kon′trə·dik′shən) *n.* **1** The contradicting of oneself or itself. **2** A statement, proposition, etc., that contradicts itself. —**self′-con′tra·dic′to·ry** *adj.*

self-con·trol (self′kən·trōl′) *n.* Control of one's impulses, emotions, etc.

self-de·fense (self′di·fens′) *n.* Defense of oneself, one's property, one's reputation, etc. —**self′-de·fen′sive** *adj.*

self-de·ni·al (self′di·nī′əl) *n.* The restraining of one's desires, impulses, etc. —**self′-de·ny′ing** *adj.*

self-de·ter·mi·na·tion (self′di·tûr′mə·nā′shən) *n.* **1** The principle of free will; decision by oneself without extraneous force or influence. **2** Decision by the people of a country or section as to its future political status. —**self′-de·ter′mined, self′-de·ter′min·ing** *adj.*

self-de·vo·tion (self′di·vō′shən) *n.* The devoting of oneself to the service of a person or a cause.

self-ed·u·cat·ed (self′ej′oo·kā′tid) *adj.* Educated through one's own efforts with little or no formal instruction. —**self′-ed′u·ca′tion** *n.*

self-es·teem (self′es·tēm′) *n.* **1** A good or just opinion of oneself. **2** An overestimate of oneself; conceit.

self-ev·i·dent (self′ev′ə·dənt) *adj.* Requiring no proof of its truth or validity. —**self′-ev′i·dence** *n.* —**self′-ev′i·dent·ly** *adv.*

self-ex·ist·ence (self′ig·zis′təns) *n.* Existence that is in-

dependent, without external cause. —**self′-ex·ist′ent** *adj.*

self-ex·plan·a·to·ry (self′ik·splan′ə·tôr·ē, -tō′rē) *adj.* Explaining itself; needing no explanation.

self-ex·pres·sion (self′ik·spresh′ən) *n.* Expression of one's own personality or individuality, as in art.

self-fer·til·i·za·tion (self′fûr′təl·ə·zā′shən, -ī·zā′shən) *n.* Fertilization of an organism by its own sperm or pollen.

self-gov·ern·ment (self′guv′ərn·mənt, -ər·mənt) *n.* **1** Self-control. **2** Government of a country or region by its own people. —**self′-gov′ern·ing, self′-gov′erned** *adj.*

self-heal (self′hēl′) *n.* A weedy perennial herb reputed to cure disease.

self-im·age (self′im′ij) *n.* The image or idea one has of oneself or of one's position in life.

self-im·por·tance (self′im·pôr′təns) *n.* An excessively high appraisal of one's own importance; conceit. —**self′-im·por′tant** *adj.*

self-in·duced (self′in·dyo͞ost′) *adj.* **1** Induced by oneself or by itself. **2** Produced by self-induction.

self-in·duc·tion (self′in·duk′shən) *n.* The production of an induced voltage in a circuit by the variation of the current in that circuit.

self-in·ter·est (self′in′trist, -in′tər·ist) *n.* Personal interest or advantage, or concern for it; selfishness. —**self′-in′ter·est·ed** *adj.*

self-ish (sel′fish) *adj.* **1** Motivated by personal needs and desires to the disregard of the welfare or wishes of others. **2** Proceeding from or characterized by undue concern for self. —**self′ish·ly** *adv.* —**self′ish·ness** *n.*

self-less (self′lis) *adj.* Having, showing, or prompted by a lack of concern for self. —**Syn.** unselfish, altruistic, self-sacrificing, self-denying.

self-load·ing (self′lō′ding) *adj.* Automatically reloading: said of a gun using the energy of recoil to eject and reload.

self-love (self′luv′) *n.* Love of oneself; the desire or tendency to seek to promote one's own well-being.

self-made (self′mād′) *adj.* **1** Having attained honor, wealth, etc., by one's own efforts. **2** Made by oneself.

self-pol·li·na·tion (self′pol′ə·nā′shən) *n.* Pollen transfer from stamens to pistils of the same flower, plant, or clone. —**self′-pol′li·na·ted** *adj.*

self-pos·ses·sion (self′pə·zesh′ən) *n.* The full possession or control of one's powers or faculties; presence of mind; self-control. —**self′-pos·sessed′** *adj.*

self-pres·er·va·tion (self′prez′ər·vā′shən) *n.* **1** The protection of oneself from injury or death. **2** The instinctive drive to protect oneself.

self-pro·nounc·ing (self′prə·noun′sing) *adj.* Having marks of pronunciation and stress applied to a word without phonetic alteration of the spelling.

self-re·li·ance (self′ri·lī′əns) *n.* Reliance on one's own abilities, resources, or judgment. —**self′-re·li′ant** *adj.* —**self′-re·li′ant·ly** *adv.*

self-re·spect (self′ri·spekt′) *n.* A proper respect for oneself, one's standing, position, etc. —**self′-re·spect′ing, self′-re·spect′ful,** *adj.* —**self′-re·spect′ful·ly** *adv.*

self-re·straint (self′ri·strānt′) *n.* Restraint imposed by the force of one's own will; self-control. —**self′-re·strained′** *adj.*

self-right·eous (self′rī′chəs) *adj.* Having or showing a high, usu. smug, opinion of one's own moral superiority. —**self′-right′eous·ly** *adv.* —**self′-right′eous·ness** *n.*

self-ris·ing (self′rī′zing) *adj.* Rising without the addition of leaven, as some flours.

self-sac·ri·fice (self′sak′rə·fīs) *n.* The subordination of one's self or one's personal welfare or wishes for others' good, for duty, etc. —**self′-sac′ri·fic′ing** *adj.*

self-same (self′sām′) *adj.* Exactly the same; identical. —**self′same′ness** *n.*

self-sat·is·fac·tion (self′sat′is·fak′shən) *n.* Satisfaction with one's own actions, characteristics, etc.; conceit. —**self′-sat′is·fied** *adj.* —**self′-sat′is·fy′ing** *adj.*

self-seek·ing (self′sē′king) *adj.* Given to the exclusive pursuit of one's own interests or gain. —*n.* Such a pursuit; selfishness. —**self′-seek′er** *n.*

self-ser·vice (self′sûr′vis) *adj.* Designating a particular type of café, restaurant, or store where patrons serve themselves.

self-serv·ing (self′sûr′ving) *adj.* Tending to justify or advance oneself, often at the expense of others.

self-start·er (self′stär′tər) *n.* **1** An engine or device with an automatic or semi-automatic starting mechanism; also, such a mechanism. **2** *Slang* One who requires no outside stimulus to start or accomplish work. —**self′-start′ing** *adj.*

self-styled (self′stīld′) *adj.* Characterized (as such) by oneself: a *self-styled* gentleman.

self-suf·fi·cient (self′sə·fish′ənt) *adj.* **1** Able to support or maintain oneself without aid or cooperation from others. **2** Having too much confidence in oneself. Also **self′-suf·fic′ing** (-sə·fī′sing). —**self′-suf·fi′cien·cy** *n.*

self-sup·port·ing (self′sə·pôrt′ing) *adj.* **1** Capable of supporting itself or its own weight. **2** Able to provide for oneself, as with money, lodging, clothing, etc.

self-will (self′wil′) *n.* Persistent adherence to one's own will or wish, esp. with disregard of the wishes of others; obstinacy. —**self′-willed′** *adj.*

self-wind·ing (self′wīn′ding) *adj.* Having an automatic winding mechanism, as some watches.

sell (sel) *v.* **sold, sell·ing** *v.t.* **1** To transfer (property) to another for a consideration; dispose of by sale. **2** To deal in; offer for sale. **3** To deliver, surrender, or betray in violation of duty or trust: often with *out*: to *sell* one's country. **4** *Informal* To cause to accept or approve something: They *sold* him on the scheme. **5** *Informal* To cause or promote the acceptance, approval, or sale of. **6** *Slang* To deceive; cheat. —*v.i.* **7** To engage in selling. **8** To be on sale or be sold. **9** To work as a salesperson. **10** To be popular with buyers, customers, etc. —**sell out 1** To get rid of (one's goods, etc.) by sale. **2** *Informal* To betray one's trust, cause, associates, etc. —*n.* **1** *Slang* A trick; joke; swindle. **2** An act or instance of selling. [< OE *sellan* give]

sell·er (sel′ər) *n.* **1** One who sells. **2** An item that is being sold, considered in reference to its sales.

sell-out (sel′out′) *n. Informal* **1** An act of selling out. **2** A performance for which all seats have been sold.

selt·zer (selt′sər) *n.* An artificially prepared mineral water that contains carbon dioxide. [< SELTZER]

Selt·zer (selt′sər) *n.* An effervescing mineral water. Also **Seltzer water.** [< Nieder *Selters,* a village in sw Prussia]

sel·vage (sel′vij) *n.* The edge of a woven fabric so finished that it will not ravel. Also **sel′vedge.** [< SELF + EDGE]

Sem. Seminary; Semitic.

se·man·tic (si·man′tik) *adj.* **1** Of or pertaining to meaning. **2** Of, relating to, or according to semantics. [< Gk. *sēmainein* signify]

se·man·tics (si·man′tiks) *n. pl. (construed as sing.)* **1** *Ling.* The study of the meanings of speech forms, esp. of the development and changes in meaning of words and word groups. **2** *Logic* The study of the relation between signs or symbols and what they signify. —**se·man′ti·cist** *n.*

sem·a·phore (sem′ə·fôr, -fōr) *n.* An apparatus for giving signals, as with movable arms, disks, flags, or lanterns. —*v.t.* To send by semaphore. [< Gk. *sēma* a sign + *pherein* carry] —**sem′a·phor′ic** (-fôr′ik, -for′ik) or **·i·cal** *adj.*

sem·blance (sem′bləns) *n.* **1** An outward, sometimes deceptive appearance; look. **2** A representation, likeness, or resemblance. **3** The barest trace; modicum. [< OF *sembler* seem]

se·men (sē′mən) *n.* The sperm-containing fluid of male animals. [< L *serere* sow]

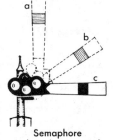

Semaphore
a. clear. b. approach.
c. stop.

se·mes·ter (si·mes′tər) *n.* Either of the two periods of approximately 18 weeks into which an academic year is divided. [< L *sex* six + *mensis* month] —**se·mes′tral** *adj.*

semi- *prefix* **1** Partly; not fully: *semicivilized.* **2** Exactly half: *semicircle.* **3** Occurring twice (in the period specified): *semiweekly.* [< L]

sem·i·an·nu·al (sem′ē·an′yo͞o·əl, sem′ī-) *adj.* Occurring, issued, etc., twice a year or every six months. —**sem′i·an′·nu·al·ly** *adv.*

sem·i·breve (sem′ē·brēv′, sem′ī-) *n. Music* WHOLE NOTE.

sem·i·cir·cle (sem′i·sûr′kəl, sem′ē-) *n.* 1 A half-circle; an arc of 180°. 2 Anything formed or arranged in a half-circle. —**sem′i·cir′cu·lar** *adj.* —**sem′i·cir′cu·lar·ly** *adv.*

semicircular canal Any of three fluid-filled tubes in the inner ear which serve as the organ of balance. •See EAR.

sem·i·civ·i·lized (sem′ē·siv′ə·līzd, sem′ī-) *adj.* Partly civilized.

sem·i·co·lon (sem′i·kō′lən, sem′ē-) *n.* A mark (;) of punctuation, indicating a greater degree of separation than the comma but less than the period.

sem·i·con·duc·tor (sem′ē·kən·duk′tər, sem′ī-) *n.* 1 One of a class of crystalline solids, as germanium or silicon, having an electrical conductivity intermediate between conductors and insulators, used in making transistors and related devices. 2 A transistor or related device.

sem·i·con·scious (sem′ē·kon′shəs, sem′ī-) *adj.* Partly conscious; not fully aware or responsive. —**sem′i·con′scious·ly** *adv.* —**sem′i·con′scious·ness** *n.*

sem·i·de·tached (sem′ē·di·tacht′, sem′ī-) *adj.* Joined to another on one side only, as two houses built side by side with one common wall.

sem·i·fi·nal (sem′ē·fī′nəl, sem′ī-) *adj.* Next before the final, as in a series of competitions. —*n.* 1 A semifinal match. 2 A semifinal round. —**sem′i·fi′nal·ist** *n.*

sem·i·flu·id (sem′ē·floo′id, sem′ī-) *adj.* Fluid, but thick and viscous. —*n.* A thick, viscous fluid.

sem·i·liq·uid (sem′ē·lik′wid, sem′ī-) *adj. & n.* SEMIFLUID.

sem·i·month·ly (sem′ē·munth′lē, sem′ī-) *adj.* Taking place, issued, etc., twice a month. —*n. pl.* ·**lies** A publication issued twice a month. —*adv.* Twice monthly.

sem·i·nal (sem′ə·nəl) *adj.* 1 Of, pertaining to, or containing seed or semen. 2 Like seed in having or contributing to the potential for future development. [< L *semen* semen, seed] —**sem′i·nal·ly** *adv.* —**Syn.** 2 original, originative, germinal, germinative.

sem·i·nar (sem′ə·när′) *n.* 1 A group of students at a college or university, meeting regularly with a professor for informal discussion of research problems. 2 A course thus conducted. 3 A room in which such a course is conducted. 4 Any informal meeting to discuss a particular topic, problem, etc. [< L *seminarium* seed plot]

sem·i·nar·y (sem′ē·ner′ē) *n. pl.* ·**nar·ies** 1 A school of theology. 2 A boarding school, esp. for young women. 3 A place where anything is nurtured. [< L *seminarium* a seed plot]

sem·i·na·tion (sem′ə·nā′shən) *n.* 1 The act of sowing or spreading seeds. 2 Propagation. [< L *semen* a seed, semen]

sem·i·nif·er·ous (sem′ə·nif′ər·əs) *adj.* 1 Carrying or containing semen. 2 Seed-bearing.

Sem·i·nole (sem′ə·nōl) *n. pl.* ·**noles** or ·**nole** One of a Florida tribe of North American Indians of Muskhogean linguistic stock.

sem·i·of·fi·cial (sem′ē·ə·fish′əl, sem′ī-) *adj.* Having partial official authority or sanction; official to some extent. —**sem′i·of·fi′cial·ly** *adv.*

sem·i·per·me·a·ble (sem′ē·pûr′mē·ə·bəl, sem′ī-) *adj.* Selectively permeable; preventing passage of larger molecules, as membranes in osmosis.

sem·i·pre·cious (sem′ē·presh′əs, sem′ī-) *adj.* Designating a gem that is not as valuable as one classified precious.

sem·i·pri·vate (sem′ē·prī′vit, sem′ī-) *adj.* Partly private: said esp. of a hospital room with two, three, or four beds.

sem·i·pro (sem′ē·prō′, sem′ī-) *adj. & n.* SEMIPROFESSIONAL.

sem·i·pro·fes·sion·al (sem′ē·prə·fesh′ən·əl, sem′ī-) *adj.* 1 Taking part in a sport or other activity for pay but not on a full-time basis. 2 Engaged in by semiprofessional players. —*n.* A semiprofessional player, etc.

sem·i·qua·ver (sem′ē·kwā′vər, sem′ī-) *n.* SIXTEENTH NOTE.

sem·i·skilled (sem′ē·skild′, sem′ī-) *adj.* Partly skilled.

sem·i·sol·id (sem′ē·sol′id, sem′ī-) *adj.* Partly solid; highly viscous. —*n.* A semisolid substance.

Sem·ite (sem′īt, *esp. Brit.* sē′mīt) *n.* 1 A person considered as a descendant of Shem. 2 One of a people of sw Asia, now represented by the Jews and Arabs, but originally including the ancient Babylonians, Assyrians, Arameans, Phoenicians, etc.

Se·mit·ic (sə·mit′ik) *adj.* Of, pertaining to, or characteristic of the Semites or their languages. —*n.* 1 The Semitic family of languages. 2 Any of these languages, including Arabic, Hebrew, Amharic, Aramaic, etc.

Sem·i·tism (sem′ə·tiz′əm) *n.* 1 A Semitic word or idiom. 2 Semitic practices, opinions, or customs collectively. 3 Any political or economic policy favoring the Jews.

sem·i·tone (sem′ē·tōn′, sem′ī-) *n. Music* 1 The tone at an interval equal to half a tone in the standard diatonic scale. 2 Such an interval; a half step. —**sem′i·ton′ic** (-ton′ik) *adj.*

sem·i·trop·i·cal (sem′ē·trop′i·kəl, sem′ī-) *adj.* Somewhat characteristic of the tropics.

sem·i·vow·el (sem′i·vou′əl) *n.* A vowellike sound used as a consonant, as (w), (y), and (r).

sem·i·week·ly (sem′ē·wēk′lē, sem′ī-) *adj.* Issued, occurring, done, etc., twice a week. —*n. pl.* ·**lies** A publication issued twice a week. —*adv.* Twice a week.

sem·o·li·na (sem′ə·lē′nə) *n.* Coarse-ground wheat flour, used in making pasta. [< L *simila* fine flour]

sem·per fi·de·lis (sem′pər fi·dā′lis) *Latin* Always faithful: motto of the U.S. Marine Corps.

sem·per pa·ra·tus (sem′pər pə·rä′təs, -pə·rā′-) *Latin* Always prepared: motto of the U.S. Coast Guard.

sem·pi·ter·nal (sem′pə·tûr′nəl) *adj.* Enduring or existing to all eternity; everlasting. [< L *semper* always] —**sem′pi·ter′nal·ly** *adv.* —**sem′pi·ter′ni·ty** *n.*

sen (sen) *n.* A Japanese coin or unit of currency, equal to ¹/₁₀₀ of a yen.

Sen., sen. senate; senator; senior.

sen·ate (sen′it) *n.* 1 *Usu. cap.* The upper branch of many national or state legislative bodies, as in the U.S. 2 A legislative body, as at a university; council. 3 A body of distinguished or venerable men often possessing legislative functions. 4 The highest governing body of the ancient Roman state. [< L *senatus*, lit., a council of old men]

sen·a·tor (sen′ə·tər) *n.* A member of a senate. —**sen′a·to′ri·al** *adj.* —**sen′a·to′ri·al·ly** *adv.* —**sen′a·tor·ship′** *n.*

send (send) *v.* **sent, send·ing** *v.t.* 1 To cause or enable to go: to *send* a messenger; to *send* one's daughter to medical school. 2 To cause to be conveyed; transmit; forward: to *send* a letter. 3 To cause to issue; emit or discharge, as heat, smoke, etc.: with *forth, out,* etc. 4 To drive by force; impel. 5 To cause to come, happen, etc.; grant: God *send* us peace. 6 To bring into a specified state or condition: The decision *sent* him into a panic. 7 To transmit, as an electric or magnetic signal. 8 *Slang* To thrill or delight. —*v.i.* 9 To dispatch an agent, messenger, or message. —**send for** To summon or order by a message or messenger. —**send packing** To dismiss abruptly or roughly. [< OE *sendan*] —**send′er** *n.*

send-off (send′ôf′, -of′) *n.* 1 The act of sending off; a start given to someone or something. 2 *Informal* A demonstration of friendship, enthusiasm, etc., toward someone beginning a new venture.

send-up (send′up′) *n. Brit. Slang* A parody; takeoff.

Sen·e·ca (sen′ə·kə) *n.* One of a tribe of North American Indians of Iroquoian stock, the largest tribe of the Five Nations, still living in New York and Ontario.

se·nes·cent (si·nes′ənt) *adj.* Growing old. [< L *senex* old] —**se·nes′cence** *n.*

sen·e·schal (sen′ə·shəl) *n.* A steward or major-domo in charge of the household of a medieval prince or noble. [< OF]

se·nile (sē′nīl, sen′īl) *adj.* Of, pertaining to, proceeding from, or characteristic of old age, esp. pertaining to or exhibiting certain mental infirmities often resulting from old age. [< L *senex* old] —**se′nile·ly** *adv.* —**se·nil·i·ty** (sə·nil′ə·tē) *n.*

sen·ior (sēn′yər) *adj.* 1 Older in years; elder; after personal names (usu. abbreviated *Sr.*), to denote the elder of two related persons of the same name, esp. a father and

his son. **2** Longer in service or superior in rank or dignity. **3** Of or pertaining to a senior or seniors. —*n.* **1** One older in years, longer in office, or more advanced in rank or dignity than another. **2** Any elderly person. **3** A member of a graduating class. [< L *senior* older]

senior citizen An elderly person, esp. one of or over the age of retirement.

sen·ior·i·ty (sēn·yôr′ə·tē, -yor′-) *n. pl.* **·ties 1** The state or condition of being senior. **2** The status or priority one achieves by length of service (as in a business firm).

sen·na (sen′ə) *n.* **1** A cathartic obtained from certain species of cassia. **2** Any of various cassia plants. [< Ar. *sanā*]

se·ñor (sā·nyôr′) *n. pl.* **·ño·res** (-nyō′rās) *Spanish* **1** A title of courtesy equivalent to *Mr.* or *Sir.* **2** A man; gentleman.

se·ño·ra (sā·nyō′rä) *n. Spanish* **1** A title of courtesy equivalent to *Mrs.* or *Madam.* **2** A woman; lady.

se·ño·ri·ta (sā′nyō·rē′tä) *n. Spanish* **1** A title of courtesy equivalent to *Miss.* **2** An unmarried woman; young lady.

sen·sa·tion (sen·sā′shən) *n.* **1 a** A mental event due to stimulation of a sense organ, as hearing, taste, etc. **b** The capacity to respond to such stimulation. **2** A state of mind induced by indeterminate stimuli: a *sensation* of fear. **3** A state of interest or excitement. **4** That which produces such a state of interest or excitement. [< L *sensus* sense]

sen·sa·tion·al (sen·sā′shən·əl) *adj.* **1** Of or pertaining to the senses or sensation. **2** Causing excitement; startling; thrilling. **3** Tending to shock, startle, etc., esp. by lurid or melodramatic details, techniques, etc. **4** *Informal* Excellent, great, etc. —**sen·sa′tion·al·ly** *adv.*

sen·sa·tion·al·ism (sen·sā′shən·əl·iz′əm) *n.* **1** *Philos.* The theory that all knowledge has a sensory basis. **2** The use of details, techniques, etc., that are intended to shock, or startle, as in literature, motion pictures, etc. —**sen·sa′tion·al·ist** *n.* —**sen·sa′tion·al·is′tic** *adj.*

sense (sens) *n.* **1** Any of the faculties of man and animals, specialized to receive and transmit external or internal stimuli, as sound, hunger, etc.; sight, touch, taste, hearing, and smell. **2** A perception or feeling produced by the senses. **3** A special capacity to perceive, appreciate, estimate, etc.: a *sense* of humor. **4** A somewhat vague perception or feeling: a *sense* of danger. **5** Rational perception or discrimination; awareness; realization: a *sense* of wrong. **6** Normal power of mind or understanding: The fellow has no *sense.* **7** That which is in accord with reason and good judgment: to talk *sense.* **8** Signification; meaning. **9** One of several meanings of the same word or phrase. **10** The opinion or judgment, as of a majority: the *sense* of the meeting. —*v.t.* **sensed, sens·ing 1** To perceive; become aware of. **2** *Informal* To comprehend; understand. [< L *sensus* perception, p.p. of *sentire* feel]

sense·less (sens′lis) *adj.* **1** Unconscious; incapable of feeling or perception. **2** Devoid of good sense, knowledge, or meaning: a *senseless* remark. **3** Without apparent cause or reason: a *senseless* crime. —**sense′less·ly** *adv.* —**sense′·less·ness** *n.*

sense organ A structure specialized to receive sense impressions, as the eye, nose, ear, etc.

sen·si·bil·i·ty (sen′sə·bil′ə·tē) *n. pl.* **·ties 1** The power to receive physical sensations. **2** A special susceptibility or sensitiveness to outside influences or mental impressions, as of pleasure or pain. **3** An awareness of and ability to respond to something (as an emotion or moral value). **4** Discriminating or excessive sensitivity in taste and emotion, with especial responsiveness to pathos.

sen·si·ble (sen′sə·bəl) *adj.* **1** Possessed of good mental perception; wise. **2** Capable of physical sensation; sensitive: *sensible* to pain. **3** Perceptible through the senses: *sensible* heat. **4** Perceptible to the mind. **5** Emotionally or mentally sensitive; aware. **6** Great enough to be perceived; appreciable. [< L *sensus*, p.p. of *sentire* feel, perceive] —**sen′si·ble·ness** *n.* —**sen′si·bly** *adv.*

sen·si·tive (sen′sə·tiv) *adj.* **1** Of or pertaining to the senses or sensation. **2** Receptive and responsive to sensations. **3** Responding readily to sensations, esp. of a particular kind: a *sensitive* ear. **4** Acutely receptive or responsive to the quality or strength of attitudes, feelings, or relationships. **5** Capable of appreciating aesthetic or intellec-

tual subtleties. **6** Easily irritated; tender: *sensitive* skin. **7** Hurt; sore. **8** Reacting excessively, as to an agent or substance: *sensitive* to insect bites. **9** Apt to take offense on slight provocation; touchy. **10** Capable of indicating very slight changes or differences; delicate: a *sensitive* barometer. **11** Readily fluctuating or tending to fluctuate: a *sensitive* stock market. [< L *sensus* sense] —**sen′si·tive·ly** *adv.* —**sen′si·tive·ness, sen′si·tiv′i·ty** *n.*

sensitive plant A tropical species of mimosa whose leaves close at a touch.

sen·si·tize (sen′sə·tīz) *v.t.* **·tized, ·tiz·ing 1** To make sensitive, esp., in photography, to make sensitive to light, as a plate or film. **2** *Med.* To make susceptible to an allergen. —**sen′si·ti·za′tion, sen′si·tiz′er** *n.*

sen·so·ri·um (sen·sôr′ē·əm, -sō′rē-) *n. pl.* **·ri·a** (-ē·ə) The entire sensory apparatus of an organism. [< L *sensus* sense]

sen·so·ry (sen′sər·ē) *adj.* **1** Of or pertaining to the senses or sensation. **2** AFFERENT. Also **sen·so·ri·al** (sen·sôr′ē·əl, -sō′rē-).

sen·su·al (sen′shoo·əl) *adj.* **1** Of or pertaining to the senses or their gratification; fleshly; carnal. **2** Unduly indulgent to the appetites or senses. **3** Caused by or preoccupied with bodily or sexual pleasure. [< L *sensus* perception] —**sen′su·al·ly** *adv.*

sen·su·al·ism (sen′shoo·əl·iz′əm) *n.* **1** Frequent or excessive indulgence in sensual pleasures. **2** *Philos.* A system of ethics holding that sensual pleasures are the highest good. —**sen′su·al·ist** *n.* —**sen′su·al·is′tic** *adj.*

sen·su·al·i·ty (sen′shoo·al′ə·tē) *n.* **1** The state of being sensual. **2** Sensual indulgence; lewdness; lasciviousness.

sen·su·al·ize (sen′shoo·əl·īz′) *v.t.* **·ized, ·iz·ing** To make sensual. *Brit. sp.* **sen′su·al·ise′.** —**sen′su·al·i·za′tion** *n.*

sen·su·ous (sen′shoo·əs) *adj.* **1** Of, pertaining or appealing to, or perceived or caused by the senses. **2** Keenly appreciative of or susceptible to the pleasures of sensation. —**sen′su·ous·ly** *adv.* —**sen′su·ous·ness** *n.*

sent (sent) *p.t. & p.p.* of SEND.

sen·tence (sen′təns) *n.* **1** A determination; opinion, esp. one expressed formally. **2** A final judgment, esp. one pronounced by a court. **3** The penalty pronounced upon a convicted person. **4** *Gram.* A word or group of words expressing a complete thought in the form of a declaration, a question, a command, a wish or an exclamation, usu. beginning with a capital letter and concluding with proper end punctuation. —*v.t.* **·tenced, ·tenc·ing** To pass sentence upon; condemn to punishment. [< L *sententia* opinion< *sentire* feel, be of opinion] —**sen′tenc·er** *n.* —**sen·ten·tial** (sen·ten′shəl) *adj.*

sen·ten·tious (sen·ten′shəs) *adj.* **1** Saying much in few words; terse; pithy. **2** Habitually using or full of aphoristic language. **3** Habitually using or full of moralistic language. [< L *sententia* opinion] —**sen·ten′tious·ly** *adv.* —**sen·ten′tious·ness** *n.*

sen·ti·ent (sen′shē·ənt, -shənt) *adj.* Possessing the powers of feeling or perception. [< L *sentire* feel] —**sen′ti·ence** *n.* —**sen′ti·ent·ly** *adv.*

sen·ti·ment (sen′tə·mənt) *n.* **1** Noble, tender, or refined feeling; delicate sensibility, esp. as expressed in a work of art. **2** A complex of opinions and feelings used as a basis for judgment or action. **3** A mental attitude, judgment, or thought often conditioned by feeling more than reason. **4** SENTIMENTALITY. **5** The meaning of something said, as distinguished from its expression. **6** A thought or wish phrased in conventional language, as a toast. [< L *sentire* feel]

sen·ti·men·tal (sen′tə·men′təl) *adj.* **1** Of, pertaining to, caused by, having, or showing sentiment. **2** Experiencing, displaying, or given to sentiment in an extravagant or maudlin manner. —**sen′ti·men′tal·ism, sen′ti·men′tal·ist** *n.* —**sen′ti·men′tal·ly** *adv.*

sen·ti·men·tal·i·ty (sen′tə·men·tal′ə·tē) *n. pl.* **·ties. 1** The state or quality of being overly sentimental, esp. in a superficial or maudlin way. **2** An expression of this.

sen·ti·men·tal·ize (sen′tə·men′təl·īz) *v.* **·ized, ·iz·ing** *v.t.* **1** To regard or treat with sentiment. —*v.i.* **2** To behave sentimentally.

sen·ti·nel (sen′tə·nəl) *n.* A guard, esp. a sentry. —*v.t.* **·neled** or **·nelled, ·nel·ing** or **·nel·ling 1** To watch over as a

sentinel. **2** To protect or furnish with sentinels. **3** To station or appoint as a sentinel. [< LL *sentinare* avoid danger < *sentire* perceive]

sen·try (sen′trē) *n. pl.* **·tries 1** A guard, esp. a soldier placed on guard to see that only authorized persons pass his post and to give warning of approaching danger. **2** The guard kept by a sentry. [? var. of SENTINEL]

Sep. September; Septuagint.

sep. sepal; separate; separated.

se·pal (sē′pəl) *n. Bot.* Any of the individual leaves of a calyx. [< NL *sepa* covering + *petalum* a petal] —**sep·a·line** (sep′-ə·lin, -līn), **sep′a·lous**, **se′paled**, **se′palled** *adj.*

Sepals of flower

sep·a·ra·ble (sep′ər·ə·bəl, sep′·rə-) *adj.* Capable of being separated or divided. —**sep′a·ra·bil′i·ty**, **sep′a·ra·ble·ness** *n.* —**sep′a·ra·bly** *adv.*

sep·a·rate (sep′ə·rāt) *v.* **·rat·ed, ·rat·ing** *v.t.* **1** To set apart; sever; disjoin. **2** To keep apart; divide: The Hudson River *separates* New York from New Jersey. **3** To divide into components, parts, etc. **4** To isolate or obtain from a compound, mixture, etc.: to *separate* the wheat from the chaff. **5** To consider separately; distinguish between. **6** *Law* To part by separation. —*v.i.* **7** To become divided or disconnected; draw apart. **8** To part company; sever an association. **9** To cease living together as man and wife. **10** To break up into component parts, as a mixture. —*adj.* (sep′ər·it, -′rit) **1** Existing or considered apart from others; distinct; individual. **2** Detached; disunited. **3** Existing independently; not related. —*n.pl.* Garments to be worn in various combinations, as skirts and blouses. [< L *se-* apart + *parare* prepare] —**sep′a·rate·ly** *adv.* —**sep′a·rate·ness**, **sep·a·ra′tor** *n.* —**sep′a·ra′tive** (-rā′tiv, -ə·rə·tiv) *adj.*

sep·a·ra·tion (sep′ə·rā′shən) *n.* **1** The act or process of separating. **2** The state of being separated. **3** A gap or dividing line. **4** *Law* Relinquishment of cohabitation between husband and wife by mutual consent.

sep·a·ra·tist (sep′ər·ə·tist, sep′rə-) *n.* One who advocates or upholds separation, esp. political, racial, or religious separation. Also **sep′a·ra′tion·ist.** —**sep′a·ra·tism** *n.*

Sep·a·ra·tist (sep′ər·ə·tist, sep′rə-) *n. Can.* One who believes in or supports the withdrawal of a province, esp. Quebec, from Confederation.

Se·phar·dim (si·fär′dim) *n. pl.* The Spanish and Portuguese Jews or their descendants. Also **Se·phar′a·dim** (-ə·dim). [< Hebrew *sephārādhīm* < *Sepharadh, Obad.* 1:20, a country identified with Spain] —**Se·phar′dic** *adj.*

se·pi·a (sē′pē·ə) *n.* **1** A reddish brown pigment prepared from the ink of certain cuttlefish. **2** The color of this pigment. **3** A picture done in this color. —*adj.* Executed in or colored like sepia. [< Gk. *sēpia* cuttlefish]

se·poy (sē′poi) *n.* Formerly, a native Indian soldier in the British or other European army. [< Pers. *sipāh* army]

sep·sis (sep′sis) *n.* The presence of pathogenic microorganisms or their toxins in the blood or tissues. [< Gk. *sēpein* make putrid]

sep·ta (sep′tə) *n. pl.* of SEPTUM.

Sep·tem·ber (sep·tem′bər) *n.* The ninth month of the year, containing 30 days. [< L *septem* seven]

sep·te·nar·y (sep′tə·ner′ē) *adj.* Consisting of, pertaining to, or being seven. —*n. pl.* **·nar·ies** A group of seven things of any kind. [< L *septeni* seven each]

sep·ten·ni·al (sep·ten′ē·əl) *adj.* **1** Recurring every seven years. **2** Continuing or capable of lasting seven years. —**sep·ten′ni·al·ly** *adv.*

sep·tet (sep·tet′) *n.* **1** A group or set of seven, esp. seven musical performers. **2** *Music* A composition for such a group. Also **sep·tette′.** [< L *septem* seven]

sep·tic (sep′tik) *adj.* **1** Of, pertaining to, or caused by sepsis. **2** Productive of putrefaction; putrid. Also **sep′ti·cal.**

sep·ti·ce·mi·a (sep′tə·sē′mē·ə) *n.* BLOOD POISONING. Also **sep′ti·cae′mi·a.** [< Gk. *sēptikos* putrefactive + *haima* blood] —**sep′ti·ce′mic** (-sē′mik) *adj.*

septic tank A tank in which sewage is held until decomposed by anaerobic bacteria.

sep·til·lion (sep·til′yən) *n. & adj.* See NUMBER. [< L *sept(em)* + F *(m)illion* a million] —**sep·til′lionth** *adj., n.*

sep·tu·a·ge·nar·i·an (sep′tᵛoo·ə·jə·nâr′ē·ən, sep′tə·wäj′ə-) *n.* A person 70 years old, or between 70 and 80. [< L *septuaginta* seventy]

Sep·tu·a·ges·i·ma (sep′tə·wə·jes′ə·mə, -jā′zə-) *n.* The third Sunday before Lent. Also **Septuagesima Sunday.** [< L, seventieth]

Sep·tu·a·gint (sep′tᵛoo·ə·jint′, sep′tə·wə-) *n.* An ancient Greek version of the Old Testament, made between 280 and 130 B.C. [< L *septuaginta* seventy < a tradition that it was produced in 70 days by a group of 72 scholars]

sep·tum (sep′təm) *n. pl.* **·ta** (-tə) A partition between two masses of tissue or two cavities: the nasal *septum.* [< L *sepes* a hedge] —**sep′tal** *adj.*

sep·tu·ple (sep′tᵛoo·pəl, sep·tᵛoo′-) *adj.* **1** Consisting of seven; sevenfold. **2** Multiplied by seven; seven times repeated. —*v.t. & v.i.* **·pled, ·pling** To multiply by seven. —*n.* A number or sum seven times as great as another. [< L *septem* seven]

sep·ul·cher (sep′əl·kər) *n.* **1** A burial place; tomb; vault. **2** A receptacle for relics, esp. in an altar slab. —*v.t.* **·chered** or **·chred, ·cher·ing** or **·chring** To place in a grave; entomb; bury. Also **sep′ul·chre** (-kər). [< L *sepulcrum*]

se·pul·chral (si·pul′krəl) *adj.* **1** Of a sepulcher. **2** Dismal in color or aspect. **3** Low or melancholy in sound. —**se·pul′chral·ly** *adv.*

seq. sequel.

seq., seqq. the following (L *sequens, sequentia*).

se·quel (sē′kwəl) *n.* **1** Something which follows; a continuation; development. **2** A narrative which, though entire in itself, develops from a preceding one. **3** A consequence; result. [< L *sequi* follow]

se·quence (sē′kwəns) *n.* **1** The process or fact of following in space, time, or thought; succession or order. **2** Order of succession; arrangement. **3** A number of things following one another, considered collectively; a series. **4** An effect or consequence. **5** A section of motion-picture film presenting a single episode, without time lapses or interruptions. [< L *sequi* follow]

se·quent (sē′kwənt) *n.* That which follows; a consequence; result. —*adj.* **1** Following in the order of time; succeeding. **2** Consequent; resultant. [< L *sequi* follow]

se·quen·tial (si·kwen′shəl) *adj.* **1** Characterized by or forming a sequence, as of parts. **2** SEQUENT. —**se·quen·ti·al·i·ty** (si·kwen′shē·al′ə·tē) *n.* —**se·quen′tial·ly** *adv.* —Syn. **1** consecutive, orderly, serial.

se·ques·ter (si·kwes′tər) *v.t.* **1** To place apart; separate. **2** To seclude; withdraw: often used reflexively. **3** *Law* To take (property) into custody until a controversy, claim, etc., is settled. **4** In international law, to confiscate and control (enemy property) by preemption. [< LL *sequestrare* remove, lay aside] —**se·ques′tered** *adj.*

se·ques·trate (si·kwes′trāt) *v.t.* **·trat·ed, ·trat·ing** SEQUESTER. —**se·ques·tra·tor** (sē′·kwes·trā′tər, si·kwes′trā·tər) *n.*

se·quin (sē′kwin) *n.* A spangle or small coinlike ornament sewn on clothing. —*v.t.* **se·quined** or **se·quinned, se·quin·ing** or **se·quin·ning** To decorate with sequins. [< Ar. *sikka* a coining-die]

se·quoi·a (si·kwoi′ə) *n.* Either of two species of gigantic coniferous evergreen trees of the western U.S. [< *Sikwayi,* 1770?–1843, American Indian who invented the Cherokee alphabet]

ser. serial; series; sermon.

se·ra (sir′ə) A *pl.* of SERUM.

se·ra·glio (si·ral′yō, -räl′-) *n. pl.* **·glios 1** That part of a sultan's palace where his harem lives. **2** The palace of a sultan. Also **se·rail** (se·rāl′). [< Ital. *serraglio* an enclosure]

Sequoia

se·ra·pe (se·rä′pē) *n.* A shawl or blanketlike outer garment worn in Latin America. [Sp.]

ser·aph (ser′əf) *n. pl.* **ser·aphs** or **ser·a·phim** (ser′ə·fim) An angel of the highest order, usu. represented as having six wings. [< Heb. *serāphīm*, pl.] **—se·raph·ic** (si·raf′ik) *adj.* **—se·raph′i·cal·ly** *adv.*

Ser·bo-Cro·a·tian (sûr′bō·krō·ā′shən) *n.* **1** The South Slavic language of Yugoslavia. **2** Any person whose native tongue is Serbo-Croatian. **—adj.** Of this language or people.

sere (sir) *adj.* Withered; dried up.

ser·e·nade (ser′ə·nād′) *n.* An evening piece, usu. the song of a lover beneath his lady's window. **—v.t. & v.i.** **·nad·ed, ·nad·ing** To entertain with a serenade. [< L *serenus* clear, serene] **—ser′e·nad′er** *n.*

Serape

ser·en·dip·i·ty (ser′ən·dip′ə·tē) *n.* The faculty of making fortunate discoveries by accident. [Coined by Horace Walpole (1754) after fairy tale characters] **—ser′en·dip′i·tous** *adj.*

se·rene (si·rēn′) *adj.* **1** Clear, bright, and fair; cloudless; untroubled. **2** Tranquil; calm; peaceful. **3** *Usu. cap.* Of exalted rank: used chiefly in royal titles: His *Serene* Highness. [< L *serenus*] **—se·rene′ly** *adv.* **—se·ren·i·ty** (si·ren′ə·tē), **se·rene′ness** *n.* **—Syn.** **2** composed, collected, placid.

serf (sûrf) *n.* **1** In feudal times, a person attached to the estate on which he lived. **2** Any person in servile subjection. [< L *servus* a slave] **—serf′dom, serf′age, serf′hood** *n.*

serge (sûrj) *n.* **1** A strong twilled woolen fabric woven with a diagonal rib on both sides. **2** A twilled silk or synthetic lining fabric. [< L *serica (lana)* (wool) of the Seres, an eastern Asian people]

ser·geant (sär′jənt) *n.* **1** See GRADE. **2** A police officer of rank next below a captain or lieutenant. **3** SERGEANT AT ARMS. [< L *servire* serve] **—ser′gean·cy, ser′geant·cy, ser′geant·ship** *n.*

sergeant at arms *pl.* **sergeants at arms** An officer in a legislative body, court, etc. who enforces order.

sergeant major *pl.* **sergeants major** See GRADE.

se·ri·al (sir′ē·əl) *adj.* **1** Of, like, or arranged in a series. **2** Published or presented in a series at regular intervals. **3** Of a serial or serials. **4** Of, pertaining to, or being atonal music consisting of a fixed series of tones based on the twelve-tone chromatic scale. **—n.** **1** A novel or other story regularly presented in successive installments, as in a magazine, on radio or television, or in motion pictures. **2** A periodical. **—se′ri·al·ly** *adv.*

se·ri·al·ism (sir′ē·əl·izm) *n.* Serial music. **—se′ri·al·ist** *n.*

se·ri·al·ize (sir′ē·əl·īz′) *v.t.* **·ized, ·iz·ing** To present in serial form. **—se′ri·al·i·za′tion** *n.*

serial number An identifying number assigned to a person, object, item of merchandise, etc.

se·ri·a·tim (sir′ē·ā′tim, ser′ē-) *adv.* One after another; in connected order; serially. [< L *series* series]

se·ries (sir′ēz) *n. pl.* **se·ries** **1** An arrangement or connected succession of related things placed in space or happening in time one after the other: a *series* of games; a *series* of lakes. **2** *Math.* The indicated sum of any finite set of terms or of an ordered infinite set of terms. **3** *Chem.* A group of related compounds or elements showing an orderly succession of changes in composition or structure. **4** *Electr.* An arrangement of electric devices in which the current flows through each in order. [L < *serere* join]

ser·if (ser′if) *n. Printing* A light line or stroke crossing or projecting from the end of a main line or stroke in a letter. [< L *scribere* write]

se·ri·o·com·ic (sir′ē·ō·kom′ik) *adj.* Mingling the comic with the serious. Also **se′ri·o·com′i·cal.** **—se′ri·o·com′i·cal·ly** *adv.*

se·ri·ous (sir′ē·əs) *adj.* **1** Grave and earnest in quality, feeling, or disposition; thoughtful; sober. **2** Being or done in earnest; not jesting or joking. **3** Involving much work, thought, difficulty, etc.: a *serious* problem. **4** Of grave importance; weighty. **5** Attended with considerable danger or loss: a *serious* accident. [< L *serius*] **—se′ri·ous·ly** *adv.* **—se′ri·ous·ness** *n.* **—Syn.** **1** sedate, staid, solemn, grim. **3** complex, complicated, involved, hard, troublesome.

ser·jeant (sär′jənt) *n. Brit.* SERGEANT.

ser·mon (sûr′mən) *n.* **1** A discourse, usu. based on a passage or text of the Bible, delivered as part of a church service. **2** Any serious talk or exhortation, as on duty, morals, etc. [< L *sermo* talk] **—ser·mon·ic** (sər·mon′ik) *adj.*

ser·mon·ize (sûr′mən·īz) *v.t. & v.i.* **·ized, ·iz·ing** To deliver sermons (to). **—ser′mon·iz′er** *n.*

Sermon on the Mount The discourse of Jesus found recorded in *Matt.* 5–7.

se·rol·o·gy (si·rol′ə·jē) *n.* The science of serums and their actions. [< SER(UM) + -LOGY] **—se·ro·log·i·cal** (sir′ə·loj′i·kəl) *adj.*

se·rous (sir′əs) *adj.* Pertaining to, producing, or resembling serum.

ser·pent (sûr′pənt) *n.* **1** A snake, esp. a poisonous or large one. **2** A treacherous person. [< L *serpere* to creep]

ser·pen·tine (sûr′pən·tīn, -tēn) *adj.* **1** Of or like a serpent. **2** Winding; zigzag. **3** Subtle; cunning. **—n.** A massive or fibrous, often mottled green or yellow, magnesium silicate.

ser·rate (ser′āt, -it) *adj.* Having sawlike teeth, as the margins of certain leaves. Also **ser′rat·ed.** [< L *serra* a saw] • See LEAF.

ser·ra·tion (se·rā′shən) *n.* **1** The state of being edged as with saw teeth. **2** A single projection of a serrate edge, or a series of such projections. Also **ser·ra·ture** (ser′ə·chər). [< L *serra* a saw]

ser·ried (ser′ēd) *adj.* Compacted in rows or ranks, as soldiers in company formation. [< LL *serrare* to lock]

se·rum (sir′əm) *n. pl.* **se·rums** or **se·ra** (sir′ə) **1** The fluid constituent of blood. **2** The serum of the blood of an animal which has developed immunity to a specific pathogen. **3** WHEY. **4** Any watery plant or animal secretion. [L, whey]

ser·vant (sûr′vənt) *n.* **1** A person employed to assist in domestic matters, sometimes living within the employer's house. **2** A government worker. [< OF *servir* to serve]

serve (sûrv) *v.* **served, serv·ing** *v.t.* **1** To work for as a servant. **2** To be of service to; wait on. **3** To promote the interests of; aid; help: to *serve* one's country. **4** To obey and give homage to: to *serve* God. **5** To satisfy the requirements of; suffice for. **6** To perform the duties connected with, as a public office. **7** To go through (a period of enlistment, term of punishment, etc.). **8** To furnish or provide, as with a regular supply. **9** To offer or bring food or drink to (a guest, etc.); wait on at table. **10** To bring and place on the table or distribute among guests, as food or drink. **11** To operate or handle; tend: to *serve* a cannon. **12** To copulate with: said of male animals. **13** In tennis, etc., to put (the ball) in play by hitting it to one's opponent. **14** *Law* **a** To deliver (a summons or writ) to a person. **b** To deliver a summons or writ to. **15** *Naut.* To wrap (a rope, stay, etc.), as with wire, cordage, etc., so as to strengthen or protect. **—v.i.** **16** To be a servant. **17** To perform the duties of any employment, office, etc. **18** To go through a term of service, as in the army or navy. **19** To offer or give food or drink, as to guests. **20** To wait on customers. **21** To be suitable or usable, as for a purpose; perform a function. **22** To be favorable, as weather. **23** In tennis, etc., to put the ball in play. **—n.** In tennis, etc.: **a** The delivering of the ball by striking it toward an opponent. **b** The turn of one who serves. [< L *servus* a slave]

serv·er (sûr′vər) *n.* **1** One who serves, as an attendant aiding a priest at low mass. **2** That which is used in serving, as a tray.

ser·vice (sûr′vis) *n.* **1** The act or occupation of serving. **2** The manner in which one serves or is served. **3** A division of employment, esp. of public or governmental employment: the diplomatic *service*. **4** Any branch of the armed forces. **5** A facility for meeting some public need: electric *service*. **6** Installation, maintenance, and repair provided for the buyer of something. **7** Assistance; aid; benefit: to be of *service*. **8** Often *pl.* A useful result or product of labor which is not a tangible commodity: a doctor's *services*. **9** Often *pl.* A public exercise of worship. **10** A religious or civil ritual: the marriage *service*. **11** The music for a liturgical office or rite. **12** A set of articles for a particular purpose: a tea *service*. **13** *Naut.* The protective wire, cordage, etc., wrapped around a rope. **14** *Law* The legal com-

munication of a writ, process, or summons to a designated person. **15** In animal husbandry, the copulation of a female. —*adj.* **1** Pertaining to or for service. **2** Of, for, or used by servants or tradespeople: a *service* entrance. **3** Of, pertaining to, or belonging to a military service: a *service* flag. **4** For rough or everyday usage. —*v.t.* **·viced, ·vic·ing** **1** To maintain or repair: to *service* a car. **2** To supply service to. **3** SERVE (def. 12). [< L *servus* a slave]

ser·vice·a·ble (sûr′vis·ə·bəl) *adj.* **1** That can serve a useful purpose; beneficial. **2** Capable of rendering long service; durable. —**ser′vice·a·ble·ness, ser′vice·a·bil′i·ty** *n.* —**ser′vice·a·bly** *adv.* —**Syn.** **1** practical, practicable, utilitarian, helpful.

ser·vice·man (sûr′vis·man′) *n. pl.* **·men** (-men′) **1** A member of one of the armed forces. **2** A man who performs services of maintenance, supply, repair, etc.: also **service man.**

service station **1** A place for supplying motor vehicles with gasoline, oil, etc., and often for doing auto maintenance and repair work. **2** A place for adjusting, repairing, or supplying parts for electrical and mechanical appliances.

ser·vi·ette (sûr′vē·et′, -vyet′) *n.* A table napkin. [< MF *servir* serve]

ser·vile (sûr′vil, -vil) *adj.* **1** Having the spirit of a slave; slavish; abject. **2** Of, pertaining to, or appropriate for slaves or servants: *servile* employment. [< L *servus* a slave] —**ser′vile·ly** *adv.* —**ser·vil′i·ty, ser′vile·ness** *n.* —**Syn.** **1** obsequious, fawning, groveling, cowering, submissive, cringing.

serv·ing (sûr′ving) *n.* **1** A portion of food for one person. **2** The act of one who or that which serves. —*adj.* Used for dealing out food.

ser·vi·tor (sûr′və·tər) *n.* One who waits upon and serves another; an attendant; follower; servant.

ser·vi·tude (sûr′və·t(y)o͞od) *n.* **1** The condition of a slave; slavery; bondage. **2** Enforced service as a punishment for crime: penal *servitude*. [< L *servus* a slave]

ser·vo·mech·a·nism (sûr′vō·mek′ə·niz′əm) *n.* Any of various devices using feedback in which a small input is amplified and used to control a machine, operation, process, etc. [< L *servus* slave + MECHANISM]

ses·a·me (ses′ə·mē) *n.* An East Indian plant bearing edible, oily seeds (**sesame seed**) that yield an oil (**sesame oil**) used in cooking. [< Gk. *sēsamon*]

ses·qui·cen·ten·ni·al (ses′kwi·sen·ten′ē·əl) *adj.* Of or pertaining to a century and a half. —*n.* A 150th anniversary, or its celebration. [< L *sesqui-* one half more + CEN-TENNIAL]

ses·sile (ses′il, -əl) *adj.* **1** *Bot.* Attached without a stalk, as a leaf. **2** *Zool. & Anat.* Attached at the base; sedentary. [< L *sessilis* sitting down, stunted] —**ses·sil′i·ty** *n.*

ses·sion (sesh′ən) *n.* **1** The sitting together of a legislative assembly, court, etc., for the transaction of business. **2** A single meeting or series of meetings of an assembly, court, etc. **3** In some schools, a term. **4** Any period of some specified activity: a *session* with the boss. [< L *sessus,* p.p. of *sedere* sit] —**ses′sion·al** *adj.* —**ses′sion·al·ly** *adv.*

ses·tet (ses·tet′) *n.* **1** The last six lines of a sonnet; also, any six-line stanza. **2** *Music* SEXTET. [< L *sextus* sixth]

set[1] (set) *v.* **set, set·ting** *v.t.* **1** To put in a certain place or position; place. **2** To put into a fixed, firm, or immovable position, condition, or state: to *set* brick; to *set* one's jaw. **3** To bring to a specified condition or state: *Set* your mind at ease; He *set* the barn afire; She has *set* her heart on being a doctor. **4** To restore to proper position for healing, as a broken bone. **5** To place in readiness for use: to *set* a trap. **6** To adjust according to a standard: to *set* a clock. **7** To adjust (an instrument, dial, etc.) to a particular calibration or position. **8** To place knives, forks, etc., on (a table) for a meal. **9** To bend the teeth of (a saw) to either side alternately. **10** To appoint or establish; prescribe: to *set* boundaries, regulations, fashions, etc. **11** To fix or establish a time for: We *set* our departure for noon. **12** To assign for performance, completion, etc.; to *set* a task. **13** To assign to some specific duty or function; appoint; sta-

tion: to *set* a guard. **14** To cause to sit. **15** To present or perform so as to be copied or emulated: to *set* the pace. **16** To give a specified direction to: He *set* his course for the Azores. **17** To put in place so as to catch the wind: to *set* the jib. **18** To place in a mounting or frame, as a gem. **19** To stud or adorn with gems: to *set* a crown with rubies. **20** To place (a hen) on eggs to hatch them. **21** To place (eggs) under a fowl or in an incubator for hatching. **22** To place (a price or value): with *by* or *on*: to *set* a price on an outlaw's head. **23** To arrange (hair), as with curlers, lotions, etc. **24** *Printing* **a** To arrange (type) for printing; compose. **b** To put into type, as a sentence, manuscript, etc. **25** *Music* To compose music for (words) or write words for (existing music). **26** To describe (a scene) as taking place: to *set* the scene in Monaco. **27** In the theater, to arrange (a stage) so as to depict a scene. **28** In some games, as bridge, to defeat. —*v.i.* **29** To go or pass below the horizon, as the sun; to wane; decline. **31** To sit on eggs, as fowl. **32** To become firm; solidify; congeal. **33** To become fast, as a dye. **34** To begin to move, as on a journey: with *forth, out, off,* etc. **35** To begin: *Set* to work. **36** To have a specified direction; tend. **37** To hang or fit, as clothes. **38** To mend, as a broken bone. **39** *Regional* To sit. **40** *Bot.* To begin development or growth, as a rudimentary fruit. —**set against 1** To balance; compare. **2** To make unfriendly to; prejudice against. —**set off 1** To put apart by itself. **2** To serve as a contrast or foil for; enhance. **3** To make begin; set in motion. **4** To cause to explode. —**set out 1** To display; exhibit. **2** To lay out or plan. **3** To begin a journey. **4** To begin any enterprise. **5** To plant. —**set to 1** To start; begin. **2** To start fighting. —**set up 1** To place in an upright or high position. **2** To raise. **3** To place in power, authority, etc. **4 a** To construct or build. **b** To put together; assemble. **c** To found; establish. **5** To provide with the means to start a new business. **6** To cause to be heard: to *set up* a cry. **7** To propose or put forward (a theory, etc.). **8** To cause. **9** To work out a plan for. **10** To claim to be. **11 a** To pay for the drinks, etc., of; treat. **b** To pay for (drinks, etc.). **12** To encourage; exhilarate. —**set upon** To attack; assail. —*adj.* **1** Established by authority or agreement; prescribed; appointed: a *set* time or method. **2** Customary; conventional: a *set* phrase. **3** Deliberately and systematically conceived; formal: a *set* speech. **4** Fixed and motionless; rigid. **5** Firm in consistency. **6** Fixed in opinion or disposition; obstinate. **7** Formed; built; made: deep-*set* eyes. **8** Ready; prepared: to get *set*. —*n.* **1** The act or condition of setting. **2** Permanent change of form, as by bending, pressure, strain, etc. **3** The arrangement, tilt, or hang of a garment, hat, sail, etc. **4** Carriage or bearing: the *set* of his shoulders. **5** The sinking of a heavenly body below the horizon. **6** The direction of a current or wind. **7** A young plant ready for setting out. **8** Inclination of the mind; bent. **9** *Psychol.* A temporary condition assumed by an organism preparing for a particular response or activity. **10** An arrangement of the hair, as by curling. **11** In tennis, a group of games completed when one side wins six games, or, if tied at five games, wins either two more games consecutively or wins a tie breaker. [< OE *settan* cause to sit]

set[2] (set) *n.* **1** A number of persons regarded as associated through status, common interests, etc.: a new *set* of customers. **2** A social group having some exclusive character; coterie; clique: the fast *set*. **3** A number of things belonging together or customarily used together: a *set* of instruments. **4** A group of books or periodicals issued together or related by common authorship, subject, etc. **5** In jazz performances, the music played during one period of time without an intermission; also, the period of time. **6** In the theatre, motion pictures, etc., the complete assembly of properties, structures, etc., required in a scene. **7** Radio or television receiving equipment assembled for use. **8** *Math.* Any collection of elements, objects, or numbers. [< L *secta* a sect]

se·ta (sē′tə) *n. pl.* **·tae** (-tē) *Biol.* A bristle or bristlelike process. [< L] —**se·ta·ceous** (si·tā′shəs), **se′tose** *adj.*

set·back (set′bak′) *n.* **1** A misfortune or reversal, as in

progress. 2 An indentation or steplike arrangement of the upper levels of a tall building.

Seth (seth) In the Bible, the third son of Adam.

set·off (set′ôf′, -of′) *n.* 1 Something that offsets, balances, or compensates for something else. 2 Something that contrasts with or sets off something else. 3 A counterclaim or the discharge of a debt by a counterclaim. 4 *Archit.* A ledge; offset.

set piece 1 Something, as a passage in literature, music, etc., aimed at creating a brilliant effect. 2 A fireworks display. 3 A piece of scenery for the stage.

set·screw (set′skrōō′) *n.* 1 A screw so made that it can be screwed tightly against or into another surface to prevent movement. 2 A screw for regulating the tension of a spring or the opening of a valve.

set·tee (se·tē′) *n.* 1 A long wooden seat with a high back. 2 A sofa suitable for two or three people. [?< SETTLE]

set·ter (set′ər) *n.* 1 One who or that which sets. 2 One of a breed of medium-sized, silky-coated dogs trained to indicate the location of game birds while standing rigid.

set·ting (set′ing) *n.* 1 The position, degree, etc., at which something is set. 2 A frame or mounting, as for a jewel. 3 Physical environment or surroundings. 4 The scene, time, background, etc., as of a novel or play. 5 A number of eggs placed together for hatching. 6 The music composed for a poem, set of words, etc. 7 The tableware set out for one person.

set·tle (set′l) *v.* **·tled**, **·tling** *v.t.* 1 To put in order; set to rights; to *settle* affairs. 2 To establish or fix permanently or as if permanently: He *settled* himself on the couch. 3 To calm; quiet: to *settle* one's nerves. 4 To cause (sediment or dregs) to sink to the bottom. 5 To make firm or compact: to *settle* dust or ashes. 6 To make clear or transparent, as by causing sediment or dregs to sink. 7 To make quiet or orderly: One blow *settled* him. 8 To decide or determine finally, as an argument, legal case, etc. 9 To pay, as a debt; satisfy, as a claim. 10 To establish residents or residence in (a country, town, etc.). 11 To establish as residents. 12 To establish in a permanent occupation, home, etc. 13 *Law* To make over or assign (property) by legal act: with *on* or *upon.* —*v.i.* 14 To come to rest. 15 To sink gradually; subside. 16 To become clear by the sinking of sediment. 17 To become more firm by sinking. 18 To become established or located: The pain *settled* in his arm. 19 To establish one's abode or home. 20 To come to a decision; determine; resolve: with *on, upon,* or *with.* 21 To pay a bill, etc. —**settle down** 1 To start living a regular, orderly life, esp. after a period of wandering or irresponsibility. 2 To become quiet or orderly. —*n.* A long, wooden, high-backed bench, usu. with arms and sometimes having a chest from seat to floor. [< OE *setl* a seat]

Settle

set·tle·ment (set′l·mənt) *n.* 1 The act of settling or the condition of being settled. 2 An area newly colonized. 3 A small, usu. remote village. 4 *Law* **a** The act of assigning property, money, etc., to someone. **b** That which is thus assigned. 5 An agreement or adjustment, as of differences. 6 An urban welfare institution that provides various educational or recreational services to a community or neighborhood: also **settlement house.**

set·tler (set′lər) *n.* 1 One who establishes himself in a colony or new country. 2 One who settles or decides.

set·tlings (set′lingz) *n.pl.* Dregs; sediment.

set-to (set′tōō′) *n.* A bout at fighting, arguing, etc.

set-up (set′up′) *n.* 1 A system or plan, as of a business operation, etc. 2 The arrangement or assembly of a machine, piece of equipment, etc. 3 The elements or circumstances of a situation or plan. 4 Carriage of the body; posture. 5 Ice, soda water, etc., provided for those who furnish their own liquor. 6 A table setting. 7 *Informal* **a** A contest or match arranged so as to result in an easy victory. **b** Anything easy to accomplish.

sev·en (sev′ən) *n.* 1 The sum of six plus one; 7; VII. 2 A set or group of seven members. [< OE *seofon*] —**sev′en** *adj., pron.*

seven deadly sins Pride, lust, envy, anger, covetousness, gluttony, and sloth.

sev·en·fold (sev′ən·fōld′) *adj.* 1 Seven times as many or as great. 2 Made up of seven; septuple. 3 Folded seven times. —*adv.* In sevenfold manner or degree.

seven seas All the oceans of the world.

sev·en·teen (sev′ən·tēn′) *n.* 1 The sum of 16 plus 1; 17; XVII. 2 A set or group of 17 members. —**sev′en·teen′** *adj., pron.*

sev·en·teenth (sev′ən·tēnth′) *adj. & adv.* Next in order after the 16th. —*n.* 1 The element of an ordered set that corresponds to the number 17. 2 One of seventeen equal parts.

sev·enth (sev′ənth) *adj. & adv.* Next in order after the sixth. —*n.* 1 The element of an ordered set that corresponds to the number seven. 2 One of seven equal parts. 3 *Music* The interval between any tone and the seventh tone above or below in the diatonic scale. —*adv.* In the seventh order, place, or rank: also, in formal discourse, **sev′enth·ly.**

seventh heaven The highest condition of happiness. [< the highest heaven according to certain ancient cosmologies]

sev·en·ti·eth (sev′ən·tē·ith) *adj. & adv.* Tenth in order after the 60th. —*n.* 1 The element of an ordered set that corresponds to the number 70. 2 One of seventy equal parts.

sev·en·ty (sev′ən·tē) *n. pl.* **·ties** 1 The product of seven and ten; 70; LXX. 2 A set or group of 70 members. 3 *pl.* The numbers, years, etc., between 70 and 80. —**sev′en·ty** *adj., pron.*

sev·er (sev′ər) *v.t.* 1 To put or keep apart; separate. 2 To cut or break into two or more parts. 3 To break off; dissolve, as a relationship. —*v.i.* 4 To come or break apart or into pieces. 5 To go away or apart; separate. [< L *separare* separate] —**sev′er·a·ble** *adj.* —**sev′er·er** *n.*

sev·er·al (sev′ər·əl, sev′rəl) *adj.* 1 Being of an indefinite number, more than one or two, yet not large; divers. 2 Considered individually; single; separate. 3 Individually different; various or diverse. [< L *separ* separate]

sev·er·al·ly (sev′ər·əl·ē, sev′rəl·ē) *adv.* 1 Individually; separately. 2 Respectively.

sev·er·ance (sev′ər·əns, sev′rəns) *n.* The act of severing, or the condition of being severed.

severance pay Additional pay sometimes given to an employee who has been discharged.

se·vere (si·vir′) *adj.* **·ver·er**, **·ver·est** 1 Difficult; trying. 2 Unsparing; harsh; merciless: a *severe* punishment. 3 Conforming to rigid rules; extremely strict or accurate. 4 Serious and austere in disposition or manner; grave. 5 Austerely plain and simple, as in style, design, etc. 6 Causing sharp pain or anguish; extreme: *severe* hardship. —**se·vere′ness** *n.* [< L *severus*] —**se·vere′ly** *adv.*

se·ver·i·ty (si·ver′ə·tē) *n. pl.* **·ties** The quality or condition of being severe.

sew (sō) *v.* **sewed, sewed** or **sewn, sew·ing** *v.t.* 1 To make, mend, or fasten with needle and thread. 2 To enclose or secure by sewing. —*v.i.* 3 To work with needle and thread. —**sew up** 1 To mend by sewing. 2 *Informal* **a** To achieve absolute control or use of. **b** To make or be totally successful. [< OE *siwan, siowian*]

sew·age (sōō′ij) *n.* The waste matter carried off in sewers. [< SEW(ER) + -AGE]

sew·er (sōō′ər) *n.* 1 A conduit, usu. laid underground, to carry off drainage and excrement. 2 Any large public drain. [< OF *seuwiere* a channel from a fish pond]

sew·er·age (sōō′ər·ij) *n.* 1 A system of sewers. 2 Systematic draining by sewers. 3 SEWAGE.

sew·ing (sō′ing) *n.* 1 The act, business, or occupation of one who sews. 2 Material worked with needle and thread; needlework.

sewing circle A group of women meeting periodically to sew, usu. for some charitable purpose.

sewing machine A machine for stitching or sewing cloth, leather, etc.

sewn (sōn) A *p.p.* of SEW.

sex (seks) *n.* 1 Either of two divisions, male and female, by which organisms are distinguished with reference to the reproductive functions. 2 Males or females collectively. 3 The character of being male or female. 4 The activity or phenomena of life concerned with sexual de-

sire or reproduction. **5** *Informal* Any act affording sexual gratification, as sexual intercourse. —*adj. Informal* SEX-UAL. [< L *sexus*]

sex·a·ge·nar·i·an (sek'sə·jə·nâr'ē·ən) *adj.* Sixty years old, or between sixty and seventy. —*n.* A person of this age. [< L *sexageni* sixty each]

Sex·a·ges·i·ma (sek'sə·jes'ə·mə, -jā'zə-) *n.* The second Sunday before Lent. [L, sixtieth]

sex·a·ges·i·mal (sek'sə·jes'ə·məl) *adj.* Of or based on the number 60. [< L *sexagesimus < sexaginta* sixty]

sex appeal A physical quality or charm which attracts sexual interest.

sex chromosome Either of a pair of chromosomes associated with the determination of sex in plants and animals.

sex·ism (seks'iz·əm) *n.* Prejudice or discrimination against women. [< SEX + -ISM, on analogy with *racism*] —**sex'ist** *n, adj.*

sex·less (seks'lis) *adj.* **1** Having no sex; neuter. **2** Without sexual interest or qualities. —**sex'less·ly** *adv.* —**sex'less·ness** *n.*

sex linkage The presence on a sex chromosome of genes for certain nonsexual characteristics, resulting in the development of those characteristics in one sex only. —**sex-linked** (seks'lingkt') *adj.*

sex·ol·o·gy (seks·ol'ə·jē) *n.* The study of human sexual behavior. —**sex·o·log·ic** (sek'sə·loj'ik) or **·i·cal** *adj.* —**sex·ol'o·gist** *n.*

sex·ploi·ta·tion (seks'ploi·tā'shən) *n.* The commercial exploitation of interest in sex, as by means of pornography. [Blend of SEX + EXPLOITATION]

sex·pot (seks'pot) *n. Slang* A very sexy woman.

sext (sekst) *n.* One of the canonical hours; the office for the sixth hour or noon. [< L *sex* six]

sex·tant (seks'tənt) *n.* An instrument for measuring the angular distance between two objects, as between a heavenly body and the horizon, used esp. in determining latitude at sea. [< L *sextus* sixth]

Sextant
a. eyepiece.

sex·tet (seks·tet') *n.* **1** A group of six musical performers. **2** A musical composition for such a group. **3** Any collection of six persons or things. Also **sex·tette'.** [Alter. of SESTET]

sex·til·lion (seks·til'yən) *n. & adj.* See NUMBER. [< L *sex* six + F *(m)illion* a million]

sex·ton (seks'tən) *n.* An officer of a church having charge of maintenance and also of ringing the bells, overseeing burials, etc. [< Med. L *sacristanus* sacristan]

sex·tu·ple (sek·st^yōō'pəl, -stup'-, seks'too·pəl) *adj.* **1** Sixfold. **2** Multiplied by six; six times repeated. **3** *Music* Having six beats to the measure. —*v.t.* **·pled, ·pling** To multiply by six. —*n.* A number or sum six times as great as another. [< L *sextus* sixth] —**sex'tu·ply** *adv.*

sex·tu·plet (seks·tup'lit, -t^yōō'plit, seks'too·plit) *n.* **1** A set of six similar things. **2** One of six offspring produced at a single birth.

sex·u·al (sek'shōō·əl) *adj.* **1** Of, pertaining or peculiar to, characteristic of, or affecting sex, the sexes, or the organs or functions of sex. **2** Characterized by or having sex. [< L *sexus* sex] —**sex'u·al'i·ty** (-al'ə·tē) *n.* —**sex'u·al·ly** *adv.*

sexual intercourse 1 The sexual act, esp. between humans, in which the erect penis is introduced into the vagina for the ejaculation of semen and sexual gratification. **2** Any act of sexual connection, esp. between humans.

sex·y (sek'sē) *adj.* **sex·i·er, sex·i·est 1** *Informal* Provocative of sexual desire: a *sexy* dress; a *sexy* woman. **2** *Informal* Concerned in large or excessive degree with sex: a *sexy* novel. **3** *Slang* Interesting, exciting, or stimulating: Crime was the *sexiest* issue of the political campaign.

sf., sfz. sforzando.

sfor·zan·do (sfôr·tsän'dō) *adj. & adv. Music* Accented with sudden explosive force. —*n.* A sforzando note or chord. Also **sfor·za'to** (-tsä'tō). [Ital. < *sforzare* to force]

sg. s.g. senior grade; specific gravity.

sgd. signed.

Sgt. Sergeant.

sh (sh) *interj.* An exclamation requesting silence.

sh. share; sheep; sheet; shilling.

Shab·bat (shä·bät', shä'bəs) *n. pl.* **Shab·bat·im** (-bä'təm, -bô'səm) The Jewish Sabbath. [< Heb. *shabbāth*]

shab·by (shab'ē) *adj.* **·bi·er, ·bi·est 1** Threadbare, ragged. **2** Characterized by worn or ragged garments. **3** Mean; paltry. [< OE *sceabb* a scab] —**shab'bi·ly** *adv.* —**shab'bi·ness** *n.*

Sha·bu·oth (shä·vōō'ōth, shə·vōō'əs) *n.* The Jewish festival of Pentecost.

shack (shak) *n.* **1** A crudely built cabin or hut. **2** *Informal* A poorly built or designed house. —*v.i. Slang* To live or stay, usu. briefly, at a specific place. [?]

shack·le (shak'əl) *n.* **1** A bracelet or fetter for encircling and confining a limb or limbs. **2** *Usu. pl.* Any impediment or restraint. **3** One of various forms of fastenings, as a link for coupling railway cars. —*v.t.* **·led, ·ling 1** To restrain or confine with shackles; fetter. **2** To keep or restrain from free action or speech. **3** To connect or fasten with a shackle. [< OE *sceacul*] —**shack'ler** *n.*

Shackles

shad (shad) *n. pl.* **shad** Any of various anadromous fish related to the herring. [< OE *sceadd*]

shad·ber·ry (shad'ber'ē) *n. pl.* **·ries 1** SHADBUSH. **2** The fruit of the shadbush.

shad·bush (shad'bŏŏsh') *n.* Any of various early-blooming shrubs with white flowers and edible purple berries. Also **shad'blow'** (-blō). [So called because it flowers when the shad appear in U.S. rivers]

shade (shād) *v.* **shad·ed, shad·ing** *v.t.* **1** To screen from light or heat. **2** To make dim with or as with a shadow; darken; **3** To screen or protect with or as with a shadow. **4** To cause to change, pass, blend, or soften, by gradations. **5 a** To represent (degrees of shade, colors, etc.) by gradations of light or shading. **b** To represent varying shades, colors, etc., in (a picture of painting). **6** To make slightly lower, as a price. —*v.i.* **7** To change or vary by degrees. —*n.* **1** Relative darkness caused by the interception or partial absence of rays of light. **2** A place having such relative darkness. **3** That part of a drawing, painting, etc. represented as being relatively dark or in shadow. **4** A gradation of darkness or blackness in a color. **5** A minute difference, variation, or degree: *shades* of meaning. **6** A screen or cover that partially or totally shuts off light: a lamp *shade.* **7** A ghost or phantom. **8** *pl. Slang* SUNGLASSES. —**in** (or **into**) **the shade 1** In or into a shady place. **2** In or into a condition of inferiority, defeat, obscurity, etc. [< OE *sceadu* a shade]

shad·ing (shā'ding) *n.* **1** Protective against light or heat. **2** The representation pictorially of darkness, color, or depth. **3** A slight difference or variation.

shad·ow (shad'ō) *n.* **1** A comparative darkness within an illuminated area caused by the interception of light by an opaque body. **2** The dark figure or image thus produced on a surface: the *shadow* of a man. **3** The shaded portion of a picture. **4** A mirrored image: to see one's *shadow* in a pool. **5** A phantom, ghost, etc. **6** A faint representation or indication; a symbol: the *shadow* to things to come. **7** A remnant; vestige: *shadows* of his former glory. **8** An insignificant trace or portion: not a *shadow* of evidence. **9** Gloom or a saddening influence. **10** An inseparable companion. **11** One who trails or follows another, as a detective or spy. **12** A slight growth of beard, esp. in the phrase **five o'clock shadow.** —*v.t.* **1** To cast a shadow upon; shade. **2** To darken or make gloomy. **3** To represent or foreshow dimly or vaguely: with *forth* or *out.* **4** To follow closely or secretly; spy on. **5** To shade in painting, drawing, etc. —*adj.* Of or pertaining to a shadow cabinet. [< OE *sceadu* a shade] —**shad'ow·er** *n.*

shad·ow·box (shad'ō·boks') *v.i.* To spar with an imaginary opponent as a form of exercise. —**shad'ow·box'ing** *n.*

shadow box A small, open, framed cabinet, usu. hung on a wall to display knickknacks, etc.

shadow cabinet In the British or other parliamentary government, a group of opposition leaders who would assume specific cabinet positions if the government in power should fall.

shad·ow·y (shad′ō·ē) *adj.* **·ow·ier, ·ow·i·est** **1** Dark; shady. **2** Vague; dim. **3** Unreal; ghostly. **—shad′ow·i·ness** *n.*

shad·y (shā′dē) *adj.* **shad·i·er, shad·i·est** **1** Full of shade; casting a shade. **2** Shaded or sheltered. **3** Morally questionable; suspicious. **4** Quiet; hidden. **—shad′i·ness** *n.*

shaft (shaft, shäft) *n.* **1** The long narrow rod of an arrow, spear, lance, harpoon, etc. **2** An arrow or spear. **3** Something hurled like or having the effect of an arrow or spear: *shafts* of ridicule. **4** A beam of light. **5** A long handle, as of a hammer, ax, etc. **6** *Mech.* A long and usu. cylindrical bar, esp. if rotating and transmitting motion. **7** *Archit.* **a** The portion of a column between capital and base. **b** A slender column, as an obelisk. **8** The stem of a feather. **9** The slender portion of a bone or the portion of a hair from root to the end. **10** A tall, narrow building or spire. **11** A narrow, vertical passage, as the entrance to a mine or an opening through a building for an elevator. **12** A conduit for the passage of air, heat, etc. **13** *Slang* Malicious or abusive treatment: with *the*, esp. in the phrases **get the shaft, give (someone) the shaft.** **—v.t.** *Slang* To act maliciously or abusively toward. [< OE *sceaft*]

shag (shag) *n.* **1** A rough coat or mass, as of hair. **2** A long, rough nap on cloth. **3** Cloth having a rough or long nap. **4** A coarse, strong tobacco: also **shag tobacco.** **—v. shagged, shag·ging** *v.t.* **1** To make shaggy or rough. **—v.i.** **2** To become shaggy or rough. [< OE *sceacga* wool]

shag·bark (shag′bärk′) *n.* **1** A species of hickory with rough, flaking bark. **2** Its edible nut. **3** Its wood.

shag·gy (shag′ē) *adj.* **·gi·er, ·gi·est** **1** Having, consisting of, or resembling rough hair or wool. **2** Covered with any rough, tangled growth; fuzzy. **3** Unkempt. **—shag′gi·ly** *adv.* **—shag′gi·ness** *n.*

sha·green (shə·grēn′) *n.* **1** An abrasive leather made of the skin of various sharks and rays. **2** A rough-grained rawhide. [< Turk. *sāghrī* horse's hide]

shah (shä) *n.* An eastern ruler, esp. of Iran. [< Pers.]

shake (shāk) *v.* **shook, shak·en, shak·ing** *v.t.* **1** To cause to move to and fro or up and down with short, rapid movements. **2** To affect by or as by vigorous action: with *off, out, from*, etc.: to *shake* out a sail; to *shake* off a tackler. **3** To cause to tremble or quiver; vibrate: The blows *shook* the door. **4** To cause to stagger or totter. **5** To weaken or disturb: to *shake* one's determination. **6** To agitate or rouse; stir: often with *up*. **7** *Informal* To get rid of or away from. **8** To clasp (hands) as a form of greeting, agreement, etc. **9** *Music* TRILL. **—v.i.** **10** To move to and fro or up and down in short, rapid movements. **11** To be affected by vigorous action: with *off, out, from*, etc. **12** To tremble or quiver, as from cold or fear. **13** To become unsteady; totter. **14** To clasp hands. **15** *Music* TRILL. **—shake down 1** To cause to fall by shaking. **2** To cause to settle by shaking. **3** To test or become familiar with (new equipment, etc.). **4** *Slang* To extort money from. **—shake up 1** To mix or blend by shaking. **2** To agitate or rouse; stir. **3** To jar or jolt. **4** To effect or cause rather extensive changes or reorganization in. **5** *Slang* To cause to lose one's composure; disconcert. **—n.** **1** The act or an instance of shaking: a *shake* of the hand. **2** A tight fissure in rock or timber. **3** *pl. Informal* A fit of bodily shaking or trembling: usu. with *the*. **4** MILKSHAKE. **5** *Informal* EARTHQUAKE. **6** *Informal* An instant; jiffy. **7** *Informal* A deal: to get a fair *shake*. **8** *Music* TRILL. **—give (someone or something) the shake** To get away from (someone or something). [< OE *scacan*]

shake·down (shāk′doun′) *n.* **1** A thorough search. **2** *Slang* Extortion of money. **3** A testing or becoming familiar with something, as with a new ship. **—adj.** For the purpose of testing mechanical parts or familiarizing personnel: a *shakedown* cruise.

shak·er (shā′kər) *n.* One who or that which shakes: a *saltshaker*, cocktail *shaker*, etc.

Shak·er (shā′kər) *n.* One of a sect practicing celibacy and communal living: so called from their trembling movements during religious meetings. **—Shak′er·ism** *n.*

Shake·spear·i·an (shāk·spir′ē·ən) *adj.* Of, pertaining to, or characteristic of Shakespeare, his work, or his style. **—n.** A specialist on Shakespeare or his writings. Also **Shake·spear′e·an.**

shake-up (shāk′up′) *n.* A rather extensive change or reorganization, as in a business office, etc.

shak·o (shak′ō, shāk′-, shäk′-) *n. pl.* **·os** A high, stiff military headdress, having a visor and an upright plume. [< Hung. *csākó*]

shak·y (shā′kē) *adj.* **shak·i·er, shak·i·est** **1** Not firm or solid. **2** Not well founded, thought out, etc.: a *shaky* theory. **3** Not dependable or reliable. **4** Characterized by shaking. **5** Weak; unsound, as in body. **— shak′i·ly** *adv.* **—shak′i·ness** *n.*

shale (shāl) *n.* A rock resembling slate, with fragile, uneven layers. [< G *Schale* shale] **—shal′y** *adj.*

Shako

shall (shal) *v. p.t.* **should.** Used now only as an auxiliary, *shall* expresses: **1** Simple futurity: I *shall* go next week. **2** That which seems inevitable or certain: I know I *shall* never leave. **3** Determination, promise, threat, or command: They *shall* not pass; You *shall* pay for this; You *shall* have it. **4** In laws, resolutions, etc., that which is obligatory: It *shall* be required to have identification. [< OE *sceal* I am obliged] **• shall, will** The traditional rule is that to express simple futurity *shall* is used with the first person and the auxiliary *will* with the second and third. To express determination, obligation, command, etc., *will* is used with the first person and *shall* with the second and third. This rule is now widely ignored, both in speech and in writing. *Will*, by far the more common auxiliary, occurs with all subjects and in all contexts. *Shall* is still often used with the first person, less so with the second and third, where its use is likely to appear stilted.

shal·lop (shal′əp) *n.* An open boat propelled by oars or sails. [< Du. *sloep* sloop]

shal·lot (shə·lot′, shal′ət) *n.* **1** A mild, onionlike vegetable allied to garlic. **2** SCALLION. [< OF *eschalotte*]

shal·low (shal′ō) *adj.* **1** Lacking depth. **2** Not extending far inwards or outwards: a *shallow* room. **3** Lacking intellectual depth; superficial. **—n.** *Usu. pl. but construed as sing. or pl.* A shallow place in a body of water; shoal. **—v.t. & v.i.** To make or become shallow. [ME *schalowe*] **—shal′low·ly** *adv.* **—shal′low·ness** *n.*

shalt (shalt) *v.* Archaic second person singular, present tense of SHALL: used with *thou*.

sham (sham) *adj.* False; pretended; counterfeit; mock. **— n.** **1** A person who shams. **2** A hoax; deception. **3** An imitation; counterfeit. **4** Cheap artificiality or pretension. **5** A decorative cover or the like for use over a household article: a pillow *sham*. **—v. shammed, sham·ming** *v.t.* **1** To counterfeit; feign. **—v.i.** **2** To make false pretenses; feign something. [? dial. var. of SHAME]

sha·man (shä′mən, shā′-, sham′ən) *n.* A priest of shamanism. [< Skt. *śamana* ascetic]

sha·man·ism (shä′mən·iz′əm, shā′-, sham′ən-) *n.* **1** A religion of NE Asia holding that supernatural spirits, etc., work for the good or ill of mankind only through the shamans. **2** Any similar religion, such as that practiced by certain Indians of the American Northwest. **—sha′man·ist** *n.* **—sha′man·is′tic** *adj.*

sham·ble (sham′bəl) *v.i.* **·bled, ·bling** To walk with shuffling or unsteady gait. [?]

sham·bles (sham′bəlz) *n.pl.* (*usu. construed as sing.*) **1** SLAUGHTERHOUSE. **2** Any place of carnage or execution. **3** A place marked by great destruction, disorder, or confusion. [< OE *scamel* a bench.]

shame (shām) *n.* **1** A painful feeling caused by a sense of guilt, unworthiness, impropriety, etc. **2** Disgrace; humiliation. **3** A person or thing causing disgrace or humiliation. **4** Misfortune; outrage: It's a *shame* they didn't go. **—put to shame 1** To disgrace; make ashamed. **2** To surpass or eclipse. **—v.t. shamed, sham·ing 1** To cause to feel shame. **2** To bring shame upon; disgrace. **3** To impel by a sense of shame: with *into* or *out of*. [< OE *scamu*]

shame·faced (shām′fāst′) *adj.* **1** Showing shame; ashamed. **2** Bashful; modest. [< OE *scamfæst* abashed] **—**

shame·fac·ed·ly (shām′fā′sid·lē, shām′fāst′lē) *adv.* — **shame′fac′ed·ness** *n.*

shame·ful (shām′fəl) *adj.* **1** Bringing shame or disgrace; disgraceful; scandalous. **2** Indecent. —**shame′ful·ly** *adv.* —**shame′ful·ness** *n.* —**Syn. 1** disreputable, dishonorable, ignoble, ignominious, base, despicable, contemptible, deplorable, vile, odious.

shame·less (shām′lis) *adj.* **1** Impudent; brazen; immodest. **2** Done without shame, indicating a want of decency. —**shame′less·ly** *adv.* —**shame′less·ness** *n.*

sham·my (sham′ē) *n.* CHAMOIS.

sham·poo (sham·pōō′) *v.t.* **1** To lather and wash (the hair and scalp) thoroughly. **2** To cleanse by rubbing. —*n.* The act or process of shampooing, or a preparation used for it. [< Hind. *chāmpnā* to press] —**sham·poo′er** *n.*

sham·rock (sham′rok) *n.* Any of several plants, with trifoliate leaves, accepted as the national emblem of Ireland, esp. the wood sorrel. [< Irish *seamar* trefoil]

shang·hai (shang′hī, shang·hī′) *v.t.* **·haied**, **·hai·ing 1** To drug or render unconscious and kidnap for service aboard a ship. **2** To cause to do something by force or deception. [< *Shanghai*]

Shamrock (wood sorrel)

Shan·gri-la (shang′grē·lä′) *n.* Any imaginary hidden utopia or paradise. [< *Shangri-la,* name of a utopian place in James Hilton's novel *Lost Horizon,* 1933]

shank (shangk) *n.* **1** The leg between the knee and the ankle. **2** The entire leg. **3** A cut of meat from the leg of an animal; the shin. **4** The stem, as of a tobacco pipe, key, anchor, etc. **5** The part of a tool connecting the handle with the working part; shaft. **6** The projecting piece or loop in the back of some buttons by which they are attached. **7** *Printing* The body of a type. **8** The narrow part of a shoe sole in front of the heel. • See SHOE. —**shank of the evening** *Informal* The early part of the evening. [< OE *sceanca*] —**shanked** *adj.*

shanks' mare One's own legs as a means of conveyance.

shan't (shant, shänt) Contraction of *shall not.*

shan·tung (shan′tung, shan·tung′) *n.* A fabric with a rough, nubby surface, originally made in China of silk, now often made of synthetic or cotton fiber. [< *Shantung,* China]

shan·ty[1] (shan′tē) *n. pl.* **·ties** A small, rickety shack or cabin. [< F (Canadian) *chantier* lumberer's shack]

shan·ty[2] (shan′tē) *n.* CHANTEY.

shape (shāp) *n.* **1** Outward form or contour. **2** Appearance of a body with reference only to its contour; figure. **3** Something that gives or determines shape, as a pattern or mold. **4** An assumed aspect or appearance; guise. **5** A developed or final expression or form: to put an idea into *shape.* **6** Any embodiment or form in which a thing may exist: the *shape* of a novel. **7** A ghost or phantom. **8** *Informal* The condition of a person or thing as regards health, orderliness, etc. —**in shape** In good physical condition or appearance. —**out of shape** In bad physical condition or appearance. —**take shape** To begin to have or assume definite form. —*v.* **shaped, shap·ing** *v.t.* **1** To give shape to; mold; form. **2** To adjust or adapt; modify. **3** To devise; prepare. **4** To give direction or character to: to *shape* one's course of action. **5** To put into or express in words. —*v.i.* **6** To take shape; develop; form: often with *up* or *into.* —**shape up 1** To develop fully or appropriately; work out. **2** *Informal* To do, work, behave, etc., properly. [< OE *gesceap* creation] —**shap′er** *n.*

SHAPE (shāp) Supreme Headquarters Allied Powers, Europe.

shape·less (shāp′lis) *adj.* **1** Having no definite shape. **2** Lacking a pleasing shape or symmetry. —**shape′less·ly** *adv.* —**shape′less·ness** *n.*

shape·ly (shāp′lē) *adj.* **·li·er, ·li·est** Having a pleasing shape; well-formed. —**shape′li·ness** *n.*

shape-up (shāp′up′) *n.* The selection of a work crew, usu. on a day-to-day basis, from among a number of men assembled for a work shift.

shard (shärd) *n.* **1** A broken piece of a brittle substance, as of an earthen vessel. **2** *Zool.* A stiff covering, as the wing cover of a beetle. [< OE *sceard*]

share (shâr) *n.* **1** A portion alloted or due to a person or contributed by a person. **2** One of the equal parts into which the capital stock of a company or corporation is divided. **3** An equitable part of something used, done, or divided in common. —*v.* **shared, shar·ing** *v.t.* **1** To divide and give out in shares or portions; apportion. **2** To enjoy, use, participate in, endure, etc., in common. —*v.i.* **3** To have a part; participate: with *in.* **4** To divide something in equal parts: with *out* or *with.* [< OE *scearu*] —**shar′er** *n.*

share·crop·per (shâr′krop′ər) *n.* A tenant farmer who pays a share of his crop as rent for his land.

share·hold·er (shâr′hōl′dər) *n.* An owner of a share or shares of a company's stock.

sha·rif (shə·rēf′) *n.* SHERIF.

shark[1] (shärk) *n.* Any of a large order of mostly marine fishes having a cartilaginous skeleton, lateral gill slits, and a tough skin. —*v.i.* To fish for sharks. [?]

Great white shark

shark[2] (shärk) *n.* **1** A dishonest person, esp. a swindler. **2** *Slang* A person of exceptional skill or ability. [?< SHARK[1]]

shark·skin (shärk′skin′) *n.* **1** Leather made of a shark's skin. **2** A summer fabric with a smooth surface. **3** A fabric with a pebbly surface.

sharp (shärp) *adj.* **1** Having a keen edge or an acute point; capable of cutting or piercing. **2** Not rounded; pointed; angular: *sharp* features. **3** Abrupt in change of direction: a *sharp* curve. **4** Distinct; well-defined: a *sharp* contrast. **5** Keen or quick in perception or discernment. **6** Keen or acute, as in seeing or hearing. **7** Shrewd, as in bargaining. **8** Quickly aroused; harsh: a *sharp* temper. **9** Heated; fiery: a *sharp* debate. **10** Vigilant; attentive: a *sharp* watch. **11** Quick; vigorous. **12** Keenly felt: *sharp* hunger pangs. **13** Intense or penetrating in effect; incisive to the point of being unsettling or wounding: a *sharp* look; a *sharp* tongue. **14** Shrill: a *sharp* sound. **15** Having an acid or pungent taste or smell. **16** *Slang* Stylishly dressed or well groomed. **17** *Music* Being above the proper or indicated pitch. —*adv.* **1** In a sharp manner. **2** Promptly; exactly: at 4 o'clock *sharp.* **3** *Music* Above the proper pitch. —*n.* **1** *Music* A character (♯) used on a natural degree of the staff to make it represent a tone a half-step higher; also, the tone so indicated. **2** A sewing needle of long, slender shape. **3** A cheat; sharper: a *cardsharp.* —*v.t.* **1** *Music* To raise in pitch, as by a half-step. —*v.i.* **2** *Music* To sing, play, or sound above the right pitch. [< OE *scearp*] —**sharp′ly** *adv.* —**sharp′ness** *n.*

sharp·en (shär′pən) *v.t. & v.i.* To make or become sharp. —**sharp′en·er** *n.*

sharp·er (shär′pər) *n.* A swindler; cheat.

sharp·ie (shär′pē) *n.* **1** A long, flat-bottomed sailboat having a centerboard and one or two masts. **2** *Informal* A shrewd, clever person, esp. in bargaining. [< SHARP]

sharp·shoot·er (shärp′shōō′tər) *n.* A skilled marksman. —**sharp′shoot′ing** *n.*

sharp-sight·ed (shärp′sī′tid) *adj.* Having keen vision. —**sharp′-sight′ed·ly** *adv.* —**sharp′-sight′ed·ness** *n.*

sharp-tongued (shärp′tungd′) *adj.* Bitter or caustic in speech.

sharp-wit·ted (shärp′wit′id) *adj.* Acutely intelligent; discerning.

Shas·ta daisy (shas′tə) A cultivated, daisylike variety of chrysanthemum having white-rayed flowers. [< Mt. *Shasta,* California]

shat·ter (shat′ər) *v.t.* **1** To break into pieces suddenly, as by a blow. **2** To break the health or well-being of, as the body or mind. **3** To damage or demolish. —*v.i.* **4** To break into pieces; burst. —*n. pl.* Shattered pieces or fragments, esp. in the phrase **in shatters.** [ME *scateren* to scatter]

shave (shāv) *v.* **shaved, shaved** or **shav·en, shav·ing** *v.i.* **1** To

cut hair or beard close to the skin with a razor. —*v.t.* **2** To remove hair or beard from (the face, head, etc.) with a razor. **3** To cut (hair or beard) close to the skin with a razor: often with *off*. **4** To trim closely as if with a razor: to *shave* a lawn. **5** To cut thin slices or pieces from. **6** To touch or scrape in passing; graze; come close to. **7** *Informal* To lower or deduct from (a price, amount, etc.). —*n.* **1** The act or operation of shaving with a razor. **2** A thin slice or piece; shaving. **3** *Informal* The act of barely grazing something. [< OE *scafan*]

shav·en (shā'vən) A *p.p.* of SHAVE. —*adj.* **1** Shaved; also, tonsured. **2** Trimmed closely.

shav·er (shā'vər) *n.* **1** One who shaves. **2** An instrument for shaving: an electric *shaver*. **3** *Informal* A lad.

shave·tail (shāv'tāl') *n.* *Slang* A second lieutenant, esp. one recently commissioned. [In allusion to young, unbroken army mules with bobbed tails]

Sha·vi·an (shā'vē·ən) *n.* An admirer of George Bernard Shaw, his writings, or his theories. —*adj.* Of or characteristic of George Bernard Shaw or his work.

shav·ing (shā'ving) *n.* **1** The act of one who or that which shaves. **2** A thin paring shaved from anything.

shawl (shôl) *n.* A wrap, as a square cloth, or large broad scarf, worn over the head or shoulders. [< Pers. *shāl*]

Shaw·nee (shô·nē') *n.* One of a tribe of North American Indians of Algonquian stock, formerly living in Tennessee and South Carolina, now in Oklahoma. [< Algon.]

shay (shā) *n.* A light carriage; chaise. [Back formation < CHAISE, mistaking it for a plural]

she (shē) *pron.* **1** The female person or being previously mentioned or understood, in the nominative case. **2** Any woman. **3** Something personified as female: *She* is a great little car. —*n.* A female person or animal: often used in combination: a *she-lion*. [< OE *sēo*]

sheaf (shēf) *n.* *pl.* **sheaves** (shēvz) **1** Stalks of cut grain or the like, bound together. **2** Any collection of things, as papers, held together by a band or tie. —*v.t.* To bind in a sheaf; sheave. [< OE *scēaf*]

shear (shir) *n.* **1** Either of the blades of a pair of shears. **2** A cutting machine for sheet metal. **3** *Physics* **a** A deformation of a solid body, equivalent to a sliding over each other of adjacent layers. **b** A force or system of forces tending to cause this. **4** The act or result of shearing. —*v.* sheared (*Archaic* shore), sheared or shorn, shear·ing *v.t.* **1** To cut the hair, fleece, etc., from. **2** To remove by cutting or clipping: to *shear* wool. **3** To deprive; strip, as of power or wealth. **4** To cut or clip with shears or other sharp instrument: to *shear* a cable. —*v.i.* **5** To use shears or other sharp instrument. **6** To slide or break from a shear (def. 3). **7** To proceed by or as by cutting a way: with *through*. [< OE *sceran* to shear] —**shear'er** *n.*

shears (shirz) *n.pl.* Any large cutting or clipping instrument worked by the crossing of cutting edges. Also **pair of shears.**

shear·wa·ter (shir'wô'tər, -wot'ər) *n.* Any of various web-footed, far-ranging sea birds that usu. skim the water when flying.

sheath (shēth) *n.* **1** An envelope or case, as for a sword; scabbard. **2** *Biol.* Any structure that enfolds or encloses. [< OE *scæth*]

sheathe (shēth) *v.t.* sheathed, sheath·ing **1** To put into a sheath. **2** To plunge (a sword, etc.) into flesh. **3** To draw in, as claws. **4** To protect or conceal, as by covering: to *sheathe* plasterboard; to *sheathe* one's anger.

sheath·ing (shē'thing) *n.* **1** An outer covering, as of a building or ship's hull. **2** The material used for this. **3** The act of one who sheathes.

sheave¹ (shēv) *v.t.* sheaved, sheav·ing To gather into sheaves; collect.

sheave² (shēv) *n.* A grooved pulley wheel; also, a pulley wheel and its block. [ME]

sheaves (shēvz) *n.pl.* of SHEAF.

she·bang (shi·bang') *n.* *Slang* Matter; concern; affair: tired of the whole *shebang*. [?]

shed¹ (shed) *v.* shed, shed·ding *v.t.* **1** To pour forth in drops; emit, as tears or blood. **2** To cause to pour forth. **3** To send forth or abroad; radiate: to *shed* light on a subject. **4** To throw off without allowing to penetrate, as rain; repel. **5** To cast off by natural process, as hair, skin, a shell, etc.

—*v.i.* **6** To cast off or lose hair, skin, etc., by natural process. **7** To fall or drop, as leaves or seed. —*n.* That which sheds, as a sloping surface or watershed. [< OE *scēadan* separate, part]

shed² (shed) *n.* **1** A small low building or lean-to, used for storage, etc. **2** A large hangarlike building, often with open front or sides. [Var. of SHADE]

she'd (shēd) Contraction of *she had* or *she would*.

shed·der (shed'ər) *n.* **1** One who sheds. **2** An animal that molts.

sheen (shēn) *n.* **1** A glistening brightness, as if from reflection. **2** Bright, shining attire. —*v.i.* To shine; gleam; glisten. [< OE *scēne* beautiful] —**sheen'y** *adj.*

sheep (shēp) *n.* *pl.* **sheep** **1** Any of a genus of woolly, medium-sized ruminants, esp. domesticated species grown for their fleece, flesh, and hide. **2** A meek or timid person. [< OE *scēap*]

Sheep

sheep·cote (shēp'kōt') *n.* SHEEPFOLD. Also **sheep'cot'** (-kot').

sheep dip Any insecticidal, medicinal, or cleansing solution used to bathe sheep.

sheep dog Any dog trained to guard and control sheep.

sheep·fold (shēp'fōld') *n.* A pen for sheep.

sheep·herd·er (shēp'hûr'dər) *n.* A herder of sheep. —**sheep'herd'ing** *n.*

sheep·ish (shē'pish) *adj.* **1** Embarrassed; chagrined. **2** Meek; timid. —**sheep'ish·ly** *adv.* —**sheep'ish·ness** *n.*

sheep·skin (shēp'skin') *n.* **1** A sheep's hide, or anything made from it, as parchment, an outdoor coat, etc. **2** A document written on parchment. **3** *Informal* A diploma.

sheep sorrel A low-growing weed related to buckwheat.

sheer¹ (shir) *v.i.* **1** To swerve from a course; turn aside. —*v.t.* **2** To cause to swerve. —*n.* **1** *Naut.* **a** The slight rise of the lengthwise lines of a vessel's hull. **b** A position of a vessel that enables it to swing clear of a single anchor. **2** A swerving course. [< SHEAR]

sheer² (shir) *adj.* **1** Having no modifying conditions; absolute; utter: *sheer* folly. **2** Exceedingly thin and fine: said of fabrics. **3** Perpendicular; steep: a *sheer* precipice. **4** Pure; pellucid. —*n.* Any very thin fabric used for clothes. —*adv.* **1** Entirely; utterly. **2** Perpendicularly. [ME *schere*] —**sheer'ly** *adv.* —**sheer'ness** *n.*

sheet (shēt) *n.* **1** A thin, broad, usu. rectangular piece of any material, as metal, glass, etc. **2** A broad, flat surface or expanse: a *sheet* of flame. **3** A large, usu. rectangular piece of cotton, linen, silk, etc., used as bedding. **4** A usu. rectangular piece of paper, used esp. for writing, printing, etc. **5** *Usu. pl.* *Printing* A printed signature for a book. **6** *Informal* A newspaper. **7** A sail: a literary use. **8** *Naut.* A rope or chain attached to the lower corner of a sail, used to regulate the angle of the sail to the wind. **9** The large, unseparated block of stamps printed by one impression of a plate. —*v.t.* To cover with, wrap in, or form into a sheet or sheets. —*adj.* Formed or cut into sheets: *sheet* metal. [< OE *scēte* linen cloth]

sheet anchor 1 An anchor used only in emergency. **2** A person or thing depended upon in an emergency.

sheet·ing (shē'ting) *n.* **1** Material for bed sheets. **2** Any material used for lining or covering a surface.

sheet metal Metal rolled and pressed into sheets.

sheet music Music printed on unbound sheets of paper.

sheik (shēk, shāk) *n.* The chief of an Arab tribe or family. Also **sheikh.** [< Ar. *shakha* grow old] —**sheik'dom, sheikh'-dom** *n.*

shek·el (shek'əl) *n.* **1** An ancient, esp. Hebrew unit of weight. **2** A coin having this weight. **3** *pl.* *Slang* Money; riches.

shel·drake (shel'drāk') *n.* **1** Any of various Old World wild ducks with varicolored plumage. **2** MERGANSER. [< dial. E *sheld* dappled + DRAKE]

shelf (shelf) *n.* *pl.* **shelves** (shelvz) **1** A piece of material set horizontally into or against a wall, cabinet, closet, etc., to support articles. **2** The contents of a shelf. **3** Any flat projecting ledge, as of rock. **4** A reef; shoal. [< LG *schelf* set of shelves]

shell (shel) *n.* **1** The hard outer covering of a mollusk,

lobster, egg, nut, etc. • See OYSTER. **2** Something like a shell in shape or function, as the outer framework of a building, a ship's hull, a hollow pastry or pie crust for filling, etc. **3** A sleeveless blouse or sweater. **4** A very light, long, and narrow racing rowboat. **5** A hollow metallic projectile filled with an explosive or chemical. **6** A metallic or paper cartridge case containing the powder, bullet, or shot for breechloading small arms. **7** Any case used to contain the explosives of fireworks. **8** A reserved or impersonal attitude: to come out of one's *shell.* —*v.t.* **1** To divest of or remove from a shell, husk, or pod. **2** To separate from the cob, as Indian corn. **3** To bombard with shells, as a fort. **4** To cover with shells. —*v.i.* **5** To shed or become freed from the shell or pod. **6** To fall off, as a shell or scale. [< OE *scell* shell] —**shell'er** *n.* —**shell'y** *adj.* (**·i·er, ·i·est**)

she'll (shēl) Contraction of *she will* or *she shall.*

shel·lac (shə·lak′) *n.* **1** A purified lac in the form of thin flakes, used in varnish, insulators, etc. **2** A varnish made of shellac dissolved in alcohol. —*v.t.* **·lacked, ·lack·ing 1** To cover or varnish with shellac. **2** *Slang* **a** To beat. **b** To defeat utterly. Also **shel·lack′.** [< SHELL + LAC[1]]

shel·lack·ing (shə·lak′ing) *n. Slang* **1** A beating; assault. **2** A thorough defeat.

shell·back (shel′bak′) *n.* **1** A veteran sailor. **2** Anyone who has crossed the equator on a ship.

shell·bark (shel′bärk′) *n.* SHAGBARK.

shell·fire (shel′fīr′) *n.* The firing of artillery shells.

shell·fish (shel′fish′) *n. pl.* **·fish** or **·fish·es** An aquatic mollusk or crustacean, esp. if edible, as a clam, shrimp, etc.

shell game **1** A swindling game in which the victim bets on the location of a pea covered by one of three nutshells; thimblerig. **2** Any game in which the victim cannot win.

shell·proof (shel′prōōf′) *adj.* Built to resist the destructive effect of projectiles and bombs.

shell shock COMBAT FATIGUE. —**shell-shocked** (shel′-shokt′) *adj.*

shel·ter (shel′tər) *n.* **1** That which covers or shields from exposure, danger, etc. **2** The state of being covered, protected, or shielded. —*v.t.* **1** To provide protection or shelter for; shield, as from danger or inclement weather. —*v.i.* **2** To take shelter. [?] —**shel′ter·er** *n.*

shelve (shelv) *v.* **shelved, shelv·ing** *v.t.* **1** To place on a shelf. **2** To postpone indefinitely; put aside. **3** To retire. **4** To provide or fit with shelves. —*v.i.* **5** To incline gradually.

shelves (shelvz) *n. pl.* of SHELF.

shelv·ing (shel′ving) *n.* **1** Shelves collectively. **2** Material for the construction of shelves.

Shem (shem) In the Bible, the eldest son of Noah.

Shem·ite (shem′īt) *n.* SEMITE.

she·nan·i·gan (shi·nan′ə·gən) *n. Usu. pl. Informal* **1** Trickery; foolery. **2** Deceitful or underhanded actions. [?]

She·ol (shē′ōl) *n.* In the Old Testament, a place where the dead were believed to go. [< Heb. *shā′al* dig]

shep·herd (shep′ərd) *n.* **1** A keeper or herder of sheep. **2** Figuratively, a pastor, leader, or guide. —*v.t.* To herd, guide, protect, or direct, as a shepherd. [< OE *scēaphyrde*] —**shep′herd·ess** *n. Fem.*

shepherd dog SHEEP DOG.

shepherd's purse A common weed related to mustard, bearing small white flowers and pouchlike pods.

Sher·a·ton (sher′ə·tən) *adj.* Denoting a style of furniture characterized by simplicity and pleasing proportions. [< T. *Sheraton,* 1751–1806, English designer]

sher·bet (shûr′bit) *n.* **1** A frozen dessert, usu. fruit-flavored, made with water or milk, gelatin, etc. **2** Originally, a Turkish drink, made of fruit juice sweetened and diluted with water. Also **sher′bert** (-bərt). [< Ar. *sharbah* a drink]

she·rif (shə·rēf′) *n.* **1** A member of a princely Muslim family which claims descent from Mohammed. **2** The chief magistrate of Mecca. **3** An Arab chief. [< Ar. *sharīf* noble]

sher·iff (sher′if) *n.* **1** The chief law-enforcement officer of a county, who executes the mandates of courts, keeps order, etc. **2** In Canada, an official whose job is to enforce minor court orders, such as the eviction of persons for

nonpayment of rent. [< OE *scīr-gerēfa* shire reeve] —**sher′-iff·dom** *n.*

sher·ry (sher′ē) *n. pl.* **·ries** A fortified wine originally made in Spain. [< *Xeres,* former name of Jerez, Spain]

she's (shēz) Contraction of *she is* or *she has.*

Shet·land pony (shet′lənd) A small, shaggy breed of pony originally bred on the Shetland Islands.

shew (shō) *n. & v. Archaic* SHOW.

shew·bread (shō′bred′) *n.* Unleavened bread formerly placed as an offering in Jewish temples.

SHF, S.H.F., shf, s.h.f. superhigh frequency.

shib·bo·leth (shib′ə·leth) *n.* A test word or pet phrase of a party; a watchword. [< Heb. *shibbōleth,* a word mispronounced by certain Hebrew spies, betraying them as aliens. *Judges* 12:4–6]

shied (shīd) *p.t. & p.p.* of SHY.

shield (shēld) *n.* **1** A broad piece of defensive armor, commonly carried on the left arm; a large buckler. **2** Anything that protects or defends. **3** Any of various devices that afford protection, as from machinery, electricity, radiation, etc. **4** Anything shaped like a shield, as a policeman's badge, decorative emblem, etc. **5** A heraldic escutcheon. —*v.t.* **1** To protect from danger; defend; guard. **2** To hide or screen from view. —*v.i.* **3** To act as a shield or safeguard. —**shield′er** *n.*

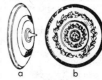

Shields.
a. Anglo-Saxon.
b. Greek.

shield·ing (shēld′ing) *n.* A protective device or screen: radiation *shielding.*

shi·er (shī′ər) Comparative of SHY.

shi·est (shī′ist) Superlative of SHY.

shift (shift) *v.t.* **1** To change or move from one position, arrangement, place, etc., to another. **2** To change for another or others of the same class. —*v.i.* **3** To change position, place, attitude, etc. **4** To manage or get along. **5** To evade; equivocate. —*n.* **1** The act of shifting. **2** A change in position, place, direction, etc. **3** A change in attitude, loyalty, etc. **4** An action or recourse taken in an emergency; expedient. **5** A trick or evasion. **6** GEARSHIFT. **7** A relay of workers or their period of work: the night *shift.* **8** A woman's dress that is not belted or fitted at the waist. **9** *Archaic* A chemise or undergarment. [< OE *sciftan* divide] —**shift′er** *n.*

shift·less (shift′lis) *adj.* **1** Unable or unwilling to work or accomplish something; inefficient or lazy. **2** Inefficiently or incompetently done. —**shift′less·ly** *adv.* —**shift′-less·ness** *n.*

shift·y (shif′tē) *adj.* **shift·i·er, shift·i·est 1** Characterized by or showing deceit or trickery. **2** Full of expedients; resourceful. —**shift′i·ly** *adv.* —**shift′i·ness** *n.*

shill (shil) *n. Slang* The ally of a sidewalk peddler or gambler who makes a purchase or bet to encourage onlookers to buy or bet. [?]

shil·le·lagh (shi·lā′lē, -lə) *n.* In Ireland, a stout cudgel made of oak or blackthorn. Also **shil·la′lah, shil·lea′lah, shil·le′lah.** [< *Shillelagh,* a town in Ireland famed for its oaks]

shil·ling (shil′ing) *n.* **1** A current silver coin of Great Britain, equal to five (new) pence or 1/20 of a pound. **2** A former colonial American coin, varying in value from 12 to 16 cents. [< OE *scilling*]

shil·ly-shal·ly (shil′ē·shal′ē) *v.i.* **·lied, ·ly·ing** To act with indecision; vacillate. —*adj.* Irresolute; hesitating. —*n.* Weak or foolish vacillation; irresolution. —*adv.* In an irresolute manner. [Redupl. of *Shall I?*] —**shil′ly-shal′li·er** *n.*

shim (shim) *n.* A thin wedge of metal, wood, etc., used to fill out space. —*v.t.* **shimmed, shim·ming** To wedge up, fill out, or level by inserting a shim. [?]

shim·mer (shim′ər) *v.i.* To shine faintly; give off or emit a tremulous light; glimmer. —*n.* A tremulous shining or gleaming; glimmer. [< OE *scimerian*] —**shim′mer·y** *adj.*

shim·my (shim′ē) *n. pl.* **·mies 1** A jazz dance accompanied by shaking movements. **2** Undesired oscillation or vibration, as of automobile wheels. —*v.i.* **·mied, ·my·ing 1** To

vibrate or wobble. **2** To dance the shimmy. [Alter. of CHE-MISE]

shin (shin) *n.* **1** The front part of the leg below the knee; also, the shinbone. **2** The lower foreleg: a *shin* of beef. — *v.t. & v.i.* **shinned, shin·ning** To climb (a pole) by gripping with the hands or arms and the shins or legs: usu. with *up.* [< OE *scinu*]

shin·bone (shin'bōn') *n.* TIBIA.

shin·dig (shin'dig) *n. Slang* A dance or noisy party. [?]

shine (shīn) *v.i.* **shone** or (*esp. for def. 5*) **shined, shin·ing 1** To emit light; beam; glow. **2** To show or be conspicuous. **3** To excel; be preeminent. —*v.t.* **4** To cause to shine. **5** To brighten by rubbing or polishing. —*n.* **1** Radiance; luster; sheen. **2** Fair weather; sunshine. **3** *Informal* A liking or fancy. **4** *Informal* A smart trick or prank. **5** A gloss or polish, as on shoes. [< OE *scīnan*]

shin·er (shī'nər) *n.* **1** One who or that which shines. **2** Any of various species of minnows with silvery scales. **3** *Slang* A black eye.

shin·gle[1] (shing'gəl) *n.* **1** A thin, tapering piece of wood or other material, used in courses to cover roofs. **2** A small signboard bearing the name of a doctor, lawyer, etc., and placed outside his office. **3** A short haircut. —*v.t.* **·gled, ·gling 1** To cover (a roof, building, etc.) with shingles. **2** To cut (the hair) short. [< L *scandula* a shingle] —**shin'gler** *n.*

shin·gle[2] (shing'gəl) *n.* **1** Rounded, stones, coarser than gravel, found on the seashore. **2** A place strewn with shingle, as a beach. [?] —**shin'gly** *adj.*

shin·gles (shing'gəlz) *n. pl. (construed as sing.)* A painful viral disease marked by inflammation of sensory nerves and blistering, chiefly affecting the torso. [< L *cingulum* girdle]

shin·ing (shī'ning) *adj.* **1** Emitting or reflecting a continuous light; gleaming. **2** Of unusual excellence; conspicuous. —**shin'ing·ly** *adv.*

shin·ny[1] (shin'ē) *n.* A game resembling hockey, or one of the sticks or clubs used by the players. Also **shin'ney.** [< *shin ye*, a cry used in the game]

shin·ny[2] (shin'ē) *v.i* **·nied, ·ny·ing** *Informal* To climb using one's shins: usu. with *up.*

Shin·to (shin'tō) *n.* The primary religion of Japan, consisting chiefly in ancestor worship, and formerly in the worship of the Emperor as a divinity. Also **Shin'to·ism.** [< Chin. *shin* god + *tao* way] —**Shin'to·ist** *n.*

shin·y (shī'nē) *adj.* **shin·i·er, shin·i·est 1** Glistening; glossy; polished. **2** Full of sunshine; bright. —**shin'i·ness** *n.*

ship (ship) *n.* **1** Any large vessel suitable for deep-water navigation. **2** The crew and officers of such a vessel. **3** An aircraft or spacecraft. —*v.* **shipped, ship·ping** *v.t.* **1** To transport by ship. **2** To send by any means of transportation, as by rail, truck, or air. **3** To hire and receive for service on board a vessel, as sailors. **4** To draw (oars) inside a boat. *Naut.* To receive over the side: to *ship* a wave. —*v.i.* **6** To go on board ship; embark. **7** To enlist as a seaman. [< OE *scip*]

-ship *suffix* **1** The state or quality of: *friendship.* **2** Office, rank, or dignity of: *kingship.* **3** The art or skill of: *marksmanship.* [< OE *-scipe*]

ship biscuit A hard, crackerlike biscuit; hardtack.

ship·board (ship'bôrd', -bōrd') *n.* A ship. —**on ship·board** In or on a ship.

ship·build·er (ship'bil'dər) *n.* One who designs or works at building ships. —**ship'build'ing** *n.*

ship·load (ship'lōd') *n.* A load that a ship can carry.

ship·mas·ter (ship'mas'tər, -mäs'-) *n.* The captain or master of a merchant ship.

ship·mate (ship'māt') *n.* A fellow sailor.

ship·ment (ship'mənt) *n.* **1** The act of shipping. **2** Goods shipped; a consignment.

ship·per (ship'ər) *n.* One who ships goods.

ship·ping (ship'ing) *n.* **1** The act, process, or business of shipping goods. **2** Ships collectively, esp. with respect to nationality or tonnage.

ship·shape (ship'shāp') *adj.* Trim; orderly; neat. —*adv.* In a seamanlike manner; neatly.

ship·worm (ship'wûrm') *n.* Any of various wormlike marine mollusks that undermine wooden piers, ships, etc., by boring into them.

ship·wreck (ship'rek') *n.* **1** A ship or parts of it after being wrecked. **2** The partial or total destruction of a ship at sea. **3** Utter destruction; ruin. —*v.t.* **1** To wreck, as a vessel. **2** To bring to disaster; destroy.

ship·wright (ship'rīt') *n.* One whose work is to construct or repair ships.

ship·yard (ship'yärd') *n.* An enclosure where ships are built or repaired.

shire (shīr) *n.* A territorial division of Great Britain; a county. [< OE *scīr*]

shirk (shûrk) *v.t.* **1** To avoid doing (something that should be done). —*v.i.* **2** To avoid work or evade obligation. —*n.* One who shirks: also **shirk'er.** [?]

shirr (shûr) *v.t.* **1** To gather (cloth) by parallel rows of small stitches. **2** To bake with crumbs in a buttered dish, as eggs. —*n.* A gathering of cloth made by shirring. [?]

shirt (shûrt) *n.* **1** A garment for the upper part of the body, usu. having a collar and cuffs and buttoning along the front. **2** UNDERSHIRT. —**lose one's shirt** *Slang* To lose everything. [< OE *scyrte* shirt, short garment]

shirt·ing (shûr'ting) *n.* Material used for making shirts, blouses, etc.

shirt·sleeve (shûrt'slēv') *adj.* **1** Not wearing a jacket or coat; informally dressed: a *shirt-sleeve* audience. Also **shirt-sleeved. 2** Straightforward; plain; simple and direct in technique, approach, manner, etc.: *shirt-sleeve* diplomacy.

shirt·waist (shûrt'wāst') *n.* A tailored blouse or shirt worn by women.

Shi·va (shē'və) SIVA.

shiv·er[1] (shiv'ər) *v.i.* To tremble, as with cold or fear. — *n.* The act of shivering; a shaking or quivering. —**shiv'·er·y** *adj.* [ME *shiveren*]

shiv·er[2] (shiv'ər) *v.t. & v.i.* To break suddenly into fragments; shatter. —*n.* A splinter; silver. [ME *schivere*]

shlock (shlok) *n.* SCHLOCK. —**shlock'y** *adj.* (**·i·er, ·i·est**)

shoal[1] (shōl) *n.* **1** A shallow place in any body of water. **2** A bank or bar of sand, esp. one seen at low water. —*v.i.* To become shallow. [< OE *sceald* shallow]

shoal[2] (shōl) *n.* **1** A thing or school, as of fish. —*v.i.* To gather in shoals. [< OE *scolu* shoal of fish.]

shoat (shōt) *n.* A young hog. [ME *shote*]

shock[1] (shok) *n.* **1** A violent collision or concussion; impact; blow. **2** The result of such a collision. **3** A sudden, severe effect on the mind or emotions; jolt: the *shock* of recognition. **4** Something causing such an effect. **5** An acute impairment of vital functions associated with failure of the circulatory system following grave trauma such as burns, poisoning, brain injury, massive bleeding, etc. **6** Involuntary muscular contraction caused by the passage of an electric current through the body. —*v.t.* **1** To disturb the emotions or mind of; horrify; disgust. **2** To subject to an electric shock. **3** To shake by sudden collison; jar. [< OF *choc*] —**shock'er** *n.* —**Syn.** *v.* **1** appall, take aback, surprise, astound.

shock[2] (shok) *n.* A number of sheaves of grain, stalks of corn, or the like, stacked for drying upright in a field. — *v.t. & v.i.* To gather (grain) into a shock or shocks. [ME *schokke*] —**shock'er** *n.*

shock[3] (shok) *adj.* Shaggy; bushy. —*n.* A coarse, tangled mass, as of hair. [?]

shock absorber *Mech.* A device designed to absorb the energy of sudden impacts, as in the suspension of an automobile.

shock·ing (shok'ing) *adj.* Causing sudden and violent surprise, horror, etc.: *shocking* news. —**shock'ing·ly** *adv.*

shock therapy A method of treating mental illness by inducing convulsions and unconsciousness with electric current or certain drugs. Also **shock treatment.**

shock wave *Physics* A powerful compression wave produced by a body moving faster than the speed of sound.

shod (shod) *p.t. & p.p.* of SHOE.

shod·dy (shod'ē) *n. pl.* **·dies 1** Reclaimed wool obtained by shredding waste materials. **2** Fiber or cloth manufactured of inferior material. **3** Vulgar display; sham. **4** Refuse; waste. —*adj.* **·di·er, ·di·est 1** Poorly made; inferior. **2** Made of or containing shoddy. **3** Cheaply pretentious; vulgar. **4** Nasty; mean: a *shoddy* remark. [?] —**shod'di·ly** *adv.* —**shod'di·ness** *n.* —**Syn.** *adj.* **1** tawdry, cheap, sloppy, second-rate.

shoe (shōo) *n.* **1** An outer covering, usu. of leather, for the human foot. **2** Something resembling a shoe in position or use. **3** A rim or plate of iron to protect the hoof of an animal. **4** The tread or outer covering of a pneumatic tire. **5** A braking device that stops or retards the motion of an object. —*v.t.* **shod** or **shoed, shoe·ing** To furnish with shoes or the like. [< OE *scōh*] —**sho′er** *n.*

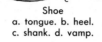

Shoe
a. tongue. b. heel.
c. shank. d. vamp.

shoe·horn (shōo′hôrn′) *n.* A smooth curved implement as of metal, horn, etc., shaped to aid in putting on a shoe.

shoe·lace (shōo′lās) *n.* A cord or string used to fasten a shoe.

shoe·mak·er (shōo′mā′kər) *n.* One who makes or repairs shoes. —**shoe′mak′ing** *n.*

shoe·shine (shōo′shīn′) *n.* The waxing and polishing of a pair of shoes.

shoe·string (shōo′string) *n.* SHOELACE. —**on a shoe·string** With meager or inadequate financial resources.

shoe·tree (shōo′trē′) *n.* A rigid form inserted in a shoe to hold its shape or to stretch it.

sho·far (shō′fär) A ram's horn used in Jewish ritual, sounded on solemn occasions. [< Heb. *shōphār*]

sho·gun (shō′gun) *n.* The hereditary commander in chief of the Japanese army until 1868. [< Chin. *chiang-chün* leader of an army] —**sho′gun·ate** (-it, -āt) *n.*

shone (shōn, shon) *p.t.* & *p.p.* of SHINE.

shoo (shōo) *interj.* Get away! —*v.t.* **1** To drive away by crying "shoo." —*v.i.* **2** To cry "shoo."

shoo-in (shōo′in′) *n. Informal* One who is virtually certain to win, as an election.

shook (shŏŏk) *p.t.* of SHAKE.

shoot (shōot) *v.* **shot, shoot·ing** *v.t.* **1** To hit, wound, or kill with a missile discharged from a weapon. **2** To discharge (a missile or weapon): to *shoot* an arrow or a gun. **3** To send forth, as questions, glances, etc. **4** To pass over or through swiftly: to *shoot* rapids. **5** To photograph or film. **6** To thrust out; dart; flick: with *out*: He *shot* out an arm in gesture. **7** To push into or out of the fastening, as the bolt of a door. **8** To propel, discharge, or dump, as down a chute or from a container. **9** *Slang* To inject (a drug, esp. a narcotic). **10** In games: **a** To score (a goal, point, total score, etc.). **b** To play (golf, craps, pool, etc.). **c** To propel (a basketball, puck, marble, etc.) to attempt a score. **d** To cast (dice). —*v.i.* **11** To discharge a missile from a firearm, bow, etc. **12** To go off; discharge. **13** To move swiftly; dart. **14** To extend or project. **15** To put forth buds, leaves, etc. **16** To record photographically. **17** In games, to make a play by propelling the ball, puck, etc., in a certain manner. —**shoot at** (or **for**) *Informal* To strive for; seek to attain. —**shoot the works** *Informal* To risk everything. —*n.* **1** A young branch or growth; offshoot. **2** The process of early growth. **3** A narrow passage in a stream; a rapid. **4** An inclined passage down which anything may be shot. **5** The act of shooting; a shot. **6** A shooting match, hunting party, etc. [< OE *scēotan*] —**shoot′er** *n.*

shooting star METEOR.

shoot-out (shōot′out′) *n.* A battle involving an exchange of gunfire.

shop (shop) *n.* **1** A place where goods and services are sold at retail: also **shoppe.** **2** A place for the carrying on of any skilled work: a machine *shop.* —**talk shop** To discuss one's work. —*v.i.* **shopped, shop·ping** To visit shops or stores to purchase or look at goods. [< OE *sceoppa* booth] —**shop′per** *n.* • *Shoppe* is an archaic spelling but is still used in the names of some establishments to suggest a quaint, old-fashioned character. However, the spelling *shop* has been in use since at least 1600, so it is hardly a novelty.

shop·keep·er (shop′kē′pər) *n.* One who owns or runs a shop.

shop·lift·er (shop′lif′tər) *n.* One who steals goods displayed for sale in a shop. —**shop′lift′ing** *n.*

shopping center A group of retail stores, restaurants, etc., including an ample parking area, usu. built as a unit and accessible chiefly by automobile.

shop steward A union worker elected to represent the union in conferences, etc., with management.

shop·worn (shop′wôrn′, -wōrn′) *adj.* **1** Soiled or damaged from having been handled or on display in a store. **2** Lacking freshness or originality: *shopworn* ideas.

sho·ran (shôr′an, shō′ran) *n.* A short-range electronic navigation system for ships and aircraft. [< *sho(rt) ra(nge) n(avigation)*]

shore[1] (shôr, shōr) *n.* **1** The land adjacent to an ocean, sea, lake, or large river. **2** Land, as distinguished from a body of water. [ME]

shore[2] (shôr, shōr) *v.t.* **shored, shor·ing** To prop, as a wall, by a vertical or sloping timber: usu. with *up.* —*n.* A beam set endwise as a prop, as against the side of a building. [ME *shoren*]

shore bird Any of various birds that feed and nest along the edges of lakes, oceans, rivers, etc.

shore·line (shôr′līn′, shōr′-) *n.* The line or contour of a shore.

shore patrol A detail of the U.S. Navy, Coast Guard, or Marine Corps assigned to police duties ashore.

shore·ward (shôr′wərd, shōr′-) *adj.* & *adv.* Toward the shore. Also **shore′wards.**

shor·ing (shôr′ing, shō′ring) *n.* **1** The act of propping, as with shores. **2** Shores or their manner of use.

shorn (shôrn, shōrn) A *p.p.* of SHEAR.

short (shôrt) *adj.* **1** Having relatively little linear extension; not long. **2** Being below the average stature; not tall. **3** Having relatively little extension in time; brief. **4** Of no great distance: a *short* trip. **5** Less than the usual or standard duration, quantity, extent, etc.: on *short* notice; a *short* letter. **6** Having few items: a *short* list. **7** Not reaching or attaining a goal or requirement: an effort *short* of the mark. **8** Not retentive: a *short* memory. **9** Abrupt in manner; curt. **10** Having an inadequate supply: *short* of cash. **11** Quickly aroused or agitated: a *short* temper. **12** *Phonet.* **a** Of relatively brief duration. **b** Describing any vowel sound that contrasts with a long vowel, as the vowel sound in *mat* contrasted with that in *mate.* **13** In finance: **a** Not having in one's possession when selling, as stocks or commodities. **b** Describing a sale of stocks or commodities that the seller does not possess but anticipates procuring subsequently at a lower price for delivery as contracted. **14** In English prosody, unaccented. **15** Flaky or crisp: pastry made *short* with lard. —**for short** For brevity and ease of expression: The University of Connecticut is called Uconn *for short.* —**in short** In summary; briefly. —**in short order** Without delay; forthwith; promptly. —*n.* **1** Something short, as a garment, vowel, syllable, etc. **2** *pl.* Short trousers extending to the knee or above the knee. **3** *pl.* A man's undergarment resembling short trousers. **4** SHORT CIRCUIT. **5** SHORT SUBJECT. —*adv.* **1** Abruptly: to stop *short.* **2** In a curt manner. **3** So as to be short of a goal or mark. **4** By means of a short sale. —*v.t.* & *v.i.* **1** To give (someone) less than the amount due. **2** SHORT-CIRCUIT. [< OE *sceort*] —**short′ness** *n.*

short·age (shôr′tij) *n.* An inadequate supply; deficiency.

short·bread (shôrt′bred′) *n.* A rich, dry cake or cooky made with shortening.

short·cake (shôrt′kāk′) *n.* A dessert consisting of a cake or biscuit served with fruit and often topped with whipped cream.

short·change (shôrt′chānj′) *v.t.* **·changed, ·chang·ing 1** To give less change than is due to. **2** To give less than what is rightfully due; cheat. —**short′chang′er** *n.*

short-cir·cuit (shôrt′sûr′kit) *v.t.* & *v.i.* To make a short circuit (in).

short circuit *Electr.* An electrical connection of low resistance or impedance, esp. when accidental or unintended.

short·com·ing (shôrt′kum′ing) *n.* A defect; imperfection.

short·cut (shôrt′kut′) *n.* **1** A route between two places

shorter than the regular way. 2 A means or method that saves time, effort, etc.

short·en (shôr′tən) v.t. 1 To make short or shorter; reduce; lessen. 2 To make flaky or crisp, as pastry. —v.i. 3 To become short or shorter. —**short′en·er** n.

short·en·ing (shôr′tən·ing, shôrt′ning) n. 1 Edible fat, esp. as used in bakery products. 2 An abbreviation.

short·fall (shôrt′fôl′) n. 1 A failure to meet an expectation or requirement. 2 The amount or extent of such a failure: a *shortfall* of 20 percent.

short·hand (shôrt′hand′) n. 1 Any of various systems of recording speech by writing symbols, abbreviations, etc.; stenography. 2 Any method of quick communication. —adj. 1 Written in shorthand. 2 Using shorthand.

short·hand·ed (shôrt′han′did) adj. Not having a sufficient number of assistants or workmen.

short·horn (shôrt′hôrn′) n. One of a breed of cattle with short horns.

short·lived (shôrt′līvd′, -livd′) adj. Living or lasting but a short time.

short·ly (shôrt′lē) adv. 1 In a short time; soon. 2 In few words; briefly. 3 Curtly; abruptly.

short shrift Little or no mercy or delay in dealing with a person or disposing of a matter.

short·sight·ed (shôrt′sī′tid) adj. 1 NEARSIGHTED. 2 Resulting from or characterized by lack of foresight. —**short′·sight′ed·ly** adv. —**short′·sight′ed·ness** n.

short·stop (shôrt′stop′) n. In baseball, an infielder stationed between second and third bases.

short story A narrative prose story shorter than a novel or novelette.

short subject A relatively brief film, as a documentary or animated cartoon.

short·tem·pered (shôrt′tem′pərd) adj. Easily aroused to anger.

short·term (shôrt′tûrm′) adj. Payable a short time after issue, as securities.

short ton 2,000 pounds avoirdupois.

short wave A radio wave having a wavelength of about 100 meters or less. —**short′·wave′** adj.

short·wind·ed (shôrt′win′did) adj. Becoming easily out of breath. —**short′·wind′ed·ness** n.

Sho·sho·ne (shō·shō′nē) n. One of a large tribe of North American Indians, formerly occupying parts of Wyoming, Idaho, Nevada, and Utah. Also **Sho·sho′ni**.

Sho·sho·ne·an (shō·shō′nē·ən, shō′shə·nē′ən) n. The largest branch of the Uto-Aztecan linguistic family of North American Indians. —adj. Of or pertaining to this linguistic branch. Also **Sho·sho′ni·an**.

shot¹ (shot) n. 1 The act of shooting, as a firearm. 2 Something likened to a shot, as a cutting remark. 3 pl. **shot** a Any of the lead pellets that comprise ammunition for a shotgun; also, the pellets collectively. b A solid missile, as a ball of iron, fired from a cannon or other gun. 4 A solid metal ball thrown for distance in sports competitions. 5 The range of a projectile. 6 One who shoots; a marksman. 7 A single effort, attempt, or opportunity to do a specific thing: to have a *shot* at getting the job. 8 In certain sports and games, the act or manner of shooting the ball, puck, etc., as in attempting a score. 9 A conjecture; guess. 10 A hypodermic injection, as of a drug, or the dose so administered. 11 An action or scene recorded on film. 12 The taking of a photograph; also, a photograph. 13 A blast, as in mining. —**like a shot** Very quickly. —adj. 1 Having a changeable or variegated appearance: purple fabric *shot* with gold. 2 Informal Utterly exhausted or ruined; washed-up. [< OE *scot*]

shot² (shot) p.t. & p.p. of SHOOT.

shote (shōt) n. SHOAT.

shot·gun (shot′gun′) n. A smoothbore gun, often double-barreled, adapted for the discharge of shot at short range. —adj. Coerced with, or as with, a shotgun.

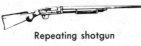

Repeating shotgun

should (shŏŏd) 1 p.t. of SHALL. 2 An auxiliary expressing: **a** Obligation: You *should* write that letter. **b** Condition: If I *should* go, he would go too. **c** Futurity, as viewed from the past: She wondered how she *should* dress for the

party. **d** Expectation: I *should* be at home by noon. **e** Politeness or modesty in requests or statements of doubt: I *should* hardly think so. [< OE *scolde*, p.t. of *sculan* owe]

shoul·der (shōl′dər) n. 1 The part of the trunk between the neck and the arm or forelimb. 2 The joint connecting the arm or forelimb with the body. 3 pl. The area of the upper back including both shoulders. 4 The shoulders considered as a support for burdens or the seat of responsibility. 5 The part of a garment designed to cover the shoulder. 6 The forequarter of an animal. 7 Something resembling a shoulder in form, as the broadened part of a bottle below the neck. 8 Either edge of a road or highway. —**straight from the shoulder** Informal Candidly; straightforwardly. —v.t. 1 To assume as something to be borne: to *shoulder* the blame. 2 To bear upon the shoulders. 3 To push with or as with the shoulder. —v.i. 4 To push with the shoulder. —**shoulder arms** To rest a rifle against the shoulder, holding the butt with the hand on the same side. [< OE *sculder* shoulder]

shoulder blade SCAPULA.

should·n't (shŏŏd′nt) Contraction of *should not*.

shout (shout) n. A sudden and loud outcry. —v.t. 1 To utter with a shout; say loudly. —v.i. 2 To utter a shout; cry out loudly. [ME *shouten*] —**shout′er** n.

shove (shuv) v.t. & v.i. **shoved, shov·ing** 1 To push, as along a surface. 2 To press forcibly (against); jostle. —**shove off** 1 To push along or away, as a boat. 2 Informal To depart. —n. The act of pushing or shoving. [< OE *scūfan*] —**shov′er** n.

shov·el (shuv′əl) n. A flattened scoop with a handle, as for digging, lifting earth, rock, etc. —v. **·eled** or **·elled, ·el·ing** or **·el·ling** v.t. 1 To take up and move or gather with a shovel. 2 To toss hastily or in large quantities as if with a shovel. 3 To clear or clean with a shovel, as a path. —v.i. 4 To work with a shovel. [< OE *scofl*] —**shov′el·er, shov′el·ler, shov′el·ful** n.

show (shō) v. **showed, shown** or **showed, show·ing** v.t. 1 To cause or permit to be seen; present to view. 2 To cause or allow (something) to be understood or known; explain. 3 To make known by behavior or expression; reveal: to *show* emotion. 4 To cause (someone) to understand or see; explain something to. 5 To confer; bestow: to *show* favor. 6 To make evident by the use of logic; prove. 7 To guide; lead, as into a room: Please *show* them in. 8 To enter in a show or exhibition. —v.i. 9 To become visible or known. 10 To appear; seem. 11 To make one's or its appearance. 12 To give a theatrical performance; appear. 13 In racing, to finish third or better. —**show off** To exhibit proudly; display ostentatiously. —**show up** 1 To expose or be exposed, as faults. 2 To be evident or prominent. 3 To make an appearance. 4 Informal To be better than. —n. 1 A presentation, as of a film, television program, or live entertainment, for viewing by spectators. 2 An exhibition, as of merchandise or art. 3 A competition at which certain animals, as dogs, are displayed and judged. 4 Someone or something regarded as a spectacle to be viewed, as in wonder or amusement. 5 An act of showing; display or manifestation: a *show* of strength. 6 Pretense or semblance; also, ostentation: mere *show*. 7 A sign of metal, oil, etc., in a mining or drilling operation. 8 In racing, a finish of third place or better. [< OE *scēawian*] —**show′er** n. —**Syn.** v. 1 exhibit, manifest, display. 4 convince, teach. n. 1 viewing, showing. 5 mark, sign, indication.

show biz Slang SHOW BUSINESS.

show·boat (shō′bōt′) n. A boat on which an acting troupe gives performances in river towns.

show business The entertainment industry, esp. the theater, motion pictures, and television.

show·case (shō′kās′) n. A glass case for exhibiting and protecting articles for sale.

show·down (shō′doun′) n. Informal Any action that forces a resolution of an issue or dispute.

show·er (shou′ər) n. 1 A fall of rain, hail, or sleet, esp. of short duration. 2 A copious fall, as of tears, sparks, or other small objects. 3 A bath in which water is sprayed from an overhead nozzle: also **shower bath**. 4 A party for the giving of gifts, as to a bride. —v.t. 1 To sprinkle or wet with or as with showers. 2 To discharge in a shower; pour out. 3 To bestow upon in large numbers; overwhelm: to

shower her with gifts. —*v.i.* **4** To fall as in a shower. **5** To take a shower bath. [< OE *scūr*] —**show'er·y** *adj.*

show·ing (shō'ing) *n.* **1** An act of presenting for public view, as a film. **2** A result of being shown, as in competition; record: a fine *showing*. **3** Presentation; statement, as of a subject.

show·man (shō'mən) *n. pl.* **·men** (-mən) **1** One who exhibits or produces shows. **2** One who is skilled at the art of effective performance. —**show'man·ship** *n.*

shown (shōn) *p.p.* of SHOW.

show·off (shō'ôf') *n.* One who makes a pretentious display of himself.

show·piece (shō'pēs') *n.* A prized object considered worthy of special exhibit.

show·place (shō'plās') *n.* A place exhibited or noted for its beauty, historic interest, etc.

show·room (shō'rōōm') *n.* A room for the display of merchandise.

show·y (shō'ē) *adj.* **show·i·er, show·i·est 1** Striking; splendid; brilliant. **2** Brilliant or conspicuous in a superficial or tasteless way; gaudy; meretricious. —**show'i·ly** *adv.* —**show'i·ness** *n.*

shpt. shipment.

shrank (shrangk) *p.t.* of SHRINK.

shrap·nel (shrap'nəl) *n. pl.* **·nel 1** A projectile for use against personnel, containing metal balls and a charge that expels them in mid-air. **2** Shell fragments. [< Henry *Shrapnel*, 1761–1842, British artillery officer]

shred (shred) *n.* **1** A long, irregular strip torn or cut off. **2** A fragment; particle. —*v.t.* **shred·ded** or **shred, shred·ding** To tear or cut into shreds. [< OE *scrēade* cutting] —**shred'der** *n.*

shrew (shrōō) *n.* **1** Any of numerous tiny mouselike mammals having a long pointed snout and soft fur. **2** A vexatious or nagging woman. [< OE *scrēawa*] —**shrew'ish** *adj.* —**shrew'ish·ly** *adv.* —**shrew'ish·ness** *n.*

Shrew

shrewd (shrōōd) *adj.* **1** Having keen insight, esp. in practical matters; clever; able. **2** Artful; sly. [< ME *shrew* malicious person] —**shrewd'ly** *adv.* —**shrewd'ness** *n.*

shriek (shrēk) *n.* A sharp, shrill cry or scream. —*v.i.* **1** To utter a shriek. —*v.t.* **2** To utter with a shriek. [< ON *skrækja*] —**shriek'er** *n.*

shrift (shrift) *n. Archaic* The act of shriving; confession. [< OE *scrift*]

shrike (shrīk) *n.* Any of various predatory birds with hooked bill and a slim tail. [< OE *scrīc* thrush]

shrill (shril) *adj.* **1** High-pitched and piercing, as a sound. **2** Emitting a sharp, piercing sound. **3** Harsh and immoderate: *shrill* criticism. —*v.t.* **1** To cause to utter a shrill sound. —*v.i.* **2** To make a shrill sound. [ME *shrille*] —**shrill'ness** *n.* —**shrill'y** *adv.* —**Syn. 1** penetrating. **3** intemperate, hysterical, bitter.

shrimp (shrimp) *n. pl.* **shrimp** or **shrimps 1** Any of numerous small, long-tailed crustaceans having ten legs and a fused head and thorax covered with a carapace, esp. various edible marine species. **2** *Informal* A small or insignificant person. [ME *shrimpe*]

Shrimp

shrine (shrīn) *n.* **1** A receptacle for sacred relics. **2** A sacred tomb or chapel. **3** A thing or spot made sacred by historic or other association. [< L *scrinium* case]

shrink (shringk) *v.* **shrank** or **shrunk, shrunk** or **shrunk·en, shrink·ing** *v.i.* **1** To draw together; contract as from heat, cold, etc. **2** To become less or smaller; diminish. **3** To draw back, as from disgust or horror; recoil: with *from.* —*v.t.* **4** To cause to shrink, contract, or draw together. —*n.* **1** The act of shrinking. **2** *Slang* A psychiatrist or psychoanalyst. [< OE *scrincan*] —**shrink'a·ble** *adj.* —**shrink'er** *n.*

shrink·age (shringk'ij) *n.* **1** The act or process of shrinking; contraction. **2** The amount lost by contraction. **3** Decrease in value; depreciation.

shrive (shrīv) *v.* **shrove** (shrōv) or **shrived, shriv·en** (shriv'-) or **shrived, shriv·ing** *Archaic v.t.* **1** To receive the confession of and give absolution to. —*v.i.* **2** To make confession. **3** To hear confession. [< OE *scrīfan*] —**shriv'er** *n.*

shriv·el (shriv'əl) *v.t. & v.i.* **·eled** or **·elled, ·el·ing** or **·el·ling 1** To contract into wrinkles; shrink and wrinkle. **2** To make or become helpless or impotent; wither. [?]

shroud (shroud) *n.* **1** A cloth used to wrap a corpse for burial. **2** Something that envelops or conceals. **3** *Naut.* One of a set of ropes or wires stretched from a masthead to the sides of a ship, serving to strengthen the mast laterally. —*v.t.* **1** To clothe in a shroud. **2** To envelop or conceal; block from view. [< OE *scrūd* a garment]

shrove (shrōv) *p.t.* of SHRIVE.

Shrove·tide (shrōv'tīd') *n.* The three days immediately preceding Ash Wednesday, on which confession is made in preparation for Lent.

shrub (shrub) *n.* A woody perennial of low stature, usu. with several stems. [< OE *scrybb* brushwood] —**shrub'bi·ness** *n.* —**shrub'by** *adj.* (·bi·er, ·bi·est)

shrub·ber·y (shrub'ər·ē) *n. pl.* **·ber·ies** A group of shrubs, as in a garden.

shrug (shrug) *v.t. & v.i.* **shrugged, shrug·ging** To draw up (the shoulders), as in displeasure, doubt, surprise, etc. —*n.* The act of shrugging the shoulders. [?]

shrunk (shrungk) *p.t. & p.p.* of SHRINK.

shrunk·en (shrungk'ən) *p.p.* of SHRINK. —*adj.* Contracted and atrophied.

shtick (shtik) *n. Slang* Something contrived to make one's personality distinct or memorable, as an actor's characteristic mannerism or a comedian's routine. [< Yiddish < G *stück* piece, bit]

sh. tn. short ton.

shuck (shuk) *n.* **1** A husk, shell, or pod, as of corn. • See WALNUT. **2** A shell of an oyster or a clam. **3** *Informal* Something of little or no value: not worth *shucks.* —*v.t.* **1** To remove the husk or shell from (corn, oysters, etc.). **2** *Informal* To take off or cast off, as an outer covering. [?] —**shuck'er** *n.*

shucks (shuks) *interj. Informal* A mild exclamation of annoyance, disgust, etc.

shud·der (shud'ər) *v.i.* To tremble or shake, as from fright or cold. —*n.* A convulsive shiver, as from horror or fear. [ME *shudren*] —**Syn.** *v.* shiver, quake. *n.* tremor.

shuf·fle (shuf'əl) *v.* **·fled, ·fling** *v.t.* **1** To shift about so as to mix up or confuse; disorder. **2** To change the order of by mixing, as cards in a pack. **3** To move (the feet) along with a dragging gait. **4** To change or move from one place to another. —*v.i.* **5** To scrape the feet along. **6** To change position; shift ground. **7** To resort to indirect or deceitful methods; prevaricate. **8** To shuffle cards. —*n.* **1** A dragging of the feet. **2** The act of shuffling, as cards. **3** A deceitful or evasive course; artifice. [< LG *schuffeln*] —**shuf'fler** *n.*

shuf·fle·board (shuf'əl·bôrd', -bōrd') *n.* A game in which disks are slid by means of a pronged cue along a smooth surface toward numbered spaces.

shun (shun) *v.t.* **shunned, shun·ning** To keep clear of; avoid. [< OE *scunian*] —**shun'ner** *n.*

shunt (shunt) *v.t.* **1** To turn aside. **2** In railroading, to switch, as a train or car, from one track to another. **3** *Electr.* **a** To connect a shunt in parallel with. **b** To be connected as a shunt for or of. **4** To put off on someone else, as a task. —*v.i.* **5** To move to one side. **6** *Electr.* To be diverted by a shunt: said of current. **7** To move back and forth; shuttle. —*n.* **1** The act of shunting. **2** A railroad switch. **3** *Electr.* A conductor joining two points in a circuit and diverting part of the current. —**shunt'er** *n.*

shush (shush) *interj.* Keep quiet! —*v.t.* To try to quiet.

shut (shut) *v.* **shut, shut·ting** *v.t.* **1** To bring into such position as to close an opening. **2** To close (an opening) so as to prevent passage or movement in or out. **3** To close and fasten securely, as with a lock. **4** To keep from entering or leaving: with *out* or *in.* **5** To close, fold, or bring together, as extended parts: to *shut* an umbrella. —*v.i.* **6** To be or become closed or in a closed position. —**shut down 1** To cease from operating, as a factory. **2** To lower;

come down close: The fog *shut down.* —**shut off 1** To cause to stop operating: to *shut off* a light. **2** To separate: usu. with *from: shut off* from all companionship. —**shut out** In sports, to keep (an opponent) from scoring during the course of a game. —**shut up 1** *Informal* To stop talking or cause to stop talking. **2** To close all the entrances to, as a house. **3** To imprison; confine. —*adj.* **1** Made fast or closed. **2** *Regional* Freed, as from something disagreeable; rid: with *of.* [< OE *scyttan*]

shut·down (shut′doun′) *n.* The closing of a mine, industrial plant, etc.

shut·eye (shut′ī′) *n. Slang* Sleep.

shut·in (shut′in′) *n.* An invalid who has to stay at home. —*adj.* **1** Obliged to stay at home. **2** Inclined to avoid people.

shut·out (shut′out′) *n.* In sports, a game in which one side is prevented from scoring.

shut·ter (shut′ər) *n.* **1** A hinged screen or cover, as for a window. **2** *Phot.* A mechanism for momentarily admitting light through a camera lens to a film or plate. **3** One who or that which shuts. —*v.t.* To furnish, close, or divide off with shutters.

shut·tle (shut′l) *n.* **1** A device used in weaving to carry the weft to and fro between the warp threads. **2** A similar device in a sewing machine. **3** A system of transportation for moving goods or passengers in both directions between two nearby points; also, the vehicle, as a bus, train, or airplane, operating between these points, usu. frequently. —*v.t. & v.i.* **·tled, ·tling** To move back and forth frequently or like a shuttle. [< OE *scytel* missile]

shut·tle·cock (shut′l·kok′) *n.* A rounded piece of cork, with a crown of feathers, that is hit back and forth in the game of badminton.

shy¹ (shī) *adj.* **shy·er, shy·est,** or **shi·er, shi·est 1** Easily frightened or startled; timid. **2** Uneasy in the company of others; bashful; reserved. **3** Circumspect; watchful; wary. **4** Expressing or suggesting diffidence or reserve: a *shy* look. **5** *Informal* Having less than is called for or expected; short. —*v.t.* **shied, shy·ing 1** To start suddenly to one side, as a horse. **2** To draw back, as from doubt or caution: with *off* or *away.* —*n.* A starting aside, as in fear. [< OE *scēoh* timid] —**shy′ly** *adv.* —**shy′ness** *n.*

Shuttlecock

shy² (shī) *v.t. & v.i.* **shied, shy·ing** To throw with a swift, sidelong motion. —*n. pl.* **shies** A careless throw; a fling. [?]

shy·ster (shīs′tər) *n. Informal* Anyone, esp. a lawyer, who conducts his business in an unscrupulous or tricky manner. [?]

SI International System of Units (Le Système International d'Unités).

Si silicon.

Si·am (sī·am′) *n.* The former name for THAILAND. —**Si·a·mese** (sī′ə·mēz′, -mēs′) *adj., n.*

Siamese cat A breed of short-haired cat, typically fawn-colored or pale cream, with dark ears, tail, feet, and face, and blue eyes.

Siamese twins Any twins conjoined at birth. [< Eng and Chang (1811–74), conjoined twins born in Siam.]

sib (sib) *n.* **1** A blood relation, esp. a brother or sister. **2** Kinsmen collectively; relatives. —*adj.* Related by blood; akin. [< OE *sibb*]

sib·i·lant (sib′ə·lənt) *adj.* **1** Hissing. **2** *Phonet.* Describing those consonants which are uttered with a hissing sound, as (s), (z), (sh), and (zh). —*n. Phonet.* A sibilant consonant. [< L *sibilare* to hiss] —**sib′i·lance** *n.* —**sib′i·lant·ly** *adv.*

sib·ling (sib′ling) *n.* A brother or sister. [< OE, a relative]

sib·yl (sib′əl) *n.* **1** In ancient Greece and Rome, any of several women who prophesied future events. **2** A fortune-teller; sorceress. —**si·byl·ic** (si·bil′ik) or **si·byl′lic, sib′yl·line** (-īn) *adj.*

sic¹ (sik) *adv.* So; thus: used within brackets after something quoted, to indicate that the quotation is exactly reproduced, even though questionable or incorrect. [L]

sic² (sik) *v.t.* **sicked, sick·ing 1** To urge to attack: to *sic* a dog on a burglar. **2** To seek out or attack: used in the imperative esp. to a dog. [Var. of SEEK]

sick¹ (sik) *adj.* **1** Affected with disease; ill; ailing. **2** Of or used by sick persons. **3** Affected by nausea; nauseated. **4**

Sickly; weak: a *sick* laugh. **5** Mentally or emotionally upset or ill: *sick* with grief. **6** Disposed to find offensive or wearisome from being surfeited: with *of: sick* of hearing transistor radios in public places. [< OE *sēoc*] —**sick′ish** *adj.* —**sick′ish·ly** *adv.* —**sick′ish·ness** *n.*

sick² (sik) *v.t.* SIC².

sick·bay (sik′bā′) *n.* That part of a ship or naval base set aside for the care of the sick.

sick·bed (sik′bed′) *n.* The bed upon which a sick person lies.

sick·en (sik′ən) *v.t. & v.i.* To make or become sick or disgusted. —**sick′en·er** *n.*

sick·en·ing (sik′ən·ing) *adj.* Disgusting; nauseating. —**sick′en·ing·ly** *adv.*

sick headache MIGRAINE.

sick·le (sik′əl) *n.* A cutting or reaping implement with a long, curved blade mounted on a short handle. —*v.t.* **·led, ·ling** To cut with a sickle, as grass, hay, etc. [< OE *sicel*]

sick·le-cell anemia (sik′əl·sel′) A severe, hereditary anemia occurring among the offspring of parents who both have sickle-cell trait.

sickle-cell trait A tendency in erythrocytes to become deformed into a sickle shape and to clog small blood vessels, occurring chiefly among Negroes and due to the presence of a genetic hemoglobin abnormality inherited from one parent. Also **sickl·e·mi·a** (sik′əl·ē′mē·ə).

Sickle

sick·ly (sik′lē) *adj.* **·li·er, ·li·est 1** Habitually ailing; unhealthy; feeble. **2** Marked by the prevalence of sickness. **3** Nauseating; disgusting; sickening. **4** Of or characteristic of sickness: a *sickly* appearance. **5** Lacking in conviction; weak; unconvincing: a *sickly* excuse. **6** Faint; pallid. —*adv.* In a sick manner; poorly. —*v.t.* **·lied, ·ly·ing** To make sickly, as in color. —**sick′li·ly** *adv.* —**sick′li·ness** *n.*

sick·ness (sik′nis) *n.* **1** The state of being sick; illness. **2** A particular form of disease. **3** Nausea. **4** Any disordered and weakened state.

side (sīd) *n.* **1** Any of the boundary lines of a surface or any of the surfaces of a solid: the *side* of a box. **2** A boundary line or surface, distinguished from the top and bottom or front and back. **3** Either of the surfaces of an object of negligible thickness, as a sheet of paper or a coin. **4** The right half or the left half of a human body, esp. of the torso, or of any animal. **5** The space beside someone. **6** A lateral part of a surface or object: the right *side* of a room. **7** The lateral half of a slaughtered animal: a *side* of beef. **8** One of two or more contrasted surfaces, parts, or places: the far *side* of a river. **9** A slope, as of a mountain. **10** An opinion, aspect, or point of view: the conservative *side* of the issue. **11** A group of competitors or partisans of a point of view. **12** Family connection, esp. by descent through one parent: my father's *side.* —**on the side** In addition to the main part or chief activity. —**side by side 1** Alongside one another. **2** In a spirit of cooperation; together. —**take sides** To give one's support to one of two sides engaged in a dispute. —*adj.* **1** Situated at or on one side. **2** Being from one side: a *side* glance. **3** Incidental: a *side* issue. **4** Being in addition to the main dish: a *side* order. —*v.t.* To provide with a side or sides. —**side with** To range oneself on the side of; support, esp. in a dispute. [< OE]

side arms Weapons worn at the side, as pistols.

side·board (sīd′bôrd′, -bōrd′) *n.* **1** A piece of dining-room furniture for holding tableware. **2** *pl. Brit.* SIDEBURNS.

side·burns (sīd′bûrnz′) *n.pl.* **1** Whiskers grown on the cheeks; burnsides. **2** The hair growing on the sides of a man's face in front of the ears.

side·car (sīd′kär′) *n.* A one-wheeled passenger car attached to the side of a motorcycle.

side effect A secondary, often harmful effect, as of a drug.

side·kick (sīd′kik′) *n. Slang* A faithful subordinate or friend.

side·light (sīd′līt′) *n.* **1** A light coming from the side. **2** Incidental illustration or information.

side·line (sīd′līn′) *n.* **1** An auxiliary line of goods. **2** Any additional or secondary work differing from one's main job. **3** One of the lines bounding the two sides of an athletic

field or court, as in football or tennis. **4** *pl.* The area just outside these lines. —*v.t.* **·lined**, **·lin·ing** To make unfit or unavailable for active participation: Injuries *sidelined* him.

side·long (sīd'lông', -long') *adj.* Inclining or tending to one side; lateral. —*adv.* **1** In a lateral or oblique direction. **2** On the side.

side·man (sīd'man') *n. pl.* **·men** (-men') One of the supporting musicians, as distinguished from the featured performers, of a band, esp. a jazz band.

si·de·re·al (sī·dir'ē·əl) *adj.* **1** Of or relating to the stars. **2** Measured by means of the stars: *sidereal* time. [< L *sidus* star] —**si·de·re·al·ly** *adv.*

sid·er·ite (sid'ə·rīt) *n.* **1** A glassy ferrous carbonate mineral. **2** An iron meteorite. [< Gk. *sidēros* iron] —**sid'er·it'ic** (-rit'ik) *adj.*

side·sad·dle (sīd'sad'l) *n.* A saddle for a woman wearing skirts, designed to be ridden facing sideways, with both legs on the same side of the horse.

side·show (sīd'shō') *n.* **1** A small show incidental to a major one, as in a circus. **2** Any subordinate issue or attraction.

side·split·ting (sīd'split'ing) *adj.* Provoking wild laughter; hilarious.

side·step (sīd'step') *v.* **·stepped**, **·step·ping** *v.i.* **1** To step to one side. **2** To avoid responsibility. —*v.t.* **3** To avoid, as an issue; dodge. —**side'step'per** *n.*

side step A step or movement to one side.

side·swipe (sīd'swīp') *v.t. & v.i.* **·swiped**, **·swip·ing** To strike or scrape along the side: to *sideswipe* a car while passing it. —*n.* **1** A glancing collision along the side. **2** *Informal* An oblique or parenthetical criticism.

side·track (sīd'trak') *v.t. & v.i.* **1** To move to a siding, as a railroad train. **2** To divert from the main issue or subject. —*n.* A railroad siding.

side·walk (sīd'wôk') *n.* A pavement at the side of the street for pedestrians.

side·ward (sīd'wərd) *adj.* Directed or moving toward or from the side; lateral. —*adv.* Toward or from the side: also **side'wards.**

side·ways (sīd'wāz') *adv.* **1** From one side. **2** So as to incline with the side forward: Hold it *sideways.* **3** Toward one side; askance; obliquely. —*adj.* Moving to or from one side. Also **side'way'**, **side'wise'** (-wīz').

side·wheel (sīd'ʰwēl') *adj.* Describing a steamboat having a paddle wheel on either side. —**side'-wheel'er** *n.*

sid·ing (sī'ding) *n.* **1** A railway track by the side of the main track. **2** A material used to cover the side of a frame building, as paneling or shingles.

si·dle (sīd'l) *v.i.* **·dled**, **·dling** To move sideways, esp. in a cautious or stealthy manner. —*n.* A sideways step or movement. [< obs. *sidling* sidelong] —**si'dler** *n.*

siege (sēj) *n.* **1** The surrounding of a town or fortified place in an effort to seize it, as after a blockade. **2** A steady attempt to win something. **3** A trying time: a *siege* of illness. —*v.t.* **sieged**, **sieg·ing** BESIEGE. [< L *sedere* sit]

si·en·na (sē·en'ə) *n.* **1** A yellowish brown pigment consisting of clay containing oxides of iron and manganese. **2** A yellowish brown color. **3** BURNT SIENNA. [< Ital. *(terra di) Siena* (earth of) Siena]

si·er·ra (sē·er'ə) *n.* A mountain range or chain, esp. one having a jagged outline. [< L *serra* a saw]

Si·er·ra Le·one (sē·er'rä lē·ōn', sir'ə-) An independent member of the Commonwealth of Nations in w Africa, 27,925 sq. mi., cap. Freetown. • See map at AFRICA.

si·es·ta (sē·es'tə) *n.* A nap or rest taken in the afternoon. [Sp.< L *sexta (hora)* sixth (hour), noon]

sieve (siv) *n.* A utensil or apparatus for sifting, consisting of a frame provided with a bottom of mesh wire. —*v.t. & v.i.* **sieved**, **siev·ing** To sift. [< OE *sife* sieve]

Sieve

sift (sift) *v.t.* **1** To pass through a sieve in order to separate the fine parts from the coarse. **2** To scatter by or as by a sieve. **3** To examine carefully. **4** To separate as if with a sieve; distinguish: to *sift* fact from fiction.

—*v.i.* **5** To use a sieve. **6** To fall or pass through or as through a sieve: The light *sifts* through the trees. [< OE *siftan*] —**sift'er** *n.*

Sig., **sig.** signal; signature; signor.

sigh (sī) *v.i.* **1** To draw in and exhale a deep, audible breath, as in expressing sorrow, weariness, pain, or relief. **2** To make a sound suggestive of a sigh, as the wind. **3** To yearn; long: with *for.* —*v.t.* **4** To express with a sigh. —*n.* **1** The act of sighing. **2** A sound of sighing or one suggestive of sighing. [ME *sighen*] —**sigh'er** *n.*

sight (sīt) *n.* **1** The act or faculty of seeing; vision. **2** Something seen; an image perceived by the eye; spectacle: an inspiring *sight;* an ugly *sight.* **3** A view; glimpse: to catch *sight* of someone. **4** The range or scope of vision. **5** *Informal* Something remarkable or strange in appearance. **6** *Usu. pl.* A place or thing of particular interest, as to a tourist: seeing the *sights.* **7** A point of view; estimation. **8** Mental perception or awareness: Don't lose *sight* of the facts. **9** A device to assist aiming, as a gun or a leveling instrument. **10** An aim or observation taken with a telescope or other sighting instrument. —**at** (or **on**) **sight 1** As soon as seen. **2** On presentation for payment. —**out of sight 1** Beyond range of sight. **2** *Informal* Beyond expectation; too great or too much. **3** *Slang* Extraordinarily good. —*v.t.* **1** To catch sight of; discern with the eyes: to *sight* shore. **2** To look at through a sight, as a telescope; observe. **3** To adjust the sights of, as a gun. **4** To take aim with. —*v.i.* **5** To take aim. **6** To make an observation or sight. —*adj.* **1** Understood or performed on sight without previous familiarity or preparation: *sight* reading of music. **2** Payable when presented: a *sight* draft. [< OE *gesiht*]

sight·ed (sīt'əd) *adj.* Having (a specified kind of) sight or vision: *far-sighted.*

sight·less (sīt'lis) *adj.* **1** Blind. **2** Invisible. —**sight'less·ly** *adv.* —**sight'less·ness** *n.*

sight·ly (sīt'lē) *adj.* **·li·er**, **·li·est 1** Pleasant to the view; comely. **2** Affording a grand view. —**sight'li·ness** *n.*

sight·see·ing (sīt'sē'ing) *n.* The practice of going to see places or things of interest, as in touring. —*adj.* Engaged in or for the purpose of sightseeing. —**sight'se'er** *n.*

sig·ma (sig'mə) *n.* The 18th letter in the Greek alphabet (Σ, σ, ς).

sign (sīn) *n.* **1** Anything that directs the mind or attention toward something: a *sign* of aging; a *sign* of intelligence. **2** A telltale mark or indication; trace: the first *sign* of spring. **3** A motion or action used to communicate a thought, desire, or command. **4** A symbol; token: black armbands as a *sign* of grief. **5** A conventional written or printed symbol representing a word or relation: $ is a dollar *sign;* = is an equal *sign.* **6** Information, directions, advertising, etc., publicly displayed. **7** A structure on which such information is printed or posted. **8** An occurrence taken to be miraculous and proof of divine commission. **9** One of the twelve equal divisions of the zodiac. —*v.t.* **1** To write one's signature on, esp. in acknowledging or attesting to the validity of a document. **2** To write (one's name). **3** To indicate or represent by a sign. **4** To mark or consecrate with a sign, esp. with a cross. **5** To engage by obtaining the signature of to a contract. **6** To hire (oneself) out for work: often with *on.* —*v.i.* **7** To write one's signature. **8** To make signs or signals. —**sign off** To announce the end of a program from a broadcasting station and stop transmission. —**sign up** To enlist, as in a branch of military service. [< L *signum*] —**sign'er** *n.* —**Syn.** *n.* **2** vestige, evidence, spoor.

sig·nal (sig'nəl) *n.* **1** A sign or event agreed upon or understood as a call to action. **2** Any device, sound, gesture, etc., used to convey information or give direction or warning. **3** An event that incites to action or movement: His yawn was our *signal* to leave. **4** *Telecom.* A flow of energy that varies so as to transmit information. —*adj.* **1** Out of the ordinary; notable; distinguished. **2** Used to signal. —*v.* **·naled** or **·nalled**, **·nal·ing** or **·nal·ling** *v.t.* **1** To inform or notify by signals. **2** To communicate by signals. —*v.i.* **3** To make a signal or signals. [< L *signum* sign] —**sig'nal·er** or **sig'nal·ler** *n.*

sig·nal·ize (sig′nəl·īz) v.t. ·ized, ·iz·ing 1 To make notable or distinguished. 2 To point out with care.

sig·nal·ly (sig′nəl·ē) adv. In a signal manner; extraordinarily.

sig·nal·man (sig′nəl·mən) n. pl. ·men (-mən) One who operates or is responsible for signals, as for a railroad.

sig·na·to·ry (sig′nə·tôr′ē, -tō′rē) n. pl. ·ries One who has signed or is bound by a document, esp. a nation so bound. —adj. Being a signatory. [< L signum a sign]

sig·na·ture (sig′nə·chər) n. 1 The name of a person written by himself. 2 The act of signing one's name. 3 Any identifying mark or sign, as a musical theme to signal the beginning and end of a television show. 4 Printing a A distinguishing mark or number on the first page of each sheet of pages to be gathered as a guide to the binder. b A printed sheet that when folded and trimmed constitutes a section of a book, as 32 pages. 5 Music A symbol or group of symbols at the beginning of a staff, indicating time or key. [< L signum sign]

sign·board (sīn′bôrd′, -bōrd′) n. A board displaying a sign, as an advertisement.

sig·net (sig′nit) n. 1 A seal used instead of a signature on a document to indicate its official nature. 2 An impression made by or as if by a seal. —v.t. To mark wth a signet or seal. [< L signum sign]

signet ring A finger ring bearing a signet, as a monogram.

sig·nif·i·cance (sig·nif′ə·kəns) n. 1 Importance; consequence. 2 That which is signified or intended to be expressed; meaning. 3 The state or character of being significant. Also **sig·nif′i·can·cy.**

sig·nif·i·cant (sig·nif′ə·kənt) adj. 1 Having or expressing a meaning; esp., rich in meaning: significant details. 2 Important; momentous. —**sig·nif′i·cant·ly** adv. —Syn. 1 meaningful, suggestive. 2 weighty, consequential.

sig·ni·fi·ca·tion (sig′nə·fə·kā′shən) n. 1 That which is signified; meaning; sense; import. 2 The act of signifying; communication.

sig·nif·i·ca·tive (sig·nif′ə·kā′tiv) adj. 1 Signifying. 2 Conveying a meaning; significant.

sig·ni·fy (sig′nə·fī) v. ·fied, ·fy·ing v.t. 1 To represent; mean; suggest. 2 To make known by signs or words; express. —v.i. 3 To have some meaning or importance; matter. [< L signum sign + -FY] —**sig′ni·fi′er** n.

sign language A system of communication by means of signs, largely manual.

si·gnor (sēn·yôr′) n. pl. **si·gno·ri** (-ē) or **si·gnors** Italian 1 A title of courtesy equivalent to Mr. or Sir. 2 A man; gentleman. Also **si·gnior′.** [< L senior senior]

si·gno·ra (sē·nyō′rä) n. pl. **si·gno·re** (-rā) or ·ras Italian 1 A title of courtesy equivalent to Mrs. or Madam. 2 A woman; lady.

si·gno·ri·na (sē′nyō·rē′nä) n. pl. ·ri·ne (-nā) or ·nas Italian 1 A title of courtesy equivalent to Miss. 2 An unmarried woman; young lady.

sign·post (sīn′pōst′) n. A post bearing a sign.

Sikh (sēk) n. An adherent of a religion of India characterized by monotheism and the rejection of caste. —adj. Of or pertaining to the Sikhs. [Hind., lit., disciple] —**Sikh′·ism** n.

si·lage (sī′lij) n. Succulent fodder stored in a silo.

si·lence (sī′ləns) n. 1 Absence of sound; stillness. 2 Abstinence from speech or from making any sound. 3 Failure to mention; oblivion; secrecy. —v.t. ·lenced, ·lenc·ing 1 To make silent. 2 To stop the activity or expression of; put to rest. —interj. Be silent. [< L silere be silent]

si·lenc·er (sī′lən·sər) n. 1 A device attached to the muzzle of a firearm to muffle the report. 2 One who or that which imposes silence.

si·lent (sī′lənt) adj. 1 Not making any sound or noise; noiseless. 2 Not speaking; mute. 3 Disinclined to talk; taciturn. 4 Present but not audible: silent tears. 5 Characterized by the absence of comment: His statement was silent on that point. 6 Free from activity, motion, or disturbance. 7 Written but not pronounced, as the e in bake. 8 Not accompanied by a sound track: a silent film. [< L silere be silent] —**si′lent·ly** adv. —**si′lent·ness** n.

silent partner A partner who shares in the financing of an enterprise but has no part in its management.

Silhouette of
Abraham
Lincoln

sil·hou·ette (sil′ōō·et′) n. 1 A profile drawing or portrait having its outline filled in with uniform color, usu. black. 2 The outline of a solid figure. —v.t. ·et·ted, ·et·ting To cause to appear in silhouette; outline. [< Étienne de Silhouette, 1709–1767, French minister]

sil·i·ca (sil′i·kə) n. The dioxide of silicon, occurring pure as quartz and as an important constituent of rocks, sand, and clay. [< L silex, silicis flint]

sil·i·cate (sil′ə·kāt, -i·kit) n. Any of various compounds consisting of an oxide of silicon and a metallic radical.

si·li·ceous (si·lish′əs) adj. Pertaining to or containing silica. Also **si·li′cious.**

si·lic·ic (si·lis′ik) adj. Pertaining to or derived from silica or silicon.

silicic acid Any of several gelatinous compounds of silica and water.

sil·i·con (sil′ə·kon′, -kən) n. A nonmetallic element (symbol Si) comprising about 25 percent of the earth's crust and forming many compounds analogous to those of carbon. [< L silex, silicis flint]

sil·i·cone (sil′ə·kōn′) n. Any of various synthetic compounds composed of chains of alternate silicon and oxygen atoms with hydrocarbon branches joined to the silicon.

sil·i·co·sis (sil′ə·kō′sis) n. A chronic lung disease due to inhalation of silica dust produced by stonecutting, etc.

silk (silk) n. 1 A soft, shiny fiber produced by various insect larvae, as silkworms, to form their cocoons. 2 Cloth or thread made of this fiber. 3 Anything resembling silk, as the fine strands of an ear of corn. 4 Usu. pl. A garment of silk, as the uniform of a jockey. —adj. Consisting of or like silk; silken. [< OE seoloc]

silk cotton The silky covering of the seeds of certain trees, used for filling cushions, etc.; kapok.

silk·en (sil′kən) adj. 1 Made of silk. 2 Like silk; glossy; smooth. 3 Suave; insinuating: silken speech. 4 Dressed in silk. 5 Luxurious.

silk-screen (silk′skrēn′) adj. Describing or made by a printing process which forces ink through the meshes of a silk screen prepared so that ink penetrates only in those areas to be printed. —v.t. To make or print by the silk-screen process.

silk-stock·ing (silk′stok′ing) adj. Marked by patrician elegance or extreme wealth. —n. A member of a silk-stocking social class.

silk·worm (silk′wûrm′) n. The larva of a moth that produces a dense silken cocoon.

silk·y (sil′kē) adj. **silk·i·er, silk·i·est** 1 Like silk; soft; lustrous. 2 Made or consisting of silk; silken. 3 Smooth or insinuating. —**silk′i·ly** adv. —**silk′i·ness** n.

sill (sil) n. 1 A horizontal member or beam forming the foundation, or part of the foundation, of a structure, as at the bottom of a casing in a building. 2 The horizontal part at the bottom of a door or window frame. [< OE syll]

sil·ly (sil′ē) adj. ·li·er, ·li·est 1 Showing a lack of ordinary sense or judgment; foolish. 2 Trivial; frivolous. 3 Informal Stunned; dazed, as by a blow. —n. pl. ·lies Informal A silly person. [< OE gesælig happy] —**sil′li·ly** or **sil′ly** adv. —**sil′li·ness** n.

si·lo (sī′lō) n. pl. ·los 1 A pit or tower in which fodder is stored. 2 An underground structure for the housing and launching of guided missiles. —v.t. ·loed, ·lo·ing To put or preserve in a silo. [< Gk. siros pit for corn]

silt (silt) n. 1 An earthy sediment consisting of extremely fine particles suspended in and carried by water. 2 A deposit of such sediment. —v.t. & v.i. To fill or become filled or choked with silt: usu. with up. [ME sylte] —**sil·ta·tion** (sil·tā′shən) n. —**silt′y** adj. (·i·er, ·i·est)

Si·lu·ri·an (si·lŏŏr′ē·ən, sī-) adj. & n. See GEOLOGY.

sil·van (sil′vən) adj. SYLVAN.

sil·ver (sil′vər) n. 1 A pale gray, lustrous, malleable metallic element (symbol Ag), having great electric and thermal conductivity and forming various photosensitive salts. 2 Silver regarded as a commodity or as a standard of currency. 3 Silver coin considered as money. 4 Articles, as tableware, made of or plated with silver; silverware. 5

A luster or color resembling that of silver. —*adj.* 1 Made of or coated with silver. 2 Resembling silver; having a silvery grey color. 3 Relating to, connected with, or producing silver. 4 Having a soft, clear, bell-like tone. 5 Designating a 25th wedding anniversary. 6 Favoring the use of silver as a monetary standard. —*v.t.* 1 To coat or plate with silver or something resembling silver. —*v.i.* 2 To become silver or white, as with age. [< OE *siolfor*] —**sil′·ver·er** *n.* —**sil′ver·ly** *adv.*

sil·ver·fish (sil′vər·fish′) *n. pl.* **·fish** or **·fish·es** Any of numerous silvery, wingless insects having bristles on the tail and long feelers, usu. found in damp and dark places.

silver fox 1 A fox with white-tipped black fur. 2 The fur, or a garment made of it.

silver nitrate The salt of silver and nitric acid, used in industry, photography, and in medicine as an antiseptic.

sil·ver·smith (sil′vər·smith′) *n.* A maker of silverware.

silver standard A monetary standard or system based on silver.

sil·ver·ware (sil′vər·wâr′) *n.* Articles made of or plated with silver, esp. tableware.

sil·ver·y (sil′vər·ē) *adj.* 1 Containing silver. 2 Resembling silver, as in luster or hue. 3 Having a soft, clear, bell-like tone. —**sil′ver·i·ness** *n.*

sim·i·an (sim′ē·ən) *adj.* Like or pertaining to the apes and monkeys. —*n.* An ape or monkey. [< L *simia* ape]

sim·i·lar (sim′ə·lər) *adj.* 1 Bearing resemblance to one another or to something else. 2 Having like characteristics, nature, or degree. 3 *Geom.* Shaped alike, but differing in measure. [< L *similis* like] —**sim′i·lar·ly** *adv.*

sim·i·lar·i·ty (sim′ə·lar′ə·tē) *n. pl.* **·ties** 1 The quality or state of being similar. 2 A point in which compared objects are similar.

sim·i·le (sim′ə·lē) *n.* A figure of speech expressing comparison or likeness by the use of such terms as *like* or *as.* [< L *similis* similar] • See METAPHOR.

si·mil·i·tude (si·mil′ə·t y o͞od) *n.* 1 Similarity; correspondence. 2 One who or that which is similar; counterpart. 3 A point of similarity. [< L *similis* like]

sim·i·tar (sim′ə·tər) *n.* SCIMITAR.

sim·mer (sim′ər) *v.i.* 1 To boil gently; be or stay at or just below the boiling point. 2 To be on the point of breaking forth, as with rage. —*v.t.* 3 To cook in a liquid at or just below the boiling point. —*n.* The state of simmering. [?]

si·mo·le·on (si·mō′lē·ən) *n. Slang* A dollar. [?]

Si·mon Le·gree (sī′mən li·grē′) A harsh or brutal taskmaster. [< a character in Harriet Beecher Stowe's *Uncle Tom's Cabin,* 1851]

si·mon-pure (sī′mən-py o͝or′) *adj.* Real; genuine; authentic. [< a character in Susanna Centlivre's play, *A Bold Stroke for a Wife,* 1718]

si·mo·ny (sī′mə·nē, sim′ə-) *n.* The purchase or sale of sacred things, as ecclesiastical preferment. [< *Simon* (Magus), who offered Peter money for the gift of the Holy Spirit *Acts* 8:9–24]

si·moom (si·mo͞om′, sī-) *n.* A hot, dry, dustladen, exhausting wind of the African and Arabian deserts. Also **si·moon′** (-mo͞on′). [< Ar. *samūm*]

simp (simp) *n. Slang* A simpleton.

sim·per (sim′pər) *v.i.* 1 To smile in a silly, self-conscious manner; smirk. —*v.t.* 2 To say with a simper. —*n.* A silly, self-conscious smile. —**sim′per·er** *n.* —**sim′per·ing·ly** *adv.*

sim·ple (sim′pəl) *adj.* **·pler, ·plest** 1 Easy to comprehend or do: a *simple* problem or task. 2 Not complex or complicated. 3 Without embellishment; plain; unadorned: a *simple* dress. 4 Having nothing added; mere: the *simple* truth. 5 Not luxurious or elaborate: a *simple* meal. 6 Consisting of one thing; single. 7 Free from affectation; artless: a *simple* soul. 8 Weak in intellect; silly or foolish. 9 Of humble rank or condition; ordinary. 10 *Bot.* Not divided: a *simple* leaf. —*n.* 1 One who is foolish or ignorant; simpleton. 2 A medicinal plant. [< L *simplex*] —**sim′ple· ness** *n.* —**Syn.** 4 bare, sheer. 5 frugal, austere. 7 guileless, unsophisticated.

simple fraction A fraction in which both numerator and denominator are integers.

simple interest Interest computed on the original principal alone.

simple machine Any one of certain basic mechanical devices, as the lever, the wedge, the inclined plane, the screw, the wheel and axle, and the pulley.

sim·ple-mind·ed (sim′pəl·mīn′did) *adj.* 1 Weak in intellect; foolish or feeble-minded. 2 Artless or unsophisticated. —**sim′ple-mind′ed·ly** *adv.* —**sim′ple-mind′ed·ness** *n.*

simple sentence A sentence consisting of one independent clause, without subordinate clauses.

sim·ple·ton (sim′pəl·tən) *n.* A weak-minded or silly person.

sim·plic·i·ty (sim·plis′ə·tē) *n. pl.* **·ties** 1 The state of being simple; freedom from complexity or difficulty. 2 Freedom from ornament or ostentation. 3 Freedom from affectation; artlessness; sincerity. 4 Foolishness; stupidity.

sim·pli·fy (sim′plə·fī) *v.t.* **·fied, ·fy·ing** To make more simple or less complex. —**sim′pli·fi·ca′tion, sim′pli·fi′er** *n.*

sim·plis·tic (sim·plis′tik) *adj.* Tending to ignore or overlook underlying questions, complications, or details. —**sim· plis′ti·cal·ly** *adv.*

sim·ply (sim′plē) *adv.* 1 In a simple manner. 2 Merely; only. 3 Really; absolutely: *simply* adorable.

sim·u·la·crum (sim′yə·lā′krəm, -lak′rəm) *n. pl.* **·cra** (-krə) 1 A likeness; image. 2 An imaginary or shadowy semblance. [< L, image]

sim·u·late (sim′yə·lāt) *v.t.* **·lat·ed, ·lat·ing** 1 To make a pretense of; imitate, esp. to deceive. 2 To assume or have the appearance or form of, without the reality. [< L *similis* like] —**sim′u·la′tive** *adj.* —**sim′u·la′tor** *n.*

sim·u·la·tion (sim′yə·lā′shən) *n.* 1 The act of simulating. 2 Something given the form or function of another, as in order to test or determine capability; model.

si·mul·cast (sī′məl·kast′, -käst′) *v.t.* **·cast, ·cast·ing** To broadcast by radio and television simultaneously. —*n.* A broadcast so transmitted.

si·mul·ta·ne·ous (sī′məl·tā′nē·əs, sim′əl-) *adj.* Occurring, done, or existing at the same time. [< L *simul* at the same time] —**si′mul·ta′ne·ous·ly** *adv.* —**si′mul·ta′ne·ous· ness, si′mul·ta·ne′i·ty** (-tə·nē′ə·tē) *n.*

sin (sin) *n.* 1 A transgression against moral or religious law or divine authority, esp. when deliberate. 2 The state of having thus transgressed; wickedness. 3 Any action or condition regarded as morally wrong or deplorable. —*v.* **sinned, sin·ning** *v.i.* 1 To commit a sin. 2 To do wrong. [< OE *synn*]

Si·nai (sī′nī), **Mount** The mountain where Moses received the law from God. *Ex.* 19.

since (sins) *adv.* 1 From a past time up to the present: traveling *since* last Monday. 2 At some time between the past and the present: He has *since* recovered from the illness. 3 Before now: long *since* forgotten. —*prep.* During the time following (a time in the past): Times have changed *since* you left. —*conj.* 1 During or within the time after which. 2 Continuously from the time when: She has been ill ever *since* she arrived. 3 Because of; inasmuch as. [< OE *siththan* afterwards]

sin·cere (sin·sir′) *adj.* **·cer·er, ·cer·est** Free from hypocrisy, deceit, or calculation; honest; genuine: a *sincere* friend; *sincere* regrets. [< L *sincerus* uncorrupted] —**sin· cere′ly** *adv.* —**sin·cere′ness** *n.*

sin·cer·i·ty (sin·ser′ə·tē) *n.* The state or quality of being sincere; honesty of purpose or character; freedom from hypocrisy.

sine (sīn) *n.* A function of an acute angle in a right triangle expressible as the ratio of the side opposite the angle to the hypotenuse. [< L *sinus* a bend]

si·ne·cure (sī′nə·ky o͝or, sin′ə-) *n.* A position or office providing compensation or other benefits but requiring little or no responsibility or effort. [< L *sine* without + *cura* care]

$BC/AB = $ sine of angle *a*

si·ne di·e (sī′nē dī′ē, sin′ā dē′ā) Without setting a date, as for another meeting; indefinitely: an adjournment *sine die.* [L, without a day]

---

si·ne qua non (sin′ə kwä nōn′, non′, sī′nē kwä non′) That which is absolutely indispensable; an essential element. [L, without which not]

sin·ew (sin′yo͞o) n. 1 TENDON. 2 Strength or power. 3 *Often pl.* A source of strength. —*v.t.* To strengthen, as with sinews. [< OE *sinu, seonu*] —**sin′ew·less** *adj.*

sin·ew·y (sin′yo͞o-ē) *adj.* 1 Of, like, or having sinews. 2 Having many sinews; tough. 3 Strong; brawny. 4 Vigorous; forceful.

sin·ful (sin′fəl) *adj.* Tainted with, full of, or characterized by sin. —**sin′ful·ly** *adv.* —**sin′ful·ness** *n.* —**Syn.** wicked, bad, immoral, evil.

sing (sing) *v.* sang or *(now less commonly)* sung, sung, sing·ing *v.i.* 1 To produce musical sounds with the voice. 2 To perform vocal compositions professionally or in a specified manner. 3 To produce melodious sounds, as a bird. 4 To make a continuous, melodious sound suggestive of singing, as a teakettle, the wind, etc. 5 To buzz or hum; ring: My ears are *singing.* 6 To be suitable for singing. 7 To relate or celebrate something in song or verse. 8 To compose poetry. 9 *Slang* To confess the details of a crime, esp. so as to implicate others. 10 To be joyous; rejoice. — *v.t.* 11 To perform (music) vocally. 12 To chant; intone. 13 To bring to a specified condition or place by singing: *Sing* me to sleep. 14 To relate, proclaim, praise, etc., in or as in verse or song. —*n. Informal* A singing, esp. by a group. [< OE *singan*] —**sing′a·ble** *adj.*

sing. singular.

singe (sinj) *v.t.* singed, singe·ing 1 To burn slightly. 2 To remove bristles or feathers from by passing through flame. 3 To burn the ends of (hair, etc.). —*n.* A slight or superficial burn; scorch. [< OE *sengan*] —**sing′er** *n.*

sing·er (sing′ər) *n.* 1 One who sings, esp. as a profession. 2 A poet. 3 A songbird.

Sin·gha·lese (sing′gə-lēz′, -lēs′) *adj.* Of or pertaining to a group of people in Sri Lanka or to their language. —*n.* 1 One of the Singhalese people. 2 Their language.

sin·gle (sing′gəl) *adj.* 1 Consisting of only one. 2 With no other or others; solitary; lone; alone. 3 Unmarried; also, pertaining to the unmarried state. 4 Of, pertaining to or involving only one person. 5 Consisting of only one part; simple. 6 Upright; sincere; honest. 7 Designed for use by only one person: a *single* bed. 8 *Bot.* Having only one row of petals, as a flower. —*n.* 1 One who or that which is single. 2 In baseball, a hit by which the batter reaches first base. 3 In cricket, a hit which scores one run. 4 *pl.* In tennis or similar games, a match with only one player on each side —*v.* ·gled, ·gling *v.t.* 1 To choose or select (one) from others: usually with *out.* —*v.i.* 2 In baseball, to make a single. [< L *singulus*] —**sin′gle·ness** *n.* —**sin′gly** *adv.*

sin·gle-breast·ed (sing′gəl-bres′tid) *adj.* Overlapping at the center of the front of the body just enough to allow for fastening by a single button or row of buttons.

single file 1 A line of people, animals, etc., moving one behind the other. 2 In such a line: to walk *single file.*

sin·gle-foot (sing′gəl-fo͝ot′) *n.* The gait of a horse in which the sequence in which the feet leave the ground is right hind, right fore, left hind, left fore. —*v.i.* To go at this gait.

sin·gle-hand·ed (sing′gəl-han′did) *adj.* 1 Done or working alone; without assistance; unaided. 2 Having but one hand. 3 Capable of being used with a single hand. —**sin′·gle-hand′ed·ly** *adv.*

sin·gle-heart·ed (sing′gəl-här′tid) *adj.* Sincere and undivided, as in purpose, dedication, feeling, etc. —**sin′gle-heart′ed·ly** *adv.*

sin·gle-mind·ed (sing′gəl-mīn′did) *adj.* 1 Having only one purpose or end in view. 2 Free from duplicity; ingenuous; sincere. —**sin′gle-mind′ed·ly** *adv.* —**sin′gle-mind′ed·ness** *n.*

sin·gle·stick (sing′gəl·stik′) *n.* 1 A wooden, swordlike stick used in fencing. 2 The art or an instance of fencing with such sticks.

sin·gle·ton (sing′gəl·tən) *n.* 1 A single card of a suit originally held in the hand of a player. 2 Any single thing, distinct from two or more of its group.

sin·gle-track (sing′gəl·trak′) *adj.* 1 Having only one track. 2 Having a limited scope, outlook, flexibility, etc.

sin·gle·tree (sing′gəl·trē′) *n.* WHIFFLETREE.

sing·song (sing′sông′, -song′) *n.* 1 Monotonous regularity of rhythm and rhyme in verse. 2 Verse characterized by such regularity. 3 A voice, speech tones, etc., characterized by a monotonous rise and fall of pitch. —*adj.* Having a monotonous rhythm or rise and fall of pitch.

sin·gu·lar (sing′gyə·lər) *adj.* 1 Being the only one of its type; unique; separate; individual. 2 Extraordinary; remarkable; uncommon: a *singular* honor. 3 Odd; not customary or usual. 4 *Gram.* Of, pertaining to, or being a word form which denotes one person or thing. —*n. Gram.* The singular number, or a word form having this number. —**sin′gu·lar·ly** *adv.* —**sin′gu·lar·ness** *n.* —**Syn.** 1 peculiar, distinctive. 3 strange, conspicuous.

sin·gu·lar·i·ty (sing′gyə·lar′ə·tē) *n. pl.* ·ties 1 The state or quality of being singular. 2 Something of uncommon or remarkable character.

sin·gu·lar·ize (sing′gyə·lə·rīz′) *v.t.* ·ized, ·iz·ing To make singular.

Sin·ha·lese (sin′hə·lēz′, -lēs′) *adj., n.* SINGHALESE.

sin·is·ter (sin′is·tər) *adj.* 1 Malevolent; evil: a *sinister* expression on the face. 2 Boding or attended with misfortune or disaster; inauspicious. 3 Of, pertaining to, or situated on the left side or hand. 4 *Her.* On the wearer's left, the spectator's right. [L, left, unlucky] —**sin′is·ter·ly** *adv.* —**sin′is·ter·ness** *n.*

sink (singk) *v.* sank or sunk, sunk (*Obs.* sunk·en), sink·ing *v.i.* 1 To go beneath the surface or to the bottom, as of water or snow. 2 To go down, esp. slowly or by degrees. 3 To seem to descend, as the sun. 4 To incline downward; slope gradually, as land. 5 To pass into a specified state: to *sink* into a coma. 6 To approach death: He's *sinking* fast. 7 To become less in force, volume, or degree: His voice *sank* to a whisper. 8 To become less in value, price, etc. 9 To decline in quality or condition; retrogress; degenerate: usu. with *into* or *to.* 10 To penetrate or be absorbed: The oil *sank* into the wood. 11 To be impressed or fixed, as in the heart or mind: I think that lesson will *sink* in. —*v.t.* 12 To cause to go beneath the surface or to the bottom: to *sink* a fence post. 13 To cause or allow to fall or drop; lower. 14 To cause to penetrate or be absorbed. 15 To make (a mine shaft, well, etc.) by digging or excavating. 16 To reduce in force, volume, or degree. 17 To debase or degrade. 18 To suppress or hide; restrain. 19 To defeat; ruin. 20 To invest. 21 To invest and subsequently lose. 22 To pay up; liquidate. 23 In certain sports, to cause (a ball or other object) to go through or into a receptacle or hole. —*n.* 1 A basinlike receptacle with a drainpipe and usu. a water supply. 2 A sewer or cesspool. 3 A place where corruption and vice gather or are rampant. 4 A hollow place or depression in a land surface, esp. one in which water collects or disappears by evaporation or percolation. 5 A body or mechanism by which matter or energy is absorbed or dissipated: a heat *sink.* [< OE *sincan*] —**sink′a·ble** *adj.* —**Syn.** 2 descend, dwindle, diminish, lessen.

sink·er (singk′ər) *n.* 1 One who or that which sinks. 2 A weight for sinking a fishing or sounding line. 3 *Informal* A doughnut.

sinking fund A fund accumulated to pay off a debt at maturity.

sin·less (sin′lis) *adj.* Having no sin; guiltless; innocent. —**sin′less·ly** *adv.* —**sin′less·ness** *n.*

sin·ner (sin′ər) *n.* One who has sinned.

Sino- *combining form* 1 Of or pertaining to the Chinese people, language, etc. 2 Chinese and: *Sino-Tibetan.* [< LL *Sinae* the Chinese]

Si·no-Ti·bet·an (sī′nō·ti·bet′n) *n.* A family of languages spoken over a wide area in CEN. and SE Asia, including the languages of China, Burma, Tibet, and Thailand.

sin·u·ate (sin′yo͞o·it, -āt) *adj.* 1 Winding in and out; wavy. 2 *Bot.* Having a strongly indented, wavy margin, as some leaves. —*v.i.* (sin′yo͞o·āt) ·at·ed, ·at·ing To curve in and out; turn; wind. [< L *sinus* curve] —**sin′u·ate·ly** *adv.* —**sin′u·a′tion** *n.*

sin·u·ous (sin′yo͞o·əs) *adj.* 1 Characterized by turns or curves; winding; undulating; tortuous: a *sinuous* path. 2 Devious; indirect; not straightforward. [< L *sinus* bend] —**sin′u·ous·ly** *adv.* —**sin·u·os·i·ty** (sin′yo͞o·os′ə·tē), **sin′u·ous·ness** *n.*

si·nus (sī′nəs) *n.* **1** Any of the natural cavities in the skull that contain air and usu. connect with the nostrils. **2** A dilated part of a blood vessel. **3** Any narrow opening leading to an abscess. **4** *Bot.* A recess or depression between two adjoining lobes, as of a leaf. [L, curve, hollow]

si·nu·si·tis (sī′nə·sī′tis) *n.* Inflammation of a sinus or the sinuses of the skull.

Si·on (sī′ən) *n.* ZION.

Siou·an (sōō′ən) *n. pl.* **Siouan** or **Siouans** **1** A large family of languages spoken by Indians who formerly inhabited parts of CEN. and E North America. **2** A member of any of the peoples speaking a language of this family. —*adj.* Of or pertaining to this language family.

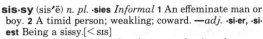

Sinuses
a. frontal.
b. maxillary.

Sioux (sōō) *n. pl.* **Sioux** One of a group of North American Indian tribes of Siouan linguistic stock formerly occupying parts of the Great Plains area in the Dakotas, Minnesota, and Nebraska.

sip (sip) *v.* **sipped, sip·ping** *v.t.* **1** To imbibe in small quantities. **2** To drink from by sips. **3** To take in; absorb. —*v.i.* **4** To drink in sips. —*n.* **1** A very small amount sipped. **2** The act of sipping. [< OE *sypian* drink in] —**sip·per** *n.*

si·phon (sī′fən) *n.* **1** A bent tube for transferring liquids from a higher to a lower level over an intervening barrier. **2** SIPHON BOTTLE. **3** *Zool.* A tubular structure in certain aquatic animals, as the squid, for drawing in or expelling liquids. —*v.t.* **1** To draw off by or cause to pass through or as through a siphon. —*v.i.* **2** To pass through a siphon. [< Gk. *siphōn*] —**si′phon·al** *adj.*

siphon bottle A bottle containing aerated or carbonated water, which is expelled through a bent tube in the neck of the bottle by the pressure of the gas when a valve in the tube is opened.

Siphon

sir (sûr) *n.* The conventional term of respectful address to a man: not followed by a proper name. [< SIRE]

Sir (sûr) *n.* A title of baronets and knights, used before the given name or the full name.

sire (sīr) *n.* **1** *Archaic* A father or forefather. **2** The male parent of an animal, esp. a domestic animal. **3** *Archaic* A man of high rank; also a form of address to a superior used esp. in addressing a king. —*v.t.* **sired, sir·ing** To beget; procreate: used chiefly of domestic animals. [< L *senior* older]

si·ren (sī′rən) *n.* **1** *Often cap. Gk. Myth.* One of a group of sea nymphs who lured sailors to destruction by their sweet singing. **2** A seductive, enticing woman. **3** A device for producing a series of loud tones, as for a warning, often consisting of a perforated rotating disk or disks through which sharp puffs of steam or compressed air are permitted to escape. —*adj.* Of or pertaining to a siren; seductive; enticing. [< Gk. *seirēn*]

Sir·i·us (sir′ē·əs) *n.* The Dog Star, the brightest star in the night sky, in the constellation of Canis Major. [< Gk. *seirios* scorching]

sir·loin (sûr′loin) *n.* A cut of meat, esp. of beef, from the upper portion of the loin. [< OF *sur-* above + *longe* loin]

si·roc·co (si·rok′ō) *n. pl.* **·cos** **1** A hot, dry, and dusty wind blowing from the Libyan deserts into S Europe, esp. to Italy, Sicily, and Malta. **2** Any hot or warm wind, esp. one blowing toward a center of low barometric pressure. [< Ar. *sharq* the east]

sir·up (sir′əp) *n.* SYRUP.

sis (sis) *n. Informal* Sister.

si·sal (sī′səl, -zəl, sis′əl) *n.* **1** A tough fiber obtained from the leaves of a species of agave. **2** The plant itself. Also **sisal hemp.** [< *Sisal,* town in Yucatán, Mexico]

sis·sy (sis′ē) *n. pl.* **·sies** *Informal* **1** An effeminate man or boy. **2** A timid person; weakling; coward. —*adj.* **·si·er, ·si·est** Being a sissy. [< SIS]

sis·ter (sis′tər) *n.* **1** A female person having the same parents as another person. **2** A female of the lower animals having one parent in common with another. **3 a** HALF SISTER. **b** SISTER-IN-LAW. **c** A foster sister. **4** A woman or girl allied to another or others by race, creed, a common interest, membership in a society, etc. **5** *Eccl.* A member of a sisterhood; nun. **6** *Chiefly Brit.* A head nurse in the ward or clinic of a hospital; also, any nurse. **7** A person or thing having similar characteristics to another. —*adj.* Bearing the relationship of a sister or one suggestive of sisterhood. [< OE *swostor*] —**sis′ter·ly** *adj.*

sis·ter·hood (sis′tər·hŏŏd) *n.* **1** A body of women united by some bond. **2** *Eccl.* A community of women forming a religious order. **3** The sisterly relationship.

sis·ter-in-law (sis′tər·in·lô′) *n. pl.* **sis·ters-in-law** **1** A sister of one's husband or wife. **2** A brother's wife. **3** A brother-in-law's wife.

Sis·y·phus (sis′ə·fəs) *Gk. Myth.* A king of Corinth, condemned in Hades forever to roll uphill a huge stone that always rolled down again.

sit (sit) *v.* **sat, sit·ting** *v.i.* **1** To rest on the buttocks or haunches; be seated. **2** To perch or roost, as a bird. **3** To cover eggs so as to give warmth for hatching. **4** To pose, as for a portrait. **5** To be in session; hold a session. **6** To occupy a seat in a deliberative body. **7** To have or exercise judicial authority. **8** To fit or hang: That dress *sits* well. **9** To rest; lie: an obligation that *sat* heavily on her. **10** To be situated or located. **11** BABY-SIT. —*v.t.* **12** To have or keep a seat or a good seat upon: to *sit* a horse. **13** To seat (oneself): *Sit* yourself down. —**sit in (on)** **1** To join; participate: to *sit in on* a game of cards or a business deal. **2** To attend or take part in a discussion or music session. **3** To take part in a sit-in. —**sit on (or upon)** **1** To belong to (a jury, commission, etc.) as a member. **2** To hold discussions about or investigate. **3** *Informal* To suppress, squelch, or delay action on or consideration of. —**sit out** **1** To remain until the end of. **2** To sit during or take no part in: They *sat out* a dance. **3** To stay longer than. —**sit up** **1** To assume a sitting position. **2** To maintain an erect posture while seated. **3** To stay up later than usual at night. **4** To be startled or show interest. [< OE *sittan*]

si·tar (si·tär′) *n.* A stringed instrument used in Hindu music, somewhat resembling the lute, having a long neck, a resonating gourd or gourds, and a variable number of strings, some of which are plucked, others vibrating sympathetically. [< Hind. *sitār*]

sit·com (sit′kom′) *n. Slang* A situation comedy. [< SIT(UATION) + COM(EDY)]

sit-down (sit′doun′) *n.* **1** A strike during which strikers refuse to work or leave their place of employment until agreement is reached: also **sit-down strike.** **2** A form of civil disobedience in which demonstrators obstruct some activity by sitting down and refusing to move.

Sitar

site (sīt) *n.* **1** A plot of ground used for or considered for some specific purpose. **2** The place, scene, or location of something: the battle *site*. [< L *situs* position]

sit-in (sit′in′) *n.* **1** SIT-DOWN (def. 2). **2** An organized demonstration in which a protesting group occupies an area prohibited to them, as by taking seats in a restricted restaurant, etc. —**sit′-in·ner** *n.*

sit·ter (sit′ər) *n.* One who sits, esp. a baby sitter.

sit·ting (sit′ing) *n.* **1** The act or position of one who sits. **2** An uninterrupted period of being seated, as for the painting of a portrait. **3** A session or term. **4** An incubation; period of hatching. **5** The number of eggs on which a bird sits at one incubation. —*adj.* That sits or is seated.

sitting duck *Informal* An easy target or victim.

sit·ting room (sit′ting·rŏŏm′, -rŏŏm′) LIVING ROOM.

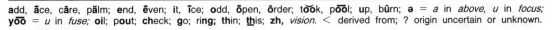

add, āce, câre, pälm; end, ēven; it, īce; odd, ōpen, ôrder; tŏŏk, pōōl; up, bûrn; ə = a in *above*, u in *focus*; yŏŏ = u in *fuse*; oil; pout; check; go; ring; thin; this; zh, *vision*. < derived from; ? origin uncertain or unknown.

sit·u·ate (sich′ōō·āt) *v.t.* **·at·ed, ·at·ing** To place in a certain position; locate. [<L *situs* a place]

sit·u·at·ed (sich′ōō·ā′tid) *adj.* **1** Having a fixed location. **2** Placed in certain circumstances or conditions, esp. financially: He is well *situated.*

sit·u·a·tion (sich′ōō·ā′shən) *n.* **1** The way in which something is situated, relative to its surroundings; position; location. **2** A locality; site. **3** Condition as modified or determined by circumstances. **4** A salaried post of employment. **5** A combination of circumstances at a specific time; state of affairs. **6** An unusual, difficult, critical, or otherwise significant state of affairs. **—sit′u·a′tion·al** *adj.*

situation comedy A television or radio show typically centered about a few characters involved in comical situations and presented in separate episodes.

Si·va (sē′və, shē′-) The Hindu god of destruction and reproduction. **—Si′va·ism** *n.* **—Si′va·is′tic** *adj.*

six (siks) *n.* **1** The sum of five plus one; 6; VI. **2** A set or group of six members. **—at sixes and sevens** In a state of confusion and indecision. [<OE] **—six** *adj., pron.*

six-pack (siks′pak′) *n.* **1** A group of six cans or bottles packaged as a unit. **2** The contents of such a unit.

six·pence (siks′pəns) *n.* **1** A British coin worth six pence. **2** The sum of six pence.

six·pen·ny (siks′pen′ē, -pən·ē) *adj.* **1** Worth, or sold for sixpence. **2** Cheap; trashy. **3** Denoting a size of nails, usu. two inches long.

six-shoot·er (siks′shōō′tər) *n.* A revolver that will fire six shots without reloading.

six·teen (siks′tēn′) *n.* **1** The sum of 15 plus 1; 16; XVI. **2** A set or group of sixteen members. **—six′teen′** *adj., pron.*

six·teenth (siks′tēnth′) *adj. & adv.* Next in order after the 15th. **—n. 1** The element of an ordered set that corresponds to the number 16. **2** One of 16 equal parts.

sixteenth note *Music* A note of one sixteenth of the time value of a whole note. • See NOTE.

sixth (siksth) *adj. & adv.* Next in order after the fifth. **—n. 1** The element of an ordered set that corresponds to the number six. **2** One of six equal parts. **3** *Music* The interval between a tone and another five steps away in a diatonic scale.

sixth sense The power of intuitive perception, thought of as independent of the five senses.

six·ti·eth (siks′tē·ith) *adj. & adv.* Tenth in order after the 50th. **—n. 1** The element of an ordered set that corresponds to the number 60. **2** One of sixty equal parts.

six·ty (siks′tē) *n. pl.* **·ties 1** The product of six and ten; 60; LX. **2** A set or group of 60 members. **3** *pl.* The numbers, years, etc., between 60 and 70. **—six′ty** *adj., pron.*

six·ty-fourth note (siks′tē-fôrth, -fōrth) *Music* A note of one sixty-fourth of the time value of a whole note. • See NOTE.

siz·a·ble (sī′zə·bəl) *adj.* Comparatively large. Also **size′a·ble. —siz′a·ble·ness** *n.* **—siz′a·bly** *adv.*

size[1] (sīz) *n.* **1** The dimensions of a thing as compared with some standard; physical magnitude or bulk. **2** Considerable amount, dimensions, etc. **3** One of a series of graded measures, as of hats, shoes, etc. **4** *Informal* State of affairs; true situation: That's the *size* of it. **—v.t. sized, siz·ing 1** To arrange or classify according to size. **2** To cut or otherwise make (an article) to a required size. **—size up** *Informal* **1** To form an opinion of. **2** To meet specifications. [<OF *assise* ASSIZE]

size[2] (sīz) *n.* A liquid preparation used to give a smooth finish to cloth, paper, or other porous surface. **—v.t. sized, siz·ing** To treat with size. [?<SIZE[1]]

size[3] (sīz) *adj.* SIZED (def. 1).

sized (sīzd) *adj.* **1** Having graded dimensions or a definite size: usu. in combination: large-*sized.* **2** Arranged according to size.

siz·ing (sī′zing) *n.* **1** SIZE[2]. **2** The act or process of adding size to a fabric, yarn, etc.

siz·zle (siz′əl) *v.* **·zled, ·zling** *v.i.* **1** To emit a hissing sound under the action of heat. **2** To seethe with rage, resentment, etc. **—v.t. 3** To cause to sizzle. **—n.** A hissing sound, as from frying. [Imit.]

S.J. Society of Jesus.

skald (skôld, skäld) *n.* A Scandinavian poet or bard of ancient times. [<ON *skáld* poet]

skate[1] (skāt) *n.* **1** A metal runner attached to a frame, with clamps or straps for fastening it to the sole of a boot or shoe, enabling the wearer to glide over ice. **2** A shoe or boot with such a runner permanently attached. **3** ROLLER SKATE. **—v.i. skat·ed, skat·ing** To glide or move over ice or some other smooth surface, on or as on skates. [<Du. *schaats*] **—skat′er** *n.*

skate[2] (skāt) *n.* Any of various flat-bodied, cartilaginous marine fishes with enlarged pectoral fins and ventral gill slits. [<ON *skata*]

skate·board (skāt′bôrd′, -bōrd′) *n.* A toy consisting of two pairs of skate wheels attached to a narrow board serving as a platform for riding. **—skate′board′er** *n.*

ske·dad·dle (ski·dad′l) *Informal v.i.* **·dled, ·dling** To flee in haste. **—n.** A hasty flight. [?]

Skate

skeet (skēt) *n.* A variety of trapshooting in which clay targets, hurled in such a way as to resemble the flight of birds, are fired at from various angles. [?]

skein (skān) *n.* **1** A fixed quantity of yarn, thread, silk, wool, etc., wound in a loose coil. **2** Something like this: a *skein* of hair. [<OF *escaigne*]

skel·e·ton (skel′ə·tən) *n.* **1** The supporting framework of a vertebrate, composed of bone and cartilage. **2** Any framework constituting the main supporting parts of a structure. **3** A mere sketch or outline of anything. **4** A very thin person or animal. **—skeleton in the closet** A secret source of shame or discredit. **—adj.** Of, pertaining to, or like a skeleton. [<Gk. *skeletos* dried up] **—skel·e·tal** *adj.*

skeleton key A key having a large part of the bit filed away to enable it to open many simple locks.

skep·tic (skep′tik) *n.* **1** A person characterized by skepticism, esp. in regard to religion. **2** A person who advocates or believes in philosophical skepticism. *Chiefly Brit. sp.* **scep′tic.** [<Gk. *skeptikos* reflective]

skep·ti·cal (skep′ti·kəl) *adj.* Of, pertaining to, characteristic of, or marked by skepticism. *Chiefly Brit. sp.* **scep′ti·cal. —skep′ti·cal·ly** *adv.* **—skep′ti·cal·ness** *n.*

skep·ti·cism (skep′tə·siz′əm) *n.* **1** A doubting or incredulous state of mind. **2** Doubt about basic religious doctrines such as immortality, revelation, etc. **3** The philosophical doctrine that absolute knowledge in any given area is unattainable, and that relative certainty can be approximated only by a continuous process of doubt, criticism, and suspended judgment. *Chiefly Brit. sp.* **scep′ti·cism.**

sketch (skech) *n.* **1** A rough or undetailed drawing or design, often done as a preliminary study. **2** A brief plan, description, or outline. **3** A short literary or musical composition. **4** A short scene, play, comical act, etc. **—v.t. 1** To make a sketch or sketches of. **—v.i. 2** To make a sketch or sketches. [<Gk. *schedios* impromptu] **—sketch′er** *n.*

sketch·book (skech′bōōk′) *n.* **1** A pad or book of drawing paper for sketching. **2** A printed volume of sketches.

sketch·y (skech′ē) *adj.* **sketch·i·er, sketch·i·est 1** Like or in the form of a sketch; roughly suggested without detail. **2** Incomplete; superficial. **—sketch′i·ly** *adv.* **—sketch′i·ness** *n.*

skew (skyōō) *v.i.* **1** To take an oblique direction. **2** To go sideways; squint. **—v.t. 3** To give an oblique form or direction to. **4** To give a bias to; misrepresent; distort. **—adj.** Placed, turned or running to one side; oblique; slanting. **2** ASYMMETRIC. **—n.** A deviation from straightness; an oblique direction or course. [<AF *eskiuer*]

skew·er (skyōō′ər) *n.* **1** A long pin of wood or metal, used for fastening meat while roasting. **2** Any of various articles of similar shape or use. **—v.t.** To run through or fasten with or as with a skewer. [?]

ski (skē, *Brit. also* shē) *n. pl.* **skis 1** One of a pair of flat, narrow runners of wood, metal, or other material, worn clamped to boots for gliding over snow. **2** WATER SKI. **—v. skied, ski·ing** *v.i.* **1** To glide or travel on skis. **—v.t. 2** To glide or travel over on skis. [Norw.<ON *skidh* snowshoe] **—ski′er** *n.*

skid (skid) *n.* **1** A log, plank, etc., often one of a pair, used to support or elevate something or as an incline on which heavy objects can be rolled or slid. **2** A low, movable platform that holds material to be moved, temporarily stored,

etc. **3** A shoe, drag, etc., used to prevent a wheel from turning. **4** A runner used in place of a wheel in the landing gear of an airplane or helicopter. **5** The act of skidding. — **on the skids** *Slang* Rapidly declining in prestige, power, etc. —*v.* **skid·ded, skid·ding** *v.i.* **1** To slide instead of rolling, as a wheel over a surface. **2** To slide due to loss of traction, as a vehicle. **3** *Aeron.* To slip sideways when turning. —*v.t.* **4** To put, drag, haul, or slide on skids. **5** To brake or hold back with a skid. [?] —**skid′der** *n.*

skid row *Slang* An urban section frequented by vagrants, derelicts, etc.

skiff (skif) *n.* **1** A light rowboat. **2** A small, light sailing vessel. [< OHG *scif* ship]

skill (skil) *n.* **1** Ability or proficiency in execution or performance. **2** A specific art, craft, trade, or job; also such an art, craft, etc., in which one has a learned competence. [< ON *skil* knowledge]

skilled (skild) *adj.* **1** Having skill. **2** Having or requiring a specialized ability, as in a particular occupation, gained by training or experience.

skil·let (skil′it) *n.* A frying pan. [ME *skelet*] • See APPLIANCE.

skill·ful (skil′fəl) *adj.* **1** Having skill. **2** Done with or requiring skill. Also **skil′ful.** —**skill′fully** *adv.* —**skill′ful·ness** *n.*

skim (skim) *v.* **skimmed, skim·ming** *v.t.* **1** To remove floating matter from the surface of (a liquid): to *skim* milk. **2** To remove (floating matter) from the surface of a liquid: to *skim* cream from milk. **3** To cover with a thin film, as of ice. **4** To move lightly and quickly across or over. **5** To cause to bounce and ricochet swiftly and lightly, as a coin across a pond. **6** To read or glance over hastily or superficially. —*v.i.* **7** To move quickly and lightly across or near a surface; glide. **8** To make a hasty and superficial perusal; glance: with *over* or *through.* **9** To become covered with a thin film. —*n.* **1** The act of skimming. **2** That which is skimmed off. **3** A thin layer or coating. —*adj.* Skimmed: *skim* milk. [< OF *escume* scum, foam] —**skim′mer** *n.*

skim milk Milk from which the cream has been removed. Also **skimmed milk.**

skimp (skimp) *v.i.* **1** To provide too little; scrimp. **2** To keep expenses at a minimum. —*v.t.* **3** To do poorly, hastily, or carelessly. **4** To be stingy in providing for. —*adj.* Scant; meager. [?] —**skimp′ing·ly** *adv.*

skimp·y (skim′pē) *adj.* **skimp·i·er, skimp·i·est** Scanty; insufficient. —**skimp′i·ly** *adv.* —**skimp′i·ness** *n.*

skin (skin) *n.* **1** The membranous outer covering of an animal body. **2** The pelt or hide of an animal. **3** A vessel for holding liquids, made of the skin of an animal. **4** Any outside layer, coat, or covering resembling skin, as fruit rind. —**by the skin of one's teeth** *Informal* Very closely or narrowly; barely. —**get under one's skin 1** To provoke one. **2** To be a source of excitement, emotion, etc., to one. —**have a thick (thin) skin** To be very insensitive (or sensitive), as to insult, criticism, etc. —**save one's skin** *Informal* To avoid harm or death. —*v.* **skinned, skin·ning** *v.t.* **1** To remove the skin of; peel. **2** To cover with or as with skin. **3** To remove as if taking off skin: to *skin* a dollar from a roll of bills. **4** *Informal* To cheat or swindle. —*v.i.* **5** To become covered with skin. **6** To climb up or down; shin. [< ON *skinn*] —**skin′ner** *n.*

skin-deep (skin′dēp′) *adj.* **1** Penetrating only as deep as the skin. **2** Of little importance; superficial.

skin diving Underwater swimming in which the swimmer is equipped with a breathing apparatus, as a snorkel, goggles, and with various other equipment as foot fins, rubber garments, etc. —**skin diver**

skin-flint (skin′flint) *n.* One who tries to get or save money in any possible way. —**Syn.** miser, niggard, scrooge.

skink (skingk) *n.* One of a group of lizards with short limbs and smooth, flat, shiny scales. [< Gk. *skinkos,* a kind of lizard]

skin·ner (skin′ər) *n.* **1** One who strips or processes the skins of animals. **2** A dealer in skins. **3** *Informal* A mule driver.

skin·ny (skin′ē) *adj.* **·ni·er, ·ni·est 1** Consisting of or like skin. **2** Without sufficient flesh; too thin. **3** Lacking the

normal or desirable quality, quantity, size, etc. —**skin′ni·ly** *adv.* —**skin′ni·ness** *n.*

skin·ny-dip (skin′ē-dip′) *Informal* *v.i.* **·dipped, ·dip·ping** To swim in the nude. —*n.* A swim in the nude. —**skin·ny-dip·per** *n.*

skin-tight (skin′tīt′) *adj.* Fitting tightly to the skin, as a garment.

skip (skip) *v.* **skipped, skip·ping** *v.i.* **1** To move with springing steps, esp. by a series of light hops on alternate feet. **2** To be deflected from a surface; ricochet. **3** To pass from one point to another without noticing what lies between. **4** *Informal* To leave or depart hurriedly; flee. **5** To be advanced in school beyond the next grade in order —*v.t.* **6** To leap lightly over. **7** To cause to ricochet. **8** To pass over or by without notice. **9** *Informal* To leave (a place) hurriedly. **10** To fail to attend a session or sessions of (church, school, etc.) **11** To cause to be advanced in school beyond the next grade in order —*n.* **1** A light bound or spring, esp. any of a series of light hops on alternate feet. **2** A passing over without notice. [Prob. < Scand.]

skip·jack (skip′jak) *n.* Any of various fishes that jump above or play along the surface of the water.

skip·per[1] (skip′ər) *n.* **1** One who or that which skips. **2** Any of various insects that make erratic, skipping movements.

skip·per[2] (skip′ər) *n.* **1** The master or captain of a vessel, esp. of a small ship or boat. **2** One who is in charge of any endeavor. —*v.t.* To act as the skipper of (a vessel, etc.) [< Du. *schip* ship]

skirl (skûrl, skirl) *v.i.* **1** To shriek shrilly, as a bagpipe. —*v.t.* **2** To play on the bagpipe. —*n.* A high, shrill sound, as of a bagpipe. [< Scand.]

skir·mish (skûr′mish) *n.* **1** A minor fight or encounter, usu. an incident in a larger conflict. **2** Any unimportant dispute, argument, etc. —*v.i.* To take part in a skirmish. [< OF *eskermir* to fence, fight] —**skir′mish·er** *n.*

skirt (skûrt) *n.* **1** That part of a dress, gown, etc., that hangs from the waist down. **2** A separate garment for women or girls that hangs from the waist down. • See PLEAT. **3** Anything that hangs or covers like a skirt: the *skirt* of a dressing table. **4** *Slang* A girl; woman. **5** The margin, border, or outer edge of anything. **6** *pl.* The border, fringe, or edge of a particular area; outskirts. —*v.t.* **1** To lie along or form the edge of; to border. **2** To surround or border: with *with.* **3** To pass around or about, usu. to avoid crossing: to *skirt* the town. —*v.i.* **4** To be on or pass along the edge or border. [< ON *skyrt* shirt]

skit (skit) *n.* **1** A short theatrical sketch, usu. humorous or satirical. **2** A short piece of writing, humorous or satirical in tone. [?]

skit·ter (skit′ər) *v.i.* **1** To glide or skip along a surface lightly and quickly. **2** To draw a lure or baited hook along the surface of the water with a skipping or twitching movement. —*v.t.* **3** To cause to skitter.

skit·tish (skit′ish) *adj.* **1** Easily frightened, as a horse. **2** Very playful or lively. **3** Unreliable; fickle. [ME] —**skit′·tish·ly** *adv.* —**skit′tish·ness** *n.*

skit·tle (skit′l) *n.* **1** *pl. (construed as sing.)* A British version of the game of ninepins, in which a wooden disk or ball is thrown to knock down the pins. **2** One of the pins used in this game. —**beer and skittles** Carefree, unruffled enjoyment: usu. with a negative: Life is not all *beer and skittles.* [?]

skiv·vy (skiv′ē) *n. pl.* **·vies** *Slang* **1** A man's T-shirt. **2** *pl.* Men's underwear. [?]

skoal (skōl) *interj.* Good health, good luck, etc.: used as a toast. [< Dan. and Norw. *skaal* cup < ON *skāl* bowl]

Skr. Sanskrit.

Skt. Sanskrit.

sku·a (skyōō′ə) *n.* A predatory sea bird. Also **skua gull.** [< ON *skūfr*]

skul·dug·ger·y (skul·dug′ər·ē) *n.* Dishonesty; trickery; underhandedness. [?]

skulk (skulk) *v.i.* **1** To move about furtively or slily; sneak. **2** *Chiefly Brit.* To shirk; evade work or responsibility. —*n.* One who skulks. [< Scand.] —**skulk′er** *n.*

---

add, āce, câre, pălm; end, ēven; it, īce; odd, ōpen, ôrder; tŏŏk, pōōl; up, bûrn; ə = *a* in *above, u* in *focus;* yōō = *u* in *fuse;* oil; pout; check; go; ring; thin; ᴛʜis; zh, *vision.* < derived from; ? origin uncertain or unknown.

skull (skul) *n.* **1** The bony framework of the head of a vertebrate animal; the cranium. **2** The head considered as the seat of intelligence; mind. [< Scand.]

skull and cross-bones A representation of the human skull over two crossed thighbones, used as a warning label on poison and, formerly, as an emblem of piracy.

skull·cap (skul'kap') *n.* A cap closely fitting the skull and having no brim or peak.

skunk (skungk) *n.* **1** A small nocturnal carnivore of North America, usu. black with a white stripe down the back, and ejecting an offensive odor when attacked. **2** *Informal* A low, contemptible person. —*v.t. Slang* To defeat, as in a contest, esp. to defeat so thoroughly as to keep from scoring. [< Algon. *seganku*]

skunk cabbage A stemless perennial herb growing in marshy terrain and having a strong, skunklike odor. Also **skunk'weed'** (-wēd').

Skunk

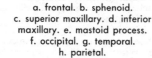

Bones of the human skull
a. frontal. b. sphenoid.
c. superior maxillary. d. inferior maxillary. e. mastoid process.
f. occipital. g. temporal.
h. parietal.

sky (skī) *n. pl.* **skies 1** The blue vault that seems to bend over the earth; the firmament. **2** *Often pl.* The upper atmosphere, esp. in regard to its appearance: cloudy *skies*. **3** The celestial regions; heaven. **4** Climate; weather. —**out of a clear** (or **blue**) **sky** Without any warning. —**to the skies** Without reservations: to praise something *to the skies*. —*v.t.* **skied** or **skyed, sky·ing** *Informal* **1** To hit, throw, bat, etc., high into the air. **2** To hang, as a picture, esp. at an exhibition, above eye level. [< ON *skȳ* cloud]

sky blue A blue like the color of the sky; azure. —**sky'·blue'** *adj.*

sky·dive (skī'dīv') *v.i.* **·dived, ·div·ing** To engage in skydiving. —**sky'div·er** *n.*

sky·div·ing (skī'dī'ving) *n.* The sport of jumping from an airplane and performing various maneuvers before opening a parachute.

sky·jack (skī'jak') *v.t.* HIJACK (def. 3). [< SKY + (HI)JACK] —**sky'jack'er** *n.*

sky·lark (skī'lärk') *n.* A lark noted for singing as it flies. —*v.i.* To indulge in hilarious or boisterous frolic. —**sky'·lark'er** *n.*

sky·light (skī'līt') *n.* A window facing skyward.

sky·line (skī'līn') *n.* **1** The line where earth and sky appear to meet; horizon. **2** The outline of buildings, trees, etc., against the sky.

sky·rock·et (skī'rok'it) *n.* A rocket that is shot high into the air. —*v.t. & v.i.* To rise or cause to rise or ascend steeply, like a skyrocket, as wages, prices, etc.

sky·sail (skī'səl, -sāl') *n. Naut.* A small sail above the royal in a square-rigged vessel.

sky·scrap·er (skī'skrā'pər) *n.* A very high building.

sky·ward (skī'wərd) *adv.* Toward the sky. Also **sky'·wards.** —**sky'ward** *adj.*

sky·writ·ing (skī'rī'ting) *n.* The forming of words in the air by the release of a substance, as a jet of vapor, from an airplane. —**sky'writ'er** *n.*

slab (slab) *n.* **1** A fairly thick, flat piece or slice, as of metal, stone, meat, etc. **2** An outer piece cut from a log. —*v.t.* **slabbed, slab·bing 1** To saw slabs from, as a log. **2** To form into a slab or slabs. [ME]

slack¹ (slak) *adj.* **1** Hanging loosely. **2** Careless; remiss; slovenly; slow. **3** Weak; loose: a *slack* mouth. **4** Lacking activity; not brisk or busy; slow or sluggish: a *slack* season. **5** Listless; limp: a *slack* grip. **6** Flowing sluggishly, as water. —*v.t.* **1** To make slack. **2** To slake, as lime. —*v.i.* **3** To be or become slack. **4** To become less active or less busy: usu. with *off.* —*n.* **1** The part of anything, as a rope, that is slack. **2** A period of inactivity. **3** A cessation of movement, as in a current. —*adv.* In a slack manner. [< OE *slæc*] —**slack'ly** *adv.* —**slack'ness** *n.*

slack² (slak) *n.* A mixture of coal dust, dirt, and small pieces of coal left after coal has been screened. [ME *sleck*]

slack·en (slak'ən) *v.t. & v.i.* To make or become slack.

slack·er (slak'ər) *n.* One who shirks his duties, esp. one who avoids military service in wartime.

slacks (slaks) *n.pl.* Trousers, esp. for informal wear.

slag (slag) *n.* **1** *Metall.* The fused residue separated in the reduction of ores. **2** Volcanic scoria. —*v.t. & v.i.* **slagged, slag·ging** To form into slag. [< MLG *slagge*] —**slag'gy** *adj.*

slain (slān) *p.p.* of SLAY.

slake (slāk) *v.* **slaked, slak·ing** *v.i.* **1** To lessen the force of; quench: to *slake* thirst or flames. **2** To mix (an oxide, as lime, etc.) with water; to hydrate. —*v.i.* **3** To become hydrated; said of lime. [< OE *slacian* retard]

slaked lime Calcium hydroxide produced by mixing calcium oxide and water.

sla·lom (slä'ləm, slä'-) *n.* In skiing, a race over a zigzag course laid out between upright obstacles. —*v.i.* To ski in or as in a slalom. [Norw.]

slam¹ (slam) *v.* **slammed, slam·ming** *v.t.* **1** To shut with violence and noise. **2** To put, dash, throw, etc., with violence. **3** *Slang* To strike with the fist. **4** *Informal* To criticize severely. —*v.i.* **5** To shut or move with force. —*n.* **1** A closing or striking with a bang; the act or noise of slamming. **2** *Informal* Severe criticism. [? < Scand.]

slam² (slam) *n.* **1** GRAND SLAM (def. 1). **2** LITTLE SLAM. [?]

slam-bang (slam'bang') *Informal adv.* Vigorously, violently, or noisily. —*adj.* Vigorous, violent, or noisy.

slan·der (slan'dər) *n.* **1** The uttering of false statements or misrepresentations which defame and injure the reputation of another. **2** Such a statement. —*v.t.* **1** To injure by uttering a false statement, etc.; defame. —*v.i.* **2** To utter slander. [< L *scandalum* scandal] —**slan'der·er** *n.* • Popularly, *slander* and *libel* are used synonomously to mean defamation. Legally, however, *slander* refers to oral defamation and *libel* to defamation by any other means, as writing, pictures, effigies, etc.

slan·der·ous (slan'dər·əs) *adj.* **1** Uttering slander. **2** Containing or constituting slander. —**slan'der·ous·ly** *adv.* —**slan'der·ous·ness** *n.*

slang (slang) *n.* **1** A type of popular language comprised of words and phrases of a vigorous, colorful, or facetious nature, which are invented or derived from the unconventional use of the standard vocabulary. **2** The special vocabulary of a certain class, group, profession, etc.; argot; jargon. [?] —**slang'i·ness** *n.* —**slang'y** *adj.*

slant (slant) *v.t.* **1** To give a sloping direction to. **2** To write or edit (news or other literary matter) so as to express a special attitude or appeal to a particular group, interest, etc. —*v.i.* **3** To have or take an oblique or sloping direction. —*adj.* Sloping —*n.* **1** A slanting direction, course, line, etc.; incline. **2** A point of view, esp. one that is personal or peculiar. [< Scand.] —**slant'ing** *adj.* —**slant'ing·ly** *adv.* —**slant'ing·ness** *n.*

slant·wise (slant'wīz') *adj.* Slanting; oblique. —*adv.* At a slant or slope; obliquely. Also **slant'ways'** (-wāz').

slap (slap) *n.* **1** A blow delivered with the open hand or with something flat. **2** The sound made by such a blow, or a sound like it. **3** An insult or rebuff. —*v.* **slapped, slap·ping** *v.t.* **1** To strike with the open hand or with something flat. **2** To put, place, throw, etc., violently or carelessly. —*adv.* **1** Suddenly; abruptly. **2** Directly; straight: *slap* into his face. [< LG *slapp*] —**slap'per** *n.*

slap-dash (slap'dash') *adj.* Done or acting in a hasty or careless way. —*n.* Something done in a hasty or careless manner. —*adv.* In a slap-dash manner.

slap-hap·py (slap'hap'ē) *adj. Slang* **1** Confused or dazed, as by blows to the head. **2** Giddy or silly.

slap·jack (slap'jak) *n.* PANCAKE.

slap·stick (slap'stik') *n.* **1** A flexible, double paddle formerly used in farces and pantomimes to make a loud report when an actor was struck with it. **2** The type of comedy which depends on farce, violent activity, etc. —*adj.* Using or suggestive of such comedy.

slash (slash) *v.t.* **1** To cut violently with or as with an edged instrument; gash. **2** To strike with a whip; lash; scourge. **3** To slit, as a garment, so as to expose ornamental material or lining in or under the slits. **4** To criticize severely. **5** To reduce sharply, as salaries. —*v.i.* **6** To make a long sweeping stroke with or as with something sharp; cut. —*n.* **1** The act of slashing. **2** The result of slashing; cut; slit; gash. **3** An ornamental slit cut in a garment. **4** An opening in a forest, covered with debris, as from cutting timber. **5** Such debris. [? < OF *esclashier* to break] —**slash′er** *n.*

slash·ing (slash′ing) *adj.* **1** Severely critical; merciless. **2** Spirited; dashing; impetuous. **3** *Informal* Tremendous; great. —*n.* A slash. —**slash′ing·ly** *adv.* —**slash′ing·ness** *n.*

slat (slat) *n.* Any thin, narrow strip of wood or metal; lath. —*v.t.* **slat·ted, slat·ting** To provide or make with slats. [< OF *esclat* splinter, chip]

slat (slāt) *n.* **1** A rock that splits readily into thin and even sheets or layers. **2** A piece, slab, or plate of slate used for roofing, writing upon, etc. **3** A list of candidates, as for nomination or election. **4** A dull bluish gray color resembling that of slate: also **slate gray.** —**a clean slate** A record unmarred by dishonor or dishonesty. —*v.t.* **slat·ed, slat·ing** **1** To cover with or as with slate. **2** To put on a political slate or a list of any sort. [< OF *esclat* a chip, splinter] —**slat′er** *n.* —**slat′y** *adj.* (**·i·er, ·i·est**)

slat·tern (slat′ərn) *n.* An untidy or slovenly woman. [?]

slat·tern·ly (slat′ərn·lē) *adj.* Of, pertaining to, characteristic of, or fit for a slattern. —*adv.* In the manner of a slattern. —**slat′tern·li·ness** *n.* —**Syn.** *adj.* untidy, dowdy, frowzy, sluttish.

slaugh·ter (slô′tər) *n.* **1** The act of killing, esp. the butchering of animals for market. **2** The wanton or savage killing of one or more human beings, esp. of a great number in battle. —*v.t.* **1** To kill for the market; butcher. **2** To kill wantonly or savagely, esp. in large numbers. [< ON *slātr* butcher's meat] —**slaugh′ter·er** *n.* —**slaugh′ter·ous** *adj.* —**slaugh′ter·ous·ly** *adv.*

slaugh·ter·house (slô′tər·hous′) *n.* A place where animals are butchered.

Slav (släv, slav) *n.* A member of any of the Slavic-speaking peoples of E, SE, or CEN. Europe.

Slav. Slavic.

slave (slāv) *n.* **1** A person who is owned by and completely subject to another; one bound by slavery. **2** A person who is totally subject to some habit, influence, etc. **3** One who labors like a slave; drudge. **4** A machine or device that is controlled by another machine or device. **5** SLAVE ANT. —*v.i.* **slaved, slav·ing** To work like a slave; toil; drudge. [< Med. L *sclavus* Slav]

slave ant An ant enslaved by members of a slave-making ant species.

slave-driv·er (slāv′drī′vər) *n.* **1** An overseer of slaves at work. **2** Any severe or exacting taskmaster.

slave·hold·er (slāv′hōl′dər) *n.* An owner of slaves. —**slave′hold′ing** *adj.* & *n.*

slav·er[1] (slā′vər) *n.* A person or a vessel engaged in the slave trade.

slav·er[2] (slav′ər) *v.i.* To dribble saliva; drool. —*n.* Saliva dribbling from the mouth. [? < ON *slafra*] —**slav′er·er** *n.*

slav·er·y (slā′vər·ē, slāv′rē) *n.* **1** The legalized social institution in which humans are held as property or chattels. **2** The condition of being a slave. **3** Submission to some habit, influence, etc. **4** Slavish toil; drudgery.

slave trade The business of dealing in slaves, esp. the procurement, transportation, and sale of black Africans.

slav·ey (slā′vē, slav′ē) *n. pl.* **slav·eys** *Chiefly Brit. Informal* A drudge, usu. a maidservant.

Slav·ic (slä′vik, slav′ik) *adj.* Of or pertaining to the Slavs or their languages. —*n.* A branch of the Indo-European language family including Byelorussian, Bulgarian, Czech, Polish, Serbo-Croatian, Slovene, Russian, and Ukrainian.

slav·ish (slā′vish) *adj.* **1** Of, pertaining to, or characteristic of a slave; servile. **2** Having no originality; imitative. —**slav′ish·ly** *adv.* —**slav′ish·ness** *n.*

slaw (slô) *n.* COLESLAW. [< Du. *sla*, short for *salade* salad]

slay (slā) *v.t.* **slew, slain, slay·ing** **1** To kill violently; slaughter. **2** *Informal* To amuse, impress, etc., in an overwhelming way. [< OE *slēan*] —**slay′er** *n.*

slea·zy (slē′zē, slā′-) *adj.* **·zi·er, ·zi·est** **1** Lacking firmness of texture or substance. **2** Cheap in character or quality; shoddy, shabby, etc.: a *sleazy* novel; a *sleazy* dress. [?] —**slea′zi·ly** *adv.* —**slea′zi·ness** *n.*

sled (sled) *n.* **1** A vehicle on runners, designed for carrying people or loads over snow and ice. **2** A small sled used esp. by children for sliding on snow and ice. —*v.* **sled·ded, sled·ding** *v.t.* **1** To convey on a sled. —*v.i.* **2** To ride on or use a sled. [< MLG *sledde*] —**sled′der** *n.*

sled·ding (sled′ing) *n.* **1** The act of using or riding on a sled. **2** The conditions under which one uses a sled. **3** *Informal* The conditions under which one pursues any goal; going; progress.

sledge[1] (slej) *n.* A vehicle mounted on low runners for moving loads, esp. over snow and ice. —*v.t.* & *v.i.* **sledg·ing** To travel or convey on a sledge. [< MDu. *sleedse*]

Sledge

sledge[2] (slej) *n.* & *v.t.*, *v.i.* **sledged, sledg·ing** SLEDGEHAMMER. [< OE *slecg*]

sledge·ham·mer (slej′ham′ər) *n.* A long, heavy hammer, usu. wielded with both hands. —*v.t.* & *v.i.* To strike with or as with such a hammer. —*adj.* Like a sledgehammer; extremely powerful; crushing.

sleek (slēk) *adj.* **1** Smooth and glossy. **2** Well-groomed or well-fed. **3** Smooth-spoken and polished in behavior, esp. in a specious way. —*v.t.* **1** To make smooth or glossy; polish. **2** To soothe; mollify. [Var. of SLICK] —**sleek′ly** *adv.* —**sleek′ness** *n.*

Sledge-hammers

sleep (slēp) *n.* **1** A natural, recurrent physiological state characterized by cessation of voluntary movement and inattention to external stimuli. **2** A period of sleep. **3** Any condition of inactivity or rest. —**last sleep** Death. —*v.* **slept, sleep·ing** *v.i.* **1** To be or fall asleep; slumber. **2** To be in a state resembling sleep. —*v.t.* **3** To rest or repose in: to *sleep* the sleep of the dead. **4** To provide with sleeping quarters; lodge: The hotel can *sleep* a hundred guests. —**sleep away** To pass or spend in sleeping. —**sleep in** To sleep in the house where one works. —**sleep off** To get rid of by sleeping: He *slept off* a headache. —**sleep on** To postpone a decision upon. [< OE *slēp*]

sleep·er (slē′pər) *n.* **1** One who or that which sleeps. **2** A railroad sleeping car. **3** A heavy beam resting on or in the ground, as a support for a roadway, rails, etc. **4** *Informal* Someone or something thought to be unpromising that unexpectedly attains value, importance, notoriety, etc.

sleeping bag A large, warmly-lined bag, usu. zippered and often padded, for sleeping in esp. outdoors.

sleeping car A passenger railroad car with accommodations for sleeping.

sleeping sickness 1 Any of several often fatal tropical diseases caused by protozoans transmitted by the bites of certain insects, as the tsetse fly in Africa, and marked by fever and progressive lethargy. **2** A form of encephalitis.

sleep·less (slēp′lis) *adj.* **1** Unable to sleep; wakeful; restless. **2** Marked by or giving no sleep. **3** Always active or moving. —**sleep′less·ly** *adv.* —**sleep′less·ness** *n.*

sleep·walk·er (slēp′wô′kər) *n.* A person who walks in his sleep; somnambulist. —**sleep′walk′ing** *n.*

sleep·y (slē′pē) *adj.* **sleep·i·er, sleep·i·est** **1** Inclined to or ready for sleep; drowsy. **2** Lethargic, inactive, sluggish, or dull. **3** Conducive to sleep. —**sleep′i·ly** *adv.* —**sleep′i·ness** *n.*

sleet (slēt) *n.* **1** A mixture of snow or hail and rain. **2** Partly frozen rain. **3** A thin coating of ice, as on rails, wires, roads, etc. —*v.i.* To pour or shed sleet. [ME *slete*] —**sleet′y** *adj.*

sleeve (slēv) *n.* **1** The part of a garment that serves as a

covering for the arm. 2 *Mech.* A tube or tubelike part surrounding another part or into which another part fits. —**up one's sleeve** Hidden but at hand —*v.t.* **sleeved, sleev·ing** To furnish with a sleeve or sleeves. [< OE *slēfe*]

sleigh (slā) *n.* A light vehicle with runners, used esp. for transporting people on snow and ice. —*v.i.* To ride or travel in a sleigh. [< Du. *slee*, contraction of *slede* sledge[1]] —**sleigh'er** *n.*

Sleigh

sleight (slīt) *n.* 1 Deftness; skill; dexterity. 2 Craft; cunning. [< ON *slægdh* slyness]

sleight of hand 1 Skill in performing magical tricks or in juggling. 2 An instance of such skill in performing.

slen·der (slen'dər) *adj.* 1 Having a small width or circumference, in proportion to length or height; long and thin. 2 Having a slim figure; attractively slight. 3 Having slight force or foundation. 4 Small or inadequate. [ME *slendre*] —**slen'der·ly** *adv.* —**slen'der·ness** *n.*

slen·der·ize (slen'də·rīz) *v.t.* & *v.i.* **·ized, ·iz·ing** To make or become slender.

slept (slept) *p.t.* & *p.p.* of SLEEP.

sleuth (slooth) *n.* 1 *Informal* A detective. 2 A bloodhound: also **sleuth'hound.** —*v.i.* To act as a detective. [< ON *slōdh* track]

slew[1] (sloo) *p.t.* of SLAY.

slew[2] (sloo) *n.* SLOUGH[1] (def. 2).

slew[3] (sloo) *n.* *Informal* A large number or amount. [< Ir. *sluagh*]

slew[4] (sloo) *v.* & *n.* SLUE[1].

slice (slīs) *n.* 1 A thin, broad piece cut off from a larger body. 2 A share or portion. 3 Any of various implements with a thin, broad blade, as a spatula. 4 **a** The course of a ball so hit that it curves in the direction of the dominant hand of the player who propels it. **b** The ball that follows such a course. —*v.* **sliced, slic·ing** *v.t.* 1 To cut or remove from a larger piece: often with *off, from,* etc. 2 To cut, separate, or divide into parts, shares, or thin, broad pieces. 3 To stir, spread, etc. with a slice. 4 To hit (a ball) so as to produce a slice. —*v.i.* 5 To cut with or as with a knife. 6 To slice a ball, as in golf. [< OHG *slizan* to slit] —**slic'er** *n.*

slick (slik) *adj.* 1 Smooth, slippery, or sleek. 2 *Informal* Deceptively clever; tricky; smooth. 3 Clever; deft; adept. 4 *Informal* Technically skillful but shallow and insignificant: a *slick* novel. 5 *Slang* Very good, attractive, enjoyable, etc. —*n.* 1 A smooth place on a surface of water, as from oil. 2 A film of oil on the surface of water. 3 *Informal* A magazine printed on glossy paper. —*adv.* *Slang* In a slick or smooth manner; deftly, cleverly, smoothly, etc. —*v.t.* 1 To make smooth, trim, or glossy. 2 *Informal* To make smart or presentable: often with *up.* [< OE *slician* make smooth]

slick·er (slik'ər) *n.* 1 A long, loose waterproof coat of oilskin. 2 *Informal* A clever, deceptive, crooked person.

slide (slīd) *v.* **slid, slid** or **slid·den, slid·ing** *v.i.* 1 To pass along a surface with a smooth movement. 2 To move smoothly over snow or ice. 3 To move or pass stealthily or imperceptibly. 4 To proceed in a natural way; drift: to let the matter *slide.* 5 To pass or fall gradually (into a specified condition). 6 To slip from a position: The cup *slid* off the saucer. 7 To slip or fall by losing one's equilibrium or foothold. 8 In baseball, to throw oneself along the ground toward a base. —*v.t.* 9 To cause to slide, as over a surface. 10 To move, put, enter, etc., with quietness or dexterity: with *in* or *into.* —*n.* 1 An act of sliding. 2 An inclined plane, channel, etc., on which persons, goods, logs, etc., slide downward to a lower level. 3 A small plate of glass on which a specimen is mounted and examined through a microscope. 4 A small plate of transparent material bearing a single image for projection on a screen. 5 A part or mechanism that slides, as the U-shaped portion of the tubing which is pushed in and out to vary the pitch of a trombone. 6 The slipping of a mass of earth, snow, etc., from a higher to a lower level. 7 The mass that slips down. [< OE *slīdan*] —**slid'er** *n.*

slide fastener ZIPPER.

slide rule A device consisting of a rigid ruler with a central sliding piece, both graduated, used in calculation.

sliding scale A schedule affecting imports, prices, or wages, varying under conditions of consumption, demand, or market price.

slight (slīt) *adj.* 1 Of small importance or degree: a *slight* illness. 2 Slender in build: a *slight* figure. 3 Frail; fragile: a *slight* structure. —*v.t.* 1 To omit due courtesy toward or respect for: to *slight* a friend. 2 To do carelessly or thoughtlessly; shirk. 3 To treat as trivial or insignificant. —*n.* An act of discourtesy or disrespect. [< ON *slēttr* smooth] —**slight'er, slight'ness** *n.* —**slight'ly** *adv.*

sli·ly (slī'lē) *adv.* SLYLY.

slim (slim) *adj.* **slim·mer, slim·mest** 1 Small in thickness in proportion to height or length. 2 Slight; meager: a *slim* chance of survival. —*v.t.* & *v.i.* **slimmed, slim·ming** To make or become thin or thinner. [< Du. *slim* bad] —**slim'ly** *adv.* —**slim'ness** *n.*

slime (slīm) *n.* 1 Soft, moist, adhesive mud or earth; muck. 2 A mucous exudation from the bodies of certain organisms. 3 An offensive, digusting substance or quality. —*v.t.* **slimed, slim·ing** 1 To smear with or as with slime. 2 To remove slime from, as fishes. [< OE *slīm*]

slim·y (slī'mē) *adj.* **slim·i·er, slim·i·est** 1 Covered with slime. 2 Containing slime. 3 Filthy; foul. —**slim'i·ly** *adv.* —**slim'i·ness** *n.*

sling (sling) *n.* 1 A strap or pocket with a string attached to each end, for hurling a stone. 2 One of various devices for holding up an injured arm. 3 A device, as a band or chain, for lifting or moving heavy objects. 4 The act of slinging; a sudden throw. 5 A drink made of sugar, liquor, and water: a gin *sling.* —*v.t.* **slung, sling·ing** 1 To fling; hurl. 2 To move or hoist, as by a rope or tackle. 3 To suspend loosely in a sling. [? < ON *slyngva* hurl] —**sling'er** *n.*

sling·shot (sling'shot') *n.* A forked stick with an elastic strap attached to the prongs for hurling small missiles.

slink (slingk) *v.* **slunk** or **slinked, slink·ing** *v.i.* To move or go furtively or stealthily. [< OE *slincan*] —**slink'ing·ly** *adv.* —Syn. creep, steal, sneak, skulk.

slink·y (slingk'ē) *adj.* **slink·i·er, slink·i·est** 1 Sneaking; stealthy. 2 *Slang* Sinuous or feline in movement or form. —**slink'i·ly** *adv.* —**slink'i·ness** *n.*

slip[1] (slip) *v.* **slipped, slip·ping** *v.t.* 1 To cause to glide or slide. 2 To put on or off easily, as a loose garment. 3 To convey slyly or secretly. 4 To free oneself or itself from. 5 To unleash, as hounds. 6 To release from its fastening and let run out, as a cable. 7 To dislocate, as a bone. 8 To escape or pass unobserved: It *slipped* my mind. —*v.i.* 9 To slide so as to lose one's footing. 10 To fall into an error. 11 To escape. 12 To move smoothly and easily. 13 To go or come stealthily: often with *off, away,* or *from.* 14 To overlook: to let an opportunity *slip.* —**let slip** To say without intending to. —**slip one over on** *Informal* To take advantage of by trickery. —**slip up** *Informal* To make a mistake. —*n.* 1 A sudden slide. 2 A slight mistake. 3 A narrow space between two wharves. 4 A pier. 5 An inclined plane leading down to the water, on which vessels are repaired or constructed. 6 A woman's undergarment approximately the length of a dress. 7 A pillowcase. 8 A leash containing a device which permits quick release of the dog. 9 Undesired relative motion, as between a wheel and the road; also, the amount of this. —**give (someone) the slip** To elude (someone). [< MLG *slippen*]

slip[2] (slip) *n.* 1 A cutting from a plant for planting or grafting. 2 A small, slender person, esp. a youthful one. 3 A small piece of something, as of paper. —*v.t.* **slipped, slip·ping** To cut off for planting; make a slip or slips of. [< MDu. *slippe*]

slip·cov·er (slip'kuv'ər) *n.* A fitted cloth cover for a piece of furniture, that can be readily removed.

slip·knot (slip'not') *n.* 1 A knot so made that it will slip along the rope or cord around which it is formed. 2 A knot easily untied by pulling. Also **slip knot.**

slip-on (slip'on', -ôn') *adj.* 1 Designating a garment or accessory that can be easily donned or taken off. 2 Designating a garment, esp. a sweater, that is put on and taken off over the head: also **slip'o'ver** (-ō'vər). —*n.* A slip-on garment, glove, shoe, etc.

slip·per (slip'ər) *n.* A low, light shoe into or out of which the foot is easily slipped. —**slip'pered** *adj.*

slip·per·y (slip′ər-ē) *adj.* ·per·i·er, ·per·i·est 1 Having a surface so smooth that bodies slip or slide easily on it. 2 That evades one's grasp; elusive. 3 Unreliable; tricky. —**slip′per·i·ness** *n.*

slippery elm 1 A species of small elm with mucilaginous inner bark. 2 Its wood or inner bark.

slip·shod (slip′shod′) *adj.* 1 Wearing shoes or slippers down at the heels. 2 Slovenly; sloppy. 3 Performed carelessly: *slipshod* work.

slip·stream (slip′strēm′) *n. Aeron.* The stream of air driven backwards by the propeller of an aircraft.

slip-up (slip′up′) *n. Informal* A mistake; error.

slit (slit) *n.* A relatively straight cut or a long, narrow opening. —*v.t.* **slit, slit·ting** 1 To make a long incision in; slash. 2 To cut lengthwise into strips. 3 To sever. [ME *slitten*] —**slit′ter** *n.*

slith·er (slith′ər) *v.i.* 1 To slide; slip, as on a loose surface. 2 To glide, as a snake. —*v.t.* 3 To cause to slither. —*n.* A sinuous, gliding movement. [< OE *slidrian*] —**slith′er·y** *adj.*

sliv·er (sliv′ər) *n.* 1 A slender piece, as of wood, cut or torn off lengthwise; a splinter. 2 Corded textile fibers drawn into a fleecy strand. —*v.t. & v.i.* To cut or be split into long thin pieces. [< ME *sliven* to cleave] —**sliv′er·er** *n.*

slob (slob) *n.* 1 Mud; mire. 2 *Slang* A careless or unclean person. [< Ir. *slab*]

slob·ber (slob′ər) *v.t.* 1 To wet with liquids oozing from the mouth. 2 To shed or spill, as liquid food, in eating. —*v.i.* 3 To drivel; slaver. 4 To talk or act gushingly. —*n.* 1 Liquid spilled as from the mouth. 2 Gushing, sentimental talk. [ME *sloberen*] —**slob′ber·er** *n.* —**slob′ber·y** *adj.*

sloe (slō) *n.* 1 A small, plumlike, astringent fruit. 2 The shrub that bears it; the blackthorn. [< OE *slā*]

sloe gin A cordial with a gin base, flavored with sloes.

slog (slog) *v.t. & v.i.* **slogged, slog·ging** 1 To slug, as a pugilist. 2 To plod (one's way). —*n.* A heavy blow. [?] —**slog′ger** *n.*

slo·gan (slō′gən) *n.* 1 A catchword or motto adopted by a political party, advertiser, etc. 2 A battle or rallying cry. [< Scot. Gael. *sluagh* army + *gairm* yell]

slo·gan·eer (slō′gə·nir′) *Informal n.* One who coins or uses slogans. —*v.i.* To coin or use slogans.

sloop (slōōp) *n.* A small sailboat with a single mast and at least one jib. [< Du. *sloep*]

slop¹ (slop) *v.* **slopped, slop·ping** *v.i.* 1 To splash or spill. 2 To walk or move through slush. —*v.t.* 3 To cause (a liquid) to spill or splash. 4 To feed (a domestic animal) with slops. —**slop over** 1 To overflow and splash. 2 *Slang* To show too much zeal, emotion, etc. —*n.* 1 Slush or watery mud. 2 An unappetizing liquid or watery food. 3 *pl.* Refuse liquid. 4 *pl.* Waste food or swill. [< ME *sloppe* mud]

slop² (slop) 1 A loose outer garment, as a smock. 2 *pl.* Articles of clothing and other merchandise sold to sailors on shipboard. [ME *sloppe*]

slope (slōp) *v.* **sloped, slop·ing** *v.i.* 1 To be inclined from the level; slant downward or upward. 2 To go obliquely. —*v.t.* 3 To cause to slope. —*n.* 1 Any slanting surface or line. 2 The degree of inclination of a line or surface from the plane of the horizon. [< OE *aslupan* slip away] —**slop′er, slop′ing·ness** *n.* —**slop′ing·ly** *adv.*

slop·py (slop′ē) *adj.* ·pi·er, ·pi·est 1 Slushy; splashy; wet. 2 Watery or pulpy. 3 Splashed with liquid or slops. 4 *Informal* Messy; slovenly; careless. 5 *Informal* Maudlin; overly sentimental. —**slop′pi·ly** *adv.* —**slop′pi·ness** *n.*

slosh (slosh) *v.t.* 1 To throw about, as a liquid. —*v.i.* 2 To splash; flounder: to *slosh* through a pool. —*n.* Slush. [Var. of SLUSH]

slot (slot) *n.* 1 A long narrow groove or opening; slit. 2 A narrow depression cut to receive some corresponding part in a mechanism. 3 *Informal* An opening or position, as in

Sloop

an organization, or a place in a sequence. —*v.t.* **slot·ted, slot·ting** To cut a slot or slots in. [< OF *esclot* the hollow between the breasts]

sloth (slōth, slôth, sloth) *n.* 1 Disinclination to exertion; laziness. 2 Any of several slow-moving, arboreal mammals of South America. [< SLOW]

sloth·ful (slōth′fəl, slôth′-, sloth′-) *adj.* Inclined to or characterized by sloth. —**sloth′ful·ly** *adv.* —**sloth′ful·ness** *n.* —**Syn.** lazy, indolent, sluggish, shiftless.

Three-toed sloth

slot machine A vending machine or gambling machine having a slot in which a coin is dropped to cause operation.

slouch (slouch) *v.i.* 1 To have a downcast or drooping gait, look, or posture. 2 To hang or droop carelessly. —*n.* 1 A drooping movement or appearance caused by depression or carelessness. 2 An awkward or incompetent person. [?] —**slouch′y** *adj.* (·i·er, ·i·est) —**slouch′i·ly** *adv.* —**slouch′i·ness** *n.*

slough¹ (slou; slōō *esp. for def. 2*) *n.* 1 A place of deep mud or mire. 2 A stagnant swamp, backwater, etc. 3 A state of great despair or degradation. [< OE *slōh*] —**slough′y** *adj.*

slough² (sluf) *n.* 1 Dead tissue separated and thrown off from living tissue. 2 The skin of a serpent that has been or is about to be shed. —*v.t.* 1 To cast off; shed. 2 To discard; shed, as a habit or a growth. —*v.i.* 3 To be cast off. 4 To cast off a slough or tissue. [ME *slouh*] —**slough′y** *adj.*

Slo·vak (slō′väk, slō′vak) *n.* 1 One of a Slavic people of NW Hungary and parts of Moravia. 2 The language spoken by the Slovaks. —*adj.* Of or pertaining to the Slovaks or to their language. Also **Slo·vak′i·an.**

slov·en (sluv′ən) *n.* One who is habitually untidy, careless, or dirty. [ME *sloveyn*]

Slo·vene (slō′vēn, slō·vēn′) *n.* One of a group of s Slavs now living in NW Yugoslavia. —*adj.* Of or pertaining to the Slovenes or to their language. —**Slo·ve′ni·an** *adj., n.*

slov·en·ly (sluv′ən·lē) *adj.* ·li·er, ·li·est Untidy and careless in appearance, work, habits, etc. —*adv.* In a slovenly manner. —**slov′en·li·ness** *n.*

slow (slō) *adj.* 1 Taking a long time to move, perform, or occur. 2 Behind the standard time: said of a timepiece. 3 Not hasty: *slow* to anger. 4 Dull in comprehending: a *slow* student. 5 Uninteresting; tedious: a *slow* drama. 6 Denoting a condition of a racetrack that retards the horses' speed. 7 Heating or burning slowly; low: a *slow* flame. 8 Not brisk; slack: Business is *slow.* —*v.t. & v.i.* To make or become slow or slower: often with *up* or *down.* —*adv.* In a slow manner. [< OE *slāw*] —**slow′ly** *adv.* —**slow′ness** *n.*

slow-mo·tion (slō′mō′shən) *adj.* 1 Moving or acting at less than normal speed. 2 Denoting a television or motion picture filmed at greater than standard speed so that the action appears slow in normal projection.

sludge (sluj) *n.* 1 Soft, water-soaked mud. 2 A slush of snow or broken or half-formed ice. 3 Muddy or pasty refuse, sediment, etc. [?] —**sludg′y** *adj.* (·i·er, ·i·est)

slue¹ (slōō) *v.* **slued, slu·ing** *v.t.* 1 To cause to swing, slide, or skid to the side. 2 To cause to twist or turn. —*v.i.* 3 To move sidewise. —*n.* The act of skidding or pivoting. [?]

slue² (slōō) *n. Informal* SLEW³.

slue³ (slōō) *n.* SLOUGH¹ (def. 2).

slug¹ (slug) *n.* 1 A bullet. 2 *Printing* **a** A strip of type metal between words or letters. **b** A metal strip bearing a line of type in one piece. 3 Any small chunk of metal; esp., one used in place of a coin in automatic machines.

slug² (slug) *n.* 1 Any of numerous land mollusks related to the snail, having an elongated body and a rudimentary shell. 2 The sluglike larvae of certain insects. [ME *slugge* a sluggard]

slug³ (slug) *Informal n.* A heavy blow, as with the fist. —*v.t.* **slugged, slug·ging** To strike heavily, as with the fist. [?] —**slug′ger** *n.*

Slug

slug[4] (slug) *n. Slang* A single drink, esp. of undiluted alcoholic liquor. [< Du. *sluck* a swallow]

slug·gard (slug′ərd) *n.* A person habitually lazy. —*adj.* Lazy; sluggish. [< SLUG[2]] **—slug′gard·ly** *adv.*

slug·gish (slug′ish) *adj.* 1 Having little motion; inactive; torpid. 2 Habitually idle and lazy. **—slug′gish·ly** *adv.* **—slug′gish·ness** *n.*

sluice (sloos) *n.* 1 Any artificial channel for conducting water. 2 A device for controlling the flow of water; a floodgate: also **sluice gate.** 3 The water held back by such a gate. 4 Something through which anything issues or flows. 5 A sloping trough in which gold is washed from sand. —*v.* **sluiced, sluic·ing** *v.t.* 1 To drench or cleanse by a flow of water. 2 To wash in or by a sluice. 3 To draw out or conduct by or through a sluice. 4 To send (logs) down a sluiceway.*—v.i.* 5 To flow out or issue from a sluice. [< L *excludere* shut out]

sluice·way (sloos′wā′) *n.* An artificial channel for the passage of water.

slum (slum) *n.* A squalid, dirty, overcrowded street or section of a city. —*v.i.* **slummed, slum·ming** To visit slums, as for reasons of curiosity. [?] **—slum′mer** *n.*

slum·ber (slum′bər) *v.i.* 1 To sleep lightly or quietly. 2 To be inactive; stagnate. —*v.t.* 3 To spend or pass in sleeping. —*n.* Quiet sleep. [< OE *slūma* sleep] **—slum′ber·er** *n.* **—slum′ber·ing·ly** *adv.*

slum·ber·ous (slum′bər·əs) *adj.* 1 Inviting to slumber. 2 Drowsy; sleepy. 3 Quiet; peaceful: a hot, *slumberous* afternoon. Also **slum·brous** (slum′brəs). **—slum′ber·ous·ly** *adv.* **—slum′ber·ous·ness** *n.*

slum·lord (slum′lôrd′) *n.* A landlord who derives high profits from run-down property, esp. housing. [< SLUM + (LAND)LORD]

slump (slump) *v.i.* 1 To fall or fail suddenly. 2 To stand, walk, or proceed with a stooping posture; slouch. —*n.* 1 The act of slumping. 2 A collapse or decline: a *slump* in the stock market. [Prob. < Scand.]

slung (slung) *p.t. & p.p.* of SLING.

slunk (slungk) *p.t. & p.p.* of SLINK.

slur (slûr) *v.t.* **slurred, slur·ring** 1 To slight; disparage; depreciate. 2 To pass over lightly or hurriedly. 3 To pronounce hurriedly and indistinctly. 4 *Music* **a** To sing or play as indicated by the slur. **b** To mark with a slur. —*n.* 1 A disparaging remark or insinuation. 2 *Music* **a** A curved line (‿ or ⁀) indicating that tones so tied are to be performed without a break between them. **b** The legato effect indicated by this mark. 3 A slurred pronunciation. [< ME *sloor* mud] **—slur′ring·ly** *adv.*

slurb (slûrb) *n. Slang* A suburban area so poorly planned and developed as to seem like a slum. [< SL(UM) + (SUB)URB]

slurp (slûrp) *v.t. & v.i. Slang* To sip noisily. [Imit.]

slush (slush) *n.* 1 Soft, sloppy material, as melting snow or soft mud. 2 Greasy material used for lubrication, etc. 3 Sentimental talk or writing. [ME *sloche*] **—slush′y** *adj.*

slush fund Money collected or spent for bribery, lobbying, political pressure, etc.

slut (slut) *n.* 1 A slatternly woman. 2 A sexually promiscuous woman; whore. 3 A female dog. [?] **—slut′tish** *adj.* **—slut′tish·ly** *adv.* **—slut′tish·ness** *n.*

sly (slī) *adj.* **sli·er** or **sly·er, sli·est** or **sly·est** 1 Artfully dexterous in doing things secretly. 2 Playfully clever; roguish. 3 Meanly or stealthily clever; crafty. 4 Done with or marked by artful secrecy: a *sly* trick. **—on the sly** In a stealthy way. [< ON *slægr*] **—sly′ly** *adv.* **—sly′ness** *n.*

Sm samarium.

smack[1] (smak) *n.* 1 A quick, sharp sound, as of the lips when separated rapidly. 2 A noisy kiss. 3 A sounding blow or slap. —*v.t.* 1 To separate (the lips) rapidly. 2 To kiss noisily. 3 To slap. —*v.i.* 4 To make a smacking noise, as in tasting, kissing, striking, etc.; slap. —*adv.* Directly; exactly: also **smack′-dab′** (-dab′). [< MDu. *smack* a blow]

smack[2] (smak) *v.i.* 1 To have a slight taste or flavor: usu. with *of.* 2 To have, keep, or disclose a slight suggestion: with *of.* —*n.* 1 A suggestive flavor. 2 A mere taste; smattering. [< OE *smæc* a taste]

smack[3] (smak) *n.* A small sailing vessel used chiefly for fishing; esp. one having a well for fish in its hold. [< Du. *smak, smacke*]

smack[4] (smak) *n. Slang* HEROIN.

smack·er (smak′ər) *n.* 1 One who or that which smacks. 2 *Slang* A dollar.

smack·ing (smak′ing) *adj.* Brisk; lively, as a breeze.

small (smôl) *adj.* 1 Not as large as other things of the same kind; little. 2 Being of slight degree, weight, or importance. 3 Ignoble; mean: a *small* nature. 4 Of humble background; poor. 5 Acting or transacting business in a limited way: a *small* shopkeeper. 6 Weak in characteristic properties: *small* beer. 7 Having little body or volume. 8 Not capital: said of letters. **—feel small** To feel humiliated or ashamed. —*adv.* 1 In a low or faint tone: to sing *small.* 2 Into small pieces. 3 In a small way; trivially. —*n.* 1 A small or slender part: the *small* of the back. 2 A small thing or quantity. [< OE *smæl*] **—small′ness** *n.*

small arms Arms that may be carried on the person, as a rifle, automatic pistol, or revolver.

small calorie See CALORIE.

small capital A capital letter cut slightly larger than the lower-case letters of a specified type and slightly smaller than the regular capital.

small fry 1 Small, young fish. 2 Young children. 3 Small or insignificant people or things.

small hours The early hours after midnight.

small-minded (smôl′mīn′did) *adj.* Having a petty mind; intolerant; ungenerous.

small potatoes *Informal* Unimportant, insignificant persons or things.

small·pox (smôl′poks′) *n.* An acute, highly contagious viral disease characterized by a rash that leaves pitted scars.

small talk Unimportant or casual conversation.

small-time (smôl′tīm′) *adj. Slang* Petty; unimportant: a *small-time* gambler.

smart (smärt) *v.i.* 1 To experience a stinging sensation. 2 To cause a stinging sensation. 3 To experience remorse, grief, hurt feelings, etc. —*v.t.* 4 To cause to smart. —*adj.* 1 Quick in thought; clever. 2 Impertinently witty. 3 Harsh; severe: a *smart* slap. 4 Brisk: to go at a *smart* pace. 5 Keen or sharp, as at trade; shrewd. 6 *Informal* or *Regional* Large; considerable: a *smart* crop of wheat. 7 Sprucely dressed. 8 Fashionable; chic. —*n.* 1 An acute stinging sensation, as from a scratch or an irritant. 2 Any mental or emotional suffering. [< OE *smeortan*] **—smart′ly** *adv.* **—smart′ness** *n.*

smart al·eck (al′ik) *Informal* A cocky, conceited person. **—smart-al·eck·y** (smärt′al′ik-ē) *adj.*

smart bomb *Slang* A bomb capable of being guided, as by a laser beam, to a target.

smart·en (smär′tən) *v.t.* 1 To improve in appearance. 2 To make alert or lively. —*v.i.* 3 To improve one's appearance: with *up.*

smart set Fashionable, sophisticated society.

smart·weed (smärt′wēd′) *n.* Any of several species of knotgrass having an acrid taste, growing usu. in wet soil.

smash (smash) *v.t.* 1 To break in many pieces suddenly. 2 To flatten; crush. 3 To dash or fling violently so as to break in pieces. 4 To strike with a sudden blow. 5 To destroy; ruin. 6 In tennis, to strike (the ball) with a hard, swift, overhand stroke. —*v.i.* 7 To be ruined; fail. 8 To move or be moved with force; collide. **—go to smash** *Informal* To be ruined; fail. —*n.* 1 An instance or sound of smashing. 2 Any disaster or sudden collapse, esp. financial ruin. 3 In tennis, a strong overhand shot. 4 *Informal* An outstanding public success. —*adj.* Outstandingly successful: a *smash* hit. [?] **—smash′er** *n.*

smash·ing (smash′ing) *adj.* 1 That smashes: a *smashing* blow. 2 *Informal* Extremely impressive; overwhelmingly good. —*interj. Chiefly Brit.* An exclamation expressing approval, enthusiasm, etc.

smash-up (smash′up′) *n.* A violent collision; a wreck.

smat·ter (smat′ər) *n.* A slight knowledge. [< ME *smateren* to dabble]

smat·ter·ing (smat′ər·ing) *n.* 1 A superficial or fragmentary knowledge. 2 A little bit or a few.

sm. c., sm. caps small capitals (printing).

smear (smir) *v.t.* 1 To rub or soil with grease, paint, dirt, etc. 2 To spread or apply in a thick layer or coating. 3 To harm the reputation of; slander. 4 *Slang* To defeat utterly. —*v.i.* 5 To become smeared. —*n.* 1 A soiled spot; stain. 2

A specimen, as of blood, tissue cells, etc., spread on a slide for microscopic examination. 3 A slanderous attack. [< OE *smeoru* grease] **—smear′y** *adj.* **—smear′i·ness** *n.*

smell (smel) *v.* **smelled** or **smelt, smell·ing** *v.t.* 1 To perceive by means of the nose and its olfactory nerves. 2 To perceive the odor of. 3 To test by odor or smell. 4 To discover or detect, as if by smelling. **—v.i.** 5 To give off a particular odor: to *smell* of roses. 6 To have an unpleasant odor. 7 To give indications of: to *smell* of treason. 8 To use the sense of smell. **—n.** 1 The sense by means of which odors are perceived. 2 That which is smelled; odor. 3 An unpleasant odor. 4 A faint suggestion; hint. 5 An act of smelling. [ME *smellen*] **—smel′ler** *n.* **—smel′ly** *adj.* (**·i·er, ·i·est**) **—Syn.** *n.* 2 aroma, fragrance, scent. 3 reek, stench, stink.

smelling salts A pungent preparation, as ammonium carbonate, used to relieve faintness, etc.

smelt[1] (smelt) *v.t.* *Metall.* 1 To reduce (ores) by fusion in a furnace. 2 To obtain (a metal) from the ore by a process including fusion. **—v.i.** 3 To melt or fuse, as a metal. [< MDu. *smelten* melt]

smelt[2] (smelt) *n. pl.* **smelts** or **smelt** Any of various small, silvery, anadromous or landlocked food fishes. [< OE]

smelt[3] (smelt) A *p.t.* & *p.p.* of SMELL.

smelt·er (smel′tər) *n.* 1 One engaged in smelting ore. 2 An establishment for smelting: also **smelt′er·y.**

smidg·en (smij′ən) *n.* *Informal* A tiny bit or part. [?]

smi·lax (smī′laks) *n.* 1 Any of a large genus of woody vines having oval leaves and globular fruit. 2 A twining plant of the lily family, with greenish flowers, used for bouquets, etc. [< Gk. *smilax* yew]

smile (smīl) *n.* 1 A pleased or amused expression of the face, formed by curling the corners of the mouth upward. 2 A favorable appearance or aspect: the *smile* of fortune. **—v.** **smiled, smil·ing** *v.i.* 1 To exhibit a smile; appear cheerful. 2 To show approval or favor: often with *upon.* **—v.t.** 3 To express by means of a smile. [ME *smilen.*] **—smil′er** *n.* **—smil′ing·ly** *adv.*

Smilax

smirch (smûrch) *v.t.* 1 To soil, as by contact with grime; smear. 2 To defame; dishonor: to *smirch* a reputation. **—n.** 1 A smutch; smear. 2 A moral stain. [ME *smorchen*]

smirk (smûrk) *v.i.* To smile in a self-complacent, affected manner. **—n.** An affected or artificial smile. [< OE *smercian*] **—smirk′er** *n.* **—smirk′ing·ly** *adv.*

smite (smīt) *v.* **smote, smit·ten** or **smote, smit·ing** *v.t.* 1 To strike (something) hard. 2 To strike a blow with (something); cause to strike. 3 To kill with a sudden blow. 4 To strike with disaster; afflict. 5 To affect or impress suddenly and powerfully. **—v.i.** 6 To strike a blow with or as if with sudden force. [< OE *smītan*] **—smit′er** *n.*

smith (smith) *n.* 1 One whose work is shaping metals, esp. a blacksmith. 2 A maker: used in combination: *gunsmith; wordsmith.* [< OE]

smith·er·eens (smith′ə·rēnz′) *n.pl.* *Informal.* Fragments produced as by a blow. Also **smith′ers.** [< Ir. *smidirin* a fragment]

smith·y (smith′ē, smith′ē) *n. pl.* **smith·ies** A blacksmith's shop.

smit·ten (smit′n) A *p.p.* of SMITE.

smock (smok) *n.* A loose outer garment worn to protect one's clothes. **—v.t.** To decorate (fabric) with smocking. [< OE *smoc*]

smock·ing (smok′ing) *n.* Shirred work; stitching that forms a gathered pattern.

smog (smog) *n.* A noxious mist resulting from the action of sunlight on atmospheric pollutants. [< SM(OKE) + (F)OG]

smoke (smōk) *n.* 1 The vaporous products of the combustion of an organic compound, as coal, wood, etc., charged with fine particles of carbon or soot. 2 Any system of solid particles dispersed in a gas. 3 The act of or time taken in smoking tobacco. 4 *Informal* A cigarette, cigar, or

Smocking

pipeful of tobacco. **—v.** **smoked, smok·ing** *v.i.* 1 To emit or give out smoke. 2 To emit smoke excessively, as a stove or lamp. 3 To inhale and exhale the smoke of tobacco. **—v.t.** 4 To inhale and exhale the smoke of (tobacco, opium, etc.). 5 To use, as a pipe, for this purpose. 6 To treat, cure, or flavor with smoke. 7 To drive away or force out of hiding by or as if by the use of smoke: *smoke* bees; *smoke* out the enemy. 8 To change the color of (glass, etc.) by darkening with smoke. [< OE *smoca*]

smoke·house (smōk′hous′) *n.* A building or room in which meat, fish, hides, etc., are smoked.

smoke·less (smōk′lis) *adj.* Having or emitting little or no smoke: *smokeless* powder.

smok·er (smō′kər) *n.* 1 One who smokes tobacco habitually. 2 A railroad car in which smoking is allowed. 3 A social gathering for men only.

smoke screen 1 A dense cloud of smoke emitted to screen an attack or cover a retreat. 2 Anything intended to conceal or mislead.

smoke·stack (smōk′stak′) *n.* An upright pipe through which combustion gases from a furnace are discharged into the air.

smok·y (smō′kē) *adj.* **smok·i·er, smok·i·est** 1 Giving forth smoke, esp. excessively or unpleasantly. 2 Containing smoke: *smoky* air. 3 Like or suggestive of smoke: a *smoky* flavor. 4 Discolored by smoke. 5 Smoke-colored. **—smok′i·ly** *adv.* **—smok′i·ness** *n.*

smol·der (smōl′dər) *v.i.* 1 To burn showing little smoke and no flame. 2 To show suppressed feeling. 3 To exist in a latent state or inwardly. **—n.** A smoldering fire or thick smoke. *Brit. sp.* **smoul′der.** [ME *smolderen*]

smolt (smōlt) *n.* A young salmon on its first descent from the river to the sea. [ME]

smooch (smōōch) *v.i.* *Slang* To kiss and caress; neck. **—smooch′er** *n.* [?]

smooth (smōōth) *adj.* 1 Having no surface irregularities; continuously even. 2 Free from obstructions, shocks, or jolts. 3 Without lumps; well blended. 4 Free from hair. 5 Flowing or moving evenly and without interruption. 6 Mild-mannered; calm. 7 Suave and flattering, usu. in a deceitful way: a *smooth* talker. 8 Pleasant-tasting; mild: a *smooth* wine. 9 *Phonet.* Having no aspiration. **—adv.** Calmly; evenly. **—v.t.** 1 To make smooth or even on the surface. 2 To free from obstructions. 3 To soften the worst features of: usu. with *over.* 4 To make calm; mollify. **—v.i.** 5 To become smooth. **—n.** 1 The smooth portion or surface of anything. 2 The act of smoothing. [< OE *smōth*] **—smooth′er, smooth′ness** *n.* **—smooth′ly** *adv.* **—Syn.** *adj.* 1 glossy, polished, sleek. 6 collected, placid, unruffled. *v.* 3 extenuate, palliate. 4 soothe.

smooth·bore (smōōth′bôr′, -bōr′) *n.* A firearm with an unrifled bore: also **smooth bore.** **—adj.** Having no rifling: said of firearms.

smooth muscle Muscle tissue consisting of flat sheets of spindle-shaped cells, by which involuntary movement is effected in blood vessels, viscera, etc.

smor·gas·bord (smôr′gəs·bôrd; *Sw.* smœr′gōs·bôrd) *n.* A Scandinavian buffet. Also **smör′gås·bord.** [Sw.]

smote (smōt) *p.t.* of SMITE.

smoth·er (smuth′ər) *v.t.* 1 To prevent (someone) from breathing. 2 To kill by such means; suffocate. 3 To cover, or cause to smolder, as a fire. 4 To hide or suppress: to *smother* a scandal. 5 To cook in a covered pan or under a blanket of some other substance. **—v.i.** 6 To be covered without vent or air, as a fire. 7 To be hidden or suppressed, as wrath. **—n.** That which smothers, as stifling vapor or dust. [< OE *smorian*] **—smoth′er·er** *n.* **—smoth′er·y** *adj.*

smudge (smuj) *v.* **smudged, smudg·ing** *v.t.* 1 To smear; soil. **—v.i.** 2 To be or become smudged. **—n.** 1 A smear; stain. 2 A smoky fire or smoke for driving away insects, preventing frost, etc. [? var. of SMUTCH] **—smudg′i·ly** *adv.* **—smudg′i·ness** *n.* **—smudg′y** *adj.* (**·i·er, ·i·est**)

smug (smug) *adj.* **smug·ger, smug·gest** 1 Self-satisfied or extremely complacent. 2 Trim; neat; spruce. [? < LG *smuk* neat] **—smug′ly** *adv.* **—smug′ness** *n.*

smug·gle (smug′əl) *v.* **·gled, ·gling** *v.t.* 1 To take (merchan-

dise) into or out of a country illegally. **2** To bring in or introduce illicitly or secretly. —*v.i.* **3** To engage in or practice smuggling. [<LG *smuggelen*] —**smug′gler** *n.*

smut (smut) *n.* **1** The blackening made by soot, smoke, etc. **2** Obscene writing, speech, or illustration. **3** Any of various fungus diseases of plants, characterized by patches of powdery black spores. **4** The parasitic fungus causing such a disease. —*v.t. & v.i.* **smut·ted, smut·ting** To make or become smutty. [<LG *schmutt* dirt]

smutch (smuch) *n.* A stain or smear. —*v.t.* To smear; smudge. [?] —**smutch·y** *adj.* (**·i·er, ·i·est**)

smut·ty (smut′ē) *adj.* **·ti·er, ·ti·est 1** Soiled with smut; stained. **2** Affected by smut: *smutty* corn. **3** Obscene; indecent. —**smut′ti·ly** *adv.* —**smut′ti·ness** *n.* —**Syn. 1** blackened, dirty. **3** coarse, earthy, suggestive.

Sn tin (L *stannum*).

Sn. sanitary.

snack (snak) *n.* A light meal. —*v.i.* To eat a snack. [< MDu. *snacken* to bite, snap]

snaf·fle (snaf′əl) *n.* A horse's bit without a curb, jointed in the middle. —*v.t.* **·fled, ·fling** To control with a snaffle. [?<Du. *snavel* muzzle]

sna·fu (sna·fōō′) *Slang adj.* In a state of utter confusion; chaotic. —*v.t.* **·fued, ·fu·ing** To put into a confused or chaotic condition. —*n.* A confused or chaotic situation. [< S(ITUATION) N(ORMAL) A(LL) F(UCKED) U(P)]

snag (snag) *n.* **1** A jagged or sharp protuberance, esp. the stumpy base of a branch left in pruning. **2** A snaggletooth. **3** The trunk of a tree fixed in a river, bayou, etc., which presents a danger to navigation. **4** Any hidden obstacle or difficulty. —*v.t.* **snagged, snag·ging** To injure, destroy, or impede by or as by a snag. [< Scand.] —**snag′gy** *adj.*

snag·gle·tooth (snag′əl·tōōth′) *n.* A tooth that is broken or out of alignment with the others. —**snag′gle-toothed′** (-tōōtht′, -tōōthd′) *adj.*

snail (snāl) *n.* **1** Any of numerous slow-moving, terrestrial or aquatic gastropod mollusks with a spiral shell. **2** A slow or lazy person. [< OE *snægl*]

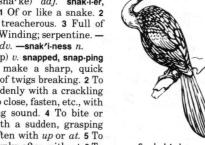

Snail

snake (snāk) *n.* **1** Any of a large variety of limbless reptiles having a scaly body, no eyelids, and a specialized swallowing apparatus. **2** A treacherous person. **3** A flexible wire used to clean clogged drains, etc. —*v.* **snaked, snak·ing** *v.t. Informal* **1** To drag or pull forcibly; haul, as a log. —*v.i.* **2** To wind or move like a snake. [< OE *snaca*]

snake·bird (snāk′bûrd′) *n.* Any of several birds with a long sinuous neck, frequenting southern U.S. swamps.

snak·y (snā′kē) *adj.* **snak·i·er, snak·i·est 1** Of or like a snake. **2** Cunning; treacherous. **3** Full of snakes. **4** Winding; serpentine. —**snak′i·ly** *adv.* —**snak′i·ness** *n.*

snap (snap) *v.* **snapped, snap·ping** *v.i.* **1** To make a sharp, quick sound, as of twigs breaking. **2** To break suddenly with a crackling noise. **3** To close, fasten, etc., with a snapping sound. **4** To bite or snatch with a sudden, grasping motion: often with *up* or *at.* **5** To speak sharply: often with *at.* **6** To move or act with sudden, neat

Snakebird

gestures: He *snapped* to attention. **7** To give way suddenly, as under mental pressure. —*v.t.* **8** To seize suddenly or eagerly; snatch: often with *up.* **9** To sever with a snapping sound. **10** To cause to make a sharp, quick sound. **11** To close, fasten, etc., with a snapping sound. **12** To take (a photograph). —**snap out of it** *Informal* **1** To recover quickly. **2** To change a mood, attitude, etc., quickly. —*n.* **1** The act of snapping or a sharp, quick sound produced by it. **2** A sudden breaking or release of anything or the sound so produced. **3** Any catch, fastener, etc., that closes or springs into place with a snapping sound. **4** A small, thin, crisp cake, esp. a gingersnap. **5** Brisk energy; zip. **6**

A brief spell: said chiefly of cold weather. **7** Any easy task or duty. **8** A snapshot. —*adj.* **1** Made or done suddenly: a *snap* judgment. **2** Fastening with a snap. **3** *Informal* Easy. —*adv.* Briskly; quickly. [<MDu. *snappen* bite at]

snap·drag·on (snap′drag′ən) *n.* Any of several varieties of plants having racemes of flowers with a saclike, double-lipped corolla.

snap·per (snap′ər) *n.* **1** One who or that which snaps. **2** Any of various voracious marine food fishes. • See RED SNAPPER. **3** A snapping turtle.

snapping turtle Any of various large voracious freshwater turtles having powerful jaws, a small plastron, and a tail with erect bony scales.

Snapping turtle

snap·pish (snap′ish) *adj.* **1** Apt to speak crossly. **2** Disposed to snap or bite, as a dog. —**snap′pish·ly** *adv.* —**snap′pish·ness** *n.*

snap·py (snap′ē) *adj.* **·pi·er, ·pi·est 1** *Informal* Brisk and energetic. **2** *Informal* Smart or stylish. **3** Snappish. —**snap′pi·ly** *adv.* —**snap′pi·ness** *n.*

snap·shot (snap′shot′) *n.* A photograph taken with a small, simple camera.

snare[1] (snâr) *n.* **1** A device, as a noose, for catching birds or other animals; a trap. **2** Anything that misleads, entangles, etc. —*v.t.* **snared, snar·ing 1** To catch with a snare; entrap. **2** To capture by trickery; entice. [< ON *snara*] —**snar′er** *n.*

snare[2] (snâr) *n.* **1** A cord that produces a rattling on a drumhead. **2** A snare drum. [< MDu. *snare* a string]

snare drum A small drum to be beaten on one head and having snares stretched across the other. • See DRUM.

snarl[1] (snärl) *n.* A sharp, angry growl. —*v.i.* **1** To growl harshly, as a dog. **2** To speak angrily and resentfully. —*v.t.* **3** To utter or express with a snarl. [< MLG *snarren* to growl] —**snarl′er** *n.* —**snarl′ing·ly** *adv.* —**snarl′y** *adj.*

snarl[2] (snärl) *n.* **1** A tangle, as of hair or yarn. **2** Any complication or entanglement. —*v.i.* **1** To become entangled or confused. —*v.t.* **2** To put into a snarl. [?< SNARE[1]] —**snarl′er** *n.* —**snarl′y** *adj.*

snatch (snach) *v.t.* **1** To seize, take, grasp, etc., suddenly or eagerly. **2** To take or obtain as the opportunity arises: to *snatch* a few hours of sleep. —*v.i.* **3** To attempt to seize swiftly and suddenly: with *at.* —*n.* **1** A hasty grab or grasp: usu. with *at.* **2** A small amount; fragment: *snatches* of a conversation. [ME *snacchen*] —**snatch′er** *n.*

snatch·y (snach′ē) *adj.* **snatch·i·er, snatch·i·est** Interrupted; spasmodic.

sneak (snēk) *v.i.* **1** To move or go in a stealthy manner. **2** To act slyly or with cowardice. —*v.t.* **3** To put, give, move, etc., secretly or stealthily. **4** *Informal* To pilfer. —**sneak out of** To avoid (work, etc.) by sly means. —*n.* **1** One who sneaks; a stealthy, despicable person. **2** *pl. Informal* Sneakers. **3** A stealthy movement. —*adj.* Stealthy; covert: a *sneak* attack. [?] —**sneak′i·ly, sneak′ing·ly** *adv.* —**sneak′i·ness** *n.* —**sneak′y** *adj.* (**·i·er, ·i·est**)

sneak·er (snē′kər) *n.* **1** *pl.* Rubber-soled canvas shoes. **2** One who sneaks; a sneak.

sneer (snir) *n.* **1** A grimace of contempt or scorn. **2** A mean or contemptuous sound, word, etc. —*v.i.* **1** To show contempt or scorn by a sneer. **2** To express contempt in speech, writing, etc. —*v.t.* **3** To utter with a sneer. [ME *sneren*] —**sneer′er** *n.* —**sneer′ing·ly** *adv.* —**Syn.** *v.* **2** gibe, jeer, scoff, taunt.

sneeze (snēz) *v.i.* **sneezed, sneez·ing** To drive air forcibly and audibly out of the mouth and nose by a spasmodic involuntary action. —**not to be sneezed at** *Informal* Entitled to consideration; not to be ignored. —*n.* An act of sneezing. [ME *fnesen*] —**sneez′er** *n.*

snick·er (snik′ər) *n.* A half-suppressed or smothered laugh, usu. scornful. —*v.i.* **1** To utter a snicker. —*v.t.* **2** To utter or express with a snicker. [Imit.]

snide (snīd) *adj.* **snid·er, snid·est** Malicious; nasty. [?] —**snide′ly** *adv.* —**snide′ness** *n.*

sniff (snif) *v.i.* **1** To breathe through the nose in short, quick, audible inhalations. **2** To express contempt, etc., by sniffing: often with *at.* **3** To inhale a scent in sniffs. —*v.t.* **4** To inhale. **5** To smell or attempt to smell with sniffs. **6** To perceive as if by sniffs. —*n.* **1** An act or the sound of

sniffing. **2** Something perceived by sniffing; an odor. [ME *sniffen*]

snif·fle (snif′əl) *v.i.* **·fled, ·fling 1** To breathe through a partially obstructed nose noisily and with difficulty. **2** To snivel or whimper. —*n.* The act of sniffling, or the sound made by it. —**the sniffles** A clogged condition of the nose caused by a cold, allergy, etc. [Freq. of SNIFF] —**snif′fler** *n.*

snig·ger (snig′ər) *n.* SNICKER. —*v.i.* SNICKER. [Var. of SNICKER] —**Syn.** *n.,v.* giggle, smirk, snort, titter.

snip (snip) *v.* **snipped, snip·ping** *v.t.* **1** To clip, remove, or cut with a short, light stroke or strokes, as of shears: often with *off.* —*v.i.* **2** To cut with small, quick strokes. —*n.* **1** An act of snipping. **2** A small piece snipped off. **3** *Informal* A small or insignificant person. [< Du. *snippen*] —**snip′per** *n.*

snipe (snīp) *n. pl.* **snipe** or **snipes** Any of various marsh and shore birds having a long, flexible bill. —*v.i.* **sniped, snip·ing 1** To hunt or shoot snipe. **2** To shoot at individuals, as of an enemy force, from a place of concealment. **3** To attack a person in an underhanded, malicious manner: with *at.* [< ON *snīpa*]

snip·er (snī′pər) *n.* One who shoots at individuals, as of an enemy force, from a place of concealment.

snip·pet (snip′it) *n.* **1** A small piece snipped off. **2** A small or insignificant person.

snip·py (snip′ē) *adj.* **·pi·er, ·pi·est** *Informal* **1** Supercilious; impertinent. **2** Fragmentary. —**snip′pi·ly** *adv.* —**snip′pi·ness** *n.*

snit (snit) *n. Informal* A state of irritability or agitation.

snitch (snich) *Slang v.t.* **1** To grab quickly; steal. —*v.i.* **2** To inform; tattle: usu. with *on.* [?]

sniv·el (sniv′əl) *v.i.* **·eled** or **·elled, ·el·ing** or **·el·ling** To cry in a snuffling manner. —*n.* The act of sniveling. [< OE (assumed) *snyflan*] —**sniv′el·er** or **sniv′el·ler** *n.*

snob (snob) *n.* **1** One who regards wealth and elevated social position as of paramount importance and who typically seeks to improve his station by associating with the rich or powerful or popular and by avoiding or behaving with condescension to those with whom association is inexpedient. **2** One who affects to be superior, as in taste or learning: an intellectual *snob.* [?] —**snob′ber·y** (*pl.* **·ies**), **snob′bish·ness** *n.* —**snob′bish** *adj.* —**snob′bish·ly** *adv.*

snood (snood) *n.* A small meshlike cap or bag worn by women to keep the hair in place at the back of the head. —*v.t.* To bind with a snood. [< OE *snōd*]

snoop (snoop) *Informal v.i.* To pry into things with which one has no business. —*n.* One who snoops. [< Du. *snoepen* eat goodies on the sly] —**snoop′er** *n.* —**snoop′y** *adj.* (**·i·er, ·i·est**)

snoot (snoot) *n. Informal* The nose or face. [Var. of SNOUT]

snoot·y (snoo′tē) *adj.* **snoot·i·er, snoot·i·est** *Informal* Haughty; snobbish. —**snoot′i·ly** *adv.* —**snoot′i·ness** *n.*

snooze (snooz) *Informal v.i.* **snoozed, snooz·ing** To sleep lightly; doze. —*n.* A short, light sleep. [?]

snore (snôr, snōr) *v.i.* **snored, snor·ing** To breathe with loud, snorting noises while asleep. —*n.* An act or sound of snoring. [Imit.] —**snor′er** *n.*

snor·kel (snôr′kəl) *n.* **1** A long ventilating tube capable of extending from a submerged submarine to the surface of the water. **2** A similar device used for underwater breathing. —*v.i.* To swim with a snorkel. [< G *Schnorchel*] —**snor′kel·er** *n.*

snort (snôrt) *v.i.* **1** To force the air violently and noisily through the nostrils, as a horse. **2** To express indignation, ridicule, etc., by a snort. —*v.t.* **3** To utter or express by snorting. —*n.* **1** The act or sound of snorting. **2** *Slang* A small drink of liquor. [ME *snorten*] —**snort′er** *n.*

snot (snot) *n.* **1** Mucus from or in the nose: a vulgar usage. **2** *Slang* A snotty person. [< OE *gesnot*]

snot·ty (snot′ē) *adj.* **·ti·er, ·ti·est 1** Dirtied with snot: a vulgar usage. **2** *Slang* Contemptible; nasty. **3** *Slang* Impudent. —**snot′ti·ly** *adv.* —**snot′ti·ness** *n.*

snout (snout) *n.* **1** The projecting muzzle of a vertebrate. **2** Some similar anterior prolongation of the head, as that of a gastropod, skate, weevil, etc. **3** A person's nose, esp. a large one. [ME *snute*]

snow (snō) *n.* **1** Precipitation in the form of ice crystals formed from water vapor in the air when the temperature is below 32° F., usu. falling in irregular masses or flakes. **2** A fall of snow. **3** Flickering light or dark spots appearing on a television or radar screen. **4** *Slang* Cocaine. —*v.i.* **1** To fall as snow. —*v.t.* **2** To cause to fall as or like snow. **3** *Slang* To overpower with insincere or flattering talk. —**snow in** To close in or obstruct with snow.

Snow crystals

—**snow under 1** To cover with snow. **2** *Informal* To overwhelm: *snowed under* with work. [< OE *snāw*]

snow·ball (snō′bôl′) *n.* **1** A small round mass of snow to be thrown. **2** A shrub related to honeysuckle, having globular clusters of sterile white flowers: also **snowball bush** or **tree.** —*v.i.* **1** To throw snowballs. **2** To gain in size, importance, etc. —*v.t.* **3** To throw snowballs at.

snow bank A large mound or heap of snow.

snow·ber·ry (snō′ber′ē) *n. pl.* **·ries** Any of various shrubs bearing white berries.

snow·bird (snō′bûrd′) *n.* **1** A junco. **2** SNOW BUNTING.

snow blindness A temporary or partial impairment of vision, caused by long exposure to the glare of snow. —**snow′-blind′** *adj.*

snow·bound (snō′bound′) *adj.* Forced to remain in a place because of heavy snow.

snow bunting A sparrowlike bird of northern regions, having white plumage with black or rust-colored markings.

snow·capped (snō′kapt′) *adj.* Having its top covered with snow, as a mountain.

snow·drift (snō′drift′) *n.* A pile of snow heaped up by the wind.

snow·drop (snō′drop′) *n.* A low, early-blooming bulbous plant bearing a single, white, drooping flower.

snow·fall (snō′fôl′) *n.* **1** A fall of snow. **2** The amount of snow that falls in a given period.

snow·flake (snō′flāk′) *n.* **1** A flake or crystal of snow. **2** Any of various plants allied to and resembling the snowdrop.

snow job *Slang* An attempt to overpower with a flow of insincere talk, esp. flattery.

snow line The limit of perpetual snow on the sides of mountains. Also **snow limit.**

snow·mo·bile (snō′mō·bēl′) *n.* A motorized vehicle used for traveling over snow, ice, etc. —**snow′mo·bil′er, snow′·mo·bil′ing** *n.*

snow·plow (snō′plou′) *n.* Any large, plowlike device for removing snow from roads, railroad tracks, etc.

snow·shoe (snō′shoo′) *n.* A device, usu. a network of sinew in a wooden frame, to be fastened on the foot and used to prevent sinking in soft snow when walking. —*v.i.* **·shoed, ·shoe·ing** To walk on snowshoes.

Snowshoe

snow·slide (snō′slīd′) *n.* An avalanche of snow.

snow·storm (snō′stôrm′) *n.* A storm with a heavy fall of snow.

snow·y (snō′ē) *adj.* **·i·er, ·i·est 1** Abounding in or covered with snow. **2** White as snow. —**snow′i·ly** *adv.* —**snow′i·ness** *n.*

snub (snub) *v.t.* **snubbed, snub·bing 1** To treat with contempt or disdain. **2** To stop or check, as the movement of a rope in running out. —*n.* **1** An act of snubbing; a deliberate slight. **2** A sudden checking, as of a running rope or cable. —*adj.* Short and slightly turned-up: said of the nose. [< ON *snubba*] —**snub′ber** *n.* —**Syn.** *v.* **1** cut, high-hat, ignore, rebuff, slight.

snub-nosed (snub′nōzd′) *adj.* Having a snub nose.

snuff¹ (snuf) *v.t.* **1** To draw in (air, etc.) through the nose.

2 To smell; sniff. —*v.i.* **3** To snort; sniff. —*n.* An act of snuffing. [?< MDu. *snuffen*] —**snuf′fi·ness** *n.* —**snuf′fy** *adj.*

snuff² (snuf) *n.* The charred portion of a wick. —*v.t.* **1** To crop the snuff from (a wick). **2** To put out or extinguish: with *out.* [ME *snoffe*]

snuff³ (snuf) *n.* **1** Pulverized tobacco to be inhaled into the nostrils. **2** The quantity of it taken at one time. —**up to snuff** *Informal* Meeting the usual standard, as in quality, health, etc. —*v.i.* To take or use snuff. [< Du. *snuf*]

snuf·fer (snuf′ər) *n.* **1** One who or that which snuffs (a candle). **2** *pl.* A scissorlike instrument for removing the snuff from a candle.

snuf·fle (snuf′əl) *v.* ·**fled**, ·**fling** *v.i.* **1** SNIFFLE. **2** To talk through the nose. —*v.t.* **3** To utter in a nasal tone. —*n.* An act of snuffling, or the sound made by it. —**the snuffles** THE SNIFFLES. See SNIFFLE. [Freq. of SNUFF¹] —**snuf′fler** *n.*

snug (snug) *adj.* **snug·ger**, **snug·gest 1** Comfortable and cozy. **2** Well-built and compact; trim: said of a ship. **3** Fitting closely, as a garment. —*v.* **snugged, snug·ging** —*v.t.* **1** To make snug. —*v.i.* **2** SNUGGLE. —**snug down** To prepare (a vessel) for a storm, as by lashing down movables. [?] —**snug′ly** *adv.* —**snug′ness** *n.*

snug·gle (snug′əl) *v.t.* & *v.i.* ·**gled**, ·**gling** To nestle; cuddle; often with *up* or *together.* [Freq. of SNUG]

so¹ (sō) *adv.* **1** To this or that or such a degree; to this or that extent: Don't talk *so* much. **2** In this, that, or such a manner: Hold the flag *so.* **3** To such a great extent: I love him *so.* **4** Just as said, directed, suggested, or implied; consequently; therefore. **5** To an extreme degree; very: He is *so* tall. **6** About as many or as much as stated; thereabouts: I shall stay a day or *so.* **7** Too; also: and *so* do I. **8** According to the truth of what is sworn to or averred: *So* help me God. —*adj.* True: It isn't *so.* —*conj.* **1** With the purpose that: often with *that.* **2** As a consequence of which: He consented, *so* they went away. —*interj.* An expression of surprise, disapproval, triumph, etc. [< OE *swā*]

so² (sō) *n.* SOL.

So. South; southern.

soak (sōk) *v.t.* **1** To place in liquid till thoroughly saturated; steep. **2** To wet thoroughly; drench. **3** *Informal* To drink, esp. to excess. **4** *Slang* To charge exorbitantly. —*v.i.* **5** To remain or be placed in liquid till saturated. **6** To penetrate; pass: with *in* or *into.* **7** *Slang* To drink to excess. —**soak up 1** To take up; absorb. **2** *Informal* To take eagerly into the mind. —*n.* **1** The process or act of soaking, or state of being soaked. **2** Liquid in which something is soaked. **3** *Slang* A hard drinker. [< OE *socian*] —**soak′er** *n.* —**soak′ing·ly** *adv.*

so-and-so (sō′ən·sō′) *n. pl.* ·**sos** An unnamed or undetermined person or thing: often a euphemism for offensive epithets.

soap (sōp) *n.* **1** *Chem.* A metallic salt of a fatty acid. **2** A cleansing agent consisting of a sodium or potassium salt of a fatty acid made by boiling a fat or oil with a lye. **3** *Slang* Money used for bribes. —**no soap** *Slang* It's not possible or acceptable. —*v.t.* To rub or treat with soap. [< OE *sāpe*] —**soap′i·ly** *adv.* —**soap′i·ness** *n.* —**soap′y** *adj.*

soap·ber·ry (sōp′ber′ē) *n. pl.* ·**ries 1** A berrylike fruit containing a substance that forms a detergent lather with water. **2** Any of various related trees of s U.S. and tropical America that yield soapberries.

soap·box (sōp′boks′) *n.* Any box or crate used as a platform by street orators. —*adj.* Of or pertaining to such orators or oratory. —*v.i.* To make a speech to a street audience.

soap opera A daytime television or radio drama presented serially and usu. dealing with highly emotional domestic themes.

soap·stone (sōp′stōn′) *n.* STEATITE.

soap·suds (sōp′sudz′) *n.pl.* Soapy water, esp. when worked into a foam.

soar (sôr, sōr) *v.i.* **1** To float aloft through the air on wings, as a bird. **2** To sail or glide through the air. **3** To rise above any usual level: Prices soared. —*n.* **1** An act of soaring. **2** A range of upward flight. [< L *ex* out + *aura* breeze, air] —**soar′er** *n.* —**soar′ing·ly** *adv.*

sob (sob) *v.* **sobbed, sob·bing** *v.i.* **1** To weep with audible, convulsive catches of the breath. **2** To make a sound like a sob, as the wind. —*v.t.* **3** To utter with sobs. **4** To bring

to a specified condition by sobbing: to *sob* oneself to sleep. —*n.* The act or sound of sobbing. [Imit.] —**sob′bing·ly** *adv.*

so·ber (sō′bər) *adj.* **1** Moderate in or abstaining from the use of alcoholic beverages. **2** Not drunk. **3** Temperate in action or thought; rational. **4** Not frivolous; straightforward. **5** Solemn; serious: a *sober* expression. **6** Of subdued or modest color. —*v.t.* **1** To make sober. —*v.i.* **2** To become sober, as after intoxication: with *up.* [< L *sobrius*] —**so′ber·ly** *adv.* —**so′ber·ness** *n.* —**Syn.** *n.* 1 abstemious. 3 calm, dispassionate, staid, steady.

so·bri·e·ty (sō·brī′ə·tē) *n. pl.* ·**ties 1** The state or quality of being moderate, serious, or sedate. **2** Abstinence from alcoholic drink.

so·bri·quet (sō′bri·kā, sō·bri·kā′) *n.* A fanciful or humorous appellation; a nickname. [F]

sob story *Slang* A sad personal narrative told to elicit pity or sympathy.

soc. socialist; society.

so-called (sō′kôld′) *adj.* **1** Popularly or generally named or known (by the following term): the *so-called* black market. **2** Called (by the following term): an ironic use, implying that the designated term is unjustified or unsuitable: his *so-called* wittiness.

soc·cer (sok′ər) *n.* A form of football in which the ball is propelled toward the opponents' goal by kicking or by striking with the body or head, but never with the hands. [Alter. of *association (football)*, original name]

so·cia·ble (sō′shə·bəl) *adj.* **1** Inclined to seek company; friendly. **2** Characterized by or affording occasion for agreeable conversation and friendliness. —*n.* An informal social gathering. [< L *socius* friend] —**so′cia·bil′i·ty, so′cia·ble·ness** *n.* —**so′cia·bly** *adv.*

so·cial (sō′shəl) *adj.* **1** Of or pertaining to society or its organization: *social* questions. **2** Friendly toward others; sociable. **3** Living in a society: *social* beings. **4** Of or pertaining to public welfare: *social* work. **5** Pertaining to or characteristic of fashionable, wealthy people: the *social* register. **6** Living in communities: *social* ants. **7** Grouping compactly, as individual plants. **8** Partly or wholly covering a large area of land: said of plant species. —*n.* An informal social gathering. [< L *socius* ally]

social disease Venereal disease: a euphemism.

so·cial·ism (sō′shəl·iz′əm) *n.* **1** The theory of public collective ownership or control of the basic means of production, distribution, and exchange, with the avowed aim of operating for use rather than for profit. **2** A political system or party advocating or practicing this theory. —**so′·cial·ist** *adj., n.* —**so′cial·is′tic** *adj.*

Socialist party A political party advocating socialism, esp. a U.S. party formed in 1901.

so·cial·ite (sō′shəl·īt) *n.* A person prominent in fashionable society.

so·cial·ize (sō′shəl·īz) *v.* ·**ized**, ·**iz·ing** *v.t.* **1** To make friendly, cooperative, or sociable. **2** To put under group control; esp. to regulate according to socialistic principles. **3** To adapt for the uses and needs of society. —*v.i.* **4** To take part in social activities. *Brit. sp.* **so′cial·ise.** —**so′cial·i·za′tion** *n.*

socialized medicine The provision of comprehensive medical services at public expense.

social register A directory of persons prominent in fashionable society.

social science 1 The body of knowledge dealing with society, its members, organizations, interrelationships, etc. **2** Any of the fields into which this body of knowledge is divided, as economics, history, sociology, politics, etc.

social security A federal program of old-age pensions, unemployment benefits, disability insurance, survivors' benefits, etc., paid jointly by workers, employers, and the U.S. government.

social work Any of various activities for improving community welfare, as services for health, rehabilitation, counseling, recreation, adoptions, etc. Also **social service.** —**social worker**

so·ci·e·ty (sə·sī′ə·tē) *n. pl.* ·**ties 1** A group of people, usu. having geographical boundaries and sharing certain characteristics, as language, culture, etc. **2** The people making up such a group. **3** The fashionable, usu. wealthy portion of a community. **4** A body of persons associated for

a common purpose; an association, club, or fraternity. **5** Association based on friendship or intimacy: to enjoy the *society* of one's neighbors. [< L *socius* a friend]

Society of Friends A Christian religious group, founded in seventeenth-century England, noted for its repudiation of ritual and its opposition to military service and to violence.

Society of Jesus The Jesuits.

socio- *combining form* **1** Society; social: *sociology*. **2** Sociology; sociological: *socioeconomic*. [< F < L *socius* a companion]

so·ci·o·bi·ol·o·gy (sō′sē·ō·bī·ol′ə·jē) *n.* The study of social behavior in animals and humans, as determined by their biological characteristics.

so·ci·o·ec·o·nom·ic (sō′sē·ō·ek′ə·nom′ik, sō′shē-, -ē′kə-) *adj.* Based upon the interrelationship of social and economic factors. —**so′ci·o·ec′o·nom′i·cal·ly** *adv.*

so·ci·o·lin·guis·tics (sō′sē·ō·ling·gwis′tiks, sō′shē-) *n. pl.* (*construed as sing.*) The study of language as a social instrument and in its social context. [< SOCIO- + LINGUISTICS] —**so′ci·o·lin·guis′tic** *adj.* —**so′ci·o·lin·guis′ti·cal·ly** *adv.*

so·ci·ol·o·gy (sō′sē·ol′ə·jē, sō′shē-) *n.* The science dealing with the origin, evolution, and development of human society and its organization, institutions, and functions. —**so′ci·o·log′i·cal** *adj.* —**so′ci·o·log′i·cal·ly** *adv.* —**so′ci·ol′o·gist** *n.*

sock[1] (sok) *n.* A short stocking reaching part way to the knee. [< L *soccus* slipper]

sock[2] (sok) *Slang v.t.* To strike or hit, esp. with the fist. —*n.* A hard blow. [?]

sock·et (sok′it) *n.* A cavity into which a corresponding part fits: an electric light *socket;* the eye *socket.* [< OF *soc* a plowshare]

sock·eye (sok′ī′) *n.* A red salmon of the Pacific coast, highly valued as a food fish. [Alter. of Salishan *sukkegh*]

So·crat·ic method (sə·krat′ik, sō-) The method of instruction by questions and answers, as adopted by Socrates in his disputations, leading the pupil either to a foreseen conclusion or to contradict himself.

sod (sod) *n.* **1** Grassy surface soil held together by the matted roots of grass and weeds. **2** A piece of such soil. —*v.t.* **sod·ded, sod·ding** To cover with sod. [< MDu. *sode* piece of turf]

so·da (sō′də) *n.* **1** Any of several sodium compounds in common use, as sodium bicarbonate, carbonate, hydroxide, etc. **2** SODA WATER **3** A soft drink containing soda water and flavoring and sometimes ice cream. [< Ital. *soda (cenere)* solid (ash)]

soda ash Anhydrous sodium carbonate.

soda cracker A thin, crisp, usu. salted wafer of flour leavened with baking soda.

soda fountain **1** An apparatus from which soda water is drawn, usu. containing receptacles for syrups, ice, and ice cream. **2** A counter at which soft drinks and ice cream are dispensed.

soda jerk *Slang* A clerk who serves at a soda fountain.

so·dal·i·ty (sō·dal′ə·tē) *n. pl.* **·ties** A brotherhood or fraternity; esp., one for devotional or charitable purposes. [< L *sodalis* companion]

soda water An effervescent drink consisting of water charged under pressure with carbon dioxide, formerly generated from sodium bicarbonate.

sod·den (sod′n) *adj.* **1** Soaked; saturated. **2** Doughy; soggy, as undercooked bread. **3** Dull or stupid, as from drink. [ME *sothen,* pp. of *sethen* seethe] —**sod′den·ly** *adv.*

so·di·um (sō′dē·əm) *n.* A soft, silver-white, highly reactive metallic element (symbol Na) whose compounds are abundant in nature and essential to life. [< Med. L *soda*]

sodium bicarbonate A white crystalline compound that reacts with acids to liberate carbon dioxide; baking soda.

sodium carbonate The strongly alkaline sodium salt of carbonic acid, in crystalline hydrated form known as washing soda.

sodium chloride Common salt.

sodium cyanide A white, very poisonous salt of hydrocyanic acid, used in electroplating, as a fumigant, etc.

sodium hydroxide A white, deliquescent compound forming a strongly alkaline solution in water; caustic soda.

sodium hypochlorite An unstable compound of sodium, oxygen, and chlorine, used in weak aqueous solution as a laundry bleach.

sodium nitrate A white compound occurring naturally and produced synthetically, used as a fertilizer and in the manufacture of nitric acid and explosives.

sodium thiosulfate A crystalline compound of sodium, sulfur, and oxygen, used in photography as a fixing agent. Also, erroneously, **sodium hyposulfite.**

Sod·om (sod′əm) *n.* In the Bible, a city on the Dead Sea, destroyed with Gomorrah because of the wickedness of its people. *Gen.* 13:10.

sod·om·ite (sod′əm·īt) *n.* A person who practices sodomy.

sod·om·y (sod′əm·ē) *n.* Anal copulation, esp. between male persons or with animals. [< LL *Sodoma* Sodom]

so·ev·er (sō·ev′ər) *adv.* To or in any degree at all. • *Soever* is usu. added to *who, which, what, where, when, how,* etc., to form the compounds *whosoever,* etc., giving them emphasis or specific force. When used separately, as in "how great *soever* he might be," *soever* tends to sound stilted and literary.

so·fa (sō′fə) *n.* A long upholstered couch having a back and arms. [< Ar. *soffah* a part of a floor raised to form a seat]

Sofa

soft (sôft, soft) *adj.* **1** Easily changed in shape by pressure. **2** Easily worked: *soft* wood. **3** Less hard than other things of the same kind: *soft* rock. **4** Smooth and delicate to the touch: *soft* skin. **5** Not loud or harsh: a *soft* voice. **6** Mild; gentle: a *soft* breeze. **7** Not glaring; subdued: *soft* colors. **8** Expressing mildness or sympathy: *soft* words. **9** Easily touched in feeling: a *soft* heart. **10** Out of condition: *soft* muscles. **11** *Informal* Weak-minded: *soft* in the head. **12** *Informal* Overly lenient: a judge *soft* on criminals. **13** Free from mineral salts that form insoluble compounds with soap: said of water. **14** Biodegradable: said of detergents. **15** Regarded as being nonaddicting and less harmful than hard narcotics: said of drugs, esp. marihuana. **16** *Phonet.* Describing *c* and *g* when articulated fricatively as in *cent* and *gibe.* **17** *Informal* Easy: a *soft* job. —*n.* That which is soft; a soft part or material. —*adv.* **1** Softly. **2** Quietly; gently. —*interj. Archaic* Hush! Stop!. [< OE *sōfte*] —**soft′ly** *adv.* —**soft′ness** *n.* —**Syn.** *adj.* **1** flexible, malleable, pliable. **5** low. **9** compassionate, kind, sympathetic.

soft·back (sôft′bak′, soft′-) *adj.* SOFT-COVER. —*n.* A soft-cover book.

soft·ball (sôft′bôl′, soft′-) *n.* **1** A variation of baseball requiring a smaller diamond and a larger, softer ball. **2** The ball used in this game.

soft-boiled (sôft′boild′) *adj.* Boiled so that the yolk and white are soft or semiliquid: said of eggs.

soft coal Bituminous coal.

soft-cov·er (sôft′kuv′ər, soft′-) *adj.* Designating a book having flexible sides, as of paper. Also **soft′bound** (-bound′).

soft drink A nonalcoholic beverage, esp. a carbonated drink.

sof·ten (sôf′ən, sof′-) *v.t. & v.i.* To make or become soft or softer. —**sof′ten·er** *n.*

soft-heart·ed (sôft′här′tid, soft′-) *adj.* Full of kindness, tenderness, and compassion. —**soft′heart′ed·ly** *adv.*

soft palate The fleshy back part of the roof of the mouth. • See MOUTH.

soft-shell (sôft′shel′, soft′-) *adj.* Having a soft shell, as a crab after shedding its shell: also **soft′-shelled′.** —*n.* A crab that has shed its shell: also **soft-shelled crab.**

soft-soap (sôft′sōp′, soft′-) *v.t. Informal* To flatter.

soft soap **1** Fluid or semifluid soap. **2** *Informal* Flattery.

---

add, āce, câre, pälm; end, ēven; it, īce; odd, ōpen, ôrder; tòòk, pōōl; up, bûrn; ə = a in *above,* u in *focus;* yōō = u in *fuse;* oil; pout; check; go; ring; thin; this; zh, *vision.* < derived from; ? origin uncertain or unknown.

soft·ware (sôft′wâr′, soft′-) *n.* In a digital computer, any of the programs designed to control various aspects of the operation of the machine, such as input and output operations.

soft·wood (sôft′wŏŏd′, soft′-) *n.* 1 A coniferous tree or its wood. 2 Any light, loosely structured wood, or any tree with such wood.

soft·y (sôf′tē, soft′-) *n. pl.* **soft·ies** *Informal* 1 An extremely sentimental person. 2 A person who is easily taken advantage of. Also **soft′ie.**

sog·gy (sog′ē) *adj.* **·gi·er, ·gi·est** 1 Saturated with water or moisture; soaked. 2 Heavy and wet: said of pastry. [< dial. E *sog* a swamp, bog] **—sog′gi·ly** *adv.* **—sog′gi·ness** *n.*

soil[1] (soil) *n.* 1 Finely divided rock mixed with decayed vegetable or animal matter, constituting the portion of the surface of the earth in which plants grow. 2 Region, land, or country. [< L *solium* a seat, mistaken for *solum* the ground]

soil[2] (soil) *v.t.* 1 To make dirty; smudge. 2 To disgrace; defile. **—v.i.** 3 To become dirty. **—n.** A spot or stain. [< L *suculus,* dim. of *sus* a pig]

soi·rée (swä·rā′) *n.* An evening party or reception. Also **soi·ree′.** [F< *soir* evening]

so·journ (sō′jûrn, sō·jûrn′) *v.i.* To stay or live temporarily. **—n.** (sō′jûrn) A temporary residence or short visit. [< OF *sojourner*] **—so′journ·er** *n.*

sol (sōl) *n. Music* In solmization, the fifth note of a diatonic scale. [See GAMUT.]

Sol (sol) *Rom. Myth.* The god of the sun. **—n.** The sun. [L]

Sol. Solomon.

sol. solicitor; soluble; solution.

sol·ace (sol′is) *v.t.* **·aced, ·ac·ing** 1 To comfort in trouble or grief; console. 2 To alleviate, as grief; soothe. **—n.** 1 Comfort in grief, trouble, or calamity. 2 Anything that supplies such comfort. [< L *solacium*] **—sol′ac·er** *n.* **—Syn. v.** 2 assuage, ease, mitigate. *n.* 1 cheer, consolation.

so·lar (sō′lər) *adj.* 1 Of, from, reckoned by, or pertaining to the sun. 2 Using energy from the sun: *solar* heat. [< L *sol* sun]

solar energy 1 Energy emitted by the sun as radiation over the entire electromagnetic spectrum. 2 Radiation from the sun, esp. in the infrared range, technologically convertible to domestic and industrial uses.

so·lar·i·um (sō·lâr′ē·əm) *n. pl.* **·i·a** (-ē·ə) or **·ums** A room, porch, etc., in which people can sit in the sun. [L]

solar plexus 1 A network of sympathetic nerves serving the abdominal viscera. 2 *Informal* The pit of the stomach.

solar system The sun and the bodies that orbit it. ● See PLANET.

sold (sōld) *p.t.* & *p.p.* of SELL.

sol·der (sod′ər) *n.* 1 An easily melted alloy used for joining metal parts. 2 Anything that unites or cements. **—v.t.** 1 To unite or repair with solder. 2 To join together; bind. **—v.i.** 3 To work with solder. 4 To be united by or as by solder. [< L *solidus* firm, hard] **—sol′der·er** *n.*

sol·dier (sōl′jər) *n.* 1 A person serving in an army. 2 An enlisted man in an army, as distinguished from a commissioned officer. 3 A brave, skillful, or experienced warrior. 4 One who serves a cause loyally. **—v.i.** 1 To be or serve as a soldier. 2 To shirk: to *soldier* on the job. [< LL *solidus*] **—sol′dier·ly** *adj.* **—sol′dier·li·ness** *n.*

soldier of fortune A soldier willing to serve any government for money or adventure.

sol·dier·y (sōl′jər·ē) *n. pl.* **·ies** 1 Soldiers collectively. 2 Military service.

sole[1] (sōl) *n.* 1 The bottom surface of the foot. 2 The bottom surface of a shoe, boot, etc. 3 The lower part or bottom of anything. **—v.t.** **soled, sol·ing** To furnish with a new sole, as a shoe. [< L *solea* a sandal]

sole[2] (sōl) *n.* Any of several marine flatfishes allied to the flounders, highly esteemed as food. [< L *solea* sole[1], fish]

sole[3] (sōl) *adj.* 1 Being the only one: a *sole* survivor. 2 Only: His *sole* desire was for sleep. 3 *Law* Unmarried; single. 4 Of or for only one person or group. 5 Acting or accomplished without another. [< L *solus* alone] **—sole′ness** *n.*

Sole

sol·e·cism (sol′ə·siz′əm) *n.* 1 A grammatical error or a violation of approved idiomatic usage. 2 Any impropriety or incongruity. [< Gk *soloikos* speaking incorrectly] **—sol′e·cist** *n.* **—sol′e·cis′tic** or **·ti·cal** *adj.*

sole·ly (sōl′lē) *adv.* 1 By oneself or itself alone; singly. 2 Completely; entirely. 3 Only.

sol·emn (sol′əm) *adj.* 1 Characterized by majesty, mystery, or power; awe-inspiring. 2 Characterized by ceremonial observances; sacred. 3 Marked by gravity; earnest. [< L *solemnis*] **—sol′emn·ly** *adv.* **—sol′emn·ness** *n.* **—Syn.** 1 impressive. 3 grave, sedate, serious, somber.

so·lem·ni·ty (sə·lem′nə·tē) *n. pl.* **·ties** 1 The state or quality of being solemn. 2 A solemn rite or observance.

sol·em·nize (sol′əm·nīz) *v.t.* **·nized, ·niz·ing** 1 To perform according to legal or ritual forms: to *solemnize* a marriage. 2 To celebrate with formal ritual. 3 To make solemn, grave, or serious. **—sol′em·ni·za′tion, sol′em·niz′er** *n.*

so·le·noid (sō′lə·noid) *n. Electr.* A conducting wire in the form of a cylindrical coil, used to produce a magnetic field. [< Gk. *sōlēn* a channel + -OID] **—so′le·noi′dal** *adj.* **—so′le·noi′dal·ly** *adv.*

Solenoid

sol·fa (sōl′fä′) *Music v.t.* & *v.i.* **-faed, -fa·ing** To sing using the sol-fa instead of words. **—n.** 1 The syllables used in solmization. 2 The act of singing them. [< Ital. *solfa.* See GAMUT.] **—sol′fa′ist** *n.*

sol·feg·gio (sōl·fej′ō) *n. pl.* **·feg·gi** (-fej′ē) or **·feg·gios** *Music* 1 A florid singing exercise using arbitrary vowels and consonants. 2 Solmization. [< Ital. *solfa* sol-fa]

so·lic·it (sə·lis′it) *v.t.* 1 To ask for earnestly; beg or entreat. 2 To seek to obtain, as by persuasion. 3 To entice (one) to an unlawful or immoral act. **—v.i.** 4 To make a petition. [< L *sollicitare* agitate] **—so·lic′i·ta′tion** *n.*

so·lic·i·tor (sə·lis′ə·tər) *n.* 1 A person who solicits money for causes, subscriptions, etc. 2 The chief law officer of a city, town, etc. 3 In England, a lawyer who may appear as an advocate in the lower courts only. **—so·lic′i·tor·ship′** *n.*

Solicitor General *pl.* **Solicitors General** 1 A law officer ranking below the Attorney General and assisting him. 2 The principal law officer in some of the states, corresponding to the Attorney General in others.

so·lic·i·tous (sə·lis′ə·təs) *adj.* 1 Full of anxiety or concern. 2 Full of eagerness. **—so·lic′i·tous·ly** *adv.* **—so·lic′i·tous·ness** *n.*

so·lic·i·tude (sə·lis′ə·ty ŏŏd) *n.* 1 The state of being solicitous. 2 That which makes one solicitous.

sol·id (sol′id) *adj.* 1 Having a definite shape and volume; resistant to stress; not fluid. 2 Filling the whole of the space occupied by its form; not hollow. 3 Of the same substance throughout: *solid* marble. 4 Three-dimensional. 5 Well-built; firm: a *solid* building. 6 United or unanimous: a *solid* base of support. 7 Financially safe; sound. 8 Continuous; unbroken: a *solid* hour. 9 Written without a hyphen: said of a compound word. 10 Carrying weight or conviction: a *solid* argument. 11 Serious; reliable: a *solid* citizen. 12 *Informal* Being on good terms: They were *solid* with the boss. 13 *Slang* Excellent. 14 *Printing* Having no leads or slugs between the lines; not open. **—n.** 1 A mass of matter that has a definite shape which resists change. 2 A three-dimensional figure or object. [< L *solidus*] **—sol′id·ly** *adv.* **—so·lid′i·ty** (*pl.* **·ties**), **sol′id·ness** *n.*

solid angle The angle formed at the vertex of a cone or subtended at the point of intersection of three or more planes.

sol·i·dar·i·ty (sol′ə·dar′ə·tē) *n. pl.* **·ties** Unity of purpose, relations, or interests, as of a race, class, etc.

solid geometry The geometry of a space of three dimensions.

so·lid·i·fy (sə·lid′ə·fī) *v.t.* & *v.i.* **·fied, ·fy·ing** 1 To make or become solid, hard, firm, or compact. 2 To bring or come together in unity. **—so·lid′i·fi·ca′tion** *n.*

solid state physics The physics of solid substances, esp. their properties and structure.

sol·i·dus (sol′ə·dəs) *n. pl.* **·di** (-dī) 1 A gold coin of the Byzantine Empire. 2 The sign (/) used to divide shillings from pence: 10/6 (10*s.* 6*d.*) or sometimes used to express fractions: 3/4. [L]

so·lil·o·quize (sə·lil′ə·kwīz) *v.i.* **·quized, ·quiz·ing** To utter

a soliloquy. **—so·lil′o·quist** (-kwist), **so·lil′o·quiz′er** n. **—so·lil′o·quiz′ing·ly** adv.

so·lil·o·quy (sə·lil′ə·kwē) n. pl. **·quies** 1 A talking to oneself. 2 A speech made by an actor while alone on the stage, revealing his thoughts to the audience. [< L solus alone + loqui to talk]

sol·ip·sism (sol′ip·siz′əm) n. The theory that only knowledge of the self is possible, that, for each individual, only the self exists, and therefore that reality is subjective. **—sol′ip·sist** n. **—sol′ip·sis′tic** adj.

sol·i·taire (sol′ə·târ′) n. 1 A diamond or other gem set alone. 2 Any of various card games played by one person. [< L solitarius solitary]

sol·i·tar·y (sol′ə·ter′ē) adj. 1 Living, being, or going alone. 2 Made, done, or passed alone: a solitary life. 3 Remote; secluded. 4 Lonesome; lonely. 5 Single; one; sole: Not a solitary soul was there —n. 1 pl. **·tar·ies** One who lives alone; a hermit. 2 Informal Solitary confinement in prison, usu. directed as a punishment. [< L solus alone] **—sol′i·tar′i·ly** adv. **—sol′i·tar′i·ness** n.

sol·i·tude (sol′ə·tyōod) n. 1 A being alone; seclusion. 2 Loneliness. 3 A deserted or lonely place. [< L solus alone] **—Syn.** 1 privacy, retirement. 2 isolation, lonesomeness.

sol·mi·za·tion (sol′mə·zā′shən) n. Music The use of syllables as names for the tones of the scale, now commonly do, re, mi, fa, sol, la, ti. [< SOL + MI]

so·lo (sō′lō) n. pl. **·los** or **·li** (-lē) 1 A musical composition or passage for a single voice or instrument, with or without accompaniment. 2 Any of several card games, esp. one in which a player plays alone against others. 3 Any performance accomplished alone or without assistance. —adj. 1 Performed or composed to be performed as a solo. 2 Done by a single person alone: a solo flight. —v.i. **·loed**, **·lo·ing** To fly an airplane alone, esp. for the first time. [< L solus alone] **—so′lo·ist** n.

Sol·o·mon (sol′ə·mən) In the Bible, king of Israel, successor to his father David. —n. Any very wise man.

Sol·o·mon's-seal (sol′ə·mənz·sēl′) n. Any of several perennial herbs of the lily family, having tubular greenish flowers.

so long Informal Good-by.

sol·stice (sol′stis) n. Either of the times of year when the sun is farthest from the celestial equator, either north or south. In the northern hemisphere the **summer solstice** occurs about June 22, the **winter solstice** about December 22. [< L solstitium] **—sol·sti·tial** (sol·stish′əl) adj.

sol·u·ble (sol′yə·bəl) adj. 1 Capable of being dissolved. 2 Capable of being solved or explained. [< L solvere solve, dissolve] **—sol′u·bil′i·ty**, **sol′u·ble·ness** n. **—sol′u·bly** adv.

sol·ute (sol′yōot, sō′lōot) n. The dissolved substance in a solution.

so·lu·tion (sə·lōo′shən) n. 1 A homogeneous mixture of varying proportions, formed by dissolving one or more substances, whether solid, liquid, or gaseous, in another substance, usu. liquid but sometimes gaseous or solid. 2 The act or process by which such a mixture is made. 3 The act or process of explaining, settling, or solving a difficulty, problem, or doubt. 4 The answer or explanation reached in such a process. [< L solutus, pp. of solvere dissolve]

solve (solv) v.t. **solved**, **solv·ing** To arrive at or work out the correct solution or the answer to; resolve. [< L solvere solve, loosen] **—sol′va·ble** adj. **—sol′va·bil′i·ty**, **sol′ver** n.

sol·vent (sol′vənt) adj. 1 Having means sufficient to pay all debts. 2 Capable of dissolving. —n. 1 That which solves. 2 A substance, usu. a liquid, capable of dissolving other substances. [< L solvere solve, loosen] **—sol′ven·cy** n.

Som. Somaliland.

So·ma·lia (sō·mä′lyə) n. A republic of E Africa, 262,000 sq. mi., cap. Mogadiscio. • See map at AFRICA. **—So·ma′li** (-lē) adj., n.

so·mat·ic (sō·mat′ik) adj. 1 Of or relating to the body; corporeal. 2 Of or pertaining to the walls of a body, as distinguished from the viscera. 3 Pertaining to those elements or processes of an organism which are concerned with the maintenance of the individual as distinguished from the reproduction of the species: somatic cells. [< Gk. sōma body] **—so·mat′i·cal·ly** adv.

som·ber (som′bər) adj. 1 Dark; gloomy. 2 Somewhat melancholy; sad. Brit. sp. **som′bre**. [< F sombre] **—som′ber·ly** adv. **—som′ber·ness** n. **—Syn.** 1 Gloomy, dusky, murky.

som·bre·ro (som·brâr′ō) n. pl. **·ros** A broad-brimmed hat, usu. of felt, worn in Spain and Latin America. [< Sp. sombra shade]

Sombrero

some (sum) adj. 1 Of indeterminate quantity: Have some candy. 2 Of an unspecified number: It happened some days ago. 3 Not definitely specified: Some people dislike cats. 4 Informal Worthy of notice; extraordinary: That was some cake. —pron. 1 A certain undetermined quantity or part: Please take some. 2 Certain ones not named: Some believe it is true. —adv. 1 Informal Approximately; about: Some eighty people were present. 2 Informal Somewhat. [< OE sum some]

-some[1] suffix of adjectives Characterized by, or tending to be: blithesome. [< OE -sum like, resembling]

-some[2] suffix of nouns A group consisting of (a specified number): twosome. [< SOME]

some·bod·y (sum′bod′ē, -bəd·ē) pron. An unknown or unnamed person. —n. pl. **·bod·ies** Informal A person of consequence or importance.

some·day (sum′dā′) adv. At some future time.

some·how (sum′hou′) adv. In some unspecified way.

some·one (sum′wun′, -wən) pron. Some person; somebody.

som·er·sault (sum′ər·sôlt) n. An acrobatic roll in which a person turns heels over head. —v.i. To perform a somersault. [< OF sobresault]

some·thing (sum′thing) n. 1 A thing not determined or stated. 2 A person or thing of importance. 3 An indefinite quantity or degree: He is something of an artist. —adv. Somewhat: something like his brother.

some·time (sum′tīm′) adv. 1 At some future time not precisely stated. 2 At some indeterminate time or occasion. —adj. 1 Former: a sometime student at Oxford. 2 Informal Occasional; sporadic: a sometime thing.

some·times (sum′tīmz′) adv. At times; occasionally.

some·way (sum′wā′) adv. In some way; somehow: also **some way**, **some′ways′**.

some·what (sum′hwot′, -hwət) adv. To some degree. —n. An uncertain quantity or degree.

some·where (sum′hwâr′) adv. 1 In, at, or to some unspecified or unknown place. 2 At some unspecified time: somewhere around noon. 3 Approximately. —n. An unspecified or unknown place.

some·wheres (sum′hwârz′) adv. Chiefly Regional Somewhere.

som·nam·bu·late (som·nam′byə·lāt) v. **·lat·ed**, **·lat·ing** v.i. To walk about while asleep. [< L somnus sleep + AMBULATE] **—som·nam′bu·la′tion** n.

som·nam·bu·lism (som·nam′byə·liz′əm) n. The act or state of walking during sleep. **—som·nam′bu·lant** (-lənt), **som·nam′bu·lis′tic** adj. **—som·nam′bu·list** n.

som·nif·er·ous (som·nif′ər·əs) adj. Tending to produce sleep; narcotic. [< L somnus sleep + -FEROUS]

som·no·lent (som′nə·lənt) adj. 1 Inclined to sleep; drowsy. 2 Tending to induce drowsiness. [< L somnus sleep] **—som′no·lence** or **·len·cy** n. **—som′no·lent·ly** adv.

son (sun) n. 1 A male child considered in his relationship to one parent or both. 2 Any male descendant. 3 One who occupies the place of a son, as by adoption, marriage, or regard. 4 Any male associated with a particular country, place, or idea: a son of liberty; a native son. 5 A familiar term of address to a young man or boy. **—the Son** Jesus Christ. [< OE sunu]

so·nant (sō′nənt) Phonet. adj. Voiced. —n. 1 A voiced speech sound. 2 A syllabic sound. [< L sonare resound]

so·nar (sō′när) n. A system or device for using underwater sound waves for sounding, range finding, detection of

---

submerged objects, communication, etc. [< *so(und) na(vigation and) r(anging)*]

so·na·ta (sə·nä′tä) *n. Music* An instrumental composition written in three or four movements. [< Ital. *sonare* to sound]

song (sông, song) *n.* **1** The act of singing. **2** Any melodious utterance, as of a bird. **3** A short musical composition for voice. **4** A short poem; a lyric or ballad. **5** Poetry; verse. —**for a song** At a very low price. —**song and dance** *Slang* A long, usu. repetitive statement or explanation, often untrue or not pertinent to the subject under discussion. [< OE]

song·bird (sông′bûrd′, song′-) *n.* Any of a large number of small, perching birds, having complex musical songs characteristic of each species.

Song of Solomon A book of the Old Testament, consisting of a dramatic love poem, attributed to Solomon. Also **Song of Songs.**

song sparrow A common North American sparrow noted for its song.

song·ster (sông′stər, song′-) *n.* **1** A person or bird given to singing. **2** A writer of songs. —**song′stress** (-stris) *n. Fem.*

son·ic (son′ik) *adj.* Of, pertaining to, determined, or affected by sound: *sonic* speed. [< L *sonus* sound]

sonic barrier *Aeron.* The effects, such as drag and turbulence, that hinder flight at or near the speed of sound.

son-in-law (sun′in·lô′) *n. pl.* **sons-in-law** The husband of one's daughter.

son·net (son′it) *n.* A poem of 14 lines in any of several fixed verse and rhyme schemes. [< Prov. *son* a sound]

son·net·eer (son′ə·tir′) *n.* A composer of sonnets. —*v.i.* To compose sonnets.

son·ny (sun′ē) *n. pl.* **·nies** *Informal* Little boy: a familiar form of address.

so·no·rous (sə·nôr′əs, -nō′rəs, son′ə·rəs) *adj.* **1** Productive or capable of producing sound vibrations. **2** Loud and full-sounding; resonant. **3** High-sounding: *sonorous* verse. [< L *sonare* resound] —**so·nor·i·ty** (sə·nôr′ə·tē, -nor-, son′-ôr′ə·tē), **so·nor′ous·ness** *n.* —**so·no′rous·ly** *adv.*

soon (sōōn) *adv.* **1** In the near future; shortly. **2** Without delay. **3** Early: He awoke too *soon.* **4** In accord with one's inclination; willingly: I would as *soon* go as not; I'd *sooner* quit than accept a demotion. —**had sooner** Would rather. —**sooner or later** Eventually; in time; sometime. [< OE *sōna* immediately]

soot (sōōt, sŏŏt) *n.* A black deposit of finely divided carbon from the incomplete combustion of wood, coal, etc. —*v.t.* To soil or cover with soot. [< OE *sōt*] —**soot′i·ness** *n.* —**soot′y** *adj.* (**·i·er, ·i·est**)

sooth (sōōth) *Archaic adj.* True; real. —*n.* Truth. —**in sooth** *Archaic* Truly. [< OE *sōth*] —**sooth′ly** *adv.*

soothe (sōōth) *v.* **soothed, sooth·ing** *v.t.* **1** To restore to a quiet or normal state; calm. **2** To mitigate, soften, or relieve, as pain or grief. —*v.i.* **3** To afford relief. [< OE *sōthian* verify] —**sooth′er** *n.* —**sooth′ing·ly** *adv.* —**Syn.** **1** compose, pacify, tranquilize. **2** allay, alleviate, ease.

sooth·say·er (sōōth′sā′ər) *n.* A person who claims to be able to foretell events. —**sooth′say′ing** *n.*

sop (sop) *v.* **sopped, sop·ping** *v.t.* **1** To dip or soak in a liquid. **2** To take up by absorption: often with *up.* —*v.i.* **3** To be absorbed; soak in. **4** To become saturated or drenched. —*n.* **1** Anything softened in liquid, as bread. **2** Anything given to pacify, as a bribe. [< OE *sopp*]

SOP, S.O.P. standard operating procedure; *(Mil.)* standing operating procedure.

sop. soprano.

soph·ism (sof′iz·əm) *n.* **1** A false argument seemingly correct but actually misleading. **2** A fallacy. [< Gk. *sophos* wise]

soph·ist (sof′ist) *n.* **1** A learned person; thinker. **2** One who argues cleverly and deviously. **3** *Often cap.* A member of a certain school of early Greek philosophy, preceding the Socratic school. **4** *Often cap.* One of the later Greek teachers of philosophy and rhetoric, skilled in subtle disputation. [< Gk. *sophos* wise] —**so·phis′tic** or **·ti·cal** *adj.* —**so·phis′ti·cal·ly** *adv.* —**so·phis′ti·cal·ness** *n.*

so·phis·ti·cate (sə·fis′tə·kāt) *v.* **·cat·ed, ·cat·ing** *v.t.* **1** To make less simple or ingenuous; render worldly-wise. **2** To

mislead or corrupt. —*v.i.* **3** To indulge in sophistry. —*n.* (-kit, -kāt) A sophisticated person. [< Gk. *sophos* wise] —**so·phis′ti·ca′tor** *n.*

so·phis·ti·cat·ed (sə·fis′tə·kā′tid) *adj.* **1** Worldly-wise. **2** Of a kind that appeals to the worldly-wise. **3** Very complicated in design, function, etc.: a *sophisticated* machine.

so·phis·ti·ca·tion (sə·fis′tə·kā′shən) *n.* **1** Worldly experience; urbanity, usu. with a loss of simplicity. **2** The state of being sophisticated. **3** Sophistry.

soph·is·try (sof′is·trē) *n. pl.* **·tries** **1** Subtly fallacious reasoning or disputation. **2** The art or methods of the Sophists.

soph·o·more (sof′ə·môr, -mōr) *n.* A second-year student in an American high school or college. —*adj.* Of or pertaining to second-year students or studies. [Earlier *sophomer* a dialectician < *sophom,* var. of SOPHISM]

soph·o·mor·ic (sof′ə·môr′ik, -mōr′-) *adj.* **1** Of, pertaining to, or like a sophomore. **2** Shallow and pretentious. **3** Immature; inexperienced. Also **soph′o·mor′i·cal.** —**soph′o·mor′i·cal·ly** *adv.*

-sophy *combining form* Knowledge or a system of knowledge: *philosophy.* [< Gk. *sophia* wisdom]

sop·o·rif·ic (sop′ə·rif′ik, sō′pə-) *adj.* **1** Causing or tending to cause sleep. **2** Drowsy; sleepy. —*n.* A medicine that produces sleep. [< L *sopor* sleep]

sop·ping (sop′ing) *adj.* Drenched; soaking.

sop·py (sop′ē) *adj.* **·pi·er, ·pi·est** Saturated and softened with moisture; soft and sloppy. —**sop′pi·ness** *n.*

so·pran·o (sə·pran′ō, -prä′nō) *n. pl.* **so·pran·os** or **so·pra·ni** (sə·prä′nē) **1** A part or singing voice of the highest range. **2** The music for such a voice. **3** A person having such a voice or singing such a part. —*adj.* Of or pertaining to a soprano voice or part. [< Ital. *sopra* above]

so·ra (sôr′ə, sō′rə) *n.* A grayish brown crake with a short yellow bill. Also **sora rail.** [? < N. Am. Ind.]

sor·cer·er (sôr′sər·ər) *n.* A wizard; magician.

sor·cer·ess (sôr′sər·es) *n.* A woman who practices sorcery; witch.

sor·cer·y (sôr′sər·ē) *n. pl.* **·cer·ies** Use of supernatural agencies; magic; witchcraft. [< L *sors* fate] —**sor′cer·ous** *adj.* —**sor′cer·ous·ly** *adv.*

sor·did (sôr′did) *adj.* **1** Of degraded character; vile; base. **2** Dirty; squalid. **3** Mercenary; selfish. [< L *sordidus* squalid] —**sor′did·ly** *adv.* —**sor′did·ness** *n.*

sore (sôr, sōr) *n.* **1** A place on an animal body where the skin or flesh is bruised, broken, or inflamed. **2** Anything that causes pain or trouble. —*adj.* **sor·er, sor·est** **1** Having a sore or sores; tender. **2** Pained or distressed. **3** Irritating; distressing. **4** Very great; extreme: in *sore* need of money. **5** *Informal* Offended; angry. —*adv. Archaic* Sorely. [< OE *sār*] —**sore′ness** *n.* —**Syn.** **n. 1** cut, scrape, wound.

sore·head (sôr′hed′, sōr′-) *n. Informal.* A disgruntled person.

sore·ly (sôr′lē, sōr′-) *adv.* **1** Grievously; distressingly. **2** Greatly: His aid was *sorely* needed.

sor·ghum (sôr′gəm) *n.* **1** A canelike tropical grass cultivated for fodder and its sugary sap. **2** Syrup prepared from the sap of the plant. [< L *Syricus* of Syria, where originally grown]

so·ror·i·ty (sə·rôr′ə·tē, -ror′-) *n. pl.* **·ties** A women's organization having chapters at colleges, universities, etc. [< L *soror* a sister]

sor·rel[1] (sôr′əl, sor′-) *n.* Any of various plants with acid leaves. [< OF *sur* sour]

sor·rel[2] (sôr′əl, sor′-) *n.* **1** A reddish brown color. **2** An animal of this color. —*adj.* Reddish brown. [< OF *sor* a hawk with red plumage]

Sorghum

sor·row (sor′ō, sôr′ō) *n.* **1** Pain or distress because of loss, injury, misfortune, or grief. **2** An event that causes such pain or distress; affliction. **3** The expression of grief; mourning. —*v.i.* To feel or express sorrow; grieve. [< OE *sorg* care] —**sor′row·er** *n.*

sor·row·ful (sor′ə·fəl, sôr′-) *adj.* **1** Full of or showing sorrow or grief. **2** Causing sorrow: a *sorrowful* occasion. —**sor′row·ful·ly** *adv.* —**sor′row·ful·ness** *n.*

sor·ry (sor′ē, sôr′ē) *adj.* ·ri·er, ·ri·est 1 Feeling or showing regret or remorse. 2 Affected by sorrow; grieved. 3 Causing sorrow; melancholy. 4 Pitiable or worthless; paltry. [< OE *sārig* < *sār* sore] —**sor′ri·ly** *adv.* —**sor′ri·ness** *n.*

sort (sôrt) *n.* 1 A collection of persons or things characterized by similar qualities; a kind. 2 Character; nature. 3 Manner; way; style. 4 A person of a certain type: He's a good *sort.* —**of sorts** Of a poor or unsatisfactory kind: an actor *of sorts.* —**out of sorts** Slightly ill or ill-humored. —**sort of** *Informal* Somewhat. —*v.t.* To arrange or separate into grades, kinds, or sizes; assort. [< L *sors* lot, condition] —**sort′er** *n.*

sor·tie (sôr′tē) *n.* 1 A sudden attack by troops from a besieged place. 2 A single trip of an aircraft on a military mission. [< F *sortir* go forth]

S O S (es′ō·es′) 1 The international signal of distress in the Morse code (...- - -...), used by airplanes, ships, etc. 2 *Informal* Any call for assistance.

so-so (sō′sō′) *adj.* Passable; mediocre. —*adv.* Indifferently; tolerably. Also **so′so′, so so.**

sot (sot) *n.* A habitual drunkard. [< OE *sott* a fool] —**sot′tish** *adj.* —**sot′tish·ly** *adv.* —**sot′tish·ness** *n.*

sot·to vo·ce (sot′ō vō′chē, *Ital.* sôt′tō vō′chā) Softly; in an undertone; privately. [Ital., lit., under the voice]

sou (sōō) *n.* 1 Any of several former French coins of varying value, esp. one equal to 12 deniers. 2 A coin equal to five centimes. [< LL *solidus,* a gold coin]

sou·brette (sōō·bret′) *n.* 1 The part of a frivolous or flirtatious young woman, often a maidservant, in a play or light opera. 2 An actress who portrays such parts. [< Prov. *soubret* shy] —**sou·bret′tish** *adj.*

sou·bri·quet (sōō′bri·kā, sōō·bri·kā′) *n.* SOBRIQUET.

souf·flé (sōō·flā′) *adj.* Made light and frothy, and fixed in that condition by heat: also **souf·fléed′** (-flād′). —*n.* A light, baked dish made of a sauce, beaten egg whites, and various flavorings and ingredients. [F < L *sub-* under + *flare* to blow]

sough (suf, sou) *v.i.* To make a sighing sound, as the wind. —*n.* A deep, murmuring sound. [< OE *swōgan* sound]

sought (sôt) *p.t.* & *p.p.* of SEEK.

soul (sōl) *n.* 1 That essence or entity of the human person which is regarded as being immortal, invisible, and the source or origin of spirituality, emotion, volition, etc. 2 The moral or spiritual part of man. 3 Emotional or spiritual force, vitality, depth, etc.: His acting lacks *soul.* 4 The most essential or vital element or quality of something: Justice is the *soul* of law. 5 The leading figure or inspirer of a cause, movement, etc. 6 Embodiment: The *soul* of generosity. 7 A person: Every *soul* trembled at the sight. 8 The disembodied spirit of one who has died. 9 Among U.S. Negroes: **a** The awareness of a black African heritage. **b** A strongly emotional pride and solidarity based on this awareness. **c** The qualities that arouse such feelings, esp. as exemplified in black culture and art. 10 SOUL MUSIC. 11 SOUL FOOD. —*adj.* Of or pertaining to soul (def. 9). [< OE *sāwol*]

soul brother A Negro male: used by other Negroes.

soul food Any of various Southern foods or dishes popular with American Negroes, as fried chicken, ham hocks, chitterlings, yams, etc.

soul·ful (sōl′fəl) *adj.* Full of emotion or feeling. —**soul′ful·ly** *adv.* —**soul′ful·ness** *n.* —**Syn.** deep-felt, heartfelt, deep, profound, moving, emotional.

soul kiss A kiss with the mouth open and the tongues touching.

soul·less (sōl′lis) *adj.* 1 Having no soul. 2 Without feeling or emotion; cold. —**soul′less·ly** *adv.* —**soul′less·ness** *n.*

soul music A type of popular music strongly emotional in character and influenced chiefly by the blues and gospel hymns.

soul-search·ing (sōl′sûrch′ing) *n.* A deep examination of one's motives, desires, actions, etc.

soul sister A Negro female: used by other Negroes.

sound¹ (sound) *n.* 1 Energy in the form of a disturbance, usually periodic, in the pressure and density of a fluid or the elastic strain of a solid, detectable by human organs of hearing when between about 20Hz and 20kHz in frequency. 2 The sensation produced by such energy. 3 Any noise, tone, voice, etc., of a specified quality or source: the *sound* of a door slamming shut. 4 Sounding or hearing distance; earshot: within *sound* of the battle. 5 Significance; implication: The story has a sinister *sound.* 6 Mere noise without significance: full of *sound* and fury. —*v.i.* 1 To give forth a sound or sounds. 2 To give a specified impression; seem: The story *sounds* true. —*v.t.* 3 To cause to give forth sound: to *sound* a bell; also, to give forth the sound of: to *sound* A on the violin. 4 To give a signal or order for or announcement of: to *sound* retreat. 5 To utter audibly; pronounce. 6 To make known or celebrated. 7 To test or examine by sound; auscultate. [< OF *son* < L *sonus*]

sound² (sound) *adj.* 1 Functioning without impairment; healthy. 2 Free from injury, flaw, or decay: *sound* timber. 3 Correct, logical, or sensible in reasoning, judgment, etc.: *sound* advice. 4 Not unorthodox; established: a *sound* belief. 5 Financially solid or solvent. 6 Stable; safe; secure: a *sound* investment. 7 Complete and effectual; thorough: a *sound* beating. 8 Deep; unbroken: *sound* sleep. 9 Legally valid. [< OE *gesund*] —**sound′ly** *adv.* —**sound′ness** *n.*

sound³ (sound) *n.* 1 A long, narrow body of water connecting larger bodies of water or separating an island from the mainland. 2 The air bladder of a fish. [< OE *sund* sea and ON *sund* a strait]

sound⁴ (sound) *v.t.* 1 To test the depth of (water, etc.), esp. by means of a lead weight at the end of a line. 2 To measure (depth) thus. 3 To explore or examine (the bottom of the sea, the atmosphere, etc.) by means of various probing devices. 4 To discover or try to discover the views and attitudes of (a person) by means of conversation, subtle questions, etc.: usu. with *out.* 5 To try to ascertain or determine (beliefs, attitudes, etc.) in such a manner. 6 *Surg.* To examine, as with a sound. —*v.i.* 7 To measure depth, as with a sounding lead. 8 To dive down suddenly and deeply, as a whale when harpooned. 9 To make investigation; inquire. —*n. Surg.* An instrument for exploring a cavity; a probe. —*adv.* Deeply: *sound* asleep. [< OF *sonder*] —**sound′a·ble** *adj.* —**sound′er** *n.*

sound barrier SONIC BARRIER.

sound effects In motion pictures, radio, on the stage, etc., the imitative sounds, as of rain, hoofbeats, fire, etc., produced by various methods.

sound·ing¹ (soun′ding) *adj.* 1 Giving forth a full sound; sonorous. 2 Noisy and empty. —**sound′ing·ly** *adv.*

sound·ing² (soun′ding) *n.* 1 Measurement of the depth of water. 2 *pl.* The depth of water as sounded. 3 Water of such depth that the bottom may be reached by sounding. 4 Measurement or examination of the atmosphere, space, etc. at various heights. 5 A sampling of public opinion.

sounding board 1 A structure over a pulpit or speaker's platform to amplify and clarify the speaker's voice. 2 A thin board, as the belly of a violin, used to increase the resonance of the sound: also **sound′board′.** 3 Any person, group, device, etc., used to propagate opinions. 4 A person or group on whom one tests the validity or effectiveness of something.

sound·less (sound′lis) *adj.* Making no sound; silent. —**sound′less·ly** *adv.* —**sound′less·ness** *n.*

sound·man (sound′man′) *n. pl.* ·men (-men′) A man who has charge of sound effects.

sound·proof (sound′prōōf′) *adj.* Resistant to the penetration or spread of sound. —*v.t.* To make soundproof.

sound track That portion along the edge of a motion-picture film which carries the sound record.

soup (sōōp) *n.* 1 A food made of meat or fish, vegetables, etc., cooked and served, either whole or puréed, in water, stock, or other liquid. 2 *Slang* A heavy fog. 3 *Slang* Nitroglycerin. —**in the soup** *Slang* In difficulties; in a quandary. —**soup up** *Slang* To supercharge or otherwise modify (an engine) for high speed. [< F *soupe*]

soup·çon (sōōp·sôṅ′) *n.* A minute quantity; a taste. [F, lit., a suspicion]

soup·y (sōō′pē) *adj.* **soup·i·er, soup·i·est** 1 Like soup in consistency. 2 Very foggy or cloudy. 3 Overly sentimental.

---

add, ăce, câre, pälm; end, ēven; it, īce; odd, ōpen, ôrder; tŏŏk, pōōl; up, bûrn; ə = a in *above,* u in *focus;* yōō = u in *fuse;* oil; pout; check; go; ring; thin; this; zh, *vision.* < derived from; ? origin uncertain or unknown.

sour (sour) *adj.* **1** Sharp, acid, or tart to the taste, like vinegar. **2** Having an acid or rancid taste or smell as the result of fermentation. **3** Of or pertaining to fermentation. **4** Cross; morose: a *sour* smile. **5** Bitterly disenchanted. **6** Bad in quality, performance, etc.: an athlete gone *sour*. **7** Wrong or unpleasant in pitch or tone: a *sour* note. **8** Unpleasant. **9** Acid: said of soil. —*v.t. & v.i.* To become or make sour. —*n.* **1** Something sour. **2** A cocktail, made usu. with lemon juice, fruit garnishes, etc.: a whiskey *sour*. [< OE *sūr*] —**sour′ly** *adv.* —**sour′ness** *n.* —**Syn. 4** dour, acid, bitter, unhappy.

source (sôrs, sōrs) *n.* **1** That from which something originates or is derived. **2** A cause or agency: a *source* of joy. **3** The spring or fountain from which a stream of water originates. **4** A person, writing, or agency from which information is obtained. [< L *surgere* to rise]

sour cream A food product made of cream soured and thickened by the action of lactic acid bacteria.

sour·dough (sour′dō′) *n.* **1** Fermented dough for use as leaven in making bread. **2** A pioneer or prospector in Alaska or Canada: from the practice of carrying fermented dough to make bread.

sour grapes That which a person affects to despise, because it is unattainable: an allusion to Aesop's fable of the fox and the grapes.

sour·gum (sour′gum′) *n.* TUPELO.

sour·puss (sour′poos′) *n. Slang* A person with a sullen, peevish expression or disposition.

souse (sous) *v.t. & v.i.* **soused, sous·ing 1** To dip or steep in a liquid. **2** To pickle. **3** To make or become thoroughly wet. **4** *Slang* To make or get drunk. —*n.* **1** Pickled meats, esp. the feet and ears of a pig. **2** A plunge in water. **3** Brine. **4** *Slang* A drunkard. [< OHG *sulza* brine]

sou·tane (sōō·tän′, -tan′) *n.* CASSOCK. [< Ital. *sottana*]

south (south) *n.* **1** The general direction to the right of sunrise. **2** The point of the compass at 180°, directly opposite north. **3** A region or point lying in this direction. —*adj.* **1** Situated in a southern direction relatively to the observer or to any given place or point. **2** Facing south. **3** Belonging to or proceeding from the south. —*v.i.* To turn southward. —*adv.* **1** Toward or at the south. **2** From the south. —**the South 1** In the U.S., those states lying south of Pennsylvania and the Ohio River and east of the Mississippi. **2** The Confederacy. [< OE *sūth*]

South Africa A republic of s Africa, 472,359 sq. mi., cap. Pretoria, legislative center Cape Town.

South African A native or citizen of South Africa, esp. an Afrikaner. —*adj.* Of or pertaining to South Africa or its people.

South African Dutch AFRIKAANS.

South America The southern continent of the western hemisphere, about 6,900,000 square miles. —**South American**

south·bound (south′bound′) *adj.* Going southward.

south·east (south′ēst′, *in nautical usage* sou′ēst′) *n.* **1** The direction or compass point midway between south and east. **2** Any region lying in this direction. —*adj.* Of, pertaining to, toward, or from the southeast. —*adv.* Toward or from the southeast. —**south′east′ern, south′east′ern·most** *adj.*

south·east·er (south′ēs′tər, *in nautical usage* sou′ēs′tər) *n.* A gale from the southeast.

south·east·er·ly (south′ēs′tər·lē, *in nautical usage* sou′·ēs′tər·lē) *adj. & adv.* **1** Toward the southeast. **2** From the southeast: said of wind.

south·east·ward (south′ēst′wərd) *adj. & adv.* Toward the southeast. —*n.* A southeastward point or direction — **south′east′ward·ly, south′east′wards** *adv.*

south·er (sou′thər) *n.* A strong wind from the south.

south·er·ly (suth′ər·lē) *adj.* **1** Situated in or tending toward the south. **2** From the south: a *southerly* wind. —*adv.* Toward or from the south. —**south′er·li·ness** *n.*

south·ern (suth′ərn) *adj.* **1** Of, in, or facing the south. **2** From the south, as a wind. **3** *Often cap.* Of, from, or characteristic of the South: *southern* cooking. —**south′ern·ly** *adv.* —**south′ern·most** *adj.*

Southern Cross A southern constellation having four bright stars in the form of a cross.

South·ern·er (suth′ərn·ər) *n.* A native or inhabitant of the s regions of the U.S.

Southern Hemisphere See HEMISPHERE.

southern lights AURORA AUSTRALIS.

Southern Yemen YEMEN, PEOPLE'S DEMOCRATIC REPUBLIC OF.

South Korea See KOREA.

south·land (south′land′) *n.* **1** A region situated to the south. **2** *Often cap.* The southern U.S. —**south′land′er** *n.*

south·paw (south′pô′) *Slang n.* **1** In baseball, a left-handed pitcher. **2** Any left-handed person or player. —*adj.* Left-handed.

South Pole The southern extremity of the earth's axis; the 90th degree of south latitude.

south-south·east (south′south′ēst′, *in nautical usage* sou′sou′ēst′) *n.* The direction or compass point midway between south and southeast. —*adj.* Of, pertaining to, toward, or from this direction. —*adv.* Toward or from this direction.

south-south·west (south′south′west′, *in nautical usage* sou′sou′west′) *n.* The direction or compass point midway between south and southwest. —*adj.* Of, pertaining to, toward, or from this direction. —*adv.* Toward or from this direction.

South Vietnam See VIETNAM.

south·ward (south′wərd, *in nautical usage* suth′ərd) *adj.* Situated in or toward the south. —*adv.* In a southerly direction: also **south′ward·ly, south′wards.** —*n.* The direction of south; also, a region to the south.

south·west (south′west′, *in nautical usage* sou′west′) *n.* **1** The direction or compass point midway between south and west. **2** Any region lying in this direction. —*adj.* Of, pertaining to, toward or from the southwest. —*adv.* Toward or from the southwest. —**the Southwest** The sw part of the U.S., generally including Oklahoma, Texas, New Mexico, Arizona, and southern California. —**south′·west′ern, south′west′ern·most** *adj.*

south·west·er (south′wes′tər, *in nautical usage* sou′·wes′tər) *n.* **1** A wind, gale, or storm from the southwest. **2** A waterproof hat of oilskin, canvas, etc., with a broad protective brim behind. Also **sou′west′er.**

south·west·er·ly (south′wes′·tər·lē, *in nautical usage* sou′wes′·tər·lē) *adj. & adv.* **1** Toward the southwest. **2** From the southwest: said of wind.

Southwester *def. 2*

south·west·ward (south′west′·wərd) *adj. & adv.* Toward the southwest. —*n.* A southwestward point or direction. — **south′west′ward·ly, south′west′wards** *adv.*

sou·ve·nir (sōō′və·nir′, sōō′və·nir) *n.* A token of remembrance; memento. [< L *subvenire* come to mind]

sov·er·eign (sov′rin, -ə·rən, -ərn, suv′-) *adj.* **1** Exercising or possessing supreme jurisdiction or power. **2** Free; independent; autonomous: a *sovereign* state. **3** Supremely excellent, great, or exalted. **4** Extremely potent or effective: a *sovereign* remedy. **5** Total; unmitigated: *sovereign* hate. **6** Of chief importance, supremacy, etc.: *sovereign* claims. —*n.* **1** One who possesses sovereign authority; a monarch. **2** A body of persons in whom sovereign power is vested. **3** An English gold coin equivalent to one pound sterling. [< L *super* above] —**sov′er·eign·ly** *adv.*

sov·er·eign·ty (sov′rin·tē, -ə·rən-, -ərn-, suv′-) *n. pl.* **·ties** **1** The state or quality of being sovereign. **2** The ultimate, supreme power in a state. **3** A sovereign state. **4** The status or power of a sovereign.

so·vi·et (sō′vē·et, sō′vē·et′, sov′ē-, -ē·it) *n.* **1** In the Soviet Union, any of the elected legislative councils existing at various governmental levels. **2** Any of various similar socialist legislative councils. [< Russ. *sovyet* a council]

So·vi·et (sō′vē·et, sō′vē·et′, sov′ē-, -ē·it) *adj.* Of or pertaining to the Union of Soviet Socialist Republics. —*n.pl.* The Soviet people, esp. the officials of the government.

so·vi·et·ize (sō′vē·ə·tīz′, sov′ē-) *v.t.* **·ized, ·iz·ing** To bring under a soviet form of government. —**so′vi·et·i·za′tion** *n.*

Soviet Russia 1 UNION OF SOVIET SOCIALIST REPUBLICS. **2** RUSSIAN SOVIET FEDERATED SOCIALIST REPUBLIC.

Soviet Union UNION OF SOVIET SOCIALIST REPUBLICS.

sow[1] (sō) *v.* **sowed, sown** or **sowed, sow·ing** *v.t.* **1** To scatter (seed) over land for growth. **2** To scatter seed over (land). **3** To disseminate; implant: to *sow* the seeds of distrust. — *v.i.* **4** To scatter seed. [< OE *sāwan*] —**sow′er** *n.*

sow[2] (sou) *n.* A female hog. [< OE *sū*]

sow·bel·ly (sou′bel′ē) *n. Informal* SALT PORK.

soy (soi) *n.* A dark brown salty liquid condiment made from fermented soybeans. Also **soy sauce.** [Japanese]

soy·bean (soi′bēn) *n.* **1** A small leguminous forage plant native to Asia. **2** Its edible bean, a source of oil, flour, and other products. Also, *esp. Brit.,* **soy·a** (soi′ə).

SP Shore Patrol; Submarine Patrol.

Sp. Spain; Spaniard; Spanish.

sp. special; specialist; species; specific; spelling; spirit(s).

s.p. without issue (L *sine prole*).

spa (spä) *n.* **1** Any locality frequented for its mineral springs. **2** A mineral spring. **3** A fashionable resort or resort hotel. [< *Spa,* a Belgian watering town]

space (spās) *n.* **1** The three-dimensional expanse that is considered as coextensive with the universe. **2** A limited or measurable distance or area, as that between or within points or objects. **3** A specific area designated for a particular purpose: landing *space.* **4** OUTER SPACE. **5** An interval or period of time. **6** One of the degrees of a musical staff between two lines. **7** *Printing* **a** A blank piece of type metal, used for spacing between lines, characters, etc. **b** The area occupied by such pieces. **8** Reserved accommodations, as on a ship or airliner. —*adj.* Of or pertaining to space, esp. to outer space. —*v.t.* **spaced, spac·ing 1** To separate by spaces. **2** To divide into spaces. [< L *spatium*] —**space′less** *adj.* —**spac′er** *n.*

space·craft (spās′kraft′, -kräft′) *n.* Any vehicle, manned or unmanned, designed for flight in outer space.

spaced-out (spāst′out′) *adj. Slang* Dazed or drugged, by or as by the use of narcotics.

space·flight (spās′flīt′) *n.* Flight in outer space.

space·ship (spās′ship′) *n.* Any vehicle designed to travel outside the earth's atmosphere.

space station A large, usu. manned satellite orbiting the earth and used for observation, experiments, as a relay station, etc.

space-time (spās′tīm′, -tīm′) *n.* A four-dimensional continuum in which each point is identified by three position coordinates and one coordinate of time. Also **space-time continuum.**

spa·cial (spā′shəl) *adj.* SPATIAL.

spac·ing (spā′sing) *n.* **1** The arrangement of spaces. **2** A space or spaces, as in a line of print.

spa·cious (spā′shəs) *adj.* **1** Of large or ample extent; not cramped or crowded; roomy. **2** Large or great in scale or scope. —**spa′cious·ly** *adv.* —**spa′cious·ness** *n.* —**Syn. 1** extensive, ample, sizable, capacious, commodious.

spack·le (spak′əl) *v.t.* **·led, ·ling** To apply Spackle to.

Spack·le (spak′əl) *n.* A powder which, moistened to form a paste, is used for filling cracks, etc. before painting: a trade name.

spade[1] (spād) *n.* An implement used for digging in the ground, heavier than a shovel and having a flatter blade. —**call a spade a spade 1** To call a thing by its right name. **2** To speak the plain truth. —*v.t.* **spad·ed, spad·ing** To dig or cut with a spade. [< OE *spadu*] —**spade′ful, spad′er** *n.*

spade[2] (spād) *n.* **1** A figure, resembling a heart with a triangular handle, on a playing card. **2** A card so marked. **3** *Usu. pl.* The suit of cards so marked. [< Gk. *spathē* broad sword]

spade·work (spād′wûrk′) *n.* Any preliminary work necessary to get a project under way.

spa·dix (spā′diks) *n. pl.* **spa·di·ces** (spā′də·sēz) *Bot.* A spike of tiny flowers on a fleshy axis, usu. enclosed within a spathe. [L, branch torn from palm tree < Gk.]

spa·ghet·ti (spə·get′ē) *n.* **1** A thin, cordlike pasta. **2** Insulated tubing through which bare wire is passed, as in a radio circuit. [< Ital. *spago* a small cord]

Spain (spān) *n.* A nominal constitutional monarchy in sw Europe, 194,368 sq. mi., capital Madrid.

spake (spāk) *Archaic p.t.* of SPEAK.

span[1] (span) *v.t.* **spanned, span·ning 1** To measure, esp. with the hand with the thumb and little finger extended. **2** To extend in time across: His influence *spanned* two centuries. **3** To extend over or from side to side of: This road *spans* the continent. **4** To provide with something that stretches across or extends over. —*n.* **1** The distance or measure between two points, ends, or extremities: the *span* of an eagle's wing. **2** The space or distance between the supports of an arch, abutments of a bridge, etc. **3** The part that spans such a space or distance: the graceful *spans* of Brooklyn Bridge. **4** A period of time or duration: life *span.* **5** The extreme space over which the hand can be expanded, usu. considered to be nine inches. [< OE *spann* distance]

span[2] (span) *n.* A pair of matched horses, oxen, etc., used as a team. [< MDu. *spannen* join together]

span·gle (spang′gəl) *n.* **1** A small bit of brilliant metal foil, plastic, etc., used for decoration, esp. on theatrical costumes. **2** Any small sparkling object. —*v.* **·gled, ·gling** *v.t.* **1** To adorn with or as with spangles; cause to glitter. —*v.i.* **2** To sparkle as spangles; glitter. [< MDu. *spang* a clasp, brooch] —**span′gly** *adj.*

Span·iard (span′yərd) *n.* A native or citizen of Spain.

span·iel (span′yəl) *n.* **1** A small or medium-sized dog having large pendulous ears and long silky hair. • See SPRINGER. **2** An obsequious follower. [< OF *espaignol* Spanish (dog)]

Span·ish (span′ish) *n.* **1** The language of Spain and many of the countries of the Western Hemisphere. **2** The people of Spain collectively: used with *the.* —*adj.* Of or pertaining to Spain, its people, their language, etc.

Spanish America Those countries of the Western Hemisphere in which Spanish is the common language. —**Span·ish-A·mer·i·can** *adj.*

Spanish American A native or inhabitant of Spanish America.

Spanish moss An epiphytic plant related to pineapple, growing in pendulous tufts on trees in s U.S. and tropical America.

spank (spangk) *v.t.* **1** To slap or strike, esp. on the buttocks with the open hand as a punishment. —*v.i.* **2** To move briskly. —*n.* A smack on the buttocks. [Imit.]

spank·er (spangk′ər) *n.* **1** One who spanks. **2** *Naut.* A fore-and-aft sail extended by a boom and a gaff from the mizzenmast of a ship or bark.

spank·ing (spangk′ing) *adj.* **1** Moving or blowing rapidly; swift; lively. **2** *Informal* Uncommonly large or fine. —*n.* A series of slaps on the buttocks. —*adv. Informal* Very: a *spanking* new bike. [?]

span·ner (span′ər) *n.* **1** One who or that which spans. **2** *Brit.* WRENCH.

spar[1] (spär) *n.* **1** *Naut.* A pole for extending a sail, as a mast, yard, or boom. **2** A similar heavy, round beam forming part of a derrick, crane, etc. **3** That part of an airplane wing which supports the ribs. —*v.t.* **sparred, spar·ring** To furnish with spars. [< ON *sparri* a beam]

spar[2] (spär) *v.i.* **sparred, spar·ring 1** To box, esp. with care and adroitness, as in practice. **2** To bandy words; wrangle. **3** To fight, as cocks, by striking with spurs. —*n.* The act or practice of boxing: also **spar′ring.** [< L *parare* prepare]

spar[3] (spär) *n.* Any of various vitreous, crystalline, easily cleavable, lustrous minerals. [< MDu.]

Spar (spär) *n.* A member of the women's reserve of the U.S. Coast Guard. Also **SPAR.** [< L *s(emper) par(atus)* always ready, the motto of the U.S. Coast Guard]

---

add, āce, câre, pälm; end, ēven; it, īce; odd, ōpen, ôrder; tŏŏk, pōōl; up, bûrn; ə = a in *above*, u in *focus*; yŏŏ = u in *fuse*; oil; pout; check; go; ring; thin; this; zh, *vision*. < derived from; ? origin uncertain or unknown.

spare (spâr) *v.* **spared, spar·ing** *v.t.* **1** To refrain from injuring, molesting, or killing; treat mercifully. **2** To free or relieve (someone) from (pain, expense, etc.): *Spare* us the sight. **3** To use frugally; refrain from using or exercising. **4** To dispense or dispense with; do without: Can you *spare* a dime? —*v.i.* **5** To be frugal. **6** To be lenient or forgiving. —*adj.* **spar·er, spar·est 1** That is over and above what is necessary, used, filled, etc.: *spare* time. **2** Held in reserve; additional; extra. **3** Thin; lean. **4** Not abundant or plentiful; scanty. **5** Not elaborate or fussy: a *spare* style of writing. —*n.* **1** A duplicate of something that has been saved for future use. **2** An extra tire usu. carried in or on a vehicle as a replacement in the event of a flat tire: also **spare tire. 3** In bowling, the act of overturning all the pins with the first two balls; also, the score thus made. [< OE *sparian* to spare] —**spare′ly** *adv.* —**spare′ness, spar′er** *n.*

spare·ribs (spâr′ribz′) *n.pl.* A cut of pork ribs somewhat closely trimmed.

spar·ing (spâr′ing) *adj.* **1** Scanty; slight. **2** Frugal; stingy. —**spar′ing·ly** *adv.* —**spar′ing·ness** *n.*

spark (spärk) *n.* **1** An incandescent particle, esp. one thrown off by a fire. **2** Any similar glistening or brilliant point or particle. **3** A small trace or indication: a *spark* of wit. **4** Anything that kindles or animates. **5** *Electr.* The luminous effect of an electric discharge, or the discharge itself. —*v.i.* **1** To give off sparks. **2** In an internal-combustion engine, to have the electric ignition operating. —*v.t.* **3** To activate or cause: The shooting *sparked* a revolution. [< OE *spearca*] —**spark′er** *n.*

spar·kle (spär′kəl) *v.i.* **·kled, ·kling 1** To give off flashes or bright points of light; glitter. **2** To emit sparks. **3** To effervesce, as certain wines, etc. **4** To be brilliant or vivacious. —*n.* **1** A spark; gleam. **2** Brilliance; vivacity. [Freq. of SPARK]

spar·kler (spär′klər) *n.* **1** One who or that which sparkles. **2** *Informal* A sparkling gem, as a diamond. **3** A thin, rodlike firework that emits sparks.

spark plug A device for igniting the charge in an internal-combustion engine by means of an electric spark.

spar·row (spar′ō) *n.* **1** Any of various small, plainly colored, passerine birds related to the finches, as the English sparrow. **2** Any of numerous similar birds, as the song sparrow. [< OE *spearwa*]

sparrow hawk 1 A small North American falcon with rufous back and tail. **2** A small European hawk.

sparse (spärs) *adj.* **spars·er, spars·est** Thinly spread or scattered; not dense: a *sparse* crowd. [< L *sparsus*, pp. of *spargere* sprinkle] —**sparse′ly** *adv.* —**sparse′ness, spar·si·ty** (spär′sə·tē) *n.*

Spar·ta (spär′tə) *n.* An ancient city in the Peloponnesus, s Greece, capital of ancient Laconia.

Spar·tan (spär′tən) *adj.* **1** Of Sparta or the Spartans. **2** Characterized by austerity, simplicity, self-denial, self-discipline, etc. **3** Heroically brave and enduring. —*n.* **1** A native or citizen of Sparta. **2** One of exceptional valor and fortitude. —**Spar′tan·ism** *n.*

spasm (spaz′əm) *n.* **1** A sudden, involuntary muscular contraction. **2** Any sudden action or effort. [< Gk. *spasmos* < *spaein* draw, pull]

spas·mod·ic (spaz·mod′ik) *adj.* **1** Of the nature of a spasm; intermittent; temporary; transitory. **2** Violent or impulsive. Also **spas·mod′i·cal.** —**spas·mod′i·cal·ly** *adv.*

spas·tic (spas′tik) *adj.* Of, pertaining to, or characterized by spasms. —*n.* A person afflicted with cerebral palsy or similar disability. —**spas′ti·cal·ly** *adv.*

spat¹ (spat) *p.t. & p.p.* of SPIT¹.

spat² (spat) *n.* **1** Spawn of a bivalve mollusk, esp. the oyster. **2** A young oyster, or young oysters collectively. [?]

spat³ (spat) *n.* **1** *Informal* A pet- ty dispute or quarrel. **2** A splash, as of rain; spatter. —*v.* **spat·ted, spat·ting** *v.i.* **1** To strike with a slight sound. **2** *Informal* To engage in a petty quarrel. —*v.t.* **3** To slap. [Imit.]

spat⁴ (spat) *n.* A short gaiter worn over a shoe and fastened underneath with a strap. [Short for SPATTERDASH]

Spats⁴

spate (spāt) *n.* **1** A flood or overflow. **2** A large amount or incidence. **3** A sudden outpouring, as of words. [?]

spathe (spāth) *n. Bot.* A large bract or pair of bracts sheathing a flower cluster, as a spadix. [< Gk. *spathē* broad sword]

spa·tial (spā′shəl) *adj.* Of, involving, occupying, or having the nature of space. [< L *spatium* space] —**spa·ti·al·i·ty** (spā′shē·al′ə·tē) *n.* —**spa′tial·ly** *adv.*

spat·ter (spat′ər) *v.t.* **1** To scatter in drops or splashes, as mud or paint. **2** To splash with such drops; bespatter. **3** To defame. —*v.i.* **4** To throw off drops or splashes. **5** To fall in a shower, as raindrops. —*n.* **1** The act of spattering or the condition of being spattered. **2** The mark or soiled place caused by spattering. **3** The sound of spattering. **4** A small amount or number. [?< OE *spatlian* spit out]

spat·ter·dash (spat′ər·dash′) *n.* A knee-high legging worn as a protection from mud, esp. when riding.

spat·u·la (spach′ōō·lə) *n.* A knifelike instrument with a dull, flexible, rounded blade, used to spread plaster, cake icing, etc. [L]

spav·in (spav′in) *n.* A laming disease of the hock joint of horses. [< OF *espavain*] —**spav′ined** *adj.*

spawn (spôn) *n.* **1** The eggs of fishes, amphibians, mollusks, etc., esp. in masses. **2** A great number of offspring: usu. derisive. **3** Any large quantity or yield. —*v.i.* **1** To produce spawn; deposit eggs or roe. **2** To come forth as or like spawn. —*v.t.* **3** To produce (spawn). **4** To give rise to; originate. [< L *expandere* expand]

spay (spā) *v.t.* To remove the ovaries from (a female animal). [< OF *espeer* cut with a sword]

S.P.C.A. Society for the Prevention of Cruelty to Animals.

speak (spēk) *v.* **spoke** (*Archaic* **spake**), **spo·ken** (*Archaic* **spoke**), **speak·ing** *v.i.* **1** To employ the vocal organs in ordinary speech; utter words. **2** To express or convey ideas, opinions, etc., in or as in speech: Actions *speak* louder than words. **3** To make a speech; deliver an address. **4** To converse. **5** To make a sound; also, to bark, as a dog. —*v.t.* **6** To express or make known in or as in speech. **7** To utter in speech: to *speak* words of love. **8** To use or be capable of using (a language) in conversation. —**so to speak** In a manner of speaking. —**speak for 1** To speak in behalf of; represent officially. **2** To reserve or request: usu. used in the passive voice: Has that appointment been *spoken for?* [< OE *specan*] —**speak′a·ble** *adj.*

speak·eas·y (spēk′ē′zē) *n. pl.* **·eas·ies** A place where liquor is sold contrary to law, esp. such a place in the U.S. during prohibition.

speak·er (spē′kər) *n.* **1** One who speaks, esp. in public. **2** The presiding officer in a legislative body. **3** LOUDSPEAKER.

speak·ing (spē′king) *adj.* **1** Able to speak. **2** Of, pertaining to, or for speech. **3** Using a specified language: a French-*speaking* colony. **4** Vividly lifelike: the *speaking* image of his father. —*n.* **1** The act or technique of one who speaks. **2** Something spoken. —**speak′ing·ly** *adv.*

spear (spir) *n.* **1** A weapon consisting of a pointed head on a long shaft. **2** A similar instrument, barbed and usu. forked, as for spearing fish. **3** A leaf or slender stalk, as of grass. —*v.t.* **1** To pierce or capture with or as with a spear. —*v.i.* **2** To pierce or wound with or as with a spear. **3** To send forth spears, as a plant. [< OE *spere*] —**spear′er** *n.*

spear·head (spir′hed′) *n.* **1** The point of a spear or lance. **2** The person, group, etc., that leads an action or undertaking. —*v.t.* To be in the lead of (an attack, etc.).

spear·man (spir′mən) *n. pl.* **·men** (-mən) A man armed with a spear. Also **spears′man.**

spear·mint (spir′mint′) *n.* An aromatic herb similar to peppermint.

spe·cial (spesh′əl) *adj.* **1** Out of the ordinary; uncommon; unique; different: a *special* problem. **2** Designed for or assigned to a specific purpose, occasion, etc.: a *special* permit. **3** Memorable; notable: a very *special* occasion. **4** Extra or additional: a *special* bonus. **5** Intimate; esteemed; beloved: a *special* favorite. —*n.* **1** Something made, detailed for, or appropriated to a specific service, occasion, etc., as a train, newspaper edition, sales item, featured dish, etc. **2** A television show produced and scheduled for a single presentation only. [< L *species* kind, species] —**spe′cial·ly** *adv.* —**Syn.** *adj.* **1** peculiar, particular, distinc-

tive, singular, original, unusual. **3** noteworthy, unforgettable, extraordinary, exceptional, rare.

special delivery Mail delivery by special courier for an additional fee.

Special Drawing Rights International monetary credit that can be drawn by member nations from the International Monetary Fund to be used in lieu of gold.

spe·cial·ist (spesh′əl·ist) *n.* A person devoted to one line of study, occupation, or professional work. —**spe′cial·ism** *n.* —**spe′cial·is′tic** *adj.*

spe·ci·al·i·ty (spesh′ē·al′ə·tē) *n. pl.* **·ties** *Chiefly Brit.* SPECIALTY.

spe·cial·ize (spesh′əl·īz) *v.* **·ized**, **·iz·ing** *v.i.* **1** To concentrate on one particular activity or subject. **2** To take on a form or forms adapted to special conditions or functions. —*v.t.* **3** To make specific or particular; particularize. **4** To adapt for or direct toward some special use or purpose. *Brit. sp.* **·ise.** —**spe′cial·i·za′tion** *n.*

spe·cial·ty (spesh′əl·tē) *n. pl.* **·ties** **1** Something, as a trade, study, activity, etc., in which one specializes. **2** A product or article possessing a special quality, excellence, character, etc.: *Fish is the* specialty *of this restaurant.* **3** A special mark, quality, or characteristic. **4** The state of being special.

spe·cie (spē′shē) *n.* Coined money; coin. —**in specie 1** In coin. **2** In kind. [< L *(in) specie* (in) kind]

spe·cies (spē′shēz, -shiz) *n. pl.* **·cies 1** A category of animals or plants subordinate to a genus and comprising similar organisms usu. with the capacity of interbreeding only among themselves. **2** A group of individuals or objects having in common certain attributes and designated by a common name. **3** A kind; sort; variety; form. **4** *Eccl.* **a** The visible form of bread or of wine retained by the eucharistic elements after consecration. **b** The consecrated elements of the Eucharist. [L, kind]

spe·cif·ic (spi·sif′ik) *adj.* **1** Distinctly and plainly set forth; explicit. **2** Special; definite; particular; distinct: *He took no* specific *action.* **3** Belonging to or distinguishing a species. **4** Having some distinct medicinal or pathological property: a *specific* germ. **5** Designating a particular property, composition, ratio, or quantity serving to identify a given substance or phenomenon: *specific* gravity. —*n.* **1** Anything adapted to effect a specific result. **2** A medicine affecting a specific condition or pathogen. **3** *Usu. pl.* A particular item or detail. [< L *species* kind + -FIC] —**spe·cif′i·cal·ly** *adv.* —**spec·i·fic·i·ty** (spes′ə·fis′ə·tē) *n.*

spec·i·fi·ca·tion (spes′ə·fə·kā′shən) *n.* **1** The act of specifying. **2** A definite and complete statement, as in a contract; also, one detail in such a statement. **3** In patent law, the detailed description of an invention. **4** *Usu. pl.* A description of dimensions, types of material, capabilities, etc., of a device, building project, etc. **5** A single item in such a description.

specific gravity The ratio of the mass of a substance to that of an equal volume of some standard substance, water in the case of solids and liquids, and air or hydrogen in the case of gases.

spec·i·fy (spes′ə·fī) *v.t.* **·fied**, **·fy·ing 1** To mention or state in full and explicit detail. **2** To include as an item in a specification.

spec·i·men (spes′ə·mən) *n.* **1** A person or thing regarded as representative of a class. **2** A sample, as of blood, sputum, etc., for laboratory analysis. **3** *Informal* A person of a specified type or character. [< L *specere* look at]

spe·cious (spē′shəs) *adj.* Apparently good, right, logical, etc., but actually without merit or foundation: *specious* reasoning. [< L *speciosus* fair] —**spe′cious·ly** *adv.* —**spe′cious·ness** *n.*

speck (spek) *n.* **1** A small spot or stain. **2** Any very small thing; particle. —*v.t.* To mark with specks. [< OE *specca*]

speck·le (spek′əl) *v.t.* **·led**, **·ling** To mark with specks. —*n.* A speck.

specs (speks) *n.pl. Informal* **1** EYEGLASSES. **2** Specifications. See SPECIFICATION (def. 4).

spec·ta·cle (spek′tə·kəl) *n.* **1** A grand or unusual sight or public display, as a pageant, parade, natural phenome-

non, etc. **2** An embarrassing or deplorable exhibition. **3** *pl.* EYEGLASSES. [< L *specere* see] —**spec′ta·cled** (-kəld) *adj.*

spec·tac·u·lar (spek·tak′yə·lər) *adj.* Of or like a spectacle; unusually wonderfully, exciting, etc. —*n.* Something spectacular, esp. a lavish television production. —**spec·tac′u·lar·ly** *adv.* —**spec·tac·u·lar′i·ty** (-lar′ə·tē) *n.*

spec·ta·tor (spek′tā·tər, spek·tā′-) *n.* **1** One who beholds; an eyewitness. **2** One who is present at and views a show, game, spectacle, etc. [< L *spectare* look at]

spec·ter (spek′tər) *n.* A phantom; apparition. Also *esp. Brit.* **spec′tre.** [< L *spectrum* vision]

spec·tra (spek′trə) A *pl.* of SPECTRUM.

spec·tral (spek′trəl) *adj.* **1** Pertaining to a specter; ghostly. **2** Pertaining to a spectrum. —**spec′tral·ly** *adv.*

spectro- *combining form* Spectrum: *spectroscope.*

spec·tro·gram (spek′trə·gram) *n.* A photograph or other record of a spectrum.

spec·tro·graph (spek′trə·graf, -gräf) *n.* A device for displaying and recording spectra.

spec·tro·scope (spek′trə·skōp) *n.* An instrument for sorting out into a spectrum the wavelengths in a beam of light or other radiation. —**spec′tro·scop′ic** (-skop′ik) or **·i·cal** *adj.* —**spec′tro·scop′i·cal·ly** *adv.*

spec·tros·co·py (spek·tros′kə·pē) *n.* **1** The science treating of the phenomena observed with the spectroscope. **2** The art of using the spectroscope.

spec·trum (spek′trəm) *n. pl.* **·tra** (-trə) or **·trums 1** The continuous band of colors observed when a beam of white light is diffracted, as by a prism, according to wavelength, ranging from red, the longest visible rays, to violet, the shortest. **2** Any array of radiant energy ordered according to a varying characteristic, as frequency, wavelength, etc. **3** A band of wave frequencies: the radio *spectrum.* **4** A series or range within limits: a wide *spectrum* of activities. [L, a vision]

spec·u·late (spek′yə·lāt) *v.i.* **·lat·ed**, **·lat·ing 1** To weigh mentally or conjecture; ponder; theorize. **2** To make a risky investment with hope of gain. [< L *speculari* look at, examine] —**spec′u·la·tor** *n.* —**spec·u·la·to·ry** (-lə·tôr′ē, -tō′rē) *adj.* —**Syn. 1** guess, presume, surmise, venture, hazard.

spec·u·la·tion (spek′yə·lā′shən) *n.* **1** The act of speculating or conjecturing. **2** A theory or conjecture. **3** An investment or business transaction involving risk with hope of large profit.

spec·u·la·tive (spek′yə·lə·tiv, -lā′tiv) *adj.* **1** Of, pertaining to, engaged in, or given to speculation or conjecture. **2** Strictly theoretical; not practical. **3** Engaging in or involving financial speculation. **4** Risky; doubtful. —**spec′u·la·tive·ly** *adv.* —**spec′u·la·tive·ness** *n.*

spec·u·lum (spek′yə·ləm) *n. pl.* **·la** (-lə) or **·lums 1** A mirror usu. of polished metal, used for telescope reflectors, etc. **2** *Med.* An instrument that dilates a passage of the body for examination. [L, mirror < *specere* see]

sped (sped) A *p.t. & p.p.* of SPEED.

speech (spēch) *n.* **1** The act of speaking; faculty of expressing thought and emotion by spoken words. **2** The power or capability of speaking. **3** That which is spoken; conversation; talk. **4** A public address. **5** A characteristic manner of speaking. **6** A particular language, idiom, or dialect: American *speech.* **7** The study or art of oral communication. [< OE *specan* speak]

speech·i·fy (spē′chə·fī) *v.i.* **·fied**, **·fy·ing** To make speeches; often used derisively. —**speech′i·fi′er** *n.*

speech·less (spēch′lis) *adj.* **1** Temporarily unable to speak because of physical weakness, strong emotion, etc.: *speechless* with rage. **2** Mute; dumb. **3** Silent; reticent. **4** Inexpressible in words: *speechless* joy. —**speech′less·ly** *adv.* —**speech′less·ness** *n.*

speed (spēd) *n.* **1** Rapidity of motion; swiftness. **2** Rate of motion: *speed* of light. **3** Rate or rapidity of any action or performance. **4** A transmission gear in a motor vehicle. **5** *Informal* A characteristic interest, life style, etc. **6** *Slang* An amphetamine drug, esp. methamphetamine. **7** *Archaic* Good luck; success: They wished him good *speed.* — *v.* **sped** or **speed·ed**, **speed·ing** *v.i.* **1** To move or go with speed. **2** To exceed the legal driving limit, esp. on high-

---

add, āce, câre, pälm; end, ēven; it, īce; odd, ōpen, ôrder; tŏŏk, pōōl; up, bûrn; ə = a in above, u in focus; yŏŏ = u in fuse; oil; pout; check; go; ring; thin; this; zh, vision. < derived from; ? origin uncertain or unknown.

ways. —*v.t.* **3** To promote the forward progress of: *speed* a letter. **4** To cause to move or go with speed. **5** To promote the success of. **6** To wish Godspeed to: *Speed* the parting guest. —**speed up** To accelerate in speed or action. —*adj.* Of, pertaining to, or indicating speed. [< OE *spēd* power]

speed·boat (spēd′bōt′) *n.* A motorboat capable of high speed.

speed·er (spē′dər) *n.* A person or thing that speeds; esp., a motorist who drives at a speed exceeding a safe or legal limit.

speed·om·e·ter (spi·dom′ə·tər) *n.* A device for indicating the speed of a vehicle.

speed·ster (spēd′stər) *n.* A speeder.

speed·up (spēd′up′) *n.* An acceleration in work, output, movement, etc.

speed·way (spēd′wā′) *n.* **1** A racetrack for automobiles or motorcycles. **2** A road for vehicles traveling at high speed.

speed·well (spēd′wel) *n.* Any of various herbs of the figwort family, usu. bearing blue or white flowers.

speed·y (spē′dē) *adj.* **speed·i·er, speed·i·est 1** Characterized by speed. **2** Without delay. —**speed′i·ly** *adv.* —**speed′·i·ness** *n.*

spe·le·ol·o·gy (spē′lē·ol′ə·jē, spel′ē-) *n.* **1** The scientific study of caves. **2** The exploration of caves. [< L *spelaeum* a cave + -LOGY] —**spe′le·o·log′i·cal** (-ə·loj′i·kəl) *adj.* —**spe′le·ol′o·gist** *n.*

spell¹ (spel) *v.* **spelled** or **spelt, spell·ing** *v.t.* **1** To pronounce or write the letters of (a word); esp., to do so correctly. **2** To form or be the letters of: C-a-t *spells* cat. **3** To signify; mean. —*v.i.* **4** To form words out of letters, esp. correctly. —**spell out 1** To read each letter of, usu. with difficulty. **2** To puzzle out and learn. **3** To make explicit and detailed. [< OF *espeler*]

spell² (spel) *n.* **1** A magical word or formula. **2** A state of enchantment. **3** An irresistible power or fascination. [< OE, story]

spell³ (spel) *n.* **1** *Informal* A period of time, usu. of short duration. **2** *Informal* A continuing type of weather. **3** *Informal* A short distance. **4** *Informal* A fit of illness, debility, etc. **5** A turn of duty in relief of another. **6** A period of work or employment. —*v.t.* **1** To relieve temporarily from some work or duty. **2** *Austral.* To give a rest to, as a horse. —*v.i.* **3** *Austral.* To take a rest. [< OE *gespelia* a substitute]

spell·bind (spel′bīnd′) *v.t.* **·bound, ·bind·ing** To bind or enthrall, as if by a spell. —**spell′bind·er** *n.*

spell·bound (spel′bound′) *adj.* Enthralled or fascinated by or as by a spell. —**Syn.** astonished, amazed, aghast, agog, bewitched, enchanted, charmed.

spell·er (spel′ər) *n.* **1** One who spells. **2** A spelling book.

spell·ing (spel′ing) *n.* **1** The act of one who spells. **2** The art of correct spelling; orthography. **3** The way in which a word is spelled.

spelling bee A spelling competition.

spelt¹ (spelt) A *p.t.* & *p.p.* of SPELL¹.

spelt² (spelt) *n.* A species of wheat. [< OE]

spe·lun·ker (spē·lung′kər) *n.* An enthusiast in the exploration and study of caves; a speleologist. [< L *spelunca* a cave]

spend (spend) *v.* **spent, spend·ing** *v.t.* **1** To pay out or disburse (money). **2** To expend by degrees; use up. **3** To apply or devote, as thought or effort, to some activity, purpose, etc. **4** To pass: to *spend* one's life in jail. **5** To use wastefully; squander. —*v.i.* **6** To pay out or disburse money, etc. [< OE *aspendan*] —**spend′er** *n.*

spend·thrift (spend′thrift′) *n.* One who is wastefully lavish of money. —*adj.* Excessively lavish; prodigal.

spent (spent) *p.t.* & *p.p.* of SPEND. —*adj.* **1** Worn out or exhausted. **2** Deprived of force.

sperm¹ (spûrm) *n.* **1** The male fertilizing fluid; semen. **2** A male reproductive cell; spermatozoon. [< Gk. *sperma* a seed]

sperm² (spûrm) *n.* **1** SPERM WHALE. **2** SPERMACETI. **3** SPERM OIL.

-sperm *combining form Bot.* A seed (of a specified kind): *gymnosperm.* [< Gk. *sperma* a seed]

sper·ma·ce·ti (spûr′mə·sē′tē, -set′ē) *n.* A white, waxy substance separated from the oil contained in the head of the sperm whale, used for making candles, ointments, etc. [< L *sperma ceti* seed of a whale]

sper·mat·ic (spûr·mat′ik) *adj.* Of or pertaining to sperm or the male sperm-producing gland.

sper·ma·to·phyte (spûr′mə·tə·fīt′) *n.* Any seed-bearing plant; an angiosperm or a gymnosperm. [< Gk. *sperma* seed + *phylos* plant] —**sper′ma·to·phyt′ic** (-fit′ik) *adj.*

sper·ma·to·zo·on (spûr′mə·tə·zō′on) *n. pl.* **·zo·a** (-zō′ə) A male reproductive cell of an animal, which carries half the complement of genetic material normal for its species. [< Gk. *sperma* seed + *zōion* an animal] —**sper′ma·to·zo′al, sper′ma·to·zo′an, sper′ma·to·zo′ic** *adj.*

sperm oil A pale yellow lubricating oil obtained from the sperm whale.

sperm whale A large, toothed whale of warm seas, having a huge truncate head containing a reservoir of sperm oil.

Sperm whale

spew (spyoo) *v.i.* **1** To throw up; vomit. **2** To come or issue forth. —*v.t.* **1** To throw up; vomit. **2** To eject or send forth. —*n.* That which is spewed. [< OE *spīwan*]

sp. gr. specific gravity.

sphag·num (sfag′nəm) *n.* **1** Any of a genus of whitish gray mosses; peat moss. **2** This moss in dried form, used by florists for potting plants, etc. [< Gk. *sphagnos* kind of moss] —**sphag′nous** *adj.*

sphe·noid (sfē′noid) *n.* An irregular, wedge-shaped bone forming part of the orbit. —*adj.* Wedge-shaped. [< Gk. *sphēn* wedge] —**sphe·noi·dal** (sfi·noid′l) *adj.* • See SKULL.

sphere (sfir) *n.* **1** A round body in which every point on its surface is equidistant from the center; globe. **2** A planet, sun, star, etc. **3** CELESTIAL SPHERE. **4** The apparent outer dome of the sky. **5** The field or place of activity, experience, influence, etc.; scope; province. **6** Social rank or position. —*v.t.* **sphered, spher·ing 1** To place in or as in a sphere; encircle. **2** To set among the celestial spheres. **3** To make spherical. [< Gk. *sphaira* a ball]

-sphere *combining form* Denoting an enveloping spherical mass: *atmosphere.*

spher·i·cal (sfer′i·kəl) *adj.* **1** Shaped like a sphere; globular. **2** Pertaining to a sphere or spheres. Also **spher′ic.** —**spher′i·cal·ly** *adv.* —**spher′i·cal·ness** *n.*

sphe·roid (sfir′oid) *n.* A body having approximately the form of a sphere; an ellipsoid. —**sphe·roi′dal** (sfi·roid′l), **sphe·roi′dic** or **·di·cal** *adj.* —**sphe·roi′dal·ly** *adv.*

sphinc·ter (sfingk′tər) *n. Anat.* A ring of muscle serving to open and close an opening in the body. [< Gk. *sphingein* to close] —**sphinc′ter·al** *adj.*

sphinx (sfingks) *n. pl.* **sphinx·es** or **sphin·ges** (sfin′jēz) **1** *Egypt. Myth* A wingless monster with a lion's body and the head of a man, a ram, or a hawk. **2** *Gk. Myth. Usu. cap.* A winged monster with a woman's head and breasts and a lion's body, that destroyed those unable to guess her riddle. **3** A mysterious or enigmatical person. [< Gk.]

sphyg·mo·ma·nom·e·ter (sfig′mō·mə·nom′ə·tər) *n.* An instrument for measuring blood pressure. Also **sphyg·mom′e·ter** (-mom′ə·tər). [< Gk. *sphygmos* pulse + MANOMETER]

Sphinx def. 2

spi·cate (spī′kāt) *adj.* **1** Arranged in spikes: said of flowers. **2** Having a spur, as the legs of some birds. Also **spi′cat·ed.** [< L *spica* spike]

spice (spīs) *n.* **1** An aromatic vegetable substance, as cinnamon, cloves, etc., used for flavoring. **2** Such substances collectively. **3** That which gives zest or adds interest. **4** An aromatic odor; an agreeable perfume. —*v.t.* **spiced, spic·ing 1** To season with spice. **2** To add zest or piquancy to. [< L *species* kind] —**spic′er** *n.*

spice·bush (spīs′boosh′) *n.* An aromatic deciduous shrub related to laurel. Also **spice′wood′** (-wood′).

spick-and-span (spik′ən·span′) *adj.* **1** Neat and clean. **2** Perfectly new, or looking as if new. Also **spic′-and-span′**. [Var. of SPICK[1] + ON *spānn* chip]

spic·ule (spik′yōōl) *n.* **1** A small, slender, sharp-pointed body; a spikelet. **2** *Zool.* One of the small, hard, needlelike growths supporting the soft tissues of certain invertebrates, as sponges. Also **spic·u·la** (spik′yə·lə). [< L *spicum* point, spike] —**spic′u·lar, spic′u·late** (-lāt, -lit) *adj.*

spic·u·lum (spik′yə·ləm) *n. pl.* **·la** (-lə) **1** SPICULE. **2** *Zool.* A small, pointed organ, as a spine of a sea urchin. [L]

spic·y (spī′sē) *adj.* **spic·i·er, spic·i·est** **1** Containing, flavored, or fragrant with spices. **2** Producing spices. **3** Full of spirit and zest; lively. **4** Somewhat improper or risqué. —**spic′i·ly** *adv.* —**spic′i·ness** *n.*

spi·der (spī′dər) *n.* **1** Any of numerous wingless arachnids capable of spinning silk into webs for the capture of prey. **2** A long-handled iron frying pan, often having legs. **3** Any of various devices with radiating, leglike projections. [< OE *spīthra*] —**spi′der·y** *adj.*

Garden spider

spider crab Any of various ocean crabs with long legs and spiny growths on the carapace.

spider monkey An arboreal Central and South American monkey with very long, slender limbs and a long prehensile tail.

spi·der·wort (spī′dər·wûrt′) *n.* Any of several plants with grasslike leaves and usu. blue, three-petaled flowers.

spiel (spēl) *Slang n.* An informal but purposeful speech or talk, usu. rehearsed, as by a politician or salesman. — *v.i.* To deliver a spiel. [< G *spielen* to play]

spi·er (spī′ər) *n.* One who spies.

spif·fy (spif′ē) *adj.* **·fi·er, ·fi·est** *Slang* Smartly dressed; spruce. —**spif′fi·ness** *n.* [?]

spig·ot (spig′ət, spik′-) *n.* **1** A plug for the bunghole of a cask. **2** A turning plug or valve fitting into a faucet; also, the faucet itself. [ME *spigote*]

spike[1] (spīk) *n.* **1** A very large, thick nail. **2** A slender, pointed piece of metal, as used along the top of an iron fence. **3** A projecting, pointed piece of metal in the soles of shoes to keep the wearer from slipping. **4** A very high, slender heel on a woman's shoe. **5** A straight, unbranched antler, as of a young deer. — *v.t.* **spiked, spik·ing** **1** To fasten with spikes. **2** To set or provide with spikes. **3** To block; put a stop to. **4** To pierce with or impale on a spike. **5** *Informal* To add alcoholic liquor to. [ME] —**spik′er** *n.* —**spik′y** *adj.*

spike[2] (spīk) *n.* **1** An ear of corn, barley, wheat, or other grain. **2** *Bot.* A flower cluster in which the flowers are closely attached to the stalk. [< L *spica* ear of grain]

spike·let (spīk′lit) *n. Bot.* A small spike.

spike·nard (spīk′nərd, -närd) *n.* **1** An ancient fragrant and costly ointment. **2** A perennial East Indian herb of the valerian family yielding this ointment. [< L *spica* spike + *nardus* nard]

spile (spīl) *n.* **1** A large timber or stake driven into the ground as a foundation; a pile. **2** A wooden spigot or plug used in a cask. **3** A spout driven into a sugar-maple tree to lead the sap to a bucket. — *v.t.* **spiled, spil·ing** **1** To pierce for and provide with a spile. **2** To drive spiles into. [< MDu., skewer]

spill[1] (spil) *v.* **spilled** or **spilt, spill·ing** *v.t.* **1** To allow or cause to fall or run out or over, as a liquid or a powder. **2** To shed, as blood. **3** *Naut.* To empty (a sail) of wind. **4** *Informal* To cause to fall, as from a horse. **5** *Informal* To divulge; make known, as a secret. — *v.i.* **6** To fall or run out or over: said of liquids, etc. — *n.* **1** The act of spilling. **2** That which is spilled. **3** *Informal* A fall to the ground, as from a horse or vehicle. **4** SPILLWAY. [< OE *spillan* destroy] —**spill′age, spill′er** *n.*

spill[2] (spil) *n.* **1** A slip of wood, or rolled strip of paper, used for lighting lamps, etc. **2** A splinter. **3** A slender peg, pin, or bar of wood, esp. for stopping up a hole. [Var. of SPILE[1]]

spill·way (spil′wā′) *n.* **1** A passageway in or about a dam

to release the water in a reservoir. **2** The paved upper surface of a dam over which surplus water escapes.

spilt (spilt) A *pt. & p.p.* of SPILL[1].

spin (spin) *v.* **spun, spin·ning** *v.t.* **1** To draw out and twist into threads; also, to draw out and twist fiber into (threads, yarn, etc.). **2** To make or produce (a web or cocoon) as if by spinning. **3** To tell, as a story or yarn. **4** To protract; prolong, as a story by additional details: with *out.* **5** To cause to whirl rapidly. — *v.i.* **6** To make thread or yarn. **7** To extrude filaments of a viscous substance from the body: said of spiders, etc. **8** To whirl rapidly; rotate. **9** To seem to be whirling, as from dizziness. **10** To move rapidly. — *n.* **1** An act or instance of spinning. **2** A rapid whirling. **3** Any rapid movement or action. **4** A ride, as in an automobile. **5** The uncontrolled, spiral descent of an airplane after a stall. [< OE *spinnan*]

spin·ach (spin′ich) *n.* **1** An edible garden plant of the goosefoot family. **2** Its edible leaves. [< Ar. *isbānah*]

spi·nal (spī′nəl) *adj.* **1** Of or pertaining to the spine or spinal cord. **2** Of or pertaining to spines or a spiny process.

spinal column A series of hollow, articulated bones that enclose the spinal cord and form the axis of the skeleton of a vertebrate animal.

spinal cord The thick, soft cord of nerve tissue enclosed by the spinal column.

spin·dle (spin′dəl) *n.* **1** In hand spinning, a notched, tapered rod used to twist into thread the fibers pulled from the distaff. **2** The slender rod in a spinning wheel by the rotation of which the thread is twisted and wound on a spool or bobbin on the same rod. **3** A small rod or pin bearing the bobbin of a spinning machine. **4** A rotating rod, pin, axis, arbor, or shaft, esp. when small and bearing something that rotates: the *spindle* of a lathe. **5** The tapering end of a vehicle axle that enters the hub. **6** A small shaft passing through the lock of a door and bearing the knobs or handles. **7** Any decorative, often tapered rod, used in the back of a chair, etc. **8** A needlelike rod mounted on a weighted base, for impaling bills, checks, etc. — *v.* **·dled, ·dling** *v.i.* **1** To grow into a long, slender stalk or body. — *v.t.* **2** To form into or as into a spindle. **3** To provide with a spindle. [< OE *spinel*]

spin·dle-leg·ged (spin′dəl·leg′id, -legd′) *adj.* Having long, slender legs. Also **spin′dle-shanked′** (-shangkt′).

spin·dle-legs (spin′dəl·legz′) *n.* **1** Long, slender legs. **2** *Informal* A person having long, slender legs. Also **spin′dle-shanks′** (-shangks′).

spin·dling (spind′ling) *adj.* SPINDLY.

spin·dly (spind′lē) *adj.* **·dli·er, ·dli·est** Of a slender, lanky growth or form, suggesting weakness.

spin·drift (spin′drift) *n.* Blown spray or scud. [Var. of SPOONDRIFT]

spine (spīn) *n.* **1** SPINAL COLUMN. **2** Any of various hard, pointed outgrowths on the bodies of certain animals, as the porcupine and starfish. **3** A thorny projection on the stems of certain plants, as the cactus. **4** The back of a bound book. **5** A projecting eminence or ridge. [< L *spina* spine, thorn]

spi·nel (spi·nel′, spin′əl) *n.* Any of various hard minerals, a red variety, the **ruby spinel,** being used as a gem. [< Ital. *spina* thorn]

spine·less (spīn′lis) *adj.* **1** Having no spine or backbone; invertebrate. **2** Lacking spines. **3** Having a very flexible backbone; limp. **4** Weak-willed; irresolute. —**spine′less·ness** *n.*

spin·et (spin′it) *n.* **1** A small harpsichord. **2** A small upright piano. **3** A small electronic organ. [< Ital. *spinetta*]

spin·na·ker (spin′ə·kər) *n. Naut.* A large jib-shaped sail set on the mainmast of a racing vessel, opposite the mainsail, and used when sailing before the wind. [?]

spin·ner (spin′ər) *n.* **1** One who or that which spins, as a spider or a machine. **2** In angling, a whirling spoon bait.

spin·ner·et (spin′ə·ret′) *n.* **1** An organ, as of spiders and silkworms, for spinning their silky threads. **2** A metal plate pierced with holes through which filaments of plastic material are forced, as in the making of rayon fibers.

spin·ning (spin′ing) *n.* **1** The action of converting fibers

into thread or yarn. **2** The product of spinning. —*adj.* That spins or is used in the process of spinning.

spinning jenny A machine for spinning more than one strand of yarn at a time.

spinning wheel A former household implement for spinning yarn or thread, consisting of a rotating spindle operated by a treadle and flywheel.

spin-off (spin′ôf′, -of′) *n.* **1** A secondary product, application, or result derived from another product or activity; by-product: industrial *spin-offs* from military technological research. **2** The distribution by a corporation to its stockholders of stocks or assets obtained from a subsidiary company. Also **spin′off′**.

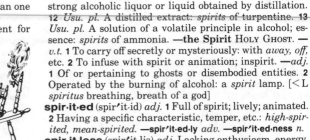

Spinning wheel

spi·nose (spī′nōs) *adj.* Bearing, armed with, or having spines. Also **spi·nous** (-nəs). —**spi′nose·ly** *adv.* —**spi·nos′i·ty** (-nos′-ə·tē) *n.*

spin·ster (spin′stər) *n.* **1** A woman who has never married, esp. an elderly one. **2** A woman who spins; a spinner. [< SPIN + -STER] —**spin′ster·hood** *n.* —**spin′ster·ish** *adj.*

spin·y (spī′nē) *adj.* **spin·i·er, spin·i·est 1** Having spines; thorny. **2** Difficult; perplexing. —**spin′i·ness** *n.*

spiny anteater ECHIDNA.

spir·a·cle (spir′ə·kəl, spī′rə-) *n.* **1** Any of numerous external openings through which air enters the tracheae of insects, etc. **2** The blowhole of a cetacean. [< L *spiraculum* airhole]

spi·ral (spī′rəl) *adj.* **1** Winding about and constantly receding from or advancing toward a center. **2** Winding and advancing; helical. **3** Winding and rising in a spire, as some springs. **4** Continuously increasing or developing. — *n. Geom.* Any plane curve formed by a point that moves around a fixed center at a distance that is always increasing. **2** A curve winding like a screw thread. **3** Something wound as a spiral or having a spiral shape. **4** A continuously developing increase or decrease: price *spirals*. —*v.* **·raled** or **·ralled, ·ral·ing** or **·ral·ling** *v.t.* **1** To cause to take a spiral form or course. —*v.i.* **2** To take a spiral form or course. **3** To increase or decrease continuously or sharply, as prices, costs, etc. [< L *spira* coil] —**spi′ral·ly** *adv.* • The use of the intransitive verb (def. 3) without any accompanying modifier almost always means "to increase," as *Prices spiraled in June.* If "to decrease" is meant, an adverb should be used to prevent ambiguity, as *Prices spiraled downward in June.*

spi·rant (spī′rənt) *n. & adj. Phonet.* FRICATIVE. [< L *spirare* breathe]

spire (spīr) *n.* **1** The tapering or pyramidal roof of a tower; also, a steeple. **2** A slender stalk or blade. **3** The summit or tapering end of anything. —*v.* **spired, spir·ing** *v.t.* **1** To furnish with a spire or spires. —*v.i.* **2** To shoot or point up in or as in a spire. **3** To put forth a spire or spires; sprout. [< OE *spīr* stem] —**spired** *adj.*

Spire

spi·re·a (spī·rē′ə) *n.* Any of a genus of ornamental shrubs of the rose family, having small, white or pink flowers. Also **spi·rae′a**. [< Gk. *speira* coil]

spir·it (spir′it) *n.* **1** The animating principle of life and energy in man and animals. **2** SOUL (def. 1). **3** That part of a human being characterized by intelligence, emotion, will, etc.; the mind. **4 a** A supernatural being without a material body, as an angel, demon, etc. **b** Such a being regarded as having a certain character, abode, effect: an evil *spirit*. **c** A supernatural being regarded as having a visible form, power of speech, etc.; ghost; specter. **5** A state of mind; mood; disposition: low *spirits*. **6** Vivacity, energy, courage, positiveness, etc.: to have *spirit*. **7** A characteristic or prevailing feeling, attitude, motivation, quality, etc.: in the *spirit* of fun; the *spirit* of the Reformation. **8** A person regarded with reference to any specific activity, characteristic, or temper: a

blithe *spirit*. **9** True intent or meaning: the *spirit* of the law. **10** Ardent loyalty or devotion: school *spirit*. **11** *pl.* A strong alcoholic liquor or liquid obtained by distillation. ~~**12** *Usu. pl.* A distilled extract: *spirits* of turpentine. **13**~~ *Usu. pl.* A solution of a volatile principle in alcohol; essence: *spirits* of ammonia. —**the Spirit** HOLY GHOST. —*v.t.* **1** To carry off secretly or mysteriously: with *away, off,* etc. **2** To infuse with spirit or animation; inspirit. —*adj.* **1** Of or pertaining to ghosts or disembodied entities. **2** Operated by the burning of alcohol: a *spirit* lamp. [< L *spiritus* breathing, breath of a god]

spir·it·ed (spir′it·id) *adj.* **1** Full of spirit; lively; animated. **2** Having a specific characteristic, temper, etc.: *high-spirited, mean-spirited*. —**spir′it·ed·ly** *adv.* —**spir′it·ed·ness** *n.*

spir·it·less (spir′it·lis) *adj.* Lacking enthusiasm, energy, or courage. —**spir′it·less·ly** *adv.* —**spir′it·less·ness** *n.*

spirit level An instrument for indicating the horizontal or perpendicular by reference to the position of a bubble of air in a tube of liquid.

spir·it·ous (spir′i·təs) *adj.* SPIRITUOUS.

spir·i·tu·al (spir′i·chōō·əl, -ich·əl) *adj.* **1** Of or pertaining to spirit, as distinguished from matter. **2** Of or consisting of spirit; incorporeal. **3** Of, pertaining to, or affecting the highest or purest moral or intellectual qualities of man; not earthly or sensual. **4** Sacred or religious; not lay or temporal. **5** Supernatural. —*n.* **1** Anything pertaining to spirit or to sacred matters. **2** A religious folk song originating among the Negroes of the s U.S. —**spir′i·tu·al′i·ty, spir′i·tu·al·ness** *n.* —**spir′i·tu·al·ly** *adv.* —**Syn.** *adj.* **3** otherworldly, unworldly, unearthly, pure, heavenly, angelic.

spir·i·tu·al·ism (spir′i·chōō·əl·iz′əm) *n.* **1** The belief that the spirits of the dead can communicate with the living, usu. through the agency of a person called a medium. **2** *Usu. cap.* A religious movement based on this belief. **3** A philosophy that identifies ultimate reality as basically spiritual. —**spir′i·tu·al·ist** *n.* —**spir′i·tu·al·is′tic** *adj.*

spir·i·tu·al·ize (spir′i·chōō·əl·īz′, -ich·ə·līz′) *v.t.* **·ized, ·iz·ing 1** To make spiritual. **2** To treat as having a spiritual meaning or sense. *Brit. sp.* **·ise.** —**spir′i·tu·al·i·za′tion, spir′·i·tu·al·iz′er** *n.*

spir·i·tu·el (spir′i·chōō·el′, *Fr.* spē·rē·tü·el′) *adj.* Characterized by esprit, or wit, and by the higher and finer qualities of the mind generally. [F] —**spir′i·tu·elle′** *adj. Fem.*

spir·i·tu·ous (spir′i·chōō·əs, -ich·əs, -ət·əs) *adj.* Containing alcohol, esp. distilled alcohol. —**spir′i·tu·ous·ness** *n.*

spiro- *combining form* Spiral; coiled: *spirochete*. [< Gk. *speira* coil]

spi·ro·chete (spī′rə·kēt) *n.* **1** Any of a genus of spiral-shaped bacteria usu. found in water. **2** Any similar microorganisms including those which cause syphilis, yaws, etc. Also **spi′ro·chaete**. [< Gk. *speira* coil + *chaitē* bristle] —**spi′ro·che′tal** *adj.* • See BACTERIUM.

spirt (spûrt) *n. & v.* SPURT.

spit[1] (spit) *v.* **spat** or **spit, spit·ting** *v.t.* **1** To eject (saliva, blood, etc.) from the mouth. **2** To throw off, eject, or utter by or as if by spitting: often with *out*: to *spit* out an oath. **3** To light, as a fuse. —*v.i.* **4** To eject saliva from the mouth. **5** To make a hissing noise, as an angry cat. **6** To fall in scattered drops or flakes, as rain or snow. —**spit on** *Informal* To treat with contempt. —*n.* **1** Spittle; saliva. **2** An act of spitting or expectorating. **3** A frothy, whitish secretion of a spittle insect; also, a spittle insect. **4** A light, scattered fall of snow or rain. **5** *Informal* SPITTING IMAGE. [< OE *spittan*] —**spit′ter** *n.*

spit[2] (spit) *n.* **1** A pointed rod on which meat is skewered and roasted before a fire. **2** A point of low land, or a long, narrow shoal, extending into the water. —*v.t.* **spit·ted, spit·ting** To transfix or impale with or as with a spit. [< OE *spitu*]

spit·ball (spit′bôl′) *n.* **1** Paper chewed in the mouth and shaped into a ball for use as a missile. **2** In baseball, an illegal pitch of a ball moistened on one side with saliva, etc.

spite (spīt) *n.* **1** Malicious bitterness or resentment, usu. resulting in mean or vicious acts. **2** That which is done in spite. —**in spite of** (or **spite of**) In defiance of; notwithstanding. —*v.t.* **spit·ed, spit·ing** To show one's spite toward; vex maliciously; thwart. [Short for DESPITE] —**spite′ful** *adj.* —**spite′ful·ly** *adv.* —**spite′ful·ness** *n.*

spit·fire (spit′fīr′) n. A quick-tempered person.

spitting image *Informal* An exact likeness or counterpart. Also **spit and image**.

spit·tle (spit′l) n. 1 SALIVA. 2 SPIT¹ n. (def. 3). [< OE *spātl*]

spittle insect Any of various jumping insects whose nymphs excrete frothy matter.

spit·toon (spi·tōōn′) n. A receptacle for spit; a cuspidor.

spitz (spits) n. One of a breed of small dogs with a tapering muzzle; a Pomeranian. Also **spitz dog**. [G, pointed]

spiv (spiv) n. *Brit. Informal* A flashy chiseler, sharper, or one who lives by his wits. [?]

splash (splash) v.t. 1 To dash or spatter (a liquid, etc.) about. 2 To spatter, wet, or soil with a liquid dashed about. 3 To make with splashes: to *splash* one's way. 4 To decorate or mark with or as with splashed colors. 5 To display prominently: His name was *splashed* all over the front page. —v.i. 6 To make a splash or splashes. 7 To move, fall, or strike with a splash or splashes. —n. 1 The act or noise of splashing liquid. 2 Something splashed, as a spot of liquid. 3 A small area or spot of color, light, etc. 4 A small amount; dash: a *splash* of bitters. 5 A brilliant or ostentatious display. —**make a splash** *Informal* To attract notice or become conspicuous, usu. briefly. [Var. of PLASH] — **splash′er** n. —**splash′y** adj. (·i·er, ·i·est)

splash·down (splash′doun′) n. The landing of a spacecraft, or a part of it, in the seas following its flight.

splat (splat) n. A thin, broad piece of wood, as that forming the middle of a chair back. [?]

splat·ter (splat′ər) v.t. & v.i. To spatter or splash. —n. A spatter; splash. [Blend of SPLASH and SPATTER]

splay (splā) adj. 1 Spread or turned outward. 2 Clumsily formed; ungainly. —n. *Archit.* A slanted surface or beveled edge. —v.t. 1 To make with a splay. 2 To open to sight; spread out. —v.i. 3 To spread out; open. 4 To slant; slope. [Var. of DISPLAY]

splay·foot (splā′fŏŏt′) n. 1 Abnormal flatness and turning outward of a foot or feet. 2 A foot so affected. —**splay′· foot′ed** adj.

spleen (splēn) n. *Anat.* 1 A highly vascular, ductless organ near the stomach of most vertebrates, which modifies, filters, and stores blood. 2 Ill temper; spitefulness: to vent one's *spleen*. [< Gk. *splēn*]

spleen·ful (splēn′fəl) adj. Irritable; peevish; ill-tempered. Also **spleen′ish**, **spleen′y**. —**spleen′ful·ly** adv.

splen·did (splen′did) adj. 1 Magnificent; imposing. 2 Conspicuously great or illustrious; glorious: a *splendid* achievement. 3 Giving out or reflecting brilliant light; shining. 4 *Informal* Very good; excellent: a *splendid* offer. [< L *splendere* to shine] —**splen′did·ly** adv. —**splen′did·ness** n. —**Syn.** 1 majestic, dazzling, sublime, superb, grand. 2 outstanding, renowned, celebrated, marvelous.

splen·dif·er·ous (splen·dif′ər·əs) adj. *Informal* Exhibiting great splendor; very magnificent: a facetious usage.

splen·dor (splen′dər) n. 1 Exceeding brillance or brightness. 2 Magnificence; greatness; grandeur. *Brit. sp.* ·**dour**. —**splen′dor·ous**, **splen′drous** adj.

sple·net·ic (spli·net′ik) adj. Fretfully spiteful; peevish; irritable. —n. A peevish person. —**sple· net′i·cal·ly** adv.

splen·ic (splen′ik, splē′nik) adj. Of or pertaining to the spleen.

splice (splīs) v.t. **spliced**, **splic·ing** 1 To unite, as two ropes or parts of a rope, so as to form one continuous piece, by intertwining the strands. 2 To connect, as timbers, by beveling, scarfing, or overlapping at the ends. 3 *Slang* To join in marriage. —n. A joining or joint made by splicing. [< MDu. *splissen*] —**splic′er** n.

splint (splint) n. 1 SPLINTER. 2 A thin, flexible strip of split wood used for basket-making, chair bottoms, etc. 3 An appliance for supporting or immobilizing a part of the body. —

Splices
a. cut. b, c. long.

v.t. To confine, support, or brace, as a fractured limb, with or as with splints. [< MDu. *splinte*]

splin·ter (splin′tər) n. 1 A thin, sharp piece of wood, glass, metal, etc., split or torn off lengthwise; a sliver. 2 SPLINTER GROUP. —v.t. & v.i. 1 To split into thin sharp pieces or fragments; shatter; shiver. 2 To separate into smaller groups or factions. [< MDu.] —**splin′ter·y** adj.

splinter group A group or faction that has broken away from a parent group or organization, usu. because of disagreements.

split (split) v. **split**, **split·ting** v.t. 1 To separate into two or more parts by or as by force. 2 To break or divide lengthwise or along the grain. 3 To divide or separate: The mountains *split* the state down the middle. 4 To divide and distribute by portions or shares. 5 To divide into groups or factions. 6 To cast (a vote) for candidates of different parties. 7 To act upon as if by splitting or breaking: Thunder *split* the air. —v.i. 8 To break apart or divide lengthwise or along the grain. 9 To become divided through disagreement, etc. 10 To share something with others. 11 *Slang* To leave quickly or abruptly. —**split off** 1 To break off by splitting. 2 To separate by or as by splitting. —**split up** 1 To separate into parts and distribute. 2 To cease association; separate. —n. 1 The act of splitting. 2 The result of splitting, as a crack, tear, rent, etc. 3 A separation into factions or groups, usu. because of disagreements. 4 A sliver; splinter. 5 A share or portion, as of loot or booty. 6 A small, usu. six-ounce, bottle of wine, soft drink, etc. 7 A wooden strip, as of osier, used in weaving baskets. 8 A confection made of a sliced banana, ice cream, syrup, chopped nuts, and whipped cream. 9 A single thickness of a skin or hide split horizontally. 10 In bowling, the position of two or more pins left standing on such spots that a spare is nearly impossible. 11 An acrobatic trick in which the legs are fully extended to the front and back and at right angles to the body. 12 *Slang* A quick departure. —adj. 1 Divided or separated longitudinally or along the grain. 2 Divided, as to agreement, unanimity, etc.: a *split* ballot; a *split* decision. [< MDu. *splitten*] —**split′ter** n.

split infinitive A verbal phrase in which the sign of the infinitive "to" is separated from its verb by an intervening word, usu. an adverb, as in "to quickly return." • Although this construction is often condemned by purists, it is sometimes justified to avoid ambiguity or awkwardness.

split-lev·el (split′lev′əl) adj. Designating a type of dwelling in which the floors of adjoining parts are at different levels, connected by short flights of stairs. —n. A split-level dwelling.

split pea A dried, hulled pea that has split naturally into two parts, used mainly for soup.

split personality A psychological condition in which a person intermittently exhibits traits, mannerisms, attitudes, etc., of two or more unrelated personalities.

split second A very small instant of time. —**split′-sec′· ond** adj.

split ticket A ballot on which the voter has distributed his vote among candidates of different parties.

split·ting (split′ing) adj. Acute or extreme in kind or degree: a *splitting* headache.

splotch (sploch) n. A spot or daub, as of ink, etc. —v.t. To soil or mark with a splotch or splotches. [?] —**splotch′y** adj.

splurge (splûrj) *Informal* n. 1 An ostentatious display. 2 An extravagant expenditure. —v.i. **splurged**, **splurg·ing** 1 To show off; be ostentatious. 2 To spend money lavishly or wastefully. [?]

splut·ter (splut′ər) v.i. 1 To make a series of slight, explosive sounds, or throw off small particles, as meat frying in fat. 2 To speak hastily, confusedly, or incoherently, as from surprise or indignation; sputter. —v.t. 3 To utter excitedly or confused; sputter. 4 To spatter or bespatter. —n. A spluttering noise or utterance. [Blend of SPLASH and SPUTTER] —**splut′ter·er** n.

spoil (spoil) v. **spoiled** or **spoilt**, **spoil·ing** v.t. 1 To impair or destroy the value, beauty, enjoyment, etc., of.

2 To weaken or impair the character or personality of, esp. by overindulgence. —*v.i.* **3** To lose normal or useful qualities; specifically, to become tainted or decayed, as food. —*n.* **1** *Usu. pl.* Plunder seized by violence; booty; loot. **2** *Usu. pl.* The jobs in government awarded by a winning political party to its faithful supporters. **3** An object of plunder. **4** Material removed in digging. [< L *spolium* booty] —**spoil′er** *n.* —**Syn.** *v.* **1** damage, injure, harm, mar, mutilate, disfigure, maim, botch, bungle. **2** indulge, humor. **3** decay, decompose, mold, rot, putrefy.

spoil·age (spoi′lij) *n.* **1** The act or process of spoiling. **2** Something spoiled. **3** Waste or loss due to spoilage.

spoils·man (spoilz′mən) *n. pl.* **·men** (-mən) One who works for a political party for spoils.

spoil·sport (spoil′spôrt′, -spōrt′) *n.* A person who spoils the pleasures of others.

spoils system The practice of giving public offices or other awards to supporters of a victorious political party.

spoke[1] (spōk) *n.* **1** One of the members of a wheel which brace the rim by connecting it to the hub. **2** One of the radial handles of a ship's steering wheel. **3** A rung of a ladder. —*v.t.* **spoked, spok·ing** To provide with spokes. [< OE *spāca*]

spoke[2] (spōk) *p.t.* & a *p.p.* of SPEAK.

spo·ken (spō′kən) *p.p.* of SPEAK. —*adj.* **1** Uttered as opposed to written. **2** Having a specified kind of speech: *smooth-spoken.*

spoke·shave (spōk′shāv′) *n.* A wheelwright's tool having a blade set between two handles, used with a drawing motion in rounding and smoothing wooden surfaces.

spokes·man (spōks′mən) *n. pl.* **·men** (-mən) One who speaks in the name and on behalf of another or others. — **spokes′wom′an** (-wŏŏm′ən) *n. Fem.*

spo·li·a·tion (spō′lē·ā′shən) *n.* **1** The act of plundering or robbing. **2** The act of spoiling or damaging. [< L *spoliare* despoil] —**spo′li·a·tor** *n.*

spon·dee (spon′dē) *n.* A metrical foot consisting of two long or accented syllables. [< Gk. *spondeios (pous)* libation (meter)] —**spon·da′ic** (-dā′ik) *adj.*

sponge (spunj) *n.* **1** Any of a phylum of plantlike animals having a fibrous skeleton and growing underwater in large colonies. **2** The light, porous, extremely absorbent skeleton of such animals, used for bathing, cleaning, etc. **3** Any of various absorbent substances or materials used to clean, soak up liquids, etc. **4** Leavened dough. **5** A porous mass of metal, as platinum. **6** *Informal* SPONGER (def. 3). —**throw** (or **toss**) **up** (or **in**) **the sponge** *Informal* To yield; give up; abandon the struggle. —*v.* **sponged, spong·ing** *v.t.* **1** To wipe, wet, or clean with a sponge. **2** To wipe out; expunge; erase. **3** To absorb; suck in, as a sponge does. **4** *Informal* To get by imposing or at another's expense. — *v.i.* **5** To be absorbent. **6** To gather or fish for sponges. **7** *Informal* To be a sponger (def. 3): often with *off* or *on.* [< OE < Gk. *spongos*] —**spong′i·ness** *n.* —**spong′y** *adj.*

sponge cake A light cake of sugar, eggs, flour, etc., but containing no shortening.

spong·er (spun′jər) *n.* **1** One who uses a sponge, as for cleaning, etc. **2** A person or vessel that gathers sponges. **3** *Informal* A person who obtains something from others by taking advantage of their generosity, good nature, etc.

spon·son (spon′sən) *n.* **1** A curved projection from the hull of a vessel or seaplane, to increase its stability or surface area. **2** A similar protuberance on a ship or tank, for storage purposes or for the training of a gun. **3** An air tank built into the side of a canoe, to improve stability and prevent sinking. [?]

spon·sor (spon′sər) *n.* **1** A person who acts as surety for another, as in a loan, debt, etc. **2** A person or group who helps establish or finance something, as a club, activity, etc. **3** GODPARENT. **4** A business firm or enterprise that assumes all or part of the costs of a radio or television program which advertises its product or service. —*v.t.* To act as a sponsor for. [< L *spondere* to pledge] —**spon·so·ri·al** (spon·sôr′ē·əl, -sō′rē-) *adj.* —**spon′sor·ship** *n.*

spon·ta·ne·i·ty (spon′tə·nē′ə·tē, -nā-) *n. pl.* **·ties** **1** The state or quality of being spontaneous. **2** Something spontaneous, as an action, manner of behavior, etc.

spon·ta·ne·ous (spon·tā′nē·əs) *adj.* **1** Acting or arising naturally and without constraint from an inner impulse, prompting, or desire; not planned or contrived. **2** Apparently arising independently without external cause, stimulus, influence, or condition. **3** Produced without human labor; wild; indigenous. [< L *sponte* of free will] —**spon·ta′ne·ous·ly** *adv.* —**spon·ta′ne·ous·ness** *n.*

spontaneous combustion Ignition resulting from the accumulation of heat generated by slow oxidation.

spontaneous generation *Biol.* ABIOGENESIS.

spoof (spōōf) *Informal v.t.* & *v.i.* **1** To deceive or hoax; joke. **2** To satirize in a good-natured manner. —*n.* **1** A deception; hoax. **2** A playful parody or satire. [< a game invented by A. Roberts, 1852-1933, English comedian]

spook (spōōk) *Informal n.* A ghost; apparition; specter. — *v.t.* **1** To haunt (a person or place). **2** To frighten, disturb, or annoy. **3** To startle or frighten (an animal) into flight, stampeding, etc. [< Du.] —**spook′ish** *adj.*

spook·y (spōō′kē) *adj.* **spook·i·er, spook·i·est** *Informal* **1** Of or like a spook; ghostly; eerie. **2** Frightened; nervous; skittish. —**spook′i·ly** *adv.* —**spook′i·ness** *n.*

spool (spōōl) *n.* **1** A cylinder having a projecting rim at each end, on which is wound thread, wire, etc., and a hole from one end to the other, as for mounting on a spindle. **2** The quantity of thread, wire, etc., held by a spool. **3** Anything resembling a spool in shape or purpose. —*v.t.* To wind on a spool. [< MLG *spole*]

spoon (spōōn) *n.* **1** A utensil having a shallow, generally ovoid bowl and a handle, used in preparing, serving, or eating food. **2** Something resembling a spoon or its bowl. **3** A metallic lure attached to a fishing line: also **spoon bait.** **4** A wooden golf club with lofted face and comparatively short, stiff shaft. —*v.t.* **1** To lift up or out with a spoon. **2** To play or hit (a ball) with a weak shoving or scooping movement. —*v.i.* **3** To spoon a ball. **4** *Informal* To kiss and caress, as lovers. [< OE *spōn* chip]

spoon·bill (spōōn′bil′) *n.* **1** A wading bird related to the ibis, having a spoon-shaped bill. **2** A duck having the bill broad and flattened; a shoveler. —**spoon′-billed′** *adj.*

Spoonbill *def. 1*

spoon·drift (spōōn′drift) *n.* SPINDRIFT. [< *spoon*, var. of SPUME + DRIFT]

spoon·er·ism (spōō′nə·riz′əm) *n.* The unintentional transposition of sounds or of parts of words in speaking, as in "half-*w*armed fish" for "half-*f*ormed *w*ish". [< W. A. *Spooner*, 1844-1930, of New College, Oxford]

spoon·feed (spōōn′fēd′) *v.t.* **·fed, ·feed·ing** **1** To feed with a spoon. **2** To pamper; spoil. **3** To present (information) in such a manner that little or no thought, initiative, etc., is required of the recipient. **4** To instruct or inform (a person or group) in this manner.

spoon·ful (spōōn′fŏŏl′) *n. pl.* **·fuls** As much as a spoon will hold.

spoon·y (spōō′nē) *adj.* **spoon·i·er, spoon·i·est** *Informal* Sentimental or silly, as in lovemaking. Also **spoon′ey.**

spoor (spōōr) *n.* Footprints, droppings, or other traces of a wild animal. —*v.t.* & *v.i.* To track by or follow a spoor. [< MDu.]

spo·rad·ic (spə·rad′ik) *adj.* **1** Occurring infrequently; occasional. **2** Not widely diffused; occurring in isolated cases: a *sporadic* infection. Also **spo·rad′i·cal.** [< Gk. *sporas* scattered] —**spo·rad′i·cal·ly** *adv.* —**spo·rad′i·cal·ness** *n.* — **Syn.** **1** irregular, fitful, spasmodic, intermittent.

spo·ran·gi·um (spô·ran′jē·əm, spō-) *n. pl.* **·gi·a** (-jē·ə) A sac or single cell in which spores are produced. [< SPOR(O)- + Gk. *angeion* a vessel] —**spo·ran′gi·al** *adj.*

spore (spôr, spōr) *n.* **1** The reproductive body in plants that bear no seeds, as bacteria, algae, ferns, etc. **2** A minute body that develops into a new individual; any minute organism; a germ. —*v.i.* **spored, spor·ing** To develop spores: said of plants. [< Gk. *spora* seed, sowing] —**spo·ra·ceous** (spô·rā′shəs, spō-) *adj.*

spore case SPORANGIUM.

sporo- *combining form* Seed; spore: *sporophyte.*

spo·ro·phyll (spôr′ə·fil, spō′rə-) *n.* A leaf, or modified leaf, which bears sporangia. Also **spo′ro·phyl.**

spo·ro·phyte (spôr′ə·fīt, spō′rə-) *n.* The spore-bearing generation in plants which have a distinct reproductive phase.

spor·ran (spor′ən, spôr′-) *n.* A skin pouch, usu. with the fur on, worn in front of the kilt by Highlanders. [< Scots Gaelic *sporan*] • See KILT.

sport (spôrt, spōrt) *n.* 1 A diversion; pastime. 2 A particular game or physical activity pursued for diversion, esp. an outdoor or athletic game, as baseball, football, track, tennis, swimming, etc. 3 A spirit of jesting or raillery. 4 An object of derision; a laughingstock; butt. 5 An animal or plant that exhibits sudden variation from the normal type; a mutation. 6 *Informal* A gambler. 7 *Informal* One who lives a fast, gay, or flashy life. 8 A person characterized by his observance of the rules of fair play, or by his ability to get along with others: a good *sport.* 9 *Archaic* Amorous or sexual play. —*v.i.* 1 To amuse oneself; play; frolic. 2 To participate in games. 3 To make sport or jest; trifle. 4 To vary suddenly or spontaneously from the normal type; mutate. 5 *Archaic & Regional* To make love, esp. in a trifling manner. —*v.t.* 6 *Informal* To display or wear ostentatiously. —*adj.* Of, pertaining to, or fitted for sports; also, appropriate for casual wear: a *sport* coat: also **sports.** [Var. of DISPORT] —**sport′ful** *adj.* —**sport′ful·ly** *adv.*

sport·ing (spôr′ting, spōr′-) *adj.* 1 Pertaining to, engaged in, or used in athletic games or field sports. 2 Characterized by or conforming to the spirit of sportsmanship. 3 Interested in or associated with gambling or betting. —**sport′ing·ly** *adv.*

sporting chance *Informal* A chance involving the likelihood of loss but also the possibility of success.

spor·tive (spôr′tiv, spōr′-) *adj.* 1 Relating to or fond of sport or play; frolicsome. 2 Interested in, active in, or related to sports. —**spor′tive·ly** *adv.* —**spor′tive·ness** *n.*

sports·man (spôrts′mən, spōrts′-) *n. pl.* **·men** (-mən) 1 One who pursues field sports, esp. hunting and fishing. 2 One who abides by a code of fair play. —**sports′man·like′, sports′man·ly** *adj.*

sports·man·ship (spôrts′mən·ship, spōrts′-) *n.* 1 The art or practice of field sports. 2 Honorable or sportsmanlike conduct.

sports·wear (spôrts′wâr′, spōrts′-) *n.* Clothes made for informal or outdoor activities.

sports·wom·an (spôrts′woŏm′ən, spōrts′-) *n. pl.* **·wom·en** (-wim′in) A woman who participates in sports.

sport·y (spôr′tē, spōr′-) *adj.* **sport·i·er, sport·i·est** *Informal* 1 Relating to or characteristic of a sport. 2 Colorful; gay; loud, as clothes. —**sport′i·ly** *adv.* —**sport′i·ness** *n.*

spor·ule (spôr′yoōl, spor′-) *n.* A little spore. [Dim. of SPORE]

spot (spot) *n.* 1 A particular place or locality. 2 Any small portion of a surface differing as in color from the rest, as a mark, speck, blotch, etc. 3 A stain or blemish on character; a fault; a reproach. 4 A food fish of the Atlantic coast of the U.S. 5 One of the figures or pips with which a playing card is marked; also, a card having (a certain number of) such marks: the five *spot* of clubs. 6 *Slang* Paper money having a specified value: a ten *spot.* 7 *Chiefly Brit.* A portion or bit: a *spot* of tea. 8 *Informal* Place or allotted time, as on a list, schedule, etc. 9 *Informal* Position, job, or situation. 10 *Informal* SPOTLIGHT. 11 *Slang* NIGHTCLUB. 12 *Informal* A brief commercial or announcement, usu. scheduled between regular radio or television programs. —**hit the spot** *Slang* To gratify an appetite or need. —**in a spot** *Slang* In a difficult or embarrassing situation; in trouble. —**on the spot** 1 At once; immediately. 2 At the very place of occurrence. 3 *Slang* a In trouble, danger, difficulty, etc. b Accountable for some action, mistake, etc. —*v.* **spot·ted, spot·ting** *v.t.* 1 To mark or soil with spots. 2 To remove spots from. 3 To place or locate in or at a designated spot or spots. 4 To recognize or detect; identify; see. 5 To sully or disgrace, as the reputation of. 6 To schedule or list. 7 To shine a spotlight on. 8 *Informal* To yield (an advantage or handicap) to someone. —*v.i.* 9 To become marked or soiled with spots. 10 To make a stain or discoloration. —*adj.* 1 Paid or ready to be paid for at

once: *spot* cash. 2 Ready for instant delivery following sale. 3 Involving cash payment only. 4 Made or selected at random or according to a prearranged plan: a *spot* check. 5 Broadcast between regular programs: a *spot* announcement. 6 Televised or broadcast on the spot or from a specific spot. [< LG] —**spot′ta·ble** *adj.*

spot·check (spot′chek′) *v.t. & v.i.* To sample or examine at random or according to a prearranged plan.

spot·less (spot′lis) *adj.* 1 Free from spots, dirt, etc.: a *spotless* house. 2 Pure; unsullied: a *spotless* life. —**spot′less·ly** *adv.* —**spot′less·ness** *n.*

spot·light (spot′līt′) *n.* 1 A bright, powerful beam of light used to illuminate a person, group, building, etc. 2 A device that produces such a light. 3 Public notice or acclaim. —*v.t.* To light up or make prominent with or as with a spotlight.

spot·ted (spot′id) *adj.* 1 Discolored in spots; soiled. 2 Characterized or marked by spots.

spotted fever Any of various infectious diseases marked by fever and skin rash.

spot·ter (spot′ər) *n.* 1 In drycleaning, one who removes spots. 2 A detective hired to watch for theft, etc., as in a department store. 3 Anyone who keeps watch for something.

spot·ty (spot′ē) *adj.* **·ti·er, ·ti·est** 1 Having many spots. 2 Uneven or irregular, as in quality, performance, etc. —**spot′ti·ly** *adv.* —**spot′ti·ness** *n.*

spous·al (spou′zəl) *adj.* Pertaining to marriage. —*n.* Marriage; espousal.

spouse (spouz, spous) *n.* A partner in marriage; one's husband or wife. [< L *sponsus,* pp. of *spondere* to promise, betroth]

spout (spout) *v.i.* 1 To pour out copiously and forcibly, as a liquid under pressure. 2 To speak pompously, somewhat angrily, or at length. —*v.t.* 3 To cause to pour or shoot forth. 4 To utter pompously, somewhat angrily, or at length. —*n.* 1 A tube, trough, etc., for the discharge of a liquid. 2 A continuous stream of fluid. [ME *spoute*] —**spout′er** *n.*

spp. species (plural).

sprain (sprān) *n.* 1 A violent straining or twisting of the ligaments surrounding a joint. 2 The condition due to such strain. —*v.t.* To cause a sprain in. [< OF *espreindre* to squeeze]

sprang (sprang) A *p.t.* of SPRING.

sprat (sprat) *n.* Any of various small herringlike fish. [< OE *sprott*]

sprawl (sprôl) *v.i.* 1 To sit or lie with the limbs stretched out ungracefully. 2 To be stretched out ungracefully, as the limbs. 3 To move with awkward motions of the limbs. 4 To spread out in a straggling manner, as handwriting, vines, etc. —*v.t.* 5 To cause to spread or extend awkwardly or irregularly. —*n.* 1 The act or position of sprawling. 2 An unplanned or disorderly group, as of houses, spread out over a broad area: urban *sprawl.* [< OE *sprēawlian* move convulsively] —**sprawl′er** *n.*

spray[1] (sprā) *n.* 1 Liquid dispersed in fine particles. 2 An instrument for discharging small particles of liquid; an atomizer. 3 Something like a spray of liquid. —*v.t.* 1 To disperse (a liquid) in fine particles. 2 To apply spray to. —*v.i.* 3 To send forth or scatter spray. 4 To go forth as spray. [< MDu. *sprayen*] —**spray′er** *n.*

spray[2] (sprā) *n.* 1 A small branch bearing dependent branchlets or flowers. 2 Any ornament or pattern like this. [ME]

spread (spred) *v.* **spread, spread·ing** *v.t.* 1 To open or unfold to full width, extent, etc., as wings, sail, a map, etc. 2 To distribute over a surface, esp. in a thin layer. 3 To cover with something. 4 To force apart or farther apart. 5 To distribute over a period of time or among a group. 6 To make more widely known, active, etc.; promulgate or diffuse: to *spread* a rumor. 7 To set (a table, etc.), as for a meal. 8 To arrange or place on a table, etc., as a meal or feast. 9 To set forth or record in full. —*v.i.* 10 To be extended or expanded; increase in size, width, etc. 11 To be distributed or dispersed, as over a surface or area; scatter.

12 To become more widely known, active, etc. **13** To be forced farther apart; separate. —*n.* **1** The act of spreading. **2** The limit, distance, or extent of spreading, expansion, etc. **3** A cloth or covering for a table, bed, etc. **4** Something used for spreading: a cheese *spread*. **5** *Informal* A feast or banquet; also, a table with a meal set out on it. **6** A prominent presentation in a periodical. **7** Two pages of a magazine or newspaper facing each other and covered by related material; also, the material itself. —*adj.* Expanded; outstretched. [<OE *spraedan*] —**spread′er** *n.*

spread·ea·gle (spred′ē′gəl) *adj.* **1** Having the arms and legs spread wide apart. **2** Extravagant; bombastic: said of excessively patriotic oratory in the U.S. —*v.* **-ea·gled, -ea·gling** *v. t.* **1** To force to assume a spread-eagle position.

spread eagle **1** The figure of an eagle with extended wings, used as an emblem of the U.S. **2** Any position or movement resembling this, as a figure in skating.

spread·sheet (spred′shēt′) *n.* A kind of computer program that processes numerical data for detailed financial calculations of various kinds.

spree (sprē) *n.* **1** A period of heavy drinking. **2** Any period of fun, activity, etc. [?]

sprig (sprig) *n.* **1** A shoot or sprout of a plant. **2** An ornament in this form. **3** An heir or offspring of a family, esp. a young man. [ME *sprigge*] —**sprig′ger** *n.*

spright·ly (sprīt′lē) *adj.* **-li·er, -li·est** Full of animation and spirits; vivacious; lively. —*adv.* Spiritedly; briskly; gaily. [<*spright*, var. of SPRITE] —**spright′li·ness** *n.* —**Syn.** *adj.* animated, brisk, bustling, cheerful, nimble, spry, quick.

spring (spring) *v.* **sprang** or **sprung, sprung, spring·ing** *v.i.*
1 To move or rise suddenly and rapidly; leap; dart. **2** To move suddenly as by elastic reaction; snap. **3** To happen or occur suddenly or immediately: An angry retort *sprang* to his lips. **4** To work or snap out of place, as a mechanical part. **5** To become warped or bent, as boards. **6** To rise above surrounding objects. **7** To come into

Springs

being: New towns have *sprung* up. **8** To originate; proceed, as from a source. **9** To develop; grow, as a plant. **10** To be descended: He *springs* from good stock. —*v.t.* **11** To cause to spring or leap. **12** To cause to act, close, open, etc., unexpectedly or suddenly, as by elastic reaction: to *spring* a trap. **13** To cause to happen, become known, or appear suddenly: to *spring* a surprise. **14** To leap over; vault. **15** To start (game) from cover; flush. **16** To explode (a mine). **17** To warp or bend; split. **18** To cause to snap or work out of place. **19** To force into place, as a beam or bar. **20** To suffer (a leak). **21** *Slang* To obtain the release of (a person) from prison or custody. —*n.* **1** *Mech.* An elastic device that yields under stress, and returns to normal form when the stress is removed. **2** Elastic quality or energy. **3** The act of flying back from a position of tension; recoil. **4** A cause of action; motive. **5** Any source or origin. **6** A flow or fountain, as of water. **7** The act of leaping up or forward suddenly; a jump; bound. **8** The season in which vegetation starts anew; in the north temperate zone, the three months of March, April, and May; in the astronomical year, the period from the vernal equinox to the summer solstice. —*adj.* **1** Of or pertaining to the season of spring. **2** Resilient; acting like or having a spring. **3** Hung on springs. **4** Coming from or housing a spring of water. [<OE *springan*]

spring·board (spring′bôrd′, -bōrd′) *n.* **1** A flexible board used to give impetus, as to a dive, acrobatic leap, etc. **2** Anything that gives impetus, as to an activity.

spring·bok (spring′bok′) *n. pl.* **·bok** or **·boks** A small African gazelle noted for its ability to leap high in the air. Also **spring′buck′** (-buk′). [<Afrikaans]

spring chicken **1** A young chicken. **2** *Informal* A young person, esp. a girl: usu. with a negative: She's no *spring chicken*.

Springbok

spring·er (spring′ər) *n.* **1** One who or that which springs. **2** A young chicken. **3** A spaniel valuable for flushing game; also **springer spaniel.**

spring fever The listlessness that overtakes a person with the first warm days of spring.

spring tide **1** A high tide occurring about new moon and full moon. **2** Any great wave of feeling, etc.

Springer spaniel

spring·time (spring′tīm′) *n.* **1** The season of spring. **2** Any early or youthful period. Also **spring′tide′** (-tīd′).

spring·y (spring′ē) *adj.* **spring·i·er, spring·i·est** **1** Elastic; resilient. **2** Having many water springs; wet. —**spring′i·ly** *adv.* —**spring′i·ness** *n.*

sprin·kle (spring′kəl) *v.* **·kled, ·kling** *v.t.* **1** To scatter in drops or small particles. **2** To scatter over or upon: *Sprinkle* the top with flour. —*v.i.* **3** To fall or rain in scattered drops. —*n.* **1** The act of sprinkling. **2** A small quantity. **3** A light rain. [ME *sprenkelen*] —**sprin′kler** *n.*

sprin·kling (spring′kling) *n.* **1** The act of one who or that which sprinkles. **2** A small amount or number: a *sprinkling* of people.

sprint (sprint) *n.* **1** The act of sprinting. **2** A short race run at top speed. **3** A brief period, as of speed. —*v.i.* To go or run fast, as in a sprint. [<Scand.] —**sprint′er** *n.*

sprit (sprit) *n.* A small spar reaching diagonally from a mast to the peak of a fore-and-aft sail. [<OE *sprēot* pole]
• See SPRITSAIL.

sprite (sprīt) *n.* **1** A fairy, elf, or goblin. **2** A small, elflike person. **3** A ghost. [<L *spiritus*]

sprit·sail (sprit′səl, sprit′sāl′) *n.* A sail extended by a sprit.

sprock·et (sprok′it) *n.* **1** A projection, as on the rim of a wheel, for engaging with the links of a chain. **2** A wheel bearing such projections: also **sprocket wheel.** [?]

sprout (sprout) *v.i.* **1** To put forth shoots; begin to grow; germinate. **2** To develop or grow rapidly. —*v.t.* **3** To cause to sprout. **4** To remove shoots from. —*n.* **1** A new shoot or bud on a plant. **2** Something like or suggestive of a sprout, as a young person. **3** *pl.* BRUSSELS SPROUTS. [<OE *sprūtan*]

a. spritsail. b. sprit.

spruce¹ (sprōōs) *n.* **1** Any of a genus of evergreen trees of the pine family, having needle-shaped leaves and pendulous cones. **2** The wood of any of these trees. [<Med. L *Prussia* Prussia]

spruce² (sprōōs) *adj.* **spruc·er, spruc·est** Smart, trim, and neat in appearance. —*v.* **spruced, spruc·ing** *v.t.* **1** To make spruce: often with *up*. —*v.i.* **2** To make oneself spruce: usu. with *up*. [<earlier *spruce*, a kind of superior Prussian leather] —**spruce′ly** *adv.* —**spruce′ness** *n.*

sprung (sprung) *p.p.* & a *p.t.* of SPRING.

spry (sprī) *adj.* **spri·er** or **spry·er, spri·est** or **spry·est** Quick and active; agile. [<Scand.] —**spry′ly** *adv.* —**spry′ness** *n.*

spt. seaport.

spud (spud) *n.* **1** A spadelike tool with narrow blade or prongs for uprooting weeds. **2** *Informal* A potato. —*v.t.* **spud·ded, spud·ding** To remove, as weeds, with a spud. [ME *spuddle*]

spume (spyōōm) *n.* Froth; foam; scum. —*v.i.* **spumed, spum·ing** To foam; froth. [<L *spuma* foam] —**spu′mous, spum′y** *adj.*

spu·mo·ni (spyōō·mō′nē) *n.* A frozen dessert of Italian origin, containing ice cream in layers of various colors and usu. candied fruit and nuts. Also **spu·mo′ne.** [<L *spuma* foam]

spun (spun) *p.t.* & *p.p.* of SPIN.

spunk (spungk) *n.* **1** A slow-burning tinder, as punk. **2** *Informal* Mettle; pluck; courage. [<L *spongia* sponge]

spunk·y (spungk′ē) *adj.* **spunk·i·er, spunk·i·est** *Informal* Spirited; courageous. —**spunk′i·ly** *adv.* —**spunk′i·ness** *n.*

spur (spûr) *n.* **1** Any of various pricking or goading instruments worn on the heel of a horseman. **2** Anything that

incites or urges; incentive. **3** A part or attachment like a spur, as a steel gaff fastened to a gamecock's leg, a climbing iron used by linemen, etc. **4** A stiff, sharp spine on the legs or wings of certain birds. **5** A crag or ridge extending laterally from a mountain or range. **6** A branch of a railroad, lode, etc. **7** A buttress or other offset from a wall. **8** A brace reinforcing a rafter or post. **9** A tubular extension of a part of a flower, usu. containing the nectar. **—on the spur of the moment** Hastily; impulsively. **—win one's spurs** To gain recognition or reward, esp. for the first time. **—v. spurred, spur·ring** v.t. **1** To prick or urge with or as with spurs. **2** To furnish with spurs. **3** To injure or gash with the spur, as a gamecock. —v.i. **4** To spur one's horse. **5** To hasten; hurry. [< OE *spura*] **—spur′rer** n.

spurge (spûrj) n. Any of several flowering shrubs yielding a milky juice of bitter taste. [< OF *espurgier* to purge]

spu·ri·ous (spyŏŏr′ē·əs) adj. **1** Seemingly real or genuine, but actually not; false; counterfeit. **2** Illegitimate, as of birth. [< L *spurius*] **—spu′ri·ous·ly** adv. **—spu′ri·ous·ness** n.

spurn (spûrn) v.t. **1** To reject with disdain; scorn. **2** To strike with the foot; kick. —v.i. **3** To reject something with disdain. —n. The act or an instance of spurning. [< OE *spurnan*] **—spurn′er** n.

spurred (spûrd) adj. Wearing or having spurs.

spurt (spûrt) n. **1** A sudden gush of liquid. **2** Any sudden, short-lived outbreak, as of anger, energy, etc. —v.i. **1** To come out in a jet; gush forth. **2** To make a sudden, forceful effort. —v.t. **3** To squirt. [< OE *spryttan* come forth]

sput·nik (spŏŏt′nik, spŭt′-) n. An artificial earth satellite, esp. the first, called Sputnik I, launched in October, 1957, by the U.S.S.R. [Russ., lit., fellow traveler]

sput·ter (sput′ər) v.i. **1** To throw off solid or fluid particles in a series of slight explosions. **2** To speak excitedly and incoherently. **3** To make crackling or popping sounds, as burning wood, frying fat, etc. —v.t. **4** To throw off in small particles. **5** To utter excitedly or incoherently —n. **1** The act or sound of sputtering; esp. excited talk; jabbering. **2** That which is thrown out in sputtering. [< Du. *sputteren*] **—sput′ter·er** n.

spu·tum (spyŏŏ′təm) n. pl. **·ta** (-tə) Mucus from the respiratory tract, usu. mixed with saliva; expectorated matter. [< L *spuere* to spit]

spy (spī) n. pl. **spies** **1** One who is hired to get secret information from or about an enemy, another government, etc.; a secret agent. **2** One who watches another or others secretly. —v. **spied, spy·ing** v.i. **1** To keep watch closely or secretly; act as a spy. **2** To make careful examination; pry: with *into*. —v.t. **3** To observe stealthily and usu. with hostile intent: often with *out*. **4** To catch sight of; see; espy. [< OF *espier* espy]

spy·glass (spī′glas′, -gläs′) n. A small telescope.

Sq. Squadron; Square (street).

sq. square; sequence; the following (L *sequentia*).

sq. ft. square foot; square feet.

sq. in. square inch(es).

sq. mi. square mile(s).

squab (skwob) n. **1** A young nestling pigeon about four weeks old. **2** A fat, short person. —adj. **1** Fat and short; squat. **2** Unfledged or but half-grown. [< Scand.]

squab·ble (skwob′əl) v.i. **·bled, ·bling** To engage in a petty quarrel; bicker. —n. A petty quarrel. [< Scand.] **—squab′·bler** n.

squad (skwod) n. **1** A small group of persons organized to do a special job; esp., the smallest tactical unit in the infantry of the U.S. Army. **2** A team: a football *squad*. — v.t. **squad·ded, squad·ding** **1** To form into a squad or squads. **2** To assign to a squad. [< L *quattuor* four]

squad car An automobile used by police for patrolling, and equipped with radiotelephone for communicating with headquarters.

squad·ron (skwod′rən) n. **1** An assemblage of war vessels smaller than a fleet. **2** A division of a cavalry regiment. **3** The basic unit of the U.S. Air Force, usu. consisting of two or more flights operating as a unit. **4** Any regularly arranged or organized group. —v.t. To arrange in a squadron or squadrons. [< Ital. *squadra* squad]

squal·id (skwol′id) adj. **1** Having a dirty, neglected, or poverty-stricken appearance. **2** Sordid; base. [< L *squalere* be foul] **—squal′id·ly** adv. **—squal′id·ness, squa·lid·i·ty** (skwo·lid′ə·tē) n. **—Syn. 1** foul, filthy, wretched, untidy.

squall[1] (skwôl) n. A loud, screaming outcry. —v.i. To cry loudly; scream; bawl. [< Scand.] **—squall′er** n.

squall[2] (skwôl) n. **1** A sudden, violent burst of wind, often accompanied by rain or snow. **2** A brief disturbance or commotion. —v.i. To blow a squall. [< Scand.] **—squall′y** adj. (**·i·er, ·i·est**)

squal·or (skwol′ər) n. The state of being squalid; wretched filth or poverty.

squa·ma (skwā′mə) n. pl. **·mae** (-mē) A thin, scalelike structure; a scale. [L] **—squa′mate** (-māt), **squa′mose, squa′mous** adj.

squan·der (skwon′dər) v.t. To spend (money, time, etc.) wastefully. —n. Prodigality; wastefulness. [?] **—squan′·der·er** n. **—squan′der·ing·ly** adv. **—Syn. v.** dissipate, waste, lavish, run through, throw away.

square (skwâr) n. **1** A parallelogram having four equal sides and four right angles. **2** Any object, part, or surface that is square or nearly so, as one of the spaces on a checkerboard. **3** An L- or T-shaped instrument by which to test or lay out right angles. **4** An open area bordered by streets or formed by their intersection. **5** A town or city block; also, the distance between one street and the next. **6** *Math.* The product of a number or element multiplied by itself. **7** *Slang* A person of excessively conventional tastes or habits. **—on the square 1** At right angles. **2** *Informal* Honest, fair, true, etc.; also, honestly, fairly, truly, etc. **—out of square** Not at right angles; obliquely. —adj. **squar·er, squar·est 1** Having four equal sides and four right angles. **2** Approaching a square or a cube in form: a *square* box. **3** Forming a right angle: a *square* nook. **4** Adapted to forming squares or computing in squares: a *square* measure. **5** Being a square with each side of specified length: two inches *square*. **6** Perfectly adjusted, aligned, balanced, etc. **7** Even; settled: said of debts, etc. **8** Tied, as a score. **9** Honest; fair; just. **10** *Informal* Solid; full; satisfying: a *square* meal. **11** Broad; solid; muscular: a *square* build. **12** *Slang* Excessively conventional or conservative; not sophisticated. **13** *Naut.* At right angles to the mast and keel. —v. **squared, squar·ing** v.t. **1** To make square. **2** To shape or adjust so as to form a right angle. **3** To mark with or divide into squares. **4** To test for the purpose of adjusting to a straight line, right angle, or plane surface. **5** To bring to a position suggestive of a right angle: *Square* your shoulders. **6** To make satisfactory settlement or adjustment of: to *square* accounts. **7** To make equal, as a game score. **8** To cause to conform; adapt: to *square* one's opinions to the times. **9** To reconcile or set right. **10** *Math.* **a** To multiply (a number or element) by itself. **b** To determine the area of. **11** *Slang* To bribe. —v.i. **12** To be at right angles. **13** To conform; agree; harmonize: with *with*. **—square away 1** *Naut.* To set (the yards) at right angles to the keel. **2** To put into good order; make ready. **3** SQUARE OFF. **—square off** To assume a position for attack or defense; prepare to fight. **—square up** To adjust or settle satisfactorily. —adv. **1** So as to be square, or at right angles. **2** Honestly; fairly. **3** Directly; firmly. [< OF *esquarre*] **—square′ness, squar′er** n. • See PARAL-LELOGRAM.

square dance Any dance, as a quadrille, in which the couples form sets in squares.

square knot A common knot, formed of two overhand knots. • See KNOT.

square·ly (skwâr′lē) adv. **1** In a direct or straight manner: He looked her *squarely* in the eyes. **2** Honestly; fairly. **3** Plainly; unequivocally. **4** In a square form: *squarely* built. **5** At right angles (to a line or plane).

square measure A unit or system of units for measuring areas. • See MEASURE.

square-rigged (skwâr′rigd′) adj. Having the principal sails extended by horizontal yards at right angles to the masts.

square-rig·ger (skwâr′rig′ər) n. A square-rigged ship.

---

add, āce, câre, pälm; end, ēven; it, īce; odd, ōpen, ôrder; tŏŏk, pōōl; up, bûrn; ə = a in above, u in focus;
yōō = u in fuse; oil; pout; check; go; ring; thin; this; zh, vision. < derived from; ? origin uncertain or unknown.

square root *Math.* A number or element whose square is equal to a given quantity.

square sail A four-sided sail usu. rigged on a horizontal yard set at right angles to the mast.

square shooter *Informal* One who acts honestly and justly.

squash[1] (skwosh) *v.t.* **1** To squeeze or press into a pulp or soft mass; crush. **2** To quell or suppress. **3** *Informal* To silence or humiliate quickly and thoroughly; squelch. — *v.i.* **4** To be smashed or squashed. **5** To make a splashing or sucking sound. —*n.* **1** A crushed mass. **2** The sudden fall of a heavy, soft, or bursting body; also, the sound made by such a fall. **3** The sucking, squelching sound made by walking through ooze or mud. **4** Either of two games played on an indoor court with rackets and a ball. In one (**squash rackets**), a slow rubber ball is used; in the other (**squash tennis**), a livelier, smaller ball. **5** *Brit.* A fruit-flavored beverage. —*adv.* With a squelching, oozy sound. [< L *ex-* thoroughly + *quassare* crush] —**squash′er** *n.*

squash[2] (skwosh) *n.* **1** Any of various edible gourds usu. cooked and served as a vegetable. **2** The plant that bears it. [< Algon.]

squash·y (skwosh′ē) *adj.* **squash·i·er, squash·i·est** **1** Soft and moist. **2** Easily squashed. —**squash′i·ly** *adv.* —**squash′·i·ness** *n.*

squat (skwot) *v.* **squat·ted** or **squat, squat·ting** *v.i.* **1** To sit on the heels or hams, or with the legs near the body. **2** To crouch or cower down, as to avoid being seen. **3** To settle on a piece of land without title or payment. **4** To settle on government land in accordance with certain government regulations that will eventually give title. —*v.t.* **5** To cause (oneself) to squat. —*adj.* **squat·ter, squat·test** **1** Short and thick. **2** Being in a squatting position. —*n.* A squatting attitude or position. [< OF *esquatir*] —**squat′ter** *n.*

squat·ty (skwot′ē) *adj.* **·ti·er, ·ti·est** Short and thickset; squat.

squaw (skwô) *n.* An American Indian woman or wife.

squawk (skwôk) *v.i.* **1** To utter a shrill, harsh cry, as a parrot. **2** *Slang* To utter loud complaints or protests. —*n.* **1** A shrill, harsh cry. **2** *Slang* A shrill complaint. [Imit.] — **squawk′er** *n.*

squeak (skwēk) *n.* **1** A thin, sharp, penetrating sound. **2** *Informal* An escape, esp. in the phrase **a narrow** (or **close**) **squeak.** —*v.i.* **1** To make a squeak. **2** *Informal* To let out information; squeal. **3** To succeed or otherwise progress after narrowly averting failure: to *squeak* through. —*v.t.* **4** To utter or effect with a squeak. **5** To cause to squeak. [Prob. < Scand.] —**squeak′y** *adj.* (**·i·er, ·i·est**) —**squeak′i·ly** *adv.* —**squeak′i·ness** *n.*

squeal (skwēl) *v.i.* **1** To utter a sharp, shrill, somewhat prolonged cry. **2** *Slang* To turn informer; betray an accomplice or a plot. —*v.t.* **3** To utter with or cause to make a squeal. —*n.* A shrill, prolonged cry, as of a pig. [Imit.] — **squeal′er** *n.*

squeam·ish (skwē′mish) *adj.* **1** Easily disgusted or shocked. **2** Overly scrupulous. **3** Nauseated; also, easily nauseated. [< AF *escoymous*] —**squeam′ish·ly** *adv.* — **squeam′ish·ness** *n.*

squee·gee (skwē′jē) *n.* **1** An implement having a straight-edged strip of rubber, etc., used for removing water from window panes, etc., after washing them. **2** *Phot.* A smaller similar implement, often made in the form of a roller, used for pressing a film closer to its mount, etc. —*v.t.* **·geed, ·gee·ing** To use a squeegee on. [Var. of SQUEEZE]

squeeze (skwēz) *v.* **squeezed, squeez·ing** *v.t.* **1** To press hard upon; compress. **2** To extract something from by pressure: to *squeeze* oranges. **3** To get or draw forth by pressure: to *squeeze* juice from apples. **4** To force, push, maneuver, etc., by or as by squeezing: He *squeezed* his car into the narrow space. **5** To oppress, as with burdensome taxes. **6** To exert pressure upon (someone) to act as one desires, as by blackmailing. **7** To embrace; hug. —*v.i.* **8** To apply pressure. **9** To force one's way; push: with *in, through,* etc. **10** To be pressed; yield to pressure. — **squeeze by, through,** etc. *Informal* To avoid failure, defeat, trouble, etc., by the narrowest margin. —*n.* **1** The act or process of squeezing; pressure. **2** A handclasp; also, an embrace; hug. **3** A quantity of something, as juice, extracted or expressed. **4** The state or condition of being

squeezed; crush. **5** A time of trouble, scarcity, difficulty, etc. **6** SQUEEZE PLAY. **7** *Informal* Pressure exerted for the extortion of money or favors; also, financial pressure. [< OE *cwēsan* to crush] —**squeez′a·ble** *adj.* —**squeez′er** *n.*

squeeze play **1** In baseball, a play in which the batter bunts the ball so that a man on third base may score by starting while the pitcher is about to deliver the ball. **2** Any attempt or maneuver to realize some end or goal by coercion.

squelch (skwelch) *v.t.* **1** To crush; squash. **2** *Informal* To subdue utterly; silence, as with a crushing reply. —*v.i.* **3** To make or move with a splashing or sucking noise. —*n.* **1** A noise, as made when walking in wet boots. **2** A heavy fall or blow. **3** *Informal* A crushing retort or reply. [Imit.] —**squelch′er** *n.*

squib (skwib) *n.* **1** A brief news item. **2** A short witty or satirical speech or writing. **3** A broken firecracker that burns with a spitting sound. —*v.* **squibbed, squib·bing** *v.i.* **1** To write or use squibs. **2** To fire a squib. **3** To explode or sound like a squib. —*v.t.* **4** To attack with squibs; lampoon. [?]

squid (skwid) *n.* One of various ten-armed marine cephalopods with a long, slender body, ink sac, and broad caudal fins. [?]

squill (skwil) *n.* **1** A bulbous plant of the lily family. **2** Its bulb, containing various medicinal and poisonous alkaloids. [< Gk. *skilla* sea onion]

squint (skwint) *v.i.* **1** To look with half-closed eyes, as into bright light. **2** To look with a side glance; look askance. **3** To be cross-eyed. **4** To incline or tend: with *toward,* etc. —*v.t.* **5** To hold (the eyes) half shut, as in glaring light. **6** To cause to squint. —*adj.* **1** Affected with strabismus. **2** Looking obliquely or askance; indirect. —*n.* **1** An affection of the eyes in which their axes are differently directed; strabismus. **2** The act or habit of squinting. [?] —**squint′er** *n.*

Squid

squire (skwīr) *n.* **1** A knight's attendant; an armor bearer. **2** In England, the chief landowner of a district. **3** In the U.S., a title applied esp. to village lawyers and justices of the peace. **4** A gentleman who escorts a lady in public; a gallant. —*v.t.* **squired, squir·ing** To be a squire to (someone); escort. [Var. of ESQUIRE]

squirm (skwûrm) *v.i.* **1** To bend and twist the body; wriggle; writhe. **2** To show signs of pain or distress. —*n.* A squirming motion. [?] —**squirm′y** *adj.* (**·i·er, ·i·est**)

squir·rel (skwûr′əl *Brit.* skwir′əl) *n.* **1** Any of various slender rodents with a long bushy tail, living mainly in trees and feeding chiefly on nuts. The **red squirrel,** the **gray squirrel,** and the **fox squirrel** are North American types. **2** One of various related rodents, as the woodchuck, ground squirrel, etc. **3** The fur of a squirrel. —*v.t.* **squir·reled** or **·relled, squir·rel·ing** or **·rel·ling** To take away and hide (something) for possible use in the future: often with *away.* [< Gk. *skia* shadow + *oura* tail]

Gray squirrel

squirt (skwûrt) *v.i.* **1** To come forth in a thin stream or jet; spurt out. —*v.t.* **2** To eject (water or other liquid) forcibly and in a jet. **3** To wet or bespatter with a squirt or squirts. —*n.* **1** The act of squirting or spurting; also, a jet of liquid squirted forth. **2** A syringe or squirt gun. **3** *Informal* A youngster, esp. a mischievous one. [ME *swirten*] —**squirt′·er** *n.*

squirt gun An instrument or toy shaped like a gun and used for squirting.

squish (skwish) *v.t.* & *v.i.* SQUASH[1]. —*n.* A squashing sound. [Var. of SQUASH[1]] —**squish′y** (**·i·er, ·i·est**) *adj.*

sq. yd. square yard(s).

Sr strontium.

Sr. Senior; Señor; Sir; Sister.

sr steradian.

Sra. Señora.

Sri Lank·a (srē langk′ə) An island south of India, an independent state of the Commonwealth of Nations, 25,-332 sq. mi., cap. Colombo: formerly Ceylon. •See map at INDIA.

S.R.O. standing room only.

Srta. Señorita.

SS, SS. Nazi special police (G *Schutzstaffel*).

SS, S.S., S/S steamship.

SS. Saints.

S.S. Sunday School; written above (L *supra scriptum*).

ss, ss., s.s. shortstop.

SSA, S.S.A. Social Security Administration.

SSB, S.S.B. Social Security Board.

SSE, S.S.E., sse, s.s.e. south-southeast.

S.Sgt., S/Sgt Staff Sergeant.

SSR, S.S.R. Soviet Socialist Republic.

SSS Selective Service System.

SST supersonic transport.

SSW, S.S.W., ssw, s.s.w. south-southwest.

St. Saint; Strait; Street.

St., st. statute(s); stratus (clouds).

st. stanza; stet; stitch; stone (weight); street.

s.t. short ton.

Sta. Santa; Station.

sta. station; stationary.

stab (stab) *v.* **stabbed, stab·bing** *v.t.* **1** To pierce with a pointed weapon; wound, as with a dagger. **2** To thrust (a dagger, etc.), as into a body. **3** To penetrate; pierce. —*v.i.* **4** To thrust or wound with or as with a pointed weapon. —*n.* **1** A thrust or wound made with a pointed weapon. **2** A sharp painful or poignant sensation: a *stab* of grief. **3** *Informal* An effort; attempt. [ME *stabbe*] —**stab'ber** *n.*

sta·bile (stā'bil, -bīl) *adj.* **1** Stable; fixed. **2** *Med.* Not affected by moderate heat. —*n.* (stā'bēl) A piece of stationary abstract sculpture, usu. of sheet metal, wood, wire, etc. [< L *stabilis*]

sta·bil·i·ty (stə·bil'ə·tē) *n. pl.* **·ties** **1** The condition of being stable; steadiness. **2** Steadfastness of purpose or resolution; constancy. **3** *Physics* The ability of an object or system to resume equilibrium after a disturbance.

sta·bi·lize (stā'bə·līz) *v.* **·lized, ·liz·ing** *v.t.* **1** To make stable. **2** To keep from fluctuating, as currency: to *stabilize* prices. —*v.i.* **3** To become stable. —**sta'bi·li·za'tion** *n.*

sta·bi·liz·er (stā'bə·lī'zər) *n.* Something that stabilizes, esp. an auxiliary airfoil of an aircraft. • See AIRPLANE.

sta·ble[1] (stā'bəl) *adj.* **·bler, ·blest** **1** Standing firmly in place; not easily moved, shaken, or overthrown; fixed. **2** Marked by firmness of purpose; steadfast. **3** Having durability or permanence; abiding. **4** Resistant to chemical change. **5** *Physics* Of, having, or exhibiting stability. [< L *stabilis*] —**sta'bly** *adv.* —**sta'ble·ness** *n.*

sta·ble[2] (stā'bəl) *n.* **1** A building for lodging and feeding horses or cattle. **2** Racehorses belonging to a particular owner; also, the personnel who take care of such racehorses. **3** *Informal* Those performers, writers, athletes, etc., who are under the same management or agency. —*v.t. & v.i.* **·bled, ·bling** To put or lodge in or as in a stable. [< L *stabulum*]

sta·ble·boy (stā'bəl·boi') *n.* A boy employed in a stable.

stac·ca·to (stə·kä'tō) *adj.* **1** *Music* Played, or to be played, with brief pauses between each note. **2** Marked by abrupt, sharp sounds or emphasis: a *staccato* style of speaking. —*adv.* So as to be staccato. —*n.* Something staccato. [< Ital. *staccare* detach]

stack (stak) *n.* **1** A large, orderly pile of unthreshed grain, hay, or straw, usu. conical. **2** Any pile or heap of things arranged somewhat neatly or systematically. **3** A group of rifles (usu. three) set upright and supporting one another. **4** *pl.* That part of a library where most of the books are shelved; also, the bookshelves. **5** A chimney; smokestack; also, a collection of such chimneys or flues. **6** *Informal* A great amount; plenty. —*v.t.* **1** To gather or pile up in a stack. **2** To plan or arrange dishonestly beforehand so as to assure a certain result or outcome. **3** To assign (an airplane) to a pattern of designated altitudes while awaiting clearance to land: often with *up.* —**stack up** **1** To total. **2** To compare: often with *against.* [< ON *stakkr*] —**stack'er** *n.*

sta·di·um (stā'dē·əm) *n. pl.* **·di·ums,** for def. 2 **·di·a** (-dē·ə) **1** A large modern structure for sports events, having seats arranged in tiers. **2** In ancient Greece and Rome: **a** A course for footraces, with banked seats for spectators. **b** A measure of length, equaling 606.75 feet. [< Gk. *stadion,* a measure of length]

staff (staf) *n. pl.* **staffs;** *also for defs. 1–3* **staves** (stāvz). **1** A stick or piece of wood carried for some special purpose, as an aid in climbing, as a cudgel, or as an emblem of authority. **2** A shaft or pole that forms a support or handle: the *staff* of a flag. **3** A stick used in measuring or testing, as a surveyor's leveling rod. **4** A group of people who function as assistants or advisors to a leader, director, president, etc. **5** A body of persons working together in some specific task, occupation, or enterprise: the hospital *staff;* the editorial *staff.* **6** *Mil.* A body of officers not having command but attached in an executive or advisory capacity to a military unit as assistants to the officer in command. **7** *Music* The five horizontal lines and the spaces between them on which notes are written. —*v.t.* To provide (an office, etc.) with a staff. [< OE *stæf* stick]

staff·er (staf'ər) *n.* A member of a staff, as of a periodical.

staff officer An officer serving on a military staff.

stag (stag) *n.* **1** The adult male of various deer, esp. the red deer. **2** A castrated bull or boar. **3** A man at a party, dance, etc., who is unaccompanied by a woman. **4** A social gathering for men only. —*adj.* Of or for men only. [< OE *stagga*]

stage (stāj) *n.* **1** The platform on which plays, operas, etc., are given. **2** The area on the adjacent sides and in back of this platform, including the wings, backstage, etc. **3** The profession of acting: with *the.* **4** Any of the activities or occupations having to do with the theater or drama: with *the.* **5** Any raised platform or floor, esp. a scaffold for workmen. **6** A horizontal level, section, or story of a building. **7** The scene of, or plan of action for, an event or events. **8** A center of attention. **9** A distinct period or step in some development, progress, or process. **10** A water level: flood *stage.* **11** A regular stopping place on a journey, esp. a journey by stagecoach. **12** STAGECOACH. **13** The distance traveled between two stopping points; leg. **14** *Electronics* One of a series of modules through which a signal passes. **15** One of the series of propulsion units used by a rocket vehicle. —*v.t.* **staged, stag·ing** **1** To put or exhibit on the stage. **2** To plan, conduct, or carry out: to *stage* a rally. **3** To organize, perform, or carry out so as to appear authentic, legitimate, or spontaneous, when actually not so: The entire incident was *staged* for the press photographers. [< OF *estage*]

stage·coach (stāj'kōch') *n.* A horse-drawn, passenger and mail vehicle having a regular route between towns.

stage·craft (stāj'kraft', -kräft') *n.* Skill in writing or staging plays.

stage door A door to a theater which leads to the stage or behind the scenes.

stage·hand (stāj'hand') *n.* A worker in a theater who handles scenery and props, etc.

stage-man·age (stāj'man'ij) *v.t.* **·aged, ·ag·ing** **1** To be a stage manager for. **2** To direct, organize, or carry out so as to achieve maximum effectiveness, publicity, etc.

stage manager One who assists a director in the production of a play and, during its performance, superintends the stage area, actors, and technicians.

stage·struck (stāj'struk') *adj.* **1** Fascinated by the theater. **2** Longing to become an actor or actress.

stage whisper A loud whisper, as one uttered on the stage for the audience to hear.

stag·fla·tion (stag'flā'shən) *n. Econ.* Inflation combined with abnormally slow economic growth, resulting in high unemployment. [< *stag(nation)* + *(in)flation*]

stag·ger (stag'ər) *v.i.* **1** To move unsteadily; totter; reel. **2** To become less confident or resolute; waver; hesitate. —*v.t.* **3** To cause to stagger. **4** To affect strongly; overwhelm, as with surprise or grief. **5** To place in alternating rows or groups. **6** To arrange or distribute so as to prevent congestion or confusion: to *stagger* lunch hours. —*n.* The

Stag head

act of staggering. **—the (blind) staggers** Any of various diseases of domestic animals marked by staggering, falling, etc. [< ON *stakra*] **—stag′ger·er** *n.* **—stag′ger·ing·ly** *adv.*

stag·ing (stā′jing) *n.* **1** A scaffolding or temporary platform. **2** The act of putting a play, opera, etc., upon the stage. **3** The act of jettisoning a rocket stage from a space vehicle. **4** The business of running stagecoaches. **5** Traveling by stagecoach.

stag·nant (stag′nənt) *adj.* **1** Standing still; not flowing: said of water. **2** Foul from long standing. **3** Dull; inert; sluggish. [< L *stagnum* a pool] **—stag′nan·cy** *n.* **—stag′nant·ly** *adv.*

stag·nate (stag′nāt) *v.i.* **·nat·ed, ·nat·ing** To be or become stagnant. **—stag·na′tion** *n.*

stag·y (stā′jē) *adj.* **stag·i·er, stag·i·est** **1** Of or suited to the stage. **2** Excessively theatrical; artificial. **—stag′i·ly** *adv.* **—stag′i·ness** *n.*

staid (stād) *adj.* Sedate; sober; serious. [Orig. p.t. and p.p. of STAY[1]] **—staid′ly** *adv.* **—staid′ness** *n.*

stain (stān) *n.* **1** A discoloration or spot from foreign matter. **2** A dye or thin pigment used in staining. **3** A moral blemish or taint. **—v.t.** **1** To make a stain upon; discolor; soil. **2** To color with a dye or stain. **3** To bring a moral stain upon; blemish. **—v.i.** **4** To take or impart a stain. [< OF *desteindre* to deprive of color] **—stain′a·ble** *adj.* **—stain′er** *n.*

stained glass Glass colored by the addition of pigments, usu. in the form of metallic oxides which are fused throughout the glass or burned onto its surface. **—stained′-glass′** *adj.*

stain·less (stān′lis) *adj.* **1** Without a stain. **2** Resistant to stain. **3** Made of stain-resistant materials. **—n.** Tableware made of stainless steel. **—stain′less·ly** *adv.*

stainless steel A corrosion-resistant steel alloyed with chromium and often other elements, esp. nickel.

stair (stâr) *n.* **1** A step, or one of a series of steps, for mounting or descending from one level to another. **2** *Usu. pl.* A series of steps. [< OE *stæger*]

stair·case (stâr′kās′) *n.* A flight of stairs, complete with the supports, balusters, etc.

stair·way (stâr′wā′) *n.* One or more flights of stairs.

stair·well (stâr′wel′) *n.* A vertical shaft enclosing a staircase.

stake (stāk) *n.* **1** A stick or post, as of wood or metal, sharpened for driving into the ground. **2** A post to which a person is bound to be burned alive; also, death by burning at the stake. **3** A post or stick set upright in the floor of a car or wagon, to confine loose material. **4** *Often pl.* Something wagered or risked, as the money bet on a race. **5** *Often pl.* A prize in a contest. **6** An interest or share, as in an enterprise. **7** GRUBSTAKE. **—at stake** In hazard or jeopardy. **—v.t. staked, stak·ing** **1** To fasten or support by means of a stake. **2** To mark the boundaries of with stakes: often with *off* or *out*. **3** *Informal* To wager; risk. **4** *Informal* To supply with money, equipment, etc.; back. [< OE *staca*]

sta·lac·tite (stə·lak′tīt′, stal′ək-) *n.* **1** An elongated, hanging cone of calcium carbonate formed by slow dripping from the roof of a cave. **2** Any similar formation. [< Gk. *stalaktitos* dripping] **—stal·ac·tit·ic** (stal′ək·tit′ik) or **·i·cal** *adj.*

sta·lag·mite (stə·lag′mīt′, stal′·əg-) *n.* **1** A usu. conical mound deposited on a cave floor by dripping from a stalactite. **2** Any similar formation. [< Gk. *stalagmos* a dripping] **—stal·ag·mit·ic** (stal′əg·mit′ik) or **·i·cal** *adj.* • See STALACTITE.

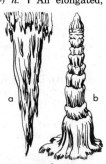

a. stalactite.
b. stalagmite.

stale (stāl) *adj.* **stal·er, stal·est** **1** Having lost freshness; slightly changed or deteriorated, as air, beer, old bread, etc. **2** Lacking in interest from age or familiarity; trite: a *stale* joke. **3** Lacking effectiveness, energy, spontaneity, etc., from too little or too much activity or practice. **—v.t. & v.i. staled, stal·ing** To make or become stale. [?] **—stale′ly** *adv.* **—stale′ness** *n.*

stale·mate (stāl′māt′) *n.* **1** In chess, a position in which a player can make no move without putting his king in check. The result is a draw. **2** Any tie, standstill, or deadlock. **—v.t. ·mat·ed, ·mat·ing** **1** To put into a condition of stalemate. **2** To bring to a standstill. [< AF *estale* a fixed position + MATE[2]]

stalk[1] (stôk) *n.* **1** The stem or axis of a plant. **2** Any support on which an organ is borne, as a pedicel. **3** A supporting part or stem: the *stalk* of a quill. **4** Any stem or main axis, as of a goblet. [ME *stalke*] **—stalked, stalk′less** *adj.*

stalk[2] (stôk) *v.i.* **1** To approach game, etc., stealthily. **2** To walk in a stiff or haughty manner. **—v.t.** **3** To approach (game, etc.) stealthily. **4** To invade or permeate: Famine *stalked* the countryside. **—n.** **1** The act of stalking game. **2** A stalking step or walk. [< OE *bestealcian* move stealthily] **—stalk′er** *n.*

stalk·ing-horse (stô′king·hôrs′) *n.* **1** A horse behind which a hunter conceals himself in stalking game. **2** Anything serving to conceal one's intention.

stall (stôl) *n.* **1** A compartment in which a horse or bovine animal is confined and fed. **2** A small booth or compartment in a street, market, etc., for the sale or display of small articles. **3** A partially enclosed seat, as in the choir of a cathedral. **4** *Brit.* A seat very near the stage of a theater. **5** A small compartment, as for showering. **6** An evasive or delaying action. **7** A condition in which a motor temporarily stops functioning. **8** A condition in which an airplane loses the air speed needed to produce sufficient lift to keep it flying. **—v.t.** **1** To place or keep in a stall. **2** To bring to a standstill; halt the progress of. **3** To stop, usu. unintentionally, the operation or motion of. **4** To put (an airplane) into a stall. **5** To cause to stick fast in mud, snow, etc. **—v.i.** **6** To come to a standstill; stop, esp. unintentionally. **7** To stick fast in mud, snow, etc. **8** To make delays; be evasive: to *stall* for time. **9** To live or be kept in a stall. **10** *Aeron.* To go into a stall. [< OE *steall*]

stall-feed (stôl′fēd′) *v.t.* **-fed, -feed·ing** To feed (cattle) in a stall so as to fatten them. **—stall′-fed′** *adj.*

stal·lion (stal′yən) *n.* An uncastrated male horse. [< OHG *stal* stable]

stal·wart (stôl′wərt) *adj.* **1** Strong and robust. **2** Resolute; determined. **3** Brave; courageous. **—n.** **1** An uncompromising partisan, as in politics. **2** One who is stalwart. [< OE *stæl* place + *wierthe* worth] **—stal′wart·ly** *adv.* **—stal′wart·ness** *n.*

sta·men (stā′mən) *n. pl.* **sta·mens** or **stam·i·na** (stam′ə·nə) One of the pollen-bearing organs of a flower, consisting of a filament supporting an anther. [L, warp, thread] **—stam·i·nal** (stam′·ə·nəl) *adj.*

stam·i·na (stam′ə·nə) *n.* Strength and endurance, as in withstanding hardship or difficulty. [L, pl. of *stamen* warp, thread] **—stam′i·nal** *adj.*

stam·i·nate (stam′ə·nit, -nāt) *adj.* **1** Having stamens but no pistil, as male flowers. **2** Having stamens.

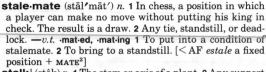

Stamen (a, b, c)
a. pollen. b. anther.
c. filament. d. pistil.

stam·mer (stam′ər) *v.t. & v.i.* To speak or utter with nervous repetitions or prolongations of a sound or syllable, and involuntary pauses. **—n.** The act or habit of stammering. [< OE *stamerian*] **—stam′mer·er** *n.*

stamp (stamp) *v.t.* **1** To strike heavily with the sole of the foot. **2** To bring down (the foot) heavily and noisily. **3** To affect in a specified manner by or as by stamping with the foot: to *stamp* out opposition. **4** To make, form, cut out, etc., with a stamp or die: often with *out*: to *stamp* out a circle from the steel. **5** To imprint or impress with a die, stamp, etc.: to *stamp* the date on a letter. **6** To fix or imprint permanently: The deed was *stamped* on his memory. **7** To characterize; brand: to *stamp* a story false. **8** To affix an official seal, stamp, etc., to. **9** To crush or pulverize, as ore. **—v.i.** **10** To strike the foot heavily on the ground. **11** To walk with heavy, resounding steps. **—n.** **1** The act of stamping. **2** A machine or tool, as a die, that cuts out or shapes a form. **3** An implement or device that imprints a design, character, mark, etc., on something; also, the design, character, mark, etc., so imprinted. **4** A printed de-

vice of paper to be attached to something to show that a tax or fee has been paid: a postage *stamp*. **5** TRADING STAMP. **6** A specific impression or effect: the *stamp* of genius. **7** Characteristic quality or form; kind; sort: I dislike men of his *stamp*. [ME *stampen*] —**stamp′er** *n*.

stam·pede (stam-pēd′) *n*. **1** A sudden starting and rushing off through panic: said primarily of a herd of cattle, horses, etc. **2** Any sudden, impulsive rush or movement of a crowd, as of a mob. **3** A spontaneous mass impulse, trend, or movement, as toward the support of a political candidate. **4** *Can.* RODEO. —*v.* ·**ped·ed**, ·**ped·ing** *v.t.* **1** To cause a stampede in. —*v.i.* **2** To engage in a stampede. [< Am. Sp. *estampar* to stamp] —**stam·ped′er** *n*.

stamping ground A favorite or habitual gathering place.

stance (stans) *n*. **1** Mode of standing; posture, esp. with reference to the placing of the feet. **2** Attitude; point of view: a moral *stance*. [< L *stans* pr. p. of *stare* to stand]

stanch (stanch, stänch) *v.t.* **1** To stop or check the flow of (blood, tears, etc.). **2** To stop the flow of blood from (a wound). **3** To check or put an end to. —*adj.* STAUNCH. [< OF *estanchier* to halt] —**stanch′er** *n*. • The spelling *stanch* is usu. preferred for the verb in both England and the U.S., and *staunch* for the adjective. Many writers, however, use one or the other spelling for both.

stan·chion (stan′shən) *n*. **1** An upright bar forming a principal support. **2** A device that fits around a cow's neck, used to restrain movement in a stall. —*v.t.* To provide, restrain, or support with stanchions. [< OF *estanchon*]

stand (stand) *v.* **stood, stand·ing** *v.i.* **1** To assume or maintain an erect position on the feet. **2** To be in a vertical position: The oars *stood* in the corner. **3** To measure a specified height when standing: He *stands* six feet. **4** To assume a specified position: to *stand* aside. **5** To be situated; have position or location; lie: The factory *stands* on a hill. **6** To have or be in a specified state, condition, or relation: We *stand* to gain everything by not fighting; He *stood* in fear of his life. **7** To assume an attitude for defense or offense: *Stand* and fight! **8** To maintain one's attitude, opinions, etc.: *Stand* firm. **9** To be or exist in a printed or written form: Photograph the letter just as it *stands*. **10** To remain unimpaired, unchanged, or valid: My decision still *stands*. **11** To collect and remain: Tears *stood* in her eyes. **12** To be of a specified rank or class: He *stands* third. **13** To stop or pause; halt. **14** *Naut.* To take a direction; steer. **15** *Brit.* To be a candidate, as for election. —*v.t.* **16** To place upright; set in an erect position. **17** To put up with; endure; tolerate. **18** To be subjected to; undergo: He must *stand* trial. **19** To withstand or endure successfully: to *stand* the test of time. **20** To carry out the duty of: to *stand* watch. **21** *Informal* **a** To treat: I'll *stand* you to a drink. **b** To bear the expense of: to *stand* a dinner. —**stand a chance** To have a chance. —**stand by 1** To stay near and be ready to help or operate. **2** To help; support. **3** To abide by; make good; adhere to. **4** To remain passive, as when help is needed. **5** *Telecom.* To keep tuned in, as for the continuance of an interrupted transmission. —**stand for 1** To represent; symbolize. **2** To put up with; tolerate. —**stand in for** To act as a substitute for. —**stand off 1** To keep at a distance. **2** To fail to agree or comply. **3** To put off; evade, as a creditor. —**stand on 1** To be based on or grounded in; rest. **2** To insist on observance of: to *stand on* ceremony. **3** *Naut.* To keep on the same tack or course. —**stand out 1** To stick out; project or protrude. **2** To be prominent or conspicuous. **3** To be outstanding, remarkable, etc. **4** To refuse to consent or agree. —**stand pat** In poker, to play one's hand as dealt, without drawing new cards. **2** To resist change. —**stand to reason** To conform to reason. —**stand up 1** To stand erect. **2** To withstand wear, criticism, analysis, etc. **3** *Slang* To fail, usu. intentionally, to keep an appointment with. —**stand up for** To side with; take the part of. —**stand up to** To confront courageously; face. —*n*. **1** The act or condition of standing, esp. of halting or stopping, as: **a** A stopping or halt, as in a retreat, to fight back or resist. **b** A stop for a performance, made by a theatrical company while on

tour; also, the place stopped at. **2** The place or location where one stands or is assigned to stand; position. **3** Any place where something stands: a taxi *stand*. **4** An opinion, attitude, point of view, etc.: to take a *stand*. **5** A structure upon which persons may sit or stand, as: **a** *Often pl.* A series of raised seats or benches, as at an athletic contest. **b** A platform: a reviewing *stand*. **c** A small platform in court from which a witness testifies. **6** A small table. **7** A rack or other structure for holding something: an umbrella *stand*. **8** A stall, counter, or the like where merchandise is displayed or sold. **9** A vertical growth of trees or plants. [< OE *standan*] —**stand′er** *n*.

stan·dard (stan′dərd) *n*. **1** A flag, ensign, or banner, used as an emblem of a government, body of men, head of state, etc. **2** A figure or image adopted as an emblem or symbol. **3** Something established and generally accepted as a model, example, or test of excellence, attainment, etc.; criterion. **4** Something established as a measure or reference of weight, extent, quantity, quality, or value. **5** In coinage, the established proportion by weight of pure gold or silver and an alloy. **6** The measurable basis of value in a monetary system. **7** An upright structure, timber, post, etc., used as a support. **8** A musical composition whose popularity has become firmly established over the years. **9** A plant growing on a vigorous, unsupported, upright stem. —*adj*. **1** Having the accuracy or authority of a standard; serving as a gauge or criterion. **2** Of recognized excellence, popularity, reliability, etc.: the *standard* repertoire of symphonies. **3** Not unusual or special in any way; ordinary; typical; regular: *standard* procedure; *standard* equipment. [< OF *estandard* banner]

stan·dard-bear·er (stan′dərd-bâr′ər) *n*. **1** The person who carries the flag or standard of a group, esp. of a regiment or other military body. **2** The official leader or representative of a group, as a presidential nominee.

standard gauge 1 A railroad track width of 56½ inches, considered as standard. **2** A railroad having such a gauge. —**stan′dard-gauge′** *adj*.

stan·dard·ize (stan′dər-dīz) *v.t.* ·**ized**, ·**iz·ing** To make conform to, regulate, or test by a standard. —**stan′dard·i·za′tion, stan′dard·iz′er** *n*.

standard of living The average manner of day-to-day living of a country, group, or person, with reference to food, housing, clothing, comforts, etc.

standard time The official time for any region or country. Mean solar time is reckoned, east or west, from the meridian of Greenwich, England, each time zone comprising a sector of 15 degrees of longitude and representing a time interval of one hour. In the conterminous U.S., the four time zones, **Eastern Standard Time, Central Standard Time, Mountain Standard Time,** and **Pacific Standard Time** represent the 75th, 90th, 105th, and 120th meridians west of Greenwich, and are accordingly 5, 6, 7, and 8 hours earlier than Greenwich time. Therefore, noon in London corresponds to 7 A.M. in New York, 6 A.M. in Chicago, 5 A.M. in Denver, and 4 A.M. in San Francisco.

stand·by (stand′bī′) *n. pl.* ·**bys 1** A person who can be relied on, as in an emergency. **2** Something that always pleases, is always effective, etc. **3** A person or thing waiting and ready to replace another person or thing; substitute.

stand·ee (stan-dē′) *n*. A person who must stand for lack of chairs or seats, as at a theater or on a train.

stand-in (stand′in′) *n*. **1** A person who substitutes for a motion-picture or television performer while lights are arranged, camera angles set, etc. **2** Any substitute for another person.

stand·ing (stan′ding) *adj*. **1** That is upright or erect. **2** Continuing for regular or permanent use; not special or temporary: a *standing* rule. **3** Stagnant; not flowing: *standing* water. **4** Begun or done while standing: a *standing* ovation; a *standing* high jump. **5** Not in use; idle: *standing* machinery. **6** Not movable. —*n*. **1** The act or condition of one who stands. **2** A place to stand in. **3** Relative place or position, as on a graded list of excellence,

achievement, etc. **4** Reputation, esp. good reputation. **5** Duration; continuance: a feud of long *standing*.

standing room Place in which to stand, as in a theater when the seats are all occupied.

stand·off (stand'ôf', -of') *n.* **1** A draw or tie, as in a game. **2** A counterbalancing or neutralizing effect. —*adj.* **1** That stands off. **2** STANDOFFISH.

stand·off·ish (stand'ôf'ish) *adj.* Aloof; cool. —**stand'off'·ish·ly** *adv.* —**stand'off'ish·ness** *n.*

stand·out (stand'out') *Informal n.* A person or thing that is unusually good or excellent. —*adj.* Unusually good or excellent.

stand·pat (stand'pat') *adj. Informal* Resistant to change; conservative. —**stand'pat'ter, stand'pat'tism** *n.*

stand·pipe (stand'pīp') *n.* A high vertical pipe or water tower, as at a reservoir, into which the water is pumped to create pressure.

stand·point (stand'point') *n.* Point of view; position; stance.

stand·still (stand'stil') *n.* A stopping; cessation; halt.

stand·up (stand'up') *adj.* **1** Having an erect or vertical position: a *stand-up* collar. **2** Done, consumed, etc., while standing.

stan·hope (stan'hōp) *n.* A light, open, one-seated carriage. [< F. *Stanhope*, 1787–1864, English clergyman]

stank (stangk) *p.t.* of STINK.

stan·nic (stan'ik) *adj. Chem.* Of, pertaining to, or containing tin, esp. in its higher valence. [< L *stannum* tin]

stan·nous (stan'əs) *adj.* Of, pertaining to, or containing tin, esp. in its lower valence. [< L *stannum* tin]

stan·za (stan'zə) *n.* A certain number of lines of verse grouped together and forming a definite division of a poem. [Ital., room, stanza] —**stan·za·ic** (stan·zā'ik) *adj.*

sta·pes (stā'pēz) *n. pl.* **sta·pes** or **sta·pe·des** (stə·pē'dēz, stā'pə·dēz) *Anat.* The innermost small bone of the middle ear of mammals. [LL, a stirrup] —**sta·pe·di·al** (stə·pē'dē·əl) *adj.*

staph (staf) *n.* STAPHYLOCOCCUS.

staph·y·lo·coc·cus (staf'ə·lō·kok'əs) *n. pl.* **·coc·ci** (-kok'sī, -sē, -ī, -ē) Any of a group of spherical bacteria occurring singly, in pairs, or in irregular clusters and often acting as infective agents. [< Gk. *staphylos* bunch of grapes + *kokkos* a berry] —**staph'y·lo·coc'cic** (-kok'sik, -kok'ik) *adj.* • See BACTERIUM.

sta·ple¹ (stā'pəl) *n.* **1** A principal commodity or product of a country or region. **2** A chief item, element, or main constituent of anything. **3** A product that is constantly sold and used, as sugar or salt. **4** Raw material. **5** The corded or combed fiber of cotton, wool, or flax, with reference to its length. **6** A source of supply; storehouse. —*adj.* **1** Regularly and constantly produced, consumed, or sold. **2** Main; chief. —*v.t.* **·pled, ·pling** To sort or classify according to length, as wool fiber. [< MDu. *stapel* market]

sta·ple² (stā'pəl) *n.* A U-shaped piece of metal or thin wire, having pointed ends and driven into a surface, as wood or paper, to serve as a fastening. —*v.t.* **·pled, ·pling** To fix or fasten by a staple or staples. [< OE *stapol* post]

sta·pler¹ (stā'plər) *n.* **1** A person who staples wool, etc. **2** A person who deals in staple goods.

sta·pler² (stā'plər) *n.* A device for driving staples into a surface.

star (stär) *n.* **1** *Astron.* Any of the numerous celestial objects that emit radiant energy, including visible light, generated by nuclear reactions. **2** Loosely, any of the luminous bodies regularly seen as points of light in the night sky. **3** A conventional figure having five or more radiating points. **4** Something resembling such a figure, as an emblem or device. **5** An asterisk (*). **6** A person of outstanding talent or accomplishment and a quality of personality that attracts wide public interest or attention. **7** A performer who plays the leading role in a play, opera, etc. **8** *Often pl.* Any of the planets or their configuration considered as influencing one's fate. **9** Fortune; destiny. —*v.* **starred, star·ring** *v.t.* **1** To set, mark, or adorn with stars. **2** To mark with an asterisk. **3** To present as a star in an entertainment. —*v.i.* **4** To be prominent or brilliant. **5** To play the leading part; be the star. —*adj.* **1** Of or pertaining to a star or stars. **2** Prominent; brilliant: a *star* football player. [< OE *steorra*] —**star'less, star'like** *adj.*

star·board (stär'bərd) *n.* The right-hand side of a vessel or aircraft as one faces the front or forward. —*adj.* Of, pertaining to, or on the starboard. —*adv.* Toward the starboard side. —*v.t.* To put, move, or turn (the helm) to the starboard side. [< OE *steorbord* steering side]

starch (stärch) *n.* **1** A complex, insoluble carbohydrate produced by photosynthesis and usu. stored in roots, tubers, seeds, etc. **2** A white, powdery substance consisting of purified starch extracted from potatoes, corn, etc. **3** Any starchy foodstuff. **4** A fabric stiffener made of starch suspended in water. **5** A stiff or formal manner. **6** *Informal* Energy; vigor. —*v.t.* To apply starch to; stiffen with or as with starch. [< OE *stearc* stiff]

starch·y (stär'chē) *adj.* **starch·i·er, starch·i·est** **1** Stiffened with starch; stiff. **2** Primly formal or stiff. **3** Containing a large proportion of starch: a *starchy* vegetable. —**starch'·i·ly** *adv.* —**starch'i·ness** *n.*

star-crossed (stär'krôst', -krost') *adj.* Doomed; ill-fated: a *star-crossed* love affair.

star·dom (stär'dəm) *n.* **1** The status of a person who is a star. **2** Stars of the stage, screen, etc., collectively.

stare (stâr) *v.* **stared, star·ing** *v.i.* **1** To gaze fixedly, usu. with the eyes open wide, as from admiration, fear, or insolence. **2** To be conspicuously or unduly apparent; glare. —*v.t.* **3** To gaze fixedly at. **4** To affect in a specified manner by a stare: to *stare* a person into silence. —**stare down** To gaze back fixedly (at a person) until he turns his eyes away. —**stare one in the face** To be perfectly plain or obvious. —*n.* A steady, fixed gaze. [< OE *starian*] —**star'er** *n.*

star·fish (stär'fish') *n. pl.* **·fish** or **·fish·es** Any of various radially symmetrical echinoderms with a star-shaped body having five or more arms.

star·gaze (stär'gāz') *v.i.* **·gazed, ·gaz·ing** **1** To gaze at or study the stars. **2** To daydream. —**star'gaz'·er** *n.*

stark (stärk) *adj.* **1** Deserted; barren; bleak: a *stark* landscape. **2** Severe; difficult: *stark* measures. **3** With little or no ornamentation, color, etc.: a *stark* room. **4** Blunt; grim; pitiless: *stark* reality. **5** Complete; utter: *stark* madness. **6** Stiff or rigid, as in death. **7** Sharp and bare, as of outline. —*adv.* **1** In a stark manner. **2** Completely; utterly: *stark* naked. [< OE *stearc* stiff] —**stark'ly** *adv.* —**stark'ness** *n.*

Starfish

star·let (stär'lit) *n. Informal* A young movie actress being prepared for stardom.

star·light (stär'līt) *n.* The light given by a star or stars. —*adj.* Lighted by or only by the stars: also **star'lit'** (-lit').

star·ling (stär'ling) *n.* **1** A chubby, gregarious, aggressive bird with iridescent black plumage, introduced from Europe and now common in North America. **2** Any of various related European birds. [< OE *stærling*]

star of David The six-pointed star used as a symbol of Judaism.

starred (stärd) *adj.* **1** Spangled or marked with stars. **2** Marked with an asterisk. **3** Affected by astral influence: used chiefly in combination: *ill-starred*. **4** Presented or advertised as the star of an entertainment.

star·ry (stär'ē) *adj.* **·ri·er, ·ri·est** **1** Set or marked with stars. **2** Shining as or like stars. **3** Star-shaped. **4** Lighted by or abounding in stars. **5** Of, from, having to do with, or like stars. —**star'ri·ness** *n.*

Star of David

star·ry-eyed (stär'ē·īd') *adj.* Excited by or given to fanciful thoughts of romance, adventure, etc.

Stars and Stripes The flag of the U.S., having 13 alternating horizontal stripes of red and white, and in the upper left-hand corner 50 white stars against a blue ground.

star-span·gled (stär'spang'gəld) *adj.* Spangled with stars or starlike spots or points.

Star-Spangled Banner **1** The flag of the U.S. **2** The national anthem of the U.S., with words written by Francis Scott Key in 1814.

start (stärt) *v.i.* **1** To make an involuntary, startled movement, as from fear or surprise. **2** To move suddenly, as with a spring, leap, or bound. **3** To begin an action, undertaking, trip, etc.: They *started* early on their vacation. **4** To become active, operative, etc.: School *starts* in the fall. **5** To be on the team, lineup, etc., that begins a game or contest. **6** To protrude; seem to bulge: His eyes *started* from his head. **7** To be displaced or dislocated; become loose, warped, etc. —*v.t.* **8** To set in motion, activity, etc.: to *start* an engine; to *start* a rumor. **9** To begin; commence: to *start* a lecture. **10** To put on the team, lineup, etc., that begins a game or contest: I'm *starting* the new players today. **11** To set up; establish. **12** To introduce (a subject) or propound (a question). **13** To displace or dislocate; loosen, warp, etc.: The collision *started* the ship's seams. **14** To rouse from cover; cause to take flight; flush, as game. **15** To draw the contents from; tap, as a cask. —**start up 1** To rise or appear suddenly. **2** To begin; come into being. **3** To begin the operation of (a motor, etc.). —**to start with** In the first place. —*n.* **1** A quick, startled movement or reaction. **2** A temporary or spasmodic action or attempt: by fits and *starts.* **3** A beginning or commencement, as of an action, undertaking, etc. **4** Advantage; lead, as in a race. **5** A place or time of beginning. **6** A loosened place or condition; crack: a *start* in a ship's planking. [ME *sterten* start, leap]

start·er (stär'tər) *n.* **1** One who or that which starts, esp.. **a** A competitor or member of a team at the start of a race or contest. **b** A person giving the starting signal for a race or contest. **c** A person whose job is to see to it that buses, trolleys, etc., leave on schedule. **d** Any mechanical device that initiates movement in an engine or the like. **2** A substance or mixture that initiates a chemical reaction, esp. in food: a *starter* for bread.

star·tle (stär'təl) *v.* **·tled, ·tling** *v.t.* **1** To arouse or excite suddenly; alarm. —*v.i.* **2** To be aroused or excited suddenly; take alarm. —*n.* A sudden fright or shock; a scare. [< OE *steartlian* to kick] —**star'tler** *n.*

star·tling (stärt'ling) *adj.* Rousing sudden surprise, alarm, or the like. —**star'tling·ly** *adv.*

star·va·tion (stär·vā'shən) *n.* **1** The act of starving. **2** The state of being starved. —*adj.* Insufficient to sustain life or to purchase basic necessities: a *starvation* diet; *starvation* wages.

starve (stärv) *v.* **starved, starv·ing** *v.i.* **1** To die or perish from lack of food. **2** To suffer from extreme hunger. **3** To suffer from lack or need: to *starve* for friendship. —*v.t.* **4** To cause to die of hunger. **5** To deprive of food. **6** To bring to a specified condition by starving: to *starve* an enemy into surrender. [< OE *steorfan* die] —**starv'er** *n.*

starve·ling (stärv'ling) *n.* A person or animal that is starving, starved, or emaciated.

stash (stash) *v.t.* *Informal* To hide or conceal (money or valuables), for future use or safe-keeping: often with *away.* —*n.* *Slang* **1** A place where things are stashed away. **2** Something stashed away. [?]

-stat *combining form* A device which stops or makes constant: *thermostat.* [< Gk. *-statēs* causing to stand]

state (stāt) *n.* **1** A mode or condition of being or existing: a *state* of war. **2** A particular physical or chemical stage or condition of something: Ice is the solid *state* of water. **3** Frame of mind: a *state* of utter peace. **4** Any extreme mental condition, as of excitement, nervousness, etc. **5** Social status or position. **6** A grand, ceremonious, or luxurious style of living or doing: to arrive in *state.* **6** A sovereign political community; nation. **7** A political and territorial unit within such a community: the *state* of Maine. —**lie in state** To be placed on public view before burial. —*adj.* **1** Of or pertaining to a state, nation, or government. **2** Intended for use on occasions of ceremony. —*v.t.* **stat·ed, stat·ing 1** To set forth explicitly in speech or writing; declare. **2** To fix; settle: to *state* terms. [< L *status* condition, state < *stare* to stand] —**state'hood** *n.* —**Syn.** *n.* **1** circumstances. **5** standing. *v.* **1** affirm, assert, aver.

state·craft (stāt'kraft', -kräft') *n.* The art of conducting affairs of state.

stat·ed (stā'tid) *adj.* **1** Regular; fixed. **2** Told; asserted: a *stated* fact. —**stat'ed·ly** *adv.*

state·house (stāt'hous') *n. Often cap.* A building used for sessions of a state legislature. Also **state house.**

state·ly (stāt'lē) *adj.* **·li·er, ·li·est 1** Dignified; majestic: a *stately* mansion. **2** Slow; measured: a *stately* march. —*adv.* Loftily. —**state'li·ness** *n.* —**Syn. 1** imposing, grand, awesome, impressive.

state·ment (stāt'mənt) *n.* **1** The act of stating. **2** That which is stated. **3** A summary of assets and liabilities, showing the balance due. **3** A major or dominant idea expressed in the composition of a creative work, as in art, music, or design; motif. **4** The expression of such an idea.

state·room (stāt'rōōm', -rŏŏm') *n.* A small private bedroom on a passenger ship or railroad train.

state's evidence Testimony for the prosecution in a U.S. federal or state court, esp. that of a criminal against his accomplices. —**turn state's evidence** To offer state's evidence.

state·side (stāt'sīd') *adj. Informal* Of or in the continental U.S. —*adv.* In or to the continental U.S.

states·man (stāts'mən) *n. pl.* **·men** (-mən) A person skilled in the science of government and prominent in national and foreign affairs. —**states'man·ly** *adv.* —**states'·man·ship** *n.*

state socialism A political theory advocating government ownership of utilities and industries.

States' rights The powers not vested in the U.S. federal government by the Constitution nor prohibited by it to the states. Also **State rights.**

states·wom·an (stāts'wŏŏm'ən) *n. pl.* **·wom·en** (-wim'in) A woman skilled in the science of government and prominent in national and foreign affairs.

state·wide (stāt'wīd') *adj. & adv.* Throughout a state.

stat·ic (stat'ik) *adj.* **1** Pertaining to bodies at rest or forces in equilibrium. **2** *Physics* Not involved in or with motion: *static* pressure. **3** *Electr.* Of or caused by stationary electric charges. **4** At rest; not active. **5** Of or pertaining to nonactive elements. **6** Dealing with fixed or stable conditions. Also **stat'i·cal.** —*n. Electronics* Electrical noise, esp. atmospheric, that interferes with radio communications. [< Gk *statikos* causing to stand] —**stat'i·cal·ly** *adv.*

stat·ics (stat'iks) *n.pl.* *(construed as sing.)* The mechanics of bodies at rest.

sta·tion (stā'shən) *n.* **1** A place where a person or thing usu. stands. **2** The headquarters of some official person or body of men: a police *station.* **3** A starting point or stopping place of a railroad or bus line. **4** A building for the accommodation of passengers or freight, as on a railroad or bus line; depot. **5** Social rank; standing. **6** *Mil.* The place to which an individual, unit, or ship is assigned for duty. **7** The installations of a radio or television broadcasting unit. —*v.t.* To assign to a station; set in position. [< L *stare* to stand]

sta·tion·ar·y (stā'shə·ner'ē) *adj.* **1** Remaining in one place. **2** Fixed; not portable. **3** Exhibiting no change of character or condition.

sta·tion·er (stā'shə·nər) *n.* A dealer in stationery and related goods. [< Med. L *stationarius* stationary, having a fixed location (for business)]

sta·tion·er·y (stā'shə·ner'ē) *n.* Paper, pens, pencils, ink, notebooks, and other related goods.

station wagon An automotive vehicle with one or more rows of seats behind the front seat and with a hinged tailgate for admitting luggage, etc.

stat·ism (stā'tiz·əm) *n.* A theory of government which advocates the concentration of economic planning, control, etc., in a centralized government. —**stat'ist** *n.*

sta·tis·tic (stə·tis'tik) *n.* Any element entering into a statistical statement. —*adj.* STATISTICAL.

sta·tis·ti·cal (stə·tis'tə·kəl) *adj.* **1** Of or pertaining to statistics. **2** Composed of statistics. —**sta·tis'ti·cal·ly** *adv.*

stat·is·ti·cian (stat'is·tish'ən) *n.* One skilled in collecting and tabulating statistical data.

sta·tis·tics (stə·tis'tiks) *n.pl.* **1** A collection of quantitative data or facts. **2** *(construed as sing.)* The branch of

mathematics that deals with the collection and analysis of quantitative data. [< L *status* position, state]

stat·u·ar·y (stach′ōō·er′ē) *n. pl.* ·ar·ies Statues collectively. —*adj.* Of or suitable for statues. [< L *statua* statue]

stat·ue (stach′ōō) *n.* A three-dimensional representation of a human or animal figure modeled in clay or wax, cast in bronze or plaster, or carved in wood or stone. [< L *status,* pp. of *stare* stand]

stat·u·esque (stach′ōō·esk′) *adj.* 1 Resembling a statue, as in grace or dignity. 2 Shapely; comely. —**stat′u·esque′ly** *adv.* —**stat′u·esque′ness** *n.*

stat·u·ette (stach′ōō·et′) *n.* A small statue. [F]

stat·ure (stach′ər) *n.* 1 The natural height of a body. 2 The height of anything, as a tree. 3 Status or reputation resulting from development or growth: artistic *stature.* [< L *status* condition, state]

sta·tus (stā′təs, stat′əs) *n.* 1 State, condition, or relation. 2 Relative position or rank. [< L *stare* to stand]

sta·tus quo (stā′təs kwō, stat′əs) The actual or existing condition or state. Also **status in quo.** [L]

stat·ute (stach′ōōt) *n.* 1 *Law* A legislative enactment. 2 An established law or regulation. [< L *statutus,* pp. of *statuere* constitute]

statute law The law as set forth in statutes.

statute mile MILE (def. 1).

statute of limitations A statute which imposes time limits upon the right of action in certain cases.

stat·u·to·ry (stach′ə·tôr′ē, -tō′rē) *adj.* 1 Pertaining to a statute. 2 Created by or based upon legislative enactment.

statutory rape See RAPE.

staunch (stônch, stänch) *adj.* 1 Firm in principle; constant; trustworthy. 2 Stout; seaworthy: a *staunch* ship. —*v.t.* STANCH. [< OF *estanchier* make stand] —**staunch′ly** *adv.* —**staunch′ness** *n.* —**Syn.** *adj.* 1 faithful, loyal, trusty. 2 sound, trim. • See STANCH.

stave (stāv) *n.* 1 A curved strip of wood, forming a part of the sides of a barrel, tub, or the like. 2 *Music* A staff. 3 A stanza; verse. 4 A rod, cudgel, or staff. 5 A rung of a rack or ladder. —*v.* **staved** or **stove, stav·ing** *v.t.* 1 To break or make (a hole) by crushing or collision. 2 To furnish with staves. —*v.i.* 3 To be broken in, as a vessel's hull. —**stave off** To ward off: to *stave off* bankruptcy. [< *staves,* pl. of STAFF]

Barrel stave

staves (stāvz) *n.* 1 A *pl.* of STAFF. 2 *pl.* of STAVE.

stay[1] (stā) *v.i.* 1 To stop; halt: *Stay* where you are. 2 To continue in a specified place or condition: to *stay* home; to *stay* healthy. 3 To remain temporarily as a guest or resident. 4 To tarry: I'll *stay* a few more minutes. 5 *Informal* To have endurance; last. 6 *Informal* To keep pace with a competitor, as in a race. —*v.t.* 7 To bring to a stop; halt. 8 To hinder; delay. 9 To put off; postpone. 10 To satisfy the demands of temporarily; appease: to *stay* the pangs of hunger. 11 To remain for the duration of: to *stay* the night. —*n.* 1 The act or time of staying: a week's *stay* at the beach. 2 A deferment or suspension of judicial proceedings: The court granted a *stay* of sentencing. 3 *Informal* Staying power; endurance. [< L *stare* stand] —**stay′er** *n.*

stay[2] (stā) *v.t.* To be a support to; prop or hold up. —*n.* 1 Anything which props or supports. 2 *pl.* A corset stiffened, as with steel strips or whalebone. [< OF *estayer*]

stay[3] (stā) *Naut.* *n.* 1 A large, strong rope or wire, used to brace a mast or spar. 2 Any rope having a similar use. —*v.t.* 1 To support with a stay or stays. 2 To put (a vessel) on the opposite tack. —*v.i.* 3 To tack: said of vessels. [< OE *stæg*]

staying power The ability to endure.

stay·sail (stā′sāl′, -səl) *n. Naut.* A sail, usu. triangular, extended on a stay.

Ste. Sainte (female) (F *Sainte*).

stead (sted) *n.* Place of another person or thing as assumed by a substitute or a successor: My sister went in my *stead.* —**stand (one) in good stead** To give (one) good service, support, etc. [< OE *stede* place]

stead·fast (sted′fast′, -fäst′, -fəst) *adj.* 1 Firmly fixed in faith or devotion to duty. 2 Directed fixedly at one point, as the gaze. [< OE *stedefæst*] —**stead′fast′ly** *adv.* —**stead′fast′ness** *n.*

stead·y (sted′ē) *adj.* **stead·i·er, stead·i·est** 1 Stable; not liable to shake or totter: a *steady* ladder. 2 Unfaltering; constant: a *steady* light; *steady* loyalty. 3 Calm; unruffled: *steady* nerves. 4 Free from intemperance and dissipation: *steady* habits. 5 Regular: a *steady* customer. 6 Of a ship, keeping more or less upright in rough seas. —**go steady** *Informal* To date exclusively. —*v.t. & v.i.* **stead·ied, stead·y·ing** To make or become steady. —*interj.* Not so fast; keep calm. —*n. Slang* A sweetheart or constant companion. [< STEAD] —**stead′i·ly** *adv.* —**stead′i·ness** *n.*

steak (stāk) *n.* A slice of meat or fish, esp. of beef, usu. broiled or fried. [< ON *steik*]

steal (stēl) *v.* **stole, sto·len, steal·ing** *v.t.* 1 To take from another without right or permission. 2 To take or obtain in a subtle manner: He has *stolen* the hearts of the people. 3 In baseball, to reach (another base) without the aid of a hit or error: said of a base runner. —*v.i.* 4 To move quietly and stealthily: to *steal* away in the night. 5 To commit theft. 6 To move secretly or furtively. —*n. Informal* 1 The act of stealing or that which is stolen. 2 Any underhanded financial deal that benefits the originators. 3 A bargain: a *steal* at $3.99. [< OE *stelan*] —**steal′er** *n.* —**Syn.** *v.* 1 filch, pilfer, purloin. 4 skulk, slink.

stealth (stelth) *n.* Secret or furtive action, movement, or behavior. [< OE *stelan* steal]

stealth·y (stel′thē) *adj.* **stealth·i·er, stealth·i·est** Marked by stealth; designed to elude notice. —**stealth′i·ly** *adv.* —**stealth′i·ness** *n.*

steam (stēm) *n.* 1 Water in the form of a gas, esp. above the boiling point of the liquid. 2 The visible mist formed by sudden cooling of hot steam. 3 Any kind of vaporous exhalation. 4 Energy or power derived from hot water vapor under pressure. 5 *Informal* Vigor; force; speed. —**let off steam** To give expression to pent-up emotions or opinions. —*v.i.* 1 To emit steam or vapor. 2 To rise or pass off as steam. 3 To become covered with condensed water vapor: often with *up.* 4 To generate steam. 5 To move or travel by the agency of steam. —*v.t.* 6 To treat with steam, as in softening, cooking, cleaning, etc. —*adj.* 1 Of, driven, or operated by steam. 2 Producing or containing steam: a *steam* boiler; a *steam* pipe. 3 Treated by steam. 4 Using steam: *steam* heat. [< OE *stēam*] —**steam′i·ness** *n.* —**steam′y** *adj.* (·**i·er, i·est**)

steam·boat (stēm′bōt′) *n.* A boat propelled by steam.

steam engine An engine that derives its force from the pressure of hot steam.

steam·er (stē′mər) *n.* 1 A steamship or steamboat. 2 A pot or container in which something is steamed.

steam·fit·ter (stēm′fit′ər) *n.* A man who sets up or repairs steam pipes and their fittings. —**steam′fit′ting** *n.*

steam·roll·er (stēm′rōl′ər) *n.* 1 A machine having a heavy roller for flattening asphalt surfaces. 2 *Informal* Any force that ruthlessly overcomes opposition. —*v. Informal v.t.* 1 To crush ruthlessly. —*v.i.* 2 To move with crushing force. Also **steam′roll′.**

steam·ship (stēm′ship′) *n.* A large vessel used for ocean traffic and propelled by steam.

steam shovel A power-operated machine for digging and excavation.

ste·ap·sin (stē·ap′sin) *n.* A pancreatic enzyme that aids in the digestion of fat. [< STEA(RIN) + (PE)PSIN]

ste·ar·ic acid (stē·ar′ik, stir′ik) A fatty acid common in solid animal fats, used in making soap. Also **ste′a·rin.** [< Gk. *stear* suet]

ste·a·tite (stē′ə·tīt) *n.* Massive talc found in extensive beds and used for electric insulation. [< Gk. *stear, steatos* suet, tallow] —**ste′a·tit′ic** (-tit′ik) *adj.*

sted·fast (sted′fast′, -fäst′, -fəst) *adj.* STEADFAST.

steed (stēd) *n.* A horse; esp., a spirited horse. [< OE *stēda* studhorse]

steel (stēl) *n.* 1 Any of various alloys of iron containing carbon in amounts up to about 2 percent, often with other components that give special properties. 2 Something made of steel, as an implement or weapon. 3 Hardness of character. 4 *Can.* A railway track or line. —*adj.* 1 Made or composed of steel. 2 Adamant; unyielding. —*v.t.* 1 To cover with steel. 2 To make strong; harden: to *steel* one's heart against misery. [< OE *stēl*] —**steel′i·ness** *n.* —**steel′y** *adj.* (·**i·er, ·i·est**)

steel wool Steel fibers matted together for use in cleaning and polishing.

steel·work·er (stēl′wûr′kər) *n.* One who works in a steel mill.

steel·yard (stēl′yärd′, stil′yərd) *n.* A device for weighing, consisting of a scaled beam, a movable counterpoise, and hooks to hold the article to be weighed. Also **steel′·yards.**

steen·bok (stēn′bok, stān′) *n. pl.* **·bok** or **·boks** A small African antelope with short horns in the male. [< MDu. *steen* stone + *boc* buck]

steep[1] (stēp) *adj.* **1** Sloping sharply; precipitous. **2** *Informal* Exorbitant; high, as a price. —*n.* A cliff; a precipitous place. [< OE *stēap*] —**steep′ly** *adv.* —**steep′ness** *n.* —**Syn.** *adj.* **1** abrupt, high, sharp, sheer.

steep[2] (stēp) *v.t.* **1** To soak in a liquid, as for softening, cleansing, etc. **2** To imbue thoroughly: *steeped* in crime. —*v.i.* **3** To undergo soaking in a liquid. —*n.* **1** The process of steeping, or the state of being steeped. **2** A liquid or bath in which anything is steeped. [< ON *steypa* pour] —**steep′er** *n.*

Steenbok

steep·en (stē′pən) *v.t. & v.i.* To make or become steep or steeper.

stee·ple (stē′pəl) *n.* A lofty structure rising above the roof of a church, usu. having a spire. [< OE *stēpel*]

stee·ple·chase (stē′pəl·chās′) *n.* **1** A race on horseback across country. **2** A race over a course with hedges, rails, and water jumps. —**stee′ple·chas′er** *n.*

stee·ple·jack (stē′pəl·jak′) *n.* A man whose occupation is to climb steeples and other tall structures to inspect or make repairs.

steer[1] (stir) *v.t.* **1** To direct the course of (a vessel or vehicle). **2** To follow (a course). **3** To direct; guide; control. —*v.i.* **4** To direct the course of a vessel, vehicle, etc. **5** To undergo guiding or steering. **6** To follow a course: to *steer* for land. —**steer clear of** To avoid; keep away from. —*n. Slang* A tip; piece of advice. [< OE *stēoran*] —**steer′er** *n.*

steer[2] (stir) *n.* **1** A young castrated bovine. **2** Any male cattle raised for beef. [< OE *stēor*]

steer·age (stir′ij) *n.* That part of an ocean passenger vessel allotted to passengers paying the lowest fares.

steers·man (stirz′mən) *n. pl.* **·men** (-mən) One who steers a boat or a ship; a helmsman.

stein (stīn) *n.* A beer mug. [G]

stein·bok (stīn′bok) *n.* STEENBOK.

stel·lar (stel′ər) *adj.* **1** Of or pertaining to the stars; astral. **2** Chief; principal: a *stellar* role in a play. [< L *stella* star]

stel·late (stel′it, -āt) *adj.* Star-shaped; having rays pointing outward from a center. Also **stel·lat·ed** (stel′ā·tid). [< L *stella* star] —**stel′late·ly** *adv.*

St. El·mo's fire (sānt el′mōz) A luminous discharge of static electricity sometimes appearing on the superstructure of ships, on the tips of airplane wings, etc. Also **St. El·mo's light.**

stem[1] (stem) *n.* **1** The main ascending axis of a plant, serving to transport water and nutrients, to hold up the leaves to air and light, etc. **2** A subsidiary stalk supporting a fruit, flower, or leaf. **3** The slender upright support of a goblet, wine glass, vase, etc. **4** In a watch, the small projecting rod used for winding the mainspring. **5** *Music* The line attached to the head of a written musical note. **6** *Ling.* The unchanged element common to all the members of a given inflection. **7** The bow of a boat. —**from stem to stern 1** From one end of a ship to the other. **2** Throughout; thoroughly. —*v.t.* **stemmed, stem·ming** To remove the stems of or from. —**stem from** To be descended or derived. [< OE *stemm, stemn*] —**stem′mer** *n.*

stem[2] (stem) *v.t.* **stemmed, stem·ming 1** To stop, hold back, or dam up, as a current. **2** To make progress against, as a current, opposing force, etc. [< ON *stemma* stop]

stem·wind·er (stem′wīn′dər) *n.* **1** A stemwinding watch. **2** *Slang* A very superior person or thing.

stem·wind·ing (stem′wīn′ding) *adj.* Wound, as a watch, by turning a knob at the outermost end of the stem.

stench (stench) *n.* A foul or offensive odor. [< OE *stenc*] —**stench′y** *adj.* —**Syn.** fetidness, miasma, reek, stink.

sten·cil (sten′səl) *n.* **1** A thin sheet or plate in which a written text or a pattern is cut through which applied paint or ink penetrates to a surface beneath. **2** Produced by stenciling. —*v.t.* **·ciled** or **·cilled, ·cil·ing** or **·cil·ling** To mark with a stencil. [< OF *estenceler*] —**sten′·cil·er** or **sten′cil·ler** *n.*

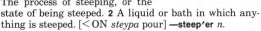

sten·o (sten′ō) *n. pl.* **sten·os 1** STENOGRAPHER. **2** STENOGRAPHY.

steno- *combining form* Tight; contracted: *stenography.* [< Gk. *stenos* narrow]

steno., stenog. stenographer; stenography.

ste·nog·ra·pher (stə·nog′rə·fər) *n.* One who is skilled in shorthand.

ste·nog·ra·phy (stə·nog′rə·fē) *n.* **1** The method of rapid writing by the use of contractions or arbitrary symbols; shorthand. **2** The act of using stenography. —**sten·o·graph·ic** (sten′ə·graf′ik) or **·i·cal** *adj.* —**sten′o·graph′i·cal·ly** *adv.*

sten·o·type (sten′ə·tīp) *n.* A keyboard-operated machine for recording on paper tape symbols representing speech.

sten·o·typ·y (sten′ə·tī′pē) *n.* A system of shorthand utilizing a keyboard-operated machine to record letters in various combinations that represent sounds, words, or phrases. —**sten′o·typ′ist** *n.*

sten·to·ri·an (sten·tôr′ē·ən, -tō′rē-) *adj.* Extremely loud. [< *Stentor,* a herald in the *Iliad,* famous for his loud voice] —**sten·to′ri·an·ly** *adv.*

step (step) *n.* **1** A change in location or position accomplished by lifting the foot and putting it down in a different place. **2** The distance passed over in making such a motion. **3** Any space easily traversed. **4** A stair or ladder rung. **5** A single action or proceeding regarded as leading to something. **6** A grade or degree: They advanced him a *step.* **7** The sound of a footfall. **8** A footprint; track. **9** *pl.* Progression by walking. **10** A combination of foot movements in dancing. **11** *Music* An interval approximately equal to that between the first two tones of a diatonic scale. —**in step 1** Walking or dancing evenly with another by taking corresponding steps. **2** Conforming; in agreement. —**out of step 1** Not in step. **2** Not conforming or agreeing. —**step by step** In slow stages. —**take steps** To adopt measures, as to attain an end. —**watch one's step** To be cautious. —*v.* **stepped, step·ping** *v.i.* **1** To move forward or backward by taking a step or steps. **2** To walk a short distance. **3** To move with measured, dignified, or graceful steps. **4** To move or act quickly or briskly. **5** To pass into a situation, circumstance, etc.: He *stepped* into a fortune. —*v.t.* **6** To take (a pace, stride, etc.). **7** To perform the steps of: to *step* a quadrille. **8** To place or move (the foot) in taking a step. **9** To measure by taking steps: often with *off.* **10** To cut or arrange in steps. —**step down 1** To decrease gradually. **2** To resign from an office or position; abdicate. —**step in** To begin to take part; intervene. —**step on** (or **upon**) **1** To tread upon. **2** To put the foot on so as to activate, as a brake or treadle. **3** *Informal* To reprove or subdue. —**step on it** *Informal* To hurry; hasten. —**step out 1** To go outside. **2** *Informal* To go out for fun or entertainment. **3** To step down. **4** To walk with long strides. —**step up** To increase; raise. [< OE *stæpe*] —**Syn.** *n.* **6** stage, level, position, notch.

step- *combining form* Related through the previous marriage of a parent or spouse, but not by blood: *stepchild.* [< OE *steop-*]

step·broth·er (step′bruth̠′ər) *n.* The son of one's stepparent by a former marriage.

step·child (step′chīld′) *n. pl.* **·chil·dren** The child of one's husband or wife by a former marriage.

step·daugh·ter (step′dô′tər) *n.* A female stepchild.

step-down (step′doun′) *adj.* **1** That decreases gradually. **2** *Electr.* Designating a transformer whose output voltage is less than its input voltage. **3** Designating a speed-reducing gear.

step·fa·ther (step′fä′thər) *n.* A man who has married one's mother after the decease or divorce of one's own father.

step-in (step′in′) *adj.* Put on, as undergarments or shoes, by being stepped into.

step·lad·der (step′lad′ər) *n.* A set of portable, usu. flat steps with a hinged frame at the back for support.

step·moth·er (step′muth′ər) *n.* A woman who has married one's father after the decease or divorce of one's own mother.

step·par·ent (step′pâr′ənt) *n.* A stepfather or stepmother.

steppe (step) *n.* **1** A vast plain devoid of forest. **2** One of the extensive plains in SE Europe and Asia. [< Russ. *step′*]

stepped-up (stept′up′) *adj. Informal* Speeded up; increased: *stepped-up* production.

step·per (step′ər) *n.* **1** One who or that which steps. **2** *Slang* A dancer.

step·ping·stone (step′ing·stōn′) *n.* **1** A stone forming a footrest, as for crossing a stream, etc. **2** That by which one advances or rises.

step·sis·ter (step′sis′tər) *n.* The daughter of one's stepparent by a former marriage.

step·son (step′sun′) *n.* A male stepchild.

step-up (step′up′) *adj.* **1** Increasing by stages. **2** Designating a transformer whose output voltage exceeds its input voltage. **3** Designating a speed-increasing gear. —*n.* An increase, as in intensity, amount, etc.

-ster *suffix of nouns* **1** One who makes or is occupied with: *songster.* **2** One who belongs or is related to: *gangster.* **3** One who is: *youngster.* [< OE *-estre*]

ster., stg. Sterling.

ste·ra·di·an (sti·rā′dē·ən) *n.* A solid angle with its vertex at the center of a sphere which encloses a surface equivalent to the square of the radius of the sphere: a unit of measure. [< Gk. *stereos* solid + RADIAN]

stere (stir) *n.* A cubic meter. [< Gk. *stereos* solid]

ster·e·o (ster′ē·ō, stir′-) *n. pl.* **·e·os** **1** A stereophonic record player, record, tape, etc. **2** Stereophonic sound. **3** STEREOTYPE (defs. 1 & 2). **4** A stereoscopic method; also, a steroscopic photograph. —*adj.* **1** STEREOPHONIC. **2** STEREOTYPED (def. 1). **3** Of or pertaining to the stereoscope; stereoscopic.

stereo- *combining form* Solid; firm; three-dimensional: *stereoscope.* [< Gk. *stereos* hard]

ster·e·o·phon·ic (ster′ē·ə·fon′ik, stir′-) *adj.* Of, for, or designating a system of sound reproduction in which two independent channels are used so as to present different sounds to each of a listener's ears. —**ster′e·o·phon′i·cal·ly** *adv.*

ster·e·o·scope (ster′ē·ə·skōp′, stir′-) *n.* An instrument for presenting different images of an object to each eye, so as to produce a three-dimensional illusion. —**ster′e·o·scop′ic** (-skop′ik) or **·i·cal** *adj.* —**ster′e·o·scop′i·cal·ly** *adv.* —**ster·e·os·co·pist** (ster′ē·os′kə·pist, stir-) *n.*

ster·e·o·type (ster′ē·ə·tīp′, stir′-) *n.* **1** A printing plate cast in metal from a matrix molded from a raised surface, as type. **2** Anything made or processed in this way. **3** A conventional or hackneyed expression, custom, or mode of thought. —*v.t.* **·typed, ·typ·ing** **1** To make a stereotype of. **2** To print from stereotypes. **3** To give a fixed or unalterable form to. —**ster′e·o·typ′er, ster′e·o·typ′ist** *n.*

ster·e·o·typed (ster′ē·ə·tīpt′, stir′-) *adj.* **1** Produced from a stereotype. **2** Hackneyed; without originality.

ster·ile (ster′əl, *Chiefly Brit.* -īl) *adj.* **1** Having no reproductive power; barren. **2** Lacking productiveness: *sterile* soil. **3** Containing no microorganisms; aseptic: a *sterile* fluid. **4** Lacking vigor or interest: *sterile* prose. **5** Without results; futile: *sterile* hopes. [< L *sterilis*] —**ster′ile·ly** *adv.* —**ste·ril·i·ty** (stə·ril′ə·tē), **ster′ile·ness** *n.*

ster·il·ize (ster′əl·īz) *v.t.* **·ized, ·iz·ing** **1** To render incapable of reproduction, esp. by surgery. **2** To destroy microorganisms. **3** To make barren. —**ster′i·li·za′tion, ster′il·iz′er** *n.*

ster·ling (stûr′ling) *n.* **1** British money. **2** The official standard of fineness for British coins. **3** Sterling silver as used in manufacturing articles, as tableware, etc. **4** Articles made of sterling silver collectively. —*adj.* **1** Made of or payable in sterling: pounds *sterling.* **2** Made of sterling silver. **3** Having great worth; genuine: *sterling* qualities. [Prob. < OE *steorra* star + -LING]

sterling silver An alloy of 92.5 percent silver and usu. 7.5 percent copper.

stern¹ (stûrn) *adj.* **1** Marked by severity or harshness: a *stern* command. **2** Having an austere disposition: a *stern* judge. **3** Inspiring fear. **4** Resolute: a *stern* resolve. [< OE *styrne*] —**stern′ly** *adv.* —**stern′ness** *n.*

stern² (stûrn) *n.* **1** *Naut.* The aft part of a ship, boat, etc. **2** The hindmost part of any object. —*adj.* Situated at or belonging to the stern. [< ON *styra* steer] —**stern′most′** (-mōst′) *adj.*

ster·num (stûr′nəm) *n. pl.* **·na** (-nə) or **·nums** The structure of bone and cartilage that forms the ventral support of the ribs in vertebrates. [< Gk. *sternon* breast] —**stern·al** (stûr′nal) *adj.*

ster·nu·ta·tion (stûr′nyə·tā′shən) *n.* **1** The act of sneezing. **2** A sneeze or the noise produced by it. [< L *sternuere* to sneeze] —**ster·nu·ta·to·ry** (ster·nyōō′tə·tôr′ē, -tō′ri) *adj.*

stern-wheel·er (stûrn′hwē′lər) *n.* A steamboat propelled by one large paddle wheel at the stern.

ster·oid (ster′oid) *n.* Any of a large group of structurally similar organic compounds found in plants and animals, including many hormones and the precursors of certain vitamins. [< STER(OL) + -OID]

ster·ol (ster′ōl, -ol) *n.* Any of a class of steroids comprising solid, fat-soluble alcohols, as cholesterol. [Contraction of CHOLESTEROL]

ster·tor·ous (stûr′tər·əs) *adj.* Characterized or accompanied by a snoring sound: *stertorous* breathing. [< L *stertere* to snore] —**ster′tor·ous·ly** *adv.* —**ster′tor·ous·ness** *n.*

stet (stet) Let it stand: a direction used in proofreading to indicate that a word, letter, etc., marked for omission is to remain. —*v.t.* **stet·ted, stet·ting** To mark for retention with the word *stet.* [< L *stare* to stand]

steth·o·scope (steth′ə·skōp) *n.* An apparatus for conducting sounds from the human body to the ears of an examiner. [< Gk. *stēthos* breast + -SCOPE] —**steth′o·scop′ic** (-skop′ik) *adj.* —**steth′o·scop′i·cal·ly** *adv.* —**ste·thos·co·py** (ste·thos′kə·pē) *n.*

stet·son (stet′sən) *n. Often cap.* A man's hat, usu. of felt, with a high crown and a broad brim, popular in the w U.S. [< *Stetson,* a trade name]

ste·ve·dore (stē′və·dôr, -dōr) *n.* One whose business is loading or unloading ships. —*v.t. & v.i.* **·dored, ·dor·ing** To load or unload (a vessel or vessels). [< L *stipare* compress, stuff]

stew (st^yōō) *v.t. & v.i.* **1** To boil slowly and gently. **2** *Informal* To worry. —*n.* **1** Stewed food, esp. a preparation of meat or fish and vegetables cooked by stewing. **2** *Informal* Mental agitation; worry. [< OF *estuver*]

stew·ard (st^yōō′ərd) *n.* **1** A person entrusted with the management of the affairs of others. **2** A person put in charge of services for a club, ship, railroad train, etc. **3** On shipboard, a person who waits on table and takes care of passengers' staterooms. **4** SHOP STEWARD. [< OE *stī* hall + *weard* ward, keeper] —**stew′ard·ship** *n.*

stew·ard·ess (st^yōō′ər·dis) *n.* A woman whose occupation is that of a steward, esp. one who is employed on an airplane to attend passengers.

stewed (st^yōōd) *adj.* **1** Cooked by stewing. **2** *Slang* Drunk.

stge. storage.

stick (stik) *n.* **1** A stiff shoot or branch cut or broken off from a tree or bush. **2** Any relatively long and thin piece of wood. **3** A piece of wood fashioned for a specific use: a walking *stick;* a hockey *stick.* **4** Anything resembling a stick in form: a *stick* of dynamite. **5** A piece of wood of any size, cut for fuel, lumber, or timber. **6** *Aeron.* The lever of an airplane that controls pitching and rolling. **7** A poke, stab, or thrust with a stick or pointed implement. **8** The state of being stuck together; adhesion. **9** *Informal* A stiff, inert, or dull person. —**the sticks** *Informal* An obscure rural district. —*v.* **stuck, stick·ing** *v.t.* **1** To pierce or penetrate with a pointed object. **2** To stab. **3** To thrust or force, as a sword or pin, into or through something else. **4** To force the end of (a nail, etc.) into something. **5** To fasten

in place with or as with pins, nails, etc. **6** To cover with objects piercing the surface: a paper *stuck* with pins. **7** To impale; transfix. **8** To put or thrust: He *stuck* his hand into his pocket. **9** To fasten to a surface by or as by an adhesive substance. **10** To bring to a standstill: We were *stuck* in Rome. **11** *Informal* To smear with something sticky. **12** *Informal* To baffle; puzzle. **13** *Slang* To cheat. **14** *Slang* To force great expense, an unpleasant task, responsibility, etc., upon. —*v.i.* **15** To be or become fixed in place by being thrust in: The pins are *sticking* in the cushion. **16** To adhere; cling. **17** To come to a standstill; halt. **18** *Informal* To be baffled or disconcerted. **19** To hesitate; scruple: with *at* or *to*. **20** To persevere, as in a task or undertaking: with *at* or *to*. **21** To remain faithful, as to an ideal or bargain. **22** To protrude: with *out, through, up,* etc. —**be stuck on** *Informal* To be enamored of. —**stick around** *Slang* To remain near or near at hand. —**stick by** To remain loyal to. —**stick it out** To persevere to the end. —**stick up** *Slang* To stop and rob. —**stick up for** *Informal* To take the part of; defend. [< OE *sticca*]

stick·er (stik'ər) *n.* **1** One who or that which sticks. **2** A gummed label. **3** *Informal* Anything that confuses; a puzzle. **4** A prickly stem, thorn, or bur.

sticking plaster An adhesive material for covering slight cuts, etc.

stick·le (stik'əl) *v.i.* **·led, ·ling 1** To contend about trifles. **2** To hesitate for petty reasons. [< OE *stihtan* arrange]

stick·le·back (stik'əl·bak') *n.* Any of various small, nest-building fresh- or salt-water fishes having sharp dorsal spines.

Stickleback

stick·ler (stik'lər) *n.* **1** One who insists upon exacting standards, as of behavior: with *for:* a *stickler* for punctuality. **2** A baffling problem.

stick·pin (stik'pin') *n.* An ornamental pin for a necktie.

stick-to-it·ive·ness (stik'tōō'ə·tiv·nis) *n. Informal* Perseverance; diligence.

stick·up (stik'up') *n. Slang* A robbery or hold-up.

stick·y (stik'ē) *adj.* **stick·i·er, stick·i·est 1** Adhering to a surface; adhesive. **2** Warm and humid. **3** *Informal* Unpleasant or complicated: a *sticky* situation. —**stick'i·ly** *adv.* — **stick'i·ness** *n.* —**Syn. 1** gluey, mucilaginous, viscous.

stiff (stif) *adj.* **1** Resistant to bending; rigid. **2** Not easily worked or moved: a *stiff* bolt. **3** Moving with difficulty or pain: a *stiff* back. **4** Not natural, graceful, or easy: a *stiff* bow. **5** Taut; tightly drawn: a *stiff* rope. **6** Strong and steady: a *stiff* breeze. **7** Thick; viscous: a *stiff* batter. **8** Harsh; severe: a *stiff* penalty. **9** High; dear: *stiff* prices. **10** Difficult; hard: a *stiff* examination. **11** Stubborn; unyielding: *stiff* resistance. **12** Awkward or noticeably formal; not relaxed or easy; wooden. **13** Strong; potent: a *stiff* drink. **14** Difficult; arduous: a *stiff* climb. —*n. Slang* **1** A corpse. **2** An awkward or unresponsive person. **3** A person; fellow: a working *stiff*. **4** A rough person. [< OE *stif*] —**stiff'ly** *adv.* —**stiff'ness** *n.*

stiff·en (stif'ən) *v.t. & v.i.* To make or become stiff or stiffer. —**stiff'en·er** *n.*

stiff-necked (stif'nekt') *adj.* **1** Suffering from a stiff neck. **2** Stubborn; obstinate.

sti·fle (stī'fəl) *v.* **·fled, ·fling** *v.t.* **1** To kill by stopping respiration; choke. **2** To suppress or repress, as sobs. —*v.i.* **3** To die of suffocation. **4** To experience difficulty in breathing, as in a stuffy room. [ME *stuflen*] —**sti'fler** *n.* —**sti'fling·ly** *adv.*

stig·ma (stig'mə) *n. pl.* **stig·ma·ta** (stig·mä'tə, stig'mə·tə) or (*esp. for def. 2*) **stig·mas 1** A mark of disgrace. **2** *Bot.* That part of a pistil which receives the pollen. **3** *Biol.* Any spot or small opening. **4** A spot or scar on the skin. **5** *Med.* Any physical sign of diagnostic value. **6** *pl.* The wounds that Christ received at the Crucifixion. [L, mark, brand] —**stig·mat·ic** (·mat'ik) *adj.* —**Syn. 1** blemish, blot, stain.

stig·ma·tize (stig'mə·tīz) *v.t.* **·tized, ·tiz·ing 1** To characterize as disgraceful. **2** To mark with a stigma. *Brit. sp.* **stig'ma·tise.** —**stig'ma·ti·za'tion, stig'ma·tiz'er** *n.*

stile (stīl) *n.* A step, or series of steps, on each side of a fence or wall to enable one to climb over. [< OE *stigel*]

Stile

sti·let·to (sti·let'ō) *n. pl.* **·tos** or **·toes** A small dagger with a slender blade. —*v.t.* **·toed, ·to·ing** To pierce with a stiletto; stab. [< Ital. *stilo* dagger]

still[1] (stil) *adj.* **1** Being without movement; motionless. **2** Free from disturbance or agitation. **3** Making no sound; silent. **4** Low in sound; hushed. **5** Subdued; soft. **6** Dead; inanimate. **7** Having no effervescence: said of wines. **8** *Phot.* Not capable of showing movement. —*n.* **1** Absence of sound or noise. **2** *Phot.* A still photograph; esp. one taken on a motion-picture set, for advertising purposes. —*adv.* **1** Up to this or that time; yet: He is *still* here. **2** After or in spite of something; nevertheless. **3** In increasing degree; even yet: *still* more. **4** *Archaic* or *Regional* Always; constantly. —*conj.* Nevertheless. —*v.t.* **1** To cause to be still or calm. **2** To silence or hush. **3** To allay, as fears. —*v.i.* **4** To become still. [< OE *stille*] —**still'ness** *n.* —**Syn.** *adj.* **2** peaceful, tranquil, undisturbed. *v.* **1** soothe, tranquil-lize. **2** quiet.

Still[2]

still[2] (stil) *n.* **1** An apparatus for distilling liquids, esp. alcoholic liquors. **2** DISTILLERY. —*v.t. & v.i.* To distill. [< L *stilla* a drop]

still·born (stil'bôrn') *adj.* Dead at birth. —**still'birth'** (-bûrth') *n.*

still life *pl.* **lifes 1** In painting, the representation of inanimate objects. **2** A picture of such objects. —**still'-life'** *adj.*

Still·son wrench (stil'sən) A wrench resembling a monkey wrench, but with one serrated jaw capable of slight angular movement, so that the grip is tightened by pressure on the handle: a trade name. [< D. *Stillson,* its U.S. inventor in 1869]

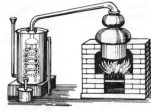
Stillson wrench

still·y (stil'ē) *adj.* **·i·er, ·i·est** Quiet; calm. —*adv.* (stil'lē) Calmly; quietly.

stilt (stilt) *n.* **1** One of a pair of slender poles made with a projection above the ground to support the foot in walking. **2** A tall post or pillar used as a support for a dock or building. **3** Any of various shore birds with thin bills and long legs. [ME *stilte*]

stilt·ed (stil'tid) *adj.* Excessively formal or stuffy: *stilted* prose. —**stilt'ed·ly** *adv.* —**stilt'ed·ness** *n.*

stim·u·lant (stim'yə·lənt) *n.* **1** A drug that stimulates the rate or intensity of vital functions, esp. in the central nervous system. **2** Something that stimulates one to activity.

stim·u·late (stim'yə·lāt) *v.* **·lat·ed, ·lat·ing** *v.t.* **1** To rouse to activity; spur. **2** To increase action in by applying some form of stimulus: to *stimulate* the heart. **3** To affect by intoxicants. —*v.i.* **4** To act as a stimulus or stimulant. [< L *stimulus* a goad] —**stim'u·lat'er, stim'u·la'tor, stim'u·la'tion** *n.*

stim·u·la·tive (stim'yə·lā'tiv) *adj.* Having the power to stimulate. —*n.* Something that stimulates.

stim·u·lus (stim'yə·ləs) *n. pl.* **·li** (-lī, -lē) **1** Anything that rouses to activity, as a stimulant, incentive, etc. **2** Any agent that influences activity in an organism. [< L]

sting (sting) *v.* **stung, sting·ing** *v.t.* **1** To pierce or prick painfully: The bee *stung* me. **2** To cause to suffer sharp, smarting pain. **3** To cause to suffer mentally: to be *stung* with remorse. **4** To stimulate or rouse as if with a sting; goad. **5** *Slang* To overcharge. —*v.i.* **6** To have or use a sting, as a bee. **7** To suffer a sharp, smarting pain. **8** To suffer mental distress. —*n.* **1** A sharp offensive or defensive or-

gan, as of a bee, capable of introducing an allergen or a venom into a victim's skin. **2** The act of stinging. **3** A wound made by a sting. **4** The pain caused by such a wound. **5** Any sharp, smarting sensation. **6** A keen stimulus; spur. [< OE *stingan*] —**sting'er** *n.* —**sting'ing·ly** *adv.*

sting ray Any of various flat-bodied fishes with a whiplike tail having one or more stinging spines. Also **sting'ray, sting·a·ree** (sting'ə·rē, sting'rē')

Sting ray

stin·gy (stin'jē) *adj.* **·gi·er, ·gi·est** **1** Extremely penurious or miserly. **2** Scanty; meager: a *stingy* portion. [?] —**stin'gi·ly** *adv.* —**stin'gi·ness** *n.* —**Syn. 1** avaricious, niggardly, parsimonious, tightfisted.

stink (stingk) *n.* A strong, foul odor; stench. —*v.* **stank** or **stunk, stunk, stink·ing** *v.i.* **1** To give forth a foul odor. **2** To be extremely offensive or hateful. —*v.t.* **3** To cause to stink. [< OE *stincan*] —**stink'er** *n.* —**stink'ing·ly** *adv.* —**stink'y** *adj.* (**·i·er, ·i·est**)

stink·bug (stingk'bug') *n.* Any of certain hemipterous insects with a sickening odor.

stink·weed (stingk'wēd') *n.* Any of various plants with foul-smelling flowers or leaves.

stint (stint) *v.t.* **1** To limit, as in amount. —*v.i.* **2** To be frugal or sparing. —*n.* **1** A task to be performed within a specified time: a weekly *stint.* **2** A bound; restriction. [< OE *styntan* stupefy] —**stint'er** *n.* —**stint'ing·ly** *adv.*

stipe (stīp) *n.* A stalklike support, esp. that of a fern frond, a pistil, or a mushroom cap. [< L *stipes* branch]

sti·pend (stī'pend, -pənd) *n.* A regular, fixed allowance or salary. [< L *stips* payment in coin + *pendere* weigh, pay out]

sti·pen·di·a·ry (stī·pen'dē·er'ē) *adj.* **1** Receiving a stipend. **2** Performing services for a fixed payment. —*n. pl.* **·ar·ies** One who receives a stipend.

stip·ple (stip'əl) *v.t.* **·pled, ·pling** To draw, paint, or engrave with dots. —*n.* **1** In painting, etching, etc., a method of representing light and shade by employing dots instead of lines. **2** The effect resulting from this method. **3** Stippled work. Also **stip'pling.** [< Du. *stip* dot] —**stip'pler** *n.*

stip·u·late (stip'yə·lāt) *v.* **·lat·ed, ·lat·ing** *v.t.* **1** To specify as the terms of an agreement, contract, etc. **2** To specify as a requirement for agreement. —*v.i.* **3** To demand something as a requirement or condition. [< L *stipulari* to bargain] —**stip'u·la'tor** *n.* —**stip'u·la·to·ry** (-lə·tôr'ē, -tō'rē) *adj.*

stip·u·la·tion (stip'yə·lā'shən) *n.* **1** The act of stipulating. **2** An agreement or contract.

stip·ule (stip'yōol) *n.* One of a pair of leaflike appendages at the base of the petiole of certain leaves. [< L *stipula* stalk] —**stip'u·lar, stip'u·late, stip'u·lat·ed** *adj.*

stir[1] (stûr) *v.* **stirred, stir·ring** *v.t.* **1** To mix thoroughly by giving a circular motion to, as with a spoon, fork, etc.: to *stir* soup. **2** To cause to move, esp. slightly. **3** To move vigorously; bestir: *Stir* yourself! **4** To rouse, as from sleep, indifference, or inactivity. **5** To incite; provoke: often with *up.* **6** To affect strongly; move with emotion. —*v.i.* **7** To move, esp. slightly: The log wouldn't *stir.* **8** To be active; move about. **9** To take place; happen. **10** To undergo stirring: This molasses *stirs* easily. —*n.* **1** The act of stirring. **2** Movement. **3** Public interest; excitement. **4** A poke; nudge. [< OE *styrian*] —**stir'rer** *n.*

stir[2] (stûr) *n. Slang* A jail; prison. [?]

stir·ring (stûr'ing) *adj.* **1** Stimulating; inspiring. **2** Full of activity. —**stir'ring·ly** *adv.* —**Syn. 1** exciting, rousing. **2** animated, lively, sprightly.

stir·rup (stûr'əp, stir'-) *n.* **1** A loop of metal or wood suspended from a saddle to support a horseback rider's foot. **2** A similar device used as a support, as for a beam. [< OE *stigrāp* mounting rope] • See SADDLE.

stirrup bone STAPES.

stitch (stich) *n.* **1** A single passage of a threaded needle or other implement through fabric and back again, as in sewing. **2** A single turn of thread or yarn around a needle or other implement, as in knitting or crocheting. **3** Any individual arrangement of a thread or threads used in sewing: a chain *stitch.* **4** A sharp sudden pain. **5** *Informal* A garment: I haven't a *stitch* to wear. —**be in stitches** To

be overcome with laughter. —*v.t.* **1** To join together with stitches. **2** To ornament with stitches. —*v.i.* **3** To make stitches; sew. [< OE *stice* prick]

sti·ver (stī'vər) *n.* **1** A small Dutch coin, 1/20 of a guilder. **2** Anything of little value.

St. Johns·wort (sānt jonz'wûrt') Any of various small, woody perennials, usu. with yellow flowers. Also **Saint Johnswort, St. John's-wort.**

stk. stock.

sto·a (stō'ə) *n. pl.* **sto·ae** (stō'ē) or **sto·as** In Greek architecture, a covered colonnade, portico, cloister, or promenade. [Gk., porch]

stoat (stōt) *n. pl.* **stoats** or **stoat** The ermine, esp. in its brown summer coat. [ME *stote*]

stock (stok) *n.* **1** The goods a store or merchant has on hand. **2** A quantity of something acquired or kept for future use: a *stock* of provisions. **3** LIVESTOCK. **4** The original, as a man, race, or language, from which others are descended or derived. **5** A line of familial descent. **6** An ethnic group; race. **7** A related group of plants or animals. **8** A group of related languages; also, a language family. **9** The trunk or main stem of a tree or other plant. **10 a** A plant stem from which cuttings are taken for grafting. **b** A plant stem upon which a graft is made. **11** In finance: **a** The capital raised by a corporation through the sale of shares that entitle the holder to interest or dividends. **b** The part of this capital credited to an individual stock holder. **c** The certificate or certificates indicating this. **12** A fund or debt owed (as by a nation, city, etc.) to individuals who receive a fixed interest rate. **13** The part of a device that functions as a support and to which other parts are attached, as the wooden portion or handle of a firearm, whip, etc. **14** Raw material: paper *stock.* **15** The broth from boiled vegetables, meat, or fish, used in preparing soups, gravies, etc. **16** Something lacking life, feeling, or motion. **17** The group of plays produced by a theatrical company at one theater. **18** A broad, heavily starched band, formerly worn as a cravat. —**in stock** Available for purchase. —**out of stock** Not available; all sold out. — **stock in trade** One's abilities, talents, or resources. — **take stock 1** To take an inventory. **2** To size up a situation. —**take stock in** *Informal* To have trust or belief in. —**the stocks 1** A former device for public punishment consisting of a timber frame for confining the ankles, or the ankles and wrists. **2** The timber frame on which a ship or boat is built. —*v.t.* **1** To supply with cattle, as a farm. **2** To supply (a store) with merchandise. **3** To keep for sale: to *stock* avocados. **4** To supply with wildlife: to *stock* a pond. **5** To put aside for future use. **6** To provide with a handle or stock. —*v.i.* **7** To lay in supplies or stock: often with *up.* —*adj.* **1** Kept on hand: a *stock* size. **2** Banal; commonplace: a *stock* phrase. **3** Of or pertaining to the breeding and raising of livestock. **4** Employed in handling or caring for the stock: a *stock* clerk. **5** Of or pertaining to a stock or stocks (def. 9). [< OE *stocc*]

stock·ade (sto·kād') *n.* **1** A defense consisting of a strong, high barrier of upright posts, stakes, etc. **2** The area enclosed by such a barrier. **3** A similar area used to confine prisoners, esp. in military installations. —*v.t.* **·ad·ed, ·ad·ing** To surround or fortify with a stockade. [< OF *estaque* a stake]

stock·bro·ker (stok'brō'kər) *n.* One who buys and sells stocks or securities for others.

stock car 1 An automobile, usu. a sedan, modified for racing. **2** A railroad car used for transporting cattle.

stock company 1 An incorporated company that issues stock. **2** A theatrical company under one management that presents a series of plays.

stock exchange 1 A place where securities are bought and sold. **2** An association of stockbrokers.

stock farm A farm that specializes in the breeding of livestock.

stock·hold·er (stok'hōl'dər) *n.* One who holds stocks or shares in a company.

stock·i·net (stok'i·net') *n.* An elastic knitted fabric used chiefly for undergarments. [< STOCKING]

stock·ing (stok'ing) *n.* **1** A close-fitting knitted covering for the foot and leg. **2** Something resembling such a covering. [< STOCK, in obs. sense of "a stocking"]

stocking cap A long knitted cap, tapered and often having a pompon or tassel at the end.

stock·man (stok′mən) *n. pl.* **·men** (-mən) **1** One who raises or owns livestock; a cattleman. **2** A man having charge of goods, as in a warehouse.

stock market 1 STOCK EXCHANGE. **2** The business transacted in such a place: The *stock market* was active.

stock·pile (stok′pīl′) *n.* A storage pile of materials or supplies. Also **stock pile.** —*v.t. & v.i.* **·piled, ·pil·ing** To accumulate a supply or stockpile (of).

stock raising The breeding and raising of livestock.

stock·room (stok′rōōm′, -rŏŏm′) *n.* A room where reserve stocks of goods are stored.

stock·still (stok′stil′) *adj.* Completely motionless.

stock·y (stok′ē) *adj.* **stock·i·er, stock·i·est** Short and stout. —**stock′i·ly** *adv.* —**stock′i·ness** *n.*

stock·yard (stok′yärd′) *n.* A large yard with pens, stables, etc., where cattle are kept ready for shipping, slaughter, etc.

stodg·y (stoj′ē) *adj.* **stodg·i·er, stodg·i·est 1** Dull; boring. **2** Indigestible; heavy. [?] —**stodg′i·ly** *adv.* —**stodg′i·ness** *n.*

sto·gy (stō′gē) *n. pl.* **·gies** A long, slender, inexpensive cigar. Also **sto′gie.** [< *Conestoga,* Pennsylvania]

sto·ic (stō′ik) *n.* A person apparently unaffected by pleasure or pain. —*adj.* Indifferent to pleasure or pain; impassive: also **sto′i·cal.** [< STOIC] —**sto′i·cal·ly** *adv.* —**sto′i·cal·ness** *n.*

Sto·ic (stō′ik) *n.* A member of a school of Greek philosophy founded by Zeno about 308 B.C., holding the belief that wisdom lies in being superior to passion, joy, grief, etc. —*adj.* Of or pertaining to the Stoics or Stoicism. [< Gk. *Stoa,* the colonnade at Athens where Zeno taught]

sto·i·cism (stō′ə·siz′əm) *n.* Indifference to pleasure or pain.

Sto·i·cism (stō′ə·siz′əm) *n.* The doctrines of the Stoics.

stoke (stōk) *v.t.* **stoked, stok·ing 1** To supply (a furnace) with fuel. **2** To stir up; intensify. —*v.i.* **3** To tend a fire. [Back formation < STOKER]

stoke·hole (stōk′hōl′) *n.* **1** The space about the mouth of a furnace; the fireroom. **2** The mouth of a furnace.

stok·er (stō′kər) *n.* **1** A person who tends a furnace or boiler. **2** A mechanical device for feeding coal to a furnace. [< Du. *stoken* stir a fire]

STOL, S.T.O.L. short takeoff and landing.

stole[1] (stōl) *n.* **1** *Eccl.* A long, narrow band, usu. of decorated silk or linen, worn about the shoulders by priests and bishops. **2** A fur, scarf, or garment resembling a stole, worn by women. [< Gk. *stolē* a garment] —**stoled** *adj.*

stole[2] (stōl) *p.t.* of STEAL.

sto·len (stō′lən) *p.p.* of STEAL.

stol·id (stol′id) *adj.* Expressing no feeling; impassive. [< L *stolidus* dull] —**sto·lid·i·ty** (stə·lid′ə·tē), **stol′id·ness** *n.* —**stol′id·ly** *adv.*

sto·ma (stō′mə) *n. pl.* **sto·ma·ta** (stō′mə·tə, stom′ə·tə) or **sto·mas** A small, mouthlike opening, esp. any of the minute epidermal breathing pores on a plant leaf. Also **sto′mate** (stō′māt′). [< Gk. *stoma* mouth] —**sto′ma·tal** *adj.*

Stole

stom·ach (stum′ək) *n.* **1** A pouchlike dilation of the alimentary canal, situated in most vertebrates next to the esophagus and serving as one of the principal organs of digestion. **2** Any digestive cavity, as of an invertebrate. **3** The abdomen; belly. **4** Desire for food; appetite. **5** Any desire or inclination. —*v.t.* **1** To put up with; endure. **2** To take into and retain in the stomach; digest. [< Gk. *stoma·chos*] —**stom′ach·al** *adj.* —**sto·mach·ic** (stō·mak′ik), **sto·mach′i·cal** *adj., n.* • See LIVER.

stom·ach·er (stum′ək·ər) *n.* A former article of clothing worn, esp. by women, over the breast and stomach.

stomp (stomp) *v.t. & v.i.* To stamp; tread heavily (upon).

—*n.* A jazz dance involving heavy stamping. [Var of STAMP] —**stomp′er** *n.*

stone (stōn) *n. pl.* **stones** or *for def. 8* **stone 1** ROCK (def. 3). **2** A small piece of rock, as a pebble. **3** A piece of shaped or hewn rock, as a gravestone. **4** A jewel; gem. **5** Something like a stone in shape or hardness: a *hailstone.* **6** An abnormal, hard concretion in the body. **7** The hard inner part of a drupe. **8** *Brit.* A measure of weight equal to 14 pounds. —**cast the first stone** To be the first to blame (someone). —**leave no stone unturned** To do everything within possibility. —*adj.* **1** Made of stone: a *stone* ax. **2** Made of coarse, hard earthenware: a *stone* bottle. —*v.t.* **stoned, ston·ing 1** To hurl stones at. **2** To kill by throwing stones at. **3** To remove the stones or pits from. **4** To furnish or line with stone. [< OE *stān*] —**ston′er** *n.*

Stone Age The earliest known period of human cultural evolution, marked by the creation of stone implements.

stone-blind (stōn′blīnd′) *adj.* Completely blind.

stone-broke (stōn′brōk′) *adj.* *Informal* Without any money; having no funds. Also **ston′y-broke′.**

stone·crop (stōn′krop′) *n.* SEDUM.

stone-cut·ter (stōn′kut′ər) *n.* One who or that which cuts stone; esp. a machine for facing stone. —**stone′cut′· ting** *n.*

stoned (stōnd) *adj.* *Slang* **1** Drunk. **2** Under the influence of a drug or narcotic.

stone-deaf (stōn′def′) *adj.* Completely deaf.

stone·ma·son (stōn′mā′sən) *n.* One whose trade is to prepare and lay stones in building. —**stone′ma′son·ry** *n.*

stone's throw (stōnz) **1** The distance a stone may be cast by hand. **2** A short distance.

stone·wall (stōn′wôl′) *Slang v.i.* **1** To act in a calculatedly obstructive way, as by lying or failing to respond to inquiry. —*v.t.* **2** To respond to in such a way.

stone·ware (stōn′wâr′) *n.* A very hard, glazed pottery, made from siliceous clay or clay mixed with flint or sand.

stone·work (stōn′wûrk′) *n.* **1** The art or process of cutting or setting stone. **2** Work built or made of stone. **3** *pl.* A place where stone is shaped. —**stone′work′er** *n.*

ston·y (stō′nē) *adj.* **ston·i·er, ston·i·est 1** Abounding in stone or stones. **2** Made or consisting of stone. **3** Hard as stone; unfeeling. **4** Like stone. **5** *Slang* Having no money. —**ston′i·ly** *adv.* —**ston′i·ness** *n.* —**Syn. 3** chilly, cold, pitiless.

stood (stŏŏd) *p.t. & p.p.* of STAND.

stooge (stōōj) *n.* **1** *Informal* An actor who feeds lines to the principal comedian, acts as a foil for his jokes, etc. **2** Anyone who acts as or is the tool or dupe of another. —*v.i.* **stooged, stoog·ing** To act as a stooge: usu. with *for.* [?]

stool (stōōl) *n.* **1** A backless and armless seat intended for one person. **2** A low bench or portable support for the feet or for kneeling. **3** A seat or place used as a toilet. **4** The matter evacuated from the bowels; feces. **5** A stump or root from which suckers or sprouts shoot up. [< OE *stōl*]

stool pigeon 1 A living or artificial pigeon used to decoy others into a trap. **2** *Slang* An informer, as for the police.

stoop[1] (stōōp) *v.i.* **1** To lean the body forward and down. **2** To stand or walk with the upper part of the body habitually bent forward; slouch. **3** To bend: said of trees, cliffs, etc. **4** To lower or degrade oneself. —*v.t.* **5** To bend (one's head, shoulders, etc.) forward. —*n.* **1** A downward and forward bending of the body. **2** A habitual forward inclination of the head and shoulders. [< OE *stūpian*]

stoop[2] (stōōp) *n.* A small porch or platform at the entrance to a house. [< Du. *stoep*]

stop (stop) *v.* **stopped, stop·ping** *v.t.* **1** To bring (something in motion) to a halt: *stop* an automobile. **2** To prevent the doing or completion of: *stop* a revolution. **3** To prevent (a person) from doing something; restrain. **4** To withhold or cut off, as wages or supplies. **5** To cease doing: *Stop* that! **6** To check, as a flow of blood from a wound. **7** To obstruct (a passage, road, etc.). **8** To fill in or otherwise close, as a hole, cavity, etc. **9** To close (a bottle, barrel, etc.) with a cork, plug, etc. **10** To order a bank not to pay or honor: to *stop* a check. **11** *Music* To press down (a string) or close (a finger hole) to change the pitch of. **12** In boxing, etc., to parry. —*v.i.* **13** To come to a halt; cease progress

or motion. **14** To cease doing something. —**stop off** To stop for a brief stay before continuing on a trip. —**stop over** *Informal* To stop briefly, as for a visit or a rest during a journey. —*n.* **1** The act of stopping, or the state of being stopped. **2** That which stops or limits the range or time of a movement; an obstruction. **3** *Music* **a** The pressing down of a string or the closing of an aperture to change the pitch. **b** A key, lever, or handle for stopping a string or an aperture. **4** *Music* In an organ, a set of pipes producing tones of the same timbre. **5 a** *Brit.* A punctuation mark; a period. **b** In cables, etc., a period. **6** *Phonet.* **a** Complete blockage of the breath stream, as with the lips or tongue, followed by a sudden release. **b** A consonant so produced, as *p, b, t, d, k,* and *g.* —**put a stop to** To end; terminate. [< OE *-stoppian*] —**Syn** *v.* **2** deter, quash. **4** discontinue.

stop·cock (stop′kok′) *n.* A faucet or valve.

stop·gap (stop′gap′) *n.* A person or thing serving as a temporary substitute. —*adj.* Being a stopgap.

stop·o·ver (stop′ō′vər) *n.* The act of stopping over, or permission to stop over on a journey and continue later, using the ticket issued for the whole journey.

stop·page (stop′ij) *n.* **1** The act of stopping or the state of being stopped. **2** A blocking or obstruction.

stop·per (stop′ər) *n.* **1** One who or that which stops or brings to a stop. **2** A plug or cork for a container, as a bottle. —*v.t.* To secure or close with a stopper.

stop·ple (stop′əl) *n.* A stopper, plug, cork, or bung. —*v.t.* **·pled, ·pling** To close with or as with a stopple. [< ME *stop·pen* stop]

stop·watch (stop′woch′) *n.* A watch with a hand indicating fractions of a second which may be stopped or started instantly, used for timing races, etc.

stor·age (stôr′ij, stō′rij) *n.* **1** The depositing of articles in a place for their safekeeping. **2** Space for storing goods. **3** A charge for storing. **4** A section of a computer in whch data is held for later use; memory.

storage battery A connected group of two or more electrolytic cells that can be reversibly charged and discharged.

store (stôr, stōr) *v.t.* **stored, stor·ing 1** To put away for future use. **2** To furnish or supply; provide. **3** To place in a warehouse or other place for safekeeping. —*n.* **1** That which is stored or laid up against future need. **2** *pl.* Supplies, as of food, arms, or clothing. **3** A storehouse; warehouse. **4** A place where merchandise of any kind is kept for sale; a shop. —**in store** Set apart for the future; impending. —**set store by** To value or esteem. [< L *instaurare* restore, erect]

store·front (stôr′frunt′, stōr′-) *n.* **1** The front or facade of a store, usu. opening directly out onto a pedestrian sidewalk. **2** A public service or other facility, often temporary, situated on the site of a former store. —*adj.* Characteristic of or being a storefront.

store·house (stôr′hous′, stōr′-) *n.* A place in which goods are stored; depository.

store·keep·er (stôr′kē′pər, stōr′-) *n.* A person who keeps a retail store or who is in charge of supplies.

store·room (stôr′rōōm′, -rōōm′, stōr′-) *n.* A room in which things are stored.

sto·rey (stôr′ē, stōr′ē) *n. pl.* **·reys** *Chiefly Brit.* STORY².

sto·ried¹ (stôr′ēd, stōr′ēd) *adj.* Having or consisting of stories: a *six-storied* house.

sto·ried² (stôr′ēd, stōr′ēd) *adj.* **1** Having a notable history. **2** Ornamented with designs representing scenes from history or story.

stork (stôrk) *n.* A large wading bird with a long neck and long legs, related to the herons. [< OE *storc*]

storm (stôrm) *n.* **1** A disturbance of the atmosphere that creates strong winds, often with heavy precipitation of rain, snow, dust, etc. **2** Any heavy, prolonged precipitation of snow, rain, etc. **3** Anything similar to a storm: a *storm* of missiles. **4** A violent outburst: a *storm* of applause. **5** A violent and rapid assault. —*v.i.* **1** To blow with violence; rain, snow,

White stork

hail, etc., heavily. **2** To be very angry; rage. **3** To rush with violence or rage: He *stormed* about the room. —*v.t.* **4** To attack: to *storm* a fort. [< OE]

storm cellar An underground shelter adapted for use during cyclones, hurricanes, etc.

storm door An additional outer door used to conserve heat during cold weather.

storm petrel Any of certain petrels thought to portend storm.

storm troops A Nazi party militia unit, the *Sturmabteilung,* established in 1924. —**storm trooper**

storm window An extra window outside the ordinary one for greater insulation against cold.

storm·y (stôr′mē) *adj.* **storm·i·er, storm·i·est 1** Characterized by storms; turbulent. **2** Violent; rough. —**storm′i·ly** *adv.* —**storm′i·ness** *n.* —**Syn. 1** blustery, tempestuous. **2** disturbed, passionate, vehement.

stormy petrel 1 STORM PETREL. **2** A person thought to portend or foment trouble.

sto·ry¹ (stôr′ē, stōr′ē) *n. pl.* **·ries 1** A narrative or recital of an event, or a series of events. **2** A narrative intended to entertain a reader or hearer. **3** An account of the facts relating to a particular person, thing, or incident. **4** A news article in a newspaper or magazine. **5** The material for a news article. **6** An anecdote. **7** *Informal* A lie; falsehood. **8** The series of events in a novel, play, etc. —*v.t.* **·ried, ·ry·ing 1** *Archaic* To relate as a story. **2** To adorn with designs representing scenes from history, legend, etc. [< L *historia*]

sto·ry² (stôr′ē, stōr′ē) *n. pl.* **·ries 1** A division in a building comprising the space between two successive floors. **2** All the rooms on one level of a building. [< Med. L *historia* story (painted on a row of windows)]

sto·ry·tell·er (stôr′ē·tel′ər, stōr′ē-) *n.* **1** One who relates stories or anecdotes. **2** *Informal* A prevaricator; fibber. —**sto′ry·tell′ing** *n., adj.*

stoup (stōōp) *n.* **1** *Eccl.* A basin for holy water at the entrance of a church. **2** A flagon, tankard, or large drinking glass. [< ON *staup* bucket]

stout (stout) *adj.* **1** Fat; thick-set. **2** Firmly built; strong: a *stout* fence. **3** Courageous: a *stout* heart. **4** Stubborn; unyielding: a *stout* denial. —*n.* **1** A stout person. **2** *Usu. pl.* Clothing made for stout or big people. **3** A strong, very dark porter or ale. [< OF *estout* bold, strong] —**stout′ly** *adv.* —**stout′ness** *n.*

stout·heart·ed (stout′här′tid) *adj.* Brave; courageous. —**stout′heart′ed·ly** *adv.* —**stout′heart′ed·ness** *n.*

stove¹ (stōv) *n.* An apparatus, usu. of metal, in which fuel is consumed for heating or cooking. [< OE *stofa* a heated room]

stove² (stōv) A *p.t. & p.p.* of STAVE.

stove·pipe (stōv′pīp′) *n.* **1** A pipe for conducting the smoke from a stove to a chimney flue. **2** *Informal* A tall silk hat: also **stovepipe hat.**

stow (stō) *v.t.* **1** To place or arrange compactly; pack. **2** To fill by packing. —**stow away 1** To put in a place of safekeeping, hiding, etc. **2** To be a stowaway. [< OE *stōw* a place]

stow·age (stō′ij) *n.* **1** The act of stowing. **2** Space for stowing goods. **3** Charge for stowing goods. **4** The goods stowed.

stow·a·way (stō′ə·wā′) *n.* One who conceals himself on a ship, train, airplane, etc., to obtain free passage, to escape, or to cross a border illegally.

STP (es′tē′pē′) *n.* A hallucinogenic drug chemically related to mescaline and amphetamine. [< STP, a trade name for a gasoline additive supposed to increase engine power.]

STP standard temperature and pressure.

str. steamer; strait; string(s).

stra·bis·mus (strə·biz′məs) *n.* Inability to focus the eyes simultaneously on the same spot because of a disorder of the eye muscles. [< Gk. *strabizein* to squint] —**stra·bis′mal, stra·bis′mic** or **·mi·cal** *adj.*

strad·dle (strad′l) *v.* **·dled, ·dling** *v.i.* **1** To stand, walk, or sit with the legs spread apart. **2** To be spread wide apart: said of the legs. **3** *Informal* To appear to favor both sides of an issue. —*v.t.* **4** To stand, walk, or sit with the legs on either side of. **5** To spread (the legs) wide apart. **6** *Informal* To appear to favor both sides of (an issue). —*n.* **1** The act

of straddling. **2** The distance between the legs in straddling. **3** *Informal* A noncommittal position on an issue. [Freq. of STRIDE] —**strad′dler** *n.* —**strad′dling·ly** *adv.*

Strad·i·var·i·us (strad′i·vâr′ē·əs) *n.* One of the violins, cellos, etc., made by Antonio Stradivari (1644–1737), Italian violin maker.

strafe (strāf, sträf) *v.t.* **strafed, straf·ing 1** To attack (troops, emplacements, etc.) with machine-gun fire from low-flying airplanes. **2** To bombard or shell heavily. **3** *Slang* To punish. [< G *strafen* punish] —**straf′er** *n.*

strag·gle (strag′əl) *v.i.* **·gled, ·gling 1** To wander from the road, main body, etc.; stray. **2** To wander aimlessly about; ramble. **3** To occur at irregular intervals. [ME *straglen*] —**strag′gler** *n.* —**strag′gling·ly** *adv.* —**strag′gly** *adj.* (**·i·er, ·i·est**)

straight (strāt) *adj.* **1** Extending uniformly in the same direction without curve or bend. **2** Free from kinks; not curly, as hair. **3** Not stooped; erect. **4** Not deviating from truth, fairness, or honesty. **5** Free from obstruction; uninterrupted. **6** Correctly ordered or arranged. **7** Sold without discount for number or quantity taken. **8** *Informal* Accepting the whole, as of a plan, party, or policy: a *straight* ticket. **9** In poker, consisting of five cards forming a sequence. **10** Having nothing added: *straight* whiskey. **11** *Slang* Conforming to what is accepted as usual, normal, or conventional, esp. according to middle-class standards. **12** *Slang* HETEROSEXUAL. —*n.* **1** A straight part or piece. **2** The part of a racecourse between the winning post and the last turn. **3** In poker, a numerical sequence of five cards. **4** *Slang* A conventional person. **5** *Slang* HETEROSEXUAL. —*adv.* **1** In a straight line or a direct course. **2** Closely in line; correspondingly. **3** At once: Go *straight* to bed. **4** Uprightly: to live *straight*. **5** Correctly: I can't think *straight*. **6** Without restriction or qualification: Tell it *straight*. —**go straight** To reform after having led the life of a criminal. —**straight away** or **off** At once; right away. [< OE *streht*, pp. of *streccan* stretch] —**straight′ness** *n.*

straight angle An angle of 180°.

straight·a·way (strāt′ə·wā′) *adj.* Having no curve or turn. —*n.* A straight course or track. —*adv.* At once; straightway.

straight·en (strāt′n) *v.t.* **1** To make straight. —*v.i.* **2** To become straight. —**straighten out** To restore order to; rectify. —**straighten up 1** To make neat; tidy. **2** To stand in erect posture. **3** To reform. —**straight′en·er** *n.*

straight face A sober, expressionless, or unsmiling face. —**straight-faced** (strāt′fāst′) *adj.*

straight·for·ward (strāt′fôr′wərd) *adj.* **1** Candid; honest. **2** Proceeding in a straight course. —*adv.* In a straight course or direct manner: also **straight′for′wards** (-wərdz). —**straight′for′ward·ly** *adv.* —**straight′for′ward·ness** *n.* —**Syn. 1** aboveboard, frank, open, sincere. **2** direct.

straight man *Informal* An entertainer who acts as a foil for a comedian.

straight-out (strāt′out′) *adj. Informal* **1** Unreserved; unrestrained. **2** Thorough; complete.

straight·way (strāt′wā′) *adv.* Immediately.

strain[1] (strān) *v.t.* **1** To pull or draw tight. **2** To exert to the utmost. **3** To injure by overexertion; sprain. **4** To deform in structure or shape as a result of stress. **5** To stretch beyond the true intent, proper limit, etc.: to *strain* a point. **6** To embrace tightly; hug. **7** To pass through a strainer. **8** To remove by filtration. —*v.i.* **9** To make violent efforts; strive. **10** To be or become wrenched or twisted. **13** To filter, trickle, or percolate. —**strain at 1** To push or pull with violent efforts. **2** To strive for. **3** To scruple or balk at accepting. —*n.* **1** An act of straining or the state of being strained. **2** Any very taxing demand on strength, emotions, etc.: the *strain* of city life. **3** Any violent effort or exertion. **4** The injury resulting from excessive tension or effort. **5** *Physics* The change of shape or structure of a body produced by the action of a stress. [< L *stringere* bind tight]

strain[2] (strān) *n.* **1** Line of descent, or the individuals, collectively, in that line. **2** Inborn or hereditary disposition; natural tendency. **3** A line of plants or animals selectively bred to perpetuate distinctive traits. **4** *Often pl.* A

melody; tune. **5** Prevailing tone, style, or manner. [< OE *strēon* offspring]

strain·er (strā′nər) *n.* A utensil or device that filters, strains, or sifts.

strait (strāt) *n.* **1** *Often pl.* A narrow passage of water connecting two larger bodies of water. **2** Any narrow pass or passage. **3** *Often pl.* Distress; embarrassment: financial *straits*. —*adj. Archaic* **1** Narrow. **2** Strict. [< L *strictus*, p.p. of *stringere* bind tight.] —**strait′ly** *adv.* —**strait′ness** *n.*

strait·en (strāt′n) *v.t.* **1** To make strait or narrow; restrict. **2** To embarrass, or restrict, as in finances.

strait·jack·et (strāt′jak′it) *n.* **1** A jacket with long, closed sleeves for confining the arms of a violent patient or prisoner. **2** Anything that unduly confines or restricts. —*v.t.* To confine in or as if in a straitjacket.

strait-laced (strāt′lāst′) *adj.* **1** Formerly, tightly laced, as corsets. **2** Strict, esp. in morals or manners; prudish.

strand[1] (strand) *n.* A shore or beach, esp. on the ocean. —*v.t. & v.i.* **1** To drive or run aground, as a ship. **2** To leave or be left in difficulties or helplessness: *stranded* in a strange city. [< OE]

strand[2] (strand) *n.* **1** Any of the fibers, wires, or threads twisted or plaited together to form a rope, cable, cord, etc. **2** A single hair or similar filament. **3** Any of various rope-like objects: a *strand* of pearls. —*v.t.* To break a strand of (a rope). [ME *strond*]

strange (strānj) *adj.* **strang·er, strang·est 1** Previously unknown, unseen, or unheard of. **2** Peculiar; out of the ordinary: a *strange* experience. **3** Foreign; alien. **4** Out of place: to feel *strange* in a new school. **5** Inexperienced: *strange* to a new job. [< L *extraneus* foreign] —**strange′ly** *adv.* —**strange′ness** *n.* —**Syn. 1** unfamiliar. **2** odd, queer, unusual. **4** unaccustomed.

stran·ger (strān′jər) *n.* **1** One who is not an acquaintance. **2** An unfamiliar visitor; guest. **3** A foreigner. **4** One unacquainted with something specified: with *to*: a *stranger* to higher mathematics.

stran·gle (strang′gəl) *v.* **·gled, ·gling** *v.t.* **1** To choke to death; throttle. **2** To repress; suppress. —*v.i.* **3** To suffer or die from strangulation. [< Gk. *strangalaein*] —**stran′gler** *n.*

stran·gle·hold (strang′gəl·hōld′) *n.* **1** In wrestling, an illegal hold which chokes one's opponent. **2** Anything that chokes freedom or progress.

stran·gu·late (strang′gyə·lāt) *v.t.* **·lat·ed, ·lat·ing 1** STRANGLE. **2** *Pathol.* To constrict so as to cut off circulation of the blood. [< L *strangulare*] —**stran′gu·la′tion** *n.*

strap (strap) *n.* **1** A long, narrow, and flexible strip of leather, webbing, etc., for binding or fastening things together. **2** A razor strop. **3** Something used as a strap: a shoulder *strap*. —*v.t.* **strapped, strap·ing 1** To fasten or bind with a strap. **2** To beat with a strap. **3** To sharpen or strop. **4** To embarrass financially. [Var. of STROP]

strap·hang·er (strap′hang′ər) *n. Informal* A standing passenger on a bus or train who keeps his balance by holding on to a strap, bar, etc.

strap·ping (strap′ing) *adj. Informal* Large and muscular; robust.

stra·ta (strā′tə, strat′ə) *n.pl.* of STRATUM.

strat·a·gem (strat′ə·jəm) *n.* **1** A maneuver designed to deceive or outwit an enemy. **2** Any device or trick for obtaining advantage. [< Gk. *stratēgēma* piece of generalship] —**Syn. 2** artifice, deception, ruse, trick.

stra·te·gic (strə·tē′jik) *adj.* **1** Of or based on strategy. **2** Important in strategy. **3** Having to do with materials essential for conducting a war. **4** Assigned to destroy important enemy installations: a *strategic* air force. Also **stra·te′gi·cal.** —**stra·te′gi·cal·ly** *adv.*

strat·e·gist (strat′ə·jist) *n.* One skilled in strategy.

strat·e·gy (strat′ə·jē) *n. pl.* **·gies 1** The science of planning and conducting military campaigns on a broad scale. **2** Any plan based on this. **3** The use of stratagem or artifice, as in business, politics, etc. **4** Skill in management. **5** An ingenious plan or method. [< Gk. *stratēgos* general]

strat·i·fy (strat′ə·fī) *v.* **·fied, ·fy·ing** *v.t.* **1** To form or arrange in strata or layers. —*v.i.* **2** To form in strata. **3** To

be formed in strata. [< L *stratum* layer + -FY] —**strat′i·fi·ca′tion** *n.*

stra·to·cu·mu·lus (strāt′ō-kyōō′myə-ləs, strat′-) *n. pl.* **·li** (-lī) *Meteorol.* A type of dark, low-lying cloud, characterized by horizontal bases and high, rounded summits.

strat·o·sphere (strat′ə-sfir) *n. Meteorol.* The portion of the atmosphere beginning at about six miles above the earth, where a more or less uniform temperature prevails. —**strat′o·spher′ic** (-sfer′ik) or **·i·cal** *adj.*

stra·tum (strā′təm, strat′əm) *n. pl.* **·ta** (-tə) or **·tums** 1 A natural or artificial layer. 2 *Geol.* A more or less homogeneous layer of rock. 3 A level of society, having similar educational, cultural, and usu. economic backgrounds. [< L *stratus,* p.p. of *sternere* to spread]

Rock strata

stra·tus (strā′təs, strat′əs) *n. pl.* **·ti** (-tī) *Meteorol.* A low-lying, foglike cloud. [L, orig. p.p. of *sternere* to spread]

straw (strô) *n.* 1 A dry stalk of grain. 2 Stems or stalks of grain after being threshed, used for fodder, etc. 3 A mere trifle. 4 A slender tube made of paper, glass, etc., used to suck up a beverage. —**catch** (or **grab**) **at a straw** To try anything as a last resort. —**straw in the wind** A sign of the course of future events. —*adj.* 1 Made of or like straw, as in color. 2 Worthless; sham. [< OE *strēaw* straw]

straw·ber·ry (strô′ber′ē, -bər·ē) *n. pl.* **·ries** 1 Any of a genus of stemless perennials of the rose family, with trifoliolate leaves, usu. white flowers and slender runners by which it propagates: also **strawberry vine.** 2 Its edible fruit, consisting of a red, fleshy receptacle bearing many achenes. [< STRAW + BERRY]

strawberry blond A person having reddish blond hair.

straw boss *Informal* A worker acting as an assistant foreman.

straw vote An unofficial test vote.

stray (strā) *v.i.* 1 To wander from the proper course; roam. 2 To deviate from right or goodness; go astray. —*adj.* 1 Having strayed; straying: a *stray* dog. 2 Irregular; occasional: He made a few *stray* remarks. —*n.* A domestic animal that has strayed. [< L *extra vagare* wander outside] —**stray′er** *n.*

streak (strēk) *n.* 1 A long, narrow mark or stripe: a *streak* of lightning. 2 A trace or characteristic: a *streak* of meanness. 3 A layer or strip: meat with a *streak* of fat and a *streak* of lean. 4 *Informal* A period or interval: a winning *streak.* 5 *Slang* The act or an instance of streaking (*v.* def. 3). —**like a streak** *Informal* As rapidly as possible. —*v.i.* 1 To form a streak or streaks. 2 To move at great speed. 3 *Slang* To appear naked in a public place, usu. briefly and esp. while running, as for a thrill. —*v.t.* 4 To form streaks in or on. 5 *Slang* To appear naked in (a public place), usu. briefly and esp. while running, as for a thrill. [< OE *strica*] —**streak′y** *adj.* (**·i·er, ·i·est**) —**streak′i·ly** *adv.* —**streak′er, streak′i·ness** *n.*

stream (strēm) *n.* 1 A current or flow of water, esp. a small river. 2 Any continuous flow or current: a *stream* of invective. —*v.i.* 1 To pour forth or issue in a stream. 2 To pour forth in a stream: eyes *streaming* with tears. 3 To proceed uninterruptedly, as a crowd. 4 To float with a waving movement, as a flag. 5 To move with a trail of light, as a meteor. 6 To come or arrive in large numbers. [< OE *strēam*] —**Syn.** *n.* 1 brook, course, creek, rill, rivulet.

stream·er (strē′mər) *n.* 1 An object that streams forth, or hangs extended. 2 A long, narrow flag or standard. 3 A stream or shaft of light. 4 A newspaper headline that runs across the whole page.

stream·let (strēm′lit) *n.* RIVULET.

stream·line (strēm′līn′) *n.* 1 A line in a mass of fluid such that each of its tangents coincides with the local velocity of the fluid. 2 Any shape or contour designed to lessen resistance to motion of a solid in a fluid. —*adj.* 1 Designating an uninterrupted flow or drift. 2 Denoting a

form or body designed to minimize turbulence in the flow of fluid around it. —*v.t.* **·lined, ·lin·ing** 1 To design with a streamline shape. 2 To make more up-to-date, esp. by reorganization.

stream·lined (strēm′līnd′) *adj.* 1 STREAMLINE. 2 Improved in efficiency; modernized.

street (strēt) *n.* 1 A public way in a city, town, or village, usu. with buildings on one or both sides. 2 Such a public way as set apart for vehicles: Don't play in the *street.* 3 *Informal* The people living on a specific street. —*adj.* 1 Working in the streets: a *street* musician. 2 Opening onto the street: a *street* door. 3 Performed or taking place on the street: *street* crime. 4 Habituated to the ways of life in the streets, esp. in cities: *street* people. [< LL *strata (via)* paved (road)]

street Arab A homeless or outcast child who lives in the streets; gamin.

street·car (strēt′kär′) *n.* A passenger car that runs on rails laid on the surface of the streets.

street people Young people, esp. of the late 1960s, usu. without a permanent residence and having a life style marked by the rejection of middle-class values and by the use of drugs.

street·walk·er (strēt′wô′kər) *n.* A prostitute who solicits in the streets. —**street′walk′ing** *n.*

strength (strength) *n.* 1 The quality or property of being physically strong: the *strength* of a weight lifter. 2 The capacity to sustain the application of force without yielding or breaking. 3 Effectiveness: the *strength* of an argument. 4 Binding force or validity, as of a law. 5 Vigor or force of style: a drama of great *strength.* 6 Available numerical force in a military unit or other organization. 7 Degree of intensity, as of color, light, or sound. 8 Potency, as of a drug, chemical, or liquor; concentration. 9 A support; aid: He is our *strength.* —**on the strength of** Relying on; on the basis of. [< OE *strang* strong] —**Syn.** 1 force, power, vigor. 2 solidity, tenacity, toughness.

strength·en (streng′thən) *v.t.* 1 To make strong. 2 To encourage; hearten. —*v.i.* 3 To become or grow strong or stronger. —**strength′en·er** *n.*

stren·u·ous (stren′yōō-əs) *adj.* Necessitating or marked by strong effort or exertion. [< L *strenuus*] —**stren′u·ous·ly** *adv.* —**stren′u·ous·ness** *n.*

strep throat (strep) A streptococcal throat infection.

strep·to·coc·cus (strep′tə-kok′əs) *n. pl.* **·coc·ci** (-kok′sī, -sē, -ī, -ē) Any of a large group of spherical bacteria that grow together in long chains, including a few pathogens. [< Gk. *streptos* twisted + COCCUS] —**strep′to·coc′cal** (-kok′əl), **strep′to·coc′cic** (-kok′sik, -kok′ik) *adj.*

strep·to·my·cin (strep′tō-mī′sin) *n.* A potent antibiotic isolated from a mold. [< Gk. *streptos* twisted + *mykēs* fungus]

stress (stres) *n.* 1 Special weight, importance, or significance. 2 Physical or emotional tension. 3 *Mech.* A force tending to deform a body on which it acts. 4 Emphasis. 5 In pronunciation, the relative force with which a sound, syllable, or word is uttered. —*v.t.* 1 To subject to stress. 2 To accent, as a syllable. 3 To give emphasis or weight to. [< L *strictus,* p.p. of *stringere* draw tight] —**stress′ful** *adj.*

-stress *suffix of nouns* Feminine form of -STER: *songstress.*

stretch (strech) *v.t.* 1 To extend or draw out, as to full length or width. 2 To draw out forcibly, esp. beyond normal or proper limits. 3 To cause to reach, as from one place to another. 4 To put forth, hold out, or extend (the hand, an object, etc.). 5 To tighten, strain, or exert to the utmost: to *stretch* every nerve. 6 To adjust or adapt to meet specific needs, circumstances, etc.: to *stretch* the truth; to *stretch* food. 7 *Slang* To fell with a blow. —*v.i.* 8 To reach or extend from one place to another. 9 To become extended, esp. beyond normal limits. 10 To extend one's body or limbs, as in relaxing. 11 To lie down: usu. with *out.* —*n.* 1 An act of stretching, or the state of being stretched. 2 Extent to which something can be stretched. 3 A continuous extent of space or time: a *stretch* of woodland; a *stretch* of two years. 4 In racing, the straight part of the track. 5 *Slang* A term of imprisonment. —*adj.* Capable of being easily stretched, as clothing: *stretch* socks. [< OE *streccan* stretch] —**stretch′i·ness** *n.* —**stretch′y** *adj.*

stretch·er (strech′ər) *n.* 1 Any device for stretching: a

shoe *stretcher.* 2 A portable, often webbed frame for carrying the injured, sick, or dead.

stretch-out (strech′out′) *n. Informal* A system of industrial operation in which employees are required to perform more work per unit of time worked, usu. without increase in pay.

strew (strōō) *v.t.* **strewed, strewed** or **strewn, strew·ing** 1 To spread about at random; sprinkle. 2 To cover with something scattered or sprinkled. 3 To be scattered over (a surface). [< OE *strēawian*]

stri·at·ed (strī′ā·tid) *adj.* Striped, grooved, or banded: *striated* muscle. [< L *striatus*, p.p. of *striare* to groove] — **stri′a·tion** *n.*

strick·en (strik′ən) *adj.* 1 Struck down by injury, disease, calamity, remorse, etc. 2 Advanced or far gone, as in age: *stricken* in years. [< OE *stricen*, p.p. of *strican* to strike]

strict (strikt) *adj.* 1 Observing or enforcing rules exactly: a *strict* church. 2 Containing severe rules or provisions; exacting. 3 Harsh; stern: a *strict* teacher. 4 Exactly defined or applied: the *strict* truth. 5 Devout; orthodox: a *strict* Catholic. 6 Absolute: in *strict* confidence. [< L *strictus*, p.p. of *stringere* draw tight] —**strict′ly** *adv.* —**strict′·ness** *n.*

stric·ture (strik′chər) *n.* 1 Severe criticism. 2 Something that checks or restricts. 3 Closure or narrowing of a duct or passage of the body. [< L *strictus* strict]

stride (strīd) *n.* 1 A long and measured step. 2 The space passed over by such a step. —**hit one's stride** To attain one's normal speed. —**make rapid strides** To make quick progress. —**take (something) in one's stride** To do or accept (something) without undue effort or without becoming upset. —*v.* **strode, strid·den, strid·ing** *v.i.* 1 To walk with long steps, as from haste. —*v.t.* 2 To walk through, along, etc., with long steps. 3 To pass over with a single stride. 4 To straddle; bestride. [< OE *strīdan* to stride] —**strid′er** *n.*

stri·dent (strīd′nt) *adj.* Having a loud and harsh sound; grating. [< L *stridere* to creak] —**stri′dence, stri′den·cy** *n.* —**stri′dent·ly** *adv.*

strid·u·late (strij′ōō·lāt) *v.i.* **·lat·ed, ·lat·ing** To make a chirping, nonvocal noise, as a cricket, etc. [< L *stridere* to rattle, rasp] —**strid′u·la′tion** *n.* —**strid′u·la·to′ry** (-lə·tôr′ē, -tō′rē) *adj.* —**strid′u·lous** *adj.*

strife (strīf) *n.* 1 Angry contention; fighting. 2 Any contest or rivalry. 3 The act of striving; strenuous endeavor. [< OF *estriver* strive]

strike (strīk) *v.* **struck, struck** (*chiefly Archaic* **strick·en**), **strik·ing** *v.t.* 1 To hit with a blow; deal a blow to. 2 To crash into: The car *struck* the wall. 3 To deal (a blow, etc.). 4 To cause to hit forcibly: He *struck* his hand on the table. 5 To attack; assault. 6 To ignite (a match, etc.) 7 To form by stamping, printing, etc. 8 To announce; sound: The clock *struck* two. 9 To reach: A sound *struck* his ear. 10 To affect suddenly or in a specified manner: He was *struck* speechless. 11 To occur to: An idea *strikes* me. 12 To impress in a specified manner. 13 To attract the attention of: The dress *struck* her fancy. 14 To assume: to *strike* an attitude. 15 To cause to enter deeply or suddenly: to *strike* dismay into one's heart. 16 To lower or haul down, as a sail or a flag. 17 To cease working in order to compel compliance to a demand, etc. 18 To make and confirm, as a bargain. —*v.i.* 19 To come into violent contact; crash; hit. 20 To deal or aim a blow or blows. 21 To make an assault or attack. 22 To sound from a blow or blows. 23 To be indicated by the sound of blows or strokes: Noon has just *struck.* 24 To ignite. 25 To lower a flag in token of surrender. 26 To take a course; start and proceed: to *strike* for home. 27 To cease work in order to enforce demands, etc. 28 To snatch at or swallow the lure: said of fish. —**strike camp** To take down the tents of a camp. —**strike down** 1 To fell with a blow. 2 To incapacitate completely. — **strike dumb** To astonish; amaze. —**strike home** 1 To deal an effective blow. 2 To have telling effect. —**strike it rich** 1 To find a valuable pocket of ore. 2 To come into wealth or good fortune. —**strike off** 1 To remove or take off by or as by a blow or stroke. 2 To deduct. —**strike oil**

1 To find oil while drilling. 2 *Slang* To meet with unexpected good fortune. —**strike out** 1 To aim a blow or blows. 2 To cross out or erase. 3 To begin; start. 4 In baseball, to put out (the batter) by pitching three strikes. —**strike up** 1 To begin to play, as a band. 2 To start up; begin, as a friendship. —*n.* 1 An act of striking. 2 In baseball, an unsuccessful attempt by the batter to hit the ball. 3 In bowling, the knocking down of all the pins with the first bowl. 4 The quitting of work by a body of workers to secure some demand from management. 5 A new discovery, as of oil or ore. 6 Any unexpected or complete success. 7 The sudden rise and taking of the bait by a fish. —**on strike** Refusing to work in order to secure higher pay, better working conditions, etc. [< OE *strican* stroke, move]

strike·break·er (strīk′brā′kər) *n.* One who takes the place of a worker on strike or who seeks to intimidate or replace the strikers with other workers. —**strike′break′ing** *n.*

strik·er (strī′kər) *n.* 1 One who or that which strikes. 2 An employee who is on strike.

strik·ing (strī′king) *adj.* 1 Notable; impressive: a *striking* girl. 2 On strike. 3 That strikes: a *striking* clock. —**strik′ing·ly** *adv.* —**strik′ing·ness** *n.*

string (string) *n.* 1 A slender line, thinner than a cord and thicker than a thread, used for tying parcels, lacing, etc. 2 A cord of catgut, nylon, wire, etc., for musical instruments, bows, tennis rackets, etc. 3 A stringlike formation, as of certain vegetables. 4 A series of things hung on a small cord: a *string* of pearls. 5 A connected series or succession, as of things, acts, or events. 6 A drove or small collection of stock, esp. of saddle horses. 7 *pl.* Stringed instruments, esp., the section of violins, cellos, etc., in a symphony orchestra. 8 In sports, a group of contestants ranked as to skill. 9 *Informal Often pl.* A condition or restriction attached to an offer or gift. —**on a string** Under control or domination. —**pull strings** 1 To control the actions of others, usu. secretly. 2 To influence others to gain an advantage. —*v.* **strung, string·ing** *v.t.* 1 To thread, as beads, on or as on a string. 2 To fit with a string or strings, as a guitar or bow. 3 To bind, fasten, or adorn with a string or strings. 4 To tune the strings of (a musical instrument). 5 To brace; strengthen. 6 To make tense or nervous. 7 To arrange or extend like a string. 8 To remove the strings from (vegetables). —*v.i.* 9 To extend or proceed in a line or series. 10 To form into strings. —**string along** *Slang* 1 To cooperate with. 2 To deceive; cheat. 3 To keep (someone) on tenterhooks. —**string out** *Informal* To protract; prolong: to *string out* an investigation. —**string up** *Informal* To hang. [< OE *streng* string]

string bean 1 The unripe edible seed pod of several varieties of bean. 2 The plants bearing these pods. 3 *Informal* A tall, skinny person.

stringed instrument (stringd) A musical instrument provided with strings or wires, as a violin, guitar, etc.

strin·gent (strin′jənt) *adj.* 1 Rigid; severe, as regulations. 2 Hampered by scarcity of money: said of a market. 3 Convincing; forcible. [< L *stringens*, pr.p of *stringere* draw tight] —**strin′gen·cy, strin′gent·ness** *n.* —**strin′gent·ly** *adv.*

string·er (string′ər) *n.* 1 One who strings. 2 A heavy timber supporting other members of a structure. 3 A newsman employed on a free-lance basis, often in out-of-town or foreign locations. 4 A person having a specific rating as to excellence, skill, etc.: used in combination: a *second-stringer.*

string·halt (string′hôlt′) *n.* In horses, lameness marked by spasmodic movement of the hind legs.

string·y (string′ē) *adj.* **string·i·er, string·i·est** 1 Of or like a string or strings: *stringy* hair. 2 Containing fibrous strings. 3 Forming in strings, as thick glue; ropy. 4 Tall and wiry in build. —**string′i·ly** *adv.* —**string′i·ness** *n.*

strip[1] (strip) *n.* 1 A narrow piece, comparatively long, as of cloth, wood, etc. 2 A number of stamps attached in a row. 3 A narrow piece of land used as a runway for airplanes. 4 A comic strip. [?]

strip[2] (strip) *v.* **stripped** or **stript, strip·ping** *v.t.* 1 To pull the

covering, clothing, leaves, etc., from; lay bare. **2** To pull off (the covering, etc.). **3** To rob or plunder; spoil. **4** To make bare or empty. **5** To take away. **6** To deprive of something; divest. **7** To damage the teeth, thread, etc., of (a gear, bolt, etc.). —*v.i.* **8** To undress. [< OE *bestrȳpan* plunder]

stripe[1] (strīp) *n.* **1** A line, band, or long strip of material differing in color or finish from its adjacent surfaces. **2** Distinctive quality or character: a man of artistic *stripe*. **3** Striped cloth. **4** *pl.* Prison uniform. **5** A piece of material or braid on a uniform to indicate rank. —*v.t.* **striped, strip·ing** To mark with a stripe or stripes. [< MDu.]

stripe[2] (strīp) *n.* **1** A blow struck with a whip or rod. **2** A weal or welt on the skin caused by such a blow. [Prob. < LG]

strip·ling (strip′ling) *n.* A mere youth; a lad. [?]

strip mine A mine, esp. a coal mine, the seams of which are close to the surface of the earth and which is worked by stripping away the topsoil and the material beneath it. —**strip′·mine**′ *v.t.* (**-mined, -min·ing**) —**strip miner**

strip·per (strip′ər) *n.* **1** One who or that which strips. **2** *Slang* A female performer of a striptease.

strip·tease (strip′tēz′) *n.* An act, usu. in burlesque, in which a female performer gradually disrobes before an audience. —**strip′teas′er** *n.*

strive (strīv) *v.i.* **strove, striv·en** (striv′ən) or **strived, striv·ing** **1** To make earnest effort. **2** To engage in strife; fight: to *strive* against an enemy. [< OF *estriver*] —**striv′er** *n.* — **Syn. 1** endeavor, try. **2** contend, struggle.

strobe (strōb) *n.* **1** STROBOSCOPE. **2** An electronically controlled device that emits light in very brief, brilliant flashes, used in photography, in the theater, etc.: also **strobe light.**

strob·o·scope (strōb′ə·skōp) *n.* An instrument for studying the motion of an object by making the object appear to be stationary, as by periodic instantaneous illumination or observation. [< Gk. *strobos* twirling + -SCOPE] —**strob′o·scop′ic** (-skop′ik) or **·i·cal** *adj.* —**strob·os·co·py** (strō·bos′kə·pē) *n.*

strode (strōd) *p.t.* of STRIDE.

stroke (strōk) *n.* **1** The act or movement of striking. **2** One of a series of recurring movements, as of oars, arms in swimming, a piston, etc. **3** A rower who sets the pace for the rest of the crew. **4** A single movement of a pen or pencil. **5** A mark made by such a movement. **6** Any ill effect: a *stroke* of misfortune. **7** APOPLEXY. **8** A sound of a striking mechanism, as of a clock. **9** A sudden or brilliant mental act: a *stroke* of wit. **10** A light caressing movement; a stroking. —**keep stroke** To make strokes simultaneously, as oarsmen. —*v.t.* **stroked, strok·ing** **1** To pass the hand over gently or caressingly. **2** To set the pace for (a rowboat or its crew). [< OE *strācian* strike] —**strok′er** *n.*

stroll (strōl) *v.i.* **1** To walk in a leisurely manner; saunter. **2** To go from place to place. —*n.* A leisurely walk. [?]

stroll·er (strō′lər) *n.* **1** A small, light baby carriage, often collapsible. **2** One who strolls. **3** An actor who travels from place to place to perform.

strong (strông, strong) *adj.* **1** Physically powerful; muscular. **2** Healthy; robust: a *strong* constitution. **3** Resolute; courageous. **4** Mentally powerful or vigorous. **5** Especially competent or able: *strong* in mathematics. **6** Abundantly supplied: *strong* in trumps. **7** Solidly made or constituted: *strong* walls. **8** Powerful, as a rival or combatant. **9** Easy to defend: a *strong* position. **10** In numerical force: an army 20,000 *strong*. **11** Well able to exert influence, authority, etc. **12** Financially sound: a *strong* market. **13** Powerful in effect: *strong* poison. **14** Not diluted or weak: *strong* coffee. **15** Containing much alcohol: a *strong* drink. **16** Powerful in flavor or odor: a *strong* breath. **17** Intense in degree or quality: a *strong* light. **18** Loud and firm: a *strong* voice. **19** Firm; tenacious: a *strong* will. **20** Fervid: a *strong* desire. **21** Cogent; convincing: *strong* evidence. **22** Distinct; marked: a *strong* resemblance. **23** Extreme: *strong* measures. **24** Emphatic: *strong* language. **25** Moving with great force: said of a wind, stream, or tide. **26** *Phonet.* Stressed. **27** *Gram.* Of verbs, indicating changes in tense by means of vowel changes, rather than by inflectional endings, as *drink, drank, drunk.* —*adv.* In a firm, vigorous manner. [< OE] —**strong′ly** *adv.* —**strong′ness** *n.*

strong-arm (strông′ärm′, strong′-) *Informal adj.* Using physical or coercive power: *strong-arm* tactics. —*v.t.* **1** To use physical force upon; assault. **2** To coerce; compel.

strong·box (strông′boks′, strong′-) *n.* A chest or safe for keeping valuables.

strong drink Alcoholic liquors.

strong·hold (strông′hōld′, strong′-) *n.* A strongly defended place; fortress.

strong·man (strông′man′, strong′-) *n. pl.* **·men** (-mən) A political leader having preeminent power, as from a military coup or other extralegal means.

strong-mind·ed (strông′mīn′did, strong′-) *adj.* **1** Having an active, vigorous mind. **2** Determined; resolute. — **strong′-mind′ed·ly** *adv.* —**strong′-mind′ed·ness** *n.*

strong-willed (strông′wild′, strong•-) *adj.* Having a strong will; obstinate.

stron·ti·um (stron′chē·əm, -chəm, -tē·əm) *n.* A metallic element (symbol Sr) chemically resembling calcium, used in pyrotechnics. [< *Strontian,* Argyll, Scotland, where first discovered] —**stron′tic** (-tik) *adj.*

strop (strop) *n.* A strip of leather on which to sharpen a razor. —*v.t.* **stropped, strop·ping** To sharpen on a strop. [< Gk. *strophos* band]

stro·phe (strō′fē), *n.* **1** In ancient Greece, the verses sung by the chorus in a play while moving from right to left. **2** A stanza of a poem. [< Gk. *strophē* a turning, twist] —**stroph·ic** (strof′ik, strō′fik) or **·i·cal** *adj.*

strove (strōv) *p.t.* of STRIVE.

struck (struk) *p.t. & p.p.* of STRIKE.

struc·tur·al (struk′chər·əl) *adj.* **1** Of, pertaining to, or characterized by structure. **2** Used in or essential to construction. —**struc′tur·al·ly** *adv.*

structural steel Rolled steel shaped and adapted for use in construction.

struc·ture (struk′chər) *n.* **1** That which is constructed, as a building. **2** Something based upon or organized according to a plan or design: the political *structure* of a republic. **3** The manner of such organization: a hierarchical *structure.* **4** The arrangement and relationship of the parts of a whole, as organs in a plant or animal, atoms in a molecule, etc. —*v.t.* **·tured, ·tur·ing** **1** To form or organize into a structure; build. **2** To conceive as a structural whole. [< L *structus,* p.p. of *struere* build]

stru·del (strōōd′l) *n.* A kind of pastry with a filling of fruit, nuts, etc. [G, lit., eddy]

strug·gle (strug′əl) *n.* **1** A violent effort or series of efforts. **2** A war; battle. —*v.i.* **·gled, ·gling** **1** To contend with an adversary in physical combat; fight. **2** To strive: to *struggle* against odds. **3** To make one's way by violent efforts: to *struggle* through mud. [ME *strogelen*] —**strug′· gler** *n.* —**strug′gling·ly** *adv.*

strum (strum) *v.t. & v.i.* **strummed, strum·ming** To play idly or carelessly (on a stringed instrument). —*n.* The act of strumming. [Prob. Imit.] —**strum′mer** *n.*

strum·pet (strum′pit) *n.* A whore; prostitute. [ME]

strung (strung) *p.t. & p.p.* of STRING.

strung out *Slang* **1** Sick or in weakened health from prolonged use of drugs. **2** Addicted to narcotics.

strut (strut) *n.* **1** A proud or pompous step or walk. **2** A supporting piece in a framework, keeping two others from approaching nearer together. —*v.* **strut·ted, strut·ting** *v.i.* **1** To walk pompously and affectedly. —*v.t.* **2** To brace or support with a brace or strut. [< OE *strūtian* be rigid, stand stiffly] —**strut′ter** *n.* —**strut′ting·ly** *adv.*

strych·nine (strik′nīn, -nən, -nēn) *n.* A poisonous alkaloid obtained from nux vomica, used in medicine as a stimulant. Also **strych′ni·a** (-nē·ə) [< Gk. *strychnos* nightshade] —**strych′nic** *adj.*

stub (stub) *n.* **1** Any short remnant, as of a pencil, candle, cigarette, cigar, or broken tooth. **2** In a checkbook, the short piece on which the amount of a check is recorded and that remains when the check is detached. **3** A tree stump. —*v.t.* **stubbed, stub·bing** **1** To strike, as the toe, against a low obstruction or projection. **2** To clear or remove the stubs or roots from. [< OE *stubb*] —**stub′ber** *n.*

stub·ble (stub′əl) *n.* **1** The stubs of plants covering a field after reaping. **2** The field itself. **3** Any surface or growth resembling stubble, as short bristly hair or beard. [< L *stipula* stalk] —**stub′bly** *adj.* (**·bli·er, ·bli·est**)

Strop

stub·born (stub′ərn) *adj.* **1** Inflexible in opinion or intention. **2** Determined to have one's own way. **3** Not easily handled, bent, or overcome. **4** Characterized by perseverance or persistence: *stubborn* fighting. [ME *stoborne*] — **stub′born·ly** *adv.* —**stub′born·ness** *n.* —**Syn.** **1** opinionated, unyielding. **2** headstrong, obdurate, obstinate.

stub·by (stub′ē) *adj.* **·bi·er**, **·bi·est** **1** Short, stiff, and bristling: a *stubby* beard. **2** Short and thick: a *stubby* pencil. **3** Short and thick-set: a *stubby* man. —**stub′bi·ly** *adv.* — **stub′bi·ness** *n.*

stuc·co (stuk′ō) *n. pl.* **·coes** or **·cos** **1** Any plaster or cement used for the external coating of buildings. **2** Work done in stucco: also **stuc′co·work.** —*v.t.* **·coed**, **·co·ing** To apply stucco to; decorate with stucco. [Ital.] —**stuc′co·er** *n.*

stuck (stuk) *p.t. & p.p.* of STICK.

stuck-up (stuk′up′) *adj. Informal* Conceited; very vain.

stud¹ (stud) *n.* **1** Any of a series of small knobs, round-headed nails, or small protuberant ornaments. **2** A small, removable button such as is used in a shirt front. **3** A post to which laths are nailed in a building frame. **4** STUD POKER. —*v.t.* **stud·ded**, **stud·ding** **1** To set thickly with small points, projections, or knobs. **2** To be scattered over: Daisies *stud* the meadows. **3** To support or stiffen by means of studs or upright props. [< OE *studu* post]

stud² (stud) *n.* **1** A collection of horses and mares for breeding, riding, hunting, or racing. **2** The place where they are kept. **3** A stallion. —**at stud** Available for breeding purposes: said of male animals. —*adj.* Of or pertaining to a stud. [< OE *stōd*]

stu·dent (st*y*ōōd′nt, -ənt) *n.* **1** A person engaged in a course of study, esp. in an educational institution. **2** One who closely examines or investigates. [< L *studere* be eager, apply oneself, study]

stud·horse (stud′hôrs′) *n.* A stallion kept for breeding. Also **stud horse.**

stud·ied (stud′ēd) *adj.* **1** Deliberately planned; premeditated: a *studied* insult. **2** Acquired or prepared by study. —**stud′ied·ly** *adv.* —**stud′ied·ness** *n.*

stu·di·o (st*y*ōō′dē·ō) *n. pl.* **·di·os** **1** The workroom of an artist, photographer, etc. **2** A place where motion pictures are filmed. **3** A room or rooms where radio or television programs are broadcast or recorded. **4** A room or place in which music is recorded. [< L *studere* apply oneself, be diligent]

stu·di·ous (st*y*ōō′dē·əs) *adj.* **1** Given to or fond of study. **2** Considerate; careful; attentive. —**stu′di·ous·ly** *adv.* — **stu′di·ous·ness** *n.*

stud poker A game of poker in which the cards of the first round are dealt face down and the rest face up.

stud·y (stud′ē) *v.* **stud·ied**, **stud·y·ing** *v.t.* **1** To acquire a knowledge of: to *study* physics. **2** To examine; search into: to *study* a problem. **3** To scrutinize: to *study* one's reflection. **4** To memorize, as a part in a play. —*v.i.* **5** To apply the mind in acquiring knowledge. **6** To be a student. — **study up on** To acquire more complete information concerning. —*n. pl.* **stud·ies** **1** The process of acquiring information. **2** A particular instance or form of mental work. **3** A branch or department of knowledge. **4** A specific product of studious application: his *study* of plankton. **5** An examination or consideration of a problem, proposal, etc. **6** In art, a first sketch. **7** A careful literary treatment of a subject. **8** A room set aside for study, reading, etc. **9** A thoughtful state of mind: a brown *study.* **10** *Music* A composition designed to develop technique; an étude. [< L *studium* zeal] —**Syn.** *v.* **1** grasp, learn. **2** investigate, ponder, analyze.

stuff (stuf) *v.t.* **1** To fill completely; pack. **2** To plug. **3** To obstruct or stop up. **4** To fill with padding, as a cushion. **5** To fill (a fowl, roast, etc.) with stuffing. **6** In taxidermy, to fill the skin of (a bird, animal, etc.) with a material preparatory to mounting. **7** To fill too full; cram: He *stuffed* himself with cake. **8** To fill with knowledge, ideas, or attitudes, esp. unsystematically. —*v.i.* **9** To eat to excess. —*n.* **1** The material or matter out of which something is or may be shaped or made. **2** The fundamental element of anything: the *stuff* of genius. **3** *Informal* A

specific skill, field of knowledge, etc.: That editor knows her *stuff.* **4** Personal possessions generally. **5** Unspecified material, matter, etc.: They carried away tons of the *stuff.* **6** A miscellaneous collection of things. **7** Nonsense; foolishness. **8** Woven material, esp. of wool. **9** Any textile fabric. [< OF *estoffer* cram] —**stuff′er** *n.*

stuffed shirt *Informal* A pretentious, pompous person.

stuff·ing (stuf′ing) *n.* **1** The material with which anything is stuffed. **2** A mixture, as of crumbs with seasoning, used in stuffing fowls, etc. **3** The process of stuffing anything.

stuff·y (stuf′ē) *adj.* **stuff·i·er**, **stuff·i·est** **1** Badly ventilated. **2** Filled up so as to impede respiration: a *stuffy* nose. **3** Dull; uninspired: a *stuffy* speech. **4** Strait-laced; stodgy. — **stuff′i·ly** *adv.* —**stuff′i·ness** *n.*

stul·ti·fy (stul′tə·fī′) *v.t.* **·fied**, **·fy·ing** **1** To cause to appear absurd. **2** To make useless or futile. [< L *stultus* foolish + -FY] —**stul′ti·fi·ca′tion, stul′ti·fi′er** *n.*

stum·ble (stum′bəl) *v.* **·bled**, **·bling** *v.i.* **1** To miss one's step in walking or running; trip. **2** To speak or act in a blundering manner: The student *stumbled* through his recitation. **3** To happen upon something by chance: with *across*, *on*, *upon*, etc. **4** To do wrong; err. —*v.t.* **5** To cause to stumble. —*n.* The act of stumbling. [ME *stumblen*] —**stum′bler** *n.* — **stum′bling·ly** *adv.*

stum·bling-block (stum′bling-blok′) *n.* Any obstacle or hindrance.

stump (stump) *n.* **1** That portion of the trunk of a tree left standing when the tree is felled. **2** The part of a limb, etc., that remains when the main part has been removed. **3** *pl. Informal* The legs. **4** A place or platform where a political speech is made. **5** A short, thick-set person or animal. **6** A heavy step; a clump. —**take the stump** To electioneer in a political campaign. —**up a stump** In trouble or in a dilemma. —*adj.* **1** Being or resembling a stump. **2** Of or pertaining to political oratory or campaigning: a *stump* speaker. —*v.t.* **1** To reduce to a stump; lop. **2** To remove stumps from (land). **3** To canvass (a district) by making political speeches. **4** *Informal* To bring to a halt by real or fancied obstacles. **5** To stub, as one's toe. —*v.i.* **6** To walk heavily. [< MLG] —**stump′i·ness** *n.* —**stump′y** *adj.*

stun (stun) *v.t.* **stunned**, **stun·ning** **1** To render unconscious or incapable of action. **2** To astonish; astound. **3** To daze or overwhelm. —*n.* The act of stunning or the condition of being stunned. [< OF *estoner*]

stung (stung) *p.t. & p.p.* of STING.

stunk (stungk) *p.p.* and alternative *p.t.* of STINK.

stun·ner (stun′ər) *n.* **1** A person or blow that stuns. **2** *Slang* A person or thing of extraordinary qualities, such as beauty.

stun·ning (stun′ing) *adj.* **1** That stuns or astounds. **2** *Informal* Surprising; impressive; beautiful. —**stun′ning·ly** *adv.*

stunt¹ (stunt) *v.t.* To check the natural development of; dwarf; cramp. —*n.* **1** A check in growth, progress, or development. **2** A stunted animal or person. [< OE, dull, foolish] —**stunt′ed·ness** *n.*

stunt² (stunt) *Informal n.* **1** A sensational feat, as of bodily skill. **2** Any remarkable feat. —*v.i.* **1** To perform a stunt or stunts. —*v.t.* **2** To perform stunts with (an airplane, etc.). [?]

stunt man In motion pictures, a person employed to substitute for an actor when dangerous jumps, falls, etc., must be made.

stu·pe·fac·tion (st*y*ōō′pə·fak′shən) *n.* The act of stupefying or state of being stupefied.

stu·pe·fy (st*y*ōō′pə·fī′) *v.t.* **·fied**, **·fy·ing** **1** To dull the senses or faculties of; stun. **2** To amaze; astound. [< L *stupere* be stunned + -FY] —**stu′pe·fi′er** *n.*

stu·pen·dous (st*y*ōō·pen′dəs) *adj.* **1** Of prodigious size, bulk, or degree. **2** Astonishing; marvelous. [< L *stupere* be stunned] —**stu·pen′dous·ly** *adv.* —**stu·pen′dous·ness** *n.*

stu·pid (st*y*ōō′pid) *adj.* **1** Very slow in understanding; lacking in intelligence; dull-witted. **2** Affected with stupor; stupefied. **3** Dull and profitless; tiresome: to regard rote learning as *stupid.* **4** Resulting from slowness in un-

derstanding or a lack of intelligence. **5** *Informal* Annoying; bothersome: This *stupid* nail won't go in straight. [< L *stupidus* struck dumb] **—stu·pid·i·ty** (stŷoo·pid′ə·tē) (*pl.* **·ties**) **stu′pid·ness** *n.* **—stu′pid·ly** *adv.*

stu·por (stŷoo′pər) *n.* **1** Abnormal lethargy due to shock, drugs, etc. **2** Extreme intellectual dullness. [< L *stupere* be stunned] **—stu′por·ous** *adj.*

stur·dy (stûr′dē) *adj.* **·di·er**, **·di·est 1** Possessing rugged health and strength. **2** Firm and resolute: a *sturdy* defense. [< OF *estourdir* stun, amaze] **—stur′di·ly** *adv.* **—stur′di·ness** *n.* **—Syn. 1** hardy, lusty, robust, vigorous. **2** determined, unyielding.

stur·geon (stûr′jən) *n.* Any of various large edible fishes of northern regions, valued as the source of caviar. [< Med. L *sturio*]

Sturgeon

stut·ter (stut′ər) *v.t. & v.i.* To utter or speak with spasmodic repetition, blocking, and prolongation of sounds and syllables. **—n.** The act or habit of stuttering. [Freq. of ME *stutten* stutter] **—stut′ter·er** *n.* **—stut′ter·ing·ly** *adv.*

St. Vi·tus's dance (sānt vī′təs·iz) CHOREA. Also **St. Vitus dance.** [< *St. Vitus,* third-century Christian child martyr]

sty[1] (stī) *n. pl.* **sties 1** A pen for swine. **2** Any filthy habitation. [< OE *stī, stig*]

sty[2] (stī) *n. pl.* **sties** A pustule on the edge of an eyelid. Also **stye.** [< OE *stīgan* rise + *ye* eye]

Styg·i·an (stij′ē·ən) *adj.* **1** Pertaining to or like the river Styx or the lower world. **2** Dark and gloomy.

style (stīl) *n.* **1** A fashionable manner or appearance: to be in *style*. **2** Fashion: the latest *style* in shirts. **3** A particular fashion in clothing. **4** A distinctive form of expression: a florid *style*. **5** An effective way of expression: His drawings have *style*. **6** Manner: a church in the Romanesque *style* of architecture. **7** A way of living or behaving: Domestic life is not his *style*. **8** A pointed instrument for marking or engraving. **9** An indicator on a dial. **10** *Printing* The typography, spelling, design, etc., used in a given published text. **11** *Bot.* The slender part of a carpel between stigma and ovary. **12** A system of arranging the calendar years so as to average that of the true solar year. Our calendar, adopted in 1752, is called **New Style,** while **Old Style** dates are 13 days earlier.**—v.t. styled, styl·ing 1** To name; give a title to: Richard I was *styled* "the Lion-Hearted." **2** To cause to conform to a specific style: to *style* a manuscript. [< L *stylus* writing instrument] **—styl′er** *n.*

style·book (stīl′book′) *n.* A book setting forth rules of capitalization, punctuation, etc., for the use of printers, writers, and editors. Also **style manual.**

styl·ish (stī′lish) *adj.* **1** Having style. **2** Very fashionable. **—styl′ish·ly** *adv.* **—styl′ish·ness** *n.*

styl·ist (stī′list) *n.* **1** One who is a master of style: a literary *stylist*. **2** An adviser on or a creator of styles: a hair *stylist*. **—sty·lis′tic** *adj.* **—sty·lis′ti·cal·ly** *adv.*

styl·ize (stī′līz) *v.t.* **·ized, ·iz·ing** To conform to or create in a distinctive or specific style. *Brit. sp.* **styl′ise. —styl′i·za′·tion** (stī′lə·zā′shən), **styl′iz·er** *n.*

sty·lus (stī′ləs) *n. pl.* **·lus·es** or **·li** (lī) **1** An ancient instrument for writing on wax tablets. **2** A tiny, usu. jewel-tipped needle whose vibrations in tracing the groove in a phonograph record transmit sound. [L]

sty·mie (stī′mē) *n.* A condition in golf in which an opponent's ball lies in the line of the player's putt on the green. **—v.t.** **·mied, ·my·ing 1** To block (an opponent) by or as by a stymie. **2** To baffle or perplex. [?]

styp·tic (stip′tik) *adj.* Tending to halt bleeding; astringent: also **styp′ti·cal. —n.** A styptic substance. [< Gk. *styp sis* a contraction] **—styp·tic·i·ty** (stip·tis′ə·tē) *n.*

Sty·ro·foam (stī′rə·fōm) *n.* A lightweight, rigid, cellular material formed from a synthetic hydrocarbon polymer: a trade name.

Styx (stiks) *n. Gk. Myth.* The river across which the dead were ferried to Hades.

sua·sion (swā′zhən) *n.* The act of persuading: usu. in the phrase **moral suasion.** [< L *suadere* persuade] **—sua·sive** (swā′siv), **sua·so·ry** (swā′sər·ē) *adj.* **—sua′sive·ly** *adv.* **—sua′sive·ness** *n.*

suave (swäv) *adj.* Smooth and pleasant in manner, often superficially so. [< L *suavis* sweet] **—suave′ly** *adv.* **—suave′ness, suav′i·ty** (*pl.* **·ties**) *n.*

sub (sub) *n. Informal* **1** SUBSTITUTE. **2** A subordinate or subaltern. **3** SUBMARINE. **—v.i.** **subbed, sub·bing** To act as a substitute for someone.

sub- *prefix* **1** Under; beneath; below: *subcutaneous.* **2** Almost; nearly: *subtropical.* **3** Further; again: *subdivide.* **4** Lower in rank or grade: *subaltern.* **5** Having less importance; secondary: *subtitle.* **6** Forming a further division: *subcommittee.* [< L *sub* under] • See TAXONOMY.

sub. subaltern; submarine; subscription; substitute; suburb; suburban.

sub·al·tern (sub·ôl′tərn, *esp. Brit.* sub′əl·tərn) *adj.* **1** *Brit. Mil.* Ranking below a captain. **2** Of inferior rank or position. **—n. 1** A person of subordinate rank or position. **2** *Brit. Mil.* An officer ranking below a captain. [< L *sub-* under + *alternus* alternate]

sub·ant·arc·tic (sub′ant·ärk′tik, -är′tik) *adj.* Denoting or pertaining to a region surrounding the Antarctic Circle.

sub·arc·tic (sub·ärk′tik, -är′tik) *adj.* Denoting or pertaining to a region surrounding the Arctic Circle.

sub·a·tom·ic (sub′ə·tom′ik) *adj.* **1** Of or pertaining to the constituent parts of an atom. **2** Smaller than an atom.

sub·com·mit·tee (sub′kə·mit′ē) *n.* A small committee appointed from a larger committee for special work.

sub·con·scious (sub·kon′shəs) *adj.* **1** Only dimly conscious; not fully aware. **2** Not attended by full awareness, as an automatic action. **—n.** That portion of mental activity not in the focus of consciousness. **—sub·con′scious·ly** *adv.* **—sub·con′scious·ness** *n.*

sub·con·tract (sub·kon′trakt) *n.* A contract subordinate to another contract and assigning part of the work to a third party. **—v.t. & v.i.** (sub′kən·trakt′) To make a subcontract (for). **—sub·con·trac·tor** (sub′kon′trak′tər, sub′·kən·trak′-) *n.*

sub·cul·ture (sub′kul·chər) *n.* A group having specific patterns of behavior that set it off from other groups within a culture or society.

sub·cu·ta·ne·ous (sub′kyoo·tā′nē·əs) *adj.* Situated or applied beneath the skin. [< L *sub-* under + *cutis* skin] **—sub′cu·ta′ne·ous·ly** *adv.*

subd. subdivision.

sub·deb (sub′deb′) *n. Informal* **1** A young girl during the period before she becomes a debutante. **2** Any young girl of the same age.

sub·di·vide (sub′di·vīd′, sub′di·vīd′) *v.t. & v.i.* **·vid·ed, ·vid·ing 1** To divide again. **2** To divide (land) into lots for sale or improvement.

sub·di·vi·sion (sub′di·vizh′ən, sub′di·vizh′ən) *n.* **1** Division following upon division. **2** A part, as of land, resulting from subdividing.

sub·due (sub·dŷoo′) *v.t.* **·dued, ·du·ing 1** To gain dominion over, as by war or force. **2** To overcome by training, influence, or persuasion. **3** To repress (emotions, impulses, etc.). **4** To reduce the intensity of. [< L *subducere* lead away] **—sub·du′ed·ly** *adv.* **—sub·du′er** *n.* **—Syn. 1** conquer, subjugate, vanquish. **2** master, tame. **4** lessen, soften.

sub·group (sub′groop′) *n.* A subdivision of a group.

sub·head (sub′hed′) *n.* **1** A heading or title of a subdivision of a chapter, etc. **2** A subordinate title. Also **sub′·head·ing.**

sub·hu·man (sub·hyoo′mən) *adj.* Less than or imperfectly human.

subj. subject; subjective; subjunctive.

sub·ja·cent (sub·jā′sənt) *adj.* Situated underneath; underlying. [< L *sub-* under + *jacere* to lie] **—sub·ja′cen·cy** *n.* **—sub·ja′cent·ly** *adv.*

sub·ject (sub′jikt) *adj.* **1** Being under the power of another. **2** Exposed: *subject* to criticism. **3** Having a tendency: *subject* to colds. **4** Conditional upon: *subject* to your consent. **—n. 1** One who is under the governing power of another, as of a ruler. • See CITIZEN. **2** One who or that which is employed or treated in a specified way, as in an experiment. **3** The theme or topic of a discussion. **4** Something described or depicted in a literary or artistic work. **5** *Gram.* The word, phrase, or clause of a sentence about which something is stated or asked in the predicate. **6**

Music The melodic phrase on which a composition or a part of it is based. **7** A branch of learning. —*v.t.* (səb·jekt′) **1** To bring under dominion or control; subjugate. **2** To cause to undergo some experience or action. **3** To make liable; expose: *His inheritance was subjected to heavy taxation.* [<L *sub-* under + *jacere* throw] —**sub·jec′tion** *n.*

sub·jec·tive (səb·jek′tiv) *adj.* **1** Of or belonging to that which is within the mind and not subject to independent verification. **2** Expressing very personal feelings or opinions: *a subjective piece of writing.* **3** Highly influenced by the emotions or by prejudice. **4** *Med.* Of the kind of which only the patient is aware: said of symptoms. **5** *Gram.* Designating the case and function of the subject of a sentence. —**sub·jec′tive·ly** *adv.* —**sub·jec′tive·ness, sub·jec·tiv·i·ty** (sub′jek·tiv′ə·tē) *n.*

sub·join (sub·join′) *v.t.* To add at the end; affix. [<L *sub-* in addition + *jungere* join] —**sub·join′der** (-dər) *n.*

sub·ju·gate (sub′jōō·gāt) *v.t.* **·gat·ed, ·gat·ing 1** To bring under dominion; conquer. **2** To make subservient or submissive. [<L *sub-* under + *jugum* a yoke] —**sub′ju·ga′tion, sub′ju·ga′tor** *n.*

sub·junc·tive (səb·jungk′tiv) *Gram. adj.* Of or pertaining to that mood of the finite verb that is used to express a future contingency, a supposition, or a wish or desire. —*n.* **1** The subjunctive mood. **2** A verb form or construction in this mood. [<L *subjunctus.* p.p. of *subjungere* subjoin] —**sub·junc′tive·ly** *adv.*

sub·lease (səb·lēs′) *v.t.* **·leased, ·leas·ing** To obtain or let (property) on a sublease. —*n.* (sub′lēs′) A lease of property from a tenant.

sub·let (sub·let′, sub′let′) *v.t.* **·let, ·let·ting 1** To let to another (property held on a lease). **2** To let (work that one has contracted to do) to a subordinate contractor. —*n.* Property, esp. dwellings, that is subleased or available for subleasing.

sub·li·mate (sub′lə·māt) *v.* **·mat·ed, ·mat·ing** *v.t.* **1** To refine; purify. **2** *Psychol.* To convert (a primitive impulse) into socially acceptable behavior. **3** *Chem.* SUBLIME. —*v.i.* **4** To undergo or engage in sublimation. —*adj.* Sublimated; refined. —*n. Chem.* The product of sublimation. [<L *sub-limis* uplifted, sublime]

sub·li·ma·tion (sub′lə·mā′shən) *n.* **1** The act or process of sublimating. **2** *Chem.* A change of state from solid to vapor or from vapor to solid without liquefaction.

sub·lime (sə·blīm′) *adj.* **1** Characterized by or eliciting feelings of grandeur, nobility, or awe. **2** *Informal* Outstandingly excellent; supreme: *a sublime meal.* —*v.* **·limed, ·lim·ing** *v.t.* **1** To make sublime; ennoble. **2** *Chem.* To purify by the process of sublimation. —*v.i.* **3** *Chem.* To undergo sublimation. [<L *sublimis* lofty] —**sub·lime′ly** *adv.* —**sub·lim·i·ty** (sə·blim′ə·tē), sub·lime′ness** *n.* —**Syn.** *adj.* **1** grand, magnificent, solemn. **2** noble.

sub·lim·i·nal (sub·lim′ə·nəl) *adj.* **1** Below or beyond the threshold of consciousness: *a subliminal stimulus.* **2** Too slight or weak to be felt or perceived. [<L *sub-* under + *limen* threshold] —**sub·lim′i·nal·ly** *adv.*

sub·ma·chine gun (sub′mə·shēn′) A lightweight, automatic or semi-automatic gun, designed for firing from the shoulder or hip.

sub·mar·gin·al (sub·mär′jən·əl) *adj.* **1** Below the margin. **2** Not productive enough to develop, cultivate, etc.: *submarginal* land.

sub·ma·rine (sub′mə·rēn′) *adj.* Existing, done, or operating beneath the surface of the sea. —*n.* (sub′mə·rēn) **1** A vessel, usu. a warship, designed to operate both on and below the surface of the water. **2** HERO (def. 5).

sub·max·il·lar·y (sub·mak′sə·ler′ē) *adj.* Of, pertaining to, or situated in the lower jaw. —*n. pl.* **·lar·ies** A submaxillary salivary gland, nerve, artery, etc.

sub·merge (səb·mûrj′) *v.* **·merged, ·merg·ing** *v.t.* **1** To place under or plunge into water. **2** To cover; hide. —*v.i.* **3** To sink or dive beneath the surface of water. [<L *sub-* under + *mergere* to plunge] —**sub·mer′gence** *n.*

sub·merse (səb·mûrs′) *v.t.* **·mersed, ·mers·ing** SUBMERGE. [<L *submergere* submerge] —**sub·mer′sion** *n.*

sub·mers·i·ble (səb·mûr′sə·bəl) *adj.* That may be sub-

merged. —*n.* **1** SUBMARINE (def. 1). **2** Any of various, usu. small, underwater craft used for naval observation, scientific study, etc.

sub·mis·sion (səb·mish′ən) *n.* **1** A yielding to the power or authority of another. **2** Acquiescence or obedience. **3** The act of referring a matter of controversy to consideration, arbitration, etc. —**Syn. 1** surrender. **2** compliance, humbleness.

sub·mis·sive (səb·mis′iv) *adj.* Willing or inclined to submit; docile. —**sub·mis′sive·ly** *adv.* —**sub·mis′sive·ness** *n.*

sub·mit (səb·mit′) *v.* **·mit·ted, ·mit·ting** *v.t.* **1** To place under or yield to the authority of another. **2** To present for the consideration of others; refer. **3** To present as one's opinion; suggest. —*v.i.* **4** To give up; surrender. **5** To be obedient. [<L *sub-* under + *mittere* send] —**sub·mit′tal** *n.*

sub·nor·mal (sub·nôr′məl) *adj.* Below the normal; of less than normal intelligence, development, etc. —*n.* A subnormal individual. —**sub·nor·mal·i·ty** (sub′nôr·mal′ə·tē) *n.* —**sub·nor′mal·ly** *adv.*

sub·or·di·nate (sə·bôr′də·nit) *adj.* **1** Secondary; minor. **2** Lower in rank. **3** Subject or subservient to another. **4** *Gram.* Used within a sentence as a noun, adjective, or adverb: said of a clause. —*n.* One who or that which is subordinate. —*v.t.* (-nāt) **·nat·ed, ·nat·ing 1** To assign to a lower order or rank. **2** To make subject or subservient. [<L *sub-* under + *ordinare* to order] —**sub·or′di·nate·ly** *adv.* —**sub·or′di·nate·ness, sub·or′di·na′tion** *n.*

sub·orn (sə·bôrn′) *v. t.* **1** To bribe (someone) to commit perjury. **2** To incite or instigate to an evil act. [<L *sub-* secretly + *ornare* equip] —**sub·orn′er, sub·or·na·tion** (sub′ôr·nā′shən) *n.*

sub·poe·na (sə·pē′nə) *n.* A writ requiring a person to appear at court at a specified time and place. —*v.t.* **·naed, ·na·ing** To summon by subpoena. Also **sub·pe′na.** [<L *sub-* under + *poena* penalty]

sub·ro·gate (sub′rō·gāt) *v.t.* **·gat·ed, ·gat·ing** To substitute (one person, esp. one creditor) for another. [<L *sub-* in place of + *rogare* ask] —**sub′ro·ga′tion** *n.*

sub ro·sa (sub rō′zə) Confidentially; in secret. [L, under the rose, a symbol of silence]

sub·rou·tine (sub′rōō·tēn′) *n.* A part of a computer program, especially a sequence of instructions to perform a specific task.

sub·scribe (səb·skrīb′) *v.* **·scribed, ·scrib·ing** *v.t.* **1** To write, as one's name, at the end of a document; sign. **2** To sign one's name to as an expression of assent. **3** To promise, esp. in writing, to pay or contribute (a sum of money). —*v.i.* **4** To write one's name at the end of a document. **5** To give approval; agree. **6** To promise to contribute money. **7** To pay in advance for a series of periodicals, tickets to performances, etc. with *to.* [<L *sub-* under + *scribere* write] —**sub·scrib′er** *n.*

sub·script (sub′skript) *adj.* **1** Written following and slightly beneath, as a small letter or number. —*n.* A subscript number, symbol, or letter, as the 2 in H_2O. [<L *subscriptus,* p.p. of *subscribere* subscribe]

sub·scrip·tion (səb·skrip′shən) *n.* **1** The act of subscribing; confirmation or agreement. **2** That which is subscribed; a signed paper or statement. **3** A signature written at the end of a document. **4** The total subscribed for any purpose. **5** The purchase in advance of a series of periodicals, tickets to performances, etc.

sub·sec·tion (sub·sek′shən, sub′sek′shən) *n.* A subdivision of a section.

sub·se·quent (sub′sə·kwənt) *adj.* Following in time, place, or order, or as a result. —**subsequent to** Following; after. [<L *sub-* next below + *sequi* follow] —**sub·se·quence** (sub′sə·kwəns), sub′se·quen·cy, sub′se·quent·ness** *n.* —**sub′·se·quent·ly** *adv.*

sub·serve (səb·sûrv′) *v.t.* **·served, ·serv·ing 1** To be of use or help in furthering (a process, cause, etc.); promote. **2** To serve as a subordinate to (a person). [<L *sub-* under + *servire* serve]

sub·ser·vi·ent (səb·sûr′vē·ənt) *adj.* **1** Servile; obsequious; truckling. **2** Adapted to promote some end or purpose, esp. in a subordinate capacity. —*n.* One who or that which

subserves. **—sub·ser′vi·ent·ly** *adv.* **—sub·ser′vi·ent·ness, sub·ser′vi·ence, sub·ser′vi·en·cy** *n.*

sub·set (sub′set) *n. Math.* A set comprising some or all of the elements of another set.

sub·side (səb·sīd′) *v.i.* **·sid·ed, ·sid·ing 1** To sink to a lower level. **2** To become calm or quiet; abate. **3** To sink to the bottom, as sediment; settle. [< L *sub-* under + *sidere* to settle] **—sub·sid·ence** (səb·sīd′ns, sub′sə·dəns) *n.* **—Syn. 1** fall. **2** decrease, diminish, ebb, wane.

sub·sid·i·ar·y (səb·sid′ē·er′ē, -sid′ə·rē) *adj.* **1** Assisting; supplementary; auxiliary. **2** Of, pertaining to, or in the nature of a subsidy. **—n. pl. ·ar·ies 1** One who or that which furnishes supplemental aid or supplies. **2** A business enterprise with over half of its assets or stock owned by another company. **—sub·sid·i·ar·i·ly** (səb·sid′ē·er′ə·lē) *adv.*

sub·si·dize (sub′sə·dīz) *v.t.* **·dized, ·diz·ing 1** To grant a regular allowance or financial aid to. **2** To obtain the assistance of by a subsidy. *Brit. sp.* **sub′si·dise. —sub′si·di·za′tion, sub′si·diz′er** *n.*

sub·si·dy (sub′sə·dē) *n. pl.* **·dies 1** Financial aid directly granted by government to a person or commercial enterprise whose work is deemed beneficial to the public. **2** Any financial assistance granted by one government to another. [< L *subsidium* auxiliary forces, aid < *subsidere* subside]

sub·sist (səb·sist′) *v.i.* **1** To continue to exist. **2** To remain alive; manage to live: to *subsist* on a meatless diet. **3** To continue unchanged; abide. [< L *sub-* under + *sistere* cause to stand] **—sub·sist′er** *n.*

sub·sis·tence (səb·sis′təns) *n.* **1** The act of subsisting. **2** That on which or by which one subsists; sustenance; livelihood. [< LL *subsistentia* < *subsistere* SUBSIST] **—sub·sis′·tent** *adj.*

sub·soil (sub′soil′) *n.* The stratum of earth just beneath the surface soil.

sub·son·ic (sub·son′ik) *adj.* Designating those sound waves beyond the lower limits of human audibility.

subst. substantive; substitute.

sub·stance (sub′stəns) *n.* **1** The material of which anything is made or constituted. **2** The essential meaning of anything said or written. **3** Material possessions; wealth; property. **4** The quality of stability or solidity: an argument lacking *substance*. **5** A distinct but unidentified kind of matter: a gaseous *substance*. **6** Essential components or ideas: The *substance* of the two arguments is the same. **—in substance 1** Essentially; chiefly. **2** Really; actually. [< L *substare* be present]

sub·stan·dard (sub·stan′dərd) *adj.* **1** Below an accepted standard; inferior: *substandard* housing. **2** Lower than the established legal standard. **3** Not conforming to the standard language usage of educated speakers and writers: "He don't want none" is *substandard*.

sub·stan·tial (səb·stan′shəl) *adj.* **1** Solid; strong; firm: a *substantial* bridge. **2** Of real worth and importance: a *substantial* profit. **3** Possessed of wealth or sufficient means. **4** Having real existence; not illusory. **5** Containing or conforming to the essence of a thing: in *substantial* agreement. **6** Ample and nourishing: a *substantial* meal. **—sub·stan′ti·al′i·ty** (-shē·al′ə·tē), **sub·stan′tial·ness** *n.* **—sub·stan′tial·ly** *adv.*

sub·stan·ti·ate (səb·stan′shē·āt) *v.t.* **·at·ed, ·at·ing 1** To establish by evidence; verify. **2** To give form or substance to. [< L *substantia* substance] **—sub·stan′ti·a′tion** *n.* **—sub·stan′ti·a′tive** *adj.*

sub·stan·tive (sub′stən·tiv) *n.* **1** A noun or pronoun. **2** A verbal form, phrase, or clause used in place of a noun. **—adj. 1** Capable of being used as a noun. **2** Expressive of or denoting existence: The verb "to be" is called the *substantive* verb. **3** Having substance or reality. **4** Being an essential part or constituent. **5** Having distinct individuality. **6** Independent. [< L *substantia* substance] **—sub·stan·ti·val** (sub′stən·tī′vəl) *adj.* **—sub′stan·ti′val·ly, sub′stan·tive·ly** *adv.* **—sub′stan·tive·ness** *n.*

sub·sta·tion (sub′stā′shən) *n.* A subsidiary station, as for electric power or postal service.

sub·sti·tute (sub′stə·tyōōt) *v.* **·tut·ed, ·tut·ing** *v.t.* **1** To put in the place of another person or thing. **2** To take the place of. **—v.i. 3** To act as a substitute. **—n.** One who or that which takes the place of another. **—adj.** Situated in or

taking the place of another: a *substitute* teacher. [< L *sub-* in place of + *statuere* set up]

sub·sti·tu·tion (sub′stə·tyōō′shən) *n.* **1** The act of substituting, or the state of being substituted. **2** A substitute. **—sub′sti·tu′tion·al** *adj.* **—sub′sti·tu′tion·al·ly** *adv.*

sub·stra·tum (sub·strā′təm, -strat′əm) *n. pl.* **·stra·ta** (-strā′tə, -strat′ə) or **·stra·tums 1** An underlying stratum or layer, as of earth or rock. **2** A foundation or basis. [< L, p.p. neut. of *substernere* spread underneath] **—sub·stra′tal, sub·stra′tive** *adj.*

sub·struc·ture (sub′struk′chər, sub·struk′-) *n.* A structure serving as a foundation. **—sub·struc′tur·al** *adj.*

sub·ten·ant (sub·ten′ənt) *n.* A person who rents or leases from a tenant. **—sub·ten′an·cy** *n.*

sub·tend (səb·tend′) *v.t.* **1** *Geom.* To extend under or opposite to, as the chord of an arc or the side of a triangle opposite to an angle. **2** *Bot.* To enclose in its axil: A leaf *subtends* a bud. [< L *sub-* underneath + *tendere* stretch]

sub·ter·fuge (sub′tər·fyōōj′) *n.* Any plan or trick to escape something unpleasant. [< L *subter-* below, in secret + *fugere* flee, take flight]

sub·ter·ra·ne·an (sub′tə·rā′nē·ən) *adj.* **1** Situated or occurring below the surface of the earth. **2** Hidden. Also **sub′ter·ra′ne·ous.** [< L *sub-* under + *terra* earth] **—sub′ter·ra′ne·an·ly, sub′ter·ra′ne·ous·ly** *adv.*

sub·tile (sut′l, sub′til) *adj.* **1** Elusive; subtle. **2** Crafty; cunning. [< L *subtilis*] **—sub′tile·ly** *adv.* **—sub′tile·ness, sub·til·i·ty** (sub·til′ə·tē) *n.*

sub·ti·tle (sub′tīt′l) *n.* **1** A subordinate or explanatory title, as in a book, play, or document. **2** *pl.* In motion pictures, printed translations of foreign-language dialogue, usu. appearing at the bottom of the screen.

sub·tle (sut′l) *adj.* **sub·tler** (sut′lər, sut′l·ər), **sub·tlest 1** Not easily detected; elusive; delicate: a *subtle* aroma. **2** Characterized by or requiring keenness of mind, vision, hearing, etc.: *subtle* humor; *subtle* variations in sound. **3** Very skillful or ingenious: a *subtle* craftsman. **4** Not direct or obvious: a *subtle* hint. [< L *subtilis* fine] **—sub′tle·ness** *n.* **—sub′tly** *adv.*

sub·tle·ty (sut′l·tē) *n. pl.* **·ties 1** The state or quality of being subtle. **2** Something that is subtle.

sub·tract (səb·trakt′) *v.t. & v.i.* To take away or deduct, as a portion from the whole, or one quantity from another. [< L *sub-* away + *trahere* draw] **—sub·tract′er, sub·trac′tion** *n.* **—sub·trac′tive** *adj.*

sub·tra·hend (sub′trə·hend) *n. Math.* That which is to be subtracted from a number or quantity to give the difference.

sub·treas·ur·y (sub·trezh′ər·ē) *n. pl.* **·ur·ies 1** A branch office of the U.S. Treasury Department. **2** Any branch treasury. **—sub·treas′ur·er** *n.*

sub·trop·i·cal (sub·trop′i·kəl) *adj.* Of, pertaining to, or designating regions adjacent to the tropical zone. Also **sub·trop′ic. —sub·trop′ics** *n.pl.*

sub·urb (sub′ûrb) *n.* **1** A district or town adjacent to a city. **2** Outlying districts; environs. **—the suburbs** Residential areas near or within commuting distance of a city. [< L *sub-* near to + *urbs* a city]

sub·ur·ban (sə·bûr′bən) *adj.* Of or pertaining to a suburb or its residents.

sub·ur·ban·ite (sə·bûr′bən·īt) *n.* A resident of a suburb.

sub·ur·ban·ize (sə·bûr′bə·nīz) *v.t.* **·ized, ·iz·ing** To make suburban or give a suburban character to. **—sub·ur′ban·i·za′tion** *n.*

sub·ur·bi·a (sə·bûr′bē·ə) *n.* **1** The social and cultural world of suburbanites. **2** Suburbs or suburbanites collectively.

sub·ven·tion (səb·ven′shən) *n.* A grant of money made, esp. by a government, to an institution, cause, or study; subsidy. [< L *subvenire*] **—sub·ven′tion·ar·y** (-er′ē) *adj.*

sub·ver·sion (səb·vûr′shən, -zhən) *n.* **1** The act of subverting; demolition; overthrow. **2** A cause of ruin. **—sub·ver′sion·ar·y** (-er′ē) *adj.*

sub·ver·sive (səb·vûr′siv) *adj.* Tending to subvert or overthrow. **—n.** A person regarded as desiring to weaken or overthrow a government, organization, etc. **—sub·ver′sive·ly** *adv.* **—sub·ver′sive·ness** *n.*

sub·vert (səb·vûrt′) *v.t.* **1** To overthrow from the very foundation; destroy utterly. **2** To corrupt; undermine the

principles or character of. [< L *subvertere* overturn] —**sub·vert′er** *n.*

sub·way (sub′wā) *n.* **1** A passage below the surface of the ground. **2** An underground railroad beneath city streets for local transportation; also, the tunnel through which it runs. **3** UNDERPASS.

suc·ceed (sək·sēd′) *v.i.* **1** To accomplish what is attempted or intended. **2** To come next in order or sequence. **3** To come after another into office, ownership, etc. —*v.t.* **4** To be the successor or heir of. **5** To come after in time or sequence; follow. [< L *succedere* go under, follow after] —**suc·ceed′er** *n.*

suc·cess (sək·ses′) *n.* **1** A favorable course or termination of anything attempted. **2** The gaining of position, fame, wealth, etc. **3** A person or thing that is successful. **4** The degree of succeeding: Did you have any *success* in getting an appointment? [< L *succedere* succeed] —**Syn. 1** achievement, satisfaction. **2** prosperity, eminence, station.

suc·cess·ful (sək·ses′fəl) *adj.* **1** Having achieved success. **2** Ending in success: a *successful* venture. —**suc·cess′ful·ly** *adv.* —**suc·cess′ful·ness** *n.*

suc·ces·sion (sək·sesh′ən) *n.* **1** The act of following consecutively. **2** A group of things that succeed in order; a series or sequence. **3** The act or right of legally or officially coming into a predecessor's office, possessions, position, etc. **4** A group or hierarchy of persons having the right to succeed. —**in succession** One after another. —**suc·ces′sion·al** *adj.* —**suc·ces′sion·al·ly** *adv.*

suc·ces·sive (sək·ses′iv) *adj.* Following in succession; consecutive. —**suc·ces′sive·ly** *adv.* —**suc·ces′sive·ness** *n.*

suc·ces·sor (sək·ses′ər) *n.* One who or that which follows in succession; esp. a person who succeeds to an office, position, or property.

suc·cinct (sək·singkt′) *adj.* Reduced to a minimum number of words; concise; terse. [< L *sub-* underneath + *cingere* gird] —**suc·cinct′ly** *adv.* —**suc·cinct′ness** *n.*

suc·cor (suk′ər) *n.* **1** Help rendered in danger, difficulty, or distress. **2** One who or that which affords relief. —*v.t.* To go to the aid of; help. *Brit. sp.* **suc′cour.** [< L *sub-* up from under + *currere* to run] —**suc′cor·er** *n.* —**Syn.** *n.* **1** aid, rescue, relief, support.

suc·co·tash (suk′ə·tash) *n.* A dish of corn kernels and beans, usu. lima beans, cooked together. [< Algon.]

suc·cu·bus (suk′yə·bəs) *n. pl.* **·bi** (-bī, -bē) One of a class of demons in female form fabled to have intercourse with sleeping men. [< LL *succuba* a strumpet]

suc·cu·lent (suk′yə·lənt) *adj.* **1** Juicy; full of juice. **2** *Bot.* Composed of fleshy, juicy tissue: a *succulent* leaf. **3** Absorbing; interesting. —*n.* A succulent plant. [< L *succus* juice] —**suc′cu·lence, suc′cu·len·cy** *n.* —**suc′cu·lent·ly** *adv.*

suc·cumb (sə·kum′) *v.i.* **1** To give way; yield, as to force or persuasion. **2** To die. [< L *sub-* underneath + *cumbere* lie]

such (such) *adj.* **1** Being the same or similar in kind or quality; of a kind mentioned or indicated: a book *such* as this; screws, bolts, and other *such* items. **2** Indicated but not specified: some *such* place. **3** Extreme in degree, quality, etc.: *such* an uproar. —**such as** As an example or examples of the kind indicated: flowers *such as* dandelions. —*pron.* **1** Such a person or thing or such persons or things. **2** The same as implied or indicated: *Such* was the result. —**as such** As the particular thing or kind it is, regardless of others: People *as such* deserve compassion. —*adv.* **1** So: *such* destructive criticism. **2** Especially; very: She's in *such* good spirits today. [< OE *swelc, swylc*]

such and such Understood to be specific but not specified: to consult *such and such* an expert.

such·like (such′līk′) *adj.* Of a like or similar kind. —*pron.* Persons or things of that kind.

suck (suk) *v.t.* **1** To draw into the mouth by means of a partial vacuum created by action of the lips and tongue. **2** To draw in or take up by suction. **3** To draw liquid or nourishment from with the mouth: to *suck* an orange or a lollipop. **4** To take and hold in the mouth as if to do this: to *suck* one's thumb. **5** To pull or draw into an association: with *in* or *into:* The lure of quick profits *sucked* him in. —

v.i. **6** To draw in liquid, air, etc., by suction. **7** To draw in milk from a breast or udder by sucking. **8** To make a sucking sound. —*n.* **1** The act or sound of sucking. **2** That which is sucked. [< OE *sūcan*]

suck·er (suk′ər) *n.* **1** One who or that which sucks. **2** Any of various freshwater fishes having thick, fleshy lips. **3** A mouth adapted for clinging and sucking, as that of a leech, tapeworm, etc. **4** *Slang* A person easily deceived. **5** *Bot.* An adventitious shoot. **6** A tube or pipe used for suction. **7** A lollipop. —*v.t.* **1** To strip (a plant) of suckers. —*v.i.* **2** To form or send out suckers or shoots.

Sucker *def.* 2

suck·le (suk′əl) *v.* **·led, ·ling** *v.t.* **1** To nourish at the breast; nurse. **2** To bring up; nourish. —*v.i.* **3** To suck at the breast. —**suck′ler** *n.*

suck·ling (suk′ling) *n.* An unweaned mammal.

su·cre (sōō′krā) *n.* The monetary unit of Ecuador.

su·crose (sōō′krōs) *n.* The sweet, soluble, crystalline carbohydrate familiar as the common white sugar of commerce, and consisting of fructose and glucose in chemical combination. [< F *sucre* sugar]

suc·tion (suk′shən) *n.* **1** The act or process of sucking. **2** The production of a partial vacuum in a space connected with a fluid or gas under reduced pressure. —*adj.* Creating or operating by suction.

suc·to·ri·al (suk·tôr′ē·əl, -tōr′-) *adj.* **1** Adapted for sucking or suction. **2** *Zool.* Living by sucking; having organs for sucking.

Su·dan (sōō·dan′) *n.* A republic of NE Africa, 967,500 sq. mi., cap. Khartoum. —**Su·da·nese** (sōō′də·nēz′) *adj., n.* • See map at AFRICA.

sud·den (sud′n) *adj.* **1** Happening quickly and without warning. **2** Causing surprise; unexpected: a *sudden* development. **3** Hurried; hasty; rash. —**all of a sudden** Without warning; suddenly. [< L *subitus,* p.p. of *subire* come or go stealthily] —**sud′den·ly** *adv.* —**sud′den·ness** *n.*

suds (sudz) *n.pl.* **1** Soapy water. **2** Froth; foam. **3** *Slang* Beer. [< MDu. *sudde, sudse* a marsh] —**suds′y** *adj.*

sue (sōō) *v.* **sued, su·ing** *v.t.* **1** To institute legal proceedings against, as for the redress of some wrong. **2** To prosecute (a legal action). —*v.i.* **3** To institute legal proceedings. **4** To seek to persuade someone by entreaty: with *for:* to *sue* for peace. [< AF *suer* pursue, sue] —**su′er** *n.*

suede (swād) *n.* Leather or a fabric having a napped surface. Also **suède.** [< F *gants de Suède* Swedish gloves]

su·et (sōō′it) *n.* The white, solid fatty tissue of beef, lamb, etc. [< L *sebum* fat] —**su′et·y** *adj.*

suf., suff. suffix.

suf·fer (suf′ər) *v.i.* **1** To feel pain or distress. **2** To sustain loss, injury, or detriment. **3** To undergo punishment, esp. death. —*v.t.* **4** To have inflicted on one; sustain, as an injury or loss: to *suffer* a fracture of the arm; to *suffer* a business reversal. **5** To undergo; pass through, as change. **6** To bear; endure: He never could *suffer* incompetence. **7** To allow; permit. [< L *sub-* up from under + *ferre* bear] —**suf′fer·a·ble** *adj.* —**suf′fer·a·bly** *adv.* —**suf′fer·er** *n.*

suf·fer·ance (suf′ər·əns, suf′rəns) *n.* **1** Permission given or implied by failure to prohibit. **2** The capacity for suffering or tolerating pain or distress. —**on sufferance** Tolerated or suffered but not encouraged.

suf·fer·ing (suf′ər·ing, suf′ring) *n.* **1** The state of anguish or pain of one who suffers. **2** The pain suffered; loss; injury.

suf·fice (sə·fīs′, -fīz′) *v.* **·ficed, ·fic·ing** *v.i.* To be sufficient or adequate. [< L *sub-* under + *facere* make]

suf·fi·cien·cy (sə·fish′ən·sē) *n. pl.* **·cies 1** The state of being sufficient. **2** That which is sufficient; esp., adequate means or income.

suf·fi·cient (sə·fish′ənt) *adj.* Being all that is needed; adequate; enough. [< L *sufficere* substitute, suffice] —**suf·fi′cient·ly** *adv.* —**Syn.** ample, satisfactory, fitting.

suf·fix (suf′iks) *n.* A letter or letters added to the end of a word or root, forming a new word or functioning as an inflectional element, as *-ful* in faithful and *-ed* in loved.

—*v.t.* To add as a suffix. [< L *suffixus,* p.p. of *suffigere* fasten underneath] —**suf′fix·al** *adj.*

suf·fo·cate (suf′ə·kāt′) *v.* ·**cat·ed,** ·**cat·ing** *v.t.* **1** To kill by obstructing respiration in any manner. **2** To cause distress in by depriving of an adequate supply or quality of air. **3** To stifle or smother, as a fire. —*v.i.* **4** To die from suffocation. **5** To be distressed by an inadequate supply or quality of air. [< L *sub-* under + *fauces* throat] —**suf′fo·cat′ing·ly** *adv.* —**suf′fo·ca′tion** *n.* —**suf′fo·ca′tive** *adj.*

suf·fra·gan (suf′rə·gən, -jən) *n.* **1** An auxiliary or assistant bishop. **2** Any bishop subordinate to an archbishop. —*adj.* Assisting; auxiliary. [< L *suffragium* vote] —**suf′fra·gan·ship′** *n.*

suf·frage (suf′rij) *n.* **1** A vote in support of someone or something. **2** The right or privilege of voting; franchise. **3** Any short intercessory prayer. [< L *suffragium* a vote]

suf·fra·gette (suf′rə·jet′) *n.* A woman who advocates female suffrage. —**suf′fra·get′tism** *n.*

suf·fra·gist (suf′rə·jist) *n.* An advocate of suffrage, esp. for women.

suf·fuse (sə·fyo͞oz′) *v.t.* ·**fused,** ·**fus·ing** To spread over, as with a fluid, light, or color. [< L *suffusus,* p.p. of *suffundere* pour underneath] —**suf·fu′sion** *n.* —**suf·fu′sive** *adj.*

sug·ar (sho͝og′ər) *n.* **1** A sweet, crystalline foodstuff obtained chiefly from sugar cane and sugar beets; sucrose. **2** Any of a large class of mostly sweet and water-soluble carbohydrates widely distributed in plants and animals, as lactose, glucose, fructose, etc. —*v.t.* **1** To sweeten, cover, or coat with sugar. **2** To make less distasteful, as by flattery. —*v.i.* **3** To make maple sugar by boiling down maple syrup: usu. with *off.* **4** To form or produce sugar; granulate. [< Ar. *sukkar*] —**sug′ar·less** *adj.*

sugar beet A variety of beet cultivated as a commercial source of sugar.

sugar cane A tall tropical grass with a solid jointed stalk rich in sugar.

sug·ar-coat (sho͝og′ər·kōt′) *v.t.* **1** To cover with sugar. **2** To cause to appear attractive or less distasteful. —**sug′ar-coat′ing** *n.*

sug·ar-cured (sho͝og′ər·kyo͝ord′) *adj.* Treated with a sweetened brine, as ham or pork.

sug·ar·plum (sho͝og′ər·plum′) *n.* A small ball or disk of candy.

sug·ar·y (sho͝og′ər·ē) *adj.* **1** Of, like, or composed of sugar; sweet. **2** Honeyed or complaisant; esp., excessively sweet or sentimental. —**sug′ar·i·ness** *n.*

sug·gest (səg·jest′, sə·jest′) *v.t.* **1** To bring or put forward for consideration, action, or approval; propose. **2** To arouse in the mind by association or connection: Gold *suggests* wealth. **3** To give a hint of; intimate: Her gesture *suggested* indifference. [< L *suggerere* carry underneath, suggest] —**sug·gest′er** *n.*

sug·gest·i·ble (səg·jes′tə·bəl, sə-) *adj.* **1** That can be suggested. **2** Responding readily to suggestions; easily led. —**sug·gest′i·bil′i·ty** *n.*

sug·ges·tion (səg·jes′chən, sə·jes′-) *n.* **1** The act of suggesting. **2** Something suggested. **3** A hint; trace; touch: a *suggestion* of irony. **4** An association of thoughts or ideas, esp. if based upon incidental or fortuitous similarities rather than a logical or rational relationship.

sug·ges·tive (səg·jes′tiv, sə-) *adj.* **1** Tending to suggest; stimulating thought or reflection. **2** Suggesting or hinting at something improper or indecent. —**sug·ges′tive·ly** *adv.* —**sug·ges′tive·ness** *n.*

su·i·cide (so͞o′ə·sīd) *n.* **1** The intentional taking of one's own life. **2** One who takes or tries to take one's own life. **3** Personal or professional ruin brought on by one's own actions. [< L *sui* of oneself + *caedere* kill] —**su·i·ci·dal** (so͞o′ə·sīd′l) *adj.* —**su′i·ci′dal·ly** *adv.*

su·i gen·e·ris (so͞o′ī jen′ər·is, so͞o′ē, gen′-) Of his (her, its) particular kind; unique. [L]

suit (so͞ot) *n.* **1** A set of garments worn together; esp., a coat and trousers or skirt, made of the same fabric. **2** An outfit or garment for a particular purpose: a bathing *suit.* **3** A group of like things; a set. **4** Any of the four sets of thirteen cards each that make up a deck of cards. **5** A proceeding in a court of law for the recovery of a right or the redress of a wrong. **6** The courting of a woman. — **follow suit 1** To play a card identical in suit to the card

led. **2** To follow an example set by another. —*v.t.* **1** To meet the requirements of or be appropriate to; befit. **2** To please; satisfy. **3** To render appropriate; adapt. **4** To furnish with clothes. —*v.i.* **5** To agree; accord. **6** To be or prove satisfactory. **7** To put on a protective suit or uniform: with *up:* ballplayers *suiting up* before a game. [< OF *sieute* < L *sequi* follow]

suit·a·ble (so͞o′tə·bəl) *adj.* Appropriate; proper; fitting. —**suit′a·bil′i·ty, suit′a·ble·ness** *n.* —**suit′a·bly** *adv.*

suit·case (so͞ot′kās′) *n.* A case for carrying clothing, etc., esp. one that is flat and rectangular.

suite (swēt; *for def.* 2, *also* so͞ot) *n.* **1** A set of things intended to go or be used together, as a number of connected rooms forming an apartment or leased as a unit in a hotel. **2** A set of matched furniture. **3** A company of attendants; a retinue. **4** *Music* An instrumental composition consisting of a series of short pieces. [< OF *sieute.* See SUIT.]

suit·ing (so͞o′ting) *n.* Cloth used in making suits of clothes.

suit·or (so͞o′tər) *n.* **1** One who institutes a suit in court. **2** A man who courts a woman. **3** A petitioner.

su·ki·ya·ki (so͞o′kē·yä′kē, skē·yä′kē) *n.* A Japanese dish of thinly sliced meat and vegetables fried together and served with condiments. [Jap.]

Suk·koth (so͝ok′ōth, so͝ok′ōs) *n.* A Jewish holiday, originally a harvest festival, occurring in late September or in October. Also **Suk′kos, Suk′kot.** [< Hebrew *sūkōth* tabernacles, booths]

sulfa- *combining form Chem.* Sulfur; related to or containing sulfur. Also **sulf-, sulfo-.** [< SULFUR]

sul·fa drug (sul′fə) Any of various sulfonamide derivatives effective in the treatment of certain bacterial infections.

sul·fate (sul′fāt) *n.* A salt of sulfuric acid. —*v.* ·**fat·ed,** ·**fat·ing** *v.t.* **1** To convert into a sulfate. **2** To treat with a sulfate or sulfuric acid. **3** *Electr.* To form a coating of lead sulfate on (the plate of a storage battery). —*v.i.* **4** To become sulfated. Also **sul′phate.** [< L *sulfur* sulfur] —**sul·fa′tion** *n.*

sul·fide (sul′fīd) *n.* A compound of sulfur with an element or radical. Also **sul′phide.**

sul·fite (sul′fīt) *n.* A salt or ester of sulfurous acid. Also **sul′phite.** —**sul·fit′ic** (-fit′ik) *adj.*

sul·fon·a·mide (sul·fon′ə·mīd, -mid) *n.* Any of a group of organic sulfur compounds containing a univalent amide radical.

sul·fur (sul′fər) *n.* **1** An industrially important, abundant nonmetallic element (symbol S), occurring in three allotropic forms and found in both free and combined states. **2** Any of various small yellow butterflies. Also, and for def. 2 always, **sul′phur.** —**sul′fur·y** *adj.*

sul·fu·rate (sul′fyə·rāt) *v.t.* ·**rat·ed,** ·**rat·ing** SULFURIZE. —**sul′fu·ra′tion** *n.*

sulfur dioxide A colorless gas with a sharp odor, very soluble in water, used in manufacturing sulfuric acid, in bleaching, etc.

sul·fu·re·ous (sul·fyo͝or′ē·əs) *adj.* **1** Of or like sulfur. **2** Greenish yellow.

sul·fu·ret (sul′fyə·ret) *v.t.* ·**ret·ed** or ·**ret·ted,** ·**ret·ing** or ·**ret·ting** SULFURIZE. —*n.* SULFIDE.

sul·fu·ric (sul·fyo͝or′ik) *adj.* Pertaining to or derived from sulfur, esp. in its higher valence.

sulfuric acid A colorless, exceedingly corrosive, syrupy liquid with a strong affinity for water, used extensively in the chemical industry.

sul·fur·ize (sul′fyə·rīz) *v.t.* ·**ized,** ·**iz·ing** To impregnate, treat with, or subject to the action of sulfur. —**sul′fur·i·za′tion** *n.*

sul·fur·ous (sul′fər·əs, *for def. 1 esp.* sul·fyo͝or′əs) *adj.* **1** Pertaining to or derived from sulfur, esp. in its lower valence. **2** Resembling burning sulfur; fiery. **3** Biting; vitriolic: *sulfurous* criticism. **4** Blasphemous, as language. —**sul′fur·ous·ly** *adv.* —**sul′fur·ous·ness** *n.*

sulfurous acid (sul·fyo͝or′əs) An unstable acid formed by dissolving sulfur dioxide in water.

sulk (sulk) *v.i.* To be sullen in mood and tend to shun others. —*n.* A sulky mood or humor. [Back formation < SULKY]

sulk·y¹ (sul′kē) *adj.* **sulk·i·er, sulk·i·est** Sulking or tending

to sulk. [? < OE *(ā)seolcan* be weak or slothful]—**sulk′i·ly** *adv.*—**sulk′i·ness** *n.*

sulk·y² (sul′kē) *n. pl.* **sulk·ies** A light, two-wheeled, one-horse vehicle for one person. [< SULKY¹; so called because one rides alone]

Sulky

sul·len (sul′ən) *adj.* **1** Showing ill-humor, as from dwelling upon a grievance; morose; glum. **2** Depressing; somber: *sullen* clouds. **3** Slow; sluggish. **4** Melancholy; mournful. [< AF *solein* sullen, alone] —**sul′len·ly** *adv.*—**sul′len·ness** *n.* —**Syn. 1** gloomy, sad, sulky, moody.

sul·ly (sul′ē) *v.* **·lied, ·ly·ing** *v.t.* To mar the brightness or purity of; soil; defile. [< MF *souiller* to soil]

sulph- For all words so spelled, see SULF-.

sul·tan (sul′tən) *n.* A Muslim ruler. [< Ar. *sultān* a sovereign, dominion]

sul·tan·a (sul·tan′ə, -tä′nə) *n.* **1** A sultan's wife, daughter, sister, or mother. **2** A white, seedless variety of grape or raisin.

sul·tan·ate (sul′tən·āt, -it) *n.* **1** The authority of a sultan. **2** The domain of a sultan. Also **sul′tan·ship.**

sul·try (sul′trē) *adj.* **·tri·er, ·tri·est 1** Hot, moist, and still; close: said of weather. **2** Oppressively hot; burning. **3** Inflamed with passion. **4** Expressing or tending to excite sexual interest; sensual. [< obs. *sulter,* var. of SWELTER] —**sul′tri·ly** *adv.*—**sul′tri·ness** *n.*

sum (sum) *n.* **1** An amount of money. **2** The result obtained by the addition of numbers or quantities. **3** A problem in arithmetic. **4** The entire quantity, number, or substance; the whole: The *sum* of his effort came to naught. **5** Essence or core; summary: In *sum,* the issue is one of trust; the *sum* of an argument. **6** The highest or furthest point; summit. —*v.* **summed, sum·ming** *v.t.* **1** To present as a summary; recapitulate; summarize: usu. with *up.* **2** To add into one total: often with *up.* —*v.i.* **3** To give a summary; recapitulate: usu. with *up.* **4** To calculate a sum: often with *up.* [< L *summa (res)* highest (thing)]

su·mac (sōō′mak, shōō′-) *n.* **1** Any of a genus of woody plants related to the cashew. **2** A species of sumac with hairy red fruit and compound leaves turning brilliant red in autumn: also **smooth sumac. 3** The dried and powdered leaves of certain species of sumac, used for tanning and dyeing. Also **su′mach.** [< Ar. *summāq*]

sum·ma cum lau·de (soom′ə koom lou′də, -dē, sōō′mə, sum′ə kum lô′dē) *Latin* With the greatest praise: to be graduated *summa cum laude.*

sum·ma·rize (sum′ə·rīz) *v.t.* **·rized, ·riz·ing** To make a summary of. *Brit. sp.* **·rise.** —**sum′ma·ri·za′tion** *n.*

sum·ma·ry (sum′ər·ē) *n. pl.* **·ries** A brief account of the substance or essential points of something spoken or written; recapitulation. —*adj.* **1** Giving the substance or essential points; concise. **2** Performed without ceremony or delay; instant: *summary* execution. [< L *summa.* See SUM.] —**Syn.** *n.* condensation, abridgment, epitome, précis, compendium. —**sum·ma·ri·ly** (sə·mer′ə·lē, sum′ər·ə·lē) *adv.*

sum·ma·tion (sum·ā′shən) *n.* **1** The act or operation of obtaining a sum; addition. **2** A sum or total. **3** A summing up of the main points of an argument, as the final speech in behalf of one of the parties in a court trial.

sum·mer (sum′ər) *n.* **1** The warmest season of the year, including, in the northern hemisphere, June, July, and August. **2** A year of life. **3** A bright or prosperous period. —*v.i.* **1** To pass the summer. —*v.t.* **2** To keep or care for through the summer. —*adj.* **1** Of, pertaining to, or occurring in summer. **2** Used or intended for use in the summer: a *summer* house. [OE *sumor, sumer*] —**sum′mer·y** *adj.*

sum·mer·sault (sum′ər·sôlt) *n. & v.i.* SOMERSAULT.

summer squash Any of various small squashes with a soft rind, usu. eaten before they ripen.

sum·mer·time (sum′ər·tīm′) *n.* Summer; the summer season.

sum·mit (sum′it) *n.* **1** The highest part; the top; vertex.

2 The highest degree; maximum. **3** The highest level or office, as of a government or business organization. **4** A meeting of executives of the highest level, as heads of government. —*adj.* Of or involving those at the highest level: a *summit* conference. [< L *summus* highest]

sum·mit·ry (sum′it·rē) *n.* **1** Meetings of officials of the highest rank, as heads of government. **2** The use or dependency upon such meetings to solve international problems.

sum·mon (sum′ən) *v.t.* **1** To order to come; send for. **2** To call together; cause to convene, as a legislative assembly. **3** To order (a person) to appear in court by a summons. **4** To call forth or into action; arouse: usu. with *up:* to *summon* up courage. **5** To call on for a specific act. [< L *summonere* suggest, hint]—**sum′mon·er** *n.*

sum·mons (sum′ənz) *n. pl.* **sum·mons·es 1** An order or call to attend or act at a particular place or time. **2** *Law* **a** A notice to a defendant summoning him to appear in court. **b** A notice to appear in court as a witness or as a juror. [< OF *somondre* summon]

su·mo (sōō′mō) *n.* A highly stylized form of wrestling popular in Japan. [< Japanese *sumō*]

sump (sump) *n.* A pit or reservoir in which liquids are received by drainage, as a cesspool. [< MDu. *somp, sump* a marsh]

sump·ter (sump′tər) *n.* A pack animal. [< OF *sometier* a driver of a pack horse]

sump·tu·ar·y (sump′chōō·er′ē) *adj.* Limiting or regulating expenditure. [< L *sumptus* expenditure < *sumere* take]

sump·tu·ous (sump′chōō·əs) *adj.* **1** Involving or showing lavish expenditure. **2** Luxurious; magnificent. [< L *sumptus* expense] —**sump′tu·ous·ly** *adv.*—**sump′tu·ous·ness** *n.*

sun (sun) *n.* **1** The star that is the gravitational center and the main source of energy for the solar system, about 93,000,000 miles distant from the earth, with a diameter of 864,000 miles and a mass 332,000 times that of the earth. **2** Any star, esp. one with a planetary system. **3** The light and heat from the sun; sunshine. **4** Anything brilliant and magnificent; a source of splendor. **5** A day or a year. —*v.* **sunned, sun·ning** *v.t.* **1** To expose to the light or heat of the sun. —*v.i.* **2** To bask in the sun; sun oneself. [< OE *sunne*]

Sun. Sunday.

sun·bathe (sun′bāth′) *v.i.* **-bathed, -bath·ing** To bask in the sun. —**sun′-bath′er** *n.*

sun·beam (sun′bēm′) *n.* A ray or beam of the sun.

Sun·belt (sun′belt′) *n.* The southeastern and southwestern states of the U.S., ranging from Virginia south to Florida and west to California.

sun·bon·net (sun′bon′it) *n.* A wide-brimmed bonnet sometimes having a flap covering the neck.

sun·burn (sun′bûrn′) *n.* Injury to the skin by ultraviolet radiation from the sun. —*v.t. & v.i.* **-burned** or **-burnt** (bûrnt), **-burn·ing** To affect or be affected with sunburn.

sun·dae (sun′dē) *n.* Ice cream topped with crushed fruit, flavoring, syrup, nuts, etc. [? < *Sunday*]

Sun·day (sun′dē, -dā) *n.* The first day of the week; the Christian Sabbath. [< OE *sunnan dæg* day of the sun]

Sunday school A school meeting on Sundays for religious instruction, esp. of the young.

sun·der (sun′dər) *v.t. & v.i.* To break apart; sever. [< OE *syndrian, sundrian*]

sun·di·al (sun′dī′əl, -dīl) *n.* A device that shows the time of day by the shadow of a style or gnomon cast on a dial in sunlight.

sun·down (sun′doun′) *n.* SUNSET (def. 2).

sun·dries (sun′drēz) *n. pl.* Various or miscellaneous articles. [< SUNDRY]

sun·dry (sun′drē) *adj.* Various; several; miscellaneous. [< OE *syndrig* separate]

sun·fish (sun′fish′) *n. pl.* **·fish** or

Sundial

·**fish·es** 1 Any of several North American freshwater perchlike fishes, usu. with narrow bodies. 2 Any of various large fishes of warm seas, having a deep compressed body.

sun·flow·er (sun′flou′ər) n. Any of a genus of tall plants with large leaves and large composite flower heads encircled with a ring of bright yellow ray flowers.

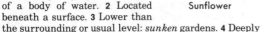

Sunflower

sung (sung) p.p. of SING.

sun·glasses (sun′glas′iz, -gläs′-) n.pl. Eyeglasses having colored lenses that protect the eyes from the glare of the sun.

sunk (sungk) p.p. & a p.t. of SINK.

sunk·en (sung′kən) A p.p. of SINK. —adj. 1 Lying at the bottom of a body of water. 2 Located beneath a surface. 3 Lower than the surrounding or usual level: sunken gardens. 4 Deeply depressed or fallen in: sunken cheeks.

sun·lamp (sun′lamp′) n. An electric lamp radiating ultraviolet rays, used esp. for therapeutic treatments.

sun·less (sun′lis) adj. Dark; cheerless. —sun′less·ness n.

sun·light (sun′līt′) n. The light of the sun.

sun·lit (sun′lit′) adj. Lighted by the sun.

sun·ny (sun′ē) adj. ·ni·er, ·ni·est 1 Characterized by bright sunlight. 2 Filled with sunlight: a sunny room. 3 Cheerful; genial: a sunny smile. —sun′ni·ly adv. —sun′ni·ness n.

sun parlor A room enclosed in glass and having a sunny exposure. Also **sun porch, sun room.**

sun·rise (sun′rīz′) n. 1 The daily first appearance of the sun above the horizon. 2 The time at which the sun rises.

sun·set (sun′set′) n. 1 The apparent daily descent of the sun below the horizon. 2 The time at which the sun sets. 3 A final period or decline, as of life.

sun·shade (sun′shād′) n. Something used as protection from the sun, as a parasol or as an awning.

sun·shine (sun′shīn′) n. 1 The direct light of the sun. 2 The light and warmth of sunlight. 3 Brightness or warmth, as of feeling. —sun′shin′y adj.

sun·spot (sun′spot′) n. One of many dark irregular spots appearing sometimes on the surface of the sun.

sun·stroke (sun′strōk′) n. Prostration and fever induced by heat and exposure to the sun. —sun′struck′ (-struk′) adj.

sun·tan (sun′tan′) n. A darkened coloration of the skin induced by exposure to ultraviolet light. —sun′tanned′ (-tand′) adj.

sun·up (sun′up′) n. SUNRISE.

sun·ward (sun′wərd) adj. Facing toward the sun. —adv. Toward the sun: also **sun′wards.**

sup[1] (sup) v.t. & v.i. supped, sup·ping To take (fluid food) a little at a time; sip. —n. A mouthful or sip of liquid or semiliquid food. [< OE sūpan drink]

sup[2] (sup) v. supped, sup·ping v.i. To eat supper. [< OF soper < soupe soup]

sup. above (L supra); superior; superlative; supplement; supplementary; supply.

su·per (sōō′pər) adj. 1 Surpassing others of its class, as in power or size: a super bomb; a super city. 2 Informal Outstanding; superb: a super performance. 3 Slang Great; wonderful: He's super! 4 More than normal or warranted. —n. 1 A superintendent (def. 2). 2 SUPERNUMERARY (esp. def. 2). 3 An article of superior size or quality.

super- prefix 1 Above in position; over: superstructure. 2 More than; above or beyond: supersonic. 3 More than normal or warranted; inordinate or inordinately: superintelligent; superpatriot. 4 Surpassing others in its class, as in power, size, or skill; superior: superhighway. 5 Extra: supertax. [< L super above, beyond] • See TAXONOMY.

su·per·a·ble (sōō′pər·ə·bəl) adj. That can be surmounted, overcome, or conquered. [< L superare overcome < super over] —su′per·a·bil′i·ty n. —su′per·a·bly adv.

su·per·a·bound (sōō′pər·ə·bound′) v.i. To abound to excess. [< L super- exceedingly + abundare overflow]

su·per·a·bun·dant (sōō′pər·ə·bun′dənt) adj. More than sufficient; excessive. [< LL superabundare to superabound] —su′per·a·bun′dance n. —su′per·a·bun′dant·ly adv.

su·per·an·nu·at·ed (sōō′pər·an′yōō·wāt′id) adj. 1 Relieved of active work on account of age; retired. 2 Set aside or discarded as obsolete or too old. [< L super beyond + annus a year]

su·perb (sōō·pûrb′, sōō-) adj. 1 Extraordinarily good; excellent: a superb wine. 2 Having grand, impressive beauty; majestic: a superb cathedral. 3 Luxurious; elegant. [< L superbus proud] —su·perb′ly adv. —su·perb′ness n.

su·per·block (sōō′pər·blok′) n. A large block of commercial buildings or residences from which motor traffic is barred, often landscaped as a unit and joined by pedestrian walks.

su·per·car·go (sōō′pər·kär′gō) n. pl. ·goes or ·gos An officer on board ship in charge of the cargo and its sale and purchase.

su·per·charge (sōō′pər·chärj′) v.t. ·charged, ·charg·ing 1 To adapt (an engine) to develop more power, as by fitting with a supercharger. 2 To charge excessively, as with emotion.

su·per·charg·er (sōō′pər·chär′jər) n. A compressor for supplying extra air or fuel mixture to an internal-combustion engine.

su·per·cil·i·ous (sōō′pər·sil′ē·əs) adj. Haughtily contemptuous; arrogant. [< L supercilium eyebrow, pride] —su′per·cil′i·ous·ly adv. —su′per·cil′i·ous·ness n.

su·per·con·duc·ting (sōō′pər·kən·duk′ting) adj. Having the property, when cooled to temperatures near absolute zero, of conducting electricity continuously without resistance: said of certain metals and alloys. —su′per·con·duc′tive adj. —su′per·con·duc·tiv′i·ty (-kon′duk·tiv′ə·tē) n. su′per·con·duc′tor n.

su·per·e·go (sōō′pər·ē′gō, -eg′ō) n. pl. ·gos Psychoanal. A largely unconscious element of the personality, acting principally as conscience and critic.

su·per·er·o·ga·tion (sōō′pər·er′ə·gā′shən) n. The performance of an act in excess of the demands or requirements of duty. [< L super- above + erogare pay out]

su·per·e·rog·a·to·ry (sōō′pər·ə·rog′ə·tôr′ē, -tō′rē) adj. 1 Of the nature of supererogation. 2 SUPERFLUOUS.

su·per·fi·cial (sōō′pər·fish′əl) adj. 1 Of, lying near, or on the surface: a superficial wound. 2 Of or pertaining to only the ordinary and the obvious; not profound; shallow. 3 Hasty; cursory: a superficial examination. 4 Apparent only; not real or genuine. [< L super- above + facies a face] —su′per·fi·ci·al′i·ty (-fish′ē·al′ə·tē), su′per·fi′cial·ness n. — su′per·fi′cial·ly adv.

su·per·fine (sōō′pər·fīn′) adj. 1 Of the best quality; very fine and delicate. 2 Unduly elaborate. —su′per·fine′ness n.

su·per·flu·i·ty (sōō′pər·flōō′ə·tē) n. pl. ·ties 1 The state of being superfluous. 2 That, or that part, which is superfluous.

su·per·flu·ous (sōō·pûr′flōō·əs) adj. Exceeding what is needed; surplus. [< L super- above + fluere to flow] —su·per′flu·ous·ly adv. —su·per′flu·ous·ness n.

su·per·heat (sōō′pər·hēt′) v.t. 1 OVERHEAT. 2 To raise the temperature of (a vapor not in contact with its liquid) above the saturation point for a given pressure. 3 To heat (a liquid) above the boiling point without conversion into vapor. —su′per·heat′er n.

su·per·het·er·o·dyne (sōō′pər·het′ər·ə·dīn′) adj. Electronics Pertaining to or designating radio reception in which the incoming signals are converted to an intermediate frequency, and are then amplified and demodulated. —n. A radio receiver of this type. [< SUPER(SONIC) + HETERODYNE]

su·per·high·way (sōō′pər·hī′wā′) n. A highway for high-speed traffic, usu. with four or more lanes.

su·per·hu·man (sōō′pər·hyōō′mən) adj. 1 Above and beyond what is human; miraculous; divine. 2 Beyond normal human ability or power. —su′per·hu′man·ly adv. — su′per·hu′man·ness n.

su·per·im·pose (sōō′pər·im·pōz′) v.t. ·posed, ·pos·ing 1 To lay or impose upon something else. 2 To add as an incidental or superfluous feature. —su′per·im·po·si′tion (-im′pə·zish′ən) n.

su·per·in·duce (sōō′pər·in·dyōōs′) v.t. ·duced, ·duc·ing To introduce additionally. [< L super- over + inducere lead in] —su′per·in·duc′tion (-duk′shən) n.

su·per·in·tend (sōō′pər·in·tend′) v.t. To have the charge and direction of; supervise. [< LL super- over + intendere

direct, aim at] **—su′per·in·ten′dence, su′per·in·ten′den·cy** n.

su·per·in·ten·dent (soō′pər·in·ten′dənt) n. 1 One who has charge of an institution or undertaking; director. 2 One responsible for the maintenance and repair of a building. **—adj.** Superintending.

su·pe·ri·or (sə·pir′ē·ər, soō-) adj. 1 Higher in rank, quality, or degree; better or excellent: superior vision; superior talent. 2 Greater in quantity: a superior supply. 3 Higher in relation to other things; upper. 4 Printing Set above the line, as 1 in x¹. 5 Serenely unaffected or indifferent: with to: superior to pettiness. 6 Affecting or suggesting an attitude of contemptuous indifference or disdain: superior airs. **—n.** 1 One who is superior, as in rank or excellence. 2 The head of an abbey, convent, or monastery. [< L superus higher < super above] **—su·pe·ri·or·i·ty** (sə·pir′ē·ôr′ə·tē, -or′-, soō-) n. **—su·pe′ri·or·ly** adv.

su·per·la·tive (sə·pûr′lə·tiv, soō-) adj. 1 Being of the highest degree; most excellent or eminent. 2 Gram. Expressing the highest or extreme degree of the quality expressed by the positive degree of an adjective or adverb: "Wisest" is the superlative form of "wise." 3 Exaggerated. **—n.** 1 That which is superlative. 2 The highest degree; apex. 3 Gram. a The superlative degree. b A form in the superlative degree. [< L superlatus excessive < super- above + latus carried] **—su·per′la·tive·ly** adv. **—su·per′la·tive·ness** n.

su·per·man (soō′pər·man′) n. pl. ·men (-men′) 1 A man of superhuman powers. 2 An intellectually and morally superior man.

su·per·mar·ket (soō′pər·mär′kit) n. A large, chiefly self-service store selling food and household supplies.

su·per·nal (soō·pûr′nəl) adj. 1 Heavenly; celestial. 2 Coming from above or from the sky. [< L supernus < super over] **—su·per′nal·ly** adv.

su·per·nat·u·ral (soō′pər·nach′ər·əl, -rəl) adj. 1 Existing or occurring through some agency beyond the known forces of nature. 2 Of or concerning phenomena of this kind: supernatural tales. 3 Believed to be miraculous or divine. 4 Suggestive of ghosts, demons, or other agents unconstrained by natural law. **—n.** That which is supernatural. [< L super- above + natura nature] **—su′per·nat′u·ral·ism, su′per·nat′u·ral·ness** n. **—su′per·nat′u·ral·ist** adj., n. **—su′per·nat′u·ral·is′tic** adj. **—su′per·nat′u·ral·ly** adv.

su·per·nu·mer·ar·y (soō′pər·nyoō′mə·rer′ē) adj. 1 Being beyond a fixed or usual number. 2 Beyond a necessary number; superfluous. **—n.** pl. ·ar·ies 1 A supernumerary person or thing. 2 A stage performer without any speaking part. [< L super over + numerus a number]

su·per·pa·tri·ot (soō′pər·pā′trē·ət, -ot) n. A person who is or claims to be a great patriot, often one whose patriotic fervor is marked by a readiness to regard dissent as unpatriotic or subversive. **—su′per·pa′tri·ot′ic** adj. **—su′per·pa′·tri·ot·ism** n.

su·per·pose (soō′pər·pōz′) v.t. ·posed, ·pos·ing To lay over or upon something else. **—su′per·pos′a·ble** adj. **—su′·per·po·si′tion** (-pə·zish′ən) n.

su·per·pow·er (soō′pər·pou′ər) n. One of a few great, dominant nations characterized by superior economic or military strength and by large population.

su·per·sat·u·rate (soō′pər·sach′oō·rāt) v.t. ·rat·ed, ·rat·ing To cause (a solution) to hold more of a solute than it can normally hold at the given temperature. **—su′per·sat′u·ra′tion** n.

su·per·scribe (soō′pər·skrīb′) v.t. ·scribed, ·scrib·ing 1 To write or engrave on the outside or on the upper part of. 2 To address, as a letter. [< L super- over + scribere write] **—su′per·scrip′tion** (-skrip′shən) n.

su·per·script (soō′pər·skript′) adj. Written above or overhead. **—n.** A letter, index, or other mark following and above a letter or figure, as in a³ or c′. [< LL superscriptus, p.p. of superscribere superscribe]

su·per·sede (soō′pər·sēd′) v.t. ·sed·ed, ·sed·ing 1 To take the place of, as by reason of superiority or right; replace. 2 To put something in the place of; set aside. [< L super- above + sedere sit] **—su′per·sed′er, su′per·se′dure** (-sē′jər) n.

su·per·son·ic (soō′pər·son′ik) adj. 1 Of or capable of moving at a speed greater than that of sound. 2 Moving at such a speed. 3 ULTRASONIC. **—su′per·son′i·cal·ly** adv.

su·per·star (soō′pər·stär′) n. A public performer, as an actor, singer, or professional athlete, regarded as one of the best or most popular. **—su′per·star′dom** n.

su·per·sti·tion (soō′pər·stish′ən) n. 1 An ignorant or irrational belief, often provoked by fear, and based upon assumptions of cause and effect contrary to known scientific facts and principles. 2 Any practice inspired by such belief. 3 Any unreasonable belief or impression. [< L superstitio excessive fear of the gods, amazement]

su·per·sti·tious (soō′pər·stish′əs) adj. 1 Disposed to believe in or be influenced by superstitions. 2 Of, based upon, or manifesting superstition. **—su′per·sti′tious·ly** adv. **—su′·per·sti′tious·ness** n.

su·per·struc·ture (soō′pər·struk′chər) n. 1 Any structure above the basement or considered in relation to its foundation. 2 Any structure built on top of another. 3 The parts of a ship's structure above the main deck.

su·per·tank·er (soō′pər·tangk′ər) n. A very large tanker capable of carrying a vast cargo, as of oil.

su·per·tax (soō′pər·taks′) n. An extra tax in addition to the normal tax; a surtax.

su·per·vene (soō′pər·vēn′) v.i. ·vened, ·ven·ing To follow closely upon something as an extraneous or additional circumstance. [< L super- over and above + venire come] **—su′per·ven′ient** (-vēn′yənt) adj. **—su′per·ven′tion** (-ven′·shən) n.

su·per·vise (soō′pər·vīz′) v.t. ·vised, ·vis·ing To have charge of; direct. [< L super- over + videre see] **—Syn.** manage, run, oversee, superintend.

su·per·vi·sion (soō′pər·vizh′ən) n. The act or process of supervising; direction, control, or guidance.

su·per·vi·sor (soō′pər·vī′zər) n. 1 One who supervises; a superintendent or manager. 2 In education, an official supervising teachers and responsible for curricula, etc., in a particular subject. **—su′per·vi′sor·ship** n. **—su·per·vi·sor·y** (soō′pər·vī′zər·ē) adj.

su·pine (soō·pīn′, sə-) adj. 1 Lying on the back, or with the face turned upward. 2 Having no interest or care; listless. [< L supinus] **—su·pine′ly** adv. **—su·pine′ness** n.

supp., suppl. supplement; supplementary.

sup·per (sup′ər) n. 1 The last meal of the day; the evening meal. 2 A social event including the serving of supper: a church supper. [< OF soper sup] **—sup′per·less** adj.

sup·plant (sə·plant′, -plänt′) v.t. 1 To take the place of, as of something inferior or out of date; displace. 2 To take the place of (someone) by scheming, treachery, etc. 3 To replace (one thing) with another: to supplant naive expectations with realistic goals. [< L supplantare trip up] **—sup·plan·ta·tion** (sup′lan·tā′shən), **sup·plant′er** n.

sup·ple (sup′əl) adj. ·pler (sup′lər, -əl·ər), ·plest 1 Easily bent; flexible; pliant: supple leather. 2 Agile or graceful in movement; limber. 3 Yielding readily to the wishes of others; compliant. 4 Servile; obsequious. 5 Quick to respond or adjust, as the mind; adaptable. **—v.t. & v.i.** ·pled, ·pling To make or become supple. [< L supplex, lit., bending under] **—sup′ple·ly** (sup′əl·ē, sup′lē) or **sup′ply** (sup′lē) adv. **—sup′ple·ness** n. **—Syn.** 2 lithe, deft, nimble.

sup·ple·ment (sup′lə·mənt) n. 1 Something added that supplies a deficiency. 2 An addition to a publication, as a section providing additional information added to a book. **—v.t.** To make additions to; provide for what is lacking in. [< L supplere. See SUPPLY.] **—sup·ple·men·tal** (sup′lə·men′·təl) adj. • Both supplement and complement refer to something added to make up for a lack or deficiency. Complement (not to be confused with compliment, an expression of praise) emphasizes the correction or adjustment of something unfinished or imperfect, and often implies a balancing of elements: The design of the housing project called for low buildings to complement the high-rises. In the case of supplement, the fact of being added is more emphatic, and the expected result is one of improvement rather than completion: Student teachers supplemented the regular teaching staff, freeing them to give more individual help to slow learners.

sup·ple·men·ta·ry (sup′lə·men′tər·ē, -trē) adj. Added as a supplement; additional.

sup·pli·ant (sup′lē·ənt) adj. Entreating earnestly and humbly. —n. One who supplicates. [< L supplicare supplicate] —**sup′pli·ant·ly** adv. —**sup′pli·ant·ness** n.

sup·pli·cant (sup′lə·kənt) n. One who supplicates. —adj. Asking or entreating humbly. [< L supplicare supplicate]

sup·pli·cate (sup′lə·kāt) v. ·cat·ed, ·cat·ing v.t. 1 To ask for humbly or by earnest prayer. 2 To beg something of; entreat. —v.i. 3 To make an earnest request. [< L sub- under + plicare bend, fold] —**sup′pli·ca′tion** n. —**sup′pli·ca·to′ry** (-kə·tôr′ē, -tō′rē) adj.

sup·ply (sə·plī′) v. ·plied, ·ply·ing v.t. 1 To make available; provide or furnish: to supply electricity to a remote area. 2 To furnish with what is needed: to supply an army with weapons. 3 To provide for adequately; satisfy. 4 To make up for; compensate for. 5 To fill (the place of another). —v.i. 6 To take the place of another temporarily. —n. pl. ·plies 1 That which is or can be supplied. 2 A store or quantity on hand. 3 pl. Accumulated stores, as for an army. 4 The amount of a commodity offered at a given price or available for meeting a demand. 5 The act of supplying. [< L supplere < sub- up from under + plere fill] —**sup·pli′er** n.

sup·port (sə·pôrt′, -pōrt′) v.t. 1 To bear the weight of, esp. from underneath; hold in position; keep from falling, sinking, etc. 2 To bear or sustain (weight, etc.). 3 To provide money or necessities for; provide with the means of subsistence. 4 To give approval or assistance to; uphold. 5 To serve to uphold or corroborate; substantiate: His testimony supports our position. 6 To endure patiently; tolerate. 7 To provide with the means to endure; keep from collapsing or yielding: Faith supported her. 8 To carry on; keep up: to support a war. 9 In the theater, etc., to act in a subordinate role to. —n. 1 The act of supporting. 2 One who supports. 3 That which supports, as a brace or girdle for the body. [< L sub- up from under + portare carry] —**sup·port′a·ble** adj. —**sup·port′a·bly** adv. —**Syn.** 4 advocate, endorse, help, aid, assist. 5 verify, bear out. 6 bear, suffer. 7 sustain.

sup·port·er (sə·pôr′tər, -pōr′-) n. 1 One who or that which supports. 2 An elastic or other support for some part of the body.

sup·por·tive (sə·pôr′tiv, -pōr′-) adj. 1 Tending or intended to support. 2 Contributing importantly to the stability of one's physical or emotional health: supportive treatment. —**sup·por′tive·ly** adv.

sup·pose (sə·pōz′) v. ·posed, ·pos·ing v.t. 1 To believe to be true or probable; presume. 2 To assume as true for the sake of argument or illustration. 3 To expect: I am supposed to follow. 4 To presuppose; imply: Mercy supposes a sense of compassion. —v.i. 5 To make a supposition. [< L supponere substitute, put under] —**sup·pos′a·ble** adj. —**sup·pos′a·bly** adv. —**sup·pos′er** n.

sup·posed (sə·pōzd′) adj. 1 Accepted as genuine; believed. 2 Imagined only, instead of actually experienced. —**sup·pos·ed·ly** (sə·pō′zid·lē) adv.

sup·po·si·tion (sup′ə·zish′ən) n. 1 Something supposed; a conjecture or hypothesis. 2 The act of supposing. —**sup′po·si′tion·al** adj. —**sup′po·si′tion·al·ly** adv.

sup·pos·i·to·ry (sə·poz′ə·tôr′ē, -tō′rē) n. pl. ·ries A small mass of a usu. medicated substance that melts at body temperature, for introduction into a body cavity, as the rectum or vagina. [< LL suppositorius placed underneath or up < L supponere put under]

sup·press (sə·pres′) v.t. 1 To put an end to or stop to; crush, as a rebellion. 2 To stop or prohibit the activities of. 3 To withhold from knowledge or publication, as a book, news, etc. 4 To hold back or repress. 5 To stop or check (a hemorrhage, etc.). [< L suppressus, p.p. of supprimere press down] —**sup·press′er, sup·pres′sor** n. —**sup·press′i·ble, sup·pres′sive** adj.

sup·pres·sion (sə·presh′ən) n. 1 The act of suppressing, or the state of being suppressed. 2 The deliberate exclusion from consciousness of unacceptable ideas, memories, etc.

sup·pu·rate (sup′yə·rāt) v.i. ·rat·ed, ·rat·ing To discharge or generate pus. [< L sub- under + pus, puris pus] —**sup′·pu·ra′tion** n. —**sup′pu·ra·tive** (-rə·tiv, -rā′-) adj.

su·pra (soo′prə) adv. Above. [L]

supra- prefix Above; beyond: supranational. [< L supra above, beyond]

su·pra·na·tion·al (soo′prə·nash′ə·nəl) adj. Of or concerning several or a number of nations; involving more than one nation. —**su′pra·na′tion·al·ism** n. —**su′pra·na′tion·al·ist** adj., n.

su·pra·re·nal (soo′prə·rē′nəl) adj. Situated above the kidneys; adrenal. —n. An adrenal gland. [< L supra-above + renalis renal]

su·prem·a·cy (sə·prem′ə·sē, soo-) n. pl. ·cies 1 The state of being supreme. 2 Supreme power or authority.

su·preme (sə·prēm′, soo-) adj. 1 Highest in power or authority; dominant. 2 Highest or greatest, as in degree; utmost: supreme devotion. 3 Ultimate; last and greatest. [< L supremus, superl. of superus < super above] —**su·preme′ly** adv. —**su·preme′ness** n.

Supreme Being God.

Supreme Court 1 The highest Federal court. 2 The highest court in many states.

Supreme Soviet The legislature of the Soviet Union.

supt. superintendent.

sur- prefix Over; beyond: surtax. [< OF sur- < L super-]

su·rah (soor′ə) n. A soft, usu. twilled, silk or silk and rayon fabric. [< Surat, India]

sur·base (sûr′bās′) n. A border or molding above the top of a base, as of a pedestal.

sur·cease (sûr·sēs′, sûr′sēs) n. Cessation; end. —v.t. & v.i. ·ceased, ·ceas·ing To end. [< AF surseoir to refrain < L supersedere to sit above]

sur·charge (sûr′chärj′) n. 1 An additional amount charged or imposed. 2 An excessive burden, load, or charge. 3 OVERCHARGE. 4 A new valuation or something additional printed on a postage or revenue stamp. —v.t. (sûr·chärj′) ·charged, ·charg·ing 1 OVERCHARGE. 2 To fill or load to excess. 3 To imprint a surcharge on (postage stamps). —**sur·charg′er** n.

sur·cin·gle (sûr′sing·gəl) n. A strap encircling the body of a horse, for holding a saddle, blanket, etc. [< SUR- + L cingulum a belt]

sur·coat (sûr′kōt′) n. An outer coat or garment, esp., in the Middle Ages, one worn over armor.

Surcoat

surd (sûrd) n. 1 Math. An irrational number, esp. an indicated root, as $\sqrt{2}$. 2 Phonet. A voiceless speech sound. —adj. 1 Math. IRRATIONAL. 2 Phonet. VOICELESS. [< L surdus deaf, silent]

sure (shoor) adj. sur·er, sur·est 1 Not subject to uncertainty or doubt; beyond all question; indisputable. 2 Characterized by freedom from doubt or uncertainty; firm: sure convictions; a sure grasp of his subject. 3 Certain or confident; positive: I was sure I had seen her before. 4 Not liable to fail or disappoint; reliable; sound: a sure memory. 5 Bound to happen or be: a sure winner. 6 Obs. Safe; secure. —adv. Informal Surely; certainly. —**for sure** Certainly; beyond all question. —**to be sure** Indeed; certainly; quite so. [< L securus] —**sure′ness** n. —**Syn.** 1 unquestionable, unimpeachable, indubitable. 4 trustworthy, dependable, true.

sure-foot·ed (shoor′foot′id) adj. Not liable to fall or stumble. —**sure′foot′ed·ly** adv. —**sure′foot′ed·ness** n.

sure·ly (shoor′lē) adv. 1 In a sure manner. 2 Without doubt; certainly. 3 Really; certainly: used as an intensive to express strong probability: He surely knew that.

sure·ty (shoor′ə·tē, shoor′tē) n. pl. ·ties 1 The state of being sure; certainty. 2 Security against loss or damage. 3 One who assumes the debts, responsibilities, etc., of another; a guarantor. [< L securus secure] —**sure′ty·ship** n.

surf (sûrf) n. 1 The swell of the sea that breaks upon a shore. 2 The foam caused by the billows. —v.i. To ride the surf on a surfboard; engage in surfing. —**surf′er** n.

sur·face (sûr′fis) n. 1 The outer part or face of an object. 2 That which has area but not thickness. 3 A superficial

aspect; external appearance. —*v.* **·faced, ·fac·ing** *v.t.* **1** To put a surface on; esp., to make smooth, even, or plain. **2** To cause to rise to the surface, as a submarine. —*v.i.* **3** To rise to the surface. **4** To come to public notice, esp. something formerly kept secret. [< SUR- + FACE] —**sur′fac·er** *n.*

sur·face-ac·tive (sûr′fis·ak′tiv) *adj.* Effective in changing the properties of a substance, esp. surface tension, at the area of contact with another substance: *surface-active* detergents.

surface tension That property of a liquid by which the surface molecules exert a strong cohesive force, thus forming an elastic skin that tends to contract.

sur·fac·tant (sûr·fak′tənt) *n.* A surface-active substance, as a detergent. [< SURF(ACE)-ACT(IVE) + -ANT]

surf·board (sûrf′bôrd′, -bōrd′) *n.* A long, narrow board used in surfing. —*v.i.* SURF. —**surf′board′er** *n.*

surf·boat (sûrf′bōt′) *n.* A boat of extra strength and buoyancy, for launching and landing through surf.

sur·feit (sûr′fit) *v.t.* **1** To feed or supply to fullness or to excess. —*v.i.* **2** To overindulge in food or drink. —*n.* **1** Excess in eating or drinking. **2** The result of such excess; satiety. **3** Any excessive amount: a *surfeit* of praise. [< OF *surfaire* overdo]

surf·ing (sûrf′ing) *n.* A water sport in which a person standing on a surfboard is borne by the surf toward the shore. Also **surf·rid·ing** (sûrf′rī′ding).

surg. surgeon; surgery; surgical.

surge (sûrj) *v.* **surged, surg·ing** *v.i.* **1** To rise and roll with a powerful, swelling motion, as waves. **2** To be tossed about by waves. **3** To move or go in a powerful, wavelike motion: The mob *surged* through the square. **4** To increase or vary suddenly, as an electric current. —*n.* **1** A large swelling wave; billow. **2** A great swelling or rolling movement, as of waves. **3** *Electr.* A sudden, transient rise in current flow. **4** Any sudden, sharp increase. [< L *surgere*]

sur·geon (sûr′jən) *n.* One who practices surgery. [< OF *cirurgie* surgery] —**sur′geon·cy** (-sē) *n.*

sur·ger·y (sûr′jər·ē) *n. pl.* **·ger·ies** **1** The treatment of disease, injury, etc., by manual and operative means. **2** The branch of medicine concerned with surgical treatment. **3** A place where surgery is performed; an operating room. **4** *Brit.* A physician's office. [< Gk. *cheirourgia* a handicraft < *cheir* the hand + *ergein* to work] —**sur·gi·cal** (sûr′ji·kəl) *adj.* —**sur′gi·cal·ly** *adv.*

sur·ly (sûr′lē) *adj.* **·li·er, ·li·est** Rude and ill-humored, esp. in response; gruff or insolent. [Earlier *sirly* like a lord < *sir* a lord] —**sur′li·ly** *adv.* —**sur′li·ness** *n.*

sur·mise (sər·mīz′) *v.* **·mised, ·mis·ing** *v.t. & v.i.* To infer (something) on slight evidence; guess. —*n.* (sər·mīz′, sûr′mīz) A conjecture made on slight evidence; supposition. [< OF *surmettre* accuse < *sur-* upon + *mettre* put] —**Syn.** *v.* suppose, assume, conjecture.

sur·mount (sər·mount′) *v.t.* **1** To overcome; prevail over (a difficulty, etc.). **2** To mount to the top or cross to the other side of, as an obstacle. **3** To be or lie over or above. **4** To place something above or on top of; cap. [< L *super-* over + *mons, montis* a hill, mountain]

sur·name (sûr′nām′) *n.* **1** A last name; family name. **2** A name added to one's real name, as Ethelred *the Unready*. —*v.t.* (sûr′nām′, sûr·nām′) **·named, ·nam·ing** To give a surname to; call by a surname. [< OF *sur-* above, beyond + *nom* a name]

sur·pass (sər·pas′, -päs′) *v.t.* **1** To go beyond or past in degree or amount; exceed or excel. **2** To be beyond the reach or powers of; transcend. —**sur·pass′a·ble** *adj.* —**sur·pass′er** *n.* —**Syn.** **1** eclipse, outdo, outstrip.

sur·pass·ing (sər·pas′ing, -päs′-) *adj.* Exceptional; excellent. —**sur·pass′ing·ly** *adv.*

sur·plice (sûr′plis) *n.* A loose white vestment with full sleeves, worn over the cassock by the clergy and choristers of some churches. [< Med. L *superpellicium (vestimentum)* an overgarment]

Surplice

sur·plus (sûr′plus) *n.* **1** That which remains over and above what is used or required. **2** Assets in excess of liabilities. —*adj.* Being in excess of what is used or needed. [< L *super-* over and above + *plus* more] —**sur′plus·age** (-ij) *n.*

sur·prise (sər·prīz′, sə-) *v.t.* **·prised, ·pris·ing** **1** To cause to feel wonder or astonishment, esp. because unusual or unexpected. **2** To come upon suddenly or unexpectedly; take unawares. **3** To attack suddenly and without warning. **4** To lead unawares, as into doing something not intended: with *into.* —*n.* **1** The state of being surprised; astonishment. **2** Something that causes surprise, as a sudden and unexpected event. **3** A sudden attack or capture. [< L *super-* over + *prehendere* take] —**sur·pris′er** *n.*

sur·pris·ing (sər·prī′zing, sə-) *adj.* Causing surprise or wonder. —**sur·pris′ing·ly** *adv.* —**Syn.** amazing, startling.

sur·re·al·ism (sə·rē′əl·iz′əm) *n.* A 20th-century movement in art and literature characterized chiefly by the incongruous juxtaposition or use of dreamlike elements, in theory an expression of the unconscious mind. —**sur·re′al·ist** *adj., n.* —**sur·re·al·is′tic** *adj.* —**sur·re·al·is′ti·cal·ly** *adv.*

sur·ren·der (sə·ren′dər) *v.t.* **1** To yield possession of or power over to another because of demand or compulsion. **2** To give up or relinquish, esp. in favor of another; resign; abandon. **3** To give (oneself) over to a passion, influence, etc. —*v.i.* **4** To give oneself up, as to an enemy in warfare. —*n.* The act of surrendering. [< OF *surrendre* < *sur-* over + *rendre* give, render]

sur·rep·ti·tious (sûr′əp·tish′əs) *adj.* **1** Accomplished by secret or improper means; clandestine. **2** Acting secretly or by stealth. [< L *subreptus,* p.p. of *subripere* steal] —**sur′rep·ti′tious·ly** *adv.* —**sur′rep·ti′tious·ness** *n.*

sur·rey (sûr′ē) *n.* A vehicle having two seats facing forward and sometimes a top. [< *Surrey,* England]

Surrey

sur·ro·gate (sûr′ə·gāt, -git) *n.* **1** Someone or something taking the place of another; substitute. **2** In some U.S. states, a probate court judge. —*v.t.* (sûr′ə·gāt) **·gat·ed, ·gat·ing** To put in the place of another; deputize or substitute. [< L *subrogare* < *sub-* in place of another + *rogare* ask]

sur·round (sə·round′) *v.t.* **1** To extend or place completely around; encircle or enclose. **2** To enclose on all sides so as to cut off communication or retreat. **3** To be or cause something to become a significant part of the environment or experience of: *surrounded* by lies; to *surround* oneself with the best legal talent. —*n. Chiefly Brit.* That which surrounds, as a border. [< LL *super-* over + *undare* rise in waves]

sur·round·ings (sə·roun′dingz) *n.pl.* The conditions, objects, etc., that constitute one's environment.

sur·tax (sûr′taks′) *n.* An extra or additional tax.

sur·tout (sər·tōō′, sûr·tōō′) *n.* A man's long, close-fitting overcoat. [F < *sur-* above + *tout* all]

sur·veil·lance (sər·vā′ləns, -vāl′yəns) *n.* A careful watching of someone or something, usu. carried on secretly or discreetly: to keep a suspect under *surveillance.* [F < *sur-* over + *veiller* watch] —**sur·veil′lant** *adj.*

sur·vey (sər·vā′, sûr′vā) *v.t.* **1** To look at in its entirety; view comprehensively, as from a height. **2** To look at carefully and minutely; scrutinize. **3** To determine accurately the area, contour, or boundaries of according to the principles of geometry and trigonometry. **4** To make a survey of. —*v.i.* **5** To survey land. —*n.* (*usu.* sûr′vā) **1** The operation, act, process, or results of surveying land. **2** A systematic inquiry to collect data for analysis, used esp. for the preparation of a comprehensive report or summary. **3** The result of such an inquiry; a comprehensive report. **4** A

general or overall view; overview: a *survey* of contemporary theater. [< L *super-* over + *videre* look]

sur·vey·ing (sər·vā′ing) *n.* **1** The science and art of surveying portions of the surface of the earth and representing them on maps. **2** The work of one who surveys.

sur·vey·or (sər·vā′ər) *n.* One who surveys, esp. one engaged in land surveying.

sur·viv·a·ble (sûr·vī′və·bəl) *adj.* Not precluding survival: a *survivable* accident. **—sur·viv′a·bil′i·ty** *n.*

sur·viv·al (sər·vī′vəl) *n.* **1** The act or fact of surviving; a continuation of life or existence. **2** The fact of living or lasting beyond another. **3** One who or that which survives.

sur·vive (sər·vīv′) *v.* **·vived, ·viv·ing 1** *v.i.* To live or continue beyond the death of another, the occurrence of an event, etc.; remain alive or in existence. **—***v.t.* **2** To live or exist beyond the death, occurrence, or end of; outlive or outlast. **3** To go on living after or in spite of: to *survive* a flood. [< L *super-* above, beyond + *vivere* live] **—sur·vi′vor, sur·viv′er** *n.*

sus·cep·ti·ble (sə·sep′tə·bəl) *adj.* **1** Readily affected; especially subject or vulnerable: with *to: susceptible* to infection; lax supervision *susceptible* to abuse. **2** Capable of being influenced or determined; liable: with *of* or *to: susceptible* of proof. **3** Easily affected in feeling or emotion; sensitive. [< L *suscipere* receive, undertake] **—sus·cep·ti·bil·i·ty** (sə·sep′tə·bil′ə·tē), **sus·cep′ti·ble·ness** *n.* **—sus·cep′ti·bly** *adv.* **—Syn. 1** unresistant, open. **2** admitting. **3** tender, impressionable.

sus·pect (sə·spekt′) *v.t.* **1** To think (a person) guilty without evidence or proof. **2** To have distrust of; doubt: to *suspect* one's motives. **3** To have an inkling or suspicion of; think possible. **—***v.i.* **4** To have suspicions. **—***adj.* (sus′pekt, sə·spekt′) Suspected; exciting suspicion. **—***n.* (sus′pekt) A person suspected, esp. of a crime. [< F *suspecter* < L *suspectus,* p.p. of *suspicere* look under, mistrust] **—sus·pect′er** *n.*

sus·pend (sə·spend′) *v.t.* **1** To bar for a time from a privilege or office as a punishment. **2** To cause to cease for a time; interrupt: to *suspend* telephone service. **3** To withhold or defer action on: to *suspend* a sentence. **4** To hang from a support so as to allow free movement. **5** To keep in suspension, as dust particles in the air. **—***v.i.* **6** To stop for a time. **7** To fail to meet obligations; stop payment. [< L *sub-* under + *pendere* hang]

sus·pend·er (sə·spen′dər) *n.* **1** One who or that which suspends. **2** *pl.* A pair of straps for supporting trousers. **3** *Brit.* A garter.

sus·pense (sə·spens′) *n.* **1** Anxiety caused by an uncertainty, as to the outcome of an event. **2** Excited interest caused by the progressive unfolding of events or information leading to a climax or resolution. **3** The state of being uncertain or indecisive. [< L *suspensus,* p.p. of *suspendere* suspend]

sus·pen·sion (sə·spen′shən) *n.* **1** The act of suspending, or the state of being suspended. **2** A temporary removal from office or position or withdrawal of privilege. **3** An interruption; cessation: *suspension* of normal procedure. **4** A deferment of action. **5** The state of hanging freely from a support. **6** A dispersion in a liquid or gas of insoluble particles that slowly settle on standing; also, a substance in this condition. **7** *Mech.* A system, as of springs or other absorbent parts, by which the chassis and body of a vehicle is insulated against shocks when moving. **8 a** *Music* The prolongation of one or more tones of a chord into the succeeding chord, causing a transient dissonance. **b** The note so prolonged.

suspension bridge A bridge having its roadway suspended from cables supported by towers and anchored at either end.

sus·pen·sive (sə·spen′siv) *adj.* **1** Tending to suspend or keep in suspense. **2** Suspending or deferring operation or effect: a *suspensive* veto. **—sus·pen′sive·ly** *adv.*

sus·pen·so·ry (sə·spen′sər·ē) *adj.* **1** Acting to support or sustain. **2** Suspending or delaying. **—***n. pl.* **·ries** Something that supports or sustains, esp. a truss for the scrotum.

sus·pi·cion (sə·spish′ən) *n.* **1** The act of suspecting; an uncertain but often tenacious feeling or belief in the likelihood of another's guilt, wrongdoing, etc., without evidence or proof. **2** *Informal* A slight amount; trace, as

of a flavor. **—***v.t. Regional* To suspect. [< L *suspicere.* See SUSPECT.]

sus·pi·cious (sə·spish′əs) *adj.* **1** Tending to arouse suspicion; questionable. **2** Having or disposed to have suspicions. **3** Indicating suspicion. **—sus·pi′cious·ly** *adv.* **—sus·pi′cious·ness** *n.*

sus·tain (sə·stān′) *v.t.* **1** To keep up or maintain; keep in effect or being. **2** To maintain by providing with food and other necessities. **3** To keep from sinking or falling, esp. by bearing up from below. **4** To endure without succumbing; withstand. **5** To suffer, as a loss or injury; undergo. **6** To uphold or support as being true or just. **7** To prove the truth or correctness of; confirm. [< L *sub-* up from under + *tenere* to hold] **—sus·tain′a·ble** *adj.* **—sus·tain′er, sus·tain′ment** *n.* **—Syn. 7** corroborate, establish.

sus·te·nance (sus′tə·nəns) *n.* **1** The act or process of sustaining; esp., maintenance of life or health; subsistence. **2** That which sustains, as food. **3** Means of support; livelihood.

sut·ler (sut′lər) *n.* Formerly, a peddler or tradesman who followed an army to sell goods and food to the soldiers. [< Du. *soeteler*] **—sut′ler·ship** *n.*

sut·tee (su·tē′, sut′ē) *n.* **1** The former custom in which a Hindu woman willingly cremated herself on the funeral pyre of her husband: also **sut·tee′ism. 2** The widow so cremated. [< Hind. *satī* < Skt., faithful wife, fem. of *sat* good, wise]

su·ture (sōō′chər) *n.* **1** The junction of two edges by or as by sewing. **2** *Anat.* The fusion of two bones at their edges, as in the skull. **3** *Surg.* **a** The act or operation of joining the edges of an incision, wound, etc. **b** The thread, wire, or other material used in this operation. **—***v.t.* **·tured, ·tur·ing** To unite by means of sutures; sew together. [< L *sutus,* p.p. of *suere* sew] **—su′tur·al** *adj.* **—su′tur·al·ly** *adv.*

su·ze·rain (sōō′zə·rin, -rān) *n.* **1** A feudal lord. **2** A nation having paramount control over a locally autonomous state. [< L *susum* upwards] **—su′ze·rain·ty** *n.* (*pl.* **·ties**)

svelte (svelt) *adj.* **1** Slender; willowy: a *svelte* fashion model. **2** Sophisticated; smart; chic. [< Ital. *svelto* stretched, slender]

SW, S.W., sw, s.w. southwest; southwestern.

Sw. Sweden; Swedish.

swab (swob) *n.* **1** A soft, absorbent substance, as of cotton or gauze, usu. secured at the end of a small stick, for applying medication, cleansing a body surface, etc. **2** *Med.* A specimen of mucus, etc., taken for examination with a swab. **3** A mop for cleaning decks, floors, etc. **4** A cylindrical brush for cleaning firearms. **5** *Slang* An oaf; lout. **—***v.t.* **swabbed, swab·bing** To clean or apply with a swab. [< MDu. *zwabben* swab] **—swab′ber** *n.*

swad·dle (swod′l) *v.t.* **·dled, ·dling 1** To wrap (an infant) in swaddling clothes. **2** To wrap with or as if with a bandage; swathe; bind. **—***n.* A band or cloth used for swaddling. [< OE *swathian* swathe]

swaddling clothes Bands or strips of linen or cloth formerly wound around a newborn infant. Also **swaddling bands.**

swag (swag) *n.* **1** A curved decoration, as a hanging fastened at either end or a carved motif on a building. **2** *Slang* Property obtained by robbery or theft; plunder. **3** *Austral.* A bundle or pack containing belongings. **4** A swaying; a lurch. [? < Scand.]

swage (swāj) *n.* A tool or form for shaping metal by hammering or pressure. **—***v.t.* **swaged, swag·ing** To shape (metal) with or as with a swage. [< OF *souage*]

swag·ger (swag′ər) *v.i.* **1** To walk with an air of conspicuous self-satisfaction and usu. of masculine vanity. **2** To behave in a blustering or self-satisfied manner. **3** To boast; brag. **—***n.* **1** A swaggering gait or manner. **2** Verve; dash; bravado. **—***adj.* Showy or stylish; smart. [< SWAG] **—swag′ger·er** *n.* **—swag′ger·ing·ly** *adv.*

swagger stick A short, lightweight stick, usu. tipped with metal, carried by some military officers as a mark of elegance or authority.

Swa·hi·li (swä·hē′lē) *n. pl.* **·hi·li** or **·hi·lis 1** One of a Bantu people of Zanzibar and the adjacent coast. **2** The language of this people, now widely used in E and central Africa.

swain (swān) *n.* **1** A rustic youth. **2** A lover; wooer. [< ON *sveinn* a boy, servant]

swal·low[1] (swol′ō) *v.t.* **1** To cause (food, etc.) to pass from the mouth into the stomach by means of muscular action of the esophagus. **2** To take in or engulf in a manner suggestive of this; absorb; envelop: often with *up.* **3** To put up with or endure; submit to, as insults. **4** To refrain from expressing; suppress: to *swallow* one's pride. **5** To take back: to *swallow* one's words. **6** *Informal* To believe (something improbable or incredible) to be true. —*v.i.* **7** To perform the act or the motions of swallowing. —*n.* **1** The act of swallowing. **2** An amount swallowed at once; a mouthful. [< OE *swelgan* swallow] —**swal′low·er** *n.*

swal·low[2] (swol′ō) *n.* **1** Any of various small birds with short bill, long, pointed wings, and forked tail, noted for swiftness of flight and migratory habits. **2** A similar bird, as the swift. [< OE *swealwe*]

swal·low·tail (swol′ō·tāl′) *n.* **1** A man's dress coat with two long, tapering skirts or tails. **2** A butterfly having a tapering prolongation on each hind wing. —**swal′low-tailed′** *adj.*

swam (swam) *p.t.* of SWIM.

swa·mi (swä′mē) *n. pl.* **·mis** Master; lord: a Hindu title of respect, esp. for a religious teacher.

swamp (swomp, swômp) *n.* A tract or region of low land saturated with water; a bog. Also **swamp′land′** (-land′). —*v.t.* **1** To drench or submerge with water or other liquid. **2** To overwhelm with difficulties; crush; ruin. **3** To sink or fill (a boat) with water. —*v.i.* **4** To sink in water, etc.; become swamped. [? < LG] —**swamp′y** *adj.* (**·i·er, ·i·est**)

swamp fever MALARIA.

swan (swon, swôn) *n.* Any of several large, web-footed, long-necked birds allied to but heavier than the goose. [< OE]

swan dive A dive performed with the head tilted back and the arms held sideways and brought together as the water is entered.

swank (swangk) *n.* **1** Ostentatious display, as in taste or manner; swagger. **2** Stylishness; smartness. —*adj.* **1** Ostentatiously fashionable. **2** Stylish; smart. —*v.i.* *Slang* To swagger; bluster. [< MHG *swanken* sway]

Trumpeter swan

swank·y (swangk′ē) *adj.* **swank·i·er, swank·i·est** *Informal* Ostentatiously or extravagantly fashionable. —**swank′i·ly** *adv.* —**swank′i·ness** *n.*

swan's-down (swonz′doun′, swônz′-) *n.* **1** The down of a swan, used for trimming, powder puffs, etc. **2** Any of various fine, soft fabrics, usu. with a nap. Also **swans′·down′.**

swan song A last work, utterance, or performance, as before retirement or death. [< the ancient fable that the swan sings a last song before dying]

swap (swop) *v.t. & v.i.* **swapped, swap·ping** *Informal* To exchange (one thing for another); trade. —*n.* The act or an instance of swapping. [< ME *swappen* strike (a bargain), slap] —**swap′per** *n.*

sward (swôrd) *n.* Land thickly covered with grass; turf. —*v.t.* To cover with sward. [< OE *sweard* a skin]

swarm[1] (swôrm) *n.* **1** A large number of bees moving together with a queen to form a new colony. **2** A hive of bees. **3** A large crowd or mass, esp. one in apparent overall movement; throng. —*v.i.* **1** To leave the hive in a swarm: said of bees. **2** To come together, move, or occur in great numbers: The crowd *swarmed* out of the stadium; gnats *swarming* about. **3** To be crowded or overrun; teem: with *with: swarming* with tourists. —*v.t.* **4** To fill with a swarm or crowd. [< OE *swearm*] —**swarm′er** *n.*

swarm[2] (swôrm) *v.t. & v.i.* To climb (a tree, etc.) by clasping it with the hands and limbs. [?]

swart (swôrt) *adj.* Swarthy. [< OE *sweart*] —**swart′ness** *n.*

swarth·y (swôr′thē) *adj.* **swarth·i·er, swarth·i·est** Having a dark complexion; tawny. [Var. of obs. *swarty* < SWART] —**swarth′i·ly** *adv.* —**swarth′i·ness** *n.*

swash (swosh, swôsh) *v.i.* **1** To move with a splashing sound, as waves. —*v.t.* **2** To splash (water, etc.). **3** To splash

or dash water, etc., upon or against. —*n.* The splash of a liquid. [Imit.] —**swash′er** *n.* —**swash′ing·ly** *adv.*

swash·buck·ler (swosh′buk′lər, swôsh′-) *n.* A swaggering soldier, adventurer, daredevil, etc. [< SWASH + BUCK-LER] —**swash′buck′ler·ing** *n.* —**swash′buck′ling** *adj., n.*

swas·ti·ka (swos′ti·kə) *n.* **1** A primitive ornament or symbol in the form of a cross with arms of equal length, bent at the ends at right angles. **2** Such a figure with the arms extended clockwise, used as the emblem of the Nazis. Also **swas′ti·ca.** [< Skt. *sú* good + *astí* being < *as* be]

Nazi swastika

swat (swot) *v.t.* **swat·ted, swat·ting** To hit with a sharp, quick, or violent blow. —*n.* A sharp, quick, or violent blow. [Var. of SQUAT] —**swat′ter** *n.* —**Syn** *v.* smack, strike, whack.

swatch (swoch) *n.* A strip, as of fabric, esp. one cut off for a sample. [?]

swath (swoth, swôth) *n.* **1** A row or line of cut grass or grain. **2** The space cut by a machine or implement in a single course. **3** A strip, track, row, etc. —**cut a wide swath** To make a fine impression. [< OE *swæth* a track]

swathe[1] (swāth, swäth) *v.t.* **swathed, swath·ing 1** To bind or wrap, as in bandages; swaddle. **2** To envelop; enwrap. —*n.* A bandage for swathing. [< OE *swathian*] —**swath′er** *n.*

swathe[2] (swāth, swäth) *n.* SWATH.

sway (swā) *v.i.* **1** To swing from side to side or to and fro; oscillate. **2** To bend or incline to one side. **3** To incline in opinion, sympathy, etc. **4** To control; rule. —*v.t.* **5** To cause to swing from side to side. **6** To cause to bend or lean to one side. **7** To cause (a person, opinion, etc.) to tend in a given way; influence. **8** To deflect or divert, as from a course of action. —*n.* **1** Power; influence. **2** A sweeping, swinging, or turning from side to side. [Prob. < ON *sveigja* bend] —**Syn.** *v.* **2** lean, veer. **4** govern, influence. *n.* **1** control, dominion.

sway·back (swā′bak′) *n.* A hollow or sagging condition of the back, as in a horse. —*adj.* Having such a back: also **sway′backed′** (-bakt).

Swa·zi·land (swä′zē·land) *n.* An independent kingdom of the Commonwealth of Nations in SE Africa, 6,704 sq. mi., cap. Mbabane. • See map at AFRICA.

swear (swâr) *v.* **swore, sworn, swear·ing** *v.i.* **1** To make a solemn affirmation with an appeal to God or some other deity or to something held sacred. **2** To make a vow. **3** To use profanity; curse. **4** *Law* To give testimony under oath. —*v.t.* **5** To affirm or assert solemnly by invoking sacred beings or things. **6** To promise with an oath; vow. **7** To declare or affirm, earnestly or emphatically: I *swear* he's a liar. **8** To take or utter (an oath). —**swear by 1** To appeal to by oath. **2** To have complete confidence in. —**swear in** To administer a legal oath to. —**swear off** *Informal* To promise to give up: to *swear off* drink. —**swear out** To obtain (a warrant for arrest) by making a statement under oath. [< OE *swerian*] —**swear′er** *n.*

swear·word (swâr′wûrd′) *n.* A word used in profanity or cursing.

sweat (swet) *v.* **sweat** or **sweat·ed, sweat·ing** *v.i.* **1** To exude or excrete salty moisture from the pores of the skin; perspire. **2** To exude moisture in drops. **3** To gather and condense moisture in drops on its surface. **4** To pass through pores or interstices in drops. **5** To ferment, as tobacco leaves. **6** To come forth, as through a porous surface; ooze. **7** *Informal* To work hard; toil; drudge. **8** *Informal* To suffer, as from anxiety. —*v.t.* **9** To exude (moisture) from the pores or a porous surface. **10** To gather or condense drops of (moisture). **11** To soak or stain with sweat. **12** To cause to sweat. **13** To cause to work hard. **14** *Informal* To force (employees) to work for low wages and under unfavorable conditions. **15** To heat (solder, etc.) until it melts. **16** To join, as metal objects with solder. **17** *Metall.* To heat so as to extract an element that is easily fusible; also, to extract thus. **18** To subject to fermentation, as hides or tobacco. **19** *Slang* To subject to torture or rigorous interrogation to extract information. —**sweat (something) out** *Slang* To

wait through anxiously; endure. —*n.* 1 Moisture in minute drops on the skin. 2 The act or state of sweating. 3 Hard labor; drudgery. 4 *Informal* Impatience, anxiety, or hurry. [< OE *swætan*] —**sweat′i·ly** *adv.* —**sweat′i·ness** *n.* —**sweat′y** *adj.* (**·i·er, ·i·est**)

sweat·band (swet′band′) *n.* 1 A band, usu. of leather, inside a hat to protect it from sweat. 2 An absorbent cloth band worn over the forehead or around the wrist.

sweat·er (swet′ər) *n.* 1 One who or that which sweats. 2 A knitted or crocheted garment with or without sleeves.

sweat gland One of the numerous minute subcutaneous glands that secrete sweat.

sweat shirt A loose-fitting, usu. long-sleeved pullover of soft, absorbent material, sometimes hooded.

sweat·shop (swet′shop′) *n.* A place where work is done under poor conditions, for insufficient wages, and for long hours.

sweat·suit (swet′soot′) *n.* A sweat shirt and matching pants (**sweat pants**) worn esp. by athletes when warming up or just after competing.

Swed. Sweden; Swedish.

Swede (swed) *n.* A native or citizen of Sweden.

Swe·den (swe′dən) *n.* A constitutional monarchy of N Europe, 173,577 sq. mi., cap. Stockholm.

Swed·ish (swe′dish) *adj.* Of or pertaining to Sweden, the Swedes, or their language. —*n.* 1 The North Germanic language of Sweden. 2 The inhabitants of Sweden collectively: with *the.*

sweep (swep) *v.* **swept, sweep·ing** *v.t.* 1 To collect or clear away with a broom, brush, etc. 2 To clear or clean with a broom, etc.: to *sweep* a floor. 3 To touch or brush with a motion as of sweeping: to *sweep* the strings of a harp. 4 To pass over swiftly: The searchlight *swept* the sky. 5 To move, carry, bring, etc., with force: The flood *swept* the bridge away. 6 To move over or through with force: The gale *swept* the bay. 7 To drag the bottom of (a body of water, etc.). 8 To win totally or overwhelmingly. —*v.i.* 9 To clean a floor or other surface with a broom, etc. 10 To move or go strongly and evenly: The train *swept* by. 11 To walk with great dignity: She *swept* into the room. 12 To trail, as a skirt. 13 To extend with a long reach or curve: The road *sweeps* along the lake shore on the north. —*n.* 1 The act or result of sweeping. 2 A long stroke or movement: a *sweep* of the hand. 3 The act of clearing out or getting rid of. 4 An unbroken stretch or extent: a *sweep* of beach. 5 A total or overwhelming victory, as in an election. 6 The range, area, or compass reached by sweeping. 7 One who sweeps chimneys, streets, etc. 8 A curving line; flowing contour. 9 A long, heavy oar. 10 A long pole on a pivot, having a bucket suspended from one end, for use in drawing water. 11 *pl.* Sweepings. 12 *pl. Informal* Sweepstakes. [< OE *swāpan*] —**sweep′er** *n.*

sweep·ing (swe′ping) *adj.* 1 Extending in a long line or over a wide area: a *sweeping* glance. 2 Covering a wide area; comprehensive: *sweeping* reforms. —*n.* 1 The action of one who or that which sweeps. 2 *pl.* Things swept up, as refuse. —**sweep′ing·ly** *adv.* —**sweep′ing·ness** *n.*

Sweep *def.* 10

sweep·stakes (swep′staks′) *n. pl.* **·stakes** (*construed as sing. or pl.*) 1 A type of lottery in which all the sums staked may be won by one or by a few of the betters, as in a horse race. 2 A race, contest, etc., to determine the outcome of such a lottery. 3 A prize in such a lottery. Also **sweep′stake′.**

sweet (swet) *adj.* 1 Having a flavor like that of sugar, often due to the presence of sugar in some form. 2 Not salted, sour, rancid, or spoiled. 3 Gently pleasing to the senses; agreeable to the taste, smell, etc. 4 Agreeable or delightful to the mind or the emotions. 5 Having gentle, pleasing, and winning qualities. 6 Sound; rich; productive: said of soil. —*n.* 1 The quality of being sweet; sweetness. 2 Something sweet, agreeable, or pleasing. 3 *Usu. pl.* Confections, preserves, candy, etc. 4 A beloved person. 5 *Brit.* DESSERT. [< OE *swēte*] —**sweet′ly** *adv.* —**sweet′ness** *n.*

sweet alyssum A small plant related to mustard having spikes of fragrant white blossoms.

sweet·bread (swet′bred′) *n.* The pancreas (**stomach sweetbread**) or the thymus (**neck sweetbread** or **throat sweetbread**) of a calf or other animal, when used as food.

sweet·bri·er (swet′brī′ər) *n.* A species of rose with dense, prickly branches and fragrant leaves. Also **sweet′bri′ar.**

sweet clover Any of several leguminous forage plants having fragrant white or yellow flowers.

sweet corn Any of several varieties of maize rich in sugar, cultivated for use as a vegetable.

sweet·en (swet′n) *v.t.* 1 To make sweet or sweeter. 2 To make more endurable; alleviate; lighten. 3 To make pleasant or gratifying. —**sweet′en·er** *n.*

sweet·en·ing (swet′n·ing) *n.* 1 The act of making sweet. 2 That which sweetens.

sweet flag A marsh-dwelling plant with sword-shaped leaves and a fragrant rhizome.

sweet gum 1 A large North American tree with maplelike leaves and bark exuding a fragrant gum. 2 The balsam or gum yielded by it.

sweet·heart (swet′härt′) *n.* 1 Darling: a term of endearment. 2 A lover.

sweetheart contract An agreement made between an employer and union officials, the terms of which are disadvantageous to union members. Also **sweetheart agreement.**

sweet·meat (swet′met′) *n. Usu. pl.* A highly sweetened food, as candy, cake, candied fruit, etc.

sweet pea A climbing leguminous plant cultivated for its fragrant, varicolored flowers.

sweet pepper A mild variety of capsicum used for pickling and as a vegetable.

sweet potato 1 A perennial tropical vine of the morning-glory family, with a fleshy tuberous root. 2 The sweet yellow or orange root, eaten as a vegetable.

sweet-talk (swet′tôk′) *Informal v.t.* 1 To persuade by coaxing or flattering. —*v.i.* 2 To flatter or coax someone. —**sweet talk**

sweet tooth *Informal* A fondness for candy or sweets.

sweet wil·liam (wil′yəm) A perennial species of pink with fragrant, closely clustered flowers. Also **sweet William.**

swell (swel) *v.* **swelled, swelled** or **swol·len, swell·ing** *v.i.* 1 To increase in size or volume, as by inflation with air or by absorption of moisture. 2 To increase in amount, degree, force, intensity, etc. 3 To rise above the usual or surrounding level, surface, etc. 4 To rise in waves or swells, as the sea. 5 To bulge. 6 *Informal* To become puffed up with pride. —*v.t.* 7 To cause to increase in size or volume. 8 To cause to increase in amount, degree, force, intensity, etc. 9 To cause to bulge. 10 To puff with pride. —*n.* 1 The act, process, or effect of swelling. 2 A long continuous wave without a crest. 3 A rise of, or undulation in, the land. 4 Any bulge or protuberance. 5 *Music* A crescendo and diminuendo in succession; also, the signs (< >) indicating it. 6 A device by which the loudness of an organ may be varied. 7 *Informal* A person who is very fashionable, elegant, or social. —*adj.* 1 *Informal* Very fashionable, elegant, or social. 2 *Slang* Very fine; first-rate; excellent. [< OE *swellan*] —**Syn.** *v.* 1 bulge, dilate, distend, enlarge, expand.

swell·ing (swel′ing) *n.* 1 The act or process by which a person or thing swells. 2 The condition of being swollen. 3 Something swollen, esp. an abnormal enlargement of a part of the body. —*adj.* That swells; increasing; bulging; puffing up, etc.

swel·ter (swel′tər) *v.i.* 1 To perspire or suffer from oppressive heat. —*v.t.* 2 To cause to swelter. —*n.* A swelter-

ing condition; oppressive heat. [< OE *sweltan* die] **—swel′-ter·ing·ly** *adv.*

swept (swept) *p.t. & p.p.* of SWEEP.

swept·back (swept′bak′) *adj. Aeron.* Having the front edge (of a wing) tilted backward from the lateral axis, as an airplane.

swerve (swûrv) *v.t. & v.i.* **swerved, swerv·ing** To turn or cause to turn aside from a course; deflect. **—n.** The act of swerving; a sudden turning aside. [< OE *sweorfan* file or grind away]

swift[1] (swift) *adj.* **1** Moving with great speed; rapid; quick. **2** Capable of quick motion; fleet. **3** Happening, coming, finished, etc., in a brief time. **4** Quick to act or respond; prompt. **—adv.** In a swift manner. [< OE] **—swift′ly** *adv.* **—swift′ness** *n.*

swift[2] (swift) *n.* Any of various swallowlike birds with extraordinary powers of flight, as the chimney swift. [< SWIFT[1]]

swig (swig) *n. Informal* A great gulp; deep draft. **—v.t. & v.i.** **swigged, swig·ging** *Informal* To take swigs (of). [?]

swill (swil) *v.t.* **1** To drink greedily or to excess. **2** To drench, as with water; rinse; wash. **3** To fill with, as drink. **—v.i.** **4** To drink greedily or to excess. **—n.** **1** Semiliquid food for domestic animals, as the mixture of edible refuse and liquid fed to pigs. **2** Garbage. **3** Unappetizing food. **4** A great gulp; swig. [< OE *swillan* to wash]

Chimney swift

swim[1] (swim) *v.* **swam** (*Regional* **swum**), **swum, swim·ming** *v.i.* **1** To move through water by working the legs, arms, fins, etc. **2** To float. **3** To move with a smooth or flowing motion. **4** To be flooded. **—v.t.** **5** To cross or traverse by swimming. **6** To cause to swim. **—n.** **1** The action or pastime of swimming. **2** The distance swum or to be swum. **3** The air bladder of a fish: also **swim bladder, swimming bladder.** **—in the swim** Active in current affairs, esp. those involved with fashion, socializing, etc. [< OE *swimman*] **—swim′mer** *n.*

swim[2] (swim) **swam** (*Regional* **swum**), **swum, swim·ming** *v.i.* **1** To be dizzy. **2** To seem to go round; reel. [< OE *swima* dizziness]

swimming hole A deep hole or pool in a stream, used for swimming.

swim·ming·ly (swim′ing·lē) *adv.* Easily and successfully.

swim·suit (swim′sōōt′) *n.* A garment designed to be worn while swimming.

swin·dle (swin′dəl) *v.* **-dled, -dling** *v.t.* **1** To cheat; defraud. **2** To obtain by such means. **—v.i.** **3** To practice fraud. **—n.** The act or process of swindling. [< G *schwindeln* cheat] **—swin′dler** *n.* **—Syn.** *v.* **1** deceive, dupe, rook.

swine (swīn) *n. pl.* **swine** **1** A pig or hog: usu. used collectively. **2** A low, greedy, or vicious person. [< OE *swīn*] **—swin′ish** *adj.* **—swin′ish·ly** *adv.* **—swin′ish·ness** *n.*

swine·herd (swīn′hûrd′) *n.* A tender of swine.

swing (swing) *v.* **swung, swing·ing** *v.i.* **1** To move to and fro or backward and forward rhythmically, as something suspended. **2** To ride in a swing. **3** To move with an even, swaying motion. **4** To turn; pivot: We *swung* around and went home. **5** To be suspended; hang. **6** *Informal* To be executed by hanging. **7** *Slang* To be very up-to-date and sophisticated, esp. in one's amusements and pleasures. **8** *Informal* To sing or play with or to have a compelling, usu. jazzlike rhythm. **9** *Slang* To be sexually promiscuous. **—v.t.** **10** To cause to move to and fro or backward and forward. **11** To brandish; flourish: to *swing* an ax. **12** To cause to turn on or as on a pivot or central point. **13** To lift, hoist, or hang: They *swung* the mast into place. **14** *Informal* To bring to a successful conclusion: to *swing* a deal. **15** *Informal* To sing or play in the style of swing (*n.,* def. 8). **—n.** **1** The action process, or manner of swinging. **2** A free swaying motion. **3** A contrivance of hanging ropes with a seat on which a person may move to and fro through the air. **4** Freedom of action. **5** The arc or range of something that swings. **6** A swinging blow or stroke. **7**

A trip or tour: a *swing* through the west. **8** A type of jazz music played by big bands, achieving its effect by lively, compelling rhythms, contrapuntal styles, and arranged ensemble playing: also **swing music.** **—in full swing** In full and lively operation. [< OE *swingan* scourge, beat up]

swinge (swinj) *v.t.* **swinged, swinge·ing** *Archaic* To flog; chastise. [< OE *swengan* shake, beat] **—swing′er** *n.*

swinge·ing (swin′jing) *adj. Chiefly Brit. Informal* Very large, good, or first-rate. [< SWINGE]

swing·er (swing′ər) *n. Slang* **1** A lively and up-to-date person. **2** A person who indulges freely in sex.

swing·ing (swing′ing) *adj. Slang* **1** Lively and compelling in effect: a *swinging* jazz quartet. **2** Modern; modish.

swin·gle (swing′gəl) *n.* A large, knifelike wooden implement for beating and cleaning flax: also **swing′knife.** **—v.t.** **·gled, ·gling** To cleanse, as flax, by beating with a swingle. [< MDu. *swinghel*]

swin·gle·tree (swing′gəl·trē′) *n.* WHIFFLETREE.

swing shift An evening work shift, usu. lasting from about 4 p.m. to midnight. **—swing shifter**

swipe (swīp) *v.* **swiped, swip·ing** **—v.t.** **1** *Informal* To strike with a sweeping motion. **2** *Slang* To steal; snatch. **—v.i.** **3** To hit with a sweeping motion. **—n.** *Informal* A hard blow. [Var. of SWEEP]

swirl (swûrl) *v.t. & v.i.* To move or cause to move along in irregular eddies; whirl. **—n.** **1** A whirling along, as in an eddy. **2** A curl or twist; spiral. [ME *swyrl*] **—swirl′y** *adj.*

swish (swish) *v.i.* **1** To move with a hissing or whistling sound. **—v.t.** **2** To cause to swish. **—n.** **1** A swishing sound. **2** A movement producing such a sound. [Imit.]

Swiss (swis) *n.* **1** A citizen or native of Switzerland. **2** The people of Switzerland collectively: used with *the.* **—adj.** Of or pertaining to Switzerland or its people.

Swiss chard Chard.

Swiss cheese A pale yellow cheese with many large holes, originally made in Switzerland.

Swiss steak A cut of steak floured and cooked, often with a sauce of tomatoes, onions, etc.

Swit., Switz., Swtz. Switzerland.

switch (swich) *n.* **1** A small flexible rod, twig, or whip. **2** A tress of false hair, worn by women in building a coiffure. **3** A mechanism for shifting a railway train from one track to another. **4** The act or operation of switching, shifting, or changing. **5** The tuft of hair at the end of the tail in certain animals, as a cow. **6** *Electr.* A device used to start or stop a flow of current. **7** A blow with or as with a switch. **—v.t.** **1** To whip or lash. **2** To move, jerk, or whisk suddenly or sharply. **3** To turn aside or divert; shift. **4** To exchange: They *switched* plates. **5** To shift, as a railroad car, to another track. **6** *Electr.* To connect or disconnect with a switch. **—v.i.** **7** To turn aside; change; shift. **8** To swing back and forth or from side to side. **9** To shift from one track to another. [?] **—switch′er** *n.*

switch·back (swich′bak′) *n.* **1** A zigzag road or railroad up a steep incline. **2** *Brit.* ROLLER COASTER.

switch·board (swich′bôrd′, -bōrd′) *n.* A panel bearing switches or controls for several electric circuits, as a telephone exchange.

switch·man (swich′mən) *n. pl.* **·men** (-mən) One who handles switches, esp. on a railroad.

switch·yard (swich′yärd′) *n.* A railroad yard in which trains are stored, maintained, assembled, etc.

Swit·zer·land (swit′sər·lənd) *n.* A republic of CEN. Europe, 15,940 sq. mi., cap. Bern. • See map at ITALY.

swiv·el (swiv′əl) *n.* **1** A coupling or pivot that permits parts, as of a mechanism, to rotate independently. **2** Anything that turns on a pin or headed bolt. **3** A cannon that swings on a pivot: also **swivel gun. —v.** **·eled** or **·elled, ·el·ing** or **·el·ling** *v.t.* **1** To turn on or as on a swivel. **2** To provide with or secure by a swivel. **—v.i.** **3** To turn or swing on or as on a swivel. [< OE *swīfan* revolve]

swivel chair A chair whose seat turns freely on a swivel.

swob (swob) *n. & v.* **swobbed, swob·bing** SWAB.

swol·len (swō′lən) A *p.p.* of SWELL.

swoon (swōōn) *v.i.* To faint. **—n.** A fainting fit. [< OE *swōgan* suffocate]

swoop (swo̅o̅p) *v.i.* 1 To drop or descend suddenly, as a bird pouncing on its prey. —*v.t.* 2 To take or seize suddenly; snatch. —*n.* The act of swooping. [< OE *swāpan* sweep]

swop (swop) *n. & v.* **swopped, swop·ping** SWAP.

sword (sôrd, sōrd) *n.* A weapon consisting of a long blade fixed in a hilt. —**at swords' points** Very unfriendly; hostile. —**cross swords** 1 To quarrel; argue. 2 To fight. —**put to the sword** To kill with a sword. —**the sword** 1 Military power. 2 War. [< OE *sweord*]

sword·fish (sôrd′fish′, sōrd′-) *n. pl.* **·fish** or **·fish·es** A large fish of the open sea having the upper jaw elongated into a swordlike process.

Swordfish

sword·grass (sôrd′gras′, -gräs′, sōrd′-) *n.* Any of several grasses or sedges with serrated or swordlike leaves.

sword·knot (sôrd′not′, sōrd′-) *n.* An ornamental tassel of leather, cord, etc., tied to a sword hilt.

sword play The act, technique, or skill of using a sword, esp. in fencing. —**sword′-play′er** *n.*

swords·man (sôrdz′mən, sōrdz′-) *n. pl.* **·men** (-mən) One skilled in the use of or armed with a sword, esp. a fencer. Also **sword′man.** —**swords′man·ship, sword′man·ship** *n.*

swore (swôr, swōr) *p.t.* of SWEAR.

sworn (swôrn, swōrn) *p.p.* of SWEAR.

swot (swot) *n. & v.* **swot·ted, swot·ting** SWAT.

swounds (zwoundz, zoundz) *interj.* ZOUNDS.

swum (swum) *p.p. & regional p.t.* of SWIM.

swung (swung) *p.t. & p.p.* of SWING.

syb·a·rite (sib′ə·rīt) *n.* A person devoted to luxury or sensuality; voluptuary. [< *Sybaris,* an ancient Greek city in southern Italy] —**syb·a·rit·ic** (sib′ə·rit′ik), **syb′a·rit′i·cal** *adj.* —**syb′a·rit′i·cal·ly** *adv.*

syc·a·more (sik′ə·môr, -mōr) *n.* 1 A medium-sized tree of Syria and Egypt allied to the fig. 2 Any of various plane trees widely distributed in North America. 3 An ornamental maple tree: also **sycamore maple.** [< Gk. *sykon* a fig + *moron* a mulberry]

syc·o·phant (sik′ə·fənt, -fant) *n.* A servile flatterer; toady. [< Gk. *sykon* fig + *phainein* to show] —**syc′o·phan·cy** (-sē) (*pl.* **·cies**) *n.* —**syc′o·phan′tic** (-fan′tik), **syc′o·phan′ti·cal** *adj.* —**syc′o·phan′ti·cal·ly** *adv.*

syl·la·bar·y (sil′ə·ber′ē) *n. pl.* **·bar·ies** A list of syllables; esp., a list of written characters representing syllables.

syl·lab·ic (si·lab′ik) *adj.* 1 Of, pertaining to, or consisting of syllables. 2 *Phonet.* Designating a consonant capable of forming a complete syllable, as *l* in *middle* (mid′l). 3 Having every syllable distinctly pronounced. Also **syl·lab′i·cal.** —*n. Phonet.* A syllabic sound. —**syl·lab′i·cal·ly** *adv.*

syl·lab·i·cate (si·lab′ə·kāt) *v.t.* **·cat·ed, ·cat·ing** SYLLABIFY. —**syl·lab′i·ca′tion** *n.*

syl·lab·i·fy (si·lab′ə·fī) *v.t.* **·fied, ·fy·ing** To form or divide into syllables. —**syl·lab′i·fi·ca′tion** *n.*

syl·la·ble (sil′ə·bəl) *n.* 1 *Phonet.* A word or part of a word uttered in a single vocal impulse. 2 A part of a written or printed word corresponding to the spoken division. 3 The least detail or mention: Please don't repeat a *syllable* of what you've heard here. —*v.* **·bled, ·bling** *v.t.* 1 To pronounce the syllables of. —*v.i.* 2 To pronounce syllables. [< Gk. *syn-* together + *lambanein* take]

syl·la·bus (sil′ə·bəs) *n. pl.* **·bus·es** or **·bi** (-bī) A concise statement or outline, esp. of a course of study. [< Gk. *sittyba* label on a book] —**Syn.** abstract, epitome, synopsis.

syl·lo·gism (sil′ə·jiz′əm) *n.* 1 *Logic* A form of reasoning consisting of three propositions. The first two propositions, called *premises,* have one term in common furnishing a relation between the two other terms, which are linked in the third, called the *conclusion.* Example: All men are mortal *(major premise);* kings are men *(minor premise);* therefore, kings are mortal *(conclusion).* 2 Reasoning that makes use of this form; deduction. [< Gk. *syn-* together + *logizesthai* infer] —**syl′lo·gis′tic, syl′lo·gis′ti·cal** *adj.* —**syl′lo·gis′ti·cal·ly** *adv.*

sylph (silf) *n.* 1 A being, mortal but without a soul, living in and on the air. 2 A slender, graceful young woman or girl. [< NL *sylphus*]

syl·van (sil′vən) *adj.* 1 Of, pertaining to, or located in a forest or woods. 2 Composed of or abounding in trees or woods. —*n.* A person or animal living in or frequenting forests or woods. [< L *silva* a wood]

sym. symbol; symmetrical; symphony.

sym·bi·o·sis (sim′bī·ō′sis, -bē-) *n.* An intimate and mutually advantageous partnership of dissimilar organisms, as of algae and fungi in lichens. [< Gk. *syn-* together + *bios* life] —**sym′bi·ot′ic** (-ot′ik) or **·i·cal** *adj.* —**sym′bi·ot′i·cal·ly** *adv.*

sym·bol (sim′bəl) *n.* 1 Something chosen to stand for or represent something else, as an object used to typify a quality, idea, etc.: The lily is a *symbol* of purity. 2 A character, mark, abbreviation, letter, etc., that represents something else. —*v.t.* **sym·boled** or **·bolled, sym·bol·ing** or **·bol·ling** SYMBOLIZE. [< Gk. *syn-* together + *ballein* throw]

sym·bol·ic (sim·bol′ik) *adj.* 1 Of, pertaining to, or expressed by a symbol. 2 Used as a symbol: with *of.* 3 Characterized by or involving the use of symbols or symbolism: *symbolic* poetry. Also **sym·bol′i·cal.** —**sym·bol′i·cal·ly** *adv.* —**sym·bol′i·cal·ness** *n.*

sym·bol·ism (sim′bəl·iz′əm) *n.* 1 The use of symbols to represent things; the act or art of investing things with a symbolic meaning. 2 A system of symbols or symbolical representation. 3 Symbolic meaning or character.

sym·bol·ist (sim′bəl·ist) *n.* One who uses symbols or symbolism, esp. an artist or writer skilled in the use of symbols.

sym·bol·is·tic (sim′bəl·is′tik) *adj.* Of or pertaining to symbolism or symbolists. —**sym′bol·is′ti·cal·ly** *adv.*

sym·bol·ize (sim′bəl·īz) *v.* **·ized, ·iz·ing** *v.t.* 1 To be a symbol of; represent symbolically; typify. 2 To represent by a symbol or symbols. 3 To treat as symbolic or figurative. —*v.i.* 4 To use symbols. *Brit. sp.* **sym′bol·ise.** —**sym′bol·i·za′·tion, sym′bol·i·zer** *n.*

sym·me·try (sim′ə·trē) *n. pl.* **·tries** 1 Corresponding arrangement or balancing of the parts or elements of a whole in respect to size, shape, and position on opposite sides of an axis or center. 2 The element of beauty and harmony in nature or art that results from such arrangement and balancing. 3 *Math.* An arrangement of points in a system such that the system appears unchanged after certain partial rotations. [< Gk. *syn-* together + *metron* a measure] —**sym·met·ric** (si·met′rik), **sym·met′ri·cal** *adj.* —**sym·met′ri·cal·ly** *adv.* —**sym·met′ri·cal·ness** *n.*

sym·pa·thet·ic (sim′pə·thet′ik) *adj.* 1 Pertaining to, expressing, or proceeding from sympathy. 2 Having a compassionate feeling for others; sympathizing. 3 Being in accord or harmony; congenial. 4 Of, proceeding from, or characterized by empathy. 5 Referring to sounds produced by responsive vibrations. Also **sym′pa·thet′i·cal.** —**sym′pa·thet′i·cal·ly** *adv.*

sympathetic nervous system The part of the autonomic nervous system that controls such involuntary actions as the dilation of pupils, constriction of blood vessels and salivary glands, and increase of heartbeat.

sym·pa·thize (sim′pə·thīz) *v.i.* **·thized, ·thiz·ing** 1 To experience or understand the sentiments or ideas of another. 2 To feel or express compassion, as for another's sorrow or affliction: with *with.* 3 To be in harmony or agreement. *Brit. sp.* **sym′pa·thise.** —**sym′pa·thiz′er** *n.* —**sym′pa·thiz′ing·ly** *adv.*

sym·pa·thy (sim′pə·thē) *n. pl.* **·thies** 1 The fact or condition of an agreement in feeling: The *sympathy* between husband and wife was remarkable. 2 A feeling of compassion for another's sufferings. 3 Agreement or accord: to be in *sympathy* with an objective. 4 Support; loyalty; approval: trying to enlist my *sympathies.* [< Gk. *syn-* together + *pathos* a feeling, passion] —**Syn.** 1 affinity, concord. 2 commiseration, condolence, pity.

sympathy strike A strike in which the strikers support the demands of another group of workers. Also **sympathetic strike.**

sym·pho·ny (sim′fə·nē) *n. pl.* **·nies** 1 A harmonious or agreeable mingling of sounds. 2 Any harmony or agreeable blending, as of color. 3 A composition for orchestra, consisting usu. of four extensive movements. 4 SYMPHONY ORCHESTRA. [< Gk. *syn-* together + *phōnē* a sound] —**sym·phon·ic** (sim·fon′ik) *adj.* —**sym·phon′i·cal·ly** *adv.*

symphony orchestra A large orchestra composed usu. of string, brass, woodwind, and percussion instruments.

sym·po·si·um (sim·pō′zē-əm) *n. pl.* **·si·ums, ·si·a** (-zē-ə) **1** A meeting for discussion of a particular subject or subjects. **2** A collection of comments, opinions, essays, etc. on the same subject. [< Gk. *syn-* together + *posis* drinking] — **sym·po′si·ac** (-ak) *adj.*

symp·tom (simp′təm) *n.* **1** An organic or functional condition indicating the presence of disease, esp. when regarded as an aid in diagnosis. **2** A sign or indication that serves to point out the existence of something else: *symptoms* of civil unrest. [< Gk. *syn-* together + *piptein* fall] — **symp′to·mat′ic** (-tə-mat′ik), **symp′to·mat′i·cal** *adj.* —**symp′·to·mat′i·cal·ly** *adv.* —**Syn. 2** earmark, mark, signal, token.

syn- *prefix* With; together; associated; at the same time: *syncarp.* [< Gk. *syn* together]

syn. synchronize; synonym; synonymous; synonymy.

syn·a·gogue (sin′ə-gôg, -gog) *n.* **1** A place of meeting for Jewish worship and religious instruction. **2** A Jewish congregation or assemblage for religious instruction and observances. Also **syn′a·gog.** [< Gk. *synagōgē* an assembly]

syn·apse (sin′aps′, sə-naps′) *n.* The junction point of two neurons, across which a nerve impulse passes. Also **syn·ap·sis** (sə-nap′səs) *pl.* **·ap·ses** (-sēz). [< Gk. *syn-* together + *hapsis* a joining] —**syn·ap·tic** (-nap′tik) *adj.*

sync (singk) *n. & v.* **synced, sync·ing** SYNCH.

syn·carp (sin′kärp) *n.* A multiple or fleshy aggregate fruit, as the blackberry. [< Gk. *syn-* together + *karpos* a fruit] — **syn·car·pous** (sin-kär′pəs) *adj.*

synch (singk) *Slang v.i. & v.t.* **synched, synch·ing** To synchronize or cause to be synchronized. —*n.* Synchronization: usu. in phrases **in synch** and **out of synch.** [< SYNCHRONIZATION]

syn·chro·mesh (sing′krō-mesh′, sin′-) *n. Mech.* **1** A gear system in which parts are synchronized before engagement. **2** The synchronizing mechanism thus used.

Syncarp (blackberry)

syn·chro·nism (sing′krə-niz′əm, sin′-) *n.* **1** The state of being synchronous; concurrence. **2** A grouping of historic personages or events according to their dates. —**syn′chro·nis′tic, syn′chro·nis′ti·cal** *adj.* —**syn′chro·nis′ti·cal·ly** *adv.*

syn·chro·ni·za·tion (sing′krə-nə-zā′shən) *n.* **1** The state of being synchronous. **2** The act of synchronizing, or the state of being synchronized.

syn·chro·nize (sing′krə-nīz, sin′-) *v.* **·nized, ·niz·ing** *v.i.* **1** To occur at the same time; coincide. **2** To move or operate in unison. —*v.t.* **3** To cause to operate synchronously: to *synchronize* watches. **4** To cause (the appropriate sound of a motion picture) to coincide with the action. **5** To assign the same date or period to; make contemporaneous. [< SYNCHRONOUS] —**syn′chro·niz′er** *n.*

syn·chro·nous (sing′krə-nəs, sin′-) *adj.* **1** Occurring at the same time; concurrent; simultaneous. **2** *Physics* Having the same period or frequency. **3** *Electr.* Normally operating at a speed proportional to the frequency of the current in the power line, as a motor. Also **syn′chro·nal.** [< Gk. *syn-* together + *chronos* time] —**syn′chro·nous·ly** *adv.* —**syn′chro·nous·ness** *n.*

syn·cline (sin′klīn) *n. Geol.* A trough or fold of stratified rock in which the layers dip downward on each side toward the axis of the fold. [< Gk. *syn-* together + *klinein* to incline] —**syn·cli′nal** (sin-klī′nəl) *adj.*

syn·co·pate (sing′kə-pāt, sin′-) *v.t.* **·pat·ed, ·pat·ing 1** To contract, as a word, by syncope. **2** *Music* To treat or modify (a rhythm, melody, etc.) by syncopation. [< LL *syncope* syncope]

syn·co·pa·tion (sing′kə-pā′shən, sin′-) *n.* **1** The act of syncopating or state of being syncopated; also, that which is syncopated. **2** *Music* The suppression of an expected rhythmic accent by the continuation of an unaccented tone that begins just before it. **3** Any music featuring syncopation, as ragtime, jazz, etc. **4** Syncope of a word, or an example of it.

syn·co·pe (sing′kə-pē, sin′-) *n.* **1** The elision of a sound or syllable in the middle part of a word, as *e'er* for *ever.* **2** *Music* Syncopation. **3** Temporary loss of consciousness; fainting. [< Gk. *syn-* together + *koptein* to cut] —**syn′co·pal, syn·cop·ic** (sin-kop′ik) *adj.*

syn·cre·tize (sin′krə-tīz, sing′-) *v.t.* **·tized, ·tiz·ing** To attempt to blend and reconcile. [< Gk. *synkrētizein* combine] —**syn′cre·tism** *n.*

syn·dic (sin′dik) *n.* **1** The business agent of a university or other corporation. **2** A government official, as a civil magistrate, with varying powers in different countries. [< Gk. *syn-* together + *dikē* judgment] —**syn′di·cal** *adj.*

syn·di·cal·ism (sin′di·kəl·iz′əm) *n.* A social and political theory proposing the taking over of the means of production by federations of labor unions through the staging of general strikes, etc. [< F *(chambre) syndicale* a labor union] —**syn′di·cal·ist** *n.* —**syn′di·cal·is′tic** *adj.*

syn·di·cate (sin′də·kit) *n.* **1** An association of individuals united to negotiate some business or to engage in some enterprise, often one requiring large capital. **2** An association for purchasing feature articles, etc., and selling them again to a number of periodicals, as newspapers, for simultaneous publication. **3** The office or jurisdiction of a syndic; also, a body of syndics. —*v.t.* (-kāt) **·cat·ed, ·cat·ing 1** To combine into or manage by a syndicate. **2** To sell for publication in many newspapers or magazines. [< F *syndic* syndic] —**syn′di·ca′tion, syn′di·ca′tor** *n.*

syn·drome (sin′drōm) *n.* **1** The aggregate of symptoms and signs characteristic of a specific disease or condition. **2** A group of traits regarded as being characteristic of a certain type, condition, etc. [< Gk. *syn-* together + *dramein* run] —**syn·drom·ic** (sin-drom′ik) *adj.*

sy·nec·do·che (si-nek′də-kē) *n.* A figure of speech in which a part stands for a whole or a whole for a part, a material for the thing made of it, etc., as *bronze* for a *statue.* [< Gk. *syn-* together + *ekdechesthai* take from]

syn·er·gism (sin′ər·jiz′əm) *n.* The mutually reinforcing action of separate substances, organs, agents, etc., which together produce an effect greater than that of all of the components acting separately. Also **syn′er·gy.** [< Gk. *synergos* working together] —**syn′er·gis′tic** or **·ti·cal** *adj.*

syn·fu·el (sin′fyoō′el) *n.* Synthetic fuel.

syn·od (sin′əd, -od) *n.* **1** An ecclesiastical council. **2** Any assembly, council, etc. [< Gk. < *syn-* together + *hodos* a way]

sy·nod·i·cal (si-nod′i·kəl) *adj.* **1** Of, pertaining to, or of the nature of a synod; transacted in a synod. **2** *Astron.* Pertaining to the conjunction of two celestial bodies or to the interval between two successive conjunctions of the same celestial bodies. Also **syn·od·al** (sin′ə·dəl, si·nod′əl), **sy·nod′ic.** —**sy·nod′i·cal·ly** *adv.*

syn·o·nym (sin′ə·nim) *n.* **1** A word having the same or almost the same meaning as some other or others in the same language. **2** A word used in metonymy to substitute for another. [< Gk. *syn-* together + *onyma* a name] — **syn′o·nym′ic, syn′o·nym′i·cal** *adj.* —**syn′o·nym′i·ty** *n.*

sy·non·y·mous (si-non′ə·məs) *adj.* Being equivalent or similar to meaning. —**sy·non′y·mous·ly** *adv.*

sy·non·y·my (si-non′ə·mē) *n. pl.* **·mies 1** The quality of being synonymous. **2** The study of synonyms. **3** The discrimination of synonyms. **2** A list or collection discriminating the meanings of synonyms or of allied terms.

sy·nop·sis (si-nop′sis) *n. pl.* **·ses** (-sēz) A general view or condensation, as of a story, book, etc.; summary. [< Gk. *syn-* together + *opsis* a view] —**Syn.** abridgment, abstract, digest, précis.

sy·nop·tic (si-nop′tik) *adj.* **1** Giving a general view. **2** Presenting the same or a similar point of view: said of the first three Gospels (**Synoptic Gospels**). Also **sy·nop′ti·cal.** —**sy·nop′ti·cal·ly** *adv.*

sy·no·vi·a (si-nō′vē-ə) *n.* The viscid, transparent, lubricating fluid secreted by a membrane in the interior of joints. [< Gk. *syn-* together + L *ovum* an egg] —**sy·no′vi·al** *adj.*

---

syn·tax (sin′taks) *n.* **1** The arrangement and interrelationship of words in grammatical constructions. **2** The branch of grammar which deals with this. [< Gk. *syn-* together + *tassein* arrange] —**syn·tac·tic** (sin·tak′tik), **syn·tac′ti·cal** *adj.* —**syn·tac′ti·cal·ly** *adv.*

syn·the·sis (sin′thə·sis) *n. pl.* **·ses** (-sēz) **1** The assembling of separate or subordinate parts into a new form. **2** The complex whole resulting from this. **3** *Chem.* The building up of a compound by the direct union of its elements or of simpler compounds. [< Gk. *syn-* together + *tithenai* to place] —**syn′the·sist** *n.*

syn·the·size (sin′thə·sīz) *v.t.* **·sized**, **·siz·ing 1** To unite or produce by synthesis. **2** To apply synthesis to. *Brit. sp.* **syn′the·sise.**

syn·the·siz·er (sin′thə·sīz′ər) *n.* Any of various complex electronic devices by which a musician can create and manipulate a wide variety of tones.

syn·thet·ic (sin·thet′ik) *adj.* **1** Of, pertaining to, or using synthesis. **2** Produced artificially by chemical synthesis. **3** Artificial; spurious. Also **syn·thet′i·cal.** —*n.* Anything produced by synthesis, esp. by chemical synthesis, as a material. [< Gk. *syn-* together + *tithenai* to place] —**syn·thet′i·cal·ly** *adv.*

syph·i·lis (sif′ə·lis) *n.* An infectious, chronic, venereal disease caused by a spirochete transmissible by direct contact or congenitally. [< *Syphilus,* a shepherd in a 16th-century Latin poem who had the disease] —**syph·i·lit·ic** (sif′ə·lit′ik) *adj., n.*

syphon (sī′fən) *n. & v.* SIPHON.

Syr. Syria; Syriac; Syrian.

syr. syrup (pharmacy).

Syr·i·a (sir′ē·ə) *n.* A republic of sw Asia, 72,234 sq. mi., cap. Damascus. • See map at JORDAN.

Syr·i·ac (sir′ē·ak) *n.* The language of the ancient Syrians, a dialect of Aramaic.

Syr·i·an (sir′ē·ən) *adj.* Of or pertaining to Syria, its people, or their language. —*n.* **1** A citizen or native of Syria. **2** The Arabic dialect spoken in modern Syria.

sy·rin·ga (si·ring′gə) *n.* **1** LILAC (defs. 1 and 2) **2** MOCK ORANGE. [< Gk. *syrinx* a pipe]

syr·inge (si·rinj′, sir′inj) *n.* **1** An instrument used to remove fluids from or inject fluids into body cavities. **2** HYPODERMIC SYRINGE. —*v.t.* **·inged**, **·ing·ing** To spray, cleanse, inject, etc. with a syringe. [< Gk. *syrinx* a pipe]

syr·inx (sir′ingks) *n. pl.* **sy·rin·ges** (sə·rin′jēz), **syr·inx·es 1** A modification of the windpipe in songbirds serving as the vocal organ. **2** *pl.* PANPIPES. [Gk., a pipe] —**sy·rin·ge·al** (si·rin′jē·əl) *adj.*

syr·up (sir′əp) *n.* A thick, sweet liquid, as the boiled juice of fruits, sugar cane, etc. [< OF sirop < Turkish *sharbat* sherbet] —**syr′up·y** *adj.*

syst. system; systematic.

sys·tem (sis′təm) *n.* **1** A group or arrangement of parts, facts, phenomena, etc., that relate to or interact with each other in such a way as to form a whole: the solar *system;* the nervous *system.* **2** Any orderly group of logically related facts, principles, beliefs, etc.: the democratic *system.* **3** An orderly method, plan, or procedure: a betting *system* that really works. **4** A method of classification, organization, arrangement, etc.: books classified according to the Dewey decimal *system.* **5** The body, considered as a functional whole. —**the system** The dominant political, economic, and social institutions and their leaders, regarded as resistant to change or to effective influence. [< Gk. *systēma* an organized whole]

sys·tem·at·ic (sis′tə·mat′ik) *adj.* **1** Of, pertaining to, or characterized by system or classification. **2** Acting by or carried out with system or method; methodical. **3** Forming or based on a system. Also **sys′tem·at′i·cal.** —**sys′tem·at′i·cal·ly** *adv.* —**Syn. 2** orderly, organized, procedural, routine. **3** organizational, bureaucratic.

sys·tem·a·tize (sis′tə·mə·tīz′) *v.t.* **·tized**, **·tiz·ing** To make into a system; organize methodically. Also **sys′tem·ize.** *Brit. sp.* **sys′tem·a·tise′.** —**sys′tem·a·ti·za′tion, sys′tem·i·za′tion** *n.* —**sys′tem·a·tiz′er, sys′tem·iz′er** *n.*

sys·tem·ic (sis·tem′ik) *adj.* **1** Of or pertaining to a system; systematic. **2** Pertaining to or affecting the body as a whole: a *systemic* poison. —**sys·tem′i·cal·ly** *adv.*

systems analysis The technique of reducing complex processes, as of industry, government, research, etc., to basic operations that can be treated quantitatively and reordered into sequences amenable to control.

sys·to·le (sis′tə·lē) *n.* **1** The rhythmic contraction of the heart, esp. of the ventricles, that impels the blood outward. **2** The shortening of a syllable that is naturally or by position long. [< Gk. *syn-* together + *stellein* send] —**sys·tol·ic** (sis·tol′ik) *adj.*

T

T, t (tē) *n. pl.* **T's, t's** or **Ts, ts, tees** (tēz) **1** The 20th letter of the English alphabet. **2** Any spoken sound representing the letter *T* or *t.* **3** Something shaped like a T. —**to a T** Precisely; perfectly. —*adj.* Shaped like a T.

't Contraction of IT: used initially, as in *'tis,* and finally, as in *on't.*

-t Inflectional ending used to indicate past participles and past tenses, as in *bereft, lost, spent:* equivalent to -*ed.*

T Technician; temperature (absolute); tension (surface); time (of firing or launching).

T. tablespoon (s); Testament; Tuesday.

t. in the time of (L *tempore*); teaspoon(s); time; ton(s); transitive; troy.

Ta tantalum.

tab[1] (tab) *n.* A flap, strip, tongue, or projection of something, as a garment, file card, etc. —*v.t.* **tabbed, tab·bing** To provide with a tab or tabs. [?]

tab[2] (tab) *n. Informal* **1** A check or bill; also, the total cost of something. **2** Close watch: to keep *tabs* on someone's activities. [? Short for TABULATION]

tab. table(s); tablet(s).

tab·ard (tab′ərd) *n.* **1** Formerly, a short, sleeveless or short-sleeved outer garment. **2** A

Tabard *def.* 3

knight's cape or cloak, worn over his armor and emblazoned with his own arms. **3** A similar garment worn by a herald and embroidered with his lord's arms. [< OF]

Ta·bas·co (tə·bas′kō) *n.* A pungent sauce made from capsicum: a trade name.

tab·by (tab′ē) *n. pl.* **·bies 1** A silk taffeta, esp. one that is striped or watered. **2** A brown or gray domestic cat with dark stripes. **3** Any domestic cat, esp. a female. **4** A gossiping woman. —*adj.* **1** Of, pertaining to, or made of tabby. **2** Brindled. [< *Attabi,* a quarter of Baghdad where it was manufactured]

tab·er·nac·le (tab′ər·nak′əl) *n.* **1** A tent or similar temporary structure. **2** *Usu. cap.* In the Old Testament, the portable sanctuary used by the Israelites in the wilderness. **3** *Usu. cap.* The Jewish temple. **4** Any house of worship, esp. one of large size. **5** The human body as the dwelling place of the soul. **6** The ornamental receptacle for the consecrated eucharistic elements. [< L *taberna* shed] —**tab·er·nac·u·lar** (tab′ər·nak′yə·lər) *adj.*

ta·ble (tā′bəl) *n.* **1** An article of furniture with a flat top, usu. fixed on legs. **2** Such a table on which food is set for a meal. **3** The food served at a meal. **4** The persons present at a meal. **5** A gaming table, as for roulette. **6** A collection of related numbers, values, signs, or items of any kind, arranged for ease of reference or comparison, often in parallel columns. **7** A compact listing: *table* of contents. **8** A tableland; plateau. **9** Any flat horizontal rock, surface,

tableau 749 **tag**

etc. **10** A tablet or slab bearing an inscription. **—the Tables** Laws inscribed on tablets, as the Ten Commandments. **—turn the tables** To reverse a situation. **—v.t. ·bled, ·bling 1** To place on a table. **2** To postpone discussion of (a resolution, bill, etc.). [< L *tabula* board]

tab·leau (tab′lō, ta-blō′) *n. pl.* **·leaux** (-lōz) or **·leaus** (-lōz) **1** Any picture or picturesque representation. **2** A scene reminiscent of a picture, usu. presented by persons motionless on a stage. [F, lit., small table]

ta·ble·cloth (tā′bəl·klôth′, -kloth′) *n.* A cloth covering for a table.

ta·ble d'hôte (tab′əl dōt′, tä′bəl) *pl.* **tab·les d'hote** (tab′· əlz dōt′, tä′bəlz) A complete meal of several specified courses, served in a restaurant at a fixed price. [F, lit., table of the host]

ta·ble·land (tā′bəl·land′) *n.* A broad, level, elevated region; a plateau.

ta·ble·spoon (tā′bəl·spoon′, -spoon′) *n.* **1** A measuring spoon with three times the capacity of a teaspoon. **2** A tablespoonful.

ta·ble·spoon·ful (tā′bəl·spoon·fool′, -spoon-) *n. pl.* **·fuls** The amount a tablespoon will hold; ½ fluid ounce.

tab·let (tab′lit) *n.* **1** A small, flat or nearly flat piece of some prepared substance, as a drug. **2** A pad, as of writing paper or note paper. **3** A small flat surface designed for or containing an inscription or design. **4** A thin leaf or sheet of ivory, wood, etc., for writing, painting, or drawing. **5** A set of such leaves joined together at one end. [< OF *tablete*, lit., small table]

table tennis A game resembling tennis in miniature, played indoors with a small celluloid ball and wooden paddles on a large table.

ta·ble·ware (tā′bəl·wâr′) *n.* Dishes, knives, forks, spoons, etc., used to set a table.

tab·loid (tab′loid) *n.* A newspaper, usu. one half the size of an ordinary newspaper, in which the news is presented concisely, often sensationally, and with many pictures. —*adj.* Compact; concise. [< TABL(ET) + -OID]

ta·boo (tə·boo′, ta-) *n. pl.* **·boos 1** A religious or social prohibition against touching or mentioning someone or something or doing something because such persons or things are considered sacred, dangerous, etc. **2** The practice of such prohibitions. **3** Any restriction or ban based on custom or convention. —*adj.* Restricted, prohibited, or excluded by taboo, custom, or convention. —*v.t.* **1** To place under taboo. **2** To avoid as taboo. Also **ta·bu′.** [< Tongan]

ta·bor (tā′bər) *n.* A small drum on which a fife player beats his own accompaniment. Also **ta′bour.** [< Pers. *tabīrah* drum]

tab·o·ret (tab′ə·ret′, -rā′) *n.* **1** A small tabor. **2** A stool or small seat, usu. without arms or back. **3** A small table or stand. **4** An embroidery frame. Also **tab′ou·ret.**

tab·u·lar (tab′yə·lər) *adj.* **1** Of, pertaining to, or arranged in a table or list. **2** Computed from or with a mathematical table. **3** Having a flat surface. —**tab′u·lar·ly** *adv.*

tab·u·late (tab′yə·lāt) *v.t.* **·lat·ed, ·lat·ing** To arrange in a table or list. —*adj.* Having a flat surface or surfaces; broad and flat. —**tab′u·la′tion, tab′u·la′tor** *n.*

tac·a·ma·hac (tak′ə·mə·hak′) *n.* **1** A resinous substance with a strong odor, used in ointments and incense. **2** Any of the trees producing this substance. Also **ta′ca·ma·hac′a** (-hak′ə), **tac′ma·hack′.** [< Nahuatl *tecomahca*]

ta·chom·e·ter (tə·kom′ə·tər) *n.* A device for indicating the speed of rotation of an engine, centrifuge, etc. [< Gk. *tachos* speed + -METER]

tach·y·car·di·a (tak′i·kär′dē·ə) *n.* Abnormal rapidity of the heartbeat. [< Gk. *tachys* swift + *kardia* heart]

tac·it (tas′it) *adj.* **1** Existing, inferred, or implied without being directly stated. **2** Not spoken; silent. **3** Emitting no sound. [< L *tacitus*, pp. of *tacere* be silent] —**tac′it·ly** *adv.*

tac·i·turn (tas′ə·tûrn) *adj.* Habitually silent or reserved. [< L *tacitus*. See TACIT.] —**tac·i·tur·ni·ty** (tas′ə·tûr′nə·tē) *n.* —**tac′i·turn·ly** *adv.* —**Syn.** uncommunicative, reticent.

tack (tak) *n.* **1** A small sharp-pointed nail, usu. with a relatively broad, flat head. **2** *Naut.* **a** A rope which holds down the lower outer corner of some sails. **b** The corner

so held. **c** The direction in which a vessel sails when sailing closehauled, considered in relation to the position of its sails. **d** A change in a ship's direction made by a change in the position of its sails. **3** A policy or course of action. **4** A temporary fastening, as any of various stitches in sewing. —*v.t.* **1** To fasten or attach with tacks. **2** To secure temporarily, as with long stitches. **3** To attach as supplementary; append. **4** *Naut.* **a** To change the course of (a vessel) by turning into the wind. **b** To navigate (a vessel) to windward by making a series of tacks. —*v.i.* **5** *Naut.* **a** To tack a vessel. **b** To sail to windward by a series of tacks. **6** To change one's course of action. **7** ZIGZAG. [< OF *tache* a nail] —**tack′er** *n.*

tack·le (tak′əl) *n.* **1** A rope and pulley or combination of ropes and pulleys, used for hoisting or moving objects. **2** The rigging of a ship. **3** The equipment used in any work or sport; gear. **4** The act of tackling. **5** In football, either of two linemen stationed between the guard and end. —*v.t.* **·led, ·ling 1** To fasten with or as if with tackle. **2** To harness (a horse). **3** To undertake to master, accomplish, or solve: *tackle* a problem. **4** To seize suddenly and forcefully. **5** In football, to seize and stop (an opponent carrying the ball). [< MLG *taken* seize] —**tack′ler** *n.*

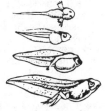

Tackles

tack·y¹ (tak′ē) *adj.* **tack·i·er, tack·i·est** Slightly sticky, as partly dried varnish. [< TACK, *v.*]

tack·y² (tak′ē) *adj.* **tack·i·er, tack·i·est 1** *Informal* Unfashionable; in bad taste. **2** Without good breeding; common. [?]

ta·co (tä′kō) *n. pl.* **·cos** A fried tortilla folded around any of several fillings, as chopped meat or cheese. [< Sp., wad]

tact (takt) *n.* **1** A quick or intuitive appreciation of what is fit, proper, or right; facility in saying or doing the proper thing. **2** A delicate sense of discrimination, esp. in aesthetics. [< L *tactus* sense of touch, pp. of *tangere* touch]

tact·ful (takt′fəl) *adj.* Having or showing tact. —**tact′ful·ly** *adv.* —**tact′ful·ness** *n.*

tac·ti·cal (tak′ti·kəl) *adj.* **1** Of or pertaining to tactics. **2** Showing adroitness in planning and maneuvering. —**tac′· ti·cal·ly** *adv.*

tac·ti·cian (tak·tish′ən) *n.* An expert in tactics.

tac·tics (tak′tiks) *n.pl.* **1** *(construed as sing.)* The science and art of handling troops in securing military and naval objectives. **2** Any adroit maneuvering to gain an end. [< Gk. *taktikos* suitable for arranging]

tac·tile (tak′təl, -tīl) *adj.* **1** Of, pertaining to, or having the sense of touch. **2** That may be touched; tangible. [< L *tactus*. See TACT.] —**tac·til·i·ty** (tak·til′ə·tē) *n.*

tact·less (takt′lis) *adj.* Showing or characterized by a lack of tact. —**tact′less·ly** *adv.* —**tact′less·ness** *n.*

tad·pole (tad′pōl) *n.* The aquatic larva of an amphibian, as a frog or toad, having gills and a tail. [< ME *tadde* toad + *pol* head, poll]

tael (tāl) *n.* **1** Any of several units of weight of E Asia. **2** A Chinese monetary unit. [< Pg. < Malay *tahil*]

taf·fe·ta (taf′ə·tə) *n.* A fine, glossy, somewhat stiff fabric woven of silk, rayon, nylon, etc. —*adj.* Made of or resembling taffeta. [< Pers. *tāftah*]

taff·rail (taf′rāl) *n.* The rail around a vessel's stern. [< MDu. *tafereel* panel, lit., small table]

taf·fy (taf′ē) *n. pl.* **taf·fies 1** A chewy confection made usu. of brown sugar or molasses, boiled down, and pulled until it cools. **2** *Informal* Flattery; blarney. [?]

tag¹ (tag) *n.* **1** Something attached to something else, to identify, price, classify, etc.; a label. **2** A loose, ragged edge, esp. of a piece of cloth. **3** The metal sheath at the end of a lace, cord etc. **4** The final lines of a speech, song, or poem. —*v.* **tagged, tag·ging** *v.t.* **1** To supply, adorn, fit,

Development of a tadpole

mark, or label with a tag. 2 *Informal* To follow closely or persistently. —*v.i.* 3 *Informal* To follow closely at one's heels: with *along, behind,* etc. [? < Scand.]

tag² (tag) *n.* A children's game in which a player, called "it," chases other players until he touches one of them, that person in turn becoming the one who must pursue another. —*v.t.* **tagged, tag·ging** To overtake and touch, as in the game of tag. [?]

Ta·ga·log (tə·gäl'əg, -gä'lôg) *n.* 1 A member of a people native to the Philippines. 2 The Austronesian language of this people, the official language of the Philippines.

tail¹ (tāl) *n.* 1 The rear end of an animal's body, esp. when prolonged to form a flexible appendage. 2 Anything similar in appearance, as a pigtail. 3 *Astron.* The luminous cloud extending from a comet. 4 The hind, back, or inferior portion of anything. 5 *Often pl. Informal* The reverse side of a coin. 6 A body of persons in single file. 7 A group of attendants; retinue. 8 *Aeron.* A system of airfoils placed some distance to the rear of the main bearing surfaces of an airplane. 9 *pl. Informal* A man's full-dress suit; also, a swallow-tailed coat. 10 *Informal* A person, as a detective, who follows another in surveillance. 11 *Informal* A trail or course, as one taken by a fugitive. —*v.t.* 1 To furnish with a tail. 2 To cut off the tail of. 3 To be the tail or end of. 4 To join (one thing) to the end of another. 5 To insert and fasten by one end. 6 *Informal* To follow secretly and stealthily; shadow. —*v.i.* 7 To form or be part of a tail. 8 *Informal* To follow close behind. 9 To diminish gradually: with *off.* —*adj.* 1 Rearmost; hindmost: the *tail* end. 2 Coming from behind: a *tail* wind. [< OE *tægl*]

tail² (tāl) *Law adj.* Restricted in some way, as to particular heirs: an estate *tail.* —*n.* A limiting of the inheritance of an estate, as to particular heirs. [< OF *taillié*, p.p. of *taillier* to cut]

tail·gate (tāl'gāt') *n.* A hinged or removable board or gate closing the back end of a truck, wagon, etc. Also **tail·board** (tāl'bôrd', -bōrd'). —*v.t. & v.i.* **-gat·ed, -gat·ing** To drive too close for safety behind (another vehicle).

tail·light (tāl'līt') *n.* A warning light, usu. red, attached to the rear of a vehicle. Also **tail lamp.**

tai·lor (tā'lər) *n.* One who makes or repairs garments. —*v.i.* 1 To do a tailor's work. —*v.t.* 2 To fit with garments. 3 To make, work at, or style by tailoring. 4 To form or adapt to meet certain needs or conditions. [< LL *taliare* split, cut] —**tai'lor·ing** *n.*

tai·lor·bird (tā'lər·bûrd') *n.* Any of various small birds of Asia and Africa that stitch leaves together so as to conceal the nest. • See NEST.

tai·lor-made (tā'lər·mād') *adj.* 1 Made by or looking as if made by a tailor. 2 Right or suitable for a particular person, specific conditions, etc.

tail·piece (tāl'pēs') *n.* 1 Any endpiece or appendage. 2 In a violin or similar instrument, a piece of wood at the sounding-board end, having the strings fastened to it. 3 *Printing* An ornamental design at the end of a chapter or the bottom of a short page. 4 A short beam or rafter tailed into a wall.

tail·spin (tāl'spin') *n.* 1 *Aeron.* The uncontrolled descent of an airplane along a helical path at a steep angle. 2 *Informal* A sudden, sharp, mental or emotional upheaval.

tail wind A wind blowing in the same direction as the course of an aircraft or ship.

taint (tānt) *v.t.* 1 To affect with decay or contamination. 2 To render morally corrupt. —*v.i.* 3 To be or become tainted. —*n.* A cause or result of contamination or corruption. [< OF *teint,* pp. of *teindre* to tinge, color]

take (tāk) *v.* **took, tak·en, tak·ing** *v.t.* 1 To lay hold of; grasp. 2 To get possession of; seize; capture; catch. 3 To gain, capture, or win, as in a game or in competition. 4 To choose; select. 5 To buy. 6 To rent or hire; lease. 7 To subscribe to, as a periodical. 8 To assume occupancy of: to *take* a chair. 9 To assume the responsibilities of: to *take* office. 10 To accept into some relation to oneself: He *took* a wife. 11 To assume as a symbol or badge: to *take* the veil. 12 To subject oneself to: to *take* a vow. 13 To remove or carry off: with *away.* 14 To steal. 15 To remove by death. 16 To subtract or deduct. 17 To be subjected to; undergo: to *take* a beating. 18 To submit to; accept passively: to *take* an insult. 19 To become affected with; contract: He *took*

cold. 20 To affect: The fever *took* him at dawn. 21 To captivate; charm or delight: The dress *took* her fancy. 22 To react to: How did she *take* the news? 23 To undertake to deal with; contend with; handle: to *take* an examination. 24 To consider; deem: I *take* him for an honest man. 25 To understand; comprehend: I couldn't *take* the meaning of her remarks. 26 To hit: The blow *took* him on the forehead. 27 *Informal* To aim or direct: He *took* a shot at the target. 28 To carry with one: *Take* your umbrella! 29 To lead: This road *takes* you to town. 30 To escort. 31 To receive into the body, as by eating, inhaling, etc.: *Take* a deep breath. 32 To accept or assume as if due or granted: to *take* credit. 33 To require: it *takes* courage. 34 To let in; admit; accommodate: The car *takes* only six people. 35 To occupy oneself in; enjoy: to *take* a nap. 36 To perform, as an action: to *take* a stride. 37 To confront and get over: The horse *took* the hurdle. 38 To avail oneself of (an opportunity, etc.). 39 To put into effect; adopt: to *take* measures. 40 To use up or consume: The piano *takes* too much space. 41 To make use of; apply: to *take* pains. 42 To travel by means of: to *take* a train. 43 To seek: to *take* cover. 44 To ascertain by measuring, computing, etc.: to *take* a census. 45 To obtain or derive from some source. 46 To write down or copy: to *take* notes. 47 To obtain (a likeness or representation of) by photographing. 48 To conceive or feel: She *took* a dislike to him. 49 *Slang* To cheat; deceive. 50 *Gram.* To require by construction or usage: The verb *takes* a direct object. —*v.i.* 51 To get possession. 52 To engage; catch, as mechanical parts. 53 To begin to grow; germinate. 54 To have the intended effect: The vaccination *took.* 55 To gain favor, as a play. 56 To detract: with *from.* 57 To become (ill or sick). —**take after** 1 To resemble. 2 To follow in pursuit. —**take amiss** To be offended by. —**take back** To retract. —**take down** 1 To humble. 2 To write down. —**take for** To consider to be. —**take in** 1 To admit; receive. 2 To lessen in size or scope. 3 To include; embrace. 4 To understand. 5 To cheat or deceive. 6 To visit. —**take it** To endure hardship, abuse, etc. —**take off** 1 To mimic; burlesque. 2 To rise from a surface, esp. to begin a flight, as an airplane or rocket. 3 To leave; depart. 4 To begin: often used to refer to that point in an economic venture when growth becomes a self-generating and self-sustaining process. —**take on** 1 To hire; employ. 2 To undertake to deal with. 3 *Informal* To exhibit violent emotion. —**take over** To assume control of (a business, nation, etc.) —**take place** To happen. —**take to** 1 To become fond of. 2 *Informal* To adopt a way of doing, using, etc.: He has *taken* to walking to work. 3 To flee: to *take* to the hills. —**take up** 1 To make smaller or less; shorten or tighten. 2 To pay, as a note or mortgage. 3 To accept as stipulated: to *take up* an option. 4 To begin or begin again. 5 To occupy, engage, or consume, as space or time. 6 To develop an interest in or devotion to: to *take up* a cause. —**take up with** *Informal* To become friendly with; associate with. —*n.* 1 The act of taking or that which is taken. 2 *Slang* An amount of money received; receipts; profit. 3 A quantity collected at one time: the *take* of fish. 4 An uninterrupted run of the camera in photographing a movie or television scene. 5 A scene so photographed. 6 The process of making a sound recording. 7 A recording made in a single recording session. [< OE *tacan* < ON *taka*] —**tak'er** *n.* • See BRING.

take-home pay (tāk'hōm') Net wages after tax and other deductions.

take·off (tāk'ôf', -of') *n.* 1 *Informal* A satirical representation; caricature. 2 The act of taking off, as in flight. 3 The place from which one takes off. 4 A point at which something begins.

take·o·ver (tāk'ō'vər) *n.* The act or an instance of taking over, esp. the assumption of power in a business, nation, etc.

tak·ing (tā'king) *adj.* Fascinating; captivating. —*n.* 1 The act of one who takes. 2 The thing or things taken; catch. 3 *pl.* Receipts, as of money. —**tak'ing·ly** *adv.* —**tak'ing·ness** *n.*

talc (talk) *n.* A soft mineral magnesium silicate, used in making talcum powder, lubricants, etc. —*v.t.* **talcked** or **talced, talck·ing** or **talc·ing** To treat with talc. [< Ar. *talq*]

tal·cum (tal'kəm) *n.* TALC.

talcum powder Finely powdered, purified, and usu. perfumed talc, used as a face and body powder.

tale (tāl) *n.* 1 A story that is told or written; a narrative of real or fictitious events. 2 An idle or malicious piece of gossip. 3 A lie. 4 *Archaic* A tally or amount; total. [< OE *talu* speech, narrative]

tale·bear·er (tāl'bâr'ər) *n.* One who gossips, spreads rumors, tells secrets, etc. **—tale'bear'ing** *adj., n.* **—Syn.** gossip, scandalmonger, newsmonger.

tal·ent (tal'ənt) *n.* 1 *pl.* A person's natural abilities. 2 A particular aptitude for some special work, artistic endeavor, etc. 3 A person, or people collectively with skill or ability. 4 Any of various ancient weights and denominations of money, used in ancient Greece, Rome, and the Middle East. [< L *talentum*, a sum of money] **—tal'ent·ed** *adj.*

ta·ler (tä'lər) *n.* A former German silver coin. [< G *Taler*]

tales·man (tālz'mən) *n. pl.* **·men** (-mən) One summoned to fill a vacancy in a jury when the regular panel has become deficient in number. [< ML *tales (de circumstantibus)* such (of the bystanders) + MAN]

tale·tell·er (tāl'tel'ər) *n.* 1 RACONTEUR. 2 TALEBEARER. **—tale'tell'ing** *adj., n.*

ta·li (tā'lī) *n.pl.* of TALUS¹.

tal·i·pes (tal'ə·pēz) *n.* Congenital deformity of one or both feet. [< L *talus* ankle + *pes* foot]

tal·i·pot (tal'ə·pot) *n.* An East Indian palm crowned by large leaves often used as fans, umbrellas, etc. Also **talipot palm.** [< Skt. *tālī* fan palm + *pattra* leaf]

tal·is·man (tal'is·mən, -iz-) *n. pl.* **·mans** 1 An object, as a ring or amulet, supposed to ward off evil, bring good luck, etc. 2 Anything supposed to have a magical effect. [< LGk. *telesma* a sacred rite] **—tal'is·man'ic** (·man'ik) *adj.*

talk (tôk) *v.i.* 1 To express or exchange thoughts in audible words; speak or converse. 2 To communicate by means other than speech: to *talk* with one's fingers. 3 To chatter. 4 To confer; consult. 5 To gossip. 6 To make sounds suggestive of speech. 7 *Informal* To give information; inform. — *v.t.* 8 To express in words; utter. 9 To converse in: to *talk* Spanish. 10 To discuss: to *talk* business. 11 To bring to a specified condition or state by talking: to *talk* one into doing something. **—talk back** To answer impudently. **—talk down** To silence by talking. **—talk down to** To speak to patronizingly. **—talk shop** To talk about one's work. — *n.* 1 The act of talking; conversation; speech. 2 A speech, either formal or informal. 3 Report; rumor: *talk* of war. 4 A subject of conversation. 5 A conference or discussion. 6 Mere words; empty conversation, discussion, etc. 7 A special kind of speech; lingo: baseball *talk.* 8 Sounds suggestive of speech, as made by a bird or animal. [Prob. < OE *talian* reckon, tell]

talk·a·thon (tô'kə·thon') *n. Informal* A prolonged session of talking, debating, etc. [< TALK + (MAR)ATHON]

talk·a·tive (tô'kə·tiv) *adj.* Given to or fond of much talking. **—talk'a·tive·ly** *adv.* **—talk'a·tive·ness** *n.* **—Syn.** garrulous, loquacious, voluble, windy.

talk·ie (tô'kē) *n.* Formerly, a motion picture with a sound track, as distinguished from a silent film.

talk·ing-to (tô'king·tōō') *n. pl.* **·tos** *Informal* A scolding.

tall (tôl) *adj.* 1 Having more than average height; high. 2 Having a specified height: five feet *tall.* 3 *Informal* Extravagant; boastful; exaggerated: a *tall* story. 4 Large; extensive: a *tall* order. *—adv. Informal* Proudly: to walk *tall.* [< OE *getæl* swift, prompt] **—tall'ish** *adj.* **—tall'ness** *n.*

tal·lith (tal'ith, tä'lis) *n. pl.* **tal·li·thim** (tal'ə·sēm', -thēm) A fringed shawl worn by Jewish men during morning prayer. [< Heb. *tallīth* cover]

tal·low (tal'ō) *n.* Solid, rendered animal fats, as of beef or mutton, refined for making candles, soaps, etc. *—v.t.* To smear with tallow. [< MLG *talg, talch*] **—tal'low·y** *adj.*

tal·ly (tal'ē) *n. pl.* **·lies** 1 A piece of wood on which notches or scores are cut as marks of number. 2 A score or mark. 3 A reckoning; account. 4 A counterpart; duplicate. 5 A mark indicative of number. 6 A label; tag. *—v.* **·lied, ·ly·ing** *v.t.* 1 To score on a tally; mark. 2 To reckon; count: often with *up.* 3 To register, as points in a game; score.

4 To cause to correspond. *—v.i.* 5 To make a tally. 6 To agree precisely: His story *tallies* with yours. 7 To keep score. 8 To score, as in a game. [< L *talea* rod, cutting] **—tal'li·er** *n.*

tal·ly·ho (tal'ə·hō') *interj.* A huntsman's cry to hounds when the quarry is sighted. *—n.pl.* **·hos** 1 The cry of "tallyho." 2 A kind of coach drawn by four horses. *—v.t.* 1 To urge on, as hounds, with the cry of "tallyho." *—v.i.* 2 To cry "tallyho." [? < F *taïaut*, a hunting cry]

Tal·mud (tal'mud, täl'mōōd) *n.* The written body of Jewish civil and religious law. [< Heb. *talmūdh* instruction] **—Tal·mud'ic** or **·i·cal** *adj.* **—Tal'mud·ist** *n.*

tal·on (tal'ən) *n.* 1 The claw of a bird or other animal, esp. a bird of prey. 2 A human finger or hand thought of as resembling a claw. [< L *talus* heel] **—tal'oned** *adj.*

ta·lus¹ (tā'ləs) *n. pl.* **·li** (-lī) or **·lus·es** 1 The upper, pivotal bone of the ankle. 2 The entire ankle. [L, ankle]

ta·lus² (tā'ləs, tal'əs) *n.* 1 A slope, as of a tapering wall. 2 *Geol.* The sloping mass of rock fragments at the foot of a cliff. 3 The slope given to the face of a wall, as in a fortification. [F < L *talutium* slope bearing signs of the presence of gold]

tam (tam) *n.* TAM-O'-SHANTER.

ta·ma·le (tə·mä'lē) *n.* A Mexican dish of ground meat seasoned with red pepper, rolled in cornmeal, wrapped in corn husks, and steamed. [< Nahuatl *tamalli*]

tam·a·rack (tam'ə·rak) *n.* 1 A species of larch common in N North America. 2 Its wood. [< Algon.]

tam·a·rind (tam'ə·rind) *n.* 1 A tropical tree of the bean family, with yellow flowers. 2 The edible fruit of this tree, a pod with acid pulp. [< Ar. *tamr hindi* Indian date]

tam·bour (tam'bŏŏr) *n.* 1 A drum. 2 A light wooden frame, usu. circular, esp. a set of two hoops between which fabric is stretched for embroidering. *—v.t. & v.i.* To embroider on a tambour. [< Ar. *tanbūr* drum]

tam·bou·rine (tam'bə·rēn') *n.* A musical instrument like the head of a drum, with metal disks in the rim, played by striking it with the hand. [F, lit., small tambour]

tame (tām) *adj.* **tam·er, tam·est** 1 Having lost its native wildness; domesticated. 2 Docile; tractable; subdued; submissive. 3 Lacking in spirit; uninteresting; dull. *—v.t.* **tamed, tam·ing** 1 To make tame; domesticate. 2 To bring into subjection or obedience. 3 To tone down; soften. [< OE *tam*] **—tam'a·ble** or **tame'a·ble** *adj.* **—tame'ly** *adv.* **—tame'ness, tam'er** *n.*

tame·less (tām'lis) *adj.* Untamable or not tamed.

Tam·il (tam'əl) *n.* 1 A member of a Dravidian people of s India and N Sri Lanka. 2 Their language.

Tam·ma·ny (tam'ə·nē) *n.* A fraternal society in New York City (founded 1789) serving as the central organization of the city's Democratic party, located in **Tammany Hall.** [< *Tamanend*, a 17th c. Delaware Indian chief]

tam-o'-shan·ter (tam'ə·shan'tər) *n.* A Scottish cap with a round flat top, sometimes with a center pompon. [< the hero of a poem by Robert Burns]

tamp (tamp) *v.t.* 1 To force down or pack closer by repeated blows. 2 In blasting, to pack matter around a charge in order to increase the explosive effect. [Back formation < TAMPION] **—tam'per** *n.*

tam·per (tam'pər) *v.i.* 1 To meddle; interfere: usu. with *with.* 2 To make changes, esp. so as to damage, falsify, etc.: with *with.* 3 To use secret or improper measures, as bribery. [Var. of TEMPER] **—tam'per·er** *n.*

tam·pi·on (tam'pē·ən) *n.* A plug or cover for the muzzle of a gun. [< *tapon, tape* a bung]

tam·pon (tam'pon) *n.* A plug of absorbent material for insertion in a body cavity or wound to stop bleeding or absorb secretions. *—v.t.* To plug up, as a wound, with a tampon. [< OF *tapon, tape* a bung]

tan (tan) *v.* **tanned, tan·ning** *v.t.* 1 To convert into leather, as hides or skins, by treating with tannin. 2 To darken, as the skin, by exposure to sunlight. 3 *Informal.* To thrash; flog. *—v.i.* 4 To become tanned. *—n.* 1 TANBARK. 2 TANNIN. 3 A yellowish brown color tinged with red. 4 A dark coloring of the skin, resulting from exposure to the sun. *—adj.*

---

add, āce, câre, pälm; end, ēven; it, īce; odd, ōpen, ôrder; tōōk, pōōl; up, bûrn; ə = *a* in *above, u* in *focus;* yōō = *u* in *fuse;* oil; pout; check; go; ring; thin; ṯhis; zh, *vision.* < derived from; ? origin uncertain or unknown.

1 Of the color tan. **2** Of, pertaining to, or used for tanning. [< Med. L *tanum* tanbark]

tan tangent.

tan·a·ger (tan′ə·jər) *n.* Any of a family of American song-birds related to finches and noted for the brilliant plumage of the male. [< Pg. *tangara* < Tupi] —**tan′a·grine** (-grēn) *adj.*

tan·bark (tan′bärk′) *n.* **1** The bark of certain trees used as a source of tannin. **2** Shredded bark from which the tannin has been removed, used on circus rings, racetracks, etc.

tan·dem (tan′dəm) *adv.* One behind the other. —*n.* **1** A team, as of horses, harnessed one behind the other. **2** A two-wheeled carriage drawn in such a way. **3** A bicycle with two or more seats one behind the other. —*adj.* Having parts or things arranged one behind another. [L, at length (of time)]

Tandem bicycle

tang (tang) *n.* **1** A sharp, penetrating taste, flavor or odor. **2** Any distinctive quality or flavor. **3** A trace or hint. **4** A slender shank or tongue projecting from the end of a sword blade, chisel, etc., for fitting into a handle, hilt, etc. [< ON *tongi* a point] —**tang′y** *adj.* (**·i·er**, **·i·est**)

tan·gent (tan′jənt) *adj.* **1** *Geom.* Coinciding at a point or along a line without intersection, as a curve and line, surface and plane, etc. **2** Touching; in contact. —*n.* **1** *Geom.* A line tangent to a curve at any point. **2** *Trig.* A function of an angle, equal to the quotient of its sine divided by its cosine. **3** A sharp change in course or direction. —**fly** (or **go**) **off on a tangent** *Informal* To make a sharp or sudden change, as in a course of action or train of thought. [< L *tangere* to touch] —**tan·gen·cy** (tan′jən·sē) *n.*

tan·gen·tial (tan·jen′shəl) *adj.* **1** Of, pertaining to, like, or in the direction of a tangent. **2** Touching slightly. **3** Divergent. —**tan·gen′ti·al·i·ty** (-shē·al′ə·tē) *n.* —**tan·gen′tial·ly** *adv.*

tan·ger·ine (tan′jə·rēn′, tan′jə·rēn′) *n.* **1** A variety of orange with a loose skin and easily separated segments. **2** A burnt orange color like that of the tangerine. [< *Tangier,* a city in Morocco]

tan·gi·ble (tan′jə·bəl) *adj.* **1** Perceptible by touch. **2** Not elusive or unreal; objective; concrete: *tangible* evidence. **3** Having value that can be appraised. —*n. pl.* Things having value that can be appraised. [< L *tangere* to touch] —**tan′gi·bil′i·ty, tan′gi·ble·ness** *n.* —**tan′gi·bly** *adv.*

tan·gle (tang′gəl) *v.* **·gled, ·gling** *v.t.* **1** To twist in a confused and not readily separable mass. **2** To ensnare as in a tangle; trap; enmesh. **3** To involve in such a way as to confuse, obstruct, etc. —*v.i.* To be or become entangled. —**tangle with** *Informal* To become involved or fight with. —*n.* **1** A confused intertwining, as of threads or hairs; a snarl. **2** State of confusion or complication. **3** A state of bewilderment. [Prob. < Scand.] —**tan′gler** *n.*

tan·go (tang′gō) *n. pl.* **·gos 1** A Latin American dance characterized by deliberate gliding steps and low dips. **2** The music for such a dance. —*v.i.* To dance the tango. [< Sp.]

tank (tangk) *n.* **1** A large vessel, basin, or receptacle for holding a fluid. **2** A natural or artificial pool or pond. **3** An armored combat vehicle that rides on treads and has mounted guns. **4** *Slang* A jail cell, esp. one for receiving prisoners. —*v.t.* To place or store in a tank. [? < Pg. *estanque*]

tank·age (tangk′ij) *n.* **1** The act or process of

U.S. Army tank

storing in tanks. **2** The price for storage in tanks. **3** The capacity or contents of a tank. **4** Slaughterhouse waste from which the fat has been rendered in tanks, used, when dried, as fertilizer or feed.

tank·ard (tangk′ərd) *n.* A large, one-handled drinking cup, often with a cover. [ME]

tank·er (tangk′ər) *n.* **1** A cargo ship for the transport of oil or other liquids. **2** A cargo plane used to carry gasoline and to refuel other planes in flight.

tank farm An area where oil is stored in tanks.

tan·ner (tan′ər) *n.* One who tans hides.

tan·ner·y (tan′ər·ē) *n. pl.* **·ner·ies** A place where leather is tanned.

tan·nic (tan′ik) *adj.* Of, pertaining to, or derived from tannin or tanbark.

tan·nin (tan′in) *n.* A yellowish, astringent substance extracted from tanbark, gallnut, etc., used in dyeing, tanning, etc. Also **tannic acid.** [< F *tanin* < *tanner* to tan]

tan·sy (tan′zē) *n. pl.* **·sies** Any of a genus of coarse perennial herbs, esp. a species with yellow flowers and pungent foliage. [< Gk. *athanasia* immortality]

tan·ta·lize (tan′tə·līz′) *v.t.* **·lized, ·liz·ing** To tease or torment by promising or showing something desirable and then denying access to it. *Brit. sp.* **·lise**′. [< TANTALUS] —**tan′ta·li·za′tion, tan′ta·liz′er** *n.* —**tan′ta·liz′ing·ly** *adv.*

tan·ta·lum (tan′tə·ləm) *n.* A hard, corrosion-resistant metallic element (symbol Ta). [< TANTALUS, from its inability to react with most acids]

Tan·ta·lus (tan′tə·ləs) *Gk. Myth.* A king who was punished in Hades by being made to stand in water that receded when he tried to drink and under fruit-laden branches he could not reach.

tan·ta·mount (tan′tə·mount) *adj.* Equivalent: with *to.* [< L *tantus* as much + OF *amonter* to amount]

tan·trum (tan′trəm) *n.* A violent fit of temper. [?]

Tan·za·ni·a (tan′zə·nē′ə) *n.* A republic of the Commonwealth of Nations in E Africa, 362,800 sq. mi., cap. Dar es Salaam. —**Tan′za·ni′an** *adj., n.* • See map at AFRICA.

Ta·o·ism (dou′iz·əm, tou′-) *n.* One of the principal religions or philosophies of China, founded in the sixth century B.C. by Lao-tse. [< Chin. *tao* way] —**Tao′ist** *adj., n.* —**Tao·is′tic** *adj.*

tap¹ (tap) *n.* **1** A spout through which liquid is drawn, as from a cask. **2** FAUCET. **3** A plug or stopper to close an opening, as in a cask. **4** Liquor drawn from a tap, esp. of a particular quality or brew. **5** A tool for cutting internal screw threads. **6** A point of connection for an electrical circuit. **7** The act or an instance of wiretapping. —**on tap 1** Contained in a cask; ready for tapping: beer *on tap.* **2** *Informal* Available; ready. —*v.t.* **tapped, tap·ping 1** To provide with a tap or spigot. **2** To pierce or open so as to draw liquid from. **3** To draw (liquid) from a container, body cavity, etc. **4** To make connection with: to *tap* a gas main. **5** To draw upon; utilize: to *tap* new sources of energy. **6** To make connection with secretly: to *tap* a telephone wire. **7** To make an internal screw thread in with a tap. [< OE *tæppa*]

tap² (tap) *v.* **tapped, tap·ping** *v.t.* **1** To touch or strike gently. **2** To strike gently with. **3** To make or produce by tapping. **4** To apply a tap to (a shoe) —*v.i.* **5** To strike a light blow or blows, as with the finger tip. **6** To walk with a light, tapping sound. **7** TAP-DANCE. —*n.* **1** The act or sound of striking gently. **2** Leather, metal, etc., affixed to a shoe sole or heel, for repair or tap-dancing. **3** *pl.* A military signal sounded on a trumpet or drum for the extinguishing of all lights in soldiers' quarters. [< OF *taper*]

ta·pa (tä′pä) *n.* **1** The inner bark of an Asian tree related to the mulberry. **2** A cloth made of this bark: also **tapa cloth.** [< native Polynesian name]

tap-dance (tap′dans′, -däns′) *v.i.* **-danced, -danc·ing** To dance a tap dance. —**tap′-danc′er** *n.*

tap dance A dance in which the dancer taps out a rhythm with the heels and toes of shoes.

tape (tāp) *n.* **1** A narrow strip of woven fabric. **2** Any long, narrow, flat strip of paper, metal, plastic, etc., as the magnetic strip used in a tape recorder. **3** TAPE MEASURE. **4** A string stretched across the finishing point of a racetrack and broken by the winner of the race. —*v.t.* **taped, tap·ing 1** To wrap or secure with tape. **2** To measure with a tape

measure. **3** To record on magnetic tape. [< OE *tæppe* strip of cloth] **—tap′er** *n.*

tape deck An assembly of magnetic head, tape reels, and drive for tape recording and playback.

tape measure A tape marked in inches, feet, etc., for measuring. Also **tape·line** (tāp′līn′) *n.*

ta·per (tā′pər) *n.* **1** A slender candle. **2** A long wax-coated wick used to light candles, lamps, etc. **3** A weak light. **4** A gradual diminution of size in an elongated object; also, any tapering object, as a cone. **5** Any gradual decrease. — *v.t.* & *v.i.* **1** To make or become smaller or thinner toward one end. **2** To lessen gradually: with *off.* —*adj.* Growing smaller toward one end. [< OE]

tape-re·cord (tāp′ri·kôrd′) *v.t.* TAPE (*v.*, def. 3).

tape recorder An electromagnetic apparatus which can record sound on magnetic tape and play it back.

tap·es·try (tap′is·trē) *n. pl.* **·tries 1** A heavy woven textile with a pictorial design, used for hangings, upholstery, etc. **2** Something like this, as in complexity of design. —*v.t.* **·tried, ·try·ing 1** To hang or adorn with tapestry. **2** To depict or weave in a tapestry. [< Gk. *tapētion,* dim. of *tapēs* rug]

tape·worm (tāp′wûrm′) *n.* Any of various long flat-worms parasitic in the intestines of man and various animals.

tap·i·o·ca (tap′ē·ō′kə) *n.* A starchy, granular foodstuff obtained from cassava, used in puddings, as a thickener for soups, etc. [< Tupi *tipioca*]

ta·pir (tā′pər) *n.* Any of various hoofed, herbivorous mammals of tropical America and SE Asia, having short stout limbs and a flexible snout. [< Tupi *tapy′ra*]

tap·room (tap′rōōm′, -rŏŏm′) *n.* BARROOM.

tap·root (tap′rōōt′, -rŏŏt′) *n.* A type of plant root having one main descending part. **—tap′root′ed** *adj.*

tar[1] (tär) *n.* A dark, usu. pungent, viscid mixture of hydrocarbons obtained by the dry distillation of wood, coal, etc. —*v.t.* **tarred, tar·ring** To cover with or as with tar. **—tar and feather** To smear with tar and then cover with feathers as a punishment. —*adj.* Made of, derived from, or resembling tar. [< OE *teru*]

tar[2] (tär) *n. Informal* A sailor. [Short for TARPAULIN]

tar·an·tel·la (tar′ən·tel′ə) *n.* **1** A lively Neapolitan dance. **2** Music for this dance. [< *Taranto,* a port in SE Italy]

ta·ran·tu·la (tə·ran′chōō·lə, -tə·lə) *n. pl.* **·las** or **·lae** (-lē) **1** A large, hairy, venomous spider of s Europe. **2** Any of various large, hairy American spiders capable of inflicting a painful but not dangerous bite. [< *Taranto,* Italy]

Tarantula *def. 1*

tar·dy (tär′dē) *adj.* **·di·er, ·di·est 1** Not coming, happening, etc., at the scheduled or proper time. **2** Moving, acting, etc., at a slow pace. [< L *tardus* slow] **—tar′di·ly** *adv.* **—tar′di·ness** *n.* **—Syn. 1** late, dilatory, overdue, delayed. **2** slow, sluggish, leisurely, torpid.

tare[1] (târ) *n.* **1** In the Bible, a weed that grows among wheat, supposed to be the darnel. **2** Any one of various species of vetch. [?]

tare[2] (târ) *n.* **1** The deduction of the weight of a container, used to calculate the weight of its contents if the gross weight of the container and contents is determined. **2** The weight of the container. —*v.t.* **tared, tar·ing** To weigh, as a vessel or package, in order to determine the tare. [< Ar. *tarhah*]

tar·get (tär′git) *n.* **1** An object presenting a usu. marked surface that is to be aimed and shot at, as in archery practice. **2** Anything that is shot at. **3** One who or that which is made an object of ridicule, criticism, etc.; butt. **4** A goal; objective. **5** A small round shield. —*v.t.* **1** To make a target of. **2** To establish as a goal. [< OF *targe* shield] — **tar′get·a·ble** *adj.*

tar·iff (tar′if) *n.* **1** A schedule of government-imposed duties to be paid for the importation or exportation of goods. **2** A duty of this kind, or its rate. **3** Any schedule of charges, prices, etc. —*v.t.* **1** To make a list of duties on. **2** To fix a price or tariff on. [< Ar. *ta′rif* information]

tarn (tärn) *n.* A small mountain lake. [< ON *tjörn*]

tar·nish (tär′nish) *v.t.* **1** To dim the luster of. **2** To sully, mar, debase, etc. —*v.i.* **3** To become tarnished. —*n.* **1** The condition of being tarnished; stain, blemish, loss of luster, etc. **2** The thin discolored film on the surface of tarnished metal. [< OF *ternir*] **—tar′nish·a·ble** *adj.*

ta·ro (tä′rō, tar′ō) *n. pl.* **·ros** Any of several tropical plants having starchy, edible rootstocks. [< native Polynesian name]

tar·ot (tar′ō, -ət, tar·ō′) *n.* Any of a set of old Italian figured playing cards, now used chiefly in fortunetelling.

tar·pau·lin (tär·pô′lin, tär′pə-) *n.* A waterproof material, esp. canvas, used as a covering for exposed objects. [?< TAR[1] + *palling,* pr.p. of PALL[1]]

tar·pon (tär′pon, -pən) *n. pl.* **·pon** or **·pons** A large game fish of the West Indies and the coast of Florida. [?]

tar·ra·gon (tar′ə·gon) *n.* **1** A European perennial plant allied to wormwood. **2** The fragrant leaves of this plant, used for seasoning. [< Ar. *tarkhun*]

tar·ry[1] (tar′ē) *v.* **·ried, ·ry·ing** *v.i.* **1** To put off going or coming; linger. **2** To remain in the same place; stay. **3** To wait. —*v.t.* **4** *Archaic* To wait for. [< L *tardare* to delay]

tar·ry[2] (tär′ē) *adj.* **tar·ri·er, tar·ri·est** Of, like, or covered with tar. **—tar′ri·ness** *n.*

tar·sal (tär′səl) *adj.* Of, pertaining to, or situated near the tarsus or ankle. —*n.* A tarsal part, as a bone.

tar·si·er (tär′sē·ər) *n.* A small, arboreal, nocturnal East Indian primate with large eyes and ears, long tail, and elongated digits. [< F < *tarse* tarsus]

tar·sus (tär′səs) *n. pl.* **·si** (-sī) **1** *Anat.* **a** The ankle. **b** In man, the seven bones of the ankle and heel. **2** *Zool.* **a** The shank of a bird's leg. **b** The distal part of the leg of certain arthropods. [< Gk. *tarsos* flat of the foot, any flat surface]

Tarsier

tart[1] (tärt) *adj.* **1** Having a sharp, sour taste. **2** Severe; caustic: a *tart* remark. [< OE *teart*] **—tart′ly** *adv.* **—tart′ness** *n.* **—Syn. 1** acid, bitter. **2** cutting, biting, acrimonious, sarcastic.

tart[2] (tärt) *n.* **1** A small open pastry shell filled with fruit, jelly, custard, etc. **2** *Slang* A girl or woman of loose morality. [< OF *tarte*]

tar·tan (tär′tən) *n.* **1** A woolen plaid fabric, esp. one with a pattern distinctive to a particular clan of the Scottish Highlands. **2** A fabric made to look like this. **3** Any plaid. —*adj.* Made of or like tartan. [? < OF *tiretaine* linsey-woolsey] • See PLAID.

tar·tar[1] (tär′tər) *n.* **1** A hard deposit of potassium tartrate that forms in wine casks. **2** A yellowish incrustation on teeth, chiefly calcium phosphate. [< Med. Gk. *tartaron*] — **tar·tar′e·ous** *adj.*

tar·tar[2] (tär′tər) *n.* A person of intractable or violent disposition.

Tar·tar (tär′tər) *n.* TATAR. —*adj.* Of or pertaining to the Tatars or Tatary.

tartar emetic A poisonous tartrate of antimony and potassium, used in medicine and in dyeing.

tar·tar·ic (tär·tar′ik, -tär′ik) *adj.* Pertaining to or derived from tartar or a tartaric acid.

tartaric acid A white, crystalline organic acid present in grapes and other fruits.

Tar·ta·rus (tär′tər·əs) *Gk. Myth.* **1** The abyss below Hades where Zeus confined the Titans. **2** HADES (def. 2).

Tar·ta·ry (tär′tər·ē) *n.* TATARY.

task (task, täsk) *n.* **1** A piece of work, esp. one imposed by authority or required by duty or necessity. **2** Any unpleasant or difficult assignment; burden. **—take to task** To reprove; lecture. —*v.t.* **1** To assign a task to. **2** To burden. [< L *taxare* appraise]

task force 1 A military unit specially trained to execute a specific mission. **2** Any group assigned to handle a specific task.

task·mas·ter (task′mas′tər, täsk′mäs′tər) *n.* One who assigns tasks, esp. burdensome ones.

---

add, āce, câre, pälm; end, ēven; it, īce; odd, ōpen, ôrder; tŏŏk, pōōl; up, bûrn; ə = *a* in *above, u* in *focus;* yōō = *u* in *fuse;* oil; pout; check; go; ring; thin; this; zh, *vision.* < derived from; ? origin uncertain or unknown.

tas·sel (tas′əl) *n.* **1** A tuft of loosely hanging threads or cords used as an ornament for curtains, cushions, etc. **2** Something resembling a tassel, as the inflorescence on Indian corn. —*v.* **·seled** or **·selled, ·sel·ing** or **·sel·ling** *v.t.* **1** To provide or adorn with tassels. **2** To form in a tassel or tassels. —*v.i.* **3** To put forth tassels, as Indian corn. [< OF, clasp]

taste (tāst) *v.* **tast·ed, tast·ing** *v.t.* **1** To perceive the flavor of (something) by taking into the mouth or touching with the tongue. **2** To eat or drink a little of. **3** To recognize by the sense of taste. **4** To experience. —*v.i.* **5** To recognize a flavor by the sense of taste. **6** To take a small quantity into the mouth: usu. with *of.* **7** To have experience or enjoyment: with *of: taste* of great sorrow. **8** To have a specified flavor when in the mouth: Sugar *tastes* sweet. —*n.* **1** The sensation associated with stimulation of the taste buds by foods or other substances. **2** The quality thus perceived; flavor. **3** A small quantity tasted. **4** A slight experience; sample. **5** Special fondness and aptitude; inclination: a *taste* for music. **6** Appreciation of the beautiful in nature, art, and literature. **7** Style or form with respect to the rules of propriety or etiquette. **8** Individual preference or liking. **9** The act of tasting. [< L *taxare* touch, handle, appraise]

taste bud Any of numerous clusters of receptors located on the tongue and capable of stimulation by sweet, salt, sour or bitter substances.

taste·ful (tāst′fəl) *adj.* Having, showing, or conforming to good taste. —**taste′ful·ly** *adv.* —**taste′ful·ness** *n.* —**Syn.** elegant, aesthetic, artistic, graceful.

taste·less (tāst′lis) *adj.* **1** Having no flavor; insipid; dull. **2** Uninteresting; dull. **3** Lacking or showing a lack of good taste. —**taste′less·ly** *adv.* —**taste′less·ness** *n.*

tast·er (tās′tər) *n.* **1** One who tastes, esp. to test the quality of something. **2** A device for testing or sampling, as the small, shallow, metal vessel used in testing wines.

tast·y (tās′tē) *adj.* **tast·i·er, tast·i·est** **1** Having a fine flavor. **2** Tasteful. —**tast′i·ly** *adv.* —**tast′i·ness** *n.*

tat (tat) *v.* **tat·ted, tat·ting** *v.t.* **1** To make (edging) by tatting. —*v.i.* **2** To make tatting. [Back formation < TATTING] —**tat′ter** *n.*

Ta·tar (tä′tər) *n.* **1** A member of any of the Mongolian and Turkic tribes that invaded much of w Asia and e Europe in the Middle Ages. **2** A member of a chiefly Turkic people now living in the Russian Soviet Federated Socialist Republic and Soviet Central Asia. **3** Any of the Turkic languages of the Tatars, as Uzbek. —*adj.* Of or pertaining to the Tatars or Tatary. —**Ta·tar′i·an** (tä·târ′ē·ən) *adj., n.* —**Ta·tar′ic** *adj.*

Ta·ta·ry (tä′tər·ē) *n.* A region of indefinite extent in Asia and e Europe invaded and inhabited by Tatars in the Middle Ages.

tat·ter (tat′ər) *n.* **1** A torn and hanging shred; rag. **2** *pl.* Ragged clothing. —*v.t.* **1** To tear into tatters. —*v.i.* **2** To become ragged. [< ON *töturr* rags]

tat·ting (tat′ing) *n.* **1** A kind of lace made by looping and knotting a single thread that is wound on a shuttle. **2** The act or process of making it. [?]

tat·tle (tat′l) *v.* **·tled, ·tling** *v.i.* **1** To talk idly; chatter. **2** To tell secrets, plans, etc.; gossip. —*v.t.* **3** To reveal by gossiping. —*n.* Idle talk or gossip. [< MDu. *tatelen*] —**tat′tler** *n.*

tat·tle·tale (tat′l·tāl′) *n.* A talebearer; tattler. —*adj.* Revealing; betraying.

tat·too[1] (ta·tōō′) *v.t.* **·tooed, ·too·ing** **1** To mark (the skin) in patterns with indelible pigments. **2** To mark the skin with (designs, etc.) in this way. —*n. pl.* **·toos** **1** A pattern or design so made. **2** The act of tattooing or the condition of being tattooed. [< Polynesian] —**tat·too′er** *n.*

tat·too[2] (ta·tōō′) *n. pl.* **·toos** **1** A continuous beating or drumming. **2** A signal by drum or bugle to soldiers to repair to quarters. —*v.t. & v.i.* **·tooed, ·too·ing** To beat or rap on (a drum, etc.). [< Du. < *tap* tap, faucet + *toe* shut]

tau (tou) *n.* The nineteenth letter in the Greek alphabet (T, τ).

taught (tôt) *p.t. & p.p.* of TEACH.

taunt (tônt) *n.* A sarcastic, biting remark; insult; jibe. —*v.t.* **1** To reproach or challenge with sarcastic or contemptuous words. **2** To provoke with taunts. [? < OF *tanter* provoke] —**taunt′er** *n.* —**taunt′ing·ly** *adv.*

taupe (tōp) *n.* The color of moleskin; dark brownish gray. [< L *talpa* mole]

Tau·rus (tôr′əs) *n.* A constellation and the second sign of the zodiac; the Bull. [L, bull] • See ZODIAC.

taut (tôt) *adj.* **1** Stretched tight. **2** In proper shape; trim; tidy. **3** Tense; tight: *taut* muscles. [? < OE *togian*, to pull, tow] —**taut′ly** *adv.* —**taut′ness** *n.*

tau·tog (tô·tôg′, -tog′) *n.* Any of various blackish, edible fishes of the North American Atlantic coast. [< Algon.]

tau·tol·o·gy (tô·tol′ə·jē) *n. pl.* **·gies** **1** Unnecessary repetition of the same idea in different words. **2** An instance of this. [< Gk. *tautos* identical + *logos* discourse] —**tau·to·log·ic** (tô′tə·loj′ik) or **·i·cal** *adj.* —**tau′to·log′i·cal·ly** *adv.*

tav·ern (tav′ərn) *n.* **1** An inn. **2** A place licensed to sell liquor, beer, etc., to be drunk on the premises. [< OF < L *taberna* hut, booth]

taw (tô) *n.* **1** A game of marbles. **2** The line from which marble players shoot. **3** A fancy marble used for shooting. [?]

taw·dry (tô′drē) *adj.* **·dri·er, ·dri·est** Pretentiously showy without taste or quality. [< *St. Audrey,* designating a cheap type of lace sold at St. Audrey's Fair at Ely, England] —**taw′dri·ly** *adv.* —**taw′dri·ness** *n.* —**Syn.** cheap, gaudy, meretricious, flashy.

taw·ny (tô′nē) *adj.* **·ni·er, ·ni·est** Tan-colored; brownish yellow. —*n.* The color tan or brownish yellow. [< OF *tanner* to tan] —**taw′ni·ness** *n.*

tax (taks) *n.* **1** A compulsory contribution levied upon persons, property, or business for the support of government. **2** A heavy demand, as on one's powers or resources; a burden. —*v.t.* **1** To impose a tax on. **2** To settle or fix (amounts) chargeable in any judicial matter. **3** To impose a burden upon; task. **4** To charge; blame: usu. with *with.* [< L *taxare* estimate, appraise]

tax·a·ble (taks′ə·bəl) *adj.* Liable to be taxed: *taxable* income. —**tax′a·bil′i·ty** *n.*

tax·a·tion (tak·sā′shən) *n.* **1** The act of taxing. **2** The amount assessed as a tax. **3** Revenue raised from taxes.

tax·i (tak′sē) *n. pl.* **tax·is** or **tax·ies** TAXICAB. —*v.* **tax·ied, tax·i·ing** or **tax·y·ing** *v.i.* **1** To ride in a taxicab. **2** To move along the ground or on the surface of the water, as an airplane before taking off or after landing. —*v.t.* **3** To cause (an airplane) to taxi.

tax·i·cab (tak′sē·kab′) *n.* A passenger vehicle, usu. fitted with a taximeter, available for hire. [< TAXIMETER + CAB]

tax·i·der·my (tak′sə·dûr′mē) *n.* The art of stuffing and mounting the skins of dead animals to simulate their appearance when alive. [< Gk. *taxis* arrangement + *derma* skin] —**tax′i·der′mal, tax′i·der′mic** *adj.* —**tax′i·der′·mist** *n.*

tax·i·me·ter (tak′si·mē′tər) *n.* An instrument for recording fares in a taxicab. [< F < *taxe* tariff + *mètre* a meter]

tax·on·o·my (tak·son′ə·mē) *n.* **1** The laws and principles of classification. **2** *Biol.* The systematic classification of plant and animal life into successive subgroups, as kingdom, phylum or division, class, order, family, genus, and species. [< Gk. *taxis* arrangement + *nomos* law] —**tax·o·nom·ic** (tak′sə·nom′ik) or **·i·cal** *adj.* —**tax′o·nom′i·cal·ly** *adv.* —**tax·on′o·mist** *n.* • The prefixes *sub-,* meaning next below, and *super-,* meaning next above, are often used with the taxonomic categories specified in def. 2. Thus a *suborder* ranks next below an order but above a family (or a *superfamily*), whereas a *superorder* ranks above an order but below a class (or a *subclass*).

tax·pay·er (taks′pā′ər) *n.* One who pays or is liable to pay taxes.

TB, T.B., tb, t.b. tubercle bacillus; tuberculosis.

Tb terbium.

tbs. tbsp. tablespoon(s).

Tc technetium.

Te tellurium.

tea (tē) *n.* **1** An evergreen Asian plant having white flowers. **2** The prepared leaves of this plant, or an infusion of them used as a beverage. **3** A similar potable infusion of plant leaves or animal extract: beef *tea.* **4** *Brit.* A light evening or afternoon meal. **5** A social gathering at which tea is served. **6** *Slang* MARIHUANA. [< dial. Chinese *t'e*]

tea bag A small porous sack of cloth or paper containing tea leaves, which is immersed in water to make tea.

teach (tēch) v. **taught, teach·ing** v.t. 1 To give instruction to: *teach* a class. 2 To give instruction in: *teach* French. 3 To train by example, practice, or exercise. —v.i. 4 To act as a teacher; impart knowledge or skill. [< OE *tæcan*] — **teach′a·bil′i·ty, teach′a·ble·ness** n. —**teach′a·ble** adj.

teach·er (tē′chər) n. One who teaches, esp. as an occupation.

teach-in (tēch′in′) n. An extended meeting, as at a college or university, during which faculty and students participate in lectures, discussions, etc., on a controversial issue, esp. as a form of social protest.

teach·ing (tē′ching) n. 1 The act or occupation of a teacher. 2 That which is taught.

teaching machine Any of various mechanical devices that present educational material to a student, enabling him to learn at his own rate by a system of corrective feedback.

tea·cup (tē′kup′) n. 1 A small cup suitable for serving tea. 2 The amount a teacup will hold: also **tea′cup·ful′** (-fool′)

teak (tēk) n. 1 A large tree of SE Asia yielding a hard, durable timber highly prized for furniture, etc. 2 The wood of this tree: also **teak′wood.** [< Pg. *teca* < Malayalam *tēkka*]

tea·ket·tle (tē′ket′l) n. A kettle with a spout, used for boiling water.

teal (tēl) n. Any of several small, short-necked, wild ducks. [ME *tele*]

team (tēm) n. 1 Two or more beasts of burden harnessed together. 2 A group of people working or playing together as a unit, esp. a group forming one side in a contest. —v.t. 1 To convey with a team. 2 To harness together in a team. —v.i. 3 To drive a team. 4 To form or work as a team: to *team* up. [< OE *tēam* offspring, team]

team·mate (tēm′māt′) n. A fellow player on a team.

team·ster (tēm′stər) n. One who drives a team or a truck, esp. as an occupation.

team·work (tēm′wûrk′) n. 1 Work done by a team. 2 Unity of action, as by the players on a team.

tea·pot (tē′pot′) n. A vessel with a spout, handle, and lid, in which tea is brewed and from which it is served.

tear¹ (târ) v. **tore, torn, tear·ing** v.t. 1 To pull apart, as cloth; rip. 2 To make by tearing: *tear* a hole in. 3 To injure or lacerate. 4 To divide or disrupt: a party *torn* by dissension. 5 To distress or torment: The sight *tore* his heart. —v.i. 6 To become torn or rent. 7 To move with haste and energy. —**tear down** 1 To demolish, as a building. 2 To take apart, as a machine for repair. 3 *Informal* To attack or abuse verbally. —**tear into** To attack violently or with impetuous haste. —n. 1 The act of tearing. 2 A fissure made by tearing. 3 *Slang* A spree; frolic. 4 A rushing motion. 5 A violent outburst, as of anger. [< OE *teran*]

tear² (tir) n. 1 A drop of the saline liquid that normally lubricates the eyeball and in weeping flows from the eyes. 2 Something resembling this. 3 pl. Sorrow. 4 pl. The act of weeping: to burst into *tears*. —v.i. To fill with tears. [< OE *tēar*] —**tear′less, tear′y** adj.

tear·drop (tir′drop′) n. A tear. —adj. Shaped like a falling tear: a *teardrop* earring.

tear·ful (tir′fəl) adj. 1 Weeping. 2 Causing tears. 3 Accompanied by tears: a *tearful* confession. —**tear′ful·ly** adv. —**tear′ful·ness** n. —Syn. 1 sobbing, crying, blubbering. 2 sad, pathetic, mournful.

tear gas (tir) A gas or other agent that causes the eyes to tear.

tear-jerk·er (tir′jûr′kər) n. *Slang* A story, play, film, etc., charged with sentimental sadness.

tea·room (tē′room′, -room′) n. A restaurant serving tea and other light refreshments.

tease (tēz) v. **teased, teas·ing** v.t. 1 To annoy or harass; pester. 2 To raise the nap, as with teasels. 3 To coax or beg. 4 To comb or card, as wool or flax. 5 To comb (hair) in such a way as to form fluffy layers. —v.i. 6 To annoy a person in a facetious or petty way. —n. 1 One who teases. 2 The act of teasing or the state of being teased. [< OE *tæsan* tease, pluck apart] —**teas′er** n. —**teas′ing·ly** adv.

tea·sel (tē′zəl) n. 1 Any of various coarse, prickly herbs having the flower heads covered with hooked bracts, esp. the **full·er's teasel.** 2 The dried flower head of this plant, or a mechanical substitute, used to raise a nap on cloth. —v.t. **·seled** or **·selled, ·sel·ing** or **·sel·ling** To raise the nap of with a teasel. Also **tea′zel, tea′zle.** [< OE *tæsel*] —**tea′sel·er** or **tea′sel·ler** n.

Teasel

tea·spoon (tē′spoon′, -spoon′) n. 1 A small spoon used for stirring tea, etc. 2 The amount a teaspoon will hold, 1/3 of a tablespoon: also **tea′spoon·ful** (-fool′).

teat (tit, tēt) n. 1 The protuberance on the breast or udder of most female mammals, through which milk is drawn; a nipple. 2 A small protuberance like a teat. [< OF *tete*]

teched (techt) adj. TETCHED.

tech·ne·ti·um (tek·nē′shē·əm) n. A synthetic radioactive metallic element (symbol Tc) occupying a former gap after molybdenum in the periodic table. [< Gk. *technētos* artificial]

tech·nic (tek′nik) n. TECHNIQUE. —adj. TECHNICAL.

tech·ni·cal (tek′ni·kəl) adj. 1 Of or pertaining to some particular art, science, or trade, esp. to the practical arts or applied sciences. 2 Of, characteristic of, used or skilled in a particular art, science, profession, etc. 3 Of, in, or exhibiting technique. 4 According to an accepted body of rules and regulations: a *technical* defeat. [< Gk. *technē* art] —**tech′ni·cal·ly** (-kə·lē, -klē) adv. —**tech′ni·cal·ness** n.

tech·ni·cal·i·ty (tek′ni·kal′ə·tē) n. pl. **·ties** 1 The state or quality of being technical. 2 A technical point peculiar to some art, trade, etc. 3 A petty, formal, or highly specialized distinction or detail.

technical sergeant See GRADE.

tech·ni·cian (tek·nish′ən) n. One skilled in carrying out operations in a specific field.

tech·ni·col·or (tek′ni·kul′ər) n. Brilliant or realistic color. [< *Technicolor*] —**tech′ni·col′ored** adj.

Tech·ni·col·or (tek′ni·kul′ər) n. A process used in making color films: a trade name. Also **tech′ni·col′or.**

tech·nics (tek′niks) n.pl. (construed as sing.) The principles or study of an art or of the arts, esp. the industrial or mechanical arts.

tech·nique (tek·nēk′) n. 1 The way in which an artist, craftsman, scientist, etc., handles technical details or uses basic skills. 2 The degree of excellence in doing these things. 3 Any method of accomplishing something. [< Gk. *technikos* technical]

tech·noc·ra·cy (tek·nok′rə·sē) n. pl. **·cies** A government controlled by technicians, as scientists, engineers, etc. — **tech′no·crat** (tek′nə·krat) n. —**tech′no·crat′ic** adj.

tech·nol·o·gy (tek·nol′ə·jē) n. 1 The sum total of the technical means employed to meet the material needs of a society. 2 Applied science. 3 The technical terms used in a science, art, etc. [< Gk. *technē* skill + -LOGY] —**tech′no·log′ic** or **·i·cal** adj. —**tech′no·log′i·cal·ly** adv. —**tech·nol′o·gist** n.

tec·ton·ics (tek·ton′iks) n.pl. (construed as singular) 1 The science or art of constructing buildings or things. 2 The branch of geology relating to the continuing structural evolution of the earth's crust. [< Gk. *tektōn* carpenter] —**tec·ton′ic** adj. —**tec·ton′i·cal·ly** adv.

ted (ted) v.t. **ted·ded, ted·ding** To scatter or spread for drying, as newly mown grass. [? < ON *tethja* spread manure]

ted·dy bear (ted′ē) A toy bear. [< *Teddy*, a nickname for Theodore Roosevelt, 26th U.S. president, 1858–1919]

Te De·um (tē dē′əm) 1 An ancient Christian hymn beginning with the words *Te Deum*. 2 The music for this hymn. [< L *Te Deum (laudamus)* (we praise) Thee, O God]

te·di·ous (tē′dē·əs) adj. Fatiguing or boring, as because of lack of interest or repetitiousness. [< L *taedium* tedium] —**te′di·ous·ly** adv. —**te′di·ous·ness** n.

te·di·um (tē′dē·əm) n. The quality or state of being boring, wearisome, monotonous, etc. [< L *taedere* vex, weary]

tee[1] (tē) n. 1 The letter T. 2 Something resembling the form of the letter T. —adj. Shaped like a T. —**to a tee** Exactly; precisely.

tee[2] (tē) n. 1 A little peg or cone-shaped mound on which a golf ball is placed in making the first play to a hole. 2 In golf, the area from which a player makes his first stroke at the beginning of play for each hole. —v.t. & v.i. **teed, tee·ing** To place (the ball) on the tee before striking it. —**tee off 1** To strike (a golf ball) in starting play. 2 To begin. 3 Slang To make angry or resentful. [?]

tee[3] (tē) n. In certain games, a mark toward which the balls, quoits, etc., are directed. [?<TEE[1]]

teem (tēm) v.i. To be full to overflowing; abound. [<OE tīeman]

teen-age (tēn'āj') adj. Of, being in, or related to the years from 13 to 19 inclusive. —**teen'ag·er** n.

teens (tēnz) n. pl. 1 The numbers from 13 to 19 inclusive. 2 The years of one's age from 13 to 19 inclusive. [<OE tēne ten]

tee·ny (tē'nē) adj. **·ni·er, ·ni·est** Informal Tiny. [Alter. of TINY]

teen·y·bop·per (tē'nē·bop'ər) n. Slang A modern, hip teen-ager of the 1960's, esp. a girl. [<TEEN(-AGE) + -Y[3] + bop fight + -ER[1]]

tee·pee (tē'pē) n. TEPEE.

tee shirt (tē) T-SHIRT.

tee·ter (tē'tər) v.i. 1 SEESAW. 2 To walk or move with a swaying or tottering motion. 3 To vacillate; waver. —v.t. 4 To cause to teeter. —n. SEESAW. [?<ON titra tremble]

tee·ter-tot·ter (tē'tər·tot'ər) n. SEESAW.

teeth (tēth) n. pl. of TOOTH.

teethe (tēth) v.i. **teethed, teeth·ing** To develop teeth; cut one's teeth.

tee·to·tal (tē'tōt'l) adj. 1 Of, pertaining to, or practicing total abstinence from alcoholic beverages. 2 Total; entire. [<TOTAL, with emphatic repetition of initial letter] —**tee·to'tal·ism** n. —**tee·to'tal·ly** adv.

tee·to·tal·er (tē·tōt'l·ər) n. One who abstains totally from alcoholic beverages. Also **tee·to'tal·ist, tee·to'tal·ler.**

Tef·lon (tef'lon) n. A tough, slippery, heat-resistant, chemically inert, synthetic polymer having many industrial and household applications: a trade name.

tel. telegram; telegraph; telephone.

tele- combining form 1 At, from, over, or to a distance; distant: telegraph. 2 Of, in, pertaining to, or transmitted by television: telecast. [<Gk. tēle far]

tel·e·cast (tel'ə·kast, -käst) v.t. & v.i. **·cast** or **·cast·ed, ·cast·ing** To broadcast by television. —n. A program broadcast by television.

tel·e·com·mu·ni·ca·tion (tel'ə·kə·myoo'nə·kā'shən) n. The technology of communicating at a distance, as in radio, television, telegraphy, etc. Also **tel'e·com·mu'ni·ca'· tions** (construed as sing. or pl.).

tel·e·com·mut·ing (tel'ə·kə·myoot'ing) n. Working at home by means of a home computer terminal connected by telephone line to a main computer.

tel·e·gram (tel'ə·gram) n. A message sent by telegraph.

tel·e·graph (tel'ə·graf, -gräf) n. Any of various devices, systems, or processes for transmitting messages to a distance, esp. by means of coded electric impulses conducted by wire. —v.t. 1 To send (a message) by telegraph. 2 To communicate with by telegraph. —v.i. 3 To transmit a message by telegraph. —**te·leg·ra·pher** (tə·leg'rə·fər) n.

tel·e·graph·ic (tel'ə·graf'ik) adj. 1 Of, pertaining to, or transmitted by the telegraph. 2 Concise, as a telegram. Also **tel'e·graph'i·cal.** —**tel'e·graph'i·cal·ly** adv.

te·leg·ra·phy (tə·leg'rə·fē) n. 1 The process of conveying messages by telegraph. 2 The technology used in doing this.

Te·lem·a·chus (tə·lem'ə·kəs) Gk. Myth. The son of Odysseus and Penelope, who helped his father kill his mother's suitors.

te·lem·e·ter (tel'ə·mē'tər, tə·lem'ə·tər) n. An apparatus for indicating or measuring various quantities and for transmitting the data to a distant point. —v.t. & v.i. To transmit by telemeter. —**te·lem'e·try** n. —**tel·e·met·ric** (tel'-e·met'rik) adj. [<TELE- + -METER]

tel·e·ol·o·gy (tel'ē·ol'ə·jē, tē'lē-) n. 1 The study of final causes. 2 The belief that natural phenomena can be explained in terms of an overall design as well as by me-

chanical causes. 3 The study of evidence supporting this belief. 4 The explanation of nature in terms of utility or purpose. [<Gk. telos, teleos end + -LOGY] —**tel'e·o·log'i·cal** (-ə·loj'i·kəl) adj. —**tel'e·ol'o·gist** n.

te·lep·a·thy (tə·lep'ə·thē) n. The supposed communication of one mind with another by other than normal sensory means. —**tel'e·path·ic** (tel'ə·path'ik) adj. —**tel'e·path'i·cal·ly** adv. —**te·lep'a·thist** n.

tel·e·phone (tel'ə·fōn) n. An instrument for reproducing sound or speech at a distant point, using electric impulses transmitted by wire. —v. **·phoned, ·phon·ing** —v.t. 1 To send by telephone, as a message. 2 To communicate with by telephone. —v.i. 3 To communicate by telephone. —**tel'e·phon'ic** (-fon'ik) adj. —**tel'e·phon'i·cal·ly** adv.

te·leph·o·ny (tə·lef'ə·nē) n. The technology of telephone communication.

tel·e·pho·to (tel'ə·fō'tō) adj. 1 Denoting a system of lenses which produces a large image of a distant object in a camera. 2 Of, pertaining to, or being telephotography.

tel·e·pho·to·graph (tel'ə·fō'tə·graf, -gräf) n. 1 A picture transmitted by wire or radio. 2 A picture made with a telephoto lens. —v.t. & v.i. To take or transmit (photographs) by telephotography. —**tel'e·pho'to·graph'ic** adj.

tel·e·pho·tog·ra·phy (tel'ə·fə·tog'rə·fē) n. 1 The technique of producing magnified photographs of distant objects. 2 The transmission of photographs or other visual material by radio or wire.

tel·e·proc·ess·ing (tel'ə·pros'es·ing) n. Data processing by a computer which collects data from distant locations by means of communications lines.

Tel·e·promp·ter (tel'ə·promp'tər) n. A prompting device for television whereby a magnified script, unseen by the audience, is unrolled for a speaker or performer, line by line: a trade name.

tel·e·scope (tel'ə·skōp) n. An optical instrument for enlarging the image of a distant object. —v. **·scoped, ·scop·ing** v.t. 1 To put together so that one part fits into another. 2 To shorten, condense, or compress. —v.i. 3 To slide or be forced one into another, as the cylindrical tubes of a collapsible telescope or railroad cars in a collision.

tel·e·scop·ic (tel'ə·skop'ik) adj. 1 Of, pertaining to, or done with a telescope. 2 Visible through or obtained by a telescope. 3 Visible only through a telescope. 4 Farseeing. 5 Having sections that slide within or over one another. Also **tel'e·scop'i·cal.**

te·les·co·py (tə·les'kə·pē) n. The technology of using or making telescopes. —**te·les'co·pist** n.

Refracting telescope

tel·e·text (tel'ə·tekst') n. A communications system that transmits information over a television broadcast signal, to be viewed on a television screen.

tel·e·thon (tel'ə·thon) n. A long telecast, usu. to raise funds for a charity. [<TELE- + (MARA)THON]

Tel·e·type (tel'ə·tīp) n. A teletypewriter: a trade name.

tel·e·type·writ·er (tel'ə·tīp'rī'tər) n. A telegraphic instrument resembling a typewriter, by which the work done on one is simultaneously typed on others, electrically connected but a distance away.

tel·e·view (tel'ə·vyoo) v.t. & v.i. To observe by means of television. —**tel'e·view'er** n.

tel·e·vise (tel'ə·vīz) v.t. & v.i. **·vised, ·vis·ing** To transmit or receive by television.

tel·e·vi·sion (tel'ə·vizh'ən) n. 1 An optical and electric system for continuous transmission of visual images and sound that may be instantaneously received at a distance. 2 The technology of television transmission. 3 A television receiving set. 4 Television as an industry, an art form, or a medium of communication. 5 A show transmitted by television: to watch television.

tel·ex (tel'eks) n. 1 A communication system using teletypewriters connected by wire through exchanges

which operate automatically. **2** A message sent by such a system. —*v.t.* To send by telex. [< TEL(ETYPEWRITER) + EX(CHANGE)]

tell (tel) *v.* **told, tell·ing** *v.t.* **1** To relate in detail; narrate, as a story. **2** To make known by speech or writing; express in words; communicate; utter; say. **3** To divulge; reveal; disclose: to *tell* secrets. **4** To decide; ascertain: I cannot *tell* who is to blame. **5** To distinguish; recognize: to *tell* right from wrong. **6** To command; direct; order: I *told* him to go home. **7** To let know; report to; inform. **8** To state or assure emphatically: It's cold out, I *tell* you! **9** To count; enumerate: to *tell* one's beads. —*v.i.* **10** To give an account or description: usu. with *of.* **11** To serve as indication or evidence: with *of:* Their rags *told* of their poverty. **12** To produce a marked effect: Every blow *told.* —**tell off 1** To count and set apart. **2** *Informal* To reprimand severely. —**tell on 1** To wear out; tire; exhaust. **2** *Informal* To tattle on; inform against. [< OE *tellan*] —**Syn. 1** recount, recite. **2** state, aver. **4** discriminate.

tell·er (tel'ər) *n.* **1** One who tells, as a story; narrator. **2** One who receives or pays out money, as in a bank. **3** One who counts, esp. one appointed to count votes.

tell·ing (tel'ing) *adj.* Producing a great effect. —**tell'ing·ly** *adv.* —**Syn.** striking, effective, impressive, forceful.

tell·tale (tel'tāl') *adj.* Betraying or revealing. —*n.* **1** One who gives information about others; a tattler. **2** That which conveys information; an outward sign or indication. **3** An instrument or device for giving or recording information, as a time clock.

tel·lu·ri·um (te·loor'ē·əm, tel·yoor'-) *n.* A rare, very poisonous, semimetallic element (symbol Te) resembling sulfur and selenium. [< L *tellus* the earth]

tel·ly (tel'ē) *n. pl.* **tel·lies** *Chiefly Brit. Informal* Television.

Tel·star (tel'stär') *n.* Any of several U.S. comsats, the first of which was launched July 10, 1962.

te·mer·i·ty (tə·mer'ə·tē) *n.* Foolish boldness; rashness; foolhardiness. [< L *temeritas*] —**Syn.** audacity, heedlessness, recklessness, presumption, venturesomeness.

temp. temperature; temporary; in the time of (L *tempore*).

tem·per (tem'pər) *n.* **1** A fit of anger; rage. **2** A tendency to become easily angered. **3** State of mind or feeling; mood. **4** TEMPERAMENT (def. 1). **5** Equanimity; self-control: now only in the phrases **lose** (or **keep**) **one's temper. 6** The hardness and strength of a metal, esp. when produced by heat treatment. **7** Something used to temper a substance or mixture. —*v.t.* **1** To moderate or make suitable, as by adding another quality; free from excess; mitigate: to *temper* justice with mercy. **2** To bring to the proper consistency, texture, etc., by moistening and working: to *temper* clay. **3** To bring (metal) to a required hardness and elasticity by controlled heating and cooling. **4** To make experienced; toughen, as by difficulties, hardships, etc. **5** *Music* To tune (an instrument) by temperament. —*v.i.* **6** To be or become tempered. [< L *temperare* combine in due proportion] —**tem'per·a·bil'i·ty** *n.* —**tem'per·a·ble** *adj.*

tem·per·a (tem'pər·ə) *n.* **1** An aqueous painting medium in which the pigment is laid down in a matrix of casein, size, egg, etc. **2** The method of painting in this medium; also a painting done in tempera. **3** A water-soluble paint used for posters. [< Ital. *temperare* to temper]

tem·per·a·ment (tem'pər·ə·mənt, -prə-) *n.* **1** The characteristic nature or disposition of a person. **2** A nature or disposition that is exceedingly dramatic, excitable, moody, etc. **3** *Music* The tuning of an instrument of fixed intonation to a slightly modified chromatic scale so that it is in tune for all keys. [< L *temperamentum* proper mixture]

tem·per·a·men·tal (tem'pər·ə·men'təl, -prə-) *adj.* **1** Of or pertaining to temperament. **2** Exceedingly excitable, moody, capricious, etc. **3** Unpredictable or erratic, as in performance. —**tem'per·a·men'tal·ly** *adv.*

tem·per·ance (tem'pər·əns) *n.* **1** Habitual moderation and self-control, esp. in the indulgence of any appetite. **2** The principle and practice of moderation or total abstinence from intoxicants. —*adj.* Of, relating to, practicing, or promoting total abstinence from intoxicants. [< L *temperare* mix in due proportions]

tem·per·ate (tem'pər·it, tem'prət) *adj.* **1** Characterized by moderation or the absence of extremes; not excessive. **2** Calm; restrained; self-controlled. **3** Observing moderation or self-control, esp. in the use of intoxicating liquors. **4** Moderate as regards temperature; mild. [< L *temperare* mix in due proportions] —**tem'per·ate·ly** *adv.* —**tem'per·ate·ness** *n.*

temperate zone Either of two zones of the earth, the one between the Tropic of Capricorn and the Antarctic Circle and the other between the Tropic of Cancer and the Arctic Circle. • See ZONE.

tem·per·a·ture (tem'pər·ə·chər, -prə-) *n.* **1** The degree of heat in the atmosphere as measured on a thermometer.

TEMPERATURE CONVERSION TABLE

This table provides approximate conversion figures from the Fahrenheit to the Celsius temperature scales and vice versa. On the Celsius scale, water boils at about 100° and freezes at about 0°. On the Fahrenheit scale, water boils at about 212° and freezes at about 32°. One Fahrenheit degree = 5/9° Celsius. To convert from Fahrenheit to Celsius, subtract 32 from the Fahrenheit reading, multiply by 5, and divide the product by 9. *Example:* 65°F − 32 = 33; 33 × 5 = 165; 165 ÷ 9 = 18.3°C. To convert from Celsius to Fahrenheit, multiply the Celsius reading by 9, divide the product by 5, and add 32. *Example:* 35°C × 9 = 315; 315 ÷ 5 = 63; 63 + 32 = 95°F.

Fahrenheit	*Celsius*	*Fahrenheit*	*Celsius*
500	260.0	0	−17.8
400	204.4	−10	−23.3
300	149.0	−20	−28.9
212	100.0	−30	−34.4
200	93.3	−40	−40.0
100	37.8	−50	−45.6
90	32.2	−60	−51.1
80	26.7	−70	−56.7
70	21.1	−80	−62.2
60	15.6	−90	−67.8
50	10.0	−100	−73.3
40	4.4	−200	−129.0
32	0.0	−300	−184.0
30	−1.1	−400	−240.0
20	−6.6	−459.4*	−273.0
10	−12.2		*Absolute zero.*

Celsius	*Fahrenheit*	*Celsius*	*Fahrenheit*
500	932	0	32
400	752	−10	14
300	572	−20	−4
200	392	−30	−22
100	212	−40	−40
90	194	−50	−58
80	176	−60	−76
70	158	−70	−94
60	140	−80	−112
50	122	−90	−130
40	104	−100	−148
30	86	−200	−328
20	68	−273*	−459.4
10	50		*Absolute zero.*

2 The degree or intensity of heat in a living body; also, the excess of this above the normal. **3** The intensity of heat or cold in any substance. [< L *temperatura* due measure]

tem·pered (tem'pərd) *adj.* **1** Having a particular kind of temper: used mostly in combination: *quick-tempered, ill-tempered.* **2** Moderated or changed by the addition of something else: love *tempered* with discipline. **3** *Music* Adjusted in pitch to some temperament. **4** Having the right degree of hardness, elasticity, etc.

tem·pest (tem'pist) *n.* **1** An extensive and violent wind, usu. attended with rain, snow, or hail. **2** A violent commotion or tumult. [< L *tempestas* space of time, weather < *tempus* time]

tem·pes·tu·ous (tem·pes'chōō·əs) *adj.* Stormy; turbulent; violent. —**tem·pes'tu·ous·ly** *adv.* —**tem·pes'tu·ous·ness** *n.*

Tem·plar (tem′plər) *n.* KNIGHT TEMPLAR.

tem·plate (tem′plit) *n.* **1** A pattern, as of wood or metal, used as a guide in shaping or making something. **2** In building, a stout stone or timber for distributing weight or thrust. [< OF *temple* small timber]

tem·ple[1] (tem′pəl) *n.* **1** An edifice consecrated to the worship of one or more deities. **2** An edifice dedicated to public worship; esp., in the U.S.: **a** A synagogue. **b** A Mormon church. **3** Any usu. large or imposing building dedicated or used for a special purpose: a *temple* of learning. [< L *templum* temple]

tem·ple[2] (tem′pəl) *n.* The region on each side of the head above the cheek bone. [< L *tempus* temple]

tem·po (tem′pō) *n. pl.* **·pos** or **·pi** (-pē) **1** *Music* Relative speed at which a composition is played or is supposed to be played. **2** Characteristic rate of speed; pace. [< L *tempus* time]

tem·po·ral[1] (tem′pər·əl) *adj.* **1** Of or pertaining to the present as opposed to a future life. **2** Worldly; material, as opposed to spiritual. **3** Ephemeral; transitory, as opposed to eternal. **4** Of or relating to time. **5** *Gram.* Of, pertaining to, or denoting time: *temporal* conjunctions. [< L *tempus, temporis* time] —**tem·po·ral·i·ty** (tem′pə·ral′ə·tē), **tem′po·ral·ness** *n.* —**tem′po·ral·ly** *adv.*

tem·po·ral[2] (tem′pər·əl) *adj.* Of, pertaining to, or situated at the temple or temples of the head.

temporal bone The compound bone forming either side of the skull. • See SKULL.

tem·po·rar·y (tem′pə·rer′ē) *adj.* Lasting, to be used, etc., for a time only; not permanent. [< L *tempus, temporis* time] —**tem′po·rar·i·ly** *adv.* —**tem′po·rar′i·ness** *n.*

tem·po·rize (tem′pə·rīz) *v.i.* **·rized**, **·riz·ing 1** To act evasively so as to gain time or put off commitment. **2** To comply with or yield to the situation, circumstances, etc.; compromise. [< L *tempus, temporis* time] —**tem′po·ri·za′· tion**, **tem′po·riz′er** *n.* —**tem′po·riz′ing·ly** *adv.*

tempt (tempt) *v.t.* **1** To attempt to persuade (a person) to do wrong, as by promising pleasure or gain. **2** To be attractive to; invite: Your offers do not *tempt* me. **3** To provoke or risk provoking: to *tempt* fate. **4** To incline or dispose: They were *tempted* to leave at once. [< L *temptare, tentare* test, try] —**tempt′a·ble** *adj.* —**tempt′er** *n.* —**tempt′ress** *n. Fem.*

temp·ta·tion (temp·tā′shən) *n.* **1** That which tempts. **2** The state of being tempted.

tempt·ing (temp′ting) *adj.* Alluring; attractive; seductive. —**tempt′ing·ly** *adv.* —**tempt′ing·ness** *n.*

tem·pu·ra (tem·poōr′ə, tem′poōr′ə, -poō·rä′) *n.* A Japanese dish of seafood or vegetables, dipped in batter and deep-fried. [Jap., fried food]

tem·pus fu·git (tem′pəs fyoō′jit) *Latin* Time flies.

ten (ten) *n.* **1** The sum of nine plus one; 10; X. **2** A set or group of ten members. [< OE *tēne*] —**ten** *adj., pron.*

ten. tenement; tenor; tenuto (music).

ten·a·ble (ten′ə·bəl) *adj.* Capable of being held, maintained, or defended. [< L *tenere* to hold] —**ten′a·bil′i·ty**, **ten′a·ble·ness** *n.* —**ten′a·bly** *adv.*

te·na·cious (ti·nā′shəs) *adj.* **1** Having great cohesiveness; tough. **2** Adhesive; sticky. **3** Stubborn; obstinate; persistent. **4** Strongly retentive: a *tenacious* memory. [< L *tenax* holding fast] —**te·na′cious·ly** *adv.* —**te·na′cious·ness**, **te·nac·i·ty** (tə·nas′ə·tē) *n.*

ten·an·cy (ten′ən·sē) *n. pl.* **·cies 1** The holding of lands or estates by any form of title; occupancy. **2** The period of being a tenant. **3** The property occupied by a tenant.

ten·ant (ten′ənt) *n.* **1** A person who rents a house, land, etc., for his own use. **2** One who holds or possesses lands or property by any kind of title. **3** A dweller in any place; an occupant. —*v.t.* **1** To hold as tenant; occupy. —*v.i.* **2** To be a tenant. [< F *tenir* to hold] —**ten′ant·a·ble** *adj.*

tenant farmer One who farms land owned by another and pays rent either in cash or in a share of the crops.

ten·ant·ry (ten′ən·trē) *n. pl.* **·ries 1** Tenants collectively. **2** The state of being a tenant.

ten-cent store (ten′sent′) FIVE-AND-TEN-CENT STORE.

Ten Commandments In the Old Testament, the ten rules of conduct given by God to Moses on Mount Sinai.

tend[1] (tend) *v.i.* **1** To have an aptitude, tendency, or disposition; incline. **2** To lead or conduce: Education *tends* to

refinement. **3** To go in a certain direction. [< L *tendere* extend, tend]

tend[2] (tend) *v.t.* **1** To attend to the needs or requirements of; take care of; minister to: to *tend* children. **2** To watch over or be in charge of: to *tend* a store. —*v.i.* **3** To be in attendance; serve or wait: with *on* or *upon.* **4** To give attention or care: with *to.* [Alter. of ATTEND]

ten·den·cy (ten′dən·sē) *n. pl.* **·cies 1** Inclination; propensity; bent: a *tendency* to lie. **2** A movement or course toward some purpose, end, or result. **3** The purpose or trend of a speech or story. [< L *tendere* extend, tend] —**Syn. 1** aptitude, proclivity, disposition, leaning, predilection.

ten·den·tious (ten·den′shəs) *adj.* Disposed to promote a particular view or opinion; lacking in detachment. —**ten·den′tious·ly** *adv.* —**ten·den′tious·ness** *n.*

ten·der[1] (ten′dər) *adj.* **1** Easily crushed, bruised, broken, etc.; delicate; fragile. **2** Easily chewed or cut: said of food. **3** Physically weak; not strong or hardy. **4** Youthful and delicate; not strengthened by maturity: a *tender* age. **5** Characterized by gentleness, care, consideration, etc.: a *tender* respect for the aged. **6** Kind; affectionate; loving: a *tender* father. **7** Sensitive to impressions, feelings, etc.: a *tender* conscience. **8** Sensitive to pain, discomfort, roughness, etc.: a *tender* skin. **9** Of delicate quality: a *tender* color. **10** Capable of arousing sensitive feelings; touching: *tender* memories. **11** Requiring deft or delicate treatment; ticklish; touchy: a *tender* subject. —*v.t.* To make tender; soften. [< L *tener*] —**ten′der·ly** *adv.* —**ten′der·ness** *n.*

ten·der[2] (ten′dər) *v.t.* **1** To present for acceptance, as a resignation; offer. **2** To proffer, as money, in payment of a debt, etc. —*n.* **1** The act of tendering; an offer. **2** That which is offered as payment, esp. money. [< L *tendere* extend, tend] —**ten′der·er** *n.*

tend·er[3] (ten′dər) *n.* **1** A boat used to bring supplies, passengers, and crew to and from a ship anchored near the shore. **2** A vessel that services ships at sea, lighthouses, seaplanes, etc. **3** A vehicle attached to the rear of a steam locomotive to carry fuel and water for it. **4** One who tends or ministers to.

ten·der·foot (ten′dər·foot′) *n. pl.* **·feet** (-fēt′) or **·foots 1** A newcomer, esp. to a rough or unsettled region. **2** Any inexperienced person or beginner. **3** A Boy Scout in the beginning group. —*adj.* Inexperienced.

ten·der·heart·ed (ten′dər·här′tid) *adj.* Compassionate; sympathetic. —**ten′der·heart′ed·ly** *adv.* —**ten′der·heart′ed· ness** *n.*

ten·der·ize (ten′də·rīz) *v.t.* **·ized**, **·iz·ing** To make (meat) tender by some process or substance that softens the tough fibers and connective tissues. —**ten′der·iz′er** *n.*

ten·der·loin (ten′dər·loin′) *n.* **1** The tender part of the loin of beef, pork, etc., that lies parallel to the backbone. **2** *Often cap.* A city district noted for its high incidence of crime, corruption, and police leniency.

ten·don (ten′dən) *n.* One of the bands of tough, fibrous tissue attaching a voluntary muscle to a bone. [< Gk. *tenōn* a sinew < *tenein* stretch] —**ten′di·nous** *adj.*

ten·dril (ten′dril) *n.* One of the slender, threadlike, usu. coiling organs serving to attach a climbing plant to a supporting surface. [< OF *tendron* sprout] —**ten′driled** or **ten′drilled, ten′dril·ous** *adj.*

ten·e·ment (ten′ə·mənt) *n.* **1** A room, or set of rooms, designed for one family; apartment; flat. **2** TENEMENT HOUSE. **3** *Law* Anything, as land, houses, offices, franchises, etc., held of another by tenure. [< LL *tenementum* tenure < L *tenere* to hold] —**ten′e·men′ta·ry** (-men′tər·ē), **ten′e·men′tal** (-men′təl) *adj.*

tenement house A run-down building or house, usu. an apartment house, situated in a poor section of a city.

ten·et (ten′it, tē′nit) *n.* A principle, dogma, or doctrine, esp. one held by a group or profession. [L, he holds]

ten·fold (ten′fōld′) *adj.* **1** Made up of ten. **2** Ten times as many or as much. —*adv.* In a tenfold manner or degree.

Tenn. Tennessee.

ten·nis (ten′is) *n.* **1** A game in which two opposing players or pairs of players strike a ball with rackets over a low net on a court (**tennis court**), as of clay or synthetic materials, usu. outdoors. **2** An old form of tennis played in an interior space: also **court tennis**. [< AF *tenetz* take, receive, imperative of *tenir* hold]

ten·on (ten′ən) *n.* A projection on the end of a timber, etc., for inserting into a mortise to form a joint. —*v.t.* **1** To form a tenon on. **2** To join by a mortise and tenon. [< OF *tenir* to hold] • See MORTISE.

ten·or (ten′ər) *n.* **1** General intent or purport; substance: the *tenor* of the speech. **2** General course or tendency: the even *tenor* of their ways. **3** General character or nature. **4** A man's voice singing higher than a baritone and lower than an alto; also, a singer having, or a part to be sung by, such a voice. —*adj.* **1** Of or pertaining to a tenor. **2** Having a range of or similar to a tenor voice. [< L, a course < *tenere* to hold]

ten·pins (ten′pinz′) *n.pl.* (*construed as sing.*) A game of bowling in which the players attempt to bowl down ten pins. **2** The pins.

tense[1] (tens) *adj.* **tens·er, tens·est** **1** Stretched tight; taut. **2** Under mental or nervous strain; apprehensive. **3** *Phonet.* Pronounced with the tongue and its muscles taut, as (ē) and (o͞o). —*v.t. & v.i.* **tensed, tens·ing** To make or become tense. [< L *tensus*, pp. of *tendere* to stretch] —**tense′ly** *adv.* —**tense′ness** *n.* —**Syn. 2** anxious, nervous, restless, jittery, restive, fidgety.

tense[2] (tens) *n.* **1** Any of the forms of a verb that indicate when or how long the expressed action took place or the state of being existed. **2** A specific set of such verb forms: the past *tense* of *to see.* [< L *tempus* time, tense]

ten·sile (ten′sil, *Brit.* ten′sīl) *adj.* **1** Of or pertaining to tension. **2** Capable of tension. —**ten·sil·i·ty** (ten·sil′ə·tē) *n.*

tensile strength The resistance of a material to forces of rupture and longitudinal stress: usu. expressed in pounds or tons per square inch.

ten·sion (ten′shən) *n.* **1** The act of stretching or the condition of being stretched tight; tautness. **2** Mental or nervous strain or anxiety. **3** Any strained relation, as between governments. **4** *Physics* **a** A stress that tends to lengthen a body. **b** The condition of a body when acted on by such stress. **5** A device to regulate the tightness or tautness of something, esp. the thread in a sewing machine. **6** A condition of balance or symmetry produced by opposing elements, as in an artistic work. **7** Electric potential. —**ten′sion·al** *adj.*

ten·sor (ten′sər, -sôr) *n.* Any muscle that makes tense or stretches a part.

tent (tent) *n.* A shelter of canvas or the like, supported by poles and fastened by cords to pegs (called **tent pegs**) driven into the ground. —*v.t.* **1** To cover with or as with a tent. —*v.i.* **2** To pitch a tent; camp out. [< L *tendere* stretch]

ten·ta·cle (ten′tə·kəl) *n.* **1** *Zool.* Any of various long, slender, flexible appendages of animals, esp. invertebrates, functioning as organs of touch, motion, etc. • See SEA ANEMONE. **2** *Bot.* A sensitive hair, as on the leaves of some plants. [< L *tentaculum* < *tentare* to touch, try] —**ten·tac′u·lar** (ten·tak′yə·lər) *adj.*

ten·ta·tive (ten′tə·tiv) *adj.* **1** Not definite or final; subject to change. **2** Somewhat uncertain or timid: a *tentative* glance. [< L *tentatus*, pp. of *tentare* to try, probe] —**ten′ta·tive·ly** *adv.* —**ten′ta·tive·ness** *n.*

tent caterpillar The gregarious larva of several moths that form colonies in large silken webs in the branches of trees, etc.

ten·ter (ten′tər) *n.* A frame or machine for stretching cloth to prevent shrinkage while drying. [< L *tentus* extended]

ten·ter·hook (ten′tər·ho͝ok′) *n.* A sharp hook for holding cloth while being stretched on a tenter. —**be on tenterhooks** To be in a state of anxiety or suspense.

tenth (tenth) *adj. & adv.* Next in order after the ninth. —*n.* **1** The element of an ordered set that corresponds to the number ten. **2** One of ten equal parts.

ten·u·ous (ten′yo͞o·əs) *adj.* **1** Without much substance; slight; weak: *tenuous* arguments. **2** Thin; slender. **3** Having slight density; rare. [< L *tenuis* thin] —**ten′u·ous·ly** *adv.* —**ten′u·ous·ness, ten·u·i·ty** (te·nyo͞o′ə·tē, tə-) *n.*

ten·ure (ten′yər) *n.* **1** The act, right, length of time, or manner of holding something, as land, elected office, or a position. **2** The permanent status of a teacher, civil servant, etc., after fulfilling certain requirements. [< L *tenere* to hold] —**ten′ured, ten·u·ri·al** (ten·yo͝or′ē·əl) *adj.* —**ten·u′ri·al·ly** *adv.*

te·pee (tē′pē) *n.* A conical tent of the North American Plains Indians, usu. covered with skins.

tep·id (tep′id) *adj.* **1** Moderately warm, as a liquid. **2** Not enthusiastic. [< L *tepere* be lukewarm] —**te·pid·i·ty** (tə·pid′ə·tē), **tep′id·ness** *n.* —**tep′id·ly** *adv.*

te·qui·la (tə·kē′lə) *n.* A Mexican alcoholic liquor made from the maguey. [< *Tequila,* a district in Mexico]

ter., terr. terrace; territorial; territory.

Tepee

ter·a·tism (ter′ə·tiz′əm) *n. Biol.* A monstrosity, esp. a malformed human or animal fetus. [< Gk. *teras* monster]

ter·a·to·gen·ic (ter′ə·tō·jen′ik) *adj.* Tending to cause malformations, as in a developing fetus.

ter·bi·um (tûr′bē·əm) *n.* A rare-earth metal (symbol Tb). [< *Ytterby,* a town in Sweden] —**ter′bic** *adj.*

ter·cen·te·nar·y (tûr′sen·ten′ər·ē, -sent′ən·er′ē) *adj.* Of or pertaining to a 300th anniversary. —*n. pl.* **·nar·ies** The 300th anniversary. Also **ter·cen·ten·ni·al** (tûr′sen·ten′ē·əl).

ter·gi·ver·sate (tər·jiv′ər·sāt′, -giv′-) *v.i.* **·sat·ed, ·sat·ing** **1** To be evasive; equivocate. **2** To change sides, attitudes, etc.; apostatize. [< L *tergum* back + *versare* to turn] —**ter′gi·ver·sa′tor, ter′gi·ver·sa′tion** *n.*

ter·i·ya·ki (ter′ē·yä′kē) *n.* A Japanese dish of meat or fish marinated in soy sauce, ginger, etc., then fried, broiled, or grilled. [< Jap.]

term (tûrm) *n.* **1** A word or expression used to designate some definite thing in a science, profession, art, etc.: a medical *term.* **2** *Often pl.* Any word or expression conveying some conception or thought: a *term* of reproach; to speak in general *terms.* **3** *pl.* The conditions or stipulations according to which something is to be done or acceded to: the *terms* of a contract; peace *terms.* **4** *pl.* Mutual relations; footing: usu. preceded by *on* or *upon:* to be on friendly *terms.* **5** *Math.* **a** The numerator or denominator of a fraction. **b** One of the units of an algebraic expression that are connected by the plus and minus signs. **6** *Logic* **a** In a proposition, either of the two parts, the subject and predicate, which are joined by a copula. **b** Any of the three elements of a syllogism. **7** A fixed or definite period of time, esp. of duration: a *term* of office. **8** A school semester or quarter. **9** End; conclusion. **10** *Law* **a** One of the prescribed periods of the year during which a court may hold a session. **b** A specific extent of time during which an estate may be held. **c** A space of time allowed a debtor to meet his obligation. **11** *Med.* The time for the normal termination of a pregnancy. —**in terms of** With respect to; as relating to. —*v.t.* To designate by means of a term; name or call. [< L *terminus* a limit]

term. terminal; termination; terminology.

ter·ma·gant (tûr′mə·gənt) *n.* A scolding or abusive woman; shrew. —*adj.* Violently abusive and quarrelsome; vixenish. [< ME < *Termagant,* an imaginary Muslim deity] —**ter′ma·gan′cy** *n.*

term·er (tûr′mər) *n.* A person serving or attending a certain term, as in a prison or school: used in combination: a *second-termer.*

ter·mi·na·ble (tûr′mə·nə·bəl) *adj.* That may be terminated; not perpetual. —**ter′mi·na·bil′i·ty, ter′mi·na·ble·ness** *n.* —**ter′mi·na·bly** *adv.*

ter·mi·nal (tûr′mə·nəl) *adj.* **1** Situated at or forming the end, limit, or boundary of something: a *terminal* bus station. **2** Situated or occurring at the end of a series or period of time; final: a *terminal* experiment. **3** At, undergoing, or causing the termination of life: *terminal* cancer; a *terminal* patient. **4** Of or occurring regularly in or at the end of a term or period of time: *terminal* payments. **5**

Borne at the end of a stem or branch. —*n.* **1** A terminating point or part; termination; end. **2 a** Either end of a railroad line, bus line, airline, etc. **b** A passenger or freight station located at these end points. **c** Any large passenger or freight station serving an area of considerable size. **3 a** A point in an electric circuit at which it is usual to make or break a connection. **b** A connector designed to facilitate this. **4** An electronic device by means of which a user may communicate with a computer, usually including a cathode-ray tube, a keyboard, and a printer. [<L *terminus* boundary] —**ter′mi·nal·ly** *adv.*

ter·mi·nate (tûr′mə·nāt) *v.* ·nat·ed, ·nat·ing *v.t.* **1** To put an end or stop to. **2** To form the conclusion of; finish. **3** To bound or limit. —*v.i.* **4** To have an end; come to an end. [<L *terminus* a limit] —**ter′mi·na′tive** *adj.*

ter·mi·na·tion (tûr′mə·nā′shən) *n.* **1** The act of terminating or the condition of being terminated. **2** That which bounds or limits in time or space; close; end. **3** Outcome; result; conclusion. **4** The final letters or syllable of a word; a suffix. —**ter′mi·na′tion·al** *adj.*

ter·mi·na·tor (tûr′mə·nā′tər) *n.* **1** One who or that which terminates. **2** *Astron.* The boundary between the illuminated and dark portions of the moon or of a planet.

ter·mi·nol·o·gy (tûr′mə·nol′ə·jē) *n. pl.* ·gies The technical terms relating to a particular subject, as a science, art, trade, etc. [<L *terminus* a limit + -LOGY] —**ter′mi·no·log′i·cal** (-nə·loj′i·kəl) *adj.* —**ter′mi·no·log′i·cal·ly** *adv.*

ter·mi·nus (tûr′mə·nəs) *n. pl.* ·nus·es or ·ni (-nī, -nē) **1** The final point or goal; end; terminal. **2** Either end of a railroad or bus line, airline, etc.; also, a town or station located at either end [L]

ter·mite (tûr′mīt) *n.* Any of an order of whitish, soft-bodied insects resembling ants and noted for boring into and destroying wooden structures, furniture, etc. [<L *termes, termitis*]

tern (tûrn) *n.* Any of several birds resembling gulls, but smaller, with a sharply pointed bill and a deeply forked tail. [<Scand.]

ter·na·ry (tûr′nər·ē) *adj.* **1** Formed or consisting of three; grouped in threes. **2** Third in order, importance, etc. —*n. pl.* ·ries A group of three; a triad. [<L *terni* by threes]

ter·pene (tûr′pēn) *n.* Any of various isomeric hydrocarbons contained in essential oils, resins, etc. [<*terp(entin)*, earlier form of TURPENTINE + -ENE]

Terp·sich·o·re (tûrp·sik′ə·rē) *Gk. Myth.* The Muse of dancing. [<Gk. *terpsis* enjoyment + *choros* dance]

terp·si·cho·re·an (tûrp′si·kə·rē′ən, -sə·kôr′ē-, -kō′rē-) *adj.* Of or relating to dancing. Also **terp′si·cho·re′al.**

ter·race (ter′is) *n.* **1** A raised level space, as of lawn, usu. with sloping sides; also, such levels collectively. **2** A raised street supporting a row of houses; also, the houses occupying such a street. **3** A flat roof, esp. of an Oriental or Spanish house. **4** An open, paved area connected to a house, apartment, or building, usu. with places for seating, plantings, etc. **5** A balcony. **6** A parklike area extending down the middle of a wide street or boulevard. **7** A relatively narrow step in the face of a steep natural slope. —*v.t.* ·raced, ·rac·ing To form into or provide with a terrace or terraces. [<L *terra* earth]

ter·ra cot·ta (ter′ə kot′ə) **1** A hard, kiln-burnt clay, reddish brown and usu. unglazed, used for pottery, sculpture, etc. **2** A statue made of this clay. **3** A brownish red color. [Ital., lit, cooked earth]

ter·ra fir·ma (ter′ə fûr′mə) Solid ground, as distinguished from the sea or the air. [L]

ter·rain (te·rān′, ter′ān) *n.* **1** Battleground, or a region suited for defense, fortifications, etc. **2** A land area viewed with regard to some particular characteristic: marshy *terrain*. [<L *terrenus* earthen < *terra* earth]

Ter·ra·my·cin (ter′ə·mī′sin) *n.* An antibiotic effective against a wide variety of pathogenic organisms: a trade name.

ter·ra·pin (ter′ə·pin) *n.* **1** One of the several North American edible tortoises, esp. the diamond-back. **2** Its flesh. [<Algon.]

ter·rar·i·um (te·râr′ē·əm) *n. pl.* ·rar·i·ums or ·rar·i·a (-râr′ē·ə) **1** A glass enclosure for growing a collection of small plants. **2** A

Terrapin

vivarium for small land animals. [<L *terra* earth + -arium, on analogy with *aquarium*]

ter·res·tri·al (tə·res′trē·əl) *adj.* **1** Belonging to the planet earth. **2** Pertaining to land or earth. **3** Living on or growing in earth. **4** Belonging to or consisting of land, as distinct from water, air, etc. **5** Worldly; mundane. —*n.* An inhabitant of the earth. [<L *terra* land] —**ter·res′tri·al·ly** *adv.*

ter·ret (ter′it) *n.* One of two metal rings on a harness, through which the reins are passed. [<OF *touret* small wheel]

ter·ri·ble (ter′ə·bəl) *adj.* **1** Causing extreme fear, dread, or terror. **2** Severe; extreme: a *terrible* headache. **3** Awesome: a *terrible* burden of guilt. **4** Very bad; dreadful; awful: a *terrible* play. [<L *terribilis* < *terrere* terrify] —**ter′ri·ble·ness** *n.* —**ter′ri·bly** *adv.*

ter·ri·er (ter′ē·ər) *n.* Any of several breeds of small, active, wiry dogs, formerly used to hunt burrowing animals. [<L *terrarius* pertaining to earth]

ter·rif·ic (tə·rif′ik) *adj.* **1** Arousing great terror or fear; frightening. **2** *Informal* **a** Very great; extraordinary; tremendous. **b** Unusually good; excellent. —**ter·rif′i·cal·ly** *adv.*

ter·ri·fy (ter′ə·fī) *v.t.* ·fied, ·fy·ing To fill with terror; frighten severely. [<L *terrere* frighten + -FY]

ter·ri·to·ri·al (ter′ə·tôr′ē·əl, -tō′rē-) *adj.* **1** Of or pertaining to a territory or territories. **2** Of, restricted to, or under the jurisdiction of a particular territory, region, or district. **3** *Often cap.* Organized or intended primarily for home defense: the British *Territorial* Army. —**ter′ri·to′ri·al·ism′, ter′ri·to′ri·al·ist** *n.* —**ter′ri·to′ri·al·ly** *adv.*

ter·ri·to·ri·al·i·ty (ter′ə·tôr′ē·al′ə·tē, -tō′rē-) *n.* Territorial condition, status, or position.

ter·ri·to·ry (ter′ə·tôr′ē, -tō′rē) *n. pl.* ·ries **1** The domain over which a nation, state, etc., exercises jurisdiction. **2** Any considerable tract of land; a region; district. **3** A region having a certain degree of self-government, but not having the status of a state or province. **4** A special sphere or province of activity, knowledge, etc. **5** A specific area used by or assigned to a person, group, etc.: a salesman's *territory*. [<L *terra* earth]

ter·ror (ter′ər) *n.* **1** Overwhelming fear. **2** A person or thing that causes extreme fear. **3** *Informal* A difficult or annoying person, esp. a child. **4** TERRORISM. [<L *terrere* frighten]

ter·ror·ism (ter′ə·riz′əm) *n.* The act or practice of terrorizing, esp. by violence committed for political purposes, as by a government seeking to intimidate a populace or by revolutionaries seeking to overthrow a government, compel the release of prisoners, etc. —**ter′ror·ist** *n.* —**ter′ror·is′tic** *adj.*

ter·ror·ize (ter′ə·rīz) *v.t.* ·ized, ·iz·ing **1** To reduce to a state of terror; terrify. **2** To coerce or intimidate through terrorism. —**ter′ror·i·za′tion, ter′ror·iz′er** *n.*

ter·ry (ter′ē) *n. pl.* ·ries A very absorbent pile fabric in which the loops are uncut, used for towels, etc. Also **terry cloth.** [?]

terse (tûrs) *adj.* **ters·er, ters·est** Short and to the point; succinct. [<L *tersus*, pp. of *tergere* rub off, rub down] —**terse′ly** *adv.* —**terse′ness** *n.* —**Syn.** brief, concise, pithy, curt, laconic.

ter·tian (tûr′shən) *adj.* Recurring every other day: said of a fever or disease causing such a fever, as certain forms of malaria. [<L *tertius* third (recurring every third day, reckoned inclusively)]

ter·ti·ar·y (tûr′shē·er′ē, -shə·rē) *adj.* Third in point of time, importance, rank, or value. —*n. pl.* ·ar·ies Any of the third row of wing feathers of a bird. [<L *tertius* third]

Ter·ti·ar·y (tûr′shē·er′ē, -shə·rē) *n. & adj.* See GEOLOGY.

tes·sel·late (tes′ə·lāt) *v.t.* ·lat·ed, ·lat·ing To lay or adorn with small squares or mosaic tiles, as pavement. —*adj.* Adorned or laid with mosaic patterns: also **tes′sel·lat′ed.** [<L *tessellatus* checkered] —**tes′sel·la′tion** *n.*

tes·si·tu·ra (tes′i·tŏŏr′ə) *n.* The average range of a melody or vocal composition. [Ital., lit., texture]

test (test) *v.t.* **1** To subject to an examination or proof; try. —*v.i.* **2** To undergo or give an examination or test: usu. with *for*: to *test* for accuracy. **3** To receive a rating as a result of testing: The alcohol *tested* 75 percent. —*n.* **1** An examination or observation to find out the real nature of

something or to prove or disprove its value or validity. **2** A method or technique employed to do this. **3** A criterion or standard of judgment or evaluation. **4** An undergoing of or subjection to certain conditions that disclose the character, quality, nature, etc., of a person or thing: a *test* of will. **5** A series of questions, problems, etc., intended to measure knowledge, aptitudes, intelligence, etc. **6** *Chem.* **a** A reaction by means of which a compound or ingredient may be identified. **b** Its agent or the result. [< L *testum* an earthen vessel < *testa* potsherd, shell] —**test'a·ble** *adj.* —**test'er** *n.*

Test. Testament.

tes·ta (tes'tə) *n. pl.* **·tae** (-tē) The outer, usu. hard and brittle coat of a seed. [L, shell]

tes·ta·ment (tes'tə·mənt) *n.* **1** The written declaration of one's last will: now usu. in the phrase **last will and testament.** **2** A statement testifying to some belief or conviction; credo. **3** Proof; evidence: a *testament* to their courage. **4** In Biblical use, a covenant; dispensation. [< L *testari* testify] —**tes'ta·men'tal, tes'ta·men'ta·ry** (-men'tər·ē) *adj.*

Tes·ta·ment (tes'tə·mənt) *n.* Either of the two parts of the Bible, distinguished as the **Old** and the **New Testament.**

tes·tate (tes'tāt) *adj.* Having made a will before decease. [< L *testari* be a witness]

tes·ta·tor (tes·tā'tər, tes'tā·tər) *n.* One who has died leaving a will. [< L] —**tes·ta'trix** (-triks) *n. Fem.*

tes·ti·cle (tes'ti·kəl) *n.* One of the two sex glands of the male which secrete sex hormones and spermatozoa. [< L *testiculus,* dim. of *testis* testicle]

tes·ti·fy (tes'tə·fī) *v.* **·fied, ·fy·ing** *v.i.* **1** To make solemn declaration of truth or fact. **2** *Law* To give testimony; bear witness. **3** To serve as evidence or indication. —*v.t.* **4** To bear witness to; affirm. **5** *Law* To state or declare on oath or affirmation. **6** To be evidence or indication of. **7** To make known publicly; declare. [< L *testis* witness + -FY] —**tes'ti·fi·ca'tion, tes'ti·fi'er** *n.*

tes·ti·mo·ni·al (tes'tə·mō'nē·əl) *n.* **1** A statement, often a letter, recommending the character, value, etc., of a person or thing. **2** An act, statement, event, etc., that gives public acknowledgment of esteem or appreciation. —*adj.* Pertaining to or constituting testimony or a testimonial.

tes·ti·mo·ny (tes'tə·mō'nē) *n. pl.* **·nies** **1** An oral statement of a witness under oath in a court, usu. made in answer to questioning by a lawyer or judge. **2** Any public acknowledgment or declaration, as of a religious experience. **3** Proof of something; evidence. [< L *testimonium* < *testis* a witness]

tes·tis (tes'tis) *n. pl.* **·tes** (-tēz) TESTICLE. [L]

tes·tos·ter·one (tes·tos'tə·rōn) *n.* A natural or synthetic male sex hormone. [< TESTIS + STER(OL) + -ONE]

test-tube (tes'tyoob') *adj.* **1** Experimental in nature. **2** Produced by artificial insemination.

test tube A tubular glass vessel used in making chemical or biological tests.

tes·ty (tes'tē) *adj.* **·ti·er, ·ti·est** Irritable; touchy. [< AF *testif* heady < OF *teste* head] —**tes'ti·ly** *adv.* —**tes'ti·ness** *n.* —**Syn.** irascible, peevish, petulant, querulous, snappish, crabby, grouchy.

tet·a·nus (tet'ə·nəs) *n.* An acute and often fatal infectious bacterial disease marked by spasmodic contraction of voluntary muscles, esp. the muscles of the jaw. [< Gk. *tetanos* spasm < *teinein* to stretch] —**te·tan·ic** (ti·tan'ik) *adj.*

tetched (techt) *adj. Regional* Slightly unbalanced mentally. [Alter. of *touched*]

tetch·y (tech'ē) *adj.* **tetch·i·er, tetch·i·est** Irritable; peevish; touchy. [< OF *teche* mark, quality] —**tetch'i·ly** *adv.* —**tetch'i·ness** *n.*

tête-à-tête (tāt'ə·tāt', *Fr.* tet·à·tet') *adj.* Confidential, as between two persons. —*n.* **1** A confidential chat between two persons. **2** An S-shaped sofa on which two persons may face each other. —*adv.* In private or personal talk. [F, lit., head to head]

teth·er (teth'ər) *n.* **1** Something used to check or confine, as a rope for fastening an animal. **2** The limit of one's

powers or field of action. —**at the end of one's tether** At the extreme limit of one's resources, patience, etc. [< Scand.]

tetra- *combining form* Four; fourfold: *tetrachloride.* [< Gk.]

tet·ra·chlo·ride (tet'rə·klôr'īd, -id, -klō'rīd, -rid) *n.* A compound containing four atoms of chlorine per molecule.

tet·ra·eth·yl lead (tet'rə·eth'il led) A poisonous organic antiknock compound.

tet·ra·he·dron (tet'rə·hē'drən) *n. pl.* **·drons** or **·dra** (-drə) A solid bounded by four plane triangular faces. [< Gk. *tetra-* four + *hedra* base] —**tet'ra·he'dral** *adj.*

Tetrahedron

te·tral·o·gy (te·tral'ə·jē, -tral'-) *n. pl.* **·gies** **1** A group of four dramas presented together at the festivals of Dionysus at Athens. **2** Any series of four related novels, plays, operas, etc. [< TETRA + -LOGY]

te·tram·e·ter (te·tram'ə·tər) *n.* In English verse, a line having four metrical feet. [< TETRA + -METER]

tet·rarch (tet'rärk, tē'trärk) *n.* **1** In the Roman Empire, the governor of one of four divisions of a province. **2** A subordinate ruler. [< Gk. *tetra-* four + *archos* ruler] —**tet·rar·chy** (tet'rär·kē, tē'trär-), **tet·rarch·ate** (tet'rär·kāt, -kit, tē'trär-) *n.*

tet·ra·va·lent (tet'rə·vā'lənt) *adj.* QUADRIVALENT. —**tet'ra·va'lence, tet'ra·va'len·cy** *n.*

te·trox·ide (te·trok'sīd, -sid) *n.* Any oxide having four atoms of oxygen per molecule. [< TETR(A)- + OXIDE]

Teu·ton (tyoot'n) *n.* **1** One of an ancient German tribe that dwelt in Jutland north of the Elbe, appearing in history as **Teu·to·nes** (tyoo'tə·nēz). **2** One belonging to any of the Teutonic peoples, esp. a German.

Teu·ton·ic (tyoo·ton'ik) *adj.* **1** Of or pertaining to the Teutons. **2** Of or pertaining to Germany or the Germans. **3** Of or pertaining to the peoples of northern Europe, including the English, Scandinavians, Dutch, etc. —**Teu·ton'i·cal·ly** *adv.*

Tex. Texan; Texas.

Texas leaguer In baseball, a looping fly ball that falls safe between an infielder and an outfielder.

text (tekst) *n.* **1** The actual or original words of an author or speaker, as distinguished from notes, commentary, illustrations, etc. **2** Any of the written or printed versions or editions of a piece of writing. **3** The main body of written or printed matter of a book or a single page, as distinguished from notes, indexes, illustrations, etc. **4** The words of a song, opera, etc. **5** A verse of Scripture, esp. when cited as the basis of a sermon. **6** Any subject of discourse; a topic; theme. **7** One of several styles of letters or types. **8** TEXTBOOK. [< L *textus* fabric, structure < *texere* to weave]

text·book (tekst'book') *n.* A book used as a standard work or basis of instruction in any branch of knowledge; schoolbook; manual.

tex·tile (teks'tīl, -til) *adj.* **1** Pertaining to weaving or woven fabrics. **2** Such as may be woven; manufactured by weaving. —*n.* **1** A fabric, esp. if woven or knitted; cloth. **2** Material, as a fiber, yarn, etc., capable of being woven. [< L *textus* fabric. See TEXT.]

tex·tu·al (teks'choo·əl) *adj.* **1** Pertaining to, contained in, or based on a text. **2** Literal; word for word. —**tex'tu·al·ly** *adv.*

tex·ture (teks'chər) *n.* **1** The arrangement or characteristics of the threads, etc., of a fabric: a tweed having a rough *texture.* **2** The arrangement or characteristics of the constituent elements of anything, esp. as regards surface appearance or tactile qualities: the *texture* of bread. **3** The overall or characteristic structure, form, or interrelatedness of parts of a work of art, music, literature, etc.: the tightly-knit *texture* of his poems. **4** The basic nature or structure of something: the *texture* of rural life. [< L *textus* fabric. See TEXT.] —**tex'tur·al** *adj.* —**tex'tur·al·ly** *adv.*

T-group (tē'groop) *n.* A group of people, often business or industrial personnel, who meet with a trained leader

---

add, āce, câre, pälm; end, ēven; it, īce; odd, ōpen, ôrder; took, pool; up, bûrn; ə = a in above, u in focus; yoo = u in fuse; oil; pout; check; go; ring; thin; this; zh, vision. < derived from; ? origin uncertain or unknown.

whose function is to guide them to a more insightful awareness of themselves and others through the free and uninhibited expression of their thoughts, feelings, prejudices, etc. [< *t(raining) group*]

-th¹ *suffix of nouns* 1 The act or result of the action: *growth.* 2 The state or quality of being or having: *health.* [< OE *-thu, -tho*]

-th² *suffix* Used in ordinal numbers: *tenth.* Also **-eth.** [< OE *-tha, -the*]

-th³ See -ETH¹.

Th thorium.

Th., Thur., Thurs. Thursday.

Thai (tī) *n.* 1 *pl.* **Thai** or **Thais a** A native or citizen of Thailand. **b** A member of the majority ethnic group of Thailand. 2 Any one of a group of related languages used in Thailand. —*adj.* Of or pertaining to Thailand, its people, or their languages.

Thai·land (tī′land) *n.* A constitutional monarchy in SE Asia, 198,404 sq. mi., cap. Bangkok. ● See map at INDO-CHINA.

thal·a·mus (thal′ə·məs) *n. pl.* **·mi** (-mī, mē) 1 A mass of gray matter at the base of the brain, involved in sensory transmission. 2 The receptacle of a flower. [< Gk. *thalamos* chamber] —**tha·lam·ic** (thə·lam′ik) *adj.*

Tha·li·a (thə·lī′ə, thä′lē·ə, thäl′yə) *Gk. Myth.* 1 The Muse of comedy and pastoral poetry. 2 One of the three Graces. [< Gk. *thallein* to bloom]

thal·li·um (thal′ē·əm) *n.* A soft, rare, highly poisonous metallic element (symbol Tl), used in rat poison, insecticides, and in making optical glass. [< Gk. *thallos* a green shoot; from the bright green line in its spectrum]

thal·lo·phyte (thal′ə·fīt) *n.* Any of a major division of plants without roots, stems, or leaves, comprising the bacteria, fungi, algae, and lichens. [< THALLUS + -PHYTE] —**thal′lo·phyt′ic** (-fit′ik) *adj.*

thal·lus (thal′əs) *n. pl.* **·lus·es** or **·li** (-ī) *Bot.* A plant body without true root, stem, or leaf, as in thallophytes. [< Gk. *thallos* a shoot]

than (than, *unstressed* thən) *conj.* 1 When, as, or if compared with: after an adjective or adverb to express comparison between what precedes and what follows: I am stronger *than* he (is); I know her better *than* (I know) him. 2 Except; but: used after *other, else,* etc: no other *than* you. 3 When: usu. used after *scarcely, hardly, barely:* Scarcely had we got settled *than* we had to leave. —*prep.* Compared to: used only in the phrases *than whom, than which:* An eminent judge *than whom* no other is finer. [< OE *thanne*] ● The case of a word following *than* can be either nominative or objective, depending on the word's function in the elliptical clause introduced by *than: You owe him more money than I (owe him)* or *You owe him more money than (you owe) me.* However, in informal writing and speech, the objective case is acceptable following *than* whether or not it agrees with the ellipsis: *He is younger than me.*

thane (thān) *n.* 1 In Anglo-Saxon England, a man who ranked above an ordinary freeman but below an earl or nobleman and who held land of the king or a noble in exchange for military service. 2 The chief of a Scottish clan, a baron in the service of the king. [< OE *thegn*]

thank (thangk) *v.t.* 1 To express gratitude to; give thanks to. 2 To hold responsible; blame: often used ironically: We have him to *thank* for this mess. —**thank you** An expression of gratitude or in acknowledgment of a service rendered. [< OE *thancian*]

thank·ful (thangk′fəl) *adj.* Feeling or manifesting thanks or gratitude; grateful. —**thank′ful·ly** *adv.* —**thank′ful·ness** *n.*

thank·less (thangk′lis) *adj.* 1 Not feeling or expressing gratitude; ungrateful. 2 Not gaining or likely to gain thanks; unappreciated. —**thank′less·ly** *adv.* —**thank′less·ness** *n.*

thanks (thangks) *n.pl.* An expression of gratitude or appreciation. —*interj.* I thank you. —**thanks to** 1 Thanks be given to. 2 Because of.

thanks·giv·ing (thangks′giv′ing) *n.* 1 The act of giving thanks. 2 A manner of expressing thanks, as a prayer, public celebration, etc.

Thanksgiving Day 1 In the U.S., the fourth Thursday in November, set apart as a legal holiday for giving thanks for the year's blessings. Also **Thanksgiving.** 2 In Canada, a similar holiday celebrated the second Monday in October.

that (that, *unstressed* thət) *adj. pl.* **those** 1 Pertaining to some person or thing previously mentioned, understood, or specifically designated: *that* man. 2 Denoting something more remote in place, time, or thought than the thing with which it is being compared: This winter was colder than *that* one. —*pron. pl.* **those** 1 As a demonstrative pronoun: **a** The person or thing implied, mentioned, or understood. **b** The thing further away or more remote: This will happen sooner than *that* will. 2 As a relative pronoun, *that* is used to introduce restrictive clauses and, as such, has a variety of meanings, as *who, whom, which, where, at which, with which,* etc.: The man *that* (whom) I saw is not here; The house *that* (which) you lived in was torn down. 3 Something: There is *that* to be said for him. —*adv.* 1 To that extent; so: I can't see *that* far. 2 *Informal* In such a manner or degree: It really is *that* bad! —*conj. That* is used primarily to connect a subordinate clause with its principal clause, with the following meanings: 1 As a fact that: introducing a fact: I tell you *that* it is so. 2 So that; in order that: I tell you *that* you may know. 3 For the reason that; because: She wept *that* she was growing old. 4 As a result: introducing a result, consequence, or effect: He bled so profusely *that* he died. 5 At which time; when: It was only yesterday *that* I saw him. 6 Introducing an exclamation: O *that* he would come! —**so that** 1 To the end that. 2 With the result that. 3 Provided. [< OE *thæt*] ● See WHO.

thatch (thach) *n.* 1 A covering of reeds, straw, etc., arranged on a roof so as to shed water. 2 Any of various palm leaves or coarse grasses so used. Also **thatching.** —*v.t.* To cover with a thatch. [< OE *thæc* cover] —**thatch′er** *n.* —**thatch′y** *adj.* (**thatch·i·er, thatch·i·est**)

thau·ma·tur·gy (thô′mə·tûr′jē) *n.* Magic; the performance or working of wonders or miracles. [< Gk. *thauma* wonder + *ergon* work] —**thau′ma·turge, thau′ma·tur′gist** *n.* —**thau′ma·tur′gic** or **·gi·cal** *adj.*

thaw (thô) *v.i.* 1 To melt or dissolve, as snow or ice. 2 To lose the effects of coldness or of having been frozen: often with *out.* 3 To rise in temperature so as to melt ice and snow: said of weather: It *thawed* last night. 4 To become less aloof, unsociable, rigid in opinions, etc. —*v.t.* 5 To cause to thaw. —*n.* 1 The act of thawing. 2 Warmth of weather such as melts things frozen. 3 A becoming less aloof, unsociable, etc. [< OE *thāwian*] —**thaw′er** *n.*

Th.B. Bachelor of Theology.

Th.D. Doctor of Theology.

the¹ (*stressed* thē; *unstressed before a consonant* thə; *unstressed before a vowel* thē, thi) *definite article. The* is opposed to the indefinite article *a* or *an,* and is used specifically: 1 When reference is made to a particular person, thing, or group: *The* children are getting restless; He left *the* room. 2 To give an adjective substantive force, or render a notion abstract: *the* quick and *the* dead; *the* doing of the deed. 3 Before a noun to make it generic: *The* dog is a friend of man. 4 With the force of a possessive pronoun: He kicked me in *the* (my) leg. 5 To give distributive force: equivalent to *a, per, each,* etc.: a dollar *the* bushel. 6 To designate the whole of a specific time period: in *the* Middle Ages; in *the* forties. 7 To designate a particular one as emphatically outstanding: usu. stressed in speech and italicized in writing: He is *the* officer for the command. 8 As part of a title: *The* Duke of York. 9 Before the name of a well-known place, thing, etc.: *the* Grand Canyon; *the* Eiffel Tower. [< OE]

the² (thə) *adv.* By that much; to this extent: *the* more, *the* merrier: used to modify words in the comparative degree. [< OE *thȳ*]

the·a·ter (thē′ə·tər) *n.* 1 A structure for the indoor or outdoor presentation of plays, operas, motion pictures, etc. 2 A place resembling such a structure, used for lectures, surgical demonstrations, etc. 3 The theatrical world and everything relating to it, esp.: **a** The legitimate stage, as distinguished from motion pictures, television, etc. **b** The works written for or the arts connected with the theater. 4 Theatrical effectiveness: The play was not good *theater.* 5 Any place that is the scene of events or action:

a *theater* of war operations. Also **the'a·tre.** [< Gk. *theatron* < *theasthai* behold]

the·a·ter-in-the-round (thē'ə·tər·in·thə·round') *n.* A theater having a central stage and no proscenium, with seats surrounding the stage.

theater of the absurd A form of drama that concerns itself with the tragic or comic absurdities of man's condition and his futile efforts to deal with or resolve such absurdities.

the·at·ri·cal (thē·at'ri·kəl) *adj.* **1** Of or pertaining to the theater or things of the theater, as plays, actors, costumes, etc. **2** Dramatically effective or compelling. **3** Artificially dramatic, esp. in a pretentious or showy way. Also **the·at'ric.** —*n.pl.* Dramatic performances, esp. when given by amateurs. —**the·at'ri·cal·ism, the·at'ri·cal'i·ty** *n.* —**the·at'ri·cal·ly** *adv.*

the·at·rics (thē·at'riks) *n.pl.* **1** *(construed as sing.)* The art of the theater. **2** Exaggeratedly dramatic or showy behavior, mannerisms, etc.

thee (thē) *pron.* **1** The objective case of *thou.* **2** Thou: used generally by Quakers with a verb in the third person singular: *Thee* knows my mind. [< OE *thē*]

theft (theft) *n.* **1** The act or an instance of stealing; larceny. **2** That which is stolen. [< OE *thēoft*]

the·ine (thē'ən) *n.* The alkaloid identical with caffeine, found in tea. [< NL *thea* tea]

their (thâr) *pronominal adj.* The possessive case of the pronoun *they* used attributively; belonging or pertaining to them: *their* homes. [< ON *theirra* of them]

theirs (thârz) *pron.* **1** The possessive case of *they,* used predicatively; belonging or pertaining to them: That house is *theirs.* **2** The things or persons belonging or relating to them: our country and *theirs.* —**of theirs** Belonging or pertaining to them.

the·ism (thē'iz·əm) *n.* **1** Belief in a god or gods. **2** Belief in a personal God as creator and supreme ruler of the universe. [< Gk. *theos* god] —**the'ist** *n.* —**the·is'tic** or **·ti·cal** *adj.* —**the·is'ti·cal·ly** *adv.*

them (them, *unstressed* thəm) *pron.* The objective case of *they.* [< ON *theim*]

theme (thēm) *n.* **1** A main subject or topic, as of a poem, novel, play, speech, etc. **2** A short essay, often written as an exercise. **3** In a musical composition, a melodic, harmonic, or rhythmic subject or phrase, usu. developed with variations. **4** THEME SONG. [< Gk. *thema*] —**the·mat'ic** (-mat'ik) or **·i·cal** *adj.* —**the·mat'i·cal·ly** *adv.*

theme song **1** A musical motif recurring in a film, television presentation, etc. **2** The brief melody identifying a radio or television presentation, a dance band, etc.

them·selves (them'selvz', *unstressed* thəm-) *pron.* A form of the third person, plural pronoun, used: **1** As a reflexive: They forced *themselves* to go. **2** As an intensive: They *themselves* are responsible. **3** As an indication of their normal, true, or proper selves: They were not *themselves* when they said it.

then (then) *adv.* **1** At that time. **2** Soon afterward; next in time: We dressed and *then* ate. **3** Next in space or order: Add the flour, *then* the butter. **4** At another time: often introducing a sequential statement following *now, at first,* etc.: At first she laughed, *then* she cried. —*conj.* **1** For that reason; as a consequence; accordingly: If we leave now, *then* you can go to bed. **2** In that case: I will *then,* since you won't. —*adj.* Being or acting in, or belonging to, that time: the *then* secretary of state. —*n.* A specific time already mentioned or understood; that time: We will be gone by *then.* [< OE *thanne*]

thence (thens) *adv.* **1** From that place. **2** From the circumstance, fact, or cause; therefore. **3** From that time; after that time. [< OE *thanon* from there]

thence·forth (thens'fôrth', -fôrth') *adv.* From that time on; thereafter. Also **thence'for'ward** (-fôr'wərd), **thence'·for'wards.**

theo- *combining form* God or a god: *theocracy.* [< Gk. *theos* a god]

the·o·cen·tric (thē'ə·sen'trik) *adj.* Having God for its center; proceeding from God.

the·oc·ra·cy (thē·ok'rə·sē) *n. pl.* **·cies** **1** A state, polity, or group of people that claims a deity as its ruler. **2** Government by a priestly class claiming to have divine authority, as in the Papacy. [< Gk. *theos* god + *krateein* rule] —**the·o·crat** (thē'ə·krat) *n.* —**the·o·crat·ic** (thē'ə·krat'ik) or **·i·cal** *adj.* —**the'o·crat'i·cal·ly** *adv.*

the·od·o·lite (thē·od'ə·līt) *n.* A surveying instrument having a small telescope for measuring angles. [?]

theol. theologian; theological; theology.

the·o·lo·gi·an (thē'ə·lō'jən) *n.* One versed in theology.

the·o·log·i·cal (thē'ə·loj'i·kəl) *adj.* Of, pertaining to, based on, or teaching theology. Also **the'o·log'ic.** —**the'o·log'i·cal·ly** *adv.*

the·ol·o·gize (thē·ol'ə·jīz) *v.* **·gized, ·giz·ing** *v.t.* **1** To devise or fit (something) into a system of theology. —*v.i.* **2** To reason theologically.

the·ol·o·gy (thē·ol'ə·jē) *n. pl.* **·gies** **1** The study of God, his attributes, and his relationship with man and the universe, esp. such studies as set forth by a specific church, religious group, or theologian. **2** The study of religion and religious doctrine, culminating in a synthesis or philosophy of religion. [< Gk. *theos* god + *logos* discourse]

the·o·rem (thē'ər·əm, thir'əm) *n.* **1** A proposition demonstrably true or so universally acknowledged as such as to become part of a general theory. **2** *Math.* A proposition to be proved or which has been proved. [< Gk. *theōrēma* sight, theory] —**the·o·re·mat·ic** (thē'ər·ə·mat'ik) *adj.*

the·o·ret·i·cal (thē'ə·ret'i·kəl) *adj.* **1** Of, relating to, or consisting of theory. **2** Existing only in theory; not applied; speculative; hypothetical. **3** Addicted to theorizing. Also **the'o·ret'ic.** —**the'o·ret'i·cal·ly** *adv.*

the·o·re·ti·cian (thē'ər·ə·tish'ən) *n.* One who theorizes. Also **the·o·rist** (thē'ər·ist).

the·o·rize (thē'ə·rīz) *v.i.* **·rized, ·riz·ing** To form or express theories; speculate. —**the'o·ri·za'tion, the'o·riz'er** *n.*

the·o·ry (thē'ər·ē, thir'ē) *n. pl.* **·ries** **1** A plan, scheme, or procedure used or to be used as a basis or technique for doing something. **2** A merely speculative or an ideal circumstance, principle, mode of action, etc.: often with *in:* In *theory,* the plan worked. **3** A body of fundamental or abstract principles underlying a science, art, etc.: a *theory* of modern architecture. **4** A proposed explanation or hypothesis designed to account for any phenomenon. **5** Loosely, mere speculation, conjecture, or guesswork. [< Gk. *theōria* view, speculation]

theos. theosophical; theosophist; theosophy.

the·os·o·phy (thē·os'ə·fē) *n.* **1** Any of several religious or philosophical systems claiming to have mystical insight into the nature of God and the universe. **2** *Usu. cap.* The religious system of a modern religious sect (**Theosophical Society**) that is strongly Buddhist or Brahmanic in character and claims to have and to be able to teach such mystical insights. [< Gk. *theos* god + *sophos* wise] —**the·o·soph·ic** (thē'ə·sof'ik) or **·i·cal** *adj.* —**the'o·soph'i·cal·ly** *adv.* —**the·os'o·phist** *n.*

ther·a·peu·tic (ther'ə·pyoo'tik) *adj.* **1** Having healing qualities; curative. **2** Pertaining to therapeutics. Also **ther'a·peu'ti·cal.** [< Gk. *therapeuein* serve, take care of] —**ther'a·peu'ti·cal·ly** *adv.*

ther·a·peu·tics (ther'ə·pyoo'tiks) *n.pl.* *(construed as sing.)* The branch of medicine that treats of remedies for disease. —**ther'a·peu'tist** *n.*

ther·a·py (ther'ə·pē) *n. pl.* **·pies** **1** The treatment of disease or any bodily disorder or injury by drugs, physical exercise, etc. **2** PSYCHOTHERAPY. [< Gk. *therapeuein* take care of] —**ther'a·pist** *n.*

there (thâr) *adv.* **1** In or at that place; in a place other than that of the speaker. **2** To, toward, or into that place; thither. **3** At that stage or point of action or proceeding. **4** In that respect, relation, or connection. —*n.* That place, position, or point: We moved it from *there* to here. [< OE *thǣr*] • *There* is also used: **a** As a pronominal expletive introducing a clause or sentence, the subject usually following the verb: *There* once lived three bears. **b** With independent phrases or clauses, as an equivalent of *that,* expressing encouragement, approval, etc.: *There's* a little

dear. **c** As an exclamation expressing triumph, etc.: *There!* I told you so.

there·a·bouts (thâr′ə·bouts′, thâr′ə·bouts′) *adv.* Near that number, quantity, degree, place, or time; approximately. Also **there′a·bout′** (-bout′).

there·af·ter (thâr′af′tər, -äf′-) *adv.* **1** Afterward; from that time on. **2** Accordingly.

there·at (thâr′at′) *adv.* At that event, place, or time; at that incentive; upon that.

there·by (thâr′bī′, thâr′bī′) *adv.* **1** Through the agency of that. **2** Connected with that. **3** Conformably to that. **4** Nearby; thereabout. **5** By it or that; into possession of it or that: How did you come *thereby?*

there·for (thâr′fôr′) *adv.* For this, that, or it; in return or requital for this or that: We return thanks *therefor.*

there·fore (thâr′fôr′, -fōr′) *adv. & conj.* **1** For that or this reason. **2** Consequently: He did not run fast enough; *therefore* he lost the race.

there·from (thâr′frum′, -from′) *adv.* From this, that, or it; from this or that time, place, state, event, or thing.

there·in (thâr′in′) *adv.* **1** In that place. **2** In that time, matter, or respect.

there·in·af·ter (thâr′in·af′tər, -äf′-) *adv.* In a subsequent part of that (book, document, speech, etc.).

there·in·to (thâr′in·tōō′, thâr·in′tōō) *adv.* Into this, that, or it.

there·of (thâr′uv′, -ov′) *adv.* **1** Of or relating to this, that, or it. **2** From or because of this or that cause or particular; therefrom.

there·on (thâr′on′, -ôn′) *adv.* **1** On this, that, or it. **2** Thereupon; thereat.

there's (thârz) Contraction of *there is.*

there·to (thâr′tōō′) *adv.* **1** To this, that, or it. **2** In addition; furthermore. Also **there·un·to** (thâr′un′tōō, -un·tōō′).

there·to·fore (thâr′tə·fôr′, -fōr′, thâr′tə·fôr′, -fōr′) *adv.* Before this or that; previously to that.

there·un·der (thâr′un′dər) *adv.* **1** Under this or that. **2** Less, as in number. **3** In a lower or lesser status or rank.

there·up·on (thâr′ə·pon′, -pôn′, thâr′ə·pon′, -ə·pôn′) *adv.* **1** Upon that; upon it. **2** Following upon or in consequence of that. **3** Immediately following; at once.

there·with (thâr′with′, -with′) *adv.* **1** With this, that, or it. **2** Thereupon; thereafter; immediately afterward.

there·with·al (thâr′with·ôl′) *adv.* With all this or that; besides.

ther·mal (thûr′məl) *adj.* **1** Of, coming from, or having hot springs. **2** Of, relating to, or caused by heat. **3** Hot or warm: a *thermal* draft. **4** Aiding to conserve body heat: *thermal* fabrics. Also **ther′mic.** —*n.* A rising current of warm air in the atmosphere. [< Gk. *thermē* heat]

thermo- *combining form* Heat; of, related to, or caused by heat: *thermodynamics.* [< Gk. *thermos* heat, warmth]

ther·mo·dy·nam·ics (thûr′mō·dī·nam′iks, -di-) *n.pl.* *(construed as sing.)* The branch of physics that deals with the relations between heat, other forms of energy, and work. —**ther′mo·dy·nam′ic** or **·i·cal** *adj.* —**ther′mo·dy·nam′i·cist** (-nam′ə·sist) *n.*

ther·mo·e·lec·tric·i·ty (thûr′mō·i·lek′tris′ə·tē) *n.* Electricity generated by heat. —**ther′mo·e·lec′tric** or **·tri·cal** *adj.* —**ther′mo·e·lec′tri·cal·ly** *adv.*

ther·mo·gram (thûr′mə·gram) *n.* The record made by a thermograph.

ther·mo·graph (thûr′mə·graf, -gräf) *n.* **1** An instrument for detecting and recording temperature gradations across a surface. **2** A self-registering thermometer.

ther·mog·ra·phy (thər·mog′rə·fē) *n.* **1** The process of recording temperature variations with a thermograph. **2** A process that produces raised lettering on paper, as on stationery, by applying a powder to the lettering and then subjecting it to heat. —**ther·mo·graph·ic** (thûr′mə·graf′ik) *adj.*

ther·mom·e·ter (thər·mom′ə·tər) *n.* An instrument for measuring temperature, often consisting of a tube with a bulb containing a liquid which expands or contracts so that its height in the tube is proportional to the temperature. —**ther·mo·met·ric** (thûr′mō·met′rik) or **·ri·cal** *adj.* —**ther′mo·met′ri·cal·ly** *adv.*

ther·mo·nu·cle·ar (thûr′mō·nyōō′klē·ər) *adj.* Physics Pertaining to or characterized by reactions involving the fusion of light atomic nuclei subjected to very high temperatures.

ther·mo·plas·tic (thûr′mō·plas′tik) *adj.* Becoming soft when heated, as certain synthetic resins. —*n.* A thermoplastic substance or material.

Ther·mop·y·lae (thər·mop′ə·lē) *n.* A narrow mountain pass in Greece; scene of a battle, 480 B.C., in which the Spartans held off the Persians and finally died to the last man rather than yield.

ther·mos (thûr′məs) *n.* A container having two walls separated by a vacuum which serves to retard transfer of heat to or from the contents. Also **thermos bottle.** [< *Thermos,* a trade name]

ther·mo·set·ting (thûr′mō·set′ing) *adj.* Permanently assuming a fixed shape when heated, as certain synthetic resins.

ther·mo·stat (thûr′mə·stat) *n.* An automatic control device used to maintain a desired temperature. [< THERMO- + Gk. *statos* standing] —**ther′mo·stat′ic** *adj.* —**ther′mo·stat′i·cal·ly** *adv.*

ther·mot·ro·pism (thər·mot′rə·piz′əm) *n.* *Biol.* Movement or growth in a direction determined by the location of a heat source. —**ther·mo·trop·ic** (thûr′mō·trop′ik) *adj.* —**ther′mo·trop′i·cal·ly** *adv.*

the·sau·rus (thi·sôr′əs) *n. pl.* **·sau·ri** (-sôr′ī) or **sau′rus·es** **1** A book containing words and their synonyms grouped together. **2** A book containing words or facts dealing with a specific subject or field. [< Gk. *thēsauros* treasure]

these (thēz) *pl.* of THIS.

The·seus (thē′sōōs, -sē·əs) *Gk. Myth.* The chief hero of Attica, celebrated chiefly for killing the Minotaur, and for unifying Attica with Athens as its capital. —**The′se·an** (-sē·ən) *adj.*

the·sis (thē′sis) *n. pl.* **·ses** (-sēz) **1** A proposition, esp. a formal proposition advanced and defended by argumentation. **2** A formal treatise on a particular subject, esp. a dissertation presented by a candidate for an advanced academic degree. **3 a** *Logic* An affirmative proposition. **b** An unproved premise or postulate, as opposed to a hypothesis. [< Gk., a placing, proposition]

thes·pi·an (thes′pē·ən) *adj. Often cap.* Of or relating to drama; dramatic. —*n.* An actor or actress. [< *Thespis,* 6th-c. B.C. Gk. poet]

Thess. Thessalonians.

Thes·sa·lo·ni·ans (thes′ə·lō′nē·ənz) *n.pl.* *(construed as sing.)* Either of two epistles in the New Testament (**First** and **Second Thessalonians**) written by St. Paul to the Christians of Thessalonica.

Thes·sa·lo·ni·ca (thes′ə·lə·nī′kə, -lon′i·kə) *n.* An ancient city of N Greece.

the·ta (thā′tə, thē′tə) *n.* The eighth letter in the Greek alphabet (Θ, ϑ, θ).

thew (thyōō) *n.* **1** A sinew or muscle. **2** *pl.* Bodily strength or vigor. [< OE *thēaw* habit, characteristic quality]

they (thā) *pron.* **1** The persons, beings, or things previously mentioned or understood: the nominative plural of *he, she, it.* **2** People in general: *They* say that the fishing is excellent in this area. [< ON *their*]

they'd (thād) Contraction of *they had* or *they would.*

they'll (thāl) Contraction of *they shall* or *they will.*

they're (thâr) Contraction of *they are.*

they've (thāv) Contraction of *they have.*

T.H.I., T.-H.I. temperature-humidity index.

thi·a·mine (thī′ə·min, -mēn) *n.* Vitamin B_1, a compound found in cereal grains, liver, egg yolk, etc., and also made synthetically. Also **thi′a·min** (-min). [< THI(O)- + -AMINE]

thick (thik) *adj.* **1** Relatively large in depth or extent from one surface to its opposite; not thin. **2** Having a specified dimension of this kind, whether great or small: an inch *thick.* **3** Having the constituent or specified elements growing, packed, arranged, etc., close together: a field *thick* with daisies. **4** Viscous in consistency: a *thick* sauce. **5** Heavy; dense: a *thick* fog. **6** Foggy, hazy, smoky, etc. **7** Very dark; impenetrable: a *thick* gloom. **8** Indistinct; muffled; guttural, as speech. **9** Very noticeable; decided: a *thick* German accent. **10** *Informal* Dull; stupid. **11** *Informal* Very friendly; intimate. **12** *Informal* Going beyond what is tolerable; excessive. —*adv.* In a thick manner. —

n. The thickest or most intense time or place of anything: the *thick* of the fight. [< OE *thicce*] —**thick′ish** *adj.* —**thick′ly** *adv.* —**thick′ness** *n.*

thick·en (thik′ən) *v.t. & v.i.* 1 To make or become thick or thicker. 2 To make or become more intricate or intense: The plot *thickens.* —**thick′en·er** *n.*

thick·en·ing (thik′ən·ing) *n.* 1 The act of making or becoming thick. 2 Something added to a liquid to make it thicker. 3 That part which is or has been thickened.

thick·et (thik′it) *n.* A thick growth, as of underbrush. [< OE *thiccet* < *thicce* thick]

thick·head (thik′hed′) *n.* A stupid person. —**thick′head′·ed** *adj.* —**thick′head′ed·ness** *n.*

thick·set (thik′set′) *adj.* 1 Having a short, thick body; stocky. 2 Closely planted.

thick-skinned (thik′skind′) *adj.* 1 Having a thick skin, as a pachyderm. 2 Insensitive; callous to hints or insults.

thick-wit·ted (thik′wit′id) *adj.* Stupid; obtuse.

thief (thēf) *n. pl.* **thieves** (thēvz) One who takes something belonging to another, esp. secretly. [< OE *thēof*]

thieve (thēv) *v.* **thieved, thiev·ing** *v.t.* To take by theft; purloin; steal. —*v.i.* To be a thief; commit theft. [< OE *thēofian*]

thiev·er·y (thē′vər·ē) *n. pl.* **·er·ies** The practice or act of thieving; theft; also, an instance of thieving. —**thiev′ish** *adj.* —**thiev′ish·ly** *adv.* —**thiev′ish·ness** *n.*

thigh (thī) *n.* 1 The human leg between the hip and the knee. 2 The corresponding portion in other animals. [< OE *thēoh*]

thigh·bone (thī′bōn′) *n.* FEMUR. Also **thigh bone.**

thim·ble (thim′bəl) *n.* 1 In sewing, a pitted cover worn to protect the finger that pushes the needle. 2 Any similar device, esp. a ring on a rope to prevent chafing. [< OE *thȳmel* < *thūma* thumb]

thin (thin) *adj.* **thin·ner, thin·nest** 1 Having opposite surfaces relatively close to each other; being of little depth or width; not thick. 2 Lean and slender of figure. 3 Having the component parts or particles scattered or diffused; rarefied: a *thin* gas. 4 Not large or abundant, as in number: a *thin* audience. 5 Lacking thickness of consistency: a *thin* sauce. 6 Not dense or heavy: a *thin* fog. 7 Having little intensity or richness: a *thin* red. 8 Having little volume or resonance; shrill, as a voice. 9 Of a loose or light texture: *thin* clothing. 10 Insufficient; flimsy: a *thin* excuse. 11 Lacking essential ingredients or qualities: *thin* blood. 12 Meager; scant: *thin* hair. 13 Lacking vigor, force, substance, complexity, etc.; superficial; slight: *thin* humor. —*adv.* In a thin way: Slice the sausage *thin.* —*v.t. & v.i.* **thinned, thin·ning** To make or become thin or thinner. [< OE *thynne*] —**thin′ly** *adv.* —**thin′ness** *n.*

thine (thīn) *pron.* Archaic The things or persons belonging to thee: thou and *thine.* —*pronominal adj.* Archaic Thy: *thine* eyes. [< OE *thīn*]

thing (thing) *n.* 1 That which exists or is conceived to exist as a separate entity: all the *things* in the world. 2 That which is designated, as contrasted with the word or symbol used to denote it. 3 A matter or circumstance: *Things* have changed. 4 An act, deed, event, etc.: That was a shameless *thing* to do. 5 A procedure or step, as in an ordered course or process: the first *thing* to do. 6 An item, particular, detail, etc.: each *thing* on the schedule. 7 A statement or expression; utterance: to say the right *thing.* 8 An idea; opinion; notion: Stop putting *things* in her head. 9 A quality; attribute; characteristic: Kindness is a precious *thing.* 10 An inanimate object. 11 An object that is not or cannot be described or particularized: What kind of *thing* is that? 12 A person, regarded in terms of pity, affection, or contempt: that poor *thing.* 13 *pl.* Possessions; belongings: to pack one's *things.* 14 *pl.* Clothes; esp. outer garments. 15 A piece of clothing, as a dress: not a *thing* to wear. 16 A piece of literature, art, music, etc.: He read a few *things* by Byron. 17 The proper or befitting act or result: with *the:* That was not the *thing* to do. 18 The important point, attitude, etc.: with *the:* The *thing* one learns from travel is how to combat fatigue. 19 *Informal* A point; issue; case: He always makes a big *thing* out of

dividing up the bill. 20 *Informal* A strong liking, disliking, fear, attraction, etc.: to have a *thing* for tall girls. 21 *Law* A subject or property or dominion, as distinguished from a person. —**do one's (own) thing** *Slang* To express oneself by doing what one wants to do or can do well or is in the habit of doing. [< OE, thing, cause, assembly]

thing·a·ma·bob (thing′ə·mə·bob′) *n. Informal* THING-AMAJIG. Also **thing′um·a·bob′, thing′um·bob.**

thing·a·ma·jig (thing′ə·mə·jig′) *n. Informal* A thing the specific name of which is unknown or forgotten. Also **thing′um·a·jig′.**

think[1] (thingk) *v.* **thought** (thôt), **think·ing** *v.t.* 1 To produce or form in the mind; conceive mentally: to *think* evil thoughts. 2 To examine in the mind; meditate upon, or determine by reasoning: to *think* a plan through. 3 To believe; consider: I *think* him guilty. 4 To expect; anticipate: They did not *think* to meet us. 5 To bring to mind; remember; recollect: I cannot *think* what he said. 6 To have the mind preoccupied by: to *think* business morning, noon, and night. 7 To intend; purpose: Do they *think* to rob me? —*v.i.* 8 To use the mind or intellect in exercising judgment, forming ideas, etc.; engage in rational thought; reason. 9 To have a particular opinion, sentiment, or feeling: I don't *think* so. —**think of** (or **about**) 1 To bring to mind; remember; recollect. 2 To conceive in the mind; invent; imagine. 3 To have a specified opinion or attitude toward; regard. 4 To be considerate of; have regard for. —**think over** To reflect upon; ponder. —**think up** To devise, arrive at, or invent by thinking. —*n. Informal* The act of thinking. [< OE *thencan*] —**think′er** *n.*

think[2] (thingk) *v.i.* To seem; appear: now obsolete except with the pronoun as indirect object in the combinations *methinks, methought.* [< OE *thyncan* seem]

think·a·ble (thingk′ə·bəl) *adj.* 1 Susceptible of being thought; conceivable. 2 Possible.

think·ing (thingk′ing) *adj.* Using or given to using the mind; intellectually active. —*n.* 1 The act or process of using the mind to think. 2 A result of thought; opinion or position. —**think′ing·ly** *adv.*

think tank *Informal* 1 A group of people (**think tank·ers**), usu. academics, business executives, or government employees, organized for the investigation and study of social, scientific, and technological problems. 2 The place in which such a group works.

thin·ner (thin′ər) *n.* One who or that which thins, esp. a liquid added to a viscid substance to thin it.

thin-skinned (thin′skind′) *adj.* 1 Having a thin skin. 2 Easily offended; sensitive.

thio- *combining form* Containing sulfur: *thiosulfate.* [< Gk. *theion* sulfur]

thi·o·sul·fate (thī′ō·sul′fāt) *n.* Any salt of thiosulfuric acid, esp. sodium thiosulfate.

thi·o·sul·fu·ric acid (thī′ō·sul·fyŏŏr′ik) An unstable acid, known chiefly by its salts, which are used in bleaching and photography.

third (thûrd) *adj. & adv.* 1 Next in order after the second. 2 Being one of three equal parts. —*n.* 1 The element of an ordered set that corresponds to the number three. 2 One of three equal parts. 3 *Music* The interval between any tone and another two steps away in a diatonic scale. 4 In baseball, the third base. [< OE *thridda*]

third-class (thûrd′klas′, -kläs′) *adj.* 1 Ranking next below the second or second best. 2 Of, pertaining to, or belonging to a class next below the second: *third-class* mail. —*adv.* By third-class accommodations or mail.

third degree *Informal* Severe or brutal examination of a prisoner for the purpose of securing information or a confession.

third estate The common people, traditionally ranked after the nobility and the clergy.

third·ly (thûrd′lē) *adv.* Third.

third person The form of the pronoun, as *he, she, it,* to indicate the person or thing spoken of, or the grammatical form of the verb referring to such person or thing.

third rail An insulated rail on an electric railway for supplying current to the trains or cars.

---

add, āce, câre, pälm; end, ēven; it, īce; odd, ōpen, ôrder; tŏŏk, pōōl; up, bûrn; ə = a in above, u in focus; yōō = u in fuse; oil; pout; check; go; ring; thin; this; zh, vision. < derived from; ? origin uncertain or unknown.

third-rate (thûrd'rāt') *adj.* **1** Third in rating or class. **2** Of poor quality; inferior.

third world 1 Any or all of the underdeveloped countries in the world, esp. such countries in Asia or Africa that are not aligned with either the Communist or non-Communist nations. **2** Those not resident in the countries of the third world but collectively identified with their peoples, as because of ideology, ethnic background, or disadvantaged status. Also **Third World.**

thirst (thûrst) *n.* **1** Discomfort or distress due to a need for water. **2** A craving or taste for any specified liquid: a *thirst* for alcohol. **3** Any longing or craving: a *thirst* for glory. — *v.i.* **1** To feel thirst; be thirsty. **2** To have an eager desire or craving. [< OE *thurst*] —**thirst'er** *n.*

thirst·y (thûrs'tē) *adj.* **thirst·i·er, thirst·i·est 1** Affected with thirst. **2** Lacking moisture; arid; parched. **3** Eagerly desirous. **4** *Informal* Causing thirst. [< OE *thurstig*] —**thirst'i·ly** *adv.* —**thirst'i·ness** *n.*

thir·teen (thûr'tēn') *n.* **1** The sum of 12 plus 1; 13; XIII. **2** A set or group of 13 members. [< OE *thrēotēne*] —**thir'·teen'** *adj., pron.*

thir·teenth (thûr'tēnth') *adj. & adv.* Next in order after the 12th. —*n.* **1** The element of an ordered set that corresponds to the number 13. **2** One of 13 equal parts.

thir·ti·eth (thûr'tē·ith) *adj. & adv.* Tenth in order after the 20th. —*n.* **1** The element of an ordered set that corresponds to the number 30. **2** One of 30 equal parts.

thir·ty (thûr'tē) *n. pl.* **·ties 1** The product of three and ten. **2** A set or group of 30 members. **3** *pl.* The numbers, years, etc. from 30 to 40. [< OE *thrītig*] —**thir'ty** *adj., pron.*

thir·ty-sec·ond note (thûr'tē·sek'ənd) *Music* A note having one thirty-second of the time value of a whole note. • See NOTE.

this (this) *adj. pl.* **these 1** That is near or present, either actually or in thought: *This* house is for sale; I shall be there *this* evening. **2** That is understood or has just been mentioned: *This* offense justified my revenge. **3** That is nearer than or contrasted with something else: opposed to *that: This* tree is still alive, but that one is dead. —*pron. pl.* **these 1** The person or thing near or present, being understood or just mentioned: *This* is where I live; *This* is the guilty man. **2** The person or thing nearer than or contrasted with something else: opposed to *that: This* is a better painting than that. **3** The idea, statement, etc., about to be made clear: I will say *this:* he is a hard worker. —*adv.* To this degree; thus or so: I was not expecting you *this* soon. [< OE]

this·tle (this'əl) *n.* Any of various prickly plants with cylindrical or globular heads of composite flowers. [< OE *thistel*] —**this'tly** *adj.*

this·tle·down (this'əl·doun') *n.* The silky fibers of the ripening flower of a thistle.

thith·er (thith'ər, thith'-) *adv.* To that place; in that direction. —*adj.* Situated or being on the other side; more distant. [< OE *thider*]

thith·er·to (thith'ər·tōō', thith'-) *adv.* Up to that time.

Thistle

thith·er·ward (thith'ər·wərd, thith'-) *adv.* In that direction; toward that place. Also **thith'er·wards.**

tho (thō) *conj. & adv.* THOUGH.

thole (thōl) *n.* A pin or pair of pins serving as a fulcrum for an oar in rowing. Also **thole pin.** [< OE *thol*]

Tho·mism (tō'miz·əm) *n.* The theological and philosophical doctrines of St. Thomas Aquinas. [< St. *Thomas* Aquinas] —**Tho'mist** *adj., n.*

thong (thông, thong) *n.* **1** A narrow strip, usu. of leather, as for fastening. **2** A lash of a whip. [< OE *thwang* thong]

Thor (thôr, tôr) *Norse Myth.* The god of war and thunder and son of Odin.

tho·rax (thôr'aks, thō'raks) *n. pl.* **tho·rax·es** or **tho·ra·ces** (thôr'ə·sēz, thō'rə-) **1** The part of the body between the neck and the abdomen, enclosed by the ribs. **2** The middle segment between the head and abdomen of an insect. • See INSECT. [< Gk. *thōrax*] —**tho·rac·ic** (thô·ras'ik) *adj.*

tho·ri·um (thôr'ē·əm, thō'rē-) *n.* A rare, radioactive, metallic element (symbol Th) used as a fuel in certain nuclear reactors. [< THOR] —**tho'ric** *adj.*

thorn (thôrn) *n.* **1** A sharp, rigid outgrowth from a plant stem. **2** Any of various thorn-bearing shrubs or trees. **3** A cause of discomfort, pain, or annoyance. **4** The name of the Old English rune þ, equivalent to *th*, as in *thorn*, from which it derives its name. —*v.t.* To pierce or prick with a thorn. [< OE] —**thorn'less** *adj.*

thorn apple 1 JIMSONWEED. **2** HAW².

thorn·y (thôr'nē) *adj.* **thorn·i·er, thorn·i·est 1** Full of thorns; spiny. **2** Sharp like a thorn. **3** Full of difficulties or trials; painful; vexatious. —**thorn'i·ness** *n.*

tho·ron (thôr'on, thō'ron) *n.* A radioactive isotope of radon, resulting from the disintegration of thorium and having a half-life of 54.5 seconds.

thor·ough (thûr'ō, thûr'ə) *adj.* **1** Complete; exhaustive: a *thorough* search. **2** Attentive to details and accuracy; painstaking: a *thorough* worker. **3** Completely (such and such); through and through: a *thorough* nincompoop. [Emphatic var. of THROUGH] —**thor'ough·ly** *adv.* —**thor'ough·ness** *n.* —Syn. **1** comprehensive, sweeping, out-and-out, total. **2** exact, precise, meticulous, careful, conscientious. **3** absolute, downright, utter, unmitigated, perfect.

thor·ough·bred (thûr'ə·bred') *adj.* **1** Bred from pure stock; pedigreed. **2** Possessing or showing excellence, as in training, education, manners, culture, etc.; first-rate. —*n.* **1** A thoroughbred animal. **2** A person of culture and good breeding.

Thor·ough·bred (thûr'ə·bred') *n.* A breed of English race horse, originally developed by mating Arabian stallions with English mares.

thor·ough·fare (thûr'ō·fâr', thûr'ə-) *n.* **1** A much frequented road or street through which the public have unobstructed passage. **2** A passage: now chiefly in the phrase **no thoroughfare.** [< OE *thurh* through + *faru* going]

thor·ough·go·ing (thûr'ō·gō'ing, thûr'ə-) *adj.* **1** Characterized by extreme thoroughness or efficiency. **2** Unmitigated; out-and-out.

those (thōz) *adj. & pron. pl.* of THAT. [< OE *thās*]

thou (thou) *pron.* The person spoken to, as denoted in the nominative case: archaic except in religious or poetic language, or in certain dialects. [< OE *thū*]

though (thō) *conj.* **1** Notwithstanding the fact that; although: *Though* he was sleepy, he stayed awake. **2** Granting that; even if: *Though* she may win, she will have lost her popularity. **3** And yet; still; however: I am well, *though* I do not feel very strong. —*adv.* Notwithstanding; nevertheless: It's not a good play, but I like it *though.* [< ON *thō*]

thought¹ (thôt) *n.* **1** The act or process of thinking. **2** The product of thinking, as an idea, concept, judgment, opinion, or the like. **3** Intellectual activity of a specific kind, time, place, etc.: Greek *thought.* **4** Consideration; attention; heed: Give the plan some *thought.* **5** Intention; plan; design: All *thought* of returning was abandoned. **6** Expectation; anticipation: He had no *thought* of finding her there. **7** A trifle; a small amount: Be a *thought* more cautious. [< THOUGHT²]

thought² (thôt) *p.t. & p.p.* of THINK. [< OE *thōht*]

thought·ful (thôt'fəl) *adj.* **1** Full of thought; meditative. **2** Showing, characterized by, or promoting thought. **3** Attentive; careful, esp. manifesting regard for others; considerate. —**thought'ful·ly** *adv.* —**thought'ful·ness** *n.*

thought·less (thôt'lis) *adj.* **1** Manifesting lack of thought or care; careless. **2** Not considerate of others. **3** Giddy; flighty. —**thought'less·ly** *adv.* —**thought'less·ness** *n.*

thou·sand (thou'zənd) *n.* **1** The product of ten times a hundred. **2** *Usu. pl.* An indefinitely large number. —*adj.* Consisting of a hundred times ten. [< OE *thūsend*] —**thou'sand·fold'** (-fōld') *adj., adv.*

thou·sandth (thou'zəndth) *adj.* **1** Last in a series of a thousand. **2** Being one of a thousand equal parts. —*n.* **1** The element of an ordered set that corresponds to the number 1000. **2** One of a thousand equal parts.

thrall (thrôl) *n.* **1** A person in bondage; a slave; serf. **2** One controlled by a passion or vice. **3** Slavery. [< ON *thræl*]

thrall·dom (thrôl'dəm) *n.* **1** The state of being a thrall. **2** Any sort of bondage or servitude. Also **thral'dom.**

thrash (thrash) *v.t.* **1** To thresh, as grain. **2** To beat as if with a flail; flog; whip. **3** To move or swing with flailing,

violent motions. **4** To defeat utterly. —*v.i.* **5** To move or swing about with flailing, violent motions. **6** To make one's way by thrashing. —**thrash out** (or **over**) To discuss fully and usu. come to a conclusion. —*n.* The act of thrashing. [Dial. var. of THRESH]

thrash·er[1] (thrash′ər) *n.* **1** One who or that which thrashes. **2** A machine for threshing grain. **3** THRESHER (def. 2).

thrash·er[2] (thrash′ər) *n.* Any of several long-tailed American songbirds resembling the thrushes and related to the mockingbirds. [?< THRUSH[1]]

thread (thred) *n.* **1** A very slender cord or line composed of two or more filaments, as of flax, cotton, silk, nylon, etc., twisted together. **2** A filament of metal, glass, etc. **3** A fine beam: a *thread* of light. **4** Something that runs a continuous course through a series or whole: the *thread* of his discourse. **5** *Mech.* The helical ridge of a screw. —*v.t.* **1** To pass a thread through the eye of: to *thread* a needle. **2** To string on a thread, as beads. **3** To cut a thread on or in, as a screw. **4** To make one's way through or over: to *thread* a maze. **5** To make (one's way) carefully. —*v.i.* **6** To make one's way carefully. **7** To fall from a fork or spoon in a fine thread: said of boiling syrup. [< OE *thræd*] —**thread′er** *n.*

thread·bare (thred′bâr′) *adj.* **1** Worn so that the threads show, as a rug or garment. **2** Clad in worn garments. **3** Commonplace; hackneyed. —**thread′bare′ness** *n.* —**Syn. 2** shabby. **3** common, stale, stereotyped, trite.

thread·y (thred′ē) *adj.* **thread·i·er, thread·i·est** **1** Like a thread; stringy. **2** Forming threads, as some liquids. **3** Weak; lacking vigor: a *thready* pulse. —**thread′i·ness** *n.*

threat (thret) *n.* **1** A declaration of an intention to inflict injury or pain. **2** Any menace or danger. [< OE *threat* crowd, oppression]

threat·en (thret′n) *v.t.* **1** To utter threats against. **2** To be menacing or dangerous to. **3** To portend (something unpleasant or dangerous). **4** To utter threats of (injury, vengeance, etc.). —*v.i.* **5** To utter threats. **6** To have a menacing aspect; lower. —**threat′en·er** *n.* —**threat′en·ing·ly** *adv.*

three (thrē) *n.* **1** The sum of two plus one; 3, III. **2** A set or group of three members. [< OE *thrī*] —**three** *adj., pron.*

three-D (thrē′dē′) *adj.* THREE-DIMENSIONAL. —*n.* A technique, medium, or process giving the appearance of three dimensions to visual images. Also **3-D.**

three-deck·er (thrē′dek′ər) *n.* **1** A vessel having three decks or gun decks. **2** Anything having three levels.

three-di·men·sion·al (thrē′də·men′shən·əl) *adj.* **1** Of or having three dimensions. **2** Appearing to have depth as well as height and width.

three·fold (thrē′fōld′) *adj.* **1** Made up of three parts. **2** Having three times as many or as much. —*adv.* Triply; in a threefold manner.

three-mile limit (thrē′mīl′) A distance of three geographic miles from the shore line seaward, allowed by international law for territorial jurisdiction.

three·pence (thrip′əns, threp′-, thrup′-) *n.* *Brit.* **1** The sum of three pennies. **2** A small coin of Great Britain worth three pennies: also **thrip′pence** (thrip′əns).

three-ply (thrē′plī′) *adj.* Consisting of three thicknesses, strands, layers, etc.

three R's Reading, writing, and arithmetic.

three·score (thrē′skôr′, -skōr′) *adj. & n.* Sixty.

three·some (thrē′səm) *n.* **1** A group of three people. **2** A game played by three people; also, the players.

thren·o·dy (thren′ə·dē) *n. pl.* **·dies** An ode or song of lamentation; a dirge. Also **thren′ode** (-ōd). [< Gk. *thrēnos* lament + *ōidē* song] —**thre·nod·ic** (thri·nod′ik) *adj.* —**thren′o·dist** *n.*

thresh (thresh) *v.t.* **1** To beat stalks of (ripened grain) with a flail so as to separate the grain from the husks. —*v.i.* **2** To thresh grain. **3** To move or thrash about. —**thresh out** To discuss fully and to a conclusion. —**thresh over** To discuss over and over. [< OE *therscan*]

thresh·er (thresh′ər) *n.* **1** One who or that which threshes, esp. a machine for threshing. **2** A large shark having an extremely long tail: also **thresher shark.**

thresh·old (thresh′ōld, -hōld) *n.* **1** The plank, timber, or stone lying under the door of a building; doorsill. **2** The entering point or beginning of anything: the *threshold* of the 20th century. **3** The minimum degree of stimulation necessary to produce a response or to be perceived. [< OE *therscold*]

threw (thrōō) *p.t.* of THROW.

thrice (thrīs) *adv.* **1** Three times. **2** Fully; extremely. [< OE *thriwa* thrice]

thrift (thrift) *n.* Care and wisdom in the management of one's resources; frugality. [< ON] —**thrift′less** *adj.* — **thrift′less·ly** *adv.* —**thrift′less·ness** *n.*

thrift·y (thrif′tē) *adj.* **thrift·i·er, thrift·i·est** **1** Displaying thrift or good management; frugal. **2** Prosperous; thriving. —**thrift′i·ly** *adv.* —**thrift′i·ness** *n.* —**Syn 1** economical, provident, prudent, saving.

thrill (thril) *v.t.* **1** To cause to feel a great or tingling excitement. —*v.i.* **2** To feel a sudden wave of emotion. **3** To vibrate or tremble; quiver. —*n.* **1** A feeling of excitement. **2** A thrilling quality. **3** A pulsation; quiver. [< OE *thyrlian* pierce] —**thrill′ing·ly** *adv.*

thrill·er (thril′ər) *n.* **1** One who or that which thrills. **2** *Informal* An exciting book, play, etc.

thrive (thrīv) *v.i.* **throve** (thrōv) or **thrived, thrived** or **thriv·en** (thriv′ən), **thriv·ing** **1** To prosper; be successful. **2** To flourish. [< ON *thrīfast* reflexive of *thrīfa* grasp] —**thriv′er** *n.* —**thriv′ing·ly** *adv.*

throat (thrōt) *n.* **1** The front part of the neck. **2** The passage extending from the back of the mouth and containing the epiglottis, larynx, trachea, and pharynx. **3** Any narrow passage resembling a throat. —**jump down one's throat** To scold or criticize with sudden violence. — **lump in the throat** A feeling of tightness in the throat, as from strong emotion. —**stick in one's throat** To be difficult or painful to say. [< OE *throte*]

Throat
a. soft palate. b.
pharynx. c. epiglottis.
d. esophagus.
e. trachea.

throat·y (thrō′tē) *adj.* **throat·i·er, throat·i·est** Uttered in the throat; guttural. —**throat′i·ly** *adv.* —**throat′i·ness** *n.*

throb (throb) *v.i.* **throbbed, throb·bing** **1** To pulsate rhythmically, as the heart. **2** To feel or show emotion by trembling. —*n.* **1** The act or state of throbbing. **2** A pulsation, esp. one caused by excitement or emotion. [Imit.] —**throb′ber** *n.*

throe (thrō) *n.* **1** A violent pang or pain. **2** *pl.* The pains of death or childbirth. **3** Any agonized or agonizing activity. [< OE *thrawe*]

throm·bin (throm′bin) *n.* An enzyme in blood serum that promotes clotting. [< Gk. *thrombos* clot]

throm·bo·sis (throm·bō′sis) *n.* The formation of a blood clot inside the heart or a blood vessel. [< Gk. *thrombos* clot] —**throm·bot·ic** (-bot′ik) *adj.*

throne (thrōn) *n.* **1** The chair occupied by a king, pope, etc., on state occasions. **2** The rank or authority of a king, queen, etc. —*v.t. & v.i.* **throned, thron·ing** To enthrone; exalt. [< Gk. *thronos* seat]

throng (thrông, throng) *n.* **1** A closely crowded multitude. **2** Any numerous collection. —*v.t.* **1** To crowd into and occupy fully; jam. **2** To crowd upon. —*v.i.* **3** To collect or move in a throng. [< OE *gethrang*] —**Syn.** *n.* **1** crowd, host, jam, mass, press.

throt·tle (throt′l) *n.* **1** A valve controlling the supply of fuel or steam to the cylinders of an engine: also **throttle valve.** **2** The lever which operates the throttle valve: also **throttle lever.** —*v.t.* **·tled, ·tling** **1** To strangle, choke, or suffocate. **2** To silence, stop, or suppress. **3** To reduce or shut off the flow of (steam or fuel to the cylinders of an engine). **4** To reduce the speed of by means of a throttle. —*v.i.* **5** To suffocate; choke. [Dim. of ME *throte* throat] —**throt′tler** *n.*

through (thrōō) *prep.* **1** From end to end, side to side, or limit to limit of; into at one side, end, or point, and out of at another. **2** Covering, entering, or penetrating all parts

of; throughout. **3** From the first to the last of: *through* the day. **4** Here and there upon or in. **5** By way of: He departed *through* the door. **6** By the instrumentality or aid of. **7** Having reached the end of: He got *through* his examinations. —*adv.* **1** From one end, side, surface, etc., to or beyond another. **2** From beginning to end. **3** To a termination or conclusion: to pull *through*. **4** Completely; entirely: He is wet *through*. —**through and through** Thoroughly; completely. —*adj.* **1** Going to its destination without stops: a *through* train. **2** Usable or valid for an entire trip: a *through* ticket. **3** Extending from one side or surface to another. **4** Allowing unobstructed or direct passage: a *through* road. **5** Finished: Are you *through* with my pen? [< OE *thurh*]

through·out (thrōō·out′) *adv.* Through or in every part. —*prep.* All through; everywhere in.

throve (thrōv) *p.t.* of THRIVE.

throw (thrō) *v.* **threw** (thrōō), **thrown, throw·ing** *v.t.* **1** To propel through the air by means of a sudden straightening or whirling of the arm. **2** To propel or hurl. **3** To put hastily or carelessly: He *threw* a coat over his shoulders. **4** To direct or project (light, shadow, a glance, etc.). **5** To bring to a specified condition or state: to *throw* the enemy into a panic. **6** To cause to fall: The horse *threw* its rider. **7** In wrestling, to force the shoulders of (an opponent) to the ground. **8** To cast (dice). **9** To make (a specified cast) with dice. **10** To shed; lose: The horse *threw* a shoe. **11** *Informal* To lose purposely, as a race. **12** To move, as a lever or switch. **13** *Slang* To give (a party, etc.). **14** In ceramics, to shape on a potter's wheel. —*v.i.* **15** To cast or fling something. —**throw away 1** To cast off; discard. **2** To squander. —**throw cold water on** To discourage. — **throw off 1** To reject; spurn. **2** To rid oneself of. **3** To do or utter in an offhand manner. **4** To emit; discharge. **5** To confuse; mislead. **6** To elude (a pursuer). —**throw oneself at** To strive to gain the affection or love of. —**throw oneself into** To take part in vigorously. —**throw oneself on** (or **upon**) To rely on utterly. —**throw open 1** To open suddenly, as a door. **2** To free from restrictions or obstacles. —**throw out 1** To emit. **2** To discard; reject. **3** To utter as if accidentally: to *throw out* hints. **4** In baseball, to retire (a runner) by throwing the ball to the base toward which he is advancing. —**throw over 1** To overturn. **2** To jilt. —**throw together** To put together carelessly. — **throw up 1** To vomit. **2** To erect hastily. **3** To give up. **4** *Informal* To mention (something) repeatedly and reproachfully; taunt. —*n.* **1** An act of throwing. **2** The distance over which a missile may be thrown: a long *throw*. **3** A cast of dice, or the resulting number. **4** A scarf or other light covering. **5** In wrestling, a flooring of one's opponent so that both his shoulders touch the mat simultaneously for ten seconds. [< OE *thrāwan* to turn, twist, curl] — **throw′er** *n.* —**Syn.** *v.* **1** fling, heave, hurl, pitch.

throw·back (thrō′bak′) *n.* **1** An atavism. **2** A throwing back.

thru (thrōō) *adj., adv. & prep.* THROUGH.

thrum (thrum) *v.* **thrummed, thrum·ming** *v.t.* **1** To play on (a stringed instrument), esp. idly; strum. **2** To drum on monotonously with the fingers. —*v.i.* **3** To strum a stringed instrument. —*n.* The sound made by thrumming. [Prob. imit.]

thrush¹ (thrush) *n.* Any of many species of migratory songbirds, usu. having long wings and spotted under parts, as the **hermit thrush,** the **wood thrush,** the robin, and the bluebird. [< OE *thrysce*]

thrush² (thrush) *n.* A disease of the mouth, lips, and throat caused by a yeastlike fungus. [?]

thrust (thrust) *v.* **thrust, thrust·ing** *v.t.* **1** To push or shove with force. **2** To pierce with a sudden forward motion, as with a sword. **3** To interpose. —*v.i.* **4** To make a sudden push or thrust. **5** To force oneself on or ahead: to *thrust* through a crowd. —*n.* **1** A sudden and forcible push, esp. with a pointed weapon. **2** A vigorous attack; sharp onset. **3** A force that drives or propels. **4** Salient force or mean-

Wood thrush

ing: the *thrust* of his remarks. [< ON *thrȳsta*] —**thrust′er** *n.* —**Syn.** *v.* **1** lunge. **2** stab, stick. *n.* **4** import, intention, significance, sense, gist.

thru·way (thrōō′wā′) *n.* EXPRESSWAY.

thud (thud) *n.* **1** A dull, heavy sound. **2** A blow causing such a sound; a thump. —*v.i.* **thud·ded, thud·ding** To strike or fall with a thud. [< OE *thyddan* strike, thrust, press]

thug (thug) *n.* **1** Formerly, one of an organization of religious assassins in India. **2** Any assassin or ruffian. [< Skt. *sthaga* swindler]

thu·li·um (thōō′lē·əm) *n.* A metallic element (symbol Tm) of the lanthanide series. [< *Thule*, the northernmost limit of the habitable world in ancient geography]

thumb (thum) *n.* **1** The short, thick digit of the human hand. **2** A similar part in certain animals. **3** The division in a glove or mitten that covers the thumb. —**all thumbs** Clumsy with the hands. —**thumbs down** A signal of negation or disapproval. —**thumbs up** A signal of approval. —**under one's thumb** Under one's influence or power. — *v.t.* **1** To rub, soil, or wear with the thumb in handling. **2** To handle clumsily. **3** To run through the pages of (a book, etc.) rapidly. —**thumb a ride** To get a ride by signaling with the thumb. [< OE *thūma*]

thumb index A series of scalloped indentations cut along the front edge of a book and labeled to indicate its various sections. —**thumb′-in′dex** *v.t.*

thumb·nail (thum′nāl′) *n.* **1** The nail of the thumb. **2** Anything as small as a thumbnail. —*adj.* Very brief: a *thumbnail* sketch.

thumb·screw (thum′skrōō′) *n.* **1** A screw to be turned by thumb and fingers. • See SCREW. **2** An instrument of torture for compressing the thumb or thumbs.

thumb·tack (thum′tak′) *n.* A broad-headed tack that may be pushed in with the thumb.

thump (thump) *n.* **1** A blow with a blunt or heavy object. **2** The sound made by such a blow; a thud. —*v.t.* **1** To beat or strike so as to make a heavy thud or thuds. **2** *Informal* To beat or defeat severely. —*v.i.* **3** To strike with a thump. **4** To pound or throb, as the heart. [Imit.] —**thump′er** *n.*

thun·der (thun′dər) *n.* **1** The sound that accompanies lightning, caused by the explosive effect of the electric discharge. **2** Any loud noise resembling thunder. **3** A vehement or powerful utterance. —**steal one's thunder** To undermine the effectiveness of an opponent by anticipating his next move, argument, etc. —*v.i.* **1** To give forth peals of thunder: It is *thundering.* **2** To make a noise like thunder. **3** To utter vehement denunciations. —*v.t.* **4** To utter or express with a noise like thunder: The cannon *thundered* defiance. [< OE *thunor*] —**thun′der·er** *n.*

thun·der·bolt (thun′dər·bōlt′) *n.* **1** A lightning flash accompanied by a clap of thunder. **2** A person or thing acting with great force, speed, or destructiveness.

thun·der·clap (thun′dər·klap′) *n.* **1** A sharp, violent detonation of thunder. **2** Anything violent or sudden.

thun·der·cloud (thun′dər·kloud′) *n.* A dark, heavy mass of electrically charged cloud.

thun·der·head (thun′dər·hed′) *n.* A rounded mass of silvery cumulus cloud, often developing into a thundercloud.

thun·der·ous (thun′dər·əs) *adj.* Producing or emitting thunder or a sound like thunder. —**thun′der·ous·ly** *adv.*

thun·der·show·er (thun′dər·shou′ər) *n.* A shower of rain with thunder and lightning.

thun·der·storm (thun′dər·stôrm′) *n.* A local storm accompanied by lightning and thunder.

thun·der·struck (thun′dər·struk′) *adj.* Amazed, astonished, or confounded. Also **thun′der·strick′en** (-strik′ən).

Thur., Thurs. Thursday.

thu·ri·ble (thōōr′ə·bəl) *n.* CENSER. [< L *thus, thuris* frankincense]

Thurs·day (thûrz′dē, -dā) *n.* The fifth day of the week. [< OE *Thunres dæg* day of Thor]

thus (thus) *adv.* **1** In this or that or the following way. **2** To such degree or extent; so: *thus* far. **3** In this case; therefore. [< OE]

thwack (thwak) *v.t.* To strike heavily with something flat; whack. —*n.* A blow with something flat. [Prob. imit.] — **thwack′er** *n.*

thwart (thwôrt) *v.t.* To obstruct (a plan, a person, etc.) as

by interposing an obstacle; frustrate. —*n.* **1** An oarsman's seat extending athwart a boat. **2** A brace athwart a canoe. —*adj.* Lying, moving, or extending across something; transverse. —*adv. & prep.* Athwart. [< ON *thvert,* neut. of *thverr* transverse] —**thwart′er** *n.*

thy (thī) *pronominal adj.* Belonging or pertaining to thee: *Thy* kingdom come. [< OE *thīn* THINE]

thyme (tīm) *n.* **1** Any of various small shrubby plants of the mint family, having aromatic leaves. **2** The dried leaves of certain thyme plants, used for seasoning in cookery. [< Gk. *thymon*] —**thy·mic** (-mik), **thym′y** *adj.*

thy·mus (thī′məs) *n.* A ductless glandlike structure situated at the root of the neck and nus. becoming atrophied after early childhood. [< Gk. *thymos*] • See THYROID.

thy·roid (thī′roid) *adj.* **1** Of or pertaining to the cartilage of the larynx which forms the Adam's apple. **2** Of, pertaining to, or describing a large ductless gland situated near the larynx on each side of the trachea and secreting thyroxin. —*n.* **1** The thyroid cartilage. **2** The thyroid gland. [< Gk. *thyreoeidēs* shield-shaped]

thy·rox·in (thī·rok′sin) *n.* **1** A vital hormone, secreted by the thyroid gland, which regulates growth and metabolism. **2** A white, crystalline compound, obtained from the thyroid glands of animals and also made synthetically, used in the treatment of thyroid disorders. Also **thy·rox′ine** (-sēn, -sin).

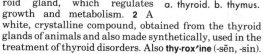

a. thyroid. b. thymus.

thyr·sus (thûr′səs) *n. pl.* **·si** (-sī, -sē) A staff wreathed in ivy and crowned with a pine cone or a bunch of ivy leaves, borne by Dionysus and the satyrs. [< Gk. *thyrsos*]

thy·self (thī·self′) *pron.* Emphatic or reflexive form of *thou:* I love thee for *thyself.*

ti (tē) *n. Music* In solmization, the seventh note of a diatonic scale. [Ital. See GAMUT.]

Ti titanium.

ti·ar·a (tē·âr′ə, -är′ə) *n.* **1** The pope's triple crown. **2** The upright headdress worn by the ancient Persian kings. **3** A jeweled head ornament or coronet worn by women on very formal or state occasions. [Gk., Persian headdress]

Ti·bet·an (ti·bet′n) *adj.* Of or pertaining to Tibet, the Tibetans, or to their language. —*n.* **1** An inhabitant or citizen of Tibet. **2** The language of Tibet.

tib·i·a (tib′ē·ə) *n. pl.* **tib·i·as** or **tib·i·ae** (tib′-ē·ē, -ē·ī) The inner and larger of the two bones of the leg below the knee; the shinbone. —**tib′i·al** *adj.*

tic (tik) *n.* Any involuntary, recurrent muscular spasm. [F]

tick[1] (tik) *n.* **1** A light recurring sound made by a watch, clock, etc. **2** *Informal* The time elapsing between two ticks of a clock; an instant. **3** A mark, as a dot or dash, used in checking off something. —*v.i.* **1** To sound a tick or ticks. —*v.t.* **2** To mark or check with ticks. [Prob. imit.]

tick[2] (tik) *n.* **1** Any of numerous small, bloodsucking arachnids, parasitic on warm-blooded animals and often harboring and transmitting pathogenic microorganisms. **2** Any of certain usu. wingless parasitic insects. [< OE *ticia*]

tick[3] (tik) *n.* **1** The stout outer covering of a mattress; also, the material for such covering. **2** *Informal* Ticking. [< Gk. *thēke* a case]

tick[4] (tik) *n. Brit. Informal* Credit; trust: to buy merchandise on *tick.* [Short for TICK-ET]

tick·er (tik′ər) *n.* **1** One who or that which ticks. **2** Formerly, a telegraphic instrument that printed stock quotations on paper ribbon (**ticker tape**). **3** *Slang* The heart.

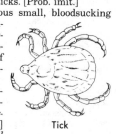

Tick

Tibia

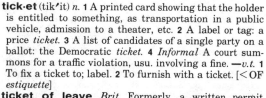

tick·et (tik′it) *n.* **1** A printed card showing that the holder is entitled to something, as transportation in a public vehicle, admission to a theater, etc. **2** A label or tag: a price *ticket.* **3** A list of candidates of a single party on a ballot: the Democratic *ticket.* **4** *Informal* A court summons for a traffic violation, usu. involving a fine. —*v.t.* **1** To fix a ticket to; label. **2** To furnish with a ticket. [< OF *estiquette*]

ticket of leave *Brit.* Formerly, a written permit granted to a convict to be at large before the expiration of his sentence.

tick·ing (tik′ing) *n.* A strong, closely woven cotton or linen fabric, used for mattress covering, awnings, etc. [< TICK[3]]

tick·le (tik′əl) *v.* **·led, ·ling** *v.t.* **1** To excite the nerves of by touching or scratching on some sensitive spot, producing a sensation resulting in spasmodic laughter or twitching. **2** To please: Compliments *tickle* our vanity. **3** To amuse or entertain; delight. **4** To move, stir, or get by tickling. —*v.i.* **5** To have a tingling sensation: My foot *tickles.* **6** To be ticklish. —*n.* **1** The sensation produced by tickling. **2** The touch or action producing such sensation. [ME *tikelen*]

tick·ler (tik′lər) *n.* **1** One who or that which tickles. **2** A memorandum book or file used as a reminder to attend to matters on certain dates in the future.

tick·lish (tik′lish) *adj.* **1** Sensitive to tickling. **2** Liable to be upset. **3** Easily offended; sensitive. **4** Requiring tact in handling; delicate: a *ticklish* situation. —**tick′lish·ly** *adv.* —**tick′lish·ness** *n.*

tick-tock (tik′tok′) *n.* The oscillating sound of a clock. —*v.i.* To make this sound. [Imit.]

tick·y tack·y (tik′ē tak′e) *Slang* **1** Shoddy, inferior materials; rows of little houses built of *ticky tacky.* **2** Dull, tedious uniformity. —**tick′y-tack′y** *adj.*

tid·al (tīd′l) *adj.* **1** Of, pertaining to, or influenced by the tides. **2** Dependent on the tide.

tidal wave **1** A great incoming rise of waters along a shore, caused by heavy winds and very high tides. **2** TSUNAMI. **3** A great upsurge, as of popular sentiment.

tid·bit (tid′bit′) *n.* A choice bit, as of food. [< dial. E *tid* a small object + BIT[1]]

tide (tīd) *n.* **1** The periodic rise and fall of the surface of the ocean caused by the gravitational attraction of moon and sun. **2** Anything that comes like the tide at flood. **3** The natural drift or tendency of events. **4** A current; stream: the *tide* of public feeling. **5** Season; time: *Easter-tide.* —**turn the tide** To reverse a condition completely. —*v.i.* **tid·ed, tid·ing** To ebb and flow like the tide. —**tide over** **1** To give or act as temporary help, as in a difficulty. **2** To surmount. [< OE *tīd* a period, season]

tide·land (tīd′land′) *n.* **1** Land alternately covered and uncovered by the tide. **2** *Often pl.* Offshore land lying completely under the ocean, but within the limits of a nation's territorial waters.

tide·wa·ter (tīd′wô′tər, -wot′ər) *n.* **1** Water affected by the tide on the seacoast or in a river. **2** A region in which water is affected by the tide. —*adj.* Pertaining to or along a tidewater.

ti·dings (tī′dingz) *n.pl. (sometimes construed as sing.)* Information; news. [< OE *tīdung*]

ti·dy (tī′dē) *adj.* **·di·er, ·di·est** **1** Neat in appearance; orderly: a *tidy* desk. **2** Keeping things in order: a *tidy* housekeeper. **3** *Informal* Moderately large: a *tidy* sum. **4** *Informal* Fairly good. —*v.t. & v.i.* **ti·died, ti·dy·ing** To put (things) in order. —*n. pl.* **·dies** An antimacassar. [< OE *tīd* time] —**ti′di·ly** *adv.* —**ti′di·ness** *n.* —**Syn.** *adj.* **1** shipshape, spruce, trim, well-kept.

tie (tī) *v.* **tied, ty·ing** *v.t.* **1** To fasten with cord, rope, etc., the ends of which are then knotted. **2** To draw the parts of together by a cord fastened with a knot: to *tie* one's shoes. **3** To form (a knot). **4** To form a knot in, as string. **5** To fasten, or join in any way. **6** To restrict; bind. **7 a** To equal (a competitor) in score or achievement. **b** To equal (a competitor's score). **8** *Informal* To unite in marriage. **9** *Music* To unite by a tie. —*v.i.* **10** To make a tie or connection. **11** To make the same score; be equal. —**tie down** To hinder;

restrict. **—tie up 1** To fasten with rope, string, etc. **2** To wrap, as with paper, and fasten with string, cord, etc. **3** To moor (a vessel). **4** To block; hinder. **5** To be previously committed, so as to be unavailable: His money is *tied up* in real estate. **—n. 1** A flexible bond or fastening secured by drawing the ends into a knot or loop. **2** Any bond or obligation. **3** In a contest, a draw; also, the point at which this occurs. **4** Something that is tied or intended for tying, as a shoelace, necktie, etc. **5** *Engin.* A structural member fastening parts together. **6** *Music* A curved line joining two notes of the same pitch to make them represent one tone. **7** One of a set of timbers laid crosswise on the ground as supports for railroad tracks. **8** *pl.* Low shoes with laces. [< OE *tīgan* bind] **—ti′er** *n.*

tie-dye (tī′dī′) *v.t.* **-dyed, -dye-ing** To create designs on fabric by tying parts of it in clumps that will not absorb the dye. **—n. 1** The process of decorating fabrics by tie-dyeing. **2** Fabric so decorated; also, a design so made.

tie-in (tī′in′) *n.* Something that connects or associates.

tier (tir) *n.* A rank or row in a series of things placed one above another. **—v.t. & v.i.** To place or rise in tiers. [< OF, a sequence]

tierce (tirs) *n.* **1** Formerly, a third of anything. **2** The third canonical hour. [< OF, a third < L *tertius*]

tie-up (tī′up′) *n.* **1** A temporary stoppage of services, operations, progress of traffic, etc. **2** *Informal* Connection; linkage.

tiff (tif) *n.* A slight quarrel; a spat. **—v.i.** To be in or have a tiff. [?]

tif-fin (tif′ən) *Brit. n.* Midday luncheon. **—v.i.** To lunch. [< Anglo-Indian *tiffing* drinking]

ti-ger (tī′gər) *n.* **1** A large carnivorous feline of Asia, with black stripes on a tawny body. **2** A fiercely determined, spirited, or energetic person or quality. [< Gk. *tigris*] **—ti′gress** *n. Fem.* **—ti′ger-ish, ti′grish** *adj.*

tiger beetle Any of certain active, usu. striped or spotted beetles having larvae that feed on other insects.

ti-ger-eye (tī′gər-ī′) *n.* A semiprecious stone, usu. shimmering yellow and brown. Also **ti′ger's-eye′.**

tiger lily Any of various lilies having orange flowers with recurved petals spotted with black. • See LILY.

tiger moth A stout-bodied moth with striped or spotted wings.

tight (tīt) *adj.* **1** Impervious to fluids; not leaky: often used in combination: *watertight.* **2** Firmly fixed or fastened in place; secure. **3** Fully stretched; taut: *tight* as a drum. **4** Strict; stringent: a *tight* schedule. **5** Fitting closely; esp. too closely: *tight* shoes. **6** *Informal* Difficult to cope with; troublesome: a *tight* spot. **7** *Informal* Stingy. **8** *Slang* Intoxicated. **9** Evenly matched: said of a race or contest. **10** Difficult to obtain because of scarcity or financial restrictions: said of money or of commodities. **—adv. 1** Firmly; securely: Hold on *tight.* **2** With much constriction: The dress fits too *tight.* **—sit tight** To remain firm in one's position or opinion. [?< ON *thēttr* dense] **—tight′ly** *adv.* **—tight′ness** *n.*

tight-en (tīt′n) *v.t. & v.i.* To make or become tight or tighter. **—tight′en-er** *n.*

tight-fist-ed (tīt′fis′tid) *adj.* Stingy.

tight-lipped (tīt′lipt′) *adj.* **1** Having the lips held tightly together. **2** Reticent; uncommunicative.

tight-rope (tīt′rōp′) *n.* A tightly stretched rope on which acrobats perform. **—adj.** Pertaining to or performing on a tightrope.

tights (tīts) *n.pl.* A close-fitting garment for the lower torso and legs, worn by dancers, acrobats, etc.

tight-wad (tīt′wod′) *n. Slang* A miser.

tike (tīk) *n.* TYKE.

til-bur-y (til′ber-ē) *n. pl.* **-bur-ies** A light, two-wheeled carriage seating two persons. [< *Tilbury,* 19th-c. London coachmaker]

til-de (til′də, -dē) *n.* A sign (˜) used in Spanish over *n* to indicate the sound of *ny,* as in *cañon,* canyon. [Sp.< L *titulus* superscription, title]

tile (tīl) *n.* **1** A thin piece of baked clay, stone, etc., used for covering roofs, floors, etc., and as an ornament. **2** A thin piece of linoleum, plastic, cork, etc., for covering walls and floors. **3** A short earthenware pipe, as used in forming sewers. **4** Tiles collectively; tiling. **5** Any of the pieces in

the game of mah jong. **—v.t. tiled, til-ing** To cover with tiles. [< L *tegula* < *tegere* to cover] **—til′er** *n.*

til-ing (tī′ling) *n.* **1** The work of one who covers with tiles. **2** Tiles collectively. **3** Something made of or faced with tiles.

till[1] (til) *v.t. & v.i.* To put and keep (soil) in order for the production of crops, as by plowing, hoeing, etc.; cultivate. [< OE *tilian* strive, cultivate] **—till′er** *n.*

till[2] (til) *prep & conj.* UNTIL. [< OE *til*] • *Till* and *until* have exactly the same meaning and may usu. be used interchangeably. However, *until* is the preferred form at the beginning of a sentence: *Until today, the weather has been bad; It won't be long till winter.*

till[3] (til) *n.* **1** A money drawer behind the counter of a store. **2** The money in such a drawer; also, available cash. **3** Formerly, a drawer for holding valuables. [ME *tillen*]

till-age (til′ij) *n.* **1** The cultivation of land. **2** The state of being tilled. **3** Land that has been tilled. **4** Crops growing on such land. [< TILL[1] + -AGE]

till-er (til′ər) *n.* **1** A lever to turn a rudder. **2** A means of guidance. [< Med. L *telarium* a weaver's beam]

tilt (tilt) *v.t.* **1** To cause to rise at one end or side; slant. **2** To aim or thrust, as a lance. **3** To charge or overthrow in a tilt or joust. **—v.i. 4** To incline at an angle; lean. **5** To contend with the lance; joust. **6** To argue; debate. **—n. 1** A slant or slope. **2** The act of tilting something. **3** A medieval sport in which mounted knights, charging with lances, endeavored to unseat each other. **4** A quarrel or dispute. **5** *Can.* In certain provinces, a seesaw. **—at full tilt** At full speed. [ME *tylten* be overthrown, totter] **—tilt′er** *n.*

tilth (tilth) *n.* **1** The act of tilling; cultivation. **2** Cultivated land.

tim-bal (tim′bəl) *n.* A kettledrum. [< Ar. *aṭ ṭabl* the drum]

tim-bale (tim′bəl, *Fr.* taṅ-bál′) *n.* **1** A dish made of chicken, fish, cheese, or vegetables, mixed with eggs, sweet cream, etc., cooked in a drum-shaped mold. **2** A small cup made of fried pastry, in which food may be served. [F, timbal]

tim-ber (tim′bər) *n.* **1** Wood suitable for building or constructing things. **2** Growing or standing trees; forests. **3** A single piece of squared wood prepared for use or already in use. **4** Any principal beam in a ship. **—v.t.** To provide or shore with timber. [< OE] **—tim′ber-er** *n.*

timber hitch A knot by which a rope is fastened around a spar, post, etc.

tim-ber-land (tim′bər-land′) *n.* Land covered with forests.

timber line The boundary of tree growth on mountains and in arctic regions; the line above which no trees grow. **—tim′ber-line′** (-līn′) *adj.*

timber wolf The large gray wolf of northern forest areas. • See WOLF.

tim-bre (tam′bər, tim′-; *Fr.* taṅ′br′) *n.* The distinctive quality of sound, produced chiefly by overtones, that characterizes or identifies a singing voice, a musical instrument, or a voiced speech sound. [F < L *tympanum* a kettledrum]

tim-brel (tim′brəl) *n.* An ancient Hebrew instrument resembling a tambourine. [< OF *timbre,* a small bell]

time (tīm) *n.* **1** The general idea, relation, or fact of continuous or successive existence; the past, present, and future. **2** A definite moment, hour, period, etc.: The *time* is 3:30. **3** Epoch; era: the *time* of the Vikings. **4** The portion of duration allotted to some specific happening, condition, etc. **5** Leisure: He has no *time* to play golf. **6** Experience on a specific occasion: to have a good *time.* **7** A point in duration; occasion: Your *time* has come! **8** A period considered as having some quality of its own: *Times* are hard. **9** A system of reckoning or measuring duration: daylight-saving *time.* **10** A case of recurrence or repetition: three *times* a day. **11** *Music* The division of a musical composition into measures; meter. **12** Period during which work has been or remains to be done; also, the amount of pay due one: *time* and a half for overtime. **13** Rate of movement, as in dancing, marching, etc.; tempo. **14** Fit or proper occasion: This is no *time* to quibble. **—against time** As quickly as possible so as to finish within the allotted time. **—at the same time 1** At the same moment. **2**

Despite that; nevertheless. —**at times** Now and then. —**behind the times** Out-of-date; passé. —**for the time being** For the present time. —**from time to time** Now and then; occasionally. —**in good time** 1 Soon. 2 At the right time. —**in time** 1 While time permits or lasts. 2 Ultimately. —**keep time** 1 To indicate time correctly, as a clock. 2 To make regular or rhythmic movements in unison with another or others. 3 To render a musical composition in proper time or rhythm. 4 To make a record of the number of hours worked by an employee. —**on time** 1 Promptly. 2 Paid for, or to be paid for, later or in installments. —**time after time** Again and again. —*adj.* 1 Of or pertaining to time. 2 Devised so as to operate, explode, etc., at a specified time: a *time* bomb, *time* lock. 3 Payable at, or to be paid for at, a future date. —*v.t.* **timed, tim·ing** 1 To record the speed or duration of: to *time* a race. 2 To cause to correspond in time: They *timed* their steps to the music. 3 To arrange the time or occasion for: He *timed* his arrival for five o'clock. 4 To mark the rhythm or measure of. [<OE *tīma*]

time·card (tīm′kärd′) *n.* A card for recording the arrival and departure times of an employee.

time clock A clock equipped to record times of arrival and departure of employees.

time exposure A long film exposure made by two separate manual operations of the shutter.

time-hon·ored (tīm′on′ərd) *adj.* Honored or accepted because of long-established usage or custom.

time·keep·er (tīm′kē′pər) *n.* 1 One who or that which keeps time. 2 TIMEPIECE.

time·less (tīm′lis) *adj.* 1 Eternal; unending. 2 Not assigned or limited to any special time, era, or epoch. —**time′less·ly** *adv.* —**time′less·ness** *n.*

time·ly (tīm′lē) *adj.* **·li·er, ·li·est** Being or occurring in good or proper time. —**time′li·ness** *n.* —**Syn.** convenient, fitting, opportune, suitable.

time·piece (tīm′pēs′) *n.* A clock or watch.

tim·er (tī′mər) *n.* 1 A timekeeper. 2 A stopwatch. 3 A device similar to a stopwatch for timing various processes: a kitchen *timer.* 4 A device that begins operations in sequence or after measured intervals of time.

times (tīmz) *prep.* Multiplied by: four *times* two is eight.

time·serv·ing (tīm′sûr′ving) *adj.* Conducting oneself so as to conform to the demands and opinions of the times and of those in power, usu. for personal advantage. —*n.* The actions of a timeserving person. —**time′serv′er** *n.*

time-shar·ing (tīm′shâr′ing) *n.* The simultaneous use of a single large computer by many people at once, by means of individual terminals.

time signature A sign, usu. two numerals placed one above the other on a musical staff, to indicate meter.

time·ta·ble (tīm′tā′bəl) *n.* A schedule showing the times at which trains, boats, airplanes, buses, etc., arrive and depart.

time-worn (tīm′wôrn, -worn′) *adj.* Made worn and ineffective by long existence or use.

time zone One of the 24 established divisions or sectors into which the earth is divided for convenience in reckoning time: each sector represents 15 degrees of longitude, or a time interval of 1 hour.

tim·id (tim′id) *adj.* 1 Easily frightened; fearful. 2 Lacking self-confidence. [<L *timere* to fear] —**ti·mid·i·ty** (ti·mid′ə·tē), **tim′id·ness** *n.* —**tim′id·ly** *adv.* —**Syn.** 2 retiring, shrinking, shy, timorous.

tim·ing (tī′ming) *n.* The art or act of regulating the speed at which something is performed to secure maximum effects.

tim·or·ous (tim′ər·əs) *adj.* Fearful and anxious; timid. [<L *timor* fear] —**tim′or·ous·ly** *adv.* —**tim′or·ous·ness** *n.*

tim·o·thy (tim′ə·thē) *n.* A perennial fodder grass having its flowers in a dense cylindrical spike. Also **timothy grass.** [<*Timothy* Hanson, who took the seed from New York to the Carolinas about 1720]

Tim·o·thy (tim′ə·thē) A convert and companion of the apostle Paul. —*n.* Either of two epistles in the New Testament, written to Timothy by Paul.

tim·pa·ni (tim′pə·nē) *n. pl. (construed as sing. or pl.)* Kettledrums. [<Ital., pl. of *timpano* a kettledrum <L *tympanum* a drum] —**tim′pa·nist** *n.*

tin (tin) *n.* 1 A soft, silvery white, corrosion-resistant metallic element (symbol Sn) usu. found combined with oxygen; used in making alloys. 2 Tin plate. 3 *Chiefly Brit.* A can, as of preserved food. —*v.t.* **tinned, tin·ning** 1 To coat or cover with tin, solder, or tin plate. 2 *Chiefly Brit.* To pack or preserve (food) in cans. —*adj.* Made of tin. [<OE]

tinc·ture (tingk′chər) *n.* 1 A medicinal solution, usu. in alcohol. 2 A tinge of color; tint. 3 A slight trace. [<L *tinctura* a dyeing]

tin·der (tin′dər) *n.* Any dry, readily combustible substance that will ignite on contact with a spark. [<OE *tynder*] —**tin′der·y** *adj.*

tin·der·box (tin′dər·boks′) *n.* 1 A box containing tinder, flint, and steel for starting a fire. 2 A highly flammable mass of material. 3 An excitable, temperamental person.

tine (tīn) *n.* A spike or prong, as of a fork or of an antler. [<OE *tind*] —**tined** *adj.*

tin·foil (tin′foil′) *n.* 1 Tin or an alloy of tin made into very thin sheets. 2 A similar sheeting made of rolled aluminum, commonly used as wrapping material.

ting (ting) *n.* A high metallic sound, as of a small bell.

tinge (tinj) *v.t.* **tinged, tinge·ing** or **ting·ing** 1 To imbue with a faint trace of color. 2 To impart a slight trace of a quality to. —*n.* 1 A faint trace of added color. 2 A slight trace, as of a quality. [<L *tingere* to dye] —**Syn.** *n.* 1, 2 dash, hint, soupçon, tincture, touch.

tin·gle (ting′gəl) *v.* **·gled, ·gling** *v.i.* 1 To experience a prickly, stringing sensation. 2 To cause such a sensation. 3 To jingle; tinkle. —*v.t.* 4 To cause to tingle. —*n.* 1 A prickly, stinging sensation. 2 A jingle or tinkling. [Appar. var. of TINKLE] —**tin′gler** *n.* —**tin′gly** *adj.*

tin·horn (tin′hôrn′) *adj. Slang* Cheap, vulgar, and pretentious: a *tinhorn* politician. [With ref. to the fine appearance but poor sound of a tin horn]

tink·er (tingk′ər) *n.* 1 A mender of pots and pans, etc. 2 A clumsy workman; a botcher. 3 Work done hastily and carelessly. —*v.i.* 1 To work as a tinker. 2 To work in a clumsy, makeshift fashion. 3 To potter; fuss. —*v.t.* 4 To mend as a tinker. 5 To repair clumsily or inexpertly. [Var. of earlier *tinekere* a worker in tin]

tinker's damn *Slang* Any useless or worthless thing: usu. in the phrase **not worth a tinker's damn.** Also **tinker's dam.** [<TINKER + DAMN; with ref. to the reputed profanity of tinkers]

tin·kle (ting′kəl) *v.* **·kled, ·kling** *v.i.* 1 To produce slight, sharp, metallic sounds, as a small bell. —*v.t.* 2 To cause to tinkle. 3 To summon or signal by a tinkling. —*n.* A sharp, clear, tinkling sound. [Imit.] —**tin′kly** (**·kli·er, ·kli·est**) *adj.*

tin·ner (tin′ər) *n.* 1 A miner employed in tin mines. 2 A tinsmith.

tin·ni·tus (ti·nī′təs) *n.* A ringing, buzzing, or clicking sound in the ears, not caused by external stimuli. [<L *tinnire* to ring]

tin·ny (tin′ē) *adj.* **·ni·er, ·ni·est** 1 Made of or containing tin. 2 Like tin in cheapness and brightness. 3 Having a thin, flat sound like that of tin being struck. —**tin′ni·ly** *adv.* —**tin′ni·ness** *n.*

Tin Pan Alley 1 A section of a city, esp. New York, frequented by musicians, song writers, and publishers of popular music. 2 The musicians, writers, publishers, etc., of popular music.

tin plate Sheet iron or steel plated with tin. —**tin′-plate′** (**-plat·ed, -plat·ing**) *v.t.* —**tin′-plat′er** *n.*

tin·sel (tin′səl) *n.* 1 Very thin glittering bits of metal or plastic used for display and ornament. 2 Anything sparkling and showy, but with little real worth. —*adj.* 1 Made or covered with tinsel. 2 Like tinsel; superficially brilliant. —*v.t.* **·seled** or **·selled, ·sel·ing** or **·sel·ling** 1 To adorn or decorate with or as with tinsel. 2 To give a false attractiveness to. [<L *scintilla* a spark]

tin·smith (tin′smith′) *n.* One who works with tin or tin plate.

---

add, āce, dâre, pälm; end, ēven; it, īce; odd, ōpen, ôrder; tŏŏk, pōōl; up; bûrn; ə = a in *above*, u in *focus*; yōō = u in *fuse*; oil; pout; check; go; ring; thin; **th**is; zh, *vision.* < derived from; ? origin uncertain or unknown.

tint (tint) *n.* **1** A variety of color; tinge: red with a blue *tint*. **2** A gradation of a color made by dilution with white. **3** A pale or delicate color. **4** In engraving, uniform shading produced by parallel lines or hatching. —*v.t.* To give a tint to. [< L *tinctus* a dyeing] —**tint′er** *n.*

tin·tin·nab·u·la·tion (tin′ti·nab′yə·lā′shən) *n.* The pealing, tinkling, or ringing of bells. [< L *tintinnare* to ring]

tin·type (tin′tīp′) *n.* An old type of photograph taken on a sensitized plate of enameled tin or iron.

tin·ware (tin′wâr′) *n.* Articles made of tin plate.

ti·ny (tī′nē) *adj.* **·ni·er**, **·ni·est** Very small; minute. [< obs. *tine* a small amount, bit] —**ti′ni·ness** *n.*

-tion *suffix of nouns* **1** Action or process of: *rejection*. **2** Condition or state of being: *completion*. **3** Result of: *connection*. [< L *-tio, -tionis*]

tip[1] (tip) *n.* A slanting position; a tilt. —*v.* **tipped**, **tip·ping** *v.t.* **1** To cause to lean; tilt. **2** To put at an angle: to *tip* one's hat. **3** To overturn or upset: often with *over*. —*v.i.* **4** To become tilted; slant. **5** To overturn; topple: with *over*. [ME *tipen* overturn] —**tip′per** *n.*

tip[2] (tip) *v.t.* **tipped**, **tip·ping** **1** To strike lightly; tap. **2** In baseball, to strike (the ball) a light, glancing blow. —*n.* A tap; light blow. [Prob. < LG *tippe*]

tip[3] (tip) *n.* **1** A small gift of money for services rendered. **2** A helpful hint. **3** A piece of confidential information: a *tip* on a horse race. —*v.* **tipped**, **tip·ping** *v.t.* **1** To give a small gratuity to. **2** *Informal* To give secret information to, as in betting, etc. —*v.i.* **3** To give gratuities. —**tip off** *Informal* **1** To give secret information to. **2** To warn. [? < TIP[2]] —**tip′per** *n.*

tip[4] (tip) *n.* **1** The point or extremity of anything tapering: the *tip* of the tongue. **2** A piece made to form the end of something, as a nozzle, ferrule, etc. **3** The uppermost part; top: the *tip* of a flagpole. —*v.t.* **tipped**, **tip·ping** **1** To furnish with a tip. **2** To form the tip of. **3** To cover or adorn the tip of. [Prob. < MDu., a point]

tip-off (tip′ôf′, -of′) *n. Informal* A hint or warning, usu. given confidentially.

tip·pet (tip′it) *n.* **1** Formerly, a long hanging strip of cloth attached to the sleeve or hood. **2** A covering, usu. of fur, velvet, etc., for the neck and shoulders, hanging well down in front. [Prob. dim. of TIP[4]]

tip·ple (tip′əl) *v.t. & v.i.* **·pled**, **·pling** To drink (alcoholic beverages) frequently and habitually. —*n.* Liquor consumed in tippling. [< earlier *tipler* bartender]

tip·ster (tip′stər) *n. Informal* One who sells tips for betting, as on a race.

tip·sy (tip′sē) *adj.* **·si·er**, **·si·est** **1** Mildly intoxicated. **2** Shaky; unsteady. [< TIP[1]] —**tip′si·ly** *adv.* —**tip′si·ness** *n.*

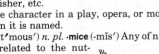

Tippet *def. 1*

tip·toe (tip′tō′, -tō′) *n.* The tip of a toe, or the tips of all the toes. —**on tiptoe 1** On one's tiptoes. **2** Expectantly; eagerly. **3** Stealthily; quietly. —*v.i.* **·toed**, **·toe·ing** To walk on tiptoe; go stealthily or quietly. —*adv.* On tiptoe.

tip·top (tip′top′) *adj.* **1** At the very top. **2** *Informal* Best of its kind; first-rate. —*n.* The highest point. —**tip′-top′per** *n.*

ti·rade (tī′rād, tī·rād′) *n.* A prolonged declamatory outpouring, as of censure. [< Ital. *tirata* a volley]

tire[1] (tīr) *v.* **tired**, **tir·ing** *v.t.* **1** To reduce the strength of, as by exertion. **2** To reduce the interest or patience of, as with monotony. —*v.i.* **3** To become weary or exhausted. **4** To lose patience, interest, etc. —**tire of** To become bored or impatient with. —**tire out** To weary completely. [< OE *tīorian*] —**Syn.** **1** exhaust, fag, fatigue, wear out, weary.

tire[2] (tīr) *n.* **1** A band or hoop surrounding the rim of a wheel. **2** A tough, flexible tube, usu. of inflated rubber, set around the rims of the wheels of automobiles, bicycles, etc. —*v.t.* **tired**, **tir·ing** To put a tire on. *Brit. sp.* **tyre**. [Prob. < obs. *tire* to attire]

tired (tīrd) *adj.* Weary; fatigued. [Orig. pp. of TIRE[1]] —**tired′ly** *adv.* —**tired′ness** *n.*

tire·less (tīr′lis) *adj.* **1** Not becoming easily fatigued; untiring. **2** Ceaseless; *tireless* zeal. —**tire′less·ly** *adv.* —**tire′less·ness** *n.*

tire·some (tīr′səm) *adj.* Tending to tire, or causing one to tire; tedious. —**tire′some·ly** *adv.* —**tire′some·ness** *n.*

ti·ro (tī′rō) *n.* TYRO.

'tis (tiz) Contraction of *it is*.

tis·sue (tish′ōō) *n.* **1** Any light or gauzy textile fabric. **2** *Biol.* An aggregate of cells and intercellular material having a particular function: nerve *tissue*. **3** A network; chain: a *tissue* of lies. **4** TISSUE PAPER. **5** A disposable square of soft absorbent paper for use as a handkerchief, etc. [< OF *tistre* to weave]

tissue paper Very thin, unsized, translucent paper for wrapping delicate articles, protecting engravings, etc.

tit[1] (tit) *n.* A titmouse, titlark, etc.

tit[2] (tit) *n.* Teat; breast; nipple. [< OE *titt*]

ti·tan (tīt′n) *n.* Any person having gigantic strength or size; a giant. —**ti·tan′ic** *adj.* [< TITAN]

Ti·tan (tīt′n) *n.* *Gk. Myth.* One of a race of giant gods, who were succeeded by the Olympian gods. —**Ti·tan′ic** *adj.*

Ti·ta·ni·a (ti·tā′nē·ə, tī-, -tan′yə) In folklore, the queen of fairyland and wife of Oberon.

ti·ta·ni·um (tī·tā′nē·əm) *n.* A widely distributed lightweight metallic element (symbol Ti) resembling aluminum in appearance, used to make tough, heat-resistant alloys. [< L *Titani* the Titans]

tit·bit (tit′bit′) *n.* TIDBIT.

tit for tat Retaliation in kind; blow for blow. [?]

tithe (tīth) *n.* **1** One tenth. **2** *Usu. pl.* A tax of one tenth part of yearly income arising from lands and from the personal industry of the inhabitants, for the support of the clergy and the church. **3** A small part. **4** Loosely, any tax or levy. —*v.t.* **tithed**, **tith·ing** **1** To give or pay a tithe, or tenth part of. **2** To tax with tithes. [< OE *tēotha, tēogotha* a tenth] —**tith′er** *n.*

ti·tian (tish′ən) *n.* A reddish yellow color much used by Titian, esp. in painting women's hair. —*adj.* Having the color titian. [< *Titian*, Venetian artist, 1477–1576]

tit·il·late (tit′ə·lāt) *v.t.* **·lat·ed**, **·lat·ing** **1** To cause a tickling sensation in. **2** To excite pleasurably. [< L *titillare* to tickle] —**tit′il·lat′er**, **tit′il·la′tion** *n.* —**tit′il·la′tive** *adj.*

tit·i·vate (tit′ə·vāt) *v.t. & v.i.* **·vat·ed**, **·vat·ing** *Informal* To smarten; dress up. Also **tit′ti·vate**. [Earlier *tidivate* ? < TIDY, on analogy with *cultivate*] —**tit′i·va′tion**, **tit′i·va′tor** *n.*

tit·lark (tit′lärk′) *n.* A pipit. [ME *tit* a little thing + LARK]

ti·tle (tīt′l) *n.* **1** The name of a book, play, motion picture, song, etc. **2** A title page, as of a book. **3** A descriptive name; epithet. **4 a** An appellation showing rank, office, profession, station in life, etc. **b** In some countries, a designation of nobility or one conferred for unusual distinction. **5** In some sports, championship: to win the *title*. **6** *Law* **a** The legal right to own property. **b** Legal evidence of such a right. **c** A document setting forth such evidence. —*v.t.* **·tled**, **·tling** To give a name to; entitle. [< L *titulus* a label, inscription]

ti·tled (tīt′ld) *adj.* Having a title, esp. of nobility.

title page A page containing the title of a work, its author, its publisher, etc.

title role The character in a play, opera, or motion picture for whom it is named.

tit·mouse (tit′mous′) *n. pl.* **·mice** (-mīs′) Any of numerous small birds related to the nuthatches. [< ME *tit-* little + *mose* < OE *mase* a titmouse]

ti·trate (tī′trāt) *v.t. & v.i.* **·trat·ed**, **·trat·ing** To analyze (a substance) by titration. [< F *titrer*]

ti·tra·tion (tī·trā′shən, ti-) *n.* Quantitative analysis of a substance in solution by the completion of a specific reaction with a measured volume of a standard solution.

Titmouse

tit·ter (tit′ər) *v.i.* To laugh in a suppressed way. —*n.* The act of tittering. [Imit.] —**tit′ter·er** *n.* —**tit′ter·ing·ly** *adv.* —**Syn.** *v.* chuckle, giggle, snicker, snigger, snort.

tit·tle (tit′l) *n.* **1** The minutest quantity; iota. **2** A very small diacritical mark in writing, as the dot over an *i*, etc. [< L *titulus* title]

tit·tle-tat·tle (tit′l·tat′l) *n.* **1** Trivial talk; gossip. **2** An idle talker. —*v.i.* **·tled, ·tling** To gossip; chatter. [Reduplication of TATTLE]

tit·u·lar (tich′o͞o·lər, tit′yə-) *adj.* **1** Existing in name or title only: a *titular* ruler. **2** Pertaining to a title. **3** Having a title. [< L *titulus* a title] —**tit′u·lar·ly** *adv.*

Ti·tus (tī′təs) A disciple of the apostle Paul. —*n.* The epistle in the New Testament addressed to Titus and attributed to Paul.

tiz·zy (tiz′ē) *n. pl.* **·zies** *Slang* A bewildered or excited state of mind; a dither. [?]

TKO, T.K.O., t.k.o. technical knockout.

Tl thallium.

T.L. trade last.

T/L time loan.

Tm thulium.

TN Tennessee (P.O. abbr.).

Tn thoron.

tn. ton; train.

tng. training.

TNT, T.N.T. trinitrotoluene.

to (to͞o, *unstressed* tə) *prep.* **1** Toward or terminating in: going *to* town. **2** Opposite or near: face *to* face; Hold me *to* your breast. **3** Intending or aiming at: Come *to* my rescue. **4** Resulting in: frozen *to* death. **5** Belonging with; of: the key *to* the barn. **6** In honor of: Drink *to* our victory. **7** In comparison with: 9 is *to* 3 as 21 is *to* 7. **8** Until: five minutes *to* one. **9** For the utmost duration of: a miser *to* the end of his days. **10** Concerning: blind *to* her faults. **11** In close application toward: Get down *to* work. **12** For: The contest is open *to* everyone. **13** Noting action toward: Give the ring *to* me. **14** By: known *to* the world. **15** From the point of view of: It seems *to* me. **16** About; involved in: That's all there is *to* it. **17** On; against: Nail the sign *to* the post. **18** In: four quarts *to* a gallon. **19** Into: The house was reduced *to* ashes. —*adv.* **1** Forward: He wore his sweater back side *to*. **2** In a direction or position, esp. closed: Pull the door *to*. **3** Into a normal condition or consciousness: She soon came *to*. **4** Into action or operation: They fell *to* eagerly. —**to and fro** In opposite or different directions; back and forth. [< OE *tō*] • *To* is also used before a verb to indicate the infinitive: It is good *to* see you; You can go if you want *to* (go).

toad (tōd) *n.* **1** Any of various tailless, jumping, insectivorous amphibians resembling the frog but usu. having a warty skin and resorting to water only to breed. **2** A contemptible or loathsome person. [< OE *tādige*]

toad·fish (tōd′fish′) *n. pl.* **·fish** or **·fish·es** Any of a family of fishes with scaleless skin and a toadlike head.

toad·stool (tōd′sto͞ol′) *n.* An inedible or poisonous mushroom.

Toad

toad·y (tō′dē) *n. pl.* **·ies** An obsequious flatterer; a sycophant. —*v.t. & v.i.* **toad·ied, toad·y·ing** To act the toady (to). [< earlier *toad-eater*, a charlatan's attendant who pretended to eat toads] —**toad′y·ism** *n.*

to-and-fro (to͞o′ən-frō′) *adj.* Moving back and forth or from one position to another. —*adv.* In a to-and-fro motion.

toast¹ (tōst) *v.t.* **1** To brown the outside of (a piece of bread, etc.) by heating in an oven, toaster, etc. **2** To warm thoroughly. —*v.i.* **3** To become warm or toasted. —*n.* Toasted bread. [< L *tostus* < *torrere* parch, roast]

toast² (tōst) *n.* **1** The act of drinking to someone's health or to some thing. **2** The person or thing thus named. —*v.t. & v.i.* To drink a toast or toasts (to). [< TOAST¹, from a custom of flavoring a drink with a spiced piece of toast] —**toast′er** *n.*

toast·er (tōst′ər) *n.* An electrical device for toasting bread.

toast·mas·ter (tōst′mas′tər, -mäs′tər) *n.* A person who, at public dinners, announces the toasts, calls upon the speakers, etc.

Tobacco plant

to·bac·co (tə·bak′ō) *n. pl.* **·cos** or **·coes 1** Any of various plants of the nightshade family, with large sticky leaves and yellow, white, or purple flowers. **2** The leaves of several of these plants, processed for smoking, chewing, etc. **3** The various products prepared from tobacco leaves, as cigarettes, cigars, etc. [< Sp. *tabaco*]

to·bac·co·nist (tə·bak′ə·nist) *n. Brit.* One who deals in tobacco.

To·bit (tō′bit) *n.* A book of the Apocrypha of the Old Testament. Also **To·bi·as** (tō·bī′əs).

to·bog·gan (tə·bog′ən) *n.* A long sledlike vehicle without runners, consisting of thin boards curved upward in front. —*v.i.* **1** To coast on a toboggan. **2** To descend swiftly: Wheat prices *tobogganed*. [< Algon.] —**to·bog′gan·er, to·bog′gan·ist** *n.*

to·by (tō′bē) *n. pl.* **·bies** *Often cap.* A mug or jug for ale or beer, often made in the form of an old man wearing a three-cornered hat. Also **toby jug.** [< *Toby*, dim. of the name *Tobias*]

toc·ca·ta (tə·kä′tə, *Ital.* tôk·kä′tä) *n.* An elaborate composition for piano, organ, etc. often preceding a fugue. [Ital., lit., a touching]

To·char·i·an (tō·kâr′ē·ən, -kär′-) *n.* **1** One of an ancient people who inhabited central Asia in the first Christian millennium. **2** The language of the Tocharians, two dialects of which are known.

to·coph·er·ol (tō·kof′ə·rōl, -rol) *n.* Vitamin E. [< Gk. *tokos* offspring + *pherein* to bear]

toc·sin (tok′sin) *n.* **1** A signal sounded on a bell; alarm. **2** An alarm bell. [< Prov. *tocar* to strike, touch + *senh* a bell]

to·day (tə·dā′) *adv.* **1** On or during this present day. **2** At the present time. —*n.* The present day or age. Also **to·day′.** [< OE *tō* to + *daeg* day]

tod·dle (tod′l) *v.i.* **·dled, ·dling** To walk unsteadily and with short steps, as a little child. —*n.* The act of toddling. —**tod′dler** *n.*

tod·dy (tod′ē) *n. pl.* **·dies 1** A drink made with whiskey, brandy, etc., and hot water and sugar. **2** The fermented sap of certain East Indian palms (**toddy palms**). [< Skt. *tāla* a palm tree]

to-do (tə·do͞o′) *n. Informal* A stir; fuss. —*Syn.* bustle, commotion, confusion, disturbance.

toe (tō) *n.* **1** One of the five digits of the foot. **2** The forward part of the foot. **3** That portion of a shoe, boot, sock, etc., that covers or corresponds to the toes. **4** Anything resembling a toe in contour, function, position, etc. —**on one's toes** Alert. —**tread on (someone's) toes** To trespass on (someone's) feelings, prejudices, etc. —*v.* **toed, toe·ing** *v.t.* **1** To touch or kick with the toes. **2** To furnish with a toe. **3** To drive (a nail or spike) obliquely. **4** To attach by nails driven thus. —*v.i.* **5** To stand or walk with the toes pointing in a specified direction: to *toe* out. —**toe the mark** (or **line**) **1** To touch a certain line with the toes preparatory to starting a race. **2** To conform to a discipline or a standard. [< OE *tā*]

toed (tōd) *adj.* **1** Having (a specified kind or number of) toes: used in combination: *pigeon-toed; three-toed.* **2** Fastened or fastening by obliquely driven nails. **3** Driven in obliquely, as a nail.

toe dance Dancing on the tips of the toes, as in ballet. —**toe′-dance′ (-danced, -danc·ing)** *v.i.* —**toe′-danc′er** *n.*

toe·hold (tō′hōld′) *n.* **1** A climbing, a small space which supports the toes. **2** Any means of entrance, support, or the like; a footing. **3** A hold in which a wrestler bends back the foot of his opponent.

toe·nail (tō′nāl′) *n.* **1** The nail growing on a toe. **2** A nail driven obliquely. —*v.t.* To fasten with obliquely driven nails.

tof·fee (tôf′ē, tof′ē) *n.* TAFFY. Also **tof′fy.**

tog (tog) *Informal n. pl.* Clothes. —*v.t.* **togged, tog·ging** To clothe: often with *up* or *out*. [< L *toga* toga]

to·ga (tō′gə) *n. pl.* **·gas** or **·gae** (-gī) **1** The loose, flowing outer garment worn in public by a citizen of ancient Rome. **2** Any robe characteristic of a calling. [< L < *tegere* to cover] —**to′·gaed** (tō′gəd) *adj.*

to·geth·er (tōō·geth′ər, tə-) *adv.* **1** In company: We were sitting *together*. **2** In or into one group, mass, unit, etc.: They put the jigsaw puzzle *together*. **3** Into contact with each other: Glue these two pieces *together*. **4** Simultaneously: Let's sing it *together*. **5** With one another; mutually: They discussed it *together*. **6** In agreement or harmony: The tie and shirt go well *together*. **7** Considered collectively: He has more courage than all of us *together*. **8** Without cessation: He talked for hours *together*. —**get it all together** *Slang* To achieve a positive outlook on life; free oneself from anxiety. —**together with** Along with. [< OE *tōgædere*]

Roman toga

tog·ger·y (tog′ər·ē) *n. Informal* Clothing; togs.

tog·gle (tog′əl) *n.* **1** A pin, or short rod, properly attached in the middle, as to a rope, and designed to be passed through a hole or eye and turned. **2** A toggle joint. —*v.t.* **·gled, ·gling** To fix, fasten, or furnish with a toggle or toggles. [?]

toggle joint A joint having a central hinge like an elbow, and operable by applying the force at the junction, thus changing the direction of motion.

toggle switch *Electr.* A switch connected to its actuating lever by a toggle joint loaded by a spring.

To·go (tō′gō) *n.* A republic of w Africa, 21,500 sq. mi., cap. Lomé. —**To′go·lese′** (-lēs, -lēz) *adj., n.* • See map at AFRICA.

Toggle joint

toil¹ (toil) *n.* **1** Fatiguing work; labor. **2** Any work accomplished by great labor. —*v.i.* **1** To work strenuously and tiringly. **2** To make one's way laboriously: to *toil* up a hill. —*v.t.* **3** To accomplish with great effort: to *toil* one's way. [< L *tudiculare* stir about] —**toil′er** *n.* —**Syn.** *v.* **1** drudge, labor, slave, travail.

toil² (toil) *n.* **1** *Archaic* A net, snare, or other trap. **2** *pl.* Anything that binds or entraps: the *toils* of remorse. [< L *tela* a web]

toi·let (toi′lit) *n.* **1** A fixture in the shape of a bowl, used for urination and defecation and equipped with a device for flushing and discharging with water. **2** A room containing such a fixture or fixtures. **3** PRIVY. **4** The act or process of bathing, grooming, and dressing oneself. **5** Formerly, a woman's attire or costume: also **toi·lette** (twa·let′). —*adj.* Used in dressing or grooming: *toilet* articles. [< F *toilette* orig. a cloth dressing gown, dim. of *toile* cloth]

toi·let·ry (toi′lit·rē) *n. pl.* **·ries** Soap, powder, cologne, etc., used in bathing and grooming oneself.

toilet water A scented liquid applied after the bath, after shaving, etc.

toil·some (toil′səm) *adj.* Involving hard work; laborious; difficult. —**toil′some·ly** *adv.* —**toil′some·ness** *n.*

toil·worn (toil′wôrn′, -wōrn′) *adj.* Exhausted by toil; showing the effects of toil.

To·kay (tō·kā′) *n.* **1** A large, sweet grape originally from Tokay, Hungary. **2** A wine made from it.

to·ken (tō′kən) *n.* **1** A visible sign; indication: This gift is a *token* of my affection. **2** Some tangible proof or evidence of one's identity, authority, etc. **3** A keepsake; souvenir. **4** A characteristic mark or feature. **5** A piece of metal issued as currency and having a face value greater than its actual value: a bus *token*. —**by the same token** Moreover; furthermore. —**in token of** As a sign or evidence of. —*adj.* **1** Having only the appearance of; nominal; minimal: *token* resistance; *token* integration. **2** Partial or very small: a *token* payment. [< OE *tācen*]

to·ken·ism (tō′kən·iz·əm) *n.* The policy of attempting to meet certain obligations or conditions by partial, symbolic, or token efforts.

To·khar·i·an (tō·kâr′ē·ən, -kär′-) *n.* TOCHARIAN.

told (tōld) *p.t. & p.p.* of TELL.

To·le·do (tə·lē′dō) *n. pl.* **·dos** A sword or sword blade from Toledo, Spain. Also **to·le′do.**

tol·er·a·ble (tol′ər·ə·bəl) *adj.* **1** Endurable; bearable. **2** Fairly good: *tolerable* health. [< L *tolerare* endure] —**tol′·er·a·ble·ness** *n.* —**tol′er·a·bly** *adv.*

tol·er·ance (tol′ər·əns) *n.* **1** The character, state, or quality of being tolerant. **2** Freedom from prejudice; open-mindedness. **3** The act of enduring, or the capacity for endurance. **4** An allowance for variations from specified measure, as of machine parts. **5** *Med.* Ability to withstand large or increasing amounts of a specified substance or stimulus.

tol·er·ant (tol′ər·ənt) *adj.* **1** Of a long-suffering disposition. **2** Indulgent; liberal. **3** *Med.* Resistant to the effects of a specific substance or stimulus. [< L *tolerare* endure] —**tol′er·ant·ly** *adv.*

tol·er·ate (tol′ə·rāt) *v.t.* **·at·ed, ·at·ing 1** To allow without opposition. **2** To concede, as the right to opinions or participation. **3** To bear or be capable of bearing. **4** *Med.* To be tolerant. [< L *tolerare* endure] —**tol′er·a·tive** *adj.* —**tol′·er·a′tion, tol′er·a′tor** *n.* —**Syn.** **1** permit. **3** endure, sustain.

toll¹ (tōl) *n.* **1** A tax or charge for some privilege granted, esp. for passage on a bridge or turnpike. **2** The right to levy such a charge. **3** A charge for a special service, as for a long-distance telephone call. **4** The number or amount lost, as in a disaster: The wreck took a *toll* of nine lives. —*v.t.* **1** To take as a toll. —*v.i.* **2** To exact a toll. [< OE]

toll² (tōl) *v.t.* **1** To sound (a church bell) slowly and at regular intervals. **2** To announce (a death, funeral, etc.) by tolling a church bell. **3** To call or summon by tolling. —*v.i.* **4** To sound slowly and at regular intervals. —*n.* **1** The act of tolling. **2** The sound of a bell rung slowly and regularly. [ME *tollen*] —**toll′er** *n.*

toll bridge A bridge at which toll for passage is paid.

toll call A long-distance telephone call.

toll·gate (tōl′gāt′) *n.* A gate at the entrance to a bridge, or on a road, at which toll is paid.

toll·keep·er (tōl′kē′pər) *n.* One who collects the tolls at a tollgate.

Tol·tec (tol′tek, tōl′-) *n.* Any of certain ancient Nahuatlan tribes that dominated Mexico about 900–1100 before the Aztecs. —*adj.* Of or pertaining to the Toltecs: also **Tol′tec·an.**

tol·u·ene (tol′yōō·ēn) *n.* A hydrocarbon obtained from coal tar, used in making dyes, drugs, and explosives. Also **tol′u·ol** (-yōō·wôl, -wōl).

tom (tom) *n.* **1** The male of various animals, esp. the cat. **2** *Often cap. Slang* UNCLE TOM. —*adj.* Male: a *tom* turkey.

tom·a·hawk (tom′ə·hôk) *n.* An ax used as a tool and as a war weapon by the Algonquian Indians. —*v.t.* To strike or kill with a tomahawk. [< Algon.]

to·ma·to (tə·mā′tō, -mä′-) *n. pl.* **·toes 1** The pulpy edible berry, yellow or red when ripe, of a tropical American plant related to the potato, used as a vegetable. **2** The plant itself. **3** *Slang* An attractive girl or woman. [< Nah. *tomatl*]

tomb (tōōm) *n.* **1** A burial place; grave. **2** A tombstone or monument. —**the tomb** Death. —*v.t.* To entomb; bury. [< Gk. *tymbos* a mound]

North American Indian tomahawks

tom·boy (tom′boi′) *n.* A young girl who behaves like a lively, active boy. [< TOM + BOY] —**tom′boy′ish** *adj.* —**tom′boy′ish·ness** *n.*

tomb·stone (tōōm′stōn′) *n.* A stone, usu. inscribed, marking a place of burial.

tom·cat (tom′kat′) *n.* A male cat. —*v.i.* **·cat·ted, ·cat·ting** *Slang* To engage in sexual relations indiscriminately: said of a man. [< *Tom*, hero of *The Life and Adventures of a Cat*, 1760, a popular anonymous work]

tome (tōm) *n.* A large, heavy book. [< Gk. *tomos* a fragment, volume]

tom·fool (tom′fōōl′) *n.* An idiotic or silly person. —*adj.* Foolish; stupid. [< *Tom Fool,* a name formerly applied to mental defectives]

tom·fool·er·y (tom′fōō′lər·ē) *n. pl.* **·er·ies** Nonsensical behavior; silliness.

tom·my (tom′ē) *n. pl.* **·mies** A British soldier. Also **Tom′. my.** [Short for TOMMY ATKINS]

Tommy At·kins (at′kinz) A British private of the regular army. [< *Thomas Atkins,* a name used on British Army specimen forms]

Tommy gun *Informal* A type of submachine gun. [< J. *Thompson,* d. 1940, U.S. army officer]

to·mor·row (tə-môr′ō, -mor′ō) *adv.* On or for the next day after today. —*n.* The next day after today. Also **to-mor′row.** [< OE *tō* to + *morgen* morning, morrow]

Tom Thumb 1 In English folklore, a hero as big as his father's thumb. 2 Any midget or dwarf.

tom·tit (tom′tit′) *n.* A titmouse or other small bird. [< the name *Tom* + TIT¹]

tom-tom (tom′tom′) *n.* Any of various drums, as of American Indian and African tribes, usu. beaten with the hands. [< Hind. *tamtam,* imit.]

-tomy *combining form* A cutting of a (specified) part or tissue: *lobotomy.* [< Gk. *tomē* a cutting]

ton (tun) *n.* 1 Any of several measures of weight; esp. the **short ton** of 2000 pounds avoirdupois; the **long ton** of 2240 pounds; or the **metric ton** of 1000 kilograms. 2 A unit for reckoning the displacement of vessels, equal to 35 cubic feet, or about one long ton of sea water: called **displacement ton.** 3 A unit for reckoning the freight capacity of a ship, usu. equivalent to 40 cubic feet of space: called **freight ton, measurement ton.** 4 A unit for reckoning the capacity of merchant vessels for purposes of registration, equivalent to 100 cubic feet or 2.832 cubic meters: called **register ton.** 5 *Informal* Any large amount, weight, etc. [Var. of TUN]

to·nal (tō′nəl) *adj.* 1 Of or pertaining to tone or tonality. 2 Having a keynote or tonic. —**to′nal·ly** *adv.*

to·nal·i·ty (tō-nal′ə-tē) *n. pl.* **·ties** 1 The existence of a keynote or tonic in music; also a key or mode. 2 The general color scheme or collective tones of a painting.

tone (tōn) *n.* 1 A vocal or musical sound; also, the quality of such a sound. 2 *Music* **a** A sound having a definite pitch, loudness, and timbre. **b** WHOLE STEP. 3 A predominating disposition; mood. 4 Characteristic tendency; quality: a want of moral *tone.* 5 Style or elegance: The party had *tone.* 6 Vocal inflection: a *tone* of pity. 7 The acoustical pitch, or change in pitch, of a phrase or sentence: A question is indicated by a rising *tone.* 8 The effect of light, shade, and color as combined in a picture. 9 A shade of a particular color: a deep *tone* of yellow. 10 Tonicity. —*v.* **toned, ton·ing** *v.t.* 1 To give tone to; modify in tone. 2 IN-TONE. —*v.i.* 3 To assume a certain tone or hue. 4 To blend or harmonize, as in tone or shade. —**tone down** 1 To subdue the tone of. 2 To moderate in quality or tone. —**tone up** 1 To raise in quality or strength. 2 To elevate in pitch. 3 To gain in vitality. [< Gk. *tonos* a pitch of voice, a stretching] —**ton′er** *n.*

tone·less (tōn′lis) *adj.* Lifeless; flat: a *toneless* voice. —**tone′less·ly** *adv.* —**tone′less·ness** *n.*

tong (tông, tong) *n.* 1 A Chinese association or closed society. 2 In the U.S., a former secret society composed of Chinese. [< Chin. *t'ang* a hall, meeting place]

Ton·ga (tong′gə) *n.* An independent kingdom in the Commonwealth of Nations situated on an archipelago E of Fiji, 270 sq. mi., cap. Nukualofa.

Ton·gan (tong′gən) *n.* 1 One of the Polynesian inhabitants of Tonga. 2 The language of Tonga.

tongs (tôngz, tongz) *n.pl. (sometimes construed as sing.)* An implement for grasping, holding, or lifting objects, consisting usu. of a pair of pivoted levers. Also **pair of tongs.** [< OE *tange*]

tongue (tung) *n.* 1 A muscular organ attached to the floor of the mouth of most vertebrates, important in masticating and tasting food, and in man as an organ of speech. • See MOUTH. 2 A similar organ in various insects, etc. 3 An animal's tongue, as of beef,

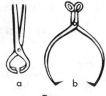

Tongs
a. blacksmith's.
b. ice.

prepared as food. 4 The power of speech: Have you lost your *tongue?* 5 Manner or style of speaking: a smooth *tongue.* 6 Utterance; talk. 7 A language or dialect. 8 Anything resembling a tongue in appearance, shape, or function. 9 A slender projection of land. 10 A long narrow bay or inlet. 11 A jet of flame. 12 A strip of leather for closing the gap in front of a laced shoe. • See SHOE. 13 The free or vibrating end of a reed in a wind instrument. 14 The clapper of a bell. 15 The harnessing pole of a horse-drawn vehicle. 16 The projecting edge of a tongue-and-groove joint. —**hold one's tongue** To keep silent. —**on the tip of one's tongue** On the verge of being remembered or uttered. —**with tongue in cheek** Facetiously, insincerely, or ironically. —*v.* **tongued, tongu·ing** *v.t.* 1 To use the tongue to attack or separate (notes) in playing a wind instrument. 2 To touch or lap with the tongue. 3 In carpentry: **a** To cut a tongue on (a board). **b** To join by a tongue-and-groove joint. —*v.i.* 4 To use the tongue to attack or separate notes in playing a wind instrument. 5 To extend as a tongue. [< OE *tunge*]

tongue-and-groove joint (tung′ən-grōōv′) In carpentry, a joint in which a projecting edge, or tongue, of one board is inserted into a corresponding groove of another board.

tongue-in-cheek (tung′ən-chēk′) *adj.* Said or meant insincerely, ironically, or facetiously.

tongue-tie (tung′tī′) *n.* Abnormal shortness of the membrane under the tongue, whereby its motion is impeded. —*v.t.* **·tied, ·ty·ing** 1 To deprive of speech or the power of speech. 2 To bewilder or amaze so as to render speechless.

Tongue-and-groove joint

tongue twister A word or phrase difficult to articulate quickly: "Miss Smith's fish-sauce shop" is a *tongue-twister.*

ton·ic (ton′ik) *adj.* 1 Having power to invigorate or build up; bracing. 2 Pertaining to tone or tones; in music, of the principal tone of a scale or tonal system. 3 *Physiol.* Of or pertaining to tension, esp. muscular tension. 4 *Pathol.* Rigid; unrelaxing: *tonic* spasm. 5 Of or pertaining to musical intonations or modulations of words, sentences, etc. 6 *Phonet.* Accented or stressed. —*n.* 1 *Med.* A medicine that promotes physical well-being. 2 Whatever imparts vigor or tone. 3 The basic tone of a key or tonal system. [< Gk. *tonos* sound, tone]

to·nic·i·ty (tō-nis′ə-tē) *n.* 1 The state of being tonic; tone. 2 The normal tension of muscle tissue. 3 Health and vigor.

to·night (tə-nīt′) *adv.* In or during the present or coming night. —*n.* The night that follows this day; also, the present night. Also **to-night′.** [< OE *tō* to + *niht* night]

ton·nage (tun′ij) *n.* 1 Weight, as expressed in tons. 2 Capacity, as of a vessel or vessels, expressed in tons. 3 A tax levied at a given rate per ton. [< OF *tonne* a ton, tun]

ton·neau (tu-nō′) *n. pl.* **·neaus** (-nōz′) or **·neaux** (-nōz′) The rear part of an early type of automobile enclosing the seats for passengers. [F, lit., barrel]

ton·sil (ton′səl) *n.* Either of two oval lymphoid organs situated on either side of the passage from the mouth to the pharynx. [< L *tonsillae* tonsils] —**ton′sil·lar, ton′sil·ar** *adj.* • See MOUTH.

ton·sil·lec·to·my (ton′sə-lek′tə-mē) *n. pl.* **·mies** Removal of the tonsils by surgery.

ton·sil·li·tis (ton′sə-lī′tis) *n.* Inflammation of the tonsils. —**ton′sil·lit′ic** (-lit′ik) *adj.*

ton·so·ri·al (ton-sôr′ē-əl, -sō′rē-) *adj.* Pertaining to a barber or to barbering: chiefly humorous. [< L *tonsor* a barber]

ton·sure (ton′shər) *n.* 1 The shaving of the head, or of the crown of the head, as of a priest or monk. 2 That part of a priest's or monk's head left bare by shaving. —*v.t.* **·sured, ·sur·ing** To shave the head of. [< L *tonsura* a shearing]

ton·tine (ton′tēn, ton-tēn′) *n.* A form of collective life annuity, the individual profits of which increase as the number of survivors diminishes, the final survivor taking

the whole. —*adj.* Of or pertaining to such an annuity. [< Lorenzo *Tonti,* a 17th-c. Neapolitan banker]

to·nus (tō′nəs) *n. Physiol.* The slightly contracted state of a muscle at rest. [L, tone]

ton·y (tō′nē) *adj.* **ton·i·er, ton·i·est** *Informal* Aristocratic; fashionable. [< TONE]

too (tōō) *adv.* **1** In addition; also. **2** In excessive quantity or degree: *too* long. **3** Very; extremely: I am *too* happy for you. **4** *Informal* Indeed: an intensive: You are *too* going! [< OE *tō* to]

took (tōōk) *p.t.* of TAKE.

tool (tōōl) *n.* **1** A simple implement, as a hammer, saw, spade, chisel, etc., used in work. **2** A power-driven apparatus used for cutting, shaping, boring, etc. **3** The active part of such an apparatus. **4** *Often pl.* Something necessary to the performance of a profession, vocation, etc.: Paints and brushes are an artist's *tools.* **5** A person used to carry out the designs of another or others, esp. when such designs are unethical or unlawful. —*v.t.* **1** To shape or work with a tool. **2** To provide, as a factory, with machinery and tools. **3** In bookbinding, to ornament or impress designs upon with a tool. —*v.i.* **4** To work with a tool. **5** *Informal* To drive or travel in a vehicle: usu. with *along.* **6** To install, as in a factory, equipment, tools, etc; usu. with *up.* [< OE *tōl*] —**tool′er** *n.* —**Syn.** *n.* **1** appliance, device, instrument, utensil. **5** dupe, stooge.

tool·ing (tōō′ling) *n.* Ornamentation or work done with tools.

toot (tōōt) *v.i.* **1** To blow a horn, whistle, etc., with short blasts. **2** To give forth a short blast. —*v.t.* **3** To sound (a horn, etc.) with short blasts. **4** To sound (a blast, etc.). —*n.* **1** A short blast on a horn, whistle, etc. **2** *Slang* A drinking spree. [? < MLG *tūten*] —**toot′er** *n.*

tooth (tōōth) *n. pl.* **teeth** (tēth) **1** One of the hard, dense

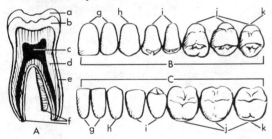

Teeth of human adult

A. cross-section of a molar. B. left upper jaw. C. left lower jaw. A.a. crown. b. enamel. c. pulp cavity. d. dentine. e. cement. f. roots. B. & C. g. incisors. h. canines. i. bicuspids. j. molars. k. wisdom teeth.

structures in the mouth of most vertebrates, used for seizing and chewing food, as offensive and defensive weapons, etc. **2** One of various hard bodies of the oral or gastric regions of invertebrates. **3** Something resembling a tooth in form or use, as a projection on a saw, comb, rake, or gearwheel. **4** Appetite or taste (for something): She has a sweet *tooth.* —**armed to the teeth** Completely or heavily armed. —**in the teeth of** Counter to or in defiance of. —**put teeth into** To make effective: to *put teeth into* a law. —**tooth and nail** With all one's strength and skill. —*v.t.* **1** To supply with teeth, as a rake or saw. **2** To give a serrated edge to; indent. —*v.i.* **3** To become interlocked, as gearwheels. [< OE *tōth*]

tooth·ache (tōōth′āk′) *n.* Pain in a tooth or in the nearby area.

tooth·brush (tōōth′brush′) *n.* A small brush used for cleaning the teeth.

toothed (tōōtht, tōōthd) *adj.* **1** Having (a specified type or number of teeth): used in combination: *sharp-toothed.* **2** Notched; serrated.

tooth·paste (tōōth′pāst′) *n.* A paste applied to a toothbrush and used in cleaning the teeth.

tooth·pick (tōōth′pik′) *n.* A small sliver, as of wood, used for removing particles of food from between the teeth.

tooth·some (tōōth′səm) *adj.* Having a pleasant taste. —**tooth′some·ly** *adv.* —**tooth′some·ness** *n.* —**Syn.** appetizing, delicious, savory, tasty.

too·tle (tōōt′l) *v.i.* **·tled, ·tling 1** To toot lightly or continuously, as on a flute, whistle, etc. —*v.t.* **2** To toot (a flute, whistle, etc.) lightly and continuously. —*n.* The sound of tootling. [Freq. of TOOT]

top[1] (top) *n.* **1** The uppermost or highest part: the *top* of a hill. **2** The higher or upper surface: the *top* of a bureau. **3** A lid or cover: a bottle *top.* **4** The roof of a vehicle, as an automobile. **5** The crown of the head. **6** *pl.* The above-ground part of a root vegetable. **7** The highest degree or reach: at the *top* of one's voice. **8** The most prominent place or rank: at the *top* of one's profession. **9** One who is highest in rank: the *top* of one's class. **10** The choicest or best part: the *top* of the crop. **11** The upper part of a shoe or boot. —**blow one's top** *Slang* To break out in a rage. —**from top to toe 1** From head to foot. **2** Completely. —**on top 1** Successful. **2** With success; victoriously. —**over the top** Over the upper edge of a trench so as to attack. —*adj.* **1** Of or pertaining to the top. **2** Forming or comprising the top. **3** Most important; chief: *top* authors. **4** Greatest in amount or degree: *top* prices; *top* speed. —*v.* **topped, top·ping** *v.t.* **1** To remove the top of; prune: to *top* a tree. **2** To provide with a top, cap, etc. **3** To form the top of. **4** To reach the top of; surmount: to *top* a wave. **5** To surpass or exceed: Can you *top* this? **6** In golf, tennis, etc., to hit the upper part of (the ball) in making a stroke. —*v.i.* **7** To top someone or something. —**top off** To complete, esp. with a finishing touch. [< OE]

top[2] (top) *n.* A toy of wood, plastic, metal, etc., with a point on which it is made to spin, as by the unwinding of a string. [< OE]

to·paz (tō′paz) *n.* **1** A yellow or brownish yellow crystalline mineral, valued as a gemstone. **2** A yellow sapphire. **3** A yellow variety of quartz resembling topaz. [< Gk. *topazos*]

top boot A boot with a high top, sometimes ornamented with materials different from the rest of the boot. —**top′-boot′ed** *adj.*

top·coat (top′kōt′) *n.* A lightweight overcoat.

top-drawer (top′drôr′) *adj. Informal* Of the highest quality, rank, or status.

top·flight (top′flīt′) *adj. Informal* Of the highest quality; outstanding; superior.

top·gal·lant (top′gal′ənt, tə·gal′ənt) *Naut. n.* The mast, sail, yard, or rigging immediately above the topmast and topsail. —*adj.* Pertaining to the topgallants.

top hat A man's formal hat, usu. black and made of silk, having a tall, cylindrical crown.

top·heav·y (top′hev′ē) *adj.* **·heav·i·er, ·heav·i·est 1** Too heavy at the top and liable to topple: a *topheavy* bookcase. **2** Having too many in positions of high rank, as an organization. —**top′heav′i·ly** *adv.* —**top′heav′i·ness** *n.*

top·ic (top′ik) *n.* **1** A subject treated of in speech or writing. **2** A theme for discussion. **3** A subdivision of an outline or a treatise. [< L *Topica,* title of a work by Aristotle] —**Syn.** **1** issue, matter, point, question.

top·i·cal (top′i·kəl) *adj.* **1** Of or belonging to a place or spot; local. **2** Of or relating to matters of present or local interest; limited in relevance to a time or place. **3** Of or pertaining to a topic. **4** *Med.* Pertaining to a restricted area of the body. —**top′i·cal·ly** *adv.*

top kick *Slang* A top sergeant.

top·knot (top′not′) *n.* **1** A tuft or knot of hair or feathers on the top of the head. **2** A bow or other ornament worn as a headdress.

top·less (top′lis) *adj.* **1** Lacking a top. **2** Nude from the waist up. **3** Being without a covering for the breasts. **4** Presenting topless waitresses, dancers, etc., as a bar. **5** So high that no top can be seen. —**top′less·ness** *n.*

top-lev·el (top′lev′əl) *adj.* Of the highest rank or importance.

top-loft·y (top′lôf′tē) *adj.* **·i·er, ·i·est** Very proud or haughty. —**top′-loft′i·ness** *n.*

top·mast (top′mast′, -məst) *n. Naut.* The mast next above the lower mast.

top·most (top′mōst′) *adj.* Being at the very top.

top·notch (top′noch′) *adj. Informal* Best or highest, as in quality, merit, or performance. —**top′-notch′er** *n.*

to·pog·ra·phy (tə·pog′rə·fē) *n. pl.* **·phies 1** The art of representing on a map or chart the physical features of

a place, as mountains, lakes, canals, usu. with indications of elevation. 2 The physical features of a region. 3 Topographic surveying. [< Gk. *topos* place + -GRAPHY] —**to·pog′ra·pher** *n.* —**top·o·graph·ic** (top′ə·graf′ik) or ·**i·cal** *adj.* —**top′o·graph′i·cal·ly** *adv.*

top·per (top′ər) *n.* 1 One who or that which tops. 2 *Slang* One who or that which is of supreme quality. 3 *Informal* A top hat. 4 *Informal* A topcoat.

top·ping (top′ing) *adj.* 1 Towering high above. 2 Eminent; distinguished. 3 *Brit. Informal* Excellent; first-rate. —*n.* That which forms a top.

top·ple (top′əl) *v.* ·**pled**, ·**pling** *v.i.* 1 To fall, top foremost, by or as if by its own weight. 2 To seem to be about to fall; totter. —*v.t.* 3 To cause to totter or fall. 4 To cause to collapse; overthrow: to *topple* a government. [Freq. of TOP¹, *v.*]

tops (tops) *adj. Slang* Excellent; first-rate.

top·sail (top′sāl′, -səl) *n. Naut.* 1 In a square-rigged vessel, a square sail set next above the lowest sail of a mast. 2 In a fore-and-aft-rigged vessel, a sail above the gaff of a lower sail.

top-se·cret (top′sē′krit) *adj.* Designating information requiring the strictest secrecy.

top sergeant *Informal* FIRST SERGEANT. See GRADE.

top·side (top′sīd′) *n.* 1 The portion of a ship above the main deck. 2 *pl.* The side of a ship above the waterline. —*adv.* To or on the upper parts of a ship.

top·soil (top′soil′) *n.* The surface soil of land.

top·sy-tur·vy (top′sē·tûr′vē) *adv.* 1 Upside down. 2 In utter confusion. —*adj.* 1 Being in an upset or disordered condition. 2 Upside-down. —*n.* A state of being topsy-turvy; disorder. [Earlier *topsy-tervy,* ? < TOP¹ + obs. *terve* overturn] —**top′sy-tur′vi·ly** *adv.* —**top′sy-tur′vi·ness** *n.*

toque (tōk) *n.* 1 A small, close-fitting, brimless hat worn by women. 2 TUQUE. [< Sp. *toca*]

To·rah (tôr′ə, tō′rə) *n.* In Judaism: 1 The Pentateuch. 2 A scroll, as of parchment, containing the Pentateuch. 3 The whole of Jewish law, including the Old Testament and the Talmud. [< Hebrew *tōrāh* an instruction, law]

torch (tôrch) *n.* 1 A stick of wood or some material dipped in tallow or oil and set ablaze at the end to provide a light that can be carried about. 2 Anything that illuminates or brightens. 3 A portable device giving off an intensely hot flame and used for burning off paint, melting solder, etc. 4 *Brit.* A flashlight. [< OF *torche*]

torch·bear·er (tôrch′bâr′ər) *n.* 1 One who carries a torch. 2 One who conveys knowledge, truth, etc. 3 A leader of a cause or movement.

torch·light (tôrch′līt′) *n.* The light of a torch or torches. —*adj.* Lighted by torches.

torch song A popular love song, usu. melancholy and expressing hopeless yearning. —**torch singer**

tore (tôr, tōr) *p.t.* of TEAR¹.

tor·e·a·dor (tôr′ē·ə·dôr′, tō′rē-) *n.* One who engages in a bullfight, esp. on horseback. [< Sp. < *toro* a bull]

to·ri·i (tôr′ē·ē, tōr′-) *n. pl.* **to·ri·i** The gateway of a Shinto shrine. [Jap.]

tor·ment (tôr′ment, -mənt) *n.* 1 Intense bodily pain or mental anguish. 2 A source of pain or anguish, or a persistent annoyance. 3 The inflicting of torture. —*v.t.* (tôr·ment′) 1 To subject to intense or persistent physical or mental pain; make miserable. 2 To harass or vex. 3 To disturb; agitate; stir up. [< L *tormentum* a rack] —**tor·men′tor, tor·men′ter** *n.*

Japanese torii

—Syn. *n.* 1 agony, torture, suffering, misery.

torn (tôrn, tōrn) *p.p.* of TEAR¹.

tor·na·do (tôr·nā′dō) *n. pl.* ·**does** or ·**dos** 1 A whirling wind of exceptional force and violence, accompanied by a funnel-shaped cloud marking the narrow path of greatest destruction. 2 Any hurricane or violent windstorm. [Alter. of Sp. *tronada* a thunderstorm < *tronar* to thunder] —**tor·nad′ic** (-nad′ik) *adj.*

tor·pe·do (tôr·pē′dō) *n. pl.* ·**does** 1 A self-propelled, tube-shaped underwater missile with an explosive warhead. 2 Any of various devices containing an explosive, as a submarine mine. —*v.t.* ·**doed**, ·**do·ing** 1 To damage or sink (a vessel) with a torpedo. 2 *Informal* To destroy utterly; demolish: Publicity could *torpedo* the agreement. 3 ELECTRIC RAY. [L, stiffness, numbness < *torpere* be numb]

torpedo boat A swift, lightly armed boat equipped to discharge torpedoes.

tor·pid (tor′pid) *adj.* 1 Having lost sensibility or power of motion, partially or wholly, as a hibernating animal; dormant; numb. 2 Slow to act or respond; sluggish. 3 Apathetic; spiritless; dull. [< L *torpidus* < *torpere* be numb] —**tor·pid·i·ty** (tôr·pid′ə·tē), **tor′pid·ness** *n.* —**tor′pid·ly** *adv.*

tor·por (tôr′pər) *n.* 1 Complete or partial loss of sensibility or power of motion; stupor. 2 Apathy; listlessness; dullness. [< L *torpere* be numb] —**tor·po·rif·ic** (tôr′pə·rif′ik) *adj.*

torque (tôrk) *n.* That which causes or tends to cause twisting or rotational acceleration; the moment of a force. [< L *torquere* to twist]

tor·rent (tôr′ənt, tor′-) *n.* 1 A stream of liquid, esp. water, flowing rapidly and turbulently. 2 Any violent or tumultuous flow; a gush: a *torrent* of abuse. [< L *torrens,* lit., boiling, burning, pr.p. of *torrere* parch]

tor·ren·tial (tô·ren′shəl, to-) *adj.* 1 Of, like, or resulting in a torrent. 2 Resembling a torrent —**tor·ren′tial·ly** *adv.*

tor·rid (tôr′id, tor′-) *adj.* 1 Parched or hot from exposure to heat, esp. of the sun. 2 Intensely hot and dry; scorching. 3 Passionate. [< L *torridus* < *torrere* parch] —**tor·rid·i·ty** (tô·rid′ə·tē, to-), **tor′rid·ness** *n.* —**tor′rid·ly** *adv.*

torrid zone That part of the earth's surface on both sides of the equator between the tropics of Cancer and Capricorn. • See ZONE.

tor·sion (tôr′shən) *n.* 1 The act of twisting, or the state of being twisted. 2 *Mech.* Deformation or stress caused by twisting. [< L *tortus,* p.p. of *torquere* twist] —**tor′sion·al** *adj.* —**tor′sion·al·ly** *adv.*

tor·so (tôr′sō) *n. pl.* ·**sos** or ·**si** (-sē) 1 The trunk of a human body. 2 The part of a sculptured human figure corresponding to the trunk, esp. when the head and limbs are missing. [Ital., a stalk, trunk of a body]

tort (tôrt) *n. Law* Any civil wrong by act or omission for which a suit can be brought, exclusive of a breach of contract. [< L *tortus* twisted]

torte (tôrt, tôr′tə) *n. pl.* **tortes** or **tor·ten** (tôr′tən) A rich cake variously made of butter, eggs, fruits, and nuts. [G]

tor·til·la (tôr·tē′ə) *n.* A small, flat cake made of coarse cornmeal and baked on a griddle, common in Mexico. [Sp., dim. of *torta* a cake]

tor·toise (tôr′təs) *n.* A turtle, esp. one living on land. [< Med. L *tortuca*]

tortoise shell 1 The mottled yellow and brown shell of certain turtles, formerly used to make eyeglass frames, combs, etc. 2 A plastic imitation of this. —**tor′toise-shell′** *adj.*

Giant tortoise

tor·tu·ous (tôr′chō̄·əs) *adj.* 1 Abounding in bends, twists, or turns; winding. 2 Not straightforward; devious: *tortuous* logic. [< L *tortus* twisted. See TORSION.] —**tor′tu·ous·ly** *adv.* —**tor′tu·ous·ness** *n.*

tor·ture (tôr′chər) *n.* 1 The infliction of extreme pain on one held captive, as in punishment, to obtain a confession or information, or to deter others from a course of action. 2 Intense physical or mental suffering; agony. 3 Something that causes severe pain. 4 *Informal* Something intensely annoying, embarrassing, or intolerable: Sitting through his speech was sheer *torture.* —*v.t.* ·**tured**, ·**tur·ing** 1 To inflict extreme pain upon; subject to torture. 2 To cause to suffer keenly in body or mind. 3 To twist or turn into an abnormal form; distort; wrench. [< L *tortura,* lit., a twisting < *tortus.* See TORSION.] —**tor′tur·er** *n.*

To·ry (tôr′ē, tō′rē) n. pl. **To·ries 1** A historical English political party, opposed to the Whigs, now called the Conservative party. **2** One who adhered to the British cause at the time of the American Revolution. **3** A very conservative person: also **tory.** —**To′ry·ism** n.

toss (tôs, tos) v.t. **1** To throw, pitch, or fling about: tossed in a small boat on the open sea. **2** To throw or cast upward or toward another: to toss a ball. **3** To throw, heave, casually or indifferently: to toss clothes on a chair. **4** To remove from abruptly or violently: with out: He was tossed out of a job. **5** To throw (a coin) in the air to decide a question by comparing the side facing up, upon landing, with a previous call. **6** To lift with a quick motion, as the head. **7** To insert or interject casually or carelessly: to toss in impressive but irrelevant statistics. **8** To utter, write, or do easily or in an offhand manner: with off. **9** To bandy about, as something discussed. **10** To turn over and mix the contents of: to toss a salad. **11** To make restless; agitate. **12** To drink at one draft: often with off. —v.i. **13** To be moved or thrown about, as a ship in a storm. **14** To roll about restlessly or from side to side, as in sleep. **15** To go quickly or angrily, as with a toss of the head. **16** To toss a coin. —n. **1** The act of tossing, as a throw or pitch. **2** A quick movement, as of the head. **3** The state of being tossed. **4** TOSS-UP (def. 1). [Prob. < Scand.] —**toss′er** n. —**Syn.** v. **2** flip, flick, hurl. **12** quaff, swallow, gulp.

toss-up (tôs′up′, tos′-) n. **1** The tossing of a coin to decide a question. **2** An even chance.

tot[1] (tot) n. A little child; toddler. [Prob. < Scand.]

tot[2] (tot) v. **tot·ted, tot·ting** Informal v.t. **1** To add; total: with up. —v.i. **2** To add. [Short for TOTAL]

to·tal (tōt′l) n. The whole sum or amount. —adj. **1** Constituting or comprising a whole. **2** Complete: a total loss. —v. **·taled** or **·talled, ·tal·ing** or **·tal·ling** v.t. **1** To ascertain the total of. **2** To come to or reach as a total; amount to. **3** Slang To wreck completely; demolish, esp. a car. —v.i. **4** To amount: often with to. [< L totus all] —**to′tal·ly** adv.

to·tal·i·tar·i·an (tō·tal′ə·târ′ē·ən) adj. **1** Designating or characteristic of a government controlled exclusively by one party or faction that suppresses political dissent by force or intimidation and whose power to control the economic, social, and intellectual life of the individual is virtually unlimited. **2** Tyrannical; despotic. —n. An adherent of totalitarian government. —**to·tal′i·tar′i·an·ism** n.

to·tal·i·ty (tō·tal′ə·tē) n. pl. **·ties 1** A total amount; aggregate; sum. **2** The state of being whole or entire.

tote (tōt) Informal v.t. **tot·ed, tot·ing 1** To carry or bear on the person; transport; haul. **2** To carry habitually: He totes a gun. —n. **1** The act of toting. **2** A load or haul. [?] —**tot′er** n.

tote bag A large handbag for personal articles, carried esp. by women.

to·tem (tō′təm) n. **1** An animal, plant, or other natural object believed to be ancestrally related to a tribe, clan, or family group, and serving as its emblem, as among the North American Indians. **2** A representation of such an emblem. [< Algon.] —**to·tem·ic** (tō·tem′ik) adj. —**to′·tem·ism** n.

totem pole A pole carved or painted with totemic symbols, erected outside the houses of Indians along the NW coast of North America.

tot·ter (tot′ər) v.i. **1** To shake or waver, as if about to fall; be unsteady. **2** To walk unsteadily. —n. An unsteady or wobbly manner of walking. [Prob. < Scand.] —**tot′ter·er** n. —**tot′ter·ing·ly** adv. —**tot′ter·y** adj.

tou·can (tōō′kan, tōō·kän′) n. A fruit-eating bird of tropical America with brilliant plumage and a very large beak. [< Tupi tucana]

touch (tuch) v.t. **1** To place the hand, finger, or other body part in contact with; perceive by feeling. **2** To be or come in contact with. **3** To bring into contact with something else. **4** To hit or strike lightly; tap. **5** To lay the hand or hands on: Please don't touch the paintings. **6** To border on; adjoin. **7** To come to; reach: The temperature touched 90°. **8** To rival or equal: As a salesman, nobody could touch him. **9** To color slightly: The sun touched the clouds with gold. **10** To

Toucan

affect the emotions of, esp. so as to feel compassion or gratitude; move: She was touched by their concern for her health. **11** To hurt the feelings of. **12** To relate to; concern; affect: The war touches us all. **13** To have to do with, use, or partake of: He never touches anything stronger than ginger ale. **14** To affect injuriously; taint: vegetables touched by frost. **15** Slang To borrow money from. —v.i. **16** To touch someone or something. **17** To come into or be in contact. —**touch at** To stop briefly at (a port or place) in the course of a journey or voyage. —**touch down** To land after flight. —**touch off 1** To cause to explode; detonate; fire. **2** To provoke or initiate, esp. a violent reaction. —**touch on** (or **upon**) **1** To relate to; concern: That touches on another question. **2** To treat or discuss briefly or in passing. —**touch up** To add finishing touches or corrections to, as a work of art or writing. —n. **1** The act or fact of touching; a coming into contact, as a tap. **2** The sense stimulated by touching; the tactile sense by which a surface or its characteristics, as of pressure or texture, may be perceived. **3** A sensation conveyed by touching: a silky touch. **4** Communication or contact: Let's keep in touch. **5** A distinctive manner or style, as of an artist, author, or craftsman: a master's touch. **6** Delicate sensitivity, appreciation, or understanding: a fine touch for collecting rare china. **7** Any slight or delicate detail that helps to finish or perfect something, as a work of art or writing: to apply the finishing touches. **8** A trace; hint: a touch of irony. **9** A slight attack; twinge: a touch of rheumatism. **10** A small quantity; dash: a touch of perfume. **11** The resistance to motion offered by the keys of a piano, typewriter, etc. **12** The manner in which something is struck or touched, as the keys of a piano. **13** Slang Borrowed money, or a request to borrow money. **14** Slang A person from whom money may be borrowed, esp. easily: a soft touch. [< OF tochier] —**touch′a·ble** adj. —**touch′er** n.

touch and go An uncertain, risky, or precarious state of things. —**touch′-and-go′** adj.

touch·back (tuch′bak′) n. In football, the act of touching the ball to the ground behind the player's own goal line when the ball was propelled over the goal line by an opponent.

touch·down (tuch′doun′) n. **1** A scoring play in football in which a player has possession of the ball on or over the opponent's goal line. **2** The act of touching down, as an aircraft or spacecraft.

tou·ché (tōō·shā′) interj. A term used in fencing to indicate a touch scored by one's opponent, and otherwise to acknowledge the wit or effectiveness of a point made in argument or conversation. [F]

touched (tucht) adj. **1** Affected emotionally; moved. **2** Slightly unbalanced in mind; crack-brained.

touch·ing (tuch′ing) adj. Appealing to the emotions; esp., inspiring tenderness or sympathy. —prep. With regard to; concerning. —**touch′ing·ly** adv. —**touch′ing·ness** n.

touch-me-not (tuch′mē·not′) n. Any of various plants, the ripe seed capsules of which explode when touched.

touch·stone (tuch′stōn′) n. **1** A dark stone formerly used to test the purity of gold by the color of the streak made on the stone by the metal. **2** Any criterion or standard by which quality or value may be tested.

touch·wood (tuch′wood′) n. PUNK[1] (def. 1).

touch·y (tuch′ē) adj. **touch·i·er, touch·i·est 1** Apt to take offense on very little provocation. **2** Liable to cause hurt feelings or contention: a touchy subject. —**touch′i·ly** adv. —**touch′i·ness** n. —**Syn. 1** sensitive, thin-skinned, volatile. **2** delicate, sensitive.

tough (tuf) adj. **1** Capable of bearing tension or strain without breaking, esp. because strong in texture or composition. **2** Difficult to cut or chew. **3** Strong in body or mind, esp. in resisting or enduring stress. **4** Requiring determined or intense effort; difficult: a tough assignment. **5** Resolute; unyielding; inflexible: a tough stand in the negotiations. **6** Severe; harsh: a tough punishment. **7** Given to or characterized by violence or rowdyism: a tough neighborhood. **8** Informal Unfortunate; regrettable. **9** Slang Great; fine. —n. A ruffian; rowdy. —v.t. Informal To manage to get through; endure: often with out: to tough out a recession. [< OE tōh] —**tough′ly** adv. —**tough′·ness** n. —**Syn. 5** uncompromising, stubborn, militant.

tough·en (tuf′ən) *v.t. & v.i.* To make or become tough or tougher. —**tough′en·er** *n.*

tou·pee (tōō·pā′) *n.* A man's small wig worn to cover a bald spot. [< OF *toup, top* a tuft of hair]

tour (tōōr) *n.* 1 An excursion or journey, as for sightseeing. 2 A trip, usu. over a planned course, as to conduct business, present theatrical performances, etc. 3 A set period of time, as of service in a particular place; turn or shift. 4 A brief survey; circuit: a *tour* of the grounds. —*v.t.* 1 To make a tour of; travel. 2 To present on a tour: to *tour* a play. —*v.i.* 3 To go on a tour. [< OF *tor* a turn < L *tornus* a lathe]

tour de force (tōōr də fôrs′) *pl.* **tours de force** (tōōr) A remarkable feat, as of skill, creativity, or industry. [F, lit., feat of strength]

touring car An old type of large, open automobile with a capacity for five or more passengers.

tour·ism (tōōr′iz·əm) *n.* 1 Recreational travel, considered esp. as an industry or source of income. 2 The organization and guidance of tourists. —**tour·is′tic** *adj.*

tour·ist (tōōr′ist) *n.* One who makes a tour or a pleasure trip. —*adj.* Of or suitable for tourists. —**tour′ist·y** *adj.*

tour·ma·line (tōōr′mə·lən, -lēn′) *n.* A complex mineral with a vitreous to resinous luster, found in various colors and valued in its transparent varieties as a gemstone. Also **tour′ma·lin** (-lin). [< F]

tour·na·ment (tûr′nə·mənt, tōōr′-) *n.* 1 A series of competitive sports events or games for prizes or cash awards and often for a championship: a golf or bridge *tournament.* 2 In medieval times, a pageant in which two opposing parties of men in armor contended on horseback with blunted weapons, esp. lances. [< OF < *torneier* to tourney]

tour·ney (tûr′nē, tōōr′-) *v.i.* To take part in a tournament. —*n.* TOURNAMENT. [< OF *torneier*]

tour·ni·quet (tōōr′nə·kit, tûr′-) *n.* A device for controlling arterial bleeding by tightening a nooselike bandage. [< F *tourner* to turn]

tou·sle (tou′zəl) *v.t.* **·sled, ·sling** To disarrange or dishevel; rumple. —*n.* A tousled mass, esp. of hair. [Freq. of ME *tousen*]

tout (tout) *Informal v.i.* 1 To solicit patronage, customers, votes, etc. 2 To sell information, as to a bettor, about horses entered in a race. —*v.t.* 3 To solicit; importune. 4 To praise highly or proclaim: *touted* as the world's fastest human. 5 To sell information concerning (a race horse). —*n.* 1 One who touts. 2 One who solicits business. [< OE *tōtian, tȳtan* peep, look out]

tout à fait (tōō tà fe′) *French* Entirely; quite.

tout de suite (tōōt swēt) Immediately; at once. [F]

tout en·sem·ble (tōō täṅ säṅ′bl′) *French* All in all; everything considered.

tow¹ (tō) *n.* A short, coarse hemp or flax fiber prepared for spinning. [Prob. < OE *tōw-* spinning]

tow² (tō) *v.t.* To pull or drag, as by a rope or chain. —*n.* 1 The act of towing, or the state of being towed. 2 That which is towed, as a barge. 3 TOWLINE. —**in tow** 1 In the condition of being towed. 2 Drawn along as if being towed: a film star with her fans *in tow.* 3 Under one's protection or care: took the orphan *in tow.* [< OE *togian*]

tow·age (tō′ij) *n.* 1 The charge for towing. 2 The act of towing.

to·ward (tôrd, tōrd, tə·wôrd′) *prep.* 1 In the direction of; facing. 2 With respect to; regarding. 3 In anticipation of or as a contribution to; for: He is saving *toward* his education. 4 Near in point of time; approaching: *toward* evening. 5 Tending or designed to result in. Also **to·wards′.** —*adj.* (tôrd, tōrd) Impending or imminent. [< OE *tō* to + *-weard* -ward] —**to·ward′ness** *n.*

tow·el (toul, tou′əl) *n.* A cloth or paper for drying anything by wiping. —*v.t.* **·eled** or **·elled, ·el·ing** or **·el·ling** To wipe or dry with a towel. [< OF *toaille*]

tow·el·ing (tou′ling, tou′əl·ing) *n.* Material for towels. Also **tow·el·ling.**

tow·er (tou′ər) *n.* 1 A structure very tall in proportion to its other dimensions, and either standing alone or forming part of a building. 2 A place of security or defense; citadel. 3 Someone or something likened to a tower in strength or command. —*v.i.* To rise or stand like a tower; extend to a great height. [< L *turris*]

tow·er·ing (tou′ər·ing) *adj.* 1 Very high or very great: a *towering* figure in modern drama. 2 Rising to a high pitch of violence or intensity: a *towering* rage.

tow·head (tō′hed′) *n.* 1 A head of very light-colored or flaxen hair. 2 A person having such hair. [< TOW¹ + HEAD] —**tow′·head′ed** *adj.*

tow·hee (tō′ē, tō′hē) *n.* Any of various American finches related to the buntings and the sparrows. Also **towhee bunting.** [Imit.]

tow·line (tō′līn′) *n.* A line, rope, or chain used in towing.

town (toun) *n.* 1 Any collection of dwellings and other buildings larger than a village and smaller than a city. 2 A closely settled urban district, as contrasted with less populated or suburban areas or with the open country. 3 A city of any size. 4 The inhabitants or voters of a town. 5 TOWNSHIP. 6 Those residents of a town who are not associated educationally or administratively with a college or university situated in the town: *town* and gown. —**go to town** *Slang* To work or proceed with dispatch; get busy. —**on the town** *Slang* On a round of bars, nightclubs, etc., in the city in search of diversion or excitement. —**paint the town red** *Slang* To go on a spree; carouse. —*adj.* Of, situated in, or for a town. [< OE *tūn, tuun* an enclosure, group of houses]

Towhee

town clerk An official who keeps the records of a town.

town crier Formerly, a person appointed to make proclamations through the streets of a town.

town hall A building in a town containing the public offices and often a place for meetings.

town house 1 A residence in a town or city, esp. when owned by one who also owns a house in the country. 2 A two- or three-story house, usu. for one family, contiguous to one or more similar houses.

town meeting A meeting of residents or voters of a town for the purpose of transacting town business.

town·ship (toun′ship) *n.* 1 In the U.S. and Canada, a territorial subdivision of a county with certain corporate powers of municipal government for local purposes. 2 In New England, a local political unit governed by a town meeting.

towns·man (tounz′mən) *n. pl.* **·men** (-mən) 1 A resident of a town. 2 A fellow citizen of a town. 3 A permanent resident of a town, as contrasted with a student or teacher in a school or college situated in the town.

towns·peo·ple (tounz′pē′pəl) *n.pl.* People who live in towns or in a particular town or city. Also **towns′folk′** (-fōk′).

town·y (toun′ē) *n. pl.* **town·ies** *Informal* TOWNSMAN (def. 3). Also **town′ie.**

tow·path (tō′path′, -päth′) *n.* A path along a river or canal used by men, horses, or mules towing boats.

tow·rope (tō′rōp′) *n.* A heavy rope or cable for towing.

tow truck A truck equipped to tow other vehicles.

tox·e·mi·a (tok·sē′mē·ə) *n.* The presence in the blood of toxins from a local source of infection. Also **tox·ae′mi·a.** [< TOX(IC) + Gk. *haima* blood] —**tox·e′mic** *adj.*

tox·ic (tok′sik) *adj.* 1 Poisonous. 2 Due to or caused by poison or a toxin. [< Gk. *toxicon (pharmakon)* (a poison) for arrows < *toxon* a bow] —**tox′i·cal·ly** *adv.* —**tox·ic′i·ty** (-sis′ə·tē) *n.*

toxico- *combining form* Poison; of or pertaining to poison or poisons: *toxicology.* Also **toxic-.** [< Gk. *toxicon* poison]

tox·i·col·o·gy (tok′sə·kol′ə·jē) *n.* The science that deals with poisons, their detection, antidotes, etc. —**tox′i·co·log′ic** (-kə·loj′ik) or **·i·cal** *adj.* —**tox′i·co·log′i·cal·ly** *adv.* —**tox′i·col′o·gist** *n.*

tox·in (tok′sin) *n.* 1 Any of various poisonous compounds produced by living organisms and acting as causative agents in many diseases. 2 Any toxic matter generated in living or dead organisms. [< TOX(IC) + -IN]

toy (toi) n. 1 Something designed or serving as a plaything for children. 2 Something trifling or unimportant. 3 An ornament; trinket. 4 A small animal, esp. one of a breed characterized by small size. —v.i. 1 To act or consider something without seriousness or conviction; trifle: to *toy* with an idea. 2 To use someone or something for one's amusement. 3 To act flirtatiously. —adj. 1 Designed as a toy. 2 Resembling a toy; esp., of miniature size: a *toy* dog. [Prob. < ME *toye* flirtation, sport] —**toy'er** n.

tp. township.

tpk. turnpike.

tr. translated; translation; translator; transpose; transitive; treasurer.

trace[1] (trās) n. 1 A vestige or mark left by some past event or by a person or thing no longer present. 2 An imprint or mark indicating the passage of a person or thing, as a footprint, etc. 3 A path or trail beaten down by men or animals. 4 A barely detectable quantity, quality, or characteristic. 5 A lightly drawn line; something traced. —v. **traced, trac·ing** v.t. 1 To follow the tracks or trail of. 2 To follow the course or development of, esp. by investigation of a series of events. 3 To find out or determine by investigation. 4 To follow (tracks, a course of development, etc.). 5 To draw; sketch. 6 To copy (a drawing, etc.) on a superimposed transparent sheet. 7 To form (letters, etc.) painstakingly. —v.i. 8 To have its origin; go back in time. 9 To follow a track, course of development, etc. [< OF *tracier* to trace] —**trace'a·bil'i·ty, trace'a·ble·ness** n. —**trace'a·ble** adj. —**trace'a·bly** adv. —**Syn.** 1 remnant, sign, aftermath, token, clue.

trace[2] (trās) n. One of two side straps or chains connected to a draft animal's harness and to the vehicle to be pulled. —**kick over the traces** To throw off control; become unmanageable. [< OF *trait* a dragging, a leather harness]

trac·er (trā'sər) n. 1 One who or that which traces. 2 An inquiry forwarded from one point to another, to trace missing mail, etc. 3 A substance, as a radioisotope, introduced into a system in minute amount as an indicator of the course of a process, reaction, disease, etc. 4 A bullet or shell that indicates its course by leaving a trail of smoke or fire.

trac·er·y (trā'sər·ē) n. pl. **·er·ies** 1 Ornamental stonework formed of branching lines, as in a Gothic window. 2 Any delicate ornamentation resembling this.

tra·che·a (trā'kē·ə) n. pl. **·che·ae** (-kē·ē, -kē·ī) or **·che·as** 1 In vertebrates, the duct by which air passes from the larynx to the bronchi and the lungs; the windpipe. 2 Any of the air passages in air-breathing arthropods. [< Gk. *(artēria) tracheia* a rough (artery)] —**tra'che·al** adj.

tra·che·ot·o·my (trā'kē·ot'ə·mē) n. pl. **·mies** Surg. An incision into the trachea. Also **tra'che·ost'·o·my** (-ost'ə·mē).

Trachea

tra·cho·ma (trə·kō'mə) n. A contagious virus disease of the eye characterized by granular excrescences on the inner surface of the eyelids. [< Gk. *trachōma* roughness] —**tra·chom·a·tous** (trə·kom'ə·təs) adj.

trac·ing (trā'sing) n. 1 The act of one who traces. 2 Something traced, as a copy made by tracing on transparent paper. 3 A record made by a self-registering instrument.

track (trak) n. 1 A mark or trail left by the passage of anything, as a series of footprints. 2 A path or way marked or worn out by the repeated passage of people, animals, or vehicles. 3 Any course or path, esp. one describing movement: the *track* of a missile or a comet. 4 A pair of parallel rails, usu. including the ties, that guide the wheels of a train, trolley, etc. 5 A usu. elliptical course for racing. 6 A sport in which footraces of various distances are held on a track. 7 TRACK AND FIELD. 8 A sequence of events; a succession of ideas. 9 Awareness of the progress or sequence; count; record: to lose *track* of an old friend; to keep *track* of expenses. 10 An endless metal belt, usu. one of a pair, by means of which certain vehicles are capable of moving over soft, slippery, or uneven surfaces. 11 The distance between the front or rear wheels of a vehicle, usu. measured from the center of the treads. 12 SOUND TRACK. 13 In education, any of two or more classes covering the same course of study in which students are placed according to their preparation and ability. —**in one's tracks** Right where one is; on the spot. —**make tracks** *Informal* To run away in haste; hurry. —**on** (or **off**) **the track** Keeping in view (or losing sight of) the subject or objective. —v.t. 1 To follow the tracks of; trail. 2 To discover or apprehend by following up marks, clues, or other evidence: with *down*: to *track* down a suspect; to *track* down a shipment of contaminated canned food. 3 To observe or plot the course of (an aircraft, spacecraft, etc.). 4 To make tracks upon or with: to *track* mud into a house. 5 To go through or traverse, as on foot: to *track* the wilderness. 6 To furnish with rails or tracks. —v.i. 7 To measure a certain distance between front or rear wheels. 8 To run in the same track or groove; be in alignment. 9 To leave tracks. —adj. Pertaining to or performed on a track, esp. a track for racing: *track* events. [< OF *trac*] —**track'er** n. —**track'less** adj.

track·age (trak'ij) n. 1 Railroad tracks collectively. 2 The right of one company to use the tracks of another. 3 The charge for this right.

track and field A sport consisting of footraces on a track and contests on a field, as in hurling, throwing, or leaping. —**track'-and-field'** adj.

trackless trolley TROLLEY BUS.

track record *Informal* A record of achievements.

tract[1] (trakt) n. 1 An extended area, as of land or water; stretch or expanse. 2 A system of parts or organs in an animal, having a distinct function: the alimentary *tract*. [< L *tractus* a drawing out < *trahere* draw]

tract[2] (trakt) n. A short treatise or pamphlet, as on religion or morals. [< L *tractatus* a handling]

tract·a·ble (trak'tə·bəl) adj. 1 Easily led or controlled; docile. 2 Readily worked or handled; malleable. [< L *tractare* handle, freq. of *trahere* draw] —**tract'a·bly** adv. —**tract'a·ble·ness, tract'a·bil'i·ty** n. —**Syn.** 1 manageable, compliant, mild, submissive.

trac·tile (trak'til, tīl) adj. That can be drawn out; ductile. [< L *tractus*. See TRACT[1].] —**trac·til'i·ty** n.

trac·tion (trak'shən) n. 1 The act of drawing, as by motive power over a surface. 2 The state of being pulled or drawn: to place a fractured limb in *traction*. 3 The power employed in pulling or drawing. 4 Adhesive or rolling friction, as of tires on a road. [< L *tractus*. See TRACT[1].] —**trac'tion·al, trac·tive** (trak'tiv) adj.

trac·tor (trak'tər) n. 1 A powerful, self-propelled vehicle used to pull farm machinery. 2 An automotive vehicle with a driver's cab, used to haul trailers, etc. 3 An airplane with the propeller or propellers situated in front of the lifting surfaces. [< L *tractus*. See TRACT[1].]

Tractor *def. 1*

trad (trad) adj. *Slang* Traditional: *trad* jazz.

trade (trād) n. 1 A business or occupation. 2 A skilled or specialized line of work, as a craft. 3 The people or companies engaged in a particular business. 4 The buying and selling or exchange of commodities; also, an instance of such commerce. 5 A firm's customers. 6 An exchange of personal articles; swap. 7 Any exchange of things or people having negotiable value: a baseball *trade*. 8 Usu. pl. TRADE WIND. —adj. 1 Of or pertaining to a trade. 2 Used by or intended for the members of a particular trade: a *trade* journal. —v.t. **trad·ed, trad·ing** 1 To give in exchange for something else. 2 To barter or exchange. —v.i. 3 To engage in commerce or in business transactions. 4 To make an exchange. 5 *Informal* To do one's shopping: with *at*: to *trade* at a store. —**trade in** To give in exchange as payment or part payment. —**trade off** To match or correlate, as incompatible elements or objectives, in the process of reaching a solution or compromise. —**trade on** To take advantage of. [< MLG, a track] —**trad'er** n.

trade-in (trād'in') n. Used merchandise accepted in payment or part payment for other, esp. new, merchandise.

trade-last (trād'last', -läst') n. *Informal* A favorable re-

mark that one has heard and offers to repeat to the person complimented in return for a similar remark.

trade·mark (trād′märk′) *n.* **1** A name, symbol, design, device, or word used by a merchant or manufacturer to identify his product and distinguish it from that of others. **2** Any distinctive or characteristic feature. —*v.t.* **1** To label with a trademark. **2** To register and bring under legal protection as a trademark.

trade name 1 The name by which an article, process, etc., is designated in trade. **2** A name given by a manufacturer to designate a proprietary article, sometimes having the status of a trademark. **3** The name of a business concern.

trade-off (trād′ôf′, -of′) *n.* **1** A giving up of something, as an objective or advantage, in exchange for something else: a *trade-off* of higher pay for longer vacations. **2** The relationship that characterizes such an exchange; a compromise or adjustment between opposing elements or positions: the *trade-off* between taxation and improved public services.

trade school A school where practical skills or trades are taught.

trades·man (trādz′mən) *n. pl.* **·men** (-mən) A retail dealer; shopkeeper. —**trades′wom·an** *n. Fem.*

trade union LABOR UNION. Also **trades union.** —**trade unionism** —**trade unionist**

trade wind Either of two steady winds blowing toward the equator, one from the northeast on the north, the other from the southeast on the south side of the equatorial line.

trading post A building or small settlement in unsettled territory used as a station for barter, as for furs.

trading stamp A stamp of fixed value given as a premium with a purchase and exchangeable, in quantity, for merchandise.

tra·di·tion (trə-dish′ən) *n.* **1** The transmission of knowledge, opinions, customs, practices, etc., from generation to generation, esp. by word of mouth and by example. **2** The body of beliefs and usages so transmitted; also, any particular story, belief, or usage of this kind. **3** A custom so long continued that it has almost the force of a law. [< L *traditus,* p.p. of *tradere* deliver] —**tra·di′tion·al** *adj.* —**tra·di′tion·al·ly** *adv.*

tra·duce (trə-dyo͞os′) *v.t.* **·duced, ·duc·ing** To misrepresent willfully the conduct or character of; defame; slander. [< L *traducere* transport, bring into disgrace] —**tra·duce′·ment, tra·duc′er** *n.*

traf·fic (traf′ik) *n.* **1** The passing of pedestrians, vehicles, aircraft, messages, etc., in a limited space or between certain points. **2** The people, vehicles, messages, etc., so moving. **3** The business of buying and selling commodities; trade. **4** Unlawful or improper trade: *traffic* in stolen goods. **5** The people or freight transported by a carrier, as a railroad. **6** The business of transportation. **7** Communication or contact; connection. —*v.i.* **·ficked, ·fick·ing 1** To engage in buying and selling illegally: with *in:* to *traffic* in narcotic drugs. **2** To have dealings: with *with.* [< MF < Ital. *traffico*] —**traf′fick·er** *n.*

traffic light A set of colored signal lights used to control the passage of automotive traffic.

tra·ge·di·an (trə-jē′dē-ən) *n.* **1** An actor of tragedy. **2** A writer of tragedies.

tra·ge·di·enne (trə-jē′dē-en′) *n.* An actress of tragedy.

trag·e·dy (traj′ə-dē) *n. pl.* **·dies 1** A form of drama in which the protagonist comes to disaster, as through a flaw in character, and in which the ending is usu. marked by sorrow or pity. **2** A play, film, etc., of this kind. **3** Any tragic or disastrous incident or series of incidents. **4** *Informal* A misfortune. [< Gk. *tragōidia*]

trag·ic (traj′ik) *adj.* **1** Of or having the nature of tragedy. **2** Appropriate to or suggestive of tragedy: a *tragic* manner. **3** Causing or likely to cause suffering, sorrow, or death: a *tragic* accident. [< Gk. *tragikos* pertaining to tragedy] —**trag′i·cal·ly** *adv.*

trag·i·com·e·dy (traj′i·kom′ə·dē) *n. pl.* **·dies 1** A drama having characteristics of both tragedy and comedy. **2** An

incident or series of incidents of this nature. —**trag′i·com′ic** or **·i·cal** *adj.* —**trag′i·com′i·cal·ly** *adv.*

trail (trāl) *v.t.* **1** To draw along lightly over a surface. **2** To drag or draw after: to *trail* oars; to *trail* an injured leg. **3** To follow the track of; trace: to *trail* game. **4** To be or come along behind. **5** To follow behind, as in pursuit or to keep under surveillance: to *trail* a suspect. —*v.i.* **6** To hang or extend loosely so as to drag over a surface. **7** To grow extensively and usu. irregularly along the ground or over rocks, etc. **8** To be or come along behind. **9** To move or walk heavily or ponderously; trudge. **10** To lag behind: to *trail* by 30,000 votes; to *trail* in the development of auto safety standards. **11** To flow or extend, as in a stream. —*n.* **1** The track left by something that has moved or been drawn or dragged over a surface. **2** The track, scent, etc., indicating the passage of someone or something. **3** The path worn by persons or by animals, esp. through a wilderness. **4** Something that trails or is trailed behind, as the train of a dress or the track of a meteor. **5** A sequence of results or conditions following after something: left a *trail* of broken hearts. [< AF *trailler* haul, tow a boat]

trail·er (trā′lər) *n.* **1** One who or that which trails. **2** A vehicle drawn by a cab or tractor having motive power. **3** A vehicle usu. drawn by an automobile or truck and equipped to serve as living quarters. **4** PREVIEW (def. 2).

trailing arbutus A prostrate evergreen shrub bearing clusters of fragrant pink flowers.

train¹ (trān) *n.* **1** A series of connected railway cars, often drawn by a locomotive. **2** Anything drawn along behind, as a trailing part of a skirt. **3** A line or group of followers; retinue. **4** A moving line of people, animals, vehicles, etc.; procession. **5** A series, succession, or set of connected things; sequence: a *train* of thought. **6** Something, as a period of time or set of circumstances, following after something else; aftermath: The argument left bitter feelings in its *train.* **7** *Mech.* A series of parts acting on each other, as for transmitting motion. —*v.t.* **1** To bring to a desired standard by careful instruction; esp., to guide in morals or manners. **2** To make skillful or proficient: to *train* soldiers. **3** To make obedient to orders or capable of performing tricks, as an animal. **4** To lead into taking a particular course; develop into a fixed shape: to *train* a plant on a trellis; to *train* the hair to lie flat. **5** To put or point in an exact direction; aim: to *train* a rifle or a gaze on someone. —*v.i.* **6** To undergo a course of training. [< OF *trahiner* to draw] —**train′a·ble** *adj.* —**train′er** *n.* —**Syn.** *v.* **1** educate, instruct, rear, bring up, mold.

train² (trān) *n. Can.* A large sled, having a shape like a toboggan. [< F *traineau* sled]

train·ee (trā·nē′) *n.* One who is being trained, as a new employee.

train·ing (trā′ning) *n.* **1** Systematic instruction and drill. **2** The method or action of one who trains, as for an athletic contest.

train·man (trān′mən) *n. pl.* **·men** (-mən) A railway employee serving on a train.

traipse (trāps) *v.i.* **traipsed, traips·ing** To walk or wander about; gad. —*n.* The act of traipsing. [Prob. < OF *trapasser,* var. of *trespasser* trespass]

trait (trāt) *n.* A distinguishing feature or quality, as of character. [< L *tractus* a drawing out < *trahere* draw]

trai·tor (trā′tər) *n.* **1** One who commits treason. **2** One who betrays a trust or acts deceitfully and disloyally. [< L *tradere* betray] —**trai′tress** (-tris) *n. Fem.*

trai·tor·ous (trā′tər·əs) *adj.* **1** Of, constituting, or resembling treason. **2** Of or characteristic of a traitor; treacherous. —**trai′tor·ous·ly** *adv.* —**trai′tor·ous·ness** *n.*

tra·jec·to·ry (trə·jek′tər·ē) *n. pl.* **·ries** The path described by an object or body moving in space, as of a comet or a bullet. [< L *trajectus,* p.p. of *trajicere* throw over]

tram (tram) *n.* **1** *Brit.* STREETCAR. **2** An open vehicle running on rails, used to carry coal in a mine. Also **tram′car′** (-kär′). [< dial. *tram* a rail]

tram·mel (tram′əl) *n.* **1** *Usu. pl.* That which limits freedom or activity; hindrance. **2** A fetter or shackle, esp. one used in teaching a horse to amble. **3** An instrument for

drawing ellipses. **4** An adjustable hook used to suspend cooking pots from a fireplace crane. **5** A net formed of three layers, the central one of finer mesh, to trap fish passing through either of the others: also **trammel net.** — *v.t.* **·meled** or **·melled, ·mel·ing** or **·mel·ling 1** To hinder or obstruct; restrict. **2** To entangle in or as in a snare; imprison. [< LL *tremaculum* net < L *tri-* three + *macula* a mesh] —**tram′mel·er** or **tram′mel·ler** *n.*

tramp (tramp) *v.i.* **1** To walk or wander about, esp. as a tramp or hobo. **2** To walk heavily or firmly. —*v.t.* **3** To walk or wander through. **4** To walk on heavily; trample. —*n.* **1** One who travels from place to place, usu. on foot and destitute and dependent on charity for a living. **2** The sound of heavy marching or walking. **3** A long stroll; hike. **4** A steam vessel that goes from port to port picking up freight wherever it can: also **tramp steamer. 5** *Slang* A sexually promiscuous woman. [ME *trampen*] —**tramp′er** *n.* — **Syn** *n.* **1** vagrant, vagabond, hobo, bum.

tram·ple (tram′pəl) *v.* **·pled, ·pling** *v.i.* **1** To tread heavily, esp. so as to crush. **2** To injure or encroach upon someone or something by or as by tramping: with *on:* to *trample* on someone's rights. —*v.t.* **3** To tread heavily or ruthlessly on. —*n.* The sound of treading under foot. [< ME *trampen* tramp] —**tram′pler** *n.*

tram·po·line (tram′pə·lēn′, tram′pə·lēn′) *n.* A heavy canvas stretched to a frame by springs and used for its resiliency in tumbling. Also **tram′po·lin.** [< Ital. *trampoli* stilts]

tram·way (tram′wā′) *n. Brit.* A streetcar line.

trance (trans, träns) *n.* **1** A state in which one appears to be unable to act consciously, as though hypnotized or governed by a supernatural force. **2** A dreamlike or sleepy state, as that induced by hypnosis. **3** A state of profound concentration marked by lack of awareness of one's surroundings; deep abstraction. [< OF *transir* pass, die]

tran·quil (trang′kwil) *adj.* **1** Free from agitation or disturbance; calm: a *tranquil* mood. **2** Quiet and motionless: a *tranquil* scene. [< L *tranquillus* quiet] —**tran′quil·ly** *adv.* —**tran′quil·ness** *n.* —**Syn.** **1** relaxed, serene. **2** placid.

tran·quil·ize (trang′kwəl·īz) *v.t.* & *v.i.* **·ized, ·iz·ing** To make or become tranquil, esp. by using a drug. Also **tran′·quil·lize.** *Brit. sp.* **·lise.** —**tran′quil·i·za′tion** *n.*

tran·quil·iz·er (trang′kwəl·ī′zər) *n.* **1** One who or that which tranquilizes. **2** Any of various drugs that calm mental agitation without impairing consciousness. Also **tran′·quil·liz′er.**

tran·quil·li·ty (trang·kwil′ə·tē) *n.* The state of being tranquil; peacefulness; quiet. Also **tran·quil′i·ty.**

trans- *prefix* **1** Across; beyond; on the other side of: *transatlantic; transmigrate.* **2** Through: *transfix.* **3** Through and through; changing completely: *transform.* [< L *trans* across, beyond, over]

trans. transactions; transferred; transitive; translated; translation; translator.

trans·act (trans·akt′, tranz-) *v.t.* **1** To carry through; accomplish; do. —*v.i.* **2** To do business. [< L *transactus,* p.p. of *transigere* drive through, accomplish] —**trans·ac′tor** *n.*

trans·ac·tion (trans·ak′shən, tranz-) *n.* **1** The act or process of transacting. **2** Something transacted; esp., a business deal. **3** *pl.* Published reports, as of a society. —**trans·ac′tion·al** *adj.*

trans·at·lan·tic (trans′ət·lan′tik, tranz′-) *adj.* **1** Across or crossing the Atlantic Ocean: a *transatlantic* flight. **2** On the other side of the Atlantic.

tran·scend (tran·send′) *v.t.* **1** To go or pass beyond the limits of: knowledge that *transcends* reason. **2** To rise above in excellence or degree. —*v.i.* **3** To be surpassing; excel. [< L *trans-* beyond, over + *scandere* to climb]

tran·scen·dent (tran·sen′dənt) *adj.* **1** TRANSCENDENTAL (def. 1). **2** *Theol.* Existing apart from and above the material universe: said of God. [< L *transcendere* transcend] — **tran·scen′dence, tran·scen′den·cy** *n.* —**tran·scen′dent·ly** *adv.*

tran·scen·den·tal (tran′sen·den′təl) *adj.* **1** Rising above or going beyond ordinary limits; surpassing. **2** Beyond natural experience; supernatural. **3** Of or pertaining to transcendentalism. —**tran′scen·den′tal·ly** *adv.*

tran·scen·den·tal·ism (tran′sen·den′təl·iz′əm) *n.* The philosophical doctrine that man can attain knowledge which goes beyond or transcends appearances or sensory phenomena. —**tran′scen·den′tal·ist** *adj., n.* —**tran′scen·den′·tal·is′tic** *adj.*

transcendental number An irrational number, such as pi, that cannot result from any finite set of algebraic equations having rational coefficients.

trans·con·ti·nen·tal (trans′kon·tə·nen′təl) *adj.* Extending or passing across a continent.

tran·scribe (tran·skrīb′) *v.t.* **·scribed, ·scrib·ing 1** To write over again; copy from an original. **2** To make a record of in handwriting or typewriting, as of something spoken. **3** To translate (shorthand notes, etc.) into standard written form. **4** To make a recording of for use in a later broadcast. **5** To adapt (a musical composition) for a change of instrument or voice. [< L *trans-* over + *scribere* write] —**tran·scrib′er** *n.*

tran·script (tran′skript) *n.* **1** Something transcribed, as from a stenographer's notes. **2** Any copy, esp., an official copy of a student's academic record. [< L *transcribere* transcribe]

tran·scrip·tion (tran·skrip′shən) *n.* **1** The act of transcribing. **2** Something transcribed; a copy; transcript. **3** A recording made for a later broadcast. **4** *Music* The adaptation of a composition for a different instrument or voice. —**tran·scrip′tion·al** *adj.*

tran·sept (tran′sept) *n.* A projecting part of a cruciform church crossing at right angles to the longer part and situated between the nave and choir; also, its projecting ends. [< L *transversus* transverse + *septum* an enclosure] —**tran·sep′tal** *adj.*

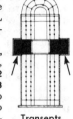

Transepts

trans·fer (trans·fûr′, trans′fər) *v.* **·ferred, ·fer·ring** *v.t.* **1** To carry, or cause to pass, from one person, place, etc., to another. **2** To make over possession of to another. **3** To convey (a drawing) from one surface to another. —*v.i.* **4** To transfer oneself. **5** To be transferred. **6** To change from one vehicle or line to another. —*n.* (trans′fər) **1** The act of transferring, or the state of being transferred. **2** That which is transferred, as a design conveyed from one surface to another. **3** A place, method, or means of transfer. **4** A ticket entitling a passenger on one vehicle to ride on another. **5** A delivery of title or property from one person to another. **6** A person transferred from one organization or position to another. [< L *trans-* across + *ferre* carry] —**trans·fer′a·bil′i·ty, trans·fer′ence, trans·fer′rer** *n.* —**trans·fer′a·ble, trans·fer′ra·ble** *adj.*

trans·fer·al (trans·fûr′əl) *n.* The act or an instance of transferring. Also **trans·fer′ral.**

trans·fig·ur·a·tion (trans′fig·yə·rā′shən) *n.* A change in shape or appearance. —**the Transfiguration 1** The supernatural transformation of Christ on the mount. **2** A festival commemorating this, August 6.

trans·fig·ure (trans·fig′yər) *v.t.* **·ured, ·ur·ing 1** To change the outward form or appearance of. **2** To make glorious. [< L *trans-* across + *figura* shape] —**trans·fig′ure·ment** *n.*

trans·fix (trans·fiks′) *v.t.* **1** To pierce through, as with a pointed implement; impale. **2** To fix in place by impaling. **3** To make motionless, as with horror, amazement, etc. [< L *trans-* through, across + *figere* fasten] —**trans·fix′ion** (-fik′shən) *n.*

trans·form (trans·fôrm′) *v.t.* **1** To change the form or appearance of. **2** To change the nature or character of; convert. **3** *Electr.* To subject to the action of a transformer. —*v.i.* **4** To be or become changed in form or character. [< L *trans-* over + *forma* a form] —**trans·form′a·ble, trans·form′a·tive** *adj.*

trans·for·ma·tion (trans′fər·mā′shən) *n.* **1** The act of transforming or the state of being transformed. **2** *Ling.* Any of the systematic processes by which grammatical sentences of a language may be derived from underlying constructions. —**trans′for·ma′tion·al** *adj.*

trans·form·er (trans·fôr′mər) *n.* **1** One who or that which transforms. **2** *Electr.* A device that couples electricity from one alternating-current circuit to another by electromagnetic induction, often with a change in the ratio of current to voltage and always with a small power loss.

trans·fuse (trans·fyōōz′) *v.t.* **·fused, ·fus·ing 1** To cause to

flow or pass from one person or thing to another. **2** *Med.* **a** To transfer (blood, plasma, etc.) from one person or animal to another. **b** To give a transfusion to. **3** To pass into; permeate. [< L *transfusus*, p.p. of *transfundere*] —**trans·fus′er** *n.* —**trans·fus′i·ble, trans·fu·sive** (trans·fyōō′siv) *adj.*

trans·fu·sion (trans·fyōō′zhən) *n.* **1** The act or an instance of transfusing. **2** *Med.* The introduction of a fluid, as saline solution, blood, blood plasma, etc., into the blood stream.

trans·gress (trans·gres′, tranz-) *v.t.* **1** To disregard and go beyond the bounds of, as a divine or traditional law; violate. **2** To pass beyond or over (limits); exceed. —*v.i.* **3** To break a law; sin. [< L *transgressus*, p.p. of *transgredi* step across] —**trans·gres′sor** *n.*

trans·gres·sion (trans·gresh′ən, tranz-) *n.* The act or an instance of transgressing, esp. a sin.

tran·ship (tran·ship′) *v.t.* **·shipped, ·shipping** TRANSSHIP. —**tran·ship′ment** *n.*

tran·sient (tran′shənt, tranch′ənt, tranz′ē·ənt) *adj.* **1** Occurring or existing only for a time; not permanent; transitory. **2** Brief; fleeting; momentary. **3** Residing or staying in a place temporarily: a large *transient* population. —*n.* One who or that which is transient, esp. a temporary resident. [< L *transire* go across] —**tran′sience, tran′sien·cy** *n.* —**tran′sient·ly** *adv.* —**Syn. 1** temporary, passing. **2** ephemeral, fugitive, evanescent. **3** casual.

tran·sis·tor (tran·zis′tər, -sis′-) *n.* *Electronics* **1** A semiconductor device having three terminals and the property that the current between one pair of them is a function of the current between another pair. **2** A transistorized radio. [< TRANS(FER) (RES)ISTOR]

tran·sis·tor·ize (tran·zis′tər·īz, -sis′-) *v.t.* **·ized, ·iz·ing** To equip with transistors. —**tran·sis′tor·i·za′tion** *n.*

tran·sit (tran′sit, -zit) *n.* **1** The act of passing over or through; passage. **2** The process of change; transition. **3** The act of carrying across or through; conveyance. **4** Transportation, esp. for carrying large numbers of people, as in a city: public *transit.* **5** *Astron.* **a** The passage of one celestial body over the disk of another. **b** The passage of a celestial body across the meridian. **6** A surveying instrument resembling a theodolite. [< L *transire* go across]

tran·si·tion (tran·sish′ən, tranz-) *n.* **1** Passage from one place, condition, or stage to another; change. **2** Something, as a period of time or a situation, that leads from one stage or period to another. **3** *Music* A passage or modulation connecting sections of a composition. —**tran·si′tion·al** *adj.* —**tran·si′tion·al·ly** *adv.*

tran·si·tive (tran′sə·tiv) *adj.* **1** *Gram.* Having, requiring, or completed by a direct object: said of a verb. **2** Of or pertaining to transition. —*n.* *Gram.* A transitive verb. [< L *transitus* transit] —**tran′si·tive·ly** *adv.* —**tran′si·tive·ness, tran′si·tiv′i·ty** *n.*

tran·si·to·ry (tran′sə·tôr′ē, -tō′rē) *adj.* **1** Existing for a short time only; soon extinguished or annulled. **2** Brief; ephemeral. —**tran′si·to′ri·ly** *adv.* —**tran′si·to′ri·ness** *n.*

trans·late (trans·lāt′, tranz-, trans·lāt′, tranz′-) *v.* **·lat·ed, ·lat·ing** *v.t.* **1** To change into another language. **2** To change from one form, condition, or place to another. **3** To explain in other words; interpret. **4** *Mech.* To change the position of in space, esp. without rotation. —*v.i.* **5** To change the words of one language into those of another, esp. as an occupation. **6** To admit of translation. [< L *translatus*, lit., carried across] —**trans·lat′a·ble** *adj.* —**trans·la′tor** *n.*

trans·la·tion (trans·lā′shən, tranz-) *n.* **1** The act of translating, or the state of being translated. **2** Something translated; esp., a reproduction of a work in a language different from the original. **3** *Mech.* Motion in which all the parts of a body follow identical courses. —**trans·la′tion·al** *adj.*

trans·lit·er·ate (trans·lit′ə·rāt, tranz-) *v.t.* **·at·ed, ·at·ing** To represent, as a word, by the characters of another alphabet. [< TRANS- + L *litera* a letter] —**trans·lit′er·a′tion** *n.*

trans·lu·cent (trans·lōō′sənt, tranz-) *adj.* Allowing the passage of light, but not permitting a clear view of any object. [< L *trans-* through, across + *lucere* to shine] —**trans·lu′cence, trans·lu′cen·cy** *n.* —**trans·lu′cent·ly** *adv.*

trans·mi·grate (trans·mī′grāt, tranz-, trans′mī-, tranz′·mī-) *v.i.* **·grat·ed, ·grat·ing** **1** To pass into another body, as the soul at death. **2** To migrate, as from one country or jurisdiction to another. —**trans·mi·gra·tion** (trans′mī·grā′shən, tranz′-), **trans·mi′gra·tor** *n.* —**trans·mi′gra·to·ry** (-mī′·grə·tôr′ē, -tō′rē) *adj.*

trans·mis·si·ble (trans·mis′ə·bəl, tranz-) *adj.* Capable of being transmitted. —**trans·mis′si·bil′i·ty** *n.*

trans·mis·sion (trans·mish′ən, tranz-) *n.* **1** The act of transmitting, or the state of being transmitted. **2** That which is transmitted. **3** *Mech.* A device that transmits power from its source to its point of application, as from the engine of an automobile to the wheels. —**trans·mis′sive** *adj.*

trans·mit (trans·mit′, tranz-) *v.t.* **·mit·ted, ·mit·ting** **1** To send from one place or person to another; convey. **2** To pass on (a gene, a virus, etc.) from one organism to another. **3** To cause (light, sound, etc.) to pass through space or a medium. **4** To send out, as by means of radio waves. **5** To serve as a medium of passage for; conduct: Iron *transmits* heat. **6** *Mech.* To convey (force, motion, etc.) from one part or mechanism to another. [< L *trans-* across + *mittere* send] —**trans·mit′ta·ble** *adj.* —**trans·mit′tal, trans·mit′tance** *n.*

trans·mit·ter (trans·mit′ər, tranz-) *n.* **1** One who or that which transmits. **2** The part of a telephone into which a person talks. **3** The part of a telegraph for sending messages. **4** *Telecom.* A device that modulates a carrier with a signal and sends the carrier forth, as in radio, telephony, or telegraphy.

trans·mog·ri·fy (trans·mog′rə·fī, tranz-) *v.t.* **·fied, ·fy·ing** To make into something altogether different; transform radically: often used humorously. [?] —**trans·mog′ri·fi·ca′tion** *n.*

trans·mu·ta·tion (trans′myōō·tā′shən, tranz′-) *n.* **1** The act of transmuting, or the state of being transmuted. **2** The conversion of an atom of an element into an atom of a different element, as by radioactive decay, nuclear fission, etc. **3** The supposed conversion of a base metal into gold or silver. —**trans′mu·ta′tion·al, trans·mut·a·tive** (trans·myōō′tə·tiv, tranz-) *adj.*

trans·mute (trans·myōōt′, tranz-) *v.t.* **·mut·ed, ·mut·ing** To change in nature or form. Also **trans·mu′tate.** [< L *trans-* across + *mutare* to change] —**trans·mut′a·ble** *adj.* —**trans·mut′a·bil′i·ty, trans·mut′a·ble·ness, trans·mut′er** *n.* —**trans·mut′a·bly** *adv.*

trans·o·ce·an·ic (trans′ō·shē·an′ik, tranz′-) *adj.* **1** Crossing or traversing the ocean. **2** Lying beyond or over the ocean.

tran·som (tran′səm) *n.* **1** A horizontal piece framed across an opening; a lintel. **2** A small window above and often hinged to such a bar, usu. situated above a door. **3** The horizontal crossbar of a gallows or cross. [< L *transtrum* a crossbeam] —**tran′somed** *adj.*

transp. transportation.

trans·pa·cif·ic (trans′pə·sif′ik) *adj.* **1** Across or crossing the Pacific Ocean. **2** On the other side of the Pacific.

trans·par·en·cy (trans·pâr′ən·sē, -par′-) *n.* *pl.* **·cies** **1** The state or quality of being transparent. **2** Something whose transmission of light defines an image, esp. a piece of photographic film, often mounted as a slide and viewed by projecting its image on a screen or other surface.

trans·par·ent (trans·pâr′ənt, -par′-) *adj.* **1** Allowing the passage of light and of clear views of objects beyond. **2** Having a texture fine enough to be seen through; diaphanous. **3** Easy to understand. **4** Without guile; frank; candid. **5** Easily detected; obvious: a *transparent* lie. [< L *trans-* across + *parere* appear, be visible] —**trans·par′ent·ly** *adv.* —**trans·par′ence, trans·par′ent·ness** *n.*

tran·spi·ra·tion (trans′pə·rā′shən) *n.* A transpiring or exhalation, as the loss of water from a plant by evaporation.

tran·spire (trans·pīr′) *v.* **·spired, ·spir·ing** *v.t.* **1** To give off through permeable tissues, as of the skin and lungs or of

add, āce, câre, pälm; end, ēven; it, īce; odd, ōpen, ôrder; tŏŏk, pōōl; up, bûrn; ə = *a* in *above*, *u* in *focus*; yōō = *u* in *fuse*; oil; pout; check; go; ring; thin; this; zh, *vision*. < derived from; ? origin uncertain or unknown.

leaf surfaces. —*v.i.* **2** To be emitted, as through the skin; be exhaled, as moisture or odors. **3** To become known. **4** To happen; occur. [< L *trans-* across, through + *spirare* breathe] • An accepted meaning of *transpire* is to become known or leak out: *It transpired that he had died penniless.* The word is more commonly used today, however, with the sense of "to happen": *We shall never know what transpired at that meeting.* The latter usage still strikes the more traditionally inclined as improper or ignorant. That judgment may be unduly harsh, but as a matter of style the usage is almost always inelegant and often pretentious.

trans·plant (trans-plant′) *v.t.* **1** To remove and plant in another place. **2** To remove and settle for residence in another place. **3** *Surg.* To transfer (an organ or tissue) from its original site to another part of the body or to another individual. —*v.i.* **4** To admit of being transplanted. —*n.* (trans′plant′) **1** That which is transplanted, as a seedling or an organ of the body. **2** The act of transplanting. —**trans′plan·ta′tion, trans·plant′er** *n.*

trans·port (trans-pôrt′, -pōrt′) *v.t.* **1** To carry or convey from one place to another. **2** To carry away with emotion, as with delight; enchant. **3** To banish to another country. —*n.* (trans′pôrt, -pōrt) **1** The act or a means of transporting; transportation. **2** A state of emotional rapture; intense delight. **3** A ship, train, truck, etc., used to transport troops, supplies, etc. **4** A system of transportation. **5** A deported convict. [< L *trans-* across + *portare* carry] — **trans·port′a·bil′i·ty, trans·port′er** *n.* —**trans·port′able** *adj.*

trans·por·ta·tion (trans′pər·tā′shən) *n.* **1** The act of transporting. **2** A means of transporting or traveling. **3** The conveying of passengers or freight, esp. as an industry. **4** Money, a pass, etc., used for being transported.

trans·pose (trans-pōz′) *v.t.* **·posed, ·pos·ing 1** To reverse the order or change the place of: to *transpose* two numerals or a word in a sentence. **2** *Math.* To transfer (a term) from one side of an algebraic equation to the other with reversed sign. **3** *Music* To write or play in a different key. [< L *trans-* over + OF *poser* put] —**trans·pos′a·ble** *adj.* —**trans·po′sal, trans·pos′er, trans·po·si·tion** (trans′pə·zish′ən) *n.*

trans·sex·u·al (trans-sek′shōō·əl, -sek′shəl) *n.* A person who is genetically and physically of one sex but who identifies psychologically with the other and may seek treatment by surgery or with hormones to bring the physical sexual characteristics into conformity with the psychological preference. —*adj.* Of, for, or characteristic of transsexuals. —**trans·sex′u·al·ism** *n.*

trans·ship (trans-ship′) *v.t. & v.i.* **·shipped, ·ship·ping** To transfer from one conveyance or means of transport to another for further shipment. —**trans·ship′ment** *n.*

tran·sub·stan·ti·ate (tran′səb·stan′shē·āt) *v.t.* **·at·ed, ·at·ing 1** To change from one substance into another; transmute; transform. **2** *Theol.* To change the substance of (bread and wine) in the rite of transubstantiation.

tran·sub·stan·ti·a·tion (tran′səb·stan′shē·ā′shən) *n.* In the Roman Catholic and Eastern Orthodox churches, the conversion of the substance of the bread and wine of the Eucharist into that of Christ's body and blood.

trans·u·ra·ni·um (trans′yōō·rā′nē·əm, tranz′-) *adj.* Of or pertaining to elements having an atomic number greater than that of uranium. Also **trans′u·ran′ic** (-ran′ik).

trans·ver·sal (trans-vûr′səl, tranz-) *adj.* TRANSVERSE. —*n. Geom.* A straight line intersecting a system of lines.

trans·verse (trans-vûrs′, tranz-) *adj.* Lying or being across or from side to side. —*n.* (*also* trans′vûrs, tranz′-) That which is transverse. [< L *transversus* lying across] — **trans·verse′ly** *adv.*

trans·ves·tite (trans-ves′tīt, tranz-) *n.* One who wears the clothes of the opposite sex. [< L *trans-* over + *vestire* to clothe + -ITE] —**trans·ves′tism, trans·ves′ti·tism** (-ves′tə·tiz′əm) *n.*

trap¹ (trap) *n.* **1** A device for catching game or other animals, as a pitfall or a baited contrivance set to spring shut on being slightly jarred or moved. **2** A devious plan or trick by which a person may be caught or taken unawares. **3** A device for hurling clay pigeons into the air, used in trapshooting. **4** Any of various devices that collect residual material or that form a seal to stop a return flow

of noxious gas, etc., as a water-filled U- or S-bend in a pipe. **5** In golf, an obstacle or hazard: a sand *trap.* **6** TRAPDOOR. **7** A light, two-wheeled carriage suspended by springs. **8** *pl.* Percussion instruments, as drums, cymbals, etc. **9** *Slang* The mouth. —*v.* **trapped, trap·ping** *v.t.* **1** To catch in or as if in a trap. **2** To provide with a trap. **3** To stop or hold by the formation of a seal. **4** To catch (a ball) just as or after it strikes the ground. —*v.i.* **5** To set traps for game; be a trapper. [< OE *træppe*]

trap² (trap) *n. Geol.* A dark, fine-grained igneous rock, often of columnar structure, as basalt. Also **trap′rock′.** [< Sw. *trappa* a stair]

trap·door (trap′dôr′, -dōr′) *n.* A door, hinged or sliding, to cover an opening, as in a floor or roof.

tra·peze (tra·pēz′, trə-) *n.* A short swinging bar suspended by two ropes, for gymnastic exercises and acrobatic stunts. [< NL *trapezium* a trapezium]

tra·pe·zi·um (trə·pē′zē·əm) *n. p.* **·zi·ums** or **·zi·a** (-zē·ə) *Geom.* **1** A four-sided plane figure of which no two sides are parallel. **2** *Brit.* TRAPEZOID (def. 1). [< Gk. *trapeza* a table, lit., a four-footed (bench)]

Trapezium def. 1   Trapezoid def. 1

trap·e·zoid (trap′ə·zoid′) *n. Geom.* **1** A quadrilateral of which two sides are parallel. **2** *Brit.* TRAPEZIUM (def. 1). [< Gk. *trapeza* a table + *eidos* form] —**trap′e·zoi′dal** *adj.*

trap·per (trap′ər) *n.* One whose occupation is the trapping of fur-bearing animals.

trap·pings (trap′ingz) *n. pl.* **1** An ornamental covering or harness for a horse; caparison. **2** Adornments of any kind; embellishments. **3** The superficial signs or perquisites; marks: the *trappings* of success. [< ME *trappe*]

Trap·pist (trap′ist) *n.* A monk belonging to an ascetic order noted for silence. —*adj.* Of this order. [< *La Trappe*, France, site of the order's establishment in 1664]

trap·shoot·ing (trap′shōō′ting) *n.* The sport of shooting clay pigeons sent up from spring traps. —**trap′shoot′er** *n.*

trash (trash) *n.* **1** Worthless or waste matter; rubbish. **2** That which is broken or lopped off, as twigs and branches. **3** Foolish or idle talk. **4** Anything worthless, shoddy, or without merit: literary *trash.* **5** A person regarded as worthless or of no account. —*v.t. & v.i. Slang* To wreck or destroy (something) purposefully but often indiscriminately as an expression of alienation or rebellion. [?] — **trash′i·ness** *n.* —**trash′y** (·i·er, ·i·est) *adj.*

trau·ma (trou′mə, trô′-) *n. pl.* **·mas** or **·ma·ta** (-mə·tə) **1** Any physical injury resulting from force. **2** A severe emotional shock having a deep effect upon the personality. [< Gk., a wound] —**trau·mat·ic** (trou·mat′ik, trô-) *adj.* —**trau·mat′i·cal·ly** *adv.*

trau·ma·tize (trô′mə·tīz) *v.t.* **·tized, ·tiz·ing** To cause trauma to or in.

trav·ail (trə·vāl′, trav′āl) *n.* **1** Pain, anguish, or distress encountered in an effort or achievement. **2** Labor in childbirth. **3** Hard or wearisome labor. **4** Physical agony. —*v.i.* **1** To suffer the pangs of childbirth. **2** To toil; labor. [< OF < *travailler* to labor, toil]

trav·el (trav′əl) *v.* **trav·eled** or **·elled, trav·el·ing** or **·el·ling** *v.i.* **1** To go from one place to another or from place to place; make a journey or tour. **2** To proceed; advance. **3** To go about from place to place as a traveling salesman. **4** *Informal* To move with speed. **5** To pass or be transmitted, as light, sound, etc. **6** *Mech.* To move in a fixed path, as a machine part. **7** In basketball, to commit the infraction of failing to dribble while moving with the ball. —*v.t.* **8** To move or journey across or through: traverse. —*n.* **1** The act of traveling. **2** *Often pl.* A journey or tour, usu. extensive. **3** Passage to, over, or past a certain place. **4** Distance traveled, as by a machine part. [< OF *travailler* to travail]

trav·eled (trav′əld) *adj.* **1** Having made many journeys. **2** Frequented or used by travelers. Also **trav′elled.**

trav·e·logue (trav·ə·lôg, -log) *n.* **1** A documentary film about a traveled place. **2** A lecture or talk on travel, usu. illustrated pictorially. Also **trav′e·log.**

tra·verse (trə·vûrs′, tra-) *v.* **·ersed, ·ers·ing** *v.t.* **1** to pass over, across, or through. **2** To move back and forth over or

along. **3** To examine carefully; scrutinize. **4** To oppose; thwart. **5** *Law* To make denial of. —*v.i.* **6** To move back and forth. **7** To move across; cross. —**trav·erse** (trav′ərs) *n.* **1** Something that traverses, as a crosspiece of a machine or structure. **2** Something serving as a screen or barrier. **3** The act of traversing or denying; a denial. —*adj.* (trav′· ərs) Lying or being across; transverse. [< L *transversus* transverse] —**tra·vers′a·ble** *adj.* —**tra·vers′al, tra·vers′er** *n.*

trav·erse rod (trav′ərs) A curtain rod equipped with a sliding mechanism for drawing a pair of curtains together or apart with a cord.

trav·es·ty (trav′is·tē) *n. pl.* **·ties 1** A grotesque imitation, as of a lofty subject; burlesque. **2** A distorted or absurd rendering or example, as if in mockery: a *travesty* of justice. —*v.t.* **·tied, ·ty·ing** To make a travesty of; burlesque; parody. [< Ital. *travestire* to disguise]

trawl (trôl) *n.* **1** A large net for towing on the bottom of the ocean by a fishing boat. **2** A stout fishing line, anchored and buoyed, from which many lines bearing baited hooks may be secured. —*v.i.* **1** To fish with a trawl. —*v.t.* **2** To drag, as a net, to catch fish. [?]

trawl·er (trô′lər) *n.* A boat used for trawling.

tray (trā) *n.* **1** A flat, shallow utensil with raised edges, used to hold or carry several or a number of articles, as dishes. **2** A tray and the articles on it. **3** A shallow, topless box serving as a compartment, as in a tool or sewing box. [< OE *trēg* a wooden board] —**tray′ful** (-fŏŏl′) *n.*

treach·er·ous (trech′ər·əs) *adj.* **1** Likely to betray allegiance or confidence; untrustworthy. **2** Of the nature of treachery; perfidious. **3** Apparently safe or secure, but in fact dangerous or unreliable: *treacherous* footing. —**treach′er·ous·ly** *adv.* —**treach′er·ous·ness** *n.*

treach·er·y (trech′ər·ē) *n. pl.* **·er·ies** Violation of allegiance, confidence, or faith; treason. [< OF *tricher* cheat]

trea·cle (trē′kəl) *n.* **1** Molasses, esp. that obtained in refining sugar. **2** Saccharine speech or sentiments. **3** Formerly, a compound used as an antidote for poison. [< Gk. *thēriakē* a remedy for poisonous bites] —**trea′cly** *adj.*

tread (tred) *v.* **trod, trod·den** or **trod, tread·ing** *v.t.* **1** To step or walk on, over, along, etc. **2** To press with the feet; trample. **3** To crush or oppress harshly. **4** To accomplish in walking or in dancing: to *tread* a measure. **5** To copulate with: said of male birds. —*v.i.* **6** To place the foot down; walk. **7** To press the ground or anything beneath the feet: usu. with *on*. —**tread water** In swimming, to keep the body erect and the head above water by moving the feet and arms. —*n.* **1** The act, manner, or sound of treading; a walking or stepping. **2** The part of a wheel or automobile tire that comes into contact with the road or rails. **3** The impression made by a foot, a tire, etc. **4** The horizontal part of a step in a stairway. [< OE *tredan*] —**tread′er** *n.*

tread·le (tred′l) *n.* A lever operated by the foot, usu. to cause rotary motion. —*v.i.* **·led, ·ling** To work a treadle. [< OE *tredel* < *tredan* tread] • See POTTER'S WHEEL.

tread·mill (tred′mil′) *n.* **1** A mechanism rotated by the walking motion of one or more persons or animals. **2** Monotonous routine; tedious and unrewarding effort.

treas. treasurer; treasury.

trea·son (trē′zən) *n.* **1** Betrayal, treachery, or breach of allegiance toward a sovereign or government. **2** A breach of faith; treachery. [< L *traditio* a betrayal, delivery] —**trea′son·ous** *adj.* —**trea′son·ous·ly** *adv.*

trea·son·a·ble (trē′zən·ə·bəl) *adj.* Of, involving, or characteristic of treason. —**trea′son·a·ble·ness** *n.* —**trea′son·a·bly** *adv.*

treas·ure (trezh′ər) *n.* **1** Riches accumulated or possessed, as a store of precious metals, jewels, or money. **2** Someone or something very precious. —*v.t.* **·ured, ·ur·ing 1** To set a high value upon; prize. **2** To lay up in store; accumulate. [< L *thesaurus*] —**Syn.** *v.* **1** cherish, esteem, value, venerate. **2** hoard.

treas·ur·er (trezh′ər·ər) *n.* **1** An officer authorized to receive, care for, and disburse revenues, as of a government, business corporation, or society. **2** A similar custodian of the funds of a society or a corporation.

treas·ure-trove (trezh′ər·trōv′) *n.* **1** *Law* Money, gold, etc., found hidden, the owner being unknown. **2** Any rich or rewarding discovery. Also **treasure trove.** [< AF *tresor* treasure + *trover* to find]

treas·ur·y (trezh′ər·ē) *n. pl.* **·ur·ies 1** A place of receipt and disbursement of public revenue or private funds. **2** The revenue or funds. **3** The place where a treasure is stored. **4** A department of government concerned with finances, the issuance of money, etc. [< OF *tresor* treasure]

treat (trēt) *v.t.* **1** To conduct oneself toward (a person, animal, etc.) in a specified manner. **2** To look upon or regard in a specified manner: They *treat* it as a childhood prank. **3** To give medical or surgical attention to. **4** To deal with in writing or speaking. **5** To depict or express artistically in a specified style. **6** To pay for the entertainment, food, or drink of. —*v.i.* **7** To deal with a subject in writing or speaking: usu. with *of.* **8** To carry on negotiations; negotiate. **9** To pay for another's entertainment. —*n.* **1** Something that gives unusual pleasure. **2** Entertainment of any kind furnished gratuitously to another. **3** *Informal* One's turn to pay for refreshment or entertainment. [< OF *tretier, traitier*] —**treat′er** *n.*

trea·tise (trē′tis) *n.* A formal, systematic, written exposition of a serious subject: a *treatise* on labor relations. [< OF *traitier*]

treat·ment (trēt′mənt) *n.* **1** The act, manner, or process of treating anything. **2** The therapeutic measures designed to cure a disease or abnormal condition.

trea·ty (trē′tē) *n. pl.* **·ties** A formal agreement or compact between two or more nations. [< OF *traitié,* p.p. of *traitier* treat]

treb·le (treb′əl) *v.t. & v.i.* **·led, ·ling** To multiply by three; triple. —*adj.* **1** Threefold. **2** *Music* **a** Of the highest range. **b** Soprano. —*n.* **1 a** *Music* A part or instrument of the highest range. **b** A soprano singer. **2** High, piping sound. [< L *triplus* triple] —**treb′ly** *adv.*

tree (trē) *n.* **1** A woody perennial plant having a distinct trunk with branches and foliage at some distance above the ground. **2** Any shrub or plant with a treelike shape or dimensions. **3** Something whose outline resembles the spreading branches of a tree, as a diagram: a genealogical *tree.* **4** A timber, post, or piece of wood used for a particular purpose. —*v.t.* **treed, tree·ing 1** To force to climb or take refuge in a tree: to *tree* an opossum. **2** *Informal* To get the advantage of; corner. [< OE *trēow*]

tree fern Any of various treelike ferns with woody trunks.

tree frog Any of various arboreal frogs having adhesive disks on the toes. Also **tree toad.**

tree·nail (trē′nāl′, tren′əl, trun′əl) *n.* A wooden peg or nail of dry, hard wood which swells when moist, used for fastening timbers.

tree of heaven AILANTHUS.

tree surgery The treatment of damaged trees by pruning, cementing cavities, etc. —**tree surgeon**

Trefoil
def. 2

tre·foil (trē′foil) *n.* **1** Any of various plants having threefold leaves, as clover. **2** An architectural ornament having the form of a three-lobed leaf. [< L *trifolium*]

trek (trek) *v.* **trekked, trek·king** *v.i.* **1** To move along with effort or slowly, esp. on foot. **3** In South Africa, to travel by ox wagon. —*v.t.* **4** To transport. **5** In South Africa, to draw (a vehicle or load): said of an ox. —*n.* **1** A journey or a stage in a journey. **2** The act of trekking. **3** In South Africa, an organized migration. [< Du. *trekken* draw, travel < MDu. *trecken*] —**trek′ker** *n.*

trel·lis (trel′is) *n.* A grating or lattice, often of wood, used as a screen or a support for vines, etc.

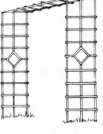

Trellis

—*v.t.* **1** To interlace so as to form a trellis. **2** To furnish with or fasten on a trellis. [< L *trilix* of three threads]

trem·a·tode (trem′ə·tōd, trē′mə-) *n.* Any of a class of parasitic flatworms, as the liver fluke. [< Gk. *trēma* a hole + *eidos* form] —**trem′a·toid** (-toid) *adj.*

trem·ble (trem′bəl) *v.i.* **·bled, ·bling 1** To shake involuntarily, as with fear or weakness. **2** To move slightly or vibrate, as from some jarring force: The building *trembled.* **3** To feel anxiety or fear. **4** To quaver, as the voice. —*n.* The act or state of trembling. [< LL *tremulus* tremulous] —**trem′bler** *n.* —**trem′bling·ly** *adv.* —**trem′bly** *adj.* — **Syn.** *v.* **2** quiver, shake, totter, quake.

tre·men·dous (tri·men′dəs) *adj.* **1** Extraordinarily large or extensive; enormous; great. **2** Causing astonishment by its magnitude, force, etc.; awe-inspiring. **3** *Informal* Wonderful; marvelous. [< L *tremendus* to be trembled at] —**tre·men′dous·ly** *adv.* —**tre·men′dous·ness** *n.*

trem·o·lo (trem′ə·lō) *n. pl.* **·los** *Music* **1** A rapid, periodic variation in the loudness of a tone. **2** The mechanism for causing this in organ tones. [Ital., trembling]

trem·or (trem′ər, trē′mər) *n.* **1** A quick, vibratory movement; a shaking. **2** Any involuntary quivering or trembling, as of a muscle. **3** A state of agitation or excitement, as in anticipation of something. [< OF *tremour* fear, a trembling]

trem·u·lous (trem′yə·ləs) *adj.* **1** Characterized or affected by trembling: *tremulous* speech. **2** Showing timidity and irresolution. **3** Characterized by mental excitement. Also **trem′u·lant.** [< L *tremulus*] —**trem′u·lous·ly** *adv.* —**trem′u·lous·ness** *n.*

tre·nail (trē′nāl, tren′əl, trun′əl) *n.* TREENAIL.

trench (trench) *n.* **1** A long narrow ditch, esp. one lined with a parapet of the excavated earth, to protect troops. **2** A long, narrow region much deeper than the adjacent surfaces, as along the ocean floor. —*v.t.* **1** To dig a trench or trenches in. **2** To fortify with trenches. **3** To cut deep furrows in. —*v.i.* **4** To cut or dig trenches. **5** To cut; carve. **6** To encroach. [< OF *trenchier* to cut] —**trench′er** *n.*

trench·ant (tren′chənt) *adj.* **1** Clear, vigorous, and effective: a *trenchant* rebuttal. **2** Cutting, as sarcasm; biting. **3** Incisive; sharp; keen: *trenchant* wit. **4** *Archaic* Cutting deeply and quickly: a *trenchant* sword. [< OF *trenchier*] — **trench′an·cy** *n.* —**trench′ant·ly** *adv.*

trench coat A raincoat with a belt, straps on the shoulders, and several pockets.

trench·er (tren′chər) *n.* A wooden plate or board used to serve food or as a surface for cutting it. [< OF *trenchier* to cut]

trench·er·man (tren′chər·mən) *n. pl.* **·men** (-mən) A person who eats heartily.

trench fever A relapsing fever transmitted by body lice.

trench foot A foot condition resembling frostbite, due to continued dampness and cold.

trench mouth A mildly contagious disease of the gums, and sometimes the larynx and tonsils, caused by a soil bacillus.

trend (trend) *n.* **1** A prevailing or probable tendency; predominant or likely course or direction; drift: a *trend* toward smaller families; investment *trends;* to study *trends* in education. **2** A popular preference or inclination: fashion *trends.* **3** The general course or direction, as of a coast; bent. —*v.i.* **1** To have or follow a general course or direction. **2** To exhibit a tendency; move: wheat prices *trending* upward. [< OE *trendan* to roll]

trend·y (tren′dē) *adj. Slang* **trend·i·er, trend·i·est** In step with current fashion; voguish. —*n. pl.* **trend·ies** *Chiefly Brit.* A trendy person or thing. —**trend′i·ness** *n.*

tre·pan (tri·pan′) *n.* **1** An early form of the trephine. **2** A large rock-boring tool. —*v.t.* **·panned, ·pan·ning** To use a trepan upon. [< Gk. *trypanon* a borer] —**trep·a·na·tion** (trep′ə·nā′shən), **tre·pan′ner** *n.*

tre·phine (tri·fīn′, -fēn′) *n. Surg.* A cylindrical saw for removing a disk of tissue, as from the skull, cornea, etc. —*v.t.* **·phined, ·phin·ing** To operate on with a trephine. [< L *tres fines* three ends]

trep·i·da·tion (trep′ə·dā′shən) *n.* **1** Tremulous agitation caused by fear; apprehension. **2** *Archaic* An involuntary trembling; tremor. [< L *trepidare* hurry, be alarmed]

tres·pass (tres′pəs, -pas′) *v.i.* **1** To violate the personal or property rights of another; esp., to go unlawfully onto another's land. **2** To go beyond the bounds of what is right or proper; transgress. **3** To intrude; encroach: to *trespass* on one's privacy. —*n.* **1** *Law* **a** Any act accompanied by actual or implied force in violation of another's person, property, or rights. **b** An action for injuries sustained because of this. **2** Any transgression of law or moral duty. **3** An intrusion; encroachment. [< Med. L *trans-* across, beyond + *passare* to pass] —**tres′pass·er** *n.*

tress (tres) *n.* **1** A lock or curl of human hair. **2** *pl.* The hair of a woman or girl, esp. when long and worn loose. [< OF *tresce*] —**tressed** (trest) *adj.*

tres·tle (tres′əl) *n.* **1** A beam or bar braced by two pairs of divergent legs, used to support tables, platforms, etc. **2** A braced framework functioning like a bridge in supporting a roadway or railway over a short span. [< L *transtrum* crossbeam]

trey (trā) *n.* A card, domino, or die having three spots or pips. [< L *tres* three]

trfd. transferred.

tri- *prefix* **1** Three; threefold; thrice: *tricycle.* **2** *Chem.* Containing three atoms, radicals, groups, etc.: *trioxide.* **3** Occurring three times within a (specified) interval: *triweekly.* [< L *tri-* threefold]

tri·ad (trī′ad) *n.* **1** A group of three persons or things. **2** *Music* A chord of three tones, esp. a tone with its third and fifth. [< Gk. *trias* < *treis* three] —**tri·ad′ic** *adj., n.*

tri·al (trī′əl, trīl) *n.* **1** The examination in a court of law, often before a jury, of the facts of a case in order to determine its disposition. **2** The act of testing or proving by experience or use. **3** The state of being tried or tested. **4** An experience, person, or thing that puts strength, patience, or faith to the test. **5** An attempt or effort to do something. **6** Hardship; difficulty: the *trials* of poverty. — **on trial** In the process of being tried or tested. —**trial and error** The trying of one thing after another until something succeeds. —*adj.* **1** Of or pertaining to a trial or trials. **2** Made or used in the course of trying or testing. [< AF < *trier* to try] —**Syn.** *n.* **2** examination, experiment. **5** endeavor. **6** misfortune, trouble.

trial balance In double-entry bookkeeping, a draft of the debit and credit balances of each account in the ledger.

trial jury A jury of 12 persons impaneled to decide a civil or criminal case; petit jury.

tri·an·gle (trī′ang·gəl) *n.* **1** *Geom.* A figure, esp. a plane figure, bounded by three sides, and having three angles. **2** Something resembling such a figure in shape. **3** A situation involving three persons: the eternal *triangle.* **4** *Music* A percussion instrument consisting of a resonant metal bar bent into a triangle and sounded by striking with a small metal rod. [< L *tri-* three + *angulus* an angle]

Triangles
a. equilateral. b. isosceles.
c. scalene. d. right-angle.

tri·an·gu·lar (trī·ang′gyə·lər) *adj.* **1** Pertaining to, like, or bounded by a triangle. **2** Concerned with or pertaining to three things, parties, or persons. —**tri·an′gu·lar′i·ty** (-lar′ə·tē) *n.* —**tri·an′gu·lar·ly** *adv.*

tri·an·gu·late (trī·ang′gyə·lāt) *v.t.* **·lat·ed, ·lat·ing 1** To divide into triangles. **2** To measure or determine by means of trigonometry. **3** To give triangular shape to. —*adj.* Marked with triangles. —**tri·an·gu·la′tion** *n.*

Tri·as·sic (trī·as′ik) *adj. & n.* See GEOLOGY. [< LL *trias* triad]

tri·bal·ism (trī′bəl·iz′əm) *n.* Tribal organization, culture, or relations.

tribe (trīb) *n.* **1** A group of people, under one chief or ruler, united by common ancestry, language, and culture. **2** In ancient Israel, any of the 12 divisions of the Hebrews. **3** In ancient Rome, any of the three clans making up the Roman people. **4** A number of persons of any class or profession taken together: often contemptuous. **5** *Biol.* **a** A group of closely related genera. **b** Any group of plants or animals. [< L *tribus*] —**tri′bal** *adj.* —**tri′bal·ly** *adv.*

tribes·man (trībz′mən) *n. pl.* **·men** (-mən) A member of a tribe.

trib·u·la·tion (trib′yə·lā′shən) *n.* **1** A condition of distress; suffering. **2** The cause of such distress. [< L *tribulare* thrash] —**Syn. 1** misery, oppression, sorrow, trouble.

tri·bu·nal (trī·byōō′nəl, tri-) *n.* **1** A court of justice. **2** Any judicial body, as a board of arbitrators. **3** The seat set apart for judges, magistrates, etc. [< L *tribunus* tribune]

trib·une[1] (trib′yōōn, trib·yōōn′) *n.* **1** In ancient Rome, a magistrate chosen by the plebeians to protect them against patrician oppression. **2** Any champion of the people. [< L *tribunus*, lit., head of a tribe < *tribus* a tribe] —**trib′u·nar′y** (-yə·ner′ē), **trib′u·ni′tial** (-yə·nish′əl) *adj.*

trib·une[2] (trib′yōōn) *n.* A rostrum or platform. [< L *tribunal* a tribunal]

trib·u·tar·y (trib′yə·ter′ē) *adj.* **1** Supplying a larger body, as a stream flowing into a river. **2** Paying tribute. —*n. pl.* **·tar·ies 1** A stream flowing into a larger one. **2** A person or state paying tribute. [< L *tributum*. See TRIBUTE.]

trib·ute (trib′yōōt) *n.* **1** Money or other valuables paid by one state to another as the price of peace and protection, or by virtue of some treaty. **2** Any obligatory payment, as a tax. **3** Anything given that is due to worth, affection, or duty: a *tribute* of praise. [< L *tributum*, neut. p.p. of *tribuere* pay, allot]

trice (trīs) *v.t.* **triced, tric·ing** To raise with a rope: usu. with *up.* —*n.* An instant: only in the phrase **in a trice.** [< MDu. *trisen* to hoist]

tri·ceps (trī′seps) *n. pl.* **·cep·ses** (-sep·sēz) or **·ceps** The large muscle at the back of the upper arm which straightens the arm when it contracts. [L, three-headed]

tri·chi·na (tri·kī′nə) *n. pl.* **·nae** (-nē) or **·nas** A roundworm whose larvae cause trichinosis. [< Gk. *trichinos* of hair]

Triceps

trich·i·no·sis (trik′ə·nō′sis) *n.* A disease usu. resulting from eating undercooked infected pork and marked by encysted trichina larvae in the muscles. Also **trich′i·ni·a·sis** (-nī′ə·sis). —**trich′i·nosed** (-nōzd, -nōst), **trich′i·nous** (-ə·nəs) *adj.*

trick (trik) *n.* **1** A deception; a petty artifice. **2** A malicious or annoying act: a dirty *trick.* **3** A practical joke; prank. **4** A particular characteristic; trait: a *trick* of tapping her foot. **5** A peculiar skill or knack. **6** A feat of jugglery. **7** In card games, the whole number of cards played in one round. **8** A turn or spell of duty. **9** *Informal* A child or young girl. —**do** (or **turn**) **the trick** *Slang* To produce the desired result. —*v.t.* **1** To deceive or cheat; delude. —*v.i.* **2** To practice trickery or deception. [< OF *trichier* cheat] —**trick′er** *n.* —**Syn. n. 1** ruse, stratagem, subterfuge, device.

trick·er·y (trik′ər·ē) *n. pl.* **·er·ies** The practice of tricks; artifice; wiles.

trick·le (trik′əl) *v.* **·led, ·ling** *v.i.* **1** To flow or run drop by drop or in a very thin stream. **2** To move, come, go, etc., bit by bit. —*v.t.* **3** To cause to trickle. —*n.* **1** The act or state of trickling. **2** A thin stream. [ME *triklen*]

trick·ster (trik′stər) *n.* One who plays tricks.

trick·y (trik′ē) *adj.* **trick·i·er, trick·i·est 1** Given to tricks; crafty; deceitful. **2** Intricate; requiring adroitness or skill. —**trick′i·ly** *adv.* —**trick′i·ness** *n.*

tri·col·or (trī′kul′ər) *adj.* Having or characterized by three colors: also **tri′col′ored.** —*n.* The French national flag. *Brit. sp.* **tri′col′our.**

tri·corn (trī′kôrn) *n.* A hat with the brim turned up on three sides. —*adj.* Three-horned; three-pronged. [< L *tricornis* three-horned]

tri·cot (trē′kō, trī′kət) *n.* **1** A hand-knitted or woven fabric, or a machine-made imitation thereof. **2** A soft ribbed cloth. [< F *tricoter* knit]

tri·cus·pid (trī·kus′pid) *adj.* **1** Having three cusps or points, as a molar tooth: also **tri·cus′pi·date. 2** Having three segments, as the valve between the right auricle and right ventricle of the heart: also **tri·cus′pi·dal.** [< L *tricuspis* three-pointed]

tri·cy·cle (trī′sik·əl) *n.* A three-wheeled vehicle worked by pedals, esp. one used by children.

tri·dent (trīd′nt) *n.* A three-pronged implement or weapon, the emblem of Neptune (Poseidon). —*adj.* Having three teeth or prongs: also **tri·den·tate** (trī·den′tāt), **tri·den′tat·ed.** [< L *tri-* three + *dens* a tooth]

tried (trīd) *p.t.* & *p.p.* of TRY. —*adj.* **1** Tested; trustworthy. **2** Freed of impurities.

tri·en·ni·al (trī·en′ē·əl) *adj.* **1** Taking place every third year. **2** Lasting three years. —*n.* **1** A ceremony celebrated every three years. **2** A plant lasting three years. [< L *tri-* three + *annus* year] —**tri·en′ni·al·ly** *adv.*

tri·fle (trī′fəl) *v.* **·fled, ·fling** *v.i.* **1** To treat or speak of something as of no value or importance: with *with.* **2** To play; toy. —*v.t.* **3** To spend (time, money, etc.) idly and purposelessly: He *trifled* away his entire fortune. —*n.* **1** Anything of very little value or importance. **2** A dessert, popular in England, made of layers of macaroons or ladyfingers with sugared fruit, custard, and meringue or whipped cream. **3** A small amount: It costs only a *trifle.* —**a trifle** Slightly; to a small extent: a *trifle* short. [< OF *truffer* deceive, jeer at] —**tri′fler** *n.*

tri·fling (trī′fling) *adj.* **1** Frivolous. **2** Insignificant. —**tri′·fling·ly** *adv.*

tri·fo·cal (trī·fō′kəl) *adj. Optics* Of or describing a lens with three segments, for near, intermediate, and far vision respectively. —*n.* A trifocal lens.

tri·fo·li·ate (trī·fō′lē·it, -āt) *adj. Bot.* Having three leaves or leaflike processes. Also **tri·fo′li·at′ed.**

tri·fo·li·o·late (trī·fō′lē·ə·lāt′) *adj. Bot.* Having three leaflets, as a clover leaf.

tri·fo·ri·um (trī·fôr′ē·əm, -fō′rē-) *n. pl.* **·fo·ri·a** (-fôr′ē·ə, -fō′rē·ə) *Archit.* A gallery above the arches of the nave or transept in a church. [< L *tri-* three + *foris* a door] —**tri·fo′ri·al** *adj.*

trig[1] (trig) *adj.* **1** Characterized by tidiness; trim; neat. **2** Strong; sound; firm. —*v.t.* **trigged, trig·ging** To make trig or neat; often with *out* or *up.* [< ON *tryggr* true, trusty] —**trig′ly** *adv.* —**trig′ness** *n.*

Triforium

trig[2] (trig) *n.* TRIGONOMETRY.

trig., trigon. trigonometric; trigonometry.

trig·ger (trig′ər) *n.* **1** A lever of a gun activating the firing mechanism when moved by a finger. •See REVOLVER. **2** Any one of various devices designed to activate other devices or systems. —**quick on the trigger 1** Quick to shoot a gun. **2** Quick-witted; alert. —*v.t. Informal* To cause or set off (an action). [< Du. *trekken* pull, tug at]

trigonometric functions *Math.* Any of various functions of an angle or arc, principally the sine, cosine, tangent, cotangent, secant, and cosecant.

trig·o·nom·e·try (trig′ə·nom′ə·trē) *n.* The branch of mathematics based on the use of trigonometric functions, as in studying the relations of the sides and angles of triangles. [< Gk. *trigōnon* a triangle + *metron* measure] —**trig·o·no·met·ric** (trig′ə·nə·met′rik) or **·ri·cal** *adj.* —**trig′o·no·met′ri·cal·ly** *adv.*

tri·he·dron (trī·hē′drən) *n. pl.* **·dra** (-drə) *Geom.* A figure having three plane surfaces meeting at a point. [< Gk. *tri-* three + *hedra* a base] —**tri·he′dral** *adj.*

tri·lat·er·al (trī·lat′ər·əl) *adj.* Having three sides. [< L *tri-* three + *latus, lateris* a side] —**tri·lat′er·al·ly** *adv.*

trill (tril) *v.t.* **1** To sing or play in a quavering or tremulous tone. **2** *Phonet.* To articulate with a trill. —*v.i.* **3** To utter a quavering or tremulous sound. **4** *Music* To execute a trill. —*n.* **1** A tremulous utterance of successive tones, as of certain insects or birds; a warble. **2** *Music* A quick alternation of two notes either a tone or a semitone apart. **3** *Phonet.* A rapid vibration of a speech organ, as of the tip of the tongue. **4** A consonant or word so uttered. [< Ital. *trillare*] —**trill′er** *n.*

tril·lion (tril′yən) *n.* & *adj.* See NUMBER. [< MF *tri-* three + *million* million] —**tril′lionth** *adj.*

tril·li·um (tril′ē·əm) *n.* Any of a genus of perennial plants of the lily family, bearing a whorl of three leaves and a solitary flower. [< L *tri-* three]

tri·lo·bate (trī·lō′bāt, trī′lə·bāt) *adj.* Having three lobes. Also **tri·lo′bal, tri·lo′bat·ed, tri·lobed** (trī′lōbd′).

tri·lo·bite (trī′lə·bīt) *n.* Any of various fossilized extinct marine arthropods found in abundance in Paleozoic rocks, characterized by two lengthwise grooves forming three ridges. [< Gk. *tri-* three + *lobos* a lobe] —**tri′lo·bit′ic** (-bit′ik) *adj.*

tril·o·gy (tril′ə·jē) *n. pl.* **·gies** A group of three literary or dramatic compositions, each complete in itself, but connected into a whole through theme and subject matter. [< Gk. *tri-* three + *logos* a discourse]

trim (trim) *v.* **trimmed, trim·ming** *v.t.* **1** To make neat by clipping, pruning, etc. **2** To remove by cutting: usu. with *off* or *away.* **3** To put ornaments on; decorate. **4** In carpentry, to smooth; dress. **5** *Informal* **a** To chide; rebuke. **b** To punish. **c** To defeat. **6** *Naut.* **a** To adjust (sails or yards) for sailing. **b** To cause (a ship) to sit well in the water by adjusting cargo, ballast, etc. **7** To bring (an airplane) to stable flight by adjusting controls. —*v.i.* **8** *Naut.* **a** To be or remain in equilibrium. **b** To adjust sails or yards for sailing. **9** To act so as to appear to favor opposing sides in a controversy. —*n.* **1** State of adjustment or preparation; fitting condition. **2** Good physical condition: in *trim* to play tennis. **3** *Naut.* Fitness for sailing. **4** *Naut.* Actual or comparative degree of immersion. **5** The moldings, etc., as about the doors of a building. **6** Ornament, as on a dress; trimming. **7** The attitude of an aircraft in flight. —*adj.* **trim·mer, trim·mest** Having a smart appearance; spruce. —*adv.* In a trim manner: also **trim′ly.** [< OE *trȳman* arrange, strengthen] —**trim′ness** *n.* —**Syn.** *v.* **1** cut, lop. **2** pare. **3** adorn, garnish.

tri·mes·ter (trī·mes′tər, trī′mes·tər) *n.* **1** A three-month period; quarter, as of an academic year. **2** Any of the three three-month periods used to identify the progress of a pregnancy. [< L *trimestris* < *tri-* three + *mensis* a month] —**tri·mes′tral, tri·mes′tri·al** *adj.*

trim·e·ter (trim′ə·tər) *adj.* In prosody, consisting of three measures or of lines containing three measures. —*n.* A line of verse having three measures.

trim·ming (trim′ing) *n.* **1** Something added for ornament or to give a finished appearance or effect. **2** *pl. Informal* The proper accompaniments or condiments of an article or food. **3** Parts or pieces trimmed away. **4** A severe reproof or a chastisement. **5** *Informal* A defeat.

tri·month·ly (trī·munth′lē) *adj. & adv.* Done or occurring every third month.

Trin·i·dad and To·ba·go (trin′ə·dad, tō·bā′gō) An independent member of the Commonwealth of Nations on two islands N of Venezuela, 1,980 sq. mi., cap. Port-of-Spain.

Trin·i·tar·i·an (trin′ə·târ′ē·ən) *adj.* **1** Of or pertaining to the Trinity. **2** Holding or professing belief in the Trinity. —*n.* A believer in the doctrine of the Trinity. —**Trin′i·tar′i·an·ism** *n.*

tri·ni·tro·tol·u·ene (trī·nī′trō·tol′yōō·ēn) *n.* An explosive made by treating toluene with nitric acid. Also **tri·ni′tro·tol′u·ol** (-yōō·ōl, -ol). [< TRI- + NITRO- + TOLUENE]

trin·i·ty (trin′ə·tē) *n. pl.* **·ties** **1** The state or character of being three. **2** The union of three parts or elements in one; a triad. [< L *trinitas* a triad]

Trin·i·ty (trin′ə·tē) *n.* In Christian theology, the union in one divine nature of Father, Son, and Holy Spirit.

trin·ket (tring′kit) *n.* **1** Any small ornament, as of jewelry. **2** A trifle; trivial object. [< AF *trenquet*]

tri·no·mi·al (trī·nō′mē·əl) *adj.* **1** *Biol.* Of, having, or employing three terms or names. **2** *Math.* Expressed as a sum of three terms. —*n.* **1** *Math.* A trinomial expression in algebra. **2** A trinomial name. Also **tri·nom′i·nal** (-nom′ə·nəl). [< TRI- + (BI)NOMIAL] —**tri·no′mi·al·ly** *adv.*

tri·o (trē′ō) *n. pl.* **tri·os** **1** Any three things grouped or associated together. **2** *Music* **a** A composition for three performers. **b** A group of three musicians who perform trios. [< Ital. *tre* three]

tri·ox·ide (trī·ok′sīd) *n.* An oxide containing three atoms of oxygen per molecule.

trip (trip) *n.* **1** A journey; excursion. **2** A misstep or stumble. **3** An active, nimble step or movement. **4** A catch or similar device for starting or stopping a movement, as in a mechanism. **5** A sudden catch of the legs or feet to make

a person fall. **6** A blunder; mistake. **7** *Slang* **a** The hallucinations and other sensations experienced by a person taking a psychedelic drug. **b** Any intense, usu. personal experience. —*v.* **tripped, trip·ping** *v.i.* **1** To stumble. **2** To move quickly and lightly. **3** To make an error. **4** To run past the nicks or dents of the ratchet escape wheel of a timepiece. **5** *Slang* To experience the effects of a psychedelic drug: often with *out.* —*v.t.* **6** To cause to stumble or make a mistake: often with *up.* **7** To perform (a dance) lightly. **8** *Mech.* To activate by releasing a catch, trigger, etc. —**trip it** To dance. [< OF *treper, triper* leap, trample] —**Syn.** *n.* **1** jaunt, tour, sojourn, voyage.

tri·par·tite (trī·pär′tīt) *adj.* **1** Divided into three parts. **2** Having three corresponding parts or copies. **3** Made between three persons: a *tripartite* pact. [< L *tri-* three + *partitus,* p.p. of *partiri* to divide] —**tri·par′tite·ly** *adv.* —**tri′·par·ti′tion** (-tish′ən) *n.*

tripe (trīp) *n.* **1** A part of the stomach wall of a ruminant used for food. **2** *Informal* Contemptible or worthless stuff; nonsense. [< OF]

trip·ham·mer (trip′ham′ər) *n.* A heavy power hammer that is raised mechanically and allowed to drop by a tripping action.

tripl. triplicate.

tri·ple (trip′əl) *v.* **·led, ·ling** *v.t.* **1** To make threefold in number or quantity. —*v.i.* **2** To be or become three times as many or as large. **3** In baseball, to make a triple. —*adj.* **1** Consisting of three things united. **2** Multiplied by three; thrice said or done. —*n.* **1** A set or group of three. **2** In baseball, a fair hit that enables the batter to reach third base without the help of an error. [< Gk. *triploos* threefold] —**trip′ly** *adv.*

triple play In baseball, a play during which three men are put out.

trip·let (trip′lit) *n.* **1** A group of three of a kind. **2** Any of three children born at one birth. **3** *Music* A group of three notes that divide the time usu. taken by two. [< TRIPLE]

triple time *Music* A rhythm having three beats to the measure with the accent on the first beat.

trip·li·cate (trip′lə·kit) *adj.* Threefold; made in three copies. —*n.* One of three precisely similar things. —**in triplicate** In three identical copies. —*v.t.* (-kāt) **·cat·ed, ·cat·ing** To make three times; triple. [< L *triplicare* to triple] —**trip′li·cate·ly** *adv.* —**trip′li·ca′tion** *n.*

tri·pod (trī′pod) *n.* A three-legged frame or stand, as for supporting a camera, etc. [< Gk. *tri-* three + *pous* foot] —**trip·o·dal** (trip′ə·dəl), **tri·pod·ic** (trī·pod′ik) *adj.*

trip·per (trip′ər) *n.* **1** A person or thing that trips. **2** *Brit. Informal* A tourist or traveler. **3** *Mech.* A trip or tripping mechanism, as a cam, pawl, etc. **4** *Slang* A person who frequently uses psychedelic drugs.

trip·ping (trip′ing) *adj.* Light; nimble. —**trip′ping·ly** *adv.*

Tripod

trip·tych (trip′tik) *n.* **1** A picture, carving, or work of art on three panels side by side. **2** A writing tablet in three sections. [< Gk. *tri-* three + *ptyx, ptychos* a fold]

tri·reme (trī′rēm′) *n.* An ancient warship with three banks of oars on each side. [< L *tri-* three + *remus* an oar]

tri·sect (trī·sekt′) *v.t.* To divide into three parts, esp., as in geometry, into three equal parts. [< TRI- + L *sectus,* p.p. of *secare* to cut] —**tri·sec′tion** (-sek′shən), **tri·sec′tor** *n.*

triste (trēst) *adj.* Sorrowful; sad. [F]

tri·syl·la·ble (trī·sil′ə·bəl) *n.* A word of three syllables. —**tri·syl·lab·ic** (trī·si·lab′ik) *adj.* —**tri′syl·lab′i·cal·ly** *adv.*

trite (trīt) *adj.* **trit·er, trit·est** Made commonplace or hackneyed by frequent repetition. [< L *tritus,* p.p. of *terere* to rub] —**trite′ly** *adv.* —**trite′ness** *n.* —**Syn.** stale, stereotyped, threadbare, cliché, shopworn, tired, stock.

trit·i·um (trit′ē·əm, trish′ē·əm) *n.* The radioactive hydrogen isotope of atomic mass 3, having a half-life of 12.5 years. [< Gk. *tritos* third]

tri·ton (trīt′n) *n.* A marine snail with a trumpet-shaped shell. [< TRITON]

Triton

Tri·ton (trīt′n) *Gk. Myth.* A sea god having a man's head and upper body and a dolphin's tail.

trit·u·rate (trich′ə·rāt) *v.t.* **·rat·ed, ·rat·ing** To reduce to a fine powder or pulp by grinding or rubbing; pulverize. —*n.* That which has been triturated. [< L *tritura* a rubbing, threshing < *tritus.* See TRITE.] *adj.* **—trit′u·ra′tor, trit′u·ra′·tion** *n.*

tri·umph (trī′əmf) *v.i.* **1** To win a victory. **2** To be successful. **3** To rejoice over a victory; exult. —*n.* **1** A victory or conquest: a *triumph* of will power. **2** An important success: the *triumphs* of modern medicine. **3** Exultation over a victory. **4** In ancient Rome, a pageant welcoming a victorious general. [< Gk. *thriambos* a processional hymn to Dionysus] **—tri·um·phal** (trī·um′fəl) *adj.* **—tri·um′phal·ly** *adv.* **—tri′umph·er** *n.*

tri·um·phant (trī·um′fənt) *adj.* **1** Exultant for or as for victory. **2** Crowned with victory; victorious. **—tri·um′phant·ly** *adv.*

tri·um·vir (trī·um′vər) *n. pl.* **·virs** or **·vi·ri** (-və·rī′, -rē′) In ancient Rome, one of three men united in public office or authority. [< L *trium virorum* of three men] **—tri·um′vi·ral** *adj.*

tri·um·vi·rate (trī·um′vər·it, -və·rāt) *n.* **1** A group or coalition of three men who govern. **2** The office of a triumvir. **3** The triumvirs collectively. **4** A group of three persons; a trio. [< L *triumvir* triumvir]

tri·une (trī′yo͞on) *adj.* Three in one: said of the Godhead. [< TRI- + L *unus* one] **—tri·un·i·ty** (trī·yo͞o′nə·tē) *n.*

tri·va·lent (trī·vā′lənt) *adj. Chem.* Having a valence or combining value of three. [< TRI- + L *valens,* pr.p. of *valere* be strong] **—tri·va′lence, tri·va′len·cy** *n.*

triv·et (triv′it) *n.* A short, usu. three-legged stand for holding cooking vessels in a fireplace, a hot dish on a table, or a heated iron. [< L *tri-* three + *pes, pedis* a foot]

triv·i·a (triv′ē·ə) *n.pl.* Insignificant or unimportant matters; trifles. [< L *trivialis* trivial]

triv·i·al (triv′ē·əl) *adj.* **1** Of little value or importance; insignificant. **2** *Archaic* Ordinary; commonplace. [< L *trivialis* of the crossroads, commonplace] **—triv′i·al·ism** *n.* **—triv′i·al·ly** *adv.* **—Syn. 1** slight, mean, paltry, inconsiderable, piddling.

triv·i·al·i·ty (triv′ē·al′ə·tē) *n. pl.* **·ties 1** The state or quality of being trivial. **2** A trivial matter.

triv·i·al·ize (triv′ē·ə·līz) *v.t.* **·ized, ·iz·ing** To treat as or make trivial; regard as unimportant. **—triv′i·al·i·za′tion** *n.*

tri·week·ly (trī·wēk′lē) *adj. & adv.* **1** Occurring three times a week. **2** Done or occurring every third week. —*n. pl.* **·lies** A triweekly publication.

tro·che (trō′kē) *n.* A small medicated lozenge, usu. circular. [< Gk. *trochiskos* a small wheel, a lozenge]

tro·chee (trō′kē) *n.* In prosody, a foot comprising a long and short syllable (¯ ˘), or an accented syllable followed by an unaccented one. [< Gk. *trochaios (pous)* a running (foot) < *trechein* to run] **—tro·cha·ic** (trō·kā′ik) *adj.*

trod (trod) *p.t. & alternative p.p.* of TREAD.

trod·den (trod′n) *p.p.* of TREAD.

trog·lo·dyte (trog′lə·dīt) *n.* **1** A prehistoric cave man. **2** A person with primitive habits. **3** A hermit. [< Gk. *trōglodytēs*] **—trog′lo·dyt′ic** (-dit′ik), **trog′lo·dyt′i·cal** *adj.*

Tro·jan (trō′jən) *n.* **1** A native of Troy. **2** A brave, persevering person. —*adj.* Of or pertaining to ancient Troy or to its people.

Trojan horse 1 *Gk. Myth.* During the Trojan War, a large, hollow wooden horse filled with Greek soldiers and brought within the walls of Troy, thus bringing about the downfall of the city. **2** *Mil.* The infiltration of military men into enemy territory to commit sabotage against industry and military installations.

Trojan War *Gk. Myth.* The ten years' war waged by the Greeks against the Trojans to recover Helen, the wife of Menelaus, who had been abducted by Paris.

troll[1] (trōl) *v.t.* **1** To sing in succession, as in a round. **2** To sing in a full, hearty manner. **3** To fish for with a moving lure, as from a moving boat. —*v.i.* **4** To roll; turn. **5** To sing a tune, etc., in a full, hearty manner. **6** To fish with a moving lure. —*n.* **1** A song taken up at intervals by several voices; round. **2** A rolling movement or motion. **3** In fishing, a spoon or other lure. [?] **—troll′er** *n.*

troll[2] (trōl) *n.* In Scandinavian folklore, a giant or dwarf living in caves or underground. [< ON]

trol·ley (trol′ē) *n. pl.* **·leys 1** A device that rolls or slides along an electric conductor to carry current to an electric vehicle. **2** A trolley car; also, a system of trolley cars. **3** A small truck or car suspended from an overhead track and used to convey material, as in a factory, mine, etc. —*v.t. & v.i.* To convey or travel by trolley. [< TROLL[1]]

trolley bus A passenger conveyance operating without rails, propelled electrically by current taken from an overhead wire by means of a trolley.

trolley car A car arranged with a trolley and motor for use on an electric railway.

trol·lop (trol′əp) *n.* **1** A slatternly woman. **2** A prostitute. [?]

trom·bone (trom·bōn′, trom′bōn) *n.* A brass wind instrument of the trumpet family in the tenor range, usu. equipped with a slide for changing pitch. [< Ital. *tromba* a trumpet] **—trom·bon′ist** *n.*

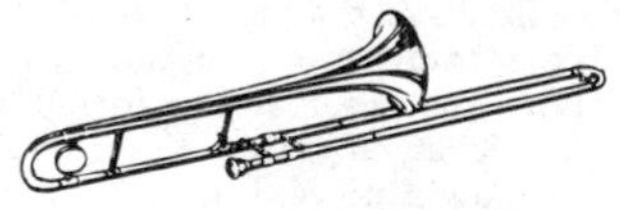

Trombone

troop (tro͞op) *n.* **1** A gathering of people. **2** A flock or herd, as of animals. **3** A unit of cavalry having 60 to 100 men and corresponding to a company in other military branches. **4** *pl.* Soldiers. **5** A unit of Boy Scouts or Girl Scouts. —*v.i.* **1** To move along as a group: shoppers *trooping* through a store. **2** To go: to *troop* across the street. —*v.t.* **3** To form into troops. [< LL *troppus* a flock] **—Syn. 1** company, crowd, multitude, throng.

troop·er (tro͞o′pər) *n.* **1** A cavalryman. **2** A mounted policeman. **3** A troop horse. **4** *Informal* A state policeman.

troop·ship (tro͞op′ship′) *n.* A ship for carrying troops.

trope (trōp) *n.* **1** The figurative use of a word or phrase. **2** A figure of speech. **3** Figurative language in general. [< L *tropus* a figure of speech < Gk. *tropos* a turn]

tro·phy (trō′fē) *n. pl.* **·phies 1** Anything taken from an enemy and displayed or treasured in proof of victory. **2** A prize representing victory or achievement: a tennis *trophy.* **3** An animal skin, mounted head, etc., kept to show skill in hunting. **4** Any memento. [< Gk. *tropē* a defeat, turning] **—tro′phied** *adj.*

trop·ic (trop′ik) *n.* **1** *Geog.* Either of two parallels of latitude, the **tropic of Cancer** at 23° 27′ north of the equator and the **tropic of Capricorn** 23° 27′ south of the equator, between which lies the torrid zone. **2** *Astron.* Either of two corresponding parallels in the celestial sphere similarly named, and respectively 23° 27′ north or south from the celestial equator. **3** *pl.* The regions in the torrid zone. —*adj.* Of or pertaining to the tropics; tropical. [< Gk. *tropikos (kyklos)* the tropical (circle), pertaining to the turning of the sun at the solstice.]

-tropic *combining form* Having a (specified) tropism: *geotropic.* [< Gk. *tropos* a turn]

trop·i·cal (trop′i·kəl) *adj.* **1** Of, pertaining to, or characteristic of the tropics. **2** Of the nature of a trope or metaphor. **—trop′i·cal·ly** *adv.*

tropical fish Any of various small, usu. brightly colored fishes originating in the tropics and adapted to living in an aquarium **(tropical aquarium)** kept at a constant warm temperature.

tro·pism (trō′piz·əm) *n.* **1** A tendency in an organism to grow or move toward or away from a given stimulus. **2** An instance of such growth or movement. [< Gk. *tropē* a turning] **—tro·pis·tic** (trō·pis′tik) *adj.*

-tropism *combining form* A (specified) tropism: *phototropism.* Also **-tropy.**

trop·o·sphere (trōp′ə·sfir, trop′-) *n. Meteorol.* The region of the atmosphere extending from six to twelve miles above the earth's surface, characterized by decreasing temperature with increasing altitude. [< Gk. *tropos* a turning + SPHERE]

trot (trot) *n.* **1** The gait of a quadruped, in which each

diagonal pair of legs is moved alternately. **2** The sound of this gait. **3** A slow running gait of a person. **4** A little child. **5** *Informal* A literal translation of a foreign-language text, used by students, often dishonestly. —**the trots** *Slang* Diarrhea. —*v.* **trot·ted, trot·ting** *v.i.* **1** To go at a trot. **2** To go quickly; hurry. —*v.t.* **3** To cause to trot. **4** To ride at a trotting gait. —**trot out** *Informal* To bring forth for inspection, approval, etc. [< OHG *trottōn* to tread]

troth (trôth, trōth) *n.* **1** Good faith; fidelity. **2** The act of pledging fidelity. **3** Truth; verity. —**plight one's troth** To promise to marry or be faithful to. [< OE *trēowth* truth]

Trot·sky·ism (trot′skē·iz′əm) *n.* The doctrines of Trotsky and his followers who opposed Stalin and believed that Communism to succeed must be international. [< L. *Trotsky*, 1879–1940, Russian Bolshevist leader] — **Trot′sky·ist, Trot′sky·ite** *n., adj.*

trot·ter (trot′ər) *n.* **1** One who or that which trots; a trotting horse, esp. one trained to trot in races. **2** *Informal* An animal's foot: a pig's *trotters.*

trou·ba·dour (trōō′bə·dôr, -dōr, -dōōr) *n.* One of a class of lyric poets, sometimes including wandering minstrels, flourishing in parts of France, Italy, and Spain during the 12th and 13th centuries. [< Prov. *trobador* < *trobar* compose, invent]

trou·ble (trub′əl) *n.* **1** The state of being distressed or worried. **2** A person, circumstance, or event that occasions difficulty or perplexity. **3** A condition of difficulty: to be in *trouble* at school; money *troubles.* **4** A disease or ailment: heart *trouble.* **5** Bother; effort: They took the *trouble* to drive me home. **6** Agitation; unrest: *trouble* in the streets. —*v.* **·led, ·ling** *v.t.* **1** To distress; worry. **2** To stir up or roil, as water. **3** To inconvenience. **4** To annoy. **5** To cause physical pain or discomfort to. —*v.i.* **6** To take pains; bother. [< OF *turbler* to trouble] —**troub′ler** *n.*

troub·le·mak·er (trub′əl·mā′kər) *n.* One who habitually stirs up trouble for others.

troub·le·shoot·er (trub′əl·shōō′tər) *n.* **1** A skilled workman able to analyze and repair breakdowns in machinery, electronic equipment, etc. **2** A person assigned to eliminate sources of difficulty or to mediate disputes, esp. in diplomacy and politics. —**troub′le·shoot′ing** *n.*

troub·le·some (trub′əl·səm) *adj.* **1** Causing trouble; trying. **2** Difficult: a *troublesome* task. —**troub′le·some·ly** *adv.* —**troub′le·some·ness** *n.* —**Syn.** **1** burdensome, disturbing, galling, harassing.

troub·lous (trub′ləs) *adj.* **1** Uneasy; restless: *troublous* times. **2** Troublesome.

trough (trôf, trof) *n.* **1** A long, narrow receptacle for food or water for animals. **2** A similarly shaped receptacle, as for mixing dough. **3** A long, narrow depression, as between waves. **4** A gutter for rain water fixed under the eaves of a building. **5** *Meteorol.* An elongated region of relatively low atmospheric pressure. [< OE *trog*]

trounce (trouns) *v.t.* **trounced, trounc·ing** **1** To beat or thrash severely; punish. **2** *Informal* To defeat. [?]

troupe (trōōp) *n.* A company of actors or other performers. —*v.i.* **trouped, troup·ing** To travel as one of a company of actors or entertainers. [< OF *trope* troop]

troup·er (trōōp′ər) *n.* **1** A member of a theatrical company. **2** An older actor of long experience.

trou·sers (trou′zərz) *n.pl.* A two-legged garment, covering the body from the waist to the ankles or knees. [Blend of obs. *trouse* breeches and DRAWERS]

trous·seau (trōō′sō, trōō·sō′) *n.* *pl.* **·seaux** (-sōz, -sōz′) or **·seaus** A bride's outfit, esp. of clothing. [F < OF, dim. of *trousse* a packed collection of things]

trout (trout) *n.* Any of various fishes of the salmon family found mostly in fresh waters and esteemed as a game and food fish. [< OE *trūht*]

trow·el (trou′əl, troul) *n.* **1** A flat-bladed, sometimes pointed implement, used by masons, plasterers, and molders. **2** A small concave scoop with a handle, used in digging about small plants. —*v.t.* **·eled** or **·elled, ·el·ing** or **·el·ling** To apply, smooth, or dig

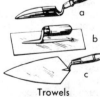

Trowels
a. garden. b. plastering. c. brick.

with a trowel. [< L *trulla*, dim. of *trua* a stirring spoon] —**trow′el·er** or **trow′el·ler** *n.*

troy (troi) *adj.* Measured or expressed in troy weight. [< *Troyes*, France; with ref. to a weight used at a fair held there]

troy weight A system of weights in which 12 ounces or 5,760 grains equal a pound, and the grain is identical with the avoirdupois grain. • See MEASURE.

tru·ant (trōō′ənt) *n.* **1** A pupil who stays away from school without leave. **2** A person who shirks responsibilities or work. —**play truant 1** To be absent from school without leave. **2** To shirk responsibilities or work. —*adj.* **1** Being truant; idle. **2** Relating to or characterizing a truant. [< OF, a vagabond] —**tru·an·cy** (trōō′ən·sē) *n.* (*pl.* **·cies**)

truce (trōōs) *n.* **1** An agreement for a temporary suspension of hostilities; an armistice. **2** A temporary stopping, as from pain, etc.; respite. [< OE *truwa* faith, a promise]

Tru·cial States (trōō′shəl) A group of sheikdoms, bound by treaties with Great Britain, in E Arabia, 32,300 sq. mi.

truck[1] (truk) *n.* **1** Any of several types of strongly built motor vehicles designed to transport heavy loads, bulky articles, freight, etc. **2** A two-wheeled barrowlike vehicle for moving barrels, boxes, etc., by hand. **3** A small wheeled vehicle used for moving baggage, goods, etc. **4** A disk at the upper extremity of a mast or flagpole through which the halyards of signals are run. **5** A small wheel. —*v.t.* **1** To carry on a truck. —*v.i.* **2** To carry goods on a truck. **3** To drive a truck. [< Gk. *trochos* a wheel]

truck[2] (truk) *v.t. & v.i.* To exchange or barter. —*n.* **1** Commodities for sale. **2** Garden produce for market. **3** *Informal* Rubbish; worthless articles. **4** Barter. **5** *Informal* Dealings: I will have no *truck* with him. [< OF *troquer* to barter]

truck·age (truk′ij) *n.* **1** The conveyance of goods on trucks. **2** The charge for this. [< TRUCK[1]]

truck·er (truk′ər) *n.* One who drives or supplies trucks or moves commodities in trucks.

truck farm A farm on which vegetables are produced for market. —**truck farmer, truck farming**

truck·ing (truk′ing) *n.* The act or business of transportation by trucks.

truck·le (truk′əl) *v.* **·led, ·ling** *v.i.* **1** To yield or submit weakly: with *to.* **2** To move on rollers or casters. —*v.t.* **3** To cause to move on rollers or casters. —*n.* A small wheel. [< L *trochlea* system of pulleys] —**truck′ler** *n.*

truckle bed TRUNDLE BED.

truck·man (truk′mən) *n. pl.* **·men** (mən) **1** A truck driver. **2** One engaged in the business of trucking.

tru·cu·lent (truk′yə·lənt) *adj.* Of savage character; cruel; ferocious. [< L *trux, trucis* fierce] —**truc·u·lence** (truk′yə·ləns), **truc·u·len·cy** *n.* —**truc′u·lent·ly** *adv.* —**Syn.** barbarous, brutal, fierce, ruthless, vicious.

trudge (truj) *v.i.* **trudged, trudg·ing** To walk wearily or laboriously; plod. —*n.* A tiresome walk or tramp. [?] —**trudg′er** *n.*

true (trōō) *adj.* **tru·er, tru·est 1** Faithful to fact or reality. **2** Being real; genuine, not counterfeit: *true* gold. **3** Faithful to friends, promises, or principles; loyal. **4** Exact: a *true* copy. **5** Accurate, as in shape, or position: a *true* fit. **6** Faithful to the requirements of law or justice; legitimate: the *true* king. **7** Faithful to truth; honest: a *true* man. **8** Faithful to the promise or predicted event: a *true* sign. **9** *Biol.* Possessing all the attributes of its class: a *true* root. **10** *Music* Exactly in tune. —**come true** To turn out as hoped for or imagined. —*n.* The state or quality of being true; also, something that is true: usu. with *the.* —**in** (or **out of**) **true** In (or not in) line of adjustment. —*adv.* **1** In truth; truly. **2** Within proper tolerances: The wheel runs *true.* —*v.t.* **trued, tru·ing** To bring to conformity with a standard or requirement: to *true* a frame. [< OE *trēowe*] —**true′ness** *n.*

true bill *Law* A bill of indictment found by a grand jury to be sustained by the evidence.

true-blue (trōō′blōō′) *adj.* Staunch; faithful.

true·love (trōō′luv′) *n.* One truly beloved; a sweetheart.

truf·fle (truf′əl, trōō′fəl) *n.* Any of various fleshy underground edible fungi regarded as a delicacy. [< OF *truffe*]

tru·ism (trōō′iz·əm) *n.* An obvious or self-evident truth; a platitude.

trull (trul) *n.* A prostitute. [< G *Trolle*]

tru·ly (trōō′lē) *adv.* 1 In conformity with fact. 2 With accuracy. 3 With loyalty.

trump (trump) *n.* 1 In various card games, a card of the suit selected to rank above all others temporarily. 2 The suit thus determined. 3 *Informal* A fine, reliable person. —*v.t.* 1 To take (another card) with a trump. 2 To surpass; excel; beat. —*v.i.* 3 To play a trump. —**trump up** To invent for a fraudulent purpose. [Alter. of TRIUMPH]

trump·er·y (trum′pər·ē) *n. pl.* **·er·ies** 1 Worthless finery. 2 Rubbish; nonsense. —*adj.* Having a showy appearance, but valueless. [< OF *tromper* to cheat]

trum·pet (trum′pit) *n.* 1 A soprano brass wind instrument with a flaring bell and a long metal tube. 2 Something resembling a trumpet in form. 3 A tube for collecting and conducting sounds to the ear; an ear trumpet. 4 A loud penetrating sound like that of a trumpet. —*v.t.* 1 To sound or publish abroad. —*v.i.* 2 To blow a trumpet. 3 To give forth a sound as if from a trumpet, as an elephant. [< OF *trompette*]

Trumpet

trum·pet·er (trum′pə·tər) *n.* 1 One who plays a trumpet. 2 One who publishes something loudly abroad. 3 A large South American bird, related to the cranes. 4 A large North American wild swan having a clarionlike cry: also **trumpeter swan.** • See SWAN. 5 A breed of domestic pigeons.

trun·cate (trung′kāt) *v.t.* **·cat·ed, ·cat·ing** To cut the top or end from. —*adj. Biol.* Ending abruptly, as though cut off: a *truncate* leaf. [< L *truncare*] —**trun′cate·ly** *adv.* —**trun·ca′tion** (trung·kā′shən) *n.*

trun·cheon (trun′chən) *n.* 1 A short, heavy stick, esp. a policeman's club. 2 Any baton of office or authority. —*v.t.* To beat as with a truncheon; cudgel. [< OF *tronchon* a stump]

trun·dle (trun′dəl) *n.* 1 A small broad wheel, as of a caster. 2 The act, motion, or sound of trundling. 3 TRUNDLE BED. —*v.* **·dled, ·dling** *v.t.* 1 To propel by rolling along: to *trundle* a wheelbarrow. 2 To haul or carry in a wheeled vehicle. —*v.i.* 3 To move ahead by revolving. 4 To progress on wheels. [< OE *trendel* a circle] —**trun′dler** *n.*

trundle bed A bed with very low frame resting upon casters, so that it may be rolled under another bed.

trunk (trungk) *n.* 1 The main stem or stock of a tree. 2 An animal or human body, apart from the head and limbs; the torso. 3 The thorax of an insect. 4 The main stem of a nerve, blood vessel, or lymphatic. 5 A main line of communication or transportation, as the circuit connecting two telephone exchanges. 6 A proboscis, as of an elephant. 7 A large box or case used for packing and carrying clothes or other articles. 8 *pl.* Very short, close-fitting trousers worn by swimmers, athletes, etc. 9 *Archit.* The shaft of a column. 10 A compartment in an automobile, opposite the end housing the motor, for carrying luggage, tools, etc. —*adj.* Being or belonging to a trunk or main body: a *trunk* railroad. [< L *truncus* stem, trunk]

trunk·fish (trungk′fish′) *n. pl.* **·fish** or **·fish·es** Any of a family of fishes characterized by a body covering of hard, bony plates.

truss (trus) *n.* 1 A supporting framework, as for a roof or bridge. 2 A bandage or support for a hernia. 3 A bundle or package. 4 *Naut.* A heavy iron piece by which a lower yard is attached to a mast. —*v.t.* 1 To tie or bind; fasten: often with *up.* 2 To support or brace (a roof, bridge, etc.) with trusses. 3 To fasten the wings of (a fowl) before cooking. [< OF *trousser, trusser* pack up, bundle] —**truss′er** *n.*

trust (trust) *n.* 1 A reliance on the integrity, veracity, or reliability of a person or thing. 2 Something committed to one's care for use or safekeeping. 3 The state or position of one who has received an important charge. 4 Confident expectation; hope. 5 In commerce, credit. 6 *Law* a The confidence reposed in a person to whom the legal title to property is conveyed for the benefit of another. b The property or thing held in trust. c The relation subsisting between the holder and the property so held. 7 A combination of business firms formed to control production and prices of some commodity. —**in trust** In the charge or care of another or others. —**on trust** 1 On credit. 2 Without investigating: to accept a statement *on trust.* —*v.t.* 1 To rely upon. 2 To commit to the care of another; entrust. 3 To commit something to the care of: with *with.* 4 To allow to do something without fear of the consequences. 5 To expect; hope. 6 To believe. 7 To allow business credit to. —*v.i.* 8 To place trust or confidence; rely: with *in.* 9 To allow business credit. —**trust to** To depend upon; confide in. —*adj.* Held in trust: *trust* property. [< ON *traust,* lit., firmness] —**trust′er** *n.* —**Syn.** *n.* 1 confidence, credence, faith.

trus·tee (trus·tē′) *n.* 1 One who is entrusted with the property of another. 2 One of a body of persons, often elective, who hold the property and manage the affairs of a company or institution.

trus·tee·ship (trus·tē′ship) *n.* 1 The post or function of a trustee. 2 Supervision and control of a trust territory by a country or countries commissioned by the United Nations.

trust·ful (trust′fəl) *adj.* Disposed to trust. —**trust′ful·ly** *adv.* —**trust′ful·ness** *n.*

trust fund Money, securities, or similar property held in trust.

trust·ing (trus′ting) *adj.* Having trust; trustful. —**trust′ing·ly** *adv.* —**trust′ing·ness** *n.*

trust territory An area, usu. a former colonial possession, governed by a member state of the United Nations.

trust·wor·thy (trust′wûr′thē) *adj.* Worthy of confidence; reliable. —**trust′wor′thi·ly** (-wûr′thə·lē) *adv.* —**trust′wor′thi·ness** *n.*

trust·y (trus′tē) *adj.* **trust·i·er, trust·i·est** 1 Faithful to duty or trust. 2 Staunch; firm. —*n. pl.* **trust·ies** A trustworthy person; esp. a convict to whom special privileges are granted. —**trust′i·ly** *adv.* —**trust′i·ness** *n.*

truth (trōōth) *n. pl.* **truths** (trōōthz, trōōths) 1 The state or character of being true. 2 That which is true. 3 Conformity to fact or reality. 4 The quality of being true; fidelity; constancy. —**in truth** Indeed; in fact. [< OE *treowe* true]

truth·ful (trōōth′fəl) *adj.* 1 Conforming to fact; veracious. 2 Telling the truth. —**truth′ful·ly** *adv.* —**truth′ful·ness** *n.*

try (trī) *v.* **tried, try·ing** *v.t.* 1 To make an attempt to do or accomplish. 2 To make experimental use or application of: to *try* a new pen. 3 To subject to a test; put to proof. 4 To put severe strain upon; tax: to *try* one's patience. 5 To subject to trouble or tribulation. 6 To extract by rendering or melting; refine. 7 *Law* To determine the guilt or innocence of by judicial trial. —*v.i.* 8 To make an attempt; put forth effort. 9 To make an examination or test. —**try on** To put on (a garment) to test it for fit or appearance. —**try out** 1 To attempt to qualify: He *tried out* for the team. 2 To test the result or effect of. —*n. pl.* **tries** The act of trying; trial. [< OF *trier* sift, pick out] —**tri′er** *n.* • **try and, try to** These constructions are both standard in modern English: *Try and meet me at six; Try to finish your work on time.* However, *try to* is usu. preferable in precise, formal writing.

try·ing (trī′ing) *adj.* Testing severely; hard to endure. —**try′ing·ly** *adv.* —**try′ing·ness** *n.* —**Syn.** arduous, difficult, onerous, troublesome.

try·out (trī′out′) *n. Informal* A test of ability, as of an actor or athlete.

tryp·sin (trip′sin) *n.* A pancreatic enzyme that helps to digest proteins. [< Gk. *tripsis* a rubbing + (PEP)SIN] —**tryp′tic** (-tik) *adj.*

try square A device for marking off right angles and testing the accuracy of anything square.

tryst (trist, trīst) *n.* 1 An appointment to meet at a specified time or place. 2 The meeting place agreed upon. 3 The

meeting so agreed upon. [< OF *triste, tristre* an appointed station in hunting]

tsar (zär, tsär) *n.* CZAR.

tset·se (tset′sē, tsē′tsē) *n.* Any of several bloodsucking flies of Africa, including species that carry and transmit pathogenic organisms to humans and animals. Also **tsetse fly.** [< Bantu]

T. Sgt., T/Sgt Technical Sergeant.

T-shirt (tē′shûrt′) *n.* A knitted cotton undershirt with short sleeves.

tsp. teaspoon(s); teaspoonful(s).

T-square (tē′skwâr′) *n.* A device used to measure out right angles or parallel lines, consisting usu. of a flat strip with a shorter head at right angles to it.

tsu·na·mi (tsŏō·nä′mē) *n.* An immense wave generated by a submarine earthquake. [Jap. < *tsu* port, harbor + *nami* wave]

Tu., Tues. Tuesday.

tub (tub) *n.* 1 A broad, open-topped vessel of metal, wooden staves, etc., for washing and bathing. 2 A bathtub. 3 *Informal* A bath taken in a tub. 4 The amount that a tub contains. 5 Anything resembling a tub, as a broad, clumsy boat. 6 *Informal* A small cask. —*v.t. & v.i.* **tubbed, tub·bing** To wash or bathe in a tub. [< MDu. *tubbe*] —**tub′ber** *n.*

tu·ba (t^yŏō′bə) *n. pl.* **·bas** or **·bae** (-bē) A large bass instrument of the bugle family. [< L, a war trumpet]

tub·by (tub′ē) *adj.* **·bi·er, ·bi·est** Resembling a tub in form; round and fat. —**Syn.** chubby, chunky, corpulent, rotund.

tube (t^yŏōb) *n.* 1 A long hollow cylindrical body of metal, glass, rubber, etc., generally used to convey or hold a liquid or gas. 2 Any device having a tube or tubelike part, as a telescope. 3 *Biol.* Any elongated hollow part or organ. 4 A subway or subway tunnel. 5 An electron tube. 6 A collapsible metal or plastic cylinder for containing paints, toothpaste, glue, and the like. —**the tube** *Slang* Television. —*v.t.* **tubed, tub·ing** 1 To fit or furnish with a tube. 2 To make tubular. [< L *tubus*] —**tu′bal** *adj.*

tu·ber (t^yŏō′bər) *n.* 1 A short, thickened portion of an underground stem, as a potato. 2 A tubercle. [L, a swelling]

tu·ber·cle (t^yŏō′bər·kəl) *n.* 1 A small rounded eminence or nodule. 2 *Bot.* A small wartlike swelling, usu. due to symbiotic microorganisms, as on the roots of certain legumes. 3 *Pathol.* A small granular tumor within an organ. [< L *tuber* a swelling]

tubercle bacillus The rod-shaped bacterium that causes tuberculosis.

tu·ber·cu·lar (t^yŏō·bûr′kyə·lər) *adj.* 1 Affected with tubercles. 2 Tuberculous. —*n.* One affected with tuberculosis.

tu·ber·cu·lin (t^yŏō·bûr′kyə·lin) *n.* A substance derived from tubercle bacilli, used in a diagnostic test for tuberculosis. [< L *tuberculum* TUBERCLE + -IN]

tu·ber·cu·lo·sis (t^yŏō·bûr′kyə·lō′sis) *n.* A communicable disease caused by the tubercle bacillus and characterized by tubercles in the lungs or other organs or tissues of the body. —**tu·ber′cu·lous** (t^yŏō·bûr′kyə·ləs) *adj.*

tube·rose (t^yŏōb′rōz′, t^yŏō′bə·rōs′) *n.* A bulbous plant of the amaryllis family, bearing a spike of fragrant white flowers. [< L *tuberosus* knobby < *tuber* a swelling]

tu·ber·ous (t^yŏō′bər·əs) *adj.* 1 Bearing projections or prominences. 2 Resembling tubers. 3 *Bot.* Bearing tubers: also **tu′ber·ose.** —**tu·ber·os·i·ty** (t^yŏō′bə·ros′ə·tē) *n.* (*pl.* **·ties**)

tub·ing (t^yŏō′bing) *n.* 1 Tubes collectively. 2 A piece of tube or material for tubes.

tu·bu·lar (t^yŏō′byə·lər) *adj.* 1 Having the form of a tube. 2 Of or pertaining to a tube or tubes.

tuck (tuk) *v.t.* 1 To thrust or press in the ends or edges of: to *tuck* in a blanket. 2 To wrap or cover snugly. 3 To thrust or press into a close place; cram. 4 To make tucks in, by folding and stitching. —*v.i.* 5 To contract; draw together. 6 To make tucks. —*n.* 1 A fold sewed into a garment. 2 Any inserted or folded thing. 3 A position in diving in which the knees are bent and the upper legs pressed against the chest. [< OE *tūcian* ill-treat, lit., tug]

tuck·er[1] (tuk′ər) *n.* 1 One who or that which tucks. 2 A

covering of muslin, lace, etc., formerly worn over the neck and shoulders by women. 3 A device on a sewing machine to make tucks.

tuck·er[2] (tuk′ər) *v.t. Informal* To weary completely; exhaust: usu. with *out.* [?]

Tu·dor (t^yŏō′dər) *adj.* 1 Of or pertaining to the English royal family (1485–1603) descended from Sir Owen Tudor. 2 Designating or pertaining to the architecture, poetry, etc., developed during the reigns of the Tudors.

Tues·day (t^yŏōz′dē, -dā) *n.* The third day of the week. [< OE *tīwesdæg* day of Tiw, a god of war]

tuft (tuft) *n.* 1 A collection or bunch of small, flexible parts, as hair, grass, or feathers, held together at the base. 2 A clump or knot. —*v.t.* 1 To provide (a mattress, upholstery, etc.) with tightly drawn tufts or buttons to keep the padding in place. 2 To cover or adorn with tufts. —*v.i.* 3 To form or grow in tufts. [< OF *tuffe*] —**tuft′er** *n.*

tuft·ed (tuf′tid) *adj.* 1 Having or adorned with a tuft or crest. 2 Forming a tuft or dense cluster.

tug (tug) *v.* **tugged, tug·ging** *v.t.* 1 To pull at with effort; strain at. 2 To pull or drag with effort. 3 To tow with a tugboat. —*v.i.* 4 To pull strenuously: to *tug* at an oar. 5 To strive; struggle. —*n.* 1 A violent pull. 2 A strenuous contest. 3 A tugboat. 4 A trace of a harness. [< OE *tēon* tow] —**tug′ger** *n.* —**Syn.** *v.* 2 draw, haul, heave, lug.

tug·boat (tug′bōt′) *n.* A small, compact, ruggedly built vessel designed for towing or pushing barges and larger vessels.

tug of war 1 A contest in which a number of persons at one end of a rope pull against a like number at the other end. 2 A laborious effort; supreme contest. Also **tug-of-war** (tug′uv·wôr′, tug′ə-) *n.* (*pl.* **tugs-of-war**).

tu·i·tion (t^yŏō·ish′ən) *n.* 1 The act or business of teaching. 2 The charge or payment for instruction. [< L *tuitio* a guard, guardianship] —**tu·i′tion·al, tu·i′tion·ar′y** (-er′ē) *adj.*

tu·la·re·mi·a (tŏō′lə·rē′mē·ə) *n.* An acute bacterial infection that can be transmitted to man from infected rabbits, squirrels, or other animals by the bite of certain flies or by direct contact. Also **tu′la·rae′mi·a.** [< *Tulare* County, California + Gk. *haima* blood]

tu·lip (t^yŏō′lip) *n.* 1 Any of numerous bulbous plants of the lily family, bearing variously colored cup-shaped flowers. 2 A bulb or flower of this plant. [< Turkish *tuliband* turban]

tulip tree A large North American forest tree related to magnolia, with greenish cup-shaped flowers.

tu·lip·wood (t^yŏō′lip·wŏŏd′) *n.* 1 The soft, light wood of the tulip tree. 2 Any of several ornamental cabinet woods. 3 Any of the trees yielding these woods.

tulle (tŏōl, *Fr.* tül) *n.* A fine, silk, open-meshed material, used for veils, etc. [< *Tulle*, a city in sw France]

tum·ble (tum′bəl) *v.* **·bled, ·bling** *v.i.* 1 To roll or toss about. 2 To perform acrobatic feats, as somersaults, etc. 3 To fall violently or awkwardly. 4 To move in a careless or headlong manner; stumble. 5 *Informal* To understand; comprehend: with *to.* —*v.t.* 6 To toss carelessly; cause to fall. 7 To throw into disorder; rumple. —*n.* 1 The act of tumbling; a fall. 2 A state of disorder or confusion. [< OE *tumbian* fall, leap]

tum·ble·bug (tum′bəl·bug′) *n.* Any of several beetles that roll up a ball of dung to enclose their eggs.

tum·ble-down (tum′bəl·doun′) *adj.* Rickety, as if about to fall in pieces; dilapidated.

tum·bler (tum′blər) *n.* 1 A drinking glass without a foot or stem; also, its contents. 2 One who or that which tumbles, as an acrobat or contortionist. 3 One of a breed of domestic pigeons noted for turning somersaults during flight. 4 In a lock, a latch that engages and immobilizes a bolt unless raised by the key bit. 5 A revolving device the contents of which are tumbled about, as certain dryers for clothes.

tum·ble·weed (tum′bəl·wēd′) *n.* Any of various plants which break off in autumn and are driven about by the wind.

tum·brel (tum′bril) *n.* 1 A farmer's cart. 2 A rude cart in which prisoners were taken to the guillotine during the French

Tumbrel

Revolution. **3** A military cart for carrying tools, ammunition, etc. Also **tum′bril.** [< OE *tomberel*]

tu·me·fy (t⁷o͞o′mə·fī) *v.t. & v.i.* **·fied,** **·fy·ing** To swell or puff up. [< L *tumere* swell + *facere* make] —**tu·me·fac·tion** (t⁷o͞o′mə·fak′shən) *n.*

tu·mes·cent (t⁷o͞o·mes′ənt) *adj.* Swelling; somewhat tumid. [< L *tumescere* to swell up] —**tu·mes′cence** *n.*

tu·mid (t⁷o͞o′mid) *adj.* **1** Swollen; enlarged, protuberant. **2** Inflated or pompous. [< L *tumidus* < *tumere* swell] —**tu·mid′i·ty,** **tu′mid·ness** *n.*

tum·my (tum′ē) *n. pl.* **-mies** *Colloq.* The stomach or abdomen.

tu·mor (t⁷o͞o′mər) *n.* A local swelling on or in the body, esp. from growth of tissue having no physiological function. *Brit. sp.* **tu′mour.** [< L *tumere* to swell] —**tu′mor·ous** *adj.*

tu·mult (t⁷o͞o′mult) *n.* **1** The commotion, disturbance, or agitation of a multitude; an uproar. **2** Any violent commotion. **3** Mental or emotional agitation. [< L *tumultus* < *tumere* swell] —**Syn.** ferment, hubbub, racket, turbulence.

tu·mul·tu·ous (t⁷o͞o·mul′cho͞o·əs) *adj.* **1** Characterized by tumult; disorderly; violent. **2** Greatly agitated or disturbed. **3** Stormy; tempestuous. —**tu·mul′tu·ous·ly** *adv.* —**tu·mul′tu·ous·ness** *n.*

tun (tun) *n.* **1** A large cask. **2** A varying measure of capacity for wines, etc., usu. equal to 252 gallons. —*v.t.* **tunned,** **tun·ning** To put into a cask or tun. [< OE *tunne*]

tu·na (t⁷o͞o′nə) *n. pl.* **tu·na** or **tu·nas** Any of various large marine food and game fishes related to mackerel. Also **tuna fish.** [Am. Sp., ult. < *thunnus* tunny]

tun·dra (tun′drə, to͞on′-) *n.* A rolling, treeless, often marshy plain of Siberia, arctic North America, etc. [Russ.]

tune (t⁷o͞on) *n.* **1** A coherent succession of musical tones; a melody or air. **2** Correct musical pitch or key. **3** Fine adjustment: the *tune* of an engine. **4** State of mind; humor: He will change his *tune*. **5** Concord; agreement: to be out of *tune* with the times. —**sing a difficult tune** To assume a different style or attitude. —**to the tune of** *Informal* To the amount of: *to the tune of* ten dollars. —*v.* **tuned,** **tun·ing** *v.t.* **1** To put into tune; adjust precisely. **2** To adapt to a particular tone, expression, or mood. **3** To bring into harmony or accord. —*v.i.* **4** To be in harmony. —**tune in 1** To adjust a radio or television receiver to (a station, program, etc.). **2** *Slang* To become or cause to become aware, knowing, or sophisticated. —**tune out 1** To adjust a radio or television receiver to exclude (interference, a station, etc.). **2** *Slang* To turn one's interest or attention away from. —**tune up 1** To bring (musical instruments) to a common pitch. **2** To adjust (a machine, engine, etc.) to proper working order. [< ME *tone* tone] —**tun′er** *n.*

tune·ful (t⁷o͞on′fəl) *adj.* Melodious; musical. —**tune′ful·ly** *adv.* —**tune′ful·ness** *n.*

tune·less (t⁷o͞on′lis) *adj.* **1** Not being in tune. **2** Lacking in melody. —**tune′less·ly** *adv.* —**tune′less·ness** *n.*

tune-up (t⁷o͞on′up′) *n.* A precise adjustment of an engine or other device.

tung oil (tung) A fast-drying oil extracted from the seeds of the subtropical **tung tree,** used in paints, varnishes, etc. [Chin. *t'ung* the tung tree]

tung·sten (tung′stən) *n.* A hard, heavy metallic element (symbol W), having a high melting point, used to make filaments for electric lamps and various alloys. [Sw. < *tung* weighty + *sten* stone]

tu·nic (t⁷o͞o′nik) *n.* **1** Among the ancient Greeks and Romans, a loose body garment, with or without sleeves, reaching to the knees. **2** A modern outer garment gathered at the waist, as a short overskirt or a blouse. **3** A short coat worn as part of a uniform. **4** *Biol.* A mantle of tissue covering an organism or a part: also **tu′ni·ca** (-kə) [< L *tunica*]

tuning fork A fork-shaped piece of steel that produces a fixed tone when struck.

Tu·ni·sia (t⁷o͞o·nē′zhə, -nish′ə, -nish′ē·ə) *n.* A republic of N Africa, 48,195 sq. mi., cap. Tunis. —**Tu·ni′sian** *adj., n.* • See map at AFRICA.

tun·nage (tun′ij) *n. Brit.* TONNAGE.

tun·nel (tun′əl) *n.* **1** An underground passageway or gallery, as for a railway or roadway. **2** Any similar passageway under or through something. **3** A burrow. —*v.* **·neled** or **·nelled, ·nel·ing** or **·nel·ling** *v.t.* **1** To make a tunnel or similar passage through or under. **2** To proceed by digging or as if by digging a tunnel. —*v.i.* **3** To make a tunnel. [< OF *tonne* a cask] —**tun′nel·er** or **tun′nel·ler** *n.*

tun·ny (tun′ē) *n. pl.* **·nies** or **·ny** TUNA. [< Gk. *thynnos*]

tup (tup) *n.* A ram, or male sheep. —*v.t. & v.i.* **tupped, tup·ping** To copulate with (a ewe). [Prob. < Scand.]

tu·pe·lo (t⁷o͞o′pə·lō) *n. pl.* **·los** Any of several North American gum trees having smooth, oval leaves and brilliant red autumn foliage. [< Muskhogean]

Tu·pi (to͞o′pē′, ‑to͞o′pē′) *n. pl.* **Tu·pis** or **Tu·pi 1** A member of any of a group of South American Indian tribes comprising the N branch of the Tupian stock. **2** The language spoken by the Tupis: also **Tu·pi′-Gua·ra·ni′** (‑gwä·rä·nē′) .

Tu·pi·an (to͞o·pē′ən) *adj.* Of or pertaining to the Tupis or their language. —*n.* A large linguistic stock of South American Indians.

tup·pence (tup′əns) *n.* TWOPENCE.

tuque (t⁷o͞ok) *n. Can.* A knitted stocking cap. [F (Canadian) < F *toque* < Sp. *toca*]

tur·ban (tûr′bən) *n.* **1** A head covering consisting of a sash or shawl, twisted about the head or about a cap, worn by men in the Orient. **2** Any similar headdress. [< Pers. *dulband* < *dul* a turn + *band* a band] —**tur′baned** (-bənd) *adj.*

tur·bid (tûr′bid) *adj..* **1** Muddy or opaque: a *turbid* stream. **2** Dense; heavy: *turbid* clouds of smoke. **3** Confused; disturbed. [< L *turbidus* < *turbare* to trouble] —**tur′bid·ly** *adv.* —**tur·bid·ness, tur·bid·i·ty** (tûr·bid′ə·tē) *n.* • **turbid, turgid** Because these words sound alike, they are often confused: *Turbid* usu. refers to water, smoke, etc., so filled with sediment or particles as to be opaque. *Turgid* means abnormally swollen or inflated.

tur·bine (tûr′bin, -bīn) *n.* An engine consisting of one or more rotary units, mounted on a shaft and provided with a series of vanes, actuated by steam, water, gas, or other fluid under pressure. [< L *turbo* a whirlwind, top]

turbo- *combining form* Pertaining to, consisting of, or driven by a turbine: *turbojet.* [< L *turbo* a top]

tur·bo·fan (tûr′bō·fan′) *n. Aeron.* A jet engine with turbine-driven fans that augment its thrust.

tur·bo·jet (tûr′bō·jet′) *n. Aeron.* A jet engine that uses a gas turbine to drive the air compressor.

tur·bo·prop (tûr′bō·prop′) *n. Aeron.* A jet engine in which part of the thrust is produced by a turbine-driven propeller.

tur·bot (tûr′bət) *n. pl.* **·bot** or **·bots 1** A large, edible European flatfish. **2** Any of various flatfishes, as the flounder, halibut, etc. [< OF *tourbout*]

tur·bu·lent (tûr′byə·lənt) *adj.* **1** Violently disturbed or agitated: a *turbulent* sea. **2** Inclined to rebel; insubordinate. **3** Having a tendency to disturb. [< L *turbulentus* full of disturbance] —**tur′bu·lence, tur′bu·len·cy** *n.* —**tur′bu·lent·ly** *adv.* —**Syn. 1** stormy, tumultuous, wild. **2** obstreperous, unruly.

tu·reen (t⁷o͞o·rēn′) *n.* A large, deep, covered dish, as for soup. [< F *terrine*]

turf (tûrf) *n. pl.* **turfs** (*Archaic* **turves**) **1** A mass of grass and its matted roots. **2** A plot of grass. **3** Peat. **4** *Slang* **a** A home territory, esp. that of a youthful street gang, defended against invasion by rival gangs. **b** Any place regarded possessively as the center of one's activity or interest: Philadelphia is his home *turf*. —**the turf 1** A racecourse. **2** Horse racing. —*v.t.* To cover with turf; sod. [< OE]

turf·man (tûrf′mən) *n. pl.* **·men** (-mən) A man who is connected with horseracing.

tur·ges·cent (tur·jes′ənt) *adj.* Being or becoming swollen or inflated. [< L *turgere* swell] —**tur·ges′cence, tur·ges′cen·cy** *n.* —**tur·ges′cent·ly** *adv.*

tur·gid (tûr′jid) *adj.* **1** Unnaturally distended; swollen. **2** Using high-flown laguage; bombastic: *turgid* prose. [< L *turgere* swell] —**tur·gid·i·ty** (tər·jid′ə·tē), **tur′gid·ness** *n.* —**tur′gid·ly** *adv.* • See TURBID.

Turk (tûrk) *n.* A citizen or native of Turkey.

Turk. Turkey; Turkish.

Turkey

tur·key (tûr′kē) *n. pl.* ·**keys** **1** A large North American bird related to the pheasant, having the head naked and a spreading tail. **2** The edible flesh of this bird. **3** *Slang* A play or a motion picture that fails. [From mistaken identification with a guinea fowl originating in *Turkey*]

Tur·key (tûr′kē) *n.* A republic of s Eurasia, 296,108 sq. mi., cap. Ankara.

turkey buzzard A black vulture of temperate and tropical America with a naked red head and neck. Also **turkey vulture.**

Turk·ic (tûr′kik) *n.* A subfamily of the Altaic family of languages. —*adj.* Pertaining to this linguistic subfamily, or to any of the peoples speaking its languages.

Turk·ish (tûr′kish) *n.* The language of Turkey. —*adj.* Of or pertaining to Turkey, its people, or their language.

Turkish bath A bath in which sweating is induced by exposure to high temperature, usu. in a room heated by steam.

Turkish Empire OTTOMAN EMPIRE.

Turkish towel A heavy, rough towel with loose, uncut pile. Also **turkish towel.**

tur·mer·ic (tûr′mər·ik, tyōō′mə·rik) *n.* **1** The orange-red, aromatic root of an East Indian plant; used as a condiment, dyestuff, etc. **2** The plant. **3** Any of several plants resembling turmeric. [? < F *terre mérite* deserving earth]

tur·moil (tûr′moil) *n.* Confused motion; disturbance; tumult. [?]

turn (tûrn) *v.t.* **1** To cause to rotate, as about an axis. **2** To change the position of, as by rotating: to *turn* a trunk on its side. **3** To move so that the upper side becomes the under: to *turn* a page. **4** To reverse the arrangement or order of; cause to be upside down. **5** To ponder: often with *over.* **6** To sprain or strain: to *turn* one's ankle in running. **7** To make sick or disgusted: The sight *turns* my stomach. **8** To shape in a lathe. **9** To give rounded or curved form to. **10** To give graceful or finished form to: to *turn* a phrase. **11** To perform by revolving: to *turn* cartwheels. **12** To bend, curve, fold, or twist. **13** To bend or blunt (the edge of a knife, etc.). **14** To change or transform: to *turn* water into wine. **15** To translate: to *turn* French into English. **16** To exchange for an equivalent: to *turn* stocks into cash. **17** To cause to become as specified: The sight *turned* him sick. **18** To make sour or rancid; ferment or curdle. **19** To change the direction of. **20** To change the direction or focus of (thought, attention, etc.). **21** To deflect or divert: to *turn* a blow. **22** To repel: to *turn* a charge. **23** To go around: to *turn* a corner. **24** To pass or go beyond: to *turn* twenty-one. **25** To compel to go; drive: to *turn* a beggar from one's door. —*v.i.* **26** To rotate; revolve. **27** To move completely or partially on or as if on an axis: He *turned* and ran. **28** To change position, as in bed. **29** To take a new direction: We *turned* north. **30** To reverse position; become inverted. **31** To reverse direction or flow: The tide has *turned.* **32** To change the direction of one's thought, attention, etc.: Let us *turn* to the next problem. **33** To depend; hinge: with *on* or *upon.* **34** To be affected with giddiness; whirl, as the head. **35** To become upset, as the stomach. **36** To change attitude, sympathy, or allegiance: to *turn* on one's neighbors. **37** To become transformed; change: The water *turned* into ice. **38** To become as specified: His hair *turned* gray. **39** To change color: said esp. of leaves. **40** To become sour or fermented, as milk or wine. —**turn against** To become or cause to become opposed or hostile to. —**turn down 1** To diminish the flow, volume, etc., of: *Turn down* the gas. **2** *Informal.* **a** To reject or refuse, as a proposal, or request. **b** To refuse the request, proposal, etc., of. —**turn in 1** To fold or double. **2** To bend or incline inward. **3** To deliver; hand over. **4** *Informal* To go to bed. —**turn off 1** To stop the operation, flow, etc., of. **2** To leave the direct road; make a turn. **3** To deflect or

divert. **4** *Slang* To cause (a person) to lose interest in or liking for. —**turn on 1** To set in operation, flow, etc.: to *turn on* an engine. **2** *Slang* To experience the effects of taking a psychedelic drug. **3** *Slang* To arrange for (someone) to take such a drug. **4** *Slang* To evoke in (someone) a profound or rapt response. —**turn out 1** To turn inside out. **2** To eject or expel. **3** To bend or incline outward. **4** To produce or make. **5** To come or go out: to *turn out* for a meeting. **6** To prove (to be). **7** To equip or fit; dress. **8** *Informal* To get out of bed. —**turn over 1** To change the position of. **2** To upset; overturn. **3** To hand over; transfer. **4** To do business to the amount of. **5** To invest and get back (capital). —**turn to 1** To set to work. **2** To seek aid from. **3** To refer or apply to. —**turn up 1** To fold the under side upward. **2** To incline upward. **3** To find or be found: to *turn up* new evidence. **4** To increase the flow, volume, etc., of. **5** To arrive. —*n.* **1** The act of turning, or the state of being turned. **2** A change to another direction or position: a *turn* of the tide. **3** A deflection from a course; a bend. **4** The point at which a change takes place: a *turn* for the better. **5** A rotation or revolution: the *turn* of a crank. **6** A regular time or chance in some sequence of action: It's his *turn* at bat. **7** Characteristic form or style. **8** Disposition; tendency: a humorous *turn.* **9** A deed: an ill *turn.* **10** A walk or drive: a *turn* in the park. **11** A round in a skein or coil. **12** *Music* An ornament in which the main tone alternates with the seconds above and below. **13** *Informal* A spell of dizziness or nervousness: The explosion gave me quite a *turn.* **14** A variation or difference in type or kind. **15** A short theatrical act. **16** A twist, as of a rope, around a tree or post. **17** A business transaction. —**at every turn** On every occasion; constantly. —**by turns 1** In alternation or sequence: also **turn by turn.** **2** At intervals. —**in turn** One after another. —**out of turn** Not in proper order or sequence. —**to a turn** Just right: meat browned *to a turn.* —**take turns** To act, play, etc. in proper order. [< L *tornare* turn in a lathe < *turnus* a lathe] —**turn′er** *n.*

turn·a·bout (tûrn′ə·bout′) *n.* **1** The act of turning about so as to face the opposite direction. **2** An about-face in allegiance, opinion, etc.

turn·a·round (tûrn′ə·round′) *n.* **1** The time required for maintenance, refueling, discharging or loading cargo, etc., during a round trip of a ship, aircraft, etc. **2** A space, as in a driveway, large enough for the turning around of a vehicle. **3** A shift or reversal of a trend, procedure, development, etc.

turn·buck·le (tûrn′buk′əl) *n. Mech.* A threaded coupling that receives a threaded rod at each end so that it may be turned to regulate the distance between them.

turn·coat (tûrn′kōt′) *n.* One who goes over to the opposite side or party; a renegade.

turn·down (tûrn′doun′) *adj.* Folded down or able to be folded down, as a collar. —*n.* **1** A rejection. **2** A decline: a *turndown* in prices.

turn·ing (tûr′ning) *n.* **1** The art of shaping wood, metal, etc., in a lathe. **2** *pl.* Spiral shavings produced by turning wood or metal on a lathe. **3** A winding; bend.

turning point The point of decisive change, as in progress, decline, etc.

tur·nip (tûr′nip) *n.* **1** The fleshy, yellow or white edible root of certain plants related to cabbage. **2** Any of these plants. [< Earlier *turnepe*]

turn·key (tûrn′kē′) *n.* One who has charge of the keys of a prison; a jailer. —*adj.* Of, pertaining to, or being, by prearrangement with a buyer, a product or service in complete readiness for use when purchased: a *turnkey* housing project.

turn·out (tûrn′out′) *n.* **1** A turning out. **2** An assemblage of persons, as at a meeting: a good *turnout.* **3** A quantity produced; output. **4** Array; equipment; outfit. **5** A railroad siding. **6** A carriage or wagon with its horses and equipage.

turn·o·ver (tûrn′ō′vər) *n.* **1** An upset. **2** A change or revolution: a *turnover* in affairs. **3** A tart made by covering half of a circular crust with fruit, jelly, etc., and turning the other half over on top. **4** The amount of money taken in and paid out in a business within a given period. **5** The selling out and restocking of goods, as in a store. **6** The rate at which persons hired within a given period are

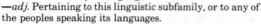

replaced by others; also, the number of persons hired. —
adj. Turning over, or capable of being turned over.

turn·pike (tûrn′pīk′) *n.* **1** A road on which there are, or
formerly were, tollgates: also **turnpike road. 2** TOLLGATE.
[ME *turnpyke* a spiked road barrier < TURN, *v.* + PIKE[1]]

turn·stile (tûrn′stīl′) *n.* A kind of gate consisting of a
vertical post and horizontal arms which by revolving permit persons to pass.

turn·stone (tûrn′stōn′) *n.* A ploverlike migratory bird
that turns over stones when searching for food.

turn·ta·ble (tûrn′tā′bəl) *n.* **1** A rotating platform, usu.
circular, on which to turn a locomotive or other vehicle
around. **2** The revolving disk of a phonograph on which
records are played.

tur·pen·tine (tûr′pən·tīn) *n.* **1** A resinous, oily liquid obtained from any of several coniferous trees. **2** The colorless essential oil (**oil of turpentine**) formed when turpentine is distilled, widely used in industry, medicine, and in
mixing paints. —*v.t.* **·tined, ·tin·ing** To treat or saturate
with turpentine. [< L *terebinthus* a Mediterranean tree]

tur·pi·tude (tûr′pə·t^yōōd) *n.* Inherent baseness; depravity. [< L *turpis* vile] —**Syn.** corruption, degeneracy,
vileness, wickedness.

tur·quoise (tûr′koiz, -kwoiz) *n.* **1** A blue or blue-green
stone, esteemed as a gemstone when highly polished. **2** A
light, greenish blue: also **turquoise blue.** —*adj.* Light,
greenish blue. [< MF *(pierre) turquoise* Turkish (stone)]

tur·ret (tûr′it) *n.* **1** A small projecting tower, usu. at the
corner of a building. **2** *Mil.* A rotating armed structure
containing guns and gunners, forming part of a warship
or tank. **3** A structure for a gunner on a combat airplane,
usu. enclosed in transparent plastic material. [< OF *tor*
tower] —**tur′ret·ed** *adj.*

tur·tle (tûr′təl) *n.* **1** Any of numerous four-limbed, terrestrial or aquatic reptiles having a
toothless beak and a soft body en-
cased in a shell. **2** The edible flesh
of certain turtles. —**turn turtle**
To overturn; capsize. [?< Sp. *tor-*
tuga < Med. L *tortuca* tortoise]
• See SNAPPING TURTLE.

tur·tle·dove (tûr′təl·duv′) *n.* **1** A
dove noted for its plaintive coo-
ing. **2** The mourning dove. [< L
turtur turtledove]

Turtle

tur·tle·neck (tûr′təl·nek′) *n.* **1** A
pullover sweater or knitted shirt with a high, close-fitting,
turnover collar. **2** Such a collar.

tusk (tusk) *n.* A long, projecting tooth, as in the boar,
walrus, or elephant. —*v.t.* To use the tusks to gore, root
up, etc. [< OE *tūx*]

tus·sah (tus′ə) *n.* **1** An Asian silkworm that spins large
cocoons of brownish or yellowish silk. **2** The silk, or the
fabric woven from it. [< Skt. *tasara* a shuttle]

tus·sle (tus′əl) *v.t.* & *v.i.* **·sled, ·sling 1** To scuffle or struggle. **2** To argue. —*n.* **1** A scuffle or struggle. **2** An argument. [Var. of TOUSLE]

tus·sock (tus′ək) *n.* **1** A tuft or clump of grass or sedge.
2 A tuft, as of hair or feathers. [?] —**tus′sock·y** *adj.*

tut (tut) *interj.* An exclamation to express impatience.

tu·te·lage (t^yōō′tə·lij) *n.* **1** The state of being under the
care of a tutor or guardian. **2** The act or office of a guardian. **3** The act of tutoring; instruction. [< L *tutela* a watching, guardianship]

tu·te·lar·y (t^yōō′tə·ler′ē) *adj.* **1** Watching over; protecting.
2 Of or pertaining to a guardian. Also **tu′te·lar.** —*n.* *pl.*
·ar·ies A guardian spirit, divinity, etc.

tu·tor (t^yōō′tər) *n.* **1** A private teacher. **2** A college teacher
who gives individual instruction. **3** *Brit.* A college official
entrusted with the tutelage and care of undergraduates
assigned to him. —*v.t.* **1** To act as tutor to; train. **2** To treat
sternly; discipline. —*v.i.* **3** To do the work of a tutor. **4** To
be tutored or instructed. [< L, a watcher, guardian]

tu·to·ri·al (t^yōō·tôr′ē·əl) *adj.* Of or involving tutors, or
based upon their participation: the *tutorial* system. —*n.*
A small class of students guided by a tutor.

tut·ti (tōō′tē) *Music adj.* All: used to indicate that all performers take part. —*n.* A passage or section to be performed by all the voices and instruments together. [< Ital.
tutto all]

tut·ti-frut·ti (tōō′tē-frōō′tē) *n.* A confection, chewing
gum, ice cream, etc., made or flavored with mixed fruits.
—*adj.* Flavored with mixed fruits. [Ital., all fruits]

tu·tu (tōō′tōō; *Fr.* tü′tü) *n.* A short, projecting, layered
skirt worn by ballet dancers. [F]

tux·e·do (tuk·sē′dō) *n. pl.* **·dos 1** A man's semiformal dinner or evening jacket without tails. **2** The suit of which the
jacket is a part. Also **Tux·e′do.** [< *Tuxedo* Park, N.Y.]

TV (tē′vē′) *n.* TELEVISION.

TV terminal velocity.

TVA, T.V.A. Tennessee Valley Authority.

TV dinner A frozen meal in a partitioned tray, ready to
be heated and served.

twad·dle (twod′l) *v.t.* & *v.i.* **·dled, ·dling** To talk foolishly
and pretentiously. —*n.* Pretentious, silly talk. [?] —**twad′-**
dler *n.*

twain (twān) *adj.* & *n.* *Archaic* Two. [< OE *twēgen* two]

twang (twang) *v.t.* & *v.i.* **twanged, twang·ing 1** To make or
cause to make a sharp, vibrant sound. **2** To utter or speak
with a harsh, nasal sound. —*n.* **1** A sharp, vibrating
sound. **2** A sharp, nasal sound of the voice. **3** A sound
resembling these. [Imit.] —**twang′y** *adj.* (**·i·er, ·i·est**)

tweak (twēk) *v.t.* To pinch and twist sharply. —*n.* A twisting pinch. [< OE *twiccan* twitch]

tweed (twēd) *n.* **1** A woolen fabric often woven in two or
more colors to effect a check or plaid pattern. **2** *pl.* Clothes
made of tweed. [< Scot. *tweel,* var. of TWILL]

twee·dle (twēd′l) *v.* **·dled, ·dling** *v.t.* **1** To play (a musical
instrument) casually or carelessly. —*v.i.* **2** To produce a
series of shrill tones. **3** To play a musical instrument casually or carelessly. —*n.* A sound so produced. [Imit. of the
sound of a reed pipe]

tweet (twēt) *v.i.* To utter a thin, chirping note. —*n.* A
twittering or chirping. [Imit.]

tweet·er (twē′tər) *n.* A loudspeaker specially designed to
reproduce only high-frequency sounds.

tweeze (twēz) *v.t.* **tweezed, tweez·ing** *Informal* To handle,
pinch, pluck, etc., with tweezers.

tweez·ers (twē′zərz) *n.pl.* (*construed as sing. or pl.*)
Small pincers for picking up or extracting tiny objects.
Also **pair of tweezers.** [< F *étui* a small case]

twelfth (twelfth) *adj.* & *adv.* Next in order after the 11th.
—*n.* **1** The element of an ordered set that corresponds to
the number 12. **2** One of 12 equal parts. [< OE *twelfta*]

Twelfth Day The twelfth day after Christmas; Epiphany.

twelve (twelv) *n.* **1** The sum of eleven plus one; 12; XII.
2 A set or group of 12 members. —**the Twelve** The twelve
apostles. [< OE *twelf*] —**twelve** *adj., pron.*

Twelve Apostles The twelve original disciples of
Jesus.

twelve·month (twelv′munth′) *n.* A year.

twelve-tone (twelv′tōn′) *adj. Music* Of, pertaining to, or
composed in a system in which any series of all twelve
tones of the chromatic scale is used as the basis of composition.

twen·ti·eth (twen′tē·ith) *adj.* & *adv.* Tenth in order after
the tenth. —*n.* **1** The element of an ordered set that corresponds to the number 20. **2** One of 20 equal parts.

twen·ty (twen′tē) *n. pl.* **·ties 1** The sum of 19 plus 1; 20;
XX. **2** A set or group of 20 members. **3** The numbers, years,
etc., from 20 to 30. [< OE *twentig*] —**twen′ty** *adj., pron.*

twen·ty-one (twen′tē-wun′) *n.* BLACKJACK (def. 3).

twice (twīs) *adv.* **1** Two times. **2** In double measure; doubly. [< OE *twiga*]

twid·dle (twid′l) *v.* **·dled, ·dling** *v.t.* **1** To twirl idly; play
with. —*v.i.* **2** To toy with something idly. **3** To be busy
about trifles. —**twiddle one's thumbs 1** To rotate one's
thumbs around each other. **2** To do nothing; be idle. —*n.*
A gentle twirling. [Prob. < ON *tridla* stir] —**twid′dler** *n.*

twig (twig) *n.* A small shoot or branch of a woody plant.
[< OE *twigge*]

---

add, āce, câre, pälm; end, ēven; it, īce; odd, ōpen, ôrder; tŏŏk, pōōl; up, bûrn; ə = a in *above,* u in *focus;*
yōō = u in *fuse;* oil; pout; check; go; ring; thin; <u>th</u>is; zh, *vision.* < derived from; ? origin uncertain or unknown.

twi·light (twī′līt′) *n.* **1** The light diffused over the sky after sunset and before sunrise. **2** The period during which this light prevails. **3** Any faint light; shade. **4** An obscure condition following the waning of past glory, achievements, etc. —*adj.* Pertaining or peculiar to twilight. [< OE < *twa* two + LIGHT]

twilight sleep A light anesthesia induced by morphine and scopolamine, formerly used in childbirth.

twill (twil) *n.* **1** Cloth woven in such a way as to produce diagonal, parallel ribs or lines. **2** The pattern formed by such weaving. —*v.t.* To weave (cloth) with a twill. [< OE *twili* a twilled fabric]

Twill

twin (twin) *n.* **1** Either of two young produced at the same birth. **2** Either of two persons or things greatly alike. —**the Twins** GEMINI. —*adj.* **1** Being a twin or twins: *twin* boys. **2** Being one of a pair of similar and closely related people or things. —*v.* twinned, twin·ning *v.i.* **1** To bring forth twins. **2** To be matched or equal. —*v.t.* **3** To bring forth as twins. **4** To couple; match. [< OE *twinn, getwinn*]

twine (twīn) *v.* twined, twin·ing *v.t.* **1** To twist together, as threads. **2** To form by such twisting. **3** To coil or wrap about something. **4** To encircle by winding or wreathing. —*v.i.* **5** To interlace. **6** To proceed in a winding course; meander. —*n.* **1** A string composed of two or more strands twisted together. **2** The act of twining or entwining. **3** A thing produced by twining. [< OE *twīn* a twisted double thread < *twa* two] —**twin′er** *n.* —**twin′ing·ly** *adv.*

twinge (twinj) *v.t.* & *v.i.* twinged, twing·ing To affect with or suffer a sudden pain. —*n.* **1** A sharp, darting, local pain. **2** A mental pang. [< OE *twengan* pinch] —**Syn.** *n.* **1** ache, cramp, throe.

twin·kle (twing′kəl) *v.* ·kled, ·kling *v.i.* **1** To shine with fitful, intermittent gleams. **2** To be bright, as with amusement: Her eyes *twinkled*. **3** To wink or blink. **4** To move rapidly to and fro; flicker: *twinkling* feet. —*v.t.* **5** To cause to twinkle. **6** To emit (light) in fitful, intermittent gleams. —*n.* **1** A tremulous gleam of light; glimmer. **2** A quick or repeated movement of the eyelids. **3** An instant; a twinkling. [< OE *twinclian*] —**twin′kler** *n.*

twin·kling (twing′kling) *n.* **1** The act of something that twinkles. **2** A wink or twinkle. **3** An instant; moment. —**twink′ling·ly** *adv.*

twirl (twûrl) *v.t.* & *v.i.* **1** To whirl or rotate rapidly. **2** To twist or curl. **3** In baseball, to pitch. —*n.* **1** A whirling motion. **2** A curl; twist; coil. [?] —**twirl′er** *n.*

twist (twist) *v.t.* **1** To wind (strands, etc.) around each other. **2** To form by such winding: to *twist* thread. **3** To give a spiral shape to. **4** To deform or distort, esp. by means of torque. **5** To distort the meaning of. **6** To confuse; perplex. **7** To wreathe, twine, or wrap. **8** To cause to revolve or rotate. **9** To impart spin to (a ball) so that it moves in a curve. —*v.i.* **10** To become twisted. **11** To move in a winding course. **12** To squirm; writhe. —*n.* **1** The act, manner, or result of twisting. **2** The state of being twisted. **3** *Physics* A torsional strain. **4** A curve; turn; bend. **5** A wrench; strain, as of a joint or limb. **6** A peculiar inclination or attitude: a mind with a criminal *twist*. **7** An unexpected turn or development. **8** A variant or novel approach or method: a mystery novel with a new *twist*. **9** Thread or cord made of tightly twisted or braided strands. **10** A twisted roll of bread. **11** A spin given to a ball by a certain stroke or throw. [< OE *-twist* a rope]

twist·er (twis′tər) *n.* **1** One who or that which twists. **2** In baseball, a curve. **3** A tornado; cyclone.

twit (twit) *v.t.* twit·ted, twit·ting To taunt. —*n.* A taunting allusion; reproach. [< OE *ætwitan*] —**twit′ter** *n.* —**Syn.** *v.* gibe, jeer, scoff, tease.

twitch (twich) *v.t.* **1** To pull sharply; pluck with a jerky movement. —*v.i.* **2** To move with a quick, spasmodic jerk, as a muscle. —*n.* **1** A sudden involuntary contraction of a muscle. **2** A sudden jerk or pull. [ME *twicchen*]

twit·ter (twit′ər) *v.i.* **1** To utter a series of light chirping or tremulous notes, as a bird. **2** To titter. **3** To be excited.

—*v.t.* **4** To utter or express with a twitter. —*n.* **1** A succession of light, tremulous sounds. **2** A state of excitement. [Imit.]

'twixt (twikst) *prep.* Betwixt.

two (tōō) *n.* **1** The sum of one plus one; 2; II. **2** A set or group of two members. —**in two** Bisected; asunder —**put two and two together** To draw an obvious conclusion by considering the facts. [< OE *twā, tū*] —**two** *adj., pron.*

two-base hit (tōō′bās′) In baseball, a hit in which the batter reaches second base without benefit of an error. Also **two′-bag′ger** (-bag′ər).

two-bit (tōō′bit′) *adj. Slang* Cheap; small-time: a *two-bit* gambler.

two bits *Informal* Twenty-five cents.

two-by-four (tōō′bī-fôr′, -fōr′) *adj.* **1** Measuring two inches by four inches. **2** *Slang* Narrow or cramped: a *two-by-four* kitchen. —*n.* (tōō′bī-fôr′, -fōr′) A timber measuring two inches in thickness and four inches in width before finishing.

two-edged (tōō′ejd′) *adj.* **1** Having an edge on each side; cutting both ways. **2** Having a double meaning.

two-faced (tōō′fāst′) *adj.* **1** Having two faces. **2** Double-dealing; insincere. —**two′-fac′ed·ly** (-fā′sid·lē, -fāst′lē) *adv.* —**two′fac′ed·ness** *n.*

two·fer (tōō′fər) *n.* **1** An article sold at two for the price of one. **2** A free coupon entitling the holder to buy two theater tickets for the price of one.

two·fold (tōō′fōld′) *adj.* Double. —*adv.* In a twofold manner or degree; doubly.

two-hand·ed (tōō′han′did) *adj.* **1** Requiring the use of both hands at once. **2** Constructed for use by two persons: a *two-handed* saw. **3** Ambidextrous. **4** Having two hands. **5** Played by two people: a *two-handed* card game.

two·pence (tup′əns) *n. Brit.* **1** Two pennies. **2** A silver coin of the same value, now issued only for alms money on Maundy Thursday. **3** A trifle; small amount.

two·pen·ny (tup′ən·ē) *adj. Brit.* **1** Of the value of two-pence. **2** Cheap; worthless.

two-ply (tōō′plī′) *adj.* **1** Woven double: a *two-ply* carpet. **2** Made of two strands or thicknesses of material.

two·some (tōō′səm) *n.* **1** Two persons together. **2** A game played by two persons. **3** The players.

two-step (tōō′step′) *n.* **1** A ballroom dance step in 2/4 time. **2** The music for it. —*v.i.* To do the two-step.

two-time (tōō′tīm′) *v.t.* -timed, -tim·ing *Slang* **1** To be unfaithful to. **2** DOUBLE-CROSS. —**two′-tim′er** *n.*

two-way (tōō′wā′) *adj.* **1** Permitting vehicles to go in opposite directions simultaneously: a *two-way* street. **2** Involving mutual or reciprocal exchanges, duties, obligations, etc.: a *two-way* agreement. **3** Involving two persons, groups, etc.: a *two-way* contest. **4** Capable of both sending and receiving communications: a *two-way* radio. **5** Made or fashioned so as to be used or worn in two ways: a *two-way* jacket.

twp. township.

TX Texas (P.O. abbr.).

-ty[1] *suffix of nouns* The state or condition of being: *sanity*. [< L *-tas*]

-ty[2] *suffix* Ten; ten times: used in numerals, as *thirty, forty*, etc. [< OE *-tig* ten]

Ty. Territory.

ty·coon (tī-kōōn′) *n.* **1** *Informal* A wealthy and powerful business leader. **2** A Japanese shogun. [< Japanese *taikun* a mighty lord]

ty·ing (tī′ing) *pr.p.* of TIE.

tyke (tīk) *n.* **1** A mongrel dog. **2** *Informal* A small mischievous child. [< ON *tik* bitch]

tym·pa·ni (tim′pə·nē) *n.pl.* TIMPANI.

tympanic membrane The membrane separating the middle ear from the external ear; the eardrum.

tym·pa·nist (tim′pə·nist) *n.* One who plays the timpani.

tym·pa·num (tim′pə·nəm) *n. pl.* **·na** (-nə) or **·nums** **1** *Anat.* **a** The cavity of the middle ear lined with the tympanic membrane. **b** TYMPANIC MEMBRANE. **2** A drum. **3** *Archit.* **a** A recessed, usu. triangular, space bounded by the sides of a pediment or gable at the end of a building. **b** A similar space over a door or window, between the lintel and the arch. [< Gk. *tympanon* a drum] —**tym·pan·ic** (tim·pan′ik) *adj.*

typ., typo., typog. typographer; typographic; typography.

type (tīp) *n.* **1** A class or group having traits and characteristics in common: an old *type* of car. **2** A standard or model. **3** The characteristic plan, form, style, etc., of a given class or group. **4** A person, animal, or object embodying the characteristics of a class or group. **5** *Printing* **a** A piece or block of metal or of wood bearing, usu. in relief, a letter or character for use in printing. **b** Such pieces collectively. **6** Typewritten or printed letters and numerals. **7** The characteristic device on either side of a medal or coin. —*v.* **typed, typ·ing** *v.t.* **1** To represent; typify. **2** To determine the type of; identify: to *type* a blood sample. **3** TYPEWRITE. **4** To prefigure. —*v.i.* **5** TYPEWRITE. [< Gk. *typos* an impression, figure, type]

-type *combining form* **1** Representative form; stamp; type: *prototype.* **2** Used in or produced by duplicating processes or by type: *Linotype.* [< Gk. *typos* stamp]

type·face (tīp′fās′) *n.* **1** A set of type of a particular design. **2** The face or impression of a type.

type·set·ter (tīp′set′ər) *n.* **1** One who sets type. **2** A machine for setting type. —**type′set′ting** *adj., n.*

type·write (tīp′rīt′) *v.t. & v.i.* **·wrote, ·writ·ten, ·writ·ing** To write with a typewriter.

type·writ·er (tīp′rī′tər) *n.* **1** A keyboard machine for producing characters, as letters, numbers, etc., that have the appearance of printer's type. **2** A typist.

ty·phoid (tī′foid) *adj.* **1** Pertaining to or resembling typhoid fever: also **ty·phoi′dal. 2** Resembling typhus. —*n.* TYPHOID FEVER.

typhoid fever A serious infectious disease caused by a bacillus transmitted in contaminated water or food and characterized by high fever, severe intestinal disturbances, and prostration.

ty·phoon (tī·fōōn′) *n.* A violent tropical storm, occurring in the W Pacific. [< Chin. *tai feng,* lit., big wind]

ty·phus (tī′fəs) *n.* Any of a group of contagious rickettsial diseases marked by high fever, a rash, nervous and mental disorders, and extreme prostration. [< Gk. *typhos* smoke, a stupor] —**ty′phous** *adj.*

typ·i·cal (tip′i·kəl) *adj.* **1** Having the nature or character of a type: a *typical* schoolboy. **2** Characteristic or representative of a group, class, etc.: *typical* middle-class values. [< Gk. *typos* TYPE] —**typ′i·cal·ly** *adv.* —**typ′i·cal·ness** *n.*

typ·i·fy (tip′ə·fī) *v.t.* **·fied, ·fy·ing 1** To represent by a type. **2** To serve as a characteristic example of. —**typ′i·fi·ca′tion** (-fə·kā′shən), **typ′i·fi′er** *n.*

typ·ist (tī′pist) *n.* **1** One who uses a typewriter. **2** A person whose work is operating a typewriter.

ty·po (tī′pō) *n. pl.* **ty·pos** *Informal* An error made by a printer or a typist. [< *typo(graphical error)*]

ty·pog·ra·pher (tī·pog′rə·fər) *n.* An expert in typography, esp. a printer or compositor.

ty·po·graph·i·cal (tī′pə·graf′i·kəl) *adj.* Of or pertaining to printing. Also **ty′po·graph′ic.** —**ty′po·graph′i·cal·ly** *adv.*

ty·pog·ra·phy (tī·pog′rə·fē) *n.* **1** The arrangement, style, and appearance of printed matter. **2** The act or art of composing and printing from types.

typw. typewriter; typewritten.

ty·ran·ni·cal (ti·ran′i·kəl, tī-) *adj.* Of or like a tyrant; despotic; arbitrary. Also **ty·ran′nic.** —**ty·ran′ni·cal·ly** *adv.* —**ty·ran′ni·cal·ness** *n.*

ty·ran·ni·cide (ti·ran′ə·sīd, tī-) *n.* **1** The slayer of a tyrant. **2** The slaying of a tyrant.

tyr·an·nize (tir′ə·nīz) *v.* **·nized, ·niz·ing** *v.i.* **1** To exercise power cruelly or unjustly. **2** To rule as a tyrant; have absolute power. —*v.t.* **3** To treat tyrannically; domineer. —**tyr′an·niz′er** *n.*

tyr·an·nous (tir′ə·nəs) *adj.* Despotic; tyrannical. —**tyr′an·nous·ly** *adv.* —**tyr′an·nous·ness** *n.*

tyr·an·ny (tir′ə·nē) *n. pl.* **·nies 1** The office, power, or jurisdiction of a tyrant. **2** A government or ruler having absolute power; despot or despotism. **3** Power used in a cruel or oppressive manner. **4** Harsh rigor; severity. **5** A tyrannical act. [< L *tyrannus* a tyrant]

ty·rant (tī′rənt) *n.* **1** One who rules oppressively or cruelly; a despot. **2** Any person who exercises power or authority in a harsh, cruel manner. [< Gk. *tyrannos* a master, a usurper]

tyre (tīr) *n. Brit. sp.* of TIRE[2].

Tyre (tīr) *n.* A port and capital of ancient Phoenicia, now in SW Lebanon.

ty·ro (tī′rō) *n. pl.* **·ros** One who is beginning to learn or study something; novice. [< L *tiro* a recruit]

tzar (tsär) *n.* CZAR.

tzet·ze (tset′sē) *n.* TSETSE.

tzi·gane (tsē·gän′) *n.* A Gypsy, esp. a Hungarian Gypsy. [F < Hung. *czigány*]

U

U, u (yōō) *n. pl.* **U's, u's, Us, us** (yōōz) **1** The twenty-first letter of the English alphabet. **2** Any spoken sound representing the letter *U* or *u.* **3** Something shaped like a U. —*adj.* Shaped like a U.

U uranium.

U., u. uncle; union; unit; university.

U.A.R. United Arab Republic.

UAW, U.A.W. United Automobile Workers; (officially) United Automobile, Aerospace, and Agricultural Implement Workers of America.

u·biq·ui·tous (yōō·bik′wə·təs) *adj.* Existing, or seeming to exist, everywhere at once; omnipresent. —**u·biq′ui·tous·ly** *adv.* —**u·biq′ui·tous·ness** *n.*

u·biq·ui·ty (yōō·bik′wə·tē) *n.* The state of being or seeming to be everywhere at the same time; omnipresence, real or seeming. [< L *ubique* everywhere]

U-boat (yōō′bōt′) *n.* A German submarine. [< G *U-boot,* contraction of *Unterseeboot,* lit., undersea boat]

u.c. upper case (printing).

ud·der (ud′ər) *n.* A large, pendulous, milk-secreting gland having nipples or teats for the suckling of offspring, as in cows. [< OE *ūder*]

UFO (yōō′ef·ō′) *n. pl.* **UFOs, UFO's** Any of various unidentified flying objects alleged to have been seen traveling at speeds and following courses that would be impossible for any aircraft to duplicate. [< *u(nidentified) f(lying) o(bject)*]

U·gan·da (yōō·gan′də, ōō·gän′dä), *n.* An independent member of the Commonwealth of Nations in CEN. Africa, 93,981 sq. mi., cap. Kampala. • See map at AFRICA.

ugh (ug, ukh, u, ōōkh, ōō) *interj.* An exclamation of repugnance or disgust. [Imit.]

ug·li·fy (ug′lə·fī′) *v.t.* **·fied, ·fy·ing** To make ugly. —**ug′li·fi·ca′tion** (-fə·kā′shən) *n.*

ug·ly (ug′lē) *adj.* **·li·er, ·li·est 1** Distasteful in appearance; unsightly. **2** Distasteful to any of the senses. **3** Morally revolting or repulsive. **4** Bad in character or consequences, as a rumor or a wound. **5** Ill-tempered; quarrelsome. **6** Portending storms; threatening. [< ON *uggligr* dreadful < *uggr* fear] —**ug′li·ly** *adv.* —**ug′li·ness** *n.* —**Syn. 1** homely, ill-looking, unlovely, unseemly. **2** repulsive, repellent, repugnant, revolting, abhorrent, disgusting. **5** ill-humored, irascible, irritable, testy, querulous.

ugly duckling Any ill-favored or unpromising child who unexpectedly grows into a beauty or a wonder. [< *The Ugly Duckling,* a story by Hans Christian Andersen]

U·gri·an (ōō′grē·ən, yōō′-) *n.* **1** A member of any of the Finno-Ugric peoples of Hungary and W Siberia. **2** UGRIC.

—*adj.* Of or pertaining to the Ugrians or their languages.

U·gric (ōō′grik, yōō′-) *n.* A branch of the Finno-Ugric subfamily of languages including Magyar (Hungarian). — *adj.* UGRIAN.

UHF, U.H.F., uhf, u.h.f. ultrahigh frequency.

uit·land·er (īt′län·dər, oit′-; *Afrikaans* œit′län·dər) *n.* Often *cap.* A foreigner; outlander. [Afrikaans]

U.K. United Kingdom.

u·kase (yōō·kās′, -kāz′, yōō′kās, ōō·koz′) *n.* 1 In imperial Russia, an edict or decree of the czar. 2 Any official decree. [< Russ. *ukaz*]

U·krain·i·an (yōō·krā′nē·ən, -krī′-) *adj.* Of or pertaining to the Ukraine, its people, or their language. —*n.* 1 A native or inhabitant of the Ukraine. 2 An East Slavic language spoken in the Ukraine.

u·ku·le·le (yōō′kə·lā′lē; *Hawaiian* ōō′kōō·lā′lä) *n.* A small, guitarlike musical instrument having four strings. [Hawaiian < *uku* insect + *lele* jump; from the movements of the fingers in playing]

ul·cer (ul′sər) *n.* 1 An open sore on skin or mucous membrane with disintegration of tissue. 2 Any evil or corrupt condition or vice. [< L *ulcus, ulceris*] —**ul′cer·ous** *adj.* —**ul′cer·ous·ly** *adv.*

ul·cer·ate (ul′sə·rāt) *v.t. & v.i.* **·at·ed, ·at·ing** To make or become ulcerous. —**ul′cer·a′tion** *n.* —**ul′cer·a′tive** *adj.*

Ukulele

-ule *suffix* Small; little: used to form diminutives: *granule*. [< L *-ulus*]

-ulent *suffix* Abounding in; full of (what is indicated in the main element): *opulent, truculent.* [< L *-ulentus*]

ul·na (ul′nə) *n. pl.* **·nae** (-nē) or **·nas** 1 The larger of the two bones of the forearm on the same side as the little finger. 2 The homologous bone in the foreleg of a quadruped. [< L, elbow] —**ul′nar** *adj.* • See HUMERUS.

ul·ster (ul′stər) *n.* A long, loose overcoat, sometimes belted at the waist, made originally of Irish frieze. [< *Ulster,* Ireland]

ult. ultimate; ultimately.

ul·te·ri·or (ul·tir′ē·ər) *adj.* 1 Not so pertinent as something else: *ulterior* considerations. 2 Intentionally unrevealed; hidden: *ulterior* motives. 3 Later in time, or secondary in importance; following; succeeding. 4 Lying beyond or on the farther side of a certain bounding line. [< L, compar. of *ulter* beyond] —**ul·te′ri·or·ly** *adv.*

ul·ti·ma (ul′tə·mə) *n.* The last syllable of a word. [< L, fem. of *ultimus* last]

ul·ti·mate (ul′tə·mit) *adj.* 1 Beyond which there is no other; maximum, greatest, utmost, etc. 2 Last; final, as of a series. 3 Most distant or remote; farthest. 4 Not susceptible of further analysis; elementary; primary. —*n.* The best, latest, most fundamental, etc., of something. [< L *ultimus* farthest, last, superl. of *ulter* beyond] —**ul′ti·mate·ness** *n.*

ul·ti·mate·ly (ul′tə·mit·lē) *adv.* In the end; at last; finally.

ul·ti·ma Thu·le (ul′tə·mə thōō′lē, tōō′lē) 1 In ancient geography, Thule, the northernmost habitable regions of the earth. 2 Any distant, unknown region. 3 The farthest possible point, degree, or limit.

ul·ti·ma·tum (ul′tə·mā′təm, -mä′-) *n. pl.* **·tums** or **·ta** (-tə) A final statement of terms, demands, or conditions, the rejection of which usu. results in a breaking off of all negotiations, a resorting to force, etc. [< L *ultimus* last, ultimate]

ul·ti·mo (ul′tə·mō) *adv.* In the month preceding the present month. [L]

ul·tra (ul′trə) *adj.* Going beyond the bounds of moderation; extreme. —*n.* One who holds extreme opinions. [< L, beyond, on the other side]

ultra- *prefix* 1 On the other side of; beyond in space: *ultramarine.* 2 Going beyond the limits or range of: *ultrasonic.* 3 Beyond what is usual or natural; extremely or excessively; *ultraconservative.*

ul·tra·high frequency (ul′trə·hī′) Any wave frequency between 300 and 3,000 megahertz.

ul·tra·ist (ul′trə·ist) *n.* One who goes to extremes in opinions, conduct, etc.; extremist. —*adj.* Radical; extreme: also **ul′tra·is′tic.** —**ul′tra·ism** *n.*

ul·tra·ma·rine (ul′trə·mə·rēn′) *n.* 1 A deep purplish blue pigment. 2 The color of ultramarine. —*adj.* Beyond or across the sea. [< L *ultra* beyond + *mare* sea]

ul·tra·mi·cro·scope (ul′trə·mī′krə·skōp′) *n.* A microscope in which objects too small to be seen by the transmitted light of an ordinary microscope are examined against a dark background by means of refracted light.

ul·tra·mi·cro·scop·ic (ul′trə·mī′krə·skop′ik) *adj.* 1 Too minute to be seen by an ordinary microscope. 2 Relating to the ultramicroscope. Also **ul′tra·mi′cro·scop′i·cal.** —**ul′tra·mi·cros′co·py** (-mī′kros′kə·pē) *n.*

ul·tra·mod·ern (ul′trə·mod′ərn) *adj.* Extremely modern, as in tastes, design, etc. —**ul′tra·mod′ern·ist** *n.*

ul·tra·son·ic (ul′trə·son′ik) *adj.* Pertaining to or designating sound waves having a frequency above the limits of audibility.

ul·tra·vi·o·let (ul′trə·vī′ə·lit) *adj.* Having wavelengths shorter than those of visible violet light and longer than those of X-rays.

ul·u·late (ul′yə·lāt′, yōōl′yə·lāt′) *v.i.* **·lat·ed, ·lat·ing** To howl, hoot, or wail. [< L *ululare*] —**ul′u·lant** *adj.* —**ul′u·la′·tion** *n.*

U·lys·ses (yōō·lis′ēz) ODYSSEUS.

um·bel (um′bəl) *n.* A flower cluster having pedicels arising from a single point. [< L *umbella* a parasol, dim. of *umbra* shadow] —**um·bel·late** (um′bə·lit, -lāt), **um′bel·lat′ed** *adj.*

um·ber (um′bər) *n.* 1 A chestnut- to liver-brown iron oxide earth, used as a pigment. 2 The color of umber, either in its natural state (**raw umber**), or heated, so as to produce a reddish brown (**burnt umber**). —*adj.* 1 Of or pertaining to umber. 2 Of the color of umber. —*v.t.* To color with umber. [< F *(terre d′)ombre* < Ital. *ombra* < L *umbra* shade, shadow]

um·bil·i·cal (um·bil′i·kəl) *adj.* 1 Pertaining to or situated near the umbilicus. 2 Placed near the navel; central. —*n.* 1 A long, flexible tube that serves as a connecting device, conduit for air, power, communication, etc., for an astronaut or aquanaut when outside the craft. 2 A similar device used as a source of fuel, etc., for a spacecraft before launching. [< L *umbilicus* navel]

umbilical cord 1 The ropelike structure connecting the navel of a fetus with the placenta. 2 UMBILICAL *(n.)*.

um·bil·i·cus (um′bə·lī′kəs, -bil′i-) *n. pl.* **·ci** (-kī, -sī) 1 NAVEL. 2 A navel-shaped depression. [< L]

um·bra (um′brə) *n. pl.* **·bras** or **·brae** (-brē, -brī) 1 A shadow. 2 The cone of shadow cast at all times by a celestial body in the solar system. When the umbra of the moon strikes the earth, it creates an area of total solar eclipse. 3 The inner dark portion of a sunspot. [L, shadow]

um·brage (um′brij) *n.* 1 A feeling of anger or resentment, esp. in the phrase **take umbrage,** to have such feelings. 2 That which gives shade, as a leafy tree. 3 Shade or shadow. [< L *umbraticus* shady < *umbra* shade] —**um·bra′geous** (-brā′jəs) *adj.* —**um·bra′geous·ly** *adv.*

um·brel·la (um·brel′ə) *n.* 1 A light portable canopy on a folding frame, carried as a protection against sun or rain. 2 A usu. radial formation of military aircraft, used as a protective screen for operations on the ground or on water. 3 Something serving as a cover or shield, or as a means of linking together various things under a common name or sponsor: the expanding *umbrella* of nuclear power. [< L *umbella* parasol, dim. of *umbra* shadow]

umbrella tree A magnolia of the s U.S., with white flowers and umbrellalike whorls of leaves at the ends of the branches.

u·mi·ak (ōō′mē·ak′) *n.* A large, open boat made of skins on a wooden frame. Also **u′mi·ack.** [Eskimo]

Umiak

um·laut (ōōm′lout) *n.* **1** *Ling.* **a** The change in quality of a vowel sound caused by its partial assimilation to a vowel or semivowel (often later lost) in the following syllable. **b** A vowel which has been so altered, as *ä, ö,* and *ü* in German. **2** In German, the two dots (ö) put over a vowel modified by umlaut. —*v.t.* To modify by umlaut. [G, change of sound < *um* about + *laut* sound]

um·pir·age (um′pīr·ij, -pə·rij) *n.* The office, function, or decision of an umpire. Also **um′pire·ship.**

um·pire (um′pīr) *n.* **1** A person called upon to settle a disagreement or dispute. **2** In various games, as baseball, a person chosen to enforce the rules of the game and to settle disputed points. —*v.t. & v.i.* **·pired, ·pir·ing** To act as umpire (of or in). [Alter. of ME *noumpere*]

ump·teen (ump′tēn′) *adj. Slang* Indeterminately large in number; very many. —**ump′teenth′** *adj.*

UMW, U.M.W. United Mine Workers.

un-[1] *prefix* Used in forming adjectives, adverbs, and less often nouns, to indicate: **1** Not; opposed or contrary to: *unable, unmannerly.* **2** Lack of: *unease.* [< OE] • See UN-[2].

un-[2] *prefix* Used in forming verbs to indicate: **1** Reversal of an action: *untie.* **2** Removal from something: *unearth.* **3** Deprivation of a condition or quality: *unman; unnerve.* **4** Intensification: *unloose.* [< OE *un-, on-,* and-] • Beginning at the bottom of this page is a partial list of words formed with **un-**[1] and **un-**[2]. Other words formed with these prefixes, having strongly positive, specific, or special meanings, will be found in vocabulary place.

UN, U.N. United Nations.

un·a·ble (un·ā′bəl) *adj.* **1** Not able; incompetent. **2** Helpless; ineffectual.

un·ac·count·a·ble (un′ə·koun′tə·bəl) *adj.* **1** Impossible to be explained or accounted for; inexplicable. **2** Not responsible. —**un′ac·count′a·ble·ness** *n.* —**un′ac·count′a·bly** *adv.*

un·ac·cus·tomed (un′ə·kus′təmd) *adj.* **1** Not accustomed or familiar: usu. with *to: unaccustomed* to hard-

ship. **2** Not common; strange: an *unaccustomed* sight. —**un′ac·cus′tomed·ness** *n.*

un·ad·vised (un′əd·vīzd′) *adj.* **1** Not having received advice. **2** Rash or imprudent. —**un′ad·vis′ed·ly** (-vī′zid·lē) *adv.* —**un′ad·vis′ed·ness** *n.*

un·af·fect·ed (un′ə·fek′tid) *adj.* **1** Not showing affectation; natural; sincere. **2** Not influenced or changed. —**un′·af·fect′ed·ly** *adv.* —**un′af·fect′ed·ness** *n.*

un·A·mer·i·can (un′ə·mer′ə·kən) *adj.* Not American, esp. not consistent with or opposed to the institutions, ideals, objectives, etc. of the U.S. —**un′-A·mer′i·can·ism** *n.*

u·nan·i·mous (yōō·nan′ə·məs) *adj.* **1** Sharing the same views or sentiments. **2** Showing or resulting from the assent of all concerned: the *unanimous* voice of the jury. [< L *unus* one + *animus* mind] —**u·na·nim·i·ty** (yōō′nə·nim′ə·tē) *n.* —**u·nan′i·mous·ly** *adv.*

un·ap·proach·a·ble (un′ə·prō′chə·bəl) *adj.* **1** Not easy to know or contact; aloof; reserved. **2** Inaccessible. —**un′ap·proach′a·bil′i·ty, un′ap·proach′a·ble·ness** *n.* —**un′ap·proach′·a·bly** *adv.*

un·armed (un·ärmd′) *adj.* Having no firearms, esp. on one's person.

un·as·sail·a·ble (un′ə·sāl′ə·bəl) *adj.* **1** That cannot be disproved or contested successfully. **2** Resistant to attack; impregnable. —**un′as·sail′a·ble·ness, un′as·sail′a·bil′i·ty** *n.* —**un′as·sail′a·bly** *adv.*

un·as·sum·ing (un′ə·sōō′ming) *adj.* Not pretentious; modest. —**un′as·sum′ing·ly** *adv.*

un·at·tached (un′ə·tacht′) *adj.* **1** Not attached. **2** Not connected with any particular group; independent. **3** Not married or engaged. **4** *Law* Not held or seized, as in satisfaction of a judgment.

un·a·vail·ing (un′ə·vā′ling) *adj.* Not effective; futile. —**un′a·vail′ing·ly** *adv.*

un·a·void·a·ble (un′ə·voi′də·bəl) *adj.* That cannot be avoided; inevitable. —**un′a·void′a·ble·ness** *n.* —**un′a·void′a·bly** *adv.*

unabashed	unarguable	unbloody	unchastity	unconfirmed	uncreated
unabated	unarm	unboastful	unchecked	uncongeal	uncredited
unabridged	unarmored	unboned	unchewed	uncongealed	uncritical
unaccented	unashamed	unbought	unchilled	uncongenial	uncross
unacceptable	unashamedly	unbound	unchivalrous	unconnected	uncrowded
unaccommodating	unasked	unbranched	unchlorinated	unconnectedly	uncrown
unaccompanied	unaspirated	unbranded	unchristened	unconquerable	uncrowned
unaccredited	unassailable	unbreakable	unclaimed	unconquerably	uncrystalline
unachievable	unassailably	unbreathable	unclassifiable	unconquered	uncrystallizable
unacknowledged	unassignable	unbridgeable	unclassified	unconscientious	uncrystallized
unacquainted	unassigned	unbridle	uncleaned	unconsecrated	uncultivated
unadorned	unassimilable	unbudging	unclear	unconsenting	uncultured
unadulterated	unassimilated	unburied	unclench	unconsoled	uncurbed
unadvisable	unassisted	unburnt	unclog	unconsolidated	uncurdled
unaesthetic	unathletic	unbusinesslike	unclogged	unconstituted	uncured
unaffiliated	unattainable	uncage	unclouded	unconstrained	uncurl
unafraid	unattained	uncalculating	uncoated	unconsumed	uncurled
unaggressive	unattempted	uncalendered	uncock	uncontaminated	uncurtained
unaided	unattended	uncanceled	uncoerced	uncontested	uncushioned
unaligned	unattested	uncared-for	uncoined	uncontradicted	undamaged
unalike	unattractive	uncaring	uncollectable	uncontrite	undamped
unallied	unauthenticated	uncarpeted	uncollected	uncontrollable	undated
unalloyed	unauthorized	uncastrated	uncollectible	uncontrollably	undecayed
unalluring	unavailable	uncaught	uncolored	uncontrolled	undecaying
unalterable	unavenged	uncaused	uncombed	unconversant	undecipherable
unaltered	unavowed	unceasing	uncomforted	unconverted	undeciphered
unambiguous	unavowedly	unceasingly	uncommercial	unconvinced	undeclared
unambitious	unawakened	uncensored	uncommissioned	unconvincing	undeclinable
unamusing	unawed	uncensured	uncommitted	uncooked	undeclined
unannealed	unbacked	uncertified	uncompetitive	uncooperative	undecomposed
unannounced	unbaked	unchallenged	uncomplaining	uncoordinated	undecorated
unanswerable	unbanked	unchangeable	uncompleted	uncorked	undefaced
unanswerably	unbaptized	unchanged	uncomplicated	uncorrected	undefeated
unanswered	unbeaten	unchanging	uncomplimentary	uncorroborated	undefended
unanticipated	unbelt	unchangingly	uncomprehending	uncorrupt	undefiled
unapparent	unbetrayed	unchaperoned	uncomprehendingly	uncorrupted	undefinable
unappeasable	unbetrothed	uncharged	uncompressed	uncounseled	undefined
unappeased	unbleached	uncharted	uncompromised	uncountable	undeformed
unappetizing	unblemished	unchartered	uncomputed	uncourteous	undelayed
unappreciative	unblest	unchaste	unconcealable	uncourtly	undeliverable
unappropriated	unblinking	unchastened	unconcealed	uncovered	undelivered
unapproved	unblinkingly		unconfined		

un·a·ware (un′ə·wâr′) *adj.* 1 Not aware or cognizant, as of something specified. 2 Carelessly unmindful; inattentive; heedless. —*adv.* UNAWARES.

un·a·wares (un′ə·wârz′) *adv.* 1 Unexpectedly. 2 Without premeditation; unwittingly.

un·bal·ance (un·bal′əns) *v.t.* ·anced, ·anc·ing 1 To deprive of balance. 2 To disturb or derange mentally. —*n.* The state or condition of being unbalanced.

un·bal·anced (un·bal′ənst) *adj.* 1 Not in a state of equilibrium. 2 In bookkeeping, not adjusted so as to balance. 3 Lacking mental balance; unsound; erratic.

un·bar (un·bär′) *v.t.* ·barred, ·bar·ring To remove the bar from.

un·bear·a·ble (un′bâr′ə·bəl) *adj.* Not to be borne; intolerable; insufferable. —**un′bear′a·bly** *adv.*

un·beat·a·ble (un·bēt′ə·bəl) *adj.* 1 Not to be defeated. 2 *Slang* First-rate; excellent.

un·be·com·ing (un′bi·kum′ing) *adj.* 1 Not becoming or appropriate, as a dress. 2 Not fitting or decorous; improper. —**un′be·com′ing·ly** *adv.* —**un′be·com′ing·ness** *n.*

un·be·known (un′bi·nōn′) *adj.* Unknown: used with *to.* Also **un′be·knownst′** (-nōnst′).

un·be·lief (un′bi·lēf′) *n.* 1 Absence of positive belief; incredulity. 2 A refusal to believe; disbelief, as in religion.

un·be·liev·a·ble (un′bə·lēv′ə·bəl) *adj.* Too unusual or astonishing to be believed; incredible. —**un′be·liev′a·bly** *adv.* —**Syn.** inconceivable, untenable, staggering, improbable.

un·be·liev·er (un′bi·lē′vər) *n.* 1 One who does not believe; skeptic; doubter. 2 One who has no religious belief.

un·be·liev·ing (un′bi·lē′ving) *adj.* Doubting; skeptical. —**un′be·liev′ing·ly** *adv.* —**un′be·liev′ing·ness** *n.*

un·bend (un·bend′) *v.* ·bent, ·bend·ing *v.t.* 1 To relax, as from exertion or formality. 2 To straighten (something bent or curved). 3 To relax, as a bow, from tension. 4 *Naut.* To loose or detach, as a rope or sail. —*v.i.* 5 To become free of restraint or formality; relax. 6 To become straight or nearly straight again.

un·bend·ing (un·ben′ding) *adj.* 1 Not bending easily. 2 Resolute; firm. 3 Not relaxed socially; stiff. —**un·bend′ing·ly** *adv.* —**un·bend′ing·ness** *n.*

un·bi·ased (un·bī′əst) *adj.* Having no bias; not prejudiced; impartial. Also **un·bi′assed.** —**un·bi′ased·ly** *adv.* —**un·bi′ased·ness** *n.*

un·bid·den (un·bid′n) *adj.* 1 Not commanded or invited. 2 Spontaneous: *unbidden* thoughts.

un·blush·ing (un·blush′ing) *adj.* Not blushing; immodest; shameless. —**un·blush′ing·ly** *adv.*

un·born (un·bôrn′) *adj.* 1 Not yet born. 2 Of a future time or generation; future. 3 Not in existence.

un·bos·om (un·boõz′əm, -boõ′zəm) *v.t.* 1 To reveal, as one's thoughts or secrets: often used reflexively. —*v.i.* 2 To say what is troubling one; tell one's thoughts, feelings, etc.

un·bound·ed (un·boun′did) *adj.* 1 Having no bounds or limits; boundless. 2 Going beyond bounds; unrestrained. —**un·bound′ed·ly** *adv.* —**un·bound′ed·ness** *n.*

un·bowed (un·boud′) *adj.* 1 Not bent or bowed. 2 Not broken or subdued by defeat or adversity.

un·brace (un·brās′) *v.t.* ·braced, ·brac·ing 1 To free from bands or braces. 2 To free from tension; loosen. 3 To weaken.

un·bri·dled (un·brīd′ld) *adj.* 1 Having no bridle on. 2 Without restraint; unrestrained: an *unbridled* tongue.

un·bro·ken (un·brō′kən) *adj.* 1 Not broken; whole; entire. 2 Not violated: an *unbroken* promise. 3 Uninterrupted; continuous. 4 Not tamed or trained. 5 Not bettered or surpassed. 6 Not disarranged or thrown out of order.

un·bur·den (un·bûr′dən) *v.t.* 1 To free from a burden. 2 To relieve (oneself, one's mind, etc.) from cares, worries, etc. 3 To make known (one's cares, worries, guilt, etc.) in order to gain relief.

un·called-for (un·kôld′fôr′) *adj.* 1 Not needed; unnecessary. 2 Not justified by circumstances; unprovoked.

un·can·ny (un·kan′ē) *adj.* 1 Weird; unnatural; eerie. 2 So

undemocratic	undissected	unendurable	unexported	unforgetful	ungrammatical
undemonstrable	undisseminated	unenforceable	unexposed	unforgetting	ungrammatically
undemonstrative	undissolved	unenforced	unexpressed	unforgivable	ungranted
undenominational	undistilled	unenfranchised	unexpressive	unforgiven	ungratified
undependable	undistinguished	unengaged	unexpurgated	unforgiving	ungrounded
underived	undistracted	unengaging	unextended	unforgotten	ungrudging
underserved	undistributed	un-English	unextinguished	unformed	unguided
undeservedly	undisturbed	unenjoyable	unfaded	unformulated	unhackneyed
undeserving	undiversified	unenlightened	unfading	unforsaken	unhampered
undesignated	undiverted	unenlivened	unfallen	unfortified	unhang
undesigned	undivided	unenriched	unfaltering	unfought	unhanged
undesirable	undivorced	unenrolled	unfashionable	unfound	unharbored
undesirably	undocking	unenslaved	unfashionably	unfractured	unharmed
undesired	undogmatic	unentangled	unfastened	unframed	unharnessed
undesirous	undomesticated	unentered	unfathomable	unfranchised	unharrowed
undetached	undoubting	unenterprising	unfavored	unfree	unharvested
undetected	undramatic	unenthralled	unfeared	unfreedom	unhasty
undetermined	undramatized	unenthusiastic	unfearing	unfrozen	unhatched
undeterred	undrape	unenthusiastically	unfeasible	unfruitful	unhealed
undeveloped	undraped	unenviable	unfed	unfulfilled	unhealthful
undeviating	undreamed	unenvied	unfederated	unfunded	unheated
undifferentiated	undreamt	unenvious	unfelt	unfunny	unheeded
undiffused	undried	unequipped	unfeminine	unfurnished	unheedful
undigested	undrinkable	unerased	unfenced	unfussy	unheeding
undignified	undutiful	unerotic	unfermented	ungallant	unheedingly
undilated	undyed	unestablished	unfertilized	ungarnished	unhelpful
undiluted	uneatable	unethical	unfetter	ungenerous	unheralded
undiminished	uneaten	unexaggerated	unfettered	ungentle	unheroic
undimmed	uneconomic	unexalted	unfilled	ungentlemanly	unhesitating
undiplomatic	uneconomical	unexamined	unfilmed	ungently	unhesitatingly
undirected	unedifying	unexcavated	unfiltered	ungenuine	unhindered
undiscernible	uneducable	unexcelled	unfinished	ungifted	unhired
undiscerning	uneducated	unexchangeable	unfired	ungird	unhistoric
undischarged	unelectrified	unexcited	unfixed	ungirt	unhomogeneous
undisciplined	unembarrassed	unexciting	unflattered	unglazed	unhonored
undisclosed	unembellished	unexcused	unflattering	unglossed	unhousebroken
undiscouraged	unemotional	unexpanded	unflavored	unglove	unhoused
undiscoverable	unemotionally	unexpended	unfocus	ungloved	unhurried
undiscovered	unemphatic	unexpiated	unforbidden	unglue	unhurt
undiscriminating	unencumbered	unexpired	unforced	ungoverned	unhusk
undiscussed	unendangered	unexplainable	unfordable	ungraced	unhygienic
undisguised	unending	unexplained	unforeseeable	ungraceful	unhyphenated
undismayed	unendingly	unexploded	unforetold	ungraded	unhypocritical
undispelled	unendorsed	unexploited	unforfeited	ungrafted	unidentified
undisputed	unendowed	unexplored	unforged	ungrained	unidiomatic

good as to seem almost supernatural in origin: *uncanny* accuracy. —**un·can'ni·ly** *adv.* —**un·can'ni·ness** *n.*

un·cer·e·mo·ni·ous (un'ser·ə·mō'nē·əs) *adj.* 1 Not ceremonious; informal. 2 Abruptly rude or discourteous. —**un'cer·e·mo'ni·ous·ly** *adv.* —**un'cer·e·mo'ni·ous·ness** *n.*

un·cer·tain (un·sûr'tən) *adj.* 1 Not yet determined; indefinite: The date is *uncertain.* 2 Not to be relied upon; unpredictable: *uncertain* weather. 3 Not definitely or exactly known. 4 Not sure or convinced; doubtful; dubious. 5 Not constant; fitful; changeable. 6 Not clear, forceful, steady, etc.: His delivery of the speech was very *uncertain.* —**un·cer'tain·ly** *adv.*

un·cer·tain·ty (un·sûr'tən·tē) *n. pl.* **·ties** 1 The state of being uncertain; doubt. 2 Something uncertain.

un·char·i·ta·ble (un·char'ə·tə·bəl) *adj.* Not forgiving or charitable, as in judgment; censorious. —**un·char'i·ta·ble·ness** *n.* —**un·char'i·ta·bly** *adv.*

un·char·ted (un·chär'tid) *adj.* 1 Not marked or charted on a map. 2 Not explored; unknown.

un·chris·tian (un·kris'chən) *adj.* 1 Not according with Christian principles, attitudes, etc. 2 Not Christian.

un·church (un·chûrch') *v.t.* 1 To deprive of membership in a church; excommunicate. 2 To deny the status of a church to (a sect, etc.).

un·cir·cum·cised (un·sûr'kəm·sīzd) *adj.* 1 Not circumcised. 2 Not Jewish; Gentile.

un·civ·il (un·siv'əl) *adj.* Wanting in civility; discourteous; ill-bred. —**un·civ'il·ly** *adv.*

un·civ·i·lized (un·siv'ə·līzd) *adj.* 1 Not civilized; barbarous. 2 Uncouth; rude; gross. 3 Remote from civilization. —**Syn.** 1 savage, brutish, brutal, ferocious. 2 crude, cross, boorish, churlish, vulgar, coarse.

un·clad (un·klad') *adj.* Without clothes; naked.

un·cle (ung'kəl) *n.* 1 The brother of one's father or mother. 2 The husband of one's aunt. 3 *Informal* An elderly man; used in direct address. 4 *Slang* A pawnbroker. [< L *avunculus* a mother's brother]

un·clean (un·klēn') *adj.* 1 Not clean; foul. 2 Morally impure. 3 Ceremonially impure. —**un·clean'ness** *n.*

un·clean·ly[1] (un·klen'lē) *adj.* 1 Lacking cleanliness. 2 Morally impure. —**un·clean'li·ness** *n.*

un·clean·ly[2] (un·klēn'lē) *adv.* In an unclean manner.

Uncle Sam The personification of the government or the people of the U.S., represented as a tall, lean man with chin whiskers, wearing a plug hat, blue swallow-tailed coat, and red-and-white striped pants.

Uncle Tom *Informal* A Negro who acts in an obsequious or servile manner towards whites: a contemptuous term. —*v.i.* **Uncle Tommed, Uncle Tom·ming** To behave like an Uncle Tom. [< *Uncle Tom,* the faithful Negro slave in H. B. Stowe's *Uncle Tom's Cabin*] —**Uncle Tom'ism** *n.*

un·cloak (un·klōk') *v.t.* 1 To remove the cloak or covering from. 2 To unmask; expose.

un·close (un·klōz') *v.t. & v.i.* **·closed, ·clos·ing** 1 To open or set open. 2 To reveal; disclose.

un·clothe (un·klōth') *v.t.* **·clothed** or **·clad, ·cloth·ing** 1 To remove the clothes from; undress. 2 To divest; uncover.

un·com·fort·a·ble (un·kum'fər·tə·bəl, -kumf'tə·bəl) *adj.* 1 Not at ease; feeling discomfort. 2 Causing uneasiness; disquieting. —**un·com'fort·a·ble·ness** *n.* —**un·com'fort·a·bly** *adv.*

un·com·mon (un·kom'ən) *adj.* 1 Not usual or common. 2 Strange; remarkable. —**un·com'mon·ly** *adv.* —**un·com'mon·ness** *n.*

un·com·mu·ni·ca·tive (un'kə·myōō'nə·kə·tiv, -kāt'iv) *adj.* Not communicative; not disposed to talk, to give information, etc.; reserved; taciturn. —**un'com·mu'ni·ca·tive·ly** *adv.* —**un'com·mu'ni·ca·tive·ness** *n.*

un·com·pro·mis·ing (un·kom'prə·mī'zing) *adj.* Making or admitting of no compromise; inflexible; strict. —**un·com'pro·mis'ing·ly** *adv.* —**Syn.** resolute, steadfast, firm, indomitable, inexorable, tenacious, obstinate.

un·con·cern (un'kən·sûrn') *n.* 1 Lack of anxiety, concern, or worry. 2 Lack of interest; indifference.

---

unilluminated	unintentional	unlisted	unmold	unorthodox	unplanted
unillumined	unintentionally	unlit	unmolested	unostentatious	unplayed
unillustrated	uninteresting	unliteral	unmollified	unostentatiously	unpleasing
unimaginable	uninterpreted	unliveliness	unmortgaged	unowned	unpledged
unimaginably	uninterrupted	unlively	unmotivated	unoxidized	unplowed
unimaginative	unintimidated	unlocked	unmounted	unpacified	unplucked
unimagined	unintoxicated	unlovable	unmourned	unpaginated	unplugged
unimbued	uninvited	unloved	unmoved	unpaid	unpoetic
unimitated	uninviting	unlovely	unmown	unpaired	unpoetical
unimmunized	uninvoked	unloving	unmuffle	unpalatable	unpointed
unimpaired	uninvolved	unlubricated	unmusical	unpardonable	unpolarized
unimpeded	unissued	unmagnified	unmuzzle	unpardonably	unpolished
unimportance	unitemized	unmanageable	unmuzzled	unparliamentary	unpolitical
unimportant	unjaded	unmanful	unnamable	unparted	unpolluted
unimposing	unjoined	unmanicured	unnameable	unpartisan	unpopulated
unimpressed	unjointed	unmannerly	unnamed	unpasteurized	unposted
unimpressionable	unjustifiable	unmarked	unnaturalized	unpatched	unpractical
unimpressive	unjustifiably	unmarketable	unnavigable	unpatented	unpredictable
unincorporated	unkennel	unmarred	unnavigated	unpatriotic	unpredictably
unindemnified	unkept	unmarriageable	unneeded	unpaved	unprejudiced
unindustrialized	unkindled	unmarried	unneighborly	unpeaceable	unpremeditated
uninfected	unkissed	unmasculine	unnoted	unpeaceful	unprepared
uninfested	unknowable	unmastered	unnoticed	unpedigreed	unprepossessing
uninflammable	unknowing	unmatched	unobjectionable	unpensioned	unpressed
uninflected	unlabeled	unmated	unobliging	unpeopled	unpretentious
uninfluenced	unlabored	unmatted	unobservant	unperceived	unpretentiously
uninformed	unladylike	unmeant	unobserved	unperfected	unpretentiousness
uninhabitable	unlamented	unmechanical	unobserving	unperforated	unpriced
uninhabited	unlash	unmedicated	unobstructed	unperformed	unprimed
uninhibited	unlasting	unmemorable	unobtainable	unpersuaded	unprinted
uninitiated	unlaundered	unmercenary	unobtrusive	unpersuasive	unprivileged
uninjured	unleaded	unmerited	unobtrusively	unperturbed	unprocessed
uninspired	unleased	unmethodical	unobtrusiveness	unphilosophical	unproductive
uninspiring	unlevel	unmilitary	unoffending	unphonetic	unprofitable
uninstructed	unlevied	unmilled	unoffered	unphotogenic	unprofitably
uninsurable	unlicensed	unmindful	unoiled	unphysical	unprogramed
uninsured	unlifelike	unmistaken	unopen	unpicturesque	unpromising
unintellectual	unlighted	unmixed	unopened	unpile	unpronounceable
unintelligent	unlikable	unmodified	unopposed	unpitying	unpropitious
unintelligible	unlikeable	unmodish	unoppressed	unplaced	unprosperous
unintelligibly	unlined	unmodulated	unordained	unplait	unprotected
unintended	unlink	unmoistened	unoriginal	unplanned	unproved

---

add, āce, câre, pălm; end, ēven; it, īce; odd, ōpen, ôrder; tōōk, pōōl; up, bûrn; ə = a in *above*, u in *focus*; yōō = u in *fuse*; oil; pout; check; go; ring; thin; this; zh, *vision.* < derived from; ? origin uncertain or unknown.

un·con·cerned (un'kən·sûrnd') *adj.* **1** Not anxious or worried. **2** Not interested; indifferent. —**un'con·cern'ed·ly** (-sûr'nid·lē) *adj.* —**un'con·cern'ed·ness** *n.*

un·con·di·tion·al (un'kən·dish'ən·əl) *adj.* Limited by no conditions; absolute. —**un'con·di'tion·al·ly** *adv.*

un·con·di·tioned (un'kən·dish'ənd) *adj.* **1** Not restricted; unconditional. **2** *Psychol.* Not acquired; natural.

un·con·scion·a·ble (un·kon'shən·ə·bəl) *adj.* **1** Unbelievably bad, wrong, inequitable, etc.: an *unconscionable* error. **2** Wholly unscrupulous. —**un·con'scion·a·ble·ness** *n.* —**un·con'scion·a·bly** *adv.*

un·con·scious (un·kon'shəs) *adj.* **1** Temporarily deprived of consciousness. **2** Not cognizant; unaware: with *of: unconscious* of his charm. **3** Not produced or accompanied by conscious effort; not intended or known: an *unconscious* pun. **4** Not endowed with consciousness or a mind. **5** Of or having to do with the unconscious. —*n.* That area of the psyche which is not in the immediate field of awareness and whose content may become manifest through dreams, morbid fears and compulsions, etc.: with *the.* —**un·con'scious·ly** *adv.* —**un·con'scious·ness** *n.*

un·con·sti·tu·tion·al (un'kon·sti·t$\overline{oo}$'shən·əl) *adj.* Contrary to or violating the precepts of a constitution. —**un'·con·sti·tu'tion·al'i·ty** *n.* —**un'con·sti·tu'tion·al·ly** *adv.*

un·con·ven·tion·al (un'kən·ven'shən·əl) *adj.* Not adhering to conventional rules, practices, etc.; informal; free. —**un'con·ven'tion·al·i·ty** *n.* —**un'con·ven'tion·al·ly** *adv.*

un·count·ed (un·koun'tid) *adj.* **1** Not counted. **2** Beyond counting; innumerable.

un·cou·ple (un·kup'əl) *v.t.* **·led**, **·ling** **1** To disconnect or unfasten. **2** To set loose; unleash (dogs). —**un·coup'led** (-kup'əld) *adj.*

un·couth (un·k$\overline{oo}$th') *adj.* **1** Marked by awkwardness or oddity; outlandish. **2** Coarse, boorish, or unrefined, as in manner or speech. [< OE *uncūth* unknown] —**un·couth'ly** *adv.* —**un·couth'ness** *n.*

un·cov·er (un·kuv'ər) *v.t.* **1** To remove a covering from.

2 To make known; disclose. —*v.i.* **3** To remove a covering. **4** To raise or remove the hat, as in token of respect.

unc·tion (ungk'shən) *n.* **1** The act of anointing, as for religious or medicinal purposes. **2** A substance used in anointing, as oil. **3** Anything that soothes or palliates. **4** A quality of speech, esp. in religious discourse, that awakens or is intended to awaken deep sympathetic feeling. **5** Excessive or affected sincerity or sympathy in speech or manner. [< L *unctio* < *ungere* anoint]

unc·tu·ous (ungk'ch$\overline{oo}$·əs) *adj.* **1** Like an unguent; greasy. **2** Greasy or soapy to the touch, as certain minerals. **3** Characterized by excessive or affected sincerity, sympathy, concern, etc. **4** Unduly smooth or suave in speech or manner. **5** Having plasticity, as clay. [< L *unctum* ointment, orig. neut. p.p. of *ungere* anoint] —**unc'tu·ous·ly** *adv.* —**unc'tu·ous·ness, unc'tu·os'i·ty** (-ch$\overline{oo}$·os'ə·tē) *n.*

un·cut (un·kut') *adj.* **1** Not cut. **2** In bookbinding, having untrimmed margins. **3** Not ground, as a gem. **4** Not shortened or abridged.

un·daunt·ed (un·dôn'tid, -dän'-) *adj.* Not daunted; fearless; intrepid. —**un·daunt'ed·ly** *adv.* —**un·daunt'ed·ness** *n.*

un·de·cid·ed (un'di·sī'did) *adj.* **1** Not having the mind made up; irresolute. **2** Not decided upon or determined. —**un'de·cid'ed·ly** *adv.*

un·de·ni·a·ble (un'di·nī'ə·bəl) *adj.* **1** That cannot be denied; indisputably true. **2** Unquestionably good; excellent: His reputation was *undeniable*. —**un'de·ni'a·bly** *adv.*

un·der (un'dər) *prep.* **1** Beneath; covered by: dust *under* the rug. **2** In a place lower than; at the foot or bottom of: *under* the hill. **3** Beneath the shelter of: *under* the paternal roof. **4** Beneath the concealment, guise, or assumption of: *under* a false name. **5** Less than in number, degree, age, value, or amount: *under* 10 tons. **6** Inferior to in quality, character, or rank. **7** Beneath the domination of; subordinate or subservient to: *under* the British flag. **8** Subject to the guidance, tutorship, or direction of: He studied *under* Mendelssohn. **9** Subject to the moral obligation of: a state-

unproven	unrelieved	unrevealed	unscholarly	unsinkable	unstitched
unprovided	unremarkable	unrevenged	unschooled	unsized	unstopped
unprovoked	unremarked	unrevised	unscientific	unskeptical	unstopper
unpruned	unremedied	unrevoked	unscratched	unslaked	unstrap
unpublishable	unremembered	unrewarded	unscreened	unsling	unstratified
unpublished	unremitted	unrhymed	unsealed	unsmiling	unstressed
unpunctual	unremorseful	unrhythmic	unseamed	unsmilingly	unstriated
unpunished	unremunerated	unrhythmical	unseasoned	unsmoked	unstriped
unpurified	unremunerative	unrighted	unseaworthy	unsnobbish	unstructured
unpuritanical	unrenewed	unripened	unseconded	unsocial	unstuck
unqualifying	unrented	unrisen	unsecret	unsoiled	unstudied
unquenchable	unrepaid	unroasted	unsecretive	unsold	unstuffed
unquestioning	unrepairable	unromantic	unsectarian	unsoldierly	unsubsidized
unrated	unrepaired	unromantically	unsecured	unsolicited	unsubstantiated
unratified	unrepealed	unroof	unseeing	unsolicitous	unsubtle
unreachable	unrepeatable	unruled	unseen	unsoluble	unsuccessful
unreadable	unrepentant	unsafe	unsegmented	unsolvable	unsuccessfully
unrealizable	unrepented	unsafely	unselected	unsolved	unsuited
unrealized	unrepenting	unsafeness	unselective	unsorted	unsullied
unrebuked	unreplaced	unsaintly	unself-conscious	unsought	unsupportable
unreceipted	unreplenished	unsalability	unselfish	unsown	unsupported
unreceivable	unreported	unsalable	unselfishly	unspecialized	unsuppressed
unreceived	unrepresentative	unsalaried	unselfishness	unspecified	unsure
unreceptive	unrepresented	unsaleability	unsent	unspectacular	unsurmountable
unreciprocated	unrepressed	unsaleable	unsentimental	unspent	unsurpassed
unreclaimed	unrequested	unsalted	unserviceable	unspilled	unsurprising
unrecognizable	unrequited	unsalvageable	unset	unspiritual	unsurveyed
unrecognized	unresented	unsanctified	unsew	unspoiled	unsurvivable
unreconciled	unreserve	unsanctioned	unsewn	unspoken	unsusceptible
unrecorded	unresigned	unsanitary	unsexual	unsponsored	unsuspected
unrecounted	unresistant	unsated	unshaded	unsportsmanlike	unsuspecting
unredeemed	unresisting	unsatiated	unshakable	unstack	unsuspicious
unrefined	unresistingly	unsatiating	unshaken	unstained	unswathe
unreflecting	unresolved	unsatisfactorily	unshaven	unstamped	unswear
unreflective	unrespectful	unsatisfactory	unsheathed	unstandardized	unsweetened
unreformable	unresponsive	unsatisfied	unsheltered	unstarched	unswept
unreformed	unresting	unsatisfying	unshod	unstarred	unsworn
unrefreshed	unrestless	unsaved	unshorn	unstartling	unsymmetrical
unregistered	unrestrained	unsayable	unshrinkable	unstatesmanlike	unsympathetic
unregretted	unrestrainedly	unscaled	unshriven	unstemmed	unsympathetically
unregulated	unrestraint	unscanned	unshrouded	unstereotyped	unsystematic
unrehearsed	unrestricted	unscarred	unshut	unsterile	untack
unrelated	unretentive	unscenic	unsifted	unsterilized	untactful
unrelaxed	unretracted	unscented	unsighted	unstick	untactfully
unrelievable	unreturned	unscheduled	unsigned	unstimulating	untainted

ment *under* oath. **10** With the liability or certainty of incurring: *under* penalty of the law. **11** Subject to the influence or pressure of: *under* the circumstances. **12** Swayed or impelled by: *under* fear of death. **13** Driven or propelled by: *under* sail. **14** Included in the group or class of; found in the matter titled or headed: See *under* History. **15** Being the subject of: the matter *under* discussion. **16** During the period of; in the reign of. **17** By virtue of; authorized, substantiated, attested, or warranted by: *under* his own signature. **18** In conformity to or in accordance with; having regard to. **19** Planted or sowed with: an acre *under* wheat. —*adv.* **1** In or into a position below something; underneath. **2** In or into an inferior or subordinate condition, rank, etc. **3** So as to be covered or hidden. **4** Less in amount, value, time, etc.: We did it in ten minutes or *under*. —*adj.* **1** Situated or moving under something else; lower or lowermost: an *under* layer. **2** Subordinate; lower in rank or authority. **3** Less than usual, standard, or prescribed. **4** Held in subjection or restraint: used predicatively. [< OE]

under- *combining form* **1** Below in position; situated or directed beneath; on the underside: *undercarriage.* **2** Below or beneath another surface or covering: *undergarment.* **3** Inferior in rank or importance; subordinate: *undergraduate.* **4** Less than is usual or proper; not enough; insufficient(ly): *underdeveloped.* **5** At a lower rate; less in degree or amount: *underpay.*

un·der·a·chieve (un′dər·ə·chēv′) *v.i.* **·chieved, ·chiev·ing** To fail to achieve the approximate level of performance, esp. in school studies, commensurate with one's abilities as indicated by testing. —**un′der·a·chieve′ment, un′der·a·chiev′er** *n.*

un·der·act (un′dər·akt′) *v.t. & v.i.* To perform (a role, scene, etc.) in a somewhat less dramatic or emphatic way than might naturally be expected.

un·der·age (un′dər·āj′) *adj.* Not of a requisite or legal age.

untaken	untranslated	unwarlike
untalented	untrapped	unwarmed
untamable	untraveled	unwarned
untame	untraversed	unwarranted
untameable	untread	unwashed
untamed	untreatable	unwasted
untangled	untreated	unwatched
untaped	untried	unwavering
untapped	untrim	unwaveringly
untarnished	untrodden	unweakened
untasted	untroubled	unweaned
untaxable	untrustworthy	unwearable
untaxed	untuck	unweary
unteachable	untufted	unwearying
untechnical	untuned	unweathered
untempered	untuneful	unweave
untenable	unturned	unwed
untenanted	untwilled	unwedded
untended	untwisted	unweeded
untenured	untypical	unwelcome
untested	unusable	unwelded
untether	unutilized	unwhetted
unthatched	unuttered	unwhipped
untheatrical	unvaccinated	unwilled
unthinkable	unvalued	unwished
unthoughtful	unvanquished	unwithered
unthreshed	unvaried	unwitnessed
unthrifty	unvarying	unwomanly
unthrone	unvaryingly	unwooded
untilled	unveiled	unwooed
untinged	unventilated	unworkable
untired	unverifiable	unworked
untiring	unverified	unworkmanlike
untiringly	unversed	unworldly
untitled	unvitrified	unworn
untouched	unvocal	unworshiped
untracked	unvoiced	unwounded
untrained	unvolatilized	unwoven
untrammeled	unvulcanized	unwrinkled
untransferable	unwakened	unwrought
untransferred	unwalled	unyielding
untranslatable	unwanted	unzealous

un·der·arm (un′dər·ärm′) *adj.* **1** Situated, placed, or used under the arm. **2** UNDERHAND (def. 2). —*n.* ARMPIT.

un·der·bid (un′dər·bid′) *v.t.* **·bid, ·bid·ding 1** To bid lower than, as in a competition. **2** In bridge, to fail to bid the full value of (a hand). —**un′der·bid′der** *n.*

un·der·brush (un′dər·brush′) *n.* Small trees and shrubs growing beneath forest trees; undergrowth. Also **un′der·bush′** (-boosh′).

un·der·buy (un′dər·bī′) *v.t.* **·bought, ·buy·ing 1** To buy at a price lower than that paid by (another). **2** To pay less than the value for. **3** To buy less of (something) than is required.

un·der·car·riage (un′dər·kar′ij) *n.* **1** The framework supporting the body of a structure, as an automobile. **2** The principal landing gear of an aircraft.

Undercarriage *def. 2*

un·der·charge (un′dər·chärj′) *v.t.* **·charged, ·charg·ing 1** To make an inadequate charge for. **2** To load with an insufficient charge, as a gun. —*n.* (un′dər·chärj′) An inadequate or insufficient charge.

un·der·class·man (un′dər·klas′mən, -kläs′-) *n. pl.* **·men** (-mən) A freshman or sophomore.

un·der·clothes (un′dər·klōz′, -klōthz′) *n.pl.* UNDERWEAR. Also **un′der·cloth′ing.**

un·der·coat (un′dər·kōt′) *n.* **1** A coat worn under another. **2** A layer of paint, varnish, etc., beneath another layer; also, a protective coating applied to the undersurface of a vehicle: also **un′der·coat′ing.** —*v.t.* To provide with an undercoat (def. 2).

un·der·cov·er (un′dər·kuv′ər) *adj.* Secret; surreptitious; esp., engaged in spying.

un·der·cur·rent (un′dər·kûr′ənt) *n.* **1** A current, as of water or air, below another or below the surface. **2** A hidden drift or tendency, as of popular sentiments.

un·der·cut (un′dər·kut′) *n.* **1** The act or result of cutting away a part, section, etc., from the lower or under surface of something. **2** *Brit.* TENDERLOIN. **3** A notch cut in the side of a tree so that it will fall toward that side when sawed through. **4** In sports, a cut or backspin imparted to the ball by an underhand stroke. —*v.t.* (un′dər·kut′) **·cut, ·cut·ting 1** To cut away the underpart of. **2** To cut away a lower portion of so as to leave a part overhanging. **3** To work or sell for lower payment than (a rival). **4** In sports, to hit (a ball) with an oblique downward or underhand stroke so as to give the ball a backspin. **5** To lessen or destroy the effectiveness or impact of; undermine. —*adj.* **1** Having the parts in relief cut under. **2** Done by undercutting.

un·der·de·vel·oped (un′dər·di·vel′əpt) *adj.* **1** Not sufficiently developed. **2** Below a normal or adequate standard in the development of industry, resources, agriculture, etc.: an *underdeveloped* country.

un·der·dog (un′dər·dôg′, -dog′) *n.* **1** The one that is losing, has lost, or is at a disadvantage in a contest. **2** The weaker, subservient, or exploited person.

un·der·done (un′dər·dun′) *adj.* Not cooked to the fullest degree.

un·der·em·ployed (un′dər·əm·ploid′) *adj.* Employed only part of the time or for too few hours to assure an adequate income. —**un′der·em·ploy′ment** *n.*

un·der·es·ti·mate (un′dər·es′tə·māt′) *v.t.* **·mat·ed, ·mat·ing** To put too low an estimate or valuation upon (things or people). —*n.* (-mit) An estimate below the just value, expense, opinion, etc. —**un′der·es′ti·ma′tion** *n.*

un·der·ex·pose (un′dər·ik·spōz′) *v.t.* **·posed, ·pos·ing** *Phot.* To expose (a film) to less light than is required for a clear image. —**un′der·ex·po′sure** (-spō′zhər) *n.*

un·der·feed (un′dər·fēd′) *v.t.* **·fed, ·feed·ing** To feed insufficiently.

un·der·foot (un′dər·foot′) *adv.* **1** Beneath the feet; down on the ground. **2** In the way.

un·der·gar·ment (un′dər·gär′mənt) *n.* A garment to be worn beneath outer garments.

un·der·go (un′dər·gō′) *v.t.* **·went, ·gone, ·go·ing 1** To be

subjected to; have experience of; suffer. **2** To bear up under; endure.

un·der·grad·u·ate (un′dər-graj′ōō-it) *n.* A student of a university or college who has not taken the bachelor's degree. —*adj.* Of, being, or for an undergraduate.

un·der·ground (un′dər-ground′) *adj.* **1** Situated, done, or operated beneath the surface of the ground. **2** Done in secret; clandestine. **3** Of, relating to, or characterized by the underground (defs. 3 and 4), their works, actions, etc. —*n.* **1** That which is beneath the surface of the ground, as a passage or space. **2** *Brit.* SUBWAY. **3** A group secretly organized to resist or oppose those in control of a government or country: usu. with *the.* **4** An avant-garde movement in art, cinema, journalism, etc., generally considered to be in opposition to conventional culture or society and whose works are usu. experimental, erotic, or radical in style, content, or purpose: usu. with *the.* —*adv.* (un′dər-ground′) **1** Beneath the surface of the ground. **2** In or into hiding, secrecy, etc.

Underground Railroad A system of cooperation among antislavery people, before 1861, for assisting fugitive slaves to escape to Canada and the free states.

un·der·growth (un′dər-grōth′) *n.* UNDERBRUSH.

un·der·hand (un′dər-hand′) *adj.* **1** Done or acting in a sly or treacherously secret manner. **2** In certain sports, done or delivered with the hand and forearm lower than the elbow or shoulder. —*adv.* **1** In a secret, sly manner. **2** With an underhand motion.

un·der·hand·ed (un′dər-han′did) *adj. & adv.* UNDERHAND. —*un′der·hand′ed·ly adv.* —*un′der·hand′ed·ness n.*

un·der·lay (un′dər-lā′) *v.t.* **·laid**, **·lay·ing** **1** To place (one thing) under another. **2** To furnish with a base or lining. **3** To support or elevate with something placed beneath. —*n.* (un′dər-lā′) Something laid beneath something else, esp., in printing, a piece of paper, etc., placed under type, etc., in order to raise it.

un·der·lie (un′dər-lī′) *v.t.* **·lay**, **·lain**, **·ly·ing** **1** To lie below or under. **2** To be the basis or reason for: What motives *underlie* his refusal to go? **3** To constitute a first or prior claim or lien over.

un·der·line (un′dər-līn′) *v.t.* **·lined**, **·lin·ing** **1** To mark with a line underneath; underscore. **2** To emphasize. —*n.* A line underneath a word or passage, as for emphasis.

un·der·ling (un′dər-ling) *n.* A subordinate; inferior.

un·der·ly·ing (un′dər-lī′ing) *adj.* **1** Lying under: *underlying* strata. **2** Basic; fundamental: *underlying* principles. **3** Not obvious, but implicit: *underlying* reasons.

un·der·mine (un′dər-mīn′, un′dər-mīn′) *v.t.* **·mined**, **·min·ing** **1** To excavate beneath; dig a mine or passage under. **2** To weaken by wearing away at the base. **3** To weaken or impair secretly, insidiously, or by degrees.

un·der·most (un′dər-mōst′) *adj.* Having the lowest place or position.

un·der·neath (un′dər-nēth′) *adv.* **1** In a place below. **2** On the under or lower side. —*prep.* **1** Beneath; under; below. **2** Under the form or appearance of. **3** Under the authority of; in the control of. —*adj.* Lower. —*n.* The lower or under part or side. [< OE *underneothan*]

un·der·nour·ish (un′dər-nûr′ish) *v.t.* To provide with insufficient nourishment. —*un′der·nour′ished adj.* —*un′der·nour′ish·ment n.*

un·der·pass (un′dər-pas′, -päs′) *n.* A road, passageway, etc., that runs beneath something, esp. a road that passes under railway tracks or under another road.

un·der·pay (un′dər-pā′) *v.t.* **·paid**, **·pay·ing** To pay insufficiently.

un·der·pin·ning (un′dər-pin′ing) *n.* **1** Material or framework used to support a wall or building from below. **2** *Often pl.* Something used or functioning as a basis or foundation: the *underpinnings* of guilt in our society.

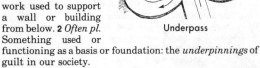

Underpass

un·der·play (un′dər-plā′) *v.t. & v.i.* **1** UNDERACT. **2** To behave, react to, etc., in a deliberately restrained manner.

un·der·priv·i·leged (un′dər-priv′ə-lijd) *adj.* **1** Deprived socially and economically of enjoying certain fundamental rights theoretically possessed by all members of a community or nation. **2** Of or pertaining to people who are underprivileged.

un·der·rate (un′dər-rāt′) *v.t.* **·rat·ed**, **·rat·ing** To rate too low; underestimate.

un·der·score (un′dər-skôr′, -skōr′) *v.t.* **·scored**, **·scor·ing** To draw a line below, as for emphasis; underline. —*n.* (un′dər-skôr′, -skōr′) A line drawn beneath a word, etc., as for emphasis.

un·der·sea (un′dər-sē′) *adj.* Being, carried on, or designed for use beneath the surface of the sea. —*adv.* (un′dər-sē′) Beneath the surface of the sea: also **un·der·seas** (un′dər-sēz′).

under secretary The assistant secretary of a principal secretary in government.

un·der·sell (un′dər-sel′) *v.t.* **·sold**, **·sell·ing** **1** To sell at a lower price than. **2** To present or promote, as a point of view or commodity, in an understated manner.

un·der·shirt (un′dər-shûrt′) *n.* A collarless undergarment, usu. without sleeves, worn beneath a shirt.

un·der·shoot (un′dər-shōōt′) *v.* **·shot**, **·shoot·ing** *v.t.* **1** To shoot short of or below (a target). **2** To land an airplane short of (the runway). —*v.i.* **3** To shoot or land short of the mark.

un·der·shot (un′dər-shot′) *adj.* **1** Propelled by water that flows underneath, as a water wheel. **2** Having a projecting lower jaw or teeth.

un·der·side (un′dər-sīd′) *n.* The lower or under side or surface.

un·der·signed (un′dər-sīnd′) *n.* The person or persons who have signed their names at the end of a document, letter, etc.

un·der·sized (un′dər-sīzd′) *adj.* Of less than the normal, legal, or average size.

Undershot water wheel

un·der·slung (un′dər-slung′) *adj.* Having the springs fixed to the axles from below, as certain automobiles.

un·der·stand (un′dər-stand′) *v.* **·stood**, **·stand·ing** *v.t.* **1** To come to know the meaning or import of. **2** To perceive the nature or character of: I do not *understand* her. **3** To have comprehension or mastery of: Do you *understand* German? **4** To be aware of; realize: She *understands* her position. **5** To have been told; believe: I *understand* that she went home. **6** To take or interpret: How am I to *understand* that remark? **7** To accept as a condition or stipulation: It is *understood* that the tenant will provide his own heat. —*v.i.* **8** To have understanding; comprehend. **9** To grasp the meaning, significance, etc., of something. **10** To believe or assume something to be the case. **11** To have a sympathetic attitude or tolerance toward something. [< OE *under-* under + *standan* stand] —*un′der·stand′a·ble adj.* —*un′der·stand′a·bly adv.*

un·der·stand·ing (un′dər-stan′ding) *n.* **1** An intellectual grasp of something; comprehension. **2** The power or capacity to think, acquire and retain knowledge, interpret experience, etc.; intelligence. **3** An agreement or settlement of differences. **4** An informal or confidential compact or agreement. **5** An individual viewpoint, interpretation, or opinion. **6** A sympathetic comprehension of or tolerance for the feelings, actions, attitudes, etc., of others. —*adj.* Possessing or characterized by comprehension, compassion, etc. —*un′der·stand′ing·ly adv.*

un·der·state (un′dər-stāt′) *v.t.* **·stat·ed**, **·stat·ing** **1** To state with less force than the actual truth warrants. **2** To state or describe in a deliberately restrained manner in order to achieve greater force or effectiveness. —*un′der·state′ment n.*

un·der·stat·ed (un′dər-stāt′əd) *adj.* Stated, executed, designed, etc., in an unemphatic, restrained, or simple manner.

un·der·stood (un′dər-stōōd′) *p.t. & p.p.* of UNDERSTAND. —*adj.* **1** Grasped mentally; comprehended. **2** Taken for granted. **3** Agreed upon by all.

un·der·stud·y (un'dər·stud'ē) v.t. & v.i. **·stud·ied, ·stud·y·ing 1** To study (a part) in order to be able, if necessary, to substitute for the actor playing it. **2** To act as an understudy to (another actor). —n. pl. **·stud·ies 1** An actor or actress who can substitute for another actor in a given role. **2** A person prepared to perform the work or fill the position of another.

un·der·take (un'dər·tāk') v.t. **took, tak·en, tak·ing 1** To take upon oneself; agree or attempt to do. **2** To contract to do; pledge oneself to. **3** To guarantee or promise. **4** To take under charge or guidance.

un·der·tak·er (un'dər·tā'kər for def. 1; un'dər·tā'kər for def. 2) n. **1** One who undertakes any work or enterprise; esp. a contractor. **2** One whose business it is to prepare a dead person for burial and to conduct funerals.

un·der·tak·ing (un'dər·tā'king, esp. for def. 3; un'dər·tā'king) n. **1** The act of one who undertakes any task or enterprise. **2** The thing undertaken; an enterprise; task. **3** The business of an undertaker (def. 2). **4** An engagement, promise, or guarantee.

un·der·tone (un'dər·tōn') n. **1** A low or subdued tone, esp. a vocal tone, as a whisper. **2** A subdued color, esp. one with other colors imposed on it. **3** A meaning, suggestion, quality, etc., that is implied but not expressed.

un·der·tow (un'dər·tō') n. A flow of water beneath and in a direction opposite to the surface current, esp. such a flow moving seaward beneath surf.

un·der·val·ue (un'dər·val'yōō) v.t. **·ued, ·u·ing 1** To value or rate below the real worth. **2** To regard or esteem as of little worth. —un'der·val'u·a'tion n.

un·der·wa·ter (un'dər·wô'tər, -wot'ər) adj. **1** Being, occurring, used, etc., below the surface of a body of water: underwater research. **2** Below the water line of a ship. —adv. Below the surface of water.

under way 1 In progress: The meeting was already under way. **2** Into operation or motion: to get the fund drive under way.

un·der·wear (un'dər·wâr') n. Garments worn underneath the ordinary outer garments.

un·der·weight (un'dər·wāt') adj. Having less than the normal, desired, or permitted weight. —n. Weight less than normal, permitted, or desired.

un·der·went (un'dər·went') p.t. of UNDERGO.

un·der·wood (un'dər·wŏŏd') n. UNDERBRUSH.

un·der·world (un'dər·wûrld') n. **1** The mythical abode of the dead; Hades. **2** The world of organized crime and vice.

un·der·write (un'dər·rīt') v. **·wrote, ·writ·ten, ·writ·ing** v.t. **1** To write beneath or sign something, as a document. **2** To agree or subscribe to, esp. to agree to pay for (an enterprise, etc.). **3** In insurance: **a** To sign one's name to (an insurance policy), thereby assuming liability for certain designated losses or damage. **b** To insure. **c** To assume (a risk or a liability for a certain sum) by way of insurance. **4** To engage to buy, at a determined price and time, all or part of the stock in (a new enterprise or company) that is not subscribed for by the public. —v.i. **5** To act as an underwriter; esp., to issue a policy of insurance.

un·der·writ·er (un'dər·rī'tər) n. **1** A person or company in the insurance business; also, an insurance employee who determines the risks involved, the amount of the premiums, etc., for a specific applicant or policy. **2** One who underwrites something.

un·de·sir·a·ble (un'di·zīr'ə·bəl) adj. Not desirable; objectionable. —n. An undesirable person. —un'de·sir'a·bil'i·ty n. —un'de·sir'a·bly adv.

un·do (un·dōō') v.t. **·did, ·done, ·do·ing 1** To cause to be as if never done; reverse, annul, or cancel. **2** To loosen or untie. **3** To unfasten and open. **4** To bring to ruin; destroy. **5** To disturb emotionally. [< OE undōn] —un·do'er n.

un·do·ing (un·dōō'ing) n. **1** A reversal of what has been done. **2** Destruction; ruin; disgrace; also, the cause of such ruin or disgrace. **3** The action of unfastening, loosening, opening, etc.

un·done[1] (un·dun') adj. **1** Untied; unfastened. **2** Ruined; disgraced. **3** Extremely disturbed or upset. [Orig. p.p. of UNDO]

un·done[2] (un·dun') adj. Not done.

un·doubt·ed (un·dou'tid) adj. **1** Not doubted; assured; certain. **2** Not viewed with distrust; unsuspected. —un·doubt'ed·ly adv.

un·draw (un·drô') v.t. & v.i. **·drew, ·drawn, ·draw·ing** To draw open, away, or aside.

un·dreamed-of (un·drēmd'uv', -dremt'-) adj. Never imagined; wholly unforeseen: undreamed-of joy. Also **un·dreamt'-of** (-dremt'-).

un·dress (un·dres') v.t. **1** To divest of clothes; strip. **2** To remove the dressing or bandages from, as a wound. **3** To divest of special attire; disrobe. —v.i. **4** To remove one's clothing. —n. **1** The state of being nude or in only partial attire, as in undergarments, dressing robe, etc. **2** The military or naval uniform worn by officers when not in full dress.

un·due (un·dyōō') adj. **1** Excessive; immoderate. **2** Not justified by law; illegal. **3** Not yet due, as a bill. **4** Not appropriate; improper.

un·du·lant (un'dyə·lənt, -jə-) adj. Undulating; fluctuating.

undulant fever A persistent bacterial disease usu. transmitted to man by contact with infected cattle and characterized by recurrent fever, exhaustion, neuralgic pains, etc.

un·du·late (un'dyə·lāt, -jə-) v. **·lat·ed, ·lat·ing** v.t. **1** To cause to move like a wave or in waves. **2** To give a wavy appearance or surface to. —v.i. **3** To move like a wave or waves. **4** To have a wavy form or appearance. —adj. (-lit, -lāt) Having a wavelike appearance, surface, or markings: also **un'du·lat·ed.** [< L unda wave]

un·du·la·tion (un'dyə·lā'shən, -jə-) n. **1** A waving or sinuous motion. **2** An appearance as of waves; a gentle rise and fall. —un'du·la·to'ry (-lə·tôr'ē, -tō'rē) adj.

un·du·ly (un·dyōō'lē) adv. **1** Excessively. **2** Improperly; unjustly.

un·dy·ing (un·dī'ing) adj. Immortal; eternal.

un·earned (un·ûrnd') adj. **1** Not earned by labor, skill, etc. **2** Undeserved.

unearned increment An increase in the value of land or property independent of any efforts of the owner, as through an increase of population that creates demand.

un·earth (un·ûrth') v.t. **1** To dig or root up from the earth. **2** To reveal; discover.

un·earth·ly (un·ûrth'lē) adj. **1** Not, or seemingly not, of this earth. **2** Supernatural; terrifying; weird; terrible. **3** Informal Ridiculous, absurd, preposterous, etc. —un·earth'li·ness n.

un·ease (un·ēz') n. Mental or emotional discomfort, dissatisfaction, anxiety, etc.

un·eas·y (un·ē'zē) adj. **·eas·i·er, ·eas·i·est 1** Deprived of ease; disturbed; unquiet. **2** Not comfortable; causing discomfort. **3** Showing embarassment or constraint; strained. **4** Not stable or secure; precarious: an uneasy peace. —un·eas'i·ly adv. —un·eas'i·ness n.

un·em·ploy·a·ble (un'əm·ploi'ə·bəl) adj. Not employable because of illness, age, physical incapacity, etc. —n. An unemployable person.

un·em·ployed (un'əm·ploid') adj. **1** Having no employment; out of work. **2** Not put to use or turned to account; idle. —**the unemployed** People who have no jobs. —un'em·ploy'ment n.

un·e·qual (un·ē'kwəl) adj. **1** Not equal in size, importance, weight, ability, duration, etc. **2** Inadequate; insufficient: with to. **3** Not balanced or uniform; variable; irregular. **4** Involving poorly matched competitors or contestants: an unequal contest. —un·e'qual·ly adv.

un·e·qualed (un·ē'kwəld) adj. Not equaled or matched; unrivaled. Also **un·e'qualled.**

un·e·quiv·o·cal (un'i·kwiv'ə·kəl) adj. Understandable in only one way; not ambiguous; clear. —un'e·quiv'o·cal·ly adv. —un'e·quiv'o·cal·ness n.

un·err·ing (un·ûr'ing, -er'-) adj. **1** Making no mistakes. **2** Certain; accurate; infallible. —un·err'ing·ly adv.

UNESCO (yōō·nes'kō) United Nations Educational, Scientific, and Cultural Organization.

---

un·es·sen·tial (un′ə·sen′shəl) *adj.* Not essential; not needed. —*n.* Something not essential; an extra.

un·e·ven (un·ē′vən) *adj.* 1 Not even, smooth, or level; rough. 2 Not straight, parallel, or perfectly horizontal. 3 Not equal or even, as in length, width, etc. 4 Not balanced or matched equally. 5 Not uniform; variable; fluctuating. 6 Not fair or just. 7 Not divisible by two without remainder; odd: said of numbers. —**un·e′ven·ly** *adv.* —**un·e′ven·ness** *n.*

un·e·vent·ful (un′i·vent′fəl) *adj.* Devoid of any noteworthy or unusual events or incidents; quiet. —**un′e·vent′·ful·ly** *adv.* —**un′e·vent′ful·ness** *n.*

un·ex·am·pled (un′ig·zam′pəld) *adj.* Without a parallel example; unprecedented; unique.

un·ex·cep·tion·a·ble (un′ik·sep′shən·ə·bəl) *adj.* That cannot be objected to; without any flaw; irreproachable. —**un′ex·cep′tion·a·bly** *adv.*

un·ex·cep·tion·al (un′ik·sep′shən·əl) *adj.* 1 Not unusual or exceptional; ordinary. 2 Subject to no exception.

un·ex·pect·ed (un′ik·spek′tid) *adj.* Coming without warning; not expected; unforeseen. —**un′ex·pect′ed·ly** *adv.* —**un′ex·pect′ed·ness** *n.* —**Syn.** unanticipated, sudden.

un·fail·ing (un·fā′ling) *adj.* 1 Giving or constituting a supply that never fails; inexhaustible: an *unfailing* spring. 2 Always fulfilling requirements or expectation. 3 Sure; infallible. —**un·fail′ing·ly** *adv.* —**un·fail′ing·ness** *n.*

un·fair (un·fâr′) *adj.* 1 Marked by injustice, deception, or bias; not fair. 2 Not honest or ethical in business affairs. —**un·fair′ly** *adv.* —**un·fair′ness** *n.*

un·faith·ful (un·fāth′fəl) *adj.* 1 Not faithful to or abiding by a vow, agreement, duty, etc.; disloyal. 2 Not accurate or exact; unreliable. 3 Not true to marriage vows; adulterous. —**un·faith′ful·ly** *adv.* —**un·faith′ful·ness** *n.*

un·fa·mil·iar (un′fə·mil′yər) *adj.* 1 Not knowing well or at all: with *with: unfamiliar* with his plays. 2 Not familiarly known; strange: an *unfamiliar* face. —**un′fa·mil′i·ar′·i·ty** (-mil′ē·ar′ə·tē) *n.* —**un′fa·mil′iar·ly** *adv.*

un·fast·en (un·fas′ən, -fäs′-) *v.t.* To untie or undo; loosen or open.

un·fa·vor·a·ble (un·fā′vər·ə·bəl) *adj.* 1 Not favorable; adverse. 2 Not propitious. —**un·fa′vor·a·bly** *adv.*

un·feel·ing (un·fē′ling) *adj.* 1 Not sympathetic; hard; callous. 2 Having no feeling or sensation. —**un·feel′ing·ly** *adv.* —**un·feel′ing·ness** *n.*

un·feigned (un·fānd′) *adj.* Not feigned; sincere; genuine. —**un·feign′ed·ly** (-fān′id·lē) *adv.*

un·fit (un·fit′) *v.t.* **·fit·ed** or **·fit, ·fit·ting** To deprive of requisite fitness, skill, etc.; disqualify. —*adj.* 1 Not able to meet the requirements or needs; unsuitable. 2 Not physically or mentally sound or fit. 3 Not appropriate or proper for a given purpose. —**un·fit′ly** *adv.* —**un·fit′ness** *n.*

un·fix (un·fiks′) *v.t.* 1 To unfasten; loosen; detach. 2 To unsettle.

un·flag·ging (un·flag′ing) *adj.* Not diminishing or failing; tireless. —**un·flag′ging·ly** *adv.*

un·flap·pa·ble (un·flap′ə·bəl) *adj. Informal* Characterized by unshakable composure; imperturbable. —**un·flap′·pa·bil′i·ty** *n.*

un·fledged (un·flejd′) *adj.* 1 Not yet fledged, as a young bird. 2 Inexperienced or immature.

un·flinch·ing (un·flin′ching) *adj.* Done without shrinking; steadfast. —**un·flinch′ing·ly** *adv.*

un·fold (un·fōld′) *v.t.* 1 To open or spread out (something folded). 2 To unwrap. 3 To reveal or make clear, as by explaining or disclosing gradually. 4 To develop. —*v.i.* 5 To become opened; expand. 6 To become manifest or develop fully.

un·fore·seen (un′fôr·sēn′, -fôr-) *adj.* Unexpected.

un·for·get·ta·ble (un′fər·get′ə·bəl) *adj.* Difficult or impossible to forget; memorable. —**un′for·get′ta·bly** *adv.*

un·for·tu·nate (un·fôr′chə·nit) *adj.* 1 Not fortunate or lucky. 2 Causing, attended by, or resulting from misfortune; disastrous. 3 Not suitable or proper; bad; regrettable: an *unfortunate* thing to say. —*n.* One who is unfortunate. —**un·for′tu·nate·ly** *adv.* —**un·for′tu·nate·ness** *n.*

un·found·ed (un·foun′did) *adj.* 1 Not based on fact; groundless; baseless. 2 Not established.

un·fre·quent·ed (un′frī·kwen′tid) *adj.* Rarely or never visited or frequented.

un·friend·ly (un·frend′lē) *adj.* 1 Not friendly or sympathetic. 2 Not favorable or propitious. —**un·friend′li·ness** *n.*

un·frock (un·frok′) *v.t.* 1 To remove a frock or gown from. 2 To depose, as a priest, from ecclesiastical rank.

un·furl (un·fûrl′) *v.t. & v.i.* 1 To unroll, as a flag; spread out. 2 To unfold. —**un·furled′** *adj.*

un·gain·ly (un·gān′lē) *adj.* 1 Awkward; clumsy. 2 Not attractive. —**un·gain′li·ness** *n.*

un·glued (un·glōōd′) *adj.* No longer glued together; separated. —**come unglued** *Slang* To become mentally or emotionally upset.

un·god·ly (un·god′lē) *adj.* 1 Without reverence for God; impious. 2 Unholy; sinful. 3 *Informal* Outrageous. —*adv. Informal* Outrageously. —**un·god′li·ness** *n.*

un·gov·ern·a·ble (un·guv′ər·nə·bəl) *adj.* That cannot be governed; wild; unruly. —**un·gov′ern·a·bly** *adv.*

un·gra·cious (un·grā′shəs) *adj.* 1 Lacking in graciousness of manner; unmannerly. 2 Not pleasing; offensive. —**un·gra′cious·ly** *adv.* —**un·gra′cious·ness** *n.* —**Syn.** 1 discourteous, rude, impolite, uncivil, ill-mannered, ill-bred.

un·grate·ful (un·grāt′fəl) *adj.* 1 Feeling or showing a lack of gratitude; not thankful. 2 Not pleasant; disagreeable. 3 Unrewarding; yielding no return. —**un·grate′ful·ly** *adv.* —**un·grate′ful·ness** *n.*

un·guard·ed (un·gär′did) *adj.* 1 Having no guard; unprotected. 2 Thoughtless; careless. 3 Without guile; direct; open. —**un·guard′ed·ly** *adv.*

un·guent (ung′gwənt) *n.* An ointment or salve. [< L *unguere* anoint] —**un′guen·tar′y** (-gwən·ter′ē) *adj.*

un·guis (ung′gwis) *n. pl.* **·gues** (-gwēz) A hoof, claw, nail, or talon. [L, nail]

un·gu·late (ung′gyə·lit, -lāt) *adj.* Having hoofs. —*n.* A hoofed mammal. [< L *ungula* hoof]

un·hand (un·hand′) *v.t.* To remove one's hand from; release from the hand or hands; let go.

un·hand·y (un·han′dē) *adj.* **·di·er, ·di·est** 1 Hard to get to or use; inconvenient. 2 Clumsy; lacking in manual skill. —**un·hand′i·ly** *adv.*

un·hap·py (un·hap′ē) *adj.* **·pi·er, ·pi·est** 1 Sad; depressed. 2 Causing or constituting misery, unrest, or dissatisfaction: *unhappy* circumstances. 3 Unfortunate; unpropitious. 4 Exhibiting lack of tact or judgment; inappropriate. —**un·hap′pi·ly** *adv.* —**un·hap′pi·ness** *n.*

un·health·y (un·hel′thē) *adj.* **·health·i·er, ·health·i·est** 1 Lacking health, vigor, or wholesomeness; sickly. 2 Causing sickness; injurious to health. 3 Morally harmful. 4 Dangerous; risky. —**un·health′i·ly** *adv.* —**un·health′i·ness** *n.*

un·heard (un·hûrd′) *adj.* 1 Not perceived by the ear. 2 Not granted a hearing. 3 Obscure; unknown.

un·heard-of (un·hûrd′uv′, -ov′) *adj.* 1 Not known of before; unknown or unprecedented. 2 Outrageous; unbelievable.

un·hinge (un·hinj′) *v.t.* **hinged, hing·ing** 1 To take from the hinges. 2 To remove the hinges of. 3 To detach; dislodge. 4 To throw into confusion; unsettle, as the mind.

un·hitch (un·hich′) *v.t.* To unfasten.

un·ho·ly (un·hō′lē) *adj.* **·ho·li·er, ·ho·li·est** 1 Not hallowed. 2 Wicked; sinful. 3 *Informal* Frightful; outrageous. —**un·ho′li·ly** *adv.* —**un·ho′li·ness** *n.*

uni- *combining form* One; single; one only: *unifoliate.* [< L *unus* one]

U·ni·ate (yōō′nē·at, -it) *n.* A member of any community of Eastern Christians that acknowledges the supremacy of the pope at Rome, but retains its own liturgy, ceremonies, and rites. —*adj.* Of the Uniates or their faith. Also **U′ni·at** (-it).

u·ni·cam·er·al (yōō′nə·kam′ər·əl) *adj.* Consisting of but one chamber, as a legislature.

UNICEF (yōō′nə·sef) United Nations Children's Fund. [< *U(nited) N(ations) I(nternational) C(hildren's) E(mergency) F(und)*, its former name]

u·ni·cel·lu·lar (yōō′nə·sel′yə·lər) *adj.* Consisting of a single cell, as a protozoan.

u·ni·corn (yōō′nə·kôrn′) *n.* A mythical, horselike animal with

Unicorn

one horn growing from the middle of its forehead. [< L *unicornis* one-horned]

u·ni·cy·cle (yōō′nə·sī′kəl) *n.* A bicyclelike vehicle having only a single wheel propelled by pedals.

u·ni·form (yōō′nə·fôrm′) *adj.* **1** Being always the same or alike; not varying: *uniform* temperature. **2** Having the same form, color, character, etc. as others: a line of *uniform* battleships. **3** Being the same throughout in appearance, color, surface, etc.: a *uniform* texture. **4** Consistent in effect, action, etc.: a *uniform* law for all drivers. —*n.* A distinctive dress or suit worn, esp. when on duty, by members of the same organization, service, etc., as soldiers, sailors, postmen, etc. —*v.t.* To put into or clothe with a uniform. [< L *unus* one + *forma* form] —**u′ni·form·ly** *adv.*

u·ni·form·i·ty (yōō′nə·fôr′mə·tē) *n. pl.* ·**ties 1** The state or quality of being uniform. **2** An instance of it.

u·ni·fy (yōō′nə·fī) *v.t.* ·**fied**, ·**fy·ing** To cause to be one; make uniform; unite. [< L *unus* one + *facere* make] —**u′ni·fi·ca′tion** (-fə·kā′shən), **u′ni·fi′er** *n.*

u·ni·lat·er·al (yōō′nə·lat′ər·əl) *adj.* **1** Of, relating to, or affecting one side only; one-sided. **2** Made, undertaken, done, or signed by only one of two or more people or parties. **3** Growing on or turning toward one side only. —**u′ni·lat′er·al·ism** *n.* —**u′ni·lat′er·al·ly** *adv.*

un·im·peach·a·ble (un′im·pē′chə·bəl) *adj.* Not impeachable; beyond question as regards truth, honesty, etc.; faultless; blameless. —**un′im·peach′a·bly** *adv.*

un·im·proved (un′im·prōovd′) *adj.* **1** Not improved; not bettered or advanced. **2** Having no improvements; not cleared, cultivated, or built upon. **3** Not made anything of; unused.

un·in·tel·li·gi·ble (un′in·tel′ə·jə·bəl) *adj.* Impossible to understand; incomprehensible. —**un′in·tel′li·gi·bil′i·ty** *n.* —**un′in·tel′li·gi·bly** *adv.*

un·in·ter·es·ted (un·in′tər·is·tid, -tris-) *adj.* Not interested; indifferent; unconcerned. ● See DISINTERESTED.

un·ion (yōon′yən) *n.* **1** The act or an instance of uniting two or more things into one, as: **a** A political joining together, as of states or nations. **b** Marriage; wedlock. **2** The condition of being united or joined; junction. **3** Something formed by uniting or combining parts, as: **a** A confederation, coalition, or league, as of nations, states, or individuals. **b** LABOR UNION. **4** A device for joining mechanical parts, esp. a coupling device for pipes or rods. **5** A college or university organization that provides facilities for recreation, meetings, light meals, etc.: also **student union. 6** A device emblematic of union used in a flag or ensign, as the blue field with white stars in the flag of the U.S. —*adj.* Of, being, or relating to a union. —**the Union** The United States of America. [< L *unus* one]

un·ion·ism (yōon′yən·iz′əm) *n.* **1** The principle of union. **2** Labor unions collectively; also, their principles and practices. —**un′ion·ist** *n.* —**un′ion·is′tic** *adj.*

Un·ion·ism (yōon′yən·iz′əm) *n.* During the U.S. Civil War, the advocacy of political union between the States, as opposed to secession. —**Un′ion·ist** *n.*

un·ion·ize (yōon′yən·īz) *v.* ·**ized**, ·**iz·ing** *v.t.* To cause to join or to organize into a labor union. —*v.i.* To become a member of or organize a labor union. —**un′ion·i·za′tion** *n.*

Union Jack The British national flag.

Union of Soviet Socialist Republics A federal union of 15 republics in N Eurasia, 8,646,400 sq. mi., cap. Moscow.

union shop A factory, office, hospital, etc., in which only members of a labor union are employed.

union suit A one-piece, man's or boy's undergarment consisting of shirt and drawers.

u·nique (yōo·nēk′) *adj.* **1** Being the only one of its kind; single; sole. **2** Being without equal; unparalleled. **3** Very

unusual or remarkable; exceptional, extraordinary, etc. [< L *unicus* < *unus* one] —**u·nique′ly** *adv.* —**u·nique′ness** *n.*

u·ni·sex (yōō′nə·seks′) *Informal adj.* For, appropriate to, or having characteristics of both sexes: *unisex* fashions. —*n.* The embodiment or integration of qualities, characteristics, etc., of both sexes, as in appearance, clothes, or activities.

u·ni·sex·u·al (yōō′nə·sek′shōō·əl) *adj.* **1** Of only one sex; dioecious: a *unisexual* plant. **2** *Informal* Of or having to do with unisex. —**u′ni·sex′u·al′i·ty** *n.* —**u′ni·sex′u·al·ly** *adv.*

u·ni·son (yōō′nə·sən, -zən) *n.* **1** A condition of perfect agreement and accord; harmony. **2** *Music* **a** The interval between tones of identical pitch. **b** The simultaneous sounding of the same tones by two or more parts. —**in unison 1** So that identical tones are sounded simultaneously by two or more parts. **2** So that identical words or sounds are uttered simultaneously. **3** In perfect agreement. [< L *unisonus* having a single sound]

u·nit (yōō′nit) *n.* **1** A predetermined quantity, as of time, length, work, value, etc., used as a standard of measurement or comparison. **2** A fixed amount of work or classroom hours used in calculating a scholastic degree. **3** The quantity, as of a drug or antigen, required to produce a given effect or result. **4** A person or group considered both singly and as a constituent part of a whole: a military *unit.* **5** Something, as a mechanical part or device, having a specific function and serving as part of a whole: the electrical *unit* of a percolator. **6** *Math.* A quantity whose measure is represented by the number 1. —*adj.* Of or being a unit: the *unit* value of an article of merchandise. [Short for UNITY]

U·ni·tar·i·an (yōō′nə·târ′ē·ən) *n.* A member of a Protestant denomination which rejects the doctrine of the Trinity, but accepts the ethical teachings of Jesus and emphasizes complete freedom of religious opinion and the independence of each local congregation. —*adj.* Pertaining to the Unitarians, or to their teachings. —**U′ni·tar′i·an·ism** *n.*

u·ni·tar·y (yōō′nə·ter′ē) *adj.* **1** Of a unit or units. **2** Characterized by, based on, or pertaining to unity. **3** Having the nature of or used as a unit.

u·nite (yōō·nīt′) *v.* **u·nit·ed**, **u·nit·ing** *v.t.* **1** To join together so as to form a whole; combine. **2** To bring into close connection, as by legal, physical, marital, social, or other ties: to be *united* in marriage; allies *united* by a common interest. **3** To have or possess in combination: to *unite* courage with wisdom. **4** To cause to adhere; combine. —*v.i.* **5** To become or be merged into one; be consolidated by or as if by adhering. **6** To join together for action. [< L *unus* one]

u·nit·ed (yōō·nī′tid) *adj.* **1** Incorporated into one; combined. **2** Of or resulting from joint action. **3** Harmonious; in agreement. —**u·nit′ed·ly** *adv.* —**u·nit′ed·ness** *n.*

United Kingdom A constitutional monarchy located on several islands off the coast of N Europe, comprising Great Britain, Northern Ireland, and nearby islands, 94,284 sq. mi., cap. London.

United Nations 1 A coalition to resist the military aggression of the Axis Powers in World War II, formed of 26 national states in January, 1942. **2** An international organization of sovereign states (originally called the **United Nations Organization**) created by the United Nations Charter adopted at San Francisco in 1945.

United Kingdom

United States of America A federal republic including 50 states (49 in North America, and Hawaii, an archipelago in the Pacific Ocean), and the District of Columbia, 3,615,222 sq. mi., cap. Washington, D.C.

u·ni·ty (yōō′nə·tē) *n. pl.* **·ties 1** The state or quality of being one or united; oneness. **2** The product or result of being one or united. **3** Singleness of purpose or action. **4** A state of mutual understanding. **5** The quality or fact of being a whole through the unification of separate or individual parts. **6** In a literary or artistic production, a combination of parts that exhibits a prevailing oneness of purpose, thought, spirit, and style; also, the cohesive or harmonious effect so produced. **7** *Math.* **a** The number one. **b** The element of a number system that leaves any number unchanged under multiplication. [< L *unus* one]

Univ. Universalist; University.

univ. universal; universally; university.

u·ni·va·lent (yōō′nə·vā′lənt) *adj. Chem.* Having a valence or combining value of one; monovalent. —**u′ni·va′·lence, u′ni·va′len·cy** *n.*

u·ni·valve (yōō′nə·valv′) *adj.* Having the shell in one piece, as a snail. Also **u′ni·val′vate, u′ni·valved′.** —*n.* **1** A mollusk having a univalve shell; a gastropod. **2** A shell of a single piece. —**u′ni·val′vu·lar** (-val′vyə·lər) *adj.*

u·ni·ver·sal (yōō′nə·vûr′səl) *adj.* **1** Prevalent or common everywhere or among all things or persons. **2** Of, applicable to, for, or including all things, persons, cases, etc., without exception. **3** Accomplished or interested in a vast variety of subjects, activities, etc.: Leonardo da Vinci was a *universal* genius. **4** Adapted or adaptable to a great variety of uses, shapes, etc. **5** *Logic* Including or designating all the members of a class. —*n.* **1** *Logic* A universal proposition. **2** Any general or universal notion or idea. **3** A behavioral trait common to all men or cultures. —**u′ni·ver′sal·ly** *adv.* —**u′ni·ver′sal·ism, u′ni·ver′sal·ness** *n.*

u·ni·ver·sal·i·ty (yōō′nə·vər·sal′ə·tē) *n.* **1** The quality, condition, or an instance of being universal. **2** Limitlessness, as of range, occurrence, etc.

u·ni·ver·sal·ize (yōō′nə·vûr′səl·īz) *v.t.* **·ized, ·iz·ing** To make universal. —**u′ni·ver′sal·i·za′tion** *n.*

universal joint *Mech.* A coupling for connecting two shafts, etc., so as to permit angular motion in all directions. Also **universal coupling.**

u·ni·verse (yōō′nə·vûrs) *n.* **1** The aggregate of all existing things; the whole creation embracing all celestial bodies and all of space; the cosmos. **2** In restricted sense, the earth. **3** Something regarded as being a universe in its comprehensiveness, as a field of thought or activity. [< L *universus* turned, combined into one < *unus* one + *versus,* p.p. of *vertere* turn]

u·ni·ver·si·ty (yōō′nə·vûr′sə·tē) *n. pl.* **·ties 1** An educational institution for higher instruction, usu., in the U.S., an institution that includes an undergraduate college or colleges and professional schools granting advanced degrees in law, medicine, the sciences, academic subjects, etc. **2** The buildings, grounds, etc., of a university. **3** The students, faculty, and administration of a university.

un·just (un·just′) *adj.* Not legitimate, fair, or just; wrongful. —**un·just′ly** *adv.*

un·kempt (un·kempt′) *adj.* **1** Not combed: said of hair. **2** Not neat or tidy. **3** Without polish; rough. [< UN-[1] + *kempt* combed, p.p. of *kemb,* dial. var. of COMB]

un·kind (un·kīnd′) *adj.* Lacking kindness; unsympathetic; harsh; cruel. —**un·kind′ly** *adj.* **(·li·er, ·li·est)** & *adv.* —**un·kind′li·ness, un·kind′ness** *n.*

un·known (un·nōn′) *adj.* **1** Not known; not apprehended mentally; not recognized, as a fact or person. **2** Not determined or identified: an *unknown* substance. —*n.* An unknown person, thing, or quantity.

un·lace (un·lās′) *v.t.* **·laced, ·lac·ing** To loosen or unfasten the lacing of; untie.

un·law·ful (un·lô′fəl) *adj.* **1** Contrary to or in violation of law; illegal. **2** Not moral or ethical. —**un·law′ful·ly** *adv.* —**un·law′ful·ness** *n.*

un·learn (un·lûrn′) *v.t.* **·learned** or **·learnt, ·learn·ing 1** To dismiss from the mind (something learned); forget. **2** To attempt to abandon the habit of.

un·learn·ed (un·lûr′nid) *adj.* **1** Not possessed of or characterized by learning; illiterate; ignorant. **2** Characterized by lack of knowledge, professional skill, etc. **3** (un·lûrnd′) Not acquired by learning or study.

un·leash (un·lēsh′) *v.t.* To set free from or as from a leash: He *unleashed* his rage.

un·less (un·les′) *conj.* If it be not a fact that; except that: *Unless* we persevere, we shall lose. —*prep.* Save; except; excepting: with an implied verb: *Unless* a miracle, he'll

not be back in time. [Earlier *onlesse (that)* in a less case < ON + LESS]

un·let·tered (un·let′ərd) *adj.* Not educated; not lettered; illiterate.

un·like (un·līk′) *adj.* Having little or no resemblance; different. —*prep.* 1 Not like; different from. 2 Not characteristic of: It's *unlike* her to complain. —**un·like′ness** *n.*

un·like·ly (un·līk′lē) *adj.* 1 Improbable. 2 Not inviting or promising success. —*adv.* Improbably. —**un·like′li·hood, un·like′li·ness** *n.*

un·lim·it·ed (un·lim′it·id) *adj.* 1 Having no limits in space, number, or time. 2 Not restricted or limited.

un·load (un·lōd′) *v.t.* 1 To remove the load or cargo from. 2 To take off or discharge (cargo, etc.). 3 To relieve of something burdensome or oppressive. 4 To withdraw the charge of ammunition from. 5 *Informal* To dispose of, esp. by selling in large quantities. —*v.i.* 6 To discharge freight, cargo, etc.

un·lock (un·lok′) *v.t.* 1 To unfasten (something locked). 2 To open; release. 3 To lay open; reveal or disclose. —*v.i.* 4 To become unlocked.

un·looked-for (un·lŏŏkt′fôr′) *adj.* Not anticipated; unexpected.

un·loose (un·lōōs′) *v.t.* **·loosed, ·loos·ing** To make loose; set free; undo, release, etc. Also **un·loos′en** (-lōō′sən).

un·luck·y (un·luk′ē) *adj.* **·luck·i·er, ·luck·i·est** 1 Not favored by luck; unfortunate. 2 Resulting in or attended by ill luck; disastrous. 3 Likely to prove unfortunate; inauspicious. —**un·luck′i·ly** *adv.* —**un·luck′i·ness** *n.*

un·make (un·māk′) *v.t.* **·made, ·mak·ing** 1 To reduce to the original condition or form. 2 To ruin; destroy. 3 To deprive of rank, power, etc.

un·man (un·man′) *v.t.* **·manned, ·man·ning** 1 To cause to lose courage; dishearten. 2 To deprive of manly qualities; make weak or timid. 3 To castrate; emasculate.

un·man·ly (un·man′lē) *adj.* Not manly; weak, cowardly, effeminate, etc. —**un·man′li·ness** *n.*

un·mask (un·mask′, -mäsk′) *v.t.* 1 To remove a mask from. 2 To expose the true nature of. —*v.i.* 3 To remove one's mask or disguise.

un·mean·ing (un·mē′ning) *adj.* 1 Having no meaning: an *unmeaning* speech. 2 Having no expression: an *unmeaning* stare. —**un·mean′ing·ly** *adv.* —**un·mean′ing·ness** *n.*

un·men·tion·a·ble (un·men′shən·ə·bəl) *adj.* Not fit to be mentioned or discussed; embarrassing. —*n.pl.* Things not ordinarily mentioned or discussed, esp. undergarments. —**un·men′tion·a·ble·ness** *n.* —**un·men′tion·a·bly** *adv.*

un·mer·ci·ful (un·mûr′sə·fəl) *adj.* 1 Showing no mercy; cruel; pitiless. 2 Extreme; exorbitant. —**un·mer′ci·ful·ly** *adv.* —**un·mer′ci·ful·ness** *n.*

un·mis·tak·a·ble (un′mis·tā′kə·bəl) *adj.* That cannot be mistaken for something else; evident; obvious. —**un′mis·tak′a·bly** *adv.*

un·mit·i·gat·ed (un·mit′ə·gā′tid) *adj.* 1 Not relieved or lessened: *unmitigated* sorrow. 2 Absolute; thoroughgoing: an *unmitigated* liar. —**un·mit′i·gat′ed·ly** *adv.*

un·mor·al (un·môr′əl, -mor′-) *adj.* 1 Incapable of distinguishing between right and wrong; not guided by moral considerations. 2 Outside the realm of morality or ethics. —**un·mo·ral·i·ty** (un′mə·ral′ə·tē) *n.* • *Unmoral, amoral,* and *immoral* are alike in meaning not moral. However, *unmoral* and *amoral* are synonomous in referring to objects or acts (or people involved with such objects or acts) which stand outside the realm of morality whereas *immoral* infers a conflict with accepted standards of morality.

un·nat·u·ral (un·nach′ər·əl, -nach′rəl, un′-) *adj.* 1 Contrary to the norm. 2 Contrary to the common laws of morality or decency; monstrous; inhuman. 3 Contrived; artificial. —**un·nat′u·ral·ly** *adv.* —**un·nat′u·ral·ness** *n.*

un·nec·es·sary (un·nes′ə·ser′ē, un′-) *adj.* Not required; not necessary. —**un·nec·es·sar·i·ly** (un′nes′ə·ser′ə·lē) *adv.*

un·nerve (un·nûrv′) *v.t.* **·nerved, ·nerv·ing** 1 To deprive of strength, firmness, courage, etc. 2 To make nervous.

un·num·bered (un·num′bərd) *adj.* 1 Not counted. 2 Innumerable. 3 Not numbered.

un·oc·cu·pied (un·ok′yə·pīd′, un′-) *adj.* 1 Empty; unin-

habited: an *unoccupied* house. 2 Idle; unemployed; at leisure.

un·of·fi·cial (un·ə·fish′əl) *adj.* Not official; not authoritative. —**un·of·fi′cial·ly** *adv.*

un·or·gan·ized (un·ôr′gən·īzd) *adj.* 1 Not organized. 2 Without form or structure. 3 Not unionized.

un·pack (un·pak′) *v.t.* 1 To open and take out the contents of. 2 To take out of the container, as something packed. —*v.i.* 3 To take the contents out of a suitcase, etc.

un·par·al·leled (un·par′ə·leld) *adj.* Without parallel; unmatched; unprecedented.

un·peg (un·peg′) *v.t.* **·pegged, ·peg·ging** To unfasten by removing the peg or pegs from.

un·peo·ple (un·pē′pəl) *v.t.* **·pled, ·pling** To depopulate; deprive of inhabitants.

un·per·son (un′pûr′sən) *n.* One reduced to a state of oblivion, as by official action or the loss of position, after a period of fame or public importance.

un·pin (un·pin′) *v.t.* **·pinned, ·pin·ning** 1 To remove a pin or pins from. 2 To unfasten by removing pins.

un·pleas·ant (un·plez′ənt) *adj.* Disagreeable; objectionable. —**un·pleas′ant·ly** *adv.* —**un·pleas′ant·ness** *n.*

un·plug (un·plug′) *v.t.* **·plugged, ·plug·ging** 1 To remove a plug from. 2 To remove an obstruction from, as a drain. 3 To break an electrical connection by pulling out a plug.

un·plumbed (un·plumd′) *adj.* Not measured or explored fully; unfathomed; unknown.

un·polled (un·pōld′) *adj.* 1 Not cast or registered: said of a vote. 2 Not canvassed in a poll.

un·pop·u·lar (un·pop′yə·lər) *adj.* Generally disliked, unaccepted, etc. —**un·pop′u·lar·ly** *adv.* —**un·pop′u·lar′i·ty** (-lar′ə·tē) *n.*

un·prac·ticed (un·prak′tist) *adj.* 1 Not skilled; inexperienced. 2 Not used or tried.

un·prec·e·dent·ed (un·pres′ə·den′tid) *adj.* Being without precedent; preceded by no similar case; novel.

un·prej·u·diced (un·prej′ŏŏ·dist) *adj.* 1 Free from prejudice or bias; impartial. 2 Not impaired, as a right.

un·prin·ci·pled (un·prin′sə·pəld) *adj.* Without moral principles; unscrupulous.

un·print·a·ble (un·prin′tə·bəl) *adj.* Not fit for printing, esp. because of profanity, obscenity, etc.

un·pro·fes·sion·al (un′prə·fesh′ən·əl) *adj.* 1 Not pertaining to, characteristic of, or belonging to a particular profession. 2 Violating the standards, ethical code, etc., of a profession. —**un′pro·fes′sion·al·ly** *adv.*

un·qual·i·fied (un·kwol′ə·fīd) *adj.* 1 Being without the proper qualifications; unfit. 2 Without limitation or restrictions; absolute: *unqualified* approval.

un·ques·tion·a·ble (un·kwes′chən·ə·bəl) *adj.* Too certain or sure to be open to question, doubt, etc.; indisputable. —**un·ques′tion·a·bly** *adv.*

un·qui·et (un·kwī′ət) *adj.* 1 Turbulent; agitated; tumultuous. 2 Disturbed physically, mentally or emotionally; restless; uneasy. —**un·qui′et·ly** *adv.* —**un·qui′et·ness** *n.*

un·quote (un·kwōt′) *v.t. & v.i.* **·quot·ed, ·quot·ing** To close (a quotation).

un·rav·el (un·rav′əl) *v.* **·eled** or **·elled, ·el·ing** or **·el·ling** *v.t.* 1 To separate the threads of, as a tangled skein or knitted article. 2 To unfold; explain, as a mystery or a plot. —*v.i.* 3 To become unraveled.

un·read (un·red′) *adj.* 1 Having read very little; uninformed; unlearned. 2 Not yet read or examined.

un·read·y (un·red′ē) *adj.* Not ready; unprepared, as for speech, action, etc. —**un·read′i·ly** *adv.* —**un·read′i·ness** *n.*

un·re·al (un·rē′əl, -rēl′) *adj.* 1 Having no reality, actual existence, or substance. 2 Not true or sincere; false. 3 Fanciful; imaginary. —**un·re·al·i·ty** (un′rē·al′ə·tē) *n.*

un·rea·son·a·ble (un·rē′zən·ə·bəl, -rēz′nə-) *adj.* 1 Acting without or contrary to reason. 2 Immoderate; exorbitant. —**un·rea′son·a·ble·ness** *n.* —**un·rea′son·a·bly** *adv.*

un·rea·son·ing (un·rē′zən·ing) *adj.* Marked by the absence of reason; irrational. —**un·rea′son·ing·ly** *adv.*

un·reel (un·rēl′) *v.t. & v.i.* To unwind from a reel.

un·re·gen·er·ate (un′ri·jen′ər·it) *adj.* 1 Not changed spiritually by regeneration; unrepentant. 2 Not convinced

by or converted to a particular doctrine, theology, cause, etc. 3 Stubborn; recalcitrant.

un·re·lent·ing (un'ri·lent'ing) *adj.* 1 Not relenting; inflexible. 2 Not diminishing in pace, effort, speed, etc. —**un're·lent'ing·ly** *adv.*

un·re·li·a·ble (un'ri·lī'ə·bəl) *adj.* Not to be relied upon; undependable. —**un're·li·a·bil'i·ty**, **un're·li·a·ble·ness** *n.* —**un're·li·a·bly** *adv.*

un·re·lig·ious (un'ri·lij'əs) *adj.* 1 IRRELIGIOUS. 2 Not related to or connected with religion.

un·re·mit·ting (un'ri·mit'ing) *adj.* Incessant; not stopping or relaxing. —**un're·mit'ting·ly** *adv.* —**un're·mit'ting·ness** *n.*

un·re·served (un'ri·zûrvd') *adj.* 1 Not qualified; unrestricted. 2 Not reticent; informal; open. 3 Not set aside, as seats. —**un·re·serv·ed·ly** (un'ri·zûr'vid·lē) *adv.* —**un're·serv'·ed·ness** *n.*

un·rest (un'rest', un'rest') *n.* 1 Restlessness, esp. of the mind. 2 Angry dissatisfaction, bordering on revolt.

un·rid·dle (un·rid'l) *v.t.* ·dled, ·dling To solve, as a mystery.

un·right·eous (un·rī'chəs) *adj.* 1 Not righteous; wicked; sinful. 2 Unfair; inequitable. —**un·right'eous·ly** *adv.* —**un·right'eous·ness** *n.*

un·ripe (un·rīp') *adj.* 1 Not arrived at maturity; not ripe; immature. 2 Not ready; not prepared. —**un·ripe'ness** *n.*

un·ri·valed (un·rī'vəld) *adj.* Having no rival; peerless.

un·roll (un·rōl') *v.t.* 1 To spread or open (something rolled up). 2 To exhibit to view. —*v.i.* 3 To become unrolled.

un·ruf·fled (un·ruf'əld) *adj.* 1 Not disturbed or agitated; calm. 2 Not ruffled; smooth.

un·ru·ly (un·rōō'lē) *adj.* Disposed to resist rule or discipline; ungovernable. —**un·ru'li·ness** *n.*

un·sad·dle (un·sad'l) *v.* ·dled, ·dling *v.t.* 1 To remove a saddle from. 2 To remove from the saddle. —*v.i.* 3 To take the saddle off a horse.

un·said (un·sed') *adj.* Not said; not spoken.

un·sat·u·rat·ed (un·sach'ə·rā'tid) *adj.* 1 Capable of dissolving more solute. 2 Having at least one free or multiple valence bond available for direct union with an atom or radical: said of organic compounds.

un·sa·vor·y (un·sā'vər·ē) *adj.* 1 Having a disagreeable taste or odor. 2 Having no savor; tasteless. 3 Disagreeable or offensive, esp. morally. —**un·sa'vor·i·ness** *n.*

un·say (un·sā') *v.t.* ·said, ·say·ing To retract (something said).

un·scathed (un·skāthd') *adj.* Not injured.

un·scram·ble (un·skram'bəl) *v.t.* ·bled, ·bling *Informal* To resolve the confused, scrambled, or disordered condition of.

un·screw (un·skrōō') *v.t.* 1 To remove the screw or screws from. 2 To remove or detach by withdrawing screws, or by turning. —*v.i.* 3 To become unscrewed or permit of being unscrewed.

un·scru·pu·lous (un·skrōō'pyə·ləs) *adj.* Not scrupulous; having no scruples; unprincipled. —**un·scru'pu·lous·ly** *adv.* —**un·scru'pu·lous·ness** *n.*

un·seal (un·sēl') *v.t.* 1 To break or remove the seal of. 2 To open (that which has been sealed or closed).

un·search·a·ble (un·sûr'chə·bəl) *adj.* That cannot be searched into or explored; mysterious. —**un·search'a·ble·ness** *n.* —**un·search'a·bly** *adv.*

un·sea·son·a·ble (un·sē'zən·ə·bəl) *adj.* 1 Not suitable to the season: *unseasonable* weather. 2 Untimely; inopportune. —**un·sea'son·a·ble·ness** *n.* —**un·sea'son·a·bly** *adv.*

un·seat (un·sēt') *v.t.* 1 To remove from a seat. 2 To throw (a rider) from a horse. 3 To deprive of office or rank; depose.

un·seem·ly (un·sēm'lē) *adj.* ·li·er, ·li·est Unbecoming, indecent, unattractive, or inappropriate. —*adv.* In an unseemly fashion. —**un·seem'li·ness** *n.*

un·set·tle (un·set'l) *v.* ·tled, ·tling *v.t.* 1 To move from a fixed or settled condition. 2 To confuse, upset, or disturb. —*v.i.* 3 To become unsettled. —**un·set'tling·ly** *adv.*

un·sex (un·seks') *v.t.* To deprive of sex, sexual power, or the distinctive qualities of one's sex.

un·shack·le (un·shak'əl) *v.t.* ·led, ·ling 1 To unfetter; free from shackles. 2 To free, as from restraint.

un·sheathe (un·shēth') *v.t.* ·sheathed, ·sheath·ing To take from or as from a scabbard or sheath; bare.

un·ship (un·ship') *v.t.* ·shipped, ·ship·ping To unload from a ship or other vessel.

un·sight·ly (un·sīt'lē) *adj.* ·li·er, ·li·est Offensive to the sight; ugly. —**un·sight'li·ness** *n.*

un·skilled (un·skild') *adj.* 1 Without special skill or training: an *unskilled* worker. 2 Requiring no special skill or training.

un·skill·ful (un·skil'fəl) *adj.* Lacking or not evincing skill; awkward; incompetent. Also **un·skil'ful.** —**un·skill'ful·ly** *adv.* —**un·skill'ful·ness** *n.*

un·snap (un·snap') *v.t.* ·snapped, ·snap·ping To undo the snap or snaps of.

un·snarl (un·snärl') *v.t.* To undo snarls; disentangle.

un·so·cia·ble (un·sō'shə·bəl) *adj.* 1 Not sociable; not inclined to seek the society of others. 2 Lacking or not conducive to sociability. —**un·so·cia·bil·i·ty** (un·sō'shə·bil'ə·tē), **un·so'cia·ble·ness** *n.* —**un·so'cia·bly** *adv.*

un·sol·der (un·sod'ər) *v.t.* 1 To take apart (something soldered). 2 To separate; divide.

un·so·phis·ti·cat·ed (un'sə·fis'tə·kā'tid) *adj.* 1 Showing inexperience or naiveté; artless. 2 Genuine; pure. 3 Not complicated; simple. —**un'so·phis'ti·cat·ed·ly** *adv.* —**un'so·phis'ti·cat·ed·ness, un'so·phis'ti·ca'tion** *n.*

un·sound (un·sound') *adj.* 1 Not strong or solid: *unsound* construction. 2 Unhealthy in body or mind. 3 Untrue or logically invalid: *unsound* arguments. 4 Not deep; disturbed: said of sleep. —**un·sound'ly** *adv.* —**un·sound'ness** *n.*

un·spar·ing (un·spâr'ing) *adj.* 1 Not sparing or saving; lavish. 2 Showing no mercy. —**un·spar'ing·ly** *adv.* —**un·spar'ing·ness** *n.*

un·speak·a·ble (un·spē'kə·bəl) *adj.* 1 That cannot be expressed; unutterable: *unspeakable* joy. 2 Extremely bad or objectionable: an *unspeakable* crime. —**un·speak'a·ble·ness** *n.* —**un·speak'a·bly** *adv.*

un·sta·ble (un·stā'bəl) *adj.* 1 Lacking in stability or firmness; liable to move, sway, shake, etc. 2 Having no fixed purpose; easily influenced: an *unstable* character. 3 Emotionally unsteady. 4 Liable to change; fluctuating; variable: an *unstable* economy. 5 *Chem.* Easily decomposed, as certain compounds. —**un·sta'ble·ness** *n.* —**un·sta'bly** *adv.*

un·stead·y (un·sted'ē) *adj.* ·stead·i·er, ·stead·i·est Not steady, as: **a** Not stable; liable to move or shake. **b** Variable; fluctuating. **c** Undependable or irregular. —**un·stead'i·ly** *adv.* —**un·stead'i·ness** *n.*

un·stop (un·stop') *v.t.* ·stopped, ·stop·ping 1 To remove a stopper from. 2 To open by removing obstructions; clear.

un·stop·pa·ble (un·stop'ə·bəl) *adj.* Impossible to stop or check. —**un·stop'pa·bly** *adv.*

un·strap (un·strap') *v.t.* ·strapped, ·strap·ping To undo or loosen the strap or straps of.

un·string (un·string') *v.t.* ·strung, ·string·ing 1 To remove from a string, as pearls. 2 To take the string or strings from. 3 To loosen the string or strings of, as a bow or guitar. 4 To make unstable or nervous.

un·struc·tured (un·struk'chərd) *adj.* Not having a definite organization or plan.

un·strung (un·strung') *adj.* 1 Having the strings removed or loosened. 2 Emotionally upset.

un·stud·ied (un·stud'ēd) *adj.* 1 Not stiff or artificial; natural; unaffected. 2 Not acquainted through study.

un·sub·stan·tial (un'səb·stan'shəl) *adj.* 1 Lacking solidity or strength; unstable; weak. 2 Having no valid basis in fact. 3 Unreal; fanciful. —**un'sub·stan'tial·ly** *adv.* —**un'sub·stan'ti·al'i·ty** (-shē·al'ə·tē) *n.*

un·suit·a·ble (un·s'ōō'tə·bəl) *adj.* Not suitable; unfitting. —**un·suit·a·bil·i·ty** (un's'ōō·tə·bil'ə·tē), **un·suit'a·ble·ness** *n.* —**un·suit'a·bly** *adv.*

un·sung (un·sung') *adj.* 1 Not celebrated, as in song or poetry; obscure. 2 Not sung.

un·swerv·ing (un·swûr'ving) *adj.* 1 Not changing or wavering; consistent: *unswerving* loyalty. 2 Not swerving from a path or course. —**un·swerv'ing·ly** *adv.*

un·tan·gle (un·tang'gəl) *v.t.* ·gled, ·gling 1 To free from tangles; disentangle. 2 To clear up or straighten out (a perplexing or confused situation, etc.)

un·taught (un·tôt') *adj.* 1 Not having been instructed; ignorant. 2 Known without having been taught; natural.

un·thank·ful (un·thangk'fəl) *adj.* 1 Not grateful. 2 Not appreciated. —**un·thank'ful·ly** *adv.* —**un·thank'ful·ness** *n.*

un·think·ing (un·thingk′ing) *adj.* Lacking thoughtfulness, care, or attention. —**un·think′ing·ly** *adv.* —**un·think′ing·ness** *n.*

un·thread (un·thred′) *v.t.* **1** To remove the thread from, as a needle. **2** To unravel; disentangle. **3** To find one's way out of, as a maze.

un·ti·dy (un·tī′dē) *adj.* ·di·er, ·di·est Not tidy; messy; disorderly. —**un·ti′di·ly** *adv.* —**un·ti′di·ness** *n.*

un·tie (un·tī′) *v.* ·tied, ·ty·ing *v.t.* **1** To loosen or undo, as a knot. **2** To free from that which binds or restrains. —*v.i.* **3** To become loosened or undone.

un·til (un·til′) *prep.* **1** Up to the time of; till: We will wait *until* midnight. **2** Before: used with a negative: The music doesn't begin *until* nine. —*conj.* **1** To the time when: *until* I die. **2** To the place or degree that: Walk east *until* you reach the river. **3** Before: with a negative: He couldn't leave *until* the car came for him. [< ME *und-* up to, as far as + TILL] • See TILL².

un·time·ly (un·tīm′lē) *adj.* Coming before time or not in proper time; premature or inopportune. —*adv.* Before time or not in the proper time; inopportunely.

un·to (un′tōō) *prep.* *Archaic* **1** To. **2** Until. [< ME *und-* up to, as far as + TO, on analogy with *until*]

un·told (un·tōld′) *adj.* **1** Not told, revealed, or described. **2** Of too great a number or extent to be counted or measured.

un·touch·a·ble (un·tuch′ə·bəl) *adj.* **1** Inaccessible to the touch; out of reach. **2** Forbidden to the touch. **3** Unpleasant, disgusting, or dangerous to touch. —*n.* In India, formerly, a member of the lowest caste.

un·to·ward (un·tôrd′, -tōrd′, -tə·wôrd′) *adj.* **1** Causing or characterized by difficulty or unhappiness; unfavorable. **2** Not easily managed; refractory. **3** Improper; unseemly. —**un·to·ward′ly** *adv.* —**un·to·ward′ness** *n.*

un·true (un·trōō′) *adj.* **1** Not true; false or incorrect. **2** Not conforming to rule or standard. **3** Disloyal; faithless. —**un·tru′ly** *adv.*

un·truth (un·trōōth′, un′trōōth′) *n. pl.* ·truths (-trōōths, -trōōthz) **1** The quality or character of being untrue. **2** Something that is not true; a falsehood; lie.

un·truth·ful (un·trōōth′fəl) *adj.* **1** Not truthful; not telling the truth. **2** Not consistent with the truth. —**un·truth′ful·ly** *adv.* —**un·truth′ful·ness** *n.*

un·tu·tored (un·t⁽y⁾ōō′tərd) *adj.* Not educated; untaught.

un·twine (un·twīn′) *v.* ·twined, ·twin·ing *v.t.* **1** To undo (something twined); unwind by disentangling. —*v.i.* **2** To become undone.

un·twist (un·twist′) *v.t.* **1** To separate by a movement the reverse of twisting; untwine. —*v.i.* **2** To become untwined.

un·used (un·yōōzd′) *adj.* **1** Not used. **2** Never having been used. **3** Not accustomed: with *to.*

un·u·su·al (un·yōō′zhōō·əl) *adj.* Not usual; odd, rare, or extraordinary. —**un·u′su·al·ly** *adv.* —**un·u′su·al·ness** *n.*

un·ut·ter·a·ble (un·ut′ər·ə·bəl) *adj.* Too great, deep, etc., to be expressed or described in words. —**un·ut′ter·a·ble·ness** *n.* —**un·ut′ter·a·bly** *adv.*

un·var·nished (un·vär′nisht) *adj.* **1** Not varnished. **2** Not embellished or adorned; simple: the *unvarnished* truth.

un·veil (un·vāl′) *v.t.* **1** To remove the veil or covering from; disclose to view; reveal. —*v.i.* **2** To remove one's veil; reveal oneself.

un·war·rant·a·ble (un·wôr′ən·tə·bəl, -wor′-) *adj.* That cannot be justified; inexcusable; indefensible. —**un·war′rant·a·bly** *adv.*

un·war·y (un·wâr′ē) *adj.* ·war·i·er, ·war·i·est Not careful; incautious. —**un·war′i·ly** *adv.* —**un·war′i·ness** *n.* —Syn. careless, heedless, reckless, unguarded.

un·well (un·wel′) *adj.* Sick; ailing.

un·wept (un·wept′) *adj.* **1** Not lamented or wept for. **2** Not shed, as tears.

un·whole·some (un·hōl′səm) *adj.* **1** Harmful to physical, mental, or moral health. **2** Sickly in health or in appearance. —**un·whole′some·ly** *adv.* —**un·whole′some·ness** *n.*

un·wield·y (un·wēl′dē) *adj.* ·i·er, ·i·est Difficult to move, manage, or control, as because of great size or awkward shape. —**un·wield′i·ly** *adv.* —**un·wield′i·ness** *n.*

un·will·ing (un·wil′ing) *adj.* **1** Not willing; reluctant; loath. **2** Done, said, granted, etc., with reluctance. —**un·will′ing·ly** *adv.* —**un·will′ing·ness** *n.*

un·wind (un·wīnd′) *v.* ·wound, ·wind·ing *v.t.* **1** To reverse the winding of; untwist or wind off. **2** To disentangle. —*v.i.* **3** To become disentangled or untwisted. **4** To free oneself from tension or anxieties; relax.

un·wise (un·wīz′) *adj.* Acting with, or showing, lack of wisdom or good sense. —**un·wise′ly** *adv.*

un·wit·ting (un·wit′ing) *adj.* **1** Having no knowledge or awareness; ignorant; unconscious. **2** Not intentional. —**un·wit′ting·ly** *adv.*

un·wont·ed (un·wôn′tid, -won′-) *adj.* Not ordinary or customary; unusual; uncommon. —**un·wont′ed·ly** *adv.* —**un·wont′ed·ness** *n.*

un·wor·thy (un·wûr′thē) *adj.* **1** Not worthy or deserving: often with *of.* **2** Not befitting or becoming: usu. with *of:* conduct *unworthy* of a gentleman. **3** Lacking worth or merit. **4** Not deserved or merited. —**un·wor′thi·ly** *adv.* —**un·wor′thi·ness** *n.*

un·wrap (un·rap′) *v.t.* ·wrapped, ·wrap·ping To take the wrapping from; open; undo.

un·writ·ten (un·rit′n) *adj.* **1** Not written down; traditional. **2** Having no writing upon it; blank.

unwritten law A law or rule of conduct, procedure, etc., whose authority stems from custom and tradition rather than from a written command, decree, or statute.

un·yoke (un·yōk′) *v.t.* ·yoked, ·yok·ing **1** To release from a yoke. **2** To separate; part.

up (up) *adv.* **1** Toward a higher place or level. **2** In or on a higher place. **3** To or at that which is literally or figuratively higher, as: **a** To or at a higher price: Barley is going *up.* **b** To or at a higher rank: people who have come *up* in the world. **c** To or at a greater size or amount: to swell *up.* **d** To or at a greater degree, intensity, volume, etc.: Turn *up* the radio. **e** To or at a place regarded as higher *up:* north. **f** To a position above the horizon: when the sun comes *up.* **g** To a later point in time or life: from her childhood *up* to her teens. **4** In or into a vertical position; on one's feet. **5** Out of bed: to get *up.* **6** So as to be level or even (with) in time, degree, amount, etc.: *up* to the brim. **7** In or into commotion or activity: to be *up* in arms. **8** Into or in a place of safekeeping: to lay *up* provisions. **9** Completely; wholly: Houses were burned *up.* **10** In baseball, at bat. **11** In some sports: **a** In the lead. **b** Apiece; alike: said of a score. **12** So as to be compact, secure, etc.: Fold *up* the linen. **13** In or into view, existence, etc.: to bring *up* a subject; It will turn *up.* **14** *Naut.* Shifted to windward, as a tiller. **15** Into an aggregate number or quantity: Add *up* these figures. **16** To a source, conclusion, etc.: to follow *up* a rumor. —**be up against** *Informal* To meet with something to be dealt with. —**be up against it** *Informal* To be in trouble, usu. financial trouble. —**be up to 1** *Informal* To be doing or about to do: What is he *up to?* **2** To be equal to or capable of: I'm not *up to* playing golf today. **3** To be incumbent upon: It's *up to* her to help us. —*adj.* **1** Moving or directed upward. **2** In, at, or to a high level, condition, etc.: Is the river *up* today? **3** Above the ground or horizon: The jonquils are *up.* **4** In a raised or erect position or condition: The new school is finally *up.* **5** At an end: Your time is *up.* **6** *Informal* Going on; taking place: What's *up?* **7** *Informal* Informed; up-to-date: *up* on the newest movies. **8** Characterized by or showing agitation or excitement: Tempers are *up.* **9** In baseball, at bat. **10** *Informal* Alert; ready: to be *up* for a meeting. —**up and doing** Busy; bustling. —**up for 1** Being considered or presented for: *up for* reelection. **2** Charged with or on trial for: *up for* manslaughter. —*prep.* **1** To, toward, or at a higher point, position, etc., on or along: monkeys scampering *up* a tree; *up* the social ladder. **2** To or at a point farther above or along: The farm is *up* the road. **3** From the coast toward the interior of (a country). **4** From the mouth toward the source of (a river). —*n.* Usu. *pl.* **1** An ascent or upward movement. **2** A state of prosperity. —**on the up and up**

add, āce, câre, pälm; end, ēven; it, īce; odd, ōpen, ôrder; tōōk, pōōl; up, bûrn; ə = *a* in *above, u* in *focus;* yōō = *u* in *fuse;* oil; pout; check; go; ring; thin; this; zh, *vision.* < derived from; ? origin uncertain or unknown.

Slang Honest; genuine. **—ups and downs** Changes of fortune or circumstance. **—v. upped, up·ping** *Informal v.t.* 1 To increase; cause to rise: to *up* one's price. 2 To put, lift, or take up. **—vi.** 3 To rise. 4 To do quickly and abruptly: usu. followed by another verb: Then she *up* and left. [OE]

up-and-coming (up′ən·kum′ing) *adj.* Enterprising; energetic; promising.

u·pas (yōō′pəs) *n.* 1 A tall Asian and East Indian tree related to mulberry, with an acrid, milky, poisonous juice. 2 The sap of this tree, used to make arrow poison. [< Malay *(phon)* *upas* poison (tree)]

up·beat (up′bēt′; *for adj., also* up′bēt′) *n. Music* An unaccented beat, esp. the last beat in a measure. **—adj.** Optimistic; confident.

up·braid (up·brād′) *v.t* To reproach for some wrongdoing; scold. [< OE *up-* up + *bregdan* weave; twist] **—up·braid′er** *adj.* **—up·braid′ing·ly** *adv.* **—Syn.** admonish, chastise, rebuke, reprimand.

up·bring·ing (up′bring′ing) *n.* Rearing and training received during childhood.

up·chuck (up′chuk′) *Informal v.t. & v.i.* To vomit. **—n.** Vomit.

up·coun·try (up′kun′trē) *Informal n.* Inland country. **—adj.** In, from, or characteristic of inland places. **—adv.** (up′kun′trē) In, into or toward the interior.

up·date (up′dāt′) *v.t.* **·dat·ed, ·dat·ing** To bring up to date, as a textbook or manual.

up·end (up′end′) *v.t. & v.i.* To stand on end.

up·front (up′frunt′) *adj. Colloq.* Out in the open; unconcealed.

up·grade (up′grād′; *for v., also* up′grād′) *n.* An upward incline or slope. **—vt. ·grad·ed, ·grad·ing** To raise to a higher rank, responsibility, value, importance, etc., as an employee or job.

up·heav·al (up·hē′vəl) *n.* 1 The act of upheaving, or the state of being upheaved. 2 A violent change or disturbance, as of the established social order.

up·heave (up·hēv′) *v.* **·heaved** *or* **·hove, ·heav·ing** *v.t.* 1 To heave or raise up. **—v.i.** 2 To be raised or lifted.

up·hill (up′hil′) *adv.* Up or as up a hill or an ascent. **—adj.** 1 Going up hill or an ascent; sloping upward. 2 Attended with difficulty or exertion. 3 Situated on high ground. **—n.** (up′hil′) An upward slope; rising ground; a steep rise.

up·hold (up·hōld′) *v.t.* **·held, ·hold·ing** 1 To hold up; keep from falling or sinking. 2 To raise; lift up. 3 To aid, encourage, sustain, or confirm. **—up·hold′er** *n.*

up·hol·ster (up·hōl′stər) *v.t.* To fit, as furniture, with coverings, cushioning, springs, etc. [ult. < ME *upholder* tradesman] **—up·hol′ster·er** *n.*

up·hol·ster·y (up·hōl′stər·ē, ·strē) *n. pl.* **·ster·ies** 1 The materials used in upholstering. 2 The act, art, or business of upholstering.

UPI, U.P.I. United Press International.

up·keep (up′kēp′) *n.* 1 The act of keeping in good condition. 2 The state of being kept in good condition. 3 The cost of keeping in good condition.

up·land (up′lənd, ·land′) *n.* High land, esp. such land located far from the sea. **—adj.** Pertaining to or situated in an upland.

up·lift (up·lift′) *v.t.* 1 To lift up, or raise aloft; elevate. 2 To put on a higher plane, mentally, morally, culturally, or socially. **—n.** (up′lift′) 1 The act of lifting up raising. 2 An elevation to a higher mental, spiritual, moral, or social plane. 3 A social movement aiming to improve, esp. morally or culturally. 4 A brassiere designed to lift and support the breasts. **—up·lift′er** *n.*

up·most (up′mōst′) *adj.,* UPPERMOST.

up·on (ə·pon′, ə·pôn′) *prep.* On: *upon* the throne. **—adv.** On: The paper has been written *upon*. • *Upon* no longer differs in meaning from *on*, but it is sometimes preferred for reasons of euphony. When *upon* has its original meaning of *up + on*, it is written and pronounced as two words: *Let's go up on the roof.*

up·per (up′ər) *adj.* 1 Higher, as in location or position. 2 Higher in station, rank, authority, etc.: the *upper* house. 3 *Geol. Usu. cap.* Being a later division of a specified period or series. **—n.** 1 Something that is above another similar or related thing, part, etc., as an upper berth. 2 That part of a boot or shoe above the sole. 3 *Slang* Any of various drugs that stimulate the central nervous system, as amphetamines. **—on one's uppers** *Informal* 1 Having worn out the soles of one's shoes. 2 At the end of one's resources; destitute. [ME, orig. compar. of UP]

up·per·case (up′ər·kās′) *adj.* Of, in, or designating capital letters. **—v.t.** **·cased, ·cas·ing** To set in capital letters.

upper case 1 A case in which are kept capital letters and some auxiliary type for use in printing. 2 Capital letters.

upper class The socially or economically superior group in any society. **—up′per-class′** (-klas′, -kläs′) *adj.*

up·per·class·man (up′ər·klas′mən, -kläs′-) *n. pl.* **·men** (-mən) A junior or senior in a high school or college.

up·per·cut (up′ər·kut′) *n.* In boxing, a swinging blow directed upward, as to an opponent's jaw. **—v.t & v.i.** **·cut, ·cut·ting** To strike with an uppercut.

upper hand The advantage; control.

Upper House The branch, in a bicameral legislature, where membership is more restricted, as the U.S. Senate.

up·per·most (up′ər·mōst′) *adj.* Highest in place, rank, authority, importance, etc.; foremost. **—adv.** In the highest place, rank, importance, etc.

Upper Vol·ta (vol′tə) A republic of w Africa, 105,900 sq. mi., cap. Ouagadougou. • See map at AFRICA.

up·pish (up′ish) *adj. Informal* UPPITY. **—up′pish·ly** *adv.* **—up′pish·ness** *n.*

up·pi·ty (up′ə·tē) *adj. Informal* Arrogant; snobbish; haughty. **—up′pi·ti·ness** *n.*

up·raise (up·rāz′) *v.t.* **·raised, ·rais·ing** To lift up; elevate.

up·right (up′rīt′) *adj.* 1 Being in a vertical position; erect. 2 Righteous; just. **—n.** 1 The state of being upright: a post out of *upright*. 2 Something having an upright position, as a vertical timber. 3 An upright piano. 4 In a football, a goal post. **—adv.** In an upright position; vertically. [< OE *up-* up + *riht* right] **—up′right′ly** *adv.* **—up′right′ness** *n.*

upright piano A piano having the strings mounted vertically within a rectangular, upright case.

up·ris·ing (up′rī′zing) *n.* 1 The act of rising up; esp., a revolt or insurrection. 2 An ascent; upward slope; acclivity.

up·roar (up′rôr′, -rōr′) *n.* 1 A state of confusion, disturbance, excitement, tumult, etc. 2 A loud, boisterous noise; din. [< Du. *op-* up + *roeren* stir]

up·roar·i·ous (up·rôr′ē·əs, -rō′·rē-) *adj.* 1 Accompanied by or making uproar. 2 Very loud and boisterous. 3 Provoking loud laughter. **—up·roar′i·ous·ly** *adv.* **—up·roar′ous·ness** *n.*

up·root (up·rōōt′, -rŏŏt′) *v.t.* 1 To tear up by the roots. 2 To destroy utterly; eradicate. **—up·root′er** *n.*

up·set (up·set′) *v.* **·set, ·set·ting** *v.t.* 1 To overturn. 2 To throw into confusion or disorder. 3 To disconcert, derange, or disquiet. 4 To defeat (an opponent favored to win): The amateur team *upset* the professionals. **—v.i.** 5 To become overturned. **—adj.** (*also* up′set′) 1 Overturned. 2 Physically ill or mentally disturbed. **—n.** (up′set′) 1 The act of overturning. 2 A physical or emotional disorder. 3 A defeat of an opponent favored to win. **—up·set′ter** *n.*

up·shot (up′shot′) *n.* The outcome; result.

up·side (up′sīd′) *n.* The upper side or part.

upside down 1 So that the upper part is underneath: to turn a table *upside down.* 2 In or into disorder or confusion: to turn a room *upside down* looking for something.

up·si·lon (yōōp′sə·lon, up′sə·lon) *n.* The twentieth letter in the Greek alphabet (Υ, υ). [< Gk. *u* u + *psilon* simple]

up·stage (up′stāj′) *adj.* 1 Of or pertaining to the back half of a stage. 2 *Informal* Conceited; haughty; snobbish. **—adv.** Toward or at the back half of a stage. **—v.** (up′stāj′) **·staged, ·stag·ing** 1 To force (a fellow actor) to face away from the audience by moving or remaining upstage. 2 To try to outdo (someone), as in a professional or social encounter.

up·stairs (up′stârz′) *adj.* Of or on an upper story. **—n.** The part of a building above the ground floor; an upper story or stories. **—adv.** To or on an upper story.

up·stand·ing (up·stan′ding) *adj.* 1 Standing up; erect. 2 Honest, straightforward, etc. **—up·stand′ing·ness** *n.*

up·start (up′stärt′) *n.* A person who has suddenly risen from a humble position to one of consequence; esp., such

a person who behaves in a way that is presumptuous, arrogant, etc.

up·state (up′stāt′) *adj.* Of, from, or designating that part of a state lying outside, usu. north, of a principal city. — *n.* The outlying, usu. northern, sections of a state. —*adv.* In or toward the outlying or northern sections of a state. —**up′stat′er** *n.*

up·stream (up′strēm′) *adv. & adj.* Toward or at the upper part or source of a stream.

up·sweep (up′swēp′) *n.* 1 A sweeping up or upward. 2 A hairdo in which the hair is piled on the top of the head and held there by pins or combs.

up·swing (up′swing′) *n.* 1 A swinging upward. 2 An increase or improvement.

up·take (up′tāk′) *n.* 1 The act of lifting or taking up. 2 Mental comprehension; understanding.

up·thrust (up′thrust′) *n.* 1 An upward thrust. 2 A sharp upward movement of rock in the earth's crust.

up·tight (up′tīt′) *adj. Slang* Uneasy, anxious, or nervous. Also **up′-tight′, up tight.** —**up′tight′ness** *n.*

up-to-date (up′tə-dāt′) *adj.* 1 Extending to the present; including the latest information, data, etc.: an *up-to-date* census report. 2 Abreast of the latest fashions, ideas, outlook, etc. —**up′-to-date′ness** *n.*

up·town (up′toun′) *adj. & adv.* Of, in, to, or toward the upper part of a town or city. —*n.* An uptown area.

up·turn (up′tûrn′, up′tûrn′) *v.t.* To turn up or over. —*n.* (up′tûrn′) A turn upward, as to improved business conditions.

up·ward (up′wərd) *adv.* 1 In or toward a higher place, position, or part. 2 Toward a source or interior part. 3 In the upper parts. 4 To or toward a higher, greater, or better condition. Also **up′wards.** —**upward of** or **upwards of** Higher than or in excess of. —*adj.* Turned, directed toward, or located in a higher place. —**up′ward·ly** *adv.*

u·rae·mi·a (yoo-rē′mē-ə) *n.* UREMIA.

U·ral-Al·ta·ic (yoor′əl-al-tā′ik) *n.* A family of languages of Europe and N Asia, comprising the Uralic and Altaic subfamilies. —*adj.* Of or pertaining to these languages or the peoples speaking them.

U·ral·ic (yoo-ral′ik) *n.* A family of languages comprising the Finno-Ugric and Samoyedic subfamilies. —*adj.* Of or pertaining to this linguistic family. Also **U·ra·li·an** (yoo-rā′lē-ən).

U·ra·ni·a (yoo-rā′nē-ə) *Gk. Myth.* The Muse of astronomy.

u·ra·ni·um (yoo-rā′nē-əm) *n.* A heavy, radioactive, metallic element (symbol U), found only in combination and in association with radium, used in the generation of atomic energy. [< URANUS]

U·ra·nus (yoor′ə-nəs, yoor-ā′nəs) *Gk. Myth.* The son and husband of Gaea (Earth) and father of the Titans, Furies, and Cyclopes. —*n.* The planet of the solar system seventh in distance from the sun. • See PLANET. —**U·ra′ni·an** *adj.*

ur·ban (ûr′bən) *adj.* 1 Of, pertaining to, characteristic of, constituting, or including a city. 2 Living or located in a city or cities. [See URBANE.]

ur·bane (ûr-bān′) *adj.* Characterized by or having refinement, esp. in manner; polite; courteous; suave. [< L *urbs, urbis* a city] —**ur·bane′ly** *adv.* —**ur·bane′ness** *n.*

ur·ban·ism (ûr′bən-iz′əm) *n.* 1 Life in the cities. 2 The study of urban life. 3 The advocacy of living in a city. — **ur′ban·ist** *n.* —**ur′ban·is′tic** *adj.*

ur·ban·ite (ûr′bən-īt) *n.* One who lives in a city.

ur·ban·i·ty (ûr·ban′ə·tē) *n. pl.* **·ties** 1 The character or quality of being urbane. 2 *pl.* Urbane acts or behavior; courtesies, amenities, etc.

ur·ban·i·za·tion (ûr′bə-nə-zā′shən) *n.* 1 The act or process of urbanizing an area or a rural group of people. 2 The quality or state of being urbanized. *Brit. sp.* **·i·sa′tion.**

ur·ban·ize (ûr′bən-īz) *v.t.* **·ized, ·iz·ing** 1 To cause (an area) to assume the characteristics of a city. 2 To cause (people) to adopt an urban life style. *Brit. sp.* **·ise.**

ur·ban·ol·o·gy (ûr′bə-nol′ə-jē) *n.* The study of problems peculiar to cities. —**ur′ban·ol′o·gist** *n.*

urban renewal A program for rebuilding or replacing substandard housing and improving public facilities in distressed urban areas.

urban sprawl The uncontrolled spread of urban housing, shopping centers, etc., into rural or undeveloped areas close to a city.

ur·chin (ûr′chin) *n.* 1 A roguish, mischievous child. 2 A ragged street child. 3 HEDGEHOG. 4 SEA URCHIN. [< L *ericius* hedgehog]

Ur·du (oor′doo, oor-doo′, ûr′doo) *n.* An Indic language, a variety of Hindi that is the official language of Pakistan and is also spoken by some of the population of India.

-ure *suffix of nouns* 1 The act, process, or result of: *pressure.* 2 The condition of being: *exposure.* 3 The function, rank, or office of: *prefecture.* 4 The means or instrument of: *ligature.* [< L *-ura*]

u·re·a (yoo-rē′ə) *n.* A soluble colorless crystalline compound excreted in urine and also made synthetically; used in the making of plastics. [< L *urina* urine] —**u·re′al** *adj.*

u·re·mi·a (yoo-rē′mē-ə) *n.* A toxic condition of the blood due to the presence of substances ordinarily excreted by the kidneys. —**u·re′mic** *adj.*

u·re·ter (yoor′ə-tər, yoo-rē′-) *n.* The duct by which urine passes from the kidney to the bladder or the cloaca. [< Gk *ourein* urinate] —**u·re·ter·al** (yoo-rē′tə-rəl), **u·re·ter·ic** (yoor′ə-ter′ik) *adj.* • See KIDNEY.

u·re·thra (yoo-rē′thrə) *n. pl.* **·thrae** (-thrē), **·thras** The duct by which urine is discharged from the bladder and which, in males, carries the seminal discharge. [< Gk. *ouron* urine] —**u·re′thral** *adj.*

urge (ûrj) *v.* **urged, urg·ing** *v.t.* 1 To drive or force forward. 2 To plead with or entreat earnestly: He *urged* them to accept the plan. 3 To advocate earnestly: to *urge* reform. 4 To move or force to some course or action. —*v.i.* 5 To present or press arguments, claims, etc. 6 To exert an impelling or prompting force. —*n.* 1 A strong impulse to perform a certain act. 2 The act of urging. [< L *urgere* to drive, urge] —**Syn.** *v.* 1 impel, press. 2 exhort, importune.

ur·gen·cy (ûr′jən-sē) *n. pl.* **·cies** 1 The quality of being urgent; insistence: the *urgency* of her plea. 2 Something urgent: to prepare for any possible *urgencies.*

ur·gent (ûr′jənt) *adj.* 1 Requiring prompt attention; pressing; imperative. 2 Eagerly importunate or insistent. [< L *urgere* drive] —**ur′gent·ly** *adv.*

-urgy *combining form* Development of or work with a (specified) material or product: *metallurgy.* [< Gk. *ergon* work]

u·ric (yoor′ik) *adj.* Of, relating to, or derived from urine.

uric acid A white, odorless substance found in small quantity in urine.

u·ri·nal (yoor′ə-nəl) *n.* 1 A fixture for men's use in urination; also, a place containing such a fixture or fixtures. 2 A receptacle for urine.

u·ri·nal·y·sis (yoor′ə-nal′ə-sis) *n. pl.* **·ses** (-sēz) Chemical analysis of the urine.

u·ri·nar·y (yoor′ə-ner′ē) *adj.* Of or pertaining to urine or to the organs concerned in its production and excretion.

u·ri·nate (yoor′ə-nāt) *v.i.* **·nat·ed, ·nat·ing** To void or pass urine. —**u′ri·na′tion** *n.*

u·rine (yoor′in) *n.* A usu. fluid substance secreted by the kidneys of vertebrates and some invertebrates and containing nitrogenous and saline wastes. [< L *urina*]

u·ri·no·gen·i·tal (yoor′ə-nō·jen′ə-təl) *adj.* UROGENITAL.

urn (ûrn) *n.* 1 A vase, usu. having a foot or pedestal, variously used as a receptacle for the ashes of the dead, or ornament, etc. 2 A vase-shaped receptacle having a faucet, designed to make and serve tea, coffee, etc. [< L *urna*]

uro- *combining form* Urine; pertaining to urine or to the urinary tract: *urology.* [< Gk. *ouron* urine]

u·ro·gen·i·tal (yoor′ō·jen′ə·təl) *adj.* Of or pertaining to the urinary and genital organs and their functions.

Urn

---

add, āce, câre, pälm; end, ēven; it, īce; odd, ōpen, ôrder; took, pool; up, bûrn; ə = a in *above, u* in *focus;* yoo = u in *fuse;* oil; pout; check; go; ring; thin; this; zh, *vision.* < derived from; ? origin uncertain or unknown.

u·rol·o·gy (yōō·rol'ə·jē) *n.* The branch of medicine relating to the urogenital or urinary system. —**u·ro·log·ic** (yōōr'·ə·loj'ik) or **·i·cal** *adj.* —**u·rol'o·gist** *n.*

u·ros·co·py (yōō·ros'kə·pē) *n.* Examination of the urine, as for diagnosis. —**u·ro·scop·ic** (yōōr'ə·skop'ik) *adj.* —**u·ros'·co·pist** *n.*

Ur·sa Ma·jor (ûr'sə) *Astron.* The Great Bear, a large northern constellation containing seven conspicuous stars, including two which point to the polestar. [L]

Ursa Minor *Astron.* The Little Bear, a northern constellation including the polestar. [L]

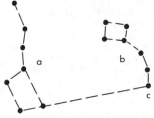

Ursa Major and Ursa Minor
a. Ursa Major. b. Ursa Minor.
c. Polaris.

ur·sine (ûr'sīn, -sin) *adj.* Of, pertaining to, or like a bear. [<L *ursus* bear]

ur·ti·car·i·a (ûr'tə·kâr'ē·ə) *n.* A skin eruption of systemic origin characterized by evanescent wheals and itching; hives. [<L *urtica* nettle] —**ur'ti·car'i·al, ur'ti·car'i·ous** *adj.*

Uru. Uruguay.

U·ru·guay (yōōr'ə·gwā, *Sp.* ōō'rōō·gwī) *n.* A republic of SE South America, 72,172 sq. mi., cap. Montevideo. —**U'ru·guay'an** *adj., n.* • See map at ARGENTINA.

us (us) *pron.* The objective case of WE. [<OE *ūs*]

US, U.S. United States.

USA, U.S.A. United States of America; United States Army.

us·a·ble (yōō'zə·bəl) *adj.* 1 Capable of being used. 2 That can be used conveniently. Also **use'a·ble.** —**us'a·ble·ness** *n.* —**us'a·bly** *adv.*

USAF, U.S.A.F. United States Air Force.

us·age (yōō'sij, -zij) *n.* 1 The act or manner of using; treatment. 2 Customary or habitual practice; custom; habit. 3 The accepted and established way of using words, speech patterns, etc.

USCG, U.S.C.G. United States Coast Guard.

use (yōōz) *v.* **used, us·ing** *v.t.* 1 To put into service: to *use* a hammer. 2 To borrow; avail oneself of: May I *use* your pen? 3 To put into practice or employ habitually: to *use* diligence in business. 4 To conduct oneself toward; treat: to *use* one badly. 5 To partake of: He does not *use* tobacco. 6 To take advantage of; exploit: to *use* one's friends. 7 To expend, exhaust, or consume: usu. with *up*. —*v.i.* 8 To be accustomed: used in the past tense with an infinitive: We *used* to go to the theater regularly. —*n.* (yōōs) 1 The act of using, or the state of being used. 2 Function: He has lost the *use* of his legs. 3 Way or manner of using: to make good *use* of one's time. 4 Habitual practice or employment; custom; usage. 5 The ability or right to use, or the privilege of using. 6 Advantage; benefit; usefulness. 7 The purpose for which something is used. 8 *Law* The benefit or profit of property to which legal title is vested in another in trust for the beneficiary. —**have no use for** 1 To have no need of. 2 To have dislike or contempt for. —**in use** Being used or occupied. —**make use of** To have occasion to use; use. —**put to use** To utilize; employ. [<L *usus*, pp. of *uti* to use] —**us'er** *n.*

used (yōōzd) *adj.* 1 That has been employed in some way. 2 SECONDHAND. 3 Accustomed; experienced. —**used to** (yōōst) Accustomed to; habituated.

use·ful (yōōs'fəl) *adj.* Capable of being used; serviceable; helpful. —**use'ful·ly** *adv.* —**use'ful·ness** *n.*

use·less (yōōs'lis) *adj.* Being of or having no use; serving no function. —**use'less·ly** *adv.* —**use'less·ness** *n.*

us·er-friend·ly (yōō'zər-frend'lē) *adj.* of a computer, program, software, etc., easy to use.

ush·er (ush'ər) *n.* 1 One who acts as doorkeeper, as of a court. 2 One who conducts persons to seats, etc., as in a church or theater. —*v.t.* 1 To act as an usher to; escort; conduct. 2 To precede as a harbinger; be a forerunner of. [<L *ostiarius* doorkeeper]

USM, U.S.M. United States Mail; United States Mint.

USMA, U.S.M.A. United States Military Academy.

USMC, U.S.M.C. United States Marine Corps; United States Maritime Commission.

USN, U.S.N. United States Navy.

USNA, U.S.N.A. United States Naval Academy.

USNG, U.S.N.G. United States National Guard.

USNR, U.S.N.R. United States Naval Reserve.

USO, U.S.O. United Service Organizations.

USS United States Ship, Steamer, or Steamship.

U.S.S. United States Senate.

USSR, U.S.S.R. Union of Soviet Socialist Republics.

usu. usual; usually.

u·su·al (yōō'zhōō·əl) *adj.* Such as occurs in the ordinary course of events; customary; common. [<L *usus* use] — **u'su·al·ly** *adv.* —**u'su·al·ness** *n.* —**Syn.** everyday, general, ordinary, prevalent.

u·su·fruct (yōō'zə·frukt, yōō'sə-) *n. Law* The right of using the fruits or profits of another's property. [<L *usus et fructus* use and fruit]

u·su·rer (yōō'zhər·ər) *n.* One who practices usury. [<L *usura* use, usury]

u·su·ri·ous (yōō·zhōōr'ē·əs) *adj.* 1 Practicing usury. 2 Of, relating to, or having the nature of usury. —**u·su'ri·ous·ly** *adv.* —**u·su'ri·ous·ness** *n.*

u·surp (yōō·sûrp', -zûrp') *v.t.* To seize and hold (an office, rights, powers, etc.) without right or legal authority; take possession of by force. [<L *usurpare* make use of, usurp]

u·sur·pa·tion (yōō'sər·pā'shən, -zər-) *n.* The act of usurping, esp. the unlawful seizure of sovereign power.

u·su·ry (yōō'zhər·ē) *n. pl.* **·ries** 1 The act or practice of lending money and charging interest that is excessive or unlawfully high. 2 Interest that is excessive or unlawfully high. [<L *usura* < *usus*, pp. of *uti* to use]

UT Utah (P.O. abbr.).

Ut. Utah.

u·ten·sil (yōō·ten'səl) *n.* A vessel, tool, implement, etc., serving a useful purpose, esp. for domestic or farming use. [<L *utensilis* fit for use]

u·ter·ine (yōō'tər·īn, -in) *adj.* 1 Of or pertaining to the uterus. 2 Born of the same mother, but having a different father. [<LL *uterinus* born of the same mother]

u·ter·us (yōō'tər·əs) *n. pl.* **u·ter·i** (yōō'tər·ī), **u·ter·us·es** The organ of a female mammal in which the fertilized ovum is deposited and develops until birth; womb. [L] • See OVARY.

u·til·i·tar·i·an (yōō·til'ə·târ'ē·ən) *adj.* 1 Of or pertaining to utility; esp., placing utility above beauty, the amenities of life, etc. 2 Of, pertaining to, or advocating utilitarianism. —*n.* An advocate of utilitarianism.

u·til·i·tar·i·an·ism (yōō·til'ə·târ'ē·ən·iz'əm) *n.* 1 The doctrine that holds usefulness to be the end and criterion of action. 2 The doctrine that the greatest happiness of the greatest number should be the sole end and criterion of all action.

u·til·i·ty (yōō·til'ə·tē) *n. pl.* **·ties** 1 Fitness for some desirable, practical purpose; usefulness. 2 Fitness to supply the needs of people. 3 Something useful. 4 A public service, as a telephone system, gas, water, etc. 5 A company that provides such a service. [<L *utilis* useful < *uti* use]

u·til·ize (yōō'təl·īz) *v.t.* **·ized, ·iz·ing** To make use of. *Brit. sp.* **u'til·ise.** —**u'til·i·za'tion, u'til·iz'er** *n.*

ut·most (ut'mōst) *adj.* 1 Of the highest or greatest degree. 2 Being at the farthest limit or most distant point; most remote; extreme. —*n.* The most possible. [<OE *ūtmost*]

U·to-Az·tec·an (yōō'tō·az'tek·ən) *n.* One of the chief linguistic stocks of North American Indians formerly occupying NW and SW U.S., Mexico, and Central America. —*adj.* Of or pertaining to this linguistic stock.

u·to·pi·a (yōō·tō'pē·ə) *n.* 1 Any state, condition, or place of ideal perfection. 2 A visionary, impractical scheme for social improvement. [<UTOPIA] —**u·to'pi·an** *adj., n.* —**u·to'pi·an·ism** *n.*

U·to·pi·a (yōō·tō'pē·ə) *n.* An imaginary island described as the seat of a perfect social and political life in the book by Sir Thomas More, published in 1516. [<Gk. *ou* not + *topos* a place] —**U·to'pi·an** *adj., n.*

u·tri·cle (yōō'tri·kəl) *n.* A small sac or cavity. [<L *uter* skin bag] —**u·tric·u·lar** (yōō·trik'yə·lər) *adj.*

ut·ter[1] (ut'ər) *v.t.* 1 To say, express, give out, or send forth,

as in words or sounds. **2** To put in circulation; esp., to deliver or offer (something forged or counterfeit). [< ME *out* say, speak out] —**ut′ter·er** *n.*

ut·ter² (ut′ər) *adj.* **1** Complete; absolute; total: *utter* misery. **2** Unqualified; final: an *utter* denial. [< OE *ūttra,* orig. compar. of *ūt* out] —**ut′ter·ly** *adv.*

ut·ter·ance (ut′ər·əns) *n.* **1** The act of uttering. **2** A manner of speaking. **3** A thing uttered.

ut·ter·most (ut′ər·mōst′) *adj. & n.* UTMOST.

U-turn (yōō′tûrn′) *n.* A complete turn which reverses the direction of movement, as of a vehicle on a road.

u·vu·la (yōō′vyə·lə) *n. pl.* **·las** or **·lae** (-lē) The pendent fleshy portion of the soft palate in the back of the mouth. [LL, dim. of *uva* grape] • See MOUTH.

u·vu·lar (yōō′vyə·lər) *adj.* **1** Pertaining to the uvula. **2** *Phonet.* Articulated with the back of the tongue near the uvula. —*n. Phonet.* A uvular sound.

ux. wife (L *uxor*).

ux·o·ri·ous (uk·sôr′ē·əs, -sō′rē-, ug·zôr′ē-, -zō′rē-) *adj.* Excessively devoted to or dominated by one's wife. [< L *uxor* wife] —**ux·o′ri·ous·ly** *adv.* —**ux·o′ri·ous·ness** *n.*

Uz·bek (ōōz′bek, uz′-) *n.* **1** A member of a Turkic people living in the Uzbek S.S.R. **2** The Turkic language of the Uzbeks.

V

V,v (vē) *n. pl.* **V's, v's, Vs, vs** (vēz) **1** The 22nd letter of the English alphabet. **2** Any spoken sound representing the letter *V* or *v.* **3** Something shaped like a V. **4** In Roman notation, the symbol for five. —*adj.* Shaped like a V.

V vanadium; vector; velocity; victory; volume.

V.,v. volt; volume.

v. valve; verb; verse; version; versus; vicar; village; vocative; voice; voltage; von.

VA Virginia (P.O. abbr.).

VA, V.A. Veterans Administration.

Va. Virginia.

vacan·cy (vā′kən·sē) *n. pl.* **·cies 1** The state of being vacant; emptiness. **2** An apartment, room, etc., that is available for rent. **3** An unoccupied post, place, or office.

va·cant (vā′kənt) *adj.* **1** Containing or holding nothing; empty. **2** Not lived in or occupied. **3** Not being used; free: a *vacant* hour. **4** Being or appearing without intelligence: a *vacant* stare. **5** Having no incumbent, officer, or possessor. [< L *vacans* prp. of *vacare* be empty] —**va′cant·ly** *adv.* —**va′cant·ness** *n.* —**Syn. 1** blank, void. **4** vapid, dull, vacuous, witless, obtuse, blank.

va·cate (vā′kāt, vā·kāt′) *v.* **·cat·ed, ·cat·ing** *v.t.* **1** To make vacant, as a dwelling, position, etc. **2** To set aside; annul. —*v.i.* **3** To leave an office, dwelling, place, etc. **4** *Informal* To go away; leave. [< L *vacare* be empty]

va·ca·tion (vā·kā′shən) *n.* A time set aside from work, study, etc., for recreation or rest; a holiday. —*v.i.* To take a vacation. [See VACATE.] —**va·ca′tion·er, va·ca′tion·ist** *n.*

vac·ci·nate (vak′sə·nāt) *v.* **·nat·ed, ·nat·ing** *v.t.* **1** To inoculate with a vaccine as a preventive or therapeutic measure; esp., to inoculate against smallpox. —*v.i.* **2** To perform the act of vaccination. —**vac′ci·na′tor** *n.*

vac·ci·na·tion (vak′sə·nā′shən) *n.* **1** The act or process of vaccinating. **2** A scar produced at the site of inoculation with a vaccine.

vac·cine (vak·sēn′, vak′sēn) *n.* **1** The virus of cowpox, as prepared for inoculation to produce immunity to smallpox. **2** Any modified virus or bacterium used to give immunity against a specific disease. [< L *vaccinus* pertaining to a cow] —**vac′ci·nal** (-sə·nəl) *adj.*

vac·il·late (vas′ə·lāt) *v.i.* **·lat·ed, ·lat·ing 1** To move one way and the other; waver. **2** To waver in mind; be irresolute. [< L *vacillare* waver] —**vac′il·la′tion** *n.* —**vac′il·la·to′ry** (-ə·lə·tô′rē, -tō′rē) *adj.* —**Syn. 1** fluctuate, oscillate, sway.

va·cu·i·ty (va·kyōō′ə·tē) *n. pl.* **·ties 1** The state of being a vacuum; emptiness. **2** Vacant space; a void. **3** Lack of intelligence; stupidity. **4** An inane or stupid thing, statement, etc. [< L *vacuus* empty]

vac·u·ole (vak′yōō·ōl) *n.* A small cavity within a cell containing air or fluid or food particles. [< L *vacuus* empty]

vac·u·ous (vak′yōō·əs) *adj.* **1** Having no contents; empty. **2** Lacking intelligence; blank. [< L *vacuus*] —**vac′u·ous·ly** *adv.* —**vac′u·ous·ness** *n.*

vac·u·um (vak′yōō·əm, -yōōm) *n. pl.* **·u·ums** or **·u·a** (-yōō·ə) **1** *Physics* A space devoid, or nearly devoid, of matter. **2** A reduction of the pressure in a space below atmospheric pressure. **3** A void; an empty feeling. **4** *Informal* A vacuum cleaner. —*v.t. & v.i. Informal* To clean with a vacuum cleaner. [L, neut. of *vacuus* empty]

vacuum bottle THERMOS.

vacuum cleaner A machine for cleaning floors, carpets, etc., by means of suction.

vacuum pump A pump designed to remove gas or air from a sealed space.

vacuum tube *Electronics* An electron tube containing a negligible amount of gas.

va·de me·cum (vā′dē mē′kəm) Anything carried for constant use, as a guidebook, manual, etc. [L, go with me]

vag·a·bond (vag′ə·bond) *n.* **1** One who wanders from place to place without visible means of support; a tramp. **2** A shiftless, irresponsible person. —*adj.* **1** Wandering; nomadic. **2** Having no definite residence; irresponsible. **3** Driven to and fro; aimless. [< L *vagus* wandering] —**vag′·a·bond′age, vag′a·bond′ism** *n.*

va·gar·y (vā′gə·rē, və·gâr′ē) *n. pl.* **·gar·ies** A wild fancy; extravagant notion. [< L *vagari* wander]

va·gi·na (və·jī′nə) *n. pl.* **·nas** or **·nae** (-nē) **1** The canal leading from the external genital orifice in female mammals to the uterus. **2** A sheath or sheathlike covering. [L, a sheath] —**vag·i·nal** (vaj′ə·nəl) *adj.*

va·gran·cy (vā′grən·sē) *n. pl.* **·cies 1** The condition of being a vagrant. **2** The offense of being a vagrant: arrested for *vagrancy.*

va·grant (vā′grənt) *n.* A person who wanders from place to place without a settled home or job and who exists usu. by begging or stealing; a tramp. —*adj.* **1** Wandering about aimlessly; wayward. **2** Pertaining to or characteristic of a vagrant. [< OF *wacrer* to walk, wander] —**va′grant·ly** *adv.* —**va′grant·ness** *n.*

vague (vāg) *adj.* **vagu·er, vagu·est 1** Lacking definiteness; not clearly stated: *vague* rumors; *vague* promises. **2** Indistinct; hard to perceive: *vague* shapes in the fog. **3** Not thinking or expressing oneself clearly. [< L *vagus* wandering] —**vague′ly** *adv.* —**vague′ness** *n.*

va·gus (vā′gəs) *n. pl.* **·gi** (-jī) *Anat.* Either of the pair of cranial nerves sending branches to the lungs, heart, stomach, and most of the abdominal viscera. Also **vagus nerve.** [L, wandering]

vain (vān) *adj.* **1** Having or showing excessive pride in oneself; conceited. **2** Unproductive; useless: *vain* efforts. **3** Without substantial foundation; unreal. —**in vain 1** To no purpose; without effect. **2** Irreverently: to take the Lord's name *in vain.* [< L *vanus* empty] —**vain′ly** *adv.* —**vain′ness** *n.* —**Syn. 1** boastful, egotistical, narcissistic.

vain·glo·ry (vān′glôr′ē, -glōr′-, vān·glôr′ē) *n.* **1** Excessive or groundless vanity; boastfulness. **2** Empty, showy pomp. [< Med. L *vana gloria* empty pomp, show] —**vain·glo′ri·ous** *adj.* —**vain·glo′ri·ous·ly** *adv.* —**vain·glo′ri·ous·ness** *n.*

val·ance (val′əns, vā′ləns) *n.* **1** A drapery hanging from the tester of a bedstead. **2** A short, full drapery across the top of a window. [Prob. < OF *avaler* descend] —**val′anced** *adj.* • See CANOPY.

vale[1] (vāl) n. VALLEY. [< L vallis]

va·le[2] (vā′lē) interj. Farewell. [L, lit., be in good health]

val·e·dic·tion (val′ə·dik′shən) n. 1 A bidding farewell. 2 VALEDICTORY. [< L valedicere say farewell]

val·e·dic·to·ri·an (val′ə·dik·tôr′ē·ən, -tō′rē-) n. A student, usu. the highest in scholastic rank, who delivers a valedictory at the graduating exercises of an educational institution.

val·e·dic·to·ry (val′ə·dik′tər·ē) adj. Pertaining to a leave-taking. —n. pl. ·ries A parting address, as by a member (ordinarily the first in rank) of a graduating class.

va·lence (vā′ləns) n. Chem. The combining capacity of an atom or radical as measured by the number of electrons gained or lost or shared in forming a bond with another atom or radical. [< L valens, pr.p. of valere be well, be strong]

val·en·tine (val′ən·tīn) n. 1 A card or small gift sent as a token of affection on Valentine's Day. 2 A sweetheart.

Valentine's Day February 14, a day observed in honor of St. Valentine, and on which valentines are sent to sweethearts, etc.

va·le·ri·an (və·lir′ē·ən) n. 1 Any of various plants with small pink or white flowers and a strong odor. 2 A sedative derived from the roots of some of these plants. [< Med. L valeriana]

val·et (val′it, val′ā, val·ā′) n. 1 A man's personal servant. 2 A manservant in a hotel who cleans and presses clothes. —v.t. & v.i. To act as a valet. [F < OF vaslet, varlet, dim. of vasal vassal]

val·e·tu·di·nar·i·an (val′ə·tyōō′də·nâr′ē·ən) n. 1 A chronic invalid. 2 A person unduly concerned about his health. —adj. 1 Infirm; ailing. 2 Unduly concerned about one's health. [< L valetudo, health, ill health < valere be well] —val′e·tu′di·nar′i·an·ism n.

Val·hal·la (val·hal′ə) n. Norse Myth. The great hall in which the souls of heroes, borne by the Valkyries, are received and feasted by Odin.

val·iant (val′yənt) adj. 1 Strong and intrepid; powerful and courageous. 2 Performed with valor; heroic. [< OF valoir be strong] —val′iant·ly adv. —val′i·an·cy or val′i·ance, val′iant·ness n.

val·id (val′id) adj. 1 Based on facts or evidence; sound: a valid argument. 2 Legally binding: a valid will. [< L validus powerful] —val′id·ly adv. —va·lid·i·ty (və·lid′ə·tē), val′id·ness n.

val·i·date (val′ə·dāt) v.t. ·dat·ed, ·dat·ing 1 To confirm by facts or authority. 2 To declare legally valid; legalize. —val′i·da′tion n.

va·lise (və·lēs′) n. A traveling bag; suitcase. [< Ital. valigia]

Val·kyr·ie (val·kir′ē, val′kir·ē) n. pl. ·ky·ries or ·ky·rie Norse Myth. One of the maidens who ride through the air and choose heroes from among those slain in battle, and carry them to Valhalla. Also **Val′kyr** (-kir). —**Val·kyr′i·an** adj.

val·ley (val′ē) n. 1 A long, wide area drained by a large river system: the Hudson valley. 2 Low land lying between mountains or hills. 3 Any hollow or depression shaped like a valley. [< L vallis]

val·or (val′ər) n. Marked courage; personal heroism; bravery. Brit. sp. val′our. [< L valere be strong] —val′or·ous adj. —val′or·ous·ly adv. —val′or·ous·ness n.

val·or·i·za·tion (val′ər·ə·zā′shən, -ī·zā′-) n. The maintenance by governmental action of an artificial price for any product. [< Pg. valor value] —val·or·ize (val′ə·rīz) v.t.

val·u·a·ble (val′yōō·ə·bəl, val′yə·bəl) adj. 1 Having financial worth, price, or value. 2 Very costly. 3 Worthy; estimable: a valuable friend. —n. Usu. pl. An article of value, as a piece of jewelry. —val′u·a·ble·ness n. —val′u·a·bly adv.

val·u·a·tion (val′yōō·ā′shən) n. 1 The act of estimating the value of something; evaluation. 2 Estimated value; appraisement. —val′u·a′tion·al adj.

val·ue (val′yōō) n. 1 The desirability or worth of a thing; merit: the value of self-discipline. 2 Something regarded as desirable, worthy, or right, as a belief or ideal. 3 Worth in money; market price. 4 A bargain. 5 Purchasing power: a decline in the value of the dollar. 6 Exact meaning: the value of a word. 7 Music The relative length of a tone. 8 Math. The number assigned to or represented by a symbol or expression. 9 In art, the relative lightness or darkness of a color. 10 The relation, as of light and shade, of one part to another in a work of art. —v.t. ·ued, ·u·ing 1 To assess; appraise. 2 To regard highly; prize. 3 To place a relative estimate of value upon: to value health above all else. [< L valere] —val′u·er n.

val·ue-add·ed tax (val′yōō·ad′id) A tax levied on each stage of a product's manufacture and marketing, from the raw material to the final retailer, the ultimate burden being placed on the consumer in the form of higher prices.

val·ued (val′yōōd) adj. 1 Highly esteemed: a valued friend. 2 Having a specified value: valued at ten dollars.

val·ue·less (val′yōō·lis) adj. Having no value; worthless. —val′ue·less·ness n.

valve (valv) n. 1 Mech. Any device used to block, direct, or otherwise control motion of a fluid. 2 Anat. A membranous structure inside a vessel or other organ, allowing fluid to flow in one direction only. 3 Zool. One of the parts of a shell, as of a clam, etc. 4 Bot. One of the parts into which a seed capsule splits. —v.t. valved, valv·ing To control the flow of by means of a valve. [< L valva leaf of a door]

val·vu·lar (val′vyə·lər) adj. 1 Pertaining to valves, as of the heart. 2 Having valves. 3 Having the form of a valve.

Gate valve in closed position (cross section)

va·moose (va·mōōs′) v.t. & v.i. ·moosed, ·moos·ing Slang To leave or depart hastily. Also **va·mose′** (-mōs′) [< Sp. vamos let us go]

vamp[1] (vamp) n. 1 The piece of leather forming the upper front part of a boot or shoe. • See SHOE. 2 Something added to give an old thing a new appearance. —v.t. 1 To provide with a vamp. 2 To repair or patch. [< OF avant before + pied foot] —vamp′er n.

vamp[2] (vamp) Slang n. A seductive woman who entices and exploits men. —v.t. & v.i. To seduce (a man) by acting as a vamp. [Short for VAMPIRE]

vam·pire (vam′pīr) n. 1 In folklore, a reanimated corpse that rises from its grave at night to suck the blood of persons who are asleep. 2 A person who preys upon those of the opposite sex; esp. a woman who degrades or impoverishes her lover. 3 A bat of tropical America that drinks the blood of mammals: also **vampire bat. 4** An insect- or fruit-eating bat mistakenly thought to suck blood: also **false vampire.** [< Slavic] —**vam′pir·ism** n.

van[1] (van) n. 1 A large covered wagon or truck for transporting furniture, household goods, etc. 2 Brit. A closed railway car for luggage, etc. [Short for CARAVAN]

van[2] (van) n. VANGUARD. [Short for VANGUARD]

va·na·di·um (və·nā′dē·əm) n. A rare, silver-white metallic element (symbol V), used to produce **vanadium steel,** a tough, resilient alloy. [L < ON Vanadīs, a name of the Norse goddess Freya]

Van Al·len belt (van al′ən) An extensive region of intense radiation consisting of charged atomic particles trapped by the earth's magnetic field and surrounding the earth in inner and outer belts. [< J. A. Van Allen, 1914–, U.S. physicist]

van·dal (van′dəl) n. One who engages in vandalism. [< VANDAL]

Van·dal (van′dəl) n. A member of a Germanic people that laid waste to Gaul, Spain, and North Africa in the fifth century and conquered Rome in 455.

van·dal·ism (van′dəl·iz′əm) n. Willful destruction or defacement of public or private property.

Van·dyke beard (van·dīk′) A small pointed beard. [< Anthony Van Dyck, 1599–1641, Flemish painter]

vane (vān) n. 1 A thin plate, pivoted on a vertical rod, to indicate the direction of the wind; a weathercock. 2 An arm or blade, as of a windmill, propeller, projectile, turbine, etc. 3 The web, or flat portion, of a feather. [< OE fana a flag] —**vaned** (vānd) adj.

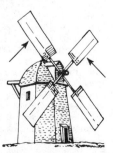

Windmill vanes

van·guard (van′gärd) *n.* **1** The forward part of an advancing army. **2** The foremost position in a movement, trend, etc. **3** The leaders of a movement, trend, etc. [< OF *avant* before + *garde* guard]

va·nil·la (və·nil′ə) *n.* **1** Any of a genus of tall climbing orchids of tropical America. **2** The long seed capsule of one species: also **vanilla bean**. **3** A flavoring extracted from these capsules or made synthetically. [< Sp. *vaina* sheath, pod] —**va·nil′lic** *adj.*

va·nil·lin (və·nil′in) *n.* The organic compound which gives vanilla flavoring its distinct odor and taste.

van·ish (van′ish) *v.i.* **1** To disappear; fade away. **2** To pass out of existence. [< L *evanescere* fade away] —**van′ish·er** *n.*

Vanilla
a. flower. b. bean.
c. pod.

vanishing point **1** In perspective, the point at which receding parallel lines appear to meet. • See PERSPECTIVE. **2** The point at which something approaches an end.

van·i·ty (van′ə·tē) *n. pl.* **·ties** **1** Excessive pride in one's talents, looks, possessions, etc. **2** Worthlessness; futility. **3** Something that is worthless or futile. **4** A low table with an attached mirror, for use while dressing the hair or putting on makeup. **5** VANITY CASE. [< L *vanus* empty, vain]

vanity case A small case holding face powder, rouge, puff, mirror, etc. Also **vanity box**.

van·quish (vang′kwish, van′-) *v.t.* **1** To defeat in battle; conquer. **2** To suppress or overcome (a feeling): to *vanquish* fear. **3** To defeat in any encounter. [< L *vincere*] — **van′quish·er** **van′quish·ment** *n.* —**Syn.** **1** beat, overcome, overpower, overwhelm, upset.

van·tage (van′tij) *n.* **1** Superiority, as over a competitor; advantage. **2** A position, place, situation, etc., that gives superiority or an advantage. [< OF *avantage* advantage]

vantage ground A position or condition which gives one an advantage.

van·ward (van′wərd) *adj. & adv.* Toward or in the front.

vap·id (vap′id, vā′pəd) *adj.* **1** Having lost sparkle and flavor. **2** Flat; insipid. [< L *vapidus* insipid] —**va·pid·i·ty** (və·pid′ə·tē), **vap′id·ness** *n.* —**vap′id·ly** *adv.*

va·por (vā′pər) *n.* **1** Moisture in the air; esp. visible floating moisture, as light mist. **2** Any cloudy substance in the air, as smoke. **3** The gaseous phase of any substance. **4** Something that is fleeting and unsubstantial. **5** A remedial agent applied by inhalation. —**the vapors** *Archaic* Depression of spirits. —*v.t.* **1** VAPORIZE. —*v.i.* **2** To emit vapor. **3** To pass off in vapor; evaporate. *Brit. sp.* **va′pour.** [< L *vapor* steam] —**va′por·er** *n.*

va·por·ize (vā′pə·rīz) *v.t. & v.i.* **·ized, ·iz·ing** To convert or be converted into vapor. —**va′por·i·za′tion** *n.*

va·por·iz·er (vā′pə·rī′zər) *n.* **1** One who or that which vaporizes. **2** A device for boiling water or a medicated liquid to form a vapor for inhalation.

va·por·ous (vā′pər·əs) *adj.* **1** Of or like vapor; misty. **2** Emitting or forming vapor. **3** Whimsical; fanciful. —**va·por·os·i·ty** (vā′pə·ros′ə·tē), **va′por·ous·ness** *n.*

va·que·ro (vä·kā′rō) *n. pl.* **·ros** (-rōz, *Sp.* -rōs) A herdsman; cowboy. [< Sp. *vaca* cow]

var. variant; variation; variety; various.

var·i·a·ble (vâr′ē·ə·bəl, var′-) *adj.* **1** Having the capacity of varying; alterable. **2** Having a tendency to change; not constant. **3** Having no definite value as regards quantity. **4** *Biol.* Prone to deviate from a type. —*n.* **1** That which is liable to change. **2** *Math.* **a** A quantity that may be equal to any one of a specified set of numbers. **b** A symbol representing such a quantity. **3** A shifting wind. —**var′i·a·bil′i·ty, var′i·a·ble·ness** *n.* —**var′i·a·bly** *adv.* —**Syn.** *adj.* **2** fluctuating, unstable, unsteady, wavering.

variable zone TEMPERATE ZONE.

var·i·ance (vâr′ē·əns, var′-) *n.* **1** The act of varying or the state of being varied. **2** Discrepancy; difference. **3** A dispute; quarrel. **4** A license or official permission to do something contrary to official regulations. —**at variance** Not in agreement; disagreeing.

var·i·ant (vâr′ē·ənt, var′-) *adj.* **1** Varying; differing, esp. differing from a standard or type. **2** *Archaic* Variable; changeable. —*n.* **1** A person or thing that differs from another in form only. **2** One of several different spellings, pronunciations, or forms of the same word.

var·i·a·tion (vâr′ē·ā′shən, var′-) *n.* **1** The act or process of varying; modification. **2** The extent to which a thing varies. **3** A thing changed in form from others of the same type. **4** *Music* A repetition of a theme or melody with changes in key, rhythm, harmony, etc. **5** *Biol.* Deviation from the typical structure or function. —**var′i·a′tion·al** *adj.*

var·i·col·ored (vâr′i·kul′ərd, var′-) *adj.* Variegated in color; parti-colored.

var·i·cose (var′ə·kōs) *adj.* **1** Abnormally dilated, as veins. **2** Having or resulting from varicose veins: *varicose ulcer*. [< L < *varix* a varicose vein] —**var′i·cos′i·ty** (-kos′ə·tē) *n.*

var·ied (vâr′ēd, var′-) *adj.* **1** Consisting of diverse sorts; assorted. **2** Altered; changed. —**var′ied·ly** *adv.*

var·i·e·gate (vâr′ē·ə·gāt′, var′-) *v.t.* **·gat·ed, ·gat·ing** **1** To mark with different colors; dapple; streak. **2** To make varied; diversify. —*adj.* VARIEGATED. [< L *varius* various + *agere* to drive, do] —**var′i·e·ga′tion** *n.*

var·i·e·gat·ed (vâr′ē·ə·gā′tid, var′-) *adj.* **1** Varied in color, as with streaks or blotches. **2** Having or exhibiting different forms, styles, or varieties.

va·ri·e·ty (və·rī′ə·tē) *n. pl.* **·ties** **1** Absence of sameness or monotony; diversity; variation; difference. **2** Sort; kind: a sweet *variety* of pickle. **3** A collection of diverse kinds; assortment: a *variety* of flowers. **4** A subdivision of a species. **5** Vaudeville: also **variety show.** [< L *varius* various]

va·ri·o·la (ver′ē·ō′lə, və·rī′ə·lə) *n.* SMALLPOX. [< L *varius* speckled] —**va·ri′o·lar** *adj.*

var·i·o·rum (vâr′ē·ôr′əm, -ō′rəm, var′-) *n.* **1** An edition of a work containing various versions of the text. **2** An edition of a work with notes by different critics or editors. —*adj.* Of or pertaining to such an edition. [< L *(cum notis) variorum* (with the notes) of various persons]

var·i·ous (vâr′ē·əs, var′-) *adj.* **1** Characteristically different from one another; diverse: *various* customs. **2** Being more than one and easily distinguishable; several: *various* friends. **3** Separate; particular; identifiable: He shook hands with *various* people. **4** Differing in nature or appearance; dissimilar. **5** Versatile; multifaceted. [< L *varius*] —**var′i·ous·ly** *adv.* —**var′i·ous·ness** *n.*

var·let (vär′lit) *n. Archaic* A scoundrel. [OF, a groom] — **var′let·ry** *n.*

var·mint (vär′mənt) *n. Regional* Any person or animal considered as troublesome, esp. vermin. [Alter. of VERMIN]

var·nish (vär′nish) *n.* **1** A solution of certain gums or resins in alcohol, linseed oil, etc., used to produce a shining, transparent coat on a surface. **2** The glossy, hard finish made by this solution when dry. **3** Any substance or finish resembling varnish. **4** Outward show; deceptive appearance. —*v.t.* **1** To cover with varnish. **2** To give a glossy appearance to. **3** To hide by a deceptive appearance; gloss over. [< Med. L *vernicium*, a kind of resin] —**var′nish·er** *n.*

var·si·ty (vär′sə·tē) *n. pl.* **·ties** *Informal* **1** *Brit.* UNIVERSITY. **2** The team that represents a university, college, or school in any competition. [Alter. of UNIVERSITY]

var·y (vâr′ē, var′-) *v.* **var·ied, var·y·ing** *v.t.* **1** To change the form, nature, substance, etc., of; modify. **2** To cause to be different from one another. **3** To diversify. **4** *Music* To systematically alter (a melody or other thematic element). —*v.i.* **5** To become changed in form, substance, etc. **6** To differ. **7** To deviate; depart: with *from.* **8** To alternate. **9** *Math.* To be subject to change. **10** *Biol.* To show variation. [< L *varius* various, diverse] —**var′y·ing·ly** *adv.*

vas (vas) *n. pl.* **va·sa** (vā′sə) *Biol.* A vessel or duct. [L, vessel, dish] —**va′sal** *adj.*

vas·cu·lar (vas′kyə·lər) *adj.* Of, pertaining to, or having vessels or ducts, as blood vessels, phloem tissue, etc. [< L *vasculum*, dim. of *vas* vessel] —**vas′cu·lar′i·ty** (-lar′ə·tē) *n.* —**vas′cu·lar·ly** *adv.*

---

vas def·er·ens (vas def′ər·ənz) The duct by which spermatozoa pass from the testicle to the penis. [<L *vas* vessel + *deferens* leading down]

vase (vās, vāz, väz) *n.* An urnlike vessel used as an ornament or for holding flowers. [<L *vas* vessel]

va·sec·to·my (və·sek′tə·mē) *n. pl.* **·to·mies** Surgical removal of a portion of the vas deferens, thus producing sterilization by preventing semen from reaching the seminal vesicles. [<VAS(O)- + -ECTOMY]

Vas·e·line (vas′ə·lēn, vas·ə·lēn′) *n.* PETROLATUM: a trade name.

vaso- *combining form* A vessel, esp. a blood vessel: *vasomotor.* [<L *vas* a vessel]

vas·o·mo·tor (vas′ō·mō′tər) *adj.* Producing contraction or dilation of blood vessels.

vas·sal (vas′əl) *n.* 1 In feudalism, a man who held land from a superior lord to whom he rendered, in return, military or other service. 2 A person who is in a position that is subordinate, lowly, servile, slavish, etc. —*adj.* Of or pertaining to a vassal. [<LL *vassus* a servant]

vas·sal·age (vas′əl·ij) *n.* 1 The condition, duties, and obligations of a vassal. 2 A position of servitude, dependence, or subjection.

vast (vast, väst) *adj.* 1 Of great extent; immense: a *vast* desert. 2 Very great in number, quantity, or amount. 3 Very great in degree, intensity, or importance. [<L, waste, empty, vast] —**vast′ly** *adv.* —**vast′ness** *n.* —Syn. 1, 2 enormous, extensive, huge, tremendous.

vat (vat) *n.* A large vessel, tub, or cistern, esp. for holding liquids during some process, as heating, fermenting, etc. —*v.t.* **vat·ted, vat·ting** To treat in a vat. [<OE *fæt*]

VAT value-added tax.

Vat. Vatican.

vat dye Any of a class of fast dyes in which the color develops, as by oxidation in air, subsequent to treatment of the fabric in a usu. colorless dye solution. —**vat′dyed′** *adj.*

Vat·i·can (vat′ə·kən) *n.* 1 The papal palace in Vatican City, Rome. 2 The papal government.

Vatican City A sovereign papal state included in Rome, 108.7 acres.

vau·de·ville (vô′də·vil, vōd′vil) *n.* A theatrical entertainment consisting of short dramatic sketches, songs, dances, acrobatic feats, etc.; a variety show. [<F *(chanson de) Vau de Vire* (song of) the valley of the Vire river (in Normandy)]

vault[1] (vôlt) *n.* 1 An arched roof or ceiling, usu. of masonry. 2 Any vaultlike covering, as the sky. An arched passage or room. 4 An underground room or compartment for storage. 5 A place for keeping valuables: bank *vault.* 6 A burial chamber. —*v.t.* 1 To cover with or as with a vault. 2 To construct in the form of a vault. [<OF *volte, vaute*]

Vaults
a. barrel. b. groined.

vault[2] (vôlt) *v.i.* 1 To leap, as over an object, by the use of one's hands on the object or by the use of a pole. —*v.t.* 2 To leap over. —*n.* 1 The act of vaulting. 2 A leap. [<OF *volter* to leap, gambol] —**vault′er** *n.*

vault·ing[1] (vôl′ting) *n.* The construction that forms a vault.

vault·ing[2] (vôl′ting) *adj.* 1 That leaps or leaps over. 2 Unduly confident or presumptuous. 3 Used for leaping and leaping over.

vaunt (vônt, vänt) *v.i.* 1 To boast. —*v.t.* 2 To boast of. —*n.* A brag or boast. [<LL *vanitare* brag <L *vanus* empty, vain] —**vaunt′er** *n.* —**vaunt′ing·ly** *adv.*

vb. verb; verbal.

V.C. Victoria Cross; Vietcong.

VD, V.D., v.d. venereal disease.

VDT Video (or visual) display terminal, a computer terminal with attached keyboard for the display of data; cathode-ray tube; terminal.

veal (vēl) *n.* 1 A calf, esp. one grown or suitable for food. 2 The flesh of a calf as food. [<L *vitellus,* dim. of *vitulus* calf]

vec·tor (vek′tər) *n.* 1 *Math.* A quantity defined by its magnitude and direction. 2 *Med.* An insect or other living carrier of pathogenic organisms from one host to another. [<L, carrier <*vehere* carry]

Ve·da (vā′də, vē′-) *n.* Any of four collections of ancient Hindu sacred writings. [Skt., knowledge] —**Ve·da·ic** (vi·dā′ik), **Ve′dic** *adj.* —**Ve·da·ism** (vā′də·iz′əm, vē′-) *n.*

V-E Day (vē′ē′) May 8, 1945, the official date of the Allied victory in Europe in World War II.

veep (vēp) *n. Slang* A vice president, esp. the vice president of the U.S. [<*V.P.,* abbr. of vice president]

veer (vir) *v.i.* 1 To shift or turn in position or direction: The wind *veered* to the east. 2 To shift from one opinion, belief, etc., to another. —*v.t.* 3 To change the direction of. —*n.* A change in direction. [<F *virer* to turn]

veer·y (vir′ē) *n. pl.* **veer·ies** A melodious tawny thrush that breeds in CEN. North America. [Prob. imit.]

veg. vegetable; vegetation.

Ve·ga (vē′gə, vā′-) *n.* A bright star in the constellation Lyra. [<Ar. *(al-Nasr) al-Waqi* the falling (vulture)]

veg·e·ta·ble (vej′ə·tə·bəl, vej′tə-) *n.* 1 A plant, esp. one cultivated for food. 2 The edible part of a plant, raw or cooked. 3 *Informal* A person who is mindless, apathetic, or passive. —*adj.* 1 Pertaining to plants, as distinct from animals: the *vegetable* kingdom. 2 Derived from, of the nature of, or resembling plants. 3 Made from or pertaining to edible vegetables: *vegetable* soup. 4 *Informal* Showing little mental activity; apathetic, passive, etc. [<L *vegetus* vigorous, lively < *vegere* be lively]

veg·e·tal (vej′ə·təl) *adj.* 1 Of or pertaining to plants or vegetables. 2 Pertaining to nonreproductive aspects of plant life.

veg·e·tar·i·an (vej′ə·târ′ē·ən) *n.* A person whose diet is made up of vegetables, fruits, grain, nuts, and sometimes animal products, as milk, eggs, etc. —*adj.* 1 Pertaining to or advocating the eating of only vegetable foods. 2 Made up exclusively of vegetables, fruits, grain, etc. —**veg′e·tar′i·an·ism** *n.*

veg·e·tate (vej′ə·tāt) *v.i.* **·tat·ed, ·tat·ing** 1 To grow, as a plant. 2 To live in a monotonous, passive way.

veg·e·ta·tion (vej′ə·tā′shən) *n.* 1 The process or condition of vegetating. 2 Plant life in the aggregate. —**veg′e·ta′tion·al** *adj.*

veg·e·ta·tive (vej′ə·tā′tiv) *adj.* 1 Of or pertaining to vegetation and plant growth. 2 Growing or capable of growing as plants; productive. 3 VEGETABLE (def. 4). 4 Concerned with nonreproductive life processes.

ve·he·ment (vē′ə·mənt) *adj.* 1 Arising from or marked by strong feeling or passing. 2 Acting with great force; violent. [<L *vehemens, -entis* impetuous, rash] —**ve′he·mence, ve′he·men·cy** *n.* —**ve′he·ment·ly** *adv.* —Syn. 1 ardent, fervent, zealous, fierce. 2 energetic, forceful, intense, powerful.

ve·hi·cle (vē′ə·kəl, vē′hi-) *n.* 1 Any device for carrying or transporting persons or things, as a car, spacecraft, etc. 2 A neutral medium for administering a medicine, etc. 3 The medium with which pigments are mixed in painting. 4 Any means by which thoughts or ideas are transmitted or communicated. [<L *vehiculum* < *vehere* to carry, ride] —**ve·hic·u·lar** (vi·hik′yə·lər) *adj.*

veil (vāl) *n.* 1 A piece of thin and light fabric, worn over the face or head for concealment, protection, or ornament. 2 A piece of cloth, as a curtain, that covers, conceals, etc. 3 Anything that conceals or covers. —**take the veil** To become a nun. —*v.t.* 1 To cover with a veil. 2 To conceal, cover, hide, disguise, etc. [<L *velum* piece of cloth, sail] —**veil′er** *n.*

veil·ing (vā′ling) *n.* 1 The act of covering with a veil. 2 Material for veils. 3 A veil.

vein (vān) *n.* 1 Any of the tubular vessels that convey blood to the heart. 2 One of the radiating supports of an insect's wing. 3 One of the slender vascular bundles that form the framework of a leaf. 4 LODE. 5 A long, irregular, colored streak, as in wood, marble, etc. 6 A distinctive tendency or disposition. —*v.t.* 1 To furnish or fill with veins. 2 To streak or ornament with veins. 3 To extend over or throughout as veins. [<L *vena* blood vessel]

Veining of maple leaf

veined (vānd) *adj.* **1** Having veins, esp. many veins. **2** Marked with streaks of another color: *veined* marble.

vein·ing (vā′ning) *n.* **1** A vein or network of veins. **2** A streaked or veined surface.

vein·let (vān′lit) *n.* A small vein.

ve·lar (vē′lər) *adj.* **1** Of or pertaining to a velum, esp. the soft palate. **2** *Phonet.* Formed with the back of the tongue touching or near the soft palate, as (k) in *cool.* —*n. Phonet.* A velar sound. [< L *velum* sail, curtain]

veld (velt, felt) *n.* In South Africa, open country having few shrubs or trees. Also **veldt.** [< MDu. *velt* field]

vel·lum (vel′əm) *n.* **1** Fine parchment made from the skins of calves; used for expensive binding, printing, etc. **2** A manuscript written on vellum. **3** Paper or cloth made to resemble vellum. [< OF *veel, viel* calf]

ve·loc·i·pede (və·los′ə·pēd) *n.* **1** An early form of bicycle or tricycle. **2** A child's tricycle. [< L *velox* swift + -PEDE]

ve·loc·i·ty (və·los′ə·tē) *n. pl.* **·ties** **1** Quickness of motion; speed; swiftness. **2** *Physics* A vector representing the rate of change of position of a body. [< L *velox* swift]

ve·lour (və·lŏŏr′) *n. pl.* **·lours** **1** A soft, velvetlike, cotton or wool fabric having a short, thick pile. **2** A type of felt with a velvety nap, used esp. for hats. Also **ve·lours** (və·lŏŏr′. [See VELURE.]

ve·lum (vē′ləm) *n. pl.* **·la** (-lə) **1** SOFT PALATE. **2** A thin membranous covering or partition. [L, veil]

ve·lure (və·l ̇yŏŏr′) *n. Archaic* A heavy fabric resembling velvet, formerly used for hangings, etc. [< F *velours* < L *villosus* shaggy]

vel·vet (vel′vit) *n.* **1** A fabric of silk, rayon, nylon, etc., having on one side a short, smooth pile. **2** Something resembling velvet. **3** *Slang* Unexpected profit or gain. —*adj.* **1** Made of velvet. **2** Smooth and soft to the touch like velvet. [Ult. < L *villus* shaggy hair] —**vel′vet·y** *adj.*

vel·vet·een (vel′və·tēn′) *n.* **1** A fabric, usu. of cotton, with a short, close pile like velvet. **2** Clothes, esp. slacks, made of velveteen.

Ven. Venerable; Venice; Venus.

ve·na ca·va (vē′nə kā′və) *pl.* **ve·nae ca·vae** (vē′nē kā′vē) Either of the two great veins that deliver blood to the right auricle of the heart. [< L, hollow vein] • See HEART.

ve·nal (vē′nəl) *adj.* **1** Capable of being corrupted or bribed. **2** Characterized by corruption or bribery. [< L *venum* sale] —**ve·nal·i·ty** (vē·nal′ə·tē) *n.* —**ve′nal·ly** *adv.*

ve·na·tion (ve·nā′shən, vē-) *n.* **1** Veins collectively. **2** NERVATION. [< L *vena* a vein]

vend (vend) *v.t.* **1** To sell, as by peddling. **2** To sell by means of a vending machine. **3** To give expression to in public —*v.i.* **4** To sell merchandise. [< L *vendere*] —**Syn.** *v.t.* **1** dispense, hawk, market, peddle.

ven·dee (ven·dē′) *n.* The person or party to whom something is sold.

ven·det·ta (ven·det′ə) *n.* Private warfare or feud, as in revenge for a murder, injury, etc. [< L *vindicta* vengeance]

vend·i·ble (ven′də·bəl) *adj.* Salable; marketable. —*n.* A thing for sale. —**vend′i·bil′i·ty, vend′i·ble·ness** *n.* —**vend′i·bly** *adv.*

vending machine A machine that makes candy, stamps, etc., available when a coin is inserted.

ven·dor (ven′dər) *n.* **1** One who vends; seller. **2** VENDING MACHINE. Also **vender.**

ve·neer (və·nir′) *n.* **1** A thin layer, as of choice wood, upon a cheaper surface. **2** Mere surface or outside show: a *veneer* of politeness. —*v.t.* **1** To cover (a surface) with veneers. **2** To conceal, as something disagreeable or coarse, with an attractive and deceptive surface. [< G *furnieren* inlay < F *fournir* furnish] —**ve·neer′er** *n.*

ven·er·a·ble (ven′ər·ə·bəl) *adj.* Meriting or commanding veneration because of dignity, age, religious or historical associations, etc. [< L *venerari* revere] —**ven′er·a·bil′i·ty, ven′er·a·ble·ness** *n.* —**ven′er·a·bly** *adv.*

ven·er·ate (ven′ə·rāt) *v.t.* **·at·ed, ·at·ing** To regard with respect and deference; revere. [< L *venerari* revere]

ven·er·a·tion (ven′ə·rā′shən) *n.* **1** Profound respect combined with awe. **2** The act of worshiping; worship.

ve·ne·re·al (və·nir′ē·əl) *adj.* **1** Pertaining to or proceeding from sexual intercourse. **2** Communicated by sexual relations with an infected person: a *venereal* disease. **3** Pertaining to or curative of diseases so communicated. **4** Infected with syphilis, gonorrhea, or other venereal disease. [< L *Venus* goddess of love] —**ve·ne′re·al·ly** *adv.*

venereal disease Any of several diseases transmitted by sexual intercourse, as syphilis, gonorrhea, etc.

ven·er·y[1] (ven′ər·ē) *n.* The pursuit of sexual gratification. [< L *Venus*, goddess of love]

ven·er·y[2] (ven′ər·ē) *Archaic n. pl.* **·er·ies** The hunting of game; the chase. [< L *venari* to hunt]

Ve·ne·tian (və·nē′shən) *adj.* Pertaining to Venice or to its people. —*n.* A citizen or inhabitant of Venice.

Venetian blind A flexible window screen having movable, overlapping slats so fastened on webbing or tape as to exclude or admit light.

Ven·e·zue·la (ven′ə·zwā′lə, -zōō·ē′lə) *n.* A republic of N South America, 352,143 sq. mi, cap. Caracas. —**Ven′e·zue′lan** *adj., n.*

ven·geance (ven′jəns) *n.* The infliction of a deserved penalty; retributive punishment. —**with a vengeance 1** With great force or violence. **2** Extremely; to an unusual extent. [< L *vindicare* defend, avenge]

venge·ful (venj′fəl) *adj.* Seeking to inflict vengeance; vindictive. —**venge′ful·ly** *adv.* —**venge′ful·ness** *n.*

ve·ni·al (vē′nē·əl, vēn′yəl) *adj.* So slight or trivial as to be overlooked, as a fault. [< L *venia* forgiveness, mercy] —**ve′ni·al′i·ty** (-al′ə·tē), **ve′ni·al·ness** *n.* —**ve′ni·al·ly** *adv.* —**Syn.** excusable, forgivable, pardonable.

ve·ni·re (vi·nī′rē) *n. Law* A panel of people from which a jury is selected. [< L *venire facias* that you cause to come]

ve·ni·re·man (vi·nī′rē·mən) *n. pl.* **·men** (-mən) A member of a venire.

ven·i·son (ven′ə·zən, -sən) *n.* The flesh of a wild animal, esp. a deer, used for food. [< L *venari* to hunt]

ve·ni, vi·di, vi·ci (vā′nē, vē′dē, vē′chē; wā′nē, wē′dē, wē′kē) *Latin* I came, I saw, I conquered: Julius Caesar's report to the Roman Senate of a victory.

ven·om (ven′əm) *n.* **1** The poison secreted by certain reptiles, insects, etc., which is transferred to a victim by a bite or sting. **2** Ill will; spite. [< L *venenum* poison] —**Syn. 2** hate, malice, rancor, spitefulness.

ven·om·ous (ven′əm·əs) *adj.* **1** Able to give a poisonous sting. **2** Malicious; spiteful. —**ven′om·ous·ly** *adv.* —**ven′om·ous·ness** *n.*

ve·nous (vē′nəs) *adj.* **1** Of, pertaining to, contained, or carried in a vein or veins. **2** Designating the blood carried by the veins back to the heart and lungs. **3** Marked with or having veins: also **ve′nose.** [< L *vena* vein] —**ve′nous·ly** *adv.* —**ve·nos·i·ty** (vē·nos′ə·tē, və-), **ve′nous·ness** *n.*

vent (vent) *n.* **1** An outlet; means of escape. **2** An opening for the passage of liquids, gases, etc. **3** A slit in a garment, as a coat. **4** *Zool.* An opening through which wastes are eliminated. —**give vent to** To utter or express: to *give vent* to one's anger. —*v.t.* **1** To give expression to. **2** To permit to escape at a vent, as a gas. **3** To make a vent in. [< OF < *fendre* cleave < L *findere* split]

ven·ti·late (ven′tə·lāt) *v.t.* **·lat·ed, ·lat·ing** **1** To produce a free circulation of air in, as by means of open windows, doors, etc. **2** To provide with a vent. **3** To expose to examination and discussion. **4** To oxygenate, as blood. [< L *ventus* wind] —**ven′ti·la′tion** *n.* —**ven′ti·la′tive** *adj.*

ven·ti·la·tor (ven′tə·lā′tər) *n.* **1** One who or that which ventilates. **2** A device or opening for replacing stale air with fresh air.

ven·tral (ven′trəl) *adj.* Toward, near, in, or on the abdomen. [< L *venter, ventris* belly] —**ven′tral·ly** *adv.*

ven·tri·cle (ven′trə·kəl) *n.* Any cavity in the body, esp. either of the two lower chambers of the heart, from which blood is forced into the arteries. [< L *venter, ventris* belly] —**ven·tric·u·lar** (-trik′yə·lər) *adj.* • See HEART.

---

add, āce, câre, pälm; end, ēven; it, īce; odd, ōpen, ôrder; tŏŏk, pōōl; up, bûrn; ə = *a* in *above, u* in *focus;* yōō = *u* in *fuse;* oil; pout; check; go; ring; thin; this; zh, *vision.* < derived from; ? origin uncertain or unknown.

ven·tril·o·quism (ven·tril′ə·kwiz′əm) *n.* The art of speaking in such a way that the sound seems to come from some source other than the person speaking. Also **ven·tril′·o·quy** (-kwē). [< L *venter* belly + *loqui* speak] —**ven·tri·lo·qui·al** (ven′trə·lō′kwē·əl), **ven·tril′o·quis′tic** *adj.* —**ven′tril·o′·qui·al·ly** *adv.* —**ven·tril′o·quist** *n.* —**ven·tril′o·quize′** (-kwīz) (·quized, ·quiz·ing) *v.i. & v.t.*

ven·ture (ven′chər) *v.* **·tured, ·tur·ing** *v.t.* **1** To expose to chance or risk; stake. **2** To run the risk of. **3** To express at the risk of denial or refutation: to *venture* a suggestion. **4** To place or send on a chance, as in a speculative investment. —*v.i.* **5** To take risk in going, coming, etc.: to *venture* into deep water. —*n.* **1** A risk; hazard. **2** An undertaking attended with risk. **3** That which is ventured, esp. property risk. —**at a venture** At random; haphazardly. [Alter. of ADVENTURE] —**ven′tur·er** *n.*

ven·ture·some (ven′chər·səm) *adj.* **1** Bold; daring. **2** Involving hazard; risky. —**ven′ture·some·ly** *adv.* —**ven′ture·some·ness** *n.*

ven·tur·ous (ven′chər·əs) *adj.* **1** Adventurous; bold. **2** Hazardous; risky; dangerous. —**ven′tur·ous·ly** *adv.* —**ven′·tur·ous·ness** *n.*

ven·ue (ven′yōō) *n. Law* **1** The place or neighborhood where a crime is committed or a cause of action arises. **2** The county or political division from which the jury must be summoned and in which the trial must be held. — **change of venue** The change of the place of trial, for good cause shown, from one county to another. [< OF *venir* come]

Ve·nus (vē′nəs) *Rom. Myth.* The goddess of love and beauty. —*n.* **1** A beautiful woman. **2** The planet of the solar system second in distance from the sun. • See PLANET.

Venus fly·trap (flī′trap′) An insectivorous plant of the SE U.S., with a basal rosette of leaves that entrap anything that touches certain sensitive hairs on their surface. Also **Ve′nus′s-fly′trap** (vē′nəs·iz-).

ver. verse(s); version.

ve·ra·cious (və·rā′shəs) *adj.* **1** Speaking the truth; truthful. **2** True; accurate. [< L *verus* true] —**ve·ra′cious·ly** *adv.* —**ve·ra′·cious·ness** *n.*

Venus flytrap

ve·rac·i·ty (və·ras′ə·tē) *n. pl.* **·ties 1** Honesty; truthfulness. **2** Accuracy; trueness. **3** That which is true; truth. [< L *verax*] — **Syn. 1** candor, frankness, integrity.

ve·ran·da (və·ran′də) *n.* An open porch, usu. roofed, along one or more sides of a building. Also **ve·ran′dah.** [< Pg. *varanda* railing, balustrade]

verb (vûrb) *n. Gram.* **1** One of a class of words which express existence, action, or occurrence, or that function as a copula or an auxiliary. **2** Any word or construction functioning similarly. [< L *verbum* word]

ver·bal (vûr′bəl) *adj.* **1** Of, in, or pertaining to words: a *verbal* contract; a *verbal* image. **2** Of, pertaining to, or concerned with words rather than the ideas they convey. **3** Word for word; verbatim; literal: a *verbal* translation. **4** *Gram.* **a** Partaking of the nature of or derived from a verb: a *verbal* noun. **b** Used to form verbs: a *verbal* prefix. **5** *Informal* Adept at using words, as in choice or range of vocabulary: She's very *verbal* for her age. —*n. Gram.* A noun directly derived from a verb, in English often having the form of the present participle, as, "There shall be *weeping* and *wailing* and *gnashing* of teeth"; also, an infinitive used as a noun, as, "*To err* is human": also **verbal noun.** [< L *verbum* word] —**ver′bal·ly** *adv.* • See ORAL.

ver·bal·ism (vûr′bəl·iz′əm) *n.* **1** A verbal phrase or expression. **2** A meaningless form of words; verbiage.

ver·bal·ist (vûr′bəl·ist) *n.* **1** One who is skilled in the use and meanings of words. **2** A person overly concerned with words rather than facts or concepts.

ver·bal·ize (vûr′bəl·īz) *v.* **·ized ·iz·ing** *v.t.* **1** *Gram.* To change (a noun, etc.) into a verb. **2** To express in words. —*v.i.* **3** To speak or write verbosely. —**ver′bal·i·za′tion, ver′bal·iz′er** *n.*

ver·ba·tim (vər·bā′tim) *adj. & adv.* In the exact words; word for word. [< L *verbum* word]

ver·be·na (vər·bē′nə) *n.* Any of a genus of plants having

spikes of showy, often fragrant flowers. [< L, foliage, vervain]

ver·bi·age (vûr′bē·ij) *n.* **1** Use of too many words. **2** Manner of verbal expression. [< F *verbe* word]

ver·bose (vər·bōs′) *adj.* Using or containing an unnecessary number of words; wordy. [< L *verbum* word] —**ver·bose′ly** *adv.* —**ver·bose′ness, ver·bos′i·ty** (-bos′ə·tē) *n.* — **Syn.** garrulous, long-winded, prolix.

ver·bo·ten (vər·bōt′n, fər-) *adj. German* Forbidden.

ver·dant (vûr′dənt) *adj.* **1** Green with vegetation; fresh. **2** Immature in experience. [< F *verdoyer* grow green] — **ver′dan·cy** *n.* —**ver′dant·ly** *adv.*

ver·dict (vûr′dikt) *n.* **1** The decision of a jury in an action. **2** A conclusion expressed; an opinion. [< L *vere dictum* truly said]

ver·di·gris (vûr′də·grēs, -gris, -grē) *n.* **1** A green or greenish blue acetate of copper obtained by treating copper with acetic acid. **2** The blue-green crust formed by corrosion of copper, bronze, or brass in air, sea water, etc. [< OF *vert de Grece*, lit., green of Greece]

ver·dure (vûr′jər) *n.* **1** The fresh greenness of growing vegetation. **2** Green vegetation. [< F *verd* green]

verge¹ (vûrj) *n.* **1** The extreme edge; brink: on the *verge* of bankruptcy. **2** A bounding or enclosing line surrounding something. —*v.i.* **verged, verg·ing 1** To be contiguous or adjacent. **2** To form the limit or verge. [< L *virga* twig]

verge² (vûrj) *v.i.* **verged, verg·ing 1** To come near; approach: a remark *verging* on rudeness. **2** To tend; incline. [< L *vergere* to bend, turn]

ver·i·fi·ca·tion (ver′ə·fə·kā′shən) *n.* **1** The act of verifying, or the state of being verified. **2** A proof or confirmation, as by examination. —**ver′i·fi·ca′tive** *adj.*

ver·i·fy (ver′ə·fī) *v.t.* **·fied, ·fy·ing 1** To prove to be true or accurate; confirm. **2** To test the accuracy or truth of. **3** *Law* To affirm under oath. [< L *verus* true + *facere* make] —**ver′i·fi′er** *n.* —**Syn. 1** authenticate, corroborate, substantiate. **2** ascertain.

ver·i·ly (ver′ə·lē) *adv.* In truth; certainly. [< VERY]

ver·i·sim·i·lar (ver′ə·sim′ə·lər) *adj.* Appearing or seeming to be true; likely; probable. [< L *verus* true + *similis* like] —**ver′i·sim′i·lar·ly** *adv.*

ver·i·si·mil·i·tude (ver′ə·si·mil′ə·tyōōd) *n.* **1** Appearance of truth; likelihood. **2** That which resembles truth. [< L *verisimilitudo*]

ver·i·ta·ble (ver′ə·tə·bəl) *adj.* Genuine; true; real. [< F *vérité* truth] —**ver′i·ta·ble·ness** *n.* —**ver′i·ta·bly** *adv.*

ver·i·ty (ver′ə·tē) *n. pl.* **·ties 1** Truth; correctness. **2** A true statement; a fact. [< L *veritas* truth < *verus* true]

vermi- *combining form* A worm; of or related to a worm: *vermicide*. [< L *vermis* a worm]

ver·mi·cel·li (vûr′mə·chel′ē, -sel′ē) *n.* A food paste made into slender wormlike cords thinner than spaghetti. [Ital., lit., little worms]

ver·mi·cide (vûr′mə·sīd) *n.* Any substance that kills worms, esp. a drug destructive of intestinal worms. — **ver′mi·cid′al** *adj.*

ver·mi·form (vûr′mə·fôrm) *adj.* Like a worm in shape.

vermiform appendix A slender, wormlike sac protruding from the large intestine. • See INTESTINE.

ver·mi·fuge (vûr′mə·fyōōj′) *n.* Any remedy that destroys intestinal worms. [< L *vermis* a worm + *fugare* expel]

ver·mil·ion (vər·mil′yən) *n.* **1** A brilliant, durable red pigment obtained from cinnabar or made synthetically. **2** An intense orange-red color. —*adj.* Of a bright orange-red color. —*v.t.* To color with vermilion. [< OF *vermeil*]

ver·min (vûr′min) *n. pl.* **·min 1** Noxious small animals or parasitic insects, as lice, worms, mice, etc. **2** *Brit.* Certain animals injurious to game, as weasels, owls, etc. **3** A repulsive person or persons. [< L *vermis* a worm] —**ver′min·ous** *adj.* —**ver′min·ous·ly** *adv.* —**ver′min·ous·ness** *n.*

ver·mouth (vər·mōōth′) *n.* A fortified white wine flavored with aromatic herbs. [< G *Wermuth* wormwood]

ver·nac·u·lar (vər·nak′yə·lər) *n.* **1** The native language of a locality. **2** The common daily speech of any people. **3** The specialized vocabulary of a profession or trade. **4** An idiomatic word or phrase. —*adj.* **1** Belonging to one's native land; indigenous: said of a language, idiom, etc. **2** Using the colloquial native tongue: *vernacular* poets. **3** Written in the language indigenous to a people: a *vernacu-*

lar translation of the Bible. [< L *vernaculus* domestic, native] **—ver·nac'u·lar·ly** *adv.*

ver·nal (vûr'nəl) *adj.* 1 Belonging to, appearing in, or appropriate to spring. 2 Youthful; fresh. [< L *vernus* belonging to spring] **—ver'nal·ly** *adv.*

vernal equinox The equinox that occurs on or about March 21.

ver·ni·er (vûr'nē·ər) *n.* A small, movable, auxiliary scale for obtaining fractional parts of the subdivisions of a main scale. Also **vernier scale.** [< Pierre *Vernier,* 1580–1637, French mathematician]

Ver·o·nal (ver'ə·nəl) *n.* BARBITAL: a trade name.

ve·ron·i·ca (və·ron'i·kə) *n.* SPEEDWELL. [< St. *Veronica,* a legendary follower of Christ]

ver·sa·tile (vûr'sə·til, -tīl) *adj.* 1 Having many aptitudes or talents. 2 Having many uses: a *versatile* fabric. 3 Movable in more than one direction, as the toe of a bird. 4 *Bot.* Turning about freely on the support to which it is attached: said of an anther. [< L *versare,* freq. of *vertere* turn] **—ver'sa·tile·ly** *adv.* **—ver'sa·til'i·ty** (-til'ə·tē) *n.*

verse (vûrs) *n.* 1 A single line of a poem. 2 A group of lines in a poem; stanza. 3 Metrical composition as distinguished from prose; poetry. 4 A specified type of metrical composition: iambic *verse.* 5 One of the short divisions of a chapter of the Bible. [< L *versus* a turning, a verse]

versed (vûrst) *adj.* Having ready skill and knowledge; proficient. [< L *versari* occupy oneself] **—Syn.** experienced, practiced, seasoned, skillful.

ver·si·fy (vûr'sə·fī) *v.* **·fied, ·fy·ing** *v.t.* 1 To turn prose into verse. 2 To narrate or treat in verse. **—***v.i.* 3 To write poetry. **—ver·si·fi·ca·tion** (vûr'sə·fə·kā'shən), **ver'si·fi'er** *n.*

ver·sion (vûr'zhən, -shən) *n.* 1 A translation or rendition from one language into another. 2 A description of an event, occurrence, etc., from a personal viewpoint. [< Med. L *versio* a turning < L *vertere* to turn] **—ver'sion·al** *adj.*

vers li·bre (ver lē'br') *French* Free verse. **—vers li·brist** (lē'brist).

ver·so (vûr'sō) *n. pl.* **·sos** 1 A left-hand page of a book, leaflet, etc. 2 The reverse of a coin or medal. [< L *verso (folio)* a turned (leaf)]

verst (vûrst) *n.* A Russian measure of distance equal to about two thirds of a mile. [< Russ. *versta*]

ver·sus (vûr'səs) *prep.* 1 In law, sports, and contests, against. 2 Considered as the alternative of: free trade *versus* high tariffs. [L, toward, turned toward]

ver·te·bra (vûr'tə·brə) *n. pl* **·brae** (-brē, -brā) or **·bras** Any of the individual bones of the spinal column. [L, a joint, vertebra < *vertere* to turn] **—ver'te·bral** *adj.*

ver·te·brate (vûr'tə·brit, -brāt) *adj.* 1 Having a backbone or spinal column. 2 Pertaining to or characteristic of vertebrates. 3 Pertaining to, having, or composed of vertebrae. **—***n.* Any of a division of animals characterized by a spinal column, as fishes, birds, and mammals. [< L *vertebratus* jointed] **—ver'te·brat'ed** *adj.*

ver·tex (vûr'teks) *n. pl.* **·tex·es** or **·ti·ces** (-tə·sēz') 1 The highest point of anything; apex. 2 *Astron.* **a** ZENITH. **b** The point in the sky toward or from which a group of stars appears to be moving. 3 *Geom.* **a** The point of intersection of the sides of an angle. **b** The point farthest from the base. [L, the top < *vertere* to turn]

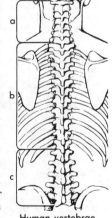

Human vertebrae
a. cervical.
b. thoracic. c. lumbar.

ver·ti·cal (vûr'ti·kəl) *adj.* 1 Perpendicular; upright. 2 Of or pertaining to the vertex. 3 Occupying a position directly overhead; at the highest point. 4 Of or pertaining to a business concern that undertakes a process from raw material to consumer: a *vertical* trust. **—***n.* 1 A vertical line, plane, or circle. 2 An upright beam or rod in a truss. **—ver'ti·cal'i·ty** (-kal'ə·tē), **ver'ti·cal·ness** *n.* **—ver'ti·cal·ly** *adv.*

vertical angle Either one of two angles which lie on opposite sides of two intersecting lines.

ver·tig·i·nous (vər·tij'ə·nəs) *adj.* 1 Affected by vertigo; dizzy. 2 Turning round; whirling. 3 Liable to cause giddiness. **—ver·tig'i·nous·ly** *adv.* **—ver·tig'i·nous·ness** *n.*

ver·ti·go (vûr'tə·gō') *n. pl.* **·goes** or **ver·tig·i·nes** (vər·tij'ə·nēz) A disorder in which a person or his surroundings seem to whirl about in such a way as to make the person dizzy and usu. sick. [L, lit., a turning around]

ver·vain (vûr'vān) *n.* A species of verbena supposedly having medicinal properties. [< L *verbena* verbena]

verve (vûrv) *n.* Enthusiasm or energy. [< L *verba,* pl. of *verbum* a word] **—Syn.** élan, liveliness, spirit, vigor.

ver·y (ver'ē) *adv.* 1 In a high degree; extremely: *very* generous. 2 Exactly: They both had the *very* same thought. **—***adj.* **ver·i·er, ver·i·est** 1 Absolute; complete: the *very* truth. 2 Suitable; right: the *very* tool we need. 3 Unqualified; complete: a *very* scoundrel. 4 Selfsame; identical: my *very* words. 5 The (thing) itself: used as an intensive: The *very* stones cry out. [< L *verus* true]

very high frequency Any wave frequency from 30 to 300 megahertz.

very low frequency Any wave frequency from 3 to 30 kilohertz.

ves·i·cant (ves'i·kənt) *adj.* Blister-producing. **—***n.* That which produces blisters, esp. a chemical warfare agent which attacks the skin on contact or lung tissue if inhaled. [< L *vesica* a blister, bladder]

ves·i·cate (ves'i·kāt) *v.* **·cat·ed, ·cat·ing** *v.t.* 1 To raise blisters on. **—***v.i.* 2 To blister, as the skin. **—ves'i·ca'tion** *n.*

ves·i·ca·to·ry (ves'i·kə·tôr'ē, və·sik'ə·tôr'ē, -tō'rē) *adj., n. pl.* **·ries** VESICANT.

ves·i·cle (ves'i·kəl) *n.* Any small bladderlike cavity, cell, cyst, or blister. [< L *vesica* a bladder] **—ve·sic·u·lar** (və·sik'yə·lar) *adj.* **—ve·sic'u·lar·ly** *adv.*

ves·per (ves'pər) *n. Archaic* EVENING. **—***adj.* Of or pertaining to evening. [L, the evening star]

Ves·per (ves'pər) *n.* EVENING STAR. [L]

ves·pers (ves'pərz) *n.pl. Often cap. Eccl.* 1 The sixth in order of the canonical hours. 2 A service of worship in the late afternoon or evening.

ves·sel (ves'əl) *n.* 1 A hollow receptacle capable of holding a liquid, as a pot, tub, pitcher, etc. 2 A ship or large boat. 3 Any of several aircraft. 4 *Biol.* A duct or canal for containing or transporting a fluid. [< L *vas* a vessel]

vest (vest) *n.* 1 A short sleeveless jacket worn, esp. under a suit coat, by men. 2 A similar garment worn by women. 3 A vestee. 4 *Chiefly Brit.* UNDERSHIRT. **—***v.t.* 1 To confer (ownership, authority, etc.) upon some person or persons. 2 To place ownership, control, or authority with (a person or persons). 3 To clothe or robe, as with church vestments. **—***v.i.* 4 To clothe oneself, as in vestments. 5 To be or become legally vested, as property. [< L *vestis* clothing, a garment]

Ves·ta (ves'tə) *Rom. Myth.* The goddess of the hearth and the hearth fire.

ves·tal (ves'təl) *n.* 1 One of the virgin priestesses of Vesta: also **vestal virgin.** 2 A chaste woman, esp. a virgin. **—***adj.* 1 Of or relating to Vesta or her priestesses. 2 Chaste. [< L *Vesta* Vesta]

vest·ed (ves'tid) *adj.* 1 Wearing clothes, esp. church vestments. 2 Not dependent on any contingency; fixed; inalienable; absolute: a *vested* right.

vested interest 1 A special interest, as in an economic or political system or arrangement, often pursued by the holder at the expense of others. 2 A person or group that pursues such an interest.

vest·ee (ves·tē') *n.* A garment worn by women to fill in the neckline of a jacket, blouse, etc. [Dim. of VEST]

ves·ti·bule (ves'tə·byool) *n.* 1 A small antechamber leading into a building or another room. 2 An enclosed passage from one railway passenger car to another. 3 *Anat.* Any cavity leading to another cavity: the *vestibule* of the

ear. —*v.t.* **·buled, ·bul·ing** To provide with a vestibule or vestibules. [< L *vestibulum* an entrance hall] —**ves·tib′u·lar** (-tib′yə·lər) *adj.*

ves·tige (ves′tij) *n.* **1** A trace of something absent, lost, or gone. **2** *Biol.* A remnant of an organ that is no longer functional. [< F < L *vestigium* a footprint] —**Syn. 1** hint, remnant, tinge, touch.

ves·tig·i·al (ves·tij′ē·əl) *adj.* Of, or of the nature of a vestige; surviving in small or degenerate form. —**ves·tig′i·al·ly** *adv.*

vest·ment (vest′mənt) *n.* **1** An article of clothing. **2** Any of several ritual garments of the clergy. [< L *vestire* clothe] —**vest·ment·al** (vest·men′təl) *adj.*

vest-pock·et (vest′pok′it) *adj.* **1** Small enough to fit in a vest pocket. **2** Much smaller than standard or usual size: a *vest-pocket* battleship.

vest-pocket park A small urban park, often on a vacant lot.

ves·try (ves′trē) *n. pl.* **·tries 1** In a church, a room where vestments are put on or kept. **2** A room in a church used for Sunday school, meetings, etc. **3** In the Anglican and Episcopal churches, a body administering the affairs of a parish or congregation. [< L *vestis* a garment]

ves·try·man (ves′trē·mən) *n. pl.* **·men** (-mən) A member of a vestry.

ves·ture (ves′chər) *n. Archaic* **1** Garments; clothing. **2** A covering or envelope. —*v.t.* **·tured, ·tur·ing** To cover or clothe. [< L *vestire* clothe] —**ves′tur·al** *adj.*

vet[1] (vet) *Informal n.* VETERINARIAN. —*v.t. & v.i.* **vet·ted, vet·ting** To treat (animals) as a veterinarian does. [Short for VETERINARIAN]

vet[2] (vet) *n. Informal* A veteran.

vet. veteran; veterinarian; veterinary.

vetch (vech) *n.* Any of a genus of trailing, leguminous vines grown for fodder. [< L *vicia*]

vet·er·an (vet′ər·ən, vet′rən) *n.* **1** An experienced soldier or an ex-soldier. **2** A member of the armed forces who has been in active service. **3** A person with long experience in an occupation, calling, etc. —*adj.* **1** Having had long experience or practice. **2** Of, pertaining to, or for veterans. [< L *vetus, veteris* old]

Veterans Day The fourth Monday in October, a U.S. holiday honoring veterans of the armed forces, formerly celebrated November 11.

vet·er·i·nar·i·an (vet′ər·ə·nâr′ē·ən, vet′rə-) *n.* A practitioner of medical and surgical treatment of animals.

vet·er·i·nar·y (vet′ər·ə·ner′ē, vet′rə-) *adj.* Of, pertaining to, or designating the science or practice of preventing, curing, or alleviating the diseases and injuries of animals, esp. domestic animals. —*n. pl.* **·nar·ies** VETERINARIAN. [< L *veterinarius* pertaining to beasts of burden < *veterina* beasts of burden]

ve·to (vē′tō) *v.t.* **·toed, ·to·ing 1** To refuse approval of (a bill passed by a legislative body). **2** To forbid or refuse to consent to. —*n. pl.* **·toes 1** The right of one branch of government to cancel, prohibit, postpone, etc., the projects of another branch; esp., the right of a chief executive, as the president or a governor, to refuse to approve a legislative enactment by withholding his signature. **2** A message giving the reasons of a chief executive for refusing to approve a bill. **3** The exercise of the right to veto. **4** Any authoritative prohibition. [< L, I forbid] —**ve′to·er** *n.*

vex (veks) *v.t.* **1** To annoy by petty irritations. **2** To trouble or afflict. **3** To baffle, puzzle, or confuse. [< L *vexare* to shake] —**vex·ed·ly** (vek′sid·lē) *adv.* —**vex′ed·ness, vex′er** *n.* —**Syn. 1** chagrin, irritate, pester, pique.

vex·a·tion (vek·sā′shən) *n.* **1** The act of vexing, or the state of being vexed. **2** Trouble, annoyance, affliction, etc.

vex·a·tious (vek·sā′shəs) *adj.* Annoying; harassing. —**vex·a′tious·ly** *adv.* —**vex·a′tious·ness** *n.*

VFW, V.F.W. Veterans of Foreign Wars.

VHF, V.H.F., vhf, v.h.f. very high frequency.

VI Virgin Islands (P.O. abbr.).

V.I. Virgin Islands.

v.i. see below (L *vide infra*); verb intransitive.

vi·a (vī′ə, vē′ə) *prep.* **1** By way of; by a route passing through. **2** By means of. [< L *via* a way]

vi·a·ble (vī′ə·bəl) *adj.* **1** Capable of living and developing normally, as a newborn infant, a seed, etc. **2** Workable; practicable: a *viable* plan. [< L *vita*] —**vi′a·bil′i·ty** *n.* —**vi′a·bly** *adv.*

vi·a·duct (vī′ə·dukt) *n.* A bridgelike structure, esp. a large one of arched masonry, to carry a road or railroad over a valley, section of a city, etc. [< L *via* a way + (AQUE)DUCT]

vi·al (vī′əl) *n.* A small bottle, usu. of glass, for medicines and other liquids. [< Gk. *phialē* a shallow cup]

vi·a me·di·a (vī′ə mē′dē·ə, vē′ə mä′-) *Latin* A middle way.

vi·and (vī′ənd) *n.* **1** An article of food, esp. meat. **2** *pl.* Provisions; food. [< OF *viande*]

Viaduct

vi·at·i·cum (vī·at′ə·kəm) *n. pl.* **·ca** (-kə) or **·cums 1** *Often cap.* The Eucharist, as given on *the verge of death.* **2** The provisions needed for a journey. [L, traveling money < *via* a way]

vibes (vībz) *n.pl. (usu. construed as sing. for def. 2) Slang* **1** Vibrations. See VIBRATION (def. 3). **2** VIBRAPHONE.

vi·brant (vī′brənt) *adj.* **1** Having, showing, or resulting from vibration; resonant. **2** Throbbing; pulsing: *vibrant* with enthusiasm. **3** Energetic; vigorous. **4** *Phonet.* VOICED (def. 3). —*n. Phonet.* A voiced sound. [< L *vibrare* to shake] —**vi′bran·cy** (-sē) *n. (pl.* **·cies)** —**vi′brant·ly** *adv.*

vi·bra·phone (vī′brə·fōn) *n.* A musical instrument like the marimba in which a vibrato is produced by rotating disks in electrically powered resonators.

vi·brate (vī′brāt) *v.* **·brat·ed, ·brat·ing** *v.i.* **1** To move back and forth, as a pendulum. **2** To move back and forth rapidly. **3** To resound: The note *vibrates* on the ear. **4** To be emotionally moved. —*v.t.* **5** To cause to move back and forth. **6** To cause to quiver. **7** To send forth (sound, etc.) by vibration. [< L *vibrare* to shake]

vi·bra·tile (vī′brə·til, -til) *adj.* **1** Pertaining to vibration. **2** Capable of vibration. **3** Having a vibratory motion. —**vi′bra·til′i·ty** (-til′ə·tē) *n.*

vi·bra·tion (vī·brā′shən) *n.* **1** The act of vibrating; oscillation. **2** *Physics* **a** A periodic, back-and-forth motion of a particle or body. **b** Any physical process characterized by cyclic changes in a variable, as wave motion. **c** A single cycle of such a process. **3** *pl. Slang* One's emotional response to an aura felt to surround a person or thing, esp. when considered in or out of harmony with oneself. —**vi·bra′tion·al** *adj.*

vi·bra·to (vē·brä′tō) *n. pl.* **·tos** *Music* A cyclic variation in the pitch of a tone. [Ital. < *vibrare* vibrate]

vi·bra·tor (vī′brā·tər) *n.* **1** One who or that which vibrates. **2** An electrically operated massaging apparatus.

vi·bra·to·ry (vī′brə·tôr′ē, -tō′rē) *adj.* **1** Pertaining to, causing, or characterized by vibration. **2** That vibrates or is capable of vibration.

vi·bur·num (vī·bûr′nəm) *n.* **1** Any of a genus of shrubs or small trees related to honeysuckle. **2** The bark of several species, used medicinally. [L, the wayfaring tree]

Vic. Victoria.

vic. vicar; vicarage; vicinity.

vic·ar (vik′ər) *n.* **1** One who is authorized to perform functions in the stead of another; deputy. **2** In the Anglican Church, the priest of a parish of which the main revenues are appropriated by a layman, the priest himself receiving a salary. **3** In the Roman Catholic Church, a representative of a bishop or the pope. **4** In the Protestant Episcopal Church, the clergyman who is the head of a chapel. [< L *vicarius* a substitute < *vicis* a change]

vic·ar·age (vik′ər·ij) *n.* **1** The benefice, office, or duties of a vicar. **2** A vicar's residence.

vic·ar-gen·er·al (vik′ər·jen′ər·al, -jen′rəl) *n.* **1** In the Roman Catholic Church, a priest appointed by the bishop as assistant in administering a diocese. **2** In the Anglican church, an official assisting the bishop or archbishop.

vi·car·i·ous (vī·kâr′ē·əs, vi-) *adj.* **1** Suffered or done in place of another: a *vicarious* sacrifice. **2** Felt through identifying with another's experience: *vicarious* pleasure in his wife's talent. **3** Filling the office of or acting for another. **4** Delegated: *vicarious* authority. [< L *vicarius*] —**vi·car′i·ous·ly** *adv.* —**vi·car′i·ous·ness** *n.*

vice[1] (vīs) *n.* **1** Moral depravity; evil. **2** An immoral action,

trait, etc. **3** A habitual, usu. trivial, failing or defect; short-coming. [<L *vitium* a fault] —**Syn. 1** corruption, dissoluteness, profligacy.

vice[2] (vīs) *n.* & *v.t.* **viced, vic·ing** *Chiefly Brit.* VISE.

vi·ce[3] (vī′sē) *prep.* Instead of; in place of. [<L *vicis* change]

vice- *prefix* One who acts for or takes the place of. [<L *vice,* abl. of *vicis* change]

vice admiral See GRADE. —**vice′-ad′mir·al·ty** (-mər·əl·tē) *n.*

vice-con·sul (vīs′kon′səl) *n.* A person who acts as a substitute for or a subordinate to a consul. —**vice-con·su·lar** (vīs′kon′sə·lər) *adj.* **vice-con·su·late** (vīs′kon′sə·lit), **vice′-con′sul·ship** *n.*

vice·ge·rent (vīs·jir′ənt) *n.* One duly authorized to exercise the powers of another; a deputy. —*adj.* Acting in the place of another. [<L *vice* + *gerere* carry, manage] —**vice·ge′ren·cy** (-sē) *n.* (*pl.* **·cies**)

vice president 1 An officer ranking next below a president, and acting, on occasion, in his place. **2** In the U.S. government, an officer of this rank designated by the Constitution to succeed the president if necessary. —**vice-pres·i·den·cy** (vīs′prez′·ə·dən·sē) (*pl.* **·cies**) *n.* —**vice′-pres′i·den′tial** (-prez′ə·den′shəl) *adj.*

vice·re·gal (vīs·rē′gəl) *adj.* Of or relating to a viceroy. —**vice·re′gal·ly** *adv.*

vice·re·gent (vīs′rē′jənt) *n.* A person who acts in the place of a regent when necessary. —*adj.* Of or pertaining to a vice-regent. —**vice′-re′gen·cy** *n.*

vice·roy (vīs′roi) *n.* One who rules a country, colony, or province by the authority of his sovereign. [<VICE- + F *roi* a king] —**vice·roy′al** (-roi′əl) *adj.* —**vice′roy′al·ty** (*pl.* **·ties**), **vice′roy·ship′** *n.*

vice squad A police division charged with combating prostitution, gambling, and other vices.

vi·ce ver·sa (vī′sē vûr′sə, vī′sə vûr′sə, vīs′vûr′sə) With the relation of terms being reversed; conversely. [L]

vi·chy·ssoise (vē′shē·swäz′, vē′shē·swäz′, vish′-) *n.* A potato cream soup flavored with leeks, celery, etc., usu. served cold with a sprinkling of chives. [<*Vichy,* France]

Vi·chy water (vish′ē) **1** The effervescent mineral water from the springs at Vichy, France. **2** Any mineral water resembling it.

vi·cin·i·ty (vi·sin′ə·tē) *n. pl.* **·ties 1** A region adjacent or near; neighborhood. **2** Nearness; proximity. [<L *vicinus* nearby]

vi·cious (vish′əs) *adj.* **1** Corrupt in conduct or habits; depraved; immoral. **2** Of the nature of vice: *vicious* acts. **3** Unruly or dangerous, as an animal: a *vicious* dog. **4** Marked by evil intent; malicious; spiteful: a *vicious* lie. **5** Worthless or invalidated because defective; full of errors or faults: *vicious* arguments. **6** *Informal* Unusually severe or punishing: a *vicious* blow. **7** *Informal* Savage; heinous: a *vicious* crime. [<OF < L *vitiosus* < *vitium* a fault] —**vi′cious·ly** *adv.* —**vi′cious·ness** *n.*

vicious circle 1 The predicament that arises when the solution of a problem creates a new problem, etc. **2** *Logic* A fallacy in reasoning created when a conclusion is based upon a premise which depends upon the conclusion.

vi·cis·si·tude (vi·sis′ə·t[y]ood) *n.* **1** *Usu. pl.* Irregular changes or variations, as of conditions or fortune: the *vicissitudes* of life. **2** A change or alteration; also, the condition or quality of being changeable. [<L *vicis* a turn, change] —**vi·cis·si·tu·di·nary** (və·sis′ə·t[y]ood′ə·ner′ē), **vi·cis′·si·tu′di·nous** *adj.*

vic·tim (vik′tim) *n.* **1** A person injured or killed by circumstances beyond his control: a *victim* of a flood. **2** A sufferer from any diseased condition: a *victim* of arthritis. **3** One who is swindled; a dupe. **4** A living creature killed as a sacrifice to a deity. [<L *victima* a beast for sacrifice]

vic·tim·ize (vik′tim·īz) *v.t.* **·ized, ·iz·ing 1** to make a victim of; cause suffering to. **2** To cheat; dupe: *victimized* by loan sharks. —**vic·tim·i·za·tion** (vik′tə·mə·zā′shən) *n.* —**vic′·tim·iz′er** *n.*

vic·tor (vik′tər) *n.* One who wins any struggle or contest. —*adj.* Victorious: the *victor* nation. [<L *victus,* p.p. of *vin·cere* conquer]

vic·to·ri·a (vik·tôr′ē·ə, -tō′rē·ə) *n.* A low, light, four-wheeled carriage, with a folding top, a seat for two persons, and a raised driver's seat. [<*Victoria,* 1819–1901, Queen of England]

Victoria Cross The highest British military decoration, awarded for outstanding valor.

Victoria Day In Canada, a national holiday celebrated on the first Monday preceding May 25th.

Victoria

Vic·to·ri·an (vik·tôr′ē·ən, -tō′rē-) *adj.* **1** Of or relating to Queen Victoria of England, or to her reign. **2** Pertaining to or characteristic of the standards of morality and taste prevalent during that era. **3** Prudish; prim; priggish. —*n.* A person living during the time of Queen Victoria's reign; also, a person exhibiting the characteristic qualities, behavior, etc., of her era. —**Vic·to′ri·an·ism** *n.*

vic·to·ri·ous (vik·tôr′ē·əs, -tō′rē-) *adj.* **1** Having won victory; triumphant. **2** Characterized by or relating to victory. —**vic·to′ri·ous·ly** *adv.* —**vic·to′ri·ous·ness** *n.*

vic·to·ry (vik′tər·ē) *n. pl.* **ries 1** The overcoming of an enemy or adversary; triumph, as in war. **2** An overcoming of any difficulty or obstacle, considered as an achievement earned through effort. [<L *victor* victor]

vict·ual (vit′l) *n.* **1** Food fit for consumption by man. **2** *pl.* Food prepared for consumption. **3** *pl.* A supply of food; provisions. [<L *victualis* of food < *victus* food]

vi·cu·ña (vi·kōon′yə, -kyōo′nə, vī-) *n.* **1** A small llamalike ruminant of the Andes having fine wool. **2** A textile made from this wool or some substitute: also **vicuña cloth.** Also **vi·cu′na.** [<Quechua]

Vicuña

vi·de (vī′dē, vē′dā′) *v.* See: used to direct attention to: *vide* p. 36. [L, imperative sing. of *videre* see]

vi·de in·fra (vī′dē in′frə) *Latin* See below.

vi·de·li·cet (vi·del′ə·sit, vī-, vi·dā′li·ket′) *adv.* That is to say; namely. [L < *videre licet* it is permitted to see]

vid·e·o (vid′ē·ō) *adj.* **1** Of or pertaining to television, esp. to the picture. **2** Producing a signal convertible to a television picture: a *video* cassette. —*n.* Television image or the electric signal corresponding to it. [L, I see]

vid·e·o·disc (vid′ē·ō·disk′) *n.* A disc for recording both image and sound for replay through a television.

vid·e·o·tape (vid′ē·ō·tāp′) *n.* A recording of a television program on magnetic tape. —*v.t.* **·taped, ·tap·ing** To make such a recording.

vid·e·o·text (vid′ē·ō·tekst′) *n.* A communications system with which a personal computer user may interact, by telephone or two-way cable lines. Users may make reservations, shop, bank, vote, etc.

vi·de su·pra (vī′dē sōo′prə) *Latin* See above.

vie (vī) *v.* **vied, vy·ing** *v.i.* To put forth effort to excel or outdo others. [<MF *envier* invite, challenge] —**vi′er** *n.*

Vi·en·nese (vē′ə·nēz′, -nēs′) *adj.* Of or pertaining to Vienna, its inhabitants, culture, etc. —*n. pl.* **·ese 1** A native or inhabitant of Vienna. **2** The German dialect spoken in Vienna.

Vi·et·nam (vē·et·näm′) *n.* A country of SE Asia, divided into: **Democratic Republic of Vietnam,** 63,344 sq. mi., cap. Hanoi: also **North Vietnam;** and **Republic of Vietnam,** 65,749 sq. mi., cap. Saigon: also **South Vietnam.** • See map at INDOCHINA.

Vi·et·nam·ese (vēet′nəm·ēz′, vyet′-, -ēs′) *adj.* Of or pertaining to Vietnam, its people, or their language. —*n. pl.* **·ese 1** a native or citizen of Vietnam. **2** The language of Vietnam.

view (vyōo) *n.* **1** The act of seeing or examining; survey; examination; inspection. **2** Range of vision. **3** Something seen: a *view* of the harbor. **4** A representation of a scene,

esp. a landscape. **5** Something regarded as the object of action; purpose. **6** Opinion; judgment; belief: What are your *views* on this subject? **7** The immediate or forseeable future: no end in *view*. —**in view of** In consideration of. —**on view** Set up for public inspection. —**with a view to** With the aim or purpose of. —*v.t.* **1** To look at; behold. **2** To scrutinize; examine. **3** To survey mentally; consider. **4** To regard in a certain way. [< OF *veoir* see < L *videre*]

view·er (vyōō′ər) *n.* **1** One who views; esp., one who watches television. **2** A device for viewing, esp. one for viewing photographic transparencies.

view·less (vyōō′lis) *adj.* **1** That cannot be viewed. **2** Having no opinions. —**view′less·ly** *adv.*

view·point (vyōō′point′) *n.* The position from which one views or evaluates something; point of view.

vi·ges·i·mal (vī·jes′ə·məl) *adj.* **1** Of, pertaining to, or based on the number 20. **2** Twentieth. [< L *vicesimus*]

vig·il (vij′əl) *n.* **1** An act or period of keeping awake. **2** An act or period of keeping watch. **3** *Eccl.* **a** The eve of a holy day. **b** *pl.* Religious devotions on such an eve. [< L *vigil* awake]

vig·i·lance (vij′ə·ləns) *n.* The quality of being vigilant; alertness to threat or danger.

vigilance committee A body of men self-organized and without official legal sanction, with the professed purpose of maintaining order and punishing crime.

vig·i·lant (vij′ə·lənt) *adj.* Alert to danger; wary. [< L *vigilare* keep awake < *vigil* awake] —**vig′i·lant·ly** *adv.* —**Syn.** cautious, circumspect, heedful, watchful.

vig·i·lan·te (vij′ə·lan′tē) *n.* A member of a vigilance committee. —**vig′i·lant′ism** *n.*

vi·gnette (vin·yet′) *n.* **1** A short, subtly wrought picture in words; sketch. **2** A decorative design before the title page of a book, at the end or beginning of a chapter, etc. **3** An engraving, photograph, etc., that shades off gradually into the background. —*v.t.* **·gnet·ted**, **·gnet·ting** To finish, as an engraving or photograph, in the manner of a vignette. [< F *vigne* a vine]

vig·or (vig′ər) *n.* **1** Active bodily or mental strength; energy. **2** Vital or natural growth, as in a healthy plant. **3** Intensity or force. **4** Legal force; validity. *Brit. sp.* **vig′·our.** [< L < *vigere* be lively, thrive]

vig·or·ous (vig′ər·əs) *adj.* Possessing, characterized by, or done with vigor. —**vig′or·ous·ly** *adv.* —**vig′or·ous·ness** *n.*

vi·king (vī′king) *n. Often cap.* One of the Scandinavian sea rovers who harried the coasts of Europe from the eighth to the tenth centuries.

vil. village.

vile (vīl) *adj.* **vil·er**, **vil·est** **1** Morally base; corrupt. **2** Disgusting; loathsome. **3** Very bad: *vile* food. [< L *vilis* cheap] —**vile′ly** *adv.* —**vile′ness** *n.*

vil·i·fy (vil′ə·fī) *v.t.* **·fied**, **·fy·ing** To speak of abusively or slanderously; defame. [< L *vilis* cheap + *facere* make] —**vil′i·fi·ca′tion** (-fə·kā′shən), **vil′i·fi′er** *n.* —**Syn.** denigrate, malign, revile, traduce.

vil·la (vil′ə) *n.* A house, usu. large and imposing, in the country or suburbs or at the seashore. [L, a country house, farm]

vil·lage (vil′ij) *n.* **1** A collection of houses in a rural district, smaller than a town but larger than a hamlet. **2** Such a settlement incorporated as a municipality. **3** The inhabitants of a village, collectively. [< L *villaticus* pertaining to a villa < *villa* a villa]

vil·lag·er (vil′ij·ər) *n.* One who lives in a village.

vil·lain (vil′ən) *n.* **1** One who has committed crimes or evil deeds; scoundrel: now often used humorously. **2** A character in a novel, play, etc., who is the opponent of the hero. **3** VILLEIN. [< OF *vilain* a farm servant]

vil·lain·ous (vil′ən·əs) *adj.* **1** Wicked; evil. **2** *Informal* Very bad; abominable. —**vil′lain·ous·ly** *adv.* —**vil′lain·ous·ness** *n.* —**Syn.** 1 detestable, heinous, notorious, shameful.

vil·lain·y (vil′ən·ē) *n. pl.* **·lain·ies** **1** The quality or condition of being villainous. **2** A villainous act; crime.

vil·lein (vil′ən) *n.* In feudal England, a member of a class of serfs who, by the 13th century, were regarded as freemen in their legal relations with all persons except their lord. [< OF *vilain.* See VILLAIN.] —**vil′lein·age, vil′len·age** *n.*

vil·lus (vil′əs) *n. pl.* **vil·li** (vil′ī, -ē) **1** *Anat.* Any of numerous tiny projections from mucous membrane, as the absorp-

tive processes in the small intestine. **2** *Bot.* Any of the soft hairs on the surface of certain plants. [L, a tuft of hair, shaggy hair] —**vil′lous** *adj.*

vim (vim) *n.* Force or vigor; energy; spirit. [L, accusative of *vis* power]

vin (van) *n. French* Wine.

vi·na·ceous (vī·nā′shəs) *adj.* **1** Of or pertaining to wine or grapes. **2** Wine-colored; red. [< L *vinum* wine]

vin·ai·grette (vin′ə·gret′) *n.* **1** An ornamental box or bottle for holding vinegar, smelling salts, etc. **2** Vinaigrette sauce. [< F *vinaigre* vinegar]

vinaigrette sauce A sauce made of vinegar and oil with herbs, onions, parsley, etc., served usu. on cold meats or fish.

Vin·cent's infection (vin′sənts) TRENCH MOUTH. Also Vincent's angina, Vincent's disease. [< J. H. *Vincent*, 1862–1950, French physician]

vin·ci·ble (vin′sə·bəl) *adj.* That can be conquered or overcome; conquerable. [< L *vincere* conquer] —**vin′ci·bil′i·ty, vin′ci·ble·ness** *n.*

vin·di·ca·ble (vin′də·kə·bəl) *adj.* That can be vindicated; justifiable.

vin·di·cate (vin′də·kāt) *v.t.* **·cat·ed**, **·cat·ing** **1** To clear of accusation, censure, suspicion, etc. **2** To defend or maintain, as a right or claim, against challenge or attack and show to be just, right, and reasonable. **3** To provide justification for; justify. [< L *vindicare* avenge, claim] —**vin·di·ca·tive** (vin·dik′ə·tiv, vin′də·kā′tiv), **vin′di·ca·to·ry** (-kə·tôr′ē, -tō′rē) *adj.* —**vin′di·ca′tor** *n.*

vin·di·ca·tion (vin′də·kā′shən) *n.* **1** The act of vindicating, or the state of being vindicated. **2** A justification; defense.

vin·dic·tive (vin·dik′tiv) *adj.* Having or characterized by a vengeful spirit. [< L *vindicta* a revenge] —**vin·dic′tive·ly** *adv.* —**vin·dic′tive·ness** *n.* —**Syn.** retaliatory, revengeful, spiteful.

vine (vīn) *n.* **1** Any climbing plant. **2** The flexible stem of such a plant. **3** GRAPEVINE (def. 1). [< L *vinum* wine]

vin·e·gar (vin′ə·gər) *n.* **1** A variously flavored solution of acetic acid obtained by the fermentation of cider, wine, etc., and used as a condiment and preservative. **2** Acerbity, as of speech. [< OF *vin* wine + *aigre* sour] —**vin′e·gar·y** *adj.*

vin·er·y (vī′nər·ē) *n. pl.* **·er·ies** A building or area where vines are grown.

vine·yard (vin′yərd) *n.* An area devoted to the growing of grapevines. [< OE *wīngeard*] —**vine′yard·ist** *n.*

vingt-et-un (van·tā·œn′) *n.* BLACKJACK (def. 3). [F, twenty-one]

vin·i·cul·ture (vin′ə·kul′chər) *n.* The cultivation of grapes for making wine. [< L *vinum* wine] —**vin′i·cul′tur·al** *adj.*

vi·nous (vī′nəs) *adj.* **1** Pertaining to, characteristic of, or having the qualities of wine. **2** Caused by, affected by, or addicted to wine. [< L *vinum* wine] —**vi·nos·i·ty** (vī·nos′ə·tē) *n.*

vin·tage (vin′tij) *n.* **1** The yield of grapes or wine from a vineyard or wine-growing district for one season. **2** The harvesting of a vineyard and the making of wine; also, the season when these things are done. **3** Wine, esp. fine wine of a particular region and year. **4** The year or the region in which a particular wine is produced. **5** *Informal* The type or kind current at a particular time: a joke of ancient *vintage.* —*adj.* Of a fine vintage: *vintage* wines. [< OF *vendage* < L *vinum* wine + *demere* remove]

vint·ner (vint′nər) *n.* **1** A wine merchant. **2** A maker of wine. [< OF *vin* wine]

vin·y (vī′nē) *adj.* **·i·er**, **·i·est** Pertaining to, like, of, full of, or yielding vines.

vi·nyl (vī′nəl) *n.* An organic radical derived from ethylene and entering into the composition of numerous plastics. [< L *vinum* wine + -YL]

vi·ol (vī′əl, -ōl′) *n.* Any of a family of stringed musical instruments, predecessors of the violin family. [< Med. L *vidula, vitula*]

vi·o·la (vē·ō′lə, vī-) *n.* A four-stringed musical instrument of the violin family, somewhat larger than the violin, and tuned a fifth lower. [Ital., orig., a viol]

vi·o·la·ble (vī′ə·lə·bəl) *adj.* That can or is likely to be vi-

olated. **—vi′o·la·ble·ness, vi′o·la·bil′i·ty** *n.* **—vi′o·la·bly** *adv.*

vio·la da gam·ba (vē·ō′lə·də·gäm′bə) An early bass of the viol family, held between the legs, and having a range similar to that of the cello. [Ital., viola of the leg]

vi·o·late (vī′ə·lāt) *v.t.* **·lat·ed, ·lat·ing** 1 To break or infringe, as a law, oath, agreement, etc. 2 To profane, as a holy place. 3 To break in on; interfere with: to *violate* one's privacy. 4 To ravish; rape. 5 To offend or treat contemptuously: to *violate* a person's beliefs. [< L *violare* use violence < *vis* force] **—vi′o·la′tion, vi′o·la′tor** *n.* **—vi′o·la′tive** *adj.* **—Syn.** 2 desecrate, pollute. 3 disturb; interrupt.

vi·o·lence (vī′ə·ləns) *n.* 1 Physical force exercised to injure, damage, or destroy. 2 An instance of such exercise of physical force; an injurious or destructive act. 3 Intensity; severity; force: the *violence* of a tornado. 4 Injury or damage, as by irreverence, distortion, or alteration: editing that did *violence* to the original text.

vi·o·lent (vī′ə·lənt) *adj.* 1 Proceeding from or marked by great physical force or activity. 2 Caused by or exhibiting intense emotional or mental excitement; passionate: a *violent* rabble-rouser. 3 Characterized by intensity of any kind: *violent* heat. 4 Marked by the unjust or illegal exercise of force: to take *violent* measures. 5 Resulting from external force or injury; unnatural: a *violent* death. [< L *violentus* < *vis* force] **—vi′o·lent·ly** *adv.*

vi·o·let (vī′ə·lit) *n.* 1 Any of a widely distributed genus of perennial herbs, bearing irregular flowers usu. of a bluish purple color. 2 Any of several plants having violet-colored flowers. 3 A bluish purple color. **—adj.** Bluish purple. [< L *viola*]

vi·o·lin (vī′ə·lin′) *n.* 1 A musical instrument having four strings and a sounding box of wood, and played by means of a bow. 2 A violinist, esp. in an orchestra. [< Ital. *viola* a viola]

vi·o·lin·ist (vī′ə·lin′ist) *n.* One who plays the violin.

vi·ol·ist (vī′əl·ist) *n.* 1 One who plays the viol. 2 (vē·ō′list) One who plays the viola.

vi·o·lon·cel·lo (vī′ə·lən·chel′ō, vē′ə·) *n.* *pl.* **·los** CELLO. [< Ital. *violone* a bass viol, aug. of *viola*] **— vi′o·lon·cel′list** *n.*

VIP, V.I.P. *Informal* very important person.

vi·per (vī′pər) *n.* 1 Any of a family of venomous Old World snakes, including the African puff adder. 2 Any of a family of typically American poisonous snakes, the **pit vipers,** including the rattlesnake, copperhead, etc., which are characterized by a small depression between the nostril and the eye. 3 Any poisonous or allegedly poisonous snake. 4 A malicious, treacherous, or spiteful person. [< L *vipera*] **—vi·per·ine** (vī′pə·rīn) *adj.*

vi·per·ous (vī′pər·əs) *adj.* 1 Of, pertaining to, or composed of vipers. 2 Malicious, treacherous, or spiteful. **— vi′per·ous·ly** *adv.*

vi·ra·go (vi·rä′gō, -rā′-, vī-) *n.* *pl.* **·goes** or **·gos** A loud, ill-tempered woman; shrew; scold. [L, manlike woman]

vi·ral (vī′rəl) *adj.* Of, pertaining to, or caused by a virus.

vir·e·o (vir′ē·ō) *n.* *pl.* **·os** Any of various inconspicuous, insectivorous songbirds of North America. [L, a kind of small bird]

vi·res·cent (vī·res′ənt) *adj.* Greenish or becoming green. [< L *virescere* grow green] **—vi·res′cence** *n.*

vir·gin (vûr′jin) *n.* 1 A person, esp. a young woman, who has never had sexual intercourse. 2 A maiden or unmarried woman. **—adj.** 1 Being a virgin. 2 Consisting of virgins: a *virgin* band. 3 Pertaining or suited to a virgin; chaste; maidenly. 4 Uncorrupted; pure; clean: *virgin* whiteness. 5 Not hitherto used, touched, tilled, or worked upon: *virgin* forest. 6 Not previously processed or manufactured; new: *virgin* wool. 7 Occurring for the first time; initial: a *virgin* effort. [< L *virgo* a maiden]

Vir·gin (vûr′jin) VIRGIN MARY. **—n.** VIRGO.

vir·gin·al[1] (vûr′jin·əl) *adj.* 1 Of, pertaining to, like, or suited to a virgin; modest; maidenly. 2 Pure; pristine; unsullied. **—vir′gin·al·ly** *adv.*

vir·gin·al[2] (vûr′jin·əl) *n.* *Often pl.* A small, rectangular harpsichord with no legs. Also **pair of virginals.**

Virginal

virgin birth *Usu. cap. Theol.* The doctrine that Jesus Christ was conceived by divine agency and born without impairment of the virginity of his mother Mary.

Vir·gin·i·a cowslip (vər·jin′yə) A perennial herb of the E U.S. with clusters of blue or purple tubular flowers. Also **Virginia bluebell.**

Virginia creeper A woody vine of the grape family, with compound leaves, small green flowers, and inedible blue berries.

Virginia deer WHITE-TAILED DEER.

Virginia reel 1 A country dance performed by couples who stand initially in two parallel lines facing one another. 2 The music for such a dance.

vir·gin·i·ty (vər·jin′ə·tē) *n.* *pl.* **·ties** 1 The state of being a virgin; maidenhood; virginal chastity. 2 The state of being fresh, untouched, etc.

Virgin Mary Mary, the mother of Jesus.

vir·gin′s-bow·er (vûr′jinz·bou′ər) *n.* A species of clematis bearing white flowers in leafy clusters.

Vir·go (vûr′gō) *n.* A constellation and the sixth sign of the Zodiac; the Virgin. • See ZODIAC.

vir·gule (vûr′gyool) *n.* A slanting line (/) used to indicate a choice between two alternatives, as in the phrase *and/or.* [< L *virga* a rod]

vir·i·des·cent (vir′ə·des′ənt) *adj.* Greenish; turning green. [< L *viridis* green] **—vir′i·des′cence** *n.*

vir·ile (vir′əl, il) *adj.* 1 Having the characteristics of manhood. 2 Having the vigor or strength of manhood. 3 Able to procreate. [< L *vir* a man] **—vi·ril·i·ty** (və·ril′ə·tē) *n.*

vi·rol·o·gy (və·rol′ə·jē, vī-) *n.* The study of viruses, esp. in relation to disease. **—vi·rol′o·gist** *n.*

vir·tu (vər·too′, vûr′too) *n.* 1 Rare, curious, or artistic quality: often in the phrase **objects** (or **articles**) **of virtu.** 2 A taste for or knowledge of such objects. 3 Such objects collectively. [< L *virtus*]

vir·tu·al (vûr′choo·əl) *adj.* Being so in essence or effect, but not in form or fact. [< Med. L *virtualis* < L *virtus* strength] **—vir′tu·al′i·ty** (-al′ə·tē) *n.* **—vir′tu·al·ly** *adv.*

vir·tue (vûr′choo) *n.* 1 General moral excellence; uprightness; goodness. 2 A particular moral excellence. 3 Any admirable quality or merit: Patience is a *virtue.* 4 Sexual purity; chastity. 5 Efficacy; potency, as of a medicine. **—by** (or **in**) **virtue of** By or through the force or authority of. **—make a virtue of necessity** To do willingly what one has to do anyhow. [< L *virtus* strength, bravery < *vir* man] **—Syn.** 1 integrity, rectitude, righteousness, worthiness.

vir·tu·os·i·ty (vûr′choo·os′ə·tē) *n.* *pl.* **·ties** The technical mastery of an art, as music.

vir·tu·o·so (vûr′choo·ō′sō) *n.* *pl.* **·si** (-sē) or **·sos** 1 A master of technique in some fine art, esp. in musical performance. 2 A knowledgeable collector or lover of curios or works of art. **—adj.** Of or characteristic of a virtuoso. [< LL *virtuosus* full of excellence]

vir·tu·ous (vûr′choo·əs) *adj.* 1 Righteous; upright; dutiful. 2 Pure and chaste. **—vir′tu·ous·ly** *adv.* **—vir′tu·ous·ness** *n.*

vir·u·lent (vir′yə·lənt) *adj.* 1 Extremely harmful; noxious; deadly. 2 Severe and rapid in its progress: said of a disease. 3 Very infectious: said of a pathogenic microorganism. 4 Full of bitter hatred; hostile. [< L *virulentus* full of poison < *virus* a poison] **—vir′u·lence, vir′u·len·cy** *n.* **—vir′u·lent·ly** *adv.*

vi·rus (vī′rəs) *n.* 1 Any of a class of ultramicroscopic filter-

passing pathogens capable of reproduction only within specific living cells. **2** Venom, as of a snake. **3** Any evil influence: the *virus* of greed. [L, poison, slime]

vis (vis) *n. pl.* **vi·res** (vī′rēz) Force. [L]

Vis., Visc., Visct. Viscount; Viscountess.

vi·sa (vē′zə) *n.* An official endorsement on a passport certifying that it has been examined and that the bearer may enter or pass through the country which has granted the endorsement. —*v.t.* **·saed, ·sa·ing 1** To put a visa on. **2** To give a visa to. [F< L < p.p. of *videre* see]

vis·age (viz′ij) *n.* **1** The face. **2** Appearance; aspect; look. [< L *visus* a look] —**vis′aged** *adj.*

vis-à-vis (vēz′ə-vē′, vēs-, -ä-vē′) *adj. & adv.* Face to face. —*prep.* **1** Opposite. **2** In relation to; toward. [F, face to face]

vis·cer·a (vis′ər-ə) *n.pl. sing.* **vis·cus** (vis′kəs) **1** The internal organs of the body, as the stomach, lungs, heart, etc. **2** Commonly, the intestines. [L, pl. of *viscus* an internal organ]

vis·cer·al (vis′ər-əl) *adj.* **1** Of or pertaining to the viscera. **2** Instinctive or emotional: a *visceral* reaction. —**vis′cer·al·ly** *adv.*

vis·cid (vis′id) *adj.* Glutinous in consistency; adhesive; syrupy; viscous. [< L *viscum* birdlime] —**vis·cid·i·ty** (vi·sid′ə·tē), **vis′cid·ness** *n.* —**vis′cid·ly** *adv.*

vis·cose (vis′kōs) *n.* A viscid substance produced from cellulose as a step in the manufacture of rayon, cellophane, etc. —*adj.* **1** VISCOUS. **2** Of, pertaining to, containing, or made from viscose.

vis·cos·i·ty (vis·kos′ə·tē) *n. pl.* **·ties 1** The property of fluids by which they offer resistance to flow or to change in the arrangement of their molecules. **2** The measure of this property.

vis·count (vī′kount) *n.* A nobleman ranking below an earl or count and above a baron. [< OF *visconte*] —**vis′·count·cy, vis′count·ship, vis′count·y** *n.*

vis·count·ess (vī′koun·tis) *n.* The wife of a viscount, or a peeress holding the title in her own right.

vis·cous (vis′kəs) *adj.* **1** Greatly resistant to flow; of high viscosity. **2** VISCID. [< L *viscum* birdlime] —**vis′cous·ly** *adv.* —**vis′cous·ness** *n.*

vise (vīs) *n.* A clamping device, usu. of two jaws made to be closed together with a screw, lever, or the like, for grasping and holding a piece of work. —*v.t.* **vised, vis·ing** To hold, force, or squeeze in or as in a vise. [< OF *vis* a screw < L *vitis* vine]

vi·sé (vē′zā) *n., v.t.* **vi·séed** or **vi·séd, vi·sé·ing** VISA.

Vish·nu (vish′nōō) In Hindu theology, the second god of the trinity (Brahma, Vishnu, and Siva), known as "the Preserver."

Machinist's vise (cross section)

vis·i·bil·i·ty (viz′ə·bil′ə·tē) *n. pl.* **·ties 1** The fact, condition, or degree of being visible. **2** *Meteorol.* The clearness of the atmosphere in terms of the distance at which objects can be seen distinctly.

vis·i·ble (viz′ə·bəl) *adj.* **1** Capable of being seen. **2** That can be perceived mentally; evident. [< L *visus*, p.p. of *videre* see] —**vis′i·ble·ness** *n.* —**vis′i·bly** *adv.* —**Syn. 1** perceptible. **2** clear, distinct, obvious, plain.

Vis·i·goth (viz′ə·goth) *n.* A member of the western Goths, a Teutonic people that invaded the Roman Empire in the late fourth century and established a monarchy in France and Spain. —**Vis′i·goth′ic** *adj.*

vi·sion (vizh′ən) *n.* **1** The act or power of seeing; sense of sight. **2** That which is seen. **3** A beautiful person, landscape, etc. **4** A mental representation of external objects or scenes, as in sleep. **5** A conception in the imagination; mental image: *visions* of power and wealth. **6** The ability to perceive, discern, and anticipate; foresight; imagination. —*v.t.* To see in or as in a vision. [< L *visus*, p.p. of *videre* see] —**vi′sion·al** *adj.* —**vi′sion·al·ly** *adv.*

vi·sion·ar·y (vizh′ən·er′ē) *adj.* **1** Not founded on fact; existing in the imagination; imaginary. **2** Able or disposed to see visions; affected by fantasies; dreamy. **3** Impractical, speculative, utopian, etc. **4** Of, pertaining to, characterized by, or seen in a vision or visions. —*n. pl.* **·ar·ies 1** One who has visions. **2** One whose plans, projects, etc., are

unrealistic or impractical; dreamer. —**vi′sion·ar′i·ness** *n.*

vis·it (viz′it) *v.t.* **1** To go or come to see (a person) from friendship, courtesy, on business, etc. **2** To go or come to (a place, etc.), as for transacting business or for touring: to *visit* the Louvre. **3** To be a guest of; stay with temporarily: I *visited* them for several days. **4** To come upon or afflict. **5** To inflict upon. —*v.i.* **6** To pay a visit; call. **7** To stay with someone temporarily. **8** *Informal* To converse; chat. —*n.* **1** The act of visiting a person, place, or thing. **2** A social call or short stay. **3** *Informal* A friendly chat. **4** An official call, as for inspection, medical examination, etc. [< L *visare* < *visus*, p.p. of *videre* see]

vis·i·tant (viz′ə·tənt) *n.* **1** A visitor. **2** A migratory bird at a particular region for a limited period.

vis·i·ta·tion (viz′ə·tā′shən) *n.* **1** The act of visiting; esp., an official inspection, examination, etc. **2** A dispensation of punishment or reward, as by God. —**the Visitation 1** The visit of the Virgin Mary to her cousin, Elizabeth. *Luke* 1:39–56. **2** A church feast, observed on July 2, commemorating this event. —**vis′i·ta′tion·al** *adj.*

visiting card CALLING CARD.

vis·i·tor (viz′ə·tər) *n.* One who visits; guest.

vi·sor (vī′zər) *n.* **1** A projecting piece on a cap shielding the eyes. **2** In armor, the front piece of a helmet which protected the upper part of the face and could be raised or lowered. **3** A movable device over the inside of the windshield of a car, serving to reduce glare. [< OF *vis* face] —**vi′sored** (-zərd) *adj.*

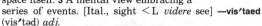

Visor def. 2

vis·ta (vis′tə) *n.* **1** A view, esp. one seen through a long, narrow space, as along an avenue, between rows of trees, etc. **2** The space itself. **3** A mental view embracing a series of events. [Ital., sight < L *videre* see] —**vis′taed** (vis′təd) *adj.*

vis·u·al (vizh′ōō·əl) *adj.* **1** Of or pertaining to the sense of sight. **2** Perceptible by sight; visible. **3** Done or perceived by sight only. **4** Instructing through the sense of sight: *visual* aids. [< L *visus* a sight < *videre* see] —**vis′u·al·ly** *adv.*

visual aids Charts, diagrams, slides, motion pictures, etc., used as aids in teaching and lecturing.

vis·u·al·ize (vizh′ōō·əl·īz′, vizh′əl-) *v.* **·ized, ·iz·ing** *v.t.* **1** To form a mental image of; picture in the mind. —*v.i.* **2** To form mental images. *Brit. sp.* **vis·u·al·ise.** —**vis′u·al·i·za′tion, vis′u·al·iz′er** *n.*

vi·tal (vīt′l) *adj.* **1** Of or pertaining to life. **2** Essential to or supporting life. **3** Affecting life in a destructive way; fatal: a *vital* wound. **4** Of the utmost importance or interest. **5** Full of life; vigorous; energetic; dynamic. —*n.pl.* **1** The organs necessary to life, as the brain, heart, etc. **2** The necessary parts of anything. [< L *vitalis* < *vita* life] —**vi′tal·ly** *adv.*

vi·tal·ism (vīt′l·iz′əm) *n.* The doctrine that the life and functions of a living organism depend upon a vital force that differs in kind from all chemical and physical forces. —**vi′tal·ist** *n.* —**vi′tal·is′tic** *adj.*

vi·tal·i·ty (vī·tal′ə·tē) *n.* **1** The power to live and develop. **2** Power of continuing in force or effect. **3** Physical or mental energy; vigor; strength.

vi·tal·ize (vīt′l·īz) *v.t.* **·ized, ·iz·ing** To make vital; endow with life or energy; animate. —**vi′tal·i·za′tion, vi′tal·iz′er** *n.*

vital statistics Data relating to births, deaths, marriages, health, etc.

vi·ta·min (vī′tə·min) *n.* Any of a group of organic substances whose presence in the diet in minute quantities is essential for the maintenance of specific physiological functions. [< L *vita* life + AMINE] —**vi′ta·min′ic** *adj.*

vitamin A The fat-soluble vitamin essential to vision and occurring in all animal tissues and many vegetables.

vitamin B complex A varied group of water-soluble vitamins having distinct functions.

vitamin B₁ THIAMINE.

vitamin B₂ RIBOFLAVIN.

vitamin B₆ PYRIDOXINE.

vitamin B₁₂ A vitamin normally produced in the intestine and essential for the production of erythrocytes.

vitamin C ASCORBIC ACID.

vitamin D A substance essential in the formation of bone

and the metabolism of calcium, occurring in fish-liver oils and formed from sterols in the skin when exposed to sunshine.

vitamin E An oily substance present in most foods and essential to fertility in experimental animals.

vitamin G RIBOFLAVIN.

vitamin H BIOTIN.

vitamin K₁ A vitamin, found in green leafy vegetables, which promotes the clotting of blood.

vitamin K₂ A form of vitamin K₁ prepared from fishmeal.

vitamin P A factor present in citrus juices that promotes the normal permeability of capillary walls.

vi·ti·ate (vish′ē·āt) *v.t.* **·at·ed, ·at·ing 1** To impair the use or value of; spoil. **2** To debase or corrupt. **3** To render weak, ineffective, legally invalid, etc.: Fraud *vitiates* a contract. [< L *vitium* a fault] —**vi′ti·a′tion, vi′ti·a′tor** *n.*

vit·i·cul·ture (vit′ə·kul′chər, vī′tə-) *n.* The science and art of grape-growing; cultivation of grapes. [< L *vitis* a vine + CULTURE] —**vit′i·cul′tur·al** *adj.* —**vit′i·cul′tur·er, vit′i·cul′tur·ist** *n.*

vit·i·li·go (vit′ə·lī′gō) *n.* A skin disorder characterized by partial loss of pigment resulting in white spots. [L, a vesicular skin disease]

vit·re·ous (vit′rē·əs) *adj.* **1** Of, pertaining to, or like glass; glassy. **2** Obtained from glass. **3** Of or pertaining to the vitreous humor. [< L *vitrum* glass] —**vit′re·os′i·ty** (-os′ə·tē), **vit′re·ous·ness** *n.*

vitreous humor The transparent jellylike tissue that fills the eyeball. Also **vitreous body.**

vit·ri·fy (vit′rə·fī) *v.t. & v.i.* **·fied, ·fy·ing** To change into glass or a vitreous substance; make or become vitreous. [< L *vitrum* glass + *facere* make] —**vit′ri·fac′tion** (-fak′-shən), **vit′ri·fi·ca′tion** *n.*

vit·ri·ol (vit′rē·ol, -əl) *n.* **1** Any sulfate of a heavy metal, as **green vitriol** (iron); **blue vitriol** (copper); **white vitriol** (zinc). **2** Sulfuric acid: also **oil of vitriol. 3** Anything sharp or caustic, as sarcasm. —*v.t.* **·oled** or **·olled, ·ol·ing** or **·ol·ling** To subject (anything) to the agency of vitriol. [< L *vitrum* glass]

vit·ri·ol·ic (vit′rē·ol′ik) *adj.* **1** Of, like, or derived from vitriol. **2** Biting, sharp, or caustic: *vitriolic* remarks.

vit·tle (vit′l) *n.* VICTUAL.

vi·tu·per·ate (vī·t⁽y⁾oo′pə·rāt, vi-) *v.t.* **·at·ed, ·at·ing** To find fault with abusively; rail at; berate; scold. [< L *vituperare* blame, scold < *vitium* a fault + *parare* prepare] —**vi·tu′per·a′tion, vi·tu′per·a′tor** *n.* —**vi·tu′per·a′tive** *adj.* —**vi·tu′per·a′tive·ly** *adv.*

viv. *Music* lively (It. *vivace*).

vi·va (vē′vä) *interj.* Live; long live (the person or thing specified): used in acclamation. [Ital. < *vivere* live < L]

vi·va·ce (vē·vä′chā) *adv. Music* Lively; quickly; briskly. [< L *vivax*]

vi·va·cious (vi·vā′shəs, vī-) *adj.* Full of life and spirits; lively; active. [< L *vivax* < *vivere* live] —**vi·va′cious·ly** *adv.* —**vi·va′cious·ness** *n.* —Syn. animated, brisk, cheerful, sparkling, spirited.

vi·vac·i·ty (vi·vas′ə·tē, vī-) *n. pl.* **·ties 1** The state or quality of being vivacious. **2** A vivacious act, expression, etc.

vi·var·i·um (vī·vâr′ē·əm) *n. pl.* **·var·i·a** (-vâr′ē·ə) or **·var·i·ums** A place for keeping or raising animals or plants for observation or research. Also **viv·a·ry** (viv′ər·ē). [< L *vivus* alive < *vivere* live]

vi·va vo·ce (vī′və vō′sē, vē′və vō′chā) By spoken word; orally or oral. [L]

vive (vēv) *interj. French* Live; long live (the person or thing specified): used in acclamation.

viv·id (viv′id) *adj.* **1** Having an appearance of vigorous life; lively; spirited. **2** Very strong; intense: said of colors. **3** Producing or suggesting lifelike images. **4** Producing a sharp impression on the senses: a *vivid* description. [< L *vividus* lively < *vivere* to live] —**viv′id·ly** *adv.* —**viv′id·ness** *n.*

viv·i·fy (viv′ə·fī) *v.t.* **·fied, ·fy·ing 1** To give life to; animate; vitalize. **2** To make more vivid or striking. [< L *vivus* alive + *facere* make] —**viv′i·fi·ca′tion** (-fə·kā′shən), **viv′i·fi′er** *n.*

vi·vip·a·rous (vī·vip′ər·əs) *adj.* Bringing forth young that have developed from eggs within the mother's body. [< L *vivus* alive + *parere* bring forth] —**vi·vip′a·rous·ly** *adv.* —**vi·vip′a·rous·ness, viv·i·par·i·ty** (viv′ə·par′ə·tē) *n.*

viv·i·sect (viv′ə·sekt) *v.t.* **1** To perform vivisection on. —*v.i.* **2** To practice vivisection. —**viv′i·sec′tor** *n.*

viv·i·sec·tion (viv′ə·sek′shən) *n.* Cutting, dissection, or other operation on a living animal, esp. in experiments designed to promote knowledge of physiological and pathological processes. [< L *vivus* living, alive + *sectio* a cutting] —**viv′i·sec′tion·al** *adj.* —**viv′i·sec′tion·ist** *n., adj.*

vix·en (vik′sən) *n.* **1** A female fox. **2** A turbulent, quarrelsome woman; shrew. [< ME *fixen* a she-fox] —**vix′en·ish** *adj.* —**vix′en·ly** *adj., adv.*

viz, viz. namely (L *videlicet*).

viz·ard (viz′ərd) *n.* A mask or visor. [Alter. of VISOR]

vi·zier (vi·zir′) *n.* A high official of a Muslim country, as in the old Turkish Empire. Also **vi·zir′.** [< Ar. *wazīr* a counselor]

vi·zor (vī′zər) *n.* VISOR.

V-J Day (vē′jā′) Sept. 2, 1945, the official date of the Allied victory over Japan in World War II.

VL, V.L. Vulgar Latin.

VLF, V.L.F., vlf, v.l.f. very low frequency.

V-mail (vē′māl′) *n.* Mail transmitted overseas in World War II on microfilm, and enlarged at point of reception for final delivery. [< V(ICTORY) + MAIL¹]

V.M.D. Doctor of Veterinary Medicine (L *Veterinariae Medicinae Doctor*).

vo. verso.

voc. vocative.

vocab. vocabulary.

vo·ca·ble (vō′kə·bəl) *n.* A word viewed as a combination of sounds and letters apart from its meaning. [< L *vocabulum* a name, appellation < *vocare* to call]

vo·cab·u·lar·y (vō·kab′yə·ler′ē) *n. pl.* **·lar·ies 1** A list of words or of words and phrases, esp. one arranged in alphabetical order and defined or translated; a lexicon; glossary. **2** All the words of a language. **3** All the words used or understood by a particular person, class, profession, etc. **4** The range of expression at a person's disposal, esp. in art. [< L *vocabulum.* See VOCABLE.]

vo·cal (vō′kəl) *adj.* **1** Of or pertaining to the voice or the production of the voice. **2** Having voice; able to speak or utter sounds: *vocal* creatures. **3** Composed for, uttered by, or performed by the voice: a *vocal* score. **4** Full of voices or sounds; resounding: The air was *vocal* with their cries. **5** Freely expressing oneself in speech: the *vocal* segment of the populace. [< L *vocalis* speaking, sounding] —**vo·cal·i·ty** (vō·kal′ə·tē), **vo′cal·ness** *n.* —**vo′cal·ly** *adv.*

vocal cords Two ligaments extending across the larynx, which, when tense, are caused to vibrate by the passage of air, thereby producing voice.

vo·cal·ic (vō·kal′ik) *adj.* **1** Of, pertaining to, or like a vowel sound. **2** Characterized by or consisting of vowel sounds.

vo·cal·ist (vō′kəl·ist) *n.* A singer.

vo·cal·ize (vō′kəl·īz) *v.* **·ized, ·iz·ing** *v.t.* **1** To make vocal; utter, say, or sing. **2** *Phonet.* **a** To change to or use as a vowel: to *vocalize* y. **b** To voice. —*v.i.* **3** To produce sounds with the voice, as in speaking or singing. **4** *Phonet.* To be changed to a vowel. —**vo′cal·i·za′tion, vo′cal·iz′er** *n.*

Vocal cords
a. open. b. closed.
c. voice. d. whisper.

vo·ca·tion (vō·kā′shən) *n.* **1** A stated or regular occupation. **2** A call to, or fitness for, a certain career. **3** The work or profession for which one has or believes one has a special fitness. [< L *vocare* to call] —**vo·ca′tion·al** *adj.* —**vo·ca′tion·al·ly** *adv.*

voc·a·tive (vok′ə·tiv) *Gram. adj.* In some inflected languages, denoting the case of a noun, pronoun, or adjective used in direct address. —*n.* **1** The vocative case. **2** A word in this case. [< L *vocare* to call]

vo·cif·er·ant (vō·sif′ər·ənt) *adj.* Vociferous; uttering loud cries. —**vo·cif′er·ance** *n.*

---

vo·cif·er·ate (vō·sif′ə·rāt) v.t. & v.i. ·at·ed, ·at·ing To cry out with a loud voice; shout. [< L vox a voice + ferre carry] —vo·cif′er·a′tion, vo·cif′er·a′tor n. —Syn. bawl, bellow, clamor, scream, yell.

vo·cif·er·ous (vō·sif′ər·əs) adj. Making or characterized by a loud outcry; noisy; clamorous. —vo·cif′er·ous·ly adv. —vo·cif′er·ous·ness n.

vod·ka (vod′kə) n. A colorless alcoholic liquor originally made in Poland and Russia, distilled from a mash, as of rye, wheat, or potatoes. [< Russ. voda water]

vogue (vōg) n. 1 Fashion or style. 2 Popular favor; popularity. [F, fashion, orig., rowing] —vogu′ish adj.

voice (vois) n. 1 The sound produced by the vocal organs of a vertebrate, esp. by a human being in speaking, singing, etc. 2 The quality or character of such sound: a melodious voice. 3 The power or ability to make such a sound: to lose one's voice. 4 Something suggesting the sound of vocal utterance: the voice of the wind. 5 Expressed opinion, choice, etc. 6 The right to express an opinion, choice, etc. 7 A person or agency by which the thought, wish, or purpose of another is expressed: This journal is the voice of the teaching profession. 8 Expression: to give voice to one's ideals. 9 Phonet. The sound produced by vibration of the vocal cords, as heard in the utterance of vowels and certain consonants, as b, d, and z. 10 A singer: Caruso was a great voice. 11 In a musical composition, a part for a singer or an instrument. 12 Gram. A form of a verb which indicates whether its subject is active or passive. —in voice Having the voice in good condition for singing and speaking. —lift up one's voice 1 To shout or sing loudly. 2 To protest. —with one voice With one accord; unanimously. —v.t. voiced, voic·ing 1 To put into speech; give expression to; utter. 2 Music To regulate the tones of, as the pipes of an organ. 3 Phonet. To utter with voice. [< L vox, vocis] • When the subject of a verb performs the action, the verb is in the active voice: My aunt baked a chocolate cake; Her father gave her a bicycle. When the subject of a verb is acted upon, the verb is in the passive voice: The chocolate cake was baked by my aunt; She was given a bicycle by her father.

voiced (voist) adj. 1 Having a voice or a specified kind of voice: often used in combination: high-voiced, soft-voiced. 2 Expressed by voice. 3 Phonet. Uttered with vibration of the vocal cords, as (b), (d), (z).

voice·less (vois′lis) adj. 1 Having no voice, speech, or vote. 2 Phonet. Produced without voice, as (p), (t), (s). — voice′less·ly adv. —voice′less·ness n.

voice-o·ver (vois′ō′vər) n. In motion pictures and television programs, the voice of a narrator or announcer speaking off camera.

voice·print (vois′print′) n. A graphic representation of the sound of a person's voice, consisting of a complex pattern of wavy lines corresponding to the various pitches used in the utterance.

void (void) adj. 1 Containing nothing; without content; empty. 2 Having no legal force or validity; not binding. 3 Producing no effect; useless. —void of Lacking; without. —n. 1 An empty space; vacuum. 2 The quality or condition of feeling empty, lonely, lost, etc. —v.t. 1 To make void or of no effect; annul. 2 To empty or remove (contents); evacuate. —v.i. 3 To eliminate waste from the body; urinate or defecate. [< L vacuus empty] —void′er, void′ness n. —void′ly adv.

voi·là (vwà·là′) interj. French There! behold! literally, see there.

voile (voil) n. A fine, sheer fabric, as of cotton, silk, wool, or rayon. [< OF veile veil]

vol. volcano; volume; volunteer.

vo·lant (vō′lənt) adj. 1 Flying, or capable of flying. 2 Agile; quick; nimble. 3 Her. Represented as flying, as a bird or bee. [< L volare to fly]

vol·a·tile (vol′ə·til; chiefly Brit. -tīl) adj. 1 Evaporating rapidly; capable of being vaporized. 2 Inconstant; changeable. 3 Transient; fleeting. [< L volatilis < volare fly] —vol′a·tile·ness, vol·a·til·i·ty (vol′ə·til′ə·tē) n.

vol·a·til·ize (vol′ə·til·īz′) v.t. & v.i. ·ized, ·iz·ing To pass off or cause to pass off in vapor. —vol′a·til·i·za′tion n.

vol·can·ic (vol·kan′ik) adj. 1 Of, pertaining to, produced by, or characterized by a volcano or volcanoes. 2 Like a volcano; explosive; violent. —vol·can′i·cal·ly adv. —vol·can·ic·i·ty (vol′kə·nis′ə·tē) n.

vol·can·ism (vol′kən·iz′əm) n. The power or action of volcanoes.

vol·ca·no (vol·kā′nō) n. pl. ·noes or ·nos Geol. An opening in the earth's surface from which hot matter is or has been ejected, often surrounded by a hill or mountain of ejected material. [< L Vulcanus Vulcan]

vole (vōl) n. Any of various short-tailed, mouselike or rat-like rodents. [Short for earlier vole mouse field mouse]

vo·li·tion (və·lish′ən) n. 1 The act of willing; exercise of the will. 2 The power of willing; willpower. [< L velle to will] —vo·li′tion·al, vo·li′tion·ar·y (-ən·er·ē), vol·i·tive (vol′ə·tiv) adj. —vo·li′tion·al·ly adv.

vol·ley (vol′ē) n. 1 A simultaneous discharge of many guns. 2 A discharge of many bullets, stones, arrows, etc. 3 Any discharge of many things at once: a volley of oaths. 4 In tennis, the flight of the ball before it touches the ground; also, a return of the ball before it touches the ground. —v.t. & v.i. ·leyed, ·ley·ing 1 To discharge or be discharged in a volley. 2 In tennis, to return (the ball) without allowing it to touch the ground. [< MF voler to fly] —vol′ley·er n.

vol·ley·ball (vol′ē·bôl′) n. 1 A game in which a number of players on both sides of a high net use their hands to hit a ball back and forth over the net without letting it drop. 2 The ball used in this game.

vol·plane (vol′plān) v.i. ·planed, ·plan·ing To glide down in an airplane with the engine turned off. —n. An airplane glide. [< F vol plané gliding flight]

vols. volumes.

volt[1] (vōlt) n. A unit equal to the difference of electric potential which, when steadily applied to a conductor whose resistance is one ohm, will produce a current of one ampere. [< A. Volta, 1745–1827, Italian physicist]

volt[2] (vōlt) n. 1 In horse-training, a gait in which the horse moves sidewise round a center with the head turned out. 2 In fencing, a sudden leap to avoid a thrust. [< Ital. volta, p.p. fem. of volvere to turn]

volt·age (vōl′tij) n. Electromotive force expressed in volts.

vol·ta·ic (vol·tā′ik) adj. Pertaining to electricity developed through chemical action; galvanic.

voltaic battery A set of voltaic cells which operate as a unit.

voltaic cell A cell that generates electricity by a chemical reaction and that cannot be efficiently recharged.

volt·me·ter (vōlt′mē′tər) n. An instrument for measuring differences of electric potential.

vol·u·ble (vol′yə·bəl) adj. Having a flow of words or fluency in speaking; talkative. [< L volubilis easily turned < volutus, p.p. of volvere to turn] —vol′u·bil′i·ty (vol′yə·bil′·ə·tē), vol′u·ble·ness n. —vol′u·bly adv.

vol·ume (vol′yōōm, -yəm) n. 1 A collection of sheets of paper bound together; a book. 2 A book that is part of a set. 3 A quantity or amount: a large volume of sales. 4 A measure of quantity in terms of space occupied, as cubic inch, cubic centimeter, liter, pint, etc. 5 Acoustics Fullness or quantity of sound or tone. —speak volumes To be full of meaning; express a great deal. [< L volumen a roll, scroll] —vol′umed adj.

vol·u·met·ric (vol′yə·met′rik) adj. Of, based on, or pertaining to measurement of substances by volume. Also vol′u·met′ri·cal. —vol′u·met′ri·cal·ly adv.

vo·lu·mi·nous (və·lōō′mə·nəs) adj. 1 Consisting of or capable of filling volumes: a voluminous correspondence. 2 Writing or speaking much. 3 Having great volume or bulk; large. [< L volumen a roll] —vo·lu·mi·nos·i·ty (və·lōō′mə·nos′ə·tē), vo·lu′mi·nous·ness n. —vo·lu′mi·nous·ly adv.

vol·un·tar·y (vol′ən·ter′ē) adj. 1 Done, made, or given by one's own free will or choice: a voluntary contribution. 2 Endowed with or exercising will or free choice. 3 Acting without constraint: a voluntary donor. 4 Subject to or directed by the will, as a muscle or movement. 5 Intentional; volitional: voluntary manslaughter. —n. pl. ·tar·ies 1 Voluntary action or work. 2 A solo, usu. on the organ, often played before, during, or after a church service. [< L voluntas will] —vol·un·tar·i·ly (vol′ən·ter′ə·lē, vol′ən·ter′-) adv. —vol′un·tar′i·ness n.

vol·un·teer (vol'ən·tir') *n.* **1** One who enters into any service of his own free will. **2** One who voluntarily enters military service. —*adj.* **1** Of, pertaining to, or composed of volunteers; voluntary. **2** Serving as a volunteer. —*v.t.* **1** To offer or give voluntarily: to *volunteer* one's services. —*v.i.* **2** To enter or offer to enter into some service or undertaking of one's free will. [< OF *voluntaire* voluntary]

vo·lup·tu·ar·y (və·lup'choo·er'ē) *n. pl.* **·ar·ies** One addicted to luxury and sensual indulgence. [< L *voluptas* pleasure] —**Syn.** hedonist, sensualist, sybarite.

vo·lup·tu·ous (və·lup'choo·əs) *adj.* **1** Pertaining to, inclining to, producing, or produced by sensuous or sensual gratification. **2** Devoted to the enjoyment of pleasures or luxuries. **3** Suggesting the satisfaction of sensual desire. [< L *voluptas* pleasure] —**vo·lup'tu·ous·ly** *adv.* —**vo·lup'tu·ous·ness** *n.*

vo·lute (və·lōōt') *n.* **1** *Archit.* A spiral scroll-like ornament, as in Ionic capitals. **2** *Zool.* One of the whorls or turns of a spiral shell. **3** A spiral or twisted form. —*adj.* Having a spiral form; scroll-shaped. [< L *voluta* a scroll < p.p. of *volvere* to turn] —**vo·lut'ed** *adj.* —**vo·lu'tion** *n.*

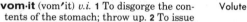

Volute

vom·it (vom'it) *v.i.* **1** To disgorge the contents of the stomach; throw up. **2** To issue with violence from any hollow place; be ejected. —*v.t.* **3** To disgorge (the contents of the stomach). **4** To discharge or send forth copiously or forcibly: The volcano *vomited* smoke. —*n.* **1** The act of vomiting. **2** Matter ejected from the stomach in vomiting. [< L *vomere*] —**vom'it·er** *n.*

vom·i·tive (vom'ə·tiv) *adj.* Of, pertaining to, or causing vomiting. —*n.* EMETIC.

von (von; *Ger.* fôn, *unstressed* fən) *prep. German* Of; from: used in German and Austrian family names as an attribute of nobility.

voo·doo (vōō'dōō) *n.* **1** A primitive religion of African origin, found among Haitian and West Indian Negroes and the Negroes of the s U.S., characterized by belief in sorcery and the use of charms, fetishes, witchcraft, etc. **2** A person who practices voodoo. **3** A voodoo charm or fetish. —*adj.* Of or pertaining to the beliefs, ceremonies, etc., of voodoo. —*v.t.* To practice voodoo upon; bewitch. Also **vou'dou.** —**voo'doo·ism, voo'doo·ist** *n.* —**voo'doo·is'tic** *adj.*

vo·ra·cious (vô·rā'shəs, vō-, və-) *adj.* **1** Eating with greediness; ravenous. **2** Very eager, as in some desire; insatiable. **3** Immoderate: a *voracious* appetite. [< L *vorax* < *vorare* devour] —**vo·ra'cious·ly** *adv.* —**vo·rac·i·ty** (-ras'ə·tē), **vo·ra'cious·ness** *n.*

-vorous *combining form* Consuming; eating or feeding upon: *omnivorous, carnivorous*. [< L *vorare* devour]

vor·tex (vôr'teks) *n. pl.* **·tex·es** or **·ti·ces** (-tə·sēz) **1** A mass of rotating or whirling fluid, esp. one spiraling in toward a center; a whirlpool or whirlwind. **2** Something resembling a vortex, as an activity or situation from which it is difficult to escape. [< L, var. of *vertex* top, point] —**vor'ti·cal** (-ti·kəl) *adj.* —**vor'ti·cal·ly** *adv.*

vo·ta·ry (vō'tər·ē) *n. pl.* **·ries** **1** One who is bound by vows, as a nun or priest. **2** One devoted to some particular worship, pursuit, study, etc. Also **vo'ta·rist.** —*adj.* **1** Of, pertaining to, or like a vow. **2** Consecrated by a vow. [< L *votus*, p.p. of *vovere* vow]

vote (vōt) *n.* **1** A formal expression of choice or opinion, as in electing officers, passing resolutions, etc. **2** That by which such choice or opinion is expressed, as the ballot, a show of hands, etc. **3** The number of ballots cast, hands raised, etc., to indicate such choice or opinion. **4** The votes of a specified group; also, the group itself. **5** The right to vote. **6** A voter. —*v.* **vot·ed, vot·ing** *v.t.* **1** To enact or determine by vote. **2** To cast one's vote for: to *vote* the Democratic ticket. **3** To elect or defeat by vote. **4** *Informal* To declare by general agreement: to *vote* a concert a success. —*v.i.* **5** To cast one's vote. —**vote down** To defeat or suppress by voting against. —**vote in** To elect. [< L *votum* a vow, wish, orig. p.p. neut. of *vovere* vow]

vot·er (vōt'ər) *n.* **1** A person who votes. **2** A person having the right to vote.

vo·tive (vō'tiv) *adj.* Performed, offered, lit, etc., as fulfillment of a vow, as an act of worship, in gratitude, etc. [< L *votum*. See VOTE.] —**vo'tive·ly** *adv.* —**vo'tive·ness** *n.*

vouch (vouch) *v.i.* **1** To give one's own assurance or guarantee: with *for*: I will *vouch* for their honesty. **2** To serve as assurance or proof: with *for*: The evidence *vouches* for his innocence. —*v.t.* **3** To bear witness to; attest or affirm. **4** To cite as support or justification, as a precedent, authority, etc. **5** To uphold by satisfactory proof or evidence; substantiate. [< L *vocare* call < *vox, vocis* a voice]

vouch·er (vou'chər) *n.* **1** A document that serves to vouch for the truth of something, or attest an alleged act, esp. the expenditure or receipt of money. **2** One who vouches for another; a witness.

vouch·safe (vouch·sāf') *v.* **·safed, ·saf·ing** *v.t.* **1** To grant, as with condescension; permit; deign. —*v.i.* **2** To condescend; deign. [< VOUCH + SAFE] —**vouch'safe'ment** *n.*

vous·soir (vōō·swär') *n. Archit.* A wedge-shaped stone in an arch. [< OF *vausoir, volsoir* curvature of a vault]

vow (vou) *n.* **1** A solemn promise, as to God or a god. **2** A pledge of faithfulness: marriage *vows*. **3** A solemn and emphatic affirmation. —**take vows** To enter a religious order. —*v.t.* **1** To promise solemnly. **2** To declare with assurance or solemnity. **3** To make a solemn promise or threat to do, inflict, etc. —*v.i.* **4** To make a vow. [< L *votum*. See VOTE.] —**vow'er** *n.*

vow·el (vou'əl, voul) *n.* **1** *Phonet.* A voiced speech sound produced by the relatively unimpeded passage of air through the mouth. **2** A letter indicating such a sound, as *a, e, i, o,* or *u*. —*adj.* Of or pertaining to a vowel or vowels. [< L *vocalis (littera)* vocal (letter)]

vox pop. voice of the people (L *vox populi*).

vox po·pu·li (voks pop'yə·lī, -lē) The voice of the people; public sentiment. [L]

voy·age (voi'ij) *n.* **1** A journey by water, esp. by sea. **2** Any journey, as one by aircraft. —*v.* **·aged, ·ag·ing** *v.i.* **1** To make a voyage; travel. —*v.t.* **2** To traverse. [< L *viaticum*] —**voy'ag·er** *n.* —**Syn.** *n.* **1** crossing, cruise, sail, trip.

vo·ya·geur (vwà·yà·zhœr') *n. pl.* **·geurs** (-zhœr') *Can.* Formerly, a man engaged by a fur company to carry men, supplies, etc., between remote trading posts. [F]

vo·yeur (vwä·yûr') *n.* One who is sexually gratified by looking at sexual objects or acts. [< F *voir* see] —**vo·yeur'ism** *n.*

V.P. Vice President.

vs. versus.

v.s. see above (L *vide supra*).

VSS versions.

VT Vermont (P.O. abbr.).

Vt. Vermont.

v.t. verb transitive.

VTOL vertical takeoff and landing.

Vul., Vulg. Vulgate.

Vul·can (vul'kən) *Rom. Myth.* The god of fire and of metallurgy. —**Vul·ca·ni·an** (-kā'nē·ən) *adj.*

vul·can·ite (vul'kən·īt) *n.* A dark-colored, hard, vulcanized rubber. [< VULCAN]

vul·can·ize (vul'kən·īz) *v.t. & v.i.* **·ized, ·iz·ing** To heat (natural rubber) with sulfur in order to increase strength and elasticity. [< VULCAN] —**vul'can·i·za'tion, vul'can·iz'er** *n.*

vul·gar (vul'gər) *adj.* **1** Lacking good manners, taste, etc.; coarse; unrefined. **2** Offensive or obscene in expression: a *vulgar* usage. **3** Of or pertaining to the common people; general; popular. **4** Written in or translated into the common language or dialect; vernacular. [< L *vulgus* the common people] —**vul'gar·ly** *adv.* —**Syn.** **1** boorish, crude, tasteless. **2** indecent, taboo. **3** ordinary, plebeian.

vul·gar·i·an (vul·gâr'ē·ən) *n.* A person of vulgar tastes or manners; esp., a wealthy person with coarse habits.

vul·gar·ism (vul'gə·riz'əm) *n.* **1** A word, phrase, or expression generally considered to be incorrect or coarse and indicative of ignorance or ill breeding on the part of the user. **2** VULGARITY.

vul·gar·i·ty (vul·gar′ə·tē) *n. pl.* **·ties 1** The state, quality, or character of being vulgar. **2** Something vulgar, as an act or expression.

vul·gar·ize (vul′gə·rīz) *v.t.* **·ized, ·iz·ing** To make vulgar. *Brit. sp.* **vul′gar·ise.** —**vul′gar·i·za′tion, vul′gar·iz′er** *n.*

Vulgar Latin The popular, informal speech of the ancient Romans, considered to be the chief source of the Romance languages.

vul·gate (vul′gāt) *adj.* Popular; accepted. —*n.* **1** Everyday speech. **2** A popularly accepted text. [< L *vulgare* make common < *vulgus* the common people]

Vul·gate (vul′gāt) *n.* A Latin version of the Bible, translated in the 4th century, since revised and used as the authorized version by Roman Catholics. —*adj.* Of or in the Vulgate.

vul·ner·a·ble (vul′nər·ə·bəl) *adj.* **1** That may be wounded; capable of being hurt. **2** Open to attack; assailable. **3** In contract bridge, having won one game of a rubber, and therefore subject to doubled penalities if contract is not fulfilled. [< L *vulnerare* to wound < *vulnus* a wound] —**vul′ner·a·bil′i·ty, vul′ner·a·ble·ness** *n.* —**vul′ner·a·bly** *adv.*

vul·pine (vul′pin, -pīn) *adj.* **1** Of or pertaining to a fox. **2** Like a fox; sly; crafty; cunning. [< L *vulpes* a fox]

vul·ture (vul′chər) *n.* **1** Any of various large birds related to hawks and falcons, having a naked head and dark plumage, and feeding on carrion. **2** Something or someone that preys upon others. [< L *vultur*] —**vul′tur·ous** *adj.*

Vulture

vul·va (vul′və) *n. pl.* **·vae** (-vē) The external genital parts of the female. [L, a covering, womb] — **vul′val, vul′var, vul′vi·form** (-və·fôrm) *adj.*

vy·ing (vī′ing) *pr.p.* of VIE. —*adj.* That vies or competes. —**vy′ing·ly** *adv.*

W

W, w (dub′əl·yōō, -yōō) *n. pl.* **W's, w's, Ws, ws** (dub′əl·yōōz, -yōōz) **1** The 23rd letter of the English alphabet. **2** Any spoken sound representing the letter *W* or *w.* **3** Something shaped like a W. —*adj.* Shaped like a W.

W tungsten (G *wolfram*).

W, W., w, w. watt; west; western.

w. warden; week(s); weight; wife; with; word; work.

WA Washington (P.O. abbr.).

wab·ble (wob′əl) *n., v.t. & v.i.* **·bled, ·bling** WOBBLE. [Var. of WOBBLE] —**wab′bler** *n.* —**wab′bly** *adj.*

Wac (wak) *n.* A member of the **WAC,** the women's division of the U.S. Army. [< W(omen's) A(rmy) C(orps)]

wack·y (wak′ē) *adj.* **wack·i·er, wack·i·est** *Slang* Extremely irrational or erratic; crazy. Also **whack′y.** [Prob. < WHACK] —**wack′i·ly** *adv.* —**wack′i·ness** *n.*

wad (wod) *n.* **1** A small compact mass of any soft or flexible substance, esp. as used for stuffing, packing, or lining. **2** A lump; mass: a *wad* of tobacco. **3** A small plug used to hold in a charge of powder in a muzzleloading gun. **4** A pasteboard or paper disk to hold powder and shot in place in a shotgun shell. • See CARTRIDGE. **5** Fibrous material for stopping up breaks, leakages, etc.; wadding. **6** *Informal* A large amount, esp. of money. **7** *Informal* A roll of banknotes. —*v.* **wad·ded, wad·ding** *v.t.* **1** To press (fibrous substances, as cotton) into a mass or wad. **2** To roll or fold into a tight wad, as paper. **3** To pack or stuff with wadding for protection, as valuables. **4** To place a wad in (a gun, etc.). **5** To hold in place with a wad. —*v.i.* **6** To form into a wad. [?] —**wad′der** *n.*

wad·ding (wod′ing) *n.* **1** Wads collectively. **2** Any substance used as wads.

wad·dle (wod′l) *v.i.* **·dled, ·dling 1** To walk with short steps, swaying from side to side. **2** To move clumsily; totter. —*n.* A clumsy rocking walk, like that of a duck. [Freq. of WADE] —**wad′dler** *n.* —**wad′dly** *adj.*

wade (wād) *v.* **wad·ed, wad·ing** *v.i.* **1** To walk through water or any substance more resistant than air, as mud, sand, etc. **2** To proceed slowly or laboriously: to *wade* through a lengthy book. —*v.t.* **3** To pass or cross, as a river, by walking on the bottom; walk through; ford. —**wade in** (or **into**) *Informal* To attack or begin energetically or vigorously. —*n.* An act of wading. [< OE *wadan* go]

wad·er (wā′dər) *n.* **1** One who wades. **2** A long-legged wading bird, as a snipe, plover, or stork. **3** *pl.* High waterproof boots or pants, worn esp. by anglers.

wa·di (wä′dē) *n. pl.* **·dies 1** In Arabia and N Africa, a ravine containing the bed of a watercourse, usu. dry except in the rainy season. **2** The stream of water flowing through a wadi. Also **wa′dy.** [< Ar. *wādī*]

Waf (waf, wäf) *n.* A member of the **WAF,** the women's division of the U.S. Air Force. [< W(omen in the) A(ir) F(orce)]

wa·fer (wā′fər) *n.* **1** A very thin crisp biscuit, cooky, or cracker; also, a small disk of candy. **2** *Eccl.* A small flat disk of unleavened bread, used in the Eucharist in some churches. **3** A thin hardened disk of dried paste, gelatin, etc., used for sealing letters, attaching papers, or receiving the impression of a seal. —*v.t.* To attach, seal, or fasten with a wafer. [< AF *wafre* < MLG *wafel*]

waf·fle[1] (wof′əl, wô′fəl) *n.* A batter cake, crisper than a pancake, baked in a waffle iron. [< Du. *wafel* a wafer]

waf·fle[2] (wof′əl, wô′fəl) *v.i.* **·fled, ·fling 1** *Chiefly Brit. Informal* To speak or write nonsense. **2** *Informal* To avoid giving a direct answer; hedge. —*n. Chiefly Brit. Informal* Nonsense; twaddle. [< obs. *woff, waff* to yelp]

waffle iron A utensil for cooking waffles, consisting of two indented metal griddles, hinged together, between which the waffle is baked.

waft (waft, wäft) *v.t.* **1** To carry or bear gently or lightly over air or water; float. **2** To convey as if on air or water. —*v.i.* **3** To float, as on the wind. **4** To blow gently, as a breeze. —*n.* **1** The act of one who or that which wafts. **2** A breath or current of air. **3** A passing sound or odor. **4** A waving motion. [< Du. *wachten* to guard] —**waft′er** *n.*

wag (wag) *v.* **wagged, wag·ging** *v.t.* **1** To cause to move lightly and quickly from side to side or up and down, as a dog's tail. **2** To move (the tongue) in talking. —*v.i.* **3** To move lightly and quickly from side to side or up and down. **4** To move busily in animated talk or gossip: said of the tongue. —*n.* **1** The act or motion of wagging: a *wag* of the head. **2** A droll or humorous person; wit. [Prob. < Scand.]

wage (wāj) *n.* **1** *Often pl.* Payment for service rendered, esp. such payment calculated by the hour, day, or week, or for a certain amount of work. **2** *Usu. pl.* (construed as *sing.* or *pl.*) Reward: the *wages* of sin. —*v.t.* **waged, wag·ing** To engage in and maintain vigorously; carry on: to *wage* war. [< AF *wagier* pledge] —**Syn.** *n.* **1** compensation, earnings, pay, remuneration.

wage earner One who works for wages.

wa·ger (wā′jər) *v.t. & v.i.* To bet. —*n.* **1** A bet. **2** The thing bet on. [< AF *wagier*] —**wa′ger·er** *n.*

wage·work·er (wāj′wûr′kər) *n.* An employee receiving wages. —**wage′work′ing** *n., adj.*

wag·ger·y (wag′ər·ē) *n. pl.* **·ger·ies 1** Mischievous joking. **2** A practical joke. [< WAG]

wag·gish (wag′ish) *adj.* **1** Being or acting like a wag; humorous. **2** Said or done as a joke. —**wag′gish·ly** *adv.* — **wag′gish·ness** *n.* —**Syn.** **1** droll, facetious, funny, jocose.

wag·gle (wag′əl) *v.* **·gled, ·gling** *v.t.* To wag; swing: The duck *waggles* its tail. —*n.* The act of waggling. [Freq. of WAG] —**wag′gling·ly** *adv.* —**wag′gly** *adj.* (·i·er, ·i·est)

Wag·ne·ri·an (väg·nir′ē·ən) *adj.* **1** Of or pertaining to Richard Wagner or to his music, style, or theories. **2** Specializing in the performance of Wagner's music. —*n.* One

who admires the music or the theories of Richard Wagner.

wag·on (wag′ən) *n.* **1** Any of various four-wheeled, usu. horse-drawn vehicles for carrying heavy loads. **2** A child's open, four-wheeled cart, pulled and steered by a long handle. **3** PATROL WAGON. **4** STATION WAGON. **5** *Brit.* A railway freight car. **6** A stand on wheels or casters for serving food or drink: a tea *wagon.* **—on** (or **off**) **the (water) wagon** *Informal* Abstaining (or no longer abstaining) from alcoholic beverages. **—fix (someone's) wagon** *Slang* To even scores with; get revenge on. **—*v.t.*** To carry or transport in a wagon. *Brit. sp.* **wag′gon.** [< Du. *wagen*]

Wagon

wag·on·er (wag′ən·ər) *n.* One whose business is driving wagons. *Brit. sp.* **wag·gon·er.**

wag·on·load (wag′ən·lōd′) *n.* The amount that a wagon can carry. *Brit. sp.* **wag·gon·load.**

wagon train A line of wagons traveling together.

wag·tail (wag′tāl′) *n.* Any of various birds that habitually jerk the tail, as certain pipits.

Wa·ha·bi (wä·hä′bē) *n.* A member of a strict orthodox Muslim sect. Also **Wah·ha′bi. —Wa·ha′bism, Wah·ha′bism** (-biz·əm) *n.*

waif (wāf) *n.* **1** A homeless, neglected person, esp. a child. **2** A stray animal. [Prob. < Scand.]

wail (wāl) *v.i.* **1** To grieve with mournful cries; lament. **2** To make a mournful, crying sound, as the wind. **—*v.t.*** **3** To mourn; lament. **4** To cry out in sorrow. **—*n.*** **1** A prolonged, high-pitched sound of lamentation. **2** Any mournful sound, as of the wind. [< ON *vei* woe] **—wail′er** *n.* **—wail′ful** *adj.* **—wail′ful·ly, wail′ing·ly** *adv.*

Wailing Wall A high wall in Jerusalem reputedly containing fragments of Solomon's temple and traditionally a place for Jews to pray and mourn.

wain (wān) *n.* An open, four-wheeled wagon for hauling heavy loads. [< OE *wægn, wæn*]

wain·scot (wān′skət, -skŏt, -skot) *n.* **1** A facing for inner walls, usu. of paneled wood. **2** The lower part of an inner wall, when finished with material different from the rest of the wall. **—*v.t.*** **·scot·ed** or **·scot·ted, ·scot·ing** or **·scot·ting** To face or panel with wainscot. [< MLG *wagen* a wagon + *schot* a wooden partition]

wain·scot·ing (wān′skət·ing, -skot-) *n.* **1** WAINSCOT. **2** Material for a wainscot. Also **wain′scot·ting.**

wain·wright (wān′rīt) *n.* A maker of wagons.

waist (wāst) *n.* **1** The part of the body between the lower ribs and the hips. **2** The middle part of any object, esp. if narrower than the ends: the *waist* of a violin. **3** That part of a woman's dress covering the body from the waistline to the shoulders. **4** BLOUSE. **5** WAISTLINE (def. 2). [ME *wast*]

waist·band (wāst′band′) *n.* A band encircling the waist, esp. such a band inside a skirt or trousers.

waist·coat (wes′kit, wāst′kōt′) *n. Chiefly Brit.* VEST (def. 1).

waist·line (wāst′līn′) *n.* **1** The so-called line that encircles the middle of the waist. **2** That part of a garment covering this line or extending above or below it according to the dictates of fashion.

wait (wāt) *v.i.* **1** To stay in expectation, as of an anticipated action or event: with *for, until,* etc. **2** To be or remain in readiness. **3** To remain temporarily neglected or undone. **4** To perform duties of personal service; esp. to act as a waiter or waitress. **—*v.t.*** **5** To stay or remain in expectation of: to *wait* one's turn. **6** *Informal* To put off or postpone: Don't *wait* breakfast for me. **—wait on** (or **upon**) **1** To act as a clerk or attendant to. **2** To go to see; visit. **3** To attend as a result or consequence. **—wait up 1** To delay going to bed in anticipation of someone's arrival or

of something happening. **2** *Informal* To stop until someone catches up. **—*n.*** The act of waiting, or the time spent in waiting; delay. **—lie in wait** To remain hidden in order to make a surprise attack. [< AF *waitier*] **—Syn.** *v.* **1** abide, linger, remain, tarry.

wait·er (wā′tər) *n.* **1** A man employed to wait on table, as in a restaurant. **2** One who awaits something. **3** A tray for dishes, etc.

wait·ing (wā′ting) *n.* The act of one who waits. **—in waiting** In attendance, esp. at court.

waiting room A room for the use of persons waiting, as for a train, a doctor, etc.

wait·ress (wā′tris) *n.* A woman employed to wait on table, as in a restaurant.

waive (wāv) *v.t.* **waived, waiv·ing 1** To give up or relinquish a claim to. **2** To refrain from insisting upon or taking advantage of; forgo. **3** To put off; postpone; delay. [< OF *gaiver* abandon]

waiv·er (wā′vər) *n. Law* **1** The voluntary relinquishment of a right, privilege, or advantage. **2** The instrument which evidences such relinquishment. [< AF *weyver* abandon, waive]

wake¹ (wāk) *v.* **woke** or **waked, waked** (*Regional* **wok·en**), **wak·ing** *v.i.* **1** To emerge from sleep: often with *up.* **2** To be or remain awake. **3** To become aware or alert. **4** *Regional* To keep watch at night; esp., to hold a wake. **—*v.t.*** **5** To rouse from sleep or slumber; awake: often with *up.* **6** To rouse or stir up; excite. **7** To make aware; alert. **8** *Regional* To hold a wake over. **—*n.*** A vigil, esp. a watch over the body of a dead person through the night, just before the burial. [Fusion of OE *wacan* awaken and *wacian* be awake]

wake² (wāk) *n.* **1** The trail of turbulence left by a moving ship, aircraft, etc. **2** Any course passed over. **—in the wake of** Following close behind. [< ON *vök* an opening in ice]

wake·ful (wāk′fəl) *adj.* **1** Not sleeping or sleepy. **2** Watchful; alert. **3** Sleepless; restless: a *wakeful* time. **—wake′·ful·ly** *adv.* **—wake′ful·ness** *n.* **—Syn.** **1** awake. **2** cautious, vigilant, wary.

wak·en (wā′kən) *v.t.* **1** To rouse from sleep; awake. **2** To rouse or urge to alertness or activity. **—*v.i.*** **3** To cease sleeping; wake up. [< OE *wacnian*] **—wak′en·er** *n.*

wake-rob·in (wāk′rob′in) *n.* **1** TRILLIUM. **2** JACK-IN-THE-PULPIT.

Wal·dorf salad (wôl′dôrf) A salad made of chopped celery, apples, walnuts, and mayonnaise. [< the first *Waldorf*-Astoria Hotel, New York City]

wale (wāl) *n.* **1** WELT (def. 1). **2** A ridge or rib on the surface of cloth, as on corduroy. **3** *Usu. pl.* One of several planks on the outer sides of a wooden ship. **—*v.t.*** **waled, wal·ing 1** To raise wales on by striking. **2** To manufacture (cloth) with ridges or ribs. [< OE *walu*]

walk (wôk) *v.i.* **1** To advance on foot in such a manner that one part of a foot is always on the ground, or, in quadrupeds, that two or more feet are always on the ground. **2** To go on foot for exercise or amusement. **3** To move in a manner suggestive of walking, as certain inanimate objects. **4** To act or live in some manner: to *walk* in peace. **5** In baseball, to advance to first base after being pitched four balls. **—*v.t.*** **6** To pass through, over, or across at a walk: to *walk* the floor. **7** To lead, ride, or drive at a walk: to *walk* a horse. **8** To force or help to walk. **9** To accompany on a walk: I'll *walk* you to school. **10** To bring to a specified condition by walking. **11** To cause to move with a motion resembling a walk: to *walk* a trunk on its corners. **12** In baseball, to allow to advance to first base by pitching four balls. **—walk away from 1** To outrun or outdo (someone). **2** To sustain little or no injury in an accident. **—walk off 1** To depart, esp. abruptly. **2** To get rid of (fat, etc.) by walking. **—walk off with 1** To win, esp. with little difficulty. **2** To steal. **—walk out** *Informal* **1** To go out on strike. **2** To depart suddenly. **—walk out on** *Informal* To forsake; desert. **—walk over 1** To defeat easily. **2** To treat with contempt. **—*n.*** **1** The act of walking, as for enjoyment. **2** Manner of walking; gait. **3** A place prepared for

walking, as a sidewalk. **4** The distance covered or time spent in walking. **5** A piece of ground set apart for the feeding and exercise of domestic animals. **6** In baseball, the act of walking a batter; also, a being walked. —**walk of life** One's social or financial status. [< OE *wealcan* roll, toss] —**walk′er** *n.* —**Syn.** *v.* **1** saunter, step, stride, tread.

walk·a·way (wôk′ə·wā′) *n. Informal* A contest won without serious opposition. Also **walk′o·ver** (-ō′vər).

walk·ie-talk·ie (wô′kē·tô′kē) *n.* A portable radio transmitting and receiving set.

walking papers *Informal* Notice of dismissal from employment, office, etc.

walking stick 1 A staff or cane. **2** Any of various insects having legs and body resembling twigs.

walk-on (wôk′on′, -ôn′) *n.* A very small, usu. non-speaking role in a play, etc.

walk·out (wôk′out′) *n. Informal* A workmen's strike.

walk-up (wôk′up′) *Informal n.* **1** An apartment house or building of two or more stories having no elevator. **2** An apartment located higher than the ground floor in such an apartment house.

wall (wôl) *n.* **1** A continuous structure designed to enclose an area, to be the surrounding exterior of a building, or to be a partition between rooms or halls. **2** A fence of stone or brickwork, surrounding or separating yards, fields, etc. **3** *Usu. pl.* A barrier or rampart constructed for defense. **4** A sea wall; levee. **5** A barrier enclosing a cavity, vessel, or receptacle: the *wall* of the abdomen. **6** Something suggestive of a wall: a *wall* of bayonets. —**drive (push** or **thrust) to the wall** To force (one) to an extremity; crush. —**drive (or send) up the wall** *Informal* To make extremely nervous, tense, etc. —*v.t.* **1** To provide, surround, protect, etc., with or as with a wall or walls. **2** To fill or block with a wall: often with *up*. —*adj.* **1** Of or pertaining to a wall. **2** Hanging from, growing on, or built into a wall. [< OE *weall* < L *vallum* a rampart]

wal·la·by (wol′ə·bē) *n. pl.* **·bies** Any of various small to medium-sized kangaroos. [< Australian *wolaba*]

wall·board (wôl′bôrd′, -bōrd′) *n.* A material of varied composition pressed into sheets and used for walls, ceilings, etc.

wal·let (wol′it) *n.* A small, usu. folding case, as of leather, for holding paper money, cards, etc., and sometimes change, carried in a pocket or purse. [ME *walet*]

wall·eye (wôl′ī′) *n.* **1** An eye with a light-colored or white iris. **2** A kind of strabismus in which the eyes diverge. **3** Any of several walleyed fishes. [Back formation < WALL-EYED]

wall·eyed (wôl′īd′) *adj.* **1** Having a walleye or walleyes. **2** Having large, staring eyes, as certain fish. [< ON *vagl* a film on the eye + *auga* eye]

walleyed pike A large freshwater game fish of North America. Also **walleyed perch.**

wall·flow·er (wôl′flou′ər) *n.* **1** Any of various cultivated perennials related to mustard having fragrant yellow, orange, or red flowers. **2** *Informal* A person who because of unpopularity or shyness does not participate in some social activity, as a party or dance.

Wal·loon (wo·lōōn′) *n.* **1** One of a people of s Belgium and adjoining regions of France. **2** Their language, a dialect of French. —*adj.* Of or pertaining to the Walloons or their dialect.

wal·lop (wol′əp) *Informal v.t.* **1** To beat soundly; thrash. **2** To hit with a hard blow. —*n.* A hard blow. [< AF *waloper*] —**wal′lop·er** *n.*

wal·lop·ing (wol′əp·ing) *Informal adj.* Very large; whopping. —*n.* A beating; whipping or crushing defeat.

wal·low (wol′ō) *v.i.* **1** To roll about, as in mud, snow, etc. **2** To move with a heavy, rolling motion, as a ship in a storm. **3** To indulge oneself wantonly: to *wallow* in sensuality. —*n.* **1** The act of wallowing. **2** A depression or hollow made by wallowing. [< OE *wealwian*] —**wal′low·er** *n.*

wall·pa·per (wôl′pā′pər) *n.* Decorative paper for covering walls. —*v.t.* To cover with wallpaper.

Wall Street 1 A street in lower Manhattan, New York City, famous as the financial center of the U.S. **2** The U.S. financial world.

wall-to-wall (wôl′tə·wôl′) *adj.* Completely covering a floor: *wall-to-wall* carpeting.

wal·nut (wôl′nut′, -nət) *n.* **1** Any of various deciduous trees cultivated as ornamental shade trees and valued for their timber and their edible nuts. **2** The wood or nut of any of these trees. **3** The shagbark or its nut. **4** The color of the wood of any of these trees, esp. of the black walnut, a very dark brown: also **walnut brown.** [< OE *wealh* foreign + *hnutu* a nut]

Wal·pur·gis Night (väl·pŏŏr′gis) The night before May 1, thought to be the occassion of a gathering of witches for demonic rites and orgies. [< St. *Walpurga*, 8th-cent. English missionary in Germany]

Black walnut
a. shuck. b. nut.

wal·rus (wôl′rəs, wol′-) *n.* A very large, seallike mammal of arctic seas, with flexible hind limbs, projecting tusklike canines in the upper jaw, a bushy, bristly mustache on the muzzle, and a very tough hide. —*adj.* **1** Belonging or pertaining to a walrus. **2** Designating a type of bushy mustache drooping at the ends. [< Scand.]

waltz (wôlts) *n.* **1** A dance to music in triple time. **2** Music for or in the style of such a dance. —*v.i.* **1** To dance a waltz. **2** To move quickly: She *waltzed* out of the room. —*v.t.* **3** To cause to waltz. —*adj.* Pertaining to the waltz. [< G *walzen* to waltz, roll] —**waltz′er** *n.*

Walrus

wam·pum (wom′pəm, wôm′-) *n.* **1** Beads made of shells, formerly used as jewelry and currency among North American Indians. **2** *Informal* Money. [< Algon. *wampom(peag)*, lit., a white (string of beads)]

wan (won) *adj.* **wan·ner, wan·nest 1** Pale, as from sickness; careworn. **2** Faint; feeble: a *wan* smile. [< OE *wann* dark, gloomy] —**wan′ly** *adv.* —**wan′ness** *n.* —**Syn. 1** ashen, livid, pallid. **2** weak.

wand (wond) *n.* **1** A slender, flexible rod waved by a magician. **2** Any rod symbolizing authority, as a scepter. **3** A musician's baton. [< ON *vöndr*]

wan·der (won′dər) *v.i.* **1** To travel about without destination or purpose; roam. **2** To go casually or by an indirect route; stroll. **3** To twist or meander. **4** To stray. **5** To deviate in conduct or opinion; go astray. **6** To be delirious. —*v.t.* **7** To wander through or across. [< OE *wandrian*] —**wan′der·er** *n.* —**wan′der·ing·ly** *adv.* —**Syn. 1** range, rove.

wan·der·lust (won′dər·lust′) *n.* An impulse to travel; restlessness. [< G *wandern* to travel + *Lust* joy]

wane (wān) *v.i.* **waned, wan·ing 1** To diminish in size and brilliance. **2** To decline or decrease gradually. **3** To draw to an end. —*n.* **1** A waning or decreasing. **2** The period of such decrease. —**on the wane** Decreasing; declining. [< OE *wanian* lessen]

wan·gle (wang′gəl) *v.* **·gled, ·gling** *Informal v.t.* **1** To obtain or make by indirect, manipulative, or dishonest methods; finagle. —*v.i.* **2** To resort to indirect, irregular, or dishonest methods. [?] —**wan′gler** *n.*

Wan·kel engine (väng′kəl, wäng′-) A light, compact type of internal-combustion engine having combustion chambers bounded by the wall of a shallow cylinder and the sides of a triangular piston that rotates in one direction inside it. Also **Wan′kel.** [< F. *Wankel*, 1902–, German inventor]

want (wont, wônt) *v.t.* **1** To feel a desire or wish for. **2** To wish; desire: used with the infinitive: to *want* to help. **3** To be deficient in, esp. to a required or customary extent. **4** To desire to see, speak to, arrest, etc.: He *wants* you on the phone; *wanted* by the police. **5** *Chiefly Brit.* To need; require. —*v.i.* **6** To have need: usu. with *for.* **7** To be needy or destitute. —*n.* **1** Lack; scarcity; shortage. **2** Poverty; destitution. **3** Something lacking; a need or craving. [Prob. < ON *vanta* be lacking] —**want′er** *n.* —**Syn.** *n.* **1** dearth, deficiency, insufficiency. **2** indigence, privation.

want ad *Informal* A classified advertisement, as in a newspaper, for something wanted, as an employee, a job, a lodging, etc.

want·ing (won'ting, wôn'-) *adj.* 1 Missing; lacking: One juror is still *wanting.* 2 Not coming up to some standard, need, or expectation: He was found *wanting.* —**wanting in** Deficient in. —*prep.* 1 Lacking; without. 2 Less; minus.

wan·ton (won'tən) *adj.* 1 Licentious; lewd; lustful. 2 Heartless or unjust; malicious: *wanton* savagery. 3 Unprovoked; senseless: a *wanton* murder. 4 Extravagant; unrestrained: *wanton* speech. 5 Not bound or tied; loose: *wanton* curls. 6 Capricious; frolicsome. —*v.i.* 1 To act in a wanton manner; be wanton. —*v.t.* 2 To waste or squander carelessly. —*n.* A lewd or licentious person. [< OE *wan* deficient + *tēon* bring up, educate] —**wan'ton·ly** *adv.* —**wan'ton·ness** *n.*

wap·i·ti (wop'ə·tē) *n. pl.* **·tis** or **·ti** A large North American deer; the American elk. [< Algon.] • See ELK.

war (wôr) *n.* 1 Armed strife or conflict between nations or states, or between different parties in the same nation. 2 Any act or state of conflict, struggle, or strife: a *war* against poverty. 3 Military science or strategy. —*v.i.* **warred, war·ring** 1 To wage war; fight or take part in a war. 2 To be in any state of active opposition. —*adj.* Of, pertaining to, used in, or resulting from war. [< OHG *werra* strife, confusion]

War Between the States CIVIL WAR.

war·ble (wôr'bəl) *v.* **·bled, ·bling** *v.t.* 1 To sing (something) with trills and runs or with tremulous vibrations. —*v.i.* 2 To sing with trills, etc. 3 To make a liquid, murmuring sound, as a stream. 4 YODEL. —*n.* The act or sound of warbling. [< OF *werble* a warble]

war·bler (wôr'blər) *n.* 1 One who or that which warbles. 2 Any of a family of small, mostly Old World birds noted for their song. 3 Any of a large and varied family of small, migratory, New World birds, usu. having brilliant springtime plumage and distinctive songs.

war bonnet The ceremonial headdress of the North American Plains Indians.

war crime *Usu. pl.* Any of various crimes committed during or as a result of war, as maltreatment of prisoners, atrocities against civilians, genocide, etc. —**war criminal**

war cry A rallying cry or slogan used by combatants in a war, or by participants in any contest.

ward (wôrd) *n.* 1 In a hospital: **a** A large room for six or more patients. **b** A division for specific illnesses or groups of patients: the children's *ward.* 2 A division of a city for administrative or electoral purposes. 3 *Law* A person, as a minor, who is in the charge of a guardian or court. 4 The act of guarding or the state of being guarded. 5 A division or subdivision of a prison. 6 Any means of defense or protection. —*v.t.* To repel or turn aside, as a thrust or blow: usu. with *off.* [< OE *weardian* to watch, guard]

-ward *suffix* Toward; in the direction of: *upward, homeward.* Also **-wards.** [< OE *-weard*]

war dance A dance of certain tribes before going to war or in celebration of a victory.

war·den (wôr'dən) *n.* 1 A supervisor or custodian of something: a game *warden;* prison *warden.* The head of certain colleges. 3 CHURCHWARDEN (def 1). [< AF *wardein*] —**war'den·ry** (*pl.* **·ries**), **war'den·ship** *n.*

ward·er (wôr'dər) *n.* 1 A guard or sentinel. 2 *Chiefly Brit.* A prison official; warden. [< OF *guarder* guard, keep]

ward heeler *Slang* A hanger-on of a political boss in a ward or other local area, who does minor tasks, canvasses votes, etc.

ward·robe (wôrd'rōb') *n.* 1 A large upright cabinet for wearing apparel. 2 All the garments belonging to any one person. 3 The clothes for a particular season: a spring *wardrobe.* 4 The costumes of a theater, theatrical troupe, motion-picture company, etc.; also, the place where such costumes are kept. [< AF *warder* keep + *robe* a robe]

ward·room (wôrd'rōom', -rŏŏm') *n.* 1 On a warship, the eating or living quarters allotted to the commissioned officers, excepting the commander. 2 These officers regarded as a group.

ward·ship (wôrd'ship) *n.* 1 The state of being a ward of a guardian or court. 2 Custody; guardianship.

ware (wâr) *n.* 1 Articles of the same class: used collectively in compounds: *glassware.* 2 *pl.* Articles for sale; merchandise. 3 Pottery; earthenware. [< OE *waru*]

ware·house (wâr'hous') *n.* 1 A storehouse for goods or merchandise. 2 *Chiefly Brit.* A large wholesale shop. —*v.t.* **·housed** (-houzd'), **·hous·ing** (-hou'zing) To place or store in a warehouse.

ware·house·man (wâr'hous'mən) *n. pl.* **·men** (-mən) One who owns or works in a warehouse.

war·fare (wôr'fâr') *n.* 1 The waging or carrying on of war. 2 Struggle; strife.

war game 1 *pl.* Practice maneuvers imitating the conditions of actual warfare. 2 A simulated military conflict organized to test tactical procedures and concepts by discussion and analysis.

war·head (wôr'hed') *n.* The chamber in the nose of a bomb, guided missile, etc., containing an explosive, incendiary, or chemical charge.

war horse 1 A heavy horse used in warfare. 2 *Informal* A veteran of many struggles or contests, esp. political contests.

war·like (wôr'līk') *adj.* 1 Fond of or ready for war. 2 Relating to, used in, or suggesting war. 3 Threatening war. —**Syn.** 1 bellicose, belligerent. 2 martial, military.

war·lock (wôr'lok') *n.* 1 A male witch; sorcerer. 2 A magician or conjurer. [< OE *wǣr* a covenant + *lēogen* lie, deny]

warm (wôrm) *adj.* 1 Moderately hot; having heat somewhat greater than temperate: *warm* water; a *warm* climate. 2 Imparting heat: a *warm* fire. 3 Imparting or preserving warmth: a *warm* coat. 4 Having the natural temperature of most living persons or animals: *warm* blood. 5 Heated, as from exertion. 6 Ardent; enthusiastic; fervent: *warm* interest. 7 Lively; agitated: a *warm* argument. 8 Cordial; friendly: a *warm* welcome. 9 Amorous; loving: a *warm* glance. 10 Excitable; fiery: a *warm* temper. 11 Having predominating tones of red or yellow. 12 Recently made; fresh: a *warm* trail. 13 Near to finding a hidden object or fact, as in certain games. 14 *Informal* Uncomfortable by reason of annoyances or danger: They made the town *warm* for him. —*v.t.* 1 To make warm. 2 To make ardent or enthusiastic; interest. 3 To fill with kindly feeling. —*v.i.* 4 To become warm. 5 To become ardent or enthusiastic: often with *up* or *to.* 6 To become kindly disposed or friendly: with *to* or *toward.* —**warm up** 1 To warm. 2 To exercise the body, voice, etc., as before a game or performance. 3 To run an engine, etc., in order to attain correct operating temperature. —*n. Informal* A warming or being warm. [< OE *wearm*] —**warm'er,** **warm'ness** *n.* —**warm'ly** *adv.*

warm-blood·ed (wôrm'blud'id) *adj.* 1 Having a nearly uniform and warm body temperature, whatever the surrounding medium. 2 Enthusiastic; ardent; passionate.

warm-heart·ed (wôrm'här'tid) *adj.* Kind; affectionate.

warming pan A closed metal pan with a long handle, containing live coals or hot water, used for warming a bed.

war·mon·ger (wôr'mung'gər, -mong'-) *n.* One who favors or tries to incite war. —**war'mon'ger·ing** *adj., n.*

warmth (wôrmth) *n.* 1 The state, quality, or sensation of being warm. 2 Ardor or excitement of disposition or feeling. 3 Sympathetic friendliness, affection, or understanding. 4 The effect produced by warm colors.

warm-up (wôrm'up') *n.* The act or an instance of warming up.

warn (wôrn) *v.t.* 1 To make aware of possible harm; caution. 2 To advise; counsel. 3 To give notice in advance. 4 To notify (a person) to go or stay away. —*v.i.* 5 To give warning. [< OE *wearnian*] —**warn'er** *n.*

warn·ing (wôr'ning) *n.* 1 The act of one who warns or the state of being warned. 2 That which warns. —*adj.* Serving as a warning. —**warn'ing·ly** *adv.* —**Syn.** *n.* 2 admonition, advice, recommendation.

War of 1812 A war between the U.S. and Great Britain (1812–15).

War of Independence AMERICAN REVOLUTION.

---

add, āce, câre, pälm; end, ēven; it, īce; odd, ōpen, ôrder; tŏŏk, pōōl; up, bûrn; ə = *a* in *above, u* in *focus;* yōō = *u* in *fuse;* oil; pout; check; go; ring; thin; ṭẖis; zh, *vision.* < derived from; ? origin uncertain or unknown.

warp (wôrp) *v.t.* **1** To turn or twist out of shape, as by shrinkage or heat. **2** To corrupt; pervert: a mind *warped* by bigotry. **3** *Naut.* To move (a vessel) by hauling on a rope or line fastened to something stationary. —*v.i.* **4** To become turned or twisted out of shape, as wood in drying. **5** To deviate from a correct or proper course: go astray. **6** *Naut.* To move by means of ropes fastened to a pier, anchor, etc. —*n.* **1** The state of being warped, twisted out of shape, or biased. **2** The threads that run the long way of a fabric, crossing the woof. **3** *Naut.* A rope or line used for warping. [< OE *weorpan* to throw] —**warp′er** *n.*

war paint **1** Paint applied to faces and bodies of primitive peoples as a sign of going to war. **2** *Informal* Cosmetics, as rouge, lipstick, etc. **3** *Informal* Official garb or regalia.

war·path (wôr′path′, -päth′) *n.* The route taken by an attacking party of American Indians. —**on the warpath** **1** On a warlike expedition. **2** Ready for a fight; thoroughly angry.

war·plane (wôr′plān′) *n.* An airplane used in war.

war·rant (wôr′ənt, wor′-) *n.* **1** *Law* A judicial writ or order authorizing arrest, search, seizure, etc. **2** Something which assures or attests; guarantee. **3** That which gives authority for some course or act; sanction; justification. **4** A certificate of appointment given to a naval or military warrant officer. **5** A document giving a certain authority, esp. for the receipt or payment of money. —*v.t.* **1** To assure or guarantee the quality, accuracy, certainty, or sufficiency of: to *warrant* a title to property. **2** To guarantee the character or fidelity of; pledge oneself for. **3** To guarantee against injury, loss, etc. **4** To be sufficient grounds for; justify. **5** To give legal authority or power to; authorize. **6** *Informal* To say confidently; feel sure. [< AF *warant*] —**war′rant·er** *n.*

war·ran·tee (wôr′ən·tē′, wor′-) *n.* *Law* The person to whom a warranty is given.

warrant officer See GRADE.

war·ran·tor (wôr′ən·tôr, wor′-) *n.* *Law* One who makes or gives a warranty to another.

war·ran·ty (wôr′ən·tē, wor′-) *n. pl.* **·ties** **1** *Law* A guarantee by the seller of property, a product, etc., that whatever is sold is or shall be as represented. **2** An official authorization or warrant. [< AF *warant* a warrant]

war·ren (wôr′ən, wor′-) *n.* **1** A place where rabbits live and breed. **2** Any building or area overcrowded with people. [< AF *warenne* a game park, a rabbit warren]

war·ri·or (wôr′ē·ər, wôr′yər, wor′-) *n.* A man engaged in or experienced in warfare or conflict.

war·ship (wôr′ship′) *n.* Any vessel used in naval combat.

wart (wôrt) *n.* **1** A small, usu. hard, benign excrescence on the skin, caused by a virus. **2** Any of various natural protuberances on certain plants and animals. [< OE *wearte*] —**wart′y** *adj.* (**·i·er**, **·i·est**)

wart hog An African wild hog having large tusks and warty excrescences on the face.

war whoop A yell, as made by American Indians, as a signal for attack, etc.

war·y (wâr′ē) *adj.* **war·i·er**, **war·i·est** **1** Carefully watching and guarding. **2** Shrewd; wily. [< OE *wær*] —**war′i·ly** *adv.* —**war′i·ness** *n.*

Wart hog

was (woz, wuz, *unstressed* wəz) First and third person sing., past indicative of BE. [< OE *wæs*]

wash (wosh, wôsh) *v.t.* **1** To cleanse with water or other liquid, as by immersing, scrubbing, etc. **2** To wet or cover with water or other liquid. **3** To flow against or over: a beach *washed* by the ocean. **4** To remove or carry by the use or action of water: with *away*, *off*, *out*, etc. **5** To form or wear by erosion. **6** To purify, as gas, by passing through a liquid. **7** To coat with a thin layer of color. **8** To cover with a thin coat of metal. **9** *Mining* **a** To subject (gravel, earth, etc.) to the action of water so as to separate the ore, etc. **b** To separate (ore, etc.) thus. —*v.i.* **10** To wash oneself. **11** To wash clothes, etc., in water or other liquid. **12** To withstand the effects of washing: That calico will *wash*. **13** *Informal* To undergo testing successfully: That story won't *wash*. **14** To flow with a lapping sound, as waves. **15** To be carried away or removed by the use or action of

water: with *away*, *off*, *out*, etc. **16** To be eroded by the action of water. —**wash out** *Slang* To fail and be dropped from a course, esp. in military flight training. —*n.* **1** The act or an instance of washing. **2** A number of articles, as of clothing, set apart for washing. **3** Liquid or semiliquid refuse; swill. **4** Any preparation used in washing or coating, as a mouthwash. **5** A paint, as water color, spread lightly on a surface. **6** The breaking of a body of water upon the shore, or the sound made by this. **7** Erosion of soil or earth by the action of running water. **8** Material collected and deposited by water, as along a river bank. **9** Agitation or turbulence in water or air caused by something passing through it. **10** An area washed by a sea or river; a marsh; bog. **11** In the w U.S., the dry bed of a stream. —*adj.* Washable without injury: *wash* fabrics. [< OE *wascan*]

Wash. Washington.

wash·a·ble (wosh′ə·bəl, wôsh′-) *adj.* That can be washed without damage.

wash-and-wear (wosh′ən-wâr′, wôsh′-) *adj.* Designating a garment or fabric so treated as to require little or no ironing after washing.

wash·board (wosh′bôrd, -bōrd′, wôsh′-) *n.* A board having a corrugated surface on which to rub clothes while washing them.

wash·bowl (wosh′bōl, wôsh′-) *n.* A basin or bowl used for washing the hands and face. Also **wash′ba·sin** (-bā′sən).

wash·cloth (wosh′klôth′, -kloth′, wôsh′-) *n.* A small cloth used for washing the body.

washed-out (wosht′out′, wôsht′-) *adj.* **1** Faded; pale. **2** *Informal* Exhausted; tired.

washed-up (wosht′up′, wôsht′-) *adj.* *Informal* **1** Finished; done with; through. **2** Exhausted.

wash·er (wosh′ər, wô′shər) *n.* **1** One who washes. **2** *Mech.* A small, flat, perforated disk of metal, rubber, etc., used to make a nut or joint tight. **3** WASHING MACHINE.

wash·er·wom·an (wosh′ər·wŏŏm′ən, wô′shər-) *n. pl.* **·wom·en** (-wim′in) LAUNDRESS.

Washer
def 2

wash·ing (wosh′ing, wô′shing) *n.* **1** The act of one who or that which washes. **2** Things (as clothing) washed or to be washed at one time. **3** A thin coating of metal: forks with only one *washing* of silver. **4** That which is obtained by washing: a *washing* of ore.

washing machine A machine that washes and usu. rinses automatically, used to clean clothes, linens, etc.

washing soda SODIUM CARBONATE.

Washington's Birthday (wash′ing·tənz, wô′shing-) The third Monday in February, a U.S. holiday observed in honor of the anniversary of George Washington's birth, February 22.

wash·out (wosh′out′, wôsh′-) *n.* **1** A considerable erosion of earth by the action of water; also, the excavation thus made. **2** *Slang* A hopeless or total failure.

wash·room (wosh′rōom′, -rŏŏm′, wôsh′-) *n.* A restroom or lavatory.

wash·stand (wosh′stand′, wôsh′-) *n.* **1** A stand for washbowl, pitcher, etc. **2** A bathroom sink.

wash·tub (wosh′tub′, wôsh′-) *n.* A usu. stationary tub used for laundry.

wash·wom·an (wosh′wŏŏm′ən, wôsh′-) *n. pl.* **·wom·en** (-wim′in) LAUNDRESS.

wash·y (wosh′ē, wô′shē) *adj.* **wash·i·er**, **wash·i·est** **1** Watery; diluted. **2** Weak; feeble.

was·n't (woz′ənt, wuz′-) Contraction of *was not*.

wasp (wosp, wôsp) *n.* Any of numerous insects related to bees, having membranous wings, biting mouth parts, and effective stings, and including both social and solitary species. [< OE *wæsp*]

WASP (wosp, wôsp) *n.* *Slang* A white Protestant American, esp. one of N European ancestry. Also **Wasp.** [< *w(hite) A(nglo)-S(axon) P(rotestant)*] —**WASP′ish, Wasp′ish** *adj.*

wasp·ish (wos′pish, wôs′-) *adj.* **1** Of or like a wasp. **2** Irritable; bad-tempered. —**wasp′ish·ly** *adv.* —**wasp′ish·ness** *n.*

Thailand Dancers
—American President Lines

Prayer before a Buddhist statue in India
—California Texas Oil Co.

ncing the Tarantella in Sicily
—Sheridan H. Garth

Women and children in the Belgian Congo, Africa

A procession of virgins in Bali
—Sheridan H. Garth

spring festival in Nidwalden, Switzerland, when cows are driven to upper Alpine pastures.
—Swiss Tourist

Croatian women of Yugoslavia dressed for church in embroidered peasant costumes.
—Sheridan H. Garth

COSTUMES

PARTHENON, Doric style building on the Acropolis, Athens, Greece.
—Greek Line

PONT DU GARD, an aqueduct over the river Gard in the south of France constructed by the Romans.
—California-Texas Oil Co. Ltd.

ERECHTHEUM, Ionic style building on the Acropolis, Athens, erected as a temple of the Gods.
—American Export L

COLOSSEUM at Rome which to a large degree still stands. The work of Vespasian and Titus in the first century after the birth of Christ.
—Italian Consu

POMPEII
—American Export Lines

AMPHITHEATRE at Delphi

ARCHAEOLOGY

The Mausoleum. Erected as a monument to the memory of Mausolus, king of Caria, by his wife Artemisia, at Halicarnassus in Asia Minor, 350 B.C.

The Pharos at Alexandria. A lighthouse completed about 200 B.C. by Ptolemy Philadelphus, king of Egypt; built of richly ornamented white stone; beacon fires on its apex guided vessels into the harbor at night; its inscription read: "King Ptolemy to the gods, the saviors, for the benefit of sailors."

The Colossus of Rhodes. A statue of the sun-god Helios, built of bronze in 292-280 B.C.; it stood until 224 B.C. when it fell into the harbor during an earthquake; the metal was later retrieved and sold by the Saracens about A.D. 653.

THE SEVEN

WONDERS

OF THE

ANCIENT WORLD

—Hulton Picture Library

The Pyramids of Egypt. Seventy-five in all of varying sizes; monumental works built as tombs for the mummies of Egyptian kings and royal families. The Great Pyramid of Khufu, the largest, near Giza on the west bank of the Nile, originally measured 768 feet at the base and 482 feet high; built in the 28th century B.C.

The Temple of Diana at Ephesus. The fifth temple on the site, begun before 350 B.C., completed about 300 B.C.; stood until burned and sacked by the Goths in A.D. 262.

e Hanging Gardens of Babylon. e enchanting gardens arranged terraces one above the other h walls fifty feet high and each :ompassing four acres; built for legendary Queen Semiramis.

The Statue of Zeus by Phidias. Completed and erected in the Temple of Zeus at Olympia about 433 B.C.; richly ornamented with gold and ivory.

Dryptosaurus

Agathaumus-Monoclonius

Allosaurus

Brontosaurus

Stegosaurus

Trachodon

DINOSAURS

Courtesy The American Museum of Natural History. Paintings (except Stegosaurus) by Charles R. Knight

OHIPPUS — Eocene — Europe, North America. Size: m fox terrier to collie. Four toes on fore feet, 3 on hind et.

HYPOHIPPUS — Middle Miocene — Asia, Europe, North America. Size: Shetland pony. Broad, hoofed middle toe with 2 side toes.

ESOHIPPUS — Oligocene — North America. Size: from vote to sheep. Large middle toe with 2 slender side toes.

HIPPARION — Upper Miocene and Pliocene — Asia, Europe, North Africa, North America. Size: antelope.

UUS SCOTTI — Pleistocene — Asia, Africa, Europe, rth America. Size: modern horse.

PLIOHIPPUS — Pliocene — North America. Size: nearly that of the modern horse. One-toed hoofed feet with vestigial side toes.

AMERICAN SADDLE HORSES

THE ENGLISH THOROUGHBRED

THE EVOLUTION OF THE HORSE

Paintings by Charles R. Knight

Courtesy The American Museum of Natural History

ASIA

Balinese women before
a shrine in Indonesia.
—Ewing Galloway

Summer Palace grounds, Peiping, Ch
—Ewing Gallo

Nijo Castle
Kyoto, Japan

Khyber Pass, between India
and Afghanistan.
—British Information Services

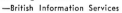

Knights Hall with Parliament Buildings, The Hague

Alhambra, Granada, Spain

EUROPE

(Left) Hilden Autobahn, Germany; (center) Piccadilly Circus showing Regent Street right and Piccadilly left, London; (right) Notre Dame Cathedral across the Seine, Paris; (below) Edinburgh, Scotland.

—British information Services   —Aerofilms Ltd.   —A.C.K. Ware

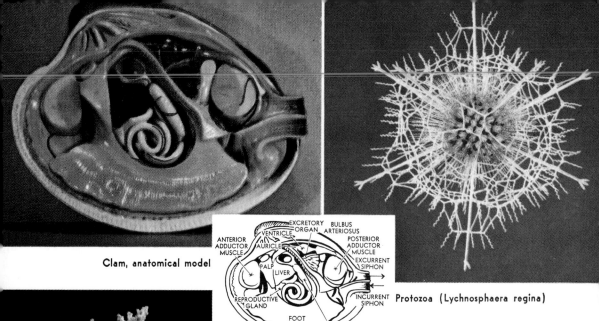

Clam, anatomical model

ANTERIOR ADDUCTOR MUSCLE
VENTRICLE
EXCRETORY ORGAN
BULBUS ARTERIOSUS
AURICLE
POSTERIOR ADDUCTOR MUSCLE
EXCURRENT SIPHON
PALP
LIVER
REPRODUCTIVE GLAND
INCURRENT SIPHON
FOOT
INTESTINE

Protozoa (Lychnosphaera regina)

Tridacna shell with coral growth

Sea Anemone

Sponge   *Courtesy The American Museum of Natural History*

Stalk Medusa (Halyclistis auricula)

INVERTEBRATES (Glass Models)

DIAMOND-BACK RATTLESNAKE

WATER MOCCASIN OR COTTON-MOUTH

HARLEQUIN OR CORAL SNAKE

BLUE RACER

COMMON GARTER SNAKE

PRAIRIE RATTLESNAKE

EASTERN COPPERHEAD

SOFT-SHELLED TURTLE

PAINTED TERRAPIN

COMMON BOX TURTLE

COMMON HORNED LIZARD

GILA MONSTER

SNAPPING TURTLE

ALLIGATOR

REPTILES OF NORTH AMERICA

Guilford L. Beck, Designer

AFRICA

Victoria Falls (above).

(Top to bottom right)—

Cape Town showing Table Mountain.

Sphinx and Pyramid in Egypt.

Bull elephant killed in the Belgian Congo.

AUSTRALIA and NEW ZEALAND

Wellington, New Zealand (right).

Aborigines of Australia (below).

Sydney business section showing a part of the residential section in the foreground (right below).

Sheep Ranch, New South Wales (bottom right).

"Champagne Pool" Geyser, New Zealand (bottom left).

—British Information Services

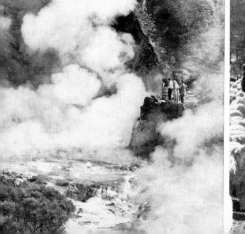

Amethyst

Aquamarine

Bloodstone

Chrysolite

Diamond

Emerald

Garnet

Jade

Lapis Lazuli

Onyx

Opal

Pearl

Rose Quartz

Ruby

Sapphire

Star Sapphire

Topaz

Tourmaline

Turquoise

Zircon

RARE AND PRECIOUS STONES

SHELLS

1. Polymita muscarum (Cuba)   2. Turbo petholatus (Philippines)   3. Pecten irradian (Senegal, Africa)   4. Vermetus spirata (Florida)   5. Polymita picta (Cuba)   6. Ianthina violacea (Australia)   7. Patella cymbiola (Madagascar)   8. Delphinula formosa (China)   9. Pterocera chiragra (Society Islands)   10. Ranella perca (Japan)   11. Haliotis excavata (Australia)   12. Pecten hericius (California)   13. Patella exarata (Sandwich Islands)   14. Spondylus gussoni (Sicily)   15. Balanus amphitrite (Florida)   16. Lima squamosa (Japan)   17. Eburna spirata (Ceylon)   18. Murex tenuispina (Eastern Seas)   19. Cypraea argus (Philippines)   20. Melongena corona (Gulf of Mexico)   21. Voluta ellioti (Australia)   22. Thais patula (Philippines)   23. Murex monodon (Australia)   24. Terebra suulata (Society Islands)   25. Conus episcopus (Ceylon)   26. Oliva porphyria (Panama)

THE TOWER BRIDGE OVER THE RIVER THAMES IN LONDON
(A Bascule Bridge)

THE QUEBEC BRIDGE   —Photo Courtesy of W. B. Edwards
(A Cantilever Bridge)

THE GOLDEN GATE BRIDGE, SAN FRANCISCO
(A Suspension Bridge)

FAMOUS BRIDGES

ocumulus with outstanding wave
ud

Altocumulus

Mammato-Cumulus during thunderstorm preceding warm front in Aberdeen, South Dakota

mulus with shower in progress out-
e Manila, Republic of Philippines

Cumulo-nimbus just grown from cumu-lus at Mount Wilson, California.

Cumulus associated with fracto cumulus Monroe County, West Virginia.

mulus and altocumulus hovering over
rida Island off Guadalcanal.
Official U. S. Navy Photo

Cumulus over harbor in moonlight

Orographic formation of cumulus and cirrus off Greenland

Altocumulus inactive

Cumulus

Lower scattered cumulus

Tornado

CLOUD FORMATIONS

Courtesy U. S. Weather Bureau

Bronze face mask, Benin, West Africa

Mask of young man, Haida, Northwest Coast Indians, North America

Twisted face mask, Iroquois, Cayuga Tribe, New York State

Spirit Mask, Ibo Tribe, Southern Nigeria

Deer mask, Tibet

Devil dancer's mask Ceylon

Pascola Dancers, Yaqui, Mexico

Noh Mask, Japanese Theatre

Dramatic Mask, Java

MASKS OF MANY LANDS
—Courtesy The American Museum of Natural History

wasp waist A very slim, narrow waist. **—wasp-waist-ed** (wosp′wās′tid, wôsp′-) *adj.*

was-sail (wos′əl, was′-, wo-sāl′) *n.* **1** An ancient toast, esp. to one's health. **2** The spiced drink, usu. ale and wine, prepared for a wassail. **3** An occasion of much drinking; a carousal. —*v.i.* **1** To take part in a wassail; carouse. — *v.t.* **2** To drink the health of; toast. [< ON *ves heill* be whole] **—was′sail-er** *n.*

Was-ser-mann test (wäs′ər-mən) A diagnostic test for syphilis, based on the detection of certain antibodies in the blood. Also **Wassermann reaction.** [< August von *Wassermann*, 1866–1925, German bacteriologist]

wast (wost, *unstressed* wəst) *Archaic* Were: used with **THOU.**

wast-age (wās′tij) *n.* That which is lost by leakage, waste, etc.

waste (wāst) *v.* **wast-ed, wast-ing** *v.t.* **1** To use or expend thoughtlessly; squander. **2** To make weak or feeble. **3** To use up; consume. **4** To fail to use or take advantage of, as an opportunity. **5** To lay waste; devastate. **6** *Slang* To kill; destroy. —*v.i.* **7** To lose strength, vigor, or bulk: often with *away.* **8** To diminish or dwindle gradually. **9** To pass gradually: said of time. —*n.* **1** Thoughtless or unnecessary expenditure, consumption, etc. **2** Failure to benefit or gain from something, as an opportunity. **3** A desolate or devastated place or region; wilderness; desert. **4** A continuous, gradual wearing away of strength, vigor, or substance. **5** Something discarded or rejected as worthless or unneeded, esp. tangled spun cotton thread. **6** Something that escapes without being used, as steam. **7** Garbage; rubbish; trash. **8** Something excreted from the body, as urine or excrement. **—lay waste** To destroy or devastate. —*adj.* **1** Cast aside as worthless; discarded. **2** Excreted from the body. **3** Not cultivated or inhabited; wild; barren. **4** Superfluous: *waste* energy. **5** Containing or conveying waste products. [< L *vastare* lay waste] **—wast′er** *n.* **—Syn.** *v.* **1** dissipate. **2** debilitate, enfeeble.

waste-bas-ket (wāst′bas′kit, -bäs′-) *n.* A container for paper scraps and other waste. Also **wastepaper basket.**

waste-ful (wāst′fəl) *adj.* **1** Prone to waste; extravagant. **2** Causing waste. **—waste′ful-ly** *adv.* **—waste′ful-ness** *n.*

waste-land (wāst′land′) *n.* A barren or desolate land.

waste-pa-per (wāst′pā′pər) *n.* Paper thrown away as worthless. Also **waste paper.**

waste pipe A pipe for carrying off waste water, etc.

wast-ing (wās′ting) *adj.* **1** Destructive; devastating. **2** Destructive to health; enfeebling.

wast-rel (wās′trəl) *n.* **1** A profligate; spendthrift. **2** An idler or loafer. [Dim. of *waster* one who wastes]

watch (woch, wôch) *v.i.* **1** To look attentively; observe closely. **2** To be on the alert. **3** To wait expectantly for something: with *for.* **4** To do duty as a guard or sentinel. **5** To keep vigil. —*v.t.* **6** To look at attentively; observe. **7** To keep informed concerning. **8** To be alert for; to *watch* one's opportunity. **9** To keep watch over; guard. **—watch out** To be careful. —*n.* **1** Close and continuous attention; careful observation. **2** Service as a guard or sentry. **3** The period of time during which a guard is on duty. **4** The person or persons set to guard or watch. **5** A small, portable timepiece worn on the wrist or carried in a pocket. **6** A vigil or wake. **7** *Naut.* **a** A spell of duty on board ship, usu. four hours. **b** The division of a crew on duty during such a period. [< OE *wæccan*] **—watch′er** *n.*

watch-case (woch′kās′, wôch′-) *n.* A metal covering for the mechanism of a watch.

watch-dog (woch′dôg′, -dog′, wôch′-) *n.* **1** A dog kept to guard a building or other property. **2** A person who keeps a vigilant lookout.

watch-ful (woch′fəl, wôch′-) *adj.* Watching carefully; vigilant; alert. **—watch′ful-ly** *adv.* **—watch′ful-ness** *n.*

watch-mak-er (woch′mā′kər, wôch′-) *n.* One who makes or repairs watches.

watch-man (woch′mən, wôch′-) *n. pl.* **-men** (-mən) A man employed to guard a building, etc., at night.

watch-tow-er (woch′tou′ər, wôch′-) *n.* A tower upon which a sentinel is stationed.

watch-word (woch′wûrd′, wôch′-) *n.* **1 PASSWORD. 2** A slogan or maxim.

wa-ter (wô′tər, wot′ər) *n.* **1** The colorless liquid that covers over 70 percent of the earth's surface, is capable of wetting and dissolving many different substances, and is an essential constituent of all organisms. **2** A chemical compound of hydrogen and oxygen which occurs as a solid, a liquid, or a vapor, depending upon its temperature. **3** *Often pl.* Any body of water, as a lake, river, or a sea. **4** Any liquid or liquid secretion of the body, as perspiration, tears, urine, etc. **5** Any preparation of water holding a substance in solution: mineral *water.* **6** An undulating sheen given to certain fabrics, as silk, etc. **7** In commerce and finance, stock issued without an increase of assets or earning power to back it. **—above water** Out of danger, debt, etc.; secure. **—hold water** To be logical, valid, or dependable. **—like water** Freely; prodigally. **—of the first water** Of the finest quality. —*v.t.* **1** To provide (land, plants, etc.) with water, as by sprinkling or irrigating. **2** To provide with water for drinking. **3** To dilute or weaken with water: often with *down.* **4** To give an undulating sheen to the surface of (silk, linen, etc.). **5** To enlarge the number of shares of (a stock company) without increasing the company assets in proportion. —*v.i.* **6** To secrete or discharge water, tears, etc. **7** To fill with saliva, as the mouth, from desire for food. **8** To drink water. [< OE *wæter*] **—wa′ter-er** *n.*

Water Bearer AQUARIUS.

wa-ter-bed (wô′tər-bed′, wot′ər-) *n.* A bed with a water-filled container serving as a mattress.

water bird Any bird living on or near water.

water bomber In Canada, an aircraft equipped to drop water on forest fires. Also **fire bomber.**

wa-ter-borne (wô′tər-bôrn′, -bōrn′, wot′ər-) *adj.* **1** Floating on water. **2** Transported in a ship, etc.

wa-ter-buck (wô′tər-buk′, wot′ər-) *n.* Either of two species of large African antelope, frequenting rivers, etc.

water buffalo A large, slow, oxlike animal of s Asia with curved horns, often domesticated as a draft animal.

water chestnut 1 The hard, nutlike, edible fruit of an aquatic plant native to Asia. **2** The plant itself: also **water cal-trop** (kal′trəp).

wa-ter-clock (wô′tər-klok′, wot′ər-) *n.* A device for measuring time by the fall or flow of water.

water closet TOILET (defs. 1 & 2).

wa-ter-col-or (wô′tər-kul′ər, wot′ər-) *n.* **1** A pigment or coloring matter prepared for painting with water as the medium. **2** A painting or painting done in watercolors. Also **water color.** —*adj.* Of or painted with watercolors.

wa-ter-cool (wô′tər-kōōl′, wot′ər-) *v.t.* To cool by means of water, as by a jacket or pipe.

water cooler A vessel or apparatus for cooling and dispensing drinking water.

wa-ter-course (wô′tər-kôrs′, -kōrs′, wot′ər-) *n.* **1** A stream of water, as a river or brook. **2** A channel for a stream of water.

wa-ter-craft (wô′tər-kraft′, -kräft′, wot′ər-) *n.* **1** Skill in sailing boats or in aquatic sports. **2** A boat or ship. **3** Boats and ships collectively.

wa-ter-cress (wô′tər-kres′, wot′ər-) *n.* An edible perennial herb of the mustard family, usu. growing in running water and cultivated for use as salad.

water cure HYDROPATHY.

wa-ter-fall (wô′tər-fôl′, wot′ər-) *n.* A fall of water over a precipice.

wa-ter-fowl (wô′tər-foul′, wot′ər-) *n. pl.* **-fowl** or **-fowls** A water bird, esp. a swimming game bird.

wa-ter-front (wô′tər-frunt′, wot′ər-) *n.* **1** Property abutting on or overlooking a natural body of water. **2** That part of a town which fronts on a body of water, usu. a commercial area of docks, warehouses, etc.

water gap A deep ravine in a mountain ridge giving passage to a stream.

water gas A poisonous fuel gas containing hydrogen and carbon monoxide produced by forcing steam over white-hot coke.

---

add, āce, câre, pälm; end, ēven; it, īce; odd, ōpen, ôrder; took, pool; up, bûrn; ə = a in *above*, u in *focus*; yōō = u in *fuse*; oil; pout; check; go; ring; thin; this; zh, *vision.* < derived from; ? origin uncertain or unknown.

wa·ter·gate (wô′tər·gāt′, wot′ər-) n. FLOODGATE.

water gauge A gauge for indicating the level of water in a boiler, reservoir, etc.

wa·ter·glass (wô′tər·glas′, -gläs′, wot′ər-) n. 1 A drinking glass. 2 WATER GAUGE. 3 A glass-bottomed tube for examining objects lying under water. 4 A water-soluble silicate, as of sodium or potassium, used as an adhesive, for preserving eggs, etc. Also **water glass.**

water hole A pond or pool of water, esp. one used by animals for drinking.

water ice *Chiefly Brit.* SHERBET.

watering place 1 A place where water can be obtained, as a spring. 2 *Chiefly Brit.* A health resort having mineral springs; also, a pleasure resort near the water.

water jacket A casing containing water for cooling, as one surrounding a cylinder of an internal-combustion engine.

water level 1 The level of water in a body of water. 2 A ship's waterline.

wa·ter·lil·y (wô′tər·lil′ē, wot′ər-) n. pl. **·lil·ies** Any of various aquatic plants with large floating leaves and showy white or colored flowers.

wa·ter·line (wô′tər·līn′, wot′ər-) n. 1 *Naut.* **a** A line on the hull of a ship which shows where the water surface reaches. **b** Short, horizontal lines on a ship's hull which correspond with the surface of the water when the ship is unloaded, partly loaded, or fully loaded. 2 Any line or mark showing to what level water has risen.

Waterlily

wa·ter·logged (wô′tər·lôgd′, -logd′, wot′ər-) adj. 1 So saturated or filled with water as to be unmanageable and barely able to float, as a ship, etc. 2 Soaked with water.

Wa·ter·loo (wô′tər·lōō, wô′tər·lōō′) n. A decisive defeat, usu. in the phrase **meet one's Waterloo.** [< *Waterloo,* Belgium, scene of Napoleon's final defeat, 1815]

water main A main pipe in a system of pipes for carrying water, esp. one laid underground.

wa·ter·man (wô′tər·mən, wot′ər-) n. pl. **·men** (-mən) A boatman or oarsman.

wa·ter·mark (wô′tər·märk′, wot′ər-) n. 1 WATERLINE (def. 2). 2 A mark or design made in paper by pressure while the paper is still in a pulpy state; also, the metal pattern which produces these markings. —v.t. 1 To impress (paper) with a watermark. 2 To impress (a mark or design) as a watermark.

wa·ter·mel·on (wô′tər·mel′ən, wot′ər-) n. 1 A gourd cultivated for its large edible fruit, having a juicy, sweet, red or pink pulp. 2 The fruit.

water mill A mill operated by waterpower.

water moccasin A venomous, brownish pit viper, found along rivers, etc., of the SE U.S.

water nymph *Gk. & Rom. Myth.* A nymph dwelling in a stream, lake, etc.

water of crystallization Water that combines with certain salts to form usu. unstable hydrates of distinct crystalline structure. Also **water of hydration.**

water ouzel Any of various small diving birds related to thrushes.

water pipe 1 A pipe for carrying water. 2 HOOKAH.

water polo A game in which two teams of swimmers attempt to take or throw an inflated ball across each other's goal line.

wa·ter·pow·er (wô′tər·pou′ər, wot′ər-) n. The power derived from the kinetic energy of flowing or falling water, used for driving machinery.

wa·ter·proof (wô′tər·prōōf′, wot′ər-) adj. 1 WATERTIGHT. 2 Coated with some substance, as rubber, which prevents the passage of water. —n. 1 Waterproof fabric. 2 *Brit.* A raincoat or other waterproof garment. —v.t. To render waterproof.

water rat 1 MUSKRAT. 2 Any of various rodents that frequent lakes, streams, etc. 3 *Slang* A waterfront tough or thief.

wa·ter·shed (wô′tər·shed′, wot′ər-) n. 1 A ridge of high land that divides two areas drained by different river sys-

tems. 2 The whole region from which a river receives its supply of water. 3 A decisive turning point affecting outlook, actions, etc.

wa·ter·side (wô′tər·sīd′, wot′ər-) n. The shore of a body of water; the water's edge.

wa·ter·ski (wô′tər·skē′, wot′ər-) v.i. **-skied, -ski·ing** To glide over water on skilike runners (**water skis**) while being towed by a motorboat. —**wa′ter·ski′er** n.

water snake 1 Any of various harmless North American snakes that live chiefly in water. 2 Any aquatic snake.

wa·ter·soak (wô′tər·sōk′, wot′ər-) v.t. To saturate with water.

water softener A substance that removes dissolved minerals from water, as by precipitation, absorption, etc.

water spaniel A breed of spaniel having a water-resistant coat, used for retrieving waterfowl.

wa·ter·spout (wô′tər·spout′, wot′ər-) n. 1 A moving, whirling column of spray and mist, resulting from a tornado at sea, on a lake, etc. 2 A pipe for the free discharge of water.

water sprite A nymph, sprite, etc., living in water.

water table The surface marking the upper level of a water-saturated subterranean zone of permeable rock.

wa·ter·tight (wô′tər·tīt′, wot′ər-) adj. 1 So closely made that water cannot enter or leak through. 2 That cannot be misunderstood, found illegal or in error, etc.: a *watertight* contract. —**wat′er·tight′ness** n.

water tower 1 A tank or tower, used as a reservoir and to maintain pressure in a system of water distribution. 2 A vehicular towerlike structure from which water can be played on a burning building from a great height.

water vapor The vapor of water, esp. below the boiling point, as in the atmosphere.

wa·ter·way (wô′tər·wā′, wot′ər-) n. A river, channel, or other stream of water, esp. when navigable by boats and ships.

water wheel A wheel designed to be turned by flowing water. • See UNDERSHOT.

water wings An inflatable device used to keep a beginning swimmer afloat.

wa·ter·works (wô′tər·wûrks′, wot′ər-) n.pl. A system of buildings, pipes, pumps, etc. for furnishing a water supply, esp. for a city.

wa·ter·worn (wô′tər·wôrn′, -wōrn′, wot′ər-) adj. Worn smooth by running or falling water.

wa·ter·y (wô′tər·ē, wot′ər·ē) adj. 1 Of, containing, or like water. 2 Diluted. 3 Overly liquid; thin. 4 Tearful. 5 Weak; vapid; insipid. —**wa′ter·i·ness** n.

watt (wot) n. A unit of power equivalent to one joule per second, or about 1/746 of a horsepower. [< J. *Watt,* 1736–1819, Scottish engineer]

wat·tage (wot′ij) n. An amount of power, esp. electric power, expressed in watts.

watt·hour (wot′our′) n. Energy equivalent to one watt acting for one hour.

watt-hr. watt-hour(s).

wat·tle (wot′l) n. 1 A framework of poles and twigs woven together, used for walls, fences, etc. 2 The poles and twigs used for this. 3 A fold of skin, often wrinkled and brightly colored, hanging from the throat of a bird or lizard. 4 Any one of various acacias of Australia, Tasmania, and South Africa. —v.t. **·tled, ·tling** 1 To weave or twist, as twigs, into a network. 2 To form,, as a fence, by intertwining flexible twigs. 3 To bind together with wattles. [< OE *watul*]

Wattle of turkey

watt·me·ter (wot′mē′tər) n. An instrument for measuring electric power in watts.

wave (wāv) v. **waved, wav·ing** v.i. 1 To move freely back and forth or up and down, as a flag in the wind. 2 To signal by moving something back and forth or up and down. 3 To have an undulating shape or form: Her hair *waves.* —v.t. 4 To cause to wave: to *wave* a banner. 5 To flourish, as a weapon. 6 To give a wavy appearance to or form into waves: to *wave* one's hair. 7 To signal by waving something: He *waved* me aside. 8 To express by waving some-

thing: to *wave* farewell. —*n.* **1** A ridge or undulation moving on the surface of a liquid. **2** A similar undulation on a freely moving surface: *waves* in the tall grass. **3** A curve or curl in the hair. **4** A curved pattern or shape, as on watered silk. **5** A back-and-forth or up-and-down motion, as with the hand. **6** A more or less prolonged meteorological condition: a heat *wave*. **7** An upsurge of something: a crime *wave*; a *wave* of emotion. **8** A surging movement, as of a mass or group: a *wave* of refugees. **9** *Usu. pl.* A large body of water. **10** *Physics* A periodic disturbance propagated through a medium, characterized by a function of time that defines its frequency, amplitude, phase, and velocity. [< OE *wafian*] —**wav′er** *n.*

Wave (wāv) *n.* A member of the **WAVES**, the women's division of the U.S. Navy. [< *W(omen) A(ppointed for) V(oluntary) E(mergency) S(ervice)*]

wave·form (wāv′fôrm′) *n.* **1** The curve produced by recording, as on a graph, the varying dimensions of a wave through successive oscillations. **2** A mathematical formula for such a curve.

wave·length (wāv′length′) *n.* *Physics* The distance, along the line of propagation, between two points of like phase in consecutive cycles of a wave.

wave·let (wāv′lit) *n.* A little wave.

wa·ver (wā′vər) *v.i.* **1** To move one way and the other; flutter. **2** To be uncertain; vacillate. **3** To show signs of falling back or giving way; falter. **4** To flicker; gleam. —*n.* A wavering. [< OE *wafian* to wave] —**wa′ver·er** *n.* —**wa′ver·ing·ly** *adv.* —**Syn.** **1** oscillate, quiver, shake. **2** hesitate.

wav·y (wā′vē) *adj.* **wav·i·er**, **wav·i·est** Full of waves or curves, as hair, lines, etc. —**wav′i·ly** *adv.* —**wav′i·ness** *n.*

wax[1] (waks) *n.* **1** BEESWAX. **2** Any of various pliable plant and animal substances that are insoluble in water, that burn in air, or otherwise resemble beeswax. **3** A solid mineral substance resembling wax, as paraffin. **4** SEALING WAX. **5** A waxlike commercial product, used for polishing furniture, floors, etc. —*v.t.* To coat or polish with wax. —*adj.* Made of or pertaining to wax. [< OE *weax*]

wax[2] (waks) *v.i.* **waxed**, **waxed** (*Archaic* **wax·en**), **wax·ing 1** To increase in size: said esp. of the moon. **2** To become: to *wax* angry. [< OE *weaxan* grow]

wax bean A pale yellow variety of string bean.

wax·ber·ry (waks′ber′ē) *n. pl.* **·ries 1** The wax myrtle, or bayberry. **2** Its fruit.

wax·en (wak′sən) *adj.* **1** Consisting of or covered with wax. **2** Pale; pallid: a *waxen* complexion.

wax myrtle Any of various North American shrubs or small trees having fragrant leaves and small berries covered with white wax, often used in making candles.

wax palm Either of two South American palms yielding waxes widely used to make polishes, cosmetics, etc.

wax paper Paper coated with paraffin to render it moistureproof. Also **waxed paper.**

wax·wing (waks′wing′) *n.* Any of various crested passerine birds having soft, mainly brown plumage, and red, waxy tips on the wings.

wax·work (waks′wûrk′) *n.* **1** Work produced in wax; esp., life-size figures of notable persons. **2** *pl.* An exhibition of such figures. —**wax′work′er** *n.*

wax·y (wak′sē) *adj.* **wax·i·er, wax·i·est 1** Resembling wax in appearance, consistency, etc. **2** Pale; pallid, as wax. **3** Made of, abounding in, or polished with wax. —**wax′i·ness** *n.*

Cedar waxwing

way (wā) *n.* **1** Direction; route: Which *way* is the city? **2** A path, course, road, etc., leading from one place to another. **3** Space or room to advance or work: Make *way* for the king. **4** Distance in general: a little *way* off. **5** Direction in general: Look the other *way*. **6** Passage from one place to another: on our *way* to Europe. **7** A customary or habitual manner or style of acting or being: Do it her *way*. **8** A plan of action; procedure; method: In what *way* will you accomplish this? **9** Respect; point; particular: He erred in two

ways. **10** A course of life or experience: the *way* of sin. **11** Desire; wish: to get one's *way*. **12** *Informal* State or condition: to be in a bad *way*. **13** The range of one's experience or observation: An accident threw it in his *way*. **14** *Informal* Neighborhood or locality: out our *way*. **15** *Naut.* **a** Forward motion; headway. **b** *pl.* A tilted framework of timbers upon which a ship slides when launched. —**by the way** In passing; incidentally. —**by way of 1** With the object or purpose of; to serve as: *by way of* introduction. **2** Through; via. —**give way (to) 1** To yield or submit. **2** To collapse. —**go out of one's** (or **the**) **way** To inconvenience oneself. —**in the way** In a position that impedes or hinders. —**out of the way 1** In a position so as not to hinder or impede. **2** Out of the usual or convenient location or route. **3** Unusual. **4** Improper; wrong: Has he done anything *out of the way?* —**under way** In motion; making progress. —*adv.* *Informal* All the distance to: He went *way* to Denver. [< OE *weg*]

way·bill (wā′bil′) *n.* A statement listing or giving instructions concerning the shipping of goods.

way·far·er (wā′fâr′ər) *n.* One who travels, esp. on foot. —**way′far′ing** *n., adj.*

way·lay (wā′lā′) *v.t.* **·laid**, **·lay·ing 1** To lie in ambush for and attack. **2** To accost on the way. —**way′lay′er** *n.*

way-out (wā′out′) *adj.* *Slang* FAR-OUT.

-ways *suffix of adverbs* In a (specified) manner, direction, or position: *noways, sideways.*

ways and means 1 Means or methods of accomplishing an end or defraying expenses. **2** In legislation, methods of raising funds for the use of the government: also **Ways and Means.**

way·side (wā′sīd′) *adj.* Pertaining to or near the side of a road. —*n.* The side or edge of the road or highway.

way station Any station between principal stations, esp. on a railroad.

way train A train stopping at way stations.

way·ward (wā′wərd) *adj.* **1** Willful; headstrong. **2** Not predictable; erratic. [< ME *awei* away + -WARD] —**way′ward·ly** *adv.* —**way′ward·ness** *n.* —**Syn.** **1** disobedient, perverse, refractory, stubborn. **2** capricious.

WbN west by north.

WbS west by south.

w.c. water closet; without charge.

W.C.T.U. Women's Christian Temperance Union.

we (wē) *pron. pl.* **1** The persons speaking or writing, or a single person writing or speaking when referring to himself and one or more others. **2** A single person denoting himself, as a sovereign, editor, writer, or speaker, when wishing to give his words a formal or impersonal character. [< OE]

weak (wēk) *adj.* **1** Lacking in physical strength, energy, or vigor; feeble. **2** Incapable of resisting stress or supporting weight: a *weak* wall. **3** Lacking in strength of will or stability of character. **4** Not effective, forceful, or convincing: *weak* reasoning. **5** Lacking in power, intensity, etc.: a *weak* voice. **6** Lacking a specified component or components in the usual or proper amount: *weak* tea. **7** Lacking the power or ability to function properly: a *weak* heart. **8** Lacking mental or intellectual capability. **9** Lacking skill, experience, etc.: a *weak* player. **10** Lacking in power, influence, or authority: a *weak* state. **11** Deficient in some specified thing or quality: *weak* in languages. **12** *Gram.* Denoting a verb in English or other Germanic languages that forms its past tense and past participle by adding *d* or *t* rather than by vowel changes. **13** *Phonet.* Unstressed; unaccented, as a syllable or sound. **14** In prosody, indicating a verse ending in which the accent falls on a word or syllable otherwise without stress. **15** Characterized by declining prices: said of the stock market. [< ON *veikr*] —**Syn.** **1** slight, puny, enfeebled, frail.

weak·en (wē′kən) *v.t. & v.i.* To make or become weak or weaker. —**weak′en·er** *n.* —**Syn.** debilitate, enervate, enfeeble, sap.

weak·fish (wēk′fish′) *n. pl.* **·fish** or **·fish·es** Any of various marine food fishes, esp. several troutlike species of E U.S. coastal waters.

---

add, āce, câre, pälm; end, ēven; it, īce; odd, ōpen, ôrder; tŏŏk, pōōl; up, bûrn; ə = *a* in *above, u* in *focus;*
yōō = *u* in *fuse;* oil; pout; check; go; ring; thin; this; zh, *vision.* < derived from; ? origin uncertain or unknown.

weak-kneed (wēk′nēd′) *adj.* 1 Weak in the knees. 2 Without resolution, strong purpose, or energy; spineless.
weak-ling (wēk′ling) *n.* A feeble person or animal. —*adj.* Weak.
weak-ly (wēk′lē) *adj.* ·li·er, ·li·est Sickly; feeble; weak. —*adv.* In a weak manner. —**weak′li·ness** *n.*
weak-mind-ed (wēk′mīn′did) *adj.* 1 Not resolute or firm; indecisive. 2 FEEBLE-MINDED. —**weak′mind′ed·ly** *adv.* —**weak′mind′ed·ness** *n.*
weak-ness (wēk′nis) *n.* 1 The state, condition, or quality of being weak. 2 A characteristic indicating feebleness. 3 A slight failing; a fault. 4 A strong liking or fondness; also, the object of such a liking.
weal[1] (wēl) *n. Archaic* A sound or prosperous condition. [< OE *wela*]
weal[2] (wēl) *n.* A welt, as from a blow. [Var. of WALE]
weald (wēld) *n. Chiefly Brit.* 1 A forest area. 2 An open region; down. [OE, a forest]
wealth (welth) *n.* 1 A large amount of money or property; riches. 2 The state of being rich. 3 Great abundance of anything: a *wealth* of learning. 4 *Econ.* **a** All material objects which have economic utility. **b** All property possessing a monetary value. [ME *welthe* < *wele* weal]
wealth-y (wel′thē) *adj.* wealth·i·er, wealth·i·est 1 Possessing wealth; affluent. 2 More than sufficient; abounding. —**wealth′i·ly** *adv.* —**wealth′i·ness** *n.* —**Syn.** 1 rich, prosperous, well-to-do, well-off.
wean (wēn) *v.t.* 1 To transfer (the young of any mammal) from dependence on its mother's milk to another form of nourishment. 2 To free from usu. undesirable habits or associations: usu. with *from.* [< OE *wenian* accustom] —**wean′er** *n.*
wean-ling (wēn′ling) *adj.* Freshly weaned. —*n.* A child or animal newly weaned.
weap-on (wep′ən) *n.* 1 Any implement of war or combat, as a sword, gun, etc. 2 Any means that may be used against an adversary. 3 Any defensive organ or part of an animal or plant, as a claw, tooth, thorn, etc. [< OE *wæpen*] —**weap′on·ry** (-rē) *n.*
wear (wâr) *v.* **wore, worn, wear·ing** *v.t.* 1 To have on the person as a garment, ornament, etc. 2 To have on the person habitually: He *wears* a derby. 3 To have in one's aspect; exhibit: He *wears* a scowl. 4 To have as a characteristic: She *wears* her hair short. 5 To display or fly: A ship *wears* its colors. 6 To impair or consume by use or constant action. 7 To cause by scraping, rubbing, etc.: to *wear* a hole in a coat. 8 To bring to a specified condition by wear: to *wear* a sleeve to tatters. 9 To exhaust; weary. —*v.i.* 10 To be impaired or diminished gradually by use, rubbing, etc. 11 To withstand the effects of use, handling, etc.: These shoes *wear* well. 12 To remain sound or interesting over a period of time: a friendship that *wore* well. 13 To become as specified from use or attrition: His patience is *wearing* thin. 14 To pass gradually: with *on* or *away.* 15 To have an unpleasant or exhausting effect. —**wear down** 1 To make or become less through friction, use, etc. 2 To tire out; exhaust. 3 To overcome the resistance of by constant pressure, harassment, etc. —**wear off** To diminish gradually. —**wear out** 1 To make or become worthless by use. 2 To waste or use up gradually. 3 To tire or exhaust. —*n.* 1 The act of wearing, or the state of being worn. 2 Material or articles of dress to be worn: often in combination: *footwear, underwear.* 3 Vogue; fashion. 4 Destruction or impairment from use or time. 5 Capacity to resist use or time; durability. —**wear and tear** Loss or damage from use over a period of time. [< OE *werian*] —**wear′er** *n.*
wear-ing (wâr′ing) *adj.* 1 Fatiguing; exhausting: a *wearing* day. 2 Capable of being, or designed to be, worn. —**wear′ing·ly** *adv.*
wearing apparel Clothing; garments.
wea-ri-some (wir′ē·səm) *adj.* Causing fatigue; tiresome. —**wea′ri·some·ly** *adv.* —**wea′ri·some·ness** *n.* —**Syn.** annoying, irksome, tedious, vexatious.
wea-ry (wir′ē) *adj.* ·ri·er, ·ri·est 1 Worn out; tired; fatigued. 2 Discontented or bored: usu. with *of:* *weary* of life. 3 Indicating or characteristic of fatigue: a *weary* sigh. 4 Causing fatigue; wearisome. —*v.t. & v.i.* ·ried, ·ry·ing To make or become weary. [< OE *wērig*] —**wea′ri·ly** *adv.* —**wea′ri·ness** *n.*

wea-sel (wē′zəl) *n.* 1 Any of certain small, slender, usu. nocturnal carnivorous mammals. 2 A sly or treacherous person. —*v.i.* ·seled, ·sel·ing *Informal* 1 To fail to fulfill a promise, etc.; renege: with *out.* 2 To speak ambiguously; equivocate. [< OE *wesle*]

Weasel

weath-er (weth′ər) *n.* 1 The general atmospheric condition, as regards temperature, moisture, winds, or related phenomena. 2 Unpleasant atmospheric conditions. —**keep one's weather eye open** *Informal* To be alert. —**under the weather** *Informal* 1 Ailing; ill. 2 Suffering from a hangover. 3 Drunk. —*v.t.* 1 To expose to the action of the weather. 2 To discolor, crumble, or otherwise affect by action of the weather. 3 To pass through and survive, as a crisis. 4 *Naut.* To pass to windward of: to *weather* Cape Fear. —*v.i.* 5 To undergo changes from exposure to the weather. 6 To resist the action of the weather. —*adj.* Facing the wind. [< OE *weder*]
weath-er-beat-en (weth′ər·bēt′n) *adj.* 1 Bearing or showing the effects of exposure to weather. 2 Tanned, wrinkled, etc., by or as if by exposure to weather, as a face.
weath-er-board (weth′ər·bôrd′, -bōrd′) *n.* CLAPBOARD. —*v.t.* To fasten weatherboards on.
weath-er-bound (weth′ər·bound′) *adj.* Detained by unfavorable weather, as a ship.
weath-er-cock (weth′ər·kok′) *n.* 1 A weathervane, properly one in the form of a cock. 2 A fickle person or variable thing.
weath-er-glass (weth′ər·glas′, -gläs′) *n.* An instrument for indicating the weather, esp. a barometer.
weath-er-man (weth′ər·man′) *n. pl.* ·men (-men′) *n.* A person who reports on daily weather conditions.

Weathercock

weather map *Meteorol.* A map or chart giving weather conditions for a given region and specified time.
weath-er-proof (weth′ər·prōōf′) *adj.* Capable of withstanding snow, rain, wind, etc., without appreciable deterioration. —*v.t.* To make weatherproof.
weather station A station or office where meteorological observations are made.
weath-er-strip (weth′ər·strip′) *n.* A narrow strip of material to be placed over or in crevices, as at doors and windows, to exclude drafts, rain, etc. Also **weath′er·strip′ping.** —*v.t.* ·stripped, ·strip·ping To equip or fit with weatherstrips.
weath-er-vane (weth′ər·vān′) *n.* A vane that indicates the direction in which the wind is blowing.
weath-er-wise (weth′ər·wīz′) *adj.* Experienced in observing or predicting the weather, public opinion, etc.
weath-er-worn (weth′ər·wôrn′, -wōrn′) *adj.* Worn by exposure to the weather.
weave (wēv) *v.* **wove** or *esp. for defs.* 7, 8, & 11 **weaved, wo-ven** or *esp. for defs.* 7, 8, & 11 **weaved, weav·ing** *v.t.* 1 To make (a fabric) by interlacing threads or yarns, esp. on a loom. 2 To interlace (threads or yarns) into a fabric. 3 To form by interlacing strands, strips, twigs, etc.: to *weave* a basket. 4 To produce by combining details or elements: to *weave* a story. 5 To twist or introduce into: to *weave* ribbons through one's hair. 6 To spin (a web). 7 To make by going from one side to another: to *weave* one's way through a crowd. 8 To direct (a car, etc.) in this manner. —*v.i.* 9 To make cloth, etc., by weaving. 10 To become woven or interlaced. 11 To make one's way by moving from one side to another. —*n.* A particular method, style, or pattern of weaving. [< OE *wefan*]
weav-er (wē′vər) *n.* 1 One who weaves. 2 A person whose job is weaving. 3 WEAVERBIRD.
weav-er-bird (wē′vər·bûrd′) *n.* Any of various finchlike birds of Asia, Africa, and Australia, that weave intricate nests.
web (web) *n.* 1 Fabric being woven on a loom. 2 The net-

work of delicate threads spun by a spider or by certain insect larvae. **3** An artfully contrived trap or snare. **4** Any complex network of interwoven parts, elements, etc.: a *web* of lies; a *web* of highways. **5** *Zool.* A membrane connecting the digits, as in aquatic birds, frogs, etc. **6** The vane of a feather. **7** *Anat.* A membrane or tissue. **8** A plate or sheet, as of metal, connecting the ribs, frames, etc., of a structure. **9** *Archit.* The part of a ribbed vault between the ribs. **10** A large roll of paper, as for use in a web press. —*v.t.* **webbed, web·bing 1** To provide with a web. **2** To cover or surround with a web; entangle. [< OE]

webbed (webd) *adj.* **1** Having a web. **2** Having the digits united by a membrane.

web·bing (web′ing) *n.* **1** A woven strip of strong fiber, used for safety belts, upholstery, etc. **2** Anything forming a web or weblike structure.

we·ber (vā′bər, wē′bər) *n.* A unit equal to the magnetic flux that, interacting with a single turn of wire, induces a potential difference of one volt as it is uniformly reduced to zero in one second. [< W. E. *Weber*, 1804–91, German physicist]

web·foot (web′fŏŏt′) *n.* **1** A foot with webbed toes. **2** A bird or animal having such feet. —**web′-foot′ed** *adj.*

web press A printing press which is fed from a continuous roll of paper instead of sheets.

wed (wed) *v.* **wed·ded, wed·ded** or **wed, wed·ding** *v.t.* **1** To take as one's husband or wife; marry. **2** To join in wedlock. **3** To unite or join closely: He is *wedded* to his job. —*v.i.* **4** To take a husband or wife; marry. [< OE *weddian* to pledge]

we'd (wēd) Contraction of *we had* or *we would*.

Wed. Wednesday.

wed·ding (wed′ing) *n.* **1** The ceremony of a marriage. **2** The anniversary of a marriage: golden *wedding*. [< OE *weddian* to pledge]

wedge (wej) *n.* **1** A V-shaped piece of metal, wood, etc., used for splitting wood, raising weights, etc. **2** Anything in the form of a wedge. **3** Any action which facilitates policy, entrance, intrusion, etc. **4** An iron golf club with the face at an angle for lofting the ball. —*v.* **wedged, wedg·ing** *v.t.* **1** To force apart with a wedge. **2** To fix in place with a wedge. **3** To crowd or squeeze (something). —*v.i.* **4** To force oneself or itself in like a wedge. [< OE *wecg*]

wedg·ie (wej′ē) *n.* A woman's shoe having a wedge-shaped piece making a solid, flat sole from heel to toe.

Wedg·wood (wej′wŏŏd′) *n.* A fine English pottery, characterized by small, white, classical figures in cameo relief against a tinted background. [< J. *Wedgwood*, 1730–95, English potter]

wed·lock (wed′lok) *n.* The state of being married. [< OE *wedd* a pledge + *-lāc*, suffix of nouns of action]

Wednes·day (wenz′dē, -dā) *n.* The fourth day of the week. [< OE *Wōdnesdæg* day of Woden]

wee (wē) *adj.* **we·er, we·est** Very small; tiny. [< OE *wēg* a quantity]

weed[1] (wēd) *n.* **1** Any unwanted or unsightly plant, esp. one that hinders the growth of cultivated plants. **2** *Informal* **a** Tobacco. **b** A cigarette or cigar. **c** Marihuana; also, a marihuana cigarette. **3** A thin, ungainly person. —*v.t.* **1** To pull up and remove weeds from. **2** To remove (a weed): often with *out*. **3** To remove (anything regarded as harmful or undesirable): with *out*. **4** To rid of anything harmful or undesirable. —*v.i.* **5** To remove weeds, etc. [< OE *wēod*] —**weed′er** *n.*

weed[2] (wēd) *n.* **1** *Usu. pl.* Mourning garb, as that worn by widows. **2** A black band, as of crepe, worn by a man on his hat or sleeve as a token of mourning. [< OE *wǣd* garment]

weed·y (wē′dē) *adj.* **weed·i·er, weed·i·est 1** Abounding in weeds. **2** Of or pertaining to a weed or weeds. **3** Gawky; lanky: a *weedy* youth. —**weed′i·ly** *adv.* —**weed′i·ness** *n.*

week (wēk) *n.* **1** A period of seven successive days, esp. one beginning with Sunday. **2** The period within a week devoted to work: a 35-hour *week*. —**week in, week out** Every week. [< OE *wicu, wice*]

week·day (wēk′dā′) *n.* **1** Any day of the week except Sunday. **2** Any day other than those of the weekend.

week·end (wēk′end′) *n.* The time from Friday evening or Saturday to the following Monday morning. —*adj.* Of, for, or on a weekend. —*v.i.* To pass the weekend. —**week′end′er** *n.*

week·ly (wēk′lē) *adj.* **1** Of, pertaining to, or lasting a week. **2** Done or occurring once a week. **3** Reckoned by the week. —*adv.* **1** Once a week. **2** Every week. —*n. pl.* **·lies** A publication issued once a week.

ween (wēn) *v.t.* & *v.i. Archaic* To suppose; guess; fancy. [< OE *wēnan* think]

weep (wēp) *v.* **wept, weep·ing** *v.i.* **1** To manifest grief or other strong emotion by shedding tears. **2** To mourn; lament: with *for.* **3** To give out or shed liquid in drops. —*v.t.* **4** To weep for; mourn. **5** To shed (tears, or drops of other liquid). —*n.* **1** The act of weeping, or a fit of tears. **2** An exhudation of liquid; moisture. [< OE *wēpan*] —**weep′er** *n.* —**Syn.** *v.* **1** cry, sob. **2** bewail, grieve.

weep·ing (wē′ping) *adj.* **1** That weeps. **2** Having branches that curve downward.

weeping willow A willow, originally from China, noted for its long, drooping branches.

Weeping willow

wee·vil (wē′vəl) *n.* Any of numerous small beetles with elongated snoutlike heads, often having larvae destructive to cotton, grain, fruit, etc. [< OE *wifel* a beetle] —**wee′vil·y, wee′vil·ly** *adj.*

weft (weft) *n.* **1** The cross threads in a web of cloth; woof. **2** A woven fabric; web. [< OE]

weigh (wā) *v.t.* **1** To determine the weight of. **2** To balance or hold in the hand so as to estimate weight. **3** To measure (a quantity or quantities of something) according to weight: with *out*. **4** To consider or evaluate carefully: to *weigh* one's words. **5** To raise or hoist: now only in the phrase **weigh anchor.** —*v.i.* **6** To have a specified weight: She *weighs* ninety pounds. **7** To have influence or importance: The girl's testimony *weighed* heavily with the jury. **8** To be burdensome or oppressive: with *on* or *upon*: What *weighs* on your mind? **9** *Naut.* **a** To raise anchor. **b** To begin to sail. —**weigh down 1** To press or force down by weight or heaviness. **2** To burden or oppress. —**weigh in** To be weighed before a fight or other athletic contest. [< OE *wegan* weigh, carry, lift] —**weigh′er** *n.*

weight (wāt) *n.* **1** The quality of having heaviness. **2** The measure of this quality, expressed indefinitely or in standard units: Its *weight* is ten pounds. **3** A piece of something, usu. metal, used as a standard unit in weighing: a three-pound *weight*. **4** Any unit of heaviness, as a pound, ounce, etc.; also, a system of such units. **5** *Physics* The force of gravity exerted on any object, equal to the mass of the object multiplied by its acceleration due to gravity. **6** Any mass weighing a definite amount: a four-pound *weight* of flour. **7** Any object having heaviness and used to balance things, exert downward force, etc., as a paperweight, a counterbalance in a machine, a dumbbell for exercising, etc. **8** Burden; pressure: the *weight* of responsibility. **9** Influence; importance; consequence: the great *weight* of this decision. **10** The larger or most valuable part: the *weight* of the data is negative. **11** The comparative heaviness of clothes, as appropriate to the season: summer *weight*. —**carry weight** To be important, significant, influential, etc. —**pull one's weight** To do one's share. —**throw one's weight around** *Informal* To use one's importance or influence in an overbearing or improper manner. —*v.t.* **1** To add weight to; make heavy. **2** To oppress or burden. **3** To adulterate or treat (fabrics or other merchandise) with cheap foreign substances. [< OE *wiht, gewiht*]

weight·less (wāt′lis) *adj.* **1** Having little or no heaviness. **2** Subject to little or no gravitational force. —**weight′less·ly** *adv.* —**weight′less·ness** *n.*

weight·y (wā′tē) *adj.* **weight·i·er, weight·i·est 1** Having great importance; far-reaching; grave: a *weighty* decision.

2 Having power to move the mind; cogent; influential: a *weighty* argument. **3** Burdensome; onerous. **4** Having great weight; heavy. —**weight′i·ly** *adv.* —**weight′i·ness** *n.* —Syn. **1** momentous, serious, solemn.

weir (wir) *n.* **1** A dam placed in a stream to raise or divert the water. **2** A fence of twigs, rods, etc., in a stream, used to catch fish. [< OE *werian* dam up]

weird (wird) *adj.* **1** Manifesting or concerned with the supernatural; unearthly; uncanny. **2** Odd; bizarre; fantastic. [< OE *wyrd* fate] —**weird′ly** *adv.* —**weird′ness** *n.*

weird·o (wir′dō) *n. pl.* **·os** *Slang* A person who is strange or eccentric. Also **weird′ie, weird′y** (-dē) (*pl.* **·ies**).

welch (welch, welsh) *v.t. & v.i. Slang* WELSH. —**welch′er** *n.*

wel·come (wel′kəm) *adj.* **1** Admitted or received gladly and cordially. **2** Producing satisfaction or pleasure; pleasing: *welcome* tidings. **3** Made free to use or enjoy: She is *welcome* to our car. —*n.* The act of bidding or making welcome; a hearty greeting. —**wear out one's welcome** To come so often or to linger so long as no longer to be welcome. —*v.t.* **·comed, ·com·ing 1** To greet gladly or hospitably. **2** To receive with pleasure: to *welcome* advice. [< OE *wilcuma*] —**wel′come·ly** *adv.* —**wel′come·ness, wel′·com·er** *n.*

weld (weld) *v.t.* **1** To unite, as two pieces of metal, by the application of heat along the area of contact. **2** To bring into close association or connection. —*v.i.* **3** To be welded or capable of being welded. —*n.* The joining of pieces of metal by welding; also, the closed joint so formed. [Alter. of INKWELL[1]] —**weld′a·ble** *adj.* —**weld′er** *n.*

wel·fare (wel′fâr) *n.* **1** The condition of being happy, healthy, prosperous, etc.; well-being. **2** WELFARE WORK. **3** Money given to those in need; relief. —**on welfare** Receiving welfare (def. 3) from the government. [< ME *wel* well + *fare* a going]

welfare state A state or social system in which the government assumes a large measure of responsibility for the welfare of its members, as regards employment, health insurance, social security, etc.

welfare work Organized efforts by a government or other organization to improve the economic condition of the needy. —**welfare worker**

wel·kin (wel′kin) *n. Archaic* **1** The vault of the sky; the heavens. **2** The air. [< OE *wolcn, wolcen* a cloud]

well[1] (wel) *n.* **1** A hole or shaft sunk into the earth to obtain a fluid, as water, oil, or natural gas. **2** A place where water issues naturally from the ground. **3** A source of continued supply; fount: a *well* of learning. **4** A depression, cavity, or vessel used to hold or collect a liquid: an *inkwell.* **5** A deep vertical opening descending through floors of a building, as for light, ventilation, stairs, etc. — *v.i.* **1** To pour forth or flow up, as water in a spring. —*v.t.* **2** To gush: Her eyes *welled* tears. [< OE *weallan* boil, bubble up]

well[2] (wel) *adv.* **bet·ter, best 1** Satisfactorily; favorably: Everything goes *well.* **2** In a good or correct manner; expertly: to dance *well.* **3** Suitably; with propriety: I cannot *well* remain here. **4** Agreeably or luxuriously: He lives *well.* **5** Intimately: How *well* do you know him? **6** To a considerable extent or degree: *well* along in years. **7** Completely; thoroughly; fully: *well* aware. **8** Far: He lagged *well* behind us. **9** Kindly; graciously: to speak *well* of someone. —**as well 1** Also; in addition. **2** With equal effect or consequence: He might just *as well* have sold it. —**as well as 1** As satisfactorily as. **2** To the same degree as. **3** In addition to. —*adj.* **1** Suitable, fortunate, right, etc.: It is *well* you called first. **2** In good health. **3** Prosperous; comfortable. —*interj.* An exclamation used to express surprise, expectation, indignation, etc., or to preface a remark. [< OE *wel*] —Syn. *adv.* **2** excellently. **3** befittingly, properly. **4** comfortably. • *Well* often appears in combination with participles to form modifiers. When used after a verb such as *be, seem,* etc., such a modifier is written as two words: to be *well satisfied.* When placed before a noun, it must be hyphenated: a *well-kept* secret.

we'll (wēl) Contraction of *we shall* or *we will.*

well-ap·point·ed (wel′ə·poin′tid) *adj.* Properly equipped; excellently furnished.

well-a·way (wel′ə·wā′) *interj. Archaic* Woe is me! [< OE *wei lā wei*]

well-bal·anced (wel′bal′ənst) *adj.* **1** Evenly balanced, adjusted, or proportioned. **2** Sound mentally; sensible.

well-be·ing (wel′bē′ing) *n.* A condition of health, happiness, or prosperity.

well-born (wel′bôrn′) *adj.* Of good family.

well-bred (wel′bred′) *adj.* **1** Well brought up; polite. **2** Of good or pure stock: said of animals.

well-dis·posed (wel′dis·pōzd′) *adj.* Favorably or kindly disposed or inclined, as to a person, idea, etc.

well-done (wel′dun′) *adj.* **1** Performed skillfully or satisfactorily. **2** Thoroughly cooked.

well-fa·vored (wel′fa′vərd) *adj.* Of attractive appearance; comely; handsome.

well-fed (wel′fed′) *adj.* **1** Plump; fat. **2** Properly fed.

well-fixed (wel′fikst′) *adj. Informal* Affluent; well-to-do.

well-found (wel′found′) *adj.* Well equipped.

well-found·ed (wel′foun′did) *adj.* Based on fact or sound thinking: *well-founded* suspicions.

well-groomed (wel′grōōmd′) *adj.* **1** Carefully dressed and scrupulously neat. **2** Carefully curried, as a horse.

well-ground·ed (wel′groun′did) *adj.* **1** Adequately schooled in the elements of a subject. **2** WELL-FOUNDED.

well-heeled (wel′hēld′) *adj. Slang* Plentifully supplied with money.

well-known (wel′nōn′) *adj.* **1** Widely known. **2** Famous. **3** Thoroughly known.

well-man·nered (wel′man′ərd) *adj.* Courteous; polite.

well-mean·ing (wel′mē′ning) *adj.* **1** Having good intentions. **2** Done with or showing good intentions: also **well′·meant′** (-ment′).

well-nigh (wel′nī′) *adv.* Very nearly; almost.

well-off (wel′ôf′, -of′) *adj.* **1** In comfortable circumstances; well-to-do. **2** Fortunate.

well-pre·served (wel′pri·zûrvd′) *adj.* Not showing many signs of age.

well-read (wel′red′) *adj.* Having a wide knowledge of literature or books; having read much.

well-round·ed (wel′roun′did) *adj.* **1** Having a good and balanced variety of elements: a *well-rounded* education. **2** Having many interests, abilities, etc.: a *well-rounded* person. **3** Fully formed: a *well-rounded* figure.

well-spo·ken (wel′spō′kən) *adj.* **1** Speaking fluently, suitably, or courteously. **2** Fitly or excellently said.

well·spring (wel′spring′) *n.* **1** The source of a stream, spring, etc. **2** A source of continual supply.

well-thought-of (wel′thôt′uv′, -ov′) *adj.* In good repute; esteemed; respected.

well-to-do (wel′tə-dōō′) *adj.* In prosperous or wealthy circumstances; affluent.

well-turned (wel′tûrnd′) *adj.* **1** Gracefully shaped; shapely. **2** Expressed in a graceful or felicitous manner: a *well-turned* phrase.

well-wish·er (wel′wish′ər) *n.* One who wishes well, as to another. —**well′-wish′ing** *adj., n.*

welsh (welsh, welch) *v.t. & v.i. Slang* To fail to pay a debt or fulfill an obligation. [?] —**welsh′er** *n.*

Welsh (welsh, welch) *adj.* Pertaining to Wales, its people, or their language. —*n.* **1** The people of Wales. **2** The Celtic language of Wales.

Welsh·man (welsh′mən, welch′-) *n. pl.* **·men** (-mən) A native or citizen of Wales.

Welsh rabbit Melted cheese cooked with milk, ale, or beer and served hot on toast or crackers. • The form *rarebit* was a later development and is the result of mistaken etymology.

welt (welt) *n.* **1** A raised mark on the skin, resulting from a blow or lashing; wale. **2** A strip of material, covered cord, etc., applied to a seam to cover or strengthen it. **3** In shoemaking, a strip of leather set into the seam between the edges of the upper and the outer sole. —*v.t.* **1** To sew a welt on or in; decorate with a welt. **2** *Informal* To flog severely, so as to raise welts. [ME *welte*]

wel·ter (wel′tər) *v.i.* **1** To roll about; wallow. **2** To lie or be soaked in some fluid, as blood. —*n.* **1** A rolling movement, as of waves. **2** A turmoil; commotion. [< MDu. *welteren*]

wel·ter·weight (wel′tər·wāt′) *n.* A boxer or wrestler whose weight is between 136 and 147 pounds. [< earlier *welter* a heavyweight + WEIGHT]

Welt·schmerz (velt'shmerts) *n.* Weariness of life; melancholy. [G, lit., world pain]

wen (wen) *n.* A cyst containing sebaceous matter, occurring on the skin, esp. on the scalp. [< OE *wenn*]

wench (wench) *n. Archaic* 1 A young woman; girl: now a humorous usage. 2 A young peasant woman; also, a female servant. 3 A prostitute; strumpet. [< OE *wencel* a child, servant]

wend (wend) *v.* **wen·ded** (*Archaic* **went**), **wend·ing** *v.t.* 1 To go on (one's way); proceed. —*v.i.* 2 *Archaic* To proceed; go. [< OE *wendan*]

went (went) *p.t.* of GO.

wept (wept) *p.t.* & *p.p.* of WEEP.

were (wûr, *unstressed* wər) Plural and second person singular past indicative, and past subjunctive singular and plural of BE. [< OE *wære, wæron*]

we're (wir) Contraction of *we are.*

wer·en't (wûrnt, wûr'ənt) Contraction of *were not.*

were·wolf (wir'wŏŏlf', wûr'-) *n. pl.* **·wolves** (-wŏŏlvz') In European folklore, a person changed into a wolf or having power to assume wolf form at will. Also **wer'wolf'**. [< OE *werwulf* man-wolf]

wert (wûrt, *unstressed* wərt) *Archaic* Were: used with *thou.*

west (west) *n.* 1 The general direction in which the sun appears at sunset. 2 The point of the compass at 270°, directly opposite east. 3 Any region lying in this direction. —**the West** 1 The countries lying west of Asia and Asia Minor, including Europe and the Western Hemisphere; the Occident. 2 In the U.S.: **a** Formerly, the region west of the Allegheny Mountains. **b** The region west of the Mississippi, esp. the NW part of this region. 3 The noncommunist countries of Europe and the Western Hemisphere. —*adj.* 1 To, toward, facing, or in the west; western. 2 Coming from the west: the *west* wind. —*adv.* In or toward the west; in a westerly direction. [< OE]

west·er·ly (wes'tər·lē) *adj.* & *adv.* 1 In, toward, or of the west. 2 From the west. —**west'er·li·ness** *n.*

west·ern (wes'tərn) *adj.* 1 Of, in, directed toward, or facing the west. 2 From the west. —*n. Often cap.* A type of fiction or motion picture using cowboy and pioneer life in the western U.S. as its material.

West·ern (wes'tərn) *adj.* 1 Of, from, or characteristic of the West. 2 Belonging or pertaining to the Roman Catholic Church, as distinguished from the Eastern Orthodox Church.

west·ern·er (wes'tər·nər) *n.* 1 One who is native to or dwells in the west. 2 *Usu. cap.* One who is native to or dwells in the western U.S.

Western Hemisphere See HEMISPHERE.

west·ern·ize (wes'tər·nīz) *v.t.* **·ized**, **·iz·ing** To make western in characteristics, habits, etc. —**west'ern·i·za'tion** *n.*

Western Roman Empire The part of the Roman Empire w of the Adriatic, which existed as a separate empire from 395 until the fall of Rome in 476.

Western Sa·mo·a (sə·mō'ə) An independent state located in the w part of the islands of Samoa, 1,133 sq. mi., cap. Apia.

West Germany See GERMANY.

West·min·ster Abbey (west'min'stər) A Gothic church in Westminster, London, where English monarchs are crowned and many notable persons are buried.

west-north·west (west'nôrth'west', *in nautical usage* west'nôr·west') *n.* The direction midway between west and northwest. —*adj.* & *adv.* In, toward, or from this direction.

west-south·west (west'south'west', *in nautical usage* west'sou·west') *n.* The direction midway between west and southwest. —*adj.* & *adv.* In, toward, or from this direction.

west·ward (west'wərd) *adj.* & *adv.* Toward the west. —*n.* A westward direction or region.

west·wards (west'wərdz) *adv.* WESTWARD.

wet (wet) *adj.* **wet·ter, wet·test** 1 Moistened, saturated, or covered with water or other liquid. 2 Marked by showers or by heavy rainfall; rainy. 3 Not yet dry: *wet* varnish. 4 Permitting the manufacture and sale of alcoholic beverages: a *wet* county. 5 Preserved or bottled in a liquid. —**all wet** *Slang* Quite wrong; mistaken. —*n.* 1 Water; moisture; wetness. 2 Showery or rainy weather. 3 *Informal* One opposed to prohibition. —*v.t.* & *v.i.* **wet** or **wet·ted, wet·ting** To make or become wet. [< OE *wæt*] —**wet'ly** *adv.* —**wet'ness, wet'ter** *n.* —**Syn.** *v.* dampen, moisten, soak.

wet·back (wet'bak') *n. Informal* A Mexican who enters the U.S. illegally, esp. by swimming or wading across the Rio Grande.

wet blanket One who or that which discourages any proceedings.

wet dream *Informal* A male's involuntary expulsion of semen during sleep, usu. accompanying an erotic dream.

weth·er (weth'ər) *n.* A castrated ram. [< OE]

wet·land (wet'land') *n. Usu. pl.* Swamps, marshes, and other land areas with heavy soil moisture.

wet nurse A woman who is hired to suckle the child of another woman.

wet pack A therapeutic method consisting of wrapping the patient in wet sheets.

wet suit A skin-tight rubber garment worn by divers, surfers, etc., to retain body warmth in cold waters.

we've (wēv) Contraction of *we have.*

wf, w.f. wrong font (printing).

wh, wh., whr, whr., w.-hr. watt-hour(s).

whack (ʰwak) *v.t.* & *v.i. Informal* To strike sharply; beat; hit. —*n.* 1 *Informal* A sharp, resounding blow. 2 *Slang* A share; portion. —**have** (or **take**) **a whack at** *Slang* 1 To give a blow to. 2 To have a chance or turn at. —**out of whack** *Slang* Out of order. [?] —**whack'er** *n.*

whack·ing (ʰwak'ing) *adj. Chiefly Brit. Informal* Strikingly large; whopping.

whale¹ (ʰwāl) *n.* 1 Any of various very large, air-breathing marine mammals of fishlike form. 2 *Informal* Something extremely good or large: a *whale* of a party. —*v.i.* **whaled, whal·ing** To engage in the hunting of whales. [< OE *hwæl*]

Blue whale

whale² (ʰwāl) *v.t.* **whaled, whal·ing** *Informal* To beat; thrash; flog. [Prob. var. of WALE]

whale·back (ʰwāl'bak') *n.* A freight steamer having a rounded bow and main deck, used on the Great Lakes.

whale·boat (ʰwāl'bōt') *n.* A long, deep rowboat, sharp at both ends.

whale·bone (ʰwāl'bōn') *n.* 1 The horny, pliable substance hanging in plates from the upper jaw of certain whales. 2 A strip of whalebone, used in stiffening corsets, etc.

whal·er (ʰwā'lər) *n.* A person or a ship engaged in whaling.

whal·ing (ʰwā'ling) *n.* The industry of capturing whales. —*adj. Slang* Huge; whopping.

wham·my (ʰwam'ē) *n. pl.* **·mies** *Slang* A jinx; hex: usu. in the phrase **put a** (or **the**) **whammy on.** [< *wham*, informal interjection imit. of the sound of a hard blow]

wharf (ʰwôrf) *n. pl.* **wharves** (ʰwôrvz) or **wharfs** 1 A structure of masonry or timber erected on the shore of a harbor, river, etc., alongside which vessels may lie to load or unload cargo, passengers, etc. 2 Any pier or dock. —*v.t.* 1 To moor to a wharf. 2 To deposit or store on a wharf. [< OE *hwearf* a dam]

wharf·age (ʰwôr'fij) *n.* 1 Charge for the use of a wharf. 2 Wharf accommodations for shipping.

wharf rat 1 A rat that inhabits wharves. 2 *Slang* One who loiters about wharves, esp. with criminal intent.

what (ʰwot, ʰwut) *pron.* 1 Which specific act, thing, name, value, etc.: *What* is going on? *What* is that? 2 That which: *What* followed is a mystery. 3 How much: *What* will it cost? —**and what not** And so forth. —**but what** But that. —**what have you** What is similar or need not be mentioned. —**what if** Suppose that. —**what's what** *Informal* The actual state of affairs. —**what with** Taking into consideration. —*adj.* 1 Which or which kind of: I know *what*

things I want. **2** How surprising, great, etc.: *What* a genius! **3** How much: *What* cash has he? **4** Whatever: Take *what* books you may need. —*adv.* How or how much: *What* do you care? —*interj.* An expression of surprise, annoyance, etc.: *What!* They stole it! [< OE *hwæt*]

what·ev·er (ʰwot'ev'ər, ʰwut'-) *pron.* **1** Anything that: Say *whatever* you want to say. **2** No matter what: *Whatever* you cook will be good. **3** *Informal* What: usu. interrogative: *Whatever* are you doing? —*adj.* **1** No matter what or which: *Whatever* things are left, you can keep. **2** Of any kind, amount, etc.: He has no ability *whatever*.

what·not (ʰwot'not', ʰwut'-) *n.* An ornamental set of shelves for holding bric-a-brac, etc.

what·so·ev·er (ʰwot'sō·ev'ər, ʰwut'-) *pron. & adj.* Whatever: a slightly more formal usage.

wheal (ʰwēl) *n.* A small raised area or pimple on the skin. [Alter. of WALE]

wheat (ʰwēt) *n.* **1** Any of a genus of cereal grasses, esp. cultivated species yielding spikes of edible grain. **2** Grains of these species collectively, constituting a staple food usu. ground into flour.

wheat·en (ʰwēt'n) *adj.* **1** Made of wheat. **2** Having the pale gold color of ripe wheat.

wheat germ The embryo of the wheat kernel, used as a vitamin source.

whee·dle (ʰwēd'l) *v.* **·dled, ·dling** *v.t.* **1** To persuade or try to persuade by flattery, cajolery, etc.; coax. **2** To obtain by cajoling or coaxing. —*v.i.* **3** To use flattery or cajolery. [?] —**whee'dler** *n.* —**whee'dling·ly** *adv.*

wheel (ʰwēl) *n.* **1** A solid disk or a circular rim connected to a hub by spokes or rays capable of rotating on a central axis and used to facilitate movement, as in vehicles, or to act with a rotary motion, as in machines. **2** Anything resembling or suggestive of a wheel. **3** An instrument or device having a wheel or wheels as its distinctive characteristic, as a steering wheel, a potter's wheel, a water wheel, etc. **4** *Informal* A bicycle. **5** An old instrument of torture or execution, consisting of a wheel to which the limbs of the victim were tied and then stretched or broken. **6** A turning or rotating movement; revolution. **7** *Usu. pl.* That which imparts or directs motion or controls activity: the *wheels* of democracy. **8** *Slang* A person of influence or authority: also **big wheel.** **9** *pl.* *Slang* An automobile. —**at** (or **behind**) **the wheel 1** Steering a motor vehicle, motor boat, etc. **2** In charge or in control. —*v.t.* **1** To move or convey on wheels. **2** To cause to turn on or as on an axis; pivot or revolve. **3** To perform with a circular movement. **4** To provide with a wheel or wheels. —*v.i.* **5** To turn on or as on an axis; pivot. **6** To change one's course of action, attitudes, opinions, etc.: often with *about*. **7** To move in a circular or spiral course. **8** To move on wheels. —**wheel and deal** *Slang* To act freely, aggressively, and often unscrupulously, as in the arrangement of a business or political deal. [< OE *hwēol*]

wheel·bar·row (ʰwēl'bar'ō) *n.* A boxlike vehicle ordinarily with one wheel and two handles, for moving small loads. —*v.t.* To convey in a wheelbarrow.

wheel·base (ʰwēl'bās') *n.* The distance separating the axles of the front and rear wheels, as an automobile, etc.

wheel·chair (ʰwēl'châr') *n.* A mobile chair mounted between large wheels, for the use of invalids. Also **wheel chair.**

wheel·er (ʰwē'lər) *n.* **1** One who wheels. **2** WHEELHORSE (def. 1). **3** Something furnished with a wheel or wheels: a *side-wheeler.*

wheel·er-deal·er (ʰwē'lər-dē'lər) *n.* *Slang* One who wheels and deals. —**wheel'er-deal'er·ing** *n.*

wheel·horse (ʰwēl'hôrs') *n.* **1** A horse harnessed next to the front wheels and behind other horses. **2** A person who works hard and dependably.

wheel·house (ʰwēl'hous') *n.* PILOTHOUSE.

wheel·wright (ʰwēl'rīt') *n.* A man whose business is making or repairing wheels.

wheeze (ʰwēz) *v.t. & v.i.* **wheezed, wheez·ing** To breathe

or utter with a husky, whistling sound. —*n.* **1** A wheezing sound. **2** *Informal* A trite joke. [Prob. < ON *hvæsa* hiss] —**wheez'er, wheez'i·ness** *n.* —**wheez'i·ly, wheez'ing·ly** *adv.* —**wheez'y** *adj.* (**·i·er, ·i·est**)

whelk¹ (ʰwelk) *n.* Any of various large, spiral-shelled, marine snails, some of which are edible. [< OE *weoloc*]

whelk² (ʰwelk) *n.* A pimple or pustule. [< OE *hwelian* suppurate]

whelm (ʰwelm) *v.t.* **1** To submerge. **2** To overpower; overwhelm. [ME *whelmen*]

whelp (ʰwelp) *n.* **1** One of the young of a dog, wolf, lion, or certain other carnivores. **2** A dog. **3** A worthless young fellow. —*v.t. & v.i.* To give birth (to): said of certain carnivores. [< OE *hwelp*]

Common whelk

when (ʰwen) *adv.* **1** At what or which time: *When* did you arrive? **2** Under what circumstances: *When* do I apply the brake? **3** At an earlier time: I knew them *when.* —*conj.* **1** At which: the time *when* we went on the picnic. **2** At which or what time: They watched till midnight, *when* they fell asleep. **3** As soon as: He laughed *when* he heard it. **4** Although: He walks *when* he might ride. **5** At the time that; while: *when* we were young. **6** If it should happen that: An employee is fired *when* he is caught stealing. **7** After which; then: We had just awakened *when* you called. **8** Considering that: Why bother to ask me *when* you already know the answer? —*pron.* What or which time: since *when;* till *when.* —*n.* The time; date: to know the *when* and why of something. [< OE *hwanne, hwænne*]

whence (ʰwens) *adv.* From what place or source: *Whence* does he come? —*conj.* From what or out of which place, source, or cause: asked *whence* these sounds arise. [< OE *hwanne* when]

whence·so·ev·er (ʰwens'sō·ev'ər) *adv. & conj.* From whatever place, cause, or source.

when·ev·er (ʰwen'ev'ər) *adv. & conj.* At whatever time.

when·so·ev·er (ʰwen'sō·ev'ər) *adv. & conj.* WHENEVER.

where (ʰwâr) *adv.* **1** At or in what place, respect, or situation: *Where* is my book? *Where* am I at fault? **2** To what place or end. *Where* is this getting us? **3** From what place or source: *Where* did you get that hat? —*conj.* **1** At, in, or to which or what place: I know the hotel *where* they are. **2** At, in, or to the place, position, or situation in which: They are living *where* they are happiest. —*pron.* The place in which: from *where* we stood. —*n.* Place; locality. [< OE *hwær*]

where·a·bouts (ʰwâr'ə·bouts') *adv.* Near or at what place; about where. —*n.pl. (construed as sing. or pl.)* The place in which a person or thing is.

where·as (ʰwâr'az') *conj.* **1** Since the facts are such as they are; seeing that: often used in the preamble of a resolution, etc. **2** While on the contrary; when in truth. —*n. pl.* **·as·es** A clause or item beginning with the word "whereas."

where·at (ʰwâr'at') *adv. Archaic* At what: *Whereat* are you angry? —*conj.* At which point.

where·by (ʰwâr'bī') *adv. Archaic* By what; how. —*conj.* By which: a plan *whereby* we will win.

wher·e'er (ʰwâr'âr') *adv. & conj.* WHEREVER.

where·fore (ʰwâr'fôr', -fōr') *adv. Archaic* For what reason; why: *Wherefore* didst thou doubt? —*conj.* **1** For which. **2** THEREFORE. —*n.* The cause; reason: the whys and *wherefores.* [< WHERE + FOR]

where·from (ʰwâr'frum', -from') *adv. & conj.* From which.

where·in (ʰwâr'in') *adv.* In what way or regard: *Wherein* is the error? —*conj.* In which: a state *wherein* there is discord.

where·of (ʰwâr'uv', -ov') *adv. & conj.* Of which, whom, or what.

where·on (ʰwâr'on', -ôn') *adv. Archaic* On what or whom. —*conj.* On which: land *whereon* to build.

where·so·ev·er (ʰwâr'sō·ev'ər) *adv. & conj.* In, at, or to whatever place; wherever.

where·to (ʰwâr'tōō') *Archaic adv.* To what place or end. —*conj.* To which or to whom. Also **where'un·to'.**

where·up·on (ʰwâr'ə·pon', -ə·pôn') *adv. Archaic* Upon

what; whereon. —*conj.* Upon which or whom; in consequence of which; after which: *whereupon* they took in sail.

wher·ev·er (ʰwâr′ev′ər) *adv. & conj.* In, at, or to whatever place or situation.

where·with (ʰwâr′with′, -with′) *adv. Archaic* With what: *Wherewith* shall I do it? —*conj.* With which; by means of which: *wherewith* we abated hunger. —*pron.* That with or by which: used with an infinitive: I have not *wherewith* to do it.

where·with·al (ʰwâr′with·ôl′, -with-) *n.* The necessary means or resources, esp. money: used with *the*.

wher·ry (ʰwer′ē) *n. pl.* **·ries** 1 A light, fast rowboat built for one person and used for racing or exercise. 2 *Brit.* A very broad, light barge. —*v.t. & v.i.* **·ried, ·ry·ing** To transport in or use a wherry. [?]

whet (ʰwet) *v.t.* **whet·ed, whet·ting** 1 To sharpen, as a knife, by friction. 2 To make more keen or eager; excite; stimulate, as the appetite. —*n.* 1 The act of whetting. 2 Something that whets. [< OE *hwettan*] —**whet′ter** *n.*

wheth·er (ʰweth′ər) *conj.* 1 If it be the case that: Tell us *whether* you are going or not. 2 In case; if: *whether* he lived or died, we never heard. 3 Either: He came in first, *whether* by luck or plan. —**whether or no** Regardless; in any case. [< OE *hwæther*]

whet·stone (ʰwet′stōn′) *n.* A fine-grained stone for whetting knives, axes, etc.

whew (ʰwyōō) *interj.* An exclamation of amazement, dismay, relief, etc.

whey (ʰwā) *n.* A clear liquid that separates from the curd when milk is curdled, as in making cheese. [< OE *hwæg*] —**whey′ey, whey′ish** *adj.*

whf. wharf.

which (ʰwich) *pron.* 1 What specific one or ones: *Which* are for sale? 2 The specific one or ones that: I know *which* I bought. 3 The thing, animal, or event designated earlier: used restrictively or nonrestrictively: The flood *which* wiped us out was last year; That car, *which* is not old, no longer runs. 4 *Archaic* The person or persons designated earlier: "Our Father, *which* art in heaven," 5 WHICHEVER: Use *which* you find most convenient. 6 A thing, situation, or fact that: He decided to go, *which* was lucky. —*adj.* 1 What specific one or ones: *Which* play did you see? 2 WHICHEVER: Take *which* one you want. 3 Being the one or ones designated earlier: The clock struck one, at *which* point he left. • See WHO. [< OE *hwelc, hwilc*]

which·ev·er (ʰwich′ev′ər) *pron. & adj.* 1 Any one (of two or of several): Select *whichever* (ring) you want. 2 No matter which: *Whichever* (song) you choose, sing it well. Also **which′so·ev′er.**

whiff (ʰwif) *n.* 1 A slight gust or puff of air. 2 A gust or puff of odor: a *whiff* of onions. 3 A sudden expulsion of breath or smoke from the mouth; a puff. —*v.t.* 1 To drive or blow with a whiff or puff. 2 To smoke, as a pipe. —*v.i.* 3 To blow or move in whiffs or puffs. 4 To exhale or inhale whiffs. [Imit.] —**whiff′er** *n.*

whif·fet (ʰwif′it) *n. Informal* 1 A trifling, useless person. 2 A small, snappish dog. [?]

whif·fle (ʰwif′əl) *v.* **·fled, ·fling** *v.i.* 1 To blow with puffs or gusts, as the wind. 2 To vacillate; veer. —*v.t.* 3 To blow or dissipate with a puff. [Freq. of WHIFF] —**whif′fler** *n.*

whif·fle·tree (ʰwif′əl·trē′) *n.* A horizontal crossbar, to the ends of which the traces of a harness are attached. [Var. of WHIPPLETREE]

Whig (ʰwig) *n.* 1 An American colonist who supported the Revolutionary War in the 18th century. 2 A member of an American political party opposed to the Democratic and succeeded by the Republican party in 1856. 3 A member of a political party (later the Liberal party) in England in the 18th and 19th centuries. —*adj.* Belonging to, consisting of, or supported by the Whigs. [Prob. short for *Whiggamore*, one of a body of 17th cent. Scottish insurgents] — **Whig′ger·y, Whig′gism** *n.* —**Whig′gish** *adj.*

while (ʰwīl) *n.* A period of time: a brief *while.* —**between whiles** From time to time. —**the while** At the same time. —**worth (one's) while** Worth one's time, labor, trouble, etc. —*conj.* 1 During the time that. 2 At the same time

that; although: *While* he found fault, he also praised. 3 Whereas: This man is short, *while* that one is tall. —*v.t.* **whiled, whil·ing** To cause to pass pleasantly: usu. with *away:* to *while* away the time. [< OE *hwīl*]

whiles (ʰwīlz) *Archaic* or *Regional adv.* Occasionally; at intervals. —*conj.* WHILE.

whi·lom (ʰwī′ləm) *Archaic adj.* FORMER. —*adv.* FORMERLY. [< OE *hwīlum* at times < *hwīl* a while]

whilst (ʰwīlst) *conj. Chiefly Brit.* WHILE.

whim (ʰwim) *n.* A sudden, capricious idea, notion, or desire; fancy. [Short for earlier *whim-wham* a trifle]

whim·per (ʰwim′pər) *v.i.* 1 To cry with plaintive broken sounds. —*v.t.* 2 To utter with or as if with a whimper. —*n.* A low, broken, whining cry. [Imit.] —**whim′per·er** *n.* —**whim′per·ing·ly** *adv.*

whim·si·cal (ʰwim′zi·kəl) *adj.* 1 Capricious; fanciful; unpredictable. 2 Odd; fantastic; quaint. —**whim·si·cal′i·ty** (-kal′ə·tē) (*pl.* **·ties**), **whim′si·cal·ness** *n.* —**whim′si·cal·ly** *adv.*

whim·sy (ʰwim′zē) *n. pl.* **·sies** 1 A whim; caprice. 2 Humor that is somewhat odd, fanciful, or quaint. Also **whim′sey.** [Prob. related to WHIM]

whine (ʰwīn) *v.* **whined, whin·ing** *v.i.* 1 To utter a high, plaintive, nasal sound expressive of grief or distress. 2 To complain in a fretful or childish way. 3 To make a steady, high-pitched sound, as a machine. —*v.t.* 4 To utter with a whine. —*n.* The act or sound of whining. [< OE *hwīnan* whiz] —**whin′er** *n.* —**whin′ing·ly** *adv.* —**whin′y** *adj.*

whin·ny (ʰwin′ē) *v.* **·nied, ·ny·ing** *v.i.* 1 To neigh, esp. in a low or gentle way. —*v.t.* 2 To express with a whinny. —*n. pl.* **·nies** A low, gentle neigh. [< WHINE]

whip (ʰwip) *v.* **whipped, whip·ping** *v.t.* 1 To strike with a lash, rod, strap, etc. 2 To punish by striking thus; flog. 3 To drive or urge with lashes or blows: with *on, up, off,* etc. 4 To strike in the manner of a whip: The wind *whipped* the trees. 5 To beat, as eggs or cream, to a froth. 6 To seize, move, jerk, throw, etc., with a sudden motion: with *away, in, off, out,* etc. 7 In fishing, to make repeated casts upon the surface of (a stream, etc.). 8 To wrap or bind about something. 9 To sew, as a flat seam, with a loose overcast or overhand stitch. 10 *Informal* To defeat; overcome, as in a contest. —*v.i.* 11 To go, move, or turn suddenly and quickly: with *away, in, off, out,* etc. 12 To thrash about in the manner of a whip: pennants *whipping* in the wind. 13 In fishing, to make repeated casts with rod and line. — **whip up** 1 To excite; arouse. 2 *Informal* To prepare quickly, as a meal. —*n.* 1 An instrument consisting of a lash attached to a handle, used for discipline or punishment. 2 A whipping or thrashing motion. 3 A member of a legislative body, as congress or parliament, appointed unofficially to enforce discipline, attendance, etc.: also **party whip.** 4 A dessert containing whipped cream or beaten egg whites, flavoring, sometimes fruit, etc. [ME *wippen*] —**Syn.** *v.* 1 beat, scourge, switch, thrash.

whip·cord (ʰwip′kôrd′) *n.* 1 A strong, hard-twisted cord, used in making whiplashes. 2 A twill fabric with a pronounced diagonal rib.

whip hand 1 The hand in which a person holds the whip while driving. 2 A position or means of advantage.

whip·lash (ʰwip′lash′) *n.* 1 The flexible striking part of a whip. 2 An injury to the neck, due to a sudden snapping back and forth of the head, as in automobile accidents: also **whiplash injury.**

whip·per·snap·per (ʰwip′ər·snap′ər) *n.* A pretentious but insignificant person, esp. a young person. [?]

whip·pet (ʰwip′it) *n.* A swift dog resembling an English greyhound in miniature, used in racing, etc. [?< WHIP]

whip·ping (ʰwip′ing) *n.* 1 The act of one who or that which whips; esp. a punishment by flog-ging. 2 Material, as cord or twine, used to whip or bind.

Whippet

whipping boy Anyone who receives blame deserved by another; scapegoat.

whipping post The fixture to which those sentenced to flogging are secured.

whip·ple·tree (ʰwip'əl·trē') n. WHIFFLETREE.

whip·poor·will (ʰwip'ər·wil) n. A small nocturnal bird, allied to the goatsuckers, common in E North America. [Imit.]

whip·saw (ʰwip'sô') n. A thin, narrow, two-man ripsaw. —v.t. ·sawed, ·sawed or ·sawn, ·saw·ing 1 To saw with a whipsaw. 2 To beat (an opponent) in two ways at the same time.

whip·stitch (ʰwip'stich') v.t. To sew or gather with overcast stitches. —n. An overcast stitch.

whip·stock (ʰwip'stok') n. A whip handle.

whir (ʰwûr) v.t. & v.i. whirred, whir·ring To fly or move with a buzzing sound. —n. 1 A whizzing, swishing sound. 2 Confusion; bustle. Also whirr. [Prob. < Scand.]

whirl (ʰwûrl) v.i. 1 To turn or revolve rapidly, as about a center. 2 To turn away or aside quickly. 3 To move or go swiftly. 4 To have a sensation of spinning: My head whirls. —v.t. 5 To cause to turn or revolve rapidly. 6 To carry or bear along with a revolving motion. —n. 1 A swift rotating or revolving motion. 2 Something whirling. 3 A state of confusion. 4 A round of activities, social events, etc. 5 Informal A short drive. 6 Informal A try. [Prob. < ON hvirfla revolve] —whirl'er n.

whirl·i·gig (ʰwûr'lə·gig') n. 1 Any toy that spins. 2 A merry-go-round. 3 Anything that moves in a cycle. 4 A whirling motion. 5 Any of certain water beetles that move on the water in swift circles: also whirligig beetle. [< WHIRL + GIG]

whirl·pool (ʰwûrl'pōōl') n. 1 An eddy or vortex where water moves in a rapid whirling motion, as from the meeting of two currents. 2 Anything resembling a whirlpool, esp. in movement.

whirl·wind (ʰwûrl'wind') n. 1 A forward-moving column of air, with a rapid circular and upward spiral motion. 2 Anything resembling a whirlwind in movement, energy, or violence. —adj. Extremely swift or impetuous: a whirlwind courtship.

whish (ʰwish) v.i. To make or move with a whizzing sound. —n. Such a sound. [Imit.]

whisk (ʰwisk) v.t. 1 To brush or sweep off lightly: often with away or off. 2 To cause to move with a quick sweeping motion. 3 To beat with a quick movement, as eggs, cream, etc. —v.i. 4 To move quickly and lightly. —n. 1 A light sweeping or whipping movement. 2 A little bunch of straw, feathers, etc. for brushing. 3 A culinary instrument of wire loops for whipping (cream, etc.). [Prob. < Scand.]

whisk·broom (ʰwisk'brōōm', -brōŏm') n. A small, short-handled broom for brushing clothing, etc.

whisk·er (ʰwis'kər) n. 1 pl. The hair of a man's beard, esp. the hair that grows on the cheeks. 2 A hair from the whiskers. 3 One of the long, bristly hairs near the mouth of some animals, as the cat, mouse, etc. [< WHISK] —whisk'·ered, whisk'er·y adj.

whis·key (ʰwis'kē) n. pl. ·keys or ·kies 1 An alcoholic liquor obtained by the distillation of a fermented mash of grain, as rye, corn, barley, or wheat. 2 A drink of whiskey. —adj. Pertaining to or made of whiskey. Also whis'ky. [< Ir. uisce beathadh, lit., water of life] • In the U.S. and Ireland, whiskey is usu. spelled with an e. Scotch and Canadian whisky, however, are traditionally spelled without the e.

whis·per (ʰwis'pər) n. 1 An act or instance of breathy speech with little or no vibration of the vocal chords. 2 An utterance made with such speech. 3 A secret communication; hint; insinuation. 4 Any low, rustling sound. —v.i. 1 To speak in a low, breathy way with little or no vibration of the vocal chords. 2 To talk cautiously or furtively; plot or gossip. 3 To make a low, rustling sound, as leaves. —v.t. 4 To utter in a whisper. 5 To speak to in a whisper. [< OE hwisprian] —whis'per·er n. —whis'per·ing·ly adv. —whis'·per·y adj.

whispering campaign An organized effort to discredit a person, group, cause, etc., by rumors and gossip.

whist (ʰwist) n. A game of cards from which bridge developed, played by four persons with a full pack of 52 cards. [Alter. of earlier whisk]

whis·tle (ʰwis'əl) v. ·tled, ·tling v.i. 1 To make a sound by sending the breath through the teeth or through puckered lips. 2 To make a sharp, shrill sound by forcing air, steam, etc., through a small opening. 3 To make a similar sound by swift passage through the air, as bullets, the wind, etc. 4 To make a shrill cry, as certain animals or birds. 5 To blow or sound a whistle. —v.t. 6 To produce (a tune) by whistling. 7 To call, manage, or direct by whistling. —n. 1 An instrument for making whistling sounds: a train whistle; a toy whistle. 2 A whistling sound. 3 The act of whistling. —wet one's whistle Slang To take a drink. [< OE hwistlian a shrill pipe] —whis'tler n.

whis·tle-stop (ʰwis'əl·stop') Informal v.i. ·stopped, ·stop·ping To make whistle stops, esp. as part of a political campaign.

whistle stop Informal 1 A small town, at which formerly a train stopped only on signal. 2 Any of a series of brief stops at small communities during a tour, esp. one made by a political candidate.

whit (ʰwit) n. The smallest particle; speck: usu. with a negative: not a whit abashed. [< OE (æbig) wiht a little amount] —Syn. bit, grain, iota, jot, shred.

white (ʰwīt) adj. whit·er, whit·est 1 Having the color produced by reflection of all the rays of the solar spectrum, as the color of pure snow. 2 Light or comparatively light in color: white wine. 3 Bloodless; ashen: white with rage. 4 Very fair; blond. 5 Silvery or gray, as with age. 6 Snowy. 7 Wearing white clothing: white nuns. 8 Not malicious or harmful: a white lie. 9 Innocent; pure. 10 Unmarked by ink or print; blank. 11 Having a light-colored skin; Caucasian. 12 Of, pertaining to, or controlled by Caucasians: the white power structure. 13 Informal Fair; straightforward; honest. 14 Music Of, pertaining to, or being a tonal quality having accuracy of pitch but lacking resonance, color, and warmth. —n. 1 A white color. 2 The state or condition of being white; whiteness. 3 The white or light-colored part of something; esp., the albumen of an egg, or the white part of the eyeball. 4 Anything that is white or nearly white, as cloth, white wine, etc. 5 pl. A white uniform or outfit: the summer whites of the Navy. 6 A Caucasian. —v.t. whit·ed, whit·ing To make white; whiten. [< OE hwīt] —white'ly adv. —white'ness n.

white ant TERMITE.

white·bait (ʰwīt'bāt') n. The young of various fishes, esp. of sprat and herring, served as a delicacy.

white birch A North American birch with white bark that peels off in papery sheets.

white·cap (ʰwīt'kap') n. A wave with foam on its crest.

white cedar 1 A strong-scented evergreen tree of the cypress family, having small, scalelike leaves and growing in moist places. 2 Its soft, easily worked wood.

white clover A common variety of clover, with white flowers.

white coal Water power.

white-col·lar (ʰwīt'kol'ər) adj. Of, pertaining to, or designating usu. salaried employees, as office personnel, whose work does not often expose their clothes to soil or stain, thus enabling them to wear garments, as white shirts, etc., that are easily stained.

white corpuscle LEUKOCYTE.

whited sepulcher A corrupt or evil person who pretends to be good; hypocrite.

white elephant 1 A rare pale-gray variety of Asian elephant held sacred in E Asia. 2 Anything that is a burden and an expense to maintain.

white feather A symbol of cowardice. —show the white feather To show cowardice.

white·fish (ʰwīt'fish') n. pl. ·fish or ·fish·es 1 Any of various silvery North American food fishes, living mostly in lakes. 2 Any of various other whitish or silvery fishes.

white flag A white flag or banner used as a signal of surrender.

white gold Gold alloyed with a white metal, usu. nickel and zinc, sometimes palladium, which gives the gold a platinumlike appearance.

white heat 1 The temperature at which metal, etc., becomes white with heat. 2 A state of intense emotion, enthusiasm, etc.

white-hot (ʰwīt'hot') adj. So hot as to glow with white light.

White House, The 1 The official residence of the president of the U.S., at Washington, D.C. **2** The executive branch of the U.S. government.

white lead A poisonous white pigment composed of lead carbonate and hydrated lead oxide.

white lie A harmless, trivial lie.

white matter The whitish portion of the brain and spinal cord that is composed mainly of nerve fibers.

white meat Any light-colored meat, as the breast of chicken, turkey, etc.

whit·en (ʰwīt′n) *v.t. & v.i.* To make or become white or nearly white. **—whit′en·er** *n.* **—Syn.** blanch, bleach.

white noise Noise in which the average intensity at any frequency between two stated limits is constant.

white oak 1 Any of numerous oaks having gray or whitish bark. **2** The wood of any white oak.

white pepper Pepper ground from the white seeds inside black peppercorns.

white pine 1 A pine of E North America, with soft, bluish-green leaves in clusters of five. **2** The light, soft wood of this tree. **3** Any of several related pines.

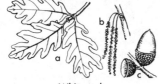

White oak
a. leaves. b. blossom. c. acorn.

white poplar A large, rapidly growing tree valued for its ornamental leaves, which are green above and silvery-white below.

white potato The common potato.

White Russian BYELORUSSIAN.

white sauce A cooked sauce of flour, butter, milk, etc.

white slave A woman forced into or held in prostitution. **—white-slave** (ʰwīt′slāv′) *adj.* **—white slaver —white slavery**

white-tailed deer (ʰwīt′tāld′) A common North American deer, having a tail white on the underside.

white tie 1 A white bow tie, worn with men's formal evening dress. **2** The formal evening dress of men.

white·wash (ʰwīt′wosh′, -wôsh′) *n.* **1** A mixture of slaked lime and water used for whitening walls, etc. **2** A suppressing or hiding of faults and defects. **3** *Informal* A defeat in which the loser fails to score. **—v.t. 1** To coat with whitewash. **2** To gloss over; hide. **3** *Informal* In games or sports, to defeat without allowing one's opponent to score. **—white′wash′er** *n.*

whith·er (ʰwith′ər) *adv. Archaic* To what place, condition, end, etc.: *Whither* are we bound? **—conj. 1** To which place, condition, end, etc.: the village *whither* we went. **2** To whatever place, condition, end, etc.: Go *whither* you will. [< OE *hwider*]

whith·er·so·ev·er (ʰwith′ər·sō·ev′ər) *adv. Archaic* To whatever place.

whit·ing[1] (ʰwī′ting) *n.* A powdered white chalk used as a pigment, for polishing, etc.

whit·ing[2] (ʰwī′ting) *n.* **1** A small European food fish related to cod. **2** A silvery-scaled hake. **3** Any of several silvery fishes, esp. the **Carolina whiting,** common on the coast of the S U.S. [< MDu. *wit* white]

whit·ish (ʰwī′tish) *adj.* Somewhat white or very light gray. **— whit′ish·ness** *n.*

Whiting[2]

whit·low (ʰwit′lō) *n.* An inflammatory, festering lesion at the edge of a fingernail. [< WHITE + FLAW]

Whit·sun (ʰwit′sən) *adj.* Of, pertaining to, or for Whitsunday or Whitsuntide.

Whit·sun·day (ʰwit′sun′dē, -dā) *n.* The seventh Sunday after Easter; Pentecost. [< OE *Hwīta Sunnandæg,* lit., white Sunday < the white robes worn by recently baptized persons on that day]

Whit·sun·tide (ʰwit′sən·tīd′) *n.* The week that begins with Whitsunday. Also **Whitsun Tide.**

whit·tle (ʰwit′l) *v.* **·tled, ·tling** *v.t.* **1** To cut or shave bits from (wood, a stick, etc.). **2** To make or shape by whittling. **3** To reduce or wear away a little at a time: with *down, off, away,* etc. **—v.i. 4** To whittle wood. [< OE *thwitan* to cut] **—whit′tler** *n.* **—Syn.** *v.* **1** carve, trim, pare.

whiz (ʰwiz) *v.* **whizzed, whiz·zing** *v.i.* **1** To make a hissing and humming sound while passing rapidly through the air. **2** To move or pass with such a sound. **—v.t. 3** To cause to whiz. **—n. 1** The sound made by whizzing. **2** *Slang* Any person or thing of extraordinary excellence or ability. Also **whizz.** [Imit.] **—whiz′zer** *n.* **—whiz′zing·ly** *adv.*

whiz kid *Slang* A young person who is extraordinarily clever, talented, or successful. [Alter. of *Quiz Kid,* a panel member of a former quiz show made up of children]

who (hōō) *pron. possessive case* whose; *objective case* whom **1** Which or what person or persons: *Who* is she? They don't know *who* I am. **2** The person or persons that; whoever: *Who* insults my friends insults me. **3** That: used as a relative to introduce a clause: the man *who* mows our lawn. **—who's who** Who the most prominent people are. **—as who should say** As if one should say; so to speak. [< OE *hwā, hwǣ*] • **who, which, that** *Who* as a relative is usu. applied only to persons, *which* only to animals or to inanimate objects, *that* to persons or things.

WHO World Health Organization.

whoa (ʰwō) *interj.* Stop! stand still! [Var. of HO]

who·dun·it (hōō·dun′it) *n. Informal* A mystery story, play, etc. [< WHO + DONE + IT]

who·ev·er (hōō·ev′ər) *pron.* **1** Any one without exception; any person who. **2** No matter who.

whole (hōl) *adj.* **1** Containing all the parts necessary to make up a total; entire; complete. **2** Not broken, injured, defective, etc.; sound; intact. **3** Being the full amount, number, duration, etc.: He failed the *whole* class. **4** In or having regained sound health; hale. **5** Having the same parents: a *whole* brother. **6** *Math.* Integral; not mixed or fractional. **—as a whole** Altogether. **—on the whole** Taking all into consideration; in general. **—n. 1** All the parts or elements making up a thing. **2** A complete unity or system. [< OE *hāl*] **—whole′ness** *n.*

whole·heart·ed (hōl′här′tid) *adj.* Done or undertaken with all earnestness, energy, dedication, etc. **—whole′-heart′ed·ly** *adv.* **—whole′heart′ed·ness** *n.*

whole note *Music* A note whose time value is the same as that of two half notes. • See NOTE.

whole number Any member of the set of numbers {. . . −3, −2, −1, 0, 1, 2, 3 . . .}; an integer.

whole·sale (hōl′sāl′) *n.* The sale of goods in large bulk or quantity, usu. for resale by retailers. **—adj. 1** Pertaining to or engaged in such selling. **2** Made or done on a large scale or indiscriminately: *wholesale* murder. **—adv. 1** In bulk or quantity. **2** Extensively or indiscriminately. **—v.t. & v.i.** **·saled, ·sal·ing** To sell (something) in large quantity, usu. for resale by retailers. [< ME *by hole sale* in large quantities] **—whole′sal′er** *n.*

whole·some (hōl′səm) *adj.* **1** Tending to promote health: *wholesome* air or food. **2** Tending to promote mental or moral well-being: a *wholesome* play. **3** Healthy: *wholesome* red cheeks. [< WHOLE + -SOME] **—whole′some·ly** *adv.* **—whole′some·ness** *n.*

whole step An interval consisting of two semitones. Also **whole tone.**

whole-wheat (hōl′ʰwēt′) *adj.* **1** Made from the entire wheat kernel: *whole-wheat* flour. **2** Made from whole-wheat flour. Also **whole wheat.**

who'll (hōōl) Contraction of *who will* or *who shall.*

whol·ly (hō′lē, hōl′lē) *adv.* **1** Completely; totally. **2** Exclusively; only.

whom (hōōm) *pron.* The objective case of WHO. [< OE *hwam*]

whom·ev·er (hōōm′ev′ər) *pron.* The objective case of WHOEVER.

whom·so·ev·er (hōōm′sō·ev′ər) *pron.* The objective case of WHOSOEVER.

whoop (hōōp, ʰwōōp, ʰwōōp) *v.i.* **1** To utter loud cries, as of excitement, rage, or exultation. **2** To hoot, as an owl. **3** To make a loud, gasping intake of breath. **—v.t. 4** To utter

with a whoop or whoops. **5** To call, urge, chase, etc., with whoops. **—whoop it** (or **things**) **up** *Slang* **1** To celebrate in a noisy, riotous manner. **2** To arouse enthusiasm. — *n.* **1** A shout of excitement, joy, derision, etc. **2** A loud, convulsive intake of breath. **3** An owl's hoot. [Imit.]

whoop·ee (ʰwo͞o′pē, ʰwo͝op′ē) *Slang interj.* An exclamation of joy, excitement, etc. **—make whoopee** To have a noisy, festive time. [< WHOOP]

whooping cough A contagious respiratory disease of bacterial origin chiefly affecting children, marked in later stages by violent coughing.

whooping crane A large white North American crane having a whooplike cry.

whop·per (ʰwop′ər) *n. Informal* **1** Something large or remarkable. **2** An outrageous falsehood.

whop·ping (ʰwop′ing) *adj.* Unusually large, great, or remarkable.

whore (hôr, hōr) *n.* A woman who engages in sexual intercourse promiscuously; esp., a prostitute. —*v.i.* **whored**, **whor·ing 1** To have illicit sexual intercourse, esp. with a whore. **2** To be or act like a whore. [< OE *hōre*]

whorl (ʰwûrl, ʰwôrl) *n.* **1** The flywheel of a spindle. **2** *Bot.* A set of leaves, etc., distributed in a circle around a stem. **3** *Zool.* A turn of a spiral shell. **4** Any of the convoluted ridges of a fingerprint. [? < WHIRL] **—whorled** *adj.*

Whorl def. 2

whor·tle·ber·ry (ʰwûr′təl·ber′ē) *n. pl.* **·ries 1** A European shrub with edible blueblack berries. **2** Its fruit. **3** HUCKLEBERRY. [< OE *horta whortleberry* + BERRY]

whose (ho͞oz) The possessive case of WHO and often of WHICH. [< OE *hwæs*, genitive of *hwā* who]

who·so (ho͞o′sō) *pron. Archaic* WHOEVER.

who·so·ev·er (ho͞o′sō·ev′ər) *pron.* WHOEVER.

why (ʰwī) *adv.* For what cause, purpose, or reason: *Why* did you go? —*conj.* **1** The reason or cause for which: I don't know *why* he went. **2** For or because of which: I know the reason *why* he went. —*n. pl.* **whys** A cause; reason. — *interj.* An exclamation expressing surprise, doubt, etc. [< OE *hwī, hwȳ*]

WI Wisconsin (P.O. abbr.).

W.I. West Indian; West Indies.

wick (wik) *n.* A strand of loosely twisted or woven fibers, as in a candle or lamp, acting by capillary attraction to convey fuel to a flame. [< OE *wēoca*] **—wick′ing** *n.*

wick·ed (wik′id) *adj.* **1** Evil; depraved. **2** Mischievous; roguish. **3** Troublesome; painful: a *wicked* headache. [< OE *wicca* a wizard] **—wick′ed·ly** *adv.* **—wick′ed·ness** *n.* — **Syn. 1** malevolent, sinful, wrong. **2** devilish.

wick·er (wik′ər) *adj.* Made of twigs, osiers, etc. —*n.* **1** A pliant young sprout or rod; twig; osier. **2** WICKERWORK. [Prob. < Scand.]

wick·er·work (wik′ər·wûrk′) *n.* A fabric or texture, as a basket, made of woven twigs, osiers, etc.

wick·et (wik′it) *n.* **1** A small door or gate often within a larger entrance. **2** A small opening in a door. **3** A small sluicegate at the end of a millrace. **4** In cricket: **a** Either of two arrangements of three upright rods set near together. **b** The level playing space between these. **c** A player's turn at bat. **5** In croquet, an arch, usu. of wire, through which one must hit the ball. [< AF *wiket*]

wick·et·keep·er (wik′it·kē′pər) *n.* In cricket, the fielder stationed right behind the wicket.

wide (wīd) *adj.* **wid·er**, **wid·est 1** Having relatively great extent between sides. **2** Extended far in every direction; spacious: a *wide* expanse. **3** Having a specified degree of width: an inch *wide*. **4** Distant from the desired or proper point, issue, etc.: *wide* of the mark. **5** Having great scope, range, inclusiveness, etc.: a *wide* variety. **6** Loose; ample; roomy: *wide* trousers. **7** Fully open; expanded or extended: *wide* eyes. **8** *Phonet.* Formed with a relatively relaxed tongue and jaw: said of certain vowels. —*n.* In cricket, a ball bowled so as not to be within the batsman's reach. — *adv.* **1** To a great distance; extensively. **2** Far from the mark, issue, etc. **3** To the greatest extent; fully open. [< OE *wīd*] **—wide′ly** *adv.* **—wide′ness** *n.* **—Syn.** *adj.* **2** ample, broad, extensive, vast.

wide-an·gle lens (wīd′ang′gəl) A type of camera lens

designed to permit an angle of view wider than that of the ordinary lens.

wide-a·wake (wīd′ə·wāk′) *adj.* **1** Totally awake. **2** Alert.

wide-eyed (wīd′īd′) *adj.* **1** With the eyes wide open. **2** Uninformed or unsophisticated.

wid·en (wīd′n) *v.t. & v.i.* To make or become wide or wider. **—wid′en·er** *n.*

wide-o·pen (wīd′ō′pən) *adj.* **1** Opened wide. **2** *Informal* Remiss in the enforcement of laws which regulate gambling, prostitution, etc.: a *wide-open* city.

wide·spread (wīd′spred′) *adj.* **1** Extending over a large space or territory. **2** Held, believed, indulged in, etc., by many people.

widge·on (wij′ən) *n.* Any of various river ducks having a short bill and wedge-shaped tail. Also **wig·eon**. [?]

wid·get (wij′it) *n. Slang* **1** A product having a unique or ingenious feature; gadget. **2** Something unnamed and used as an example in a hypothetical situation. [Alter. of GADGET]

wid·ow (wid′ō) *n.* **1** A woman who has lost her husband by death and has not remarried. **2** In some card games, an additional hand dealt to the table. **3** *Printing* A short line of type ending a paragraph at the top of a page or column; also, such a line at the end of any paragraph. —*v.t.* To make a widow of. [< OE *widewe*]

wid·ow·er (wid′ō·ər) *n.* A man who has lost his wife by death and has not remarried.

widow's mite A contribution which, although small in amount, is all or even more than the giver can afford.

widow's peak A point of hair growing down from the hairline in the middle of the forehead.

width (width) *n.* **1** Dimension or measurement of an object taken from side to side, or at right angles to the length. **2** Something that has width: a *width* of cloth. [< WIDE]

width·wise (width′wīz) *adv.* In the direction of the width. Also **width′ways′**.

wield (wēld) *v.t.* **1** To use or handle, as a weapon or instrument. **2** To exercise (authority, power, influence, etc.). [Fusion of OE *wealdan* to cause and OE *wildan* to rule] **— wield′er** *n.*

wie·ner (wē′nər) *n.* A kind of smoked sausage, similar to a frankfurter, made of beef and pork. Also **wie·ner·wurst** (wē′nər·wûrst′). [Short for *wienerwurst* < G, Vienna sausage]

wife (wīf) *n. pl.* **wives** (wīvz) **1** A woman joined to a man in lawful wedlock. **2** *Archaic* A woman: now used in combination or in certain phrases: *housewife*, old *wives'* tales. **—take to wife** To marry (a woman). [< OE *wīf*] **—wife′·dom, wife′hood** *n.*

wife·ly (wīf′lē) *adj.* **·li·er, ·li·est 1** Of or like a wife. **2** Suitable to a wife.

wig (wig) *n.* A covering of real or artificial hair for the head. —*v.t.* **wigged, wig·ging 1** To furnish with a wig or wigs. **2** *Brit. Informal* To berate or scold. [Short for PERIWIG]

wig·gle (wig′əl) *v.t. & v.i.* **·gled, ·gling** To move or cause to move quickly from side to side; wriggle. —*n.* The act of wiggling. [< MLG *wiggelen*] **—wig′gly** *adj.* **(·gli·er, ·gli·est)**

wig·gler (wig′lər) *n.* **1** One who or that which wiggles. **2** The larva of a mosquito.

Barrister's wig

wig·wag (wig′wag′) *v.t. & v.i.* **·wagged, ·wag·ging 1** To move briskly back and forth; wag. **2** To send (a message) by hand flags, torches, etc. —*n.* **1** The act of wigwagging. **2** A message sent by wigwagging. [< dial. E *wig* wiggle + WAG¹] **—wig′wag′ger** *n.*

wig·wam (wig′wom, -wôm) *n.* A dwelling or lodge of certain North American Indians, commonly a rounded or conical framework of poles covered with bark, rush matting, or hides. [< Algon.]

Wigwam

wild (wīld) *adj.* **1** Living or growing in a natural state; not tamed, domesticated, or cultivated: *wild* animals; *wild* flowers. **2** Being in the natural state without civilized inhabitants or cultiva-

tion: *wild* prairies. **3** Uncivilized; primitive: the *wild* men of Borneo. **4** Undisciplined; unruly. **5** Morally dissolute; profligate. **6** Violent; turbulent: a *wild* night. **7** Reckless; imprudent: a *wild* speculation. **8** Unusually odd or strange; extravagant; bizarre: a *wild* imagination. **9** Eager and excited: *wild* with delight. **10** Frenzied; crazed: *wild* with fury. **11** Disorderly; disarranged: a *wild* mop of hair. **12** Far from the mark aimed at; erratic: a *wild* pitch. **13** In some card games, having its value arbitrarily determined by the dealer or holder. **14** *Slang* Terrific; great: The party was *wild*. **15** *Slang* Showy; jazzy: a *wild* necktie. —*n.* Often *pl.* An uninhabited or uncultivated place; wilderness: the *wilds* of Africa. —**the wild 1** The wilderness. **2** The free, natural, wild life. —*adv.* In a wild manner: to run *wild*. [< OE *wilde*] —**wild′ly** *adv.* —**wild′ness** *n.* —**Syn.** *adj.* **3** barbarous, savage. **7** irresponsible, rash. **8** fantastic.

wild boar An Old World hog often hunted as game.

wild carrot A weed from which the cultivated carrot is derived; Queen Anne's lace.

wild·cat (wīld′kat′) *n.* **1** Any of various undomesticated felines resembling the domestic cat, but larger and stronger, as the lynx, cougar, etc. **2** An aggressive, quick-tempered person. **3** An unattached locomotive, used on special work, as when sent out to haul a train, etc. **4** A successful oil well drilled in an area previously unproductive. **5** A tricky or unsound business venture, esp. a worthless mine. Also **wild cat.** —*adj.* **1** Unsound; risky; esp. financially. **2** Made, produced, or carried on without official sanction or authorization. **3** Not running on a schedule, as a locomotive. —*v.t. & v.i.* **·cat·ted, ·cat·ting** To drill for oil in (an area not known to be productive). —**wild′cat′·ter** *n.*

wildcat strike A strike unauthorized by regular union procedure.

wilde·beest (wīld′bēst, wil′də-) *n. pl.* **·beests** or **·beest** GNU. [< Du. *wild* wild + *beeste* a beast]

wil·der·ness (wil′dər·nis) *n.* **1** An uncultivated, uninhabited, or barren region. **2** A multitudinous and confusing collection of persons or things. [< OE *wilder* a wild beast + -NESS]

wild·fire (wīld′fīr′) *n.* A raging, destructive fire that is hard to extinguish. —**like wildfire** Very quickly; uncontrollably.

wild·flow·er (wīld′flou′ər) *n.* **1** Any uncultivated plant that bears flowers. **2** The flower of such a plant. Also **wild flower.**

wild·fowl (wīld′foul′) *n. pl.* **·fowl** or **·fowls** A wild bird, esp. wild duck, pheasant, etc., hunted as game. Also **wild fowl.**

wild-goose chase (wīld′gōōs′) Pursuit of the unknown or unattainable.

wild·life (wīld′līf′) *n.* Wild animals collectively.

wild oat 1 *Usu. pl.* Any of various uncultivated grasses. **2** *pl.* Indiscretions of youth, usu. in the phrase **sow one's wild oats.**

wild rice 1 A tall aquatic grass of North America. **2** The highly esteemed, edible grain of this plant.

Wild West The w U.S. in its early period of Indian fighting, lawlessness, etc. Also **wild West**

wild·wood (wīld′wŏŏd′) *n.* Natural forest land.

wile (wīl) *n.* **1** An act or a means of cunning deception. **2** Any trick or artifice. —*v.t.* **wiled, wil·ing** To lure, beguile, or mislead. —**wile away** To pass (time) pleasantly. [< OE *wīl*] —**Syn.** *n.* **2** machination, maneuver, ruse, stratagem.

wil·ful (wil′fəl) *adj.* WILLFUL.

will[1] (wil) *n.* **1** The power to make conscious, deliberate choices or to control what one does. **2** The act or experience of exercising this power. **3** A specific desire, purpose, choice, etc.: the *will* of the people. **4** Strong determination or purpose: the *will* to succeed. **5** Self-control. **6** Attitude or inclination toward others: ill *will*. **7** *Law* The legal declaration of a person's intentions as to the disposition of his estate after his death. —**at will** As one pleases. — **with a will** Energetically. —*v.* **willed, will·ing** *v.t.* **1** To decide upon; choose. **2** To resolve upon as an action or course. **3** *Law* To bequeath by a will. **4** To control, as a

hypnotized person, by the exercise of will. **5** To decree: The king *wills* it. —*v.i.* **6** To wish; desire: as you *will*. [< OE *willa*]

will[2] (wil) *v.* Present *sing. & pl.:* **will** (*Archaic* **thou wilt**); past: **would** (*Archaic* **thou would·est** or **wouldst**) As an auxiliary verb *will* is used with the infinitive without *to*, or elliptically without the infinitive, to express: **1** Futurity: They *will* arrive by dark. **2** Likelihood: You *will* be sorry. **3** Command; order: You *will* leave immediately. **4** Willingness or disposition: Why *will* you not tell the truth? **5** Capability or capacity: The ship *will* survive any storm. **6** Custom or habit: He *will* sit for hours and brood. **7** *Informal* Probability or inference: I expect this *will* be the main street. [< OE *willan*] • See SHALL.

willed (wild) *adj.* Having a will of a given character: used in combination: *weak-willed*.

will·ful (wil′fəl) *adj.* **1** Deliberate; intentional: *willful* disregard of the law. **2** Stubborn; headstrong: a *willful* child. —**will′ful·ly** *adv.* —**will′ful·ness** *n.*

wil·lies (wil′ēz) *n.pl. Slang* Nervousness; jitters: used with *the*. [?]

will·ing (wil′ing) *adj.* **1** Having the mind favorably inclined or disposed. **2** Readily and gladly acting, responding, doing, giving, etc. **3** Readily and gladly offered, done, given, etc. —**will′ing·ly** *adv.* —**will′ing·ness** *n.* —**Syn.** **3** accommodating, compliant, obliging.

will-o'-the-wisp (wil′ə·thə·wisp′) *n.* IGNIS FATUUS. [Earlier *Will with the wisp*]

wil·low (wil′ō) *n.* **1** Any of a large genus of shrubs and trees having usu. narrow leaves and flexible shoots often used in basketry. **2** The wood of a willow. **3** *Informal* Something made of willow wood, as a cricket bat. —*adj.* Made of willow wood. [< OE *wilige, welig*] • See WEEPING WILLOW.

wil·low·y (wil′ō·ē) *adj.* **·low·i·er, ·low·i·est 1** Tall and graceful. **2** Lithe; flexible; supple. **3** Abounding in willows. — **wil′low·i·ness** *n.*

will·pow·er (wil′pou′ər) *n.* Strength to direct or control one's actions or desires; determination.

wil·ly-nil·ly (wil′ē·nil′ē) *adj.* Being or happening whether one wants it or not. —*adv.* Willingly or unwillingly. [Earlier *will I, nill I* whether I will or not]

wilt[1] (wilt) *v.i.* **1** To lose freshness; droop or become limp. **2** To lose energy and vitality; become faint or languid. **3** To lose courage or spirit. —*v.t.* **4** To cause to wilt. —*n.* **1** The act of wilting or the state of being wilted. **2** A plant disease that causes wilting. [Prob. dial. var. of obs. *welk*]

wilt[2] (wilt) *Archaic* Will: used with *thou.*

Wil·ton (wil′tən) *n.* A kind of carpet having a velvety texture. Also **Wilton carpet, Wilton rug.** [< *Wilton*, England, where first made]

wi·ly (wī′lē) *adj.* **·li·er, ·li·est** Full of or characterized by wiles; sly; cunning. —**wi′li·ly** *adv.* —**wi′li·ness** *n.*

wim·ple (wim′pəl) *n.* A cloth wrapped in folds around the neck close under the chin and over the head, exposing only the face, worn by medieval women and still by certain nuns. — *v. ·pled, ·pling v.t.* **1** To cover or clothe with a wimple. **2** To make or fold into pleats, as a veil. **3** To cause to move with slight undulations; ripple. —*v.i.* **4** To lie in plaits or folds. **5** To ripple. [< OE *wimpel*]

Wimple

win (win) *v.* **won, won, win·ning** *v.i.* **1** To gain a victory; be victorious in a contest, endeavor, etc. **2** To succeed in reaching or attaining a specified end or condition; get: often with *across, over, through*, etc. —*v.t.* **3** To be successful in; gain victory in: to *win* an argument. **4** To gain in competition or contest: to *win* the blue ribbon. **5** To gain by effort, persistence, etc.: to *win* fame. **6** To influence so as to obtain the good will or favor of: often with *over*. **7** To secure the love of; gain in marriage. **8** To succeed in reaching: to *win* the harbor. —**win out** *Informal* To succeed; triumph. —*n. Informal* A victory; success. [< OE *winnan* contend, labor] —**Syn.** *v.* **5** achieve, attain, earn, secure.

wince (wins) *v.i.* **winced, winc·ing** To shrink back; flinch. —*n.* The act of wincing. [< AF *wenchier*] —**winc′er** *n.*

winch (winch) *n.* **1** A windlass, particularly one turned by a crank and used for hoisting. **2** A crank with a handle for transmitting motion. [< OE *wince*] — **winch′er** *n.*

Win·ches·ter rifle (win′ches-tər) A type of repeating rifle, first produced in 1866: a trade name. Also **Winchester.**

Winch

wind¹ (wind) *n.* **1** Any movement of air, esp. a natural horizontal movement. **2** Any powerful or destructive movement of air, as a tornado. **3** The direction from which a wind blows. **4** Air pervaded by a scent, as in hunting. **5** The power of breathing; breath: He lost his *wind.* **6** Idle chatter. **7** Bragging; vanity; conceit. **8** *pl.* The wind instruments of an orchestra; also, the players of these instruments. **9** The gaseous product of indigestion; flatulence. —**break wind** To expel gas through the anus. —**get wind of** To receive a hint or intimation of. —**how the wind blows** (or **lies,** etc.) What is taking place, being decided, etc. —**in the teeth of the wind** Directly against the wind: also **in the wind's eye.** —**in the wind** Impending; afoot. —*v.t.* **1** To follow by scent; to catch a scent of on the wind. **2** To exhaust the breath of, as by racing. **3** To allow to recover breath by resting. **4** To expose to the wind, as in ventilating. [< OE] —**Syn.** *n.* **1** blast, breeze, gale, gust, zephyr.

wind² (wīnd) *v.* **wound** or **wind·ed, wind·ing** *v.t.* **1** To coil (thread, rope, etc.) around some object or fixed core; twine. **2** To encircle or cover with something, as by coiling or wrapping: to *wind* a spool with thread. **3** To renew the motion of, as a clock, by turning a stem, key, etc. **4** To turn in a revolving motion: to *wind* a handle. **5** To cause to turn and twist. **6** To make (one's way) by a turning and twisting course. **7** To introduce carefully or deviously; insinuate: He *wound* himself into my confidence. **8** To raise or hoist, as by means of a capstan or windlass. —*v.i.* **9** To move in a turning, twisting course; meander. **10** To coil or twine about some central object or core. **11** To move in a circular or spiral course. **12** To proceed or gain an end carefully or deviously. —**wind down** To decrease or be decreased gradually; de-escalate: to *wind down* a war. —**wind up 1** To coil or wind round and round. **2** To excite; arouse. **3** To bring to conclusion or settlement: He *wound up* his affairs. **4** In baseball, to swing the arm preparatory to pitching. **5** To hoist. —*n.* **1** The act of winding, or the condition of being wound. **2** A bend, turn, or twist. [< OE *windan*] —**wind′er** *n.*

wind³ (wīnd, wind) *v.t.* **wind·ed** or **wound, wind·ing 1** To blow, as a horn; sound. **2** To give (a call or signal), as with a horn. [< WIND¹; infl. by WIND²]

wind·age (win′dij) *n.* **1** The rush of air caused by the rapid passage of an object, as a projectile. **2** Deflection of an object, as a bullet, from its natural course by wind. **3** *Naut.* The surface offered to the wind by a vessel.

wind·bag (wind′bag′) *n. Informal* An overly talkative person who says little of significance.

wind·blown (wind′blōn′) *adj.* **1** Tossed or blown by the wind. **2** Having a permanent direction of growth as determined by prevailing winds: said of plants and trees.

wind·borne (wind′bôrn′, -bōrn′) *adj.* Carried or transported by the wind.

wind·break (wind′brāk′) *n.* Anything, as a hedge, fence, etc., that protects from or breaks the force of the wind.

wind·break·er (wind′brā′kər) *n.* A sports jacket for outer wear, having a close-fitting or elastic waistband and cuffs. [< *Windbreaker,* a trade name]

wind·bro·ken (wind′brō′kən) *adj.* Having the heaves: said of a horse.

wind·chill factor (wind′chil′) **1** A measure of air temperature modified by the chilling effect of wind of a given velocity as felt on the surface of the skin. **2** The effect of wind in reducing perceived air temperature.

wind·ed (win′did) *adj.* **1** Out of breath. **2** Having a specified kind of wind or breath: used in combination: *short-winded.*

wind·fall (wind′fôl′) *n.* **1** Something, as ripening fruit,

brought down by the wind. **2** A piece of unexpected good fortune.

wind·flow·er (wind′flou′ər) *n.* ANEMONE.

wind gauge An instrument for measuring the velocity of the wind; anemometer.

wind·hov·er (wind′huv′ər) *n. Brit.* KESTREL.

wind·ing (wīn′ding) *n.* **1** The act or condition of one who or that which winds; a turning or coiling. **2** A bend or turn, or a series of them. **3** Something that winds. —*adj.* **1** Turning spirally about an axis or core. **2** Having bends or lateral turns.

wind·ing sheet (wīn′ding) SHROUD (def. 1).

wind instrument (wind) A musical instrument whose sounds are produced by blowing air through it, esp. a portable one, as a flute, oboe, etc.

wind·jam·mer (wind′jam′ər) *n. Naut.* **1** A sailing vessel, as distinguished from a steamship. **2** A member of its crew.

wind·lass (wind′ləs) *n.* Any of several devices for hoisting or hauling, esp. one consisting of a drum turned by means of a crank so that the hoisting rope winds on the drum. [< ON *vinda* wind + *āss* a beam]

wind·mill (wind′mil′) *n.* **1** A mill having at the top a system of adjustable slats, wings, or sails which, when turned by the wind, transmit power to a pump, millstone, or the like. **2** An imaginary wrong, evil, or foe: usu. in the phrase **tilt at windmills,** an allusion to Don Quixote's combat with windmills, which he mistook for giants. • See VANE.

Differential windlass

win·dow (win′dō) *n.* **1** An opening in the wall of a building, etc., to admit light or air, usu. capable of being opened and closed, and including casements or sashes fitted with glass. **2** A windowpane or the sash or framework that encloses it. **3** Anything resembling or suggesting a window, as a transparent patch in certain envelopes. —*v.t.* To provide with a window or windows. [< ON *vindr* wind + *auga* an eye]

window box A box along a window ledge or sill, for growing plants.

window dressing 1 The act or art of arranging merchandise attractively in shop and store windows. **2** Any action, report, etc., designed to make something seem more attractive or plausible than it actually is. —**window dresser**

win·dow·pane (win′dō-pān′) *n.* A pane of glass for a window.

window seat A seat in the recess of a window.

window shade A flexible covering for the inside of a window, used to regulate light.

win·dow·shop (win′dō-shop′) *v.i.* **-shopped, -shop·ping** To look at goods shown in store windows without buying them. —**win′dow-shop′per** *n.*

win·dow·sill (win′dō-sil′) *n.* The horizontal ledge at the bottom of a window opening.

wind·pipe (wind′pīp′) *n.* TRACHEA.

wind·row (wind′rō′) *n.* **1** A long row of hay or grain raked together preparatory to building into cocks. **2** A line of dust, surf, leaves, etc. swept together by wind. —*v.t.* To rake or shape into a windrow. —**wind′row′er** *n.*

wind·screen (wind′skrēn′) *n. Brit.* WINDSHIELD.

wind·shield (wind′shēld′) *n.* A transparent screen, as of glass, across and above the dashboard of motor vehicles, power boats, etc., providing protection from the wind.

wind·sock (wind′sok′) *n.* A large, conical bag, open at both ends, mounted on a pivot, and used to indicate the direction of the wind. Also **wind sock, wind sleeve.**

Wind·sor (win′zər) Name of the royal family of Great Britain since July 27, 1917, when it was officially changed from *Saxe-Coburg-Gotha.*

Windsor chair A wooden chair, typically with a spindle back, slanting legs, and a flat or saddle seat.

Windsor knot A wide knot that can be used to tie a four-in-hand tie.

Windsor tie A wide, soft necktie tied in a loose bow.

wind·storm (wind′stôrm′) *n.* A violent wind, usu. with little or no precipitation.

wind·swept (wind′swept′) *adj.* Exposed to or propelled by the wind.

wind tunnel *Aeron.* A device in which the effects of artificially produced winds, as on airplane wings, can be studied.

wind·up (wīnd′up′) *n.* 1 The act of concluding. 2 A conclusion or culmination; end. 3 In baseball, the swing of the arm preparatory to pitching the ball.

wind·ward (wind′wərd) *adj.* 1 Of or toward the direction from which the wind blows. 2 Being on the side exposed to the wind. —*n.* The direction from which the wind blows. —*adv.* In the direction from which the wind blows.

wind·y (win′dē) *adj.* **wind·i·er, wind·i·est** 1 Of or abounding in wind; stormy; tempestuous: *windy* weather. 2 Exposed to the wind. 3 Suggestive of wind; boisterous; violent. 4 Flatulent. 5 Boastful, talkative, or pompous. 6 Idle; empty: *windy* talk. —**wind′i·ly** *adv.* —**wind′i·ness** *n.*

wine (wīn) *n.* 1 The fermented juice of the grape, used as an alcoholic beverage and in cooking. 2 The fermented juice of any of several other fruits or vegetables: dandelion *wine.* 3 The color of red wine. —*v.* **wined, win·ing** *v.t.* 1 To entertain or treat with wine. —*v.i.* 2 To drink wine. [< OE *wīn*]

wine·bib·ber (wīn′bib′ər) *n.* A person given to excessive drinking of wine. —**wine′bib′bing** *adj., n.*

wine cellar A storage space for wines; also, the wines stored.

wine·col·ored (wīn′kul′ərd) *adj.* Having the color of red wine.

wine·glass (wīn′glas′, -gläs′) *n.* A small goblet, usu. stemmed, from which to drink wine.

wine·grow·er (wīn′grō′ər) *n.* One who cultivates a vineyard and makes wine. —**wine′grow′ing** *adj., n.*

wine·press (wīn′pres′) *n.* An apparatus or a place where the juice of grapes is expressed. —**wine′press′er** *n.*

win·er·y (wī′nər·ē) *n. pl.* **·er·ies** An establishment where wine is made.

Wine·sap (wīn′sap) *n.* An American variety of red winter apple.

wine·skin (wīn′skin′) *n.* A bag made of the entire skin of an animal, as a goat, used for containing wine.

wing (wing) *n.* 1 An organ of flight; esp. one of a pair of appendages of a bird or bat, adapted for flight. 2 An analogous organ in insects and some other animals. 3 Anything resembling or suggestive of a wing in form or function. 4 *Aeron.* The (or one of the) main supporting surface(s) of an airplane. 5 *Bot.* Any thin, winglike expansion of certain stems, seeds, etc. 6 A vane, as of a windmill. 7 Anything regarded as conferring the swift motion or rapture of flight: on *wings* of song. 8 Flight by or as by wings. 9 *Archit.* A part attached to a side, esp. a projection or extension of a building on the side of the main portion. 10 An annex or separate section of a large building: the surgical *wing* of a hospital. 11 Either of two sides, unseen by the audience, of a proscenium stage; also, a piece of scenery for the side of a stage. 12 Either of two sidepieces on the back of an armchair. 13 A side section of something that shuts or folds, as a screen. 14 A tactical and administrative unit of the U.S. Air Force, larger than a group. 15 *Mil.* Either division of a military force on either side of the center. 16 An analogous formation in certain outdoor games, as hockey or football. 17 Either of two extremist groups or factions in a political organization: the left *wing.* 18 A subsidiary group of a parent organization. 19 *Slang* An arm, esp., in baseball, a pitching or throwing arm. 20 *pl.* The insignia worn by certain qualified aircraft pilots, navigators, etc. —**on** (or **upon**) **the wing** 1 In flight. 2 Departing; also, journeying. —**take wing** To fly away. —**under one's wing** Under one's protection. —*v.t.* 1 To pass over or through in flight. 2 To accomplish by flying: the eagle *winged* its way. 3 To enable to fly. 4 To cause to go swiftly; speed. 5 To transport by flight. 6 To provide with wings for flight. 7 To supply with a side body or part. 8 To wound (a bird) in a wing. 9 To disable by a

minor wound. —*v.i.* 10 To fly; soar. —**wing it** *Slang* To act, do, arrange, etc., without advance preparation; improvise. [< ON *vængr*]

wing chair A large, upholstered armchair with a high back and side pieces designed as protection from drafts.

winged (wingd, wing′id) *adj.* 1 Having wings. 2 Passing swiftly. 3 Sublime; lofty.

wing·spread (wing′spred′) *n.* The distance between the tips of the fully extended wings, as of a bird, insect, or airplane. Also **wing′span′.**

Wing chair

wink (wingk) *v.i.* 1 To close and open the eye or eyelids quickly. 2 To draw the eyelids of one eye together, as in making a sign. 3 To emit fitful gleams; twinkle. —*v.t.* 4 To close and open (the eye or eyelids) quickly. 5 To move, force, etc., by winking: with *away, off,* etc. 6 To signify or express by winking. —**wink at** To pretend not to see. —*n.* 1 The act of winking. 2 The time necessary for a wink. 3 A twinkle. 4 A hint conveyed by winking. 5 A brief bit (of sleep): I had a *wink* after lunch. —**forty winks** A short nap. [< OE *wincian* close the eyes]

wink·er (wing′kər) *n.* 1 One who winks. 2 *Slang* EYELASH.

win·ner (win′ər) *n.* 1 One who or that which wins. 2 *Informal* Someone or something likely to succeed.

win·ning (win′ing) *adj.* 1 Successful in achievement, esp. in competition. 2 Capable of charming; attractive; winsome. —*n.* 1 The act of one who wins. 2 *Usu. pl.* That which is won, as money in gambling. —**win′ning·ly** *adv.* —**win′ning·ness** *n.*

win·ning·est (win′ing·əst) *adj. Informal* Most often winning: the *winningest* team in baseball.

win·now (win′ō) *v.t.* 1 To separate (grain, etc.) from the chaff. 2 To blow away (the chaff) thus. 3 To separate (what is valuable) or to eliminate (what is valueless): to *winnow* out the good or the bad. 4 To blow upon; cause to flutter. 5 To beat or fan (the air) with the wings. 6 To scatter by blowing; disperse. —*v.i.* 7 To separate grain from chaff. 8 To fly; flap. —*n.* 1 Any device used in winnowing grain. 2 The act of winnowing. [< OE *windwian* < *wind* the wind] —**win′now·er** *n.*

win·o (wī′nō) *n. pl.* **·noes** or **·nos** *Slang* A drunkard who habitually drinks wine, esp. cheap wine. [< WINE]

win·some (win′səm) *adj.* Charming; attractive. [< OE *wyn* joy] —**win′some·ly** *adv.* —**win′some·ness** *n.* —**Syn.** amiable, appealing, engaging, pleasant, winning.

win·ter (win′tər) *n.* 1 The coldest season of the year, extending from the end of autumn to the beginning of spring. 2 A time marked by lack of life, warmth, and cheer. 3 A year as including the winter season: a man of ninety *winters.* —*v.i.* 1 To pass the winter. —*v.t.* 2 To care for, feed, or protect during the winter: to *winter* plants. —*adj.* Pertaining to, suitable for, or characteristic of winter. [< OE] —**win′ter·er** *n.*

win·ter·green (win′tər·grēn) *n.* 1 A small evergreen plant bearing aromatic oval leaves, white, bell-shaped flowers and edible red berries. 2 A colorless, volatile oil extracted from the leaves of this plant or made synthetically, used as a flavor.

win·ter·ize (win′tə·rīz) *v.t.* **·ized, ·iz·ing** To prepare or put in condition for winter, as a motor vehicle, etc.

win·ter·kill (win′tər·kil′) *v.t. & v.i.* To die or kill by exposure to extreme cold: said of plants. —*n.* The act, process, or an instance of winterkilling.

winter solstice See SOLSTICE.

winter wheat Wheat planted before snowfall and harvested the following summer.

win·try (win′trē) *adj.* **·tri·er, ·tri·est** Of or like winter; cold, bleak, cheerless, etc. Also **win′ter·y** (-tər·ē). —**win′tri·ly** *adv.* —**win′tri·ness** *n.*

win·y (wī′nē) *adj.* **win·i·er, win·i·est** Having the taste, color, smell, etc., of wine.

wipe (wīp) *v.t.* **wiped, wip·ing** 1 To subject to slight friction or rubbing, usu. with some soft, absorbent material. 2 To remove by rubbing lightly: usu. with *away* or *off.* 3 To

move or draw for the purpose of wiping: He *wiped* his hand across his brow. **4** To apply by wiping. —**wipe out** **1** To kill or murder. **2** To destroy utterly; annihilate. **3** In surfing, to be overturned by a wave. —*n.* The act of wiping. [< OE *wīpian*] —**wip′er** *n.*

wire (wīr) *n.* **1** A slender rod, strand, or thread of metal. **2** Something made of wire, as a fence, a cord to conduct an electric current, etc. **3** WIREWORK. **4** A telephone or telegraph cable. **5** The telegraph system as a means of communication. **6** TELEGRAM. **7** The screen of a papermaking machine. **8** A line marking the finish of a race. — **get (in) under the wire** To conclude or achieve something at the very last moment. —**pull wires** *Informal* To use secret or private sources of influence to attain something. —*v.* **wired, wir·ing** *v.t.* **1** To fasten or bind with wire. **2** To furnish or equip with wiring. **3** To telegraph: to *wire* an order. **4** To place on wire, as beads. —*v.i.* **5** To telegraph. [< OE *wīr*] —**wir′er** *n.*

wire gauge 1 A gauge for measuring the diameter of wire. **2** A standard system of sizes for wire.

wire-haired terrier (wīr′hârd′) A fox terrier having a wiry coat. Also **wire′hair′** (-hâr′)

wire·less (wīr′lis) *adj.* **1** Without wire or wires; having no wires. **2** *Brit.* Radio. —*n.* **1** The wireless telegraph or telephone system, or a message transmitted by either. **2** *Brit.* Radio. —*v.t.* & *v.i. Brit.* To communicate (with) by radio.

Wire·pho·to (wīr′fō′tō) *n. pl.* **·tos** An apparatus and method for transmitting and receiving photographs by wire: a trade name.

wire-pull·er (wīr′pŏŏl′ər) *n.* **1** One who pulls wires, as of a puppet. **2** One who uses secret means to control others or gain his own ends; an intriguer. —**wire′pull′ing** *n.*

wire·tap (wīr′tap′) *n.* **1** A device used to make a connection with a telephone or telegraph wire to listen to or record the message transmitted. **2** The act of wiretapping. —*v.* **·tapped, ·tap·ping** *v.t.* **1** To connect a wiretap to. **2** To monitor by the use of a wiretap. —*v.i.* **3** To use a wiretap. —**wire′tap′per** *n.*

wire·work (wīr′wûrk′) *n.* A mesh or netting made of wire.

wir·ing (wīr′ing) *n.* An entire system of wire installed for the distribution of electric power, as for lighting, heating, sound, etc.

wir·y (wīr′ē) *adj.* **wir·i·er, wir·i·est 1** Lean, but tough and sinewy: said of persons. **2** Like wire; stiff; bristly. —**wir′i·ly** *adv.* —**wir′i·ness** *n.*

Wis., Wisc. Wisconsin.

wis·dom (wiz′dəm) *n.* **1** The ability to discern what is true or right and to make sound judgments based on such discernment. **2** Insight or intuition. **3** COMMON SENSE. **4** A high degree of knowledge; learning. **5** An accumulated body of knowledge, as in philosophy, science, etc. [< OE *wīs* wise] —**Syn. 1** sapience, sagacity. **4** enlightenment, erudition.

Wisdom of Solomon A book of the Old Testament Apocrypha, consisting of a hymn in praise of wisdom.

wisdom tooth The last tooth on either side of the upper and lower jaws in man. —**cut one's wisdom teeth** To acquire mature judgment. • See TOOTH.

wise[1] (wīz) *adj.* **wis·er, wis·est 1** Having or showing wisdom (def. 1). **2** Having or showing insight, intuition, common sense, or knowledge. **3** Shrewd; calculating; cunning. **4** *Informal* Aware of: *wise* to his motives. **5** *Slang* Arrogant; fresh: a *wise* guy. —**get wise** *Slang* **1** To learn the true facts about. **2** To become arrogant or fresh. —**wise up** *Slang* To make or become aware, informed, or sophisticated. [< OE *wīs*] —**wise′ly** *adv.* —**wise′ness** *n.*

wise[2] (wīz) *n.* Way of doing; manner; method: chiefly in the phrases **in any wise, in no wise,** etc. [< OE *wīse* manner]

-wise *suffix of adverbs & nouns* **1** In a (specified) way or manner: *nowise, likewise.* **2** In a (specified) direction or position: *lengthwise, clockwise:* often equivalent to *-ways.* **3** *Informal* With reference to: *Moneywise,* the job is worth considering. [< OE *wīse* manner, fashion]

wise·a·cre (wīz′ā′kər) *n.* A person who claims to know everything. [< MDu. *wijsseggher* a soothsayer]

wise·crack (wīz′krak′) *Slang n.* A smart, insolent, or

supercilious remark. —*v.i.* To utter a wisecrack. —**wise′-crack′er** *n.*

wish (wish) *n.* **1** A desire or longing, usu. for some definite thing. **2** An expression of such a desire; petition. **3** Something wished for. —*v.t.* **1** To have a desire or longing for; want: We *wish* to be sure. **2** To desire a specified condition or state for (a person or thing): I *wish* this day were over. **3** To invoke upon or for someone: I *wished* him good luck. **4** To bid: to *wish* someone good morning. **5** To request, command, or entreat: I *wish* you would stop yelling. —*v.i.* **6** To have or feel a desire; yearn; long: usu. with *for:* to *wish* for a friend's return. **7** To make or express a wish. —**wish on** *Informal* To impose (something unpleasant or unwanted) on a person. [< OE *wȳscan*] —**wish′er** *n.*

wish·bone (wish′bōn′) *n.* The forked bone situated in front of the sternum in most birds.

wish·ful (wish′fəl) *adj.* Having or indicating a wish or desire. —**wish′ful·ly** *adv.* —**wish′ful·ness** *n.*

wishful thinking A believing that what one wants to be true is true.

wish·y-wash·y (wish′ē-wosh′ē, -wôsh′ē) *adj. Informal* **1** Thin; diluted, as liquor. **2** Lacking in purpose, effectiveness, or strength.

wisp (wisp) *n.* **1** A small bunch, as of hay, straw, or hair. **2** A small bit; a mere indication: a *wisp* of vapor. **3** A slight, delicate thing: a *wisp* of a child. **4** WILL-O′-THE-WISP. [ME *wisp, wips*] —**wisp′y** *adj.* (**·i·er, ·i·est**)

wist (wist) *Archaic p.t.* & *p.p.* of WIT[2].

wis·te·ri·a (wis·tir′ē·ə, -târ′-) *n.* Any of a genus of woody twining shrubs of the bean family, with pinnate leaves, elongated pods, and showy clusters of blue, purple, or white flowers. Also **wis·tar·i·a** (wis·târ′ē·ə). [< C. *Wistar,* 1761–1818, U.S. anatomist]

wist·ful (wist′fəl) *adj.* **1** Wishful; yearning. **2** Musing; pensive. [Appar. < obs. *wistly* intently] —**wist′ful·ly** *adv.* —**wist′ful·ness** *n.*

wit[1] (wit) *n.* **1** The power of perceiving, reasoning, knowing, etc.; intelligence. **2** *pl.* **a** The mental faculties: to use one's *wits.* **b** Such faculties in relation to their state of balance: out of one's *wits.* **3** Practical intelligence; common sense. **4** The ability to perceive unexpected analogies or incongruities and to express them in an amusing or epigrammatic manner. **5** The ability to make jokes, amusing remarks, etc. **6** A person with wit (defs. 4 & 5). **7** Speech or writing characterized by wit (defs. 4 & 5). —**at one's wits′ end** At the limit of one's devices and resources. —**live by one's wits** To make a living by using one's practical intelligence and resourcefulness, often in unscrupulous or fraudulent ways. [< OE]

wit[2] (wit) *v.t.* & *v.i.* Present indicative: I **wot,** thou **wost,** he, she, it **wot,** we, ye, they **wite(n);** *p.t.* and *p.p.* **wist;** *pr.p.* **witting** *Archaic* To be or become aware (of); learn; know. — **to wit** That is to say; namely. [< OE *witan* know]

witch (wich) *n.* **1** A woman who practices sorcery or has supernatural powers, esp. to work evil. **2** An ugly old woman; a hag. **3** A bewitching or fascinating woman or girl. —*v.t.* **1** To work an evil spell upon; effect by witchcraft. **2** To fascinate or charm. —*v.i.* **3** DOWSE[2]. [< OE *wicce* a witch, fem. of *wicca* a wizard]

witch·craft (wich′kraft′, -kräft′) *n.* **1** Black magic; sorcery. **2** Extraordinary influence or fascination.

witch doctor Among certain primitive peoples, a man skilled in counteracting evil spells.

witch·er·y (wich′ər·ē) *n. pl.* **·er·ies 1** Witchcraft; black magic; sorcery. **2** Power to charm; fascination.

witch hazel 1 Any of a genus of shrubs and small trees with usu. yellow flowers. **2** An extract derived from the bark and dried leaves of a certain witch hazel, used as a mild astringent. [< OE *wice* wych-elm + HAZEL]

witch hunt *Slang* An investigation or harassment of dissenters, often for the undeclared purpose of weakening political opposition.

witch·ing (wich′ing) *adj.* Having the power to enchant; bewitching. —**witch′ing·ly** *adv.*

with (with, with) *prep.* **1** In the company of: Walk *with* me. **2** Having; bearing: a hat *with* a feather. **3** Characterized or marked by: a man *with* brains. **4** In a manner charac-

Wisteria

terized by; exhibiting: to dance *with* grace. **5** Among, into, near to, etc.: counted *with* the others. **6** In the course of: We forget *with* time. **7** From: to part *with* the past. **8** Against: to struggle *with* an adversary. **9** In the opinion of: That is all right *with* me. **10** Because of: faint *with* hunger. **11** In or under the care, supervision, etc., of: Leave the key *with* the janitor. **12** By means or aid of: to write *with* a pencil. **13** By the use, addition, etc., of: trimmed *with* lace. **14** As an associate, member, etc., of: worked *with* her sister; played *with* an orchestra. **15** In spite of: *With* all his money, he could not buy health. **16** At the same time as: to go to bed *with* the chickens. **17** In the same direction as: to drift *with* the crowd. **18** In regard to; in the case of: I am angry *with* them. **19** Onto; to: Join this tube *with* that one. **20** In proportion to: His fame grew *with* his achievements. **21** In support of: He voted *with* the Left. **22** Of the same opinion as: I'm *with* you there! **23** Having received or been granted: With your consent I'll go now. [< OE]

with- *prefix* **1** Against: *withstand*. **2** Back; away: *withhold*. [< OE *with* against]

with·al (with·ôl′, with-) *adv.* **1** Besides; in addition. **2** Notwithstanding; nevertheless. —*prep.* *Archaic* With: used at the end of the clause: a bow to shoot *withal*. [ME *with* + *alle* all]

with·draw (with·drô′, with-) *v.* **·drew**, **·drawn**, **·draw·ing** *v.t.* **1** To draw or take away; remove. **2** To take back, as an assertion or a promise. **3** To keep from use, sale, etc. —*v.i.* **4** To draw back; retreat. **5** To remove oneself; leave, as from an activity.

with·draw·al (with·drô′əl, with-) *n.* **1** The act or process of withdrawing. **2** The act or process of overcoming one's addiction to a habit-forming drug.

withdrawal symptom Any of the symptoms caused by the withdrawal of a physically addictive drug from an addict, as tremors, sweating, chills, vomiting, and diarrhea.

with·drawn (with·drôn′, with-) *adj.* **1** Not responsive socially or emotionally; introverted. **2** Isolated; remote.

withe (with, with, with) *n.* A willowy, supple twig, used to bind or wrap. [< OE *withthe*]

with·er (with′ər) *v.i.* **1** To become limp or dry, as a plant when deprived of moisture. **2** To waste, as flesh. —*v.t.* **3** To cause to become limp or dry. **4** To abash, as by a scornful glance. [ME *widren*] —**Syn.** **1** shrink, shrivel. **4** confuse, shame.

with·ers (with′ərz) *n.pl.* The highest part of the back of the horse, ox, etc., between the shoulder blades. [< OE *withre* resistance: so called because this part presses against the harness when a horse is pulling a load]

with·hold (with·hōld′, with-) *v.* **·held**, **·hold·ing** *v.t.* **1** To hold back; restrain. **2** To refuse to grant, permit, etc. **3** To deduct (taxes, etc.) from a salary before payment. —*v.i.* **4** To refrain. —**with·hold′er** *n.*

withholding tax That part of an employee's wages or salary which is deducted as an installment on his income tax.

Withers

with·in (with·in′, with-) *adv.* **1** In the inner part; interiorly. **2** Inside the body, heart, or mind. **3** Indoors. —*prep.* **1** In the inner or interior part or parts of; inside: *within* the house. **2** In the limits, range, or compass of (a specified time, space, or distance): *within* a mile of here; *within* ten minutes' walk. **3** Not exceeding (a specified quantity): Live *within* your means. **4** In the reach, limit, or scope of: *within* my power. [< OE *with* with + *innan* in]

with-it (with′it) *adj.* *Slang* In touch with modern habits, fashions, trends, etc.; up-to-date.

with·out (with·out′, with-) *prep.* **1** Not having; lacking: *without* money. **2** In the absence of: We must manage *without* help. **3** Free from: *without* fear. **4** At, on, or to the outside of. **5** Outside of or beyond the limits of: living *without* the pale of civilization. **6** With avoidance of: He listened *without* paying attention. —*adv.* **1** In or on the outer part; externally. **2** OUTDOORS. [< OE *with* with + *ūtan* out]

with·stand (with·stand′, with-) *v.* **·stood**, **·stand·ing** *v.t.* & *v.i.* To resist, oppose, or endure, esp. successfully. [< OE *with-* against + *standan* stand]

with·y (with′ē, with′ē) *n. pl.* **with·ies** WITHE.

wit·less (wit′lis) *adj.* Lacking in wit; foolish. —**wit′less·ly** *adv.* —**wit′less·ness** *n.*

wit·ness (wit′nis) *n.* **1** A person who has seen or knows something and is therefore competent to give evidence concerning it. **2** That which serves as or furnishes evidence or proof. **3** *Law* **a** One who has knowledge of facts relating to a given cause and is subpoenaed to testify. **b** A person who has signed his name to a legal document in order that he may testify to its authenticity. **4** Evidence; testimony. —**bear witness** **1** To give evidence; testify. **2** To be evidence. —*v.t.* **1** To see or know by personal experience. **2** To furnish or serve as evidence of. **3** To give testimony to. **4** To be the site or scene of: This spot has *witnessed* many heinous crimes. **5** *Law* To see the execution of (an instrument) and subscribe to its authenticity. —*v.i.* **6** To give evidence; testify. [< OE *witnes* knowledge, testimony] —**wit′ness·er** *n.*

witness stand The platform in a courtroom from which a witness gives evidence.

wit·ted (wit′id) *adj.* Having (a specified kind of) wit: used in combination: *quick-witted*.

wit·ti·cism (wit′ə·siz′əm) *n.* A witty or clever remark. [< WITTY]

wit·ting·ly (wit′ing·lē) *adv.* Designedly; knowingly. [< WIT[2]]

wit·ty (wit′ē) *adj.* **·ti·er**, **·ti·est** Having, displaying, or full of wit. [< OE *wittig* wise] —**wit′ti·ly** *adv.* —**wit′ti·ness** *n.*

wive (wīv) *v.t.* & *v.i.* **wived**, **wiv·ing** *Archaic* To marry (a woman). [< OE *wīf* a wife, woman]

wives (wīvz) *n. pl. of* WIFE.

wiz·ard (wiz′ərd) *n.* **1** A magician or sorcerer. **2** *Informal* A very skillful or clever person. —*adj.* Of or pertaining to wizards. [< OE *wīs* wise]

wiz·ard·ry (wiz′ərd·rē) *n.* The practice or methods of a wizard.

wiz·ened (wiz′ənd) *adj.* Shriveled; dried up. [< OE *wisnian*, dry up, wither]

wk. weak; week; work.

wks. weeks; works.

WL, w.l. water line; wave length.

W. long. west longitude.

WNW, W.N.W., wnw, w.n.w. west-northwest.

WO, W.O. wait order; Warrant Officer.

woad (wōd) *n.* **1** An Old World herb related to mustard. **2** The blue dye obtained from its leaves. [< OE *wād*] —**woad′ed** *adj.*

wob·ble (wob′əl) *v.* **·bled**, **·bling** *v.i.* **1** To move or sway unsteadily. **2** To show indecision or unsteadiness; vacillate. —*v.t.* **3** To cause to wobble. —*n.* A wobbling motion. [? < LG *wabbeln*] —**wob′bler** *n.* —**wob′bling·ly** *adv.* —**wob′bly** *adj.* **(·bli·er, ·bli·est)**

woe (wō) *n.* **1** Overwhelming sorrow; grief. **2** Heavy affliction or calamity; disaster; suffering. —*interj.* Alas! [< OE *wā* misery]

woe·be·gone (wō′bi·gôn′, -gon′) *adj.* Having or exhibiting woe; mournful; sorrowful. —**Syn.** dejected, depressed, lugubrious, melancholy.

woe·ful (wō′fəl) *adj.* **1** Accompanied by or causing woe; direful. **2** Expressive of sorrow; doleful. **3** Paltry; miserable; mean; sorry. —**woe′ful·ly** *adv.* —**woe′ful·ness** *n.*

wok (wok) *n.* A Chinese cooking pan, as of iron, aluminum, or copper, with handles and a rounded bottom, usu. equipped with a separate metal ring to prevent tipping. [< Chinese]

Wok

woke (wōk) *p.t.* of WAKE[1].

wok·en (wō′kən) *Regional & alternative Brit. p.p.* of WAKE[1].

wold (wōld) *n.* An undulating tract of treeless upland. [< OE *wald* a forest]

---

add, āce, câre, pälm; end, ēven; it, īce; odd, ōpen, ôrder; to͝ok, po͞ol; up, bûrn; ə = *a* in *above*, *u* in *focus*; yo͞o = *u* in *fuse;* oil; pout; check; go; ring; thin; this; zh, *vision*. < derived from; ? origin uncertain or unknown.

wolf (wŏŏlf) n. pl. **wolves** (wŏŏlvz) 1 Any of various wild, carnivorous mammals related to the dog. 2 Any ravenous, cruel, or rapacious person. 3 *Slang* A man who zealously and aggressively pursues women. —**cry wolf** To give a false alarm. —**keep the wolf from the door** To avert want or starvation. —*v.t.* To devour ravenously: often with *down.* [< OE *wulf*]

Timber wolf

wolf·ber·ry (wŏŏlf'ber'ē) n. pl. **·ries** A shrub of the honeysuckle family, with pinkish, bell-shaped flowers and spikes of white berries.

wolf·hound (wŏŏlf'hound') n. Either of two breeds of large dogs, the **Russian wolfhound** and the **Irish wolfhound**, formerly trained to hunt wolves.

wolf·ish (wŏŏlf'ish) adj. Of or like a wolf; rapacious; savage. —**wolf'ish·ly** adv. —**wolf'ish·ness** n.

wolf·ram (wŏŏl'frəm) n. TUNGSTEN. [G]

wolf·ram·ite (wŏŏl'frəm-īt) n. A grayish black or brown mineral, an important source of tungsten. [< G *Wolfram* tungsten]

wolfs·bane (wŏŏlfs'bān') n. A species of aconite, usu. with yellow flowers. Also **wolf's-bane.**

wol·ver·ine (wŏŏl'və-rēn') n. A rapacious carnivore related to weasels, with stout body and bushy tail. Also **wol'ver·ene'.** [< WOLF]

wolves (wŏŏlvz) n. pl. of WOLF.

wom·an (wŏŏm'ən) n. pl. **wom·en** (wim'in) 1 An adult human female. 2 The female part of the human race; women collectively. 3 Womanly character; femininity: usu. with *the.* 4 A female attendant or servant. 5 A paramour or mistress. 6 *Informal* A wife. —*adj.* 1 Of or characteristic of women. 2 Female: a *woman* lawyer. [< OE *wīf* a wife + *mann* a human being] • See LADY.

wom·an·hood (wŏŏm'ən-hŏŏd) n. 1 The state of a woman or of womankind. 2 Women collectively.

wom·an·ish (wŏŏm'ən-ish) adj. 1 For or characteristic of a woman; womanly. 2 Feminine or effeminate in nature, and according ill with the qualities associated with men. —**wom'an·ish·ly** adv. —**wom'an·ish·ness** n.

wom·an·ize (wŏŏm'ən-īz) v. **·ized, ·iz·ing** *v.t.* 1 To make effeminate or womanish. —*v.i.* 2 To have affairs with many women. —**wom'an·i·zer** n.

wom·an·kind (wŏŏm'ən-kīnd') n. Women collectively.

wom·an·ly (wŏŏm'ən-lē) adj. Having the qualities natural, suited, or becoming to a woman; feminine. —**wom'an·li·ness** n.

womb (wŏŏm) n. 1 UTERUS. 2 A place where anything is engendered or brought into life. [< OE *wamb, womb* the belly]

wom·bat (wom'bat) n. Any of various burrowing Australian marsupials resembling a small bear. [< native Australian name]

wom·en (wim'in) n. pl. of WOMAN.

wom·en·folk (wim'in-fōk') n.pl. Women collectively: also **wom'·en·folks'.**

Wombat

won (wun) p.t. & p.p. of WIN.

won·der (wun'dər) n. 1 A feeling of mingled surprise, admiration, and astonishment. 2 One who or that which causes wonder. —*v.t.* 1 To have a feeling of curiosity or doubt in regard to. —*v.i.* 2 To be affected or filled with wonder; marvel. 3 To be curious or doubtful. —*adj.* Spectacularly successful: a *wonder* drug. [< OE *wundor*] —**won'der·er** n. —**won'der·ing·ly** adv.

won·der·ful (wun'dər-fəl) adj. 1 Of a nature to excite wonder; astonishing. 2 Very good; excellent. —**won'der·ful·ly** adv. —**won'der·ful·ness** n.

won·der·land (wun'dər·land') n. 1 A realm of imaginary wonders. 2 Any place of unusual beauty, astonishing sights, etc.

won·der·ment (wun'dər·mənt) n. 1 The emotion of wonder; surprise. 2 Something wonderful; a marvel.

won·drous (wun'drəs) adj. Wonderful; marvelous. —*adv.* Surprisingly. —**won'drous·ly** adv. —**won'drous·ness** n.

wont (wônt, wōnt) adj. Accustomed: He is *wont* to eat

late. —*n.* Ordinary manner of doing or acting; habit. [< OE *gewunod,* p.p. of *gewunian* be accustomed]

won't (wōnt) Contraction of *will not.*

wont·ed (wun'tid, wōn'-) adj. 1 Commonly used or done; habitual. 2 Habituated; accustomed. —**wont'ed·ness** n.

woo (wŏŏ) *v.t.* 1 To make love to, esp. so as to marry. 2 To entreat earnestly; beg. 3 To seek. —*v.i.* 4 To pay court; make love. [< OE *wōgian*] —**woo'er** n.

wood (wŏŏd) n. 1 The hard, fibrous material between the pith and bark of a tree or shrub. 2 Trees or shrubs cut for use, as for building, fuel, etc. 3 *Usu. pl.* A large, dense growth of trees; forest. 4 Something made of wood, as a woodwind or certain golf clubs having a wooden head. —*adj.* 1 Made of wood; wooden. 2 Made for burning wood: a *wood* stove. 3 Living or growing in woods. —*v.t.* 1 To furnish with wood for fuel. 2 To plant with trees. —*v.i.* 3 To take on a supply of wood. [< OE *widu, wiodu*]

wood alcohol Methanol, esp. if obtained from wood tar.

wood·bine (wŏŏd'bīn) n. 1 A climbing European honeysuckle. 2 VIRGINIA CREEPER. [< OE *wudu* wood + *bindan* bind]

wood·block (wŏŏd'blok') n. 1 A block of wood. 2 WOODCUT. Also **wood block.**

wood·chuck (wŏŏd'chuk') n. A hibernating marmot of North America; a groundhog. [Prob. < Algon.; infl. in form by WOOD and CHUCK]

Woodchuck

wood·cock (wŏŏd'kok') n. 1 A European game bird related to the snipe. 2 A smaller related North American bird.

wood·craft (wŏŏd'kraft', -kräft') n. 1 Skill in knowing how to survive in the woods by making shelters, hunting game, etc. 2 The act or art of constructing articles of wood. —**wood'crafts·man** (pl. **·men**) n.

wood·cut (wŏŏd'kut') n. 1 A block of wood engraved, as with a design, for making prints. 2 A print made from such a block.

wood·cut·ter (wŏŏd'kut'ər) n. One who cuts or chops wood. —**wood'cut'ting** n.

wood·ed (wŏŏd'id) adj. Abounding with trees.

wood·en (wŏŏd'n) adj. 1 Made of wood. 2 Stiff; awkward. 3 Dull; stupid. —**wood'en·ly** adv. —**wood'en·ness** n.

wood engraving 1 The art of cutting designs on wood for printing. 2 A block of wood with an engraving cut, as with a burin, into a surface that is perpendicular to the direction of the grain. 3 A print from such a block. —**wood engraver**

wood·en·head (wŏŏd'n-hed') n. *Informal* A stupid person; blockhead. —**wood'en·head'ed** adj. —**wood'en·head'·ed·ness** n.

wood·en·ware (wŏŏd'n-wâr') n. Dishes, vessels, bowls, etc., made of wood.

wood·land (wŏŏd'lənd, -land') n. Land covered with wood or trees; timberland. —*adj.* (-lənd) Belonging to or dwelling in the woods. —**wood'land'er** n.

wood louse Any of numerous small terrestrial flat-bodied crustaceans commonly found under old logs.

wood·note (wŏŏd'nōt') n. A simple, artless, or natural song, call, etc., as of a woodland bird.

wood nymph A nymph of the woods.

wood·peck·er (wŏŏd'pek'ər) n. Any of a large family of birds having stiff tail feathers, strong claws, and a sharp bill for drilling holes in trees in search of wood-boring insects.

wood·pile (wŏŏd'pīl') n. A pile of wood, esp. of wood cut in sizes for burning.

wood pulp Wood reduced to a pulp, used for making paper.

wood·shed (wŏŏd'shed') n. A shed for storing firewood.

woods·man (wŏŏdz'mən) n. pl. **·men** (-mən) 1 A man who lives or works in the woods. 2 A man skilled in woodcraft.

wood sorrel A creeping perennial woodland plant with cloverlike leaves containing oxalic acid. • See SHAMROCK.

Red-headed woodpecker

woods·y (wŏŏd'zē) adj. **woods·i·er, woods·i·est** Of, pertaining to, or like the woods. —**woods'i·ness** n.

wood tar A tar produced by the dry distillation of wood.

wood thrush A large, common woodland thrush with reddish brown plumage, having a bell-like song. • See THRUSH[1].

wood turning The shaping of blocks of wood by means of a lathe. —**wood turner**

wood·wind (wŏŏd′wind′) n. 1 A musical wind instrument, as the flute, clarinet, bassoon, oboe, or saxophone. 2 pl. The woodwinds of an orchestra; also, the players of these instruments.

wood·work (wŏŏd′wûrk′) n. Things made of wood, esp. certain interior parts of a house, as moldings, doors, windowsills, etc. —**wood′work′er, wood′work′ing** n.

wood·worm (wŏŏd′wûrm′) n. A worm or larva dwelling in or that bores in wood.

wood·y (wŏŏd′ē) adj. **wood·i·er, wood·i·est** 1 Made of or containing wood. 2 Resembling wood. 3 Wooded; abounding with trees. —**wood′i·ness** n.

woof[1] (wŏŏf, wōōf) n. 1 The threads that are carried back and forth across the warp in a loom. 2 The texture of a fabric. [<OE ōwef]

woof[2] (wŏŏf) n. A low barking sound or growl, esp. of a dog. —v.i. To make such a sound. [Imit.]

woof·er (wŏŏf′ər) n. A loudspeaker designed to reproduce sounds of low frequency. [<WOOF[2] + -ER]

wool (wŏŏl) n. 1 The soft, durable fiber obtained from the fleece of sheep and some allied animals, as goats, alpacas, etc. 2 Yarn or fabric made of such fibers. 3 Garments made of wool. 4 Something resembling or likened to wool. —**pull the wool over one's eyes** To delude or deceive one. —adj. Made of or pertaining to wool or woolen material. [<OE wull]

wool·en (wŏŏl′ən) adj. 1 Of or pertaining to wool. 2 Made of wool. —n. Usu. pl. Cloth or clothing made of wool. Also **wool′en.**

wool·gath·er·ing (wŏŏl′gath′ər·ing) n. Idle daydreaming; absent-mindedness. —**wool′gath′er·er** n.

wool·grow·er (wŏŏl′grō′ər) n. A person who raises sheep for the production of wool. —**wool′grow′ing** adj.

wool·ly (wŏŏl′ē) adj. **·li·er, ·li·est** 1 Consisting of, covered with, or resembling wool. 2 Not clear or sharply detailed; fuzzy. 3 Resembling the roughness and excitement of the early American West, usu. in the phrase **wild and woolly.** —n. pl. **·lies** A garment made of wool, esp. woolen underwear. Also **wool′y.** —**wool′li·ness, wool′i·ness** n.

wooz·y (wŏŏ′zē) adj. **·i·er, ·i·est** Slang Befuddled, esp. with drink. [Prob. < wooze, var. of OOZE] —**wooz′i·ly** adv. —**wooz′i·ness** n.

word (wûrd) n. 1 A speech sound or combination of sounds which has come to signify and communicate a particular idea or thought, and which functions as the smallest meaningful unit of a language when used in isolation. 2 The letters or characters that stand for such a language unit. 3 Usu. pl. Speech; talk: hard to put into words. 4 A brief remark or comment. 5 A communication or message: Send him word. 6 A command, signal, or direction: Give the word to start. 7 A promise: a man of his word. 8 Rumor, gossip, or news: What's the latest word? 9 A watchword or password. 10 pl. The text of a song: words and music. 11 pl. Language used in anger, rebuke, etc.: They had words. —**in a word** In short; briefly. —**eat one's words** To retract what one has said. —**mince words** To be evasive or overly delicate in what one says. —**take one at his word** To believe literally in what another has said and act or respond accordingly. —**word for word** In exactly the same words; verbatim. —v.t. To express in a word or words; phrase. —**the Word** 1 LOGOS (def. 2). 2 GOSPEL (def. 1). 3 The Scriptures; the Bible. [<OE]

word·age (wûr′dij) n. 1 Words collectively. 2 The number of words, as in a novel. 3 VERBIAGE. 4 WORDING.

word·book (wûrd′bŏŏk′) n. 1 A collection of words; vocabulary; lexicon; dictionary. 2 An opera libretto.

word·ing (wûr′ding) n. The style or arrangement of words; diction; phraseology.

word·less (wûrd′lis) adj. Having no words; dumb; silent.

word of mouth Spoken words; speech; oral communication. —**word-of-mouth** (wûrd′uv·mouth′) adj.

word order The sequence or arrangement of words in a sentence, phrase, or clause.

word·play (wûrd′plā′) n. 1 Clever repartee. 2 A play on words; pun.

word processing The computer-storage editing, transmittal, and reproduction of written information by means of a terminal, printer, memory, software, etc. —**word processor** n.

word·y (wûr′dē) adj. **word·i·er, word·i·est** 1 Expressed in many or too many words; verbose. 2 Of or pertaining to words; verbal. —**word′i·ly** adv. —**word′i·ness** n. —Syn. 1 long-winded, prolix, roundabout, redundant.

wore (wôr, wōr) p.t. of WEAR.

work (wûrk) n. 1 Continued physical or mental exertion or activity directed to some purpose or end; labor; toil. 2 Employment; job: to be out of work. 3 One's profession, occupation, business, trade, etc.: What is your work? 4 The place where one is employed or occupied professionally: She is at work. 5 An undertaking or task, often a part of one's job or occupation: to take work home; also, the amount of this that is accomplished or required: a day's work. 6 pl. A place where something is made, undertaken, etc.: often used in combination: the oilworks. 7 The material used or processed in manufacturing something. 8 Something that has been made, created, accomplished, etc., esp.: a An engineering structure, as a bridge. b A feat or deed: remembered for her good works. c Needlework or embroidery. d A product of the mind and imagination: the works of Beethoven. 9 Manner, quality, or style of doing something; workmanship. 10 pl. Running gear or machinery: the works of a watch. 11 The action of natural forces or the result of such action: the work of a storm. 12 Physics A transfer of energy between physical systems. —**the works** Slang 1 Everything belonging, available, etc. 2 Drastic or vicious treatment: to give someone the works. —**shoot the works** Slang 1 To risk everything. 2 To make a final, supreme effort. —v. **worked** (Archaic **wrought**), **working** v.i. 1 To perform work; labor; toil. 2 To be employed in some trade or business. 3 To perform a function; operate: The machine works well. 4 To prove effective or influential: His stratagem worked. 5 To move or progress gradually or with difficulty: He worked up in his profession. 6 To become as specified, as by gradual motion: The bolts worked loose. 7 To move from nervousness or agitation: His features worked with anger. 8 To undergo kneading, hammering, etc.; be shaped: Copper works easily. 9 To ferment. —v.t. 10 To cause or bring about: to work a miracle. 11 To direct the operation of: to work a machine. 12 To make or shape by toil or skill. 13 To prepare, as by manipulating, hammering, etc.: to work dough. 14 To decorate, as with embroidery or inlaid work. 15 To cause to be productive, as by toil: to work a mine. 16 To cause to do work: He works his employees too hard. 17 To cause to be as specified, usu. with effort: We worked the timber into position. 18 To make or achieve by effort: to work one's passage on a ship. 19 To carry on some activity in (an area, etc.); cover: to work a sales territory. 20 To solve, as a problem in arithmetic. 21 To cause to move from nervousness or excitement: to work one's jaws. 22 To excite; provoke: He worked himself into a passion. 23 To influence or manage, as by insidious means; lead. 24 To cause to ferment. 25 Informal To practice trickery upon; cheat; swindle. 26 Informal To make use of for one's own purposes; use. —**work in** To insert or be inserted. —**work off** To get rid of, as extra flesh by exercise. —**work on** (or **upon**) 1 To try to influence or persuade. 2 To influence or affect. —**work out** 1 To make its way out or through. 2 To effect by work or effort; accomplish. 3 To exhaust, as a mine. 4 To discharge, as a debt, by labor rather than by payment of money. 5 To develop; form, as a plan. 6 To solve. 7 a To prove effective or successful. b To result as specified. 8 To exercise, train, etc. —**work over** 1 To repeat. 2 Slang To treat harshly or cruelly; beat up, torture, etc. —**work up** 1 To excite; rouse, as rage or a person to

rage. **2** To form or shape by working; develop: to *work up* a new advertising campaign. **3** To make one's or its way. **4** To cause or bring about. [< OE *weorc*]

-work *combining form* **1** A product made from a (specified) material: *brickwork*. **2** Work of a (given) kind: *piecework*. **3** Work performed in a (specified) place: *housework*.

work·a·ble (wûr′kə-bəl) *adj.* **1** Capable of being worked, developed, etc. **2** Practicable, as a plan. **—work′a·bil′i·ty, work′a·ble·ness** *n.*

work·a·day (wûrk′ə-dā′) *adj.* **1** Of, pertaining to, or suitable for working days; everyday. **2** Commonplace; prosaic.

work·bench (wûrk′bench′) *n.* A bench for work, esp. that of a carpenter, machinist, etc.

work·book (wûrk′bŏŏk′) *n.* **1** A booklet based on a course of study and containing problems and exercises which a student works out directly on the pages. **2** A manual containing operating instructions. **3** A book for recording work performed or planned.

work·day (wûrk′dā′) *n.* **1** Any day, usu. not a Sunday or holiday, on which work is done. **2** The number of hours of one day spent in work. Also **working day. —adj.** WORKADAY.

work·er (wûk′kər) *n.* **1** One who or that which performs work. **2** A social insect, as a bee, ant, etc., that is sexually sterile and performs work for the colony. **3** A member of the working class.

work·fare (wûrk′fâr′) *n.* Welfare that is conditional upon assigned work or training by those receiving payments.

work·house (wûrk′hous′) *n.* **1** *Brit.* Formerly, a house for paupers able to work. **2** A prison in which petty offenders are put to work.

work·ing (wûr′king) *adj.* **1** Engaged actively in some employment. **2** That works, or performs its function: This is a *working* model. **3** Sufficient for use or action: They formed a *working* agreement. **4** Of, used in, or occupied by work: a *working* day. **5** Throbbing or twitching, as facial muscles. **—n.** **1** The act or operation of any person or thing that works. **2** *Usu. pl.* That part of a mine or quarry where excavation is going on or has gone on.

working capital That part of the finances of a business available for its operation or convertible into cash.

working class People who work for wages, esp. manual and industrial workers. **—work′ing-class′** *adj.*

work·man (wûrk′mən) *n. pl.* **·men** (-men′) **1** A male worker. **2** A man who earns his living by working with his hands or with machines. Also **work·ing·man** (wûr′king·man′).

work·man·like (wûrk′mən·līk) *adj.* Like or befitting a skilled workman; skillfully done. Also **work′man·ly.**

work·man·ship (wûrk′mən·ship) *n.* **1** The art or skill of a workman. **2** The quality of work. **3** The work produced.

work of art **1** A highly artistic product of the fine arts, esp. painting and sculpture. **2** Anything made or done with great beauty or skill.

work·out (wûrk′out′) *n.* **1** Any activity done to increase or maintain skill, physical fitness, etc. **2** Any instance of strenuous activity, disciplined work, etc.

work·room (wûrk′rōōm, -rŏŏm′) *n.* A room where work is performed.

work·shop (wûrk′shop′) *n.* **1** A building or room where any work is carried on; workroom. **2** A seminar or single session for training, discussion, etc., in a specialized field: a writers' *workshop*.

work·ta·ble (wûrk′tā′bəl) *n.* A table with drawers and other conveniences for use while working.

work·week (wûrk′wēk′) *n.* The total number of hours worked in a week; also, the number of required working hours in a week.

world (wûrld) *n.* **1** The earth. **2** The universe. **3** Any celestial body: Are there other inhabited *worlds*? **4** *Often cap.* A part of the earth: the *Old World*. **5** A specific time or period in history: the ancient *world*. **6** A division of existing or created things belonging to the earth; the animal *world*. **7** The human inhabitants of the earth; mankind. **8** A definite class of people having certain interests or activities in common: the scientific *world*. **9** Secular or worldly aims, pleasures, etc., as distinguished from religious or spiritual ones; also, those people who pursue such aims or pleasures. **10** Individual conditions or circum-

stances of a person's life: His *world* has changed. **11** A large quantity or amount: a *world* of trouble. **—come into the world** To be born. **—for all the world** **1** In every respect. **2** For any reason. **—on top of the world** *Informal* Elated. **—out of this world** *Informal* Exceptionally fine; wonderful. [< OE *weorold*]

world·ly (wûrld′lē) *adj.* **·li·er, ·li·est** **1** Pertaining to the world; mundane; earthly. **2** Devoted to secular, earthly things; not spiritual. **3** Sophisticated; worldly-wise. **—adv.** In a worldly manner. **—world′li·ness** *n.*

world·ly-mind·ed (wûrld′lē·mīn′did) *adj.* Absorbed in the things of this world. **—world′ly-mind′ed·ly** *adv.*

world·ly-wise (wûrld′lē·wīz) *adj.* Wise in the ways and affairs of the world; sophisticated.

world power A state or organization whose policies and actions have a worldwide influence.

World Series In baseball, the games played at the finish of the regular season between the champion teams of the two major U.S. leagues. Also **world series.**

World War I The war (1914–18) between the Allies and the Central Powers (Germany, Austria-Hungary, Turkey, and Bulgaria).

World War II The war (1939–45) between the United Nations and the Axis.

world-wea·ry (wûrld′wir′ē) *adj.* **·ri·er, ·ri·est** Weary of life and its conditions. **—world′-wea′ri·ness** *n.*

world·wide (wûrld′wīd′) *adj.* Extended throughout the world.

worm (wûrm) *n.* **1** *Zool.* Any of numerous limbless, elongated, soft-bodied invertebrate animals, including flatworms, roundworms, and annelids. **2** Any small animal resembling a worm, as a caterpillar, maggot, snake, shipworm, etc. **3** Something which suggests the inner, hidden gnawings of a worm: the *worm* of remorse. **4** A despicable or despised person. **5** Something conceived to be like a worm, as the thread of a screw. **6** *pl.* Any disorder due to parasitic worms in the intestines, etc. **—v.t.** **1** To move, proceed, insinuate, etc. (oneself or itself) in a wormlike manner: to *worm* one's way. **2** To draw forth by artful means, as a secret: with *out*. **3** To rid of intestinal worms. **—v.i.** **4** To move or progress slowly and stealthily. [< OE *wyrm*] **—worm′i·ness** *n.* **—worm′y** *adj.* **·i·er, ·i·est**)

worm-eat·en (wûrm′ēt′n) *adj.* **1** Eaten or bored through by worms. **2** Worn-out or decayed.

worm gear A gear having teeth shaped so as to mesh with a threaded shaft.

worm·hole (wûrm′hōl′) *n.* The hole made by a worm or a wormlike animal. **— worm′holed′** *adj.*

worm·wood (wûrm′wŏŏd′) *n.* **1** Any of various European herbs or small shrubs related to the sagebrush, esp. a species yielding a bitter oil used in making absinthe. **2** Something that embitters or is unpleasant. [< OE *wermōd*]

Worm gear

worn (wôrn, wōrn) *p.p.* of WEAR. **—adj.** **1** Affected by wear, use, continuous action, etc.; frayed, damaged, etc. **2** Showing the effects of worry, anxiety, etc. **3** Hackneyed, as a phrase.

worn-out (wôrn′out′, wōrn′-) *adj.* **1** Used until without value or usefulness. **2** Thoroughly tired; exhausted.

wor·ri·some (wûr′i·səm) *adj.* Causing worry or anxiety.

wor·ry (wûr′ē) *v.* **·ried, ·ry·ing** *v.i.* **1** To be uneasy in the mind; feel anxiety. **2** To manage despite trials or difficulties; struggle: with *along* or *through*. **—v.t.** **3** To cause to feel uneasy in the mind; trouble. **4** To bother; pester. **5** To bite, pull at, or shake with the teeth. **—n. pl.** **·ries** **1** A state of anxiety or uneasiness. **2** Something causing such a state. [< OE *wrygan* strangle] **—wor′ri·er, wor′ri·ment** *n.*

worse (wûrs) Comparative of BAD and ILL. **—adj.** **1** Bad or ill in a great degree; inferior. **2** Physically ill in a greater degree. **3** Less favorable, as to conditions, circumstances, etc. **4** More evil, corrupt, etc. **—n.** Someone or something worse. **—adv.** **1** In a worse manner, way, etc. **2** With greater intensity, severity, etc. [< OE *wyrsa*]

wors·en (wûr′sən) *v.t. & v.i.* To make or become worse.

wor·ship (wûr′ship) *n.* **1** Adoration, homage, etc., given to a deity. **2** The rituals, prayers, etc., expressing such adoration or homage. **3** Excessive or ardent admiration or

love. **4** The object of such love or admiration. **5** *Chiefly Brit.* A title of honor in addressing certain persons of station. —*v.* **·shiped** or **·shipped**, **·ship·ing** or **·ship·ping** *v.t.* **1** To pay an act of worship to; venerate. **2** To have intense or exaggerated admiration or love for. —*v.i.* **3** To perform acts or have sentiments of worship. [< OE *weorthscipe* < *weorth* worthy] —**wor′ship·er, wor′ship·per** *n.* —**Syn.** *v.* **1** exalt, praise. **2** adore, dote on, idolize.

wor·ship·ful (wûr′ship·fəl) *adj.* **1** Feeling or giving great reverence, love, etc. **2** *Chiefly Brit.* Worthy of respect by reason of character or position: applied to certain dignitaries. —**wor′ship·ful·ly** *adv.* —**wor′ship·ful·ness** *n.*

worst (wûrst) Superlative of BAD and ILL. —*adj.* **1** Bad or ill in the highest degree. **2** Least favorable, as to conditions, circumstances, etc. **3** Most evil, corrupt, etc. —**in the worst way** *Informal* Very much. —*n.* Someone or something that is worst. —**at worst** Under the worst possible circumstances or conditions. —**get the worst of it** To be defeated or put at a disadvantage. —*adv.* **1** To the greatest or most extreme degree. **2** To the greatest or most extreme degree of inferiority, badness, etc. —*v.t.* To defeat; vanquish. [< OE *wyrsta*]

wors·ted (wōōs′tid, wûr′stid) *n.* **1** Woolen yarn spun from long staple, with fibers combed parallel and twisted hard. **2** A tightly woven fabric made from such yarn. —*adj.* Consisting of or made from such yarn. [< *Worsted,* former name of a parish in Norfolk, England]

wort[1] (wûrt) *n.* A plant or herb: usu. in combination: *liver-wort.* [< OE *wyrt* a root, a plant]

wort[2] (wûrt) *n.* The unfermented infusion of malt that becomes beer when fermented. [< OE *wyrt* a root, a plant]

worth (wûrth) *n.* **1** Value or excellence of any kind. **2** The market value of something. **3** The amount of something obtainable at a specific sum: two cents′ *worth* of candy. **4** Wealth. —*adj.* **1** Equal in value (to); exchangable (for). **2** Deserving (of): not *worth* going. **3** Having wealth or possessions to the value of: He is *worth* a million. —**for all it is worth** To the utmost. —**for all one is worth** With every effort possible. [< OE *weorth*]

worth·less (wûrth′lis) *adj.* Having no worth, usefulness, virtue, etc. —**worth′less·ly** *adv.* —**worth′less·ness** *n.*

worth·while (wûrth′hwīl′) *adj.* Sufficiently important to occupy the time; of enough value to repay the effort. —**worth′while′ness** *n.*

wor·thy (wûr′the͞e) *adj.* **·thi·er, ·thi·est** **1** Possessing valuable or useful qualities. **2** Having such qualities as to deserve or merit some specified thing: *worthy* of the honor. —*n. pl.* **·thies** A person of eminent worth: sometimes used humorously. —**wor′thi·ly** *adv.* —**wor′thi·ness** *n.*

-worthy *combining form* **1** Meriting or deserving: *trustworthy.* **2** Valuable as; having worth as: *newsworthy.* **3** Fit for: *seaworthy.*

wot (wot) *p.t., first and third person singular,* of WIT[2].

would (wōōd) *p.t.* of WILL, but used chiefly as an auxiliary to express: **1** Desire: They *would* like to go. **2** Condition: They *would* go if you asked them. **3** Futurity: He said he *would* bring it. **4** Determination: The dog *would* not let go. **5** Custom or habit: He *would* walk there every day. [< OE *wolde,* p.t. of *willan* will]

would-be (wōōd′bē′) *adj.* Desiring, professing, or intended to be: a *would-be* actress.

would·n′t (wōōd′nt) Contraction of *would not.*

wound[1] (wōōnd) *n.* **1** A hurt or injury, esp. one in which the skin is torn, cut, etc. **2** A cutting or scraping injury to a tree or plant. **3** Any cause of pain or grief, as to the feelings, honor, etc. —*v.t. & v.i.* **1** To inflict a wound or wounds (upon). **2** To injure the feelings or pride of. [< OE *wund*] —**Syn.** *v.* **2** affront, hurt, offend, pique.

wound[2] (wound) *p.t. & p.p.* of WIND[2].

wove (wōv) *p.t. & a p.p.* of WEAVE.

wo·ven (wō′vən) *p.p.* of WEAVE.

wow (wou) *interj. Informal* An exclamation of wonder, surprise, pleasure, etc. —*n. Slang* A person or thing that is extraordinary, successful, etc. —*v.t. Slang* To cause to feel excitement, admiration, etc.

WPA, W.P.A. Works Progress Administration.

wrack (rak) *n.* **1** Ruin; destruction: esp. in the phrase **wrack and ruin. 2** Marine vegetation cast ashore by the sea, as seaweed. **3** A wrecked vessel; wreckage. —*v.t. & v.i.* To wreck or be wrecked. [Fusion of OE *wræc* punishment, revenge and MDu. *wrak* a wreck]

wraith (rāth) *n.* **1** An apparition of a person seen shortly before or shortly after his or her death. **2** Any specter; ghost. [?]

wran·gle (rang′gəl) *v.* **·gled, ·gling** *v.i.* **1** To argue noisily and angrily. —*v.t.* **2** To argue; debate. **3** To get by stubborn arguing. **4** To herd or round up, as livestock. —*n.* An angry dispute. [ME *wranglen*] —**wran′gler** *n.*

wrap (rap) *v.* **wrapped** or **wrapt, wrap·ping** *v.t.* **1** To surround and cover by something folded or wound about. **2** To fold or wind (a covering) about something. **3** To surround so as to blot out or conceal: a mountain *wrapped* in clouds. **4** To fold or wind. —*v.i.* **5** To be or become twined, coiled, etc.: with *about, around,* etc. —**wrap up 1** To cover with paper, etc. **2** To put on warm garments. **3** *Informal* To conclude or finish. —**wrapped up in** Involved or absorbed in: *wrapped up in* his music. —*n.* **1** A garment folded about a person. **2** *pl.* Outer garments collectively. **3** A blanket. —**keep under wraps** To keep secret. [ME *wrappen*]

wrap·a·round (rap′ə·round′) *adj.* **1** Made so as to be wrapped around the body and then fastened: a *wraparound* skirt. **2** Designed so as to curve back on each side: a *wraparound* windshield. —*n.* Anything that encircles or curves back on each side.

wrap·per (rap′ər) *n.* **1** A paper enclosing a newspaper, magazine, or similar packet for mailing or otherwise. **2** A woman's dressing gown. **3** One who or that which wraps.

wrap·ping (rap′ing) *n. Often pl.* A covering or something in which an object is wrapped.

wrap-up (rap′up′) *n. Informal* **1** A summary or conclusion: a *wrap-up* of the news. **2** The final event, action, etc., in a connected series.

wrath (rath, räth; *Brit.* rôth) *n.* **1** Violent rage, anger, or fury. **2** An act done in violent rage. [< OE *wrāth* wroth]

wrath·ful (rath′fəl, räth′-) *adj.* **1** Full of wrath; extremely angry. **2** Resulting from or expressing wrath. —**wrath′ful·ly** *adv.* —**wrath′ful·ness** *n.* —**Syn.** **1** furious, apoplectic, mad, raging.

wreak (rēk) *v.t.* **1** To inflict or exact, as vengeance. **2** To give free expression to, as a feeling or passion. [< OE *wrecan* drive, avenge]

wreath (rēth) *n. pl.* **wreaths** (rē͞thz, rēths) **1** A band, as of flowers or leaves, commonly circular, as for a crown, decoration, etc. **2** Any curled or spiral band, as of smoke, snow, etc. [< OE *writha*] —**wreath·y** (rē′the, -the) *adj.*

wreathe (rē͞th) *v.* **wreathed, wreath·ing** *v.t.* **1** To form into a wreath, as by twisting or twining. **2** To adorn or encircle with or as with wreaths. **3** To envelop; cover: His face was *wreathed* in smiles. —*v.i.* **4** To take the form of a wreath. **5** To twist, turn, or coil, as masses of cloud.

wreck (rek) *v.t.* **1** To cause the destruction of, as by a collision. **2** To bring ruin, damage, or destruction upon. **3** To tear down, as a building; dismantle. —*v.i.* **4** To suffer destruction; be ruined. **5** To engage in wrecking, as for plunder or salvage. —*n.* **1** The act of wrecking, or the condition of being wrecked. **2** That which has been wrecked or ruined by accident, collision, etc. **3** The broken remnants or remains of something wrecked. **4** SHIPWRECK. **5** The ruined, usu. stranded hulk of a ship that has been wrecked. **6** A person who is ill or under great strain. [< AF *wrec* < Scand.]

wreck·age (rek′ij) *n.* **1** The act of wrecking, or the condition of being wrecked. **2** Broken remnants or fragments from a wreck.

wreck·er (rek′ər) *n.* **1** One who causes destruction of any sort. **2** One employed in tearing down and removing old buildings. **3** A person, train, car, or machine that clears away wrecks. **4** One employed to recover disabled vessels or wrecked cargoes.

wren (ren) *n.* **1** Any of numerous small, active, usu. brown birds having short rounded wings and tail and a thin,

curved bill. **2** Any one of numerous similar birds. [<OE *wrenna*]

wrench (rench) *n.* **1** A violent twist. **2** A sprain or violent twist or pull in a part of the body. **3** A sudden surge of emotion, as of sorrow, pity, etc. **4** Any of various gripping tools for turning or twisting bolts, nuts, pipes, etc. — *v.t.* **1** To twist violently; turn suddenly by force. **2** To twist forcibly so as to cause strain or injury; sprain. **3** To cause to suffer. **4** To twist from the proper meaning, intent, or use. —*v.i.* **5** To give a twist or wrench [<OE *wrencan* to wrench]

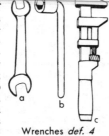

Wrenches *def. 4*
a. engineer's. b.
offset. c. monkey.

wrest (rest) *v.t.* **1** To pull or force away by violent twisting or wringing; wrench. **2** To turn from the true meaning, intent, etc.; distort. **3** To seize forcibly. **4** To gain or extract by great effort. —*n.* **1** An act of wresting. **2** A key for tuning a piano, harp, etc. [<OE *wræstan*] —**wrest′er** *n.*

wres·tle (res′əl) *v.* **·tled**, **·tling** *v.i.* **1** To engage in wrestling. **2** To struggle, as for mastery; contend. —*v.t.* **3** To contend with (someone) in wrestling. **4** To throw (a calf) and hold it down for branding. —*n.* **1** The act or an instance of wrestling. **2** A hard struggle. [<OE *wræstlian*] —**wres′tler** *n.*

wres·tling (res′ling) *n.* A sport or exercise in which each of two unarmed contestants endeavors to throw the other to the ground or force him into a certain fallen position.

wretch (rech) *n.* **1** A vile or contemptible person. **2** A miserable or unhappy person. [<OE *wrecca* an outcast]

wretch·ed (rech′id) *adj.* **1** Sunk in dejection; profoundly unhappy. **2** Causing or characterized by misery, poverty, etc. **3** Unsatisfactory in ability or quality. **4** Despicable; contemptible. —**wretch′ed·ly** *adv.* —**wretch′ed·ness** *n.* —**Syn.** **1** distressed, miserable. **3** bad, paltry, worthless.

wrig·gle (rig′əl) *v.* **·gled**, **·gling** *v.i.* **1** To twist in a sinuous manner; squirm; writhe. **2** To proceed as by twisting or crawling. **3** To make one's way by evasive or indirect means. —*v.t.* **4** To cause to wriggle. **5** To make (one's way, etc.) by evasive or sly means. —*n.* The act or motion of one who or that which wriggles. [<MLG *wriggeln*] —**wrig′gly** *adj.*

wrig·gler (rig′lər) *n.* **1** Someone or something that wriggles. **2** A mosquito larva.

wright (rīt) *n.* One who builds or creates something: used in combination: *wheelwright; playwright.* [<OE *wyrhta*]

wring (ring) *v.* **wrung**, **wring·ing** *v.t.* **1** To squeeze or compress by twisting. **2** To squeeze or press out, as water, by twisting. **3** To acquire by forcible means. **4** To distress: Her plight *wrung* their hearts. **5** To twist violently: to *wring* his neck. —*v.i.* **6** To writhe or squirm with great effort. —*n.* A twisting or wringing. [<OE *wringan*]

wring·er (ring′ər) *n.* **1** One who or that which wrings. **2** A device used to press water out of fabrics after washing.

wrin·kle[1] (ring′kəl) *n.* **1** A small ridge, as on a smooth surface; a crease; fold. **2** A small fold or crease in the skin, usu. produced by age or by excessive exposure to the elements. —*v.* **·kled**, **·kling** *v.t.* To make wrinkles in. —*v.i.* **2** To become wrinkled. [<OE *wrincle*] —**wrin′kly** *adj.*

wrin·kle[2] (ring′kəl) *n.* *Informal* A new or ingenious method, device, etc. [Prob. dim. of OE *wrenc* a trick]

wrist (rist) *n.* **1** The part of the arm that lies between the hand and the forearm; the carpus. **2** The part of a glove or garment that covers the wrist. [<OE]

wrist·band (rist′band′) *n.* **1** The band of a sleeve that covers the wrist. **2** A band for a wrist watch.

wrist·let (rist′lit) *n.* **1** A flexible band worn on the wrist for support or warmth. **2** A bracelet.

wrist pin *Mech.* A pin attaching a connecting rod to another part.

wrist watch A watch set in a band and worn at the wrist.

writ[1] (rit) *n.* **1** *Law* A written order, issued by a court, and commanding the person to do or not to do some act. **2** That which is written: now chiefly in the phrase **Holy Writ,** the Bible. [<OE *wrītan* write]

writ[2] (rit) *Archaic* or *Regional p.t. & p.p.* of WRITE.

write (rīt) *v.* **wrote** (or *Archaic* **writ**), **writ·ten· (or *Archaic* writ),** **writ·ing** *v.t.* **1** To trace or inscribe (letters, words, numbers, symbols, etc.) on a surface with pen or pencil. **2** To describe, set down, or signify in writing. **3** To communicate by letter. **4** To communicate with by letter. **5** To produce by writing; be the author or composer of. **6** To draw up; draft: to *write* a check. **7** To cover or fill with writing: to *write* two full pages. **8** To leave marks or evidence of: Anxiety is *written* on his face. **9** To underwrite: to *write* an insurance policy. **10** To store information in computer memory. —*v.i.* **11** To trace or inscribe letters, etc., on a surface, as of paper. **12** To communicate in writing. **13** To be engaged in the occupation of an author. —**write down 1** To put into writing. **2** To injure or depreciate in writing. —**write in 1** To insert in writing, as in a document. **2** To cast (a vote) for one not listed on a ballot by inserting his name in writing. —**write off 1** To cancel or remove (claims, debts, etc.) from an open account. **2** To acknowledge the loss or failure of. —**write out** To write in full or complete form. —**write up 1** To describe fully in writing. **2** To praise fully or too fully in writing. [<OE *wrītan*] • *Writ,* the archaic past participle of *write,* is now used chiefly in the phrase **writ large,** written or shown on a grand scale: *a name writ large in history.*

write-in (rīt′in) *n.* **1** The act of casting a vote for a candidate not listed on the ballot by writing in his name. **2** The name so written in. —*adj.* Of or pertaining to a write-in.

write-off (rīt′ôf, -of′) *n.* **1** A cancellation. **2** An amount canceled or noted as a loss. **3** A person or thing acknowledged to be a failure or a loss.

writ·er (rī′tər) *n.* **1** One who writes. **2** One who engages in literary composition as a profession.

write-up (rīt′up′) *n.* A written description or review.

writhe (rīth) *v.* **writhed**, **writh·ing** *v.t.* **1** To cause to twist or be distorted. —*v.i.* **2** To twist or distort the body, face, or limbs, as in pain. **3** To undergo suffering, as from embarrassment, sorrow, etc. —*n.* An act of writhing. [<OE *wrīthan*] —**writh′er** *n.*

writ·ing (rī′ting) *n.* **1** The act of one who writes. **2** HANDWRITING. **3** Anything written or expressed in letters, esp. a literary production. **4** A written form: put your request in *writing.* **5** The profession or occupation of a writer. —*adj.* **1** Used in or for writing: *writing* paper. **2** That writes.

writ·ten (rit′n) *p.p.* of WRITE.

wrong (rông) *adj.* **1** Not correct; mistaken. **2** Not appropriate: the *wrong* shoes for hiking. **3** Not morally or legally right. **4** Not in accordance with the correct or standard method: the *wrong* way to bake. **5** Not working or operating properly: What is *wrong* with the furnace? **6** Not meant to be seen, used, etc.: the *wrong* side of the fabric. **7** Not intended: a *wrong* turn. —**go wrong 1** To behave immorally. **2** To turn out badly; fail. **3** To take a wrong direction, etc. —*adv.* In a wrong direction, place, or manner; erroneously. —*n.* **1** That which is morally or socially wrong or unacceptable. **2** An injury or injustice. —**in the wrong** In error; wrong. —*v.t.* **1** To violate the rights of; inflict injury or injustice upon. **2** To impute evil to unjustly: You *wrong* him. **3** To seduce (a woman). **4** To treat dishonorably. [<Scand.] —**wrong′er, wrong′ness** *n.* —**wrong·ly** *adv.*

wrong·do·er (rông′dōō′ər, rông′-) *n.* One who does wrong. —**wrong′do′ing** *n.*

wrong·ful (rông′fəl) *adj.* **1** Characterized by wrong or injustice; injurious; unjust. **2** Unlawful; illegal. —**wrong′ful·ly** *adv.* —**wrong′ful·ness** *n.*

wrong-head·ed (rông′hed′id) *adj.* Stubbornly holding to a wrong judgment, opinion, etc. —**wrong′-head′ed·ly** *adv.* —**wrong′-head′ed·ness** *n.*

wrote (rōt) *p.t.* of WRITE.

wroth (rôth) *adj.* Filled with anger; angry. [<OE *wrāth*]

wrought (rôt) *Archaic p.t. & p.p.* of WORK. —*adj.* **1** Beaten or hammered into shape by tools: *wrought* gold. **2** Made delicately or elaborately. **3** Made; fashioned; formed. —**wrought up** Disturbed or excited; agitated. [ME *wrogt,* var. of *worht,* p.p. of *wirchen* work]

wrought iron Strong, malleable, commercially pure iron.

wrung (rung) *p.t. & p.p.* of WRING.

wry (rī) *adj.* **wri·er, wri·est 1** Bent to one side or out of position; contorted; askew. **2** Made by twisting or distorting the features: a *wry* smile. **3** Distorted or warped, as in interpretation or meaning. **4** Somewhat perverse or ironic: *wry* humor. —*v.t.* **wried, wry·ing** To twist; contort. [< OE *wrīgian* move, tend] —**wry′ly** *adv.* —**wry′ness** *n.*

wry·neck (rī′nek′) *n.* **1** A bird allied to the woodpeckers, with the habit of twisting its head and neck. **2** A spasmodic twisting of the neck.

WSW, W.S.W., wsw, w.s.w. west-southwest.

wt, wt. weight.

WV West Virginia (P.O. abbr.).

W.Va. West Virginia.

WY Wyoming (P.O. abbr.).

wy·an·dotte (wī′ən·dot) *n.* One of an American breed of chicken. [< the *Wyandot* Indians, an Iroquoian tribe]

wych-elm (wich′elm′) *n.* **1** A wide-spreading elm with large, dull-green leaves, common in N Europe. **2** Its wood. Also **witch-elm.** [< OE *wice* wych-elm + ELM]

Wyo. Wyoming.

X

X, x (eks) *n. pl.* **X's, x's, Xs, xs** (ek′siz) **1** The 24th letter of the English alphabet. **2** Any spoken sound representing the letter *X* or *x*. **3** In Roman notation, the symbol for 10. **4** An unknown quantity, result, etc. **5** A mark shaped like an X, representing the signature of one who cannot write. **6** A mark used in diagrams, maps, etc., to indicate or point out something. **7** A mark indicating one's answer on a test, one's choice on a ballot, etc. **8** A mark used to indicate a kiss. **9** A mark indicating "times" in multiplication: 4 X 2 = 8. **10** A mark indicating "by" in dimensions: 8½ X 11 inches. **11** Something shaped like an X. —*v.t.* **x-ed** or **x'd, x-ing** or **x'ing 1** To mark with an *x*. **2** To cancel or obliterate with an *x*: usu. with *out*. —*adj.* Shaped like an X.

X Christ; Christian.

xan·thic (zan′thik) *adj.* **1** Having a yellow or yellowish color. **2** Of or pertaining to xanthin or xanthine. [< Gk. *xanthos* yellow]

xan·thin (zan′thin) *n.* A yellow pigment found in plants. Also **xan′tho·phyll** (-thə·fil). [< Gk. *xanthos* yellow]

xan·thine (zan′thēn, -thin) *n.* A white, crystalline, nitrogenous compound, contained in blood, urine, and other animal secretions. [< Gk. *xanthos* yellow]

Xan·thip·pe (zan·tip′ē) The wife of Socrates, renowned as a shrew. —*n.* A shrewish, ill-tempered woman.

xan·thous (zan′thəs) *adj.* Yellow. [< Gk. *xanthos*]

x-ax·is (eks′ak′sis) *n. Math.* A coordinate axis against which the variable *x* is plotted.

X chromosome The sex chromosome that occurs in pairs in the female and is coupled with a Y chromosome in the male of humans and most animals.

X.D., x.d., x-div. ex (without) dividend.

Xe xenon.

xe·bec (zē′bek) *n.* A small, three-masted Mediterranean vessel. [< Ar. *shabbāk*]

xe·non (zē′non) *n.* A heavy, colorless, gaseous element (symbol Xe) occurring in traces in the atmosphere and rarely forming compounds. [< Gk. *xenos* a stranger]

xen·o·pho·bi·a (zen′ə·fō′bē·ə, zē′nə-) *n.* Dislike or fear of strangers or foreigners. [< Gk. *xenos* a stranger + -PHOBIA] —**xen′o·phob′ic** *adj.*

xe·rog·ra·phy (zi·rog′rə·fē) *n.* A method of copying by which a colored powder is distributed by the action of light on an electrically charged plate to form a negative, which is then transferred thermally to a paper or other surface. [< Gk. *xēros* dry + -GRAPHY] —**xe·ro·graph·ic** (zir′ə·graf′ik) *adj.*

xe·roph·i·lous (zi·rof′ə·ləs) *adj.* Thriving under arid conditions: said of plants living in dry regions, as the cactus. [< Gk. *xēros* dry + *philos* loving]

xe·ro·phyte (zir′ə·fīt) *n. Bot.* A plant adapted to arid habitats. [< Gk *xēros* dry + *phyton* plant] —**xe′ro·phyt′ic** (-fit′ik) *adj.*

Xer·ox (zir′oks) *n.* A xerographic copying process: a trade name. —*v.t.* To make or reproduce by Xerox. —*adj.* Of, for, or reproduced by Xeroxing. Also **xer′ox.**

xi (zī, sī; *Gk.* ksē) *n.* The fourteenth letter of the Greek alphabet (Ξ, ξ)

X.I., x.i., x-int. ex (without) interest.

Xmas (kris′məs, eks′məs) *n.* CHRISTMAS. [< X, abbr. for *Christ* < Gk. X, chi, the first letter of *Christos* Christ + -MAS(s)]

X-ray (eks′rā′) *n.* **1** An electromagnetic radiation having a wavelength shorter than that of ultraviolet light and longer than that of a gamma ray. **2** A photograph made with X-rays. —*adj.* Of, made by, or producing X-rays. —*v.t.* **1** To examine, diagnose, or treat with X-rays. —*v.i.* **2** To use X-rays. Also **X ray.**

x-ref. cross reference.

xy·lem (zī′ləm) *n.* The woody vascular bundles that serve as passageways for water in the roots, stems, and leaves of ferns and seed plants. [< Gk. *xylon* wood]

xy·lo·phone (zī′lə·fōn′) *n.* A musical instrument consisting of an array of wooden bars graduated in length to produce a scale, played by striking the bars with two small mallets. [< Gk. *xylon* wood + *phōnē* sound] —**xy′lo·phon′ist** *n.*

Xylophone

Y

Y, y (wī) *n. pl.* **Y's, y's, Ys, ys** (wīz) **1** The 25th letter of the English alphabet. **2** Any spoken sound representing the letter *Y* or *y*. **3** Something shaped like a Y. —*adj.* Shaped like a Y.

-y[1] *suffix* Being, possessing, or resembling what is expressed in the main element: *stony, rainy*. [< OE *-ig*]

-y[2] *suffix* **1** Quality; condition: *victory*. **2** The place or establishment where something specified happens or is made: *bakery*. **3** The entire group or body of: *soldiery*. [< L *-ia* or < Gk. *-ia, -eia*]

-y[3] *suffix* Little; small: *kitty*: often used to express endearment. [ME *-ie*]

Y (wī) *n. pl.* **Y's** or **Ys 1** YMCA or YWCA. **2** YMHA or YWHA.

Y yttrium.

y. yard(s); year(s).

yacht (yot) *n.* Any of various relatively small sailing or motor-driven ships built or fitted for private pleasure excursions or racing. —*v.i.* To cruise, race, or sail in a yacht. [< Du. *jaghte*, short for *jaghtschip* a pursuit ship]

yacht·ing (yot′ing) *n.* The act, practice, or pastime of sailing in or managing a yacht.

yachts·man (yots′mən) *n. pl.* **·men** (-mən) One who owns or sails a yacht.

---

add, āce, câre, pälm; end, ēven; it, īce; odd, ōpen, ôrder; tŏŏk, pōōl; up, bûrn; ə = a in above, u in focus; yōō = u in fuse; oil; pout; check; go; ring; thin; this; zh, vision. < derived from; ? origin uncertain or unknown.

ya·hoo (yä′hōō, yä′-) *n.* An awkward or crude person; a bumpkin. [<*Yahoo,* one of a race of brutes in Swift's *Gulliver's Travels,* 1726]

Yah·weh (yä′we) In the Old Testament, a name for God. Also **Yah·ve, Yah·veh** (yä′ve). [<Heb. *YHWH*]

yak[1] (yak) *n.* A large, shaggy wild ox of CEN. Asia, often domesticated. [<Tibetan *gyag*]

yak[2] (yak) *Slang v.i.* **yakked, yak·king** To talk or chatter a great deal. —*n.* **1** Persistent chatter or talk. **2** A boisterous laugh. **3** Something, as a joke, causing such a laugh. Also (for *v.* and *n.* def. 1) **yak·e·ty·yak** (yak′ə·tē·yak′). [Imit.] —**yak′ker** *n.*

Yak

yam (yam) *n.* **1** The fleshy, edible, tuberous root of any of a genus of climbing tropical plants. **2** Any of the plants growing this root. **3** A variety of sweet potato. [<Pg. *inhame* < a native w African name]

yam·mer (yam′ər) *v.i. Informal* **1** To complain peevishly; whine; whimper. **2** To howl; roar; shout. —*v.t.* **3** To utter in a complaining or peevish manner. —*n.* The act of yammering. [<OE *geōmrian* to lament]

yang (yang) *n.* In Chinese philosophy, the male principle and element of the universe, source of life and heat and, with yin, co-creator of everything that is. [<Chin.]

yank (yangk) *v.t. & v.i.* To jerk or pull suddenly. —*n.* A sudden sharp pull; jerk. [?]

Yank (yangk) *n. & adj. Informal* YANKEE.

Yan·kee (yang′kē) *n.* **1** A native or citizen of the U.S. **2** A native or inhabitant of the northern U.S. **3** A native or inhabitant of New England. —*adj.* Of, like, or characteristic of Yankees. [?] —**Yan′kee·dom, Yan′kee·ism** *n.*

Yankee Doo·dle (dōōd′l) A song popular in the U.S. from pre-Revolutionary times.

yap (yap) *v.i.* **yapped, yap·ping** **1** *Slang* To talk or jabber. **2** To bark or yelp, as a dog. —*n.* **1** A bark or yelp. **2** *Slang* Worthless talk; jabber. **3** *Slang* **a** A crude person. **b** The mouth. [Imit. of a dog's bark]

yard[1] (yärd) *n.* **1** A unit of length equal to 3 feet or 0.914 meter. **2** A long, slender spar set crosswise on a mast and used to support sails. [<OE *gierd* rod, yard measure]

yard[2] (yärd) *n.* **1** A plot of ground enclosed or set apart, as for some specific purpose: often in combination: *barnyard.* **2** The ground or lawn belonging and adjacent to a house, college, university, etc. **3** An enclosure used for building, selling, storing, etc.: often in combination: *shipyard; stockyard.* **4** An enclosure or piece of ground usu. adjacent to a railroad station, used for making up trains and for storage. —*v.t.* To put or collect into or as into a yard. [<OE *geard* an enclosure]

yard·age (yär′dij) *n.* The amount or length of something in yards.

yard·arm (yärd′ärm′) *n.* Either end of the yard of a square sail.

yard goods Fabric sold by the yard; piece goods.

yard·man (yärd′mən) *n. pl.* **·men** (-mən) A man employed in a yard, esp. in a railroad yard.

yard·mas·ter (yärd′mas′tər, -mäs′-) *n.* A railroad official having charge of a yard.

yard·stick (yärd′stik′) *n.* **1** A graduated measuring stick a yard in length. **2** Any measure or standard of comparison; criterion.

yar·mul·ke (yär′məl·kə) *n.* A skullcap traditionally worn by Jewish males in synagogues and often at school and in the home. Also **yar′mel·ke.** [Yiddish]

yarn (yärn) *n.* **1** Any spun fiber, as cotton, wool, or nylon, prepared for use in weaving, knitting, or crotcheting. **2** *Informal* A tale of adventure, often of doubtful truth. —*v.i. Informal* To tell a yarn or yarns. [<OE *gearn*]

yar·row (yar′ō) *n.* Any of a genus of perennial composite plants, esp. a common weed with finely divided, pungent leaves and clusters of small, usu. white flowers. [<OE *gearwe*]

yat·a·ghan (yat′ə·gan, -gən) *n.* A Turkish sword with a double-curved blade and without a handle guard. Also **yat′a·gan.**

Yataghan

yaw (yô) *v.i.* **1** To move wildly or out of its course, as a ship when struck by a heavy sea. **2** To deviate from a flight path by rotating about a vertical axis: said of spacecraft, projectiles, etc. —*v.t.* **3** To cause to yaw. —*n.* **1** The action of yawing. **2** The amount of deviation in yawing. [?]

yawl (yôl) *n.* **1** A small, fore-and-aft rigged, two-masted sailboat. **2** A ship's small boat; jollyboat. [? <Du *jol*]

yawn (yôn) *v.i.* **1** To open the mouth wide, usu. involuntarily, with a full inhalation, as the result of drowsiness, boredom, etc. **2** To stand wide open: A chasm *yawned* below. —*v.t.* **3** To express or utter with a yawn. —*n.* **1** An act of yawning. **2** A wide opening. [<OE *geonian*] —**yawn′er** *n.*

Yawl def. 1

yawp (yôp) *v.i.* **1** To bark or yelp. **2** *Informal* To talk or shout loudly. —*n.* The act or sound of yawping. [Imit.] —**yawp′er** *n.*

yaws (yôz) *n. pl.* A contagious tropical disease marked by skin lesions. [<Cariban *yáya*]

y-axis (wī′ak′sis) *n. Math.* A coordinate axis along which the variable *y* is plotted.

Yb ytterbium.

Y chromosome The smaller of the unmatched pair of sex chromosomes found in the male of humans and most animals.

y·clept (i·klept′) *adj. Archaic* Called; named. Also **y·cleped′.** [<OE *geclypod,* p.p. of *clypian* call]

yd. yard(s).

ye[1] (thē, yē) *definite article Archaic* The. [<an incorrect transliteration of the Old English thorn, properly transliterated as *th*]

ye[2] (yē) *pron. Archaic* The persons addressed; you. [<OE *gē*]

yea (yā) *adv.* **1** Yes: used in voting orally. **2** *Archaic* Not only so, but more so. **3** *Archaic* In reality; verily: a form of introduction in a sentence. —*n.* **1** An affirmative vote. **2** One who casts such a vote. [<OE *gēa*]

ye·ah (ye′ə) *adv. Informal* Yes.

yean (yēn) *v.t. & v.i.* To bring forth (young), as a goat or sheep. [<OE (assumed) *geēanian*]

yean·ling (yēn′ling) *n.* The young of a goat or sheep. —*adj.* Young; newly born.

year (yir) *n.* **1** The period of time in which the earth completes a revolution around the sun: about 365 days, 5 hours, 49 minutes, and, in the Gregorian calendar, divided into 12 months beginning January 1 and ending December 31. **2** Any period of 12 months. **3** The period of time during which a planet revolves around the sun. **4** Any part of a year devoted to some activity: the school *year.* **5** *pl.* Any extended or past period of time: the *years* before automobiles. **6** *pl.* Length or time of life; age: active for his *years.* [<OE *gēar*]

year·book (yir′bŏŏk′) *n.* A book published annually, usu. presenting information about the previous year.

year·ling (yir′ling) *n.* An animal between one and two years old. —*adj.* Being a year old.

year·long (yir′lông′, -long′) *adj.* Continuing through a year.

year·ly (yir′lē) *adj.* **1** Of a year. **2** Occurring once a year; annual. **3** Continuing for a year: a *yearly* subscription. —*adv.* Once a year; annually.

yearn (yûrn) *v.i.* **1** To desire something earnestly; long: with *for.* **2** To be deeply moved; feel sympathy. [<OE *giernan*] —**yearn′er** *n.* —**Syn.** **1** wish, want, covet, hunger, crave, pine for.

yearn·ing (yûr′ning) *n.* A strong emotion of longing or desire, esp. with tenderness.

year-round (yir′round′) *adj.* Continuing, operating, etc., throughout the entire year.

yeast (yēst) *n.* **1** Any of various single-celled fungi that produce ethyl alcohol and carbon dioxide in the process of fermenting carbohydrates. **2** A commercial preparation of certain yeasts, usu. in dry powdery form, used to leaven bread, make beer, etc. **3** Froth or spume. **4** Something causing mental or moral ferment. —*v.i.* To foam; froth. [<OE *gist*]

yeast·y (yēs'tē) *adj.* **yeast·i·er, yeast·i·est** **1** Of or resembling yeast. **2** Causing fermentation. **3** Restless; unsettled. **4** Covered with froth or foam. **5** Light or unsubstantial. —**yeast'i·ness** *n.*

yegg (yeg) *n. Slang* A burglar, esp. one who cracks safes. Also **yegg'man.** [?]

yell (yel) *v.t. & v.i.* **1** To shout; scream. **2** To cheer. —*n.* **1** A sharp, loud cry, as of pain, terror, etc. **2** A rhythmic shout by a group, as in cheering an athletic team. [< OE *giellan*] —**yell'er** *n.*

yel·low (yel'ō) *adj.* **1** Of the color yellow. **2** Changed to a sallow color by age, sickness, etc.: a paper *yellow* with age. **3** Having a yellowish or light brown complexion. **4** Cheaply or offensively sensational: said of newspapers: *yellow* journalism. **5** *Informal* Cowardly; mean; dishonorable. —*n.* **1** The color of ripe lemons or, in the spectrum, the color between green and orange. **2** Any pigment or dyestuff having such a color. **3** The yolk of an egg. —*v.t. & v.i.* To make or become yellow. [< OE *geolu*] —**yel'low·ly** *adv.* —**yel'low·ness** *n.*

yel·low·bird (yel'ō·bûrd') *n.* Any of various birds with yellow plumage, as the goldfinch.

yellow fever An acute tropical disease caused by a virus transmitted by a mosquito and characterized by jaundice and other symptoms.

yel·low·ham·mer (yel'ō·ham'ər) *n.* **1** A European bunting with bright yellow and black plumage. **2** The flicker or golden-winged woodpecker. [? < OE *geolo* yellow + *amore,* a kind of bird]

yel·low·ish (yel'ō·ish) *adj.* Somewhat yellow.

yellow jack 1 A yellow flag indicating quarantine. **2** YELLOW FEVER.

yellow jacket Any of various social wasps with bright yellow markings.

yellow peril The supposed threat to the West from the power of the peoples of E Asia.

yellow pine 1 Any of various American pines, as the loblolly. **2** Their tough, yellowish wood.

yel·low·wood (yel'ō·wŏŏd') *n.* Any of various trees having yellow or yellowish wood or yielding a yellow dye.

yel·low·y (yel'ō·ē) *adj.* Yellowish.

yelp (yelp) *v.i.* To utter a sharp or shrill cry. —*v.t.* To express by a yelp or yelps. —*n.* A sharp, shrill cry, as of a dog in distress. [< OE *gielpan* boast] —**yelp'er** *n.*

Yem·en Arab Republic (yem'ən) A country of SW Arabia, 75,000 sq. mi., cap. San'a. —**Yem·e·ni** (yem'ə·nē), **Yem'e·nite** (-nīt) *adj., n.*

Yemen, People's Democratic Republic of A republic on the S coast of Arabia, 110,000 sq. mi., cap. Madinat ash Sha'b. Also **Southern Yemen.** —**Yem'e·ni, Yem'e·nite** *adj., n.*

yen¹ (yen) *Informal n.* An ardent longing or desire. —*v.i.* **yenned, yen·ning** To yearn; long. [< Chin., opium]

yen² (yen) *n.* The basic monetary unit of Japan.

yen·ta (yen'tə) *n.* A female gossip or meddler. Also **yen'teh.** [Yiddish]

yeo·man (yō'mən) *n. pl.* **·men** (-mən) **1** A petty officer in the U.S. Navy or Coast Guard who performs clerical duties. **2** *Brit.* A farmer, esp. one who cultivates his own farm. **3** YEOMAN OF THE GUARD. **4** *Brit.* One of the attendants of a nobleman or of royalty. [? < OE *geong* young + *mann* a man]

yeo·man·ly (yō'mən·lē) *adj.* **1** Of or pertaining to a yeoman. **2** Brave; rugged. —*adv.* Like a yeoman; bravely.

Yeoman of the (Royal) Guard A member of the ceremonial bodyguard of the English royal household.

yeo·man·ry (yō'mən·rē) *n.* **1** Yeomen, as a group. **2** *Brit.* A home guard of volunteer cavalry, now part of the Territorial Army.

yeoman's service Faithful and useful support or service. Also **yeoman service.**

yep (yep) *adv. Informal* Yes.

yes (yes) *adv.* **1** As you say; truly; just so: a reply of affirmation or consent. **2** Moreover: She is willing, *yes* eager, to go. —*n. pl.* **yes·es** or **yes·ses** A reply in the affirmative. —*v.t. & v.i.* **yessed, yes·sing** To say "yes" (to). [< OE *gēa* yea + *sīe* it may be]

yes-man (yes'man') *n. pl.* **-men** (men') *Informal* A person who habitually agrees with the opinions or statements of others, esp. with those of his superiors.

yes·ter·day (yes'tər·dē, -dā') *n.* **1** The day preceding today. **2** The near past. —*adv.* **1** On the day last past. **2** At a recent time. [< OE *geostran* yesterday + *dæg* day]

yes·ter·year (yes'tər·yir') *n.* **1** Last year. **2** Recent years; recent past. **3** Time past; a past epoch: the peaceful days of *yesteryear.*

yet (yet) *adv.* **1** In addition; besides. **2** At some future time; eventually: he may *yet* succeed. **3** In continuance of a previous state or condition; still: I can hear him *yet.* **4** At the present time; now: Don't go *yet.* **5** After all the time that has or had elapsed: Are you not ready *yet?* **6** Up to the present time; heretofore: He has never *yet* lied to me. **7** Even: a *yet* hotter day. **8** Nevertheless: They are poor, *yet* happy. **9** As much as; even: He did not believe the reports, nor *yet* the evidence. —**as yet** Up to now. —*conj.* Nevertheless; but: I speak to you peaceably, *yet* you will not listen. [< OE *gīet*]

yew (yōō) *n.* **1** Any of a genus of evergreen trees and shrubs, with narrow, flat, dark green, poisonous leaves and red berrylike cones containing a single seed. **2** The hard, tough wood of the yew. [< OE *ēow, īw*]

Yid·dish (yid'ish) *n.* A language derived from 13th- and 14th-century Middle High German, now spoken primarily by Eastern European Jews and their relatives or descendants in other countries. It contains elements of Hebrew and the Slavic languages. —*adj.* Of, written, or spoken in Yiddish. [< G *jüdisch* Jewish]

yield (yēld) *v.t.* **1** To give forth by a natural process, or as a result of labor or cultivation: The field will *yield* a good crop. **2** To give in return, as for investment; furnish: The bonds *yield* five percent interest. **3** To give up, as to superior power; surrender; relinquish: often with *up:* to *yield* oneself up to one's enemies. **4** To give up one's possession of: to *yield* the right of way . —*v.i.* **5** To provide a return; produce; bear. **6** To give up; submit; surrender. **7** To give way, as to pressure or force. **8** To assent or comply, as under compulsion; consent: We *yielded* to their persuasion. **9** To give place, as through inferiority or weakness: with *to:* We will *yield* to them in nothing. —*n.* The amount yielded; product; result, as of cultivation, investment, etc. [< OE *gieldan* pay] —**yield'er** *n.*

yield·ing (yēl'ding) *adj.* **1** Productive. **2** Flexible; easily bent. **3** Obedient. —**yield'ing·ly** *adv.* —**yield'ing·ness** *n.*

yin (yin) *n.* In Chinese philosophy, the female principle and element of the universe, standing for darkness, cold, and death. [< Chin.]

yip (yip) *n.* A yelp, as of a dog. —*v.i.* **yipped, yip·ping** To yelp. [Imit.]

-yl *suffix Chem.* Used to denote a radical: *ethyl.* [< Gk. *hylē* wood, matter]

YMCA, Y.M.C.A. Young Men's Christian Association.

YMHA, Y.M.H.A. Young Men's Hebrew Association.

yock (yäk) *n. Slang* **1** A loud laugh or guffaw. **2** Something causing such a laugh. [Var. of YAK²]

yo·del (yōd'l) *v.t. & v.i.* **·deled** or **·delled, ·del·ing** or **·del·ling** To sing by changing the voice quickly from its low register to a falsetto and back. —*n.* Something yodeled, as a melody or refrain. Also **yo'dle.** [< G *jodeln,* lit., utter the syllable *jo*] —**yo'del·er, yo'del·ler, yo'dler** *n.*

yo·ga (yō'gə) *n.* **1** A Hindu mystical and ascetic discipline, the ultimate purpose of which is to gain spiritual illumination by means of a prescribed series of mental and physical exercises. **2** The exercises, esp. certain physical exercises, based on yoga techniques. [Skt., lit., union] —**yo'gic** (-gik) *adj.*

yo·gi (yō'gē) *n. pl.* **·gis** A person who practices yoga. Also **yo'gin** (-gən, -gin).

yo·gurt (yō′gərt) *n.* A semifluid food made of milk curdled with cultures of bacteria and sometimes flavored with fruit. Also **yo′ghurt.** [< Turk. *yōghurt*]

yoke (yōk) *n.* **1** A curved frame used for coupling draft animals, as oxen, usu. having a bow at each end to receive the neck of the animal. **2** Any of many similar contrivances, as a frame worn on the shoulder to balance pails of milk. **3** A pair of animals joined by a yoke. **4** Something that binds or connects; tie; bond: the *yoke* of marriage. **5** Any of various parts or pieces that connect or hold two things together. **6** Servitude; bondage. **7** A fitted part of a garment designed to support a plaited or gathered part, as at the hips or shoulders. —*v.* **yoked, yok·ing** *v.t.* **1** To attach by means of a yoke, as draft animals. **2** To join with or as with a yoke. —*v.i.* **3** To be joined or linked; unite. [< OE *geoc*]

Yoke *def. 1*

yoke·fel·low (yōk′fel′ō) *n.* A mate or companion, as in labor. Also **yoke′mate′** (-māt′).

yo·kel (yō′kəl) *n.* A country bumpkin. [?]

yolk (yōk, yōlk) *n.* **1** The yellow portion of an egg. **2** An oily exudation in unprocessed sheep's wool. [< OE *geolu* yellow] —**yolk′y** *adj.*

Yom Kip·pur (yom kip′ər, yōm, ki·pŏŏr′) The Jewish Day of Atonement, a holiday marked by prayer and fasting, celebrated in late September or in October.

yon (yon) *adj. & adv. Archaic & Regional* YONDER. [< OE *geon*]

yond (yond) *adj. & adv. Archaic & Regional* YONDER. [< OE *geond* across]

yon·der (yon′dər) *adj.* Being at a distance indicated or known. —*adv.* In that place; there. [< OE *geond, yond*]

yoo-hoo (yŏŏ′hŏŏ′) *interj.* A call used to attract the attention of someone.

yore (yôr, yōr) *n.* Time long past: in days of *yore*. [< OE *geara* formerly]

York (yôrk) *n.* A royal house of England that reigned from 1461–85.

York·shire pudding (york′shir, -shər) A batter pudding baked in meat drippings.

you (yŏŏ) *pron.* **1** The person or persons or the personified thing or things addressed: when used as a subject, always linked with a plural verb. **2** One; anyone: *You* learn by trying. [< OE *ēow,* dat. and acc. pl. of *ge* ye]

you'd (yŏŏd) Contraction of *you had* or *you would.*

you'll (yŏŏl) Contraction of *you will* or *you shall.*

young (yung) *adj.* **young·er** (yung′gər), **young·est** (yung′gist) **1** Being in the early period of life or growth; not old. **2** Not having progressed or developed far; newly formed: The day was *young*. **3** Pertaining to youth or early life. **4** Full of vigor or freshness. **5** Inexperienced; immature. **6** Denoting the younger of two persons having the same name or title; junior. **7** *Geol.* Having the characteristics of an early stage in the geological cycle: said of a river or of certain land forms. —*n.* **1** Young persons as a group. **2** Offspring, esp. of animals. —**with young** Pregnant. [< OE *geong*] —**young′ness** *n.* —**Syn. 4** lively, strong, active, spirited. **5** raw, green, unseasoned, uninitiated.

young·ber·ry (yung′ber′ē) *n. pl.* ·**ries** A dark red berry resulting from crossing a blackberry and a dewberry. [< B. M. *Young,* U.S. horticulturist of late 19th c.]

young blood 1 Young people. **2** New, fresh ideas, attitudes, etc.

young·ish (yung′ish) *adj.* Rather young.

young·ling (yung′ling) *n.* **1** A young person, animal, or plant. **2** An inexperienced person. —*adj.* Young. [< OE *geongling*]

young·ster (yung′stər) *n.* A young person, esp. a child.

Young Turk One of a group bent on seizing control of or radically altering an organization, as a political party. [Orig., a member of a 20th c. Turkish revolutionary party]

your (yôr, yŏŏr) *pronominal adj.* **1** Of, belonging to or pertaining to you: *your* fate. **2** Used before certain titles: *your* Majesty. [< OE *ēower,* genitive of *gē* ye]

you're (yŏŏr, yôr) Contraction of *you are.*

yours (yôrz, yŏŏrz) *pron. (construed as sing. or pl.)* The things or persons belonging or pertaining to you: a home as quiet as *yours*. —**of yours** Belonging or relating to you. [ME *youres*]

your·self (yôr·self′, yŏŏr-) *pron. pl.* ·**selves** (-selvz′) **1** The one who is you: used as a reflexive or emphatic form: Try not to hurt *yourself*. **2** Your normal, healthy, etc., condition: You are not *yourself* today. **3** ONESELF: It's best to take care of it *yourself*.

youth (yŏŏth) *n. pl.* **youths** (yŏŏths, yŏŏthz) **1** The state or condition of being young. **2** The period when one is young; that part of life between childhood and adulthood. **3** The early period of being or development, as of a movement. **4** A young person, esp. a young man. **5** Young people as a group: the nation's *youth*. [< OE *geoguth*]

youth·ful (yŏŏth′fəl) *adj.* **1** Of, pertaining to, or characteristic of youth. **2** Buoyant; fresh; vigorous. **3** Having youth; being still young. **4** Not far advanced; early; new. **5** *Geol.* Young. —**youth′ful·ly** *adv.* —**youth′ful·ness** *n.*

you've (yŏŏv) Contraction of *you have.*

yowl (youl) *v.i.* To howl; yell. —*n.* A loud, prolonged, wailing cry; a howl. [ME *youlen*]

yo-yo (yō′yō′) *n. pl.* ·**yos** A wheellike toy with a deep central groove around which is looped a string on which the wheel can be spun in a variety of movements. [?]

yr. year(s); younger; your.

yrs. years; yours.

Y.T. Yukon Territory.

yt·ter·bi·um (i·tûr′bē·əm) *n.* A rare metallic element (symbol Yb) of the lanthanide series. [< *Ytterby,* Sweden] —**yt·ter′bic** *adj.*

yt·tri·um (it′rē·əm) *n.* A rare metallic element (symbol Y) similar to and usu. found with ytterbium. [< *Ytterby,* Sweden]

yuc·ca (yuk′ə) *n.* **1** Any of a large genus of liliaceous American plants usu. found in dry, sandy places, having a woody stem which bears a large panicle of white flowers emerging from a crown of sword-shaped leaves. **2** The flower of this plant. [< Sp. *yuca* < Taino]

Yucca

yuck (yuk) *n. Slang* **1** A loud laugh or guffaw. **2** Something causing such a laugh. —*v.i.* To laugh uproariously. [Imit.]

Yu·go·slav (yŏŏ′gō·släv′) *adj.* Of Yugoslavia or its people: also **Yu′go·slav′ic.** —*n.* A native or citizen of Yugoslavia.

Yu·go·sla·vi·a (yŏŏ′gō·slä′vē·ə) *n.* A republic of SE Europe, 98,538 sq. mi., cap. Belgrade. —**Yu′go·sla′vi·an** *adj., n.* • See map at BALKAN STATES.

yuk (yuk) *Slang n. & v.i.* **yukked, yuk·king** YUCK.

Yule (yŏŏl) *n.* Christmas or Christmas time. [< OE *geōl*]

yule log Formerly, a large log, placed on the hearth as the foundation of the traditional Christmas Eve fire.

Yule·tide (yŏŏl′tīd′) *n.* Christmas time.

yum·my (yum′ē) *Informal adj.* ·**mi·er,** ·**mi·est** Agreeable to the senses, esp. to the taste; delicious. —*n.* Something delicious. [Imit. of the sound made when something is pleasurable to the taste]

YWCA, Y.W.C.A. Young Women's Christian Association.

YWHA, Y.W.H.A. Young Women's Hebrew Association.

Z

Z, z (zē, *Brit. & Can.* zed) *n. pl.* **Z's, z's, Zs, zs** (zēz, zedz) **1** The 26th letter of the English alphabet. **2** Any spoken sound representing the letter *Z* or *z*. **3** Something shaped like a Z. —*adj.* Shaped like a Z.

Z., z. zero; zone.

zai·bat·su (zī′bat·sōō′) *n. pl.* **zai·bat·su** The wealthy clique of Japan, representing four or five dominant families. [< Jap. *zai* property + *batsu* family]

Zaire (zīr′, zä·ir′) *n.* A republic of CEN. Africa, 904,754 sq. mi., cap. Kinshasa. • See map at AFRICA.

Zam·bi·a (zam′bē·ə) *n.* An independent member of the Commonwealth of Nations in CEN. Africa, 288,130 sq. mi., cap. Lusaka. • See map at AFRICA.

za·ny (zā′nē) *adj.* **·ni·er, ·ni·est** Absurdly funny; ludicrous. —*n. pl.* **·nies 1** In old comic plays, a clown who absurdly mimics the other performers. **2** Any ludicrous comic or buffoon. **3** A simpleton; fool. [< Ital. *zanni*] —**za′ni·ly** *adv.* —**za′ni·ness** *n.*

zap (zap) *Slang v.t.* **zapped, zap·ping 1** To kill. **2** To attack; hit; clobber. **3** To confront or impress suddenly and forcefully; astound; overwhelm. —*n.* **1** Vigorous effect; punch; vitality. **2** An attack or confrontation.

zeal (zēl) *n.* Ardor, as for a cause; fervor. [< Gk. *zēlos*] —**Syn.** enthusiasm, eagerness, devotion, passion, verve, spirit, heart.

zeal·ot (zel′ət) *n.* One who is zealous, esp. to an immoderate degree; partisan, fanatic, etc. —**zeal′ot·ry** *n.*

zeal·ous (zel′əs) *adj.* Filled with, marked by, or showing zeal; enthusiastic. —**zeal′ous·ly** *adv.* —**zeal′ous·ness** *n.*

ze·bec (zē′bek) *n.* XEBEC. Also **ze′beck.**

ze·bra (zē′brə, *Brit. & Can.* zeb′rə) *n.* Any of various African ponylike mammals having a whitish body with dark stripes. [Pg.] —**ze′brine** (-brēn, -brin), **ze′·broid** (-broid) *adj.*

ze·bu (zē′byōō) *n.* Any of various breeds of domesticated oxen of Asia and Africa, having a hump on the withers, a large dewlap, and short curved horns. [< Tibetan]

Zebra

Zech. Zechariah.

zed (zed) *n. Brit. & Can.* The letter *z.* [< Gk. *zēta*]

zeit·geist (tsīt′gīst) *n. Often cap.* The intellectual, moral, and cultural tendencies that characterize any age or epoch. [< G < *Zeit* time + *Geist* spirit]

Zen (zen) *n.* A form of Buddhism that originated in China and became widespread in Japan, that lays particular stress on deep meditation as a means of achieving an abrupt, intuitive, spiritual enlightenment. [< Jap. *zen* meditation]

Zend (zend) *n.* The ancient translation of and commentary on the Avesta. [< Pers., interpretation] —**Zend′ic** *adj.*

Zend-A·ves·ta (zend′ə·ves′tə) *n.* The sacred Zoroastrian writings including the Zend and the Avesta.

ze·nith (zē′nith) *n.* **1** The point of the celestial sphere that is exactly overhead. **2** The highest or culminating point; summit; acme. [< Ar. *samt (ar-rās)* the path (over the head)]

Zeph. Zephaniah.

zeph·yr (zef′ər) *n.* **1** The west wind. **2** Any soft, gentle wind. **3** Worsted or woolen yarn of very light weight: also **zephyr worsted.** [< Gk. *zephyros*]

zep·pe·lin (zep′ə·lin) *n.* A large, cigar-shaped dirigible. [< Count Ferdinand von *Zeppelin,* 1838–1917, German aircraft builder]

ze·ro (zir′ō, zē′rō) *n. pl.* **ze·ros** or **ze·roes 1** The numeral or symbol 0; a cipher. **2** *Math.* The element of a number system that leaves any element unchanged under addition, esp. a real number *0* such that $a + 0 = 0 + a = a$ for any real number *a.* **3** The point on a scale, as of a thermometer, from which measures are counted. **4** The temperature registered at the zero mark on a thermometer. **5** Nothing. **6** The lowest point: *Our hopes dropped to zero.* —*v.t.* **ze·roed, ze·ro·ing** To adjust (instruments) to an arbitrary zero point for synchronized readings. —**zero in 1** To move or bring into a desired position, as an airplane. **2** To adjust the sight of (a gun) or direct (ammunition) toward (a target). —**zero in on 1** To direct gunfire, bombs, etc. toward (a specific target). **2** To concentrate or focus one's energy, attention, efforts, etc., on. —*adj.* **1** Of, at, or being zero. **2** That limits vertical visibility to 50 feet or less: said of a cloud ceiling. **3** That limits horizontal visibility to 165 feet or less: said of conditions on the ground. [< Ar. *ṣifr*] • In popular usage the symbol for zero (0) is often rendered orally as (ō), as if it were the letter O.

zero hour 1 The time set for an attack. **2** Any critical moment.

zest (zest) *n.* **1** Agreeable excitement and keen enjoyment. **2** A quality that imparts such excitement. **3** Any piquant flavoring. [< F *zeste* lemon or orange peel] —**zest′·ful, zest′y** *adj.* (**·i·er, ·i·est**) —**zest′ful·ly** *adv.* —**zest′ful·ness** *n.* —**Syn. 1** delight, gusto, relish, pleasure, gratification, savor, thrill, kick.

ze·ta (zā′tə, zē′-) *n.* The sixth letter of the Greek alphabet. (Z, ζ).

Zeus (zōōs) *Gk. Myth.* The supreme deity.

zig·gu·rat (zig′ŏŏ·rat) *n.* Among the Assyrians and Babylonians, a terraced temple tower pyramidal in form, each successive story being smaller than the one below. [< Assyrian *ziqquratu,* orig., a mountain top]

Ziggurat

zig·zag (zig′zag) *n.* **1** One of a series of sharp turns or angles. **2** A path or pattern characterized by such turns or angles going from side to side. —*adj.* Having a series of zigzags. —*adv.* In a zigzag manner. —*v.t. & v.i.* **·zagged, ·zag·ging** To move in zigzags. [< G *zickzack*]

zilch (zilch) *n. Slang* Nothing; zero. [Alter. of ZERO]

zil·lion (zil′yən) *n. Informal* A very large, indeterminate number: *a zillion things to do before the plane left.* [Imit. of *million, trillion,* etc.] —**zil′lionth** *adj.*

zinc (zingk) *n.* A bluish white metallic element (symbol Zn) occurring mostly in combination, extensively used in alloys, as bronze and brass, for galvanizing, and in electric batteries. —*v.t.* **zinced** or **zincked, zinc·ing** or **zinck·ing** To coat or cover with zinc; galvanize. [< G *zink*] —**zinc′ic** (-ik), **zinc′ous** (-əs), **zinck′y, zinc′y, zink′y** *adj.*

zinc ointment A medicated ointment containing zinc oxide.

zinc oxide A white powdery compound, used as a pigment and as a mild antiseptic.

zinc white Zinc oxide used as a pigment.

zing (zing) *Informal n.* **1** A high-pitched buzzing or humming sound. **2** Energy; vitality. —*v.i.* To make a shrill, humming sound.

zin·ni·a (zin′ē·ə, zin′yə) *n.* Any of various cultivated plants having opposite entire leaves and showy, composite flowers. [< J. G. *Zinn,* 1727–59, German botanist]

Zi·on (zī′ən) *n.* **1** A hill in Jerusalem, the site of the Temple of David and his successors. **2** The Jewish people. **3** Any place or community considered to be especially under God's rule, as ancient Israel. **4** The heavenly Jerusalem; heaven. [< Heb. *tsīyōn* a hill]

---

add, āce, câre, pălm; end, ēven; it, īce; odd, ōpen, ôrder; tŏŏk, pōōl; up, bûrn; ə = *a* in *above, u* in *focus;* yōō = *u* in *fuse;* oil; pout; check; go; ring; thin; this; zh, *vision.* < derived from; ? origin uncertain or unknown.

Zi·on·ism (zī′ən·iz′əm) *n.* A movement for a resettlement of the Jews in Palestine. —**Zi′on·ist** *adj. & n.*

zip (zip) *n.* **1** A sharp, hissing sound, as of a bullet passing through the air. **2** *Informal* Energy; vitality; vim. —*v.* **zipped, zip·ping** *v.t.* **1** To fasten with a zipper: often with *up*: to *zip* up a jacket. **2** To give speed and energy to. —*v.i.* **3** *Informal* To move or act with speed and energy. **4** To move with a sharp, hissing sound. [Imit.]

zip-code (zip′kōd′) *v.t.* **-cod·ed, -cod·ing** *Sometimes cap.* To provide (mail) with a zip code.

zip code (zip) A numerical code devised to identify each postal delivery area in the U.S. Also **ZIP Code, Zip Code.** [< *z(one) i(mprovement) p(lan)*]

zip·per (zip′ər) *n.* A sliding fastener with two rows of interlocking teeth. [< *Zipper*, a trade name]

zip·py (zip′ē) *adj.* **·pi·er, ·pi·est** *Informal* Brisk; energetic.

zir·con (zûr′kon) *n.* **1** An adamantine, variously colored zirconium silicate, used as a gem in certain varieties. **2** A variety of this mineral having an artificially produced lustrous blue appearance. [< Ar. *zarqūn* cinnabar < Pers. *zargūn* golden]

zir·co·ni·um (zûr·kō′nē·əm) *n.* A metallic element (symbol Zr), used in heat-resistant alloys. [< ZIRCON] —**zir·con′·ic** *adj.*

zith·er (zith′ər, zith′-) *n.* A stringed instrument having a flat sounding board and 30 to 40 strings that are played by plucking. Also **zith′ern** (-ərn). [< Gk. *ki-thara*]

zlo·ty (zlô′tē) *n. pl.* **·tys** or **·ty** The basic monetary unit of Poland.

Zn zinc.

zo·di·ac (zō′dē·ak) *n.* **1** An imaginary belt encircling the heavens and extending about 8° on each side of the ecliptic, within which are the orbits of the moon, sun, and larger planets. It is divided into twelve parts, called **signs of the zodiac,** which formerly corre-

Zither

Signs of the zodiac (reading clockwise):
A. Vernal equinox: Aries, Taurus, Gemini.
B. Summer solstice: Cancer, Leo, Virgo.
C. Autumnal equinox: Libra, Scorpio, Sagittarius.
D. Winter solstice: Capricorn, Aquarius, Pisces.

sponded to twelve constellations. **2** Any complete circuit; round. [< Gk. *(kyklos) zōdiakos* (circle) of animals] —**zo·di·a·cal** (zō·dī′ə·kəl) *adj.*

zom·bie (zom′bē) *n.* **1** In voodoo cults, a snake deity. **2** The supernatural power by which a dead body is believed to be reanimated. **3** A corpse reactivated by such power. **4** *Slang* A person who looks weird or behaves eccentrically, mechanically, etc. **5** A strong cocktail made of several kinds of rum, fruit juices, and liqueurs. Also, esp. for defs. 1, 2, & 3, **zom′bi.** [< West African]

zo·nal (zō′nəl) *adj.* Of, pertaining to, exhibiting, or marked by a zone or zones; having the form of a zone. Also **zo′na·ry** (-nər·ē). —**zon′al·ly** *adv.*

zone (zōn) *n.* **1** One of five divisions of the earth's surface, bounded by parallels of latitude and named for the prevailing climate. These are the **torrid zone,** extending on each side of the equator 23° 27′; the **temperate** or **varia-ble zones,** included between the parallels 23° 27′ and 66° 33′ on both sides of the equator; and the **frigid zones,** within the parallels 66° 33′ and the poles. **2** *Ecol.* A belt or area delimited from others by the charac-

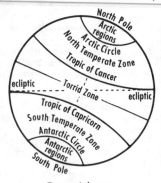

Terrestrial zones

ter of its plant or animal life, its climate, geological formations, etc. **3** A region, area, belt, etc., distinguished or set off by some special characteristic: a demilitarized *zone;* a residential *zone;* a no-parking *zone.* **4** An area, usu. circular, within which a uniform rate is charged for delivery of goods, telephone calls, etc. **5** In the U.S. postal system: **a** Any of the areas within which a uniform rate is charged for parcel post. **b** Any of the numbered postal districts in a city. **6** *Geom.* A portion of the surface of a sphere enclosed between two parallel planes. —*v.t.* **zoned, zon·ing 1** To divide into zones; esp., to divide (a city, etc.) into zones which are restricted as to types of construction and activity, as residential, industrial, etc. **2** To encircle with a zone or belt. **3** To mark with or as with zones or stripes. [< Gk. *zōnē* a girdle] —**zoned** *adj.*

zonk (zongk) *v.t. Slang* To hit, esp. on the head; clobber; brain.

zonked (zongkt) *adj. Slang* Highly intoxicated or stimulated, as by alcohol or a drug: often with *out.* [?]

zoo (zōō) *n. pl.* **zoos** A park or place where wild animals are kept for exhibition. [Short for *zoological garden*]

zoo- *combining form* Animal: *zoology*. [< Gk. *zōion* an animal]

zo·o·ge·o·graph·ic (zō′ə·jē′ə·graf′ik) *adj.* Of, pertaining to, or engaged in zoogeography. Also **zo′o·ge·o·graph′·i·cal.** —**zo′o·ge·o·graph′i·cal·ly** *adv.*

zo·o·ge·og·ra·phy (zō′ə·jē·og′rə·fē) *n.* **1** The systematic study of the distribution of animals and of the factors controlling it. **2** The study of the relations between special animal groups and the land or aquatic areas in which they predominate. —**zo′o·ge·og′ra·pher** *n.*

zo·og·ra·phy (zō·og′rə·fē) *n.* The branch of zoology that describes animals; descriptive zoology. —**zo·og′ra·pher** or **·phist** *n.* —**zo·o·graph·ic** (zō′ə·graf′ik) or **·i·cal** *adj.*

zo·oid (zō′oid) *n.* **1** An entity, usu. very small, capable of movement and independent existence, as a spermatozoon. **2** An individual member of a compound organism, as in a sponge. —*adj.* Having essentially the nature of an animal: also **zo·oi·dal** (zō·oid′l). [< zo(o)- + -OID]

zool. zoological; zoologist; zoology.

zo·o·log·i·cal (zō′ə·loj′i·kəl) *adj.* **1** Of, pertaining to, or occupied with zoology. **2** Relating to or characteristic of animals. Also **zo′o·log′ic.** —**zo′o·log′i·cal·ly** *adv.*

zoological garden zoo.

zo·ol·o·gy (zō·ol′ə·jē) *n.* **1** The science that treats of animals with reference to their structure, functions, development, nomenclature, and classification. **2** The animal life of a particular area. **3** A scientific treatise on animals. [< zoo- + -LOGY] —**zo·ol′o·gist** *n.*

zoom (zōōm) *v.i.* **1** To make a low-pitched but loud humming or buzzing sound, esp. when related to speed: The cars *zoomed* down the road. **2** To climb sharply upward, as an airplane. **3** To rise sharply, as prices. **4** To move a motion picture or TV camera rapidly or adjust the focus, as with a zoom lens, to make an image appear to come very close or become more distant: often with *in* or *out*. —*v.t.* **5** To cause to zoom. —*n.* The act of zooming. [Imit.]

zoom lens *Photog.* A lens, used chiefly on television and motion picture cameras, that permits the size of the image to be varied continuously without loss of focus.

zo·o·phyte (zō′ə-fīt) *n.* An invertebrate animal resembling a plant, as a coral or sea anemone. [< zoo- + Gk. *phyton* plant] —**zo′o·phyt′ic** (-fīt′ik) or **·i·cal** *adj.*

zo·o·spore (zō′ə-spôr, -spōr) *n.* A motile, asexual spore of certain fungi and algae, usu. provided with cilia. [< zoo- + spore] —**zo′o·spor′ic** (-spôr′ik, -spor′ik), **zo·os·po·rous** (zō-os′pər-əs) *adj.*

zo·ri (zō′rē) *n.* A flat, thonged sandal of straw or rubber. [< Japanese]

Zo·ro·as·tri·an·ism (zō′rō-as′trē-ən-iz′əm) *n.* The religious system founded in ancient Persia by Zoroaster. It recognizes two creative powers, one good and the other evil, and teaches the final triumph of good over evil.

Zou·ave (zoō-äv′, zwäv) *n.* **1** A member of a unit of the French infantry wearing a brilliant Oriental uniform. **2** A member of any volunteer regiment wearing a similar uniform. [< Ar. *Zouaoua*, a tribal name]

zounds (zoundz) *interj.* An exclamation denoting astonishment. [Short for *God's wounds*]

Zr zirconium.

zuc·chet·to (tsoōk·ket′tō) *n. pl.* **·tos** A skullcap worn by ecclesiastics in the Roman Catholic Church, black for a priest, purple for a bishop, red for a cardinal, white for the pope. [Ital. < *zucchetta*, orig. a small gourd]

zuc·chi·ni (zoō-kē′nē) *n.* An elongated summer squash having a thin green skin. [< Ital. *zucca* a gourd, squash]

Zu·lu (zoō′loō) *n. pl.* **Zu·lus** or **Zu·lu 1** A member of a Bantu nation of SE Africa. **2** The Bantu language of the Zulus. — *adj.* Of the Zulus or their language.

Zu·ñi (zoō′nyē) *n. pl.* **·ñi** or **·ñis 1** A member of a tribe of North American Indians, now living in New Mexico. **2** The language of this tribe.

zwie·back (zwī′bak, zwē′-, swī′-, swē′-, -bäk) *n.* A wheaten bread baked in a loaf and later sliced and toasted. [G, twice baked]

Zwing·li·an (zwing′lē-ən, tsving′-) *adj.* Of or pertaining to Huldreich Zwingli or his doctrines, esp. the doctrine that the Eucharist is simply a symbolic commemoration of the death of Christ. —*n.* A follower of Zwingli. —**Zwing′·li·an·ism** *n.*

zy·gote (zī′gōt, zig′ōt) *n.* **1** The product of the union of two gametes. **2** An individual developing from such a union. [< Gk *zygon* a yoke] —**zy·got·ic** (zī-got′ik) *adj.*

zy·mase (zī′mās) *n.* A mixture of enzymes that promotes fermentation by breaking down glucose and related carbohydrates into alcohol and carbon dioxide. [< Gk. *zymē* leaven]

zy·mol·o·gy (zī-mol′ə-jē) *n.* The science of fermentation. [< Gk. *zymē* leaven + -logy] —**zy·mo·log·ic** (zī′mə-loj′ik) or **·i·cal** *adj.* —**zy·mol′o·gist** *n.*

zy·mot·ic (zī-mot′ik) *adj.* Of, pertaining to, or caused by fermentation. [< Gk. *zymōtikos*]

zy·mur·gy (zī′mûr·jē) *n.* The chemistry of fermentation as applied to brewing, making of yeast, and wine making. [< Gk *zymē* leaven + -urgy]

---

add, āce, câre, pälm; end, ēven; it, īce; odd, ōpen, ôrder; toŏk, poōl; up, bûrn; ə = a in *above,* u in *focus;* yoō = u in *fuse;* oil; pout; check; go; ring; thin; this; zh, *vision.* < derived from; ? origin uncertain or unknown.

Special Signs and Symbols

ASTRONOMY

ASTRONOMICAL BODIES

⊙   1. the sun   2. Sunday
☿   1. Mercury   2. Wednesday
♀   1. Venus   2. Friday
⊕, ♁, ⊖   the earth
☾, ☽, 🌕   1. the moon   2. Monday
○, 🌕   full moon
☽, 🌕, ☽, ☽, ☽   the moon, first quarter
☾, 🌑, ☾, ☾, ☾   the moon, last quarter
●   new moon
♂   1. Mars   2. Tuesday
①, ②, ③, etc.   asteroids: in order of discovery, as ① Ceres, ② Pallas, etc.
♃   1. Jupiter   2. Thursday
♄   1. Saturn   2. Saturday
♅, ♅, ♅   Uranus
♆   Neptune
♇, P   Pluto
☄   comet
✳, ✶   star; fixed star
α, β, γ, etc.   stars (of a constellation): in order of brightness, the Greek letter followed by the Latin genitive of the name of the constellation, as α Centauri

POSITION AND NOTATION

☌   in conjunction; having the same longitude or right ascension
✶   sextile; 60° apart in longitude or right ascension
☐   quadrature; 90° apart in longitude or right ascension
△   trine; 120° apart in longitude or right ascension
☍   opposition; 180° apart in longitude or right ascension
☊   ascending node
☋   descending node
♈   vernal equinox
♎   autumnal equinox
α   right ascension
β   celestial latitude
δ   declination
λ   celestial or geographical longitude
Δ   distance
θ   sidereal time
a   mean distance
υ, ☊   longitude of ascending node
φ   1. angle of eccentricity   2. geographical latitude

SIGNS OF THE ZODIAC

♈   Aries, the Ram
♉   Taurus, the Bull   } Spring Signs
♊, Ⅱ   Gemini, the Twins

♋, ♋   Cancer, the Crab
♌   Leo, the Lion   } Summer Signs
♍   Virgo, the Virgin

♎   Libra, the Balance
♏   Scorpio, the Scorpion   } Autumn Signs
♐, ♐   Sagittarius, the Archer

♑, ♑   Capricorn, the Goat
♒   Aquarius, the Water Bearer   } Winter Signs
♓, ♓   Pisces, the Fishes

BIOLOGY

○, ⊙, ①   annual plant
⊙, ⊙, ♂   biennial plant
♃   perennial herb
△   evergreen plant
⊙   monocarpic plant
|w   plant useful to wildlife
♂, ♂   1. male organism or cell   2. staminate plant or flower
♀   1. female organism or cell   2. pistillate plant or flower
☿   hermaphroditic or perfect plant or flower
♀   neuter organism or cell
○   individual organism, especially female
☐   individual organism, especially male
∞   indefinite number
P   parental generation
F   filial generation
F_1, F_2, F_3, etc.   first, second, third, etc., filial generation

BOOKS

f°	folio
4mo, 4°	quarto
8vo, 8°	octavo
12mo, 12°	duodecimo
18mo, 18°	octodecimo
32mo, 32°	thirty-twomo

CHEMISTRY

ELEMENTS
See table of ELEMENTS.

CHEMISTRY

COMPOUNDS

Compounds are represented by the symbols for their constituent elements, each element followed by a subscript numeral if the number of atoms of it appearing in the compound is greater than one, as $NaCl$, H_2O, H_2SO_4, etc. If a radical appears more than once in a compound, the radical is enclosed in parentheses followed by a subscript numeral, as $Ca(OCl)_2$, $Al_2(SO_4)_3$, etc. Molecules consisting entirely of one element are represented by the symbol for the element followed by a subscript numeral indicating the number of atoms in the molecule, as H_2, O_2, O_3, etc. In addition: · denotes water of crystallization or hydration, as $CaSO_4 \cdot 5H_2O$.

α, β, γ, etc., *or* 1, 2, 3, etc. (in names of compounds), indicate different positions of substituted atoms or radicals.

$+$ denotes dextrorotation, as $+\,120°$.

$-$ denotes levorotation, as $-\,113°$.

[] include parentheses if one radical contains another, as $Fe_3[Fe(CN)_6]_2$.

In structural formulas:

$-$, $=$, $\equiv$, etc., *or* ., :, ⫶, etc., denotes a single, double, or triple bond, etc.

R— denotes any alkyl radical.

⬡ *or* ⬡ denotes a benzene ring.

IONS

Ions are represented by the symbols for their respective elements or by the symbols for the elements composing them, followed by a superscript symbol indicating the electric charge, as H^+, Cl^-, SO_4^{--}, etc. Thus:

$-$, $--$, $---$, etc., *or* $^{-1}$, $^{-2}$, $^{-3}$, etc., denote a single, double, triple, etc., negative charge.

$+$, $++$, $+++$, etc., *or* $^{+1}$, $^{+2}$, $^{+3}$, etc., denote a single, double, triple, etc., positive charge.

′, ″, ‴, etc., denote single, double, triple, etc., valence or charge (especially negative), as S''.

CHEMICAL REACTIONS

Chemical reactions are written in a form resembling equations, with reactants on the left and products on the right. If more than one equivalent of a compound appears, it is preceded by a coefficient. Conditions of temperature, pressure, catalysis, etc., are indicated above the arrow that shows direction. The following symbols are used:

→ *or* ← denotes "yields"; also indicates the direction of the reaction.

⇌ indicates a reversible reaction.

$+$ denotes "added to; together with."

↓ (written after a compound) denotes appearance as a precipitate.

↑ (written after a compound) denotes appearance as a gas.

$\triangle$ denotes the presence of heat.

$=$ *or* $\rightleftharpoons$ denotes equivalence of amounts in a quantitative equation.

COMMERCE AND FINANCE

@ 1. at: peaches @ $.39 per pound
   2. to: nails per pound $.50 @ $.60

$, $ dollar(s); peso(s): $100

¢ cent(s): 37¢

₱ peso(s) (Philippines)

/ shilling(s) (British): 3/

£ pound(s): £25

d penny, pence (British): 4d

¥, Y yen

R̄, R rupee(s)

Rs rupees

℗ per: 50¢ ℗ dozen

number: #60 thread

MATHEMATICS

$+$ plus (sign of addition); positive

$-$ minus (sign of subtraction); negative

$\pm$ plus or minus

$\times$ times, multiplied by (multiplication sign)

· multiplied by

$\div$ divided by (sign of division)

$\frac{2}{3}$ or $\tfrac{2}{3}$ divided by (2 divided by 3)

: is to, divided by (ratio sign)

:: equals, as (in proportion)

$<$ less than

$>$ greater than

$=$ equals

$\equiv$ identical with

$\sim$ similar to

$\cong$ congruent, equals approximately

$\leqq$ equal to or less than

$\geqq$ equal to or greater than

$\neq$ or $\neq$ not equal to

α varies directly as

∞ infinity

$\sqrt{}$ square root of

$\sqrt[n]{}$ nth root of

$\therefore$ therefore

$\parallel$ parallel to

$\perp$ perpendicular to

π pi, ratio of circumference of circle to diameter (3.14159+)

° degrees

′ minutes

″ seconds

$\angle$ angle

dx differential of x

$\triangle x$ (delta) increment of x

$\int$ integral of

Σ (sigma) summation of

$f(x), F(x), \phi(x)$ function of x

8! or $\underline{8}$ factorial 8

MISCELLANEOUS

&', & and　See AMPERSAND.
&c　et cetera
7ber, 8ber, etc.　September, October, etc.
† 　 died
% 　 percent
✕ 　 by: used in expressing dimensions, as a sheet of paper 8½″ ✕ 11″
© 　 copyright; copyrighted
♠ 　 spade
♥ 　 heart
♦ 　 diamond
♣ 　 club

MUSIC

Music is generally written on one or more staves. The pitch of each staff is indicated by a clef. The forms of the various notes and their corresponding rests indicate relative duration. In addition the following are used:

♭ 　 flat
♯ 　 sharp
♭♭ 　 double flat
✕ 　 double sharp
♮ 　 natural
C 　 common time; 4/4 meter
₵ 　 alla breve; 2/2 or 4/2 meter
~ 　 turn
~ 　 inverted turn
~ 　 mordent
~ 　 inverted mordent
>, <, ∧　accent
· ' 　 staccato
— 　 tenuto
tr 　 trill

⌢, ⌣　slur or tie
' 　 phrase or breath mark
♪ 　 grace note
< 　 crescendo
> 　 diminuendo; decrescendo
⊓ 　 down-bow
V 　 up-bow
8va 　 all' ottava; at the octave (raises the pitch of a staff one octave when written above it, lowers it when written below)
⌢, ⌣　hold

PHYSICS

α 　 alpha particle
β 　 beta particle
c 　 velocity of light
g 　 acceleration due to gravity
h 　 Planck's constant
λ 　 wavelength
v 　 frequency
j 　 square root of minus one
∿ 　 cycles (of alternating current or voltage)

RELIGION

✠, +　1. a sign of the cross used by bishops before their names 2. in some service books, an indication that the sign of the cross is to be made
* 　 in some service books, a mark used to divide psalm verses into two parts
℟ 　 response
℣, V', V,　versicle
☧, ☧, ☧　a monogram for Christ [Gk. Χρ(ιστὸς)]

Gazetteer

This section lists all of the more important political divisions and geographical features of the world, and all the urban localities in the United States and Canada having a population of 15,000 or more. The population figures given for places in the United States are from the census of 1980; those for Canada are from the census of 1976. All other population figures are rounded to the nearest thousand. Maps of virtually all countries and of other important geographical features may be found in the main section of this dictionary at the appropriate alphabetic place of entry.

Postal ZIP codes are included for places in the United States. These were not, however, available in all cases. The asterisk (*) following some ZIP codes indicates that the city is further divided into postal zones and that the number given does not adequately identify a post office. In such cases further information is available from local postal authorities.

In the table below the authorized post office abbreviations of U.S. states are listed.

Alabama	AL	Kentucky	KY	Ohio	OH
Alaska	AK	Louisiana	LA	Oklahoma	OK
Arizona	AZ	Maine	ME	Oregon	OR
Arkansas	AR	Maryland	MD	Pennsylvania	PA
California	CA	Massachusetts	MA	Puerto Rico	PR
Colorado	CO	Michigan	MI	Rhode Island	RI
Connecticut	CT	Minnesota	MN	South Carolina	SC
Delaware	DE	Mississippi	MS	South Dakota	SD
District of		Missouri	MO	Tennessee	TN
Columbia	DC	Montana	MT	Texas	TX
Florida	FL	Nebraska	NE	Utah	UT
Georgia	GA	Nevada	NV	Vermont	VT
Hawaii	HI	New Hampshire	NH	Virginia	VA
Idaho	ID	New Jersey	NJ	Virgin Islands	VI
Illinois	IL	New Mexico	NM	Washington	WA
Indiana	IN	New York	NY	West Virginia	WV
Iowa	IA	North Carolina	NC	Wisconsin	WI
Kansas	KS	North Dakota	ND	Wyoming	WY

The following abbreviations have been used throughout this section:

ab.	about	pop.	population
adm.	administrative	poss.	possession
ASSR	Autonomous Soviet	prot.	protectorate
	Socialist Republic	prov.	province
betw.	between	reg.	region
boro.	borough	RSFSR	Russian Soviet
cap(s).	capital(s)		Federated Social-
CEN.	central		ist Republic
co.	county	S	south(ern)
col.	colony	SE	southeast(ern)
ctr.	center	sq. mi.	square mile(s)
dept.	department	SSR	Soviet Socialist
dist.	district		Republic
div.	division	SW	southwest(ern)
E	east(ern)	terr.	territory
ft.	feet	twp.	township
isl(s).	island(s)	uninc.	unincorporated
mi.	mile(s)	urb.	urban
mtn(s).	mountain(s)	USSR	Union of Societ So-
N	north(ern)		cialist Republics
NE	northeaster(ern)	vill.	village
NW	northwest(ern)	W	west(ern)
penin.	peninsula		

Aachen city, W West Germany; pop. 242,971.
Aarhus co., E Denmark; 310 sq. mi.; pop. 534,000.
— city, W Aarhus co.; cap.; pop. 238,000.
Aberdeen co., NE Scotland; 1,972 sq. mi.; pop. 324,574.
— city, SE Aberdeen co.; cap.; pop. 183,000.
— city, NE South Dakota 57401*; pop. 26,476.
— city, W Washington 98520; pop. 18,739.

Abidjan city, SE Ivory Coast; cap.; pop. 500,000.
Abilene city, CEN. Texas 79600; pop. 98,315.
Acapulco city, SW Mexico; pop. 456,655.
Accra city, S Ghana; cap.; pop. 564,000.
Achaea dept., N Peloponessus, Greece; 1,146 sq. mi.; pop. 229,000; cap. Patras.
Aconcagua extinct volcano, CEN. Argentina; 22,831 ft.
Acre city, NE Israel; pop. 24,000.
Addis Ababa city, CEN. Ethiopia; cap.; pop. 1,250,000.
Addison vill. NE Illinois 60101; pop. 28,836.
Adelaide city, SE South Australia; cap.; pop. 933,350.
Aden former British col.; now part of People's Democratic Republic of Yemen.
— city, People's Democratic Republic of Yemen; pop. 264,-000.
Aden, Gulf of inlet of Arabian Sea betw. People's Democratic Republic of Yemen and Somalia.
Aden Protectorate Formerly, group of Arab tribal districts comprising a British protectorate; now part of People's Democratic Republic of Yemen.
Adirondack Mountains mtn. range, NE New York.
Adrian city, SE Michigan 49221; pop. 21,186.
Adriatic Sea inlet of the Mediterranean Sea, E of Italy.
Aegean Sea inlet of the Mediterranean Sea betw. Greece and Asia Minor.
Afghanistan republic, SW Asia; 250,000 sq. mi.; pop. 16,250,000; cap. Kabul.
Africa second largest continent, S of Europe and W of Asia; 11,710,000 sq. mi.
Afton town, NE Missouri 63123; pop. 24,067.
Agaña city, W Guam 96910; cap.; pop. 1,642.
Agawam town, W Massachusetts 01001; pop. 21,717.
Agra city, N India; site of Taj Mahal; pop. 592,000.
Aguadilla town, NW Puerto Rico 00603*; pop. 15,943.
Aguascalientes state, CEN. Mexico; 2,499 sq. mi.; pop. 338,000.
— city, CEN. Aguascalientes state; cap.; pop. 238,694.
Agulhas, Cape cape, S South Africa; southernmost point of Africa.
Ahmedabad city, W India; former cap. of Gujarat; pop. 2,515,195.
Aisne river, N France; 175 mi. long.
Ajaccio city, W Corsica; cap.; birthplace of Napoleon; pop. 41,000.
Akron city, NE Ohio 44300*; pop. 237,177.
Alabama state, SE United States; 51,609 sq. mi.; pop. 3,890,061; cap. Montgomery.
Alameda city, W California 94501*; pop. 63,852.
— vill., SE Idaho 83201; pop. 40,036.
Alamogordo town, S New Mexico 88310; site of the first atom bomb test; pop. 24,024.
Alaska state of the United States, NW North America; 586,400 sq. mi.; pop. 400,481; cap. Juneau.
Alaska, Gulf of inlet of the Pacific on the S coast of Alaska.
Alaska Highway road joining Dawson Creek, British Columbia and Fairbanks, Alaska; 1,527 mi.
Alaska Peninsula promontory of SW Alaska; ab. 400 mi. long.
Alaska Range mtn. range, CEN. Alaska.
Albania Balkan republic S of Yugoslavia; 11,100 sq. mi.; pop. 2,800,000; cap. Tirana.
Albany city, SW Georgia 31701*; pop. 73,934.
— city, E New York 12200*; cap.; pop. 101,727.
— city, W Oregon 97321; pop. 26,546.
Albemarle Sound inlet of the Atlantic, NE North Carolina.
Alberta prov., W Canada; 255,285 sq. mi.; pop. 1,838,037; cap. Edmonton.
Albert Lea city, S Minnesota 56007; pop. 19,190.
Albuquerque city, NW New Mexico 87100*; pop. 331,767.
Alcan Highway Alaska Highway: *unofficial name.*
Alderney island, N Channel Islands; 3 sq. mi.
Aleppo city, NE Syria; pop. 640,000.
Aleutian Islands isl. group, SW of Alaska Peninsula.

Alexandria N Egypt; summer cap., pop. 2,318,655.
— city, CEN. Louisiana 71301*; pop. 51,379.
— city, NE Virginia 22300*; pop. 102,494.
Algeria republic, NW Africa; 919,352 sq. mi.; pop. 20,250,000; cap. Algiers.
Algiers city, N Algeria; cap.; pop. 2,500,000.
Alhambra city, SW California 91800*; pop. 64,615.
Alicante prov., E Spain; 2,264 sq. mi.; pop. 920,000.
— city, E Alicante prov.; cap.; pop. 163,000.
Alice city, S Texas 78332; pop. 20,961.
Aliquippa boro., W Pennsylvania 15001; pop. 17,094.
Alisal vill., W California 93901; pop. 16,473.
Allahabad city N India; pop. 491,000.
Allegheny Mountains mtn. range of Appalachian system; extends from Pennsylvania through Virginia.
Allegheny River river, W New York and Pennsylvania; 325 mi. long.
Allen Park vill., SE Michigan 48101*; pop. 34,196.
Allentown city, E Pennsylvania 18100*; pop. 103,758.
Alliance city, NE Ohio 44601*; pop. 24,315.
Alma city, S Quebec, Canada; pop. 22,622.
Alma Ata city, SE Kazakh SSR; cap.; pop. 910,000.
Alps mtn. system, S Europe; extends from S coast of France to W coast of Yugoslavia.
Alsace reg. and former prov., NE France.
Alsace-Lorraine oft-disputed border reg., NE France; adjoins SW Germany.
Altadena uninc. place, SW California 91001*; pop. 42,380.
Altai Mountains mtn. system, CEN. Asia.
Altamont uninc. place, S Oregon; pop. 15,746.
Alton city, SW Illinois 62002*; pop. 34,171.
Altoona city, CEN. Pennsylvania 16601*; pop. 57,078.
Altus city, SW Oklahoma 73521*; pop. 23,101.
Alum Rock uninc. place, W California; pop. 18,355.
Amarillo city, NW Texas 79100*; pop. 149,230.
Amazon river, N South America; 3,910 mi. long; carries the largest volume of water of all rivers.
America 1 The United States of America. **2** North and South America; the western Hemisphere.
American Samoa See SAMOA.
Americus city, CEN. Georgia 31709; pop. 16,120.
Ames city, CEN. Iowa 50010*; pop. 45,775.
Amherst uninc. place, CEN. Massachusetts 01002*; pop. 33,229.
Amiens city, N France; pop. 135,992.
Amman city, CEN. Jordan; cap.; pop. 732,587.
Amoy isl. of China, Formosa Strait.
— city, Amoy isl.; pop. 224,000.
Amritsar city, W Punjab, India; pop. 407,000.
Amsterdam city, W Netherlands; cap.; pop. 957,700.
— city, CEN. New York 12010*; pop. 25,524.
Amur river, E Asia; 2,700 mi. long.
Anaheim city, SW California 92800*; pop. 221,847.
Anatolia penin. at W end of Asia; comprises most of Turkey.
Anchorage city, S Alaska 99501*; pop. 173,017.
Andalusia reg., S Spain.
Anderson city, CEN. Indiana 46010*; pop. 64,695.
— city, NW South Carolina 29621*; pop. 27,313.
Andes mtn. range, W South America; connects with the Rockies; over 4,000 mi. long.
Andorra republic betw. France and Spain; 179 sq. mi.; pop. 36,000.
— city, CEN. Andorra; cap.; pop. 2,700.
Andover town, NE Massachusetts 01810*; pop. 26,370.
Angel Falls waterfall, SE Venezuela; over 3,300 ft.
Angola republic, W Africa; 481,351 sq. mi.; pop. 7,819,000; cap. Luanda.
Anjou town, S Quebec, Canada; pop. 34,000.
Ankara city, CEN. Turkey; cap.; pop. 2,561,765.
Annandale uninc. place, NE Virginia 22003; pop. 27,428.
Annapolis city, CEN. Maryland 21400*; cap.; site of U.S. Naval Academy; pop. 31,740.
Ann Arbor city, SE Michigan 48103*; pop. 107,317.
Anniston city, NE Alabama 36201*; pop. 29,523.
Ansonia city, SW Connecticut 06401; pop. 19,039.
Antarctica continent surrounding the South Pole; over 5 million sq. mi. Also **Antarctic Continent.**
Antarctic Circle parallel of latitude at 66°33′S; the boundary of the South Frigid Zone.
Antarctic Ocean parts of Atlantic, Pacific, and Indian oceans bordering on Antarctica.
Antarctic Zone region enclosed by the Antarctic Circle.
Antigua island group of the West Indies; 171 sq. mi.; pop. 62,000; cap. St. John's.
Antilles islands of the West Indies excluding the Bahamas; comprises Greater Antilles: Cuba, Hispaniola, Jamaica, and Puerto Rico; and Lesser Antilles: Trinidad,

the Windward Islands, the Leeward Islands, and other small islands.
Antioch city, S Turkey; pop. 74,000.
— city, W California 94509; pop. 43,559.
Antwerp city, N Belgium; pop. 927,200.
Apennines mtn. range of Italy S of Po valley.
Appalachian Mountains E North America.
Appleton city, E Wisconsin 54910*; pop. 59,032.
Aquitaine reg., SW France.
Arabia penin., SW Asia, betw. the Red Sea and Persian Gulf.
Arabian Sea part of the Indian Ocean betw. Arabia and India.
Arab Republic of Egypt See EGYPT.
Aragon reg., NE Spain.
Aral Sea salt inland sea, CEN. USSR.
Ararat, Mount mtn., E Turkey; 17,011 ft.; traditional landing place of Noah's ark.
Arcadia dept., CEN. Peloponnesus, Greece; 1,168 sq. mi.; pop. 112,000; cap. Tripolis.
— city, SW California 91006*; pop. 45,994.
Arctic Circle parallel of latitude at 66°33′N; the boundary of the North Frigid Zone.
Arctic Ocean sea, N of Arctic Circle, surrounding North Pole.
Arden-Arcade uninc. place, CEN. California 95825; pop. 82,492.
Ardmore city, S Oklahoma 73401; pop. 23,689.
Arecibo town, N Puerto Rico 00612*; pop. 28,828.
Argentina republic, S South America; 1,084,362 sq. mi.; pop. 27,400,000; cap. Buenos Aires.
Argonne ridge, N France; site of battles in World Wars I and II.
Arizona state, SW United States; 113,909 sq. mi.; pop. 2,717,866; cap. Phoenix.
Arkansas state, CEN. United States; 53,104 sq. mi.; pop. 2,285,513; cap. Little Rock.
Arkhangelsk city, NW RSFSR; pop. 350,000.
Arlington town, E Massachusetts 02174; pop. 48,219;
— city, N Texas 76010*; pop. 160,123.
— city, NE Virginia 22201; pop. 174,284.
— urb. co., NE Virginia; site of **Arlington National Cemetery,** containing tomb of the Unknown Soldier.
Arlington Heights vill., NE Illinois 60004*; pop. 66,116
Armenia 1 former country, SW Asia. **2** the Armenian SSR.
Armenian SSR republic, S USSR; 11,500 sq. mi.; pop. 2,785,000; cap. Yerevan.
Arnhem city, E Netherlands; pop. 132,000.
Arvada town, CEN. Colorado 80002*; pop. 84,576.
Arvida city, CEN. Quebec, Canada; pop. 18,448.
Asbury Park city, E New Jersey 07712*; pop. 17,015.
Ascension isl. poss. of Great Britain, South Atlantic; 34 sq. mi.; pop. 750.
Asheville city, W North Carolina 28800*; pop. 53,281.
Ashland city, NE Kentucky 41101; pop. 27,064.
— city, CEN. Ohio 44805; pop. 20,326.
Ashtabula city, NE Ohio 44004*; pop. 23,449.
Asia E part of Eurasian land mass; largest of the continents; 16,900,000 sq. mi.
Asia Minor penin. of extreme W Asia, comprising most of Turkey.
Aspen city, NW Maryland 20015; pop. 16,799.
Astrakhan city, SE RSFSR; pop. 419,000.
Asunción city, SW Paraguay; cap.; pop. 437,000.
Aswan city, S Egypt; site of **Aswan Dam,** 1 1/4 mi. long; pop. 258,600.
Athens city, SE Greece; cap.; pop. 3,000,000.
— city, CEN. Georgia, 30601*; pop. 45,549.
— city, SE Ohio 45701; pop. 19,743.
Atlanta city, CEN. Georgia 30300*; cap.; pop. 425,022.
Atlantic City city, SE New Jersey 08400*; pop. 40,199.
Atlantic Ocean ocean, extending from the Arctic to the Antarctic between the Americas and Europe and Africa.
Atlas Mountains mtn. range, NW Africa.
Attleboro city, SE Massachusetts 02703; pop. 34,196.
Auburn city, CEN. Alabama 36830; pop. 28,471.
— city, SW Maine 04210; pop. 23,128.
— town, Massachusetts 01501; pop. 14,845.
— city, CEN. New York 13021*; pop. 32,548.
— city, CEN. Washington, 98002*; pop. 26,417.
Auckland city, N North Island, New Zealand; pop. 753,100.
Augsburg city, S West Germany; pop. 245,940.
Augusta city, E Georgia 30900*; pop. 47,532.
— city, S Maine 04301*; cap.; pop. 21,819.
Aurora city, CEN. Colorado 80010*; pop. 158,588.
— city, NE Illinois 60504*; pop. 81,293.

Auschwitz, German name for Oświecim, city, sw Poland; site of Nazi extermination camp in World War II; pop. 14,000.

Austin city, se Minnesota 55912; pop. 23,020.

— city, cen. Texas 78700*; cap.; pop. 345,496.

Austintown city, ne Ohio 44515; pop. 29,393.

Australasia isls. of the South Pacific, including Australia, New Zealand, and New Guinea.

Australia independent member of the Commonwealth of Nations, situated on an isl. continent in the South Pacific; 2,971,081 sq. mi.; pop. 14,900,000; cap. Canberra.

Australian Capital Territory reg., se Australia; 939 sq. mi.; contains Canberra, the capital; pop. 144,000.

Austria republic, cen. Europe; 32,375 sq. mi.; pop. 7,515,000; cap. Vienna.

Austronesia isls. of the South Pacific, including Indonesia, Melanesia, Micronesia, and Polynesia.

Avignon city, se France; pop. 86,000.

Avon river, cen. England; 96 mi. long.

Azerbaijan prov., nw Iran: **Eastern Azerbaijan:** 28,488 sq. mi.; pop. 2,600,000; cap. Tabriz; **Western Azerbaijan:** 13,644 sq. mi.; pop. 1 million; cap. Rizaiyeh.

Azerbaijan SSR republic, sw USSR; 33,590 sq. mi.; pop. 5,219,000; cap. Baku.

Azores three isl. groups of Portugal, e Atlantic; 922 sq. mi.; pop. 335,000.

Azov, Sea of inlet of the Black Sea, s USSR.

Azusa city, s California 91702; pop. 29,380.

Baden-Baden city, sw West Germany; site of famous mineral springs; pop. 40,000.

Bad Lands arid plateau, South Dakota and Nebraska. Also **Bad'lands.**

Baghdad city, cen. Iraq; cap.; pop. 225,500.

Baguio city, Luzon, n Philippines; pop. 50,000.

Bahama Islands isl. republic of the Commonwealth of Nations, se of Florida; 5,353 sq. mi.; pop. 3,205,600 ; cap. Nassau.

Bahrain isl. group, Persian Gulf near Saudi Arabia; independent emirate; 240 sq. mi.; pop. 400,000; cap. Manama.

Baikal freshwater lake, s USSR; 12,150 sq. mi.

Baker, Mount mtn., Cascade range, n Washington; 10,750 ft.

Bakersfield city, s California 93300*; pop. 101,611.

Baku city, se Azerbaijan SSR; cap.; pop. 1,550,000.

Balboa Heights adm. ctr. of Canal Zone, near Balboa; pop. 118.

Baldwin uninc. place, se New York 11510*; pop. 34,525.

— boro., sw Pennsylvania; pop. 24,598.

Baldwin Park city, sw California 91706*; pop. 50,554.

Balearic Islands isl. group, w Mediterranean; prov. of Spain; 1,935 sq. mi.; pop. 558,000; cap. Palma.

Bali isl. of Indonesia, e of Java; 2,243 sq. mi.

Balkan Mountains, mtn. range, Balkan penin.

Balkan Peninsula large penin. of se Europe.

Balkan States countries of Balkan penin.: Albania, Bulgaria, Greece, Rumania, Yugoslavia, and part of Turkey.

Baltic Sea inlet of the Atlantic in nw Europe.

Baltimore city, n Maryland 21200*; pop. 786,775.

Bamako city, cen. Mali; cap.; pop. 170,000.

Banaras Hindu sacred city, ne India; pop. 553,000. Also **Benares.**

Bandar Sari Begawan city, n Brunei; cap.; pop. 37,000.

Bandung city, w Java, Indonesia; pop. 1,282,000.

Bangalore city, e Mysore, India; cap.; pop. 4,835,000.

Bangkok city, sw Thailand; cap.; pop. 2,913,537.

Bangladesh republic, s Asia; 54,501 sq. mi.; pop. 90,700,000; cap. Dacca.

Bangor city, cen. Maine 04401*; pop. 31,643.

Bangui city, sw Central African Empire; cap.; pop. 150,000.

Banjul city, w Gambia; cap.; pop. 39,000.

Barbados isl. republic of the Commonwealth of Nations, e Caribbean; 166 sq. mi.; pop. 250,000; cap. Bridgetown.

Barberton city, ne Ohio 44203; pop. 29,751.

Barcelona prov., ne Spain; 2,985 sq. mi.; pop. 3,929,000.

— city, se Barcelona prov.; cap.; pop. 1,759,000.

Barnstable town, se Massachusetts 02630; pop. 30,898.

Barranquilla city, n Colombia; pop. 868,000.

Barrie city, s Ontario, Canada; pop. 27,676.

Barrington town, e Rhode Island 02806; pop. 16,174.

Barrow, Point extreme n point of Alaska.

Barstow city, s California 92310*; pop. 17,690.

Bartlesville city, ne Oklahoma 74003*; pop. 34,568.

Basel city, n Switzerland; pop. 235,000.

Bataan prov. s Luzon, Philippines; 517 sq. mi.; pop. 116,000; cap. Balanga; occupies **Bataan Peninsula,** scene of World War II surrender of U.S. forces to the Japanese.

Batavia city, w New York 14020*; pop. 16,703.

Bath co. boro., sw England; pop. 85,000.

Bathurst town, ne New Brunswick, Canada; pop. 16.674.

— Banjul; *the former name.*

Baton Rouge city, cen. Louisiana 70800*; cap.; pop. 219,486.

Battle Creek city, s Michigan 49014*; pop. 35,724.

Bavaria state, se West Germany; 27,235 sq. mi.; pop. 10,569,000; cap. Munich.

Bayamón town, n Puerto Rico; pop. 15,109.

Bay City city, cen. Michigan 48706*; pop. 41,593.

Bayonne city, ne New Jersey 07002*; pop. 65,047.

Baytown city, s Texas 77520*; pop. 56,923.

Bay Village city, ne Ohio; pop. 17,846.

Beaconsfield town, s Quebec, Canada; pop. 19,389.

Beaumont city, se Texas 77700*; pop. 118,102.

Beaverton city, nw Oregon 97005*; pop. 30,582.

Beckley city, s West Virginia 25801*; pop. 20,492.

Bedford city, ne Ohio 44014; pop. 15,056.

Beirut city, w Lebanon; cap.; pop. 600,000.

Belém city, n Brazil; pop. 573,000.

Belfast co. boro., and port, se N. Ireland; cap.; pop. 360,000.

Belgium kingdom, nw Europe; 11,775 sq. mi.; pop. 9,870,000; cap. Brussels.

Belgrade city e Yugoslavia; cap.; pop. 1,000,000.

Belize republic of the Commonwealth of Nations, ne Central America; 8,867 sq. mi.; pop. 160,000; cap. Belmopan.

Bell city, s California 90201*; pop. 25,450.

Bellaire city, s Texas 77401*; pop. 14,950.

Belle Glade city, se Florida 33430; pop. 16,535.

Belleville city, sw Illinois 62220*; pop. 42,150.

— town, ne New Jersey 07109; pop. 35,367.

— city, se Ontario, Canada; pop. 35,128.

Bellevue city, e Nebraska 68005; pop. 21,813.

— city, cen. Washington 98004; pop. 53,441.

Bellflower city, sw California 90706*; pop. 53,441.

Bell Gardens uninc. place, sw California 90201; pop. 34,117.

Bellingham city, nw Washington 98225; pop. 45,794.

Bellmawr boro., sw New Jersey 08030; pop. 13,721.

Bellmore uninc. place, se New York 11710*; pop. 18,431.

Bellwood vill., n Illinois 60104; pop. 19,811.

Belmont city, cen. California 94002*; pop. 24,505.

— town, e Massachusetts 02178; pop. 35,207.

Beloit city, s Wisconsin 53511*; pop. 35,207.

Bengal former prov., ne British India; divided (1947) into: **East Bengal,** now part of Bangladesh, and **West Bengal,** a state of India; 33,928 sq. mi.; pop. 44,440,000; cap. Calcutta.

Benghazi city, n Libya; one of two caps.; pop. 140,000.

Benin independent state, w Africa; 43,483 sq. mi.; pop. 3,675,000.

Benton city, cen. Arkansas 72015; pop. 17,437.

Benton Harbor city, sw Michigan 49022*; pop. 14,707.

Berea city, ne Ohio 44017; pop. 22,395.

Bergen city, sw Norway; pop. 113,000.

Bergenfield boro., ne New Jersey 07621; pop. 33,131.

Bering Sea part of the North Pacific betw. Alaska and the USSR, joined to the Arctic by **Bering Strait.**

Berkeley city, w California 94700*; pop. 103,328.

— city, cen. Missouri 63134; pop. 16,146.

Berkley city, se Michigan 48072; pop. 18,637.

Berlin city, cen. Germany; cap. prior to 1945 when divided into the British, French, Soviet, and US sectors. In 1949 the Soviet sector, **East Berlin,** was designated capital of East Germany; pop. 1,129,000. The remaining sectors formed **West Berlin,** associated with West Germany; pop. 1,905,000.

— city, n New Hampshire 03570; pop. 15,256.

Bermuda isl. group, w Atlantic; British col.; 21 sq. mi. pop. 65,000, cap. Hamilton.

Bern city, cen. Switzerland; cap.; pop. 142,800. Also **Berne.**

Berwyn city, ne Illinois 60402*; pop. 46,849.

Bessemer city, cen. Alabama 35020*; pop. 31,729.

Bethany city, cen. Oklahoma 73008; pop. 22,130.

Bethel boro., sw Pennsylvania 19507; pop. 34,791.

Bethesda uninc. area, w Maryland 20014; pop. 71,621.

Bethlehem ancient town, w Jordan; birthplace of Jesus; pop. 19,000.

— city, e Pennsylvania 18015*; pop. 70,419.

Bettendorf city, cen. Iowa 52722; pop. 27,381.

Beverly city, ne Massachusetts 01915; pop. 37,655.

Beverly Hills city, sw California, 90210*; pop. 32,367.

Bhutan kingdom, s Asia, between ne India and Tibet; 18,000 sq. mi.; pop. 1,100,000; cap. Thimphu.

Biddeford city, sw Maine 04005; pop. 19,638.
Big Spring city, w Texas 79720*; pop. 24,804.
Bikini atoll, Marshall Islands; 2 sq. mi.; site of US nuclear tests, July 1946.
Billerica town, NE Massachusetts 01821; pop. 36,727.
Billings city, CEN. Montana 59101*; pop 66,798.
Biloxi city, SE Mississippi 39530*; pop. 49,311.
Binghamton city, CEN. New York 13990*; pop. 55,860.
Birkenhead co. boro., NW England; pop. 138,000.
Birmingham co. boro., CEN. England; pop. 1,034,000.
— city, CEN. Alabama 35200*; pop. 284,413.
— city, SE Michigan 48008*; pop. 21,689.
Biscay, Bay of inlet of the Atlantic betw. w and sw France and N and NW Spain.
Bismarck city, CEN. North Dakota 58501*; cap.; pop. 44,485.
Bismarck Archipelago isl. group, Trust Territory of New Guinea; 19,200 sq. mi.
Bizerta city, N Tunisia; pop. 95,000.
Black Forest wooded mtn. reg., sw West Germany.
Black Hills mtn. reg., sw South Dakota and NE Wyoming.
Black Sea inland sea betw. Europe and Asia, connects with the Aegean via the Bosporus, the Sea of Marmara, and the Dardanelles.
Blaine vill., E Minnesota; pop. 28,558.
Bloomfield town, CEN. Connecticut 06002; pop. 18,608.
— city, NE New Jersey 07003*; pop. 47,702.
Bloomington city, CEN. Illinois 61701*; pop. 49,189.
— city, CEN. Indiana 47401*; pop. 51,646.
— city, E Minnesota 56013; pop. 81,831.
Bluefield city, s West Virginia 24701*; pop. 16,060.
Blue Island city, NE Illinois 60406; pop. 21,855.
Blue Ridge Mountains, sw part of the Appalachians.
Blytheville city, NE Arkansas 72315*; pop. 24,314.
Boardman city, NE Ohio 44512; pop. 30,852.
Boca Raton city, SE Florida 33432; pop. 49,505.
Bogalusa city, SE Louisiana 70427; pop. 18,412.
Bogotá city, CEN. Colombia; cap.; pop. 41,300,000.
Bohemia former prov., w Czechoslovakia.
Boise city, sw Idaho 83700*; cap.; pop. 102,451.
Bolivia republic, CEN. South America; 424,162 sq. mi.; pop. 5,750,000; caps. Sucre (constitutional), La Paz (de facto).
Bologna prov., CEN. Italy; 1,429 sq. mi.; pop. 837,000.
— city, cap. of Bologna prov.; pop. 493,000.
Bombay city, w India; pop. 4,152,000.
Bonn city, w German Federal Republic (West Germany); cap.; pop. 299,000.
Bophuthatswana, republic, s Africa; 15,610 sq. mi.; pop. 1,039,000; cap. Mmabatho.
Bordeaux city, sw France; pop. 267,000.
Borneo (Kalimantan) isl., betw. Java and South China seas; comprising North Borneo, Sarawak, Brunei, and Indonesian Borneo; 286,969 sq. mi.
Bosnia and Herzegovina constituent republic, CEN. Yugoslavia; 19,745 sq. mi.; pop. 3,743,000; cap. Sarajevo.
Bosporus strait, betw. the Black Sea and the Sea of Marmara.
Bossier City city, NW Louisiana 71010; pop. 49,969.
Boston city, E Massachusetts 02100*; cap.; pop. 562,994.
Botany Bay inlet of the Pacific, s of Sydney, Australia.
Botswana independent member of the Commonwealth of Nations, s Africa; 222,000 sq. mi.; pop. 750,000; cap. Gaborone.
Boucherville town, s Quebec, Canada; pop. 19,997.
Boulder city, CEN. Colorado 80301*; pop. 76,685.
Boulder Dam Hoover Dam: *the former name.*
Bountiful city, CEN. Utah 84010; pop. 32,877.
Bowie city, sw Louisiana; pop. 35,028.
Bowling Green city, s Kentucky 42101*; pop. 40,450.
— city, NW Ohio 43402; pop. 25,728.
Boynton Beach city, SE Florida 33435; pop. 35,624.
Bozeman city, sw Montana 59715; pop. 21,645.
Bradenton city, w Florida 33505*; pop. 30,170.
Braintree town, E Massachusetts 02184; pop. 35,050.
Brampton town, SE Ontario, Canada; pop. 41,211.
Brandon city, sw Manitoba, Canada; pop. 31,150.
Branford town, CEN. Connecticut 06405; pop. 20,444.
Brantford city, SE Ontario, Canada; pop. 64,421.
Brasília city, CEN. Brazil; cap.; pop. 1,000,000.
Brazil republic, NE and CEN. South America; 3,287,951 sq. mi.; pop. 127,000,000; cap. Brasília.
Brazzaville city, SE Republic of the Congo (Brazzaville) cap.; pop 156,000.
Brea city, sw California 92621; pop. 27,913.
Breed's Hill hill, near Bunker Hill. See BUNKER HILL.

Bremen state, NW West Germany, 156 sq. mi.
— city, major part of Bremen state; pop. 607,000.
Bremerhaven city, part of Bremen state, NW West Germany; pop. 149,000.
Bremerton city, w Washington 98310*; pop. 36,208.
Brenner Pass Alpine pass, Austrian-Italian border.
Brentwood uninc. place, SE New York 11717; pop. 27,-868.
Breslau Wroclaw: *the German name.*
Brest city, NW France; pop. 154,000.
— city, sw Byelorussian SSR; pop. 85,000.
Bridgeport city, sw Connecticut 06600*; pop. 142,546.
Bridgeton town, E Missouri 63044; pop. 18,445.
— city, sw New Jersey 08302*; pop. 18,795.
Brighton co. boro. and resort, sw England; pop. 166,000.
Brisbane city, SE Queensland, Australia; cap.; pop. 1,004,500.
Bristol co. boro., sw England; pop. 425,000.
— city, CEN. Connecticut 06010*; pop. 57,370.
— urb. twp., SE Pennsylvania 19007; pop. 10,867.
— town, E Rhode Island 02809; pop. 20,128.
— city, NE Tennessee 37620*; pop. 23,986.
Bristol Channel inlet of the Atlantic betw. Wales and sw England.
Britain see GREAT BRITAIN.
British Columbia prov., w Canada; 366,255 sq. mi.; pop. 2,466,608, cap. Victoria.
British Guiana former British col., NE South America. See GUYANA.
British Virgin Islands British col., E Greater Antilles; 59 sq. mi.; pop. 10,000.; cap. Road Town.
British West Indies see WEST INDIES.
Brittany reg., w France; former prov.
Brno city, CEN. Czechoslovakia; pop. 339,000.
Brockton city, E Massachusetts 02401*; pop. 95,172.
Brockville town, SE Ontario, Canada; pop. 19,765.
Bronx boro., N New York City 10400*; pop. 1,169,115. Also **the Bronx.**
Brookfield vill., NE Illinois 60513; pop. 19,395.
— city, SE Wisconsin 53005; pop. 34,035.
Brookline town, E Massachusetts 02146; pop. 55,062.
Brooklyn boro., SE New York City 11200*; pop. 31,230.
Brooklyn Center vill., SE Minnesota 55429; pop. 31,230.
Brooklyn Park vill., SE Minnesota; pop. 43,332.
Brook Park vill., N Ohio 44142; pop. 26,195.
Brossard city, s Quebec, Canada; pop. 23,452.
Browardale city, SE Florida; pop. 17,444.
Browns Village city, SE Florida 33101; pop. 23,442.
Brownsville uninc. place, NW Florida; pop. 20,294.
— city, s Texas 78520*; pop. 84,997.
Brownwood city, CEN. Texas 76801*; pop. 19,203.
Brunei sultanate under British protection, NW Borneo, 2,226 sq. mi.; pop. 150,000; cap. Bandar Sari Begawan.
Brunswick city, NE West Germany; pop. 225,000.
— city, SE Georgia 31520*; pop. 17,605.
— uninc. place, s Maine 04011; pop. 17,366.
— vill., N Ohio 44212; pop. 27,689.
Brussels city, CEN. Belgium; cap.; pop. 1,071,000.
Bryan city, CEN. Texas 77801*; pop. 44,337.
Bucharest city, s Rumania; cap.; pop. 1,488,000.
Budapest city, CEN. Hungary; cap.; pop. 2,039,000.
Buena Park city, sw California 90620*; pop. 64,165.
Buenos Aires city, E Argentina; cap.; pop. 3,500,000.
Buffalo city, w New York 14200*; pop. 357,870.
Bulgaria republic, SE Europe; 42,875 sq. mi.; pop. 8,000,-000; cap. Sofia.
Bull Run small stream, NE Virginia; site of Union defeats in the Civil War, 1861 and 1862.
Bunker Hill hill, Charlestown, Massachusetts, near which (on Breed's Hill) occurred the first organized engagement of the American Revolution, June 17, 1775.
Burbank city, sw California 91500*; pop. 84,825.
Burgundy reg., CEN. France.
Burlingame city, CEN. California 94010*; pop. 26,173.
Burlington city, SE Iowa 52601*; pop. 29,529.
— town, NE Massachusetts 01803; pop. 23,486.
— city, CEN. North Carolina 27215*; pop. 37,266.
— city, NW Vermont 05401*; pop. 37,712.
— town, SE Ontario, Canada; pop, 87,023.
Burma republic, SE Asia, betw. India and Thailand; 261,789 sq. mi.; pop. 34,483,000; cap. Rangoon.
Burma Road road betw. N Burma and sw China; a World War II supply route.
Burnsville city, SE Minnesota 55378; pop. 35,674.
Burundi kingdom, CEN. Africa; formerly part of Ruanda-Urundi; 10,747 sq. mi.; pop. 4,150,000; cap. Bujumbura.
Butler city, w Pennsylvania 16001*; pop. 17,026.

Butte city, sw Montana 59701*; pop. 37,205.
Byelorussian SSR constituent republic, USSR; 80,154 sq. mi.; pop. 9,100,000, cap. Minsk.

Cádiz city, sw Spain; pop. 138,000.
Caguas town, CEN. Puerto Rico 00625*; pop. 32,015.
Cahokia vill. sw Illinois 62206; pop. 18,904.
Cairo city, NE Egypt; cap.; pop. 3,346,000.
Calais city, N France; pop. 75,000.
Calcutta city, NE India; pop. 2,927,000.
Calgary city, s Alberta, Canada; pop. 469,917.
Caticut Kozhikode: *an alternate name.*
California state, w United States; 158,693 sq. mi.; pop. 23,668,562; cap. Sacramento.
California, Gulf of inlet of the Pacific, w Mexico, betw. Lower California and the rest of Mexico.
Calumet City city, NE Illinois 60409; pop. 39,673.
Camarillo city, sw California 93010; pop. 37,732.
Cambodia See *Kampuchea.*
Cambridge city, SE England; site of Cambridge University; pop. 99,000.
— city, E Massachusetts 02138*; pop. 95,322.
Camden city, s Arkansas 71701; pop. 15,356.
— city, sw New Jersey 08100*; pop. 84,910.
Cameroon republic, w equatorial Africa; 183,376 sq. mi.; pop. 8,650,000; cap. Yaoundé. Also **Cameroun.**
Campbell city, w California 95008; pop. 27,067.
Camp Le Jeune city, SE North Carolina 28542; pop. 34,549.
Camp Springs city, sw Maryland 20031; pop. 22,776.
Canada independent member of the Commonwealth of Nations, N North America; 3,851,809 sq. mi.; pop. 22,-992,604; cap. Ottawa.
Canal Zone US leased terr., CEN Panama; extending five miles on either side of the Panama Canal; 648 sq. mi.; pop. 41,684; adm. ctr. Balboa Heights.
Canary Islands isl. group of Spain near NW coast of Africa; 2,808 sq. mi.; pop. 1,170,000.
Canaveral, Cape cape, E Florida 32920; site of the **John F. Kennedy Space Center,** a space research and missiles installation.
Canberra city, SE Australia; cap.; pop. 195,000.
Canea city, NW Crete; pop. 120,000. Also **Khania.**
Cannes city, SE France; pop. 58,000.
Canterbury co. boro., SE England; site of famous cathedral; pop. 33,000.
Canton city, s China; pop. 2,300,000.
— town, E Massachusetts 02021; pop. 18,182.
— city, NE Ohio 44700*; pop. 94,730.
Cap-de-la-Madeleine city, s Quebec, Canada; pop. 31,-463.
Cape Girardeau city, SE Missouri 63701; pop. 34,361.
Cape Town city, s South Africa; legislative cap.; pop. 892,000. Also **Capetown.**
Cape Verde Islands republic in the CEN. Atlantic Ocean, w of Cape Verde; 1,552 sq. mi.; pop. 330,000; cap. Praia.
Capri isl. near the w coast of Italy; 4 sq. mi.
Caracas city, N Venezuela; cap.; pop. 2,950,000.
Carbondale city, s Illinois 62901; pop. 27,194.
Cardiff co. boro., SE Wales; pop. 278,000.
Caribbean Sea part of the Atlantic betw. the West Indies and Central and South America.
Carlisle boro., s Pennsylvania 17013; pop. 18,314.
Carlsbad city, SE New Mexico 88220; pop. 21,297.
Carlsbad Caverns National Park area, SE New Mexico; contains **Carlsbad Caverns,** a series of limestone caves.
Carmichael uninc. place, CEN. California 95608; pop. 37,625.
Carnegie boro., sw Pennsylvania 15106; pop. 10,099.
Carol City uninc. place, SE Florida 33054; pop. 27,361.
Caroline Islands isl. group in the Pacific, E of the Philippines; 463 sq. mi.
Carpathian Mountains mtn. range, CEN. and E Europe.
Carpentersville vill., NE Illinois 60110; pop. 23,272.
Carrara City, CEN. Italy; site of white marble quarries; pop. 65,000.
Carson uninc. place, sw California 90745*; pop. 81,221.
Carson City city, w Nevada 89701*; cap.; pop. 32,022.
Carteret boro., NE New Jersey; pop. 20,598.
Casablanca city, NW Morocco; pop. 2,220,000.
Cascade Range mtn. range in Oregon, Washington, and British Columbia.
Cashmere See KASHMIR.
Casper city, CEN. Wyoming 82601; pop. 51,016.
Caspian Sea salt-water lake in the s USSR and N Iran; 163,800 sq. mi.

Castile reg., N and CEN. Spain.
Castro Valley uninc. place, w California 94546; pop. 44,760.
Catalina Island Santa Catalina: *an alternate name.*
Catalonia reg. NE Spain.
Catania prov., E Sicily; 1,377 sq. mi.; pop. 889,000.
— city, Catania prov.; cap.; pop. 415,000.
Cataño town, N Puerto Rico; pop. 25,208.
Catonsville uninc. place, CEN. Maryland 21228; pop. 54,-812.
Catskill Mountains range of the Appalachians in SE New York.
Caucasus mtn. range betw. the Black and Caspian Seas.
— reg., sw USSR, betw. the Black and Caspian Seas. Also **Caucasia.**
Cayey town, CEN. Puerto Rico 00633; pop. 38,061.
Cedar Falls city, CEN. Iowa 50613; pop. 36,322.
Cedar Grove twp., NE New Jersey 07009; pop. 12,600.
Cedar Rapids city, E Iowa 52400*; pop. 110,243.
Celebes Sulawesi: *the former name.*
Center Point city, CEN. Alabama 35215; pop. 15,675.
Central African Empire independent state of the French Community, CEN. Africa; 238,224 sq. mi.; pop. 2,939,000; cap. Bangui.
Central America s part of North America, betw. Mexico and Colombia.
Central Falls city, NE Rhode Island 02863; pop. 16,995.
Centralia city, s Illinois 62800*; pop. 15,126.
Central Islip city, SE New York 11722; pop. 36,369.
Cerritos city, s California 90701; pop. 52,756.
Ceylon See SRI LANKA.
Chad, Lake lake, CEN. Africa; 8,000 sq. mi.
Chad, Republic of independent state of the French Community, CEN. Africa; 495,752 sq. mi.; pop. 4,650,000, cap. N'djamena.
Chambersburg boro., s Pennsylvania 17201; pop. 16,174.
Champaign city, CEN. Illinois 61820; pop. 58,133.
Champlain, Lake lake, betw. New York and Vermont, extending into Canada; 600 sq. mi.
Changchun city, NE China; pop. 975,000.
Channel Islands British isl. group, English Channel near Normandy; includes Jersey, Guernsey, Alderney, and Sark; 75 sq. mi.
Chapel Hill town, CEN. North Carolina 27514*; pop. 32,-421.
Charlesbourg city, s Quebec, Canada; pop. 33,443.
Charleston city, E Illinois 61920; pop. 19,355.
— city, SE South Carolina 29400*; pop. 69,510.
— city, CEN. West Virginia 25300*; cap.; pop. 63,968.
Charlotte city, CEN. North Carolina 28200*; pop. 314,447.
Charlotte Amalie city, s St. Thomas, Virgin Islands of the United States 00801; cap.; pop. 12,740.
Charlottesville city, CEN. Virginia 22901; pop. 45,010.
Charlottetown city, CEN. Prince Edward Island, Canada; cap.; pop. 18,427.
Chateauguay town, s Quebec, Canada; pop. 15,797.
Chateauguay-Centre town, s Quebec, Canada; pop. 17,942.
Chatham city, s Ontario, Canada; pop. 35,317.
Chattanooga city, SE Tennessee 37400*; pop. 169,565.
Cheektowaga uninc. place, w New York 14225; pop. 113,844.
Chelmsford town, NE Massachusetts 01824; pop. 31,174.
Chelsea metropolitan boro., sw London, England; pop. 47,000.
— city, E Massachusetts 02150; pop. 25,431.
Cheltenham urb. twp., SE Pennsylvania 19012; pop. 40,-238.
Cherbourg city, N France; pop. 39,000.
Chesapeake city, SE Virginia 23320*; pop. 114,226.
Chesapeake Bay inlet of the Atlantic in Virginia and Maryland.
Cheshire town, CEN. Connecticut 06410; pop. 21,788.
Chester co. boro., w Cheshire, England; cap.; pop. 63,000.
— city, SE Pennsylvania 19013*; pop. 45,794.
Cheviot Hills mtn. range, on the border betw. England and Scotland.
Cheyenne city, SE Wyoming 82001*; cap.; pop. 47,283.
Chicago city, NE Illinois 60600*; second largest city in the United States; pop. 3,005,072.
Chicago Heights city, NE Illinois 60411*; pop. 37,026.
Chico city, CEN. California 95926*; pop. 26,601.
Chicopee city, sw Massachusetts 01013*; pop. 55,112.
Chicoutimi city, s Quebec, Canada; pop. 33,893.
Chihuahua state, N Mexico; 94,830 sq. mi.; pop. 1,613,-000.

Chihuahua city, Chihuahua state; cap.; pop. 364,000.
Chile republic, w South America; 292,258 sq. mi.; pop. 11,275,000; cap. Santiago.
Chillicothe city, CEN. Ohio 45601*; pop. 23,420.
Chillum city, sw Maryland 20783; pop. 35,656.
China, People's Republic of republic, E and CEN. Asia; 3,768,377 sq. mi.; pop. 970,000,000; cap. Peking.
China, Republic of republic on Taiwan and several smaller isls.; 13,890 sq. mi.; pop. 18,000,000; cap. Taipei.
China Sea part of the Pacific bordering on China. See EAST CHINA SEA, SOUTH CHINA SEA.
Chino city, sw California 91710; pop. 40,165.
Chula Vista city, sw California 92010*; pop. 83,927.
Chung King city, CEN. China; cap. during World War II; pop. 3,500,000.
Cicero city, NE Illinois 60650; pop. 61,232.
Cincinnati city, sw Ohio 45200*; pop. 385,457.
Circassia reg., NW Caucasus, RSFSR.
Citrus Heights city, NE California 95610; pop. 21,760.
Clairton city, sw Pennsylvania 15025; pop. 12,188.
Claremont city, sw California 91711*; pop. 30,950.
Clark twp., NE New Jersey 07066; pop. 16,699.
Clarksburg city, N West Virginia 26301*; pop. 22,371.
Clarksdale city, NW Mississippi 38614; pop. 21,137.
Clarksville city, N Tennessee 37040*; pop. 54,777.
Clawson city, SE Michigan 48017; pop. 15,103.
Clayton city, E Missouri 63105; pop. 14,219.
Clearwater city, w Florida 33515*; pop. 85,450.
Cleburne city, CEN. Texas 76031; pop. 19,218.
Cleveland city, N Ohio 44100*; pop. 573,822.
— city, SE Tennessee 37311*; pop. 26,415.
Cleveland Heights city, N Ohio 44118; pop. 56,438.
Clifton city, NE New Jersey 07011*; pop. 74,388.
Clinton city, E Iowa 52732; pop. 32,828.
Clovis city, E New Mexico 88101; pop. 31,194.
Cocoa city, E Florida 32922*; pop. 16,096.
Cod, Cape penin., SE Massachusetts.
Coeur d'Alene city, N Idaho 83814; pop. 20,054.
Coffeyville city, SE Kansas 67337; pop. 15,185.
Cohoes city, E New York 12047; pop. 18,144.
College Park city, w Georgia 30022; pop. 24,632.
— city, w Maryland 20740*; pop. 23,614.
College Station city, CEN. Texas 77840*; pop. 37,272.
Collingswood boro., w New Jersey 08108; pop. 15,838.
Collinsville city, sw Illinois 62234; pop. 19,613.
Cologne city, w West Germany; pop. 866,000.
Colombia republic, NW South America; 439,519 sq. mi.; pop. 26,289,000; cap. Bogotá.
Colombo city, w Sri Lanka; cap.; pop. 512,000.
Colón city, Caribbean end of the Canal Zone; an enclave of Panama; pop. 95,000.
Colonial Heights city, CEN. Virginia, 23834; pop. 16,-509.
Colorado state, CEN. United States; 104,247 sq. mi.; pop. 2,888,834, cap. Denver.
Colorado River river flowing through Colorado, Utah, Arizona, California, and Mexico to the Gulf of California; length ab. 1,400 mi.
Colorado Springs city, CEN. Colorado 80900*; site of U.S. Air Force Academy; pop. 215,150.
Colton city, s California, 92324; pop. 19,974.
Columbia city, CEN. Missouri 65201*; pop. 62,061.
— city, CEN. South Carolina 29200*; cap.; pop. 99,296.
— city, CEN. Tennessee 38401*; pop. 25,767.
Columbia Heights city, E Minnesota 55421; pop. 20,-029.
Columbia River river, sw Canada and NW United States; 1,200 mi. long.
Columbus city, w Georgia 31900*; pop. 154,168.
— city, CEN. Indiana 47201*; pop. 30,292.
— city, E Mississippi 39701*; pop. 27,383.
— city, E Nebraska 68601; pop. 17,328.
— city, CEN. Ohio 43200*; cap.; pop. 564,871.
Commerce City town, CEN. Colorado 80022; pop. 16,-234.
Comoro Islands isl. republic in the Indian Ocean, NW of Madagascar; 838 sq. mi.; pop. 300,000; cap. Moroni.
Compton city, sw California 90220*; pop. 81,286.
Conakry city, w Guinea; cap. pop. 525,671.
Concord city, w California 94520*; pop. 103,251.
— town, NE Massachusetts 01742; pop. 16,293.
— city, NE Missouri; pop. 21,217.
— city, CEN. New Hampshire 03300*; cap.; pop. 30,400.
— city, CEN. North Carolina 28025; pop. 16,942.
Congo (Brazzaville), Republic of the independent state of the French Community, CEN. Africa; 132,000 sq. mi.; pop. 1,580,000; cap. Brazzaville.

Congo River river, CEN. Africa; 2,720 mi. long.
Connecticut state, NE United States; 5,009 sq. mi.; pop. 3,107,576; cap. Hartford.
Connersville city, E Indiana 47331; pop. 17,023.
Continental Divide ridge of the Rockies separating west-flowing and east-flowing streams in North America.
Conway city, CEN. Arkansas 72032; pop. 20,375.
Coon Rapids vill., E Minnesota 55433; pop. 35,826.
Copenhagen city, E Denmark; cap.; pop. 660,500.
Copiague uninc. place, SE New York 11726; pop. 19,578.
Coral Gables city, SE Florida 33134; pop. 43,241.
Coral Sea part of the Pacific, E of Australia and New Guinea.
Cork co., sw Ireland; 2,880 sq. mi.; pop. 352,000.
— co. boro., CEN. Cork co.; cap.; pop. 122,000.
Corner Brook city, w Newfoundland, Canada; pop. 26,-309.
Corning city, w New York 14830*; pop. 12,953.
Cornwall city, sw Ontario, Canada; pop. 47,116.
Corona city, s California 91720; pop. 37,791.
Coronado city, s California 92118; pop. 16,859.
Corpus Christi city, s Texas 78400*; pop. 231,999.
Corsica isl., N Mediterranean; a dept. of France; 3,368 sq. mi.; pop. 270,000; cap. Ajaccio.
Corsicana city, CEN. Texas 75110*; pop. 21,712.
Cortland city, CEN. New York 13045*; pop. 20,138.
Corvallis city, w Oregon 97330*; pop. 35,135.
Costa Mesa city, sw California 92626*; pop. 82,291.
Costa Rica republic, Central America; 19,690 sq. mi.; pop. 2,300,000; cap. San José.
Côte-St.-Luc city, s Quebec, Canada; pop. 24,375.
Council Bluffs city, sw Iowa 51,501*; pop. 56,449.
Coventry city and co. boro., CEN. England; pop. 335,000.
— town, CEN. Rhode Island 02816; pop. 27,065.
Covina city, sw California 91722*; pop. 33,751.
Covington city, N Kentucky 41011*; pop. 49,013.
Cranford urb. twp., E New Jersey 07016; pop. 24,573.
Cranston city, E Rhode Island 02910; pop. 71,992.
Crestwood city, E Missouri; pop. 12,815.
Crete isl., E Mediterranean; adm. div. of Greece; 3,207 sq. mi.; pop. 456,000.
Crimea penin., SE Ukrainian SSR.
Croatia constituent republic, w Yugoslavia; 21,719 sq. mi.; pop. 4,423,000; cap. Zagreb.
Crowley city, s Louisiana 70526; pop. 16,036.
Croydon co. boro., SE England; pop. 334,000.
Crystal vill., E Minnesota 55428; pop. 25,543.
Cuba isl. republic, Caribbean Sea; 44,217 sq. mi. (with the Isle of Pines); pop. 9,900,000; cap. Havana.
Cudahy city, sw California 90201; pop. 17,984.
— city, SE Wisconsin 53110; pop. 19,547.
Culver City city, sw California 90230*; pop. 38,134.
Cumberland city, NW Maryland 21501*; pop. 25,933.
— town, NE Rhode Island 02864; pop. 27,069.
Cumberland Gap passage through Cumberland Mountains, betw. Tennessee and Virginia.
Cumberland River river, Kentucky and Tennessee; flows to Ohio River.
Cupertino city, w California 95014; pop. 25,770.
Curaçao isl., w Netherlands Antilles; 171 sq. mi.; pop. 216,000; cap. Willemstad.
Cutler Ridge uninc. place, SE Florida 33157; pop. 17,-441.
Cuyahoga Falls city, NE Ohio 44221*; pop. 43,710.
Cyclades isl. group, s Aegean; a dept. of Greece; 1,023 sq. mi.; pop. 86,000; cap. Hermoupolis.
Cypress City city, sw California 90630; pop. 40,391.
Cyprus isl. republic, E Mediterranean; 3,572 sq. mi.; pop. 635,000; cap. Nicosia.
Czechoslovakia republic, CEN. Europe; 49,368 sq. mi.; pop. 15,400,000; cap. Prague.

Dacca city, CEN. Bangladesh; cap.; pop. 2,500,000.
Dachau town, SE West Germany; site of a Nazi concentration camp; pop. 25,000.
Dakar city, w Senegal; cap.; pop. 581,000.
Dallas city, N Texas 75200*; pop. 904,078.
Dalmatia reg., Croatia, w Yugoslavia; 4,954 sq. mi.; pop. 750,000; cap. Split.
Dalton city, NW Georgia 30720; pop. 20,743.
Daly City city, w California 94014*; pop. 78,519.
Damascus city, sw Syria; cap.; pop. 1,150,000.
Danbury city, sw Connecticut 06810*; pop. 60,470.
Danube river, CEN. and E Europe; 1,770 mi. long.
Danvers town, NE Massachusetts 01923; pop. 24,100.
Danville city, E Illinois 61832*; pop. 38,985.
— city, s Virginia 24540*; pop. 45,642.

Danzig city, N Poland; pop. 364,000.
Dardanelles strait, NW Turkey; connects Sea of Marmara with the Aegean.
Darien town, SW Connecticut 06820; pop. 18,892.
Darien, Gulf of inlet of the Caribbean, E coast of Panama.
Dartmouth town, SE Massachusetts 02714; pop. 23,966.
— city, S Nova Scotia, Canada; pop. 64,770.
Davenport city, E Iowa 52800*; pop. 103,264.
Davis city, CEN. California 95616; pop. 36,640.
Dayton city, SW Ohio 45400*; pop. 203,588.
Daytona Beach city, E Florida 32014*; pop. 54,176.
Dead Sea large salt lake on Israel-Jordan border; 1,292 ft. below sea level.
Dearborn city, SE Michigan 48120*; pop. 90,660.
Dearborn Heights city, SE Michigan 48127; pop. 67,706.
Death Valley desert basin, SE California; maximum depth 280 ft. below sea level.
Decatur city, N Alabama 35601*; pop. 42,002.
— city, CEN. Georgia 30030*; pop. 18,404.
— city, CEN. Illinois 62521*; pop. 94,081.
Deccan Plateau triangular tableland covering most of the penin. of India.
Dedham city, E Massachusetts 02026; pop. 25,298.
Deerfield vill., NE Illinois 60015; pop. 17,430.
Deerfield Beach town, SE Florida 33441; pop. 39,193.
Deer Park uninc. place, SE New York 11729; pop . 31,120.
Defiance city, NW Ohio 43512; pop. 16,810.
De Kalb city, N Illinois 60115; pop. 33,099.
Delaware state, E United States; 1,978 sq. mi.; pop. 595,225; cap. Dover.
— city, CEN. Ohio 43015; pop. 15,008.
Delaware River river separating Pennsylvania and Delaware from New York and New Jersey; 315 mi. long.
Del City city, CEN. Oklahoma 73115; pop. 28,424.
Delhi terr., CEN. India; 573 sq. mi.; pop. 6,196,414; contains New Delhi.
— city; Delhi terr.; cap.; pop. 3,288,000.
Delray Beach city, SE Florida 33444; pop. 34,325.
Del Rio city, SW Texas 78840; pop. 30,034.
Denison city, N Texas 75020; pop. 23,884.
Denmark kingdom, NW Europe; 16,619 sq. mi.; pop. 5,161,000; cap. Copenhagen.
Denton city, N Texas 76201; pop. 48,063.
Denver city, N Colorado 80200*; cap.; pop. 491,396.
Depew vill., W New York 14043; pop. 19,819.
Des Moines city, CEN. Iowa 50300*; cap.; pop. 191,003.
Des Plaines city, NE Illinois 60016*; pop. 53,568.
Detroit city, SE Michigan 48200*; pop. 1,203,339.
Devil's Island rocky isl. off the coast of French Guiana; formerly a penal colony.
District of Columbia federal dist., E United States; coextensive with Washington, the capital; pop. 637,651.
Dixon city N Illinois 61021; pop. 15,659.
Djibouti, republic, E Africa; 8,500 sq. mi.; pop. 116,000; cap. Djibouti.
Dnepropetrovsk city, SW Ukrainian SSR; pop. 1,066,000. Also **Dniepropetrovsk.**
Dnieper river, SW USSR; 1,420 mi. long. Also **Dnepr.**
Dneister river, SW USSR; 876 mi. long Also **Dnestr.**
Dodecanese isl. group, Aegean Sea; a dept. of Greece; 1,036 sq. mi.; pop. 120,000; cap. Rhodes.
Dolomite Alps E div. of the Alps, N Italy.
Dolton, vill., NE Illinois 60419; pop. 24,766.
Dominican Republic republic, E Hispaniola; 18,700 sq. mi.; pop. 5,580,000; cap. Santo Domingo.
Don river, SW RSFSR; 1,222 mi. long.
Donelson uninc. place, CEN. Tennessee 37214; pop 17,195.
Donets river, SW USSR; 631 mi. long.
Dorval city, S Quebec, Canada; pop. 20,469.
Dothan city, SE Alabama 36301*; pop. 48,750.
Douai town, N France; pop. 49,000.
Dover municipal boro., SE England; pop. 35,000.
— city, CEN. Delaware 19901; cap.; pop. 23,512.
— city, SE New Hampshire 03820; pop. 23,377.
— town, N New Jersey 07801; pop. 14,681.
Dover, Strait of strait at the E end of the English Channel; 21 mi. wide.
Downers Grove vill., NE Illinois 60515; pop. 39,274.
Downey city, SW California 90240*; pop. 82,602.
Dracut town, NE Massachusetts 01826; pop. 21,249.
Drayton Plains city, SE Michigan 48020; pop. 16,462.
Dresden city, S East Germany; pop. 502,000.
Drummondville city, S Quebec, Canada; pop. 31,813.
Dublin city, E Ireland; cap.; pop. 566,000.
— city, CEN. Georgia 31021; pop. 16,083.

Dubuque city, E Iowa 52001*; pop. 62,321.
Duisburg city, W West Germany; pop 458,000.
Duluth city, NE Minnesota 55800*; pop. 92,811.
Dumont boro., NE New Jersey 07628; pop. 18,334.
Duncan city, S Oklahoma 73533; pop. 22,517.
Dundalk uninc. place, CEN. Maryland 21222; pop. 85,377.
Dundas town, S Ontario, Canada; pop. 17,208.
Dundee burgh, E Scotland; pop. 182,000.
Dunedin city, W Florida 32528; pop. 30,203.
Dunkirk town, N France; scene of evacuation of British forces in World War II, May–June 1940; pop. 28,000.
— city, W New York 14048; pop. 15,310.
Dunmore boro., NE Pennsylvania 18512; pop. 16,781.
Durban city, SE South Africa; pop. 683,000.
Durham city, CEN. North Carolina 27700*; pop. 100,831.
Düsseldorf city, W West Germany; pop. 681,000.
Dutch Guiana See SURINAM.

Eagle Pass city, SW Texas 78852; pop. 21,407.
East Berlin See BERLIN.
Eastchester city, SE New York 10709; pop. 21,330.
East Chicago city, NW Indiana 46312*; pop. 39,786.
East China Sea NE part of the China Sea.
East Cleveland city, NE Ohio 44112; pop. 36,957.
East Detroit city, SE Michigan 48021; pop. 38,281.
Easter Island isl. of Chile, South Pacific; known for stone monuments found there; 45 sq. mi.
East Germany See GERMANY.
East Hartford town, CEN. Connecticut 06108; pop. 52,563.
East Haven town, S Connecticut 06512; pop. 25,028.
East Indies 1 The isls. of the Malay Archipelago. 2 SE Asia. 3 Formerly, India. Also **East India.**
Eastlake city, NE Ohio 44094; pop. 22,104.
East Lansing city, CEN. Michigan 48823*; pop. 48,309.
East Liverpool city, E Ohio 43920; pop. 16,687.
East Los Angeles uninc. place, SW California 90022; pop. 105,033.
East Massapequa city, SE New York; pop. 15,926.
East Meadow city, SE New York 11554; pop. 46,252.
East Millcreek city, NE Utah 84101; pop. 26,579.
East Moline city, NW Illinois 61244; pop. 20,907.
Easton city, S Pennsylvania 18042*; pop. 26,027.
East Orange city, NE New Jersey 07017*; pop. 77,025.
East Paterson boro., NE New Jersey 07407; pop. 22,749.
East Peoria city, CEN. Illinois 61611; pop. 22,385.
East Point city, CEN. Georgia 30044; pop. 37,486.
East Providence town, E Rhode Island 02914; pop. 50,980.
East Prussia former prov. of Prussia, NE Germany.
East Ridge town, SE Tennessee 37412; pop. 21236.
East Saint Louis city, SW Illinois 62201*; pop. 55,200.
Eastview town, SE Ontario, Canada; pop. 24,269.
Eau Claire city, CEN. Wisconsin 54701*; pop. 51.509.
Economy boro., W Pennsylvania; pop. 17,176.
Ecorse city, SE Michigan 48229; pop. 14,447.
Ecuador republic, NW South America; 109,484 sq. mi.; pop. 8,625,000; cap. Quito.
Eden city, CEN. North Carolina 27288; pop. 15,672.
Edina city, SE Minnesota 55424; pop. 46,073.
Edinburg city, S Texas 78539; pop. 24,075.
Edinburgh city, E Scotland; cap.; pop. 465,000.
Edmond city, CEN. Oklahoma 73034; pop. 34,637.
Edmonds city, NW Washington 98020; pop. 27,527.
Edmonton city, CEN. Alberta, Canada; cap.; pop. 451,635.
Egypt republic, NE Africa; 386,198 sq. mi.p pop. 43,000,000; cap. Cairo: official name **Arab Republic of Egypt.**
Eire Ireland: *the Irish Gaelic name.*
Elba isl. betw. Italy and Corsica; sovereign under the exiled Napolean Bonaparte, 1814–15.
Elbe river, CEN. Europe; 725 mi. long.
Elbrus, Mount mtn., NW Georgian SSR; 18,603 ft.
Elburz Mountains mtn. range N Iran.
El Cajon city, SW California 92020*; pop. 73,892.
El Centro city, S California 92243*; pop. 23,996.
El Cerrito city, W California 94530*; pop. 22,731.
El Dorado city, S Arkansas 71730*; pop. 26,685.
Elgin city, NE Illinois 60120*; pop. 63,798.
Elizabeth city, NE New Jersey 07200*; pop. 106,201.
Elk Grove Village vill., NE Illinois 60007; pop. 28,907.
Elkhart city, N Indiana 46514*; pop. 41,305.
Ellis Island isl., upper New York Bay; former site of US immigration station.
Elmhurst city, NE Illinois 60126*; pop. 44,251.
Elmira city, S New York 14901*; pop. 35,327.
Elmont uninc. place, SE New York 11003; pop. 28,363.
El Monte city, SW California 91731*; pop. 79,494.

Elmwood Park vill., NE Illinois 60635; pop. 24,016.
El Paso city, W Texas 79900*; pop. 425,259.
El Salvador republic, W Central America; 8,260 sq. mi.; pop. 4,750,000; cap. San Salvador.
El Segundo city, SW California 90245*; pop. 13,752.
Elwood city, SE New York 11731; pop. 15,031.
Elyria city, N Ohio 44035*; pop. 57,504.
Emporia city, CEN. Kansas 66801*; pop.25,287.
Endicott vill., S New York 13760*; pop. 14,457.
Endwell city, SW New York 13762; pop. 15,999.
Enfield town, N Connecticut 06030; pop. 42,695
England S part and largest political division of Great Britain; 50,366 sq. mi.; pop. 46,827,000; cap. London.
Englewood city, CEN. Colorado 80110; pop. 30,021
— city, NE New Jersey 07631*; pop. 23,701.
English Channel strait, betw. England and France; 20-100 mi. wide.
Enid city, N Oklahoma 73701*; pop. 50,363.
Eniwetok atoll, Marshall Islands; U.S. nuclear weapons testing area.
Enterprise city, SE Alabama 36330*; pop. 18,033.
Epsom town, SE England; site of famous racecourse; pop. 72,000.
Equatorial Guinea republic, W Africa; 10,830 sq. mi.; pop. 370,000; cap. Malabo.
Erie city, NW Pennsylvania 16500*; pop. 119,123.
Erie, Lake southernmost of the Great Lakes; 9,940 sq. mi.
Erie Canal waterway betw. Albany and Buffalo, New York; integrated with New York State Barge Canal.
Eritrea state E Africa; federated with Ethiopia; 45,000 sq. mi.; pop. 1,800,000; cap. Asmara.
Erivan see YEREVAN.
Escanaba city, NW Michigan 49829; pop. 14,355.
Escondido city, SW California 92025*; pop. 62,480.
Essen city, W West Germany; pop. 697,000.
Essex uninc. place, N Maryland 21221; pop. 38,193.
Estonian SSR constituent republic, W USSR; 17,400 sq. mi.; pop. 1,374,000; cap. Tallinn. Also **Estonia**.
Ethiopia country E Africa; 471,778 sq mi., pop. 32,000; cap. Addis Ababa.
Etna, Mount volcano, E Sicily; 10,868 ft.
Euboea isl. of Greece in the Aegean; 1,457 sq. mi.
Euclid city, NE Ohio 44117; pop. 59,999.
Eugene city, W Oregon 97401*; pop. 105,624.
Euphrates river, SW Asia; 1,740 mi. long.
Eurasia large land mass comprising Europe and Asia.
Eureka city, NW California 95501*; pop. 24,153.
Europe continent comprising the W part of the Eurasian land mass; about 4,063,000 sq. mi.
Evanston city, NE Illinois 60201*; pop. 73,706.
Evansville city, SW Indiana 47700*; pop. 130,496.
Everest mtn., E Nepal; highest point of the earth's surface; 29,028 ft.
Everett city, E Massachusetts 02149; pop. 37,195.
— city, W Washington 98201*; pop. 53,622.
Everglades large swampy reg., S Florida.
Evergreen Park vill., NE Illinois 60642; pop. 22,260.
Exeter co. boro., CEN. Devonshire, England; cap; pop. 96,000.

Fairborn city, SW Ohio 45324; pop. 29,702.
Fairfax town, N Virginia 22030; pop. 19,390.
Fairfield city, CEN California 94533*; pop. 58,099.
— town, SW Connecticut 06430*; pop. 54,849.
Fairhaven town, SE Massachusetts 02719; pop. 15,759.
Fair Lawn boro., NE New Jersey 07410*; pop. 32,229.
Fairmont city, CEN. New York; pop. 15,317.
— city, N West Virginia 26550*; pop. 23,863.
Fairview Park city, NE Ohio 44126; pop. 19,311.
Falkland Islands British col., South Atlantic; 4,618 sq. mi.; pop. 2,000; cap. Stanley.
Fall River city, SE Massachusetts 02720*; pop. 92,574
Falls urb. twp., NE Pennsylvania 18615; pop. 29,082.
Falmouth town, E Massachusetts 02540; pop. 23,640.
Farbo city, SE North Dakota 58100*; pop. 61,308.
Faribault city, SE Minnesota 55021; pop. 16,595.
Farmers Branch city, N Texas 75234; pop. 24,863.
Farmington town, NW New Mexico 87401; pop. 30,729.
Faroe Islands isl. group of Denmark, North Atlantic; 540 sq. mi.; pop. 39,000; cap. Thorshain.
Fayetteville city, NW Arkansas 72701*; pop. 36,604.
— city, CEN. North Carolina 28301*; pop. 59,507.
Federal Republic of Germany See GERMANY.
Ferguson city, E Missouri 63135; pop. 24,740.
Ferndale city, SE Michigan 48220; pop. 26,227.
Fiji Independent member of the Commonwealth of Na-

tions, South Pacific; comprises **Fiji Islands** (7,039 sq. mi.) and **Rotuma** (18 sq. mi.); pop. 625,000; cap. Suva.
Findlay city, CEN. Ohio 45840*; pop. 35,594.
Finland republic, N Europe; 130,119 sq. mi.; pop. 4,800,000; cap. Helsinki.
Finland, Gulf of part of the Baltic Sea betw. Finland and the USSR.
Fitchburg city, N Massachusetts 21420*; pop. 39,580.
Flagstaff city, CEN. Arizona 86001*; pop. 34,641.
Flanders reg., N France and S Belgium.
Flint city, SE Michigan 48500*; pop. 159,611.
Floral Park vill., SE New York 11001*; pop. 16,805.
Florence city, CEN. Tuscany, Italy; cap.; pop. 463,000.
— city, NW Alabama 35630*; pop. 37,029.
— city, E South Carolina 29501; pop. 30,062.
Florence-Graham uninc. place SW California 90001; pop. 42,895.
Florida state, SE United States; 58,560 sq. mi.; pop. 9,739,992; cap. Tallahassee.
Florida Keys isl. group SW of Florida.
Florissant city, E Missouri 63031*; pop. 55,372.
Fond du Lac town, N Wisconsin 54935*; pop. 35,515.
Fontainebleau town, N France; site of a former royal residence; pop. 20,000.
Fontana city, CEN. California 92335*; pop. 37,109.
Foochow city, SE China; pop. 616,000.
Forest Hill vill., S Ontario, Canada; pop. 23,135.
Forest Park town, CEN. Georgia 30050; pop. 18,782.
— vill., NE Illinois 60130; pop. 13,177.
— city, SW Ohio 45405; pop. 18,675.
Forestville city, SW Maryland 20028; pop. 16,152.
Formosa Taiwan: *a former name.*
Fort Benning city, W Georgia 31905; pop. 27,495.
Fort Bragg city, CEN. North Carolina 28307; pop. 46,995.
Fort Carson city, CEN. Colorado 80913; pop. 19,399.
Fort Collins city, N Colorado 80521*; pop. 64,632.
Fort Dix city, CEN. New Jersey 07024; pop. 26,290.
Fort Dodge city, CEN. Iowa 50501; pop. 29,423.
Fort Gordon city, E Georgia 30905; pop. 15,589.
Forth, Firth of estuary of the Forth River; 51 mi. long.
Fort Hood city, CEN. Texas 76544; pop. 32,597.
Forth River river, SE Scotland; 65 mi. long.
Fort Knox military reservation, N Kentucky 40120*; site of the Federal gold bullion depository.
Fort-Lamy N'djamena: *the former name.*
Fort Lauderdale city, SE Florida 33300*; pop. 153,256.
Fort Lee boro., NE New Jersey 07024*; pop. 32,449.
Fort Leonard Wood city, SE Missouri 65473; pop. 33,799.
Fort Lewis city, CEN. Washington 98433; pop. 38,054.
Fort Meade city, NW Maryland 20755; pop. 16,699.
Fort Myers city, SW Florida 33901; pop. 36,638.
Fort Pierce city, E Florida 33450*; pop. 48,802.
Fort Sill city, SW Oklahoma 73503; pop. 21,217.
Fort Smith city, W Arkansas 72901*; pop. 71,384
Fort Thomas city, N Kentucky 41075; pop. 16,012.
Fort Walton Beach city, NW Florida 32548; pop. 20,829.
Fort Wayne city, NE Indiana 46800; pop. 172,196.
Fort Worth city, N Texas 76100*; pop. 385,141.
Fostoria city, N Ohio 44830; pop. 15,743.
Fountain Valley city, SW California 92708; pop. 55,080.
Framingham town, E Massachusetts 01701; pop. 65,113.
France republic, W Europe; 212,974 sq. mi.; pop. 54,040,000; cap. Paris.
Frankfort city, CEN. Kentucky 40601; cap.; pop. 25,973.
Frankfurt (on the Main) city, CEN. West Germany; pop. 660,000.
Frankfurt (on the Oder) city, E East Germany; pop. 59,000.
Franklin town, E Massachusetts 02038; pop. 18,217.
Franklin Park vill., NE Illinois 60131; pop. 17,507.
Franklin Square uninc. place, SE New York 11010; pop. 32,156.
Frederick city, NW Maryland 21701; pop. 27,557.
Fredericton city, CEN. New Brunswick, Canada; pop. 24,254.
Freeport city, NW Bahamas, on Grand Bahama Island; pop. 26,000.
— city, N Illinois 61032*; pop. 26,406.
— vill., SE New York 11520; pop. 40,347.
Fremont city, N California 94536; pop. 131,945.
— city, E Nebraska 68025; pop. 23,979.
— city, N Ohio 43420; pop. 17,834.
French Guiana French overseas dept. NE South America; 35,000 sq. mi.; pop. 67,000; cap. Cayenne.
French Polynesia French overseas terr., South

Pacific; comprises the Society, Marquesas, Gambier, and other islands; 1,560 sq. mi.; pop. 160,000; cap. Papeete.

French Republic France, with its overseas depts. and terrs.

French West Indies isls. comprising Guadaloupe and Martinique.

Fresno city, CEN. California 93700*; pop. 218,202.

Fridley city, E Minnesota 55421; pop. 30,228.

Friesland prov., N Netherlands; 1,251 sq. mi.; pop. 528,000; cap. Leeuwarden.

Frigid Zone See NORTH FRIGID ZONE, SOUTH FRIGID ZONE.

Frisian Islands isl. group, North Sea near Germany, Denmark, and the Netherlands.

Fuji extinct volcano, Honshu, Japan; 12,389 ft.

Fullerton city, SW California 92631*; pop. 102,034.

Fundy, Bay of inlet of the Atlantic betw. Nova Scotia and new Brunswick and NE Maine.

Gabonese Republic state of the French Community, W equatorial Africa; 102,290 sq. mi.; pop. 950,000; cap. Libreville. Also **Gabon.**

Gadsden city, NE Alabama 35901*; pop. 47,565.

Gainesville city, N Florida 32601*; pop. 81,371.

— city, CEN. Georgia 30501*; pop. 15,280.

Galápagos Islands isl. group of Ecuador, South Pacific.

Galesburg city, W Illinois 61401; pop. 35,305.

Galicia reg., SE Poland and NW Ukrainian SSR.

— reg., NW Spain.

Galilee reg., N Israel.

Galilee, Sea of freshwater lake; betw. NE Israel, SW Syria, and NW Jordan; 64 sq. mi.

Gallipoli Peninsula penin., NW Turkey.

Galt city, S Ontario, Canada; pop. 38,897.

Galveston city, SE Texas 77550*; pop. 61,902.

Gambia independent member of the Commonwealth of Nations, W Africa; 4,361 sq. mi.; pop. 578,000; cap. Banjul.

Ganges river, N India and Bangladesh, sacred to Hindus; 1,560 mi. long.

Gardena city, SW California 90247*; pop. 45,165.

Garden City city, SE Michigan 48135; pop. 35,640.

— vill., SE New York 11530; pop. 22,727.

Garden Grove city, SW California 92640*; pop. 123,351.

Gardner city, N Massachusetts 01440*; pop. 17,900.

Garfield city, NE New Jersey 07026; pop. 26,803.

Garfield Heights city, NE Ohio 44125; pop. 33,380.

Garland city, N Texas 75040*; pop. 138,857.

Gary city, NW Indiana 46400*; pop. 151,953.

Gascony reg., SW France.

Gastonia city, S North Carolina 28052*; pop. 47,333.

Gatineau town, SW Quebec, Canada; pop. 22,321.

Gaza city, SW Palestine; adm. by the United Arab Republic with the **Gaza Strip,** the surrounding area; pop. 365,000.

Gdańsk port city, N Poland: formerly, as **Danzig,** cap. of the territory of the Free City of Danzig; pop. 398,000.

Gdynia city, NW Poland; pop. 190,000.

Geneva city, SW Switzerland; pop. 332,000.

— city, CEN. New York 14456; pop. 16,793.

Geneva, Lake of lake, W Switzerland; 224 sq. mi.

Genoa city, NW Italy; pop. 842,000.

Georgetown city, N Guyana; cap.; pop. 195,000.

— town, S Ontario, Canada; pop. 17,053.

Georgia state, SE United States; 58,876 sq. mi.; pop. 5,464,265; cap. Atlanta.

Georgian SSR constituent republic, SW USSR; 26,900 sq. mi.; pop. 4,730,000; cap. Tbilisi.

German Democratic Republic See GERMANY.

Germany country, CEN. Europe; divided in 1949 into the **Federal Republic of Germany** (West Germany); 95,735 sq. mi.; pop. 62,827,000; cap. Bonn; and the **German Democratic Republic** (East Germany); 41,479 sq. mi. (excluding East Berlin); pop. 16,716,000; cap. East Berlin.

Ghana republic of the Commonwealth of Nations, W Africa; 92,100 sq. mi.; pop. 11,750,000; cap. Accra.

Ghent city, NW Belgium; pop. 149,000.

Gibraltar British col. on the Rock of Gibraltar; 2.25 sq. mi.; pop. 33,000.

Gibraltar, Rock of penin., S Spain; dominates the Strait of Gibraltar.

Gibraltar, Strait of strait, betw. Spain and Africa, W Mediterranean.

Gilbert Islands See *Kiribati*

Glace Bay town, NE Nova Scotia, Canada; pop. 22,440.

Gladstone city, W Missouri 64118; pop. 24,990.

Glasgow burgh, SW Scotland; pop. 908,000.

Glastonbury city, CEN. Connecticut 06033; pop. 24,327.

Glen Burnie city, NE Maryland 21061; pop. 38,608.

Glen Cove city, SE New York 11542; pop. 24,618.

Gendale city, CEN. Arizona 85301; pop. 96,988.

— city, SW California 91200*; pop. 139,060.

Glendora city, SW California 91740; pop. 38,654.

Glen Ellyn vill., NE Illinois 60137*; pop. 23,649.

Glens Falls city, E New York 12801*; pop. 15,897.

Glenside city, SE Pennsylvania 19038; pop. 17,353.

Glenview vill., NE Illinois 60025*; pop. 30,842.

Gloucester co. boro., CEN. Gloucestershire, England; cap.; pop. 90,000.

— city, NE Massachusetts 01930*; pop. 27,768.

Gloversville city, CEN New York 12078*; pop. 17,836.

Goa former Portuguese terr., W India; annexed by India in 1961; 1,394 sq. mi.; pop. 857,000; cap. New Goa.

Gobi Desert desert, CEN. Asia; 500,000 sq. mi.

Golden Gate strait betw. San Francisco Bay and the Pacific.

Golden Valley vill., SE Minnesota 55427; pop. 22,775.

Goldsboro city, CEN. North Carolina 27530; pop. 31,871.

Good Hope, Cape of promontory, SW South Africa.

Gorki city, CEN. RSFSR; pop. 1,344,000. Also **Gorkiy, Gorky.**

Goshen city, N Indiana 46526; pop. 19,665.

Göteborg city, SW Sweden; pop. 452,000.

Gotland isl. of SE Sweden, Baltic Sea; 1,167 sq. mi.

Granada city, S Spain; pop. 170,000.

Granby city, S Quebec, Canada; pop. 34,385.

Grand Banks submarine shoal, North Atlantic; near Newfoundland.

Grand Canyon gorge of the Colorado River, NW Arizona; ab. 250 mi. long.

Grand Forks city, E North Dakota 58201*; pop. 43,765.

Grand Island city, CEN. Nebraska 68801; pop. 33,180.

Grand Junction city, W Colorado; 81501*; pop. 28,144.

Grand' Mère city CEN. Quebec, Canada; pop. 17,137.

Grand Prairie city, N Texas 75050*; pop. 71,462.

Grand Rapids city, W Michigan 49500*; pop. 181,843.

Grandview city, W Missouri 64030*; pop. 24,502.

Granite City city, SW Illinois 62040*; pop. 36,815.

Great Barrier Reef coral reef off the coast of Queensland, Australia.

Great Bend city, CEN. Kansas 67530; pop. 16,608.

Great Britain principal isl. of the United Kingdom; comprises England, Scotland, and Wales; 94,251 sq. mi.; pop. 56,387,000; cap. London.

Great Divide See CONTINENTAL DIVIDE.

Greater Antilles See ANTILLES.

Great Falls city, CEN. Montana 59401*; pop. 56,725.

Great Lakes chain of five lakes, CEN. North America; on Canada-United States border; comprises Lakes Superior, Michigan, Huron, Ontario, and Erie; total 94,710 sq. mi.

Great Plains plateau, W North America; E of the Rockies.

Great Russia CEN. and NW reg. of the USSR.

Great Salt Lake salt lake, NW Utah; ab. 2,000 sq. mi.

Great Slave Lake lake, S Northwest Territories, Canada; 11,170 sq. mi.

Great Smoky Mountains mtn. range, North Carolina and Tennessee.

Greece republic, SE Europe; 50,944 sq. mi.; pop. 9,302,000; cap. Athens.

Greeley city, N Colorado 80630*; pop. 53,006.

Green Bay city, E Wisconsin 54300*; pop. 87,899.

Greenbelt city, CEN. Maryland 20770*; pop. 16,000.

Greendale vill., SE Wisconsin 53129; pop. 16,928.

Greenfield uninc. place, NW Massachusetts 01301; pop. 18,436.

— town, SE Wisconsin 53220; pop. 31,467.

Greenfield Park town, S Quebec, Canada; pop. 15,348.

Greenland isl. of Denmark near NE North America; 840,154 sq. mi.; pop. 61,000.

Green Mountains mtn. range, CEN. Vermont.

Greensboro city, CEN. North Carolina 27400*; pop. 155,642.

Greensburg city, SW Pennsylvania 15601*; pop. 15,870.

Greenville city, W Mississippi 38701*; pop. 40,613.

— city, E North Carolina 27834*; pop. 35,740.

— city, NW South Carolina 29601*; pop. 58,242.

— city, NE Texas 75401*; pop. 22,161.

Greenwich boro., SE London; former site of the Royal Observatory; location of prime meridian; pop. 218,000.

— town, SW Connecticut 06830*; pop. 59,578.

Greenwood city, CEN. Mississippi 38930*; pop. 20,115.

— city, W South Carolina 29646*; pop. 21,613.

Grenada Independent republic, in the West Indies; 133 sq. mi.; pop. 106,000; cap. St. George's.

Gretna city, SE Louisiana 70053; pop. 24,875.

Griffin city, CEN. Georgia 30223; pop. 22,734.

Griffith town, NW Indiana 46319; pop. 18,168.

Grimsby town, S Ontario, Canada; pop. 15,770.

Grosse Pointe Park city, SE Michigan; pop. 15,585.

Grosse Pointe Woods city SE Michigan; pop. 21,878.

Groves city, SE Texas 77619; pop. 18,062.

Guadalajara city, CEN. Mexico; pop. 1,813,000.

Guadalcanal isl., British Solomons; scene of an Allied invasion in World War II, 1943.

Guadeloupe French overseas dept., Lesser Antilles; 687 sq. mi.; pop. 373,000; cap. Basse-Terre.

Guam uninc. terr. of the United States, an isl. in the Marianas; 212 sq. mi.; pop 103,000; cap. Agaña.

Guantánamo city, SE Cuba, near, **Guantánamo Bay;** pop. 125,000.

Guatemala republic, N Central America; 42,042 sq. mi.; pop. 7,470,000.

— city, CEN. Guatemala; cap.; pop. 769,000.

Guayama town, SE Puerto Rico 0065; pop. 16,913.

Guayaquil city, W Ecuador; pop. 1,100,000.

Guelph city, S Ontario, Canada; pop. 60,087.

Guernica town, N Spain; object of a German bombing, 1937.

Guernsey one of the Channel Islands; 25 sq. mi.

Guiana coastal reg., NE South America. See BRITISH GUIANA, FRENCH GUIANA, GUYANA, SURINAM.

Guinea republic, W Africa; 94,925 sq. mi.; pop. 5,115,000; cap. Conakry.

Guinea, Gulf of large bay of the Atlantic off W Africa.

Guinea-Bissau republic, W Africa; 13,948 sq. mi.; pop. 557,000; cap. Bissau.

Gulfport city, SE Mississippi 39501*; pop. 39,676.

Gulf Stream A warm ocean current flowing from the Gulf of Mexico northeastward toward Europe.

Guyana independent member of the Commonwealth of Nations, NE South America, 83,000 sq. mi.; pop 890,000; cap. Georgetown.

Haarlem city, W Netherlands; pop. 173,000.

Hacienda Heights city, S California 91745; pop. 35,969.

Hackensack city, NE New Jersey 07601*; pop. 36.039.

Haddon urb. twp., SW New Jersey; pop. 17,099.

Hagerstown city, W Maryland 21740*; pop. 35,862.

Hague, The city, W Netherlands; seat of government; pop. 6,715,000. Also **s'Gravenhage.**

Haifa city, NW Israel; pop. 227,200.

Haiti republic, W Hispaniola; 10,714 sq. mi.; pop. 5,100,000; cap. Port-au-Prince.

Halifax city, S Nova Scotia; Canada; cap.; pop. 122,035.

Hallandale city, SE Florida 33009; pop. 36,517.

Halle city, SW East Germany; pop. 257,000.

Haltom City vill., N Texas 79917; pop. 29,014.

Hamburg state and city, N West Germany; 288 sq. mi.; pop. 1,817,000.

Hamden town, S Connecticut 06514; pop. 49,357.

Hamilton city, CEN. Bermuda; cap.; pop. 3,000.

— city, SW Ohio 45010*; pop. 63,189.

— city, S Ontario, Canada; pop. 309,173.

Hammond city, NW Indiana 46320*; pop. 93,714.

Hampton city SE Virginia 23360*; pop. 122,617.

Hampton Roads channel, SE Virginia; connects several rivers with Chesapeake Bay; scene of the engagement of the "Monitor" and the "Merrimack," 1862.

Hamtramck city, SE Michigan 48212; pop. 27,245.

Hanford city, CEN. California 93230*; pop. 15,179.

Hangchow city, E China; pop. 784,000.

Hannibal city, NE Missouri 63401*; pop. 18,609.

Hannover city, CEN. West Germany; pop. 518,000.

Hanoi city, CEN. Vietnam; cap; pop 644,000.

Hanover boro., S Pennsylvania 7331; pop. 15,623.

Harbin city, NE China; pop. 1,552,000.

Harlingen city, S Texas 78550*; pop. 43,543.

Harper Woods city, SE Michigan 48236; pop. 20,186.

Harrisburg city, CEN. Pennsylvania 17101*; cap; pop. 53,264.

Hartford city, CEN. Connecticut 06100*; cap.; pop. 136,392.

Harvey city, NE Illinois 60426*; pop. 35,810.

Hastings city, S Nebraska 68901; pop. 23,580.

Hattiesburg city, SE Mississippi 39401*; pop. 40,829.

Havana city, W Cuba; cap.; pop. 2,000,000.

Haverford urb. twp., SE Pennsylvania 19041; pop. 55,-732.

Haverhill city, NE Massachusetts 01830*; pop. 46,865.

Hawaii state of the United States, North Pacific; coextensive with the Hawaiian Islands; 6,435 sq. mi.; pop. 965,000; cap. Honolulu.

— largest of the Hawaiian Islands; 4,020 sq. mi.

Hawthorne city, SW California 90250*; pop. 56,447.

— boro., NE New Jersey 07007; pop. 19,173.

Hays city, CEN. Kansas 67601*; pop. 15,396.

Hayward city, W California 94541; pop. 94,167.

Hazel Park city, SE Michigan 48030; pop. 23,784.

Hazleton city, E Pennsylvania 18201; pop. 27,318.

Hebrides isl. group off W coast of Scotland, ab. 3,000 sq. mi.

Heidelberg city, SW West Germany; pop. 122,000.

Hejaz div., W Saudi Arabia; 150,000 sq. mi.; pop 2 million; cap. Mecca.

Helena city, CEN. Montana 59601*; cap.; pop. 22,730.

Helicon mtn. range, CEN. Greece.

Helsinki city, S Finland; cap.; pop. 517,000.

Hempfield urb. twp., SW Pennsylvania; pop. 29,704.

Hempstead vill., SE New York 11550*; pop. 40,404.

Henderson city, NW Kentucky 42420; pop. 22,976.

— city, S Nevada 89015; pop. 16,395.

Hermosa Beach city, SW California 90254; pop. 17,412.

Herzegovina See BOSNIA AND HERZEGOVINA.

Hesse state, W West Germany; 8,150 sq. mi.; pop. 5,423,000; cap. Wiesbaden.

Hialeah city, SE Florida 33010; site of a famous racetrack; pop. 145,254.

Hibbing vill., NE Minnesota 55746; pop. 16,104.

Hickory city, CEN. North Carolina 28601*; pop. 20,569.

Hicksville vill., SE New York 11800*; pop. 48,075.

Highland town, NW Indiana 46322; pop. 24,935.

Highland Park city, NE Illinois 60035*; pop. 30,611.

— city, SE Michigan 48203; pop. 27,909.

High Point city, CEN. North Carolina 27260*; pop. 64,107.

Hillcrest Heights uninc. place. S Maryland; pop. 24,-037.

Hillside urb. twp., NE New Jersey 07205; pop. 21,636.

Hillo city, E Hawaii, Hawaii 96720; pop. 37,017.

Himalayas mtn. range, CEN. Asia.

Hindustan 1 loosely, the reg. of the Ganges where Hindi is spoken. **2** loosely, india.

Hingham town, E Massachusetts 02043; pop. 18,845.

Hinsdale vill., NE Illinois 60521*; pop. 15,918.

Hiroshima city, SW Honshu isl., Japan; devastated by the first atom bomb used in war, Aug. 6, 1945; pop. 542,000.

Hispaniola isl., West Indies; ab. 30,000 sq. mi.; divided into Haiti and the Dominican Republic.

Hobart city, SE Tasmania; cap; pop. 127,000.

— city, NW Indiana 46342; pop. 21,485.

Hobbs city, SE New Mexico 88240; pop. 28,794.

Hoboken city, NE New Jersey 07030*; pop. 42,460.

Ho Chi Minh City See Saigon.

Hoffman Estates city, NE Illinois 60172; pop. 38,258.

Hokkaido isl. of N Japan; ab. 29,000 sq. mi.

Holladay city, NW Utah 84117; pop. 23,014.

Holland See NETHERLANDS.

— city, SW Michigan 49422*; pop. 26,281.

Hollywood area, NW Los Angeles, California; ctr. of US motion-picture industry.

— city, SE Florida 33020*; pop. 117,188.

Holyoke city, CEN. Massachusetts 01040*; pop. 44,678.

Homewood city, CEN. Alabama 35209; pop. 21,245.

— vill., NE Illinois 60430; pop. 18.871.

Honduras republic, NE Central America; 43,277 sq. mi.; pop. 1,126,000; cap. Tegucigalpa.

Hong Kong British col., SE China; includes **Hong Kong Island** and some coastal terr.; 1,126 sq. mi.; pop. 4,727,000; cap. Victoria.

Honolulu City, SE Oahu, Hawaii 96800*; cap.; pop. 364,048.

Honshu isl. of GEN. Japan; 88,745 sq. mi.

Hood, Mount volcanic peak, Cascade Range, NW Oregon 11,245 ft.

Hoover Dam dam, Colorado River at the Arizona-Nevada border; 727 ft. high; 1,282 ft. long.

Hopewell city, SE Virginia 23860; pop. 23,471.

Hopkinsville city, SW Kentucky 42240; pop 27,318.

Horn, Cape S extremity of South America.

Hot Springs city, CEN. Arkansas 71901; pop. 35,166.

Houma city, SE Louisiana 70360*; pop. 32,602.

Houston city, SE Texas 77000*; pop. 1,594,086.

Huber city, SW Ohio 45424; pop. 18943.

Hudson uninc. place, CEN. Massachusetts 01749; pop. 16,-084.

Hudson Bay inland sea, N Canada; connected with the Atlantic by **Hudson Strait;** ab. 475,000 sq. mi.

Hudson River river, E New York; 306 mi. long.

Hull city, sw Quebec, Canada; pop. 63,580.
Hungary republic, CEN. Europe; 35,912 sq. mi.; pop. 10,725,000; cap. Budapest.
Huntington city, NE Indiana 46750; pop. 16,217.
— city, w West Virginia 25700*; pop. 63,684.
Huntington Beach city, sw California 94646*; pop. 170,505.
Huntington Park city, sw California 90255*; pop. 46,223.
Huntington Station uninc. place, SE New York 11746*; pop. 28,817.
Huntsville city, N. Alabama 35800* ; pop. 142,513.
— city, E Texas 77340*; pop. 17,610.
Huron, Lake one of the Great Lakes; betw. Michigan and Ontario; 23,010 sq. mi.
Hurst city, N Texas 76053; pop. 31,420.
Hutchinson city, CEN. Kansas 67501; pop. 36,885.
Hwang Ho river, N China; 2,900 mi. long.
Hyde Park public park, London, England.
Hyderabad city, CEN. India; pop. 1,796,000.
— city, SE Pakistan; pop. 628,310.

Iberia part of sw Europe containing Spain and Portugal.
Iceland isl., North Atlantic; a republic; 39,758 sq. mi.; pop. 235,000; cap. Reykjavik.
Idaho state, NW United States; 83,557 sq. mi.; pop. 943,935; cap. Boise.
Idaho Falls city, SE Idaho 83401*; pop. 39,590.
Ifni prov., sw Morocco; 741 sq. mi.; pop. 50,000; cap. Sidi Ifni.
Ijssel, Lake freshwater lake, CEN. Netherlands.
Illinois state, CEN. United States; 56,400 sq. mi.; pop. 11,418,461; cap. Springfield.
Imperial Beach city, sw California 92032; pop. 20,244.
Imperial Valley agricultural reg., SE California.
Independence city, w Missouri 64050*; pop. 111,806.
India republic of the Commonwealth of Nations, s Asia; 1,778,995 sq. mi.; pop. 683,810,000; cap. New Delhi.
Indiana state, CEN. United States; 36,291 sq. mi.; pop. 5,490,179; cap. Indianapolis.
— boro., CEN. Pennsylvania 15701; pop. 16,100.
Indianapolis city, CEN. Indiana 46200*; cap.; pop. 700,-807.
Indian Ocean ocean betw. Africa, Asia, Australia, and Antarctica.
Indies See EAST INDIES, WEST INDIES.
Indochina 1 SE penin. of Asia. **2** Cambodia, Laos, North and South Vietnam.
Indonesia republic, SE Asia; comprises over 100 isls. of the Malay Archipelago; 735,268 sq. mi.; pop. 155,300,000; cap. Jakarta.
Indus river, Tibet, Kashmir, and Pakistan; 1,800 mi. long.
Inglewood city, sw California 90301*; pop. 94,245.
— uninc. place, CEN. Tennessee; pop. 26,527.
Inkster vill. SE Michigan 48141; pop. 35,190.
Ionian Sea part of the Mediterranean betw. Greece and Sicily.
Iowa state, CEN. United States; 56,280 sq. mi.; pop. 2,913,387; cap. Des Moines.
Iowa City city, E Iowa 52240*; pop. 50,508.
Iraklion city, N CEN. Crete; pop. 78,000. Also **Candia, Heraklion.**
Iran republic, sw Asia; ab. 630,000 sq. mi.; pop. 37,400,000; cap. Teheran.
Iraq republic, sw Asia; 171,599 sq. mi.; pop. 13,400,000; cap. Baghdad.
Ireland westernmost of the British Isles; 31,838 sq. mi.
— republic, s Ireland; 26,600 sq. mi.; pop. 3,460,000; cap. Dublin. See NORTHERN IRELAND.
Irish Sea part of the Atlantic betw. Great Britain and Ireland.
Irkutsk city, s USSR; pop. 462,000.
Irondequoit city, w New York 14617; pop. 63,675.
Ironton city, s Ohio 45638; pop. 15,030.
Irrawaddy river, Tibet and Burma; 1,200 mi. long.
Irving city, N Texas 75060*; pop. 97,260.
Irvington town, NE New Jersey 07111; pop. 59,743.
Islamabad city, NE Pakistan; cap.; pop. 50,000.
Israel republic, E end of the Mediterranean; 7,993 sq. mi.; pop. 4,000,000; cap. Jerusalem.
Istanbul city, NE Turkey; pop. 2,990,680.
Italy republic, s Europe; 116,286 sq. mi.; pop. 57,150,000; cap. Rome.
Ithaca isl. of Greece, Ionian Sea; 36 sq. mi.
— city, CEN. New York 14850; pop. 26,226.
Ivory Coast republic, w Africa; 128,364 sq. mi.; pop. 8,500,000; cap. Abidjan.
Izmir city, w Turkey; pop. 521,000. Also **Smyrna.**

Jackson city, s Michigan 49201*; pop. 39,739.
— city, CEN. Mississippi 39200*; cap.; pop. 202,895.
— city, w Tennessee 38301*; pop. 49,131.
Jacksonville city, CEN. Arkansas 72076*; pop. 27,589.
— city, NE Florida 32200*; pop. 540,898.
— city, CEN. Illinois 62650*; pop. 20,553.
— city, E North Carolina 28540*; pop. 16,021.
Jacques-Cartier city, s Quebec, Canada; pop. 52,527.
Jakarta city, NW Java; cap. of Indonesia; pop. 4,750,000.
Jamaica independent member of the Commonwealth of Nations, isl. of the Greater Antilles; 4,411 sq. mi.; pop. 2,225,000; cap. Kingston.
Jamestown town, NW St. Helena; cap.; pop. 1,600.
— city, sw New York 14701; pop. 35,775.
— city, CEN. North Dakota 58401; pop. 15,385.
— restored vill., E Virginia 23081; site of the first English settlement in the present limits of the United States, 1607.
Jammu and Kashmir state, N India; subject of a territorial dispute with Pakistan; 85,806 sq. mi.; pop. 4,615,-000; caps. Sringar and Jammu.
Janesville city, s Wisconsin 53545*; pop. 51,071.
Japan constitutional empire; E Asia; situated on a chain of isls.; 145,711 sq. mi.; pop. 117,650,000; cap. Tokyo.
Japan, Sea of part of the Pacific betw. Japan and the Asian mainland.
Java isl. of Indonesia; SE of Sumatra; 48,842 sq. mi.
Jeannette city, sw Pennsylvania 15644; pop. 15,209.
Jefferson city, NE Virginia 22303; pop. 25,432.
Jefferson City city, CEN. Missouri 65101*; cap.; pop. 33,619.
Jefferson Heights uninc. place, SE Louisiana 70121; pop. 16,489.
Jeffersonville city, SE Indiana 47130*; pop. 20,008.
Jennings city, E Missouri 63136; pop. 19,379.
Jericho vill., w Jordan; on the site of the ancient city.
Jersey one of the Channel Islands; 45 sq. mi.
Jersey City city, NE New Jersey 07300*; pop. 223,532.
Jerusalem city, E Israel; cap.; pop. 412,000.
Jidda city, w Saudi Arabia; pop. 300,000.
Johannesburg city, NE South Africa; cap.; pop. 1,500,-000
Johnson City vill., s New York 13790; pop. 18,025.
— city, NE Tennessee 37601; pop. 39,753.
Johnston town, NE Rhode Island 02919; pop. 22,037.
Johnstown city, CEN. Pennsylvania 15901*; pop. 35,496.
Joliet city, NE Illinois 60431*; pop. 77,956.
Joliette city, s Quebec, Canada; pop. 20,127.
Jonesboro city, NE Arkansas 72401; pop. 31,530.
Jonquière city, CEN. Quebec, Canada; pop. 28,430.
Joplin city, sw Missouri 64801*; pop. 39,256.
Jordan constitutional monarchy, w Asia; 37,300 sq. mi.; pop. 3,300,000; cap. Amman.
Jordan River river, CEN. Palestine; over 200 mi. long.
Junction City city, CEN. Kansas 66441; pop. 19,018.
Juneau city, SE Alaska 99801; cap.; pop. 6,050.
Jungfrau mtn. peak, CEN. Switzerland; 13,653 ft.
Jura Mountains mtn. range, E France and w Switzerland.
Jutland penin., N Europe; comprises continental Denmark and part of Germany.

Kabul city, CEN. Afghanistan; cap.; pop. 597,000.
Kailua-Lanikai uninc. place, E Oahu, Hawaii 96734; pop. 33,783.
Kalamazoo city, sw Michigan 49001*; pop. 79,722.
Kalimantan Borneo: *the Indonesian name.*
Kaliningrad city, extreme, w USSR; pop. 331,000.
Kamchatka penin., E USSR; betw. the Bering and Okhotsk Seas.
Kampuchea country, sw Indochina peninsula, formerly Cambodia, Khmer Republic; 70,000 sq. mi.; pop. ab. 9,000,000; cap. Phnom Penh.
Kaneohe uninc. place, E Oahu, Hawaii 96744; pop. 29,-903.
Kankakee city, NE Illinois 60901; pop. 30,141.
Kannapolis uninc. place, CEN. North Carolina 28081; pop. 36,293.
Kansas state, CEN. United States; 82,276 sq. mi.; pop. 2,363,208; cap. Topeka.
Kansas City city, NE Kansas 66100*; pop. 161,087.
— city, w Missouri 64100*; pop. 448,159.
Karachi city, s Pakistan; former cap.; pop. 3,469,000.
Karelian ASSR adm. div., NW RSFSR; 66,560 sq. mi.; pop. 711,000; cap. Petrozavodsk.
Karnak vill., s Egypt; near the site of ancient Thebes.
Kashmir See JAMMU AND KASHMIR.
Kathmandu city, CEN. Nepal; cap.; pop. 195,000.

Kauai one of the Hawaiian Islands; 551 sq. mi.
Kaunas city, CEN. Lithuanian SSR; pop. 314,000.
Kazakh SSR constituent republic, CEN. USSR; 1,064,000 sq. mi.; pop. 13,070,000; cap. Alma-Ata.
Kazan city, NW Tatar ASSR; cap.; pop. 885,000.
Kearney city, CEN. Nebraska 68847; pop. 19,181.
Kearns uninc. place, N Utah 84118; pop. 17,071.
Kearny town, NE New Jersey 07032; pop. 37,585.
Keene city, SW New Hampshire 03431; pop. 20,467.
Kelowna city, S British Columbia, Canada; pop. 19,412.
Kendall city, SE Florida 33156; pop. 35,479.
Kenmore vill., W New York 14217; pop. 20,890.
Kennedy, Cape Cape Canaveral: *the former name.*
Kenner city, SE Louisiana 70062; pop. 66,382.
Kennewick city, S Washington 99336; pop. 34,399.
Kenosha city, SE Wisconsin 53140*; pop. 77,685.
Kent city, NE Ohio 44240*; pop. 26,164.
— city, CEN. Washington 98031; pop. 21,510.
Kentucky state, CEN. United States; 40,395 sq. mi.; pop. 3,661,433. cap. Frankfort.
Kentucky River river, N Kentucky; 259 mi. long.
Kentwood city, SW Michigan 49508; pop. 30,438.
Kenwood city, SW Ohio 43606; pop. 15,789.
Kenya independent member of the Commonwealth of Nations, E Africa; 224,960 sq. mi.; pop. 16,300,000; cap. Nairobi.
Kenya, Mount extinct volcano, CEN. Kenya; 17,058 ft.
Kettering city, SW Ohio 45429; pop. 61,186.
Kewanee city, NW Illinois 61443; pop. 15,762.
Key West southwesternmost of the Florida Keys.
— city, Key West Island, Florida 33040*; pop. 27,563.
Kharkov city, NE Ukrainian SSR; pop. 1,444,000.
Khartoum city, CEN. Sudan; cap.; pop. 852,000.
Khmer Republic Cambodia: an earlier name.
Khyber Pass mtn. pass betw. Afghanistan and Pakistan; ab. 30 mi. long.
Kiel city, N West Germany; pop. 269,000.
Kiel Canal ship canal betw. Kiel and the mouth of the Elbe; ab. 61 mi. long.
Kiev city, CEN. Ukrainian SSR; cap.; pop. 2,144,000.
Kilauea active crater, Mauna Loa volcano, Hawaii.
Kilimanjaro, Mount mtn., NE Tanzania; highest in Africa; 19,565 ft.
Kileen city, CEN. Texas 76540*; pop. 61,186.
Kimberley city, CEN. South Africa; pop. 96,000.
Kingsport city, NE Tennessee 37660*; pop. 37,027.
Kingston city, SE Jamaica; cap.; pop. 123,000.
— city, SE New York 12401; pop. 25,554.
— boro., CEN. Pennsylvania 18704; pop. 18,325.
— city, SE Ontario, Canada; pop. 59,047.
Kingsville city, S Texas 78363*; pop. 28,808.
Kinshasa city, W Zaire; cap.; pop. 2,500,000.
Kinston city, CEN. North Carolina 28501; pop. 25,234.
Kirghiz SSR constituent republic, S USSR; 76,640; sq. mi.; pop. 3 million; cap. Frunze.
Kiribati, republic including 3 isl. groups SW Pacific, formerly Gilbert Islands; 264 sq. mi.; pop. 60,000; cap. Bairiki.
Kirkland city, CEN. Washington 98033; pop. 15,249.
Kirksville city, N Missouri 63501; pop. 15,560.
Kirkwood city E Missouri 63122; pop. 31,890.
Kitchener city, S Ontario, Canada; pop. 111,804.
Kitty Hawk vill., NE North Carolina; site of the first sustained airplane flight, by Wilbur and Orville Wright, 1903.
Klamath Falls city, S Oregon 97601*; pop. 15,775.
Klondike reg., NW Canada in the basin of the **Klondike River.**
Knoxville city, E Tennessee 37900*; pop. 183,139.
Kobe city, S Japan; pop. 1,366,500.
Kodiak Island isl., S Alaska.
Kokomo city, CEN. Indiana 46901*; pop. 47,808.
Königsberg Kaliningrad: *the former German name.*
Korea penin., E Asia; 85,266 sq. mi.; divided into the **Democratic People's Republic of Korea** (North Korea); 47,225 sq. mi.; pop. 18,350,000; cap. Pyongyang; and the **Republic of Korea** (South Korea); 38,452 sq. mi.; pop. 38,800,000; cap. Seoul.
Korea Strait strait, betw. the Sea of Japan and the East China Sea.
Kozhikode city, S India; pop. 193,000. Also **Calicut.**
Krakatoa isl. volcano betw. Sumatra and Java, Indonesia; site of most violent volcanic eruption of modern times, 1883.
Kraków city, S Poland; pop. 583,000.
Krasnodar city, SW USSR; pop. 475,000.
Kronstadt city, W USSR; pop. 59,000.
Kuala Lumpur city, CEN. Malaya; cap. of Malaya and Malaysia; pop. 1,000,000.

Kunming city, SW China; pop. 1,700,000.
Kurdistan reg., NW Iran, NE Iraq, and SE Turkey; peopled largely by Kurds.
Kure city, SW Japan; pop. 241,000.
Kurile Islands isl. group, SE USSR; 5,700 sq. mi.
Kuwait sheikdom, NE Arabia; 7,768 sq. mi.; pop. 440,000.
— city, E Kuwait; cap.; pop. 151,000.
Kyoto city, SW Japan; pop. 1,446,000.
Kyushu isl., S Japan; 16,247 sq. mi.

Labrador terr., Newfoundland, Canada; ab. 110,000 sq. mi.; pop. 21,157.
— the penin. of North America betw. the St. Lawrence River and Hudson Bay.
La Canada-Flintridge uninc. place, SW California 91011; pop. 20,652.
Lachine city, S Quebec, Canada; pop. 44,423.
Lackawanna city, W New York 14218; pop. 28,657.
La Crosse city, W Wisconsin 54601*; pop. 47,808.
Ladoga, Lake lake, NW RSFSR; 7,100 sq. mi.
Lafayette uninc. place, W California 94549; pop. 20,484.
— city, CEN. Indiana 47901*; pop. 43,011.
— city, S. Louisiana 70501*; pop. 81,961.
Lafleche city, S Quebec, Canada; pop. 15,113.
Lagos city, SW Nigeria; cap.; pop. 4,000,000.
La Grange city, W Georgia 30240; pop. 23,301.
— vill., NE Illinois 60525; pop. 16,773.
La Grange Park vill., NE Illinois 60525; pop. 15,626.
La Habra city, SW California 90631*; pop. 45,232.
Lahore city, E Pakistan; pop. 2,165,372.
Lake Charles city, SW Louisiana 70601*; pop. 75,051.
Lake District reg., NW England; contains 15 lakes.
Lake Forest city, NE Illinois 60045; pop. 15,642.
Lakeland city, CEN. Florida 33801; pop. 47,406.
Lakes District city, CEN. Washington; pop. 48,195.
Lakewood city, SW California 90712*; pop. 74,654.
— uninc. place, CEN. Colorado 80215; pop. 112,848.
— uninc. place, E New Jersey 08701; pop. 17,874.
— city, N Ohio 44107, pop. 61,963.
Lake Worth city, SE Florida 33460; pop. 40,986.
Lamarque city, SE Texas 77568; pop. 16,131.
La Mesa city, SW California 92041*; pop. 50,342.
La Mirada city, SW California 90638; pop. 40,986.
Lancaster uninc. place, SW California 93534*; pop. 48,027.
— city, CEN. Ohio 43130*; pop. 34,953.
— city, SE Pennsylvania 17600*; pop. 54,725.
— city, SE New Brunswick, Canada; pop. 15,836.
Lanchow city, NW China; pop. 732,000.
Lansdale boro., SE Pennsylvania 19446; pop. 18,451.
Lansdowne-Baltimore Highlands uninc. place, CEN. Maryland 21227; pop. 16,976.
Lansing vill., NE Illinois 60438; pop. 29,039.
— city, CEN. Michigan 48900*; cap.; pop. 130,414.
Laos republic, NW Indochina; 91,428 sq. mi.; pop. 3,800,000; cap. Vientiane.
La Paz city, W Bolivia; de facto cap.; pop. 700,000.
Lepland reg., N Norway, Sweden, and Finland, and the NE USSR; inhabited by Lapps.
La Plata city, E Argentina; pop. 330,000.
La Porte city, NW Indiana 46350*; pop. 22,140.
La Puente city, SW California 91743*; pop. 30,882.
Laramie city, SE Wyoming 82070*; pop. 23,143.
Laredo city, S Texas 78040*; pop. 91,449.
Largo city, W Florida 33540*; pop. 58,977.
Lasalle city, S Quebec, Canada; pop. 72,912.
Las Cruces city, S New Mexico 88001*; pop. 45,086.
Las Vegas city, SE Nevada 89100*; pop. 164,674.
Latvian SSR constituent republic, NE USSR; 24,600 sq. mi.; pop. 2,400,000; cap. Riga. Also **Latvia.**
Laurel city, SE Mississippi 39440*; pop. 24,145.
Lurentian Mountains mtn. range, E Canada.
Lausanne city, W Switzerland; pop. 137,000.
Laval town, S Quebec, Canada; pop. 228,010.
Lawndale city, SW California 90260; pop. 24,825.
Lawrence town, CEN. Indiana 46226; pop. 25,591.
— city, E Kansas 66044*; pop. 52,738.
— city, NE Massachusetts 01840*; pop. 63,175.
Lawton city, SW Oklahoma 73501*; pop. 74,470.
Leaside town, S Ontario, Canada; pop. 21,250.
Leavenworth city, NE Kansas 66048; pop. 25,147.
Lebanon republic, SW Asia; 4,015 sq. mi.; pop. 3,649,000; cap. Beirut.
— city, SE Pennsylvania 17042; pop. 28,572.
Leeds city and co. boro., CEN. England; pop. 495,000.
Lees Summit city, W Missouri 64063; pop. 28,741.
Leeward Islands N isl. group, Lesser Antilles.
Leghorn city, NW Italy; pop. 175,000. Also **Livorno.**

Le Havre city, N France; pop. 200,000.
Leicester co. boro., CEN. England; pop. 284,000.
Leiden city, W Netherlands; pop. 100,000.
Leipzig city, CEN. East Germany; pop. 584,000.
Lemay city, NE Missouri 63125; pop. 40,115.
Lemon Grove uninc. place, SW California 92045; pop. 19,690.
Leningrad city, NW RSFSR; pop. 4,002,000; formerly called St. Petersburg, Petrograd.
Leominster city, CEN. Massachusetts 01453; pop. 34,508.
Leopoldville Kinshasa: *the former name.*
Lesbos isl. of Greece off NW Turkey; 623 sq. mi.
Lesotho independent member of the Commonwealth of Nations; enclave in E South Africa; 11,716 sq. mi.; pop. 1,137,000; cap. Maseru.
Lesser Antilles See ANTILLES.
Lethbridge city, S Alberta, Canada; pop. 41,217.
Lévis city, S Quebec, Canada; pop. 16,597.
Levittown vill., SE New York 11756; pop. 65,440.
Lewiston city, W Idaho 83501; pop. 27,986.
— city, SW Maine 04240*; pop. 40,481.
Lewiston Orchards uninc. place. W Idaho; pop. 26,068.
Lexington city, CEN. Kentucky 40500*; pop. 204,165.
— town, NE Massachusetts 02173; pop. 31,886.
— city, CEN. North Carolina 27292; pop. 17,205.
Leyden See LEIDEN.
Leyte isl., E Philippines, 2,875 sq. mi.
Lhasa city, S Tibet, cap.; pop. 175,000.
Liberia republic, W Africa; ab. 43,000 sq. mi.; pop. 1,920,000; cap. Monrovia.
Libreville city, W Gabon; cap.; pop. 73,000.
Libya republic, N Africa; 679,358 sq. mi.; pop. 3,100,000; cap. Tripoli.
Liechtenstein principality, CEN. Europe; 61 sq. mi.; pop. 30,000; cap. Vaduz.
Liège city, E Belgium pop. 617,000.
Lille city, N France; pop. 191,000.
Lilongwe city, CEN. Malawi; cap.; pop. 70,000.
Lima city, W Peru; cap.; pop. 2,941,000.
— city, W Ohio; 45801*; pop. 47,381.
Limerick co. boro., W Ireland; pop. 57,000.
Limoges city, CEN. France; pop. 133,000.
Lincoln city, CEN. Illinois 62656; pop. 17,582.
— city, SE Nebraska 68500*; cap.; pop. 171,932.
— town, NE Rhode Island 02865; pop. 16,182.
Lincoln Park city, SE Michigan 48146; pop. 45,105.
Linden city, NE New Jersey 07036*; pop. 37,836.
Lindenhurst vill., SE New York 11757; pop. 26,919.
Lisbon city, W Portugal; cap; pop. 861,500.
Lithuanian SSR constituent republic, NW USSR; 25,200 sq. mi.; pop. 3,200,000; cap. Vilnius. Also **Lithuania.**
Little Farms city, SW Louisiana 70052; pop. 15,713.
Little Rock city, CEN. Arkansas 72200*; cap.; pop. 158,461.
Littleton town, CEN. Colorado 80120*; pop. 28,631.
Livermore city, W California 94550*; pop. 48,349.
Liverpool co. boro., W England; pop. 607,000.
Livingston urb. twp., NE New Jersey 07039; pop. 30,127.
Livonia city, SE Michigan 48150*; pop. 104,814.
Loch Raven uninc. place, N Maryland 21204; pop. 25,000.
Lockport city, NW New York 14094; pop. 25,399.
Lodi city, CEN. California 95240*; pop. 35,221.
— boro., NE New Jersey 07644; pop. 25,213.
Lódz city, CEN. Poland; pop. 830,800.
Logan city, N Utah 84321; pop. 26,844.
Logan, Mount peak, SW Yukon Territory, Canada; 19,850 ft.
Logansport city, CEN. Indiana 46947; pop. 19,255.
Loire river, SE France; 620 mi. long.
Lombard vill., NE Illinois 60148; pop. 37,295.
Lomé city, S Togo; cap.; pop. 135,000.
Lomita uninc. place, SW California 90717; pop. 19,784.
Lompoc city, SW California 93436*; pop. 26,267.
London city and co., SE England; 1 sq. mil.; pop. 5,000 (the city proper): 117 sq. mi.; pop. 3,195,000 (the co.): 693 sq. mi.; pop. 7,379,000 (Greater London).
— city, Ontario, Canada; pop 223,222.
Long Beach city, SW California 90800*; pop. 361,334.
— city, SE New York 11561*; pop. 34,073.
Long Branch city, E New Jersey 07740*; pop. 29,819.
— city, NE Virginia; pop.
Long Island isl., SE New York; 1,723 sq. mi.
Long Island Sound inlet of the Atlantic betw. Long Island and Connecticut.
Longmeadow town, S Massachusetts 01106; pop 15,630.

Longmont city, N Colorado 80501; pop. 42,942.
Loungueuil city, SW Quebec, Canada; pop. 97,590.
Longview city, NE Texas 75601*; pop. 62,762.
— city, SW Washington 98632; pop. 31,052.
Lorain city, N Ohio 44051*; pop. 75,416.
Lorraine reg., E France.
Los Alamos town, CEN. New Mexico 87544; site of the development of the atom bomb; pop. 11,310.
Los Altos city, W California 94022; pop. 25,769.
Los Angeles city, SW California 90000*; pop. 2,966,763.
Los Gatos city, W California 95030*; pop. 26,593.
Louisiana state, S United States; 48,523 sq. mi.; pop. 4,203,972; cap. Baton Rouge.
Louisville city, N Kentucky 40200*; pop. 298,451.
Lourdes town, SW France; famous shrine; pop. 16,000.
Loveland city, N Colorado 80537; pop. 30,244.
Lower California penin., NW Mexico; betw. the Gulf of California and the Pacific. Also **Baja California.**
Lower Merion urb. twp., SE Pennsylvania; pop. 59,420.
Lowlands areas of low elevation, E and S Scotland.
Luanda city, NW Angola; cap.; pop. 600,000.
Lubbock city, NW Texas 79400*; pop. 173,979.
Lübeck city, NE West Germany; pop. 242,000.
Lucerne, Lake of lake, CEN. Switzerland; 44 sq. mi.
Lucknow city, CEN. Uttar Predesh, India; cap.; pop. 750,000.
Ludlow town, S Massachusetts 01056; pop. 17,580.
Lufkin city, E Texas 75901*; pop. 28,562.
Lumberton city, S North Carolina 28358; pop. 16,961.
Lusaka city, CEN. Zambia; cap.; pop. 415,000.
Lü-ta city, NE China; pop. 1,508,000.
Lutherville-Timonium city, NE Maryland 21093; pop. 24,055.
Luxembourg constitutional grand duchy; betw. Belgium, France, and Germany; 998 sq. mi.; pop. 340,000.
— city, CEN. Luxembourg; cap.; pop. 76,000. Also **Luxemburg.**
Luxor city, E Egypt; near the site of ancient Thebes; pop. 30,000.
Luzon isl., N Philippines; 40,420 sq. mi.
Lvov city, W Ukrainian SSR; pop. 564,000.
Lynbrook vill., SE New York 11563; pop. 23,776.
Lynchburg city, CEN. Virginia 24501*; pop. 66,743.
Lyndhurst urb. twp., NE New Jersey 07071; pop. 22,729.
— city, N Ohio 44124; pop. 19,749.
Lynn city, NE Massachusetts 01901*; pop. 78,471.
Lynnwood city, CEN. Washington 98036; pop. 16,919.
Lynwood city, SW California 90262*; pop. 48,548.
Lyon city, CEN. France; pop. 528,000.

Macao isl., Canton river delta, China.
— Portuguese overseas prov. comprising a penin. of Macao isl. and two small isls.; 6 sq. mi.; pop. 248,000.
— city; cap of Macao; pop. 161,000.
Macedonia reg., SE Europe; divided among Bulgaria, Greece, and Yugoslavia; 25,636 sq. mi.
Mackenzie river, NW Canada; 2,640 mi. long.
Mackinac, Straits of channel betw. Lakes Michigan and Huron; ab. 5 mi. wide and 40 mi. long.
Mackinac Island isl., Straits of Mackinac.
Macomb city, W Illinois 61455; pop. 19,643.
Macon city, CEN. Georgia 31200*; pop. 116,860.
Madagascar isl. republic, Indian Ocean off SE Africa; 230,035 sq. mi.; pop. 9,000,000; cap. Antananarivo: formerly called **Malagasy Republic.**
Madeira isl. group W of Morocco; an adm. dist. of Portugal; 308 sq. mi.; pop. 267,000; cap. Funchal.
Madera city, CEN. California 93637; pop. 16,044.
Madison boro., N New Jersey 07940; pop. 16,710.
— city, CEN. Wisconsin 53700*; cap.; pop. 170,616.
Madison Heights city, SE Michigan 48071; pop. 35,375.
Madisonville city, W Kentucky 42431; pop. 15,332.
Madras city, S India; pop. 2,469,000.
Madrid city, CEN. Spain; cap.; pop. 3,520,000.
Madura isl. of Indonesia E of Java; 1,762 sq. mi.
Magdeburg city, CEN. East Germany; pop. 271,000.
Magellan, Strait of channel betw. the Atlantic and Pacific, separating the South American mainland from Tierra del Fuego.
Magnitogorsk city, S RSFSR; pop. 369,000.
Maine state, NE United States; 32,562 sq. mi.; pop. 1,124,660; cap. Augusta.
Main River river, CEN. West Germany; 305 mi. long.
Majorca largest of the Balearic Islands; 1,405 sq. mi.
Malabar coastal reg., SW India. Also **Malabar Coast.**

Malacca city, w Malaya; pop. 70,000.
Malacca, Strait of strait betw. Sumatra and the Malay Peninsula.
Málaga city, s Spain; pop. 351,000.
Malagasy Republic See **Madagascar**.
Malawi independent member of the Commonwealth of Nations, SE Africa; 45,747 sq. mi.; pop. 6,125,000; cap. Lilongwe.
Malaya federation of Malay states, SE Asia; ab. 50,700 sq. mi.; pop. 9,128,000; cap. Kuala Lumpur; part of Malaysia.
Malay Archipelago isl. group off SE Asia; includes isls. of Indonesia, Malaysia, and the Philippines.
Malay Peninsula s penin. of Asia; includes Malaya, Singapore, and part of Thailand.
Malaysia federation of Malaya, Sarawak, and Sabah (North Borneo); a member of the Commonwealth of Nations; 128,328 sq. mi.; pop. 14,000,000; cap. Kuala Lumpur.
Malden city, NE Massachusetts 02148; pop. 53,386.
Maldives isl. republic, Indian Ocean s of India; 115 sq. mi.; pop. 150,000; cap. Male.
Mali republic of the French Community, w Africa; pop. 4,700,000; 464,872 sq. mi.; cap. Bamako.
Mallorca Majorca: *the Spanish name.*
Malta independent member of the Commonwealth of Nations, CEN. Mediterranean; comprises the islands of Malta, Gozo, Comino, and two islets; 122 sq. mi.; pop. 350,000; cap. Valletta.
Mamaroneck vill., SE New York 10543*; pop. 18,909.
Man, Isle of one of the British Isles, CEN. Irish Sea; 227 sq. mi.; pop. 50,000; cap. Douglas.
Managua city, sw Nicaragua; cap.; pop. 300,000.
Managua, Lake lake, sw Nicaragua; 390 sq. mi.
Manchester co. boro. and city, SE Lancashire, England; pop. 541,000.
— town, N Connecticut 06040*; pop. 47,994.
— city, s New Hampshire 03100*; pop. 90,936.
Manchuria former div., NE China.
Mandalay city, CEN. Burma; pop. 417,000.
Manhattan city, NE Kansas 66502*; pop. 32,644.
— boro., New York City 10000*; pop. 1,427,533.
Manhattan Beach city, sw California 90266; pop. 31,-542.
Manila city, sw Luzon, Philippines; pop. 1,582,000.
Manitoba prov., CEN. Canada; 246,512 sq. mi.; pop. 988,-247; cap. Winnipeg.
Manitoba, Lake lake, sw Manitoba; 1,817 sq. mi.
Manitowoc city, E Wisconsin 54220*; pop. 32,547.
Mankato city, s Minnesota 56001*; pop. 28,651.
Mansfield city, NE Connecticut 06250; pop. 19,994.
— city, CEN. Ohio 44900*; pop. 53,927.
Maple Heights city, NE Ohio 44137; pop. 29,735.
Maple Shade urb. twp., sw New Jersey 08052; pop. 16,-464.
Maplewood vill., E Minnesota 55109; pop. 26,990.
— urb. twp. NE New Jersey 07040; pop. 24,932.
Maracaibo city, NW Venezuela; pop. 845,000.
Maracaibo, Lake lake, NW Venezuela; ab. 5,000 sq. mi.
Marblehead town, NE Massachusetts 01945*; pop. 21,-295.
Marianas Islands isl. group, w Pacific; including Guam, Saipan, Tinian, and Rota; part of the UN Trust terr. of the Pacific Islands (excluding Guam); 246 sq. mi.
Marietta city, NW Georgia; 30060*; pop. 30,805.
— city, SE Ohio 45750; pop. 16,861.
Marion city, CEN. Indiana 46952*; pop. 35,874.
— city, E Iowa 52302; pop. 18,028.
— city, CEN. Ohio 43301*; pop. 37,040.
Markham vill., NE Illinois 60426; pop. 15,987.
Marlborough city, CEN. Massachusetts 01752; pop. 30,-617.
Marmara, Sea of sea betw. Europe and Asia, connecting the Bosporus and the Dardanelles. Also **Marmora.**
Marne river, NE France; 325 mi. long.
Marple urb. twp., SE Pennsylvania; pop. 19,722.
Marquesas Islands isl. group, French Polynesia; 492 sq. mi.
Marquette city, NW Michigan 49855; pop. 21,967.
Marrakesh city, sw Morocco; a traditional cap.; pop. 333,000.
Marrero city, sw Louisiana 70072; pop. 29,015.
Marseille city, SE France; pop. 914,356. Also **Marseilles.**
Marshall city, NE Texas 75607*; pop. 22,937.
Marshall Islands isl. group in Pacific; an adm. dist. of the Trust Terr. of the Pacific Islands; 66 sq. mi.; pop. 25,000; cap. Jaluit.
Marshalltown city, CEN. Iowa 50158; pop. 26,938.
Marshfield city, E Massachusetts 02050; pop. 15,223.

Marshfield city, CEN. Wisconsin 54449; pop. 15,619.
Martinez city, w California 94553*; pop. 16,506.
Martinique isl. Lesser Antilles; French overseas dept.; 421 sq. mi.; pop. 381,000; cap. Fort-de-France.
Martinsville city, s Virginia 24112*; pop. 19,653.
Maryland state, E United States; 10,577 sq. mi.; pop. 4,216,446; cap. Annapolis.
Mason City city, N Iowa 50401*; pop. 30,144.
Mason-Dixon Line boundary betw. Pennsylvania and Maryland, surveyed by Charles Mason and Jeremiah Dixon in 1763; regarded as dividing the North from the South.
Massachusetts state, NE United States; 8,257 sq. mi.; pop. 5,737,037; cap. Boston.
Massapequa uninc. place, SE New York; 11758*; pop. 26,951.
Massapequa Park vill., SE New York 11762; pop. 22,-112.
Massillon city, NE Ohio 44646; pop. 30,557.
Matsu isl. of the Republic of China, Formosa Strait; 4 sq. mi.
Matterhorn mtn. in the Alps on the Swiss-Italian border; 14,701 ft.
Mattoon city, CEN. Illinois 61938; pop. 19,681.
Maui isl. of the Hawaiian Islands; 728 sq. mi.
Maumee city, NW Ohio 43537; pop. 15,937.
Mauna Loa active volcano, CEN. Hawaii (isl.); 13,675 ft.
Mauritania republic, w Africa; 397,956 sq. mi.; pop. 1,675,000; cap. Nouakchott.
Mauritius independent member of the Commonwealth of Nations on an island in the Indian Ocean, 790 sq. mi., pop. 975,000; cap. Port Louis.
Mayagüez city, w Puerto Rico 00708; pop. 50,147.
Mayfield Heights city, N Ohio; pop. 22,139.
Maywood city, sw California 90270; pop. 16,996.
— vill., NE Illinois 60153*; pop. 27,998.
McAlester city, CEN. Oklahoma 74501*; pop. 18,802.
McAllen city, s Texas 78501*; pop. 67,042.
McKeesport city, sw Pennsylvania; 15130*; pop. 31,-012.
McKinley, Mount peak, CEN. Alaska, highest in North America; 20,300 ft.
McKinney city N Texas 75069; pop. 15,193.
McLean city, NE Virginia 22101; pop. 17,698.
Mead, Lake reservoir formed by Hoover Dam in the Colorado River, Arizona and Nevada; 246 sq. mi.
Meadville city, NW Pennsylvania 16335; pop. 16,573.
Mecca city, w Saudi Arabia; one of the caps.; birthplace of Mohammed and holy city to which Muslims make pilgrimages; pop. 500,000.
Medford city, NE Massachusetts 02155; pop. 58,076.
— city, sw Oregon 97501*; pop. 39,603.
Medicine Hat city, SE Alberta, Canada; pop. 26,518.
Medina city, w Saudi Arabia; site of Mohammed's tomb; pop. 90,000.
Mediterranean Sea sea betw. Europe, Asia, and Africa; 965,000 sq. mi.
Mekong river, SE Asia; 2,500 mi. long.
Melanesia isls. of the w Pacific s of the Equator; ab. 60,000 sq. mi.
Melbourne city, s Victoria, Australia; cap.; pop. 2,717,-600.
— city, E Florida 32901*; pop. 46,536.
Melrose city, NE Massachusetts 02176; pop. 30,055.
Melrose Park vill., NE Illinois 60160*; pop. 22,706.
Memphis city, sw Tennessee 38100*; pop. 646,356.
Menlo Park city, w California 94025*; pop. 25,673.
Menomonee Falls vill., SE Wisconsin 53051*; pop. 27,-845.
Mentor city, NE Ohio 44060; pop. 42,065.
Merced city, CEN. California 95340*; pop. 36,499.
Mercerville-Hamilton Square city, CEN. New Jersey 08619*; pop. 24,465.
Meriden city, CEN. Connecticut 06450*; pop. 57,118.
Meridian city, E Mississippi 39301*; pop. 46,577.
Merrick uninc. place, SE New York 11566; pop. 25,904.
Merrillville city, NW Indiana 46410; pop. 27,677.
Merritt Island city, CEN. Florida 32952; pop. 29,233.
Mesa city, CEN. Arizona 85201*; pop. 152,453.
Mesabi Range range of hills, NE Minnesota; site of iron ore deposits.
Mesquite city, N Texas 75149; pop. 67,053.
Messina city, NE Sicily; pop. 275,000.
Metairie city, sw Louisiana 70001; pop. 135,816.
Methuen city, NE Massachusetts 01844; pop. 35,456.
Metuchen boro., NE New Jersey 08840*; pop. 16,031.
Meuse river, w Europe; 580 mi. long.

Mexico republic s North America; 761,600 sq. mi., pop. 74,500,000.

— city, CEN Mexico; cap.; pop. 9,224,000. Also **Mexico City.**

Mexico, Gulf of inlet of the Atlantic, betw. the United States, Mexico, and Cuba; 700,000 sq. mi.

Miami city, SE Florida 33100*; pop. 346,931.

Miami Beach city SE Florida 33139; pop. 96,298.

Michigan state, N United States; 58,216 sq. mi.; pop. 9,258,344; cap. Lansing.

Michigan, Lake one of the Great Lakes; betw. Michigan and Wisconsin; 22,400 sq. mi.

Michigan City city, N Indiana 46360*; pop. 36,850.

Micronesia isls. of the w Pacific N of the equator.

Middle River uninc. place, N Maryland 21,220; pop. 19,935.

Middlesex boro., NE New Jersey 08846; pop. 15,038.

Middletown city, CEN Connecticut; 06457*; pop. 39,040.

— urb. twp., E New Jersey 07748*; pop. 54,623.

— city, SE New York 10940*; pop. 22,607.

— city, sw Ohio 45042*; pop. 43,719.

— urb. twp., SE Pennsylvania 17057; pop. 26,894.

— town, SE Rhode Island 02840; pop. 29,621.

Midi s reg. of France.

Midland city, CEN Michigan 48640*; pop. 37,250.

— city, w Texas 79701*; pop. 70,525.

Midlands counties of CEN England.

Midlothian vill., NE Illinois 60445*; pop. 15,939.

Midway Islands 2 isls. NW of Honolulu, under control of the U.S. Navy; 2 sq. mi.; scene of an important battle of World War II, June, 1942.

Midwest City city, CEN Oklahoma 73110; pop. 49,559.

Milan city, N Italy; pop. 1,714,000.

Milford city, sw Connecticut 06460*; pop. 49,101.

— uninc. place, CEN Massachusetts 01757; pop. 19,352.

Millbrae city, w California 94030*; pop. 20,781.

Millburn urb. twp., NE New Jersey 07041; pop. 21,307.

Millcreek boro., CEN Pennsylvania 17060, pop. 28,441.

Millington town, sw Tennessee 38053; pop. 21,106.

Millville city s New Jersey 08332; pop. 21,366.

Milpitas city, w California 95035; pop. 37,820.

Milton town, E Massachusetts 02186; pop. 27,190.

Milwaukee city, SE Wisconsin 53200*; pop. 636,212.

Milwaukie city, NW Oregon 97222; pop. 16,379.

Mimico town, s Ontario, Canada; pop. 19,431.

Mindanao isl. s Philippines; 36,537 sq. mi.

Mindoro isl., CEN Philippines; 3,759 sq. mi.

Mineola vill., SE New York 11501*; pop. 21,845.

Mineral Wells city, CEN Texas 76067; pop. 18,411.

Minneapolis city, E Minnesota 55400*; pop. 370,951.

Minnesota state, N United States; 84,068 sq. mi.; pop. 4,077,148; cap. St. Paul.

Minnetonka vill., E Minnesota 55343; pop. 38,683.

Minorca one of the Balearic islands; 271 sq. mi.

Minot city, N North Dakota 58701*; pop. 32,843.

Minsk city, CEN Byelorussian SSR; cap.; pop. 955,000.

Mirada Hills city, sw California; pop. 22,444.

Miramar city, SE Florida 33023; pop. 32,813.

Mishawaka city, N Indiana 46544; pop. 40,224.

Mississippi state s United States; 47,716 sq. mi.; pop. 2,520,638; cap. Jackson.

Mississippi River river, CEN United States; 2,350 mi. long.

Missoula city, w Montana 59801; pop. 33,388.

Missouri state, CEN United States; 69,674 sq. mi.; pop. 4,917,444; cap. Jefferson City.

Missouri River river, CEN United States; 2,470 mi. long.

Mobile city, sw Alabama 36600*; pop. 200,452.

Mobile Bay inlet of the Gulf of Mexico, sw Alabama.

Modesto city, CEN California 95350*; pop. 106,105.

Mojave Desert arid reg. s California; ab. 15,000 sq. mi.

Moldavian SSR constituent republic, sw USSR; 13,000 sq. mi.; pop, 3,800,000; cap. Kishinev. Also **Moldavia.**

Moline city, NW Illinois 61265*; pop. 45,709.

Molokai isl., CEN Hawaiian Islands; 259 sq. mi.

Molucca Islands isl. group of Indonesia, betw. Sulawesi and New Guines; 33,315 sq. mi.

Monaco independent principality, SE France; 368 acres: pop. 30,500.

Moncton city, SE New Brunswick, Canada; pop. 47,891.

Monessen city, sw Pennsylvania 15062; pop. 15,216.

Mongolia trh., CEN Asia; ab. 1 million sq. mi.; divided into the **Mongolian People's Republic** (formerly Outer Mongolia) in the N and w part; 604,250 sq. mi.; pop. 1,725,000; cap. Ulan Bator; and **Inner Mongolia,** a reg., N China, most of which comprises the **Inner Mongolian Autonomous Region;** ab. 400,000 sq. mi.; pop. 6,240,000; cap. Huhehot.

Monongahela River river, West Virginia and w Pennsylvania; 128 mi. long.

Monroe city, N Louisiana 71201*; pop. 57,597.

— city, SE Michigan 48161: pop. 23,894.

Monroeville boro., sw Pennsylvania 15145; pop. 30,977.

Monrovia city, E Liberia; cap.; pop. 96,226.

— city, sw California 91016*; pop. 30,531.

Montana state, NW United States; 147,138 sq. mi.; pop. 786,690; cap. Helena.

Mont Blanc highest mountain of the Alps, on the French-Italian border; 15,781 ft.; site of tunnel, 7½ mi. long, connecting France and Italy.

Montclair city, sw California 91763; pop. 22,546.

— town, NE New Jersey 07042*; pop. 38,321.

Montebello city, sw California 90640*; pop. 52,929.

Monte Carlo city, Monaco; pop. 10,000.

Montenegro constituent republic, s Yugoslavia; 5,343 sq. mi.; pop. 565,000; cap. Titograd.

Monterey city, w California 93940*; pop. 27,558.

Monterey Park city, sw California 91754*; pop. 54,338.

Monterrey city, NE Mexico; pop. 1,054,000.

Montevideo city, s Uruguay; cap.; pop. 1,229,000.

Montgomery city, CEN Alabama 36100*; cap.; pop. 178,157.

Monticello estate and residence of Thomas Jefferson, near Charlottesville, Virginia.

Montmartre dist., N Paris; former artists' quarter.

Montpelier city, CEN Vermont 05601*; cap.; pop. 8,609.

Montreal city, s Quebec, Canada; pop. 1,214,352.

Montreal-Nord city, s Quebec, Canada; pop. 89,139. Also **Montreal-North.**

Mont-Royal town, s Quebec, Canada; pop. 21,561.

Mont Saint Michel isl. off NW France; site of an ancient fortress and abbey.

Montville city, SE Connecticut 06353; pop. 15,662.

Moorehead city, CEN Oklahoma 73852; pop. 18,761.

Moorhead city, w Minnesota 56560*; pop. 29,998.

Moose Jaw city, s Saskatchewan, Canada; pop. 31,854.

Moravia reg., CEN Czechoslovakia.

Morgan City city, s Louisiana 70380; pop. 16,586.

Morgantown city, N West Virginia 26500*; pop. 27,605.

Morocco kingdom, NW Africa; ab. 172,414 sq. mi.; pop. 20,500,000; cap. Rabat.

Morristown town, CEN New Jersey 07960*; pop. 17,662.

— city, NE Tennessee 37813*; pop. 20,318.

Morton Grove vill., NE Illinois 60053; pop. 26,369.

Moscow city, w USSR; cap. USSR and RSFSR; pop. 7,635,000.

Moselle river, NE France, Luxembourg, and w West Germany; 320 mi. long.

Moss Point city, SE Mississippi 39563; pop. 19,321.

Mosul city, N Iraq; pop. 243,000.

Mountain Brook city, CEN Alabama 35223; pop. 19,474.

Mountain View city, w California 94042*; pop. 58,655.

Mount Clemens city, SE Michigan 48043*; pop. 20,476.

Mountlake Terrace city, CEN Washington 98043; pop. 16,600.

Mount Lebanon urb. twp., sw Pennsylvania 15228; pop. 39,956.

Mount Pleasant city, CEN Michigan 48858; pop. 20,504.

Mount Prospect vill., NE Illinois 60056*; pop. 52,634.

Mount Vernon home and burial place of George Washington, near Washington, D.C.

— city, s Illinois 62864; pop. 15,980.

— city, SE New York 10550*; pop. 66,713.

Mozambique republic SE Africa; 302,330 sq. mi.; pop. 10,750,000; cap. Maputo.

Muncie city, E Indiana 47302, pop. 77,216.

Mundelein vill., NE Illinois 60060; pop. 16,128.

Munhall boro., sw Pennsylvania 15120; pop. 16,674.

Munich city, SE West Germany; pop. 1,326,000.

Munster town, NW Indiana 46321; pop. 16,514.

Murfreesboro city, CEN Tennessee; 37130*; pop. 32,845.

Murmansk city, NW USSR; pop. 317,000.

Murray city, CEN Utah 84107; pop. 25,750.

Murray River river, SE Australia; 1,600 mi. long.

Muscat and Oman: Oman: *the former name.*

Muscatine city, E Iowa 52761; pop. 22,405.

Muskegon city, w Michigan 49440*; pop. 40,823.

Muskegon Heights city, w Michigan 49444; pop. 17,304.

Muskogee city, E Oklahoma 74401*; pop. 40,011.

Myrtle Grove city, CEN Florida 32506; pop. 16,186.

Mysore city, s India; pop. 254,000.

Nacogdoches city E Texas 75961*; pop. 27,149.

Nagasaki city, NW Kyushu island, Japan; largely destroyed by a U.S. atomic bomb, Aug. 9, 1945; pop. 421,000.

Nagoya city, CEN. Honshu isl., Japan; pop. 2,080,000.

Nagpur city, CEN. India; pop. 866,000.

Nairobi city, SW Kenya; cap.; pop. 863,000.

Namibia See SOUTH-WEST AFRICA.

Nampa city, SW Idaho 83651; pop. 25,112.

Nanking city, E China; cap. 1928–37; pop. 2,000,000.

Nantes city, W France; pop. 259,000.

Nantucket isl. off SE Massachusetts; 57 sq. mi.

Napa city, W California 94558*; pop. 50,879.

Naperville city, NE Illinois 60540; pop. 42,330.

Naples city, SW Italy; pop. 1,278,000.

Narragansett Bay inlet of the Atlantic, SE Rhode Island.

Nashua city, S New Hampshire 03060; pop. 67,865.

Nashville city, CEN. Tennessee 37200*; cap.; pop. 455,-651.

Nassau city, New Providence, Bahamas Islands; cap.; pop. 80,000.

Natal prov., E South Africa; 33,578 sq. mi. (including Zululand); pop. 4,246,000; cap. Pietermaritzburg.

Natchez city, W Mississippi 39120*; pop. 19,704.

Natchitoches city, CEN. Louisiana 71457; pop. 15,974.

Natick town, NE Massachusetts 01760*; pop. 31,057.

National City city, SW California 92050*; pop. 48,772.

Naugatuck town, CEN. Connecticut 06770*; pop. 26,456.

Nauru Republic, isl. W-CENT. Pacific just south of Equator; 8.2 sq. mi.; pop. 1,000; cap. Yaren.

Navarre reg. and former kingdom, N Spain and SW France.

Nazareth town, N Israel; scene of Christ's childhood; pop. 22,000.

Nebraska state, CEN. United States; 77,237 sq. mi.; pop. 1,570,006; cap. Lincoln.

Nederland city, SE Texas 77627; pop. 16,810.

Needham town, NE Massachusetts 02192; pop. 29,748.

Neenah city, CEN. Wisconsin 54956*; pop. 22,892.

Negev desert reg., S Israel; 4,700 sq. mi. Also **Negeb.**

Nejd prov., CEN. Saudi Arabia; ab. 450,000 sq. mi.; pop. 4 million; cap. Riyadh.

Nepal kingdom betw. Tibet and India; 54,362 sq. mi.; pop. 14,325,000; cap. Kathmandu.

Neptune urb. twp., E New Jersey 07753; pop. 27,863.

Netherlands kingdom, NW Europe; 15,780 sq. mi.; pop. 14,250,000; cap. Amsterdam; seat of government, The Hague.

Netherlands, Kingdom of the kingdom comprising the Netherlands, the Netherlands Antilles, and Surinam; cap. Amsterdam.

Netherlands Antilles 3 isls. N of Venezuela and 3 in the Leeward Islands group; 336 sq. mi.; pop. 216,000; cap. Willemstad.

Netherlands Guiana See SURINAM.

Nevada state, W United States; 110,540 sq. mi.; pop. 799,-184; cap. Carson city.

New Albany city, S Indiana 47150; pop. 37,103.

Newark city, W California 94560; pop. 32,126.

— city, NW Delaware 19711*; pop. 25,247.

— city, NE New Jersey 07100*; pop. 329,248.

— city, CEN. Ohio 43055*; pop. 41,200.

New Bedford city, SE Massachusetts 02740*; pop. 98,-478.

New Berlin city, SE Wisconsin 53151; pop. 30,529.

New Braunfels city, CEN. Texas 78130*; pop. 17,859.

New Brighton vill., E Minnesota 55112; pop. 19,507.

New Britain city, CEN. Connecticut 06050*; pop. 73,840.

New Brunswick city, CEN. New Jersey 08900*; pop. 41,442.

— prov., SE Canada; 27,836 sq. mi.; pop. 634,557; cap. Fredericton.

Newburgh city, SE New York 12550*; pop. 26,219.

Newburyport city, NE Massachusetts 01950*; pop. 15,-807.

New Caledonia isl. E of Australia; comprising with adjacent isls. a French overseas terr.; 7,335 sq. mi.; pop. 141,000; cap. Nouméa.

New Canaan city, SW Connecticut 06840; pop. 17,455.

New Castle city, E Indiana 47362; pop. 21,215.

— city, W Pennsylvania 16101*; pop. 33,621.

Newcastle upon Tyne city, NE England; pop. 222,000. Also **Newcastle, Newcastle on Tyne.**

New City city, SE New York, 10956; pop. 27,344.

New Delhi city, Delhi terr., India; cap. of India; pop. 302,000.

New England NE section of the United States, including Maine, New Hampshire, Vermont, Massachusetts, Rhode Island, and Connecticut.

Newfoundland prov., E Canada; comprising the island

of **Newfoundland** (43,359 sq. mi.) and Labrador on the mainland; 156,185 sq. mi.; pop. 557,725; cap. St. John's.

New Georgia isl. group, British Solomon Islands; ab. 2,000 sq. mi.

New Guinea isl., N of Australia; 304,200 sq. mi. See PAPUA NEW GUINEA, WEST NEW GUINEA.

New Hampshire state, NE United States; 9,304 sq. mi.; pop. 920,610; cap. Concord.

New Haven city, S Connecticut 06500*; pop. 126,109.

New Hebtide See *Vanuatu.*

New Hope city, SE Minnesota 55428; pop. 23,180.

New Iberia city, S Louisiana 70560*; pop. 32,766.

New Ireland volcanic isl. of the Bismarck Archipelago, S Pacific; 3,340 sq. mi.; pop. 41,100; part of Papua New Guinea.

Newington city, CEN. Connecticut 06111; pop. 26,037.

New Jersey state, E United States; 7,836 sq. mi.; pop. 7,364,158; cap. Trenton.

New Kensington city, W Pennsylvania 15068*; pop. 20,312.

New London city, SE Connecticut 06301*; pop. 28,842.

Newmarket town, S Ontario, Canada; pop. 18,941.

New Mexico state, SW United States; 121,666 sq. mi.; pop. 1,299,968; cap. Santa Fé.

New Milford boro., NE New Jersey 07646; pop. 20,201.

New Orleans city, SE Louisiana 70100*; pop. 557,482.

New Philadelphia city, CEN. Ohio 44663; pop. 15,184.

Newport city, N Kentucky 41079*; pop. 25,998.

— city, SE Rhode Island 02840*; pop. 29,259.

Newport Beach city, SW California 92660*; pop. 63,-475.

Newport News city, SE Virginia 23600*; pop. 144,903.

New Rochelle city, SE New York 10800*; pop. 70,794.

New South Wales state, SE Australia; 309,433 sq. mi.; pop. 4,590,000; cap. Sydney.

Newton city, CEN. Iowa 50208; pop. 15,619.

— city, CEN. Kansas 67114; pop. 15,439.

— city, E Massachusetts 02158; pop. 83,622.

Newtown city, SW Connecticut 06470; pop. 16,942.

New Westminster city, SW British Columbia, Canada; pop. 42,835.

New York state, NE United States; 49,576 sq. mi.; pop. 17,557,288; cap. Albany.

— city, SE New York 10000*; divided into the five boroughs of the Bronx, Brooklyn, Manhattan, Queens, and Richmond (Staten Island); 365 sq. mi.; pop. 7,071,030.

New York State Barge Canal waterway system, New York; connects the Hudson River with Lakes Erie, Champlain, and Ontario; 525 mi. long.

New Zealand self-governing member of the Commonwealth of Nations, comprising a group of isle SE of Australia; 103,416 sq. mi., excluding island territories; pop. 3,328,000; cap. Wellington.

Niagara Falls city, W New York 14300*; pop. 85,615.

— city, S Ontario, Canada; pop. 71,384.

Niagara River river betw. Ontario, Canada, and New York State, connecting Lakes Erie and Ontario; in its course occurs **Niagara Falls,** a cataract divided by Goat Island into the American Falls, ab. 167 ft. high and 1,000 ft. wide, and Horseshoe Falls on the Canadian side, ab. 160 ft. high and 2,500 ft. wide.

Nicaragua republic, Central America; ab. 50,193 sq. mi.; pop. 2,750,000; cap. Managua.

Nicaragua, Lake lake, SW Nicaragua; 3,100 sq. mi.

Nice city, SE France; pop. 346,000.

Nicobar Islands isl. terr. of India; 19 isls. in the Bay of Bengal; 754 sq. mi.; pop. 22,000.

Nicosia city, CEN. Cyprus; cap.; pop. 115,000.

Niger river, W Africa; ab. 2,600 mi. long.

Niger, Republic of republic, CEN. Africa, 489,191 sq. mi. pop. 5,550,000; cap. Naimey.

Nigeria, Federation of independent member of the Commonwealth of Nations, W Africa; 356,669 sq. mi.; pop. 79,575,000; cap. Lagos.

Nile river, E Africa; 4,130 mi. long; the longest river in the world.

Niles vill., NE Illinois 60648; pop. 30,363.

— city, NE Ohio 44446; pop. 21,581.

Norfolk city, NE Nebraska 68701; pop. 16,607.

— city, SE Virginia 23500*; pop. 266,979.

Normal town, CEN. Illinois 61761; pop. 35,672.

Norman city, CEN. Oklahoma 73069*; pop. 68,020.

Normandy reg. and former prov., NW France.

Norridge vill., NE Illinois; pop. 16,880.

Norristown boro., SE Pennsylvania 19401*; pop. 34,684.

North Adams city, NW Massachusetts 01247*; pop. 19,-195.

North America N continent of the Western Hemisphere; 9,300,000 sq. mi. (including adjacent islands).

Northampton city, w Massachusetts 01060*; pop. 29,286.
North Andover town, NE Massachusetts 01845; pop. 16,284.
North Arlington boro., NE New Jersey 07032; pop, 18,-096.
North Atlanta vill., CEN. Georgia 30319; pop. 15,000.
North Attleborough town, E Massachusetts 02760*; pop. 18,665.
North Babylon city, SE New York 11703; pop. 39,556.
North Bay city, CEN. Ontario, Canada; pop. 49,187.
North Bellmore uninc. place, SE New York 11710; pop. 22,893.
North Bergen urb. twp., NE New Jersey 07047*; pop. 47,751.
North Borneo See SABAH.
Northbrook vill., NE Illinois 60062; pop. 30,735.
North Canton vill., NE Ohio 44720; pop. 15,228.
North Cape promontory, N Norway.
North Carolina state, SE United States; 52,712 sq. mi.; pop. 5,874,429; cap. Raleigh.
North Chicago city, NE Illinois 60064*; pop. 38,774.
North Dakota state, N United States; 70,665 sq. mi.; pop. 625,695; cap. Bismarck.
Northern Ireland part of the United Kingdom in N reg. of Ireland; 5,238 sq. mi.; pop. 1,528,000; cap. Belfast.
Northern Territory reg., N Australia; 523,620 sq. mi.; pop. 71,000; cap. Darwin.
North Glen city, CEN. Colorado 80201; pop. 29,847.
North Haven city, S Connecticut 06501; pop. 22,194.
North Highlands uninc. place, CEN. California 95660; pop. 31,854.
North Island isl., N New Zealand; 44,281 sq. mi.
North Kingston town, S Rhode Island 02852*; pop. 27,-673.
North Korea See KOREA.
North Las Vegas city, SE Nevada 89030*; pop. 42,739.
North Little Rock city, CEN. Arkansas 72114*; pop. 64,419.
North Massapequa city, SE New York 11758; pop. 23,-101.
North Miami city, SE Florida 33161; pop. 42,566.
North Miami Beach city, SE Florida 33160; pop. 36,481.
North Olmsted city, N Ohio 44070; pop. 36,486.
North Park city, NE Illinois 61101; pop. 15,679.
North Plainfield boro., NE New Jersey 07060; pop. 27,-796.
North Platte city, CEN. Nebraska 69101*; pop. 19,447.
North Pole N extremity of the earth's axis.
North Providence town, NE Rhode Island; pop, 24,337.
North Richland Hills town, N Texa; pop. 30,592.
North Sea part of the Atlantic betw. Great Britain and Europe.
North Tonawanda city, NW New York 14120*; pop. 35,760.
North Vancouver city, SW British Columbia, Canada; pop. 31,847.
North Wantagh city, SE New York; pop. 15,053.
Northwest Territories adm. div., N Canada; 1,304,903 sq. mi.; pop. 42,609.
Northwest Territory reg. awarded to the United States by Britain in 1783, extending from the Great Lakes S to the Ohio River and from Pennsylvania W to the Mississippi.
Norton Shores city, SW Michigan 49444; pop. 22,271.
Norwalk city, SW California 90650*; pop. 85,232.
— city, SW Connecticut 06850*; pop. 76,767.
Norway kingdom, N Europe; 125,182 sq. mi.; pop. 4,120,-000; cap. Oslo.
Norwich co. boro., E England; pop. 122,000.
— city, SE Connecticut 06360*; pop. 38,074.
Nottingham co. boro., CEN. England; pop. 300,000.
Nova Scotia prov., E Canada; 21,425 sq. mi.; pop. 828,-571; cap. Halifax.
Novato city, W California 94947; pop. 43,916.
Novaya Zemlya two isls., Arctic Ocean, NE RSFSR; ab. 35,000 sq. mi.
Novosibirsk city, SW Asian Russian SFSR, ab. 1,700 mi. E of Moscow; pop. 1,243,000.
Nuremberg city, CEN. West Germany; pop. 477,000.
Nutley town, NE New Jersey 07110; pop. 28,998.

Oahu isl., CEN. Hawaiian Islands; 589 sq. mi.
Oak Forest city, NE Illinois 60452; pop. 26,096.
Oakland city, W California 94600*; pop. 339,288.
Oakland Park city, SE Florida 33308; pop. 16,261.

Oak Lawn vill., NE Illinois 60453*; pop. 60,590.
Oak Park vill., NE Illinois 60300*; pop. 54,887.
— city, SE Michigan 48237; pop. 31,537.
Oak Ridge city, E Tennessee 37830*; pop. 27,662.
Oakville town, S Ontario, Canada; pop. 61,483.
Ocala city, CEN. Florida 32670; pop. 37,170.
Oceania isls. of Melanesia, Micronesia, and Polynesia, and sometimes the Malay Archipelago and Australasia.
Oceanside city, SW California 92045*; pop. 76,698.
— vill., SE New York 11572; pop. 35,028.
Oder river, CEN. Europe; 563 mi. long.
Odessa city, S Ukrainian SSR; pop. 1,046,000.
— city, W Texas 79760*; pop. 90,027.
Ogden city, N Utah 84400*; pop. 64,407.
Ohio state, CEN. United States; 41,222 sq. mi.; pop. 10,-797,419; cap. Columbus.
Ohio River river, CEN. United States; 981 mi. long.
Oil City city, NW Pennsylvania 16301*; pop. 15,033.
Oildale city, CEN. California 93308; pop. 20,879.
Okhotsk, Sea of inlet of the Pacific W of Kamchatka and the Kurile Islands.
Okinawa Japanese isl., largest of the Ryukyu Islands; 554 sq. mi.; pop. 945,000; cap. Naha.
Oklahoma state, CEN. United States; 69,919 sq. mi.; pop. 3,025,266; cap. Oklahoma City.
Oklahoma City city, CEN. Oklahoma 73100*; cap.; pop. 403,213.
Okmulgee city, CEN. Oklahoma 74447; pop 15,180.
Okolona city, NW Kentucky 40291; pop. 17,643.
Olathe city, E Kansas 66061; pop. 37,258.
Old Bridge city, CEN. New Jersey 08857; pop. 25,176.
Olean city, SW New York 14760*; pop. 19,169.
Olympia city, W Washington 98501*; cap.; pop. 27,447.
Olympus, Mount mtn., N Greece; regarded in Greek mythology as the home of the gods; 9,570 ft.
Omaha city, E Nebraska 68100*; pop. 311,681.
Oman independent sultanate, SE Arabia; 82,000 sq. mi.; pop. 920,000; cap. Muscat.
Omsk city, S RSFSR; pop. 850,000.
Oneonta city, CEN. New York 13820; pop. 16,030.
Ontario city, SW California 91761*; pop. 88,820.
— prov., SE Canada; 412,582 sq. mi.; pop. 8,264,465; cap. Toronto.
Ontario, Lake easternmost of the Great Lakes; 7,540 sq. mi.
Opelika city, E Alabama 36801; pop. 19,027.
Opelousas city, CEN. Louisiana 70570; pop. 20,121.
Oporto city, W Portugal; pop. 303,000.
Opportunity uninc. place E Washington 99214; pop. 16,604.
Orange former principality, now part of SE France.
— city, SW California 92666*; pop. 91,788.
— city, NE New Jersey 07050*; pop. 31,136.
— city, E Texas 77630*; pop. 24,457.
Orange River river, S Africa; 1,300 mi. long.
Orangevale city, CEN. California 95662; pop. 16,493.
Oregon state, NW United States; 96,981 sq. mi.; pop. 2,632,663; cap. Salem.
— city, N Ohio 43616; pop. 16,563.
Orem city, CEN. Utah 84057; pop. 52,399.
Orillia town, S Ontario, Canada; pop. 24,040.
Orinoco river, Venezuela; ab. 1,700 mi. long.
Orkney Islands isl. group, N of Scotland, comprising Orkney, a co. of Scotland; 376 sq. mi.; pop. 17,000; cap. Kirkwall.
Orlando city, CEN. Florida 32800*; pop. 128,394.
Orléans city, CEN. France; pop. 96,000.
Osaka city, S Honshu, Japan; pop. 2,980,000.
Oshawa city, S Ontario, Canada; pop. 91,587.
Oshkosh city, E Wisconsin 54901*; pop. 49,678.
Oslo city, SE Norway; cap.; pop. 481,000.
Ossa mtn., E Greece; 6,490 ft. See PELION.
Ossining vill., SE New York 10562*; pop. 21,659.
Ostend city, NW Belgium; pop. 56,000.
Oswego city, N New York 13126; pop. 23,844.
Otranto, Strait of strait betw. the Adriatic and Ionian seas; ab. 43 mi. wide.
Ottawa city, N Illinois 61350; pop. 18,716.
— city, SE Ontario, Canada; cap. of Canada; pop. 394,462.
Ottumwa city, SE Iowa 52501*; pop. 27,381.
Ouagadougou city, CEN. Upper Volta; cap.; pop. 125,-000.
Outremont city, S Quebec, Canada; pop. 28,552.
Overland city, E Missouri 63114; pop. 24,949.
Overland Park uninc. place, NE Kansas 66204; pop. 81,-784.
Overlook-Page Manor city, SW Ohio 45431; pop. 19,596.

Owatonna city, s Minnesota 55060; pop. 15,341.
Owensboro city, NW Kentucky 42301*; pop. 54,450.
Owen Sound city, s Ontario, Canada; pop. 18,469.
Owosso city, CEN. Michigan 48867; pop. 17,179.
Oxford co. boro., CEN. England; pop. 109,000.
— city, SW Ohio 45056; pop. 15,868.
Oxnard city, SW California 93030*; pop. 108,195.
Ozark Mountains hilly uplands, SW Missouri, NW Arkansas, and NE Oklahoma.

Pacifica city, W California 94044; pop. 36,866.
Pacific Ocean ocean betw. the American continents and Asia and Australia; extending betw. the Arctic and Antarctic regions; ab. 70 million sq. mi.
Padua city, NE Italy; pop. 229,000.
Paducah city, W Kentucky 42001*; pop. 29,315.
Pago Pago town, SE Tutuila, American Samoa 96920; pop. 1,251.
Painesville city, NE Ohio 44077; pop. 16,536.
Pakistan republic, s Asia; 342,750 sq. mi.; pop. 85,000,000; cap. Islamabad.
Palatine vill., NE Illinois 60067; pop. 32,166.
Palau Islands isl. group, W Caroline Island; 188 sq. mi.
Palermo city, NW Sicily; cap.; pop. 664,000.
Palestine terr., E Mediterranean; 10,434 sq. mi.; cap. Jerusalem; divided (1947) by the United Nations into Israel and a terr. that became part of Jordan.
Palma city, W Majorca; cap. of the Balearic Islands, pop. 208,000.
Palm Springs city, s California 92262*; pop. 32,271.
Palo Alto city, W California 94303*; pop. 55,225.
Palomar, Mount mtn., s California; 6,126 ft.; site of Mount Palomar Observatory.
Palos Verdes Peninsula city, SW California 90274; pop. 39,616.
Pampa city, N Texas 79065*; pop. 21,726.
Panama republic, Central America; 29,306 sq. mi. (excluding Canal Zone); pop. 2,000,000.
— city, near the Pacific end of the Panama Canal; cap. of Panama; pop. 418,000.
Panama, Isthmus of isthmus connecting North and South America.
Panama Canal ship canal connecting the Atlantic and the Pacific across Panama; completed (1914) by the United States on the leased Canal Zone; 40 mi. long.
Panama Canal Zone See CANAL ZONE.
Panama City city, NW Florida 32401*; pop. 33,346.
Panay isl., CEN. Philippines; 4,446 sq. mi.
Papal States region in CEN. and NE Italy over which the Roman Catholic Church formerly had temporal power.
Papua New Guinea independent member of the Common-wealth of Nations, s Pacific, consisting of the E half of New Guinea; the isls. of the Bismarck Archipelago; Bougainville and Buka in the Solomon Isls.; and a number of smaller isls.; 183,540 sq. mi.; pop. 3,250,000; cap. Port Moresby.
Paradise town, SE Nevada 89101; pop. 24,477.
Paraguay republic, CEN. South America; 157,047 sq. mi.; pop. 3,165,000; cap. Asunción.
Paraguay River river, CEN. South America; ab. 1,300 mi. long.
Paramaribo city, N Surinam; cap.; pop. 150,000.
Paramount city, SW California 90723*; pop. 36,407.
Paramus boro., NE New Jersey 07652*; pop. 26,474.
Paraná river, CEN. South America; ab. 1,827 mi. long.
Paris city, N France; cap.; pop. 2,591,000.
— city, NE Texas 75460*; pop. 25,498.
Parkersburg city, W West Virginia 26100*; pop. 39,967.
Park Forest vill., NE Illinois 60466; pop. 26,222.
Parkland city, CEN. Washington 98444; pop. 21,012.
Park Ridge city, NE Illinois 60068; pop. 38,704.
Parkville-Carney uninc. place N Maryland 21234; pop. 33,897.
Parma city, CEN. Italy; pop. 175,000.
— city, N Ohio 44129; pop. 92,548.
Parma Heights city, NE Ohio 44129; pop. 27,192.
Parnassus, Mount mtn., CEN. Greece; anciently regarded as sacred to Apollo and the Muses; 8,062 ft.
Parsippany urb. twp., N New Jersey 07054; pop. 55,112.
Pasadena city, SW California 91100*; pop. 119,374.
— city, SE Texas 77501*; pop. 112,560.
Pascagoula city, SE Mississippi 39567; pop. 29,318.
Passaic city, NE New Jersey 07055*; pop. 52,463.
Patagonia reg. at the s tip of South America.
Paterson city, NE New Jersey 07500*; pop. 137,970.
Pawtucket city, NE Rhode Island 02860*; pop. 71,204.
Peabody city, NE Massachusetts 01960*; pop. 45,976.

Pearl City city, s Oahu, Hawaii 96782; pop. 19,552.
Pearl Harbor inlet, s Oahu, Hawaii; site of a U.S. naval base, bombed by Japanese, December 7, 1941.
Pearl River city, SE New York 10965; pop. 17,146.
Peekskill city, SE New York 10566*; pop. 18,881.
Pekin city, CEN. Illinois 61554*; pop. 33,967.
Peking city, N China; cap.; pop. 7,570,000.
Pelion mtn. range, SE Thessaly, Greece. In Greek mythology, the Titans attempted to reach heaven by piling Pelion on Ossa and both on Olympus.
Peloponnesus penin. betw. Aegean and Ionian Seas; one of the main divisions of s Greece; 8,603 sq. mi.; pop. 986,000.
Pembroke town, SE Ontario, Canada; pop. 16,544.
Pembroke Pines city, SE Florida 33023; pop. 35,776.
Penn Hills urb. twp., SW Pennsylvania 15235; pop. 51, 512.
Pennine Alps SW div. of the Alps on the Swiss-Italian border.
Pennsauken urb. twp., W New Jersey 08110; pop. 36, 394.
Penn Square city, SE Pennsylvania; pop. 20,238.
Pennsylvania state, E United States, 45,333 sp. mi.; pop. 11,866,728; cap. Harrisburg.
Pensacola city, NW Florida 32501*; pop. 57,619.
Penticton city, s British Columbia, Canada; pop. 18,146.
Peoria city, CEN. Illinois 61600*; pop. 124,160.
Persia Iran; *the former name.*
Persian Gulf inlet of the Arabian Sea betw. Iran and Arabia.
Perth city, SW Western Australia; cap. pop. 701,000.
Perth Amboy city, E New Jersey 08861*; pop. 38,951.
Peru republic, W South America; 533,916 sq. mi,; pop. 18,300,000; cap. Lima.
Petaluma city, W California 94952*; pop. 33,834.
Peterborough City, s Ontario, Canada; pop. 58,111.
Petersburg city, SE Virginia 23801*; pop. 41.055.
Pharr city, s Texas 78577; pop. 15,829.
Phenix City city, E Alabama 36867; pop. 26,928.
Philadelphia city, SE Pennsylvania 19100*; pop. 1,688,210.
Philippines, Republic of the republic occupying the Philippine Islands, a Pacific archipelago SE of China; 115,707 sq. mi.; pop 49,000,000; cap. Quezon City; seat of administration, Manila.
Phillipsburg city, W New Jersey 08865*; pop. 17,849.
Phnom Penh city, s Cen. Cambodia; cap.; pop. 20,000.
Phoenix city CEN. Arizona 85000*; cap.; pop. 764,911.
Picardy reg. and former prov., N France.
Pico Rivera city, SW California 90660*; pop. 53,459.
Piedmont reg., E United States; extends from New Jersey to Alabama E of the Appalachians; ab. 80,000 sq. mi.
Pierre city, CEN. South Dakota 57501; cap.; pop 9,699.
Pierrefonds town, s Quebec, Canada; pop. 33,010.
Pike's Peak mtn., CEN. Colorado; 14,110 ft.
Pikesville uninc. place, CEN. Maryland 21208; pop. 25, 395.
Pine Bluff city, CEN. Arkansas 71601*; pop. 56,576.
Pinellas Park city, W Florida 33565; pop. 32,811.
Pinole city, W California 94564; pop. 15,850.
Piqua city, W Ohio 45356; pop. 20,741.
Piraeus city, s Greece; pop. 184,000.
Pisa city, NW Italy; noted for its leaning tower; pop. 103, 000.
Pittsburg city, W California 94565; pop. 33,034.
— city, SE Kansas 66762*; pop. 20,171.
Pittsburgh city, SW Pennsylvania 15200*; pop. 423,938.
Pittsfield city, W Massachusetts 01200*; pop. 51,974.
Placentia city, SW California 92670; pop. 35,041.
Plainfield city, NE New Jersey 07060; pop. 45,555.
Plainview vill., SE New York 11803; pop. 32,195.
— city, NW Texas 79072*; pop. 19,096.
Plainville city, CEN. Connecticut 06062; pop. 16,733.
Plano city, CEN. Texas 75074; pop. 72,331.
Plantation city, NE Florida 33314; pop. 48,501.
Plant City city W Florida 33566; pop. 15,451.
Platte River river, s Nebraska; 310 mi. long.
Plattsburgh city, NE New York 12901*; pop. 18,715. Also Plattsburg.
Pleasant Hill uninc. place, W California 94523; pop. 25,124.
Pleasanton city, W California 94566; pop. 35,160.
Pleasure Ridge Park uninc. place, N Kentucky 40158; pop. 28,566.
Plum boro., SW Pennsylvania 15239; pop. 25,390.
Plymouth co. boro. and port, SW England; pop. 239,000.

Plymouth town, E Massachusetts 02360*; site of the first settlement in New England; pop. 18,606.
— vill., E Minnesota; pop. 31,615.
Plymouth Colony colony on the shore of Massachusetts Bay founded by the Pilgrim Fathers in 1620.
Plymouth Rock rock at Plymouth, Massachusetts, on which the Pilgrim Fathers are said to have landed in 1620.
Pocatello city, Idaho 83201*; pop. 46,340.
Pointe-aux-Trembles city, S Quebec, Canada; pop. 35,-567.
Pointe-Claire city, S Quebec, Canada; pop. 27,303.
Point Pleasant boro., E New Jersey 08742; pop. 15,968.
Poland republic, CEN. Europe; 120,359 sq. mi.; pop. 35,-900,000; cap. Warsaw.
Polynesia isls. of Oceania, CEN. and SE Pacific; E of Melanesia and Micronesia.
Pomerania former province of Prussia, N Germany; now divided between East Germany and Poland.
Pomona city N California 91766*; pop.92,742.
Pompano Beach city, SE Florida 33060*; pop. 52,618.
Pompeii ancient city, S Italy; buried in the eruption of Mount Vesuvius, A.D. 79, now ab. half excavated.
Ponca City city N Oklahoma 74601*; pop. 26,238.
Ponce city, S Puerto Rico 00731; pop. 125,926.
Pontiac city, SE Michigan 48053*; pop. 76,715.
Pont-Viau city, S Quebec, Canada; pop. 16,077.
Poona city, W India; pop. 856,000.
Poplar Bluff city, SE Missouri 63901; pop. 16,653.
Popocatepetl dormant volcano, CEN. Mexico; 17,887 ft.
Po River river, N Italy; 405 mi. long.
Portage town, NW Indiana 46368; pop. 27,409.
— city, SW Michigan 49081; pop. 38,157.
Port Angeles city, NW Washington 98362; pop. 16,367.
Port Arthur city, SE Texas 77640*; pop. 61,195.
Port-au-Prince city, S Haiti; cap.; pop. 745,000.
Port Chester vill., SE New York 10573*; pop. 25,803.
Port Colborne town, S Ontario, Canada; pop. 21,420.
Port Huron city, E Michigan 48060*; pop. 33,981.
Portland city, SW Maine 04100*; pop. 61,572.
— city, NW Oregon 97200*; pop. 366,383.
Port-of-Spain city, NW Trinidad; cap. of Trinidad and Tobago; pop. 94,000. Also **Port of Spain.**
Porto-Novo city, SE Benin; cap.; pop. 75,000.
Port Said city, NE Egypt; at the Mediterranean end of the Suez Canal; pop. 349,000.
Portsmouth co. boro., S England; site of the chief British naval station; pop. 197,000.
— city, SE New Hampshire 03801*; pop. 26,254.
— city, S Ohio 45662*; pop. 25,943.
— city, SE Virginia 23700*; pop. 104,577.
Portugal republic, SW Europe; 35,419 sq. mi.; pop. 10,000,000; cap. Lisbon.
Port Washington uninc. place, SE New York 11050; pop. 15,923
Potomac River river betw. Maryland, West Virginia, and Virginia; 287 mi. long.
Potsdam city, CEN. East Germany; scene of meeting of Allied leaders, 1945; pop. 111,000.
Pottstown boro., SE Pennsylvania 19464*; pop. 25,355.
Pottsville city, CEN. Pennsylvania 17901*; pop. 19,715.
Poughkeepsie city, SE New York 12600*; pop. 29,757.
Poznan city, W Poland; pop. 469,000.
Prague city, W Czechoslovakia; cap.; pop. 1,188,600.
Prairie Village city, NE Kansas 66208; pp. 28,138.
Pretoria city, CEN. South Africa; adm. cap.; pop. 493,000.
Prichard city, SW Alabama 36610; pop. 39,541.
Prince Albert city, CEN. Saskatchewan, Canada; pop. 28,464.
Prince Edward Island prov., NE Canada; 2,184 sq. mi.; pop. 111,641; cap. Charlottetown.
Prince George city, CEN. British Columbia, Canada; pop. 33,101.
Prince Rupert city, W British Columbia, Canada; pop. 15,747.
Provence reg. and former prov., SE France.
Providence city, NE Rhode Island 02900*; cap.; pop. 156,804.
Provo city city, CEN. Utah 84601; pop. 73,907.
Prussia former state, N Germany; dissolved, 1947.
Pueblo city, CEN. Colorado 81000*; pop. 101,686.
Puerto Rico isl., Greater Antilles; a Commonwealth of the United States 3,423 sq. mi.; pop. 2,353,297; cap. San Juan.
Puget Sound inlet of the Pacific, NW Washington.
Pulaski town, SW Virginia 24301; pop. 16,279.

Pullman city, SE Washington 99163*; pop. 20,509.
Punjab reg., NW India and E Pakistan.
Pyongyang city, W North Korea; cap.; pop. 1,500,000.
Pyrenees mtn. chain betw. France and Spain.

Qatar emirate on the W coast of the Persian Gulf; ab. 4,247 sq. mi.; pop. 230,000; cap. Doha.
Quebec prov., E Canada; 594,860 sq. mi.; pop. 6,234,445.
— city, S Quebec prov.; cap.; pop. 177,082.
Queens boro., E New York; pop. 1,891,325.
Queensland state, NE Australia; 670,500 sq. mi.; pop. 2,037,000; cap. Brisbane.
Quemoy Islands 2 isls. of the Republic of China in Formosa Strait; 54 sq. mi.
Quezon City city, CEN. Philippines; cap.; pop. 960,000.
Quincy city, W Illinois 62301*; pop. 42,352.
— city, E Massachusetts 02169; pop. 84,743.
Quito city, CEN. Ecuador; cap.; pop. 597,000.

Rabat city, N Morocco; cap.; pop. 261,000.
Racine city, SE Wisconsin 53400*; pop. 85,725.
Radnor urb. twp. SE Pennsylvania 19087; pop. 21,697.
Rahway city, NE New Jersey 07065*; pop. 26,723.
Rainier, Mount extinct volcano, Cascade Range, SW Washington; 14,408 ft.
Raleigh city, CEN. North Carolina 27600*; cap.; pop. 149,771.
Rancho Cordova uninc. place, CEN. California 95670; pop. 30,451.
Randallstown city, NE Maryland 21133; pop. 33,683.
Randolph town, E Massachusetts 02368; pop. 27,035.
Rangoon city, S Burma; cap.; pop. 2,200,000.
Rantoul vill., CEN. Illinois 61866*; pop. 25,526.
Rapid City city, SW South Dakota 57701*; pop. 46,492.
Raritan twp. CEN. New Jersey 08869; pop. 15,334.
Ravenna city, N Italy, famous for its art treasures and architecture; pop. 133,128.
Rawalpindi city, N Pakistan; pop. 340,000.
Raytown city, W Missouri 64133; pop. 31,759.
Reading town, NE Massachusetts 01867; pop. 22, 539.
— city, SE Pennsylvania 19600*; pop. 78,686.
Recife city, NE Brazil; pop. 2,346,196.
Red Deer city, CEN. Alberta, Canada: pop. 27,674.
Redding city, N California 96001*; pop. 41,995.
Redlands city, SW California 92373*; pop. 43,619.
Redondo Beach city, SW California 90277*; pop. 57,-102.
Red River river in Texas, Arkansas, and Louisiana; ab. 1,300 mi. long.
— river in N United States and S Canada; 540 mi. long.
Red Sea sea betw. Egypt and Arabia; 1,450 mi. long; ab. 170,000 sq. mi.
Redwood City city, W California 94061*; pop. 54,965.
Regina city, S Saskatchewan, Canada; cap.; pop. 139,469.
Reims city, NE France; site of a famous cathedral; pop. 179,000.
Reno city, W Nevada 89500*; pop. 100,756
Renton city, CEN. Washington 98055; pop. 30,612.
Repentigny town, S Quebec, Canada; pop. 19,520.
Réunion French overseas dept.; isl. E of Madagascar; 970 sq. mi.; pop. 446,000; cap. Saint-Denis.
Revere city, E Massachusetts 02151; pop. 42,423.
Reykjavik city, SW Iceland; cap.; pop. 84,000.
Rheims Reims: *an alternate name.*
Rhine river, CEN. Europe; 810 mi. long.
Rhode Island state, NE United States; 1,214 sq. mi.; pop. 947,154; cap. Providence.
Rhodes isl. of the Dodecanese groups; 545 sq. mi.
Rhodesia See **Zimbabwe Rhodesia.**
Rhône river, Switzerland and SE France; 504 mi. long. Also **Rhone.**
Rialto city, S California 92376; pop. 35,615.
Richardson city, N Texas 75080*; pop. 72,496.
Richfield vill., E Minnesota 55423; pop. 37,851.
Richland city, S Washington 99352; pop. 33,578.
Richmond city, W California 94800*; pop. 74,676.
— city, E Indiana 47374; pop. 41,349.
— city, CEN. Kentucky 40475*; pop. 16,861.
— boro., SW New York City; pop. 295,443.
— city, CEN. Virginia 23200*; cap.; cap. of the Confederacy 1861–65; pop.
Richmond Hill town, S Ontario, Canada; pop. 32,384.
Ridgewood urb. twp., NE New Jersey 07450*; pop. 25,-208.
Ridley urb. twp., SE Pennsylvania; pop. 35,738.
Rif mtn. range, N Morocco. Also **Riff.**
Riga city, CEN. Latvian SSR; cap.; pop. 743,000.

Rijeka City, NW Yugoslavia; including its SE suburb and officially called **Rijeka-Susak;** pop. 133,000.

Rimouski town, E Quebec, Canada; pop. 26,887.

Rio de Janeiro city, SE Brazil; former cap.; pop. 4,316,000. Also **Rio.**

Rio de la Plata estuary of the Paraná and Uruguay rivers betw. Argentina and Uruguay; 170 mi. long.

Rio de Oro terr., Spanish Sahara; 73,362 sq. mi.; pop. 157,000; cap. Villa Cisneros.

Rio Grande river betw. Texas and Mexico; 1,890 mi. long.

Riverdale vill., NE Illinois 60627; pop. 15,806.

River Rouge city, SE Michigan, 48218; pop. 15,947.

Riverside city, SW California 92501*; pop. 170,876.

Riviera coastal strip on the Mediterranean from Hyeres, France to La Spezia, Italy.

Riviera Beach town, SE Florida 33404; pop. 26,596.

Roanoke city, W Virginia 24001*; pop. 100,427.

Roanoke Island isl. off North Carolina; 12 mi. long, 3 mi. wide.

Robbinsdale city, E Minnesota 55422; pop. 16,845.

Rochester city, SE Minnesota 55901; pop. 57,855.

— city, SE New Hampshire 03867; pop. 17,938.

— city, W New York 14600*; pop. 241,741.

Rockford city, N Illinois 61100; pop. 139,712.

Rock Hill city, N South Carolina 29730*; pop. 35,344.

Rock Island city, NW Illinois 61201*; pop. 47,036.

Rockland town, E Massachusetts 02370; pop. 15,674.

Rockville city, CEN. Maryland 20850*; pop. 43,811.

Rockville Centre vill., SE New York 11570*; pop.25,-405.

Rocky Mount city, CEN. North Carolina 27801*; pop. 43,811.

Rocky Mountains mtn. system, W North America; extends from the Arctic to Mexico.

Rocky River city, N Ohio 44116; pop. 22,958.

Rolling Meadows city, NE Illinois 60008; pop. 19,178.

Romania Rumania: *an alternate form.*

Rome city, W Italy; cap.; site of the Vatican City; cap. of the former Roman republic, the Roman Empire, and the States of the Church; pop. 2,900,000.

— city, NW Georgia 30161*; pop. 29,654.

— city, CEN. New York 13440*; pop. 43,826.

Roosevelt uninc. place, SE New York 11575; pop. 15,008.

Rosario city, CEN. Argentina; pop. 672,000.

Rosedale city, NW Maryland 21237; pop. 19,417.

Roselle boro., NE New Jersey 07203 pop. 22,585.

Rosemead city, SW California 91770*; pop. 42,604.

Roseville city, CEN. California 95678; pop. 17,805.

— city SE Michigan 48066; pop. 54,311.

— vill., SE Minnesota 55113; pop. 35,820.

Roslyn city, SW Pennsylvania 19001; pop. 18,317.

Ross urb twp., SW Pennsylvania; pop. 25,952.

Rostov-on-Don city, SW RSFSR; pop. 934,000.

Roswell city, SE New Mexico 88201*; pop. 39,676.

Rotterdam city, W Netherlands; pop. 1,014,800.

— uninc. place E New York 12303; pop. 25,153.

Rouen city, N France; site of a famous cathedral; scene of the burning of Joan of Arc; pop. 120,000.

Roumania Rumania: *an alternate form.*

Rouyn city, W Quebec, Canada; pop. 17,821.

Royal Oak city, SE Michigan 48067*; pop. 70,893.

Rugby municipal boro., CEN. England; site of a boys' school; pop. 57,000.

Ruhr river, W West Germany; 142 mi. long.

— reg. S of the Ruhr, an industrial and coal-mining district. 1,770 sq. mi.

Rumania republic, SE Europe; 91,671 sq. mi.; pop.22,-500,000; cap. Bucharest.

Russia before 1917, an empire, E Europe and N Asia; cap. Saint Petersburg (Petrograd); now part of the Union of Soviet Socialist Republics.

Russian Soviet Federated Socialist Republic constituent republic, N USSR; 6,592,800 sq. mi., pop. 130,-700,000; cap. Moscow.

Ruston city, N Louisiana 71270*; pop. 17,365.

Rutherford boro., NE New Jersey 07070*; pop. 20,802.

Rutland city, CEN. Vermont 05701*; pop. 19,293.

Rwanda republic, CEN. Africa; 10,160 sq. mi.; pop. 5,200,000; cap. Kigali.

Rye city, SE New York, 10580; pop. 15,869.

Ryukyu Islands isl. group betw. Kyushu and Taiwan; 1,205 sq. mi.; pop. 1,150,000; chief isl. Okinawa; adm. by Japan.

Saar river, NE France and Germany; 152 mi. long

Saar, The state, W West Germany; 991 sq. mi.; pop. 1,129,000; cap. Saarbrücken.

Sabah part of Malaysia in N Borneo; 29,388 sq. mi.; pop. 920,000; cap. Kota Kinabalu.

Sacramento city, CEN. California; 95801*; cap.; pop. 275,741.

Sacramento River river, CEN. California; 382 mi. long.

Saddle Brook urb. twp., NE New Jersey 07662; pop. 15,098.

Saginaw city, CEN. Michigan 48601*; pop. 77,508.

Sahara desert area, N Africa; ab. 3 million sq. mi. Also **Sahara Desert.**

Saigon city, S Vietnam; formerly cap. of South Vietnam; pop. 1,761,000: also called **Ho Chi Minh City.**

Saipan one of the Mariana isls.; 47 sq. mi.; captured from Japan by U.S. forces in World War II, 1944.

Saint, Sainte See entries beginning ST., STE.

Sakhalin isl. SE RSFSR; 29,700 sq. mi.; pop. 649,000; adm. ctr. Yuzhno-Sakhalinsk.

Salem city, NE Massachusetts 01970*; pop. 38,220.

— city, SE New Hampshire 03079; pop. 20,142.

— city, NW Oregon 97301*; cap.; pop. 89,233.

— town, CEN. Virginia 24153; pop. 21,982.

Salerno city, SW Italy; scene of a battle in World War II betw. Germans and Allied landing forces, 1943; pop. 157,-000.

Salina city, CEN. Kansas 67401*; pop. 41,843.

Salinas city, W California 93901*; pop. 80,479.

Salisbury city, SE Maryland 21801; pop. 15,252.

—city, CEN. North Carolina 28144; pop. 22,515.

— city, N Zimbabwe Rhodesia; cap.; pop. 557,000.

Salonika city, NE Greece; pop. 346,000.

Salt Lake City city, CEN. Utah 84100*; cap.; pop. 163,-033.

Salvador city, E Brazil; pop. 1,766,075.

— See EL SALVADOR

Salzburg city, W Austria; birthplace of Mozart; pop. 129,-000.

Samar one of the Visayan isls., Philippines; 5,050 sq. mi.

Samarkand city, E Uzbek SSR; pop. 272,000.

Samoa isl. group, SW Pacific; 1,173 sq. mi.; divided into **American (or Eastern) Samoa,** an uninc. terr. of the United States; 76 sq. mi.; pop. 28,000; cap. Pago Pago; and **Western Samoa,** an independent state; 1,097 sq. mi.; pop. 147,000; cap. Apia.

Samos isl. of Greece, E Aegean; 184 sq. mi.

Samothrace isl. of Greece, NE Aegean; 71 sq. mi.

San Angelo city, CEN. Texas 76901*; pop. 73,240.

San Antonio city, CEN. Texas 78200*; site of the Alamo; pop. 785,410.

San Benito city, S Texas 78586; pop. 15,176.

San Bernardino city, SW California 92400*; pop. 118,-057.

San Bruno city, W California 94066*; pop. 35,417.

San Carlos city, W California 94070*; pop. 25,924.

San Clemente city, S California 92672; pop. 35,417.

San Diego city, SW California 92100*; pop. 875,504.

San Dimas city, SW California 91773; pop. 15,692.

Sandusky city, N Ohio 44870*; pop. 31,360.

San Fernando city, SW California 91340*; pop. 16,751.

Sanford city, CEN. Florida 32771; pop. 17,393.

— uninc. place, SW Maine 04073; pop. 15,812.

San Francisco city, W California 94100*; pop. 678,974.

San Francisco Bay inlet of the Pacific, W California.

San Gabriel city, SW California 91775*; pop. 30,072.

San Joaquin River river, CEN. California; 317 mi. long.

San José city, CEN. Costa Rica; cap.; pop. 211,00.

San Jose city, W California 95100*; pop. 636,550.

San Juan city, NE Puerto Rico 00900*; cap.; pop. 452,749.

San Leandro city, W California 94577*; pop. 63,952.

San Lorenzo uninc. place, W California 94580; pop. 24,-633.

San Luis Obispo city, W California 93401*; pop. 34,252.

San Marcos city, CEN. Texas 78666; pop. 18,860.

San Marino republic, an enclave in NE Italy; 24 sq. mi.; pop. 21,000.

— city, San Marino; cap.; pop. 4,000.

San Mateo city, W California 94400*; pop. 77,561.

San Pablo city, W California 94806; pop. 21,461.

San Rafael city, W California 94901*; pop. 44,700.

San Salvador city, S El Salvador; cap.; pop. 379,000.

— isl. CEN. Bahamas; site of Columbus' first landing in the western hemisphere, 1492.

Santa Ana city, SW California 92700*; pop. 203,713.

Santa Barbara city, SW California 93100*; pop. 87,746.

Santa Catalina isl. off SW California; 70 sq. mi.

Santa Clara city, W California 95050*; pop. 87,746.

Santa Cruz city, W California 95060*; pop. 41,483.

Santa Fe city, N New Mexico 87501*; cap.; pop. 74,542.

Sante Fe Trail trade route, important from 1821–80, betw. Independence, Missouri, and Santa Fe, New Mexico.

Santa Maria city, sw California 93454*; pop. 39,685.
Santa Monica city, sw California 90400*; pop. 88,314.
Santa Paula city, sw California 93060; pop. 18,001.
Santa Rosa city, w California 95401*; pop. 83,205.
Santee city, sw California 92071; pop. 21,107.
Santiago city, CEN. Chile; cap; pop. 3,850,000. Also **Santiago de Chile**.
Santo Domingo city, s Dominican Republic; cap.; pop. 1,103,400.
São Paulo city, SE Brazil; pop. 5,241,000.
Sapulpa city, CEN. Oklahoma 74066; pop. 15,159.
Sarajevo city, CEN. Yugoslavia; scene of the assassination of Archduke Franz Ferdinand, June 28, 1914; pop. 244,000.
Sarasota city sw Florida 33577*; pop. 48,868.
Saratoga city, w California 95070; pop. 29,261.
Saratoga Springs city, CEN. New York 12866; pop. 18,-845.
Sarawak part of Malaysia on NW Borneo; 47,071 sq. mi.; pop. 945,000; cap. Kuching.
Sardinia isl., CEN. Mediterranean; with adjacent isls. a reg. of Italy; 9,298 sq. mi.; pop. 1,419,000; cap. Cagliari.
Sarnia city, s Ontario, Canada; pop. 57,644.
Saskatchewan prov., CEN. Canada; 251,700 sq. mi.; pop. 926,242; cap. Regina.
Saskatoon city, CEN. Saskatchewan, Canada; pop. 126,-449.
Saudi Arabia kingdom, N and CEN. Arabia; 873,000 sq. mi.; pop. 8,650,000; caps. Mecca and Riyadh.
Saugus town, NE Massachusetts 01906; pop. 25,110.
Sault Sainte Marie city, N Michigan 49783*; pop. 15,-136.
— city, CEN. Ontario, Canada; pop. 80,332. Also **Sault Ste. Marie**.
Sault Sainte Marie Canals 3 canals that circumvent the rapids in the St. Marys River betw. Lakes Superior and Huron.
Savannah city, E Georgia 31400*; pop. 141,634.
Saxony reg. and former duchy, electorate, kingdom and prov., CEN. Germany.
Sayreville boro., E New Jersey 08872; pop. 29,969.
Scandinavia reg., NW Europe; includes Sweden, Norway, and Denmark and sometimes Finland, Iceland, and the Faroe Islands.
Scapa Flow sea basin and British naval base in the Orkney Islands, Scotland; 50 sq. mi.
Scarsdale town, SE New York 10583; pop. 19,229.
Schaumburg city, NE Illinois 60172; pop. 52,319.
Scheldt river, N France, Belgium and the Netherlands; 270 mi. long.
Schenectady city, E New York 12300*; pop. 67,972.
Schleswig-Holstein state, NE West Germany; 6,052 sq. mi.; pop. 2,529,000; cap. Kiel.
Schuylkill River river, SE Pennsylvania; 130 mi. long.
Scituate city, NE Massachusetts 02066; pop. 16,973.
Scotch Plains urb. twp., NE New Jersey 07076; pop. 22,279.
Scotland a political div. and the N part of Great Britain; a separate kingdom until 1707; 30,405 sq. mi.; pop. 5,199,000; cap. Edinburgh.
Scott urb. twp., sw Pennsylvania; pop. 19,094.
Scottsdale city, CEN. Arizona 85251*; pop. 88,364.
Scranton city, NE Pennsylvania 18500*; pop. 88,117.
Seaford uninc. place, SE New York 11783; pop. 17,379.
Seal Beach city, sw California 90740; pop. 25,975.
Seaside city, w California 93955; pop. 36,567.
Seattle city, CEN. Washington 98100*; pop. 493,846.
Sebastopol See SEVASTOPOL.
Security unic. place, CEN. Colorado 80911; pop. 15,297.
Sedalia city, CEN. Missouri 65301*; pop. 22,847.
Seguin city, CEN. Texas 78155; pop. 15,934.
Seine river, NE France; 482 mi. long.
Selma city, CEN. Alabama 36701*; pop. 26,684.
Semarang city, N Java, Indonesia; pop. 690,000.
Senegal river, NW Africa; ab. 1,000 mi. long.
Senegal, Republic of republic of the French Community, NW Africa; 76,124 sq. mi.; pop. 5,800,000.; cap. Dakar.
Seoul city, NW South Korea; cap.; pop. 5,510,000.
Sept-Iles city, E Quebec, Canada; pop. 24,320.
Serbia constituent republic, E Yugoslavia; 34,107 sq. mi.; pop. 8,860,000; cap. Belgrade.
Sevastopol city, s Crimea, USSR; pop. 236,000.
Severn river, N. Wales and w England; 210 mi. long.
Severna city, NE Maryland 21146; pop. 16,358.
Seville city, sw Spain; pop. 630,000.
Sèvres city, N France; pop. 17,000.
Shaker Heights city, N Ohio 44120; pop. 32,487.

Shaler urb. twp., sw Pennsylvania; pop. 24,939.
Shanghai city, E China; pop. 10,820,000.
Shannon river, CEN. Ireland; 224 mi. long.
Sharon city, w Pennsylvania 16146*; pop. 22,653.
Shasta, Mount extinct volcano, Cascade Range, N California; 14,162 ft.
Shawinigan city, s Quebec, Canada; pop. 27,792.
Shawnee city, NE Kansas 66103; pop. 29,653.
— city, CEN. Oklahoma 74801*; pop. 26,306.
Sheboygan city, E Wisconsin 53081*; pop. 48,085.
Sheffield co. boro., CEN. England; pop. 520,000.
Shelby city, sw North Carolina 28150; pop. 16,328.
Shelbyville city, CEN. Indiana 46176; pop. 15,094.
Shelton city, sw Connecticut 06484*; pop. 31,314.
Shenandoah river, N Virginia and NE West Virginia; 170, mi. long.
Shenyang city, NE China; pop. 3,750,000: formerly called Mukden.
Sherbrooke city, s Quebec, Canada; pop. 80,711.
Sherman city, N Texas 75090*; pop. 30,413.
Sherrelwood city, CEN. Colorado; pop. 18,868.
Shetland Islands isl. group NE of the Orkney Islands, comprising **Shetland**, a co. of Scotland; 551 mi.; pop. 17,000; cap. Lerwick.
Shikoku isl., sw Japan; 7,248 sq. mi.
Shiloh national military park, sw Tennessee; scene of a Union victory in the Civil War, 1862; 6 sq. mi.
Shively city, N Kentucky 40216; pop. 19,223.
Shorewood vill., SE Wisconsin 53211; pop. 15,576.
Shreveport city, NW Louisiana 71100*; pop. 205,815.
Shrewsbury city, CEN. Massachusetts 01545; pop. 19,-196.
Siam Thailand: *the former name.*
Siam, Gulf of part of the South China Sea betw. the Malay Peninsula and Indochina.
Siberia reg., E RSFSR; ab. 5 million sq. mi.
Sicily isl. of Italy, CEN. Mediterranean; comprises with neighboring islands a reg. of 9,926 sq. mi.; pop. 4,721,000; cap. Palermo.
Sidney city, w Ohio 45365; pop. 16,332.
Sierra Leone independent member of the Commonwealth of Nations; N Africa; 27,925 sq. mi.; pop. 3,560,000; cap. Freetown.
Sierra Nevada mtn. range, E California.
Silesia reg., CEN. Europe; divided betw. Czechoslovakia and Poland.
Silver Spring uninc. place, w Maryland 20900*; pop. 77,496.
Simi Valley city, sw California 93065; pop. 77,500.
Simla city, N India; pop. 43,000.
Simsbury city, CEN. Connecticut 06070; pop. 17,475.
Sinai penin., E Egypt, betw. the Mediterranean and the Red Sea.
Singapore isl. off the tip of the Malay Peninsula; comprises with adjacent isls. a republic of the Commonwealth of Nations; 238 sq. mi.; pop. 2,420,000.
— city, s Singapore; cap.; pop. 2,308,000.
Sinkiang-Uigur Autonomous Region div., w China; 635,829 sq. mi.; pop. ab. 8 million; cap. Urumchi (Tihwa). Also formerly **Sinkiang.**
Sioux City city, w Iowa 51100*; pop. 82,003.
Sioux Falls city, SE South Dakota 57100*; pop. 81,343.
Skokie vill., NE Illinois 60076*; pop. 60,278.
Slidell town, SE Louisiana 70458; pop. 26,718.
Slovakia reg. and former prov., E Czechoslovakia.
Slovenia constituent republic, NW Yugoslavia; 7,717 sq. mi.; pop. 1,792,000; cap. Ljubljana.
Smyrna town, CEN. Georgia 30080; pop. 19,517.
— Izmir: *an alternate name.*
Society Islands isl. group, French Polynesia; ab. 650 sq. mi.
Sofia city, w Bulgaria; cap.; pop. 1,000,000.
Solomon Islands isl. group, sw Pacific; ab. 16,500 sq. mi.; including the **British Solomon Islands**, a prot.; ab. 11,500 sq. mi.; pop. 225,000; cap. Honiara.
Somalia republic, E Africa; 246,201 sq. mi.; pop. 3,750,-000; cap. Mogadiscio. Also **Somali Democratic Republic.**
Somerset town, SE Massachusetts 02725; pop. 18,088.
Somerville city, E Massachusetts 02143; pop. 77,372.
Somme river, N France; 150 mi. long.
Soo Canals *informal* Sault Sainte Marie Canals.
Sorel city, s Quebec, Canada; pop. 19,347.
South Africa, Republic of republic, s Africa; 472,359 sq. mi.; pop. 28,115,000; seat of government Pretoria; seat of legislature Cape Town.
South America s continent of the Western Hemisphere; ab. 6,900,000 sq. mi.
Southampton co. boro., s England; pop. 215,000.

South Australia state, s Australia; 380,070 sq. mi.; pop. 1,173,000; cap. Adelaide.

South Bakersfield city, CEN. California; pop. 30,249.

South Bend city, N Indiana 46600*; pop. 109,727.

Southbridge uninc. place s Massachusetts 01550*; pop. 17,057.

South Carolina state, SE United States; 31,055 sq. mi.; pop. 3,119,208; cap. Columbia.

South Charleston city, CEN. West Virginia 25303; pop. 16,333.

South China Sea part of the Pacific betw. SE Asia and the Malay Archipelago.

South Dakota state, CEN. United States; 77,047 sq. mi.; pop. 690,178; cap. Pierre.

Southern Yemen See YEMEN, PEOPLE'S DEMOCRATIC REPUBLIC OF.

South Euclid city, NE Ohio 44121; pop. 25,713.

South Farmingdale uninc. place, SE New York 11735; pop. 20,464.

Southfield city, SE Michigan 48075*; pop. 75,568.

South Fort Polk city, SW Louisiana; pop. 15,600.

Southgate city, SE Michigan 48192; pop. 33,909.

South Gate city, SW California 90280*; pop. 66,784.

South Hadley town, GEN. Massachusetts 01075; pop. 17,033.

South Holland vill, SE Illinois 60473; pop. 23,931.

Southington uninc. place, CEN. Connecticut 06489; pop. 30,946.

South Island one of the two main isls. of New Zealand; 58,093 sq. mi.

South Kingston town, s Rhode Island; pop. 16,913.

South Korea See KOREA.

South Miami city, SE Florida 33143; pop. 19,571.

South Milwaukee city SE Wisconsin 53172; pop. 23,297.

South Orange vill., NE New Jersey 07079; pop. 16,971.

South Pasadena city, SW California 91030*; pop. 22,979.

South Plainfield boro., NE New Jersey 07080; pop. 21,142.

South Pole s extremity of the earth's axis.

South Portland city, SW Maine 04106; pop. 23,267.

South River boro., E New Jersey 08882; pop. 15,428.

South Sacramento-Frutridge uninc. place, CEN. California; pop. 28,574.

South San Francisco city, W California 94080*; pop. 49,393.

South Sea Islands isls. of the South Pacific.

South Seas waters of the Southern Hemisphere, esp. the South Pacific Ocean.

South Stickney city, NE Illinois 60459; pop. 29,900.

South Stony Brook City, SE New York; pop. 15,329.

South St. Paul city, E Minnesota 55075*; pop. 25,016.

South Valley city, CEN. New Mexico; pop. 29,389.

South-West Africa mandated terr., SW Africa; administered by the Republic of South Africa; 317,877 sq. mi.; pop. 746,000; cap. Windhoek. Also called **Namibia.**

South Whittier city, SW California 90605; pop. 46,641.

South Windsor city, CEN. Connecticut 06074; pop. 15,553.

Soviet Russia 1 Russian Soviet Federated Socialist Republic. **2** Union of Soviet Socialist Republics.

Soviet Union Union of Soviet Socialist Republics: *an alternate name.*

Spain monarchy, SW Europe; 194,368 sq. mi.; pop. 37,750,000; cap. Madrid.

Spanish America parts of the W hemisphere where Spanish is the predominant language.

Spanish Lake city, NE Missouri 63101; pop. 15,647.

Sparks city, W Nevada 89431; pop. 40,780.

Sparta city-state of ancient Greece, famous for its military power: sometimes called *Lacedaemon.*

Spartanburg city, NW South Carolina 29301*; pop. 43,968.

Speedway town, s Indiana 46224; pop. 15,056.

Spenard uninc. place s Alaska 99503; pop. 18,089.

Spitsbergen See SVALBARD.

Spokane city E Washington 99200*; pop. 171,300.

Springdale city, NW Arkansas 72764; pop. 16,783.

Springfield city, CEN. Illinois 62700*; cap.; pop. 99,637.

— city, SW Massachusetts 01100*; pop. 152,319.

— city, SW Missouri 65800; pop. 133,116.

— urb. twp., NE New Jersey 07081; pop. 15,740.

— city, CEN. Ohio 45500; pop. 72,563.

— city, W Oregon 97477; pop. 41,621.

— urb. twp., SE Pennsylvania 19064 (Delaware County); pop. 26,733.

Springfield urb. twp., SE Pennsylvania (Montgomery County); pop. 20,652.

Spring Valley city, SE California 92077; pop. 29,742.

— vill., SE New York 10977; pop. 18,112.

Sri Lanka isl. s of India, an independent state of the Commonwealth of Nations, formerly called Ceylon; 25,332 sq. mi.; pop. 15,000,000; cap. Colombo.

Stalingrad Volgograd: *the former name.*

Stamford city, SW Connecticut 06901*; pop. 102,453.

St. Ann city, E Missouri 63074; pop. 18,215.

Stanton city, SW California 90680; pop. 17,947.

State College boro., CEN. Pennsylvania 16801*; pop. 36,130.

Staten Island isl., SE New York, at the entrance to New York Harbor; coextensive with Richmond boro. 10314*; 352,121.

Statesville city, CEN. North Carolina 28677; pop. 19,996.

Staunton city, CEN. Virginia 24401*; pop. 24,504.

St.-Bruno-de-Montarville town, CEN. Quebec, Canada; pop. 15,780.

St. Catharines city, s Ontario, Canada; pop. 109,722.

St. Charles city, E Missouri 63301*; pop. 37,379.

St. Clair, Lake lake betw. s Ontario and SE Michigan; 460 sq. mi.

St. Clair Shores vill., SE Michigan 48080*; pop. 76,210.

St. Cloud city, CEN. Minnesota 56301*; pop. 42,566.

St. Croix one of the Virgin Islands of the United States; 82 sq. mi.

Ste.-Foy city, s Quebec, Canada; pop. 68,385.

Sterling city, NW Illinois 61081; pop. 16,113.

Sterling Heights city, SE Michigan 48077; pop.

Ste.-Thérèse city, s Quebec, Canada; pop. 17,175.

Stettin Szczecin: *the German name.*

Steubenville city, E Ohio 43952; pop. 26,400.

Stevens Point city, CEN. Wisconsin 54481*; pop. 23,479.

St. Helena isl., South Atlantic; British colony with Ascension Island and the Tristan da Cunha group as dependencies; 133 sq. mi.; pop. 5,000; cap. Jamestown; site of Napoleon's exile, 1815-21.

St. Hubert town, s Quebec, Canada; pop. 21,741.

St. Hyacinthe city, s Quebec, Canada; pop. 24,562.

Stillwater city, CEN. Oklahoma 74074*; pop. 31,126.

St. James city, s Manitoba, Canada; pop. 71,431.

St. Jean city, s Quebec, Canada; pop. 32,863.

St. Jérôme city, s Quebec, Canada; pop. 26,524.

St. John one of the Virgin Islands of the United States; 19 sq. mi.

— city, s New Brunswick, Canada; pop. 51,567.

St. John's city, SE Newfoundland, Canada; cap.; pop. 88,102.

St. Joseph city, NW Missouri 64500*; pop. 76,691.

St. Lambert city, s Quebec, Canada; pop. 18,616.

St. Laurent city, s Quebec, Canada; pop. 62,955.

St. Lawrence, Gulf of inlet of the Atlantic E Canada.

St. Lawrence River river, SE Canada; the outlet of the Great Lakes system; 1,900 mi. long.

St. Lawrence Seaway system of ship canals extending 114 miles along the St. Lawrence River from Montreal to Lake Ontario.

St. Leonard city, CEN. Quebec, Canada; pop. 52,040.

St. Louis city, E Missouri 63100*; pop. 453,085.

St. Louis Park vill., E Minnesota 55426; pop. 42,931.

St. Michel city, s Quebec, Canada; pop. 71,446.

Stockholm city, SE Sweden; cap.; pop. 1,477,000.

Stockton city, CEN. California 95200*; pop. 149,779.

Stoneham town, NE Massachusetts 02180; pop. 20,725.

Stoneleigh-Rodgers Forge uninc. place, N Maryland; pop. 15,645.

Stonington city, NE Connecticut 06378; pop. 15,940.

Stoughton town, E Massachusetts 02072; pop. 23,459.

Stow vill., CEN. Ohio 44224; pop. 25,303.

St. Paul city, SE Minnesota 55100*; cap.; pop. 270,230.

St. Petersburg city, W Florida 33700*; pop. 236,893.

— Leningrad: *the former name.*

Strasbourg city, NE France; pop. 253,000.

Stratford town, SE Connecticut 06497; pop. 49,775.

— city, s Ontario, Canada; pop. 24,508.

Stratford-on-Avon town, CEN. England; birthplace and burial place of Shakespeare; pop. 17,000.

Streamwood city, NE Illinois 60103; pop. 18,176.

Streator city, CEN. Illinois 61364; pop. 15,600.

Strongsville vill., N Ohio 44136; pop. 28,577.

Struthers city, E Ohio 44471; pop. 15,343.

St. Thomas one of the Virgin Islands of the United States; 28 sq. mi.; pop. 16,201.

— city, s Ontario, Canada; pop. 25,545.

Stuttgart city, SW West Germany; pop. 628,000.

Sucre city, CEN. Bolivia; cap.; pop. 85,000.
Sudan reg., N Africa S of the Sahara.
Sudan, Republic of the republic, NE Africa; 967,500 sq. mi.; pop. 19,600,000; cap. Khartoum.
Sudbury city, CEN. Ontario, Canada; pop. 90,535.
Sudetenland border dists., W Czechoslovakia.
Suez city, NE Egypt; pop. 381,000.
Suez, Gulf of inlet of the Red Sea, NE Egypt.
Suez, Isthmus of strip of land joining Asia and Africa, betw. the Gulf of Suez and the Mediterranean.
Suez Canal ship canal across the Isthmus of Suez; 107 mi.
Suitland-Silver Hills uninc. place, CEN. Maryland 20023; pop. 30,355.
Sulawesi isl. of Indonesia, E of Borneo; 87,897 sq. mi.; pop. 9,315,000.
Sulu Archipelago isl. group, SW Philippines; 1,086 sq. mi.
Sumatra isl. of Indonesia S of the Malay Peninsula; 208,-948 sq. mi.; pop. 22,934,000.
Summit city, NE New Jersey 07901; pop. 23,620.
Sumter city, CEN. South Carolina 29150*; pop. 24,435.
Sunnyvale city, W California 94086*; pop. 106,618.
Superior city, NW Wisconsin 54880*; pop. 29,571.
Superior, Lake largest of the Great Lakes; 31,820 sq. mi.
Surabaya city, NE Java, Indonesia; pop. 1,660,000.
Surinam republic, former Dutch colony NE coast of S. America; 63,251 sq. mi.; pop. 384,900; cap. Paramaribo.
Susquehanna river, New York, Pennsylvania, and Maryland; 444 mi. long.
Suwannee River river, Georgia and Florida; 250 mi. long.
Svalbard isl. group of Norway, Arctic Ocean; 23,958 sq. mi.: sometimes called *Spitsbergen.*
Swaziland independent member of the Commonwealth of Nations, SE Africa; 6,704 sq. mi.; pop. 560,000; cap. Mbabane.
Sweden kingdom, NW Europe; 173,577 sq. mi.; pop. 8,330,000; cap. Stockholm.
Sweetwater Creek city, NW Florida 33601; pop. 19,-433.
Swift Current city, SW Saskatchewan, Canada; pop. 15,-415.
Switzerland republic, CEN. Europe; 15,940 sq. mi.; pop. 6,584,000; cap. Bern.
Sydney city, NE Nova Scotia, Canada; pop. 33,230.
— city, E New South Wales, Australia; cap.; pop. 3,200,000.
Syracuse city, CEN. New York 13200*; pop. 170,105.
Syria republic, SW Asia; 71,498 sq. mi.; pop. 9,325,000; cap. Damascus.
Szczecin city, NW Poland; pop. 340,000: German name *Stettin.*

Tabriz city, NW Iran; pop. 468,000.
Tacoma city, W Washington 98400*; pop. 154,581.
Tadzhik SSR constituent republic, S USSR; 55,043 sq. mi.; pop. 3 million; cap. Dushanbe.
Tahiti isl., Society group; 402 sq. mi.; pop. 85,000.
Tahoe, Lake lake E California and W Nevada; ab. 195 sq. mi.
Taipei city, N Taiwan; cap.; pop. 2,225,000.
Taiwan isl. off SE China; comprises with the Pescadores, the Republic of China; 13,890 sq. mi.; pop. 17,350,000; cap. Taipei; formerly called *Formosa.*
Takoma Park city W Maryland 20012; pop. 18,455.
Talledaga city, CEN. Alabama 35160; pop. 17,662.
Tallahassee city, N Florida 32301*; cap.; pop. 81,548.
Tallinn city, N Estonian SSR; cap.; pop. 371,000.
Tallmadge city, NE Ohio 44278; pop. 15,274.
Tampa city, W Florida 33600*; pop. 271,523.
Tampico city, E Mexico; pop. 231,000.
Tanganyika, Lake lake, CEN. Africa; 12,700 sq. mi.
Tangier city, N Morocco; pop. 166,000.
Tanzania republic of the Commonwealth of Nations, E Africa, includes *Tanganyika* and *Zanzibar;* 362,820 sq. mi.; pop. 19,000,000; cap. Dar es Salaam.
Taranto city, SE Italy; pop. 223,000.
Tashkent city, E Uzbek SSR; cap.; pop. 1,779,000.
Tasmania isl., SE Australia; comprises a state; 26,383 sq. mi.; pop. 407,000; cap. Hobart.
Taunton city, SE Massachusetts 02780*; pop. 45,001.
Taylor city, SE Michigan 48180; pop. 77,568.
Tbilisi city, SE Georgian SSR; cap.; pop. 1,066,000.
Teaneck urb. twp., NE New Jersey 07666; pop. 42,355.
Tegucigalpa city, CEN. Honduras; cap.; pop. 268,000.
Teheran city, CEN. Iran; cap.; pop. 4,716,000.

Tel Aviv city, W Israel; includes Jaffa; pop. 383,000.
Tempe city, CEN. Arizona 85281*; pop. 106,743.
Temple city, CEN. Texas 76501; pop. 42,483.
Tennessee state, CEN. United States; 42,246 sq. mi.; pop. 4,590,750; cap. Nashville.
Tennessee River river, flowing through E Tennessee, N Alabama, W Tennessee, and SW Kentucky; 652 mi. long.
Terre Haute city, W Indiana 47801*; pop. 61,135.
Tewksbury city, NE Massachusetts 01876; pop. 22755.
Texarkana city, SW Arkansas at the Arkansas-Texas line; pop. 21,682.
— city, NE Texas; adjacent to and integrated with Texarkana, Arkansas 75501*; pop. 31,271.
Texas N state S United States; 267,339 sq. mi.; pop. 14,-228,383; cap. Austin.
Texas City city, SE Texas 77590*; pop. 41,403.
Thailand constitutional monarchy, SE Asia; 198,404 sq. mi.; pop. 48,175,000; cap. Bangkok: formerly called *Siam.*
Thames river, S England; 209 mi. long.
Thessaly div., CEN. Greece; 5,399 sq. mi.
Thetford Mines city S Quebec, Canada; pop. 22,003.
Thomasville city, S Georgia 31792; pop. 18,155.
— city, CEN. North Carolina 27360; pop. 15,230.
Thorold town, S Ontario, Canada; pop. 15,065.
Thousand Islands group of ab. 1,500 isls. in the St. Lawrence River.
Thousand Oaks city, SE California 91360; pop. 77,797.
Thrace reg., E Balkan Peninsula.
Thunder Bay city, W Ontario, Canada; pop. 113,000.
Tiber river, CEN. Italy; 245 mi. long.
Tibet adm. div., W China; ab. 470,000 sq. mi.; pop. ab. 2 million; cap. Lhasa; formerly independent.
Tientsin city, NE China; pop. 4 million.
Tierra del Fuego isl. group, S South America, included in Chile and Argentina; 7,996 sq. mi. (Argentina), 19,480 sq. mi. (Chile).
Tiffin city, CEN. Ohio 44883; pop. 21,596.
Tigris river, SW Asia, ab. 1,150 mi. long.
Tijuana city, NW Lower California, Mexico; pop. 335,000.
Timbuktu town, CEN. Mali; pop. 9,000.
Timmins town, CEN. Ontario, Canada; pop. 28,542.
Timonium-Lutherville uninc. place, CEN. Maryland 21093; pop. 24,055.
Timor isl., SE Malay Archipelago; 11,965 sq. mi.; pop. 1,356,000; W Timor has been part of Indonesia since 1949; E Timor, formerly a Portuguese overseas province, was annexed by Indonesia in 1976.
Tirana city, CEN. Albania; cap.; pop. 175,000.
Tirol See Tyrol.
Titicaca, Lake lake betw. SE Peru and W Bolivia; 3,200 sq. mi.; elevation 12,500 ft.
Titusville city, E Florida 32789; pop. 31,910.
Tobago See TRINIDAD AND TOBAGO.
Togo republic, W Africa; ab. 21,853 sq. mi.; pop. 2,600,-000; cap. Lome.
Tokyo city, E Japan; cap.; pop. 8,841,000.
Toledo city, CEN. Spain; pop. 44,000.
— city, NW Ohio 43600*; pop. 354,635.
Tomsk city, S RSFSR; pop. 386,000.
Tonawanda city, W New York 14150*; pop. 21,898.
— uninc. place, W New York; pop. 83,771.
Tonga isl. group, SE of Fiji; a Polynesian kingdom in the Commonwealth of Nations; ab. 270 sq. mi.; pop. 100,-000; cap. Nukualofa.
Topeka city, NE Kansas 66600*; cap.; pop. 132,952.
Toronto city, S Ontario, Canada; pop. 633,318.
Torrance city, SW California 90500*; pop. 131,497.
Torrington city, SW Connecticut 06790*; pop. 30,987.
Toulon city, S France; pop. 175,000.
Toulouse city, S France; pop. 371,000.
Towson uninc. place, CEN. Maryland 21204; pop. 77,809.
Trafalgar, Cape headland, SW Spain; scene of a naval victory of Nelson over the French and Spanish, 1805.
Transcaucasia reg., SE USSR; betw. the Caucasus mountains and Iran and Turkey.
Transcona town, SE Manitoba, Canada; pop. 22,490.
Transvaal province, NE South Africa; 109,621 sq. mi.; pop. 8,765,000; cap. Pretoria.
Traverse City city, NW Michigan 49684; pop. 18,048.
Trenton city, SE Michigan 48183; pop. 24,127.
— city, W New Jersey 08600*; cap.; pop. 92,124.
Trieste city, NE Italy; pop. 277,000.
Trinidad and Tobago independent member of the Commonwealth of Nations off N Venezuela; comprises isls. of **Trinidad;** 1,864 sq. mi., and **Tobago;** 116 sq. mi.; pop. 1,145,000; cap. Port-of-Spain.

Tripoli city, NW Lebanon; pop. 150,000.
— city, NW Libya; cap.; pop. 376,000.
Trois-Rivieres city, S Quebec, Canada; pop. 55,869.
Troy city, SE Michigan 48084; pop. 67,102.
— city, E New York 12180*; pop. 56,638.
— city, W Ohio 45373; pop. 17,186.
Trumbull city, SE Connecticut 06611; pop. 31,394.
Tsingtao city, E China; pop. 1,900,000.
Tucson city, SE Arizona 85700*; pop. 330,537.
Tulare city, CEN. California 93274; pop. 16,235.
Tullahoma city, CEN. Tennessee 37388; pop. 15,311.
Tulsa city, NE Oklahoma 74100*; pop. 360,919.
Tunis city, NE Tunisia; cap.; pop. 1,000,000.
Tunisia republic, N Africa; 63,170 sq. mi.; pop. 6,500,000; cap. Tunis.
Tupelo city, NE Mississippi 38801*; pop. 20,471.
Turin city, NW Italy; pop. 1,191,000.
Turkestan reg., CEN. Asia; extends from the Caspian Sea to the Gobi Desert.
Turkey republic, SW Asia; 301,382 sq. mi.; pop. 45,500,000; cap. Ankara. See ANATOLIA.
Turkmen SSR constituent republic, S USSR; 189,370 sq. mi.; pop. 2,223,000; cap. Ashkhabad.
Tuscaloosa city, CEN. Alabama 35401*; pop. 75,143.
Tustin city, SW California 92680; pop. 32,073.
Tustin-Foothills city, SW California; pop. 26,598.
Tutuila chief isl., American Samoa; 53 sq. mi.; pop. 26,000.
Twin Falls city, S Idaho 83301*; pop. 26,209.
Tyler city, E Texas 75701*; pop. 70,508.
Tyrol reg., W Austria and N Italy.

Ubangi river, CEN. Africa; 1,400 mi. long.
Uganda independent member of the Commonwealth of Nations, CEN. Africa; 91,134 sq. mi.; pop. 14,000,000; cap. Kampala.
Ukrainian SSR constituent republic SW USSR; 233,090 sq. mi.; pop. 47,496,000; cap. Kiev. Also **Ukraine**.
Ulan Bator city, CEN. Mongolian People's Republic; cap.; pop. 282,000.
Ulster former prov., N Ireland, of which the N part became Northern Ireland, 1925.
— prov., N Republic of Ireland; comprises the part of Ulster that remained after 1925; 3,093 sq. mi.; pop. 207,000.
Union urb. twp., NE New Jersey 07083*; pop. 53,077.
Union City city, NE New Jersey 07087; pop. 55,593.
Uniondale uninc. place, SE New York 11553; pop. 22,077.
Union of Soviet Socialist Republics federal union of 15 constituent republics occupying most of N Eurasia; 8,649,500 sq. mi.; pop. 266,403,000; cap. Moscow.
Uniontown city, SW Pennsylvania 15401; pop. 16,282.
United Arab Emirates reg., E Arabian Peninsula, composed of 7 sheikdoms (formerly **Trucial States**); 32,300 sq. mi.; pop. 252,000.
United Arab Republic Egypt: *the former name.*
United Kingdom constitutional monarchy comprising Great Britain, Northern Ireland, the Isle of Man, and the Channel Islands; 94,284 sq. mi.; pop. 56,387,000; cap. London: officially **United Kingdom of Great Britain and Northern Ireland.**
United States of America federal republic,, including 50 states (49 in North America, and Hawaii, an archipelago in the Pacific Ocean), and the District of Columbia (3,615,222 sq. mi.; pop. 179,323,175), and the Canal Zone, Puerto Rico, the Virgin Islands of the United States, American Samoa, and Guam, Wake, and other Pacific isls.; total 3,720,407 sq. mi.; pop. 230,000,000; cap. Washington, coextensive with the District of Columbia.
University City city, E Missouri 63130; pop. 42,738.
University Heights city, N Ohio; pop. 17,055.
University Park city, N Texas 78227; pop. 23,498.
Upland city, SW California 91786; pop. 47,647.
Upper Arlington city, CEN. Ohio 43221; pop. 35,648.
Upper Darby urb. twp., SE Pennsylvania 19082*; pop. 95,510.
Upper Moreland urb. twp., SE Pennsylvania; pop. 21,032.
Upper Volta republic, W Africa; 105,900 sq. mi.; pop. 7,100,000; cap. Ouagadougou.
Ural Mountains mtn. system in the RSFSR, extending from the Arctic Ocian to the Kasakh SSR.
Ural River river S RSFSR and W Kazakh SSR; 1,574 mi. long.
Urbana city, E Illinois 61801*; pop. 35,978.
Uruguay republic, SE South America; 68,536 sq. mi.; pop. 2,820,000; cap. Montevideo.
Uruguay River river, SE South America; 1,000 mi. long.
Utah state, CEN. United States; 84,916 sq. mi.; pop.

1,461,037; cap. Salt Lake City.
Utica city, CEN. New York 13501*; pop. 75,632.
Utrecht city, CEN. Netherlands; pop. 278,000.
Uzbek SSR constituent republic S USSR; 173,592 sq. mi.; pop. 12,300,000; cap. Tashkent.

Vacaville city, CEN. California 95688; pop. 43,367.
Val-d'Or town, W Quebec, Canada; pop. 17,421.
Valdosta city, S Georgia 31601*; pop. 37,596.
Valencia city, E Spain; pop. 770,000.
Valinda city, SE California 91744; pop. 18,837.
Vallejo city, W California 94590*; pop. 80,188.
Valleyfield city, S Quebec, Canada; pop. 30,173. Also **Salaberry de Valleyfield.**
Valley Forge locality, SE Pennsylvania, scene of Washington's winter encampment 1777–78.
Valley Station uninc. place, N Kentucky 40172; pop. 24,471.
Valley Stream vill., SE New York 11580*; pop. 35,769.
Valparaiso city, CEN. Chile; pop. 296,000.
— city, NW Indiana 46383; pop. 20,020.
Vancouver city, SW Washington 98660*; pop. 42,834.
— city, SW British Columbia, Canada; pop. 410,188.
Vancouver Island isl., off SW British Columbia, Canada; 12,408 sq. mi.
Vanuatu republic, isl. group, SW Pacific, formerly **New Hebrides;** ab. 5,700 sq. mi.; pop. 110,000; cap. Villa.
Vatican City sovereign papal state within Rome; includes the Vatican and St. Peter's Church; established June 10, 1929; 108.7 acres; pop. 1,000.
Venezuela republic, N South America; 352,143 sq. mi.; pop. 14,300,000; cap. Caracas.
Venice city, NE Italy; pop. 368,000.
Venice, Gulf of N part of the Adriatic.
Ventura city, S California 93001; pop. 55,797.
Veracruz state, SE Mexico; 28,114 sq. mi.; pop. 3,815,000; cap. Jalapa; largest city Veracruz.
Verde, Cape westernmost point of Africa; a penin.; ab. 20 mi. long.
Verdun town, NE France; scene of several battles of World War I; pop. 19,000.
— city, S Quebec, Canada; pop. 68,013.
Vermont state, NE United States; 9,609 sq. mi.; pop. 511,456; cap. Montpelier.
Vernon city, NE Connecticut 06086; pop. 27,237.
Vernon Valley uninc. place, SE New York; pop. 17,925.
Verona city, NE Italy; pop. 231,000.
— boro., NE New Jersey 07044; pop. 15,067.
Versailles city, N France; site of the palace of Louis XIV; scene of the signing of a treaty (1919) betw. the Allies and Germany after World War I; pop. 91,000.
Vesuvius active volcano, W Italy; 3,891 ft.
Vichy city, CEN. France; provisional cap. during German occupation, World War II; pop. 32,000.
Vicksburg city, W Mississippi 39180*; pop. 25,434; besieged and taken by the Union Army in the Civil War, 1863.
Victoria state, SE Australia; 87,884 sq. mi.; pop. 3,647,000; cap. Melbourne.
— city, SW British Columbia; cap.; pop. 62,551.
— city, S Hong Kong; cap.; pop. 521,000.
— city, S Texas 77901*; pop. 30,695
Victoria, Lake lake betw. Uganda, Tanganyika, and Kenya; 26,828 sq. mi. Also **Victoria Nyanza.**
Victoria Falls cataract on the Zambesi River betw. Northern and Southern Rhodesia; 343 ft. high; over a mile wide.
Victoriaville town, S Quebec, Canada; pop. 22,047.
Vienna city, NE Austria; cap.; pop. 1,628,000.
— town, NE Virginia 22180; pop. 17,152.
Vientiane city, CEN. Laos; adm cap.; pop. 130,000.
Vietnam country, SW Indochina; 126,436 sq. mi.; pop. 53,550,000; cap. Hanoi; from 1954 to 1976 divided into **North Vietnam** and **South Vietnam,** with caps. at Hanoi and Saigon, respectively.
Villa Park vill., NE Illinois 60181; pop. 25,891.
Vilnius city, SE Lithuanian SSR; cap.; pop. 386,000. Also **Vilna, Vilnyus.**
Vincennes city, SW Indiana 47591; pop. 19,867.
Vineland boro., S New Jersey 08360; pop. 53,753.
Virginia state, E United States; 40,815 sq. mi.; pop. 5,346,279; cap. Richmond.
Virginia Beach city, SE Virginia 23450*; pop. 262,199.
Virgin Islands isl. group, West Indies E of Puerto Rico. See BRITISH VIRGIN ISLANDS.
Virgin Islands of the United States uninc. terr., Virgin Islands; 133 sq. mi.; pop. 104,000; cap. Charlotte Amalie.

Visalia city, CEN. California 93277*; pop. 49,729.
Visayan Islands isl. group, CEN. Philippines; 23,621 sq. mi.
Vista uninc. place, SW California 92083; pop. 35,834.
Vistula river, CEN. and N Poland; 678 mi. long.
Vladivostok city, SE RSFSR; pop. 456,000.
Volga river, W RSFSR; 2,290 mi. long.
Volgograd city, W RSFSR; scene of a Russian victory over German forces in World War II, Sept. 1942 to Jan. 1943; pop. 929,000: from 1925–61 **Stalingrad.**
Volta river, E Ghana; 800 mi. long.
Vosges Mountains mtn. chain, E France.

Wabash river, W Ohio and Indiana; 475 mi. long.
Waco city, CEN. Texas 76700*; pop. 101,261.
Wade-Hampton city, NW South Carolina 29607; pop. 17,152.
Wahiawa city, CEN. Oahu, Hawaii 96786; pop. 17,598.
Waikiki beach on Honolulu harbor, SE Oahu, Hawaii.
Waipio city, Oahu, Hawaii 96786; pop. 22,798.
Wakefield town, E Massachusetts 01880*; pop. 25,402.
Wake Island coral atoll in the North Pacific; 4 sq. mi.; site of a U.S. naval and air base.
Wales penin., SW Britain; a principality of England; 8,018 sq. mi.; pop 2,810,000.
Walla Walla city, SE Washington 99362; pop. 25,618.
Wallingford town, CEN. Connecticut 06492; pop. 35,714.
Walnut Creek city, W California 94596*; pop. 53,643.
Walpole town, E Massachusetts 02081; pop. 18,149.
Waltham city, E Massachusetts 02154; pop. 58,200.
Wantagh vill., SE New York 11793; pop. 21,873.
Warminster urb. twp., SE Pennsylvania 18974; pop. 15,994.
Warner Robins city, CEN. Georgia 31093*; pop. 39,893.
Warren city, SE Michigan 48089*; pop. 161,134.
— city, NE Ohio 44480*; pop. 56,629.
Warrensville Heights vill., N Ohio; pop. 18,925.
Warrington uninc. place, NW Florida 32507; pop. 15,848.
Warsaw city, CEN. Poland; cap.; pop. 1,576,602.
Warwick city, CEN. Rhode Island 02886*; pop. 87,123.
Washington state, NW United States; 68,192 sq. mi.; pop. 4,130,163; cap. Olympia.
— city, E United States; coextensive with the District of Columbia 20000*; pop. 637,651.
— city, SW Pennsylvania 15301; pop. 19,827.
Waterbury city. W Connecticut 06700*; pop. 103,266.
Waterford city, NE Connecticut 06385; pop. 17,227.
Waterloo vill., CEN. Belgium; scene of Napoleon's final defeat, June 18, 1815; pop. 10,000.
— city, CEN. Iowa 50700*; pop. 75,985.
— city, S Ontario, Canada; pop. 36,677.
Watertown city, SW Connecticut 06795; pop. 18,610.
— town, E Massachusetts 02172; pop. 39,307.
— city, N New York 13601*; pp. 27,861.
— city, SE Wisconsin 53094; pop. 15,683.
Waterville city, CEN. Maine 04900*; pop. 18,192.
Waukegan city, NE Illinois 60085*; pop. 67,653.
Waukesha city, SE Wisconsin 53186*; pop. 50,319.
Wausau city, CEN. Wisconsin 54401*; pop. 32,426.
Wauwatosa city, SE Wisconsin 53213; pop. 51,308.
Waycross city, SE Georgia 31501; pop. 18,996.
Wayland city, N Massachusetts 01778; pop. 13,461.
Wayne vill., SE Michigan 48184; pop. 21,054.
— urb. twp., N New Jersey 07470*; pop. 49,141.
Waynesboro city, CEN. Virginia 22980*; pop. 16,707.
Webster Groves city, E Missouri 63119; pop. 26,995.
Weimar city, SW East Germany; pop. 64,000.
Weirton city, NW West Virginia 26062*; pop. 27,131.
Welland city, S Ontario, Canada; pop. 44,397.
Welland Canal waterway betw. Lakes Erie and Ontario.
Wellesley town. E Massachusetts 02181; pop. 28,051.
Wellington city, CEN. New Zealand; cap.; pop. 327,000.
Wenatchee city, CEN. Washington 98801*; pop. 16,912.
Weslaco city, S Texas 78596; pop. 15,313.
West Allis city, SE Wisconsin 53214; pop. 63,982.
West Bend city, SE Wisconsin 53095*; pop. 16,555.
West Berlin See BERLIN.
Westbury vill., SE New York 11590; pop. 15,362.
West Carson city, SE California; pop. 15,501.
Westchester vill., NE Illinois 60153; pop. 2,033.
West Chester boro., SE Pennsylvania 19380; pop. 19,301.
West Covina city, SW California 91790*; pop. 80,094.
West Des Moines city, CEN. Iowa 50265; pop. 16,441.
Westerly uninc. place, SW Rhode Island 02891; pop. 17,248.

Western Australia state, W Australia; 975,920 sq. mi.; pop. 737,000; cap. Perth.
Western Sahara area on the w coast of Africa, claimed by Mauritania and Morocco; 102,703 sq. mi.; pop. 152,000.
Western Samoa See SAMOA.
Westfield city, SW Massachusetts 01085; pop. 36,465.
— town, E New Jersey 07090*; pop. 33,720.
West Germany See GERMANY.
West Hartford town, CEN. Connecticut 06107; pop. 68,031.
West Haven town, S Connecticut 06516; pop. 53,184.
West Hempstead-Lakeview uninc. place, SE New York 11552; pop. 23,375.
West Hollywood uninc. place, SW California; pop. 29,448.
West Indies series of isl. groups separating the North Atlantic from the Caribbean, including Cuba, Jamaica, Hispaniola, Puerto Rico, the Bahamas, Trinidad and Tobago, and the Leeward and Windward Islands.
West Indies, the group of British cols. in the Caribbean, including the Leeward Islands (Antigua, St. Christopher-Nevis-Anguilla, Montserrat, and the British Virgin Islands) and the Windward Islands (St. Vincent, St. Lucia and Dominica).
West Islip city, SE New York 11795; pop. 16,711.
West Lafayette city, CEN. Indiana 47906; pop. 19,157.
Westlake city, N Ohio 44091; pop. 15,689.
Westland city, SE Michigan 48185; pop. 84,603.
West Memphis city, E Arkansas 72301; pop. 28,138.
West Mifflin boro., SW Pennsylvania 15120; pop. 26,279.
Westminster city and metropolitan boro., London, England; site of the Houses of Parliament and Buckingham Palace; pop. 85,000.
— city, SW California 92863; pop. 71,133.
— city, CEN. Colorado 80030; pop. 50,211.
Westmont city, SE California; pop. 29,310.
Westmount city, S Quebec, Canada; pop. 23,606.
West New Guinea prov. of Indonesia comprising the w part of New Guinea and adjacent islands; 159,375 sq. mi. pop 716,000; cap. Kotabaru, Also **West Irian.**
West New York town, NE New Jersey 07093*; pop. 39,194.
West Orange town, NE New Jersey 07052; pop. 39,510.
West Palm Beach city, SE Florida 33401*; pop. 62,530.
West Pensacola city, SW Florida 32505; pop. 20,924.
West Point U.S. military reservation, SE New York 10996; seat of the U.S. Military Academy.
Westport city, SW Connecticut 06880; pop. 27,414.
West Puente Valley city, SE California; pop. 20,733.
West Saint Paul city, E Minnesota 55118; pop. 18,799.
West Seneca uninc. place, W New York 14224; pop. 48,404.
West Springfield town, S Massachusetts 01089; pop. 28,491.
West Virginia state, E United States; 24,181 sq. mi.; pop. 1,949,644; cap. Charleston.
West Warwick town, CEN. Rhode Island 02893; pop. 24,323.
West Whittier-Los Nietos city, SE California 90606; pop. 20,845.
Wethersfield town, CEN. Connecticut 06109; pop. 26,662.
Weymouth town, E Massachusetts 02188; pop. 54,610.
Wheaton city, NE Illinois 60187*; pop. 43,043.
— uninc. place, CEN. Maryland 20902; pop. 66,247.
Wheat Ridge uninc. place, CEN. Colorado 80033; pop. 30,293.
Wheeling city, NW West Virginia 26000*; pop. 43,070.
Whitby Whitby town, S Ontario, Canada; pop. 25,324.
White Bear Lake city, E Minnesota 55110; pop. 23,313.
Whitefish Bay vill., SE Wisconsin 53217; pop. 17,394.
Whitehall city, CEN. Ohio 43213; pop. 25,263.
— boro., SW Pennsylvania 18052; pop. 16,551.
Whitehaven uninc. place, SW Tennessee 38116; pop. 19,000.
White Mountains range of the Appalachians, CEN. New Hampshire.
White Oak city, NE Maryland 29091; pop. 19,769.
White Plains city, SE New York 10600*; pop. 46,999.
White-Yardville city, CEN. New Jersey 08620; pop. 18,680.
Whitney, Mount peak, E California; 14,496 ft.
Whittier city, SW California 90601*; pop. 68,872.
Wichita city, CEN. Kansas 67200*; pop. 279,272.
Wichita Falls city, N Texas 76301*; pop. 94,201.
Wickliffe city, NE Ohio 44092; pop. 21,354.

Wight, Isle of isl. off the s coast of England; 147 sq. mi.

Wilkes-Barre city, NE Pennsylvania 18700*; pop. 51,-551.

Wilkinsburg boro., sw Pennsylvania; 15221; pop. 26,780.

Williamsburg city, E Virginia 23185; capital of Virginia (1699-1779); restored to colonial condition; pop. 9,069.

Williamsport city, CEN. Pennsylvania 17701*; pop. 33,-401.

Willoughby city, NE Ohio 44094*; pop. 18,634.

Willowbrook city, SE California; pop. 28,706.

Willow Grove city, SE Pennsylvania 19090; pop. 16,494.

Willowick city, NE Ohio 44094; pop. 21,237.

Wilmette vill., NE Illinois 60091; pop. 28,229.

Wilmington city, N Delaware; 19800*; pop. 70,195.

— city, NE Massachusetts 01887; pop. 17,102.

— city, SE North Carolina 28401*; pop. 44,000.

Wilson town, CEN. North Carolina 14172; pop. 34,424.

Wilson, Mount peak, sw California; 5,710 ft; site of a famous observatory.

Wilson Dam power dam in the Tenessee River at Muscle Shoals, NW Alabama; 137 ft. high, 4,862 ft. long.

Wimbledon town and municipal boro., s England; scene of international tennis matches; pop. 20,000.

Winchester town, E Massachusetts 01890; pop. 22,269.

Windham city, NE Connecticut 06280; pop. 19,626.

Windsor municipal boro., s England; site of **Windsor Castle,** a residence of the English sovereigns; pop. 15,000: officially **New Windsor.**

— city, SE Ontario, Canada; pop. 203,300.

Windsor Locks city, CEN. Connecticut 06096; pop. 15,-080.

Windward Islands isl. group, s Lesser Antilles.

Winnipeg city, SE Manitoba, Canada; cap.; pop. 560,000.

Winnipeg, Lake lake, s Manitoba, Canada; 9,398 sq. mi.

Winona city, SE Minnesota 55987*; pop. 27,075.

Winston-Salem city, CEN. North Carolina 27100*; pop. 131,885.

Winter Haven city, CEN. Florida 33880*; pop. 16,136.

Winter Park city, CEN. Florida 32789*; pop. 21,895.

Winthrop town, E Massachusetts 02152; pop. 20,335.

Wisconsin state, N United States; 56,154 sq. mi.; pop. 4,705,335.

Wisconsin Rapids city, CEN. Wisconsin 54494; pop. 18,587.

Woburn city, E Massachusetts 01801*; pop. 36,626.

Woodbridge urb. twp., NE New Jersey 07095; pop. 98,-944.

Woodbridge-Marumso city, NE Virginia 22191; pop. 25,412.

Woodland city, CEN. California 95695*; pop. 30,235.

Woodlawn-Woodmoor uninc. place, N Maryland 20901; pop. 28,811.

Woodmere uninc. place, SE New York 11598; pop. 19,-831.

Woodstock city, s Ontario, Canada; pop. 26,173.

Woonsocket city, NE Rhode Island 02895; pop. 45,914.

Wooster city, CEN. Ohio 44691*; pop. 18,703.

Worcester city, CEN. Massachusetts 01600*; pop. 161,-799.

Worms city, sw West Germany; pop. 78,000.

Worthington city, CEN. Ohio 43085; pop. 15,326.

Wrocław city, sw Poland; pop. 528,000: formerly called *Breslau.*

Wuhan collective name for the cities of Hankow, Hanyang, and Wuchang, CEN. China; pop. 4,250,000.

Wuppertal city, w West Germany; pop. 414,000.

Würzburg city, CEN. West Germany; pop. 120,000.

Wyandotte city, SE Michigan 48192*; pop. 34,006.

Wyckoff urb. twp., NE New Jersey 07481; pop. 16,039.

Wyoming state, NW United States; 97,914 sq. mi.; pop. 470,816; cap. Cheyenne.

— city, w Michigan 49509; pop. 59,616.

Xenia city, CEN. Ohio 45385; pop. 25,373.

Yakima city, s Washington 98901*; pop. 49,826.

Yalta city, s Crimea; scene of a conference of Roosevelt. Churchill, and Stalin in February, 1945; pop. 63,000.

Yalu river forming part of the boundary betw. NE China and Korea; 500 mi. long.

Yangtze river flowing from Tibet to the East China Sea; 3,600 mi. long.

Yellow River Hwang Ho: *an alternate name.*

Yellow Sea inlet of the Pacific betw. Korea and China; 400 mi. long, 400 mi. wide.

Yellowstone Falls 2 waterfalls of the Yellowstone River in Yellowstone National Park: **Upper Yellowstone Falls,** 109 ft.; **Lower Yellowstone Falls,** 308 ft.

Yellowstone National Park largest and oldest of the US national parks, largely in NW Wyoming; 3,458 sq. mi.; established 1872.

Yellowstone River river, NW Wyoming, SE Montana, and NW North Dakota; 671 mi. long.

Yemen, People's Democratic Republic of republic, s coast of Arabian penin.; 128,560 sq. mi.; pop. 1,950,000; cap. Aden. Also **Southern Yemen.**

Yemen Arab Republic country, sw Arabian penin.; ab. 75,000 sq. mi.; pop. 7,476,000; cap. San'a.

Yerevan city, w Armenian SSR; cap.; pop. 791,000.

Yokohama city, CEN. Honshu, Japan; pop. 2,694,500.

Yonkers city, SE New York 10700*; pop. 195,351.

York co. boro., CEN. Yorkshire, England; cap.; pop. 105,-000.

— city, s Pennsylvania 17400*; pop. 44,619.

Yosemite Valley gorge in **Yosemite National Park** (1,183 sq. mi., established 1890), CEN. California; 7 mi. long, 1 mi. wide; traversed by the Merced River that forms **Yosemite Falls:** Upper Fall, 1,430 ft.; Lower Fall, 320 ft.; with intermediate cascades, 2,425 ft.

Youngstown city, NE Ohio 44500*; pop. 115,436.

Ypres town, NW Belgium; site of three major battles of World War I, 1914, 1915, 1917; pop. 21,000.

Ypsilanti city, SE Michigan 48197; pop. 29,538.

Yucaipa city, sw California 92399; pop. 19,284.

Yucatán penin., SE Mexico and NE Central America; 70,-000 sq. mi.

Yugoslavia, Federal People's Republic of republic, SE Europe; 98,538 sq. mi.; pop. 22,550; cap. Belgrade.

Yukon terr., NW Canada; 207,076 sq. mi.; pop. 22,000; cap. Whitehorse.

Yukon River river, NW Canada and CEN. Alaska; 1,770 mi. long.

Yuma city, sw Arizona 85364; pop. 42,433.

Zagreb city, CEN. Croatia, Yugoslavia; cap.; pop. 566,000.

Zaire republic, CEN. Africa; 905,063 sq. mi.; pop. 29,450,-000; cap Kinshasa.

Zambezi river, s Africa; 1,700 mi. long.

Zambia independent member of the Commonwealth of Nations, CEN. Africa; 288,130 sq. mi.; pop. 6,000,000; cap. Lusaka.

Zanesville city, CEN. Ohio 43701*; pop. 28,655.

Zanzibar reg. of Tanzania off the coast of E Africa; comprises isls. of Zanzibar (640 sq. mi.) and **Pemba** (380 sq. mi.); pop. 354,000.

— city, w Zanzibar; cap.; pop. 58,000.

Zealand isl. of Denmark betw. the Kattegat and the Baltic Sea; 2,709 sq. mi.

Zimbabwe Rhodesia republic, s Africa; 150,804 sq. mi.; pop. 7,580,000; cap. Salisbury.

Zion city, NE Illinois 60099; pop. 17,268.

Zululand dist., NE Natal, South Africa; formerly a native kingdom; 10,362 sq. mi.; pop. 570,000.

Zurich city, NE Switzerland; pop. 423,000.

Zuyder Zee former shallow inlet of the North Sea, NW Netherlands; drainage projects have reclaimed much of the land and formed Lake Ijssel. Also **Zuider Zee.**

Biographies

Aalto, (Hugo) Alvar (Henrik), 1898–1976, Finnish architect.

Aaron, Henry, 1934–, U.S. baseball player.

Abbott, George, 1889–, U.S. theatrical director & playwright.
—William ("Budd"), 1896–1974, U.S. comedian & actor.

Abd-el-Krim, 1885?–1963, Moorish leader in Rif region of Morocco.

Abd-ul-Baha, 1844–1921, Pers. religious leader; called Abbas Effendi.

Abdul-Jabbar, Kareem, b. Lew Alcindor, 1947–, U.S. basketball player.

Abel, I(orwith) W(ilbur), 1908–, U.S. labor leader.
—Rudolph, 1902–72, Soviet spy.

Abélard, Peter, 1079–1142, Fr. theologian, philosopher, & teacher: also Abailard. See also HÉLOÏSE.

Abercombie, James 1706b–81, Brit. general.

Abernathy, Ralph D(avid), 1926–, U.S. clergyman & civil rights leader.

Abrams, Creighton W., Jr., 1914–74, U.S. general.

Abruzzi, Luigi Amedeo, Duca degli, 1873–1933, Ital. Arctic explorer.

Ace, Goodman, 1899–, U.S. comic writer & radio performer.
—Jane, 1900–74, U.S. radio performer, wife of prec.

Acheampong, Ignatius Kutu, 1932–, African military officer; president of Ghana 1972–78.

Acheson, Dean (Gooderham), 1893–1971, U.S. lawyer; secretary of state 1949–53.

Acton, John Emerich Edward Dalberg, Baron, 1834–1902, Eng. historian & author.

Adam, James, 1730–94, Scot. architect & furniture designer.
—Robert, 1728–92, Scot. architect; brother of prec.

Adams, Abigail (Smith), 1744–1818, U.S. writer.
—Ansel, 1902–, U.S. photographer.
—Brooks, 1848–1927, U.S. historian.
—Charles Francis, 1807–86, U.S. lawyer & diplomat; father of prec.
—Franklin Pierce ("F.P.A."), 1881–1960, U.S. journalist.
—Henry (Brooks), 1838–1918, U.S. historian.
—James Truslow, 1878–1949, U.S. historian.
—John, 1735–1826, 2nd U.S. president 1797–1801; husband of Abigail.
—John Quincy, 1767–1848, 6th U.S. president 1825–29; son of prec. & father of Charles Francis.
—Maude, 1872–1953, U.S. actress.
—Samuel, 1722–1803, Amer. revolutionary leader.
—Samuel Hopkins, 1871–1958, U.S. author.

Addams, Charles (Samuel), 1912–, U.S. cartoonist.
—Jane, 1860–1935, U.S. social worker.

Adderley, Julian Edwin ("Cannonball"), 1928–75, U.S. jazz musician.

Addinsell, Richard, 1904–, Eng. film composer.

Addison, Joseph, 1672–1719, Eng. essayist & poet.
—Thomas, 1793–1860, Eng. physician.

Adenauer, Konrad, 1876–1967, Ger. statesman; first chancellor of W. Germany 1949–63.

Adler, Alfred, 1870–1937, Austrian phyciatrist.
—Felix, 1851–1933, U.S. educator & reformer.
—Larry, 1914–, U.S. musician.
—Luther, 1903–, U.S. actor.
—Mortimer Jerome, 1902–, U.S. philosopher.

Adrian IV, b. Nicholas Breakspear, 1100?–59, pope 1154–59.

Adrian, Frederick 1903–59, U.S. fashion designer.

Aeschylus, 525–456 B.C., Gk. writer of tragedies.

Aesop, 6th c. B.C. Gk. writer of fables.

Aga Khan III, 1877–1957, Muslim spiritual leader.
—IV, 1936–grandson & Successor of prec.

Agassiz, Alexander, 1835–1910, U.S. zoologist.
—(Jean) Louis (Rodolphe), 1807–73, Swiss-born U.S. naturalist; father of prec.

Agee, James, 1909–55, U.S. author & critic.

Agnelli, Giovanni, 1921–, Ital. industrialist.

Agricola, Gnaeus Julius, A.D. 37–93, Roman general.

Agrippa, Marcus Vipsanius, 63–12, B.C., Roman statesman.

Agrippina, 13 B.C.-A.D. 33, mother of Caligula; called the Elder.
—A.D. 15?--59, mother of Nero; called the Younger.

Aguinaldo, Emilio, 1869–1964, Filipino statesman & revolutionary leader.

Aiken, Conrad Potter, 1889–1973, U.S. poet & author.

Ailey, Alvin, 1931–, U.S. choreographer.

Akbar, 1542–1605, Mogul emperor of Hindustan.

Akhmatova, Anna, 1888–1966, Soviet poet.

Akihito, 1933–, crown prince of Japan.

Akuffo, Frederick William Kwasi, 1937–79, African military officer; president of Ghana 1978–79.

Alarón, Pedro Antonio de, 1833–91, Sp. playwright.

Alaric, 370?–410, king of the Visigoths; sacked Rome.
—II, ?–507, king of the Visigoths.

Albanese, Licia, 1913–, Ital. soprano active in U.S.

Albee, Edward, 1928–, U.S. playwright.

Albéniz, Isaac, 1860–1909, Sp. composer & pianist.

Albers, Josef, 1888–1976, Ger.-born U.S. painter.

Albert, Prince, of Saxe-Coburg-Gotha, 1819–61, consort of Queen Victoria of England.

Albert, Carl (Bert), 1908–, U.S. politician.

Alberti, Leon Battista, 1404–72, Ital. architect & painter.

Albertus Magnus, Saint, 1200?–80, Ger. scholastic philosopher & theologian.

Albuquerque, Alfonso de, 1453–1515, Pg. viceroy in India.

Alcibiades, 450–404 B.C., Athenian general & politician.

Alcott, (Amos) Bronson, 1799–1888, U.S. educator.
—Louisa May, 1832–88, U.S. novelist, daughter of prec.

Alcuin, 735–804, Eng. theologian & scholar.

Alden, John, 1599–1687, pilgrim at Plymouth Colony.

Aldrich, Nelson W(ilmarth), 1841–1915, U.S. public official.

Aldrin, Edwin Eugene, Jr., 1930–, U.S. astronaut.

Aleichem, Sholem pseud. of Solomon Rabinowitz, 1859–1916, Russ.-born U.S. author.

Alemán Valdés, Miguel, 1902–, Mexican statesman; president of Mexico 1946–52.

Alexander II, 1818–81, Russ. czar; emancipated serfs; assassinated.

Alexander III, 356–323 B.C., king of Macedonia & conqueror of Egypt & Asia Minor; called the Great.

Alexander VI, b. Rodrigo Lanzol y Borja, 1431–1503, pope 1492–1503.

Alexander Nevski, 1220?–63, Russ. military hero & saint.

Alexander Severus, 208?–235, Roman Emperor 222–35.

Alexander, Grover Cleveland, 1887–1950, U.S. baseball player.
—Harold Rupert Leofric George (1st Earl Alexander of Tunis) 1891–1969, Brit. field marshal.

Alexanderson, Ernst F. W., 1878–1969, Swed.-born U.S. electrical engineer & inventor.

Alfieri, Count Vittorio, 1749–1803, Ital. playwright.

Alfonso XIII, 1886–1941, king of Spain 1902–31.

Alfred, 949–901, king of West Saxons: called the Great.

Alger, Horatio, 1834–99, U.S. author.

Ali, Muhammad, b. Cassius Clay, 1942–, U.S. boxer.

Alinsky, Saul David, 1909–72, U.S. social reformer.

Allen, Ethan, 1737–89, Amer. revolutionary soldier.
—Fred, 1894–1956, U.S. humorist & radio performer.
—Frederick Lewis, 1890–1954, U.S. editor & historian.
—Gracie, 1905–64, U.S. actress & comedienne.
—Stephen Valentine Patrick William (Steve), 1921–, U.S. comedian & author.
—Woody, 1935–, U.S. comedian, actor, author & film director.

Allenby, Edmund Henry, 1861–1936, Brit. field marshal.

Allende Gossens, Salvador, 1908–73, president of Chile 1970–73.

Allgood, Sara, 1883–1950, Irish-born U.S. actress.

Allport, Gordon Willard, 1897–1967, U.S. psychologist & author.

Alma-Tadema, Sir Lawrence, 1836–1912, Dutch-born Eng. painter.

Alonso, Alicia, 1921–, Cuban ballerina.

Alpini, Prospero, 1553–1617, Ital. physician & botanist.

Alsop, Joseph, 1910–, U.S. journalist & author.

—**Stewart,** 1914–74, U.S. journalist & author; brother of prec.

Altgeld, John Peter, 1847–1902, Ger.-born U.S. politician.

Altman, Benjamin, 1840–1913, U.S. merchant & art collector.

—**Robert,** 1925–, U.S. film director.

Alva, Fernando Alvarez de Toledo, Duke of, 1508–82, Sp. general in the Netherlands.

Alvarado, Pedro de, 1495?–1541, Sp. soldier in the New World.

Amara, Lucine, 1927–, U.S. soprano.

Amati, Nicola, 1596–1684, Ital. violinmaker.

Ambler, Eric, 1909–, Eng. author.

Ambrose, Saint, 340?–397, bishop of Milan.

Amenhotep III, 14th c. B.C. king of Egypt; reigned ca. 1411–1375 B.C.

Amherst, Baron Jeffrey, 1717–97, Brit. governor-general of North America.

Amin Dada, Idi, 1925?–, Ugandan general; president of Uganda 1971–79.

Amory, Cleveland, 1917–, U.S. author & critic.

Ampère, André Marie, 1775–1836, Fr. physicist.

Amundsen, Roald, 1872–1928, Norw. explorer.

Anacreon, 572?–488 B.C., Gk. poet.

Anaxagoras, 500–428 B.C., Gk. philosopher.

Anaximander, 610–546? B.C., Gk. philosopher and astronomer.

Andersen, Hans Christian, 1805–75, Dan. writer of fairy tales.

Anderson, Carl David, 1905–, U.S. physicist.

—**Jack,** 1922–, U.S. journalist.

—**Dame Judith,** 1898–, Austral.-born U.S. actress.

—**Marian,** 1902–, U.S. contralto.

—**Maxwell,** 1888–1959, U.S. playwright.

—**Sherwood,** 1876–1941, U.S. author.

Andersson, Bibi, 1935–, Swed. actress.

André, John, 1751–80, Brit. major & spy in American Revolutionary war.

Andretti, Mario Gabriel, 1940–, Ital.-born U.S. auto racer.

Andrews A family of U.S. singers incl. three sisters: **La Verne,** 1916–67; **Maxine,** 1918–, and **Patty,** 1920–.

—**Julie,** 1935–, Eng. actress & singer.

—**Roy Chapman,** 1884–1960, U.S. naturalist.

Andreyev, Leonid Nikolayevich, 1871–1919, Russ. author.

Andros, Sir Edmund, 1637–1714, Brit. governor in North America.

Angela Merici, Saint, 1474?–1540, Ital. nun & founder of Ursuline order.

Angelico, Fra, b. Giovanni da Fiesole, 1387–1455, Ital. painter.

Anglin, Margaret Mary, 1876–1958, Canadian actress active in U.S.

Ångstrom, Anders Jonas, 1814–74, Swed. physicist.

Anne, 1665–1714, queen of Great Britain 1702–14.

Anne of Cleves, 1515–57, Ger. princess; 4th wife of King Henry VIII of England.

Anouilh, Jean, 1910–, Fr. playwright.

Anselm, Saint, 1033–1109, archbishop of Canterbury.

Ansermet, Ernest, 1883–1969, Swiss conductor.

Antheil, George, 1900–59, U.S. composer.

Anthony, Saint, ca. 250–350, Egyptian monk.

—**of Padua, Saint,** 1195–1231, Ital. Franciscan monk.

Anthony, Susan B(rownell), 1820–1906, U.S. women's suffragist.

Antisthenes, 444?–371? B.C., Gk. philosopher; founder of Cynic school.

Antonescu, Ion, 1882–1946, Rumanian general & dictator; premier of Rumania 1940–44.

Antoninus Pius, A.D. 86–161, Roman emperor 131–61.

Antonio (Ruiz), 1922–, Sp. dancer.

Antonioni, Michelangelo, 1912–, Ital. film director.

Antony, Marc (L. Marcus Antonius), 83–30 B.C., Roman general & politician.

Apgar, Virginia, 1909–74, U.S. physician.

Apollinaire, Guillaume, pseud. of Wilhelm Apollinaris de Kostrowitzky, 1880–1918, Ital.-born Fr. author.

Appia, Adolphe, 1862–1928, Swiss theatrical producer & pioneer in stage lighting.

Apuleius, Lucius, 2nd c. A.D. Roman satirist.

Aquinas, Saint Thomas, 1225?–74, Ital. theologian & philosopher.

Arafat, Yasir, 1930–, Palestinian leader.

Arcaro, George Edward (Eddie), 1916–, U.S. jockey.

Archimedes, 287?–212 B.C., Gk. mathematician & inventor.

Archipenko, Alexander, 1887–1964, Russ-born U.S. sculptor.

Arden, Elizabeth, 1884–1966, Can.-born U.S. businesswoman.

Ardrey, Robert, 1908–1980, U.S. anthropologist & author.

Arendt, Hannah, 1906–75, Ger.-born U.S. political scientist & author.

Aretino, Pietro, 1492–1556, Ital. satirist.

Argentina, La, b. Antonia Mercé, 1888–1936, Argentine-born Spanish dancer.

Ariosto, Lodovico, 1474–1533, Ital. poet.

Aristarchus, 220?–150 B.C., Gk. grammarian.

—**of Samos,** 3rd c. B.C. Gk. astronomer.

Aristides, 530?–468 B.C., Athenian statesman & general: called **the Just.**

Aristippus, 435?–356? B.C., Gk. philosopher.

Aristophanes, 450?–380? B.C., Gk. playwright.

Aristotle, 384–322 B.C., Gk. philosopher.

Arkwright, Sir Richard, 1732–92, Eng. inventor & industrialist.

Arlen, Harold, 1905–, b. Hyman Arluck, U.S. composer.

Arletty, b. Léonie Bathiat, 1898–, Fr. actress.

Arliss, George, 1868–1946, Eng. actor active in U.S.

Armour, Philip Danforth, 1832–1901, U.S. industrialist.

Armstrong, Louis, 1900–71, U.S. jazz musician: called **Satchmo.**

—**Neil,** 1930–, U.S. astronaut; first on the moon.

Arno, Peter, 1904–68, U.S. cartoonist.

Arnold, Benedict, 1741–1801, Amer. revolutionary general & traitor.

—**Matthew,** 1822–88, Eng. poet & critic.

Aronson, Boris, 1900–80, Russ.-born stage designer & artist active in U.S.

Arp, Jean (or Hans), 1887–1966, Fr. sculptor & painter.

Arpad, ?–907, Hung. national hero.

Arrabal, Fernando, 1932–, Sp. playwright & author.

Arrau, Claudio, 1904–, Chilean pianist.

Arrhenius, Svante August, 1859–1927, Swed. physicist & chemist.

Arroyo, Martina, 1937–, U.S. soprano.

Artaud, Antonin, 1896–1948, Fr. playwright & director.

Arthur, 6th c. Brit. king.

Arthur, Chester Alan, 1830–86, 21st U.S. president 1881–85.

—**Jean,** 1905–, U.S. actress.

Asch, Sholem, 1880–1957, Pol.-born U.S. Yiddish author.

Ashcroft, Dame Peggy, 1907–, Eng. actress.

Ashe, Arthur (Robert), Jr., 1943–, U.S. tennis player.

Ashton, Sir Frederick, 1906–, Eng. choreographer.

Ashurbanipal, 7th c. B.C. Assyrian king.

Asimov, Isaac, 1920–, Soviet-born U.S. biochemist & author.

Asoka, ?–232, B.C., King of Magadha, India.

Aspasia, 470?–410 B.C., Gk. hetaera; consort of Pericles.

Assad, Hafiz al-, 1928–, president of Syria 1971–.

Astaire, Fred, 1899–, U.S. dancer, singer & actor.

Aston, Francis William, 1877–1945, Eng. chemist & physicist.

Astor, John Jacob, 1763–1848, U.S. financier.

Astor, Lady, b. Nancy Langhorne, 1879–1964, U.S. -born Brit. politician; first woman member of House of Commons.

—Mary, 1906–, U.S. actress & author.

Atahualpa, 1500?–33, last Inca king of Peru.

Athanasius, Saint, 296?–373, Alexandrian bishop & theologian.

Atkinson, (Justin) Brooks, 1894–, U.S. drama critic & author.

Atlas, Charles, 1894–1972, Ital.-born U.S. physical culturist.

Attila, 406?–453, king of the Huns.

Attlee, Clement Richard, Earl, 1883–1967, Eng. statesman; prime minister 1945–51.

Attucks, Crispus, 1723?–70, Negro patriot in the American Revolution.

Auden, W(ystan) H(ugh), 1907–73, Eng. -born U.S. poet.

Audubon, John James, 1785–1851, U.S. ornithologist & painter.

Auenbrugger, Leopold, 1722–1809, Austrian physician.

Augustine, Saint, 354–430, early Christian Church father, bishop of Hippo.

—Saint, ?–604, Roman monk sent to convert England to Christianity; first archbishop of Canterbury.

Augustus, b. Gaius Julius Caesar Octavianus, 63 B.C. – A.D. 14; first Roman Emperor 27 B.C. -A.D. 14: also called **Octavian.**

Aurelian (L. Lucius Domitius Aurelianus), 212?–275, Roman emperor 270–75.

Auriol, Vincent, 1884–1966, Fr. statesman; president of France 1947–54.

Austen, Jane, 1775–1817, Eng. novelist.

Austin, Stephen F(uller), 1793–1836, U.S. politician & colonizer of Texas.

Autry, (Orvon) Gene, 1907–, U.S. actor & singer.

Avedon, Richard, 1923–, U.S. photographer.

Averroes (Ar. ibn-Rushd), 1126–98, Sp.-Arab philosopher & physician.

Avicenna (Ar. ibn-Sina), 980–1037, Pers. philosopher & physician.

Avogadro, Amadeo, 1776–1856, Ital. chemist & physicist.

Axis Sally, b. Mildred Gillars, 1902–, U.S.-born German propagandist in World War II.

Ayer, Francis Wayland, 1848–1923, U.S. advertising executive.

Ayub Khan, Mohammad, 1907–74, Pakistani politician; president of Pakistan 1958–69.

Baal Shem Tov, 1700?–60, b. Israel Ben Eliezer, Jewish religious leader in Poland; founder of Chassidism.

Babbage, Charles, 1792–1871, Eng. mathematician & inventor.

Babbitt, Irving, 1865–1933, U.S. scholar & critic.

—Milton, 1916–, U.S. composer.

Babel, Isaak (Emmanuilovich), 1894–1941, Russ. author.

Baber, b. Zahir-ud-din Mohammed, 1480–1530, founder of the Mogul empire of India.

Babeuf, Francois, 1760–97, Fr. revolutionist.

Babson, Roger Ward, 1875–1967, U.S. statistician.

Bach A family of Ger. composers & musicians incl. **Johann Sebastian,** 1685–1750, & his sons: **Carl Philipp Emmanuel,** 1714–88; **Johann Christian,** 1735–82; & **Wilhelm Friedemann,** 1710–84.

Bacharach, Burt, 1929–, U.S. composer.

Bachauer, Gina, 1913-76, Gk. pianist.

Bache, Harold L., 1894–1968, U.S. business executive.

Backaus, Wilhelm, 1884–1969, Ger. pianist.

Bacon, Francis, 1561–1626, Eng. philosopher, essayist & statesman.

—Francis, 1909–, Irish-born Brit. painter.

—Roger, 1214?–92?, Eng. scientist & philosopher.

Baden-Powell, Robert (Stephenson Smyth), 1857–1941, Brit. general; founder of Boy Scouts.

Badoglio, Pietro, 1871–1956, Ital. general; premier of Italy 1943–44.

Baedeker, Karl, 1801–59, Ger. author & publisher.

Baer, Karl Ernst von, 1792–1876, Russ. embryologist active in Germany.

Baeyer, Adolf von, 1835–1917, Ger. chemist.

Baez, Joan, 1941–, U.S. folk singer.

Baffin, William, 1584?–1622, Eng. navigator & explorer.

Bahaullah, Mirza Husayn Ali, 1817–92. Pers. religious leader.

Bailey, F. Lee, 1933–, U.S. lawyer.

—Mildred, 1903–51, U.S. singer.

—Pearl (Mae), 1918–, U.S. singer.

Baird, John Logie, 1888–1946, Scot. inventor.

—William Britton (Bil), 1904–, U.S. puppeteer.

Bairnsfather, Bruce, 1888–1959, Eng. cartoonist.

Baker, George ("Father Divine"), 1877?–1965, U.S. religious leader.

—Josephine, 1906–75, U.S. entertainer.

—Russell, 1925–, U.S. jounalist & author.

Bakr, Ahmed Hassan al-, 1912–, Iraqi military officer; president & prime minister of Iraq 1968–.

Bakst, Leon Nikolaevich, 1866?–1924, Russ. painter & set designer.

Bakunin, Mikhail, 1814–76, Russ. anarchist leader.

Balaguer, Joaquin, 1902–, president of Dominican Republic 1966–78.

Balanchine, George, 1904–, Russ.-born U.S. choreographer.

Balboa, Vasco Núñez de, 1475?–1517, Sp. explorer; discovered the Pacific Ocean.

Baldwin, James, 1924–, U.S. author.

—Stanley, 1867–1947, Eng. statesman; prime minister 1923–24, 1924–29, 1935–37.

Balenciaga, Cristobal, 1896?–1972, Sp. fashion designer active in France.

Balfour, Arthur James, Earl of, 1848–1930, Eng. statesman & philosopher.

Ball, Lucille, 1911 –, U.S. actress & comedienne.

Balmain, Pierre, 1914–, Fr. fashion designer.

Balzac, Honoré de, 1799–1850, Fr. novelist.

Bancroft, Anne, 1931–, U.S. actress.

—George, U.S. historian.

Bandaranaike, Sirimavo, 1916–, prime minister of Sri Lanka 1960–65, 1970–77.

Bankhead, Tallulah (Brockman), 1903–68, U.S. actress.

Banneker, Benjamin, 1731–1806, U.S. astronomer, mathematician & inventor.

Bannister, Sir Roger, 1929–, Eng. track runner & physician.

Banting, Sir Frederick Grant, 1891–1941, Can. physiologist.

Banton, Travis, 1874–1958, U.S. costume designer.

Banzer Suarez, Hugo, 1924–, Bolivian military officer; president of Bolivia 1971–78.

Bara, Theda, 1890–1955, U.S. actress.

Baraka, Imamu Amiri, b. (Everett) LeRoi Jones, 1934–, U.S. poet, playwright & social activist.

Barber, Samuel, 1910–81, U.S. composer.

—Walter Lanier ("Red"), 1908–, U.S. sports announcer.

Barbirolli, Sir John, 1899–1970, Eng. conductor.

Bardeen, John, 1908–, U.S. physicist.

Bardot, Brigitte, 1934–, Fr. actress.

Barkley, Alben William, 1877–1956, U.S. lawyer & politician; U.S. vice-president 1949–53.

Bar Kokba, Simon, ?–A.D. 135, Jewish leader & self-proclaimed Messiah.

Barlach, Ernst, 1870–1938, Ger. sculptor & author.

Barnard, Christiaan, 1922–, South African surgeon.

—Edward Emerson, 1857–1923, U.S. astronomer.

—Frederick A(ugustus) P(orter), 1809–89, U.S. educator.

Barnes, Djuna, 1892–, U.S. author & artist.

Barnhart, Clarence L., 1900–, U.S. lexicographer.

Barnum, P(hineas) T(aylor), 1810–91, U.S. showman & circus proprietor.

Baroja, Pio, 1872–1956, Sp. novelist.

Barrault, Jean-Louis, 1910–, Fr. actor & stage director.

Barrie, Sir James M(atthew), 1860–1937, Scot, author & playwright.

Barron, Clarence Walker, 1855–1928, U.S. financial editor & publisher.

Barrow, Clyde, 1909–34, U.S. criminal.

Barry, Philip, 1896–1949, U.S. playwright.

Barrymore A family of U.S. actors incl. **Ethel**, 1879–1959; **John**, 1882–1942; **Lionel**, 1878–1954; **Maurice (Herbert Blythe)**, 1847–1905, father of Ethel, John, & Lionel.

Barth, John (Simmons), 1930–, U.S. author.

—Karl, 1886–1968, Swiss theologian.

Barthes, Roland, 1915–, Fr. author & critic.

Bartholdi, Frédéric Auguste, 1834–1904, Fr. sculptor.

Bartlett, John, 1820–1905, U.S. editor & publisher.

Bartók, Béla, 1881–1945, Hung. composer.

Bartolommeo, Fra, b. Baccio della Porta, 1475–1517, Ital. painter.

Bartolozzi, Francesco, 1727?–1815, Ital. engraver.

Barton, Bruce, 1886–1967, U.S. advertising executive & author.

—Clara, 1821–1921, U.S. civic worker; founder of the American Red Cross.

Baruch, Bernard Mannes, 1870–1965, U.S. financier & political adviser.

Baryshnikov, Mikhail, 1947–, Soviet-born ballet dancer active in U.S.

Barzun, Jacques, 1907–, Fr.-born U.S. educator & author.

Basho, 1648–94, Jap. poet.

Basie, William ("Count"), 1904–, U.S. jazz musician.

Basil, Saint (L. Basilius), 330?–379, bishop of Caesarea.

Baskerville, John, 1706–75, Eng. typographer.

Baskin, Leonard, 1922–, U.S. painter & illustrator.

Bass, Sam, 1851–78, U.S. outlaw.

Bates, Alan, 1934–, Eng. actor.

Bateson, William, 1861–1926, Eng. biologist.

Batista y Zaldivar, Fulgencio, 1901–73, Cuban soldier & political leader; president 1940–44, 1952–59.

Batu Khan, ?–1255, Mongol leader.

Baudelaire, Charles (Pierre), 1821–67, Fr. poet.

Baudouin, 1930–, king of Belgium 1951–.

Baugh, Samuel Adrian (Sammy), 1914–, U.S. football player.

Baum, L(yman) Frank, 1856–1919, U.S. author.

—Vicki, 1888–1960, Austrian-born U.S. author.

Bayes, Nora, 1880–1928, U.S. singer & actress.

Baylis, Dame Lilian, 1874–1937, Eng. theater manager.

Baylor, Elgin, 1934–, U.S. basketball player.

Bean, Roy, 1825?–1903, U.S. frontiersman.

Beard, Charles A(ustin), 1874–1958, & his wife **Mary (Ritter)**, 1876–1958, U.S. historians.

—Daniel Carter, 1850–1941, U.S. author; founder of the Boy Scouts of America.

Beardsley, Aubrey (Vincent), 1872–98, Eng. artist & illustrator.

Beaton, Cecil, 1904–1980, Eng. photographer & theatrical designer.

Beatty, Clyde, 1905–65, U.S. animal trainer & circus performer.

Beaumarchais, Pierre Augustin Caron de, 1732–99, Fr. playwright.

Beaumont, Francis, 1584–1616, Eng. playwright.

—William, 1785–1853, U.S. surgeon.

Beauregard, Pierre Gustave Toutant de, 1818–93, U.S. Confederate general.

Beauvoir, Simone de, 1908–, Fr. author.

Beaverbrook, William Maxwell Aitken, Baron, 1879–1964, Can.-born Brit. publisher & politician.

Bechet, Sidney, 1897–1959, U.S. jazz musician.

Becket, Saint Thomas à, 1118–70, Eng. Catholic martyr; archbishop of Canterbury 1162–70.

Beckett, Samuel, 1906–, Irish-born novelist & playwright.

Beckmann, Max, 1884–1950, Ger. painter.

Becquerel A family of Fr. physicists incl. **Alexandre Edmond**, 1820–91; **Antoine César**, 1788–1878, father of prec,; **Antoine Henri**, 1852–1908, son of Alexandre.

Bede, Saint, 673–735, Eng. scholar, historian, & theologian: called **the Venerable Bede**.

Beebe, Charles William, 1877–1962, U.S. naturalist.

—Lucius Morris, 1902–66, U.S. journalist & author.

Beecham, Sir Thomas, 1879–1961, Eng. conductor.

Beecher, Henry Ward, 1813–87, U.S. clergyman & writer; brother of Harriet Beecher Stowe.

—Lyman, 1775–1863, U.S. clergyman; father of prec.

Beene, Geoffrey, 1927–, U.S. fashion designer.

Beerbohm, Max, 1872–1956, Eng. author & caricaturist.

Beery, Wallace, 1886–1949, U.S. actor.

Beethoven, Ludwig van, 1770–1827, Ger. composer.

Begin, Menahem, 1913–, Pol.-born Israeli statesman; prime minister of Israel, 1977–.

Behan, Brendan (Francis), 1923–64, Irish playwright.

Behrens, Peter, 1868–1938, Ger. architect.

Behring, Emil von, 1854–1917, Ger. bacteriologist.

Behrman, S(amuel) N(athaniel), 1893–1973, U.S. playwright.

Beiderbecke, Leon Bismarck ("Bix"), 1903–31, U.S. jazz musician.

Béjart, Maurice, 1928–, Fr. dancer, choreographer, & ballet-company director.

Belafonte, Harry, 1927–, U.S. singer.

Belasco, David, 1859–1931, U.S. theatrical producer & playwright.

Belinsky, Vissarion Grigorievich, 1811–48, Russ. critic & journalist.

Bell, Alexander Graham, 1847–1922, Scot.-born U.S. physicist; inventor of the telephone.

Bellamy, Edward, 1850–98, U.S. author.

Bellinghausen, Fabian von, 1778–1852, Russ. admiral & explorer.

Bellini A family of Venetian painters incl. **Jacopo**, 1400?–70?, & his sons **Gentile**, 1429?–1507 & **Giovanni**, 1430?–1516.

—Vincenzo, 1801–35, Ital. operatic composer.

Belloc, Hilaire, 1870–1953, Eng. poet & author.

Bellow, Saul, 1915–, Can.-born U.S. novelist.

Bellows, George Wesley, 1882–1925, U.S. painter & lithographer.

Belmont, August, 1816–90, Ger.-born U.S. financier.

Belmonte, Juan, 1892–1962, Sp. bullfighter.

Bemelmans, Ludwig, 1898–1962, Austrian-born U.S. author & illustrator.

Ben Bella, Ahmed, 1918–, Algerian revolutionary leader; premier of Algeria 1962–65.

Benchley, Robert Charles, 1889–1945, U.S. humorist & author.

Bendix, Vincent, 1882–1945, U.S. inventor & manufacturer.

Benedict, Saint, 480–543, Ital. monk; founder of the Benedictine order.

Benedict, Ruth Fulton, 1887–1948, U.S. anthropologist.

Benes, Eduard, 1884–1948, Czech statesman; president of Czechoslovakia 1935–38 & 1946–48.

Benét, Stephen Vincent, 1898–1943, U.S. poet & author.

—William Rose, 1886–1950, U.S. author & editor; brother of prec.

Ben-Gurion, David, 1886–1973, Russ.-born Israeli statesman; prime minister of Israel 1948–53 & 1955–63.

Benjamin, Judah Philip, 1811–84, U.S. lawyer & Confederate cabinet member.

Bennett, (Enoch) Arnold, 1867–1931, Eng. author.

—Floyd, 1890–1928, U.S. aviator.

—James Gordon, 1795–1872, Scot-born U.S. journalist.

—Michael, 1943–, U.S. stage director & choreographer.

—Robert Russell, 1894–, U.S. composer.

Benny, Jack, 1894–1974, U.S. comedian.

Bentham, Jeremy, 1748–1832, Eng. jurist & philosopher.

Bentley, Eric Russell, 1916–, Eng.-born author & critic active in U.S.

Benton, Thomas Hart, 1889–1975, U.S. painter.

—William, 1900–73, U.S. businessman, publisher, & government official.

Berdyaev, Nikolai (Alexsandrovich), 1874–1948, Russ.-born religious philosopher resident in France.

Berenson, Bernard, 1865–1959, Lithuanian-born U.S. art critic & writer.

Berg, Alban, 1885–1935, Austrian composer.

—**Gertrude,** 1900–66, U.S. actress.

Bergen, Edgar (John), 1903–78, U.S. ventriloquist & actor.

Berger, Frank M(ilan), 1913–, Czech-born U.S. pharmacologist.

—**Hans,** 1873–1941, Ger. neurologist & psychiatrist.

Bergerac, Cyrano de, 1619–55, Fr. poet & soldier.

Bergman, Ingmar, 1918–, Swed. film director.

—**Ingrid,** 1915–, Swed.-born actress active in U.S.

Bergner, Elisabeth, 1900–, Austrian actress.

Bergson, Henri (Louis), 1859–1941, Fr. philosopher.

Beria, Lavrenti Pavlovich, 1899–1953, Soviet politician.

Bering, Vitus, 1680–1741, Dan. navigator.

Berio, Luciano, 1925–, Ital.-born composer active in U.S.

Berkeley, Busby, 1895–1976, U.S. film director & choreographer.

—**George,** 1684–1753, Irish-born Eng. prelate & philosopher.

Berle, A(dolf) A(ugustus), 1895–1971, U.S. diplomat & author.

—**Milton,** 1908–, U.S. comedian.

Berlin, Irving, 1888–, U.S. composer.

—**Sir Isaiah,** 1909–, Latvian-born Brit. historian.

Berlioz, Hector, 1803–69, Fr. composer.

Bernadette, Saint, b. Bernadette Soubirous, 1844–79, Fr. nun: called **Bernadette of Lourdes.**

Bernadotte, Folke, Count of Wisborg, 1895–1948, Swed. diplomat & mediator in Palestine; assassinated.

—**Jean Baptiste Jules,** 1763?–1844, Fr. general; king of Sweden & Norway as Charles XIV 1818–44.

Bernard, Claude, 1812–78, Fr. physiologist.

Bernard of Clairvaux, Saint, 1091–1153, Fr. Cistercian monk.

Bernbach, William, 1911–, U.S. advertising executive.

Bernhardt, Sarah, 1844–1923, Fr. actress.

Bernini, Giovanni Lorenzo, 1598–1680, Ital. sculptor & architect.

Bernoulli A family of Swiss mathematicians & scientists incl. **Daniel,** 1700–82; **Jacques,** 1654–1705; **Jean,** 1667–1748, father of Daniel & brother of Jacques.

Bernstein, Leonard, 1918–, U.S. conductor, composer & pianist.

Berra, Lawrence Peter ("Yogi"), 1925–, U.S. baseball player & manager.

Berrigan, Daniel, 1921–, U.S. priest, poet, & political activist.

—**Philip,** 1923–, U.S. priest & political activist; brother of prec.

Berry, Charles Edward (Chuck), 1926–, U.S. musician & singer.

Berryman, John, 1914–72, U.S. poet.

Bert, Paul, 1833–86, Fr. physiologist.

Bertillon, Alphonse, 1853–1914, Fr. anthropologist & criminologist.

Bertolucci, Bernardo, 1940–, Ital. film director.

Berzelius, Baron Jöns Jakob, 1779–1848, Swed. chemist.

Besant, Annie (Wood), 1847–1933, Eng. theosophist.

Bessel, Friedrich Wilhelm, 1784–1846, Ger. astronomer.

Bessemer, Sir Henry, 1813–98, Eng. engineer.

Betancourt, Romulo, 1908–1981, president of Venezuela 1959–63.

Bethe, Hans Albrecht, 1906–, Ger.-born U.S. physicist.

Bethune, Mary McLeod, 1875–1955, U.S. educator.

Betjeman, Sir John, 1906–, Eng. poet.

Bettelheim, Bruno, 1903–, Austrian-born U.S. psychologist, educator & author.

Betti, Ugo, 1892–1953, Ital. playwright.

Betz, Pauline, 1919–, U.S. tennis player.

Bevan, Aneurin, 1897–1960, Welsh labor leader & Brit. government official.

Bevin, Ernest, 1881–1951, Eng. labor leader & statesman.

Bhave, Acharya Vinoba, 1895–, Indian social reformer.

Bhutto, Zulfikar Ali, 1928–79, president of Pakistan 1971–77; executed.

Biddle, Nicholas, 1786–1844, U.S. financier.

Bienville, Sieur Jean Baptiste Lemoyne de, 1680–1768, Fr. colonial governor of Louisiana.

Bierce, Ambrose Gwinnett, 1842–1914?, U.S. author.

Bierstadt, Albert, 1830–1902, Ger.-born U.S. painter.

Biggs, E(dward George) Power, 1906–77, Eng.-born U.S. organist.

Bikila, Abebe, 1932–73, Ethiopian track runner.

Binet, Alfred, 1857–1911, Fr. psychologist.

Bing, Sir Rudolph 1902–, Austrian-born opera manager active in U.S. & in England.

Bingham, George Caleb, 1811–79, U.S. painter.

Birdseye, Clarence, 1886–1956, U.S. inventor & industrialist.

Birendra Bir Bikram Shah Dev, 1945–, king of Nepal 1972–,

Bishop, Elizabeth, 1911–1979, U.S. poet.

Bismarck, Prince Otto (Eduard Leopold) von, 1815–98, Ger. statesman; chancellor of German empire 1871–90.

Bizet, Georges, 1838–75, Fr. composer.

Björling, Jussi, 1911–60, Swed. tenor.

Björnson, Björnstjerne, 1832–1910, Norw. poet & author.

Black, Hugo L(a Fayette), 1886–1971, U.S. jurist; justice of the U.S. Supreme Court 1937–71.

—**Shirley Temple,** 1928–, U.S. actress & diplomat.

Blackett, P(atrick) M(aynard) S(tuart), 1897–1974, Eng. physicist.

Black Hawk, 1767–1838, Sac Am. Ind. chief.

Blackmun, Harry Andrew, 1908–, U.S. jurist; justice of the U.S. Supreme Court 1970–.

Blackstone, Sir William, 1723–80, Eng. jurist.

Blackwell, Elizabeth, 1821–1910, Eng.-born U.S. physician.

Blaine, James G(illespie), 1830–93, U.S. statesman.

Blake, Eugene Carson, 1906–, U.S. clergyman & social activist.

—**James Hubert ("Eubie"),** 1883–, U.S. pianist & songwriter.

—**William,** 1757–1827, Eng. poet & painter.

Blanda, George Frederick, 1927–, U.S. football player.

Blankers-Koen, Francina Eisje (Fanny), 1918–, Du. track & field athlete.

Blasco Ibáñez, Vicente, 1867–1928, Sp. author.

Blass, Bill, 1922–, U.S. fashion designer.

Blavatsky, Elena Petrovna, 1831–91, Russ. theosophist.

Blériot, Louis, 1872–1936, Fr. engineer & pioneer aviator.

Bleuler, Eugen, 1856–1939, Swiss psychiatrist.

Bligh, William, 1754–1817, Brit. naval officer.

Bloch, Ernest, 1880–1959, Swiss-born composer active in U.S.

Block, Herbert Lawrence, 1909–, U.S. political cartoonist: called **Herblock.**

Bloomer, Amelia Jenks, 1818–94, U.S. social reformer.

Bloomfield, Leonard, 1887–1949, U.S. linguist & educator.

Blücher, Gebhard Leberecht von, 1742–1819, Prussian field marshal.

Blum, Léon, 1872–1950, Fr. politician.

Boadicea, ?–A.D. 62, queen of a tribe of Britons; defeated by the Romans.

Boas, Franz, 1858–1942, Ger.-born U.S. anthropologist.

Boccaccio, Giovanni, 1313–75, Ital. writer.

Boccherini, Luigi, 1743–1805, Ital. composer.

Bode, Johann Elert, 1747–1826, Ger. astronomer.

Bodenheim, Maxwell, 1893–1954, U.S. poet.

Bodoni, Giambattista, 1740–1813, Ital. printer & type designer.

Boehm, Karl, 1894–1981, Ger. conductor.

Boethius, Anicius Manlius Severinus, 480?–524, Roman philosopher.

Bogart, Humphrey, 1899–1957, U.S. actor.

Bogdanovich, Peter, 1932–, U.S. film director.

Bohlen, Charles Eustis, 1904–74, U.S. diplomat.

Böhme, Jakob, 1575–1624, Ger. mystic.

Bohr, Niels, 1885–1962, Dan. physicist.

Boileau-Despréaux, Nicholas, 1636–1711, Fr. poet & critic.

Boito, Arrigo, 1842–1918, Ital. composer & librettist.

Bok, Edward William, 1863–1930, Du.-born U.S. editor.

Bokassa, Jean-Bedel, 1922–, African general; president of Central African Republic 1972–77; as **Bokassa I,** emperor of Central African Empire 1977–.

Bolden, Charles ("Buddy"), 1868?–1931, U.S. jazz musician.

Boleyn, Anne, 1507?–36, second wife of Henry VIII of England; mother of Elizabeth I.

Bolger, Ray, 1904–, U.S. dancer & actor.

Bolívar, Simón, 1783–1830, South American revolutionary patriot & military leader.

Böll, Heinrich (Theodor), 1917–, Ger. author.

Boltzmann, Ludwig Edward, 1844–1906, Austrian physicist.

Bonaparte, Napoleon, 1769–1821, Fr. general & emperor of France as Napoleon I 1805–14.

—(Louis) Napoleon, 1808–73, emperor of France as Napoleon III 1852–71; nephew of prec. Also **Buonaparte.**

Bonaventure, Saint, 1221–74, Ital. philosopher.

Bond, Julian, 1940–, U.S. politician & civil rights leader.

Bonheur, Rosa, 1822–99, Fr. painter.

Bonhoeffer, Dietrich, 1906–45, Ger. theologian.

Boniface VIII, b. Benedetto Caetani, 1235?–1303, pope 1294–1303.

—Saint, 680?–755, Eng. missionary in Germany.

Bonnard, Pierre, 1867–1947, Fr. painter.

Bonney, William, 1859–81, U.S. outlaw: called **Billy the Kid.**

Boole, George, 1815–64, Eng. mathematician & logician.

Boone, Daniel, 1735?–1820, Amer. frontiersman.

Boorstin, Daniel J., 1914–, U.S. historian & author.

Booth, Edwin (Thomas), 1833–93, U.S. actor.

—John Wilkes, 1838–65, U.S. actor, assassinated Abraham Lincoln, brother of prec.

—Shirley, 1907–, U.S. actress.

—William, 1829–1912, Eng. religious leader; founder of the Salvation Army.

Borah, William Edgar, 1865–1940, U.S. politician.

Bordaberry, Juan Maria, 1928–, president of Uruguay 1972–76.

Borden, Gail, 1801–74, U.S. inventor.

—Lizzie, 1860–1927, U.S. alleged murderer.

Borg, Bjorn, 1956–, Swed. tennis player.

Borges, Jorge Luis, 1900–, Argentinian poet & author.

Borgia, Cesare, 1476–1507, Ital. military & religious leader.

—Lucrezia, 1480–1519, duchess of Ferrara & art patron; sister of prec.

Borglum, Gutzon, 1867–1941, U.S. sculptor.

Bori, Lucrezia, 1887–1960, Sp. soprano active in U.S.

Borlaug, Norman Ernest, 1914–, U.S. agronomist.

Bormann, Martin Ludwig, 1900–?, Ger. Nazi politican.

Born, Max, 1882–1970, Ger. physicist.

Borodin, Alexander Porfirevich, 1834–87, Russ. composer.

Borromini, Francesco, 1599–1667, Ital. architect.

Bosch, Hieronymus, 1450?–1516, Du. painter.

Bose, Sir Jagadis Chandra, 1858–1937, Indian physicist & plant physiologist.

Boswell, James, 1740–95, Scot. author & lawyer, biographer of Samuel Johnson.

Botha, Louis, 1862–1919, Boer general; first prime minister of Union of South Africa.

Botticelli, Sandro, b. Allesandro di Mariano dei Filipepi, 1444?–1510, Florentine painter.

Botvinnik, Mikhail, 1911–, Soviet chess master.

Boucher, Francois, 1703–70, Fr. painter.

Boucicault, Dion, 1820?–90, Irish playwright & actor.

Bougainville, Louis Antoine de, 1729–1811, Fr. navigator.

Boulanger, Nadia (Juliette), 1887–1979, Fr. composer & music teacher.

Boulez, Pierre, 1925–, Swiss-born composer & conductor active in U.S.

Boult, Sir Adrian, 1889–, Eng. conductor.

Boumédiene, Houari, 1927–78, Algerian army officer; president & premier of Algeria 1965–78.

Bourguiba, Habib ben Ali, 1903–, Tunisian statesman; president of Tunisia 1957–.

Bourke-White, Margaret, 1906–1972, U.S. photographer.

Bournonville, August, 1805–79, Danish dancer & choreographer.

Bouts, Dierick, 1420?–75, Du. painter.

Bovet, Daniele, 1907–, Swiss-born Ital. pharmacologist.

Bow, Clara, 1905–65, U.S. actress.

Bowditch, Nathaniel, 1773–1838, U.S. mathematician & navigator.

Bowdler, Thomas, 1754–1825, Eng. physician & editor of Shakespeare's plays.

Bowen, Elizabeth, 1899–1973, Irish-born Brit. author.

Bowes, Edward ("Major") 1874–1946, U.S. radio personality.

Bowie, James, 1796–1836, U.S. soldier & frontiersman.

Bowker, R(ichard) R(ogers), 1848–1933, U.S. editor & publisher.

Bowles, Chester, 1901–, U.S. busines executive & diplomat.

—Jane (Sydney Auer), 1917–73, U.S. author.

—Paul, 1910–, U.S. author, composer & musicologist; husband of prec.

Boyd, William (Bill), 1898–1972, U.S. actor.

Boyer, Charles, 1899–1978, Fr. actor.

Boyle, Kay, 1903–, U.S. author.

—Robert, 1627–91, Irish-born Brit. chemist & physicist.

Bradbury, Ray Douglas, 1920–, U.S. author.

Braddock, Edward, 1695–1755, Brit. general in N. America.

Bradford, William, 1590–1657, Eng.-born Pilgrim father & governor of Plymouth Colony.

Bradley, Milton, 1836–1911, U.S. manufacturer of games.

—Omar (Nelson), 1893–1981, U.S. general.

Bradstreet, Anne, 1612–72, Eng.-born Amer. poet.

Brady, Alice, 1892–1939, U.S. actress.

—James Buchanan ("Diamond Jim"), 1856–1917, U.S. financier & philanthropist.

—Mathew, 1823?–96, U.S. photographer.

Bragg, Sir William Henry, 1862–1942, Eng. physicist.

—Sir (William) Lawrence, 1890–1971, Austral.-born Eng. physicist; son of prec.

Brahe, Tycho, 1546–1601, Dan. astronomer.

Brahms, Johannes, 1833–97, Ger. composer.

Braille, Louis, 1809–52, Fr. educator.

Brailowsky, Alexander, 1896–1976, Russ.-born pianist active in U.S.

Bramante, b. Donato d'Angelo, 1444–1514, Ital. architect.

Brancusi, Constantin, 1876–1957, Rumanian sculptor.

Brand, Max, pseud. of Frederick Schiller Faust, 1892–1944, U.S. author.

Brandeis, Louis Dembitz, 1856–1941, U.S. jurist; justice of the U.S. Supreme Court 1916–39.

Brando, Marlon, 1924–, U.S. actor.

Brandt, Willy, 1913–, W. Ger. statesman; chancellor of W. Germany 1969–74.

Braque, Georges, 1882–1963, Fr. painter.

Braudel, Fernand, 1902–, Fr. historian & author.

Bream, Julian, 1933–, Eng. guitarist & lutenist.

Brecht, Bertolt, 1898–1956, Ger. playwright & poet.

Brel, Jacques, 1929–78, Belg. singer & composer.

Brennan, William Joseph, Jr., 1906–, U.S. jurist; justice of the U.S. Supreme Court 1956–.

Breslin, James (Jimmy), 1930–, U.S. journalist & author.

Bresson, Robert, 1907–, Fr. film director.

Breton, André, 1896–1966, Fr. poet & author.

Breuer, Josef, 1842–1925, Austrian physician.

—Marcel, 1902–81, Hung.-born architect active in U.S.

Brewster, William, 1567–1644, Eng.-born Pilgrim father.

Brezhnev, Leonid Ilyich, 1906–, Soviet statesman; general secretary of the Communist Party of the Soviet Union 1966–.

Brian Boru, 926–1014, king of Ireland 1002–14.

Briand, Aristide, 1862–1932, Fr. statesman & diplomat.

Brice, Fannie, 1891–1951, U.S. singer & comedienne.

Bridger, James, 1804–81, U.S. frontiersman & scout.

Bridges, Harry, 1901–, Austral.-born U.S. labor leader.

—Robert, 1844–1930, Eng. poet.

Bridgman, Percy Williams, 1882–1961, U.S. physicist.

Bright, Richard, 1789–1858, Eng. physician.

Brill, A(braham) A(rden), 1874–1948, Austrian-born U.S. psychiatrist.

Brillat-Savarin, Anthelme, 1755–1828, Fr. writer on food & cooking.

Brinkley, David, 1940–, U.S. journalist & television news commentator.

Britten, (Edward) Benjamin, 1913–76, Eng. composer.

Broca, Pierre Paul, 1824–80, Fr. surgeon & anthropologist.

Brogan, Sir D(ennis) W(illiam), 1900–74, Eng. historian.

Bromfield, Louis, 1896–1956, U.S. author.

Bronk, Detlev W(ulf), 1897–1975, U.S. physiologist & educator.

Brontë An Eng. family incl. three sisters who were authors: **Anne,** 1820–49; **Charlotte,** 1816–55; **Emily (Jane),** 1818–48.

Bronzino, Il, b. Agnolo di Cosimo Allori, 1503?–74, Ital. painter.

Brook, Clive, 1887–1974, Eng. actor.

—Peter, 1925–, Eng. stage director & producer.

Brooke, Alan Francis, 1st Viscount Alanbrooke, 1883–1963, Brit. field marshal.

—Edward William, 1919–, U.S. senator.

—Rupert, 1887–1915, Eng. poet.

Brookings, Robert Somers, 1850–1932, U.S. businessman & philanthropist.

Brooks, Mel, 1926–, U.S. author, actor & film director.

—Phillips, 1835–93, U.S. bishop.

—Van Wyck, 1886–1963, U.S. critic & author.

Brosio, Manlio, 1897–1980, Ital. lawyer & diplomat.

Broun, (Matthew) Heywood (Campbell), 1888–1939, U.S. journalist & critic.

Browder, Earl Russell, 1891–1973, U.S. Communist Party leader.

Brown, Helen Gurley, 1922–, U.S. author & editor.

—James, 1933–, U.S. singer.

—Jim, 1936–, U.S. football player & actor.

—Joe E., 1892–1973, U.S. comedian & actor.

—John, 1800–59, U.S. abolitionist.

—Norman O(liver), 1913–, Mexican-born U.S. author & educator.

Browne, Sir Thomas 1606–82, Eng. physician & author.

Browning, Elizabeth Barrett, 1806–61, Eng. poet.

—Robert, 1812–89, Eng. poet; husband of prec.

Brown-Sequard, Charles E., 1817–94, Fr.-born Brit. physician & physiologist.

Brubeck, David Warren (Dave), (1920–, U.S. jazz musician & composer.

Bruce, Lenny, 1926–66, U.S. comedian.

Bruch, Max, 1838–1920, Ger. composer.

Bruckner, Anton, 1824–96, Austrian composer.

Brueghel A family of Flemish painters incl. **Peter,** 1525?–69 (known as **the Elder**), & his sons, **Peter,** 1564?–1638? **(the Younger),** and **Jan,** 1568–1625.

Bruhn, Erik, 1928–, Dan. ballet dancer & choreographer.

Brumel, Valery, 1942–, Soviet track athlete.

Brummell, George Bryan ("Beau"), 1778–1840, Eng. man of fashion.

Brunelleschi, Filippo, 1377–1446, Florentine architect & sculptor.

Bruno, Giordano, 1548?–1600, Ital. philosopher; burned as a heretic.

Brutus, Marcus Junius, 85–42 B.C., Roman republican leader; conspirator against Caesar.

Bryan, William Jennings, 1860–1925, U.S. statesman & orator.

Bryant, William Cullen, 1794–1878, U.S. poet.

Bryce, James Bryce, Viscount, 1838–1922, Eng. statesman & author.

Brzezinski, Zbigniew, 1928–, Pol.-born U.S. educator and government official.

Buber, Martin, 1878–1965, Austrian-born Israeli Jewish philosopher & theologian.

Buchan, John, 1st Baron Tweedsmuir, 1875–1940, Scot. author & statesman; governor-general of Canada 1935–40.

Buchanan, Jack, 1891–1957, Scot.-born actor active in England & U.S.

—James, 1791–1868, 15th U.S. president 1857–61.

Buchman, Frank Nathan Daniel, 1878–1961, U.S. evangelist.

Buchner, Eduard, 1860–1917, Ger. organic chemist.

Buchwald, Art, 1925–, U.S. journalist & author.

Buck, Frank, 1884–1950, U.S. hunter & animal collector.

—Pearl S(ydenstricker), 1892–1973, U.S. author.

Buckley, William F(rank), Jr., 1925–, U.S. author & political commentator.

Buddha, Siddhartha Gautama, 563?–483? B.C., Indian religious teacher & philosopher; founder of Buddhism.

Budge, Don(ald), 1915–, U.S. tennis player.

Buffon, Comte Georges Louis Leclerc, 1707–88, Fr. naturalist.

Bulfinch, Charles, 1763–1844, U.S. architect.

Bulganin, Nikolai Aleksandrovich, 1895–1975, premier of the U.S.S.R. 1955–58.

Bull, Ole (Bornemann), 1810–80, Norw. violinist.

Bülow, Hans von, 1830–94, Ger. conductor & pianist.

Bultmann, Rudolf Karl, 1884–1976, Ger. theologian.

Bulwer-Lytton, Edward George, 1803–73, Eng. playwright & author.

Bunche, Ralph (Johnson), 1904–72, U.S. educator & U.N. official.

Bundy, McGeorge, 1919–, U.S. government official & foundation executive.

Bunin, Ivan Alekseevich, 1870–1953, Russ. poet & author.

Bunker, Ellsworth, 1894–, U.S. diplomat.

Bunsen, Robert Wilhelm, 1811–99, Ger. chemist.

Buñuel, Luis, 1900–, Sp. film director.

Bunyan, John, 1628–88, Eng. preacher & author of *Pilgrim's Progress.*

Burbage, Richard, 1567?–1619, Eng. actor.

Burbank, Luther, 1849–1926, U.S. horticulturist.

Burchfield, Charles Ephraim, 1893–1967, U.S. painter.

—R(obert) W(illiam), 1923–, New Zealand-born Brit. lexicographer.

Burckhardt, Jacob Christoph, 1818–97, Swiss art historian.

Burger, Warren Earl, 1907–, U.S. jurist, Chief Justice of the U.S. Supreme Court 1969–.

Burgess, Anthony, 1917–, Eng. author.

—(Frank) Gelett, 1866–1951, U.S. author & illustrator.

Burgoyne, John, 1722–92, Brit. General in American Revolutionary War: known as **Gentleman Johnny.**

Burke, Edmund, 1729–97, Irish-born Brit. orator, author & statesman.

Burne-Jones, Sir Edward Coley, 1833–98, Eng. painter.

Burnett, Carol, 1934–, U.S. actress, singer & comedienne.

Burney, Fanny, 1752–1840, Eng. author & diarist.

Burns, Arthur, 1904–, Russ.-born U.S. economist.

—George, 1896–, U.S. actor & comedian.

—Robert 1759–96, Scot. poet.

Burnside, Ambrose Everett, 1824–81, U.S. Civil War general.

Burr, Aaron, 1756–1836, Amer. lawyer & statesman; U.S. vice-president 1801–05.

Burroughs, Edgar Rice, 1875–1950, U.S. author.

—John, 1837–1921, U.S. naturalist & author.

—William, 1914–, U.S. author.

Burton, Richard, 1925–, Brit. actor.

—Sir Richard Francis, 1821–90, Eng. traveler & author.

Busch, Adolphus, 1839–1913, Ger.-born U.S. business-man & philanthropist.

Bush, George, 1924–, U.S. statesman; U.S. vice-president 1981–.

—**Vannevar,** 1890–1974, U.S. electrical engineer.

Bushman, Francis X(avier), 1883–1966, U.S. actor.

Busoni, Ferruccio (Benvenuto), 1866–1924, Ital. composer & pianist.

Butler, Nicholas Murray, 1862–1947, U.S. educator.

—**Samuel,** 1612–80, Eng. satirical poet.

—**Samuel,** 1835–1902, Eng. author.

Button, Richard Totten (Dick), 1929–, U.S. figure skater.

Buxtehude, Diderik, 1637–1707, Dan.-born Ger. organist & composer.

Byrd, Richard Evelyn, 1888–1957, U.S. explorer.

Byron, George Gordon, Lord, 1788–1824, Eng. poet.

Cabell, James Branch, 1879–1958, U.S. author.

Cable, George Washington, 1844–1925, U.S. author.

Cabot, John, b. Giovanni Caboto, 1451?–98, Venetian navigator & explorer.

Cabral, Pedro Alvares, 1460?–1526, Pg. navigator.

Cabrini, Saint Frances Xavier, 1850–1917, Ital.-born U.S. nun; canonized 1946: known as **Mother Cabrini.**

Cadillac, Sieur Antoine de la Mothe, 1658–1730, Fr. explorer in N. America.

Caedmon, 7th c. Eng. poet; first to be known by name.

Caesar, Gaius Julius, 100–44 B.C., Roman general, statesman & historian.

—**Sid,** 1922–, U.S. comedian & actor.

Caetano, Marcelo, 1906–80, Pg. lawyer; premier of Portugal 1968–74.

Cage, John, 1912–, U.S. composer.

Cagliostro, Count Alessandro di, 1743–95, Ital. charlatan.

Cagney, James, 1904–, U.S. actor.

Cahn, Sammy, 1913–, U.S. lyricist.

Calder, Alexander, 1898–1976, U.S. sculptor.

Calderón de la Barca, Pedro, 1600–81, Sp. poet & playwright.

Caldwell, Erskine, 1903–, U.S. author.

—**(Janet) Taylor,** 1900–, U.S. author.

—**Sarah,** 1928–, U.S. opera director & conductor.

Calhoun, John C(aldwell), 1782–1850, U.S. lawyer & politician; U.S. vice-president 1825–32.

Caligula, b. Gaius Caesar, A.D. 12–41, Roman emperor 37–41; assassinated.

Callaghan, James, 1912–, Eng. politician; prime minister 1976–79.

—**Morley,** 1903–, Can. author.

Callas, Maria (Meneghini), 1923–77, U.S. soprano.

Callisthenes, 360?–328? B.C., Gk. philosopher & historian.

Calloway, Cab(ell), 1907–, U.S. singer & band leader.

Calvert, Sir George, 1580?–1632, Eng. statesman; founder of Maryland.

Calvin, John, 1509–64, Fr. Protestant reformer.

Cambyses, ?–522 B.C., king of Persia; son of Cyrus.

Camões, Luiz Vaz de, 1524–80, Pg. poet.

Camp, Walter Chauncey, 1859–1925, U.S. football coach.

Campbell, Mrs. Patrick, b. Beatrice Stella Tanner, 1867–1940, Eng. actress.

—**Thomas,** 1777–1844, Eng. poet.

Campion, Thomas, 1567–1620, Eng. poet & musician.

Camus, Albert, 1913–60, Algerian-born Fr. writer.

Canaletto, b. Antonio Canale, 1697–1768, Ital. painter.

Canby, Henry Seidel, 1878–1961, U.S. educator.

Candolle, Augustine Pyrame de, 1778–1841. Swiss botanist.

Cannon, Joseph Gurney ("Uncle Joe"), 1836–1926, U.S. lawyer & politician.

—**Walter Bradford,** 1871–1945, U.S. physiologist.

Canova, Antonio, 1757–1833, Ital. sculptor.

Cantor, Eddie, 1892–1964, U.S. singer & actor.

Canute, 994?–1035, king of England, Denmark & Norway.

Čapek, Karel, 1890–1938, Czech author & playwright.

Capet, Hugh, 940?–996, king of France 987–996.

Capone, Al(phonse), 1898–1947, U.S. criminal.

Capote, Truman, 1924–, U.S. author.

Capp, Al, 1909–79, U.S. cartoonist.

Capra, Frank, 1897–, Ital.-born U.S. film director.

Captain Kangaroo, pseud. of Robert James Keeshan, 1927–, U.S. TV personality.

Caracalla, b. Marcus Aurelius Antoninus Bassianus, A.D. 188–217, Roman emperor 212–17.

Caramanlis, Constantine, 1907–, premier of Greece 1974–.

Caravaggio, Michelangelo Amerighi da, 1569–1609, Ital. painter.

Cárdenas, Lázaro, 1895–1970, Mexican general; president of Mexico 1934–40.

Cardin, Pierre, 1922–, Ital.-born Fr. fashion designer.

Cardozo, Benjamin Nathan, 1870–1938, U.S. jurist; justice of U.S. Supreme Court 1932–38.

Carême, Marie Antoine, 1784–1833, Fr. chef & gastronome.

Carew, Thomas, 1595?–1645?, Eng. poet.

Carl XVI Gustaf, 1946–, king of Sweden 1973–.

Carlota, 1840–1927, Austrian-born Empress of Mexico 1864–67.

Carlyle, Thomas, 1795–1881, Scot. author.

Carman, (William) Bliss, 1861–1929, Can. poet & journalist active in U.S.

Carmichael, Hoaglund Howard ("Hoagy"), 1899–1981, U.S. song writer.

Carnap, Rudolf, 1891–1970, Ger.-born U.S. philosopher.

Carné, Marcel, 1909–, Fr. film director.

Carnegie, Andrew, 1837–1919, Scot.-born U.S. industrialist & philanthropist.

—**Dale,** 1888–1955, U.S. author & teacher of public speaking.

Carnot, Lazare Nicolas Marguerite, 1753–1823, Fr. revolutionary statesman & general.

—**Nicolas Léonard Sadi,** 1796–1832, Fr. physicist; son of prec.

Carol II, 1893–1953, king of Rumania 1930–40; abdicated.

Carpaccio, Vittore, 1460?–1525?, Ital. painter.

Carracci A family of Ital. painters incl. **Lodovico,** 1555–1619, & his nephews **Agostino,** 1557–1602, & **Annibale,** 1560–1609.

Carranza, Venustiano, 1859–1920, Mexican revolutionist & statesman; president of Mexico 1915–20.

Carrel, Alexis, 1873–1944, Fr. surgeon & biologist.

Carrington, Richard Christopher, 1826–75, Eng. astronomer.

Carroll, Charles, 1737–1832, Amer. revolutionary patriot.

—**Lewis,** pseud. of Charles Lutwidge Dodgson, 1832–98, Eng. mathematician & author of *Alice's Adventures in Wonderland.*

Carson, Christopher ("Kit"), 1809–68, U.S. frontiersman.

—**Johnny,** 1925–, U.S. comedian & television personality.

—**Rachel (Louise),** 1907–64, U.S. biologist & author.

Carter, Elliott (Cook), 1908–, U.S. composer.

Carter, Jimmy (James Earl), 1924–, politician, 39th U.S. president 1977–81.

Cartier, Jacques, 1491–1557, Fr. explorer; discoverer of the St. Lawrence River.

Cartier-Bresson, Henri, 1908–, Fr. photographer.

Cartwright, Edmund, 1743–1823, Eng. inventor of the power loom.

Caruso, Enrico, 1873–1921, Ital. tenor.

Carver, George Washington, 1864?–1943, U.S. chemist & botanist.

—**John,** 1576?–1621, Eng.-born Amer. colonist; 1st governor of Plymouth colony.

Cary, (Arthur) Joyce (Lunel), 1888–1957, Eng. author.

Casadesus, Robert, 1899–1972, Fr. pianist.

Casals, Pablo, 1876–1973, Sp. cellist & composer.

Casanova, Giovanni Giacomo, 1725–98, Ital. adventurer; known for his *Memoirs.*

Casement, Sir Roger, 1864–1916, Irish nationalist; hanged by the British for treason in World War I.

Cash, Johnny, 1932–, U.S. singer & song writer.

Caslon, William, 1692–1766, Eng. type founder.

Cassatt, Mary, 1855–1926, U.S. painter.

Cassini, Giovanni Domenico, 1625–1712, Fr. astronomer.

Cassiodorus, Flavius Magnus Aurelius, ?–575, Roman statesman & author.

Cassirer, Ernst, 1874–1945, Ger. philosopher.

Cassius Longinus, Gaius, ?–42 B.C., Roman general; conspirator against Caesar.

Catagno, Andrea del, ?–1457?, Ital. painter.

Castiglione, Count Baldassare, 1478–1529, Ital. statesman & author.

Castle, Irene, 1893–1969, U.S. dancer.

—Vernon, 1887–1918, Eng.-born U.S. dancer & aviator; husband of prec.

Castlereagh, Robert Stewart, Viscount, 1769–1822, Brit. statesman.

Castro (Ruz), Fidel, 1927– Cuban revolutionary leader; prime minister of Cuba 1959–.

Catharine of Aragon, 1485–1536, first wife of Henry VIII of England; mother of Mary I.

Cather, Willa (Sibert), 1876–1947, U.S. author.

Catherine II (Ekaterina Alekseevna), 1729–96, Ger.-born empress of Russia 1762–96; known as **Catherine the Great.**

Catiline (L. Lucius Sergius Catilina), 108?–62 B.C., Roman politician & conspirator.

Catlin, George, 1796–1872, U.S. painter & sculptor.

Cato, Marcus Porcius, 234–149 B.C., Roman statesman: known as **the Elder.**

—Marcus Porcius, 95–46 B.C., Roman statesman & philosopher; great-grandson of prec.: known as **the Younger.**

Catt, Carrie Chapman (Lane), 1859–1947, U.S. suffragist.

Catton, (Charles) Bruce, 1899–1978, U.S. journalist & historian.

Catullus, Gaius Valerius, 84?–54 B.C., Roman poet.

Cavafy, Constantinos, 1863–1933, Gk. poet.

Cavell, Edith, 1865–1915, Eng. nurse & patriot; executed by the Germans in World War I.

Cavendish, Henry, 1731?–1810, Eng. chemist & physicist.

Cavett, Dick, 1936–, U.S. TV personality & author.

Cavour, Count Camillo Benso di, 1810–61, Ital. statesman.

Caxton, William, 1422–91, first Eng. printer.

Cayce, Edgar, 1877–1945, U.S. photographer & psychic.

Cayley, Sir George, 1773–1857, Eng. engineer & aircraft designer.

Ceausescu, Nicolae, 1918–, president of Rumania 1967–.

Cecil, Lord (Edward Christian) David, 1902–, Eng. author.

—William, 1st Baron Burghley, 1520–98, Eng. statesman.

Céline, Louis Ferdinand, 1894–1961, Fr. author.

Cellini, Benvenuto, 1500–71, Ital. sculptor & goldsmith.

Celsius, Anders, 1701–44, Swed. astronomer.

Cenci, Beatrice, 1577–99, Ital. noblewoman; executed for parricide.

Cerf, Bennett (Alfred), 1895–1971, U.S. author & publisher.

Cervantes, Miguel de, 1547–1616, Sp. novelist & playwright; author of *Don Quijote de la Mancha.*

Cézanne, Paul, 1839–1906, Fr. painter.

Chabrol, Claude, 1930–, Fr. film director.

Chadwick, Sir James, 1891–1974, Eng. physicist.

Chagall, Marc, 1887–, Russ.-born painter active in France.

Chaliapin, Feodor Ivanovich, 1873–1938, Russ. basso.

Chamberlain, (Arthur) Neville, 1869–1940, Eng. statesman; prime minister 1937–40.

—Owen, 1920–, U.S. physicist.

—Wilt (on Norman), 1936–, U.S. basketball player.

Chambers, (Jay David) Whittaker, 1901–61, U.S. journalist.

Champion, Gower, 1921–80, U.S. dancer, choreographer & stage director.

—Marjorie (Marge), 1925–, U.S. dancer.

Champlain, Samuel de, 1567?–1635, Fr. explorer in America.

Champollion, Jean Francois, 1790–1832, Fr. Egyptologist.

Chandler, Raymond, 1888–1959, U.S. author.

Chanel, Gabrielle ("Coco"), 1883?–1971, Fr. fashion designer.

Chaney, Lon, 1883–1930, U.S. actor.

Chang & Eng, 1811–74, Siamese-born conjoined twins residing in U.S.; the original "Siamese twins."

Channing, William Ellery, 1780–1842, U.S. clergyman & social reformer.

Chaplin, Sir Charles Spencer (Charlie), 1889–1977, Eng.-born film actor & producer active in U.S.

Chapman, George, 1559?–1634, Eng. playwright & translator.

—John, 1774–1845, U.S. pioneer: called **Johnny Appleseed.**

Charcot, Jean Martin, 1825–93,. Fr. neurologist.

Chardin, Jean Baptiste Siméon, 1699–1779, Fr. painter.

Chardonnet, Hilaire Bernigaud, Comte de, 1839–1924, Fr. chemist & inventor.

Charlemagne, 742–814, king of the Franks 768–814 & Holy Roman Emperor 800–814: known as **Charles the Great.**

Charles I, 1600–49, king of England 1625–49; beheaded.

—II, 1630–85, king of England 1660–85.

Charles V, 1337–80, king of France 1364–80: known as **Charles the Wise.**

Charles V, 1500–58, Holy Roman Emperor; king of Spain as Charles I.

Charles XIV See BERNADOTTE, JEAN, BAPTISTE, JULES.

Charles Philip Arthur George, 1948–, Prince of Wales, heir apparent to the Brit. throne.

Charles, Jacques Alexandre César, 1746–1823, Fr. physicist.

Chase, Lucia, 1907–, U.S. ballet dancer & ballet-company director.

—Mary Ellen, 1887–1973, U.S. author & educator.

—Salmon P(ortland), 1808–73, U.S. statesman; chief justice of the U.S. Supreme Court.

Chateaubriand, François René, Vicomte de, 1768–1848, Fr. author & politician.

Chatterton, Ruth, 1893–1961, U.S. actress.

—Thomas, 1752–70, Eng. poet.

Chaucer, Geoffrey, 1340?–1400, Eng. poet.

Chávez, Carlos, 1899–1978, Mexican composer & conductor.

—Cesar (Estrada), 1927–, U.S. labor leader.

Chayefsky, Sidney ("Paddy"), 1923–81, U.S. playwright.

Cheever, John, 1912–, U.S. author.

Chekhov, Anton Pavlovich, 1860–1904, Russ. playwright & author.

Chénier, André Marie de, 1762–94, Fr. poet.

Chennault, Claire Lee, 1890–1958, U.S. Air Force general.

Cheops, Egyptian king of the 4th dynasty ca. 2650 B.C.; built the Great Pyramid at Gizeh: also known as **Khufu.**

Cherenkov, Pavel Alekseevich, 1904–, Soviet physicist.

Chernyshevski, Nikolai Gavrilovich, 1829–89, Russ. revolutionist & author.

Cherubini, (Maria) Luigi, 1760–1842, Ital. composer.

Chessman, Caryl (Whittier), 1921–60, U.S. criminal & author; executed.

Chesterfield, Philip Dormer Stanhope, Earl of, 1694–1773, Eng. statesman & author.

Chesterton, G(ilbert) K(eith), 1874–1936, Eng. author.

Chevalier, Maurice, 1888–1972, Fr. entertainer.

Chevrolet, Louis, 1878–1941, U.S. automobile manufacturer.

Chiang Ching, 1913–, Chin. government official; wife of Mao Tse-tung.

Chiang Kai-shek, 1886–1975, Chin. general & statesman; president of Republic of China (Taiwan) 1948–75.

—Madame Chiang Kai-shek See SOONG.

Chikamatsu Monzaemon, 1653?–1724, Jap. dramatist.
Child, Francis James, 1825–96, U.S. philologist & ballad editor.
—**Julia (McCormick),** 1912–, U.S. culinary expert & author.
Chippendale, Thomas, 1718–79, Eng. cabinetmaker.
Chirico, Giorgio di, 1888–1978, Ital. painter.
Chittenden, Russell Henry, 1856–1943, U.S. physiological chemist.
Chomsky, Noam, 1928–, U.S. linguist.
Chopin, Frédéric François, 1810–49, Pol. composer & pianist active in France.
Chrétien de Troyes, 12th c. Fr. poet.
Christensen, Lew, 1908–, U.S. dancer, choreographer & ballet company director.
Christians, Mady, 1900–51, Austrian actress.
Christie, Dame Agatha, 1890–1976, Eng. author.
Christoff, Boris, 1919–, Bulgarian basso.
Christophe, Henri, 1767–1820, Haitian revolutionary leader; king of Haiti 1811–20.
Christopher, Saint, 3rd c. Christian martyr.
Christy, Howard Chandler, 1873–1952, U.S. painter & illustrator.
Chrysler, Walter P(ercy), 1875–1940, U.S. automobile manufacturer.
Chuang-tzu, 4th c. B.C. Chin. philosopher.
Churchill, Lord Randolph, 1849–95, Eng. statesman.
—**Winston,** 1871–1947, U.S. author.
—**Sir Winston,** 1874–1965, Eng. statesman & author; son of Lord Randolph.
Chu Teh, 1886–1976, Chin. military leader.
Ciano, Count Galeazzo, 1903–44, Ital. diplomat.
Ciardi, John, 1916–, U.S. poet & critic.
Cibber, Colley, 1671–1757, Eng. actor & poet.
Cicero, Marcus Tullius, 106–43 B.C., Roman statesman, orator & writer.
Cid, El, b. Rodrigo Diaz de Bivar, 1044?–99, Sp. soldier & epic hero.
Cimabue, Giovanni, 1240–1302, Florentine painter.
Cimarosa, Domenico, 1749–1801, Ital. composer.
Cincinnatus, Lucius Quinctius, 5th c. B.C. Roman general & statesman.
Clair, René, 1898–1981, Fr. film director.
Claire, Ina, 1895–, U.S. actress.
Clare, Saint, 1194–1253, Ita. nun.
Clark, Bobby, 1888–1960, U.S. comedian.
—**(Charles) Joseph,** 1939–, Can. statesman; prime minister of Canada, 1979–80.
—**George Rogers,** 1752–1818, U.S. soldier & frontiersman.
—**James Beauchamp ("Champ"),** 1850–1921, U.S. politician.
—**Kenneth B(ancroft),** 1914–, U.S. psychologist.
—**Lord Kenneth M.,** 1903–, Eng. art historian.
—**Mark,** 1896–, U.S. general.
—**William,** 1770–1838, U.S. explorer.
—**(William) Ramsey,** 1927–, U.S. lawyer & politician.
Clarke, Arthur C(harles), 1917–, Eng. author.
Claudel, Paul (Louise Charles), 1868–1955, Fr. author & diplomat.
Claude (de) Lorrain, b. Claude Gellée, 1600–82, Fr. painter.
Claudius I, b. Tiberius Claudius Drusus Nero Germanicus, 10 B.C.-A.D. 54, 4th Roman emperor 41–54.
Clausewitz, Karl von, 1780–1831, Prussian general & writer on military science.
Clausius, Rudolf Julius Emanuel, 1822–88, Ger. physicist & mathematician.
Clay, Cassius Marcellus, 1810–1903, U.S. politician & abolitionist.
—**Henry,** 1777–1852, U.S. statesman & orator.
—**Lucius DuBignon,** 1897–1978, U.S. general.
Cleaver, (Leroy) Eldridge, 1935–, U.S. author & political activist.
Clemenceau, Georges (Benjamin Eugène), 1841–1929, Fr. statesman; premier of France 1906–09 & 1917–20.
Clemens, Samuel Langhorne See TWAIN, MARK.
Clement VII, b. Guilio de' Medici, 1478–1534, pope 1523–34.

Clement of Alexandria (L. Titus Flavius Clemens), A.D. 150?–220?, Gk. theologian.
Cleopatra, 69–30 B.C., queen of Egypt 51–30 B.C.
Cleveland, (Stephen) Grover, 1837–1908, 22nd & 24th U.S. president 1885–89, 1893–97.
Cliburn, Harvey Lavan (Van), 1934–, U.S. pianist.
Clinton, De Witt, 1769–1828, U.S. lawyer & statesman.
Clive, Robert (Baron Clive of Plassey), 1725–74, Brit. general in India.
Clough, Arthur Hugh, 1819–61, Eng. poet.
Clovis, I, 466?–511, Frankish king.
Clurman, Harold, 1901–80, U.S. director & drama critic.
Cobb, Irvin Shrewsbury, 1876–1944, U.S. journalist & humorist.
—**Lee J.,** 1911–76, U.S. actor.
—**Ty(rus Raymond),** 1886–1961, U.S. baseball player.
Cobbett, William, 1762–1835, Eng. political economist.
Cobden, William, 1804–65, Eng. statesman & economist.
Coca, Imogene, 1908–, U.S. comedienne & actress.
Cochise, ?–1874, Apache Am. Ind. chief.
Cochran, Jacqueline, 1912?–80, U.S. businesswoman & aviator.
Cockcroft, Sir John Douglas, 1897–1967, Eng. nuclear physicist.
Cocteau, Jean, 1891–1963, Fr. author & film director.
Cody, William Frederick, 1846–1917, U.S. plainsman, army scout & showman; known as **Buffalo Bill.**
Coe, Fred(erick), 1914–, U.S. television producer & stage & film director.
Coffin, Robert P(eter) Tristram, 1892–1955, U.S. poet & author.
Cohan, George M., 1878–1942, U.S. theatrical producer, actor & composer.
Cohn, Ferdinand Julius, 1828–98, Ger. botanist.
—**Harry,** 1891–1958, U.S. film executive.
Cohn-Bendit, Daniel, 1945–, Ger.-born anarchist & student leader: called **Danny the Red.**
Coke, Sir Edward, 1552–1634, Eng. jurist.
Colbert, Claudette, 1905–, Fr.-born U.S. actress.
—**Jean Baptiste,** 1619–83, Fr. statesman.
Cole, Nat "King", 1919–65, U.S. singer & pianist.
—**Thomas,** 1801–48, Eng.-born U.S. painter.
Coleman, Ornette, 1930–, U.S. jazz musician & composer.
Coleridge, Samuel Taylor, 1772–1834, Eng. poet.
Colet, John, 1466?–1519, Eng. theologian & scholar.
Colette, (Sidonie Gabrielle Claudine), 1873–1954, Fr. author.
Colgate, William, 1783–1857, U.S. businessman & philanthropist.
Collins, Michael, 1890–1922, Irish revolutionist.
—**(William) Wilkie,** 1824–89, Eng. author.
Colman, Ronald, 1891–1959, Eng. actor active in U.S.
Colt, Samuel, 1814–62, U.S. inventor & firearms manufacturer.
Coltrane, John, 1926–67, U.S. jazz musician & composer.
Colum, Padraic, 1881–1972, Irish poet & playwright.
Columbus, Christopher, 1446–1506, Ital. navigator; discovered America.
Comaneci, Nadia, 1962–, Romanian gymnast.
Commager, Henry Steele, 1902–, U.S. historian.
Commoner, Barry, 1917–, U.S. biologist & educator.
Como, Perry, 1913–, U.S. singer.
Compton, Arthur Holly, 1892–1962, U.S. physicist.
Compton-Burnett, Ivy, 1892–1969, Eng. author.
Comstock, Anthony, 1844–1915, U.S. social reformer.
Comte, Auguste, 1798–1857, Fr. philosopher.
Conant, James Bryant, 1893–1978, U.S. chemist & educator.
Condon, Eddie, 1905–73, U.S. jazz musician.
—**Edward U(hler),** 1902–74, U.S. physicist.
Condorcet, Marie Jean Antoine Nicolas de Caritat, Marquis de, 1743–94, Fr. philosopher, mathematician & politician.
Confucius, Latinized form of **Kung Fu-tse** 551–478 B.C., Chin. philosopher & teacher.
Congreve, William, 1670–1729, Eng. playwright.
Connelly, Marc(us Cook), 1890–, U.S. playwright.

Connolly, Cyril, 1903–74, Eng. critic & editor.
—Maureen, 1934–69, U.S. tennis player.
Connors, James Scott (Jimmy), 1952–, U.S. tennis player.
Conrad, Joseph, 1857–1924, Pol.-born Eng. author.
Constable, John, 1776–1837, Eng. painter.
Constantine I, ?–715, pope 708–715.
Constantine I, b. Flavius Valerius Aurelius, 272–337, first Christian emperor of Rome: call **the Great.**
Constantine II, 1940–, king of Greece 1964–67.
Cook, Barbara, 1927–, U.S. singer & actress.
—James, 1728–79, Eng. naval officer & explorer.
Cooke, (Alfred) Alistair, 1908–, Eng.-born U.S. author & journalist.
Cooley, Denton A., 1920–, U.S. surgeon.
Coolidge, (John) Calvin, 1872–1933, 30th U.S. president 1923–29.
Cooper, Gary, 1901–61, U.S. actor.
—Gladys, 1888–1971, Eng. actress.
—James Fenimore, 1789–1851, U.S. novelist.
—Peter, 1791–1883, U.S. manufacturer & philanthropist.
Copernicus, Nicholas, 1473–1543, Pol. astronomer.
Copland, Aaron, 1900–, U.S. composer.
Copley, John Singleton, 1738–1815, U.S. novelist.
Coppola, Francis Ford, 1939–, U.S. film director.
Coquelin, Benoît Constant, 1841–1909, Fr. actor.
Corbett, James J(ohn), 1866–1933, U.S. boxer.
Corbusier, Le, b. Charles Edouard Jeanneret, 1887–1965, Swiss architect active in France.
Corday, Charlotte, 1768–93, Fr. patriot; assassinated Marat.
Cordobés, El, b. Manuel Benitez Perez, 1936–, Sp. bullfighter.
Corelli, Arcangelo, 1653–1713, Ital. composer & violinist.
—Franco, 1924–, Ital. tenor.
Cori, Carl Ferdinand, 1896–, & his wife **Gerty Theresa (Radnitz),** 1896–1957, Czech-born U.S. biochemists.
Corio, Ann, 1914?–, U.S. stripteaser.
Corneille, Pierre, 1606–84, Fr. playwright.
Cornell, Ezra, 1807–74, U.S. financier & philanthropist.
—Katherine, 1898–1974, U.S. actress.
Cornwallis, Charles, Marquis, 1738–1805, Eng. general & statesman.
Coronado, Francisco Vasquez de, 1510?–54, Sp. explorer.
Corot, Jean Baptiste Camille, 1796–1875, Fr. painter.
Correggio, Antonio Allegri da, 1494–1534, Ital. painter.
Correll, Charles, 1890–1972, U.S. radio actor.
Cortes, Hernando, 1485–1547, Sp. conqueror of Mexico.
Cosby, Bill, 1937–, U.S. comedian & actor.
Costello, Lou, 1906–59, U.S. comedian & actor.
Cotton, John, 1584–1652, Eng.-born Puritan clergyman in America.
Coughlin, Charles Edward, 1891–1979, U.S. clergyman & political spokesman: called **Father Coughlin.**
Coulomb, Charles Augustin de, 1736–1806, Fr. physicist.
Couper, Archibald Scott, 1831–92, Scot. chemist.
Couperin, François, 1668–1733, Fr. composer.
Courbet, Gustave, 1819–77, Fr. painter.
Cournand, André Frédéric, 1895–, Fr.-born U.S. physiologist.
Courrèges, André, 1923–, Fr. fashion designer.
Court, Margaret Smith, 1942–, Austral. tennis player.
Cousin, Victor, 1792–1867, Fr. philosopher.
Cousins, Norman, 1912–, U.S. editor & author.
Cousteau, Jacques Yves, 1910–, Fr. naval officer, underwater explorer & filmmaker.
Cousy, Robert Joseph (Bob), 1928–, U.S. basketball player & coach.
Coverdale, Miles, 1488–1568, Eng. translator of the Bible.
Coward, Sir Noel, 1899–1973, Eng. playwright, composer & actor.
Cowell, Henry (Dixon), 1897–1965, U.S. composer.
Cowl, Jane, 1884–1950, U.S. actress.
Cowles, Gardner, 1903–, U.S publisher.

Cowley, Abraham, 1618–67, Eng. poet.
—Malcolm, 1898–, U.S. critic.
Cowper, William, 1731–1800, Eng. poet.
Cozzens, James Gould, 1903–78, U.S. author.
Crabbe, George, 1754–1832, Eng. poet.
—Larry ("Buster"), 1909–, U.S. swimmer & actor.
Craig, (Edward) Gordon, 1872–1966, Eng. director & stage designer.
Craigavon, James Craig, 1st Viscount, 1871–1940, Irish statesman; first prime minister of N. Ireland, 1921–40.
Craigie, Sir William Alexander, 1867–1957, Scot. philologist & lexicographer.
Cram, Ralph Adams, 1863–1942, U.S. architect & author.
Cranach, Lucas, 1472–1553, Ger. painter & engraver.
—Lucas, 1515–86, Ger. portrait painter; son of prec.: called **the Younger.**
Crane, (Harold) Hart, 1899–1932, U.S. poet.
—Stephen, 1871–1900, U.S. author & poet.
Cranko, John, 1928–73, South African-born choreographer & ballet-company director active in W. Germany.
Cranmer, Thomas, 1489–1556, archbishop of Canterbury; burned at the stake.
Crashaw, Richard, 1613–49, Eng. poet.
Crassus, Marcus Licinius, 115?–53 B.C., Roman politician.
Crater, Joseph Force, 1889–1937?, U.S. jurist.
Crawford, Cheryl, 1902–, U.S. theatrical producer.
—Joan, 1908–77, U.S. actress.
Crazy Horse, b. Tashunca-Utico, 1849?–77, Sioux Am. Ind. chief.
Crespin, Régine, 1927–, Fr. soprano.
Crèvecoeur, Michel Guillaume St. Jean de, 1735–1813 Fr.-born author active in America.
Crichton, James, 1560?–82, Scot. scholar & adventurer: called **the Admirable Crichton.**
Crick, Francis, 1916–, Eng. geneticist.
Cripps, Sir (Richard) Stafford, 1889–1952, Eng. lawyer & socialist statesman.
Croce, Benedetto, 1866–1952, Ital. philospher, statesman, critic & historian.
Crockett, David (Davy), 1786–1836, U.S. frontiersman & congressman.
Croesus, 6th c. B.C. Lydian king famed for great wealth.
Cromwell, Oliver, 1599–1658, Eng. general & statesman.
—Richard, 1626–1712, Eng. general & statesman; son of prec.
Cronin, A(rchibald) J(oseph), 1896–1981, Eng. physician & author.
Cronkite, Walter (Leland, Jr.), 1916–, U.S. journalist & TV news commentator.
Cronyn, Hume, 1911–, Can.-born U.S. actor.
Crookes, Sir William, 1832–1919, Eng. physicist.
Crosby, Harry Lillis ("Bing"), 1904–77, U.S. singer & actor.
Crouse, Russel, 1893–1966, U.S. journalist & playwright.
Cruikshank, George, 1792–1878, Eng. illustrator & caricaturist.
Cukor, George, 1899–, U.S. film director.
Culbertson, Ely, 1893–1955, Rumanian-born U.S. expert on the game of bridge.
Cummings, E(dward) E(stlin), 1894–1962, U.S. poet: usu. known as **e. e. cummings.**
Cunard, Sir Samuel, 1787–1865, Can. steamship executive.
Cunha, Tristão da, 1460?–1540, Portuguese navigator & explorer.
Cunningham, Merce, 1922–, U.S. choreographer.
Curie, Marie, b. Marja Sklodowska, 1867–1934, Pol.-born Fr. physicist & chemist.
—Pierre, 1859–1906, Fr. physicist; husband of prec.
Curley, James Michael, 1874–1958, U.S. politician.
Currier & Ives A U.S. firm of lithographers established 1835 by **Nathaniel Currier,** 1838–88; later joined by **James Merritt Ives,** 1824–95.
Curry, John Steuart, 1897–1946, U.S. painter.
Curtis, Cyrus H. K., 1850–1933, U.S. publisher & philanthropist.

Curtiss, Glenn Hammond, 1878–1930, U.S. aviator & inventor.

Curtiz, Michael, 1888–1962, Hung.-born U.S. film director.

Cushing, Harvey, 1869–1939, U.S. surgeon & author.

Cushman, Charlotte Saunders, 1816–76, U.S. actress

Custer, George Armstrong, 1839–76, U.S. general.

Cuvier, Baron Georges Léopold, 1769–1832, Fr. naturalist.

Cynewulf, 8th c. Anglo-Saxon poet.

Cyril, Saint, 827–869, Gk. missionary & apostle to the Slavs.

Cyrus, ?–529 B.C., king of Persia 550–529 B.C.; founder of the Persian Empire: called **the Great.**

Czerny, Karl, 1791–1857, Austrian composer & pianst.

de Gama, Vasco, 1469?–1524, Pg. navigator.

Daguerre, Louis Jacques Mandé, 1787–1851, Fr. inventor.

Daladier, Édouard, 1884–1970, Fr. statesman.

Daley, Richard Joseph, 1902–76, U.S. politician; mayor of Chicago 1955–76.

Dali, Salvador, 1904–, Sp.-born painter active in U.S.

Dallapicola, Luigi, 1904–75, Ital. pianist & composer.

Dalton, John, 1766–1844, Eng. chemist & physicist.

—**Robert,** 1867–92, U.S. outlaw.

Daly, (John) Augustin, 1838–99, U.S. playwright & theater manager.

D'Amboise, Jacques, 1934–, U.S. ballet dancer & choreographer.

Damien de Veuster, Joseph, 1840–89, Belg. missionary to lepers in Hawaiian Islands: called **Father Damien.**

Damrosch, Walter Johannes, 1862–1950, Ger.-born U.S. conductor.

Dana, Charles Anderson, 1819–97, U.S. newspaper editor.

—**Richard Henry,** 1815–82, U.S. lawyer & author.

Dane, Clemence, pseud. of Winifred Ashton, 1888–1965, Eng. author.

Daniel, Samuel, 1562?–1619 Eng. poet.

Danilova, Alexandra, 1906–, Russ-born ballerina active in U.S.

D'Annunzio, Gabriele, 1863–1938, Ital. author & adventurer.

Dante Alighieri, 1265–1321, Ital. poet.

Danton, Georges Jacques, 1759–94, Fr. revolutionary leader.

Da Ponte, Lorenzo, 1749–1838, Ital. librettist.

Dare, Virginia, 1587 –?, first child born in America of Eng. parents.

Darius I, 558?–486 B.C., king of Persia 521–486 B.C.: called **the Great.**

Darnley, Henry Stewart, Lord, 1545–67, Scot. nobleman: second husband of Mary, Queen of Scots; assassinated.

Darrow, Clarence Seward, 1857–1938, U.S. lawyer.

Darwin, Charles Robert, 1809–82, Eng. naturalist; founder of evolutionary theory of natural selection.

—**Erasmus,** 1731–1802, Eng. physiologist & poet; grandfather of prec.

Daubigny, Charles Francois, 1817–78, Fr. painter.

Daudet, Alphonse, 1840–97, Fr. author.

—**Léon,** 1867–1942, Fr. journalist & author; son of prec.

Daumier, Honoré, 1808–79, Fr. painer & caricaturist.

David, Gerard, 1450?–1523, Du. painter.

—**Jacques Louis,** 1748–1825, Fr. painter.

Davidson, Jo, 1883–1952, U.S. sculptor.

Davis, Adelle, 1904–74, U.S. nutritionist & author.

—**Benjamin Oliver, Jr.** 1912–, U.S. general.

—**Elmer Holmes** 1890–1958, U.S. radio news commentator.

—**Jefferson,** 1808–89, U.S. statesman; president of the Confederacy 1862–65.

—**Miles,** 1927–, U.S. jazz musician.

—**Richard Harding,** 1864–1916, U.S. war correspondent & author.

—**Ruth Elizabeth (Bette),** 1908–, U.S. actress.

—**Sammy, Jr.,** 1925–, U.S. singer & actor.

—**Stuart,** 1894–1964, U.S. painter.

Davy, Sir Humphrey, 1778–1829, Eng. chemist.

Day, Clarence Sheperd, 1874–1935, U.S. author.

—**Dorthoy,** 1897–1980, U.S. journalist & social reformer.

Dayan, Moshe, 1915–81, Israeli soldier & statesman.

Day-Lewis, C(ecil), 1904–72, Irish-born Brit. poet & author.

Dean, Jay Hanna ("Dizzy"), 1911–74, U.S. baseball player

DeBakey, Michael Ellis, 1908–, U.S. surgeon.

De Broca, Philippe, 1935–, Fr. film director.

de Broglie, Louis Victor, Prince, 1892–, Fr. physicist.

Debs, Eugene V(ictor), 1855–1926, U.S. labor leader & socialist.

Debussy, Claude Achille, 1862–1918, Fr. composer.

Debye, Peter J(oseph) W(illiam), 1884–1966, Du.-born U.S. physicist & chemist.

Decatur, Stephen, 1779–1820, U.S. naval officer.

Dee, Ruby, 1923?-, U.S. actress.

Deere, John, 1804–86, U.S. inventor.

Defoe, Daniel, 1661?–1731, Eng. author.

De Forest, Lee, 1873–1961, U.S. inventor.

Degas, (Hilaire Germain) Edgar, 1834–1917, Fr. painter & sculptor.

De Gasperi, Alcide, 1881–1954, Ital. statesman; premier of Italy 1945–53.

de Gaulle, Charles (Andrè Joseph Marie), 1890–1970, Fr. general & statesman; president of France 1945–46 & 1959–69.

De Geer, Charles, 1720–78, Swed. entomologist.

de Ghelderode, Michel, 1898–1962, Belg. playwright.

de Havilland, Oliva, 1916–, U.S. actress born in Japan.

De Kalb, Johann, 1721–80, Ger. soldier; served in Amer. revolutionary army.

Dekker, Thomas, 1572?–1632?, Eng. playwright.

de Koonig, Willem, 1904–, Du. born U.S. painter.

De Kruif, Paul, 1890–1971, U.S. bacteriologist & author.

Delacroix, (Ferdinand Victor) Eugène, 1799–1863, Fr. painter.

de la Mare, Walter, 1873–1956, Eng. poet & author.

Delaunay, Robert, 1885–1951, Fr. painter.

De La Warr, Thomas West, Lord, 1577–1618, Eng. colonial administrator in America.

Delbrück, Max, 1906–81, Ger.- born U.S. molecular geneticist.

Delibes, (Clement Philibert) Lèo, 1836–91, Fr. composer.

Delius, Frederick, 1862–1934, Eng. composer.

Dellinger, John Howard, 1886–1962, U.S. radio engineer.

Dello Joio, Norman, 1913–, U.S. composer.

Del Monaco, Mario, 1915–, Ital. tenor.

Delmonico, Lorenzo, 1813–81, Swiss-born U.S. restaurateur.

De Los Angeles, Victoria, 1923–, Sp. soprano.

Del Rio, Dolores, 1905–, Mexican-born U.S. actress.

De Mille, Agnes George, 1908–, U.S. dancer & choreographer.

—**Cecil B(lount),** 1881–1959, U.S. film director; uncle of prec.

Democritus, 460?–352? B.C., Gk. philospher.

Demosthenes, 384?–322 B.C., Athenian orator & patriot.

Dempsey, William Harrison ("Jack"), 1895–, U.S. boxer.

Demuth, Charles, 1883–1935, U.S. painter.

Deng Xiaoping, 1904–, Chin. statesman; vice-premier Chin. Communist Party 1977–.

Denis, Saint, 3rd c, first bishop of Paris & patron saint of France.

De Quincey, Thomas, 1785–1859, Eng. author.

Derain, André, 1880–1954, Fr. painter.

Desai, Morarji, 1896–, Indian political leader; prime minister of India 1977–.

Descarters, René, 1596–1650, Fr. mathematician & philosopher.

de Seversky, Alexander Prokofieff, 1894–1974, Russ.-born U.S. aeronautical engineer.

De Sica, Vittorio, 1902–74, Ital. film director, and actor.

Desmoulins, Camille, 1760–94, Fr. revolutionist.

De Soto, Hernando, 1499?–1542, Sp. explorer.

Des Prez, Josquin, 1450?–1521, Du. composer.

Dessalines, Jean Jacques, 1758?–1806, Haitian military leader; emperor of Haiti as Jacques I.

De Valera, Éamon, 1882–1975, U.S.-born Irish statesman; president of Ireland 1959–73.

de Valois, Dame Ninette, 1898–, Irish-born ballerina, teacher & impressario active in England.

De Voto, Bernard Augustine, 1897–1955, U.S. author.

de Vries, Hugo, 1848–1935, Dutch botanist.

De Vries, Peter, 1910–, U.S. author.

Dewey, George, 1837–1917, U.S. admiral.

—John, 1859–1952, U.S. philosopher, psychologist & educator.

—Melvil, 1851–1931, U.S. librarian.

—Thomas E(dmund), 1902–71, U.S. lawyer & politician.

Diaghilev, Sergei Pavlovich, 1872–1929, Russ. ballet producer active in Paris.

Diamond, John Thomas ("Legs"), 1898–1931, U.S. criminal.

Dias, Bartholomeu, 1450?–1500, Pg. navigator.

Diaz, Porfirio, 1830–1915, Mexican general & statesman; president of Mexico 1884–1911.

Dickens, Charles, 1812–70, Eng. author.

Dickey, James, 1923–, U.S. poet & author.

Dickinson, Emily (Elizabeth), 1830–86, U.S. poet.

Diderot, Denis 1713–84, Fr. critic & encyclopedist.

Diem, Ngo Dinh, 1901–63, first president of S. Vietnam 1955–63; assassinated.

Dies, Martin, 1901–72, U.S. politician.

Diesel, Rudolf, 1858–1913, Ger. mechanical engineer & inventor.

Dietrich, Marlene, 1901–, Ger.-born film actress active in U.S.

Dietz, Howard, 1896–, U.S. lyricist & film executive.

Dillard, Harrison, 1923–, U.S. track runner.

Dillinger, John, 1903–34, U.S. criminal.

Dillon, C(larence) Douglas, 1909–78, U.S. government official.

DiMaggio, Joseph Paul (Joe), 1914–, U.S. baseball player.

Dinesen, Isak, pseud. of Baroness Karen Blixen-Finecke, 1885–1962, Dan. writer.

Diocletian (L. Gaius Aurelius Valerius Diocletianus), 245–313, Roman emperor.

Diogenes, 412?–323? B.C., Gk. philosopher.

Dionysius the Areopagite, Saint, 1st c. A.D. GK. mystic & theologian.

Dior, Christian, 1905–57, Fr. fashion designer.

Dioscorides, Pedanius, 1st c. A.D. Gk. physician & botanist.

Dirac, Paul Adrien Maurice, 1902–, Eng. mathematician & physicist.

Dirksen, Everett McKinley, 1896–1969, U.S. politician.

Disney, Walt(er Elias), 1901–66, U.S. producer of animated & live films.

Disraeli, Benjamin, 1804–81, Eng. statesman & author.

Di Stefano, Giuseppe, 1921–, Ital. tenor.

Dix, Dorothea Lynde, 1802–87, U.S. social reformer.

—Dorothy, pseud. of Elizabeth Meriwether Gilmer, 1870–1951, U.S. journalist.

Dixon, Jeremiah, ?–1777, Eng. astronomer & surveyor; with Charles Mason, established the Mason-Dixon line.

Djilas, Milovan, 1911–, Yugoslav author.

Dobrynin, Anatoly, 1919–, Soviet diplomat.

Dobzhansky, Theodosius, 1900–75, Russ.-born U.S. geneticist.

Dodd, Frank Howard, 1844–1916, U.S. publisher.

Dodgson, Charles Lutwidge See CARROLL, LEWIS.

Dohnányi, Ernst von, 1877–1960, Hung. composer.

Dolin, Anton, 1904–, Eng. ballet dancer & choreographer.

Dollfuss, Engelbert, 1892–1934, Austrian statesman; chancellor of Austria 1932–34; assassinated.

Dolly, Jenny, 1892–1941, & her sister Rosie, 1892–1970, Hung.-born vaudeville performers active in U.S.

Domenichino, Il, b. Domenico Zampieri, 1581–1641, Ital. painter.

Dominguín, Luis Miguel, 1926–, Sp. bullfighter.

Dominic, Saint, 1170–1221, Sp. friar; founded the Dominican Order.

Donat, Robert, 1905–59, Eng. actor.

Donatello, b. Donato di Niccolò di Betto Bardi, 1386–1466, Ital. sculptor.

Donen, Stanley, 1924–, U.S. film director & producer.

Dönitz, Karl, 1891–, Ger. admiral.

Donizetti, Gaetano, 1797–1848, Ital. composer.

Donne, John, 1573?–1631, Eng. poet & clergyman.

Donovan, William Joseph ("Wild Bill"), 1883–1959, U.S. lawyer & military intelligence officer.

Dooley, Thomas Anthony, 1927–61, U.S. physician in Indochina.

Doolittle, Hilda ("H.D."), 1886–1961, U.S. poet. active in Europe.

—James Harold, 1896–, U.S. aviator & Air Force general.

Doppler, Christian Johann, 1803–53, Austrian physicist & mathematician.

Dorati, Antal, 1906–, Hung.-born U.S. conductor.

Doré, (Paul) Gustave, 1833–83, Fr. painter & engraver.

Dorsey, James Francis (Jimmy), 1904–57, U.S. clarinetist & band leader.

—Thomas Francis (Tommy), 1905–56, U.S. trombonist & band leader; brother of prec.

Dos Passos, John, 1896–1970, U.S. author.

Dostoevski, Feodor Mikhailovich, 1821–81, Russ. author.

Dou, Gerard, 1613–75, Du. painter.

Doubleday, Abner, 1819–93, U.S. military officer; reputed inventor of baseball.

—Frank Nelson, 1862–1934, U.S. publisher.

Douglas, Helen Gahagan, 1900–, U.S. actress, author & politician.

—Kirk, 1918–, U.S. actor.

—Melvyn, 1901–1981, U.S. actor; husband of Helen Gahagan.

—Norman, 1868–1952, Eng. author.

Stephen (Arnold), 1813–61, U.S. senator; opposed Lincoln in campaign debates.

—William O(rville), 1898–1980, U.S. jurist, justice of the U.S. Supreme Court 1939–75.

Douglass, Frederick, 1817–95, U.S. Negro leader & statesman.

Dove, Arthur Garfield, 1880–1946, U.S. painter.

Dow, Charles Henry, 1851–1902, U.S. economist & editor.

Dowland, John, 1563–1626, Eng. musician & composer.

Downes, (Edwin) Olin, 1886–1955, U.S. music critic.

Downing, Andrew Jackson, 1815–52, U.S. architect & landscape designer.

Doxiadis, Constantinos Apostolos, 1913–, Gk. architect & urban planner.

Doyle, Sir Arthur Conan, 1859–1930, Eng. physician & author; creator of Sherlock Holmes.

D'Oyly Carte, Richard, 1844–1901, Eng. operatic producer.

Draco, 7th c. B.C. Gk. lawgiver & statesman.

Drake, Alfred, 1914–, U.S. singer & actor.

—Edwin L(aurentine), 1819–80, U.S. military officer & petroleum entrepreneur.

—Sir Francis, 1540–96 , Eng. admiral & circumnavigator of the globe.

Draper, Henry, 1837–82, U.S. astronomer.

—Ruth, 1884–1956, U.S. monologuist.

Drayton, Michael, 1563–1631, Eng. poet.

Dreiser, Theodore, 1871–1945, U.S. author.

Dreisser, Samuel P., 1933–, U.S. chemist.

Dressler, Marie, 1869–1934, U.S. actress & comedienne.

Drew, John, 1826–62, Irish-born U.S. actor, & his son John, 1853–1927, U.S. actor.

Dreyer, Carl Theodore, 1889–1968, Dan. film director.

Dreyfus, Alfred, 1859–1935, Fr. army officer.

Driesch, Hans Adolf Eduard, 1867–1941, Ger. biologist & philosopher.

Dryden, John, 1631–1700, Eng. poet & playwright.

du Barry, Comtesse Marie Jeanne, 1746–93, mistress of Louis XV.

Dubček, Alexander, 1921–, Czech politician; first secretary of the Communist party of Czechoslovakia 1968–69.

Dubinsky, David, 1892–, Russ.-born U.S. labor leader.

Dubois, W(illiam) E(dward) B(urghardt), 1868–1963, U.S. historian, Negro leader & educator.

Du Bois-Reymond, Emil, 1818–96, Ger. physiologist.

Dubos, René, 1906–1982, Fr. biologist.

Dubuffet, Jean, 1901–, Fr. painter & sculptor.

Duccio (di Buoninsegna), 1255?–1319, Ital. painter.

Duchamp, Marcel, 1887–1968, Fr. painter.

Duchin, Edwin Frank (Eddy), 1909–51, U.S. pianist & band leader.

Dufy, Raoul, 1877–1953, Fr. painter.

Dujardin, Felix, 1801–60, Fr. biologist.

Duke, Benjamin Newton, 1855–1929, & his brother **James Buchanan Duke,** 1856–1925, U.S. tobacco industrialists.

—**Vernon,** 1903–, Russ.-born composer active in U.S.

Dulles, Allen (Welsh), 1893–1969, U.S. government official.

—**John Foster,** 1888–1959, U.S. statesman; secretary of state 1953–59; brother of prec.

Dumas, Alexandre (père), 1803–70, Fr. author & playwright.

—**Alexandre (fils),** 1824–95, Fr. author & playwright; son of prec.

Du Maurier, Daphne, 1907–, Eng. author.

—**George Louis,** 1834–96, Fr.-born Eng. author & illustrator, grandfather of prec.

Dunant, Jean Henri, 1828–1910, Swiss philanthropist & founder of the Red Cross.

Dunbar, Paul Laurence, 1872–1906, U.S. poet.

Duncan, David Douglas, 1916–, U.S. photographer & author.

—**Isadora,** 1878–1927, U.S. dancer.

Dunham, Katherine, 1910–, U.S. dancer & choreographer.

Dunne, Irene, 1904–, U.S. actress.

Dunois, Comte Jean de, 1403?–68, Fr. general & companion of Joan of Arc; called the **Bastard of Orleans.**

Dunsany, Edward John Plunkett, Lord, 1878–1957, Irish poet & playwright.

Duns Scotus, Johannes, 1265–1308, Scot. monk & philosopher.

du Pont, E(leuthère) I(rénée), 1771–1834, Fr.-born U.S. industrialist.

Dupré, Marcel, 1886–1971, Fr. organist.

Durant, Will(iam James), 1885–1981, U.S. historian, & his wife **Ariel,** b. Ida Kaufman, 1898–1981, Russ.-born U.S. historian.

Durante, James Francis (Jimmy), 1893–1980, U.S. comedian & actor.

Duras, Marguerite, 1914–, Fr. author.

Durbin, Deanna, 1922–, Can.-born U.S. actress.

Dürer, Albrecht, 1471–1528, Ger. painter & engraver.

Durkheim, Émile, 1858–1917, Fr. sociologist.

Durocher, Leo Ernest, 1906–, U.S. baseball player & manager.

Durrell, Gerald Malcolm, 1925–, Eng. zoologist & author.

—**Lawrence George,** 1912–, Eng. author & poet; brother of prec.

Durrenmatt, Friedrich, 1921–, Swiss playwright.

Duse, Eleanora, 1859–1924, Ital. actress.

Dutrochet, René, 1776–1847, Fr. biologist.

Dutton, Edward, 1831–1923, U.S. publisher.

Duvalier, Francois ("Papa Doc"), 1907–71, Haitian president 1957–71.

—**Jean-Claude,** 1951–, president of Haiti 1971–; son of prec.

Duvivier, Julien, 1896–1967, Fr. film director.

Dvořák, Antonin, 1841–1904, Czech composer.

Dylan, Bob, 1941–, U.S. composer & singer.

Eads, James Buchanan, 1820–87, U.S. inventor.

Eagels, Jeanne, 1894–1929, U.S. actress.

Eakins, Thomas, 1844–1916, U.S. painter & sculptor.

Eames, Charles, 1907–78, U.S. designer & film director.

Earhart, Amelia, 1898–1937, U.S. aviator.

Early, Jubal Anderson, 1816–94, U.S. Confederate general.

Earp, Wyatt, 1848–1929, U.S. frontier marshal.

Eastman, George, 1854–1932, U.S. inventor & industrialist.

—**Max (Forrester),** 1883–1969, U.S. editor & author.

Eaton, Cyrus Stephen, 1883–1979, U.S. financier.

Eban, Abba, 1915–, South African-born Israeli diplomat.

Ebbinghaus, Hermann, 1850–1909, Ger. experimental psychologist.

Eberhart, Richard, 1904–, U.S. poet.

Echeverría Alvarez, Luis, 1922–, president of Mexico 1970–76.

Eck, Johann, 1486–1543, Ger. theologian.

Eckhart, Johannes, 1260?–1327?, Ger. theologian & mystic: known as **Meister Eckhart.**

Eddington, Sir Arthur Stanley, 1884–1944, Eng. astronomer & astrophysicist.

Eddy, Mary Baker, 1821–1910, U.S. religious leader; founder of the Christian Science Church.

—**Nelson,** 1901–67, singer & actor.

Edelman, Gerald Maurice, 1919–, U.S. biochemist.

Eden, Sir (Robert) Anthony, 1897–1977, Eng. statesman; prime minister 1955–1957.

Ederle, Gertrude, 1907–, U.S. swimmer.

Edison, Thomas Alva, 1847–1931, U.S. inventor.

Edward, 1004?–66, king of England 1042–66: called **the Confessor.**

—**VII,** 1841–1910, king of Great Britain 1901–10.

—**VII,** 1894–1972, king of Great Britain 1936; abdicated; known as **Duke of Windsor** after abdication.

Edwards, Jonathan, 1703–58, Amer. theologian.

—**Ralph,** 1913–, U.S. TV personality.

Egbert, 775?–839, first king of all England 829–839.

Eglevsky, André, 1917–77, Russ.-born U.S. ballet dancer.

Ehrenberg, Christian G., 1795–1876, Ger. naturalist.

Ehrenburg, Ilya Grigorievich, 1891–1967, Soviet author.

Ehrlich, Paul, 1854–1915, Ger. bacteriologist.

—**Paul Ralph,** 1932–, U.S. biologist & author.

Eichmann, Adolf, 1906–62, Ger. Nazi official.

Eiffel, (Alexandre) Gustave, 1832–1923, Fr. engineer.

Eijkman, Christian, 1858–1930, Du. physician.

Einstein, Albert, 1878–1955, Ger.-born U.S. physicist.

—**Alfred,** 1880–1952, Ger.-born U.S. music critic.

Einthoven, Willem, 1860–1927, Du. physiologist.

Eiseley, Loren (Corey), 1907–77, U.S. anthropologist & author.

Eisenhower, Dwight D(avid), 1890–1969, U.S. general & 34th president 1953–61.

Eisenstaedt, Alfred, 1898–, Ger.-born photographer & author active in U.S.

Eisenstein, Sergei Mikhailovich, 1898–1948, Russ.-born Soviet film director & producer.

Eleanor of Aquitaine, 1122–1204, queen of France as the wife of Louis VII & queen of England as the wife of Henry II.

Elgar, Sir Edward, 1857–1934, Eng. composer.

Eliot, Charles William, 1834–1926, U.S. educator.

—**George,** pseud. of Mary Ann Evans, 1819–80, Eng. author.

—**John,** 1604–90, Amer. clergyman & missionary to Indians.

—**T(homas) S(tearns),** 1888–1965, U.S. born Brit. poet, playwright & critic.

Elizabeth I, 1533–1603, queen of England 1558–1603.

—**II,** 1926–, queen of Great Britain 1952–.

—**(Angela Marguerite Bowes-Lyon),** 1900–, queen of George VI of Great Britain & mother of Elizabeth II.

Ellington, Edward Kennedy ("Duke"), 1899–1974, U.S. jazz composer, pianist & band leader.

Elliott, Maxine, 1871–1940, U.S. actress.

—**Robert (Bob),** 1923–, U.S. comedian.

Ellis, (Henry) Havelock, 1859–1939, Eng. psychologist & author.

Ellison, Ralph, 1914–, U.S. author.

Ellsworth, Lincoln, 1880–1951, U.S. polar explorer.

Elman, Mischa, 1891–1967, Russ.-born U.S. violinist.

Elssler, Fanny, 1810–84, Austrian dancer.

Elyot, Sir Thomas, 1490?–1546, Eng. scholar & diplomat.

Elzevir, A family of Dutch printers including, **Louis,** 1540?–1617; his son, **Bonaventure,** 1583–1652; and his grandson **Abraham,** 1592?–1652.

Emerson, Ralph Waldo, 1803–82, U.S. author, poet & philosopher.

Emmet, Robert, 1778–1803, Irish nationalist & revolutionary.

Emmett, Daniel Decatur, 1815–1904, U.S. songwriter.

Endecott, John, 1589?–1665, Eng.-born Amer. colonist; first governor of Massachusetts Bay colony.

Enders, John Franklin, 1897–, U.S. bacteriologist.

Enesco, Georges, 1881–1955, Rumanian composer.

Engels, Friedrich, 1820–95, Ger. socialist & author.

Ensor, James, 1860–1949, Belg. painter & printmaker.

Epictetus, 50?–138? A.D., Gk. philosopher.

Epicurus, 341?–270 B.C., Gk. philosopher.

Epstein, Sir Jacob, 1880–1959, U.S.-born Brit. Sculptor.

Erasistratus, 304–250 B.C., Gk. physician & anatomist.

Erasmus, Desiderius, b. Gerhard Gerhards, 1466?–1536, Du. scholar & theologian.

Eratosthenes, 3rd c. B.C. Gk. mathematician & astronomer.

Erhard, Ludwig, 1897–1977 , chancellor of W. Germany 1963–66.

Ericsson, John, 1803–89, Swed.-born U.S. engineer & inventor.

—**Leif,** 11th c. Norw. explorer; son of Eric the Red.

Eric the Red, 10th c. Norw. explorer.

Erigena, Johannes Scotus, 815?–877?., Irish philosopher & theologian.

Erikson, Erik H(omburger), 1902–, Ger.-born U.S. psychologist & author.

Erlander, Tage Frithiof, 1901–, premier of Sweden 1946–69.

Erlanger, Joseph, 1874–1965, U.S. physiologist.

Ernst, Max, 1891–1976, Ger. painter active in France & U.S.

Ervin, Sam(uel) J., Jr., 1896–, U.S. politician.

Ervine, St. John (Greer), 1883–1971, Irish playwright & author.

Erving, Julius, 1950–, U.S. basketball player: called **Doctor J.**

Escoffier, Auguste, 1847–1935, Fr. chef & author.

Eshkol, Levi, 1895–1969, Russ.-born Israeli statesman; prime minister of Israel 1963–69.

Esposito, Phil(ip Anthony), 1942–, Can.-born hockey player.

Essex, Robert Devereux, 2nd Earl of, 1566–1601, Eng. courtier & soldier: beheaded.

Esterhazy, Marie Charles Ferdinand Walsin, 1847–1923, Fr. army officer.

Esterházy, Miklós József, 1714–90, Hung. prince & art patron.

Ethelred II, 968?–1016, king of England 978–1016: called **the Unready.**

Euclid, 450?–374 B.C., Gk. mathematician.

Eugénie (Marie de Montijo de Guzmán), 1826–1920, Sp.-born empress of France as wife of Napoleon III.

Euler, Leonhard, 1707–83, Swiss mathematician.

Euripides, 479? –406? B.C., Gk. playwright.

Eustachio, Bartolommeo, 1524?–74, Ital. anatomist.

Evans, Sir Arthur John, 1851–1941, Eng. archaeologist.

—**Bergen,** 1904–78, U.S. author & educator.

—**Dame Edith,** 1888–1976, Eng. actress.

—**Gil,** 1912–, Can.-born U.S. jazz musician.

—**Maurice,** 1901–, Eng.-born U.S. actor.

—**Rowland, Jr.,** 1921–, U.S. journalist.

—**Walker,** 1903–75, U.S. photographer.

—**William J. (Bill),** 1929–80, U.S. jazz pianist & composer.

Evelyn, John 1620–1706, Eng. diarist.

Everett, Edward, 1794–1865, U.S. clergyman, orator & statesman.

Evers, (James) Charles, 1922–, U.S. politician & civil rights activist.

—**Medgar (Wiley),** 1925–63, U.S. civil rights activist; murdered; brother of prec.

Evert, Chris(tine Marie), 1954–, U.S. tennis player.

Ewing, William Maurice, 1906–74, U.S. geologist.

Eysenck, Hans, 1916–, Eng. psychologist.

Faber, John Eberhard, 1822–79, Ger.-born U.S. industrialist.

Fabiola, 1928–, Sp.-born queen of King Baudouin of Belgium.

Fabius (Quintus Fabius Maximus Verrucosus Cunctator), ?–203 B.C., Roman general.

Fabre, Jean Henri, 1823–1915, Fr. entomologist.

Fabricius ab Aquapendente, Hieronymus, 1537–1619, Ital. surgeon & anatomist.

Fadiman, Clifton, 1904–, U.S. author & editor.

Fahrenheit, Gabriel Daniel, 1686–1736, Ger. physicist.

Fairbanks, Douglas, 1883–1939, U.S. actor.

—**Douglas, Jr.,** 1909–, U.S. actor; son of prec.

Faisal ibn Abdul Aziz, 1904?–75, king of Saudi Arabia 1964–75; assassinated.

Falla, Manuel de, 1876–1946, Sp. composer.

Fälldin, Thorbjörn, 1926–, Swed. politician; prime minister of Sweden 1976–.

Fallopius, Gabriel, 1523–62, Ital. anatomist.

Faneuil, Peter, 1700–43, Amer. merchant.

Fanfani, Amintore, 1908–, premier of Italy 1958–59 & 1960–62.

Faraday, Michael, 1791–1867, Eng. physicist.

Fargo, William George, 1818–81, U.S. transportation entrepreneur.

Farley, James Aloysius, 1888–1976, U.S. politician.

Farmer, Fannie Merritt, 1857–1915, U.S. culinary expert, teacher & author.

—**James Leonard,** 1920–, U.S. Negro civil rights leader.

Farouk I, 1920–65, king of Egypt 1936–52.

Farquhar, George, 1678–1707, Eng. playwright.

Farragut, David Glasgow, 1801–70, U.S. admiral.

Farrar, Geraldine, 1882–1967, U.S. soprano.

Farrell, Eileen, 1920–, U.S. soprano.

—**James T(homas),** 1904–79, U.S. author.

—**Suzanne,** 1945–, U.S. ballerina.

Fatima, 606?–632?, daughter of Mohammed.

Fauchard, Pierre, 1678–1761, Fr. dentist; founder of modern dentistry.

Faulkner, William, 1897–1962, U.S. author.

Fauré, Gabriel Urbain, 1845–1924, Fr. composer.

Fawkes, Guy, 1570–1606, Eng. conspirator; participant in the Gunpowder Plot.

Fay, Frank, 1897–1961, U.S. actor.

Faye, Alice, 1915–, U.S. actress.

Feiffer, Jules, 1929–, U.S. cartoonist & author.

Feininger, Andreas, 1906–, Fr.-born U.S. photographer.

—**Lyonel (Charles Adrian),** 1871–1956, U.S. painter; father of prec.

Feller, Robert William Andrew (Bob), 1918–, U.S. baseball player.

Fellini, Federico, 1920–, Ital. film director.

Fénelon, François de Salignac de la Mothe-, 1651–1715, Fr. prelate & author.

Fenollosa, Ernest Francisco, 1853–1908, U.S. oriental scholar & author.

Ferber, Edna, 1887–1968, U.S. author.

Ferdinand V of Castile (and II of Aragon), 1452–1516, first king of united Spain 1474–1516; ruled jointly with his wife Isabella.

Fermat, Pierre de, 1606–65, Fr. mathematician.

Fermi; Enrico, 1901–54, Ital. physicist active in U.S.

Fernandel, b. Fernand Contandin, 1903–71, Fr. actor.

Ferrier, Sir David, 1843–1928, Scot. neurologist.

—**Kathleen,** 1912–53, Eng. contralto.

Fessenden, Reginald Aubrey, 1866–1932, Can-born U.S. physicist & inventor.

Feuerbach, Ludwig Andreas, 1804–72, Ger. philosopher.

Feuermann, Emanuel, 1902–42, Pol.-born cellist active in U.S.

Feydeau, Georges, 1862–1921, Fr. playwright.

Fichte, Johann Gottlieb, 1762–1814, Ger. philosopher.

Fiedler, Arthur, 1894–, U.S. conductor.

—**Leslie,** 1917–, U.S. author & critic.

Field, Cyrus West, 1819–92, U.S. industrialist.

—**Eugene,** 1850–95, U.S. poet & journalist.

—**Marshall,** 1834–1906, U.S. businessman.

Fielding, Henry, 1707–54, Eng. author.

Fields, Dorothy, 1905–, U.S. lyricist.
—**Gracie,** 1898–1979, Eng. singer & actress.
—**W.C.,** 1879–1946, U.S. film comedian.
Filene, Edward Albert, 1860–1937, U.S. businessman & social reformer.
Fillmore, Millard, 1800–74, 13th U.S. president 1850–53.
Fink, Mike, 1700?–1823, U.S. frontiersman.
Finlay, Carlos Juan, 1833–1915, Cuban physician.
Finney, Albert, 1936–, Eng. actor.
Firbank, Ronald, 1886–1926, Eng. author.
Firdausi, pseud. of Abdul Qasim Mansur, 940?–1020?, Persian epic poet.
Firestone, Harvey Samuel, 1868–1938, U.S. industrialist.
Fischer, Robert James (Bobby), 1943–, U.S. chess master.
Fischer-Dieskau, Dietrich, 1925–, Ger. baritone.
Fish, Hamilton, 1808–93, U.S. statesman.
Fishbein, Morris, 1889–, U.S. physician, author & editor.
Fisher, Dorothy Canfield, 1879–1958, U.S. author.
—**M(ary) F(rances) K(ennedy),** 1908–, U.S. author.
Fiske, Minnie Maddern, 1865–1932, U.S. actress.
Fitch, John, 1743–98, Amer. inventor.
—**(William) Clyde,** 1865–1909, U.S. playwright.
Fitzgerald, Ella, 1918–, U.S. jazz singer.
—**F(rancis) Scott (Key),** 1896–1940, U.S. author.
—**George F.,** 1851–1901, Irish physicist.
—**Geraldine,** 1914–, Irish-born U.S. actress.
FitzGerald, Edward, 1809–83, Eng. poet & translator.
Flagg, Ernest, 1857–1947, U.S. architect.
—**James Montgomery,** 1877–1960, U.S. painter, illustrator & author.
Flagler, Henry Morrison, 1830–1913, U.S. business executive.
Flagstad, Kirsten, 1895–1963, Norw. soprano active in U.S.
Flaherty, Robert (Joseph), 1884–1951, U.S. film director.
Flammarion, Camille, 1842–1925, Fr. astronomer & author.
Flaubert, Gustave, 1821–80, Fr. author.
Fleming, Sir Alexander, 1881–1955, Eng. bacteriologist.
—**Ian (Lancaster),** 1908–64, Eng. author.
—**Victor,** 1883–1949, U.S. film director.
Flemming, Walther, 1843–1905, Ger. anatomist.
Fletcher, John, 1579–1625, Eng. playwright.
Flourens, Pierre Marie Jean, 1794–1867, Fr. anatomist & physiologist.
Flynn, Errol, 1909–59, Tasmanian-born actor active in U.S.
Foch, Ferdinand, 1851–1929, Fr. general; marshal of France.
Fokine, Michel, 1880–1942, Russ.-born U.S. choreographer.
Fokker, Anthony Herman Gerard, 1890–1939, Du.-born U.S. aircraft designer.
Folger, Henry Clay, 1857–1930, U.S. bibliophile.
Fonda, Henry, 1905–, U.S. actor.
—**Jane,** 1937–, U.S. actress & political activist: daughter of prec.
Fontanne, Lynn, 1887–, Eng.-born U.S. actress.
Fonteyn, Dame Margot, 1919–, Eng. ballerina.
Ford, Ford Madox, 1873–1939, Eng. author.
—**Gerald Rudolph,** 1913–, 38th U.S. president 1974–77.
—**Henry,** 1863–1947, U.S. auto manufacturer.
—**John,** 1586?–1638?, Eng. playwright.
—**John,** 1895–1973, U.S. film director.
Forester, C(ecil) S(cott), 1899–1966, Eng. author active in U.S.
Forman, Milos, 1932–, Czech film director active in U.S.
Forrest, Edwin, 1806–72, U.S. actor.
Forrestal, James Vincent, 1892–1949, U.S. banker & government official.
Forster, E(dward) M(organ), 1879–1970, Eng. author.
Fosdick, Harry Emerson, 1878–1969, U.S. clergyman & author.
Foss, Lukas, 1922–, Ger.-born U.S. composer.
Foster, John Stuart, Jr. 1922–, U.S. physicist.

—**Stephen (Collins),** 1836–64, U.S. composer.
Foucault, Jean Bernard Leon, 1819–68, Fr. physicist.
Fourdrinier, Henry, 1766–1854, & his brother **Sealy,** ?–1847, Eng. inventors & paper manufacturers.
Fourier, François Marie Charles, 1772–1837, Fr. socialist.
—**Jean Baptiste Joseph,** 1768–1830, Fr. mathematician & physicist.
Fowler, H(enry) W(atson), 1858–1933, Eng. lexicographer.
Fox, George, 1624–91, Eng. preacher; founded the Society of Friends.
Foxx, James Emery (Jimmy), 1907–67, U.S. baseball player.
Foy, Eddie, 1856–1928, U.S. vaudeville performer.
Foyt, A(nthony) J(oseph), Jr., 1935–, U.S. auto racer.
Fracastoro, Girolamo, 1483–1553, Ital. physician.
Fragonard, Jean Honoré, 1732–1806, Fr. painter.
France, Anatole, pseud. of Jacques Anatole Thibault, 1844–1924, Fr. author.
Francesca da Rimini, ?–1285?, Ital. noblewoman; murdered by her husband.
Francescatti, Zino, 1905–, Fr. violinist.
Francis I, 1494–1547, king of France 1515–47.
Francis of Assisi, Saint, 1182–1226, Ital. preacher; founder of Franciscan Order.
Francis, Arlene, 1908–, U.S. actress & TV personality.
Franck, César (Auguste), 1822–90, Belg.-born Fr. composer.
—**James,** 1882–1964, Ger.-born U.S. physicist.
Franco, Francisco, 1892–1975, Sp. general and dictator; chief of state of Spain 1939–75.
Frank, Anne, 1929–45, Ger.-born Du. diarist.
Frankfurter, Felix, 1882–1965, Austrian-born U.S. jurist; justice of the U.S. Supreme Court 1939–62.
Franklin, Aretha, 1942–, U.S. singer.
—**Benjamin,** 1706–90, Amer. patriot, scientist, statesman & diplomat.
—**Frederic,** 1914–, Eng.-born dancer & ballet-company director active in U.S.
Franz Ferdinand, 1863–1914, archduke of Austria; assassinated.
Franz Josef I, 1830–1916, emperor of Austria 1848–1916.
Fraser, Dawn, 1939–Austral. swimmer.
—**(John) Malcolm,** 1930–, prime minister of Australia 1975–.
—**Neale,** 1933–, Austral. tennis player.
Fraunhofer, Joseph von, 1787–1826, Ger. optician & physicist.
Frazer, Sir James (George), 1854–1941, Scot. anthropologist.
Frazier, Joe, 1944–, U.S. boxer.
—**Walt(er),** 1945–, U.S. basketball player.
Frederick I, 1121–90, king of Germany & Holy Roman Emperor 1152–90: called **Barbarossa.**
Frederick II, 1194–1250, Holy Roman Emperor, 1215–50.
Frederick II, 1712–86, king of Prussia 1740–86: called **the Great.**
Frederick IX, 1899–1972, king of Denmark 1947–72.
Frederick William, 1620–88, elector of Brandenburg: called **the Great Elector.**
Freed, Arthur, 1894–1973, U.S. film producer.
Frelinghuysen, Frederick Theodore, 1817–85, U.S. statesman.
Frémont, John Charles, 1813–90, U.S. military officer & explorer.
French, Daniel Chester, 1850–1931, U.S. sculptor.
Freneau, Philip Morin, 1752–1832, U.S. poet.
Frescobaldi, Girolamo, 1583–1643, Ital. composer.
Fresnel, Augustin Jean, 1788–1827, Fr. physicist.
Freud, Anna, 1895–, Austrian-born Eng. psychoanalyst.
—**Sigmund,** 1856–1939, Austrian neurologist; founder of modern theory of psychoanalysis; father of prec.
Frick, Henry Clay, 1849–1919, U.S. industrialist & philanthropist.
Friedan, Betty, 1921–, U.S. author & feminist.
Friedman, Milton, 1912–, U.S. economist.
Friendly, Fred W., 1915–, U.S. radio & TV executive.

Fries, Elias Magnus, 1794–1878, Swed. botanist.
Friml, Rudolf, 1879–1972, Czech-born U.S. composer.
Frisch, Frank, 1898–1973, U.S. baseball player.
—**Karl von,** 1886–, Austrian zoologist.
Frobisher, Sir Martin, 1535?–94, Eng. navigator.
Froebel, Friedrich (Wilhelm August), 1782–1852, Ger. educator.
Frohman, Charles, 1860–1915, U.S. theatrical manager.
Froissart, Jean, 1333?–1400, Fr. chronicler.
Fromm, Erich, 1900–80, Ger.-born U.S. psychoanalyst.
Frondizi, Arturo, 1908–, Argentine politician; president of Argentina 1958–62.
Frontenac, Louis de Buade, Comte de, 1620–98, Fr. general & colonial administrator in N. America.
Frost, David, 1939–, Eng. TV personality active in U.S.
—**Robert (Lee),** 1875–1963, U.S. poet.
Fry, Christopher, 1907–, Eng. playwright.
—**Roger (Eliot),** 1866–1934, Eng. painter & art critic.
Fuchs, Klaus Emil Julius, 1912–, Ger.-born spy in U.S.
Fuentes, Carlos, 1928–, Mexican author.
Fugger, Jacob, 1459–1525, Ger. merchant & banker.
Fulbright, J(ames) William, 1905–, U.S. politician.
Fuller, Alfred Carl, 1885–1973, U.S. business executive.
—**Buckminster,** 1895–, U.S. architect, designer & author.
—**(Sarah) Margaret,** 1810–50, U.S. social reformer.
Fulton, Robert, 1765–1815, U.S. inventor.
Funk, Isaac Kauffman, 1839–1912, U.S. publisher & lexicographer.
Furness, Betty, 1916–, U.S. actress & TV personality.
Furnivall, Frederick James, 1825–1910, Eng. philologist.
Furtwängler, Wilhelm, 1886–1954, Ger. conductor.

Gabin, Jean, 1904–76, Fr. actor.
Gable, Clark, 1901–60, U.S. actor.
Gabor, Dennis, 1900–79, Hung.-born Brit. physicist.
Gadsden, James, 1788–1858, U.S. military officer & diplomat.
Gagarin, Yuri Alekseyevich, 1934–68, Soviet astronaut: first to orbit the earth.
Gage, Thomas, 1721–87, Eng. general & colonial governor of Massachusetts 1774–75.
Gainsborough, Thomas, 1727–88, Eng. Painter.
Gaitskell, Hugh (Todd Naylor), 1906–63, Eng. socialist leader.
Galanos, James, 1924–, U.S. fashion designer.
Gailbraith, John Kenneth, 1908–, U.S. economist, diplomat & author.
Gale, Zona, 1874–1938, U.S. author.
Galen, Claudius, A.D. 130?–200?, Gk. physician & writer.
Galilei Galilei, 1564–1642, Ital. astronomer, mathematician & physicist.
Gallatin, (Abraham Alfonse) Albert, 1761–1849, Swiss-born U.S. financier & statesman.
Gallaudet, Thomas Hopkins, 1787–1851, U.S. educator.
Galli-Curci, Amelita, 1889–1963, Ital -born U.S. soprano.
Gallup, George (Horace), 1901–, U.S. public opinion statistician.
Galsworthy, John, 1867–1933, Eng. author & playwright.
Galton, Sir Francis, 1822–1911, Eng. scientist.
Galvani, Luigi, 1737–98, Ital. physiologist.
Gambetta, Leon, 1838–82, Fr. statesman.
Gamow, George, 1904–68, Russ-born U.S. physicist & author.
Gandhi, Indira (Nehru), 1917–, Indian stateswoman; prime minister of India 1966–77 and 1980–; daughter of Jawaharial Nehru.
—**Mohandas Karamchand,** 1869–1948, Hindu nationalist leader & social reformer; assassinated: known as **Mahatma Gandhi.**
Garamond, Claude, ?–1561, Fr. type founder.
Garand, John Cantius, 1888–1974, Can.-born U.S. inventor.
Garbo, Greta, 1905–, Swed.-born actress active in U.S.
Garcia Lorca, Federico, 1899–1936, Sp. poet, playwright & author.

Garcilaso de la Vega, 1539?–1616, Peruvian historian: called **El Inca.**
Garden, Mary, 1874–1967, Scot-born U.S. soprano.
Gardiner, Stephen, 1483?–1535, Eng. prelate & statesman.
Gardner, Erle Stanley, 1889–1970, U.S. author.
—**Isabella Stewart,** 1840–1924, U.S. social leader & art collector.
Garfield, James Abram, 1831–81, 20th U.S. president 1881; assassinated.
—**John,** 1913–52, U.S. actor.
Garibaldi, Giuseppe, 1807–82, Ital. patriot & general.
Garland, Hamlin, 1860–1940, U.S. author.
—**Judy,** 1922–69, U.S. singer & actress.
Garner, Erroll, 1923–77. U.S. jazz pianist.
—**John Nance,** 1868–1967, U.S. politician; U.S. vice-president 1933–41.
Garnett, Constance (Black), 1862–1946, Eng. translator.
—**David,** 1892–, Eng. writer; son of prec.
Garrick, David, 1717–79, Eng. actor & author.
Garrison, William Lloyd, 1805–79, U.S. abolitionist.
Garroway, Dave, 1913–, U.S. TV personality.
Garvey, Marcus, 1880–1940, W. Indian Negro leader active in the U.S.
Gascoigne, George, 1525?–77, Eng. poet.
Gaskell, Walter H., 1847–1914, Eng. biologist & neurologist.
Gates, Horatio, 1728?–1806, Amer. Revolutionary general.
—**John Warne ("Bet-a-Million"),** 1855–1911, U.S. financier.
Gatling, Richard Jordan, 1818–1903, U.S. inventor.
Gatti-Casazza, Giulio, 1869–1940, Ital. operatic manager active in U.S.
Gaudí i Cornet, Antonio, 1852–1926, Sp. architect & furniture designer.
Gauguin, Paul, 1848–1903, Fr. painter active in Tahiti after 1891.
Gauss, Karl Friedrich, 1777–1855, Ger. mathematician.
Gautier, Théophile, 1811–72, Fr. poet & critic.
Gay, John, 1685–1732, Eng. poet & playwright.
Gay-Lussac, Joseph Louis, 1778–1850, Fr. chemist.
Gaynor, Janet, 1906–, U.S. actress.
Gedda, Nicolai, 1925–, Swed. tenor.
Geddes, Norman Bel, 1893–1958, U.S. industrial & set designer.
Geer, Will, 1902–78, U.S. actor.
Gehrig, (Henry) Lou(is), 1903–41, U.S. baseball player.
Geiger, Hans W., 1882–1945, Ger. physicist.
Geisel, Ernesto, 1908–, Brazilian military officer; president of Brazil 1974–78.
Gell-Mann, Murray, 1929–, U.S. physicist.
Genauer, Emily, ?–, U.S. author, editor & critic.
Genêt, Edmond Charles Edouard, 1763–1834, Fr. diplomat; first minister of France to the U.S. 1792–94: called **Citizen Genêt.**
—**Jean,** 1909–, Fr. playwright & author.
Genghis Khan, 1162–1227, Mongol conqueror in Europe & Asia.
Geoffrey of Monmouth, 1100?–54, Eng. ecclesiastic & chronicler.
George I, 1660–1727, king of Great Britain 1714–27.
—**II,** 1683–1760, king of Great Britain 1727–60.
—**III,** 1738–1820, king of Great Britain 1760–1820.
—**IV,** 1762–1830, king of Great Britain 1820–30.
—**V,** 1865–1936, king of Great Britain 1910–36.
—**VI,** 1895–1952, king of Great Britain 1936–52.
George, Saint, ?–303?, Christian martyr; patron saint of England.
George, Grace, 1879–1961, U.S. actress.
—**Henry ,** 1839–97, U.S. economist.
—**Stefan,** 1868–1933, Ger. poet.
Gerard, John, 1545–1612, Eng. botanist & barber-surgeon.
Géricault, (Jean Louis André) Théodore, 1791–1824, Fr. painter.
Gernreich, Rudi, 1922–, Austrian-born U.S. fashion designer.

Gernsback, Hugo, 1884–1967, Luxembourg-born U.S. inventor & publisher.

Geronimo, 1829–1909, Apache Am. Ind. chief.

Gershwin, George, 1898–1937, U.S. composer.

—**Ira,** 1896–, U.S. lyricist; brother of prec.

Gesell, Arnold L(ucius), 1880–1961, U.S. child psychologist.

Getty, Jean Paul, 1892–1976, U.S. business executive resident in England.

Getz, Stan, 1927–, U.S. jazz musician.

Ghiberti, Lorenzo, 1378–1455, Florentine sculptor, painter & goldsmith.

Ghirlandaio, Domenico, 1449–94, Ital. painter.

Giacometti, Alberto, 1901–66, Swiss-born sculptor & painter active in France.

Giannini, Amadeo Peter, 1870–1949, U.S. banker.

Giap, Vo Nguyen, 1912–, N. Vietnamese general & political leader.

Gibbon, Edward, 1737–94, Eng. historian.

Gibbons, Floyd, 1887–1939, U.S. journalist & war correspondent.

Gibbs, J(osiah) Willard, 1839–1903, U.S. mathematician & physicist.

Gibran, Kahlil, 1883–1931, Lebanese poet & painter active in U.S.

Gibson, Althea, 1927–, U.S. tennis player.

—**Charles Dana,** 1867–1944, U.S. illustrator.

—**William,** 1914–, U.S. playwright & author.

Gide, André, 1869–1951, Fr. author & playwright.

Gielgud, Sir John, 1904–, Eng. actor & stage director.

Gierek, Edward, 1913–, first secretary of the Communist Party of Poland 1970–.

Gieseking, Walter, 1895–1956, Fr.-born Ger. pianist.

Gigli, Beniamino, 1980–1957, Ital. tenor.

Gilbert, Cass, 1859–1934, U.S. architect.

—**Sir Humphrey,** 1539?–83, Eng. navigator.

—**William,** 1540–1603, Eng. physician & physicist.

—**Sir W(illiam) S(chwenck),** 1836–1911, Eng. poet, librettist & lyricist.

Gilels, Emil, 1916–, Soviet pianist.

Gillespie, John Birks ("Dizzy"), 1917–, U.S. jazz musician.

Gillette, William, 1855–1937, U.S. actor.

Ginastera, Alberto, 1916–, Argentine composer.

Ginsberg, Allen, 1926–, U.S. poet.

Giorgione II, b. Giorgio Barbarelli, c. 1478–1511, Venetian painter.

Giotto (di Bondone), 1266–1337, Florentine painter & architect.

Giraudoux, Jean, 1882–1944, Fr. playwright.

Giscard d'Estaing, Valéry, 1926–, president of France 1974–.

Gish, Dorothy, 1898?–1968, U.S. actress.

—**Lillian,** 1896?–, U.S. actress; sister of prec.

Givenchy, Hubert de, 1927–, Fr. fashion designer.

Glackens, William James, 1870–1938, U.S. painter & illustrator.

Gladstone, William Ewart, 1809–98, Eng. statesman; prime minister 1868–74, 1880–85, 1886 & 1892–94.

Glaser, Donald Arthur, 1926–, U.S. physicist.

Glasgow, Ellen (Anderson Gholson), 1874–1945, U.S. author.

Glazunov, Aleksandr Konstantinovich, 1865–1936, Russ. composer.

Gleason, Herbert John ("Jackie"), 1916–, U.S. comedian & actor.

Glenn, John Herschel, 1921–, U.S. astronaut & politician.

Glière, Reinhold, 1875–1956, Russ. composer.

Glinka, Mikhail Ivanovich, 1803–57, Russ. composer.

Gluck, Alma, 1884–1938, Rumanian-born U.S. soprano.

—**Christoph Willibald,** 1714–87, Ger. composer.

Gobbi, Tito, 1915–, Ital. baritone.

Godard, Jean-Luc, 1930–, Fr. film director.

Goddard, Henry Herbert, 1866–1957, U.S. psychologist.

—**Robert Hutchings,** 1882–1945, U.S. physicist.

Godey, Louis Antoine, 1804–78, U.S. magazine publisher.

Godfrey of Bouillon, 1061?–1100, Fr. crusader.

Godfrey, Arthur (Michael), 1903–, U.S. radio & TV personality.

Godolphin, Sidney, 1st Earl of Godolphin, 1645–1712, Eng. statesman.

Godowsky, Leopold, 1870–1938, Pol. pianist.

Godunov, Boris Fyodorovich, 1551?–1605, czar of Russia 1598–1605.

Godwin, Mary Wollstonecraft, 1759–97, Eng. feminist & author.

Goebbels, Joseph Paul, 1897–1945, Ger. Nazi propagandist.

Goes, Hugo van der, 1440?–82, Du. painter.

Goethals, George Washington, 1858–1928, U.S. military officer & engineer.

Goethe, Johann Wolfgang von, 1749–1832, Ger. poet, playwright & statesman.

Gofman, John William, 1918–, U.S. physician & biophysicist.

Gogol, Nikolai Vasilevich, 1809–52, Russ. author.

Goldberg, Arthur Joseph, 1908–, U.S. lawyer, jurist & diplomat.

—**Reuben Lucius (Rube),** 1883–1970, U.S. cartoonist.

Golden, Harry (Lewis), 1902–81, U.S. journalist & author.

Golding, William, 1911–, Eng. author.

Goldman, Edwin Franko, 1878–1956, U.S. bandmaster & composer.

—**Emma,** 1869–1940, Lithuanian-born U.S. anarchist.

Goldoni, Carlo, 1707–93, Ital. playwright.

Goldsmith, Oliver, 1728–74, Eng. author.

Goldstein, Eugen, 1850–1931, Ger. physicist.

Goldwater, Barry, 1909–, U.S. senator & political leader.

Goldwyn, Samuel, 1882–1974, Pol.-born U.S. film producer.

Golgi, Camillo, 1844–1926, Ital. physician & histologist.

Gompers, Samuel, 1850–1924, U.S. labor leader.

Gomulka, Wladyslaw, 1905–, first secretary of the Communist Party of Poland 1956–70.

Goncourt, Edmond, 1822–96, & his brother **Jules,** 1830–70, Fr. diarists & authors.

Gonzalez, Pancho, 1928–, U.S. tennis player.

Goodenough, Florence Laura, 1886–1959, U.S. psychologist.

Goodman, Benjamin David (Benny), 1909–, U.S. musician.

—**Paul,** 1911–72, U.S. author & educator.

Goodson Mark, 1916–, U.S. TV producer.

Goodyear, Charles, 1800–60, U.S. inventor.

Gordon, Charles George, 1833–85, Brit. military officer: called **Chinese Gordon.**

—**Max,** 1892–1978, U.S. theatrical producer.

—**Ruth** 1896–, U.S. actress & author.

Goren, Charles Henry, 1901–, U.S. bridge player & author.

Gorgas, William Crawford, 1854–1920, U.S. sanitation engineer.

Göring, Hermann Wilhelm, 1893–1946, Ger. Nazi politician.

Gorki, Maxim, 1868–1936, Russ. author & playwright.

Gorky, Arshile, 1904–48, Turkish-born U.S. painter.

Gosden, Freeman, 1899–, U.S. radio actor.

Gottschalk, Louis Moreau, 1829–69, U.S. pianist & composer.

Gottwald, Klement, 1896–1953, Czech communist leader.

Goudy, Frederic William, 1865–1947, U.S. type designer.

Gould, Chester, 1900–, U.S. cartoonist.

—**Glenn,** 1932–, Can. pianist.

—**Jason (Jay),** 1836–92, U.S. financier.

—**Morton,** 1913–, U.S. composer & conductor.

—**Shane,** 1954–, Austral. swimmer.

Goulding, Ray, 1922–, U.S. comedian.

Gounod, Charles Francois, 1818–93, Fr. composer.

Gourmont, Rémy de, 1858–1915, Fr. poet, author & critic.

Gowon, Yakubu, 1934–, head of state of Nigeria 1966–75.

Goya, Francisco José de, 1746–1828, Sp. painter & etcher.

Graaf, Regnier de, 1641–73, Du. physician.
Grable, Betty, 1916–73, U.S. actress, singer & dancer.
Gracchus, Gaius Sempronius, 153–121 B.C., & his brother **Tiberius Sempronius,** 163–133 B.C., Roman statesmen.
Grace, Princess, b. Grace Patricia Kelly, 1929–, U.S.-born actress & wife of Prince Rainier III of Monaco.
Graham, Katherine, 1917–, U.S. publisher.
—**Martha,** 1893?–, U.S. choreographer & dancer.
—**Sheilah,** 1905?–, Eng.-born U.S. journalist & author.
—**Thomas,** 1805–69, Scot. physical chemist.
—**William Franklin (Billy),** 1918–, U.S. evangelist
Grahame, Kenneth, 1859–1932, Eng. author.
Grainger, Percy Aldridge, 1882–1961, Austral.-born pianist & composer active in U.S.
Gram, Hans Christian Joachim, 1853–1938, Dan. bacteriologist.
Granados, Enrique, 1867–1916, Sp. composer.
Grange, Harold ("Red"), 1903–, U.S. football player.
Grant, Cary, 1904–, Eng.-born U.S. actor.
—**Ulysses S(impson),** 1822–85, U.S. Civil War general & 18th U.S. president 1869–77.
Granville-Barker, Harley Granville, 1877–1946, Eng. actor, playwright & producer.
Grappelli, Stéphane, 1908–, Fr. jazz violinist.
Grass, Günter, 1927–, Ger. author.
Gratian (L. Flavius Gratianus), 359–383, Roman emperor 375–83.
Graves, Robert, 1895–, Eng. poet & author.
Gray, Asa, 1810–88, U.S. botanist.
—**Thomas,** 1716–71, Eng. poet.
Graziano, Rocco ("Rocky"), 1922–, U.S. boxer.
Greco, El, b. Domenikos Theotokopoulos, 1541?–1614?, Cretan-born painter active in Italy & Spain.
Greco, José, 1919–, Ital.-born U.S. dancer.
Greeley, Horace, 1811–72, U.S. editor & political leader.
Green, Adolph, 1915–, U.S. lyricist.
—**Henrietta Robinson (Hetty),** 1835–1916, U.S. financier.
—**Henry,** pseud. of Henry Vincent Yorke, 1905–, Eng. author.
—**Martyn,** 1899–1975, Eng. actor & singer active in U.S.
—**William,** 1873–1952, U.S. labor leader.
Greenberg, Henry (Hank), 1911–, U.S. baseball player.
Greene, Graham, 1904–, Eng. author.
—**Nathanael,** 1742–86, Amer. Revolutionary general.
—**Robert,** 1558–92, Eng. poet & playwright.
Greenstreet, Sydney, 1879–1954, Eng. actor active in U.S.
Gregory I, Saint, 540?–604, pope 590–640; known as the Great.
—**XIII,** 1502–85, pope 1572–85.
Gregory, Lady Augusta (Persse), 1859?–1932, Irish playwright & theater director.
—**Dick,** 1932–, U.S. comedian & social activist.
Gresham, Sir Thomas, 1519?–79, Eng. financier.
Greuze, Jean Baptiste, 1725–1805, Fr. painter.
Grey, Beryl, 1927–, Eng. dancer & ballet-company director.
—**Lady Jane,** 1537–54, Eng. noblewoman; beheaded.
—**Zane,** 1875–1939, U.S. author.
Grieg, Edvard (Hagerup), 1843–1907, Norw. composer.
Griffith D(avid) W(ark), 1875–1948; U.S. film director & producer.
Grigorovitch, Yuri, 1927–, Soviet choreographer & ballet-company director.
Grimaldi, Francesco Maria, 1618–63, Ital. physicist.
Grimm, Jacob Ludwig Karl, 1785–1862, & his brother **Wilhelm Karl,** 1786–1859, Ger. philologists & collectors of fairy tales.
Gris, Juan, 1887–1927, Sp. painter.
Grisi, Carlotta, 1819–99, Ital. ballerina.
Grofé, Ferde, 1892–1972, U.S. composer & conductor.
Grolier de Servières, Jean, 1479–1565, Fr. diplomat & bibliophile.
Gromyko, Andrei Andreivich, 1909–, Soviet economist & diplomat.
Groote, Gerhard, 1340–84, Du. religious reformer.

Gropius, Walter, 1883–1969, Ger. architect active in U.S. after 1937.
Gropper, William, 1897–1977, U.S. painter.
Grosz, George, 1893–1959, Ger. painter & illustrator.
Grotius, Hugo, 1583–1645. Du. jurist & statesman.
Grove, Sir George, 1820–1900, Eng. musicologist & author.
—**Robert ("Lefty"),** 1900–75, U.S. baseball player.
Groves, Leslie Richard, 1896–1970, U.S. general.
Grünewald, Mathias, 1480?–1528?, Ger. painter.
Guardi, Francesco, 1712–93, Ital. painter.
Guarneri, Giuseppe Antonia, 1683–1745, Ital. violin-maker.
Gueden, Hilde, 1917–, Austrian soprano.
Guest, Edgar A(lbert), 1881–1959, U.S. poet & journalist.
Guevara, Ernesto ("Che"), 1928–67, Argentinian-born Cuban revolutionary leader.
Guggenheim A family of U.S. industrialists & philanthropists incl. **Meyer,** 1828–1905, & his sons **Benjamin,** 1865–1912; **Daniel,** 1856–1930; **Issac,** 1854–1922; **Murry,** 1858–1939; **Simon,** 1867–1941; **Solomon R.,** 1861–1949; & **William,** 1868–1941.
—**Peggy,** 1898–, U.S. art collector, patron & author.
Guido d'Arezzo, 990?–1050?, Ital. monk & musician.
Guinness, Sir Alec, 1914–, Eng. actor.
Guitry, Sacha, 1885–1957, Fr. film director.
Gunther, John, 1901–70, U.S. author.
Gustaf VI, 1882–1973, king of Sweden 1950–73.
Gustavus Adolphus (Gustaf II), 1594–1632, king of Sweden 1611–32.
Gutenberg, Johann, 1400?–1468?, Ger. printer & reputed inventor of movable type.
Guthrie, Sir Tyrone, 1900–71, Eng. stage director active in U.S.
—**Woodrow Wilson (Woody),** 1912–67, U.S. folk singer.
Gwynne, Nell, 1650–87, Eng. actress; mistress of Charles II.

Haakon VII, 1872–1957, king of Norway 1905–57.
Haber, Fritz, 1868–1934, Ger. chemist.
Hachette, Louis, 1800–64, Fr. publisher & bookseller.
Hadrian (L. Publius Aelius Hadrianus), A.D. 76-138, Roman emperor, A.D. 117–138.
Haechkel, Ernst Heinrich, 1834–1919, Ger. biologist.
Hafiz, pseud. of Shams ud-din Mohammed, 14th c. Persian poet.
Hagen, Walter Charles, 1892–1969, U.S. golfer.
Haggard, sir (Henry) Rider, 1856–1925, Eng. author.
Hague, Frank, 1876–1956, U.S. politician.
Hahn, Otto, 1879–1968, Ger. physical chemist.
Haig, Alexander Meigs, Jr., 1924–, U.S. general and statesman; secretary of state 1981–.
Haile Selassie, 1891–1975, emperor of Ethiopia 1930–74.
Hailey, Arthur, 1920–, Eng author.
Hakluyt, Richard, 1552–1616, Eng. geographer & historian.
Halas, George Stanley, 1895–, U.S. football player, coach, and owner.
Haldane, J(ohn) B(urdon) S(anderson), 1892–1964, Eng. biologist.
—**John Scott,** 1860–1936, Eng physiologist.
—**Richard Burdon,** 1856–1928, Eng. philosopher & statesman.
Hale, Edward Everett, 1822–1909, U.S. clergyman & author.
—**George Ellery,** 1868–1938, U.S. astronomer.
—**Nathan,** 1755–76, Amer. revolutionary officer; hanged as a spy by the Bristish.
Hales, Stephen, 1677–1761, Eng. botanist & chemist.
Halévy, Jacques, 1799–1862, Fr. composer.
—**Ludovic,** 1834–1908, Fr. playwright & author; nephew of prec.
Halifax, Edward Frederick Lindley Wood, Earl of, 1881–1959, Eng. statesman & diplomat.
Hall, James Norman, 1887–1951, U.S. author.
Halley, Edmund, 1656–1742, Eng. astronomer.
Halliburton, Richard, 1900–1939, U.S. explorer & author.
Hals, Frans, 1850?–1666, Du. painter.

Halsey, William Frederick ("Bull"), 1882–1959, U.S. admiral.

Halsted, William Stewart, 1852–1922, U.S. surgeon.

Hambro, Carl Joachim, 1885–1964, Norw. statesman.

Hamilcar Barca, 270?–228 B.C., Carthaginian general; father of Hannibal.

Hamilton, Alexander, 1757–1804, Amer. statesman.

—**Edith,** 1867–1963, U.S. classicist & author.

—**Lady Emma,** 1761?–1815, mistress of Lord Nelson.

Hammarskjöld, Dag, 1905–61, Swed. statesman; secretary general of the U.N. 1953–61.

Hammerstein, Oscar, 1847?–1919, U.S. theatrical manager.

—**Oscar II,** 1895–1960, U.S. lyricist; nephew of prec.

Hammett, Dashiell, 1894–1961, U.S. author.

Hammurabi, 18th. c., B.C., Babylonian king & lawgiver.

Hampden, John, 1594–1643, Eng. statesman.

—**Walter,** 1879–1955, U.S. actor.

Hampton, Lionel, 1913–, U.S. jazz musician.

—**Wade,** 1818–1902, U.S. politician & Confederate general.

Hamsun, Knut, 1859–1952, Norw. author.

Hancock, John, 1737–93, Amer. statesman.

Hand, Learned, 1872–1961, U.S. jurist.

Handel, George Frederick, 1685–1759, Ger. composer active in England.

Handler, Philip, 1917–81, U.S. educator.

Handlin, Oscar, 1915–, U.S. historian & sociologist.

Handy, W(illiam) C(hristopher), 1873–1958, U.S. jazz musician & composer.

Hanna, Marcus Alonzo (Mark), 1837–1904, U.S. businessman & politician.

Hannibal, 247–183 B.C., Carthaginian general; invaded Italy by crossing the Alps.

Hansard, Luke, 1752–1828, Eng. printer.

Hanson, Howard, 1896–1981, U.S. composer & conductor.

Harbach, Otto Abels, 1873–1963, U.S. playwright & lyricist.

Harburg, E(dgar) Y. ("Yip"), 1898–1981, U.S. lyricist.

Harden, Sir Arthur, 1865–1940, Eng. biochemist.

Harding, Warren Gamaliel, 1865–1923, 29th U.S. president 1921–23.

Hardwick, Elizabeth, 1916–, U.S. author & critic.

Hardwicke, Sir Cedric (Webster), 1893–1964, Eng. actor.

Hardy, Oliver (Nowell), 1892–1957, U.S. comedian.

—**Thomas,** 1840–1928, Eng. author & poet.

Hargreaves, James, 1722?–78, Eng. inventor of the spinning jenny.

Harington, Sir John, 1561–1612, Eng. author & translator.

Harkness, Rebekah West, 1915–, U.S. composer & ballet patron.

Harlan, John Marshall, 1833–1911, & his grandson **John Marshall Harlan II,** 1899–1971, U.S. jurists.

Harlow, Jean, 1911–37, U.S. actress.

Harold II, 1022?–66, last Saxon king of England 1066.

Haroun-al-Rashid, 764?–809, Caliph of Baghdad 786–809.

Harper, James, 1795–1869, & his brothers: **John,** 1797–1875, **(Joseph) Wesley,** 1801–70 & **Fletcher,** 1806–77, U.S. printers & publishers.

Harriman, Edward Henry, 1848–1909, U.S.industrialist.

—**W(illiam) Averell,** 1891–, U.S. businessman, statesman & diplomat.

Harrington, (Edward) Michael, 1928–, U.S. author.

Harriot, Thomas, 1560–1621, Eng. mathematician.

Harris, Frank, 1854–1931, Irish-born U.S. editor & author.

—**Jed,** 1900–79, Austrian-born U.S. theatrical producer.

—**Joel Chandler,** 1848–1908, U.S. author.

—**Julie,** 1925–, U.S. actress.

—**Louis,** 1921–, U.S. public opinion statistician.

—**Roy,** 1898–1979, U.S. composer.

—**Townsend,** 1804–78, U.S. businessman & diplomat.

Harrison, Benjamin, 1833–1901, 23rd U.S. president 1889–93.

—**George,** 1943–, Eng. composer & musical performer.

—**Rex,** 1908–, Eng. actor active in U.S.

—**Ross Granville,** 1870–1959, U.S. biologist.

—**William Henry,** 1773–1841, U.S. general & 9th U.S. president 1841; grandfather of Benjamin.

Hart, Lorenz, 1895–1943, U.S. lyricist.

—**Moss,** 1904–61, U.S. playwright.

—**William S(urrey),** 1872–1946, U.S. actor.

Harte, Francis Brett (Bret), 1836–1902, U.S. author.

Hartford, Huntingdon, 1911–, U.S. financier & art patron.

Hartley, Marsden, 1877–1943, U.S. painter.

Harvard, John, 1607–38, Eng. clergyman active in U.S.

Harvey, William, 1578–1657, Eng. physician & anatomist.

Hassam, Childe, 1859–1935, U.S. painter & etcher.

Hassan II, 1929–, king of Morocco 1961–.

Hassler, Hans Leo, 1564–1612, Ger. composer.

Hastings, Thomas, 1860–1929, U.S. architect.

—**Warren,** 1732–1818, Eng. statesman active in India.

Hauptmann, Gerhart, 1862–1946, Ger. author & playwright.

Haussmann, Baron Georges Eugène, 1809–91, Fr. prefect & city planner.

Hawkins, Sir John, 1532–95, Eng. admiral.

Hawks, Howard, 1896–1977, U.S. film director.

Hawthorne, Nathaniel, 1804–64, U.S. author.

Hay, John Milton, 1838–1905, U.S. statesman & author; secretary of state 1898–1905.

Haya de la Torre, Victor Raúl, 1895–1979, Peruvian political leader.

Haydn, Franz Joseph, 1732–1809, Austrian composer.

Hayes, Helen, 1900–, U.S. actress.

—**Robert (Bob),** 1942–, U.S. track runner & football player.

—**Roland,** 1887–1977, U.S. tenor.

—**Rutherford B(irchard),** 1822–93, 19th U.S. president 1877–81.

Hays, Arthur Garfield, 1881–1954, U.S. lawyer.

Hayward, Leland, 1902–71, U.S. theatrical producer.

—**Susan,** 1919–75, U.S. actress.

Hayworth, Rita, 1919–, U.S. actress.

Hazlitt, William, 1778–1830, Eng. author.

Head, Edith, 1907–1981, U.S. costume designer.

Hearn, Lafcadio, 1850–1904, Gk.-born Irish author active in Japan.

Hearts, William Randolph, 1863–1951, U.S. publisher.

Heath, Edward, 1916–, Eng. politician; prime minister 1970–74.

Heatter, Gabriel, 1890–1972, U.S. journalist & radio commentator.

Heaviside, Oliver, 1850–1925, Eng. physicist & electrician.

Hecht, Ben, 1894–1964, U.S. journalist, author & playwright.

Hefner, Hugh Marston, 1926–, U.S. editor & publisher.

Hegel, Georg Wilhelm Friedrich, 1770–1831, Ger. philosopher.

Heidegger, Martin, 1889–1976. Ger. philospher.

Heiden, Eric, 1958–, Olympic speed skater.

Heifetz, Jascha, 1901–, Lithuanian-born U.S. violinist.

Heine, Heinrich, 1797–1856, Ger. poet.

Heinz, Henry John, 1844–1919, U.S. food processor.

Heisenberg, Werner, 1901–76, Ger. physicist.

Held, Anna, 1873?–1918, Fr.-born singer & actress active in U.S.

—**John, Jr.** 1889–1958, U.S. illustrative & author.

Heliogabalus, 204–222, Roman emperor 218–22.

Heller, Joseph, 1923–, U.S. author.

Hellinger, Mark, 1903–47, U.S. journalist & theatrical producer.

Hellman, Lillian, 1905–, U.S. playwright.

Helmholtz, Hermann Ludwig Ferdinand von, 1821–94, Ger. physiologist & physicist.

Helmont, Jan Baptista van, 1577–1644, Flemish physician & chemist.

Héloïse, 1101?–64?, Fr. abbess; pupil, mistress & later, wife of Abélard.

Helpmann, Robert, 1909–, Austral.-born dancer, choreographer & actor active in Great Britain.

Helvétius, Claude Adrien, 1715–71, Fr. philosopher.

Hemingway, Ernest, 1899–1961, U.S. author.

Henderson, (James) Fletcher, 1897–1952, U.S. jazz musician.

Hendrix, Jimi, 1942–70, U.S. musician & singer.

Hengist, 5th c. Jute invader of Great Britain.

Henie, Sonja, 1913–69, Norw.-born ice skater & actress active in U.S.

Henri, Robert, 1865–1929, U.S. painter.

Henry II, 1133–89, king of England 1154–89.

—IV, 1367–1413, king of England 1399–1413.

—V, 1387–1422, king of England 1413–22.

—VIII, 1491–1547, king of England 1509–47; established Church of England.

Henry IV (of Navarre), 1553–1610, king of France 1589–1610.

Henry the Navigator, 1394–1460, Pg. prince & promoter of navigation.

Henry, O., pseud. of William Sidney Porter, 1862–1910, U.S. author.

—Patrick, 1736–99, Amer. patriot, statesman & orator.

Hensen, Victor, 1835–1924, Ger. marine biologist.

Henze, Hans Werner, 1926–, Ger. composer.

Hepburn, Audrey, 1929–, Belg.-born actress active in U.S.

—Katharine, 1909–, U.S. actress.

Hepplewhite, George, ?–1786, Eng. furniture designer.

Hepworth, Dame Barbara, 1903–75, Eng. sculptor.

Heraclitus, ca. 5th c. B.C. Gk. philospher.

Herbert, George, 1593–1633, Eng. poet & Clergyman.

—Victor, 1859–1924, Irish-born U.S. composer.

—William, 1580–1630, Eng. statesman & poet.

Herder, Johann Gottfried von, 1744–1803, Ger. philosopher & author.

Heredia, José Maria de, 1842–1905, Cuban-born Fr. poet.

Herman, Woodrow Charles (Woody), 1913–, U.S. jazz musician.

Herod, 73?–4 B.C., king of Judea 37–4 B.C.: called the Great.

—Antipas, 4 B.C.–A.D. 39, governor of Galilee; son of prec.

Herodotus, 484?–424? B.C., Gk. historian.

Herophilus, 4th c. B.C., Gk. anatomist.

Herrick, Robert, 1591–1674, Eng. poet.

Herschel, Sir William, 1738–1822, & his son **Sir John Frederick William Herschel,** 1792–1871, Eng. astronomers.

Hersey, John Richard, 1914–, U.S. author.

Hershey, Milton Snavely, 1857–1945, U.S. businessman & philanthropist.

Herskovits, Melville Jean, 1895–1963, U.S. anthropologist.

Hertz, Heinrich Rudolph, 1857–94, Ger. physicist.

Herzl, Theodor, 1860–1904, Hung.-born Austrian journalist; founder of the Zionist movement.

Hesiod, , ca. 8th c. B.C., Gk. poet.

Hess, Dame Myra, 1890–1965, Eng. pianist.

—Victor Franz, 1883–1964, Austrian physicist.

—Walter Rudolf, 1881–1973, Swiss physiologist.

—(Walther Richard) Rudolf, 1894–, Ger. Nazi politician.

Hesse, Hermann, 1877–1962, Ger. author.

Heydrich, Reinhard, 1904–42, Ger. Nazi administrator: known as **the Hangman.**

Heyerdahl, Thor, 1914–, Norw. anthropologist & author.

Heyward, DuBose, 1885–1940, U.S. author.

Hiawatha, 16th c. Mohawk Am. Ind. chief.

Hickok, James Butler ("Wild Bill"), 1837–76, U.S. scout & marshal.

Hicks, Edward, 1780–1849, U.S. painter.

—Granville, 1901–, U.S. author & critic.

Hidalgo y Costilla, Miguel, 1753–1811, Mexican priest & revolutionary.

Highet, Gilbert, 1906–78, Scot.-born U.S. author & educator.

Hill, George Washington, 1884–1946, U.S. businessman.

—Graham, 1929–75, Eng. auto racer.

—Joe, 1872?–1915, Swed.-born U.S. labor organizer & songwriter.

Hillary, Sir Edmond, 1919–, New Zealand explorer & mountain-climber.

Hilel, 60 B.C.?–A.D. 10, Babylonian teacher of biblical law.

Hiller, Wendy, 1912–, Eng. actress.

Hillman, Sidney, 1887–1946, Lithuanian-born U.S. labor leader.

Hilton, Conrad Nicholson, 1887–1979, U.S. businessman.

—James, 1900–54, Eng. author.

Himmler, Heinrich, 1900–45, Ger. Nazi politician.

Hindemith, Paul, 1895–1963, Ger. composer active in U.S.

Hindenburg, Paul von, 1847–1934, Ger. field marshal; president of Germany 1925–34.

Hine, Lewis Wickes, 1874–1940, U.S. photographer.

Hines, Duncan, 1880–1959, U.S food expert, author & publisher.

—Earl ("Fatha"), 1905–, U.S. jazz musician.

Hippocrates, 460?–377 B.C., Gk. physician.

Hires, Charles Elmer, 1851–1937, U.S. businessman.

Hirohito, 1901–, Emperor of Japan 1926–.

Hiroshige, Ando, 1797–1858, Jap. painter.

Hirsch, Elray ("Crazy Legs"), 1923–, U.S. football player.

Hirschfeld, Al(bert), 1903–, U.S. cartoonist.

Hirshhorn, Joseph, 1899–1981, Latvian-born U.S. mining executive, entrepreneur & art collector.

Hiss, Alger, 1904–, U.S. government official.

Hitchcock, Alfred, 1899–1980, Eng. film director active in U.S.

—Henry-Russell, 1903–, U.S. art historian.

Hitler, Adolf, 1889–1945, Austrian-born Nazi dictator of Germany 1933–45.

Hoban, James, 1762?–1831, Irish-born U.S. architect.

Hobbema, Meindert, 1638–1709, Du. painter.

Hobbes, Thomas, 1588–1679, Eng. philospher.

Hobby, Oveta Culp, 1905–, U.S. journalist & government official.

Ho Chi Minh, 1890?–1969, president of N. Vietnam 1945–69.

Hoffa, James Riddle, 1913–75?, U.S. labor leader.

Hoffer, Eric, 1902–, U.S. philosopher & author.

Hoffman, Malvina, 1887–1966, U.S. sculptor.

Hoffmann, E(rnst) T(heodor) A(madeus), 1776–1822, Ger. author & illustrator.

Hofmann, Hans, 1880–1966, Ger.-born U.S. painter.

—Josef Casimir, 1876–1957, Pol. pianist.

Hofmannsthal, Hugo von, 1874–1929, Austrian poet & playwright.

Hofstadter, Richard, 1916–70, U.S. historian.

Hogan, Ben W., 1912–, U.S. golfer.

Hogarth, William, 1697–1764, Eng. painter & engraver.

Hokinson, Helen, 1899?–1949, U.S. cartoonist.

Hokusai, Katsuhika, 1760–1849, Jap. painter & engraver.

Holbein, Hans, 1460?–1524, (called **the Elder**), and his son, **Hans,** 1497–1543, **(the Younger),** Ger. painters.

Hölderlin, (Johann Christian) Friedrich, 1770–1843, Ger. poet.

Holiday, Billie, 1915–59, U.S. jazz singer.

Holinshed, Raphael, ?–1580?, Eng. chronicler.

Holley, Robert W., 1922–, U.S. biochemist.

Holiday, Judy, 1921–65, U.S. actress.

Holmes, Oliver Wendell, 1809–94, U.S. physician & poet.

—Oliver Wendell, 1841–1935, U.S. jurist; justice of U.S. Supreme Court 1902–32; son of prec.

Holst, Gustav Theodore, 1874–1934, Eng. composer.

Homer, ca. 8th c. B.C. Gk. epic poet; traditional author of the *Iliad* & the *Odyssey.*

Homer, Winslow, 1836–1910, U.S. painter.

Honecker, Erich, 1912–, 1st secretary of E. German Communist party 1971–.

Honegger, Arthur 1892–1955, Fr. composer.

Hood, Raymond, 1881–1934, U.S. architect.

Hooke, Robert, 1635–1703, Eng. philospher & scientist.

Hooker, Thomas, 1586?–1647, Eng.-born clergyman; founder of Connecticut colony.

Hooton, Earnest Albert, 1887–1954, U.S. anthropologist.

Hoover, Herbert (Clark), 1874–1964, 31st U.S. president 1929–33.

Hoover, J(ohn) Edgar 1895–1972, U.S. criminologist; director of the FBI 1924–72.

Hope, Leslie Townes ("Bob"), 1903–, Eng.-born U.S. actor & comedian.

Hopkins, Gerard Manley, 1844–89, Eng. poet.

—**Harry Lloyd**, 1890–1946, U.S. politician & administrator.

—**Johns**, 1795–1873, U.S. financier & philanthropist.

—**Mark**, 1802–87, U.S. educator.

Hopkinson, Francis, 1737–91, U.S. lawyer & author.

Hoppe, William Frederick (Willie), 1887–1959, U.S. billiards player.

Hopper, Edward, 1882–1967, U.S. painter.

—**Hedda**, 1890–1966, U.S. actress & columnist.

Horace (L. Quintus Horatius Flaccus), 65–8 B.C., Roman poet.

Horne, Lena, 1917–, U.S. singer & actress.

—**Marilyn**, 1934–, U.S. mezzo-soprano.

Horney, Karen, 1885–1952, Ger.-born U.S. psychiatrist.

Hornsby, Rogers, 1896–1963, U.S. baseball player.

Horowitz, Vladimir, 1904–, Russ.-born U.S. pianist.

Horsa, ?–455, Jute invader of Great Britain.

Houdini, Harry, 1874–1926, U.S. magician.

Houphouët-Boigny, Félix, 1905–, president of Ivory Coast 1960–.

House, Col. Edward Mandell, 1858–1938, U.S. diplomat.

Houseman, John, 1902–, U.S. producer, director, actor & author for theater, TV & films.

Housman, A(lfred) E(dward), 1859–1936, Eng. poet & classical scholar.

Houston, Sam(uel), 1793–1863, U.S. statesman & general; president of Republic of Texas 1836–38 & 1841–44.

Howard, Catherine, 1520?–42, 5th wife of King Henry VIII of England.

—**Henry, Earl of Surrey**, 1517?–47, Eng. soldier & poet.

—**Leslie**, 1893–1943, Eng. actor active in U.S.

—**Roy W.**, 1883–1964, U.S. editor & publisher.

—**Sidney Coe**, 1891–1939, U.S. playwright.

—**Trevor**, 1916–, Eng. actor.

Howe, Elias, 1819–67, U.S. inventor of the sewing machine.

—**Gordon (Gordie)**, 1928–, Can. hockey player.

—**James Wong**, 1899–1976, Chin.-born U.S. cinematographer.

—**Julia Ward**, 1819–1910, U.S. suffragist & author.

—**Mark Anthony DeWolf**, 1864–1960, U.S. author.

—**Richard, Earl**, 1726–99, Eng. naval officer.

Howells, William Dean, 1837–1920, U.S. author & editor.

Hoxha, Enver, 1908–, 1st secretary of Albanian Labor (Communist) Party 1945–.

Hoyle, Edmond, 1672–1769, Eng. writer on games.

—**Sir Fred**, 1915–, Eng. astronomer.

Hu Yaobang, 1915–, Chin. statesman; chairman Chin. Communist Party 1981.

Hubble, Edwin Powell, 1889–1953, U.S. astronomer.

Hudson, Henry, ?–1611, Eng. explorer.

Huggins, Sir William, 1824–1910, Eng. astronomer.

Hughes, Charles Evans, 1862–1948, U.S. jurist; Chief Justice of the U.S. Supreme Court 1930–41.

—**Howard Robard**, 1905–76, U.S. businessman.

—**(James) Langston**, 1902–67, U.S. author & poet.

Hugo, Victor (Marie), 1802–85, Fr. poet, author & playwright.

Huizinga, Johan, 1872–1945, Du. historian.

Hull, Cordell, 1871–1955, U.S. statesman; secretary of state 1933–44.

—**Robert Marvin (Bobby)**, 1939–, Can. hockey player.

Humboldt, Baron (Friedrich Heinrich) Alexander von, 1769–1859, Ger. naturalist & traveler.

Hume, David, 1711–76, Scot. historian & philosopher.

Humperdinck, Engelbert, 1854–1921, Ger. composer.

Humphrey, Doris, 1895–1958, U.S. choreographer & dancer.

—**Hubert Horatio**, 1911–78, U.S. senator & political leader; U.S. vice president 1965–69.

Hunt, H(aroldson) L(afayette), 1889–1974, U.S. businessman.

—**(James Henry) Leigh**, 1784–1859, Eng. author.

—**Richard Morris**, 1828–96, U.S. architect.

Hunter, John, 1728–93, Eng. surgeon.

Huntley, Chester Robert (Chet), 1911–74, U.S. news analyst & commentator.

Hunyadi, János, 1387?–1456, Hung. soldier & national hero.

Hurok, Sol, 1888–1974, Russ.-born U.S. impresario.

Husak, Gustav, 1913–, general secretary of the Communist party of Czechoslovakia 1969–& president 1975–.

Huss, John, 1369–1415, Bohemian religious reformer.

Hussein I, 1935–, king of Jordan 1952–.

Husserl, Edmund, 1859–1938, Ger. philosopher; founder of phenomenology.

Huston, John, 1906–, U.S. film director & actor.

—**Walter**, 1884–1950, Can.-born U.S. actor; father of prec.

Hutchins, Robert Maynard, 1899–1977, U.S. educator.

Hutchinson, Anne (Marbury), 1591–1643, U.S. religious leader.

—**Thomas**, 1711–80, U.S. colonial administrator.

Huxley A family of Eng. scientists & writers incl. **Aldous (Leonard)**, 1894–1963, author, **Sir Julian (Sorell)**, 1887–1975, biologist, brother of prec., **Thomas Henry**, 1825–95, biologist, grandfather of Aldous & Julian.

Huxtable, Ada Louise 1921–, U.S. architecture critic & journalist.

Huygens, Christian, 1629–95, Du. mathematician, physicist & astronomer.

Huysman, Joris Karl, 1848–1907, Fr. author.

Ibert, Jacques, 1890–1962, Fr. composer.

ibn-Khaldun, 1332–1406, Arab historian.

ibn Saud, Abdul Aziz, 1880–1953, king of Saudi Arabia 1932–53.

Ibsen, Henrik, 1828–1906, Norw. playwright & poet.

Ickes, Harold LeClair, 1874–1952, U.S. Lawyer & government official.

Ictinus, 5th. B.C. Gk. architect.

Ikeda, Hayato, 1899–1965, premier of Japan 1960–64.

Ikhnaton, king of Egypt 1375–1358 B.C.: also known as **Akhnaton, Amenhotep IV.**

Indy, Vincent d', 1851–1931, Fr. composer.

Inge, William, 1913–73, U.S. playwright.

Ingenhousz, Jan, 1730–99, Du. physician & plant physiologist.

Ingersoll, Robert Green, 1833–99, U.S. lawyer, author & lecturer.

Ingres, Jean Auguste Dominique, 1780–1867, Fr. painter.

Inman, Henry, 1801–46, U.S. painter.

Inness, George, 1825–94, U.S. painter.

Innocent III, b. Giovanni Latario de'Conti, 1161–1216, pope 1198–1216.

Inönü, Ismet, 1884–1973, first premier of Turkey; president 1938–50.

Insull, Samuel, 1859–1938, Eng.-born U.S. utilities executive.

Ionesco, Eugene, 1912–, Rumanian-born Fr. playwright.

Iqbal, Mohammed, 1873–1938, Moslem leader & national hero of Pakistan.

Irving, Sir Henry, 1838–1905, Eng. actor.

—**John**, 1942–, U.S. novelist.

—**Washington**, 1783–1859, U.S. author.

Isaacs, Alick, 1921–67, Eng. biologist.

Isabella I, 1451–1504, queen of Castile & wife of Ferdinand V; sponsored the voyages of Columbus.

Isherwood, Christopher (William Bradshaw), 1904–, Eng.-born U.S. author.

Ismail Pasha, 1830–95, khedive of Egypt 1863–79.

Iturbi, José, 1895–1980, Sp. pianist & conductor active in U.S.

Ivan III, 1440–1505, grand duke of Muscovy & founder of Russ. Empire: called **the Great.**

—**IV**, 1530–84, grand duke of Muscovy & first czar of Russia: called **the Terrible.**

Ives, Burl, 1909–, U.S. singer & actor.

—**Charles**, 1874–1954, U.S. composer.

Jackson, Andrew, 1767–1845, U.S. general & 7th U.S. president 1829–37.

—**Glenda**, 1936–, Eng. actress.

Jackson, Henry M(artin), 1912–, U.S. politician.
—**Jesse,** 1941–, U.S. Negro civil rights leader.
—**Mahalia,** 1911–72, U.S. gospel singer.
—**Thomas Jonathan ("Stonewall"),** 1824–63, U.S. Confederate general.
Jacobs, Henry (Hull), 1908–, U.S. tennis player.
Jacquard, Joseph Marie, 1752–1834, Fr. inventor.
Jagger, Mick, 1944–, Eng. singer & musician.
James I, 1566–1625, king of England 1603–25; also called **James** as king of Scotland 1567–1625.
—**II,** 1633–1701, king of England 1685–88; deposed.
James, Harry, 1916–, U.S. bandleader.
—**Henry,** 1843–1916, U.S. author & critic active in England.
—**Jesse (Woodson),** 1847–82, U.S. outlaw.
—**William,** 1842–1910, U.S. psychologist, philosopher, educator & author; brother of Henry.
Jamison, Judith, 1944–, U.S. dancer.
Janaček, Leoš, 1854–1928, Czech composer.
Janis, Elsie, 1889–1956, U.S. actress.
Jannings, Emil, 1887?–1950, Swiss-born actor active in Germany.
Jansen, Cornelis, 1585–1638, Du. theologian.
Jacques-Dalcroze, Émile, 1865–1590, Swiss composer & educator.
Jarrell, Randall, 1914–65, U.S. poet.
Jaspers, Karl, 1883–1969, Ger. philosopher.
Jastrow, Robert, 1925–, U.S. physicist.
Jaurès, Jean Léon, 1859–1914, Fr. socialist leader.
Jay, John, 1745–1829, Amer. statesman & first Chief Justice of the U.S. Supreme Court.
Jean, Grand Duke, 1921–, ruler of Luxembourg 1964–.
Jeans, Sir James Hopwood, 1877–1946, Eng. mathematician, astronomer, physicist & author.
Jeffers, (John) Robinson, 1887–1961, U.S. poet.
Jefferson, Joseph, 1829–1905, U.S. actor.
—**Thomas,** 1743–1826, Amer. statesman & 3rd. U.S. president 1801–09; drafted the Declaration of Independence.
Jellicoe, John Rushworth, (1st Earl Jellicoe), 1859–1935, Brit. admiral.
Jenner, Bruce, 1949–, U.S. decathlon athlete.
—**Edward,** 1749–1823, Eng. physician.
Jerome, Saint, 340?–420; early Church father & religious scholar.
Jespersen, (Jens) Otto (Harry), 1860–1943, Dan. linguist.
Jessel, George Albert, 1898–1981, U.S. comedian.
Jesus, 6? B.C.–A.D. 29, religious leader & founder of Christianity; also called **Jesus Christ & Jesus of Nazareth.**
Jewett, Sarah Orne, 1849–1909, U.S. author.
Joachim, Joseph, 1831–1907, Hung. violinist.
Joan of Arc, Saint, 1412–31, Fr. heroine; burned as a heretic: Fr. **Jeanne d'Arc;** also called **the Maid of Orleans.**
Jodl, Alfred, 1892?–1946, Ger. general.
Joffre, Joseph Jacques Césaire, 1852–1931, Fr. field marshal.
Joffrey, Robert, 1930–, U.S. choreographer & ballet-company director.
John, 1166?–1216, Eng. king 1199–1216; signed Magna Carta 1215.
John XXIII, Angelo Roncalli, 1881–1963, pope 1958–63.
John of Austria, Don, 1547–78, Sp.-born general.
John of the Cross, Saint, b. Juan de Yepis y Álvarez, 1542–91, Sp. mystic.
John of Gaunt, 1340–99, Eng. prince.
John, Augustus Edwin, 1878–1961, Eng. painter.
John Paul I, b. Albino Luciani, 1912–78, pope 1978.
John Paul II, b. Karol Wojtyla, 1920–, pope 1978–.
Johnson, Andrew, 1808–75, 17th U.S. president 1865–69.
—**Celia,** 1908–, Eng. actress.
—**Harold ("Chic"),** 1891–1962, U.S. comedian.
—**Howard (Deering),** 1896?–1972, U.S. businessman.
—**Jack (Arthur),** 1878–1946, U.S. boxer.
—**James Weldon,** 1871–1938, U.S. poet & author.
—**(Jonathan) Eastman,** 1824–1906, U.S. painter.
—**Lyndon Baines,** 1908–73, 36th U.S. president 1963–69.

Johnson, Philip (Cortelyou), 1906–, U.S. architect.
—**Samuel,** 1709–84, Eng. author, critic & lexicographer.
—**Virginia (Eshelman),** 1925–, U.S. sex researcher.
—**Walter Perry,** 1887–1946, U.S. baseball player.
Joliot-Curie, Frèderic, 1900–58 & his wife, **Irène** (daughter of Marie & Pierre Curie), 1897–1956, Fr. physicists.
Jolliet, Louis, 1645–1700, Can. explorer in America. Also **Joliet.**
Jolson, Al, 1886–1950, Russ.-born U.S. singer & actor.
Jones, Ernest, 1879–1958, Welsh-born Brit. psychoanalyst & author.
—**Inigo,** 1573–1652, Eng. architect & stage designer.
—**James,** 1921–77, U.S. author.
—**James Earl,** 1931–, U.S. actor.
—**John Luther ("Casey"),** 1864–1900, U.S. railroad engineer.
—**John Paul,** 1747–92, Scot.-born Amer. naval commander.
—**Robert Tyre, Jr. (Bobby),** 1902–71, U.S. golfer.
Jonson, Ben, 1572–1637, Eng. poet & playwright.
Joplin, Janis, 1943–70, U.S. singer.
—**Scott,** 1868–1917, U.S. jazz musician & composer.
Jordaens, Jacob, 1593–1678, Flemish painter.
Joseph, b. Hinmatonyalakit, 1840?–1904, Nez Percé Am. Ind. chief.
Josephine, 1763–1814, wife of Napoleon I 1796–1809 & empress of France 1804–09.
Josephus, Flavius, A.D. 37–100?, Jewish historian.
Joule, James Prescott, 1818–89, Eng. physicist.
Jouvet, Louis, 1887–1951, Fr. actor & stage director.
Jowett, Benjamin, 1817–93, Eng. classical scholar.
Joyce, James, 1882–1941, Irish author & poet.
—**William,** 1906–46, U.S.-born Brit. traitor during World War II; executed: called **Lord Haw-Haw.**
Juan Carlos I, 1938–, king of Spain 1975–.
Juarez, Benito Pablo, 1806–72, Mexican patriot; president of Mexico 1867–72.
Julian (L. Flavius Claudius Julianus), 331–363, Roman emperor: called **the Apostate.**
Juliana, 1909–, queen of the Netherlands 1948–.
Julius II, b. Giuliano della Rovere, 1443–1513, pope 1503–13.
Jung, Carl Gustav, 1875–1961, Swiss psychologist.
Junkers, Hugo, 1859–1935, Ger. airplane designer.
Jussieu, Antoine Laurent de, 1748–1836, Fr. botanist.
Justinian I, 483–565, Byzantine emperor; codifier of Roman law.
Juvenal, (L. Decimus Junius Juvenalis), A.D. 60?–140?, Roman poet.

Kadar, János, 1912–, first secretary of the Communist party of Hungary 1956–.
Kael, Pauline, 1919–, U.S. film critic.
Kafka, Franz, 1883–1924, Czech-born Austrian author.
Kagawa, Toyohiko, 1888–1960, Jap. Christian social reformer & author.
Kahn, Louis I., 1901–74, Estonian-born U.S. architect.
—**Otto Herman,** 1867–1934, Ger.-born U.S. banker, art patron & philanthropist.
Kaiser, Henry J(ohn), 1882–1967, U.S. industrialist.
Kalmar, Bert, 1884–1947, U.S. lyricist & librettist.
Kaltenborn, H(ans) V(on), 1878–1965, U.S. news commentator.
Kamehameha, 1758?–1819, king of Hawaii 1795–1819.
Kamerlingh Onnes, Heike, 1853–1926, Du. physicist.
Kandinski, Vasili, 1866–1944, Russ. painter active in Germany.
Kanin, Garson, 1912–, U.S. playwright & stage director.
Kano A family of 15th–17th c. Jap. painters, incl. **Masanobu,** 1453–90, & his sons, **Motonobu,** 1476–1559, & **Yokinobu,** 1513–75.
Kant, Immanuel, 1724–1804, Ger. philosopher.
Kantor, MacKinlay, 1904–77, U.S. writer.
Kapitza, Pyotr Leonidovich, 1894–, Russ. physicist.
Karajan, Herbert von, 1908–, Austrian conductor.
Karinska, (Barbara), 1886–, Russ.-born U.S. costume designer & maker.

Karloff, Boris, 1887–1969, Eng.-born actor active in U.S.

Karsavina, Tamara, 1885–1978, Russ. ballerina.

Karsh, Yousuf, 1908–, Armenian-born Can. photographer.

Kasavubu, Joseph, 1910–69, first president of the Congolese Republic (now Zaire) 1960–65.

Kassem, Abdul Karim, 1914–63, Iraqi general; premier of Iraq 1958–63; executed.

Kaufman, George, 1889–1961, U.S. playwright.

Kaunda, Kenneth David, 1924–, president of Zambia 1968–.

Kawabata, Yasunari, 1899–1972, Jap. author.

Kay, Ulysses S(impson), 1917–, U.S. composer.

Kaye, Danny, 1913–, U.S. comedian & actor.

Kazan, Elia, 1909–, Turkish-born U.S. stage & film director & author.

Kazantzakis, Nikos, 1885–1957, Gk. poet & author.

Kean, Edmund, 1787–1833, Eng. actor.

Keaton, Buster, 1895–1966, U.S. film actor & director.

Keats, John, 1795–1821, Eng. poet.

Keeler, Ruby, 1910–, Can.-born U.S. singer, dancer & actress.

Kefauver, Estes, 1903–63, U.S. politician.

Keino, Kipchoge, 1940–, Kenyan track runner.

Keitel, Wilhelm, 1882–1946, Ger. field marshal.

Kekkonen, Urho Kaleva, 1900–, president of Finland 1956–.

Kekulé von Stradonitz, Friedrich August, 1829–96, Ger. chemist.

Keller, Helen (Adams), 1880–1968, U.S. author & lecturer, blind and deaf from infancy.

Kelley, Clarence M., 1911–, U.S. government official; director of the FBI 1973–77.

Kellogg, Frank Billings, 1856–1937, U.S. statesman.

—**Will Keith,** 1860–1951, U.S. businessman.

Kelly, Alvin A. ("Shipwreck"), 1893–1952, U.S. flagpole sitter.

—**Ellsworth,** 1923–, U.S. painter & sculptor.

—**Emmett,** 1898–1979, U.S. circus clown.

—**Gene (Curran),** 1912–, U.S. dancer, singer, actor & choreographer.

—**George,** 1887–1971, U.S. playwright.

—**Walt(er),** 1913–73, U.S. cartoonist.

Kelvin, Lord (William Thompson), 1824–1907, Eng. physicist.

Kemal Atatürk, Mustafa, 1881–1938, Turkish general; president of Turkey 1923–38.

Kemble, Frances Anne (Fanny), 1809–93; Eng. actress.

Kempff, Wilhelm, 1895–, Ger. pianist.

Kempis, Thomas à, 1380–1471, Ger. mystic.

Kempton, (James) Murray, 1918–, U.S. journalist & social critic.

Kendall, Edward Calvin, 1886–1972, U.S. biochemist.

Kennan, George (Frost), 1904–, U.S. statesman & author.

Kennedy A U.S. family prominent in politics, incl. **Joseph Patrick,** 1888–1969, businessman & diplomat, his wife **Rose Fitzgerald,** 1890–, & their sons, **Edward (Moore),** 1932–, U.S. senator; **John Fitzgerald,** 1917–63, U.S. senator, 35th U.S. president 1961–63, assassinated; & **Robert Francis,** 1925–68, U.S. senator, assassinated.

Kennelly, Arthur Edwin, 1861–1939, Indian-born U.S. electrical engineer.

Kenner, (William) Hugh, 1923–, Can. author & critic active in U.S.

Kenny, Elizabeth, 1886–1952, Austral. nurse & physiotherapist; called **Sister Kenny.**

Kent, Rockwell, 1882–1971, U.S. painter & illustrator.

Kenton, Stan, 1912–79, U.S. jazz musician.

Kenyatta, Jomo, 1893?–1978, African nationalist leader & first president of Kenya 1963–1978.

Keokuk, 1788?–1848, Sauk Am. Ind. leader.

Kepler, Johannes, 1571–1630, Ger. astronomer.

Kerensky, Alexander Feodorovich, 1881–1970, Russ. revolutionary leader & prime minister of Soviet provisional government 1917.

Kern, Jerome (David), 1885–1945, U.S. composer.

Kerouac, Jack, 1922–69, U.S. author.

Kerr, Walter, 1913–, U.S. drama critic & author.

Kesselring, Albert, 1887–1960, Ger. field marshal.

Kettering, Charles Franklin, 1876–1958, U.S. electrical engineer & inventor.

Key, Francis Scott, 1780?–1843, U.S. lawyer; wrote "The Star-Spangled Banner."

Keynes, John Maynard, 1883–1946, Eng. economist.

Khachaturian, Aram, 1903–78, Armenian-born Soviet composer.

Khama, Sir Seretse, 1921–, president of Botswana 1965–.

Khomeini, Ayatollah Ruhollah, 1899?-, Iranian religious and political leader.

Khorana, Har Gobind, 1922–, Indian-born U.S. biochemist.

Khrushchev, Nikita Sergeyevich, 1894–1971, premier of the Soviet Union 1953–64.

Kidd, Michael, 1919–, U.S. choreographer.

—**Captain William,** 1645? –1701, Eng. privateer & pirate; hanged.

Kieran, John Francis, 1892–1981, U.S. author & journalist.

Kierkegaard, Soren Aabye, 1813–55, Dan. philosopher & theologian.

Kiesinger, Kurt Georg, 1904–, W. German politician; chancellor of W. Germany 1966–69.

Kilgallen, Dorothy, 1913–65, U.S. journalist.

Killy, Jean-Claude, 1943–, Fr. skier.

Kilmer, (Alfred) Joyce, 1886–1918, U.S. poet.

Kim Il Sung, 1912–, Korean military leader; premier of N. Korea 1948–.

King, Billie Jean, 1943–, U.S. tennis player.

—**Dennis,** 1897–1971, Eng. actor & singer.

—**Martin Luther, Jr.,** 1929–68, U.S. clergyman & Negro civil rights leader; assassinated.

—**(William Lyon) Mackenzie,** 1874–1950, prime minister of Canada 1921–26, 1926–30, & 1935–48.

Kingsley, Charles, 1819–75, Eng. clergyman & author.

—**Sidney,** 1906–, U.S. playwright.

Kinsey, Alfred Charles, 1894–1956, U.S. zoologist; pioneered in studies of human sexual behavior.

Kipling (Joseph) Rudyard, 1865–1936, Indian-born Eng. author.

Kipnis, Alexander, 1891–1978, Russ.-born U.S. basso.

—**Igor,** 1930–, Ger.-born U.S. harpsichordist; son of prec.

Kirchner, Ernst Ludwig, 1880–1938, Ger. painter.

Kirkland, Gelsey, 1953–, U.S. ballerina.

Kirov, Sergei Mironovich, 1888–1934, Russ. revolutionary.

Kirstein, Lincoln, 1907–, U.S. author, dance promoter & ballet-company director.

Kirsten, Dorothy, 1919–, U.S. soprano.

Kissinger, Henry A(lfred), 1923–, Ger.-born U.S. foreign-policy adviser; U.S. secretary of state 1973–77.

Kitchener, Horatio Herbert, (1st Earl Kitchener), 1850–1916, Brit. field marshal & statesman.

Kittredge, George Lyman, 1860–1941, U.S. Shakespeare scholar & editor.

Klee, Paul, 1879–1940, Swiss painter.

Kleist, Heinrich von, 1777–1811, Ger. playwright.

Klemperer, Otto, 1885–1973, Ger. conductor.

Kliegl, Anton T., 1872–1927, & his brother **John H.,** 1869–1959, Ger.-born U.S. lighting experts.

Klimt, Gustav, 1862–1918, Austrian painter.

Kline, Franz (Joseph), 1919–62, U.S. painter.

Klopstock, Friedrich Gottlieb, 1724–1803, Ger. poet.

Knievel, Robert ("Evel"), 1938–, U.S. motorcycle stunt man.

Knopf, Alfred A(braham), 1892–, U.S. publisher.

Knox, John, 1507?–72, Scot. Protestant clergyman & religious reformer.

Koch, John, 1909–78, U.S. painter.

—**Robert,** 1843–1910, Ger. bacteriologist.

Kocher, Emil Theodor, 1841–1917, Swiss surgeon.

Kodály, Zoltan, 1882–1967, Hung. composer.

Koestler, Arthur, 1905–, Hung.-born Eng. author.

Koffka, Kurt, 1886–1941, Ger.-born U.S. psychologist.

Kohler, Wolfgang, 1887–1967, Russ.-born U.S. psychologist.

Kokoschka, Oskar, 1886–1980, Austrian-born Brit. painter.

Kollwitz, Käthe, 1867–1945, Ger. painter, etcher & lithographer.

Konoye, Prince Fumimaro, 1891–1945, premier of Japan 1937–39 & 1940–41.

Koo, V(i) K(uyuin) Wellington 1887–, Chin. Statesman & diplomat.

Kooweskoowe, b. John Ross, 1790–1866, Cherokee Am. Ind. leader.

Korda, Alexander, 1893–1956, Hung.-born Brit. film director.

Korngold, Erich Wolfgang, 1897–1957, Austrian-born U.S. composer, conductor & pianist.

Korsakov, Sergei, 1853–1900, Russ. neurologist & psychiatrist.

Korzybski, Alfred (Habdank Skarbek), 1879–1950, Pol.-born U.S. linguist.

Kosciusko, Thaddeus, 1746–1817, Pol. patriot in the Amer. Revolution.

Kosinski, Jerzy, 1933–, Pol.-born U.S. novelist.

Kossel, Albrecht, 1853–1927, Ger. biochemist.

Kossuth, Louis, 1802–94, Hung. patriot.

Kostelanetz, André, 1901–80, Russ.-born U.S. conductor.

Kosygin, Alexei Nikolayevich, 1904–, Soviet statesman; premier of the Soviet Union 1964–.

Koufax, Sanford ("Sandy"), 1935–, U.S. baseball player.

Koussevitsky, Serge, 1874–1951, Russ.-born U.S. conductor.

Kovalevski, Alexander Onufriyevich, 1840–1901, Russ. embryologist.

Krafft-Ebing, Baron Richard von, 1840–1902, Ger. neurologist.

Kramer, Jack, 1921–, U.S. tennis player.

—Stanley, 1913–, U.S. film director.

Krebs, Sir Hans Adolf, 1900–81, Ger.-born Brit. biochemist.

Krehbiel, Henry Edward, 1854–1923, U.S. music critic.

Kreisky, Bruno, 1911–, Austrian politician; chancellor of Austria 1970–.

Kreisler, Fritz, 1875–1962, Austrian-born U.S. violinist.

Kresge, S. S., 1867–1966, U.S. merchant.

Kress, Samuel Henry, 1863–1955, U.S. businessman, art collector & philanthropist.

Krips, Josef, 1902–74, Austrian conductor.

Krishna Menon, V(engalil) K(rishnan), 1896–1974, Indian statesman.

Krock, Arthur, 1886–1974, U.S. journalist.

Kroeber, Alfred Louis, 1876–1960, U.S. anthropologist.

Kropotkin, Prince Pyotr Alekseevich, 1842–1921, Russ. geographer & revolutionary.

Kruger, Paul, 1825–1904, South African statesman; president of Transvaal 1883–1900.

Krupa, Gene, 1909–73, U.S. jazz musician.

Krupp, Alfred, 1912–87, Ger. munitions manufacturer.

Krupskaya, Nadezhda Konstantinovna, 1869–1939, Russ. social worker & revolutionist; wife of Nikolai Lenin.

Krutch, Joseph Wood, 1893–1970, U.S. critic & author.

Kubelik, Rafael, 1914–, Czech conductor & composer.

Kublai Khan, 1214–94, founder of the Mongol dynasty of China.

Kubrick, Stanley, 1928–, U.S. film director.

Kühne, Willy, 1837–1900, Ger. physiologist.

Kun, Béla, 1885–1937, Hung. communist leader.

Küng, Hans, 1928–, Swiss theologian.

Kunitz, Stanley, 1905–, U.S. poet.

Kunstler, William M., 1919–, U.S. lawyer.

Kurosawa, Akira, 1910–, Jap. film director.

Kurusu, Saburo, 1888–1954, Jap. diplomat.

Kusch, Polykarp, 1911–, Ger.-born U.S. physicist & educator.

Kutuzov, Mikhail Ilarionovich, 1745–1813, Russ. field marshal.

Kuznets, Simon, 1901–, Russ.-born U.S. economist.

Kyd, Thomas, 1558–94, Eng. playwright.

La Bruyère, Jean de, 1645–96, Fr. author.

LaChaise, François d'Aix de, 1624–1709, Fr. Jesuit priest.

Lachaise, Gaston, 1882–1935, Fr.-born U.S. sculptor.

Laemmle, Carl, 1867–1939, Ger.-born U.S. film producer.

Laënnec, René, 1781–1826, Fr. physician.

La Farge, John, 1835–1910, U.S. painter & stained-glass craftsman.

—Oliver (Hazard Perry), 1901–63, U.S. anthropologist & author.

Lafayette, Marie Joseph du Motier, Marquis de, 1757–1834, Fr. general & patriot; served in Amer. revolutionary army.

Lafitte, Jean, 1780?–1825?, Fr. pirate active in U.S.

La Follette, Robert M(arion), 1855–1925, U.S. senator & Progressive Party presidential candidate.

La Fontaine, Jean de, 1621–95, Fr. poet & writer of fables.

Lagerkvist, Pär, 1891–1974, Swed. author, poet & playwright.

Lagerlöf, Selma, 1858–1940, Swed. author.

Lagrange, Joseph Louis, 1736–1813, Fr. mathematician & astronomer.

La Guardia, Fiorello H(enry), 1882–1947, U.S. politician; mayor of New York City 1934–45.

Lahr, Bert, 1895–1967, U.S. comedian & actor.

Laine, ("Papa") Jack, 1873–1966, U.S. jazz musician.

Laing, R(onald) D., 1927–, Scot. psychoanalyst & author.

Lalo, Édouard (Victor Antoine), 1823–92, Fr. composer.

Lamarck, Jean Baptiste de Monet, Chevalier de, 1744–1829, Fr. naturalist.

Lamarr, Hedy, 1915–, Austrian-born U.S. actress.

Lamartine, Alphonse Marie Louis de Prat de, 1790–1869, Fr. poet.

Lamb, Charles, 1775–1834, Eng. author: pseud. **Elia.**

—Mary, 1764–1847, Eng. author; sister of prec.

Land, Edwin Herbert, 1909–, U.S. inventor & industrialist.

Landau, Lev Davidovich, 1908–68, Soviet physicist.

Landers, Ann, pseud. of Esther Pauline Friedman, 1918–, U.S. columnist.

Landis, Kenesaw Mountain, 1866–1944, U.S. jurist & baseball commissioner.

Landon, Alf(red Mossman), 1887–, U.S. politician.

Landor, Walter Savage, 1775–1864, Eng. poet & author.

Landowska, Wanda, 1879–1959, Pol. harpsichordist active in U.S. after 1941.

Landru, Henri, 1869–1922, Fr. murderer; executed: known as the modern Bluebeard.

Landseer, Sir Edwin Henry, 1802–73, Eng. painter.

Landsteiner, Karl, 1968–1943, Austrian-born U.S. pathologist.

Lane, Burton, 1912–, U.S. composer.

Lang, Andrew, 1844–1912, Scot. poet, scholar & author.

—Fritz, 1890–1976, Austrian-born U.S. film director.

Langdon, Harry, 1884–1944, U.S. vaudeville performer.

Lange, Dorothea, 1895–1965, U.S. photographer.

Langer, Susanne, 1895–, U.S. philosopher & educator.

Langland, William, 1332?–1400, Eng. poet.

Langley, John Newport, 1851–1925, Eng. physiologist.

—Samuel Pierpont, 1834–1906, U.S. astronomer.

Langmuir, Irving, 1881–1957, U.S. chemist.

Langtry, Lillie, 1853–1929, Eng. actress.

Lanier, Sidney, 1842–81, U.S. poet.

Lankester, Sir Edwin Ray, 1847–1929, Eng. zoologist.

Lansky, Meyer, 1902–, U.S. criminal.

Lao-tse, 604?–531? B.C., Chin. philosopher & mystic; founder of Taoism.

Laplace, Pierre Simon, Marquis de, 1749–1827, Fr. mathematician & astronomer.

Lapp, Ralph E(ugene), 1917–, U.S. physicist.

Lardner, Ring(gold Wilmer), 1885–1933, U.S. author.

La Rochefoucauld, Duc Francois de, 1613–80, Fr. writer.

Larousse, Pierre Athanase, 1817–75, Fr. grammarian & lexicographer.

La Salle, Sieur Robert, Cavalier de, 1643–87, Fr. explorer.

Lashley, Karl Spencer, 1890–1958, U.S. psychologist.

Lasker, Albert Davis, 1880–1952, Ger.-born U.S. businessman & philanthropist.
—**Emanuel,** 1868–1941, Ger. mathematician & chess master.
Laski, Harold Joseph, 1893–1950, Eng. Political scientist.
Latimer, Hugh, 1485?–1555, Eng. Protestant martyr.
La Tour, Georges de, 1593–1652, Fr. painter.
Latrobe, Benjamin Henry, 1764–1820, Eng.-born U.S. architect & engineer.
Lattimore, Owen, 1900–, U.S. author & oriental expert.
Lauder, Sir Harry, 1870–1950, Scot. singer.
Laue, Max Theodor Felix von, 1879–1960, Ger. physicist.
Laughton, Charles, 1899–1962, Eng.-born U.S. actor.
Laurel, (Arthur) Stan(ley), 1890–1965, Eng.-born U.S. comedian & actor.
Laurencin, Marie, 1885–1956, Fr. painter.
Laurier, Sir Wilfrid, 1841–1919, Can. statesman.
Laval, Pierre, 1883–1945, Fr. lawyer & politician.
LaValliére, Louise LeBlanc, Duchesse de, 1644–1710, mistress of Louis XIV.
Laver, Rod(ney George), 1938–, Austral. tennis player.
Laveran, Charles Louis Alphonse, 1845–1922. Fr. physician.
Lavoisier, Antoine Laurent, 1743–94, Fr. chemist & physicist.
Lavrovsky, Leonid M., 1905–67, Soviet choreographer.
Law, John, 1671–1729, Scot. financier & speculator.
Lawes, Lewis Edward, 1883–1947, U.S. penologist.
Lawrence, David, 1888–1973, U.S. journalist.
—**D(avid) H(erbert),** 1885–1930, Eng. author & poet.
—**Ernest O(rlando),** 1901–58, U.S. physicist.
—**Gertrude,** 1898–1952, Eng. actress active in U.S.
—**Sir Thomas,** 1769–1830, Eng. painter.
—**T(homas) E(dward),** 1888–1935, Eng. Soldier, archaeologist & author: known as **Lawrence of Arabia.**
Laxness, Halldór Kiljan, 1902–, Icelandic author.
Layne, Robert, 1926–, U.S. footabll player.
Lazarus, Emma, 1849–87, U.S. poet & author.
Leacock, Stephen Butler, 1869–1944, Can. economist & humorist.
Leadbelly, b. Huddie Ledbetter, 1888?–1949, U.S. folk singer.
Leahy, William Daniel, 1875–1959, U.S. admiral.
Leakey, Louis S(eymour) B(azett), 1903–72, and his wife **Mary Nicol Leakey,** 1913–, Brit. anthropologists.
Lean, David, 1908–, Eng. film director.
Lear, Edward, 1812–88, Eng. poet, painter & illustrator.
—**William Powell,** 1902–78, U.S. engineer & manufacturer.
Leavis, F(rank) R(aymond), 1895–1978, Eng. critic.
Le Brun, Charles, 1619–90, Fr. painter.
Le Carré, John, pseud. of David J. M. Cornwell, 1931–, Eng. author.
Leconte de Lisle, Charles Marie, 1818–94, Fr. poet.
Lederberg, Joshua, 1925–, U.S. geneticist.
Lee, Ann, 1736–84, Eng. mystic; founder of the Shaker movement in America.
—**Francis Lightfoot,** 1734–97, Amer. revolutionary patriot.
—**Gypsy Rose,** 1914–70, U.S. stripteaser & author.
—**Henry,** 1756–1818, Amer. revolutionary soldier & statesman: known as **Light-Horse Harry Lee.**
—**Peggy,** 1920–, U.S. singer.
—**Richard Henry,** 1732–94, Amer. revolutionary patriot.
—**Robert E(dward),** 1807–70, commander in chief of the Confederate Army; son of Henry.
—**Tsung-Dao,** 1926–, Chin.-born U.S. physicist.
Leeuwenhoek, Anton van, 1632–1723, Du. naturalist.
Le Gallienne, Eva, 1899–, Eng.-born U.S. actress.
—**Richard,** 1866–1947, Eng. author; father of prec.
Léger, Ferdinand, 1881–1955, Fr. painter.
Lehár, Franz, 1870–1948, Austrian composer.
Lehman, Herbert H(enry), 1878–1963, U.S. banker & politician.
Lehmann, Lili, 1848–1929, Ger. soprano.
—**Lotte,** 1888–1976, Ger. soprano.
Lehmbruck, Wilhelm, 1881–1919, Ger. sculptor.
Leibniz, Baron Gottfried Wilhelm von, 1646–1716. Ger.

philosopher & mathematician.
Leicester, Robert Dudley, 1st Earl of, 1532?–88, Eng. Eng. courtier.
Leider, Frida, 1888–1975, Ger. soprano.
Leigh, Vivien, 1913–67, Indian-born Eng. actress.
Leinsdorf, Erich, 1912–, Austrian-born U.S. conductor.
LeMay, Curtis E(merson), 1906–, U.S. air force officer.
Lemnitzer, Lyman L., 1899–, U.S. general.
Lenard, Phillip E. A., 1862–1947, Ger. physicist.
Lenclos, Ninon de, 1620–1705, Fr. courtesan & wit.
L'Enfant, Pierre Charles, 1754–1825, Fr. architect; planned Washington, D.C.
Lenglen, Suzanne, 1899–1938, Fr. tennis player.
Lenin, Nikolai, b. Vladimir Ilich Ulyanov, 1870–1924, Russ. revolutionary leader; premier of Soviet Union 1918–24.
Lennon, John, 1940–80, Eng. composer & musical performer.
Lenya, Lotte, 1900–81, Austrian singer & actress active in U.S.
Lenz, Heinrich F. E., 1804–65, Russ. physicist.
Leo I, Saint, 390?–461, pope 440–461: called **the Great.**
—**III, Saint,** 750?–816, pope 795–816.
—**X,** b. Giovanni de' Medici, 1475–1521, pope 1513–21.
Leonardo da Vinci, 1452–1519, Ital. Painter, sculptor, architect, engineer, inventor, musician, scientist & natural philosopher.
Leoncavallo, Ruggiero, 1858–1919, Ital. composer & librettist.
Leone, Giovanni, 1908–, Ital. politician; president of Italy 1971–78.
Leonidas, 5th c. B.C. Gk. military leader: king of Sparta 490?–480 B.C.
Leontief, Wassily W., 1906–, Russ.-born U.S. economist & author.
Leopardi, Count Giacomo, 1798–1837, Ital. poet.
Lepidus, Marcus Aemilius, ?–13 B.C., Roman statesman.
Lermontov, Mikhail Yurievich, 1814–41, Russ. poet & author.
Lerner, Alan Jay, 1918–, U.S. playwright & lyricist.
—**Max,** 1902–Russ.-born U.S. author & journalist.
Le Roy, Mervyn, 1900–, U.S. film director.
Leschetizky, Theodor, 1830–1915, Russ. pianist & composer.
Lesseps, Count Ferdinand de, 1805–94, Fr. engineer; built Suez Canal.
Lessing, Doris, 1919–, Iranian-born Brit. author.
—**Gotthold Ephraim,** 1729–81, Ger. playwright & critic.
Lester, Richard, 1932–Eng. film director.
Leutze, Emanuel, 1816–68, Ger.-born U.S. painter.
Levant, Oscar, 1906–72, U.S. pianist, composer & author.
Levene, Phoebus A. T., 1869–1940, Russ.-born U.S. chemist.
—**Sam,** 1905–, Russ.-born U.S. actor.
Leverrier, Urbain Jean Joseph, 1811–77, Fr. astronomer.
Levertov, Denise, 1923–, Eng.-born U.S. poet.
Levine, Jack, 1915–, U.S. painter.
—**Joseph E.,** 1905–, U.S. film producer.
Lévi-Strauss, Claude, 1908–, Belg.-born Fr. anthropologist.
Lewin, Kurt, 1890–1947, Ger.-born U.S. psychologist.
Lewis, Anthony, 1927–, U.S. journalist.
—**Cecil Day** See DAY-LEWIS, CECIL.
—**C(live) S(taples),** 1898–1963, Eng. author.
—**Gilbert N.,** 1875–1946, U.S. chemist.
—**Jerry,** 1926–, U.S. actor & comedian.
—**John L(lewellyn),** 1880–1969, U.S. labor leader.
—**Meriwether,** 1774–1809, U.S. explorer.
—**Oscar,** 1914–70, U.S. sociologist & author.
—**(Percy) Wyndham,** 1884–1957, Eng. painter & author.
—**Sinclair,** 1885–1951, U.S. author.
Lewisohn, Ludwig, 1883–1955, Ger.-born U.S. author & critic.
Lhevinne, Joseph, 1874–1944, Russ.-born U.S. pianist.
Li, Choh Hao, 1913–, Chin.-born U.S. biochemist.
Libby, W(illard) F(rank), 1908–80, U.S. chemist.

Lichtenstein, Roy, 1923–, U.S. artist.

Liddell Hart, Basil Henry, 1895–1970, Eng. military scientist.

Lie, Trygve, 1896–1968, Norw. statesman; first secretary general of the U.N. 1946–53.

Liebig, Baron Justus von, 1803–73, Ger. chemist.

Lifar, Serge, 1905–, Russ. dancer.

Ligeti, György, 1923–, Hung. composer.

Lilienthal, David Eli, 1899–1981, U.S. lawyer & administrator.

Lillie, Beatrice, 1898–, Can.-born comedienne & actress active in England & the U.S.

Lilly, John C., 1915–, U.S. neurophysiologist & biophysicist.

Limón, José, 1908–72, Mexican-born U.S. dancer, choreographer & dance-company director.

Lincoln, Abraham, 1809–65, 16th U.S. president 1861–65; assassinated.

Lind, James 1716–94, Scot. physician.

—Jenny, 1820–87, Swed. soprano.

Lindbergh, Anne Morrow, 1906–, U.S. author.

—Charles A(ugustus), 1902–74, U.S. aviator; made first transatlantic nonstop solo flight 1927; husband of prec.

Lindsay, Howard, 1889–1968, U.S. playwright.

—John Vliet, 1921–, U.S. politician.

—(Nicholas) Vachel, 1879–1931, U.S. poet.

Linklater, Eric, 1899–1974, Eng. author.

Linnaeus, Carolus, b. Carl von Linné, 1707–78, Swed. botanist & taxonomist.

Lin Biao, 1907–71, Chin. political leader.

Lin Yutang, 1895–1976, Chin. philologist & author.

Lipchitz, Jacques, 1891–1973, Lithuanian-born sculptor active in U.S.

Li Po, 700?–762, Chin. poet.

Lippi, Fra Filippo (Lippo), 1406?–69, & his son **Filippino,** 1457?–1504, Ital. painters.

Lippmann, Walter, 1889–1974, U.S. journalist.

Lipset, Seymour Martin, 1922–, U.S. sociologist.

Lipton, Sir Thomas Johnstone, 1850–1931, Eng. merchant & yachtsman.

Lissajous, Jules A., 1822–80, Fr. physicist.

Lister, Joseph, 1827–1912, Eng. surgeon.

Liszt, Franz, 1811–86, Hung. composer & pianist.

Littlewood, Joan, 1916–, Eng. theater director.

Litvinov, Maxim Maximovich, 1876–1951, Russ. revolutionary & statesman.

Liu Shaogi, 1898–1973, Chin. government official.

Livingstone, David, 1813–73, Scot. missionary & explorer in Africa.

—Mary, 1916–, U.S. radio personality.

Livy (Titus Livius), 59 B.C. – A.D. 17, Roman historian.

Lloyd George, David, 1863–1945, Brit. statesman; prime minister 1916–22.

Lloyd, Harold (Clayton), 1894–1971, U.S. actor & film producer.

Lobachevski, Nikolai Ivanovich, 1793–1856, Russ. mathematician.

Locke, John, 1632–1704, Eng. philosopher.

Lodge, Henry Cabot, 1902–, U.S. politician & diplomat.

Loesser, Frank, 1910–69, U.S. composer & lyricist.

Loewe, Frederick, 1904–, Austrian-born U.S. composer.

Loewi, Otto, 1873–1961, Ger.-born U.S. pharmacologist.

Loewy, Raymond (Fernand), 1893–, Fr.-born U.S. industrial designer.

Lofting, Hugh (John), 1886–1947, Eng.-born U.S. author & illustrator.

Logan, Joshua, 1908–, U.S. stage & film director, producer & author.

Lomax, John Avery, 1867–1948, & his son **Alan,** 1915–, U.S. folk-song collectors.

Lombard, Carole, 1909–42, U.S. actress.

Lombardi, Vince(nt Thomas), 1913–70, U.S. football coach.

Lombardo, Guy Albert, 1902–77, Can.-born U.S. bandleader.

Lombrosso, Cesare, 1836–1909, Ital. criminologist & physician.

London, George, 1920–, Can. bass-baritone.

—Jack, 1876–1916, U.S. author.

Long, Crawford Williamson, 1815–78, U.S. surgeon.

—Huey Pierce, 1893–1935, U.S. lawyer & politician, assassinated.

Longfellow, Henry Wadsworth, 1807–82, U.S. poet.

Longstreet, James, 1821–1904, U.S. Confederate general.

Lon Nol, 1913–, Cambodian general; president of the Khmer Republic 1970–75.

López Portillo, José, 1920–, president of Mexico 1976–1982.

Loren, Sophia, 1934–, Ital. actress.

Lorentz, Hendrik Antoon, 1853–1928, Du. physicist & author.

Lorenz, Konrad (Zacharias), 1903–, Austrian zoologist.

Lorre, Peter, 1904–64, Hung.-born actor active in U.S.

Losey, Joseph, 1909–, U.S. film director active in England.

Louis IX (Saint Louis), 1214–70, king of France 1226–70.

—XIII, 1601–43, king of France 1610–43.

—XIV, 1638–1715, king of France 1643–1715; son of prec.

—XV, 1710–74, king of France 1715–74; great-grandson of prec.

—XVI, 1754–93, king of France 1774–92; guillotined; grandson of prec.

—XVIII, 1755–1824, king of France 1814–15 & 1815–24; brother of prec.

Louis Philippe, 1773–1850, king of France 1830–48.

Louis, Joe, 1914–1981, U.S. boxer.

Lovecraft, H(oward) P(hillips), 1890–1937, U.S. author.

Lovelace, Richard, 1618–58, Eng. poet.

Lovell, Sir (Alfred Charles) Bernard, 1913–, Eng. astronomer.

Low, Sir David, 1891–1963, New Zealand-born Brit. cartoonist.

—Juliette Gordon, 1860–1927, U.S. founder of the Girl Scouts.

Lowell, Amy, 1874–1925, U.S. poet & critic.

—James Russell, 1819–91, U.S. poet & author.

—Percival, 1855–1916, U.S. astronomer; brother of Amy.

—Robert (Traill Spence, Jr.), 1917–77, U.S. poet.

Lowry, Malcolm, 1909–57, Eng. author.

Loy, Myrna, 1905–, U.S. actress.

Loyola, Saint Ignatius, b. Iñigo de Oñez y Loyola, 1491–1556, Sp. soldier & priest; founder with Francis Xavier of the Society of Jesus.

Lubitsch, Ernst, 1892–1947, Ger.-born U.S. film director.

Lübke, Heinrich, 1894–1972, W. German government official; president of W. Germany 1959–69.

Lucas, George, 1944–, U.S. film director.

Luce, Clare Boothe, 1903–, U.S. writer & diplomat.

—Henry R(obinson), 1898–1967, U.S. editor & publisher; husband of prec.

Luckman, Sid(ney), 1916–, U.S. football player.

Lucretius, 96?–55 B.C., Roman poet & philosopher.

Lucullus, Lucius Licinius, 1st c. B.C. Roman general & epicure.

Luening, Otto, 1900–, U.S. composer.

Lugosi, Bela, 1884–1956, Rumanian-born actor active in U.S.

Lukas, J. Anthony, 1933–, U.S. journalist.

—Paul, 1894–1971, Hung.-born actor active in U.S.

Lully, Jean Baptiste, 1633?–87, Ital.-born Fr. composer.

Lumet, Sidney, 1924–, U.S. film director.

Lumumba, Patrice, 1925–61, first prime minister of the Congolese Republic (now Zaire) 1960–61; assassinated.

Lunt, Alfred, 1892–1977, U.S. actor.

Lupino, Ida, 1918–, Eng.-born U.S. actress.

Luria, Salvador Edward, 1912–, Ital.-born U.S. microbiologist.

Luther, Martin, 1483–1546, Ger. monk, theologian & leader of the Protestant Reformation.

Luthuli, Albert J., 1899–1967, South African civil-rights leader.

Luxemburg, Rosa, 1870–1919, Ger. socialist leader.

Lycurgus, 7th c. B.C. Spartan lawgiver.

Lyell, Sir Charles, 1797–1875, Eng. geologist.

Lyly, John, 1554?–1606, Eng. author.

Lynch, Charles, 1736–96, U.S. justice of the peace.

Lynd, Robert Staughton, 1892–1970, & his wife Helen Merrell, 1897–, U.S. sociologists.

Lysenko, Trofim Denisovich, 1898–1976, Soviet agronomist.

Mabuse, Jan, b. Jan Gossaert, 1478?–1533?, Flemish painter.

MacArthur, Charles, 1895–1956, U.S. playwright.

—Douglas, 1880–1964, U.S. general & commander in chief of Allies in sw Pacific, World War II.

Macaulay, Thomas Babington, 1800–59, Eng. historian, author & statesman.

Macbeth, ?–1057, king of Scotland 1040–57.

Maccabeus, Judas, ?–150? B.C., Jewish patriot.

MacDiarmid, Hugh, pseud. of Christopher Murray Grieve, 1892–, Scot. poet.

MacDonald, George, 1824–1905, Scot. author.

—Dwight, 1906–, U.S. critic & author.

—(James) Ramsey, 1866–1937, Eng. statesman.

—Jeanette, 1906–65, U.S. actress & singer.

MacDowell, Edward Alexander, 1861–1908, U.S. composer.

Macfadden, Bernarr, 1868–1955, U.S. physical culturist & publisher.

Mach, Ernst, 1838–1916, Austrian physicist.

Machiavelli, Niccolò, 1469–1527, Florentine statesman & political theorist.

MacIver, Robert Morrison, 1882–1970, Scot.-born U.S. sociologist.

Mack, Connie, 1862–1956, U.S. baseball player & manager.

Mackenzie, William Lyon, 1795–1861, Scot.-born Can. insurgent leader.

MacLeish, Archibald, 1892–, U.S. poet.

Maclennan, Hugh, 1907–, Can. author.

Macleod, John James Rickard, 1876–1935, Scot. physiologist.

MacMahon, Aline, 1899–, U.S. actress.

—Comte Marie Edmé Patrice, 1808–93, Fr. general; president of France 1873–79.

Macmillan, Kenneth, 1930–, Eng. dancer, choreographer & ballet-company director.

—(Maurice) Harold, 1894–, Eng. statesman; prime minister 1957–63.

MacNeice, Louis, 1907–63, Irish-born Brit. poet.

Madison, Dolley, b. Dorothea Payne, 1768–1849, U.S. first lady & hostess.

—James, 1751–1836, 4th U.S. president 1809–17, husband of prec.

Maecenas, Gaius Cilnius, 73?–8 B.C., Roman statesman & patron of Horace & Virgil.

Maes, Nicolaes, 1632–93, Du. painter.

Maeterlinck, Maurice, 1862–1949, Belg. poet & playwright.

Magellan, Fernando, 1480–1521, Pg. explorer.

Magendie, François, 1783–1855, Fr. physiologist.

Maginot, Andre, 1877–1932, Fr. politician.

Magnani, Anna, 1908–73, Ital. actress.

Magritte, René, 1898–1967, Belg. painter.

Magsaysay, Ramón, 1907–57, Filipino statesman; president of the Philippines 1953–57.

Mahan, Alfred Thayer, 1840–1914, U.S. naval officer & historian.

Maharishi Mahesh Yogi, 1911?–, Indian guru.

Mahavira, Vardhamana Jnatiputra, ca. 6th c. B.C., Indian religious leader; founder of Jainism.

Mahler, Gustav, 1860–1911, Austrian composer.

Mailer, Norman, 1923–, U.S. author.

Maillol, Aristide, 1861–1944, Fr. sculptor.

Maimonides, 1135–1204, Sp. rabbi & philosopher.

Maintenon, Francoise d'Aubigné, Marquise de, 1635–1719, second wife of Louis XIV of France.

Makarios III, 1913–77, Cypriot Greek Orthodox archbishop; president of Cyprus 1960–74 & 1975–77.

Makarova, Natalya, 1940–, Soviet-born ballerina active in U.S.

Malamud, Bernard, 1914–, U.S. author.

Malan, Daniel F., 1874–1959, Afrikaner statesman.

Malcolm X, b. Malcolm Little, 1925–65, U.S. Negro leader; assassinated.

Malenkov, Georgi Maximilianovich, 1902–, premier of the Soviet Union 1953–55.

Malinowski, Bronislaw Kasper, 1884–1942, Pol.-born U.S. anthropologist.

Mallarmé, Stéphane, 1842–98, Fr. poet.

Malle, Louis, 1932–, Fr. film director.

Mallon, Mary, 1870?–1938, U.S. domestic servant & typhoid carrier: called Typhoid Mary.

Malory, Sir Thomas, ?–1470?, Eng. writer; translated Arthurian legends into English.

Malpighi, Marcello, 1628–94, Ital. anatomist.

Malraux, André, 1901–76, Fr. author & government official.

Malthus, Thomas Robert, 1766–1834, Eng. political economist.

Mamoulian, Rouben, 1897–, Russ.-born U.S. stage director.

Mancini, Henry, 1924–, U.S. composer & pianist.

Manes, 216?–276?, Pres. prophet; founder of Manicheism.

Manet, Édouard, 1832–83, Fr. painter.

Maney, Richard, 1891–1968, U.S. press agent.

Mankiewicz, Joseph L., 1909–, U.S. film director & screenwriter.

Mann, Horace, 1796–1859, U.S. educator.

—Thomas, 1875–1955, Ger. author active in U.S.

Mannes, Marya, 1904–, U.S. author & journalist.

Manolete, b. Manuel Laureano Rodríguez y Sánchez, 1917–47, Sp. bullfighter.

Mansart, Jules Hardouin, 1646?–1708, Fr. architect.

Mansfield, Katherine, 1888–1923, New Zealand-born Brit. author.

—Michael Joseph (Mike), 1903–, U.S. senator.

—Richard, 1854–1907, Eng. actor active in U.S.

Mantegna, Andrea, 1431–1506, Ital. painter & engraver.

Mantle, Mickey (Charles), 1931–, U.S. baseball player.

Mantovani, Annunzio, 1905–, Ital. conductor.

Manulis, Martin, 1915–, U.S. radio & TV producer.

Manutius, Aldus, b. Teobaldo Manucci, 1450–1515, Ital. printer & classical scholar.

Manzoni, Alessandro Francesco, 1785–1873, Ital. author.

Mao Zedong (Tse-tung), 1893–1976, Chin. statesman; chairman of the People's Republic of China 1954–76.

Marat, Jean Paul, 1743–93, Fr. revolutionary leader; assassinated by Charlotte Corday.

Marble, Alice, 1913–, U.S. tennis player.

Marc, Franz, 1880–1916, Ger. painter.

Marceau, Marcel, 1923–, Fr. mime.

March, Fredric, 1897–1975, U.S. actor.

Marciano, Rocky, 1924–69, U.S. boxer.

Marconi, Guglielmo, 1874–1937, Ital. inventor of wireless telegraphy.

Marcos, Ferdinand Edralin, 1917–, Filipino politician; president of the Philippines 1965–.

Marcus Aurelius, A.D. 121–180, Roman emperor & philosopher.

Marcuse, Herbert, 1898–1979, Ger.-born U.S. philosopher.

Margaret, 1353–1412, Queen of Denmark, Norway & Sweden.

Margaret Rose, 1930–, Eng. princess, the sister of Queen Elizabeth II.

Margrethe II, 1940–, queen of Denmark 1972–.

Maria Theresa, 1717–80, queen of Hungary & Bohemia.

Marie Antoinette, 1755–93, Austrian-born queen of Louis XVI of France; guillotined.

Marignac, Jean de, 1817–94, Swiss chemist.

Marin, John Cheri, 1870–1953, U.S. painter.

Marini, Marino, 1901–80, Ital. sculptor.

Marion, Francis, 1732?–95, Amer. revolutionary commander: called the Swamp Fox.

Maritain, Jacques, 1882–1973, Fr. philosopher.

Markevich, Igor, 1912–, Russ.-born Swiss conductor.

Markham, (Charles) Edwin, 1852–1940, U.S. poet.

Markova, Alicia, 1910–, Eng. ballerina.

Marlborough, John Churchill, Duke of, 1650–1722,

Eng. general & statesman.

Marlowe, Christopher, 1564–93, Eng. playwright.

—**Julia,** 1866–1950, Eng.-born U.S. actress.

Marquand, J(ohn) P(hilips), 1893–1960, U.S. author.

Marquette, Jacques, 1637–75, Fr. explorer of America.

Marquis, Don(ald Robert Perry), 1878–1937, U.S. journalist & humorist.

Marsh, Dame Ngaio, 1899–1982, New Zealand author.

—**Reginald,** 1898–1954, U.S. painter.

Marshall, George C(atlett), 1880–1959, U.S. general & statesman; chief of staff of U.S. Army in World War II.

—**John,** 1755–1835, U.S. statesman & jurist; Chief Justice of the U.S. Supreme Court 1801–35.

—**Thurgood,** 1908–, U.S. jurist; justice of the U.S. Supreme Court 1967–.

Martel, Charles, 688?–741, Frankish king 715–741; grandfather of Charlemagne.

Marti, José (Julian), 1853–95, Cuban lawyer & revolutionary.

Martial, (L. Marcus Valerius Martialis), A.D. 40?–104?, Roman poet.

Martin, John, 1893–, U.S. dance critic.

—**Mary,** 1913–, U.S. singer & actress.

Martin du Gard, Roger, 1881–1958, Fr. author.

Martinelli, Giovanni, 1885–1969, Ital. tenor active in U.S.

Martini, Simone, 1283?–1344, Ital. painter.

Marvell, Andrew, 1621–78, Eng. poet.

Marx A family of U.S. actors & comedians. four brothers: **Arthur ("Harpo"),** 1893–1964; **Herbert ("Zeppo"),** 1901–1979; **Julius ("Groucho"),** 1895–1977, **Leonard ("Chico"),** 1891–1961.

—**Karl,** 1818–83, Ger. socialist writer; author of *Das Kapital.*

Mary I, 1516–58 queen of England 1553–58; known as **Bloody Mary** or **Mary Tudor.**

—**II,** 1662–94, queen of England 1689–94; co-ruler with her husband, William III.

Mary, Queen of Scots (Mary Stuart), 1542–87, queen of Scotland 1561–67; beheaded.

Masaccio, b. Tommaso Guidi, 1402–38, Florentine painter.

Masaryk, Jan Garrigue, 1886–1948, Czech diplomat & politician.

—**Thomas,** 1850–1937, first president of Czechoslovakia 1918–35; father of prec.

Mascagni, Pietro, 1863–1945, Ital. composer.

Masefield, John, 1878–1967, Eng. poet.

Maslow, Abraham, 1908–, U.S. author & psychologist.

Mason, Charles, 1730–87, Eng. astronomer & surveyor; with Jeremiah Dixon, established Mason-Dixon line.

—**James,** 1909–, Eng.-born actor active in U.S.

Massasoit, 1580?–1661, Am. Ind. chief of the Wampanoag tribes of Massachusetts.

Massenet, Jules, 1842–1912, Fr. composer.

Massey, Raymond, 1896–, Can.-born U.S. actor.

Massine, Leonide, 1896–1979, Russ.-born U.S. choreographer & dancer.

Masters, Edgar Lee, 1869–1950, U.S. poet.

—**William Howell,** 1915–, U.S. physician & sex researcher.

Masterson, William Barclay ("Bat"), 1853–1921, U.S. frontier peace officer & journalist.

Mastroianni, Marcello, 1924–, Ital. actor.

Mather, Cotton, 1663–1728, Amer. theologian.

Mathewson, Christopher (Christy), 1880–1925, U.S. baseball player.

Mathias, Robert Bruce (Bob), 1930–, U.S. decathlon athlete & politician.

Matisse, Henri, 1869–1954, Fr. painter.

Matsuoka, Yosuke, 1880–1946, Jap. statesman.

Maugham, W(illiam) Somerset, 1874–1965, Eng. author & playwright.

Mauldin, William H. (Bill), 1921–, U.S. cartoonist.

Maupassant, Guy de, 1850–93, Fr. author.

Mauriac, Francois, 1885–1970, Fr. author.

Maurois, André, 1885–1967, Fr. author.

Mauser, Peter Paul, 1838–1914, & his brother, **Wilhelm,** 1834–82, Ger. inventors.

Maverick, Samuel Augustus, 1803–70, U.S. cattle rancher & public official.

Maxim, Sir Hiram Stevens, 1840–1916, U.S.-born Brit. inventor.

Maxim, Hudson, 1853–1927, U.S. inventor & explosives expert; brother of prec.

Maximilian (Ferdinand Joseph), 1832–67, Austrian archduke, emperor of Mexico 1864–67; executed.

Maxwell, Elsa, 1883–1963, U.S. columnist & noted hostess.

—**James Clerk,** 1831–79, Scot. physicist.

May, Elaine, 1932–, U.S. actress & film director.

—**Rollo,** 1909–, U.S. psychoanalyst & philosopher.

Mayakovsky, Vladimir (Vladimirovich), 1893–1930, Russ. poet & playwright.

Mayer, Jean, 1920–, Fr. nutritionist active in U.S.

—**Louis B(urt),** 1885–1958, Russ.-born U.S. film producer.

Mayo, Charles Horace, 1865–1939, U.S. surgeon.

—**William James,** 1861–1939, U.S. surgeon; brother of prec.

Mays, Willie (Howard), 1931–, U.S. baseball player.

Mazzini, Giuseppe, 1805–72, Ital. patriot & revolutionary.

Mboya, Thomas J. (Tom), 1930–69, Kenyan political leader.

McBride, Mary Margaret, 1899–1976, U.S. radio personality.

—**Patricia,** 1942–, U.S. ballerina.

McCarey, Leo, 1898–1969, U.S. film director.

McCarthy, Eugene Joseph, 1916–, U.S. politician.

—**Joseph Raymond,** 1908–57, U.S. politician.

—**Mary,** 1912–, U.S. author & critic.

McCartney, Paul, 1942–, Eng. composer & musical performer.

McClellan, George Brinton, 1826–85, U.S. general.

McClintic, Guthrie, 1893–1961, U.S. theater director.

McClure, Samuel Sidney, 1857–1949, Irish-born U.S. editor & publisher.

McCormack, John, 1884–1945, Irish-born U.S. tenor.

—**John William,** 1891–1980, U.S. politician.

McCormick, Cyrus Hall, 1809–84, U.S. inventor of the reaping machine.

—**Joseph Medill,** 1877–1925, U.S. newspaper publisher.

—**Robert Rutherford,** 1880–1955, U.S. newspaper publisher; brother of prec.

McCullers, Carson, 1917–67, U.S. novelist.

McEnroe, John, 1959–, U.S. tennis player.

McGill, James, 1744–1813, Scot.-born Can. businessman & philanthropist.

McGinley, Phyllis, 1904–78, U.S. poet.

McGovern, George Stanley, 1922–, U.S. politician.

McGraw, John Joseph, 1873–1934, U.S. baseball player & manager.

McGuffey, William Holmes, 1800–73, U.S. educator.

McKenna, Siobhan, 1923–, Irish actress.

McKim, Charles Follen, 1847–1909, U.S. architect.

McKinley, William, 1843–1901, 25th U.S. president 1897–1901; assassinated.

McKuen, Rod (Marvin), 1933–, U.S. composer & poet.

McLaglen, Victor, 1886–1959, Eng. actor active in U.S.

McLuhan, (Herbert) Marshall, 1911–, Can. educator & author.

McMillan, Edwin Mattison, 1907–, U.S. chemist.

McNamara, Robert S(trange), 1916–, U.S. government official & president of World Bank 1968–.

McPherson, Aimee Semple, 1890–1944, Can.-born U.S. evangelist.

McQueen, Steve, 1930–80, U.S. actor.

Mead, Margaret, 1901–78, U.S. anthropologist.

Meade, George Gordon, 1815–72, U.S. Civil War general.

Meany, George, 1894–1980, U.S. labor leader; president of the AFL-CIO 1955–.

Medici, Catherine de, 1519–89, Florentine-born queen of Henry II of France.

—**Cosimo I de,** 1519–74, Duke of Florence & Grand Duke of Tuscany: called **the Great.**

—**Lorenzo de,** 1448?–92, Florentine prince, statesman & patron of the arts; called **the Magnificent.**

Medici, Emilio Garrastazu, 1905–, Brazilian military officer; president of Brazil 1969–74.

Mehta, Zubin, 1936–, Indian-born conductor active in the U.S.

Meir, Golda, 1898–1978, Russ-born Israeli stateswoman; prime minister of Israel 1969–74.

Meiss, Millard, 1904–75, U.S. art historian.

Meitner, Lise, 1878–1968, Ger. physicist.

Melba, Dame Nellie, 1861–1931, Austral. soprano.

Melchoir, Lauritz, 1890–1973, Dan. baritone.

Mellon, Andrew William 1855–1937, U.S. financier.

Melville, Herman, 1819–91, U.S. author.

Memling, Hans, 1430–95, Flemish painter.

Menander, 343?–291? B.C., Gk. playwright.

Mencken, H(enry) L(ouis), 1880–1956, U.S. author, editor & critic.

Mendel, Gregor Johann, 1822–84, Austrian monk & botanist.

Mendeleyev, Dimitri Ivanovich, 1834–1907, Russ. chemist.

Mendelssohn, Felix, 1808–47, Ger. composer.

Mendès-France, Pierre, 1907–, Fr. politician.

Menken, Helen, 1902–66, U.S. actress.

Menninger, Karl Augustus, 1893–, U.S. psychiatrist.

Menotti, Gian Carlo, 1911–, Ital.-born U.S. composer.

Menuhin, Yehudi, 1916–, U.S. violinist.

Menzies, Sir Robert Gordon, 1894–1978, Austral. statesman.

Mercator, Gerhard, 1512–94, Flemish geographer & cartographer.

Mercer, Johnny, 1909–1976, U.S. lyricist.

—**Mabel,** 1900–, Eng.-born U.S. singer.

Meredith, George, 1828–1909, Eng. author & poet.

Mergenthaler, Ottmar, 1854–99, Ger.-born U.S. inventor of the Linotype machine.

Mérimée, Prosper, 1803–70, Fr. author.

Merman, Ethel, 1909–, U.S. singer & actress.

Merrick, David, 1912–, U.S. theatrical producer.

Merrill, Robert, 1919–, U.S. baritone.

Merton, Thomas, 1915–68, Fr.-born U.S. monk & author.

Merwin, W(illiam) S(tanley), 1927–, U.S. poet.

Mesmer, Friedrich Anton, 1734–1815, Austrian physician.

Messalina, Valeria, ?–A.D. 48, third wife of Emperor Claudius.

Messerschmitt, Willy, 1898–1978, Ger. aircraft designer & manufacturer.

Mesta, Perle, 1891–1975, U.S. hostess & diplomat.

Mestrovic, Ivan, 1883–1962, Yugoslav-born U.S. sculptor.

Metaxas, Joannes, 1871–1941, Gk. general & dictator.

Metchnikoff, Élie, 1845–1916, Russ. zoologist & bacteriologist.

Metternich, Prince Klemens von, 1773–1858, Austrian statesman.

Meyer, Adolf, 1866–1950, Swiss-born U.S. psychiatrist.

—**Julius L.,** 1830–95, Ger. chemist.

Meyerbeer, Giacomo, 1791–1864, Ger. composer active in France.

Meyerhof, Otto, 1884–1951, Ger. physiologist.

Meyerhold, Vsevolod Emilievich, 1874–1940, Russ. theatrical director & producer.

Michelangelo (Buonarroti), 1475–1564, Ital. sculptor, architect, painter & poet.

Michelet, Jules, 1798–1874, Fr. historian.

Michelson, Albert Abraham, 1852–1931, Ger.-born U.S. physicist.

Michener, James A(lbert), 1907–, U.S. author.

—**Roland,** 1900–, Can. politician; governor-general of Canada 1967–74.

Midler, Bette, 1945–, U.S. singer & comedienne.

Mielziner, Jo, 1901–76, Fr.-born set designer active in U.S.

Mies van der Rohe, Ludwig, 1886–1969, Ger.-born U.S. architect.

Mikan, George (Larry), 1924–, U.S. basketball player.

Miki, Takeo, 1907–, prime minister of Japan 1974–76.

Mikoyan, Anastas Ivanovich, 1895–1978, president of U.S.S.R. 1964–65.

Milanov, Zinka, 1906–, Yugoslav opertic soprano active in U.S.

Milburn, Rodney, 1950–, U.S. track athlete.

Milestone, Lewis, 1895–1980, U.S. film director.

Milhaud, Darius, 1892–1974, Fr. composer.

Mill, John Stuart, 1806–73, Eng. philospher & political economist.

Millay, Edna St. Vincent, 1892–1950, U.S. poet.

Miller, Arthur, 1915–, U.S. playwright.

—**Glenn,** 1904–44. U.S. bandleader & arranger.

—**Henry,** 1891–1980, U.S. author.

—**Joseph (Joe),** 1684–1738, Eng. comedian.

—**Perry (Gilbert Eddy),** 1905–63, U.S. scholar & critic.

Miles, Carl (Wilhelm Emil), 1875–1955, Swed.-born U.S. sculptor.

Millet, Jean Francois, 1814–75, Fr. painter.

Millikan, Robert Andrews, 1868–1953, U.S. physicist.

Mills, John, 1908–, Eng. actor.

Milne, A(lan) A(lexander), 1882–1956, Eng. author.

Milstein, Nathan, 1904–, Russ. violinist.

Miltiades, 540?–489? B.C., Athenian general.

Milton, John, 1608–74, Eng. poet.

Mindszenty, Jozsef Cardinal, 1892–1975, Hung. Roman Catholic prelate.

Mingus, Charles (Charlie), 1922–79, U.S. jazz musician.

Minh, Duong Van, 1916–, S. Vietnamese general; president of S. Vietnam 1975; called **Big Minh.**

Minkowski, Hermann, 1864–1909, Russ.-born mathematician active in Germany.

Minnelli, Liza, 1946–, U.S. singer & actress.

—**Vincente,** 1913–, U.S. film director, father of prec.

Minnesota Fats, b. Rudolf Walter Wanderone, Jr., 1913–, U.S pool player.

Minuit, Peter, 1580–1638, first Du. director-general of New Netherland (including New York).

Mirabeau, Gabriel Honoré de Riquetti, Comte de, 1749–91, Fr. revolutionary orator & statesman.

Miranda, Carmen, 1917–1955, Pg.-born actress & singer active in U.S.

Miró, Joan, 1893–, Sp. painter.

Mishima, Yukio, 1925–70, Jap. novelist.

Mistral, Gabriela, 1889–1957, Chilean poet.

Mitchell, Arthur, 1934–, U.S. ballet dancer, choreographer & ballet-company director.

—**Margaret,** 1900–49, U.S. author.

—**William ("Billy"),** 1879–1936, U.S. general & air force advocate.

Mitford, Jessica, 1917–, Eng. author.

—**Nancy,** 1904–73, Eng. author; sister of prec.

Mithridates, VI, c. 132–63 B.C., king of Pontus: called **the Great.**

Mitropoulos, Dmitri, 1896–1960, Gk.-born U.S. conductor.

Mitterand, François, 1916–, Fr. statesman; President 1981–.

Mix, Thomas Edwin (Tom), 1880–1940, U.S. actor.

Mizoguchi, Kenji, 1898–1956, Jap. film director.

Möbius, August Ferdinand, 1790–1868, Ger. mathematician.

Mobutu Sese Seko, b. Joseph Desiré Mobutu, 1930–, president of Zaire 1964–.

Modigliani, Amadeo, 1844–1920, Ital. painter & sculptor active in France.

Modjeska, Helena (Opid), 1840–1909, Pol.-born actress active in U.S.

Mohammed, 570–632. Arabian religious & military leader, founder of Islam & author of the Koran.

Mohammed Reze Pahlavi, 1919–1980, shah of Iran 1941–79.

Moholy-Nagy, Laszlo, 1895–1946, Hung. painter, designer & photographer active in Germany & U.S.

Mohorovicic, Andrija, 1857–1936, Yugoslav geologist.

Moiseyev, Igor, 1906–, Soviet choreographer & dance-company director.

Molière, pseud. of Jean Baptiste Poquelin, 1622–73, Fr. playwright.

Molnár, Ferenc, 1878–1952, Hung. playwright & author.

Molotov, Vyacheslav Mikhailovich, 1890–, Soviet statesman; foreign minister of the Soviet Union 1939–49 & 1953–56.

Moltke, Count Helmuth von, 1800–91, Prussian field marshal.

Molyneux, Edward, 1894–1974, Eng. fashion designer.

Mondale, Walter F(rederick) 1928–, U.S. statesman; U.S. vice-president 1977–1981.
Mondrian, Piet, 1872–1944, Du. painter.
Monet, Claude, 1840–1926, Fr. painter.
Monk, Julius, 1912–, U.S. nightclub producer & director.
—**Thelonious,** 1920–82, U.S. jazz musician.
Monmouth, James Scott, Duke of, 1649–85, Eng. rebel & claimant to throne; illegitimate son of Charles II.
Monnet, Jean, 1888–1978, Fr. political economist & statesman.
Monod, Jacques Lucien, 1910–76, Fr. biochemist & author.
Monroe, Harriet, 1860–1936, U.S. poet & editor.
—**James,** 1758–1831, 5th U.S. president 1817–25.
—**Marilyn,** 1926–62, U.S. film actress.
Montagu, Lady Mary Wortley, 1689–1762, Eng. letter writer.
—**(Montague Francis) Ashley,** 1905–, Eng.-born U.S. anthropologist.
Montaigne, Michel Eyquem de, 1533–92, Fr. author.
Montand, Yves, 1921–, Ital.-born Fr. actor & singer.
Montcalm, Joseph Louis, 1712–59, Fr. general.
Montefiore, Sir Moses Haim, 1734–1885, Ital.-born Brit. financier & philanthropist.
Montespan, Françoise Athenaïs Rochechouart, Marquise de, 1641–1707, mistress of Louis XIV of France.
Montesquieu, Baron de la Brède et de, title of Charles de Secondat, 1689–1755, Fr. jurist, philosopher & historian.
Montessori, Maria, 1870–1952, Ital. educator.
Monteux, Pierre, 1875–1964, Fr.-born U.S. conductor.
Monteverdi, Claudio, 1567–1643, Ital. composer.
Montez, Lola, 1818–61, Irish-born dancer & adventuress.
Montezuma II, 1479?–1520, Aztec Indian emperor of Mexico.
Montgolfier, Joseph Michel, 1740–1810, & his brother **Jacques Etienne,** 1745–99, Fr. inventors & balloonists.
Montgomery, Bernard Law, 1st Viscount, 1887–1976, Eng. field marshal.
—**Robert,** 1904–1981, U.S. actor & film & television producer.
Montherlant, Henri (Millon) de, 1896–1972, Fr. author.
Moody, Dwight Lyman, 1837–99, U.S. evangelist.
—**Helen Wills,** 1905–, U.S. tennis player.
Moore, Clement Clarke, 1779–1863, U.S. lexicographer & poet.
—**Douglas,** 1893–1969, U.S. composer.
—**George,** 1852–1933, Irish author, critic & playwright.
—**Grace,** 1901–47, U.S. soprano & actress.
—**Henry,** 1898–, Eng. sculptor.
—**Marianne,** 1887–1972, U.S. poet.
—**Mary Tyler,** 1937–, U.S. actress.
—**Thomas,** 1779–1852, Irish poet.
—**Victor,** 1876–1962, U.S. actor.
Moorehead, Agnes, 1906–74, U.S. actress.
Moravia, Alberto, pseud. of Alberto Pincherle, 1907–, Ital. author.
More, Sir Thomas, 1478–1535, Eng. statesman & writer; beheaded; canonized 1935.
Moreau, Gustave, 1826–98, Fr. painter.
—**Jeanne,** 1928–, Fr. actress.
Morgan, Helen, 1900–41, U.S. singer & actress.
—**Henry,** 1915–, U.S. TV personality.
—**Sir Henry,** 1635?–88, Eng. buccaneer.
—**John Hunt,** 1825–64, U.S. Confederate cavalry officer.
—**J(ohn) Pierpont,** 1837–1913, U.S. financier.
—**Lewis Henry,** 1818–81, U.S. anthropologist.
—**Michèle,** 1920–, Fr. actress.
—**Thomas Hunt,** 1866–1945, U.S. geneticist.
Morgenthau, Henry, 1891–1967, U.S. government official.
Morison, Samuel Eliot, 1887–1976, U.S. historian.
—**Stanley,** 1889–1968, Eng. type designer.
Morisot, Berthe, 1841–95, Fr. painter.
Morita, Akio, 1921–, Jap. physicist & business executive.
Morley, Christopher Darlington, 1890–1957, U.S. author.
—**Edward Williams,** 1838–1923, U.S. chemist & physicist.

Morley, Robert, 1908–, Eng. actor.
Morphy, Paul, 1837–84, U.S. chess master.
Morris, Gouverneur, 1752–1816, U.S. statesman & diplomat.
—**Robert** 1734–1806, U.S. financier & statesman.
—**William,** 1834–96, Eng. painter, craftsman & poet.
Morse, Samuel F(inley) B(reese), 1791–1872, U.S. artist & inventor of the telegraph.
Morton, Ferdinand Joseph ("Jelly Roll"), 1885–1941, U.S. jazz musician.
—**William T. G.,** 1819–68, U.S. dentist.
Mosconi, Willie, 1913–, U.S. billiards player.
Moseley, Henry Gwyn-Jeffreys, 1887–1915, Eng. physicist.
Moses, Anna Mary Robertson, 1860–1961, U.S. painter: called **Grandma Moses.**
—**Robert,** 1888–1981, U.S. public official.
Mosley, Sir Oswald Ernald, 1896–, Eng. fascist politician.
Mossadegh, Mohammed, 1881–1967, Pers. statesman; prime minister of Iran 1951–53.
Mössbauer, Rudolf Ludwig, 1929–, Ger.-born U.S. physicist.
Mostel, Sam ("Zero"), 1915–77, U.S. actor.
Motherwell, Robert, 1915–, U.S. painter.
Mott, Charles Stewart, 1875–1973, U.S. industrialist.
—**Lucretia (Coffin),** 1798–1880, U.S. social reformer.
Mountbatten, Louis, Earl, 1900–79, Eng. admiral & governor general of India 1947–48.
Moussorgsky, Modest Petrovich, 1835–81, Russ. composer.
Moynihan, Daniel Patrick, 1927–, U.S. sociologist & government official.
Mozart, Wolfgang Amadeus, 1756–91, Austrian composer.
Mubarak, Hosni, 1929–, Egyptian statesman and president 1981–.
Muggeridge, Malcolm, 1903–, Eng. editor & author.
Muhammad, Elijah, b. Elijah Poole, 1897–1975, U.S. religious leader.
Muir, John, 1838–1914, U.S. naturalist.
Muller, Herman J., 1890–1967, U.S. geneticist.
Müller, Paul, 1899–1965, Swiss chemist.
Mulligan, Gerald Joseph (Gerry), 1927–, U.S. jazz musician.
Mumford, Lewis, 1895–, U.S. author.
Munch, Charles, 1891–1968, Fr.-born U.S. conductor.
—**Edvard,** 1863–1944, Norw. painter.
Münchausen, Baron Karl Friedrich von, 1720–97, Ger. soldier & adventurer.
Muni, Paul, 1895–1967, U.S. actor.
Muñoz Marín, Luis, 1898–1980, governor of Puerto Rico 1948–64.
Murasaki, Lady, 11th c. Jap. novelist.
Murdoch, (Jean) Iris, 1919–, Irish-born Brit author & philosopher.
Murieta, Joaquin, ?–1853?, Mexican bandit in Amer. Southwest.
Murillo, Bartolomé Esteban, 1617–82, Sp. painter.
Murnau, Friedrich W., 1899–1931, Ger. film director.
Murray, Arthur, 1895–, & his wife **Kathryn,** 1906–, U.S. dancing teachers.
—**Sir James Augustus Henry,** 1837–1915, Eng. lexicographer.
—**John Courtney,** 1904–67, U.S. theologian.
—**Mae,** 1885–1965, U.S. actress.
Murrow, Edward R., 1908–65, U.S. news analyst.
Musial, Stan(ley Frank), 1920–, U.S. baseball player.
Muskie, Edmund Sixtus, 1914–, U.S. politician.
Mussolini, Benito, 1883–1945, Ital. Fascist leader & premier; executed: called **Il Duce.**
Muybridge, Eadweard, b. Edward James Muggeridge, 1830–1904, Eng.-born U.S. photographer.
Muzio, Claudia, 1889–1936, Ital. soprano.
Muzorewa, Abel Tendekayi, 1925–, African religious and political leader; prime minister of Zimbabwe 1979–.
Myrdal, Gunnar, 1898–, Swed, sociologist & economist.
Myron, 5th c. B.C. Gk. sculptor.

Nabokov, Vladimir, 1899–1977, Russ.-born U.S. author.
Nader, Ralph, 1934–, U.S. lawyer & consumer advocate.
Nagurski, Bronko, 1908–, Can.-born U.S. football player.
Nagy, Imre, 1895?–1958, premier of Hungary 1953–55; executed.
Naismith, James, 1861–1939, Can.-born U.S. athletic coach; originator of basketball.
Namath, Joseph William (Joe), 1943–, U.S. football player.
Nanak, 1469–1538, founder of the Sikh faith in India.
Nansen, Fridtjof, 1861–1930, Norw. Arctic explorer.
Napier, John, 1550–1617, Scot. mathematician.
Napoleon I and III See BONAPARTE.
Nash, Ogden, 1902–71, U.S. poet.
—Thomas, 1567–1601, Eng. playwright.
Nasser, Gamal Abdel, 1918–70, Egyptian revolutionary leader; president of the United Arab Republic 1958–70.
Nast, Thomas, 1840–1902, Ger.-born U.S. cartoonist.
Nathan, George Jean, 1882–1958, U.S. critic.
Nation, Carry (Amelia), 1846–1911, U.S. temperance reformer.
Natwick, Mildred, 1908–, U.S. actress.
Nazimova, Alla, 1879–1945, Russ.-born actress active in U.S.
Nebuchadnezzar II, ?–562? B.C., king of Babylon 605–562 B.C., conqueror of Jerusalem.
Nefertiti, 14th c. B.C., Egyptian queen.
Nehru, Jawaharlal, 1889–1964, Indian nationalist leader; prime minister of India 1947–64.
Neill, A(lexander) S(utherland), 1883–1973, Eng. educator & author.
Nelson, Viscount Horatio, 1758–1805, Eng. admiral.
—(John) Byron, 1912–, U.S. golfer.
—Oswald George ("Ozzie"), 1907–75, U.S. bandleader, actor & TV producer.
Nemerov, Howard, 1920–, U.S. poet.
Nenni, Pietro, 1891–1980, Ital. socialist leader & journalist.
Nernst, Hermann W., 1864–1941, Ger. physical chemist.
Nero, A.D., 37–68, Roman emperor 54–68.
Neruda, Pablo, 1904–73, Chilean poet.
Nerva, Marcus Cocceius, A.D. 35?–98, Roman emperor 96–98.
Nervi, Pier Luigi, 1891–1979, Ital. architect.
Neutra, Richard Joseph, 1892–1970, Austrian-born U.S. architect.
Nevelson, Louise, 1900–, Russ.-born U.S. sculptor.
Nevins, Allan, 1890–1971, U.S. historian.
Newcombe, John, 1944–, Austral. tennis player.
Newhouse, Samuel, 1895–1979, U.S. publisher.
Ne Win, U, 1911–, Burmese military leader; prime minister of Burma 1962–74; president 1974–.
Newlands, John A. R., 1838–98, Eng. chemist.
Newman, John Henry, Cardinal, 1801–90, Eng. theologian & author.
—Paul, 1925–, U.S. actor.
Newton, Sir Isaac, 1642–1727, Eng. mathematician & physicist.
—Robert, 1905–56, Eng. actor.
Nicholas I, 1796–1855, czar of Russia 1825–55; called the Great.
—II, 1868–1918, czar of Russia 1894–1917; executed.
Nicholas, Saint, 4th c. prelate; patron saint of Russia, seamen, and children.
Nichols, Mike, 1931–, Ger.-born U.S. comedian & stage & film director.
Nicholson, Ben, 1894–1982, Eng. artist.
—Jack, 1936–, U.S. actor.
Nicklaus, Jack W., 1940–, U.S. golfer.
Nicolle, Charles J. H., 1866–1936, Fr. physician.
Nicolson, Sir Harold George, 1886–1968, Eng. diplomat, author & journalist.
Niebuhr, Reinhold, 1892–1971, U.S. Protestant clergyman & theologian.
Nielsen, Carl, 1865–1931, Dan. composer.
Niemeyer Soares, Oscar, 1907–, Brazilian architect.
Niemöller, Martin, 1892–, Ger. theologian.
Nietzsche, Friedrich Wilhelm, 1844–1900, Ger. philosopher & author.

Nightingale, Florence, 1820–1910, Eng. nurse in the Crimean War; considered the founder of modern nursing.
Nijinska, Bronislava, 1891–1972, Pol. dancer & choreographer.
Nijinsky, Vaslav, 1890–1950, Russ.-born ballet dancer & choreographer; brother of prec.
Nikolais, Alwin, 1912–, U.S. choreographer & dance-company director.
Nilsson, Birgit, 1918–, Swed. soprano.
Nimeiry, Gaafar al-, 1929–, Sudanese military officer; president of Sudan 1971–.
Nimitz, Chester William, 1885–1966, U.S. admiral.
Nin, Anais, 1903–77, Fr.-born U.S. author.
Nirenberg, Marshall Warren, 1927–, U.S. biochemist.
Niven, David, 1910–, Scot.-born actor active in U.S.
Nixon, Richard M(illhouse), 1913–, 37th U.S. president 1969–74; resigned.
Nizer, Louis, 1902–, Eng.-born U.S. lawyer & author.
Nkrumah, Kwame, 1909–72, president of Ghana 1960–66.
Nobel, Alfred Bernhard, 1833–96, Swed. industrialist & philanthropist.
Nock, Albert Jay, 1870–1945, U.S. author.
Noguchi, Hideyo, 1876–1928, Jap. bacteriologist active in U.S.
—Isamu, 1904–, U.S. sculptor.
Nolde, Emil, pseud. of Emil Hansen, 1867–1956, Ger. painter.
Nomura, Kichisaburo, 1877–1964, Jap. admiral & diplomat.
Nordica, Lillian, 1857–1914, U.S. soprano.
Norell, Norman, 1900–72, U.S. fashion designer.
Normand, Mabel, 1894–1930, U.S. actress.
Norris, (Benjamin) Frank(lin), 1870–1902, U.S. author.
—George W., 1861–1944, U.S. politician.
Norstad, Lauris, 1907–, U.S. general.
North, Alex, 1910–, U.S. composer.
—Frederick, Lord, 1732–92, Eng. statesman; prime minister 1770–82.
Norton, Charles Eliot, 1827–1908, U.S. author & educator.
Nostradamus, b. Michel de Notredame, 1503–66, Fr. physician & astrologer.
Novaes, Guiomar, 1895–1979, Brazilian pianist.
Novak, Robert (David Sanders), 1931–, U.S. journalist.
Novalis, pseud. of Friedrich von Hardenberg, 1772–1801, Ger. poet.
Novarro, Ramon, 1899–1968, Mexican-born U.S. actor.
Novello, Ivor, 1893–1951, Eng. playwright, composer & actor.
Novotna, Jarmila, 1911–, Czech-born U.S. soprano.
Novotny, Antonin, 1904–75, president of Czechoslavakia 1957–68.
Noyes, Alfred, 1880–1958, Eng. poet.
Nu, U, 1907–, prime minister of Burma 1948–58 & 1960–62.
Nureyev, Rudolf, 1938–, Soviet-born ballet dancer & choreographer.
Nurmi, Paavo, 1897–1973, Finnish track runner.
Nyerere, Julius K., 1922–, African statesman & first president of Tanzania 1965–.

Oakley, Annie, 1860–1926, U.S. markswoman.
Oates, Joyce Carol, 1938–, U.S. author.
—Titus, 1649–1705, Eng. conspirator.
Oberon, Merle, 1911–79, Tasmanian-born U.S. actress.
Oboler, Arch, 1909–, U.S. writer.
Obote, (Apollo) Milton, 1926–, president of Uganda 1967–71.
Obregón, Alvaro, 1880–1928, Mexican soldier & politician; president of Mexico 1920–24 & 1928; assassinated.
O'Brien, Lawrence Francis, 1917–, U.S. politician & government official.
—Margaret, 1937–, U.S. actress.
—Pat(rick), 1899–, U.S. actor.
O'Casey, Sean, 1880–1964, Irish playwright.
Ochoa, Severo, 1905–, Sp.-born U.S. biochemist.

Ochs, Adolph Simon, 1858–1935, U.S. newspaper pubisher.

Ockham, William of, 1285?–1349?, Eng. philosopher.

O'Connell, Daniel, 1775–1847, Irish nationalist leader.

O'Connor, Flannery, 1925–64, U.S. author.

—**Frank,** pseud. of Michael John O'Donovan, 1903–66, Irish author.

—**Sandra Day,** 1930–, U.S. jurist; justice of U.S. Supreme Court, 1981–.

—**Thomas P. ("Tay Pay"),** 1848–1929, Irish journalist & nationalist.

O'Day, Anita, 1920–, U.S. jazz singer.

Odets, Clifford, 1906–63, U.S. actor & playwright.

Odetta, b. Odetta Holmes, 1930–, U.S. folk singer.

Oenslager, Donald, 1902–75, U.S. set designer.

Oersted, Hans C., 1777–1851, Dan. physicist.

Oerter, Alfred, 1936–, U.S. discus thrower.

O'Faoláin, Sean, 1900–, Irish author.

Offenbach, Jacques, 1819–80, Fr. composer.

O'Flaherty, Liam, 1896–, Irish author.

Ogden, C(harles) K(ay), 1889–1957, Eng. phycologist & semanticist.

Ogilvy, David MacKenzie, 1911–, Eng. advertising executive active in U.S.

Oglethorpe, James Edward, 1696–1785, Eng. general & philanthropist; founder of Georgia colony.

O'Hara, John, 1905–70, U.S. author.

O'Higgins, Bernardo, 1778–1842, Chilean soldier & statesman.

Ohm, Georg Simon, 1787–1854, Ger. physicist.

Oistrakh, David Fyodorovich, 1908–74, Soviet violinist.

O'Keeffe, Georgia, 1887–, U.S. painter.

Olav V, 1903–, king of Norway 1957–.

Oldenburg, Claes Thure, 1929–, Swed.-born U.S. sculptor.

Oldfield, Berna Eli ("Barney"), 1878–1946, U.S. automobile racer.

Olds, Ransom Eli, 1864–1950, U.S. automobile manufacturer.

Oliver, Edna May, 1883–1942, U.S. actress.

—**Joe ("King"),** 1885–1938, U.S. jazz musician.

Olivier, Lord (Laurence), 1907–, Eng. actor & director.

Olmsted, Frederick Law, 1822–1903, U.S. landscape architect.

Omar Khayyám, ?–1123?, Pers. poet & astronomer.

Onassis, Aristotle Socrates, 1906–75, Turk.-born Gk. shipping magnate.

O'Neill, Eugene (Gladstone), 1888–1953, U.S. playwright.

—**Thomas Philip,** 1912–, U.S. statesman.

Onions, Charles Talbut, 1873–1965, Eng. lexicographer.

Onsager, Lars, 1903–76, Norw.-born U.S. physical chemist.

Oparin, Aleksandr I., 1894–, Soviet biochemist.

Oppenheimer, J(ulius) Robert, 1904–67, U.S. physicist.

Ophuls, Max, 1902–57, Fr. film director.

Orczy, Baroness Emmuska, 1865–1947, Hung.-born Eng. author.

Orff, Carl, 1895–, Ger. composer.

Origen, A.D. 185?–254?, Gk. writer & church father.

Ormandy, Eugene, 1899–, Hung.-born U.S. conductor.

Orozco, José Clemente, 1883–1949, Mexican painter.

Orr, Robert Gordon (Bobby), 1948–, Can. hockey player.

Ortega y Gasset, José, 1883–1955, Sp. philosopher & author.

Orwell, George, pseud. of Eric Arthur Glair, 1903–50, Eng. author & social critic.

Osborne, John (James), 1929–, Eng. playwright.

Osceola, 1804–38, Seminole Am. Ind. chief.

Osler, Sir William, 1849–1919, Can. physician.

Osman I, 1259–1326, Turkish founder of the Ottoman Empire.

Oswald, Lee Harvey, 1939–63, U.S. alleged assassin of President John F. Kennedy; murdered.

Otis, Elisha Graves, 1811–61, U.S. inventor.

O'Toole, Peter, 1932–, Irish actor.

Ouspenskaya, Maria, 1876–1949, Russ. actress active in U.S.

Ovid (L. Publius Ovidius Naso), 43 B.C.–A.D. 17, Roman poet.

Owen, Robert, 1771–1858, Welsh social reformer.

—**Wilfred,** 1893–1918, Eng. poet.

Owens, Jesse, 1913–1980, U.S. track athlete.

Paar, Jack, 1918–, U.S. TV personality.

Pabst, Georg W., 1885–1967, Ger. film director.

Paderewski, Ignace Jan, 1860–1941, Pol. pianist, composer & statesman.

Paganini, Niccolò, 1782–1840, Ital. violinist & composer.

Page, Geraldine, 1924–, U.S. actress.

Paget, Sir James, 1814–99, Eng. surgeon & pathologist.

Pagnol, Marcel, 1895–1974, Fr. playwright & film producer.

Paige, Leroy David ("Satchel"), 1906–, U.S. baseball player.

Paine, Thomas, 1737–1809, Eng.-born Amer. revolutionary patriot, political philosopher & author.

Palestrina, Giovanni Pierluigi da, 1526?–94, Ital. composer.

Paley, William S(amuel), 1901–, U.S. radio & TV executive.

Palladio, Andrea, 1508–80, Ital. architect.

Palme, Olof, 1927–, premier of Sweden 1969–76.

Palmer, Arnold (Daniel), 1929–, U.S. golfer.

—**Daniel David,** 1845–1913, Can. founder of chiropractic medicine.

Palmerston, Henry John Temple, 3rd Viscount, 1784–1865, Eng. statesman; prime minister 1885–58 & 1859–65.

Pandit, Madame Vijaya Lakshmi, 1900–, Indian diplomat & president of U.N. general assembly 1953–54.

Panini, 4th c. B.C. Indian Sanskrit grammarian.

Pankhurst, Emmeline (Goulden), 1858–1928, Eng. suffragist.

Panofsky, Erwin, 1892–1968, Ger.-born U.S. art historian.

Papadopoulos, George, 1919–, Gk. military officer; premier of Greece 1967–73.

Papandreou, George, 1888–1968, Gk. politician & opposition leader.

Papanicolaou, George Nicholas, 1883–1962, Gk.-born U.S. physician.

Papas, Irene, 1925–, Gk. actress.

Papp, Joseph, 1921–, U.S. theatrical producer.

Paracelsus, pseud. of Theophrastus von Hohenheim, 1493–1541, Swiss physician & alchemist.

Paré, Ambroise, 1510–90, Fr. surgeon.

Pareto, Vilfredo, 1848–1923, Ital. economist & sociologist.

Park Chung Hee, 1917–79, president of South Korea 1961–79.

—**Robert Ezra,** 1864–1944, U.S. sociologist.

Parker, Bonnie, 1910–34, U.S. criminal.

—**Charles Christopher, Jr.,** 1920–55, U.S. jazz musician: called **Bird.**

—**Dorothy,** 1893–1967, U.S. author.

Parkman, Francis, 1823–93, U.S. historian.

Parks, Bert, 1915–, U.S. TV personality.

—**Gordon,** 1912–1979, U.S. photographer & film director.

Parmigianino, Il, b. Girolamo Mazzuoli, 1503–40, Ital. painter.

Parnell, Charles Stewart, 1846–91, Irish statesman.

Parr, Catherine, 1512–48, sixth wife of Henry VIII of England.

Parrington, Vernon Louis, 1871–1929, U.S. historian.

Parrish, Maxfield, 1870–1966, U.S. painter.

Parsons, Estelle, 1927–, U.S. actress.

—**Louella O(ettinger),** 1893–1972, U.S. columnist.

—**Talcott,** 1902–1979, U.S. sociologist.

Partridge, Eric H., 1894–1979, Eng. lexicographer & critic.

Pascal, Blaise, 1623–62, Fr. mathematician & philosopher.

Pasionaria, La (Dolores Ibarruri), 1895–, Sp. revolutionist & founder of Spain's Communist Party.

Pasolini, Pier Paolo, 1922–75, Ital. film director.
Pasternak, Boris, 1890–1960, Soviet poet & novelist.
Pasteur, Louis, 1822–95, Fr. chemist & bacteriologist.
Pastor, Antonio (Tony), 1837–1908, U.S. actor & theater manager.
Pater, Walter (Horatio), 1839–94, Eng. essayist & critic.
Paton, Alan Stewart, 1903–, South African author.
Patrick, Saint, 389?–461, Brit. missionary to and patron saint of Ireland.
Patterson, Eleanor Medill ("Cissy"), 1884–1948, and her brother **Joseph M.,** 1879–1946, U.S. publishers.
Patti, Adelina, 1843–1919, Sp.-born Ital. soprano.
Patton, George Smith, 1885–1945, U.S. general.
Pauker, Ana (Rabinsohn), 1889?–1960, Rumanian communist.
Paul, Saint, A.D.?–67?, b. Saul, a Jew of Tarsus who became the apostle of Christianity to the Gentiles; author of various New Testament books.
Paul VI, b. Giovanni Battista Montini, 1897–1978, pope 1963–78.
Pauli, Wolfgang, 1900–58, Swiss-Austrian physicist.
Pauling, Linus Carl, 1901–, U.S. chemist.
Pausanias, 2nd c. A.D. Gk. traveler & geographer.
Pavese, Cesare, 1908–50, Ital. author.
Pavlov, Ivan Petrovich, 1849–1936, Russ. physiologist.
Pavlova, Anna, 1885–1931, Russ. ballerina active in France.
Paxinou, Katina, 1900–73, Gk. actress active in U.S.
Peale A family of U.S. painters incl. **Charles Willson,** 1741–1827; his brother **James,** 1749–1831; and **Rembrandt,** 1778–1860, son of Charles.
—Norman Vincent, 1898–, U.S. clergyman & author.
Pearson, Andrew Russell (Drew), 1897–1969, U.S. columnist.
—Lester B(owles), 1897–1972, Can. statesman; prime minister of Canada 1963–68.
Peary, Robert Edwin, 1856–1920, U.S. Arctic explorer.
Peck, Gregory, 1916–, U.S. actor.
Peckinpah, Sam, 1925–, U.S. film director.
Peel, Sir Robert, 1788–1850, Eng. statesman & founder of Irish police force.
Peerce, Jan, 1904–, U.S. tenor.
Pegler, (James) Westbrook, 1894–1969, U.S. columnist.
Péguy, Charles, 1873–1914, Fr. poet & author.
Pei, I(eoh) M(ing), 1917–, Chin.-born U.S. architect.
Peirce, Benjamin, 1809–80, U.S. mathematician & astronomer.
—Charles Sanders, 1839–1914, U.S. physicist & mathematician; son of prec.
Pélé, b. Edson Arantes do Nascimento, 1940–, Brazilian soccer player.
Pendergast, Thomas J., 1872–1945, U.S. politician.
Penfield, Wilder G., 1891–1976, U.S.-born Can. neurosurgeon.
Penn, Irving, 1917–, U.S. photographer.
—William, 1644–1718, Eng. Quaker; founder of Pennsylvania.
Penney, J(ames) C(ash), 1875–1971, U.S. merchant.
Pepin the Short, 714?–768, king of the Franks 751–768.
Pepys, Samuel, 1633–1703, Eng. author.
Percy, Sir Henry, 1364–1403, Eng. soldier: called **Hotspur.**
Perelman, S(idney) J(oseph), 1904–79, U.S. author.
Peretz, Isaac Loeb, 1851–1915, Pol. poet & author.
Perez, Carlos Andres, 1922–, president of Venezuela 1974–.
Perez de Cuellar, Javiera, 1920–, Peruvian diplomat and secretary-general of the U.N. 1982–.
Pergolesi, Giovanni Battista, 1710–36, Ital. composer.
Pericles, ?–429 B.C., Athenian statesman & general.
Perkins, Frances, 1882–1965, U.S. social worker; first woman Cabinet member; secretary of labor 1933–45.
—Maxwell, 1884–1947, U.S. editor.
—(Richard) Marlin, 1905–, U.S. zoo director.
Perls, Frederick (Fritz), 1893–1970, Ger.-born U.S. psychologist.
Perón, Juan Domingo, 1895–1974, Argentinian political leader; president 1946–55 & 1973–74.

Perón, Maria Estela (Isabel) Martinez de, 1931–, president of Argentina 1974–76; wife of prec.
Perrault, Charles, 1628–1703, Fr. writer & compiler of fairy tales.
Perry, Antoinette, 1888–1946, U.S. stage actress, director & producer.
—Matthew Calbraith, 1794–1858, U.S. commodore.
—Oliver Hazard, 1785–1819, U.S. naval commander; brother of prec.
Perse, St. John, pseud. of Alexis Saint-Léger Léger, 1887–1975, Fr. poet & diplomat.
Pershing, John Joseph, 1860–1948, U.S. general.
Perugino, Il, b. Pietro Vannucci, 1446–1523, Ital. painter.
Pestalozzi, Johann Heinrich, 1746–1827, Swiss educator.
Pétain, Henri Philippe, 1856–1951, Fr. political leader; premier 1940–44.
Peter I, 1672–1725, czar of Russia 1689–1725; called **the Great.**
Peter, Saint, b. Simon,? –A.D. 67?, 1st pope A.D.42?–67?
Peterson, Oscar, 1925–, U.S. jazz pianist.
—Roger Tory, 1908–, U.S. ornithologist & author.
Petrarch, Francesco, 1304–74, Ital. scholar & poet.
Petrie, Sir (William Matthew) Flinders, 1853–1942, Eng. archaeologist.
Petronius, Gaius, A.D.?–66?, Roman satirist.
Pevsner, Sir Nikolaus, 1902–, Ger.-born Brit. art historian.
Pham Van Dong, 1906–, premier of N. Vietnam 1955–.
Phidias, 500?–432? B.C., Gk. sculptor & architect.
Philby, Harold A. R., 1911–, Eng.-born spy for the U.S.S.R.
Philip II, 382–336 B.C., king of Macedonia & conqueror of Thessaly & Greece; father of Alexander the Great.
Philip II, 1527–98, king of Spain 1556–98.
Philip, Prince (Duke of Edinburgh), 1921–, husband of Queen Elizabeth II.
Philip the Good, 1396–1467, Duke of Burgunday 1419–67.
Philip (Metacomet), 1639?–76, sachem of the Wampanoag Amer. Indians.
Philippe, Gerard, 1922–57, Fr. actor.
Phillips, Wendell, 1811–84, U.S. orator & reformer.
Philo Judaeus, 20 B.C.?–A.D. 50?, Jewish Platonist philosopher.
Phumiphon Aduldet, 1927–, king of Thailand 1946–.
Phyfe, Duncan, 1768–1854, Scot.-born U.S. cabinetmaker.
Piaf, Edith, 1912–63, Fr. singer.
Piaget, Jean, 1896–1980, Swiss psychologist & author.
Piatigorski, Gregor, 1903–, Ukrainian-born U.S. cellist.
Picabia, Francis, 1878–1953, Fr. painter.
Picard, Jean, 1620–82, Fr. astronomer.
Picasso, Pablo, 1881–1973, Sp. artist active in France.
Piccard, Auguste, 1884–1962, Swiss physicist.
Pickett, George Edward, 1825–75, U.S. Confederate general.
Pickford, Mary, 1893–1979, Can.-born U.S. actress.
Picon, Molly, 1898–, U.S. actress.
Pierce, Franklin, 1804–69, 14th U.S. president 1853–57.
Piero della Francesca, 1418?–92, Ital. painter.
Pike, Zebulon Montgomery, 1779–1813, U.S. general & explorer.
Pilate, Pontius, 1st c. A.D. Roman governor of Judea A.D. 26–36?; delivered Jesus to be crucified.
Pillsbury, Charles Alfred, 1842–99, U.S. businessman.
Pindar, 522?–443, B.C., Gk. poet.
Pinel, Philippe, 1745–1826, Fr. physician & psychologist.
Pinero, Sir Arthur Wing, 1855–1934, Eng. playwright & actor.
Pinkerton, Allan, 1819–84, Scot.-born detective active in U.S.
Pinkham, Lydia (Estes), 1819–83, U.S. businesswoman.
Pinter, Harold, 1930–, Eng. playwright.
Pinturicchio, b. Bernardino Betti, 1454–1513, Ital. painter.
Pinza, Ezio, 1892–1957, Ital.-born U.S. basso.
Pirandello, Luigi, 1867–1936, Ital. playwright & author.

Piranesi, Giambattista, 1720–78, Ital. architect & engraver.
Pisano, Giovanni, 1245–1314, Ital. sculptor.
—**Nicola,** 1220–84, Ital. sculptor; father of prec.
Piscator, Erwin, 1893–1966, Ger. theater director.
Pissarro, Camille, 1830–1903, Fr. painter.
Piston, Walter, 1894–1976, U.S. composer.
Pitcher, Molly, b. Mary Ludwig, 1754–1832, Amer. revolutionary heroine.
Pitman, Sir Isaac, 1813–97, Eng. phoneticist; invented a system of shorthand.
Pitt, William, 1708–78, Eng. statesman.
—**William,** 1759–1806, Eng. prime minister 1783–1801 & 1804–06; son of prec.: called **the Younger.**
Pius XII, b. Eugenio Pacelli, 1876–1958, pope 1939–58.
Pizarro, Francisco, 1475?–1541, Sp. soldier & conqueror of Peru.
Planck, Max, 1858–1947, Ger. physicist.
Plath, Sylvia, 1932–63, U.S. poet resident in England.
Plato, 427?–347? B.C., Gk. philosopher.
Plautus, Titus Maccius, 254?–184 B.C., Roman playwright.
Plimpton, George Ames, 1927–, U.S. author and editor.
Plimsoll, Samuel, 1824–98, Eng. shipping reformer.
Pliny (L. Gaius Plinius Secundus), A.D. 23–79, Roman naturalist & writer: called **the Elder.**
—(L. Gaius Plinius Caecilius), A.D., 62–113, Roman statesman; nephew of prec.: called **the Younger.**
Plisetskaya, Maya, 1925–, Soviet ballerina.
Plotinus, 205?–270, Egyptian-born Roman philosopher.
Plummer, Christopher, 1929–, Can. actor active in U.S.
Plutarch, A.D. 46?–120?, Gk. historian.
Pocahontas, 1595?–1617, Am. Ind. princess; daughter of Powhatan.
Podgorny, Nikolai Viktorovich, 1903–, Soviet politician; president of U.S.S.R. 1966–.
Poe, Edgar Allan, 1809–49, U.S. author, critic & poet.
Poincaré, Jules Henri, 1854–1912, Fr. mathematician.
Poinsett, Joel Roberts, 1779–1851, U.S. diplomat & amateur botanist.
Poisson, Simeon D., 1781–1840, Fr. mathematician.
Poitier, Sidney, 1924–, U.S. actor.
Polanski, Roman, 1933–, Pol. film director active in U.S.
Politian, b. Angelo Poliziano, 1454–94, Ital. classical scholar & poet.
Polk, James Knox, 1795–1849, 11th U.S. president 1845–49.
Pollock, Jackson, 1912–56, U.S. painter.
Polo, Marco, 1254?–1324?, Venetian traveler & author.
Polycleitus, 5th c. B.C. Gk. sculptor & architect.
Pompadour, Jeanne Antoinette Poisson, Marquise de, 1721–64, mistress of Louis XV.
Pompey (L. Gnaeus Pompeius Magnus), 106–48 B.C., Roman general & statesman.
Pompidou, Georges, 1911–74, president of France 1969–74.
Ponce de Leon, Juan, 1460–1521, Sp. discoverer of Florida.
Pons, Lily, 1904–76, Fr.-born U.S. soprano.
Ponselle, Rosa Melba, 1897–1981, U.S. soprano.
Ponti, Carlo, 1913–, Ital. film director.
Pontiac, ?–1769, Ottowa Am. Ind. chief.
Pontormo, Jacopo da, b. Jacopo Carrucci, 1494–1557, Ital. painter.
Pope, Alexander, 1688–1744, Eng. poet & essayist.
Porter, Cole, 1893–1964, U.S. composer & lyricist.
—**Katherine Anne,** 1890–1980, U.S. author.
Post, Charles William, 1854–1914, U.S. breakfast-food manufacturer.
—**Emily (Price),** 1873?–1960, U.S. writer on etiquette.
—**Marjorie Merriweather,** 1887–1973, U.S. philanthropist.
—**Wiley,** 1898–1935, U.S. aviator.
Potemkin, Grigori Aleksandrovich, 1739–91, Russ. statesman & general.
Potter, Beatrix, 1866?–1943, Eng. author & illustrator of children's books.
Poulenc, Francis, 1899–1963, Fr. composer.

Pound, Ezra (Loomis), 1885–1972, U.S. poet resident in Italy.
Poussin, Nicholas, 1594–1665, Fr. painter.
Powell, Adam Clayton, 1908–72, U.S. clergyman & politician.
—**Anthony,** 1905–, Eng. author.
—**Dick,** 1904–63, U.S. actor & singer.
—**Eleanor,** 1912–82, U.S. dancer & actress.
—**John Wesley,** 1834–1902, U.S. geographer & explorer.
—**Lewis F(ranklin), Jr.,** 1907–, U.S. jurist; justice of the U.S. Supreme Court 1972–.
—**William,** 1892–, U.S. actor.
Power, Tyrone, 1913–58, U.S. actor.
Powhatan, 1550?–1618, Algonquin Am. Ind. chief.
Praxiteles, 4th c. B.C. Athenian sculptor.
Prefontaine, Steve(n Roland), 1951–75, U.S. track runner.
Preminger, Otto (Ludwig), 1906–, Austrian-born U.S. film director & producer.
Presley, Elvis Aron, 1935–77, U.S. singer & actor.
Pretorius, Andries Wilhelmus Jacobus, 1799–1853, and his son **Marthinus Wessels,** 1819–1901, Du. colonizers & soldiers in South Africa.
Previn, André, 1929–, Ger.-born U.S. composer, conductor & pianist.
Price, George, 1901–, U.S. cartoonist.
—**Leontyne,** 1927–, U.S. soprano.
—**Vincent,** 1911–, U.S. actor.
Priestley, J(ohn) B(oynton), 1894–, Eng. author.
—**Joseph,** 1733–1804, Eng. chemist.
Primrose, William, 1904–, Scot.-born U.S. violinist.
Primus, Pearl, 1919–, Trinidad-born dancer & choreographer active in U.S.
Prince, Harold, 1928–, U.S. theatrical producer & director.
Princip, Gavrilo, 1895–1918, Serbian political agitator & assassin of Archduke Franz Ferdinand.
Pritchett, V(ictor) S(awdon), 1900–, Eng. author.
Prokofiev, Sergei, 1891–1953, Soviet composer.
Proudhon, Pierre Joseph, 1809–65, Fr. author & political leader.
Proust, Joseph Louis, 1754–1826, Fr. chemist.
—**Marcel,** 1871–1922, Fr. author.
Ptolemy, 2nd c. A.D. Alexandrian astronomer, mathematician & geographer.
Ptolemy I, 367?–283? B.C., Macedonian general of Alexander the Great & founder of the ruling dynasty of Egypt; king of Egypt 305–285 B.C.
—**II,** 309?–246 B.C., king of Egypt 285–246 B.C.; son of prec.
Pucci, Emilio, 1914–, Ital. fashion designer.
Puccini, Giacomo, 1858–1924, Ital. operatic composer.
Pulaski, Count Casimir, 1748?–79, Pol. soldier & Amer. revolutionary general.
Pulitzer, Joseph, 1847–1911, Hung.-born U.S. publisher & philanthropist.
Pullman, George Mortimer, 1831–97, U.S. inventor.
Pupin, Michael Idvorsky, 1858–1935, Yugoslav-born U.S. physicist & inventor.
Purcell, Henry, 1658–95, Eng. composer.
Purkinje, Johannes Evangelista, 1787–1869, Czech physiologist.
Pushkin, Alexander Sergeyevich, 1799–1837, Russ. poet.
Putnam, George, 1814–72, U.S. publisher.
Puvis de Chavannes, Pierre, 1824–98, Fr. painter & muralist.
Pyle, Ernest Taylor (Ernie), 1900–45, U.S. journalist & war correspondent.
—**Howard,** 1853–1911, U.S. author & illustrator.
Pythagoras, 6th c. B.C. Gk. philosopher.

Qaddafi, Muammar al-, 1942–, Libyan military officer; head of state of Libya 1969–.
Quant, Mary, 1934–, Eng. fashion designer.
Quantrill, William Clarke, 1837–65, U.S. Confederate guerrilla leader.
Quasimodo, Salvatore, 1901–68, Ital. poet & critic.
Quayle, Anthony, 1913–, Eng. actor.

Queen, Ellery, pseud. of cousins **Frederic Dannay,** 1905–, & **Manfred Bennington Lee,** 1905–71, U.S. authors.

Queensbury, John Sholto Douglas, Marquis of, 1844–1900, Scot. boxing patron.

Quercia, Jacopo della, 1378?–1438, Ital. sculptor.

Quezon, Manuel Luis, 1878–1944, Filipino statesman; first president of the Philippines 1935–44.

Quiller-Couch, Sir Arthur Thomas, 1863–1944, Eng. author; pseud. **Q.**

Quincy, Josiah, 1744–75, Amer. lawyer & revolutionary patriot.

Quinn, Anthony, 1915–, Mexican-born U.S. actor.

Quintero, Jose, 1924–, Panamanian-born U.S. stage director.

Quisling, Vidkun, 1887–1945, Norw. traitor during World War II.

Rabelais, François, 1494?–1553, Fr. writer & satirist.

Rabi, Isadore Isaac, 1898–, Austrian-born U.S. physicist.

Rabin, Yitzhak, 1922–, prime minister of Israel 1974–77.

Rachmaninoff, Sergei Vassilievich, 1873–1943, Russ.-born pianist & composer in U.S. after 1918.

Racine, Jean, 1639–99, Fr. playwright.

Rackham, Arthur, 1867–1939, Eng. illustrator.

Radcliffe, Ann (Ward), 1764–1823, Eng. author.

Raemaekers, Louis, 1869–1956, Du. cartoonist.

Raffles, Sir (Thomas) Stanford, 1781–1825, Eng. colonial administrator in East Indies.

Raft, George, 1903–80, U.S. actor.

Raimondi, Marcantonio, 1475?–1534, Ital. engraver.

Raimu, b. Jules Auguste Muraire, 1883–1946, Fr. actor.

Rainier III (Louis Henri Maxence Bertrand), 1923–, prince of Monaco.

Rains, Claude, 1889–1967, Eng.-born U.S. actor.

Raitt, John, 1917–, U.S. singer & actor.

Raleigh, Sir Walter, 1552–1618, Eng. statesman & poet; beheaded. Also **Ralegh.**

Ramakrishna, 1834–86, Hindu yogi.

Raman, Sir Chandrasekhara Venkata, 1888–1970, Indian physicist.

Rambert, Dame Marie, 1888–, Pol.-born ballet dancer, teacher & impresario active in Great Britain.

Rameau, Jean Philippe, 1683–1764, Fr. composer.

Ramon y Cajal, Santiago, 1852–1934, Sp. histologist.

Ramsay, Sir William, 1852–1916, Scot. chemist.

Ramses A dynasty of Egyptian kings incl. **Ramses I,** founder of the dynasty in the 14th c. B.C., and **Ramses II,** ?–1225 B.C.

Rand, Ayn, 1905–82, Russ.-born U.S. author.

—Sally, 1904–79, U.S. dancer.

Randolph, A(sa) Philip, 1889–1979, U.S. labor leader.

Rank, Otto, 1884–1939, Austrian psychoanalyst.

Rankin, Jeannette, 1880–1973, U.S. feminist & first U.S. Congresswoman.

Ransom, John Crowe, 1888–1974, U.S. poet & educator.

Raphael, b. Raffaello Santi, 1483–1520, Ital. painter.

Rasmussen, Knud (Johan Victor), 1879–1933, Dan. explorer & ethnologist.

Rasputin, Gregori Efimovich, 1871?–1916, Russ. mystic in the court of Czar Nicholas II; assassinated.

Rathbone, Basil, 1892–1967, South African-born U.S. actor.

Rathenau, Walter, 1867–1922, Ger. industrialist & statesman; assassinated.

Rauschenberg, Robert, 1925–, U.S. artist.

Ravel, Maurice (Joseph), 1875–1937, Fr. composer.

Rawls, Elizabeth Earle (Betsy), 1928–, U.S. golfer.

Ray, Man, 1890–, U.S. artist & photographer.

—Satyajit, 1921–, Indian film director.

Rayburn, Sam(uel Taliaferro), 1882–1961, U.S. politician.

Rayleigh, John William Strutt, Baron, 1842–1919, Eng. physicist.

Read, Sir Herbert, 1893–1968, Eng. art critic & author.

Reagan, Ronald W(ilson), 1911–, U.S. statesman; 40th U.S. president 1981–.

Réaumur, René Antoine Ferchault de, 1683–1757, Fr. physicist.

Récamier, Jeanne Françoise Julie Adélaïde Bernard, 1779–1849, Fr. social leader & patron of literature.

Red Cloud, 1822–1909, Oglala Sioux Am. Ind. chief.

Redford, Robert, 1937–, U.S. actor.

Redgrave, Sir Michael, 1908–, Eng. actor.

—Vanessa, 1937–, Eng. actress; daughter of prec.

Redon, Odilon, 1840–1916, Fr. painter.

Reed, Sir Carol, 1906–76, Eng. film director.

—John, 1887–1920, U.S. journalist & poet.

—Rex, 1940–, U.S. author, critic & journalist.

—Walter, 1851–1902, U.S. Army surgeon & bacteriologist.

—Willis, 1942–, U.S. basketball player.

Rehnquist, William H(ubbs), 1924–, U.S. jurist; justice of the U.S. Suprene Court 1972–.

Reich, Wilhelm, 1897–1957, Austrian-born psychiatrist active in U.S.

Reichstein, Tadeus, 1897–, Pol.-born Swedish chemist.

Reid, Ogden M., 1882–1947, U.S. newspaper publisher.

Reik, Theodor, 1888–1969, Austrian-born U.S. psychologist & author.

Reiner, Carl, 1922–, U.S. comedian.

—Fritz, 1888–1963, Hung.-born U.S. conductor.

Reinhardt, Jean Baptiste ("Django"), 1910–53, Belg.-born jazz guitarist active in France.

—Max, 1873–1943, Austrian theatrical director & producer active in Germany & U.S.

Reisz, Karel, 1926–, Eng. film director.

Réjane, b. Gabrielle Réju, 1857–1920, Fr. actress.

Remarque, Erich Maria, 1898–1970, Ger.-born U.S. author.

Rembrandt (Harmenszoon) van Rijn, 1606–69, Du. painter & etcher.

Remington, Frederic, 1861–1909, U.S. painter & sculptor.

Reni, Guido, 1575–1642, Ital. painter.

Renoir, Jean, 1894–1979, Fr. film director.

—Pierre Auguste, 1841–1919, Fr. painter; father of prec.

Renwick, James, 1818–95, U.S. architect.

Resnais, Alain, 1922–, Fr. film director.

Resnik, Regina, 1924–, U.S. mezzo-soprano.

Respighi, Ottorino, 1879–1936, Ital. composer.

Reston, James, 1909–, Scot.-born U.S. journalist.

Reszke, Jean de, 1850–1925, Pol. tenor.

Retz, Gilles de, 1404?–40, Fr. feudal lord & soldier: thought to be the original **Bluebeard.**

Reuter, Baron Paul Julius, 1816–99, Ger.-born Eng. news agency founder.

Reuther, Walter (Philip), 1907–70, U.S. labor leader.

Revels, Hiram Rhoades, 1822–1901, U.S. clergyman, educator & congressman.

Revere, Paul, 1735–1818, Amer. revolutionary patriot.

Revson, Charles Haskell, 1906–75, U.S. business executive.

Rexroth, Kenneth, 1905–, U.S. author & critic.

Reynolds, Sir Joshua, 1723–92, Eng. painter.

—Richard S., Jr., 1908–80, U.S. business executive.

Rhee, Syngman, 1875–1965, first president of Republic of Korea 1948–60.

Rhine, Joseph Banks, 1895–1980, U.S. parapsychologist.

Rhodes, Cecil (John), 1853–1902, Eng.-born South African financier & statesman.

Rhys, Jean, 1895–1979, British novelist.

Ribbentrop, Joachim von, 1893–1946, Ger. diplomat.

Ribera, Jusepe de, 1588–1652, Sp. painter & etcher: called **Lo Spagnoletto.**

Ribicoff, Abraham A., 1910–, U.S. politician.

Ricardo, David, 1772–1823, Eng. political economist.

Rice, Elmer, 1892–1967, U.S. playwright.

—Grantland, 1880–1954, U.S. sportswriter.

—Thomas Dartmouth, 1808–60, U.S. minstrel show pioneer.

Richard I, 1157–99, king of England 1189–99; called **the Lion-Hearted.**

—II, 1367–1400, king of England 1377–99.

—III, 1452–85, king of England 1483–85.

Richard, (Joseph Henri) Maurice, 1921–, Can. hockey player.

Richards, Dickinson Woodruff, 1895–, U.S. physcian.

—I(vor) A(rmstrong), 1893–1979, Eng. critic & author.

Richardson, H(enry) H(obson), 1838–86, U.S. architect.

—Sir Owen Williams, 1879–1959, Eng. physicist.

—Sir Ralph, 1902–, Eng. actor.

—Samuel, 1689–1761, Eng. novelist.

Richelieu, Armand Jean du Plessis, Duc de, 1585–1642, Fr. cardinal & statesman.

Richter, Sviatoslav, 1914–, Soviet pianist.

Richthofen, Manfred, Baron von, 1892–1918, Ger. military aviator; called **the Red Baron.**

Rickard, George Lewis ("Tex"), 1871–1929, U.S. boxing promoter.

Rickenbacker, Edward Vernon, 1890–1973, U.S. aviator.

Ricketts, Howard Taylor, 1871–1910, U.S. pathologist.

Rickey, Branch, 1881–1965, U.S. baseball manager.

Rickover, Hyman George, 1900–, U.S. admiral.

Ridgway, Matthew B(unker), 1895–, U.S. general.

Riefenstahl, Leni, 1902–, Ger. film director.

Riemann, Georg Friedrich Bernhard, 1826–66, Ger. mathematician.

Riemenschneider, Tilman, 1460?–1531, Ger. sculptor.

Rienzi, Cola di, 1313–54, Ital. revolutionary statesman.

Riesman, David, 1909–, U.S. sociologist & author.

Riggs, Robert Larimore (Bobby), 1918–, U.S. tennis player.

Riis, Jacob (August), 1849–1914, Dan.-born U.S. journalist & social reformer.

Riley, James Whitcomb, 1849–1916, U.S. poet.

Rike, Rainer Maria, 1875–1926, Czech-born Ger. poet.

Rimbaud, Arthur, 1854–91, Fr. poet.

Rimsky-Korsakov, Nikolai Andreyevich, 1844–1908, Russ. composer.

Rinehart, Mary Roberts, 1876–1958, U.S. author.

Ringling A family of U.S. circus owners incl. five brothers; **Albert,** 1852–1916; **Alfred,** 1861–1919; **Charles,** 1863–1926; **John,** 1866–1936; & **Otto,** 1858–1911.

Ripley, Robert L(eRoy), 1893–1949, U.S. cartoonist.

Ristori, Adelaide, 1822–1906, Ital. actress.

Rittenhouse, David, 1732–96, U.S. astronomer & instrument maker.

Rivera, Diego, 1886–1957, Mexican painter.

Rivera y Orbaneja, Miguel Primo de, 1870–1930, Sp. general; dictator 1925–30.

Rivers, Larry, 1923–, U.S. artist.

Rizal, José (Mercado), 1861–96, Filipino patriot.

Riza Pahlevi, 1877–1944, shah of Iran 1925–41.

Robards, Jason, Jr., 1922–, U.S. actor.

Robbe-Grillet, Alain, 1922–, Fr. author.

Robbins, Harold, 1916–, U.S. author.

—Jerome, 1918–, U.S. dancer & choreographer.

Robert I, 1274–1329, king of Scotland 1306–29: called **the Bruce.**

Robert, Henry Martyn, 1837–1923, U.S. engineer, soldier & parliamentarian.

Roberts, Elizabeth Madox, 1886–1941, U.S. poet & novelist.

—(Granville) Oral, 1918–, U.S. evangelist.

—Kenneth, 1885–1957, U.S. author.

Robertson, Oscar, 1938–, U.S. basketball player.

Robeson, Paul LeRoy, 1898–1976, U.S. singer & actor.

Robespierre, Maximilien François Marie Isidore de, 1758–94; Fr. revolutionary; guillotined.

Robinson, Bill ("Bojangles"), 1878–1949, U.S. dancer & actor.

—Edward G., 1893–1973, Rumanian-born U.S. actor.

—Edwin Arlington, 1869–1935, U.S. poet.

—Edwin Arlington, 1869–1935, U.S. poet.

—Jack Roosevelt (Jackie), 1919–72, U.S. baseball player.

—Ray ("Sugar Ray"), 1920–, U.S. boxer.

Robson, Dame Flora, 1902–, Eng. actress.

Rochambeau, Jean Baptiste de Vimeur, Comte de, 1725–1807, Fr. marshal; commanded Fr. allies in Amer. Revolution.

Roche, Kevin, 1922–, U.S. architect.

Rockefeller A family of U.S. oil magnates & philanthropists incl. **David,** 1915–, business executive; **John D(avison),** 1839–1937, grandfather of prec; **John D(avison), Jr.,** 1874–1960, son of prec.; **Nelson Aldrich,** 1908–79, governor of New York 1958–73, vice president of the U.S. 1974–77, son of prec. & brother of David.

Rockne, Knute (Kenneth), 1881–1931, Norw.-born U.S. football coach.

Rockwell, Norman, 1894–1978, U.S. painter & illustrator.

Rodgers, Richard, 1902–1979, U.S. composer.

Rodin, Auguste, 1840–1917, Fr. sculptor.

Rodzinski, Artur, 1894–1958, Yugolsav-born U.S. conductor.

Roebling, John Augustus, 1806–69, Ger.-born U.S. engineer & bridge-builder.

—Washington Augustus, 1837–1926, U.S. engineer; sone of prec.

Roebuck, Alvah Curtis, 1863–1948, U.S. businessman.

Roelants, Gaston, 1937–, Belg. track runner.

Roentgen, Wilhelm Konrad, 1845–1923, Ger. physicist; discoverer of X-rays.

Roethke, Theodore, 1908–63, U.S. poet.

Rogers, Carl R., 1902–, U.S. psychologist.

—Ginger, 1911–, U.S. actress.

—Will(iam Penn Adair), 1879–1935, U.S. humorist & actor.

Roget, Peter Mark, 1779–1869, Eng. physician & author of the *Thesaurus of English Words and Phrases.*

Rolland, Romain, 1866–1944, Fr. author.

Rölvaag, Ole Edvart, 1876–1931, Norw.-born educator & author active in U.S.

Romains, Jules, pseud. of Louis Farigoule, 1885–1972, Fr. author.

Romano, Giulio, 1499–1546, Ital. painter & architect.

Romanov, Mikhail Feodorovich, 1596–1645, czar of Russia 1613–45.

Romberg, Sigmund, 1887–1951, Hung.-born U.S. composer.

Rome, Harold, 1908–, U.S. composer.

Rommel, Erwin, 1891–1944, Ger. general.

Romney, George, 1734–1802, Eng. painter.

Romulo, Carlos, 1901–, Filipino statesman.

Ronsard, Pierre de, 1524–85, Fr. poet.

Rooney, Mickey, 1920–, U.S. actor.

Roosevelt, (Anna) Elenor, 1884–1962, U.S. lecturer, author, stateswoman & humanitarian.

—Franklin Delano, 1882–1945, 32nd U.S. president 1933–45; husband of prec.

—Theodore, 1858–1919, 26th U.S. president 1901–09.

Root, Elihu, 1845–1937, U.S. lawyer & statesman.

Rorem, Ned, 1923–, U.S. composer.

Rorschach, Hermann, 1844–1922, Swiss psychiatrist.

Rosa, Salvator, 1615–73, Ital. painter & poet.

Rosario (Perez), 1920–, Sp. dancer.

Rosay, Françoise, 1891–1974, Fr. actress.

Roscius, Quintus, 126?–62? B.C., Roman actor.

Rose, Billy, 1899–1966, U.S. theatrical producer & lyricist.

—Pete(r Edward), 1942–, U.S. baseball player.

Rosenberg, Julius, 1918–53, & his wife **Ethel,** 1915–53, U.S. radicals; executed as spies for the U.S.S.R.

Rosenthal, Jean, 1912–69, U.S. theatrical lighting designer.

Rosenwald, Julius, 1862–1932, U.S. merchant & philanthropist.

Rosewall, Ken, 1934–, Austral. tennis player.

Ross, Betsy, 1752–1836, Amer. patriot; made first Amer. flag.

—Harold W(allace), 1892–1957, U.S. editor.

—Sir James Clark, 1800–62, & his uncle **Sir John,** 1777–1856, Scot. polar explorers.

Rossellini, Roberto, 1906–77, Ital. film director.

Rossetti, Christina (Georgina), 1830–94, Eng. poet.

Dante Gabriel, 1828–82, Eng. painter & poet; brother of prec.

Rossini, Gioacchino Antonio, 1792–1868, Ital. composer.

Rostand, Edmond, 1868–1918, Fr. playwright & poet.

Rostropovich, Mstislav Leopoldovitch, 1927–, Soviet-born cellist & conductor active in U.S.

Roth, Lillian, 1910–1980, U.S. singer & actress.

—**Philip,** 1933–, U.S. author.

Rothko, Mark, 1903–70, Russ.-born U.S. painter.

Rothschild A family of Ger. bankers incl. **Meyer Amschel,** 1743–1812, & his sons: **Anselm Meyer,** (1773–1855; **James,** 1792–1868; **Karl,** 1788–1855; **Nathan Meyer,** 1777–1836; & **Solomon,** 1774–1855.

Roualt, Georges, 1871–1958, Fr. painter.

Rouget de Lisle, Claude Joseph, 1760–1836, Fr. poet; author & composer of the *Marseillaise.*

Rousseau, Henry, 1844–1910, Fr. painter.

—**Jean Jacques,** 1712–78, Fr. philosopher & author.

Rowlandson, Thomas, 1756–1827, Eng. artist & caricaturist.

Roxas y Acuña, Manuel, 1892–1948, Filipino statesman.

Royce, Josiah, 1855–1916, U.S. philosopher.

Rozsa, Miklos, 1907–, Hung.-born U.S. composer.

Rubens, Peter Paul, 1577–1646, Flemish painter.

Rubenstein, Helena, 1882?–1965, Pol.-born U.S. businesswoman.

Rubinstein, Anton, 1829–94, Russ. pianist & composer.

—**Artur,** 1889–, Pol.-born pianist active in U.S.

Ruby, Harry, 1895–1959, U.S. composer.

Rudolf I, 1218–91, Holy Roman Emperor 1273–91.

Rudolph, Paul, 1918–, U.S. architect.

—**Wilma,** 1940 –, U.S. track runner.

Ruggles, Carl, 1876–1971, U.S. composer.

Ruisdael, Jacob, 1628?–82, & his uncle **Salomon,** 1600?–70, Du. painters.

Rundstedt, Karl Rudolf Gerd van, 1875–1953, Ger. field marshal.

Runyon, (Alfred) Damon, 1880–1946, U.S. author.

Rush, Benjamin, 1745–1813, U.S. physcian.

Rusher, William A., 1923–, U.S. publisher.

Ruskin, John, 1819–1900, Eng. critic & author.

Russell, Bertrand (Arthur William), 1872–1970, Eng. mathematician & philosopher.

—**Charles (Marion),** 1864–1926, U.S. artist.

—**Ken,** 1927–, Eng. film director.

—**Lillian,** 1861–1922, U.S. singer & actress.

—**Richard B.,** 1897–1971, U.S. politician.

—**Rosalind,** 1911–76, U.S. actress.

—**William Felton (Bill),** 1934–, U.S. basketball player & coach.

Rustin, Bayard, 1910–, U.S. Negro civil rights leader.

Ruth, George Herman ("Babe"), 1895–1948, U.S. baseball player.

Rutherford, Sir Ernest, 1871–1937, New Zealand-born Eng. physicist.

—**Margaret,** 1892–1972, Eng. actress.

Ruysbroeck, Jan van, 1293–1381, Flemish mystic & theologian.

Ryan, Robert, 1913–73, U.S. actor.

—**Thomas Fortune,** 1851–1928, U.S. businessman.

Ryder, Albert Pinkham, 1847–1917, U.S. painter.

Ryun, James (Jim), 1947–, U.S. track runner.

Saarinen, Aline Bernstein, 1914–72, U.S. author & art critic.

—**Eero,** 1910–61, U.S. architect; husband of prec.

—**Eliel,** 1873–1950, Finnish-born U.S. architect; father of prec.

Sabbatai Zevi, 1626–76, Turkish-born Jewish mystic & self-proclaimed Messiah.

Sabin, Albert B(ruce), 1906–, Russ.-born U.S. physician & bacteriologist.

Sacajawea, 1787–1812, Soshone Am. Ind. guide and interpreter for the Lewis and Clark expedition.

Sacco, Nicola, 1891–1927, Ital. anarchist in the U.S.; executed with Bartolomeo Vanzetti for murder.

Sacher-Masoch, Leopold von, 1835–95, Austrian writer.

Sachs, Nelly, 1891–1970, Ger.-born Swed. poet.

Sackville-West, Victoria Mary (Vita), 1892–1962, Eng. author.

Sadat, Anwar, 1918–81, president of Egypt 1970–81; assassinated.

Sade, Comte Donatien Alphonse Francois, 1740–1814, Fr. author; known as **Marquis de Sade.**

Safire, William 1929–, U.S. author & journalist.

Sagan, Carl, 1934–, U.S. astronomer.

—**Francoise,** pseud. of Francoise Quoirez, 1935–, Fr. author.

Sage, Russell, 1816–1906, U.S. financier.

Sahl, Mort, 1927–, Can.-born U.S. comedian.

Sainte-Beuve, Charles Augustin, 1804–69, Fr. poet, critic & historian.

Saint-Exupéry, Antoine de, 1900–44, Fr. author & aviator.

Saint-Gaudens, Augustus, 1848–1907, Irish-born U.S. sculptor.

Saint-Just, Louis Antoine Leon de, 1767–94, Fr. revolutionary.

Saint-Laurent, Yves (1936–, Fr. fashion designer.

Saint-Saëns, (Charles) Camille, 1835–1921, Fr. composer.

Saintsbury, George Edward Bateman, 1845–1933, Eng. critic.

Saint-Simon, Claude Henri de Rouvroy, Comte de, 1760–1825, Fr. philosopher & author.

—**Louis de Rouvroy, Duc de,** 1675–1755, Fr. statesman & author.

Saint-Subber, Arnold, 1918–, U.S. theatrical producer.

Sakel, Manfred, 1906–57, Austrian-born U.S. psychiatrist.

Sakharov, Andrei Dimitrievich, 1921–, Soviet physicist.

Saki, pseud. of Hector Hugh Munro, 1870–1916, Scot. author.

Saladin, 1137?–93, sultan of Egypt & Syria.

Salant, Richard, 1914–, U.S. radio & TV executive & lawyer.

Salazar, Antonio de Oliveira, 1889–1970, Pg. statesman; premier 1928–68.

Salinger, J(erome) D(avid), 1919–U.S. author.

Salisbury, Harrison E., 1908–, U.S. journalist.

Salk, Jonas E(dward), 1914–, U.S. bacteriologist.

Sallust (L. Gaius Sallustius Crispus), 86–34 B.C., Roman historian & politician.

Salomon, Haym, 1740?–85, Amer. revolutionary patriot & banker.

Samuelson, Paul, 1915–, U.S. economist & author.

Sand, George, pseud. of Amandine Aurore Lucie Dudevant, 1803–76, Fr. author.

Sandburg, Carl, 1878–1967, U.S. poet.

Sangallo, Antonio da, b. Antonio Cordiani, 1485–1546, Ital. architect.

—**Giuliano da,** 1445–1516, Ital. architect & sculptor.

Sanger, Fredrick, 1918–, Eng. chemist.

—**Margaret,** 1883–1966, U.S. pioneer in birth-control education.

San Martin, José de, 1778–1850, Argentinian-born S. Amer. revolutionary leader & general.

Sansovino, Jacopo, 1486–1570, Ital. sculptor & architect.

Santayana, George, 1863–1952, Sp.-born U.S. philosopher & author.

Sapir, Edward, 1884–1939, U.S. anthropologist.

Sappho, 7th c. B.C. Gk. poet.

Sarazen, Gene, 1901–, U.S. golfer.

Sardi, Vincent, Jr., 1915–U.S. restaurateur.

Sardou, Victorien, 1831–1908, Fr. playwright.

Sargent, John Singer, 1856–1925, U.S. painter.

Sarnoff, David, 1891–1971, Russ.-born U.S. radio & TV executive.

—**Robert,** 1918–, U.S. communications executive; son of prec.

Saroyan, William 1908–1981, U.S. author.

Sarto, Andrea del, 1487–1531, Florentine painter.

Sartre, Jean Paul, 1905–1980, Fr. philosopher, author, playwright & critic.

Sasetta, c. 1400–50, Ital. painter.

Sassoon, Siegfried, 1886–1967, Eng. poet.

—**Vidal,** 1928–, Eng.-born U.S. coiffeur.

Satie, (Alfred) Erik (Leslie), 1866–1925, Fr. composer.

Sa'ud Ibn Abdul, 1902–69, king of Saudi Arabia 1953–64.

Saul Hebrew name of the apostle PAUL.

Saussure, Ferdinand de, 1857–1913, Swiss linguist.

Savonarola, Girolamo, 1452–98, Ital. monk & reformer; burned for heresy.

Sayao, Bidu, 1908–, Brazilian soprano active in U.S.

Sayers, Dorothy Leigh, 1893–1957, Eng. author.

Scanderbeg (Iskender Bey), b. George Castriota, 1403?–68, Albanian chieftain.

Scarlatti, Alessandro, 1659–1725, and his son **Domenico,** 1683–1757, Ital. composers.

Schary, Dore, 1905–1980, U.S. film producer, writer & director.

Scheff, Fritzi, 1879–1954, Austrian singer & actress active in U.S.

Schelling, Friedrich Wilhelm Joseph von, 1775–1854, Ger. philosopher.

Scherman, Thomas, 1917–, U.S. conductor.

Schiaparelli, Giovanni Virginio, 1835–1910, Ital. astronomer.

—**Elsa,** 1890–1973, Ital.-born Fr. fashion designer.

Schick, Bela, 1877–1967, Hung.-born U.S. pediatrician.

Schiff, Dorothy, 1903–, U.S. publisher.

—**Jacob H.,** 1847–1920, U.S. businessman.

Schildkraut, Joseph, 1895–1964, Austrian actor.

Schiller, Johann Friedrich von, 1759–1805, Ger. poet & playwright.

Schipa, Tito, 1889–1965, Ital. tenor.

Schippers, Thomas, 1930–77, U.S. conductor.

Schirmer, Gustav, 1829–93, Ger.-born U.S. music publisher.

Schlegel, August Wilhelm von, 1767–1845, Ger. author.

—**Friedrich von,** 1772–1829, Ger. philosopher & author; brother of prec.

Schleiden, Matthias Jakob, 1804–81, Ger. botanist.

Schlesinger, Arthur M., Sr., 1888–1965, and his son **Arthur M., Jr.,** 1917–, U.S. historians.

—**James Rodney,** 1929–, U.S. government official.

—**John,** 1926–, Eng. film director.

Schliemann, Heinrich, 1822–90, Ger. archaeologist.

Schmeling, Max(imilian), 1905–, Ger.-born boxer active in U.S.

Schmidt, Helmut, 1918–, chancellor of W. Germany 1974–.

Schnabel, Arthur, 1882–1951, Austrian-born pianist active in U.S.

Schnitzler, Arthur, 1862–1931, Austrian physician & playwright.

Schönberg, Arnold, 1874–1951, Austrian composer & conductor active in U.S.

Schonberg, Harold C., 1915–, U.S. music critic.

Schongauer, Martin, 1445?–91, Ger. painter & engraver.

Schopenhauer, Arthur, 1788–1860, Ger. philosopher.

Schrödinger, Erwin, 1887–1961, Austrian physicist.

Schubert, Franz(Peter), 1797–1828, Austrian composer.

Schuller, Gunther, 1925–, U.S. composer.

Schultz, Dutch, b. Arthur Flegenheimer, 1902–35, U.S. criminal.

Schulz, Charles M(onroe), 1922–, U.S. cartoonist.

Schuman, Robert, 1886–1963, Fr. statesman.

—**William Howard,** 1910–, U.S. composer.

Schumann, Clara, 1819–96, Ger. pianist & composer.

—**Elisabeth,** 1885–1952, Ger. soprano.

—**Robert (Alexander),** 1810–56, Ger. composer; husband of Clara.

Schumann-Heink, Ernestine, 1861–1936, Austrian contralto.

Schurz, Carl, 1829–1906, Ger.-born U.S. politician, military officer & author.

Schütz, Heinrich, 1585–1672, Ger. composer.

Schwab, Charles Michael, 1862–1939, U.S. industrialist.

Schwann, Theodor, 1810–82, Ger. physiologist.

Schwarzkopf, Elisabeth, 1915–, Ger. soprano.

Schweitzer, Albert, 1875-1965, Alsatian medical missionary, musician & theologian in Africa.

Scipio Africanus, Publius Cornelius, 237–183 B.C., Roman general: called **the Elder.**

Scofield, Paul, 1922–, Eng. actor.

Scopes, John Thomas, 1900–73, U.S. educator.

Scott, Dred, 1795–1858, U.S. Negro slave.

—**George C.,** 1927–, U.S. actor & director.

—**Robert Falcon,** 1868–1912, Eng. Antarctic explorer.

—**Sir Walter,** 1771–1832, Scot. author & poet.

Scotti, Antonio, 1866–1936, Ital. baritone.

Scriabin, Alexander, 1872–1915, Russ. composer.

Scribner, Charles, 1821–71, U.S. publisher.

Scripps, Edward W., 1854–1926, U.S. newspaper publisher.

Seaborg, Glenn Theodore, 1912–, U.S. chemist.

Seabury, Samuel, 1920–96, U.S. religious leader.

Searle, Ronald, 1920–, Eng. cartoonist.

Sears, Richard Warren, 1862–1914, U.S. merchant.

Seeger, Pete, 1919–, U.S. folk singer.

Seferis, George, pseud. of Giorgios Seferiades, 1900–71, Gk. diplomat & poet.

Segal, George, 1924–, U.S. sculptor.

Segovia, Andrés, 1894–, Sp. guitarist.

Segrè, Emilio, 1905–, Ital.-born U.S. physicist.

Sékou Touré, Ahmed, 1922–, African political leader; first president of Guinea 1958–.

Seldes, Gilbert Vivian, 1893–1970, U.S. author & critic.

Seleucus I, 358?–280 B.C., founder of Gk. dynasty in Syria.

Selfridge, Harry Gordon, 1857–1947, U.S.-born merchant & businessman active in Great Britain.

Sellers, Peter, 1925–1980, Eng. actor.

Selznick, David, 1902–65, U.S. film director.

Semmelweis, Ignaz P., 1818–65, Hung. physician.

Sendak, Maurice, 1928–, U.S. writer & illustrator.

Seneca, Lucius Annaeus, 3? B.C.-A.D. 65, Roman philosopher, statesman & playwright.

Senghor, Léopold Sédar, 1906–, African poet & stateman; president of Senegal 1960–.

Sennett, Mack, 1884–1960, Can.-born U.S. film director.

Sequoya, 1770?–1843, Cherokee Indian scholar.

Sergeyev, Konstantin, 1910–, Soviet choreographer & ballet-company director.

Serkin, Rudolf, 1903–, Czech pianist active in U.S.

Serling, Rod, 1924–75, U.S. TV writer & producer.

Serra, Junipero, 1713–84, Sp. missionary in Mexico & California.

Service, Robert W(illiam), 1874–1958, Can. author.

Sesshu, 1420?–1506, Jap. painter.

Sessions, Roger, 1896–, U.S. composer.

Seton, Saint Elizabeth Ann, b. Elizabeth Bayley, 1774–1821, U.S. religious leader.

Seurat, Georges, 1859–91, Fr. painter.

Seuss, Dr., pseud. of Theodore Seuss Geisel, 1904–, U.S. author & illustrator of children's books.

Sevareid, (Arnold) Eric, 1912–, U.S. news analyst & radio & TV commentator.

Sévigné, Marie de Rabutin-Chantal, Marguise de, 1626–96, Fr. writer.

Seward, William Henry, 1801–72, U.S. statesman; U.S. secretary of state 1861–69.

Seymour, Jane, 1509?–37, third wife of Henry VIII of England.

Sforza, Count Carlo, 1872–1952, Ital. statesman.

Shackleton, Sir Ernest Henry, 1874–1922, Eng. Antarctic explorer.

Shah Jehan, 1592–1666, Mogul emperor of Hindustan 1628–58; builder of the Taj Mahal.

Shahn, Ben, 1898–1969, Lithuanian-born U.S. painter.

Shakespeare, William, 1564–1616, Eng. poet & playwright.

Shankar, Ravi, 1920–, Indian musician.

Shankara, c. 788–820, Indian philosopher.

Shapiro, Karl Jay, 1913–, U.S. poet.

Shapley, Harlow, 1885–1972, U.S. astronomer.

Shastri, Shri Lal Bahadur, 1904–66, Indian politician; prime minister of India 1964–66.

Shaw, Artie, 1910–, U.S. musician.
—**George Bernard,** 1856–1950, Irish-born Brit. playwright, critic & reformer.
—**Robert,** 1927–78, Eng. actor, playwright & author.
—**Robert (Lawson),** 1916–, U.S. conductor & choral director.
Shawn, Edwin Meyers (Ted), 1891–1972, U.S. dancer & choreographer.
Shays, Daniel, 1747?–1825, Amer. revolutionary & rebel.
Shearer, Norma, 1905–, Can.-born U.S. actress.
Shearing, George, 1919–, Eng.-born U.S. jazz musician.
Sheean, (James) Vincent, 1899–1975, U.S. journalist & author.
Sheen, Fulton J(ohn), 1895–1979, U.S. religious leader & author.
Shelley, Mary Wollstonecraft (Godwin), 1797–1851, Eng. author.
—**Percy Bysshe,** 1792–1822, Eng. poet; husband of prec.
Shepard, Alan (Bartlett), Jr.; 1923–, U.S. astronaut.
Sheraton, Thomas, 1751–1806, Eng. furniture designer & cabinetmaker.
Sheridan, Ann, 1916?–67, U.S. actress.
—**Philip Henry,** 1831–88, U.S. Civil War general.
—**Richard Brinsley,** 1715–1816, Irish-born Brit. playwright & politician.
Sherman, Roger, 1721–93, U.S. jurist & statesman.
—**William Tecumseh,** 1820–91, U.S. Civil War general.
Sherrington, Sir Charles Scott, 1857–1952, Eng. physiologist.
Sherwood, Robert E(mmet), 1896–1955, U.S. playwright.
Shirer, William L(awrence), 1904–, U.S. journalist & author.
Shockley, W(illiam) B(radford), 1910–, Eng. -born U.S. physicist.
Shoemaker, William Lee (Willie), 1931–, U.S. jockey.
Sholes, Christopher Lathan, 1819–90, U.S. inventor.
Sholokhov, Mikhail Aleksandrovich, 1905–, Soviet author.
Shore, Dinah, 1917–, U.S. singer & actress.
Short, Bobby, 1936–, U.S. singer.
Shorter, Frank, 1947–, Ger. -born U.S. track runner.
Shostakovich, Dmitri, 1906–75, Soviet composer.
Shubert A family of U.S. theater managers and producers incl. three brothers: **Lee,** 1875–1953; **Jacob J.,** 1880–1963; and **Sam S.,** 1876–1905.
Shumlin, Herman, 1898–1979, U.S. theatrical producer & film director.
Shute, Nevil, 1899–1960, Eng. engineer & author.
Sibelius, Jean, 1865–1957, Finnish composer.
Siddons, Sarah Kemble, 1755–1831, Eng. actress.
Sidgwick, Nevil V., 1873–1952, Eng. chemist.
Sidney, Sir Philip, 1554–86, Eng. soldier, statesman & poet.
Siegel, Benjamin ("Bugsy"), 1906–47, U.S. criminal.
Sienkiewicz, Henryk, 1846–1916, Pol. author.
Siepi, Cesare, 1923–, Ital. basso.
Signorelli, Luca, 1441?–1523, Ital. painter.
Signoret, Simone, 1921–, Fr. actress.
Sihanouk, Prince Norodom, 1922–, chief of state of Cambodia 1964–70.
Sikorsky, Igor Ivan, 1889–1972, Russ.-born U.S. aeronautical engineer.
Silliphant, Sterling, 1918–, U.S. playwright.
Sills, Beverly, 1929–, U.S. soprano.
Silone, Ignazio, pseud. of Secondo Tranquilli, 1900–78, Ital. author.
Silvers, Phil, 1911–, U.S. comedian.
Simenon, Georges, 1903–, Belg.-born Fr. author.
Simeon Stylites, Saint, 390?–459, Syrian ascetic.
Simon, Michel, 1895–1975, Swiss actor active in France.
—**Neil,** 1927–, U.S. playwright.
Simpson, George Gaylord, 1902–, U.S. paleontologist.
—**O(renthal) J(ames),** 1947–, U.S. football player.
Sinatra, Francis Albert (Frank), 1917–, U.S. singer & actor.
Sinclair, Harry Ford, 1876–1956, U.S. businessman.
—**Upton Beall,** 1878–1968, U.S. author & politician.
Singer, Isaac Bashevis, 1904–, Pol.-born U.S. author.

Singer, Isaac Merrit, 1811–75, U.S. inventor.
Siqueiros, David Alfaro, 1898–, Mexican painter & muralist.
Sisler, George, 1893–1973, U.S. baseball player.
Sisley, Alfred, 1839–99, Eng.-born painter active in France.
Sitting Bull. 1834?–90, Sioux Am. Ind. chief.
Sitwell A family of Eng. writers incl. **Dame Edith,** 1887–1964; and her brothers **Sir Osbert,** 1892–1969; and **Sacheverell,** 1897–; all poets, essayists, critics & authors.
Sjöström, Victor, 1879–1960, Swed. film director.
Skelton, John, 1460?–1529, Eng. poet.
—**Red,** 1913–, U.S. actor & comedian.
Skinner, B(urrhus) F(rederic), 1904–, U.S. psychologist.
—**Cornelia Otis,** 1901–79, U.S. actress & author.
—**Otis,** 1858–1942, U.S. actor; father of prec.
Skouras, Spyros P(anagiotes), 1893–1971, U.S. film executive.
Skulnik, Menasha, 1898–1970, Pol.-born U.S. actor.
Sloan, John French, 1871–1951, U.S. printer.
Smetana, Bedřich, 1824–84, Czech composer.
Smith, Adam, 1723–90, Scot. economist.
—**Alfred E(manuel),** 1873–1944, U.S. politician.
—**Bessie,** 1894–1937, U.S. blues singer.
—**David,** 1906–65, U.S. sculptor.
—**Howard K(ingsbury),** 1914–, U.S. radio & TV news commentator.
—**Ian Douglas,** 1919–, prime minister of Rhodesia 1964–79.
—**Capt. John,** 1579–1631, Eng. adventurer; president of the Virginia Colony 1608.
—**Joseph,** 1805–44, U.S. founder of the Mormon Church.
—**Kathryn Elizabeth (Kate),** 1909–. U.S. singer.
—**Maggie,** 1934–, Eng. actress.
—**Oliver,** 1918–, U.S. set designer, theatrical producer & ballet-company director.
—**Walter Wellesley ("Red"),** 1905–81, U.S. sports columnist.
—**William,** 1769–1839, Eng. geologist.
Smithson, James, 1865–1829, Eng. chemist & mineralogist.
Smollett, Tobias (George), 1721–71, Eng. author.
Smuts, Jan Christiaan, 1870–1950, South African statesman & general.
Snead, Samuel J. (Sam), 1912–, U.S. golfer.
Snell, Peter, 1938–, New Zealand track runner.
Snow, Sir C(harles) P(ercival), 1905–80, Eng. author & physicist.
Socrates, 469?–399 B.C., Athenian philosopher.
Soddy, Frederick, 1877–1956, Eng. chemist.
Sodoma, Il, b. Giovanni Antonio de' Bazzi, 1477?–1549, Ital. painter.
Soleri, Paolo, 1912–, Ital. architect active in U.S.
Solon, 638?–558? B.C., Athenian statesman & lawgiver.
Solti, Sir Georg, 1912–, Hung.-born conductor active in U.S.
Solzhenitsyn, Alexander, 1918–, Soviet author resident in Switzerland.
Somoza Debayle, Anastasio, 1925–80, president of Nicaragua 1967–79.
Sondheim, Stephen, 1930–, U.S. composer.
Sontag, Susan, 1933–, U.S. critic, author & film director.
Soong A Chin. family active in politics & banking, incl. **T(se) V(en),** 1891–1971; and his sisters **Ching-ling,** 1890–1981, widow of Sun Yat-sen; and **Mei-ling,** 1898–, widow of Chiang Kai-shek.
Sophocles, 495?–406 B.C., Gk. playwright.
Sorel, Georges, 1847–1922, Fr. journalist & philosopher.
Sørensen, Søren P.L., 1868–1939, Dan. chemist.
Sorokin, Pitirim Aleksandrovich, 1889–1968, Russ.-born U.S. sociologist.
Sousa, John Philip, 1854–1932, U.S. composer.
Southey, Robert, 1774–1843, Eng. poet.
Soutine, Chaim, 1774–1843, Lithuanian-born painter active in France.
Souvanna Phouma, Prince, 1901–, prime minister of Laos, 1962–75.

Soyer, Moses, 1899–1974 & his twin brother **Raphael,** 1899–, Russ.-born U.S. painters.

Spaak, Paul Henri, 1899–1972, Belg. lawyer & statesman; secretary general of NATO 1957–61.

Spahn, Warren Edward, 1921–, U.S. baseball player.

Spalding, Albert Goodwill, 1850–1915, U.S. baseball player & sporting-goods manufacturer.

Spallanzani, Lazzaro, 1729–99, Ital. biologist.

Spark, Muriel, 1918–, Eng. author.

Spartacus, ?–71 B.C., Thracian leader of slaves in an uprising against Rome 73–71 B.C.

Spassky, Boris, 1937–, Soviet chess master.

Speaker, Tris, 1888–1958, U.S. baseball player.

Spellman, Francis Joseph, Cardinal, 1889–1967, U.S. religious leader.

Spencer, Herbert, 1820–1903, Eng. philosopher.

Spender, Stephen, 1909–, Eng. poet.

Spengler, Oswald, 1880–1936, Ger. philosopher.

Spenser, Edmund, 1552–99, Eng. poet.

Sperry, Elmer Ambrose, 1860–1930, U.S. inventor.

Spiegel, Sam(uel) P., 1904?–, U.S. film producer.

Spillane, Frank Morrison ("Mickey"), 1918–, U.S. author.

Spinoza, Baruch, 1632–77, Du. philosopher.

Spitz, Mark, 1950–, U.S. swimmer.

Spock, Benjamin, 1903–, U.S. pediatrician & political activist.

Spode, Josiah, 1754–1827, Eng. potter.

Spohr, Ludwig, 1784–1859, Ger. composer, conductor & violinist.

Springer, Axel, 1917–, Ger. publisher.

Spyri, Johanna (Heusser), 1827–1901, Swiss author.

Squanto, ?–1622, Am. Ind. friend of the Pilgrims.

Squibb, Edward Robinson, 1819–1900, U.S. physician & manufacturer.

Staël, Mme. Anne Louise (Necker) de, 1766–1817, Fr. writer.

Stagg, Amos Alonzo, 1862–1965, U.S. football coach.

Stalin, Joseph, b. Iosif Vissarionovich Djugashvili, 1879–1953, Soviet dictator 1927–53.

Standish, Miles, 1584?–1656, Eng.-born, soldier & military leader of the Pilgrims in America.

Stanford, Leland, 1824–93, U.S. railroad builder & public official.

Stanislavsky, Constantin, 1863–1938, Soviet actor, director, producer & teacher.

Stanley, Francis Edgar, 1849–1918, & his twin brother **Freelan,** 1849–1940, U.S. inventors & automobile manufacturers.

—**Sir Henry Morton,** 1841–1904, Eng. explorer & author.

—**Wendell Meredith,** 1904–71, U.S. biochemist.

Stanton, Elizabeth Cady, 1815–1902, U.S. suffragist.

—**Frank,** 1908–, U.S. radio & TV executive.

Stanwyck, Barbara, 1907–, U.S. actress.

Stapleton, Maureen, 1925–, U.S. actress.

Stare, Frederick John, 1910–, U.S. nutritionist & biochemist.

Stark, Johannes, 1874–1957, Ger. physicist.

Starr, Ringo, 1940–, Eng. composer & musical performer.

Stassen, Harold Edward, 1907–, U.S. lawyer & politician.

Statler, Ellsworth Milton, 1863–1928, U.S. hotel executive.

Staudinger, Hermann, 1881–1965, Ger. chemist.

Stauffenberg, Count Claus Schenk von, 1907–44, Ger. staff officer; led abortive plot against Hitler.

St. Cyr, Lili, 1917?–, U.S. stripteaser.

St. Denis, Ruth, 1877?–1968, U.S. dancer & choreographer.

Steegmuller, Francis, 1906–, U.S. biographer.

Steele, Sir Richard, 1672–1729, Irish-born Brit. author & playwright.

Stefan, Joseph, 1835–93, Austrian physicist.

Stefansson, Vihjalmur, 1879–1962, Can. Arctic explorer.

Steffens, (Joseph) Lincoln, 1866–1936, U.S. journalist & author.

Steichen, Edward, 1879–1973, Luxembourg-born U.S. photographer.

Stein, Gertrude, 1874–1946, U.S. writer active in France.

Steinbeck, John (Ernest), 1902–68, U.S. author.

Steinberg, Saul, 1914–, Rumanian-born U.S. cartoonist.

—**William,** 1899–1978, Ger. conductor active in U.S.

Steinem, Gloria, 1936–, U.S. author & feminist leader.

Steiner, George, 1929–, Fr.-born U.S. critic.

—**Max,** 1888?–1971, Austrian-born U.S. film composer.

—**Rudolf,** 1861–1925, Austrian-born U.S. educator.

Steinmetz, Charles (Proteus), 1865–1923, Ger.-born U.S. electrical engineer & inventor.

Steinway, Henry Englehard, 1797–1871, Ger.-born U.S. piano manufacturer.

Stella, Frank Philip, 1936–, U.S. painter.

Stendhal, pseud. of Marie Henri Beyle, 1783–1842, Fr. author.

Stengel, Charles Dillon ("Casey"), 1890–1975, U.S. baseball player & manager.

Stephens, James, 1882–1950, Irish poet & author.

Stephenson, George, 1781–1848, Eng. inventor.

Stern, Isaac, 1920–, Russ.-born U.S. violinist.

—**Otto,** 1888–1969, Ger.-born U.S. physicist.

Sternberg, Josef von, 1894–1969, U.S. film director.

Sterne, Laurence, 1713–68, Irish-born Brit. author.

Stetson, John Batterson, 1830–1906, U.S. hat manufacturer.

Steuben, Baron Friedrich Wilhelm von, 1730–94, Prussian army officer; served in Amer. Revolution.

Stevens, George, 1904–75, U.S. film director.

—**John Paul,** 1920–, U.S. jurist; justice of the U.S. Supreme Court 1976–.

—**Rise,** 1913–, U.S. mezzo soprano.

—**Wallace,** 1879–1955, U.S. poet.

Stevenson, Adlai E(wing), 1900–65, U.S. statesman.

—**Robert Louis,** 1850–94, Scot. author.

Stevinus, Simon, 1548–1620, Belg. mathematician.

Stewart, Ellen, 1931–, U.S. theater director.

—**James,** 1908–, U.S. actor.

—**Potter,** 1915–, U.S. jurist; justice of the U.S. Supreme Court 1958–.

Stieglitz, Alfred, 1864–1946, U.S. photographer.

Still, William Grant, 1895–, U.S. composer.

Stilwell, Joseph Warren, 1883–1946, U.S. general.

Stimson, Henry Louis, 1867–1950, U.S. statesman.

St. Laurent, Louis Stephen, 1882–1973, Can. lawyer; prime minister of Canada 1948–57.

Stockhausen, Karlheinz, 1928–, Ger. composer.

Stoker, Bram, 1847–1912, Eng. author.

Stokowski, Leopold, 1882–1977, Eng.-born U.S. conductor.

Stone, Edward Durell, 1902–78, U.S. architect.

—**Harlan Fiske,** 1872–1946, U.S. jurist.

—**Irving,** 1903–, U.S. author.

—**I(sidor) F(einstein),** 1907–, U.S. journalist.

—**Lucy,** 1818–93, U.S. social reformer & women's suffragist.

Stoney, George J. 1826–1911, Irish physicist.

Stout, Rex (Todhunter), 1886–1975, U.S. author.

Stowe, Harriet Beecher, 1811–96, U.S. author.

Strachey, (Giles) Lytton, 1880–1932, Eng. author.

Stradivari, Antonio, 1644–1737, Ital. violinmaker.

Strand, Paul, 1890–1976, U.S. photographer.

Strasberg, Lee, 1901–82, Austrian-born U.S. drama teacher & actor.

Straus, Isidor, 1845–1912, & his brother **Nathan,** 1848–1931, U.S. merchants & philanthropists.

—**Oskar,** 1870–1954, Austrian-born Fr. composer.

Strauss A family of Austrian composers incl. **Johann,** 1804–49 (called **the Elder**), and his sons: **Johann,** 1825–99 (**the Younger**); and **Josef,** 1827–70.

—**Levi,** 1829?–1902, U.S. clothing manufacturer.

—**Richard,** 1864–1949, Ger. composer & conductor.

Stravinsky, Igor (Fedorovich), 1882–1971, Russ.-born composer active in the U.S.

Streisand, Barbara, 1942–, U.S. singer & actress.

Strindberg, (John) August, 1849–1912, Swed. playwright & author.

Sroessner, Alfredo, 1912–, president of Paraguay 1958–.

Stroheim, Erich von, 1885–1957, Austrian-born U.S. actor & film director.

Stroud, Robert, 1890–1963, U.S. convict & ornithologist.

Strougal, Lubomir, 1935–, premier of Czechoslovakia 1970–.

Struve, Friedrich G. W., 1793–1864, Ger. astronomer.

—**Otto,** 1897–1963, Russ.-born U.S. astronomer.

Stuart, Charles Edward, 1720–88, pretender to the throne of Great Britain: called Bonnie Prince Charlie & the Young Pretender.

—**Gilbert (Charles),** 1755–1828, U.S. painter.

—**James Edward,** 1688–1766, Eng. prince; father of Charles: called **the Old Pretender.**

—**James Ewell Brown ("Jeb"),** 1833–64, U.S. Confederate general.

Studebaker, Clement, 1831–1901, U.S. carriage manufacturer.

Sturges, Preston, 1898–1959, U.S. film director.

Stutz, Harry Clayton, 1876–1930, U.S. automobile manufacturer.

Stuyvesant, Peter, 1592–1672, last Du. governor of New Amsterdam (now New York).

Styne, Jule, 1905–, Eng.-born U.S. composer.

Styron, William, 1925–, U.S. author.

Suharto, 1921–, Indonesian general; president of Indonesia 1968–.

Sukarno, 1902–70, Indonesian statesman; first president of the republic of Indonesia 1950–67.

Suleiman I, 1496?–1566, Turkish sultan of the Ottoman empire: called **the Magnificent.**

Sullavan, Margaret, 1911–60, U.S. actress.

Sullivan, Sir Arthur (Seymour), 1842–1900, Eng. composer.

—**Ed(ward Vincent),** 1902–74, U.S. jornalist & TV personality.

—**Harry Stack,** 1892–1949, U.S. psychiatrist.

—**John L(awrence),** 1856–1924, U.S. architect.

Sulzberger, Arthur Hays, 1891–1968, U.S. publisher.

Summerson, Sir John, 1904–, Eng. art historian.

Sumner, Charles, 1811–74, U.S. statesman & orator.

Sunday, William Ashley (Billy), 1862–1935, U.S. evangelist.

Sun Yat-sen, 1865–1925, Chin. revolutionary leader & president of the republic of China 1911–12.

Susann, Jacqueline, 1921–74, U.S. author.

Susskind, David, 1920–, U.S. TV producer.

Sutherland, Joan, 1926–, Austral. soprano.

Sutter, John Augustus, 1803–80, Ger.-born pioneer in California.

Suzuki, D(aisetz) T(eitaro), 1870–1966, Jap. Buddhist scholar.

—**Zenko,** 1911–, Jap. statesman and prime minister 1980–.

Svoboda, Ludvik, 1895–1979, president of Czechoslovakia 1968–75.

Swanson, Gloria, 1899–, U.S. actress.

Swarthout, Gladys, 1904–69, U.S. mezzo-soprano.

Swedenborg, Emmanuel, 1688–1772, Swed. religious mystic, philosopher & scientist.

Swift, Gustavus Franklin, 1839–1903, U.S. meat packer.

—**Jonathan,** 1667–1745, Irish-born Brit. satirist.

Swinburne, Algernon Charles, 1837–1909, Eng. poet & critic.

Swope, Herbert Bayard, 1882–1958, U.S. journalist.

Sydenham, Thomas, 1624–89, Eng. physician.

Sydow, Max von, 1929–, Swed. actor.

Symington, (William) Stuart, 1901–, U.S. politician.

Synge, John Millington, 1871–1909, Irish playwright & poet.

Szell, George, 1897–1970, Hung.-born U.S. conductor.

Szent-Györgyi von Nagyrapolt, Albert, 1893–, Hung. chemist.

Szewinska, Irena, 1946–, Pol. track runner.

Szigeti, Joseph, 1892–1973, Hung. violinist.

Szilard, Leo, 1898–1964, Hung.-born U.S. physicist.

Szold, Henrietta, 1860–1945, U.S. Zionist; founder of Hadassah.

Tacitus, Gaius Cornelius, A.D. 55?–117?, Roman historian.

Taft, Robert (Alphonso), 1889–1953, U.S. senator 1939–53.

—**William Howard,** 1857–1930, 27th U.S. president 1906–13; Chief Justice of the U.S. Supreme Court 1921–30; father of prec.

Tagliavini, Ferruccio, 1913–, Ital. tenor.

Taglioni, Marie, 1804–84, Ital. ballerina.

Tagore, Sir Rabindranath, 1861–1941, Hindu poet.

Taine, Hippolyte Adolphe, 1828–93, Fr. philosopher & critic.

Takamine, Jokichi, 1854–1922, Jap. chemist & industrialist active in U.S.

Talese, Gay, 1932–, U.S. journalist & author.

Tallchief, Maria, 1925–, U.S. ballerina.

Talleyrand-Perigord, Charles Maurice de, 1754–1838, Fr. statesman.

Talma, Francois Joseph, 1763–1826, Fr. actor.

Talmadge, Norma, 1897–1957, U.S. actress.

Tamayo, Rufino, 1899–, Mexican painter.

Tamerlane, 1336?–1405, Tatar conqueror of Asia. Also **Tamburlaine.**

Tamm, Igor Yevgenievich, 1895–1971, Soviet physicist.

Tanaka, Kakuei, 1918–, premier of Japan 1972–74.

Tancred, 1078?–1112, Norman leader in the first crusade.

Tandy, Jessica, 1909–, Eng.-born U.S. actress.

Tanguay, Eva, 1878–1947, Can.-born U.S. actress.

Tanguy, Yves, 1900–55, Fr.-born U.S. artist.

Tanner, Alain, 1920–, Swiss film director.

Tarbell, Ida Minerva, 1857–1944, U.S. author.

Tarkington, Booth, 1869–1946, U.S. author.

Tarquin, (L. Lucius Tarquinius Superbus), 6th c. B.C. king of Rome.

Tartini, Giuseppe, 1692–1770, Ital. violinist & composer.

Tasman, Abel Janszoon, 1603–59, Du. navigator & explorer.

Tasso, Torquato, 1544–95, Ital. poet.

Tate, (John Orley) Allen, 1899–1979, U.S. poet, critic & biographer.

Tati, Jacques, 1908–, Fr. actor, author & film director.

Tatum, Art, 1901–56, U.S. jazz musician.

—**Edward Lawrie,** 1909–75, U.S. biochemist.

Tauber, Richard, 1892–1948, Austrian tenor.

Tawney, R(ichard), H(enry), 1880–1962, Eng. economic historian.

Taylor, Deems, 1885–1966, U.S. composer & music critic.

—**Elizabeth,** 1932–, Eng.-born U.S. actress.

—**Laurette,** 1884–1946, U.S. actress.

—**Maxwell D(avenport),** 1901–, U.S. general.

—**Paul,** 1930–, U.S. dancer & choreographer.

—**Robert,** 1911–69, U.S. actor.

—**Zachary,** 1784–1850, U.S. general & 12th U.S. president 1849–50.

Tchaikovsky, Peter Ilyich, 1840-93, Russ. composer.

Tcheitchew, Pavel, 1898–1957, Russ.-born U.S. painter.

Teach, Edward, ?–1718, Eng. pirate: known as **Blackbeard.**

Teagarden, Jack, 1905–64, U.S. jazz musician.

Teale, Edwin Way, 1899–1980, U.S. naturalist & author.

Teasdale, Sara, 1884–1933, U.S. poet.

Tebaldi, Renata, 1922–, Ital. soprano.

Tecumseh, 1768?–1813, Shawnee Am. Ind. chief.

Teilhard de Chardin, Pierre, 1881–1955, Fr. paleontologist, geologist & philosopher.

Telemann, Georg Philipp, 1681?–1767, Ger. composer.

Teller, Edward, 1908–, Hung.-born U.S. physicist.

Temple, Shirley See BLACK, SHIRLEY TEMPLE.

Templeton, Alec, 1910–63, Welsh-born U.S. composer & musician.

Tenniel, Sir John, 1820–1914, Eng. illustrator.

Tennyson, Alfred, 1809–92, Eng. poet.

Tenzing Norgay, 1914–, Nepalese Sherpa mountain climber.

Ter-Arutunian, Rouben, 1920–, Soviet-born U.S. set & costume designer.

Ter Borch, Gerard, 1617–81, Du. painter.

Terence (L. Publius Terentius Afer), 190?–159 B.C., Roman playwright.

Tereshkova, Valentina Vladimirovna, 1937–, Soviet cosmonaut; first woman in space.

Terhune, Albert Payson, 1872–1942, U.S. author.

Terman, L(ewis) M(adison), 1877–1956, U.S. psychologist.

Terry, Dame Ellen (Alicia), 1847–1928, Eng. actress.

Terry-Thomas, 1911–, Eng. comedian & actor.

Tertullian (L. Quintus Septimius Florens Tertullianus), A.D. 160?–230?, Roman theologian.

Tesla, Nikola, 1857–1943, Yugoslav-born U.S. inventor.

Tetley, Glen, 1926–, U.S. choreographer.

Tetrazzini, Luisa, 1874–1940, Ital. soprano.

Tetzel, Johann, 1465?–1519, Ger. Dominican monk.

Thackeray, William Makepeace, 1811–63, Eng. author.

Thalberg, Irving G(rant), 1899–1936, U.S. film producer.

Thales, 640?–546 B.C., Gk. philosopher.

Thant, U, 1909–74, Burmese diplomat & secretary general of the U.N. 1961–71.

Thatcher, Margaret, 1925–, Eng. political leader; prime minister 1979–.

Thebom, Blanche, 1918–, U.S. mezzo-soprano.

Themistocles, 527?–460? B.C., Athenian general & statesman.

Theocritus, 3rd c. B.C. Gk. poet.

Theodora, ?–548, Byzantine empress; co-ruler with her husband, Justinian I.

Theodorakis, Mikis, 1925–, Gk. composer.

Theophrastus, 372?–287? B.C., Gk. philosopher & naturalist.

Theresa of Avila, Saint, 1515–82, Sp. Carmelite nun.

Thespis, 6th c. B.C. Gk. poet & dramatist.

Thieu, Nguyen Van, 1923–, president of South Vietnam 1967–75.

Thomas, Ambroise, 1811–96, Fr. composer.

—**Dylan (Marlais),** 1914–53, Welsh poet.

—**Lowell (Jackson),** 1892–1981, U.S. news commentator & author.

—**Norman,** 1884–1968, U.S. socialist leader & author.

—**Seth,** 1785–1859, U.S. clock manufacturer.

Thomas of Erceldoune, 13th c. Scot. poet.

Thompson, Benjamin, Count Rumford, 1753–1814, Amer.-born Eng. statesman & scientist.

—**Dorothy,** 1894–1961, U.S. journalist.

—**Francis,** 1859–1907, Eng. poet.

—**J(ames) Walter,** 1847–1928, U.S. advertising executive.

Thomson, Sir George, 1892–1975, Eng. physicist.

—**Sir Joseph John,** 1856–1940, Eng. physicist; father of prec.

—**Virgil,** 1896–, U.S. composer & music critic.

Thoreau, Henry David, 1817–62, U.S. author & naturalist.

Thorndike, Edward Lee, 1874–1949, U.S. psychologist.

—**Dame Sybil,** 1882–1976, Eng. actress.

Thorpe, James Francis (Jim), 1888–1953, U.S. football player & track athlete.

Thucydides, 471?–399 B.C., Athenian statesman & historian.

Thurber, James (Grover), 1894–1961, U.S. author & artist.

Thurmond, J. Strom, 1902–, U.S. politician.

Tibbett, Lawrence Mervil, 1896–1960, U.S. baritone.

Tiberius Claudius Nero Ceasar, 42 B.C.–A.D. 37, Roman emperor A.D. 14–37.

Tiepolo, Giovanni Battista, 1696–1770, Venetian painter.

Tiffany, Charles Lewis, 1812–1902, U.S. jeweler.

—**Louis,** 1848–1933, U.S. decorative designer; son of prec.

Tiglath-pileser III, ?–727 B.C., king of Assyria 745–727 B.C.

Tilden, William (Bill), 1893–1953, U.S. tennis player.

Tillich, Paul (Johannes), 1886–1965, Ger.-born U.S. theologian.

Tillstrom, Burr, 1917–, U.S. puppeteer.

Tinbergen, Jan, 1903–, Du. economist.

Tinbergen, Nikolaas, 1907–, Du. zoologist; brother of prec.

Tindemans, Leo, 1922–, premier of Belgium 1974–78.

Tintoretto, b. Jacopo Robusti, 1518–94, Venetian painter.

Tiomkin, Dimitri, 1894–1979, Russ.-born U.S. composer.

Tirso de Molina, pseud. of Gabriel Téllez, 1571?–1648, Sp. playwright.

Titchener, Edward Bradford, 1867–1927, Eng.-born U.S. psychologist.

Titian, b. Tiziano Vecelli, 1477–1576, Venetian painter.

Tito, b. Josip Broz, 1892–, Yugoslav patriot & statesman; president of Yugoslavia 1953–.

Tittle, Y(elverton) A(braham), Jr., 1926–, U.S. football player.

Titus Flavius Sabinus Vespasianus, A.D. 40?–81, Roman emperor 79–81.

Tobey, Mark, 1890–1976, U.S. painter.

Tocqueville, Alexis (Charles Henri Maurice Clerel) de, 1805–59, Fr. statesman & political writer.

Todd, Sir Alexander Robertus, 1907–, Eng. chemist.

Todman, William, 1916–, U.S. TV producer.

Togliatti, Palmiro, 1893?–1964, Ital. communist leader.

Togo, Shigenori, 1882–1950, Jap. diplomat.

Tojo, Hideki, 1885–1948, Jap. general & politician.

Tokyo Rose, b. Iva d'Aquino, 1916–, U.S.-born propagandist for Japan in World War II.

Tolbert, William Richard, 1913–, president of Liberia 1971–.

Tolkien, J(ohn) R(onald) R(euel), 1892–1973, Eng. author.

Tolstoy, Count Leo Nikolayevich, 1828–1919, Russ. author & social reformer.

Tommasini, Vicenzo, 1880–1950, Ital. composer.

Tone, (Theobald) Wolfe, 1763–98, Irish revolutionary.

Torelli, Giacomo, 1608–78, Ital. stage designer.

Tormé, Mel(vin Howard), 1925–, U.S. singer.

Torquemada, Tomás de, 1420–98, Sp. monk & inquisitor.

Torre-Nilsson, Leopoldo, 1924–, Argentine film director.

Torricelli, Evangelista, 1608–47, Ital. physicist.

Toscanini, Arturo, 1867–1957, Ital. conductor active in U.S.

Toulouse-Lautrec, Henri Marie Raymond de, 1864–1901, Fr. painter & lithographer.

Tourel, Jennie, 1910–73, Can.-born U.S. mezzo-soprano.

Toussaint L'Ouverture, Dominique Francois, 1743–1803, Haitian Negro revolutionary leader & general.

Tovey, Donald Francis, 1875–1940, Eng. musicologist & composer.

Townes, Charles Hard, 1915–, U.S. physicist.

Townsend, Sir John S. E., 1868–1957, Irish physicist.

Toynbee, Arnold J(oseph), 1889–1975, Eng. historian.

Tracy, Spencer, 1900–67, U.S. actor.

Trajan (L. Marcus Ulpius Trajanus), A.D. 52?–117, Roman emperor 98–117.

Traubel, Helen, 1899–1972, U.S. soprano.

Traynor, Harold Joseph ("Pie"), 1899–1972, U.S. baseball player.

Tree, Sir (Herbert) Beerbohm, 1853–1917, Eng. actor-manager.

Treigle, Norman, 1927–75, U.S. basso.

Treitschke, Heinrich von, 1834–96, German historian and political writer.

Tremayne, Les, 1913–, Eng.-born U.S. radio actor.

Trevelyan, George Macaulay, 1876–1962, Eng. historian.

Trevino, Lee, 1939–, U.S. golfer.

Trigère, Pauline, 1912–, Fr.-born U.S. fashion designer.

Trilling, Diana (Rubin), ?–, U.S. critic & author.

—**Lionel,** 1905–75, U.S. critic & author: husband of prec.

Trollope, Anthony, 1815–82, Eng. author.

Trotsky, Leon, b. Lev Davidovich Bronstein, 1879–1940, Soviet revolutionary leader; assassinated.

Trudeau, Pierre Elliott, 1919–, Can. statesman; prime minister of Canada 1968–79 and 1980–.

Trudeau, Gary, 1948–, U.S. cartoonist and satirist.

Truffaut, François, 1932–, Fr. film director.

Trujillo Molina, Rafael Leonidas, 1891–1961, Domini-

can general; president of the Dominican Republic 1930–38 & 1940–52; assassinated.

Truman, Harry S, 1884–1972, 33rd U.S. president 1944–53.

Trumbo, Dalton, 1905–, U.S. author.

Truth, Sojourner, b. Isabella Van Wagener, 1797?–1883, U.S. social reformer.

Tshombe, Moise K., 1919–69, Africa political leader.

Tsiolkovsky, Konstantin Eduardovich, 1857–1935, Russ. physicist.

Tsvett, Mikhail Semenovich, 1872–1920, Ital.-born Russ. botanist.

Tubman, Harriet, 1820?–1913, U.S. abolitionist.

—**William V(acanarat) S(hadrach),** 1895–1971, president of Liberia 1943–71.

Tuchman, Barbara, 1912–, U.S. historian.

Tucker, Richard, 1914–75, U.S. tenor.

—**Sophie,** 1884–1966, Russ.-born U.S. singer & actress.

Tudor, Antony, 1908–, Eng. choreographer.

Tu Fu, 712–770, Chin. poet.

Tugwell, Rexford Guy, 1891–1979, U.S. economist & political adviser.

Tunney, James Joseph ("Gene"), 1898–1978, U.S. boxer.

Tureck, Rosalyn, 1914–, U.S. pianist & harpsichordist.

Turgenev, Iva Sergeyevich, 1818–83, Russ. author.

Turner, Frederick Jackson, 1861–1932, U.S. historian.

—**J(oseph) M(allord) W(illiam),** 1775–1851, Eng. painter.

—**Nat,** 1800–31, U.S. Negro slave; leader of an unsuccessful revolt.

Turpin, Dick, 1706–36, Eng. highwayman.

Tussaud, Mme. Marie (Gresholtz), 1760–1850, Swiss-born wax modeler active in England.

Tutankhamen, 14th c. B.C. Egyptian king; tomb discovered 1922.

Twain, Mark, pseud of Samuel Langhorne Clemens, 1835–1910, U.S. author.

Tweed, William Marcy ("Boss"), 1823–78, U.S. politician.

Twort, Frederick Wiliam, 1877–1950, Eng. Bacteriologist.

Tyler, John, 1790–1862, 10th U.S. president 1841–45.

—**Wat,** ?–1381, Eng. leader of Pesant Revolt against taxation.

Tyndale, William, 1484–1536, Eng. religious reformer; translated new Testament; executed for heresy.

Tyndall, John 1820–93, Irish-born Brit. physicist.

Tzara, Tristan, 1896–1963, Rumanian poet & author; one of the founders of Dadaism.

Uccello, Paolo, b. Paolo di Dono, 1397–1475, Ital. painter.

Ulanova, Galina, 1910–, Soviet ballerina.

Ulbricht, Walter, 1893–1973, E. German political leader; first secretary of Socialist Unity Party 1950–71.

Ullmann, Liv, 1939–, Norw. actress active in Sweden and the U.S.

Umberto I, 1844–1900, king of Italy 1878–1900.

Unamuno y Jugo, Miguel de, 1864–1936, Sp. philosopher & author.

Uncas, 1588?–1683, Pequot Am. Ind. chief.

Undset, Sigrid, 1882–1949, Norw. author.

Unitas, John, 1933–, U.S. football player.

Untermeyer, Louis, 1885–1977, U.S. poet & editor.

Updike, John, 1932–, U.S. author.

Upjohn, Richard, 1802–78, Eng.-born U.S. architect.

Urban, Joseph, 1872–1933, Austrian-born U.S. architect & set designer.

Urey, Harold, 1893–1981, U.S. chemist.

Uris, Leon Marcus, 1924–, U.S. author.

Ussachevsky, Vladimir, 1911–, U.S. composer born in China.

Ussher, James, 1581–1656, Irish archbishop.

Ustinov, Peter, 1921–, Eng. actor, director, producer & author.

Utamaro,Kitagawa, 1753?–1806, Jap. printmaker.

Utrillo, Maurice, 1883–1955, Fr. painter.

Valentine, Saint, 3rd c. Roman Christian martyr.

Valentino, Rudolph, 1895–1926, Ital.-born U.S. actor.

Valéery, Paul (Ambroise), 1871–1945, Fr. poet & philosopher.

Vallee, Hubert Prior ("Rudy"), 1901–, U.S. singer & actor.

Van Allen, James Alfred, 1914–, U.S. physicist.

Van Brocklin, Norm(an), 1926–, U.S. football player & coach.

Vanbrugh, Sir John, 1664–1726, Eng. architect & playwright.

Van Buren, Abby, pseud. of Pauline Esther Friedman, 1918–, U.S. columnist.

—**Martin,** 1782–1862, 8th U.S. president 1837–41.

Vancouver, George, 1757–98, Eng. navigator & explorer.

Van de Graaff, Robert Jemison, 1901–67, U.S. physicist.

Vandenberg, Arthur Hendrick, 1884–1951, U.S. journalist & politician.

Vanderbilt, Alfred G., 1912–, U.S. horse breeder & sportsman.

—**Amy,** 1908–74, U.S. writer on etiquette.

—**Cornelius ("Commodore"),** 1794–1877, U.S. capitalist & industrialist.

—**Gloria,** 1924–, U.S. poet, artist & fabric designer.

Van der Waals, Johannes D. 1837–1923, Du. physicist.

Van Dine, S. S., pseud. of Willard Huntington Wright, 1888–1939, U.S. author.

Van Doren, Carl, 1885–1950, U.S. author.

—**Mark,** 1894–1972, U.S. author; brother of prec.

Van Dyck, Anthony, 1599–1641, Flemish painter. Also **Van Dyke.**

Van Eyck, Hubert, 1366?–1426?, & his brother **Jan,** 1389?–1441?, Flemish painters.

Van Goh, Vincent, 1853–1900, Du. painter.

Van Heusen, James (Jimmie), 1913–, U.S. composer.

Van Horne, Harriet, 1920–, U.S. journalist.

van't Hoff, Jacobus Hendricus, 1852–1911, Du. physical chemist.

Vanzetti, Bartolomeo, 1888–1927, Ital. anarchist in the U.S; executed with Nicola Sacco for murder.

Varda, Angès, 1928–, Fr. film director.

Vare, Glenna Collett, 1903–, U.S. golfer.

Varèse, Edgard, 1885–1965, Fr.-born U.S. composer.

Varnay, Astrid, 1918–, Swed.-born U.S. soprano.

Vasari, Giorgio, 1511-74, Ital. painter, architect & writer.

Vauban, Sébastien Le Prestre, Marquis de, 1633–1707, Fr. military engineer & architect.

Vaughan, Henry, 1622–95, Eng. poet.

Vaughan Williams, Ralph, 1872–1958, Eng. composer.

Vaux, Calvert, 1824–95, Eng.-born U.S. landscape architect.

Veblen, Thorstein (Bunde), 1857–1929, U.S. political economist & sociologist.

Veeck, William Louis, Jr. (Bill) 1914–, U.S. sports promoter.

Vega, Lope de, 1562–1635, Sp. playwright & poet.

Velázquez, Diego Rodriguez de Silva y, 1599–1660, Sp. painter.

Venturi, Robert, 1925–, U.S. architect.

Venuti, Giuseppe (Joe), 1903–78, U.S. jazz violinist.

Vercingetorix, 72?–46? B.C., Gallic chieftain defected by Julius Caesar.

Verdi, Biuseppe, 1813–1901, Ital. composer.

Verlaine, Paul. 1844–96, Fr. poet.

Vermeer, Jan, 1632–75, Du. painter.

Verne, Jules, 1828–1905, Fr. author.

Vernier, Pierre, 1580?–1637, Fr. mathematician.

Veronese, Paolo, 1528–88, Venetian painter.

Verrazano, Giovanni da, 1480?–1528?, Ital. navigator.

Verrett, Shirley, 1931–, U.S. mezzo-soprano.

Verrocchio, Andrea del, 1435–88, Florentine sculptor & painter.

Verwoerd, Hendrik Frensch, 1901–66, prime minister of Republic of South Africa 1958–66; assassinated.

Vesalius, Andreas, 1514–64, Belg. anatomist.

Vesey, Denmark, 1762–1822, U.S. slave & insurrectionist.

Vespasian (L. Titus Flavius Sabinus Vespasianus), A.D. 9–79, Roman emperor 69–79.

Vespucci, Amerigo, 1451–1512, Ital. navigator.

Vico, Giovanni Battista (Giambattista), 1668–1744, Ital. philosopher & historian.

Victor Emmanuel II, 1820–78, king of Sardinia 1849–61 & first king of Italy 1861–78.

—**III,** 1869–1947, king of Italy 1900–46; grandson of prec.

Victoria, 1819–1901, queen of Great Britian 1837–1901.

Vidal, Gore, 1925–, U.S. novelist, playwright & critic.

Vidor, King (Wallis), 1894–, U.S. film director.

Vigny, Comte Alfred Victor de, 1797–1863, Fr. author.

Vigo, Jean, 1905–34, Fr. film director.

Villa, Francisco ("Pancho"), 1877–1923, Mexican revolutionary leader.

Villa-Lobos, Heitor, 1887–1959, Brazilian composer.

Villard, Henry, 1835–1900, U.S. journalist & financier.

Villella, Edward, 1936–, U.S. ballet dancer.

Villon, François, 1431–85?. Fr. poet.

Vincent de Paul, Saint, 1581?–1660, Fr. priest.

Viollet-le-Duc, Eugène Emmanuel, 1814–79, Fr. architect & restorer.

Virgil (L. Publius Vergilius Maro), 70–19 B.C., Roman poet. Also **Vergil.**

Virtanen, Artturi Ilmari, 1895–1973, Finnish biochemist.

Visconti, Luchino, 1906–76, Ital. film director.

Vishinsky, Andrei Y., 1883–1954, Soviet jurist & diplomat.

Vishnevskaya, Galina, 1926–, Soviet-born soprano.

Vitruvius Pollio, Marcus, 1st c. B.C. Roman architect & engineer.

Vitti, Monica, 1933–, Ital. actress.

Vivaldi, Antonio, 1675?–1743, Ital. composer.

Vlaminck, Maurice de, 1876–1958, Fr. painter.

Volstead, Andrew John, 1860–1947, U.S. politician & prohibitionist.

Volta, Count Alessandro, 1745–1827, Ital. physicist.

Voltaire, b. François Marie Arouet, 1694–1778, Fr. writer & philosopher.

Von Braun, Wernher, 1912–77, Ger.-born U.S. aerospace engineer.

Vonnegut, Kurt, Jr., 1922–, U.S. author.

Von Neumann, John, 1903–57, Hung.-born U.S. mathematician.

Voroshilov, Kliment Efremovich, 1881–1969, Soviet marshal & politician.

Vorster, Balthazar Johannes (John), 1915–, prime minister of Republic of South Africa 1966–78.

Vought, Chance Milton, 1890–1930, U.S. aeronautical engineer & designer.

Vuillard, (Jean) Édouard, 1868–1940, Fr. painter.

Wagner, Geroge Raymond, 1915?–63, U.S. wrestler: known as **Gorgeous George.**

—**John Peter ("Honus"),** 1874–1955, U.S. baseball player.

—**Richard,** 1813–83, Ger. composer & critic.

—**Robert F(erdinand),** 1910–, U.S. politician.

Wajda, Andrzej, 1926–, Pol. film director.

Waksman, Selman Abraham, 1888–1973, Ukrainian-born U.S. microbiologist.

Wald, George, 1906–, U.S. biologist.

—**Lillian D.** 1867–1940, U.S. social worker.

Waldheim, Kurt 1918–, Austrian diplomat & secretary general of the U.N. 1972–1982.

Walesa, Lech, 1943–, Polish labor leader.

Waley, Arthur, 1889–1966, Eng. oriental scholar & translator.

Walgreen, Charles Rudolph, 1873–1939, U.S. pharmacist & merchant.

Walker, James John ("Jimmy"), 1881–1946, U.S. politician; mayor of New York City 1926–32.

—**Nancy,** 1922–, U.S. actress.

Wallace, Alfred Russel, 1823–1913, Eng. naturalist.

—**DeWitt,** 1889–1981 U.S. publisher.

—**George Corley,** 1919–, U.S. governor & political leader.

Wallace, Henry Agard, 1888–1965, U.S. agriculturist & politician; U.S. vice-president 1941–45.

—**Irving,** 1916–, U.S. author.

—**Lila Bell Acheson,** 1889–, Can.-born U.S. publisher & patron of the arts; wife of DeWitt.

—**Mike,** 1918–, U.S. TV interviewer & commentator.

Waller, Edmund, 1606–87, Eng. poet.

—**Thomas ("Fats"),** 1904–43, U.S. jazz musician.

Wallis, Hal B(rent), 1899–, U.S. film producer.

Walpole, Horace, (4th Earl of Orford), 1717–97, Eng. author.

—**Sir Hugh Seymour,** 1884–1941, Eng. author.

Walsh, Raoul, 1892–1981, U.S. film director.

Walter, Bruno, 1876–1962, Ger. conductor active in U.S.

Walters, Barbara, 1931–, U.S. TV personality.

Walther von der Vogelweide, 1170–1230, Ger. poet.

Walton, Izaak, 1593–1683, Eng. author.

—**Sir William Turner,** 1902–, Eng. composer.

Wanamaker, John, 1883–1922, U.S. merchant.

Wanger, Walter, 1894–1968, U.S. film producer.

Wang Wei, 699–759, Chin. painter, poet & musician.

Wankel, Felix, 1902–, Ger. engineer & inventor.

Warburg, Aby, 1866–1929, Ger. art historian.

—**James P.,** 1896–1969, U.S. financier.

—**Otto Heinrich,** 1883–1970, Ger. physiologist.

Ward, Aaron Montgomery, 1843–1913, U.S. merchant.

—**Artemus,** pseud. of Charles Farrar Browne, 1834–67, U.S. humorist.

—**Barbara (Lady Jackson),** 1914–1981, Eng. economist & author.

—**Clara,** 1924–73, U.S. gospel singer.

Warfield, William Caesar, 1920–, U.S. baritone.

Warhol, Andy, 1927–, U.S. painter & filmmaker.

Waring, Fred, 1900–, U.S. bandleader.

Warmerdam, Cornelius, 1915–, U.S. pole vaulter.

Warner A family of U.S. film executives incl. three brothers: **Albert,** 1884–1967; **Harry M(orris),** 1881–1957; & **Jack L(eonard),** 1892–1978.

—**Glenn Scobey ("Pop"),** 1871–1954, U.S. football coach.

Warren, Earl, 1891–1974, U.S. jurist; Chief Justice of the U.S. Supreme Court 1953–69.

—**Leonard,** 1911–60, U.S. baritone.

—**Robert Penn,** 1905–, U.S. poet & author.

Washington, Booker T(aliaferro), 1856–1915, U.S. Negro educator & author.

—**George,** 1732–99, Amer. general & statesman; first U.S. president 1789–97.

Wassermann, August von, 1866–1925, Ger. bacteriologist.

Waterfield, Robert Staton (Bob), 1920–, U.S. football player & coach.

Waterman, Lewis Edson, 1837–1901, U.S. inventor & manufacturer.

Waters, Ethel, 1900–77, U.S. singer & actress.

Watson, James Dewey, 1928–, U.S. biochemist.

—**John B(roadus),** 1878–1958, U.S. psychologist.

—**Thomas John,** 1874–1956, U.S. businessman.

Watt, James, 1736–1819, Scot. engineer & inventor.

Watteau, Jean Antoine, 1684–1721, Fr. painter.

Watts, Alan (Witson), 1915–73, Eng.-born U.S. religious philosopher & author.

—**André,** 1946–, Ger.-born U.S. pianist.

—**Isaac,** 1674–1748, Eng. theologian & poet.

Waugh, Evelyn (Arthur St. John), 1903–66, Eng. author.

Wayne, Anthony, 1745–96, Amer. revolutionary general.

—**John,** 1907–79, U.S. actor.

Weaver, Robert Clifton, 1907–, US. economist & government official.

—**Sylvester L., Jr. ("Pat"),** 1908–, U.S. TV executive.

Webb, Beatrice, 1858–1943, & her husband **Sidney,** 1859–1947; Eng. socialist reformers & economists.

—**Clifton,** 1891–1966, U.S. actor.

Weber, Carl Maria (Friedrich Ernst) von, 1786–1826, Ger. composer.

—**Max,** 1864–1930, Ger. economist & sociologist.

—**Max,** 1881–1961, Russ.-born U.S. painter.

Webern, Anton (von), 1883–1945, Austrian composer.
Webster, Daniel, 1782–1852, U.S. statesman.
—**John,** 1580?–1625, Eng. playwright.
—**Margaret,** 1905–72, U.S. actress & stage director.
—**Noah,** 1758–1843, U.S. lexicographer.
Wechsler, David, 1896–, U.S. pyschologist.
—**James A.,** 1915–, U.S. journalist & editor.
Wedekind, Frank, 1864–1918, Ger. playwright.
Wedgwood, Josiah, 1730–95, Eng. potter.
Wegener, Alfred L., 1880–1930, Ger. geologist.
Weidman, Charles, 1901–75, U.S. dancer & choreographer.
Weill, Kurt, 1900–50, Ger.-born U.S. composer.
Weingartner, Felix, 1863–1942, Austrian conductor.
Weismann, August, 1834–1914, Ger. biologist.
Weissmuller, John, 1905–, U.S. swimmer & actor.
Weizmann, Chaim, 1874–1952, Russ.-born Israeli chemist & Zionist leader; first president of Israel 1949–52.
Welch, Joseph Nye, 1890–1960, U.S. lawyer.
—**Robert H. W., Jr.,** 1899–, U.S. manufacturer & political activist.
Welitsch, Ljuba, 1913–, Bulgarian soprano.
Welk, Lawrence, 1903–, U.S. bandleader.
Welles, Orson, 1915–, U.S. film director & actor.
Wellington, Arthur Wellesley, Duke of, 1769–1852, Irish-born Brit. statesman & general.
Wellman, William, 1896–1975, U.S. film director.
Wells, Henry, 1805–78, U.S. transportation entrepreneur.
—**H(erbert) G(eorge),** 1866–1946, Eng. author.
—**Mary,** 1928–, U.S. advertising executive.
Welty, Eudora, 1909–, U.S. author.
Wenceslaus, 1361–1419, king of Germany & Holy Roman Emperor 1378–1400 & king of Bohemia 1378–1419.
Werfel, Franz, 1890–1945, Ger. author.
Wertheimer, Max, 1880–1943, Ger. psychologist.
Wertmüller, Lina, 1931–, Ital. film director.
Wesker, Arnold, 1932–, Eng. author & playwright.
Wesley, Charles, 1707–88, Eng. Methodist preacher & poet.
—**John,** 1703–91, Eng. clergyman; founder ot Methodism; brother of prec.
West, Benjamin, 1738–1820, Amer. painter active in England.
—**Jerome Allen (Jerry),** 1938–, U.S. basketball player.
—**Mae,** 1892–1980, U.S. actress.
—**Nathanael,** 1903–40, U.S. author.
—**Rebecca,** pseud. of Cicily Isabel Fairfield, 1892–, Eng. author & critic.
Westinghouse, George, 1846–1914, U.S. inventor.
Westmore, Perc, 1904–70, U.S. cosmetician & businessman.
Westmoreland, William C., 1914–, U.S. general.
Weston, Edward, 1886–1958, U.S. photographer.
Weyden, Rogier van der, 1399?–1464, Flemish painter.
Weyer, Johann, 1515–88, Belg. physician.
Weyerhaeuser, Frederick, 1834–1914, Ger.-born U.S. businessman.
Wharton, Edith (Newbold Jones), 1862–1937, U.S. author.
Wheatley, Phillis, 1753?–84, African-born Amer. poet.
Wheatstone, Sir Charles, 1802–75, Eng. physicist.
Wheelock, John Hall, 1886–1978, U.S. poet.
Whistler, James Abbott McNeill, 1834–1903, U.S. painter active in England & France.
White, Byron R(aymond), 1917–, U.S. jurist; justice of the U.S. Supreme Court 1962–.
—**E(lwyn) B(rooks),** 1899–, U.S. author & editor.
—**George,** 1890–1968, U.S. theatrical producer & director.
—**Josh,** 1908–69, U.S. folk singer.
—**Patrick,** 1912–, Austral. author born in England.
—**Pearl,** 1889–1938, U.S. actress.
—**Stanford,** 1853–1906, U.S. architect.
—**Theodore H.,** 1915–, U.S. political analyst & author.
—**Walter Francis,** 1893–1955, U.S. Negro civil rights leader & author.
—**William Allen,** 1868–1944, U.S. journalist & author.
Whitehead, Alfred North, 1861–1947, Eng. mathematician & philosopher active in U.S.

Whiteman, Paul, 1891–1967, U.S. conductor.
Whitman, Marcus, 1802–47, & his wife **Narcissa (Prentice),** 1808–47, U.S. missionaries & pioneers.
—**Walt(er),** 1819–92, U.S. poet & journalist.
Whitney, Eli, 1765–1825, U.S. inventor of the cotton gin.
Whittier, John Greenleaf, 1807–92, U.S. poet.
Whitty, Dame May, 1865–1948, Eng. actress.
Wicker, Thomas Grey (Tom), 1926–, U.S. journalist & author.
Widor, Charles Marie, 1845–1937, Fr. organist & composer.
Wien, Wilhelm, 1864–1928, Ger. physicist.
Wiener, Norbert, 1894–1964, U.S. mathematician.
Wiesner, Jerome Bert, 1915–, U.S. engineer.
Wiggin, Kate Douglas (Smith), 1856–1923, U.S. educator & author.
Wightman, Hazel Hotchkiss, 1886–1974, U.S. tennis player.
Wigman, Mary, 1889–1973, Ger. dancer.
Wigner, Eugene Paul, 1902–, Hung.-born U.S. physicist.
Wiberforce, William, 1759–1833, Eng. abolitionist & philanthropist.
Wilbur, Richard (Purdy), 1921–, U.S. poet.
Wilcox, Ella Wheeler, 1850–1919, U.S. poet.
Wilde, Oscar (Fingall O'Flahertie Wills), 1856–1900, Irish playwright & poet.
—**Patricia,** 1928–, Can.-born U.S. ballerina.
Wilder, Samuel ("Billy"), 1906–, Austrian-born U.S. film director.
—**Thornton (Niven),** 1897–1975, U.S. author & playwright.
Wilhelmina, 1880–1962, queen of the Netherlands 1890–1948.
Wilkes, John, 1727–97, Eng. political reformer.
Wilkins, Roy, 1901–1981, U.S. Negro civil rights leader.
Willard, Jess, 1883–1968, U.S. boxer.
William I, 1027–87, Norman invader of England; king of England 1066–87; known as **the Conqueror.**
—**III,** 1650–1702, king of England 1689–1702; co-ruler with his wife Mary II 1689–94.
William I, 1533–84, Prince of Orange; founder of the Dutch republic: known as the **the Silent.**
William II, 1859–1941, emperor of Germany & king of Prussia 1888–1918: known as **Kaiser Wilhelm.**
Williams, Edward Bennett, 1920–, U.S. lawyer.
—**Esther,** 1923–, U.S. swimmer & actress.
—**Roger,** 1603?–85, Eng. clergyman; founder of Rhode Island.
—**Tennessee,** 1914–, U.S. playwright.
—**Theodore Samuel (Ted),** 1918–, U.S. baseball player.
—**William Carlos,** 1883–1963, U.S. poet, author & physician.
Williamson, Nicol, 1938–, Brit. actor.
Willis, Thomas, 1621–75, Eng. anatomist & physician.
Willkie, Wendell Lewis, 1892–1944, U.S. lawyer, businessman & politician.
Willstätter, Richard, 1872–1942, Ger. chemist.
Willys, John North, U.S. automobile manufacturer.
Wilson, Charles E(rwin), 1890–1961, U.S. industrialist & government official.
—**Charles Thomson Rees,** 1869–1959, Scot. physicist.
—**Edmund,** 1895–1972, U.S. author, critic & journalist.
—**Harold,** 1916–, Eng. politician; prime minister 1964–70 & 1974–76.
—**Samuel,** 1766–1854, U.S. merchant: known as **Uncle Sam.**
—**Teddy,** 1912–, U.S. jazz musician.
—**(Thomas) Woodrow,** 1856–1924, 28th U.S. president 1913–21.
Winchell, Walter, 1897–1972, U.S. journalist & radio broadcaster.
Winchester, Oliver Fisher, 1810–80, U.S. firearms manufacturer.
Winckelmann, Johann Joachim, 1717–68, Ger. archaeologist.
Windaus, Adolf, 1876–1959, Ger. chemist.
Windsor, Duchess of, (Wallis Warfield Simpson),

1896–, U.S.-born wife of Edward VIII.
—**Duke of** See EDWARD VIII.
Winters, Jonathan, 1925–, U.S. comedian.
Winthrop, John, 1588–1649, Eng.-born Puritan; governor of Masssachusetts.
Wise, Isaac Mayer, 1819–1900, Austrian-born U.S. religious leader; founder of Reform Judaism in the U.S.
—**Stephen Samuel,** 1874–1949, Hung.-born U.S. rabbi & Zionist leader.
Wister, Owen, 1860–1938, U.S. author.
Withers, Jane, 1926–, U.S. actress.
Wittgenstein, Ludwig, 1889–1951, Austrian philosopher active in England.
Wittkower, Rudolph, 1901–, Ger.-born Brit. art historian.
Wodehouse, Sir P(elham) G(renville), 1881–1975, Eng.-born U.S. author.
Woffington, Margaret (Peg), 1714?–60, Irish actress.
Wöhler, Friedrich, 1800–82, Ger. chemist.
Wolf, Hugo, 1860–1903, Austrian composer.
Wolfe, James, 1727–59, Eng. general.
—**Thomas (Clayton),** 1900–38, U.S. author.
Wolff, Kaspar Friedrich, 1733–94, Ger. antomist.
Wolf-Ferrari, Ermanno, 1876–1948, Ital.-born Ger. composer.
Wolfflin, Heinrich, 1864–1945, Swiss art historian.
Wolfram von Eschenbach, 1170?–1220?, Ger. poet.
Wollaston, William Hyde, 1766–1828, Eng. chemist & physicist.
Wollstonecraft, Mary, 1759–97, Eng. feminist & author.
Wolsey, Thomas, 1475?–1530, Eng. cardinal & statesman.
Wood, Grant, 1892–1942, U.S. painter.
—**Sam,** 1883–1949, U.S. film director.
Woodbridge, Frederick J(ames) E(ugene), 1867–1940, Can.-born U.S. philosopher.
Woodcock, Leonard, 1911–, U.S. labor leader.
Woodhull, Victoria Clafin, 1838–1927, U.S. feminist.
Woodward, C(omer) Vann, 1908–, U.S. historian.
—**Joanne,** 1930–, U.S. actress.
—**Robert Burns,** 1917–1979, U.S. chemist.
Woolf, (Adeline) Virginia (Stephen), 1882–1941, Eng. author & critic.
—**Leonard Sidney,** 1880–1969, Eng. author & critic; husband of prec.
Woollcott, Alexander, 1887–1943, U.S. journalist & critic.
Woolworth, Frank Winfield 1852–1919, U.S. merchant.
Worcester, Joseph Emerson, 1784–1865, U.S lexicorgrapher.
Wordsworth, William, 1770–1850, Eng. poet.
Worth, Charles Frederick, 1825–95, Eng. fashion designer active in France.
Wouk, Herman, 1915–, U.S. author.
Wren, Sir Christopher, 1632–1723, Eng. architect.
Wright, Eizur, 1804–85, U.S. abolitionist.
—**Frank Lloyd,** 1867–1959, U.S. architect.
—**Mary Kathryn (Mickey),** 1935–, U.S. golfer.
—**Orville,** 1871–1948, & his brother **Wilbur,** 1867–1912, U.S. aviation pioneers.
—**Richard,** 1908–60, U.S. author.
Wrigley, William, Jr., 1861–1932, U.S. businessman.
Wunderlich, Fritz, 1930–66, Ger. tenor.
Wundt, Wilhelm, 1832–1920, Ger. physiologist & psychiatrist.
Wuorinen, Charles, 938–, U.S. composer.
Wyatt, Sir Thomas, 1503–43, Eng. poet & diplomat.
Wycherly, William, 1640?–1716, Eng. playwright & poet.
Wyclif, John 1324?–84. Eng. religious reformer; translator of the Bible into English.
Wyeth, Andrew (Newell), 1917–, U.S. painter.
—**N(ewell) C(onvers),** 1882–1945, U.S. painter & illustrator, father of prec.
Wyler, William, 1902–1981, U.S. film director.
Wylie, Elinor Morton, 1885–1928, U.S. poet.
—**Philip,** 1902–71, U.S. author.
Wynn, Ed, 1886–1966, U.S. comedian & actor.

Xanthippe, 5th c. B.C., wife of Socrates.
Xavier, Saint Francis, 506–52, Sp. Jesuit missionary in the Orient; founder, with Ignatius of Loyola, of the Society of Jesus.
Xenakis, Iannis, 1922–, Rumanian-born composer, architect & engineer active in France.
Xenophon, 435?–355? B.C., Gk. historian & soldier.
Xerxes I, 519?–465 B.C., king of Persia 486–465 B.C.

Yale, Elihu, 1649–1721, Eng.-born Amer. merchant & philanthropist.
—**Linus,** 1821–68, U.S. inventor & lock manufacturer.
Yamamoto, Isoroku, 1884–1943, Jap. admiral.
Yamasaki, Minoru, 1912–, U.S. architech.
Yamashita, Tomoyuki, 1885–1946, Jap. general.
Yang, Chen Ning, 1922–, Chin. physicist.
Yeats, William Butler, 1865–1939, Irish poet, playwright & essayist.
Yerby, Frank Garvin, 1916–, U.S. author.
Yerkes, Charles Tyson, 1837–1905, U.S. financier.
—**Robert Mearns,** 1876–1956, U.S. psychologist.
Yesenin, Sergey, 1895–1925, Russ. poet.
Yevtushenko, Yevgeny, 1933–, Soviet poet.
York, Alvin Cullum, 1887–1964, U.S. soldier: known as Sergeant York.
Yoshida, Shigeru, 1878–1967, Jap. prime minister 1946–54.
Youmans, Vincent, 1898–1946, U.S. composer.
Young, Brigham, 1801–77, U.S. Mormon leader.
—**Denton, True ("Cy"),** 1867–1955, U.S. baseball player.
—**Lester, (Willis),** 1909–59, U.S. jazz musician.
—**Loretta,** 1913–, U.S. actress.
—**Murat Bernard ("Chic"),** 1901–73, U.S. cartoonist.
—**Stark,** 1881–1963, U.S. author & magazine editor.
—**Thomas,** 1773–1829, Eng. physicist & physician.
—**Victor,** 1900–56, U.S. composer.
—**Whitney M(oore),** 1921–71, U.S. Negro civil rights leader.
Younger, (Thomas) Cole(man), 1844–1916, U.S. outlaw.
Youngman, Henny, 1906–, Eng.-born U.S. comedian.
Youskevitch, Igor, 1912–, Russ.-born U.S. ballet dancer
Yukawa, Hideki, 1907–1981, Jap. physicist.
Yurka, Blance, 1887–1974, U.S. actress.

Zadkine, Ossip, 1890–, Russ.-born Fr. sculptor.
Zaharias, Mildred Didrikson ("Babe"), 1914–56, U.S. athlete.
Zangwill, Israel, 1864–1926, Eng. author & playwright.
Zanuck, Darryl, 1902–1979, U.S. film producer.
Zapata, Emiliano, 1877?–1919, Mexican revolutionary leader.
Zatopek, Emil, 1922–, Czech track runner.
Zeeman, Pieter, 1865–1943, Du. physicist.
Zeffirelli, Franco, 1922–, Ital. stage, opera & film director.
Zenger, John Peter, 1697–1746, Ger.-born Amer. journalist & publisher.
Zeno, 342?–270? B.C., Gk. philosopher: called **the Stoic.**
Zeppelin, Count Ferdinand von, 1838–1917, Ger. general & aviation pioneer.
Zernicke, Frits, 1888–1966, Du. physicist.
Zetterling, Mai, 1925–, Swed. film actress & director.
Zhdanov, Andrei Aleksandrovich, 1896–1948, Soviet politician & general.
Zhivkov, Todor, 1911–, head of state of Bulgaria 1971–.
Zhou Enlai, 1898–1976, Chin. statesman; premier & foreign minister of People's Republic of China 1949–76.
Zhukov, Georgi Konstantinovich, 1894–1974, Soviet marshal.
Ziegfeld, Florenz, 1869–1932, theatrical producer & playwright.
Zimbalist, Efrem, 1889–, Russ.-born U.S. violinist.
Zinnemann, Fred, 1907–, U.S. film director.
Zinoviev, Grigori Evseevich, 1883–1936, Soviet Communist leader.
Zinsser, Hans, 1878–1940, U.S. bacteriologist.

Zola, Emile, 1840–1902, Fr. author.

Zorach, William, 1887–1966, Lithuanian-born U.S. painter & sculptor.

Zorn, Anders Leonhard, 1860–1920, Swed. painter, etcher & sculptor.

Zoroaster, ca. 6th c. B.C. Pers. founder of Zoroastrianism: also called **Zarathustra.**

Zsigmondy, Richard, 1865–1929, Ger. chemist.

Zukor, Adolph, 1873–1976, Hung.-born U.S. film producer & executive.

Zurbarán, Francisco, 1598–1664, Sp. painter.

Zweig, Arnold, 1887–1968, Ger. author.

—**Stefan,** 1881–1942, Austrian-born Brit. author.

Zwingli, Huldreich, 1484–1531, Swiss religious reformer.

Zworykin, Vladimir Cosma, 1889– , Russ.-born U.S. engineer & inventor.

Given Names

Aar·on (âr'ən, ar'ən) ? Enlightener. [< Hebrew]

A·bel (ā'bəl) Breath. [< Hebrew]

A·bi·el (ā'bē·el, ə·bī'əl) Strong father. [< Hebrew]

Ab·ner (ab'nər) Father of light. [< Hebrew]

A·bra·ham (ā'brə·ham; *Fr.* à·brà·àm'; *Ger.* ä'brä·häm) Exalted father of multitudes. [< Hebrew] Also *Sp.* **A·bra·hán** (ä'brä·än'). Dims. **Abe, A'bie.**

A·bram (ā'brəm; *Fr.* à·brän'; *Sp.* ä·bräm') Exalted father. [< Hebrew]

Ab·sa·lom (ab'sə·ləm) The father is peace. [< Hebrew]

Ad·am (ad'əm) Red; man of red earth. [< Hebrew]

Ad·el·bert (ad'l·bûrt, ə·del'bûrt) Var. of ALBERT.

Ad·olph (ad'olf, ā'dolf) Noble wolf. [< Gmc.] Also *Dan., Du., Ger.* **A·dolf** (ä'dôlf), *Fr.* **A·dolphe** (à·dôlf'), *Ital., Sp.* **A·dol·fo** (*Ital.* ä·dôl'fō; *Sp.* ä·thôl'fō), *Lat.* **A·dol·phus** (ə·dol'fəs), *Pg.* **A·dol·pho** (ə·thôl'fōō).

A·dri·an (ā'drē·ən) Of Adria: from the name of two Italian cities, or the Adriatic Sea. [< L] Also *Fr.* **A·dri·en** (à·drē·añ'), *Ital.* **A·dri·a·no** (ä'drē·ä'nō), *Lat.* **A·dri·a·nus** (ā'drē·ā'nəs).

Af·fon·so (ə·fôn'sōō) Pg. form of ALPHONSO.

Al·an (al'ən) Handsome. [< Celtic] Also **Al'lan, Al'len.** Dim. **Al.**

Al·a·ric (al'ə·rik) All-ruler. [< Gmc.]

Al·as·tair (al'əs·tər) Scot. contr. of ALEXANDER. Also **Al'is·ter.**

Al·ban (ôl'bən, al'-) White; of Alba: from the name of several Italian cities. [< L] Also **Al'bin.**

Al·bert (al'bûrt; *Fr.* àl·bâr'; *Ger., Sw.* äl'bert) Nobly bright. [< F < Gmc.] Also *Ital.,* **Al·ber·to** (äl·ber'tō), *Lat.* **Al·ber·tus** (al·bûr'təs). Dims. **Al, Alb, Bert.**

Al·den (ôl'dən) Old friend. [OE]

Al·do (al'dō) Meaning uncertain. [< Gmc. or Hebrew]

Al·dous (ôl'dəs, al'-) From the old place. [OE] Also **Al'dis, Al'dus.**

Al·ex·an·der (al'ig·zan'dər, -zän'-; *Du., Ger.* ä'lek·sän'dər) Defender of men. [< Gk.] Also *Fr.* **A·lex·an·dre** (à·lek·säñ'dr'), *Modern Gk.* **A·le·xan·dros** (ä·lä'ksän·drōs), *Ital.* **A·les·san·dro** (ä'läs·sän'drō), *Pg.* **A·le·xan·dre** (ə·lē·shañn'drə), *Russ.* **A·le·ksandr** (ə·lyi·ksän'dər), *Sp.* **A·le·jan·dro** (ä'lä·hän'drō). Dims. **Al'ec, Al'eck, Al'ex, San'der, San'dy.**

A·lex·is (ə·lek'sis) Defender. [< Gk.]

Al·fon·so (äl·fôn'sō) Ital. and Sp. form of ALPHONSO. Also *Dan., Ger.* **Al·fons** (äl'fôns).

Al·fred (al'frid; *Ger.* äl'frät; *Fr.* àl·fred') Elf counselor; hence, wise. [OE] Also *Ital., Sp.* **Al·fre·do** (*Ital.* äl·frā'dō; *Sp.* äl·frā'tho), *Lat.* **Al·fre·dus** (al·frē'dəs) or **Al·u·re·dus** (al'yōō·rē'dəs). Dims **Al, Alf, Fred.**

Al·ger (al'jər) Noble spear. [< Gmc.]

Al·ger·non (al'jər·nən) Mustached. [< OF] Dims. **Al·gie, Al·gy** (al'jē).

Al·len (al'ən) Var. of ALAN. Also **Al'lan.**

A·lon·zo (ə·lon'zō) Var. of ALPHONSO. Also *Ital., Sp.* **A·lon·so** (ä·lôn'sō).

A·loy·sius (al'ō·ish'əs) Lat. form of LOUIS. Also **A·lois** (ə·lois').

Al·phon·so (al·fon'zō, -sō) Nobly ready. [< Sp. < Gmc.] Also *Fr.* **Al·phonse** (àl·fôns'). Dims. **Al, Alph, Al'phy.**

Al·va (al'və; *Sp.* äl'vä) White. [< L]

Al·vin (al'vin) Noble friend. [< Gmc.] Also **Al·win** (al'win; *Ger.* äl'vēn), **Al'van,** *Fr.* **A·luin** (à·lwañ), *Ital.* **Al·vi·no** (äl·vē'nō), *Sp.* **A·lui·no** (ä·lwē'nō).

Am·brose (am'brōz) Divine; immortal. [< Gk.] Also *Fr.* **Am·broise** (äñ·brwäz'), *Lat.* **Am·bro·si·us** (am·brō'zhē·əs, -zē·əs).

A·me·ri·go (ä'mā·rē'gō) Ital. form of EMERY.

A·mos (ā'məs) Burden. [< Hebrew]

An·a·tole (an'ə·tōl; *Fr.* à·nà·tôl') Sunrise. [< Gk.]

An·drew (an'drōō) Manly. [< Gk.] Also **An·dre·as** (an'drē·əs, an·drē'əs; *Dan.* än·drā'əs; *Du., Ger.* än·drā'äs; *Lat.* an'drē·əs), *Fr.* **An·dré** (äñ·drā'), *Ital.* **An·dre·a** (än·drā'ä), *Russ.* **An·drei** (än·drā'), *Sp.* **An·drés** (än·drās'). Dims. **An'dy, Drew.**

An·gus (ang'gəs) Singular. [< Celtic]

An·selm (an'selm; *Ger.* än'zelm) Divine helmet. [< Gmc.] Also **An·sel** (an'səl), *Fr.* **An·selme** (äñ·selm'), *Ital., Sp.* **An·sel·mo** (an'sel·mō), *Lat.* **An·sel·mus** (an·sel'məs).

An·tho·ny (an'thə·nē, -tə-) Inestimable: from the name of a Roman clan. Also **An·to·ny** (an'tə·nē), *Fr.* **An·toine** (äñ·twän'), *Ger., Lat.* **An·to·ni·us** (*Ger.* än·tō'nē·ōōs; *Lat.* an·tō'nē·əs), *Ital., Sp.* **An·to·nio** (än·tō'nyō). Dim. **To'ny.**

An·ton (än'tōn) Dan., Du., Ger. and Sw. form of ANTHONY.

Ar·chi·bald (är'chə·bôld) Nobly bold. [< Gmc.] Dims. **Ar'chie, Ar'chy.**

Ar·mand (är'mänd; *Fr.* àr·män') Fr. form of HERMAN.

Ar·min·i·us (är·min'ē·əs) Lat. form of HERMAN.

Ar·nold (är'nəld; *Ger.* är'nôlt) Eagle power. [< Gmc.] Also *Fr.* **Ar·naud** (àr·nō'), *Ital.* **Ar·nol·do** (är·nôl'dō), *Sp.* **Ar·nal·do** (är·näl'thō). Dims. **Arn, Ar'nie.**

Ar·te·mas (är'tə·məs) He of Artemis. [< Gk.] Also **Ar'te·mus.**

Ar·thur (är'thər; *Fr.* àr·tōōr') He-bear: from a totemic or royal title suggesting valor, strength, and nobility. [< Celtic] Also *Ital.* **Ar·tu·ro** (är·tōō'rō). Dims. **Art, Art'ie.**

A·sa (ā'sə) Healer. [< Hebrew]

Ash·ley (ash'lē) Dweller among ash trees: from a surname. [< Gmc.]

Ath·el·stan (ath'əl·stan) Noble stone or jewel. [OE] Also **Ath'el·stane** (-stän).

Au·brey (ô'brē) Elf ruler. [< F < Gmc.]

Au·gus·tine (ô'gəs·tēn, ô·gus'tin) Dim. of AUGUSTUS. Also **Au·gus·tin** (ô·gus'tən; *Fr.* ō·güs·tàn'; *Ger.* ou'gōōs·tēn'), *Ital.* **A·go·sti·no** (ä'gō·stē'nō), *Lat.* **Au·gus·ti·nus** (ô'gəs·tī'nəs), *Pg.* **A·gos·ti·nho** (ə·gōōsh·tē'nyōō), *Sp.* **A·gus·tín** (ä'gōōs·tēn').

Au·gus·tus (ô·gus'təs) Venerable. [< L] Also **Au·gust** (ô'gəst; *Ger.* ou'gōōst), *Fr.* **Au·guste** (ō·güst').

Au·re·li·us (ô·rē'lē·əs, ô·rēl'yəs) The golden one. [< L]

Aus·tin (ôs'tən) Contr. of AUGUSTINE.

A·ver·y (ā'vər·ē, ā'vrē) Courageous. [< Gmc.] Also **A·ver·il, A·ver·ill** (ā'vər·əl, ā'vrəl).

Bald·win (bôld'win) Bold friend. [< Gmc.] Also *Fr.* **Bau·doin** (bō·dwań').

Bal·tha·zar (bäl·thä'zər, -thaz'ər) Bel's or Baal's prince [< Chaldean], or splendid prince [< Persian]. Also **Bal·tha'sar** (-zər).

Bap·tist (bap'tist) Baptizer. [< Gk.] Also *Fr.* **Bap·tiste** (bà·tēst').

Bar·na·bas (bär'nə·bəs) Son of consolation [< Hebrew], or prophetic son [< Aramaic]. Also **Bar·na·by** (bär'nə·bē). Dim. **Bar'ney.**

Bar·nard (bär'nərd) Var. of BERNARD.

Bar·ney (bär'nē) Dim. of BARNABAS or BERNARD.

Bar·ry (bar'ē) Spear; hence, straightforward. [< Celtic]

Bar·thol·o·mew (bär·thol'ə·myōō) Son of furrows. [< Hebrew] Also *Fr.* **Bar·thé·le·my** (bàr·tāl·mē'), *Ger.* **Bar·tho·lo·mä·us** (bär'tō·lō·mä'ōōs), *Ital.* **Bar·to·lo·me·o** (bär·tō'lō·mā'ō), *Lat.* **Bar·thol·o·mae·us** (bär·tol'ə·mē'əs), *Sp.* **Bar·to·lo·mé** (bär·tō'lō·mā'). Dims. **Bart, Bat.**

Bas·il (baz'əl, bā'zəl) Kingly. [< Gk.]

Bax·ter (bak'stər) Baker. [< Gmc.]

Bay·ard (bā'ərd, bī'-, -ärd) From a surname. [< OF]

Ben·e·dict (ben'ə·dikt) Blessed. [< L] Also **Ben'e·dick,** *Fr.* **Be·noît** (bə·nwà'), *Ger.* **Be·ne·dikt** (bā'nä·dikt), *Ital.* **Be·ne·det·to** (bā'nä·dāt'tō) or **Be·ni·to** (bā·nē'tō), *Lat.* **Ben·e·dic·tus** (ben'ə·dik'təs), *Sp.* **Be·ni·to** (bā·nē'tō).

Ben·ja·min (ben'jə·mən; *Fr.* bañ·zhà·mañ'; *Ger.* ben'yä·mēn) Son of the right hand; hence, favorite son. [< Hebrew] Also *Ital.* **Ben·ia·mi·no** (ben'yä·mē'nō), *Sp.* **Ben·ja·mín** (ben'hä·mēn'). Dims. **Ben, Ben'jy, Ben'ny.**

Ben·net (ben'it) Var. of BENEDICT. Also **Ben'nett.**

Ber·nard (bûr'nərd, bər·närd'; *Fr.* ber·nàr') Bear-brave: probably from a totemic title. [< Gmc.] Also *Ger.* **Bern·hard** (bern'härt), *Ital., Sp.* **Ber·nar·do** (*Ital.* bär·när'dō; *Sp.* ber·när'tho), *Lat.* **Ber·nar·dus** (bər·när'dəs). Dims. **Bar'ney, Ber'ney, Ber'nie.**

Bert (bûrt) Dim. of ALBERT, BERTRAM, GILBERT, HERBERT, and HUBERT. Also **Ber·tie** (bûr'tē).

Ber·tram (bûr'trəm) Bright raven. [< Gmc.] Also **Ber·trand** (bûr'trənd; *Fr.* ber·träñ'). Dim. **Bert.**

Bill (bil) Dim. of WILLIAM. Also **Bil'ly.**

Bob (bob) Dim. of ROBERT. Also **Bob'bie, Bob'by.**

Bo·ris (bôr'is, bō'ris; *Russ.* bə·ryēs') Warrior. [< Russ.]

Boyd (boid) Yellow-haired. [< Celtic]

Bri·an (brī'ən) Strong. [< Celtic] Also **Bry'an, Bry·ant** (brī'ənt).

Brice (brīs) Meaning uncertain. [? < Celtic] Also **Bryce.**

Bruce (brōōs) From a Norman Fr. surname; orig. a place name.

Bru·no (brōō'nō) The brown one. [< Gmc.]

Bur·gess (bûr'jis) Citizen. [< Gmc.]

By·ron (bī'rən) From a Fr. surname; orig. a place name. Also **Bi'ron.**

Cad·wal·la·der (kad·wol'ə·dər) Battle arranger. [< Welsh] Also **Cad·wal'a·der.**

Cae·sar (sē'zər) Long-haired: ? symbolic title suggesting royalty or holiness. [< L] Also **Ce'sar,** *Fr.* **Cé·sar** (sā·zàr'), *Ital.* **Ce·sa·re** (chā'zä·rā).

941

Ca·leb (kā′ləb)   Dog; hence, loyal.   [< Hebrew]
Cal·vin (kal′vin)   Bald: from a Roman name.   [< L]   Dim. **Cal.**
Carl (kärl)   English form of KARL.
Car·ol (kar′əl)   English form of CAROLUS.
Car·o·lus (kar′ə·ləs)   Lat. form of CHARLES.
Car·y (kãr′ē)   ? Dim. of CAROL. Also **Car′ey.**
Cas·per (kas′pər)   English form of KASPAR. Also **Cas′par** (-pər).
Ce·cil (sē′səl, ses′əl)   Blind: from the name of a Roman clan.
Ced·ric (sed′rik, sē′drik)   War chief.   [< Celtic]
Charles (chärlz; *Fr.* shàrl)   Manly.   [< F < Gmc.] Also *Ital.* **Car·lo** (kär′lō), *Lat.* **Car·o·lus** (kar′ə·ləs), *Sp.* **Car·los** (kär′lōs).   Dims. **Char′ley, Char′lie, Chuck.**
Chaun·cey (chôn′sē, chän′-)   Chancellor.   [< OF]
Ches·ter (ches′tər)   Dweller in camp; hence, soldier: from a surname.   [< L]   Dims. **Ches, Chet.**
Chris·tian (kris′chən; *Ger.* kris′tē·än)   Christian.   [< L < Gk.] Also *Fr.* **Chré·tien** (krā·tyaṅ′).   Dim. **Chris.**
Chris·to·pher (kris′tə·fər)   Bearer of Christ.   [< Gk.] Also *Fr.* **Chris·tophe** (krēs·tôf′), *Ger.* **Chris·toph** (kris′tôf), *Ital.* **Chri·sto·fo·ro** (krēs·tô′fō·rō), *Sp.* **Cris·tó·bal** (krēs·tō′väl).   Dims. **Chris, Kit.**
Clar·ence (klar′əns)   From the name of an English dukedom.
Claude (klôd; *Fr.* klōd)   Lame: from the name of a Roman clan. Also *Ital., Sp.* **Clau·di·o** (*Ital.* klou′dyō; *Sp.* klou′·thyō), *Lat.* **Clau·di·us** (klô′dē·əs).
Clay·ton (klā′tən)   From an English surname; orig. a place name.
Clem·ent (klem′ənt)   Merciful.   [< L]   Dim. **Clem.**
Clif·ford (klif′ərd)   From an English surname; orig. a place name. Dim. **Cliff.**
Clif·ton (klif′tən)   From an English surname; orig. a place name.
Clin·ton (klin′tən)   From an English surname; orig. a place name. Dim. **Clint.**
Clive (klīv)   Cliff; cliff-dweller: from an English surname.
Clyde (klīd)   From a Scot. surname; orig. the river *Clyde.*
Col·in (kol′ən, kō′lən)   Dove.   [< Scot. < L]
Con·rad (kon′rad)   Bold counsel.   [< Gmc.]
Con·stant (kon′stənt; *Fr.* kôṅ·stäṅ′)   Var. of CONSTANTINE.
Con·stan·tine (kon′stən·tīn, -tēn)   Constant; firm.   [< L]
Cor·nel·ius (kôr·nēl′yəs; *Ger.* kôr·nä′lē·ŏŏs)   ? Horn: from the name of a Roman clan. Dims. **Con, Con′nie, Neil.**
Craig (krāg)   Crag; crag-dweller: from a Scot. surname.
Cris·pin (kris′pin)   Curly-headed.   [< L] Also *Lat.* **Cris·pi·nus** (kris·pī′nəs) or **Cris·pus** (kris′pəs).
Cur·tis (kûr′tis)   Courteous.   [< OF]
Cuth·bert (kuth′bərt)   Notably brilliant.   [OE]
Cyr·il (sir′əl)   Lordly.   [< Gk.]
Cy·rus (sī′rəs)   The sun.   [< Persian]   Dim. **Cy.**

Dan (dan)   Judge.   [< Hebrew]
Dan·iel (dan′yəl; *Fr.* dà·nyel′; *Ger.* dä′nē·el)   God is my judge.   [< Hebrew]   Dims. **Dan, Dan′ny.**
Da·ri·us (də·rī′əs)   Wealthy.   [< Persian]
Da·vid (dā′vid; *Fr.* dà·vēd′; *Ger.* dä′vēt)   Beloved.   [< Hebrew]   Dims. **Dave, Da′vey, Da′vie, Da′vy.**
Dean (dēn)   From an ancient religious or military title.   [< OF < LL]   Also **Deane.**
De·me·tri·us (di·mē′trē·əs)   He of Demeter.   [< Gk.] Also *Russ.* **Dmi·tri** (dmyē′trē).
Den·nis (den′is)   Var. of DIONYSIUS. Also **Den′is**, *Fr.* **De·nis** or **De·nys** (də·nē′).   Dim. **Den′ny.**
Der·ek (der′ik)   Du. dim. of THEODORIC. Also **Der′rick, Direck** (dûrk; *Du.* dirk), **Dirk.**
DeWitt (də·wit′)   From a surname. Also **De Witt.**
Dex·ter (dek′stər)   Right; right-handed; hence, fortunate or skillful.   [< L]
Dick (dik)   Dim. of RICHARD.
Dolph (dolf)   Dim. of ADOLPH or RUDOLPH. Also **Dolf.**
Dom·i·nic (dom′ə·nik)   Of the Lord.   [< L] Also **Dom′i·nick.**   Dim. **Dom.**
Don·ald (don′əld)   World chief.   [< Celtic]   Dims. **Don, Don′nie.**
Doug·las (dug′ləs)   Dark.   [< Celtic]   Dims. **Doug, Doug′ie.**
Drew (drōō)   Skilled one [< Gmc.], or dim. of ANDREW.
Duane (dwān, dōō·än′)   Poem.   [< Celtic]
Dud·ley (dud′lē)   From an English surname; orig. a place name.
Duke (dōōk, dyōōk)   From the title.   [< OF]
Dun·can (dung′kən)   Brown warrior.   [< Celtic]
Dun·stan (dun′stən)   From an English place name.
Dwight (dwīt)   Meaning uncertain.   [< Gmc.]

Earl (ûrl)   From the title.   [OE] Also **Earle.**
Eb·en·e·zer (eb′ə·nē′zər)   Stone of help.   [< Hebrew]   Dim. **Eb·en** (eb′ən).
Ed·gar (ed′gər)   Rich spear; hence, fortunate warrior.   [OE]   Dims. **Ed, Ed′die, Ned.**

Ed·mund (ed′mənd; *Ger.* et′mŏŏnt)   Rich protector.   [OE] Also **Ed·mond** (ed′mənd; *Fr.* ed·môṅ′).   Dims. **Ed, Ed′die, Ned.**
Ed·ward (ed′wərd)   Rich guardian.   [OE] Also *Fr.* **É·dou·ard** (ā·dwär′), *Ger.* **E·du·ard** (ā′dōō·ärt), *Sp.* **E·duar·do** (ā·thwär′thō).   Dims. **Ed, Ed′die, Ned, Ted, Ted′dy.**
Ed·win (ed′win)   Rich friend.   [OE]   Dims. **Ed, Ed′die.**
Eg·bert (eg′bərt)   Bright sword; hence, skilled swordsman.   [OE]   Dims. **Bert, Bert′ie.**
El·bert (el′bərt)   Var. of ALBERT.
El·dred (el′drid)   Mature counsel.   [OE]
El·e·a·zar (el′ē·ā′zər)   God has helped.   [< Hebrew] Also **El′e·a′zer.**
E·li (ē′lī)   The highest one.   [< Hebrew]
E·li·as (i·lī′əs)   Var. of ELIJAH.
E·li·hu (el′ə·hyōō)   Var. of ELIJAH.
E·li·jah (i·lī′jə)   Jehovah is God.   [< Hebrew]
E·li·ot (el′ē·ət)   God's gift.   [< Hebrew] Also **El′li·ot, El′li·ott.**
E·li·sha (i·lī′shə)   God is salvation.   [< Hebrew]
El·lis (el′is)   Var. of ELIAS.
El·mer (el′mər)   Nobly famous.   [OE]
El·ton (el′tən)   From an English surname; orig. a place name.
El·vin (el′vin)   Of the elves.   [OE] Also **El·win** (el′win).
E·man·u·el (i·man′yōō·əl)   Var. of IMMANUEL. Also **Em·man′u·el.**
Em·er·y (em′ər·ē)   Work ruler.   [< Gmc.] Also **Em·er·ic** (em′ər·ik), **Em′o·ry.**
É·mile (ā·mēl′)   From the name of a Roman clan. Also *Fr.* **É·mile** (ā·mēl′), *Ger.* **E·mil** (ā′mēl), *Ital.* **E·mi·lio** (ā·mē′lyō).
Em·mett (em′it)   Ant; hence, industrious.   [OE] Also **Em′met.**
E·ne·as (i·nē′əs)   Praiseworthy.   [< Gk.]
E·noch (ē′nək)   Dedicated.   [< Hebrew]
E·nos (ē′nəs)   Man.   [< Hebrew]
En·ri·co (än·rē′kō)   Ital. form of HENRY.
E·phra·im (ē′frē·əm, ē′frəm)   Doubly fruitful.   [< Hebrew]
E·ras·mus (i·raz′məs)   Lovable.   [< Gk.]
E·ras·tus (i·ras′təs)   Lovable.   [< Gk.]   Dim. **Ras·tus** (ras′·təs).
Er·ic (er′ik)   Honorable king.   [< Scand.] Also **Er′ich, Er′ik.**
Er·man·no (er·män′nō)   Ital. form of HERMAN.
Er·nest (ûr′nist)   Earnest.   [< Gmc.] Also *Ger.* **Ernst** (ernst).   Dims. **Ern, Er′nie.**
Er·win (ûr′win)   Var. of IRVING.
Es·te·ban (äs·tā′bän)   Sp. form of STEPHEN.
E·than (ē′thən)   Firmness.   [< Hebrew]
Eth·el·bert (eth′əl·bûrt)   Nobly bright.   [OE]
Eth·el·red (eth′əl·red)   Noble council.   [< Gmc.]
É·tienne (ā·tyen′)   Fr. form of STEPHEN.
Eu·gene (yōō·jēn′)   Well-born.   [< Gk.]   Dim. **Gene.**
Eus·tace (yōōs′tis)   Good harvest.   [< Gk.]
Ev·an (ev′ən)   Welsh form of JOHN.
Ev·e·lyn (ēv′lin, ev′ə·lin)   Ancestor.   [< OF < Gmc.]
Ev·er·ard (ev′ər·ärd)   Strong as a boar.   [< Gmc.] Also **Ev·er·art** (ev′ər·ärt).
Ev·er·ett (ev′ər·it)   Var. of EVERARD. Also **Ev′er·et.**
E·ze·ki·el (i·zē′kē·əl, -kyəl)   God gives strength.   [< Hebrew]   Dim. **Zeke** (zēk).
Ez·ra (ez′rə)   Helper.   [< Hebrew]

Fë·dor (fyô′dər)   Russ. form of THEODORE. Also **Fe·o·dor** (fyi·ô′dər).
Fe·li·pe (fā·lē′pā)   Sp. form of PHILIP.
Fe·lix (fē′liks)   Happy; fortunate.   [< L]
Fer·di·nand (fûr′də·nand; *Fr.* fer·dē·näṅ′; *Ger.* fer′dē·nänt)   Peaceful courage.   [< Gmc.] Also *Sp.* **Fer·nan·do** (fer·nän′dō), **Her·nan·do** (her·nän′dō).   Dim. **Fer′die.**
Floyd (floid)   Var. of LLOYD.
Fran·cis (fran′sis, frän′-)   Free.   [< Gmc.] Also *Fr.* **Fran·çois** (fräṅ·swà′), *Ger.* **Franz** (fränts), *Ital.* **Fran·ce·sco** (frän·chā′skō), *Sp.* **Fran·cis·co** (frän·thēs′kō).   Dim. **Frank, Frank′ie.**
Frank (frangk)   Dim. of FRANCIS or FRANKLIN. Also **Frank′ie.**
Frank·lin (frangk′lin)   Freeman.   [ME]   Dims. **Frank, Frank′ie.**
Fred (fred)   Dim. of ALFRED, FREDERICK, or WILFRED. Also **Fred′die, Fred′dy.**
Fred·er·ick (fred′ər·ik, fred′rik)   Peace ruler.   [< Gmc.] Also **Fred′er·ic, Fred′ric, Fred′rick,** *Fr.* **Fré·dé·ric** (frā·dā·rēk′), *Ger.* **Frie·drich** (frē′drikh), *Sp.* **Fe·de·ri·co** (fā′dā·rē′kō).   Dims. **Fred, Fred′die, Fred′dy, Fritz.**
Fritz (frits)   Ger. dim. of FREDERICK.

Ga·bri·el (gā′brē·əl; *Fr.* gà·brē·el′; *Ger.* gä′brē·el)   Man of God.   [< Hebrew]   Dim. **Gabe** (gāb).
Ga·ma·li·el (gə·mā′lē·əl, -mäl′yəl)   Reward of God.   [< Hebrew]

Gar·di·ner (gärd′nər, gär′də·nər) From an English surname. Also **Gar′de·ner, Gard′ner.**
Gar·ret (gar′it) Var. of GERARD. Also **Gar′rett.**
Gar·y (gâr′ē) Dim. of GARRET.
Gas·par (gas′pər) Var. of CASPER. Also *Fr.* **Gas·pard** (gàs·pär′).
Gas·ton (gas′tən; *Fr.* gàs·tôṅ′) Meaning uncertain.
Gau·tier (gō·tyá′) Fr. form of WALTER.
Gene (jēn) Dim. of EUGENE.
Geof·frey (jef′rē) English form of Fr. *Geoffroi*; var. of GODFREY. Dim. **Jeff.**
George (jôrj) Earthworker; farmer. [< Gk.] Also *Fr.* **Georges** (zhôrzh), *Ger.* **Ge·org** (gā·ôrkh′), *Ital.* **Gior·gio** (jôr′jō), *Russ.* **Ge·or·gi** (gyi·ôr′gyi). Dim. **Georg′ie, Geor′die.**
Ger·ald (jer′əld) Spear ruler. [< Gmc.] Also *Fr.* **Gé·raud** (zhā·rō′) or **Gi·raud** (zhē·rō′). Dims. **Ger′ry, Jer′ry.**
Ge·rard (ji·rärd′; *Brit.* jer′ärd) Hard spear. [< Gmc.] Also *Fr.* **Gé·rard** (zhā·ràr′), *Ger.* **Ger·hard** (gär′härt). Dims. **Ger′ry, Jer′ry.**
Ge·ro·ni·mo (jā·rō′nē·mō) Ital. form of JEROME.
Gia·co·mo (jä′kō·mō) Ital. form of JAMES.
Gid·e·on (gid′ē·ən) Hewer. [< Hebrew]
Gi·e·ron·y·mus (jē′ə·ron′i·məs) Lat. form of JEROME.
Gif·ford (gif′ərd, jif′-) Meaning uncertain. [< Gmc.]
Gil·bert (gil′bərt; *Fr.* zhēl·bâr′) Bright wish. [< Gmc.] Dims. **Bert, Gil.**
Giles (jīlz) From the name of the goddess Athena's shield; hence, shield or protection. [< OF < Gk.]
Gio·van·ni (jō·vän′nē) Ital. form of JOHN.
Giu·lio (jōō′lyō) Ital. form of JULIUS.
Giu·sep·pe (jōō·zep′pä) Ital. form of JOSEPH.
Glenn (glen) From a Celtic surname; orig. a place name. Also **Glen.**
God·dard (god′ərd) Divine resoluteness. [< Gmc.]
God·frey (god′frē) Peace of God. [< Gmc.] Also *Ger.* **Gott·fried** (gôt′frēt).
God·win (god′win) Friend of God. [OE]
Gor·don (gôr′dən) From a Scot. surname.
Gra·ham (grā′əm) From an English surname; orig. a place name.
Grant (grant) From a Norman Fr. surname.
Greg·o·ry (greg′ər·ē) Vigilant. [< Gk.] Dim. **Greg.**
Grif·fin (grif′in) Var. of GRIFFITH.
Grif·fith (grif′ith) Red-haired. [< Celtic]
Gro·ver (grō′vər) Grove-dweller. [< Gmc.]
Gual·te·ri·o (gwäl·tä′rē·ō) Sp. form of WALTER.
Gu·gliel·mo (gōō·lyel′mō) Ital. form of WILLIAM.
Guil·laume (gē·yōm′) Fr. form of WILLIAM.
Guil·ler·mo (gē·lyer′mō, gē·yer′mō) Sp. form of WILLIAM.
Gus (gus) Dim. of AUGUSTUS or GUSTAVUS.
Guy (gī; *Fr.* gē) Leader [< F < Gmc.] Also *Ital.* **Gui·do** (gwē′dō).

Hal (hal) Dim. of HAROLD or HENRY.
Ham·il·ton (ham′əl·tən) From a surname.
Hank (hangk) Dim. of HENRY.
Han·ni·bal (han′ə·bəl) Grace of Baal. [< Phoenician]
Hans (häns) Ger. dim. of JOHANNES. See JOHN.
Har·ley (här′lē) From an English surname; orig. a place name.
Har·old (har′əld) Chief of the army. [OE < Scand.] Dim. **Hal.**
Har·ry (har′ē) Dim. of HAROLD or var. of HENRY.
Har·vey (här′vē) Army battle. [< F < Gmc.]
Hec·tor (hek′tər) He who holds fast; defender. [< Gk.]
Hen·ry (hen′rē) Home ruler. [< F < Gmc.] Also *Du.* **Hen·drik** (hen′drik), *Fr.* **Hen·ri** (äṅ·rē′), *Ger.* **Hein·rich** (hīn′rikh). Dims. **Hal, Hank, Har′ry, Hen.**
Her·bert (hûr′bərt) Glory of the army. [OE] Dims. **Bert, Bert′ie, Herb.**
Her·man (hûr′mən) Man of the army. [< Gmc.] Also *Ger.* **Her·mann** (her′män).
Her·mes (hûr′mēz) Of the earth. [< Gk.]
Her·nan·do (er·nän′dō) Sp. form of FERDINAND.
Hez·e·ki·ah (hez′ə·kī′ə) God strengthens. [< Hebrew]
Hil·a·ry (hil′ər·ē) Joyful. [< L] Also *Fr.* **Hi·laire** (ē·lâr′).
Hi·ram (hī′rəm) Honored brother. [< Hebrew] Dims. **Hi, Hy.**
Ho·bart (hō′bərt, -bärt) Var. of HUBERT.
Hodge (hoj) Dim. of ROGER. Also **Hodg′kin.**
Ho·mer (hō′mər) Pledge, or blind one. [< Gk.]
Ho·no·ré (ô·nô·rā′) Honored. [< F < L]
Hor·ace (hôr′is, hor′-) Var. of HORATIO.
Ho·ra·ti·o (hə·rā′shē·ō, -shō) From the name of a Roman clan.
Ho·se·a (hō·zē′ə, -zā′ə) Salvation. [< Hebrew]
How·ard (hou′ərd) From an English surname. Dim. **How′ie.**
Hu·bert (hyōō′bərt) Bright spirit or mind. [< F < Gmc.]
Hugh (hyōō) Mind; intelligence. [< OF < Gmc.] Also **Hu·go** (hyōō′gō), *Fr.* **Hugues** (üg). Dim. **Hugh′ie.**

Hum·bert (hum′bərt) Bright support. [< OF < Gmc.]
Hum·phrey (hum′frē) Peaceful stake or support. [< OF < Gmc.] Also **Hum′frey, Hum′phry.**

I·an (ē′ən, ī′ən) Scot. form of JOHN.
Ich·a·bod (ik′ə·bod) ? Inglorious. [< Hebrew]
Ig·na·ti·us (ig·nā′shē·əs, -shəs) Fiery. [< Gk.] Also *Fr.* **I·gnace** (ē·nyàs′), *Ger.* **Ig·naz** (ig′näts), *Ital.* **I·gna·zio** (ē·nyä′tsyō).
Im·man·u·el (i·man′yōō·əl) God with us. [< Hebrew]
I·ra (ī′rə) Vigilant. [< Hebrew]
Ir·ving (ûr′ving) From a Scot. surname; orig. a place name. Also **Ir·vin** (ûr′vin).
Ir·win (ûr′win) Var. of IRVING.
I·saac (ī′zək) Laughter. [< Hebrew] Dim. **Ike** (īk).
I·sa·iah (ī·zā′ə, ī·zī′ə) Salvation of God. [< Hebrew]
Is·i·dore (iz′ə·dôr, -dōr) Gift of Isis. [< Gk.] Also **Is′a·dore, Is′a·dor, Is′i·dor.** Dim. **Iz·zy** (iz′ē).
Is·ra·el (iz′rē·əl) Contender with God. [< Hebrew]
I·van (ī′vən; *Russ.* i·vän′) Russ. form of JOHN.

Ja·bez (jā′biz) Sorrow. [< Hebrew]
Jack (jak) English form of Fr. **Jacques**; dim. of JOHN.
Ja·cob (jā′kəb) He who seizes by the heel; hence, successor. [< LL < Hebrew] Also *Ger.* **Ja·kob** (yä′kôb). Dims. **Jack, Jake** (jāk), **Jock** (jok).
Jacques (zhàk) Fr. form of JACOB. [< OF < LL]
James (jāmz) English form of Sp. *Jaime*; var. of JACOB. [< Sp. < LL] Also *Sp.* **Jai·me** (hī′mä). Dims. **Jam·ie** (jā′mē), **Jem, Jem′my, Jim, Jim′mie, Jim′my.**
Jan (yän) Du., Ger., and Pol. form of JOHN.
Já·nos (yä′nōsh) Hung. form of JOHN.
Ja·pheth (jā′fith) Enlarged; hence, powerful or honored. [< Hebrew] Also **Ja′phet** (-fit).
Jar·ed (jâr′id) Descent. [< Hebrew]
Jar·vis (jär′vis) From a Norman Fr. surname. Also **Jer·vis** (jûr′vis; *Brit.* jär′vis).
Ja·son (jā′sən) Healer. [< Gk.]
Jas·per (jas′pər) Treasury lord [< OF, ? < Persian], or from the name of the jewel.
Jay (jā) ? Jay bird. [? < OF]
Jean (jēn; *Fr.* zhäṅ) French form of JOHN.
Jef·frey (jef′rē) Var. of GEOFFREY. Dim. **Jeff.**
Je·hu (jē′hyōō) Jehovah is he. [< Hebrew]
Jeph·thah (jef′thə) Opposer. [< Hebrew]
Jer·e·mi·ah (jer′ə·mī′ə) God's chosen. [< Hebrew] Also **Jer·e·my** (jer′ə·mē). Dim. **Jer′ry.**
Je·rome (jə·rōm′; *Brit.* jer′əm) Holy name. [< Gk.] Also *Fr.* **Jé·rôme** (zhā·rôm′), *Sp.* **Je·ró·ni·mo** (hā·rō′nē·mō).
Jer·ry (jer′ē) Dim. of GERALD, GERARD, JEREMIAH, or JEROME.
Jes·se (jes′ē) Meaning uncertain. [< Hebrew] Also **Jess.**
Je·sus (jē′zəs) English form of Lat. *Josua*; var. of JOSHUA.
Jeth·ro (jeth′rō) Abundant or excellent. [< Hebrew]
Jim (jim) Dim. of JAMES. Also **Jim′mie, Jim′my.**
Jo·ab (jō′ab) Jehovah is father. [< Hebrew]
Jo·a·chim (jō′ə·kim) Jehovah will judge. [< Hebrew] Also *Sp.* **Joa·quín** (hwä·kēn′).
João (zhwouṅ) Pg. form of JOHN.
Job (jōb) Persecuted. [< Hebrew]
Jock (jok) Scot. form of JACK.
Joe (jō) Dim. of JOSEPH. Also **Jo′ey.**
Jo·el (jō′əl) Jehovah is God. [< Hebrew]
John (jon) God is good. [< Hebrew] Also *Ger.* **Jo·hann** (yō′hän) or **Jo·han·nes** (yō·hän′əs). Dims. **Jack, Jack′ie, Jack′y, Jock, John′nie, John′ny.**
Jon (jon) Var. of JOHN, or dim. of JONATHAN.
Jo·nah (jō′nə) Dove. [< Hebrew] Also **Jo·nas** (jō′nəs).
Jon·a·than (jon′ə·thən) God has given. [< Hebrew] Dims. **Jon, Jon′nie, Jon′ny.**
Jor·ge (*Pg.* zhôr′zhə; *Sp.* hôr′hä) Pg. and Sp. form of GEORGE.
Jo·seph (jō′zəf; *Fr.* zhō·zef′; *Ger.* yō′zef) God shall give (a son). [< Hebrew] Also *Lat.* **Jo·se·phus** (jō·sē′fəs), *Pg.*, *Sp.* **Jo·sé** (*Pg.* zhōō·ze′; *Sp.* hō·sā′). Dims. **Jo, Joe, Jo′ey.**
Josh·u·a (josh′ōō·ə) God is salvation. [< Hebrew] Also *Fr.* **Jo·sué** (zhō·zwä′), *Lat.* **Jos·u·a** (jos′ōō·ə). Dim. **Josh.**
Jo·si·ah (jō·sī′ə) God supports. [< Hebrew] Also *Lat.* **Jo·si·as** (jō·sī′əs).
Jo·tham (jō′thəm) God is perfection. [< Hebrew]
Juan (hwän) Sp. form of JOHN.
Ju·dah (jōō′də) Praised. [< Hebrew] Also **Jude** (jōōd; *Fr.* zhüd), *Lat.* **Ju·das** (jōō′dəs).
Jules (jōōlz; *Fr.* zhül) Fr. form of JULIUS.
Jul·ian (jōōl′yən) Var. of JULIUS.
Jul·ius (jōōl′yəs) Downy-bearded; youthful: from the name of a Roman clan. Also *Sp.* **Ju·lio** (hōō′lyō). Dims. **Jule** (jōōl), **Jul·ie** (jōō′lē).
Jun·ius (jōōn′yəs, jōō′nē·əs) Youthful: from the name of a Roman clan.
Jus·tin (jus′tin) Just. [< L] Also **Jus·tus** (jus′təs).

Karl (kärl) Ger. form of CHARLES.
Kas·par (käs′pär) Ger. form of JASPER.
Keith (kēth) From a Scot. surname; orig. a place name.
Kel·vin (kel′vin) From a Celtic surname.
Ken·neth (ken′ith) Handsome. [< Celtic] Dims. **Ken, Ken′nie, Ken′ny.**
Kent (kent) From an English surname; orig. a place name.
Kev·in (kev′ən) Handsome birth. [< Celtic]
Kit (kit) Dim. of CHRISTOPHER.
Kon·rad (kôn′rät) Ger. form of CONRAD.

La·ban (lā′bən) White. [< Hebrew]
La·fay·ette (lä′fē·et′, laf′ē·et′; Fr. là·fà·yet′) From a Fr. surname. Dim. **Lafe** (lāf).
Lam·bert (lam′bərt) The land's brightness. [< F < Gmc.]
Lance (lans, läns) Of the land. [< Gmc.]
Lan·ce·lot (lan′sə·lot, län′-; Fr. län·slō′) Fr. dim. of LANCE. Also **Laun·ce·lot** (lôn′sə·lot, lan′-, län′-).
Lars (lärz; Sw. lärs) Sw. form of LAURENCE.
Lau·rence (lôr′əns, lor′-) Laureled; hence, prophetic or poetic. [< L] Also **Law′rence,** Fr. **Lau·rent** (lō·rän′), Ger. **Lo·renz** (lō′rents). Dims. **Lar·ry** (lar′ē), **Lau·rie** or **Law·rie** (lôr′ē).
Laz·a·rus (laz′ə·rəs) God has helped. [< Hebrew] Also Fr. **La·zare** (là·zàr′), Ital. **Laz·za·ro** (läd′dzä·rō).
Le·an·der (lē·an′dər) Lion man. [< Gk.]
Lee (lē) From an English surname.
Leif (lēf) Loved one. [< Scand.]
Leigh (lē) From an English surname.
Lem·u·el (lem′yōō·əl) Belonging to God. [< Hebrew] Dim. **Lem.**
Le·o (lē′ō) Lion. [< L < Gk.]
Le·on (lē′on, -ən) Lion. [< L < Gk.] Also Fr. **Lé·on** (lā·ôn′).
Leon·ard (len′ərd) Lion-strong. [< Gmc.] Also Fr. **Lé·o·nard** (lā·ō·nàr′), Ger. **Le·on·hard** (lā′ōn·härt), Ital. **Le·o·nar·do** (lā′ō·när′dō). Dims. **Len, Len′ny.**
Le·on·i·das (lē·on′ə·dəs) Lionlike. [< Gk.]
Le·o·pold (lē′ə·pōld; Ger. lā′ō·pōlt) The people's strong one. [< Gmc.]
Le·roy (lə·roi′, lē′roi) Royal. [< OF]
Les·lie (les′lē, lez′-) From an English surname. Dim. **Les.**
Les·ter (les′tər) From an English surname; orig. the place name Leicester. Dim. **Les.**
Le·vi (lē′vī) He who unites. [< Hebrew]
Lew·is (lōō′is) Var. of LOUIS. Dims. **Lew, Lew′ie.**
Lin·coln (ling′kən) From an English surname.
Li·nus (lī′nəs) Meaning uncertain. [< Gk.]
Li·o·nel (lī′ə·nəl, -nel) Young lion. [< F < L]
Lisle (līl) Var. of LYLE.
Llew·el·lyn (lōō·el′ən) Meaning uncertain. [< Welsh]
Lloyd (loid) Gray. [< Welsh]
Lo·ren·zo (lə·ren′zō; Ital. lō·ren′tsō; Sp. lō·rän′thō) Var. of LAURENCE.
Lot (lot) Veiled. [< Hebrew] Also **Lott.**
Lou·is (lōō′is, lōō′ē; Fr. lwē) War famous. [< OF < Gmc.] Also **Lew′is,** Du. **Lo·de·wijk** (lō′də·vīk), Ger. **Lud·wig** (lōōt′·viKH), Ital. **Lu·i·gi** (lōō·ē′jē), or **Lo·do·vi·co** (lō′dō·vē′kō), Pg. **Lu·iz** (lōō·ēsh′), Sp. **Lu·is** (lōō·ēs′). Dims. **Lew, Lou.**
Low·ell (lō′əl) Beloved. [OE] Also **Lov·ell** (luv′əl).
Lu·cas (lōō′kəs) Light. [< L]
Lu·cian (lōō′shən) Var. of LUCIUS. [< L Lucianus] Also **Lu·cien** (lōō′shən; Fr. lü·syän′).
Lu·ci·fer (lōō′sə·fər) Light-bearer. [< L]
Lu·cius (lōō′shəs) Light. [< L]
Lu·cre·tius (lōō·krē′shəs, -shē·əs) Shining or wealthy. [< L]
Luke (lōōk) English form of LUCAS.
Lu·ther (lōō′thər) Famous warrior. [< Gmc.] Also Fr. **Lo·thaire** (lō·târ′), Ital. **Lo·ta·rio** (lo·tä′ryō).

Mac (mak) Son. [< Celtic] Also **Mack.**
Mal·a·chi (mal′ə·kī) Messenger. [< Hebrew]
Mal·colm (mal′kəm) Servant of (St.) Columba. [< Celtic]
Ma·nu·el (mä·nwel′) Sp. form of IMMANUEL.
Mar·cel·lus (mär·sel′əs) Dim. of MARCUS. Also Fr. **Mar·cel** (mär·sel′), Ital. **Mar·cel·lo** (mär·chel′lō).
Mar·cus (mär′kəs) Of Mars. [< L]
Mar·i·on (mar′ē·ən, mâr′-) Of Mary. [< F]
Mark (märk) English form of MARCUS. Also Fr. **Marc** (märk), Ital. **Mar·co** (mär′kō).
Mar·ma·duke (mär′mə·dōōk, -dyōōk) Meaning uncertain. [? < Celtic]
Mar·shal (mär′shəl) From the title. [< Gmc.] Also **Mar′shall.**
Mar·tin (mär′tən; Fr. màr·tan′; Ger. mär′tēn) Of Mars. [< L] Dims. **Mart, Mar′ty.**
Mar·vin (mär′vin) Sea friend. [< Gmc.]
Ma·son (mā′sən) Stoneworker. [< Gmc.]
Mat·thew (math′yōō) Gift of God. [< Hebrew] Fr. **Ma·thieu** (mà·tyœ′), Ital. **Mat·te·o** (mät·tā′ō), Sp. **Ma·te·o** (mä·tā′ō). Dims. **Mat, Matt.**

Mat·thi·as (mə·thī′əs) Var. of MATTHEW. [< Gk.]
Mau·rice (mə·rēs′, môr′is, mor′is; Fr. mô·rēs′) Moorish; dark. [< F < L]
Max (maks; Ger. mäks) Dim. of MAXIMILIAN.
Max·i·mil·ian (mak′sə·mil′yən; Ger. mäk′sē·mē′lē·än) Prob. coined by Frederick III from the Roman names Maximus and Aemilianus. Dim. **Max.**
May·nard (mā′nərd, -närd) Powerful strength. [< Gmc.]
Mel·vin (mel′vin) High protector. [OE] Dim. **Mel.**
Mer·e·dith (mer′ə·dith) Sea protector. [< Welsh]
Mer·vin (mûr′vin) Var. of MARVIN.
Mi·cah (mī′kə) Who is like God? [< Hebrew]
Mi·chael (mī′kəl; Ger. mi′KHä·el) Who is like God? [< Hebrew] Also Fr. **Mi·chel** (mē·shel′), Ital. **Mi·che·le** (mē·kā′lä), Sp., Pg. **Mi·guel** (mē·gel′). Dims. **Mike** (mīk), **Mick·ey** or **Mick·y** (mik′ē), **Mik·ey** (mī′kē).
Mi·klós (mī′klōsh) Hung. form of NICHOLAS.
Miles (mīlz) Meaning uncertain. [< Gmc.] Also **Myles.**
Mi·lo (mī′lō; Ital. mē′lō) Ital. var. of MILES.
Mil·ton (mil′tən) From an English surname; orig. a place name. [< Gmc.] Dim. **Milt.**
Mitch·ell (mich′əl) Var. of MICHAEL. Dim. **Mitch.**
Mon·roe (mən·rō′, Brit. mun′rō) From a Celtic surname; orig. a place name.
Mon·ta·gue (mon′tə·gyōō) From a Norman Fr. surname; orig. a place name. Dim. **Mon′ty.**
Mont·gom·er·y (mont·gum′ər·ē) From a Norman Fr. surname; orig. a place name. Dim. **Mon′ty.**
Mor·gan (môr′gən) Sea-dweller. [< Welsh]
Mor·ris (môr′is, mor′-) Var. of MAURICE.
Mor·ti·mer (môr′tə·mər) From a Norman Fr. surname; orig. a place name. Dims. **Mort, Mor′ty.**
Mor·ton (môr′tən) From an English surname; orig. a place name. Dim. **Mort, Mor′ty.**
Mo·ses (mō′zis, -ziz) ? Son. [< Hebrew, ? < Egyptian] Dim. **Moe** (mō), **Moi·she** (moi′shə), **Mose** (mōz).
Moss (môs, mos) Var. of MOSES.
Mur·dock (mûr′dok) Seaman. [< Celtic] Also **Mur′doch.**
Mur·ray (mûr′ē) From a Scot. surname, or var. of MAURICE.
Myles (mīlz) Var. of MILES.

Na·hum (nā′əm) Consolation. [< Hebrew]
Na·po·le·on (nə·pō′lē·ən) Of the new city. [< F < Gk.] Also Fr. **Na·po·lé·on** (nà·pô·lā·ôñ′), Ital. **Na·po·le·o·ne** (nä·pō′lā·ō′nä).
Na·than (nā′thən) Gift. [< Hebrew] Dims. **Nat** (nat), **Nate** (nāt).
Na·than·iel (nə·than′yəl) Gift of God. [< Hebrew] Also **Na·than′a·el.** Dims. **Nat, Nate.**
Ned (ned) Dim. of EDGAR, EDMUND, or EDWARD. Also **Ned′dy.**
Ne·he·mi·ah (nē′hə·mī′ə) Comfort of God. [< Hebrew]
Neil (nēl) Champion. [< Celtic] Also **Neal.**
Nel·son (nel′sən) Neal's son: from an English surname.
Ne·ro (nir′ō) Strong: from the name of a Roman clan.
Nev·ille (nev′il, -əl) From a Norman Fr. surname; orig. a place name. Also **Nev′il, Nev′ile, Nev′ill.**
New·ton (nōōt′n, nyōōt′n) From an English surname; orig. a place name.
Nich·o·las (nik′ə·ləs) The people's victory. [< Gk.] Also **Nic′o·las,** Fr. **Ni·co·las** (nē·kô·lä′), Ital. **Nic·co·lò** (nēk′kō·lô′), Lat. **Ni·co·la·us** (nik′ō·lā′əs), Russ. **Ni·ko·lai** (nyi·kə·lī′), Sp. **Ni·co·lás** (nē′kō·läs′). Dims. **Nick, Nick′y.**
Ni·gel (nī′jəl) Noble. [< Celtic]
No·ah (nō′ə) Comfort. [< Hebrew]
No·el (nō′əl) Christmas. [< OF < L] Also Fr. **No·ël** (nō·el′).
Nor·bert (nôr′bərt) Brightness of Njord. [< Gmc.]
Nor·man (nôr′mən) Northman. [< Scand.] Dim. **Norm.**

O·ba·di·ah (ō′bə·dī′ə) Servant of God. [< Hebrew]
Oc·ta·vi·us (ok·tā′vē·əs) The eighth (born). [< L]
O·laf (ō′läf; Dan., Norw. ō′läf; Sw. ōō′läf) Ancestor's heirloom. Also **O′lav** [< Scand.]
Ol·i·ver (ol′ə·vər) Of the olive tree. [< F < L] Dims. **Ol′lie, Ol′ly.**
Or·lan·do (ôr·lan′dō; Ital. ôr·län′dō) Ital. form of ROLAND.
Os·bert (ôz′bərt) Divine brilliance. [OE]
Os·car (os′kər) Divine spear. [OE]
Os·wald (oz′wəld, -wôld) Divine power. [OE] Also **Os′wold.**
Ot·to (ot′ō; Ger. ôt′ō) Rich. [< Gmc.]
O·wen (ō′ən) Young warrior [< Welsh]

Pat·rick (pat′rik) Patrician; aristocratic. [< L] Dims. **Pad′dy, Pat, Pat′sy.**
Paul (pôl; Fr. pôl; Ger. poul) Little: from a given name of the Aemiliani, a Roman clan. Also Ital. **Pa·o·lo** (pä′ō·lō), Lat. **Pau·li·nus** (pô·lī′nəs) or **Pau·lus** (pô′ləs), Pg. **Pau·lo** (pou′lōō), Sp. **Pa·blo** (pä′vlō).

Per·ci·val (pûr′sə·vəl) Meaning uncertain. [< OF] Also **Per′ce·val.**
Per·cy (pûr′sē) From a Norman Fr. surname; orig. a place name.
Per·ry (per′ē) Of the pear tree: from an English surname.
Pe·ter (pē′tər; *Du., Ger., Norw., Sw.* pā′tər) A rock. [< Gk.] Also *Dan.* **Pe·der** (pā′thər), *Du.* **Pie·ter** (pē′tər), *Fr.* **Pierre** (pyâr), *Modern Gk.* **Pe·tros** (pā′trôs), *Ital.* **Pie·tro** (pyā′trō), *Pg., Sp.* **Pe·dro** (*Pg.* pā′thrōō; *Sp.* pā′thrō), *Russ.* **Pëtr** (pyô′tər). Dim. **Pete.**
Phi·lan·der (fi·lan′dər) Lover of men. [< Gk.]
Phi·le·mon (fi·lē′mən) Loving. [< Gk.]
Phil·ip (fil′ip) Lover of horses. [< Gk.] Also *Fr.* **Phi·lippe** (fē·lēp′), *Ger.* **Phi·lipp** (fē′lip). Dims. **Phil, Pip.**
Phin·e·as (fin′ē·əs) Mouth of brass: prob. an oracular priest's title. [< Hebrew]

Quen·tin (kwen′tin) The fifth (born). [< L] Also **Quin·tin** (kwin′tən).
Quin·cy (kwin′sē) ? var. of QUENTIN. [< OF]
Ralph (ralf; *Brit.* rāf) Wolf-wise. [< Gmc.] *Fr.* **Ra·oul** (rä·ōōl′).
Ran·dal (ran′dəl) Shield wolf. [OE] Also **Ran′dall.**
Ran·dolph (ran′dolf) Shield wolf. [OE] Dim. **Ran′dy.**
Ra·pha·el (rā′fē·əl, raf′ē·əl) God has healed. [< Hebrew]
Ray (rā) Dim. of RAYMOND.
Ray·mond (rā′mənd; *Fr.* rā·môn′) Wise protection. [< Gmc.] Also **Ray′mund,** *Sp.* **Rai·mun·do** (rī·mōōn′dō) or **Ra·món** (rä·mōn′). Dim. **Ray.**
Reg·i·nald (rej′ə·nəld) Judicial ruler. [< Gmc.] Also *Fr.* **Re·gnault** (rə·nyō′) or **Re·naud** (rə·nō′), *Ital.* **Ri·nal·do** (rē·näl′dō), *Sp.* **Rey·nal·do** (rā·näl′thō). Dims. **Reg** (rej), **Reg′gie, Rex.**
Re·né (rə·nā′) Reborn. [< F < L]
Reu·ben (rōō′bin) Behold, a son! [< Hebrew] Dim. **Rube.**
Rex (reks) King [< L], or dim. of REGINALD.
Rey·nard (rā′nərd, ren′ərd) Brave judgment. [< Gmc.]
Reyn·old (ren′əld) Var. of REGINALD. [< OF]
Rich·ard (rich′ərd; *Fr.* rē·shâr′; *Ger.* rikh′ärt) Strong king. [< OF < Gmc.] Also *Ital.* **Ric·car·do** (rēk·kär′dō), *Sp.* **Ri·car·do** (rē·kär′thō). Dims. **Dick, Dick′ie, Dick′y, Rich, Rich′ie, Rick, Rick′y.**
Ro·ald (rō′äl) Famous power. [< Norw. < Gmc.]
Rob·ert (rob′ərt; *Fr.* rô·bâr′) Bright fame. [< Gmc.] Also *Ital., Sp.* **Ro·ber·to** (rō·ber′tō). Dims. **Bob, Bob′by, Dob, Dob′bin, Rob, Rob′bie, Rob′in.**
Rod·er·ick (rod′ər·ik) Famous king. [< Gmc.] Also **Rod′er·ic, Rod·rick** (rod′rik), *Fr.* **Ro·drigue** (rô·drēg′), *Ital., Sp.* **Ro·dri·go** (*Ital.* rō·drē′gō; *Sp.* rō·thrē′gō). Dims. **Rod, Rod′dy.**
Rod·ney (rod′nē) From an English surname; orig. a place name. Dim. **Rod.**
Ro·dolph (rō′dolf) Var. of RUDOLPH. Also **Ro·dol·phus** (rō·dol′fəs).
Rog·er (roj′ər; *Fr.* rô·zhā′) Famous spear. [< OF < Gmc.] Dims. **Hodge, Hodg′kin, Rodge.**
Ro·land (rō′lənd; *Fr.* rô·län′) Country's fame. [< Celtic < Gmc.] Also **Row′land.**
Rolf (rolf) Dim. of RUDOLPH. Also **Rolph.**
Rol·lo (rol′ō) Dim. of RUDOLPH.
Ron·ald (ron′əld; *Norw.* rō·näl′) Old Norse form of REGINALD.
Ro·ry (rôr′ē, rō′rē) Red. [< Celtic]
Ros·coe (ros′kō) From an English surname; orig. a place name.
Ross (rôs) From an English surname; orig. a place name.
Roy (roi) King. [< OF]
Ru·dolph (rōō′dolf) Famous wolf. [< Gmc.] Also **Ru′·dolf, Ru·dol·phus** (rōō·dol′fəs), *Fr.* **Ro·dolphe** (rô·dôlf′), *Ital.* **Ro·dol·pho** (rō·dôl′fō), *Sp.* **Ro·dol·fo** (rō·thôl′fō). Dims. **Rol′lo, Ru′dy.**
Ru·fus (rōō′fəs) Red-haired. [< L] Dim. **Rufe.**
Ru·pert (rōō′pərt) Var. of ROBERT. [< G] Also *Ger.* **Ru·precht** (rōō′prekht).
Rus·sell (rus′əl) Red: from an English surname. [OE < OF] Dim. **Russ.**

Sal·o·mon (sal′ə·mən) Var. of SOLOMON.
Sam·son (sam′sən) The sun. [< Hebrew] Also **Samp′·son** (samp′sən, sam′-).
Sam·u·el (sam′yōō·əl) Name of God. [< Hebrew] Dims. **Sam, Sam′my.**
San·dy (san′dē) Dim. of ALEXANDER. Also **San·der** (san′dər, sän′-).
Saul (sôl) Asked (of God). [< Hebrew]
Schuy·ler (skī′lər) Shelter. [< Du.]
Scott (skot) The Scot: from an English surname.
Seam·us (shā′məs) Irish form of JAMES.
Sean (shôn, shan) Irish form of JOHN.
Se·bas·tian (si·bas′chən) Venerable. [< Gk.]
Seth (seth) Appointed. [< Hebrew]

Sew·ard (sōō′ərd) ? Sow-herder: from an English surname.
Sey·mour (sē′môr, -mōr) From an English surname; orig. a place name. Dims. **Cy, Sy.**
Shawn (shôn) Irish form of JOHN. Also **Shaun.**
Shel·don (shel′dən) From an English surname; orig. a place name.
Shir·ley (shûr′lē) From an English surname; orig. a place name.
Sid·ney (sid′nē) St. Denis: from an English surname. Dim. **Sid.**
Sieg·fried (sēg′frēd; *Ger.* zēk′frēt) Victorious peace. [< Gmc.]
Sig·is·mund (sij′əs·mənd, sig′-) Victorious protection. [< Gmc.]
Sig·mund (sig′mənd; *Ger.* zekh′mōōnt) Var. of SIGISMUND.
Si·las (sī′ləs) Meaning uncertain. [< Gk.] Dim. **Si** (sī).
Sil·va·nus (sil·vā′nəs) From the name of the Roman god of woods and crops.
Sil·ves·ter (sil·ves′tər) Of the woods; rustic. [< L]
Sim·e·on (sim′ē·ən) He who is heard (widely); hence, famous. [< Hebrew] Dim. **Sim** (sim).
Si·mon (sī′mən) Var. of SIMEON.
Sin·clair (sin·klâr′, sin′klâr) St. Clair: from a Norman Fr. surname.
Sol·o·mon (sol′ə·mən) Peaceful. [< Hebrew] Dim. **Sol.**
Stan·ley (stan′lē) From an English surname; orig. a place name. Dim. **Stan.**
Ste·phen (stē′vən) Crown. [< Gk.] Also **Ste′ven,** *Ger.* **Ste·phan** or **Ste·fan** (shte′fän), *Ital.* **Ste·fa·no** (stā′fä·nō), *Russ.* **Ste·pan** (styi·pän′). Dims. **Steve, Ste′vie.**
Stew·art (stōō′ərt, styōō′-) Steward: from an English surname. Also **Stu′art.** Dims. **Stew, Stu.**
Sum·ner (sum′nər) Summoner: from an English surname.
Syd·ney (sid′nē) Var. of SIDNEY.
Syl·va·nus (sil·vā′nəs) Var. of SILVANUS.
Syl·ves·ter (sil·ves′tər) Var. of SILVESTER.

Taf·fy (taf′ē) Welsh dim. of DAVID.
Tad (tad) Dim. of THEODORE or THADDEUS.
Ted (ted) Dim. of EDWARD or THEODORE. Also **Ted′dy.**
Ter·ence (ter′əns) From the name of a Roman clan. Also **Ter′rence.** Dim. **Ter′ry.**
Thad·de·us (thad′ē·əs) Praised. [< Aramaic] Dims. **Tad, Thad, Tha′dy, Thad′dy.**
The·o·bald (thē′ə·bôld, tib′əld) The people's brave one. [< Gmc.]
The·o·dore (thē′ə·dôr, -dōr) Gift of God. [< Gk.] Also *Fr.* **Thé·o·dore** (tā·ô·dôr′), *Ger.* **The·o·dor** (tā′ō·dôr), *Modern Gk.* **The·o·do·ros** (thē·ô′tho·rôs), *Ital.,* **Te·o·do·ro** (*Ital.* tā′ō·dô′rō; *Sp.* tā′ō·thô′rō). Dims. **Tad, Ted, Ted′dy, Dode** (dōd).
Thom·as (tom′əs; *Fr.* tô·mä′; *Ger.* tō′mäs) Twin. [< Aramaic] Also *Ital.* **Tom·ma·so** (tōm·mä′zō), *Sp.* **To·más** (tō·mäs′). Dims. **Tom, Tom′my.**
Thurs·ton (thûrs′tən) Thor's stone. [< Scand.]
Tim·o·thy (tim′ə·thē) Honor of God. [< Gk.] Also *Fr.* **Ti·mo·thée** (tē·mô·tā′), *Ital.* **Ti·mo·te·o** (tē·mô′tā·ō). Dims. **Tim, Tim′my.**
Ti·tus (tī′təs) Meaning uncertain. [< L]
To·bi·as (tō·bī′əs) God is good. [< Hebrew] Also **To·bi·ah** (tō·bī′ə). Dim. **To·by** (tō′bē).
Tod (tod) Fox: from an English surname. Also **Todd.**
To·ny (tō′nē) Dim. of ANTHONY.
Tris·tan (tris′tan; -tən) Confusion. [< Celtic] Also **Tris·tram** (tris′trəm). Dim. **Tris.**
Tyb·alt (tib′əlt) Var. of THEOBALD.

U·lys·ses (yōō·lis′ēz) ? Hater: Lat. form of Gk. *Odysseus.*
Um·ber·to (ōōm·ber′tō) Ital. form of HUMBERT.
Ur·ban (ûr′bən) Of the city. [< L]
U·ri·ah (yōō·rī′ə) God is light. [< Hebrew] Also **U·ri·as** (yōō·rī′əs).
U·ri·el (yōōr′ē·əl) Light of God. [< Hebrew]

Val·en·tine (val′ən·tīn) Strong; healthy. [< L] Dim. **Val.**
Van (van) From an English surname, or from the Ger. or Du. name element *von, van,* indicating residence or origin.
Va·si·li (və·syē′lyē) Russ. var. of BASIL.
Ver·gil (vûr′jəl) Var. of VIRGIL.
Ver·non (vûr′nən) Meaning uncertain. [< L or F] Dim. **Vern.**
Vic·tor (vik′tər; *Fr.* vēk·tôr′) Conqueror. [< L] Also *Ital.* **Vit·to·rio** (vit·tô′ryō). Dims. **Vic, Vick.**
Vin·cent (vin′sənt; *Fr.* van·sän′) Conquering. [< L] Also *Ger.* **Vin·cenz** (vin′tsents), *Ital.* **Vin·cen·zo** (vēn·chen′tsō), *Sp.* **Vi·cen·te** (vē·thān′tā). Dims. **Vin, Vince, Vin′ny.**
Vir·gil (vûr′jəl) Flourishing: from the name of a Roman clan. Also **Ver′gil.** Dims. **Virge, Vir′gie.**
Viv·i·an (viv′ē·ən, viv′yən) Lively. [< F] Also **Viv·i·en** (viv′ē·ən; *Fr.* vē·vyàn′).

Wal·do (wôl′dō, wol′-) Ruler. [< Gmc.]
Wal·lace (wol′is) Welsh(man): from a Scot. surname. Also
Wal′lis. Dim. **Wal′ly.**
Wal·ter (wôl′tər; *Ger.* väl′tər) Ruler of the army. [<
Gmc.] Also *Ger.* **Wal·ther** (väl′tər). Dims. **Walt, Wal′ly.**
Ward (wôrd) Guard: from an English surname.
War·ren (wôr′ən, wor′-) From an English surname.
Wayne (wān) From an English surname. [< Celtic]
Wes·ley (wes′lē; *Brit.* wez′lē) From an English surname;
orig. a place name. Dim. **Wes.**
Wil·bur (wil′bər) Bright will. [< Gmc.] Also **Wil′ber.**
Wil·fred (wil′frid) Resolute peace. [< Gmc.] Also **Wil′-**
frid. Dim. **Fred.**
Wil·lard (wil′ərd) From an English surname.
Wil·liam (wil′yəm) Resolute protection. [< Gmc.] Also
Du. **Wil·lem** (vil′əm), *Ger.* **Wil·helm** (vil′helm). Dims. **Bill,
Bil′ly, Will, Wil′lie, Wil′ly.**
Wil·lis (wil′is) Willie's son: from an English surname.

Win·fred (win′frid) Friend of peace. [OE] Also **Win′frid.**
Dims. **Win, Win′nie.**
~~**Win·ston** (win′stən) From an English surname; orig. a
place name.~~
Wy·att (wī′ət) Dim. of GUY. [< OF]
Wys·tan (wis′tən) Battle stone. [OE]

Zach·a·ri·ah (zak′ə·rī′ə) Remembrance of God. [< He-
brew] Also **Zach·a·ri·as** (zak′ə·rī′əs). Dims. **Zach** (zak),
Zack.
Zach·a·ry (zak′ər·ē) Var. of ZACHARIAH.
Zeb·a·di·ah (zeb′ə·dī′ə) Gift of God. [< Hebrew]
Zeb·e·dee (zeb′ə·dē) Contr. of ZEBADIAH.
Zech·a·ri·ah (zek′ə·rī′ə) Var. of ZACHARIAH.
Zeke (zēk) Dim. of EZEKIEL.
Zeph·a·ni·ah (zef′ə·nī′ə) Protected by God. [< Hebrew]
Dim. **Zeph.**

FEMININE NAMES

Ab·i·gail (ab′ə·gāl) Father's joy. [< Hebrew] Dims. **Ab′-**
by, Ab′bie.
A·da (ā′də) Joyful; flourishing. [< Gmc.]
A·dah (ā′də) Beauty. [< Hebrew] Also **A′da.**
Ad·e·la (ad′ə·lə; *Sp.* ä·thä′lä) Noble. [< Gmc.] Also
A·dele (ə·del′), *Fr.* **A·dèle** (à·del′), *Ger.* **A·de·le** (ä·dā′lə).
Ad·e·laide (ad′ə·lād) Nobility. [< Gmc.] Also *Fr.* **A·dé-**
la·ide (à·dā·là·ēd′), *Ger.* **A·del·heid** (ä′dəl·hīt), *Ital.* **A·de·la-**
i·de (ä′dä·lä′ē·dä). Dims. **Ad′die, Ad′dy.**
Ad·e·line (ad′ə·līn; *Fr.* àd·lēn′) Of noble birth. [< Gmc.]
Also **Ad′a·line, Ad·e·li·cia** (ad′ə·lish′ə), **Ad·e·li·na** (ad′ə·
li′nə). Dims. **Ad′die, Ad′dy.**
A·dri·enne (ā′drē·en; *Fr.* à·drē·en′) Fem. of ADRIAN. [< F]
Ag·a·tha (ag′ə·thə) Good; kind. [< Gmc.] Also *Fr.* **A·gathe**
(à·gàt′), *Ger.* **A·ga·the** (ä·gä′tə). Dim. **Ag′gie.**
Ag·nes (ag′nis; *Ger.* äg′nes) Pure; sacred. [< Gk.] Also
Fr. **A·gnès** (à·nyâs′). Dim. **Ag′gie.**
A·i·da (ä·ē′də, ä′də) From the heroine of Verdi's opera.
Ai·leen (ā·lēn′; *Irish* ī·lēn′) Var. of EILEEN.
Ai·mée (ā·mā′) French form of AMY.
Al·ber·ta (al·bûr′tə) Fem. of ALBERT. Also **Al·ber·ti·na**
(al′bər·tē′nə), **Al·ber·tine** (al′bər·tēn).
A·le·the·a (al′ə·thē′ə, ə·lē′thē·ə) Truth. [< Gk.]
Al·ex·an·dra (al′ig·zan′drə, -zän′-) Fem. of ALEXANDER.
Also **Al·ex·an·dri·na** (al′ig·zan·drē′nə, -zän-), *Fr.* **A·lex·an-**
drine (à·lek·sän·drēn′), *Ital.* **A·les·san·dra** (ä′läs·sän′drä),
Sp. **A·le·jan·dra** (ä′lā·hän′drä) or **A·le·jan·dri·na** (ä′lä·hän-
drē′nä). Dims. **A·lex·a** (ə·lek′sə), **Al·ex·in·a** (al′ig·zē′nə),
Al·ix (al′iks), **San·dra** (san′drə).
A·lex·is (ə·lek′sis) Fem. of ALEX. Also **A·lex·i·a** (ə·lek′sē·ə).
Al·fre·da (al·frē′də) Fem. of ALFRED.
Al·ice (al′is; *Fr.* à·lēs′; *Ger.* ä·lē′sə; *Ital.* ä·lē′chä) Truth. [<
OF < Gmc.] Also **Al′lis, Al′yce, Al′ys.** Dim. **Al′lie.**
A·li·cia (ə·lish′ə, ə·lish′ē·ə) Var. of ALICE. [< L]
A·line (ə·lēn′, al′ēn) Var. of ADELINE.
Al·i·son (al′ə·sən) Of sacred memory. [< Gmc.] Also
Al′li·son.
Al·ix (al′iks) Dim. of ALEXANDRA.
Al·le·gra (ə·lā′grə) Spirited. [< Ital. < L]
Al·ma (al′mə) Providing; gracious. [< L]
Al·mi·ra (al·mī′rə) Lofty; princess. [< Arabic]
Al·the·a (al·thē′ə) Healer. [< Gk.]
Al·vi·na (al·vī′nə, al·vē′nə) Fem. of ALVIN.
Am·a·bel (am′ə·bel) Lovable. [< L] Also **Am′a·belle.**
Dim. **Mab** (mab).
A·man·da (ə·man′də) Lovable. [< L] Also *Fr.* **A·man-**
dine (à·män·dēn′). Dim. **Man′dy.**
Am·a·ran·tha (am′ə·ran′thə) Immortal. [< Gk.]
Am·a·ryl·lis (am′ə·ril′əs) Country sweetheart. [< L]
A·mel·ia (ə·mēl′yə, ə·mē′lē·ə; *Ital.* ä·mâ′lyä; *Sp.* ä·mä′lyä)
Industrious. [< Gmc.] Also *Fr.* **A·mé·lie** (à·mä·lē′). Dim.
Mil′lie, Mil′ly.
Am·i·ty (am′ə·tē) From the abstract noun.
A·my (ā′mē) Beloved. [< L]
An·as·ta·sia (an′ə·stā′zhə, -shə) Able to live again. [< L]
An·dre·a (an′drē·ə; *Ital.* än·drā′ä) Fem. of ANDREW.
An·ge·la (an′jə·lə) Angel. [< L] Also **An·ge·li·na** (an′-
jə·lē′nə, -lī′-), *Fr.* **An·gèle** (än·zhel′).
An·gel·i·ca (an·jel′i·kə; *Ital.* än·jâ′lē·kä) Angelic. [< Gk.]
Also *Fr.* **An·gé·lique** (än·zhä·lēk′).
A·ni·ta (ə·nē′tə) Dim. of ANNA. [< Sp.] Also **A·ni·tra**
(ə·nē′trə).
Ann (an) Grace. [< Hebrew] Also *Sp.* **A·na** (ä′nä).
Dims. **An′nie, Nan, Nan′cy, Ni′na.**
An·na (an′ə; *Ger.* ä′nä) Var. of HANNAH. Dim. **An′nie.**
An·na·bel (an′ə·bel) Gracefully fair. [< Hebrew] Also
An·na·bel·la (an′ə·bel′ə), **An′na·belle.**

Anne (an) Var. of ANN.
An·nette (ə·net′; *Fr.* à·net′) Dim. of ANNE. [< F]
An·the·a (an·thē′ə) Flowery. [< Gk.]
An·toi·nette (an′twə·net′; *Fr.* än·twà·net′) Fr. form of AN-
TONIA. Also *Ital.* **An·to·niet·ta** (än′tō·nyet′tä). Dims. **Net′-**
tie, Net′ty, To′ni.
An·to·ni·a (an·tō′nē·ə, an′tō·nē′ə) Fem. of ANTHONY. [<
L] Also *Ital., Sp.* **An·to·ni·na** (än′tō·nē′nä).
A·pril (ā′prəl) From the name of the month.
Ar·i·ad·ne (ar′ē·ad′nē) Most pure. [< Gk.]
Ar·lene (är·lēn′) Meaning and origin uncertain. Also **Ar-**
leen (är·lēn′), **Ar·line** (är·lēn′).
As·pa·sia (as·pā′zhə, -zhē·ə) Welcome. [< L < Gk.]
As·trid (as′trid) God's power. [< Scand.]
A·the·na (ə·thē′nə) From the name of the Greek goddess of
wisdom. Also **A·the·ne** (ə·thē′nē).
Au·drey (ô′drē) Noble might. [< OF < Gmc.]
Au·gus·ta (ô·gus′tə; *Ger.* ou·gŏŏs′tä; *Ital.* ou·gŏŏs′tä) Fem.
of AUGUSTUS. Also **Au·gus·ti·na** (ô′gəs·tē′nə), **Au·gus·tine**
(ô′gəs·tēn). Dims. **Gus′sie, Gus′ta.**
Au·rel·ia (ô·rēl′yə) Golden. [< L]
Au·ro·ra (ô·rôr′ə, ô·rō′rə) From the name of the Roman
goddess of the dawn.
A·va (ā′və) Meaning and origin uncertain.
Av·e·line (av′ə·lēn, -lin) Hazel. [< F]
A·vis (ā′vis) Bird. [< L]

Ba·bette (ba·bet′) Fr. dim. of ELIZABETH.
Bap·tis·ta (bap·tis′tə) Fem. of BAPTIST. Also *Ital.* **Bat·tis-**
ta (bät·tēs′tä).
Bar·ba·ra (bär′bər·ə, -brə) Foreign; strange. [< Gk.]
Dims. **Bab, Bab′bie, Babs, Barb, Bar′bie, Bob′bie.**
Bath·she·ba (bath·shē′bə, bath′shi·bə) Daughter of the
promise. [< Hebrew]
Be·a·ta (bē·ä′tə) Blessed. [< L]
Be·a·trice (bē′ə·tris; *Ital.* bä′ä·trē′chä) She who makes
happy. [< L] Also **Be·a·trix** (bē′ə·triks; *Ger.* bä·ä′triks), *Fr.*
Bé·a·trice or **Bé·a·trix** (bā·à·trēs′). Dims. **Bea, Bee, Trix,
Trix′ie, Trix′y.**
Beck·y (bek′ē) Dim. of REBECCA.
Be·lin·da (bə·lin′də) Serpent: title of an oracular priestess.
[< Gmc.] Dim. **Lin′da.**
Bel·la (bel′ə) Dim. of ARABELLA or ISABELLA. Also **Bell.**
Belle (bel) Beautiful. [< F]
Ben·e·dic·ta (ben′ə·dik′tə) Fem. of BENEDICT. Also *Ital.*
Be·ne·det·ta (bā′nā·dät′tä), *Sp.* **Be·ni·ta** (bā·nē′tä).
Ber·e·nice (ber′ə·nīs′) Victorious. [< Gk.]
Ber·na·dette (bûr′nə·det′, *Fr.* ber·nà·det′) Fem. of BER-
NARD. [< F]
Ber·nar·dine (bûr′nər·dēn) Fem. of BERNARD. [< F] Al-
so **Ber·nar·di·na** (bûr′nər·dē′nə).
Ber·nice (bər·nēs′, bûr′nis) Var. of BERENICE.
Ber·tha (bûr′thə; *Du.*, *Ger.*, *Sw.* ber′tä) Bright; famous.
[< Gmc.] Also *Fr.* **Berthe** (bert), *Ital., Sp.* **Ber·ta** (ber·tä).
Dims. **Ber′tie, Ber′ty.**
Ber·yl (ber′əl) From the name of the jewel.
Bess (bes) Dim. of ELIZABETH. Also **Bes′sie, Bes′sy.**
Beth (beth) Dim. of ELIZABETH.
Beth·el (beth′əl) House of God. [< Hebrew]
Bet·sy (bet′sē) Dim. of ELIZABETH.
Bet·ti·na (bə·tē′nə) Dim. of ELIZABETH. [< Ital.]
Bet·ty (bet′ē) Dim. of ELIZABETH. Also **Bet′te** (bet′ē, bet).
Beu·lah (byŏŏ′lə) Married. [< Hebrew] Also **Beu′la.**
Bev·er·ly (bev′ər·lē) From an English surname; orig. a
place name. Also **Bev′er·ley.** Dim. **Bev.**
Bid·dy (bid′ē) Dim. of BRIDGET.
Blanche (blanch, blänch; *Fr.* bläṅsh) White; shining. [<

F < Gmc.] Also **Blanch**, *Ital.* **Bian·ca** (byäng'kä), *Sp.* **Blan·ca** (bläng'kä).

Bon·ny (bon'ē) Good. [< F] Also **Bon'nie**.

Bren·da (bren'də) Sword or torch. [< Gmc.]

Bridg·et (brij'it) High; august. [< Celtic] Also **Brig·id** (brij'id, brē'id). Dims. **Bid'dy, Bri·die** (brī'dē).

Ca·mel·lia (kə·mēl'yə) From the name of the flower.

Ca·mil·la (kə·mil'ə; *Ital.* kä·mēl'lä) Attendant at a sacrifice. [< L] Also *Fr.* **Ca·mille** (kȧ·mēl'), *Sp.* **Ca·mi·la** (kä·mē'lä).

Can·dice (kan'dis) Radiant. [< L] Also **Can·da·ce** (kan'də·sē, kan·dā'sē).

Can·di·da (kan'di·də) White; pure. [< L]

Ca·ra (kär'ə) Loved one. [< L]

Car·la (kär'lə) Fem. of CARLO.

Car·lot·ta (kär·lot'ə; *Ital.* kär·lôt'tä) Ital. form of CHARLOTTE. Also *Sp.* **Car·lo·ta** (kär·lō'tä). Dims. **Lot'ta, Lot'tie, Lot'ty.**

Car·mel (kär'məl) Garden. [< Hebrew] Also **Car·mel·a** (kär·mel'ə). Dim. **Car·me·li·ta** (kär'mə·lē'tə).

Car·men (kär'mən) Song. [< L]

Car·ol (kar'əl) From CAROL, masc., var. of CHARLES. Also **Car·o·la** (kar'ə·lə), **Car'ole, Kar'ol.**

Car·o·line (kar'ə·līn, -lin; *Fr.* kȧ·rô·lēn') Fem. of CHARLES. Also **Car·o·lyn** (kar'ə·lin), **Car·o·li·na** (kar'ə·lī'nə; *Ital., Sp.* kä'rō·lē'nä). Dim. **Car'rie.**

Cas·san·dra (kə·san'drə) From the name of the Trojan prophetess in the *Iliad.* [< Gk.] Dims. **Cass, Cas'sie.**

Cath·er·ine (kath'ər·in, kath'rin, *Fr.* kȧ·trēn') Purity. [< Gk.] Also **Kath'er·ine, Cath·a·rine, Cath·a·ri·na** (kath'ə·rē'nə), *Ital., Sp.* **Ca·ta·ri·na** (kä'tä·rē'nä) or **Ca·te·ri·na** (kä'tä·rē'nä). Dims. **Cath'y, Kate, Kath'y, Kath'ie, Ka'tie, Kay, Kit, Kit'ty.**

Cath·leen (kath'lēn, kath·lēn') Var. of KATHLEEN.

Ce·cil·ia (si·sil'yə, -sēl'yə) Fem. of CECIL. Also **Ce·cel'ia, Ce·cile** (si·sēl'), **Cec·i·ly** (ses'ə·lē), *Fr.* **Cé·cile** (sā·sēl'). Dims. **Cis, Cis'sie, Cis'sy.**

Ce·leste (si·lest') Heavenly. [< F < L] Also **Ce·les·tine** (si·les'tin, sel'is·tīn), *Fr.* **Cé·les·tine** (sā·les·tēn').

Cel·ia (sēl'yə, sēl'ē·ə; *Ital.* chä'lyä) From the name of a Roman clan. Also *Fr.* **Cé·lie** (sā·lē').

Cha·ris·sa (kə·ris'ə) Love; grace. [< Gk.]

Char·i·ty (char'ə·tē) From the abstract noun. Dim. **Cher'ry.**

Char·lene (shär·lēn') Fem. of CHARLES.

Char·lotte (shär'lət; *Fr.* shȧr·lôt'; *Ger.* shär·lôt'ə) Fem. of CHARLES. [< F] Dims. **Car'ry, Lot'ta, Lot'tie, Lot'ty.**

Cher·yl (cher'əl) Meaning and origin uncertain.

Chlo·e (klō'ē) Bud; sprout. [< Gk.]

Chris·ta·bel (kris'tə·bel) The fair anointed. [< L] Also **Chris·ta·bel'la, Chris'ta·belle.**

Chris·ti·an·a (kris'tē·an'ə) Fem. of CHRISTIAN. Also *Ger.* **Chri·sti·a·ne** (kris'tē·ä'nə).

Chris·ti·na (kris·tē'nə) Var. of CHRISTIANA. Also **Chris·tine** (kris·tēn'; *Fr.* krēs·tēn'; *Ger.* kris·tē'nə). Dims. **Chris, Chris'sie, Chris'ta, Chris'tie, Ti'na.**

Cic·e·ly (sis'ə·lē) Var. of CECILIA.

Cin·dy (sin'dē) Dim. of LUCINDA.

Claire (klâr) Var. of CLARA. [< F] Also **Clare.**

Clar·a (klar'ə, klâr'ə; *Ger., Sp.* klä'rä) Bright; illustrious. [< L]

Clar·i·bel (klar'ə·bel) Brightly fair. [< L] Also **Clar'a·belle.**

Cla·rice (klə·rēs', klar'is) Derived from CLARA. Also **Cla·ris·sa** (klə·ris'ə), **Cla·risse** (klə·rēs').

Cla·rin·da (klə·rin'də) Derived from CLARA.

Clau·dette (klô·det'; *Fr.* klô·det') Fem. of CLAUDE. [< F]

Clau·di·a (klô'dē·ə) Fem. of *Claudius*, Lat. form of CLAUDE.

Clem·en·tine (klem'ən·tēn, -tīn) Fem. of CLEMENT. [< F]

Cle·o·pa·tra (klē'ə·pat'rə, -pä'trə, -pā'trə) Celebrated for her country. [< Gk.] Dim. **Cle·o** (klē'ō).

Cli·o (klī'ō, klē'ō) From the name of the Greek muse of history.

Clo·til·da (klō·til'də) Famous in war. [< Gmc.] Also **Clo·thil'da, Clo·thil'de**, *Fr.* **Clo·tilde** (klô·tēld').

Co·lette (kō·let'; *Fr.* kô·let') Fem. of NICHOLAS. [< F]

Col·leen (kol'ēn, ko·lēn') Girl. [< Irish]

Con·stance (kon'stəns, *Fr.* kôṅ·stäṅs') Constant; firm. [< L] Dims. **Con'nie, Con'ny.**

Con·sue·lo (kən·swā'lō; *Sp.* kōn·swä'lō) Consolation. [< Sp.]

Co·ra (kôr'ə, kō'rə) Maiden. [< Gk.]

Cor·del·ia (kôr·dēl'yə, -dēl'ē·ə) Meaning uncertain. [< L]

Co·rin·na (kə·rin'ə) Maiden. [< Gk.] Also **Co·rinne** (kə·rin', -rēn'; *Fr.* kô·rēn').

Cor·nel·ia (kôr·nēl'yə, -nēl'ē·ə) Fem. of CORNELIUS. [< L]

Cris·ti·na (krēs·tē'nä) Ital. and Sp. form of CHRISTINA.

Crys·tal (kris'təl) From the common noun.

Cyn·thi·a (sin'thē·ə) Of Mount Cynthius: an epithet of the Greek goddess Artemis; poetically, the moon.

Dag·mar (dag'mär) Bright day. [< Dan.]

Dai·sy (dā'zē) From the name of the flower.

Dale (dāl) From the common noun.

Daph·ne (daf'nē) Laurel. [< Gk.]

Dar·leen (där·lēn') Beloved. [OE] Also **Dar·lene', Dar·line'.**

Dawn (dôn) From the common noun.

Deb·o·rah (deb'ər·ə, deb'rə) Queen bee. [< Hebrew] Dims. **Deb, Deb'by.**

Deir·dre (dir'drə) From the name of a heroine of Irish myth.

Del·ia (dēl'yə) Of Delos: an epithet of the Greek goddess Artemis. [< Gk.]

De·li·lah (di·lī'lə) Delicate; languid. [< Hebrew]

Del·la (del'ə) Var. of ADELA.

Del·phin·i·a (del·fin'ē·ə) Of Delphi. [< Gk.] Also *Fr.* **Del·phine** (del·fēn').

De·nise (də·nēz', -nēs') Fem. of *Denis*, Fr. form of DENNIS.

Des·i·ree (dez'ə·rē) Desired. [< F] Also *Fr.* **Dé·si·rée** (dā·zē·rā').

Di·an·a (dī·an'ə) From the name of the Roman goddess of the moon. Also **Di·ane** (dī·an';, *Fr.* dyȧn). Dim. **Di** (dī).

Di·nah (dī'nə) Judged. [< Hebrew]

Do·lo·res (də·lôr'is, -lō'ris; *Sp.* dō·lō'rās) Our Lady of Sorrows: a title of the Virgin Mary. [< Sp.] Dim. **Lo·la** (lō'lə).

Dom·i·nique (dom'ə·nēk; *Fr.* dô·mē·nēk') Fr. fem. of DOMINIC. Also **Dom·i·ni·ca** (dom'ə·nē'kə, də·min'ə·kə).

Don·na (don'ə) Lady. [< Ital.]

Do·ra (dôr'ə, dō'rə) Dim. of DOROTHY, EUDORA, or THEODORA.

Dor·cas (dôr'kəs) Gazelle. [< Gk.]

Do·reen (dô·rēn', dôr'ēn, dō-) Irish dim. of DORA.

Do·rin·da (dô·rin'də) Gift. [< Gk.]

Dor·is (dôr'is, dor'-) Dorian woman. [< Gk.]

Dor·o·thy (dôr'ə·thē, dor'-) Gift of God. [< Gk.] Also **Dor·o·the·a** (dôr'ə·thē'ə, dor'-; *Ger.* dō'rō·tā'ä), *Fr.* **Do·ro·thée** (dô·rô·tā'). Dims. **Doll, Dol'lie, Dol'ly, Do'ra, Dot'Dot'ty.**

Dru·sil·la (drōō·sil'ə) She who strengthens. [< L] Also **Dru·cil'la.**

E·dith (ē'dith) Prosperous in war. [OE] Also *Lat.* **Ed·i·tha** (ed'i·thə, ē'di·thə). Dim. **E·die** or **Ea·die** (ē'dē).

Ed·na (ed'nə) Rejuvenation. [< Hebrew]

Ed·wi·na (ed·wē'nə, -win'ə) Fem. of EDWIN.

Ef·fie (ef'ē) Dim. of EUPHEMIA.

Ei·leen (ī·lēn') Irish form of HELEN.

E·ka·te·ri·na (yə·kȧ·tyi·ryē'nə) Russ. form of CATHERINE.

E·laine (i·lān', ē·lān') Var. of HELEN. [< OF] Also **E·layne'.**

El·ber·ta (el·bûr'tə) Fem. of ELBERT.

El·ea·nor (el'ə·nər, -nôr) Var. of HELEN. [< F] Also **El'i·nor, El·ea·no·ra** (el'ə·nôr'ə, -nō'rə, el'ē·ə-), *Fr.* **É·lé·o·nore** (ā·lā·ô·nôr'), *Ger.* **E·le·o·no·re** (ā'lā·ō·nō'rə), *Ital.* **E·le·o·no·ra** (ā'lā·ō·nō'rä). Dims. **El'la, El'lie, Nell, Nel'lie, Nel'ly.**

E·lec·tra (i·lek'trə) Shining; golden-haired. [< Gk.] Also **E·lek'tra.**

E·le·na (el'ə·nə, ə·lē'nə; *Ital.* â'lä·nä) Var. of HELEN. [< Ital.]

E·li·za (i·lī'zə) Dim. of ELIZABETH. Also *Fr.* **É·lise** (ā·lēz').

E·liz·a·beth (i·liz'ə·bəth) Consecrated to God. [< Hebrew] Also **E·lis·a·beth** (i·liz'ə·bəth; *Ger.* ā·lē'zä·bet), *Fr.* **É·li·sa·beth** (ā·lē·zȧ·bet'), *Ital.* **E·li·sa·bet·ta** (ā·lē'zä·bät'tä). Dims. **Bess, Bes'sie, Beth, Bet'sy, Bet'te, Bet'ty, El'sa, El'sie, Lib'by, Li'sa, Liz, Liz'beth, Liz'zie, Liz'zy.**

El·la (el'ə) Dim. of ELEANOR. Also **El'lie.**

El·len (el'ən) Var. of HELEN.

E·lo·i·sa (el'ō·ē'zä) Ital. form of LOUISE.

E·lo·ise (el'ō·ēz', el'ō·ēz) Var. of LOUISE. [< F]

El·sa (el'sə; *Ger.* el'zä) Dim. of ELIZABETH. Also **El·sie** (el'sē).

El·speth (el'spəth) Scot. form of ELIZABETH.

El·va (el'və) Elf. [< Gmc.]

El·vi·ra (el·vī'rə, -vir'ə) Elf ruler. [< Sp. < Gmc.]

Em·e·line (em'ə·līn, -lēn) Derived from EMILY. Also **Em'me·line.**

Em·i·ly (em'ə·lē) Fem. of EMIL. Also **Em'i·lie**, *Fr.* **É·mi·lie** (ā·mē·lē'), *Ger.* **E·mi·li·e** (e·mē'lē·ə), *Ital., Sp.* **E·mi·lia** (ā·mē'lyä). Dim. **Em.**

Em·ma (em'ə) Grandmother. [< Gmc.] Dims. **Em, Em'mie.**

E·nid (ē'nid) Chastity; purity. [< Celtic]

Er·i·ca (er'i·kə) Fem. of ERIC. Also **Er'i·ka.**

Er·ma (ûr'mə) Dim. of ERMENGARDE.

Er·men·garde (ûr'mən·gärd) Great guardian. [< Gmc.]

Er·men·trude (ûr'mən·trōōd) Great strength. [< Gmc.]

Er·nes·tine (ûr'nəs·tēn) Fem. of ERNEST.

Es·me·ral·da (ez'mə·ral'də) Emerald. [< Sp.]

Es·telle (es·tel') Star. [< L] Also **Es·tel·la** (es·tel'ə).

Es·ther (es'tər) Star. [< Pers.] Dims. **Es'sie, Het'ty.**

Eth·el (eth'əl) Noble. [< Gmc.]

Et·ta (et/ə)   Dim. of HENRIETTA.
Eu·do·ra (yōō-dôr/ə, -dō/rə)   Good gift.   [< Gk.]
Eu·ge·ni·a (yōō-jē/nē-ə, -jēn/yə)   Fem. of EUGENE.   Also **Eu·ge·nie** (yōō-jē/nē), *Fr.* **Eu·gé·nie** (œ·zhä·nē/).   Dims. **Gene, Ge/nie.**
Eu·la·li·a (yōō-lā/lē-ə, -lāl/yə)   Fair speech.   [< Gk.]   Also **Eu·la·lie** (yōō/lə·lē; *Fr.* œ·là·lē/).
Eu·nice (yōō/nis; *Lat.* yōō·nī/sē)   Good victory.   [< Gk.]
Eu·phe·mi·a (yōō-fē/mē-ə)   Of good repute.   [< Gk.]   Also *Fr.* **Eu·phé·mie** (œ·fä·mē/).   Dims. **Ef·fie** (ef/ē), **Phe/mie.**
E·va (ē/və; *Ger., Ital., Sp.* ä/vä)   Var. of EVE.   [< L]
E·van·ge·line (i·van/jə·lin, -līn, -lēn)   Bearer of glad tidings.   [< Gk.]
Eve (ēv; *Fr.* ev)   Life.   [< Hebrew]
Ev·e·lyn (ev/ə·lin; *Brit.* ēv/lin)   Hazelnut.   [< L]   Also **Ev·e·li·na** (ev/ə·lī/nə, -lē/-).
E·vi·ta (ā·vē/tä)   Sp. dim. of EVA.

Faith (fāth)   From the abstract noun.   Dim. **Fay.**
Fan·ny (fan/ē)   Dim. of FRANCES.   Also **Fan/nie.**
Faus·ti·na (fôs·tī/nə, -tē/-)   Lucky.   [< L]   Also **Faus·tine** (fôs·tēn/; *Fr.* fôs·tēn/).
Fawn (fôn)   From the name of the animal.
Fay (fā)   Fairy or faith.   [OF]   Also **Fae, Faye.**
Fe·li·cia (fə·lish/ə, -lish/ē-ə, -lē/shə)   Happy.   [< L]   Also **Fe·lice** (fə·lēs/), **Fe·lic/i·ty** (-lis/ə·tē).
Fern (fûrn)   From the common noun.
Fer·nan·da (fer·nän/dä)   Fem. of *Fernando*, Sp. form of FERDINAND.
Fi·del·ia (fi·dēl/yə, -dē/lē-ə)   Faithful.   [< L]
Fi·o·na (fē·ō/nə)   Fair or white.   [< Celtic]
Fla·vi·a (flā/vē-ə)   Blonde.   [< L]
Flo·ra (flôr/ə, flō/rə)   Flower.   [< L]
Flor·ence (flôr/əns, flor/-; *Fr.* flō·räns/)   Blooming.   [< L]   Dims. **Flo** (flō), **Flor·rie** (flôr/ē, flor/ē), **Flos·sie** (flos/ē).
Fran·ces (fran/sis, frän/-)   Fem. of FRANCIS.   Also *Fr.* **Fran·çoise** (frän·swäz/) or **Fran·cisque** (frän·sēsk/), *Ital.* **Fran·ces·ca** (frän·chäs/kä).   Dims. **Fan/nie, Fan/ny, Fran, Fran/cie, Frank, Fran/nie.**
Fran·cine (fran·sēn/)   Derived from FRANCES.   Also **Fran·cene/.**
Fred·er·i·ca (fred/ə·rē/kə, fred·rē/kə)   Fem. of FREDERICK.   Dim. **Fred/die.**
Frie·da (frē/də)   Peace.   [< G]   Also **Fre/da.**

Ga·bri·elle (gā/brē·el/, gab/rē-; *Fr.* gà·brē·el/)   Fem. of GABRIEL.   Also **Ga·bri·el·la** (gā/brē·el/ə).   Dim. **Ga·by** (gä·bē/).
Gail (gāl)   Short for ABIGAIL.   Also **Gale.**
Gay (gā)   From the adjective.
Gen·e·vieve (jen/ə·vēv, jen/ə·vēv/)   White wave.   [< F < Celtic]   Also *Fr.* **Ge·ne·viève** (zhen·vyev/).
Ge·nev·ra (ji·nev/rə)   Var. of GUINEVERE.   [< Ital.]   Also **Ge·ne·va** (ji·nē/və).
Geor·gia (jôr/jə)   Fem. of GEORGE.
Geor·gi·an·a (jôr/jē·an/ə)   Fem. of GEORGE.   Also **Geor·gi·na** (jôr·jē/nə), *Fr.* **Geor·gine** (zhôr·zhēn/) or **Geor·gette** (zhôr·zhet/).
Ger·al·dine (jer/əl·dēn)   Fem. of GERALD.   Dims. **Ger/ry, Jer/ry.**
Ger·maine (jər·mān/)   German.   [< F < L]
Ger·trude (gûr/trōōd, *Fr.* zher·trüd/)   Spear maid.   [< Gmc.]   Also *Ger.* **Ger·trud** (ger/trōōt).   Dims. **Ger/tie, Ger/ty, Tru/da, Tru/dy.**
Gil·ber·ta (gil·bûr/tə)   Fem. of GILBERT.   Also **Gil·ber·tine** (gil/bər·tēn), *Fr.* **Gil·berte** (zhēl·bert/).
Gil·da (gil/də)   Servant of God.   [< Celtic]
Gil·li·an (jil/ē·ən, jil/yən)   Var. of JULIANA.
Gi·nev·ra (ji·nev/rə)   Var. of GUINEVERE.   [< Ital.]
Gin·ger (jin/jer)   From the plant name.
Gio·van·na (jō·vän/nä)   Fem. of *Giovanni*, Ital. form of JOHN.
Gi·sele (zhē·zel/)   Pledge or hostage.   [< F < Gmc.]   Also **Gi·selle/.**
Giu·lia (jōō/lyä)   Ital. form of JULIA.
Glad·ys (glad/is)   Welsh fem. form of CLAUDIUS.
Glen·na (glen/ə)   Fem. of GLENN.   Also **Glen·nis** (glen/is), **Glyn·is** (glin/is).
Glo·ri·a (glôr/ē-ə, glō/rē-ə)   Glory.   [< L]
Grace (grās)   Grace; favor.   [< L]   Also **Gra·ci·a** or **Gra·ti·a** (grā/shē-ə, -shə).
Gret·a (gret/ə, grē/tə; *Ger.* grā/tə)   Dim. of MARGARET.   [< G]   Also **Gre·tel** or **Gre·thel** (grā/təl).
Gretch·en (grech/ən; *Ger.* grāt/khən)   Dim. of MARGARET.   [< G]
Gri·sel·da (gri·zel/də)   Stony or unbeatable heroine.   [< Gmc.]   Also **Gris·sel** (gris/əl), **Griz·el** (griz/əl).
Gus·sie (gus/ē)   Dim. of AUGUSTA.   Also **Gus·ta** (gus/tə).
Gwen·do·lyn (gwen/də·lin)   White-browed.   [< Celtic]   Also **Gwen/do·len, Gwen/do·line** (-lin, -lēn).   Dims. **Gwen, Gwenn, Wen·dy** (wen/dē).

Gwen·eth (gwen/ith)   Fair or blessed.   [< Celtic]   Also **Gwen/ith, Gwyn·eth** (gwin/ith), **Gyn·eth** (gin/ith).
Gwyn (gwin)   Fair or white.   [< Celtic]   Also **Gwynne.**

Han·nah (han/ə)   Grace.   [< Hebrew]   Also **Han/na.**
Har·ri·et (har/ē-ət)   Fem. of HARRY.   Dims. **Hat/tie, Hat/ty.**
Ha·zel (hā/zəl)   From the plant name.
Heath·er (heth/ər)   From the plant name.
Hed·da (hed/ə)   War.   [< Gmc.]
Hed·wig (hed/wig)   War.   [< Gmc.]
Hel·en (hel/ən)   Light; a torch.   [< Gk.]   Also *Fr.* **Hé·lène** (ā·len/).   Dims. **Nell, Nel/lie, Nel/ly.**
Hel·e·na (hel/ə·nə)   Var. of HELEN.   Dim. **Le·na** (lē/nə).
Hel·ga (hel/gə)   Holy.   [< Gmc.]
Hé·lo·ïse (ā·lō·ēz/)   Fr. form of ELOISE.
Hen·ri·et·ta (hen/rē·et/ə)   Fem. of HENRY.   Also *Fr.* **Hen·ri·ette** (än·ryet/).   Dims. **Et/ta, Et/tie, Hat/tie, Hat/ty, Het/ty, Net/tie, Ret/ta.**
Heph·zi·bah (hep/zə·bə)   She who is my delight.   [< Hebrew]
Her·mi·o·ne (hər·mī/ə·nē)   Fem. of HERMES.
Hes·ter (hes/tər)   Var. of ESTHER.   Also **Hes/ther.**   Dim. **Het/ty.**
Het·ty (het/ē)   Dim. of ESTHER, HENRIETTA, or HESTER.
Hil·a·ry (hil/ər·ē)   Joyful.   [< L]
Hil·da (hil/də)   Battle maiden.   [OE]
Hil·de·garde (hil/də·gärd)   Guardian battle maiden.   [< Gmc.]   Also **Hil/de·gard.**
Hol·ly (hol/ē)   From the plant name.
Ho·no·ra (hō·nôr/ə, -nō/rə)   Honor.   [< L]   Also **Ho·no·ri·a** (hō·nôr/ē-ə, -nō/rē-ə)   Dims. **No/ra, No/rah.**
Hope (hōp)   From the abstract noun.
Hor·tense (hôr/tens; *Fr.* ôr·täns/)   Gardener: from the name of a Roman clan.   [<·F < L]   Also *Lat.* **Hor·ten·si·a** (hôr·ten/shē-ə).

I·da (ī/də)   Happy; godlike.   [< Gmc.]
I·lo·na (i·lō/nə)   Radiantly beautiful.   [< Hung. < Gk.]
Il·se (il/sə; *Ger.* il/zə)   Dim. of ELIZABETH.   [< G]
Im·o·gene (im/ə·jēn)   Meaning and origin uncertain.   Also **Im·o·gen** (im/ə·jən).
I·na (ī/nə)   From Lat. suffix for fem. names.
I·nez (ī/nez, ē/nez; *Sp.* ē·nāth/)   Var. of AGNES   [< Sp. & Pg.]
In·grid (ing/grid)   Daughter of Ing (a god in Gmc. mythology).   [< Gmc.]   Also **In·ga** (ing/gə).
I·rene (ī·rēn/)   Peace.   [< Gk.]
I·ris (ī/ris)   Rainbow   [< Gk.], or from the name of the flower.
Ir·ma (ûr/mə)   Var. of ERMA.
Is·a·bel (iz/ə·bel; *Sp.* ē/sä·bel/)   Oath of Baal.   [< Hebrew]   Also **Is·a·bel·la** (iz/ə·bel/ə; *Ital.* ē/zä·bel/lä), **Is·a·belle** (iz/ə·bel; *Fr.* ē·zà·bel/), **Is/o·bel,** *Fr.* **I·sa·beau** (ē·zà·bō/).   Dims. **Bell, Bel/la, Belle.**
Is·a·do·ra (iz/ə·dôr/ə, -dō/rə)   Fem. of ISIDORE.
I·vy (ī/vē)   From the plant name.

Jac·que·line (jak/wə·lin, -lēn, jak/ə-; *Fr.* zhä·klēn/)   Fem. of *Jacques,* Fr. form of JACOB.   Dim. **Jac/kie.**
Jane (jān)   Var. of JOAN.   [< OF]
Jan·et (jan/it, jə·net/)   Dim. of JANE.
Jan·ice (jan/is)   Var. of JANE.
Jas·mine (jaz/min, jas/-)   From the name of the flower.
Jean (jēn)   Var. of JOAN.   [< F]
Jeanne (jēn, *Fr.* zhän)   Fr. form of JOAN.
Jean·nette (jə·net/)   Dim. of JEANNE.
Je·mi·ma (jə·mī/mə)   Dove.   [< Hebrew]
Jen·ni·fer (jen/ə·fər)   Var of GUINEVERE.   Dims. **Jen/ny, Jin/ny.**
Jer·ry (jer/ē)   Dim. of GERALDINE.
Jes·si·ca (jes/i·kə)   Fem. of JESSE.   Dims. **Jess, Jes/sie, Jes/sy.**
Jew·el (jōō/əl)   From the common noun.
Jill (jil)   Short for JULIA.
Jo (jō)   Dim. of JOSEPHINE.
Joan (jōn, jō·an/)   Fem. of JOHN.   Also **Jo·an·na** (jō·an/ə), **Jo·anne** (jō·an/).
Joc·e·lyn (jos/ə·lin)   Playful; merry.   [< L]   Also **Joc/e·lin, Joc/e·line** (-lin).
Jo·han·na (jō·han/ə; *Ger.* yō·hän/ä)   Ger. form of JOAN.
Jo·se·pha (jō·sē/fə)   Var. of JOSEPHINE.
Jo·se·phine (jō/sə·fēn, -zə-)   Fem. of JOSEPH.   [< F]   Dims. **Jo, Jo/sie, Jo/zy.**
Joy (joi)   From the abstract noun.
Joyce (jois)   Joyful.   [< L]
Jua·na (wä/nə; *Sp.* hwä/nä)   Fem. of *Juan,* Sp. form of JOHN.
Jua·ni·ta (wä·nē/tə; *Sp.* hwä·nē/tä)   Sp. dim. of JUANA.
Ju·dith (jōō/dith)   Praised.   [< Hebrew]   Dim. **Ju/dy.**
Ju·li·a (jōōl/yə)   Fem. of JULIUS.   Also **Ju·lie** (jōō/lē; *Fr.* zhü·lē/).

Ju·li·an·a (jōō'lē·an'ə, -ä'nə)   Fem. of JULIAN.   Also *Fr.* **Ju·li·enne** (zhü·lyen').
Ju·li·et (jōō'lē·et, jōō'lē·et')   Dim. of JULIA.
June (jōōn)   From the name of the month.
Jus·ti·na (jus·tī'nə, -tē'-)   Fem. of JUSTIN.   Also **Jus·tine** (jus·tēn'; *Fr.* zhüs·tēn').

Kar·en (kâr'ən; *Dan., Norw.* kä'rən)   Var. of CATHERINE. [< Dan. & Norw.]
Kate (kāt)   Dim. of CATHERINE.   Also **Ka'tie**.
Kath·a·rine (kath'ə·rin, kath'rin)   Var. of CATHERINE.   Also **Kath'er·ine, Kath'ryn.**
Kath·leen (kath'lēn, kath·lēn')   Irish form of CATHERINE.
Kath·y (kath'ē)   Dim. of CATHERINE.
Ka·tri·na (kə·trē'nə)   Var. of CATHERINE.   Also **Kat·rine** (kat'rin, -rēn).   Dim. **Tri·na** (trē'nə).
Kay (kā)   Dim. of CATHERINE.
Kir·sten (kûr'stən; *Norw.* khish'tən, khir'stən)   Norw. form of CHRISTINE.
Kit·ty (kit'ē)   Dim. of CATHERINE.   Also **Kit**.
Kla·ra (klä'rä)   Ger. form of CLARA.

Lau·ra (lôr'ə)   Laurel. [< L]   Also *Fr.* **Laure** (lôr).   Dims. **Lau'rie, Lol'ly.**
Lau·ret·ta (lô·ret'ə)   Dim. of LAURA.   Also **Lau·rette'.**
Lau·rin·da (lô·rin'də)   Derived from LAURA.
La·verne (lə·vûrn')   From the name of the Roman goddess of spring and grain.
La·vin·i·a (lə·vin'ē·ə)   Purified. [< L]
Le·ah (lē'ə)   Gazelle. [< Hebrew]   Also **Le'a**.
Lei·la (lē'lä)   Dark night or dark beauty. [< Arabic]
Le·na (lē'nə)   Dim. of HELENA or MAGDALENE.
Le·no·ra (lə·nôr'ə, -nō'rə)   Var. of ELEANOR.   Also **Le·nore** (lə·nôr').
Le·o·na (lē·ō'nə)   Fem. of LEO and LEON.   Also *Fr.* **Lé·o·nie** (lā·ō·nē').
Le·o·ra (lē·ôr'ə, -ō'rə)   Var. of LEONORA.
Les·lie (les'lē, lez'-)   From LESLIE, masc.   Also **Les'ley**.
Le·ti·ti·a (li·tish'ə)   Joy. [< L]   Dim. **Let·ty** (let'ē).
Lib·by (lib'ē)   Dim. of ELIZABETH.
Li·la (lī'lə, lē'-)   Var. of LILIAN.
Lil·i·an (lil'ē·ən, lil'yən)   Lily. [< L]   Also **Lil'li·an**.   Dims. **Lil, Lil'ly, Lil'y.**
Lil·y (lil'ē)   From the name of the flower; also, dim. of LILIAN.
Lin·da (lin'də)   Pretty [< Sp.], or short for BELINDA or MELINDA.
Li·sa (lī'zə, lē'-)   Dim. of ELIZABETH.   Also **Li'za**, *Ger.* **Li·se** (lē'zə).
Li·sette (lē·zet')   Fr. dim. of ELIZABETH.   Also **Li·zette'.**
Liz·beth (liz'bəth)   Dim. of ELIZABETH.
Liz·zie (liz'ē)   Dim. of ELIZABETH.   Also **Liz'zy, Liz.**
Lo·is (lō'is)   Desirable. [< Gk.]
Lo·la (lō'lə; *Sp.* lō'lä)   Dim. of DOLORES. [< Sp.]   Dim. **Lo·li·ta** (lō·lē'tə; *Sp.* lō·lē'tä).
Lor·ene (lô·rēn')   Var. of LAURA.   Also **Laur·een', Laur·ene', Lor·een'.**
Lor·et·ta (lô·ret'ə, lō-)   Dim. of LAURA.   Also **Lor·ette** (lô·ret').
Lo·rin·da (lô·rin'də, lə-)   Var. of LAURINDA.
Lor·na (lôr'nə)   Lost. [OE]
Lor·raine (lə·rān')   Var. of LAURA.
Lot·tie (lot'ē)   Dim. of CHARLOTTE.   Also **Lot'ta, Lot'ty.**
Lou·el·la (lōō·el'ə)   Var. of LUELLA.
Lou·ise (lōō·ēz')   Fem. of LOUIS. [< F]   Also **Lou·i·sa** (lōō·ē'zə).   Dims. **Lou, Lou'ie, Lu, Lu'lu.**
Lu·cia (lōō'shə; *Ital.* lōō·chē'ä)   Fem. of LUCIUS.
Lu·cille (lōō·sēl')   Var. of LUCIA. [< F]   Also **Lu·cile'.**
Lu·cin·da (lōō·sin'də)   Derived from LUCY.   Dim. **Cin·dy** (sin'dē).
Lu·cre·tia (lōō·krē'shə, -shē·ə)   Fem. of LUCRETIUS.   Also *Fr.* **Lu·crèce** (lü·kres'), *Ital.* **Lu·cre·zia** (lōō·krā'tsyä).
Lu·cy (lōō'sē)   Var. of LUCIA.   Also *Fr.* **Lu·cie** (lü·sē').
Lu·el·la (lōō·el'ə)   Meaning and origin uncertain.   Also **Lou·el'la.**
Lu·i·sa (lōō·ē'zä)   Ital. form of LOUISA.   Also *Ger.* **Lu·i·se** (lōō·ē'zə).
Lu·lu (lōō'lōō)   Dim. of LOUISE.
Lyd·i·a (lid'ē·ə)   She of Lydia. [< Gk.]

Ma·bel (mā'bəl)   Short for AMABEL.   Dim. **Mab** (mab).
Mad·e·leine (mad'ə·lin, -lān, *Fr.* mà·dlen')   Var. of MAGDALENE. [< F]   Also **Mad·e·line** (mad'ə·lin, -lēn).
Madge (madj)   Dim. of MARGARET.
Mae (mā)   Var. of MAY.
Mag (mag)   Dim. of MARGARET.   Also **Mag'gie.**
Mag·da·lene (mag'də·lēn, mag'də·lē'nē)   Woman of Magdala. [< Hebrew]   Also **Mag·da·len** (mag'də·lən), **Mag·da·le·na** (mag'də·lē'nə; *Sp.* mäg'thä·lā'nä).   Dims. **Le·na** (lē'nə), **Mag·da** (mag'də).
Mai·sie (mā'zē)   Dim. of MARGARET. [< Scot.]

Mal·vi·na (mal·vī'nə, -vē'-)   Meaning and origin uncertain.
Ma·mie (mā'mē)   Dim. of MARGARET.
Man·dy (man'dē)   Dim. of AMANDA.
Mar·cel·la (mär·sel'ə)   Fem. of MARCELLUS.   Also *Fr.* **Mar·celle** (mär·sel').
Mar·cia (mär'shə)   Fem. of *Marcius*, var. of MARCUS.
Mar·ga·ret (mär'gə·rit, mär'grit)   Pearl. [< Gk.]   Also *Ger.* **Mar·ga·re·te** (mär'gä·rā'tə), *Ital.* **Mar·ghe·ri·ta** (mär'gä·rē'tä), *Ital., Sp.* **Mar·ga·ri·ta** (mär'gä·rē'tä).   Dims. **Gret'a, Gretch'en, Madge, Mag, Mag'gie, Ma'mie, Meg, Me'ta, Peg, Peg'gy, Ri'ta.**
Marge (märj)   Dim. of MARJORIE.   Also **Mar'gie, Marj.**
Mar·ger·y (mär'jər·ē)   Var. of MARGARET.
Mar·got (mär'gō; *Fr.* màr·gō')   Var. of MARGARET. [< F]   Also **Mar'go.**
Mar·gue·rite (mär'gə·rēt'; *Fr.* mär·gə·rēt')   Var. of MARGARET. [< F]
Ma·ri·a (mə·rī'ə, -rē'ə; *Ger., Ital.* mä·rē'ä)   Var. of MARY. [< L]   Also *Sp.* **Ma·rí·a** (mä·rē'ä).
Mar·i·an (mar'ē·ən, mâr'-)   Var. of MARION.
Mar·i·anne (mar'ē·an')   From MARY and ANNE.   Also **Mar·i·an·na** (mâr'ē·an'ə).
Ma·rie (mə·rē'; *Fr.* mà·rē')   Var. of MARY. [< F]
Mar·i·et·ta (mâr'ē·et'ə, mar'-)   Dim. of MARIA.
Mar·i·gold (mar'ə·gōld, mâr'-)   From the name of the flower.
Mar·i·lyn (mar'ə·lin, mâr'-)   Var. of MARY.
Mar·i·on (mar'ē·ən, mâr'-)   Var. of MARY.
Mar·jo·rie (mär'jər·ē)   Var. of MARGARET.   Also **Mar'jo·ry.**   Dims. **Marge, Mar'gie, Marj.**
Mar·lene (mär·lēn'; *Ger.* mär·lā'nə)   Var. of MAGDALENE.
Mar·sha (mär'shə)   Var. of MARCIA.
Mar·tha (mär'thə)   Lady. [< Aramaic]   Also *Fr.* **Marthe** (màrt), *Ital., Sp.* **Mar·ta** (mär'tä).   Dims. **Mar'ty, Mat'tie, Mat'ty.**
Mar·y (mâr'ē)   Meaning uncertain. [< Hebrew]   Dims. **May, Min'nie, Moll'y, Pol'ly.**
Ma·til·da (mə·til'də)   Mighty battle maiden. [< Gmc.]   Also **Ma·thil·da** (mə·til'də), *Ger.* **Ma·thil·de** (mä·til'də).   Dims. **Mat'tie, Mat'ty, Pat'ty, Til'da, Til'lie, Til'ly.**
Maud (môd)   Contr. of MAGDALENE.   Also **Maude.**
Mau·ra (môr'ə)   Irish form of MARY.   Also **Maur·ya** (môr'yə).
Mau·reen (mô·rēn')   Dim. of MAURA.
Ma·vis (mā'vis)   From the name of the bird, or the Irish fairy queen Maeve or Mab.
Max·ine (mak·sēn', mak'sēn)   Fem. of MAX. [< F]
May (mā)   Dim. of MARY.
Meg (meg)   Dim. of MARGARET.
Mel·a·nie (mel'ə·nē)   Black. [< Gk.]
Me·lin·da (mə·lin'də)   Var. of BELINDA.
Me·lis·sa (mə·lis'ə)   Bee. [< Gk.]
Mer·ce·des (mər·sā'dēz, -sē'-, mûr'sə·dēz; *Sp.* mer·thā'thäs)   Mercies. [< Sp.]
Mer·cy (mûr'sē)   From the abstract noun.
Me·ta (mā'tə, mē'-)   Dim. of MARGARET. [< G]
Mi·gnon (min'yon, *Fr.* mē·nyôn')   Dainty. [< F]
Mil·dred (mil'drid)   Moderate power. [OE]   Dims. **Mil'lie, Mil'ly.**
Mil·li·cent (mil'ə·sənt)   Power to work. [< Gmc.]   Also **Mil'i·cent.**
Mi·mi (mē'mē)   Fr. dim. of WILHELMINA.
Mi·na (mē'nə)   Dim. of WILHELMINA.
Mi·ner·va (mi·nûr'və)   From the name of the Roman goddess of wisdom.
Min·na (min'ə)   Dim. of WILHELMINA.
Min·nie (min'ē)   Memory or love [< Gmc.]; also, dim. of MARY.
Mi·ran·da (mi·ran'də)   Admirable. [< L]
Mir·i·am (mir'ē·əm)   Var. of MARY. [< Hebrew]
Moi·ra (moi'rə)   Var. of MAURA.
Mol·ly (mol'ē)   Dim. of MARY.   Also **Moll.**
Mo·na (mō'nə)   Noble. [< Irish]
Mon·i·ca (mon'ə·kə)   Adviser. [< L]
Mu·ri·el (myŏŏr'ē·əl)   Myrrh. [< Gk.]
Myr·na (mûr'nə)   Meaning and origin uncertain.
Myr·tle (mûrt'l)   From the plant name.

Na·dine (nā·dēn', nə-; *Fr.* nà·dēn')   Hope. [< F < Russ.]
Nan (nan)   Dim. of ANN.
Nan·cy (nan'sē)   Dim. of ANN.
Nan·nette (na·net')   Dim. of ANN. [< F]   Also **Na·nette'.**
Na·o·mi (nā·ō'mē, nā'ō·mē)   Pleasant. [< Hebrew]
Nat·a·lie (nat'ə·lē)   Christmas child. [< L]   Also *Russ.* **Na·ta·sha** (nä·tä'shä).
Nell (nel)   Dim. of ELEANOR, ELLEN, or HELEN.   Also **Nel'lie, Nel'ly.**
Net·tie (net'ē)   Dim. of ANTOINETTE, HENRIETTA, or JEANNETTE.   Also **Net'ty.**
Ni·cole (ni·kōl'; *Fr.* nē·kōl')   Fem. of *Nicolas*, Fr. form of NICHOLAS.
Ni·na (nī'nə, nē'-)   Dim. of ANN. [< Russ.]

Ni·ta (nē′tə; *Sp.* nē′tä) Dim. of JUANITA. [< Sp.]
No·na (nō′nə) Ninth. [< L]
No·ra (nôr′ə, nō′rə) Dim. of ELEANOR, HONORA, LEONORA. Also **No′rah.**
No·reen (nôr′ēn, nô·rēn′) Irish dim. of NORA.
Nor·ma (nôr′mə) Pattern. [< L]

Oc·ta·vi·a (ok·tā′vē·ə) Fem. of OCTAVIUS.
Ol·ga (ol′gə) Holy. [< Russ. < Scand.]
O·live (ol′iv) Var. of OLIVIA.
O·liv·i·a (ō·liv′ē·ə) She of the olive tree: prob. an epithet of the goddess Athena. [< L] Dims. **Liv′i·a, Liv′ie.**
O·lym·pi·a (ō·lim′pē·ə) She of Olympus. [< L < Gk.]
O·pal (ō′pəl) From the name of the gem.
O·phel·ia (ō·fēl′yə) Help. [< Gk.]
Ot·ti·lie (ot′ə·lē) Fem. of OTTO. [< Ger.]

Pam·e·la (pam′ə·lə) ? Invented by Sir Philip Sidney. Dim. **Pam.**
Pan·sy (pan′zē) From the name of the flower.
Pa·tience (pā′shəns) From the abstract noun.
Pa·tri·cia (pə·trish′ə) Fem. of PATRICK. Dims. **Pat, Pat′sy, Pat′ty.**
Paul·a (pô′lə) Fem. of PAUL.
Pau·lette (pô·let′) Fr. fem. dim. of PAUL.
Pau·line (pô·lēn′) Fem. of PAUL. [< F] Also *Lat.* **Pau·li·na** (pô·lī′nə).
Pearl (pûrl) From the name of the jewel.
Peg (peg) Dim. of MARGARET. Also **Peg′gy.**
Pe·nel·o·pe (pə·nel′ə·pē) Weaver. [< Gk.] Dim. **Pen′ny.**
Per·sis (pûr′sis) She of Persia. [< Gk.]
Phi·lip·pa (fi·lip′ə, fil′ə·pə) Fem. of PHILIP.
Phoe·be (fē′bē) Bright; shining: an epithet of Artemis. [< Gk.] Also **Phe′be.**
Phyl·lis (fil′is) Green bough or leaf. [< Gk.] Also **Phil′·lis.**
Pol·ly (pol′ē) Dim. of MARY.
Pop·py (pop′ē) From the name of the flower.
Por·tia (pôr′shə, pôr′-) Fem. of *Porcius*, name of a Roman clan. [< L]
Pris·cil·la (pri·sil′ə) Ancient. [< L]
Pru·dence (prōōd′ns) From the abstract noun. Dim. **Prue.**

Queen·ie (kwē′nē) Derived from QUEEN, used as dim. of REGINA.

Ra·chel (rā′chəl; *Fr.* rà·shel′) Ewe or lamb. [< Hebrew] Dims. **Rae, Ray.**
Ra·mo·na (rə·mō′nə) Fem. of *Ramón*, Sp. form of RAYMOND.
Re·ba (rē′bə) Short for REBECCA.
Re·bec·ca (ri·bek′ə) Ensnarer. [< Hebrew] Dim. **Beck′y.**
Re·gi·na (ri·jē′nə, -jī′-) Queen. [< L]
Re·née (rə·nā′, rā′nē, rē′nē) Reborn. [< F]
Rhe·a (rē′ə) From the name of the Greek goddess.
Rho·da (rō′də) Rose. [< Gk.]
Ri·ta (rē′tə) Dim. of *Margarita*, Ital. and Sp. form of MARGARET.
Ro·ber·ta (rə·bûr′tə) Fem. of ROBERT. Dims. **Bert, Bob′·bie, Bob′by.**
Rob·in (rob′in) From the name of the bird, or from the masc. name.
Ro·chelle (rə·shel′) Stone or small rock. [< F]
Ron·ny (ron′ē) Dim. of VERONICA. Also **Ron′nie.**
Ro·sa (rō′zə) Var. of ROSE. [< L]
Ro·sa·bel (rō′zə·bel) Beautiful rose. [< L]
Ro·sa·lie (rō′zə·lē) Little rose. [< L] Also **Ro·sal·ia** (rō·zāl′yə, -zā′lē·ə).
Ros·a·lind (roz′ə·lind) Fair rose. [< Sp.] Also **Ros·a·lin·da** (roz′ə·lin′də).
Ros·a·line (roz′ə·lin, -līn, -lēn, rō′zə-) Var. of ROSALIND. Also **Ros′a·lyn** (-lin).
Ros·a·mond (roz′ə·mənd, rō′zə-) Famous protector. [< Gmc.] Also **Ros′a·mund, Ro·sa·mun·da** (rō′zə·mun′də).
Ros·anne (rōz·an′) From ROSE and ANNE. Also **Ros·an·na** (rōz·an′ə), **Rose·anne′, Rose·an′na.**
Rose (rōz) From the name of the flower. Also **Ro·sa** (rō′zə; *Fr.* rō·zà′; *Ger.* rō′zä; *Ital.* rô′zä; *Sp.* rō′sä).
Rose·mar·y (rōz′mâr′ē, -mə·rē) From the plant name. Also **Rose·ma·rie** (rōz′mə·rē).
Row·e·na (rō·ē′nə) ? From the name of an ancient Celtic goddess.
Rox·an·a (rok·san′ə) Dawn of day. [< Persian] Also **Rox·an′na,** *Fr.* **Rox·ane** (rôk·sàn′). Dim. **Rox′y.**
Ru·by (rōō′bē) From the name of the jewel.
Ruth (rōōth) Companion. [< Hebrew]

Sa·bi·na (sə·bī′nə) A Sabine woman. [< L]
Sa·die (sā′dē) Dim. of SARAH.
Sal·ly (sal′ē) Dim. of SARAH.
Sa·lo·me (sə·lō′mē) Peace. [< Hebrew]

San·dra (san′drə, sän′-) Dim. of ALEXANDRA.
Sar·ah (sâr′ə) Princess. [< Hebrew] Also **Sar·a** (sâr′ə). Dims. **Sa′die, Sal′ly.**
Sel·ma (sel′mə) Fair [< Celtic], or a fem. dim. of ANSELM.
Se·re·na (sə·rē′nə) Serene. [< L]
Shar·on (shar′ən, shâr′-) Of Sharon. [< Hebrew]
Shei·la (shē′lə) Irish form of CECILIA.
Shir·ley (shûr′lē) From an English surname; orig. a place name.
Sib·yl (sib′əl) Prophetess. [< Gk.] Also **Syb′il.**
Sid·ney (sid′nē) From an English surname. Also **Syd′ney.**
Sig·rid (sig′rid; *Ger.* zē′grit; *Norw.* sē′grē) Conquering counsel. [< Gmc.]
Sil·vi·a (sil′vē·ə) Var. of SYLVIA.
Si·mone (sē·mōn′) Fr. fem. of SIMON.
So·fi·a (sō·fē′ä) Ger., Ital., and Sw. form of SOPHIA.
Son·ia (sōn′yə) Russ. dim. of SOPHIA. Also **Son′ya.**
So·phi·a (sō·fī′ə, -fē′ə) Wise. [< Gk.] Also **So·phie** (sō′fē; *Fr.* sô·fē′). Dims. **So′phie, So′phy.**
So·phro·ni·a (sə·frō′nē·ə) Prudent. [< Gk.]
Sta·cie (stā′sē) Orig. dim. of ANASTASIA. Also **Sta′cy.**
Stel·la (stel′ə) Star. [< L]
Steph·a·nie (stef′ə·nē) Fem. of STEPHEN. Also **Steph·a·na** (stef′ə·nə), *Fr.* **Sté·pha·nie** (stā·fà·nē′).
Su·san (sōō′zən) Var. of SUSANNAH. Dims. **Sue, Su′sie, Su′zy.**
Su·san·nah (sōō·zan′ə) Lily. [< Hebrew] Also **Su·san′·na, Su·zanne** (sōō·zan′; *Fr.* sü·zàn′). Dims. **Sue, Su·ky** (sōō′kē), **Su′sie, Su′zy.**
Syb·il (sib′əl) Var. of SIBYL.
Syl·vi·a (sil′vē·ə) Of the forest. [< L] Also **Sil′vi·a.**

Tab·i·tha (tab′ə·thə) Gazelle. [< Aramaic]
Te·re·sa (tə·rē′sə, -zə); *Ital.* tā·rā′zä; *Sp.* tā·rā′sä) Var. of THERESA. [< Ital. & Sp.] Dims. **Ter′ry, Tess, Tes′sie.**
Thal·ia (thāl′yə, thal′-) Flourishing; blooming. [< Gk.]
The·a (thē′ə) Goddess. [< Gk.]
Thel·ma (thel′mə) ? Var. of SELMA.
The·o·do·ra (thē′ə·dôr′ə, -dō′rə) Fem. of THEODORE. Dims. **Do′ra, The′da, The′o.**
The·o·do·sia (thē′ə·dō′shə) Gift of God. [< Gk.]
The·re·sa (tə·rē′sə, -zə) She who reaps. [< Gk.] Also *Fr.* **Thé·rèse** (tā·râz′) Dims. **Ter′ry, Tess, Tes′sie.**
Til·da (til′də) Dim. of MATILDA.
Til·ly (til′ē) Dim. of MATILDA. Also **Til′lie.**
Ti·na (tē′nə) Dim. of CHRISTINA.
Tri·na (trē′nə) Dim. of KATRINA.
Trix·ie (trik′sē) Dim. of BEATRICE or BEATRIX. Also **Trix, Trix′y.**
Tru·dy (trōō′dē) Dim. of GERTRUDE.

U·na (yōō′nə) One. [< L]
Un·dine (un·dēn′, un′dēn) She of the waves. [< L]
U·ra·ni·a (yōō·rā′nē·ə) From the name of the Greek goddess of heaven, the muse of astronomy.
Ur·su·la (ûr′syə·lə, -sə-) Little she-bear. [< L]

Va·le·ri·a (və·lir′ē·ə) Fem. of *Valerius*, name of a Roman clan. Also **Val·er·ie** or **Val·er·y** (val′ər·ē), *Fr.* **Va·lé·rie** (và·lā·rē′). Dim. **Val.**
Va·nes·sa (və·nes′ə) Butterfly. [< Gk.]
Ve·ra (vir′ə) Faith [< Slavic], or truth [< L].
Ver·na (vûr′nə) Short for *Laverna*, var. of LAVERNE.
Ve·ron·i·ca (və·ron′i·kə) True image. [< LL] Also *Fr.* **Vé·ro·nique** (vā·rō·nēk′). Dim. **Ron′nie, Ron′ny.**
Vic·to·ri·a (vik·tôr′ē·ə, -tō′rē·ə) Victory. [< L] Also *Fr.* **Vic·toire** (vēk·twàr′). Dim. **Vick′y.**
Vi·o·la (vī′ō·lə, vī·ō′lə, vē-) Violet. [< L]
Vi·o·let (vī′ə·lit) From the name of the flower.
Vir·gin·ia (vər·jin′yə) Fem. of *Virginius*, name of a Roman clan. Also *Fr.* **Vir·gi·nie** (vēr·zhē·nē′). Dim. **Gin′ny.**
Viv·i·an (viv′ē·ən, viv′yən) Lively. [< L] Also **Viv′i·en,** *Fr.* **Vi·vienne** (vē·vyen′).

Wan·da (wän′də) Shepherdess or roamer. [< Gmc.]
Wen·dy (wen′dē) Dim. of GWENDOLYN.
Wil·hel·mi·na (wil′hel·mē′nə, wil′ə-; *Ger.* vil′hel·mē′nä) Fem. of *Wilhelm*, Ger. form of WILLIAM. Dims. **Mi′na, Min′na, Wil′la, Wil′ma.**
Wil·la (wil′ə) Dim. of WILHELMINA.
Wil·ma (wil′mə) Dim. of WILHELMINA.
Win·i·fred (win′ə·frid, -fred) White wave or stream. [< Welsh] Dim. **Win′nie.**

Yo·lan·da (yō·lan′də) Meaning uncertain. [? < OF] Also **Yo·lan′de** (-də).
Y·vonne (i·von′, ē-) Meaning uncertain. [< F]

Ze·no·bi·a (zi·nō′bē·ə) She who was given life by Zeus. [< Gk.]
Zo·e (zō′ē) Life. [< Gk.]

Grammar and Usage Handbook

WORD USAGE AND WORD RELATIONSHIPS

Agreement of Subject and Verb

It may seem needless to say that a singular subject takes a singular verb, while a plural subject takes a plural verb; however, when phrases or other elements come between the subject and the verb, the agreement may not be clear.

> The small table around which the children play *was* in the hall.
> The small tables owned by the church *were* in the hall.
> The men, as well as the policeman, *were* aghast at the sight.

The following words are generally considered singular and take singular verbs: *each, either, neither, one, someone, anyone, everybody, nobody, somebody, much, anybody, everyone.*

The following words are plural and take plural verbs: *both, few, many, several.*

The following pronouns may be singular or plural depending on the meaning intended: *all, most, some, every, none, any, half, more.*

When one is referring to two or more persons who are of different sexes, or to a group of people whose gender one has no way of determining, the pronouns *they, them,* and *their* are often used to refer to *anyone, each, everybody,* etc., in order to avoid the awkward *he or she, him or her, his or her.*

Either – Or; Neither – Nor

Neither always takes *nor; either* takes *or.*

When a subject is compounded with *neither . . . nor* or *either . . . or,* the verb is normally singular if the nouns joined are singular, and plural if they are plural. If, however, one noun is singular and one plural, the verb agrees with the second or nearer subject.

> Either Bill or Ralph *is* lying.
> Neither she nor her sisters *skate* well.

Collective Nouns

A collective noun, such as *class, company, club, crew, jury, committee,* takes a singular verb when the whole is considered as a unit, and a plural verb when members of the whole are being considered separately.

> The jury *has* deliberated for six hours.
> The crew *were* near exhaustion after their many hours of exposure.

Some collective nouns, as *police* and *cattle,* are used only in the plural form; others, as *mankind* and *wildlife,* are generally used in the singular form.

> The cattle *were* almost destroyed by the severe storm.
> The New England wildlife *has* been protected.

Agreement of Pronoun with Its Antecedent

If the antecedent is singular, the pronoun is singular, if the antecedent is plural, the pronoun is likewise plural.

> The *boy* did *his* best in the contest.
> The *boys* in the school did *their* best.
> The *boy and* the *girl* did *their* best.
> *Neither one* of the boys did *his* best.

CAPITALIZATION

Conventions governing the use of capital letters are quite clear.

Capitalize the first word of every sentence.

The first person singular pronoun *I* and the vocative *O* are generally capitalized.

Unless style requires a different form, *a.m.* and *p.m.* are set in small letters without a space between them. Capital letters are used for B.C. and A.D. but, again, there is no space between them.

> 9:30 a.m.   10:30 p.m.
> A.D. 1760 *or* 1760 A.D.
> 76 B.C.

Note: Although A.D. should technically precede the number of the year, popular usage permits it to follow the date. In printed matter B.C., A.D., a.m., and p.m. usually appear in small capitals (B.C., A.D., A.M., P.M.).

The first letter of a line of conventional poetry is capitalized. Much modern poetry, however, ignores this convention.

> Hickory, dickory, dock
> The mouse ran up the clock.

The first word after a colon should be capitalized only when it begins a complete sentence.

> The candidate made only one promise: If elected, he would fight for better conditions.
> The list contained these items: five pounds of flour, two dozen eggs, and a pound of butter.

Every direct quotation should begin with a capital, except where the quoted passage is grammatically woven into the text preceding it.

> The announcer shouted, "There it goes, over the back wall for a home run!"
> The announcer shouted that the ball was going "over the back wall for a home run."

Capitalize the first letters of all important words in the titles of books, newspapers, magazines, chapters, poems, articles. Short conjunctions and prepositions are generally not capitalized.

> How to Win Friends and Influence People

Geographical divisions and regions require capitals.

| Arctic Circle | the Atlantic Seaboard |
| the Orient | the Great Plains |

Compass points are capitalized when they are part of a generally accepted name, but not when they denote direction or locality.

Middle East   eastern New York
Old South   Head west for twenty-five miles.

Capitalize names of streets, parks, buildings, but not the general categories into which they fall.

Fifth Avenue
Which avenue is widest?
General Post Office
We went to the post office.

Religions, religious leaders, the various appellations for God and the Christian Trinity require capitalization, as do all names for the Bible and its parts.

the Father, the Son, and the Holy Ghost
Virgin Mary, the Immaculate Virgin
Yahweh, Jehovah, Saviour, Messiah
Buddhism, Shintoism, Taoism
New Testament
Exodus
Sermon on the Mount
Ten Commandments

Capitalize the names of political parties, classes, clubs, organizations, movements, and their adherents. Use small letters for the terms that refer generally to ideology (bolshevism, fascism, socialism).

Democratic Party
the Right Wing
Farm Bloc
Boy Scouts of America

Political divisions are capitalized.

Holy Roman Empire   the Colonies
French Republic   Suffolk County
the Dominion   Eighth Election District

Government bodies, departments, bureaus, and courts are capitalized.

the Supreme Court   the Cabinet
House of Representatives   Census Bureau
Department of Labor   British Parliament

Capitalize the titles of all high-ranking government officials, and all appellations of the President of the United States. Many publishers, it should be pointed out, prefer small letters for titles that are not accompanied by the name of the official.

President   Commander-in-Chief
Secretary of State   Chief Justice
Undersecretary   Prime Minister
Ambassador to India   Minister of War

Capitalize the names of treaties, documents, and important events.

Second World War   Declaration of Independence
Treaty of Versailles   Boston Tea Party

Family designations, when used without a possessive pronoun, take a capital letter.

I sent Mother home by taxi.
I sent my mother home by taxi.

Capitalize seasons only when they are personified. All personifications require capitals.

The frosty breath of Winter settled on the land.
The voice of Envy whispered in her ear.
Necessity is the mother of Invention.
When Headquarters commands, we jump.
He saw Mother Nature's grim visage.

Names and epithets of peoples, races, and tribes are capitalized.

Caucasian   Sioux
Negro   Cliff Dwellers

Articles and prepositions are generally capitalized in the names of Englishmen and Americans, and are not capitalized in French, Italian, Spanish, German, and Dutch names, unless otherwise specified by family usage.

Thomas De Quincey   Ludwig van Beethoven
Martin Van Buren   Leonardo da Vinci
Fiorello La Guardia   San Juan de la Cruz

Capitalize the names of holidays and festivals.

Christmas   Shrove Tuesday
Yom Kippur   New Year's Day

Capitalize such parts of a book as the Glossary, Contents, Index, and Preface.

Capitalize the first and last words in the salutation in business letters, and all titles.

My dear Sir   Dear Doctor Brown
My dear Reverend Lothrop   Dear Reverend Father

Capitalize only the first word of the complimentary close of a letter.

Very truly yours   Sincerely yours

SPELLING

General Suggestions

When in doubt as to the correct spelling of a word, consult the dictionary; do not take anything for granted.

Keep a list of your spelling errors and study them.

Learn the most commonly misspelled words in the lists below.

Learn to spell by syllables, carefully pronouncing each syllable. Faulty spelling is often due to faulty pronunciation.

Use newly acquired words and make them part of your oral and written vocabulary.

Do not use the simplified or modern forms of spelling in business correspondence, as *thru* for *through*.

Learn some basic spelling rules such as the following.

cede, ceed, and sede endings According to the Government Style Manual, there is only one word which ends in *sede — supersede,* and three that end in *ceed — proceed, exceed, succeed.* All other words having this sound end in *cede — precede, secede, recede,* etc.

ie and ei a. After *c,* when the sound is long *e* (ē), the *e* usually precedes the *i: receive, deceive, ceiling, receipt.*

b. After most other letters, the *i* precedes the *e: thief, grief, believe, achieve, lien.*

c. When the sound is *not* long *e* (ē); and especially if the sound is long *a* (ā), the *e* precedes the *i: sleigh, veil.*

The exceptions must be learned, since they follow no rule: *neither, leisure, weird, seize.*

Beginnings and Endings of Words (Prefixes and Suffixes)

a. As a general rule, drop the final *e* in the base word when a suffix beginning with a vowel is added.

decide — deciding; write — writer; type — typist

b. As a rule, retain the final *e* in the base word when a suffix beginning with a consonant is added.

remote—remotely; care—carefully; infringe—infringement

c. In applying the rule for adding *ed* or *ing*, the accent (or lack of it) may serve as a guide. Words of one syllable (and most words of more than one syllable) that end in a single consonant (except *f, h,* or *x*), preceded by a single vowel, double the final consonant *if the accent falls on the last syllable.*

plan—planned, planning; whet—whetted, whetting transfer—transferred, transferring; control—controlled, controlling

When the word is *not* accented on the last syllable, the consonant is usually not doubled.

travel—traveled, traveler; profit—profited, profiteer

d. When the endings *ness* and *ly* are added to a word not ending in *y*, the base word rarely changes. In most words ending in *y*, the *y* changes to *i* when *ly* is added.

natural—naturally; similar—similarly; genuine—genuineness; blessed—blessedness; hazy—hazily; body—bodily

If the base word ends in *n* and the suffix *ness* is added, the *n* is doubled.

sudden—suddenness; mean—meanness; vain—vainness

e. In regard to the word endings *ise, ize, yze,* the most common form is *ize,* but here the dictionary should be consulted if there is doubt.

legalize, fraternize, criticize, jeopardize
advertise, merchandise, surmise, enterprise
paralyze, analyze

In British English *ise* is sometimes used for *ize,* as *realise* for *realize.*

f. When adding the suffix *ful,* the *l* is single except when *ly* is also added *(fully).*

care—careful—carefully; hope—hopeful—hopefully

g. When the word beginnings (prefixes) *in, en, im, em, un, dis, mis, be, de, re, il,* and *over* are added to a word, the spelling of the base word is not changed.

inactive, enjoy, impending, embrace, uneasy, dismiss, mistrust, beguile, degrade, retreat, illegal, overhaul

Forming the Plurals of Nouns

a. Most nouns form the plural by simply adding *s.*

table—tables; house—houses

b. Some nouns, especially those ending in *s,* form the plural by adding *es.*

class—classes; fox—foxes

c. Words ending in *y* preceded by a consonant form the plural by changing the *y* to *i* and adding *es.*

candy—candies; study—studies; secretary—secretaries

d. Words ending in *y* preceded by a vowel form the plural by adding *s* but without any other change in the word.

key—keys; boy—boys

e. Nouns ending in *o* preceded by a vowel form the plural by adding *s.*

rodeo—rodeos; radio—radios

When the *o* is preceded by a consonant, the plural is formed by adding *es.*

hero—heroes; torpedo—torpedoes

f. Nouns referring to music which end in *o* preceded by a consonant form the plural by simply adding *s.*

piano—pianos; oratorio—oratorios; contralto—contraltos; soprano—sopranos

g. Some few nouns follow none of the above rules but form the plural in an unusual way.

child—children; tooth—teeth; mouse—mice; ox—oxen

h. Compound nouns (more than one word) form the plural from the main word.

trade union—trade unions; father-in-law—fathers-in-law

i. When a solid compound ends in *ful,* the plural is formed at the end of the solid compound and not within the word.

basketful—basketfuls; pocketful—pocketfuls

j. When the words in compounds are of almost equal importance, both parts of the compound are pluralized.

head of department—heads of departments; woman operator—women operators

k. Words taken from another language sometimes form the plural as they would in the original language.

stratum—strata; addendum—addenda; datum—data

SUMMARY OF SPELLING RULES*

	RULE	EXAMPLES	EXCEPTIONS

IE and **EI**	I before E, except after C.	ach*ie*ve, but c*ei*ling	1. Use *EI* when:
			  a. Sounded as *ā*: n*ei*ghbor, w*ei*gh
			  b. Sounded as *ĭ*: counterf*ei*t
			  c. Sounded as *ī*: h*ei*ght
			2. Use *IE* for almost all other sounds: fr*ie*nd, l*ie*utenant.
			3. If *i* and *e* do not form a digraph, rules do not apply: f*ie*ry, d*ei*ty.

Final Silent **E**	1. **Drop** before suffix beginning with a vowel. 2. **Retain** before suffix beginning with a consonant.	grieve—grievance absolute—absolutely	1. Retain *e* after soft *c* and soft *g* before suffixes beginning with *a* or *o*: peaceable, manageable.
Final **Y**	1. **Change** final *y* to *i* if *y* is **preceded** by a **consonant** and **followed** by any **suffix** except one beginning with *i*. 2. **Retain** final *y* if it is **preceded** by a **vowel**.	beauty—beautiful BUT carry—carrying boy—boys; valley—valleys	dry—dryness; sly—slyness. day—daily; pay—paid
Final Consonants	**Double** final consonants when: 1. Preceded by a single vowel. 2. Followed by a suffix beginning with a vowel. 3. The consonant terminates a monosyllabic word. 4. The consonant terminates a polysyllabic word accented on the last syllable.	1. drop—dropped; beg—beggar 2. quit—quitting; swim—swimmer 3. hit—hitter; run—running 4. omit—omitted; transfer—transferred	Final consonant is not doubled if: 1. Accent shifts to preceding syllable when suffix is added: con-fer′—confer′ring BUT con′ference. 2. Final consonant is preceded by a consonant: start—started. 3. Final consonant is preceded by two vowels: beat—beating; boil—boiling.
k added to words ending in **c**	**Add** *k* to words ending in *c* before a suffix beginning with *e, i, y*.	frolic—frolicking—frolicked; picnic—picnicking—picnicked	
-cede **-ceed** **-sede**	Except for super*sede*, ex*ceed*, pro*ceed*, suc*ceed*, all words having this sound end in *-cede*.	accede, precede, recede, concede	

Plurals	1. Regular noun plurals add *-s* to the singular.
	2. Irregular plurals:
	  a. Add *-es* if noun ends in *o* preceded by consonant.
	  b. Change *y* to *i* and add *-es* if noun ends in *y* preceded by consonant.
	  c. Add *-s* if noun ends in *y* preceded by vowel.
		boy—boys; book—books
		
		a. echo—echoes; Negro—Negroes
		b. sky—skies; enemy—enemies
		
		c. play—plays; day—days
			a. piano—pianos; zero—zeros; solo—solos.

*From *Business Letter Writing Made Simple*, revised ed., by Irving Rosenthal and Harry W. Rudman, Copyright © 1955, 1968 by Doubleday & Co., Inc.

	RULE	EXAMPLES	EXCEPTIONS

Possessives	1. Don't confuse contractions with possessive pronouns.	*Contraction Possessive*
		 1. it's (it is) its
		    they're their
		    (they are)	

	2. Use no apostrophes with possessive or relative pronouns.	2. *his, hers, ours, yours, theirs, whose*	
	3. If singular or plural noun **does not** end in *s*, add **apostrophe** and *s*.	3. child's (Sing.), children's (Plur.)	
	4. If singular or plural noun **does** end in *s*, add **apostrophe**	4. hostess' (Sing.), hostesses' (Plur.), princes' (Plur.)	

SPELLING LISTS. List of Words Most Frequently Misspelled by High School Seniors.

The list of words below* contains 149 words most frequently misspelled by high school seniors. These words and word-groups (those which are variants of the same word, as *acquaint* and *acquaintance*), were compiled by Dean Thomas Clark Pollock of New York University from 14,651 examples of misspelling submitted by 297 teachers in the United States, Canada and Hawaii. Each of the words represented was misspelled twenty times or more, and yet these words, comprising fewer than three per cent of the original list of 3,811 words, account for thirty per cent of the total misspellings.

NOTE: The trouble spots in each word are italicized. Numbers beside the words indicate how frequently each word is misspelled.

their	179	all right	91	its	52
receive	163	separate	91	it's	22
too	152	until	88		
		privilege	82	occur	9
writer	11	definite	78	occurred	52
writing	81	there	78	occurrence	10
written	13	believe	77	occurring	2
describe	28	study	1	probably	33
description	38	studied	3	speech	33
		studies	3	argument	32
tragedy	64	studying	34		

* The list compiled by Dr. Pollock appears in the *Teachers' Service Bulletin in English* (Macmillan, November, 1952).

decide	48	convenience	5	image	3
decision	15	convenient	33	imagine	7
				imaginary	5
occasion	54	difference	15	imagination	17
occasionally	8	different	23		
				quiet	32
succeed	25	than	38	then	32
success	22	athletic	37		
successful	12	to	37	prejudice	30
		business	36	sense	30
interest	56			similar	30
beginning	55	equipped	21		
		equipment	14	your	2
immediate	3	principal	18	you're	28
immediately	51	principle	18		
				appearance	29
coming	53	prophecy	35	conscious	29
embarrass	48	prophesy	35	pleasant	29
grammar	47				
		benefit	16	stop	1
humor	2	beneficial	5	stopped	24
humorous	45	benefited	11	stopping	4
		benefiting	1		
exist	3			surprise	29
existence	43	develop	34		
		environment	34	excite	1
lose	28	recommend	34	excited	7
losing	15	fascinate	33	excitement	13
		finally	33	exciting	7
disappoint	42				
rhythm	41	necessary	24	experience	28
		necessity	9	government	27
acquaint	17			laboratory	27
acquaintance	9	foreign	14	tried	27
		foreigners	9		
affect	26			familiar	21
accept	25	performance	23	escape	21
accommodate	25	together	23	meant	21
excellent	25	descend	13	where	21
opportunity	25	descendant	9	chief	20

{ marry	4	during	22	{ hero	10	maintenance	referred	
{ marries	6	forty	22	{ heroes	9	marriage	relieve	
{ marriage	15	woman	22	{ heroine	1	mischievous	rhythm	
		certain	21			noticeable	schedule	
				lonely	20	occasion	seize	
character	24	{ commit	4	opinion	20	occurred	separate	
complete	24	{ committed	12	parliament	20	occurrence	shining	
friend	24	{ committing	5	possess	20	o'clock	stationery	
truly	24	criticism	21	professor	20	omitted	strength	
accidentally	23	disappear	21	restaurant	20	parallel	succeed	
doesn't	23	exaggerate	21	villain	20			

perhaps	superintendent
principal	supersede
principles	tragedy
privilege	tries
proceed	truly
pronunciation	villain
quiet	Wednesday
quite	weird
received	whether
recommend	woman

List of 100 Words Most Frequently Misspelled by College Freshmen.

absence	conscientious	forth
accidentally	conscious	forty
across	coolly	fourth
aggravate	council	friend
all right	counsel	government
amateur	criticism	grammar
argument	deceive	grievance
around	definite	hadn't
athletic	desert	height
believed	dessert	indispensable
benefited	dining	interested
business	disappointed	its
busy	doesn't	it's
capital	don't	knowledge
cemetery	effect	laboratory
choose	eighth	latter
chosen	embarrassed	literature
coming	environment	loose
committee	exercise	lose
competition	February	losing

List of Words Frequently Misspelled on Civil Service Examinations.

accident	municipal	society
all right	principal	simplified
auxiliary	principle	technicality
athletic	promotional	tendency
buoyant	president	their
catalogue		thousandth
career	precede	transferred
comptroller	proceed	transient
criticise	promissory	truly
dividend	recommend	villain
	personnel	
embarrass	purchasable	Wednesday
expedient	responsibility	writ
government	received	whether
inveigle	regrettable	yield
monetary	supersede	

CONFUSING WORDS

accept See EXCEPT.

addition, edition *Addition* means the process of joining together or finding the sum of. *Edition* refers to the form in which a book, magazine, or other literary work is published: first *edition*.

advice, advise *Advice* is the noun: to give *advice*. *Advise* is the verb: to *advise* a person.

affect See EFFECT.

all ready See ALREADY.

all right, alright *All right* is the only spelling to be used: It is *all right* to do so. The spelling *alright* is not yet considered acceptable and should not be used.

allude, elude *Allude* means to make indirect or casual reference to: He *alluded* to one of Shakespeare's sonnets. *Elude* means to avoid or escape: The meaning *eludes* me.

already, all ready *Already* means before or by this time or the time mentioned: The group has *already* gone. *All ready* (two words) means that everyone is ready to do a given thing: We are *all ready* to go.

among, between *Among* is used when referring to more than two persons or things. *Between* is usually preferable when referring to only two persons or things.

appraise, apprise *Appraise* means to make an official valuation of. *Apprise* means to notify or inform.

ascent, assent *Ascent* means rising, soaring, or climbing: the *ascent* of the mountain. *Assent* means agreement, consent, sanction: *assent* to a course of action.

between See AMONG.

can See MAY.

capital, capitol *Capital* means a city that is important in some special way: Albany is the *capital* of New York. *Capitol* means a building in which a State legislature meets: The *capitol* is on Chamber Street.

censor, censure *Censor* means (*n.*) an official examiner of manuscripts, plays, etc.; (*v.*) to act as a censor; delete; suppress. *Censure* means (*v.*) to express disapproval of; (*n.*) the expression of disapproval or blame.

census See SENSES.

cite, sight, site *Cite* means to mention or bring forward: to *cite* an incident. *Sight* (*n.*) means a view, a vision: a beautiful *sight*. *Site* means a place or location: the *site* of the church.

compliment, complement *Compliment* (*n.*) means praise or congratulation. *Complement* (*n.*) means one of two parts that mutually complete each other.

consul See COUNCIL.

council, counsel, consul *Council* (*n.*) means an assembly convened for consultation. *Counsel* (*n.*) means guidance, advice; also, a lawyer. *Consul* (*n.*) means an officer residing in a foreign country to protect his own country's interests.

creditable, credible *Creditable* means deserving credit or esteem; praiseworthy: a *creditable* project for reducing poverty. *Credible* means capable of being believed; reliable: a *credible* alibi.

decent, descent, dissent *Decent* means proper; respectable. *Descent* means the act of descending or going downward. *Dissent* means (*v.*) to disagree; (*n.*) a disagreement.

devise, device *Devise* (*v.*) means to invent, contrive, or plan. *Device* (*n.*) is something devised; invention; contrivance.

dissent See DECENT.

edition See ADDITION.

effect, affect *Effect,* common as both a noun and a verb, means (*v.*) to bring about; to cause or achieve: The treatments will *effect* an early cure; and (*n.*) result, outcome. *Affect,* in common use a verb only, means to influence or act upon: Fear *affects* the mind.

effective, effectual *Effective* means producing a desired result: *Effective* action averted the strike. *Effectual* means having the power to produce a desired result: *effectual* legal steps.

elicit, illicit *Elicit* means to bring to light: to *elicit* the truth. *Illicit* means unlawful or unauthorized.

elude See ALLUDE.

eminent, imminent *Eminent* means high in station; distinguished; prominent: an *eminent* statesman. *Imminent* means about to happen (said especially of danger): an *imminent* calamity.

except, accept *Except* (*v.*) means to take or leave out: to *except* no one from the restrictions. *Accept* means to receive or agree to; acknowledge: to *accept* an invitation.

formerly, formally *Formerly* means some time ago; once: He was *formerly* a judge. *Formally* means with formality or with regard to form: *formally* dressed.

illicit See ELICIT.

imminent See EMINENT.

lay, lie See note under LAY¹ in the body of this dictionary.

learn See TEACH.

lesson, lessen *Lesson* refers to instructive or corrective example. *Lessen* means to make less; decrease.

loose, lose *Loose* means not fastened or attached. *Lose* means to mislay or be deprived of.

may, can *May* expresses permission: The child *may* play in the yard. *Can* expresses ability to do: The child *can* do better than he is doing at present.

past, passed *Past* means (*adj.*) ended or finished: His hopes are *past;* and (*n.*) time gone by: He dreams of the *past. Passed,* the past tense and past participle of *pass,* means went (or gone) beyond or farther than: The car, which was going at high speed, *passed* him easily.

persecute, prosecute *Persecute* means to maltreat or oppress; to harass. *Prosecute,* generally used in a legal sense, means to bring suit against.

personal, personnel *Personal* pertains to a person: *personal* matters, *personal* opinions. *Personnel* pertains to a body or group of persons: *personnel* problems, *personnel* department.

practical, practicable *Practical* pertains to actual use and experience. *Practicable* means feasible or usable.

prosecute See PERSECUTE.

senses, census *Senses,* the plural of *sense,* refers to awareness and rationality or to the faculty of sensation: to come to one's *senses;* Her *senses* were dulled by the accident. *Census* refers to an official count of the people of a country or district, etc.

shall, will See note under SHALL in the body of this dictionary.

sight See CITE.

site See CITE.

stationery, stationary *Stationery* refers to writing supplies. *Stationary* means remaining in one place.

sweet, suite *Sweet* means having a taste like sugar. *Suite* refers to a set or series of things intended to be used together: *suite* of rooms, *suite* of furniture.

teach, learn *Teach* means to impart knowledge; *learn* means to acquire knowledge. The teacher *teaches;* the student *learns.*

will, shall See note under SHALL in the body of this dictionary.

SAMPLE BUSINESS LETTERS*

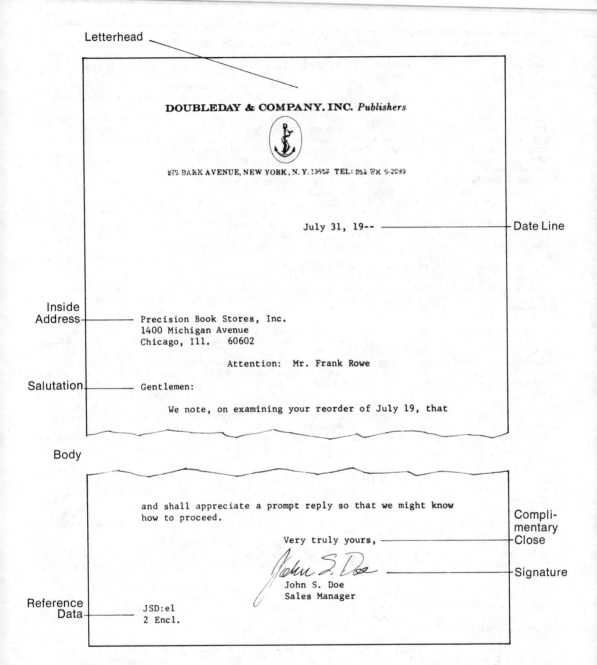

Letterhead

DOUBLEDAY & COMPANY, INC. *Publishers*

277 PARK AVENUE, NEW YORK, N.Y. 10017 TEL: 212 PL 5-2099

July 31, 19-- ─────────── **Date Line**

Inside Address

Precision Book Stores, Inc.
1400 Michigan Avenue
Chicago, Ill. 60602

Attention: Mr. Frank Rowe

Salutation Gentlemen:

We note, on examining your reorder of July 19, that

Body

and shall appreciate a prompt reply so that we might know
how to proceed.

Very truly yours, ───────── **Complimentary Close**

John S. Doe ───────── **Signature**

John S. Doe
Sales Manager

Reference Data JSD:el
2 Encl.

This model letter includes in standard form all the elements normally employed in the business letter.

*From *Business Letter Writing Made Simple*, revised ed., by Irving Rosenthal and Harry W. Rudman, Copyright © 1955, 1968 by Doubleday & Co., Inc.

The "Modified Block" Form

February 28, 19

Mr. John Jones
1492 Columbus Avenue
Louisville, Kentucky 40216

Dear Mr. Jones:

I was very pleased to receive your prompt response to

and I look forward to seeing you on your next trip to
the city.

Sincerely yours,

George Sabrin

All the letter's contents, with the exception of the date, the complimentary close, the signature, are aligned on the left hand margin. This is still the most widely employed form.

Full Indention

---

19 Elm Street
Oswego, New York
April 5, 19

Mr. Gilbert Kahn
67 Wren Road
Miami, Florida 33138

My dear Mr. Kahn:

                In undertaking the assignment you gave me
when I was in your office last Thursday, I made it clear

nevertheless intend to do the best job I can.

Sincerely yours,

Lucille Graham

This form is all but obsolete, and there seems little doubt that in time it will cease entirely to be used.

Additional Sheets

Mr. John Jones -- page 2 -- January 14, 19

therefore feel that we cannot accept the return of the

merchandise at this late date. We like to cooperate

with all our accounts. . . .

It was necessary, because of its length, to continue this letter on an additional sheet. The additional sheet is headed by the addressee's name, the page number, and the date. There is the requisite minimum of three lines of text, in addition to complimentary close and signature.

The "Full Block" Form

February 28, 19

Mr. John Jones
1492 Columbus Avenue
Louisville, Kentucky 40216

Dear Mr. Jones:

I was very pleased to receive your prompt response to my

and I look forward to seeing you on your next trip to the city.

Sincerely yours,

George Sabrin

In the "full block" form all the letter's contents are aligned on the left hand margin.

FORMS OF ADDRESS

President of the United States
Address: Business: The President
The White House
Washington, D.C.
Social: The President
and Mrs. Roberts
The White House
Washington, D.C.
Salutation: Formal: Mr. President:
Informal: Dear Mr. President:
Closing: Formal: Most respectfully yours,
Informal: Sincerely yours,
In Conversation: Mr. President or Sir
Title of Introduction: The President or Mr. Roberts

Vice President of the United States
Address: Business: The Vice President
United States Senate
Washington, D.C.
Social: The Vice President
and Mrs. Hope
Home Address
Salutation: Formal: Mr. Vice President:
Informal: Dear Mr. Vice President:
Closing: Formal: Very truly yours,
Informal: Sincerely yours,
In Conversation: Mr. Vice President or Sir
Title of Introduction: The Vice President or
Mr. Hope

Chief Justice of The United States
Address: Business: The Chief Justice
The Supreme Court
Washington, D.C.
Social: The Chief Justice
and Mrs. Page
Home Address
Salutation: Formal: Sir:
Informal: Dear Mr. Chief Justice:
Closing: Formal: Very truly yours,
Informal: Sincerely yours,
In Conversation: Mr. Chief Justice or Sir
Title of Introduction: The Chief Justice

Associate Justice of the Supreme Court
Address: Business: Mr. Justice Katsaros
The Supreme Court
Washington, D.C.
Social: Mr. Justice Katsaros
and Mrs. Katsaros
Home Address
Salutation: Formal: Sir:
Informal: Dear Mr. Justice Katsaros:
Closing: Formal: Very truly yours,
Informal: Sincerely yours,
In Conversation: Mr. Justice or Mr. Justice
Katsaros or Sir
Title of Introduction: Mr. Justice Katsaros

Cabinet Officer
Address: Business: The Honorable Gary George
Gussin
Secretary of the Treasury or
Attorney General of the United
States
Washington, D.C.
Social: The Secretary of the Treasury
and Mrs. Gussin
Home Address
or (for a woman cabinet member)
The Honorable Beatrice Schwartz

or (if she is married)
Mr. and Mrs. Henry Leo Woods
Salutation: Formal: Sir: or Dear Sir: or Madam:
Informal: Dear Mr. Secretary: or
Dear Madam Secretary:
Closing: Formal: Very truly yours,
Informal: Sincerely yours,
In Conversation: Mr. Secretary or Madam Secretary
or Mr. Attorney General or
Mr. (or Miss or Mrs.) Smith
Title of Introduction: The Secretary of the Treasury,
Mr. Smith or
The Attorney General of the
United States, Mr. Smith

Former President
Address: Business: The Honorable Alfred Edward
Work
Office Address
Social: The Honorable and Mrs. Alfred
Edward Work
Home Address
Salutation: Formal: Sir:
Informal: Dear Mr. Work:
Closing: Formal: Very truly yours,
Informal: Sincerely yours,
In Conversation: Mr. Work or Sir
Title of Introduction: The Honorable Alfred Edward
Work

United States Senator
Address: Business: The Honorable John Wandzilak
United States Senate
Washington, D.C.
Social: The Honorable and Mrs. John
Wandzilak
Home Address
or (for a woman senator)
The Honorable Marguerite
Sanders
or (if she is married)
Mr. and Mrs. John Row Doe
Salutation: Formal: Sir: or Madam:
Informal: Dear Senator Wandzilak:
Closing: Formal: Very truly yours,
Informal: Sincerely yours,
In Conversation: Senator or Senator Wandzilak or
Sir
Title of Introduction: Senator Wandzilak

Speaker of the House of Representatives
Address: Business: The Honorable Walter Fry
The Speaker of the House of
Representatives
Washington, D.C.
Social: The Speaker of the House of
Representatives and Mrs. Fry
Home Address
Salutation: Formal: Sir:
Informal: Dear Mr. Speaker:
Closing: Formal: Very truly yours,
Informal: Sincerely yours,
In Conversation: Mr. Speaker or Sir
Title of Introduction: The Speaker of the House of
Representatives or
The Speaker, Mr. Fry

Member of the House of Representatives
Address: Business: The Honorable Henry Cobb
Wellcome
United States House of
Representatives
Washington, D.C.

Social: The Honorable and Mrs. Henry
Cobb Wellcome
Home Address
or (for a woman member)
The Honorable Ann Davenport
or (if she is married)
Mr. and Mrs. John Knox Jones
Salutation: Formal: Sir: *or* Madam:
Informal: Dear Mr. Wellcome:
Closing: Formal: Very truly yours,
Informal: Sincerely yours,
In Conversation: Mr. Wellcome *or* Miss Davenport *or*
Mrs. Jones *or* Sir *or* Madam
Title of Introduction: Representative Wellcome

Ambassador of the United States

Address: Business: The Honorable John Wilson
Smith
The Ambassador of the United
States
American Embassy
London, England
Social: The Honorable and Mrs. John
Wilson Smith
Home Address
or (for a woman ambassador)
The Honorable Janet Lund
or (if she is married)
Mr. and Mrs. Joseph Leeds
Walker
Salutation: Formal: Sir: *or* Madam:
Informal: Dear Mr. Ambassador: *or* Dear
Madam Ambassador:
Closing: Formal: Very truly yours,
Informal: Sincerely yours,
In Conversation: Mr. Ambassador *or* Madam
Ambassador *or* Sir *or* Madam
Title of Introduction: The American Ambassador *or*
The Ambassador of the
United States

Minister Plenipotentiary of the United States

Address: Business: The Honorable James Lee Row
The Minister of the United States
American Legation
Oslo, Norway
Social: The Honorable and Mrs. James
Lee Row
Home Address
or (for a woman minister)
The Honorable Eugenia Carlucci
or (if she is married)
Mr. and Mrs. Arthur Johnson
Salutation: Formal: Sir: *or* Madam:
Informal: Dear Mr. Minister *or* Dear
Madam Minister:
Closing: Formal: Very truly yours,
Informal: Sincerely yours,
In Conversation: Mr. Row *or* Miss Carlucci *or*
Mrs. Johnson
Title of Introduction: Mr. Row, the American
Minister

Consul of the United States

Address: Business: Mr. John Smith
American Consul
Rue de Quelque Chose
Paris, France
Social: Mr. and Mrs. John Smith
Home Address
Salutation: Formal: Sir: *or* Dear Sir:
Informal: Dear Mr. Smith:

Closing: Formal: Very truly yours,
Informal: Sincerely yours,
In Conversation: Mr. Smith
Title of Introduction: Mr. Smith

Ambassador of a Foreign Country

Address: Business: His Excellency, Juan Luis Ortega
The Ambassador of Mexico
Washington, D.C.
Social: His Excellency
The Ambassador of Mexico and
Señora Ortega
Home Address
Salutation: Formal: Excellency:
Informal: Dear Mr. Ambassador:
Closing: Formal: Very truly yours,
Informal: Sincerely yours,
In Conversation: Mr. Ambassador *or* Sir
Title of Introduction: The Ambassador of Mexico

Minister of a Foreign Country

Address: Business: The Honorable
Carluh Matti
The Minister of Kezeah
Washington, D.C.
Social: The Honorable and Mrs. Carluh
Matti
Home Address
Salutation: Formal: Sir:
Informal: Dear Mr. Minister:
Closing: Formal: Very truly yours,
Informal: Sincerely yours,
In Conversation: Mr. Minister *or* Sir
Title of Introduction: The Minister of Kezeah

Governor of a State

Address: Business: The Honorable Joseph L. Marvin
Governor of Idaho
Boise, Idaho
Social: The Honorable and Mrs. Joseph L.
Marvin
Home Address
or (for a woman governor)
The Honorable Katherine Marvin
or (if she is married)
Mr. and Mrs. Walter O'Reilly
Salutation: Formal: Sir:
Informal: Dear Governor Marvin:
Closing: Formal: Very truly yours,
Informal: Sincerely yours,
In Conversation: Governor Marvin *or* Sir *or* Madam
Title of Introduction: The Governor *or* The
Governor of Idaho

State Senators and Representatives are addressed
in the same manner as U.S. Senators and Representatives.

Mayor

Address: Business: Honorable Roger Shute
Mayor of Easton
City Hall
Easton, Maryland
Social: The Honorable
and Mrs. Roger Shute
Home Address
or (for a woman mayor)
The Honorable Martha Wayne
or (if she is married)
Mr. and Mrs. Walter Snow
Salutation: Formal: Sir: *or* Madam:
Informal: Dear Mayor Shute:

Closing: Formal: Very truly yours,
          Informal: Sincerely yours,
In Conversation: Mr. Mayor or Madam Mayor
Title of Introduction: Mayor Shute

Judge
Address: Business: The Honorable Carson Little
                    Justice, Appellate Division
                    Supreme Court of the State of
                    New York
                    Albany, New York
          Social: The Honorable and Mrs. Carson
                    Little
                    Home Address
                    or (for a woman judge)
                    The Honorable Josefina Gonzalez
                    or (if she is married)
                    Mr. and Mrs. Rafael Montoya
Salutation: Formal: Sir:
              Informal: Dear Judge Little:
Closing: Formal: Very truly yours,
          Informal: Sincerely yours,
In Conversation: Mr. Justice or Madam Justice
Title of Introduction: Justice Little

Protestant Bishop
Address: Business: The Right Reverend John S.
                    Bowman
                    Bishop of Rhode Island
                    Providence, Rhode Island
          Social: The Right Reverend and
                    Mrs. John S. Bowman
Salutation: Formal: Right Reverend Sir:
              Informal: Dear Bishop Bowman:
Closing: Formal: Respectfully yours,
          Informal: Sincerely yours,
In Conversation: Bishop Bowman
Title of Introduction: Bishop Bowman

Protestant Clergyman
Address: Business: The Reverend David Dekker
                    or (if he holds the degree)
                    The Reverend David Dekker,
                    D.D.
                    Address of his church
          Social: The Reverend and Mrs. David
                    Dekker
                    Home Address
Salutation: Formal: Dear Sir:
              Informal: Dear Mr. (or Dr.) Dekker:
Closing: Formal: Sincerely yours,
          Informal: Sincerely yours,
In Conversation: Mr. (or Dr.) Dekker
Title of Introduction: Mr. (or Dr.) Dekker

Rabbi
Address: Business: Rabbi Paul Aaron Fine
                    or (if he holds the degree)
                    Dr. Paul Aaron Fine, D.D.
                    Address of his synagogue
          Social: Rabbi (or Dr.) and Mrs. Paul
                    Aaron Fine
                    Home Address
Salutation: Formal: Dear Sir:
              Informal: Dear Rabbi (or Dr.) Fine:
Closing: Formal: Sincerely yours,
          Informal: Sincerely yours,
In Conversation: Rabbi (or Dr.) Fine
Title of Introduction: Rabbi (or Dr.) Fine

The Pope
Address: His Holiness Pope Paul VI
          or His Holiness the Pope
          Vatican City

Salutation: Your Holiness:
Closing: Your Holiness' most humble servant,
In Conversation: Your Holiness
Title of Introduction: One is presented to: His
                        Holiness or The Holy Father

Cardinal
Address: His Eminence Alberto Cardinal Vezzetti
          Archbishop of Baltimore
          Baltimore, Maryland
Salutation: Formal: Your Eminence:
              Informal: Dear Cardinal Vezzetti:
Closing: Your Eminence's humble servant,
In Conversation: Your Eminence
Title of Introduction: One is presented to: His
                        Eminence, Cardinal Vezzetti

Roman Catholic Archbishop
Address: The Most Reverend Preston Lowen
          Archbishop of Philadelphia
          Philadelphia, Pennsylvania
Salutation: Formal: Your Excellency: or Most
                    Reverend Sir:
              Informal: Dear Archbishop Lowen:
Closing: Your Excellency's humble servant,
In Conversation: Your Excellency
Title of Introduction: One is presented to: The Most
                        Reverend
                        The Archbishop of Philadelphia

Roman Catholic Bishop
Address: The Most Reverend Matthew S. Borden
          Address of his church
Salutation: Formal: Your Excellency: or Most
                    Reverend Sir:
              Informal: Dear Bishop Borden:
Closing: Formal: Your obedient servant,
          Informal: Sincerely yours,
In Conversation: Your Excellency
Title of Introduction: Bishop Borden

Monsignor
Address: The Right Reverend Monsignor Ryan
          Address of his church
Salutation: Formal: Right Reverend Monsignor:
              Informal: Dear Monsignor Ryan:
Closing: Formal: I remain, Right Reverend
                  Monsignor, yours faithfully,
          Informal: Faithfully yours,
In Conversation: Monsignor Ryan
Title of Introduction: Monsignor Ryan

Priest
Address: The Reverend John Matthews (and the
          initials of his order)
          Address of his church
Salutation: Formal: Reverend Father:
              Informal: Dear Father Matthews:
Closing: Formal: I remain, Reverend Father, yours
                  faithfully,
          Informal: Faithfully yours,
In Conversation: Father or Father Matthews
Title of Introduction: The Reverend Father
                        Matthews

Member of Religious Order
Address: Sister Angelica (and initials of order) or
          Brother James (and initials)
          Address
Salutation: Formal: Dear Sister: or Dear Brother:
              Informal: Dear Sister Angelica: or Dear
                        Brother James:
Closing: Formal: Respectfully yours,

Informal: Faithfully yours,
In Conversation: Sister Angelica *or* Brother James
Title of Introduction: Sister Angelica *or* Brother
James

University Professor
Address: Business: Professor Robert Knowles
Office Address
Social: Professor *or* Mr.
or (if he holds the degree)
Dr. and Mrs. Robert Knowles
Home Address
or (for a woman professor)
Professor or Miss (*or* Dr.)
Catherine Stone
or (if she is married)
Mr. and Mrs. Wallace Bryant
Salutation: Formal: Dear Professor (*or* Dr.) Knowles:
Informal: Dear Mr. (*or* Miss *or* Mrs. *or*
Ms.) Knowles:
Closing: Formal: Very truly yours,
Informal: Sincerely yours,
In Conversation: Professor (*or* Dr. *or* Mr. *or* Miss
or Mrs.) Knowles
Title of Introduction: Professor (*or* Dr.) Knowles

Physician
Address: Business: William L. Barnes, M.D. *or*
Dr. William L. Barnes
Office Address
Social: Dr. and Mrs. William L. Barnes
Home Address
Salutation: Dear Dr. Barnes:
Closing: Formal: Very truly yours,
Informal: Sincerely yours,
In Conversation: Dr. Barnes
Title of Introduction: Dr. Barnes

CANADA

Prime Minister
Address: Business: The Right Hon. John Smith,
P.C., M.P.
Prime Minister of Canada
Parliament Building
Ottawa, Ontario
Social: The Hon. and Mrs. John Smith
Home Address
Salutation: Formal: Sir: *or* Dear Sir:
Informal: Dear Mr. Prime Minister: *or*
Dear Mr. Smith:
Closing: Formal: Yours very truly,
Informal: Yours very sincerely,
In Conversation: Mr. Prime Minister *or* Mr. Smith
or Sir

Governor General – The Commonwealth
Address: Business: His Excellency
John Smith (or his personal title)
Government House
Ottawa, Ontario
Social: Their Excellencies
The Governor General and
Mrs. John Smith
Home Address
Salutation: Formal: Sir: *or* Dear Sir:
Informal: Dear Mr. Smith:
Closing: Formal: Your Excellency's obedient servant,
Informal: Yours very sincerely,
In Conversation: Your Excellency

Former Prime Minister
Address: The Honourable (*or* Right Honourable)
John Smith
Home Address (*or* Office Address)

Cabinet Officer
Address: Business: The Hon. John Smith, P.C., M.P.
Minister of Forestry
Ottawa, Ontario
Social: The Hon. and Mrs. John Smith
Home Address
or (for a woman cabinet member)
The Hon. Mary Jones
(*or, if she is married*)
Mr. and Mrs. John Smith
Salutation: Formal: Sir: *or* Dear Sir: *or* Madam:
or Dear Madam:
Informal: Dear Mr. Smith: *or* Dear
Mrs. Smith:
Closing: Formal: Yours very truly,
Informal: Yours very sincerely,
In Conversation: Sir *or* Madam (*formally*); Mr. *or*
Mrs. Smith *or* Mr. Minister
(*informally*)

Judges
Judges of the following federal and provincial courts have the title The Honourable.

Supreme Court of Canada, Exchequer Court of Canada, Courts of appeal of the provinces of British Columbia, Manitoba, and Saskatchewan, Court of Chancery of the province of Prince Edward Island, Courts of Queen's Bench of the Provinces of Manitoba, Quebec, and Saskatchewan, Superior Court of the province of Quebec, Supreme courts of the provinces of Alberta, British Columbia, New Brunswick, Nova Scotia, Ontario, Prince Edward Island, and Newfoundland; and the territorial courts.
Address: Business: The Hon. Mr. Justice John Smith
Social: The Hon. Mr. Justice John Smith
and Mrs. Smith
Salutation: Formal: Sir:
Informal: Dear Mr. Justice Smith:
Closing: Formal: Yours very truly,
Informal: Yours very sincerely,
In Conversation: Sir (*formally*); Mr. Justice
(*informally*)

Mayor
Address: His Worship
The Mayor of St. Lazare
Salutation: Formal: Dear Sir:
Informal: Dear Mr. Mayor:
Closing: Formal: Yours very truly,
Informal: Yours very sincerely,
In Conversation: Sir (*formally*); Mr. Mayor
(*informally*)

Member of Parliament
Address: John Smith, Esq., M.P.
House of Commons
Ottawa, Ontario
Salutation: Formal: Dear Sir: *or* Dear Madam:
Informal: Dear Mr. (*or* Miss *or* Mrs.) Smith
Closing: Formal: Yours very truly,
Informal: Yours very sincerely,
In Conversation: Sir *or* Madam (*formally*): Mr. (*or*
Miss *or* Mrs.) Smith (*informally*)

Greek and Latin Elements in English

The following list contains a selection of English words, listed alphabetically, each of which is shown with a corresponding combining form, prefix, or suffix of Greek or Latin derivation. The list will prove of great assistance in word study and the enrichment of one's vocabulary, and will give some insight into the origins and general range of meaning of new and unfamiliar words.

COMBINING FORMS

abdomen Gk. coelo-, gastro-; L. ventro-.
agriculture Gk. agro-.
air Gk. aero-; L. aeri-. See also BREATH, WIND.
aircraft Gk. aero-.
all Gk. pan-, panto-; L. omni-. See also WHOLE.
ancient Gk. archeo-, paleo-.
angle Gk. -gon, gonio-.
animal Gk. zoo-.
appearance Gk. -opsis.
arm Gk. brachio-.
art Gk. techno-.
artery Gk. arterio-.
back Gk. noto-; L. dorsi-, dorso-.
bad Gk. caco-, dys-; L. mal-. See also DIFFICULT.
bag Gk. asco-. See also BLADDER, VESSEL.
bare Gk. gymno-; L. nudi-.
beautiful Gk. calli-.
bearing L. -fer, -ferous, -gerous, -parous. See also PRODUCING.
bent Gk. ankylo-; L. flexi-. See also CURVED.
berry L. bacci-.
berry-shaped Gk. & L. cocci-, -coccus.
big See GREAT.
bile Gk. chole-, cholo-.
bird Gk. ornitho-; L. avi-.
birth Gk. toco-; L. nati-. See also CHILD.
bitter Gk. picro-.
black Gk. melano-; L. nigri-.
bladder Gk. cysto-; L. vesico-. See also BAG, VESSEL.
blind Gk. typhlo-.
blood Gk. -emia (condition or disease), hema-, hemato-; L. sangui-.
bluish Gk. cyano, glauco-.
body Gk. somato-, -soma, -some.
bone Gk. osteo-; L. ossi-.
book Gk. biblio-.
both Gk. amphi-; L. ambi-.
brain Gk. encephalo-, phreno-; L. cerebro-. See also MIND.
brass See COPPER.
breast Gk. masto-.
breath Gk. pneumato-; L. spiro-. See also AIR, WIND.
bristle L. seti-.
broad Gk. eury-; L. lati-. See also FLAT.
bronze See COPPER.
bud Gk. blasto-, -blast; L. gemmi-.
burning See FIRE.
carbon L. carbo-, carboni-.
carrying See BEARING.
cartilage Gk. chondro-.
carved, carving Gk. glypto-, -glyph.
cattle Gk. tauro-; L. bovi-.
cave Gk. & L. speleo-.
cavity Gk. -cele.
cell Gk. cyto-, -plast.
center Gk. centro-; L. centri-.
chemical Gk. chemo-.
chest Gk. stetho-.
chief Gk. arch-, archi-.

child Gk. pedo-, toco-.
Chinese L. Sino-.
chlorine Gk. chloro-.
circle Gk. cyclo-, gyro-, -cyclic.
class See NATION, ORDER, SPECIES, TYPE.
clear See VISIBLE.
climate Gk. climato-.
closed Gk. cleisto-.
cloud Gk. nepho-.
cold Gk. cryo-, psychro-.
colon Gk. colo-.
color Gk. chromato-, chromo-, -chrome; L. colori-.
comb Gk. cteno-.
common Gk. ceno-.
complete See FINAL.
cone Gk. cono-.
copper Gk. chalco-; L. cupro-.
cornea Gk. kerato-.
corpse Gk. necro-.
correct Gk. ortho-.
country Gk. choro-.
covered See HIDDEN.
craving Gk. -mania, -maniac.
crest Gk. lopho-.
cross Gk. stauro-; L. cruci-.
crystal Gk. crystallo-.
cup Gk. scypho-; L. scyphi-.
curly L. cirro-.
current Gk. rheo-.
curved L. curvi-.
custom Gk. nomo-.
cut Gk. tomo-, -tomy; L. -sect, -section. See also KNIFE, SPLIT.
cyanogen Gk. cyano-.
cyst Gk. cysto-.
dance Gk. choreo-, choro-.
darkness Gk. scoto-.
death Gk. thanato-. See also CORPSE.
decompose Gk. sapro-.
deep, depth Gk. batho-, bathy-.
diaphragm Gk. phreno-.
different Gk. hetero-; L. vari-, vario-. See also FOREIGN, OTHER.
difficult Gk. dys-.
disease Gk. noso-, patho-, -iasis, -osis, -pathy. See also PAIN.
dissolving Gk. lyo-, lysi-, -lysis, -lyte.
divide See CUT, SPLIT.
divining Gk. -mancy, -mantic.
double Gk. diplo-.
dream Gk. oneiro-.
drug Gk. pharmaco-.
dry Gk. xero-.
dung Gk. copro-, scato-; L. sterco-, stercori-.
duodenum L. duodeno-.
dust Gk. conio-.
ear Gk. oto-.
early, earliest Gk. eo-. See also ANCIENT, FIRST, PRIMITIVE.
earth Gk. geo-; L. terri-.
earthquake Gk. seismo-.
eat Gk. phago-, -phage, -phagous, -phagy; L. -vorous. See also FOOD, NOURISHMENT.
egg Gk. oo-; L. ovi-, ovo-.
eight Gk. & L. octa-, octo-.

electric Gk. & L. electro-. See also CURRENT.
embryo Gk. embryo-.
end See FINAL.
English L. Anglo-.
equal Gk. iso-; L. equi-, pari-. See also LIKE, SAME.
existence Gk. onto-.
external Gk. ecto-, exo-; L. extra-.
extremity See TIP.
eye Gk. ophthalmo-, -opia; L. oculo-. See also SIGHT.
eyelid Gk. blepharo-.
false Gk. pseudo-.
far Gk. tele-, telo-.
fat, fatty Gk. lipo-; L. sebi-, sebo-.
father L. patri-.
fear Gk. -phobia.
feather See WING.
feed See EAT, NOURISHMENT.
female See WOMAN.
fermentation Gk. zymo-.
fever L. febri-.
few Gk. oligo-.
fibrous L. fibro-.
field See AGRICULTURE.
fight Gk. -machy.
filament See THREAD.
fin L. pinni-.
final Gk. teleo-, telo-.
finger Gk. dactylo-; L. digiti-.
fire Gk. pyro-; L. igni-.
first Gk. proto-; L. primi-.
fish Gk. ichthyo-; L. pisci-.
five Gk. penta-; L. quinque-.
flat Gk. platy-; L. plano-.
flee L. -fugal, -fuge.
flesh Gk. sarco-.
flow Gk. -rrhea, -rrhagia, -rrhagic. See also CURRENT.
flower Gk. antho-; L. -florous.
fluorescence L. fluo-, fluoro-.
fluorine L. fluo-, fluoro-.
food Gk. sito-. See also EAT, NOURISHMENT.
foot Gk. -pod, -podous; L. pedi-, -ped, -pede.
fond of See LOVE.
force See POWER.
foreign Gk. xeno-. See also DIFFERENT, OTHER.
foretelling See DIVINING.
form Gk. morpho-, -morphic, -morphous. See also APPEARANCE, IMAGE, LIKE.
four Gk. tetra-; L. quadri-, quadru-.
French L. Gallo-.
front, frontal L. fronto-.
fruit Gk. carpo-, -carpous.
fungus Gk. myco-, -mycete; L. fungi-.
gamete Gk. gameto-.
ganglion Gk. ganglio-.
gas Gk. aero-.
genital L. genito-.
gigantic Gk. giganto-.
gills Gk. branchio-, -branch.
gland Gk. adeno-.
glass Gk. hyalo-; L. vitri-.
god Gk. theo-.
gold Gk. chryso-.
good Gk. eu-.
govern Gk. -archy, -cracy, -crat.

grain	L. grani-.	man	Gk. andro-, anthropo-, -androus.
gray matter	Gk. polio-.		
great	Gk. mega-, megalo-; L. magni-. See also LARGE, LONG.	manifestation	Gk. -phany.
		many	Gk. poly-, myria- (very many); L. multi-.
Greek	L. Greco-.	marriage	Gk. -gamy.
green	Gk. chloro-.	material, matter	Gk. hylo-, -plasm.
groin	L. inguino-.		
growth	Gk. -plasia, -plasis. See also BUD, TUMOR.	measure	Gk. metro-, -meter, -metry.
		medicine	Gk. iatro-, -iatrics, -iatry; L. medico-.
hair	Gk. chaeto-, tricho-.		
half	Gk. hemi-; L. demi-, semi-.	membrane	Gk. hymeno-.
		middle	Gk. meso-; L. medio-.
hand	Gk. chiro-.	milk	Gk. galacto-; L. lacto-.
hard	Gk. sclero-. See also SOLID.	mind	Gk. phreno-, psycho-. See also SPIRIT.
hate	Gk. miso-.	monster	Gk. terato-.
head	Gk. cephalo-, -cephalic, -cephalous. See also SKULL.	moon	Gk. seleno-; L. luni-.
		mother	L. matri-.
healing	See MEDICINE.	motion pictures	Gk. cine-.
hear	Gk. acous-; L. audio-.		
heart	Gk. cardio-.	mountain	Gk. oro-.
heat	Gk. thermo-. See FIRE.	mouth	Gk. stomato-, -stome, -stomous; L. oro-.
the heavens	Gk. urano-.		
hernia	Gk. -cele; L. hernio-.	movement	Gk. kinesi-, kineto-, -kinesis.
hidden	Gk. crypto-.		
high, height	Gk. hypso-; L. alti-, alto-.	mucus	L. muco-, muci-. See also SLIMY.
hollow	See CAVITY.	much	See MANY.
holy	See SACRED.	muscle	Gk. myo-.
horn	Gk. kerato-.	myth	Gk. mytho-.
horse	Gk. hippo-.	naked	See BARE.
hundred	Gk. hecto-; L. centi-.	narrow	Gk. steno-.
hysteria	Gk. hystero-.	nation	Gk. ethno-. See also SPECIES.
idea	Gk. ideo-.		
ileum	L. ileo-.	nature	Gk. physio-.
image	Gk. icono-.	near	Gk. para-; L. juxta-.
individual	Gk. idio-.	neck	L. cervico-.
inflammation	Gk. -itis.	needle	See POINT.
inhabiting	L. -colous.	nerve	Gk. neuro-.
insect	Gk. entomo-.	new	Gk. neo-.
interior	Gk. endo-, ento-; L. intra-, intro-.	night	Gk. nycto-; L. nocti-.
		nine	Gk. ennea-.
intestine	Gk. entero-. See also COLON, DUODENUM, ILEUM, RECTUM, VISCERA.	nitrogen	Gk. azo-; L. nitro-.
		nose	Gk. rhino-; L. naso-.
		nourishment	Gk. tropho-, -trophy. See also EAT, FOOD.
iodine	Gk. iodo-.	nucleus	Gk. karyo-; L. nucleo-.
iris (of eye)	Gk. irido-.	observation	Gk. -scope, -scopy.
iron	Gk. sidero-; L. ferro-, ferri-.	oil	L. oleo-.
		old age	Gk. geronto-.
jaw	Gk. gnatho-, -gnathous.	one	Gk. mono-; L. uni-.
joint	Gk. arthro-.	opening	Gk. -stomy (surgical).
kidney	Gk. nephro-; L. reni-.	orchid	Gk. orchido-.
kill	L. -cidal, -cide.	order	Gk. -taxis, -taxy.
knife	Gk. -tome.	organ, organic	Gk. organo-.
knowledge of	Gk. -gnomy, -gnosis, -sophy.	other	Gk. allo-. See also DIFFERENT, FOREIGN.
large	Gk. macro-. See also GREAT, LONG.	outside	Gk. ecto-, exo-; L. extra-.
larynx	Gk. laryngo-.	ovary	Gk. gyno-.
law	Gk. nomo-.	oxygen	Gk. oxy-.
lead (metal)	L. plumbo-.	pain	Gk. -algia, -odynia. See also DISEASE, SUFFERING.
leading	Gk. -agog, -agogue.		
leaf, leafy	Gk. phyllo-, -phyllous; L. -folious.	pair	Gk. zygo-. See also DOUBLE, TWO.
left	L. levo-.	palm	L. palmi-.
level	See FLAT.	paralysis	Gk. -plegia.
life	Gk. bio-, -biosis.	part	Gk. mero-, -mere, -merous.
light	Gk. photo-; L. luci-, lumini-; Gk. actino- (light ray).	path	See WAY.
		pelvis	Gk. pyelo-; L. pelvi-.
like	Gk. homeo-, homoio-, -oid, -ode; L. quasi-. See also APPEARANCE, EQUAL, FORM, SAME.	people	Gk. demo-. See also NATION.
		perpendicular	See UPRIGHT.
lime	L. calci-.	pharynx	Gk. pharyngo-.
lip	Gk. chilo-; L. labio-.	physics	Gk. physico-.
list	Gk. -logy.	pillar	Gk. stylo-.
little	See SMALL.	pistil	See OVARY.
liver	Gk. hepato-.	place	Gk. topo-.
long	Gk. macro-; L. longi-.	plant	Gk. phyto-, -phyte.
love	Gk. philo-, -phile; -philia, -phily (morbid love).	plate	See SCALE.
		pleura	Gk. pleuro-.
lung	Gk. pneumo-; L. pulmo-.	point	L. acu-. See also SPINY.
lymph	L. lympho-, lymphato-.	poison	Gk. toxico-.
magnet	L. magneto-.	position	Gk. stato-.
making	Gk. -plastic, -poietic. See also PRODUCING.	power	Gk. dyna-, dynamo-.

pressure	Gk. piezo-, baro- (atmospheric pressure).
primitive	Gk. archi-.
producing	Gk. -gen, -genous, -geny, -gony. See also BEARING, MAKING.
pulse	Gk. sphygmo-.
pus	Gk. pyo-.
race	See NATION, SPECIES.
radiant energy	L. radio-.
radiate	Gk. actino-.
radio	L. radio-.
radioactive	L. radio-.
rain	Gk. hyeto-, ombro-; L. pluvio-.
ray	See LIGHT.
recent	Gk. -cene (geology and anthropology).
rectum	Gk. procto-; L. recto-.
red	Gk. erythro-.
region	See COUNTRY, PLACE.
reproduction	Gk. gono-.
rib	L. costo-.
right	L. dextro-.
river	L. fluvio-.
rock	See STONE.
root	Gk. rhizo-.
rot	See DECOMPOSE.
rough	Gk. trachy-.
row	Gk. -stichous.
rule	See GOVERN.
run	Gk. -drome, -dromous.
sacred	Gk. hagio-, hiero-.
sacrum	L. sacro-.
salt	Gk. halo-.
same	Gk. homo-, tauto-. See also EQUAL, LIKE.
scale	Gk. lepido-; L. lamelli-.
science of	Gk. -logy, -logical, -nomy.
sea	Gk. halo-, thalasso-.
seaweed	Gk. phyco-.
second (adj.)	Gk. deutero-.
seed	Gk. spermato-, -gonium, -sperm, -spermous. See also SPORE.
seizure	Gk. -lepsy.
self	Gk. auto-.
serum	L. sero-.
seven	Gk. hepta-; L. septi-.
sexual union	Gk. gamo-.
sharp	Gk. oxy-.
short	Gk. brachy-; L. brevi-.
side	Gk. pleuro-, -hedral, -hedron (geometry).
sight	Gk. -opia, -opsia.
silicon	L. silico-.
simple	Gk. haplo-; L. simplici-.
single	Gk. haplo-.
six	Gk. hexa-; L. sex-.
skin	Gk. dermato-, dermo-, -derm.
skull	Gk. cranio-.
sleep	Gk. hypno-; L. somni-.
slender	Gk. lepto-.
slimy	Gk. myxo-.
slope	Gk. clino-, -cline (geology).
slow	Gk. brady-.
small	Gk. micro-. See also FEW.
snake	Gk. ophio-.
society	L. socio-.
soft	Gk. malaco-.
solid	Gk. stereo-.
sound	Gk. phono-, -phone, -phony.
speech	Gk. logo-, -phasia (defective).
species	Gk. phylo-.
spectrum	L. spectro-.
spermatozoa	Gk. spermato-.
sphere	Gk. -sphere.
spinal cord	Gk. myelo-.
spiny	Gk. acantho-, echino-; L. spini-.
spiral	Gk. helico-, spiro-.
spirit	Gk. pneumato-, psycho-. See also MIND.

spleen	Gk. spleno-.	thread	Gk. nemato-.	vessel	Gk. angio-; L. vaso-. See also BAG, BLADDER, CUP.
split	Gk. schisto-, schizo-; L. fissi-, -fid.	three	L. ter-, tri-.		
		throat	See LARYNX, PHARYNX, TRACHEA.	viscera	Gk. splanchno-.
spore	Gk. sporo-, -sporous.	thyroid	Gk. thyro-.	visible	Gk. phanero-.
sprout	See BUD.	time	Gk. chrono-.	voice	See SOUND.
stamen	Gk. andro-; L. stamini-.	tip	Gk. acro-.	walking	L. -grade.
star	Gk. aster-, astro-; L. sidero-, stelli-.	tissue	Gk. histo-.	water	Gk. hydro-; L. aqui-.
		toe	See FINGER.	wave	Gk. cymo-.
starch	Gk. amylo-.	tone	Gk. tono-.	wax	Gk. cero-.
stomach	Gk. gastero-, gastro-.	tongue	Gk. glosso-.	way	Gk. hodo-, odo-, -ode.
stone	Gk. litho-, petro-, -lith.	tooth	Gk. odonto-, -odont; L. denti-.	web	L. pinni-.
stop	Gk. -stat.			wealth	Gk. pluto-.
straight	Gk. ortho-; L. recti-.	top	See TIP.	wedge	Gk. spheno-.
strange	See FOREIGN.	torpor	Gk. narco-.	weight	Gk. baro-.
style	Gk. stylo- (biology).	trachea	Gk. broncho-, tracheo-.	wet	Gk. hygro-.
substitute	L. vice-.	tree	Gk. dendro-, -dendron; L. arbori-.	white	Gk. leuko-.
suffering	Gk. patho-, -pathy.			whole	Gk. holo-; L. toti-.
sugar	Gk. saccharo-.	tribe	See SPECIES.	wide	See BROAD.
sulfur	Gk. thio-; L. sulfa-, sulfo-.	tumor	Gk. -cele, -oma.	wind	Gk. anemo-. See also AIR, BREATH.
		turned	Gk. -tropous, -tropy.		
sun	Gk. helio-.	twelve	Gk. dodeca-.	wine	L. vini-.
sweet	Gk. glyco-.	two	Gk. di-; L. bi-, duo-.	wing	Gk. ptero-, -pterous; L. -pennate.
swift	Gk. tachy-.	type	Gk. typo-.		
sword	Gk. xiphi-.	united	Gk. gamo-.	woman	Gk. gyneco-, gyno-.
tail	Gk. uro-.	universe	Gk. cosmo-.	wood	Gk. xylo-; L. ligni-.
technical	Gk. techno-.	upright	Gk. ortho-.	word	Gk. logo-.
ten	Gk. deca-.	urethra	Gk. urethro-.	work	Gk. ergo-.
a tenth	L. deci-.	urine	Gk. uro-, -uria; L. urino-.	world	See UNIVERSE.
terrible	Gk. dino-.			worm	L. vermi-.
testicle	Gk. orchio-.	uterus	Gk. hystero-, metro-; L. utero-.	write	Gk. grapho-, -gram, -graph, -graphy.
thick	Gk. pachy-.				
thorax	Gk. thoraco-.	vagina	L. vagino-.	yellow	Gk. xantho-.
thousand, thousandth	L. milli-.	vein	Gk. phlebo-; L. veni-.	yoke	Gk. zygo-.

PREFIXES

about	See AROUND.	behind	See AFTER.	on this side of	L. cis-.
above	Gk. hyper-; L. super-, supra-. See also ON.	beside	Gk. para-; L. juxta-.	out	Gk. & L. ex- (e-, ec-, ef-).
		between	L. inter-.	outside	Gk. exo-; L. extra-. See also BEYOND.
across	L. trans-. See also THROUGH.	beyond	Gk. meta-; L. preter-, ultra-.		
				over	See ABOVE, ON, BEYOND, VERY.
after	Gk. meta-; L. post-.	changed	Gk. meta-.		
again	Gk. ana-; L. re-. See also BACK.	down	Gk. cata- (cath-); L. de-.	thoroughly	Gk. ana-, cata- (cath-); L. com- (co-, col-, con-, cor-), per-.
		excessively	See ABOVE.		
against	Gk. anti-; L. contra-, in- (il-, im-, ir-), ob- (oc-, of-, op-).	for	L. pro-.		
		forward	Gk. & L. pro-.	through	Gk. dia-; L. per-.
		from	L. ab- (a-, abs-). See also DOWN.	to, toward	L. ad- (ac-, af-, ag-, al-, an-, ap-, ar-, as-, at-).
among	See BETWEEN, WITHIN.				
apart	L. dis- (di-), se-. See also AWAY, FROM.	in, into	Gk. en- (el-, em-); L. in- (il-, im-, ir-), intro-. See also WITHIN.	under	Gk. hypo-; L. sub- (suc-, suf-, sug-, sum-, sup-, sur-, sus-), subter-.
around	Gk. peri-; L. circum-.				
at	See BESIDE, NEAR, TO.	not	Gk. a- (an-); L. de-, in- (il-, im-, ir-), non-.	up	Gk. ana-.
away	Gk. apo-. See also APART, FROM.	off	See APART, AWAY, FROM.	very	Gk. peri-; L. per-. See also THOROUGHLY.
back	L. retro-. See also AGAIN.	on	Gk. epi- (eph-); L. in- (il-, im-, ir-).	with	Gk. sym- (sy-, syl-, syn-).
badly	L. mal-, mis-.	on that side of	L. trans-. See also BEYOND.	within	Gk. endo-; L. intra-.
before	Gk. pro-; L. ante-, pre-.			without	See NOT, OUTSIDE.

SUFFIXES OF ADJECTIVES

able to, able to be	L. -able, -ile (-il).	coming from	L. -an.	related to	See PERTAINING TO.
adhering to or following	L. -an.	doing	L. -ant, -ent.	tending to	L. -able, -ive.
		full of	L. -ose, -ous.	worthy of	See ABLE TO.
affected by	L. & Gk. -ac.	like, of the nature of	L. -ine (-in), -ive, -ory, -ose.		
beginning to	L. -escent.				
belonging to	L. -an (in zoology).	making	See CAUSING.		
capable of	See ABLE TO.	originating in	See COMING FROM.		
causing	L. -fic.	pertaining to	Gk. & L. -ac, -ic; L. -aceous, -al, -ar, -ary, -ile (-il), -ine, -ory.	Many adjectives so formed are also used as nouns, as *animal*, *human*, etc. These nouns mean generally a person or thing related to or described by the adjective.	
characterized by	L. -al, -ate, -id. See also PERTAINING TO.				

SUFFIXES OF NOUNS

act, action	L. -al, -ion (-cion, -sion, -tion), -ment, -ure.	descendant of	Gk. -ite.	practitioner	L. -ary, -ist, -or -aster (inferior), -trix (female).
		example	See INSTANCE.		
advocate or adherent	Gk. -ist, -ite.	function	See OFFICE.		
		instance	L. -al.	result	L. -ate, -ion (-cion, -sion, -tion), -ment, -mony, -ure.
art	Gk. -ic, -ics. See also SYSTEM.	instrument	L. -ment, -ory, -ure.		
		methods	See SYSTEM.		
collection	L. -ana.	native	L. -ite.	state	See CONDITION.
condition	L. -ion (-cion, -sion, -tion), -ment, -mony, -tude.	office	L. -ate, -ure.	student	L. -ist.
		place	L. -arium, -ary, -orium, -ory.	study	See ART.
				system	Gk. -ics.

SUFFIXES OF VERBS

become	Gk. -ize; L. -fy.	combine with	L. -ate.	practice	Gk. -ize.
begin	L. -esce.	make	Gk. -ize; L. -fy.	treat with	Gk. -ize; L. -ate.

The Library Research Paper

BY WILLIAM W. WATT

What is research? In recent years the word has filtered out of the ivory tower and spread like an epidemic in the marketplace. Loose popular usage has worn the sharp edges from its meaning and threatened to deface its value. To many people *research* refers loosely to the act of looking up or checking up on anything, anywhere, in any way. Political polls, television ratings, the detection of factual errors in unpublished magazine articles, traffic counts at intersections, questionnaires on consumer habits, comparison shopping to price silk stockings—all are called *research*. The transitive verb ("I'll research it for you") appears to be catching up with the noun in popularity, and the well-drilled team is crowding out the lonely adventurer.

Though the weakening of a noble word may be disturbing, it is a useful reminder that the natural human passion for discovering, recording, and evaluating data is not—and never was—the special province of the academic expert in the library, laboratory, museum, geological quarry, or archaeological digging. The scholar's methods may be more systematic and his conclusions more profound. He may have a more sincere faith in the freedom that lies in the pursuit of truth for its own sake—in "pure" research. But he has no monopoly on the activity of research.

Of the infinite varieties, none is more generally useful than the experience that begins as a hunting expedition in a library and ends when the last period is typed on the finished paper. The library research paper is an inevitable academic assignment. Commonly known as the *term paper*, it regularly serves as a sort of commencement exercise at the end of the course or year. For the secondary school student who goes on to college, or for the college undergraduate who proceeds to graduate professional school, there is always another commencement, another beginning of a new research paper. But though the project may become increasingly ambitious and the process more complex, the essential discipline does not change with academic advancement. The basic rules remain the same. The student who forms scholarly habits of research in school will find them invaluable later, whether under the discipline of further formal education or the self-discipline of his vocation, his avocation, or a civic activity. Because the responsible adult is a student all his life, the word *student* will have no chronological limits in this article.

The experience of writing even a single research paper pays educational dividends to any serious student. It encourages him to develop a personal interest in a subject of his own choice. It offers an opportunity for genuine independent study. It introduces him to the resources of whatever library he is privileged to use. It shows him the excitement of tracking down knowledge that is not neatly packaged in a textbook or on a blackboard. It offers him the satisfaction of completing a task more thorough than any routine writing sssignment. (The word *re-search* suggests thoroughness: a *searching again*, checking *and* double-checking.)

The task demands discriminating reading at various speeds and levels, accurate note-taking, intelligent summarizing, honest and systematic acknowledgment of intellectual indebtedness, and a more intricate organization than is ever required on a short composition. The process of separating truth from error and facts from judgments, of compiling and selecting evidence to support a credible conclusion, is a general application of *scientific* method; the problem of organizing the results on paper so that they will instruct and even intrigue a reader belongs to the province of *art*. In first-rate research the "two cultures" meet.

Ideally, then, the library research paper is the product of both critical thinking and creative writing. It should reflect the enthusiasm of an alert mind, not the methodical digging of a reluctant mole. But the most talented and enthusiastic student cannot even approach the ideal unless he is aware from the start that rigorous scholarly method (not pedantic methodology) is the foundation of success. To present an elementary understanding of that method is the purpose of this article.

FINDING AND LIMITING A SUBJECT

Unless the student has a specific assignment thrust upon him by a teacher, his first problem is to choose a subject for investigation. (He is luckier, or course, if the subject has chosen him.) Selecting a suitable subject should not be a haphazard process like rolling dice at random until the right combination pays off. As soon as the writer knows that he is faced with a research deadline—usually a comfortable number of weeks away—he should do some preliminary prowling in the library, along the open stacks if that is permitted, to see what, if anything, it contains within his spheres of general interest. If a teacher has restricted the choice to the limits of a single course, he should be on the alert for clues in the unfinished business of the required reading or class discussion. A good discussion in class is full of loose ends that need to be tied together or of questions that require more time and information to answer. A good teacher will always start more game than he can bring to earth; few mortals irritate him more than the student who, after weeks of classroom suggestions, both explicit and implicit ("This would make a good subject for a research paper") comes staggering toward the deadline still fumbling around for "something to write about."

The first rule for finding a subject is hallowed by age. Two thousand years ago the Roman poet Horace put it this way: "Choose a subject, ye who write, suited to your strength." This does not mean that a student should regard a research assignment only as another chance to ride a familiar hobby. It means that the beginner's reach should not so far exceed his grasp that he will quickly become bogged down in learned technicalities that defy translation.

The second rule is that even a subject well suited to the writer's taste and talent should be strictly limited in accordance with the proposed or required length of the paper. Overly ambitious intentions usually lead to unsuccessful research papers because the student cannot possibly treat his subject adequately within the allotted space and time.

The tentative choice of a subject may be nothing more than a general idea of the territory to be explored, but before the student has ventured far he should become aware of the boundaries so that he won't waste precious hours wandering off limits. Sometimes during the early stages of research a large, nebulous subject will rapidly assume a clearly defined shape, if only because of the limitations of a particular library. More often the reverse is true: a general topic divides and subdivides and the student, who thought he had focused on a subject, finds himself helplessly confused. It is best to limit the subject in advance and avoid this predicament, especially when there is a deadline to meet.

The problem of limiting a subject for research is no different in kind from the routine dilemma of channeling an ambitious idea into a short composition. The same writer who struggles to capture the significance of "Love" or "Ambition" or "The Beat Generation" in 500 words is just as likely to propose a research paper of 3,000 on "The Poetry of Robert Browning" or "The History of Television." Certainly "Browning's Dramatic Monologues" or "Educational Television" would be preferable. Making the necessary allowances for the experience of the writer and the resources of the library, "Browning's Dramatic Monologues on Renaissance Painters" or "Closed Circuit Television in the High School Science Class" would be even better. Nothing more quickly betrays the limitations of a writer's knowledge than his inability to limit his subject.

A more specific way of limiting is to begin with a definite *thesis*—a proposition to prove, perhaps even a side to defend in a hypothetical pro and con debate: to presume to show, for example, that Browning's failure to achieve success in the theater was largely the fault of the Victorian audience, or that classroom television costs more money than it's worth. Such a proposition gives direction to the research and provides a convenient mold for the paper. But the pre-fabricated

968

thesis has caused many dangerous detours from the truth. When a writer has flown effortlessly to a conclusion, it is hard for him to persuade himself that he ought to go back and trudge over the land on foot. It is a human weakness, even among scholars, to warp the truth to accommodate a foregone conclusion, casually ignoring the stubborn facts that won't conform. Moreover, many useful subjects for research do not lend themselves to a thesis statement: they involve explanation, narrative, analysis, or revelation—but not necessarily proof. On the whole, unless a writer is already something of an expert on his subject at the start, he should postpone the choice of a thesis until he has done most of the digging.

He might, like a scientist, begin with a *working hypothesis*, a tentative proposition to serve as a guidepost. But he should always be careful not to mistake a hunch for a fact, or a prejudice for an opinion. Objectivity is at the heart of genuine scholarship. Any researcher would do well to remember Thomas Henry Huxley's definition of a tragedy: "the slaying of a beautiful hypothesis by an ugly fact."

Whatever the subject, there should be no misconceptions about the requirements of the job. Though no two subjects require identical treatment, *the final paper should make it clear that the writer has reflected on the material and marshaled it as evidence to support one or more convincing conclusions.* Many beginners honestly believe that research is only an exercise in genteel plagiarism: tracking down information and transferring it—in great chunks or little snippets—from print to typescript by way of hastily jotted notes—producing a result that could have been achieved more efficiently with a Gillette blade and a roll of Scotch tape. Many failing papers are little more than anthologies of unfamiliar quotations or patchwork quilts of paraphrase. To be sure, the novice is not required to aim at the goal of the ideal Ph.D. dissertation: "an original contribution to knowledge." He is not expected to be an authority on his subject and should not presume to be. Most of his material will have been carefully sifted by more experienced hands, but this does not exempt him from the duty of critical thinking. If he understands this from the start, he will not arbitrarily divide his labor into a physical act of compilation and a mental act of composition. From the first visit to the library he will be reflecting carefully upon the material, not just thoughtlessly jotting down notes. The final product will be a transfusion, not a series of transplants.

USING THE LIBRARY

Because no two libraries are identical, no general instruction on "how to use the library" is custom-tailored to the individual in Azusa or Zanesville. The best way for a reader to get familiar with the machinery of a particular library is to make himself at home there. He should not stride directly to the delivery desk and say to whoever is in charge: "Do you have any books on closed circuit television?" Though the librarian—especially a trained reference librarian—may provide indispensable help at a later stage of the investigation, the student should begin with a declaration of inde-

pendence. Given the run of the stacks in a small or middle-sized library, he can get off to a good start by going at once to the general territory of his subject (he can find *English Literature* or *American History* on a chart without memorizing the Dewey Decimal System). Wandering up and down the aisles from A to Z, he can get a preliminary view of the land by merely scanning the backbones of books.

But such freedom is not usually permitted in a large library, where the student may have to spend many minutes at the delivery desk waiting to receive the books he has requested. Moreover, a good research paper is not the end-product of aimless browsing. The student will save both himself and the librarian time and trouble by learning the names of the standard reference guides, where to find them, and how to use them. To do this is to practice one of the fundamental principles of research: *Always take pains in the present to avoid panic in the future.*

Regardless of the subject, three reference guides will probably prove indispensable: (1) the card catalogue; (2) a comprehensive encyclopedia; and (3) the *Reader's Guide to Periodical Literature.*

The Card Catalogue

The proper use of a card catalogue requires both imagination and persistence. (Serendipity—the ability to discover treasures that you are not looking for—is probably more of a reward for alertness and patience than a native gift.) In a complete catalogue any book in the library may be listed alphabetically on at least three cards: by subject, author (last name first), and title. Other cards serve as cross-references.

For example, a student planning a paper on "Closed Circuit Television in the High School Science Class" might begin by looking up "Television." He should find a number of subject cards with this label at the top (probably typed in red), each alphabetically arranged by author. As he shuffles further, he should find other cards with more specific subject labels. "Television—apparatus and supplies" may interest him; "Television—law and legislation" may not. A group of books catalogued under "Television in education" certainly will. The student is on his way.

A single card, like a single dictionary entry, contains a wealth of information, some of which is essential for a bibliography. Consider the scope of the data on a typical subject card of the kind disseminated throughout the country by the Library of Congress (*below*).

A Comprehensive Encyclopedia

The reader digging for a research paper should ordinarily regard a complete encyclopedia as an indispensable guide, not an ultimate goal. The writer whose footnotes and bibliography show that he has quarried his material from a half dozen competing encyclopedias—however reputable—is easily identified as an explorer who has never left his safe home in the reference room.

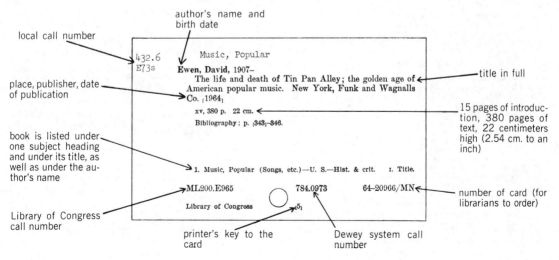

author's name and birth date

local call number

place, publisher, date of publication

book is listed under one subject heading and under its title, as well as under the author's name

Library of Congress call number

432.6	Music, Popular
E73s	**Ewen, David,** 1907–
	The life and death of Tin Pan Alley; the golden age of American popular music. New York, Funk and Wagnalls Co. ₁1964₁
	xv, 380 p. 22 cm.
	Bibliography: p. ₁343₁–346.

title in full

15 pages of introduction, 380 pages of text, 22 centimeters high (2.54 cm. to an inch)

1. Music, Popular (Songs, etc.)—U. S.—Hist. & crit.   I. Title.

ML200.E965   784.0973   64–20966/MN

Library of Congress   ₁5₁

number of card (for librarians to order)

printer's key to the card

Dewey system call number

For the conscientious student a good encyclopedia article has two main virtues: (1) it provides an authoritative and comprehensive view of a general subject, probably one in which he has staked out a more restricted claim; (2) it supplies bibliographical references which the student may not have discovered in the card catalogue. Let us take one possible example. The 1963 printing of the *Encyclopaedia Britannica* has an article on "Television" that runs to 19 large double-column pages, complete with photographs and diagrams. As the key to the contributors' initials reveals in the index volume, it is an authoritative article written by the Director of the Research Division of the Philco Corporation. But less than half a column is devoted to the applications of closed circuit TV in education. On the other hand, the article is followed by a list of six more extensive treatments of the general subject, any one of which might find a place in the student's final bibliography. Moreover, if the reader turns to "television" in the index volume, he will find other references to "educational television" that do not appear in the general entry. By consulting several good encyclopedias on a subject the student may choose one which he feels will best help him construct a firm foundation for a research paper.

The *Reader's Guide*

Neither the card catalogue nor the most complete encyclopedia can pretend to give a comprehensive listing of magazine articles that have not been corralled in a book. Even in these days of prolific publishing, many interesting subjects of limited appeal have never been fully treated in book form. New developments, especially in science, are arriving and changing with such speed that even an encyclopedia publishing an annual supplement can never be completely up-to-date. On almost any subject of general interest the first place to hunt for magazine articles is the *Reader's Guide to Periodical Literature*.

The *Reader's Guide* has been indexing current contributions to the best-known American magazines since 1901 and now includes references to more than 125 publications. The semimonthly issues (monthly in July and August) are conveniently bound in volumes that cover periods of one to four years. Articles are listed by author and subject. If a student's chosen subject relates to a specific event since 1901 ("The Hamlet of John Barrymore," "The Attack on Pearl Harbor"), he can begin at that date and work toward the present. If not, especially if he has no clues to authors, he should start with the subject entries in the most recent issues and hunt backward through the bound volumes. On looking up "Television," for example, in the volume for March 1963–February 1964, he would find three articles listed under "TELEVISION, Closed circuit" and twenty-one under "TELEVISION in education." (Any abbreviations in the entries can be understood easily by referring to a key at the front of the volume.) And these would be only a selection of the articles for one year in popular magazines: a glance at the *Education Index* (see below) would uncover many more in professional journals. It is no wonder that teachers turn gray when students report that they "can't find any material" on an obvious subject in an adequate library.

The reader with limited time and facilities cannot expect to locate every one of these articles. It is one of the inevitable frustrations of research to find that the article with the most promising title of all appears in a periodical to which the library does not subscribe. The reader should not compound the frustration by vainly wandering in the stacks. On turning to the list of periodicals at the front of each volume in the *Reader's Guide*, he may find that the ones on the premises have been ticked off in ink. If not, he should have easy access to a list of periodicals in the library without riffling through the card catalogue.

After consulting the card catalogue, several encyclopedias, and the *Reader's Guide*, the student may have enough clues to books and articles—depending always on the subject and scope of his research—to keep him busy for several weeks of digging. No amateur can be expected to play the scholar's game by all the rules—traveling for months, or even years, from library to library, borrowing books and articles at long distance through interlibrary loans, examining others on photostats or microfilms, tracking down the most infinitesimal detail to its final hiding place. But any reader can vicariously experience the excitement of such sleuthing on a smaller scale. Even the beginner should be familiar with more than three guides to research. Some of these tools

can prove indispensable to him for detecting clues to possible sources of information on his topic.

Of the innumerable research tools in a great library—including reference guides to reference books and bibliographies of bibliography—the following list contains only a generous sample.

Catalogues and Bibliographies

Books in Print (1948–   ). An annual author and title index to the *Publishers' Trade List Annual*. Lists the books still available from more than 1,100 American publishers. *Subject Guide to Books in Print* (1957–   ) lists them annually by subject.

Library of Congress Catalog (1942–   ). A complete catalogue by authors, showing facsimiles of the cards in the great library in Washington, D.C. A similar catalogue arranges books by subject.

Periodical Indexes

General

Book Review Digest (1905–   ). A monthly collection of excerpts from current book reviews indexed by author, subject, and title. It helps the reader to get a quick general picture of whether the first greetings were favorable, unfavorable, or lukewarm. More important, it directs him to reviews that he may want to read *in toto*.

International Index to Periodicals (1907–   ). A key to articles in scholarly journals that are not indexed in the *Reader's Guide*, which is limited to more popular magazines.

New York Times Index (1913–   ). A detailed index (now published twice a month) to a distinguished newspaper. Indispensable for a writer whose subject is related to any newsworthy event since the year before World War I. Even if the library does not have the complete file of the *Times* (now available in microfilm), he can make extensive use of the index to pin down exact dates, establish the chronological order of events, and find leads to news in any paper that may be available.

Poole's Index to Periodical Literature (1802–1906). Though much less thorough than the *Reader's Guide*, this annual subject index is a useful key to articles in English and American magazines in the nineteenth century.

Special

Agricultural Index (1916–   ).
Applied Science and Technology Index (1858–   ).
Art Index (1929–   ).
Dramatic Index (1909–   ).
Education Index (1929–   ).
Essay and General Literature Index (1900–   ).
Industrial Arts Index (1913–1957).
Public Affairs Information Service (1915–   ).
Short Story Index (1953–   ).

Dictionaries

Language (general)

Of all reference books, the general reader should be most familiar with his own desk dictionary, which to him may be "the dictionary." But if he is writing a paper on some aspect of English or American usage, or trying to pin down an accurate or comprehensive definition of a particular term at a particular time, he will find more complete or specialized information in the following works:

Dictionary of American English on Historical Principles. 4 vols. Chicago, 1936–1944. Supplemented by *A Dictionary of Americanisms*, 1951.

New "Standard" Dictionary. rev. ed. New York, 1959. A revision of an unabridged dictionary published by Funk and Wagnalls since 1913.

Oxford English Dictionary. 12 vols. and supplement. London and New York, 1933. When a writer is summoning up remembrance of things past, few records are more suggestive than the changing history of a word's meaning through the years. The great OED supplies such a record by citing the use of words in passages of prose and poetry, arranged in chronological order from the earliest occurrences. Once published as the *New English Dictionary* (NED).

Webster's Third New International Dictionary. Springfield, Mass., 1961. "Webster's Third" contains many new words and meanings not included in the second edition of 1934 and illustrates them profusely in actual contexts. Based on recent linguistic theory, it records—often without restrictive labels—many usages that are widely frowned on.

Language (special)

Evans, Bergen and Cornelia. *A Dictionary of Contemporary American Usage.* New York, 1957.
Fowler, H. W. *A Dictionary of Modern English Usage.* London, 1926.
Nicholson, Margaret. *A Dictionary of American-English Usage.* New York, 1957. Based on Fowler.
Roget's International Thesaurus. 3rd ed., New York, 1962.
Webster's Dictionary of Synonyms. Springfield, Mass., 1942.

Biography

Dictionary of American Biography. 20 vols. and supplements. New York, 1928–   . The DAB contains lives of dead Americans.
Dictionary of National Biography. 22 vols. and supplements. London, 1885–   . The DNB has lives of dead Britons.
International Who's Who. London, 1936–   . Annual.
Kunitz, Stanley J. and Howard Haycraft. *Twentieth Century Authors.* New York, 1942. Supplement, 1945.
Webster's Biographical Dictionary. Springfield, Mass., 1943.
Who's Who. London, 1849–   . An annual dictionary of living Britons.
Who's Who in America. Chicago, 1899–   . A biennial dictionary of living Americans.

Encyclopedias and Surveys

General

There are many good, comprehensive encyclopedias which are following an editorial program of constant revision. Any good library should have several such encyclopedias of recent copyright. These encyclopedia publishers also supply yearbooks or supplemental material to make the most recent information promptly available to the researcher.

Special

Bailey, Liberty Hyde, ed. *Cyclopedia of American Agriculture.* 4 vols. New York, 1908–1909.
Baldwin, James M., and B. Rand, eds. *Dictionary of Philosophy and Psychology.* new ed. 3 vols. New York, 1949.
Bartlett's Familiar Quotations. 13th ed. Boston, 1955.
Blom, Eric., ed. *Grove's Dictionary of Music and Musicians.* 5th ed. 10 vols. London, 1954. Supplement, 1961.
Cambridge Ancient History. 17 vols., including plates. Cambridge, 1928–1939.
Cambridge Medieval History. 16 vols., including maps and plates. Cambridge, 1911–1936.
Cambridge Modern History. 2nd ed. 13 vols. and atlas. Cambridge, 1902–1926.
Cambridge Bibliography of English Literature. 5 vols. Cambridge, 1941. Supplement 1957.
Cambridge History of American Literature. 4 vols. New York, 1917–1921.
Cambridge History of English Literature. 15 vols. Cambridge, 1907–1927.
Catholic Encyclopedia. rev. ed. 17 vols. New York, 1936–   .
Dictionary of American History. rev. ed. 5 vols. and index. New York, 1946.
Encyclopedia of World Art. New York, 1958–   . In progress.
Feather, Leonard. *Encyclopedia of Jazz.* rev. ed. New York, 1960.
Fletcher, Sir Banister. *A History of Architecture.* 17th ed. New York, 1961.
Good, C. V. *Dictionary of Education.* 2nd ed. New York, 1959.
Harper's Encyclopedia of Art. 2 vols. New York, 1937. Reissued as *New Standard Encyclopedia of Art,* 1939.
Hart, James D. *Oxford Companion to American Literature.* 3rd ed. New York, 1956.
Harvey, Sir Paul, ed. *Oxford Companion to Classical Literature.* 3rd ed. New York, 1956. *Oxford Companion to English Literature.* 3rd ed. New York, 1946.

Hastings, James, ed. *Encyclopedia of Religion and Ethics.* new ed. 13 vols. New York, 1951.
Kirk, Raymond E., and Donald F. Othmer. *Encyclopedia of Chemical Technology.* 15 vols. and supplements. New York, 1947–
Langer, William L., ed. *Encyclopedia of World History.* rev. ed. Boston, 1952.
McGraw-Hill Encyclopedia of Science and Technology. 15 vols. New York, 1960.
McLaughlin, Andrew C., and A. B. Hart, eds. *Cyclopedia of American Government.* 3 vols. New York, 1914.
Monroe, Walter S., ed. *Encyclopedia of Educational Research.* 3rd ed. by Chester Harris. New York, 1960.
Munn, Glenn G. *Encyclopedia of Banking and Finance.* rev. ed. L. Garcia. Boston, 1962.
Oxford History of English Literature. 12 vols. projected. Oxford, 1947–
Sarton, George. *Introduction to the History of Science.* 3 vols. Baltimore, 1927–1948.
Seligman, Edwin R. A., and A. Johnson, eds. *Encyclopedia of the Social Sciences.* 15 vols. New York, 1930–1935. Reissued in 8 vols., 1948.
Singer, Charles, ed. *History of Technology.* 5 vols. New York, 1956–1958.
Smith, Horatio, ed. *Columbia Dictionary of Modern European Literature.* New York, 1947.
Spiller, Robert E., ed. *A Literary History of the United States.* 3 vols. New York, 1948. rev. ed. 1 vol. 1953. Supplement by R. M. Ludwig, 1959.
Stevenson, Burton. *The Home Book of Quotations.* 9th ed. New York, 1959. Organized by subjects.
Thompson, Oscar, and N. Slonimsky, eds. *International Cyclopedia of Music and Musicians.* new ed. 3 vols. New York, 1940.
Tweney, C. F., and L. E. C. Hughes, eds. *Chambers's Technical Dictionary.* 3rd rev. ed. New York, 1958.
Universal Jewish Encyclopedia. 10 vols. and index. New York, 1939–1944.
Van Nostrand's Scientific Encyclopedia. 3rd ed. New York, 1958.

Yearbooks

In addition to the yearbooks made available by encyclopedia publishers, the following may be found useful.

American Year Book (1910–   ).
The New International Year Book (1907–   ).
Statesman's Year Book (1864–   ).
World Almanac and Book of Facts (1868–   ).

THE WORKING BIBLIOGRAPHY

At the very beginning of his search for materials the reader should be armed with a dependable pen and a supply of 3 x 5 index cards. (Pencils may smudge and encourage illegible scribbling; items jotted in notebooks or on miscellaneous scraps of paper are harder to organize and easier to overlook.) Though the search through the reference guides will turn up some material that will later prove unavailable or useless, it will pay at this stage to make a written record of every title that may conceivably bear on the chosen subject. When arranged in alphabetical form—with no more than one title on a card—these entries will form a tentative list of sources: a working bibliography. When the actual reading of sources begins, some of the cards will be jettisoned, and—as new references turn up in the reading—others will be added. The final bibliography, compiled after the paper is written, may have only a general family resemblance to its pioneering ancestor. But it is far less trouble to tear up a card that has not proved useful than it is to remember an unrecorded title or to return repeatedly to the reference guides.

To avoid trouble later on, the student should write down *the same facts in the same form* that will be required in the final bibliography. Authorities differ about the formal details, but if every researcher were permitted to follow his own fancy, whether through careless indifference or conscious resistance to tradition, the useful shorthand of scholarship would soon degenerate into chaos. The forms illustrated here for both bibliography and footnotes (pp. 1024–1026) are those recommended in *The MLA Style Sheet* (revised edition), compiled by William Riley Parker for the Modern Language Association after consulting with the editors of 109 journals and 34 university presses. No prudent beginner would ignore

such an expert jury to accommodate his own whims. Accurate scholarly form demands *the right facts in the right order with the right punctuation*. Though the standard may seem pedantic to the novice, even the substitution of a semicolon for a colon is not acceptable.

Here are some sample entries for bibliography cards. (Other varieties appear in the specimen bibliography on page 1026.)

For a book with one author:

Galbraith, John K. *The Affluent Society*. Boston, 1958.

Notice that the entry contains four parts in the following order: (1) Author's name, last name first—for alphabetizing; (2) full title—underlined (italicized); (3) place of publication; (4) date of publication. Periods separate the parts except for the comma between place and date. A period also comes at the end of the entry. Unless a different form of an author's name is well known (Eliot, T. S., or Maugham, W. Somerset), give the first name and any initials. Nobody wants to search through a large catalogue for Brown, J.

Some authorities insist on including the name of the publisher. It comes after the place of publication and is preceded by a colon and followed by a comma:

Galbraith, John K. *The Affluent Society*. Boston: Houghton Mifflin, 1958.

For a book with more than one author:

Sledd, James H., and Gwin J. Kolb. *Dr. Johnson's Dictionary*. Chicago, 1955.

Because the second name does not determine the alphabetical placing of the entry, it follows the normal order. If a book has more than two authors, it is sufficient to give the name of the first and add "and others."

For a periodical article:

Lippmann, Walter. "Cuba and the Nuclear Risk," *Atlantic*, CCXI (February 1963), 55–58.

The standard form has five parts in this order: (1) Author's name, last name first (the title comes first if the author is not known); (2) full title of article—in quotes; (3) name of periodical—underlined (italicized); (4) volume—in Roman numerals—and date—in parentheses; (5) page numbers. Except for the period after the author's name, the parts are separated by commas. Notice that this form differs from that of the *Reader's Guide*, where the entry reads:

Cuba and the nuclear risk. Atlan 211:55–8 F '63.

Such an abbreviated form should not be copied onto bibliography cards.

For a newspaper article:

New York *Times*, December 28, 1964, p. 6.

The place of publication is not ordinarily underlined, and the page number is preceded by the standard abbreviation for *page* (lower case p.). If a newspaper has two or more sections with separate paging, the section number is included after the date:

New York *Times*, January 3, 1965, sec. 4, p. 7.

For an encyclopedia article:

Fink, Donald G. "Television," *Encyclopaedia Britannica* (1963), XXI, 910A–913.

In addition to this minimum of information, the student should allow room in the upper left-hand corner of the card for the call number. This will save unnecessary trips to the card catalogue. If the library is large and unfamiliar and the stacks are open, it is helpful to add a further note about the location:

613.84   Neuberger, Maurine B. *Smoke Screen:*
N478s   *Tobacco and the Public Welfare*. Engle-
(2nd floor,   wood Cliffs, N.J., 1963.
north stack)

EVALUATING SOURCES

As soon as the student turns from the cards of his working bibliography to the actual pages of the sources, he can begin to evaluate the material. Often a quick glance at a book or article will assure him that it is not appropriate; the card, in this case, may be torn up at once. Though other sources will require more careful attention, the researcher should always be ready to change his reading pace, slowing down when the material is complicated or difficult, and speeding up when it is readily comprehensible. The independent reading for research will give him an incomparable opportunity to practice whatever he knows about the difference between skimming and thorough reading. Bacon's proverbial wisdom will become a practical reality: "Some books are to be tasted, others to be swallowed, and some few to be chewed and digested...." "A man," said Samuel Johnson, "will turn over half a library to make one book." But not, the Doctor might have added, if the man plods through all the reading at the same unchanging pace.

Only a seasoned expert in a field can know for certain what authors to respect as authorities or disregard as quacks. But even the beginner can show some intelligent discrimination. The inexperienced reader can learn to evaluate sources just as the scholar does, by asking a few questions based on *external* and *internal evidence*. For example:

External Evidence

Who wrote the book or article? What's in a name? To a conscientious scholar, a great deal. If a name turns up again and again during the investigation—especially if others explicitly refer to the owner as an authority—it is a reasonable, though not a foolproof, assumption that he is more dependable than an obscure author. If the author has a pedigree in one or more standard biographical dictionaries, so much the better, though it must not be forgotten that the elect compile their own pedigrees. A Civil War historian in a great university probably knows more about the battle of Gettysburg than a feature writer commemorating the anniversary for a small town newspaper. A professional folklorist should have a more accurate knowledge of the history of the popular ballad than an itinerant guitar strummer.

Who published it? Though it is risky to make odious comparisons in the mushrooming world of publishing, a reader with some experience will be safer in trusting a reputable imprint of long standing than a new and untested brand name. A scholarly book published by a university press is probably a safer, if duller, guide to a specialized subject than a popular best-seller concocted for the trade. A sober account in the New York *Times* should be fitter to quote than a sensational exposé in a cheap tabloid.

When was it written? Is the material first-hand, second or third? A newspaper extra printed on December 8, 1941 might capture the confused excitement of the attack on Pearl Harbor, but an unbiased study published ten years later would probably be a more reliable source for the facts. An estimate of Winston Churchill published in 1919 would lack the perspective of a book written after the Battle of Britain. A student writing on a subject that is changing as swiftly as "Space Travel" or "Jet Propulsion" will naturally look for the latest word; a scholar delving into the past will be eager to uncover the earliest. The investigator with limited time and experience will lack the scholar's opportunities for tracking down a subject to its *primary sources*—burrowing beyond the printed page to the original manuscript. But he can share the scholar's desire for getting as near as possible to the first-hand truth of an event, the actual wording of a text or document. If he is writing about Shakespeare's treatment of the theme of mercy, he doesn't have to summarize a paraphrase of Portia's speech from a student cram book when a reputable text of *The Merchant of Venice* is close at hand. Nor should he quote a critic from the *Book Review Digest* when the original review is on a nearby shelf.

Internal Evidence

What does the actual text of the book or article reveal about the reliability of the author? The experienced reader will find it easier to answer such a question than the novices but it does not take much sophistication to distinguish between critical thinking and slanted writing (is the author's

manner analytical or emotional, are the words neutral or loaded?); or between a disinterested search on all sides of the truth and an argument that is mere propaganda; or between a thorough investigation leading to conclusions founded on facts and a superficial survey resulting in unsupported conjectures.

Considering the amount of piffle on paper, no experienced reader has an ingenuous faith in the sanctity of print for its own sake. But many a reader who ought to know better, eager to accumulate evidence to support a thesis, will gather material at random without the slightest attention to the quality or reliability of his sources. The true scholar does not snap up ill-considered trifles; he is a discriminating reader and a natural skeptic. He not only wants to be shown, he insists on being convinced.

TAKING NOTES

It is sometimes convenient to jot down a general note about a book or article on one of the 3 x 5 bibliography cards. "A comprehensive survey with no recent evidence on the subject." "A jazzy sketch to amuse the reader, not inform him." But more specific or extensive notes should be on separate cards. Because they will not be shuffled in the same deck with the bibliography, these note cards need not be of the same size. Most scholars recommend 4 x 6 note cards (or slips of paper); some prefer half sheets ($5\frac{1}{2}$ x 8). Here convenience is more important than tradition. Note cards should be small enough to sort handily, large enough to allow room for legible notes, but not so large as to invite wholesale transcribing.

Note-taking is a useful art, whether in routine reading, lectures, class discussions, or meetings of clubs and committees. In research it assumes some of the dimensions of an exact science. The individual may eventually derive a personal method that suits him best. The following are some hints and warnings:

Do not take too many notes. Note-taking should be an aid to discriminating reading, not an opportunity for voluminous writing. The reader who postpones all his mental sorting until he begins to go through his note cards to write the paper is making his task unnecessarily difficult.

Restrict each note to one point on one side of the card. The definition of *point* is always arbitrary. It may be a sharp point like a brief direct quotation or a broad point like a short summary of a paragraph or a whole article. But do not clutter up a note with a miscellaneous scattering of quota-

tions and reactions scribbled at random on both sides. The careful assignment of points to cards is another step in the winnowing process that accompanies research from start to finish. Organizing a research paper is not unlike playing a hand of bridge. If aces could not be quickly distinguished from deuces, or face-up cards from face-down, the game would be impossible.

Identify each card accurately at the top with a brief caption for the note and a key to the source, including the exact page number or numbers. If the complete information on the source appears, as it should, on a bibliography card, all that is necessary on a note card is the author's name and the page —or, if he is responsible for more than one source, a short title: Muir, p. 61 or *The Present Age*, pp. 158–159. If a direct quotation extends from one page to another, carefully indicate the division with a slant line (/) at the appropriate point.

Take notes with meticulous care. Note-taking is not jotting. Even when reading rapidly, come to a full stop at any important intersection. If necessary, look back and ahead to avoid the common distortion that comes from ripping a passage hastily out of its context. Remember that a careless glance may change *psychology* to *physiology*, and a single illegible word in a key quotation may later require an emergency trip to the library to revisit a book that somebody else has since withdrawn. Get it right the first time.

Take pains to distinguish between direct quotation and paraphrase and between the author's ideas and your own reactions to them. (The word *paraphrase* is used here in its general sense to mean any rewriting of another's material in your own words, whether it expands, contracts (summarizes), or keeps to the scale of the original.)

Nothing is more confusing and annoying to the reader of a research paper than the writer's failure to make these distinctions clear. Wholesale transgressions of this kind may represent conscious plagiarism. More often they result from ignorance of the meaning of research or of the rules of literary ethics. Because the problem sometimes arises at the writing stage, it is discussed in more detail on page 1024. But often a bad research paper–like a failing examination–can be traced back to poor or carelessly taken notes. Any passage taken word-for-word from the text, even a clause or unusual phrase, should appear in the notes in bold quotation marks. The student who "forgot to put in the quotes" is either dishonest, naive, or inexcusably careless. If the note-taker temporarily abandons direct quotation for paraphrase, he should carefully close the quotes and open them again when the paraphrase is finished. If he makes an independent comment of his own

IV. 2. a   "Social Balance"   Galbraith, 251-269

We ignore need for balance between private production and public services. Inadequate services in cities, blighted and polluted countryside, neglected education and recreation, inadequate housing -- vs. more and more cars, T.V. sets, comic books, switchblade knives, gimmicks and gadgets. "Social balance," which would bring greater enjoyment to life, hindered by power of private advertising," the truce on inequality," tendency to inflation.
[This published in 1958. How much progress since?]

in the middle of a quotation or paraphrase, he should enclose it in square brackets [thus], not parentheses (thus). He might even go so far as to identify it with his own initials.

Take particular pains to copy quotations precisely. Any scholar will quote much more than he finally uses, but even at the note-taking stage, it is wise to limit direct quotations to short passages *precisely* transcribed. Precisely means word for word, spelling for spelling (except for obvious typographical errors), punctuation mark for punctuation mark. Any omission from a quotation should be carefully identified with three spaced periods (. . .) followed by the period at the end of the sentence where appropriate. Every theater-lover is familiar with the way a press agent can play fast and loose with a critic's review. The reviewer may write: "My final judgment is that, except for the acting, the play is brilliant." With the dots carefully omitted, the advertisement reads: "My final judgment is that the play is brilliant." The scholar's rule is not pedantry, but simple honesty.

Examine each of the sample note cards carefully. The first note, conceivably for a paper on "The Economics of American Poverty," presents a brief summary of an entire chapter in John Kenneth Galbraith's *The Affluent Society*. (The code number in the upper left-hand corner has presumably been supplied later when the cards were organized to match an outline for the paper.) Because the phrases "Social Balance" and "the truce on inequality" are, at least in this context, Galbraith's own, they are put in quotation marks. The reader's reaction is carefully segregated in square brackets.

Even the liveliest argument can't move ahead in a straight line without a well-articulated skeleton.

Though the traditional outline form can at times become a strait jacket for a writer, it has a number of virtues: (1) It tells the writer where he has been, where he is, and where he is going; (2) It reminds the writer that the reader demands the same information, suggesting the need for topic sentences (expressed or implied) and adequate transitions; (3) It avoids unnecessary repetition; (4) It emphasizes the importance of symmetry and proportion; (5) It requires the writer to coordinate his main points, subordinate his subpoints, and relegate trivia to limbo.

A formal outline should follow the accepted method of subordination:

I.
  A.
    1.
    2.
      a.
      b.
  B.

The writer should use either a *topic outline* (limited to words or phrases) or a *sentence outline* (with complete sentences). According to strict rule, the two types should not be mixed. The sentence outline has the advantage of requiring specific assertions (which may turn into topic sentences) instead of ambiguous catchall topics. But with many kinds of material, sustaining a sentence outline is an artificial struggle.

11.3.4   *Services*   Galbraith, pp. 258-259

Residential housing can't be limited to private sector. "It is improbable that the housing industry is greatly more incompetent or inefficient in the United States than in those countries -- [Scandinavia, Holland, or (for the most part) England -- where slums have been largely eliminated and where <u>minimum</u> standards of cleanliness and comfort are well above our own. As the experience of these countries shows . . . the housing industry functions well only in combination with a large, complex, and costly array of public services." Land purchase, clearance, city planning, zoning, research and architectural services, public assistance for poor.

A passage of direct quotation has been sandwiched between two short pieces of paraphrase in the second note. Notice the slant line marking the transition from page 258 to 259, the parentheses (Galbraith's, not the note-taker's), the line under *minimum* to represent Galbraith's italics, and the three spaced periods to mark an omission from the quotation. Were the omission at the end of a sentence, a fourth spaced period would follow (. . . .).

THE OUTLINE

When a student has made the last of his notes and carefully read them all through to get a bird's-eye view of the land, he is finally ready to plan the actual writing of the paper. Teachers of writing differ about the value of a formal outline for a short composition, but for a research paper of 2,000 words or more, some sort of blueprint is indispensable.

Common errors in outlining should be strictly avoided; examples of these are given below.

The meaningless category

"Introduction," "Body," and "Conclusion," for example, are often too general to be useful. Oftentimes a writer can do better by ignoring the introduction entirely and plunging his pen right into the body.

Illogical coordination

I. Athletics
  A. Football
  B. Baseball
  C. Basketball
  D. Team sports

Improper subordination

Placing a topic under the wrong heading:

I. Athletics
   A. Football
   B. Baseball
      1. Good sportsmanship

Or putting a main point in a subordinate position:

I. School life
   A. Athletics
      1. Major sports
      2. Minor sports
   B. Classroom activities
      1. Discussion
      2. Learning

Single subdivision

If *I* is divided at all, it should have at least two subheads, A and B. If A is divided, it should have at least two subheads, 1 and 2. And so forth. The temptation to use a single sub-head can be resisted by following a heading with a colon and a qualifying phrase. A. Athletics: a cause of student failure.

Here is a topic outline displaying the organization of this article: (Because details can be tucked in place as the writing progresses, a practical working outline might be simpler than this. The small bones are supplied here to help the reader in studying and reviewing the article.)

The Library Research Paper

I. The meaning of research
   A. A fashionable word
   B. A popular human activity
   C. The value of the research paper

II. Choosing and limiting a subject
   A. How and where to look
   B. Over-sized subjects
   C. Ways of reducing
      1. From general to specific
      2. The thesis: use and abuse
      3. The working hypothesis
   D. Keeping the end in view

III. Using the library
   A. Browsing in the stacks
   B. Consulting reference works
      1. Three indispensable guides
         a. The card catalogue
         b. A comprehensive encyclopedia
         c. The *Reader's Guide*
      2. Other research tools
         a. Catalogues and bibliographies
         b. Periodical indexes
         c. Dictionaries
         d. Encyclopedias and surveys
         e. Yearbooks

IV. The working bibliography
   A. The value of cards and completeness
   B. The proper forms
      1. For a book
      2. For a periodical article
      3. For a newspaper article
      4. For an encyclopedia article
   C. Evaluating sources
      1. Shifting reading speed
      2. External evidence
         a. Who wrote it?
         b. Who published it?
         c. When was it written?
      3. Internal evidence: the necessity for skepticism

V. Taking notes
   A. Hints and warnings
      1. Taking too many
      2. One to a card
      3. Identifying cards
      4. Meticulous care
      5. Quotation, paraphrase, comment
      6. Precise copying
   B. Samples

VI. The outline
   A. The uses of outlining
   B. The accepted form
      1. Proper subordination
      2. Topic and sentence outlines
   C. Common errors
      1. The meaningless category
      2. Illogical coordination
      3. Improper subordination
      4. Single subdivision
   D. A sample

VII. Writing the paper
   A. Style: English vs. Acadamese
   B. Tone
   C. Quotation and paraphrase revisited
      1. Short quotation
      2. Long quotation
      3. Partial paraphrase
      4. Complete paraphrase
      5. Half-baked paraphrase
   D. Footnotes
      1. For a book
      2. For a periodical article
      3. For a newspaper article
      4. For an encyclopedia article
      5. Shortened footnotes
   E. Abbreviations
   F. The final bibliography
   G. The final draft

WRITING THE PAPER

Except for the greater complexity of organiztion and the special problems of quotation, paraphrase, and proper acknowledgment, "writing up" the results of research is not essentially different from writing any other kind of paper. Whatever laws govern grammar and diction, spelling and punctuation, sentence and paragraph structure, none of them is suspended for research. The freedom to experiment with language may be more limited; the premium on clarity and accuracy is even higher. There is less room for the infinite riches of rhetoric: the drama and poetry of narrative and description are usually replaced by the humbler virtues of clear exposition. But good writing is good writing regardless of its habitat.

Illusions about research die hard. Even students who are convinced that the paper should be composed, not compiled, often assume that the art of composition requires a special style—freighted with *Academese*—and a special tone—impersonal, stuffy, and deadly dull.

Academese is only one kind of jargon. There is also *Pedagese*, the jargon of educationists, and *Scientese*, the jargon of would-be scientists, *Legalese*, *Commercialese*, and *Officialese*. All these dialects share the traits of jargon: involved sentence structure; unnecessary repetition and interminable circumlocution; a pseudotechnical vocabulary. Such writing has been called *gobbledygook* or—suggesting that it is often contrived to impress or even confuse—*bafflegab*. It might be better to revive the old-fashioned word *crabbed*—pronounced slowly with two syllables. A crabbed style suggests an animal that can move its imposing armaments forward only by slow, sideways slithering.

An expert talking to other experts will inevitably use the technical terms of his trade. Nobody writing on a technical subject, whether the propulsion of a rocket or the scansion of a poem, can entirely avoid technical language. But the problem is to explain it, not exploit it, to understand it, not merely parrot it. Genuine technical language is concise, concrete, and clear; it serves to identify and limit a phenomenon—a *paramecium*, not a *wiggly beasty*, *iambic pentameter*, not *words with a regular beat*. Pseudotechnical language is pulpy, abstract, and cryptic—*the intellectual confrontation in an interpersonal situation* instead of *the meeting of human minds*. The proliferation of such jargon by scholars does not make it scholarly.

The style and tone appropriate to a research paper will vary, of course, with the subject, the writer, and the intended reader. A style can be formal without being involved, or informal without being casual and careless. For the general writer who does not pretend to expert knowledge, the best advice on style is simply this: Relax but don't be lax; say simple things simply in your own language; do not write anything, even a quotation or a borrowed idea, in words that

you do not understand yourself; be as concrete as possible; remember that, of all the virtues of good writing, the greatest is *clarity*.

The tone of a research paper can be serious without solemnity, dignified without stuffiness. The goal is not a charming personal essay; the reader is presumably interested in the subject, not the personality of the middle man. But the studied effort to be impersonal—and therefore ostensibly disinterested—often results in writing without either personality or interest. Though practice varies, it is better for a writer to use the first person, *I*, than to get tangled in the circumlocutions—the passive voice, for example—of the impersonal manner. Humor and irony may be useful if they grow naturally out of the subject instead of being thrust upon it. Irrelevant wisecracking is taboo. Jokes will not improve stale prose. The essential rule for tone is that all good writing more nearly reflects the living sound of a human voice, than the metallic chatter of a computer.

Quotation and Paraphrase Revisited

One special writing problem—anticipated in the discussion of note-taking—requires expansion here: the proper use of quotation and paraphrase. Make a careful comparison of the following samples:

(1) Short quotation

Leo Stein once said this about composition: "Every personal letter one writes, every personal statement one makes, may be creative writing if one's interest is to make it such."

(A short quotation in a research paper, as in any other paper, is introduced by a colon, or a comma, and carefully enclosed in quotation marks.)

(2) Long quotation

Talking about how to teach the proper use of language, Leo Stein said:

There is no difficulty in teaching them the routine of expression . . . but it is good to make them realize that there is no essential difference between them and those who write, except interest, use and purpose—that creativity in writing means nothing more than fitting words accurately and specifically to what one specifically and accurately intends. Shakespeare certainly intended more than most and had exceptional gifts, but anyone who has anything to say and wants to interest the receiver has a like object. Every personal letter one writes, every personal statement one makes, may be creative writing if one's interest is to make it such. Most people do not have this interest; what they write in ordinary communications is as dull as they can make it. They have never been taught to think of all writing as in its degree *writing* and all speaking *speaking*, and so they write in rubber stamps [clichés] and speak in the current routine of slang, as though writing and speaking were something reserved for the elect.

(Because the quotation is long—meaning, according to a common rule, five lines or more of typescript—it is set off in a separate paragraph, indented, and typed single-space without quotation marks. The student has represented Stein's italics (*writing, speaking*) by underlining. The three spaced periods in the first sentence stand for a deletion by the writer of the paper, and the bracketed word [clichés] is his addition.)

(3) Partial paraphrase

Leo Stein maintains that creative writing is "nothing more than fitting words accurately and specifically to what one specifically and accurately intends." That Shakespeare had greater intentions and gifts does not, he insists, alter the rule. "Every personal letter one writes, every personal statement one makes, may be creative writing if one's interest is to make it such." A person who has no interest in writing or speaking, who mistakenly assumes that they are "reserved for the elect," will inevitably settle for dullness couched in clichés.

(To compress Stein's passage while preserving some of the original flavor, the writer of the paper uses an acceptable blend of paraphrase and direct quotation. Restricting the paraphrase to his own words and carefully setting off Stein's exact words in quotation marks, he weaves the two into a single tapestry.)

(4) Complete paraphrase

Leo Stein argues that creativity is not a special gift awarded to writers and speakers and denied to ordinary mortals. If he has something to say and is interested in saying it well, anyone, even in a personal letter, can be a creative writer.

(The summary, entirely in the student's own words, reproduces Stein's essential meaning but loses some of the flavor. It has the advantage of brevity.)

All four techniques are acceptable, depending on the purpose and scope of the paper. One *unacceptable* technique is far too common: a confusing mixture of the words of the source and the words of the student without proper distinction between them. It has been called *half-baked paraphrase*.

(5) Half-baked paraphrase

Stein says that students ought to be taught that people in general just don't bother to take advantage of their creativity, which only means in writing fitting words accurately and specifically to what one specifically and accurately intends. Shakespeare intended more than most and had exceptional gifts, but anyone who has anything to say and wants to interest the receiver has a like object. People in general are dull with words because they couldn't care less. They don't bother to think of all writing as in its degree writing and all speaking speaking, and so they use rubber stamps and slang.

(Though they are mixed clumsily with some comment of his own, the student has appropriated appreciable amounts of Stein's own wording without identifying it in quotation marks. A footnote or a bibliographical entry does not excuse this common practice. Whether it results from carelessness, laziness, or dishonesty, it is plagiarism.)

To quote or not to quote? No sacred formula answers the question. A historian working with original documents will resort to frequent quotation. A literary scholar cannot adequately analyze the work of a poet without reproducing excerpts from the poems, line by line, exactly as they appear in the original. But many inexperienced students quote too much: their research papers are merely collections of quotes loosely tethered by incidental interruptions. Generally speaking, direct quotation is useful to clinch an important point, to preserve some of the authentic flavor of the source, or to reproduce a passage that is particularly well written or peculiarly inept. A student should never quote at length unless the passage is especially important for his purpose.

FOOTNOTES

Footnotes should be carefully supplied during the writing process, not superimposed later as an afterthought. In the first draft they can be included temporarily in the text itself. Even in the final draft, short notes may be conveniently inserted in the text in parentheses (*Hamlet* III. ii.61–64) if the source is clearly identified and they do not clutter up the page with too many interruptions. Otherwise, footnotes are usually placed at the bottom of the page, not at the end of the paper. They are keyed to the text with Arabic numerals—not asterisks or other symbols—and should be numbered consecutively throughout the paper. The number in the text should be raised slightly above the line, and placed after any mark of punctuation and at the end—not the beginning—of any quotation, long or short. The number should not be enclosed in parentheses or followed by a period, either in the text or at the bottom of the page. At the foot of the page each note should begin with a capital letter on a new line—with the number raised and indented—and end with a period.

Occasionally a footnote is useful to supply an interesting detail or incidental comment that does not fit conveniently into the text. But in a research paper most footnotes are supplied to acknowledge specific borrowings from sources. Unlike the bibliography, which is a general listing of sources, they usually provide exact page references. With that exception, a complete footnote furnishes the same essential information as a bibliographical entry, but with a different system of punctuation and in a slightly different order.

A footnote is always used to acknowledge a direct quotation unless its exact source is made clear in the text or is familiar (like the Gettysburg Address) to any educated reader. But in spite of a common illusion, the student's responsibility does not end there. He should also use a footnote (1) to acknowledge the use of another writer's idea or opinion *even if it is completely paraphrased*, and (2) as a receipt for the loan of any facts, statistics, or other illustrative material that he has not acquired by original observation.

Here is a representative group of complete footnotes: (Compare them with the bibliographical entries on page 1026,

observing the differences in punctuation and order of their parts.)

For a book with one author:

[1]John K. Galbraith, *The Affluent Society* (Boston, 1958), p. 23.

For a book with more than one author:

[2]James H. Sledd and Gwin J. Kolb, *Dr. Johnson's Dictionary* (Chicago, 1955), pp. 49–50.

For a periodical article:

[3]Walter Lippmann, "Cuba and the Nuclear Risk," *Atlantic*, CCXI (February 1963), 57.

For a newspaper article:

[4]New York *Times*, December 28, 1964, p. 6.

[4]New York *Times*, January 3, 1965, sec. 4, p. 7.

For an encyclopedia article:

[5]Donald G. Fink, "Television," *Encyclopaedia Britannica* (1963), XXI, 912.

Whenever a source is used for the first time, the student should give a complete footnote even though most of the information will be repeated in the bibliography. If, however, some of the details appear in the text—the author's name, for example, or the title—it is unnecessary to repeat them at the foot of the page. After the first footnote, an abbreviated form may be used if the complete note is not buried too far back. The easiest short form is the author's last name:

[6]Galbraith, p. 29.

If previous notes refer to more than one work by the same author, a shortened title should be added:

[7]Galbraith, *Affluent Society*, p. 29.

The popularity of the following Latin abbreviations is on the wane, partly because they have led to widespread misunderstanding. Though the writer may never be required to use them, he should understand their meaning in the footnotes of others: (They are sometimes italicized because of their foreign origin.)

Ibid.	short for *ibidem*, meaning "in the same place." Refers to the same page of the same source cited in the footnote *immediately preceding*.
Ibid., p. 57.	another page of the same source cited in the footnote *immediately preceding*.
Galbraith, *op. cit.*, p. 59.	short for *opere citato*, meaning "in the work cited." Refers here to page 59 of the opus by Galbraith cited in a recent footnote. Obviously has no advantage over the use of the author's name alone or author and short title.
Op. cit., p. 59.	may be used if the author's name is made clear in the text.
Loc. cit.	short for *loco citato*, meaning "in the place cited"—that is, the same passage as in a recent footnote. Never used with a page number. Not used at all by many modern scholars.

Because documentation is intended to help the reader, not impress or confuse him, discretion is the better part of valor. If, for example, a number of short quotations from the same source appear in one paragraph of the paper, or if the writer is indebted to one authority for a tissue of small facts, it is unnecessary to present the reader with a whole flock of ibids. On occasion a single covering note may be sufficient:

[1]My main authority for the facts about the charge of the Light Brigade is Cecil Woodham-Smith, *The Reason Why* (New York, 1953), pp. 207–257.

As Frank Sullivan once observed, if you give a footnote an inch it will take a foot.

The student may find the following abbreviations useful in either footnotes or bibliography:

Abbreviations Commonly Used in Footnotes and Bibliographies

anon.—anonymous

c. or ca.—from Latin *circa*, meaning "about." Used with approximate dates (c. 1340).

cf.—compare (cf. p. 47). Should not be used interchangeably with *see* (see p. 79).

ch., chs., chap., chaps.—chapter(s)

col., cols.—column(s)

ed., eds.—editor(s), edition(s)

f., ff.—and the following page(s) or line(s). 76f. or 76ff. 76–78 and 76–87 are more exact.

l., ll.—line(s)

n., nn.—note(s). For example, p. 69, n. 3 refers to the third footnote on page 69. Also p. 69*n* (italicized without the period).

n.d.—no date. Inserted in square brackets when date of publication is not given.

no., nos.—number(s)

par., pars.—paragraph(s)

passim—here and there throughout the work

pseud.—pseudonym

rev.—review, reviewed (by), revised (by), revision

sc.—scene in a play. Unnecessary in short notes if acts are put in large Roman numerals, scenes in small Roman numerals, lines in Arabic (IV.iii.27–46).

sic—Latin for "thus" or "so." Inserted in square brackets to make a succinct comment on something in a quotation such as an error in logic or spelling [sic].

vol., vols.—volume(s)

THE FINAL BIBLIOGRAPHY

If exact indebtedness to sources is carefully acknowledged throughout the footnotes, a final bibliography may not be required. In scholarly publishing, a full-length book is usually supplied with one, an article is not. A teacher will often insist on a bibliography as an exercise in formal acknowledgment and a convenient map of the ground actually covered in preparing the paper. Ordinarily it should be no more than a *selected bibliography*. A complete inventory of all the discoverable sources may be useful to a specialist, but only an ingenuous student would expect extra credit for his ability to transcribe the card catalogue and the *Reader's Guide*. A selected bibliography contains only those items on the bibliography cards that have proved useful in writing the paper. The length of the list is roughly proportionate to the paper's scope. In a long list it may be convenient to have two or more groupings, separating books from articles, or sourses of special importance from sources of general interest. For most research papers a single alphabetical listing is sufficient. Note that each entry in the following specimen contains the same information in the same order as on a bibliography card. If a book or article does not have an author, it is usually listed alphabetically under the first important word of the title.

Selected Bibliography

Ashworth, John. "Olivier, Freud, and Hamlet," *Atlantic*, CLXXXIII (May 1949), 30–33.

Brown, John R., "Theatrical Research and the Criticism of Shakespeare and His Contemporaries," *Shakespeare Quarterly*, XIII (1962), 451–461.

Hankins, John E. "Caliban the Bestial Man," PMLA, LXII (September 1947), 793–801.

Knight, G. Wilson. "The Embassy of Death: An Essay on Hamlet," *The Wheel of Fire* (London, 1949), 17–30.

Littleton, Taylor, and Robert R. Rea, eds. *To Prove a Villain: The Case of King Richard III.* New York, 1964.

Raysor, Thomas M., ed. *Coleridge's Shakespearean Criticism.* 2 vols. Cambridge, Mass., 1930.

"Shakespeare at 400," *Life*, LVI (April 24, 1964), 58–99.

Shakespeare, William. *The Complete Works*, ed. George Lyman Kittredge. Boston, 1936.

Tillyard, E. M. W. *The Elizabethan World Picture.* London, 1943.

Traversi, D. A. *An Approach to Shakespeare.* 2nd rev. ed. New York, 1956.

THE FINAL DRAFT

The final draft of the research paper should be typed—double-spaced—on one side of heavy white paper (not onion skin) 8½ x 11 inches and unlined. Footnotes and long indented quotations should be single-spaced. Two spaces should appear between footnotes and three between the text and the first note. The pages should be numbered with Arabic numerals, either centered at the top or in the upper right-hand corner. Whether held in a binder or merely with a paper clip, the pages should be kept flat, not folded as in a shorter composition. Margins should be at least an inch wide all around. The title should appear on both the first page (about two inches from the top) and on a separate title page, which should also include the author's name, the date, and the name of the course, if any. Corrections in the final draft should be strictly limited, preferably made by neat erasing and retyping. A sloppy paper inevitably suggests a sloppy mind. Besides, it is absurd for the writer to stumble in haste over the final barrier after he has taken so long to come so far.

ABBREVIATIONS COMMONLY IN USE

The following alphabetical list of abbreviations with their meanings includes those that are commonly employed in reference works, textbooks, journals, and newspapers. Where two or more forms of an abbreviation are shown, as by capital letter or lower-case letter, or with a following period or without such period, each form is in recognized use. Where an abbreviation covers two or more meanings, each meaning is given in alphabetical sequence, and where, in such listing, a given abbreviation is sometimes used in a form which applies to one meaning only, that separate usage is shown in parentheses following the meaning to which it applies. In abbreviations of foreign words, as Latin, the meaning of the abbreviation is first given, followed by the word or phrase, in brackets, in the language of origin. Many of the abbreviations here given are not capitalized when used independently; but in combination with proper names they are properly capitalized, as *ft.* (fort) in Ft. Henry; *mt.* (mount) in Mt. Shasta; *coll.* (college) in Claverling Coll.; *dept.* (department) in Dept. of Biology.

A

a. about; alto; ampere; are (measure); area; argent; before [L *ante*]; year [L *anno*].
a., a assists (baseball).
a., A acre.
A. Absolute (temperature).
A argon.
A, A angstrom (unit).
AA, A.A. Alcoholics Anonymous; anti-aircraft.
AAA, A.A.A. American Automobile Association.
A.A.A.L. American Academy of Arts and Letters.
AAAS, A.A.A.S. American Academy of Arts and Sciences; American Association for the Advancement of Science.
AAE, A.A.E. American Association of Engineers.
AAF, A.A.F. (formerly) Army Air Forces.
A. and M. Agricultural and Mechanical (College).
Aar. Aaron.
A.A.U. Amateur Athletic Union.
a.b., ab (times) at bat.
a.b., A.B. able-bodied (seaman).
Ab alabamine.
A.B. Bachelor of Arts [L *Artium Baccalaureus*].
AB adapter booster; airborne.
ABA American Bar Association.
a & b assault and battery.
aband. abandoned.
abbr., abbrev. abbreviation.
ABC the alphabet; American Broadcasting System; Audit Bureau of Circulation.
ab ex. from without [L *ab extra*].
ab init. from the beginning [L *ab initio*].
abl. ablative.
ABM antiballistic missile.
abp. arterial blood pressure.
abr. abridged; abridgment.
abs. absent; absolute (temperature); absolutely; abstract.
abstr. abstract; abstracted.
a.c., A.C. alternating current.
a/c, A/C account; account current.
Ac actinium.
AC, A.C. Air Corps.
A.C. after Christ.
a.c. before meals [L *ante cibum*].
acad. academic; academy.
acc. acceptance; accompanied; account; accountant.
acc., accus. accusative.
ACC, A.C.C. Air Coordinating Committee.
accel. accelerando; accelerate.
acct. account; accountant.
ack. acknowledge; acknowledgment.
A.C.P. American College of Physicians.
acpt. acceptance.
ACS, A.C.S. American Chemical Society.
A/cs Pay. accounts payable.
A/cs Rec. accounts receivable.
act. active.
actg. acting.
ACTH adrenocorticotropic hormone.
ad. advertisement.
a.d. before the day [L *ante diem*].
A.D. year of our Lord [L *anno domini*].
ADA, A.D.A. American Dental Association; Americans for Democratic Action.
A.D.C., a.d.c. aide-de-camp.
add. addenda; addendum; addition; additional; address.
ad fin. at the end; to one end [L *ad finem*].
ad inf. to infinity [L *ad infinitum*].
adj. adjacent; adjective; adjourned; adjunct; adjustment.
Adj., Adjt. Adjutant.
ad lib. to the amount desired [L *ad libitum*].
adm. administrative; administrator; admitted.
Adm. Admiral; Admiralty.
adv. adverb; adverbial; advertisement.
ad val. according to value [L *ad valorem*].
advt. advertisement.
ae., aet., aetat., of age [L *aetatis*].
A.E.A. Actors' Equity Association.
A.E. and P. Ambassador Extraordinary and Plenipotentiary.
AEC, A.E.C. Atomic Energy Commission.
AEF, A.E.F. American Expeditionary Force.
aeron. aeronautics.
a.f., A.F., AF, a-f audio frequency.
Af. Africa; African.
AF, A.F. Air Force.
A.F.A.M., A.F.&A.M. Ancient Free and Accepted Masons.
AFB Air Force Base.
Afg., Afgh. Afghanistan.
AFL, A.F.L., A.F. of L. American Federation of Labor.
AFL-CIO, A.F.L.-C.I.O. American Federation of Labor—Congress of Industrial Organizations.
A.F.M. American Federation of Musicians.
Afr. Africa; African.
A.F.T.R.A. American Federation of Television and Radio Artists.
A.F.T. American Federation of Teachers.
Ag. August.
Ag silver [L *argentum*].
AG, A.G. Adjutant General; Attorney General.
agcy. agency.
agr., agri., agric. agricultural; agriculture; agriculturist.
agt., Agt. agent; agreement.
AHQ, A.HQ. Army Headquarters.
A.I. in the year of the discovery [L *anno inventionis*].
AK Alaska (P.O. abbr.).
a.k.a. also known as.
A.K.C. American Kennel Club.
al. other things (persons) [L *alia, alii*].
AL, A.L. Aviation Electronicsman.
AL Alabama (P.O. abbr.).
Al aluminum.
Ala. Alabama.
ALA, A.L.A. American Library Association.
Alas. Alaska.
Alb. Albania; Albanian; Albany; Alberta.
Alba. Alberta (Canada).
Ald., Aldm. Alderman.
alg. algebra.
Alg. Algeria; Algerian.
A.L.P. American Labor Party.
alt. alteration; alternate; altitude; alto.
Alta. Alberta (Canada).
alum. aluminum.
a.m., A.M. before noon [L *ante meridiem*].
Am. America.
Am americium.
AM, am. amplitude.
am. ammeter.
AM, A.M., a-m, a.m. amplitude modulation.
Am. alabamine; America; American.
A.M. Air Mail; in the year of the world [L *anno mundi*]; Master of Arts [L *Artium Magister*].
A.M.A. American Management Association; American Medical Association.
Amb. Ambassador.
A.M.D.G., AMDG to the greater glory of God [L *ad majorem Dei gloriam*].
A.M.E. African Methodist Episcopal.
Amer. America; American.
AMG, A.M.G. Allied Military Government (of Occupied Territory).
Am. Ind. American Indian.
amp. ampere; amperage.
amp-hr. ampere-hour.
amt. amount.
amu atomic mass unit.
AMVETS American Veterans (of World War II and the Korean War).
an. anonymous; before [L *ante*].
anal. analogous; analogy; analysis; analytic(al).
anat. anatomical; anatomy.
anc. ancient; anciently.
and. moderately slow [It. *andante*].
And. Andorra.
Ang. Anglican; Angola.
Angl. Anglican; Anglicized.
anim. animated [It. *animato*].
ann. annals; annual; annuities; annuity; years [L *anni*].
anon., Anon. anonymous.
ans. answer; answered.
ant. antenna; antiquarian; antiquity; antonym.
Ant. Antarctic; Antarctica.
anthrop., anthropol. anthropological; anthropology.
antilog. antilogarithm.
antiq. antiquarian; antiquities.
a/o, A/O account of.
AOL, A.O.L., a.o.l. absent over leave.
Ap. apostle; April.
ap. apothecary.
AP, A.P., a.p. antipersonnel.
A.P., AP Associated Press.
APB all points bulletin.
apmt. appointment.
APO, A.P.O. Army Post Office.
Apoc. Apocalypse; Apocrypha; Apocryphal.
app. apparatus; apparent; appended; appendix; apprentice.
appar. apparatus; apparent.
approx. approximate; approximately.
Apr., Apr April.
APS, A.P.S. Army Postal Service.
apt(s). apartment(s).
aq., Aq. aqueous; water [L *aqua*].
AQ, A.Q. achievement quotient.
a.r. in the year of the reign [L *anno regni*].
Ar. argon; silver [L *argentum*].
ar. argent; aromatic; arrival; arrive.
Ar., Arab. Arabia; Arabian; Arabic.
AR Arkansas (P.O. abbr.).
Aram. Aramaic.
ARC, A.R.C. American Red Cross.
arch. archaic; archaism; archery; archipelago; architect.
Arch., Archbp. Archbishop.
archaeol., archeol. archaeology; archeology.
Archd. Archdeacon; Archduke.
archit. architecture.
archt. architect.
arg. argent; silver [L *argentum*].
Arg. Argentina; Argyll.
arith. arithmetic; arithmetical.
Ariz. Arizona.
Ark. Arkansas.
Arm. Armenia; Armenian.
Ar.M. Master of Architecture [L *Architecturae Magister*].
arr. arrange; arranged; arrangements; arrival; arrive; arrived.
art. article; artificial; artist.
A.R.V. American Revised (Standard) Version (of the Bible).
AS anti-submarine.
AS, AS., A.S. Anglo-Saxon.
as., asym. asymmetric.
As arsenic.
ASA, A.S.A. American Standards Association.
asb. asbestos.
ASCAP, A.S.C.A.P. American Society of Composers, Authors and Publishers.
asgd. assigned.
A.S.P.C.A. American Society for the Prevention of Cruelty to Animals.
ass. assistant; association.
Ass., Assyr. Assyrian.
assd. assigned.
assn. association.
assoc. associate; association.
asst., Asst. assistant.
Assyr. Assyria; Assyrian.
astr., astron. astronomer; astronomical; astronomy.
astrol. astrologer; astrological; astrology.
AT, A.T. anti-tank.
at. atmosphere; atomic.
At astatine.
ATC, A.T.C. Air Transport Command.
athl. athlete; athletic; athletics.
Atl. Atlantic.
atm. atmosphere; atmospheric.
at. no. atomic number.
ATS, A.T.S. Army Transport Service; Auxiliary Territorial Service.
att., attn., atten. attention.
att., atty. attorney.
attrib. attribute; attributive; attributively.
Atty. Gen. Attorney General.
at. wt. atomic weight.
a.u., A.u., A.U. angstrom unit.
Au gold [L *aurum*].
A.U.C. from (the year of) the building of the city (of Rome) [L *ab urbe condita*].
aud. audible; audit; auditor.
Aug. August **(Aug)**; Augustan; Augustus.
AUS, A.U.S. Army of the United States.
Aus., Aust. Austria.
Aus., Austl. Australia.
auth. authentic; author; authority; authorized.
Auth. Ver. Authorized Version (of the Bible).
auto. automatic; automotive.
aux., auxil. auxiliary.
A.V. Authorized Version (of the Bible).
a.v., a/v, A/V according to value [L *ad valorem*].
Av. avenue.
av., avdp. avoirdupois.
av., avg. average.
AVC, a.v.c. automatic volume control.
ave. avenue.
avg. average.
avn. aviation.
avoir. avoirdupois.
A/W actual weight; all water.
AWL, A.W.L., a.w.l. absent with leave.
AWOL, A.W.O.L., a.w.o.l., awol absent without leave.
AWVS, A.W.V.S. American Women's Volunteer Services.
ax. axis; axiom.
AZ Arizon (P.O. abbr.).
az. azimuth; azure.

B

b., b base; base hit; baseman.
b., B. bachelor; balboa (coin); base; bass; basso; bat; battery; bay; bench; bicuspid; bolivar (coin); boliviano; book; born; brass; breadth; brother.
B. bacillus; Bible; British; Brotherhood.
B bishop (chess); boron.
B/- bag; bale.
Ba barium.
B.A. Bachelor of Arts [L *Baccalaureus Artium*]; British Academy.
bach. bachelor.
bact., bacteriol. bacteriological; bacteriologist; bacteriology.
B.A.E. Bachelor of Aeronautical Engineering; Bachelor of Arts in Education.
B. Ag., B. Agr. Bachelor of Agriculture.
B. Ag. Sc. Bachelor of Agricultural Science.
bal. balance; balancing.
Balt. Baltic.
Bap., Bapt. Baptist.
bapt. baptized.
bar. barometer; barometric; barrel; barrister.
BAR, B.A.R. Browning automatic rifle.
B. Ar., B. Arch. Bachelor of Architecture.
barit. baritone.
Bart. Baronet.
B.A.S., B.A.Sc. Bachelor of Agricultural Science; Bachelor of Applied Science.
bat., batt. battalion; battery.
b.b., bb base(s) on balls.
B.B.A., B.Bus. Ad. Bachelor of Business Administration.
BBC, B.B.C., British Broadcasting Corporation.
bbl, bbl. barrel; barrels.
B.C. Bachelor of Chemistry; Bachelor of Commerce; before Christ; British Columbia.
B.C.E. Bachelor of Chemical Engineering; Bachelor of Civil Engineering.
bch. bunch.
B.C.L. Bachelor of Civil Law.
B.C.P. Book of Common Prayer.
B.C.S. Bachelor of Chemical Science.
bd. board; bond; bound; bundle.
B.D. Bachelor of Divinity.
b.d., B/D bank draft; bills discounted; brought down.
bd. ft. board feet.
bdg. binding.
bdl., bdle. bundle.
B.D.S. Bachelor of Dental Surgery.
bds. bundles; (bound in) boards.
BDSA Business and Defense Services Administration.
Be beryllium.
B.E. Bachelor of Education; Bachelor of Engineering; Bank of England; Board of Education.
B.E., B/E, b/e bills of exchange.
BEC Bureau of Employees' Compensation.
B.E.E. Bachelor of Electrical Engineering.
bef. before.
BEF., B.E.F. British Expeditionary Force(s).
Bel., Belg. Belgian; Belgium.
Beng. Bengal; Bengali.
B. ès L. Bachelor of Letters [F *Bachelier ès Lettres*].
B. ès S. Bachelor of Sciences [F *Bachelier ès Sciences*].
bet., betw. between.
bev, BEV billion electron volts.
BEW, B.E.W. Board of Economic Warfare.
b.f., bf. bold face.
b.f., B/F brought forward.
B.F. Bachelor of Finance; Bachelor of Forestry.
B.F.A. Bachelor of Fine Arts.
BFDC Bureau of Foreign and Domestic Commerce.
bg. bag(s).
B.G. Brigadier General.
bhp brake horsepower.
Bi bismuth.
Bib. Bible; Biblical.
bibl., Bibl. biblical; bibliographical.
bibliog. bibliography.
bicarb. bicarbonate of soda.
b.i.d. twice a day [L *bis in die*].
biochem. biochemistry.
biog. biographer; biographical; biography.
biol. biological; biologist; biology.
BIS, B.I.S. British Information Services.
B.J. Bachelor of Journalism.
Bk berkelium.
bk. bank; block; book.
bkg. banking.
bkkpg. bookkeeping.
bklr. black letter.
bkpt. bankrupt.
bks., Bks. barracks; books.
bkt. basket(s); bracket.
b.l., B/L bill of lading.
bl. bale; barrel; black; blue.
B.L., B.LL. Bachelor of Laws.
B.L.A. Bachelor of Liberal Arts.
bld bold face.
bldg., blg. building.
B.L.E. Brotherhood of Locomotive Engineers.
B. Lit., B. Litt. Bachelor of Letters (Literature) [L *Baccalaureus Litterarum*].
blk. black; block.
bln., bln balloon.
bls. bales; barrels.
BLS Bureau of Labor Statistics.
B.L.S. Bachelor of Library Science; Bachelor of Library Service.
blvd. boulevard.
b.m. board measure.
BM, B.M. Bureau of Mines.
B.M. Bachelor of Medicine [L *Baccalaureus Medicinae*]; Bachelor of Music [L *Baccalaureus Musicae*].
B.M.E. Bachelor of Mechanical Engineering; Bachelor of Mining Engineering.
B. Mech. E. Bachelor of Mechanical Engineering.
BMEWS Ballistic Missile Early Warning System.
BMR basal metabolic rate.
B. Mus. Bachelor of Music.
Bn., bn. battalion.
B.N. bank note.
B.N.A. Basel Anatomical Nomenclature [L *Basle Nomina Anatomica*]; British North

America.
b.o. back order; body odor; box office; branch office; broker's order; buyer's option.
BO, B.O. Board of Ordnance.
B/O brought over.
Boh., Bohem. Bohemia; Bohemian.
Bol. Bolivia.
bor. borough.
bot. botanical; botanist; botany; bottle.
B.O.T. Board of Trade.
bp, b.p. below proof; boiling point.
b.p. B/P bill of parcels; bills payable.
B.P. Bachelor of Pharmacy.
B.P., B.Ph., B.Phil. Bachelor of Philosophy [L *Baccalaureus Philosophiae*].
bp. birthplace; bishop.
B.Pd., B.Pe. Bachelor of Pedagogy.
B.P.E. Bachelor of Physical Education.
B.P.H. Bachelor of Public Health.
BPI, B.P.I. Bureau of Public Inquiries.
B.P.O.E. Benevolent and Protective Order of Elks.
BPPC Brussels Pact Permanent Commission.
br. branch; brand; brief; bridge; brig; bronze; brother.
Br. Breton, Britain, British.
Br bromine.
B.R., B/R Bill of Rights.
b.r., B/R bills receivable.
Braz. Brazil; Brazilian.
Brazil. Brazilian.
B.R.C.S. British Red Cross Society.
B.Rec., b.rec. bills receivable.
brev. brevet; brevetted.
Br. Hond. British Honduras.
Brig. Brigade; Brigadier.
Brig. Gen. Brigadier General.
Brit. Britain; Britannia; Britannica; British.
bro. brother.
bros. brothers.
b.s. balance sheet.
b.s., B/S bill of sale.
B.S. Bachelor of Surgery.
B/S bags; bales.
B.S., B.Sc. Bachelor of Science [L *Baccalaureus Scientiae*].
B.S.A. Bachelor of Scientific Agriculture; Bibliographical Society of America; Boy Scouts of America.
B.S.Ed. Bachelor of Science in Education.
bsh. bushel(s).
BSM Bronze Star Medal.
B.S.S., B.S.Sc. B.S. in S.S. Bachelor of (Science in) Social Sciences.
Bt. Baronet.
B.T., B.Th. Bachelor of Theology.
B.T.U., BTU, B.th.u., Btu British thermal unit.
Btry. battery.
bu. bureau.
bu., bu bushel; bushels.
buck. buckram.
bul., bull. bulletin.
Bulg. Bulgaria; Bulgarian.
B.V. Blessed Virgin [L *Beata Virgo*]; farewell [L *bene vale*].
B.V.M. Blessed Virgin Mary [L *Beata Virgo Maria*].
bvt. brevet; brevetted.
bx. box.
Bz. benzene.

C

C carbon; constant; Roman numeral for 100.
C., c. about [L *circa*]; calends; candle; capacity (electrical); cape; carton; case; catcher (baseball); cathode; cent; centime; cents; century; chapter; chief; child; church; copyright; cost; cubic; current.
c., c, C., C centigrade; centimeter.
C. Catholic; Celtic; Chancellor; Congress; Conservative; Court.
c.a., C.A. chief accountant; claim agent; commercial agent; consular agent; controller of accounts.
ca. about [L *circa*]; cathode; centiare.
Ca calcium.
C.A. Catholic Action; Central America; Coast Artillery; Confederate Army.
CA, C.A. chronological age.
CA California (P.O. abbr.).
C/A commercial account; credit account; current account.
CAA, C.A.A. Civil Aeronautics Administration (Authority).
CAB, C.A.B. Civil Aeronautics Board.
C.A.F., c.a.f. cost and freight; cost, assurance and freight.
cal. calendar; calends; caliber; calomel; small calorie (**cal**).
Cal., Cal caliber; large calorie.
Calif., Cal. California.
Cam camouflage.
can. canon; canto.
Can. Canada; Canadian.
Canad. Canadian.
canc. cancel; cancellation; canceled.
cant. canton; cantonment.
Cant. Canterbury; Canticles; Cantonese.
Cantab. Cambridge [L *Cantabrigia*].
cap. capital; capitalize; chapter [L *caput*].
CAP, C.A.P. Civil Air Patrol.
caps capital letters.
Capt. Captain.
car. carat.
CAR, C.A.R. Civil Air Regulations.
Card. Cardinal.
CARE Cooperative for American Remittances Everywhere.
cat. catalog; catechism.
cath. cathedral.
Cath. Catholic.
CATV community antenna television.
cav. cavalier; cavalry.
CAVU, C.A.V.U. ceiling and visibility unlimited.
c.b. center of buoyancy; confined to barracks.
Cb columbium; cumulonimbus.
CB Construction Battalion.
C.B. Bachelor of Surgery [L *Baccalaureus Chirurgiae*].
CBC, C.B.C. Canadian Broadcasting Corporation.
C.B.D., c.b.d. cash before delivery.
CBS, C.B.S. Columbia Broadcasting System.
c.c., C.C. carbon copy; cash credit; cashier's check; chief clerk; circuit court; city council; city councilor; civil court; common councilman; company clerk; company commander; consular clerk; contra credit; county clerk; county commissioner; county council; county court; current account [F *compte courant*].
cc. chapters.
cc, cc., c.c. cubic centimeter.
Cc cirrocumulus.
CC cyanogen chloride (poison gas).
CCA Commission for Conventional Armaments.
C.C.A. Chief Clerk of the Admiralty; Circuit Court of Appeals.
CCC, C.C.C. Civilian Conservation Corps; Commodity Credit Corporation.
CCF, C.C.F. Cooperative Commonwealth Federation (of Canada).
CCS, C.C.S. Combined Chiefs of Staff.
cd candela.
c.d. cash discount.
cd., cd cord.
Cd cadmium.
c/d, C/D carried down.
C.D. Civilian Defense.
cd. ft. cord foot (feet).
CDR, Cdr. Commander.
CE Council of Europe; Corps of Engineers.
C.E. Chemical Engineer; Chief Engineer; Church of England; Civil Engineer.
Ce cerium.
CEA Council of Economic Advisers.
CED Committee for Economic Development.
Celt. Celtic.
cen., cent. central; century.
cent. centered; centigrade; centimeter; one hundred [L *centum*].
CERN European Council for Nuclear Research [F *Centre Européen des Recherches Nucléaires*].
cert. certificate; certify.
certif. certificate; certificated.
cet. par. other things being equal [L *ceteris paribus*].
Cey. Ceylon.
c.f., cf center field(er).
c.f., C.F. cost and freight.
cf. compare [L *confer*].
Cf californium.
c/f, C/F carried forward.
c.f.i., C.F.I. cost, freight, and insurance.
cfm, c.f.m. cubic feet per minute.
CFR, C.F.R. Code of Federal Regulations.
cfs, c.f.s. cubic feet per second.
c.g., C.G. center of gravity; consul general.
cg., cg, cgm. centigram(s).
CG Commanding General.
C.G. Coast Guard.
C.G.H. Cape of Good Hope.
cgs, CGS, c.g.s. centimeter–gram–second.
c.h., C.H. clearing-house; courthouse; customhouse.
C.H. Companion of Honor.
Ch. Chaldean; Chaldee; China; Chinese.
ch. chain; champion; chargé d'affaires; check (chess); chestnut; chervonets; chief; child; children; chirurgeon; church; of surgery [L *chirurgiae*].
ch., chap. chaplain; chapter.
c.-h., c-hr. candle-hour.
Chanc. Chancelor; Chancery.
char. character; charter.
Ch.B. Bachelor of Surgery [L *Chirurgiae Baccalaureus*].
Ch. Clk. Chief Clerk.
Ch.E., Che.E. Chemical Engineer.
chem. chemical; chemist; chemistry.
chg. charge.
chgd. charged.
Chin. Chinese.
Ch.J. Chief Justice.
Ch.M. Master of Surgery [L *Chirurgiae Magister*].
chm. checkmate.
chm., chmn. chairman.
Chr. Christ; Christian.
chron., chronol. chronological; chronology.
Chron. Chronicles.
chs. chapters.
Ci cirrus.
CIA Central Intelligence Agency.
Cia., cia. company [Sp. *Compania*].
CIAA Coordinator of Inter-American Affairs.
CIC, C.I.C. Counter-Intelligence Corps.
C.I.D. Criminal Investigation Department (Brit.).
Cie., cie. company [F *compagnie*].
c.i.f., C.I.F. cost, insurance, and freight.
C. in C., C in C, CINC, Cinc Commander in Chief.
CIO, C.I.O. Congress of Industrial Organizations.
cir., circ. about [L *circa, circiter, circum*]; circular; circulation; circumference.
cit. citation; cited; citizen.
civ. civil; civilian.
C.J. body of law [L *corpus juris*]; Chief Judge; Chief Justice.
ck. cask; check; cook.
Cl chlorine.
c.l. carload; carload lots; center line; civil law; craft loss (insurance).
cl. centiliter(s); claim; class; classification; clause; clearance; clergyman; clerk; cloth.
clar. clarinet.
class. classic; classical; classification; classified; classify.
cler. clerical.
climatol. climatological; climatology.
clin. clinic; clinical.
clk. clerk; clock.
clm. column.
C.L.U. Chartered Life Underwriter.
CM court martial.
c.m. church missionary; circular mil; common meter; corresponding member.
C.M. Master of Surgery [L *Chirurgiae Magister*].
cm., cm centimeter(s)
CM curium.
Cmdr. Commander.
C.M.G. Companion (of the Order) of St. Michael and St. George.
cml. commercial.
CMTC, C.M.T.C. Citizens' Military Training Camp.
c.n., C/N circular note; credit note.
CNO Chief of Naval Operations.
Cn cumulonimbus.
CNS, C.N.S. central nervous system.
CO Colorado (P.O. abbr.).
C.O. commanding officer; conscientious objector.
co., Co. company; county.
c/o, C/O, c.o. care of; carried over; cash order.
Co cobalt.
coad. coadjutor.
c.o.d., C.O.D. cash on delivery; collect on delivery.
Cod., cod. codex.
Codd., codd. codices.
coef. coefficient.
C. of C. Chamber of Commerce.
C. of S. Chief of Staff.
cog., cogn. cognate.
col. collected; collector; college; colonial; colony; color; colored; column.
Col. Colombia; Colonel; Colorado; Columbia.
Col., Col, Coloss. Colossians.
coll. colleague; collect; collection; collective; collector; college; colloquial.
collab. collaborated; collaboration; collaborator.
collat. collateral.
colloq. colloquial; colloquialism; colloquially.
Colo., Col. Colorado.
colog cologarithm.
com. comedy; comic; comma; commentary; commerce; commercial; common; commonly; commune; communication; community.
Com. Commission; Commissioner; Committee; Commodore; Communist.
Com., Comdr. Commander; Commodore.
Com., Como., COMO, Commodore.
comb. combination.
comdg. commanding.
Comdt. Commandant.
Com. in Ch., Cominch Commander in Chief.
coml. commercial.
comm. commander; commentary; commerce; commercial; commissary; commission; committee; commonwealth; commutator.
COMO, Como Commodore.
comp. companion; compare; compilation; compiled; complete; composition; compositor; compound; comprising.
compar. comparative.
compt. compartment; comptometer.
Comr. Commissioner.
Com. Ver. Common Version (of the Bible).
con. against [L *contra*]; concerto; conclusion; condense; conduct; connection; consols; consolidate; continued; wife [L *conjunx*].
Con. Conformist; Consul.
conc. concentrate; concentrated; concentration; concerning.
Confed. Confederate; Confederation.
cong. gallon [L *congius*].
Cong. Congregational; Congress; Congressional.
conj. conjugation; conjunction; conjunctive.
Conn. Connecticut.
cons. consecrated; conserve; consigned; consignment; consolidated; consonant; construction; consulting.
cons., Cons. constable; constitution; constitutional; consul.
consol. consolidated.
const., Const. constable; constant; constitution.
constr. construction; construed.
cont. containing; contents; continent; continue; contract; contraction; contrary; control.
Cont. Continental.
contd. continued.
contemp. contemporary.
contg. containing.
contin. continued; let it be continued [L *continuetur*].
contr. contract; contralto; control.
contrib. contribution; contributor.
CONUS Continental United States.
coop., co-op. cooperative.
cop. copper; copyright; copyrighted.
Cop. Copernican; Coptic.
cor. corner; cornet; coroner; corpus; correct; corrected; correction; correlative; correspondence; correspondent; corresponding; corrupt.
Cor. Corinthians.
corol., coroll. corollary.
Corp. Corporal.
corp., corpn. corporation.
corr. correct; corrected; correspond; correspondence; correspondent; corresponding; corrupt; corrupted; corruption.
correl. correlative.
corresp. correspondence.
c.o.s., C.O.S. cash on shipment.
cos. companies; counties.
cos cosine.
cosec cosecant.
cosh hyperbolic cosine.
cot cotangent.
coth hyperbolic cotangent.
covers coversed sine.
c.p., C.P. chemically pure; court of probate.
CP command post.
cp. compare.
cp, c.p. candlepower.
C.P. Canadian Press; Cape Province; center of pressure; Chief Patriarch; Common Prayer; Communist Party.
C.P.A. Certified Public Accountant.
cpd. compound.
C.P.H. Certificate in Public Health.
Cpl. corporal.
cpm, c.p.m. cycles per minute.
CPO, C.P.O., c.p.o. Chief Petty Officer.
cps, c.p.s. cycles per second.
cpt. counterpoint.
CPTP, C.P.T.P. Civil Pilot Training Program.
CQ Charge of Quarters.
cr. created; credit; creditor; crescendo; creek; crown(s).
Cr chromium.
CR Construction Recruit.
C.R. Costa Rica.
craniol. craniological; craniology.
craniom. craniometry.
cres., cresc. crescendo.
crim.con. criminal conversation.
crit. critic; critical; criticism.
crs. credits; creditors.
CRT cathode-ray tube.
cryst. crystalline; crystallography; crystals.
Cs cesium; cirrostratus.
C.S. Christian Science; Christian Scientist; Confederate States.
C.S., c.s. capital stock; civil service.
C/S, cs. case; cases.
C.S.A. Confederate States of America.
csc cosecant.
CSC Civil Service Commission.
C.S.C. Conspicuous Service Cross.
csch hyperbolic cosecant.
csk. cask; countersink.
CSO, C.S.O. Chief Signal Officer (CSigO); Chief Staff Officer.
CSS Commodity Stabilization Service.
C.S.T., CST, c.s.t. central standard time.
CT Communications Technician.
C.T., CT, c.t. central time.
ct. cent(s); certificate; county; court.
Ct. Connecticut; Count.
CTC, C.T.C. Citizens' Training Camp.
ctg. cartridge.
ctn cotangent.
ctnh hyperbolic cotangent.
ctr. center.
cts. centimes; cents; certificates.
cu., cu cubic.
Cu copper [L *cuprum*]; cumulus.
cu. cm., cu cm cubic centimeter(s).
cu.ft. cubic foot; cubic feet.
cu.in. cubic inch(es).
cur. currency; current.
cu.yd. cubic yard(s).
C.V. Common Version (of the Bible).
cv., cvt. convertible.
cw, CW continuous wave.
CWA, C.W.A. Civil Works Administration.
C.W.O., c.w.o. cash with order.
CWO, C.W.O. Chief Warrant Officer; Commissioned Warrant Officer.
CWS Chemical Warfare Service.
cwt. hundredweight.
cy. capacity; currency; cycles.
cyc. cyclopedia; cyclopedic.
cyl cylinder.
CYO, C.Y.O. Catholic Youth Organization.
C.Z. Canal Zone.

D

d. date; daughter; day(s); dead; decree; degree; delete; democrat(ic); deputy; diameter; died; director; dividend; dollar; door; dose; dyne; give [L *da*].
d penny; pence [L *denarius, denarii*].
D. December; Department; Dutch; God [L *Deus*]; Lord [L *Dominus*].
D deuterium; Roman numeral for 500.
da. daughter; day(s).
D.A. District Attorney; Delayed Action.
DA Dental Apprentice.

D.A.B., DAB Dictionary of American Biography.
D.A.E., DAE Dictionary of American English.
dal., dal decaliter.
Dak. Dakota.
Dan. Daniel; Danish.
Danl. Daniel.
D.A.R., DAR Daughters of the American Revolution.
dat. dative.
dau. daughter.
DAV, D.A.V. Disabled American Veterans.
Dav. David.
D.B. Domesday Book.
d.b. daybook.
db, db. decibel; decibels.
d.b.a. doing business as.
D.B.E. Dame (Commander, Order) of the British Empire.
d.b.h. diameter at breast height *(forestry)*.
D. Bib. Douai Bible.
dbl. double.
DC Dental Corps; Disarmament Commission.
d.c., d–c, dc, d c, D.C., D–C, DC, D C direct current.
D.C. District of Columbia; Doctor of Chiropractic; from the beginning [It. *da capo*].
D.C.L. Doctor of Canon Law; Doctor of Civil Law.
D.C.M. Distinguished Conduct Medal (Brit.).
D.C.S. Deputy Clerk of Sessions; Doctor of Christian Sci-
dd., d/d. delivered.
DD Department of Defense.
D.D. Doctor of Divinity [L
ence; Doctor of Commercial Science.
d.d., D/D demand draft.
d.d., D/d, D/D days after date; days' date.
Divinitatis Doctor].
D.D.S. Doctor of Dental Science (or Surgery).
D.D.Sc. Doctor of Dental Science.
DE Delaware (P.O. abbr.); Destroyer Escort; Doctor of Engineering; Doctor of Entomology.
deb., deben. debenture.
Deb. Deborah.
dec. deceased; declaration; declension; declination; decrease; decrescendo.
dec., decim. decimeter.
Dec., Dec December.
decd. deceased.
decl. declension.
decoct. decoction.
decresc. decrescendo.
ded., dedic. dedication.
def. defective; defendant; defense; deferred; defined; definite; definition.
deg. degree(s).
del. delegate; delete; deliver; he (she) drew it [L *delineavit*].
Del. Delaware.
deliq. deliquescent.
Dem. Democrat; Democratic.
demon. demonstrative.
Den. Denmark.
denom. denomination.
dent. dental; dentist; dentistry.
dep. departs; departure; deposed; deposit; depot.
Dep. dependency.
dep., dept. department; deponent; deputy.
der., deriv. derivation; derivative; derive; derived.
dermatol. dermatological; dermatologist; dermatology.
desc. descendant.
descr. descriptive.
D. ès L. Doctor of Letters [F *Docteur ès Lettres*].
D. ès S. Doctor of Sciences [F *Docteur ès Sciences*].
det. detach; detachment; detail.
Deu, Deut. Deuteronomy.
devel. development.
D.F. Dean of the Faculty; Defender of the Faith [L *Defensor Fidei*]; Federal District [Pg. *Districto Federal;* Sp. *Distrito Federal*].
DF, D/F, D.F. direction finding.
D.F.C., DFC Distinguished Flying Cross.
D.G. by the grace of God [L *Dei gratia*].
dg., dg decigram(s).
dh designated hitter (baseball).
d.h. deadhead; that is to say [G *das heisst*].
DHQ Division Headquarters.
di., dia. diameter.
Di didymium.
diag., diagr. diagram.
dial. dialect; dialectic; dialectical.
diam. diameter.
dict. dictation; dictator; dictionary.
diet. dietetics.
diff. difference; different; differential.
dil. dilute.
dim. dimension.
dim., dimin. diminuendo; diminutive.
din. dinar.
dioc. diocesan; diocese.
dipl. diplomat; diplomatic.
dir. director.
dis. distance; distant.
disc. discount; discover; discovered.
disch. discharged.
diss. dissertations.
dist. discount; distance; distant; distinguish; distinguished; district.
Dist. Atty. District Attorney.
distr. distribute; distributed; distribution; distributive; distributor.
div. divergence; diversion; divide; divided; dividend; divine; division; divisor; divorced.
Div. Divinity.
DK Disbursing Clerk.
dk. deck; dock.
dkg., dkg dekagram(s).
dkl., dkl dekaliter(s).
dkm., dkm dekameter(s).
dks., dks dekastere(s).
dl., dl deciliter(s).
D/L demand loan.
D.Lit., D.Litt. Doctor of Letters (Literature) [L *Doctor Lit(t)erarum*].
dlr. dealer.
D.L.S. Doctor of Library Science.
dm., dm decameter(s); decimeter(s).
D.M. Deputy Master.
DM., Dm. Deutschemark.
DM Draftsman.
DMB Defense Mobilization Board.
D.M.D. Doctor of Dental Medicine [L *Dentariae Medicinae Doctor*].
D.Mus. Doctor of Music.
D.N. our Lord [L *Dominus noster*].
DNA deoxyribonucleic acid.
DNB, D.N.B. Dictionary of National Biography (British).
do. ditto.
D.O. Doctor of Osteopathy.
D.O.A. dead on arrival.
doc. document.
dol. dolce; dollar; dollars **(dols.)**.
Dom. Dominica; Dominican.
dom. domestic; dominion.
Dor. Dorian; Doric.
Dow. Dowager.
doz., doz dozen(s).
DP, D.P. degree of polymerization; diametrical pitch; displaced person.
D.P.H. Doctor of Public Health.
D.P.Hy. Doctor of Public Hygiene.
D.Ph., D.Phil. Doctor of Philosophy.
dpt. department; deponent.
D.P.W. Department of Public Works.
D.R., D/R, d.r. dead reckoning; deposit receipt.
dr. debtor; dram(s).
Dr. doctor; drive.
dram. pers. dramatis personae.
d.s. daylight saving; days after sight; document signed.
ds., ds decistere(s).
Ds dysprosium.
D.S., d.s. (repeat) from this sign [It. *dal segno*].
D.S., D.Sc. Doctor of Science.
D.S.C. Distinguished Service Cross.
D.S.M., DSM Distinguished Service Medal.
D.S.O. Brit. Distinguished Service Order; District Staff Officer.
d.s.p. died without issue [L *decessit sine prole*].
DSRD, D.S.R.D. Department of Scientific Research and Development.
DST, D.S.T. Daylight Saving Time.
D.S.T. Doctor of Sacred Theology.
DT Dental Technician.
d.t. delirium tremens **(d.t's)**; double time.
D.T., D.Th., D.Theol. Doctor of Theology.
Du. Duke; Dutch.
dup., dupl. duplicate.
D.V. Douay Version (of the Bible).
D.v., D.V. God willing [L *Deo volente*].
D.V.M. Doctor of Veterinary Medicine.
D.V.M.S. Doctor of Veterinary Medicine and Surgery.
D/W dock warrant.
D.W.S. Department of Water Supply.
d.w.t. dead weight tons.
dwt. pennyweight [L *denarius* weight].
DX, D.X. distance; distant.
Dy dysprosium.
dyn., dynam. dynamics.
dz. dozen.

E

e., E., E English.
e., e error(s).
e., E., E east, eastern.
e, e. erg.
E., E English.
E. Earl; Earth.
ea. each.
e. and o.e. errors and omissions excepted.
Eb erbium.
EbN east by north.
EbS east by south.
E.C. Engineering Corps; Established Church.
ECA Economic Cooperation Administration.
ECAFE Economic Commission for Asia and the Far East.
eccl., eccles. ecclesiastical.
Ecc, Eccl., Eccles. Ecclesiastes.
Ecclus. Ecclesiasticus.
ECE Economic Commission for Europe.
ECLA Economic Commission for Latin America.
ECME Economic Commission for the Middle East.
ecol. ecological; ecology.
econ. economic; economics; economy.
ECOSOC Economic and Social Council (of the United Nations).
ECSC European Coal and Steel Community.
Ecua. Ecuador.
ed. edited; edition; editor.
Ed.B. Bachelor of Education.
EDC European Defense Community.
Ed.D. Doctor of Education.
edit. edited; edition; editor.
Ed.M. Master of Education.
E.D.T., e.d.t. eastern daylight time.
educ. education; educational.
E.E. Early English; Electrical Engineer; Electrical Engineering; Envoy Extraordinary.
e.e. errors excepted.
E.E.C. European Economic Community.
E.E. & M.P. Envoy Extraordinary & Minister Plenipotentiary.
EEDC Economic Employment and Development Commission.
EEG electroencephalogram.
eff. efficiency.
efflor. efflorescent.
e.g. for example [L *exempli gratia*].
Eg. Egypt; Egyptian.
Egyptol. Egyptology.
EHF, E.H.F., ehf, e.h.f. extremely high frequency.
EHFA, E.H.F.A. Electric Home and Farm Authority.
E.I., E.Ind. East Indian; East Indies.
EIB, E.I.B. Export-Import Bank.
EKG electrocardiogram.
el., elev. elevation.
elec., elect. electric; electrical; electrician.
elem. elementary; elements.
elev. elevation.
ellipt. elliptical.
elong. elongation.
e. long. east longitude.
E.M. Engineer of Mines.
EM Electrician's Mate; enlisted man (men).
Em., eman. emanation (chemistry).
emb., embryol. embryology.
e.m.f., emf, E.M.F., EMF electromotive force.
Emp. Empire; Emperor; Empress.
emph. emphasis; emphatic.
e.m.u., emu, E.M.U. electromagnetic units.
emul. emulsion.
enc., encl. enclosed; enclosure.
ency., encyc., encycl. encyclopedia.
ENE, E.N.E., ene, e.n.e. east-northeast.
eng. engine; engineer; engineering; engraved; engraver; engraving.
Eng. England; English.
Eng.D. Doctor of Engineering.
engin. engineering.
engr. engineer; engraved; engraver; engraving.
enl. enlarged; enlisted.
Ens. Ensign.
entom., entomol. entomological; entomology.
env. envelope.
e.o. from office [L *ex officio*].
e.p. en passant (chess).
EP extended play.
Ep., Epis., Epist. Epistle(s).
Eph., Eph, Ephes. Ephesians.
epil. epilogue.
Epiph. Epiphany.
Epis., Episc. Episcopal.
epit. epitaph; epitome.
EPU European Payments Union.
E.Q., EQ educational quotient.
eq. equal; equalizer; equation; equator; equivalent **(equiv.)**.
e.r., er earned runs.
E.R. King Edward [L *Eduardus Rex*]; Queen Elizabeth [L *Elizabeth Regina*].
Er erbium.
E.R.A. Educational Research Association; Emergency Relief Administration **(ERA)**.
ERP, E.R.P. European Recovery Program.
erron. erroneous; erroneously.
E.R.V. English Revised Version (of the Bible).
Es einsteinium.
ESA Economic Stabilization Administration.
ESC Economic and Social Council.
eschat. eschatology.
Esd. Esdras.
ESE, E.S.E., ese, e.s.e. east-southeast.
Esk. Eskimo.
esp., espec. especially.
ESP extrasensory perception.
Esq., Esqr. Esquire.
est. estate; estimated; estuary.
EST, E.S.T., e.s.t. eastern standard time.
Est. Estonia.
estab. established.
Esth. Esther.
e.s.u., esu electrostatic unit.
ET Electronics Technician.
e.t.a., ETA estimated time of arrival.
et al. and others [L *et alii*]; and elsewhere [L *et alibi*].
etc. and so forth; and others [L *et ceteri, ceterae,* or *cetera*].
eth. ether; ethical; ethics.
Eth. Ethiopia; Ethiopian; Ethiopic.
ethnog. ethnographical; ethnography.
ethnol. ethnological; ethnology.
ETO European Theater of Operations.
et seq. and the following; and what follows [L *et sequens, et sequentes* or *sequentia*].
ety., etym., etymol. etymological; etymology.
Eu europium.
euphem. euphemism; euphemistic.
Eur. Europe; European.
E.V. English Version (of the Bible).
e.v., ev electron volt(s).
evac. evacuation.
evan., evang. evangelical; evangelist.
Evang. Evangelical.
evap. evaporation.
ex. examination; examine; examined; example; except; excepted; exception; exchange; excursion; executed; executive.
Ex., Ex, Exod. Exodus.
exam. examination; examined; examinee; examinor.
exc. excellent; except; excepted; exception; excursion.
Exc. Excellency.
exch. exchange; exchequer.
excl. exclusive.
excl., exclam. exclamation.
exec. executive; executor.
ex int. without interest.
ex lib. from the library (of) [L *ex libris*].
ex off. from office [L *ex officio*].
exp. expenses; expiration; expired; export; exportation; exported; exporter; express.
exper. experimental.
expt. experiment.
exptl. experimental.
exr. executor.
ext. extension; external; extinct; extra; extract.
Ez., Ez, Ezr. Ezra.
Eze., Eze, Ezek. Ezekiel.

F

F fluorine.
f activity coefficient.
f. farthing; fathom; feet; female; feminine; fine; fluid (ounce); folio; following; foot; formed; forte; franc; frequency; from; let it be made [L *fiat*]; strong [L *forte*].
f., F function (of).
f., f, F., F farad.
f., f foul(s).
f, f/, f:, F, F/, F: F number (photography).
F. fahrenheit; February; Fellow; France; French; Friday; son [L *filius*].
FA Field Artillery
F.A. Fine Arts; Food Administration.
f.a. fire alarm; freight agent.
f.a., F.A. free alongside; freight agent.
F.A.A.A.S. Fellow of the American Association for the Advancement of Science.
fac. facsimile; factor; factory.
F.A.C.D. Fellow of the American College of Dentists.
F.A.C.P. Fellow of the American College of Physicians.
F.A.C.S. Fellow of the American College of Surgeons.
Fah., Fahr. Fahrenheit.
F.A.I.A. Fellow of the American Institute of Architects.
fam. familiar; family.
F.A.M., F. & A.M. Free and Accepted Masons.
FAO, F.A.O. Food and Agricultural Organization (of the United Nations).
F.A.P.S. Fellow of the American Physical Society.
f.a.s., F.A.S. free alongside ship.
F.A.S.A. Fellow of the Acoustical Society of America.
fasc. a bundle [L *fasciculus*].
fath. fathom.
f.b. freight bill.
f.b., fb fullback.
F.B.A. Fellow of the British Academy.
FBI, F.B.I. Federal Bureau of Investigation.
fbm feet board measure (board feet).
f.c. follow copy (printing).
Fc fractocumulus.
FCA, F.C.A. Farm Credit Administration.
F.C.C. Federal Communications Commission **(FCC)**; Federal Council of Churches; First Class Certificate; Food Control Committee.
FCDA Federal Civil Defense Administration.
FCIC, F.C.I.C. Federal Crop Insurance Corporation.
fcp. foolscap.
F.D. Defender of the Faith [L *Fidei Defensor*]; Fire Department.
FDA, F.D.A. Food and Drug Administration; Food Distribution Administration.
FDIC, F.D.I.C. Federal Deposit Insurance Corporation.
Fe iron [L *ferrum*].
FEB Fair Employment Board.
Feb., Feb February.
FEC Far Eastern Commission.
fec. he (or she) made it [L *fecit*].
fed. federal; federated; federation.
fem. female; feminine.
FEPC, F.E.P.C. Fair Employment Practices Committee.
FERA, F.E.R.A. Federal Emergency Relief Administration.
feud. feudal; feudalism.
ff. folios; following; fortissimo.
f.f. fixed focus.
f.f.a., F.F.A. free foreign agent; free from alongside.
F.F.A. Future Farmers of America.
F.F.V. First Families of Virginia.
F.G.S.A. Fellow of the Geological Society of America.
FHA Federal Housing Administration.
FHLBB Federal Home Loan Bank Board.
f.h.p. friction horsepower.
fid. fidelity; fiduciary.
fifo, FIFO first in, first out.
fig. figuratively; figure(s).
F.I.L. Fellow of the Institute of Linguists.
filo, FILO first in, last out.
fin. finance; financial; finished.
Fin. Finland; Finnish.
fl. floor; florin(s); flower; fluid; flute.
fl fluid.
Fl. Flanders; Flemish.
Fl fluorine.

FL Florida (P.O. abbr.)
Fla. Florida.
FLB Federal Land Bank.
fl. dr. fluid dram(s).
Flem. Flemish.
flex. flexible.
fl. oz. fluid ounce(s).
F.M. Field Manual: Field Marshal.
Fm fermium.
fm. fathom; from.
FM frequency modulation.
FMCS Federal Mediation and Conciliation Service.
FNMA Federal National Mortgage Association.
F.O. field officer; Foreign Office.
f.o.b., F.O.B. free on board.
F.O.E. Fraternal Order of Eagles.
fol. folio; following.
foll. following.
f.o.r., F.O.R. free on rails.
for. foreign; forestry.
fort. fortification; fortified.
f.p. fireplug; fire policy; floating policy; fully paid.
f.p., fp forward pass.
f.p., fp, fp. freezing point.
f.p., F.P., fp foot-pound(s).
fp forte piano (Ital.).
fp. foolscap.
FPA, F.P.A. Food Products Administration; Foreign Press Association.
FPC, F.P.C. Federal Power Commission.
FPHA, F.P.H.A. Federal Public Housing Administration.
fpm, f.p.m. feet per minute.
FPO fleet post office.
fps, f.p.s. feet per second; foot-pound-second (system).
f.r. right-hand page [L *folio recto*].
fr. fragment; franc; from.
Fr. Brother [L *Frater*]; Father; France; French; Friday; wife [G *Frau*].
Fr francium.
Frl. Miss [G *Fräulein*].
F.R.B., FRB Federal Reserve Bank; Federal Reserve Board.
FRC, F.R.C. Federal Radio Commission; Federal Relief Commission.
F.R.C.P. Fellow of the Royal College of Physicians.
F.R.C.S. Fellow of the Royal College of Surgeons.
freq. frequency; frequently; frequentative.
F.R.G.S. Fellow of the Royal Geographical Society.
Fr. Gui. French Guiana.
Fri. Friday.
Frl. Fräulein.
F.R.S. Federal Reserve System **(FRS)**; Fellow of the Royal Society.
F.R.S.A. Fellow of the Royal Society of Arts.
frt. freight.
F.S. Field Service; Fleet Surgeon.
f.s. foot-second.
Fs fractostratus.
FSA, F.S.A. Farm Security Administration; Federal Security Agency.
FSCC, F.S.C.C. Federal Surplus Commodities Corporation.
FSH follicle-stimulating hormone.
FSR, F.S.R. Field Service Regulations.
ft. feet; foot; fort; fortification; fortified.
FT Fire Control Technician.
FTC, F.T.C. Federal Trade Commission.
ft.-c. foot-candle.
fth., fthm. fathom.
ft.-l. foot-lambert.
ft.-lb. foot-pound.
fur. furlong.
furl. furlough.
furn. furnished; furniture.
fut. future.
f.v. on the back of the page [L *folio verso*].
FWA, F.W.A. Federal Works Agency.
fwd. forward.
FY fiscal year.
F.Z.S. Fellow of the Zoological Society.

G

g. gender; general; genitive; grand; guide.
g., G. conductance; gauge; gold; gourde **(gde.)**; grain(s); guilder(s); guinea(s); gulf.
g., g goal(s); goalie; goalkeeper.
g., g, G., G gram(s).
g general intelligence; (specific) gravity.
G gun.
G, G. German.
G. Germany; (specific) gravity.
g.a., G.A., G/A general average.
Ga. Georgia.
Ga gallium.
G.A. General Agent; General Assembly.
GA Georgia (P.O. abbr.)
Gael. Gaelic.
gal., gall. gallon(s).
Gal. Galatians; Galen.
galv. galvanic; galvanism; galvanized.
GAO General Accounting Office.
G.A.R., GAR Grand Army of the Republic.
GATT General Agreement on Tariffs and Trade.
G.A.W. guaranteed annual wage.
gaz. gazette; gazetteer.
G.B. Great Britain.
G.B.E. (Knight or Dame) Grand (Cross or Order) of the British Empire.
GCA, G.C.A. ground control approach (radar).
g-cal. gram calorie(s).
G.C.B. (Knight) Grand Cross of the Bath.
G.C.D. g.c.d., gcd, greatest common divisor.
g.c.f., gcf, G.C.F. greatest common factor.
GCI ground controlled interception (aircraft).
G.C.L.H. Grand Cross of the Legion of Honor.
GCM General Court Martial.
g.c.m., gcm, G.C.M. greatest common measure.
GCT, G.C.T., G.c.t. Greenwich civil time.
G.C.V.O. (Knight) Grand Cross of the (Royal) Victorian Order.
G.D. Grand Duchess; Grand Duchy; Grand Duke.
Gd gadolinium.
gds. goods.
Ge germanium.
geb. born [G *geboren*].
gel. gelatinous.
gen. gender; genera; general; generally; generator; generic; genitive; genus.
Gen. General; Genesis; Geneva; Genevan.
geneal. genealogical; genealogy.
genit. genitive.
genl. general.
gent. gentleman; gentlemen.
geod. geodesy; geodetic.
geog. geographer; geographic; geographical; geography.
geol. geologic; geological; geologist; geology.
geom. geometer; geometric; geometrical; geometry.
ger. gerund.
Ger., Germ. German; Germany.
gest. died [G *gestorben*].
G.F.T.U. General Federation of Trade Unions.
g.gr. great gross.
GHA Greenwich hour angle.
GHQ, G.H.Q. General Headquarters.
g.i., GI, G.I. gastrointestinal.
GI, G.I. general issue; government issue.
gi. gill(s).
Gib. Gibraltar.
Gk. Greek.
Gl glucinum.
gl. glass; gloss.
gld. guilder(s).
gloss. glossary.
gm. gram(s).
G.M. general manager; Grand Master.
GM Gunner's Mate.
G.m.a.t. Greenwich mean astronomical time.
Gmc. Germanic.
G.m.t. GMT, G.M.T. Greenwich mean time.
GNP, G.N.P. gross national product.
GO general orders.
G.O.P. Grand Old Party (Republican party).
Goth. gothic; Gothic.
gov., govt. government.
Gov. Governor.
G.P. general practitioner; Graduate in Pharmacy; general paresis.
g.p.m. gallons per minute.
GPO, G.P.O. General Post Office; Government Printing Office.
g.p.s. gallons per second.
GQ, G.Q., g.q. general quarters.
G.R. King George [L *Georgius Rex*].
gr. grade; grain(s); gram(s); grammar; great; gross; group.
Gr. Grecian; Greece; Greek.
grad. graduate; graduated.
gram. grammar; grammarian; grammatical.
Gr.Br., Gr.Brit. Great Britain.
gro. gross.
gr.wt. gross weight.
GS German silver.
G.S. General Secretary; General Staff; Girl Scouts.
GSA General Services Administration.
G.S.A. Girl Scouts of America.
GSC, G.S.C. General Staff Corps.
GSO, G.S.O. General Staff Officer.
gt. gilt; great.
g.t.c., G.T.C. good till canceled.
gtd. guaranteed.
gtt. a drop [L *gutta*].
g.u., g.-u. genitourinary.
guar. guaranteed.
Guat. Guatemala.
Guin. Guinea.
gun. gunnery.
guttat. by drops [L *guttatim*].
g.v. gravimetric volume.
gym. gymnasium; gymnastics.
gyn., gynecol. gynecological; gynecology.

H

h. harbor; hard; hardness; heavy sea; height; hence; high; horns (music); hour(s); hundred; husband.
h., h hit(s).
h, hy henry *(electr.)*.
H hydrogen; intensity of magnetic field.
h.a. this year [L *hoc anno*].
ha hectare(s).
Hab., Hab Habakkuk.
hab. corp. have the body [L *habeas corpus*].
Hag., Hag Haggai.
Hal halogen.
Hb hemoglobin.
hb., hb halfback.
H.B.M. His (Her) Britannic Majesty.
H.C. House of Commons.
hcap., hcp. handicap.
h.c.f., hcf, H.C.F. highest common factor.
hd. hand; head.
hdbk. handbook.
hdkf., hkf. handkerchief.
hdqrs. headquarters.
He helium.
H.E. His Eminence; His Excellency.
HE, H.E. high explosive.
Heb., Heb, Hebr. Hebrew; Hebrews.
her. heraldic; heraldry.
herp., herpetol. herpetology.
hex. hexachord; hexagon; hexagonal.
h.f., h-f, HF high frequency.
hf. half.
Hf hafnium.
hf.bd. half-bound (bookbinding).
hf.mor. half-morocco (bookbinding).
HG, H.G. High German.
H.G. His (Her) Grace; Home Guard.
hg hectogram(s); heliogram.
Hg mercury [L *hydrargyrum*].
hgt. height.
H.H. His (Her) Highness; His Holiness.
hhd hogshead.
HHFA Housing and Home Finance Agency.
HI Hawaii (P.O. abbr.).
H.I.H. His (Her) Imperial Highness.
H.I.M. His (Her) Imperial Majesty.
Hind. Hindi; Hindu; Hindustan; Hindustani.
hist. histology; historian; historical; history.
H.J. here lies [L *hic jacet*].
H.J.S. here lies buried [L *hic jacet sepultus*].
hkf. handkerchief.
hl, hl. hectoliter(s).
H.L. House of Lords.
HL mustard-lewisite (poison gas).
HLBB Home Loan Bank Board.
h.m. in this month [L *hoc mense*].
hm hectometer(s).
H.M. His (Her) Majesty.
H.M.S. His (Her) Majesty's Service (Ship, Steamer).
HN nitrogen mustard gas.
H.O. head office; Home Office.
ho. house.
Ho holmium.
HOLC, H.O.L.C. Home Owners' Loan Corporation.
hon. honorably; honorary.
Hon. Honorable.
Hond. Honduras.
hor. horizon; horizontal.
horol. horology.
hort., hortic. horticultural; horticulture.
Hos., Hos Hosea.
hosp. hospital.
HP, H.P. high power.
hp, HP, h.p., H.P. high pressure; horsepower.
hp.-hr. horsepower-hour.
h.q. look for this [L *hoc quaere*].
HQ, H.Q., hq, h.q. headquarters.
h.r., hr home run(s).
hr. hour(s).
Hr. Mister [G *Herr*].
H.R. Home Rule; House of Representatives.
H.R.E. Holy Roman Empire.
H.R.H. His (Her) Royal Highness.
H.R.I.P. here rests in peace [L *hic requiescat in pace*].
hrs. hours.
H.S. here is buried [L *hic sepultus*]; here lies [L *hic situ*]; High School; Home Secretary (Brit.); in this sense [L *hoc sensu*].
H.S.H. His (Her) Serene Highness.
H.S.M. His (Her) Serene Majesty.
h.t. at this time [L *hoc tempore*]; in or under this title [L *hoc titulo*].
ht. heat; height.
Hts. Heights.
HUD, H.U.D. Housing and Urban Development.
Hun., Hung. Hungarian; Hungary.
H.V., h.v., hv high voltage.
h.w. high water.
hyd., hydros. hydrostatics.
hydraul. hydraulic; hydraulics.
hyg. hygiene; hygroscopic.
hyp., hypoth. hypotenuse; hypothesis; hypothetical.

I

i. incisor; interest; intransitive; island.
I. Island(s); Isle(s).
I iodine; Roman numeral for 1.
IA Iowa (P.O. abbr.).
Ia. Iowa.
IADB Inter-American Defense Board.
IAEA International Atomic Energy Agency (of the United Nations).
IATA International Air Transport Association.
ib., ibid. in the same place [L *ibidem*].
IBRD International Bank for Reconstruction and Development.
IBT International Brotherhood of Teamsters.
ICA International Cooperation Administration.
ICAO International Civil Aviation Organization.
ICBM Intercontinental ballistic missile.
ICC Indian Claims Commission.
I.C.C. Interstate Commerce Commission.
Ice., Icel. Iceland; Icelandic.
ICES International Council for the Exploration of the Sea.
ICFTU International Confederation of Free Trade Unions.
ichth. ichthyology.
ICJ International Court of Justice.
ICNAF International Commission for Northwest Atlantic Fisheries.
i.c.w. interrupted continuous wave.
id. the same [L *idem*].
Id. Idaho.
ID, I.D., i.d. inside diameter.
I.D. identification; Infantry Division; Intelligence Department.
ID Idaho (P.O. abbr.).
Ida. Idaho.
i.e. that is [L *id est*].
I.E., IE Indo-European.
IF, I.F. i.f., i-f intermediate frequency.
IFCTU International Federation of Christian Trade Unions.
IFF Identification friend or foe (British radar device).
IG, I.G. amalgamation [G *Interessengemeinschaft*]; Indo-Germanic; Inspector General.
ign. ignites; ignition; unknown [L *ignotus*].
IHP, I.H.P. ihp, i.h.p., i.-hp. indicated horsepower.
I.H.S., IHS Jesus: often, incorrectly, Jesus Savior of Men [L *Iesus hominum salvator*] or, in this sign [L *in hoc signo*].
Il illinium.
IL Illinois (P.O. abbr.).
ILA International Longshoremen's Association.
I.L.G.W.U. International Ladies' Garment Workers' Union.
ill., illus., illust. illustrate; illustrated; illustration; illustrator.
Ill. Illinois.
illit. illiterate.
ILO, I.L.O. International Labor Organization (of the United Nations).
I.L.P. Independent Labour Party (Brit.).
ILS instrument landing system.
IMF International Monetary Fund.
imit. imitation; imitative.
immun. immunology.
IMO International Meteorological Organization.
imp. imperative; imperfect; imperial; impersonal; import; important; imported; importer; imprimatur; improper.
Imp. Imperator.
imper. imperative.
imperf. imperfect; imperforate.
impers. impersonal.
impf. imperfect.
imp. gal. imperial gallon.
impv. imperative.
in. inch(es).
In indium.
IN Indiana (P.O. abbr.).
inbd. inboard.
inc. inclosure; including; inclusive; income; incorporated; increase.
inch., incho. inchoative.
incl. inclosure; including.
incog. incognito.
incor., incorp. incorporated.
incorr. incorrect.
incr. increased; increasing.
I.N.D. in the name of God [L *in nomine Dei*].
ind. independence; independent; index; indicated; indicative; indigo; indirect; industrial.
Ind. India; Indian; Indiana; Indies.
indecl. indeclinable.
indef. indefinite.
inden., indent. indention (printing).
indic. indicating; indicative; indicator.
individ. individual.
induc. induction.
ined. not published.
in ex. at length [L *in extenso*].
in f. at the end [L *in fine*].
inf. below [L *infra*]; inferior; infinitive; information.
Inf. Infantry.
infin. infinitive.
infl. influence; influenced.
init. initial; in the beginning [L *initio*].
inj. injection.
in.-lb. inch-pound.
in lim. at the outset (on the threshold) [L *in limine*].
in loc. in its place [L *in loco*].
in loc. cit. in the place cited [L *in loco citato*].
inorg. inorganic.
I.N.R.I. Jesus of Nazareth, King of the Jews [L *Iesus Nazarenus Rex Iudaeorum*].
ins. inches; inspector; insular; insulated; insulation; insurance.
I.N.S., INS International News Service.
insc., inscr. inscribe; inscribed; inscription.
insep. inseparable.
insol. insoluble.
insp. inspected; inspector.
inst. instant; instantaneous; instrument.
Inst. Institute; Institution.
instr. instruction, instructor; instrument.
insur. insurance.
int. intelligence; interest; interior; interjection; internal; interval; intransitive.
intens. intensive.
inter. intermediate.
interj. interjection.
internat. international.
interp. interpreter.
Interpol. International Police Organization.
interrog. interrogative.
intr., intrans. intransitive.
in trans. on the way [L *in transitu*].
Int. Rev. Internal Revenue.
introd. introduction; introductory.
inv. invented; invention; inventor; invoice.
invert. invertebrate.
invt. inventory.
Io ionium.
I.O.B.B. Independent Order of B'nai B'rith.

.O.O.F. Independent Order of Odd Fellows.
.O.U., IOU I owe you.
p. in passing (chess).
.p., ip innings pitched.
.P.A., IPA International Phonetic Alphabet (Association).
PI International Press Institute.
PPC International Penal and Penitentiary Commission.
.P.R. Institute of Pacific Relations.
ps, i.p.s. inches per second.
q. the same as [L *idem quod*].
Q, I.Q. intelligence quotient.
q.e.d. what was to be proved [L *id quod erat demonstrandum*].
r. Ireland; Irish.
r iridium.
.R.A. Irish Republican Army.
ran. Iranian; Iranic.
RBM intermediate range ballistic missile.
re. Ireland.
RO International Refugee Organization.
rreg. irregularly.
RS Internal Revenue Service.
s. island(s); isle(s).
s., Is, Isa. Isaiah.
sl. island(s).
so. isotropic.
som. isometric.
soth. isothermal.
sr. Israel.
sth. isthmus.
t., ital. italic; italics.
t., Ital. Italian; Italy.
.T.A., i/t/a Initial Teaching Alphabet.
in. itinerant; itinerary.
TO International Trade Organization.
TU International Telecommunication Union; International Typographical Union.
U, I.U. international unit(s).
WW, I.W.W. Industrial Workers of the World.

J

joule (physics).
. Judge; Justice.
a., j/a, J.A., J/A joint account.
A, J.A. Judge Advocate.
a., Jan., Jan January.
.A.G. Judge Advocate General.
am. Jamaica.
ap. Japan; Japanese.
as., Jas James.
.C.D. Doctor of Canon Law [L *Juris Canonici Doctor*]; Doctor of Civil Law [L *Juris Civilis Doctor*].
CS Joint Chiefs of Staff.
t., jctn. junction.
.D. Doctor of Laws [L *Jurum Doctor*].
e., Je June.
er, Jer. Jeremiah.
g., jg junior grade.
July.
n John.
on Jonah.
os. Joseph; Joshua **(Jos)**; Josiah.
our. journal; journalist; journeyman.
.P. Justice of the Peace.
., Jr. junior.
u, Judg. Judges.
ul., Jul July.
un., Jun June.
n., Jun. junior.
nc., junct. junction.
ur.D. Doctor of Law [L *Juris Doctor*].
urisp. jurisprudence.
us., just. justice.
v. juvenile.
v. junior varsity.
wlr. jeweler.
y. July.

K

potassium [L *kalium*].
capacity; carat; constant.
., K. calends [L *kalendae*]; karat (carat); kilogram; king; king (chess); knot (naut.); kopeck; koruna; krone.
kilo.
a. kathode (cathode).
A Kansas (P.O. abbr.).
al. kalends (calends).
an., Kans., Kas. Kansas.
.B. King's Bench; Knight Bachelor.
B king's bishop (chess).
BP king's bishop's pawn (chess).
c., kc kilocycle(s).
.C. King's Counsel; Knight Commander; Knights of Columbus.
cal kilocalorie.
.C.B. Knight Commander (of the Order) of the Bath.
.C.V.O. Knight Commander of the (Royal) Victorian Order.
Ken. Kentucky.
kg., kg keg(s); kilogram(s).
K.G. Knight (of the Order) of the Garter.
KGB, K.G.B. Commission of State Security (Russian *Komitet Godsudarstvennoi Bezopasnost'i*).
Ki Kings (book of the Bible).
kilo. kilogram(s); kilometer(s).
kilog. kilogram(s).
kilol. kiloliter(s).
kilom. kilometer(s).
kingd. kingdom.
K.K.K., KKK Ku Klux Klan.
kl., kl kiloliter(s).
km., km kilometer(s).
kn. kronen.
KN king's knight (chess).
KNP king's knight's pawn (chess).
KO, K.O., k.o. knockout.
K. of C. Knight (Knights) of Columbus.
K. of P. Knight (Knights) of Pythias.
kop. kopeck(s).
K.P. Knight (of the Order of St.) Patrick; Knights of Pythias.
KP king's pawn (chess).
KP, K.P. kitchen police.
kr., Kr. krona; krone.
Kr krypton.
KR king's rook (chess).
KRP king's rook's pawn (chess).
kt. karat (carat).
K.T. Knight (Knights) Templar.
kv., kv kilovolt(s).
kva, kv.-a. kilovolt-ampere.
kvar reactive kilovolt-ampere.
kw., kw kilowatt(s).
K.W.H., kw-h, kw.-hr., kw-hr kilowatt-hour(s).
Ky. Kentucky.
KY Kentucky (P.O. abbr.).

L

L., l. book [L *liber*]; lake; land; lat; latitude; law; leaf; league; left; lempira; length; leu; lev; lex; line; link; lira; lire; lit; low; place [L *locus*].
l, l. liter(s).
l., l (games) lost.
L. Latin; licentiate; Linnaeus.
L, £, l. pound (sterling) [L *libra*].
L Latin.
L length; lewisite; longitude.
L, l coefficient of inductance.
La. Louisiana.
La lanthanum.
L.A. Legislative Assembly; Library Association; Local Agent.
LA Louisiana (P.O. abbr.).
lab. laboratory.
L.A.M. Master of Liberal Arts [L *Liberalium Artium Magister*].
lam. laminated.
Lam., Lam Lamentations.
lang. language.
laryngol. laryngological; laryngology.
lat. latitude.
Lat. Latin; Latvia.
Latv. Latvia.
lb. pound [L *libra*].
L.B. Bachelor of Letters [L *Litterarum Baccalaureus*]; Local Board.
lb.ap. pound, apothecary.
lb.av. pound, avoirdupois.
lbs. pounds.
lb.t. pound, troy.
l.c. left center; lower case (printing); in the place cited [L *loco citato*].
l/c, L/C letter of credit; lower case.
L.C. Library of Congress.
L.C.D., l.c.d., lcd lowest common denominator.
l.c.m., lcm, L.C.M. lowest, or least, common multiple.
ld. lead (printing).
Ld. Lord.
L.D., LD., LD Low Dutch.
ldg. landing; leading; loading.
L.Div. Licentiate in Divinity.
ld. lmt. load limit.
ldry. laundry.
L.D.S. Licentiate in Dental Surgery.
l.e., le left end.
lea. league; leather; leave.
lect. lecture; lecturer.
led. ledger.
leg. legal; legate; legato; legislation.
legis. legislation; legislative; legislature.
LEM lunar excursion module.
L. ès S. Licentiate in Sciences [F *Licencié ès Sciences*].
Lev., Lev, Levit. Leviticus.
lex. lexicon.
l.f., lf. lightface (printing).
l.f., lf left field(er); left forward.
l.f., l-f, LF, L.F. low frequency.
l.g., lg left guard.
LG, LG., L.G. Low German.
lg., lge. large.
LGk. Late Greek.
lgth. length.
LH luteinizing hormone.
l.h., L.H., LH left hand.
l.h., lh, l.h.b., lhb left halfback.
LHA local hour angle.
L.H.D. Doctor of Humanities [L *Litterarum Humaniorum Doctor*].
Li lithium.
L.I. Long Island.
LI Lithographer.
lib. book [L *liber*]; librarian; library.
Lib. Liberal; Liberia.
Lieut. Lieutenant.
lifo, LIFO last in, first out.
lilo, LILO last in, last out.
lin. lineal; linear.
ling. linguistics.
linim. liniment.
Linn. Linnaeus; Linnean.
lino. linotype.
liq. liquid; liquor.
li.qts. liquid quarts.
lit. liter; literal; literally; literary; literature.
Lit. B., Litt. B. Bachelor of Letters (Literature) [L *Lit(t)erarum Baccalaureus*].
Lit.D., Litt.D. Doctor of Letters (Literature) [L *Lit(t)erarum Doctor*].
lith., litho., lithog. lithograph; lithography.
Lith. Lithuania; Lithuanian.
Lk Luke.
ll. leaves; lines.
LL, L.L. Late Latin; Legal Latin; Low Latin.
LL.B. Bachelor of Laws [L *Legum Baccalaureus*].
LL.D. Doctor of Laws [L *Legum Doctor*].
LL.M. Master of Laws [L *Legum Magister*].
LM Legion of Merit; lunar (excursion) module.
L.M. Licentiate in Medicine (or Midwifery).
LMT local mean time.
LNG liquefied natural gas.
loc. local; location.
local. localism.
loc. cit. in the place cited [L *loco citato*].
log, log. logarithm.
long. longitude.
loq. he (she, it) speaks [L *loquitur*].
lox liquid oxygen.
l.p. large paper; long primer.
l.p., lp, L.P., LP low pressure; long playing (phonograph record).
L.P.S. Lord Privy Seal.
L.S. Licentiate in Surgery; place of the seal [L *locus sigilli*].
l.s.c. in the place cited above [L *loco supra citato*].
LSD Landing Ship, Dock; lysergic acid diethylamide.
£.s.d. pounds, shillings, pence (British).
L.S.S., LSS Lifesaving Service (U. S.).
LST. Landing Ship, Tank.
l.t., l.tn. long ton.
l.t., lt left tackle.
Lt. Lieutenant.
ltd., Ltd. limited.
L.Th. Licentiate in Theology.
Lt. Inf. Light Infantry.
Ltjg. Lieutenant, Junior Grade.
Lu lutetium.
lubric. lubricate; lubrication.
Luth. Lutheran.
Lux. Luxemburg.
lv. leave(s).
lw lawrencium.
l.w.l. load waterline.
l.w.m. low watermark.
LXX Septuagint.
lyr. lyric; lyrical.

M

m., m meter(s); noon [L *meridies*].
m. majesty; male; manual; mark; married; masculine; mass; measure; medicine; medium; member; meridian; mile; mill; minim; minute; month; moon; morning; mountain; noon [L *meridies*].
M. handful [L *manipulus*]; Master [L *magister*]; monsieur; of medicine [L *medicinae*].
M Medieval; middle; Roman numeral for 1,000.
M.A. Master of Arts [L *Magister Artium*]; Military Academy.
MA Machine Accountant; Maritime Administration; Massachusetts (P.O. abbr.).
MA, M.A. mental age.
Ma masurium.
MAC mean aerodynamic chord.
Mac., Macc. Maccabees.
Maced. Macedonia; Macedonian.
mach., machin. machine; machinery; machinist.
Mad., Madm. Madam.
mag. magazine; magnet; magnetism; magnitude.
M. Agr., M. Agric. Master of Agriculture.
maj. majority.
Maj. Major.
Mal, Mal. Malachi; Malay; Malayan; Malta.
malac. malacology.
Man. manila (paper); Manitoba.
Manch. Manchukuo; Manchuria.
manuf. manufacture; manufactured; manufacturer; manufacturing.
mar. marine; maritime; married.
Mar., Mar March.
March. Marchioness.
marg. margin; marginal.
Marq. Marquis.
mas., masc. masculine.
Mass. Massachusetts.
mat. matinée; matins; maturity.
MATS Military Air Transport Service.
math. mathematical; mathematician; mathematics.
matr., matric. matriculate; matriculation.
Matt. Matthew.
max. maximum.
Max. Maximilian.
M.B. Bachelor of Medicine [L *Medicinae Baccalaureus*].
M.B.A. Master in (or of) Business Administration.
MBS Mutual Broadcasting System.
mc, m.c., mc. megacycle; millicurie.
M.C. Maritime Commission; Master Commandant; Master of Ceremonies; Medical Corps; Member of Congress.
M.Ch. Master of Surgery [L *Magister Chirurgiae*].
M.C.L. Master of Civil Law.
Md mendelevium.
Md. Maryland.
M.D. Doctor of Medicine [L *Medicinae Doctor*]; Medical Department; mentally deficient.
MD Maryland (P.O. abbr.).
MD, M.D. Middle Dutch.
M/D, m/d memorandum of deposit; months' date.
M.D.S. Master of Dental Surgery.
mdse. merchandise.
MDu. Middle Dutch.
m.e. marbled edges (bookbinding).
Me. Maine.
Me methyl.
M.E. Mechanical (Military, Mining) Engineer; Methodist Episcopal.
ME Maine (P.O. abbr.).
ME, ME., M.E. Middle English.
meas. measure; measurable.
mech., mechan. mechanical; mechanics; mechanism.
med. medical; medicine; medieval; medium.
M.Ed. Master of Education.
Med.Gk. Medieval Greek.
Medit. Mediterranean.
Med.L Medieval Latin.
meg. megacycle; megohm.
mem. member; memoir; memorandum; memorial.
memo. memorandum.
mensur. mensuration.
m.e.p. mean effective pressure.
mer. meridian; meridional.
merc. mercantile; mercurial; mercury.
Messrs., Messrs Messieurs.
met. metaphor; metaphysics; meteorological; metronome; metropolitan.
metal., metall. metallurgical; metallurgy.
metaph. metaphor; metaphorical; metaphysics.
metath. metathesis; metathetical.
meteor., meteorol. meteorological; meteorology.
meth. method; methylated.
Meth. Methodist.
meton. metonymy.
metrol. metrological; metrology.
metrop. metropolitan.
mev, Mev, MEV, m.e.v. million electron volts.
Mex. Mexican; Mexico.
MF, M.F., mf, m.f. medium frequency.
mf, mf. mezzoforte; millifarad.
mf, mf., mfd microfarad.
MF., MF Middle French.
mfg. manufacturing.
M.Flem. Middle Flemish.
mfr. manufacture; manufacturer.
MG Military Government.
mg., mg, mgm milligram(s).
Mg magnesium.
Mgr. Manager; Monseigneur; Monsignor.
mgt. management.
MH Medal of Honor.
mh, mh. millihenry.
MHG, MHG., M.H.G. Middle High German.
MI Michigan (P.O. abbr.).
mi., mi mile(s).
Mic., Mic Micah.
Mich. Michigan.
micros. microscope; microscopic; microscopy.
mid. middle; midshipman.
Mid.Dan. Middle Danish.
Mid.Sw. Middle Swedish.
mil. mileage; military; militia; million.
milit. military.
mim., mimeo. mimeograph; mimeographed.
min. mineralogical; mineralogy; minim(s); minimum; mining; minor; minute(s).
mineral. mineralogy.
Minn. Minnesota.
m.i.p. marine insurance policy; mean indicated pressure.
MIr. Middle Irish.
MIRV multiple independently targetable reentry vehicle.
misc. miscellaneous; miscellany.
Miss. Mississippi.
mk. mark; markka.
Mk Mark.
mkd. marked.
m.k.s., mk., M.K.S. meter-kilogram-second (system).
mkt. market.
ml., ml milliliter(s).
M.L., ML., ML Medieval (or Middle) Latin.
ML Molder.
M.L.A. Modern Language Association; Member of the Legislative Assembly.
MLD, M.L.D., m.l.d. minimum lethal dose.
MLG, M.L.G., MLG. Middle Low German.
Mlle., Mlle Mademoiselle.
Mlles., Mlles Mesdemoiselles.
M.L.S. Master of Library Science.
m.m. with the necessary changes [L *mutatis mutandis*].
mm., mm millimeter(s); thousands [L *millia*].
MM. Messieurs.
MM Machinist's Mate.
Mme., Mme Madame.
Mmes., Mmes Mesdames.
m.m.f. magnetomotive force.
mmfd. micromicrofarad.
m.n. the name being changed [L *mutato nomine*].
MN Minnesota (P.O. abbr.).
Mn manganese.
mo. month(s); monthly.
Mo. Missouri; Monday.
Mo molybdenum.
M.O. mail order; Medical Officer; money order.
MO Missouri (P.O. abbr.).
mod. moderate; moderato; modern.
Mod.Gr. Modern Greek.
Mod. L Modern Latin.
Moham. Mohammedan.
M.O.I. Ministry of Information.
mol. molecular; molecule.
mol.wt. molecular weight.
mon. monastery; monetary.
Mon. Monday; Monsignor.
Mong. Mongolia; Mongolian.
monocl. monoclinic.
monog., monogr. monograph.
Mons. Monsieur.
Monsig. Monsignor.
Mont. Montana.
mor. morocco (bookbinding).
Mor. Morocco.
morn. morning.
morph., morphol. morphological; morphology.
mort. mortuary.
MOS military occupational specialty.
mos. months.
mot. motor, motorized.
mp, m.p., M.P. melting point.
MP, M.P. Member of Parliament; Military Police.
mp moderately soft (It. *mezzo piano*).
M.Pd. Master of Pedagogy.
M.P.E. Master of Physical

Education.
mph, m.p.h., MPH miles per hour.
M.P.P.D.A., MPPDA Motion Picture Producers and Distributors of America, Inc.
MR Machinery Repairman; motivational research.
Mr. Mister.
M.R.A. Moral Re-Armament.
MRC Metals Reserve Company.
Mrs. Mistress.
m.s., M/S months after sight.
ms., ms, MS., MS manuscript.
M.S. Master of Science [L *Magister Scientiae*]; sacred to the memory of [L *memoriae sacrum*]; mine sweeper.
MS Mississippi (P.O. abbr.).
MSA Mutual Security Agency.
M.Sc. Master of Science.
msg. message.
Msgr. Monsignor.
M.Sgt., M/Sgt Master Sergeant.
m.s.l., M.S.L. mean sea level.
mss., mss, MSS., MSS manuscripts.
MST, M.S.T., m.s.t. mountain standard time.
mt. mount; mountain.
m.t. mean time; metric ton; motor transport; mountain time.
Mt Matthew.
MT Montana (P.O. abbr.).
mtg. meeting; mortgage.
mtge. mortgage.
mtl. material.
m.t.l., M.T.L. mean tidal level.
mtn. mountain.
MTO Mediterranean Theater of Operations.
Mt. Rev. Most Reverend.
mts. mountains.
MU Musician.
mun. municipal; municipality.
mus. museum; music; musician.
Mus.B., Mus.Bac. Bachelor of Music [L *Musicae Baccalaureus*].
Mus.D., Mus.Doc., Mus.Dr. Doctor of Music [L *Musicae Doctor*].
Mus.M. Master of Music [L *Musicae Magister*].
mut. mutilated; mutual.
mv., mv millivolt(s).
m.v. softly (It. *mezzo voce*).
Mv mendelevium.
MVA, M.V.A. Missouri Valley Authority.
MVD Soviet Ministry of Internal Affairs [Russian *Ministerstvo Vnutrennikh Del*].
M.W. Most Worshipful; Most Worthy.
MY May.
mya. myriare(s).
mycol. mycological; mycology.
myg. myriagram(s).
myl. myrialiter(s).
mym. myriameter(s).
myth., mythol. mythological; mythology.

N

n. name; net; neuter; new; nominative; noon; normal; note; noun; number; born [L *natus*]; our [L *noster*].
n neutron.
N. Nationalist; Navy; Norse; November.
N., N, n. north; northern.
N knight (chess); nitrogen.
Na sodium [L *natrium*].
N.A. National Army; North America.
N.A.A. National Aeronautic Association; National Automobile Association.
N.A.A.C.P., NAACP National Association for the Advancement of Colored People.
NAC North Atlantic Council.
NACA National Advisory Committee for Aeronautics.
N.A.D. National Academy of Design.
Nah., Nah Nahum.
N.Am. North American.
N.A.M. National Association of Manufacturers.
NASA National Aeronautics and Space Administration.
nat. national; native; natural; naturalist.
nat.hist. natural history.
natl. national.
NATO North Atlantic Treaty Organization.
NATS National Air Transport Service.
naut. nautical.
nav. naval; navigable; navigation.
navig. navigation; navigator.
n.b., N.B. note well [L *nota bene*].
N.B. New Brunswick.
Nb niobium.
NBA, N.B.A. National Boxing Association.
NBC National Broadcasting Company.
NbE north by east.
NBS, N.B.S. National Bureau of Standards.
NbW north by west.
n.c., N.C. nitrocellulose.
N.C., N.Car. North Carolina.
NC North Carolina (P.O. abbr.).
NCAA, N.C.A.A. National Collegiate Athletic Association.
NCO, N.C.O., n.c.o. non-commissioned officer.
N.D., n.d. no date.
Nd neodymium.
N.D., N.Dak. North Dakota.
ND North Dakota (P.O. abbr.).
NDRC, N.D.R.C. National Defense Research Committee.
NE, N.E., ne, n.e. northeast; northeastern.
Ne neon.
N.E. New England.
NE Nebraska (P.O. abbr.).
NEA, N.E.A. National Education Association.
Neb., Nebr. Nebraska.
N.E.C., NEC National Electric Code; National Emergency Council.
n.e.c. not elsewhere classified.
NED, N.E.D. New English Dictionary (Oxford English Dictionary).
neg. negative; negatively.
Neh., Neh Nehemiah.
n.e.i. not elsewhere indicated.
neol. neologism.
NEP, Nep., nep. New Economic Policy.
n.e.s. not elsewhere specified (or stated).
Neth. Netherlands.
neur., neurol. neurological; neurology.
neut. neuter; neutral.
Nev. Nevada.
Newf. Newfoundland.
New M. New Mexico.
New Test. New Testament.
n.f. noun feminine.
N.F. National Formulary; Newfoundland; Norman French.
N.F., n/f. no funds.
n.g., N.G. no good.
NG, N.G. National Guard; New Guinea.
NGk, N.Gk., NGk. New Greek.
N.H. New Hampshire.
NH New Hampshire (P.O. abbr.).
NHA, N.H.A. National Housing Administration (Agency).
NHG, NHG., N.H.G. New High German.
NHI National Health Insurance (Brit.).
n.h.p. nominal horsepower.
Ni nickel.
N.I., N.Ire. Northern Ireland.
NIA National Intelligence Authority.
Nic., Nicar. Nicaragua.
Nig. Nigeria; Nigerian.
NIRA, N.I.R.A. National Industrial Recovery Act.
N.J. New Jersey.
NJ New Jersey (P.O. abbr.).
NKVD People's Commissariat of Internal Affairs [Russ. *Narodnyi Komissariat Vnutrennikh Del*].
n.l. new line (printing); north latitude; not clear [L *non liquet*]; not far [L *non longe*]; not lawful [<L *non licet*].
NL, NL., N.L. New Latin.
N.lat. north latitude.
NLRB, N.L.R.B. National Labor Relations Board.
n.m. nautical mile; noun masculine.
N.M., N.Mex. New Mexico.
NM New Mexico (P.O. abbr.).
N.M.U., NMU National Maritime Union.
NNE, N.N.E, nne, n.n.e. north-northeast.
NNW, N.N.W., nnw, n.n.w. north-northwest.
No nobelium.
no., No. north; northern; number.
nob. for (or on) our part [L *nobis*].
nol. pros. unwilling to prosecute [L *nolle prosequi*].
nom. nomenclature; nominal; nominative.
nomin. nominative.
noncom. non-commissioned officer.
non cul. not guilty [L *non culpabilis*].
non dest. notwithstanding [L *non destante*].
non obs., non obst. notwithstanding [<L *non obstante*].
non pros. he (or she) does not prosecute [L *non prosequitur*].
non seq. it does not follow [L *non sequitur*].
nor., Nor. north; northern.
Nor. Norman; Norway; Norwegian.
norm normal.
Norw. Norway; Norwegian.
nos., Nos. numbers.
nov. novelist.
Nov., Nov November.
n.p. net proceeds; new paragraph; no paging; no place (of publication).
Np neptunium.
N.P. no protest; Notary Public; unless before [L *nisi prius*].
NP knight's pawn (chess); neuropsychiatric.
NPN non-protein nitrogen.
n.p. or d. no place or date.
n.p.t., N.P.T. normal pressure and temperature.
nr. near.
NRA, N.R.A. National Recovery Administration.
n.s. near side (shipping); new series; new style.
N.S., n.s. not specified.
Ns nimbostratus.
N.S. New Style; Nova Scotia.
NSA National Shipping Authority.
NSC National Security Council.
NSF National Science Foundation.
N.S.F., N/S/F not sufficient funds.
N.S.P.C.A. National Society for the Prevention of Cruelty to Animals.
N.S.P.C.C. National Society for the Prevention of Cruelty to Children.
NSRB National Security Resources Board.
nt. net.
Nt niton.
NT., N.T. New Testament.
n.t.p., N.T.P. normal temperature and pressure.
nt.wt. net weight.
num. number(s); numeral(s).
Num., Num, Numb. Numbers.
NV Nevada (P.O. abbr.).
numis., numism. numismatic; numismatics.
nv. non-voting (stock).
NW, N.W., nw, n.w. northwest; northwestern.
N.W.T. Northwest Territories (Canada).
N.Y. New York.
NY New York (P.O. abbr.).
NYA, N.Y.A. National Youth Administration.
N.Y.C. New York City.
N.Z., N.Zeal. New Zealand.

O

o. off; only.
o., O. octavo; old; order; pint [L *octavius*].
o ohm.
o- ortho-.
O. Ocean; October; Ohio; Ontario; Oregon.
O Old; oxygen.
OAPC, O.A.P.C. Office of Alien Property Custodian.
OAr., O.Ar. Old Arabic.
OAS Organization of American States.
ob. he (or she) died [L *orbit*]; in passing [L *obiter*]; obstetrical; obstetrics.
Ob., Ob, Obad. Obadiah.
obb. obbligato.
obdt., obt. obedient.
O.B.E. Officer (of the Order) of the British Empire.
obit. obituary.
obj. object; objection; objective.
obl. oblique; oblong.
obs. obscure; observation; observatory; obsolete; obsolescence.
obsol., obsoles. obsolescent.
ob.s.p. died without issue [L *obiit sine prole*].
obstet. obstetrical; obstetrics.
obt. obedient.
obv. obverse.
o.c. in the work cited [L *opere citato*].
Oc., oc. ocean.
o/c old charter; overcharge.
O.C., OC Office of Censorship; Officer Commanding; original cover.
OCAS Organization of Central American States.
occ. occasion; occasionally; occident; occidental.
occult. occultism.
OCD, O.C.D. Office of Civilian Defense.
oceanog. oceanography.
OCS Office of Contract Settlement; Officer Candidate School.
oct. octavo.
Oct, Oct. October.
octupl. octuplicate.
o.d. olive drab; on demand; outside diameter.
O.D. Doctor of Optometry; Officer of the Day; Ordnance Department; overdraft; overdrawn.
ODan. Old Danish.
OD., OD, ODu. Old Dutch.
ODM Office of Defense Mobilization.
OE, OE., O.E. Old English.
O.E.D. Oxford English Dictionary.
OEEC Organization for European Economic Cooperation.
O.E.S. Office of Economic Stabilization **(OES)**; Order of the Eastern Star.
OF, OF., O.F. Old French.
off. offered; office; official; officinal.
O.G. Officer of the Guard; original gum (philately).
OH Ohio (P.O. abbr.).
OHE Office of the Housing Expediter.
OHG, OHG., O.H.G. Old High German.
O.H.M.S. On His (Her) Majesty's Service.
OIAA Office of Inter-American Affairs.
OIC Office of Information and Culture (of the State Department).
O.Ir. Old Irish.
OIT Office of International Trade.
OK Oklahoma (P.O. abbr.).
Okla. Oklahoma.
OL, O.L. Old Latin.
Old Test. Old Testament.
oleo. oleomargarine.
O.M. Order of Merit (Brit.).
ON, ON., O.N. Old Norse.
ONI Office of Naval Intelligence.
ONorm.Fr. Old Norman French.
onomat. onomatopoeia; onomatopoeic.
Ont. Ontario.
OOD, O.O.D. Officer of the Day; Officer of the Deck.
O.P., OP, o.p., op out of print; overprint; overproof.
OP observation post.
op. operation; opposite; work [L *opus*]; works [L *opera*].
OPA, O.P.A. Office of Price Administration.
op. cit. in the work cited [L *opere citato*].
OPEC Organization of Petroleum Exporting Countries.
OPer. Old Persian.
ophthal. ophthalmology.
opp. oppose; opposed; opposite.
opt. optative; optical; optics.
OR, O.R. Operating room.
orat. oratorical; oratory.
ORC, O.R.C. Officers' Reserve Corps.
orch. orchestra; orchestral.
ord. ordained; order; ordinal; ordinance; ordinary; ordnance.
OR Oregon (P.O. abbr.).
ordn. ordnance.
Ore., Oreg. Oregon.
org. organic; organism; organized.
orig. original; originally.
Ork. Orkney (Islands).
ornith., ornithol. ornithological; ornithologist; ornithology.
Orth. Orthodox.
orth. orthopedic; orthopedics.
O.S. ordinary seaman.
O.S., o/s, O/S Old Style.
OS, OS., O.S Old Saxon.
Os osmium.
O.S.A. Order of St. Augustine.
O.S.B. Order of St. Benedict.
OSD Office of the Secretary of Defense.
O.S.D. Order of St. Dominic.
osc. oscillating; oscillator.
OSerb. Old Serbian.
O.S.F. Order of St. Francis.
OSlav. Old Slavic.
O.Sp. Old Spanish.
OSRD, O.S.R.D. Office of Scientific Research and Development.
OSS, O.S.S. Office of Strategic Services.
osteo. osteopath; osteopathy.
O.T. Old Testament; on truck; overtime.
OTC, O.T.C. Officer's Training Corps.
otol. otology.
OTS, O.T.S. Officer Trainin[g] School.
ott. octave [It. *ottava*].
OWI, O.W.I. Office of War In[-]formation.
Oxon. Oxford [L *Oxonia*].
oz, oz. ounce(s).
oz.ap. ounce, apothecary.
oz.av. ounce, avoirdupois.
ozs. ounces.
oz.t. ounce, troy.

P

p. after [L *post*]; by [L *per*]; b[y] weight [L *pondere*]; first [L *primus*]; for [L *pro*]; in par[t] [L *partim*]; page; part; participle; past; penny; perc[h] (measure); period; perishable peseta **(pta)**; peso; pint; pipe pole (measure); population post; power; pressure.
p, p. pitcher; softly [It. *piano*]
P. bishop [L *pontifex*]; fathe[r] [F *père*; L *pater*]; pastor; pengö people [L *populus*], peso piaster; pope [L *papa*]; president; priest; prince; prompte[r] (theater).
P parental; phosphorus; pressure; prisoner; pawn (chess)
p- para- (chemistry).
P- pursuit (military).
p.a. for the year [L *pro anno*] participial adjective; particula[r] average (insurance); public address; yearly [L *per annum*]
pa. paper.
Pa. Pennsylvania.
Pa protoactinium.
P.A. Passenger Agent; Petroleum Administration **(PA)**; Pos[t] Adjutant; Purchasing Agent.
P.A., P/A power of attorney private account.
PA Pennsylvania (P.O. abbr.) physician's assistant; press agent public-address (system).
PABA, paba para-aminobenzoi[c] acid.
Pac., Pacif. Pacific.
P.A.C. Pan-American Congress Political Action Committe[e] **(PAC)**.
p. ae. equal parts [L *parte[s] aequales*].
Pal. Palestine.
paleob. paleobotany.
paleog. paleography.
paleontol. paleontology.
palm. palmistry.
pam., pamph. pamphlet.
Pan. Panama.
P. and L. profit and loss.
pap. paper.
par. paragraph; parallel; parenthesis.
Par., Para. Paraguay.
paren. parenthesis.
parens. parentheses.
parl. parliamentary.
part. participle; particular.
pass. everywhere [L *passim*] passage; passenger; passive.
pat. patent; patented; patrol pattern.
patd. patented.
path., pathol. pathology.
Pat. Off. Patent Office.
pat.pend. patent pending.
P.A.U., PAU Pan America[n] Union.
P.A.Y.E. pay as you earn; pa[y] as you enter.
payt. payment.
P.B. Pharmacopoeia Britannica prayer book.
PBA Public Buildings Administration.
PBS Public Buildings Service.
PBX, P.B.X. private branc[h] (telephone) exchange.
p.c. after meals [L *post cibos*] postcard.
p.c., Pc., P.C., PC. percent percentage.
pc. piece; price.
p/c, P/C petty cash; price current.
P.C. Police Constable; Post Commander; Privy Council; professional corporation.
PCA Progressive Citizens o[f] America.
Pcs. preconscious.
pct. percent.
p.d., P.D. by the day [L *pe[r] diem*]; potential difference.
pd. paid.
Pd palladium.
P.D. Police Department.
PD phenyl dichloride.
Pd.B. Bachelor of Pedagogy [L *Pedagogiae Baccalaureus*].
Pd.D. Doctor of Pedagogy [L *Pedagogiae Doctor*].
Pd.M. Master of Pedagogy [L *Pedagogiae Magister*].
P.E. Petroleum Engineer; Pre

siding Elder; printer's error; probable error; Protestant Episcopal.
ped. pedal; pedestal; pedestrian.
P.E.I. Prince Edward Island.
pen. peninsula; penitent; penitentiary.
P.E.N. (International Association of) Poets, Playwrights, Editors, Essayists, and Novelists.
Penn., Penna. Pennsylvania.
penol. penology.
per. period; person.
per an., per ann. by the year [L *per annum*].
perd., perden. dying away [It. *perdendo*].
perf. perfect; perforated; performer.
perh. perhaps.
perm. permanent.
perp. perpendicular; perpetual.
pers. person; personal.
Pers. Persia; Persian.
persp. perspective.
pert. pertaining.
Peru., Peruv. Peruvian.
pet. petroleum.
petn. petition.
petrog. petrography.
petrol. petrology.
p.f. louder [It. *più forte*]; power factor.
pf. pfennig.
pg. page.
Pfc, Pfc. Private, first class.
pfd. preferred.
pfg. pfennig.
Pg. Portugal; Portuguese.
P.G. Past Grand (Master); paying guest; postgraduate.
PGA, P.G.A. Professional Golfers Association.
PH, P.H. Purple Heart.
ph. phrase.
Ph phenyl.
PHA Public Housing Administration.
phar., pharm. pharmaceutical; pharmacist; pharmacy.
Phar. B. Bachelor of Pharmacy [L *Pharmaciae Baccalaureus*].
Phar. D. Doctor of Pharmacy [L *Pharmaciae Doctor*].
Phar. M. Master of Pharmacy [L *Pharmaciae Magister*].
pharmacol. pharmacology.
Ph.B. Bachelor of Philosophy [L *Philosophiae Baccalaureus*].
Ph.C. Pharmaceutical Chemist.
Ph.D. Doctor of Philosophy [L *Philosophiae Doctor*].
phil., philos. philosopher; philosophical; philosophy.
Phil. Philippians; Philippines.
Phila. Philadelphia.
philol. philology.
philos. philosopher; philosophical; philosophy.
phon. phonetic; phonetics; phonology.
phonet. phonetic; phonetics.
phot., photog. photograph; photographic; photography.
photom. photometrical; photometry.
phr. phrase.
phren., phrenol. phrenological; phrenology.
PHS Public Health Service.
phys. physical; physician; physicist; physics.
physiol. physiological; physiology.
Pi., pias. piaster.
pict. pictorial; picture.
pil. pill [L *pilula*].
pinx. he (or she) painted [L *pinxit*].
pizz. plucked (music) [It. *pizzicato*].
pk. pack; park; peak; peck.
pkg. package(s).
pkt. packet.
pl. place; plate; plural.
plat. plateau; platform; platoon.
plen. plenipotentiary.
plf., plff. plaintiff.
plu. plural.
plup., plupf. pluperfect.
plur. plural; plurality.
p.m., P.M. after death [L *post mortem*]; afternoon [L *post meridiem*]; post-mortem.
P.M. Pacific Mail; Past Master; Paymaster; Police Magistrate; Postmaster; Prime Minister; Provost Marshal.
PM Postmaster; Provost Marshal.
Pm promethium.
PMA Production and Marketing Administration.
pmk. postmark.
pmkd. postmarked.
p.n., P/N promissory note.
pneum. pneumatic; pneumatics.
p.n.g. a person who is not acceptable [L *persona non grata*].
pnxt. he (or she) painted [L *pinxit*].
p.o., po put-out(s).
p.o., P.O. personnel officer; petty officer; postal order; post office.
Po polonium.
P.O.D. pay on delivery **(p.o.d.)**; Post Office Department.
Pod.D. Doctor of Podiatry.
P.O.E. Port of Embarkation; Port of Entry.
poet. poetic; poetical; poetry.
pol., polit. political; politics.
Pol. Poland; Polish.
pol. econ., polit. econ. political economy.
POP Point of Purchase.
pop. popular; population.
p.o.r. pay on return.
port. portrait.
Port. Portugal; Portuguese.
pos., posit. position; positive.
poss. possession; possessive; possible; possibly.
post. postal.
pot. potential.
P.O.W., POW Prisoner of War.
p.p., P.P. parcel post; parish priest; postpaid.
pp., p.p. past participle.
pp. pages; privately printed.
pp pianissimo.
PP pellagra preventive (factor).
pour prendre congé].
p.p.c., P.P.C. to take leave [F
ppd. postpaid; prepaid.
pph. pamphlet.
p.p.i. policy proof of interest.
PPI plan position indicator.
ppl. participle.
ppm., p.p.m. parts per million.
ppp. pianississimo.
ppr., p.pr. present participle.
p.p.s., P.P.S. additional postscript [L *post postscriptum*].
p.q. previous question.
P.Q. Province of Quebec.
pr. pair; pairs; paper; power; preferred; preposition; present; price; priest; prince; printing; pronoun.
PR public relations; Puerto Rico (P.O. abbr.).
Pr praseodymium.
P.R. Puerto Rico; proportional representation.
preb. prebend; prebendary.
prec. preceeding.
pred. predicate; predication; predicative; prediction.
pref. preface; prefatory; preference; preferred; prefix.
prelim. preliminary.
prem. premium.
prep. preparation; preparatory; prepare; preposition.
Pres. President.
pres. present; presidency; president; presumptive.
Presb., Presbyt. Presbyter; Presbyterian.
pret. preterit.
prev. previous; previously.
prim. primary; primitive.
prin. principal; principally; principle.
print. printer; printing.
priv. private; privately; privative.
P.R.O., PRO public relations officer.
pro. professional.
prob. probable; probably; problem.
proc. proceedings; process; proclamation.
prod. produce; produced; product.
prof. professor.
prog. progress; progressive.
prom. promenade; promontory.
pron. pronoun; pronounced; pronunciation.
pronom. pronominal.
prop. proper; properly; property; proposition; proprietor; proprietary.
propr. proprietor; proprietary.
pros. prosody.
Prot. Protectorate; Protestant.
pro tem. for the time being [L *pro tempore*].
prov. proverbial; providence; provident; province; provincial; provision; provost.
Prov, Prov. Proverbs.
prox. next (month) [L *proximo*].
prs. pairs.
prtd. printed.
prtg. printing.
Prus., Pruss. Prussia; Prussian.
p.r.v., P.R.V. to return a call [F *pour rendre visite*].
p.s., P.S. passenger steamer; permanent secretary; postscript; prompt side (theater); public sale.
ps. pieces; pseudonym.
Ps., Ps, Psa. Psalms.
P.S. Police Sergeant; Privy Seal; Public School.
pseud. pseudonym.
p.s.f., psf pounds per square foot.
p.s.i., psi pounds per square inch.
P.S.R.O. Professional Standards Review Organization.
p.ss., P.SS. postscripts.
PST, P.S.T., P.s.t. Pacific standard time.
psych., psychol. psychological; psychologist; psychology.
psychoanal. psychoanalysis.
p.t. for the time being [L *pro tempore*]; post town; postal telegraph.
pt. part; payment; pint(s); point(s); port; preterit.
Pt platinum.
P.T. Physical Training.
P.T.A., PTA Parent-Teachers' Association.
pta. peseta.
ptbl. portable.
ptg. printing.
pts. parts; payments; pints.
pty. proprietary.
Pu plutonium.
pub. public; publication; published; publisher.
publ. publication; published; publisher.
pulv. pulverized.
punct. punctuation.
pur., purch. purchaser; purchasing.
p.v. par value; post village; priest vicar.
Pvt. Private.
P.W., PW Prisoner of War.
PWA, P.W.A. Public Works Administration.
pwr. power.
pwt. pennyweight.
PX post exchange.
pymt. payment.

Q

q. quart; quarter; quarterly; quarto; query; question; queen.
Q. Quebec.
Q queen (chess).
q., Q. quarto.
q.b., qb quarterback.
Q.B. Queen's Bench.
QB queen's bishop (chess).
QBP queen's bishop's pawn (chess).
Q.C. Quartermaster Corps; Queen's Counsel.
q.d. as if one should say [L *quasi dicat*]; as if said [L *quasi dictum*]; as if he had said [L *quasi dixisset*].
q.e. which is [L *quod est*].
Q.E.D. which was to be demonstrated [L *quod erat demonstrandum*].
Q.E.F. which was to be done [L *quod erat faciendum*].
Q.E.I., q.e.i. which was to be found out [L *quod erat inveniendum*].
q.l. as much as you please [L *quantum libet*].
ql. quintal.
qlty. quality.
QM, Q.M. Quartermaster.
QMC, Q.M.C. Quartermaster Corps.
QMG, Q.M.G., Q.M.Gen. Quartermaster General.
qn. question.
QN queen's knight (chess).
QNP queen's knight's pawn (chess).
QP queen's pawn (chess).
q.pl., Q.P. as much as you wish [L *quantum placeat*].
Qq. quartos.
qq.v. which see (plural) [L *quos vide*].
qr. quarter; quarterly; quire.
QR queen's rook (chess).
QRP queen's rook's pawn (chess).
qrs. farthings [L *quadrantes*]; quarters; quires.
qrtly. quarterly.
q.s. as much as suffices [L *quantum sufficit*]; quarter section.
qt., qt quart.
qt. quantity.
q.t. quiet.
qto. quarto.
qts., qts quarts.
qu. quart; queen; query; question.
quad. quadrangle; quadrant; quadrat; quadrilateral; quadruple.
quar., quart. quarter; quarterly.
Que. Quebec.
ques. question.
quin., quint. quintuple; quintuplet.
quor. quorum.
quot. quotation; quoted.
q.v. as much as you will [L *quantum vis*]; which see [L *quod vide*].
qy. query.

R

r. range; rare; received; recipe; residence; resides; retired; right; right-hand page [L *recto*]; rises; rod; rubber; ruble.
r roentgen(s).
r., r run(s).
r., R. commonwealth [L *res publica*]; king [L *rex*]; queen [L *regina*]; rabbi; railroad; railway; rector; redactor; river; road; royal; ruble; rupee; take [L *recipe*].
r, R resistance (electrical); royal; ruble.
R gas constant (chemistry); radical (chemistry); radius; ratio; Réaumur; Republican; respond or response (ecclesiastical); ring (chemistry); rook (chess).
Ra radium.
R.A. Rear Admiral; right ascension; Royal Academy.
RA, R.A. Regular Army.
rad. radical; radio; radius; root [L *radix*].
RAF, R.A.F. Royal Air Force.
ral., rall. gradually slower [It. *rallentando*].
r and d, R & D, R and D research and development.
R.A.R. radio acoustic ranging.
RB Renegotiation Board.
Rb rubidium.
r.b.i., rbi run(s) batted in.
R.C. Red Cross; Reserve Corps; Roman Catholic.
RCAF, R.C.A.F. Royal Canadian Air Force.
R.C.Ch. Roman Catholic Church.
rcd. received.
R.C.M.P. Royal Canadian Mounted Police.
RCP Royal College of Physicians.
rcpt. receipt.
RCS Royal College of Surgeons.
Rct. Recruit.
rd. rod; round.
rd., Rd. reduce; rix-dollar; road.
RD Research and Development.
R.D. Rural Delivery.
Rd radium.
r.e., re right end.
Re. rupee.
Re rhenium.
R.E. real estate; Reformed Episcopal; Right Excellent; Royal Engineers.
REA, R.E.A. Rural Electrification Administration.
react. reactance (electricity).
rec. receipt; received; recipe; record; recorded; recorder; recording.
recd. received.
recip. reciprocal; reciprocity.
recit. recitative.
rec. sec. recording secretary.
rect. receipt; rectified; rector; rectory.
rec't receipt.
red. reduced; reduction.
redisc. rediscount.
redup., redupl. reduplicated; reduplication.
ref. referee; reference; referred; refining; reformation; reformed.
Ref.Ch. Reformed Church.
refl. reflection; reflective; reflectively; reflex; reflexive.
refrig. refrigeration.
reg. regent; regiment; region; register; registered; registrar; registry; regular; regularly; regulation; regulator.
Reg. Queen [L *regina*].
regt. regent; regiment.
rel. relating; relative; relatively; released; religion; religious.
rel. pron. relative pronoun.
rem. remittance.
REM rapid eye movement.
rep. repair; repeat; report; reporter; representative; reprint; republic.
Rep. Representative; Republic; Republican.
repr. representing; reprinted.
Repub. Republic; Republican.
req. required; requisition.
res. research; reserve; residence; resides; residue; resigned; resistance; resistor; resolution.
resp. respective; respiration; respondent.
restr. restaurant.
Resurr. Resurrection.
ret. retain; retired; returned.
retd. retained; returned.
retrog. retrogressive.
rev. revenue; reverse; reversed; review; revise; revised; revision; revolution; revolving.
Rev, Rev. Revelation; Reverend.
Rev. Ver. Revised Version (of the Bible).
r.f., rf right field(er); right forward.
r.f., R.F., RF radio frequency; range finder; rapid fire; right field.
R.F.A. Royal Field Artillery.
R.F.C. Reconstruction Finance Corporation **(RFC)**; Royal Flying Corps.
RFD, R.F.D. Rural Free Delivery.
r.g., rg right guard.
r.h. relative humidity; right hand.
r.h., rh, r.h.b., rhb right halfback.
Rh Rhesus (blood factor); rhodium.
R.H. Royal Highness.
rhap. rhapsody.
rhbdr. rhombohedral.
rhet. rhetoric; rhetorical.
rhin., rhinol. rhinology.
rhomb. rhombic.
r.h.p. rated horsepower.
R.I. King and Emperor [L *Rex et Imperator*]; Queen and Empress [L *Regina et Imperatrix*]; Rhode Island.
RI Rhode Island (P.O. abbr.).
R.I.P. may he (she, or they) rest in peace [L *requiescat*, or *requiescant, in pace*].
rip. supplementary (music) [It. *ripieno*].
rit. retarded (music) [It. *ritardando*].
riv. river.
rkva reactive kilovolt-ampere.
rm. ream; room.
Rm., R.M., RM, r.m. Reichsmark(s).
rms. reams; rooms.
rms, r.m.s. root mean square.
Rn radon.
R.N. registered nurse; Royal Navy.
RNA ribonucleic acid.
R.N.R. Royal Naval Reserve.
R.N.W.M.P. Royal Northwest Mounted Police.
ro. recto; rood.
ROK Republic of Korea.
rom. roman (type).
Rom. Roman; Romance; Romania; Romanian; Romans **(Rom)**.
R.O.P. record of production.
rot. rotating; rotation.
ROTC, R.O.T.C. Reserve Officers' Training Corps (Camp).
roul. roulette (philately).
Roum. Roumania; Roumanian.
roy. royal.
R.P. Reformed Presbyterian; Regius Professor.
R.P.D. Doctor of Political Science [L *Rerum Politicarum Doctor*].
rpm, r.p.m. revolutions per minute.
R.P.O. Railway Post Office.
rps, r.p.s. revolutions per second.
rpt. report.
R.R. railroad **(RR.)**; Right Reverend.
rr. very rarely [L *rarissime*].
rs, RS. reis; rupees.
R.S. Recording Secretary; Reformed Spelling; Revised Statutes.
R.S.F.S.R., RSFSR Russian Soviet Federated Socialist Republic.
R.S.V., RSV Revised Standard Version (Bible).
r.s.v.p., R.S.V.P. please reply [F *répondez s'il vous plaît*].
r.t., rt right tackle.
rt. right.
Rt. Hon. Right Honorable.
Rt. Rev. Right Reverend.
Rts. rights.
Ru Ruth; ruthenium.
rub. ruble.
Rum. Rumania; Rumanian.
Rus., Russ. Russia; Russian.
RV recreational vehicle.
R.V. Revised Version (Bible).
rva, RVA reactive volt-ampere.
R.W. Right Worshipful; Right Worthy.
Ry., ry. railway.

S

s. sacral; second; section; see; semi-; series; set; shilling [L *solidus*]; sign; signed; silver; singular; sire; solo; son; south-

ern: stem; stock; substantive; sun; surplus.
s., S. buried [L *sepultus*]; fellow [L *socius* or *sodalis*]; lies [L *situs*]; saint; school; scribe; secondary; senate; singular; socialist; society; soprano; steel.
s stere(s).
S., S, s., s south; southern.
s- symmetrical (chemistry).
S. Sabbath; Saturday; Saxon; Senate; September; Signor; Sunday.
S., Sig. signature.
S Seaman; sulfur; knight (in chess) [G *Springer*].
S.A. Salvation Army; sex appeal; South Africa; South America.
Sa samarium; Samuel.
SA Seaman Apprentice.
Sab. Sabbath.
SAC Strategic Air Command.
S.A.E., SAE Society of Automotive Engineers.
S.Afr. South Africa; South African.
SALT, S.A.L.T. Strategic Arms Limitation Talks.
S.Am., S.Amer. South America; South American.
SAM surface-to-air missile.
Sans., Sansk. Sanskrit.
S.ap. apothecary's scruple.
SAR, S.A.R. Sons of the American Revolution.
Sask. Saskatchewan.
sat. saturated; saturation.
Sat. Saturday; Saturn.
SAT Scholastic Aptitude Test.
sav. savings.
s.b., sb stolen base(s).
S.B. Bachelor of Science [L *Scientiae Baccalaureus*]; Shipping Board.
sb. substantive.
Sb. antimony [L *stibium*].
SBA Small Business Administration.
SbE south by east.
SbW south by west.
s.c. salvage charges; sized and calendered; small capitals (printing); supercalendered.
S.C. Signal Corps; South Carolina; Supreme Court.
SC Security Council (of the United Nations).
sc. he (she) carved or engraved it [L *sculpsit*]; namely [L *scilicet*]; scale; scene; science; screw; scruple (weight).
Sc scandium; stratocumulus.
Scan., Scand. Scandinavia; Scandinavian.
s.caps small capitals (printing).
Sc.B. Bachelor of Science [L *Scientiae Baccalaureus*].
Sc.D. Doctor of Science [L *Scientiae Doctor*].
sch. school; schooner.
sched. schedule.
schol. scholar; scholastic.
sci. science; scientific.
sci. fa. show cause [L *scire facias*].
scil. namely [L *scilicet*].
Sc.M. Master of Science [L *Scientiae Magister*].
Scot. Scotland; Scots; Scottish.
scr. scrip; script; scruple (weight).
Script. Scriptural; Scriptures.
sculp., sculpt. he (or she) carved it [L *sculpsit*]; sculptor.
SD Steward.
s.d. indefinitely (without date) [L *sine die*].
s.d., S.D. standard deviation.
S.D. Doctor of Science [L *Scientiae Doctor*].
SD South Dakota (P.O. abbr.).
S.D., S.Dak. South Dakota.
SDR, S.D.R., SDRs, S.D.R.s Special Drawing Rights.
Se selenium.
SE, S.E., se, s.e. southeast; southeastern.
SEATO Southeast Asia Treaty Organization.
sec. according to [L *secundum*]; secant (**see**); second(s); secondary; secretary; section(s); sector.
SEC, S.E.C. Securities and Exchange Commission.
sec.-ft. second-foot.
sech hyperbolic secant.
sec.leg. according to law [L *secundum legem*].
sec.reg. according to rule [L *secundum regulam*].
secs. seconds; sections.
sect. section; sectional.
secy. secretary.
seg. segment.
seismol. seismology.
sel. selected; selection(s).
Sem. Seminary; Semitic.
sen., Sen. senate; senator; senior.
sent. sentence.
sep. sepal; separate.
Sep., Sept. September (**Sep**); Septuagint.
seq. sequel.
seq., seqq. the following [L *sequens, sequentia*].
ser. serial; series; sermon.
serv. servant; service.
sess. session.
sf., sforz., sfz. with emphasis (music) [It. *sforzando, sforzato*].
S.F.S.R. Soviet Federated Socialist Republic.
s.g. specific gravity.
sg, s.g. senior grade.
sgd. signed.
Sgt. Sergeant.
sh. share; sheet; shilling(s); shunt.
SHAEF Supreme Headquarters, Allied Expeditionary Forces.
Shak. Shakespeare.
SHAPE Supreme Headquarters Allied Powers (Europe).
SHF, S.H.F., shf, s.h.f. superhigh frequency.
shipt., shpt. shipment.
shtg. shortage.
sh.tn. short ton.
Si silicon.
S.I. Staten Island (N.Y.).
Sib. Siberia; Siberian.
sig., Sig. signal; signature; signor; signore; signori.
sigill. seal [L *sigillum*].
sim. simile.
sin sine.
sing. singular.
sinh hyperbolic sine.
sist. sister.
s.j. under consideration [L *sub judice*].
S.J. Society of Jesus [L *Societas Jesu*].
S.J.D. Doctor of Juridical Science [L *Scientiae Juridicae Doctor*].
sk. sack.
Skr., Skt. Sanskrit.
s.l. without place (of publication) [L *sine loco*].
s.l.a.n. without place, date, or name [L *sine loco, anno, vel nomine*].
S. lat. south latitude.
Slav. Slavic; Slavonian.
sld. sailed; sealed.
SLIC, S.L.I.C. Savings and Loan Insurance Corporation.
s.l.p. without lawful issue [L *sine legitima prole*].
sm. small.
Sm samarium.
S.M. Master of Science [L *Scientiae Magister*]; Sergeant Major; State Militia.
sm.c., sm.caps small capitals.
smorz. dying away (music) [It. *smorzando*].
s.m.p. without male issue [L *sine mascula prole*].
s.n. without name [L *sine nomine*].
Sn tin [L *stannum*].
s.o., so struck out.
s.o. seller's option.
So. south; southern.
soc. socialist; society.
sociol. sociological; sociology.
sol. solicitor; soluble; solution.
Sol. Solomon.
soln. solution.
Som. Somaliland.
son. sonata.
SOP, S.O.P. standard operating procedure.
sop. soprano.
sos., sost., sosten. sustained (music) [It. *sostenuto*].
s.p. single phase; single pole; without issue [L *sine prole*].
SP shore patrol; shore police.
sp. special; species; specific; specimen; spelling; spirit(s).
Sp. Spain; Spaniard; Spanish.
S.P.A.S. Fellow of the American Philosophical Society [L *Societatis Philosophiae Americanae Socius*].
S.P.C.A. Society for the Prevention of Cruelty to Animals.
S.P.C.C. Society for the Prevention of Cruelty to Children.
spec. special; specification; speculation.
specif. specifically.
spg. spring.
sp. gr. specific gravity.
sp. ht. specific heat.
sph. spherical.
spp. species (plural).
S.P.R. Society for Psychical Research.
spt. seaport.
sq. square; sequence; the following [L *sequentia*].
Sq. Squadron; Square (street).
sq. ft. square foot; square feet.
sq. in. square inch(es).
sq. m., sq. mi. square mile(s).
sq. rd. square rod(s).
sq. yd. square yard(s).
sr steradian.
Sr. Senior; Señor; Sir; Sister.
Sr strontium.
Sra. Señora.
S.R.O. standing room only.
Srta. Señorita.
s.s., ss., ss shortstop.
ss namely (in law) [L *scilicet*].
SS. Saints.
S.S. Silver Star; Sunday School; written above [L *supra scriptum*].
SS, S.S., S/S steamship.
SS., SS Nazi guards [G *Schutzstaffeln*].
SSA, S.S.A. Social Security Act (Administration).
SSB, S.S.B. Social Security Board.
SSE, S.S.E., sse, s.s.e. south-southeast.
S.Sgt., S/Sgt Staff Sergeant.
SSR, S.S.R. Soviet Socialist Republic.
SSS Selective Service System.
SST supersonic transport.
SSW, S.S.W., ssw, s.s.w. south-southwest.
s.t. short ton.
st. stand; stanza; stere; stet; stitch; stone (weight); street; strophe.
st., St. statute(s); street.
St. Saint; Straight; Strait.
St stratus (clouds).
sta. station; stationary; stator.
Sta. Santa; Station.
stac., stacc. staccato.
stan. stanchion.
Staph. staphylococcus.
stat. immediately [L *statim*]; static; stationary; statistics; statuary; statute; statutes.
S.T.B. Bachelor of Sacred Theology [L *Sacrae Theologiae Baccalaureus*].
stbd. starboard.
std. standard.
S.T.D. Doctor of Sacred Theology [L *Sacrae Theologiae Doctor*].
Ste. Sainte.
steno., stenog. stenographer; stenography.
ster., stg. sterling.
St.Ex. Stock Exchange.
stge. storage.
stip. stipend; stipendiary; stipulation.
Stir. Stirling; Stirlingshire.
stk. stock.
STOL, S.T.O.L. short take-off and landing.
stor. storage.
S.T.P. Professor of Sacred Theology [L *Sacrae Theologiae Professor*].
stp. stamped.
STP standard temperature and pressure.
str. steamer; strait; string(s).
Strep. streptococcus.
stud. student.
sub. subaltern; submarine; subscription; substitute; suburb; suburban; understand (or supply) [L *subaudi*].
subd. subdivision.
subj. subject; subjective; subjunctive.
subs. subscription; subsidiary.
subseq. subsequent; subsequently.
subst. substantive; substitute.
succ. successor.
suf., suff. suffix.
sug., sugg. suggested; suggestion.
Sun., Sund. Sunday.
sup. above [L *supra*]; superfine; superior; superlative; supplement; supplementary; supply; supreme.
super. superfine; superintendent; superior; supernumerary.
superl. superlative.
supp., suppl. supplement; supplementary.
supr. supreme.
supt., Supt. superintendent.
sur. surcharged; surplus.
surg. surgeon; surgery; surgical.
surr. surrender; surrendered.
surv. survey; surveying; surveyor; surviving.
susp. suspended.
s.v. sailing vessel; under this word [L *sub verbo*].
S.V. Holy Virgin [L *Sancta Virgo*].
SW, S.W., sw, s.w. southwest; southwestern.
Sw., Swe., Swed. Sweden; Swedish.
S.W.A., S.W.Afr. South-West Africa.
Swit., Switz., Swtz. Switzerland.
syl., syll. syllable.
sym. symbol; symmetrical; symphony.
syn. synchronize; synonym; synonymous; synonymy.
syr. syrup (pharmacy).
Syr. Syria; Syriac; Syrian.
syst. system; systematic.

T

t. in the time of [L *tempore*]; tare; target; teaspoon(s); telephone; temperature; tempo; tenor; tense (grammar); terminal; territory; time; tome; ton(s); town; township; transit; transitive; troy (weight); volume [L *tomus*].
T. tablespoon(s); Testament; Tuesday; Trinity; Turkish.
T tantalum; Technician; temperature (absolute); tension (surface); time.
Ta tantalum.
TAB Technical Assistance Board.
tab. table(s).
TAC Tactical Air Command; Technical Assistance Committee.
tal. qual. as they come (or average quality) [L *talis qualis*].
tan tangent.
tanh hyperbolic tangent.
TAP Technical Assistance Program.
tart. tartaric.
taut. tautological; tautology.
t.b. trial balance.
TB, T.B., Tb., Tb, t.b., tb tubercle bacillus; tuberculosis.
Tb terbium.
tbs., tbsp. tablespoon(s); tablespoonful(s).
TC Trusteeship Council (of the United Nations).
Tc technetium.
tc. tierce(s).
tchr. teacher.
td., td, TD touchdown.
TD Tank Destroyer; Tradevman.
TD, T.D. Traffic Director; Treasury Department.
t.d.n. total digestible nutrients.
Te tellurium.
tech. technical; technological; technology.
technol. technology.
tel. telegram; telegraph; telegraphic; telephone.
telecom. telecommunication(s).
teleg. telegram; telegraph; telegraphic; telegraphy.
temp. in the time of [L *tempore*]; temperature; temporary.
ten. tenement; tenor; tenuto (music).
Tenn. Tennessee.
ter., terr. terrace; territorial; territory.
term. terminal; termination; terminology.
test. testamentary; testator.
Test. Testament.
tetr., tetrag. tetragonal.
Teut. Teuton; Teutonic.
Tex. Texas; Texan.
tfr. transfer.
t.g. type genus.
tgt. target.
Th., Thur., Thurs. Thursday.
Th thorium.
Th.B. Bachelor of Theology [L *Theologiae Baccalaureus*].
Th.D. Doctor of Theology [L *Theologiae Doctor*].
Th-Em thoron (thorium emanation).
theol. theologian; theological; theology.
theor. theorem.
theos. theosophical; theosophist; theosophy.
therm. thermometer.
thermochem. thermochemical; thermochemistry.
thermodynam. thermodynamics.
Thess. Thessalonians; Thessaly.
T.H.I., T.-H.-I. temperature-humidity index.
Ti titanium.
t.i.d. three times daily [L *ter in die*].
tinct. tincture.
tit. title.
Tit., Tit Titus.
tk. truck.
TKO, t.k.o., T.K.O. technical knockout.
Tl thallium.
T/L time loan.
T.L. trade-last.
t.m. true mean.
Tm thulium.
TN Tennessee (P.O. abbr.).
tn. ton; train.
Tn thoron.
tng. training.
TNT, T.N.T. trinitrotoluene; trinitrotoluol.
t.o. turnover; turn over.
tonn. tonnage.
top., topog. topographical; topography.
t.p. title page.
tp. township; troop.
t.p.r. temperature, pulse, respiration.
tps. townships.
Tr terbium.
Tr. Troop.
tr. tare; tincture; trace; train; transitive; translated; translation; translator; transpose; treasurer; trust.
trag. tragedy; tragic.
trans. transactions; transfer; transferred; transitive; translated; translation; translator; transportation; transpose; transverse.
transf. transfer; transference; transferred.
transl. translated; translation(s).
transp. transparent; transportation.
trav. traveler; travels.
treas. treasurer; treasury.
trf, t.r.f., t-r-f tuned radio frequency.
trfd. transferred.
tricl. triclinic (crystal).
trig., trigon. trigonometric; trigonometry.
trim. trimetric (crystal).
tripl. triplicate.
trit. triturate.
trop. tropic; tropical; tropics.
t.s. tensile strength.
T.Sgt., T/Sgt Technical Sergeant.
tsp. teaspoon(s); teaspoonful(s).
Tu., Tues. Tuesday.
Tu thulium.
T.U. Trade Union; Training Unit.
T.U.C., TUC Trades Union Congress.
Turk. Turkey; Turkish.
TV television; terminal velocity.
TVA, T.V.A. Tennessee Valley Authority (Administration).
twp. township.
TX Texas (P.O. abbr.).
Ty. Territory.
typ., typo., typog. typographer typographic; typography.
typw. typewriter; typewritten.

U

u. and [G *und*].
u., U. uncle; university; upper.
U uranium.
UAW, U.A.W. United Automobile, Aircraft and Agricultura Implement Workers; United Automobile Workers of America.
u.c. upper case (printing).
UCMJ Uniform Code of Military Justice.
UFO, ufo unidentified flying object(s).
UHF, U.H.F., uhf, u.h.f. ultra-high frequency.
U.J.D. Doctor of Civil and Canon Law [L *Utriusque Juris Doctor*].
U.K. United Kingdom.
Ukr. Ukraine.
ult. ultimate; ultimately.
ult., ulto. last month [L *ultimo*].
UMT Universal Military Training.
UMTS Universal Military Training Service (System).
UMW, U.M.W. United Mine Workers of America.
UN, U.N. United Nations.
unabr. unabridged.
unb., unbd. unbound (book binding).
undsgd. undersigned.
undtkr. undertaker.
UNEDA United Nations Economic Development Administration.
UNESCO, Unesco United Nations Educational, Scientific and Cultural Organization.
ung. ointment [L *unguentum*].
UNICEF United Nations Children's Fund.
Unit. Unitarian; Unitarianism.
univ. universal; universally; university.
Univ. Universalist.
UNKRA United Nations Korean Reconstruction Agency.
unl. unlimited.
unm. unmarried.
UNO United Nations Organization.
unof. unofficial.
unp. unpaged.
unpub. unpublished.
UNREF United Nations Refu

ee Emergency Fund.

NRRA United Nations Relief and Rehabilitation Administration.

NRWA United Nations Relief and Works Agency.

NSCOB United Nations Special Committee on the Balkans.

P., UP Union Pacific (Railroad); United Press.

PI, U.P.I. United Press International.

r uranium.

ol. urology.

ru. Uruguay.

s. in the place mentioned above [L *ubi supra*]; as above. [L *ut supra*].

S, U.S. United States.

SA, U.S.A. United States of America; United States Army.

SAF, U.S.A.F. United States Air Force.

SAFI, U.S.A.F.I. United States Armed Forces Institute.

S.C. & G.S. United States Coast and Geodetic Survey.

SCG, U.S.C.G. United States Coast Guard.

SDA, U.S.D.A. United States Department of Agriculture.

SES, U.S.E.S. United States Employment Service.

SHA, U.S.H.A. United States Housing Authority (Administration).

SIA, U.S.I.A. United States Information Agency.

SIBA United States International Book Association.

SIS, U.S.I.S. United States Information Service.

SM, U.S.M. United States Mail; United States Marines; United States Mint.

SMA, U.S.M.A. United States Military Academy.

SMC, U.S.M.C. United States Marine Corps; United States Maritime Commission.

SN, U.S.N. United States Navy.

SNA, U.S.N.A. United States National Army; United States Naval Academy.

SNG, U.S.N.G. United States National Guard.

SNR, U.S.N.R. United States Naval Reserve.

SO, U.S.O. United Service Organizations.

SP, U.S.P. United States Patent; United States Pharmacopoeia (**U. S. Pharm.**).

S.P.H.S., USPHS United States Public Health Service.

S.P.O. United States Post Office.

S.S. United States Senate; United States Ship (Steamer)

(USS).

U.S.S.B., USSB United States Shipping Board.

U.S.S.Ct. United States Supreme Court.

U.S.S.R., USSR Union of Soviet Socialist Republics.

usu. usual; usually.

u.s.w., usw and so forth [G *und so weiter*].

U.S.W.A. United Steel Workers of America.

u.t. universal time.

ut. utility.

Ut. Utah.

UT Utah (P.O. abbr.).

ut dict. as directed [L *ut dictum*].

ut sup. as above [L *ut supra*].

U.T.W.A. United Textile Workers of America.

ux. wife [L *uxor*].

V

v. of [G *von*]; see [L *vide*]; valve; ventral; verb; verse; version; versus; vicar; vice–; village; vision; vocative; voice; voltage; volunteer(s); von.

v., V. volt; volume.

V. Venerable; Viscount.

V vanadium; vector; velocity; victory; volume.

v.a. verb active; verbal adjective.

va volt-ampere(s).

Va. Virginia.

V.A. Veterans Administration (**VA**); Vicar Apostolic; Vice Admiral; (Order of) Victoria and Albert.

VA Virginia (P.O. abbr.).

vae. vacuum.

val. valentine; valuation; value.

var. variant; variation; variety; various.

var reactive volt-ampere.

Vat. Vatican.

VAT value-added tax.

v. aux. verb auxiliary.

vb. verb; verbal.

vb. n. verbal noun.

V.C. Veterinary Corps; Vice Chairman; Vice Chancellor; Vice Consul; Victoria Cross.

v.d. vapor density; various dates.

Vd vanadium.

V.D., VD, v.d. venereal disease.

veg. vegetable; vegetation.

vel. vellum (bookbinding).

Ven. Venerable; Venice; Venus.

Venez. Venezuela.

vent. ventilating; ventilation; ventilator.

ver. verse(s); version.

vers versed sine, versine.

vert. vertebra; vertebrate; vertical.

ves. vessel; vestry; vesicle; vesicular.

vet. veteran; veterinarian; veterinary.

veter. veterinary.

VFW, V.F.W. Veterans of Foreign Wars.

V.G. Vicar General.

v.g for example [L *verbi gratia*].

VHF, V.H.F., vhf, v.h.f. very high frequency.

v.i. see below [L *vide infra*]; verb intransitive.

V.I. Virgin Islands.

Vi virginium.

VI Virgin Islands (P.O. abbr.).

vie. vicar; vicarage.

Vic., Viet. Victoria; Victorian.

vid. for example (see) [L *vide*].

v.imp. verb impersonal.

VIP, V.I.P. very important person.

v.irr. verb irregular.

vis. visibility; visual.

Vis., Visc., Visct. Viscount; Viscountess.

viv. lively (music) [It. *vivace*].

viz., viz namely [L *videlicet*].

VL, V.L. Vulgar Latin.

VLF, V.L.F., vlf, v.l.f. very low frequency.

vm. voltmeter.

V.M.D. Doctor of Veterinary Medicine [L *Veterinariae Medicinae Doctor*].

v.n., v.neut. verb neuter.

vo. verso.

vocab. vocabulary.

vol. volcano; volume; volunteer.

vole. volcanic; volcano.

vols. volumes.

vox pop. voice of the people [L *vox populi*].

voy. voyage.

v.p. various pagings; various places; verb passive; voting pool (stocks).

V.P. Vice President.

V.R. Queen Victoria [L *Victoria Regina*].

v.r. verb reflexive.

V. Rev. Very Reverend.

v.s. see above [L *vide supra*]; vibration seconds (sound); volumetric solution.

vs. versus.

V.S. Veterinary Surgeon.

VSS versions.

VT Vermont (P.O. abbr.).

v.t. verb transitive.

Vt. Vermont.

VTOL Vertical takeoff and landing.

Vul., Vulg. Vulgate.

vulg. vulgar; vulgarity.

v.v. vice versa.

vv. verses; violins.

W

w. wanting; warden; warehousing; week(s); weight; wide; width; wife; with; word; work.

W, W., w, w. watt; west; western.

w., w won.

W. Wales; Washington; Wednesday; Welsh.

W tungsten [G *wolfram*].

WA Washington (P.O. abbr.).

WAC, W.A.C. Women's Army Corps.

w.a.e. when actually employed.

WAF, W.A.F. Women in the Air Force.

war. warrant.

Wash. Washington.

WASP, W.A.S.P. Women's Air Force Service Pilots.

watt–hr watt-hour(s).

WAVES, W.A.V.E.S. Women Appointed for Voluntary Emergency Service.

w.b. warehouse book; water ballast; westbound.

W.B., W/B, W/b, W.b. waybill.

WbN west by north.

WbS west by south.

w.c. water closet; without charge.

W.C.T.U. Women's Christian Temperance Union.

Wed. Wednesday.

w.f., wf wrong font (printing).

W.Flem. West Flemish.

WFTU, W.F.T.U. World Federation of Trade Unions.

WGme., W.Ger. West Germanic.

wh, wh., whr, whr., w.-hr. watt-hour(s).

whf. wharf.

WHO World Health Organization.

w.i. when issued (stocks); wrought iron.

W.I. West Indies; West Indian.

WI Wisconsin (P.O. abbr.).

W.Ind. West Indies.

Wis., Wisc. Wisconsin.

wk. weak; week; work.

wkly. weekly.

wks. weeks; works.

w.l., WL water line; wavelength.

wldr. welder.

W. long. west longitude.

wm wattmeter.

wmk. watermark.

WMO World Meteorological Organization.

WNW, W.N.W., wnw, w.n.w. west-northwest.

WO, W.O. wait order; Warrant Officer.

w.p., W.P. weather permitting; wire payment.

WPA, W.P.A. Work Projects Administration; Works Progress Administration.

WRAC, W.R.A.C. Women's Royal Army Corps.

WRAF, W.R.A.F. Women's Royal Air Force.

WREN, W.R.N.S. Women's Royal Naval Service.

wrnt. warrant.

WSW, W.S.W., wsw, w.s.w. west-southwest.

wt., wt weight.

WV West Virginia (P.O. abbr.).

W.Va. West Virginia.

WVS, W.V.S. Women's Volunteer Service (Brit.).

WY Wyoming (P.O. abbr.).

Wyo. Wyoming.

X

x symbol for an unknown quantity.

X Christ; Christian; a ten-dollar bill; xenon.

x.c., X.C. ex-coupon.

x.d., X.D., x-div. ex-dividend.

Xe xenon.

xi., X.I., x-int. ex-interest.

Xmas Christmas.

Xn. Christian.

Xnty., Xty. Christianity.

x-ref. cross-reference.

X-rts. ex-rights.

Xtian. Christian.

xyl. xylograph.

Y

y. yard(s); year(s); younger; youngest.

Y. Young Men's (Women's) Christian Association.

Y yttrium.

Yb ytterbium.

yd. yard(s).

yds. yards.

Yid. Yiddish.

Y.M., Y.M.C.A., YMCA Young Men's Christian Association.

Y.M.H.A., YMHA Young Men's Hebrew Association.

Y.P.S.C.E. Young People's Society of Christian Endeavor.

yr. year(s); younger; your.

yrs. years; yours.

Y.T. Yukon Territory.

Yt yttrium.

Y.W., Y.W.C.A., YWCA Young Women's Christian Association.

Y.W.H.A., YWHA Young Women's Hebrew Association.

Z

z., Z. zone.

Z zenith distance.

Zec, Zech. Zechariah.

Zep, Zeph. Zephaniah.

Z/F zone of fire.

Zn zinc.

zool. zoological; zoologist; zoology.

Zr zirconium.

Vocabulary and Spelling Improvement

BY ALBERT H. MARCKWARDT

IMPROVING YOUR VOCABULARY

Why Study Words?

The author of a recent book on the English language asks the question and then proceeds to answer it as follows: "The fact is that, if we are going to be able to talk about anything very far beyond our day-to-day, bread and butter living, if we are going to associate in an easy manner with cultivated people, if we are going to read books which such people have found to be important and significant, then we must have at our command a great many words that the man in the street and the man with the hoe neither know nor use."[1]

This is a direct and convincing answer to the question, but it is by no means the only reason for improving your vocabulary. The needs of society must be considered as well as those of the individual. If it were not for language, human society could not function; language makes it possible for human beings to cooperate and to create a social order. This is true even of the very simple, the most primitive societies. Throughout the entire twentieth century our societies have been growing more and more complex; the problems which they face both internally and externally are vastly more complicated and difficult than they were in the days of our grandparents. This places a greater burden upon the language, and thus places a greater responsibility upon every one of us to use the language as effectively as he can. Accordingly, vocabulary improvement becomes a responsibility of the man in the street as well as the man in the library.

There is, moreover, a large element of personal satisfaction in being able to use words effectively. The fluent speaker and the exact writer are widely admired for being able to express their thoughts and feelings in a manner that is both precise and direct. Precision and fluency are the qualities for which we must strive in our command of words, tempered always by a sense of what is suitable for the audience to whom our language is directed. Almost everyone of us has a dual task: to learn more words than we now know, and to use both those which we now know and the new ones that we learn as exactly as we can.

The English Lexicon

Let us set out immediately to add a new word to the total stock of many who will read this passage. *Lexicon* is often used as a term for the totality of words in a language. The few who know Greek will recognize its origin in *lexis*, the Greek for "word" or "speech." The many who know English may have encountered the words *lexical* or *lexicography*. At any rate here *lexicon* gives us a convenient alternate for *vocabulary*, although the two words do not have exactly the same range of meaning.

The point to be made, however, is that the English lexicon poses certain peculiar problems for anyone who is trying to improve his mastery of it. For one thing, it consists of two classes of words, learned and popular. As one writer has described the situation, "First, there are those words with which we become acquainted in ordinary conversation—which we learn . . . from the members of our own families and from our familiar associates, and which we should know and use even if we could not read or write. They concern the common things of life and are the stock in trade of all who speak the language. Such words may be called 'popular,' since they belong to the people at large and are not the exclusive possession of a limited class."

The author then goes on to say, "On the other hand, our language includes a multitude of words which are comparatively seldom used in ordinary conversation. Their meanings are known to every educated person, but there is little occasion to employ them at home or in the market-place. Our first acquaintance with them comes not from our mother's lips or from the talk of our schoolmates, but from the books that we read, lectures that we hear, or the more formal conversation of highly educated speakers, who are discussing some particular topic in a style appropriately elevated above the habitual level of everyday life. Such words we call 'learned' and the distinction between them and 'popular' words is of great importance to a right understanding of linguistic process."[2] He then goes on to cite the words *lively* and *vivacious* as examples of the popular and learned classes respectively.

Not all of us would necessarily agree with the author that the learned words are known to every educated person, but there can be little question over the existence in English of two sectors of the vocabulary. It is also true that these two sectors are farther apart from each other in English than in most other languages. Consequently, a manner of speaking or writing that uses learned words to the exclusion of the popular is often felt as artificial or pretentious. There is little point in saying, "There was general rejoicing over the cessation of hostilities," when we might as well say, "People were glad that the war was over." At the same time, we must recognize that the chemist who wrote, "Neuraminic acid in the form of its alkali-stable methoxy derivative was first isolated by Klenk from gangliosides and more recently from bovine sub-maxillary gland mucin," could not have expressed his ideas in the popular vocabulary.

The popular vocabulary consists of short words, native words, words which often have many meanings. The learned vocabulary for the most part contains long words, words of foreign origin, often though not always somewhat more precise in their meanings. The problem for each of us is to acquire the learned words which are necessary and useful to us in our reading, in the exercise of our professions, and in carrying on the affairs of our society, but to use them with discretion, with a feeling for our audience.

The Individual Vocabulary

Because of the very existence of the two sectors of our lexicon, the English language has a very large stock of words. The larger dictionaries generally record about 450,000, almost half a million words, and there are others, of course, that never get into the dictionary for various reasons. Some authorities on language have expressed the opinion that perhaps our language is too richly endowed, that there are too many words that almost duplicate one another in meaning. The opposing view is that a large vocabulary makes it possible to give to words a great many shades of emotion as well as of meaning, and that individual styles may thus be developed. The net result, however, is that the average individual commands a smaller proportion of the total wordstock of English than is the case with speakers of many other languages. This also creates a problem for anyone who wants to improve his vocabulary.

We must also recognize the distinction between what is called a *passive* or *recognition* vocabulary and an *active* or *use* vocabulary. The recognition vocabulary is composed of those words which you recognize when you see or hear them. The active vocabulary consists of the words which you, yourself, employ. The recognition vocabulary is by far the larger. According to some estimates, it is about three times the size of the active vocabulary.

Enlarging Your Vocabulary

We have seen that the English language contains a large number of words, divided into two fairly well-defined layers, the learned and the popular. The total lexicon of the language is vastly greater than that of any person who speaks it. Every speaker has a passive and an active vocabulary, the

[1] Thomas Pyles, *The Origins and Development of the English Language*, Harcourt, Brace, and World, Inc., New York, 1964, p. 302.

[2] J. B. Greenough and G. L. Kittredge, *Words and Their Ways in English Speech*, Macmillan, N.Y., 1901, p. 19.

former more extensive than the latter. Anyone who wants to increase his word power must do so within this context, concentrating especially upon three phases of it:

1. He must increase the range and extent of his recognition vocabulary.
2. He must transfer words from his recognition to his active or use vocabulary.
3. He must develop the ability to form new words as he needs them, particularly by using the rich supply of prefixes and suffixes in the language.

Increasing the Passive Vocabulary

How do we come to learn new words, even when we are not consciously trying to add to our stock of them? Generally we do so through reading or hearing them and then coming to some conclusion about their meaning from the context in which they appear.

Suppose, for example, you did not know what a Cape Cod lighter was, and you heard someone say that he had just bought one and luckily it was working very well. At this point you may conjecture that it is some kind of operational device, either for the purpose of illumination or kindling a fire. The next time you encountered the word was when you heard someone say that he had bought some kerosene for his Cape Cod lighter. Since illumination by kerosene is relatively rare, you eliminate the light-giving function and conclude that it must have something to do with getting a fire started. Upon your third encounter with the word you learn from the speaker that he keeps his Cape Cod lighter near the fireplace but occasionally uses it for his outdoor grill. By this time you have formed a clear idea of its function; you do not yet have an idea about its size and shape, or how it actually works. Other contextual clues will furnish this information, if you have not already seen or acquired one by that time. But this is the way that much of our adult knowledge of words comes about and, of course, all of our pre-reading knowledge.

Vocabulary enlargement through reading comes about in much the same way. Our first contact with a new word may be in a context which is not particularly suggestive or revealing. Suppose, for example, a reader's earliest encounter with *commendatory* is in the sentence, "It was a commendatory speech about our economic administration." Unless he connects this word with *commend* or *commendation*, which he may well do, he concludes, perhaps, that it refers to some quality which a speech may possess, but he gets little more out of it than just that. But when he then comes upon the sentence, "The official sent a commendatory letter to the chief of police for the excellent manner in which he quelled the riot," he is able to deduce that the kind or quality is a favorable one.

But we do have resources beyond these very general contextual clues, and we must learn to be sensitive to them. For example, words are often paired with others of similar though not identical meaning. Suppose we come upon *utilize* in a sentence such as the following: "Certainly it should be regarded as a preeminent quality of true genius to *utilize and transform to its own purposes* the rich resources of the world in which it reaches." From this we sense that *utilize* is, if not equivalent, at least not unrelated and possibly even similar to *transform to its* own *purposes*. A similar pairing, "to improve and utilize each opportunity," will give us a further notion of the positive meaning of the word, and finally when we come upon, "They must either *nullify or utilize* the mouth of the Danube," our concept of positive effort and beneficial result is strengthened by seeing the word in opposition to a strong negative. Then, when we encounter, "Let all physical exertion be utilized," and "Her services could not be utilized for missions," our sense of the meaning of the word is fairly complete.

It is also helpful to form the habit of seeing words in relation to others which are built upon the same base forms. It has already been suggested that the connection of *commendatory* with *commend*, *commendation*, and even *recommend* and *recommendation* would shed some light upon its meaning. *Preeminent*, in the phrase, "a preeminent quality of true genius," also quoted above, should bring to mind both *eminent* and *eminence*. *Utilize*, which has just been discussed, has obvious connections with *utility* and *utilitarian*. The recognition of such groups and families is bound to increase not only the knowledge of meanings but a sensitivity to the shades of feeling which they convey.

Using the Dictionary

The obvious source of information for the meanings of words that you do not know is your dictionary. Yet there are times in the course of reading even a paragraph of moderate difficulty that you will come upon a half-dozen words that are unfamiliar to you. If you were to look up every one of them, you would not only increase the reading time of the passage by five or six minutes, but you would have broken the train of thought six times. This is clearly a nuisance and tends to make reading a chore rather than a pleasure. In the long run you will profit more by reading for enjoyment and enjoying what you read. This does not mean that you should avoid what is intellectually challenging. Tackle it. Get the most out of your dictionary by using it selectively and intelligently, only after you find that contextual clues and word relationships seem not to be helpful in giving you an idea about the meaning of a word or the way in which it is being used.

When you do turn to the dictionary for the meaning of a word, it is important that you get all it has to give. Suppose, for example, that you are confronted with the following: "Precocity flames up in a brief moment, and drawing only from within, quickly burns itself out; but genius, growing with what it feeds on, its natural powers reinforced through union with congenial elements from without, glows with increasing warmth until it reaches its full potential strength." Let us assume that you are reasonably certain about the meaning of every word in the passage except the very first, *precocity*. You know that the passage is about the poet Keats, who died as a young man. You also recognize that in this passage *precocity* is somehow being contrasted with *genius*, but this is not enough for your purpose. Stupidity and mediocrity could also be contrasted with genius. You need a dictionary explanation for *precocity* if the sentence in which it occurs is to mean much of anything.

Go to the dictionary. In this dictionary you will find that *precocity* is not given a main entry. It is one of the derivatives listed under the main entry *precocious*. There are two meanings given under the main entry. One shows the word in a favorable sense: "Unusually forward or advanced, especially mentally." The other nontechnical definition is less so: "Developing before the natural season." Going back to our passage, we recognize that in it precocity is being contrasted rather unfavorably with genius, hence it is the more neutral definition that more nearly fits the case.

At the same time, we should not overlook the etymology. From it we learn that the adjective *precocious* comes from Latin *prae*, "before," combined with *coquere*, "cook." This suggests, of course, the combination *pre-cook* in our present-day speech, and if we stop to think we might also recall that the slang phrase *half-baked* makes use of virtually the same figure of speech. All of this suggests that if a single difficult word is thus carefully studied and considered, there is a far greater likelihood that it will remain in your memory than any six words hastily looked up.

To conclude, try to recognize words in their context. You will make some mistakes, as does everyone else. Look up only those words necessary to the meaning. When you do look up a word, get everything that the dictionary treatment has to offer. Interest yourself in these words. Become word conscious in a wholesome, not in a picayunish manner. When Sir Francis Bacon wrote, more than two hundred and fifty years ago, "Reading maketh a full man," this was part of what he had in mind.

From Recognition to Use

Bacon followed his statement about reading with the assertion that "conference," that is to say speaking, produces a ready man. A ready man is one who thinks clearly and swiftly, and can express his thoughts easily. He is articulate. It has already been suggested that this comes about in part by putting words to work, transferring them from the passive to the active vocabulary. "Use a word six times and it is yours," so the saying is. The number varies, all the way from three to ten, but the advice is sound on the surface. Certainly practice is necessary to bring about vocabulary increase. The question is how one goes about it.

The best suggestion is to keep reading and speaking in close relationship with each other. Talking with others about what you read is the best way to create opportunities to put into use the words you encounter in the course of your reading. It does not matter whether your reading is in connection with your occupation, your outside interests, or if it is purely

recreational. The principle is valid in any event. Certainly one must avoid the difficulty which plagued Leora, the wife of Martin Arrowsmith, in Sinclair Lewis's novel. After an afternoon spent in reading about modern painting in order to impress her husband's associates, she found herself unable to maneuver the evening's conversation in that direction.

It is here that writing comes to our aid. To a degree at least, we can, when we write, choose the subject which will allow us to use our newly acquired words. Far too often we tend to shy away from opportunities to express ourselves on paper. When we sit in a meeting, we leave it to someone else to frame a resolution or a motion. If we are asked for suggestions or to frame a plan for action, we often content ourselves by making a few scattered notations instead of a well-formed and coherent statement. It is in thinking through an idea, in phrasing it in such a way that it cannot be misunderstood or misinterpreted that we call upon our vocabulary reserves and put them to use. Muscles do not develop without exercise; the same may be said of anyone's vocabulary. The third part of Bacon's statement was that "Writing maketh an exact man."

Synonyms and Antonyms

One way of achieving both precision and variety in language is to develop an awareness of the many words in English which may be used to express a particular idea, words which have nearly the same meaning. These are called synonyms, and most dictionaries will discuss the differences in shades of meaning within a group of related words, such as *postpone, adjourn, defer, delay,* and *procrastinate.* The entry in this dictionary for this group of words runs as follows: "*Adjourn* signifies literally to put off to another day, and, hence, to any future time. A deliberative assembly may *adjourn* to another day or to another hour of the same day, and resume business where it left off, as if there had been no interval; or it may *adjourn* to a definite later date or, when no day can be fixed, to meet at the call of the president or other officer. In common usage, to *adjourn* a matter is to hold it in abeyance until it may be more conveniently or suitably attended to; in such use *defer* and *postpone* are close synonyms of *adjourn*; *defer* is simply to lay or put aside temporarily; to *postpone* is strictly to lay or put aside until after something else occurs, or is done, known, obtained or the like; but *postpone* is often used without such limitation. *Adjourn, defer,* and *postpone* all imply definite expectation of later consideration or action; *delay* is much less definite, while *procrastinate* is hopelessly vague. One who *procrastinates* gives no assurance that he will ever act."

The foregoing illustration dealt with a group of words easily interchanged but which, nevertheless, are by no means identical in meaning. The problem here is to know under what circumstances they may be substituted for one another and when such a substitution would be inappropriate. Note the following examples:

1. *amateur, connoisseur, dilettante.* Etymologically, the *amateur* is the one who loves, the *connoisseur* one who knows. The *amateur* practices to some extent that in regard to which he may not be well informed; the *connoisseur* is well informed in regard to that which he may not practice at all. *Dilettante,* which had originally the sense of *amateur,* has come to denote one who is superficial, pretentious, and affected, whether in theory or practice.

2. *forgery, counterfeiting.* Imitating or altering a coin or note which passes as currency or money is *counterfeiting;* the making of a fraudulent writing, or the material alteration of a genuine writing with intent to defraud, is *forgery.* . . .

Sometimes in speaking of writing we are at a loss for words which indicate the opposite of one we have in mind. The technical term for these is *antonym.* Again the dictionary helps us here by listing these as part of the synonymy. For example, the treatment of *despair,* quoted above, is followed by the listing *hope, expectation, confidence*—words suggesting positive or healthy attitudes. Information of this kind can also be found in a thesaurus, a kind of glossary which lists and organizes words according to the classes of ideas they express. For most people, however, the dictionary is easier to use.

Prefixes and Suffixes

Many of the words in English consist of a base form or root to which prefixes and suffixes may be added. Every speaker and writer of the language forms words in this fashion, even when he has not heard them before. Let us suppose that a particular child of ten has, in his lifetime, encountered and learned the words *gladness, hardness, softness, happiness, sadness,* and *smoothness.* Out of this experience he will have learned, though he doesn't know it, that *-ness* is added to adjectives to form abstract nouns. Consequently, when he needs to form a word meaning "the quality of being rough," he merely extends the *-ness* pattern to the adjective *rough* and comes up with *roughness.* He may never have heard or read the word before, or he may have heard it and forgotten it. The process works unconsciously and automatically. In the same way, he will be able to interpret other formations with *-ness,* new to him, when he meets them in conversation or reading. This process is called word derivation. It is most useful in expanding our individual vocabularies.

In general the common prefixes and suffixes give us very little trouble, partly because they are so universally applied. Almost any verb can take the suffix *-er* to refer to the person who performs the action or undergoes the state which the meaning of the verb suggests: *work, worker; bake, baker; sit, sitter; think, thinker.* The prefix *un-* is almost equally common in its application to adjectives which suggest a state of affairs: *unwell, unhappy, unusual, unclean.* Most native speakers have a built-in set of restrictions which prevent them from concocting such unacceptable formations as *unold, smoothen,* or *coolth.* But these prefixes and suffixes are all native; they belong to the familiar part of our vocabulary.

Because of the great number of borrowed words in English and the frequency with which they are used, some foreign prefixes and suffixes have also become part of the working mechanism of the English language. Certain of these, such as *-able* (*lovable, passable*) and *-ess* (*huntress, princess*) are common and cause no difficulty. Those from Latin and Greek, however, do give trouble and will be taken up in some detail here.

Prefixes In general, prefixes tend only to modify the meanings of the words to which they are attached; they do not change the grammatical function. It is merely necessary, therefore, to associate the Latin or Greek prefix with its meaning in English. The table of prefixes on page 971 is designed to help you make these associations. The prefixes are listed according to the meaning in English which they convey.

Suffixes It is grammatical function rather than meaning which is affected by the addition of a suffix. The meaning of the base form *coma* is still present in the combination *comatose,* but the word has changed from noun to adjective. The same would be true of *development* (noun) from *develop* (verb) or *beautify* (verb) from *beauty* (noun). Thus, suffixes serve as a means of making the language flexible. Quite often the suffix is added not to an independent word but to a base form which does not normally stand alone: *sanctify, contrary, aviatrix.* The tables of suffixes on page 971 will give you a start toward the analysis of words, but only a start. Developing a sense for the way in which suffixes are added and what they do to the base forms is a study worth pursuing with your dictionary. This awareness will enhance your feeling for the language.

IMPROVING YOUR SPELLING

Americans have always placed a high value upon the ability to spell correctly. The blue-backed spelling book was a fixture of the colonial schoolroom and sold literally millions of copies. The spelling bee was for a long period a favorite school and even community activity, and recently newspapers, radio, and television have developed it on a national scale. Despite all this, business men constantly complain about secretaries who are unable to spell; college professors make the same charge against their students.

The very complaints bear witness to our awareness of spelling; the actual situation is not as bad as it is often painted. Recent studies have shown that the average high-school graduate spells correctly most of the words that he uses. Most of the spelling difficulties of college students are caused by no more than 250 words out of the ten thousand or so that they are likely to use. Poor spelling is seldom something that cannot be remedied if the ailing victim is determined to improve and will go about it in a systematic way.

Why We Misspell

Some of the principal reasons for our difficulties with English spelling lie in the nature of the English language and certain aspects of its history. English has always had from twelve to sixteen distinct vowel sounds, not to mention the diphthongs or vowel combinations. At the same time, there have been only five vowel characters—or seven at most, if *w* and *y* are counted—to spell them with. This is a problem which, as we shall see, has been dealt with in several ways during the twelve hundred years we have been using the Roman alphabet, but no one of them has been carried out consistently. The reduction of vowels in unstressed syllables, as in *Cuba, custom, circus, outrageous*, where *a, o, u*, and *ou* all represent the same pronunciation, has created another problem.

In addition, many of the thousands of English words which have come into English from other languages have kept the spellings which they had in those languages, sometimes a far cry from the characteristic patterns of English spelling. Finally, it was about the year 1500 when printing replaced manuscript copying, as a result of which spelling became relatively fixed. But since that time many changes in pronunciation, not only of individual words but of entire classes of words, have occurred, and this has only served to increase the distance, already great enough, between spelling and pronunciation. Therefore we have "silent" letters such as *b* in *dumb* and *gh* in *thought*, fossilized remains of sounds which are no longer pronounced. We also have various ways of spelling the same vowel sound, as in *meat* and *meet*, where the spelling once served to indicate a distinction in pronunciation no longer present.

We have discussed these matters briefly neither to excuse or justify bad spelling nor to make the task of spelling improvement seem hopelessly difficult, but rather to explain why our rules for spelling seem to have such frequent exceptions.

Ways of Indicating Vowel Length

As a background which will help us to understand some of the spelling rules, we must first notice three devices which have been developed throughout the history of our language to differentiate certain pairs of sounds. One of the earliest of these was to double the vowel letter, with a single letter indicating a short or lax sound and the doubled character signaling a long or tense sound. We still do this in pairs like *cop, coop; rot, root; met, meet; fed, feed*. Today the practice is confined to the letters *e* and *o*.

A second way of showing vowel length was to place an unpronounced final *-e* after a syllable when the vowel in it was long, but to close the syllable with a consonant when the vowel was short. Thus we have *cap* contrasting with *cape, bed* with *bede* (the Middle English form of *bead*), *bit* with *bite, hop* with *hope, us* with *use*. Notice that the *-e* has no value in and of itself; it merely signals something about the preceding vowel letter.

Finally, a doubled consonant may be used to signal a preceding short vowel, whereas a single consonant suggests the long-vowel quality usually associated with the spelling. Thus *latter* contrasts with *later, bitter* with *biter, mopping* with *moping*, and *cutter* with *cuter*. Usually this device is employed when a syllable is joined to the one in which the length of the vowel needs to be specified.

All of these devices are centuries old. Each of them has a certain logic behind it. Unfortunately no one of them has been carried out consistently. Much of our spelling difficulty arises from not knowing which device or practice to apply. But understanding just this much about them leads one to see something of a system, a kind of consistency in the use of single or double consonants and whether the final *-e* is lost or kept.

Loss of Final -e

Final *-e* is lost before a suffix beginning with a vowel. It is kept before a suffix beginning with a consonant.

We have already seen that final *-e* was used to indicate the length of a preceding vowel, as in *hope*. When a suffix like *-ful*, beginning with a consonant, is added to *hope*, we still need the *-e* to show that the *o* is long; thus our spelling is *hopeful*. On the other hand, any vowel letter can serve the purpose of suggesting the long sound; hence we can spell *hoping* without it. Note the following:

	Suffix Beginning With a Vowel	Suffix Beginning With a Consonant
hate	hating	hateful
love	lovable	lovely
bore	boring	boredom
like	likable	likely
achieve	achievable	achievement
use	usage	useful

There are certain exceptions to this rule which a careful speller should remember:

1. After *c* or *g*, final *e* is kept before *a* and *o* in order to maintain the soft sound of the consonant: *noticeable, traceable, vengeance, outrageous*. This is not necessary when *c* or *g* is followed by *i*: *noticing, tracing*.

2. Final *e* is dropped after *g* in such combinations as *judgment, acknowledgment, abridgment*. In England the *-e* is usually retained in the spelling of these words.

3. A few other common words do not follow this pattern: *argument, awful, duly, truly, hoeing, singeing, dyeing* ("the process of coloring"), *wholly, mileage*.

Doubling of Consonants

We have already seen that our spelling system provides for such contrasts as *hop, hope, fat, fate, sit* and *site*. But when we add suffixes beginning with a vowel, the scheme is likely to break down: we need to be able to distinguish between *hop + ing* and *hope + ing*. We do it by doubling the consonant after the short vowel:

hope	hoping	hoped
hop	hopping	hopped
plane	planing	planed
plan	planning	planned
snipe	sniping	sniped
snip	snipping	snipped

Some further observations:

1. Note that when vowel length is indicated by a doubled vowel character or a combination of vowel characters, the consonant is not doubled: *stooping, reader, sleeping, boating*.

2. Thus far, we have applied the rule about doubling of consonants only to words of one syllable, when a suffix is added. In words of more than one syllable, we must notice which syllable is stressed. Compare these pairs:

adMIT	adMITTING	adMITTED
EDit	EDiting	EDited
deFER	deFERRING	deFERRED
DIFfer	DIFfering	DIFfered

Note also the position of the stress and the spelling of the following: *réference*, but *reférring; préference*, but *preférred; regrétting, fócused, prohíbitive, overlápping, devéloped*.

Spelling the Long e Sound

There is probably no sound in the English language that is spelled in quite so many ways. There are at least six that are used quite frequently, and certain others which appear from time to time. Note: *cedar, ease, agree, receive, achieve, antique, people, key, quay, Caesar*. The two spellings which are most often confused are *ie* and *ei*. A two-line jingle makes the spelling rule easy to remember:

Spell *i* before *e*
Except after *c*.

ie: achieve, believe, chief, grief, niece, piece, relieve
cei: ceiling, conceit, conceive, deceive, perceive, receive, receipt

There are two kinds of exceptions to this rule. First, certain words pronounced with a long *e* sound behave in direct opposition to the rule:

ei: either, leisure, neither, seize, weird
cie: financier, species

Moreover, there are certain *ei* spellings which are pronounced with a sound other than long *e*, usually with long *a*

or with the vowel of *care: weigh, neighbor, veil, reign, freight, heir, their.*

Y as a Vowel

Y sometimes represents a consonant sound (*year, yet, your, youth*), usually at the beginning of a word or syllable. Y, in final position and preceded by a consonant, normally represents a vowel. This creates a problem when we want to spell such combinations as *dry + ed* or *study + es*, since it would be difficult at times to tell whether the *y* was indicating a vowel or consonant value. For this reason:

1. Final *y* preceded by a consonant is usually changed to *i* before all suffixes except those beginning with *i*:

cry	cried	crying
dry	drier	drying
fly	flies	flying
	flier	
bury	burial	burying
copy	copies	copying
	copied	
mercy	mercies	
	merciful	
forty	fortieth	fortyish
noisy	noisier	
	noisily	

2. Final *y* preceded by a vowel generally retains the *y* when a suffix is added.

buy	buyer	buying
delay	delays	delaying
	delayed	
joy	joys	
	joyful	
play	played	playing
obey	obeys	obeying
sway	swayed	swaying
valley	valleys	

Exceptions: *daily, gaily, gaiety, laid, paid, said.*

Plural of Nouns Ending in o

1. Nouns ending in *o* preceded by a consonant usually form their plurals by adding *-es*:

echo	hero	potato	tornado
echoes	heroes	potatoes	tornadoes
embargo	Negro	tomato	veto
embargoes	Negroes	tomatoes	vetoes

2. Proper names ending in *o* add *s* only:

Eskimo	Filipino	Romeo
Eskimos	Filipinos	Romeos

3. Many nouns clearly of foreign origin and others that are seldom used in the plural or seldom used at all add only *s*: *albino, credo, crescendo, dynamo, embryo, kimono, magneto, octavo, photo, piano, silo, solo, soprano, tyro.*

4. Nouns ending in *o* preceded by a vowel add *s* only:

carabao	radio	zoo
carabaos	radios	zoos
cameo	kangaroo	duo
cameos	kangaroos	duos

Vowels in Unstressed Syllables

One of the characteristic features of English is the reduction of vowels in unstressed syllables to a neutral sound which is indicated in this dictionary by the symbol ə. Yet this reduced vowel may be spelled with any one of the five vowel letters: *sofa, silent, charity, kingdom, circus.* Naturally, this causes a great deal of confusion; unstressed syllables are a frequent source of misspelling. For example, *a, e,* and *i* become indistinguishable in the endings *-ate* and *-ite, -able* and *-ible, -ance* and *-ence, -ant* and *-ent.* Associating the word in question with a closely related one will sometimes be helpful in suggesting the correct spelling. If you are uncertain about *definite,* think of *finish* and *definition. Separation* will suggest the *a* in *separate,* as will *ultimAtum* in *ultimate.* If you know that the verb *freQUENT* is pronounced with the vowel of *let,* this will help you with the spelling of *frequent* when the stress is on the first syllable.

Unfortunately, this device will help you with only a limited number of words; for many others no such help is available. The following are particularly likely to give some trouble:

   a: accept*able,* accept*ance,* attend*ance,* brilli*ant,* perform*ance*
   e: consist*ent,* excell*ence,* exist*ence,* experi*ence,* independ*ent,* persist*ent,* occurr*ence*
   i: irresist*ible,* plaus*ible,* poss*ible,* suscept*ible*

Confusion of Prefixes

Some spelling difficulties arise from the confusion of prefixes which look alike, are pronounced similarly, but are so different in meaning that they cannot be attached to the same roots. The following are especially troublesome:

ante, "before": *antedate*	*anti,* "against": *antidote*
de, "from, down, away": *debate*	*di,* "twice": *diploma*
dis, "separation": *disgrace*	*dys,* "hard, ill": *dystrophy*
per, "through": *perform*	*pre,* "before": *prescribe*

Pronunciation and Spelling

Some spelling errors arise from the tendency to leave out the vowels of unstressed syllables in pronunciation, or to omit one of a combination of consonants. Reasonable care in the pronunciation of the following, and words like them, may help in creating a more accurate word image:

recoGnize	liAble
quanTity	probAbly
environMent	sophomore
governMent	boundAry
diPHthong	libRary

There is always a question as to how far to go in the cultivation of pronunciations which consciously match the spelling. For example, in the case of *February,* some dictionaries recognize pronunciations with or without the first *r.* In this instance, if a pronunciaton with the *r* will help you to remember the spelling, there can be no objection to adopting it. In the case of *Wednesday,* however, where no dictionary sanctions the pronunciation of the *d,* and it is employed only by a few overzealous radio and television announcers, there is little excuse for adopting it.

There are other instances of confusion where it is difficult to say if the faulty spelling is the cause of the mispronunciation or the other way around. All that can be done is to try to straighten out both spelling and pronunciation. Words of this kind are:

cavAlry	grIEvous
irRElevant	mischIEvous
reMUNeration	heighT

Words Similar in Spelling But Different in Meaning

Some words need attention because they sound somewhat alike but differ in spelling, meaning, and origin. Here are listed some of the most troublesome pairs and triplets:

accept	aisle	altogether
except	isle	all together
adapt	alley	angel
adopt	ally	angle
advice	already	ascent
advise	all ready	assent
affect	altar	bare
effect	alter	bear

baring	gamble	rain
barring	gambol	reign
bearing		rein
	holly	
born	holy	right
borne	wholly	rite
bourn		write
	hoping	
breath	hopping	serf
breathe		surf
	instance	
canvas	instants	shone
canvass		shown
	its	
capital	it's	sole
capitol		soul
	loath	
censor	loathe	staid
censure		stayed
	loose	
cite	lose	stake
site		steak
sight	metal	
	medal	stationary
clothes		stationery
cloths	morn	
	mourn	steal
compliment		steel
complement	passed	
	past	than
consul		then
council	peace	
counsel	piece	there
		their
corps	personal	they're
corpse	personnel	
		to
costume	plain	too
custom	plane	two
dairy	planed	villain
diary	planned	villein
decent	precede	wander
descent	proceed	wonder
dissent	procedure	
		weak
desert	precedence	week
dessert	precedents	
		weather
dual	presence	whether
duel	presents	
		who's
formally	principal	whose
formerly	principle	
		your
forth	quiet	you're
fourth	quite	

enquire	manoeuvre	theater
inquire	maneuver	theatre
analog	naturalise	orthopaedic
analogue	naturalize	orthopedic
catalog	gray	practice
catalogue	grey	practise
fledgeling	mediaeval	encase
fledgling	medieval	incase

Words Often Misspelled

Even though spelling seems to present a whole series of problems, studies of the words most frequently misspelled have shown that these constitute a relatively small group. The list which follows includes most of them, except for those which have been discussed previously. You will find the list useful for drills and practice. Study it carefully.

absence	Britain	disappear
abundance	bulletin	disappoint
acceptable	calendar	disastrous
accessible	capitalism	disciple
accidentally	career	discriminate
acclaim	careless	dissatisfied
accommodate	carrying	dominant
accompanied	category	efficient
accomplish	ceiling	embarrass
accustom	cemetery	eminent
achievement	challenge	emphasize
acknowledgment	changeable	entertain
acquaintance	character	entirely
acquire	choose	entrance
acquitted	comfortable	environment
across	coming	equipped
actually	committed	erroneous
address	comparative	escape
adequate	competition	exaggerate
adolescence	completely	excellent
aggressive	conceive	exercise
allotted	concentrate	exhilarate
all right	condemn	existence
analyze	conscience	expense
anxiety	conscious	experience
apology	consensus	explanation
apparatus	considerably	extremely
apparent	consistency	fallacy
appearance	continuously	familiar
appreciate	controlling	fascinate
approach	controversial	finally
argument	convenience	fictitious
arrangement	cooly	foreign
arouse	counsel	friend
article	courageous	fulfill
athletic	courteous	fundamental
attended	criticism	further
audience	curiosity	government
authority	curriculum	grammar
balance	deceive	group
ballot	decision	guarantee
bargain	definite	handled
basically	despair	happened
basis	dependent	happiness
beginning	description	height
behavior	desirability	heroine
belief	develop	hindrance
beneficial	difference	humorous
brilliance	dilemma	hundred

Dual Spellings

Some words have at least two acceptable spellings. In some cases there is a difference between American and British practice. With certain other words, both spellings are current in the United States. If you have already mastered one correct spelling, there is generally little point in taking the trouble to learn another. Nevertheless, it is better if you spell consistently all of the words in the same class or group: if you spell *labor* and not *labour*, then spell *humor* and not *humour*. Your dictionary will list variant spellings and often will indicate where the variants are used. The list below will give some idea of the nature and extent of the problem.

adviser	program	reflection
advisor	programme	reflexion
center	gipsy	enrolment
centre	gypsy	enrollment
enclose	odor	smolder
inclose	odour	smoulder
endorse	pretence	caliber
indorse	pretense	calibre

hungrily	merely	preferred	sergeant	summary	tyranny
hypocrisy	mileage	prejudice	separate	suppose	unanimous
idea	miniature	prepare	shining	suppress	undoubtedly
ignorant	mortgage	prevalent	significance	surprising	unnecessary
imagine	mysterious	privilege	similar	surround	unusual
immediate	narrative	probably	speech	susceptible	useful
incidentally	naturally	professor	sponsor	technique	vacuum
independence	necessity	prominent	strictly	temperament	valuable
indispensable	ninety	propaganda	studying	theory	variety
inevitable	noticeable	prophecy	substantial	thorough	vengeance
influential	occasion	prove	subsistence	together	warrant
ingenious	occurrence	psychology	subtle	tragedy	weather
initiative	operate	pursue	success	transferred	weird
inseparable	opinion	quantity	sufficient	tremendous	yield
intelligent	opportunity	readily			
interest	oppose	really			
interpretation	optimist	realistically			

Use Your Dictionary

The dictionary is your best help. Irregular spellings of noun plurals, verb participles, and past tenses, all of which can cause trouble, are usually given in connection with the treatment of the individual word. If you are in doubt about such a spelling, look it up.

We have already seen that it is helpful to know the parts which go to make up related words. The dictionary helps you to learn these by listing all the derived forms that a word may have. Sometimes the origin of a word, its etymology, will give you useful information. Finding a Latin form such as *cura* in the etymology of *cure* will help you to understand why the English derivative is *curable* and not *curible*.

The dictionary performs another useful service in indicating whether compound words are written solid, with a hyphen, or as two words. The spelling of compounds in English is inconsistent. There are no simple rules, and no one can be expected to remember the spelling of every word combination he is likely to use. Form the habit of checking the spelling of every compound that you use in your writing.

Most experienced writers use the dictionary to check the spelling of foreign terms and of particularly difficult words. Form the dictionary habit. Looking up words when you are writing does take a little time but amply repays your efforts in the correctness it helps you to attain.

interrupt	origin
involve	paid
irrelevant	pamphlets
jealousy	parallel
knowledge	paralyze
laboratory	particular
laid	performance
leisure	permanent
license	phenomenon
likelihood	philosophy
loneliness	physical
losing	plausible
magazine	pleasant
magnificence	politician
maintenance	possess
marriage	possible
mathematics	practical
medieval	practice

receive
recommend
referring
relieve
religion
repetition
response
rhythm
ridiculous
sacrifice
safety
satire
satisfied
scarcity
scene
schedule
seize
senses

Quotations

The following pages contain more than 1600 significant sayings, epigrams, and thoughts of all ages, including our own. The quotations are grouped under 178 subject headings —from *Ability* to *Youth*—and following each is the author's name, his birth and death dates, and, in most cases, the source from which the quotation was obtained.

Most of the selections come from familiar sources—Shakespeare, Emerson, Bacon, Cervantes, Cicero, La Rochefoucauld, Aristotle, Thomas Jefferson, the Old and New Testaments, etc. Many additional selections, however, have been made from the ranks of contemporary thinkers, world leaders, and authors. Among those quoted are Lyndon B. Johnson, John F. Kennedy, Pope John XXIII, Winston Churchill, Arthur Miller, Eleanor Roosevelt, Jacques Maritain, and Edith Hamilton.

ABILITY

Natural abilities are like natural plants, that need pruning by study.
— FRANCIS BACON (1561–1620) *Essays: Of Studies*

I add this also, that natural ability without education has oftener raised man to glory and virtue than education without natural ability.
— CICERO (106–43 B.C.) *Oratio Pro Licinio Archia*

Skill to do comes of doing.
— RALPH WALDO EMERSON (1803–1882) *Society and Solitude*

A man who qualifies himself well for his calling, never fails of employment.
— THOMAS JEFFERSON (1743–1826)

It is a great ability to be able to conceal one's ability.
— FRANÇOIS DE LA ROCHEFOUCAULD (1613–1680) *Maxims*

Better be proficient in one art than a smatterer in a hundred.
— JAPANESE PROVERB

So long as a man imagines that he cannot do this or that, so long is he determined not to do it; and consequently so long is it impossible to him that he should do it.
— BENEDICT SPINOZA (1632–1677) *Ethics*

They are able because they think they are able.
— VERGIL (70–19 B.C.) *Aeneid*

ABSENCE

But ay the tear comes in me ee,
To think on him that's far awa.
— ROBERT BURNS (1759–1796) *The Bonnie Lad That's Far Awa*

Our hours in love have wings; in absence crutches.
— COLLEY CIBBER (1671–1757) *Xerxes*

To him that absent is All things succeed amiss
— CERVANTES (1547–1616) *Don Quixote*

Friends, though absent, are still present.
— CICERO (106–43 B.C.) *De Amicitia*

Absence from whom we love is worse than death
And frustrate hope severer than despair
— WILLIAM COWPER (1731–1800) *Despair at his Separation*

Love reckons hours for months, and days for years;
And every little absence is an age.
— JOHN DRYDEN (1631–1700) *Amphitryon*

Out of sight, out of mind
— HOMER (c. 10th–8th C. B.C.) *Odyssey*

Friendship, like love, is destroyed by long absence, though it may be increased by short intermissions.
— SAMUEL JOHNSON (1709–1784) *The Idler*

But O the heavy change, now thou art gone,
Now thou art gone, and never must return!
— JOHN MILTON (1608–1674) *Lycidas*

Two evils, monstrous either one apart
Possessed me, and were long and loath at going:
A cry of Absence, Absence, in the heart,
And in the wood the furious winter blowing.
— JOHN CROWE RANSOM (1888–1974) *Winter Remembered*

Hast thou no care of me? shall I abide
In this dull world, which in thy absence is
No better than a sty?
— SHAKESPEARE (1564–1616) *Antony and Cleopatra*, IV, xiii, 60

The Lord watch between me and thee, when we are absent one from another.
— OLD TESTAMENT: *Genesis*, xxxi, 49

Greater things are believed of those who are absent.
— TACITUS (c. 55–117) *Histories*

ACTION

I am perplexed . . . whether to act or not to act.
— AESCHYLUS (525–456 B.C.) *Suppliant Maidens*

Of every noble action the intent
Is to give worth reward, vice punishment.
— FRANCIS BEAUMONT (1584–1616) and JOHN FLETCHER (1579–1625) *The Captain*

The end of man is an action, not a thought.
— THOMAS CARLYLE (1795–1881) *Sartor Resartus*

Action may not always bring happiness; but there is no happiness without action.
— BENJAMIN DISRAELI (1804–1881) *Lothair*

A man's action is only a picture book of his creed.
— RALPH WALDO EMERSON (1803–1882)

Brave actions never want a Trumpet.
— THOMAS FULLER (1608–1681) *Gnomologia*

The great end of life is not knowledge, but action.
— T. H. HUXLEY (1825–1895) *Technical Education*

We would often be ashamed of our finest actions if the world understood all the motives which produced them.
— FRANÇOIS DE LA ROCHEFOUCAULD (1613–1680) *Maxims*

Actions speak louder than words.
— PROVERB

One hour of life, crowded to the full with glorious action, and filled with noble risks, is worth whole years of those mean observances of paltry decorum.
— SIR WALTER SCOTT (1771–1832) *Count Robert of Paris*

If it were done when 'tis done, then 'twere well
It were done quickly.
— SHAKESPEARE (1564–1616) *Macbeth*, I, vii, i

Heaven n'er helps the men who will not act.
— SOPHOCLES (495–406 B.C.) *Fragment*

No sooner said than done.
— TERENCE (c. 190–150 B.C.) *Eunuchus*

We cannot think first and act afterwards. From the moment of birth we are immersed in action, and can only fitfully guide it by taking thought.
— ALFRED NORTH WHITEHEAD (1861–1947)

ADVERSITY

The virtue of prosperity is temperance; the virtue of adversity is fortitude . . . .
— FRANCIS BACON (1561–1620) *Essays*

Hope and patience are two sovereign remedies for all, the surest reposals, the softest cushions to lean on in adversity.
— ROBERT BURTON (1577–1640) *Anatomy of Melancholy*

Adversity is sometimes hard upon a man; but for one man who can stand prosperity there are a hundred that will stand adversity.
— THOMAS CARLYLE (1795–1881) *Heroes and Hero-Worship*

Friendship, of itself a holy tie,
Is made more sacred by adversity.
— JOHN DRYDEN (1631–1700) *The Hind and the Panther*

In time of prosperity friends will be plenty;
In time of adversity not one in twenty.
— JAMES HOWELL (1594?–1666) *Proverbs*

Mishaps are like knives, that either serve us or cut us, as we grasp them by the blade or the handle.
— HERMAN MELVILLE (1819–1891) *Cambridge Thirty Years Ago*

In adversity a man is saved by hope.
— MENANDER (342–291 B.C.) *Fragments*

It is a kingly action, believe me, to come to the help of those who are fallen.
— OVID (43 B.C.–A.D. 18?) *Epistulae ex Ponto*

Great men rejoice in adversity just as brave soldiers triumph in war.
— SENECA (4? B.C.–A.D. 65) *De Providentia*

Trial is the true test of mortal men.
— PINDAR (*c.* 522–442 B.C.) *Olympian Odes*

Of one ill comes many.
— SCOTTISH PROVERB

Sweet are the uses of adversity,
Which like the toad, ugly and venomous,
Wears yet a precious jewel in his head.
— SHAKESPEARE (1564–1616) *As You Like It*, II, i, 12

The worst is not
So long as we can say, "This is the worst."
— SHAKESPEARE (1564–1616) *King Lear*, IV, i, 28

It is the duty of all persons, when affairs are the most prosperous, then in especial to reflect within themselves in what way they are to endure adversity.
— TERENCE (*c.* 190–150 B.C.) *Phormio*

In the day of prosperity be joyful, but in the day of adversity consider.
— OLD TESTAMENT: *Ecclesiastes*, viii

A friend loveth at all times, and a brother is born for adversity.
— OLD TESTAMENT: *Proverbs*, xvii, 17

ADVICE

A fool sometimes gives weighty advice.
— NICHOLAS BOILEAU (1636–1711)

Who cannot give good counsel? 'Tis cheap, it costs them nothing.
— ROBERT BURTON (1577–1640) *Anatomy of Melancholy*

A woman's advice is not worth much, but he who doesn't heed it is a fool.
— PEDRO CALDERÓN (1600–1681) *El medico de su honra*

No one can give you better advice than yourself.
— CICERO (106–43 B.C.) *Ad Atticum*

We ask advice, but we mean approbation.
— CHARLES C. COLTON (1780?–1832) *Lacon*

When Thales was asked what was difficult, he said, "To know one's self." And what was easy, "To advise another."
— DIOGENES LAERTIUS (2nd or 3rd C.)

'Tis easier to advise the suffering than to bear suffering.
— EURIPIDES (480–406 B.C.) *Alcestis*

Don't give your advice before you are called upon.
— DESIDERIUS ERASMUS (1466–1536) *Adagia*

Whatever advice you give, be short.
— HORACE (B.C. 65–8) *Ars Poetica*

Advice is offensive, —because it shows us that we are known to others as well as to ourselves.
— SAMUEL JOHNSON (1709–1784) *The Rambler*

Advice is least heeded when most needed.
— ENGLISH PROVERB

Never advise anyone to go to war or to marry.
— SPANISH PROVERB

Many receive advice, only the wise profit by it.
— PUBLILIUS SYRUS (1st C. B.C.)

The only thing to do with good advice is to pass it on. It is never of any use to oneself.
— OSCAR WILDE (1854–1900) *An Ideal Husband*

AGE

Age appears to be the best in four things—old wood best to burn, old wine to drink, old friends to trust, and old authors to read.
— FRANCIS BACON (1561–1620) *Apothegms*, No. 97

He lives long that lives till all are weary of him.
— HENRY GEORGE BOHN (1797–1884) *Handbook of Proverbs*

Grow old along with me!
The best is yet to be,
The last of life, for which the first was made.
— ROBERT BROWNING (1812–1889) *Rabbi Ben Ezra*

Let age approve of youth, and death complete the same.
— ROBERT BROWNING (1812–1889) *Rabbi Ben Ezra*

Young men think old men are fools; but old men *know* young men are fools.
— GEORGE CHAPMAN (1559?–1634?) *All Fools*, Act V

I am ready to meet my Maker. Whether my Maker is prepared for the great ordeal of meeting me is another matter.
— WINSTON CHURCHILL (1874–1965) remark on eve of his 75th birthday

For as I like a young man in whom there is something of the old, so I like an old man in whom there is something of the young.
— CICERO (106–43 B.C.) *De Senectute*

No one is so old as to think he cannot live one more year.
— CICERO (106–43 B.C.) *De Senectute*

A man is as old as he's feeling
A woman as old as she looks.
— MORTIMER COLLINS (1827–1876) *How Old Are You?*

Folly in youth is sin, in age is madness.
— SAMUEL DANIEL (1562–1619)

Age is like love; it cannot be hid.
— THOMAS DEKKER (1570?–1632) *Old Fortunatus*, Act II

Youth is a blunder; Manhood a struggle;
Old Age a regret.
— BENJAMIN DISRAELI (1804–1881) *Coningsby*

A woman is as old as she looks to a man that likes to look at her.
— FINLEY PETER DUNNE (1867–1936) *Old Age*

We do not count a man's years until he has nothing else to count.
— RALPH WALDO EMERSON (1803–1882)

Forty is the old age of youth; fifty is the youth of old age.
— VICTOR HUGO (1802–1885)

Whenever a man's friends begin to compliment him about looking young, he may be sure that they think he is growing old.
— WASHINGTON IRVING (1783–1859)

It was near a miracle to see an old man silent, since talking is the disease of age.
— BEN JONSON (1572–1637)

We hope to grow old, and we fear old age: that is to say, we love life and flee death.
— JEAN DE LA BRUYÈRE (1645–1696) *Caractères*

Of middle age the best that can be said is that a middle-aged person has likely learned how to have a little fun in spite of his troubles.
— DON MARQUIS (1878–1932) *The Almost Perfect State*

He who is of a calm and happy nature will hardly feel the pressure of Age, but to him who is of an opposite disposition, youth and age are equally a burden.
— PLATO (428–347 B.C.) *The Republic*

He whom the gods favour dies in youth.
— PLAUTUS (*c.* 254–184 B.C.) *Bacchides*

When men grow virtuous in old age, they only make a sacrifice to God of the devil's leavings.
— ALEXANDER POPE (1664–1721) *Thoughts on Various Subjects*

To the old cat give a tender mouse.
— ITALIAN PROVERB

Before old age my care was to live well; in old age, to die well.
— SENECA (4? B.C.–A.D. 65)

Age cannot wither her, nor custom stale
Her infinite variety.
— SHAKESPEARE (1564–1616) *Antony and Cleopatra*, II, ii, 243

No wise man ever wished to be younger.
— JONATHAN SWIFT (1667–1745)

To love is natural in a young man, a shame in an old one.
— PUBLILIUS SYRUS (1st C. B.C.)

Nobody loves life like an old man.
— SOPHOCLES (495–406 B.C.) *Acrisius*, Frag. 63

In the days of my youth I remembered my God,
And He hath not forgotten my age.
— ROBERT SOUTHEY (1774–1843) *The Old Man's Comforts*

We are always the same age inside.
— GERTRUDE STEIN (1874–1946)

A fool at forty is a fool indeed.
— EDWARD YOUNG (1683–1765) *Love of Fame*

AMBITION

Every eel hopes to become a whale.
— GERMAN PROVERB

The same ambition can destroy or save,
And makes a patriot as it makes a knave.
— ALEXANDER POPE (1688–1744) *Essay on Man*

All ambitions are lawful except those which climb upward on the miseries or credulities of mankind.
— JOSEPH CONRAD (1857–1924) *Personal Record*

'Tis a laudable Ambition, that aims at being better than his Neighbours.
— BEN FRANKLIN (1706–1790) *Poor Richard's Almanack*

A man without ambition is like a woman without beauty.
— FRANK HARRIS (1856–1931) *Montes the Matador*

Ambition is a vice, but it may be the father of virtue.
— QUINTILIAN (40–*c.* 100)

The slave has but one master; the man of ambition has as many as there are people useful to his fortune.
— JEAN DE LA BRUYÈRE (1645–1696) *Caractères*

Ambition and suspicion always go together.
— GEORG CHRISTOPH LICHTENBERG (1742–1799)

The very substance of the ambitious is merely the shadow of a dream.
— SHAKESPEARE (1564–1616) *Hamlet*, II, ii, 268

AMERICA

Driven from every other corner of the earth, freedom of thought and the right of private judgment in matters of conscience direct their course to this happy country as their last asylum.
— SAMUEL ADAMS (1722–1803) Speech at Philadelphia, 1776

The South! the South! God knows what will become of her.
— JOHN C. CALHOUN (1782–1850) on his deathbed.

Our country! in her intercourse with foreign nations may she always be in the right; but our country, right or wrong!
— STEPHEN DECATUR (1779–1820) Toast at a dinner, 1816

I feel that you are justified in looking into the future with true assurance, because you have a mode of living in which we find the joy of life and the joy of work harmoniously combined. Added to this is the spirit of ambition which pervades your very being, and seems to make the day's work like a happy child at play.
— ALBERT EINSTEIN (1879–1955) *New Year's Greeting*, 1931

America means opportunity, freedom, power.
— RALPH WALDO EMERSON (1803–1882) *Essays, Second Series*

We must meet our duty and convince the world that we are just friends and brave enemies.
— THOMAS JEFFERSON (1743–1826)

The citizens of America have explored the sea and air. They have given open-handed hospitality and employment to people immigrating from every land. America has continued to overcome with courage the various difficulties that have arisen from time to time and to render her legislation ever more in keeping with the dignity of the human person.
— POPE JOHN XXIII (1881–1963), March 17, 1963

If we are to keep our system secure and our society stable, we must all begin to work where all of us work best—and that is in the communities where we all live.
— LYNDON B. JOHNSON (1908–1973) Speech, August, 1964

I am willing to love all mankind, except an American.
— SAMUEL JOHNSON (1709–1784) in Boswell's *Life*

And so, my fellow Americans: Ask not what your country can do for you—ask what you can do for your country.
— JOHN F. KENNEDY (1917–1963) Inauguration Speech, 1961

A citizen, first in war, first in peace, and first in the hearts of his countrymen.
— GENERAL HENRY "LIGHT-HORSE HARRY" LEE (1756–1818)

Intellectually I know that America is no better than any other country; emotionally I know she is better than every other country.
— SINCLAIR LEWIS (1885–1951) Interview in Berlin, 1930

In the wars of the European powers in matters relating to themselves we have never taken any part, nor does it comport

with our policy so to do. It is only when our rights are invaded or seriously menaced that we resent injuries or make
preparation for our defence.
— JAMES MONROE (1758–1831) Message to Congress, 1823

The United States never lost a war or won a conference.
— WILL ROGERS (1879–1935)

There is a homely adage which runs, "Speak softly and carry
a big stick; you will go far." If the American nation will
speak softly and yet build and keep at a pitch of the highest
training the Monroe Doctrine will go far.
— THEODORE ROOSEVELT (1858–1919)

Every American takes pride in our tradition of hospitality,
to men of all races and all creeds. We must be constantly
vigilant against the attacks of intolerance and injustice. We
must scrupulously guard the civil rights and civil liberties
of all citizens, whatever their background.
— FRANKLIN D. ROOSEVELT (1882–1945)

Yesterday, December 7, 1941—a date that will live in infamy
—the United States of America was suddenly and deliberately attacked by naval and air forces of the Empire of
Japan.
— FRANKLIN D. ROOSEVELT, 1941

In the four quarters of the globe, who reads an American
book? or goes to an American play? or looks at an American
picture or statue? What does the world yet owe to American
physicians or surgeons? . . . What have they done in mathematics? Who drinks out of American glasses? . . . or wears
American coats and gowns? . . . Finally, under which of the
old tyrannical governments of Europe is every sixth man a
slave . . . ?
— SIDNEY SMITH (1771–1845) in the *Edinburgh Review*, 1820

Liberty and Union, now and forever, one and inseparable!
— DANIEL WEBSTER (1782–1852) Speech, 1830

The Americans, like the English, probably make love worse
than any other race.
— WALT WHITMAN (1819–1892) *An American Primer*

Our whole duty, for the present at any rate, is summed up in
the motto: America first.
— WOODROW WILSON (1856–1924) Speech, 1915

America is God's crucible, the great Melting-Pot where all
the races of Europe are melting and re-forming.
— ISRAEL ZANGWILL (1864–1926) *The Melting-Pot*

ANGER

I was angry with my friend:
I told my wrath, my wrath did end.
I was angry with my foe;
I told it not, my wrath did grow.
— WILLIAM BLAKE (1757–1827) *Christian Forbearance*

Anger begins with folly and ends with repentance.
— HENRY GEORGE BOHN (1796–1884) *Handbook of Proverbs*

Truly to moderate your mind and speech when you are angry,
or else to hold your peace, betokens no ordinary nature.
— CICERO (106–43 B.C.) *Epistolae Quintum Fratrem*

Beware the fury of a patient man.
— JOHN DRYDEN (1631–1700) *Absalom and Achitophel*

Anger and folly walk cheek by jowl;
repentance treads on both their heels.
— BEN FRANKLIN (1706–1790) *Poor Richard's Almanack*

Two things a man should never be angry at: what he can
help, and what he cannot help.
— THOMAS FULLER (1608–1681) *Historie of the Holy Warre*

Temper: a quality that, at critical moments, brings out the
best in steel and the worst in people.
— OSCAR HAMMLING (1890–   ) *Laconics*

Let anger's fire be slow to burn.
— GEORGE HERBERT (1593–1633) *Jacula Prudentum*

When I am angry I can write, pray, and preach well, for then
my whole temperament is quickened, my understanding
sharpened, and all mundane vexations and temptations
depart.
— MARTIN LUTHER (1483–1546) *Table-Talk*

The best answer to anger is silence.
— GERMAN PROVERB

A soft answer turneth away wrath; but grievous words stir
up anger.
— OLD TESTAMENT: *Proverbs*, xv, i

APRIL See MONTHS

ART

It is the glory and good of Art,
That Art remains the one way possible
Of speaking truth. . . .
— ROBERT BROWNING (1812–1889) *The Ring and the Book*

Art imitates nature as well as it can, as a pupil follows his
master; thus is it a sort of grandchild of God.
— DANTE (1265–1321) *Inferno*, Canto xi

In life beauty perishes, but not in art.
— LEONARDO DA VINCI (1452–1519) *Notebook*

Great art is the contempt of a great man for small art.
— F. SCOTT FITZGERALD (1896–1940) *Notebooks*

Nobody, I think, ought to read poetry, or look at pictures
or statues, who cannot find a great deal more in them than
the poet or artist has actually expressed.
— NATHANIEL HAWTHORNE (1804–1864) *The Marble Faun*

Rules and models destroy genius and art.
— WILLIAM HAZLITT (1778–1830) *On Taste*

Life is short, the art long, opportunity fleeting, experience
treacherous, judgment difficult.
— HIPPOCRATES (460?–377? B.C.) *Aphorisms*

Art may make a suit of clothes; but Nature must produce a
man.
— DAVID HUME (1711–1776) *Essays: The Epicurean*, 15

Art is nothing more than the shadow of humanity.
— HENRY JAMES (1843–1916) *Lectures*

Art hath an enemy called ignorance.
— BEN JONSON (1574–1637)

The true work of art is but a shadow of the divine perfection.
— MICHELANGELO (1475–1564)

To have faithfully studied the honorable arts, softens the
manners and keeps them free from harshness.
— OVID (43 B.C.–A.D. 18?) *Epistles*

There are three arts which are concerned with all things:
one which uses, another which makes, and a third which
imitates them.
— PLATO (428–347 B.C.) *The Republic*

True artists are almost the only men who do their work
with pleasure.
— AUGUSTE RODIN (1840–1917)

When love and skill work together expect a masterpiece.
— JOHN RUSKIN (1819–1900)

Art is not a handicraft; it is the transmission of feeling the
artist has experienced.
— LEO TOLSTOY (1828–1910) *What is Art?*

A work of art is a corner of creation seen through a temperament.
— ÉMILE ZOLA (1840–1902) *Mes Haines*

An artist may visit a museum, but only a pedant can live
there.
— GEORGE SANTAYANA (1853–1952) *Life of Reason*

AUGUST See MONTHS

AUTUMN

Autumn wins you best by this, its mute
Appeal to sympathy for its decay.
— ROBERT BROWNING (1812–1889) *Paracelsus*

All-cheering Plenty, with her flowing horn,
Led yellow Autumn, wreath'd with nodding corn.
— ROBERT BURNS (1759–1796) *The Brigs of Ayr*

The melancholy days are come, the saddest of the year,
Of wailing winds, and naked woods, and meadows brown
and sear.
— WILLIAM CULLEN BRYANT (1794–1878) *The Death of the
Flowers*

She loves the bare, the withered tree;
She walks the sodden pasture lane.
— ROBERT FROST (1875–1963) *My November Guest*

Dread autumn, harvest-season of the Goddess of Death.
— HORACE (65–8 B.C.) *Satires*

A solemn land of long-fulfilled desires
Is this, and year by year the self-same fires
Burn in the trees.
— MARY WEBB (1881–1927) *The Plain in Autumn*

AVARICE

Be not penny-wise; riches have wings, and sometimes they
fly away of themselves, sometimes they must be set flying
to bring in more.
— FRANCIS BACON (1561–1620) *Essays: Of Riches*

If you would abolish avarice, you must abolish its mother,
luxury.
— CICERO (106–43 B.C.) *De Oratore*

Would'st thou both eat thy cake and have it?
— GEORGE HERBERT (1593–1633) *The Size*

It is sheer madness to live in want in order to be wealthy
when you die.
— JUVENAL (*c.* 60–*c.* 130) *Satires*

The beautiful eyes of my money-box!
He speaks of it as a lover of his mistress.
— MOLIÈRE (1622–1673) *L'Avare*

They are greedy dogs which can never have enough.
— OLD TESTAMENT: *Isaiah, lvi, 11*

BABY See CHILDREN

BEAUTY

Beauty is a gift of God.
— ARISTOTLE (384–322 B.C.) *Apothegm*

There is no excellent beauty that hath not some strangeness
in the proportion.
— FRANCIS BACON (1561–1620) *Essays: Of Beauty*

Beauty is not caused. It is.
— EMILY DICKINSON (1830–1886) *Further Poems*

No Spring, nor Summer beauty hath such grace,
As I have seen in one Autumnal face.
— JOHN DONNE (1572–1631) *Elegies*

Beauty is in the eye of the beholder.
— MARGARET W. HUNGERFORD (1855?–1897)

A thing of beauty is a joy forever;
Its loveliness increases; it will never
Pass into nothingness . . . .
— JOHN KEATS (1795–1821) *Endymion*

"Beauty is truth, truth beauty," that is all
Ye know on earth, and all ye need to know.
— JOHN KEATS (1795–1821) *Ode on a Grecian Urn*

Euclid alone
Has looked on Beauty bare.
— EDNA ST. VINCENT MILLAY (1892–1951) *Sonnets*

Beauty and wisdom are seldom found together.
— PETRONIUS ARBITER (1st C. A.D.) *Satyricon*

It is the beautiful bird that gets caged.
— CHINESE PROVERB

Beauty provoketh thieves sooner than gold.
— SHAKESPEARE (1564–1616) *As You Like It*, I, iii, 13

O how can beautie maister the most strong!
— EDMUND SPENSER (1552?–1599) *Faerie Queene*

BOY See CHILDREN

CHILDREN

It is a great happiness to see our children rising round us,
but from that good fortune spring the bitterest woes of man.
— AESCHYLUS (525–456 B.C.) *Agamemnon*

Cornelia kept her in talk till her children came from school,
"And these," said she, "are my jewels."
— ROBERT BURTON (1557–1640) *Anatomy of Melancholy*

Respect the child. Be not too much his parent.
Trespass not on his solitude.
— RALPH WALDO EMERSON (1803–1882)

To a father waxing old nothing is dearer than a daughter.
Sons have spirits of higher pitch, but less inclined to sweet,
endearing fondness.
— EURIPIDES (480–406 B.C.)

An undutiful Daughter will prove an unmanageable Wife.
— BEN FRANKLIN (1706–1790) *Poor Richard's Almanack*

It is a wise child that knows his own father.
— HOMER (10th–8th C. B.C.) *Odyssey*

Children have more need of models than of critics.
— JOSEPH JOUBERT (1754–1824) *Pensées*, No. 261

Between the dark and the daylight,
When the night is beginning to lower,
Comes a pause in the day's occupations
That is known as the children's hour.
— HENRY W. LONGFELLOW (1807–1882) *The Children's Hour*

Suffer the little children to come unto me, and forbid them
not; for such is the kingdom of God.
— NEW TESTAMENT: *Mark*, x, 14; *Luke*, xviii, 16

It were better for him that a millstone were hanged about
his neck, and he cast into the sea, than that he should offend
one of these little ones.
— NEW TESTAMENT: *Luke*, xvii, 2

Out of the mouths of babes and sucklings hast thou ordained
strength.
— OLD TESTAMENT: *Psalms*, viii, 2

The wildest colts make the best horses.
— PLUTARCH (46–120)

A wise son maketh a glad father.
— OLD TESTAMENT: *Proverbs*, x, 1

Even a child is known by his doings.
— OLD TESTAMENT: *Proverbs*, xx, 11

Behold the child, by nature's kindly law,
Pleased with a rattle, tickled with a straw.
— ALEXANDER POPE (1688–1744) *Essay on Man*

Lacking all sense of right and wrong, a child can do nothing
which is morally evil, or which merits either punishment or
reproof.
— JEAN-JACQUES ROUSSEAU (1712–1778) *Emile*

At first the infant,
Mewling and puking in the nurse's arms.
And then the whining school-boy, with his satchel,
And shining morning face, creeping like snail
Unwillingly to school.
— SHAKESPEARE (1564–1616) *As You Like It*, II, viii, 143

I do not love him because he is good, but because he is my little child.
— SIR RABINDRANATH TAGORE (1861–1841) *The Crescent Moon*

A child tells in the street what its father and mother say at home.
— THE TALMUD

A babe in a house is a well-spring of pleasure.
— MARTIN FARQUHAR TUPPER (1810–1889) *Of Education*

Heaven lies about us in our infancy.
— WILLIAM WORDSWORTH (1770–1850) *Intimations of Immortality*

The child is father of the man.
— WILLIAM WORDSWORTH (1770–1850) *My Heart Leaps up When I Behold*

CIVILIZATION

Civilization degrades the many to exalt the few.
— BRONSON ALCOTT (1799–1888) *Table-Talk*

Increased means and increased leisure are the two civilizers of man.
— BENJAMIN DISRAELI (1804–1881) Speech, 1872

The true test of civilization is not the census, nor the size of cities, nor the crops, —no, but the kind of man the country turns out.
— RALPH WALDO EMERSON (1803–1882) *Essays: Society and Solitude.*

No one is so savage that he cannot become civilized, if he will lend a patient ear to culture.
— HORACE (65–8 B.C.) *Epistles*

Things have their day, and their beauties in that day. It would be preposterous to expect any one civilization to last forever.
— GEORGE SANTAYANA (1863–1952) *Character and Opinion in the United States*

A civilization which develops only on its material side, and not in corresponding measure on its mental and spiritual side, is like a vessel with a defective steering gear . . . .
— ALBERT SCHWEITZER (1875–1965) *The Decay and Restoration of Civilization*

COMMON SENSE

If a man can have only one kind of sense, let him have common sense. If he has that and uncommon sense too, he is not far from genius.
— HENRY WARD BEECHER (1813–1887)

Nothing astonishes men so much as common sense and plain dealing.
— RALPH WALDO EMERSON (1803–1882) *Art*

Where sense is wanting, everything is wanting.
— BEN FRANKLIN (1706–1790) *Poor Richard's Almanack*

Common sense is only a modification of talent. Genius is an exaltation of it.
— EDWARD BULWER-LYTTON (1803–1873)

Common sense is not so common.
— VOLTAIRE (1694–1778) *Philosophical Dictionary*

COMPENSATION

For every thing you have missed, you have gained something else; and for every thing you gain, you lose something.
— RALPH WALDO EMERSON (1803–1882) *Compensation*

For all our works a recompense is sure:
'Tis sweet to think on what was hard t'endure.
— ROBERT HERRICK (1591–1674) *Hesperides*

It is a comfort that the medal has two sides. There is much vice and misery in the world, I know; but more virtue and happiness, I believe.
— THOMAS JEFFERSON (1743–1826)

Whoever tries for great objects must suffer something.
— PLUTARCH (46?–120?) *Lives*

There is no evil without its compensation. Avarice promises money; luxury, pleasure; ambition, a purple robe.
— SENECA (4? B.C.–A.D. 65) *Epistulae ad Lucillium*

Give unto them beauty for ashes, the oil of joy for mourning, the garment of praise for the spirit of heaviness.
— OLD TESTAMENT: *Isaiah*, lxi, 3

CONCEIT See EGOTISM

CONSCIENCE

Conscience and reputation are two things. Conscience is due to yourself, reputation to your neighbor.
— ST. AUGUSTINE (354–430)

There is another man within me that's angry with me.
— SIR THOMAS BROWNE (1605–1682) *Religio Medici*

Conscience, good my lord,
Is but the pulse of reason.
— SAMUEL TAYLOR COLERIDGE (1772–1834) *Zapolya*

The still small voice.
— WILLIAM COWPER (1731–1800) *The Task*

A good conscience is a continual Christmas.
— BEN FRANKLIN (1706–1790) *Poor Richard's Almanack*

The man who acts never has any conscience; no one has any conscience but the man who thinks.
— GOETHE (1749–1832)

That fierce thing
They call a conscience.
— THOMAS HOOD (1799–1845) *Lamia*

The sting of conscience, like the gnawing of a dog at a bone, is mere foolishness.
— FRIEDRICH NIETZSCHE (1844–1900) *Human All-too-Human*

There is no witness so terrible, no accuser so potent, as the conscience that dwells in every man's breast.
— POLYBIUS (c. 204–122 B.C.) *Histories*

The worm of conscience keeps the same hours as the owl.
— SCHILLER (1759–1805) *Kabale und Liebe*

The play's the thing
Wherein I'll catch the conscience of the king.
— SHAKESPEARE (1564–1616) *Hamlet*, II, ii, 641

Trust that man in nothing who has not a conscience in everything.
— LAURENCE STERNE (1713–1768) *Tristram Shandy*

Conscience is, in most men, an anticipation of the opinion of others.
— SIR HENRY TAYLOR (1800–1886) *The Statesman*

Conscience and cowardice are really the same thing.
— OSCAR WILDE (1854–1900) *The Picture of Dorian Gray*

CONSERVATISM

The absurd man is one who never changes.
— AUGUSTE BARTHELEMY (1796–1867) *Nemesis*

Conservative: A statesman who is enamored of existing evils, as distinguished from the Liberal who wishes to replace them with others.
— AMBROSE BIERCE (1842–1914?) *The Devil's Dictionary*

A conservative government is an organized hypocrisy.
— BENJAMIN DISRAELI (1804–1881)

A conservative is a man who is too cowardly to fight and too fat to run.
— ELBERT HUBBARD (1856–1915) *Epigrams*

What is conservatism? Is it not adherence to the old and tried, against the new and untried?
— ABRAHAM LINCOLN (1809–1865) *Cooper Union Address*, 1860

Be not the first by whom the new are tried,
Nor yet the last to lay the old aside.
— ALEXANDER POPE (1688–1744) *Essay on Criticism*

The man for whom the law exists—the man of forms, the Conservative, is a tame man.
— HENRY DAVID THOREAU (1817–1862) *An Essay on Civil Disobedience*

CONSTANCY AND INCONSTANCY

Without constancy there is neither love, friendship, nor virtue in the world.
— JOSEPH ADDISON (1672–1719)

It is as absurd to say that a man can't love one woman all the time as it is to say that a violinist needs several violins to play the same piece of music.
— HONORÉ DE BALZAC (1799–1850) *Physiology of Marriage*

A good man it is not mine to see. Could I see a man possessed of constancy, that would satisfy me.
— CONFUCIUS (*c.* 551–478 B.C.) *Analects*

What is there in this vile earth that more commendeth a woman than constancy?
— JOHN LYLY (1554?–1606) *Euphues*

There are two sorts of constancy in love—one rises from continually discovering in the loved person new subjects for love, the other arises from our making a merit of being constant.
— FRANÇOIS DE LA ROCHEFOUCAULD (1613–1680) *Maxims*

But I am constant as the northern star,
Of whose true-fix'd and resting quality
There is no fellow in the firmament.
— SHAKESPEARE (1564–1616) *Julius Caesar*, III, i, 58

There is nothing in this world constant but inconstancy.
— JONATHAN SWIFT (1667–1745)

CONTEMPT

Familiarity breeds contempt, while rarity wins admiration.
— APULEIUS (2nd C.) *De Deo Socratis*

None but the contemptible are apprehensive of contempt.
— FRANÇOIS DE LA ROCHEFOUCAULD (1613–1680) *Maxims*

Here is another man with whom I cannot get angry, because I despise him.
— BENITO MUSSOLINI (1883–1945)

Man is much more sensitive to the contempt of others than to self-contempt.
— FRIEDRICH NIETZSCHE (1844–1900) *Human All-too-Human*

Contempt penetrates even the shell of the tortoise.
— PERSIAN PROVERB

CONTENT AND DISCONTENT

No form of society can be reasonably stable in which the majority of the people are not fairly content. People cannot be content if they feel that the foundations of their lives are wholly unstable.
— JAMES TRUSLOW ADAMS (1878–1949) *Record of America*

Be content with your lot; one cannot be first in everything.
— AESOP (6th C. B.C.) *The Peacock and Juno*

A perverse and fretful disposition makes any state of life unhappy.
— CICERO (106–43 B.C.) *De Senectute*

Who is rich? He that is content. Who is that? Nobody.
— BEN FRANKLIN (1706–1790) *Poor Richard's Almanack*

Unhappy man! He frets at the narrow limits of the world.
— JUVENAL (*c.* 60–*c.* 130 A.D.)

When we cannot find contentment in ourselves it is useless to seek it elsewhere.
— FRANÇOIS DE LA ROCHEFOUCAULD (1613–1680) *Maxims*

Discontent is the first step in the progress of a man or nation.
— OSCAR WILDE (1854–1900) *A Woman of No Importance*

Poor in abundance, famish'd at a feast.
— EDWARD YOUNG (1683–1765) *Night Thoughts*

I have learned, in whatsoever state I am, therewith to be content.
— NEW TESTAMENT: *Hebrews*, iv, 11

COURAGE

Often the test of courage is not to die but to live.
— VITTORIO ALFIERI (1749–1903) *Oreste*

But where life is more terrible than death, it is then the truest valor to dare to live.
— SIR THOMAS BROWNE (1663–1704) *Religio Medici*

Courage is that virtue which champions the cause of right.
— CICERO (106–43 B.C.) *De Officiis*

Every man of courage is a man of his word.
— PIERRE CORNEILLE (1606–1684) *Le Menteur*

Courage consists in equality to the problem before us.
— RALPH WALDO EMERSON (1803–1882) *Society and Solitude*

Courage may be taught as a child is taught to speak.
— EURIPIDES (480–406 B.C.) *The Suppliant Women*

A decent boldness ever meets with friends.
— HOMER (*c.* 10th C.–8th C. B.C.) *Iliad*

Nothing is too high for the daring of mortals; we storm Heaven itself in our folly.
— HORACE (65–8 B.C.) *Odes*

It is better to die on your feet than to live on your knees.
— LA PASIONARIA (1895–   ) Speech at Paris, 1936

True courage is to do, without witnesses, everything that one is capable of doing before all the world.
— FRANÇOIS DE LA ROCHEFOUCAULD (1613–1680) *Maxims*

What though the field be lost?
All is not lost; th'unconquerable will,
And study of revenge, immortal hate,
And courage never to submit or yield.
— JOHN MILTON (1608–1674) *Paradise Lost*

The strongest, most generous, and proudest of all virtues is true courage.
— MICHEL DE MONTAIGNE (1533–1592) *Essays*

Be of good cheer: it is I; be not afraid.
— NEW TESTAMENT: *Matthew*, xiv, 27

We shall attack and attack until we are exhausted, and then we shall attack again.
— GENERAL GEORGE S. PATTON (1885–1945) Address to his troops before the invasion of North Africa, 1942

The smallest worm will turn being trodden on,
And doves will peck in safeguard of their brood.
— SHAKESPEARE (1564–1616) *III Henry VI*, II, ii, 17

Why, courage then! What cannot be avoided
'Twere childish weakness to lament or fear.
— SHAKESPEARE (1564–1616) *Henry VI*, V, iv, 37

COURTSHIP

Those marriages generally abound most with love and constancy that are preceded by a long courtship.
— JOSEPH ADDISON (1672–1719) *The Spectator*

He that will win his dame must do
As love does when he draws his bow;
With one hand thrust the lady from,
And with the other pull her home.
— SAMUEL BUTLER (1612–1680) *Hudibras*

Courtship to marriage is but as the music in the playhouse till the curtain's drawn.
— WILLIAM CONGREVE (1670–1729) *The Old Bachelor*

If I am not worth the wooing, I am surely not worth the winning.
— HENRY W. LONGFELLOW (1807–1882) *Courtship of Miles Standish*

Had we but world enough and time
This coyness, lady, were no crime.
— ANDREW MARVELL (1621–1678) *To His Coy Mistress*

I will now court her in the conqueror's style;
"Come, see, and overcome."
— PHILIP MASSINGER (1583–1640) *Maid of Honor*

We cannot fight for love, as men may do;
We should be woo'd and were not made to woo.
— SHAKESPEARE (1564–1616) *Midsummer Night's Dream*, II, i, 241

The weather is usually fine when people are courting.
— R. L. STEVENSON (1850–1894) *Virginibus Puerisque*

A man always chases a woman until she catches him.
— UNKNOWN

COURTESY

If a man be gracious and courteous to strangers it shows he is a citizen of the world.
— FRANCIS BACON (1561–1620) *Essays*

Politeness. The most acceptable hypocrisy.
— AMBROSE BIERCE (1842–1914?) *Devil's Dictionary*

'Tis ill talking of halters in the house of a man that was hanged.
— CERVANTES (1547–1616) *Don Quixote*, Pt. i

Politeness is the ritual of society, as prayers are of the church.
— RALPH WALDO EMERSON (1803–1882) *English Traits*

Be civil to all; sociable to many; familiar with few.
— BEN FRANKLIN (1706–1790) *Poor Richard's Almanack*

He was so generally civil, that nobody thanked him for it.
— SAMUEL JOHNSON (1709–1784) in Boswell's *Life*

Civility is a desire to receive it in turn, and to be accounted well bred.
— FRANÇOIS DE LA ROCHEFOUCAULD (1613–1680) *Maxims*

Politeness costs nothing and gains everything.
— LADY MARY WORTLEY MONTAGU (1689–1762) Letters

It is one of the greatest blessings that so many women are so full of tact. The calamity happens when a woman who has all the other riches of life just lacks that one thing.
— SIR WILLIAM OSLER (1848–1919)

True politeness consists in being easy one's self, and in making every one about one as easy as one can.
— ALEXANDER POPE (1688–1744) *Table-Talk*

To speak kindly does not hurt the tongue.
— FRENCH PROVERB

Dissembling courtesy! How fine this tyrant
Can tickle where she wounds!
— SHAKESPEARE (1564–1616) *Cymbeline*, I, i, 84

The greater man the greater courtesy.
— TENNYSON (1809–1882) *The Last Tournament*

COWARDICE

Coward. One who in a perilous emergency thinks with his legs.
— AMBROSE BIERCE (1842–1914?) *Devil's Dictionary*

To see what is right and not do it is want of courage.
— CONFUCIUS (551–478 B.C.) *Analects*

The coward never on himself relies,
But to an equal for assistance flies.
— GEORGE CRABBE (1754–1832) *The Gentleman Farmer*

Many would be cowards if they had courage enough.
— THOMAS FULLER (1608–1681) *Gnomologia*

Ever will a coward show no mercy.
— SIR THOMAS MALORY (f. 1470) *Morte d'Arthur*

It is the act of a coward to wish for death.
— OVID (43 B.C.-A.D. 18?) *Metamorphoses*

The coward calls himself cautious.
— PUBLILIUS SYRUS (1st C. B.C.) *Sententiae*

A cowardly cur barks more fiercely than it bites.
— QUINTUS CURTIUS RUFUS (c. 2nd C. A.D.) *De Rebus Gestis Alexandri Magni*

When all the blandishments of life are gone,
The coward sneaks to death, the brave live on.
— GEORGE SEWELL (d. 1726)

A coward, a most devout coward, religious in it.
— SHAKESPEARE (1564–1616) *Twelfth Night*, III, iv, 427

Cowards die many times before their deaths;
The valiant never taste of death but once.
— SHAKESPEARE (1564–1616) *Julius Caesar*, II, ii, 32

CRITICISM

Criticism is a disinterested endeavour to learn and propagate the best that is known and thought in the world.
— MATTHEW ARNOLD (1822–1888) *Essays in Criticism*

As the arts advance towards their perfection, the science of criticism advances with equal pace.
— EDMUND BURKE (1729–1797) *On the Sublime and Beautiful*

Let dull critics feed upon the carcasses of plays; give me the taste and the dressing.
— LORD CHESTERFIELD (1694–1773) *Letters to his Son*

Critics—murderers!
— SAMUEL TAYLOR COLERIDGE (1772–1834)

Those who write ill, and they who ne'er durst write,
Turn critics out of mere revenge and spite.
— JOHN DRYDEN (1631–1700) *Conquest of Granada*

Blame where you must, be candid where you can,
And be each critic the Good-natured Man.
— OLIVER GOLDSMITH (1728–1774) *Good-Natured Man*

Criticism is the art wherewith a critic tries to guess himself into a share of the artist's fame.
— GEORGE JEAN NATHAN (1882–1958) *House of Satan*

Damn with faint praise, assent with civil leer
And without sneering teach the rest to sneer.
— ALEXANDER POPE (1688–1744) *Epistle to Dr. Arbuthnot*

They damn what they do not understand.
— QUINTILIAN (c. 40–100 A.D.) *De Institutione Oratoria*

Critic: a man who writes about things he doesn't like.
— UNKNOWN

Really to stop criticism they say one must die.
— VOLTAIRE (1694–1778)

CURIOSITY

This disease of curiosity.
— ST. AUGUSTINE (354–430) *Confessions*

The first and simplest emotion which we discover in the human mind is curiosity.
— EDMUND BURKE (1729–1797) *The Sublime and Beautiful*

Shun the inquisitive person, for he is also a talker.
— HORACE (65–8 B.C.) *Epistles*

Curiosity is one of the most permanent and certain characteristics of a vigorous intellect.
— SAMUEL JOHNSON (1709–1784) *The Rambler*

Curiosity killed the cat.
— AMERICAN PROVERB

He that pryeth into every cloud may be struck by a thunderbolt.
— JOHN RAY (1627?–1705) *English Proverbs*

You know what a woman's curiosity is. Almost as great as a man's!
— OSCAR WILDE (1854–1900) *An Ideal Husband*

Curiosity. The reason why most of us haven't committed suicide long ago.
— UNKNOWN

DANGER

Dangers bring fears, and fears more dangers bring.
— RICHARD BAXTER (1615–1691) *Love Breathing Thanks*

Danger, the spur of all great minds.
— GEORGE CHAPMAN (1559?–1634?) *Bussy d'Ambois*

Moving of the earth brings harms and fears.
Men reckon what it did and meant.
But trepidation of the spheres
Though greater far, is innocent.
— JOHN DONNE (1573–1631) *Valediction Forbidding Mourning*

As soon as there is life there is danger.
— RALPH WALDO EMERSON (1803–1882) *Lectures*

Great perils have this beauty, that they bring to light the fraternity of strangers.
— VICTOR HUGO (1802–1885) *Les Misérables*

Out of this nettle, danger, we pluck this flower, safety.
— SHAKESPEARE (1564–1616) *I Henry IV*, II, iii, 10

Better face a danger once than be always in fear.
— PROVERB

DARKNESS See NIGHT

DAUGHTER See CHILDREN

DAWN See DAY

DAY

Day is a snow-white Dove of heaven
That from the East glad message brings.
— THOMAS BAILEY ALDRICH (1836–1907) *Day and Night*

Day!
O'er nights brim, day boils at last;
Boils, pure gold, o'er the cloud-cup's brim.
— ROBERT BROWNING (1812–1889) *Pippa Passes*

One day well spent is to be preferred to an eternity of error.
— CICERO (106–43 B.C.) *Tusculanarum Disputationum*

He is only rich who owns the day. There is no king, rich man, fairy, or demon who possesses such power as that. . . . The days are made on a loom whereof the warp and woof are past and future time.
— RALPH WALDO EMERSON (1803–1882) *Society and Solitude*

Rosy-fingered Dawn.
— HOMER (10th–8th? C. B.C.) *Iliad*

The day has eyes; the night has ears.
— PROVERB

Wait till it is night before saying it has been a fine day.
— FRENCH PROVERB

My days are swifter than a weaver's shuttle.
— OLD TESTAMENT: *Job*, vii, 6

Listen to the Exhortation of the Dawn!
Look to this Day! For it is Life,
The very Life of Life.
— *Salutation of the Dawn* (SANSKRIT)

The glow-worm shows the matin to be near,
And 'gins to pale his uneffectual fire.
— SHAKESPEARE (1564–1616) *Hamlet*, I, v, 89

Night's candles are burnt out, and jocund day
Stands tiptoe on the misty mountaintops.
— SHAKESPEARE (1564–1616) *Romeo and Juliet*, III, v, 9

DEATH

Death is a black camel, which kneels at the gates of all.
— ABD-EL-KADER (1807?–1883)

It is good to die before one has done anything deserving death.
— ANANANDRIDES (4th C. B.C.) *Fragment*

Men fear death as children fear to go in the dark; and as that natural fear in children is increased with tales, so is the other.
— FRANCIS BACON (1561–1620) *Essays: Of Death*

He that unburied lies wants not his hearse,
For unto him a Tomb's the Universe.
— SIR THOMAS BROWNE (1605–1682) *Religio Medici*

We all labor against our own cure, for death is the cure of all diseases.
— SIR THOMAS BROWNE (1605–1682) *Religio Medici*

The fear of death is worse than death.
— ROBERT BURTON (1577–1640) *Anatomy of Melancholy*

Ah, surely nothing dies but something mourns!
— LORD BYRON (1788–1824) *Don Juan*

Death levels all things.
— CLAUDIAN (c. 395) *De Raptu Proserpinae*

These have not the hope of death.
— DANTE (1265–1321) *Inferno*

Death, be not proud, though some have called thee
Mighty and dreadful, for thou art not so:
For those, whom thou think'st thou dost overthrow,
Die not, poor Death. . .
— JOHN DONNE (1572–1631) *Divine Poems: Holy Sonnet*

There were some who said that a man at the point of death was more free than all others, because death breaks every bond, and over the dead the united world has no power.
— FÉNELON (1651–1715) *Telemachus*

Death is Nature's expert advice to get plenty of Life.
— GOETHE (1749–1832)

We die ourselves a little every time we kill in others something that deserved to live.
— OSCAR HAMMLING (1890–   ) *Laconics*

I have been half in love with easeful death,
Call'd him soft names in many a mused rhyme.
— JOHN KEATS (1795–1821) *Ode to a Nightingale*

So now he is a legend when he would have preferred to be a man.
— MRS. JACQUELINE KENNEDY (1929–   ) in a tribute to her husband, Nov. 1964

Wheresoever ye be, death will overtake you, although ye be in lofty towers.
— THE KORAN

A man's dying is more the survivors' affair than his own.
— THOMAS MANN (1875–1955) *The Magic Mountain*

The grave's a fine and private place,
But none, I think, do there embrace.
— ANDREW MARVELL (1621–1678) *To His Coy Mistress*

Death has a thousand doors to let out life.
I shall find one.
— PHILIP MASSINGER (1584–1640) *A Very Woman*

Whom the gods love dies young.
— MENANDER (342–291 B.C.)

Dead men tell no tales.
— ENGLISH PROVERB

To die at the will of another is to die twice.
— PUBLILIUS SYRUS (*b.* 1st C. B.C.) *Sententiae*

Death seems to provide the minds of the Anglo-Saxon race with a greater fund of innocent amusement than any other single subject.
— DOROTHY L. SAYERS (1893–1957)

I have a rendezvous with Death
At some disputed barricade . . .
— ALAN SEEGER (1888–1916) *I Have a Rendezvous with Death*

Death is a punishment to some, to some a gift, and to many a favor.
— SENECA (4? B.C.–A.D. 65)

Nothing in his life became him like the leaving it . . . .
— SHAKESPEARE (1564–1616) *Macbeth*, I, iv, 7

Imperious Caesar, dead and turn'd to clay,
Might stop a hole to keep the wind away.
— SHAKESPEARE (1564–1616) *Hamlet*, V, i, 235

  To die, —to sleep,
No more, and by that sleep to say we end
The heart-ache and the thousand natural shocks
That flesh is heir to . . . .
— SHAKESPEARE (1564–1616) *Hamlet*, III, i, 60

Say nothing but good of the dead.
— SOLON (638–559 B.C.)

Do not go gentle into that good night,
Old age should burn and rave at close of day;
Rage, rage against the dying of the light.
— DYLAN THOMAS (1914–1953) *Poem to My Father*

I saw him now going the way of all flesh.
— JOHN WEBSTER (1580–1625) *Westward Ho!*, Act II

O death, where is thy sting? O grave, where is thy victory?
— NEW TESTAMENT: *I Corinthians*, xv, 55

I looked and beheld a pale horse: and his name that sat on him was Death.
— NEW TESTAMENT: *Revelation*, vi, 8

Dust thou art, and unto dust shalt thou return.
— OLD TESTAMENT: *Genesis*, iii, 19

DECEIT

God is not averse to deceit in a holy cause.
— AESCHYLUS (525–456 B.C.)

We are never deceived; we deceive ourselves.
— GOETHE (1749–1832)

Hateful to me as the gates of hell,
Is he, who, hiding one thing in his heart,
Utters another.
— HOMER (*c.* 10th–8th C. B.C.) *Iliad*

It is a double pleasure to deceive the deceiver.
— JEAN DE LA FONTAINE (1621–1695) *Fables*

The surest way to be deceived is to think one's self more clever than others.
— FRANÇOIS DE LA ROCHEFOUCAULD (1613–1680) *Maxims*

You can fool some of the people all of the time, and all of the people some of the time, but you cannot fool all of the people all of the time.
— ABRAHAM LINCOLN (1809–1865)

Listen at the key-hole and you'll hear news of yourself.
— PROVERB

Oh, what a tangled web we weave,
When first we practise to deceive!
— SIR WALTER SCOTT (1771–1832) *Marmion*

Sigh no more, ladies, sigh no more,
Men were deceivers ever.
— SHAKESPEARE (1564–1616) *Much Ado About Nothing*, II, iii, 65

DECEMBER See MONTHS

DECISION AND INDECISION

There is grief in indecision.
— CICERO (106–43 B.C.) *De officiis*

The wavering mind is but a base possession.
— EURIPIDES (480–406 B.C.)

There is no more miserable human being than one in whom nothing is habitual but indecision.
— WILLIAM JAMES (1842–1910) *Psychology*

Decide not rashly. The decision made
Can never be recalled.
— HENRY W. LONGFELLOW (1807–1882) *Masque of Pandora*

Once to every man and nation comes the moment to decide . . . .
— JAMES RUSSELL LOWELL (1819–1891) *The Present Crisis*

To be or not to be, that is the question . . . .
— SHAKESPEARE (1564–1616) *Hamlet*, III, i, 56

I am at war twixt will and will not.
— SHAKESPEARE (1564–1616) *Measure for Measure*, II, ii, 32

Quick decisions are unsafe decisions.
— SOPHOCLES (495–406 B.C.) *Oedipus Tyrannus*

DEMOCRACY

If liberty and equality, as is thought by some, are chiefly to be found in democracy, they will be best attained when all persons alike share in the government to the utmost.
— ARISTOTLE (384–322 B.C.) *Politics*

The tyranny of a multitude is a multiplied tyranny.
— EDMUND BURKE (1729–1797) Letter to Thomas Mercer

Democracy means government by the uneducated, while aristocracy means government by the badly educated.
— G. K. CHESTERTON (1874–1936) Interview, 1931

The tendency of democracies is, in all things, to mediocrity.
— JAMES FENIMORE COOPER (1789–1851) *American Democrat*

Only if basically the democracy of our day satisfies the mental, moral, and physical wants of the masses living under it, can it continue to exist.
— DWIGHT D. EISENHOWER (1890–1969) *Crusade in Europe*

The world is weary of statesmen whom democracy has degraded into politicians.
— BENJAMIN DISRAELI (1805–1881)

Democracy has another merit. It allows criticism, and if there isn't public criticism there are bound to be hushed-up scandals.
— E. M. FORSTER (1879–1970) *I Believe*

Democracy is based upon the conviction that there are extraordinary possibilities in ordinary people.
— HARRY EMERSON FOSDICK (1878–1969) *Democracy*

The republican is the only form of government which is not eternally at open or secret war with the rights of mankind.
— THOMAS JEFFERSON (1743–1826) Reply to Address

If we fail now, then we will have forgotten in abundance what we learned in hardship: that democracy rests on faith, that freedom asks more than it gives, and the judgment of God is harshest on those who are most favored.
— LYNDON B. JOHNSON (1908–1973) Inaugural Address, Jan. 1965

The world is very different now. For man holds in his mortal hands the power to abolish all forms of human poverty and all forms of human life. And yet the same revolutionary beliefs for which our forebears fought are still at issue around the globe . . .
— JOHN F. KENNEDY (1917–1963), Inaugural Address, Jan. 1961

All creatures are members of the one family of God.
— THE KORAN

Democracy gives to every man
The right to be his own oppressor.
— JAMES RUSSELL LOWELL (1819–1891) *Bigelow Papers*

We must define democracy as that form of government and of society which is inspired above every other, with the feeling and consciousness of the dignity of man.
— THOMAS MANN (1875–1955) *The Coming Victory of Democracy*

We must be the great arsenal of democracy.
— FRANKLIN D. ROOSEVELT (1882–1945) Radio Address, 1940

Democracy is unfinished business, not fulfilment; it is a process of always advancing toward fulfilment.
— RAYMOND GRAM SWING (1887–1968)

Democracy is the recurrent suspicion that more than half of the people are right more than half of the time.
— E. B. WHITE (1899–   )

I believe in democracy because it releases the energies of every human being.
— WOODROW WILSON (1856–1924) Address to Congress, 1917

The world must be made safe for democracy. Its peace must be planted upon the tested foundations of political liberty.
— WOODROW WILSON (1856–1924) Address to Congress, 1917

DEPENDENCE AND INDEPENDENCE

Each man for himself.
— GEOFFREY CHAUCER (1340?–1400) *Canterbury Tales*

The greatest man living may stand in need of the meanest, as much as the meanest does of him.
— THOMAS FULLER (1608–1681)

Even in the common affairs of life, in love, friendship, and marriage, how little security have we when we trust our happiness in the hands of others!
— WILLIAM HAZLITT (1778–1830) *On Living to Oneself*

The strongest man in the world is he who stands most alone.
— HENRIK IBSEN (1828–1906) *An Enemy of the People*

No degree of knowledge attainable by man is able to set him above the want of hourly assistance.
— SAMUEL JOHNSON (1709-1784)

To be independent is the business of a few only; it is the privilege of the strong.
— FRIEDRICH NIETZSCHE (1844–1900) *Beyond Good and Evil*

Independence? That's middle class blasphemy. We are all dependent on one another, every soul of us on earth.
— GEORGE BERNARD SHAW (1856–1950) *Pygmalion*

Without the help of thousands of others, any one of us would die, naked and starved.
— ALFRED E. SMITH (1873–1944)

Dependence is a perpetual call upon humanity, and a greater incitement to tenderness and pity than any other motive whatever.
— WILLIAM MAKEPEACE THACKERAY (1811–1863)

DESIRE

He begins to die that quits his desires.
— GEORGE HERBERT (1593–1633) *Outlandish Proverbs*

Naked I seek the camp of those who desire nothing.
— HORACE (65–8 B.C.) *Odes*

We live in our desires rather than in our achievements.
— GEORGE MOORE (1852–1933) *Ave*

We desire most what we ought not to have.
— PUBLILIUS SYRUS (1st C. B.C.) *Sententiae*

If wishes were horses, beggars would ride.
— SCOTTISH PROVERB

Can one desire too much of a good thing?
— SHAKESPEARE (1564–1616) *As You Like It*, IV, i, 129

The fewer desires, the more peace.
— THOMAS WILSON (1663–1755)

Desire accomplished is sweet to the soul.
— OLD TESTAMENT: *Proverbs*, xiii, 19

DESPAIR

I want to be forgotten even by God.
— ROBERT BROWNING (1812–1889) *Easter Day*

The name of the Slough was Despond.
— JOHN BUNYAN (1628–1688) *Pilgrim's Progress*

Despair is the damp of hell, as joy is the serenity of heaven.
— JOHN DONNE (1572–1631)

Despondency is not a state of humility. On the contrary, it is the vexation and despair of a cowardly pride . . . .
— FÉNELON (1651–1715)

Then black despair,
The shadow of a starless night, was thrown
Over the world in which I moved alone.
— PERCY B. SHELLEY (1792–1822) *Revolt of Islam*

The only refuge from despair is to project one's ego into the world.
— LEO TOLSTOY (1828–1910)

When we have lost everything, including hope, life becomes a disgrace and death a duty.
— VOLTAIRE (1694–1778) *Merope*

Out of the depths have I cried unto Thee, O Lord.
— OLD TESTAMENT: *Psalms*, cxxx, 1

DESPOTISM See TYRANNY

DESTINY See FATE

DISCONTENT See CONTENT

DISCRETION AND INDISCRETION

An indiscreet man is more hurtful than an ill-natured one; for the latter will only attack his enemies, and those he wishes ill to; the other injures indifferently both friends and foes.
— JOSEPH ADDISON (1672–1719) *The Spectator*

He knows not when to be silent who knows not when to speak.
— PUBLILIUS SYRUS (1st C. B.C.)

Least said, soonest mended.
— CHARLES DICKENS (1812–1870) *David Copperfield*

For good and evil in our actions meet;
Wicked is not much worse than indiscreet.
— JOHN DONNE (1572–1631)

A demi-vierge is a woman for whom chastity, from being a
temporary asset, has become a permanent liability.
— OSCAR HAMMLING (1890–   )

Let your discretion be your tutor; suit the action to the word,
the word to the action.
— SHAKESPEARE (1564–1616) *Hamlet*, III, ii, 18

The better part of valour is discretion; in the which better
part I have saved my life.
— SHAKESPEARE (1564–1616) *I Henry IV*, V, iv, 121

Be swift to hear, slow to speak, slow to wrath.
— NEW TESTAMENT: *James*, i, 19

DOUBT

Doubt whom you will, but never doubt yourself.
— CHRISTIAN NESTELL BOVEE (1820–1904)

Doubting charms me not less than knowledge.
— DANTE (1265–1321) *Inferno*, canto xii, l. 93

Just think of the tragedy of teaching children not to doubt.
— CLARENCE DARROW (1857–1938)

Scepticism is the first step on the road to philosophy.
— DENIS DIDEROT (1713–1784)

To believe with certainty we must begin with doubting.
— STANISLAUS LESCYNSKI (1677–1766)

I respect faith, but doubt is what gets you an education.
— WILSON MIZNER (1876–1933)

Doubt makes the mountain which faith can move.
— UNKNOWN

Our doubts are traitors
And make us lose the good we oft might win
By fearing to attempt.
— SHAKESPEARE (1564–1616) *Measure for Measure*, I, iv, 77

DREAMS

The more a man dreams, the less he believes.
— H. L. MENCKEN (1880–1956) *Prejudices*

Dreams are the true interpreters of our inclinations, but art
is required to sort and understand them.
— MICHEL DE MONTAIGNE (1533–1592) *Essays*

Those dreams are true which we have in the morning, as the
lamp begins to flicker.
— OVID (43 B.C.–A.D. 18?) *Epistles*

All that we see or seem
Is but a dream within a dream.
— EDGAR ALLAN POE (1809–1849) *A Dream Within a Dream*

To sleep; perchance to dream: ay, there's the rub;
For in that sleep of death what dreams may come,
When we have shuffled off this mortal coil
Must give us pause.
— SHAKESPEARE (1564–1616) *Hamlet*, III, i, 65

We are such stuff
As dreams are made on, and our little life
Is rounded out with a sleep.
— SHAKESPEARE (1564–1616) *The Tempest*, IV, i, 156

We rest. A dream has power to poison sleep;
We rise. One wandering thought pollutes the day.
— PERCY B. SHELLEY (1792–1822) *Mutability*

But I, being poor, have only my dreams;
I have spread my dreams under your feet;
Tread softly, for you tread on my dreams.
— WILLIAM BUTLER YEATS (1865–1939) *The Cloths of Heaven*

Your old men shall dream dreams, your young men shall see
visions.
— OLD TESTAMENT: *Joel*, II, 28

DUTY

In doing what we ought we deserve no praise, because it is
our duty.
— ST. AUGUSTINE (354–430)

The fulfilment of spiritual duty in our daily life is vital to
our survival.
— WINSTON CHURCHILL (1874–1965) Speech, 1949

Do your duty and leave the rest to heaven.
— PIERRE CORNEILLE (1606–1684) *Horace*

The reward of one duty is the power to fill another.
— GEORGE ELIOT (1819–1880) *Daniel Deronda*

Fear God, and keep his commandments; for this is the whole
duty of man.
— OLD TESTAMENT: *Ecclesiastes*, xii, 13

Up to a certain point it is good for us to know that there are
people in the world who will give us love and unquestioned
loyalty to the limit of their ability. I doubt, however, if it
is good for us to feel assured of this without the accompanying obligation of having to justify this devotion by our behavior.
— ELEANOR ROOSEVELT (1884–1962) *This is My Story*

There is no duty we underrate so much as the duty of being
happy.
— R. L. STEVENSON (1850–1894) *Virginibus Puerisque*

He who eats the fruit should at least plant the seed.
— HENRY DAVID THOREAU (1817–1862)

Duty is what one expects from others.
— OSCAR WILDE (1854–1900) *Woman of No Importance*

EDUCATION See LEARNING

EGOTISM (See also VANITY)

Self-conceit may lead to self-destruction.
— AESOP (6th C. B.C.) *The Frog and the Ox*

Why should I be angry with a man, for loving himself better
than me?
— FRANCIS BACON (1561–1620) *Essays*

Conceit is God's fit to little men.
— BRUCE BARTON (1886–1967) *Conceit*

I've never had any pity for conceited people, because I think
they carry their comfort about with them.
— GEORGE ELIOT (1819–1880) *The Mill on the Floss*

We reproach people for talking about themselves; but it is
the subject they treat best.
— ANATOLE FRANCE (1844–1924)

We would rather speak ill of ourselves than not talk of ourselves at all.
— FRANÇOIS DE LA ROCHEFOUCAULD (1613–1680) *Maxims*

There is not enough love and goodness in the world to throw
any of it away on conceited people.
— FRIEDRICH NIETZSCHE (1844–1900)

If you love yourself over much, nobody else will love you at
all.
— PROVERB

Every bird loves to hear himself sing.
— GERMAN PROVERB

Who loves himself need fear no rival.
— LATIN PROVERB

Conceit may puff a man up, but never prop him up.
— JOHN RUSKIN (1819–1900) *True and Beautiful*

Self-love, in nature rooted fast,
Attends us first, and leaves us last.
— JONATHAN SWIFT (1667–1745) *Cadenus and Vanessa*

We are interested in others when they are interested in us.
— PUBLILIUS SYRUS (1st C. B.C.) *Sententiae*

From his cradle to his grave a man never does a single thing which has any first and foremost object save one—to secure peace of mind, spiritual comfort, for himself.
— MARK TWAIN (1835–1910) *What is Man?*

All men think all men mortal but themselves.
— EDWARD YOUNG (1683–1765) *Night Thoughts*

ENEMY

Wise men learn much from their enemies.
— ARISTOPHANES (444–380 B.C.) *The Birds*

Every man is his own greatest enemy, and as it were his own executioner.
— SIR THOMAS BROWNE (1605–1682) *Religio Medici*

You shall judge a man by his foes as well as by his friends.
— JOSEPH CONRAD (1857–1924) *Lord Jim*

Though thy enemy seems a mouse, yet watch him like a lion.
— PROVERB

One enemy can do more hurt than ten friends can do good.
— JONATHAN SWIFT (1667–1745) Letter, 1710

He makes no friend who never made a foe.
— TENNYSON (1809–1892) *Idylls of the King*

Rejoice not over thy greatest enemy being dead, but remember that we die all.
— APOCRYPHA: *Ecclesiasticus*

A man's foes shall be they of his own household.
— NEW TESTAMENT: *Matthew* x, 36

Love your enemies, bless them that curse you, do good to them that hate you ....
— NEW TESTAMENT: *Matthew,* v, 44

ENVY

Those that are not envied are never wholly happy.
— AESCHYLUS (525–456 B.C.) *Agamemnon*

Envy not greatness: for thou mak'st thereby
Thyself the worse, and so the distance greater.
— GEORGE HERBERT (1593–1633) *The Church*

All the tyrants of Sicily never invented a worse torment than envy.
— HORACE (65–8 B.C.) *Epistles*

No man likes to be surpassed by those of his own level.
— LIVY (59 B.C.–A.D. 17) *Annales*

Since we cannot attain to greatness, let us revenge ourselves by railing at it.
— MICHEL DE MONTAIGNE (1533–1592) *Essays*

It is a nobler fate to be envied than to be pitied.
— PINDAR (c. 522–442 B.C.) *Pythian Odes*

The truest mark of being born with great qualities is being born without envy.
— FRANÇOIS DE LA ROCHEFOUCAULD (1613–1680) *Maxims*

  No metal can,
No, not the hangman's axe, bear half the keenness
Of thy sharp envy.
— SHAKESPEARE (1564–1616) *Merchant of Venice*, IV, i, 123

Where envying and strife is, there is confusion, and every evil work.
— NEW TESTAMENT: *James*, iii, 16

EQUALITY AND INEQUALITY

The only stable state is the one in which all men are equal before the law.
— ARISTOTLE (384–322 B.C.) *Politics*

We hold these truths to be self-evident—that all men are created equal; that they are endowed by their Creator with certain inalienable rights; that among these are life, liberty, and the pursuit of happiness.
— DECLARATION OF INDEPENDENCE

Before God we are all equally wise—equally foolish.
— ALBERT EINSTEIN (1879–1955) *Cosmic Religion*

Men are made by nature unequal. It is vain, therefore, to treat them as if they were equal.
— JAMES ANTHONY FROUDE (1818–1894)

Though all men are made of one metal, yet they were not cast all in the same mold.
— THOMAS FULLER (1608–1681) *Gnomologia*

That all men are equal is a proposition to which at ordinary times no sane individual has ever given his assent.
— ALDOUS HUXLEY (1894–1963) *Proper Studies*

And our sorrowing gaze turns also to the other children of God everywhere, suffering because of race and economic conditions, at once complex and giving reason for anxiety, or through the limitation on the exercise of their natural and civil rights.
— POPE JOHN XXIII (1881–1963) April 17, 1960

All animals are created equal—but some animals are created more equal than others.
— GEORGE ORWELL (1903–1950) *Animal Farm*

The only real equality is in the cemetery.
— GERMAN PROVERB

Nature knows no equality; its sovereign law is subordination and dependence.
— MARQUIS DE VAUVENARGUES (1715–1747) *Reflections*

ERROR

There is many a slip
'Twixt the cup and the lip
— RICHARD HARRIS BARHAM (1788–1845) *Ingoldsby Legends*

I can pardon everybody's mistakes except my own.
— MARCUS CATO (234–149 B.C.)

Who errs and mends, to God himself commends.
— CERVANTES (1547–1616) *Don Quixote*

Mistake, error, is the discipline through which we advance.
— WILLIAM ELLERY CHANNING (1780–1842)

It is the nature of every man to err, but only the fool perseveres in error.
— CICERO (106–43 B.C.) *Philippicae*

The cautious seldom err.
— CONFUCIUS (c. 551–478 B.C.) *Analects*

Errors, like straws, upon the surface flow;
He who would search for pearls must dive below.
— JOHN DRYDEN (1631–1700) *All for Love*

Even a mistake may turn out to be the one thing necessary to a worthwhile achievement.
— HENRY FORD (1863–1947) Interview. 1938

Dark Error's other hidden side is truth.
— VICTOR HUGO (1802–1885) *Legend of the Centuries*

The man who makes no mistakes does not usually make anything.
— BISHOP W. C. MAGEE (1821–1891)

To err is human, to forgive divine.
— ALEXANDER POPE (1688–1744) *Essay on Criticism*

The wise course is to profit from the mistakes of others.
— TERENCE (*c.* 190–150 B.C.)

I fear our mistakes far more than the strategy of our enemies.
— THUCYDIDES (471?–400? B.C.) *Funeral Oration*

The progress of the rivers to the ocean is not so rapid as that of man to error.
— VOLTAIRE (1694–1778) *Philosophical Dictionary*

EVENING See NIGHT

EVIL

Evil events from evil causes spring.
— ARISTOPHANES (444–380 B.C.)

Better suffer a great evil than do a little one.
— HENRY GEORGE BOHN (1796–1884) *Handbook of Proverbs*

Often the fear of one evil leads us into a worse.
— NICOLAS BOILEAU (1636–1711) *The Poetic Art*

God bears with the wicked, but not forever.
— CERVANTES (1547–1616) *Don Quixote*

Evil to him who thinks evil. [Honi soit qui mal y pense.]
— EDWARD III (1327–1377) Motto of the Order of the Garter

A wicked man is his own hell.
— THOMAS FULLER (1606–1661) *Gnomologia*, No. 460

Don't let us make imaginary evils, when you know we have so many real ones to encounter.
— OLIVER GOLDSMITH (1730–1774)

The source of all wars, the source of all evil, lies in us.
— PIERRE LECOMTE DU NOÜY (1883–1947) *Human Destiny*

The evil best known is the most tolerable.
— LIVY (59 B.C.–A.D. 17) *History of Rome*

An evil life is a kind of death.
— OVID (43 B.C.–A.D. 18?) *Epistulae ex Ponto*

No evil can happen to a good man, either in life or after death.
— SOCRATES (470?–399 B.C.)

Every one that doeth evil hateth the light.
— NEW TESTAMENT: *John*, iii, 20

I have seen the wicked in great power, and spreading himself like the green bay tree. Yet he passed away, and lo, he was not.
— OLD TESTAMENT: *Isaiah*, lv, 7

Fret not thyself because of evildoers . . . for they shall soon be cut down like the grass, and wither as the green herb.
— OLD TESTAMENT: *Psalms*, xxxvii, 1–2

EXPERIENCE

All experience is an arch to build upon.
— HENRY ADAMS (1838–1918) *Education of Henry Adams*

It is costly wisdom that is bought by experience.
— ROGER ASCHAM (1515–1568) *Schoolmaster*

Thou shalt know by experience how salt the savor is of another's bread, and how sad a path it is to climb and descend another's stairs.
— DANTE (1265–1321) *Paradiso*

Experience keeps a dear school, but fools will learn in no other.
— BEN FRANKLIN (1706–1790) *Poor Richard's Almanack*

The finished man of the world must eat of every apple once.
— RALPH WALDO EMERSON (1803–1882) *Conduct of Life*

Happy is he who gains wisdom from another's mishap.
— PUBLILIUS SYRUS (1st C. B.C.) *Sententiae*

Experience is the name everyone gives to his mistakes.
— OSCAR WILDE (1854–1900) *Lady Windermere's Fan*

FAITH

Faith is a higher faculty than reason.
— PHILIP JAMES BAILEY (1816–1902)

I believe in the incomprehensibility of God.
— HONORÉ DE BALZAC (1799–1850)

To me, faith means not worrying.
— JOHN DEWEY (1859–1952)

Faith is not belief. Belief is passive. Faith is active. It is vision which passes inevitably into action.
— EDITH HAMILTON (1867–1963) *Witness to the Truth*

Faith may be defined briefly as an illogical belief in the occurrence of the improbable.
— H. L. MENCKEN (1880–1956) *Prejudices*, Series iii

Faith is like love; it cannot be forced.
— ARTHUR SCHOPENHAUER (1788–1860)

Faith is the antiseptic of the soul.
— WALT WHITMAN (1819–1892) *Leaves of Grass*, preface

We walk by faith, not by sight.
— NEW TESTAMENT: *II Corinthians*, v, 7

If ye have faith as a grain of mustard seed, ye shall say unto this mountain, Remove hence to yonder place; and it shall remove: and nothing shall be impossible unto you.
— NEW TESTAMENT: *Matthew*, xvii, 20

FALL See AUTUMN

FAMILY See MARRIAGE, FATHER.

FATE

Nor sitting at his hearth at home doth man escape his appointed doom.
— AESCHYLUS (525–456 B.C.) *The Choephorae*

Destiny is not a matter of chance, it is a matter of choice; it is not a thing to be waited for, it is a thing to be achieved.
— WILLIAM JENNINGS BRYAN (1860–1925) Speech, 1899

'Tis fate that flings the dice, and as she flings
Of kings makes peasants, and of peasants kings.
— JOHN DRYDEN (1631–1700) *Jupiter Cannot Alter the Decrees of Fate*

The moving finger writes; and having writ
Moves on; nor all your Piety nor Wit
Shall lure it back to cancel half a Line.
— EDWARD FITZGERALD (1809–1883) tr.: *Rubáiyát of Omar Khayyám*

Man supposes that he directs his life and governs his actions, when his existence is irretrievably under the control of destiny.
— GOETHE (1749–1832)

That which God writes on thy forehead, thou wilt come to it.
— THE KORAN

Our hour is marked, and no one can claim a moment of life beyond what fate has predestined.
— NAPOLEON BONAPARTE (1811–1884)

This generation of Americans has a rendezvous with destiny.
— FRANKLIN D. ROOSEVELT (1882–1945) Address, 1936

Fate leads the willing, and drags along those who hang back.
— SENECA (4? B.C.–A.D. 65)

There is a divinity that shapes our ends,
Rough-hew them how we will.
— SHAKESPEARE (1564–1616) *Hamlet*, V, ii, 10

All things come alike to all: there is one event to the righteous, and to the wicked; to the good and to the clean, and to the unclean . . . .
— OLD TESTAMENT: *Ecclesiastes*, ix, 2

FATHER

Diogenes struck the father when the son swore.
— ROBERT BURTON (1577–1640) *Anatomy of Melancholy*

He that has his father for judge goes safe to the trial.
— CERVANTES (1547–1616) *Don Quixote*

One father is more than a hundred schoolmasters.
— GEORGE HERBERT (1593–1633) *Jacula Prudentum*

If a man strike his father his hand shall be cut off.
— *The Code of Hammurabi*

It is a wise father that knows his own child.
— SHAKESPEARE (1564–1616) *Merchant of Venice*, II, ii, 80

A wise son maketh a glad father.
— OLD TESTAMENT: *Proverbs*, x, i

He that honoureth his father shall have a long life.
— APOCRYPHA: *Ecclesiasticus*, iii, 6

FAULTS

What an absurd thing it is to pass over all the valuable parts of a man, and fix our attention on his infirmities.
— JOSEPH ADDISON (1672–1719)

The greatest of faults, I should say, is to be conscious of none.
— THOMAS CARLYLE (1795–1881) *Heroes and Hero-Worship*

Men ought to be most annoyed by the sufferings which come from their own faults.
— CICERO (106–43 B.C.) *Epistolae ad Fratrem*

The defects of great men are the consolation of dunces.
— ISAAC D'ISRAELI (1766–1848)

All his faults were such that one loved him still the better for them.
— OLIVER GOLDSMITH (1730–1774) *The Good-Natur'd Man*

A fault confessed is more than half amended.
— SIR JOHN HARINGTON (1561–1612)

If we had no faults, we should not take so much pleasure in remarking them in others.
— FRANÇOIS DE LA ROCHEFOUCAULD (1613–1680) *Maxims*

He who loves not the loved one's faults does not truly love.
— SPANISH PROVERB

The fault, dear Brutus, is not in our stars,
But in ourselves, that we are underlings.
— SHAKESPEARE (1564–1616) *Julius Caesar*, I, ii, 140

FEAR

No one loves the man whom he fears.
— ARISTOTLE (384–322 B.C.)

We listen'd and look'd sideways up!
Fear at my heart, as at a cup,
My life-blood seem'd to sip.
— SAMUEL TAYLOR COLERIDGE (1772–1834) *Ancient Mariner*

Fear always springs from ignorance.
— RALPH WALDO EMERSON (1803–1882) *The American Scholar*

Fear is the parent of cruelty.
— JAMES ANTHONY FROUDE (1818–1894)

Many may not love us, but all shall fear us.
— HEINRICH HIMMLER (1900–1945)

Let us never negotiate out of fear. But let us never fear to negotiate.
— JOHN F. KENNEDY (1917–1963), Inaugural Address, 1961

Apprehensions are greater in proportion as things are unknown.
— LIVY (B.C. 59–A.D. 17) *Annales*

Fear is a feeling that is stronger than love.
— PLINY THE YOUNGER (62–113) *Letters*

The only thing we have to fear is fear itself.
— FRANKLIN D. ROOSEVELT (1882–1945) Inaugural Address, 1933

His flight was madness; when our actions do not,
Our fears do make us traitors.
— SHAKESPEARE (1564–1616) *Macbeth*, IV, ii, 3

To him who is in fear everything rustles.
— SOPHOCLES (495–406 B.C.)

Fear, like pain, looks and sounds worse than it feels.
— REBECCA WEST (1892–   )

FEBRUARY See MONTHS

FIDELITY AND INFIDELITY

Give me a man that is capable of a devotion to anything, rather than a cold, calculating average of all the virtues.
— BRET HARTE (1838–1902) *Two Men of Sandy Bar*

The fidelity of most men is merely an invention of self-love to win confidence . . . .
— FRANÇOIS DE LA ROCHEFOUCAULD (1613–1680) *Maxims*

Fidelity bought with money is overcome by money.
— SENECA (4? B.C.–A.D. 65) *Agamemnon*

Oh, where is loyalty?
If it be banish'd from the frosty head,
Where shall it find a harbour in the earth?
— SHAKESPEARE (1564–1616) *II Henry IV*, V, i, 166

To God, thy countrie, and thy friend be true.
— HENRY VAUGHAN (1622–1695) *Rules and Lessons*

Be thou faithful unto death.
— NEW TESTAMENT: *Revelation*, ii, 10

FLATTERY

A flatterer is a friend who is your inferior or pretends to be so.
— ARISTOTLE (384–322 B.C.) *Nicomachean Ethics*

We sometimes think that we hate flattery, but we only hate the manner in which it is done.
— FRANÇOIS DE LA ROCHEFOUCAULD (1613–1680) *Maxims*

'Tis hard to find a man of great estate,
That can distinguish flatterers from friends.
— HORACE (65–8 B.C.)

When flatterers meet, the Devil goes to dinner.
— JOHN RAY (1627?–1705) *English Proverbs*

But when I tell him he hates flatterers,
He says he does, being then most flattered.
— SHAKESPEARE (1564–1616) *Julius Caesar*, II, i, 208

They do abuse the king that flatter him:
For flattery is the bellows blows up sin.
— SHAKESPEARE (1564–1616) *Pericles*, I, ii, 38

A flattering mouth worketh ruin.
— OLD TESTAMENT: *Proverbs*, xxvi, 28

FLOWERS See GARDEN

FOLLY AND FOOLS

The folly of one man is the fortune of another.
— FRANCIS BACON (1561–1620) *Essays: Of Fortune*

A sucker is born every minute.
— P. T. BARNUM (1810–1891)

The hours of folly are measur'd by the clock; but of wisdom, no clock can measure.
— WILLIAM BLAKE (1757–1827) *Marriage of Heaven and Hell*

A fool always finds one still more foolish to admire him.
— NICOLAS BOILEAU (1636–1711) *The Poetic Art*

And fools cannot hold their tongue.
— GEOFFREY CHAUCER (1340?–1400) *Romaunt of the Rose*

The first degree of folly is to conceit one's self wise; the second to profess it; the third to despise counsel.
— BEN FRANKLIN (1706–1790) *Poor Richard's Almanack*

When lovely woman stoops to folly,
And finds too late that men betray,
What charm can soothe her melancholy?
What art can wash her guilt away?
— OLIVER GOLDSMITH (1730–1774) *Vicar of Wakefield*

I am always afraid of a fool. One cannot be sure that he is not a knave as well.
— WILLIAM HAZLITT (1778–1830) *Characteristics*

Folly pursues us in every period of life. If any one appears wise, it is only because his follies are proportioned to his age and fortune.
— FRANÇOIS DE LA ROCHEFOUCAULD (1613–1680) *Maxims*

There is no fool like an old fool.
— JOHN LYLY (1554?–1606)

I enjoy vast delight in the folly of mankind; and, God be praised, that is an inexhaustible source of entertainment.
— LADY MARY WORTLY MONTAGU (1689–1762) *Letter*

Fools rush in where angels fear to tread.
— ALEXANDER POPE (1688–1744) *An Essay on Criticism*

If every fool wore a crown, we'd all be kings.
— WELSH PROVERB

The fool doth think he is wise, but the wise man knows himself to be a fool.
— SHAKESPEARE (1564–1616) *As You Like It*, V, i, 34

Give me the young man who has brains enough to make a fool of himself.
— R. L. STEVENSON (1850–1894) *Virginibus Puerisque*

A fool and his money are soon parted.
— UNKNOWN

The best way to silence any friend of yours whom you know to be a fool is to induce him to hire a hall.
— WOODROW WILSON (1856–1924) *Speech, 1916*

The wise man's eyes are in his head, but the fool walketh in darkness.
— OLD TESTAMENT: *Ecclesiastes*, ii, 14

FORGETFULNESS

A man must get a thing before he can forget it.
— OLIVER WENDELL HOLMES (1809–1894) *Medical Essays*

Blessed are the forgetful; for they get the better of even their blunders.
— FRIEDRICK NIETZSCHE (1844–1900) *Beyond Good and Evil*

We have all forgotten more than we remember.
— PROVERB

  We bury love,
Forgetfulness grows over it like grass;
That is a thing to weep for, not the dead.
— ALEXANDER SMITH (1830–1867) *City Poems*

If I forget thee, O Jerusalem, let my right hand forget her cunning.
— OLD TESTAMENT: *Psalms*, cxxxvii, 5

FORESIGHT See PRUDENCE

FORGIVENESS

You may pardon much to others, nothing to yourself.
— AUSONIUS (*f.* 4th C. A.D.) *Epigrams*

Those who forgive most shall be most forgiven.
— PHILIP JAMES BAILEY (1816–1902) *Festus*

He who forgives readily only invites offense.
— PIERRE CORNEILLE (1606–1684) *Cinna*

God may forgive you, but I never can.
— QUEEN ELIZABETH I (1533–1603) to the Countess of Nottingham

It is often easier to forgive those who have wronged us than those whom we have wronged.
— OSCAR HAMMLING (1890–   ) *Laconics*

Know all and you will pardon all.
— THOMAS À KEMPIS (1380–1471) *Imitation of Christ*

We pardon in proportion as we love.
— FRANÇOIS DE LA ROCHEFOUCAULD (1613–1680) *Maxims*

We read that we ought to forgive our enemies; but we do not read that we ought to forgive our friends.
— COSIMO DE' MEDICI (1519–1574)

If the injured one could read your heart, you may be sure he would understand and pardon.
— R. L. STEVENSON (1850–1894) *Truth of Intercourse*

There is nothing so advantageous to a man than a forgiving disposition.
— TERENCE (*c.* 190–150 B.C.) *Adelphi*

Father, forgive them; for they know not what they do.
— NEW TESTAMENT: *Luke*, xxiii, 34

A woman may consent to forget and forgive, but she never will drop the habit of referring to the matter now and then.
— UNKNOWN

FORTUNE

Fortune is a god and rules men's lives.
— AESCHYLUS (525–456 B.C.) *The Choephorae*

Every man is the architect of his own fortune.
— APPIUS CLAUDIUS (*f.* 312 B.C.)

All fortune is to be conquered by bearing it.
— FRANCIS BACON (1561–1620) *Advancement of Learning*

I am not now in fortune's power;
He that is down can fall no lower.
— SAMUEL BUTLER (1612–1680) *Hudibras*

Fortune hath somewhat the nature of a woman; if she be too much wooed, she is the farther off.
— EMPEROR CHARLES V (1500–1588)

It is fortune, not wisdom, that rules man's life.
— CICERO (106–43 B.C.)

Ill fortune seldom comes alone.
— JOHN DRYDEN (1631–1700) *Cymon and Iphigenia*, Act I

Fortune never seems so blind as to those upon whom she confers no favors.
— FRANÇOIS DE LA ROCHEFOUCAULD (1613–1680) *Maxims*

Not many men have both good fortune and good sense.
— LIVY (59 B.C.–A.D. 17) *History of Rome*

The wheel goes round and round
And some are up and some are on the down
And still the wheel goes round.
— JOSEPHINE POLLARD (1843–1892) *Wheel of Fortune*

Fortune can take from us nothing but what she gave us.
— PUBLILIUS SYRUS (1st C. B.C.) *Sententiae*

Fear of the future is worse than one's present fortune.
— QUINTILIAN (40 –*c.* 100)

Everyone is the architect of his own fortune.
— ABBÉ REGNIER (1794–?) *Satire*

Fortune, that arrant whore
Ne'er turns the key to the poor.
— SHAKESPEARE (1564–1616) *King Lear*, II, iv, 52

FREEDOM

The cause of freedom is the cause of God.
— WILLIAM LISLE BOWLES (1762–1850) To EDMUND BURKE

A man can be free even within prison walls. Freedom is
something spiritual. Whoever has once had it, can never
lose it. There are some people who are never free outside a
prison.
— BERTOLD BRECHT (1898–1956) *A Penny for the Poor*

Hereditary bondsmen! Know ye not
Who would be free themselves must strike the blow?
— LORD BYRON (1788–1824) *Childe Harold*

Perfect freedom is reserved for the man who lives by his own
work and in that work does what he wants to do.
— ROBIN GEORGE COLLINGWOOD (1889–1943) *Speculum
Mentis*

I am as free as nature first made man.
Ere the base laws of servitude began,
When wild in woods the noble savage ran.
— JOHN DRYDEN (1631–1700) *Conquest of Granada*

Freedom from fear and injustice and oppression will be ours
only in the measure that men who value such freedom are
ready to sustain its possession—to defend it against every
thrust from within or without.
— DWIGHT D. EISENHOWER (1890–1969) *Crusade in Europe*

No man is free who is not master of himself.
— EPICTETUS (1st C. A.D.) *Discourses*

No man is wholly free. He is a slave to wealth, or to fortune,
or the laws, or the people restrain him from acting according
to his will alone.
— EURIPIDES (480–406 B.C.) *Hecuba*

The right to personal freedom comes second in importance to
the duty of maintaining the race.
— ADOLF HITLER (1889–1945) *Mein Kampf*

Who then is free? the wise man who is lord over himself;
Whom neither poverty nor death, nor chains alarm, strong
to withstand his passions and despise honors, and who is
completely finished and founded off in himself.
— HORACE (65–8 B.C.) *Satires*

Every man has a right to utter what he thinks truth, and
every other man has a right to knock him down for it.
— SAMUEL JOHNSON (1709–1784) in Boswell's *Life*

The most unfree souls go west and shout of freedom. Men
are freest when they are most unconscious of freedom. The
shout is a rattling of chains.
— D. H. LAWRENCE (1885–1930) *Studies in Classic American
Literature*

Those who deny freedom to others deserve it not for themselves, and, under a just God cannot long retain it.
— ABRAHAM LINCOLN (1809–1865) Letter, 1859

If I have freedom in my love,
And in my soul am free,
Angels alone, that soar above,
Enjoy such liberty.
— RICHARD LOVELACE (1618–1658) *To Althea from Prison*

There is only one cure for the evils which newly acquired
freedom produces, and that is more freedom.
— THOMAS MACAULAY (1800–1859) *Essay on Milton*

In the modern social order, the *person* is sacrificed to the
individual. The individual is given universal suffrage, equality of rights, freedom of opinion; while the person, isolated,
naked, with no social armor to sustain and protect him, is
left to the mercy of all the devouring forces which threaten
the life of the soul . . . .
— JACQUES MARITAIN (1882–1973) *Three Reformers*

Oh, Lord, I want to be free, want to be free;
Rainbow round my shoulder, wings on my feet.
— UNKNOWN, American Negro Spiritual

Is any man free except the one who can pass his life as he
pleases?
— PERSIUS (34–62) *Satires*

The people who settled in New England came here for religious freedom, but religious freedom to them meant freedom
only for their kind of religion . . . . This attitude seems to be
our attitude in many situations today.
— ELEANOR ROOSEVELT (1884–1962)

Man is born free—and everywhere he is in irons.
— JEAN JACQUES ROUSSEAU (1712–1778) *Social Contract*

No one can be perfectly free till all are free.
— HERBERT SPENCER (1820–1903) *Social Statics*

There are times in the lives of all people when freedom is
the twin of duty, sacrifice the companion of happiness, and
when courage—parent of fortitude, endurance, determination
—is the first virtue.
— DOROTHY THOMPSON (1894–1961) *On the Record*

I would rather sit on a pumpkin and have it all to myself,
than to be crowded on a velvet cushion.
— HENRY DAVID THOREAU (1817–1862) *Walden*

I disapprove of what you say, but I will defend to the death
your right to say it.
— Attributed to VOLTAIRE by a later biographer

Freedom exists only where the people take care of the government.
— WOODROW WILSON (1856–1924) Speech, 1912

FRIENDS

One friend in a lifetime is much; two are many; three are
hardly possible. Friendship needs a certain parallelism of
life, a community of thought, a rivalry of aim.
— HENRY ADAMS (1838–1918) *Education of Henry Adams*

Beast knows beast; birds of a feather flock together.
— ARISTOTLE (384–322 B.C.) *Rhetoric*

Thy friendship oft has made my heart to ache:
Do be my enemy—for friendship's sake.
— WILLIAM BLAKE (1757–1827) *To H.*

Friendships multiply joys and divide griefs.
— HENRY GEORGE BOHN (1796–1884) *Handbook of Proverbs*

I have loved my friends as I do virtue, my soul, my God.
— SIR THOMAS BROWNE (1605–1682) *Religio Medici*

Tell me what company thou keepest, and I'll tell thee what
thou art.
— CERVANTES (1547–1616) *Don Quixote*

Endeavor, as much as you can, to keep company with people
above you.
— LORD CHESTERFIELD (1694–1773) *Letters*

Never injure a friend, even in jest.
— CICERO (106–43 B.C.) *De Amicitia*

Friendship often ends in love; but love in friendship, never.
— CHARLES C. COLTON (1780?–1832) *Lacon*

Chance makes our parents, but choice makes our friends.
— JACQUES DELILLE (1738–1813) *Pitié*

Animals are such agreeable friends—they ask no questions,
they pass no criticisms.
— GEORGE ELIOT (1819–1880)

The dearest friends are separated by impassable gulfs.
— RALPH WALDO EMERSON (1803–1882) *Essays*

The only way to have a friend is to be one.
— RALPH WALDO EMERSON (1803–1882) *Essays*

Men who know the same things are not long the best company for each other.
— RALPH WALDO EMERSON (1803–1882)

In prosperity it is very easy to find a friend; in adversity, nothing is so difficult.
— EPICTETUS (1st C. A.D.) *Encheiridion*

Real friends are our greatest joy and our greatest sorrow. It were almost to be wished that all true and faithful friends should expire on the same day.
— FÉNELON (1651–1715)

If you have one true friend you have more than your share.
— THOMAS FULLER (1608–1681) *Gnomologia*

There is no better looking-glass than an old friend.
— THOMAS FULLER (1608–1681) *Gnomologia*

'Tis thus that on the choice of friends
Our good or evil name depends.
— JOHN GAY (1688–1732) *Old Woman and Her Cats*

There is no desert like being friendless.
— BALTASAR GRACIÁN (1601–1658)

To have a great man for an intimate friend seems pleasant to those who have never tried it; those who have, fear it.
— HORACE (65–8 B.C.) *Epistulae*

I never considered a difference of opinion in politics, in religion, in philosophy, as cause for withdrawing from a friend.
— THOMAS JEFFERSON (1743–1826) Letter, 1800

An injured friend is the bitterest of foes.
— THOMAS JEFFERSON (1743–1826)

I find as I grow older that I love those most whom I loved first.
— THOMAS JEFFERSON (1743–1826) Letter, 1787

I live in the crowds of jollity, not so much to enjoy company as to shun myself.
— SAMUEL JOHNSON (1709–1784) *Rasselas*

If my friends are one-eyed, I look at them in profile.
— JOSEPH JOUBERT (1754–1824) *Pensées*

In friendship, as in love, we are often more happy from the things we are ignorant of than from those we are acquainted with.
— FRANÇOIS DE LA ROCHEFOUCAULD (1613–1680) *Maxims*

If you want to make a dangerous man your friend, let him do you a favor.
— LEWIS E. LAWES (1883–1947)

The vulgar estimate friends by the advantage to be derived from them.
— OVID (43 B.C.–A.D. 18?)

It is better to be alone than in ill company.
— GEORGE PETTIE (1548–1589)

Histories are more full of examples of the fidelity of dogs than of friends.
— ALEXANDER POPE (1688–1744) Letter, 1709

A friend in need is a friend indeed.
— ENGLISH PROVERB

It is fun to be in the same decade with you.
— FRANKLIN D. ROOSEVELT (1882–1945) in a cable to WINSTON CHURCHILL

He that goeth to bed with dogs ariseth with fleas.
— JAMES SANDFORD (*f.* 1572) *Hours of Recreation*

The principal task of friendship is to foster one's friends' illusions.
— ARTHUR SCHNITZLER (1862–1931) *Anatole*

Friendship always benefits; love sometimes injures.
— SENECA (4? B.C.–A.D. 65) *Epistulae ad Lucilium*

To lose a friend is the greatest of all evils, but endeavour rather to rejoice that you possessed him than to mourn his loss.
— SENECA (4? B.C.–A.D. 65) *Epistulae ad Lucilium*

Keep thy friend under thine own life's key.
— SHAKESPEARE (1564–1616) *All's Well that Ends Well*, I, i, 74

Those friends thou hast, and their adoption tried,
Grapple them to thy soul with hoops of steel;
But do not dull thy palm with entertainment
Of each new-hatch'd, unfledg'd comrade.
— SHAKESPEARE (1564–1616) *Hamlet*, I, iii, 59

　　To wail friends lost
Is not by much so wholesome—profitable,
As to rejoice at friends but newly found.
— SHAKESPEARE (1564–1616) *Love's Labour Lost*, V, ii, 759

I am not of that feather to shake off
My friend when he must need me.
— SHAKESPEARE (1564–1616) *Timon of Athens*, I, i, 100

The most I can do for my friend is simply to be his friend.
— HENRY DAVID THOREAU (1817–1862) *Journal*, 1841

God save me from my friends. I can protect myself from my enemies.
— MARSHAL DE VILLARS (1653–1734)

Friendship's the wine of life.
— EDWARD YOUNG (1683–1765) *Night Thoughts*

A faithful friend is a strong defense: and he that hath found such an one hath found a treasure.
— APOCRYPHA: *Ecclesiasticus*, vi, 14

Greater love hath no man than this, that a man lay down his life for his friends.
— NEW TESTAMENT: *John*, xv, 13

Saul and Jonathan were lovely and pleasant in their lives, and in their death they were not divided.
— OLD TESTAMENT: *II Samuel*, i, 23

A friend is one who dislikes the same people that you dislike.
— UNKNOWN

FUTURE

We are always doing something for Posterity, but I would fain see Posterity do something for us.
— JOSEPH ADDISON (1672–1719) *The Spectator*

You can never plan the future by the past.
— EDMUND BURKE (1729–1797) Letter

For my part, I think that a knowledge of the future would be a disadvantage.
— CICERO (106–43 B.C.) *De Devinatione*

I never think of the future. It comes soon enough.
— ALBERT EINSTEIN (1879–1955)

The future is a convenient place for dreams.
— ANATOLE FRANCE (1844–1924)

I know of no way of judging the future but by the past.
— PATRICK HENRY (1736–1799) Speech, 1775

Trust no future, howe'er pleasant!
Let the dead Past bury its dead!
— HENRY W. LONGFELLOW (1801–1882) *Psalm of Life*

The mind that is anxious about the future is miserable.
— SENECA (4? B.C.–A.D. 65) *Epistulae ad Lucilium*

We know what we are, but know not what we may be.
— SHAKESPEARE (1564–1616) *Hamlet*, IV, v, 43

Take no thought for the morrow: for the morrow shall take thought for the things of itself.
— NEW TESTAMENT: *Matthew*, vi, 34

GARDEN AND FLOWERS

Who loves a garden still his Eden keeps . . . .
— AMOS BRONSON ALCOTT (1799–1888)

Ah, Sunflower, weary of time,
Who countest the steps of the sun;
Seeking after that sweet golden clime,
Where the traveller's journey is done . . . .
— WILLIAM BLAKE (1757–1827) *The Sunflower*

God the first garden made, and the first city Cain.
— ABRAHAM COWLEY (1618–1667) *The Garden*

Loveliest of trees, the cherry now
Is hung with bloom along the bough,
And stands about the woodland ride
Wearing white for Eastertide.
— A. E. HOUSMAN (1859–1936)

Your sacred plants, if here below,
Only among the plants will grow.
Society is all but rude,
To this delicious solitude.
— ANDREW MARVELL (1621–1678) *The Garden*

Many things grow in the garden that were never sowed there.
— PROVERB

Lilies that fester smell far worse than weeds.
— SHAKESPEARE (1564–1616) *Sonnets*, xciv

Consider the lilies of the field, how they grow; they toil not, neither do they spin: And yet I say unto you, that even Solomon in all his glory was not arrayed like one of these.
— NEW TESTAMENT: *Matthew*, vi, 28

The Lord God planted a garden eastward in Eden; and there He put the man whom He had formed.
— OLD TESTAMENT: *Genesis*, ii, 8

GENEROSITY See GIFTS AND GIVING

GENIUS

Doing easily what others find difficult is talent; doing what is impossible for talent is genius.
— HENRI-FREDERIC AMIEL (1828–1881) *Journal*

Genius is mainly an affair of energy.
— MATTHEW ARNOLD (1822–1888) *Essays in Criticism*

I have known no man of genius who had not to pay, in some affliction or defect either physical or spiritual, for what the gods had given him.
— MAX BEERBOHM (1872–1956) *The Pines*

Patience is a necessary ingredient of genius.
— BENJAMIN DISRAELI (1805–1881) *Contarini Fleming*

Genius is one percent inspiration and ninety-nine percent perspiration.
— THOMAS E. EDISON (1847–1931) Newspaper interview

Every man of genius sees the world at a different angle from his fellows, and there is his tragedy.
— HAVELOCK ELLIS (1859–1939) *Dance of Life*

Genius is the power of lighting one's own fire.
— JOHN FOSTER (1770–1843)

A man of genius makes no mistakes. His errors are volitional and are the portals of discovery.
— JAMES JOYCE (1882–1941) *Ulysses*

Gift, like genius, I often think only means an infinite capacity for taking pains.
— JANE ELLICE HOPKINS (1836–1904)

Genius is a promontory jutting out into the infinite.
— VICTOR HUGO (1802–1885) *William Shakespeare*

Genius begets great works; labor alone finished them.
— JOSEPH JOUBERT (1754–1824) *Pensées*

One science only will one genius fit;
So vast is art, so narrow human wit.
— ALEXANDER POPE (1668–1744) *Essay on Criticism*

The poets' scrolls will outlive the monuments of stone.
Genius survives; all else is claimed by death.
— EDMUND SPENSER (1552?–1599) *Shepherd's Calendar*

There is a certain characteristic common to all those whom we call geniuses. Each of them has a consciousness of being a man apart.
— MIGUEL DE UNAMUNO (1864–1936) *Essays and Soliloquies*

GIFTS AND GIVING

It is easy to become generous with other people's property.
— LATIN PROVERB

The most important thing in any relationship is not what you get but what you give. . . . In any case, the giving of love is an education in itself.
— ELEANOR ROOSEVELT (1884–1963)

You must be fit to give before you can be fit to receive.
— JAMES STEPHENS (1882–1950)

I fear the Greeks, even when they bring gifts.
— VERGIL (70–19 B.C.) *Aeneid*

It is more blessed to give than to receive.
— NEW TESTAMENT: *Acts*, xx, 35

Or what man is there of you, whom if his son ask bread, will he give him a stone?
— NEW TESTAMENT: *Matthew*, vii, 9

GIRL See CHILDREN

GOD

God's mouth knows not to utter falsehood, but he will perform each word.
— AESCHYLUS (525–456 B.C.) *Prometheus*

Nature herself has imprinted on the minds of all the idea of God.
— CICERO (106–43 B.C.) *De Natura Deorum*

Earth with her thousand voices, praises God
— SAMUEL TAYLOR COLERIDGE (1772–1834)

God moves in a mysterious way
His wonders to perform.
— WILLIAM COWPER (1731–1800) *Light Shining out of Darkness*

Father expected a great deal of God. He didn't actually accuse God of inefficiency, but when he prayed his tone was loud and angry, like that of a disatisfied guest in a carelessly managed hotel.
— CLARENCE DAY (1874–1935) *God and My Father*

God tempers the cold to the shorn lamb.
— HENRI ESTIENNE (*d.* 1520) *Premises*

There is no God but God.
— THE KORAN, Bk. iii

I live and love in God's peculiar light.
— MICHELANGELO (1475–1564)

God never shuts one door but he opens another.
— IRISH PROVERB

Had I but served my God with half the zeal
I served my king, he would not in mine age
Have left me naked to mine enemies.
— SHAKESPEARE (1564–1616) *Henry VIII*, III, ii, 456

Man proposes, but God disposes.
— THOMAS À KEMPIS (1380–1471) *Imitation of Christ*

If God didn't exist, man would have to invent Him.
— VOLTAIRE (1694–1778)

If God be for us, who can be against us?
— NEW TESTAMENT: *Romans*, viii, 31

God is our refuge and our strength, a very present help in trouble.
— OLD TESTAMENT: *Psalms*, xlvi, i

The heavens declare the glory of God; and the firmament showeth his handiwork.
— OLD TESTAMENT: *Psalms*, xix, i

GOODNESS

Goodness is easier to recognize than to define; only the greatest novelists can portray good people.
— W. H. AUDEN (1907–1973) *I Believe*

It is as hard for the good to suspect evil, as it is for the bad to suspect good.
— CICERO (106–43 B.C.)

Good and bad men are each less so than they seem.
— SAMUEL TAYLOR COLERIDGE (1772–1834) *Table-Talk*

True goodness springs from a man's own heart. All men are born good.
— CONFUCIUS (c. 551–479 B.C.) *Analects*

The ground that a good man treads is hallowed.
— GOETHE (1749–1832) *Torquato Tasso*

Let them be good that love me, though but few.
— BEN JONSON (1572–1637) *Cynthia's Revels*

The greatest pleasure I know is to do a good action by stealth, and to have it found out by accident.
— CHARLES LAMB (1775–1834)

There is no man so good, who, were he to submit all his thoughts and actions to the laws, would not deserve hanging ten times in his life.
— MICHEL DE MONTAIGNE (1533–1592) *Essays*

Goodness is a special kind of truth and beauty. It is truth and beauty in human behavior.
— HARRY ALLEN OVERSTREET (1895–1970)

The good die young.
— ENGLISH PROVERB

He is so good that he is good for nothing.
— ITALIAN PROVERB

The evil that men do lives after them;
The good is oft interred with their bones.
— SHAKESPEARE (1564–1616) *Julius Caesar*, III, ii, 81

The good man is his own friend.
— SOPHOCLES (495–406 B.C.) *Oedipus Coloneus*

Be good, and you will be lonesome.
— MARK TWAIN (1835–1910)

GOVERNMENT

The marvel of history is the patience with which men and women submit to burdens unnecessarily laid upon them by their governments.
— WILLIAM E. BORAH (1865–1940) Speech in U.S. Senate

And having looked to Government for bread, on the very first scarcity they will turn and bite the hand that fed them.
— EDMUND BURKE (1729–1797)

A thousand years scarce serve to form a state;
An hour may lay it in the dust.
— LORD BYRON (1788–1824) *Childe Harold*

Self-government is the natural government of man.
— HENRY CLAY (1777–1852) Speech, 1818

No man has any right to rule who is not better than the people over whom he rules.
— CYRUS THE ELDER (600?–529 B.C.)

I can retain neither respect nor affection for a Government which has been moving from wrong to wrong in order to defend its immorality.
— MOHANDAS K. GANDHI (1869–1948)

The spirit of resistance to government is so valuable on certain occasions that I wish it to be always kept alive.
— THOMAS JEFFERSON (1743–1826) to Abigail Adams

No man is good enough to govern another man without that other's consent.
— ABRAHAM LINCOLN (1809–1865) Speech, 1854

That is the best government which desires to make the people happy, and knows how to make them happy.
— THOMAS B. MACAULAY (1800–1859)

If men be good, government cannot be bad.
— WILLIAM PENN (1644–1718) *Fruits of Solitude*

Oligarchy: A government resting on a valuation of property, in which the rich have power and the poor man is deprived of it.
— PLATO (428–347 B.C.) *The Republic*

That form of government is best which includes monarchy, aristocracy, and democracy.
— POLYBIUS (205?–125 B.C.) *Histories*

Any government, like any family, can for a year spend a little more than it earns. But you and I know that a continuance of that habit means the poorhouse.
— FRANKLIN D. ROOSEVELT (1882–1945) Radio Speech, 1932

GRATITUDE AND INGRATITUDE

Gratitude is the sign of noble souls.
— AESOP (6th C. B.C.) *Androcles*

Earth produces nothing worse than an ungrateful man.
— AUSONIUS (*f.* 4th C. B.C.) *Epigrams*

Next to ingratitude, the most painful thing to bear is gratitude.
— HENRY WARD BEECHER (1813–1887)

Words are but empty thanks.
— COLLEY CIBBER (1671–1757) *Women's Wit*

When I'm not thanked at all I'm thanked enough.
— HENRY FIELDING (1707–1754)

A man is very apt to complain of the ingratitude of those who have risen far above him.
— SAMUEL JOHNSON (1709–1784) in Boswell's *Life*

A man who is ungrateful is often less to blame than his benefactor.
— FRANÇOIS DE LA ROCHEFOUCAULD (1613–1680) *Maxims*

The gratitude of most men is but a secret desire of receiving greater benefits.
— FRANÇOIS DE LA ROCHEFOUCAULD (1613–1680) *Maxims*

Gratitude is the least of virtues, but ingratitude the worst of vices.
— PROVERB

Blow, blow, thou winter wind,
Thou art not so unkind
As man's ingratitude ....
— SHAKESPEARE (1564–1616) *As You Like It*, II, vii, 174

How sharper than a serpent's tooth it is
To have a thankless child.
— SHAKESPEARE (1564–1616) *King Lear*, I, iv, 312

Do you like gratitude? I don't. If pity is akin to love, gratitude is akin to the other thing.
— GEORGE BERNARD SHAW (1856–1950) *Arms and the Man*

Alas! the gratitude of men
Hath often left me mourning.
— WILLIAM WORDSWORTH (1770–1850) *Simon Lee*

GREATNESS

When the dust of death has choked
A great man's voice, the common words he said
Turn oracles.
— ELIZABETH BARRETT BROWNING (1812–1861)

The price of greatness is responsibility.
— WINSTON CHURCHILL (1874–1965) Speech, 1943

The world cannot live at the level of its great men.
— SIR JAMES FRAZER (1854–1941) The Golden Bough

No really great man ever thought himself so.
— WILLIAM HAZLITT (1778–1830) Table Talk

There would be no great ones if there were no little ones.
— GEORGE HERBERT (1593–1633)

Be not afraid of greatness. Some are born great, some achieve greatness, and some have greatness thrust upon them.
— SHAKESPEARE (1564–1616) Twelfth Night, II, v, 156

Great men are not always wise.
— OLD TESTAMENT: Job, xxxii, 9

GREED See AVARICE

GRIEF

It is dangerous to abandon one's self to the luxury of grief: it deprives one of courage, and even of the wish for recovery.
— HENRI-FREDERIC AMIEL (1828–1881) Journal, 1871

There is no grief which time does not lessen and soften.
— CICERO (106–43 B.C.) Epistles

Grief is itself a medicine.
— WILLIAM COWPER (1731–1800) Charity

Grief is the agony of an instant: the indulgence of grief the blunder of a life.
— BENJAMIN DISRAELI (1804–1881) Vivian Grey

The only cure for grief is action.
— GEORGE HENRY LEWES (1817–1878)

If our inward griefs were seen written on our brow, how many would be pitied who are now envied.
— METASTASIO (1698–1782) Guiseppe Riconosciuto

Grief is a tree that has tears for its fruit.
— PHILEMON (361?–263? B.C.) Fragment

Grief fills the room up of my absent child,
Lies in his bed, walks up and down with me,
Puts on his pretty looks, repeats his words,
Remembers me of all his gracious parts,
Stuffs out his vacant garments with his form.
— SHAKESPEARE (1564–1616) King John, III, iv, 93

GUILT

The pot calls the kettle black.
— CERVANTES (1547–1616) Don Quixote

Guilt is present in the very hesitation, even though the deed be not committed.
— CICERO (106–43 B.C.) De Officiis

Secret guilt by silence is betrayed.
— JOHN DRYDEN (1631–1700) The Hind and the Panther

Men's minds are too ready to excuse guilt in themselves.
— LIVY (59 B.C.–A.D. 17) History

He that knows no guilt can know no fear.
— PHILIP MASSINGER (1583–1640)

He confesseth himself guilty, who refuseth to come to trial.
— PROVERB

The lady doth protest too much, methinks.
— SHAKESPEARE (1564–1616) Hamlet, III, ii, 242

In other words, psychoanalysts relieve their patients from feeling guilty about things of which they are not guilty, and leave them with the sense of guilt about things of which they really are guilty.
— GREGORY ZILBOORG (1890–1959) Psychoanalysis and Religion

HABIT

Habit is a sort of second nature.
— CICERO (106–43 B.C.) De Finibus

It seems, in fact, as though the second half of a man's life is made up of nothing but the habits he has accumulated during the first half.
— FEODOR DOSTOEVSKI (1821–1881) The Possessed

Habit is a cable; we weave a thread of it every day, and at last we cannot break it.
— HORACE MANN (1796–1859)

How use doth breed a habit in a man!
— SHAKESPEARE (1564–1616) Two Gentlemen of Verona, V, iv, 1

HANDS

Living from hand to mouth, soon satisfi'd.
— GUILLAUME DU BARTAS (1544–1590) Devine Weekes

Many hands make light work.
— PROVERB

One hand washeth the other.
— SENECA (4? B.C.–A.D. 65) Apocolocyntosis

All the perfumes of Arabia will not sweeten this little hand.
— SHAKESPEARE (1564–1616) Macbeth, V, i, 57

See, how she leans her cheek upon her hand!
O, that I were a glove upon that hand,
That I might touch that cheek!
— SHAKESPEARE (1564–1616) Romeo and Juliet, II, ii, 23

Let not thy left hand know what thy right hand doeth.
— NEW TESTAMENT: Matthew, vi, 3

His hand will be against every man and every man's hand against him.
— OLD TESTAMENT: Genesis, xvi, 12

HAPPINESS

Hold him alone truly fortunate who has ended his life in happy well-being.
— AESCHYLUS (525–456 B.C.) Agamemnon

Happiness is at once the best, the noblest and the pleasantest of things.
— ARISTOTLE (384–322 B.C.) Nicomachean Ethics

What is given by the gods more desirable than a happy hour?
— CATULLUS (84?–54 B.C.) Odes

The happiness of life is made up of minute fractions—the little soon forgotten charities of a kiss or smile, a kind look, a heartfelt compliment, and the countless infinitesimals of pleasurable and genial feeling.
— SAMUEL TAYLOR COLERIDGE (1772–1834) Friend

To fill the hour—that is happiness.
— RALPH WALDO EMERSON (1803–1882) Experience

Often the greatest enemy of present happiness is past happiness too well remembered.
— OSCAR HAMMLING (1890–   )

Call no man happy till you know the nature of his death! He is at best but fortunate.
— HERODOTUS (484–424? B.C.)

And there is even a happiness
That makes the heart afraid.
— THOMAS HOOD (1799–1845) Ode to Melancholy

The supreme happiness of life is the conviction that we are loved.
— VICTOR HUGO (1802–1885) *Les Misérables*

He is happiest of whom the world says least, good or bad.
— THOMAS JEFFERSON (1743–1826) Letter to John Adams, 1786

The happiness or unhappiness of men depends no less upon their dispositions than on their fortunes.
— FRANÇOIS DE LA ROCHEFOUCAULD (1613–1680) *Maxims*

Oh, how bitter a thing it is to look into happiness through another man's eyes.
— SHAKESPEARE (1564–1616) *As You Like It*, V, ii, 48

Happiness is the shadow of things past,
Which fools still take for that which is to be!
— FRANCIS THOMPSON (1859–1907) *From the Night of Forebeing*

The sun and stars that float in the open air;
The apple-shaped earth, and we upon it—
          surely the drift of them is something grand!
I do not know what it is, except that it is grand,
          and that it is happiness.
— WALT WHITMAN (1819–1892) *Carol of Occupations*

HATRED

Now hatred is by far the greatest pleasure;
Men love in haste, but they detest at leisure.
— LORD BYRON (1788–1824) *Don Juan*

People hate those who make them feel their own inferiority.
— LORD CHESTERFIELD (1694–1773) *Letters to His Son*

There are glances of hatred that stab and raise no cry of murder.
— GEORGE ELIOT (1819–1880) *Felix Holt*

Whom men fear they hate, and whom they hate, they wish dead.
— QUINTUS ENNIUS (239–169 B.C.) *Thyestes*

How incredible it is that in this fragile existence we should hate and destroy one another. There are possibilities enough for all who will abandon mastery over others to pursue mastery over nature. There is world enough for all to seek their happiness in their own way.
— LYNDON B. JOHNSON (1908–1973) Inaugural Address, Jan. 1965

Men hate more steadily than they love.
— SAMUEL JOHNSON (1709–1784) Boswell's *Life of Johnson*

For never can true reconcilement grow,
Where wounds of deadly hate have pierced so deep.
— JOHN MILTON (1608–1674) *Paradise Lost*

There is no sport in hate when all the rage
Is on one side.
— PERCY B. SHELLEY (1792–1822) *Lines to a Reviewer*

It is characteristic of human nature to hate the man whom you have wronged.
— TACITUS (54–119) *Agricola*

As love, if love be perfect, casts out fear,
So hate, if hate be perfect, casts out fear.
— TENNYSON (1809–1892) *Idylls of the King*

HEALTH

In nothing do men more nearly approach the gods than in giving health to men.
— CICERO (106–43 B.C.) *Pro Ligario*

The health of the people is really the foundation upon which all their happiness and all their powers as a State depend.
— BENJAMIN DISRAELI (1804–1881)

Health is not a condition of matter, but of Mind.
— MARY BAKER G. EDDY (1821–1910) *Science and Health*

O health! health! the blessing of the rich! the riches of the poor! who can buy thee at too dear a rate, since there is no enjoying this world without thee?
— BEN JONSON (1572–1637) *Volpone*

Our prayers should be for a sound mind in a healthy body.
— JUVENAL (47–138) *Satires*

Life is not merely being alive, but being well.
— MARTIAL (c. A.D. 66) *Epigrams*

A man in good health is always full of advice to the sick.
— MENANDER (342–291 B.C.) *Andria*

It is part of the cure to wish to be cured.
— SENECA (8 B.C.–A.D. 65) *Hippolytus*

Measure your health by your sympathy with morning and spring. If there is no response in you to the awakening of nature, if the prospect of an early morning walk does not banish sleep, if the warble of the first bluebird does not thrill you, know that the morning and spring of your life are past, Thus may you feel your pulse.
— HENRY DAVID THOREAU (1817–1862) *Early Spring in Massachusetts*

HEART

My heart's in the Highlands, my heart is not here;
My heart's in the Highlands a-chasing the deer.
— ROBERT BURNS (1759–1796)

Maid of Athens, ere we part,
Give, oh, give me back my heart!
— LORD BYRON (1788–1824) *Maid of Athens*

Faint heart never won fair lady.
— WILLIAM CAMDEN (1551–1623) *Remains Concerning Britain*

The heart has eyes that the brain knows nothing of.
— DR. CHARLES HENRY PARKHURST (1842–1933)

And let me wring your heart; for so I shall,
If it be made of penetrable stuff.
— SHAKESPEARE (1564–1616) *Hamlet*, III, iv, 35

I will wear my heart upon my sleeve
For daws to peck at.
— SHAKESPEARE (1564–1616) *Othello*, I, i, 64

He hath a heart as sound as a bell and his tongue is the clapper, for what his heart thinks his tongue speaks.
— SHAKESPEARE (1564–1616) *Much Ado About Nothing*, III, ii, 12

My heart is a lonely hunter that hunts on a lonely hill.
— WILLIAM SHARP (1856?–1905) *The Lonely Hunter*

My true-love hath my heart, and I have his
By just exchange one for the other given
I hold his dear, and mine he cannot miss
There never was a better bargain driven.
— SIR PHILIP SIDNEY (1554–1586) *The Bargain*

Let not your heart be troubled.
— NEW TESTAMENT: *John*, xiv, 1

HEAT See WEATHER

HEAVEN

All places are distant from heaven alike.
— ROBERT BURTON (1577–1640) *Anatomy of Melancholy*

To Appreciate heaven well
'Tis good for a man to have some fifteen minutes of hell.
— WILL CARLETON (1845–1912) *Farm Ballads*

And so upon this wise I prayed,—
    Great Spirit, give to me
A heaven not so large as yours
    But large enough for me.
— EMILY DICKINSON (1830–1886) *A Prayer*

I sent my soul through the invisible,
Some letter of that after-life to spell:
   And by and by my soul return'd to me,
And answer'd, "I myself am Heav'n and Hell."
— EDWARD FITZGERALD (1809–1883) tr.: *Rubáiyát of Omar Khayyám*

All this, and Heaven too!
— MATTHEW HENRY (1662–1714) *Life of Philip Henry*

What came from the earth returns back to the earth, and the spirit that was sent from heaven, again carried back, is received into the temple of heaven.
— LUCRETIUS (96–55 B.C.) *De Rerum Natura*

Here we may reign secure; and in my choice
To reign is worth ambition, though in Hell:
Better to reign in Hell, than serve in Heav'n.
— JOHN MILTON (1608–1674) *Paradise Lost*

Heaven-gates are not so highly arch'd
As princes' palaces; they that enter there
Must go upon their knees.
— JOHN WEBSTER (1580?–1625) *The Duchess of Malfi*

In my father's house are many mansions.
— NEW TESTAMENT: *John,* xiv, 2

HELL

Hell is full of good intentions or desires.
— ST. BERNARD OF CLAIRVAUX (1091–1153)

Here sighs, plaints, and voices of the deepest woe resounded through the starless sky. Strange languages, horrid cries, accents of grief and wrath, voices deep and hoarse, with hands clenched in despair, made a commotion which whirled forever through that air of everlasting gloom, even as sand when whirlwinds sweep the ground.
— DANTE (1265–1321) *Inferno,* Canto iii

Abandon every hope, ye who enter here.
— DANTE (1265–1321) *Inferno,* Canto iii [Inscription over the gate of Hell]

I found the original of my hell in the world which we inhabit.
— DANTE (1265–1321)

Hell is a circle about the unbelieving.
— THE KORAN

Hell hath no limits, nor is circumscrib'd
In one self-place; for where we are is hell;
And where hell is, there must we ever be;
And to conclude, when all the world dissolves,
And every creature shall be purified,
All places shall be hell that are not heaven.
— CHRISTOPHER MARLOWE (1564–1593) *Dr. Faustus*

Myself am Hell;
And, in the lowest deep, a lower deep,
Still threat'ning to devour me, opens wide;
To which the hell I suffer seems a heaven.
— JOHN MILTON (1608–1674) *Paradise Lost*

HEROISM

No man is a hero to his valet.
— MLLE. AÏSSE (1694?–1733) *Letters*

Heroism is the brilliant triumph of the soul over the flesh—that is to say, over fear.... Heroism is the dazzling and glorious concentration of courage.
— HENRI-FREDERIC AMIEL (1828–1881) *Journal,* October 1, 1849

Heroism feels and never reasons and therefore is always right.
— RALPH WALDO EMERSON (1803–1882) *Heroism*

There is nothing more touching than the sight of a Nation in search of its great men, nothing more beautiful than its readiness to accept a hero on trust.
— JAMES RUSSELL LOWELL (1819–1891) *General McClellan's Report*

HISTORY

The great object in trying to understand history is to get behind men and grasp ideas.
— LORD ACTON (1834–1902) *Letters to Mary Gladstone*

Biography is the only true history.
— THOMAS CARLYLE (1795–1881) *Journal,* January 13, 1832

All history, so far as it is not supported by contemporary evidence, is romance.
— SAMUEL JOHNSON (1709–1784) Boswell's *Tour to Hebrides*

History is the witness of the times, the torch of truth, the life of memory, the teacher of life, the messenger of antiquity.
— CICERO (106–43 B.C.) *De Oratore*

History is clarified experience.
— JAMES RUSSELL LOWELL (1819–1891) *Books and Libraries*

History repeats itself.
— THUCYDIDES (471?–400? B.C.) *History,* Bk. i

HOME

You are a King by your own Fireside, as much as any Monarch on his Throne.
— CERVANTES (1547–1616) *Don Quixote*

In love of home, the love of country has its rise.
— CHARLES DICKENS (1812–1870) *Old Curiosity Shop*

Home is the place where, when you have to go there,
They have to take you in.
— ROBERT FROST (1875–1963) *The Death of the Hired Man*

Be it ever so humble, there's no place like home.
— JOHN HOWARD PAYNE (1791–1852) *Home Sweet Home*

Home is where the heart is.
— PLINY THE ELDER (23–79)

Weep no more, my lady;
   Oh, weep no more today!
We will sing one song for the old Kentucky home,
   For the old Kentucky home, far away.
— STEPHEN C. FOSTER (1812–1864) *Old Folks At Home*

It takes a heap o' livin' in a house t' make it home.
— EDGAR A. GUEST (1881–1959) *Home*

To be happy at home is the ultimate result of all ambition, the end to which every enterprise and labor tends, and of which every desire prompts the prosecution.
— SAMUEL JOHNSON (1709–1784) *Rambler*

When I was at home I was in a better place.
— SHAKESPEARE (1564–1616) *As You Like It,* II, iv, 14

As a bird that wandereth from her nest, so is a man that wandereth from his place.
— OLD TESTAMENT: *Proverbs,* xxvii, 8

HONESTY

A trustee is held to something stricter than the morals of the market place. Not honesty alone, but the punctilio of an honor the most sensitive, is then the standard of behavior.
— BENJAMIN N. CARDOZO (1870–1938)

Make yourself an honest man, and then you may be sure that there is one rascal less in the world.
— THOMAS CARLYLE (1795–1881)

Honesty is the best policy.
— CERVANTES (1547–1616) *Don Quixote*

   If he were
To be made honest by an act of parliament
I should not alter in my faith of him.
— BEN JONSON (1572–1637) *Devil is an Ass*

An honest man is the noblest work of God.
— ALEXANDER POPE (1688–1744) *Essay on Man*

You are underrating the President [Lincoln]. I grant that he lacks higher education and his manners are not in accord with European conceptions of the dignity of a chief magistrate. He is a well-developed child of nature and is not skilled in polite phrases and poses. But he is a man of profound feeling, correct and firm principles and incorruptible honesty. His motives are unquestionable, and he possesses to a remarkable degree the characteristic, God-given trait of this people, sound common sense.
— CARL SCHURZ (1829–1906) Letter, October, 1864

There is no terror, Cassius, in your threats,
For I am arm'd so strong in honesty
That they pass by me as the idle wind,
Which I respect not.
— SHAKESPEARE (1564–1616) *Julius Caesar*, IV, iii, 66

HONOR

The best memorial for a mighty man is to gain honour ere death.
— BEOWULF (8th C.)

Better a thousand times to die with glory than live without honor.
— LOUIS VI OF FRANCE (1081–1137)

I could not love thee, dear, so much,
Loved I not honor more.
— RICHARD LOVELACE (1618–1658) To Lucasta, On Going to Wars

Set honour in one eye and death i' the other
And I will look on both indifferently;
For let the gods so speed me as I love
The name of honour more than I fear death.
— SHAKESPEARE (1564–1616) *Julius Caesar*, I, ii, 86

Mine honour is my life; both grow in one;
Take honour from me and my life is done.
— SHAKESPEARE (1564–1616) *Richard II*, I, i, 182

HOPE

I live on hope and that I think do all
Who come into this world.
— ROBERT BRIDGES (1844–1930) *The Growth of Love*

To the sick, while there is life there is hope.
— CICERO (106–43 B.C.) *Epistolae Ad Atticum*

Hope is itself a species of happiness, and, perhaps, the chief happiness which this world affords.
— SAMUEL JOHNSON (1709–1784) in Boswell's *Life of Johnson*

The setting of a great hope is like the setting of the sun. The brightness of our life is gone.
— HENRY W. LONGFELLOW (1807–1882) *Hyperion*

Hopes are but the dreams of those who wake.
— PINDAR (c. 522–442 B.C.) *Fragment*

Hope springs eternal in the human breast;
Man never is, but always to be blest.
— ALEXANDER POPE (1688–1744) *Essay on Man*

Hope, dead lives nevermore,
No, not in heaven.
— CHRISTINA ROSSETTI (1830–1894) *Dead Hope*

True hope is swift, and flies with swallow's wings;
Kings it makes gods, and meaner creatures kings.
— SHAKESPEARE (1564–1616) *Richard III*, V, ii, 23

We did not dare to breathe a prayer
Or to give our anguish scope!
Something was dead in each of us,
And what was dead was hope.
— OSCAR WILDE (1854–1900) *The Ballad of Reading Gaol*

HOSPITALITY

People are either born hosts or born guests.
— MAX BEERBOHM (1872–1956)

Hospitality consists in a little fire, a little food, and an immense quiet.
— RALPH WALDO EMERSON (1803–1882) *Journal*

Then why should I sit in the scorner's seat,
Or hurl the cynic's ban?
Let me live in my house by the side of the road,
And be a friend to man.
— SAM WALTER FOSS (1858–1911) *House by the Side of the Road*

Hail Guest! We ask not what thou art:
If Friend, we greet thee, hand and heart;
If Stranger, such no longer be;
If Foe, our love shall conquer thee.
— ARTHUR GUITERMAN (1871–1943) *Old Welsh Door Verse*

True friendship's laws are by this rule express'd,
Welcome the coming, speed the parting guest.
— HOMER (c. 10th–8th C. B.C.) *The Odyssey*

Fish and guests in three days are stale.
— JOHN LYLY (1554?–1606) *Euphues*

When there is room in the heart there is room in the house.
— DANISH PROVERB

I had three chairs in my house: one for solitude, two for friendship, three for society.
— HENRY DAVID THOREAU (1817–1862) *Walden*

Be not forgetful to entertain strangers, for thereby some have entertained angels unawares.
— NEW TESTAMENT: *Hebrews*, xiii, 2

HUMILITY

Lowliness is the base of every virtue,
And he who goes the lowest builds the safest.
— PHILIP J. BAILEY (1816–1902) *Festus*

I ate umble pie with an appetite.
— CHARLES DICKENS (1812–1870) *David Copperfield*

True humility,
The highest virtue, mother of them all.
— TENNYSON (1809–1892) *Idylls of the King*

Whosoever shall smite thee on thy right cheek, turn to him the other also.
— NEW TESTAMENT: *Matthew*, v, 39: *Luke*, vi, 29

Whosoever shall compel thee to go a mile, go with him twain.
— NEW TESTAMENT: *Matthew*, vi, 41

HUNGER

Hunger is the best sauce in the world.
— CERVANTES (1547–1616) *Don Quixote*

An empty stomach is not a good political adviser.
— ALBERT EINSTEIN (1879–1955) *Cosmic Religion*

They that die by famine die by inches.
— MATTHEW HENRY (1662–1714) *Commentaries*

Death in all its shapes is hateful to unhappy man, but the worst is death from hunger.
— HOMER (c. 10th–8th C. B.C.) *Odyssey*

If thine enemy be hungry, give him bread to eat.
— OLD TESTAMENT: *Lamentations*, iv, 9

HUSBAND

We wedded men live in sorrow and care.
— GEOFFREY CHAUCER (1340?–1400) *Merchant's Tale Prologue*

It is necessary to be almost a genius to make a good husband.
— HONORÉ DE BALZAC (1799–1850) *Physiology of Marriage*

Let the husband render unto the wife due benevolence: and likewise also the wife unto the husband.
— NEW TESTAMENT: *I Corinthians*, vii, 3

IDLENESS

Idleness is only the refuge of weak minds, and the holiday of fools.
— LORD CHESTERFIELD (1694–1773) *Letters*, July 20, 1749

Absence of occupation is not rest,
A mind quite vacant is a mind distress'd.
— WILLIAM COWPER (1731–1800) *Retirement*

There is no place in civilization for the idler. None of us has any right to ease.
— HENRY FORD (1863–1947)

Laziness travels so slowly that poverty soon overtakes him.
— BEN FRANKLIN (1706–1790) *Poor Richard's Almanack*

To be idle and to be poor have always been reproaches, and therefore every man endeavors with his utmost care to hide his poverty from others, and his idleness from himself.
— SAMUEL JOHNSON (1709–1784) *The Idler*

Of all our faults, the one that we excuse most easily is idleness.
— FRANÇOIS DE LA ROCHEFOUCAULD (1613–1680) *Maxims*

For Satan finds some mischief still
For idle hands to do.
— ISAAC WATTS (1674–1748) *Divine Songs*

To do nothing at all is the most difficult thing in the world, the most difficult and the most intellectual.
— OSCAR WILDE (1854–1900) *The Critic as Artist*

Go to the ant, thou sluggard; consider her ways, and be wise.
— OLD TESTAMENT: *Proverbs*, vi, 6

IGNORANCE

Ignorance is the night of the mind, but a night without moon or star.
— CONFUCIUS (*c.* 551–478 B.C.) *Analects*

To be conscious that you are ignorant is a great step to knowledge.
— BENJAMIN DISRAELI (1804–1881) *Sybil*

To the ignorant even the words of the wise seem foolishness.
— EURIPIDES (480–406 B.C.) *The Bacchae*

No more; where ignorance is bliss,
'Tis folly to be wise.
— THOMAS GRAY (1716–1771) *On a Distant Prospect of Eton College*

Ignorance of the law excuses no man: not that all can know the law, but because 'tis an excuse everyone will plead, and no man can tell how to refute him.
— JOHN SELDEN (1584–1654) *Table Talk*

There is no darkness, but ignorance.
— SHAKESPEARE (1564–1616) *Twelfth Night*, IV, ii, 44

IMAGINATION

Only in men's imagination does every truth find an effective and undeniable existence. Imagination, not invention, is the supreme master of art as of life.
— JOSEPH CONRAD (1857–1924) *A Personal Record*

To know is nothing at all; to imagine is everything.
— ANATOLE FRANCE (1844–1924) *The Crime of Sylvestre Bonnard*

Were it not for imagination a man would be as happy in the arms of a chambermaid as of a duchess.
— SAMUEL JOHNSON (1709–1784) Boswell's *Life of Johnson*

His imagination resembled the wings of an ostrich. It enabled him to run, though not to soar.
— THOMAS B. MACAULAY (1800–1859) *On John Dryden*

The human race is governed by its imagination.
— NAPOLEON BONAPARTE (1769–1821)

IMITATION

Men often applaud an imitation, and hiss the real thing.
— AESOP (6th C. B.C.) *The Buffoon and the Countryman*

Imitation is the sincerest flattery.
— CHARLES C. COLTON (1780?–1832)

He who imitates what is evil always goes beyond the example that is set; on the contrary, he who imitates what is good always falls short.
— FRANCESCO GUICCIARDINI (1483–1540) *Story of Italy*

Agesilaus, being invited once to hear a man who admirably imitated the nightingale, declined, saying he had heard the nightingale itself.
— PLUTARCH (46?–120?) *Lives: Agesilaus*

A great part of art consists in imitation. For the whole conduct of life is based on this: that what we admire in others we want to do ourselves.
— QUINTILIAN (40–*c.* 100) *De institutio Oratoria*

Go, and do thou likewise.
— NEW TESTAMENT: *Luke*, x, 37

IMMORTALITY

Let us not lament too much the passing of our friends. They are not dead, but simply gone before us along the road which all must travel.
— ANTIPHANES (*c.* 360 B.C.) *Fragment*

After the resurrection of the body shall have taken place, being set free from the condition of time, we shall enjoy eternal life, with love ineffable and steadfastness without corruption.
— ST. AUGUSTINE (354–430) *Of the Faith and of the Creed*

If I err in my belief that the souls of men are immortal, I err gladly, and I do not wish to lose so delightful an error.
— CICERO (106–43 B.C.) *De Senectute*

My humble friend, we know not how to live this life which is so short yet seek one that never ends.
— ANATOLE FRANCE (1844–1924) *The Red Lily*

Either the soul is immortal and we shall not die, or it perishes with the flesh, and we shall not know that we are dead. Live, then, as if you were eternal.
— ANDRÉ MAUROIS (1885–1967)

INDECISION See DECISION

INDEPENDENCE See DEPENDENCE

INDISCRETION See DISCRETION

INDIVIDUALISM

What another would have done as well as you, do not do it. What another would have said as well as you, do not say it; written as well, do not write it. Be faithful to that which exists nowhere but in yourself—and thus make yourself indispensable.
— ANDRÉ GIDE (1869–1951) *Fruits of the Earth*

Whatever crushes individuality is despotism, by whatever name it may be called.
— JOHN STUART MILL (1806–1873) *On Liberty*

An individual is as superb as a nation when he has the qualities which make a superb nation.
— WALT WHITMAN (1819–1892) *Leaves of Grass*, preface

JEALOUSY

Anger and jealousy can no more bear to lose sight of their objects than love.
— GEORGE ELIOT (1819–1880) *The Mill on the Floss*

Though jealousy be produced by love, as ashes are by fire, yet jealousy extinguishes love as ashes smother the flame.
— MARGARET OF NAVARRE (1492–1549) *Heptameron*

O! beware, my lord, of jealousy
~~It is the green-eyed monster which doth mock~~
The meat it feeds on.
— SHAKESPEARE (1564–1616) *Othello*, III, iii, 166

Love is strong as death; jealousy is cruel as the grave.
— OLD TESTAMENT: *Song of Solomon*, viii, 6

JOY

Joy rises in me like a summer's morn.
— SAMUEL TAYLOR COLERIDGE (1772–1834) *Christmas Carol*

My theory is to enjoy life, but the practice is against it.
— CHARLES LAMB (1775–1834)

My candle burns at both ends,
    It will not last the night;
But ah, my foes, and oh, my friends,
    It gives a lovely light!
— EDNA ST. VINCENT MILLAY (1892–1951)

Drink and dance and laugh and lie,
    Love the reeling midnight through,
For tomorrow we shall die!
    (But, alas, we never do.)
— DOROTHY PARKER (1893–1968) *The Flaw in Paganism*

A joy that's shared is a joy made double.
— JOHN RAY (1627?–1705) *English Proverbs*

Silence is the perfectest herald of joy:
I were but little happy if I could say how much.
— SHAKESPEARE (1564–1616) *Much Ado About Nothing*, II, i, 317

    I have drunken deep of joy,
And I will taste no other wine to-night.
— PERCY B. SHELLEY (1792–1822) *The Cenci*

Weeping may endure for a night, but joy cometh in the morning.
— OLD TESTAMENT: *Psalms*, xxx, 5

JUSTICE

Heaven gives long life to the just and the intelligent.
— CONFUCIUS (*c.* 551–478 B.C.) *The Book of History*

Justice is truth in action.
— BENJAMIN DISRAELI (1804–1881) Speech, Feb. 11, 1851

He reminds me of the man who murdered both his parents, and then, when sentence was about to be pronounced, pleaded for mercy on the grounds that he was an orphan.
— ABRAHAM LINCOLN (1809–1865) attributed

Just as, in fact there can be no peace without order so there can be no order without justice. . . .
— POPE PIUS XII (1876–1958) Address on Easter Sunday, 1939

Only the actions of the just
Smell sweet and blossom in the dust.
— JAMES SHIRLEY (1596–1666) *The Contention of Ajax and Ulysses*

Thrice is he armed that hath his quarrel just,
And he but naked, though locked up in steel,
Whose conscience with injustice is corrupted.
— SHAKESPEARE (1564–1616) *Henry VI*, III, ii, 232

What's sauce for a goose is sauce for a gander.
— JONATHAN SWIFT (1667–1745) *Polite Conversation*

Judging from the main portions of the history of the world, so far, justice is always in jeopardy.
— WALT WHITMAN (1819–1892) *Democratic Vistas*

He that ruleth over men must be just.
— OLD TESTAMENT: *Samuel*, xxiii, 3

The spirit of just men made perfect.
— NEW TESTAMENT: *Hebrews*, xii, 23

KINDNESS

It is difficult to tell how much men's minds are conciliated by a kind manner and gentle speech.
— CICERO (106–43 B.C.) *De Officiis*

A kindness loses its grace by being noised abroad,
Who desires it to be remembered should forget it.
— PIERRE CORNEILLE (1606–1684) *Theodore*

It is a kindness to refuse gently what you intend to deny.
— PUBLILIUS SYRUS (1st C. B.C.) *Sententiae*

This was the unkindest cut of all.
— SHAKESPEARE (1564–1616) *Julius Caesar*, III, ii, 187

    Yet do I fear thy nature;
It is too full o' the milk of human kindness.
— SHAKESPEARE (1564–1616) *Macbeth*, I, v, 14

KNOWLEDGE

What one knows is, in youth, of little moment; they know enough who know how to learn.
— HENRY ADAMS (1838–1918) *Education of Henry Adams*

Knowledge is, indeed, that which, next to virtue, truly and essentially raises one man above another.
— JOSEPH ADDISON (1672–1719) *The Guardian*

I assure you I had rather excel others in the knowledge of what is excellent, than in the extent of my power and dominion.
— ALEXANDER THE GREAT (356–323 B.C.)

Knowledge is power.
— FRANCIS BACON (1561–1620) *De Haeresibus*

Knowledge is a comfortable and necessary retreat and shelter for us in an advanced age; and if we do not plant it while young, it will give us no shade when we grow old.
— LORD CHESTERFIELD (1694–1773) *Letters*

No technical knowledge can outweigh knowledge of the humanities, in the gaining of which philosophy and history walk hand in hand. Our inheritance of well-founded slowly conceived codes of honor, morals and manners, the passionate convictions which so many hundreds of millions share together of the principles of freedom and justice, are far more precious to us than anything which scientific discoveries can bestow.
— WINSTON CHURCHILL (1874–1965) Speech, March 31, 1949

It is the province of knowledge to speak, and it is the privilege of wisdom to listen.
— OLIVER WENDELL HOLMES (1809–1894)

Knowledge is of two kinds. We know a subject ourselves or we know where we can find information upon it.
— SAMUEL JOHNSON (1709–1784) Boswell's *Life of Johnson*

To myself I seem to have been only like a boy playing on the sea-shore, and diverting myself in now and then finding a smoother pebble, or a prettier shell than ordinary, whilst the great ocean of truth lay all undiscovered before me.
— SIR ISAAC NEWTON (1642–1727)

Then I began to think, that it is very true which is commonly said, that the one-half of the world knoweth not how the other half liveth.
— FRANÇOIS RABELAIS (1494?–1553) *Pantagruel*

    Ignorance is the curse of God,
Knowledge the wing wherewith we fly to heaven.
— SHAKESPEARE (1564–1616) *II Henry VI*, IV, vii, 78

I do not know that knowledge amounts to anything more definite than a novel and grand surprise, or a sudden revelation of the insufficiency of all that we had called knowledge before; an indefinite sense of the grandeur and glory of the universe.
— HENRY DAVID THOREAU (1817–1862) *Spring in Massachusetts*

LABOR

There is no right to strike against the public safety by anybody, anywhere, anytime.
— CALVIN COOLIDGE (1872–1933) Letter to Samuel Gompers

Each needs the other: capital cannot do without labor, nor labor without capital.
— POPE LEO XIII (1810–1903) *Rerum Novarum*

Bowed by the weight of centuries he leans
Upon his hoe and gazes on the ground,
The emptiness of the ages in his face,
And on his back the burden of the world.
— EDWIN MARKHAM (1852–1940) *Man With the Hoe*

No business which depends for existence on paying less than living wages to its workers has any right to continue in this country.
— FRANKLIN D. ROOSEVELT (1882–1945) Public statement

I am a true labourer: I earn that I eat, get that I wear, owe no man hate, envy no man's happiness, glad of other men's good.
— SHAKESPEARE (1564–1616) *As You Like It*, III, ii, 78

There is no real wealth but the labor of man. Were the mountains of gold and the valleys of silver, the world would not be one grain of corn the richer; no one comfort would be added to the human race.
— PERCY B. SHELLEY (1792–1822) *Queen Mab*, notes

The labourer is worthy of his hire.
— NEW TESTAMENT: *Luke*, x, 7

Let them be hewers of wood and drawers of water.
— OLD TESTAMENT: *Joshua*, ix, 21

LANGUAGE

You are worth as many men as you know languages.
— CHARLES V, HOLY ROMAN EMPEROR (1500–1558)

In language clearness is everything.
— CONFUCIUS (c. 551–478 B. C.) *Analects*

A man who does not know foreign languages is ignorant of his own.
— GOETHE (1749–1832) *Sprüche in Prosa*

There is no master key to the inner life of a people, but language unlocks a vast treasure house.
— EDGAR LEE HEWETT (1865–1946) *Ancient Life in Mexico*

Every language is a temple in which the soul of those who speak it is enshrined.
— OLIVER WENDELL HOLMES (1809–1894)

Language is the dress of thought.
— SAMUEL JOHNSON (1709–1784) *Lives of the Poets*

The way to learn a language is to sit down and learn it.
— WILLIAM GRAHAM SUMNER (1840–1910) *Reminiscences*

Language, as well as the faculty of speech, was the immediate gift of God.
— NOAH WEBSTER (1758–1843) *American Dictionary*, Preface

Language is not an abstract construction of the learned, or of dictionary makers, but it is something arising out of the work, needs, ties, joys, affections, tastes, of long generations of humanity, and has its bases broad and low, close to the ground.
— WALT WHITMAN (1819–1892) *Slang in America*

LAUGHTER

God hath not granted to woeful mortals even laughter without tears.
— CALLIMACHUS (c. 260–240 B.C.) *Fragments*

You no doubt laugh in your sleeve.
— CICERO (106–43 B.C.) *De Finibus*

The loud laugh that spoke the vacant mind.
— OLIVER GOLDSMITH (1730–1774) *The Deserted Village*

Laughter unquenchable arose among the blessed gods.
— HOMER (c. 10th–8th C. B.C.) *Iliad*

I laugh because I must not cry.
— ABRAHAM LINCOLN (1809–1865)

He deserves Paradise who makes his companions laugh.
— MOHAMMED (570–632) *The Koran*

Everything gives cause for either laughter or tears.
— SENECA (4? B.C.–A.D. 65) *De Ira*

The pleasantest laughter is at the expense of our enemies.
— SOPHOCLES (495–406 B.C.) *Ajax*

Laughter is not a bad beginning for a friendship, and it is the best ending for one.
— OSCAR WILDE (1854–1900) *The Picture of Dorian Gray*

Woe unto you that laugh now! for ye shall mourn and weep.
— NEW TESTAMENT: *Luke*, vi, 25

As the crackling of thorns under a pot, so is the laughter of a fool.
— OLD TESTAMENT: *Ecclesiastes*, vii, 6

LAW

Law is a pledge that the citizens of a state will do justice to one another.
— ARISTOTLE (384–322 B.C.) *Politics*

The beginning of the law is benevolence, and with benevolence it ends.
— BABYLONIAN TALMUD: *Sotah*

The laws place the safety of all before the safety of individuals.
— CICERO (106–43 B.C.) *De Finibus*

Men would be great criminals did they need as many laws as they make.
— CHARLES JOHN DARLING (1849–1936) *Scintillæ Juris*

Time is the best interpreter of every doubtful law.
— DIONYSIUS OF HALICARNASSUS (d. c. 7 B.C.) *Antiquities of Rome*

Possession is nine points of the law.
— THOMAS FULLER (1608–1681) *Holy War*

In law a man is guilty when he violates the rights of another. In ethics he is guilty if he only thinks of doing so.
— IMMANUEL KANT (1724–1804) *Lecture at Königsberg*, 1775

The purpose of law is to prevent the strong from always having their way.
— OVID (43 B.C.–A.D. 18?) *Fasti*

No man is above the law and no man is below it; nor do we ask any man's permission when we require him to obey it.
— THEODORE ROOSEVELT (1858–1919) Message, Jan. 1904

Ye shall have one manner of law, as well for the stranger, as for one of your own country.
— OLD TESTAMENT: *Leviticus*, xxiv, 22

Where is there any book of the law so clear to each man as that written in his heart?
— LEO TOLSTOY (1828–1910) *The Chinese Pilot*

He that pleads his own cause has a fool for his client.
— ENGLISH PROVERB

LEADERSHIP

I light my candle from their torches.
—ROBERT BURTON (1577–1640) *Anatomy of Melancholy*

And when we think we lead we most are led.
— LORD BYRON (1788–1824) *The Two Foscari*

The final test of a leader is that he leaves behind him in other men the conviction and the will to carry on.
— WALTER LIPPMANN (1889–1974) *Roosevelt Has Gone*

An two men ride of a horse, one must ride behind.
— SHAKESPEARE (1564–1616) *Much Ado About Nothing*, III, v, 40

Ill can he rule the great that cannot reach the small.
— EDMUND SPENSER (1552?–1599) *The Faerie Queen*

Reason and calm judgement, the qualities specially belonging to a leader.
— TACITUS (55–117) *History*

LEARNING

What one knows is, in youth, of little moment; they know enough who know how to learn.
— HENRY ADAMS (1838–1918) *Education of Henry Adams*

All men by nature desire to know.
— ARISTOTLE (384–322 B.C.)

That there should one man die ignorant who had capacity for knowledge, this I call tragedy.
— THOMAS CARLYLE (1795–1881)

Wear your learning, like your watch, in a private pocket; and do not pull it out, and strike it, merely to show that you have one.
— LORD CHESTERFIELD (1694–1773) *Letters*, February 22, 1748

A smattering of everything and a knowledge of nothing.
— CHARLES DICKENS (1812–1870) *Sketches by Boz*

Education is a controlling grace to the young, consolation to the old, wealth to the poor, and ornament to the rich.
— DIOGENES LAERTIUS (2nd or 3rd C. A.D.)

You send your child to the schoolmaster, but 'tis the schoolboys who educate him.
— RALPH WALDO EMERSON (1803–1882) *Conduct of Life*

If you have knowledge, let others light their candles at it.
— MARGARET FULLER (1810–1850)

A child's education should begin at least one hundred years before he was born.
— OLIVER WENDELL HOLMES (1809–1894)

The important thing is not so much that every child should be taught, as that every child should be given the wish to learn.
— SIR JOHN LUBBOCK (1834–1913) *Pleasures of Life*

A little learning is a dangerous thing;
Drink deep, or taste not the Pierian spring:
There shallow draughts intoxicate the brain,
And drinking largely sobers us again.
— ALEXANDER POPE (1688–1744) *An Essay On Criticism*

'Tis education forms the common mind:
Just as the twig is bent the tree's inclined.
— ALEXANDER POPE (1688–1744) *Moral Essays*

I am glad to learn, in order that I may teach.
— SENECA (4? B.C.–A.D. 65) *Ad Lucilium*

The great aim of education is not knowledge but action.
— HERBERT SPENCER (1820–1903)

There is no royal road to learning; no short cut to the acquirement of any valuable art.
— ANTHONY TROLLOPE (1815–1882) *Barchester Towers*

LEISURE

When a man's busy, why, leisure
Strikes him as wonderful pleasure;
'Faith, and at leisure once is he?
Straightway he wants to be busy.
— ROBERT BROWNING (1812–1889) *The Glove*

It is the mark of a superior man that he will take no harmful ease.
— CONFUCIUS (c. 551–478 B.C.) *Book of History*

A life of leisure and a life of laziness are two things.
— BEN FRANKLIN (1706–1790) *Poor Richard's Almanack*

Give time to your friends, leisure to your wife, relax your mind, give rest to your body, so that you may the better fulfil your accustomed occupation.
— PHAEDRUS (A.D. 1st C.) *Fables*

To be able to fill leisure intelligently is the last product of civilization.
— BERTRAND RUSSELL (1872–1970) *The Conquest of Happiness*

LIBERTY

Eternal spirit of the chainless mind!
Brightest in dungeons, Liberty! thou art.
— LORD BYRON (1788–1824) *The Prisoner of Chillon*

The condition upon which God has given liberty to man is eternal vigilance.
— JOHN PHILPOT CURRAN (1750–1817) Speech upon the Right of Election, July 10, 1790.

Those, who would give up essential liberty to purchase a little temporary safety, deserve neither liberty nor safety.
— BEN FRANKLIN (1706–1790) Historical Review of Constitution and Government of Pennsylvania

Is Life so dear or peace so sweet as to be purchased at the price of chains and slavery? Forbid it, Almighty God! I know not what course others may take, but as for me, give me liberty, or give me death.
— PATRICK HENRY (1736–1799) Speech, 1775

The God who gave us life gave us liberty at the same time.
— THOMAS JEFFERSON (1743–1826) *The Rights of British America*

It is true that liberty is precious—so precious that it must be rationed.
— NIKOLAI LENIN (1870–1924)

The inescapable price of liberty is an ability to preserve it from destruction.
— GENERAL DOUGLAS MACARTHUR (1880–1964) Speech

He that would make his own liberty secure must guard even his enemy from oppression.
— THOMAS PAINE (1737–1809) *First Principles of Government*

There is . . . no liberty but liberty under law. Law does not restrict liberty; it creates the only real liberty there is.
— WILLIAM SUMNER (1840–1910) *The Forgotten Man*

LIFE

Remember that man's life lies all within this present, as 't were but a hair's breadth of time; as for the rest, the past is gone, the future may never be. Short, therefore, is man's life, and narrow is the corner of the earth wherein he dwells.
— MARCUS AURELIUS (121–180) *Meditations*

Life is a test and this world a place of trial. Always the problems—or it may be the same problem—will be presented to every generation in different forms.
— WINSTON CHURCHILL (1874–1965) Speech 1949

I have measured out my life with coffee spoons.
— T. S. ELIOT (1888–1965) *Love Song of J. Alfred Prufrock*

The fool, with all his other faults, has this also: he is always getting ready to live.
— EPICURUS (342–270 B.C.) *Fragments*

Were it offered to my choice, I should have no objection to a repetition of the same life from its beginnings, only asking the advantages authors have in a second edition to correct some faults.
— BEN FRANKLIN (1706–1790) *Autobiography*

There is more to life than increasing its speed.
— MOHANDAS GANDHI (1869–1948)

I wish to preach, not the doctrine of ignoble ease, but the doctrine of the strenuous life.
— THEODORE ROOSEVELT (1858–1919) Speech

Life is neither a good nor an evil; it is simply the place where good and evil exist.
— SENECA (4? B.C.–A.D. 65) Epistulae ad Lucilium

Life is as tedious as a twice-told tale,
Vexing the dull ear of a drowsy man.
— SHAKESPEARE (1564–1616) King John, III, iv, 108

One man in his time plays many parts,
His acts being seven ages.
— SHAKESPEARE (1564–1616) As You Like It, II, vii, 142

The web of our life is of a mingled yarn, good and ill together.
— SHAKESPEARE (1564–1616) All's Well That Ends Well, IV, iii, 83

As for man, his days are as grass: as a flower of the field, so he flourisheth.
— OLD TESTAMENT: Psalms, viii, 15

The mass of men lead lives of quiet desperation.
— HENRY DAVID THOREAU (1817–1862) Walden

LOVE

I have never loved anyone for love's sake, except, perhaps, Josephine—a little.
— NAPOLEON BONAPARTE (1769–1821)

How do I love thee? Let me count the ways.
. . .
I love thee with a love I seemed to lose
With my lost saints, —I love thee with the breath,
Smiles, tears, of all my life!—, if God choose,
I shall but love thee better after death.
— ELIZABETH B. BROWNING (1806–1861) Sonnets from the Portuguese

God be thanked, the meanest of his creatures
Boasts two soul-sides, one to face the world with,
One to show a woman when he loves her.
— ROBERT BROWNING (1812–1889) One Word More

Oh my luve's like a red, red, rose,
    That's newly sprung in June;
Oh my luve's like the melodie
    That's sweetly played in tune.
— ROBERT BURNS (1759–1796) Red, Red Rose

To see her is to love her,
    And love but her forever;
For nature made her what she is,
    And never made anither!
— ROBERT BURNS (1759–1796) Bonny Lesley

Alas! the love of women! it is known
To be a lovely and a fearful thing.
— LORD BYRON (1788–1824) Don Juan

Let Time and Chance combine, combine!
Let Time and Chance combine, combine!
The fairest love from heaven above,
    That love of yours was mine,
        My Dear!
    That love of yours was mine.
— THOMAS CARLYLE (1795–1881) Adieu

Love and war are the same thing, and strategems and policy are as allowable in the one as in the other.
— CERVANTES (1547–1616) Don Quixote

If love be good, from whennes comth my wo?
— GEOFFREY CHAUCER (1340?–1400) Troilus and Criseyde

The Stoics define love as the endeavor to form a friendship inspired by beauty.
— CICERO (106–43 B.C.) Tusculanae Disputationes

When povertie comes in at doores, love leaps out at windowes.
— JOHN CLARK (1609–1676) Paroemiologia

Love's but a frailty of the mind,
When 'tis not with ambition joined:
A sickly flame, which, if not fed, expires,
And feeding, wastes in self-consuming fires.
— WILLIAM CONGREVE (1670–1729) Way of the World

Say what you will, 'tis better to be left
Than never to have loved.
— WILLIAM CONGREVE (1670–1729) Way of the World

We are all born for love . . . . It is the principle of existence and its only end.
— BENJAMIN DISRAELI (1804–1881) Sybil

Men and women call one another inconstant, and accuse one another of having changed their minds, when, God knows, they have but changed the object of their eye, and seen a better white or red.
— JOHN DONNE (1572–1631) Sermons

Last night, ah, yesternight, betwixt her lips and mine
There fell thy shadow, Cynara! Thy breath was shed
Upon my soul between the kisses and the wine;
And I was desolate and sick of an old passion,
Yea, I was desolate and bowed my head:
I have been faithful to thee, Cynara! in my fashion.
— ERNEST DOWSON (1867–1900) Cynara

But you must believe me when I tell you that I have found it impossible to carry the heavy burden of responsibility and to discharge my duties as King as I would wish to do without the help and support of the woman I love.
— EDWARD VIII (1894–1972) Abdication Speech

All mankind love a lover.
— RALPH WALDO EMERSON (1803–1882) Essays

He is not a lover who does not love forever.
— EURIPIDES (480–406 B.C.) Troades

Perhaps they were right in putting love into books . . .
Perhaps it could not live anywhere else.
— WILLIAM FAULKNER (1897–1962) Light in August

Love grants in a moment
What toil can hardly achieve in an age.
— GOETHE (1749–1832) Torquato Tasso

Ah! What is love? It is a pretty thing,
As sweet unto a shepherd as a king,
    And sweeter too;
For kings have cares that wait upon a crown,
And cares can make the sweetest love to frown.
— ROBERT GREENE (1560?–1592) Shepherd's Wife

To demand of love that it be without jealousy is to ask of light that it cast no shadows.
— OSCAR HAMMLING (1890–   ) Laconics

If you would be loved, love.
— HECATO (c. 550–476 B.C.) Fragments

At thy command I would change, not merely my costume, but my very soul, so entirely art thou the sole possessor of my body and my spirit. Never, God is my witness, never have I sought anything in thee but thyself; I have sought thee, and not thy gifts. I have not looked to the marriage-bond or dowry.
— HÉLOISE (1101–1164) to Abelard

Love in a hut, with water and a crust,
Is—love, forgive us!—cinders, ashes, dust.
— JOHN KEATS (1795–1821) Lamia

Come live with me and be my love,
And we will all the pleasures prove,
That valleys, groves, or hills, or fields,
Or woods and steepy mountains yields.
— CHRISTOPHER MARLOWE (1564–1593) Passionate Shepherd to his Love

If I were a king, ah love, if I were a king!
What tributary nations I would bring
To stoop before your sceptre and to swear
Allegience to your lips and eyes and hair.
— JUSTIN HUNTLY MCCARTHY (1861–1936) *If I Were King*

'Tis not love's going hurts my days,
But that it went in little ways.
— EDNA ST. VINCENT MILLAY (1892–1951) *Spring and Fall*

Take love away from life and you take away its pleasures.
— MOLIÈRE (1622–1673) *Bourgeois Gentleman*

'Tis sweet to think, that, where'er we rove,
We are sure to find something blissful and dear;
And when we're far from the lips we love,
We've but to make love to the lips we are near.
— THOMAS MOORE (1779–1852) *'Tis Sweet to Think*

But there's nothing half so sweet in life
As love's young dream.
— THOMAS MOORE (1779–1852) *Love's Young Dream*

Love that comes late oft claims a heavy toll.
— SEXTUS PROPERTIUS (50?–15 B.C.) *Elegies*

If all the world and love were young,
And truth in every shepherd's tongue,
These pretty pleasures might me move
To live with thee, and be thy love.
— SIR WALTER RALEIGH (1552?–1618)

The pleasure of love is in loving; and we are much happier
in the passion we feel than in that which we inspire.
— FRANÇOIS DE LA ROCHEFOUCAULD (1613–1680) *Maxims*

If thou remember'st not the slightest folly
That ever love did make thee run into,
Thou hast not lov'd.
— SHAKESPEARE (1564–1616) *As You Like It*, II, iv, 34

No sooner met but they looked, no sooner looked but they
loved, no sooner loved but they sighed, no sooner sighed but
they asked one another the reason.
— SHAKESPEARE (1564–1616) *As You Like It*, V, ii, 36

Where love is great, the littlest doubts are fear;
When little fears grow great, great love grows there.
— SHAKESPEARE (1564–1616) *Hamlet*, III, ii, 188

But love is blind, and lovers cannot see
The pretty follies that themselves commit.
— SHAKESPEARE (1564–1616) *Merchant of Venice*, II, vi, 344

Ay me! for aught that I ever could read,
Could ever hear by tale or history,
The course of true love never did run smooth.
— SHAKESPEARE (1564–1616) *Midsummer Night's Dream*,
I, i, 132

Speak low, if you speak love.
— SHAKESPEARE (1564–1616) *Much Ado About Nothing*, II,
i, 102

There is no creature loves me,
And if I die, no soul shall pity me.
— SHAKESPEARE (1564–1616) *Richard III*, V, iii, 200

For stony limits cannot hold love out,
And what love can do that dares love attempt.
— SHAKESPEARE (1564–1616) *Romeo and Juliet*, II, ii, 67

Give me my Romeo; and, when he shall die,
Take him and cut him out in little stars,
And he will make the face of heaven so fine,
That all the world will be in love with night,
And pay no worship to the garish sun.
— SHAKESPEARE (1564–1616) *Romeo and Juliet*, III, ii, 21

Love's not Time's fool, though rosy lips and cheeks
    Within his bending sickle's compass come;
Love alters not with his brief hours and weeks,
    But bears it out even to the edge of doom.
— SHAKESPEARE (1564–1616) Sonnet CXVI.

Common as light is love,
And its familiar voice wearies not ever,
Like the wide heaven, the all-sustaining air,
It makes the reptile equal to the god.
— PERCY B. SHELLEY (1792–1822) *Prometheus Unbound*

Love is a symbol of eternity. It wipes out all sense of time,
destroying all memory of a beginning and all fear of an end.
— MADAME DE STAËL (1766–1817) *Corinne*

And blessings on the falling out
That all the more endears,
When we fall out with those we love,
And kiss again with tears.
— TENNYSON (1809–1892) *The Princess*

To say that you can love one person all your life is just like
saying that one candle will continue burning as long as you
live.
— LEO TOLSTOY (1828–1910) *Kreutzer Sonata*

Yet each man kills the thing he loves,
By each let this be heard,
Some do it with a bitter look,
Some with a flattering word,
The coward does it with a kiss,
The brave man with a sword.
— OSCAR WILDE (1854–1900) *Ballad of Reading Gaol*

Whom the Lord loveth he chasteneth.
— NEW TESTAMENT: *Hebrews*, xii, 6

Who love too much, hate in the like extreme.
— HOMER (c. 10th–8th C. B.C.) *Odyssey*

Greater love hath no man than this, that a man lay down his
life for his friends.
— NEW TESTAMENT: *John*, xv, 13

There is no fear in love; but perfect love casteth out fear.
— NEW TESTAMENT: *I John*, iv, 8

Whither thou goest, I will go; and where thou lodgest, I will
lodge: thy people shall be my people, and thy God my God.
— OLD TESTAMENT: *Ruth*, i, 16

Many waters cannot quench love, neither can the floods
drown it.
— OLD TESTAMENT: *Songs of Solomon*, viii, 7

LUXURY

Luxury and avarice—these pests have been the ruin of every
state.
— CATO (234–149 B.C.) In support of the Oppian Law

Faint-hearted men are the fruit of luxurious countries. The
same soil never produces both luxuries and heroes.
— HERODOTUS (484–424 B.C.) *History*

Fell luxury! more perilous to youth
Than storms or quicksands, poverty, or chains
— HANNAH MORE (1745–1833) *Belshazzar*

People have declaimed against luxury for 2000 years, in verse
and in prose, and people have always delighted in it.
— VOLTAIRE (1694–1778) *Philosophical Dictionary*

On the soft beds of luxury most kingdoms have expired.
— EDWARD YOUNG (1683–1765) *Centaur*

MAJORITY AND MINORITY

The oppression of a majority is detestable and odious: the
oppression of a minority is only by one degree less detestable
and odious.
— WILLIAM EWART GLADSTONE (1809–1898) Speech

It is my principle that the will of the majority should always
prevail.
— THOMAS JEFFERSON (1743–1826) Letter to James Madison

One, of God's side, is a majority.
— WENDELL PHILLIPS (1811–1884) Speech on John Brown

MALICE

Malice is cunning.
— CICERO (106–43 B.C.) *De Natura Deorum*

Malice hath a strong memory.
— THOMAS FULLER (1608–1681) *Pisgah Sight*

With malice toward none; with charity for all; with firmness in the right, as God gives us to see the right, let us strive on to finish the work we are in.
— ABRAHAM LINCOLN (1809–1865) *Second Inaugural Address*

MAN

This Being of mine, whatever it really is, consists of a little flesh, a little breath and the ruling Reason.
— MARCUS AURELIUS (121–180) *Meditations*

No man is an Iland, intire of it selfe; everyman is a piece of the Continent, a part of the maine, if a Clod bee washed away by the Sea, Europe is the lesse, as well as if a Promontorie were, as well as if a Mannor of thy friends or of thine owne were; any mans death diminishes me, because I am involved in Mankinde; and therefore never send to know for whom the bell tolls; it tolls for thee.
— JOHN DONNE (1572–1631) *Devotions*

Man is a fallen god who remembers the heavens.
— ALPHONSE DE LAMARTINE (1790–1869) *Meditations*

He's not the finest character that ever lived. But he's a human being, and a terrible thing is happening to him. So attention must be paid. He's not to be allowed to fall into his grave like an old dog.
— ARTHUR MILLER (1915–   ) *Death of a Salesman*

Man is a rope stretched between the animal and the superman—a rope over an abyss.
— FRIEDRICH W. NIETZSCHE (1844–1900) *Thus Spake Zarathustra*

What a chimera, then, is man! What a novelty! What a monster, what a chaos, what a contradiction, what a prodigy! Judge of all things, feeble worm of the earth, depositary of truth, a sink of uncertainty and error, the glory and the shame of the universe.
— BLAISE PASCAL (1623–1662) *Pensées*

Placed on this isthmus of a middle state
A being darkly wise and rudely great
Created half to rise and half to fall
Great lord of all things, yet prey to all.
Sole judge of truth in endless error hurled,
The glory, jest and riddle of the world.
— ALEXANDER POPE (1688–1744) *Essay on Man*

What a piece of work is a man! how noble in reason! how infinite in faculty! in form and moving how express and admirable! in action how like an angel! in apprehension how like a god! the beauty of the world! the paragon of animals! And, yet, to me, what is this quintessence of dust? man delights not me: no, nor woman neither, though by your smiling, you seem to say so.
— SHAKESPEARE (1564–1616) *Hamlet*, II, 2, 313

Man's capacities have never been measured; nor are we to judge of what he can do by any precedents, so little has been tried.
— HENRY DAVID THOREAU (1817–1862) *Walden*

Man is the only animal that blushes. Or needs to.
— MARK TWAIN (1835–1910) *Pudd'nhead Wilson's New Calendar*

Who shall enumerate the many ways in which that costly piece of fixed capital, a human being, may be employed! More of him is wanted everywhere! Hunt, then, for some situation in which your humanity may be used.
— ALBERT SCHWEITZER (1875–1965) *Civilization and Ethics*

He was a man, take him for all in all,
I shall not look upon his like again.
— SHAKESPEARE (1564–1616) *Hamlet*, I, ii, 187

How beauteous mankind is! O brave new world,
That has such people in 't!
— SHAKESPEARE (1564–1616) *The Tempest*, V, i, 183

Thou hast made him a little lower than the angels.
— OLD TESTAMENT: *Psalms*, viii, 5

MARRIAGE

He that hath a wife and children hath given hostages to fortune; for they are impediments to great enterprises, either of virtue or mischief.
— FRANCIS BACON (1561–1626) *Marriage and Single Life*

Cursed be the man, the poorest wretch in life,
The crouching vessel, to the tyrant wife,
Who has no will but her high permission;
Who has not sixpence but in her possession;
Who must to her his dear friend's secret tell;
Who dreads a curtain lecture worse than hell.
Were such the wife had fallen to my part,
I'd break her spirit or I'd break her heart.
— ROBERT BURNS (1759–1796) *Henpecked Husband*

Marriage and hanging go by destiny; matches are made in heaven.
— ROBERT BURTON (1577–1640) *Anatomy of Melancholy*

The first bond of society is marriage; the next, our children; then the whole family and all things in common.
— CICERO (106–43 B.C.) *De Officiis*

Like blood, like goods, and like age,
Make the happiest marriage.
— JOHN CLARKE (1609–1676) *Paroemiologia*

Thus grief still treads upon the heels of pleasure,
Marry'd in haste, we may repent at leisure.
— WILLIAM CONGREVE (1670–1729) *Old Bachelor*

Happy and thrice happy are they who enjoy an uninterrupted union, and whose love, unbroken by any complaints, shall not dissolve until the last day.
— HORACE (65–8 B.C.) *Carmina*

Marriages are made in heaven.
— MIDRASH: *Genesis Rabbah*, lxviii

Hail, wedded love, mysterious law; true source
Of human offspring.
— JOHN MILTON (1608–1674) *Paradise Lost*

If you would marry wisely, marry your equal.
— OVID (43 B.C.–A.D. 18?) *Heroides*

All happy families resemble one another; every unhappy family is unhappy in its own fashion.
— LEO TOLSTOY (1828–1910) *Anna Karenina*

When a man marries again it is because he adored his first wife.
— OSCAR WILDE (1854–1900) *Picture of Dorian Gray*

MEMORY

To be ignorant of what happened before you were born is to be ever a child. For what is man's lifetime unless the memory of past events is woven with those of earlier times.
— CICERO (106–43 B.C.) *De Oratore*

There is no greater sorrow than to recall, in misery, the time when we were happy.
— DANTE (1265–1321) *Inferno*

Memory is the treasure-house of the mind.
— THOMAS FULLER (1608–1681) *The Holy State: Memory*

A retentive memory is a good thing, but the ability to forget is the true token of greatness.
— ELBERT HUBBARD (1856–1915) *Epigrams*

The leaves lie thick upon the way
Of Memories.
— JAMES JOYCE (1882–1941) *Chamber Music*

Better by far you should forget and smile,
Than that you should remember and be sad.
— CHRISTINA ROSSETTI (1830–1894) *A Birthday*

Things that were hard to bear are sweet to remember.
— SENECA (4? B.C.–A.D. 65) *Hercules Furens*

Hamlet: Methinks I see my father.
Horatio: O! Where, my lord?
Hamlet: In my mind's eye, Horatio.
— SHAKESPEARE (1564–1616) *Hamlet*, I, ii, 184

Remember thee!
Ay, thou poor ghost, while memory holds a seat
In this distracted globe. Remember thee!
Yea, from the fable of my memory
I'll wipe away all trivial fond records.
— SHAKESPEARE (1564–1616) *Hamlet*, I, v, 97

When to the sessions of sweet silent thought
I summon up remembrance of things past,
I sigh the lack of many a thing I sought,
And old woes new wail my dear time's waste.
— SHAKESPEARE (1564–1616) *Sonnets*, xxx

I shall remember while the light lives yet,
And in the night-time I shall not forget.
— ALGERNON CHARLES SWINBURNE (1837–1909) *Erotion*

MERCY

The quality of mercy is not strain'd
It droppeth as the gentle rain from heaven
Upon the place beneath: it is twice blest;
It blesseth him that gives and him that takes;
'Tis mightiest in the mightiest; it becomes
The throned monarch better than his crown;
His sceptre shows the force of temporal power,
The attribute to awe and majesty,
Wherein doth sit the dread and fear of kings;
But mercy is above this sceptred sway;
It is enthroned in the hearts of kings,
It is an attribute to God himself;
And earthly power doth show likest God's
When mercy seasons justice.
— SHAKESPEARE (1564–1616) *Merchant of Venice*, IV, i, 184

Blessed are the merciful: for they shall obtain mercy.
— NEW TESTAMENT: *Matthew*, v, 7

What doth the Lord require of thee, but to do justly, and to
love mercy, and to walk humbly with thy God.
— OLD TESTAMENT: *Micah*, iv, 4

Mercy and truth are met together; righteousness and peace
have kissed each other.
— OLD TESTAMENT: *Psalms*, lxxxv, 10

To hide the fault I see:
That mercy I to others show
That mercy show to me.
— ALEXANDER POPE (1688–1744) *Universal Prayer*

MONTHS

Pale January lay
In its cradle day by day,
Dead or living, hard to say.
— ALFRED AUSTIN (1835–1913) *Primroses*

That blasts of January
Would blow you through and through.
— SHAKESPEARE (1564–1616) *Winter's Tale*, IV, iv, 3

Late February days; and now, at last,
Might you have thought that Winter's woe was past;
So fair the sky and so soft the air.
— WILLIAM MORRIS (1834–1896) *Earthly Paradise*

Menallo: I would chuse March, for I would come in like a
Lion.
Tony: But you'd go out like a Lamb when you went to
hanging.
— JOHN FLETCHER (1579–1625) *Wife for a Month*

April is the cruelest month, breeding
Lilacs out of the dead land, mixing
Memory and desire, stirring
Dull roots with spring rain.
— T. S. ELIOT (1888–1965) *The Waste Land*

Oh, to be in England
Now that April's here.
— ROBERT BROWNING (1812–1889) *Home Thoughts*

He has a hard heart who does not love in May.
— GUILLAUME DE LORRIS (d. *c.* 1235) *Roman de la Rose*

And what is so rare as a day in June?
Then, if ever, come perfect days;
Then Heaven tries earth if it be in tune,
And over it softly her warm ear lays.
— JAMES RUSSELL LOWELL (1819–1891) *Vision of Sir Launfa*

The Summer looks out from her brazen tower,
Through the flashing bars of July.
— FRANCIS THOMPSON (1859–1907) *Corymbus for Autumn*

Hot July brings cooling showers,
Apricots and gillyflowers.
— SARA COLERIDGE (1802–1852) *Pretty Lessons in Verse*

Never return in August to what you love;
Along the leaves will rust
And over the hedges dust,
And in the air vague thunder and silence burning . . .
Choose some happier time for your returning.
— BERNICE LESBIA KENYON (1897–   ) *Return*

I'm not a chicken; I have seen
Full many a chill September.
— OLIVER WENDELL HOLMES (1809–1894) *September Gale*

The skies they were ashen and sober;
The leaves they were crisp and sere—
The leaves they were withering and sere;
It was night in the lonesome October
Of my most immemorial year.
— EDGAR ALLAN POE (1809–1849) *Ulalume*

When chill November's surly blast
Made fields and forests bare.
— ROBERT BURNS (1759–1796) *Man Was Made to Mourn*

In a drear-nighted December,
Too happy, happy brook,
Thy bubblings ne'er remember
Apollo's summer look;
But with a sweet forgetting,
They stay their crystal fretting,
Never, never petting
About the frozen time.
— JOHN KEATS (1795–1821) *Stanzas*

When we shall hear
The rain and wind beat dark December, how
In this our pinching cave, shall we discourse
The freezing hours away.
— SHAKESPEARE (1564–1616) *Cymbeline*, III, iii, 36

MUSIC

Music, the greatest good that mortals know,
And all of heaven we have below.
— JOSEPH ADDISON (1672–1719) *Song for St. Cecilia's Day*

Music exalts each joy, allays each grief,
Expels diseases, softens every pain,
Subdues the rage of poison, and the plague.
— JOHN ARMSTRONG (1709–1779) *Preserving Health*

Who hears music, feels his solitude
Peopled at once.
— ROBERT BROWNING (1812–1889) *Balaustion's Adventure*

Music is well said to be the speech of angels.
— THOMAS CARLYLE (1795–1881) *Essays: The Opera*

Music hath charms to soothe the savage breast,
To soften rocks, or bend a knotted oak.
— WILLIAM CONGREVE (1670–1729) *The Mourning Bride*

Heard melodies are sweet, but those unheard
Are sweeter: therefore, ye soft pipes, play on;
Not to the sensual ear, but, more endear'd,
Pipe to the spirit ditties of no tone.
— JOHN KEATS (1795–1821) *Ode to a Grecian Urn*

NATION

How much more are men than nations!
— RALPH WALDO EMERSON (1803–1882) *Letters and Social Aims*

It is because nations tend to stupidity and baseness that mankind moves so slowly; it is because individuals have a capacity for better things that it moves at all.
— GEORGE GISSING (1857–1903) *Private Papers of Henry Ryecroft*

The first panacea for a mismanaged nation is inflation of the currency; the second is war. Both bring a temporary prosperity; both bring a permanent ruin. But both are the refuge of political and economic opportunists.
— ERNEST HEMINGWAY (1898–1961) *Notes on the Next War*

There is no such thing as a little country. The greatness of a people is no more determined by their number than the greatness of a man is determined by his height.
— VICTOR HUGO (1802–1885)

The political life of a nation is only the most superficial aspect of its being. In order to know its inner life, the source of its action, one must penetrate to its soul by literature, philosophy and the arts, where are reflected the ideas, the passions, the dreams of a whole people.
— ROMAIN ROLLAND (1866–1945) *Musicians of the Past*

That nation is worthless which does not joyfully stake everything in defense of its honor.
— SCHILLER (1759–1805) *Maid of Orleans*

It is a maxim founded on the universal experience of mankind that no nation is to be trusted farther than it is bound by its interest.
— GEORGE WASHINGTON (1732–1799) Letter to Congress, 1778

No nation is fit to sit in judgment upon any other nation.
— WOODROW WILSON (1856–1924)

And hath made of one blood all nations of men for to dwell on all the face of the earth.
— NEW TESTAMENT: *Acts*, xvii, 26

A little one shall be come a thousand and a small one a strong nation.
— OLD TESTAMENT: *Isaiah*, ix, 22

NATURE

The study of Nature is intercourse with the Highest Mind. You should never trifle with Nature.
— JEAN LOUIS AGASSIZ (1807–1873) *Agassiz at Penikese*

Believe one who knows: you will find something greater in woods than in books. Trees and stones will teach you that which you can never learn from masters.
— ST. BERNARD OF CLAIRVAUX (1091–1153) *Epistles*

Whatever befalls in accordance with Nature shall be accounted good.
— CICERO (106–43 B.C.) *De Senectute*

Nor rural sounds alone, but rural sounds,
Exhilarate the spirit, and restore
The tone of languid Nature.
— WILLIAM COWPER (1731–1800) *The Task*

Hast thou named all the birds without a gun;
Loved the wood-rose, and left it on its stalk?
— RALPH WALDO EMERSON (1803–1882) *Forbearance*

Never does Nature say one thing and Wisdom another.
— JUVENAL (*c.* 60–130 A.D.) *Satires*

So Nature deals with us, and takes away
Our playthings one by one, and by the hand
Leads us to rest.
— HENRY W. LONGFELLOW (1807–1882) *Nature*

All that thy seasons, O Nature, bring is fruit for me!
All things come from thee, subsist in thee, go back to thee.
— MARCUS AURELIUS (121–180) *Meditations*

In those vernal seasons of the year, when the air is calm and pleasant, it were an injury and sullenness against Nature not to go out and see her riches and partake in her rejoicing with heaven and earth.
— JOHN MILTON (1608–1674) *Tractate of Education*

The perfections of Nature show that she is the image of God; her defects show that she is only his image.
— BLAISE PASCAL (1623–1662) *Pensées*

All Nature is but Art, unknown to thee;
All Chance, Direction, which thou canst not see.
— ALEXANDER POPE (1688–1744) *Essay on Man*

Nature abhors a vacuum.
— FRANÇOIS RABELAIS (1494?–1553) *Gargantua*

And this our life, exempt from public haunt,
Finds tongues in trees, books in the running brooks,
Sermons in stones, and good in everything.
— SHAKESPEARE (1564–1616) *As You Like It*, II, i, 15

One touch of nature makes the whole world kin.
— SHAKESPEARE (1564–1616) *Troilus and Cressida*, III, iii, 175

I inhale great draughts of space,
The east and the west are mine, and the north and the south are mine.
I am larger than I thought,
I did not know I held so much goodness.
— WALT WHITMAN (1819–1892) *Song of the Open Road*

NEIGHBOR

Reprove thy neighbor before thou threaten.
— BEN SIRA (*c.* 190 B.C.) *Book of Wisdom*

You must ask your neighbour if you shall live in peace.
— JOHN CLARK (1609–1676) *Paroemiologia*

Good fences make good neighbors.
— ROBERT FROST (1875–1963) *Mending Wall*

Love your neighbour, yet pull not down your hedge.
— GEORGE HERBERT (1593–1633) *Jacula Prudentum*

A bad neighbor is as great a plague as a good one is a blessing; he who enjoys a good neighbor has a precious possession.
— HESIOD (*c.* 735 B.C.) *Works and Days*

There is an idea abroad among moral people that they should make their neighbors good. One person I have to make good: myself. But my duty to my neighbor is much more nearly expressed by saying that I have to make him happy—if I may.
— R. L. STEVENSON (1850–1894) *A Christmas Sermon*

Love thy neighbour as thyself.
— NEW TESTAMENT: *Matthew*, xix, 19

Better is a neighbour that is near than a brother far off.
— OLD TESTAMENT: *Proverbs*, xxvii, 10

NIGHT

I linger yet with Nature, for the night
Hath been to me a more familiar face
Than that of man; and in her starry shade
Of dim and solitary loveliness
I learn'd the language of another world.
— LORD BYRON (1788–1824) *Manfred*, III, iv

The night . . . giveth truce to all labours, and by sleeping maketh sweet all pains and travail.
— WILLIAM CAXTON (1422?–1491) *Eneydos*

Dark was the night as pich, or as the cole.
— GEOFFREY CHAUCER (1340?–1400) *Canterbury Tales*

Every evening we are poorer by a day.
— ARTHUR SCHOPENHAUER (1788–1860)

Come, seeling night,
Scarf up the tender eye of pitiful day;
And with thy bloody and invisible hand
Cancel and tear to pieces that great bond
Which keeps me pale.
— SHAKESPEARE (1564–1616) *Macbeth*, III, ii, 46

In the night there is peace for the old and hope for the young.
— GEORGE BERNARD SHAW (1856–1950) *Heartbreak House*

Press close, bare-bosom'd night—press close, magnetic nourishing night!
Night of south winds—night of the large few stars!
Still nodding night—mad naked summernight.
— WALT WHITMAN (1819–1882) *Song of Myself*

The night cometh when no man can work.
— NEW TESTAMENT: *John*, ix, 4

Watchman, what of the night?
— OLD TESTAMENT: *Isaiah*, xxi, ii

NOBILITY

The nobleman is he whose noble mind
Is filled with inborn worth, unborrowed from his kind.
— GEOFFREY CHAUCER (1340?–1400) *Canterbury Tales*

Send your noble Blood to Market, and see what it will buy.
— THOMAS FULLER (1608–1681) *Gnomologia*

To live as one likes is plebeian; the noble man aspires to order and law.
— GOETHE (1749–1832)

Hereditary nobility is due to the presumption that we shall do well because our fathers have done well.
— JOSEPH JOUBERT (1754–1824) *Pensées*

Noblesse oblige.
— FRANÇOIS GASTON DE LÉVIS (1720–1787) *Maxims*

True nobility is exempt from fear.
— SHAKESPEARE (1564–1616) *II Henry VI*, IV, i, 129

There is
One great society alone on earth;
The Noble Living and the Noble Dead.
— WILLIAM WORDSWORTH (1770–1850) *Prelude*

OATH

An oath sworn with the clear understanding in one's mind that it should be performed must be kept.
— CICERO (106–43 B.C.) *De Officiis*

A liar is always prodigal with oaths.
— PIERRE CORNEILLE (1606–1684) *The Liar*

We mutually pledge to each other our lives, our fortunes, and our sacred honor.
— THOMAS JEFFERSON (1743–1826) *Declaration of Independence*

Ease would recant
Vows made in pain, as violent and void.
— JOHN MILTON (1608–1674) *Paradise Lost*

'Tis not the many oaths that make the truth,
But the plain single vow that is vow'd true.
— SHAKESPEARE (1564–1616) *All's Well that Ends Well*, IV, ii, 21

I write a woman's oaths in water.
— SOPHOCLES (B.C. 495–406) *Fragment*

OBEDIENCE

The fear of some divine and supreme power keeps men in obedience.
— ROBERT BURTON (1577–1640) *Anatomy of Melancholy*

All arts his own, the hungry Greekling counts;
And bid him mount the skies, the skies he mounts.
— JUVENAL (*c.* 60–130) *Satires*

Obedience,
Bane of all genius, virtue, freedom, truth,
Makes slaves of men, and, of the human frame,
A mechanized automaton.
— PERCY B. SHELLEY (1792–1822) *Queen Mab*

Learn to obey before you command.
— SOLON (638–559 B.C.)

Theirs not to make reply,
Theirs not to reason why,
Theirs but to do and die.
— TENNYSON (1809–1892) *Charge of the Light Brigade*

Obedience is the courtesy due to kings.
— TENNYSON (1809–1892) *Idylls of the King*

We ought to obey God rather than men.
— NEW TESTAMENT: *Acts*, v, 29

OPINION

The man who never alters his opinion is like standing water, and breeds reptiles of the mind.
— WILLIAM BLAKE (1757–1827) *Proverbs of Hell*

He that complies against his will
Is of his own opinion still.
— SAMUEL BUTLER (1612–1680) *Hudibras*

No well-informed person has declared a change of opinion to be inconstancy.
— CICERO (106–43 B.C.) *Ad Atticum*

The only sin which we never forgive in each other is difference of opinion.
— RALPH WALDO EMERSON (1803–1882) *Society and Solitude*

Men will die for an opinion as soon as for anything else.
— WILLIAM HAZLITT (1778–1830) *Characteristics*

With effervescing opinions, as with the not yet forgotten champagne, the quickest way to let them get flat is to let them get exposed to the air.
— JUSTICE OLIVER WENDELL HOLMES (1841–1935) *Opinion*

For a thousand heads, a thousand tastes.
— HORACE (65–8 B.C.) *Satires*

The foolish and dead alone never change their opinion.
— JAMES RUSSELL LOWELL (1819–1891) *My Study Windows*

You are young, my son, and as the years go by, time will change, and even reverse many of your present opinions. Refrain therefore, awhile from setting yourself up as a judge of the highest matters.
— PLATO (428–347 B.C.) *Laws*

Some praise at morning what they blame at night,
But always think the last opinion right.
— ALEXANDER POPE (1688–1744) *Essay on Criticism*

A plague of opinion! a man may wear it on both sides, like a leather jerkin.
— SHAKESPEARE (1564–1616) *Troilus and Cressida*, III, iii, 268

It were not best that we should all think alike; it is difference of opinion that makes horse-races.
— MARK TWAIN (1835–1910) *Pudd'nhead Wilson's Calendar*

Public opinion is stronger than the legislature, and nearly as strong as the Ten Commandments.
— CHARLES D. WARNER (1829–1900) *My Summer in a Garden*

OPPORTUNITY

A wise man makes more opportunities than he finds.
— FRANCIS BACON (1561–1620)

When one door is shut, another opens.
— CERVANTES (1547–1616) *Don Quixote*

He who seizes the (right) moment is the right man.
— GOETHE (1749–1832) *Faust*

I knock unbidden once at every gate!
If sleeping, wake; if feasting, rise before
I turn away. It is the hour of fate.
— JOHN JAMES INGALLS (1833–1900) *Opportunity*

Four things come not back:
The spoken word; The sped arrow;
Time past; The neglected opportunity.
— OMAR IBN (c. 581–644) *Sayings*

O Opportunity, thy guilt is great!
'Tis thou that execut'st the traitor's treason;
Thou set'st the wolf where he the lamb may get;
Whoever plots the sin, thou point'st the season.
— SHAKESPEARE (1564–1616) *The Rape of Lucrece*

OPTIMISM

Optimism. The doctrine or belief that everything is beautiful, including what is ugly.
— AMBROSE BIERCE (1842–1914?) *Devil's Dictionary*

God's in his Heaven—
All's right with the world!
— ROBERT BROWNING (1812–1889) *Pippa Passes*

A man that could look no way but downwards with a muck-rake in his hand.
— JOHN BUNYAN (1628–1688) *Pilgrim's Progress*

The optimist proclaims that we live in the best of all possible worlds; and the pessimist fears this is true.
— JAMES BRANCH CABELL (1879–1958) *Silver Stallion*

An optimist is a guy that has never had much experience.
— DON MARQUIS (1878–1937) *Maxims of Archy*

The refuge from pessimism is the good men and women existing at any time in the world—they keep faith and happiness alive.
— CHARLES E. NORTON (1827–1908)

All is for the best in the best of all possible worlds.
— VOLTAIRE (1694–1778) *Candide*

ORATORY

He can best be described as one of those orators who, before they get up, do not know what they are going to say; when they are speaking, do not know what they are saying; and, when they have sat down, do not know what they have said.
— WINSTON CHURCHILL (1874–1965)

When his words fell soft as snowflakes on a winter's day, then could no mortal man beside vie with Odysseus.
— HOMER (c. 10th–8th C. B.C.) *Iliad*

Oratory is the power of beating down your adversary's arguments, and putting better in their place.
— SAMUEL JOHNSON (1709–1784) Boswell's *Life of Johnson*

Fear not, my lord, I'll play the orator
As if the golden fee for which I plead
Were for myself.
— SHAKESPEARE (1564–1616) *Richard III*, III, v, 95

It is not the powerful arm,
But soft enchanting tongue that governs all.
— SOPHOCLES (495–406 B.C.) *Philoctetes*

If ever a woman feels proud of her lover, it is when she sees him as a successful public speaker.
— HARRIET BEECHER STOWE (1811–1896)

ORDER

Order means light and peace, inward liberty and free command over oneself; order is power.
— HENRI-FRÉDÉRIC AMIEL (1828–1881) *Journal*

Order is Heav'ns first law.
— ALEXANDER POPE (1688–1744) *Essay on Man*

A place for everything and everything in its place.
— SAMUEL SMILES (1812–1904) *Thrift*

Order governs the world. The Devil is the author of confusion.
— JONATHAN SWIFT (1667–1745) Letter to Stella

Have a place for everything and keep the thing somewhere else. This is not advice, it is merely custom.
— MARK TWAIN (1835–1910) *Diaries*

Let all things be done decently and in order.
— NEW TESTAMENT: *I Corinthians*, xiv, 40

PAIN

Pleasure must succeed to pleasure, else past pleasure turns to pain.
— ROBERT BROWNING (1812–1889) *La Saisiaz*

Real pain can alone cure us of imaginary ills.
— JONATHAN EDWARDS (1703–1757) *Resolutions*

He has seen but half the universe who never has been shewn the house of Pain.
— RALPH WALDO EMERSON (1803–1882)

The gods have so spun the thread for wretched mortals that they must live in pain.
— HOMER (c. 10th–8th C. B.C.) *Iliad*

Those who do not feel pain seldom think that it is felt.
— SAMUEL JOHNSON (1709–1784) *The Rambler*

There is a certain pleasure which is akin to pain.
— METRODORUS (f. 168 B.C.)

Pain is perfect misery, the worst of evils,
And excessive, overturns all patience.
— JOHN MILTON (1608–1674) *Paradise Lost*

Ay, but I fear you speak upon the rack,
Where men enforced do speak anything.
— SHAKESPEARE (1564–1616) *Merchant of Venice*, III, ii, 32

PARADISE

A book of Verses underneath the Bough,
A Jug of Wine, a Loaf of Bread—and Thou
Beside me singing in the Wilderness—
Oh, Wilderness were Paradise enow!
— EDWARD FITZGERALD (1809–1883) *Rubaiyat*

Man and Woman may only enter Paradise hand in hand. Together, the myth tells us, they left it and together must they return.
— RICHARD GARNETT (1835–1906) *De Flagello Myrteo*

Paradise is a dwelling place promised the faithful.
— MOHAMMED (570–632) *The Koran*

The loves that meet in Paradise shall cast out fear,
And Paradise hath room for you and me and all.
— CHRISTINA ROSSETTI (1830–1894) *Saints and Angels*

PARENTS

Reverence for parents—this standeth written third among the statutes of Justice to whom supreme honor is due.
— AESCHYLUS (525–456 B.C.) *Suppliants*

There are three degrees of filial piety. The highest is being a credit to our parents, the second is not disgracing them; the lowest is being able simply to support them.
— CONFUCIUS (c. 551–478 B.C.) *Book of Rites*

It used to be believed that the parent had unlimited claims on the child and rights over him. In a truer view of the matter, we are coming to see that the rights are on the side of the child and the duties on the side of the parent.
— WILLIAM G. SUMNER (1840–1910) *Forgotten Man's Almanac*

He argued that the principal duty which a parent owed to a child was to make him happy.
— ANTHONY TROLLOPE (1815–1882) *Doctor Thorne*

Children begin by loving their parents; as they grow older they judge them; sometimes they forgive them.
— OSCAR WILDE (1854–1900) *Dorian Gray*

Honour thy father and mother; that thy days may be long upon the land which the Lord thy God giveth thee.
— OLD TESTAMENT: *Exodus*, XX, 12

PARTING

Go from me. Yet I feel that I shall stand
Henceforward in thy shadow.
— ELIZABETH B. BROWNING (1806–1861) *Sonnets from Portuguese*

Parting is all we know of heaven,
And all we need of hell.
— EMILY DICKINSON (1830–1886) *Poems*

They who go
Feel not the pain of parting; it is they
Who stay behind that suffer.
— HENRY W. LONGFELLOW (1807–1882) *Michael Angelo*

Good night! Good night! parting is such sweet sorrow
That I shall say good night till it be morrow.
— SHAKESPEARE (1564–1616) *Romeo and Juliet*, II, ii, 185

PAST

Think only of the past as its remembrance gives you pleasure.
— JANE AUSTEN (1775–1817) *Pride and Prejudice*

I have small patience with the antiquarian habit which magnifies the past and belittles the present.... Change is inevitable, at once a penalty and a privilege.
— JOHN BUCHAN (1875–1940) *Memory Hold-the-Door*

He seems
To have seen better days, as who has not
Who has seen yesterday?
— LORD BYRON (1788–1824) *Age of Bronze*

Oh! leave the past to bury its own dead.
— WILLIAM S. BLUNT (1840–1922) *To One Who Would Make a Confession*

Historic continuity with the past is not a duty, it is only a necessity.
— JUSTICE OLIVER WENDELL HOLMES (1841–1935)

Tomorrow I will live, the fool does say;
Today itself's too late; the wise lived yesterday.
— MARTIAL (*c.* 66 A.D.) *Epigrams*

Those who cannot remember the past are condemned to repeat it.
— GEORGE SANTAYANA (1863–1952) *Life of Reason*

PATIENCE

There is a limit at which forbearance ceases to be a virtue.
— EDMUND BURKE (1729–1797) *Observations*

Beware the fury of a patient man.
— JOHN DRYDEN (1631–1700) *Absalom and Achitophel*

Patience, that blending of moral courage with physical timidity.
— THOMAS HARDY (1840–1928) *Tess of the D'Urbervilles*

All men commend patience, although few be willing to practise it.
— THOMAS À KEMPIS (1380–1471) *Imitation of Christ*

Forbearance is a part of justice.
— MARCUS AURELIUS (121–180) *Meditations*

They also serve who only stand and wait.
— JOHN MILTON (1608–1674) *On His Blindness*

It's a long lane that has no turning.
— SAMUEL RICHARDSON (1689–1761) *Clarissa*

'Tis all men's office to speak patience
To those who wring under the load of sorrow;
But no man's virtue nor sufficiency
To be so moral when he shall endure
The like himself.
— SHAKESPEARE (1564–1616) *Much Ado About Nothing*, V, i, 27

Ye have heard of the patience of Job.
— NEW TESTAMENT: *James*, v, ii

In your patience possess ye your souls.
— NEW TESTAMENT: *Luke*, xxi, 18

PATRIOTISM

The die was now cast; I had passed the Rubicon. Swim or sink, live or die, survive or perish with my country was my unalterable determination.
— JOHN ADAMS (1735–1826)

The country of every man is that one where he lives best.
— ARISTOPHANES (444–380 B.C.) *Plutus*

No man can be a patriot on an empty stomach.
— WILLIAM C. BRANN (1855–1898) *Iconoclast*

He who loves not his country can love nothing.
— LORD BYRON (1788–1824) *Two Foscari*

Our country! In her intercourse with foreign nations, may she always be in the right; but our country, right or wrong.
— STEPHAN DECATUR (1779–1820)

My affections are first for my own country, and then, generally, for all mankind.
— THOMAS JEFFERSON (1743–1826) Letter to Thomas Law

My country is the world, and my religion is to do good.
— THOMAS PAINE (1737–1809) *Rights of Man*

If I were an American, as I am an Englishman, while a foreign troop was landed in my country I never would lay down my arms, never! never! never!
— WILLIAM PITT (1708–1778) Speech, 1777

We should behave toward our country as women behave toward the men they love. A loving wife will do anything for her husband except stop criticizing and trying to improve him. We should cast the same affectionate but sharp glance at our country.
— J. B. PRIESTLEY (1894–   )

Where is the man who owes nothing to the land in which he lives? Whatever the land may be, he owes to it the most precious thing possessed by man, the morality of his actions and the love of virtue.
— JEAN-JACQUES ROUSSEAU (1712–1778) *Émile*

Breathes there a man with soul so dead,
Who never to himself hath said,
This is my own, my native land!
— SIR WALTER SCOTT (1771–1832) *Lay of the Last Minstrel*

I do love
My country's good with a respect more tender,
More holy and profound, than my own life.
— SHAKESPEARE (1564–1616) *Coriolanus*, III, iii, 111

The proper means of increasing the love we bear our native country is to reside some time in a foreign one.
— WILLIAM SHENSTONE (1714–1763) *Of Men and Manners*

Our country, right or wrong. When right, to be kept right; when wrong, to be put right.
— CARL SCHURZ (1829–1906) Speech, 1872

The more I see of other countries, the more I love my own.
— MADAME DE STAËL (1766–1817) *Corinne*

PEACE

He makes a solitude, and calls it—peace!
— LORD BYRON (1788–1824) *Bride of Abydos*

We have preserved peace in our time.
— NEVILLE CHAMBERLAIN (1869–1940) Speech, 1938

Peace rules the day, where reason rules the mind.
— WILLIAM COLLINS (1720–1756) *Hassan*

The gentleman (Josiah Quincy) cannot have forgotten his own sentiment, uttered even on the floor of this House, "Peaceably if we can, forcibly if we must."
— HENRY CLAY (1777–1852) Speech, 1813

Peace at any price.
— ALPHONSE DE LAMARTINE (1790–1869)

Peace will come soon and come to stay, and so come as to be worth keeping in all future time. It will then have been proved that among free men there can be no successful appeal from the ballot to the bullet, and that they who take such appeal are sure to lose their cases and pay the cost.
— ABRAHAM LINCOLN (1809–1865)

We supplicate all rulers not to remain deaf to the cry of mankind. Let them do everything in their power to save peace. By so doing they will spare the world the horrors of a war that would have disastrous consequences, such as nobody can foresee.
— POPE JOHN XXIII (1881–1963) Oct. 25, 1962

We will have to want Peace, want it enough to pay for it, before it becomes an accepted rule.
— ELEANOR ROOSEVELT (1884–1964)

A peace is of the nature of a conquest;
For then both parties nobly are subdued
And neither party loser.
— SHAKESPEARE (1564–1616) *Henry IV*, IV, ii, 89

Peace be to you. [Pax vobiscum.]
— OLD TESTAMENT: *Genesis*, xliii, 23

Go in peace. [Vade in pace.]
— OLD TESTAMENT: *Exodus*, iv, 18

The peace of God, which passeth all understanding.
— NEW TESTAMENT: *Philippians*, iv, 7

Blessed are the peace-makers.
— NEW TESTAMENT: *Matthew*, v, 9

Glory to God in the highest, and on earth peace, good will toward men.
— NEW TESTAMENT: *Luke*, ii, 14

They shall beat their swords into ploughshares, and their spears into pruning-hooks; nation shall not lift up sword against nation, neither shall they learn war any more.
— OLD TESTAMENT: *Isaiah*, ii, 4

PEOPLE

A people's voice is dangerous when charged with wrath.
— AESCHYLUS (525–456 B.C.) *Agamemnon*

The individual is foolish; the multitude, for the moment is foolish, when they act without deliberation; but the species is wise, and, when time is given to it, as a species it always acts right.
— EDMUND BURKE (1729–1797)

The rabble estimate few things according to their real value, most things according to their prejudices.
— CICERO (106–43 B.C.) *Oratio Pro Quinto Roscio Comaedo*

Your people, sir, is nothing but a great beast!
— ALEXANDER HAMILTON (1757–1804) Argument with Thomas Jefferson

The Lord prefers common-looking people. That is the reason He made so many of them.
— ABRAHAM LINCOLN (1809–1865)

The people is Everyman, everybody.
Everybody is you and me and all others.
What everybody says is what we all say.
— CARL SANDBURG (1878–1967) *The People, Yes*

PERFECTION

There never was such beauty in another man,
Nature made him, and broke the mould.
— LODOVICO ARIOSTO (1474–1533) *Orlando Furioso*

The more a thing is perfect, the more it feels pleasure and likewise pain.
— DANTE (1265–1321) *Inferno*

In this broad earth of ours,
Amid the measureless grossness and the slag,
Enclosed and safe within its central heart,
Nestles the seed Perfection.
— WALT WHITMAN (1819–1892) *Song of the Universal*

Be ye therefore Perfect, even as your Father which is in heaven is perfect.
— NEW TESTAMENT: *Matthew*, v, 48

PHILANTHROPY

He who bestows his goods upon the poor,
Shall have as much again, and ten times more.
— JOHN BUNYAN (1628–1688) *Pilgrim's Progress*

In nothing do men more nearly approach the gods than in doing good to their fellow men.
— CICERO (106–43 B.C.) *Pro Ligario*

The most acceptable service to God is doing good to man.
— BEN FRANKLIN (1706–1790) *Autobiography*

I expect to pass through this world but once. Any good therefore that I can do, or any kindness that I can show to any fellow creature, let me do it now. Let me not defer or neglect it, for I shall not pass this way again.
— STEPHEN GRELLET (1773–1855)

The hands that help are holier than the lips that pray.
— ROBERT GREEN INGERSOLL (1833–1899)

To pity distress is but human: to relieve it is Godlike.
— HORACE MANN (1796–1859) *Lectures on Education*

Benevolence is the distinguishing characteristic of man. As embodied in man's conduct, it is called the path of duty.
— MENCIUS (372?–289 B.C.) *Discourses*

I am a man, and nothing in man's lot can be indifferent to me.
— TERENCE (c. 190–150 B.C.) *Heautontimoroumenos*

Myself not ignorant of adversity, I have learned to befriend the unhappy.
— VERGIL (70–19 B.C.) *Aeneid*

I was a stranger, and ye took me in.
— NEW TESTAMENT: *Matthew*, xxv, 35

PHILOSOPHY

What I have gained from philosophy is the ability to feel at ease in any society.
— ARISTIPPUS (425?–366? B.C.)

The Philosopher is he to whom the Highest has descended, and the Lowest has mounted up; who is the equal and kindly brother of all.
— THOMAS CARLYLE (1795–1881) *Sartor Resartus*

Philosophy as a fellow once said to me is only thinking. Thinking is an instrument of adjustment to the conditions of life—but it becomes an end in itself.
— JUSTICE OLIVER WENDELL HOLMES (1841–1935)

Philosophy is an attitude toward life, based on a greater or lesser, but always limited comprehension of the universe as far as we happen to know it.
— LIN YUTANG (1895-   ) *I Believe*

Philosophy is toleration, and it is only one step from toleration to forgiveness.
— ARTHUR W. PINERO (1855–1934) *Second Mrs. Tanqueray*

The greater the philosopher, the harder it is for him to answer the questions of common people.
— HENRYK SIENKIEWICZ (1846–1916) *Quo Vadis*

Men of Athens, I honor and love you; but I shall obey God rather than you, and while I have life and strength I shall never cease from the practise and teaching of philosophy.
— SOCRATES (470–399? B.C.) in Plato's *Apology*

Philosophers must deal with ideas, but the trouble with most nineteenth century poets is too much philosophy; they are nearer to being philosophers than poets, without being in the true sense either.
— ALLEN TATE (1899-   ) *Reactionary Essays*

POETRY

Poetry is simply the most beautiful, impressive and widely effective mode of saying things, and hence its importance.
— MATTHEW ARNOLD (1822–1888) *Essays*

Poetry has been to me an exceeding great reward; it has soothed my affliction; it has multiplied and refined my enjoyments; it has endeared my solitude; and it has given me the habit of wishing to discover the Good and the Beautiful in all that meets and surrounds me.
— SAMUEL TAYLOR COLERIDGE (1772–1834)

Poetry is not a turning loose of emotion, but an escape from emotion; it is not the expression of personality, but an escape from personality. But, of course, only those who have personality and emotions know what it means to want to escape from these things.
— T. S. ELIOT (1888–1965) *Tradition and the Individual Talent*

Writing free verse is like playing tennis with the net down.
— ROBERT FROST (1875–1963) Address

Do you suppose we owe nothing to Pope's deformity? —He said to himself, "If my person be crooked, my verses shall be straight."
— WILLIAM HAZLITT (1778–1830)

I have reared a monument more enduring than bronze and loftier than the royal pyramids, one that no wasting rain, no unavailing north wind can destroy; no, not even the unending years nor the flight of time itself. I shall not wholly die. The greater part of me shall escape oblivion.
— HORACE (65–8 B.C.) *Odes*

A poet is a nightingale who sits in darkness and sings to cheer its own solitude with sweet sounds.
— PERCY B. SHELLEY (1792–1822) *Defense of Poetry*

Verse without rhyme is a body without a soul.
— JONATHAN SWIFT (1667–1745) *Advice to a Young Poet*

POLITICS

Politics make strange bedfellows.
— JOHN S. BASSETT (1867–1928) *Life of Jackson*

Politics. The conduct of public affairs for private advantage.
— AMBROSE BIERCE (1842–1914?) *Devil's Dictionary*

I shall not help crucify mankind upon a cross of gold. I shall not aid in pressing down upon the bleeding brow of labor this crown of thorns.
— WILLIAM JENNINGS BRYAN (1860–1925) Speech

We are Republicans, and we don't propose to leave our party and identify ourselves with the party whose antecedents have been rum, Romanism and rebellion.
— REV. S. D. BURCHARD (1812–1891) Speech, 1884

When I was called upon to be Prime Minister, now nearly two years ago, there were not many applicants for the job. Since then perhaps the market has improved.
— WINSTON CHURCHILL (1874–1965) Speech, Jan. 1942

Damn your principles. Stick to your party.
— BENJAMIN DISRAELI (1804–1881)

Every time I bestow a vacant office I make a hundred discontented persons and one ingrate.
— LOUIS XIV OF FRANCE (1638–1715)

The various admirable movements in which I have been engaged have always developed among their members a large lunatic fringe.
— THEODORE ROOSEVELT (1858–1919)

PRAYER

"Oh, God, if I were sure I were to die tonight I would repent at once." It is the commonest prayer in all languages.
— JAMES M. BARRIE (1860–1937) *Sentimental Tommy*

He prayeth well who loveth well
Both man and bird and beast;
He prayeth best who loveth best
All things both great and small
For the dear God who loveth us,
He made and loveth all.
— SAMUEL TAYLOR COLERIDGE (1772–1834) *Ancient Mariner*

We, on our side, are praying to Him to give us victory, because we believe we are right; but those on the other side pray to Him, too, for victory, believing they are right. What must He think of us?
— ABRAHAM LINCOLN (1809–1865)

God grant me the serenity to accept the things I cannot change, courage to change things I can, and wisdom to know the difference.
— REINHOLD NIEBUHR (1892–1971)

More things are wrought by prayer
Than this world dreams of.
— TENNYSON (1809–1892) *Morte d'Arthur*

I have never made but one prayer to God, a very short one: "O Lord, make my enemies ridiculous." And God granted it.
— VOLTAIRE (1694–1778)

Therefore I say unto you, What things soever ye desire, when ye pray, believe that ye receive them, and ye shall receive them.
— NEW TESTAMENT: *Mark*, XI, 23, 24

Ask, and it shall be given you; seek, and ye shall find, knock, and it shall be opened unto you.
— NEW TESTAMENT: *Matthew*, vii, 7

PRIDE

Pride is the beginning of sin.
— BEN SIRA (c. 190 B.C.) *Book of Wisdom*

Pride, Envy, Avarice—these are the sparks
Have set on fire the hearts of all men.
— DANTE (1265–1321) *Inferno*

The readiness with which we admit a fault or acknowledge a weakness may be only our pride masquerading as humility.
— OSCAR HAMMLING (1890-   )

In pride, in reas'ning pride, our error lies;
All quit their sphere, and rush into the skies!
Pride still is aiming at the bless'd abodes,
Men would be angels, Angels would be Gods.
— ALEXANDER POPE (1688–1744) *Essay on Man*

War is the child of pride, and pride the daughter of riches.
— JONATHAN SWIFT (1667–1745) *Battle of the Books*

Pride goeth before destruction, and an haughty spirit before a fall.
— OLD TESTAMENT: *Proverbs*, xvi, 18

PRUDENCE

Make haste slowly.
— AUGUSTUS CAESAR (63 B.C.–A.D. 14)

Put your trust in God, my boys, and keep your powder dry.
— OLIVER CROMWELL (1599–1658)

The greatest good is prudence; a more precious thing even than philosophy; from it spring all the other virtues.
— EPICURUS (342–270 B.C.) *Letter to Menaeceus*

That man is prudent who neither hopes nor fears anything from the uncertain events of the future.
— ANATOLE FRANCE (1844–1924) *Procurator of Judea*

Beware of rashness, but with energy and sleepless vigilance go forward and give us victories.
— ABRAHAM LINCOLN (1809–1865) Letter to Gen. Hooker

Let every man be swift to hear, slow to speak.
— NEW TESTAMENT: *James*, i, 19

READING

Reading is to the Mind, what Exercise is to the Body.
— JOSEPH ADDISON (1672–1719) *The Tatler*

To read a book for the first time is to make the acquaintance of a new friend; to read it a second time is to meet an old one.
— SELWYN G. CHAMPION (1875–1950) *Racial Proverbs*

Some read to think—these are rare; some to write—these are common; and some to talk—and these form the great majority.
— CHARLES C. COLTON (1780?–1832) *Lacon*

There is an art of reading, as well as an art of thinking, and an art of writing.
— ISAAC D'ISRAELI (1766–1848) *Literary Character*

. man ought to read just as inclination leads him; for what e reads as a task will do him little good. A young man should ead five hours in a day, and so may acquire a great deal of nowledge.
— SAMUEL JOHNSON (1709–1784) Boswell's *Life*

I'm quite illiterate, but I read a lot.
— J. D. SALINGER (1919–   ) *Catcher in the Rye*

He hath never fed of the dainties that are bred in a book.
— SHAKESPEARE (1564–1616) *Love's Labour's Lost*, IV, ii, 25

The habit of reading is the only enjoyment in which there is no alloy; it lasts when all other pleasures fade.
— ANTHONY TROLLOPE (1815–1882)

REASON

Reason is a light that God has kindled in the soul.
— ARISTOTLE (384–322 B.C.) *Art of Rhetoric*

He who will not reason is a bigot; he who cannot is a fool; and he who dares not is a slave.
— WILLIAM DRUMMOND (1585–1649) *Academical Question*

It is wise even in adversity to listen to reason.
— EURIPIDES (480–406 B.C.) *Hecuba*

The soul of man is divided into three parts, intelligence, reason and passion. Intelligence and passion are possessed by other animals, but reason by man alone.... Reason is immortal, all else mortal.
— PYTHAGORAS (582–500 B.C.)

REGRET

Regret not that which is past; and trust not to thine own righteousness.
— ST. ANTHONY (*c.* 250–350)

O lost days of delight, that are wasted in doubting and waiting!
O lost hours and days in which we might have been happy!
— HENRY W. LONGFELLOW (1807–1882) *Tales of a Wayside Inn*

Of all sad words of tongue or pen,
The saddest are these: "It might have been."
— JOHN GREENLEAF WHITTIER (1807–1892) *Maud Muller*

RESPECT

Respect is what we owe; love, what we give.
— PHILIP JAMES BAILEY (1816–1902) *Festus*

He removes the greatest ornament of friendship, who takes away from it respect.
— CICERO (106–43 B.C.) *De Amicitia*

A man's real life is that accorded to him in the thoughts of other men by reason of respect or natural love.
— JOSEPH CONRAD (1857–1924) *Under Western Eyes*

Deference is the instinctive respect which we pay to the great and good; the unconscious acknowledgment of the superiority or excellence of others.
— TRYON EDWARDS (1809–1894)

Even a nod from a person who is esteemed is of more force than a thousand arguments or studied sentences from others.
— PLUTARCH (46?–120?) *Lives: Phocion*

There is no respect of persons with God.
— NEW TESTAMENT: *Romans*, ii, 11

RETIREMENT

Don't think of retiring from the world until the world will be sorry that you retire. I hate a fellow whom pride or cowardice or laziness drive into a corner, and who does nothing when he is there but sit and growl. Let him come out as I do, and bark.
— SAMUEL JOHNSON (1709–1784)

Let me caution persons grown old in active business, not lightly, nor without weighing their own resources, to forego their customary employment all at once, for there may be danger in it.
— CHARLES LAMB (1775–1834) *Superannuated Man*

  I could be well content
To entertain the lag-end of my life
With quiet hours.
— SHAKESPEARE (1564–1616) *I Henry IV*, V, i, 23

SCIENCE

Science bestowed immense new powers on man and at the same time created conditions which were largely beyond his comprehension and still more beyond his control.
— WINSTON CHURCHILL (1874–1965) Speech, March 31, 1949

In science we must be interested in things, not in persons.
— MARIE CURIE (1867–1934)

What art was to the ancient world, science is to the modern.
— BENJAMIN DISRAELI (1804–1881) *Coningsby*

Why does this magnificent applied science, which saves work and makes life easier, bring us little happiness? The simple answer runs, because we have not yet learned to make sensible use of it.
— ALBERT EINSTEIN (1879–1955) Address, 1931

Science is the knowledge of consequences, and dependence of one fact upon another.
— THOMAS HOBBES (1588–1679) *Leviathan*

In science the credit goes to the man who convinces the world, not to the man to whom the idea first occurs.
— SIR WILLIAM OSLER (1849–1919)

SEA

Roll on, thou deep and dark blue ocean, roll.
Ten thousand fleets sweep over thee in vain:
Man marks the earth with ruin, —his control
Stops with the shore.
— LORD BYRON (1788–1824) *Childe Harold*

The sea possesses a power over one's moods that has the effect of a will. The sea can hypnotize. Nature in general can do so.
— HENDRIK IBSEN (1828–1906) *Lady from the Sea*

Comrades! now that we have established our peace on land, let us conquer the freedom of the seas.
— NAPOLEON BONAPARTE (1769–1821)

Any one can hold the helm when the sea is calm.
— PUBLILIUS SYRUS (1st C. B.C.) *Sententiae*

The sea folds away from you like a mystery. You can look and look at it and mystery never leaves it.
— CARL SANDBURG (1878–1967) *Remembrance Rock*

Full fathom five thy father lies;
  Of his bones are coral made;
Those are pearls that were his eyes;
  Nothing of him that doth fade
But doth suffer a sea-change
  Into something rich and strange.
— SHAKESPEARE (1564–1616) *Tempest*, I, ii, 394

All the rivers run into the sea; yet the sea is not full.
— OLD TESTAMENT: *Ecclesiastes*, i, 7

SEASON

To everything there is a season, and a time to every purpose under the heaven.
— OLD TESTAMENT: *Ecclesiastes*, iii, 1

SELF-CONTROL

One of the most important, but one of the most difficult things for a powerful mind is, to be its own master. A pond may lie quiet in a plain; but a lake wants mountains to compass and hold it in.
— JOSEPH ADDISON (1672–1719)

I count him braver who overcomes his desires than him who conquers his enemies; for the hardest victory is the victory over self.
— ARISTOTLE (384–322 B.C.) *Stobaeus: Florilegium*

Conquer thyself. Till thou hast done this, thou art but a slave for it is almost as well to be subjected to another's appetite as to thine own.
— ROBERT BURTON (1577–1640) *Anatomy of Melancholy*

Nothing gives one person so much advantage over another as to remain always cool and unruffled under all circumstances.
— THOMAS JEFFERSON (1743–1826)

No conflict is so severe as his who labors to subdue himself.
— THOMAS À KEMPIS (1380–1471) *Imitation of Christ*

He that is slow to anger is better than the mighty; and he that ruleth his spirit than he that taketh a city.
— OLD TESTAMENT: *Proverbs*, xvi, 32

SELFISHNESS

People often grudge others what they cannot enjoy themselves.
— AESOP (6th C. B.C.) *Dog in the Manger*

This is the plain truth: every one ought to keep a sharp eye for the main chance.
— PLAUTUS (*c.* 254–184 B.C.) *Asinaria*

We have always known that heedless self-interest was bad morals; we know now that it is bad economics.
— FRANKLIN D. ROOSEVELT (1882–1945) Second Inaugural

There's plenty of boys that will come hankering and gruvelling around when you've got an apple, and beg the core off you; but when *they've* got one, and you beg for the core, and remind them how you give them a core one time, they make a mouth at you, and say thank you most to death, but there ain't a-going to *be* no core.
— MARK TWAIN (1835–1910) *Tom Sawyer Abroad*

Selfishness is the only real atheism; aspiration, unselfishness, the only real religion.
— ISRAEL ZANGWILL (1864–1926) *Children of the Ghetto*

SELF-RESPECT

The reverence of a man's self is, next to religion, the chiefest bridle of all vices.
— FRANCIS BACON (1561–1620) *New Atlantis*

Few men survey themselves with so much severity as not to admit prejudices in their own favor.
— SAMUEL JOHNSON (1709–1784) *The Rambler*

I care not so much what I am in the opinion of others as what I am in my own; I would be rich of myself and not by borrowing.
— MICHEL DE MONTAIGNE (1533–1592) *Essays*

If ye would go up high, then use your own legs! Do not get yourselves *carried* aloft; do not seat yourselves on other's backs and heads!
— FRIEDRICH NIETZSCHE (1844–1900) *Thus Spake Zarathustra*

To have a respect for ourselves guides our morals; and to have a deference for others governs our manners.
— LAURENCE STERNE (1713–1768)

SERENITY

Remember to preserve an even mind in adverse circumstance and likewise in prosperity a mind free from overweening joy.
— HORACE (65–8 B.C.) *Odes*

Calm of mind, all passion spent.
— JOHN MILTON (1608–1674) *Samson Agonistes*

He who is of a calm and happy nature will hardly feel the pressure of age, but to him who is of an opposite disposition youth and age are equally a burden.
— PLATO (428–347 B.C.) *The Republic*

SILENCE

Silence gives consent.
— CANON LAW: *Decretals*

Silence is the unbearable repartee.
— G. K. CHESTERTON (1874–1936) *Dickens*

Silence is true wisdom's best reply.
— EURIPIDES (480–406 B.C.) *Fragments*

There is an eloquent silence: it serves sometimes to approve, sometimes to condemn; there is a mocking silence; there is a respectful silence.
— FRANÇOIS DE LA ROCHEFOUCAULD (1613–1680) *Reflections*

He has occasional flashes of silence, that make his conversation perfectly delightful.
— SYDNEY SMITH (1771–1845) *Speaking of Macaulay*

Even a fool, when he holdeth his peace, is counted wise.
— OLD TESTAMENT: *Proverbs*, xvii, 28

SLEEP

We sleep, but the loom of life never stops and the pattern which was weaving when the sun went down is weaving when the sun comes up tomorrow.
— HENRY WARD BEECHER (1813–1887) *Life Thoughts*

Sleep is a death; oh, make me try
By sleeping, know what it is to die,
And as gently lay my head
On my grave, as now my bed.
— THOMAS BROWNE (1605–1682) *Religio Medici*

Our life is two-fold: Sleep hath its own world,
A boundry between the things misnamed
Death and existence: Sleep hath its own world.
And a wide realm of wild reality.
— LORD BYRON (1788–1824) *The Dream*

Now blessings light on him that first invented this same sleep!
It covers a man all over, thoughts and all, like a cloak; 'tis
meat for the hungry, drink for the thirsty, heat for the cold,
and cold for the hot. 'Tis the current coin that purchases all
the pleasures of the world cheap; and the balance that sets
the king and the shepherd, the fool and the wise man even.
— CERVANTES (1547–1616) *Don Quixote*

O Sleep, thou rest of all things, Sleep, gentlest of the gods,
peace of the soul, who puttest care to flight.
— OVID (43 B.C.–A.D. 18?) *Metamorphoses*

Our foster-nurse of nature is repose,
The which he lacks; that to provoke in him,
Are many simples operative, whose power
Will close the eye of anguish.
— SHAKESPEARE (1564–1616) *King Lear*, IV, iv, 12

Sleep that knits up the ravell'd sleave of care,
The death of each day's life, sore labour's bath,
Balm of hurt minds, great nature's second course,
Chief nourisher in life's feast.
— SHAKESPEARE (1564–1616) *Macbeth*, II, ii, 36

Thou hast been called, O sleep! the friend of woe;
But 'tis the happy that have called thee so.
— ROBERT SOUTHEY (1774–1843) *Curse of Kehama*

Yet a little sleep, a little slumber, a little folding of the hands
to sleep.
— OLD TESTAMENT: *Proverbs*, vi, 10

SMILE

What sunshine is to flowers, smiles are to humanity. They
are but trifles, to be sure; but, scattered along life's pathway,
the good they do is inconceivable.
— JOSEPH ADDISON (1672–1719)

There is a smile of Love,
And there is a smile of Deceit,
And there is a smile of smiles
In which these two smiles meet.
— WILLIAM BLAKE (1757–1827) *Smile and Frown*

A smile is ever the most bright and beautiful with a tear upon
it. What is the dawn without the dew? The tear is rendered
by the smile precious above the smile itself.
— WALTER S. LANDOR (1775–1864)

SOLDIER

It were better to be a soldier's widow than a coward's wife.
— THOMAS B. ALDRICH (1836–1907) *Mercedes*

I love a brave soldier who has undergone the baptism of fire.
— NAPOLEON BONAPARTE (1769–1821)

The army is a school in which the miser becomes generous,
and the generous prodigal; miserly soldiers are like monsters,
very rarely seen.
— CERVANTES (1547–1616) *Don Quixote*

How sleep the brave, who sink to rest,
By all their country's wishes blest!
— WILLIAM COLLINS (1721–1759) *Ode Written in 1746*

For it's Tommy this, an' Tommy that, an'
    "Chuck 'im out, the brute!"
But it's the "Saviour of 'is country" when
    the guns begin to shoot.
— RUDYARD KIPLING (1865–1936) *Tommy*

But in a larger sense, we cannot dedicate, we cannot consecrate, we cannot hallow this ground. The brave men living
and dead, who struggled here, have consecrated it far above
our poor power to add or detract. The world will little note,
nor long remember, what we say here, but it can never forget
what they did here.
— ABRAHAM LINCOLN (1809–1865) Gettysburg Address

"Companions," said he [Saturninus], "you have lost a good
captain, to make of him a bad general."
— MICHEL DE MONTAIGNE (1533–1592) *Essays*

Your son, my lord, has paid a soldier's debt:
He only lived but till he was a man;
The which no sooner had his prowess confirm'd
In the unshrinking station where he fought,
But like a man he died.
—SHAKESPEARE (1564–1616) *Macbeth*, V, vii, 68

The proper qualities of a general are judgment and deliberation.
— TACITUS (c. 55–117) *History*

The combat infantryman should combine the arts of a successful poacher, a cat-burglar and a gunman.
— FIELD MARSHAL EARL WAVELL (1885–1950)

SON See CHILDREN

SORROW

There is no sorrow which length of time does not diminish
and soften.
— CICERO (106–43 B.C.) *De Finibus*

I have had sorrows . . . but I have borne them ill.
I have broken where I should have bent.
— CHARLES DICKENS (1812–1870) *Barnaby Rudge*

When sorrows come, they come not single spies,
But in battalions.
— SHAKESPEARE (1564–1616) *Hamlet*, IV, v, 78

SUMMER

Heat, ma'am! It was so dreadful here that I found nothing
left for it but to take off my flesh and sit in my bones.
— SYDNEY SMITH (1771–1845) in Lady Holland's *Memoirs*

Shall I compare thee to a summer's day?
—SHAKESPEARE (1564–1616) *Sonnets*, xviii

Today the summer has come at my window with its sighs and
murmurs; and the bees are plying their minstrelsy at the
court of the flowering grove.
— RABINDRANATH TAGORE (1861–1941) *Gitanjali*

SYMPATHY

   The man who melts
With social sympathy, though not allied,
Is of more worth than a thousand kinsmen.
— EURIPIDES (480–406 B.C.) *Orestes*

Sympathy is a virtue much cultivated by those who are
morally uplifted by the sufferings and misfortunes of others.
— OSCAR HAMMLING (1890–   )

As man laughs with those that laugh, so he weeps with those
that weep; if thou wish me to weep, thou must first shed tears
thyself; then thy sorrows will touch me.
— HORACE (65–8 B.C.) *De Arte Poetica*

It is better to be generous than just. It is sometimes better
to sympathize instead of trying to understand.
— PIERRE LECOMTE DE NOÜY (1883–1947) *Human Destiny*

TALENT

Doing easily what others find difficult is talent . . . .
— HENRI-FRÉDÉRIC AMIEL (1828–1881) *Journal*

Every man hath his proper gift of God, one after this manner
and another after that.
— NEW TESTAMENT: *I Corinthians*, vii, 7

TASTE

Happy is the man possessing
The superior holy blessing
Of a judgment and a taste
Accurate, refined and chaste.
— ARISTOPHANES (444–380 B.C.) *The Frogs*

Love of beauty is Taste. . . . The creation of beauty is Art.
— RALPH WALDO EMERSON (1803–1882)

TEACHER AND TEACHING

A teacher affects eternity; he can never tell where his influence stops.
— HENRY ADAMS (1838–1918) *Education of Henry Adams*

The true teacher defends his pupils against his own personal influence.
— AMOS BRONSON ALCOTT (1799–1888) *Orphic Sayings*

To know how to suggest is the great art of teaching.
— HENRI-FRÉDÉRIC AMIEL (1828–1881) *Journal*

What nobler employment, or more valuable to the state, than that of the man who instructs the rising generation?
— CICERO (106–43 B.C.) *De Divinatione*

The secret of teaching is to appear to have known all your life what you learned this afternoon.
— UNKNOWN

THRIFT

A man's ordinary expenses ought to be but half of his receipts, and if he think to wax rich, but to the third part.
— FRANCIS BACON (1561–1620)

He will always be a slave, who does not know how to live upon a little.
— HORACE (65–8 B.C.) *Epistulae*

Resolve not to be poor; whatever you have, spend less.
— SAMUEL JOHNSON (1709–1784) Boswell's *Life*

Thrift is care and scruple in the spending of one's means. It is not a virtue, and it requires neither skill nor talent.
— IMMANUEL KANT (1724–1804) Lecture

TIME

Go, sir, gallop, and don't forget that the world was made in six days. You can ask me for anything you like except time.
— NAPOLEON BONAPARTE (1769–1821) To one of his aides

Never the time and the place
And the loved one all together!
— ROBERT BROWNING (1812–1889) *Never the Time and Place*

There is no remembrance which time does not obliterate, nor pain which death does not end.
— CERVANTES (1547–1616) *Don Quixote*

For though we sleep or wake, or roam, or ride,
Aye fleets the time, it will no man abide.
— GEOFFREY CHAUCER (1340?–1400) *Canterbury Tales*

Dost thou love life? Then do not squander time, for that is the stuff life is made of.
— BEN FRANKLIN (1706–1790) *Poor Richard's Almanack*

Gather ye rosebuds while ye may,
  Old Time is still a-flying,
And this same flower that smiles today,
  Tomorrow will be dying.
— ROBERT HERRICK (1591–1674) *To the Virgins*

Stand still, you ever moving spheres of heaven,
That time may cease, and midnight never come.
— CHRISTOPHER MARLOWE (1564–1593) *Dr. Faustus*

The time which we have at our disposal every day is elastic; the passions that we feel expand it, those that we inspire contract it; and habit fills up what remains.
— MARCEL PROUST (1871–1922) *Remembrance of Things Past*

Time flies on restless pinions—constant never.
Be constant—and thou chainest time forever.
— JOHANN SCHILLER (1759–1805) *Epigram*

Make use of time, let not advantage slip;
Beauty within itself should not be wasted:
Fair flowers that are not gather'd in their prime,
Rot and consume themselves in little time.
— SHAKESPEARE (1564–1616) *Venus and Adonis*. 129

There is . . . a time to be born, and a time to die; a time to plant, and a time to pluck up that which is planted; A time to kill, and a time to heal; a time to break down, and a time to build up; A time to weep, and a time to laugh; a time to mourn, and a time to dance; . . . A time to love and a time to hate.
— OLD TESTAMENT: *Ecclesiastes*, iii, 1

TOLERANCE AND INTOLERANCE

He knows not how to wink at human frailty,
Or pardon weakness that he never felt.
— JOSEPH ADDISON (1672–1719) *Cato*

Toleration is good for all or it is good for none.
— EDMUND BURKE (1729–1797) Speech, 1773

I have seen gross intolerance shown in support of toleration.
— SAMUEL TAYLOR COLERIDGE (1772–1834) *Biographia*

Give to every other human being every right you claim for yourself.
— ROBERT GREEN INGERSOLL (1833–1899) *Limitations of Toleration*

Shall I ask the brave soldier, who fights by my side
In the cause of mankind, if our creeds agree!
Shall I give up the friend I have valued and tried,
If he kneel not before the same altar with me.
— THOMAS MOORE (1779–1852) *Come, Send Round the Wine*

It is easy to be tolerant when you do not care.
— CLEMENT F. ROGERS (1866–   ) *Verify Your References*

It is now no more that toleration is spoken of, as if it were by the indulgence of one class of people that another enjoyed the exercise of their inherent rights.
— GEORGE WASHINGTON (1732–1799) Letter to Hebrew Congregation of Newport, R. I.

TRUTH

Truth is within ourselves; it takes no rise
From outward things, whate'er you may believe
There is an inmost centre in us all
Where truth abides in fulness.
— ROBERT BROWNING (1812–1889) *Paracelsus*

Truth, crushed to earth, shall rise again;
  The eternal years of God are hers;
But error, wounded, writhes in pain,
  And dies among his worshippers.
— WILLIAM CULLEN BRYANT (1794–1878) *Living Lost*

'Tis strange, but true; for truth is always strange,—
Stranger than fiction.
— LORD BYRON (1788–1824) *Don Juan*

The greatest friend of truth is Time, her greatest enemy is Prejudice, and her constant companion is Humility.
— CHARLES C. COLTON (1780?–1832) *Lacon*

God offers to every mind its choice between truth and repose. Take which you please—you can never have both.
— RALPH WALDO EMERSON (1803–1882) *Essays*

If the truth hurts most of us so badly that we don't want it told, it hurts even more grievously those who dare to tell it. It is a two-edged sword, often deadly dangerous to the user.
— JUDGE BEN LINDSEY (1869–1943) *Revolt of Modern Youth*

The smallest atom of truth represents some man's bitter toil and agony; for every ponderable chunk of it there is a brave truth-seeker's grave upon some lonely ash-dump and a soul roasting in hell.
— H. L. MENCKEN (1880–1956) *Prejudices*

Truth often suffers more by the heat of its defenders, than from the arguments of its opposers.
— WILLIAM PENN (1644–1718) *Fruits of Solitude*

'Tis not enough your counsel still be true;
Blunt truths more mischief than nice falsehoods do.
— ALEXANDER POPE (1688–1744) *Essay on Criticism*

We know the truth has been
Told over to the world a thousand times;—
But we have had no ears to listen yet
For more than fragments of it; we have heard
A murmur now and then, an echo here
And there.
— EDWIN ARLINGTON ROBINSON (1869–1935) *Captain Orsig*

A thing is not necessarily true because a man dies for it.
— OSCAR WILDE (1854–1900) *Portrait of Mr. W. H.*

That witty and eloquent old Dr. Oliver Wendell Holmes once
said . . . "You needn't fear to handle the truth roughly; she
is no invalid."
— WOODROW WILSON (1856–1924) Address, 1918

If you shut up truth and bury it under the ground, it will but
grow, and gather to itself such explosive power that the day it
bursts through, it will blow up everything in its way.
— ÈMILE ZOLA (1840–1902) *J'accuse*

Ye shall know the truth, and the truth shall make you free.
— NEW TESTAMENT: *John*, viii, 32

TYRANNY

I have sworn upon the altar of God eternal hostility against
every form of tyranny over the mind of man.
— THOMAS JEFFERSON (1743–1826)

They [the people in lands with dictators] have forgotten the
lessons of history that the ultimate failures of dictatorships
cost humanity far more than any temporary failures of democracy.
— FRANKLIN D. ROOSEVELT (1882–1945) Address, 1937

Like the form of a seen and unheard prowler,
like a slow and cruel violence,
is the known unspoken menace:
do what we tell you or go hungry;
listen to us or you don't eat.
— CARL SANDBURG (1878–1967) *The People, Yes*

And the little screaming fact that sounds through all history:
repression works only to strengthen and knit the repressed.
— JOHN STEINBECK (1902–1968) *Grapes of Wrath*

VALOR See COURAGE

VANITY

An ostentatious man will rather relate a blunder or an ab-
surdity he has committed, than be debarred from talking of
his own dear person.
— JOSEPH ADDISON (1672–1719)

One will rarely err if extreme actions be ascribed to vanity,
ordinary actions to habit, and mean actions to fear.
— FRIEDRICH NIETZSCHE (1844–1900)

Vanity as an impulse has without doubt been of far more
benefit to civilization than modesty has ever been.
— WILLIAM E. WOODWARD (1874–1950) *George Washington*

Vanity of vanities, saith the Preacher, vanity of vanities; all
is vanity.
— OLD TESTAMENT: *Ecclesiastes*, i, 2

WAR

In war there are no winners.
— NEVILLE CHAMBERLAIN (1869–1940) Speech, 1938

Little did we guess that what has been called the Century of
the Common Man would witness as its outstanding feature
more common men killing each other with greater facilities
than any other five centuries together in the history of the
world.
— WINSTON CHURCHILL (1874–1965) Speech, 1949

If, however, there is to be a war of nerves let us make sure
our nerves are strong and are fortified by the deepest convictions of our hearts.
— WINSTON CHURCHILL (1874–1965) Speech, Mar. 31, 1949

I wisht it cud be fixed up, so' th' men that starts th' wars
could do th' fightin'.
— FINLEY PETER DUNNE (1867–1936) *War and War Makers*

So long as mankind shall continue to lavish more praise upon
its destroyers than upon its benefactors war shall remain the
chief pursuit of ambitious minds.
— EDWARD GIBBON (1737–1794) *Decline and Fall of the
Roman Empire*

It must be thoroughly understood that the lost land will
never be won back by solemn appeals to the good God, nor by
hopes in any League of Nations, but only by the force of arms.
— ADOLF HITLER (1889–1945) *Mein Kampf*

If—which God prevent—a new war breaks out, nothing else
will await or confront all peoples . . . but appalling destruction and ruin, and this whether they are victor or vanquished.
— POPE JOHN XXIII (1881–1963) July 2, 1959

War is the greatest plague that can afflict mankind. . . . Any
scourge is preferable to it.
— MARTIN LUTHER (1483–1546) *Table-Talk*, No. 821

War ought to be the only study of a prince.
— NICCOLO MACHIAVELLI (1469–1527) *The Prince*

They shall not pass.
— MARSHAL HENRI PÉTAIN (1856–1951) Battle of Verdun,
1916

And after the strife of war begins the strife of peace.
— CARL SANDBURG (1878–   ) *The People, Yes*

And Caesar's spirit, ranging for revenge,
With Ate by his side come hot from hell,
Shall in these confines with a monarch's voice,
Cry "Havoc" and let slip the dogs of war.
— SHAKESPEARE (1564–1616) *Julius Caesar*, III, i, 270

In peace there's nothing so becomes a man
As modest stillness and humility;
But when the blast of war blows in our ears,
Then imitate the action of the tiger:
Stiffen the sinews, summon up the blood.
— SHAKESPEARE (1564–1616) *Henry V*, III, ii, 3

In the arts of life man invents nothing: but in the arts of
death he outdoes Nature herself, and produces by chemistry
and machinery all the slaughter of plague, pestilence and
famine.
— GEORGE BERNARD SHAW (1856–1950) *Man and Superman*,
Act III

It [War] is all hell. . . . I look upon war with horror.
— WILLIAM TECUMSEH SHERMAN (1820–1891) Address, 1880

To be prepared for war is one of the most effectual means of
preserving peace.
— GEORGE WASHINGTON (1732–1799) Speech, 1790

The war to end wars.
— H. G. WELLS (1860–1946) Attributed

Wars and rumours of wars.
— NEW TESTAMENT: *Matthew*, xxiv, 6

WEATHER

For the man sound in body and serene of mind there is no
such thing as bad weather! every sky has its beauty, and
storms which whip the blood do but make it pulse more
vigorously.
— GEORGE GISSING (1857–1903)

We may achieve climate, but weather is thrust upon us.
— O. HENRY (1862–1910) *Fog in Santone*

Climate is theory. Weather is a condition.
— OLIVER HERFORD (1865–1935)

I wonder that any human being should remain in a cold
country who could find room in a warm one.
— THOMAS JEFFERSON (1743–1826) Letter

The fog comes
on little cat feet.
It sits looking
over the harbor and city
on silent haunches
and then, moves on.
— CARL SANDBURG (1878–1967) *Fog*

When it is evening, ye say, It will be fair weather: for the
sky is red. And in the morning, It will be foul weather today: for the sky is red and lowring.
— NEW TESTAMENT: *Matthew*, xvi, 2–3

WIFE

Helmer: Before all else you are a wife and a mother.
Nora: That I no longer believe. I think that before all
else I am a human being.
— HENRIK IBSEN (1828–1906) *Doll's House*

If you want peace in the house, do what your wife wants.
— AFRICAN PROVERB

A good wife should be as a looking glass to represent her
husband's face and passion; if he be pleasant, she should be
merry; if he laugh, she should smile; if he look sad, she
should participate of his sorrow.
— PLUTARCH (46?–120?) *Moralia: Advice to a Bride*

She looketh well to the ways of her household, and eateth
not the bread of idleness.
— OLD TESTAMENT: *Proverbs*, xxxi, 27

WISDOM

Wise men, though all laws were abolished, would lead the
same lives.
— ARISTOPHANES (444–380 B.C.)

Make wisdom your provision for the journey from youth to
old age, for it is a more certain support than all other possessions.
— BIAS (*f.* 570 B.C.)

A man doesn't begin to attain wisdom until he recognizes
that he is no longer indispensable.
— ADMIRAL RICHARD E. BYRD (1888–1957) *Alone*

Wisdom is full of pity, and thereby
Men pay for too much wisdom with much pain.
— EURIPIDES (480–406 B.C.) *Electra*

Wisdom is not finally tested in the schools,
Wisdom cannot be passed from one having it to another not
having it,
Wisdom is of the soul, is not susceptible of proof, is its own
proof.
— WALT WHITMAN (1819–1892) *Song of the Open Road*

The fear of the Lord is the beginning of wisdom.
— OLD TESTAMENT: *Psalms*, cxi, 10

WOOING See COURTSHIP

WRITING

I don't wait for moods. You accomplish nothing if you do
that. Your mind must know it has got to get down to work.
— PEARL BUCK (1892–1973) *Reader's Digest*

Writing a long and substantial book is like having a friend
and companion at your side, to whom you can always turn
for comfort and amusement, and whose society becomes
more attractive as a new and widening field of interest is
lighted in the mind.
— WINSTON CHURCHILL (1874–1965) *Gathering Storm*

Composition is for the most part, an effort of slow diligence
and steady perseverence, to which the mind is dragged by
necessity or resolution.
— SAMUEL JOHNSON (1709–1784) *The Adventurer*

The chief glory of every people arises from its authors.
— SAMUEL JOHNSON (1709–1784) *Preface to Dictionary*

The writers who have nothing to say are the ones you can
buy; the others have too high a price.
— WALTER LIPPMANN (1889–1974) *Preface to Politics*

The impulse to create beauty is rather rare in literary men . . .
Far ahead of it comes the yearning to make money. And
after the yearning to make money comes the yearning to
make a noise.
— H. L. MENCKEN (1880–1956) *Prejudices*

YOUTH

Young men are fitter to invent than to judge; fitter for execution than for counsel; and fitter for new projects than for
settled business.
— FRANCIS BACON (1561–1626) *Of Youth and Age*

They shall not grow old, as we that are left grow old;
Age shall not weary them, nor the years condemn.
At the going down of the sun, and in the morning,
We shall remember them.
— LAURENCE BINYON (1869–1943) *For the Fallen*

Blow out, you bugles, over the rich Dead!
There's none of these so lonely and poor of old,
But dying, has made us rarer gifts than gold.
These laid the world away: poured out the red
Sweet wine of youth; gave up the years to be
Of work and joy, and that unhoped serene
That men call age, and those who would have been
Their sons, they gave their immortality.
— RUPERT BROOKE (1887–1915) *The Dead* (1914)

Ah! happy years! once more who would not be a boy!
— LORD BYRON (1788–1824) *Childe Harolde*

Youth is to all the glad season of life; but often only by
what it hopes, not by what it attains, or what it escapes.
— THOMAS CARLYLE (1795–1881) *Essays*

As I approve of a youth that has something of the old man
in him, so I am no less pleased with an old man that has something of the youth. He that follows this rule may be old in
body, but can never be so in mind.
— CICERO (106–43 B.C.) *Cato*

There is a feeling of Eternity in youth which makes us
amends for everything. To be young is to be as one of the
Immortals.
— WILLIAM HAZLITT (1778–1830) *Table Talk*

When all the world is young, lad,
And all the trees are green;
And every goose a swan, lad,
And every lass a queen;
Then hey, for boot and horse, lad,
And round the world away;
Young blood must have its course, lad,
And every dog his day.
— CHARLES KINGSLEY (1819–1875) *Water Babies*

How different from the present man was the youth of
earlier days!
— OVID (43 B.C.–A.D. 18) *Heroides*

We think our fathers fools, so wise we grow;
Our wiser sons, no doubt, will think us so.
— ALEXANDER POPE (1688–1744) *Essay on Criticism*

My salad days;
When I was green in judgement.
— SHAKESPEARE (1564–1616) *Antony and Cleopatra*, I, v, 73

Through all the lying days of my youth
I swayed my leaves and flowers in the sun;
Now I may wither into the truth.
— WILLIAM BUTLER YEATS (1865–1939) *The Coming of Wis-
dom with Time*

Youth is not rich in time; it may be poor;
Part with it as with money, sparing; pay
No moment but in purchase of its worth,
And what it's worth, ask death-beds; they can tell.
— EDWARD YOUNG (1684–1765) *Night Thoughts*

The World's Religions

BY JOHN B. NOSS

Man's religions reflect his human need to feel at home in the universe and comfortable among his neighbors. He has always sensed that he cannot stand alone; that good workable relations with his neighbors matter to him; that since mysterious powers in Nature and Society will not let him alone but affect him at every step, he must be in harmony either with them, with the great lords and kings among them, or with the one originative being that has brought the whole world into being and in some sovereign way commands all its processes.

The religions of the past (not treated in this article) have all reflected these human needs and concerns. The Neanderthal Man and his talented successors, the Cro-Magnon men of France, Spain, and Africa, very evidently sought good relations with nonhuman powers that pervaded the natural world and affected human destiny. The great national religions of the past in Egypt, Mesopotamia, Greece, Rome, and Northern Europe were constantly concerned with great lords and kings among the spirits and powers operating on earth and in the heavens, and they showed an equal concern as to the destiny of man in this life and the next.

We shall see that the living religions of man today are similarly motivated.

PRIMITIVE RELIGIONS

Religions of peoples who live close to nature, in relatively isolated societies not yet penetrated by the technology and culture of highly organized industrial societies, are said to be primitive. They include the Australian aborigines, the pygmies of Africa, the jungle tribes of India and Southeast Asia, the natives of New Guinea and of portions of the South Seas, the Indians of the Upper Amazon and of Central America, and certain Eskimo tribes.

Many primitive groups of a generation ago are now undergoing transformation through cultural, educational, and technological changes that are breaking up the established patterns of the past; but primitives are in general resistant to such changes. The traditional customs and beliefs are their means of adaptation to environment; furthermore, they unify the tribe, are comfortable for the individual in that they provide each group member with a role to play that is approved in advance, and are above all sacred, because hallowed by ancestors and divine powers, and therefore binding. Besides this, they satisfy basic biological and psychological needs. Many primitive customs and beliefs strike persons trained in scientific method as naive and superstitious, but they in fact reflect the kind of realism and common sense which follow from taking sensations at face value—a characteristic of primitives in general. Moreover the individual seldom questions what the group feels or senses to be the case. Hence, while primitives have beliefs and practices that the experimental methods of science would seem to discredit, they find them quite true and necessary. Some common features of primitive belief and practice may be discerned, as follows:

Reverence for the Sacred Events, persons, and places in any degree uncanny, mysterious, or creditable with supernatural power are sacred or holy. Included in this very large category are most rites and ceremonies and those who conduct or commandingly participate in them. The traditions of the tribe are hallowed by the ancestors who passed them on. Many places and objects are sacred, such as groves of trees or fetishes (objects thought to embody spirits or magic powers). The most common reason for considering a person, place, or action *taboo* or to be abstained from is that it is sacred and has the power to cause quick good or ill. The presence of the sacred, because it arouses anxiety, is also the chief cause of religious and magical rituals seeking reassurance and favorable outcomes.

Intermingling of Magic and Religion Religious rituals are persuasive in intent, while magical rituals seek to be coercive. But in most primitive ceremonies it is hard to disentangle the magical and religious elements; the words may be persuasive in form, but taken together they may carry the guarantee of a compulsive effect on gods and spirits, while, on the other hand, magical rites may mingle prayers with commands. This should be borne in mind when considering the topics that follow.

Veneration and Worship of Many Powers and Spirits Primitives reverence and at times worship multitudes of powers and spirits, some of which have the status of gods. Venerated or worshiped are stones, plants, trees, many kinds of animals and reptiles, fire, volcanoes, rivers and lakes, sun, moon, stars, mountains, and many other animate and inanimate things. These objects may be regarded as themselves alive with power in every part; or they may be considered the residences of separable individual spirits and powers. In the former case they may be full of *mana*, an indwelling power that causes action of an extraordinary kind; in the latter case, they are objects (bodies) containing souls capable of thought, feeling, and action of an individual kind, able to leave the body they have entered and to survive its death or destruction. Belief in the latter is called *animism*.

Recognition of High Gods There is widespread belief among primitives that there exists a great god far up in the sky, or at a distance, who has made everything—gods, men, and animals—and who is the ultimate lawgiver and overseer. But he is usually so far removed as to be beyond the reach of prayer, and certainly immune to magical coercion.

Types of Magic Magic is resorted to when danger or uncertainty attends an activity and the utterance of set words or the performance of set acts, or both, promise a favorable result. Magic rites may be variously classified. *Preventive magic* wards off happenings and *productive magic* brings them about. Thus corn or fertility dances are productive of favorable growth of grain, while a dance in which a black cloud is threatened with a spear turns aside a thunderstorm. *Sympathetic magic* presumes that like produces like or that severed portions of a body retain sympathy with the organism to which they once belonged. Thus spearing an image during a hunting dance insures success in the following hunt, and doing magic with severed hair and nails affects the person who is in the body from which they have been severed. *Black magic*, which seeks to harm, has its roots in sympa-

thetic magic; thus, if one makes an image in wax of an enemy and pierces it to the heart with pins, the enemy will die. Another form of magic accompanies *fetishism*; it uses the powers in inanimate objects, such as distinctive stones or stuffed antelope horns. *Shamanism* makes use of the magic powers possessed by certain persons, such as medicine men and sorcerers; this is done to cure or inflict disease, to induce spirits into persons or exorcize them. Shamans are able to guide souls after death into the next world and are besought to leave their bodies temporarily in order to do so.

Attitudes to the Dead; Ancestor Worship Death is usually animistically viewed as the departure of a soul from the body that it had animated and directed. Disembodied souls are regarded with fear unless they depart to a distance; should they remain near, they are constantly appeased. If not placated, they may become demonic; this is assumed to be the case with persons killed by violence or left for any cause unburied without the customary funeral rites. Many different precautions are taken to keep the dead from harassing the living, the most common being to leave food at the grave. But not all of the dead are inimical; for ancestral spirits, if remembered, praised, and fed, may help the living in many ways, not only by warding off evil spirits, but also by bringing good fortune to their descendants.

Totemism The myths and rituals connected with this cultic practice recognize a mystical bond or relationship between various human groups and their totems—which are certain animals, plants, or objects intimately related to these groups and graphically represented by them in their religious art. The totem is sacred to the group that regards it as theirs. Sometimes a myth tells of a common ancestor of the totem and its human counterparts. The members of a totem group must marry outside of the group (a practice called exogamy); and the totem may not be eaten by members of the totem group except at a sacramental feast where the bond between them and the totem is recognized.

Other Features of primitive belief and practice are purification rites, rites of passage (i.e., rites which attend important events in an individual's life, such as birth, initiation into adulthood, marriage, and death), divination, sacrifice, war dances, and fertility rites.

In general, the primitive world abounds with ills caused by powers and spirits in the air and underground, powers immanent in every kind of natural object, beast, plant, and human being. The problem is to divine the presence of threatening powers and to take preventive action through magic, sacrifice, and prayer. Appropriate action may convert the threatened evil into productive good; but this can be achieved only by constant vigilance and care. The best course is to follow faithfully the traditional procedures of the group without deviation. But primitive life is not utterly fearful and anxious. It should be said that when all goes well, the primitive is as capable of joy and high spirits as human beings in general.

HINDUISM

The term Hinduism applies to a very complex body of traditions accumulated through at least thirty centuries. These traditions are followed today by nearly 400 million people, who, in spite of divergence in details of belief and practice, are conscious of a common heritage.

Origins The two principal contributors to early Hinduism were: (1) the light-skinned Indo-Europeans who invaded India through the Khyber Pass about 1500 B.C. and (2) the people they conquered, the dark-skinned creators of the Indus culture of western and central India. The former brought with them some forty gods and goddesses bearing names common to Indo-European cultures, such as Dyaus Pitar (Jupiter, Zeus), Prithivi Matar (Demeter), Mitra (Mithra), Varuna (Uranus), Agni (Ignis) and others. The latter supplied more earthy elements: a god presiding over reproduction (later known as Shiva), mother goddesses concerned with fertility, and (possibly) the beliefs in reincarnation and the Law of Karma.

After the invaders had established themselves in Western India, they produced an extensive oral literature, the four *Vedas* (the Rig-, Yajur-, Sama-, and Atharva-Vedas) which are still the basic scriptures of Hinduism. These were followed after 800 B.C. by a written literature in Sanskrit, the

classical language of India. Based on the Vedas, the principal components of this literature were priestly treatises called the *Brahmanas* and philosophical conversations, the *Upanishads*.

One of the social effects of the Indo-European invasion was the establishment of a color barrier (*varna*) to control miscegenation between the light-skinned conquerors and their darker-skinned vassals. This resulted in the early fixed *castes*, the Brahmins (priests), the Kshatriyas (warriors and princes), the Vaishyas (artisans and peasants) and the Shudras (servants). These castes were forbidden to intermarry, sleep, or eat together. Their diets differed. In the course of centuries they subdivided further until there were 2,000 subcastes. Outside the pale were the outcastes and unclean persons, the untouchables. It is only recently, under the stress of social and economic change, that this complex system has begun to break down.

Dharma and the Way of Works What makes a Hindu feel he is a Hindu and therefore different from non-Hindus? The most comprehensive answer to this question is that it is the *Dharma*, the pattern of life which Hindus have followed for centuries as their religious and moral duty; in other words, it is the Way of Works (*Karma Marga*) laid down in tradition, the duties owing to the gods, the ancestors, priests, the family, the caste, the community, animals, and so on. Specifically, the Dharma governs the household life. The typical Hindu home begins its day with adoration of the rising sun. The household deity—Shiva, Vishnu, or some other god or perhaps goddess—is welcomed to the new day and the household with a morning ritual. In the evening another ritual puts the deity to rest for the night. At the birth of a child, and at its name giving, its first taking out to see the sun, its first feeding with boiled rice (weaning), its first hair cutting, there is a ceremony. For boys of the three highest castes, there is the rite of initiation into manhood, comparable to the bar mitzvah of Jews and the confirmation of Christians. For both sexes there are the rites of betrothal, marriage, death, and disposal of the dead (commonly by cremation). There are also the periodic *shraddha* rites for the spirits of the dead. The Dharma also includes visiting temples and going on pilgrimages to distant holy places. Nor is the subhuman world left out. The principle of *ahimsa* or noninjury to any sentient being calls for the practice of nonviolence toward the whole subhuman world, especially toward the cow. "The cow to me," said Mahatma Gandhi, "means the entire sub-human world . . . . She is the mother to millions of Indian mankind. The cow is a poem of pity."

But there is yet another dimension to the Dharma. The next life depends on how the Dharma is practiced in this. Reincarnation (*samsara*) is a universal belief in India. Hindus believe that all souls in bodies—whether of gods, men, animals, reptiles, insects, plants, or souls in hell—are subject to death and rebirth. Births are not always on the same level. If one has accumulated favorable *karma* ("deeds") by obedience to the Dharma, birth will be at a higher level; if evil has been done, the birth will be lower: one may become an insect or a being in hell. This is governed by an inflexible law, the *Law of Karma* which determines whether one rises or falls in the scale of existence.

To follow the Way of Works (i.e., to perform what is called for by the Dharma) is one of the three ways of salvation. It will not get one into Nirvana, but it will procure a better rebirth, and may even get one to heaven. Salvation through the Way of Works is not so difficult as salvation through the Way of Knowledge.

Brahmanism and the Way of Knowledge Brahmanism is a convenient term for a form of Hinduism originating in the post-Vedic period. In its first phase, beginning about 800 B.C., a vast body of sacrificial rituals honoring the various gods was created. They are contained in the ancient priestly manuals, the *Brahmanas*, and are no longer performed in their entirety. In the second and more lasting phase, Brahmanism turned to philosophy and provided a basis for the Way of Knowledge (*Jnana Marga*). Talented men and women of the Brahmin and Kshatriya castes began to speculate that the gods were symbolic of a single reality seen from various angles. All things—men, beasts, gods, all objects—had come from this One Thing or Being and would return to It. After calling It by various names, they finally settled on a neuter noun, *Brahman*. Brahman, they said, is the sole real existent; there is no second thing whatsoever. In a series of treatises called the *Upanishads* (Secret Knowledge),

which were in the form of conversations, these conclusions were set forth with great subtlety.

According to the majority view, synthesized by Shankara in the eighth century A.D., That One Thing (Brahman) extrudes from itself millions of souls (each called an *atman*) and along with them a creative being called *Ishvara* ("Lord," Brahman in the form of a personal god, known to men by various names). There are thus two modes of Brahman: the unmanifested and unknowable *Nirguna Brahman* (Brahman without attributes) and the knowable personal god *Saguna Brahman* (Brahman with attributes). As for the individual soul or self, each is Brahman in the form of an individual self; consequently, full realization of this fact leads the earnest thinker to see the *identity* of himself with Brahman, an experience not fully gained without a trance of oneness (*yoga*) coming at the end of concentrated meditation, with backbone rigid, eyes gazing down the nose. The best name for the ultimate reality is therefore Brahman-Atman, and each soul must say of itself *Tat tvam asi* ("THAT is what *you* are!").

Along with this goes another realization. Ishvara, the personal god, has had from the first a magic power (*maya*) to create appearances, the millions of things in the world perceived by individual atmans. The world is therefore in every part a kind of deception of the senses, an illusion. It is only our ignorance (*avidya*, nonseeing) that causes us to consider it as real as it appears to be. Acceptance of maya entails being "bound to the ever-turning wheel" of *samsara*, i.e., it entails being reborn from one life to another endlessly. If, on the other hand, one subdues his senses by yoga exercises until he ceases to accept maya and goes into a trance of oneness with Brahman (which is what *Nirvana* means), then one has reached salvation by following the Way of Knowledge.

Bhakti and the Way of Devotion This is the third way of salvation and is distinctly religious, for *bhakti* is ardent and hopeful devotion to a particular god or goddess in gratitude for aid received or promised. Whereas the Way of Works is basically legalistic and the Way of Knowledge philosophic, the Way of Devotion involves the religious act of surrender to a deity. The first way seeks a better rebirth, the second entrance into Nirvana, the third union with a deity who may grant admission to heaven or enable one to make gigantic strides toward Nirvana in this or the next life. The classic literary expression of the way of bhakti is the *Bhagavad Gita*, an episode in the great epic, the *Mahabharata*. In the Gita the god Krishna, who is an earthly form of Vishnu, explains to a hesitant warrior, Arjuna, his duty in its cosmic setting. He tells Arjuna that if he is not able to do his caste duty (fighting) or pursue the way of knowledge, he should rely in utter faith and devotion on himself (Krishna) and enjoy the god's loving assistance and saving power.

In the lives of millions of Hindus, bhakti is of primary importance. It has led to the erection of temples to gods great and small, the proliferation of holy places, including sacred cities like Benares and Puri, the practice of going on pilgrimages to sacred shrines along the holy Ganges River, and the celebration of festivals (*utsavas*) at religious fairs to which millions throng in the hope of heavenly benefit. Bhakti also enters into the family rites centering in the patron deity of the house, whether Vishnu, Shiva, Krishna, or some other deity.

The Trimurti Although the polytheism of India embraces thousands of gods, goddesses, demons, ghosts, and powerful spirits, three manifestations of godhead are recognized as chief. They are Brahmā the Creator, Shiva the Destroyer, and Vishnu the Preserver. When Brahman manifests Itself as Ishvara, creation follows, and along with creation the eternal processes of preservation on the one hand and destruction on the other. The three gods symbolize these three phases of natural process. Each has a consort and associates. Brahmā does not have many temples erected to him, because he did his work long ago and now rides aloof on the back of a wild white goose, with his four heads attentively reading the Vedas. Shiva is a nearer presence, a name for decay and renewal, life, death, and reproduction. His feminine counterparts are called *shaktis* ("energies") and go by various names; some are benevolent like Uma and Parbati, others dour like Durga and Kali. His associates are Ganesha, his elephant-headed son, and Nandi the sacred bull. His symbol is the *lingam*, a phallic column. Vishnu is more consistently benevolent,

standing as he does for conservation of the good and necessary. Although he does not himself leave his heavenly seat, in times of need he comes to earth in *avataras* ("descents"), ten being generally listed. Two of these are of prime importance, Rama, the perfect hero described in the epic, the *Ramayana*, and Krishna, the god-hero of the *Mahabharata*. They are separately worshiped. Vishnu's consort is the goddess of beauty and fortune, Lakshmi. She strokes his feet in wifely devotion as he reclines on the cosmic sea serpent, Shesha. He also uses Garuda, a great bird, as his vehicle. (This last is separately worshiped on the island of Bali.)

The Four Acceptable Ways of Life Within the general scheme of rebirth there are different qualities of existence. Hindus consider that men may justifiably follow four ways of life, that is, if they act with integrity at the level they choose. Beginning with the lowest level, these are: (1) the way of *kama* or sensuous pleasure, (2) the way of *artha* or pursuit of wealth and power, (3) the way of the *dharma* or fulfilling one's moral obligations, and (4) the way of *moksha* or salvation, with its twin aims of escape from illusion and entrance into Nirvana. It is expected that anyone who begins at either of the first two levels will find them less than fully satisfactory and will ascend to the third and fourth levels, either in this or a following life.

The Darshanas or Six Acceptable Systems of Philosophy During a period of 1500 years of unhurried philosophical discussion six systems of philosophy emerged as orthodox: (1) the *Nyaya*, concerned with logical reasoning ("things to be proved"); (2) the *Vaiseshika*, conceiving the world as a combination of atoms, souls, and an "unseen force of deity" that is the cause of the world of composite things; (3) the *Sankhya*, rejecting monism (Brahman) and accepting two ultimate principles, *prakriti* (the natural world) and *purusha* (the infinite number of selves or spirits); (4) *Yoga*, a system of mental and physical self-discipline aiming at liberation of the soul from earthly bonds; (5) the *Purva-Mimansa*, a moral philosophy derived from the four Vedas and the Brahmanas regarded as the ultimate authorities on the Dharma; and (6) the *Vedanta*, literally "the conclusion of the Vedas," a point of view including several philosophical systems of a monistic kind much like that described above as the majority view in Brahmanism. The great name here is that of Shankara (788–830 A.D. or earlier): His "unqualified non-dualism" (i.e. monism) was modified by Ramanuja (died 1137) and Madhva (1199–1276) to allow greater independent reality to the universe and its souls.

Sects The two major sectarian groups are the Shaivites, devotees of Shiva, and the Vaishnavites, devotees of Vishnu. The literature of the former is contained in numerous Hindu *Tantras* ("Threads") and in six books of the *Puranas* ("Ancient Stories"), while that of the latter is found principally in the *Bhagavad Gita*, mentioned above, and in six *Puranas* other than those devoted to Shiva. From about the eighth century A.D. on, teachers of the masses began to appear trying to meet the need for images and symbols that would enable ordinary folk to understand the chief features of reality and give expression to their adoration (bhakti). In Shaivism the *lingam* became the chief symbol of the god. Groups of *shaktas* (followers of the shaktis) formed. Some were the so-called right-handed shaktas (the Dakshinacharins), who looked upon the lingam as a significant symbol of the principle of life. The left-handed shaktas (the Vamacharins) practiced secret rites, seeking to exhaust and subdue desire for meat, liquor, and sex by ritually indulging in them. The shaktas picture Shiva as half-woman on his left side and half-man on his right. The Lingayats, founded in the 12th century, carry with them at all times a soapstone lingam wrapped in a red scarf and will not be without it, They stress, however, the ascetic aspect of Shiva, remembering the time he was a *sannyasin* (holy man). The Vaishnavites are far less severe and give honor to the compassion of the kindly god who incarnates himself to save mankind from danger. Ramanuja, Madhva, and Ramananda (12th, 13th and 14th centuries) are their greatest thinkers.

Hinduism and the West The British rulers of India brought Hindus face-to-face with Western culture, science, and religion. The first result of this was a liberal movement of rapprochement with the West, started by Ram Mohun Rai and called the *Brahmo Samaj*. It welcomed insights from all religions, renounced idolatry, and proclaimed mono-

theism. More strictly Hindu in spirit was the *Arya Samaj* founded by Swami Dayanand. Its principles of reform come from "going back to the Vedas," the all-sufficient scriptures, in which monotheism and the basic tenets of science are found. Broad tolerance and all-inclusiveness were taught by the 19th century Hindu saint Ramakrishna, whose followers developed the world-ranging *Ramakrishna Movement*. Secularism or the acceptance of science and humanism as the sole sources of truth, with a consequent rejection of the Dharma and all religion, is widespread in India today. On the other hand, Mahatma Gandhi distrusted Western technology as threatening India's village economy and found in Hinduism an expression of religion wholly suited to his needs, although he felt all religions convey truth to their adherents in about equal measure.

JAINISM

Based in its present form on the life and presumed teachings of Mahavira or Great Hero (sixth century B.C.), this religion has rejected monistic Brahmanism on philosophical grounds. But this would not make it a heresy; its heresy consists in its rejection of the Vedas, the sacrificial system of the priests, and the caste system. "Man, you are your own friend; why do you wish for a friend beyond yourself?" Mahavira is reported to have said. In other words, a man is not saved by gods or priests but by his own efforts. Mahavira achieved *moksha* (salvation) by severe asceticism. He also zealously practiced *ahimsa* (nonviolence), never injuring any living thing because of the soul in it. He avoided stepping on or crushing any live thing and would not eat raw (i.e., live) fruit or vegetables, relying on food cooked by someone else and left over. He begged his food from strangers and wandered naked.

His followers became a new group because of their rejection of the Hindu Dharma. They believed that Mahavira had descended from heaven to enter his mother's womb, and that he was the last of 24 *Tirthankaras* ("Finders of the river ford"), all of whom are now reverenced. Historically, Mahavira did have one predecessor, Parshva, the founder of the ascetic group which Mahavira joined in his youth. Later followers divided into two main groups, the Digambaras, whose mendicants went about naked ("clad in atmosphere") and the Shvetambaras, who in public wore a single white garment. The Jains' principal influence on India has been through their practice of ahimsa. They now number about two million, most of them in the Bombay area.

BUDDHISM

Buddhists have been regarded by Hindus as a "dissenting group" (i.e., heretical). Their philosophical doctrines do not disqualify them, for Hindus allow absolute freedom of thought. But like the Jains they have renounced the Hindu Dharma and substituted one of their own; they have rejected the Vedas, the Brahmins as agents of salvation, and the Hindu caste system.

Gautama Buddha: His Life and Teachings The founder of Buddhism was born about 560 B.C. into the Kshatriya caste and was destined to be a ruling prince, but in his late twenties he left his parents, wife, and son to seek release from the misery of existence by entrance into Nirvana. His first teachers were Brahmins, but he rejected their views as unenlightening. He then turned for five years to the practice of an extreme asceticism much like that of Mahavira (who was probably unknown to him). But he found this debilitating rather than enlightening. Under a tree, later known as the Bo tree (from *bodhi*, or enlightenment, tree), at a place renamed for him Budhgaya (the place of the Enlightenment), he sat alone pondering the reasons for his failure. The ways of salvation as people practiced them were certainly all ways out of human misery; but what was the *cause* of this misery, he asked. Suddenly the answer came. It was *tanha* (desire, thirst, passion, wanting what was not possessed). Indeed the very intensity of his desire for release was a cause of his present misery. To get rid of every desire would be to get rid of every misery. Realizing that he was then utterly without desire, he went into an ecstasy, without losing "mindfulness," and experienced *bodhi*, enlightenment. Nirvana, he concluded, was exactly such a state of desirelessness and utter peace. Now he would be reborn no more; he had achieved deliverance. He was a *buddha* ("an enlightened one").

In the deer park near Benares he found five ascetics with whom he had earlier been associated, and preached to them his first sermon; it was on the Middle Way between sensuality and ascetic self-torture. He explained how control of desire would enable them to live in the world without being overcome by its passions. Together they formed the *Sangha* or Buddhist monastic order. In the 45 years remaining to him (he died about 480 B.C. at 80 years of age), the Buddha and his disciples spread the Sangha through northern India. Members of all castes and of both sexes were admitted to the order as brothers and sisters. All alike shaved their heads and wore yellow robes. They subscribed to a simple creed: "I take refuge in the Buddha, I take refuge in the Dhamma (Dharma), I take refuge in the Sangha." They used the word Dharma in a sense different from that of the Hindus, meaning by it primarily the Teaching or Doctrine. Included, of course, were such instructions concerning conduct as the Ten Precepts forbidding monks and nuns to take life, indulge in sexual intercourse, steal, tell lies, eat after noon, look on at dancing, singing, or dramatic spectacles, use garlands or perfumes, sleep on high or broad beds, accept gold or silver. But a central element in the Dharma was the *Four Noble Truths:* (1) all life is permeated with misery, (2) the cause of such misery is desire, (3) the cure of misery lies in the overcoming of desire, (4) the overcoming of desire comes from following the Noble Eightfold Path, which may be called the road leading to no-desire. It requires right beliefs, right aspirations, right speech, right conduct, right means of livelihood, right effort, right mindfulness, and right meditation. Desire for these is misery-reducing.

The philosophical context of the Buddhist ethical code is the conviction that all the constituents of any living person and the whole live world are in constant flux; nothing remains immune to change except Nirvana; the permanence of the world and the self is thus an illusion. The Wheel of Time and Rebirth is ever turning. It is set spinning by a *Chain of Causation*, beginning in a previous existence, carrying through this, and going on into the next existence. The operative causes are linked in a "dependent origination," each rising from the one before. They are: a basic ignorance of the impermanence of selves and all objects, the predispositions brought into this life as a result of such ignorance, the acceptance in infancy of the world and self as real, expression of individuality as a value, exercise of the mind and senses in such expression, making contact with other selves and with things, indulging the feelings when doing so, developing desires thereby, and at last clinging to existence and throwing oneself into the processes of becoming with its misery-producing entailments, old age, disease, and death. The Buddha taught that all selves suffer from three defects of their existence: (1) transitoriness (*anicca*), (2) the basic unreality of the self (*anatta*), and (3) consequent misery (*dukkha*). In these circumstances it is best to give up the world, to renounce love for individuals, and to seek freedom from dependence and desire, until at last one attains freedom even from the desire for no-desire; which is to be in Nirvana. At the same time one must hate no one and love all without loving any *one*.

Theravada or Hinayana Buddhism After the Buddha's death the monks of the Sangha came together to recite and give final form to his teachings. An oral tradition in the Pali language was thus formed. It is called the Theravada or Teaching of the Elders. Some years passed before it was written down. The Pali tradition was divided into three *pitakas* ("baskets"): (1) the *Vinaya Pitaka*, which contains the disciplinary rules for the Sangha; (2) the *Sutta Pitaka* or remembered discourses of the Buddha, and (3) the *Abhidamma Pitaka* or further expositions of the Doctrine. Each pitaka is subdivided into important individual treatises like the *Majjhima Nikaya* and *Digha Nikaya* of the second and the *Dhammapada* and *Jataka* of the third.

An important accession to Buddhism occurred with the conversion of the Emperor Asoka (264–223 B.C.). He sent missionaries into all parts of India and into Ceylon, Burma, and the Near East. The so-called Southern Buddhism (Theravada, or Hinayana) thus came into existence and spread farther to Thailand, Cambodia, and other areas of Southeast Asia. To this day in these areas the highest aim is becoming an *arhat* or enlightened monk intent on getting himself into Nirvana. The temples, as for example those in Rangoon and Bangkok, are elaborate and filled with gold-plated images of the Buddha, but it is understood by the informed that prayers to the Buddha, while meritorious, do

not reach him, since he is in Nirvana. The layman should acquire merit by learning scripture and giving gifts to the Sangha in order that he may be reborn as a monk. The monk on his part should compassionately instruct laymen in the right path.

Mahayana Buddhism Mahayana Buddhism is self-named. *Yana* means "vehicle," e.g., a carriage or a ferry, and *maha* means "great." Hence this type of Buddhism is consciously "the great ferry," the ferry for the many, across the river between this world and Nirvana. (Because the Mahayanists named their "vehicle" the large one, the older Buddhism came to be called, not much to its adherents' liking, the Hinayana, i.e., the small or one-at-a-time ferry. No wonder they now prefer to be called Theravadins.) The Mahayana is sometimes called Northern Buddhism, for it spread into China, Korea and Japan from the south, into Mongolia by way of the passes from northwest India into central Asia, and into Tibet from Nepal.

The literature of this movement was in Sanskrit rather than Pali, and was produced not only in India but also in China and Japan. Among the hundreds of works the *Diamond-Cutter*, the *Lotus of the Good Law*, the *Prajna-Paramita Sutras*, and the *Pure Land Sutras* were especially influential.

The transition from original Buddhism to the Mahayana was made in northwest India. First it was asked whence Gautama Buddha had come. The answer: he must have been in the heavens, specifically the Tusita heaven, and came down out of compassion for suffering mankind to be born from a woman. How did he get to the Tusita heaven? He rose to it after many existences as a benevolent and self-sacrificial being, sometimes human, sometimes animal. Before his appearance on earth he was, therefore, a *bodhisattva*, a Buddha-to-be. The next steps followed swiftly. There is a bodhisattva in the heavens now, waiting for his time; because he is full of brotherly love (*maitri*), his name is Maitreya. There have also been predecessors of Gautama, buddhas who came in past ages. There must also be buddhas who never leave the heavens, although they send their holy spirits to earth; these are the buddhas who preside over special heavens to which they admit the faithful who call to them. There are thus three types of buddhas: (1) the *manushi* buddhas who have come in history and are gone to Nirvana, (2) the *bodhisattvas*, those who are preparing for future buddhahood, and (3) the *dhyani* buddhas who live in the heavens in serene contemplation (*dhyana*) yet graciously bring others to their side. The Mahayanists are prepared to name names. In addition to Maitreya there are powerful bodhisattvas who make a career of aiding persons who pray to them; among them are Avalokitesvara, who appears in China, Korea, and Japan as a mother goddess, Kwan Yin or Kannon; Manjusri, a champion of the Dharma; Samantabhadra, a bringer of happiness; and Kshitigarbha, who guides travelers and transfers souls from hell to heaven. Of the dhyani buddhas three are widely worshiped: Vairocana, the buddha of the sun; Bhaisajyaguru, the healing buddha; and Amitabha, the kindly buddha of the Pure Land, a paradise in the western sky, whom millions have adored in China and Japan by the names Omito and Amida.

The bodhisattvas are notable for one thing: they have postponed their entrance into Nirvana indefinitely in order to be helpful to all suffering and needy souls. This same unselfishness is potential in everyone; there is a Buddha-nature in all souls. Hence, anyone, man or woman, can make a vow to be a bodhisattva, to accumulate merit through many future existences for the use of others, "until the last blade of grass is saved"—a startlingly far-looking aim!

For this mythology and ethics the Buddhist philosophers and theologians supplied a cosmic setting and a profound theory of knowledge. The Madhyamika School founded by Nagarjuna in the second century A.D. held that the world and the self known to the senses are phantasmal and void (*sunya*), that is, devoid of the qualities sense and reason assign to them; but the thing-in-itself (*svabhava*) underlying the phantasms is real, although totally unknowable to a mind not yet liberated into the world of absolute truth (Nirvana). The Yogacara School, founded by the brothers Asanga and Vasubandhu, taught that the reality constituting all things is consciousness, and that there is an all-inclusive reservoir of consciousness (*alaya-vijnana*) from which all phenomena experienced by the individual mind flow as mental events. In a parallel development the ultimate consciousness was named the *Bhutatathata* ("that which is such as it is"), i.e., that which is ultimately real but which finite

minds misconceive as the phenomenal world and its selves. In the *Prajna-Paramita Sutras* it is maintained that when the individual consciousness has experienced "the Wisdom gone to the Other Shore," it will cast away (as having had only provisional value) Buddhism, the Buddha, and the notion of Nirvana itself. The Alaya-Vijnana or the Bhutatathata takes on a distinctly theological dimension when it is regarded as a Buddha-essence (an Adi- or Originative-Buddha) at the heart of the universe producing Buddhas and Bodhisattvas as an essential part of its nature, which in this light becomes a love principle.

The Mahayana sects are numerous. They may conveniently be grouped as follows:

The Pure Land Sects Here the motive is getting into the heaven of Amitabha Buddha. Of prime importance is faith in the grace of Amitabha. Such faith is best shown in constant repetition of the formula "All hail to Amitabha Buddha" (in China *Namu Omito Fo*, in Japan *Nembutsu*). The chief sect in China bears the name *Ching-t'u*, while in Japan the *Jodo* and *Shin* sects both have large followings.

The Knowledge Sects The meditation (dhyana) leading to the trance of enlightenment requires, according to these sects, the preparation provided by reading, study, and discussion, as well as performance of ceremonies and rituals. In China the T'ien-t'ai and in Japan the Tendai sects have represented this view.

The Intuition Sects: Ch'an and Zen Dhyana was pronounced ch'an in China, zen in Japan. In these sects systematic study and discussion are rejected, the emphasis lying principally on the individual experience of enlightenment through an intuitive flash of insight, known in Japan as *satori*. The individual must free himself from dependence on, although he is encouraged to have some knowledge of, Buddhist literature and of Ch'an and Zen "masters." The oneness of the universe and the self is presupposed; all phenomena are alike in their Buddha-essence. The flash of insight reveals one's own Buddha-essence. Zen in particular tries to shock the seeker by presenting him with logical paradoxes (*koans*) that will make him give up logical explanations and wait for the intuition of his own Buddha-essence.

The Mystery or True-Word Sects These sects combine philosophy, the idea of a regnant deity (Buddha Vairocana) and right-handed Tantrism (see paragraph on Hindu sects, p. 1015). They emphasize a secret or true word which can be known only by immediate intuition. There is use of rituals, gestures, allegory and symbols, and these have, at least for the common man, a magical power to promote health and prosperity. In China the chief sect was the *Chen Yen*, in Japan the *Shingon*.

The Nichiren Sect This is a Japanese sect, founded in the 13th century by Nichiren, a fiery patriot who thought he had discovered original Buddhism in the *Lotus of the Good Law*. He thought the other Buddhist sects had missed the true way. The implicit patriotism of this sect is seen in its three vows: "I will be a pillar of Japan; I will be eyes to Japan; I will be a great ship for Japan." The contemporary militant *Soka Gakkai* movement is a revival of the Nichiren sect, even to the constant repetition of the *daimoku* formula: *Namu Myoho Renge Kyo*, "Hail to the Lotus of the Good Law!"

The Vajrayana of Tibet This variety of Buddhism is also called the Mantrayana, because of its heavy use of *mantras* (efficacious verses of scripture). An older but inadequate name, coined by Western scholars, was Lamaism. Vajrayana means "Vehicle of the Thunderbolt (or of the Diamond)." Coming late to Tibet (seventh century), Buddhism was slow even then in taking hold, and when it did, it came in a Tantric form. A typical theological formulation provided five celestial Buddhas, one at the zenith and the others in the four quarters of the heavens. Since, according to Tantric conceptions, natural forces are a union of male and female elements, each of these Buddhas was paired with a mate (a *prajna*, "wisdom"). All five are emanations of the Adi-Buddha, the originative Buddha-reality, and they gave rise in their turn to bodhisattvas, and these in turn to earthly incarnations. Thus, according to one view, the Adi-Buddha has produced as one of his spiritual sons Amitabha, and the latter has brought into being Avalokitesvara, who in turn

has had as his earthly incarnation Gautama Buddha. These beings are said to have a magical and irresistible substance or power (*vajra*) like that of a thunderbolt and a hardness like that of a diamond, besides which all other things appear soft. If the human devotee can identify himself with any one of these heavenly beings, he will himself gain magical substance and power and will know what Nirvana is. In the meantime he can ward off evil by magical gestures and by repeating, sometimes with the aid of prayer wheels, such potent formulae as *Om mani padme hum!* ("Hail to the jewel in the lotus, hum!"), which is likely an address to Avalokitesvara.

Buddhism Today Vajrayana Buddhism is presently obscured behind the Chinese "bamboo curtain." But the Theravada and the Mahayana are experiencing a resurgence. The former is supported by a new national pride in Ceylon, Burma, Thailand, Cambodia, Laos, and Vietnam. The Mahayana is undergoing revival in Japan and Korea, although it is at an ebb in China, Mongolia, and North Vietnam. The ecumenical spirit has appeared in the Buddhist world; the Theravadins and the Mahayanists have made approaches to each other in the growing conviction that their doctrinal divergences have been logical and natural and presuppose a common heritage. A new spirit of proselytism is also in evidence, which with greater Buddhist unity would pose as its task conversion of the non-Buddhist world.

SIKHISM

One of the youngest religions of the world, Sikhism was founded in the 16th century by Nanak, a native of the Punjab. Though his parents were Hindus, he was in constant association with Muslims and felt that there must be a True Name for God differing from Allah, Brahma, Vishnu, Shiva, etc. One day while in the forest he had a vision of "the one God whose name is True" and began to preach on the theme that if men followed the True Name, they would cease to be divided into Hindus and Muslims but be one as *Sikhs* (Disciples). He dressed in a garb combining Hindu and Muslim elements and proclaimed a monotheism that owed something to both Hinduism and Islam. He subscribed to the Hindu doctrine of *maya*, accepted reincarnation and the Law of Karma, and at the same time taught that the one sovereign and omnipotent True Name predestinated all creatures, a clearly Muslim teaching. He did away with the Hindu taboo against eating meat by saying that God has ordained that man is to be served by the lower creation. He condemned idolatry and distrusted all rites and ceremonies, preferring instead the simple repetition of the True Name. His quietism and pacifism were followed by the first four *gurus* (teachers) who succeeded him as leaders of the Sikhs; but the fifth head, Guru Arjan in the 16th century, finding that the liberal emperor Akbar's successor, Jahangir, was determined to constrain the Sikhs by force, advised his son Har Govind to arm his followers. Guru Har Govind did so. His son, on his accession, named himself Guru Govind Singh ("Govind the Lion"). To change the spirit of the Sikhs, he added to the hymns of the *Granth* (the Sikh scriptures) a collection of militant chants. For his male followers he provided a Baptism of the Sword, a war cry, and an honorific title, "The Lions of the Punjab." After many battles, the Sikhs gained control of the Punjab, a control which they relinquished only to the British (1849). The British employed them widely as soldiers and police. Today their plight has worsened. In the partition of India in 1947 their home territory was divided between Pakistan and India. They have petitioned for "home rule," but so far their pleas have been denied.

TAOISM

One of the two native religions of China, Taoism is rooted, as is Confucianism, in the religious beliefs and practices of ancient China.

Beliefs of Ancient China The ancient Chinese believed that their country was centrally located under the bowl of Heaven and that it stood to benefit most from harmony between Heaven and Earth. All things and all natural processes were thought to be the result of the interaction between a masculine, positive energy mode, the *yang*, and a feminine, passive mode, the *yin*. The day, the air, the sun,

the good spirits (*shen*) including ancestors, are full of yang; night, water, soil, evil spirits (*kwei*) are full of yin. Many objects exhibit yin when at rest, yang when active. Yin and yang alternate as dominant energies in events and persons, as when night alternates with day. This occurs naturally in response to a principle of order and law called the *Tao* ("way" or "proper course"). Each separate thing has its Tao and Earth and Heaven as totalities obey an all-encompassing Tao. When any animate thing conforms to its Tao, it becomes perfect in its kind. If all things in Heaven and on Earth would follow the Tao, harmony and order would be seen everywhere. In other words, when men and animals behave naturally, according to their true nature, they enjoy health and the blessing of Heaven. But, of course, evil spirits and reckless men act contrary to the Tao, and so there are droughts, floods, famines, wars, pestilence. There is great evil in the world and it is due to the rebelliousness of multitudes of demons, devils, and dangerous spirits.

Taoism as a Philosophy The legendary Lao-tzu is usually credited with founding Taoism in the sixth century B.C. and writing the famous *Tao-Te-Ching* ("Treatise on the Tao and Its Power"). It seems certain, however, that this work was composed in the fourth rather than the sixth century B.C. According to it, the term Tao is a convenient name for a reality that has brought the universe into being out of nonbeing. All things come out of nonbeing into being and return to nonbeing. The way of the Tao is the natural way. Men should not oppose their own will to it. They should let nature take its course and not interfere. They should practice *wu-wei* or nonmeddlesomeness, and behave with instinctive spontaneity. When they do, they find themselves getting along with their neighbors and in harmony with heaven and earth; love, sincerity, and goodness will arise, and men will enjoy health and long life; wars will cease and there will be no traveling where one has no business to be and no desire to dominate others. If governments would practice noninterference, the people would spontaneously right themselves. As for the sages, they know that all things come from and blend into One and that they are themselves one with all things in the One.

In the fourth century B.C. the philosopher Chuang-tzu expounded and illustrated this point of view in a series of brilliant and witty essays that still make good reading. "In the days when natural instincts prevailed," he said, "men moved quietly and gazed steadily.... Their virtue could not go astray."

Taoism as Magic Both the Tao-Te-Ching and Chuang-tzu said that the Taoist sage possessed the secret of long life. In later times Taoism turned into a search for the means to prolong life magically. Pills of immortality were diligently compounded. Taoists used the alchemy furnace in order to make gold eatable, so that it might confer immortality on those who would eat it. Much speculation was spent on the whereabouts of the Three Isles of Immortality and tales multiplied about the Eight Immortals, humans who by eating the right substances had conferred immortality on themselves. Secret societies were formed to obtain immortality by meditative practices and the swallowing of potions. Some of these societies acquired great if temporary political power. To the populace, Taoist priests were diviners and doctors of thaumaturgy who were to be consulted at many critical junctures in family life.

Taoism as Religion By the second century A.D. official sacrifices were being offered to Lao-tzu in temples built in his honor. By the seventh century he was surrounded with Taoist gods and spirits gathered into a pantheon in imitation of Buddhist models. Among them were Chinese deities long known to the people, like the god of the hearth, the guardians of the door, and the city god. Heaven and hell were added to the theological scheme. Lao-tzu was elevated to a position in the Three Purities, a trinity serving the supreme deity, the Jade Emperor. But this religion, largely a patchwork, lacked real vitality and ceased to function as a living faith by the beginning of the 20th century.

CONFUCIANISM

Taoists advised a way of life away from the cities and the complexities and problems of organized social life, but this advice seemed wrong to the Confucians. They did not think

that society should be decentralized; it should be better established and improved, according to its own *Tao*, i.e., its own laws of order and harmony. Their founder was Kung-fu-tzu (Confucius), who was born about 551 B.C. Left fatherless at three, Confucius was given an aristocratic training by his devoted mother and early aspired to government office. After her death he turned his home into a private school, where he taught the Six Disciplines in which he himself had been trained (history, poetry, manners, government, divination, and music). He broke with tradition by admitting poor boys to his school. He wished to train them for responsible participation in government. The feudal system established 500 years earlier by the Chou Dynasty was disintegrating, and there seemed only one way to avoid disaster and that was to reestablish *li*, the manners and morals of the sages of olden times, and to inculcate *jen*, the kindly inward disposition that led men to show "human-heartedness." Men should exhibit *shu*, mutuality, or doing as one would be done by. The higher type of man (the *chün-tzu*) was unfailingly correct in his behavior and profoundly generous and just. Confucius believed that the climate of society was set by the rulers: "the prince is like the wind and the people like grass; it is the nature of grass to bend with the wind."

Confucius encouraged ancestor worship and the domination of the family by its elders. Each member of society should know his place in it. With the ideal definition of his place and function in mind (the principle of "the rectification of names"), he should measure up: the emperor should be benevolent and just, the subject loyal; the father wise and kind, the son filially pious; the husband righteous, the wife submissive; the elder brother considerate, the younger brothers deferent; friends instilled with mutuality. This would assure justice, freedom to do easily what is required of one, and happiness arising from social cooperation and harmony.

Confucius felt that he was designated by Heaven to teach his doctrines, and to this extent he was religious, despite a skepticism about gods and spirits that allowed only a low-key recognition of supernatural influences.

After Confucius' death, his disciples formed the Confucian school. They preserved the textbook materials he used in his teaching and these became the *Five Classics*. By recording his sayings, they created the *Analects*, one of the four Confucian Books, the others being the *Great Learning*, the *Doctrine of the Mean*, and the *Essays of Mencius*. But for some time they met with strong opposition from the Taoists, the Legalists, and the followers of Mo-tzu. The last were a tightly organized group of proto-communists, who taught that universal love was superior to Confucian filial piety and hard work in the fields more necessary to social order than education. The Legalists were, on the other hand, a proto-fascist group who demanded unquestioning obedience to rulers as possessors of awesome authority (*shih*). They succeeded in motivating the Duke of Ch'in to conquer all the provinces and install himself as Shih Huang-ti ("The First Emperor"). He turned on the Confucians and burned their books; but with his death his dynasty fell, and the Han emperors who succeeded him sought to restore peace and order by a resort to Confucian principles.

Meanwhile, Confucianism had undergone development. Mencius (371–289 B.C.), the greatest writer of the Confucian school, urged that men are born with a good nature and are corrupted by their environment. Hsün-tzu (298–238 B.C.), on the other hand, maintained with the Legalists that man is born with an evil nature that must be controlled firmly; so he advocated strict Confucian training to recondition man into behaving for the general good.

The Han emperors instituted the Confucian academies to prepare students for imperial examinations in the Confucian literature, a measure designed to sift out scholars worthy to be placed in high office. Centuries later, when Buddhism and Taoism had much diminished Confucian influence, the Neo-Confucians (11th and succeeding centuries), especially Chu Hsi and Wang Yang-ming, reinterpreted Confucianism and restored its prestige. The system of examinations in the Confucian classics continued to the beginning of the 20th century, but was discontinued with the Revolution of 1912. Confucianism has been in decline for the past half-century. The present Communist regime opposes it as feudal and reactionary.

SHINTO

The Japanese native religion is centered entirely on Japan, its topography, its gods, its dead, its imperial family, and its people. Its central myth, as told in the *Kojiki*, describes how Izanagi and Izanami came down the bridge of Heaven and made an island on which they bred the great islands of Japan and their first inhabitants, who were, of course, all gods (*Kami*) in the "land of the gods." Upon Izanami's death, Izanagi followed her to the underworld; on emerging he cleansed from his right eye Amaterasu the sun goddess, from his left eye Tsukiyomi the moon god, and from his nostrils Susanowo the storm god. Amaterasu lived in the heavens and her grandson Ninigi on earth; Ninigi's great-grandson was Jimmu Tenno, the first human emperor, from whom the present emperor is lineally descended. The Japanese people have meanwhile descended from the other gods. So, according to the myth, Japan is a divine land, sprung from the womb of a goddess, and is filled with gods and their descendants.

The Shinto shrines are wooden structures of an ancient design, with unique gateways called *torii*. They honor the sun goddess and a host of other deities reflecting Japan's geography, climate, and plant and animal life. Ancestors and heroes are also venerated, and in times past the emperor also.

Shinto received its name when Japan was undergoing transformation under Chinese influences in the sixth to eighth centuries A.D. The name is derived from *shen-tao* ("the Way of the Gods"). During the period of Buddhist influence, the Shinto deities were declared to be the "appearances" of the buddhas and bodhisattvas when they came to Japan. In the 17th century, when Shinto experienced a revival, this formulation was discouraged, but with little success. In the 19th century, after the visit of U.S. Admiral Perry, the Japanese systematically brought about a second transformation of Japan to accord with their desire to become a modern world power. In the 1930's, during the Japanese Army's attempt to establish control over the Far East, the Shinto myth was invoked to intensify emperor-worship and secure unqualified obedience to the national program of war and conquest. Men of the armed forces were committed by solemn vows never to surrender to an enemy. The medieval Bushido or *samurai* code was revived, and suicide in repelled attack or hopeless defence (*hara-kiri*) was elevated to a moral principle.

Since 1945 the emperor has "descended from his divinity" and lives among the people as a fully human being. The nation has renounced war as an instrument of national policy, and the Shinto shrines formerly maintained by the government have been turned over to private control. The Shinto sects are proliferating into hundreds more, many of them seeking syncretizing solutions to religious need. It is a highly fluid situation, with an uncertain future.

ZOROASTRIANISM

Zoroastrianism was founded in ancient Iran by a prophet—its only one—probably in the seventh century B.C. His name was Zoroaster (Zarathustra), and his purpose seems to have been to reform the religion of his people, probably because it was excessively priest-ridden and demanded animal sacrifices that the agricultural economy could not afford. After experiencing a trance, during which, through the mediation of divine Good Thought (*Vohu Manah*), he was taken into the presence of God the Wise Lord (*Ahura Mazda*), the creator of the good earth and of men and cattle, he began to get revelations in the form of hymns. These became the *Gathas*, the first scripture of Zoroastrianism. He believed Ahura Mazda operated through such powerful agencies as the Good Spirit (*Spenta Mainyu*), Piety, Power, Right, Good Thought, and Immortality (all later personalized as archangels). But the good God was opposed by *Angra Mainyu*, the Evil Spirit, later known as Shaitin, and by his associates, Druj (the Lie) and many evil demons (the *daevas*). Each man, Zoroaster taught, must decide whom he will serve. After death the soul will go either to the House of Song (Paradise) or the House of the Lie (Hell). The struggle between God and Devil now convulses the world, but God will triumph in the end and there will be a Last Judgment in which the Devil and all who serve him will be finally punished.

After Zoroaster's death the reform he had instituted—a reform of the old Iranian faith, brought in by invading Indo-Europeans akin to those who invaded India—became the faith of the Achaemenian dynasty of Persia and was carried into Babylonia by Cyrus the Great. In becoming the faith of the Mesopotamian peoples it underwent significant changes. Zoroaster was transfigured into a magical personage whose birth was attended by miracle. His repre-

sentative, the Saoshyant, a Messianic figure (the first in history), was to come at the end of earthly history, before the Last Judgment. Many gods and goddesses of older religions were turned into angels and divine helpers of Ahura Mazda. Thus Ishtar, the sex goddess of Mesopotamia, became Anahita, the Spotless One; and Mithra of the old Iranian religion became Ahura Mazda's right-hand agent. Attention shifted from ethics to magical cleansing from pollution by the use of *manthras* (verses of scripture). Fire was reverenced as the chief symbol of Ahura Mazda, whether in the sun or on the altar.

The Sassanian dynasty (221–651 A.D.) was overthrown by the Muslims in the seventh century, and Zoroastrians found themselves increasingly in disfavor. Thousands fled to India after the eighth century, where they became known as *Parsees* (Persians). Concentrated in the Bombay area, they maintain Fire Temples and Towers of Silence (*dakhmas*). The latter are walled-in enclosures where the dead are laid exposed to air and vultures, so that their fluids will not pollute the earth. Recent leaders of the Zoroastrian community, many of them highly educated, have started a movement "back to the Gathas," in which they see a challenge to live a good life of faith and constructive social action.

JUDAISM

Judaism arose out of a context in which there was a continuous interpenetration of the cultures of many peoples, e.g., the Canaanites, Philistines, Egyptians, Assyrians, Babylonians, Greeks and Romans. In its beginnings it was the faith of the Hebrews, a term which is derived from *Hapiru* or *Hibri*, names applied by Egyptians and Mesopotamians about 1500 B.C. to Semitic wanderers ("boundary crossers" or "desert raiders") pushing their way into Palestine. One group among these desert tribes came from the borders of Egypt and called themselves "children of Israel" because they claimed descent from the twelve sons of Israel (Jacob) whose father was Isaac and grandfather Abraham. On entering Palestine they were joined by non-Israelite Hebrews who eventually adopted their faith and national identity.

The Hebrew Faith (1250–587 B.C.) About 1250 B.C. (a much-debated date) Moses, while serving as a shepherd in Midian, had a religious experience on Mt. Sinai as a result of which he went to Egypt with a message to the Israelites, then in bondage to the Egyptians. He told them that Yahweh (or Jehovah), identified as the god of Abraham, Isaac, and Jacob, had sent him to lead the Israelites out of their bondage and take them to Canaan, their Promised Land. The Egyptians were distracted by a crisis at the time and the Israelites seized the opportunity to flee with Moses across the Sea of Reeds. The Egyptians belatedly pursued them, but their chariots sank in the mud of the lake through which the Israelites escaped. Moses led his people to Mt. Sinai, and at its base conducted a ritual of blood covenant by which the Israelites solemnly bound themselves to Yahweh. Yahweh's will for them was conveyed by Moses and his successors in the moral and ritual precepts summarized in the Ten Commandments and amplified in a growing body of law, the Torah. After forty years of wandering during which Moses died, the Israelites broke into Canaan and gradually took it over. Scholars disagree as to how historically authentic some of the events up to this point may be; succeeding events are more widely accepted as having a definite historical basis.

Called Hebrews by their neighbors, the Israelites together with their nomadic allies soon numbered enough people to become a nation. Their first king was Saul, and he was succeeded by David and Solomon. Jerusalem became the capital. A temple to Yahweh was erected there by Solomon, with many priests to perform the morning and evening sacrifices. But the Hebrews had adopted so many of the customs of the Canaanites that the Mosaic Covenant was in danger of being replaced by the native Baalism and its accompanying fertility cults. The *baals* were Canaanite farm gods operating under a Baal of Heaven, and each baal had a female consort (a *baalah*) to whom he was annually married in fertility rites. It was to protest against disloyalty to Yahweh that the prophets (*nebiim*) arose. Elijah and Elisha appeared in the ninth century and were followed in succeeding centuries by others with stern messages prefaced by the words: "Thus says the Lord." While calling the people back to Yahweh, prophets like Amos and Hosea in the eighth century issued a summons to social justice, and made it clear that failure in

righteousness would arouse the wrath of Yahweh and bring on a Doomsday during which enemies would overrun the nation. When Assyria loomed as the Foe from the North who might be the instrument of Yahweh's wrath, Isaiah and Micah prophesied in Jerusalem, the former recalling the people to a faith that might save them, the latter declaring that Yahweh wanted, not sacrifices, but men who would be just and kind and walk in quiet fellowship with God. It was Isaiah who predicted that, should the Day of Doom come, a righteous remnant would survive to enjoy a new day under the benign rule of the Prince of Peace, a Messianic descendant of David. After the ten northern tribes (Israel) had been overrun by the Assyrians and transported to distant parts ("lost"), Judah survived as a remnant of ancient Israel, only to fall, in the time of King Manasseh, under the influence of Assyrian sun and star worship and erect an altar to Ishtar in the very precincts of the Temple. The good king Josiah, however, instituted a drastic reform, basing it upon a newfound farewell message of Moses (Deuteronomy). He sought by this "Deuteronomic Reform" to restore the Hebrew religion to its ancient purity, but he was killed during a gigantic clash between Egypt and the newly established Babylonian Empire, in which the Babylonians were victors. The Babylonians now demanded that Judah become a willing vassal state or suffer conquest. It fell to the prophet Jeremiah to undertake the thankless task of saying it was Yahweh's will that the nation submit, and when it refused to do so, of pronouncing its doom. His prophecy was quickly fulfilled. Nebuchadnezzar invested the city and obtained its surrender in 597 B.C. He ordered the king and court, all the men fit for war, and all craftsmen and smiths to be transported to the vicinity of Babylon. When rebellion broke out in Judah nine years later, he came back to loot and destroy every building in the city, tear down the walls, and take all but a handful of the people into exile. The city was so thoroughly laid waste that it was in ruins for over a century and a half. The religion of the Hebrews seemed to have received a mortal blow.

Post-Exile Judaism (539 B.C.–70 A.D.) The Babylonian Exile was in some sense a blessing in disguise. The Hebrew nation had been destroyed but the Jews (a term derived from Judeans) remained. Chastened by the national tragedy and fearful that their inherited faith was in jeopardy, they gathered up and pieced together the records of their past, and so produced the books of the Bible dealing with their history, their laws, the messages of their prophets and their devotional life (the Psalms). And two prophets appeared to prepare them for a return to their homeland, Ezekiel and Second-Isaiah. The former envisaged in detail the restored rites in the Temple, and the latter foresaw a day when the Jewish faith, purified in affliction, would become the whole world's way of life.

The Persians under Cyrus the Great overthrew the Babylonian Empire in 539 B.C. and shortly thereafter, honoring a Jewish plea, Cyrus issued an edict permitting the Jews to return to Judah. Only a few thousand at a time returned, but the process went on for three hundred years. The Temple was first restored, but not until a hundred years later in the time of Nehemiah was the city rebuilt. About that time Ezrah the Scribe gathered the people at the Water Gate and led them in making a binding covenant to "walk in the law of God given by Moses." It was in reality a new covenant—Israel's second. It established a theocratic state with power vested in the priests. Stress fell on tithing, offerings of the first fruits of a crop, sacrifices, and fixed festivals. The Jews pledged themselves not to marry outside their group. In their diet, they promised to distinguish between clean and unclean. Judaism, a clear-cut legalistic religion, was born; it was a way of life established in law and ritual, so laid upon Jewish consciences that it claimed them more and more. New meeting places, the scene of Sabbath services, appeared in the villages and came to be known later as synagogues. A new class of teachers arose, called rabbis, who expounded the Law and the Prophets.

In 332 B.C. Alexander the Great, after defeating the Persians, brought Judah under Greek control. His liking for the Jews won their gratitude and paved the way for powerful Hellenistic influences on their modes of thought and life. Open-air theaters, gymnasiums, libraries, and academies appeared for the first time in Palestine. The high-priest class in Jerusalem, the Sadducees, aped Greek dress, domestic architecture, and argumentation. But "the quiet in the land," the *hasidim* ("the pious"), resisted the Hellenistic

influence and eventually erupted into violence against the attempt of Antiochus Epiphanes, king of Syria, to force the Jews to give up their religion and worship Greek gods. In 165 B.C. Judas Maccabeus and his Jewish rebels recaptured Jerusalem and established Jewish national independence. This Jewish nation lasted until 63 B.C., when the Romans took over.

Meanwhile, during the Maccabean period, two parties had appeared among the Jews. One was the *Pharisees*, who were anti-Hellenistic and who embraced new Messianic concepts that owed much to Zoroastrian influence. They believed that when the Messiah came the dead would rise to meet the living for a Last Judgment. The second was the *Sadducees*, who combined Hellenistic tendencies with religious conservatism, maintaining that it was best to go no further than the Torah in these and other matters; assuredly the dead would not rise. When Julius Caesar made Herod king of Judea, three other parties appeared: the *Zealots* who meant to fight for recovery of national independence and acknowledged no ruler but God; the *Herodians* who thought the Roman rule should be tolerated; and the *Essenes* who withdrew from society to live in quiet awaiting the Messiah. The recently recovered "Dead Sea Scrolls" were devotional texts of one such group of Essenes.

In 66 A.D. discontent boiled into war, and four years later the Romans captured and destroyed Jerusalem. Many thousands of Jews fled to areas outside Palestine. This scattering (*diaspora*) of the Jews was intensified after 130 when the Jews still in Palestine attempted a second war and were disastrously defeated and driven from their homeland.

Rabbinic Judaism (70–1500 A.D.)

With the fall of Jerusalem in 70, the Sadducees, Essenes, and Herodians ceased to offer viable alternatives in Judaism. The Zealots struggled on to 130, but then perished. Only the Pharisees (rabbis) and and the rapidly spreading Christian "heresy" remained. The rabbis were worried. Even before the fall of Jerusalem they took measures to preserve rabbinical learning; after it, largely in secret, they produced from the *Halakah* (legal traditions) and *Haggadah* ("narratives") the *Mishnah* and the *Gemara*, which when combined became the *Talmud*. Jewish communities in Babylonia, Egypt, and cities of the Roman world found in the Talmud directives enabling them to preserve Judaism without morning and evening sacrifices. Synagogues sprang up throughout the Roman Empire to enable them to conduct Sabbath worship and perform the rituals of the festivals and fasts of the Jewish calendar. This stood them in good stead as the Roman Empire decayed and fell, followed by a time of even greater troubles.

When the Turks came from the East, the Jews in Babylonia fled to Spain (10th and 11th centuries), where they enjoyed a renaissance of literature and learning under the Moors; but with the expulsion of the Moors, those who would not turn Christian fled east again to Turkey and Syria. Their brethren in England and France had already been expelled, at least in law, in the 13th and 14th centuries, and those in Italy, Austria, and Germany were in ghettos. Northern Jews found more freedom in Poland and Russia but many perished from time to time in pogroms there. In a kind of underground fashion, they nourished their souls with the Talmud, the writings of 12th century scholars like Maimonides and Nahmanides and the esoteric mystic speculations of the *Kabbala*.

Judaism in the Modern World

The Protestant Reformation only slightly eased the Jewish situation. It was not until the Napoleonic wars that the Jews began to be freed from the ghettos, and not until the social upheavals of 1848 that they won Europe-wide equality with other men before the law. Up to that time the only haven for the Jew was the New World, and so many thousands availed themselves before World War I of the opportunity to cross the Atlantic that a numerical shift of the Jewish world to the west occurred.

A momentous turn of events occurred during World War I with the issuance of the Balfour Declaration. The Zionist cause, initiated in the closing years of the 19th century by Theodore Herzl, came to fruition in the Declaration's designation of Palestine as "a national home for the Jewish people." After World War II and Hitler's annihilation of 6 million Jews, refugees poured into Palestine. In 1947 the UN General Assembly voted to partition Palestine and create Israel as an independent state, a development which the Arab states bitterly resent.

CHRISTIANITY

Christianity emerged from Judaism but in the course of centuries has absorbed substantial elements of the Greek world-view and some doctrinal and cultic elements from the Romans. It shares with Judaism indebtedness to Canaanite, Babylonian, Zoroastrian, and Egyptian sources. Its central figure, Jesus, has been regarded as an incarnation of God the Father and the source therefore of a primary revelation.

The Life and Teachings of Jesus. Jesus was born in 4 or 6 B.C. in Bethlehem of Judea, and grew up in Nazareth of Galilee. At an early age he became interested in the prophetic tradition of his people. The times were in confusion. Galilee was the scene not only of Jewish rivalries but of extensive Greek and Roman cultural penetration. The Zealots of Galilee revolted when Jesus was about ten years old and he must have witnessed their bloody suppression. At 30 years of age he went down to the Jordan River to hear John the Baptist and be baptized by him. During his immersion he experienced a call to prophecy. After a period of solitary preparation, he appeared in Galilee proclaiming that the Kingdom of Heaven was at hand. He recruited 12 disciples to accompany him while he taught in the synagogues and to large crowds in the countryside. He modified John the Baptist's proclamation of the imminent Last Judgment by making a distinction between the "end of the age" when the Kingdom would "come in power" and the indeterminate period preceding it when the Kingdom would be a reality in the lives of those who submitted to God's rule and lived in fellowship with their neighbors. The principles to govern this interim period were set forth in his ethical teaching. Although he was reared in the Pharisaic tradition, he rejected the excessively legalistic interpretation of piety, declaring that mere externalism in religion is hypocritical and that first importance must be given to justice, love, and mercy issuing from the inner self. The Sabbath was made for man, he declared, not man for the Sabbath. The "men of old were told an eye for an eye, but I say to you love your enemies." His preaching was addressed to the plain man and was notable for its parables. Miracles of healing accompanied his ministry. Great crowds attended him at first, but the Sadducees and Pharisees reduced his influence by accusing him of blasphemously claiming to supersede the Law and the Prophets and of being an instrument of the devil. He was seized in Jerusalem during the Passover of 28 A.D., accused before Pilate the Roman procurator, and crucified on Mt. Calvary along with two criminals. His disciples began to disperse, crushed by despair.

The Apostolic Age The despair of the disciples was short-lived, however, for some of Jesus' women followers reported visions of angels in his empty tomb and of the resurrected Jesus himself. After a number of appearances to the apostles and others in Judea, Jesus met them, they said, in Galilee and ascended to heaven. They were now convinced beyond doubt that he was indeed the Christ (the Messiah) and that he had come from God and had returned to God.

At Pentecost a few weeks later, the disciples were meeting in an upper room in Jerusalem and experienced the descent of the Holy Spirit. They were now empowered to spread the Gospel throughout the world. Peter and other apostles preached the new faith in the streets of Jerusalem and were arrested. The Jewish authorities, ascertaining that they adhered to the Torah, charged them not to preach their doctrine and let them go. But their Greek-speaking Jewish converts were more radical in giving up the Law and ceasing to worship in the Temple, and one of them, Stephen, was seized and stoned to death.

A witness to Stephen's death was a man from Tarsus called Saul (Paul). As an ardent Pharisee, he was active in seeking the suppression of the Christians, but while going to Damascus to pursue this cause, he had a blinding vision and heard the voice of Jesus. Converted to the Christian faith, he became a leader in missionary work among the Gentiles. In Asia Minor, Macedonia, and Greece, he established churches to which he wrote letters full of theology and admonition. He went beyond Jewish categories in describing Jesus, calling him not only the Christ but the Lord (*kurios*, a Greek term) and saying that he preexisted in heaven before taking the form of a servant and dying on the cross. Men who were in Christ, he taught, enjoyed the freedom of the Spirit and were no longer slaves of the Jewish law. Those who were baptized were mystically buried with Christ and resurrected with him

to a new life in which Christ dwelt within them. To a culturally divided world he brought the good news that in Christ there was neither Jew nor Greek, barbarian, Scythian, freeman nor slave, or even male or female, for they were all one. A tinge of misogyny, however, common to Christianity's predecessors, remains in Paul—as when he recommends marriage only if a man can escape temptation and damnation in no other way. After taking a collection to the poor in the Jerusalem church, he was mobbed by the Jews, imprisoned, and sent to Rome for trial as a disturber of the peace. The verdict went against him and he became a Christian martyr.

The new churches needed a scripture of their own. The letters of Paul, and others credited to Peter, James, and John, were given scriptural rank. Four gospels were written: Mark, Matthew, Luke and John, probably in that order. To them was added Luke's Acts of the Apostles. An apocalyptic vision of the end of time, written in the manner of Daniel, became the Revelation of John. These works were ultimately gathered into the canon of the New Testament (more accurately, the New Covenant) to accompany the use of the Jewish scriptures (the Old Testament or Covenant).

In early apostolic times the Christians met in homes, but with the extension of the Church throughout the world (as far as India) special meeting places were built, elders and deacons were appointed, and leading elders became pastors (bishops). Children were given catechetic instruction. At length the bishops of large centers of population (Antioch, Alexandria, Byzantium, Rome) became archbishops and patriarchs, the bishop of Rome becoming a Holy Father (a *papa* or pope).

The Ancient Catholic Church (150–1054 A.D.) The early Church gained its name from its claim to be catholic or universal. In its struggle against opposition without and heresy within, it attained a definition of its doctrines. The Gnostics were the first group from which it had to differentiate itself. They asserted that Jesus came to earth in the masquerade of a body from a realm of spiritual powers centered in God the Father. He did this, they claimed, to save men's souls from the evil realm of matter (the physical world) created by a being of a lower order (Jehovah). Against these claims, the Church asserted Irenaeus' principle that the sign of a sound doctrine is its apostolicity and that the carefully titled *Apostles' Creed* contains what is to be believed. The Creed stresses that God created earth as well as heaven and that Jesus was physically born, died, and was buried. Also declared heretical were the fourth and fifth century views that Christ was a created being and not eternal (Arianism); that the Logos dwelt within a wholly human Jesus as in a temple, in which case Mary was not the mother of God but of "a man, the organ of deity" (Nestorianism); that Christ had, not two natures, one divine and one human, but one nature, because the Logos, as the reasoning principle, united with a human body containing an animating principle (Monophysitism). Arianism was rejected at the Council of Nicaea (325 A.D.) and the others at Chalcedon (451).

Meanwhile, monasticism had risen in Egypt and spread through the Catholic world. Orders were founded by St. Basil in Asia Minor and St. Benedict in Italy. After he became a monk, St. Augustine (354–430) gave prominence to the doctrine of original sin, the procession of the Holy Spirit from both the Father and the Son (*filioque*, a doctrine abhorrent to the East), and the distinction between the visible earthly church and the invisible heavenly one.

In the fourth century, Christianity triumphed with the accession of Constantine to the imperial throne and by the end of the century became the imperial state church. The superior dignity of the church of Rome as one founded by Peter and Paul was widely acknowledged; whereupon its heads, the Popes, began to claim that, since St. Peter was the first of the apostles, the church he founded should be accorded primacy among the churches. The pressing of this claim by the popes resulted in 1054 in the division of the Church between the Roman West and the Orthodox East.

The Medieval Church (1054–1517) During the Middle Ages, the sack of Constantinople in 1204 by an army of the Fourth Crusade and its capture in 1453 by the Turks deepened the sense of separation of East and West.

The Eastern churches arose originally in the Greek-speaking areas of the Roman Empire and spread southward into Egypt and northward into the Balkans and Russia. Many of their congregations could boast of being founded by an apostle. Hence, when the bishop of Rome claimed supremacy over them, they replied that they had equal claims to venerability. They differed—and continue to differ—with the West in other matters. They reject the *filioque* clause accepted by the West. They observe some of the seven sacraments differently: baptism is by triple immersion in infancy; confirmation comes immediately after baptism; communion (eucharist) is shared by all worshipers; the sick are anointed during life and not just at the point of death; celibacy is required only of monks and those who aspire to high office in the church. Churches are decorated with mosaics, paintings, and small pictures (*icons*) but are not allowed sculpture. The liturgy is sung, but without instrumental accompaniment. The various bodies of the Eastern Orthodox Church have been since medieval times virtually independent of each other, divided as they are into units more or less corresponding to national states, although they have always maintained full communion with each other.

In the West, the Papacy attained its greatest secular power in the 11th to 13th centuries. One pope, Gregory VII, forced the German emperor to plead for papal clemency by standing barefoot in the snow at Canossa; another, Innocent III, exercised temporal as well as spiritual power over kings and emperors. Among the monastic orders, the Dominican and Franciscan had enormous influence. Universities were founded and in them scholasticism devoted itself to exploring and corroborating the dogmas of the Church. The greatest of the scholastics, Thomas Aquinas, produced the *Summa Theologica*, which adapted Aristotle's methods to Christian revelation in a synthesis that is still honored as authoritative by Catholics today.

The Protestant Reformation and its Catholic Counterpart (1517–1700) The Middle Ages ended in a humanistic renaissance. With the rise of commercial towns independent of feudal barons, townsmen developed a new individualism and a daring demand for freedom and reform. The common man thirsted to hear the Bible in his own tongue. In Germany, Martin Luther (1483–1546) became convinced by his study of the scriptures that the Church had succumbed to unscriptural pomp, worldliness, and pride, and had resorted to unscriptural devices for gain. In 1517, as a protest, he nailed his 95 Theses to the church door at Wittenberg and precipitated the Protestant Reformation. His general position was that every Christian can through faith enjoy God's favor without the necessary mediation of priest or pope, and that the true Church is a community of persons who through inward change have surrendered themselves to Christ and find their ultimate authority, not in the Pope, but in the Bible made understandable by the Holy Spirit through faith. In Switzerland, Ulrich Zwingli had independently reached the conclusion that Christians are bound by and should practice only what is commanded in the Bible; the Catholic mass should therefore be radically altered to conform to the early Christian Lord's Supper; and Christian worship should get along without organs, vestments, and images. The German and Swiss reformations spread throughout northern Europe—to France, the Netherlands, and the British Isles. Calvin in Switzerland, John Knox in Scotland, Menno Simons in the Netherlands, and George Fox in England continued and reinforced the work of the early reformers. The Church of England, while Catholic in theology, had long balked at giving primacy to the papacy in Rome; Henry VIII made this view official (though for the trivial reason of justifying his private marital whims), thus establishing the Reformation in England. And the nonconformist Puritans, in pursuit of full liberty of conscience, carried the Protestant cause to the shores of New England.

The Catholics, on their part, were incited to a reformation of their own (often called the Counter Reformation). The Council of Trent, meeting over a period of 18 years (1545–1563), instituted reforms in church discipline and management, and redefined the Catholic theological position vis-à-vis the Protestant. To revive Catholic spirit and zeal, new religious orders arose, the most famous being the Jesuit Order founded by Ignatius Loyola (1491–1566).

The Church in the Modern World (since 1700). Since the Reformation, both the Protestant and Catholic churches hardened into set positions while yet developing new and vigorous forms of mission to the world. The Deism of the 18th century cooled the religious ardor of the Church of England but also led John Wesley and his associates to organize and spread to America a religious movement (dubbed the Methodist Church) that strove to restore through "conversion" the sense of the immediacy of God's presence in human lives. The missionary movement, begun by Protes-

tants in the 18th century, was greatly intensified in the 19th, both in Europe and America, and penetrated to every part of the world. The 19th century—which may be labeled the great Protestant century—saw the rise of a powerful educational effort resulting initially in Sunday Schools and then in the broad-gauge Christian education program of the 20th century. In the same century the long-delayed conflict between religion and science broke into the open, and led in the 20th century to Fundamentalism, Modernism, and Neo-Orthodoxy. The concern of the churches for the alleviation of poverty and injustice resulted in the early 20th century in the vigorous heralding of the Social Gospel, an attempt to reexplore and apply socially the references of Jesus to the Kingdom of God. The mid-20th century has been dominated by efforts toward concerted action by the various Protestant bodies, e.g., the World Council of Churches. This ecumenical concern is, in part, motivated by a realization that the 20th century is a post-Protestant, even a post-Christian, period, and therefore the churches need to unite for effectiveness and strength.

Meanwhile, the Roman Catholic Church has moved along parallel lines. In hardening into set positions, it proclaimed in 1854 the Immaculate Conception of the Virgin Mary, declared in 1870 the doctrine of papal infallibility, and in 1950 added as a dogma the assumption of the uncorrupted body of the Virgin Mary to heaven after her death. But the forces of liberalism were not by any means dead. This became apparent in the pontificate of Pope John XXIII. In 1959 he issued a summons to an ecumenical council (that is, one embracing the entire Catholic world). Several sessions of the Council were held by the mid-1960's, attended by 2,500 bishops and cardinals. Official observers from the Protestant churches were given a place. The Council ordered liturgical reforms that have put large portions of the Mass into the vernacular of the countries involved, declared that the Jews are not to be held peculiarly responsible for the death of Christ, gave the bishops greater voice in the management of the Church, and put on the agenda of future meetings a resolution dealing with religious freedom.

One of the most vivid reaffirmations of Christ's teaching in the 20th century was the devotion with which U.S. Christians, both Catholic and Protestant, both clergy and laity, actively joined the Negro civil rights movement in the 1960's. Support ranged from official proclamations rejecting segregation issued by many church bodies to lobbying, picketing, and even martyrdom—as in the case of Unitarian minister James Reeb, killed in Selma, Alabama, during 1965.

ISLAM

Islam is rooted in three religions, Zoroastrianism, Judaism, and Christianity, but it has its own distinct character as befits its Arabian origin. Islam means "submission" and its adherents are Muslims (or Moslems)—"submitters" to Allah (God).

Muhammad's Life and Teaching Muhammad (or Mohammed) was born in Mecca about 570 A.D. and was an orphan at six. A ward of his grandfather and then of his uncle, Abu Talib, he took a detached and disapproving view of Arabian polytheism and social disunity. At 25 he married a rich widow, Khadijah, and had leisure to brood on religious problems. Having learned from Judaism and Christianity, he asked himself why no prophet had yet come to the Arabians to prepare them for the Last Judgment—which haunted him. When he was 40, he began to have ecstatic experiences of conversations with the Angel Gabriel, from whom he received revelations from Allah. Muhammad was astonished to find that he himself was the needed prophet to Arabia. He was accepted as such by his wife and a few converts, but when he recited his revelations in the streets, he was ridiculed by the Meccans, then threatened. Both Khadijah and Abu Talib died at about the same time, and, feeling the loss of their protection, Muhammad accepted an invitation to come to Yathrib and made a *hijra* (or *hegira*, "withdrawal") with his followers to that city in 622 A.D., the year from which all Muslim dates are reckoned. He became the civil as well as religious leader of the town, which was renamed for him Medina an Nabi ("the City of the Prophet"). When the Meccans came to destroy him, he repulsed them; not long after, in 631, he took their city, making it and its central shrine, the Kabah, the holy center for Muslim pilgrimage.

In the preceding years his revelations had continued steadily. They defined his religious beliefs and prescribed the conduct of his followers. In a famous summary he warned: "Whoever disbelieves in Allah and his angels and his scriptures and his messengers and the Last Day, he truly has wandered far astray." The five chief Muslim beliefs are here listed. (1) Allah is the one true God and does not share his divinity with any associate. The Christian doctrine of the Trinity is thus a serious error. (2) Angels surround Allah's throne, Gabriel having the highest rank. There is also a fallen angel, Iblis (from the Greek *diabolos*), also called Shaitin, who with his minions, including some *jinn* (demons), are busy leading men astray. (3) The scriptures are four: the Torah of Moses, the Zabur (Psalms) of David, the Injil (Evangel) of Jesus, and the revelations to Muhammad, compiled after his death into the *Quran* (or *Koran*). The last corrects and gives final form to the truth in the others. (4) Allah's human messengers are the prophets, Muhammad himself and his honored predecessors, of whom the chief are Adam, Noah, Abraham, Moses, and Jesus. Of Jesus, Muhammad had a high opinion, incensed though he was by the doctrine that Jesus was the Son of God. He held that Jesus was virgin born, performed miracles, and ascended to heaven, but he denied that he had been crucified in his own person. (5) A Last Day is coming. It is vividly anticipated in Muhammad's earlier revelations. His descriptions of Hell are as terrifying as those of Paradise are enchanting.

Muhammad gave much attention to elevating the morals of his followers. He prohibited wine and gambling. He raised the status of women by giving them property rights and not allowing divorce from them without provision for their economic needs. Men who could afford it were allowed more than one wife, but not more than four. Orphans were not to be taken advantage of, on pain of hellfire. No man should scorn his parents. The divisive Arabian tribal organization, with its blood vengeance and violence, was to be transformed into a means of expressing inclusive brotherhood and respect for human rights. He substituted for tribal feuds the "holy war" (*jihad*) to be made on unbelievers, if the latter provided provocation.

Muhammad died of a fever in the year following his takeover of Mecca, and his successor (*caliph*) was his friend and father-in-law, Abu Bakr.

Muslim Consolidation and Expansion Shortly after Muhammad's death his revelations were gathered into the *Quran*, and the process of interpreting and supplementing it began, with a resulting accumulation of tradition (*hadith*). His recorded and remembered prescriptions concerning religious duties yielded the "Five Pillars" (*al-Arkan*), now so fixed in Muslim practice: (1) Repetition of the *Shahadah* or Creed: "There is no god but Allah and Muhammad is the prophet of Allah." (2) Prayer (*Salat*) on Friday at the mosque and five times a day facing Mecca. (3) Alms (*zakat*) for the needy. (4) Fasting during the month of Ramadan from dawn to dusk. (5) Pilgrimage (*hajj*) at least once in a lifetime to Mecca, either in person or by proxy. In addition, orthodox practice required women to go veiled in public, but men were to mingle freely without any racial or class discrimination, especially at times of prayer.

The major feasts and festivals of the Muslim year were worked out later and were also fixed at five: the "Little Feast" (*Id al-Fitr*) at the end of the month-long Ramadan fast; the "Great Feast" (*Id al-Adha*) during pilgrimage at Mecca, the New Year festival (*Muharram*), the festival of the Prophet's birthday (*Mawlid an-Nabi*), and the festival of the Prophet's Night Journey (*Lailat al-Miraj*) which commemorates Muhammad's ascension to the presence of Allah just before the Hijra.

As this process of coordination and consolidation was taking place the Arabs broke out of the desert and rapidly overran Syria, Palestine, Egypt, and Mesopotamia. Later they pushed on into Persia, India, and beyond the Himalayas. They also pressed through North Africa into Spain. Eventually they penetrated northward into Turkey and the Balkans and southward into central Africa. Muslims now number some 450 million, including those in the East Indies, the Philippines, Mongolia, and China.

Muslim Diversification The three chief traditional groupings among Muslims are: (1) the *Sunnis*, who follow the *Quran* and the hadith as closely as changing conditions permit; (2) the *Shiites* or "Partisans of Ali," who regard the son-in-law of Muhammad and his descendants as the only "legitimate" Imams (divinely designated leaders) after Muhammad; and (3) the *Sufis* or mystics, who overlap with the

Sunnis but modify the traditional accent on the transcendence of Allah by stressing his immanence and the possibilities of mystical communion with him. Within these groupings there is further diversification. Among the Sunnis, the two chief theologians are Ashari and Ghazzali, the former conservative, the latter liberal enough to see truth in the Sufi position. There are also among them Four Schools of Law. The Shiites fall into three main sects, the Zaidites, Twelvers, and Ismailis. The Aga Khan heads a sub-sect of Ismailis.

Recent Developments The impact of the West on Islam has led to a complicated attempt, on the one hand to appropriate the methods of Western science and technology, and on the other to set up defenses against Western religion and culture. At present the liberalism of half a century ago, inspired by Muhammad Abduh of Egypt and Sir Sayyid Ahmad Khan and Sir Muhammad Iqbal of India, has suffered a setback in the violent reaction against the establishment of Israel on what is regarded as Muslim soil. Attempts to destroy Israel are threatened. The drive toward a United Arab Republic astride "the crossroads of the world" has met serious setbacks but is persistently sought.

The Fruit of Islam, commonly known as the Black Muslims, purports to be an Islamic sect in the United States, composed exclusively of Negroes whose leader calls himself Elijah Muhammad. The Black Muslims stand for rigid separation of the races and for an independent black nation to be carved out of the United States as reparation for the enforced slavery of Negroes in the past. Religious leaders of orthodox Islam reject this movement's claims to authenticity and charge it with distortion of Muhammad's teachings.

GLOSSARY OF MYTHOLOGY

The mythological terms most commonly encountered, chiefly those of Greek or Roman origin, are to be found in the main vocabulary of the dictionary. These are indicated here by cross reference.

Aa·ru (ä·a′roo) *Egyptian* 1. Peaceful fields in which were located Ra's throne, deities, and souls of the blessed dead. 2. Peaceful crop-producing fields in the nether world of Osiris. Also *Yaaru.* Also **A·a′lu** (-loo).

Aar·vak (ôr′väk) *Norse* One of the horses of the sun; the dawn.

Ach·e·ron (ak′ə·ron) See main vocabulary.

A·chil·les (ə·kil′ēz) See main vocabulary.

A·cis (ā′sis) *Greek* See GALATEA (def. 2).

Ac·tae·on (ak·tē′ən) See main vocabulary.

A·dad (ā′däd) *Babylonian* See RAMMAN.

A·da·pa (ä′dä·pä) *Babylonian* A mortal summoned to heaven for breaking the south wind's wings. There he is presented with the bread and water of life (immortality) but rejects it on Ea's advice to beware the offer.

A·di·ti (ə·dē′tē) *Hindu* Personification of the female principle in creation, variously regarded as the mother of the world, mother of the gods, supporter of the earth or sky, or the wife or mother of Vishnu.

A·dit·yas (ə·dēt′yəz) *Hindu* The seven sons of Aditi, a group of divine moral personifications.

Ad·me·tus (ad·mē′təs) See main vocabulary.

A·don·is (ə·do′nis, ə·dōn′is) See main vocabulary.

A·dras·tus (ə·dras′təs) See main vocabulary.

Æ·gir (ē′jər, ā′jər) See main vocabulary.

Ae·gis·thus (ē·jis′thəs) See main vocabulary.

Ae·ne·as (i·nē′əs) See main vocabulary.

Ae·o·lus (ē′ə·ləs) See main vocabulary.

Aes·cu·la·pi·us (es′kyə·lā′pē·əs) See main vocabulary.

A·esh·ma (ä·esh′mə) *Persian* The most malignant of the Zoroastrian demons; a fiend of lust and outrage.

Ae·sir (ā′sir, ē′-) See main vocabulary.

Ag·a·mem·non (ag′ə·mem′non) See main vocabulary.

A·gas·tya (ə·gäs′tyə) *Hindu* A legendary holy man, son of the two gods Mitra and Varuna, and revered as the author of several Vedic hymns. He is noted for asceticism and for miracles like halting the growth of the Vindya mountains and drinking up the ocean.

Ag·dis·tis (ag·dis′tis) *Greek & Roman* A hermaphrodite whose male organs were severed by the gods in abhorrence.

A·glai·a (ə·glä′ə) See main vocabulary.

Ag·ni (äg′nē) See main vocabulary.

A·hi (ä′hē) *Hindu* The dragon from whose body the waters, blood, and sap of life were released by Indra when he killed it with a thunderbolt: also *Vritra.*

a·him·sa (ə·him′sä) See main vocabulary.

Ah·ri·man (ä′ri·mən) See main vocabulary.

A·hu·ra Maz·da (ä′hoo·rä mäz′dä) See ORMUZD in main vocabulary.

Ai·lill mac Ma·tach (a′lil mäk·mä′täk) *Irish* The king of Connacht, husband of Medb, and father of Findabair in the Ulster Cycle. He is a henpecked husband in the *Táin Bó Cuáilgne.*

Ái·ne (ôn′yə) *Irish* A banshee of Munster, legendary mother of Gerald, Earl of Munster, and primitively a minor fertility goddess.

A·jax (ā′jaks) See main vocabulary.

Akh·tya (äk′tyə) *Persian* Chief of the sorcerers (yatus) of Zoroastrianism.

A·ku·pa·ra (a′koo·pä′rə) *Hindu* The tortoise upon which the earth rests.

Al·ber·ich (äl′bər·ikh) See main vocabulary.

Al·burz (äl′bərz) *Persian* The sacred mountain of light, root of all other mountains.

Al·ces·tis (al·ses′tis) See main vocabulary.

al·far (äl′vär) *Germanic* The elves, some of whom dwell in their special realm (Alfheim) and some beneath the earth.

Al·la·tu (ä·lä′too, al′ä·too) *Sumerian & Babylonian* Another name for ERESHKIGAL.

A·lo·a·dae (ä·lō′ə·dē) *Greek* The giants Ephialtes and Otus, twin sons of Poseidon, who made war upon the gods, threatening to pile Mount Pelion upon Olympus and Mount Ossa upon Pelion to reach them. They were killed by Apollo.

Al·viss (äl′vis) *Norse* The earth-dwelling dwarf who sued for the hand of Thor's daughter Thrud, but was defeated in a riddling game.

A·ma·dán (ô′mə·dôn) *Irish* The fairy fool, whose touch produces incurable crippling or deformity.

A·mae·thon (ä·mī′thon) *Welsh* A son of Dôn in *Kulwch and Olwen* (see MABINOGION), a great tiller of fields. He is probably primitively an agricultural god or culture hero.

A·mal·thae·a (ə·mal′thē·ə) See main vocabulary.

A·mar·a·va·ti (ə·mär′ə·vä′tē) *Hindu* The capital of Indra's heaven, a blissful city reserved for those who do penance or sacrifice, or who die in battle.

A·ma·ter·a·su O·mi·ka·mi (ä·mä·ter·ä·soo ō·mē·kä·mē) *Japanese* The sun goddess.

Ama·tsu·ma·ra (ä·mä·tsoo·mä·rä) *Japanese* The one-eyed blacksmith god who helped make the mirror that was used to entice Amaterasu Omikami out of a cave.

Am·a·zon (am′ə·zon, -zən) See main vocabulary.

am·bro·sia (am·brō′zhə, -zhē·ə) See main vocabulary.

A·men (ä′mən) *Egyptian* See AMON.

A·men·ti (ə·men′tē) *Egyptian* 1. The underworld, or a hazardous stream leading to it. 2. A goddess of the underworld.

A·me·sha Spen·tas (ə·mē′shə spen′təs) *Persian* The archangels or divine attendants of Ormuzd.

Am·mit (ä′mit) *Egyptian* A frightful hybrid monster, called the Devourer, present at the "weighing of souls" to eat all those dead whose hearts did not exactly balance the feather of truth on the scales of judgment.

A·mon (ä′mən) *Egyptian* Originally, a little-known local god of Thebes. Amon eventually merged with Ra to become the supreme deity, Amon-Ra: also *Amen.* Also **Am′mon, A′mun.**

A·mon-Ra (ä′mən-rä′) *Egyptian* The supreme deity, proclaimed king of the gods; actually a combination in which the lesser god Amon assumed the qualities of the primeval sun-god Ra. Also **A′men-Ra′, A′men-Re′** (-rä), **A′mon-Re′.**

Am·phi·a·ra·us (am′fī·ərä′yoos) *Greek* One of the Seven Against Thebes.

am·ri·ta (äm·rē′tə) *Hindu* The water of life that confers immortality.

An (än) *Sumerian* God of heaven.

A·na·hi·ta (än′ə·hē′tə) *Persian* The great mother or fertility goddess of Zoroastrianism and earlier Iranian mythology.

A·nan·ga (ə·näng′gə) *Hindu* The bodiless: an epithet of Kama, the god of love.

An·an·ta (ə·nän′tə) *Hindu* The infinite: an epithet of Vishnu and several other divinities.

An·chi·ses (an·kī′sēz) See main vocabulary.

An·drom·a·che (an·drom′ə·kē) See main vocabulary.

An·drom·e·da (an·drom′ə·də) See main vocabulary.

And·var·i (änd·vär′ē) See main vocabulary.

An·gra Main·yu (äng′grə mīn′yoo) *Persian* See AHRIMAN.

An·gur·bo·da (än′goor·bō′dä) *Norse* The giantess of Utgard, mother of the Fenris wolf, the Midgard serpent, and Helle.

An·gus Og (eng′gəs ōg) See main vocabulary.

An·hur (än′hər) *Egyptian* Originally a local sun-god, his identification with Shu as Anhur-Shu evoked great popularity; also thought to be Ra personified as a warrior. Also **An′her.**

An·hur-Shu (än′hər·shoo) *Egyptian* The manifestation of the sun-god Znhur in possession of the power and influence of the higher-ranking air-god Shu.

ankh (angk) See main vocabulary.

An·kou (än′koo) *Breton* The ghost of the last person to have died in the parish during a year, which drives a cart to the house of one about to die, along with two spectral helpers.

An·nwf·n (än·noo′vən) *Welsh* The paradisiacal afterworld, variously described as a group of fortified islands or a great revolving castle on an island. Also **An·nwn** (än′noon).

An·sa (än′sə) *Hindu* One of the seven sons of Aditi, personifying bounty.

An·shar (än′shär) *Babylonian* A sky-deity born of Lahmu and Lahamu.

An·tae·us (an·tē′əs) See main vocabulary.

An·tu (än′tōo) *Sumerian* A consort of the Babylonian sky-god Anu.

A·nu (ä′nōo) See main vocabulary.

A·nu·bis (ə·nōo′bis, ə·nyōo′-) See main vocabulary.

A·nu·ket (ä·nōo′ket) *Egyptian* Nile-goddess worshiped at Elephantine; wife of Khnum.

A·nun·na·ki (ä·nōo·nä′kē) *Sumerian & Babylonian* Attendant gods. In Babylonian mythology they appeared most often as gods of earth, on a lower tier than the Igigi.

A·pe·pi (ä·pe′pē) *Egyptian* A night-serpent who led the underworld attack on Ra's passage each evening, but who was always overthrown. Also **Aph·o·bis** (ä′fō-bis).

Aph·ro·di·te (af′rə·dī′tē) See main vocabulary.

A·pis (ā′pis, ä′-) See main vocabulary.

A·pol·lo (ə·pol′ō) See main vocabulary.

Ap·su (ap′sōo) *Babylonian* The primeval sweet-water abyss personified as the husband of Tiamat.

A·rach·ne (ə·rak′nē) See main vocabulary.

A·ral·lu (ä·rä′lōo) *Sumerian & Babylonian* The nether world.

A·ra·wn (ä·roun′) *Welsh* The lord and king of Annwfn.

Ar·ca·di·an hind (är·kā′dē·ən) *Greek* The hind that Hercules captured, after a year's chase, as his third labor.

Ar·es (âr′ēz) See main vocabulary.

Ar·go·naut (är′gə·nôt) See main vocabulary.

Ar·gus (är′gəs) *Greek* 1. See main vocabulary. 2. Odysseus's dog, who recognized him on his return from his wanderings.

Ar·i·ad·ne (ar′ē·ad′nē) See main vocabulary.

Ar·i·an·rhod (är′ē·än′rōod) *Welsh* A beautiful goddess, daughter of Dôn and mother of the twins Llew Llaw Gyffes and Dylan, to whom she was deeply inimical.

Ar·is·tae·us (ar′is·tē′əs) See main vocabulary.

Ar·ju·na (är·jōo′nə) *Hindu* The most prominent of the Pandavas, a great warrior and archer and favorite of Krishna.

Ar·te·mis (är′tə·mis) See main vocabulary.

A·ru·ru (ä·rōo′rōo) *Babylonian* The goddess who fashioned the ill-fated hero, Enkidu, from mud.

Ar·ya·man (är·yä′mən) *Hindu* One of the seven sons of Aditi, personifying bosom comradeship.

A·sag (ä′säg) *Sumerian* Demon of disease and sickness, dwelling in the Kur, which was attacked and destroyed by Ninurta.

As·a·pur·na (ä·sä·pōor′nə) *Hindu* An earth or mother goddess; literally, she who fulfills desires. Also **A·sa·pur·a** (ä·sä·pōor′ə), **A·sa·pur·i** (ä·sä·pōor′ē).

As·can·i·us (as·kā′nē·əs) See main vocabulary.

As·cle·pi·us (as·klē′pē·əs) See main vocabulary.

As·gard (as′gärd, äs′-) See main vocabulary.

Ash·gir·bab·bar (äsh′gûr·bä′bär) *Sumerian* See NANNA.

A·shur (ä′shōor) See main vocabulary.

Ask (äsk) See main vocabulary.

As·tar·te (as·tär′tē) See main vocabulary.

As·vins (äs′vins) *Hindu* Twin cosmic gods, variously the deities of dawn, heaven and earth, day and night, sun and moon, morning and evening, or twilight. Also **As′wins**.

A·syn·jur (ä′sün·yōor) *Norse* The goddesses collectively.

At·a·lan·ta (at′ə·lan′tə) See main vocabulary.

A·tar (ä·tär′) *Persian* The fire god, a son of Ormuzd.

A·te (ā′tē) See main vocabulary.

A·tem (ä′tem) *Egyptian* See ATMU.

A·ten (ä′tən) *Egyptian* The solar disk itself, worshiped as the supreme (but not sole) deity during the reign of the so-called heretic king, Akhenaton. Also **A′ton**.

Ath·a·mas (ath′ə·mas) See main vocabulary.

A·the·na (ə·thē′nə) See main vocabulary.

At·las (at′las) See main vocabulary.

At·li (ät′lē) See main vocabulary.

at·man (ät′mən) See main vocabulary.

At·mu (ät′mōo) *Egyptian* Ra as the setting sun: also *Atem, Tem, Temu.*

A·tra·ha·sia (ä′trə·hä′sis) *Babylonian* A Noah-like mortal who survived a flood sent by the gods by building and loading a large boat.

A·tre·us (ā′trē·əs, ā′trōos) See main vocabulary.

At·tis (at′is) See main vocabulary.

A·tum (a′tōom) *Egyptian* An ancient god who rose out of Nun, the primeval ocean, and masturbated to form the gods Shu and Tefnut. See also PTAH.

Aud·hum·la (oud·hōom′lä) *Norse* The monstrous cow, formed of the cold from Niflheim and the heat from Muspellheim, that nourished Ymir, the first giant.

Au·ge·an stables (ô·jē′ən) See main vocabulary.

Au·tol·y·cus (ô·tol′i·kəs) See main vocabulary.

A·va·lo·ki·ta (ə·vä·lō·kē′tə) *Hindu* A Buddhist god of mercy and compassion; the Bodhisattva whose face is turned in every direction in order to save everyone. Also **A·va·lo·ki·tes·va·ra** (ə·vä·lō·kē′tes·vä′rə).

av·a·tar (av′ə·tär′) See main vocabulary.

Ba (bä) See main vocabulary.

Ba·ba (bä′bə) *Sumerian* A fertility goddess and consort of Ningirsu.

Ba·ba Ya·ga (bä′bə yä·gä′) *Russian* A forest ogress that eats human flesh, preferably that of young children.

Bab·bar (bä′bär) *Sumerian* Ancient sun-god; equivalent of the Babylonian *Shamash*.

Bac·chus (bäk′əs) See main vocabulary.

Badb (bä′ib) See main vocabulary.

Bah·ram·gor (bä·räm·gôr′) *Persian* A hero-prince of many tales, both Persian and Indian. Also **Bah·ram Gur** (bä·räm′ gōor).

Bak·ha·u (bäk′hä·ōo) *Egyptian* The mountain that supported the sky and heaven at their eastern end. See MANU.

Bal·der (bôl′dər) See main vocabulary.

Ba·li (bä′lē) *Hindu* The king of the Daityas, favored by the gods for his goodness.

Ba·lin (bä·lēn′) *Hindu* A monkey king, said to have been born from his mother's hair.

Ba·lor (bä′lôr) See main vocabulary.

Ban·ba (ban′bə) *Irish* A queen of the Tuatha Dé Danann, wife of King Mac Cuill. She wished her name to be given to the land of Ireland by the invading Milesians.

Bast (bäst) *Egyptian* A cat-headed goddess of pleasure and protectress against disease. Mummified cats were buried in her sacred city Bubastis. Also **Bas·tet** (bäs′tit).

Battle of the Trees *Welsh* A battle between Arwan and Amaethon in which trees take part as warriors. It is described in the poem *Câd Goddeu*, and is thought to be related to the ancient Celtic tree alphabet and the druidic mysteries.

Ba·u (bä′ōo) *Babylonian* A mother-goddess and healer.

Bau·cis (bô′sis) See main vocabulary.

Bé·find (bā′find) *Celtic* One of the three fairies present at the birth of every child, who predict its future and endow it with gifts. In Irish mythology she was a sister of Bóann.

Be·lit·se·ri (bā′lit·sâr′ē) *Sumerian & Babylonian* Wife of Namtar and scribe of the nether world.

Bel·ler·o·phon (bə·ler′ə·fon) See main vocabulary.

Bel·lo·na (bə·lō′nə) See main vocabulary.

Bel·Mer·o·dach (bäl′mer′ō·dak) *Babylonian* See MARDUK.

Bel·tane (byel′tə·nə) See main vocabulary.

Bel·tu (bäl′tōo) *Babylonian* A mother-goddess of high rank.

ber·ser·ker (bûr′sûr′kər) See main vocabulary.

Bes (bes) See main vocabulary.

Bha·ga (bä′gə) *Hindu* One of the seven sons of Aditi, personifying good luck, wealth, and bounty.

Bhag·a·vad·Gi·ta (bä′gä·väd·gē′tə) See main vocabulary.

Bhai·ra·va (bī·rä′və) *Hindu* Any of the eight fearful forms of Siva, worshiped as a dog, drummer, or stone.

Bhai·ra·vi (bī·rä′vē) *Hindu* See DEVI.

Bhi·ma (bē′mə) *Hindu* A strong, courageous, and coarse Pandava prince, son of the wind god Vayu.

Bhu·de·vi (bōo·dev′ē) See DHARTI MAI.

Bi·frost (bēf′rost) See main vocabulary.

Bi·le (bil′ə) *Irish* A king of Spain, one of the Milesians.

bi·li (bil′ē) *Celtic* Sacred trees, believed to be the habitations of gods and spirits.

Bish·a·mon·ten (bēsh·ä·môn·ten) *Japanese* The god of riches.

Blod·en·wedd (blod′ən·wəd) *Welsh* The dawn goddess.

Bó·ann (bō′ən) *Irish* The queen of the Tuatha Dé Danann, wife of Dagda, and mother of Angus Og.

Bodb (bōv) *Irish* The eldest son of Dagda, and himself later chosen king of the Tuatha Dé Danann.

Bo·dhi·satt·va (bō′di·sat′wə) See main vocabulary.

Book of the Dead *Egyptian* A collection of magic formulas and incantations written on papyrus and interred with the deceased to insure his safe passage through the underworld.

Bo·re·as (bôr′ē·əs, bō′rē-) See main vocabulary.

Bo tree (bō) See main vocabulary.

Bra·gi (brä′gē) See main vocabulary.

Brah·ma (brä′mə) See main vocabulary.

Brah·ma·pur·a (brä′mä·pōor′ə) *Hindu* The heaven and city of Brahma, situated on the summit of Mount Meru.

Bran (brän) See main vocabulary.

Bran·stock (brän′stôk′) *Germanic* An oak growing through the roof of the Volsungs' hall. Only Sigmund could withdraw the sword that Odin had thrust into its trunk.

Bres (bresh) See main vocabulary.

Bric·ri·u (brē′ə·krōo) *Irish* A warrior who appears in some tales as an inciter of bloodshed among the great champions of Ireland Loegaire Buadac, Conall Cearneac, and Cuchulain, but in another as an honored poet.

Brig·id (brij′id) See main vocabulary.

Bri·has·pa·ti (brē·häs·pä′tē) *Hindu* The chaplain of the gods, the lord of prayer, and wisdom incarnate. Also **Brah·man·as·pa·ti** (brä·män·äs·pä′tē).

Bri·se·is (brī·sē′is) See main vocabulary.

Bris·ing·a·men (bris′ing·gä·men′) *Germanic* The magic necklace made by the Svartalfaheim dwarfs for Freya. Loki stole it, but Heimdall recovered it after the gods had engaged in a shape-shifting contest.

Brun·hild (brōōn′hild, *Ger.* brōōn′hilt) See main vocabulary.

Brünn·hil·de (brün·hil′də) See main vocabulary.

Bryn·hild (brün′hilt) See main vocabulary.

Bu·ri (bü′rə) *Germanic* The progenitor of the gods.

Bush·yas·ta (bōōsh·yäs′tə) *Persian* The yellow demon of lethargy and sloth.

Bu·to (byōō′tō) *Egyptian* A protective goddess of Lower Egypt, portrayed as a cobra.

Ca·bir·i (kə·bir′ē) *Greek* Deities, perhaps Phoenician in origin, worshiped in many parts of the ancient world.

Câd Goddeu (kōōd god′ə) *Welsh* See BATTLE OF THE TREES.

Cad·mus (kad′məs) See main vocabulary.

Cae·ne·us (kē′nē·əs) *Greek* A Lapith who had been changed from a woman to a man, and made invulnerable to wounds. He worshiped only his own spear, and Zeus in anger caused him to be buried in fir trees by the centaurs.

Caill·e·ac (kal′yäk) *Celtic* Personification of the last sheaf as the embodiment of the field spirits; literally, old woman.

Cal·li·o·pe (kə·lī′ə·pē) See main vocabulary.

Cal·lis·to (kə·lis′tō) See main vocabulary.

Cal·y·don·i·an boar (kal′i·dō′nē·ən) See main vocabulary.

Ca·lyp·so (kə·lip′sō) See main vocabulary.

Ca·no·pic Chest (kə·nō′pik) *Egyptian* A container into which the four Canopic Jars were inserted, and which was guarded by the goddesses Isis, Nephthys, Neith and Selket.

Canopic Jars See main vocabulary.

Cap·a·neus (kap′ə·nōōs, -nyōōs, kə·pā′nē·əs) *Greek* One of the Seven Against Thebes.

Car·de·a (kär·dē′ə) *Roman* The goddess of door-hinges and protectress of children against vampire-witches.

Car·men·ta (kär·men′tə) *Roman* The goddess of prophecy and of healing. She followed her son Evander into Italy and changed the Greek alphabet into the Roman.

Car·ne·a (kär·nē′ə) 1. *Roman* The goddess of physical health. 2. *Greek* An important Spartan festival in honor of Apollo.

Cas·san·dra (kə·san′drə) See main vocabulary.

Cas·si·o·pe·ia (kas′ē·ə·pē′ə) See main vocabulary.

Cas·tor and Pol·lux (kas′tər, käs′-; pol′əks) See main vocabulary.

Cath·bad (käth′bŏŏd) *Irish* The chief druid of Ulster in the reign of Conchobar.

Ce·crops (sē′krops) See main vocabulary.

cen·taur (sen′tôr) See main vocabulary.

Ceph·a·lus (sē′fə·ləs) *Greek* The husband of Procris, daughter of Cecrops, with whom he became reconciled after each had been unfaithful, only to kill her by error as she jealously spied on him while he was hunting.

Ce·pheus (sē′fyōōs, -fē·əs) See main vocabulary.

Cer·ber·us (sûr′bər·əs) See main vocabulary.

Cer·co·pes (sûr·kō′pēz) *Greek* A race of apelike but human pygmies who were punished for trying to steal the weapons of Hercules and trying to trick Zeus.

Ce·res (sir′ēz) See main vocabulary.

Chan·di (chän′dē) *Hindu* See DEVI.

Chang Fei (chäng fā) *Chinese* A god of butchers, eight feet tall with a panther's head, a swallow's chin, and a voice of thunder.

Chang Hsien (chäng shē·en) *Chinese* A patron of child-bearing women.

Chang Kuo (chäng kōō·ô) *Chinese* One of the Eight Immortals of Taoism, a clever old man riding backwards on a white donkey. Also **Chang Kuo Lao** (lou).

Char·on (kâr′ən, kar′-) See main vocabulary.

Cha·ryb·dis (kə·rib′dis) See main vocabulary.

Ch'eng Huang (cheng hwäng) *Chinese* God of the ramparts, city walls, moats, and ditches, and spiritual magistrate of the people.

Cheng Wu (cheng wōō) *Chinese* The guardian of the North in Taoist lore.

Chi·me·ra (kə·mir′ə-, kī-) See main vocabulary.

Chi·ron (kī′ron) See main vocabulary.

Chit·ra·gup·ta (chet·rä·gōōp′tə) *Hindu* The recorder of vices and cirtues, and the judge who sends men to heaven or hell.

Chry·se·is (krī·sē′əs) *Greek* See main vocabulary.

Churning of the Ocean *Hindu* A joint project on the part of the gods and demons to recover the amrita lost at the deluge; they churned the milk-white ocean for a thousand years, after throwing in specimens of all the plants in the world, and reproduced amrita after producing all manner of things including Parijata, Surabhi, and Varuni.

Chy·a·va·na (chē·ä·vä′nə) *Hindu* An ancient sage noted for having a faithful young wife.

Cia·ban (kē′vən) *Irish* A hero who was banished from the Fianna because of his charm for women and the jealousy of his comrades. He won Clíodna's love and carried her off, only to have her drowned by a huge wave.

Cir·ce (sûr′sē) See main vocabulary.

Cli·o (klī′ō) See main vocabulary.

Clí·od·na (klē′ə·nə) *Irish* Daughter of the chief druid of Manannán mac Lir, lord of the sea.

Cod·rus (kod′rəs) *Greek* The last king of Athens, who deliberately gave his life when the oracle said the war with the Dorians would be won by the side whose king died.

Co·mus (kō′məs) See main vocabulary.

Con·all Céar·ne·ac (kun′əl kyär′näk) *Irish* One of the three first champions of Ulster and a cousin of Cuchulain.

Con·cho·bar mac Nes·sa (krōō′khŏŏr mäk·nes′ə) *Irish* King of Ulster about the beginning of the Christian era, uncle and fosterer of Cuchulain.

Con·cor·di·a (kon·kôr′dē·ə) See main vocabulary.

Con·la (kōōn′lə) *Irish* Son of Cuchulain, killed by his own father in ignorance.

Con·sen·tes Di·i (kon·sen′tēz dī′i) *Roman* The twelve major deities, six male and six female, who formed the council of Jupiter. They include Juno, Minerva, Sumanus, Vulcan, Saturn, Mars, and six others whose identities are not certain. The council was Etruscan in origin.

Con·sus (kon′səs) *Roman* An ancient god of good counsel, secret deliberation, the stored harvest, and the underworld.

Cor·mac Conn·lon·ges (kôr′môk kōn′lij·əz) *Irish* Son of Conchobar mac Nessa who went into hiding to protest the killing of the sons of Usnech, and was murdered on his way to assume the kingship of Ulster.

Cor·mac mac Airt (kôr′môk mäk′ärt) *Irish* A king famous for his wisdom, generosity, and good rule. He is now thought to be a historical ruler of the late third century.

cor·nu·co·pi·a (kôr′nə·kō′pē·ə) See main vocabulary.

Cor·ri·gan (kôr′i·gən) *Breton* A female fairy thought to have been an ancient druid, and hence malicious toward the Christian clergy.

Cot·yt·to (kô·te′tō) *Greek* The great mother goddess of Thrace, whose festival was notorious for its lewdness. Her cult spread throughout Greece and Italy. Also **Cot·ys** (kô′tēs).

Cro·nus (krō′nəs) See KRONOS in main vocabulary.

Cuch·ul·ain (kōō·khul′yən) See main vocabulary.

Cu·pid (kyōō′pid) See main vocabulary.

Cu·re·tes (kyōō′rə·tēz) *Greek* A group of demigods associated with the infant Zeus.

Cú Roi (kōō rē) *Irish* A great wizard of southern Ireland to whom the three champions of Ulster went for judgment.

Cwn An·nw·fn (kōōn′ ä·nōō′vən) *Welsh* The hounds that took part in raids on this world by inhabitants of Annwfn.

Cyb·e·le (sib′ə·lē) See main vocabulary.

Cy·clops (sī′klops) See main vocabulary.

Cyn·thi·a (sin′thē·ə) See main vocabulary.

Cyth·e·re·a (sith′ə·rē′ə) See main vocabulary.

Dac·tyls (dak′tilz) *Greek* The wonder-working smiths who dwelt on Mount Ida and were connected with the Phrygian cult of Rhea.

Daed·a·lus (ded′ə·ləs) See main vocabulary.

Dag·da (däg′də) See main vocabulary.

Daire mac Fiach·na (dir′ə mäk·firkh′nə) *Irish* A chief of Ulster, owner of the brown bull of Cuáilgne, and cause of the war described in the *Táin Bó Cuáilgne.*

Dak·sha (däk′shä) *Hindu* One of the seven sons of Aditi, personifying dexterity and skill.

Dam·ki·na (däm·kē′nə) *Babylonian* Consort of Ea; mother of Marduk.

Dam·o·cles (dam′ə·klēz) See main vocabulary.

Da·mon and Pyth·i·as (dā′mən; pith′ē·əs) See main vocabulary.

Dan·a·e (dan′i·ē) See main vocabulary.

Da·na·i·des (də·nā′ə·dēz) See main vocabulary.

Dan·a·us (dan′ē·əs) See main vocabulary.

Dan·u (than′ōō) See main vocabulary.

Daph·ne (daf′nē) See main vocabulary.

Dar·da·nus (där′də·nəs) See main vocabulary.

Dech·tir·e (dekh′tə·rə) *Irish* Sister of Conchobar and mother of Cuchulain after supernatural impregnation by Lug.

De·ia·ni·ra (dē′ə·nī′rə) See main vocabulary.

Deir·dre (dir′drə) See main vocabulary.

Del·phic oracle (del′fik) See main vocabulary.

De·me·ter (di·mē′tər) See main vocabulary.

Deu·ca·li·on (dōō·kā′lē·ən, dyōō-) See main vocabulary.

de·va (dev′ə) See main vocabulary.

Dev·a·ki (dev·ä′kē) *Hindu* The mother of Krishna, who conceived him from one of Vishnu's black hairs that he placed in her womb.

Dev·i (dev′ē) See main vocabulary.

Dhar·ma (där′mə) See main vocabulary.

Dhar·ti Mai (där′tē mī) *Hindu* The earth goddess who supports human, animal, and vegetable life, and is present everywhere in the ground: also *Bhudevi.*

Di·an·a (dī·an′ə) See main vocabulary.

Di·an·cecht (dē′ən·khäkht) *Irish* A clever physician of the Tuatha Dé Danann.

Glossary of Mythology

Diar·muid (dir′məd) *Irish* In the Finn Cycle, the young man who eloped with Grainne, promised bride of Fionn.

Di·do (dī′dō) See main vocabulary.

Dil·mun (dil′mən) *Sumerian* A land of paradise lacking sweet water. This is supplied by Enki, the water-god.

Di·o·ne (dī·ō′nē) See main vocabulary.

Di·o·ny·sus (dī·ə·nī′səs) See main vocabulary.

Di·os·cu·ri (dī′ə·skyōō′rī) See main vocabulary.

Dis (dis) See main vocabulary.

Do·do·na (dō·dō′nə) See main vocabulary.

Don (dun) *Welsh* The mother of Arianrhod, Gwydion, and other personages in the *Mabinogion*, interpreted as a fertility goddess and identified with the Irish goddess Danu.

Do·nar (dō′när) See main vocabulary.

dry·ad (drī′əd, -ad) See main vocabulary.

Du·am·u·tef (dōō·äm′ə·tef) *Egyptian* Son of Horus whose jackal-headed image serves as a stopper for the Canopic Jar containing the mummified stomach he has been assigned to guard.

Du·at (dōō·wät′) *Egyptian* Twelve regions of the underworld, representing the hours of night, through which Ra's boat passes from west to east despite opposing demons: also *Tuat.*

Du·mu·zi (dōō′mə·zē) *Sumerian* A shepherd-god who was chosen by his wife, Inanna, to be her substitute in the nether world.

Dur·ga (dōōr′gə) See DEVI.

Dval·in (dväl′in) *Germanic* **1.** The dwarf who invented runes. **2.** One of the four stags who grazed on the tree Yggdrasil.

dver·gar (dver′gär) *Norse* The dwarfs, formed by the gods from maggots in the flesh of the giant Ymir.

Dy·a·us (dē·ä′əs) *Hindu* The sky god and father whose offspring included the Adityas, Agni, Asvins, Parjanya, Surya, Indra, and others.

Dy·av·a·prith·i·vi (dē·ä′vä·prēt′ə·vē) *Hindu* Heaven and earth as one deity.

Dyl·an (dil′ən) *Welsh* One of the twin sons of Arianrhod, interpreted as a sea god or the waves of the sea.

E·a (ā′ä) See main vocabulary.

E·a·ba·ni (ā′ä·bä′nē) *Babylonian* Another name for EN-KIDU.

E·chid·na (ā·chid′nə) *Greek* The sister of Geryon, half woman and half serpent, and mother of many monsters like the Chimera, Cerberus, Scylla, the Nemean lion, and others.

E·cho (ek′ō) See main vocabulary.

Ei·lei·thy·ia (ə·lē′thē·ə) *Greek* The goddess of childbirth, early an aspect of Hera and later almost identified with Artemis.

Ein·her·i·ar (īn·her′ē·är) *Germanic* The slain warriors who were Odin's guests in Valhalla.

Eir·a (ī′rä) *Germanic* The goddess of healing, an attendant of Frigga. Also **Eir** (īr), **Eyr′a.**

E·lec·tra (i·lek′trə) See main vocabulary.

El·eu·sin·i·an mysteries (el′yōō·sin′ē·ən) See main vocabulary.

E·ly·si·um (i·lizh′ē·əm, i·liz′-) See main vocabulary.

Em·bla (em′blə) *Norse* The first woman, created from an elm tree. Also **Em·la** (em′lə), **Em·o·la** (em′ō·lə).

Em·esh (em′esh) *Sumerian* Brother of Enten, created by Enlil.

En·cel·a·dus (en·sel′ə·dəs) See main vocabulary.

En·ki (en′kē) *Sumerian* Water-god and god of wisdom, the father of Uttu. A primary figure in the Sumerian pantheon who appears in many creation and culture myths, often associated with Dilmun, the locale of some of his amorous adventures.

En·ki·du (en′kē·dōō) In Babylonian myths, a savage man formed to fight the tyrant Gilgamesh. They wrestle, become boon companions and share many adventures.

En·kim·du (en·kim′dōō) *Sumerian* A farmer-god, rival of Dumuzi for the love of Inanna.

En·lil (en·lil′) *Sumerian* Air-god and supreme deity in Sumerian pantheon but lacking absolute power.

En·mer·kar (en·mûr′kär) *Sumerian* Legendary hero.

En·ten (en′ten) *Sumerian* Brother of Emesh, created by Enlil.

En·um·a el·ish (en·ōōm′ə el′ish) *Babylonian & Assyrian* Known by its first two words ("When above" or "When on high") this important myth describes the slaying of Tiamat, the organization of the universe, and the creation of man.

E·os (ē′əs) See main vocabulary.

E·phi·al·tes (i·fē′al·tēz) See main vocabulary.

E·po·na (i·pō′nə) *Celtic* The ancient goddess of horses, donkeys, mules, and all who had to do with them.

Er·a·to (er′ə·tō) See main vocabulary.

Er·e·bus (er′ə·bəs) See main vocabulary.

E·rech·theus (i·rek′thyōōs, -thē·əs) See main vocabulary.

E·resh·ki·gal (ār·esh′kē·gäl) *Sumerian & Babylonian* The goddess of death, violently hostile toward her sister (*Inanna*

in Sumerian myths, *Ishtar* in Babylonian); the ruling deity of the nether world until overpowered by Nergal who, after threatening to kill her, married her: also *Allatu.*

E·rich·tho·ni·us (i·rik·thō′nē·əs) *Greek* A legendary king of Athens, son of Hephaestus and Ge.

E·rin·y·es (i·rin′i·ēz) See FURIES in main vocabulary.

E·ris (ir′is, er′is) See main vocabulary.

Er·i·u (ā′rōō) *Irish* A queen of the Tuatha Dé Danann, to whom the Milesians promised that her name would be the chief name of Ireland forever.

erl·king (ûrl′king′) See main vocabulary.

Er·os (ir′os, er′os) See main vocabulary.

Er·y·man·thi·an boar (er′ə·man′thē·ən) See main vocabulary.

E·ta·na (ā·tä′nä) *Babylonian* A childless mortal who ascended to heaven, borne aloft by an eagle.

E·te·o·cles (i·tē′ə·klēz) See main vocabulary.

Et·zel (et′sel) See main vocabulary.

Eu·phros·y·ne (yōō·fros′ə·nē) See main vocabulary.

Eu·ro·pa (yōō·rō′pə) See main vocabulary.

Eu·ryd·i·ce (yōō·rid′ə·sē) See main vocabulary.

Eu·rys·the·us (yōō·ris′thē·əs) See main vocabulary.

Eu·ter·pe (yōō·tûr′pē) See main vocabulary.

E·vad·ne (i·vad′nē) *Greek* **1.** The wife of Capaneus, who threw herself on his funeral pyre when he was killed in the siege of Thebes. **2.** A daughter of Poseidon and mother by Apollo of Iamus, whom she killed out of shame.

E·van·der (i·van′dər) *Roman* A son of Hermes and an Arcadian nymph, who came from his mother's country sixty years before the Trojan War and founded a colony at the foot of the Palatine hill.

Faf·nir (fäv′nir, fäf-) See main vocabulary.

Fates (fāts) See main vocabulary.

Fau·nus (fô′nəs) *Roman* A god of nature, patron of agriculture: identified with the Greek *Pan.*

Fen·ris wolf (fen′ris) *Norse* A huge wolf, son of Loki and Angur-boda, whom the gods attempted to fetter. He is tied by a silken cord that will hold until Ragnarök, when he will devour Odin and be torn apart by Vidar.

Fen·sa·lir (fen′sä·lir) *Norse* The mansion of Frigga in which happy married couples spend eternity together.

Fer·diad (fir′dyad) *Irish* Sworn brother of Cuchulain, beguiled by Medb to fight against him in the war for the brown bull of Cuáilgne. See *Táin Bó Cuáilgne.*

Fer·gus mac Roich (fir′gəs mäk·rē′əkh) *Irish* A great warrior of the Red Branch and a tutor of Cuchulain.

Fi·an·na Eire·ann (fē′ə·nə er′in) See main vocabulary.

Fim·bul·win·ter (fēm′bōōl·vēn′tər) *Norse* The three uninterrupted fierce winters preceding Ragnarök.

Fin·da·bair (fin′dhōōr) *Irish* The beautiful daughter of Ailill and Medb, beloved of Fraech.

Finn·bear·a (fin′bûr·ə) *Irish* King of the fairies of Connacht.

Finn Cycle (fin) *Irish* A body of heroic and romantic tales dealing with the exploits of Fionn macCumhail, the Fianna, Fionn's son Oisin and grandson Oscar. Also **Fen·i·an Cycle** (fē′nē·ən).

Fionn mac·Cumal (fin′məkōōl′) See main vocabulary.

Fir·bolg (fir′bul·əg) See main vocabulary.

fire-drake (fīr′drāk′) See main vocabulary.

Fjal·ar (fyä′lär) *Norse* **1.** One of the dwarfs who killed the great teacher Kvasir. **2.** The cock who will crow to announce Ragnarök.

Fod·la (fō′lhə) *Irish* One of the three queens of the Tuatha Dé Danann encountered by the invading Milesians.

Fo·mor·i·an (fə·môr′ē·ən) See main vocabulary.

For·se·ti (fôr′se·tē) See main vocabulary.

For·tu·na (fôr·tōō′nə, -tyōō′-) See main vocabulary.

Fraech (frekh) *Irish* See FODLA.

Frag·a·rach (frä′gər·äkh) *Irish* The terrible and wonderful sword called the Answerer, which Lug brought from the other world and which could cut through any armor.

Frey (frā) See main vocabulary.

Frey·a (frā′ə) See main vocabulary.

Frigg (frig) See main vocabulary. Also **Frig·ga** (frig′ə).

Fro·di (frōōd′ē) *Norse* A legendary king of Denmark, supposed to be an incarnation of Frey.

Fu Hsi (fōō shē) *Chinese* A legendary emperor and culture hero who instituted the rites, laws, and customs of marriage.

Ful·la (ful′ə) *Norse* An attendant or sister of Frigga whose lovely long hair represented the golden grain.

Fur·ies (fyōōr′ēz) See main vocabulary.

Fur·ri·na (fōōr′i·nə) *Roman* An ancient goddess whose festival survived into late Rome. She was perhaps a spirit of darkness.

Gae·a (jē′ə) See main vocabulary.

Gae Bulg (gā bul′əg) *Irish* The wonderful spear of Cuchulain, made from the bones of a sea-monster.

Ga·lar (gä′lär) *Norse* The dwarf who, along with Fjalar, killed the great teacher Kvasir.

Gal·a·te·a (gal′ə·tē′ə) **1.** See main vocabulary. **2.** *Greek* A Nereid, beloved of Polyphemus but in love with Acis, whom Polyphemus killed.

Gan·dhar·va (gän·där′və) *Hindu* **1.** The measurer of space; the sun steed. **2.** One of a group of sky-dwelling, medically skilled fertility deities. **3.** One of a group of shaggy, half-animal beings. **4.** One of a group of musicians at the banquets of the gods.

Gand·reid (gänd′rād′) *Norse* The wild hunt or spirit's ride that brings fertility to any field it passes over.

Ga·nes·a (gä·nes′ə) *Hindu* The god of wisdom, prudence, and learning, the remover of obstacles, and the leader of the troops of lesser deities; a son of Siva and Parvati. Also **Ga·nesh·a** (gä·nesh′ə), **Ga·na·pa·ti** (gä·nə·pä′tē).

Gan·y·mede (gan′ə·mēd) See main vocabulary.

Garm (gärm) *Norse* The blood-stained watchdog who guarded Hel's gate. Also **Gar·mr** (gär′mər).

Ga·ru·da (gä·rōō′də) *Hindu* The sun, represented as half man and half bird, with a golden body, white face, and red wings.

Gau·ri (gou′rē) *Hindu* See DEVI.

Ge (jē) *Greek* Gaea. See main vocabulary.

Geb (geb) *Egyptian* God of the earth, closely united with his sister/spouse Nut, the sky-goddess, until separated from her by the air-god Shu: also *Keb, Seb.*

Gef·jon (gef′yōn) *Norse* The goddess of agriculture and patroness of virgins, an attendant of Frigga.

Ger·da (gûr′dä) See main vocabulary.

Gi·bil (gi′bəl) *Sumerian & Babylonian* A fire-god.

Gi·gan·tes (jə·gän′tēz) *Greek* A race of giants that sprang from Gaea when the blood of the mutilated Uranus fell upon her. They fought the gods, and were defeated with the help of Hercules.

Gil·ga·mesh (gil′gə·mesh) See main vocabulary.

Gin·nung·a·gap (ye·nōōng′ä·gäp) *Norse* The bottomless abyss between Niflheim and Muspelheim.

Gir·ru (gir′ōō, gir′rōō) *Babylonian* A fire-god.

Gish Bar (gish bär) *Babylonian* A fire-god.

Gish·zi·da (gish·zē′dä) *Babylonian* One of a pair of heavenly gatekeepers. The other was Tammuz.

Glas Gai·bleann (glas gob′lin) *Irish* A wonderful gray cow that gave an inexhaustible supply of milk.

Goib·niu (gib′nōō) *Irish* The devine smith who made spears and arms for the Tuatha Dé Danann. His counterpart in Welsh mythology is **Go·van·non** (guv′ə·non).

golden bough In the folklore and mythology of many cultures, the mistletoe.

Golden Fleece See main vocabulary.

go·lem (gō′lem, -ləm) See main vocabulary.

Goll mac Mor·na (gul mäk·môr′nə) *Irish* Fionn mac-Cumal's greatest rival in the Finn Cycle, usually identified with Connacht.

Gor·gon (gôr′gən) See main vocabulary.

Göt·ter·däm·mer·ung (gœt′ər·dem′ər·ŏŏngk) See main vocabulary.

Gra·ces (grā′siz) See main vocabulary.

Grae·ae (grē′ē) See main vocabulary.

Grain·ne (grän′yə) *Irish* The daughter of Cormac mac Airt and promised bride of Fionn macCumal. She eloped with Diarmuid, and after he was pursued and killed, finally married Fionn.

grif·fin (grif′ən) See main vocabulary.

Grim·hild (grim′hild) *Norse* The wife of Guiki, king of the Nibelungs, and mother of Gunnar, Gudrun, and Hogni.

Gud·run (gŏŏd′rŏŏn) See main vocabulary.

Gu·i·ki (gŏŏ′ē·kē) *Norse* The king of the Nibelungs.

Gu·la (gŏŏ′lä] *Babylonian & Assyrian* Goddess of health; wife of Ninib.

Gung·nir (gŏŏng′nir) *Norse* Odin's infallible spear.

Gun·nar (gŏŏn′är) See main vocabulary.

Gu·tru·ne (gŏŏ·trŏŏ′nə) See main vocabulary.

Gwy·di·on (gwē′dē·on) *Welsh* A son of Dôn, the brother and lover of Arianrhod, and by her father of Dylan and Llew Llaw Gyffes.

Gy·ges (gī′jēz) See main vocabulary.

Ha·chi·man (hä·chē·män) *Japanese* The god of war, originally the deified Emperor Ojin of the 4th century A.D.

Ha·dad (hä′däd) *Babylonian* See RAMMAN.

Ha·des (hä′dēz) See main vocabulary.

Hag·en (hä′gən) See main vocabulary.

ham·a·dry·ad (ham′ə·drī′əd) See main vocabulary.

Han Chung·li (hän chŏŏng·lē) *Chinese* One of the eight immortals, a friend, teacher, and drinking companion of Lü Tung Pin.

Han·u·man (hän′ŏŏ·män) See main vocabulary.

Hap (häp) *Egyptian* See APIS.

Ha·pi (hä′pē) *Egyptian* A Nile-god depicted as a man with female breasts who wears a headpiece of papyrus or lotus.

Ha·py (hä′pē) *Egyptian* Son of Horus whose ape- or dog-headed image serves as a stopper for the Canopic Jar containing mummified lungs which he has been assigned to guard.

Har·akh·ti (här·äk′tē) *Egyptian* A concept of Horus as the sun, independent of his role in the Isis-Osiris myth. Later absorbed by Ra as Ra-Harakhti.

Har·pe·chru·ti (här·pə·krŏŏ′tē) *Egyptian* Manifestation of the god Horus as a child.

Har·poc·ra·tes (här·pok′rə·tēz) *Greek & Roman* The god of silence; the Egyptian god Horus as a child, adopted by the Greeks and Romans in Hellenistic times.

Har·py (här′pē) See main vocabulary.

Ha·thor (hä′thôr, hath′ôr, hät′hôr) See main vocabulary.

Hav·mand (häv′mänd) *Danish* A legendary marine creature, having the head (usually bearded and handsome) and upper body of a man, and the tail of a fish.

He·be (hē′bē) See main vocabulary.

Hec·a·te (hek′ə·tē) See main vocabulary.

Hec·u·ba (hek′yŏŏ·bə) See main vocabulary.

Heh (he) *Egyptian* Everlasting time personified as a god.

Heim·dall (hām′däl) See main vocabulary.

Hek·et (hek′ət) *Egyptian* Fertility goddess represented as a frog or a frog-headed woman.

Hel (hel) See main vocabulary.

Helen of Troy See main vocabulary.

He·li·o·gab·a·lus (hē′lē·ə·gab′ə·ləs) See main vocabulary.

He·li·os (hē′lē·os) See main vocabulary.

Hel·le (hel′ē) See main vocabulary.

Hel·len (hel′ən) See main vocabulary.

He·phaes·tus (hi·fes′təs) See main vocabulary.

He·ra (hir′ə) See main vocabulary.

Her·cu·les (hûr′kyə·lēz) See main vocabulary. Also **Her·a·cles** or **Her·a·kles** (her′ə·klēz).

Her·maph·ro·di·tus (hûr·maf′rə·dī′təs) See main vocabulary.

Her·mes (hûr′mēz) See main vocabulary.

Her·mod (her′mōd) See main vocabulary.

He·ro (hir′ō) See main vocabulary.

He·si·o·ne (hi·sī′ə·nē) See main vocabulary.

Hes·per·i·des (hes·per′ə·dēz) See main vocabulary.

Hes·ti·a (hes′tē·ə) See main vocabulary.

Him·a·vat (hēm′ə·vät) *Hindu* The personification of the Himalayan Mountains, and father of Ganga and Devi.

Hior·dis (hyor′dis) *Norse* The third wife of Sigmund and fosterer of Sigurd.

Hip·po·crene (hip′ə·krēn, hip′ə·krē′nē) See main vocabulary.

Hip·pol·y·ta (hi·pol′i·tə) See main vocabulary.

Hip·pol·y·tus (hi·pol′i·təs) See main vocabulary.

Hip·pom·e·don (hi·pom′ə·dən) *Greek* One of the Seven Against Thebes.

Hip·pom·e·nes (hi·pom′ə·nēz) See main vocabulary.

Hi·ru·ko (hi·rōō·kō) *Japanese* The first child of Izanagi and Izanami, who was cast adrift in a boat.

Ho·der (hō′dər) See main vocabulary.

Hœ·nir (hœ′nir) See main vocabulary.

Hog·ni (hŏŏg′nē) *Norse* The brother of Gunnar and Gudrun, whom Brynhilt asked to kill Sigurd; he hid the Nibelung gold in the Rhine.

Ho·rae (hō′rē) See main vocabulary.

Ho·rus (hō′rəs) See main vocabulary.

Ho·tei (hō·tī) *Japanese* The most popular of the Japanese gods of luck, represented as a very fat man.

Hou Chi (hō chē) *Chinese* The god of millet.

Hou T'u (hō tōō) *Chinese* The god of earth or soil; sovereign earth.

Hrolf Kra·ki (hrolf krä′kē) The most famous Danish king of the heroic age, identified with Hrothulf of the Old English epic *Beowulf* and celebrated in several sagas.

Hrung·nir (hrŏŏng′nir) *Norse* A famous giant who met Thor in single combat.

Hsi Wang Mu (shē wäng mōō) *Chinese* The consort of Tung Wang Kung formed from the yin principle of the purely female; the lady of the western heavens.

Huang Ti (hwäng tē) *Chinese* A legendary emperor and culture hero who was the first to unite China.

Hu·gin (hŏŏ′yen) ' *Norse* See MUNIN.

Hu·wa·wa (hŏŏ·wä′wä) *Sumerian & Babylonian* Fierce monster-guardian of the cedar forest, slain by Gilgamesh and Enkidu: also *Khumbaba.* Also **Hum·ba·ba** (hŏŏm·bä′bä).

Hy·ge·ia (hī·jē′ə) See main vocabulary.

Hy·las (hī′ləs) See main vocabulary.

Hy·men (hī′mən) See main vocabulary.

Hy·per·bo·re·an (hī′pər·bôr′ē·ən, -bō′rē·ən) See main vocabulary.

Hy·pe·ri·on (hī·pir′ē·ən) See main vocabulary.

Hyp·nos (hip′nos) See main vocabulary.

I·ac·chus (ī-ak′əs) *Greek* The principal god of the Eleusinian mysteries, and one of a triad with Demeter and Persephone.

I·am·be (ī-am′bē) *Greek* A daughter of Pan and Echo who with her jesting was able to make the grieving Demeter smile when she was in search of Persephone.

I·a·si·on (ī-ā′sē-ən) *Greek* The father of Pluto by Demeter.

I·car·i·us (i-kar′ē-əs) *Greek* An Attic Greek to whom Dionysus gave the secret of wine-making in return for hospitality; his neighbors, drunk on his wine, killed him.

Ic·a·rus (ik′ə-rəs, ī′kə-) See main vocabulary.

I·dom·e·neus (ī-dom′ə-nōos, -nyōos) See main vocabulary.

I·dun (ē′dōōn) *Norse* The wife of Bragi and keeper of the golden apples of youth.

I·gi·gi (i-gē′gē, i′gə-gē) *Babylonian* Attendant sky-gods who sometimes reversed roles with the Anunnaki.

Ig·nis (ig′nis) *Hindu* See AGNI.

Il·i·ad (il′ē-əd) See main vocabulary.

Im·ho·tep (im-hō′tep) *Egyptian* The human being who designed a famous pyramid, ultimately deified as a son of Ptah.

Im·se·ty (im-se′tē) *Egyptian* Son of Horus whose man-headed image served as a stopper for the Canopic Jar containing the mummified liver, which he was assigned to guard: also *Mesti.*

Im·su (im′sōō) *Egyptian* See MIN.

I·nan·na (i-nä′nä) *Sumerian* Omnipresent goddess of love and war who visited the nether world naked, having shed her garments at its seven gates. She almost succumbed but was saved, her husband, Dumuzi, dying instead.

In·a·ri (in-ä-rē) *Japanese* The rice or harvest god.

in·cu·bus (in′kyə-bəs, ing′-) See main vocabulary.

In·di·ge·tes (in-dij′ə-tēz) *Roman* The gods and heroes who had lived as mortals in Rome and were invoked and Worshiped as the protectors of the state; especially, the descendants of Aeneas.

In·dra (in′drə) See main vocabulary.

In·fer·i (in-fer′ē) *Greek & Roman* The gods of the lower world and the shades of the departed: distinguished from *Superi.*

Ing (ing) *Germanic* A mythical hero and eponymous ancestor of several Germanic tribes.

I·no (ī′nō) *Greek* The nurse of Dionysus and the cruel stepmother of Phrixus and Helle.

I·o (ī′ō) See main vocabulary.

Iph·i·cles (if′i-klēz) See main vocabulary.

Iph·i·ge·ni·a (if′ə-jə-nī′ə) See main vocabulary.

I·ris (ī′ris) See main vocabulary.

Ish·tar (ish′tär) See main vocabulary.

Is·i·mud (is′ə-mōōd) *Sumerian* Enki's messenger.

I·sis (ī′sis) See main vocabulary.

Ith (ē) *Irish* The first of the Milesians to visit Ireland; his death at the hands of the three kings of Ireland caused the Milesian invasion and conquest.

I·tys (ī′tis) See main vocabulary.

Ix·i·on (ik-sī′ən) See main vocabulary.

Iz·a·na·gi (i-zä-nä-gē) *Japanese* The male of the divine couple who created the eight main islands of Japan and engendered many gods.

Iz·a·na·mi (i-zä-nä-mē) *Japanese* The female of the divine couple, with Izanagi the male.

Jal·an·dhar·a (jäl-än-där′ə) *Hindu* A titan king who defeated the gods in the created spheres as a result of his extraordinary austerities, and set up a tyrannical, wicked, and selfish government.

Jam·bu·dvi·pa (jäm-bōō-dvē′pə) *Hindu* India; literally, the rose-apple island.

Ja·nus (jā′nəs) See main vocabulary.

Ja·ta·yu (jä-tä′yōō) *Hindu* The king of the vultures, a son of Garuda and the ally of Rama against Ravana.

Jim·mu Ten·no (jēm-mōō ten-nō) *Japanese* The legendary first emperor of Japan, about 660 B.C.: also *Toyomikenu.*

Ji·zo (jē-zō) *Japanese* A Bodhisattva regarded as the patron of small children travelers, pregnant women, and persons suffering from toothache.

Jo·cas·ta (jō-kas′tə) See main vocabulary.

Jord (yôrd) *Norse* A giantess, the wife of Odin and mother of Thor; a personification of the unpopulated and uncultivated earth.

Jor·mun·gan·dr (yôr′mən-gän-dər) *Norse* The Midgard serpent, son of Loki and Angur-boda, brother of the Fenris wolf and Hel.

jö·tun (yœ′tōōn) *n. pl.* **jöt·nar** (yœt′när) See main vocabulary.

Jö·tun·heim (yœ′tōōn-hām) *Norse* The home of the giants, to the northeast of Asgard.

Jove (jōv) See main vocabulary.

Jug·ger·naut (jug′ər-nôt) See main vocabulary.

Juno (jōō′nō) See main vocabulary.

Ju·pi·ter (jōō′pə-tər) See main vocabulary.

Ju·tur·na (jōō-tûr′nə) *Roman* A nymph, the personification of healing springs and wells.

Ju·ven·tas (jōō-ven′təs) *Roman* An early goddess of youth: identified with the Greek *Hebe.*

Ka (kä) *Hindu* The unknown god, an abstraction and deification of the interrogative pronoun "who."

Ka (kä) See main vocabulary.

Ka·ban·dha (kä-bän′də) *Hindu* A huge, hairy, headless Rakshasa, with a mouth in the middle of his belly and one big eye in his breast.

Kad·ru (käd′rōō) *Hindu* One of the thirteen daughters of Daksha, all of whom were married to Kasyapa.

Ka·la (kä′lə) *Hindu* The black one, the god of time, a form of Siva as the creator of the universe and its destroyer.

Ka·li (kä′lē) See main vocabulary.

Ka·li·ya (kä-lē′ə) *Hindu* The five-headed king of the serpents who lived in the river Jumna and emerged to devastate the countryside; banished by Krishna.

Kal·ki (käl′kē) *Hindu* The white horse, tenth and last incarnation of Vishnu, which will appear at the end of the present age, destroy the world, and restore purity.

Ka·ma (kä′mə) *Hindu* The god of love and desire, a beautiful young man carrying a flower bow with flower string and five flower shafts.

Kam·sa (käm′sə) *Hindu* A god and king who persecuted Krishna because it had been foretold that a child of Devaki would kill him, and was killed by Krishna.

Ka·ri (kä′rē) *Norse* A giant of tempests and lord of the storm giants.

kar·ma (kär′mə) See main vocabulary.

Kart·ti·key·a (kärt′tē-kä′ə) *Hindu* The six-faced god of war and of the planet Mars.

Ka·sy·a·pa (kä-sē-ä′pə) *Hindu* The old tortoise man, progenitor of all things living on the earth.

Ka·tha Sa·rit Sa·ga·ra (kä′tə sä′rēt sä-gä′rə) *Hindu* The ocean of the rivers of stories, a collection of popular fairy tales and romances written in Sanskrit about the beginning of the twelfth century.

Kau·ra·vas (kou-rä′vəs) *Hindu* The opponents of the Pandavas in the battles of the Mahabharata.

Keb (keb) *Egyptian* See GEB.

Keb·eh·se·nuf (keb′e-sə-nōōf′) *Egyptian* See QEBHSNUF.

kel·pie (kel′pē) See main vocabulary.

Ke·res (kē′rēz) *pl.* of **Ker** (kûr) *Greek* Malignant spirits and bringers of evil.

Khan·da·va (kän-dä′və) *Hindu* The country and forest of the Pandavas.

Khen·su (ken′sōō) *Egyptian* A healer-god identified with the moon; son of Amon and Mut: also *Khons.*

Khep·ri (kep′rī) *Egyptian* God of regeneration of life, identified with Ra, symbolized as a scarab or scarab-headed human. Also **Khep·e·ra** (kep′ə-rä).

Khnum (knōōm) See main vocabulary.

Khum·ba·ba (kōōm-bä′bä) *Babylonian & Assyrian* See HUWAWA.

Ki (kē) *Sumerian* Goddess of earth.

Kin·gu (king′gōō) *Babylonian* The consort of Tiamat, slain by Marduk. His blood was used to mold the first man.

Kin·na·ra (kēn-nä′rə) *Hindu* The heavenly musicians, followers of Kubera.

Kirt·ti·mu·kha (kirt-tē-mōō′kə) *Hindu* The face of the lion-headed monster embodying the destructive power of the universal god.

Ki·shar (kä′shär) *Babylonian* An earth deity born of Lahamu and Lahmu.

Kriem·hild (krēm′hild) See main vocabulary.

Krish·na (krish′nə) See main vocabulary.

Kro·nos (krō′nəs) See main vocabulary.

Kuan Ti (kwän tē) *Chinese* The god of war, honored because he prevents, rather than makes, war.

Kuan Yin (kwän yēn) See main vocabulary.

Ku·be·ra (kōō-ber′ə) *Hindu* The king of the Yakshas, god of wealth, and lord of the treasures of the earth.

Kuei Hsing (kwä shēng) *Chinese* An ugly dwarf associated with Wen Ch'ang; he won first prize in the emperor's examinations, but was denied the award because of his ugliness, whereupon he threw himself into the ocean, was rescued by a dragon, and set in heaven among the stars.

Kur (kûr) *Sumerian* The nether world in some myths; in others, any inimical or foreign land.

Kur·ma (kûr′mə) *Hindu* The tortoise, second avatar of Vishnu, that helped the gods recover the amrita and other precious things lost during the deluge.

Ku·ru (kûr′ōō) *Hindu* A prince of the moon race, ancestor of the Kauravas and Pandavas.

Kva·sir (kvä′sir) *Norse* A being renowned for knowledge and goodness, who went about the earth answering all questions and thus teaching mankind.

Kwan·non (kwän-nôn) *Japanese* The goddess of mercy: identified with the Chinese *Kuan Yin.*

Glossary of Mythology

Lab·y·rinth (lab′ə·rinth) See main vocabulary.

La·don (lā′dən) See main vocabulary.

La·ha·mu and Lah·mu (lä·hä′moo; lä′moo) *Babylonian* Silt deities born of the primeval sweet-water and salt-water oceans.

Lak·shma·na (läk·shmä′nə) *Hindu* The brother and faithful companion of Lama.

Lak·shmi (läk′shmē) *Hindu* The goddess lotus, spouse of Vishnu and symbol of his creative energy, symbolized by the lotus wherever it appears in Hindu art: also called *Padma*.

La·mas·su (lä·mä′soo, lä′mə·soo) *Assyrian* A winged, human-headed sculptured bull, a protective genie of palaces.

La·mi·a (lā′mē·ə) See main vocabulary.

La·o·co·on (lā·ok′ə·won, -ō·won) See main vocabulary.

La·om·e·don (lā·om′ə·don) See main vocabulary.

Lap·i·thae (lap′ə·thē) See main vocabulary.

lar·es (lâr′ēz, lā′rēz) See main vocabulary.

lar·va (lär′və) *Roman* An evil spirit that frightened and worked ill against people.

La·ti·nus (lə·tī′nəs) *Roman* The father-in-law of Aeneas, and variously the son of Faunus, Odysseus, or Hercules.

La·to·na (lə·tō′nə) See main vocabulary.

La·vin·i·a (lə·vin′ə·ə, -ē·ə) *Roman* The daughter of Latinus, won by Aeneas when he killed Turnus in a duel.

Le·an·der (lē·an′dər) See main vocabulary.

Le·da (lē′də) See main vocabulary.

Lei Kung (lā koong) *Chinese* The god of thunder.

Lei Tsu (lā tsoo) *Chinese* A culture hero, wife of Huang Ti, and the first to domesticate wild silkworms.

lep·re·chaun (lep′rə·kôn) See main vocabulary.

Le·the (lē′thē) See main vocabulary.

Le·to (lē′tō) See main vocabulary.

Li·a Fáil (lē′ə fôl) *Irish* The stone from the mythical city of Falias, which Lug took to Tara, and which would scream out under the foot of every rightful king of Ireland.

Li·at Ma·ca (lē′ət mäl′kä) *Irish* The gray of Macha, the wonderful gray horse of Cuchulain that died defending him in his last fight.

Li·ber and Li·be·ra (lī′bər; lī·ber′ə) *Roman* The ancient Italian deities of the vine, worshiped along with Ceres as fertility gods. Liber became identified with Bacchus, and Libera with Persephone.

Lif and Lif·tha·ser (lēf; lēf′thə·sər) *Norse* The man and woman who will sleep through Ragnarök and found a new race in the green and verdant earth after the disaster.

Lil·ith (lil′ith) See main vocabulary.

Li·nus (lī′nəs) *Greek* A youth who was exposed in infancy, raised by shepherds, and killed by dogs; he was celebrated in songs of vintagers and reapers, of Phoenician origin, and by festivals in various parts of Greece.

Lir (lir) *Irish* The personification of the sea, and father of the sea god Manannán.

Llew Llaw Gyf·fes (loo lô jif′əs) *Welsh* One of the marvelous twin boys born to Arianrhod, twin brother of Dylan, and interpreted as a sun god.

Lludd (lood) *Welsh* A legendary king of Britain who freed his land of three terrible plagues, including two dragons.

Loegair·e Bua·duc (leg′rə bood′ok) *Irish* One of the three first champions of Ulster, along with Cuchulain and Conall Cearnac.

Lo·gi (lō′gē) *Norse* A personification of wildfire.

Lo·ki (lō′kē) See main vocabulary.

Lu·a (loo′ə) *Roman* The ancient Italian goddess of war and calamity, the consort of Saturn in the cult.

Lu·ci·na (loo·sī′nə) See main vocabulary.

Lug (loog) See main vocabulary.

Lu·gaid mac Con (loo′ē mäk·kung′) See main vocabulary.

Lu·gal·ban·da (loo·gal·bän′də) *Babylonian* Father of Gilgamesh; slayer of the Zu-bird.

Lu·na (loo′nə) See main vocabulary.

Lung Wang (loong wäng) *Chinese* The dragon king, bringer of rain, controller of the ocean and of all storms and waters, and dweller in all lakes.

Lu Pan (loo pän) *Chinese* The patron of carpenters.

Lü·tsu (loo·tsoo) *Chinese* The patron of barbers, beggars, and pedicures.

Lü Tung Pin (loo toong pēn) *Chinese* One of the eight immortals, a man eight feet tall with a sparse beard, renowned as a killer of devils and beloved of barbers.

Ly·ca·on (lī·kā′on) See main vocabulary.

Lyg·ni (lüg′nē) *Norse* In the *Volsunga Saga*, a suitor of Hiordis who was so angry when she married Sigmund that he killed all the Volsungs; later killed by Sigmund's son Sigurd.

Maat (mät) *Egyptian* Goddess of justice and truth, represented by the feather utilized by Anubis during the weighing of souls. See WEIGHING OF SOULS.

Mab·i·no·gi·on (mab′ə·nō′gē·ən) See main vocabulary.

Mac Cecht (mäk·kyäkht′) *Irish* A king of the Tuatha Dé Danann.

Mac Cuill (mäk·kwil′) *Irish* A king of the Tuatha Dé Danann.

Mac Greine (mäk·grän′yə) *Irish* A king of the Tuatha Dé Danann.

Mach·a (mäkh′ə) *Irish* 1. One of the trio of war goddesses, with Morrigan and Neman being the others, who appeared on battlefields in the form of a crow. 2. The wife of an Ulster chieftain, gifted with enormous speed. She outran the king of Ulster's horses, even when about to give birth.

mae·nad (mē′nad) See main vocabulary.

Mag Tured, Battle of (ma too′rid) *Irish* The great battle, according to some versions fought in two parts, in which the Tuatha Dé Danann defeated the Firbolgs and the Fomorians and came to rule all of Ireland: also *Moytura*.

Ma·ha·bhar·a·ta (mä·hä′bər·ä′tə) See main vocabulary.

Ma·ha·de·va (mä·hä·dev′ə) *Hindu* Siva.

Ma·ha·de·vi (mä·hä·dev′ē) *Hindu* See DEVI.

Mai·a (mā′yə, mī′ə) See main vocabulary.

Ma·ma (mä′mä) *Babylonian* Mother-goddess.

Ma·nan·nán (man′ə·non) *Irish* The sea god, son of Lir.

Ma·na·sa (mä·nä′sə) *Hindu* A snake goddess, depicted as yellow, with four arms, sitting on a water lily, and clothed with snakes.

ma·nes (mā′nēz) See main vocabulary.

Ma·nu (mä′noo) 1. *Hindu* The hero of the deluge, who built a ship and survived to repopulate the earth. 2. *Egyptian* The mountain that supported the sky and heaven at their western end. See BAKHAU.

Mar·duk (mär′dook) See main vocabulary.

Mars (märz) See main vocabulary.

Mar·sy·as (mär·sī′əs) See main vocabulary.

Mart·tan·da (mär·tän′də) *Hindu* The eighth son of Aditi, by the sun.

Ma·ruts (mä·roots′) *Hindu* The storm gods, allies of Indra, who ride golden cars gleaming with lightning.

Ma·san (mä·sän′) *Hindu* A hideous black ghost who comes from the ashes of the funeral pyre and afflicts children with disease by throwing ashes over them.

Mat·sy·a (mät·sē′ə) *Hindu* The fish incarnation of Vishnu.

Ma Wang (mä wäng) *Chinese* The protector of horses.

Me (mē) *Sumerian* Laws that control the universe, probably in the same form as the later Babylonian Tablets of Destiny.

Medb (mäb) *Irish* The wife of Ailill mac Matach, who henpecked him.

Me·de·a (mə·dē′ə) See main vocabulary.

Mef·det (mef′det) *Egyptian* A cat-goddess worshiped as a protectress against the bites of serpents.

Me·lam·pus (mə·lam′pəs) *Greek* The first person with prophetic powers, the first mortal physician, and the first Greek to worship Dionysus.

Mele·a·ger (mel·ē·āj′ər) See main vocabulary.

Mel·pom·e·ne (mel·pom′ə·nē) See main vocabulary.

Men·e·la·us (men′ə·lā′əs) See main vocabulary.

Men·tu (men′too) *Egyptian* Ancient Theban god of war, identified with Ra, depicted as a bull- or falcon-headed human: also *Mont*.

Mer·cu·ry (mûr′kyə·rē) See main vocabulary.

Mer·o·dach (mer′ō·dak) *Babylonian* See MARDUK.

Mert·seg·er (mûrt·seg′ər) *Egyptian* A snake-goddess, primarily benevolent, of the necropolis at Thebes.

Me·ru, Mount (mä′roo) *Hindu* The mountain at the center of the earth, where the gods dwell.

Mes·khent (mes′kent) *Egyptian* Goddess of birth who eased the labor of expectant mothers and predicted the fate of newborn infants.

Mes·ti (mes′tē) *Egyptian* See IMSETY.

Mi·das (mī′dəs) See main vocabulary.

Mid·gard (mid′gärd) See main vocabulary.

Mil (mil) *Irish* The leader of the Milesians.

Mi·les·i·ans (mī·lē′zhənz) See main vocabulary.

Mi·mir (mē′mir) See main vocabulary.

Min (min) *Egyptian* Phallic god of vegetation and fertility, and patron of travelers. Also called *Imsu*.

Mi·ner·va (mi·nûr′və) See main vocabulary.

Mi·nos (mī′nəs, -nos) See main vocabulary.

Mi·no·taur (min′ə·tôr) See main vocabulary.

Mit·ra (mēt′rə) *Hindu* One of the seven sons of Aditi, personifying the light of day.

Mne·mos·y·ne (nē·mos′ə·nē, -moz′-) See main vocabulary.

Moi·rai (moi′rī) See main vocabulary.

Mon·e·ta (mon′ə·tə) *Roman* The admonisher or warner, a title of Juno. The temple of Juno Moneta later became the mint, and this event is the basis of the words "mint," "money," etc.

Mont (mont) *Egyptian* See MENTU.

Mor·phe·us (môr′fē·əs, -fyoos) See main vocabulary.

Mor·ri·gan (môr′ə·gən) *Irish* One of a group of three war goddesses, along with Macha and Neman; sometimes used as a generic term to include all three.

Moy·tu·ra (moi·tōō′rə) *Irish* See MAG TURED.
Mu (mōō) *Egyptian* A child of Ra representing physical light personified.
Mum·mu (mōō′mōō) *Babylonian* The vizier of Apsu.
Mu·nin (mōō′nēn) *Norse* One of the two ravens, Hugin being the other, that flew about all day observing, and at nightfall perched on Odin's shoulders to tell him what they had seen and heard.
Muse (myōōz) See main vocabulary.
Mus·pell·heim (mōōs′pel·hãm) *Norse* The southern abode of the fire-devils who will destroy the world at Ragnarök.
Mut (mōōt) *Egyptian* A mother-goddess whose headpiece, in the form of a vulture, symbolized maternity; wife of Amon-Ra.
My·lit·ta (mi·lit′ə) *Babylonian* Goddess in whose name every Babylonian woman was required, at least once, to submit to the embraces of a stranger in the sacred temple for a small fee.

Na·bu (nä′bōō) *Babylonian* See NEBO.
Nag·l·far (näl′fär) *Norse* A ship, made of the nail-parings of the dead, that will carry the giants to do battle against the gods at Ragnarök.
Naio·se (nē′shə) *Irish* One of the sons of Usnech, lover of Deirdre, with whom he eloped to Scotland.
Nam·mu (nä′mōō) *Sumerian* Primeval mother of heaven and earth.
Nam·tar (näm·tär′) *Sumerian & Babylonian* Messenger of Allatu, the nether-world goddess; also, a demon of disease.
Nan·di (nän′dē) *Hindu* The milk-white bull of Siva, chief of his attendants.
Nan·na (nän′nä) *Norse* The goddess of purity, blossoms, and vegetation; the wife of Balder and mother of Forseti.
Nan·na (nä′nä) *Sumerian* Moon-god and chief astral deity in the Sumerian pantheon; son of Enlil and Ninlil: also *Ashgirbabbar, Sin.*
Na·ra·da (nä·rä′də) *Hindu* A legendary sage, inventor of the lute and author of a law textbook.
Na·ra·ka (nä·rä′kə) *Hindu* A god who, in the form of an elephant, outdid the evil deeds of all other gods; he carried off 16,000 women.
Na·ra·si·nha (nä·rä·sē′nə) *Hindu* The man-lion, fourth avatar of Vishnu.
Na·ra·ya·na (nä·rä·yä′nə) *Hindu* An epithet of several gods, but especially of Brahma and Vishnu; literally, either "moving on the waters," or "son of man."
Nar·cis·sus (när·sis′əs) See main vocabulary.
Ne·bo (nā′bō) *Babylonian & Assyrian* God of wisdom: a Babylonian deity later introduced into the Assyrian pantheon, where his influence in his cult centers approached that of the great god Ashur: also *Nabu.*
Nef·er·tum (nef′r·tōōm) *Egyptian* A lotus- or lion-headed sun-god.
Ne·heb-Ka·u (ne′heb-kä′ōō) *Egyptian* A serpent-goddess symbolizing fertility and the protective mother.
Ne·ith (nē′ith) *Egyptian* Goddess of war and domestic arts; virgin-mother of Ra and other gods. Also **Net** (net).
Nekh·e·bet (nek′ə·bet) *Egyptian* Protective goddess portrayed as a vulture.
Ne·man (nem′an) *Irish* One of a group of three war goddesses, the others being Macha and Morrigan.
Ne·me·an lion (nē′mē·ən) See main vocabulary.
Neph (nef) *Egyptian* Creation-god who manifested himself also as Nun and Ptah.
Neph·e·le (nef′ə·lē) See main vocabulary.
Neph·thys (nep′this) *Egyptian* Sister-goddess of Isis and protectress of the dead: mother of Anubis.
Nep·tune (nep′tōōn, -tyōōn) See main vocabulary.
Ne·re·id (nir′ē·id) See main vocabulary.
Ner·eus (nir′ōōs, -ē·əs) See main vocabulary.
Ner·gal (när′gäl) *Sumerian & Babylonian* Originally a sky-god but ultimately lord of the nether world as husband of Ereshkigal.
Ner·thus (ner′tōōs) *Germanic* The ancient earth mother and goddess of fertility.
Nes·sus (nes′əs) See main vocabulary.
Nes·tor (nes′tər) See main vocabulary.
Ne·ti (ne′tē) *Sumerian* Chief gate-keeper of the seven gates to the nether world.
Ni·be·lung (nē′bə·lŏŏng) See main vocabulary.
Ni·be·lung·en·lied (nē′bə·lŏŏng′ən·lēt′) See main vocabulary.
nightingale legend See main vocabulary.
Ni·na (nē′nä) *Sumerian & Assyrian* Fish-goddess, corn spirit and goddess of maternity, whose name is reflected in the Sumerian city of Nina and the Assyrian city of Nineveh.
Nin·gal (nin′gal) *Sumerian* Mother of the sun-god Utu.
Nin·gir·su (nin·gûr′sōō) *Sumerian & Babylonian* See NINURTA.

Nin·hur·sag (nin·hŏŏr′sag, nin′hŏŏr-) *Sumerian* Mother-goddess, possibly derived from earlier earth-goddess Ki. Also **Nin·mah** (nin′mä), **Nin·tu** (nin′tōō).
Nin·ib (nin′ib, ni′nib) *Babylonian & Assyrian* Benevolent god of healing, and lord of battle.
Nin·i·gi-no-Mi·ko·to (nēn·ē·gē·nō·mē·kō·tō) *Japanese* The grandson of the sun-goddess Amaterasu, who descended from heaven to Japan after receiving the three imperial jewels, married a mortal woman, and is the presumed ancestor of the Japanese sovereigns.
Nin·kur (nin·kōōr′) *Sumerian* Lover of Enki and mother of Uttu the plant goddess.
Nin·lil (nin·lil′) *Sumerian* Air-goddess, wife of Enlil.
Nin·sar (nin′sär) *Sumerian* Daughter and lover of Enki; mother of Ninkur.
Nin·shu·bur (nin·shōō′bər) *Sumerian* Inanna's messenger whose timely action rescued her from death in the nether-world realm of her sister Ereshkigal.
Ni·nur·ta (ni·nōōr′tä) *Sumerian & Babylonian* God of agriculture and war whose personified weapon, the Sharur, induced him to attack Asag, the demon of sickness: also *Ningirsu.*
Ni·o·be (nī′ə·bē) See main vocabulary.
Niord (nyôrd) *Norse* The god of the sea, especially of coastal waters, and of fishing, commerce, and prosperity.
nir·va·na (nir·vä′nə, nər·van′ə) See main vocabulary.
Nit (nit) *Egyptian* Goddess of war and hunting.
Niu Wang (nyōō wäng) *Chinese* The guardian of cattle.
nix (niks) See main vocabulary.
Norn (nôrn) See main vocabulary.
Nu·a·da (nōō′ə·də) *Irish* A king of the Tuatha Dé Danann.
Nu·dim·mud (nōō·dim′ŏŏd) *Babylonian* See EA.
nu·men (nōō′mən, nyōō′-) See main vocabulary.
Nun (nōōn, nŏŏn) *Egyptian* The primeval ocean, existing prior to creation itself, from which the gods issued. Also **Nu** (nōō, nŏŏ).
Nus·ku (nōōs′kōō, nŏŏsk′ōō) *Babylonian* Fire-deity and messenger of the gods.
Nut (nōōt, nŏŏ′it) *Egyptian* Goddess of the sky, depicted as a cow or woman held aloft by her father Shu.
nymph (nimf) See main vocabulary.

Oc·nus (ok′nəs) *Greek* The personification of delay, dwelling in the underworld where he constantly twines a rope that is constantly eaten by his donkey.
O·din (ō′din) See main vocabulary.
O·dy·seus (ō·dis′yōōs, -ē·əs) See main vocabulary.
Od·ys·sey (od′ə·sē) See main vocabulary.
Oed·i·pus (ed′ə·pəs, ē′də-) See main vocabulary.
Oe·no·ne (ē·nō′nē) See main vocabulary.
Og·ma (ŏ′mä) *Irish* One of the Tuatha Dé Danann, a culture god of poetry, speech, and eloquence.
Oi·sin (ā′shin) *Irish* A son of Fionn macCumal and father of Oscar. He spent many years at Tir na n'Og and returned to Ireland, not knowing that ages had passed; as a wrinkled old man he met St. Patrick and his monks, and told them the legends of the Fianna.
Om·pha·le (om′fə·lē) See main vocabulary.
om·pha·los (om′fə·ləs) See main vocabulary.
O·nu·phis (ō·nōō′fis) *Egyptian* See APIS.
O·phi·on (ō′fē·ən) *Greek* The Titan who ruled the universe before Cronus, who overthrew him.
Ops (ops) See main vocabulary.
Or·cus (ôr′kəs) See main vocabulary.
O·res·tes (ô·res′tēz, ō-) See main vocabulary.
O·ri·on (ō·rī′ən) See main vocabulary.
Or·muzd (ôr′muzd) See main vocabulary.
Or·phe·us (ôr′fē·əs) See main vocabulary.
Os·car (os′kar) *Irish* The grandson of Fionn macCumal, and a hero of the Finn Cycle.
O·si·ris (ō·sī′ris) See main vocabulary.
Os·sa (ä′sə) *Greek* See ALOADAE.
Os·ta·ra (os′tə·rä) *Germanic* The ancient goddess of spring, a development of the primitive Indo-European goddess of dawn.
O·tus (ō′təs) *Greek* One of the Aloadae.

Pad·ma (päd′mə) *Hindu* See LAKSHMI.
Pad·ma·pa·ni (päd·mä·pä′nē) *Hindu* The universal savior of Mahayana Buddhism, greatest of the Bodhisattvas, and prototype of Kuan Yin and Kwannon.
Pal·i·nu·rus (pal′i·nŏŏr′əs) See main vocabulary.
Pan (pan) See main vocabulary.
Pan·da·vas (pän·dä′vəs) *Hindu* One of the two families whose battles are the main subject of the *Mahabharata*, the other being the Kauravas.
Pan·di·on (pan′dē′on) *Greek* A king of Athens, son of Erichthonius and a naiad, and father of Procne and Philomela.
Pan·do·ra (pan·dôr′ə, -dō′rə) See main vocabulary.

Pap·su·kal (pap·soo'kal) *Babylonian* Messenger of the gods whose timely action rescued Ishtar from death in the underworld realm of her sister Ereshkigal.

Pa·ra·su·ra·ma (pä'rä·soo·rä'mə) *Hindu* The sixth incarnation of Vishnu.

Par·cae (pär'sē) See main vocabulary.

Pa·ri·ja·ta (pä·rē·jä'tə) *Hindu* The celestial coral tree that yields all desired objects; it was first planted in Indra's heaven, then removed by Krishna, and returned after Krishna's death.

Par·is (par'is) See main vocabulary.

Par·jan·ya (pär·jän'yə) *Hindu* The god of rain and personification of the rain cloud, a son of Dyaus.

Par·the·no·pae·us (pär'thə·nō'pē·əs) *Greek* One of the Seven Against Thebes.

Par·va·ti (pär·vä'tē) *Hindu* See DEVI.

Pa·ta·la (pä·tä'lə) *Hindu* Collective name for seven infernal regions.

Pa·tro·clus (pə·trō'kləs) See main vocabulary.

Peg·a·sus (peg'ə·səs) See main vocabulary.

Pe·leus (pē'lyoos, -lē·əs) See main vocabulary.

pe·na·tes (pə·nä'tēz) See main vocabulary.

Pe·nel·o·pe (pə·nel'ə·pē) See main vocabulary.

Per·seph·o·ne (pər·sef'ə·nē) See main vocabulary.

Per·seus (pûr'syoos, -sē·əs) See main vocabulary.

Phae·dra (fē'drə) See main vocabulary.

Pha·e·thon (fā'ə·thon) See main vocabulary.

Phe·nix (fē'niks) See main vocabulary under PHOENIX.

Phi·le·mon (fī·lē'mən) See main vocabulary.

Phil·oc·te·tes (fil'ək·tē'tēz) See main vocabulary.

Phi·lo·me·la (fī·lə·mē'lə) See main vocabulary.

Phi·neus (fī'noos, -nē·əs) See main vocabulary.

Phoe·be (fē'bē) See main vocabulary.

Phoe·bus (fē'bəs) See main vocabulary.

Phoe·nix (fē'niks) See main vocabulary.

Pho·lus (fō'ləs) *Greek* An Arcadian centaur, son of Silenus, who entertained Hercules in his cave during the hunt for the Erymanthian boar, and caused a battle between Hercules and other centaurs attracted by the wine.

Phor·cus (fôr'kəs) See main vocabulary.

Phrix·us (frik'səs) See main vocabulary.

Pi·rith·o·us (pī·rith'ō·əs) See main vocabulary.

Pi·sa·cha (pē·sä'chə) *Hindu* The vilest and most malevolent of demons; literally, flesh-eater.

Pi·tris (pē'trēs') *Hindu* The sainted ancestral spirits; literally, fathers.

pix·y (piks'sē) See main vocabulary.

Plei·a·des (plē'ə·dēz, plī'-) See main vocabulary.

Plu·to (ploo'tō) See main vocabulary.

Pol·y·hym·ni·a (pol'i·him'nē·ə) See main vocabulary.

Pol·y·i·dus (pol'i·i'dəs) *Greek* A soothsayer of Argos who was able to find the body of Minos's drowned son and eventually to restore him to life.

Pol·y·ni·ces (pol'i·nī'sēz) *Greek* A son of Oedipus, and one of the Seven Against Thebes.

Pol·y·phe·mus (pol'i·fē'məs) See main vocabulary.

Po·sei·don (pō·sī'dən) See main vocabulary.

Pra·ja·pa·ti (prä·jä·pä'tē) *Hindu* Lord of creatures, an epithet of several gods including Indra, Savitri, and Soma; in later application, Brahma, as chief and father of the gods.

Pra·kri·ti (prä·krē'tē) *Hindu* The primitive matter from which the universe is evolved, as opposed to spirit or Purusa; the creative force, prototype of the female.

Pri·am (prī'əm) See main vocabulary.

Proc·ne (prok'nē) See main vocabulary.

Proc·ris (prok'ris) *Greek* See CEPHALUS.

Pro·me·theus (prə·mē'thyoos, -thē·əs) See main vocabulary.

Psy·che (sī'kē) See main vocabulary.

Ptah (tä) See main vocabulary.

pu·ca (poo'kə) *Irish* A harmless but very mischievous supernatural being of Irish folklore, often appearing in animal or half-animal form. Also **poo'ka.**

Pu·ru·sa (pə·roo'sə) *Hindu* 1. A primeval giant sacrificed by the gods to create the world; he represents the spiritual force opposed to but working with Prakriti, the material force. 2. Brahma as the creator and original male.

Pu·shan (poo·shän') *Hindu* An indistinctly defined sun god, protector and multiplier of cattle, friend and guide of travelers, guardian of paths, and patron of conjurers.

Pu·ta·na (poo·tä'nə) *Hindu* A female demon who tried to kill the infant Krishna by suckling him with her poisonous milk.

Pyg·ma·li·on (pig·mā'lē·ən, -māl'yən) See main vocabulary.

Pyr·rha (pir'ə) See main vocabulary.

Py·thon (pī'thon) *Greek* The female dragon who dwelt at Delphi and guarded the chasm; killed by Apollo.

py·tho·ness (pī'thə·nis, pith'ə-) See main vocabulary.

Qebh·snuf (keb'snoof) *Egyptian* Son of Horus whose hawk-headed image served as a stopper for the Canopic Jar containing mummified intestines, which he was assigned to guard: also *Kebehsenuf*.

Qui·ri·nus (kwi·rī'nəs) See main vocabulary.

Ra (rä) See main vocabulary.

Rag·na·rök (räg'nä·rûk) See main vocabulary.

Ra-Har·akh·ti (rä'här·äk'tē) *Egyptian* The name assumed by the sun-god Ra in absorbing the qualities and role of the sun-god Horus.

Ra·hu (rä'hoo) *Hindu* The cause of eclipses, king of meteors, and guardian of the southwest quarter; he had mischievously drunk some of the amrita produced at the Churning of the Ocean, and achieved immortality.

Rak·sha·sas (räk·shä'səs) *Hindu* Demigod demons malignantly hostile to men, capable of appearing in animal or human form, and devoted to all kinds of vileness and destruction.

Ram (räm) *Hindu* Generalized term for god or divinity.

Ra·ma (rä'mə) See main vocabulary.

Ra·ma·ya·na (rä·mä·yä'nə) See main vocabulary.

Ram·man (räm'än) *Babylonian* The storm-god, god of lightning and thunder, identified with an ancient flood myth: also *Adad, Hadad.*

Ran (rän) See main vocabulary.

Ra·va·na (rä·vä'nə) *Hindu* The king of the Rakshasas, incarnation of wickedness, breaker of laws, and ravisher of women.

Re (rä) See main vocabulary under RA.

Red Branch *Irish* The organized body of warriors around Conchobar mac Nessa, king of Ulster in the 1st century A.D.

Re·gin (rä'gin) See main vocabulary.

Ren·pet (ren'pet) *Egyptian* Goddess of youth.

Rer·et (rer'et) *Egyptian* See TAUERET.

Rhad·a·man·thus (rad'ə·man'thəs) See main vocabulary.

Rhe·a (rē·ə) See main vocabulary.

Ri·bhu (rē·boo') *Hindu* One of the three artisans of the gods, along with Vaja and Vibhu, who were deified because of their skill.

Rom·u·lus (rom'yə·ləs) See main vocabulary.

Ru·dra (roo'drə) *Hindu* The god of storms who controls the cyclone, and inflicts and heals diseases.

Sa·lus (sā'ləs) See main vocabulary.

San·cus (san'kəs) *Roman* The ancient god of oaths, treaties, hospitality, marriage, and perhaps of the sown field; sometimes identified with Apollo, sometimes with Jupiter.

Sa·ra·pis (sä·rä'pis) *Egyptian* See SERAPIS.

Sa·ti (sä'tē) *Egyptian* Goddess of the Nile; wife of Khnum. Also **Sa·tet** (sä'tet).

Sa·ti (sä'tē) *Hindu* The daughter of Daksha and wife of Rudra, who killed herself by entering the fire after a quarrel between her husband and father; this act is the mythical basis of suttee.

Sat·urn (sat'ərn) See main vocabulary.

sat·yr (sat'ər, sā'tər) See main vocabulary.

Sa·vi·tri (sä·vē'trē *Hindu* 1. A name of the sun, especially in its life-giving aspect. 2. In the *Mahabharata*, the heroine whose devotion to her husband was so great that Yama was forced to restore her husband to life.

scar·ab (skar'əb) See main vocabulary.

scorpion-man *Babylonian* A monstrous but friendly creature met by Gilgamesh in his search for Utnapishtim.

Scyl·la (sil'ə) See main vocabulary.

Seb (seb) *Egyptian* See GEB.

Seb·ek (seb'ek) *Egyptian* Crocodile-god represented in cult centers by living, pampered crocodiles. In other areas crocodiles, identified with Set, were destroyed.

Sek·er (sek'ər) *Egyptian* Funerary deity usually depicted in the shape of a human mummy: also *Sokar.*

Sekh·et (sek'et) *Egyptian* Manifestation of Hathor sent by Ra to destroy mankind.

Se·le·ne (si·lē'nē) See main vocabulary.

Sel·ket (sel'ket) *Egyptian* Scorpion-goddess who helped guard the entrails of the deceased; depicted as a woman with a scorpion atop her head or as a human-headed scorpion. Also **Ser·ket** (sûr'ket).

Sem·e·le (sem'ə·lē) See main vocabulary.

Sem·ir·a·mis (sem·ir'ə·mis) See main vocabulary.

Se·ra·pis (si·rä'pis) See main vocabulary.

Se·sha (sesh'ə) *Hindu* The world serpent who supports the seven Patalas or hells, and the world; depicted with a thousand heads, dressed in purple, and holding a plow and a pestle.

Sesh·at (sesh'at, ses'hät) *Egyptian* Ancient goddess of learning, and most important wife of Thoth.

Set (set) See main vocabulary.

Seven Against Thebes *Greek* The seven heroes (Adrastus, Amphiaraus, Capaneus, Hippomedon, Parthenopaeus, Polynices, and Tydeus) who unsuccessfully marched on

Thebes to restore Polynices to the throne, which had been usurped by his brother, Oedipus's other son, Eteocles.

Shab·ti (shăb′tē) *Egyptian* Human figurine interred with the deceased, originally as an alternate dwelling place for the spirit but ultimately as a servant: also *Ushabti.*

Sha·la (shä′lä) *Babylonian* Wife of Ramman, the storm-god.

Sha·mash (shä′mäsh) See main vocabulary.

Shang Ti (shäng tē) *Chinese* The personification of heaven, the source of imperial power; he was worshiped only by the emperor.

Shar·ur (shar′ûr) *Sumerian* Personified weapon of Ninurta.

Shen Nung (shen nŏong) *Chinese* The great culture hero who was patron of agriculture, invented the plow, taught the people planting and the medicinal properties of herbs.

Shih Wang Mu (shû wäng mŏo) *Chinese* The Taoist goddess of the western heavens.

Shu (shŏo, shŏo) *Egyptian* God of the atmosphere who brutally separated the goddess Nut from the god Geb by thrusting her skywards and holding her there.

Sid·dha (sĕd′da) *Hindu* One of the semidivine "perfect ones," 88,000 in number, dwelling between earth and sun.

Si·du·ri (sē-dŏo′rē) *Babylonian* Cupbearer of the gods, encountered by Gilgamesh in his search for the immortal Utnapishtim.

Sieg·fried (sēg′frēd, Ger. zēkh′frēt) See main vocabulary.

Sig·mund (sig′mŏond) *Norse* The father of Sigurd.

Si·gurd (sig′ŏord) See main vocabulary.

Si·le·nus (sī-lē′nas) See main vocabulary.

Sin (sin) **1.** *Sumerian* See NANNA. **2.** *Babylonian* God of wisdom and moon-god.

si·ren (sī′ran) See main vocabulary.

Si·ta (sē′ta) *Hindu* The goddess of agriculture and wife of Rama.

Sis·y·phus (sis′a-fas) See main vocabulary.

Si·va (sē′va) See main vocabulary.

Sleip·nir (slāp′nir) *Norse* Odin's eight-legged gray horse, son of a giant's stallion and Loki in the form of a mare.

Smin·theus (smin′thyŏos, -thē·as) *Greek* Apollo's epithet as the mouse god.

Sol (sol) See main vocabulary.

So·ma (sō′ma) *Hindu* The god of the soma-juice, the moon, stars, plants, and Brahmans.

so·ma (sō′ma) A plant providing an astringent narcotic juice regarded as having divine power.

Som·nus (som′nas) See main vocabulary.

Sons of Horus *Egyptian* Four gods assigned to protect mummified viscera: Imsety, Qebhsnuf, Duamutef and Hapy.

Stym·pha·li·an birds (stim-fā′lē·an) *Greek* The huge flocks of birds chased from the Stymphalian lake by Hercules as the sixth of his labors.

suc·cu·bus (suk′ya-bas) See main vocabulary.

Su·gri·va (sŏo-grē′va) *Hindu* The monkey king who was Rama's ally in his battle with Ravana.

Su·kha·va·ti (sŏo-kä-vä′tē) *Hindu* In Buddhist belief, the "happy universe of the West"; more accessible than nirvana, it is a region of universal pleasure and immeasurable life.

Su·pe·ri (sŏo′pa-rē) *Greek & Roman* The Olympians, living above the earth: distinguished from *Inferi.*

Su·ra·bhi (sŏo-rä′bē) *Hindu* The cow of plenty which grants all desires; created by Prajapati from his breath, or produced at the Churning of the Ocean.

Sur·tr (sûr′tar) *Norse* The flame giant who presides over Muspellheim, and whose fire will destroy the world at Ragnarök.

Sur·ya (sŏor′ya) *Hindu* One of the seven sons of Aditi, personifying the sun.

Su·sa·no·o (sŏo-sä-nô-ô) *Japanese* The god of wind, who sprang from Izanagi's nose.

Svart·al·far (svärt′äl-fär) *Norse* The black elves that grew from the maggots of Ymir's flesh.

Sym·ple·ga·des (sim-plē′ga-dēz) See main vocabulary.

Tablets of Destiny *Babylonian* Symbols of authority that Marduk took from Kingu and sealed to his own breast, thereby assuming the supreme position among the gods.

Táin Bó Cuáilgne (toin bō kŏol′nä) See main vocabulary.

Tam·muz (tam′ŏoz) See main vocabulary.

Tan·ta·lus (tan′ta-las) See main vocabulary.

Tash·mit (täsh′mit) *Assyrian* Wife of Nebo and intercessor with him on behalf of mortals.

Ta·uer·et (tä′wer′at) *Egyptian* Popular goddess of childbirth depicted as a hippopotamus standing on its hind legs: also *Reret.*

Tef·nut (tef′nŏot) *Egyptian* Goddess of moisture; mother of Geb and Nut.

Tel·a·mon (tel′a-mon) See main vocabulary.

Te·lem·a·chus (ta-lem′a-kas) See main vocabulary.

Tem (tem) *Egyptian* See ATMU.

Te·reus (tir′yŏos, tir′ē·as) See main vocabulary.

Ter·mi·nus (tûr′ma-nas) See main vocabulary.

Terp·sich·o·re (tûrp·sik′a·rē) See main vocabulary.

Tha·li·a (tha-lī′a) See main vocabulary.

The·seus (thē′syŏos, -sē·as) See main vocabulary.

Thor (thôr) See main vocabulary.

Thoth (thŏth, tōt) See main vocabulary.

Thrym (thrŭm) *Norse* The frost giant who stole Thor's hammer, and demanded Freya as the price of returning it. Thor disguised himself as Freya, retrieved the hammer, and killed Thrym and his giant band.

Ti·a·mat (tē·ä′mät) *Babylonian* The primeval salt sea personified as a dragon of chaos that Marduk slew and split into two pieces, one of which he used to form the sky.

Ti·re·si·as (tī·rē′sē·as) See main vocabulary.

Tir na nog (tir na nōg) *Irish* The land of youth, an otherworldly paradise on an island.

Ti·tan (tīt′n) See main vocabulary.

Tri·ton (trīt′n) See main vocabulary.

Trojan War See main vocabulary.

troll (trōl) See main vocabulary.

Tsai Shen (tsī shen) *Chinese* The god of wealth.

Tsao Chün (tsou chün) *Chinese* The god of the kitchen, stove, and hearth; annually he returns to heaven to report on the misdeeds of the family.

Ts'ao Kuo-ch'iu (tsou kwō·chyŏo) *Chinese* One of the eight immortals.

Tuatha Dé Danann (tŏo′ha dä dä′non) See main vocabulary.

Tung Wang Kung (tŏong wäng kŏong) *Chinese* The Taoist lord of the immortals, lord of the east, and prime embodiment of the male principle, yang.

Tur·nus (tûr′nas) *Roman* An Italian chief, the rival of Aeneas for the hand of Lavinia.

T'u Ti (tŏo tē) *Chinese* The god of place or locality.

Ty·che (tī′kē) See main vocabulary.

Ty·deus (tī′dyŏos, -dē·as) *Greek* One of the Seven Against Thebes.

Ty·phoe·us (tī′fē·as) See main vocabulary.

Tyr (tür, tir) See main vocabulary.

Ul·ler (ŏol′lar) *Norse* The god of winter, hunting, archery, skating, and snowshoeing.

Ulster Cycle See main vocabulary.

U·ma (ŏo′ma) *Hindu* See DEVI.

U·ra·ni·a (yŏo·rä′nē·a) See main vocabulary.

U·ra·nus (yŏor′a·nas) See main vocabulary.

Ur·Sha·na·bi (ûr-sha·nä′bē) *Babylonian* Utnapishtim's boatman who consented to ferry Gilgamesh over the waters of death.

U·shab·ti (ŏo-shäb′tē) *Egyptian* See SHABTI.

Us·nech (ish′näkh) *Irish* Father of three sons (including Naiose) who fled to Scotland with Deirdre but were lured back to Ireland by Conchobar and beheaded.

Ut·gard (ŏot′gärd) See main vocabulary.

Ut·gard-Lo·ki (ŏot′gärd-lō′kē) See main vocabulary.

Ut·na·pish·tim (ŏot-na·pish′tim) *Babylonian* The Noahlike figure of the Gilgamesh Epic who gained immortality.

Ut·tu (u′tŏo) *Sumerian* Goddess of vegetation born in the paradise-like land of Dilmun; daughter of Enki and Ninkur.

U·tu (ŏo′tŏo) *Sumerian* Sun-god born of Nanna the moongod and his wife Ningal.

Vai·ta·ra·ni (vī·ta·rä′nē) *Hindu* The river of death that flows between the land of the living and the kingdom of Yama.

Va·ja (vä′ja) *Hindu* One of the three artisans of the gods, along with Ribhu and Vibhu, who were deified for their great skill.

Val·hal·la (val·hal′a) See main vocabulary.

Va·li (vä′lē) *Norse* **1.** A son of Odin, born for the purpose of avenging the death of Balder. **2.** A son of Loki.

val·kyr·ie (val·kir′ē, val′kir·ē) See main vocabulary.

Va·nir (vä′nir) See main vocabulary.

Va·ra·ha (vä·rä′ha) *Hindu* The boar avatar of Vishnu, assumed in order to deliver the world from a demon who had seized it and carried it to the bottom of the ocean.

Va·ru·na (vä·rŏo′na) See main vocabulary.

Va·ru·ni (vä·rŏo′nē) *Hindu* The goddess of wine.

Va·su·ki (vä·sŏo′kē) *Hindu* One of the serpent kings who ruled in Patala.

Va·yu (vä′yŏo) **1.** *Hindu* The god of wind and atmosphere, and the breath of life that sprang from Purusa. **2.** *Persian* A wind god having two aspects, gentle and destructive.

Ve·da (vā′da, vē-) See main vocabulary.

Ve·dan·ta (vi·dän′ta, -dan′-) See main vocabulary.

Ve·nus (vē′nas) See main vocabulary.

Vi·bhu (vē′bŏo) *Hindu* One of the three artisans of the gods, along with Ribhu and Vaja, who were deified for their great skill.

Vi·dar (vē′där) *Norse* A son of Odin, regarded as the guardian of peace and the primeval forest, who will survive Ragnarök along with his brother Vali.

Vid·ya·dha·ra (vĕd·yä·dä′rə) *Hindu* One of a group of benevolent supernatural beings who dwell in the northern mountains and can intermarry with men.

Vi·grid (vē′grid) *Norse* The battlefield of Ragnarök.

Vi·li and Ve (vē′le; vä) *Norse* Odin's two brothers, who killed Ymir and from his body created the earth.

Vi·na·ta (vē·nä′tə) *Hindu* The mother of Garuda and one of the wives of Kasyapa.

Vi·ra·bha·dra (vē·rä·bä′drə) *Hindu* An emanation of, or the son of, Siva, created as a form of his anger.

Vish·nu (vish′nōō) See main vocabulary.

Vis·va·kar·ma (vis·vä·kär′mə) *Hindu* Originally, the epithet of a powerful god like Surya or Indra; later, the name of an independent creator-god, identified with Parjapati and having arms, face, eyes, and feet on every side.

Vis·va·va·su (vis·vä·vä′sōō) *Hindu* The king of the Siddhas.

Vol·sun·ga Sa·ga (vol′sōōng·gə sä′gə) See main vocabulary.

Vol·sungs (vol′sōōngz) See main vocabulary.

Vul·can (vul′kən) See main vocabulary.

Wal·pur·gis Night (väl·pōōr′gis) See main vocabulary.

Way·land (wā′lənd) See main vocabulary.

weighing of souls *Egyptian* A ceremony conducted in the underworld before Osiris in which the heart of the deceased was placed on a balance against Maat, the feather of truth, which it was not to outweigh.

Wen Ch'ang (wen chäng) *Chinese* The god of literature.

Wyrd (wird) *Germanic* The goddess of fate, chiefly known from English sources.

Xan·thos and Ba·li·os (zän′thōs; bə·lī′ōs) *Greek* The two immortal horses given by Poseidon to Peleus as a wedding present, and used by Achilles as chariot horses.

Yak·shas (yäk′shäs) *Hindu* Supernatural beings who seceded from the demons and took over the mountain areas.

Ya·ma (yä′mə) *Hindu* The king of the dead, and later the judge of the dead.

yang (yäng) See main vocabulary.

Yang Chin (yäng chēn) *Chinese* The goat god.

Yen Lo (yen lō) *Chinese* Lord of the fifth hell and infernal jungle.

Ygg·dra·sil (ig′drə·sil) *Norse* A huge ash tree whose roots and branches bind together heaven, earth, and hell.

Yin (yin) See main vocabulary.

Y·mir (ē′mir, ü′mir) See main vocabulary.

Zar·pan·it (zär·pan′it) *Babylonian* Consort of Marduk and mother of Nebo.

Zeus (zōōs) See main vocabulary.

Zi·u·su·dra (zē′ə·sōō′drä) *Sumerian* A hero whose Noah-like adventures antedate those of the Babylonian Utnapishtim.

Zu-bird (zōō′bûrd) *Sumerian & Babylonian* Mischief-making lesser god, slain in one. myth by Lugalbanda and in another by Marduk.

PARLIAMENTARY PROCEDURE

by John Bradley

Every day, year in and year out, thousands of small clubs or societies, such as garden clubs, church societies, building and trade associations, may be found holding their meetings. Every day, too, new clubs are being formed. The existence of this multitude of small societies is a healthy manifestation of the democratic process in action. For in our democratic way of life even the smallest society organizes itself, and conducts its meetings in accordance with a system of rules that insures full, fair and free discussion leading to a course of action determined by the majority. This system of rules, variously called parliamentary procedure or parliamentary law or rules of order, governs every democratic assembly, from the highest legislative body to the smallest village community club. The rules used in guiding a small club are, of course, fewer and less complex than those used by Congress. Consequently this article, which aims at helping those who have a practical interest in small clubs, will not attempt a comprehensive treatment of parliamentary procedure. Rather, it will concentrate on the procedure that is necessary and sufficient to establish a small society and run its meetings in a democratic and effective manner.

ORGANIZING A CLUB

Interest in forming a club is normally shared by a few people. These people should meet and carefully discuss the kind of organization they have in mind. Attention should first be given to such things as the purpose of the club, how this purpose is to be accomplished, how the club will be financed, and who will be admitted to membership. Plans should then be made for calling the first meeting. In making these plans it is important to decide on the following details: (1) Date, time, and place of the first meeting. Who will secure the accommodations? (2) Invitations to be issued to those who would probably be interested in such a club. Invitations should announce not only the place, date and hour of the meeting, but also its purpose. How should invitations be issued? By letter, telephone, word-of-mouth, radio? Who will take care of this? (3) Who will call the first meeting to order? (4) Who will explain the purpose of the meeting to the gathering?

The First Meeting

When the people gather for the first meeting the person previously designated for this task assumes the chair, raps on the table and says, "Will the meeting please come to order." When the meeting has come to order he sets about forming a temporary organization as follows: "I nominate Mr. X for temporary chairman (alternatively he may ask for nominations from the floor). Is there a second?" When this proposal or motion has been seconded he says, "All in favor will please say, 'Aye.' All opposed will say, 'No.'" Since Mr. X was nominated because of his competence and general suitability it is unlikely that he will be defeated. The result of the vote is then announced thus: "The motion is carried, and Mr. X is elected temporary chairman. Will he please take the chair." Mr. X now takes over the chair and conducts the meeting. His first business is to call for the election of a temporary secretary. The temporary secretary, who is elected in the same manner as the temporary chairman, takes a seat at the table near the chair and records the proceedings of the meeting from the beginning.

Motion to Form a Club

The temporary chairman now calls on the person chosen for this job when the meeting was planned to explain fully the purpose of the gathering. After suitable discussion of the proposed new organization a formal motion that a club of this kind be formed should be offered: "I move that this assembly form a permanent club to be known as . . . ." If this motion is seconded and receives a majority vote, someone should move that a committee be appointed to draft bylaws. It is normal for the chairman to appoint this committee. (A word to the members of the bylaws committee: First make sure that you thoroughly understand the purposes of the proposed club. Then survey the constitutions and bylaws that have been successfully used by similar organizations. Collections of such constitutions and bylaws may be consulted in most libraries.) After the bylaws committee has been appointed the chairman asks, "Is there any other business?" When all business has been completed a motion to adjourn ("I move that we adjourn") should be made and seconded. When this motion has been carried the chairman says, "This meeting is adjourned, and will meet at (time and place of the next meeting)."

Second Meeting

The principal business of the second meeting will be a consideration of the report of the bylaws committee. The temporary chairman calls the meeting to order and instructs the secretary to read the minutes of the previous meeting. As soon as the minutes have been read, corrected, if necessary, and approved, the chairman announces the report of the bylaws committee as the next business in order. The chairman of the committee then comes forward and reads the entire list of bylaws. A second complete reading of the bylaws may be dispensed with by general consent of the assembly. Then each paragraph is read and discussed and amended. No vote is taken after each separate paragraph has been dealt with. A vote is taken at the end on the acceptance or rejection of the entire list of bylaws. For the adoption of bylaws a majority vote suffices. The next order of business is the election of permanent officers. Normally the procedures for the nomination and election of officers is prescribed in the bylaws and should be strictly observed. After the election of permanent officers, unless there is other business that requires immediate attention, the meeting should be adjourned. The club has now achieved a permanent organization, and is ready to begin its regular business at the next meeting.

Quorum

No action taken in a business meeting of any organized society is legally binding unless a certain number of its members was present. That number, usually specified in the bylaws, is called a *quorum*. It is the largest number of members that may reasonably be expected to attend meetings under ordinary circumstances, and a number that would be competent to conduct business. Bylaws frequently specify a quorum of one-third or one-quarter of the members. If the bylaws do not specify a number, a quorum is a majority of the members. It is the duty of the presiding officer to determine the presence of a quorum. When a quorum is present, decisions can be officially made whether or not all present vote. For instance, a

club with a membership of 100, whose quorum is specified as one-quarter of the members, may find that though 25 members are present at a meeting only 20 vote. If the motion receives a majority vote the decision is official, even though five members did not vote. The same rule applies to decisions that require a two-thirds majority.

Order of Business

A chairman, in conducting the business of a meeting, must follow the order of business laid down in the bylaws of the club. The following order is typical:

1. Call to order.
2. Roll call. If this takes too much time, such alternatives as having the members sign their names in a roster, or having tellers check them, may be used.
3. Reading and approval of the minutes of the last meeting.
4. Reports of officers.
5. Reports of committees.
6. Unfinished business.
7. New business.
8. Announcements.
9. Adjournment.

Introducing Business

Whenever any business is brought to the attention of a meeting, the action to be taken on that business is proposed in the form of a *motion*. The member desiring to make a motion must "get the floor," i.e., he must (1) *stand*, (2) *address the chairman*, and (3) *be recognized* by him. When the member has made his motion he should take his seat. Next, the motion usually must be seconded by another member and restated by the chairman. It is then ready to be discussed by the assembly if it is a debatable motion. Any motion that is long or involved should be in writing and should be given to the secretary as soon as it has been read. Such a motion is usually called a *resolution*. A motion is proposed in the following manner:

MR. A (*standing*): Mr. (Madam) Chairman.
CHAIRMAN: Mr. A.
MR. A: I move that . . . (*or* I move to . . .)
MR. B (*seated*): I second the motion.
CHAIRMAN: It has been moved by Mr. A and seconded by Mr. B that . . . (he repeats the motion). Is there any discussion?

Discussion follows. Each person desiring to speak must first get the floor. Any person failing to observe this procedure is ruled out of order by the chairman. If two or more persons rise simultaneously and address the chairman, recognition will be given to:

1. One who has not spoken previously on the same question.
2. The one who made the motion.
3. One who is opposed to the views of the previous speaker.

Discussion

In the discussion of a question the following points should be observed:

1. No member may speak more than twice on the same question during the meeting.
2. No member may speak a second time on the same question until others who have not spoken at all have had an opportunity to speak.
3. No one may speak longer than ten minutes at one time except by general consent or a two-thirds vote.
4. Every speaker must confine his remarks to the question that is placed before the meeting by the chairman. If a speaker disregards this he is out of order.
5. Members are not allowed to address one another directly. All remarks are addressed to the chairman.
6. Any member who, in speaking from the floor, refers to another member in a discourteous manner or impugns the motives of another or uses improper language or is disorderly in any other way, should be ruled out of order. In serious cases he may be required to apologize, and if he refuses to apologize, he may be disciplined by the assembly.

7. When a speaker is ruled out of order he should take his seat immediately.
8. A person who has made a motion is not permitted to speak against it.

CLASSIFICATION AND PRECEDENCE OF MOTIONS

It should now be very clear that the device we call a "motion" has a most important role in the work of conducting a club's business. Since this is so, it follows that unless the motions themselves are governed by strict procedures, an orderly, fair, and free discussion of that business will be impossible. Consequently the various motions are governed by definite rules of precedence. In other words, there is a fixed priority or order according to which motions may be proposed, discussed and acted upon. The following four groups of motions are classified according to their purpose and precedence.

Main Motions These have the lowest rank of all motions.
Subsidiary Motions These rank immediately above main motions. They also have a fixed order of precedence among themselves.
Privileged Motions These outrank both subsidiary and main motions, and have a fixed order of precedence among themselves.
Incidental Motions As a group these rank above subsidiary motions and below privileged motions. They have no order of precedence among themselves, but take their rank from the motions to which they apply.

Order of Precedence

The following table lists the more common privileged, subsidiary, and main motions in their order of precedence.

I PRIVILEGED MOTIONS
    1. Adjourn.
    2. Take a recess.
    3. Raise a question of privilege.
    4. Call for "Orders of the Day."
II SUBSIDIARY MOTIONS
    5. Lay on the table.
    6. Close debate.
    7. Limit or extend debate.
    8. Postpone to a certain time.
    9. Refer to a committee.
    10. Amend.
    11. Postpone indefinitely.
III MAIN MOTIONS
    12. Main motions from the floor or committee.

Rules of Precedence

There are two basic rules of precedence: (1) When a motion is pending any motion that outranks it in precedence may be proposed, but no motion of lower rank may be proposed. Thus, if a motion to refer to a committee is pending (9th in order of precedence), a motion to limit or extend debate (7th in order of precedence) may be proposed. But a motion to postpone indefinitely (11th) may not be proposed. (2) Motions are considered and voted on in inverse order to their proposal. Thus, if motions ranking 12th, 10th, and 6th were proposed in that order and are all pending, the one ranking 6th is taken up and considered first, then the one ranking 10th, and finally the one ranking 12th.

Main Motions

Main motions are the most important class of motions, for they are aimed at getting some action on the primary items of business listed on the program of a business meeting. Though they are the most important, main motions are nevertheless outranked in precedence by every other motion. This shows us that precedence does not indicate importance, but simply determines the order in which the various motions are taken up and dealt with. Main motions and resolutions are identical in function, but different words are used in introducing them. A main motion begins with the form: "I move that . . ." A resolution is introduced thus: "I move the adoption of the following resolution: Resolved, that . . ." Any motion that is long or involved should be written and proposed in the form of a resolution. As soon as it has been proposed it should be given to the secretary.

Subsidiary Motions

The purpose of the various subsidiary motions is to help the assembly in considering and acting upon the main motion. Subsidiary motions outrank main motions in precedence, and have an order of precedence among themselves (see table on page 1631). Although only one main motion can be before an assembly at any given time, one or more or all of the subsidiary motions can be pending at the same time, each to be disposed of in its proper order of precedence. The subsidiary motions are outranked in precedence by the four privileged motions and are numbered accordingly in the following list.

5. Lay on the Table This is the highest ranking subsidiary motion. Its purpose is to lay aside, or postpone temporarily, the consideration of a motion until a later time.

Form: "I move that the motion (or amendment) be laid on the table." *or* "I move that the motion (or amendment) be postponed temporarily."

This motion requires: a second; majority vote. It is not debatable.

6. Close Debate This motion is also known as "Call for the Previous Question," or "Vote Immediately." Its purpose is to halt all further consideration of the questions pending and bring them to a vote.

Form: "I move that we vote immediately on the motion to . . ." *or* "I move that we vote immediately on the main motion and the motions adhering to it." *or* "I call for the 'Previous Question' on . . ."

This motion requires: a second; two-thirds vote. It is not debatable.

7. Limit or Extend Debate This motion is aimed at extending or restricting the time devoted to the discussion of a question. It is frequently adopted by unanimous consent.

Form: "I move that debate on . . . be limited to . . . minutes." *or* "I move that debate on . . . be limited to one five-minute speech by each speaker." *or* "I move that the discussion period be extended . . . minutes." *or* "I move that the discussion be extended to . . . o'clock."

This motion requires: a second; two-thirds vote. It is not debatable.

8. Postpone to a Certain Time The purpose of this motion is to suspend discussion of a question and fix a later, definite time for its further consideration. If a question is postponed to a certain time it is treated as an "order of the day" for that time and so will precede New Business.

Form: "I move to postpone consideration of the question until the next meeting (or some other specific time)."

This motion requires: a second; majority vote. Only the propriety of postponement to a certain time is debatable.

9. Refer to a Committee This motion may be made for various reasons. The proposer may feel that the matter requires more detailed study by a smaller group, or that it is too delicate for public airing, or that it should be held up for some time in committee. The proposer may specify such details as the type of committee, number of members, how members are to be selected, etc. If not, the chairman may ask the assembly for suggestions, which may be adopted by general consent or voted on.

Form: "I move to refer the motion to a committee." *or* "I move that the motion be referred to a committee consisting of Mrs. A, Mr. B and Mr. C." *or* "I move that the motion be referred to a committee of 5 (or 3 or 7) members appointed by the chair." *or* "I move that the motion be referred to the Committee on Membership (or some other standing committee)." *or* "I move that the chair appoint a committee of 3 (or 5 or 7) members to study the question of . . . and report suitable resolutions at our next regular meeting."

This motion requires: a second; majority vote. Only the propriety of referring the question to a committee is debatable.

10. Amend A motion to amend a main motion is made with the purpose of changing or modifying the main motion or resolution, so that it will more truly meet the mind of the assembly. An amendment of a main motion or resolution is called a *primary* amendment. A primary amendment may itself be amended in the same manner as a main motion. An amendment of an amendment is called a *secondary* amendment. The three common types of amendment are: (a) amendment by addition of certain words to the motion; (b) amendment by elimination of certain words from the motion; (c) amendment by the substitution of a new motion for the original motion (but the substitution must not destroy the original question).

Form: "I move to amend the motion by adding (or inserting) the words . . ." *or* "I move to amend the motion by eliminating the words . . ." *or* "I move to substitute for this motion the following motion . . ."

This motion requires: a second; majority vote. It is debatable, unless applied to an undebatable motion.

11. Postpone Indefinitely The name given to this motion is misleading. Its purpose is not to postpone consideration of a question but to kill it. It is often used by members who oppose a motion but fear they may not have sufficient votes to defeat it. A motion that has been postponed indefinitely may be brought up at a later meeting, but it must then be proposed as a new motion.

Form: "I move that the motion to . . . be postponed indefinitely." *or* "I move to postpone action on the main motion indefinitely."

This motion requires: a second; majority vote. It is debatable.

Privileged Motions

Privileged motions, unlike subsidiary motions, are not directly related to the main motion. They are motions dealing with matters of such urgency that they require immediate attention. Since they are emergency motions, privileged motions as a class have the highest order of precedence. They also have an order of precedence among themselves and are numbered accordingly in the following list:

1. Adjourn (unqualified) The purpose of this motion is to bring a meeting to an end at once. A qualified motion to adjourn ("I move we adjourn in ten minutes") is not a privileged motion; it is a main motion and as such is of the lowest rank in precedence. Although the unqualified motion to adjourn has the highest rank of any motion it is out of order when another person has the floor, or while a vote is being taken. Furthermore, the chairman should not permit the motion until announcements and important business have been disposed of, and the time and place of the next meeting settled.

Form: "I move that we adjourn."

This motion requires: a second; majority vote. It is not debatable.

2. Take a Recess The purpose of this motion is to provide an intermission within a meeting. After the recess the chairman calls the meeting to order, and business is resumed at the point where it was interrupted.

Form: "I move that we take a recess of . . . minutes (or hours)." *or* "I move that we take a recess until . . . o'clock."

This motion requires: a second; majority vote. It is not debatable.

3. Raise a Question of Privilege This motion is concerned with the rights and privileges of the assembly as a whole or the rights and privileges of an individual member. It is used in such circumstances as the following: disorderly conduct during a meeting; unsatisfactory conditions of the meeting place; charges made against the character of a member; illness. When a member raises a question of privilege the chairman will decide whether it is such or not, and will rule accordingly. Any two

members may, of course, appeal from the chairman's ruling, thus forcing the matter to a vote.

Form: MR. A: Mr. (Madam) Chairman, (*and then, without waiting to be recognized*) I rise to a question of privilege.
   CHAIRMAN: The member will please state his request.
   MR. A: I request that the visitors be asked to leave this meeting before we continue.
   CHAIRMAN: Your request is granted. Will the visitors please leave at once.

This motion requires: no second; no vote. It is not debatable.

4. **Call for "Orders of the Day"** This motion is concerned with deviations from the duly established order of business. If the chairman does not adhere to this order any member has the right to demand that he do so.

Form: "I call for 'orders of the day.' "   *or*   "I call for a return to the 'orders of the day.' "

This motion requires: no second; no vote, unless the chairman maintains there has been no deviation (majority vote needed), or contends that the deviation is justified (two-thirds vote needed). It is not debatable.

Incidental Motions

Incidental motions are so named because they arise only incidentally out of the business that is being considered by the assembly. As a group they rank in precedence above subsidiary motions and below privileged motions. Unlike all the motions discussed so far they have no fixed order of precedence among themselves. They take their rank from the motions to which they are applied. Since these motions have no precedence among themselves the order in which they are listed below is quite arbitrary.

1. **Appeal** When a decision by the chairman seems to be in error or unfair, any member may appeal from that decision. Immediately after the decision has been announced—but not later—he should rise, and without waiting to be recognized (even though another member has the floor) should make his appeal.

Form: MR. A: Mr. (Madam) Chairman, I appeal from the decision of the chair.
   CHAIRMAN: The decision of the chair has been appealed from. Will the member appealing please give his grounds for appeal.
   When the member has given his grounds for appeal the chairman may state the reasons for his decision (or he may postpone this until after discussion). The question is then put to vote as follows:
   CHAIRMAN: Those in favor of sustaining the decision of the chair say, "Aye." Those opposed, say, "No.". . . The decision of the chair is sustained (overruled).

This motion requires: a second; majority or tie vote. It is debatable.

2. **Division of a Question** When a motion has several parts a member can request that it be divided into two or more independent propositions, and each proposition considered and voted on separately. Thus it becomes possible to adopt certain parts of the motion and reject others. The chairman will decide if a motion can be divided.

Form: MR. A: I move that the question be divided and considered in two (or more) parts as follows . . . (specifying exactly how the division is made).
   CHAIRMAN: (if he decides that the question can be divided suitably) It is requested that the motion be divided into two (or more) parts. If there is no objection this will be done. The motion now before the assembly is . . .

This motion requires: no second; no vote. It is not debatable.

3. **Division of the Assembly** The purpose of this motion is to secure an accurate vote. If a vote has been taken by

voice or by a show of hands and there is a reasonable doubt as to the outcome, any member may, without rising or addressing the chair, demand a standing vote.

Form: MR. A: I call for a division.
   CHAIRMAN: A division has been called for. All in favor of the motion (he states the motion just voted on) please rise. The secretary will please count . . . Be seated . . . Those opposed, please rise . . . Be seated . . . The vote in favor of the motion is 10. The vote against the motion is 13. The motion, therefore, is defeated.

This motion requires: no second; no vote. It is not debatable.

4. **Objection to Consideration** The chairman may rule out of order any motion that is irrelevant, contentious, or embarrassing. If he fails to do so any member, even when another has the floor, may rise and object. Objections, however, must be made immediately after the motion to which it applies has been presented, and before debate has begun.

Form: MR. A: Mr. (Madam) Chairman, I object to the consideration of this question.
   CHAIRMAN: An objection has been raised to the consideration of this question. All opposed to the consideration of this question please rise . . . Be seated . . . Those in favor, please rise . . . Be seated . . . There is a two-thirds vote opposed. The question, therefore, will not be considered.

This motion requires: no second; two-thirds vote. It is not debatable.

5. **Parliamentary Inquiry** If a member desires some information on a question of procedure he should rise and, without waiting to be recognized, put his inquiry to the chairman.

Form: MR. A: I rise to a parliamentary inquiry.
   CHAIRMAN: Please state your inquiry.
   MR. A: Is an amendment in order at this time?
   CHAIRMAN: It is not.

Variations of a parliamentary inquiry are: (1) a request for information concerning the motion pending; (2) a request to ask the speaker a question.

Form (1): MR. A: Mr. (Madam) Chairman, I rise for information.
   CHAIRMAN: What is the member's question?
   MR. A: I should like to know . . .
   CHAIRMAN: (will supply the information requested)
Form (2): MR. A: Mr. (Madam) Chairman, I should like to ask the speaker a question.
   CHAIRMAN: Is the speaker willing to answer the question?
   SPEAKER: I am willing.

This motion requires: no second; no vote. It is not debatable.

6. **Point of Order** The chairman has the duty of guarding against any breach of the rules. If he does not notice a violation of the rules or disregards it, any member may draw his attention to it and insist, if necessary, that the rules be strictly enforced. In such a case the member will rise, even though another has the floor and, without waiting to be recognized, address the chair.

Form: MR. A: Mr. (Madam) Chairman, I rise to a point of order.
   CHAIRMAN: The member may state the point.

If the member is right the chairman must correct the error at once. If the chairman cannot decide whether or not there has been a violation of the rules he may: (1) ask the advice of other members he considers competent; (2) put the matter to the assembly; (3) defer a decision until he has had time to study the matter more fully.

This motion requires: no second; no vote. It is not debatable.

7. **Suspend the Rules** If an assembly finds it necessary or desirable to take some action that conflicts with the rules of order or standing rules, it may, by a two-thirds vote, suspend temporarily the rule(s) involved.

Form: MR. A: Mr. (Madam) Chairman, I move to suspend the rule(s) that interferes with . . .

CHAIRMAN: It has been moved and seconded to suspend the rule(s) that interferes with . . . All in favor please rise . . . Be seated . . . Those opposed, please rise . . . Be seated . . . There is a two-thirds vote in favor. The The rule(s) is (are), therefore suspended.

This motion requires: a second; two-thirds vote. It is not debatable.

8. **Withdraw a Motion** The author of a motion may withdraw or change his motion at any time before it is stated by the chairman. After it has been stated, however, it can be withdrawn or changed only by general consent or a vote.

Form: MR. A: Mr. (Madam) Chairman, I ask leave to withdraw (change) my motion.

CHAIRMAN: Mr. A asks leave to withdraw (change) his motion. If there is no objection, the motion is withdrawn (changed).

If anyone objects the chairman may put the question to a vote, or Mr. A or any other member may move that leave be granted to withdraw (change) the motion.

This motion requires: no second; no vote unless questioned. It is not debatable.

CONSULT STANDARD WORKS

As we observed at the beginning of this article, the foregoing explanation of parliamentary procedure is aimed at helping those who have a practical interest in starting and running a small club. It is not, nor is it meant to be, a comprehensive treatment of this complex subject. Consequently while we are confident that it will prove to be adequate for meeting its purpose in most instances, questions could arise that would require the help of a truly comprehensive treatment. In such cases the standard works on parliamentary procedure, which are readily available in most libraries, should be consulted.

BUSINESS LAW AND WILLS

by Cornelius W. Gillam

INTRODUCTION

Business law deals with the legal rules and principles of primary interest to the business community, and because of the complexity of modern business necessarily includes a wide range of topics, many of which are difficult and technical. This article is intended for maximum usefulness to laymen as a brief and convenient explanation of basic principles, which if applied to typical business transactions and relationships will reduce legal risks and warn of the need for professional advice. Because the principles of business law rest fundamentally upon the evolutionary growth of the law through court decisions rather than upon specific rules enacted by legislative bodies, this article deals with basic concepts rather than with narrow rules applicable to specific situations. A thorough grasp of these basic concepts is the only safe road to the minimization of legal risks and recognition of the need to consult counsel in important or unusual transactions.

The two branches of the law most essential to an understanding of business and personal legal matters are torts and contracts. This section consists chiefly of a basic analysis of these two subjects. Since it is much sounder and wiser to seek a firm grasp of fundamentals than to attempt a cursory survey of the necessarily large number of advanced and technical subjects with which lawyers must work daily, this article chooses to avoid the advanced and technical matters in which "a little knowledge is a dangerous thing," in favor of an adequate and accurate exposition of basic concepts. Such an approach represents the best compromise between complete ignorance of the law, at the one extreme, and professional competence at the other. It will give the thoughtful reader a grasp of the underlying policies, purposes and principles of the law, will warn him of many potential hazards, and will make him a more intelligent client.

This approach necessarily omits many important matters, such as all branches of public law (constitutional and administrative law, taxation, criminal law) and most advanced topics in private law (such as the law of negotiable instruments and commercial paper, partnerships and corporations, debtor-creditor relationships, real estate, and so on). However, a short article on *Wills* is included (p. 1741) because of its universal interest. It must be emphasized that the only legitimate purpose of these articles is to explain basic principles, to encourage behavior tending to minimize legal risks, and to warn of the need to consult counsel in reference to specific problems. As the old saying goes, "He who acts as his own lawyer has a fool for a client."

Much of this material is adapted, with permission of the publishers, from Spencer and Gillam, *A Textbook of Law and Business*, 3rd ed. (copyright 1952, McGraw-Hill, Inc.) and from Cataldo, Gillam, Kempin, Stockton and Weber, *Introducion to Law and the Legal Process* (copyright 1965, John Wiley and Sons, Inc.). Readers wishing to pursue these matters in greater detail, or to explore subjects not discussed here, should consult either of these standard texts. All quoted material in this article is taken from the public record of court decisions and other legal documents. It was felt to be unnecessary to burden the reader with footnotes referring to each particular source, since it is unlikely that anyone but a student of law or a practicing attorney would wish to investigate further the cases cited.

TORTS

General Principles

The law of torts deals with noncontractual civil wrongs. "Tort" is a French word, derived from the Latin *tortus* ("twisted," "crooked"), which means simply "a wrong." Once common also in English, our word "tort" now has become a legal term. But, unlike many other legal terms, "tort" has no precisely defined meaning. It is indeed a markedly elastic legal concept, which may be expanded (usually) or contracted (more rarely) to meet the requirements of justice and of sound social policy in situations to which other branches of the law do not apply.

What Is a Tort? This elasticity of the tort concept makes it necessary to define a tort as anything, not classifiable within some other legal category, for which a court will award damages or grant other relief. If a logically unassailable definition of torts is impossible to formulate, however, it may at least be said that the most familiar torts are readily recognizable. Automobile accidents resulting from the defendant's negligence undoubtedly represent the most common kind of tort, and perhaps the most common legal problem known to our society. But a tort may be found in any kind of accident or injury resulting from negligence; in such cases of wilful misconduct as assault, battery, false imprisonment, malicious prosecution, slander or libel, trespasses against land or goods, unreasonable invasion of privacy, unfair methods of business competition, unwarranted interference with personal or business relations, or maintaining a nuisance; or, exceptionally, in certain situations where the defendant's conduct causes loss to others although he is himself chargeable with no wrongdoing at all, either intentional or negligent. The law of torts is older than any branch of the law except that dealing with crimes. Its basic purpose is to secure the persons and property of the citizenry against the greed, aggression or indifference of society's less self-disciplined members. Only upon the base of personal and property security established by a just and effective law of torts can the domestic, social, commercial, intellectual and artistic institutions of an advanced civilization be erected.

"Social Engineering" Since it is the purpose of tort law to maintain the individual and collective security of all citizens, tort cases often require that delicate judgments be made in the adjustment of conflicting interests. Like all branches of the law, but especially significantly, the law of torts essays the wisdom of Solomon to achieve that fine balance of interests characteristic of a humane and stable society. Considerations of underlying social policy therefore appear in tort cases with notable prominence, and it is in the law of torts that the legal scholar, searching for the lodestone of justice, works his richest ore.

Tort and Contract Tort and contract law are radically different in one vital respect: The essence of contract law is the enforcement of a promise, but tort liability requires no consensual or promissory relationship. Contracts are voluntarily entered into by the parties and represent a relationship self-created for mutual advantage out of free will. But tort duties are consensual only in the remote and more or less conjectural sense that free men have entered into a "social con-

tract"—that is, have accepted certain essential limitations on their personal conduct in exchange for the amenities of a common life in a civilized society. The mandates of tort law are voluntarily accepted only in the sense that one who cannot respect them is theoretically free to dissociate himself from his fellow men and seek a solitary life on some desert island. For practical purposes tort law may be considered to establish standards of conduct which all citizens must meet, whether they like them or not and without volunteering to do so, at peril of responding in damages for losses to others attributable to their failure to meet these standards. In other words, contracts create private duties between the parties to those contracts, but tort law creates social duties between all members of society, strangers as well as brothers. Most business law, of course, is contractural in nature, but beneath the structure of commercial law there lies a firm foundation of tort principles.

Tort and Crime In many ways the law of torts has much more in common with criminal law than with contract law. Torts and crimes of course both are based upon general social duties rather than upon voluntary agreements. In very early times (in terms of the history of the common law), no distinction between torts and crimes was made. As a more refined legal system evolved it became possible to differentiate between the social injury resulting from antisocial behavior, and the individual injury resulting from antisocial behavior. The former now is the distinct province of the criminal law, which *punishes* extremes of nonconformity in the name of the state. The law of torts, whose purpose is to *compensate* individuals for their private losses caused by socially unacceptable behavior, now deals with the latter area.

Significant parallel relationships, which reflect the common history of torts and crimes, still connect the two fields of law; for example, intent as an element of liability is far more potent a factor in torts than in contracts. (Contract law has largely adopted an objective-manifestation theory of consensual intent, whereas tort law largely retains the emphasis on actual subjective intent implicit in the criminal concept of *guilt*.) Again, several torts and crimes make matching pairs and bear the same names, such as assault or trespass. On the other hand, our modern concepts of civil liberty require proof of guilt beyond a reasonable doubt in criminal trials, whereas tort cases merely require the ordinary standard of proof typical of civil suits.

The Stranger as Plaintiff Another difference between torts and contracts lies in the scope of the duties created. From the defendant's viewpoint a breach of contract exposes him to suit by a more or less limited and identifiable range of plaintiffs. To be sure, a contract may be assigned or may otherwise create a right to sue in one who is a stranger to the defendant, but the range of potential plaintiffs is finite and limited. Tort law, however, requires the plaintiff to assume the risks of his victim's unknown identity. He owes a duty, if not to the world at large, at least to a relatively broad and loosely defined group of his fellow citizens. The relationship that subsists between parties to a contract (privity of contract) does not limit his liability to those with whom he voluntarily enters into a private relationship; rather he assumes a broad potential liability to anyone injured by his tortious conduct. (The word *tortious* will be used throughout this article to mean *of the nature of or implying a tort; wrongful*.) This magnifies the risk factor in tort situations and makes it difficult to define and allocate risks in an economically rational manner. Market realities and the duty to mitigate damages, combined with the limited range of potential plaintiffs, make the probable losses from breaches of contract much more predictable and controllable than those from tortious conduct, which thus can produce surprising and disastrous results for the unwary.

Classifications of Torts

By Degree of Culpability The infinitely varied forms of behavior which the law treats as tortious may conveniently be analyzed in terms of the degree of culpability, or fault, characterizing them. Tort liability may be imposed on the basis of wilful misconduct or intentional wrong, on the basis of negligence or failure to use reasonable care, or on the basis of policy considerations which sometimes call for liability where no fault or culpability exists at all (absolute liability).

The law of torts is, of course, most closely connected with the criminal law in the area of the "intentional" torts, those

based on deliberate, wilful misconduct foreseeably likely to injure others. These are historically the oldest torts and those which most closely resemble crimes. However, it is important to realize that "intent" does not mean the same thing in the case of the intentional torts that it means in the case of criminal behavior. The criminal law necessarily places great emphasis on the defendant's state of mind because its purpose is to punish moral turpitude—what the law calls *mens rea* (diseased mind) or simply criminal intent. Intent in the sense of *mens rea* consists of the conscious choice of wrong when one knows the difference between right and wrong and exercises free will in making his choice. The essence of criminality is, in other words, the knowing and voluntary choice of evil. If one cannot tell the difference between good and evil he is (according to the traditional view) insane and thus incapable of *mens rea*; if one is not a free agent (having, for example, been forced against his will to do one evil to avoid another) the only punishable *mens rea* is that of the agent who forced his conduct.

It follows that the "intent" (*mens rea*) so essential to the criminal law must be largely subjective in character—that is, it emphasizes what state of mind the defendant was "actually" or consciously in, largely ignoring (short of insanity) the objective criteria of conduct or of the reasonableness of the state of mind actually present. Accordingly we like to say that the standards of the criminal law are essentially subjective in character, because states of mind carry more weight than objectively verifiable patterns of conduct. The civil law, on the other hand—and contract law especially—adopts objective standards of liability, and so places far more emphasis on conduct and its consequences than on the state of mind motivating conduct. To put it more simply if less precisely, the criminal law stresses *motives*, the civil law stresses *results*. Of course the separation of emphasis never is pure, and we find some (more or less anomalous, though explainable) situations in which criminal liability rests on mere behavior, or in which civil liability is based upon or expanded by subjective evil intent.

In general, when we speak of intent in the law of torts we are speaking of civil, not criminal, intent—that is, of the consequences of voluntary *behavior*, not of a purely subjective state of mind theoretically divorced from the results that it produces. For example, if the defendant points a gun at the deceased, pulls the trigger, and kills the deceased, the defendant's conduct does not constitute the crime of murder unless the state can prove (beyond reasonable doubt) that the defendant's behavior stemmed from an evil desire to kill. The killing or wounding, not merely the firing of the gun, must be intended. The law of torts, on the other hand, asks merely whether the defendant aimed and fired voluntarily and under circumstances in which he *should have* foreseen some risk to the deceased if he did so. Thus the defendant might well be held liable to pay tort damages to the deceased's survivors, without being subject to punishment for murder.

Accordingly one must not be misled by the superficial resemblance between intentional torts and the crimes with which many of them correspond. With this caution, the principal intentional torts may be enumerated as follows:

Assault. Assault consists of intentional threatening conduct the effect of which is to put the plaintiff in reasonable fear of imminent harmful or offensive bodily contact. The contact itself need not follow; it is the fear produced by the threat of such contact that is the essence of the tort.

Battery. Battery is actual, unpermitted, unprivileged intentional bodily contact. Normally assault and battery are closely connected, but either may occur without the other. (For example, battery occurs without assault where a blow is not anticipated before it is struck; assault without battery occurs where a threat of battery is not carried out.)

False Imprisonment. False imprisonment is the intentional and unjustified restriction of physical liberty.

Malicious Prosecution. Malicious prosecution consists of intentionally and without justification or probable cause charging the plaintiff with commission of a crime and setting the machinery of law enforcement into action against him. The closely related tort of *abuse of process* results from the bringing, without justification or probable cause, of a malicious civil suit.

Intentional Infliction of Mental Suffering. Gross invasions of the plaintiff's privacy, dignity, or emotional security, at

least in flagrant cases in which intent can be established, now are regarded by many courts as valid grounds of tort liability. The traditional and conservative view is that mental suffering alone, however outrageous, will not be compensated unless accompanied by some physical injury.

Defamation. Intentional interference with the plaintiff's right to his good name, by publishing or uttering messages which tend to lower the plaintiff's esteem in his community, is tortious. Usually the plaintiff must be able to prove pecuniary injury, and even then he may be subject to defenses based on truth or privilege. Defamation in printed or broadcast form is called *libel*; defamation in ordinary speech or under circumstances where it is not widely circulated is called *slander*.

Invasion of the Right of Privacy. A relatively new intentional tort, invasion of the right of privacy, now is recognized, at least to some degree, in most jurisdictions. It protects the plaintiff against serious, outrageous or indecent invasions of his personal privacy, especially where the invasion of privacy is commercially motivated. The right of privacy is limited by a privilege to publish matters subject to legitimate public interest, but has been held to cover outrageous intrusions upon physical privacy: circulation of private information, publication of the plaintiff's name or photograph, exposure to public ridicule, and the like.

Trespass. The essence of trespass is unjustified interference with the plaintiff's right to possession of land or tangible personal property.

Conversion. Conversion applies only to tangible personal property and consists not merely of interference with the plaintiff's right of possession, but of defendant's assertion of dominion or control as if he were himself the owner. The usual case of conversion is one in which the defendant has obtained or continued in possession of the goods to such a degree as to deprive the plaintiff of their whole use and value, or has sold, damaged or destroyed them. The remedy is to compel the defendant to buy the goods at their full value.

These intentional torts all are based upon voluntary conduct of the defendant which poses so great and obvious a risk of injury to the plaintiff or his property that it may fairly be said that the defendant intends the results of that conduct (whether or not he "actually" or subjectively does intend them). However, intent is not the only basis of tort liability. In addition to the various kinds of tortious intent, negligence and liability without fault may result in tort liability.

Negligence. Negligence is in a sense, or rather to a limited degree, intentional, but the tort of negligence involves a lesser degree of intent than the intentional torts discussed above (which in turn involve a lesser degree of intent than crimes). Accordingly negligence is classed as a separate kind of tort, not based on intent in the sense in which that word is used with the intentional torts, but nevertheless based on the fault or culpability of the defendant. Negligence consists of the creation of an unreasonable risk of harm to others within the zone of foreseeable danger, as the result of behavior by the defendant which, though it does not imply intent to injure others, nevertheless falls short of the standards which a reasonable man of ordinary prudence would meet under the circumstances. Acts of negligence occur in an infinite variety of forms, but always have one common feature: A culpable though "unintentional" failure to live up to the community's ideal of reasonable care. In short, negligence consists of accidents which result from someone's fault. Negligence is discussed more fully later on in this chapter.

Tort liability generally occurs only where some significant degree of fault or culpability, either intentional or negligent, characterizes the defendant's behavior. However, in extraordinary circumstances, policy considerations may require that tort liability be imposed where no fault exists.

Liability Without Fault. A third basis of tort liability, in addition to intent and negligence, is liability without fault (strict liability or absolute liability). Modern strict liability is based on policy grounds such as ability to pay, ability to absorb or spread the risk, or the feeling that profit-motivated conduct should pay its own way. An older and less controversial basis of liability without fault is ultrahazardous conduct of various kinds, such as use of explosives or other inherently dangerous materials, keeping wild or vicious animals, and setting fires or traps.

By Interest Protected The law of torts may also be considered in terms of the social purposes it serves, as well as in terms of the degree of the defendant's culpability. The law of torts protects and advances a variety of social interests whose importance to a free and civilized society is self-evident. Among these protected interests are the following:

Bodily Integrity and Freedom. The torts of assault, battery, false imprisonment, malicious prosecution and abuse of process, and often negligence, are designed to protect personal dignity and security against outrage or invasion.

Property and Economic Interests. Here trespass and conversion obviously are apropos; negligence and liability without fault also are often invoked in defense of property, and certain specialized torts such as inducing a third person to break his contract with the plaintiff, or unfair methods of business competition, have been developed to provide more complete protection for business and property interests.

Reputation and Esteem in the Community. Here the torts of defamation (libel and slander) and invasion of the right of privacy find their reason for being. An advanced and humane society obviously should protect other, more subtle interests than those of bodily and property security, and one step in this direction is recognition of a protected interest in one's relations with and regard by his fellows.

Right to Freedom from Unreasonable Invasions of Privacy or Outrageous Psychic Trauma. The law perhaps cannot go so far as to enact the Golden Rule, but scholarly and critical comment agrees that it can and should go beyond protection of person, property and reputation to deal with equally outrageous, if more novel, violations of the standards of decency and dignity. As increasingly refined concepts of justice establish themselves in the law we may expect to observe continued growth in the existing torts of invasion of the right of privacy and intentional infliction of mental suffering, and indeed the establishment of still more new torts as the needs of society develop.

What Losses Are Compensated?

From a practical standpoint the crucial question in relation to any set of legal facts always is, What remedy is available? How much can be recovered as damages? What is the price of the defendant's invasion of the plaintiff's rights? What are the plaintiff's rights worth, and how far do they extend? May consequential and intangible, as well as immediate and direct, losses be compensated?

Money Losses

Out-of-pocket Expenditures. Since the motivating principle behind a civil action for money damages is the compensation of economic loss—the restoration of the successful plaintiff to his economic status quo ante—it logically follows that out-of-pocket losses necessarily incurred as a direct and proximate consequence of the defendant's conduct may be recovered as compensable damages. Of course the plaintiff must sustain his burden of proof with respect to the actual expenditures incurred, their necessity or reasonableness under the circumstances, and their direct causal connection with the defendant's tort.

Future Expenditures and Losses. Of course the plaintiff cannot be restored to his economic position prior to the defendant's tort, unless he waits forever to bring his action, if his recovery is limited to out-of-pocket expenses, such as medical and hospital bills or the cost of auto repairs, already incurred. Future expenses and losses, perhaps continuing for many years and necessarily difficult to determine in advance, may be and often are directly caused by the defendant's tortious conduct. Such elements as the cost of continuing medical care, reduced earning power, shortened life expectancy, or loss of prospective sales and profits due to injury to the assets which would have been used to earn them are proper items to be considered in determining the total amount of the plaintiff's damages, provided always that the plaintiff sustains his burden of proof with respect to their

amount and their direct connection with the defendant's act. In determining the amount of damages to be awarded the jury may, of course, consider the discounted present value of sums due in the future, and may fix such sums net of income taxes and other adjustments.

Psychic Losses

Pain and Suffering. Out-of-pocket and prospective money losses, though often difficult to reduce to a certain sum, at least are quantitative in character and thus are logically susceptible of determination by a process of simple arithmetic. When the law of torts is confronted with losses which are essentially nonmonetary and nonquantifiable much more serious difficulties present themselves. The law allows juries to consider not only money losses but also the plaintiff's pain and suffering when determining the damages due, and often the element of pain and suffering accounts for a large proportion of the award. Yet, if the theory of a civil action is one of compensation for an economic loss, how can one justify the award of damages for purely psychic injuries over and above their actual economic cost? Two approaches are possible: (1) The law can say that to right all wrongs, to undo all that is done, is unfortunately impossible; the law, as an imperfect instrument for the approximation of justice to the extent money will buy it, can deal only with objective, quantifiable factors; the law does not pretend that this is ideal justice, but as a practical matter must limit itself to the compensation of economic losses, leaving psychic injuries, however severe or outrageous, beyond the purview of actions for money damages. Since money cannot erase the plaintiff's memory of his pain, it is futile to offer him money for his pain. (2) The logical alternative is to say that, since no amount of money will adequately compensate the plaintiff for his pain and suffering, he should, in the absence of a better remedy, be given, for whatever it is worth to him, everything the defendant has. This still does not compensate the plaintiff for the wrong done to him, but it is the best that an imperfect legal system can do for him, and the least that it should do.

In practice the law compromises between these two points of view, awarding money damages for pain and suffering as well as for out-of-pocket and prospective money losses, but confining damages for pain and suffering within limits and generally refusing to award them at all unless accompanied by some kind of money loss or physical injury. In practice the lawyer's bargaining formula in negotiating for settlement of a tort claim is: "Add incurred and prospective money losses, and multiply the sum by a factor representing the plaintiff's pain and suffering."

Loss of Consortium. The law's logical difficulty in dealing with injuries of a kind not logically translatable into monetary terms is again illustrated by the perverse rules concerning "loss of consortium" as an element of damages. By "consortium" is meant a spouse's right to the services, society and marital companionship of his (or her) mate. The damages recoverable for loss of consortium include the money expenses of caring for an injured spouse, the value of the services lost, and the psychic injury due to loss of companionship. A parent may recover damages for loss of the services of his (or her) minor child, as well as for the costs of the child's care.

Loss of consortium as an element of damages is predicated upon the master's traditional right to recover damages from third persons for acts resulting in the servant's unfitness to perform his duties. Damages for this interference with the master-servant relationship could be recovered at common law in addition to whatever damages the servant might himself recover for his own injuries, loss of wages, etc. By analogy it was determined that a husband might sue for loss of his wife's services, and "services" was extended to cover not only her domestic utility but also her affection and companionship. More recently the loss of "services" has been reduced to a purely technical requirement, so that if the plaintiff is entitled to services in some slight degree he may tack onto his minor loss of services the major element of damages, loss of consortium. A few states have carried this development to its logical conclusion by abandoning entirely the requirement that some right to and loss of services be shown. Conversely, in a few states the statutes "emancipating" married women have been held to abolish the husband's right to recover for loss of consortium, or to limit his recovery to the out-of-pocket costs of his wife's care, on the theory that these statutes abolish the common-law duty of wives to serve their husbands.

What is puzzling and paradoxical about loss of consortium as an element of damages is that a husband may recover for loss of consortium although a wife, according to common-law tradition, may not. This inconsistency stems from the fact that at common law a husband was entitled to his wife's services, but was not obligated to serve his wife. Accordingly, if a plaintiff wife was deprived of her husband's services by the defendant's tortious conduct, it was her misfortune to lose a good husband but not to lose a legal right upon the loss of which could be hung further damages for loss of companionship. In other words, a husband's right to his wife's consortium was protected by law, but a wife's interest in her husband's consortium was beneath the law's notice. The wife was of course entitled to the husband's support and the husband was obligated to support her, but support was as much as the wife was deemed to expect from the marital relationship, an injury to the husband did not terminate his duty to support his wife, and the husband himself could recover from the defendant for impairment of his earning power.

The double standard established by these rules cannot even be described as logical though unjust, for it also was illogical after development (by the end of the nineteenth century) of the wife's right to sue a third party for alienation of affections or "criminal conversation" for direct interference with the marital relationship. Yet an equally injurious indirect interference with the wife's domestic happiness, resulting from tortious injury to her husband, afforded the wife no remedy because technically it did not violate her rights.

Reflecting upon the fact that, in Holmes' deathless words, "the life of the law is not logic, but experience," it may seem unrealistic to assail this shocking—to our twentieth-century minds—example of legal misogyny merely on logical grounds. But today, at least, it is not only illogical, but inhumane and flagrantly unjust; on grounds of "experience" as well as of logic the wife's cause of action should be correlative to the husband's.

The mounting criticism by legal scholars of this double standard, emphasizing as it does that the wife's denial of recovery for loss of consortium is merely a historical accident, that the pegging of liability to "services" is an outmoded fiction, and that the wife's interest in the marital relationship is no less worthy of protection through other tort actions than through the action for alienation of affections, is beginning to take effect. A few courts have scrapped the double standard to hold that a wife has the same right to recover for loss of consortium as a husband, and others have so held where the injury to the husband is intentional or where the damages claimed extend only to out-of-pocket expenditures such as medical and funeral expenses.

It still is true, of course, that an argument for equality between husband and wife in legal actions for loss of consortium is an argument for the payment of cash "heart balm" to assuage grief or to sweeten pain rather than to compensate economic loss by restoring the plaintiff to the financial *status quo ante*. The fact is, of course, that our legal system is committed to the award of monetary "compensation" for just these purposes, among others, and that our mores not only accept the practice but indeed would be shocked at any proposal to limit damage awards to past or future economic losses.

The Roles of Jury and Judge

The inconsistencies and logical difficulties, as well as the policy issues, inherent in the theory of compensation for tort losses are in practice resolved through reliance upon the discretion of the human participants in what certainly is more of a human than a logical or mechanical process. The contribution of these human participants, most influential of whom are the jury and the judge, is that of insuring the substantial reasonableness of the result in the context of prevailing community customs relating to the monetary compensation of nonmonetary as well as of monetary losses.

These customs often are surprisingly well-defined at particular times and places. Indeed there is almost a "market" for personal-injury cases, in which the loss of a leg, say, or three months in the hospital carry a surprisingly well-defined price. Lawyers practicing in the personal-injury field are of course in close and continuous touch with this "market" and can estimate with reasonable accuracy the probable value of a particular tort claim, at a given time and in their own communities. However, the customs of various American com-

munities differ widely with respect to the proper monetary compensation for an identical injury, some jurisdictions being known for large and others for small verdicts.

Parenthetically, the differences in attitude among the various American jurisdictions are well illustrated by our "wrongful death" statutes. At common law a tort claim for personal injuries was considered personal to the plaintiff; he alone suffered the injuries and he alone could sue for them. If he died from his injuries his survivors had no cause of action for his pain and suffering, for their deprivation of his society and affection, or for the disbursements he made for medical care. Contract rights survived their owners' deaths or could be assigned between living persons, but tort claims, not being recognized as property, lacked this durability or liquidity and died with the plaintiff. This explains the saying that at common law it was better to kill the plaintiff than merely to injure him. The obvious injustice to dependent families inherent in the rule that tort claims were personal to the plaintiff has been corrected, at least in part, by "wrongful death" statutes, which create a new tort action, unknown to the common law, for causing the wrongful death of one who could himself have been a plaintiff had he been only injured. Under these statutes the deceased's estate may assert his rights against the tortfeasor. What is remarkable about these wrongful death statutes, however, is that many of them allow the estate to recover only a limited maximum sum, although the deceased, had he lived, would have been subject to no such limitation. Other statutes simply give the deceased's rights to his estate without qualification, thus enabling the estate to sue for as much as the deceased himself could have claimed. The legislatures which enacted limited wrongful-death statutes chose to compromise between the common-law position of the estate and its position under the unlimited wrongful-death statutes, and in some states having statutes of this type the recovery limit is quite low by contemporary standards, sometimes only $5,000 or $10,000.

The form of a wrongful death statute may make the difference between, say, $10,000 and $250,000 to the survivors of a deceased family breadwinner. The differences among the various jurisdictions are not likely to be this dramatic in cases not involving differing statutes, since popular conceptions of the value of personal injuries tend to change smoothly and continuously as cultural patterns evolve, rather than by the infrequent fits and starts characteristic of the legislative process. Nevertheless it is true that juries in some jurisdictions tend to be generous, while those in other jurisdictions tend to be conservative. Not only are broad regional differences apparent, but also one observes differences between cities, suburbs, and country towns in the same state. The well-known geographic differences in automobile liability insurance rates reflect these differences (as well, of course, as the varying probability of having an accident at all).

Since our legal system is committed to the principle that it is the mores *of the particular community* that the law must reinforce, and has in general entrusted to juries and legislatures rather than to lawyers and judges the task of defining the mores of the community, it follows that, once the applicable statutes are identified and interpreted, the jury plays the dominant role in quantifying the dollar value of a plaintiff's injuries (or other tort claim). In the typical suit on a tort claim it is the jury who decides what the facts are, and who translates the facts as found into a judgment for a given sum of dollars. Since the sum fixed is apt to be so largely influenced by the dollar value placed on nonmonetary losses such as pain and suffering, the jury's effective discretion obviously is always broad and often decisive.

There are, however, limits to the jury's discretion. While the jury, unless it acts irrationally or dishonestly, decides all issues of fact (unless, of course, the case is tried, by mutual consent, without a jury—which is rare in tort cases), issues of law are within the exclusive province of the judge. The question whether the jury acted rationally—that is, whether the verdict is supported by the evidence, whether reasonable men could reach the jury's verdict on the strength of the admissible and credible evidence presented—is itself a question of law to be decided by the judge. This means that the judge (under the law) fixes the limits of the jury's discretion in reaching a verdict and in assessing the damages. If the verdict is contrary to the evidence the judge is empowered to set the verdict aside and enter judgment notwithstanding the verdict. In practice this power is exercised not only to see that the side winning the verdict wins it on the basis of the evidence presented, but also to ensure that the amount of the

resulting judgment bears some reasonable relationship to the evidence and to the prevailing "market value" of the claim at the same time and place. Of course the jury still has broad discretion within these limits, but if it crosses the limits the verdict may be set aside. Just where the limits are in a particular case of course is uncertain, within a range of discretion. Under these circumstances judges often use their power to set verdicts aside and order new trials to coerce a sort of post-verdict settlement on a basis that seems reasonable to the judge in the light of the law, the evidence, and the jury's reaction to the evidence.

Suppose, for example, that a plaintiff wins a verdict of $500,000 as a result (the judge believes) of the jury's passion and prejudice, in a case in which the evidence (in the judge's opinion) can rationally support a verdict of between $50,000 and $100,000. The judge cannot tell the jury where to decide within the range of $50,000 to $100,000, but he can and will tell the plaintiff that the verdict will be set aside and a new trial will be ordered unless the plaintiff consents to a "voluntary" reduction of the verdict from $500,000 to $100,000. If the plaintiff does not like this of course he may appeal, but usually he takes the $100,000.

Thus the effective power of decision is, under our system, divided between judge and jury. The jury's power is paramount within the limits of its discretion, but the law sets limits and the judge decides when those limits have been passed in a particular case. The entire process takes place in the context of community mores and community evaluations of the dollar value of psychic trauma. The results produced by this complex procedure and subjective division of powers, though not fully consistent and certainly slow and expensive, apparently are sufficiently just in comparison with possible alternatives (such as liability without fault and the assessment of damages by professional administrative agencies, in the manner of workmens' compensation claims) so that legislatures have, so far, been disinclined to make fundamental changes in our system of defining and compensating noncontractual injuries.

Negligence

The essence of tort law is the concept of fault. Since negligence is the most common and also the most subtle form of fault, a relatively detailed analysis of negligence and of the ideas and limitations associated with it offers the clearest path toward an understanding of tort law.

Preliminarily, it is basic that the law of torts does not attempt to compensate all misfortune. It merely strives to compensate plaintiffs for losses or injuries directly caused by defendants' wrongful, or in rare cases (liability without fault) innocent but extrahazardous, conduct. Lacking fault (intentional or negligent) or the voluntary creation of an extraordinary risk, no liability is imposed on the defendant. In other words, most fortuitous losses, unavoidable accidents not directly caused by anyone's fault or creation of extraordinary risk, lie where they fall. An unintentional accident which the exercise of reasonable care would not have forestalled is legally unavoidable and does not result in tort liability, however great and however piteous the loss it produces.

The Legal Standard of Reasonableness The law of negligence, like so much of the law of contracts, must be understood primarily in terms of rational response to risk. Negligence law recognizes the inevitability of risk and the social utility of much risk-creating activity, but seeks to redistribute risk in such a way that it falls upon those best able to minimize it, or to shift it in infinitely small portions to society at large. The law simultaneously tries to minimize risk by encouraging care, and to discourage carelessness by compelling the careless to pay for the losses they cause. Negligence is defined in terms of a standard of reasonableness which appraises the defendant's conduct by balancing its social utility against the degree of risk it creates. Failure to use reasonable care under the relevant circumstances constitutes negligence; whether the defendant did or did not act with reasonable care is, usually, a question of fact to be decided by the jury. The essence of the question is whether the defendant has created an unreasonable degree of risk to others.

The question in each case is whether the defendant has conducted himself with that degree of care which would have characterized the behavior, under the same circumstances, of a hypothetical "reasonable man of ordinary prudence"

having the same physique, perception, mental capacity, information, experience, and professional skill as the defendant. The conduct expected of this abstract reasonable man represents society's basic minimum expectations of each of its members.

Acts of Omission vs. Acts of Commission While the "reasonable man" standard seems reasonable enough, it is subject to an interesting, somewhat unreasonable, and indeed paradoxical limitation—the law's distinction between acts of omission and of commission. Liability for the commission of affirmative acts of negligence ("misfeasance") extends to anyone foreseeably and unreasonably endangered; this principle was firmly established in the early common law, which necessarily had to concern itself much more with active misconduct than with mere passive quiescence. Inaction of this latter sort (nonfeasance) presented, according to the expectations of the day, no very serious problems for the early law, and as a result the distinction between misfeasance and nonfeasance became embedded in tort law, which traditionally refuses to find any general liability for nonfeasance, even to those foreseeably endangered. Only where there exists between the parties some special relationship, considered to impose a duty to act, will "mere" nonfeasance constitute negligence. Such special relationships usually involve either the assumption of a duty to serve the public as a whole (for example, by public utilities, common carriers, or innkeepers), or entrance upon a relationship motivated by the defendant's quest for profit and therefore thought to justify special obligations in return (for example, owners or occupiers of land who invite the public to enter in order to do business with them). Absent some such relationship considered to impose a duty to act, there is no general tort liability for nonfeasance.

This means that the law does not require one to be a Good Samaritan, however slight the inconvenience and however great the danger to the one in need of help. Unless the plaintiff's predicament results from the defendant's own fault, or is aggravated by his interference with the rescue efforts of others or by the ineptitude of his own assumption of the Good Samaritan's role, the defendant has no legal obligation to go to his rescue, whatever moral obligation a gentleman might perceive. Traditionally the expert swimmer may watch a man drown before his eyes if he prefers not to get wet; the doctor need not go to the aid of the stricken; the motorist need not stop to remove a dangerous object from its place in the curve of the road. The only hope of those in danger is the conscience and sense of moral obligation of those who happen to be in a position to help.

This traditional attitude is difficult to justify in an increasingly interdependent society and is generally condemned by legal scholars as morally outrageous. Nevertheless the practical difficulty of laying down workable standards of moral obligation to one's fellow man has tended to restrict liberalization of the traditional attitude to cases where there exists some kind of special relationship between the parties, such as that between railroad and passenger, employer and employee, ship and crew member, store and customer, or (by statute) victim and hit-run driver. Though even this degree of erosion of the nonfeasance principle has been very slow and cautious, it may well continue to the point of requiring the defendant, in the name of humanity, to make some effort, reasonable under the circumstances, to go to the aid of his endangered brethren.

Degrees of Negligence In general negligence is simply negligence, the law eschewing the notion of various degrees of negligence except in the sense that in any given situation the care must be commensurate with the apparent risk. Some courts, however, recognize three degrees of negligence (slight, ordinary, and gross) in some kinds of cases, especially in "bailment" situations (where the "bailor's" goods are temporarily placed in the "bailee's" possession for some purpose such as storage, repair, convenience or generosity) or where it is desired to lighten the burdens upon hospitable automobile owners by holding them liable to their guest-passengers only for particular egregious acts of (gross) negligence. In bailment cases it is customary to say that if the bailment is for the sole benefit of the bailor, the bailee need exercise only slight care to protect the goods put in his custody; that if the bailment is for the mutual benefit of both parties the bailee must exercise ordinary care; and that if the bailment is for the sole benefit of the bailee he must exercise great care. However, most courts have rejected any general attempt to establish degrees of negligence, holding simply

that reasonableness may require varying amounts of care under varying circumstances. Thus "gross negligence" becomes negligence plus a scolding.

Much of the responsibility for confusion with respect to degrees of negligence must be charged to legislative bodies, which have persistently tried to attach a special onus to "gross negligence," "wilful negligence" (a contradiction in terms!), or "criminal negligence" (another contradiction), often in automobile guest statutes, for the purpose of awarding "punitive damages" (still another contradiction), or to avoid the defense of contributory negligence (discussed below). If these epithets have no clear legal significance, they at least manifest a special sense of outrage at the defendant's conduct, sometimes amounting to his treatment as an intentional, rather than a merely negligent, wrongdoer.

Violation of Statute as Negligence A statute or ordinance often has the effect of establishing the standard of conduct considered reasonable under particular circumstances. For example, if the speed limit is 60 m.p.h. it might be unreasonable in itself, regardless of circumstances, to go faster; or if a statute requires druggists to label poisons, the sale of unlabeled poison might constitute negligence even if care were taken to warn the purchaser orally.

It is anomalous that criminal statutes imposing criminal punishments for their violation should also create civil liability, especially in cases where no criminal prosecution occurs. It may be argued that to infer civil negligence from the mere fact of technical violation of a criminal statute gives the statute an effect much broader than that contemplated by the legislature (since, for example, the unique procedural safeguards surrounding criminal trials, such as the requirement of proof of guilt beyond reasonable doubt, do not apply in civil cases). However, the prevailing view is that the courts may legitimately apply and extend the underlying policy of the statute, which is to protect society against the evils which it penalizes, by means of supplementary judicial legislation adding civil liabilities to the criminal penalties established by the legislature.

There are, however, certain limits to this extension of the effect of the statute: The plaintiff must be a member of the class of persons the statute was meant to protect, and his injury must be of the type the statute was meant to prevent. For example, a wartime regulation limiting highway speed limits to 35 m.p.h. for the purpose of conserving tires and gasoline does not automatically make it negligent to be involved in an accident at 40 m.p.h.; a statute prohibiting the operation of trains on Sunday does not automatically establish the railroad's negligence in running down the plaintiff's cow on the Sabbath; and an ordinance requiring safety devices on sawmill machinery, being intended to protect employees, does not establish the mill company's negligence with respect to others.

In general, violation of a statute designed to protect the instant plaintiff against the very type of harm which has befallen him constitutes negligence *per se* ("in itself"), conclusively establishing the defendant's negligence without other evidence thereof and without leaving the jury any question of fact to decide on the issue of negligence. In other words, violation of the statute is negligence as a matter of law, and the court must so instruct the jury. This of course bars the jury from relaxing the policy established by the legislature, and imposes a heavy burden of compliance upon the defendant. In some states, however, or generally in some types of situations, violation of the statute is merely *evidence* of negligence, which the defendant may rebut and which the jury may weigh, for whatever it considers it to be worth, along with all other relevant and competent evidence.

The Duty Theory The essential elements of a cause of action for negligence are: A legal duty to exercise reasonable care for the protection of the plaintiff, failure to exercise such reasonable care, and a "proximate" causal connection between the defendant's negligence and the plaintiff's injury. This "tort triad" or *triune nexus* of duty owing, breach of that duty, and proximate cause, taken as a whole, significantly qualifies the general principle of liability for negligence. Negligence itself now having been explained, it remains to discuss the duty theory of negligence and the general requirement (applicable to all torts, not only to negligence) of proximate cause.

The concept of tort duty is essentially a limitation upon the scope of the obligation to use reasonable care. The standard of reasonable care being imposed upon all citizens

as a matter of social policy, one would think that every citizen owes to the world at large an enforceable responsibility to act with due care. Persuasive support may be marshalled in support of this view, but in general the law says "Not so!" A duty of reasonable care is not owed to the world at large, but only to a particular class of persons, and the plaintiff's suit will not succeed unless he can establish his own membership in that class. Though the issue remains unsettled, it often is held that the duty of reasonable care is owed only to those foreseeably endangered by failure to exercise due care. This means that if the defendant's negligence causes injury, however directly, to one outside the zone of apparent danger, there is no liability as to that plaintiff, since no duty of care was owed to him even if such a duty may have been owed to others. There must be a duty to use reasonable care *with respect to the plaintiff*. The defendant must have been negligent toward this particular plaintiff, or the class of which he is a member.

The "duty" limitation upon general tort liability is well illustrated in the traditional attitude toward prenatal injuries. Until about twenty years ago it could be said with confidence that injury to a pregnant woman, resulting in deformity of or other injury to the infant apparent after its birth, gave the infant no cause of action against the defendant, because (among other reasons) the defendant owed no duty to the infant plaintiff, since legal rights and duties are recognized only between legal persons and a fetus is not a legal person. That is, if the defendant owes a duty not to the world at large but only to particular persons, the duty theory bars from suing him persons not in existence, and therefore owed no duty, at the time of his negligence. The sensible answer, of course, is that the infant exists from conception, and is recognized from that time by the criminal law (killing the fetus may be murder), by the law of property (the fetus may inherit), by the law of persons (a guardian may be appointed), and for some purposes by the law of torts (after birth, the infant may sue for the wrongful death of its parent). Legal scholars unanimously condemn the traditional rule, and today the right of an infant born alive to sue for prenatal injuries is rapidly taking hold in this country.

The duty theory still is very much with us, however, in connection with the question whether the plaintiff was within the zone of foreseeable danger. The classic case, one of the most interesting and significant decisions of the common law, and then and now one of the most hotly debated, is *Palsgraf v. Long Island Railroad Co.* The railroad's employees, boosting a breathless passenger aboard an already-moving train, negligently knocked a parcel from his arms; it contained explosives which were set off when the parcel fell under 'the wheels. The explosion overturned scales at the opposite end of the station platform, injuring the plaintiff. It was found that the railroad's employees could have foreseen injury to the boarding passenger or to his parcel but not to the plaintiff, and a divided court held, four judges (led by Cardozo) to three, that the railroad owed no duty to the plaintiff and that she therefore had no cause of action for its negligence toward the boarding passenger. Negligence and duty of care were limited to the zone of foreseeable harm; what was a wrong to another was not necessarily a wrong to the plaintiff, who must "sue in her own right for a wrong personal to her, and not as the vicarious beneficiary of a breach of duty to another."

The dissenting judges, rejecting the duty theory and asserting an obligation of reasonable care toward the world at large, argued that "Due care is an obligation imposed upon each one of us to protect society from unnecessary danger, not to protect A, B or C alone ... Every one owes to the world at large the obligation of refraining from those acts which unreasonably threaten the safety of others ... Not only is he wronged to whom harm might reasonably be expected to result, but he also who is in fact injured, even if he be outside what would generally be thought the danger zone."

The *Restatement of Torts*, which Cardozo helped draft, adopted the "duty" theory of the Palsgraf majority, but the issue continues to be debated and the various courts are fairly evenly divided in choosing sides. It is difficult to say to what extent the duty theory really is the law of the land; the best that can be said for it is that some limit of liability is needed as a matter of policy and that the duty theory fixes a limit.

For the dissenters it may be said that an admittedly negligent defendant should pay for the injuries of an admittedly innocent plaintiff, and that the defendant can fully protect himself simply by exercising reasonable care. Furthermore,

it is interesting to observe that the duty concept is peculiar to the common law, is superfluous to the (Continental) Civil Law, and is widely condemned as useless and confusing by the best English and American scholars. It is logically fallacious because the assertion that a duty does or does not exist assumes the case out of the real issue, which is whether as a matter of social policy the defendant's conduct should be regarded as a wrongful invasion of the plaintiff's rights.

Applications of the Duty Theory Whether or not the duty theory really is an established feature of our law, and whether it ought to be if it is, we may at least better understand its significance by evaluating its impact in certain specific areas. It is the purpose of this section to briefly survey the effect of the duty theory in connection with several legal relationships in which it often rears its ugly head.

Trespassers, Invitees and Licensees. The duty theory traditionally leads to a sharp differentiation between various classes of persons to whom owners or occupiers of land are potentially liable. Does the owner or occupier of land owe a duty of reasonable care to anyone present on his premises? The law answers this question in the negative, generally finding no such duty as to trespassers but a fairly onerous duty as to business invitees. Note that here, unlike the *Palsgraf* situation, the test is not geographic; it is not the position of the plaintiff in space that counts (except insofar as that may define his functional classification as trespasser, licensee or invitee), but rather the capacity in which he is present. In general the landowner (or occupier) has no duty of care to trespassers, who enter at their peril and take the premises as they find them—save only that the landowner must refrain from actively endangering a trespasser once his presence is discovered and perhaps must warn him of serious hidden dangers, that the same duty extends to undiscovered trespassers in places at which trespassing is common, and that special precautions may be required with respect to the foreseeable trespasses of children resulting in their exposure to special danger. Apart from these limited humanitarian exceptions landowners need not exert themselves for the accommodation of trespassers. Licensees, those who enter with permission but without invitation, are treated much like discovered trespassers, being entitled only to reasonable care for their discovery, for their safety from the landowner's activities, and for warning of hidden dangers. Otherwise the licensee, like the trespasser, enters at his peril: There is no general duty of care *to him*. Guests in one's automobile are treated much like licensees upon one's land.

Invitees, persons who enter at the express or implied invitation of the landowner for some purpose beneficial to him (for example, customers coming into a store), are, however, treated quite differently. As to such invitees (though only within the geographic area to which their invitations extend), the landowner is under a positive duty to exercise reasonable care for their protection. This duty requires not only that invitees be warned of danger, but also that active steps be taken to make the premises reasonably safe and to search out unknown or potential dangers. The courts vary in their definitions of an invitee to whom a duty of care is owed, some requiring potential pecuniary benefit to the landowner as the basis of the invitation, others searching only for an implied assurance of reasonable safety.

Landlord and Tenant. A landlord generally owes no duty of care to his lessee with respect to risks stemming from the condition of the premises, since the lessee is in possession, presumably is as well acquainted with the premises as the landlord, and is in the most convenient position to deal with any dangers. Similarly, the tenant owing an occupier's duty to third parties, the landlord has no duty of care toward third parties with respect either to the condition of the premises or the activities of the tenant. Exceptions to this general principle have been created in cases of known hidden dangers, the continuance of dangers threatening third parties, the known plans of the tenant to use the premises for dangerous activities, nonperformance of a promise to repair (in some states), or negligence in making repairs. The landlord remains liable as an occupier, of course, for portions of the premises continuing within his control. In the case of premises leased for purposes contemplating public use (stores, theaters, etc.) the landlord may owe to the general public a duty to deliver the premises to the lessee in safe condition. As between sellers and buyers of real estate, the seller again owes no general duty of care, but must warn of known hidden dangers

and may remain liable to third parties for some time after the sale. The buyer's duty of care to third parties generally applies to specific dangers only after he learns of them.

Suppliers of Chattels. In this type of situation the duty of reasonable care is no longer limited to those in privity of contract with the defendant, but has been extended to everyone within the zone of foreseeable danger. Thus the lender of a defective ladder might be liable to the borrower's son for injuries sustained when the ladder collapsed; the manufacturer of a new car with defective brakes might be liable to a pedestrian injured by the driver; and the seller of a pie containing a piece of broken glass would be liable to the purchaser's husband when he bites into the foreign substance. Note that in none of these cases is the *Palsgraf* rule violated: Duty still is confined within the zone of foreseeable danger.

Representations Relied upon by Third Parties. A misrepresentation may be intentional, negligent, or, in some cases to which the policy of liability without fault is deemed to apply, actionable though innocent. As another illustration of the "duty" theory one particular misrepresentation problem is considered here—that in which the defendant unintentionally but negligently makes a false statement which is communicated by its addressee to third parties and relied upon by them. Here the range of possible harm is almost infinite, and may be out of all proportion to the degree of fault involved. Accordingly it is considered wise policy to fix some limit on the scope of the duty to use reasonable care in making factual representations. Most courts hold that the duty extends only to those to whom the representation is made, or to those specific third persons to whom further communication is known to be intended. Thus mere expectation or possibility of communication to unspecified third persons imposes no duty of care as to such third persons, and attorneys, accountants, surveyors and others have been held not liable to strangers. A famous case on the point is *Ultramares Corporation v. Touche*, where the defendant accountants negligently certified a corporation's balance sheet, expecting that it might be shown to third parties in connection with various financial transactions but not having any reason to know that the plaintiff himself would rely upon it in lending money to the corporation. It was held that the accountants were not liable for negligence because they had no duty of care toward an unknown plaintiff (though liability was imposed on a theory of intentional deceit, since the accountants knew they were ignorant of essential facts they had to know before they could certify the balance sheet). Extension of the duty in this case on an intent theory of course reflects the practice of extensive business reliance on certified financial statements. The policy factors which require an exceedingly high standard of truth and accuracy in public or semipublic disseminations of financial information is apparent again in the federal Securities and Exchange Act, which establishes criminal penalties for the filing of registration statements containing false information.

"Danger Invites Rescue." Though there is no general legal duty to be a Good Samaritan and go to another's rescue, may one who responds to the moral imperative of the situation and, at some danger to himself, undertakes the rescue claim that the person responsible for the predicament of the person rescued owes a duty of reasonable care not only to the rescued but also to the rescuer? A number of cases have decided this question in the affirmative, finding that the defendant owes an independent duty of care to the rescuer, which is not limited or negated by the conduct of the person rescued. This constitutes, of course, a liberal extension of the scope of foreseeable risk. In effect the risks associated with rescue are added to the risks creating the situation which invites rescue, and even one who negligently places himself in a situation inviting rescue owes a duty of reasonable care to his own rescuer. As the great Cardozo so eloquently put it,

"Danger invites rescue. The cry of distress is the summons to relief. The law does not ignore these reactions of the mind in tracing conduct to its consequences. It recognizes them as normal. It places their effects within the range of the natural and probable. The wrong that imperils life is a wrong to the imperiled victim; it is a wrong also to his rescuer."

Proximate Cause

Liability for negligence requires not only a legal duty to the plaintiff and its breach, but also a degree of directness and closeness between the breach of duty and the plaintiff's injury. This additional requirement is called "proximate cause." It calls for a causal relationship between the defendant's conduct and the plaintiff's injury, but a causal connection is not in itself sufficient; the defendant's conduct must not only be the cause, it must be the *proximate* cause of the plaintiff's injury. There is a causal connection if the plaintiff's injury would not have occurred but for the defendant's negligence, but that negligence is the *proximate* cause of the plaintiff's injury only if a court decides, as a matter of social policy, that the connection between cause and effect is sufficiently close and direct to justify the imposition of liability upon the plaintiff.

A moment's reflection will indicate that the law cannot, as a practical matter, base liability upon causation alone. To do so would require tracing the chain of causation back through all the relevant circumstances in an attempt to identify the ultimate cause of the injury. But what, after all, is the ultimate cause of anything? How far back in time and space can the law go before the fading of memories, the conjunction of multiple causes, the intervention of other factors compel it to call a halt? Obviously a line must be drawn at some point, beyond which liability does not extend although causation may still be perceived. "Proximate cause" ends at this line, and it is only the immediate, proximate or direct cause of the plaintiff's injury to which tort liability is attached.

Because application of the standard of proximate cause involves policy decisions which are extraordinarily difficult to fit within the limits of any precise rule, the law of proximate cause is uncertain and amorphous. It is beyond the scope of this book to trace out the various factors which have entered into the numerous attempted definitions of proximate cause. We may say here that, though the chain of causation is not legally broken simply because harm to the plaintiff was beyond the defendant's expectation, the courts often are reluctant to impose liability where the injury to the plaintiff is difficult to foresee, is remote in time and space, occurs in a highly unusual manner, or constitutes harm to an interest of the plaintiff different from that apparently threatened by the defendant's conduct. An unforeseeable, independent and unusual intervening cause, producing an unforeseeable result, relieves the defendant of liability because his negligence no longer is the proximate cause of the plaintiff's injury.

The *Palsgraf* case, discussed above in connection with the "duty" theory, is equally pertinent to the question of proximate cause. Even if the railroad owed a duty of care to the plaintiff, was her injury the proximate result of the negligence of the railroad's employees? No, the majority of the court said, because it was not foreseeable that negligence toward the boarding passenger, jostling him enough to make him drop his parcel, could set in motion a chain of circumstances resulting in injury to someone several hundred feet away. The proximate cause was the extraordinary contents of the parcel, not the employees' rough handling of a passenger needing assistance to board the train. Injury to the passenger was foreseeable as a consequence of the risk created by the employees' negligence, but injury to the plaintiff simply was not part of that risk.

Contributory Negligence and Comparative Negligence. Perhaps the most common kind of intervening force which will "insulate" the defendant from liability is the plaintiff's own negligence. If the plaintiff's own lack of reasonable care qualifies as the "proximate" or legal cause of his injury, obviously the defendant's negligence is only a remote cause and results in no liability. Of course the plaintiff's own negligence bars his recovery only where it exposes him to the same risk from which his injury stems.

The policy basis for the defense of contributory negligence is the ruggedly individualistic idea that every citizen should be ever alert to protect himself from the wide variety of risks to which civilized life exposes him. Society's first line of defense against the staggering costs of carelessness necessarily must be the self-interest and instinct for survival of the individual citizen. The law therefore must motivate and encourage that prudence which daily saves each of us from the folly of others, and the strict doctrine of contributory negligence in its traditional form, barring as it does the plaintiff's recovery if his own carelessness has made even a modest contribution to his injury, is designed to do just this. The doctrine of contributory negligence also operates as a significant limitation on the discretion of juries, since where contributory negligence is shown the court may be required as a matter of law to direct a verdict for the defendant.

In its pure or traditional form the defense of contributory negligence works an extreme hardship upon the defendant because it allows of no comparison of the degree of his negligence with the degree of the plaintiff's. *Any* negligence on the part of the plaintiff, however slight in comparison with the defendant's negligence, bars the plaintiff's recovery. The manifest injustice of this traditional rule is ameliorated whenever the judge lets the case go to the jury, since the jury naturally tends to weigh the relative negligence of the parties and merely to reduce (rather than eliminate) the plaintiff's recovery, in proportion to his own degree of fault. This has seemed a much more just approach to most legal scholars, though in practice it is uncertain whether the judge will submit the entire issue of negligence to the jury or must rule that the plaintiff was to some degree negligent as a matter of law and therefore must be thrown out of court with a directed verdict for the defendant. The modern tendency is to leave the whole question to the jury whenever possible.

In countries following the Roman Civil Law, and in admiralty courts (which apply admiralty law, derived from the Civil Law) in common-law countries, the strict doctrine of contributory negligence is unknown, and negligence is apportioned between the parties and the damages adjusted accordingly. Some American states have adopted the Civil Law approach by enacting statutes providing for "comparative negligence," or the apportionment of negligence between the parties by the jury. Many states and all the Canadian provinces provide, by statute, for the apportionment of negligence in certain types of cases, and statutes abolishing the defense of contributory negligence in industrial accident cases (involving injuries to workmen) have been enacted in almost every state. Though they present certain difficulties in cases involving multiple parties, comparative-negligence statutes generally enjoy the support of critical opinion.

The "Last Clear Chance" Doctrine.

Another approach to the goal of ameliorating the harshness of the traditional contributory-negligence rule is based on the logic of proximate cause rather than on the principle of apportionment of negligence. The "last clear chance" doctrine, emphasizing the sequence of events in time, charges the injury to the party which had the "last clear chance," or the superior opportunity, to avoid it. The "last clear chance" doctrine is recognized, in varying degree, in most states, and in effect provides a counter-defense to the defense of contributory negligence in those cases where the defendant's, rather than the plaintiff's, negligence is the proximate cause of the plaintiff's injury. However, there is much logical confusion and local variation in the "last clear chance" doctrine, and it seems probable that comparative-negligence statutes offer a better means of escaping the harshness of contributory negligence.

Special Problems

Several of the most interesting features of tort law do not lend themselves to discussion within the pattern of negligence and duty which this essay largely follows. Accordingly they are briefly dealt with here, not as an afterthought but rather to emphasize their often anomalous character and the pressure of equitable justice upon the logical order of the law. Some of these problems still present burning issues; others are discussed to show how the evolution of the law has had to accommodate the practical demands of social policy.

Attractive Nuisance.

As explained earlier, a landowner generally owes no duty of care to undiscovered trespassers. Their trespasses ordinarily need not be anticipated or provided for; trespassers enter at their peril and take the premises as they find them. As between landowners and adult trespassers this principle, as modified by special rules regarding discovered trespassers and hidden dangers, doubtless represents a reasonable balancing of the interests of private property and humanitarian concern. However, this reasoning breaks down when applied to the trespasses of young children, who cannot be expected to possess either the sensitivity to property rights or the awareness of danger which adults may quite properly be called upon to demonstrate. Accordingly the law imposes upon landlords special responsibility for injuries suffered by trespassing children.

This has been accomplished in the United States by means of judicial development of the principle of "attractive nuisance," often called the "turntable doctrine" because it was first enunciated in a series of cases involving children induced to trespass by the magnetic attraction of a locomotive turntable. The element of allurement is no longer considered essential, however; in its modern form the doctrine of attractive nuisance simply imposes liability on landowners where their activities, or the condition of their property, present special hazards to children. The basis of liability is the foreseeability of special risk to children. Where such risk exists the landowner must discharge a duty of reasonable care to potential juvenile trespassers; what constitutes reasonable care is to be decided through a socially optimal balancing of the property and business interests of the landowner against the humanitarian interest of society in the welfare of children. This typically requires a higher degree of care on the part of the landowner than would be required where no special risk to children is foreseeable. In the turntable cases, for example, the "attractive nuisance" doctrine motivated the construction of child-proof fences around railroad yards.

Liability Without Fault.

The law of torts is designed generally to compensate plaintiffs for the consequences of the defendant's fault or culpability (negligent or intentional), and not to redistribute purely fortuitous losses—which are supposed to lie where they fall. However, where the defendant voluntarily engages in extrahazardous activities, especially where he does so for profit, many jurisdictions will require him to assume liability for the consequences of the special risk he has voluntarily created, even though he intended no harm and used reasonable care to avoid it. Such liability without fault is imposed as a matter of social policy, often with the expectation that the defendant will be able to shift its costs to society as a whole by adjustment of his own selling prices.

Charitable Immunity.

For various reasons of policy some defendants are immune from tort liability, at least for some purposes. The state and federal governments are immune from tort liability by reason of their sovereign character, though they often waive this immunity, at least in part, by statute. Partial immunity also extends to certain activities of municipal corporations and public officers. Infants and insane persons are immune to the extent that their disabilities prevent them from forming the intent, or recognizing the standard of due care, necessary to tort liability. The public interest in protection of the marital relationship generally prevents a suit between husband and wife upon a tort claim, though this doctrine is under attack in automobile accident cases.

A particularly interesting example of tort immunity is that traditionally associated with charities. The basis of a charity's immunity from tort claims is its public purpose, and the fear that the charity's social usefulness may be impaired through diversion of its assets into the hands of those toward whom it has been negligent. The doctrine of charitable immunity does indeed conserve the assets of the charity, but only at the expense of innocent plaintiffs who may themselves require charity as the result of a charity's negligence, and the availability of liability insurance under modern conditions suggests that the cost of such insurance should be treated as an ordinary operating cost of the charitable enterprise. Modern opinion generally sees no reason why a non-profit hospital, for example, should be any less liable for its negligence toward a patient than a proprietary institution.

A minority of states still adhere, at least in some degree, to the traditional doctrine of charitable immunity. In these states it may still make a decisive difference whether one is run down, say, by an ordinary citizen or by a hospital ambulance. However, the pluralism of contemporary life, the strong community support of many charities through broad-based fund drives such as the local Community Chest or United Fund, and the ready availability of liability insurance at reasonable cost all combine to destroy any rational basis for the doctrine of charitable immunity under contemporary conditions. Recent decisions in a substantial number of jurisdictions have repudiated the doctrine of charitable immunity, and it seems probable that this doctrine, which has generated such spectacular injustice in some situations, will soon disappear from our law.

Contractual Limitations of Tort Liability.

Though tort duties are rooted in social policy rather than in any agreement of the parties, the law of torts generally imposes duties only where the parties themselves have not agreed upon a different allocation of risks. In the relatively infrequent

cases where the parties prefer to allocate risks between themselves by mutual agreement rather than accept the duties imposed by the law of torts, nothing except the familiar principles of contract law says they may not do so. Thus one may bargain away his right to reasonable care by, for example, the parking lot where he leaves his automobile, or his landlord, or the railroad which gives him a free pass.

This, however, assumes that the agreement limiting (or extending) normal tort liability is the result of the parties' free choice exercised under conditions of genuine liberty of contract. Where a "contract of adhesion" appears to exist the agreement between the parties may fail for lack of genuine freedom of contract. Great inequality of bargaining power casts doubt upon the validity of any bartering away of rights conferred under the law of torts. Indeed some such agreements, for example employment contracts excusing employers from liability for negligence toward their employees or attempts by public utilities to condition service upon exemption from liability for negligence in rendering it, are so obviously onesided that they are considered contrary to public policy.

On the other hand, where the parties do in fact enjoy equal bargaining power, and where the terms of the agreement are actually brought home to and agreed upon by both parties, the social interest in liberty of contract requires that the wishes of the parties be respected. That is, freedom of contract, where it actually exists, is a social interest which takes priority over the social interest in charging the negligent with the consequences of their carelessness. Similarly, provisions for liquidated damages, if reasonable and genuine, will be respected. However, the courts always are suspicious of contractual limitations of tort liability and will scrutinize them carefully to see that no injustice will result from their enforcement, and these agreements will not normally be interpreted as extending to gross negligence or to intentional wrongs.

CONTRACTS

General Principles

Social Significance of Contract Contract is one of the most effective instrumentalities of a system of private capitalistic enterprise. It is through this device that the exchange processes in modern large-scale business take place, and the vast amount of credit required in modern business is created and transferred. It is contract which makes possible the assumption and shifting of risks which inevitably are present in our highly speculative economic order. But contract in its most important aspect is a device by which persons make binding arrangements for the future or buy and sell human conduct. In this respect contract is a planning device; it is per se a most important agency of control in modern business.

Freedom of Contract In an economic society dominated by a philosophy of individualism, it is assumed that there should be relatively complete freedom of persons to make contracts. The courts accordingly enforce most contracts between persons of normal capacity, except those which in their opinion are contrary to sound social policy or have been induced by fraud or duress. The doctrine of freedom of contract assumes that there is substantial bargaining equality between all persons of sound mind and legal age. However defensible this assumption may have been in earlier times, it is often inappropriate in a complex modern business system. Thus, legislatures have enacted many different types of legislation, particularly in the field of labor relations, restricting the doctrine of freedom of contract.

Subject Matter of Contract A study of contracts is a study of promises. A promise is a statement of intention, carrying assurance that the promisor (the party making the promise) will do or refrain from doing something in the future. It is a proposal of conduct. A promise must be differentiated from a *representation*, which is a statement of a past or present fact. A promise is a statement of what one proposes to do or not to do in the future. A statement in an insurance policy that a watchman is kept on the premises at night is merely a representation of fact. A statement that a watchman will be kept on the premises is a promise.

A promise must also be distinguished from a *condition*. A condition is a statement of an uncertain event, present or future, upon the happening or nonhappening of which some-

thing else depends. A promise carries with it an assurance that the event will or will not happen. A condition carries no such assurance. A statement in an insurance policy that the policy is void if the insured keeps gasoline on the insured premises is a condition. A statement by the insured that he will not keep gasoline on the premises is a promise.

Although promises are the subject matter of the law of contract, the law does not enforce all promises. There are many promises to which the law does not attach enforcibility. Promises in terms of enforcibility may be classified as "socially harmful," "socially indifferent," and "socially useful." An antisocial promise is one the performance of which not only does not assist in carrying out the ends of society but which, according to prevailing social and economic ideals, actually injures society and retards its work. Promises to kill a person, to steal property, to defame a person, or to obstruct the administration of justice are illustrations of promises which are socially harmful. A socially indifferent promise is one the performance of which is neither particularly useful nor particularly harmful to society. A promise to make a gift falls in this category. It is a matter of indifference to society whether a promise to make a gift is performed or not. A socially useful promise is one which is serviceable in the affairs of society. It is a promise which is utilized in the buying and selling of conduct, services, and goods. Generally speaking, the law enforces only those promises which are socially useful: promises which assist society in working out its ends.

Types of Promises. Promises are variously classified. These classifications possess no merit other than to emphasize certain aspects of promises.

Formal and simple promises: A promise is either formal or simple. This classification emphasizes the character of the act by which a promise is made. A formal promise derives its binding quality from the formality with which it is expressed. A promise under seal is enforcible under the common law because of the formal document which evidences it. A sealed promise may take the form of a bond, a charter, a covenant, or a deed. Sealed instruments are known as common law specialties.

Promises in the form of bills of exchange, promissory notes, and checks are also formal. The unusual rights and duties of the parties to negotiable instruments are dependent on the form in which the promise is expressed. Since the peculiar consequences attaching to negotiable instruments had their origin in the "customs of the merchants," it is usual to classify these instruments as mercantile specialties.

Other promises are simple. Promises not under seal and not in the form of a mercantile specialty are simple whether expressed by word of mouth or in writing.

Executed and executory promises: Promises are executed and executory. This classification turns on the state of performance of the obligation assumed by the promisor. If nothing at all has been done by the promisor in the performance of his promise, that promise is executory. If the promisor has done everything he undertook to do, the promise is said to be executed. If the promisor has partially performed his promise, the promise is partly executed and partly executory.

Express and implied promises: Promises are either express or implied. Emphasis here is laid on the mode of proving the expression of the promise. An express promise is one in the making of which the promisor has completely set forth his promise and has left nothing to inference. An implied promise is one which is inferred from circumstances or from the conduct of the promisor. Fundamentally, of course, an express and an implied promise are the same, differing only in the manner in which they are proved.

Void, voidable, and valid promises: Promises, according to a common classification, are void, voidable, or valid. A void promise is one which courts refuse to enforce. Courts will not, for instance, enforce a promise to commit a crime. A valid promise is a normal promise to which courts attach normal consequences. A voidable promise is one made under such circumstances that its maker enjoys the privilege of escaping liability under it. It is a promise, however, which courts will enforce unless the promisor exercises his privilege to avoid it. The promise of an infant is an illustration of a voidable promise.

Bilateral and unilateral promises: Promises are either bilateral or unilateral. This is a fundamental distinction and one which possesses practical importance. A bilateral promise is one which contemplates a promise in exchange for it. Thus, *A* promises to convey Blackacre to *B* for $5,000 if *B* will promise to pay $5,000 for the conveyance. *A*'s promise

is a bilateral promise because it calls for a promise from B. If B makes the promise asked for, his is also a bilateral promise because it is given in exchange for a promise. A unilateral promise is one which is given in exchange not for a promise, but for an act. A promises B $25 if B will repair A's automobile. A's promise is unilateral because it calls for an act. The resulting transaction is one in which there is a promise only on one side. In a bilateral transaction there is a promise on each side. The terms in question also are frequently employed to describe offers. A bilateral offer is one which calls for a promise. A unilateral offer is either an offer of an act for a promise or an offer of a promise for an act.

Whether a given promise is bilateral, calling for a promise in exchange, or unilateral, calling for an act, is a question of fact. When the parties make their intent clear, as they may by the proper choice of language, courts have no alternative but to honor that intent. In doubtful cases, however, the courts are inclined to say that a given promise is bilateral rather than unilateral. As a practical matter, business agreements almost universally are based upon bilateral promises.

Agreement

Nature of an Agreement As a general rule, although not necessarily, an agreement results from the making of a proposition by one called the "offeror" and its acceptance by the person to whom it is made, the "offeree." The discussion of the making of an agreement may be divded into three parts: (a) the nature of an agreement which courts will enforce, (b) the offer as the first step in the formation of an agreement, (c) the acceptance as the final step in the formation of an agreement.

"Meeting of Minds."—An agreement necessarily implies that each party has in some manner expressed assent to it. Ordinarily the offeror expresses his assent by making an offer and the offeree by accepting the offer. Offer and acceptance are, in other words, but modes of assenting to the terms constituting an agreement.

That each of two contracting parties must give assent before there is an agreement which courts will enforce is universally admitted. There can be no agreement unless there is a "meeting of minds." Considerable confusion has, however, been caused by the impression that a meeting of the minds is to be taken in a literal sense and that the parties must actually and inwardly be of the same mind, at the same time, and in the same manner, on the terms of the agreement. The business of the world could not be carried on if the test of the formation of an agreement were a "meeting of minds" in a literal, subjective sense.

In *Hughes* v. *Smith* Justice Blackburn accurately states the nature of an agreement which the law will enforce:

If, whatever a man's real intention may be, he so conducts himself that a reasonable man would believe he was assenting to the terms proposed by the other party, and the other party on that belief enters into a contract with him, the man thus conducting himself would be equally bound as if he had intended to agree to the other party's terms.

Justice Holmes states substantially the same principle in *Brauer* v. *Shaw*: "Knowingly to lead a person reasonably to suppose that you offer and to offer are the same thing."

An agreement is not, and in the nature of things cannot be, a concurrence of subjective intents. The law, in determining whether an agreement has been reached, is not interested in what a person actually intends but only in what he leads others reasonably to believe he intends. An agreement is not a meeting of minds in a literal sense or a concurrence of subjective intents but merely a concurrence of expressed intents. "Assent," says Justice Holmes, "in the sense of the law is a matter of overt acts, not of inward unanimity in motives, designs or the interpretation of words."

Assent Induced by Mistake.—If a person actually expresses an assent, his assent is valid and real even though he may have been induced by mistake to express it. In *Tatum* v. *Coast Lumber Co.* plaintiff wrote to defendant asking the price of certain goods. Defendant's clerk, in adding the prices of the various items, made a mistake so that he arrived at a total of $5,134 when he should have arrived at a total of $6,194. Defendant, accepting the total as correct, made an offer to sell the goods at the lower price. Plaintiff accepted the offer in good faith. The court held that there was a binding agreement in spite of the mistake, saying:

If a vendor can be heard to come into court and repudiate his contract on the ground that it had never been really consummated for the reason that he made a mistake in computing the prices of the various articles involved in the transaction, he might with equal reason insist that he had made a mistake in computing the profits he expected to realize out of the transaction.

The fact that a person is mistaken as to the value of an article, its adaptability to proposed uses, or its qualities is immaterial if he actually expresses an assent to buy the article. This is true even though the seller may be aware of the misunderstanding under which the buyer is laboring. The fact that both are mistaken as to the value of an article is likewise, by the better rule, immaterial. P sold a stone to D for $1, neither knowing that the stone was an uncut diamond worth about $700. The court held that P's assent to the sale was valid and binding.

A person's expression of assent is not the less real because he is mistaken as to the identity or location of the subject matter of a transaction. A, owning a house at 9361 Longwood, agrees to sell it to B. B's assent to the transaction is binding upon him even though he may have been thinking of a house at 9361 Winchester. Courts commonly say that an agreement does not result from the negotiations of A and B if at the time both are mistaken as to the existence or nonexistence of the subject matter of the transaction. A and B sign a contract for the sale and purchase of a house. Shortly before this, unknown to either party, the house burned. Courts say that in these circumstances there is no agreement, because of the mutual mistake of the parties as to the existence of the subject matter. In this situation, however, it seems better to say that an agreement has been made but that it is upon the implied condition that the subject matter shall be or continue in existence and that the time for performance of the agreement does not arise because the condition is not fulfilled.

Assent Induced by Fraud or Duress.—Assent deliberately expressed is none the less real because a person has been induced by fraud or duress to give it. A highwayman holds a gun at my head and gives me the choice of making a promise in his favor or of receiving a bullet. If I sign the contract, I give my assent, however unfair the inducement may have been. If A induces me to sign a contract for the purchase of Blackacre by a fraudulent misstatement that Blackacre contains a valuable mineral deposit, I assent to the terms of the agreement, notwithstanding the fact that my assent is unfairly obtained. In either case, I may avoid the agreement because of A's unfair tactics. In each case, however, I assent to the transaction and there is an agreement which courts will enforce unless I avoid it.

Mistake in Expression of Assent.—In the situation just discussed, the complaining party actually intends to express the assent which he expresses, although induced to do so by mistake, duress, or fraud. Suppose that he expresses an assent which he does not intend to express. In other words, a person intending to say one thing says an entirely different thing. Is this such an assent that courts will compel him to honor it? Tested by the principle that a person is bound by the intent which he manifests, regardless of his actual state of mind, there ought to be but one answer to the question. Some courts, however, still proceed upon the hypothesis that there must be an actual meeting of the minds of the parties: an agreement to the same thing, at the same time, and in the same manner. Other courts, in determining whether an agreement has been reached, say that an error in the expression of an assent is immaterial if the expression reasonably leads the person influenced by it to believe that it represents the acceptor's real intention.

A common illustration of the principle that a person is bound by his outward expression, regardless of his actual intention, is found in the rule that a person is bound by a writing which he signs in ignorance of its contents. In *Bates* v. *Harte* it is said:

One who has signed a contract in negligent ignorance of its contents cannot in the absence of fraud or misrepresentation, set up such ignorance in avoidance of his obligation. If he cannot read, due care for his own interest requires that he should have it read to him.

In the cases supporting this rule it commonly is said that the person signing is conclusively presumed to have known and assented to the terms of the document. This statement is meaningless. The truth of the matter is that the person is bound by the outward expression of assent, regardless of his knowledge and actual assent. Public policy as well as logic requires that a person shall be bound by a document which he signs in ignorance of its contents. A rule which ex-

cused a person in such a case would place a premium upon ignorance and neglect.

Another illustration of this principle is found in cases like *Western Union Telegraph Company* v. *Shotter*. Plaintiff delivered this message to the Telegraph Company for transmission: "Can deliver hundred turpentine at sixty-four. Immediate reply." The agent sent this: "Can deliver hundred turpentine at sixty. Immediate reply." The offeree ordered one hundred barrels of turpentine "at sixty." Plaintiff settled with the offeree on the basis of "sixty" and sued the Telegraph Company for damages sustained by the error. The liability of the Company depended upon whether the plaintiff was bound by the offer which he delivered to the Company or by the message which actually reached the offeree. The court held that the plaintiff was bound by the offer which reached the offeree.

The same principle should apply to a situation in which a typist makes an error in the typing of a letter containing an offer. In *Mummenhoff* v. *Randall*, however, the language of the court is contrary to this view. The defendant dictated a letter offering vegetables for "fifty-five cents a bushel." The typist made an error, quoting a price of "thirty-five cents a bushel." The plaintiff on receipt of the letter wired for a shipment of two or three cars of the articles at the price quoted. The court held there was no enforcible agreement, because "there was no meeting of the minds." If the plaintiff reasonably believed that the offer which came to him was an accurate expression of the intent of the defendant, the decision cannot be defended on principle.

In these cases no enforcible agreement arises in any event unless the other person reasonably thinks that the expression accurately represents the intent of the party making the mistake. If the person to whom the proposal comes knows that an error in expression has been made, it cannot be said that there is a concurrence of expressed intentions. Whatever else the proposer may have intended, the other party at least knows that the expression which comes to him was not intended by the proposer. The offeree has not been deceived, and nothing useful is gained by compelling the offeror to perform a proposal which the offeree knows to have been made erroneously. The fact that the price at which services or goods are offered is at wide variance with the market price is sufficient evidence to warrant the inference that the offeree realized that a mistake was made. In *Harron* v. *Foley* the plaintiff claimed that the defendant offered to sell him cattle at $161.50. The defendant replied that whatever he may have said, he intended to say $261.50. The court said that "there was sufficient evidence to justify a court or jury in finding that if the offer to sell at $161.50 was made, as claimed by the plaintiff and his witnesses, the plaintiff was aware that the offer on the part of the defendant was a mistake."

Mistaken Expression Caused by Other Party.—In another case, the defendant, an illiterate person, was induced to sign a note by a representation that the note was a document appointing him as a sales agent. The defendant was, of course, a victim of fraud and, as against the person who practiced the fraud upon him, might have avoided the agreement if the court had decided that there was an agreement. Was there, however, any agreement at all? Was there any concurrence of expressed intents? There was not. The person making the misrepresentation knew that the defendant's signature to the document did not mean what it seemed to mean. The court said that "the signature so obtained is of no force; and it is invalid, not merely on the ground of fraud where fraud exists, but on the ground that the mind of the signer did not accompany the signature; in other words that he never intended to sign, and therefore in contemplation of law never did sign the contract to which his name is appended."

Mistaken Expression Caused by Extrinsic Fact.—Finally, there are cases in which there is a semblance of a concurrence of expressed intentions but in which the expression of each party is erroneous because of an extrinsic fact over which neither has control. In these cases courts properly enough hold that no agreement ever comes into existence. In *Kyle* v. *Kavanagh* the plaintiff offered to sell to the defendant four lots on Prospect Street in Waltham. The defendant agreed to buy four lots on the street from the plaintiff. Unknown to the parties, there were two streets in Waltham by that name. The plaintiff had in mind one of the streets on which he owned four lots. The defendant had in mind the other street of the same name on which the plaintiff owned no property. In an action by plaintiff to recover the purchase price agreed upon, the court held that he could not recover, saying that

no agreement was reached, as the plaintiff was thinking of one thing and the defendant of another.

This is, however, an inadequate explanation of the decision in question. Even if there had been but one Prospect Street in Waltham, the plaintiff would have been thinking of one thing and the defendant of another if the latter had been mistaken as to the location of Prospect Street. And yet there is no doubt that in this event there would have been an enforcible agreement. The explanation of the decision is that, although there is a semblance of a concurrence of expressed intentions, actually there is none because of the intervention of an extrinsic factor over which neither party had control and for which neither should be held responsible.

The Offer

Offer Defined and Distinguished from Similar Statements
An offer is the offeror's expression of an intent to do or to refrain from doing something in the future, carrying an assurance, expressly or by implication, that he will or will not do the thing in question. It is a proposal of conduct made under such circumstances and couched in such language that it leads the offeree reasonably to believe that it is intended to influence his conduct to the end of purchasing the proposed conduct of the offeror.

Statements made in jest, anger, and excitement: Statements made in jest, anger, and excitement are not proposals of conduct which others are entitled to act upon and turn into binding agreements. A statement by the defendant, made while he was in deep affliction over the murder of a son and while he himself was suffering from a serious wound, that he would give $200 to any who would arrest the wrongdoer was held to be merely an expression of strong feeling and not an offer. The statement of the defendant that he would "give $100 to know who stole his harness," reasonably worth $15, "should be regarded rather as an extravagant exclamation of an excited man than as manifesting an intention to contract." In *Theiss* v. *Weiss* the court says that "a calm review of the circumstances indicate clearly, as we think, that the making of an offer to sell 20,000 barrels of flour at $4 a barrel at the same time when he actually bought 400 in good business earnest at $4.45 a barrel and the signing of a memorandum in writing of such sale, was never regarded or intended by either party as more than a mere bluff or banter without any serious intention that it should be performed."

These statements are not offers because they are not made under such circumstances as to lead others reasonably to believe that they are intended as proposals to sell conduct. It is conceivable that any of these statements might under other circumstances have been an offer. In *McKinzie* v. *Stretch* it is said that "where a person's conduct and conversation is such as to warrant a reasonably prudent person to believe that he is in earnest, he will not be permitted to say, in case he makes a bad bargain, that he was 'codding' and 'joking.'" In *Rief* v. *Page* the defendant standing in front of a burning building shouted to the crowd: "I will give $500 to any person who will bring the body of my wife out of that building, dead or alive." The court held that this was an offer even though the defendant was at the time laboring under great mental stress.

Vague promissory statements: In the course of a person's daily affairs he utters many vague statements of a promissory character. Some he makes because he intends to carry them out; others he makes without any intention of performing them, to relieve pressure which is being brought to bear upon him at the moment. Some of them may reasonably impress others and materially influence their conduct; others fall upon deaf ears and produce no impression. Courts usually say that these vague, indefinite statements, even though of a promissory character, are not offers which can be turned into enforcible agreements. A statement that a business would be continued for as long as it was profitable is too vague to be regarded as an offer. An agreement to renew a lease at the end of a term which specified neither the length of the new term nor the rental was held unenforcible because too indefinite. A promise by a stockholder of a corporation to an officer that he would divide profits with him on a liberal basis was held too indefinite to be an offer.

One explanation of the refusal of courts to treat these vague, promissory statements as offers is given in *Butler* v. *Kemmerer*, in which the court says that "to form the basis of a legal obligation, an offer must be so complete that upon acceptance an agreement is formed which contains all the terms necessary to determine whether the contract has been

performed or not." Another explanation is that vague and indefinite statements of future conduct do not lead persons to whom they are made reasonably to believe that they are to be taken seriously.

Negotiatory statements: The formation of an agreement usually is preceded by a stage of negotiations in which each party seeks to drive an advantageous bargain. A person having goods for sale sends out a general announcement to that effect and invites the attention of those interested in such goods. Someone attracted by the announcement makes a tentative proposition to the owner. The owner replies with a definite statement as to the conditions under which he is willing to part with the goods. The other person replies, suggesting changes. The owner accedes to some changes and not to others. Thus the negotiations continue until one of the parties has expressed a definite statement as to what he is willing to do in exchange for the conduct of the other. When this occurs an offer has been made.

Statements appearing in advertisements and trade circulars are seldom treated as offers. As a general rule, neither the circumstances in which they are made nor the language in which they are couched would warrant the conclusion that they are the final proposal of the publisher. In *Montgomery Ward & Company* v. *Johnson*, defendant sent out a circular stating that "we have prepared and are sending under this cover by registry post the terms and conditions upon which Iver Johnson revolvers will be supplied to the jobbing trade" and that "hereafter no order will be filled except upon the terms set forth in the enclosed document." The plaintiff put in an order in compliance with the conditions stated by defendant and contended that it was an acceptance of an offer of defendant. The court, holding that there was no contract, said:

A fair interpretation of the letter and document very plainly shows that it was not a general offer to sell to those addressed but an announcement or invitation that the defendant would receive proposals for sales on the terms and conditions stated, which the defendant might accept or reject at his option.

Quotations of prices and answers to trade inquiries even though couched in fairly definite language generally are held not to be offers. There is no magic in the terms "quotation" and "offer." "A quotation might be so expressed as to amount to an offer to provide a definite article, or to do a certain work, at a defined price." The fact that a given proposal is stated in the form of a quotation is some evidence that it is not to be taken as an offer. There are, however, more important factors to be considered in determining whether a given statement is a mere quotation or an offer. Did the defendant make the statement in response to an inquiry for a price or a quotation? Does the statement contain an expressed intention to sell at the price quoted to the person to whom the statement is made? How definitely are the terms stated in the communication? Is the maker of the statement a dealer, wholesaler, or manufacturer who would not ordinarily run the risk of incurring more obligations than he could perform by making general offers to his trade?

Closely related to quotations and answers to trade inquiries are statements inviting bids and offers from those to whom they are made. An announcement by a person stating that he will receive bids upon property to be sold is not an offer. It is merely a mode of determining what offers can be had. This is true even though it is stated that the highest bid will be accepted. Defendant may accept the highest or lowest bid or reject all bids. The statement that the highest bid will be accepted is made to stimulate bidding, and in the absence of special circumstances the courts do not treat it as an offer which can be accepted by one of the bidders.

It is universally agreed that an announcement that property will be sold at auction at a time and place specified is not an offer. If it were otherwise, there would be a contract between the person proposing the auction and every person who attended at the time and place mentioned. Such an announcement is a mere advertisement of the proposed auction and is so understood by persons interested in such sale. A person might, of course, announce a proposed auction in such language that the announcement would be construed as an offer. As a general rule, however, such announcements are intended to stimulate the attendance of prospective buyers and not to buy their attendance.

Nor is a statement that goods will be sold to the highest bidder or a statement that goods will be sold to the highest bidder without reserve an offer which (apart from statute)

binds one at all events to sell to the highest bidder. In *Anderson* v. *Wisconsin Ry. Co.* defendant advertised that it would sell property at auction "to the highest bidder without reserve." Plaintiff in good faith made a bid of $680, an increase of $5 over the previous bid. The auctioneer, refusing to consider the bid, sold the property to the previous bidder. In an action by plaintiff for breach of an alleged contract, the lower court gave him a verdict and judgment. On appeal the verdict and judgment were set aside. The court said that "a bid is an offer which is accepted when the hammer falls, and until the acceptance of the bid is signified in some manner, neither assumes any obligation to the other. At any time before the highest bid is accepted, the bidder may withdraw his offer to purchase or the auctioneer his offer to sell." In some states, by statute, an owner or auctioneer is required to sell to the highest bidder, if he advertises to sell to the highest bidder without reserve.

Agreements to be reduced to writing: Whether an informal arrangement is intended by the parties to form their final agreement or is intended only as a step in the negotiations leading to a written agreement is a question not always easy to answer. In *Bonnewell* v. *Jenkins* the defendant's agent offered certain premises to the plaintiff. The plaintiff replied with an offer of £800 for the estate. The agent wrote in reply: "We are instructed to accept your offer of £800 for these premises and have asked Mr. Jenkins' solicitor to prepare contracts." It was held that there was a completed contract between the parties even before the "contracts" had been prepared. The court said that "the mere reference to a preparation of an agreement, by which the terms agreed upon would be put into a more formal shape does not prevent the existence of a binding contract."

"If the written draft is viewed by the parties as a convenient memorial of their previous contract, its absence does not affect the binding force of the contract; if, however, it is viewed as the consummation of the negotiations, there is no contract until the written draft is fully signed. In determining which view is entertained in any particular case, several circumstances may be helpful, as: whether the contract is of that class which are usually found to be in writing; whether it is of such nature as to need a formal writing for its full expression; whether it has few or many details; whether the amount involved is large or small; whether it is a common or unusual contract; whether the negotiations themselves indicate that a written draft is contemplated as the final conclusion of the negotiations. If a written draft is proposed, suggested or referred to, during the negotiations, it is some evidence that the parties intended it to be the final closing of the contract."

Communication of Offer It is almost universally agreed that a proposal of conduct does not become operative as an offer until it has been communicated to the person for whom it is intended. The reason for this is found in the statement that the law of contract is an "endeavor of the state, a more or less imperfect one by the nature of the case, to establish a positive sanction for the expectation of good faith which has grown up in the mutual dealings of men of average rightmindedness." An uncommunicated proposal does not create any expectation of good faith on the part of a person to whom it has not come, and such person is not in a position to say that by his conduct he has earned the right to the proposed conduct of the offeror. Some courts, in cases of public offers of rewards, permit the plaintiff to recover the reward, even though at the time he performed the service he was ignorant of the offer. The best-reasoned cases, however, follow the general rule that a proposal does not operate as an offer until it has been communicated.

Mere knowledge of a proposal is not equivalent to a communication unless the knowledge comes with the authority of the offeror. In one case it is said that it is not sufficient that the alleged offeree "acquires knowledge of it unless the knowledge is acquired with the express or implied intention of the proposing party." An owner of land contemplating a sale thereof might direct his stenographer to draft a contract for sale to a particular person on specified terms. If the owner had not communicated, or intended to communicate, the proposed contract to that person, the latter, having acquired knowledge thereof, could not by acceptance bring the owner into contractual relation of sale." If, however, *A* prepares a proposal which through his negligence comes to *B*, in whose favor it is drawn, under such circumstances that *B* reasonably believes that it is intended for him, the proposal undoubtedly is an offer as to him.

The offeror may choose any available means for communicating an offer. He may communicate it by word of mouth, by written document, by mail, by telegraph, by messenger, by signs, or by gestures. He may communicate it expressly, or its communication may be implied by his conduct. Indeed, a very large proportion of contracts rests upon inference rather than upon express words. The offeror may communicate his proposal directly to a person or to him through an intermediary. He may communicate it to one person, to a class of persons, or to the public generally.

Offer Must Invite Conduct A statement of intent is not an offer which can be converted into a binding agreement unless it invites an act or a promise as the purchase price. The offeree must be led reasonably to believe that his conduct is the price which he pays for a claim on the conduct of the offeror. If *A* proposes to give *B* $500 when he attains his majority, it is natural that *B*, relying on the promise, will conduct himself in a way in which he would not have conducted himself but for the promise. Is *A*'s promise an offer because it reasonably influences *B*'s conduct? Not unless *B* is reasonably led to believe that by his conduct he is earning the right to have *A* conduct himself in the manner proposed. In *Ricketts* v. *Scothorn* an uncle, desiring to place his niece in a position of independence, promised her $2,000. The niece immediately gave up her employment. The court in discussing this proposal said:

> Her right to the money promised in the note was not made to depend upon an abandonment of her employment and future abstention from like service. Mr. Ricketts made no condition, requirement, or request. He exacted no *quid pro quo*. He gave the note as a gratuity and looked for nothing in return. So far as the evidence discloses, it was his purpose to place the plaintiff in a position of independence, where she could work or remain idle as she might choose. The abandonment by Miss Scothorn of her position as bookkeeper was altogether voluntary.

Expiration of an Offer

When Offeror Limits Offer.—The offeror has it within his power to make an offer for a long, short, or indefinite period of time. If he exercises this privilege, his offer comes to an end with the expiration of the stated time. Offers to be accepted by return post, immediately, or within thirty days are illustrations of offers which are limited in duration. These offers automatically terminate upon the expiration of the designated period of time.

When No Period of Time Is Stated.—It is not unusual for one to make an offer without indicating how long it is to continue. Courts have adopted a rule of convenience in dealing with these offers, holding that they expire after the lapse of a reasonable length of time. In *Park* v. *Whitney* the defendant by letter offered to buy stock from the plaintiff "at any time after January 1, 1886, if at that time you desire to have me do so." On July 9 the plaintiff attempted to accept the offer. The court, holding that the acceptance came too late, said that "plainly the offer was not to continue forever. The words 'at any time' do not import perpetuity; and if not, the plaintiff was entitled only to a reasonable time."

What constitutes a reasonable time is a question of fact to be answered in the light of the circumstances under which an offer is made. An acceptance on February 5 of an offer of January 31 to sell a lot in a city was held to have been made within a reasonable time. An acceptance at 8:30 on Tuesday morning of a telegraphic offer received between 8:00 and 9:00 on Monday morning to sell linseed oil was held to be too late. The court said that the "better opinion is, that what is or is not a reasonable time must depend upon the circumstances attending the negotiations, and the character of the subject-matter of the contract, and in no better way can the intention of the parties be determined. If the negotiations are in respect to an article stable in price, there is not so much reason for an immediate acceptance of the offer, and the same rule does not apply as in cases where the negotiations relate to an article subject to sudden and great fluctuations."

Death or Insanity of Offeror.—"The continuance of an offer is in the nature of things a constant repetition, which, of course, necessarily requires some one capable of making a repetition. Obviously, this can no more be done by a dead man than a contract can, in the first instance, be made by a dead man." The cases apparently take this view even in situations when at the time of the alleged acceptance the offeree is ignorant of the offeror's death. The reasoning of the court in the *Pratt* case, that the continuance of an offer necessarily requires someone capable of making a repetition of the offer. is inconsistent with the principle discussed earlier that the law is not interested in what a person actually intends but in what he seems to intend. A person communicating an offer to another during his life necessarily creates an impression of assent, and his death, if not communicated to the offeree, does not in the nature of things dissipate that impression. In any event, if the offeree does that which in law is an acceptance, it is immaterial that the offeror dies before receiving actual notice of the acceptance.

Although there is some confusion in the decisions, insanity of the offeror, under the general rule, has the same effect upon an offer as the death of the offeror. "The insanity of Dr. Beach," says the court in *Beach* v. *Methodist Church*, "rendered him in law as incapable of making a contract or of continuing or repeating an offer to the church as if he had actually been dead."

Rejection of an Offer A rejection of an offer has the effect of bringing it to an end. This rule exists for the protection of the offeror. The offeror by making an offer indicates that he is anxious to enter into a contract. If a particular offeree manifests an intention not to deal with the offeror on the basis of his offer, the offeror ought to be free immediately to begin negotiations with others without being under the necessity of revoking the previous offer.

Express Rejection.—It is well settled that a statement by the offeree that he will have nothing to do with the offeror's proposition is a rejection and brings the offer to an end. Having thus brought the offer to an end, he cannot thereafter agree to its terms and turn it into a contract, although his conduct, but for the rejection, would have been an effective acceptance.

Implied Rejection.—A rejection of an offer may be implied as well as expressed. If *A* in *B*'s presence makes an offer to *B* and *B* turns away without saying anything, *B*'s conduct under the circumstances justifies an inference that he has rejected the offer. A rejection may be implied by the fact that the offeree has, with knowledge of the offer, made a counter offer. In *Hyde* v. *Wrench* the defendant, desirous of disposing of an estate, offered it to the plaintiff for £1,000. The plaintiff replied that he would give £950 for the property. The defendant said that he would not sell at that price. Thereupon the plaintiff wrote the defendant, "I at once agree to the terms on which you offered the farm, viz., £1,000." The court held that the counter offer was a rejection of the offer and that the attempt later to accept was ineffective.

Not every statement made by an offeree in dealing with an offer operates as a rejection. A statement to operate as a rejection must be such as to indicate that the offeree will not deal on the proposed basis. In *Stevenson* v. *McLean* the defendants wrote to the plaintiffs offering to sell warrants for iron at "40*s*. per ton, net cash." The plaintiffs upon receipt of the offer telegraphed to defendants: "Please wire whether you would accept forty for delivery over two months, or if not, longest limit you could give." Defendants, after receipt of the inquiry, sold the warrants to another person. The plaintiffs before receiving notice of the sale sent a telegram of acceptance. The court held that the telegram of plaintiffs was not a rejection, "but a mere inquiry which should have been answered and not treated as a rejection of the offer."

Revocation of an Offer An offer is merely a proposal of conduct, and it is universally agreed that the offeror may change his mind at any time before the offeree has accepted. This is true even though the offeror has stated that the offer will remain open for thirty days and has promised that he will not revoke it sooner. A revocation under these circumstances, of course, comes as a shock to the offeree, who has been lulled into repose by the promise of the offeror to hold the offer open. Notwithstanding the disappointment which the revocation may cause to the offeree, the offeror may at pleasure revoke a simple offer, even though he has promised that he will not withdraw it for a given period.

Why should the offeror be permitted to revoke offers at will? It usually is said that a promise to give the offeree time within which to consider the proposal is gratuitous and is no more enforcible than any other gratuitous promise. It may also be said in justification of the privilege that it in some degree facilitates the formation of commercial transactions. An offeror typically must make many offers to secure a

Business Law and Wills

single acceptance. Since he takes the initiative in attempting to consummate a transaction, he ought to be free to pull in his line at any time and cast his bait in other directions unless, indeed, he has bound himself by contract not to do so.

Revocation of Sealed Offer.—At common law an undertaking under seal was binding because of its formal character. An offer which by its terms was to remain open for a stated period of time likewise was irrevocable if executed under seal. This principle does not have the practical value it once had, for in most jurisdictions the efficacy of seals has been destroyed by statute. In many of the jurisdictions in which seals still are recognized in private transactions, courts of equity will not grant specific enforcement of an offer merely because it is executed under seal.

Revocation of Paid-for Offers.—An offeror may revoke a simple offer at pleasure, and he may do so even though he promised not to do so. If, however, the offeree has paid or promised to pay him for keeping the offer open, he may not revoke it. A real option or paid-for offer is irrevocable. In spite of the offeror's known change of mind, the offeree may within the stated time turn the offer into a contract by acceptance. It is said by some writers that there is no such thing as an irrevocable offer and that the offeror may revoke an offer even though he has been paid for his promise to keep it open. Even if this is true, a revocation by the offeror of a paid-for offer is a breach of a contract not to revoke, for which the offeree is entitled to damages.

Revocation of Unilateral Offer after Part Performance.—When the offeree of a bilateral offer gives the promise asked for, an agreement results and the offer is merged into the agreement and in the nature of things cannot be revoked. A person to whom a unilateral offer is made may not, however, convert the offeror's proposal into a binding agreement by a promise. He may bind the promise only by doing the act asked for by the offeror. Until he does this, the proposal of the offeror remains what it was in the beginning, merely an offer.

May the offeror withdraw his offer after the offeree begins performance of the act but before he completes it? Strictly speaking, the unilateral offeror should enjoy the privilege of revoking his offer at any time before full performance of the act asked for. The offeree in such a case is not bound to do anything. He has been asked to make no promise and usually has made none. Why, then, should the offeror not be permitted to revoke the offer at any time before the act is fully performed?

The decisions of the courts as to revocation of unilateral offers after part performance are not satisfactory. Most courts are influenced by the supposed hardship which a revocation of this kind will cause to the offeree. All courts are inclined to construe an offer to be a bilateral offer if at all susceptible of such construction. This is permissible in doubtful cases. Some courts take the view that, regardless of the unilateral character of the offer, beginning performance of the act by the offeree is an acceptance which renders the promise binding. Other courts say that a revocation of this kind is inequitable and may not be made. Still other courts take a strictly legalistic view of the situation, holding that the offeror is entitled to revoke the offer at any time before it is accepted, even though the offeree may have partly performed the act in reliance on the offer.

What Constitutes a Revocation.—A revocation is in a sense a change of mind on the part of the offeror. A mere change of mind is not, however, a revocation. If an actual, literal meeting of the minds were of the essence of an enforcible agreement, an uncommunicated change of mind of the offeror would be a revocation. To enforce a promise, accepted after a change of mind, would be to force a person into an agreement to which he has not assented. It is, however, universally agreed, with an exception to be noted, that a change of mind does not operate as a revocation until brought to the knowledge of the offeree. Justice Holmes says that "it would be monstrous to allow an inconsistent act of the offeror, not known or brought to the notice of the offeree, to affect the making of a contract, for instance, a sale by an agent elsewhere one minute after the principal personally has offered goods which are accepted within five minutes by the person to whom he is speaking."

Must notice of the offeror's change of mind come to the offeree directly from the offeror? In a leading case Dodds offered to sell property to Dickinson, "the offer to be left open until Friday, 9 o'clock, A.M." two days from the day of the offer. Dodds meanwhile sold the property to Allan. Dickinson, having learned indirectly of the sale, attempted to accept the offer within the two days. In proceedings by Dickinson against Dodds and Allan, the principal question at issue was whether mere knowledge by Dickinson of the sale was tantamount to a revocation. The court held that it was, saying:

> ... just as when a man who has made an offer dies before it is accepted it is impossible that it can be accepted, so when once the person to whom the offer was made knows that the property has been sold to some one else, it is too late for him to accept the offer; and on that ground ... there was no binding contract for sale of this property by Dodds to Dickinson.

This rule, in the opinion of some writers, is of doubtful soundness. An offeree may not accept an offer, knowledge of which he has gained without the authority of the offeror. Why should a change of mind operate as a revocation, even though the offeree has indirectly acquired knowledge of it? There certainly is some embarrassment in holding that an offeree must take notice of facts and rumors concerning the offeror's change of mind which come to him indirectly.

The doctrine of *Shuey v. United States* is an exception to the general rule that a change of mind on the part of the offeror does not become operative as a revocation until it has come to the knowledge of the offeree. The court in this case held that a public offer may be revoked by a public announcement if substantially the same publicity is given to the withdrawal as was given to the offer. The court might more logically have held that an offeror may not revoke such an offer without giving actual notice to all persons to whom knowledge of it has come unless in the making of the offer he states that it may be revoked without notice. The decision cannot be defended upon the ground that the offeree "should have known that it could be revoked in the same manner in which it was made," for no one knew until this decision that an offer could be revoked by a public announcement.

The Acceptance The acceptance of a unilateral offer consists in doing the act asked for by the offeror; the acceptance of a bilateral offer consists in promissory expression of assent to the terms of the offer. In both cases, the conduct of the offeree must have been induced by the offer and given as the purchase price for the proposed conduct of the offeror. That an agreement is not reached until an acceptance of the offer has been made is obvious from what already has been said.

An acceptance has the effect of turning the promise contained in the offer into a binding obligation. An acceptance of a bilateral offer turns the negotiations into an agreement, and there is no longer an offer. If other requisites of a contract are present, both offeror and offeree immediately become bound to each other. The acceptance of a unilateral offer binds the promisor to the promisee.

By Whom Acceptance May Be Made.—"A party has a right to select and determine with whom he will contract and cannot have another person thrust upon him without his consent. It may be of importance to him who performs the contract, as when he contracts with another to paint a picture, or write a book, or furnish an article of a particular kind, or when he relies upon the character or qualities of an individual, or has, as in this case, reasons why he does not wish to deal with a particular party." It follows that no one, except the person or persons to whom an offer is made, can accept it.

Acceptance Must Be Provoked by Offer.—The acceptance of an offer, whether bilateral or unilateral, must have been provoked by the offer and have been made as a purchase price for the offeror's conduct. The performance of an act, in ignorance of an offer inviting the performance of the act, is not under the prevailing rule an acceptance. The act is not induced by the offer and may not be regarded as the purchase price for the offeror's proposed conduct. Similarly, the doing of an act, even with knowledge of the offer, is, generally speaking, not an acceptance unless the act was induced by the offer and was done by way of purchasing the conduct of the offeror. If, therefore, A, in order to ease his conscience, gives information leading to the conviction of B, his act is not an acceptance of a reward offered for the information, even though he may have been aware of the offer when he furnished the information.

Acceptance of Unilateral Offer The acceptance of a unilateral offer is a simple matter. It consists simply in doing the act asked for. The only question of difficulty which arises is whether notice of the doing of the act is a necessary part of

the acceptance. It is clear that the offeror may in any case dispense with notice if he chooses. In *Carlill* v. *Carbolic Smoke Ball Co.* the court says that "as notification of acceptance is for the benefit of the person who makes the offer, the person who makes the offer may dispense with notice to himself, if he thinks it desirable to do so. . . . And if the person making the offer expressly or impliedly intimates in his offer that it will be sufficient to act on the proposal without communicating acceptance of it to himself, performance of the condition is a sufficient acceptance without notification." It is equally clear that the maker of a unilateral offer may stipulate for notice of the doing of the act as a part of acceptance. If he does, the acceptance is not complete until notice has been given.

Notice Not Stipulated For.—If the offeror does not stipulate for notice, the general rule is that notice of the performance of the act is not necessary. "Ordinarily there is no occasion to notify the offeror of the acceptance as the promisor knows that he is bound when he sees that action has been taken on the faith of his offer." "But," says the same court, "if the act is of such a kind that knowledge of it will not quickly come to the promisor, the promisee is bound to give him notice of his acceptance within a reasonable time after doing that which constitutes the acceptance. In such cases, it is implied in the offer that, to complete the contract, notice shall be given with due diligence, so that the promisor may know that a contract has been made." In this case defendant wrote from Nova Scotia to plaintiff in Illinois, offering to repay advances which plaintiff might make to defendant's brother. The court said that, because of the situation of the parties, notice of the act would not "quickly come to the promisor" and that, therefore, plaintiff was under an obligation as a matter of fair play to send notice to defendant. Unless, however, the offeror stipulates for actual notice, the mere sending of notice in a reasonable manner is sufficient even though it never reaches the offeror.

Acceptance of Bilateral Offer: Assent

Mere Assent Not Sufficient.—The offeree must assent to the offer. Without his assent there is no agreement which courts can enforce. Mere assent of the offeree is not, however, sufficient as an acceptance. In *Prescott* v. *Jones* defendants notified plaintiff that they would reinsure his building for another year unless notified to the contrary. The plaintiff, intending that the building should be reinsured, gave no notice to the contrary. In an action by the plaintiff against the defendants for a loss by fire, the issue was whether what took place between the parties constituted a contract. The court thought not. "All the plaintiff did was merely to determine in his own mind that he would accept the offer. There was nothing whatever to indicate it by way of speech or other appropriate act. Plainly that did not create any rights in his favor as against the defendant. From the very nature of a contract this must be so; and it therefore seems superfluous to add that the universal doctrine is that an uncommunicated mental determination cannot create a binding contract."

Stipulation for Unevinced Assent.—The court in *Prescott* v. *Jones* goes even further.

If, therefore, the defendants might and did make their offer in such a way as to dispense with the communication of its acceptance to them in a formal and direct manner, they did not and could not so frame it as to render the plaintiff liable as having accepted it merely because it did not communicate his intention not to accept it. And if the plaintiff was not bound by the offer until he accepted, the defendants could not be, because "it takes two to make a bargain," and as contracts rest on mutual promises, both parties are bound, or neither is bound.

The court begs the question by concluding that the plaintiff was not bound and that, therefore, the defendants could not be bound. If the plaintiff actually assented to the arrangement, as seems to have been assumed by the court, he might have been bound if the court had wished to bind him. A better reason for the decision is the undesirability of proving assent by such an ambiguous fact as the failure of the offeree to communicate a different intention, even though the offeror has expressed his willingness to assume the risk of this precarious evidence.

Mere assent, then, is not an acceptance and cannot be, even though the offeror expressly stipulates that assent alone will be sufficient and that the offeree may prove his assent by remaining silent. To state the same thing affirmatively,

there can be no acceptance until the offeree has in some appropriate manner outwardly expressed an assent.

Expression of Assent

When Mode of Expression Is Indicated.—It is within the power of the offeror to prescribe the mode of expressing assent. He may require that assent be expressed orally or in writing, that it be given to him in person or to an agent, that it be communicated by telephone or telegraph, that it be expressed in some formal and ceremonious manner, or by a nod of the head or by a gesture of the hand. If the offeror chooses to prescribe the precise manner in which assent is to be expressed, an expression in some other manner is not sufficient. Ordinarily, an offeror does not require unnecessary and meaningless conduct, but he may do so if he desires. A person who deals with him must, whether he likes them or not, comply with the offeror's terms, however fanciful.

How far the offeror may go in dispensing with the usual elements of an acceptance is not clear. On the one hand, it seems that he is not permitted to dispense with everything except bare assent. On the other, it is well settled that he may dispense with actual notice of assent. He certainly should be permitted to waive everything except some overt act manifesting assent.

When Mode of Expression Is Not Indicated.—The offeror may provide the precise manner in which assent to his proposal must be expressed. He may within limits dispense with some elements of a normal acceptance. Very frequently, however, he does neither. In this event, what constitutes a sufficient expression of assent?

Silence as an expression of assent: A makes a proposal to B, to which B makes no reply. Is B's silence sufficient evidence to warrant a finding that he assented to A's proposition? It generally is held that mere silence is not sufficient evidence to justify an inference of assent by the jury. In *Royal Insurance Company* v. *Beatty* it is said that "instead of silence being evidence of an agreement to the thing requested, it is evidence either that the question was not heard, or that it was not intended to comply with the request."

Silence coupled with duty to speak: The relation between the parties may be such that the offeree after receiving an offer is under a duty to speak. In this event, silence is sufficient evidence of assent to go to the jury. In *Hobbs* v. *Massasoit Whip Company* the plaintiff had on several occasions sent to the defendant eelskins which the latter had accepted and paid for. On one occasion the plaintiff sent a consignment which was destroyed by fire before the defendant had taken any action with respect to it. In an action for the price of the skins, the court permitted plaintiff to recover. Justice Holmes said:

In such a condition of things, the plaintiff was warranted in sending skins to the defendant conforming to the requirements, and even if the offer was not such that the contract was made as soon as skins corresponding to its terms were sent, sending them did impose on the defendant a duty to act about them; and silence on its part, coupled with a retention of the skins for an unreasonable length of time might be found by the jury to warrant the plaintiff in assuming that they were accepted and thus to amount to an acceptance.

Overt action as expression of assent: Overt action is not a sufficient expression of assent unless it is such that in the ordinary course of events it will come to the knowledge of the offeror. In *White* v. *Corlies* defendant made this offer to plaintiff: "Upon an agreement to finish fitting up of offices, 57 Broadway, in two weeks from date, you can begin at once." Plaintiff made no reply but began performance by the purchase of lumber and by beginning to work on it. On the following day defendant sent a note to plaintiff countermanding the offer. The issue was whether what plaintiff had done before receiving the alleged revocation was a sufficient expression of assent. The court held not, saying:

We understand the rule to be that where an offer is made by one party to another when they are not together, the acceptance of it by that other must be manifested by some appropriate act. It does not need that the acceptance shall come to the knowledge of the one making the offer before he shall be bound. But though the manifestation need not be brought to his knowledge before being bound, he is not bound, if that manifestation is not put in a proper way to be in the usual course of events, in some reasonable time, communicated to him.

The act not only must be such that in the normal course of events notice of it will come to the offeror, but it must also be of such a character that it indicates to the offeror that the offeree has assented. In *White* v. *Corlies*, plaintiff had bought lumber and had begun to work on it for the offices of defendant. Since, however, he was a carpenter and might have been preparing the lumber for other work, his conduct "was no indication to the other party of an acceptance."

"When parties are conducting a negotiation through the mail," says the court in *Kemper* v. *Cohn*, "a contract is completed the moment a letter accepting the offer is posted, provided it is done with due diligence, after receipt of the letter containing the proposal, and before an intimation that the offer is withdrawn." This principle is equally applicable to a reply by other means so long as the acceptance is dispatched by the same means as that used to communicate the offer. In these situations, it is immaterial that the notice is unreasonably delayed or that it never reaches the offeror.

It may be urged that, until notice of the acceptance reaches the offeror, there can be no binding contract, because until then there is no meeting of the minds. The practical answer to this is that when negotiations are being "carried on through the mail, the offer and acceptance cannot occur at the same moment of time; nor, for the same reason, can the meeting of minds of the parties on the subject be known by each at the moment of concurrence; the acceptance must succeed the offer after the lapse of some interval of time; and, if the process is to be carried further in order to complete the bargain, and notice of the acceptance must be received, the only effect is to reverse the position of the parties, changing the knowledge of the completion from the one party to the other. It is obviously impossible, therefore, under the circumstances, ever to perfect a contract by correspondence, if a knowledge of both parties at the moment they become bound is an essential element in making out the obligation."

Justice Holmes says that "if convenience preponderates in favor of either view, that is a sufficient reason for its adoption." Commercial convenience clearly preponderates in favor of the view that an acceptance sent by the means used to communicate the offer is operative as soon as it is sent, regardless of what subsequently happens to it. Because of the efficiency of modern telegraph and mail service, relatively few communications go astray. The time saved in the formation of commercial transactions in the innumerable instances in which the communications arrive within the time contemplated more than outweighs the injustice which arises in the infrequent cases in which the expression of assent goes astray. In any event, the offeror, if he is unwilling to assume the risk incident to a delayed or lost acceptance, may always stipulate for actual notice of acceptance.

The posting of a letter is not an acceptance unless the letter is properly stamped and addressed. Actual receipt of the acceptance is required unless the offeree adopts the channel of communication designated by the offeror or adopts a reasonable mode of communication where none is designated. The channel of communication adopted by the offeror in making the offer is strong, but not conclusive, evidence of the channel of communication which he expects the offeree to adopt. If a person makes an offer by telegraph, it is a fair inference that he desires a reply in the same manner. An offer made by letter invites an acceptance by post or by some other channel equally safe and expeditious.

Consideration

General Principles The conduct of the offeror and the offeree has been examined to discover the nature of an agreement and the processes by which it is reached. Courts, however, do not enforce every agreement. The same conduct of the parties must, therefore, be examined from another angle to determine what agreements are prima facie enforcible. Heretofore we spoke of the offeror and the offeree. We shall now speak of the promisor, the maker of a promise, and the promisee, to whom a promise is made.

The problem with which we shall deal typically arises in this manner: *A* sues upon a promise made by *B*. *B* replies that *A* furnished no consideration to support the promise. The question presented is whether *A*'s conduct has been such that the law ought to enforce *B*'s promise. More fundamentally, the question is whether *A*'s conduct can be fairly regarded as a price for *B*'s conduct.

At the outset it is important to note that the term *consideration* is a legal, and not a business, term. Business men, generally speaking, do not think or talk in terms of consideration, but in terms of price. In the administration of their affairs, they enter into business agreements. Courts and lawyers then test the validity or enforcibility of these agreements by the technical doctrine of consideration. A simpler and more realistic approach to the problem would be to say that courts should enforce all socially desirable business agreements. Since, however, the enforcibility of promises is tested by consideration, it is necessary that the student of business have some appreciation of its meaning and application.

Consideration Defined.—In *Hamer* v. *Sidway* the court quotes with approval the statement that "a valuable consideration in the sense of the law may consist either in some right, interest, profit or benefit accruing to the one party, or some forbearance, detriment, loss or responsibility given, suffered or undertaken by the other." Another court says that "there must be either a benefit to the maker of the promise, or a loss, trouble or inconvenience to, or a charge or obligation resting upon, the party to whom the promise is made."

Although definitions of consideration are numerous, they are in substantial agreement that it consists either in the promisor's getting something which he wants and to which he is not already entitled or in the promisee's conducting himself in a manner in which he is not already bound to conduct himself. Except in rare cases, if the promisor gets what he wants and gets something to which he is not already entitled, the promisee necessarily will have conducted himself in a manner in which he was not already obliged to conduct himself.

As will appear from the discussion below, the requirement of consideration is a formality. The effect of the seal at common law provided a simpler and more certain formality by which promises could be made binding without actual consideration in the various instances in which this is desirable and intended. Statutory limitations of the legal effect of seals complicated the formal problem of making agreements enforcible to such a degree that legislation designed to provide a simple and effective means of making agreements enforcible without consideration when the parties so intend has been widely proposed. The Uniform Written Obligations Act, approved by the National Conference of Commissioners on Uniform State Laws in 1925 and adopted in Pennsylvania and Utah, makes written promises enforcible without consideration if accompanied by a written statement that they are intended to be legally binding. Sections 85 to 93 of the Restatement of Contracts, adopted by the American Law Institute in 1932, provide that promises to pay debts barred by the statute of limitations or discharged in bankruptcy, to perform a duty in spite of nonperformance of a condition, or to perform a voidable duty, or promises reasonably inducing definite and substantial action by the promisee which would result in injustice if the promise were not enforced, are enforcible without consideration if made with knowledge of the relevant facts. The new Uniform Commercial Code, Section 2-205, makes certain promises not to withdraw offers enforcible without consideration if expressed in a signed writing with intent to make the promise enforcible.

Consideration Not Guaranty of Exchange of Equivalent Values.—Whatever else consideration may be, it is not a guaranty of an exchange of equivalent values. "Where a party contracts for the performance of an act which will afford him pleasure, gratify his ambition, please his fancy, or express his appreciation of a service another has done for him, his estimate of value should be left undisturbed, unless, indeed, there is evidence of fraud. There is, in such cases, absolutely no rule by which the court can be guided, if once they depart from the value fixed by the promisor." "The value of all things contracted for is measured by the appetite of the contractors, and therefore the just value is that which they be contented to give." In *Barnum* v. *Barnum* defendant was held liable on his promise to buy a lottery ticket, even though the ticket by any external standard was worthless. In *Hemple* v. *Schneider* the consideration for the promise was the return of the promisee to St. Louis within fifty days. "There was a sufficient consideration," said the court, "and he [the promisor] must abide the consequence of his own bargain deliberately entered into."

The courts adopt a different view as to the adequacy of consideration when the transaction is a mere exchange of money. "A contract for the exchange of unequal sums of money at the same time, or at different times, when the element of time is no equivalent, is not binding; and in such

cases courts may and do inquire into the equality of the contract; for its subject upon both sides has not only a fixed value, but is itself the standard of all values; and so for the difference of values there is no consideration." Perhaps the explanation of the decision is that neither party under the circumstances reasonably can be regarded as having bargained for the other's conduct. If *A* presently promises to pay *B* $1,000 for *B*'s promise to pay *A* $1, it is difficult to believe that they really are buying and selling conduct. It seems clear that they are disguising a promise to make a gift by adopting the form of a contract.

Although consideration is not a guaranty of an exchange of equivalent values, and although the courts will not inquire into the adequacy of consideration, inadequacy of consideration may under some circumstances constitute evidence that a given promise was secured by fraud or duress. "Where the consideration is so grossly inadequate as to shock the conscience, courts will interfere, although there has been some exercise of judgment by the parties fixing it. But it will be found upon an analysis of the cases that courts interfere upon the ground of fraud, and not upon the ground of inadequacy of consideration."

Consideration Must Be Given as Price.—That which constitutes the consideration for a promise must be induced by it and given as price for it. If *A* returns lost property to *B* in ignorance of a reward offered by *B* for its return, *A*'s conduct has not been provoked by *B*'s promise and is not a consideration for *B*'s promise. Since the act was done before *A* knew of *B*'s offer, it was done gratuitously and there is no more reason for enforcing this than any other gratuitous promise. Neither is *A*'s act a consideration if he returns the property as a friendly act even though he is aware of the existence of the offer. *A*'s conduct still is gratuitous in spite of his knowledge of the offer.

In *Ricketts* v. *Scothorn*, a case which already has been discussed from the point of view of an offer, an uncle, regretting that his niece had to earn a living, gave her a promissory note. The niece more or less naturally gave up her employment. In an action on the note the court said that the giving up of her employment by the niece, although induced by the promise, was not a consideration for it. The court said that the uncle "gave the note as a gratuity and looked for nothing in return." "The abandonment by Miss Scothorn of her position as bookkeeper was altogether voluntary. It was not an act done in fulfillment of any contract obligation assumed when she accepted the note. The instrument in suit being given without any valuable consideration was nothing more than a promise to make a gift, in the future, of a sum of money."

For Whose Benefit Consideration Inures.—Assuming that an agreement upon a sufficient consideration has been made, who can take advantage of the consideration and sue on the promise? Obviously the promisee who furnished the consideration may sue upon the promise and normally is the one who does sue upon it.

Suppose, however, that *A* and *B* enter into an agreement by which *A* for a consideration moving from *B* promises to pay a sum of money to *C*. May *C* recover upon the promise? The objection usually made to an action by *C* is that he is not a party to the agreement and ought not to be permitted to sue upon it. This is a technical objection and ought not to prevail if practical convenience is served by permitting *C* to sue. Moreover, if consideration is regarded as the price which one person pays for the conduct of another, it should make no difference to *A* whether the person who buys the conduct or the person for whom it is bought brings the action for the failure to perform his promise.

All courts permit the beneficiary under a life insurance contract to recover. This, however, is a rule of the mercantile law and not a rule of the common law. Most courts of the United States, under limitations to be noted, permit a third person to sue on any simple promise made for his benefit. Some courts permit a third person to sue on a promise made for his benefit, even though the promise is made under seal. The leading case on the right of a third person to sue on a promise made for his benefit is *Lawrence* v. *Fox*. Holly, at the request of the defendant, loaned him $300. The defendant, in consideration of the loan, promised to pay $300 on the following day to the plaintiff, to whom Holly owed that amount. In an action by the plaintiff on the promise, the court permitted him to recover over the objection that he had given no consideration for the promise. The principle of *Lawrence* v. *Fox* was at first held to be limited to cases in which the promisee intends to benefit a third party with whom

he is in privity of contract and to whom he owes a legal duty to confer the benefit. But these limitations of intent, privity, and duty have been progressively relaxed in response to an insistent demand that third parties be permitted to enforce contracts in cases in which these limitations would not permit them to do so. This is another illustration of the tendency to whittle away at the requirement of consideration and its logical implications.

There are three types of third-party-beneficiary situations. The first includes cases in which a pecuniary obligation runs from the promisee to the beneficiary, for whose benefit the promisor makes the promise. This was the situation in *Lawrence* v. *Fox*. Courts in this country generally hold that the creditor beneficiary may recover upon a promise made for his benefit. To bring a case within this category, "it is not sufficient that the performance of the covenant may benefit a third person. It must have been entered into for his benefit, or at least such benefit must be the direct result of performance, and so within the contemplation of the parties."

The second group includes cases in which the promisee owes no legal duty to the beneficiary. The contract between the promisor and promisee is, in other words, not made for the purpose of discharging any legal obligation which the promisee owes the beneficiary but for the purpose of conferring a gift upon him. There is no good reason why the donee beneficiary should not have as strong a claim to recover upon such a promise as the creditor beneficiary, and most courts now take this view. "Whether the benefit secured to the third person is a gift, strictly so called, or one intended when realized to discharge some liability of such promisee to the third person does not change the situation. It is the exchange of promises between the immediate parties, and the operation of the law thereon, that binds the promisor to the third person."

The third group includes cases in which the contract is not made for the benefit of the third person but in which the third person incidentally will derive a benefit from its performance. A water company enters into a contract with a city to supply it with sufficient water pressure to protect against fires. It fails to do so, as a result of which *B*'s house burns. Although the contract is not made primarily for *B*'s benefit, he obviously will derive a benefit from its performance. *D* enters into a contract with his employees to furnish them with medical service. May *B*, who is called as a physician to attend one of *D*'s employees, recover on this contract? Under the prevailing rule, courts do not permit a person who will benefit incidentally from the performance of a contract to recover for its breach. He is, as the courts say, a stranger to the contract and has no legal or equitable interest in it.

Incidents of doctrine: Assuming that the beneficiary can in some cases bring action upon a promise made for his benefit, there are certain incidents of the relation which should be noted. In the first place, the courts permit the beneficiary to sue in these cases, even though he is not named in the contract and even though he may have been unaware of its existence until after its formation.

In the second place, the courts agree that the promisor and promisee cannot rescind the agreement after the beneficiary has learned of and assented to it. They are not, however, in agreement as to whether the promisor and promisee may rescind before knowledge and assent by the third person. The better view is "that the liability is as binding between the promisor and the third person as it would be if the consideration for the promise moved directly from such third person, regardless of whether the latter has any knowledge of the transaction at the time of its occurrence; that the liability being once created by the acts of the immediate parties to the transaction and the operation of law, neither one nor both of such parties can thereafter change the situation as regards the third person without his consent."

In the third place, the rights of the beneficiary are derivative and not absolute. They are derived through the promisee. In other words, any defense which is available against the promisee in an action on the contract is likewise available against the beneficiary. If the promisee by fraud induces the promisor to make the promise, the promisor can avoid it as against the beneficiary. If the performance of the promise is conditioned upon further action by the promisee, the failure by the promisee to perform that action defeats the right of the beneficiary to recover on the promise.

In the fourth place, the promisee can recover damages from the promisor for his failure to perform the promise to the beneficiary, even though the beneficiary at the time is

suing the promisor. If it be urged that it is hardship upon the promisor to be subjected to two actions, the answer is that he ought to perform his contracts.

Finally, a contract between *A* and *B* for the benefit of *C* does not discharge any obligation which *B* may owe to *C* until *A* has performed his promise to *C*. The beneficiary, even after he has learned of the promise made for his benefit and has assented to it, may bring action against the promisee on the original obligation. He may do this even though at the time he is also suing the promisor on his promise. Although the beneficiary may at the same time maintain both actions, he is, of course, entitled to but one satisfaction.

Consideration in Unilateral Agreements

Doing Act Promisee Not Bound To Do.—When the promisor calls for the action or the forbearance of the promisee, and not for a promise, the problem of consideration is simple. The promisee in this event furnishes a sufficient consideration to support the promise if in reliance on the promise he does the act asked for. The performance of the act is comparable to the giving of a *quid pro quo* which under the early law created a debt on the part of the person to whom the *quid pro quo* was given. In *Devecmon* v. *Shaw* the defendant's testator requested the plaintiff to take a European trip and promised to pay all his expenses. The court held that taking the trip in reliance on the promise was a sufficient consideration; it was no defense that the trip was a benefit to the plaintiff. The plaintiff did something that he was under no obligation to do, and the defendant's testator secured what she bargained for. In *White* v. *Poole* the plaintiff's testator promised to convey land to the defendant if the defendant would abandon her intention of going to Cuba and remain in Hanover. It was held that the abandonment of a change of residence in reliance on the promise was a sufficient consideration. In any case, the doing of an act asked for, in reliance on the promise, is a sufficient consideration to support the promise.

Doing Act Promisee Already Bound To Do.—If, however, the act is one which the promisee already is bound to perform, the doing of it is not a sufficient consideration to support a promise. A promise to pay money to a sheriff for effecting an arrest which by law the sheriff is already under a duty to effect is *nudum pactum* and unenforcible. If *A* is under a contractual duty to *B* to do an act, a promise by *B* of extra compensation if he will do the act is not, generally speaking, enforcible even though *A* proceeds to do the act in reliance on the new promise and with the expectation of getting the extra compensation. It frequently is said that these promises are not enforcible because the consideration is unreal. The reason for the rule is plain enough. By hypothesis the promisor already is entitled to the conduct of the promisee, and it would be contrary to public policy to compel him to buy it again.

Consideration in Bilateral Agreements

Promise for Promise as Consideration.—That a promise will support a promise given in exchange for it has been settled since about 1550. The enforcibility of a promise given for a promise was "placed on the ground that one promise is a good consideration for another. 'A promise against a promise,' it was said, 'will maintain an action.' Since that day it has been customary in declaring on bilateral contracts to lay one promise as having been made in consideration of the other."

It is said that the incurring of liability or disability by the promisee is that which renders the promise of the other binding. How can this be? *A* in consideration of *B*'s promise to work for him for six months agrees to pay *B* $250 a month. Immediately upon this exchange of promises each becomes bound to the other on his promise. It is said that *B*'s incurring of liability is the fact which supports *A*'s promise. If this is true, what supports *B*'s promise? The answer is that it is *A*'s incurring of liability. This, however, clearly begs the question. It is assumed that *A* becomes bound by his promise as a basis for holding that *B*'s promise is binding. It is then assumed that *B*'s promise is binding on him as a basis for holding that *A*'s promise is binding.

Whatever may be the legal phenomenon which renders one promise binding when another is given in exchange for it, the general rule which the courts purport to follow is this: *A promise to do something which a person is not already bound to do or to refrain from doing something which a person is entitled to do is a sufficient consideration to support a promise given in*

exchange for it. Apart from the legal technicalities involved, this is the understanding of the business community.

Sufficiency of Promise.—The statement, commonly made, that a promise as a consideration must be certain is not accurate. Uncertainty of terms must be considered in deciding whether the parties have reached an agreement capable of being enforced but has no bearing upon the sufficiency of the promise as a consideration. Nor is the statement accurate that the promise must be legal. Courts will not enforce an illegal promise, not because the promisee has not given a sufficient consideration but because the enforcement of an illegal promise would contravene public policy. Illegality of a promise is, generally speaking, a matter of performance and not a matter of consideration.

Assurance of conduct: "As contracts rest on mutual promises, both parties are bound, or neither is bound." In other words, an enforcible bilateral agreement is an exchange of assurances of future conduct. *A* cannot, therefore, insist upon the performance of *B*'s promise if he gives no promise in exchange for it or if the promise he gives is illusory and carries no assurance of conduct. A distiller promises to sell a quantity of whiskey to a dealer at certain prices; the dealer promises to buy the whiskey but reserves the right not to take it if for any reason he cannot use it. The court held that the distiller's promise was not binding because the dealer's promise carried no assurance of conduct. Courts take the same view as to contracts of employment in which the employer can terminate the relation at will. When he can terminate the relation only upon giving notice of fifteen days, courts generally hold that the agreement is enforcible. In this event, the employer has bound himself to employ the employee for at least some period of time.

A says to *B*: "I will sell you all the coal you may order from me during the year at $10 a ton." *B* replies: "I will accept your offer." Amplified, *B*'s alleged acceptance comes to this: "I promise to pay $10 a ton for all the coal I may order from you during the year." *B*'s promise obviously is illusory. He neither has agreed to take coal from *A* nor has agreed not to take coal from anyone else. If, however, *S* agrees to sell, and *B* to buy, all the coal which the latter may need in his business during the year, *B*'s promise does carry an assurance of conduct that, if he needs coal, he will buy it from *S* and is sufficient as a consideration to support *S*'s promise. In a case of this kind the court said:

It cannot be said that appellee was not bound by the contract. *It has no right to purchase iron elsewhere for use in its business.* If it had done so, appellant might have maintained an action for a breach of the contract. It was bound by the contract to take of the appellant at the price named its entire supply of iron for the year— that is, such a quantity of iron, in view of the situation and business of the appellee, as was reasonably required and necessary in its manufacturing business.

Value of Promise Not Material.—The value of a promise as a consideration is immaterial if it actually carries an assurance of conduct. The fact that a promisor discovers that a promise for which he bargained is not as valuable as he thought it would be does not excuse him from performing his promise. In *Baldwin* v. *Van Deusen* the court said that "the note of the infant was a sufficient consideration to uphold the promise of the defendant." "If the transaction was in all respects fair, the purchaser may, if he will, take upon himself the hazard or chance that the infant will pay the note which he has signed, and if he chooses to pay, or promises to pay therefor, he will be bound" even though the infant may decide not to keep his promise. *A*'s promise to pay for a suit of clothes to be made to his personal satisfaction is sufficient as a consideration to support *B*'s promise to make the suit, even though his promise may not be as valuable as *B*'s because its performance is contingent on a highly uncertain event—his personal satisfaction.

The fact that a person, in making a promise, refuses to assume certain risks of performance such as delays caused by strikes and breakdowns is immaterial if he actually has promised something. In *Edgar* v. *Hewitt Grain Co.* an agreement for the sale and purchase of sugar "subject to business conditions and other extraneous causes which render performance commercially impracticable" was enforced. Although in terms of the construction placed by the courts on the agreement it may be said that each party promised something, the agreement approaches the point at which the promises of the parties are illusory.

Promises Must Be Exchanged.—The promise relied upon as a consideration must have been induced by the promise

sought to be enforced and given in exchange for it. The mere fact that *A* makes a promise to *B* and *B* makes a promise to *A* is not enough to render either promise binding unless one was provoked by the other and given for it. In *Kimbro v. Wells A* and *B* entered into a contract by which *A* sold his business, including its good-will, to *B*. Later in the day *A* executed another writing to *B* in which he promised not to re-engage in the same business in the same town. The court held that this promise was not binding because there was no consideration for it. If the promise had been made as a part of the original transaction, the promise of *B* to buy the business would have been sufficient to support both promises of *A*: the promise to sell and the promise not to re-engage in the same business. The original transaction having been closed, it could not fairly be said that *A*'s second promise was induced by or given for *B*'s promise.

Problems in Consideration

Promise To Do What One Is Bound to Promisor To Do.— In *Lingenfelder* v. *Wainwright Brewing Co.* the Brewing Company employed Jungenfeld, an architect, to design plans for brewing buildings and to superintend their construction, for which the company undertook to pay him 5 percent of the cost of the buildings. After the buildings were begun, the Brewing Company awarded a contract for the installation of the refrigerating plant to a competitor of Jungenfeld. Because of this Jungenfeld threatened to break his contract. The company in this embarrassing situation promised Jungenfeld a 5 percent commission on the cost of installing the refrigerating plant if he would complete his original undertaking. He did complete it. In an action on behalf of Jungenfeld for the extra compensation the court applied the general rule that a promise to pay a person for doing that which he is already under contract to do is without consideration. "What we hold," said the court, "is that, when a party merely does that which he has already obligated himself to do, he cannot demand an additional compensation therefor; and although by taking advantage of the necessities of his adversary, he obtains a promise for more, the law will regard it as *nudum pactum*, and will not lend its process to aid the wrong."

Although a majority of courts follow the view of the *Wainwright Brewing Company* case, many courts for various reasons permit the promisee to recover on the new promise. Sometimes it is said that a person's surrender of his right to break a contract is a sufficient consideration for the promise of additional compensation. The fallacy of this contention is that a person has no right to break a contract, although, because of the imperfections of the legal machinery, he has the power to do it. Some courts say that the new agreement is per se a rescission of the old agreement. Others take the view that the new agreement is evidence of the rescission of the old agreement. In neither case, however, are the courts able to escape the embarrassing fact that the promisee, for the new promise, has done nothing more than what he was already under duty to do. In these cases, as one court says: "The obvious inference is that the party so refusing to perform his contract is seeking to take advantage of the necessities of the other to force from him a promise to pay a further sum for that which he is already entitled to receive."

All courts agree that, if the promisee in the new arrangement promises to do anything which he was not bound by the old agreement to do, his promise is a sufficient consideration. And it should be pointed out that courts eagerly seize, as a consideration, upon any change of plans which imposes additional burdens upon the promisee, even though there is no evidence that the parties themselves thought of the new things as consideration for the new promise.

Promise to Do What One Is Bound to Third Person to Do. —*A* is under a contract with *B* to do a certain thing. *C*, desiring that the thing shall be done, promises *A* $500 if he will perform or promise to perform. Is there a sufficient consideration in this case to support the promise of *C*? On the one hand, *A* promises to do nothing that he is not already bound to do, and if he does the thing, he has done nothing more than he ought to do. If, therefore, the enforcibility of *C*'s promise is tested by the conduct of *A*, there is no consideration. On the other hand, *C* gets what he bargained for —something to which he was not already entitled—the performance of the thing in question or a promise to perform the thing. If the enforcibility of *C*'s promise is tested by a receipt of a benefit by the promisor, there is a consideration for the promise. The English courts take the view that the

promise under these circumstances is enforcible. American courts generally take a contrary view.

Satisfaction of Debt by Payment of Less Sum.—*A* owes *B* the sum of $5,000. The debt is due and payable. *B* does not wish to bring action, as it is doubtful whether a judgment can be enforced if secured. *B* thereupon promises *A* that he will accept $3,500 in payment of the debt if *A* will pay that sum immediately. *A* does so. Later *B* sues *A* for $1,500, the balance of the original debt. *A* pleads the agreement to discharge him on the payment of $3,500. *B* replies that there was no consideration for the promise because *A* was at the time under an obligation to pay the whole sum immediately. At a fairly early time it was decided that "payment of a lesser sum on the day of satisfaction of a greater cannot be any satisfaction for the whole" even though the creditor agrees that the less sum shall constitute satisfaction.

Few doctrines of the common law have met with such criticism as this. Lord Blackburn, in *Foakes* v. *Beer*, says:

What principally weighs with me in thinking that Lord Coke made a mistake of fact is my conviction that all men of business, whether merchants or tradesmen, do every day recognize and act on the ground that prompt payment of a part of their demand may be more beneficial to them than it would be to insist on their right to enforce payment of the whole. Even where the debtor is perfectly solvent, and sure to pay at last, this is often so. Where the credit of the debtor is doubtful, this is more so.

The rule in question is, however, in keeping with the general theory of consideration that the doing of what one is already bound to do is not a sufficient consideration to support the promise of another. The promisee gives nothing which he is not already bound to give. The transaction amounts to nothing more than a promise on the part of the creditor to make a gift of a part of the debt to get the rest. Courts do not elsewhere enforce promises to make gifts. Why should they make an exception to the general rule in favor of the debtor in this situation? Critics of the doctrine likewise ignore the fact that any other rule would be an incentive to debtors to extort such promises from creditors.

Notwithstanding the well-nigh universal condemnation of the doctrine, most courts profess to follow it. One or two states hold that, if the creditor gives a receipt in full for the debt, the part payment received is a satisfaction. In ten or twelve states it has been provided by statute that the acceptance of a smaller sum in satisfaction of a greater discharges the debt if the new agreement is executed in writing. Moreover, courts "have seemed to seize with avidity upon any consideration to support the agreement to accept the lesser sum in satisfaction of the larger; or, in other words, to extract if possible from the circumstances of each case a consideration for the new agreement, and to substitute the new agreement in place of the old, and thus to form a defense to the action brought upon the old agreement." The giving of a note for a part of an open account constitutes a satisfaction of the debt. A partial payment made by a third person, even though at the request of the creditor, is a satisfaction of the whole debt. In other words, if the debtor is required to do anything or, indeed, if he does anything not required by the original debt, courts pounce upon the new act or forbearance as a consideration to support the promise of the creditor.

Composition Agreements.—*D* owes $500 to each of *A*, *B*, *C*, and *E*. His assets are insufficient to pay his creditors in full. He enters into an agreement with them by which they agree individually to release him from his debts if he will pay fifty cents on the dollar to his several creditors. *D* in reliance on this agreement pays each creditor the amount agreed upon. *A* thereafter brings an action against *D* for the balance of his debt. *D* pleads the composition agreement in defense. *A* replies that there was no consideration for his promise to accept less than the whole sum in satisfaction of the debt.

A composition agreement undoubtedly is useful in settling the affairs of a person who is insolvent. It bears some similarity to bankruptcy proceedings. Moreover, the danger that an unscrupulous debtor will take advantage of his creditors is not so great here as where the transaction arises between the debtor and a single creditor. Courts have, therefore, well-nigh universally held that the arrangement is binding, even though, in doing so, they have done some violence to the theory of consideration. Some courts say that a sufficient consideration is found in the mutual promises of the creditors. One difficulty of this view is that the beneficiary cannot in all jurisdictions recover upon a promise made for his benefit. Another difficulty is that the parties seldom think of their

mutual promises as being consideration in favor of the debtor. In cases in which the debtor assumes responsibility for inducing creditors to join in the composition agreement, his conduct is a sufficient consideration to support the promises of the creditors. In any event, the arrangement is a socially useful one and should be enforced.

Agreements Compromising Claims.—A injures B. A promises to pay B $500 if the latter will release him from liability with respect to the injury. B sues A on his promise. A contends that his promise is not binding because he did not injure B under such circumstances as to incur liability for the injury and that therefore his promise is without consideration. B sues A for the original injury, claiming $800 as damages. A pleads the agreement of B to release him from liability. B contends that there was no consideration for the promise because a trial of the controversy would show that the amount of damage suffered by him was more than $500. These situations raise the question whether there is consideration for a promise to compromise a doubtful claim.

Courts almost universally take the view that "the compromise of such a claim in good faith is a good consideration to pay money in settlement thereof, and when an action is brought upon such promise it is no defense to say that the claim was not in fact valid, or that the parties were mistaken either as to the law or fact." Every person has a right to sue upon a claim which he honestly and reasonably believes to exist, and his promise to forego that right is a sufficient consideration to support a promise of another to pay money or to do any other legal act. It is immaterial in these cases that the claim does not exist in the form or the amount asserted if it is asserted in good faith.

Agreements to Forbear Action.—A owes B $5,000. The amount is due. C enters into an agreement with B that he will pay the debt if B will not bring suit or will promise not to bring suit for thirty days. B, having forborne for thirty days, brings action against C on his promise. C contends that there is no consideration for his promise. Or B, before the expiration of thirty days, sues A on the debt. A pleads the agreement to forbear. B replies that there was no consideration for his promise.

In the first place, the mere act of forbearance of the creditor is not a sufficient consideration to support the promise of the third person unless the forbearance or promise to forbear follows the expressed or implied request of the debtor or third person. Otherwise, the promise of the third person is gratuitous and unenforcible. The court in the case just cited says that "as the defendants did not request plaintiff to forbear suit on the Neilson note and plaintiff did not agree to do so, the fact of forbearance does not indicate that it was in pursuance of a promise to forbear, nor does the forbearance itself imply a request." In the second place, if the debtor or the third person does expressly or impliedly request the creditor not to sue, forbearance by the creditor in reliance upon the request is a sufficient consideration to support the promise of the third person or any new promise by the debtor in connection with the debt.

In the third place, if the debtor requests a promise of the creditor to forbear, a promise to forbear is a sufficient consideration for the promise of the third person to pay the debt. This offer, however, contemplates a bilateral contract, and the creditor must, if he would bind the third person, promise to forbear or conduct himself in such manner as to prove a promise. In *Strong* v. *Sheffield* the defendant agreed to sign her husband's note as a surety in consideration of the plaintiff's promise to forbear suit on it. The plaintiff in taking the note with the defendant's signature said: "I will hold it until such time as I want my money. I will make a demand on you for it." The plaintiff actually did forbear bringing suit for two years. In an action against the defendant on the note, the defendant contended that there was no consideration for her promise. The court sustained her contention, saying: "There was no agreement to forbear for a fixed time or for a reasonable time, but an agreement to forbear for such a time as the plaintiff should elect. The consideration is to be tested by the agreement and not by what was done under it. We think the evidence failed to disclose any consideration for the defendant's indorsement."

If the debtor has requested a promise to forbear, it is not necessary that the creditor make the promise in so many words. Conduct which proves assent is sufficient so far as the promise is concerned. Actual forbearance for the time requested or for a reasonable time when no definite time is set is evidence from which the jury may infer the promise. In *Strong* v. *Sheffield*, the act of forbearance of the plaintiff

undoubtedly would have been sufficient to prove a promise not to sue but for the fact that he had made the statement that he would call for his money when he wanted it.

Subscription Agreements.—A subscription agreement is one in which a number of persons, having a common interest, individually promise to pay money for the furtherance of this interest. Since subscription agreements typically are made in furtherance of charitable or religious objects, courts resolve all doubt in favor of their enforcibility. "In this class of cases where public and charitable interests are involved, courts lean towards sustaining such contracts, sometimes on consideration which, in a purely business contract, might be regarded with suspicion." Although in some of the cases it can fairly be said that the promisor has bargained for conduct on the part of the promisee as a consideration, in a majority of them the promisor makes his promise as a gift and it is so understood by the parties.

All courts agree that, if a person signs the agreement with the request, expressed or implied, that the promisee shall do something, such as the incurring of an obligation, the payment of a debt, or the erection of a building, he is bound by his promise when the promisee does the act in question. A majority of courts hold that the promise of a subscriber binds him, even though not conditioned upon the doing of any act, if the subscription agreement actually is followed by acts in reliance upon it. Many courts say that the promise of one subscriber may be supported by the promise of his fellow-subscribers. Some courts say that a sufficient consideration is found in the implied undertaking of the promisee to keep the fund intact and to administer it for the purposes for which it was given, even though the promisee has not expressly promised to incur any obligation and has not done anything in reliance upon the subscription.

Promise To Pay for Services Rendered on Previous Request.—A requests B to repair a house. Afterward A promises to pay B $50 for his service. In an action on the promise, A contends that his promise is not binding because B's service was not induced by his promise and cannot, therefore, be a consideration for it. In some cases it is said that, although B's act is a past or executed consideration, nevertheless it is sufficient to support A's promise because of the request. Technically, there is no such thing as a past consideration, although the term is used by courts and writers. If A is bound to pay B for his service, it is not because of the subsequent promise but because of a promise implied in the request. Even if A had not made the subsequent promise, he would have been liable to B on an implied promise for the reasonable value of what B did at his request. The subsequent promise is immaterial except as evidence of A's estimate of the value of the service.

Courts do not infer a promise from every request. If I request my grocer to send a ham to my house and later agree to pay $5 for it, it is clear that a promise to pay for the article can be inferred from the request. If, however, I request my neighbor to water my flowers while I am away from home for a few days, it scarcely seems reasonable to infer a promise to pay for the service, and a promise subsequently made would be gratuitous. Justice Holmes, in *Moore* v. *Elmer*, says:

The modern authorities which speak of services rendered upon request as supporting a promise must be confined to cases where the request implies an understanding to pay, and do not mean that what was done as a mere favor can be turned into a consideration at a later time by the fact that it was asked for.

Promise to Pay Outlawed Obligations.—A is declared a bankrupt. B receives from the settlement of A's affairs $2,000 on a $5,000 debt. After receiving his discharge, A promises B to pay the balance of the debt. What is the legal effect of this promise? All courts agree that the creditor may recover the balance of the original debt but disagree as to the theory of the recovery. Most courts say that a moral obligation still rests on the debtor to pay his debts, even though discharged, and that the moral obligation is a sufficient consideration to support the new promise. In terms of what consideration usually means, the theory is meaningless. The moral obligation, assuming that there is one, is simply the motive which prompts the debtor to make the promise and cannot be a consideration in any real sense. Other courts take the view that a discharge in bankruptcy does not discharge a debt but only bars the remedy on it and that the debtor may waive this personal defense by recognizing the debt after its discharge.

A promise to pay a debt barred by a statute of limitations of actions likewise has the effect of rendering the obligation

binding. Courts differ as to whether the new promise is the binding obligation or whether it operates as a waiver of the personal defense created by the statute. The latter seems to be the better view.

Unenforcible Agreements

Agreements Based upon Imperfect Assent An agreement based upon a sufficient consideration is prima facie enforcible, but only prima facie so, as there may be some defect in the agreement enabling one of the parties successfully to resist its enforcement.

An agreement may be unenforcible because the party resisting enforcement is an infant or an insane person, because the assent of the person against whom it is sought to be enforced was secured in an unfair manner, because the party seeking to enforce it cannot produce the kind of evidence required by law, or because it is contrary to social policy.

Agreements Induced by Concealment.—A person is, generally speaking, under no obligation to give to another information which he has, even though he knows that the other would not enter into a proposed contract if he were in possession of the information. "Courts are created for the enforcement of civil contracts and are powerless to relieve against hard bargains, unless authorized to do so by some rule of civil law. From the very nature of their constitution, they must accommodate themselves to the general transactions of mankind; they cannot put parties upon an equality which does not in fact exist; they cannot deprive one of the advantage which superior judgment, greater skill, or wider information may give; nor can they be expected to enter upon an inquiry as to how the parties would have traded if each had known the same facts as to the state of the crops, the conditions of trade, a declaration of war, the signing of a treaty of peace, or any speculative matter of extrinsic fact of general or special knowledge."

There are, however, certain relations so delicate in character and so susceptible of abuse that the law exerts unusual precaution in their protection. These are relations *uberrimae fidei*: relations requiring the highest degree of good faith on the part of one of the parties in his dealings with the other. The relations between principal and agent, trustee and cestui que trust, guardian and ward, attorney and client, parent and child, principal and surety are the more common illustrations of this type of relation. If an agent enters into a contract with his principal, a trustee with the cestui que trust, or the parent with an unemancipated child, the contract is voidable at the election of the latter in each situation unless the former discloses all facts in his possession material to the transaction.

Agreements Induced by Misrepresentation.—If *A* induces *B* by a misrepresentation of material fact to enter into a contract, the enforcement of which will cause damage to *B*, it does not seem fair that *A* should be permitted to enforce the agreement. It is immaterial that *A* innocently misrepresented the fact and had no intention to harm *B*. The fact remains that *B* has been deceived and will suffer pecuniary damage if the contract is enforced. *A* certainly should not be allowed to profit by his own misrepresentations, even though he makes them innocently. Although an innocent misrepresentation does not give rise to an action in tort for damages at law, it is well settled that *B* may successfully resist the enforcement of the contract either at law or in equity by showing that it was induced by misrepresentation of the other party. In such a case, he also may get affirmative relief in equity, by rescission or cancellation.

Agreements Induced by Duress.—*B* at the point of a gun is induced by *A* to excute and deliver a note to him. Obviously, *A* ought not to be permitted to enforce the note against *B*. If *B* escapes his undertaking, is it because he has given an assent which he may avoid because of the duress used in procuring it or because he has in fact given no assent to the transaction? Although it is doubtful whether courts should do so, they usually proceed upon the theory that in such a situation the person signing the note actually has assented to the transaction but has assented under such circumstances that he may revoke his assent.

Duress of person: Duress of person is the oldest form of duress. It occurs when a person is compelled against his will to enter into a transaction. It is duress to compel a person to do something against his will by lawfully placing him in prison for an unlawful purpose, unlawfully placing him there for a lawful purpose, or unlawfully placing him there for an unlawful purpose. It is duress to compel a person to enter into a transaction by threatening to imprison him, whether for a lawful or an unlawful purpose. It is duress to force a person by physical force, violence, or threats of either to enter into an agreement. Courts do not think that assent procured in any of these ways should bind the promisor.

Duress ordinarily consists of bringing pressure to bear upon *A* to compel him to do something. But this is not always the case. It is duress to force *B* to enter into a transaction by threatening *B*'s spouse, child, or near relative.

Duress of property: In earlier cases, courts refused to recognize duress of property. They were unwilling to concede that the detention of a person's property or threats of its destruction were sufficient to overcome his will. In modern times, however, courts have come to realize that a person may love his property as much as himself or his family and, frequently, more. If *A*, in possession or control of *B*'s property, by an unjustified threat of its detention or destruction, induces *B* to enter into some agreement, the agreement is voidable by *B* because of duress to his property. In *Harris* v. *Cary*, Cary, who controlled a certain corporation, by threats that he would wreck the corporation, compelled Harris, a minority stockholder, to surrender a large part of his stock in the corporation. The court held that Harris, because of the duress practiced upon him, was entitled to the return of his stock. In *Westlake & Button Co.* v. *St. Louis* the city made an excessive demand upon the plaintiff for water service. The plaintiff paid the amount to prevent the city from carrying out its threat to shut off the water supply. The court said that "it is easy to see that in such circumstances the payments were not made voluntarily."

Standard by which duress is measured: "Anciently, duress in law could exist only where there was such a threat of danger to the object of it as was sufficient to deprive a constant, courageous man of his free will." Such a rule was inhuman and unjustifiable. Later the courts adopted a fairer rule—that whether a person's will has been overcome is to be tested by the effect which the pressure in question would have upon the will of a person of ordinary constancy and courage. In recent years the courts have taken a still more enlightened view:

The law no longer allows a person to enjoy without disturbance, the fruits of his iniquity, because his victim was not a person of ordinary courage; and no longer gauges the acts that shall be held legally sufficient to produce duress by an arbitrary standard; but holds him, who, by putting another in fear, shall have produced in him a state of mental incompetency to contract, and then takes advantage of such condition, no matter by what means such fear be caused, liable at the option of such other to make restitution to him of everything of value thereby taken from him.

Illegal Agreements

Basis of Illegality.—The illegality of an agreement may arise out of its formation or in its performance. A statute declares that no business shall be transacted on the Sabbath. A contract entered into on this day is illegal because its formation, not its performance, is forbidden by law. On the other hand, an agreement may be illegal because of the evil effects of its performance. *A* and *B* enter into an agreement to restrain trade. There is nothing bad in its formation. If the agreement is illegal, it is because of the antisocial effects of its performance. Practically all illegal agreements are of this type.

Social Consequences of Agreements.—On the one extreme are agreements which by prevailing social and economic standards are regarded as socially desirable. These are normal agreements to which the law attaches normal consequences. On the other extreme are agreements so antisocial in character that all courts agree that they should not be enforced. These agreements present no difficulty. Lying between them, however, are agreements which present considerable difficulty. These in some degree serve the ends of society and yet produce some antisocial effects. They present clashing interests. Their solution must, in the nature of things, represent a compromise. Courts in dealing with these situations usually must answer this question: Is the agreement likely on the whole to do more good than harm?

Agreements in Violation of Law

Agreements to Commit Civil or Criminal Wrongs.—Underlying every act regarded by law as a civil or criminal wrong

is the hypothesis that the act is antisocial in character—destructive of those interests which by prevailing social and economic standards are deemed legitimate and worth while. Prominent among these acts about which courts are thoroughly in accord are murder, rape, arson, robbery, burglary, larceny, assault and battery, libel, slander, trespass, conversion, fraud, and nuisance. If society has so far agreed upon the undesirability of these acts as to provide public punishment or private relief for their commission, it would be strange indeed if it opened its courts to litigants seeking to enforce agreements contemplating such acts. It is clear that an agreement contemplating the commission of a civil or a criminal wrong is illegal and unenforcible.

Agreements Violating Statutes Providing Penalties.—If a statute expressly prohibits a given transaction or declares that it shall be void, the illegality of the transaction is not open to question. Suppose, however, the statute merely provides a penalty for doing a certain act but is silent as to the legality of the act or of an agreement to perform it. Is an agreement to do the act illegal? Some courts take the view that the agreement is not necessarily illegal, that it is valid and enforcible if it can be inferred that the legislature provided the penalty in protection of its revenue laws. Most courts, however, are of the opinion that the fixing of a penalty is per se a declaration of the undesirability of the transaction and that any agreement which contemplates its performance is illegal.

Statutes Requiring License.—Statutes frequently require a person to procure a license as a condition of engaging in certain activities and provide a penalty for failure to secure the license but are silent as to the validity of the acts of one who engages in the activities without a license. The validity of an agreement falling within these statutes depends upon the purpose of a given statute. If it is designed to protect the public, the agreement is illegal and unenforcible. If it is merely for the purpose of raising revenue, the cases generally take the view that the agreement is valid. In the case just cited the court held that the fact that a corporation had failed to secure a license required of all domestic corporations did not invalidate its contracts or render its business illegal, but simply subjected it to a penalty for having violated the revenue laws of the state. "This law," said the court, "being a mere fiscal expedient, and not intended as a regulation or protection for the benefit of the public, and there being no statute invalidating contracts made by unlicensed corporations, they should be enforced, unless there was a clear legislative intent to prohibit the thing itself, rather than merely to punish for engaging in business without the license."

Statutes against Usury.—Interest is the price which a debtor pays for the use of money. It is the same in principle as the payment of rent for the use of land. Why have legislatures so universally regulated the price of money when they have not generally regulated the price for the use of land and other things?

Can we suppose that a principle of moral restraint of such uniform and universal adoption has no good sense in it? It is altogether the result of monkish prejudice? Ought we not rather to conclude that the provision is adapted to the necessities and the wants of our species, and grows out of the natural infirmity of man, and the temptation to abuse inherent in pecuniary loans. The question of interest arises constantly and intrudes itself into almost every transaction. It stimulates the cupidity for gain, and sensibly affects the heart and gradually presses upon the relation of debtor and creditor.

In a pecuniarily organized society, money is a commodity required by everyone. To permit a person to charge as much as he can get for the use of money would open a door to serious abuses of the financial system. All states accordingly have regulated the rate of interest which one may charge for the use of money. Usury statutes commonly establish a legal rate of interest, ranging from 5 to 8 percent, which governs in the absence of an agreement to the contrary. These statutes, however, provide that the parties may stipulate for higher rates of interest, ranging in the different states from the legal rate of interest to 12 percent. In a few states, parties are permitted by contract to stipulate for any rate of interest. Licensed pawnbrokers and other dealers in small loans commonly are permitted to stipulate for a nominal rate of interest as high as 3 percent monthly; in practice transactions may be arranged so as to result in a much higher rate of interest.

Usury usually is defined as "an illegal profit required and received by a lender of money from the borrower. To constitute usury, in contemplation of law, the following essential elements must be present: (*a*) there must be a loan or forbearance; (*b*) the loan must be of money or something circulating as money; (*c*) it must be payable absolutely and at all events; (*d*) something must be exacted for the use of the money in excess of the interest allowed by law."

Loan or forbearance: The question of what constitutes a loan or forbearance is one of fact, in many cases difficult of solution. "The form of the contract is not conclusive. The desire of lenders to exact more than the law permits and the willingness of borrowers to concede whatever may be demanded to obtain temporary relief from financial embarrassment have resulted in a variety of shifts and cunning devices designed to evade the law. The character of a transaction is not to be judged by the mere verbal raiment in which the parties have clothed it, but by its true character as disclosed by the whole evidence. If, when so judged, it appears to be a loan or forbearance of money for a greater rate of interest than that allowed by law, the statute is violated and its penalties incurred, no matter what device the parties may have employed to conceal the real character of their dealings."

D gives a conveyance of Blackacre to *C* for $5,000. It is agreed that *D* may repurchase Blackacre at any time within two years for the sum of $7,500. This transaction may, of course, be a sale with an option to repurchase. A contract of this kind, however, arouses suspicion. Is it not likely, reason the courts, that this is a transaction by which *C* loans *D* the sum of $5,000 for two years at an excessive rate of interest? In the case just cited the court said: "We express no opinion further than to say that whether a given transaction is a purchase of land, or a loan of money with title to the land taken as security, depends not upon the form of words used in contracting, but upon the real intent and understanding of the parties. No disguise of language can avail for covering up usury, or glossing over an usurious contract."

Loan of money: A transaction is not within the usual statute forbidding usury unless it is a loan of money. A loan of property, to be returned at a later time in an outrageously larger quantity or to be paid for in money at an exorbitant price, is not prohibited by a statute against usury. An undertaking to repay one and one-half bushels of corn within a year for one bushel advanced is not a usurious agreement. The plaintiff let six cows to the defendant in consideration of the defendant's promise to return "twelve cows with calves by their sides" within four years. "The contract was not usurious," said the court, "though the plaintiff was a very hard and unconscionable creditor." "It was uncertain in 1816 what would be the value of cows in 1823. Here were no negotiations for a loan of money. It was a bargain by which the plaintiff was pretty certain of making a handsome profit; but by which he might lose."

Loans and discounts: Generally speaking, the sale of negotiable paper is not a loan, and the fact that it is sold at a discount greater than the rate of interest allowed by statute for a loan of money is immaterial. In other words, the courts say that a negotiable instrument is a chattel or a commodity which the owner is entitled to sell in the market for the best price it will bring.

The general rule stated in the preceding paragraph requires explanation and qualification. In the first place, it is universally agreed that, when *A* gives his note to *B*, the transaction is a loan and not a sale of a chattel. If *B* receives the instrument at a discount greater than the rate of interest allowed in the jurisdiction for a loan, the transaction clearly is usurious.

In the second place, if *A* gives his note to *B* for *B*'s accommodation, which *B* transfers to *C*, the courts agree that the transaction is a mere loan and not a transfer of a chattel if *C* knows that the instrument was given to *B* for his accommodation. If, therefore, *C* takes the instrument at a discount greater than the legal rate of interest, he is subject to the same penalty to which he would have been subject if he had originally made an outright loan of money to *B* at a usurious rate of interest.

The courts are in disagreement as to the effect of the transaction if *B* sells the instrument at a discount to one who is ignorant of the accommodation character of the paper. Many courts, including the courts of New York, hold that the transaction, in spite of *C*'s good faith and lack of knowledge of the character of the paper, is a loan and not a sale of a chattel. Other courts take the view that *B*, as to purchasers without notice of the character of the paper, is selling a chattel and is entitled to sell it for any price he can get in the market. The court in the case just cited says that "the

better rule, and the one we think most consonant with reason and justice, is that if the holder, at the time he bought the paper, did not know that it was not already a valid subsisting security in the hands of the payee, there can be no intention of lending money, which is of the very essence of usury, and he may recover upon it of the maker."

In the third place, suppose an instrument has been transferred for value and is in the hands of a holder who can enforce it for its face value against prior parties. Does he borrow money or sell a chattel when he transfers it to another person at a discount greater than the legal rate of interest? All courts agree that the transaction is the sale of a chattel and not a loan if the holder transfers the instrument by delivery or under an indorsement without recourse, so that subsequent holders of the instrument have no recourse against him on the instrument.

There is, however, a considerable difference of opinion as to the effect of the transaction when the holder transfers the instrument under a general indorsement or when, in transferring the instrument, he guarantees its payment. Under either mode of transfer, the holder is liable to subsequent holders as a guarantor for the face value of the instrument. If, therefore, he sells an instrument at a discount in such manner as to incur contingent liability on the instrument, he may have to pay the face amount of the instrument, which will result in giving the transferee the debt at a discount greater than the legal rate of interest. Some courts say that the transaction is usurious and the indorsee is entitled to recover nothing on the instrument as against prior parties. Other courts, while holding that the transaction is usurious as between the indorser and the indorsee, take the view that the indorsee may enforce the instrument for its face value against all prior parties, except his indorser. A majority of courts, however, take the view that the holder may sell the instrument, as he would sell a chattel, for the best price he can get and hold that the transferee is entitled to enforce the instrument at face value against all prior parties.

Loan must be absolutely repayable: In determining whether a given transaction is usurious, the courts have differentiated outright loans from investments in a business. *A* advances $1,500 to *B*, *B* agreeing to use it in a certain way and to return the same with at least 15 percent if the venture turns out well. Is *A* a mere creditor, or does he become a partner in *B*'s business? Is *A* bargaining for the 15 percent for the use of his money or for a share in the profits of the venture? If he is bargaining for a share in the profits, he is a partner and not a creditor, and the agreement is not usurious. In *Goodrich* v. *Rogers* the court says:

We do not understand that our statute was ever intended to prevent one person from furnishing capital to another with which the two might embark in trade, although the person advancing the capital might receive profits greatly in excess of the rate of interest allowed by law.

Excessive interest: Finally, it must appear as an element of a usurious transaction that the lender stipulated for more than the legal rate of interest allowed in the jurisdiction in which the contract was made. The fact that the debtor out of the generosity of his heart gives the creditor an amount in excess of the legal rate of interest is immaterial. The test of the legality of the transaction is whether the creditor stipulates for an amount in excess of the legal rate.

Effect of Usury on Contract.—The effect of usury on the contract out of which it arises is determined by the statute which establishes the legal rate of interest. The statutes vary widely in the different states. In many states, the creditor merely forfeits the excess interest. In perhaps an equal number of states, the creditor forfeits all interest. In a few states, he forfeits twice or thrice the amount of the excess interest. In six or eight states, he forfeits the entire debt, including interest. In a few states, the taking of usurious interest, in addition to its effect upon the contract, is a misdemeanor, punishable by fine.

Under the common law, a debtor who has paid a debt, including usurious interest, is permitted to recover back the excess interest. This is an exception to the general rule that the law will assist neither party to get out of an illegal agreement after it has been executed. Courts, in making this exception to the general rule, say that the parties are not *in pari delicto.* They proceed upon the assumption that the creditor, in stipulating for usurious interest, must have taken advantage of the economic necessities of the debtor. In some states, statutes permit the debtor to recover back two or three times the amount of the excess interest.

Agreements Contrary to Public Policy The term "public policy" as a test of legality is in some disrepute because of its vagueness. Discerning courts frequently have warned that there is no magic in the term: that a conclusion is not necessarily explained by reference to public policy. Nevertheless the term is useful if its significance is appreciated.

An agreement contrary to public policy merely is a socially undesirable agreement. Public policy or the desirability of certain things always is worked out in terms of the prevailing social and economic ideals. It follows that there is no one public policy. Public policy is that which is socially desirable according to the best information we have at a given moment. It necessarily changes from time to time as social and economic beliefs change.

Agreements Influencing Conduct of Public Officials.—It is of great importance to the public that its officials, in the performance of their duties, shall be as free as possible from unfair and corrupting influences. Therefore, it is the general rule that an agreement which tends unfairly to influence the conduct of a public official is against public policy and unenforcible.

An agreement of a public officer to exercise his office in a certain manner, to appoint *A* to an office, to award a contract to *B*, to vote for or against a given measure, or to prosecute or not to prosecute a given offender is illegal and unenforcible. An agreement by an officer to accept less than the salary provided by law or assign his unearned salary is unenforcible. The tendency of these and similar agreements is prejudicially to affect the public service by destroying the independence of public officers and by exposing them to corrupting influences.

An agreement between *A* and *B* by which *B* undertakes to influence the conduct of a public official is void if it expressly or by implication contemplates the use of corrupting means. An agreement by *B* to use his personal influence to mold or modify the decision of a judge or to sway members of a legislative body for or against legislation is contrary to public policy. This is equally true of *B*'s undertaking to use his personal influence with a public officer who is about to award a contract or fill an office. In these situations, as courts frequently have pointed out, it is immaterial that wrongful means were not contemplated or used. "To legalize the traffic of such service," says the court in *Trist* v. *Child*, "would open a door at which fraud and falsehood would not fail to enter and make themselves felt at every accessible point. It would invite their presence and offer them a premium."

Courts agree, however, that it is not illegal for one to employ another to influence the conduct of public officials by the presentation of facts and arguments in an open and straightforward manner. "It is the right of every citizen, interested in any proposed legislation," says the court in *Cheeseborough* v. *Conover*, "to employ and agree to pay an agent to draft a bill and openly to explain it to a legislative committee, or to any member of the legislature, and ask to have it introduced; and contract which does not call for more, and services under which do not go further, are not against public policy." *A* may, of course, employ *B* to represent him in open court and, under the regulations of the court, to attempt to influence the decision of the judge. A person who wishes to sell property to the government may employ a salesman to negotiate with the appropriate public official if the agreement contemplates a transaction based on merits. Such an agreement, under the prevailing rule, is not illegal merely because the agent's stipend is conditioned upon success. Some courts, however, feel that a contract of this kind is bad because it tempts the agent to resort to unfair tactics.

Agreements Interfering with Administration of Justice.—For obvious reasons an agreement which materially interferes with the administration of justice is contrary to public policy and illegal. An agreement not to testify or to suppress or destroy evidence falls within this principle. A promise to pay a witness beyond the amount allowed by the state is illegal if the promise is conditional on the success of the promisor in litigation in which he is interested. An agreement by a person not to prosecute one who has committed a crime is itself a crime, and the agreement is not enforcible. A person is, however, entitled to get satisfaction for damages arising out of the commission of a crime, and the fact that he accepts a settlement from the criminal is no evidence that he has agreed not to prosecute the wrongdoer.

Agreements, the effect of which is completely to oust courts from their normal jurisdiction over controversies, are against

public policy and unenforcible. "The right to appeal to the courts for the redress of wrongs is one of those rights which is in its nature under our constitution inalienable and cannot be thrown off or bargained away." Parties may, however, validly agree to submit controversies to arbitration and to make the submission a condition precedent to a resort to the courts.

Wagering Agreements.—Every executory agreement is in a real sense a wagering agreement. *A* enters into an agreement to buy a supply of coal for the season from *B*. *A* and *B* are speculating on the future price of coal. *A* agrees to pay *B* the sum of $20 a year in consideration of *B*'s promise to pay him $5,000 in the event that his house burns during the year. The parties are speculating on the continued existence of the house. Are these agreements illegal merely because they are wagers? In answering these questions, three types of wagering agreements may be examined: *gaming agreements, speculative agreements,* and *insurance agreements.*

Gaming agreements: A gaming agreement is one by which a person undertakes to deliver to another something of value upon the happening or non-happening of an uncertain event in which neither of the parties has an interest worth protecting. *A* and *B* enter into an agreement by which *A* agrees to pay *B* $150 if Napoleon does not escape from St. Helena before the expiration of two years in consideration of *B*'s promise to pay him the same sum if Napoleon does escape within that time. *A* agrees to pay *B* $100 if *B*'s football team wins over *A*'s in consideration of *B*'s promise to pay *A* the same sum if *A*'s team wins. These are typical of gaming agreements. In each there is an agreement between the parties. In neither can the existence of consideration be questioned. In each, however, the agreement relates to an event in which neither of the parties has an interest worth protecting. It is not worth while to set in motion the expensive legal machinery of the state to enforce agreements when their enforcement will promote no social utility.

These agreements, however, are not merely unsocial; they are antisocial. In the first place, a wager laid upon an uncertain event, in which neither of the parties has an interest to protect or in connection with which neither has a legitimate risk to shift, actually creates a risk where no risk existed before. One of the problems of modern society is to reduce risks which are natural and inevitable; surely courts should not encourage the creation of new risks by enforcing these agreements. In the second place, these agreements generally are regarded as antisocial in that they tend to corrupt the morals of the community by fostering a spirit of getting something for nothing.

Speculative agreements: Although all executory agreements are speculative in character, the term "speculative agreement" has come generally to mean the buying and selling of goods for future delivery. *A*, needing corn in a milling business, enters into an agreement with *B*, who has no corn at the time, for the purchase of 5,000 bushels to be delivered within sixty days. *A* and *B* clearly are speculating on the future price of corn. In spite of this fact, however, these agreements generally are enforcible. The business of the world could not be carried on if they were not.

The seller and buyer, upon the making of the agreement, may not contemplate actual delivery of the subject matter of the agreement but may intend to settle on the basis of the difference between the contract price and the market price at the time set for performance. Such agreements, however, perform useful services in modern society. In the first place, their enforcibility makes it possible for one who does not care to speculate on fluctuations in market prices to shift those risks to another. *A*, a miller, buys 5,000 bushels of wheat at one dollar a bushel. The price of wheat may fall considerably by the time his flour is ready for the market. He is a miller and not a speculator and desires only to reap profits as a miller. He may, therefore, at the time he buys wheat for actual use sell an equal quantity of wheat, theoretically to be delivered at the time he will be selling his flour. If he enters into this "hedging" transaction, he has insured himself against fluctuations in the price of wheat and will in any event reap his legitimate profit as a miller.

In the second place, these agreements perform other useful services in our society, as pointed out by the court in the *Christie* case just cited:

> Of course, in a modern market contracts are not confined to sales for immediate delivery. People will endeavor to forecast the future and make agreements according to their prophecy. Speculation of this kind by competent men is the self-adjustment of society to

the probable. Its value is well known as a means of avoiding or mitigating catastrophes, equalizing prices and providing for periods of want.

The enforcement of these agreements is not without evil tendencies. "It is true that the success of the strong induces imitation by the weak," says the court in the *Christie* case, "and that incompetent persons bring themselves to ruin by undertaking to speculate in their turn." But the ruin of the incompetent speculator is the least of the evils which follows unenlightened speculation. The most significant and far-reaching evil of speculation by the incompetent is not so much their personal ruin as that their prophecies, proceeding from guesswork and not from expert knowledge, may mislead society in the production and consumption of economic goods.

Courts feel that on the whole speculative agreements are more useful than harmful. At the same time they feel that limits must be set to speculative trading. They accordingly have said that the test of the legality of a future contract is whether the parties at the time they enter into the contract intend to make and receive deliveries. If both *A* and *B* contemplate future deliveries, even though later they actually settle on the basis of the difference between the contract price and the market price at the time set for performance, the agreement is valid. If *A* contemplates delivery and *B* does not, the agreement is enforcible by *A* but not by *B*. If, when they enter into the agreement, they do not contemplate delivery but later agree that actual delivery shall be made, the agreement is valid.

The intent to make delivery of the goods is not a particularly efficient test for determining whether the parties are gambling or doing something useful. Nor is it the most illuminating test in terms of the social usefulness of speculative contracts. A more logical test would be: Was the contract made by a competent person under such circumstances that it can be regarded as a prophecy of the future upon which society can safely rely in guiding its economic activities? The legality of a speculative contract under this test would depend entirely upon the competency and expert knowledge of the speculator. But the practical difficulties in the administration of such a test are apparent. The courts perhaps laid down the most practicable test possible when they made the legality of the agreement depend upon the intent to deliver.

Insurance agreements: *A* enters into a contract with *B* by which he agrees to pay *B* the sum of $20 a year in consideration of *B*'s promise to pay him $5,000 if *C*'s house burns within the year. This is a pure gambling contract and is illegal. It performs no useful purpose whatsoever. What difference can it make to *A* whether *C*'s house continues in existence or burns? The agreement is not only unsocial but actually antisocial. It creates a new risk by tempting *A* to burn the house of *C*.

A enters into the same agreement with respect to his own house. The agreement still is a speculative agreement. *A* in effect wagers a certain amount against an amount wagered by *B* that the house will burn within the year. But *A* as owner of the house is confronted with serious risks. He must carry these risks or shift them to someone else. *B*, the professional risktaker, agrees to carry his risk for a reward. *B*, by concentrating a large number of risks, can carry *A*'s risk more easily than *A* can. He can spread the risks over a relatively large number of people and over a relatively long period of time. Although the enforcibility of such agreements results in an appreciable lowering of standards of care in the preservation of life and property, the courts think that the benefits to be derived from the concentration of risks in the hands of professional risktakers more than outweigh the evil tendencies and accordingly hold that a person may, through the many different types of insurance contracts, shift his risks to some third person.

Effect of Illegality A person asks the aid of a court in the enforcement of an agreement which contemplates the commission of a civil or criminal wrong, the violation of a statute, or the performance of an act contrary to public policy. How will courts deal with him and his agreement? Civil courts, into which the action necessarily will go, have no power to punish either party, even if they desire to do so. They can do nothing but pursue a policy of non-enforcement. They will not enforce the agreement if executory; they will not pry it open if executed. Although this attitude may not to any considerable extent discourage the making of illegal agreements, it is at least a refusal to prostitute the legal machinery of the state to the enforcement of illegal agreements.

Parties Not in Pari Delicto.—If the parties are not *in pari delicto*, the courts will permit the less guilty to avoid the

agreement if it has been executed. In doing this, they proceed on the assumption that to assist the more innocent of the parties will be more of a discouragement to the making of illegal agreements than to apply the general rule. In *Bell v. Campbell* the plaintiff, a woman of seventy years, inexperienced in business matters, without opportunity to consult disinterested friends, was induced by her son-in-law to execute a mortgage on her land to indemnify his bondsmen in respect to a default on his part as treasurer of St. Joseph. She brought proceedings to prevent sale of the land. It was contended that the mortgage was illegal, as part of an agreement to stifle prosecution. The court held, however, that the parties were not *in pari delicto* and that the plaintiff, being less guilty, was entitled to have the mortgage set aside.

Repentance by One Party.—A person who has paid money for the accomplishment of an illegal purpose or in pursuance of an illegal agreement may recover it back if he repents and demands the return of the money before the illegal purpose has been executed. Repentance of the party before the consummation of the wrong is the explanation of this doctrine. The courts think that to honor a bona fide repentance will be more effective in discouraging illegal agreements than to ignore it.

Legal and Illegal Promises Given for Same Consideration.—A carrier agrees to furnish cars to *B* and not to furnish them to *B*'s competitors, in consideration of *B*'s promise to pay it $5,000 a year. The promise to furnish the cars is a valid promise, but the promise not to furnish cars to *B*'s competitors is illegal. If *B* is willing to pay $5,000 for the legal promise and to waive performance of the illegal, the court will enforce the former. On the other hand, the carrier cannot enforce the promise of *B* to pay $5,000 without alleging performance of, or willingness to perform, both the legal and illegal promises; and since it has to rely upon the illegal promise to recover, courts will refuse any relief. This doctrine does not, however, "embrace cases where the objectionable stipulation is for the performance of an immoral or criminal act, for such an ingredient will taint the entire contract and render it unenforcible in all its parts, by reason of the maxim, *ex turpi causa non oritur actio.*"

Parties Affected by Illegality.—How far is *A* affected by the illegality of an agreement or transaction which he makes possible by advancing money or by renting or selling property to *B*? Clearly, *A* is entitled to recover from *B* if *B* without his knowledge intends to put the money or property to illegal uses. Just as clearly, he is not entitled to recover if he not only knows of *B*'s unlawful intent but actually directs the commission of the illegal act or enters into the transaction with the understanding that he is to share in the profits. Whether he is entitled to recover if he merely knows of the unlawful use is a question on which the courts are divided. A majority of courts in this country take the view that the plaintiff, in spite of his knowledge, may recover if he has neither directed nor sanctioned the unlawful use. "A person may loan money to his friend—to the man and not to the purpose." All courts agree, however, that the plaintiff cannot recover if he advances money with knowledge that it is to be put to some heinous or highly immoral use.

Assignment

Nature of Property in Contract.—A and B enter into an enforcible agreement. The resulting legal phenomenon is a *chose-in-action*: a thing on which an action at law or bill in equity may be brought. This is but another way of saying that the relation between *A* and *B* implies the existence of certain rights and duties between them relative to the subject matter about which they bargain. Rights are the essence of property. It follows, therefore, that an enforcible agreement is as much property to the parties as the relation of *A* or *B* to his house or cattle.

Salability of Contract Rights.—One of the most important inquiries about any form of property is: How far is it salable? To what extent may the present owner transfer his ownership to someone else? A contract is a form of property. How far is it salable? Is there anything peculiar about property in a contract, rendering a sale of it against public policy or impossible? These are some of the questions which need to be considered in the study of "assignment of contracts," the term used when one speaks of the salability of property in simple contracts.

Rights and Duties in Contract.—In considering what may be sold or assigned, a distinction between rights and duties must be made. *B* enters into an agreement to buy 100 tons of coal from *A* at $10 a ton, in consideration of *A*'s promise to sell him the coal at that price. *B* has the legal right to buy 100 tons of coal from *A* and owes a duty to pay *S* $1,000 as a purchase price. From the point of view of *A*, he has a right to the purchase price from *B* and owes a duty to deliver the coal to him.

What May Be Assigned *A*'s right to the price of the coal under the contract is a property right; his duty to sell and deliver the coal is not. Indeed, his duty to sell is conduct which he has sold to *B*. It therefore is inaccurate to speak of the sale of the duty to sell coal. *A* may induce *C* to furnish the coal to *B*; he is in no sense selling the duty to *C*. He is merely delegating to *C* the duty of performing something which he has undertaken to perform. The problem here is not how far a person may sell a duty, which in the nature of things he cannot do, but how far he may delegate to another the doing of a thing which he has bound himself to do.

Delegation of Duties.—A, who has undertaken to do something for *B*, cannot as a general rule delegate the performance of the duty to another without *B*'s express or implied consent. The reason for this is that, if *B* has bargained for the conduct of *A*, he ought not to be required to accept the conduct of another. If, however, the undertaking of the promisor is purely objective in character, if it can be as well performed by one person as by another, if it involves no personal skill, taste, judgment, or confidence on the part of the promisor, the promisor may delegate the performance of the undertaking to someone else. If *A* is under a duty to pay money to *B*, it is a matter of indifference to *B* whether the money is paid by *A* or *C*. If *A* is under a duty to sell and deliver coal to *B*, it is likewise generally a matter of indifference to *B* whether the coal is sold and delivered by *A* or *C*.

The fact that a duty has been delegated by the promisor does not relieve him of his liability for its non-performance. His delegation of the duty means nothing more than that he has employed someone to act for him. Default of the representative is default of the principal. "This, ordinarily," says the court in *Atl. and N.C. Railroad v. Railroad*, "is all the books mean when they state the proposition in general terms that a contract imposing liability cannot be assigned; that the assignment of such contract does not, as a rule, relieve the assignor from responsibility."

Sale of Rights.—"The assignability of [rights under] a contract must depend upon the nature of the contract and the character of the obligation assumed rather than the supposed intent of the parties, except as that intent is expressed in the agreement. Parties may, in terms, prohibit the assignment of any contract and declare that neither personal representatives nor assignees shall succeed to any rights in virtue of it, or be bound by its obligation. But when this has not been declared expressly or by implication, contracts other than those which are personal in their character, as promises to marry or engagements for personal services, requiring skill, science or peculiar qualifications, may be assigned, and by them the personal representatives will be bound."

Express Prohibition against Assignment.—If the parties expressly agree that rights under a contract shall not be transferable, courts will as a general rule give effect to their intention. In *Tabler v. Sheffield Co.* the defendant issued to its employees "labor tickets" which were evidence of the right of its employees to wages. Each ticket bore the statement "Payable to Employees Only. Not Transferable." The plaintiff came into the possession of some of these tickets and brought action on them. The court held that the plaintiff could not recover, saying that "they are expressly declared not to be transferable, which negatives any promise of defendant, otherwise implied, that payment would be made to any assignee or transferee of the holders."

Implied Prohibition against Assignment.—A and B agree to marry. *A* has the right to marry *B* and at the same time owes a duty to marry her. Clearly in this case the right is so personal in character and so intimately tied up with duty that the assignment of the right by *A* is unthinkable. The principle applies to all agreements involving close personal relations. *A* agrees to serve *B* as a private secretary for a year. *B* has the right to *A*'s services for the year. *B*'s assignment of the contract would bring *A* into close personal relations with another employer, to which *A* might properly object. Without *A*'s consent the right is non-assignable.

In this relation *A* has, first, the right to serve *B* for a year and, second, the right to compensation for her services. The first right is so inseparably tied up with her duty to perform that it cannot be assigned. Its very nature precludes its

assignment. But the second right, the right to compensation, whether earned or unearned, is not so intimately related to the duty to perform, and there is no sound reason why A should not be permitted to assign the right. Courts generally so hold.

Form of Assignment No set form is necessary in the assignment of a chose-in-action. Any statement, whether made orally or in writing, if it indicates an intention of the assignor to pass his interest in the chose-in-action, is sufficient. Even though the claim is evidenced by some document, such as a written contract, a note, or an insurance policy, its delivery is not essential in completing the assignment. An agreement to transfer a chose-in-action in the future must be supported by consideration. Consideration is not essential for an executed assignment, particularly if the assignment is accompanied by the delivery of a document evidencing the claim.

Partial Assignment.—A partial assignment of a chose-in-action is not operative at law. Courts in reaching this conclusion proceed upon the theory that the obligor by entering into the transaction did not intend, and should not be compelled, to answer several creditors for the same obligation. In equity, however, a partial assignment is enforcible. The chancellor, possessing more flexible remedies, can see to it that the debtor is not inconvenienced or harassed by several different actions. If a partial assignee appears demanding enforcement of his claim, the chancellor will, before proceeding further, summon all other assignees, and settle the whole matter as one transaction.

Notice of Assignment to Obligor.—As between the assignor and the assignee, notice to the obligor is not necessary to complete the assignment. There are situations, however, in which the assignee must give notice of the assignment to the obligor if he wishes to protect himself. In the first place, a settlement between the obligor and assignor will discharge the obligor if made by the latter in good faith, without knowledge of the assignment. In this event, the only recourse of the assignee is against his assignor. In the second place, the obligee may make a second assignment of the same claim. In this situation, many courts give priority, not to the first assignee, but to the assignee who first gives notice of the assignment to the obligor. Other courts, however, take the view that an assignor, having made a valid assignment, has nothing left which he can transfer to the second assignee.

Effect of Assignment

What Assignee Acquires by Assignment.—An assignee succeeds to the rights which his assignor has against the obligor but acquires no greater rights. The obligor may, in an action by the assignee against him, interpose any defense growing out of the transaction which he could have interposed if the assignor were suing. If the assignor induces the obligor by fraud to enter into an agreement, the obligor can avoid the obligation as well against the assignee as against the assignor.

Assignment Imposes No Burdens on Assignee.—The assignment of rights under a contract does not relieve the assignor of his duties to the obligor. The assignee by accepting the assignment does not incur the duties which rested upon the assignor. If he does assume those duties with the assent of the obligor, the transaction is not an assignment, but a novation: a substitution of one person for another in the contract with the consent of all concerned. The fact that the assignor not only assigns his rights but delegates his duties to the assignee does not impose the duties on the assignee. If the assignee fails to perform them, the obligor's recourse is against the assignor and not against the assignee.

Performance and Breach

Construction of Language Promises, generally speaking, are made to be performed and not to be broken. If, however, A fails to perform his promise, courts do what they can to force him to perform or to indemnify B for the loss caused by A's default. Whether A voluntarily performs or whether B is forced to seek the aid of courts, it is important to know what is involved in the performance of a promise.

The term "performance" is used in two different senses, each of which must be kept in mind. A promises to convey Blackacre to B in consideration of B's promise to pay $5,000 for the conveyance. In the first place, what must A do in the performance of his promise so that he can call upon B for the performance of his promise? In the second place, what must A do in the performance of his promise so that

the promise is discharged and so that he is not answerable to B in damages? The former issue relates to conditions in contract; the latter, to breach of promise.

Necessity for Construction of Promises.—Whether the issue in a given case relates to the fulfillment of conditions or to the performance of the promise, the language of the promise must first be construed. A promise may, of course, be so precise and unequivocal that all reasonable persons agree as to the scope of its obligation. Frequently, however, the promise is vague and ambiguous. In this event, the promise cannot be enforced until a court construes the language and gives it a definite meaning. Although courts commonly say they will not remake agreements for parties, they must in many cases place a more or less arbitrary construction on the language of the parties which may or may not represent their intentions. If courts really refused to enforce all agreements about the meaning of which there is difference of opinion, a surprisingly large number of agreements would fail of enforcement. It is more important to enforce agreements in accord with the probable intention of the parties than to insist upon complete unanimity, which is after all humanly impossible.

Rules of Construction.—In view of what has been said, it is natural that the courts should have worked out many rules of construction as aids in reaching the objective meaning of the language used by the parties. Some of these rules may be examined to illustrate the problem involved and the manner in which the courts deal with it.

Expressed intention prevails over secret: In construing an agreement, courts are seeking to arrive at the probable intention of the parties in using certain language. It should be remembered, however, that courts are not so much interested in what the parties actually intend as in what they seem to intend. It is not the secret intention which governs, but the expressed intention. In *Brewington* v. *Meesor* the court says:

It is probable under all the circumstances that the defendant intended to buy other presses than those delivered by the plaintiff, but there is nothing in the correspondence to show conclusively that the plaintiff was aware of the fact. The meeting of the minds which is essential to the formation of a contract is not determined by the secret intention of the parties but by their expressed intention, which may be wholly at variance with the former.

Agreement must be construed as a whole: When the parties have entered into a written agreement, all the writing must be considered in determining the meaning of a agreement. It would be improper for a court to put a construction on an agreement without giving due weight to every part of the writing. If the agreement is partly written and partly oral, not only all the writing but all that was said must be considered. The same principles apply when the agreement is oral. A court is not justified in ignoring the time, place, circumstances, or any of the words used by the parties in reaching what they supposed to be an enforcible agreement.

Contradictions appearing in language: The general rule that the court must give full effect to all portions of a written agreement cannot be applied when an irreconcilable conflict exists between different parts of the writing. The general rule being inapplicable, courts must resort to other rules. For instance, "when a contract contains two repugnant provisions, the one printed and the other written, it is well settled that the latter must control the interpretation of the instrument, as it is presumed to express the latest intention of the parties." On the same theory, portions of the document in typewriting prevail over printed matter, and portions in longhand, over matters in typewriting. This principle frequently is applied in cases in which there is a conflict between a statement in the letterhead and a statement in the written portion of a letter. "The words in writing will control, because they are the immediate language and terms selected by the parties themselves for the expression of their meaning."

When an instrument contains two statements inconsistent with each other, the one general and the other particular, prima facie the particular will prevail over the general. This rule is "based on the fact in human experience that usually the minds of parties are addressed specially to the particularization, and that the generalities, though broad enough to comprehend other fields, if they stood alone, are used in contemplation of that upon which the minds of the parties are centered."

If a writing contains two inconsistent statements, one accurate and the other inaccurate, courts give effect to the

accurate statement if it can be verified by competent evidence. A offered to sell his interest "in Chicago lots" to the plaintiff. In a later communication in the negotiations, he stated that seven lots were involved in the transaction. As a matter of fact, he owned an interest in only five lots. He contended that, since there was an ambiguity in the agreement, it could not be enforced. The court, holding that the agreement would be enforced as to the lots in which he did have an interest, said:

When there are two descriptions in an instrument, one of which describes the subject matter with reasonable certainty, and the other giving some additional particular is incorrect, the incorrect particulars or circumstances will be rejected as surplusage.

When an ambiguous agreement is susceptible of two constructions, one of which is legal and the other illegal, courts adopt the legal construction. This rule is based upon the hypothesis that the parties must have intended to do a legal rather than an illegal thing. The same principle is applicable to an agreement capable of two different constructions, one of which is reasonable and the other unreasonable. Courts assume that the parties intended to do a reasonable rather than an unreasonable thing.

Language construed most strongly against person using it: When other aids fail, courts construe the agreement most strongly against the person responsible for the ambiguous language. The theory of this is that a person, in drafting a contract, ought to use such language that there can be no doubt as to its meaning and that, if he has failed in this, he cannot complain if a construction unfavorable to him is placed upon his language. A and B entered into an agreement by which A was given the exclusive right in certain territory to sell "automobiles" manufactured by the defendant. Later, B began to sell taxicabs in the same territory. This, A contended, was a violation of the agreement. The defendant replied that he intended to give the plaintiff merely the right to sell automobiles, and not taxicabs. The court thought that there was no doubt but that the term "automobiles" included "taxicabs" but held, assuming there was doubt as to the meaning of the term, that the doubt should be resolved against the defendant who drew the contract.

Parol Evidence Rule.—An extremely important doctrine limiting the power of courts to discover the meaning of an agreement is the *parol evidence rule.* When the parties have reduced their agreement to a final written form, apparently unambiguous, the courts will not receive extrinsic evidence, the import of which is to vary or modify the fair effect of the written document. In other words, all evidence of the agreement outside the written document, although it may be logically relevant, is legally irrelevant. In *Century Electric Co.* v. *Detroit Brass Co.* the parties entered into a written contract for the sale and purchase of brass rods, to be manufactured of certain ingredients. The buyer brought an action to recover back the purchase price on the ground that the rods were so hard that they could not be cut by an automatic screw machine. He offered evidence to show that in their negotiations it had been orally agreed that the rods would be made so that they could be cut by machine. The court refused to receive the evidence, since it would add a term to the contract which did not appear in the written document.

What is the rationale of a rule which prevents a party from offering evidence relevant to the terms of an agreement? In the case just cited the court says that "the rule, that all previous negotiations are merged into the written agreement and that parol evidence to modify it is incompetent, rests upon the conclusive presumption that the parties have written into it every material term and item of their agreement." This, obviously enough, is but another way of saying that courts will not receive extrinsic evidence to vary the terms of an unambiguous written contract. The justification of the rule is that it is only by excluding extrinsic evidence that written agreements are secured against the fallibility of human memory and the temptation of adversaries to prove agreements by perjury. The rule is "essential to the maintenance of that certainty in human dealings, without which commerce degenerates into chicanery, and trade becomes another name for trickery."

The parol evidence rule does not preclude proof of an agreement, made subsequently to the execution of the written document, which modifies or discharges it. It merely excludes evidence of agreements, made prior to or contemporaneous with the execution of the written document, the effect of which is to show that the agreement is something other than what it appears in the writing to be. The rule does not preclude extrinsic evidence by one party to prove he was induced by fraud or duress to enter into the agreement. Nor does it preclude one of the parties from showing that typographical or clerical errors were made in the reduction of the agreement to writing.

The doctrine does not prohibit resort to extrinsic evidence to aid courts in placing an accurate, objective construction on an agreement. It is well settled that courts will receive such evidence to explain latent ambiguities in a written document. "A latent ambiguity," says one court, "is one where the writing upon its face appears clear and unambiguous, but where there is some collateral matter which may be raised by extrinsic evidence making the meaning uncertain; and the ambiguity being raised by extrinsic evidence, the same kind of evidence is admitted to remove it." In *Evans* v. *Gerry* the parties entered into a written contract for the exchange of properties. In the document one of the tracts was described as a certain lot in "block 75 in Highland Park as per a recorded plat." This was a clear and unambiguous statement. Extrinsic evidence, however, disclosed that there was no such block in the original plat. The court thereupon received extrinsic evidence to show that there was a block by that number in an addition to the original plat, "not to change the contract but to apply its provisions to certain property."

It is commonly said that courts will not receive extrinsic evidence to explain patent ambiguities—ambiguities which appear on the face of the instrument. In *Payne* v. *Commercial Bank* the defendant gave a check in which the amount in one place was stated as $5.00 and in another as $500. The court refused to hear any extrinsic evidence as to what amount was intended by the parties. All courts agree, however, that when an ambiguity appears on the face of an instrument they "will endeavor to place themselves in the position of the contracting parties, and read the instrument in the light of the circumstances surrounding them at the time it was made and of the objects which they then evidently had in view, so that they may understand the language in the sense intended by the parties using it." In *Armstrong Paint Co.* v. *Continental Can Co.* the defendant agreed to sell and the plaintiffs to buy "a minimum of $2,000 worth of tin cans or more, as *required* by them [at stated prices], which the buyers will need in their business" for the ensuing year. In a controversy between the parties, the defendant contended that the plaintiffs had been guilty of a breach of the contract because they had bought cans during the year from other manufacturers. The court, stating that the word "required" might mean one of several things, received evidence to show that the defendant knew when the written contract was made that plaintiffs had similar contracts with other manufacturers and decided that the fair construction of the agreement was that the plaintiffs were to buy at least $2,000 worth of cans from defendant and such other cans as they might wish to order from the defendant.

Courts will not receive parol evidence to give to a word or a phrase, having a fixed meaning, a meaning different from its ordinary meaning. They will, however, receive extrinsic evidence to explain a word or a phrase which does not have a fixed meaning or about the meaning of which there is doubt. They will not receive parol evidence to give to a technical word a meaning different from its technical meaning, although they will receive such evidence to translate the technical meaning into a popular meaning.

Order of Performance Having arrived at the probable meaning of the promise, is not the task of the court simply that of enforcing the promise as made and construed? This is true in general terms, and yet the task is not so simple as it at first appears. When a person has made a promise, the court has the task, not only of deciding what the language means, but also of determining whether the promise is absolute or conditional: whether the promisor has undertaken absolutely to do a thing at a certain time, whether he has undertaken to do it upon the happening or non-happening of an uncertain event, or whether he has undertaken to do it only when the promisee does something.

Condition Defined.—A promise which is not absolute is conditional. Anything in a promise, whether placed there by the parties or by the courts, which modifies the absolute character of the undertaking of the promisor is a condition. More specifically, a condition is an event upon the happening or non-happening of which the time and order of performance of the promise depend. A promises B $1,000 when the World

War ends. The end of the World War is an event which must occur before the promise of *A* can be enforced and is therefore a condition.

A promise is an undertaking of a person that he will do or refrain from doing a given act. A condition is an event the happening or non-happening of which determines when and how the undertaking will be carried out. *A* promises to pay *B* $1,000 when he is able. The undertaking to pay the money is a promise. The statement that the money will be paid when the promisor is able is a condition. *A* does not promise that he will ever become able; he simply promises to pay if he ever becomes able.

The promisor may in a given case undertake to bring about the happening of an event upon which the performance of the promise depends. *A* may say, "I will pay you $1,000 when I am able, and I will do all in my power to render myself able to pay." The ability to pay still is a condition which determines when *A* must perform. The statement, however, is also a promise in that *A* has undertaken to bring about the event. "Such a condition," says one writer, "might be defined as a promissory condition."

Frequently courts hold that a thing which appears to be merely a condition is also a promise. In *Dupont Powder Company* v. *Schlottman* the Powder Company contracted to purchase the capital stock of the Pittsburgh Fuse Company for $175,000. It promised the vendor an additional $25,000 "after we have had the property for a year, if in my judgment the property has for any reason been worth $175,000 to our company." Six months later the Dupont Company sold the property. In an action for the additional compensation, the court held that the plaintiff was entitled to recover. Operation of the plant for one year would seem to have been merely a condition which would determine whether the vendee would ever be obligated to pay the additional amount. The court, admitting that there was no express promise of the Dupont Company to operate the plant for any length of time, felt that under the circumstances a promise to operate it for a year ought to be implied.

Classification of Conditions.—Conditions are variously classified. A brief consideration of these classifications will help one to appreciate the nature and operation of conditions.

Conditions classified as to origin: In terms of origin, conditions are classified as express conditions, conditions implied in fact, and conditions implied in law. An express condition is one which the parties have in so many words incorporated into their agreement.

A condition implied in fact is one which the parties must have had in mind when they entered into the contract, although they did not express it in words. *A*, in consideration of *B*'s promise to receive and pay for certain goods, agrees to manufacture them for *B* as he needs them. Nothing in the agreement indicates that *B* is to give *A* notice of his needs. It is obvious, however, that the agreement cannot be carried out unless *B* does give *A* such notice. Under the circumstances it is reasonable to infer as a matter of fact that notice by *B* of his needs is a condition determining the time of performance by *A*.

A condition implied in law is one which courts read into an agreement to effect a more equitable relation between the parties as to a matter for which the parties have not made provision. *A* agrees to convey Blackacre to *B* on January 1. *B* agrees to receive the conveyance and pay the purchase price on the same day. There is nothing in the agreement indicating that the performance of one of these promises is conditional upon the performance of the other. *A* might, so far as the agreement is concerned, bring an action on January 2 for the purchase price without having conveyed Blackacre or tendered a conveyance. Courts, to prevent injustice likely to arise from the situation, say that it is a condition in the contract that *A* shall perform or tender performance before he may call upon *B* for performance.

Conditions classified as to operation: In terms of their operation, conditions are precedent, concurrent, or subsequent. A condition precedent is one in which the event must or must not happen, as the case may be, before the obligation of the promisor becomes fixed and absolute. *A*, in consideration of *B*'s promise to sell him Blackacre, agrees to receive the conveyance and pay the purchase price if and when he can dispose of Whiteacre. *A*'s disposition of Whiteacre is a condition precedent in that the event in question must come to pass before *A*'s obligation is fixed.

Conditions concurrent are those which in legal contemplation are to be fulfilled simultaneously. *A* agrees to convey Blackacre to *B* on January 1, in consideration of *B*'s promise to receive the conveyance and pay the purchase price on that day. The delivery of the deed and the payment of the purchase price theoretically are concurrent acts. If the parties actually perform their agreement as made, the operations presumably will be concurrent. If, however, either is compelled to seek legal relief, a different situation exists. Before either is entitled to relief, he must allege and prove as a condition precedent that he has performed or tendered performance.

A condition subsequent is said to be an event the happening or non-happening of which terminates a liability previously incurred. An illustration of this type of condition may be taken from property law. *A* conveys 100 acres of land to the University of Chicago with the provision that the land shall revert to his heirs if the University ceases to use it for educational purposes. The cessation of the use of the property for educational purposes is a condition and operates to terminate an estate previously granted.

Writers disagree as to whether in contracts there can be found a true condition subsequent. Although many conditions may be found which appear subsequent in form, most of them really are conditions precedent. An insurance policy provides for the payment of any loss caused by fire, provided action is brought on the policy for the loss within two years after its occurrence. On the theory that this provision is a condition subsequent, the liability of the insurer becomes fixed upon the happening of the fire, but the liability is terminated by the failure of the insured to bring action within two years. Some writers, however, contend that even in this situation the bringing of action within two years is a condition precedent to the absolute liability of the insurer.

Effect of Nonfulfilment of Conditions.—The performance of a promise may be conditioned upon the happening of an event over which neither party has control or upon the doing of something by the promisee. Nonfulfilment of a condition therefore occurs either if the event fails to happen or if the promisee fails to do that which he is supposed to do. What, now, is the effect of the nonfulfilment of a condition? Clearly, it does not entitle the person against whom it operates to bring an action for damages. An action for damages can be brought only for a breach of promise. Nonfulfilment of a condition merely entitles the person against whom it operates to withdraw from the contract. *A* agrees to insure *B*'s house for *B*'s promise to pay premiums. The contract provides that it shall be void if *B* keeps gasoline on the premises. *B*'s failure to pay premiums is a breach of promise, entitling *A* to recover damages. *B*'s keeping gasoline on the premises is a breach of condition. It does not entitle *A* to recover damages from *B* but merely entitles him to treat the contract as at an end.

Waiver of Nonfulfilment of Conditions.—Conditions are incorporated into contracts either because the parties desire them or because courts think they are necessary more fully to do justice between the parties. It follows that, unless the parties themselves insist upon strict observance of conditions, courts will not require all of them. In other words, a party entitled to treat an agreement as at an end because of the nonfulfilment of a condition may refuse to exercise his privilege and permit the contract to continue in existence. In the situation discussed in the preceding section, the insurer may refuse to exercise his privilege of terminating the agreement because *B* keeps gasoline on the premises. He may in other words waive the nonfulfilment or breach of a condition.

A waiver may be express, or it may be implied. It is express if the party against whom it operates declares in so many words his intention not to take advantage of the privilege to terminate the agreement. It is implied if his intention not to terminate the agreement can be inferred from circumstances. If the insurer, with knowledge that the insured is keeping gasoline on the premises in violation of the contract, continues to receive premiums from *B*, there is sufficient evidence to justify an inference that he has waived the nonfulfilment of the condition.

Express Conditions It generally is said that courts will enforce express conditions strictly because the parties have incorporated them into their agreement in express terms. However, this rule is applicable only after the court has decided what the language of the condition means.

A agrees to repair boilers for *B* in consideration of *B*'s promise to pay for the work when he is "satisfied that the boilers as changed are a success." *A* agrees to make a suit of clothes for *B*, for which *B* agrees to pay if he is satisfied with it. It is clear that there is in each case an express condition

which modifies the undertaking of the promisor. In each of the cases, however, the only question of difficulty is in determining just what is meant by "satisfaction." Does *B* have to be honestly satisfied? Does he have to be reasonably satisfied? Is he bound if a reasonable person would have been satisfied? In the first place, all courts agree that in cases of this kind the promisor cannot escape his obligation by a dishonest expression of dissatisfaction. He must in any event act in good faith.

In the second place, if the object of the agreement is to gratify taste, serve personal convenience, or satisfy individual preference, courts hold that the condition is not fulfilled unless the promisor is personally satisfied, regardless of how fanciful and unreasonable he may be in his likes and dislikes. In *Brown* v. *Foster* the plaintiff agreed to make a suit to the satisfaction of the defendant. In an action by the plaintiff for the price of the clothes, the court held that the judgment of the defendant that he was not satisfied was final, provided his expression of dissatisfaction was honest.

In the third place, if the thing to be done is of a routine, ministerial, or mechanical character, courts hold that the promisee will have to be satisfied if a reasonable person would have been satisfied with the performance of the promise. In *Duplex Safety Boiler Co.* v. *Garden* in which the plaintiff promised to repair boilers to the satisfaction of the defendant, the court said, in an action by the plaintiff for his compensation, that "that which the law will say a contracting party ought in reason to be satisfied with, that the law will say he is satisfied with."

Another group of cases illustrating the operation of express conditions relates to the production of architects' certificates in building contracts. *A* agrees to erect a building for *B* according to certain specifications. *B* agrees to pay for the work upon the production by *A* of the certificate of an architect that the work has been done according to specifications. It is clear that the production by *A* of the certificate is a condition precedent to *B*'s liability to pay for the work. But it is not clear what the condition means. What if the architect in collusion with the owner of the building withholds the certificate? What if the architect acts fraudulently in withholding it? What if he acts honestly but unreasonably in withholding it? What if he acts honestly and reasonably in withholding it? All courts agree that the contractor is under no obligation to produce the certificate if the architect and owner of the building collude to withhold it. Most American courts hold that he is under no obligation to produce it if the architect acts unreasonably, although honestly, in withholding it. The decisions undoubtedly do substantial justice between the parties, but it is obvious that the court is reading something into the condition which the parties did not place there. The contractor says: "I understand I get no compensation unless I produce the architect's certificate." Courts add: "... provided the architect acts reasonably and fairly in withholding the certificate."

Conditions Implied in Law A condition implied in law is one read into the contract by the courts. Just why courts should assume the responsibility of modifying an otherwise absolute undertaking of a party is a question which is not always easy to answer. At times courts undoubtedly read implied conditions into contracts because of a belief or custom of the community with respect to their desirability. In such cases the courts attempt, perhaps unconsciously, to effect a more equitable relationship between the parties as to some aspect of the contract which they did not provide for in so many words. It is clear, in any event, that an implied condition may or may not be based upon the intention of the parties.

For the most part conditions implied in law relate to the order of performance of mutual promises. *A* agrees to convey Blackacre to *B* on January 1. *B* agrees to pay $5,000 for the conveyance on that day. The parties have not expressly indicated whether the performance of one of these promises is dependent upon the performance of the other. Are the two undertakings mutually dependent? Is each independent of the other? Is one dependent and the other independent? May *A* call upon *B* for the purchase price without performing or tendering performance?

Rules Determining Conditions Implied in Law.—The parties may, as indeed they frequently do, expressly stipulate that one promise shall be dependent or independent. If they do, no difficulty is encountered in determining the order of performance beyond construing the language employed. Many situations, however, arise in which the parties have not

clearly expressed their intention as to the dependence or independence of their promises. The courts have developed a series of rules applicable to typical situations, some of which will be examined.

General rule: "The question whether covenants are dependent or independent must be determined in each case upon the proper construction to be placed on the language employed by the parties to express their agreement. If the language is clear and unambiguous it must be taken according to its plain meaning as expressive of the intention of the parties, and under settled principles of judicial decision should not be controlled by the supposed inconvenience or hardship that may follow such construction. If parties think proper, they may agree that the right of one to maintain an action against another shall be conditional or dependent upon the plaintiff's performance of covenants entered into on his part. On the other hand, they may agree that the performance by one shall be a condition precedent to the performance of the other. The question in each case is, which intent is disclosed by the language employed in the contract?"

Promises given for each other are prima facie mutually dependent: Courts at one time held that promises, although each was the consideration for the other, were mutually independent unless the parties expressly made them dependent. *A* agrees to convey Blackacre to *B* on January 1. *B* agrees to pay *A* $5,000 for the conveyance on January 1. Under the early rule courts held that, since the parties had not expressly made the performance of one dependent upon the performance of the other, each was an independent undertaking. At present "the general rule is that, in the absence of clear indications to the contrary, promises, each of which forms the whole consideration for the other, will not be held to be independent of one another; and a failure of one party to perform on his part will exonerate the other from liability." By the better rule this principle is applicable even though the promises occur in separate writings.

The modern rule not only does substantial justice between the parties, in that it protects *B* against having to perform without assurance that he will get performance from *A*, but also promotes economical administration of justice, in that a controversy can be settled in one proceeding instead of two. If the promises are regarded as independent of each other, when *A* sues *B*, *B* can do nothing but pay the judgment recovered against him and bring action against *A* for his failure to convey the land. If they are regarded as mutually dependent, *A* cannot recover the purchase price without alleging and proving that he has performed or tendered performance.

When by the terms of the agreement one promise is to be performed before the other, the first is independent and the second dependent: *A* agrees to convey Blackacre to *B* on January 1. *B* agrees to pay the purchase price within ninety days after the conveyance. In this case the obligation of *A* to make the conveyance on January 1 is absolute and unconditional. *B* is clearly entitled to call upon *A* for the performance of *A*'s obligation without having to allege and prove performance or tender of performance on his part. On the other hand, *A* is not entitled to call upon *B* for the purchase price unless he proves that he has performed or tendered performance.

When one promise requires time for performance and the other does not, prima facie the first is independent and the second dependent: *A* undertakes to deliver to *B* 75,000 brick at a certain place. In performance of his undertaking he delivers 21,000 brick and demands payment for them before making further deliveries. In an action by *A* to recover for the brick delivered, the court held that *A*'s promise was entire and indivisible and that a delivery of the whole quantity of brick was a condition precedent to *B*'s liability for any of the brick.

"*When the vendee of land covenants to pay by installments, and the vendor covenants to make title upon the payment of the last installment, the covenants of the vendee to pay the installments, except the last, are independent. But the covenants of the vendee to pay the last installment and of the vendor to make title, are dependent.*" *A* agrees to sell Blackacre to *B* for $10,000, in ten monthly instalments, the deed to be delivered upon the payment of the last instalment. In this situation, the obligation of *B* to pay each of the nine instalments is absolute and unconditional. *A* may recover any of these instalments without having to prove anything by way of performance on his part. But the obligation of *B* to pay the last instalment and the obligation of *A* to make the conveyance are mutually dependent. *A* may not recover the final payment without

proving performance or tender of performance on his part. Nor is *B* entitled to a conveyance without proof of the payment or tender of the last instalment. If any or all of the previous instalments are due when the last one becomes due, *A* is not entitled to recover anything under the contract without proving performance or its tender.

In contracts of personal service, the undertaking of the employer to continue the employment is conditional upon substantial performance by the employee: Absence by an employee for a substantial period from his employment, even through no fault of his own (as because of sickness or of detention by law), is a breach of condition which entitles the employer to terminate the agreement. In *Leopold* v. *Salkey* the plaintiff entered into an agreement with the defendant by which he agreed to work for the defendant for three years as a superintendent in his business as a manufacturer of and dealer in clothes. For his services, the defendant agreed to pay him $3,000 annually, in monthly instalments. During a busy season the plaintiff was placed in jail for two weeks by the federal government. Upon being released, he offered to resume work in the defendant's plant. In the meantime, the defendant had employed someone else. In an action by the plaintiff for breach of contract, the court held that his absence in the circumstances was such a substantial breach of his promise that it went to the essence of the contract and was a breach of condition, entitling the defendant to terminate the agreement. In such a case, it is a question of fact whether the absence of the employee is so serious that it constitutes a breach of condition. This must be answered in terms of the "nature and necessities of the business in which the servant is employed."

In contracts in which the obligation of one is to be performed in instalments, the obligation of the other is dependent upon substantial performance of each instalment: In *Norrington* v. *Wright* the plaintiff sold to the defendant 5,000 tons of iron rails to be delivered at the rate of about 1,000 tons a month, with the understanding that slight deficiencies in performance might be made up in the sixth month. During the first month the plaintiff shipped only 400 tons and during the second month only 885 tons. Upon learning the facts, the defendant gave notice that he would receive no further shipments under the contract. The plaintiff brought action for breach of contract. The court gave judgment for the defendant, holding that substantial performance of each instalment by the plaintiff was a condition precedent to the obligation of the defendant to continue to receive shipments.

This principle also applies in divisible contracts when the party who is to pay money in instalments defaults in the payment of an instalment. The obligation of the promisor to deliver goods or perform services in these cases is dependent upon substantial performance by the other party in the payment of the money in the amount and at the time promised.

In every contract it is a condition that neither party, before the time set for performance, will announce that he will not perform: *A* engages *B* as a guide, his services to begin at a future date. Before the time set for performance arrives, *A* notifies *B* that his services will not be required. Is *B* under the necessity of waiting until the time set for performance and seeing what *A* then does? By the well-settled rule *B* may, if he desires, terminate the agreement immediately. Courts read into the agreement the condition that *A* shall not disturb the contractual relation by announcing in advance that he will not perform. *B*, however, is under no duty to accept the breach of condition. He may wait and insist that the other party perform. In this event the contract continues in existence, but it continues for both alike. Until the injured party has accepted the breach of condition and terminated the agreement, the wrongdoer is entitled to change his mind. If he changes his mind before the other has accepted the breach, it is then too late for the other to take advantage of it.

Sufficiency of Performance in Fulfilment of Conditions

When the performance of *B*'s promise is dependent upon the performance of *A*'s promise, how far must *A* perform before he may call upon *B* for the performance of his promise? Must *A* perform literally, or may he call upon *B* for performance if he has substantially performed?

Time of Performance.—*A*'s promise, when it does not indicate the time of performance, must be performed within a reasonable length of time after it is given. What constitutes a reasonable length of time is a question of fact which must be answered in the light of all the circumstances. His promise, when it does indicate the time of performance, must be performed at the time indicated.

It does not follow, however, in determining whether *A* has performed his promise sufficiently to call upon *B* for performance, that in all cases *A* must perform within the time required by the promise. Under the early cases, time apparently was of the essence of all agreements. In the modern view, however, this is not, generally speaking, true. Failure of *A* to perform within the time stated is a breach of promise, entitling *B* to damages for the delay, but it is not a breach of condition, justifying *B* in terminating the agreement.

One may, of course, stipulate that time shall be of the essence of an agreement. In this event, performance within the time stated is a condition precedent to the right of one party to call for the performance of the other. Circumstances may be such as to justify a court in holding that time is of the essence of an agreement, even though not expressly made so, as where *A* promises to convey a house to *B* for his personal occupancy and to give him possession within sixty days. All courts agree that time is of the essence of contracts of merchants. Their storage facilities, their contracts with customers, the necessity for rapid turnovers in the making of profits require that a contract for the sale and purchase of goods be performed at the time agreed upon. Delay by the seller in delivering goods to a buyer in performance of an agreement justifies the buyer in terminating the agreement and in seeking goods elsewhere. In any case, if the delay of one party is so prolonged as to defeat the main purpose of the agreement, the other is justified in terminating it.

Substantial Performance.—*A*, in consideration of *B*'s promise to pay him $11,700, promises to do the masonry work, according to certain specifications, on two buildings being erected by *B*. *A* attempts in good faith to comply with the terms of the agreement and does substantially comply with them. There are, however, defects in *A*'s performance to the extent of about $200. In this situation, there are three possible modes of adjusting the controversy between *A* and *B*. In the first place, it may be held, as the early courts held, that strict performance of the promise by *A* is a condition precedent to his right to recover anything under the contract. In this event, *A* could recover nothing for the benefits which he conferred upon *B*. In the second place, *A* may be permitted in quasi-contract to recover the reasonable value of the benefits in question. This is the logical view of the situation, and a few courts follow it. In the third place, *A* may be permitted to recover on the contract, less such amount as will compensate *B* for the defects in performance. This view is taken by a majority of courts in cases in which a person has in good faith substantially performed his promise.

The doctrine of substantial performance is applied to contracts by which one person promises to manufacture a chattel for the special use of the buyer. The court in the case just cited said that it was "prepared to hold that the doctrine of substantial performance applies not only to building contracts; but to all contracts for the construction of chattels according to plans and specifications for a special use." Likewise, in contracts for services, substantial performance by an employee entitles him to recover on the contract, less such damages as the employer has suffered by reason of imperfect performance. The courts generally have refused to apply this doctrine to a sale of goods by description when they are not manufactured for a special use. In these cases, the seller's furnishing the article described is a condition precedent to the liability of the buyer to pay the purchase price.

Whether a person has substantially performed so that he can maintain his action against the promisor on his promise is a question of fact for the jury under the instructions of the court. If the deficiencies are such as to defeat the main purpose of the contract, the person has not substantially performed. Nor is his performance substantial within the meaning of the doctrine if the deficiencies are the result of wilfulness or negligence. He must attempt in good faith to comply with the terms of the agreement and must actually comply with them in substance.

Tender of Performance.—Tender of performance is the promisor's expression of willingness to do that which he agreed to do and present ability to do it. Generally speaking, a tender of performance by a promisor is not the equivalent of performance in discharging the promise. When, however, the performance of *A*'s promise is dependent upon the performance of *B*'s promise, a tender of performance by *B* is the equivalent of a performance insofar as it entitles *B* to call upon *A* for the performance of his promise. *B*, in consideration of *A*'s promise to convey Blackacre to him, promises to pay *A* $5,000 for the conveyance on January 1. *B*'s tender

of $5,000 on January 1 entitles him to call upon *A* for a conveyance of Blackacre but does not discharge his promise to pay the purchase price agreed upon.

Failure of Performance as Breach of Promise

Right and Power To Break Promise.—"Either party to a contract, however solemn in its character or binding its form, has the power to violate it, and courts of law give no redress to him who is injured except compensatory damages; but it is not accurate in law or in morals to say that a party has a right to break his contract. It would be to assert that it is legally right to do what is legally wrong. A person bound by contract to do or not to do a thing may find it to his advantage not to keep his engagements, for the mere obligation may be more onerous than the damages likely to be imposed for its breach, but the violation of the contract cannot be regarded as a contractual right. One party may notify the other party to the contract that he will proceed no further in its execution, and then it is for such party to accept the situation and terminate all relations, sue for the breach, or negotiate other terms for the performance of the duties imposed by the violated contract."

Breach of Promise.—A breach of condition, as has been seen, entitles the person against whom it operates to terminate the agreement, but it gives rise to no cause of action for damages unless it is also a breach of promise. A breach of promise, on the other hand, gives rise to a cause of action for damages in favor of the promisee, but it does not justify him in terminating the agreement unless the breach is so far-reaching that it goes to the essence of the contract, in which event it is a breach of condition as well as a breach of promise.

Breach may be failure to perform: Any failure of the promisor to perform his promise as construed by the court is a breach of promise, giving rise to an action for damages in favor of the promisee. In *Nolan* v. *Whitney* cited above, the contractor so far performed his promise as to be able to call upon the defendant for the contract price of his services, but slight deficiencies in his performance rendered him liable to the defendant for a breach of promise. To escape liability for a breach of promise the promisor must perform at the precise time agreed upon and must strictly comply with all terms of the agreement.

Tender of performance, generally speaking, does not discharge the promisor. If *A* has performed his obligation under a bilateral agreement and *B* has not, a valid tender of performance by *B* is the equivalent of performance, except in cases in which his obligation is one to pay money. In this event, a valid tender of the amount due stops the accrual of interest from that time forward and imposes upon the creditor the duty to pay the costs of the litigation if, refusing to accept the tender, he brings action on the claim. The tender, however, does not discharge the debt.

Breach may consist in repudiation by promisor: The promisor may announce to the promisee that he will not perform. This is a repudiation and is as much a breach of promise as if the promisor had failed utterly to perform. It may take place during performance or before performance has begun.

A is under contract with *B* to repair *B*'s property. After *A* begins work, *B* notifies him to cease. This constitutes a breach of promise. *A* is entitled immediately to bring action for damages suffered by reason of the breach. May *A* continue the work in spite of *B*'s renunciation? As a general rule, he may not but must accept the breach. *A* is not permitted to enhance damages by proceeding with performance after the promisor has changed his mind, when he might, from the point of view of society, be more profitably engaged in some other activity. Of course, if the promisee cannot secure other work in the meantime, that fact is taken into consideration in determining the damages to which he is entitled for the breach.

The promisor may, before the time set for performance arrives, inform the promisee that he does not intend to perform. In *O'Neil* v. *Supreme Council, American Legion of Honor*, cited above, the defendant, in consideration of the payment of premiums by the plaintiff, promised to pay to a designated beneficiary $5,000 upon the death of the plaintiff. Subsequently the defendant notified the plaintiff that it would not pay the money to his beneficiary upon his death. Previously it was pointed out that there is in every contract a condition implied in law that the promisor must not, before the time for performance, announce that he will not perform. Such an announcement entitles the promisee immediately to treat the contract as at an end. After the announcement the promisee is under no obligation to hold himself in readiness to perform. Is there also a breach of contract which entitles the promisee immediately to bring action for damages? Has the defendant in the case cited broken his promise? He agreed to pay money upon the death of the plaintiff. How can there be a breach of that promise until after the death of the plaintiff? The courts in practically all jurisdictions hold that the promisee is entitled not only to treat the contract as at an end but also to bring action at once for damages. It has been said, in explanation of this rule, generally described as the *doctrine of anticipatory breach*, that the promisor not only expressly promises to perform at a future date but also impliedly promises that he will not in the meantime announce that he will not perform. Whatever may be the explanation of the doctrine, the rule which permits the promisee to bring his action immediately is both just and convenient. Certainly "the man who wrongfully renounces a contract into which he has deliberately entered, cannot justly complain if he is immediately sued for a compensation in damages by the man whom he has injured."

The promisee cannot treat the statement of the promisor as a repudiation unless it is absolute and unconditional. "A mere assertion that the party will be unable, or will refuse to perform his contract, is not sufficient; it must be a distinct and absolute refusal to perform the promise, and must be treated and acted upon as such by the party to whom the promise was made."

Assuming that the promisor has unequivocally announced his intention not to perform, must the promisee accept the breach? He may refuse to do so and insist that the promisor perform. In this event, the contract remains in existence, but it remains in existence for the promisor as well as for the promisee. If circumstances arise which make it profitable for the promisor to change his mind, he may do so, provided he acts before the promisee has accepted the breach.

However, a promisee who has refused to accept an anticipatory breach is not permitted to enhance damages by making preparations for performance. Indeed, he is under a positive duty to mitigate damages by making a reasonable effort to get other employment. *A* agrees to serve *B*, the employment to begin January 1. On December 1, the defendant announces that he will not perform. The promisee, even though he is unwilling to accept the breach, is not permitted to expend time and money during the month of December making preparations for performance. Furthermore, he must seek other employment in mitigation of the damages caused by the breach.

What constitutes an acceptance of the breach? Clearly, the bringing of an action at once is an acceptance of the breach. The fact that the promisee enters into a similar contract with another person is strong, if not conclusive, evidence that he has accepted the breach. By the better rule, an unequivocal statement by the promisee that he regards the contract as at an end, even though he does not bring action or change his position, is sufficient evidence to prove an acceptance of the breach.

Waiver of Breach of Promise.—A breach of promise entitles the promisee to bring action for damages. The breach may be so serious and far-reaching that it constitutes a breach of condition, entitling the promisee to treat the contract as at an end. A promisee may waive a breach of promise as well as a breach of condition. The waiver may be express or implied. It is express if the promisee in so many words declares an intention not to sue for the breach. It is implied if from the circumstances it fairly can be inferred that it is not the intention of the promisee to sue for damages. Courts say that the conduct of the promisee, to constitute a waiver, must be such that it is inconsistent with any intent on his part to insist upon full performance of the undertaking of the promisor. The mere fact that the promisee does not terminate the contract, when the breach is so serious as to constitute a breach of condition, is not enough evidence to warrant the inference that he has waived his rights to damages. Mere delay on the part of the promisee in bringing his action for damages is not a waiver.

Excuses for Nonperformance of Promises

General Rule.—The general rule is that the risk of impossibility of performance of a promise, arising after the promise has been made, rests upon the promisor. An enforcible promise is essentially an insurance contract—a contract that a certain thing shall be done or that damages will be forthcoming if the thing is not done. The business of

the world could not be carried on if promisors were permitted to escape the consequences of their promises by showing hardship or impossibility of performance. In *Berg* v. *Erickson* the defendant in April entered into an agreement with the plaintiff by which he agreed to furnish grass and water for 1,000 head of cattle, for which the plaintiff agreed to pay the defendant $7,000. As a result of an unprecedented drought, no rain falling from May until September, the defendant was unable to perform his promise. In an action by the plaintiff for damages, the defendant contended that he was excused from performance because of impossibility caused by an act of God. The court applied the general rule that "one who makes a positive agreement to do a lawful act is not absolved from liability for a failure to fulfill his covenant by a subsequent impossibility of performance caused by an act of God, or an unavoidable accident, because he voluntarily contracts to perform it without any reservation or exception."

Exceptions to General Rule.—There are important exceptions to the general rule that the promisor assumes the risk of being unable to perform. In relieving the promisor from the absolute character of his undertaking, courts are remaking the agreement of the parties. In doing so, they proceed upon some more or less vague principle of justice that, on the whole, in these exceptional situations, the risk of impossibility of performance arising after the contract has been made, ought not to be placed upon the promisor.

Performance rendered impossible by promisee: The promisor is always excused from the performance of his promise if the promisee has made its performance impossible. The justification for this exception is clear enough. In *St. John* v. *St. John* the defendant promised $1,000 to a daughter-in-law for her undertaking to make a home for him. This she did until he remarried and went elsewhere to live. In an action for the amount promised, the court permitted the plaintiff to recover. She had performed as fully as she could and would have performed completely but for the fact that the defendant by his own act rendered further performance impossible.

Performance rendered impossible by law: The promisor is excused from the performance of his promise if its performance is rendered impossible by operation of domestic law. In *Greil* v. *Mabson* the plaintiff leased to the defendant space in a certain building for a term of five years "for occupation as a bar and not otherwise." Two years later Alabama prohibited the operation of bars and saloons. In an action upon promissory notes given for rent, the defendant contended that he was not liable because the state had made his performance impossible and that he had surrendered the lease. The court, holding that the defendant was excused, said that "where the act or thing contracted to be done is subsequently made unlawful by an act of the legislature, the promise is avoided."

Courts usually say, in justification of this exception, that it would be contrary to public policy to compel a person to perform a promise contrary to law. Public policy would be involved if courts really were compelling the promisor to perform. The application of the general rule to the situation would not compel him to perform but would only compel him to pay damages for his failure to perform. However this may be, the promisor is excused from the performance of his promise if its performance is rendered impossible by operation of domestic law after the promise is made.

Performance rendered impossible by sickness or death of promisor: "Contracts of this kind, *for the personal services,* whether of the contracting party or of a third person, requiring skill, and which can only be performed by the particular individual named, are not, in their nature, absolute obligations under all circumstances. Both parties must be supposed to contemplate the continuance of the ability of the person whose skilled services are the subject of the contract, as one of the conditions of the contract. Contracts for personal services are subject to this implied condition, that the person shall be able at the time appointed to perform them; and if he dies, or without fault on the part of the covenantor becomes disabled, the obligation to perform is extinguished."

This exception does not apply unless the undertaking is of personal character, under which the personal performance of the promisor is contemplated. A person who undertakes to convey land is not excused from his undertaking by reason of his sickness or death. The thing agreed to be done can easily enough be done by someone for him. Neither does it apply where the contract contemplates that the promise may be performed by someone other than the promisor, even though the undertaking is personal in nature. The exception is applicable only in situations in which the promisee might legally refuse to accept performance from anyone other than the promisor.

Performance rendered impossible by destruction of subject matter: "It is well settled, that when work is to be done under a contract on a chattel, or building which is not wholly the property of the contractor, or for which he is not solely accountable, as where repairs are to be made on the property of another, the agreement on both sides is upon the implied condition that the chattel or building shall continue in existence; and the destruction of it without the fault of either of the parties will excuse performance of the contract, and leave no right of recovery of damages in favor of either against the other." The contractor in cases of this kind may, however, recover the reasonable value of services performed before the destruction of the subject matter. On the other hand, if the contractor undertakes to erect a building or construct a chattel for another, the general rule is applicable and he must perform or pay damages if the subject matter is destroyed during its construction.

Performance made impossible by failure of particular mode of performance: If parties expressly or by implication contemplate a certain mode of performance, and if performance becomes impossible by reason of the failure of that mode, the promisor is excused from performance. *A* agrees to grow a crop of turnips for *B*. *A* is not excused from performance because the crop is destroyed by an unforeseen frost. *A* agrees to sell a crop of turnips grown on a particular piece of land. In this event, by the general rule, *A* is excused if the crop fails. The same principle has been applied to contracts to manufacture a given article. If the promisor undertakes generally to manufacture an article, he is not excused from performance merely because of the destruction of his plant. If, however, it is agreed that the article shall be manufactured at a certain plant, the continued existence of the plant is a condition precedent to the liability of the promisor.

Remedies for Breach

Promises are made to be performed and not to be broken. If a promisor fails or refuses to perform his promise, courts of law will, as best they can, compensate the promisee for the loss he sustains through the promisor's conduct; and courts of equity, within very narrow limits, will compel the promisor specifically to perform.

Remedies at Law.—The normal remedy against a promisor who has broken his promise is an action at law for damages. The problem which here chiefly requires attention relates to the nature and amount of damages to which a promisee is entitled. Damages are of three kinds: nominal, compensatory, and punitive. Nominal damages are awarded in a situation in which the promisee can show a breach of promise but is unable to show any actual loss as a result of the breach. Nominal damages are awarded to vindicate the rights of a promisee. Compensatory damages are those which are awarded a promisee to compensate him for actual losses which he has sustained by reason of the breach of promise. Punitive damages, damages in excess of actual losses, are awarded, not to compensate the promisee, but to punish the promisor in cases in which the promisor has acted maliciously or wilfully. With the exception of actions for breaches of promise to marry, which sound in tort, courts do not assess punitive damages in actions on contracts.

Compensatory damages: Courts say that the promisee must be compensated for the actual loss sustained by a breach of promise. But how can courts determine the actual loss sustained by a promisee? May the promisee claim as damages all injurious consequences, however remote, which flow from a breach of promise? Clearly not. In the leading case of *Hadley* v. *Baxendale* the court says in substance that the recoverable damages for the vindication of a contract, to which one party is entitled because of the breach by the other, are those which arise naturally from the breach or those damages which the parties, at the time of the making of the contract, may reasonably be supposed to have had in mind as a probable result of a breach. The plaintiff may not recover damages for losses which he could reasonably have avoided, since the purpose of allowing him to recover at all is to put him in the position he would have been in if the defendant had fully performed.

For the breach of a promise to sell real or personal property, the damage which, under the precedents, naturally flows from the breach is the difference between the contract price of the property and the market value at the time the contract

is to be performed. The damage which naturally flows from the breach of a contract of service is from the point of view of the employee the difference between the agreed stipend and what by reasonable effort he can earn in the meanwhile in mitigation of his loss. From the point of view of the employer, the damage is the difference between the agreed stipend and what he is required to pay to someone else for the same services.

A agreed to install a sprinkler system in B's building by May 1. The building was destroyed by fire on June 20, at which time the system had not been installed. The court held that the destruction of the building was not a natural consequence of the breach. "The measure of damage in such a case would be the increased cost of insurance caused by the absence of the sprinklers, or the loss of greater rent which could be had for a sprinklered building." Loss of rents is not a natural consequence of the breach of a promise to install an elevator in an office building.

Damages over and above the natural consequences of the breach may be recovered if special circumstances are brought to the attention of the promisor in such manner that it is fair to assume that the promisor made his promise with reference to the special circumstances. The defendant promised to sell flues to the plaintiff, agreeing to deliver them by July 1. The defendant failed to perform his promise. Ordinarily the plaintiff's damages in this event would be the difference between the contract price and what it would cost the plaintiff to procure the article at the time set for performance. Upon a showing, however, that the defendant knew that the flues were to be used by the plaintiff in curing his tobacco crop and that any delay in the curing process would result in serious damage to the tobacco, the court permitted the plaintiff to prove as special damages the deterioration in his tobacco crop caused by the delay in curing it. The plaintiff, acting as a realty broker, negotiated a contract between B and the defendant for the exchange of properties. The defendant refused to perform. Normally, the plaintiff's damages in such a situation would be the commissions which the defendant promised to pay him. The court, however, permitted the plaintiff to recover from the defendant an amount equal to the commissions promised by both B and the defendant upon proof that he informed the defendant that his right to commissions from B would depend upon an execution of the contract.

Liquidated damages: The task of estimating recoverable damages is a difficult matter even under favorable circumstances. In many situations, the task becomes particularly embarrassing. It is, therefore, well settled that the parties in drawing a contract may stipulate the amount of recoverable damages in the event of a breach. If the amount stipulated is reasonable under all the circumstances, courts will enforce the stipulation. In doing this courts do not lose sight "of the principle of compensation, which is the law of contract; but merely adopt the computation of the damages made by the parties as being the best and most certain mode of ascertaining the actual damage, or what sum will amount to just compensation."

If, however, the damages stipulated for bear no reasonable relation to the actual damages in the event of a breach, courts do not hesitate to deal with the stipulation as a penalty. "Where the stipulated sum is wholly collateral to the object of the contract, being evidently inserted as security for performance, it will not be allowed as liquidated damage." To discourage the practice of inserting stipulations of damages as penalties, statutes in many states declare that stipulations for liquidated damages are illegal except in cases in which accurate estimates of damages are difficult or impossible.

Remedies in Equity.—It commonly is said that courts of equity will compel a promisor's specifically to perform his promise in cases in which the promisee's remedy at law is inadequate. This statement, however, is not enlightening, as one must know the situations in which the remedy at law is inadequate to know the situations in which equity grants specific performance of promises.

Although courts of equity have granted specific performance in many different situations, they have granted it most commonly in the enforcement of contracts for the purchase and sale of real property. It usually is said that specific performance is necessary in these cases, because the promisee's remedy at law is inadequate. This may be true in some cases, but it is far from being true as a general rule. Courts of equity not only compel the grantor to convey the land, but some courts may also compel the grantee to accept the performance and pay the purchase price. Courts do this, as they say, to provide mutuality of remedies. This principle is applied to any agreement, one promise of which is specifically enforcible.

Courts of equity, generally speaking, do not specifically enforce promises to sell personal property. They are convinced that in these cases the remedies at law are adequate. In *Steinway* v. *Massey* the court refused to compel the defendant to sell a Steinway piano to the plaintiff. Courts of equity will, however, specifically enforce such a promise if the chattel is rare or unique, such as a painting, a family picture, or a piece of family jewelry. They will compel the assignment of patents and copyrights which are legally unique because they are monopolies. Under some circumstances, courts will decree the specific performance of a contract to sell corporate stock. In *Smurr* v. *Kamen* the court says that "if the shares are readily available in the open market, specific performance will not be decreed; but if the shares have no market value and cannot be easily obtained elsewhere, specific performance will be granted."

The granting of specific performance lies within the discretion of the court. A complainant cannot demand it as a matter of right. The chancellor of course will always refuse to enforce an illegal promise or a promise procured by fraud or duress. He ordinarily will deny specific performance of a promise for which the promisee gave no consideration. This has special application to promises made under seal, which in courts of law are enforced without respect to consideration, except in jurisdictions in which the legal efficacy of seals has been abolished. In no event will the chancellor decree specific performance against the promisor unless the promisee has performed or is able and willing to perform.

Discharge

By Mutual Agreement The enforcibility of a promise arises out of a mutual agreement between the parties. The parties may terminate the enforcibility of the promise in the same manner. An enforcible promise may be terminated by mutual agreement in several ways: rescission, novation, accord and satisfaction, and arbitration and award.

Rescission.—A has bound himself for a consideration to convey Blackacre to B. The promise imposes certain duties upon A and confers certain rights upon B. In this situation, a rescission simply means that by agreement between the parties B surrenders his rights and A escapes his duties.

A rescission is operative only if the promisee furnishes a sufficient consideration for the surrender by the promisor of his rights under the agreement. If there are obligations on each of two parties to an agreement, the surrender by A of his rights is a sufficient consideration to support the surrender by B of his and the surrender by B of his rights is a sufficient consideration to support the surrender by A of his. If, however, the relation at the time is unilateral, the promisee must furnish some other consideration. A pays B $200 for B's promise to paint a building. A statement by A that he releases B from his duty to paint the house does not release the obligation. B must furnish some consideration to support the surrender of rights by A.

The term "rescission," in another sense, indicates a means by which a promisor can bring a promise to an end. A promisor has been induced by fraud, duress, or undue influence to give a promise. The promise is not void, but merely voidable. It will be enforced if the promisor does not avoid it on the ground of fraud or duress. In this event it is commonly said that the promisor may rescind his promise. But rescission in this sense is unilateral and is not the result of a mutual agreement of the parties.

Novation.—Novation is another means by which a promise may be discharged by agreement of the parties. Novation is the substitution of a new agreement for an old. It may take one of two forms: the substitution of a new agreement for the old, the parties remaining the same, or substitution of a new party for an old, the agreement remaining the same. A novation of the former kind commonly is termed an "accord and satisfaction."

The substitution of one promisor for another does not differ greatly in principle from the discharge of a promise by rescission. It means simply the discharge of one promisor from his promise and the bringing in of a new promisor bound by the same promise. B owes A $100. C owes B the same amount. C agrees to pay B's debt to A in consideration of B's releasing him from the debt which he owes to B. If A assents to this arrangement, a novation takes place. C is substituted for B, who is released from his debt.

Accord and Satisfaction.—Accord and satisfaction is the substitution of one agreement for another. An accord is the making of the new agreement; the satisfaction is the performance of the new promise by the promisor in satisfaction of the original obligation. *A* owes $500 to *B*. *A* promises to deliver to *B* certain stock in satisfaction of the debt. This is an accord. *B* accepts the stock. This is a satisfaction, and *A* is discharged from further obligation under his promise.

As a general rule, the accord or the new promise is not a satisfaction of the original obligation. *A* gives a check to *B* for a debt which he owes the latter. The check is not absolute, but only conditional, payment. The original debt remains until the check is paid. However, "the rule that a promise to do another thing is not satisfaction is subject to the qualification that where the parties agree that the new promise shall itself be a satisfaction of the prior debt or duty, and the new agreement is based upon a good consideration, and is accepted in satisfaction, then it operates as such and bars the action."

Arbitration and Award.—Another way in which an enforcible promise may be discharged is by arbitration and award. *A* makes an enforcible promise to *B*. Later, a dispute arises as to what *A* promised. The parties, unable to reach an agreement, submit the controversy to one or more disinterested parties for investigation and agree to accept their findings in settlement of the controversy. In this situation, it is clear that the parties are establishing a non-official tribunal to settle their controversy. It would seem that courts would favor attempts of the parties to settle their controversies in friendly ways outside court. Strangely enough, however, courts always have viewed with suspicion any procedure which takes from them jurisdiction over controversies.

Although in modern times courts have adopted a more favorable attitude toward arbitration and award, it still is well settled that the parties cannot by their agreement completely oust the courts from their normal jurisdiction over controversies. "Parties have no more right to enter into stipulations against a resort to the courts for their remedy in a given case, than they have to provide a remedy prohibited by law; such stipulations are repugnant to the rest of the contract, and assume to divest courts of their established jurisdiction." Parties may, however, validly agree that submission to arbitration shall be a condition precedent to the institution of an action on the original claim.

Either party to an arbitration agreement may at any time before the publication of the final award revoke the authority of the arbiters to proceed with their investigation. This revocation, if unjustified, is a breach of the arbitration agreement for which the other party is entitled to damages if the agreement was based upon a sufficient consideration.

Assuming, however, that the parties allow the arbiters to publish an award, what is the effect of the award upon the original obligation of the promisor? If the original obligation was for a liquidated sum of money, it generally is held that the award does not substitute a new obligation for it but is merely a statement of what the original obligation is. If the original obligation is for an unliquidated sum of money, the award is a new obligation which is substituted for the old. In the former case, the plaintiff brings his action upon the original obligation; in the latter he brings it upon the award.

By Operation of Law

By Judgment.—If the promisee recovers a judgment against the promisor on his promise, the promise is gone. It is merged into the higher obligation of judgment.

By Death.—Generally speaking, the death of the promisor has no effect upon the enforcibility of a promise made during his lifetime. After his death the promisee may still enforce it against his estate. This is not true, however, if the promise calls for personal services or services requiring the skill and judgment of the promisor. Such a promise expires with the promisor.

By Discharge in Bankruptcy.—Promises provable under the bankruptcy act are, generally speaking, discharged by a decree in bankruptcy. It sometimes is said that the decree in bankruptcy does not discharge the obligation but simply bars the remedy. However this may be, the fact remains that after the decree in bankruptcy the promisee cannot enforce the promise unless the promisor makes a new promise to perform.

Statutes of Limitations of Actions.—In all states there are statutes which provide that, after the lapse of a stated period after a cause of action has arisen on a promise, the promisee cannot bring action thereon against the promisor. These statutes are known as "statutes of limitations of actions" and are based on the theory that the law should not assist a promisee who has not been reasonably diligent in the assertion and enforcement of his rights. Generally speaking, a statute of limitations does not discharge the promise but merely bars an action on it. Under this view, a promise to pay a debt after it has been outlawed operates as a waiver of the bar and entitles the promisee to enforce the promise as originally made. In some states, the statute expressly declares that the lapse of time shall discharge the promise and not merely bar action on it.

By Performance and Breach

Breach of Condition.—The breach or non-fulfilment of a condition does not per se discharge the promise dependent upon the condition. It merely gives to the party against whom it operates the privilege of terminating his promise. He may, as has been seen elsewhere, waive the nonfulfilment of the condition and insist upon performance by the other party. In this event, the agreement remains in existence not only for his benefit but for the benefit of the other party as well.

Breach of Promise.—A breach of promise does not discharge the promise. The promisee may, as previously seen, waive a breach of promise as well as a breach of condition. If he waives the breach, the promise continues in existence as an unbroken promise. An acceptance of the breach of promise converts the broken promise into a cause of action, which its owner may surrender by a release under seal in jurisdictions in which seals still possess their efficacy. The parties may discharge a cause of action by an accord and satisfaction. This, obviously enough, is nothing more than an exchange of the cause of action for some new consideration.

Performance of Promise.—Although substantial performance of a promise, if made in good faith, entitles one party to call upon the other for the performance of his promise, it does not discharge his promise. Nothing less than strict and literal performance of the promise as it has been construed by the court discharges it.

WILLS AND ESTATE PLANNING

Introduction

Everyone should have an up-to-date will, reflecting an estate plan adapted to individual needs and circumstances. A will is a written document which takes effect at the death of the testator (as the law calls a person making a will) for the purpose of distributing his worldly assets to those whom he desires or "wills" to have them. An estate plan is a rational plan for the arrangement of one's affairs and the distribution of one's assets in such a way as to achieve maximum realization of the testator's objectives—which may include keeping taxes at a minimum, provision of financial management for the benefit of a surviving widow and children, selection of a trusted adviser, relative or friend as executor or guardian, and so on. A proper will is the heart of any estate plan, but the estate plan may rely upon gifts, insurance and annuities, special types of contracts (for example, contracts for the purchase of a business by surviving associates), trusteeship arrangements, and other devices to accomplish the testator's purpose. Professional advice is particularly important for individuals whose assets (including sums payable under life insurance policies) exceed $60,000 (or married couples whose assets exceed $120,000), since the federal estate tax applies to these and larger estates.

You Already Have a Will Everyone has a will, whether he realizes it or not. One who dies "intestate," that is without an individual will reflecting his own wishes, automatically has provided for him by state law a kind of "standard" will reflecting the legislature's conception of the deceased's probable objectives. These intestacy laws cause one's property to pass to one's survivors according to rules fixed by the State of which one is a legal resident, but these rules never operate as thriftily as a proper will and sometimes result in serious shrinkage of the estate or indeed in a distribution of assets quite different from what the deceased probably wanted. If the estate is large disastrous litigation may follow one's death. If the estate is small it may be divided between various survivors in portions too small to help anyone. If the

deceased leaves minor children they will inherit part of his estate along with his widow. A guardian must be appointed for the children and this involves expensive and time-consuming court proceedings; the guardian must post a bond, renewable annually at a substantial premium; the guardian is supervised by the court and must account to it annually, resulting in more expense and loss of time. None of these expensive and involved procedures is altered by the fact that the guardian may be the children's mother and the deceased's widow. Political hacks may be appointed by the court as appraisers, executors or guardians—and they are entitled to substantial fees for their services. Worst of all, the intestacy laws may distribute one's assets in a manner contrary to one's own wishes. For example, these laws make it impossible for all assets to go to the widow if there are children too; they do not consider the needs of parents if a widow or child survives; they treat children equally though their needs may be quite unequal; they do not differentiate between faithful, loving spouses and mere legal mates; they treat helpless widows and spouses who are quite capable in business affairs just alike. The time and expense involved in making a sound will is infinitesimal in comparison with the least of these dangers. The "will you already have" is always inferior to the will you ought to have—even though the intestacy laws represent the state's best efforts to help those who refuse to help themselves.

Common Provision of Intestacy Laws While it *always* is highly disadvantageous to die without a proper will, it is instructive to consider the effect of the intestacy laws in certain common situations. Where the deceased leaves a widow, no children, no parents, the widow of course gets everything—after various expenses which a proper will could have avoided. Where only parents survive the parents usually take everything (though in some states brothers and sisters share in the estate), and where only children survive the children take everything—subject to similar disadvantages, which are especially acute in the case of minor children. But suppose the deceased leaves surviving him his wife and his parents? In most states the wife gets everything, even if she is financially independent and the deceased husband's aged and destitute parents have provided the basis of the husband's modest estate. In a few states, however, the parents get up to half their son's estate, regardless of the widow's needs—often the basis of a tragic family quarrel. If there are children the deceased's parents or other relatives (other than his wife, of course) take nothing. If the wife and one child survive each takes half the estate, usually—but in some states the child may take two-thirds or even virtually the entire estate in certain situations. Where the wife and two or more children survive one-third of the estate generally goes to the wife, the remaining two-thirds being equally divided between the children. Where the wife (but no children) and brothers and sisters of the deceased (but not their parents) survive, in most states the wife gets everything but in New York, for example, the deceased's brothers and sisters (or *their* surviving children) may take almost half the estate!

Obviously these provisions may work great hardship or injustice for many people, although they represent the legislature's best efforts to develop rules that will do the greatest good for the greatest number of thoughtless or irresponsible people who fail to protect their loved ones with the simplest, cheapest death benefit anyone can leave behind him—a personal will adapted to his own personal circumstances. Furthermore, the intestacy laws always are subject to change without one's knowing it, whereas a will can be changed only by the person making it (qualification: the later birth of a child, a later change in marital status, a move to another state, or a substantial change in the nature of one's estate or even in the degree of one's prosperity may partially void a will or affect its results; periodic review of one's affairs is essential, and if one's circumstances have changed a new will may be required).

The Dangers of Joint Tenancy The various forms of joint ownership are no substitute for a will, and may involve peculiar dangers of their own. While joint ownership has its proper place, it is widely misused or misunderstood. Space does not permit an adequate discussion of joint ownership here, but it must be said that joint ownership often produces results contrary to those intended, that joint ownership rarely saves taxes or other expenses and sometimes increases them dramatically, and that the whole subject of joint ownership is so confused in many states that even lawyers cannot be sure of its effects. It often is desirable to maintain checking accounts and small savings accounts in joint ownership in order to provide the survivor with ready cash upon the death of one joint owner; even if the account is frozen for a time it normally will be available to the survivor long before the assets of the deceased's estate. Perhaps primarily for sentimental reasons, it is common for husband and wife to own the family home jointly. Beyond this, joint ownership should be based upon sound legal advice—which also will extend to an overall estate plan based upon a will.

Community Property Our Western and Southwestern states follow the Roman law, rather than the English common law, with respect to property relationships between husband and wife. In its modern form this is known as the law of community property. In common-law states marriage gives husbands and wives certain rights in each other's property which often cannot be changed by a will. This is equally true in community-property states, but the rights are somewhat different. In these states half the income earned during marriage by either spouse belongs to the other. All property owned by the couple presumably is community property, of which each owns half; but property owned by either spouse before marriage and kept separate, the income from such property if also kept separate, and property acquired by one spouse individually otherwise than through productive effort to which his mate presumably contributes—for example by gift or inheritance—is the separate property of the spouse owning it. One may pass his own separate property and his half of the community property by will, but one's will does not touch a spouse's share of the community property, nor, of course, a spouse's separate property. *However*, the married couple are free to agree between themselves as to what is community property and what is the separate property of either; thus they may classify their property as community property, separate property of the husband, or separate property of the wife, as they please. Such community-property agreements, a kind of contract (contracts, unlike wills, take effect when made rather than upon death), are an essential tool of estate planning in community-property states but do not forestall the necessity of a will any more than joint tenancy does, and like joint tenancies are fraught with dangers of their own.

What Is a Will? A will is a written document, signed by the testator in the presence of witnesses, which operates at his death to distribute his property according to his directions, subject to certain limitations imposed by law. (Examples of such limitations are the duty to pay tax liabilities, debts, funeral expenses and costs of administration first; or the minimum legal rights of a surviving spouse in the deceased's estate; or the refusal on grounds of public policy to recognize provisions discouraging marriage, wasting assets, or tying up wealth for unreasonable periods of time.) A will may be very short and simple in the case of a small and uncomplicated estate—often only a page or two. But the simplicity of even a short and typical will is deceptive; for that reason no specimen will is shown here. Certain absolutely essential requirements must be met, not arbitrarily but for good reasons. It is just as impossible to draft a universally satisfactory will as to write a universally satisfactory intestacy law. Therefore "standard" wills, stationers' forms, the well-meaning advice of notaries public, real-estate brokers, insurance salesmen and other laymen, and other kinds of folk-lore must be avoided like the plague. Any competent attorney at law can prepare a simple will quickly, cheaply and perfectly. No one else can. Above all, then, a will is a vital and unique personal document prepared on the basis of *individual legal advice*.

Advantages of a Will A will allows you to dispose of your property to the persons you select, at the time you fix, in the amounts and proportions you determine, and permits you to specify how this property will be protected and who will be responsible for its protection. If you die without a will there will be unnecessary, expensive and time-consuming court procedures, impersonal and perhaps casual administration by strangers, expensive taxes and other expenses. Above all, one who dies intestate loses the vitally important right to nominate the guardian of his children and the executor of his estate.

Who May Make a Will? Anyone twenty-one years of age and mentally capable of understanding the nature of a will

and the terms of his own will may make his will. In some states or under some conditions the age requirement is reduced or waived.

What Law Governs The law of the state where the testator maintains his permanent residence governs the validity of his will with respect to his personal property; but since each state has the right to fix title to land situated within its boundaries, the law of the state where the land is located governs the validity and effect of the will with respect to real estate. Often a sound estate plan calls for avoidance of unnecessary ownership of real estate in states where the testator is a nonresident, particularly if there is any danger that two or more states may claim him as a resident and thus attempt to tax his entire estate rather than merely the local realty. Most states and indeed most countries of the world cooperate with one another by recognizing as valid a will which is valid either in the jurisdiction of which the testator is a resident, the jurisdiction in which the will was made, or (as to real estate) the jurisdiction in which the property is located. However, the extent of this mutual cooperation among the states is subject to change and may be unpredictable in certain types of situations. Therefore it is desirable that the will be consistent with the requirements of the state of residence, and one's will should be reviewed when moving to another jurisdiction. There are certain unusual types of wills which are recognized in only few states, but a proper will drawn by legal counsel will be prepared in such a way as to meet the requirements of most if not all states.

Common Disasters In the common situation where husband and wife each leave their estates to the other, the death of both in the same accident creates potential difficulty with respect to the order in which they died. Of course the estate of the first to die passes to the survivor, and upon the survivor's death the family property passes under the survivor's will or under the applicable intestacy rule. If there are children they presumably will get the property in any case, but if there are no children (or if they die earlier or in the same accident) the stage is set for a disastrous struggle between the husband's relatives and the wife's, especially where the order of their deaths is uncertain. Thus if Husband and Wife are involved in an accident which kills Husband outright and results in injuries fatal to Wife a few hours later, Husband's property passes to Wife and at Wife's death to Wife's relatives. Husband's family would take nothing, even though the property Wife owned at her death came largely from Husband or his family. Bitter conflict and expensive litigation can be avoided by a proper will containing a common disaster clause providing for the distribution of family assets in the event of simultaneous deaths or deaths resulting from the same accident.

The All-Important Executor Save only the appointment of a guardian for surviving minor children, the appointment of one's executor is the most important privilege available to one who makes his will. The loyalty and business ability of the executor, once the basic estate plan is established and the will is made in accordance with it, is the single most important factor in minimizing shrinkage of the estate. The executor, subject to supervision by and responsibility to the appropriate court, takes possession of the assets upon the testator's death, manages the estate as the deceased would himself, pays debts, taxes and expenses, retains counsel and through counsel handles all legal obligations and procedures, accounts to the court and heirs for his stewardship, and distributes the assets of the estate according to the testator's will and applicable legal requirements. Obviously business skills and judgment, diligence and the capacity to attend to details and maintain proper records are essential qualities of the executor.

The testator may nominate the executor of his choice; and alternates if he wishes. Often a surviving widow or trusted friend or relative is appointed; it generally is advisable to name the testator's legal counsel as co-executor. Or the executor may be a corporate trustee—the trust department of a bank, usually. The professional trustee, sometimes (especially in Boston) an individual but today typically a bank or trust company, has the complete facilities, the permanence and freedom from personal or business distractions, the staff and the professional skills necessary to do the work well. The widow, relative or lawyer may be appointed co-executor if it is desired to combine the close personal relationship of a trusted individual with the skills and facilities of the corporate trustee.

Of course the executor must be compensated for his services, except in the case of the relative or friend who serves out of a sense of duty or because he is a principal heir. Executor's fees are based on the size of the estate, but typically run about 2 % to $2\frac{1}{2}$ % of the gross assets.

Trusts The fiduciary services of an individual or corporate trustee may be required not only for the relatively short-run duties of the executor (six months to a year or two, typically) but also for the far longer periods required, for example, to invest the proceeds of an estate, pay the income to the widow for her life (probably with discretion to invade principal if necessary), further to devote the income to the upbringing and education of the couple's surviving children, and finally to pay the principal to the children when they reach maturity. A "trust" is a gift of property to a trustee for some specified purpose, such as investment of the trust assets for the support of a beneficiary. In such a case the trustee's most important service is the management of long-term investments; the testator (if the trust is created by will) essentially is buying investment skill. Obviously the trust device is especially appropriate for the support of widows and orphans prematurely deprived of husband, father and breadwinner. The creation of trusts necessarily requires highly specialized legal skills and emphatically is a job for experienced legal counsel. However, the thoughtfully-planned trust device is assuming increasing importance as a central feature of sound estate planning—especially in estates of medium to large size, where trusts may lead to very significant tax savings.

It is important to note that a trust may not continue indefinitely (unless it is devoted to charitable purposes).

Disposition of the Will Obviously a will must be left where it will come into the proper hands after the testator's death. His safe deposit box is not necessarily the best place for his will, since the safe deposit box will be sealed at his death, to be opened only in the presence of the tax authorities, and this may involve serious loss of time. It is best to deliver the will to the executor, to leave it with one's lawyer, or to keep it with one's personal records at home if it will be safe from prying eyes or possible tampering.

Letter of Instructions A final but important and often neglected step in a sound estate plan is the leaving of a letter of final instructions with the lawyer or executor. This letter is not part of the will and need comply with no formal requirements. Its purpose is to provide a detailed inventory of assets, instructions with respect to the location of all needed documents (birth, marriage and military discharge records, social security card, insurance policies, list of bank accounts and safe deposit boxes, title deeds, pension papers, etc.), instructions for the liquidation of business affairs, notation of the location of the will, funeral instructions, and the like. Often it also expresses the testator's wishes with respect to investment of the proceeds of his estate, the education of his children, the future plans of his widow or other family matters, and any other subjects which he wishes to mention privately (the will becomes a public record) or to express as a hope or suggestion rather than as a binding testamentary disposition.

METRIC SYSTEM AND EQUIVALENT UNITS

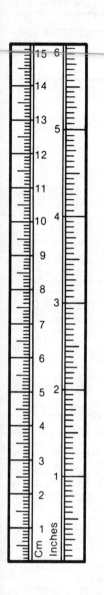

LINEAR MEASURE

10 millimeters	= 1 centimeter	= 0.3937 inch
10 centimeters	= 1 decimeter	= 3.937 inches
10 decimeters	= 1 meter	= 39.37 inches or 3.28 feet
10 meters	= 1 decameter	= 393.7 inches
10 decameters	= 1 hectometer	= 328 feet 1 inch
10 hectometers	= 1 kilometer	= 0.621 mile
10 kilometers	= 1 myriameter	= 6.21 miles

SQUARE MEASURE

100 square millimeters	= 1 square centimeter	= 0.15499 square inch
100 square centimeters	= 1 square decimeter	= 15.499 square inches
100 square decimeters	= 1 square meter	= 1,549.9 square inches or 1.196 square yards
100 square meters	= 1 square decameter	= 119.6 square yards
100 square decameters	= 1 square hectometer	= 2.471 acres
100 square hectometers	= 1 square kilometer	= 0.386 square mile

LAND MEASURE

1 square meter	= 1 centiare	= 1,549.9 square inches
100 centiares	= 1 acre	= 119.6 square yards
100 acres	= 1 hectare	= 2.471 acres
100 hectares	= 1 square kilometer	= 0.386 square mile

EQUIVALENT UNITS OF:

LENGTH																		TEMP.			
Centimeters to Inches		Inches to Centimeters		Meters to Feet		Feet to Meters		Meters to Yards		Yards to Meters		Kilometers to Miles		Miles to Kilometers		Celsius to Fahrenheit		Fahrenheit to Celsius	
cm	in	in	cm	m	ft	ft	m	m	yd	yd	m	km	miles	miles	km	°C	F°	°F	°C
1	0.39	1	2.54	1	3.28	1	0.30	1	1.09	1	0.91	1	0.62	1	1.61	10	50.00	10	-12.22
2	0.79	2	5.08	2	6.56	2	0.61	2	2.19	2	1.83	2	1.24	2	3.22	20	68.00	20	-6.67
3	1.18	3	7.62	3	9.84	3	0.91	3	3.28	3	2.74	3	1.86	3	4.83	30	86.00	30	-1.11
4	1.57	4	10.16	4	13.12	4	1.22	4	4.37	4	3.66	4	2.49	4	6.44	40	104.00	40	4.44
5	1.97	5	12.70	5	16.40	5	1.52	5	5.47	5	4.57	5	3.11	5	8.05	50	122.00	50	10.00
6	2.36	6	15.24	6	19.68	6	1.83	6	6.56	6	5.49	6	3.73	6	9.66	60	140.00	60	15.56
7	2.76	7	17.78	7	22.97	7	2.13	7	7.66	7	6.40	7	4.35	7	11.27	70	158.00	70	21.11
8	3.15	8	20.32	8	26.25	8	2.44	8	8.75	8	7.32	8	4.97	8	12.87	80	176.00	80	26.67
9	3.54	9	22.86	9	29.53	9	2.74	9	9.84	9	8.23	9	5.59	9	14.48	90	194.00	90	32.22
10	3.94	10	25.40	10	32.81	10	3.05	10	10.94	10	9.14	10	6.21	10	16.09	100	212.00	100	37.78

VOLUME MEASURE

1,000 cubic millimeters = 1 cubic centimeter = .06102 cubic inch
1,000 cubic centimeters = 1 cubic decimeter = 61.02 cubic inches
1,000 cubic decimeters = 1 cubic meter = 35.314 cubic feet

(the unit is called a *stere* in measuring firewood)

CAPACITY MEASURE

10 milliliters = 1 centiliter = 0.338 fluid ounce
10 centiliters = 1 deciliter = 3.38 fluid ounces
10 deciliters = 1 liter = 1.0567 liquid quarts or
0.9081 dry quart
10 liters = 1 decaliter = 2.64 gallons or
0.284 bushel
10 decaliters = 1 hectoliter = 26.418 gallons or
2.838 bushels
10 hectoliters = 1 kiloliter = 264.18 gallons or
35.315 cubic fcet

WEIGHTS

10 milligrams = 1 centigram = 0.1543 grain
10 centigrams = 1 decigram = 1.5432 grains
10 decigrams = 1 gram = 15.432 grains
10 grams = 1 decagram = 0.3527 ounce
10 decagrams = 1 hectogram = 3.5274 ounces
10 hectograms = 1 kilogram = 2.2046 pounds
10 kilograms = 1 myriagram = 22.046 pounds
10 myriagrams = 1 quintal = 220.46 pounds
10 quintals = 1 metric ton = 2,204.6 pounds

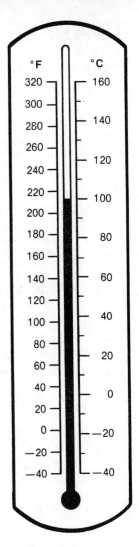

EQUIVALENT UNITS OF:

VOLUME						WEIGHT			
Millileters to Ounces	Ounces to Milliliters	Liters to Quarts	Quarts to Liters	Liters to Gallons	Gallons to Liters	Grams to Ounces	Ounces to Grams	Kilograms to Pounds	Pounds to Kilograms
ml liq oz	liq oz ml	l liq qt	liq qt l	l gal	gal l	g oz	oz g	kg lb	lb kg
10 0.34	1 29.57	1 1.06	1 0.95	1 0.26	1 3.79	1 0.04	1 28.3	1 2.20	1 0.45
20 0.68	2 59.15	2 2.11	2 1.89	2 0.53	2 7.57	2 0.07	2 56.7	2 4.41	2 0.91
30 1.01	3 88.72	3 3.17	3 2.84	3 0.79	3 11.36	3 0.11	3 85.0	3 6.61	3 1.36
40 1.35	4 118.29	4 4.23	4 3.79	4 1.06	4 15.14	4 0.14	4 113.4	4 8.82	4 1.81
50 1.69	5 147.87	5 5.28	5 4.73	5 1.32	5 18.93	5 0.18	5 141.7	5 11.02	5 2.27
60 2.03	6 177.44	6 6.34	6 5.68	6 1.59	6 22.71	6 0.21	6 170.1	6 13.23	6 2.72
70 2.37	7 207.01	7 7.40	7 6.62	7 1.85	7 26.50	7 0.25	7 198.4	7 15.43	7 3.18
80 2.71	8 236.59	8 8.45	8 7.57	8 2.11	8 30.28	8 0.28	8 226.8	8 17.64	8 3.63
90 3.04	9 266.16	9 9.51	9 8.52	9 2.38	9 34.07	9 0.32	9 255.1	9 19.84	9 4.08
100 3.38	10 295.74	10 10.57	10 9.46	10 2.64	10 37.85	10 0.35	10 283.5	10 22.05	10 4.54

TABLES OF WEIGHTS AND MEASURES

LINEAR MEASURE

1 inch	=	2.54 centimeters
12 inches = 1 foot	=	0.3048 meter
3 feet = 1 yard	=	0.9144 meter
5½ yards or 16½ feet = 1 rod (or pole or perch)	=	5.029 meters
40 rods = 1 furlong	=	201.17 meters
8 furlongs or 1,760 yards or 5,280 feet = 1 (statute) mile	=	1,609.3 meters
3 miles = 1 (land) league	=	4.83 kilometers

SQUARE MEASURE

1 square inch	=	6.452 square centimeters
144 square inches = 1 square foot	=	929 square centimeters
9 square feet = 1 square yard	=	0.8361 square meter
30¼ square yards = 1 square rod (or square pole or square perch)	=	25.29 square meters
160 square rods or 4,840 square yards or 43,560 square feet = 1 acre	=	0.4047 hectare
640 acres = 1 square mile	=	259 hectares or 2.59 square kilometers

CUBIC MEASURE

1 cubic inch	=	16.387 cubic centimeters
1,728 cubic inches = 1 cubic foot	=	0.0283 cubic meter
27 cubic feet = 1 cubic yard (in units for cordwood, etc.)	=	0.7646 cubic meter
16 cubic feet = 1 cord foot		
8 cord feet = 1 cord	=	3.625 cubic meters

CHAIN MEASURE

(for Gunter's, or surveyor's, chain)

7.92 inches = 1 link	=	20.12 centimeters
100 links or 66 feet = 1 chain	=	20.12 meters
10 chains = 1 furlong	=	201.17 meters
80 chains = 1 mile	=	1,609.3 meters

(for engineer's chain)

1 foot = 1 link	=	0.3048 meter
100 feet = 1 chain	=	30.48 meters
52.8 chains = 1 mile	=	1,609.3 meters

SURVEYOR'S (SQUARE) MEASURE

625 square links = 1 square pole	=	25.29 square meters
16 square poles = 1 square chain	=	404.7 square meters
10 square chains = 1 acre	=	0.4047 hectare
640 acres = 1 square mile or 1 section	=	259 hectares or 2.59 square kilometers
36 square miles = 1 township	=	9,324.0 hectares or 93.24 square kilometers

NAUTICAL MEASURE

6 feet = 1 fathom		= 1.829 meters
100 fathoms = 1 cable's length (ordinary)		
(In the U.S. Navy 120 fathoms or 720 feet = 1 cable's length; in the British Navy, 608 feet = 1 cable's length.)		
10 cables' lengths = 1 nautical mile (6,076.10333 feet)		= 1.852 kilometers (by international agreement, 1954)
1 nautical mile = 1.1508 statute miles		
(the length of a minute of longitude at the equator)		
(Also called geographical, sea, or air mile, and, in Great Britain, Admiralty mile.)		
3 nautical miles = 1 marine league (3.45 statute miles)		= 5.56 kilometers
60 nautical miles = 1 degree of a great circle of the earth		

DRY MEASURE

1 pint	=	33.60 cubic inches	= 0.5505 liter
2 pints = 1 quart	=	67.20 cubic inches	= 1.1012 liters
8 quarts = 1 peck	=	537.61 cubic inches	= 8.8096 liters
4 pecks = 1 bushel	=	2,150.42 cubic inches	= 35.2383 liters

1 British dry quart = 1.032 U.S. dry quarts.

According to United States government standards, the following are the weights avoirdupois for single bushels of the specified grains: for wheat, 60 pounds; for barley, 48 pounds; for oats, 32 pounds; for rye, 56 pounds; for corn, 56 pounds. Some states have specifications varying from these.

LIQUID MEASURE

1 gill = 4 fluid ounces	=	7.219 cubic inches	= 0.1183 liter
(see next table)			
4 gills = 1 pint	=	28.875 cubic inches	= 0.4732 liter
2 pints = 1 quart	=	57.75 cubic inches	= 0.9463 liter
4 quarts = 1 gallon	=	231 cubic inches	= 3.7853 liters

The British imperial gallon (4 imperial quarts) = 277.42 cubic inches = 4.546 liters. The barrel in Great Britain equals 36 imperial gallons, in the United States, usually 31½ gallons.

APOTHECARIES' FLUID MEASURE

1 minim	=	0.0038 cubic inch	= 0.0616 milliliter
60 minims = 1 fluid dram	=	0.2256 cubic inch	= 3.6966 milliliters
8 fluid drams = 1 fluid ounce	=	1.8047 cubic inches	= 0.0296 liter
16 fluid ounces = 1 pint	=	28.875 cubic inches	= 0.4732 liter

See table immediately preceding for quart and gallon equivalents. The British pint = 20 fluid ounces.

CIRCULAR (or ANGULAR) MEASURE

60 seconds (″)	= 1 minute (′)
60 minutes	= 1 degree (°)
90 degrees	= 1 quadrant or 1 right angle
4 quadrants or 360 degrees	= 1 circle

AVOIRDUPOIS WEIGHT

(The grain, equal to 0.0648 gram, is the same in all three tables of weight)

1 dram or 27.34 grains	=	1.772 grams
16 drams or 437.5 grains = 1 ounce	=	28.3495 grams
16 ounces or 7,000 grains = 1 pound	=	453.59 grams
100 pounds = 1 hundredweight	=	45.36 kilograms
2,000 pounds = 1 ton	=	907.18 kilograms

In Great Britain, 14 pounds (6.35 kilograms) = 1 stone, 112 pounds (50.80 kilograms) = 1 hundredweight, and 2,240 pounds (1,016.05 kilograms) = 1 long ton.

TROY WEIGHT

(The grain, equal to 0.0648 gram, is the same in all three tables of weight)

3.086 grains = 1 carat	= 200	milligrams
24 grains = 1 pennyweight	=	1.5552 grams
20 pennyweights or 480 grains = 1 ounce	=	31.1035 grams
12 ounces or 5,760 grains = 1 pound	=	373.24 grams

APOTHECARIES' WEIGHT

(The grain, equal to 0.0648 gram, is the same in all three tables of weight)

20 grains = 1 scruple	=	1.296 grams
3 scruples = 1 dram	=	3.888 grams
8 drams or 480 grains = 1 ounce	=	31.1035 grams
12 ounces or 5,760 grains = 1 pound	=	373.24 grams

VITAL FACTS ABOUT U. S. PRESIDENTS

	Name	Born	Birthplace	Died	Age at Death
1.	George Washington	Feb. 22, 1732	Westmoreland County, Va.	Dec. 14, 1799	67
2.	John Adams	Oct. 30, 1735	Braintree, Mass.	July 4, 1826	90
3.	Thomas Jefferson	Apr. 13, 1743	Albemarle County, Va.	July 4, 1826	83
4.	James Madison	Mar. 16, 1751	Port Conway, Va.	June 28, 1836	85
5.	James Monroe	Apr. 28, 1758	Westmoreland County, Va.	July 4, 1831	73
6.	John Quincy Adams	July 11, 1767	Braintree, Mass.	Feb. 23, 1848	80
7.	Andrew Jackson	Mar. 15, 1767	Waxhaw, S. C.	June 8, 1845	78
8.	Martin Van Buren	Dec. 5, 1782	Kinderhook, N. Y.	July 24, 1862	79
9.	William H. Harrison	Feb. 9, 1773	Berkeley, Va.	Apr. 4, 1841	68
10.	John Tyler	Mar. 29, 1790	Greenway, Va.	Jan. 18, 1862	71
11.	James K. Polk	Nov. 2, 1795	Pineville, N. C.	June 15, 1849	53
12.	Zachary Taylor	Nov. 24, 1784	Orange County, Va.	July 9, 1850	65
13.	Millard Fillmore	Jan. 7, 1800	Locke, N. Y.	Mar. 8, 1874	74
14.	Franklin Pierce	Nov. 23, 1804	Hillsboro, N. H.	Oct. 8, 1869	64
15.	James Buchanan	Apr. 23, 1791	Mercersburg, Pa.	June 1, 1868	77
16.	Abraham Lincoln	Feb. 12, 1809	Hardin County, Ky.	Apr. 15, 1865	56
17.	Andrew Johnson	Dec. 29, 1808	Raleigh, N. C.	July 31, 1875	66
18.	Ulysses S. Grant	Apr. 27, 1822	Point Pleasant, O.	July 23, 1885	63
19.	Rutherford B. Hayes	Oct. 4, 1822	Delaware, O.	Jan. 17, 1893	70
20.	James A. Garfield	Nov. 19, 1831	Orange, O.	Sept. 19, 1881	49
21.	Chester A. Arthur	Oct. 5, 1830	Fairfield, Vt.	Nov. 18, 1886	56
22.	Grover Cleveland	Mar. 18, 1837	Caldwell, N. J.	June 24, 1908	71
23.	Benjamin Harrison	Aug. 20, 1833	North Bend, O.	Mar. 13, 1901	67
24.	Grover Cleveland	Mar. 18, 1837	Caldwell, N. J.	June 24, 1908	71
25.	William McKinley	Jan. 29, 1843	Niles, O.	Sept. 14, 1901	58
26.	Theodore Roosevelt	Oct. 27, 1858	New York City	Jan. 6, 1919	60
27.	William H. Taft	Sept. 15, 1857	Cincinnati, O.	Mar. 8, 1930	72
28.	Woodrow Wilson	Dec. 28, 1856	Staunton, Va.	Feb. 3, 1924	67
29.	Warren G. Harding	Nov. 2, 1865	Morrow County, O.	Aug. 2, 1923	57
30.	Calvin Coolidge	July 4, 1872	Plymouth Notch, Vt.	Jan. 5, 1933	60
31.	Herbert Hoover	Aug. 10, 1874	West Branch, Ia.	Oct. 20, 1964	90
32.	Franklin D. Roosevelt	Jan. 30, 1882	Hyde Park, N. Y.	Apr. 12, 1945	63
33.	Harry S Truman	May 8, 1884	Lamar, Mo.	Dec. 26, 1972	88
34.	Dwight D. Eisenhower	Oct. 14, 1890	Denison, Tex.	Mar. 28, 1969	78
35.	John F. Kennedy	May 29, 1917	Brookline, Mass.	Nov. 22, 1963	46
36.	Lyndon B. Johnson	Aug. 27, 1908	Gillespie County, Tex.	Jan. 22, 1973	64
37.	Richard M. Nixon	Jan. 9, 1913	Yorba Linda, Calif.		
38.	Gerald R. Ford	July 14, 1913	Omaha, Neb.		
39.	Jimmy Carter	Oct. 1, 1924	Plains, Ga.		
40.	Ronald W. Reagan	Feb. 6, 1911	Tampico, Ill.		

	Burial Place	Served	Age on Taking Office	Party	Vice-President
1.	Mount Vernon, Va.	1789-1797	57	Federalist	John Adams
2.	Quincy, Mass.	1797-1801	61	Federalist	Thomas Jefferson
3.	Monticello, Va.	1801-1809	57	Democratic-Republican	Aaron Burr George Clinton
4.	Montpelier, Va.	1809-1817	57	Democratic-Republican	George Clinton Elbridge Gerry
5.	Richmond, Va.	1817-1825	58	Democratic-Republican	Daniel D. Tompkins
6.	Quincy, Mass.	1825-1829	57	Democratic-Republican	John C. Calhoun
7.	Hermitage, Tenn.	1829-1837	61	Democratic	John C. Calhoun Martin Van Buren
8.	Kinderhook, N. Y.	1837-1841	54	Democratic	Richard M. Johnson
9.	North Bend, O.	1841	68	Whig	John Tyler
10.	Richmond, Va.	1841-1845	51	Whig	
11.	Nashville, Tenn.	1845-1849	49	Democratic	George M. Dallas
12.	Louisville, Ky.	1849-1850	64	Whig	Millard Fillmore
13.	Buffalo, N. Y.	1850-1853	50	Whig	
14.	Concord, N. H.	1853-1857	48	Democratic	William R. King
15.	Lancaster, Pa.	1857-1861	65	Democratic	John C. Breckinridge
16.	Springfield, Ill.	1861-1865	52	Republican	Hannibal Hamlin Andrew Johnson
17.	Greeneville, Tenn.	1865-1869	56	Democratic	
18.	New York City	1869-1877	46	Republican	Schuyler Colfax Henry Wilson
19.	Fremont, O.	1877-1881	54	Republican	William A. Wheeler
20.	Cleveland, O.	1881	49	Republican	Chester A. Arthur
21.	Albany, N. Y.	1881-1885	50	Republican	
22.	Princeton, N. J.	1885-1889	47	Democratic	Thomas A. Hendricks
23.	Indianapolis, Ind.	1889-1893	55	Republican	Levi P. Morton
24.	Princeton, N. J.	1893-1897	55	Democratic	Adlai E. Stevenson
25.	Canton, O.	1897-1901	54	Republican	Garret A. Hobart Theodore Roosevelt
26.	Oyster Bay, N. Y.	1901-1909	42	Republican	Charles W. Fairbanks
27.	Arlington, Va.	1909-1913	51	Republican	James S. Sherman
28.	Washington, D.C.	1913-1921	56	Democratic	Thomas R. Marshall
29.	Marion, O.	1921-1923	55	Republican	Calvin Coolidge
30.	Plymouth, Vt.	1923-1929	51	Republican	Charles G. Dawes
31.	West Branch, Ia.	1929-1933	54	Republican	Charles Curtis
32.	Hyde Park, N. Y.	1933-1945	51	Democratic	John N. Garner Henry A. Wallace Harry S Truman
33.	Independence, Mo.	1945-1953	60	Democratic	Alben W. Barkley
34.	Abilene, Kan.	1953-1961	62	Republican	Richard M. Nixon
35.	Arlington, Va.	1961-1963	43	Democratic	Lyndon B. Johnson
36.	Stonewall, Tex.	1963-1969	55	Democratic	Hubert H. Humphrey
37.		1969-1974	56	Republican	Spiro Agnew
38.		1974-1977	61	Republican	Nelson A. Rockefeller
39.		1977-1981	53	Democrat	Walter F. Mondale
40.		1981-	69	Republican	George H. Bush

Vice-Presidents of the United States

Name	Birthplace	Served Under	Took Office
John Adams (F) (1735–1826)	Braintree, Mass.	Washington	1789
Thomas Jefferson (R) (1743–1826)	Shadwell, Va.	J. Adams	1797
Aaron Burr (R) (1756–1836)	Newark, N.J.	Jefferson	1801
George Clinton (R) (1734–1812)	Little Britain, N.Y.	Jefferson Madison	1805
Elbridge Gerry (R) (1744–1814)	Marblehead, Mass.	Madison	1813
Daniel D. Tompkins (R) (1774–1825)	Fox Meadows, N.Y.	Monroe	1817
John C. Calhoun (R) (1782–1850)	Abbeville District, S.C.	J. Q. Adams Jackson	1825
Martin Van Buren (D) (1782–1862)	Kinderhook, N.Y.	Jackson	1833
Richard M. Johnson (D) (1780–1850)	Beargrass, Ky.	Van Buren	1837
John Tyler (W) (1790–1862)	Charles City County, Va.	W. H. Harrison	1841
George M. Dallas (D) (1792–1864)	Philadelphia, Pa.	Polk	1845
Millard Fillmore (W) (1800–74)	Cayuga County, N.Y.	Taylor	1849
William R. King (D) (1786–1853)	Sampson Co., N.C.	Pierce	1853
John C. Breckinridge (D) (1821–75)	Lexington, Ky.	Buchanan	1857
Hannibal Hamlin (R) (1809–91)	Paris, Me.	Lincoln	1861
Andrew Johnson[1] (1808–75)	Raleigh, N.C.	Lincoln	1865
Schuyler Colfax (R) (1823–85)	New York, N.Y.	Grant	1869
Henry Wilson (R) (1812–75)	Farmington, N.H.	Grant	1873
William A. Wheeler (R) (1819–87)	Malone, N.Y.	Hayes	1877
Chester A. Arthur (R) (1830–86)	Fairfield, Vt.	Garfield	1881
Thomas A. Hendricks (D) (1819–85)	Muskingum Co., Ohio	Cleveland	1885
Levi P. Morton (R) (1824–1920)	Shoreham, Vt.	B. Harrison	1889
Adlai E. Stevenson (D)[2] (1835–1914)	Christian Co., Ky.	Cleveland	1893
Garret A. Hobart (R) (1844–99)	Long Branch, N.J.	McKinley	1897
Theodore Roosevelt (R) (1858–1919)	New York, N.Y.	McKinley	1901
Charles W. Fairbanks (R) (1852–1918)	Unionville Center, Ohio	T. Roosevelt	1905
James S. Sherman (R) (1855–1912)	Utica, N.Y.	Taft	1909
Thomas R. Marshall (D) (1854–1925)	N. Manchester, Ind.	Wilson	1913
Calvin Coolidge (R) (1872–1933)	Plymouth Notch, Vt.	Harding	1921
Charles G. Dawes (R) (1865–1951)	Marietta, Ohio	Coolidge	1925
Charles Curtis (R) (1860–1936)	Topeka, Kan.	Hoover	1929
John N. Garner (D) (1868–1967)	Red River Co., Texas	F. Roosevelt	1933
Henry A. Wallace (D) (1888–1966)	Adair Co., Iowa	F. Roosevelt	1941
Harry S Truman (D) (1884–1972)	Lamar, Mo.	F. Roosevelt	1945
Alben W. Barkley (D) (1877–1956)	Graves Co., Ky.	Truman	1949
Richard M. Nixon (R) (1913–)	Yorba Linda, Calif.	Eisenhower	1953
Lyndon B. Johnson (D) (1908–73)	Near Stonewall, Texas	Kennedy	1961
Hubert H. Humphrey (D) (1911–1978)	Wallace, S.D.	Johnson	1965
Spiro Agnew (R) (1918–)	Baltimore, Md.	Nixon	1969
Gerald R. Ford (R)[3] (1913–)	Omaha, Neb.	Nixon	1973
Nelson A. Rockefeller (R)[3] (1908–1979)	Bar Harbor, Me.	Ford	1974
Walter F. Mondale (D) (1928–)	Ceylon, Minn.	Carter	1977
George H. Bush (R) (1924–)	Milton, Mass.	Reagan	1981

1. Andrew Johnson: A Democrat nominated by Republicans and elected with Lincoln on the National Union ticket.
2. Adlai E. Stevenson: 23d Vice President. Grandfather of the Democratic candidate for President, 1952 and 1956.
3. Appointed Vice-President under the 25th Amendment to the Constitution.

Aaron Burr, Vice-President under President Thomas Jefferson.

—From an engraving by E. G. Williams & Brothers

John C. Breckinridge, Vice-President under President James Buchanan.

—From an engraving by A. B. Walter

THE DECLARATION OF INDEPENDENCE

In Congress, July 4, 1776. The unanimous Declaration of the thirteen united States of America.

When in the Course of human events, it becomes necessary for one people to dissolve the political bands which have connected them with another, and to assume among the powers of the earth, the separate and equal station to which the Laws of Nature and of Nature's God entitle them, a decent respect to the opinions of mankind requires that they should declare the causes which impel them to the separation.—

We hold these truths to be self-evident, that all men are created equal, that they are endowed by their Creator with certain unalienable Rights, that among these are Life, Liberty and the pursuit of Happiness.—

That to secure these rights, Governments are instituted among Men, deriving their just powers from the consent of the governed,—

That whenever any Form of Government becomes destructive of these ends, it is the Right of the People to alter or to abolish it, and to institute new Government, laying its foundation on such principles and organizing its powers in such form, as to them shall seem most likely to effect their Safety and Happiness. Prudence, indeed, will dictate that Governments long established should not be changed for light and transient causes; and accordingly all experience hath shown, that mankind are more disposed to suffer, while evils are sufferable, than to right themselves by abolishing the forms to which they are accustomed. But when a long train of abuses and usurpations, pursuing invariably the same Object evinces a design to reduce them under absolute Despotism, it is their right, it is their duty, to throw off such Government, and to provide new Guards for their future security.—

Such has been the patient sufferance of these Colonies; and such is now the necessity which constrains them to alter their former Systems of Government. The history of the present King of Great Britain is a history of repeated injuries and usurpations, all having in direct object the establishment of an absolute Tyranny over these States. To prove this, let Facts be submitted to a candid world.—

He has refused his Assent to Laws, the most wholesome and necessary for the public good.—

He has forbidden his Governors to pass Laws of immediate and pressing importance, unless suspended in their operation till his Assent should be obtained; and when so suspended, he has utterly neglected to attend to them.—

He has refused to pass other Laws for the accommodation of large districts of people, unless those people would relinquish the right of Representation in the Legislature, a right inestimable to them and formidable to tyrants only.—

He has called together legislative bodies at places unusual, uncomfortable, and distant from the depository of their public Records, for the sole purpose of fatiguing them into compliance with his measures.—

He has dissolved Representative Houses repeatedly, for opposing with manly firmness his invasions on the rights of the people.—

He has refused for a long time, after such dissolutions, to cause others to be elected; whereby the Legislative powers, incapable of Annihilation, have returned to the People at large for their exercise; the State remaining in the mean time exposed to all the dangers of invasion from without, and convulsions within.—

He has endeavoured to prevent the population of these States; for that purpose obstructing the Laws for Naturalization of Foreigners; refusing to pass others to encourage their migrations hither, and raising the conditions of new Appropriations of Lands.—

He has obstructed the Administration of Justice, by refusing his Assent to Laws for establishing Judiciary powers.—

He has made Judges dependent on his Will alone, for the tenure of their offices, and the amount and payment of their salaries.—

He has erected a multitude of New Offices, and sent hither swarms of Officers to harrass our people, and eat out their substance.—

He has kept among us in times of peace, Standing Armies without the Consent of our legislatures.—

He has affected to render the Military independent of and superior to the Civil power.—

He has combined with others to subject us to a jurisdiction foreign to our constitution, and unacknowledged by our laws; giving his Assent to their Acts of pretended Legislation:—

For quartering large bodies of armed troops among us:—

For protecting them, by a mock Trial, from punishment for any Murders which they should commit on the Inhabitants of these States:—

For cutting off our Trade with all parts of the world:—

For imposing Taxes on us without our Consent:—

For depriving us in many cases, of the benefits of Trial by Jury:—

For transporting us beyond Seas to be tried for pretended offences:—

For abolishing the free System of English Laws in a neighbouring Province, establishing therein an Arbitrary government, and enlarging its Boundaries so as to render it at once an example and fit instrument for introducing the same absolute rule in these Colonies:—

For taking away our Charters, abolishing our most valuable Laws, and altering fundamentally the Forms of our Governments:—

For suspending our own Legislatures, and declaring themselves invested with power to legislate for us in all cases whatsoever.—

He has abdicated Government here, by declaring us out of his Protection and waging War against us.—

He has plundered our seas, ravaged our Coasts, burnt our towns, and destroyed the lives of our people.—

He is at this time transporting large Armies of foreign Mercenaries to compleat the works of death, desolation and tyranny, already begun with circumstances of Cruelty & perfidy scarcely paralleled in the most barbarous ages, and totally unworthy the Head of a civilized nation.—

He has constrained our fellow Citizens taken Captive on the high Seas to bear Arms against their Country, to become the executioners of their friends and Brethren, or to fall themselves by their Hands.—

He has excited domestic insurrections amongst us, and has endeavoured to bring on the inhabitants of our frontiers, the merciless Indian Savages, whose known rule of warfare, is an undistinguished destruction of all ages, sexes and conditions.

In every stage of these Oppressions We have Petitioned for Redress in the most humble terms: Our repeated Petitions have been answered only by repeated injury. A Prince, whose character is thus marked by every act which may define a Tyrant, is unfit to be the ruler of a free people.

Nor have We been wanting in attentions to our British brethren. We have warned them from time to time of attempts by their legislature to extend an unwarrantable jurisdiction over us. We have reminded them of the circumstances of our emigration and settlement here. We have appealed to their native justice and magnanimity, and we have conjured them by the ties of our common kindred to disavow these usurpations, which, would inevitably interrupt our connections and correspondence. They too have been deaf to the voice of justice and of consanguinity. We must, therefore acquiesce in the necessity, which denounces our Separation, and hold them, as we hold the rest of mankind, Enemies in War, in Peace Friends.—

We, therefore, the Representatives of the united States of America, in General Congress, Assembled, appealing to the Supreme Judge of the world for the rectitude of our intentions, do, in the Name, and by Authority of the good People of these Colonies, solemnly publish and declare, That these United Colonies are, and of Right ought to be, Free and Independent States; that they are Absolved from all Allegiance to the British Crown, and that all political connection between them and the State of Great Britain, is and ought to be totally dissolved; and that as Free and Independent States, they have full Power to levy War, conclude Peace, contract Alliances, establish Commerce, and to do all other Acts and Things which Independent States may of right do.—

And for the support of this Declaration, with a firm reliance on the protection of divine Providence, we mutually pledge to each other our Lives, our Fortunes and our sacred Honor.

THE SIGNERS OF THE
DECLARATION OF INDEPENDENCE

Name	Born–Died	Birthplace	Age at Adoption of Declaration	Colony Represented	Profession	Later Achievements
John Adams	1735–1826	Massachusetts	40	Massachusetts	Lawyer	Vice-president of U.S. 1789–1797; President of U.S. 1797–1801
Samuel Adams	1722–1803	Massachusetts	53	Massachusetts	Businessman	Governor of Massachusetts 1794–1797
Josiah Bartlett	1729–1795	Massachusetts	46	New Hampshire	Physician	Governor of New Hampshire 1793–1794
Carter Braxton	1736–1797	Virginia	39	Virginia	Planter	Member of Virginia Council of State 1786–1791, 1794–1797
Charles Carroll	1737–1832	Maryland	38	Maryland	Lawyer-Planter	U.S. Senator from Maryland 1789–1792
Samuel Chase	1741–1811	Maryland	35	Maryland	Lawyer	Associate Justice, Supreme Court of U.S. 1796–1811
Abraham Clark	1726–1794	New Jersey	50	New Jersey	Politician	U.S. Rep. from New Jersey 1791–1794
George Clymer	1739–1813	Pennsylvania	37	Pennsylvania	Banker	Signed U.S. Constitution; U.S. Rep. from Pennsylvania 1789–1791
William Ellery	1727–1820	Rhode Island	48	Rhode Island	Lawyer	Collector of Customs, Newport, R. I. 1790–1820
William Floyd	1734–1821	New York	41	New York	Farmer	U.S. Rep. from New York 1789–1791
Benjamin Franklin	1706–1790	Massachusetts	70	Pennsylvania	Publisher	Signed U.S. Constitution
Elbridge Gerry	1744–1814	Massachusetts	31	Massachusetts	Merchant	Vice-president of U.S. 1813–1814
Button Gwinnett	1735(?)–1777	England	41	Georgia	Merchant	Acting President of Georgia 1777
Lyman Hall	1724–1790	Connecticut	52	Georgia	Physician	Governor of Georgia 1783
John Hancock	1737–1793	Massachusetts	39	Massachusetts	Merchant	Governor of Massachusetts 1780–1785, 1787–1793
Benjamin Harrison	1726–1791	Virginia	50	Virginia	Planter	Governor of Virginia 1781–1784
John Hart	1711(?)–1779	Connecticut	65	New Jersey	Farmer	Died before Independence was won
Joseph Hewes	1730–1779	New Jersey	46	North Carolina	Merchant	First executive head of American navy
Thomas Heyward, Jr.	1746–1809	South Carolina	29	South Carolina	Lawyer	Artillery officer during Revolutionary War, captured and imprisoned by British
William Hooper	1742–1790	Massachusetts	34	North Carolina	Lawyer	North Carolina State legislator 1777–1782
Stephen Hopkins	1707–1785	Rhode Island	69	Rhode Island	Merchant	Delegate to the Continental Congress 1778
Francis Hopkinson	1737–1791	Pennsylvania	38	New Jersey	Lawyer	Said to have designed U.S. Flag 1777, U.S. District Court judge 1789–1791
Samuel Huntington	1731–1796	Connecticut	45	Connecticut	Lawyer	President of Continental Congress 1779–1781 Governor of Connecticut 1786–1796

The Signers of the Declaration of Independence

Name	Born–Died	Birthplace	Age at Adoption of Declaration	Colony Represented	Profession	Later Achievements
Thomas Jefferson	1743–1826	Virginia	33	Virginia	Planter-Lawyer	U.S. Secretary of State 1789–1793, Vice-President of U.S. 1797–1801, President of U.S. 1801–1809
Francis Lightfoot Lee	1734–1797	Virginia	41	Virginia	Planter	Delegate to Continental Congress 1775–1779
Richard Henry Lee	1732–1794	Virginia	44	Virginia	Planter	President of Continental Congress 1784, U.S. Senator from Virginia 1789–1792
Francis Lewis	1713–1802	Wales	63	New York	Merchant	Retired
Philip Livingston	1716–1778	New York	60	New York	Merchant	Died before Independence was won
Thomas Lynch, Jr.	1749–1779	South Carolina	26	South Carolina	Planter-Lawyer	Died before Independence was won
Thomas McKean	1734–1817	Pennsylvania	42	Delaware	Lawyer	Governor of Pennsylvania 1799–1808
Arthur Middleton	1742–1787	South Carolina	34	South Carolina	Lawyer-Planter	Militia officer during Revolutionary War, captured and imprisoned by British
Lewis Morris	1726–1798	New York	50	New York	Landowner	Major general in state militia during Revolutionary War
Robert Morris	1734–1806	England	42	Pennsylvania	Financier	Signed U.S. Constitution, U.S. Senator from Pennsylvania 1789–1795
John Morton	1724–1777	Pennsylvania	52	Pennsylvania	Farmer	Died before Independence was won
Thomas Nelson	1738–1789	Virginia	37	Virginia	Planter-Merchant	Commander-in-chief of state militia in Revolutionary War, Governor of Virginia 1781
William Paca	1740–1799	Maryland	35	Maryland	Lawyer	Governor of Maryland 1782–1785, U.S. District Court judge 1789–1799
Robert Treat Paine	1731–1814	Massachusetts	45	Massachusetts	Lawyer	Massachusetts Supreme Court justice 1790–1804
John Penn	1740–1788	Virginia	36	North Carolina	Lawyer	Retired by ill health
George Read	1733–1798	Maryland	42	Delaware	Lawyer	Signed U.S. Constitution, U.S. Senator 1789–1793, Chief Justice of Delaware 1793–1798
Caesar Rodney	1728–1784	Delaware	47	Delaware	Planter	Commanded state militia in Revolutionary War, President of Delaware 1778–1781
George Ross	1730–1779	Delaware	46	Pennsylvania	Lawyer	Admiralty judge of Pennsylvania 1779
Benjamin Rush	1745–1813	Pennsylvania	30	Pennsylvania	Physician	Treasurer of U.S. Mint 1797–1813
Edward Rutledge	1749–1800	South Carolina	26	South Carolina	Planter-Lawyer	Governor of South Carolina 1798–1800
Roger Sherman	1721–1793	Massachusetts	55	Connecticut	Merchant-Lawyer	Signed U.S. Constitution, U.S. Senator from Connecticut 1791–1793
James Smith	1719(?)–1806	Ireland	57	Pennsylvania	Lawyer	Pennsylvania Court of Appeals judge 1781
Richard Stockton	1730–1781	New Jersey	45	New Jersey	Lawyer	Imprisoned by British during Revolutionary War
Thomas Stone	1743–1787	Maryland	33	Maryland	Lawyer	Helped frame Articles of Confederation

The Signers of the Declaration of Independence

Name	Born–Died	Birthplace	Age at Adoption of Declaration	Colony Represented	Profession	Later Achievements
George Taylor	1716–1781	Ireland	60	Pennsylvania	Iron-maker	Retired by ill health
Matthew Thornton	1714(?)–1803	Ireland	62	New Hampshire	Physician	Associate justice of New Hampshire Superior Court
George Walton	1741–1804	Virginia	35	Georgia	Lawyer	U.S. Senator from Georgia 1795–1796
William Whipple	1730–1785	Maine	46	New Hampshire	Merchant	Brigadier general during Revolutionary War
William Williams	1731–1811	Connecticut	45	Connecticut	Merchant	Helped frame Articles of Confederation
James Wilson	1742–1798	Scotland	33	Pennsylvania	Lawyer	Signed U.S. Constitution, Associate justice of Supreme Court of U.S. 1789–1798
John Witherspoon	1723–1794	Scotland	53	New Jersey	Clergyman	President, College of New Jersey (now Princeton)
Oliver Wolcott	1726–1797	Connecticut	49	Connecticut	Politician-Soldier	Governor of Connecticut 1796–1797
George Wythe	1726–1806	Virginia	50	Virginia	Lawyer	First professor of law in America, Chancellor of Virginia 1786–1806

THE CONSTITUTION OF THE UNITED STATES

We the People of the United States, in Order to form a more perfect Union, establish Justice, insure domestic Tranquility, provide for the common defence, promote the general Welfare, and secure the Blessings of Liberty to ourselves and our Posterity, do ordain and establish this Constitution for the United States of America.

Article I

Section 1. All legislative Powers herein granted shall be vested in a Congress of the United States, which shall consist of a Senate and House of Representatives.

Section 2. The House of Representatives shall be composed of Members chosen every second Year by the People of the several States, and the Electors in each State shall have the Qualifications requisite for Electors of the most numerous Branch of the State Legislature.

No Person shall be a Representative who shall not have attained to the Age of twenty five Years, and been seven Years a Citizen of the United States, and who shall not, when elected, be an Inhabitant of that State in which he shall be chosen.

Representatives and direct Taxes shall be apportioned among the several States which may be included within this Union, according to their respective Numbers, which shall be determined by adding to the whole Number of free Persons, including those bound to Service for a Term of Years, and excluding Indians not taxed, three fifths of all other Persons. The actual Enumeration shall be made within three Years after the first Meeting of the Congress of the United States, and within every subsequent Term of ten Years, in such Manner as they shall by Law direct. The Number of Representatives shall not exceed one for every thirty Thousand, but each State shall have at Least one Representative; and until such enumeration shall be made, the State of New Hampshire shall be entitled to chuse three, Massachusetts eight, Rhode-Island and Providence Plantations one, Connecticut five, New-York six, New Jersey four, Pennsylvania eight, Delaware one, Maryland six, Virginia ten, North Carolina five, South Carolina five, and Georgia three.

When vacancies happen in the Representation from any State, the Executive Authority thereof shall issue Writs of Election to fill such Vacancies.

The House of Representatives shall chuse their speaker and other Officers; and shall have the sole Power of Impeachment.

Section 3. The Senate of the United States shall be composed of two Senators from each State, chosen by the Legislature thereof, for six Years; and each Senator shall have one Vote.

Immediately after they shall be assembled in Consequence of the first Election, they shall be divided as equally as may be into three Classes. The Seats of the Senators of the first Class shall be vacated at the Expiration of the second Year, of the second Class at the Expiration of the fourth Year, and of the third Class at the Expiration of the sixth Year, so that one third may be chosen every second Year; and if Vacancies happen by Resignation, or otherwise, during the Recess of the Legislature of any State, the Executive thereof may make temporary Appointments until the next Meeting of the Legislature, which shall then fill such Vacancies.

No Person shall be a Senator who shall not have attained to the Age of thirty years, and been nine Years a Citizen of the United States, and who shall not, when elected, be an Inhabitant of that State for which he shall be chosen.

The Vice President of the United States shall be President of the Senate, but shall have no Vote, unless they be equally divided.

The Senate shall chuse their other Officers, and also a President pro tempore, in the Absence of the Vice President, or when he shall exercise the Office of President of the United States.

The Senate shall have the sole Power to try all Impeachments. When sitting for that Purpose, they shall be on Oath or Affirmation. When the President of the United States is tried, the Chief Justice shall preside: And no Person shall be convicted without the Concurrence of two thirds of the Members present.

Judgment in Cases of Impeachment shall not extend further than to removal from Office, and disqualification to hold and enjoy any Office of honor, Trust or Profit under the United States: but the Party convicted shall nevertheless be liable and subject to Indictment, Trial, Judgment and Punishment, according to law.

Section 4. The Times, Places and Manner of holding Elections for Senators and Representatives, shall be prescribed in each State by the Legislature thereof; but the Congress may at any time by Law make or alter such Regulations, except as to the Places of chusing Senators.

The Congress shall assemble at least once in every Year, and such Meeting shall be on the first Monday in December, unless they shall by Law appoint a different Day.

Section 5. Each House shall be the Judge of the Elections, Returns and Qualifications of its own Members, and a Majority of each shall constitute a Quorum to do Business; but a smaller Number may adjourn from day to day, and may be authorized to compel the Attendance of absent Members, in such Manner, and under such Penalties as each House may provide.

Each House may determine the Rules of its Proceedings, punish its Members for disorderly Behaviour, and, with the Concurrence of two thirds, expel a Member.

Each House shall keep a Journal of its Proceedings, and from time to time publish the same, excepting such Parts as may in their Judgment require Secrecy; and the Yeas and Nays of the Members of either House on any question shall, at the Desire of one fifth of those Present, be entered on the Journal.

Neither House, during the Session of Congress, shall, without the Consent of the other, adjourn for more than three days, nor to any other Place than that in which the two Houses shall be sitting.

Section 6. The Senators and Representatives shall receive a Compensation for their Services, to be ascertained by Law, and paid out of the Treasury of the United States. They shall in all Cases, except Treason, Felony and Breach of the Peace, be privileged from Arrest during their Attendance at the Session of their respective Houses, and in going to and returning from the same; and for any Speech or Debate in either House, they shall not be questioned in any other Place.

No Senator or Representative shall, during the Time for which he was elected, be appointed to any civil Office under the Authority of the United States, which shall have been created, or the Emoluments whereof shall have been encreased during such time; and no Person holding any Office

under the United States, shall be a Member of either House during his Continuance in Office.

Section 7. All Bills for raising Revenue shall originate in the House of Representatives; but the Senate may propose or concur with Amendments as on other Bills.

Every Bill which shall have passed the House of Representatives and the Senate, shall, before it become a Law, be presented to the President of the United States; If he approve he shall sign it, but if not he shall return it, with his Objections to that House in which it shall have originated, who shall enter the Objections at large on their Journal, and proceed to reconsider it. If after such Reconsideration two thirds of that House shall agree to pass the Bill, it shall be sent, together with the Objections, to the other House, by which it shall likewise be reconsidered, and if approved by two thirds of that House, it shall become a Law. But in all such Cases the Votes of both Houses shall be determined by yeas and Nays, and the Names of the Persons voting for and against the Bill shall be entered on the Journal of each House respectively. If any Bill shall not be returned by the President within ten Days (Sundays excepted) after it shall have been presented to him, the Same shall be a Law, in like Manner as if he had signed it, unless the Congress by their Adjournment prevent its Return, in which Case it shall not be a Law.

Every Order, Resolution, or Vote to which the Concurrence of the Senate and House of Representatives may be necessary (except on a question of Adjournment) shall be presented to the President of the United States; and before the Same shall take Effect, shall be approved by him, or being disapproved by him, shall be repassed by two thirds of the Senate and House of Representatives, according to the Rules and Limitations prescribed in the Case of a Bill.

Section 8. The Congress shall have Power To lay and collect Taxes, Duties, Imposts and Excises, to pay the Debts and provide for the common Defence and general Welfare of the United States; but all Duties, Imposts and Excises shall be uniform throughout the United States;

To Borrow Money on the Credit of the United States;

To regulate Commerce with foreign Nations, and among the several States, and with the Indian Tribes;

To establish an uniform Rule of Naturalization, and uniform Laws on the subject of Bankruptcies throughout the United States;

To coin Money, regulate the Value thereof, and of foreign Coin, and fix the Standard of Weights and Measures;

To provide for the Punishment of counterfeiting the Securities and current Coin of the United States;

To establish Post Offices and post Roads;

To promote the Progress of Science and useful Arts, by securing for limited Times to Authors and Inventors the exclusive Right to their respective Writings and Discoveries;

To constitute Tribunals inferior to the supreme Court;

To define and punish Piracies and Felonies committed on the high Seas, and Offences against the Law of Nations;

To declare War, grant Letters of Marque and Reprisal, and make Rules concerning Captures on Land and Water;

To raise and support Armies, but no Appropriation of Money to that Use shall be for a longer Term than two Years;

To provide and maintain a Navy;

To make Rules for the Government and Regulation of the land and naval Forces;

To provide for calling forth the Militia to execute the Laws of the Union, suppress Insurrections and repel Invasions;

To provide for organizing, arming, and disciplining, the Militia, and for governing such Part of them as may be employed in the Service of the United States, reserving to the States respectively, the Appointment of the Officers, and the Authority of training the Militia according to the discipline prescribed by Congress;

To exercise exclusive Legislation in all Cases whatsoever, over such District (not exceeding ten Miles square) as may, by Cession of particular States, and the Acceptance of Congress, become the Seat of the Government of the United States, and to exercise like Authority over all Places purchased by the Consent of the Legislature of the State in which the Same shall be for the Erection of Forts, Magazines, Arsenals, dock-Yards, and other needful Buildings;—And

To make all Laws which shall be necessary and proper for carrying into Execution the foregoing Powers, and all other Powers vested by this Constitution in the Government of the United States, or in any Department or Officer thereof.

Section 9. The Migration or Importation of such Persons as any of the States now existing shall think proper to admit, shall not be prohibited by the Congress prior to the Year one thousand eight hundred and eight, but a Tax or duty may be imposed on such Importation, not exceeding ten dollars for each Person.

The Privilege of the Writ of Habeas Corpus shall not be suspended, unless when in Cases of Rebellion or Invasion the public Safety may require it.

No Bill of Attainder or ex post facto Law shall be passed.

No Capitation, or other direct, Tax shall be laid, unless in Proportion to the Census or Enumeration herein before directed to be taken.

No Tax or Duty shall be laid on Articles exported from any State.

No Preference shall be given by any Regulation of Commerce or Revenue to the Ports of one State over those of another: nor shall Vessels bound to, or from, one State, be obliged to enter, clear, or pay Duties in another.

No Money shall be drawn from the Treasury, but in Consequence of Appropriations made by Law; and a regular Statement and Account of the Receipts and Expenditures of all public Money shall be published from time to time.

No Title of Nobility shall be granted by the United States: And no Person holding any Office of Profit or Trust under them, shall, without the Consent of the Congress, accept of any present, Emolument, Office, or Title, of any kind whatever, from any King, Prince, or foreign State.

Section 10. No State shall enter into any Treaty, Alliance, or Confederation; grant Letters of Marque and Reprisal; coin Money; emit Bills of Credit; make any Thing but gold and silver Coin a Tender in Payment of Debts; pass any Bill of Attainder, ex post facto Law, or Law impairing the Obligation of Contracts, or grant any Title of Nobility.

No State shall, without the Consent of the Congress, lay any Imposts or Duties on Imports or Exports, except what may be absolutely necessary for executing it's inspection Laws: and the net Produce of all Duties and Imposts, laid by any State on Imports or Exports, shall be for the Use of the Treasury of the United States; and all such Laws shall be subject to the Revision and Controul of the Congress.

No State shall, without the Consent of Congress, lay any Duty of Tonnage, keep Troops, or Ships of War in time of Peace, enter into any Agreement or Compact with another State, or with a foreign Power, or engage in War, unless actually invaded, or in such imminent Danger as will not admit of delay.

Article II

Section 1. The executive Power shall be vested in a President of the United States of America. He shall hold his Office during the Term of four Years, and, together with the Vice President, chosen for the same term, be elected, as follows

Each State shall appoint, in such Manner as the Legislature thereof may direct, a Number of Electors, equal to the whole Number of Senators and Representatives to which the State may be entitled in the Congress: but no Senator or Representative, or Person holding an Office of Trust or Profit under the United States, shall be appointed an Elector.

The Electors shall meet in their respective States, and vote by Ballot for two Persons, of whom one at least shall not be an Inhabitant of the same State with themselves. And they shall make a List of all the Persons voted for, and of the Number of Votes for each; which List they shall sign and certify, and transmit sealed to the Seat of the Government of the United States, directed to the President of the Senate. The President of the Senate shall, in the Presence of the Senate and House of Representatives, open all the Certificates, and the Votes shall then be counted. The Person having the greatest Number of Votes shall be the President, if such Number be a Majority of the whole Number of Electors appointed; and if there be more than one who have such Majority, and have an equal Number of Votes, then the House of Representatives shall immediately chuse by Ballot one of them for President: and if no Person have a Majority, then from the five highest on the List the said House shall in like Manner chuse the President. But in chusing the President, the Votes shall be taken by States, the Representation from each State having one Vote; A quorum for this Purpose shall consist of a Member or Members from two thirds of the States, and a Majority of all the States shall be necessary to a Choice. In every Case, after the Choice of the President, the Person having the greatest Number of Votes of the Electors shall be the Vice President. But if there should remain two or more who have equal Votes, the Senate shall chuse from them by Ballot the Vice President.

The Congress may determine the Time of chusing the Electors, and the Day on which they shall give their Votes; which Day shall be the same throughout the United States.

No Person except a natural born Citizen, or a Citizen of the United States, at the time of the Adoption of this Constitution, shall be eligible to the Office of President; neither shall any Person be eligible to that Office who shall not have attained to the Age of thirty five Years, and been fourteen Years a Resident within the United States.

In Case of the Removal of the President from Office, or of his Death, Resignation, or Inability to discharge the Powers and Duties of the said Office, the Same shall devolve on the Vice President, and the Congress may by Law provide for the Case of Removal, Death, Resignation or Inability, both of the President and Vice President, declaring what Officer shall then act as President, and such Officer shall act accordingly, until the Disability be removed, or a President shall be elected.

The President shall, at stated Times, receive for his Services, a Compensation, which shall neither be encreased nor diminished during the Period for which he shall have been elected, and he shall not receive within that Period any other Emolument from the United States, or any of them.

Before he enter on the Execution of his Office, he shall take the following Oath or Affirmation:—"I do solemnly swear (or affirm) that I will faithfully execute the Office of President of the United States, and will to the best of my Ability, preserve, protect and defend the Constitution of the United States."

Section 2. The President shall be Commander in Chief of the Army and Navy of the United States, and of the Militia of the several States, when called into the actual Service of the United States; he may require the Opinion, in writing, of the principal Officer in each of the executive Departments, upon any Subject relating to the Duties of their respective Offices, and he shall have Power to grant Reprieves and Pardons for Offences against the United States, except in Cases of Impeachment.

He shall have Power, by and with the Advice and Consent of the Senate, to make Treaties, provided two thirds of the Senators present concur; and he shall nominate, and by and with the Advice and Consent of the Senate, shall appoint Ambassadors, other public Ministers and Consuls, Judges of the supreme Court, and all other Officers of the United States, whose Appointments are not herein otherwise provided for, and which shall be established by Law: but the Congress may by Law vest the Appointment of such inferior Officers, as they think proper, in the President alone, in the Courts of Law, or in the Heads of Departments.

The President shall have Power to fill up all Vacancies that may happen during the Recess of the Senate, by granting Commissions which shall expire at the End of their next Session.

Section 3. He shall from time to time give to the Congress Information of the State of the Union, and recommend to their Consideration such Measures as he shall judge necessary and expedient; he may, on extraordinary Occasions, convene both Houses, or either of them, and in Case of Disagreement between them, with Respect to the Time of Adjournment, he may adjourn them to such Time as he shall think proper; he shall receive Ambassadors and other public Ministers; he shall take Care that the Laws be faithfully executed, and shall Commission all the Officers of the United States.

Section 4. The President, Vice President and all civil Officers of the United States, shall be removed from Office on Impeachment for, and Conviction of, Treason, Bribery, or other High Crimes and Misdemeanors.

Article III

Section 1. The judicial Power of the United States, shall be vested in one supreme Court, and in such inferior Courts as the Congress may from time to time ordain and establish. The Judges, both of the supreme and inferior Courts, shall hold their Offices during good Behaviour, and shall, at stated Times, receive for their Services, a Compensation, which shall not be diminished during their Continuance in Office.

Section 2. The judicial Power shall extend to all Cases, in Law and Equity, arising under this Constitution, the Laws of the United States, and Treaties made, or which shall be made, under their Authority;—to all Cases affecting Ambassadors, other public Ministers and Consuls;—to all Cases of admiralty and maritime Jurisdiction;—to Controversies to which the United States shall be a Party;—to Controversies between two or more States; between a State and Citizens of another State;—between Citizens of different States; —between Citizens of the same State claiming Lands under Grants of different States, and between a State, or the Citizens thereof, and foreign States, Citizens or Subjects.

In all Cases affecting Ambassadors, other public Ministers and Consuls, and those in which a State shall be Party, the supreme Court shall have original Jurisdiction. In all the other Cases before mentioned, the supreme Court shall have appellate Jurisdiction, both as to Law and Fact, with such Exceptions, and under such Regulations as the Congress shall make.

The Trial of all Crimes, except in Cases of Impeachment, shall be by Jury; and such Trial shall be held in the State where the said Crimes shall have been committed; but when not committed within any State, the Trial shall be at such Place or Places as the Congress may by Law have directed.

Section 3. Treason against the United States, shall consist only in levying War against them, or in adhering to their Enemies, giving them Aid and Comfort. No Person shall be convicted of Treason unless on the Testimony of two Witnesses to the same overt Act, or on Confession in open Court.

The Congress shall have Power to declare the Punishment of Treason, but no Attainder of Treason shall work Corruption of Blood, or Forfeiture except during the Life of the Person attainted.

Article IV

Section 1. Full Faith and Credit shall be given in each State to the public Acts, Records, and judicial Proceedings of every other State. And the Congress may by general Laws prescribe the Manner in which such Acts, Records and Proceedings shall be proved, and the Effect thereof.

Section 2. The Citizens of each State shall be entitled to all Privileges and Immunities of Citizens in the several States.

A Person charged in any State with Treason, Felony, or other Crime, who shall flee from Justice, and be found in another State, shall on Demand of the executive Authority of the State from which he fled, be delivered up, to be removed to the State having Jurisdiction of the Crime.

No Person held to Service or Labour in one State, under the Laws thereof, escaping into another, shall, in Consequence of any Law or Regulation therein, be discharged from such Service or Labour, but shall be delivered up on Claim of the Party to whom such Service or Labour may be due.

Section 3. New States may be admitted by the Congress into this Union; but no new State shall be formed or erected within the Jurisdiction of any other State; nor any State be formed by the Junction of two or more States, or Parts of States, without the Consent of the Legislatures of the States concerned as well as of the Congress.

The Congress shall have Power to dispose of and make all needful Rules and Regulations respecting the Territory or other Property belonging to the United States; and nothing in this Constitution shall be so construed as to Prejudice any Claims of the United States, or of any particular State.

Section 4. The United States shall guarantee to every State in this Union a Republican Form of Government, and shall protect each of them against Invasion; and on Application of the Legislature, or of the Executive (when the Legislature cannot be convened) against domestic Violence.

Article V

The Congress, whenever two thirds of both Houses shall deem it necessary, shall propose Amendments to this Constitution, or, on the Application of the Legislatures of two thirds of the several States, shall call a Convention for proposing Amendments, which, in either Case, shall be valid to all Intents and Purposes, as Part of this Constitution, when ratified by the Legislatures of three fourths of the several States, or by Conventions in three fourths thereof, as the one or the other Mode of Ratification may be proposed by the Congress; Provided that no Amendment which may be made prior to the Year One thousand eight hundred and eight shall in any Manner affect the first and fourth Clauses in the Ninth Section of the first Article; and that no State, without its Consent, shall be deprived of its equal Suffrage in the Senate.

Article VI

All Debts contracted and Engagements entered into, before the Adoption of this Constitution, shall be as valid

against the United States under this Constitution, as under the Confederation.

This Constitution, and the Laws of the United States which shall be made in Pursuance thereof; and all Treaties made, or which shall be made, under the Authority of the United States, shall be the supreme Law of the Land; and the Judges in every State shall be bound thereby, any Thing in the Constitution or Laws of any State to the Contrary notwithstanding.

The Senators and Representatives before mentioned, and the Members of the several State Legislatures, and all executive and judicial Officers, both of the United States and of the several States, shall be bound by Oath or Affirmation, to support this Constitution; but no religious Test shall ever be required as a Qualification to any Office or public Trust under the United States.

Article VII

The Ratification of the Conventions of nine States, shall be sufficient for the Establishment of this Constitution between the States so ratifying the Same.

DONE in Convention by the Unanimous Consent of the States present the Seventeenth Day of September in the Year of our Lord one thousand seven hundred and Eighty seven and of the Independence of the United States of America the Twelfth IN WITNESS whereof We have hereunto subscribed our Names,

G°. WASHINGTON—Presid^t
and deputy from Virginia

AMENDMENTS

(The first 10 Amendments were ratified December 15, 1791, and form what is known as the "Bill of Rights")

Amendment 1

Congress shall make no law respecting an establishment of religion, or prohibiting the free exercise thereof; or abridging the freedom of speech, or of the press; or the right of the people peaceably to assemble, and to petition the Government for a redress of grievances.

Amendment 2

A well regulated Militia, being necessary to the security of a free State, the right of the people to keep and bear Arms, shall not be infringed.

Amendment 3

No Soldier shall, in time of peace be quartered in any house, without the consent of the Owner, nor in time of war, but in a manner to be prescribed by law.

Amendment 4

The right of the people to be secure in their persons, houses, papers, and effects, against unreasonable searches and seizures, shall not be violated, and no Warrants shall issue, but upon probable cause, supported by Oath or affirmation, and particularly describing the place to be searched, and the persons or things to be seized.

Amendment 5

No person shall be held to answer for a capital, or otherwise infamous crime, unless on a presentment or indictment of a Grand Jury, except in cases arising in the land or naval forces, or in the Militia, when in actual service in time of War or public danger; nor shall any person be subject for the same offence to be twice put in jeopardy of life or limb; nor shall be compelled in any criminal case to be a witness against himself, nor be deprived of life, liberty, or property, without due process of law; nor shall private property be taken for public use, without just compensation.

Amendment 6

In all criminal prosecutions, the accused shall enjoy the right to a speedy and public trial, by an impartial jury of the State and district wherein the crime shall have been committed, which district shall have been previously ascertained by law, and to be informed of the nature and cause of the accusation; to be confronted with the witnesses against him; to have compulsory process for obtaining witnesses in his favor, and to have the Assistance of Counsel for his defence.

Amendment 7

In Suits at common law, where the value in controversy shall exceed twenty dollars, the right of trial by jury shall be preserved, and no fact tried by a jury, shall be otherwise re-examined in any Court of the United States, than according to the rules of the common law.

Amendment 8

Excessive bail shall not be required, nor excessive fines imposed, nor cruel and unusual punishments inflicted.

Amendment 9

The enumeration in the Constitution, of certain rights, shall not be construed to deny or disparage others retained by the people.

Amendment 10

The powers not delegated to the United States by the Constitution, nor prohibited by it to the States, are reserved to the States respectively, or to the people.

Amendment 11

(Ratified February 7, 1795)

The Judicial power of the United States shall not be construed to extend to any suit in law or equity, commenced or prosecuted against one of the United States by Citizens of another State, or by Citizens or Subjects of any Foreign State.

Amendment 12

(Ratified July 27, 1804)

The Electors shall meet in their respective states and vote by ballot for President and Vice-President, one of whom, at least, shall not be an inhabitant of the same state with themselves; they shall name in their ballots the person voted for as President, and in distinct ballots the person voted for as Vice-President, and they shall make distinct lists of all persons voted for as President, and of all persons voted for as Vice-President, and of the number of votes for each, which lists they shall sign and certify, and transmit sealed to the seat of the government of the United States, directed to the President of the Senate;—The President of the Senate shall, in the presence of the Senate and House of Representatives, open all the certificates and the votes shall then be counted;—The person having the greatest number of votes for President, shall be the President, if such number be a majority of the whole number of Electors appointed; and if no person have such majority, then from the persons having the highest numbers not exceeding three on the list of those voted for as President, the House of Representatives shall choose immediately, by ballot, the President. But in choosing the President, the votes shall be taken by states, the representation from each state having one vote; a quorum for this purpose shall consist of a member or members from two-thirds of the states, and a majority of all the states shall be necessary to a choice. And if the House of Representatives shall not choose a President whenever the right of choice shall devolve upon them, before the fourth day of March next following, then the Vice-President shall act as President, as in the case of the death or other constitutional disability of the President.—The person having the greatest number of votes as Vice-President, shall be the Vice-President, if such number be a majority of the whole number of Electors appointed, and if no person have a majority, then from the two highest numbers on the list, the Senate shall choose the Vice-President; a quorum for the purpose shall consist of two-thirds of the whole number of Senators, and a majority of the whole number shall be necessary to a choice. But no person constitutionally ineligible to the office of President shall be eligible to that of Vice-President of the United States.

Amendment 13

(Ratified December 6, 1865)

Section 1. Neither slavery nor involuntary servitude, except as a punishment for crime whereof the party shall have been duly convicted, shall exist within the United States, or any place subject to their jurisdiction.

Section 2. Congress shall have power to enforce this article by appropriate legislation.

Amendment 14

(Ratified July 9, 1868)

Section 1. All persons born or naturalized in the United States, and subject to the jurisdiction thereof, are citizens of the United States and of the State wherein they reside. No State shall make or enforce any law which shall abridge the privileges or immunities of citizens of the United States; nor shall any State deprive any person of life, liberty, or property, without due process of law; nor deny to any person within its jurisdiction the equal protection of the laws.

Section 2. Representatives shall be apportioned among the several States according to their respective numbers, counting the whole number of persons in each State, excluding Indians not taxed. But when the right to vote at any election for the choice of electors for President and Vice President of the United States, Representatives in Congress, the Executive and Judicial officers of a State, or the members of the Legislature thereof, is denied to any of the male inhabitants of such State, being twenty-one years of age, and citizens of the United States, or in any way abridged, except for participation in rebellion, or other crime, the basis of representation therein shall be reduced in the proportion which the number of such male citizens shall bear to the whole number of male citizens twenty-one years of age in such State.

Section 3. No person shall be a Senator or Representative in Congress, or elector of President and Vice President, or hold any office, civil or military, under the United States, or under any State, who, having previously taken an oath, as a member of Congress, or as an officer of the United States, or as a member of any State legislature, or as an executive or judicial officer of any State, to support the Constitution of the United States, shall have engaged in insurrection or rebellion against the same, or given aid or comfort to the enemies thereof. But Congress may by a vote of two-thirds of each House, remove such disability.

Section 4. The validity of the public debt of the United States, authorized by law, including debts incurred for payment of pensions and bounties for services in suppressing insurrection or rebellion, shall not be questioned. But neither the United States nor any State shall assume or pay any debt or obligation incurred in aid of insurrection or rebellion against the United States, or any claim for the loss or emancipation of any slave; but all such debts, obligations and claims shall be held illegal and void.

Section 5. The Congress shall have power to enforce, by appropriate legislation, the provisions of this article.

Amendment 15

(Ratified February 3, 1870)

Section 1. The right of citizens of the United States to vote shall not be denied or abridged by the United States or by any State on account of race, color, or previous condition of servitude.

Section 2. The Congress shall have power to enforce this article by appropriate legislation.

Amendment 16

(Ratified February 3, 1913)

The Congress shall have power to lay and collect taxes on incomes, from whatever source derived, without apportionment among the several States, and without regard to any census or enumeration.

Amendment 17

(Ratified April 8, 1913)

The Senate of the United States shall be composed of two Senators from each State, elected by the people thereof for six years; and each Senator shall have one vote. The electors in each State shall have the qualifications requisite for electors of the most numerous branch of the State legislatures.

When vacancies happen in the representation of any State in the Senate, the executive authority of such State shall issue writs of election to fill such vacancies: *Provided*, That the legislature of any State may empower the executive thereof to make temporary appointments until the people fill the vacancies by election as the legislature may direct.

This amendment shall not be so construed as to affect the election or term of any Senator chosen before it becomes valid as part of the Constitution.

Amendment 18

(Ratified January 16, 1919)

Section 1. After one year from the ratification of this article the manufacture, sale, or transportation of intoxicating liquors within, the importation thereof into, or the exportation thereof from the United States and all territory subject to the jurisdiction thereof for beverage purposes is hereby prohibited.

Section 2. The Congress and the several States shall have concurrent power to enforce this article by appropriate legislation.

Section 3. This article shall be inoperative unless it shall have been ratified as an amendment to the Constitution by the legislatures of the several States, as provided in the Constitution, within seven years from the date of the submission hereof to the States by the Congress.

Amendment 19

(Ratified August 18, 1920)

The right of citizens of the United States to vote shall not be denied or abridged by the United States or by any State on account of sex.

Congress shall have power to enforce this article by appropriate legislation.

Amendment 20

(Ratified January 23, 1933)

Section 1. The terms of the President and Vice President shall end at noon on the 20th day of January, and the terms of Senators and Representatives at noon on the 3d day of January, of the years in which such terms would have ended if this article had not been ratified; and the terms of their successors shall then begin.

Section 2. The Congress shall assemble at least once in every year, and such meeting shall begin at noon on the 3d day of January, unless they shall by law appoint a different day.

Section 3. If, at the time fixed for the beginning of the term of the President, the President elect shall have died, the Vice President elect shall become President. If a President shall not have been chosen before the time fixed for the beginning of his term, or if the President elect shall have failed to qualify, then the Vice President elect shall act as President until a President shall have qualified; and the Congress may by law provide for the case wherein neither a President elect nor a Vice President elect shall have qualified, declaring who shall then act as President, or the manner in which one who is to act shall be selected, and such person shall act accordingly until a President or Vice President shall have qualified.

Section 4. The Congress may by law provide for the case of the death of any of the persons from whom the House of Representatives may choose a President whenever the right of choice shall have devolved upon them, and for the case of the death of any of the persons from whom the Senate may choose a Vice President whenever the right of choice shall have devolved upon them.

Section 5. Sections 1 and 2 shall take effect on the 15th day of October following the ratification of this article.

Section 6. This article shall be inoperative unless it shall have been ratified as an amendment to the Constitution by the legislatures of three-fourths of the several States within seven years from the date of its submission.

Amendment 21

(Ratified December 5, 1933)

Section 1. The eighteenth article of amendment to the Constitution of the United States is hereby repealed.

The Constitution of the United States

Section 2. The transportation or importation into any State, Territory, or possession of the United States for delivery or use therein of intoxicating liquors, in violation of the laws thereof, is hereby prohibited.

Section 3. This article shall be inoperative unless it shall have been ratified as an amendment to the Constitution by conventions in the several States, as provided in the Constitution, within seven years from the date of the submission hereof to the States by the Congress.

Amendment 22

(Ratified February 27, 1951)

Section 1. No person shall be elected to the office of the President more than twice, and no person who has held the office of President, or acted as President, for more than two years of a term to which some other person was elected President shall be elected to the office of the President more than once. But this Article shall not apply to any person holding the office of President when this Article was proposed by the Congress, and shall not prevent any person who may be holding the office of President, or acting as President, during the term within which this Article becomes operative from holding the office of President or acting as President during the remainder of such term.

Section 2. This article shall be inoperative unless it shall have been ratified as an amendment to the Constitution by the legislatures of three-fourths of the several States within seven years from the date of its submission to the States by the Congress.

Amendment 23

(Ratified March 29, 1961)

Section 1. The District constituting the seat of Government of the United States shall appoint in such manner as the Congress may direct:

A number of electors of President and Vice President equal to the whole number of Senators and Representatives in Congress to which the District would be entitled if it were a State, but in no event more than the least populous State; they shall be in addition to those appointed by the States, but they shall be considered, for the purposes of the election of President and Vice President, to be electors appointed by a State; and they shall meet in the District and perform such duties as provided by the twelfth article of amendment.

Section 2. The Congress shall have power to enforce this article by appropriate legislation.

Amendment 24

(Ratified January 23, 1964)

Section 1. The right of citizens of the United States to vote in any primary or other election for President or Vice President, for electors for President or Vice President, or for Senator or Representative in Congress, shall not be denied or abridged by the United States or any State by reason of failure to pay any poll tax or other tax.

Section 2. The Congress shall have power to enforce this article by appropriate legislation.

Amendment 25

(Ratified February 10, 1967)

Section 1. In case of the removal of the President from office or his death or resignation, the Vice President shall become President.

Section 2. Whenever there is a vacancy in the office of the Vice President, the President shall nominate a Vice President who shall take the office upon confirmation by a majority vote of both houses of Congress.

Section 3. Whenever the President transmits to the President pro tempore of the Senate and the Speaker of the House of Representatives his written declaration that he is unable to discharge the powers and duties of his office, and until he transmits to them a written declaration to the contrary, such powers and duties shall be discharged by the Vice President as Acting President.

Section 4. Whenever the Vice President and a majority of either the principal officers of the executive departments or of such other body as Congress may by law provide, transmit to the President pro tempore of the Senate and the Speaker of the House of Representatives their written declaration that the President is unable to discharge the powers and duties of his office, the Vice President shall immediately assume the powers and duties of the office as Acting President.

Thereafter, when the President transmits to the President pro tempore of the Senate and the Speaker of the House of Representatives his written declaration that no inability exists, he shall resume the powers and duties of his office unless the Vice President and a majority of either the principal officers of the executive department or of such other body as Congress may by law provide, transmit within four days to the President pro tempore of the Senate and the Speaker of the House of Representatives their written declaration that the President is unable to discharge the powers and duties of his office. Thereupon Congress shall decide the issue, assembling within 48 hours for that purpose if not in session. If the Congress, within 21 days after receipt of the latter written declaration, or, if Congress is not in session, within 21 days after Congress is required to assemble, determines by two-thirds vote of both houses that the President is unable to discharge the powers and duties of his office, the Vice President shall continue to discharge the same as Acting President; otherwise, the President shall resume the powers and duties of his office.

Amendment 26

(Ratified June 30, 1971)

Section 1. The right of citizens of the United States, who are eighteen years of age or older, to vote shall not be denied or abridged by the United States or by any State on account of age.

Section 2. The Congress shall have power to enforce this article by appropriate legislation.

THE SIGNERS OF THE UNITED STATES CONSTITUTION

Name	Born–Died	Birthplace	Age at Signing of Constitution	Colony Represented	Profession	Later Achievements
Abraham Baldwin	1754–1807	Connecticut	32	Georgia	Lawyer	U.S. Senator from Georgia 1799–1807
Richard Bassett	1745–1815	Maryland	42	Delaware	Lawyer	Governor of Delaware 1799–1800
Gunning Bedford, Jr.	1747–1812	Philadelphia	40	Delaware	Lawyer	U.S. District judge 1789–1812
John Blair	1732–1800	Virginia	55	Virginia	Lawyer	Associate justice, Supreme Court of U.S. 1789–1796
William Blount	1749–1800	North Carolina	38	North Carolina	Politician	President, Tennessee state constitutional convention 1796
David Brearley	1745–1790	New Jersey	42	New Jersey	Lawyer	U.S. District judge 1789–1790
Jacob Broom	1752–1810	Delaware	35	Delaware	Businessman	Built first cotton mill in Wilmington, Del.
Pierce Butler	1744–1822	Ireland	42	South Carolina	Soldier-Planter	U.S. Senator from South Carolina 1789–1796, 1802–1806
Daniel Carroll	1730–1796	Maryland	56	Maryland	Landowner	U.S. Representative from Maryland 1789–1791
George Clymer	1739–1813	Philadelphia	48	Pennsylvania	Banker	U.S. Representative from Pennsylvania 1789–1791
Jonathan Dayton	1760–1824	New Jersey	26	New Jersey	Lawyer	U.S. Representative from New Jersey 1791–1799; U.S. Senator 1799–1805
John Dickinson	1732–1808	Maryland	54	Delaware	Lawyer	President of Delaware 1781–1782; President of Pennsylvania 1782–1785
William Few	1748–1828	Maryland	39	Georgia	Politician	U.S. Senator from Georgia 1789–1795
Thomas FitzSimons	1741–1811	Ireland	46	Pennsylvania	Businessman	U.S. Representative from Pennsylvania 1789–1795
Benjamin Franklin	1706–1790	Massachusetts	81	Pennsylvania	Publisher	Retired
Nicholas Gilman	1755–1814	New Hampshire	32	New Hampshire	Politician	U.S. Representative 1789–1797; U.S. Senator 1805–1814
Nathaniel Gorham	1738–1796	Massachusetts	49	Massachusetts	Businessman	Became a land speculator
Alexander Hamilton	1757–1804	West Indies	30/32	New York	Lawyer	Secretary of the Treasury 1789–1795
Jared Ingersoll	1749–1822	Connecticut	38	Pennsylvania	Lawyer	Federalist candidate for Vice President of U.S. in 1812
Daniel of St. Thomas Jenifer	1723–1790	Maryland	64	Maryland	Landowner	Retired
William Samuel Johnson	1727–1819	Connecticut	59	Connecticut	Lawyer-Educator	President of Columbia College 1787–1800
Rufus King	1755–1827	Massachusetts	32	Massachusetts	Lawyer	U.S. Senator from New York 1789–1796, 1813–1825

The Signers of the United States Constitution

Name	Born–Died	Birthplace	Age at Signing of Constitution	Colony Represented	Profession	Later Achievements
John Langdon	1741–1819	New Hampshire	46	New Hampshire	Shipowner	Governor of New Hampshire 1805–1809, 1810–1812
William Livingston	1723–1790	New York	63	New Jersey	Lawyer	Governor of New Jersey 1776–1790
James Madison, Jr.	1751–1836	Virginia	36	Virginia	Politician	President of U.S. 1809–1817
James McHenry	1753–1816	Ireland	33	Maryland	Physician	Secretary of War 1796–1800
Thomas Mifflin	1744–1800	Philadelphia	43	Pennsylvania	Politician	Governor of Pennsylvania 1790–1799
Gouverneur Morris	1752–1816	New York	35	Pennsylvania	Lawyer	U.S. Senator from Pennsylvania 1800–1803
Robert Morris	1734–1806	England	53	Pennsylvania	Financier	U.S. Senator from Pennsylvania 1789–1795
William Paterson	1745–1806	Ireland	42	New Jersey	Lawyer	Associate justice of Supreme Court of U.S. 1793–1806
Charles Pinckney	1757–1824	South Carolina	29	South Carolina	Lawyer	Governor of South Carolina 1789–1792; 1796–1798; 1806–1808
Charles Cotesworth Pinckney	1746–1825	South Carolina	41	South Carolina	Lawyer	Federalist candidate for President of U.S. 1804 and 1808
George Read	1733–1798	Maryland	53	Delaware	Lawyer	Chief justice of Delaware 1793–1798
John Rutledge	1739–1800	South Carolina	48	South Carolina	Lawyer	Chief justice of the United States 1795
Roger Sherman	1721–1793	Massachusetts	66	Connecticut	Merchant-Lawyer	U.S. Senator from Connecticut 1791–1793
Richard Dobbs Spaight	1758–1802	North Carolina	29	North Carolina	Politician	Governor of North Carolina 1792–1795
George Washington	1732–1799	Virginia	55	Virginia	Soldier-Planter	President of U.S. 1789–1797
Hugh Williamson	1735–1819	Pennsylvania	51	North Carolina	Physician	U.S. Representative from North Carolina 1790–1793
James Wilson	1742–1798	Scotland	44	Pennsylvania	Lawyer	Associate justice of Supreme Court of U.S. 1789–1798